W9-CHP-011

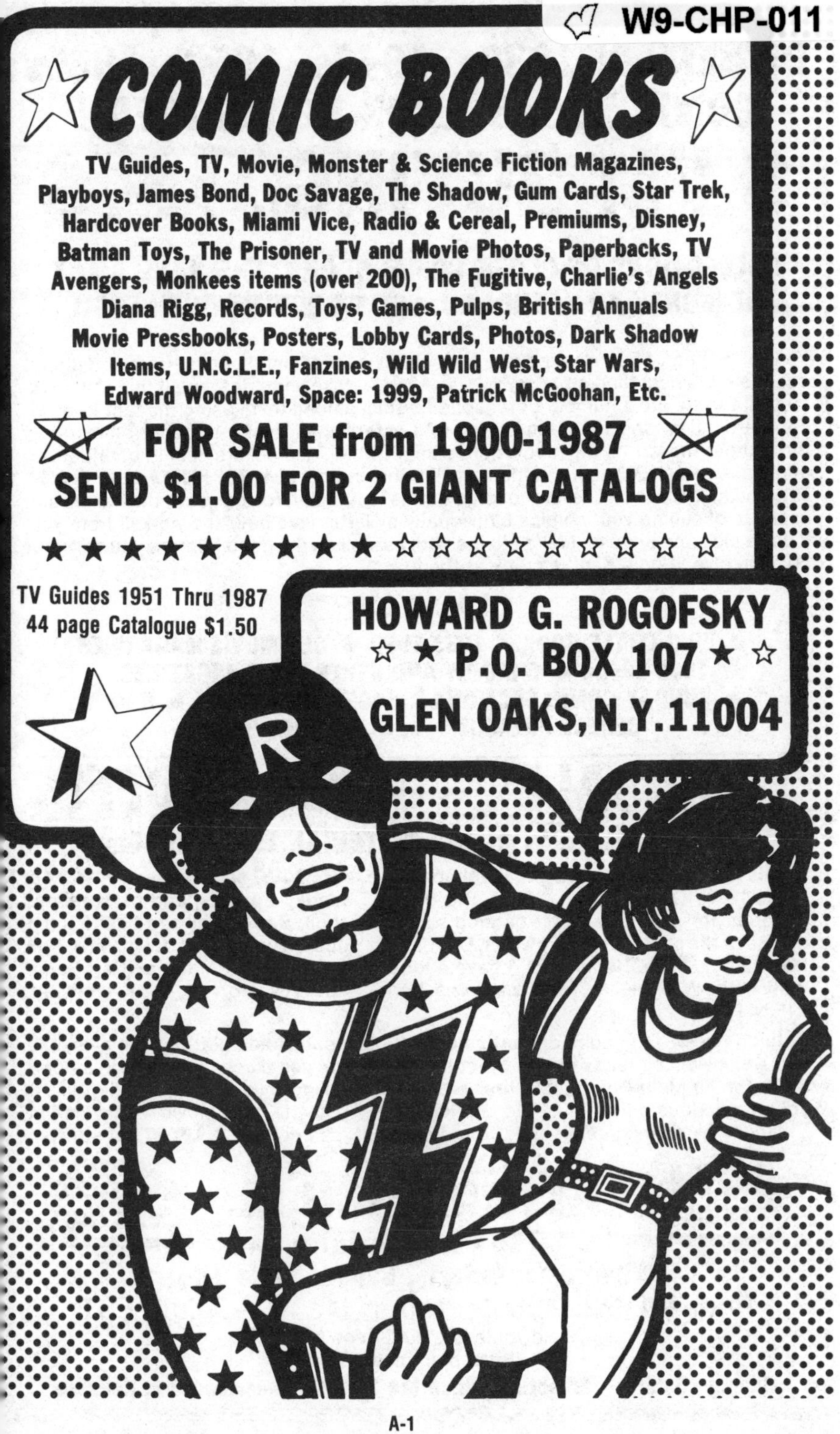

OWNERS OF 1930s - 1940s - 1950s - 1960s COMIC BOOKS: LOOK NO FURTHER!!

$ I'M BUYING. . . .$

COLLECTIONS OF OLDER COMIC BOOKS, AND HAVE A LOT OF MONEY TO SPEND! SO, LET'S DO SOME BUSINESS!!

Year after Year, I buy **more** private collections of old comic books (from collectors, dealers & laymen) than most **anybody, anywhere**! (Make enquiries: you'll find this to be factual.) There are a number of reasons for this, among them being the fact that I've been around a long time, am a very well established dealer in paper collectibles throughout the world, my reputation is impeccible, (and sellers deal in confidence), and I guarantee 100% satisfaction on all transactions. **I PAY TOP PRICES, I PAY PROMPTLY**, and no collection is ever too large for me to handle! You can save the hassle and expense of selling your comics individually by letting me buy "the works" from you. (I don't pick and choose; I take all: the bad, as well as the good.) Before you sell your comics, give "Uncle Ken" a crack at them!

I ALSO BUY:

• "BIG LITTLE BOOKS" 1933-1950 • OLD MOVIE MAGAZINES 1920-1960s • SHADOW AND OTHER PULP MAGAZINES • SUNDAY COMIC SECTIONS & PAGES 1929-1950s • RADIO, CEREAL PREMIUMS • OLD DISNEY BOOKS

FOR SALE — OLDER STUFF!

I SPECIALIZE IN OLDER MATERIAL 1900—1960's

At this time (and most always!), I probably have the **LARGEST** selection and **VARIETY** of 1920s-1960s Comic Books, "Big Little Books," Sunday Funnies, and most related material, for sale. (My latest catalog will verify this). Besides all the **GREAT** companies of the past (Timely, Fawcett, DC, Fiction House, Quality, Dell, Avon, MLJ, Fox, ME, Disney, Prize, Nedor, etc), I have a lot of Special Interest Material (Carl Barks, Walt Kelly, Walt Disney, EC's, westerns, horror, Movie/TV, Marvels, funny types, AD INFINITUM!).

Catalog No. 47 (40 pages of vintage collectibles, and Nostalgia!) is now available, and No. 48 will be ready in a few months. $2.00 gets you a copy (if you're in a hurry, $3.00 for Air-Mail) Refundable first order. An order gets you on my mailing list (if you're a serious collector of old comics, its the place to be!). Movie Magazine list, $1.00 (My catalog-content varies from list to list, as I do have a **LOT** of old stuff).

KEN MITCHELL

710 Conacher Drive
Willowdale, Ontario, Canada M2M 3N6

Phone 416:222-5808, Hours: 11a.m.—9p.m., EST

(Willowdale is a suburb of Toronto)
(By appointment only)

CBG
Customer Service Award — 1985

Buying—Selling—Collecting, since the 1940s—Experienced & Reliable

PRICE GUIDE

1987-1988

17th Edition

BOOKS FROM 1900—PRESENT INCLUDED

CATALOGUE & EVALUATION GUIDE—ILLUSTRATED

By Robert M. Overstreet

SPECIAL CONTRIBUTORS TO THIS EDITION

Terry Taylor, Tom Andrae, Bill Spicer, Bruce Hamilton, Tom Inge Ron Dias and Landon Chesney

SPECIAL ADVISORS TO THIS EDITION

**Bruce Hamilton *Hugh O'Kennon *Ron Pussell *Dave Smith *Walter Wang *John Snyder *Terry Stroud *Jon Warren *Dan Malan *Steve Geppi *Gary Colabuono *Jay Maybruck *Joe Vereneault*

THE HOUSE OF COLLECTIBLES
NEW YORK, NEW YORK 10022

Published by The House of Collectibles and distributed to the book trade by Ballantine Books, a division of Random House, Inc., New York and simultaneously in Canada by Random House of Canada Limited, Toronto.

Published and distributed to the collectors' market by Overstreet Publications, Inc., 780 Hunt Cliff Dr. N.W., Cleveland, TN 37311.

Manufactured in the United States of America

Cover Illustration by Ron Dias

ISBN 0-87637-746-0
ISSN 0891-8872
10 9 8 7 6 5 4 3 2 1

17th Edition

TABLE OF CONTENTS

ACKNOWLEDGEMENTS

Larry Bigman (Frazetta-Williamson data); Glenn Bray (Kurtzman data); Dan Malan & Charles Heffelfinger (Classic Comics data); Gary Carter (DC data); J. B. Clifford Jr. (E. C. data); Gary Coddington (Superman data); Wilt Conine (Fawcett data); Dr. S. M. Davidson (Cupples & Leon data); Al Dellinges (Kubert data); Kevin Hancer (Tarzan data); Charles Heffelfinger and Jim Ivey (March of Comics listing); R. C. Holland and Ron Pussell (Seduction and Parade of Pleasure data); Grant Irwin (Quality data); Richard Kravitz (Kelly data); Phil Levine (giveaway data); Fred Nardelli (Frazetta data); Michelle Nolan (love comics); Mike Nolan (MLJ, Timely, Nedor data); George Olshevsky (Timely data); Richard Olson (LOA data); Scott Pell ('50s data); Greg Robertson (National data); Frank Scigliano (Little Lulu data); Gene Seger (Buck Rogers data); Rick Sloane (Archie data); David R. Smith, Archivist, Walt Disney Productions (Disney data); Don and Maggie Thompson (Four Color listing); Mike Tiefenbacher, Jerry Sinkovec, and Richard Yudkin (Atlas and National data); Raymond True (Classic Comics data); Jim Vadeboncoeur Jr. (Williamson and Atlas data); Kim Weston (Disney and Barks data); Cat Yronwode (Spirit data); Andrew Zerbe and Gary Behymer (M. E. data).

My appreciation must also be extended to Dan Hering, John Snyder, Steve Geppi, Bruce Hamilton, and Jon Warren, who loaned material for photographing, and especially to Hugh and Louise O'Kennon for their support and help. Special acknowledgement is also given to Ron Pussell, Ken Mitchell, Scott Pell, C.M. Peterson and especially to Dan Stevenson for submitting an unusual amount of corrective data; to Dr. Richard Olson for rewriting grading definitions; to Larry Breed for his suggestions on re-organizing the introductory section; to Dan Malan for revamping the Classics section; to Terry Stroud, Hugh O'Kennon, Jon Warren, Dave Smith, Chuck Zepp, Rod Dyke, Jay Maybruck, Jack Mallette, Joe Vereneault, James Payette, John Snyder, Gary Carter, Bill Cole, Rick Sloane, Stephen Fishler, Jerry Wiest, Walter Wang, Steve Geppi, Richard Dell, Gary Colabuono, Mark Brown and Ron Pussell, (pricing); to Tom Inge for his "Chronology of the American Comic Book;" to Terry Taylor for his Snow White article; to Bill Spicer for his editing and layout work; to Tom Andrae for his Disney article; to Bruce Hamilton who did a lot of leg work in setting up the Disney theme for this edition; to Ron Dias for his outstanding cover art; to Landon Chesney and Dave Noah for their work on the key comic book list; to L. B. Cole, Steve Saffel, and Jerry DeFuccio for their counsel and help; to Bill Spicer and Zetta DeVoe (Western Publishing Co.) for their contribution of data; and especially to Bill for his kind permission to reprint portions of his and Jerry Bails' **America's Four Color Pastime**; to Robert Crestohl for his statistical compilation; and to Walter Presswood, Dave Noah, and Jeff Overstreet for their help in editing this volume.

I will always be indebted to Jerry Bails, Landon Chesney, and Larry Bigman whose advice and concern have helped in making **The Comic Book Price Guide** a reality; to my wife Martha for her encouragement and help in putting this reference work together; and to everyone who placed ads in this edition.

Acknowledgement is also due to the following people who have so generously contributed much needed data for this edition:

Aaron Andrade
Jeffrey Backenger
Stephen Baer
Jim Bahler
Robert Barks
Sheila Barnard
Lee J. Barrie
Jon Berk
Morris Berndt

Paul Bernhardt
Brad Bilbo
Dr. John Binder
Earl Blair
Steve Brewster
Frank Brockel
Kerry Brodsky
Andy Brown
David M. Brucas
Steven A. Carey
Bob Cherry
David Clark
L.B. Cole
Amata Crawford
Dan Crawford
David H. Curtis
Craig Delich
Edward F. Fausel
Stephen Fishler
Danny Fuchs
Dana Gabbard
Sebastien Gaudet
Leonard P. Gray
Joseph Grissell
Michael J. Gronsky
Jay E. Hadley
David Gerald C. Hamilton
Steve Haynie
John Hosier
Jerry F. Howell
Bill Hutchison
Terry Julian

Chris Khalat
David Klees
Timothy A. Krubsack
Charles N. LaPress
Rod Lewis
Martin Lock
Frank Lopiccolo, Jr.
Gregg Mackler
Don Mangus
Greg Z. Manos
Don Maris
Kevin Martz
Gary P. Marusary
Robert Mathis
John C. McGonigle
James P. McLoughlin
Jeff Melius
Ken Mitchell
Robert E. Myers
Raymond A. Ossman
David Peattie
Scott Pell
C.M. Peterson
Brian Powell
Gary P. Raber
Aaron Rakhra
Stanley Resnick
Don B. Rhoden
J. Richard
Daniel J. Ringel
David Roach

Paul Roach
Steven Rowe
Mike Sagert
Michael Sanchez
Joe Sarno
Ben Schillinger
Gary A. Shuster
Calvin Slobodian
David R. Smith
William Smith
David Sorochty
Bill Sprague
Dan Stevenson
Ray Storch
Robert Tabor
Brad Tenan
James Thompson
Peter R. Thorpe
Mike Tickal
Joe Torcivia
Jeff Walker
M.D. Warner
Lawrence Watt-Evans
Ken Wedertz
Mike Wileman
Gerald Williamson
Clint Wilcox
Dan Wright, Ph.D.
Catherine Yronwode
Randall Zbiciak
Monty Zutz

PREFACE

Comic book values listed in this reference work were recorded from convention sales, dealers' lists, adzines, and by special contact with dealers and collectors from coast to coast. Prices paid for rare comics vary considerably from one locale to another. We have attempted to list a realistic average between the lowest and highest range observed. The reader should keep in mind that the prices listed only reflect the market just prior to publication. Any new trends that have developed since the preparation of this book would not be shown.

The values listed are reports, not estimates. Each new edition of the guide is actually an average report of sales that occurred during the year; not an estimate of what we feel the books will be bringing next year. Even though many prices listed will remain current throughout the year, the wise user of this book would keep abreast of current market trends to get the fullest potential out of his invested dollar.

By the same token, many of the scarcer books are seldom offered for sale in top condition. This makes it difficult to arrive at a realistic market value. Some of the issues in this category are: Action No. 1, All-American No. 16, Batman No. 1, Black and White No. 20, Captain America No. 1, Captain Marvel No. 1, Detective No. 27, Double Action No. 2, the No-Number Feature Books, Green Giant No. 1, March of Comics No. 4, Marvel No. 1, More Fun No. 52, Motion Picture Funnies Weekly No. 1, Silver Streak No. 6, Superman No. 1, Tough Kid Squad No. 1, Whiz No. 2 (No. 1), Wonder No. 1, Amazing Man No. 5, and Wow No. 1.

Some rare comics were published in a complete black and white format; i.e., All-New No. 15, Blood Is the Harvest, Boy Explorers No. 2, Eerie No. 1, Flash Gordon No. 5, If the Devil Would Talk, Is This Tomorrow, and Stuntman No. 3. As we have learned in the case of Eerie No. 1, the collector or investor in these books would be well advised to give due consideration to the possibility of counterfeits before investing large sums of money.

This book is the most comprehensive listing of comic books ever attempted. Comic book titles, dates of first and last issues, publishing companies, origin and special issues are listed when known.

The Guide will be listing only American comic books due to space limitation. Some variations of the regular comic book format will be listed. These basically include those pre-1933 comic strip reprint books with varying size—usually with cardboard covers, but sometimes with hardback. As forerunners of the modern comic book format, they deserve to be listed despite their obvious differences in presentation. Other books that will be listed are giveaway comics—but only those that contain known characters, work by known artists, or those of special interest.

All titles are listed as if they were one word, ignoring spaces, hyphens and apostrophes. Page counts listed will always include covers.

IMPORTANT. Prices listed in this book are in U. S. currency and are for your reference only. This book is not a dealer's price list, although some dealers may base their prices on the values listed. The true value of any comic book is what you are willing to pay. Prices listed herein are an indication of what collectors (not dealers) would probably pay. For one reason or another, these collectors might want certain books badly, or else need specific issues to complete their runs and so are willing to pay more. Dealers are not in a position to pay the full prices listed, but work on a percentage depending largely on the amount of investment required and the quality of material offered. Usually they will pay from 20 to 70 percent of the list price depending on how long it will take them to sell the collection after making the investment; the higher the demand and better the condition, the more the percentage. Most dealers are faced with expenses such as advertising, travel, telephone and mailing, plus convention costs. These costs all go in before the books are sold. The high demand books usually sell right away but there are many other titles that are difficult to sell due to low demand. Sometimes a dealer will have cost tied up in this type of material for several years before finally moving it. Remember, his position is that of handling, demand and overhead. Most dealers are victims of these economics.

Everyone connected with the publication of this book advocates the collecting of comic books for fun and pleasure, as well as for nostalgia, art, and cultural values. Second to this is investment, which, if wisely placed in the best quality books (condition and contents considered), will yield dividends over the long term. The publisher of this reference work is a collector and has no comic books for sale.

TERMINOLOGY

Many of the following terms and abbreviations are used in the comic book market and are explained here:

a—Story art; **a(i)**—Story art inks; **a(p)**—Story art pencils; **a(r)**—Story art reprint.

B&W—Black and white art.

Bondage cover—Usually denotes a female in bondage.

c—Cover art; **c(i)**—Cover inks; **c(p)**—Cover pencils; **c(r)**—Cover reprint.

Cameo—When a character appears briefly in one or two panels.

Colorist—Artist that applies color to the pen and ink art.

Con—A Convention or public gathering of fans.

Cosmic Aeroplane—Refers to a large collection discovered by Cosmic Aeroplane Books.

Debut—The first time that a character appears anywhere.

Drug propaganda story—Where comic makes an editorial stand about drug abuse.

Drug use story—Shows the actual use of drugs: shooting, taking a trip, harmful effects, etc.

Fanzine—An amateur fan publication.

File Copy—A high grade comic originating from the publisher's file.

First app.—Same as debut.

Flashback—When a previous story is being recalled.

G. A.—Golden Age (1930s—1950s).

Headlight—Protruding breasts.

i—Art inks.

Infinity cover—Shows a scene that repeats itself to infinity.

Inker—Artist that does the inking.

Intro—Same as debut.

JLA—Justice League of America.

JSA—Justice Society of America.

Lamont Larson—Refers to a large high grade collection of comics. Many of the books have Lamont or Larson written on the cover.

Logo—The title of a strip or comic book as it appears on the cover or title page.

Mile High—Refers to a large NM-Mint collection of comics originating from Denver, Colorado (Edgar Church collection).

nd—No date.

nn—No number.

N. Y. Legis. Comm.—New York Legislative Committee to Study the Publication of Comics (1951).
Origin—When the story of the character's creation is given.
p—Art pencils.
Penciler—Artist that does the pencils.
POP—**Parade of Pleasure**, book about the censorship of comics.
Poughkeepsie—Refers to a large collection of Dell Comics' "file copies" believed to have originated from Poughkeepsie, N. Y.
R or r—Reprint.
Rare—10 to 20 copies estimated to exist.
Reprint comics—Comic books that contain newspaper strip reprints.
S. A.—Silver Age (1956—Present).
Scarce—20 to 100 copies estimated to exist.
Silver proof—A black & white actual size print on thick glossy paper given to the colorist to indicate colors to the engraver.
S&K—Simon and Kirby (artists).
SOTI—**Seduction of the Innocent**, book about the censorship of comics.
Splash panel—A large panel that usually appears at the front of a comic story.
Very rare—1 to 10 copies estimated to exist.
X-over—When one character crosses over into another's strip.
Zine—See Fanzine.

Marvel comic books are cover coded for the direct sales (comic shop), newsstand, and foreign markets. They are all first printings, with the special coding being the only difference. The comics sold to the comic shops have to be coded differently, as they are sold on a no-return basis while newsstand comics are not. The Price Guide has not detected any price difference between these versions.

Direct Sales
(Comic Shops)

Newsstand

Newsstand
Overseas

Marvel Reprints: In recent years Marvel has reprinted some of their comics. There has been confusion in identifying the reprints from the originals. However, in 99 percent of the cases, the reprints will list "reprint," or "2nd printing," etc. in the indicia, along with a later copyright date in some cases. The only known exceptions are a few of the movie books such as *Star Wars*, the *Marvel Treasury Editions*, and tie-in books such as *G. I. Joe*. These books were reprinted and not identified as reprints. The *Star Wars* reprints have a large diamond with no date and a blank UPC symbol on the cover. The other reprints will have some cover variation such as a date missing, different colors, etc.

Gold Key comics were sold with two different labels: Whitman and Gold Key. There are collectors who prefer the Gold Key labels to Whitman, although the Price Guide does not differentiate in the price. Beginning in 1980, all comics produced by Western carried the Whitman label.

Many of the better artists are pointed out. When more than one artist worked on a story, their names are separated by a (/). The first name did the pencil drawings and the second did the inks. When two or more artists work on a story, only the most prominent will be noted in some cases. There has been some confusion in past editions as to which artists to list and which to leave out. We wish all good artists could be listed, but due to space limitation, only the most popular can. The following list of artists are considered to be either the most collected in the comic field or are historically significant and should be pointed out. Artists designated below with an (*) indicate that only their most noted work will be listed. The rest will eventually have all their work shown as the information becomes available. This list could change from year to year as new artists come into prominence.

Adams, Neal
*Aparo, Jim
*Austin, Terry
Baker, Matt
Barks, Carl
Beck, C. C.
Brunner, Frank
*Buscema, John
Byrne, John
*Check, Sid
Cole, Jack
Cole, L. B.
Craig, Johnny
Crandall, Reed
Davis, Jack
Disbrow, Jayson
*Ditko, Steve
Eisner, Will
*Elder, Bill
Evans, George
Everett, Bill
Feldstein, Al
Fine, Lou
Foster, Harold
Fox, Matt
Frazetta, Frank
Giffen, Keith
Golden, Michael
Gottfredson, Floyd
*Guardineer, Fred
Gustavson, Paul
*Heath, Russ
Howard, Wayne
Ingels, Graham
Jones, Jeff
Kamen, Jack
Kane, Bob
*Kane, Gil
Kelly, Walt
Kinstler, E. R.
Kirby, Jack
Krenkel, Roy
Krigstein, Bernie
*Kubert, Joe
Kurtzman, Harvey
Manning, Russ
*Meskin, Mort
Miller, Frank
Moreira, Ruben
*Morisi, Pete
*Nasser, Mike
*Newton, Don
Nostrand, Howard
Orlando, Joe
Pakula, Mac (Toth inspired)
*Palais, Rudy
*Perez, George
Powell, Bob
Raboy, Mac
Raymond, Alex
Ravielli, Louis
*Redondo, Nestor
Rogers, Marshall
Schomburg, Alex
Siegel & Shuster
Simon & Kirby (S&K)
*Simonson, Walt
Smith, Barry
Smith, Paul
Stanley, John
Starlin, Jim
Steranko, Jim
Torres, Angelo
Toth, Alex
Tuska, George
Ward, Bill
Williamson, Al
Woggon, Bill
Wolverton, Basil
Wood, Wallace
Wrightson, Bernie

The following abbreviations are used with the cover reproductions throughout the book for copyright credit purposes. The companies they represent are listed here:

ACE—Ace Periodicals
ACG—American Comics Group
AJAX—Ajax-Farrell
AP—Archie Publications
ATLAS—Atlas Comics (see below)
AVON—Avon Periodicals
BP—Better Publications
C & L—Cupples & Leon
CC—Charlton Comics
CEN—Centaur Publications
CCG—Columbia Comics Group
CG—Catechetical Guild
CHES—Harry 'A' Chesler
CLDS—Classic Det. Stories
CM—Comics Magazine
DC—DC Comics, Inc.
DELL—Dell Publishing Co.
DMP—David McKay Publishing
DS—D. S. Publishing Co.
EAS—Eastern Color Printing Co.
EC—E. C. Comics
ENWIL—Enwil Associates
EP—Elliott Publications
ERB—Edgar Rice Burroughs
FAW—Fawcett Publications
FF—Famous Funnies
FH—Fiction House Magazines
FOX—Fox Features Syndicate
GIL—Gilberton
GK—Gold Key
GP—Great Publications
HARV—Harvey Publications
HILL—Hillman Periodicals
HOKE—Holyoke Publishing Co.
KING—King Features Syndicate
LEV—Lev Gleason Publications
MCG—Marvel Comics Group
ME—Magazine Enterprises
MLJ—MLJ Magazines
NOVP—Novelty Press
PG—Premier Group
PINE—Pines
PMI—Parents' Magazine Institute
PRIZE—Prize Publications
QUA—Quality Comics Group
REAL—Realistic Comics
RH—Rural Home
S & S—Street and Smith Publishers
SKY—Skywald Publications
STAR—Star Publications
STD—Standard Comics
STJ—St. John Publishing Co.
SUPR—Superior Comics
TC—Tower Comics
TM—Trojan Magazines
TOBY—Toby Press
UFS—United Features Syndicate
VITL—Vital Publications
WDC—The Walt Disney Company
WEST—Western Publishing Co.
WHIT—Whitman Publishing Co.
WHW—William H. Wise
WMG—William M. Gaines (E. C.)
WP—Warren Publishing Co.
YM—Youthful Magazines
Z-D—Ziff-Davis Publishing Co.

TIMELY/MARVEL/ATLAS COMICS. "A Marvel Magazine" and "Marvel Group" was the symbol used between December 1946 and May 1947 (not used on all titles/issues during period). The Timely Comics symbol was used between July 1942 and September 1942 (not on all titles/issues during period). The round "Marvel Comic" symbol was used between February 1949 and June 1950. Early comics code symbol (star and bar) was used between April 1952 and February 1955. The Atlas globe symbol was used between December 1951 and September 1957. The M over C symbol (beginning of Marvel Comics) was used between July 1961 until the price increased to 12¢ on February 1962.

TIMELY/MARVEL/ATLAS Publishers' Abbreviation Codes:

ACI—Animirth Comics, Inc.
AMI—Atlas Magazines, Inc.
ANC—Atlas News Co., Inc.
BPC—Bard Publishing Corp.
BFP—Broadcast Features Pubs.
CBS—Crime Bureau Stories
CIDS—Classic Detective Stories
CCC—Comic Combine Corp.
CDS—Current Detective Stories
CFI—Crime Files, Inc.
CmPI—Comedy Publications, Inc.
CmPS—Complete Photo Story
CnPC—Cornell Publishing Corp.
CPC—Chipiden Publishing Corp.
CPI—Crime Publications, Inc.
CPS—Canam Publishing Sales Corp.
CSI—Classics Syndicate, Inc.
DCI—Daring Comics, Inc.
EPC—Euclid Publishing Co.
EPI—Emgee Publications, Inc.
FCI—Fantasy Comics, Inc.
FPI—Foto Parade, Inc.
GPI—Gem Publishing, Inc.
HPC—Hercules Publishing Corp.
IPS—Interstate Publishing Corp.
JPI—Jaygee Publications, Inc.
LBI—Lion Books, Inc.
LCC—Leading Comic Corp.
LMC—Leading Magazine Corp.
MALE—Male Publishing Corp.
MAP—Miss America Publishing Corp.
MCI—Marvel Comics, Inc.
MgPC—Margood Publishing Corp.
MJMC—Marjean Magazine Corp.
MMC—Mutual Magazine Corp.
MPC—Medalion Publishing Corp.
MPI—Manvis Publications, Inc.
NPI—Newsstand Publications, Inc.
NPP—Non-Pareil Publishing Corp.
OCI—Official Comics, Inc.
OMC—Official Magazine Corp.
OPI—Olympia Publications, Inc.
PPI—Postal Publications, Inc.
PrPI—Prime Publications, Inc.
RCM—Red Circle Magazines, Inc.
SAI—Sports Actions, Inc.
SePI—Select Publications, Inc.
SnPC—Snap Publishing Co.
SPC—Select Publishing Co.
SPI—Sphere Publications, Inc.
TCI—Timely Comics, Inc.
TP—Timely Publications
20 CC—20th Century Comics Corp.
USA—U.S.A. Publications, Inc.
VPI—Vista Publications, Inc.
WFP—Western Fiction Publishing
WPI—Warwick Publications, Inc.
YAI—Young Allies, Inc.
ZPC—Zenith Publishing Co., Inc.

YOUR INFORMATION IS NEEDED: In order to make future Guides more accurate and complete, we are interested in any relevant information or facts that you might have. **Relevant and significant data includes:**

Works by the artists named elsewhere. **Caution:** Most artists did not sign their work and many were imitated by others. When submitting this data, advise whether the work was signed or not. In many cases, it takes an expert to identify certain artists—so extreme caution should be observed in submitting this data.
Issues mentioned by Wertham and others in **Seduction, Parade**...
Origin issues.
First and last appearances of strips or characters.
Title continuity information.
Beginning and ending numbers of runs.
Atomic bomb, Christmas, Flag and infinity covers.
Swipes.
Photo covers.

To record something in the Guide, **documented** facts are needed. Please send a photo copy of indicia or page in question if possible.

Non-relevent data—Most giveaway comics will not be listed. Literally thousands of titles came out, many of which have educational themes. We will only list significant collectible giveaways such as March of Comics, Disney items, communist books (but not civil defense educational comics), and books that contain illustrated stories by top artists or top collected characters.

Good Luck and Happy Hunting...

Robert M. Overstreet

Robert M. Overstreet

Advertise in the Guide

This book reaches more serious comic collectors than any other publication and has proven ad results due to its world-wide circulation and use. Your ad will pull all year long until the new edition comes out.

Display Ad space is sold in full, half, fourth, and eighth page sizes. Ad rates are set in the early fall prior to each edition's release. Write at that time for rates (between Oct.—Dec.).

PRINTED SIZES

FULL PAGE—8" long x 5" wide. HALF PAGE—4" long x 5" wide. FOURTH PAGE—4" long x 2½" wide. EIGHTH PAGE—2" long x 2½" wide. CLASSIFIED ADS will be retyped and reduced about one-half. No artwork permitted. Rate is based on your 4" typed line. DISPLAY CLASSIFIED ADS: The use of borders or bold face type or cuts or other decorations change your classified ad to display—rates same as regular display.

NOTE: Submit your ad on white paper in a proportionate version of the actual printed size. All full —Quarter page advertisers will receive a complimentary copy of the Guide. The NEW Guide will be professionally done throughout...so to reflect a consistently high quality from cover to cover, we must ask that all ads be neatly and professionally done. Full payment must be sent with all ads. All but classified ads will be run as is.

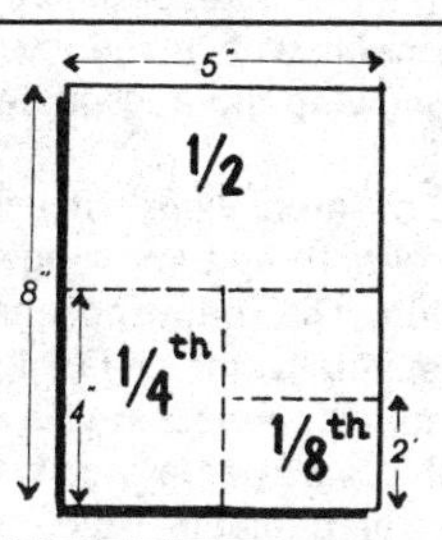

AD DEADLINE - COLOR—Nov. 15th
AD DEADLINE-Black & White—Jan. 15th

Overstreet Publications, Inc.
780 Hunt Cliff Dr. N.W.
Cleveland, Tennessee 37311

The PRICE GUIDE has become the STANDARD REFERENCE WORK in the field and is distributed to thousands of comic collectors throughout the world. Don't miss this opportunity to advertise in the Guide.

NOTICE: All advertisements are accepted and placed in the Price Guide in good faith. However, we cannot be held responsible for any losses incurred in your dealings with the advertisers. If, after receiving legitimate complaints, and there is sufficient evidence to warrant such action, these advertisers will be dropped from future editions.

SPECIAL NOTICE

If copyrighted characters are planned for your ad, the following must be done: Send a copy of your ad layout (including characters) to the company(s) or copyright owner(s) involved requesting permission for their use. A copy of this permission must be sent to us with your ad. DC Comics and Marvel Comics have indicated that you will have no problem getting permission, so if you must use their characters...write for the permission. For DC, write: Public Relations, DC Comics, Inc., 666 Fifth Ave., New York, NY, 10103. For Marvel, write: Marvel Comics, c/o Carol Kalish, 575 Madison Ave., N. Y., N.Y. 10022. Other companies such as Disney could be more of a problem. At any rate, we cannot accept any ads with copyrighted characters without a copy of the permission.

GRADING COMIC BOOKS

Before a comic book's true value can be assessed, its condition or state of preservation must be determined. In most comic books, especially in the rarer issues, the better the condition, the more desirable the book. The scarcer first and/or origin issues in PRISTINE MINT condition will bring several times the price of the same book in POOR condition. The grading of a comic book is done by simply looking at the book and describing its condition, which may range from absolutely perfect newsstand condition (PRISTINE MINT) to extremely worn, dirty, and torn (POOR). Numerous variables influence the evaluation of a comic's condition and **all** must be considered in the final evaluation. More important characteristics include tears, missing pieces, wrinkles, stains, yellowing, brittleness, tape repairs, water marks, spine roll, writing, and cover lustre. The significance of each of these will be described more fully in the grading scale definitions. As grading is the most subjective aspect of determining a comic's value, it is very important that the grader must be careful and not allow wishful thinking to influence what the eyes see. It is also very important to realize that older comics in above MINT condition are extremely scarce and are rarely advertised for sale; most of the nicer comics advertised range from VERY FINE to NEAR MINT. To the novice, grading will appear difficult at first, but as experience is gained, accuracy will improve. Whenever in doubt, consult with a reputable dealer or experienced collector in your area. The following grading guide is given to aid the panelologist.

GRADING DEFINITIONS

The hardest part of evaluating a comic is being honest and objective with yourself, and knowing what characteristics to look for in making your decision. The following characteristics should be checked in evaluating books, especially those in higher grades: degree of cover lustre, degree of color fading, staples, staple areas, spine condition, top and bottom of spine, edges of cover, centering, brittleness, browning/yellowing, flatness, tightness, interior damage, tape, tears, folds, water marks, color flaking, and general cleanliness.

VERY IMPORTANT: A book must be graded in its entirety; not by just the cover alone. A book in any of the grades listed must be in its **ORIGINAL** unrestored condition. Restored books must be graded as such; i.e., a restored book grading Fine might only be worth the same as a Very Good copy in its unrestored state. The value of an extensively restored book tends to usually be halfway between the value of its original state and the condition it appears to be after restoration. Examine books very closely for repairing before purchase. Major things to look for are: bleaching, trimming, interior spine and tear reinforcement, gluing, restapling, and recoloring. Dealers should state that a book has been restored and not expect to get as much as a book unrestored in that condition would bring. **Note:** Cleaning, stain removal, rolled spine removal, staple replacement, etc., if professionally done, would not be considered restoration as long as the printed condition of the comic has not been changed. After examining these characteristics a comic may be assigned to one of the following grades:

PRISTINE MINT (PM): Absolutely perfect in every way, regardless of age. The cover has full lustre, is crisp, and shows no imperfections of any sort. The cover and all pages are extra white and fresh; the spine is tight, flat, and clean; not even the slightest blemish can be detected around staples, along spine, at corners or edges. Arrival dates pencilled on the cover are acceptable. As comics must be truly perfect to be graded PM, they are obviously extremely scarce even on the newsstand. Books prior to 1960 in this grade bring 20 to 250 per cent more.

MINT (M): Like new or newsstand condition, as above, but with very slight loss of lustre, or a slight off-centered cover, or a minor printing error. Could have pencilled arrival dates, slight color fading, and white to extra white cover and pages. Any defects noticeable would be very minor and attributable to the cutting, folding and stapling process.

NEAR MINT (NM): Almost perfect; tight spine, flat and clean; just enough minor defects of wear noticeable with close inspection to keep it out of the MINT category; i.e., a small flake of color missing at a staple, corner or edge, or slight discoloration on inside cover or pages; near perfect cover gloss retained.

VERY FINE (VF): Slight wear beginning to show; possibly a small wrinkle or crease at staples or where cover has been opened a few times; still clean and flat with most of cover gloss retained. Slight yellowing acceptable.

FINE (FN): Tight cover with some wear, but still relatively flat, clean and shiny with no subscription crease, writing on cover, yellowed margins or tape repairs. Stress lines around staples and along spine beginning to show; minor color flaking possible at spine, staples, edges or corners. Slight yellowing acceptable.

VERY GOOD (vg): Obviously a read copy with original printing lustre and gloss almost gone; some discoloration, but not soiled; some signs of wear and minor markings, but none that deface the cover; usually needs slight repair around staples and along spine which could be rolled; cover could have a minor tear or crease where a corner was folded under or a loose centerfold; no chunks missing. Slight yellowing acceptable.

GOOD (g): An average used copy complete with both covers and no panels missing; slightly soiled or marked with possible creases, minor tears or splits, rolled spine and small color flaking, but perfectly sound and legible. A well-read copy, but perfectly acceptable with no chunks missing. **Minor** tape repairs and slight browning (no brittleness) acceptable, although tape repairs should be considered a defect and priced accordingly.

FAIR (f): Very heavily read and soiled, but complete with possibly a small chunk out of cover; tears needing repairs and multiple folds and wrinkles likely; damaged by the elements, but completely sound and legible, bringing 50-70% of good price.

POOR (p): Damaged; heavily weathered; soiled; or otherwise unsuited for collection purposes.

COVERLESS (c): Coverless comics turn up frequently, are usually hard to sell and in many cases are almost worthless. It takes ingenuity and luck to get a good price; e.g., color xerox covers will increase the salability. A cover of an expensive book is scarcer and worth more. However, certain "high demand" issues could bring up to 30 percent of the good price.

IMPORTANT: Comics in all grades with fresh extra white pages usually bring more. Books with defects such as pages or panels missing, coupons cut, torn or taped covers and pages, brown or brittle pages, restapled, taped spines, pages or covers, water-marked, printing defects, rusted staples, stained, holed, or other imperfections that distract from the original beauty, are worth less than if free of these defects.

Many of the early strip reprint comics were printed in hardback with dust jackets. Books with dust jackets are worth more. The value can increase from 20 to 50 percent depending on the rarity of book. Usually, the earlier the book, the greater the percentage. Unless noted, prices listed are without dust jackets. The condition of the dust jacket should be graded independently of the book itself.

STORAGE OF COMIC BOOKS

Acids left in comic book paper during manufacture are the primary cause of aging and yellowing. Improper storage can accelerate the aging process.

The importance of storage is proven when looking at the condition of books from large collections that have surfaced over the past few years. In some cases, an entire collection has brown or yellowed pages approaching brittleness. Collections of this type were probably stored in too much heat or moisture, or exposed to atmospheric pollution (sulfur dioxide) or light. On the other hand, other collections of considerable age (30 to 50 years) have emerged with snow white pages and little sign of aging. Thus we learn that proper storage is imperative to insure the long life of our comic book collections.

Store books in a dark, cool place with an ideal relative humidity of 50 percent and a temperature of 40 to 50 degrees or less. Air conditioning is recommended. Do not use regular cardboard boxes, since most contain harmful acids. Use acid-free boxes instead. Seal books in Mylar[1] or other suitable wrappings or bags and store them in the proper containers or cabinets, to protect them from heat, excessive dampness, ultraviolet light (use tungsten filament lights), polluted air, and dust.

Many collectors seal their books in plastic bags and store them in a cool dark room in cabinets or on shelving. Plastic bags should be changed every two to three years, since most contain harmful acids. Cedar chest storage is recommended, but the ideal method of storage is to stack your comics (preferably in Mylar[1] bags) vertically in acid-free boxes. The boxes can be arranged on shelving for easy access. Storage boxes, plastic bags, backing boards, Mylar[1] bags, archival supplies, etc. are available from dealers. (See ads in this edition.)

Some research has been done on deacidifying comic book paper, but no easy or inexpensive, clear-cut method is available to the average collector. The best and longest-lasting procedure involves soaking the paper in solutions or spraying each page with specially prepared solutions. These procedures should be left to experts. Covers of comics pose a special problem in deacidifying due to their varied composition of papers used.

Here is a list of persons who offer services in restoration or archival supplies:

—Wei T'o Associates, Inc., 21750 Main St., Unit No. 27, P.O. Drawer 40, Matteson, IL 60443. Manufactures deacidification solutions.
—Restorations, 563 N. Pine St., Nevada City, CA 95959. PH: (916) 477-5527.

[1]*Mylar is a registered trademark of the DuPont Company.*

—The Art Conservatory, Mark Wilson, P.O. Box 705, Union City, CA 94587. Restoration.
—Bill Cole, P.O. Box 60, Wollaston, MA 02170. Archival supplies, storage protection, deacidification solutions.
—The Restoration Lab, P.O. Box 632, New Town Branch, Boston, Mass. 02258. PH: (617) 924-4297.

1986 MARKET REPORT

by Bob Overstreet,

Stable national economic growth and lower interest rates provided the necessary atmosphere for another year of expansion in the comic marketplace Increases in this market continued to outdistance leading national economic indicators for the same period. Given the favorable national economic outlook, one may expect that similar type increases in the comic marketplace may be expected in the coming year.

Large collections arriving in the marketplace during the second half of the year appeared and just as quickly disappeared into private collections, and were priced significantly higher than those previously offered. Titles and issues rarely offered began appearing for the first time in many years at very high prices.

The hottest title during 1986 was *Batman* and related comics (*Detective*), probably due in part to DC's release of *Batman: The Dark Knight Returns* by Frank Miller. This new title was a smash hit, with the first three issues going into three printings each to meet demand. Number one, first printing, was selling for $20-$30 each at year's end. Consequently, interest in all early appearances of *Batman* skyrocketed in the marketplace. During the year many dealers reported being literally wiped out of early issues of *Batman* and *Detective Comics.*

The comic market of late is becoming more and more sophisticated in recognizing the rarity of certain early issues and, more particularly, of those issues in nice condition. For instance only one copy of *Action Comics* No. 1 and *Whiz Comics* No. 1 are known to exist in mint condition. The best known copy of *Detective Comics* No. 1 is in fn-vf, and No. 27 is vf-nm condition.

Those who trade in books of this caliber know that only a few copies exist in high grade (vf-nm) with possibly only one in true mint condition. This is why in some cases a vf-nm copy will sell for above the listed mint price. The person who pays this price knows he is getting probably the 2nd or 3rd best copy in existence. Such a sale occurred at the 1986 San Diego con. A vf-nm *Action* No. 1 sold for a record $30,000 cash. Another vf-nm copy brought $28,000 late in the year. If the one known mint copy of *Action* No. 1 ever sold, it would probably fetch a record price of $60,000-$80,000.

As was the case last year, one of the more active areas of the Golden Age market during the past twelve months was sales activity pertaining to "Mile High" comics. While the value of "Mile High" books has a relation to the overall market, sales of these books need be viewed as distinct; they reflect the extraordinary appeal and demand for these particular books from this particular collection. Because of the tremendous historical significance of this

[1] *With helpful assistance from Steve Geppi, Hugh O'Kennon, Ron Pussell, Jay Maybruck, Joe Vereneault, Dan Malan, Rick Sloane, John Snyder, Terry Stroud, Gary Colabuono, Walter Wang, James Payette, Jon Warren, Stephen Fishler, Bruce Hamilton, Joe Mannarino, Kathy Morby, Martin Hilland and Bill Grandey.*

collection, a "Mile High" copy will sell for far more than will an identical condition book which is not from this collection. The distinct nature of the "Mile High" collection (see the Market Report in No. 16 guide for further details) has resulted in reasonably good records of the sale and ownership of these issues. Since a collector or investor is paying a substantial premium for genuine "Mile High" issues, he would be well advised to be certain of the authenticity of any "Mile High" copy he acquires. The following individuals can, in most cases, provide ownership or authenticity information on "Mile High" comics: Chuck Rozanski of Mile High Comics, Steve Geppi of Diamond Distr., Joe Vereneault of Sparkle City Comics, John Verseil of Comic Heaven, Ron Pussell of Redbeard's Book Den, and John Snyder.

Comics from the "Mile High" collection are currently selling at between 1.75 and 3.5 times mint guide, with certain key comics, select DC, Centaur, and Timely books in particular, bringing more.

Many record prices were set during 1986 causing increased prices throughout this edition. The most newsworthy sale was the "Mile High" copy of *Marvel Comics* No. 1. A collector traded key early DCs valued at $69,000 for this book. He later traded it to another collector for $80,000 worth of key material. The actual cash value of this copy would be impossible to determine based on the two trades, but would be substantial and somewhere beyond $50,000-$60,000. The "Mile High" run of Jungle changed hands at 2.75 times mint guide.

The title of the guide has changed this year due to a change in publishers. Beginning with this edition, Ballantine Books will be distributing the guide to the bookstore trade. We are proud to be represented by such a large and prestigious firm. With Ballantine, the guide's circulation should expand dramatically.

A more detailed recap of the market follows, broken down by periods, publishers and/or genres:

1930s TITLES: As was the case last year, supplies from this period could not keep up with demand. More and more collectors are becoming aware of the rarity of many of these early books, especially in condition. The hottest 30s title was *Detective Comics* followed by other early DC titles, *More Fun* and *Adventure*. A fn copy of *Detective* No. 1 sold for $5,500; another No. 1 in fn brought $6,000. A No. 3 in good sold for $300; a No. 3 in fair sold for $500 and a No. 6 in vf brought $700. At the San Diego Con, dealers were paying multiples times guide for early issues of *Detective*. A fair-good set of *New Fun* No. 1-6 sold for 10 times guide; a *New Comics* No. 3-6 set in fair brought $65 each; a *More Fun* No. 9 in fair to good sold for $700; a No. 14 in vg brought $225. *100 Pages Of Comics* No. 1 in mint brought $750 and *Western Picture Stories* No. 1 in vf sold for $450. A *Comics Magazine* No. 1 in g + sold for $300. These prices are an indication of market demand for these key early books. Many of the 30s titles are on the move and offer excellent investment potential for the future as supplies become more exhausted.

1940s TITLES: The superhero titles remained in high demand throughout the year, along with science fiction and jungle-theme books. Most No. 1s and other key books were highly sought after. The DC Superman, Batman, Flash, All Star and Green Lantern titles were the highest in demand, followed by Timely, Centaur, Fox and MLJ. Most other genres held their own with some renewed interest in late 40s Fox and Fiction House good-girl art titles. Western comics were moderate to hot depending upon the region of the country. A *Superworld* No. 1 (Denver copy) sold for $500.

DC—Most all DC comics enjoyed good growth and remained the hottest area in comics. *Detective Comics* No. 1 and 27, *Action Comics* No. 1, *Batman* No. 1, *All-American* No. 16, *Flash Comics* No. 1 and *All Star Comics* No. 3 seemed to be the hottest single books this year. *Action* No. 1 is showing signs of reclaiming its position as the most valuable single comic book. Its value is arguably equal if not more than *Marvel* No. 1, although the guide doesn't yet show it. As mentioned earlier, *Batman* was the hottest single DC character followed by *All Star Comics, Green Lantern, Flash Comics* and *Superman. Three Batman* No. 1s in vf sold for $5000, $7300 and $7500 respectively; a *Superman* No. 1 in good brought $3100; a No. 24 in mint sold for $750; a No. 53 in vf sold for $400; a *New York World's Fair 1939* in vf sold for $1150; a *Detective* No. 27 in vg sold for $5000 and a vf for $16,500; a No. 29 in vf for $2500; a No. 33 in vf for $2990; a No. 38 in vf+ for $4400; a *Green Lantern* No. 1 in vf brought $2200; an *All-American* No. 16 in fn+ for $3500; No. 16 (Larson copy) for $4750; No. 17 (Larson copy) for $1400; a *More Fun* No. 101 in vf+ for $1250; a No. 73 in vf+ for $1350; a No. 53 in fn for $2500. *All Star* No. 1 in nm sold for $3185; a No. 3 in fn+ for $2600 & $3500; in nm for $4200; a No. 8 in nm for $2000, a No. 16 in nm for $715, a No. 16 (Mile High) for $1365; a *Wonder Woman* No. 1 (Denver copy) sold for $2700; a No. 1 in fn for $650; a *Flash Comics* No. 1 in vf for $2700, in nm for $3500, $4000 and $5000.

Detective Comics is still showing the best rate of return (34.0%), but *Flash Comics* is coming on strong with a 25.8% rate. *Adventure, Green Lantern, More-Fun, Batman, All Star, Star Spangled* and *All American* are all increasing by 20+% per year. All of the above titles show solid investment potential.

Timely—*Captain America, Marvel Mystery, Sub-Mariner* and *Human Torch* still enjoyed immense popularity in the market, selling at and around guide values. A bonafide offer of $10,000 was made for the "Mile High" copy of *Red Raven* No. 1, but was refused. Of course the "bombshell" news of the year was the aforementioned $80,000 "Mile High" *Marvel* No. 1 trade. A *Young Allies* No. 4 in nm brought $375; an *All Winners* No. 13 in nm sold for $180; three *Marvel* No. 1s brought $23,000 in vf, 18,500 in fn+ (Larson), and $19,000 in vf; a *Mystic* No. 2 in nm (Larson) sold for $1,000; a *Captain America* No. 1 in nm for $5,000. Most Timelys are increasing over 10% per year in value, which is much more than current economic indicators, and shouldn't be overlooked in your investment portfolio.

Fox—There was renewed interest in the late 40s titles: *Phantom Lady, Blue Beetle, Zoot, Rulah, Jo-Jo,* etc. The early 40s issues of *Weird, Mystery Men, Fantastic, Wonder/Wonderworld, and Blue Beetle* were in high demand, especially the first issues and those with Lou Fine covers.

Fiction House—The entire line and especially *Planet, Jumbo, Jungle, Rangers, Wings* and *Fight* sold extremely well in all grades. This company continues to show solid gains with *Jumbo* and *Jungle* increasing an average of 22.3 and 27.2% per year respectively. *Sheena, Wambi* and *Ghost* also enjoyed strong demand. Here are some examples of sales: *Jumbo* No. 1 in fn—$1,000, vg+—$500; No. 2 in vg—$600; No. 5 in vf—$600; *Jungle* No. 1 in vf+—$600, nm—$650.

Fawcett—Overall a slow to moderate demand was evident throughout the year. Early issues of *Whiz* and *Captain Marvel* were slow, with later issues moving moderately. Early issues of *Master* were scarce while *Nickel, Marvel Family, Slam Bang, Bulletman, Spy Smasher, Captain Midnite,* et al sold moderately. A vf *Whiz* No. 1 sold for $12,000. There was a lot of interest in the B&W *Flash* and *Thrill* No. 1s, with all available copies selling in the $3,000-$10,000 range. A *Captain Midnite* No. 1 in vf brought $300; a *Captain*

Marvel Jr No. 1 in vf sold for $400; a *Captain Marvel* No. 1 in fn sold for $3,800, and in good for $850. The *Whiz* No. 1 remained the rarest in high grade of the top four books.

Centaur—There was a strong demand for all titles of this early pre-Timely company with most issues selling for over guide. *Amazing-Man* No. 5 is rapidly becoming one of the top investment books exhibiting a 56.3% average annual rate of return over the past five years. In fact, the entire run of *Amazing-Man* is showing a yearly average increase of 38.7%. All Centaurs remained scarce and hard to get. *Detective Picture Stories* No. 1 (the first comic book ever of a single theme) is still undervalued and highly prized by collectors. Most Centaurs are still in the $100-$200 range and offer excellent investment opportunities for the investor. An *Amazing-Man* No. 5 in vg sold for $1,000 while a mixed run of "Mile High" copies of *Amazing Mystery Funnies* sold for 5.5 times mint guide. A *Detective Picture Stories* No. 4 in vg brought $100.

M.L.J.—Most titles of this company showed moderate interest with *Pep, Blue Ribbon, Zip, Top-Notch* and *Jackpot* the most collected. *Katy Keene* was strong with early *Archie* and related comics moderate. A *Pep* No. 1 in nm sold for $1,100; a *Blue Ribbon* No. 1 in vf sold for $475; an *Archie Annual* No. 1 brought $425; a *Shield-Wizard* No. 1 (Denver copy) sold for $750.

Quality—*Blackhawk* and *Military* enjoyed moderate demand. *Hit, Smash, Feature, Police, Plasticman, National,* etc. were slow to moderate but nice runs of these titles were not that plentiful. A *Military* No. 1 in vf sold for $1,050 and a *Police* No. 1 brought $700 in vf.

Classic Comics—Most dealers report growth in *Classics* this year. *Classics* Collectors are increasing, and more and more of them are going after every variation of original and reprint editions. More professional people seem to be entering the market with substantial availability of finances. Demand is drying up sources, and prices are rising. Most key issues sell quickly when collections come out. The hottest items are the first 44 originals, all *Classic Comic* reprints, and any reprints of key numbers such as 8, 14, 20, 21, 33, 40, 43 & 44. The demand for *Classics* giveaways, giants, gift boxes, records, educational series, and newspaper editions remained high. The interest in foreign *Classics* is also growing.

Disney—Check the *Mickey Mouse Magazine* listing which was greatly expanded this year. A few nm copies surfaced and sold for double to triple mint guide. There was a slight increase in demand for early *Comics And Stories* and *Mickey Mouse* one-shots, otherwise most Disney comics were available in ample supply to meet demand. A few mint runs of later '50s-'60s Disneys surfaced and sold easily to anxious collectors.

Gleason—Interest in *Daredevil* and *Silver Streak* seemed to pick up during the year. A *Daredevil* No. 1 (Penn. copy) sold for $1,600. Other Gleason titles enjoyed moderate sales.

Harvey—*Green Hornet, Champ* and *Champion* enjoyed good sales while the later titles, *Richie Rich*, etc. were slow.

Miscellaneous—Many other 40s titles sold well with *Airboy, Bomber, Superworld, Prize, Frankenstein, Miracle, Giggle,* and *Ha Ha* showing high demand. Love comics remained slow with most crime titles selling moderately.

1950s TITLES: Again the more reasonably priced science fiction, movie related, TV related, horror and western titles were most in demand. Most titles showed slow steady growth. Early books with Ditko art sold at a fast clip.

TV Comics—Most TV comics were published by Dell beginning with *Howdy Doody* No. 1 in 1949. Interest in this genre is growing rapidly with many titles becoming highly sought after by collectors. Most all TV westerns which had photo covers were very strong. *Rawhide* with Clint Eastwood photo covers was the hottest title. *Gunsmoke, Maverick* (Roger Moore & James Garner photo covers), *Have Gun Will Travel, Cisco Kid, The Rebel, Laramie, Cheyenne* and *Bonanza* are but a few examples of high demand titles. Jay Ward's *Rocky & Bullwinkle,* Hanna Barbera's *Flintstones,* along with *Dark Shadows,* and *The Three Stooges* were hot. Annette Funicello photo covers, *Ricky Nelson, Gomer Pyle, Andy Griffith, Captain Kangaroo, The Life Of Riley, Man From Uncle, Honey West, I Love Lucy* and a host of other TV titles sold at multiples of mint guide. DCs and St. John's *Jackie Gleason* were priced at 2.5 times guide. *Leave It to Beaver* sold at double guide and *The Real McCoys, Sea Hunt, Fury* and *Wagon Train* were in demand. This genre is on the move and shows great promise for continued growth in the future.

E.C.—A slight increase of interest was noticed in most titles, but at current price levels. The pre-trend titles continued to show slow steady growth.

Avon and Ziff-Davis—Most Avon titles held their own with renewed interest in many of the Ziff-Davis titles, especially those with Norman Saunders painted covers.

DC—Most all non-hero DC titles showed good steady growth. *Sgt. Bilko, Bob Hope, Alan Ladd, Ozzie & Harriet, Mystery in Space, Strange Adventures, and Funny Stuff* sold briskly. A *Funny Stuff* No. 1 in vf sold for $175. *Real Screen* and *Fox & the Crow* stayed in high demand. Since most DC titles are highly collected, high grade copies still couldn't meet demand and remained scarce.

Atlas—Slow, steady growth with the supply in high grade continuing to dry up. Ditko was the most collected artist.

Westerns—As outlined above, the TV westerns showed the strongest gains. All the regular Dell westerns—*Roy Rogers, Lone Ranger, Gene Autry, Red Ryder,* etc. continued their slow steady growth. The Fawcett westerns were stronger and were hard to get in high grade. *Bob Steele, Ken Maynard, Tom Mix, Hopalong Cassidy, Lash LaRue, Rocky Lane, Tex Ritter,* and *Fawcett Movie Comics* are some of the titles in demand. *Sunset Carson* remained very scarce and *John Wayne* and *Whip Wilson* showed solid gains. ME's *Straight Arrow, Tim Holt,* and *Durango Kid* received moderate interest.

Dell/Gold Key Giants—These books are very scarce in mint condition due to the stiff cardboard bound covers which are very easily damaged. Early in the year a few mint sets of these books entered the market for sale. The market's appreciation for the rarity of these books in true mint condition was slow to catch on at first. But gradually as more of these books were seen by collectors, they began to sell quite rapidly. Many record prices were set with most selling at multiples of guide, depending upon how low they were listed. Eventually all giants were selling at a minimum price of $20 each, including most of the early '60s Gold Key giants. A *Donald Duck Fun Book* No. 2 brought $150. By year's end, word was out about these giants and demand for them was high. More record prices will probably be seen in 1987 as demand continues to grow against a scarce supply. Because of the increased interest, all Dell giants now appear under the Dell Giant listing.

1960s-1970s TITLES: More activity occurred this year due to a noticeable pick-up of interest in the pre-1965 Marvels and DCs. Many of the key No. 1s remained hard to get in high grade as well as the first ten to twenty issues of most runs. Post-1965 to late 1970 comics are still in a slump with ample supply available to meet demand. *X-Men* is still king, although prices are not climbing as rapidly as in previous years.

1980s TITLES: 1986 will always be remembered as the year of *The Dark*

Knight. It has been many years since the comic book world has been impacted as much by a single title. The media attention, immediate price rise in first editions, multi-format availability of the title all caused confusion, headaches, and profits for the comic book industry across the board.

The Dark Knight is a four part *Batman* story written and drawn by Frank Miller, published by DC Comics. It was initially produced in a deluxe format in four single issues. The series received much publicity both in the comic industry as well as national attention, primarily due to the efforts of DC publicist Peggy May. The demand for the series far exceeded the initial orders and second and third printings were done for the single issues as the prices for the first printings escalated to $10 and more. The four issues were repackaged in a hardcover edition which also quickly sold out with premium prices being asked for the available copies. A trade paperback with two different covers were released by Warner Books and DC Comics and they too quickly sold out, requiring an almost immediate second printing. Finally, a hardcover signed and numbered edition of 4,000 copies was released. Because of the very small number available, this issue immediately commanded prices anywhere between $100 and $2,000.

Although *Dark Knight* was by far the biggest success for both DC and the comic industry, there were many other successful projects by DC and all the other publishers. In a concerted effort to get back on top, DC used the momentum generated by their *Crisis on Infinite Earths* series of 1985 to totally revise several of their major characters. Most notably, *Superman* was given over to John Byrne with the numbering starting over with number one. The results were as expected with *Superman* again becoming one of DC's most popular titles. George Perez took over *Wonder Woman* and the sales immediately jumped reflecting the talents of Mr. Perez as well as the lure to collectors by beginning again with number one. Similar revisions in the numbering and editorial changes are scheduled for *Flash* and *Justice League* in early 1987. DC also introduced *The Watchmen* Limited Series by Alan Moore, the winner of many awards for his work on *Swamp Thing*.

Marvel, the top seller in the comic book marketplace launched an entire new line of comics in the Summer of 1986. The New Universe consists of eight new titles outside the Marvel Universe. The concept was to create a "real world" science fiction universe that is radically different from the traditional genres of comic books. Under the editorial leadership of Marvel's Editor-in-Chief, Jim Shooter, the new line was released over the Summer of 1986. Time will tell whether we have the birth of a major market force or not. Within the Marvel Universe, much emphasis was placed on building on the successful licensed characters from 1985. Titles such as *Transformers, G.I. Joe* and *Thundercats were strong sellers for Marvel. Their best-selling title and concept continues to be X-Men* and other mutants. Marvel introduced *Classic X-Men,* a reprint title, as well as several cross-overs to capitalize on the popularity of this group.

The biggest controversy in the marketplace for 1986 has certainly been the rise and fall of the black and white, small print run comics. In January of 1986 there were only a handful of successful black and white publishers including Aardvark, Renegade, Mirage, WaRP, Kitchen Sink, Aircel, and Blackthorne. By the end of 1986, there were over one hundred small press publishers producing products of varying quality for the comic book marketplace. The amount of product was staggering and many retailers complained of the poor editorial quality of many of these newcomers. It seems inevitable that 1987 will be the year of the shakeout of small press publishers.

This dramatic increase in the popularity of the short print run black and white was an attempt by many to cash in on and imitate the success of titles such as *Teenage Mutant Ninja Turtles*. With a very small print run and limited distribution, *TMNT* No. 1 first printings are commanding prices of $100 and more. Similar low print run products caused their prices on the secondary market to jump by more than 100% overnight as collectors, retailers and distributors scrambled to satisfy the demand. This buying frenzy for low print run books attracted the attention of many would be comic book publishers and as the market swelled, the overall quality went down and with it the popularity declined. While there are many good quality titles that deserve the interest of collectors, there are too many amateurish publications which are merely capitalizing on the market and the market is due for some radical price adjustments.

1986 welcomed the return of two long time publications. Harvey Publications returned with *Richie Rich* and *Casper* and friends after a three year absence. Gladstone emerged on the comic book scene with a license to publish Walt Disney comic books. *Donald Duck, Mickey Mouse, Uncle Scrooge* and company appear once again in comics after too long an absence.

Overall, the new comic book market is stronger than it has been in recent history. With Marvel and DC battling each other for the top spot and also battling the legions of new, up-and-coming publishers for their market share, we have real competition for the available talent as well as for the consumer dollar. The results are better comics, a more responsive marketplace and generally healthier conditions for consumers, retailers, distributors and publishers.

IMPORTANT WARNING TO INVESTORS IN NEW COMICS: During the last few years there has been a virtual explosion of new publishers. This has resulted in an avalanche of new titles and publications, many of these being relatively low print run, black and white books. This renaissance in the field of comic book production has led to substantial speculation by dealers and collectors alike. Thus, the prices on comics from the last few years have been extremely volatile and unstable. These changes are reflected as accurately as possible in both this publication and in *Overstreet Comic Updates*.

The potential buyer or collector of these new titles should be certain he understands that many of these books are common. Most prices which exceed the $5.00 to $10.00 range are likely to fall as quickly as they rose. This is obviously not the case with older comic collectibles. Usually the most important factor in a comic's becoming valuable as a collectible is **consistency and long term demand** combined with true scarcity. It is not enough that a given book has a limited print run. We have already seen that many titles that become hot one year are not sustained in the following year. With a few exceptions, it is vital that a title (or character) continues to be published for a long time to sustain interest. It is also important that the publishing company remain publishing for a long period of time. Extreme caution should be excercised when speculating on new comics solely for financial gain.

BARKS ORIGINAL ART—There has never been a year when so many Carl Barks oils have changed hands as in 1986. With a few new buyers entering the market, a surge in demand for original Barks oils occurred. In 1980 a 16x20" Barks oil sold for $42,000. Between 1973 and 1976 Barks produced 122 paintings of which only 67 were 16x20" size. During the year between 35 and 40 paintings were sold. Some of these were in the $40,000-$50,000 range. A record was set when a 16x20" sold for $70,000. The latest paintings by Barks are for Another Rainbow's lithograph series. These are large 20x25" and 24x30" and a total of ten have been done. Several of these paintings sold in the $70,000-$75,000 range with one bringing a record price of $80,000.

The general art market as well as many other collectible fields saw a pick-up in sales during the year. New York auction houses are breaking dozens of price records. Sotheby's set a record in 1986 for a one-night auction at $42,372,000. Christie's broke many records as well. A Piet Mondrian's "Composition in a Square" sold for $5.06 million at Sotheby's.

The Barks preliminary idea oils (12½x10" & 9x9") sold for $6,500 to $12,000 depending on size. The 52 waterfowl water colors and four waterfowl oils done between 1978 and 1981 increased in value. In 1985 an 11x14" oil sold for $7,000. In 1986 an 11x14" oil sold for $10,000. A single figure water color brought $2,300, while an offer of $3,200 was turned down for a complex water color with multiple figures. Only about 125 Barks original pages are known to exist. A new record was set in 1986 with the sale of a single page at $4,500.

In 1985 the Barks Disney lithograph reached $1,000. It reached $1,400 in 1986. This lithograph was limited to 245 copies. The other lithos were limited (with two exceptions) to a standard 345 each for the regular edition and 100 each for the gold plate edition. The market value in 1986 for these lithos No. 2 - 9 are as follows: No. 2, "An Embarrassment of Riches"—$800; No. 3, "Ti'l Death Do Us Part"—$395 regular, $495 gold; No. 4, "A 1934 Belchfire Runabout"—$550 regular, $700 gold; No. 5, "In Uncle Walt's Collectory"—$550 regular, $700 gold; No. 6, "Return to Morgan's Island"—$600 regular, $750 gold; No. 7, "A Foul of the Flying Dutchman"—$500 regular, $650 gold; No. 8, "Dam Disaster at Money Lake"—$450 regular, $600 gold; No. 9, "Dubious Doings at Dismal Downs"—$450 regular, $600 gold. The Another Rainbow book "The Fine Art of Walt Disney's Donald Duck" by Carl Barks was selling at $400.

During the year original artwork was on exhibition in Germany with a theme of the history of animation. It started in Berlin and ended in Frankfurt. Through this and other big conventions in Erlangen and Collogne, several pieces of original art sold. Some Barks pencil cover roughs sold for DM 600 each and other comic page layout drawings sold for DM 500 to DM 800. A Winsor McCay *Little Nemo in Slumberland* Sunday page brought DM 4500. A Dutch Disney comic colored page sold for DM 600. Demand for American originals by Adams, Barks, Gottfredson and others is growing in Germany. Animation art is in demand and varies from DM 300 for a Disney animation drawing to DM 40 for a Lantz drawing.

INVESTOR'S DATA

The following table denotes the rate of appreciation of the top 50 most valuable Golden Age titles over the past year and the past five years (1982-1987). The retail value for a complete mint run of each title in 1987 is compared to its value in 1986 and 1982. The 1971 values are also included as an interesting point of reference. The rate of return for 1987 over 1986, and the yearly average rate of return for each year since 1982, is given.

For example, a complete mint run of *Detective Comics* retails at $107,328 in 1987, $83,497 in 1986, and $39,762 in 1982. The rate of increase of 1987 over 1986 can be easily calculated at 28.5%, while the average yearly increase or rate of return over the past five years is 34.0%. This means that the mint value of this title has increased an average of 34.0% each year over the past five years. However, the rate of increase would be less for fine condition and much less for good condition over the same period.

The place in rank is given for each title by year, with its corresponding mint value. This table can be very useful in forecasting trends in the market place. For instance, the investor might want to know which title is yielding the best dividend from one year to the next, or one might just be interested in seeing how the popularity of titles changes from year to year. For instance, *King Comics* was in 6th place in 1971 and has dropped to 35th place in 1987. But this title could be on the move to reclaim its original position, as it has changed from 46th place to 35th in the past five years and currently continues to show a strong price increase (1987 over 1986).

More Fun overtook *Four Color* for the number four spot, and *Classic Comics* overtook *Silver Streak* for the number 38 spot this year. *Dick Tracy* jumped from 24th to 20th spot. *Amazing Man* increased by 18.1 percent from 1986, but shows a yearly average increase of 38.7 percent. *Jungle Comics* was up 23.9 percent and *Planet Comics* up 12.9 percent.

The following tables are meant as a guide to the investor and it is hoped that they might aid him in choosing titles in which to invest. However, it should be pointed out that trends may change at anytime and that some titles can meet market resistence with a slowdown in price increases, while others can develop into real comers from a presently dormant state. In the long run, if the investor sticks to the titles that are appreciating steadily each year, he shouldn't go very far wrong.

The Silver Age titles are beginning to show movement, especially early issues of Marvel's and DC's in high grade. Golden Age titles are continuing to appreciate faster than economic inflationary values during the same period.

TOP 50 TITLES

TOP 50 TITLES & RATE OF INCREASE OVER 1986 AND 1982 GUIDE VALUES

Title	1987 Guide Rank & Value		%Change From '86 Value	Avg. Yrly. Return '82-'87	1986 Guide Rank & Value		1982 Guide Rank & Value		1971 Guide Rank & Value	
Detective Comics	1	$107,328	+28.5	+34.0	1	$83,497	3	$39,762	4	$2,747
Action Comics	2	91,230	+11.5	+18.2	2	81,788	1	47,824	7	2,354
Marvel Mystery Comics	3	73,654	+10.9	+14.6	3	66,414	2	42,600	5	2,584
More Fun Comics	4	62,048	+24.1	+22.3	5	50,004	5	29,319	3	2,816
Four Color	5	58,480	+13.5	+11.9	4	51,516	4	36,697	1	4,229
Adventure Comics	6	54,475	+17.9	+24.2	7	46,210	7	24,644	2	3,066
Superman	7	53,276	+7.0	+17.5	6	49,813	6	28,402	13	1,460
Captain America	8	36,759	+ 9.3	+14.6	8	33,624	11	21,250	17	1,303
Whiz Comics	9	35,623	+ 8.4	+11.0	9	32,865	9	22,980	14	1,357
Batman	10	34,260	+20.1	+21.7	11	28,524	13	16,428	19	1,246
All Star Comics	11	$34,128	+15.4	+23.0	10	$29,585	14	$15,890	10	$1,657
Flash Comics	12	29,902	+14.8	+25.8	13	26,045	16	13,048	15	1,344
All American Comics	13	28,853	+16.9	+23.4	14	24,685	15	13,308	24	1,189
Donald Duck	14	26,825	+ 2.6	+ 2.6	12	26,155	8	23,698	53	604
Walt Disney's C & S	15	24,233	+ 0.7	+ 2.7	15	24,069	10	21,337	12	1,487
Planet Comics	16	21,429	+12.9	+15.9	17	18,988	18	11,940	50	613
Spirit	17	21,224	+ 0.6	+ 3.6	16	21,087	12	18,024	44	645
Police Comics	18	20,467	+17.3	+12.8	18	17,449	17	12,485	30	903
World's Fair & Finest	19	18,624	+14.7	+14.5	19	16,237	21	10,808	33	841
Dick Tracy	20	17,475	+28.3	+16.7	24	13,618	23	9,520	25	1,116
Captain Marvel Advs.	21	$16,977	+ 5.8	+ 9.3	20	$16,046	19	$11,571	29	$1,009
Jumbo Comics	22	16,886	+16.5	+22.3	22	14,496	28	7,980	16	1,320
Mickey Mouse Magazine	23	16,654	+26.8	+ 9.8	28	13,139	20	11,166	18	1,252
Master Comics	24	16,094	+11.8	+14.1	23	14,394	24	9,440	28	1,021
Human Torch	25	15,956	+ 4.6	+12.6	21	15,255	22	9,781	46	632
Star Spangled Comics	26	15,326	+14.2	+20.5	26	13,419	30	7,561	35	830
Pep Comics	27	15,204	+15.0	+22.5	27	13,220	32	7,160	31	880
Submariner	28	14,408	+ 7.2	+12.6	25	13,445	25	8,835	54	601
Famous Funnies	29	14,377	+16.8	+27.6	31	12,306	36	6,035	8	2,343
Sensation Comics	30	14,358	+10.4	+17.8	29	13,004	29	7,604	41	681
Feature Book	31	$13,744	+11.5	+13.1	30	$12,323	27	$8,297	26	$1,069
Green Lantern	32	12,770	+14.4	+24.0	32	11,160	40	5,810	87	390
Wonder Woman	33	12,617	+15.3	+15.0	33	10,942	31	7,204	64	537

Title	1987 Guide Rank & Value		%Change From '86 Value	Avg.Yrly. Return '82-'87	1986 Guide Rank & Value		1982 Guide Rank & Value		1971 Guide Rank & Value	
Jungle Comics	34	12,522	+23.9	+27.2	34	10,105	49	5,306	32	861
King Comics	35	11,831	+31.3	+23.9	44	9,014	46	5,394	6	2,490
Marge's Little Lulu	36	11,305	+19.4	+23.0	37	9,468	52	5,255	135	219
Tip Top Comics	37	10,879	+ 9.8	+23.0	36	9,905	54	5,064	9	2,088
Classic Comics	38	10,780	+18.3	+19.6	40	9,111	44	5,451	189	65
Hit Comics	39	10,726	+ 8.2	+13.9	35	9,912	34	6,325	67	523
Amazing-Man Comics	40	10,695	+18.1	+38.7	41	9,055	64	3,642	108	314
Silver Streak Comics	38	$10,608	+12.3	+15.6	38	$9,447	39	$5,953	86	$394
Feature & Feature Funnies	42	10,353	+14.7	+22.1	42	9,026	55	4,919	22	1,214
Military Comics	43	10,094	+12.0	+17.9	43	9,015	47	5,330	68	520
Superboy	44	10,044	+13.2	+13.1	47	8,876	35	6,074	94	360
Target Comics	45	10,003	+11.6	+17.0	45	8,967	45	5,413	38	746
Large Feature Comic	46	9,901	+ 5.2	+ 3.1	39	9,416	26	8,581	27	1,058
National Comics	47	9,810	+10.0	+12.9	46	8,922	38	5,955	42	676
Crack Comics	48	9,675	+10.4	+16.5	48	8,762	50	5,298	50	613
Popular Comics	49	9,616	+18.5	+27.5	54	8,116	60	4,050	11	1,598
Ace Comics	50	9,097	+22.7	+23.3	60	7,414	58	4,200	23	1,212

The following table shows the rate of return of the 50 most valuable single books and the 20 most valuable Silver Age books over the past year. It also shows the average yearly rate of return over the past five years (1987-1982). Comparisons can be made in the same way as in the previous table of the Top 50 titles. Ranking in many cases is relative since so many books have the same value. These books are listed alphabetically within the same value.

50 MOST VALUABLE BOOKS AND RATE OF RETURN

Issue	1987 Guide Rank & Value		%Change From '86 Value	Avg.Yrly. Return '82-'87	1986 Guide Rank & Value		1982 Guide Rank & Value	
Marvel Comics No. 1	1	$26,000	+13.0	+12.5	1	23,000	1	$16,000
Action Comics No. 1	2	25,000	+35.1	+17.0	2	18,500	2	13,500
Superman No. 1	3	18,000	+ 0.3	+20.0	3	17,500	3	9,000
Detective Comics No. 27	4	17,500	+25.0	+26.7	4	14,000	5	7,500
Whiz Comics No. 1	5	15,000	+15.4	+18.5	5	13,000	4	7,800
Batman No. 1	6	7,600	+16.9	+10.4	6	6,500	7	5,000
Detective Comics No. 1	7	7,500	+87.5	+63.3	16	4,000	29	1,800
More Fun Comics No. 52	8	7,000	+11.1	+11.1	7	6,300	8	4,500
Double Action Comics No. 2	9	5,800	+ 0.0	+ 5.8	8	5,800	8	4,500
Captain America No. 1	10	5,700	+ 7.5	+ 7.1	9	5,400	11	4,200
Captain Marvel Advs. No. 1	10	$5,700	+ 7.5	+ 7.1	9	$5,400	11	$4,200
All American Comics No. 16	12	5,075	+20.8	+19.0	13	4,200	16	2,600
Motion Pic. Funnies Wkly. No. 1	13	5,000	+ 0.0	– 3.3	11	5,000	6	6,000
More Fun Comics No. 53	14	4,800	+20.0	+12.0	16	4,000	13	3,000
All Star Comics No. 3	15	4,760	+23.6	+36.0	18	3,850	31	1,700
Wow Comics No. 1	16	4,700	+ 4.4	+ 4.7	12	4,500	12	3,800
Action Comics No. 2	17	4,550	+ 8.3	+10.3	13	4,200	13	3,000
Detective Comics No. 28	18	4,200	+20.0	+22.0	19	3,500	24	2,000
Marvel Mystery Comics No. 2	18	4,200	+ 2.8	+10.0	15	4,085	15	2,800
Flash Comics No. 1	20	3,850	+37.5	+28.1	26	2,800	33	1,600
Detective Comics No. 33	21	$3,745	+24.8	+26.8	22	$3,000	33	$1,600
Detective Comics No. 38	21	3,745	+24.8	+33.5	22	3,000	46	1,400
New Fun Comics No. 1	23	3,500	+112.8	+57.8	60	1,645	77	900
Action Comics No. 3	24	3,400	+ 7.9	+10.9	20	3,150	21	2,200
Marvel Mystery Comics No. 5	25	3,150	+ 3.3	+ 6.3	21	3,050	19	2,400
Amazing-Man Comics No. 5	26	3,050	+24.5	+56.3	31	2,450	91	800
Human Torch No. 1	27	3,000	+ 3.4	+10.0	24	2,900	24	2,000
Superman No. 2	28	2,940	+ 5.0	+ 9.4	26	2,800	24	2,000
Walt Disney's C & S No. 1	29	2,900	+ 0.0	+ 2.3	24	2,900	16	2,600
Action Comics No. 5	30	2,800	+ 7.7	+ 9.5	28	2,600	28	1,900
All Star Comics No. 1	30	$2,800	+17.6	+23.1	35	$2,380	51	$1,300
Dick Tracy Feature Book nn	30	2,800	+16.7	+15.0	33	2,400	33	1,600
New Fun Comics No. 2	30	2,800	+100.0	+81.8	77	1,400	-	550
Daring Mystery Comics No. 1	34	2,765	+12.9	+14.6	31	2,450	33	1,600

Issue	1987 Guide Rank	1987 Guide Value	%Change From '86 Value	Avg.Yrly. Return '82-'87	1986 Guide Rank	1986 Guide Value	1982 Guide Rank	1982 Guide Value
Popeye Feature Book nn	35	2,700	+12.5	+25.0	37	2,400	55	1,200
Red Raven Comics No. 1	35	2,700	+ 8.0	+ 7.0	30	2,500	24	2,000
Donald Duck March of Comics 4	37	2,600	+ 0.0	+ 1.7	28	2,600	19	2,400
Captain America No. 2	38	2,500	+ 6.6	+ 9.4	36	2,345	31	1,700
Action Comics No. 7	39	2,450	+ 7.7	+12.7	38	2,275	43	1,500
Action Comics No. 10	39	2,450	+ 7.7	+12.7	38	2,275	43	1,500
Marvel Mystery Comics No. 3	39	$2,450	+ 4.7	+10.6	37	$2,340	33	$1,600
Mystic Comics No. 1	42	2,415	+ 9.8	+20.3	40	2,200	55	1,200
Detective Comics No. 2	43	2,400	+50.0	+40.0	62	1,600	91	800
Detective Comics No. 29	43	2,400	+20.0	+23.6	44	2,000	66	1,100
Sub-Mariner Comics No. 1	43	2,400	+ 9.1	+10.0	40	2,200	33	1,600
Action Comics No. 4	46	2,380	+ 8.2	+11.7	40	2,200	43	1,500
Batman No. 2	47	2,200	+14.3	+16.7	47	1,925	55	1,200
Whiz Comics No. 2	47	2,200	+ 0.0	+ 4.4	40	2,200	29	1,800
Detective Comics No. 31	49	2,170	+21.6	+26.9	53	1,785	76	925
Action Comics No. 6	50	2,150	+ 7.5	+13.1	44	2,000	51	1,300

20 MOST VALUABLE BOOKS (SILVER AGE)

Issue	1987 Guide Rank	1987 Guide Value	%Change From '86 Value	Avg.Yrly. Return '82-'87	1986 Guide Rank	1986 Guide Value	1982 Guide Rank	1982 Guide Value
Adventure Comics No. 247	1	$1,320	+10.0	+46.0	4	$1,200	10	$400
Fantastic Four No. 1	2	1,250	+13.6	+ 0.8	2	1,100	1	1,200
Showcase No. 4	2	1,250	+13.6	+ 2.7	2	1,100	2	1,100
Amazing Fantasy No. 15	4	1,200	+ 9.1	+ 4.0	2	1,100	2	1,100
Amazing Spider-Man No. 1	5	900	+12.5	+ 8.1	5	800	4	640
Incredible Hulk No. 1	6	630	+ 8.6	+ 0.2	6	580	5	625
Detective Comics No. 225	7	525	+12.9	+ 9.2	7	465	14	360
Brave & The Bold No. 1	8	500	+ 9.9	+ 6.7	9	455	12	375
Fantastic Four No. 2	8	500	+ 8.7	+ 2.7	8	460	8	440
Justice League No. 1	10	490	+11.4	+29.0	10	440	33	200
X-Men No. 1	11	$480	+20.0	+22.7	13	$400	30	$225
Jimmy Olsen No. 1	12	476	+13.3	+ 5.4	12	420	12	375
Tales To Astonish No. 27	13	460	+15.0	+ 7.5	13	400	18	335
Journey Into Mystery No. 83	14	450	+12.5	- 1.3	13	400	7	480
Avengers No. 1	15	440	+15.8	+ 5.9	18	380	16	340
Brave & The Bold No. 28	15	440	+25.7	+12.0	21	350	24	275
Richie Rich No. 1	15	440	+ 0.0	+ 0.0	10	440	8	440
Showcase No. 8	18	425	+10.4	+ 5.0	16	385	18	340
Flash No. 105	19	420	+20.0	+ 6.3	21	350	19	320
Showcase No. 1	19	420	+ 9.1	+ 4.0	16	385	15	350

The following table lists the really hot current titles over the past year. From one year to another, this list can change drastically.

HOT TITLES & RATE OF INCREASE 1987 GUIDE OVER 1986 GUIDE

Title	Increase
Albedo	4,447%
Grendel	1,744%
Thundermace Comics	1,300%
Crusaders	1,233%
Macross	900%
Primer	538%
Love and Rockets	500%
Adventurers, The	467%
Adolescent Radioactive BBH	327%
Samurai	322%
Flaming Carrot No. 1	317%
Realm, The	313%
Redfox	311%
Captain Confederacy	300%
Nam, The	300%
Domino Chance	288%
Usagi Yojimbo——	264%
Tales From The Aniverse	250%
Justice Machine	244%
Batman: The Dark Knight	239%
Teengae Mutant Ninja Turtles	231%
Boris The Bear	225%
Flaming Carrot	222%
Trollords	217%
Kelvin Mace	178%
Punisher	168%
Shadow, The	167%
Heroes	167%
Rion 2990	150%
Michaelangelo: TMNJ	133%
Mage	131%
Cerebus Jam	125%
Shuriken	125%
Whisper	118%

X-Factor	117%
Longshot	108%
Donatello	100%
Fugitoid	100%
Mangazine	100%
Man Of Steel	100%
Samurai Penguin	100%
Robotech: The Macross Saga	95%
Ex-Mutants	94%
Firestar	88%
D.P. 7	87%
West Coast Avengers ('84)	86%
G.I. Joe	83%
Classic X-Men	82%
Groo The Wanderer	82%
Badger, The	74%
Elflord	74%
Eb'nn The Raven	73%
Elementals	71%
Eagle	67%
Trufan Advs. Theatre	67%
Elfquest	63%
Power Pack	63%
Cosmic Boy	56%
Critters	56%

THE FIRST WAVE OF COMIC BOOKS 1933-1943 (Key books listed and ranked)

The first modern format comic book came out in 1933 and represents the beginning of comic books as we know them today. The impact of these early characters and ideas are today deeply engrained in American folklore and continue to feed and inspire this ever changing industry.

Over the years historians, collectors and bibliofiles have tried to make some sense out of this era. The question 'what are considered to be the most important books?' has been a topic of discussion and debate for many years. With certain criteria considered, how would the top key issues be ranked in order of importance? How would they relate to each other? In an attempt to answer some of these questions, the following list has been prepared. The books are grouped chronologically in the order they were published. The most important books are ranked into seven tiers, with the top six designated with stars. The more important the book is, the more stars it receives. The following criteria were used to determine the importance and placement of each book in each tier:

a. Durability of character(s)
b. Durability of title
c. Popularity of character(s)
d. First appearance anywhere of a major character
e. First issue of a title
f. Originality of character (first of a type)
g. First or most significant work of a major artist
h. Starts a trend
i. First of a genre
j. Historical significance
k. First of a publisher
l. First appearance in comic books of a character from another medium

This list was compiled by several people* and represents a collective opinion of all. The list is not perfect, not by any means. Adjustments will be made over time as more input is received. The final ranking of a book depends greatly on the overall importance and impact of that book on the comic book market. Obviously, the further you get away from the top key books, the more difficult it becomes for proper ranking. For this reason, books ranked in the lower numbered tiers could change drastically. The final rating given a book is not based entirely on the quantity of points it receives, but rather the overall weight of the points it does receive. For example, the first appearance of ***The Fighting Yank*** is not as important as the first appearance of ***Superman*** who was a trend setting character and long lasting.

In the comics market there are several comics that have become high demand, valuable books due primarily to rarity. A list of the top key books ranked due to value, demand and rarity would look entirely different than what we have here. As we have learned in coins, stamps and other hobbies, rarity is an important factor that affects value and it is not our intention to demean the collectibility of any particular book that is rare. Quite the contrary. There are many rare books that would enhance anyone's collection. Consideration of rarity, for the ranking of books in this list has been kept at a minimum.

The following list covers the period 1933 through 1943 and includes **every** key book of this period of which we are currently aware. Any omissions will be added in future lists. It should be noted that many other issues, although highly collectible, were not considered important for the purpose of this list: i.e., origin issues, early issues in a run, special cover and story themes, etc.

Special thanks is due* ***Landon Chesney* *who contributed considerable energy and thought to the individual write-ups; to* ***David Noah*** *who polished and edited, and to the following people who contributed their time and ideas to the compilation of this list: Hugh O'Kennon, Steve Geppi, Richard Halegua, John Snyder, Joe Tricarichi, Walter Wang, Jon Warren, Bruce Hamilton, Ray Belden and Chuck Wooley*

NOTE: All **first issues** are included as well as books that introduce an important new character, or has key significance in some other way.

CHRONOLOGICAL LIST OF KEY COMIC BOOKS FOR PERIOD 1933 - 1943

(All first issus listed)

GENRE CODES (Main theme)

An - Anthology (mixed)
Av - Aviation
Cr - Crime
D - Detective
F - Funny Animal
H - Costumed/Superhero
Hr - Horror
Hm - Humor
J - Jungle
Lit - Literature
Mg - Magic
M - Movie
R - Strip Reprints
Re - Religious
SF - Science Fiction
Sp - Sport
TA - Teen-Age
Tr - True Fact
W - War
Ws - Western

NOTE: The stars signify the ranking of books into seven different tiers of importance. The top (most important) books receive six stars (1st tier), dropping to no star (7th tier) as their significance diminishes. The following information is provided for each comic: 1. Ranking, 2. Title, 3. Issue number, 4. Date, 5. Publisher, 6. Genre code, 7. Description. 8. Criteria codes.

ANTEDILUVIAN PERIOD

1933 ■

★★★★ **FUNNIES ON PARADE** nn (1933, Eastern Color, R)-The very first comic book in the modern format reprinting popular strip characters. Given away to test the feasibility of demand for repackaged Sunday newspaper funnies. (An 8-page tabloid folded down to 32 pages).
(a,c,d,e,h,i,j,k,l)

★★★★ **FAMOUS FUNNIES, A CARNIVAL OF COMICS** nn (1933, Eastern Color, R)-The second comic book. Given away to test reader demand. Its success set up another test to come in the following year to see if the public would actually pay 10¢ for this type of product (an 8-page tabloid folded down to 32 pages). The first of three first issues for this title.
(a,b,c,e,f,h,j)

★ **CENTURY OF COMICS** nn (1933, Eastern Color, R)-The third comic book. A 100-pager given away with three times the contents of the previous two books.
(e,j)

1934 ■

★ **SKIPPY'S OWN BOOK OF COMICS** nn (1934, Eastern Color, R)-The fourth comic book. The first to feature a single character-this wasn't tried again until ***Superman*** No. 1.
(e,j)

★★★★ **FAMOUS FUNNIES, SERIES I** (1934, Eastern Color, R)-The first comic book sold to the general public (through chain stores). The acid test, its unprecedented success set up the beginning of the first continuous series (anthology reprint) title in comics, and started the chain reaction.
(a,b,c,e,f,h,j)

★★★★★ **FAMOUS FUNNIES** No. 1 (7/34, Eastern Color, R)-Satisfied with the public response, this issue began the series and was the first comic book sold to the general public through newsstand distribution.
(a,b,c,e,f,h,j)

★ **FAMOUS FUNNIES** No. 3 (9/34, Eastern Color, R)-This issue ushered in the famous and very popular *Buck Rogers* strip reprints. Not trend setting, but important for the survival of the run which lasted 22 years.
(a,b,c,f,i,j,l)

1935 ■

★★★★ **NEW FUN COMICS** No. 1 (2/35, DC, An)-The first prototype of the modern comic in

that it featured an anthology format of continuing characters and original rather than reprinted material. First of the DC line and the first tabloid-size book (albeit short-lived), surviving 13 years as ***More Fun Comics***.
(b,e,h,i,j,k)

★ **MICKEY MOUSE MAGAZINE** No. 1 (Sum/35, K.K., F)-Magazine-size protocomic introducing the already legendary transfer characters to the fledgling comic book market. This title first appeared in 1933 as a black & white giveaway comic, and after going through format changes, eventually led to the ultimate "funny animal" comic, ***Walt Disney's Comics & Stories***, to come five years later.
(a,b,c,e,g,j,k)

★ **NEW COMICS** No. 1 (12/35, DC, An)-DC felt enough confidence in the market to issue a second anthology title featuring original, continuing characters. It was second only to ***New Fun*** of its kind. Evolved into ***Adventure Comics***, warhorse of the DC line. DC parlayed the second most perfect comic book title (the first is ***Action***) into a forty plus year run.
(b,e,h,j)

1936 ■

MORE FUN COMICS No. 7 (1/36, DC, An)-DC cancelled the title ***New Fun*** due to the appearance of ***New Comics*** , continuing the series under this changed title.
(b,e,j)

★★★ **POPULAR COMICS** No. 1 (2/36, Dell, R)-The second anthology format title of continuing reprint strips. First of the Dell line, the third publisher to enter the field. Featuring the first comic book appearance of *Dick Tracy, Little Orphan Annie, Terry & the Pirates* and others, lasting 13 years.
(a,b,c,e,j,k,l)

BIG BOOK OF FUN COMICS (Spr/36, DC, An)-The first annual in comics (56 pages, large size; reprints from ***New Fun*** No. 1-5).
(e,h,i,j)

★★★ **KING COMICS** No. 1 (4/36, McKay, R)-Ties as the third continuous series reprint title. The first of a publisher (4th to enter the field). Showcase title of all the King Feature characters-the most popular and widely circulated in the world, featuring Segar's *Popeye* and Raymond's *Flash Gordon* series as the mainstay, lasting 16 years.
(a,b,c,e,j,k,l)

★★★ **TIP TOP COMICS** No. 1 (4/36, UFS, R)-Ties as the third continuous series reprint anthology title. The first of a publisher (5th to enter the field). Featuring the *Tarzan* and *Li'l Abner* series and surviving 25 years.
(a,b,c,e,j,k,l)

★ **COMICS MAGAZINE, THE** (Funny Pages) No. 1 (5/36, Comics Mag., An)-The third anthology format title of original material. The first of a publisher (6th to enter the field). This book is unique in that its cover and entire contents were purchased from DC. This material created gaps in the story line continuity of DC's titles ***More Fun*** and ***New Adventure*** from which it came.
(e,j,k)

WOW COMICS No. 1 (5/36, McKay, An)-The fourth anthology title of original material. McKay's second series (first with original contents), lasting only 4 issues to 11/36. The Unpublished inventory formed the basis of the Eisner/Iger shop.
(e)

NEW BOOK OF COMICS No. 1 (6-8/36, DC, An)-The second annual in comics; 100 pages, reprinting popular strips from ***More Fun*** and ***New Comics***. Second and last issue appeared in Spring of 1938.
(e)

FUNNIES, THE No. 1 (10/36, Dell, R)-Having published this title six years earlier as a tabloid, Dell brought it back as a regular comic book. Featuring more popular strip characters, this became Dell's second comic book title and ran for 6 years.
(b,e)

FUNNY PAGES No. 6 (11/36, Comics Mag., An)-Continued from ***The Comics Magazine***; introduced *The Clock*(?), the first masked hero (detective type, transition hero) in a comic book.
(a,b,c,d,e,f,h,i,j)

FUNNY PICTURE STORIES No. 1 (11/36, Comics Mag., An)-Actually this company's second title, featuring their popular original character, *The Clock*, who appeared on the cover. Title continues for 3 years.
(e)

DETECTIVE PICTURE STORIES No. 1 (12/36, Comic Mag., D)-The first anthology comic title series devoted to a single theme and the first to focus on this subject. Popular in pulps, magazines and films of the time, lasted 7 issues.
(e,h,i,j)

1937 ■

NEW ADVENTURE COMICS No. 12 (1/37, DC, An)-Title change from ***New Comics***, continues series.
(e)

STAR COMICS No. 1 (2/37, Chesler, An)-Ties as

first of a publisher. Anthology format of continuing original material, but short lived (2½ years). Large-size format.
(e,k)

STAR RANGER No. 1 (2/37, Chesler, Ws)-Ties as first of a publisher, and as the first continuous series western anthology title (see ***Western Picture Stories***). Large-size format of original material, lasting only 1 year.
(e,i,j,k)

WESTERN PICTURE STORIES No. 1 (2/37, Comics Mag, Ws)-Ties with ***Star Ranger*** as the first anthology comic title of original material to focus on this subject, the second of a single theme, not lasting out the year.
(e,i,j)

COMICS, THE No. 1 (3/37, Dell, R)-Dell's third anthology reprint title. The first comic book appearance of *Tom Mix*, lasting only one year.
(e,d)

★★★ **DETECTIVE COMICS** No. 1 (3/37, DC, D)-Inaugurated the longest run in comics. Initially a pulpy anthology of mystery men and private eyes, it emerged as the first important title on a single theme with the debut of the implacable *Batman* in '39 (Siegel and Shuster's *Slam Bradley* series is a flavorful example of title's '37-'38 period).
(a,b,c,e,f,h,i,j)

ACE COMICS No. 1 (4/37, McKay, R)-Due to the enormous success of McKay's first series, ***King Comics***, this companion title was published featuring, among others, Raymond's *Jungle Jim*, lasting 12 years.
(a,b,c,e,j,l)

WESTERN ACTION THRILLERS No. 1 (4/37, Dell, Ws)-The third title devoted to westerns. A one-shot of 100 pages.
(e)

FEATURE BOOK nn (Popeye)(1937, McKay, R)-A new concept. The first series of comic books representing a divergence from the normal anthology format. Each issue in the run is actually a one-shot devoted to a single character. More than one issue in the run can be devoted to the same character. These books began in a B&W, magazine-size format. Improvements on this concept came a year later with UFS's ***Single Series*** (in color, comic book size), and still a year later with Dell's ***Four Color*** series, the only one to last.
(a,b,c,e,h,i,j)

FEATURE FUNNIES No. 1 (10/37, Chesler, R)-Another reprint title to add to the list, surviving 13 years as ***Feature Comics***; carrying *Joe Palooka, Mickey Finn* and others.
(e)

100 PAGES OF COMICS No. 101 (1937, Dell, R)-Another 100-page reprint anthology book (Dell's 2nd) with a western cover. Only one issue.
(e)

1938 ■

ACE COMICS No. 11 (2/38, McKay, R)-First comic book appearance of *The Phantom*. Premiere mystery man and first costumed hero. The Ghost Who Walks never made the impact in comics that he enjoyed as a syndicated star.
(a,b,c,f,i,j,l)

FUNNY PAGES V2/6 (3/38, Centaur, An)-Ties with ***Funny Picture Stories***, ***Star Comics*** and ***Star Ranger*** as first of a publisher. Series picked up from Chesler, ending two years later.
(k)

FUNNY PICTURE STORIES V2/6 (3/38, Centaur, An)-Ties with ***Funny Pages***, ***Star Comics***, and ***Star Ranger*** as first of a publisher. Series picked up from Comics Magazine, ending one year later.
(k)

STAR COMICS No. 10 (3/38, Centaur, An)-Ties with ***Funny Pages***, ***Funny Picture Stories***, and ***Star Ranger*** as first of a publisher. Series picked up from Chesler, ending one year later.
(k)

STAR RANGER V2/10 (3/38, Centaur, Ws)-Ties with ***Funny Picture Stories***, ***Star Ranger***, and ***Funny Pages*** as first of a publisher. Series picked up from Chesler, lasting 2 more issues.
(k)

COMICS ON PARADE No. 1 (4/38, UFS, R)-The second title of this publisher, featuring much the same reprint strips as ***Tip Top***, their first. This series survived 17 years.
(a,b,c,e,j)

MAMMOTH COMICS No. 1 (1938, Whitman, R)-First of a publisher, in the same format as the McKay ***Feature Books***. Only one issue.
(e,k)

SUPER COMICS No. 1 (5/38, Dell, R)-A dynamic new title, Dell's fourth. Debuted with some of the heavy weights transferred from the already successful ***Popular Comics***. This new line-up of *Dick Tracy, Terry & The Pirates,* etc. proved to be a sound marketing strategy, lasting 11 years.
(a,b,c,e,j)

GOLDEN AGE PERIOD

★★★★★★ **ACTION COMICS** No. 1 (6/38, DC, H)-The ultimate refinement of the anthology, continuing character title. The first appearance of *Superman*, the quintessential hero with extraordinary powers. Arguably the most imitated character in all of fiction. Standard bearer of the DC line. The most important comic book ever published, and in tandem with ***Superman***, one of the most influential, prevailed beyond four decades.
(a,b,c,d,e,f,h,i,j)

CIRCUS COMICS No. 1 (6/38, Globe, An)-A unique short-lived title featuring a top artist line-up. Introduced Wolverton's *Spacehawks*, later to appear in ***Target Comics*** as *Spacehawk*. First of a publisher.
(d,e,f,j,k)

CRACKAJACK FUNNIES No. 1 (6/38, Dell, R)-A new Dell title, replacing the defunct ***The Comics*** with a similar but different mix of reprint strips. Lasted 4 years.
(e)

COWBOY COMICS No. 13 (7/38, Centaur, Ws)-Continued from ***Star Ranger*** and lasted only two issues. The fourth western anthology title.
(e)

KEEN DETECTIVE FUNNIES No. 8 (7/38, Centaur, An)-Continued from ***Detective Picture Stories***, this title became one of Centaur's mainstays introducing the *Masked Marvel* one year later, lasting 2 years.
(e)

LITTLE GIANT COMICS No. 1 (7/38, Centaur, An)-Small-size diversion from the regular format and short-lived (4 issues).
(e)

AMAZING MYSTERY FUNNIES No. 1 (8/38, Centaur, An)-Standard bearer of the Centaur line. Top artist line-up due to its production by the Everett shop. Ran for two years.
(e,g)

LITTLE GIANT MOVIE FUNNIES No. 1 (8/38, Centaur, An)-A miniautre-sized format comic lasting two issues. A small cartoon panel appears on the right edge of each page giving the illusion of motion when riffled (a flip book) (the cover is set up to represent a movie theater).
(e,i)

★ **FUNNY PAGES** V2/10 (9/38, Centaur, H)-First appearance of *The Arrow* who is the very first costumed hero originating in the comic book (3 months after *Superman*). A primitive percursor of the more refined archers to come, *The Arrow* executed his adversaries with the medieval bluntness his uniform suggested.
(a,b,d,f,h,i,j)

★★★ **JUMBO COMICS** No. 1 (9/38, FH, J)-Publisher of the most perused, but least read, of Golden Age comics, Fiction House did not so much initiate a trend as continue the trusty formula that sustained their line of pulps, cheesecake cast against a variety of single theme adventurous backgrounds (aviation, s/f, jungle & war). ***Jumbo*** was the pilot model of the FH line and the first of the exploitation comics. The debut of *Sheena, Queen of the Jungle* heralded hordes of jungle goddesses to follow. The line overall is perhaps best remembered as a showcase for Matt Baker's patented 'calendar girl' art which, after Caniff and Raymond, was the most pervasive of Golden Age styles, enduring 15 years.
(a,b,c,e,f,h,i,j,k,l)

DETECTIVE COMICS No. 20 (10/38, DC, H)-First appearance of *The Crimson Avenger*, a *Shadow* look-a-like, who was the second comic book costumed hero (4 months after *Superman*).
(b,c,d,f,h,i,j)

LITTLE GIANT DETECTIVE FUNNIES No. 1 (10/38, Centaur, An)-Small-size format only lasting a few issues.
(e)

STAR RANGER FUNNIES No. 15 (10/38, Centaur, An)-Links to ***Star Ranger*** and ***Cowboy Comics***, only lasting a few months. (Packaged by the Iger Shop.)
(e)

★★★ **DONALD DUCK** nn (1938, Whitman, F)-The first *Donald Duck*, as well as the first Walt Disney comic book; in the format of McKay's ***Feature Book*** (B&W with color cover), reprinting 1936 & 1937 Sunday comics. The first funny animal comic devoted to a single character. Precursor to great things to come for this character.
(a,b,c,e,f,i,j,l)

★★ **SINGLE SERIES** nn (Captain & The Kids) (1938, UFS, R)-UFS refined McKay's one-shot ***Feature Book*** format by adding color and adopting the standard comic book size, resulting in a more marketable package. Dell addopted this format for their ***Four Color*** series, which started a year later. This is UFS' third continuous series title.
(e,f,h,i,j)

COCOMALT BIG BOOK OF COMICS No. 1 (1938, Chesler, An)-A one-shot mixed anthology Charles Biro creation, packaged by the Chesler shop (top-notch art).
(e)

NICKEL COMICS No. 1 (1938, Dell, An)-A small-size divergent format one-shot, lasting only one issue.
(e)

1939 ■

ALL-AMERICAN COMICS No. 1 (4/39, DC, R)-DC finally bends to the reprint anthology format, but includes some original material for flavor. *Scribbly* by Mayer begins; a ten-year run.
(a,b,c,d,e,j)

NEW YORK WORLD'S FAIR (3-5/39, DC, H)-The first newsstand comic with a commercial tie-in, capitalizing on the enormous publicity of a real life public event, featuring DC's top characters. The thick format, as well as the title segued into ***World's Finest Comics*** two years later.
(a,c,e,i,j)

★ **MOVIE COMICS** No. 1 (4/39, DC, M)-A unique but short-lived idea. The notion of adapting films to comics in fumetti form (the panels were half-tones of stills from the films) was a good one, but didn't work any better in '39 than it does today. (The first movie adaption comic in standard comic book form and probably the first attempt at a fumetti continuity.)
(e,f,j,i)

★★★★★ **DETECTIVE COMICS** No. 27 (5/39, DC, H)-Reliable but predictable 'funny paper' cops 'n robbers anthology came into focus with the debut of *The Batman*. DC's second powerhouse set another standard for the industry to follow. The 'dynamic' hero—costumed athlete sans extraordinary powers—proved a viable alternative for the burgeoning competition to mimic, but Bob Kane broke the mold. The character's unique personna defied any but the most oblique imitation. ***Detective*** shared standard bearer honors with ***Action*** and provided the initials by which the company was known. One of the top four comics.
(a,b,c,d,f,h,j)

KEEN KOMICS V2/1 (5/39, Centaur, An)-A large size mixed anthology comic changing to regular size with number two. Packaged by the Everett shop and lasting only three issues.
(e)

★★ **WONDER COMICS** No. 1 (5/39, Fox, H)-Salutory effort of Fox (packaged by Eisner/Iger). First, and shortest-lived, of *Superman* imitations. Historically significant because the debut of Fox's *Wonder Man* prompted DC's first attempt to successfully defend their copyright on *Superman*. (A precedent that would prove decisive when the Man of Steel confronted a more formidable courtroom adversary a decade hence). Only one more issue followed.
(d,e,j,k)

★★★ **MOTION PICTURE FUNNIES WEEKLY** No.1 (5/39? Funnies, Inc., H)-Produced as a theatre giveaway, this title featured the first appearance of *Sub-Mariner*. His official newsstand debut occurred later in the year in ***Marvel Comics*** No. 1. Only seven known copies exist.
(a,c,d,e,f,g,h,i,j,k)

FEATURE COMICS No. 21 (6/39, Quality, An)-Continues from ***Feature Funnies*** of two years earlier. A discreet title change, indicating that original adventure comics were becoming a significant alternative to the formerly dominant reprints.
(b,e,k)

★★ **ADVENTURE COMICS** No. 40 (7/39, DC, H)-The *Sandman*, a transition crime fighter who stuck tenaciously to the trusty regalia of the pulp heroes. Finally, the pressure to adopt modern togs was brought to bear. The original mystery man vanished into oblivion, replaced by a swashbuckling Kirby hero.
(a,b,c,d,j)

AMAZING MYSTERY FUNNIES V2/7 (7/39, Centaur, H)-Debut of *The Fantom of the Fair*, mystery man, whose headquarters were under the World's Fair (An unexpected attraction for Fair goers). Destined for extinction with the 1940 wind-up of the Fair. Top artist line-up and exciting cover concepts.
(c,d,j)

COMIC PAGES V3/4 (7/39, Centaur, An)-A mixed anthology series continuing from ***Funny Picture Stories*** of three years earlier, lasting 3 issues.
(e)

KEEN DETECTIVE FUNNIES V2/7 (7/39, Centaur, H)-*The Masked Marvel*, super sleuth, and his three confederates began a terror campaign against lawless gangs. His big amphibian plane, secret laboratory and projected red shadow were devices used in the strip, lasting one year.
(d,j)

★★★ **MUTT AND JEFF** nn (Sum/39, DC, R)-This one shot represented a significant departure for DC. Formerly they had avoided the reprint title, preferring to develop their own original characters. This title was obviously a test to see if the market would support an entire book devoted to a single character (or in this case characters). This book has the honor of being the very first *newsstand* comic devoted to a single reprint strip. After a very slow start (four issues in four years), ***Mutt And Jeff*** was made a quarterly and soon became a popular run lasting 26 astounding years. It was the only successful reprint series of a single character to enjoy a respectible run. The syndicated *Mutt and Jeff* strip was, after *The Katzenjammer Kids*, the oldest continuously published

newspaper strip.
(a,b,c,e,j)

★★★★★ **SUPERMAN** No. 1 (Sum/39, DC, H)-This landmark issue signaled a major turning point for the industry. Argurably, the second most important comic ever published (***Action*** being the first), and possibly the most influential. *Superman* was the first original character promoted from headling an anthology title to starring in a book of his own. More importantly, this tandem exposure demonstrated to the industry that it could survive on its own original material, independent of the proven syndicated stars. As other publishers were attracted to the field in the months to come, they emulated not only *Superman*, but the tandem anthology/headline format that had contributed to his unprecedented success. A double trend setter. Contains reprint material from ***Action*** No. 1-4. Title has continued beyond four decades.
(a,b,c,e,h,i,j)

WONDERWORLD COMICS No. 3 (7/39, Fox, H)-After the *Wonder Man* debacle, Fox bounces back with a revised title and a new lead character (courtesy of the Iger shop). *The Flame* got off to a brilliant start, but was snuffed out when Iger and Fox parted company, lasting 3 years.
(a,c,d,e,j)

MAGIC COMICS No. 1 (8/39, McKay, R)-King Features' third reprint anthology (after ***King*** and ***Ace Comics***) featured such popular syndicated stars as *Mandrake, Henry,* and *Blondie*. By 1940 *Blondie* had become the most widely syndicated newspaper strip in the world, and became the prime cover feature for the balance of the run, title enduring 10½ years.
(a,b,c,e,j)

★ **MYSTERYMEN COMICS** No. 1 (8/39, Fox, H)-Fox was on firm ground with a trio of potential contenders: ***Wonderworld's*** *The Flame* and, debuting in this title, *The Blue Beetle* and *The Green Mask*. These early products of the Eisner/Iger shop are worth a second look. Potential glows from every page. Soon, due to the E/I and Fox break up, the characters sunk into hack oblivion.
(a,c,d,e,j)

SMASH COMICS No. 1 (8/39, Quality, An)-This is the first title that Quality developed entirely on their own, (previous titles having been purchased from other publishers). The series lacked originality until the debut of Lou Fine's *Ray* which began in issue No. 14.
(b,e,j)

AMAZING MAN COMICS No. 5 (9/39, Centaur, H)-Everett's *A-Man* was launched here, the first Centaur character to headline his own title. The first costumed hero to shrink (*Minimidget*) begins. (This concept was better used later in Quality's *Doll Man.*) Top artist line-up in this series which ended in early 1942. The standard bearer of the Centaur line.
(e,j)

SPEED COMICS No. 1 (10/39, Harvey, H)-First of a publisher. *Shock Gibson* is the main hero. The characters in this series lacked the charisma of the competition's best; had a few bright moments when top artists entered the line-up, surviving as an average run for 7 years.
(a,b,e,k)

BEST COMICS No. 1 (11/39, BP, H)-First of a publisher. Debut of the Red Mask. An experimental large format book that read sideways; it failed to find an audience after four issues and folded.
(e,j,k)

BLUE RIBBON COMICS No. 1 (11/39, MLJ, An)-First of a publisher. Contents unremarkable (*Rang-A-Tang, The Wonder Dog*, for example). An MLJ anthology that failed to survive beyond 1942 despite the influx of super heroes.
(e,j,k)

★★★★★ **MARVEL COMICS** No. 1 (11/39, Timely, H)-Timely, the first publisher to hit with a smash twin bill in their inaugural title (courtesy of the Everett shop). From the onset, the formula of iconoclast as hero would prove to be Timely's most successful newsstand strategy. *The Human Torch* and *Sub-Mariner* won immediate reader approval, paving the way for more marvels to come from the pre-eminent Thrill Factory of comicdom. Possibly The most sought after of all Golden Age comics. Title lasted 10 years.
(a,b,c,d,e,f,g,h,i,j,k)

CHAMPION COMICS No. 2 (12/39, Harvey, An)-Early transitional anthology title with a sports theme, changing over to costumed heroes early on. None of the characters caught on enough to sustain the run for more than four years.
(e)

FANTASTIC COMICS No. 1 (12/39, Fox, H)-Biblical character *Samson* debuts. This series is more noted for the Lou Fine covers (Iger Shop). *Stardust* begins, one of the most bizarre super heroes in comics (Almost child-like, almost surrealistic art and plotting). He assassinated wrong doers regularly.
(e)

★★ **FEATURE COMICS** No. 27 (12/39, Quality, H)-Debut of the *Dollman* (Quality's first super hero), who was the second, but most significant, with the power to shrink (See ***Amazing Man***). The stories were generally undistinguished but Quality's high standards of illustration (Eisner in this case) lent the strip a credibility that would have been lacking in lesser hands. This title lasted 11

years.
(a,b,c,d,j)

★ **SILVER STREAK COMICS** No. 1 (12/39, Lev, An)-First of a publisher. Debut of *The Claw*, one of the most bizarre villains in the annals of comics. Standing 100 feet tall with claws and fangs was the ultimate refinement of the 'yellow peril' theme from the pulps. Such a formidable figure had to have an adversary to match (See ***Silver Streak*** No. 7). The first comic book to display a metallic silver logo to insure prominence on the stands.
(a,c,d,e,f,k)

TOP-NOTCH COMICS No. 1 (12/39, MLJ, H)-*The Wizard*, one of MLJ's top characters debuted. Their second anthology title, lasting 4½ years.
(a,b,c,d,e,j)

LARGE FEATURE COMIC nn (1939, Dell, R)-Black and white, magazine size, one-shot series with color covers (identical to Mckay ***Feature Books*** of two years earlier), lasting four years.
(a,c,e)

CAPTAIN EASY nn (1939, Hawley, R)-First of a publisher. A one-shot reprint comic devoted to a single character, already proven successful by other publishers.
(a,c,e,k)

★★ **FOUR COLOR** No. 1 (Dick Tracy)(1939, Dell, R)-Exact format of UFS's ***Single Series*** of one year earlier. The most successful of the one-shot continuity titles, lasting 23 years. This series also provided a testing arena for new characters and concepts.
(a,b,c,e,j)

LONE RANGER COMICS, THE nn (1939, giveaway, Ws)-Fifth western title, first of a major character. This one-shot may have had newsstand distribution as price (10 cents) was stamped on cover.
(a,c,e)

1940 ■

★★ **BLUE BEETLE, THE** No. 1 (Wint/39-40, Fox, H)-The star of the second continuous series title devoted to a single character exemplified the pioneer 'crime fighter' of the early comics. His uniform was as simple and direct as the four-color medium itself-- unadorned, form-fitting chain mail. Disdaining cloak, cape and the cover of night, *Blue Beetle* trounced crime where he found it, usually in the street and in broad daylight. Striking figure made an indelible impression on readers and, had Fox been more committed to long term development, would have doubtless gone the distance. The series eventually succumbed to tepid scripts and lack-lustre art, but the character was of sufficient personal appeal to survive, in memory, not only the demise of his title but legions of better produced, longer tenured heroes.
(a,b,c,e,j)

DARING MYSTERY COMICS No. 1 (1/40, Timely, H)-Unusual anthology title (their second) in that each issue featured a practically new line-up of costumed heroes. Very collectible due to its quantity of vintage characters crammed into a short run. High impact covers and art.
(e)

DOUBLE ACTION COMICS No. 2 (1/40, DC, An)-A very rare complete comic book (only five known) containing pre-*Superman* material that possibly had very limited distribution. An experimental issue to see if an all B&W comic would sell (The cover was in color).
(e,j)

FIGHT COMICS No. 1 (1/40, FH, Sp)-Sports theme anthology comic produced by the Iger shop. Later adapted to a war theme, and finally to a jungle theme. The usual house style of cheesecake covers/stories was adhered to resolutely throughout. Duration 13 years.
(a,b,e)

★★★★★ **FLASH COMICS** No. 1 (1/40, DC, H)-DC reinforced its arsenal with two more dynamos: *The Flash* (first, and most significant hero with lightning speed), and *The Hawkman* (first and most significant winged hero). Both trend setters, with series lasting beyond 40 years.
(a,b,c,d,e,f,h,i,j)

★★ **FLASH COMICS** No. 1 (1/40, Faw, H)-An inhouse b&w proof produced to secure pre-publication copyright. Important changes made before the book was officially released were, a title change from ***Flash*** to ***Whiz*** (DC had already gone to press with their ***Flash Comics***), and the name of the lead character was changed from *Captain Thunder* to *Captain Marvel*. (8 known copies exist.)
(e,f,g,j,k)

THRILL COMICS No. 1 (1/40, Faw, H)-Identical to ***Flash Comics*** listed above, only a different title. Only three known copies exist.
(e,f,g,j,k)

JUNGLE COMICS No. 1 (1/40, FH, J)-The second single theme anthology series of this subject (cloned from ***Jumbo)***. The title more perfectly suggested the 'jungle' theme with format selling rather than strong characters. Third series of a publisher, lasting as long as its parent (14½ years), with no competition until six years later.
(a,b,c,d,e,j)

★★ **PEP COMICS** No. 1 (1/40, MLJ, H)-Debut of *The Shield*, the first patriotic hero, later eclipsed by Simon & Kirby's *Captain America*, the bomb-

shell of 1941. MLJ's third and longest lasting (over 40 years) anthology title. Archie eventually takes over the series.
(a,b,c,d,e,f,h,i,j)

★★★★ **PLANET COMICS** No. 1 (1/40, FH, SF)-The publisher's fourth anthology title of continuing characters. The first and by far the most successful science fiction run in comics. As with ***Jumbo*** and ***Jungle***, this title had no competition for many years. Fiction Houses's style of action-packed covers and art made up for the routine plotting, lasting 14 years.
(a,b,c,e,f,h,i,j)

MIRACLE COMICS No. 1 (2/40, Hillman, H)-A mixed anthology series similar to ***Rocket Comics*** published a month later. First of a publisher. Covers have good eye-appeal, ending with the fourth issue.
(e,k)

★★★ **MORE FUN COMICS** No. 52,53 (2,3/40, DC, H)-DC modernizes its first anthology title, introducing the ominous *Spectre* in this two-part origin series. This frightening ethereal hero was too much a match for his adversaries, but gave DC an exciting alternative to their swelling ranks of wondermen. A trend setter, lasting 4 years in this title.
(a,b,c,d,f,h,i,j)

SCIENCE COMICS No. 1 (2/40, Fox, SF)-With qualifications, the second science fiction anthology title (very few of the stories dealt with outer space). Aside from the Lou Fine covers (No. 1 & 2), the artwork was not attractive and the series died after eight issues. First *Eagle* (the second winged hero).
(e)

TARGET COMICS No. 1 (2/40, Novelty, H)-First of a publisher. An early Everett shop super hero production. First *White Streak* by Burgos (the second android super hero). Top artist line-up featuring above average covers and stories, lasting 10 years.
(b,e,k)

THRILLING COMICS No. 1 (2/40, Better, H)-The first successful anthology title by this publisher (their second series). Debut of *Dr. Strange*. Logo carried over from the pulp. The Schomburg covers are the highlight of the run. The title lasted 11 years, switching to a jungle theme near the end.
(a,b,c,e,j)

★★★★★ **WHIZ COMICS** No. 2 (2/40, Faw, H)-After ***Action***, the most significant of all hero/adventure anthologies was this late entry from Fawcett. Origin, first appearance of *Captain Marvel*, humor hero par excellence. The most accessible of miracle men came from behind to eclipse the competition's best. He also founded the industry's first character dynasty (Marvel's *Junior, Mary* and even *Bunny*), a tactic that would prove as fundamental to comics' merchandising as DC's hero team concept. Landmark first issue also introduced such secondary stalwarts as *Sivana, Old Shazam, Spy Smasher* (the definitive aviator/mystery man), and *Ibis the Invincible*, most memorable of comic book sorcerers. Flagship of the Fawcett line and a perennial favorite for 13 years.
(a,b,c,d,e,f,g,j,k)

ZIP COMICS No. 1 (2/40, MLJ, H)-MLJ's fourth anthology title (featuring *Steel Sterling*). Interesting stylized covers and art. Series lasted four years. With the exception of *Wilbur* (an Archie clone), none of the characters reached their own titles.
(a,b,c,d,j)

★★ **ADVENTURE COMICS** No. 48 (3/40, DC, H)-Debut of *The Hourman*. A substantial secondary feature that sold a few books for DC, but never received adequate creative support. Interesting premise came to dominate all the stories resulting in monotonous repetition.
(a,b,c,d,e,j)

COLOSSUS COMICS No. 1 (3/40, Sun, H)-An early esoteric book which ties to the esoteric ***Green Giant*** comic.
(e)

★★★ **DONALD DUCK FOUR COLOR** No. 4 (3/40?, Dell, F)-The first comic book devoted to this important transfer character. Still confined to one page gag strips. Full potential not yet reached.
(a,b,c,j)

MASTER COMICS No. 1 (3/40, Faw, H)-An experimental format at first (magazine size, priced at 15¢ and 52 pages). Debut of *Master Man*, an imitation of *Superman*, killed by DC after six issues; just in time for *Bulletman* to become the lead figure with issue no. 7, transferred from the defunct ***Nickel Comics***.
(b,e,j,k)

MYSTIC COMICS No. 1 (3/40, Timely, H)-Unusual anthology title (their third) in that each issue featured a practically new line-up of costumed heroes. High impact covers and art, lasting only 10 issues.
(e)

PRIZE COMICS No. 1 (3/40, Prize, H)-High quality anthology series with the debut of *Power Nelson*. First of a publisher. Dick Briefer's unique *Frankenstein* was introduced in No. 7 as well as Simon & Kirby's *Black Owl*. The covers have tremendous eye-appeal.
(a,b,e,j,k)

ROCKET COMICS No. 1 (3/40, Hillman, H)-The title is misleading. This is actually a mixed anthology title with science fiction covers; short-lived with only three issues. Companion mag to ***Miracle Comics***. The second Hillman title.
(e)

★ **SHADOW COMICS** No. 1 (3/40, S&S, H)-The venerable pulp publisher tested the comic waters with a heavyweight who had dominated both the pulp and radio markets but never quite found his metier in a medium that relied on action over ethereal atmosphere. *Doc Savage*, another renowned pulp character. debuted in this issue. A respectable but undistinguished run (9 years) probably sustained by popularity of radio program.
(a,b,c,e,f,i,j,k,l)

SLAM BANG COMICS No. 1 (3/40, Faw, An)-Fawcett's third title was an ill conceived adventure anthology starring civilian heroes. This formula had gone out two years before with the appearance of *Superman*. The title was retired after 8 issues.
(e)

SUN FUN KOMIKS No. 1 (3/40, Sun, Hm)-An esoteric one-shot printed in black and red. A satire on comic books. The first of its kind not to be fully developed until ***Mad*** of 12 years hence.
(e,i,j)

★★★★ **DETECTIVE COMICS** No. 38 (4/40, DC, H)-DC initiates yet another breakthrough concept—the apprentice costumed hero. Origin, first appearance of *Robin*, the first and most enduring juvenile aide. For the first time in popular literature, the youthful apprentice was accepted as an equal by his partner. Bob Kane set another standard for the industry to mimic. The foreboding and enigmatic *Batman* was never the same after this issue.
(a,b,c,d,f,h,i,j)

EXCITING COMICS No. 1 (4/40, Better, H)-A sister anthology title to ***Thrilling***, becoming Better's second successful series. This title launched the Black Terror in No. 9, with Schomburg doing the covers early on (a poor man's Timely). Title lasted 9 years with jungle theme covers at the end.
(b,e,j)

★★ **NEW YORK WORLD'S FAIR** (3-5/40, DC, H)-The second comic book produced for a public event, ending the series. The first book to feature *Superman* and *Batman* together on a cover, as well as the first to showcase all of a company's stars, all in one book.
(a,c,j)

SUPERWORLD COMICS No. 1 (4/40, Gernsback, SF)-Following the success of ***Planet***, this title takes the honors as the third continuous series science fiction anthology. But Gernsback soon learned that 'raw' science fiction without a unique art style or gimmick (cheesecake) wouldn't sell. Disappeared after only three issues.
(e,k)

WEIRD COMICS No. 1 (4/40, Fox, H)-Another mixed anthology title with costumed heroes. The first to capitalize on this title, which became more common a decade later. Early issues by the Iger shop. First *Birdman* (the third winged hero). First *Thor*, from Greek mythology. Title lasted 2 years.
(e)

BIG SHOT COMICS No. 1 (5/40, CCG, Av)-First *Skyman*, the second aviation hero (noted for his flying wing)(See ***Whiz***). The first of a publisher. Mixed anthology series with original and reprint strips (*Joe Palooka*), lasting 9 years.
(a,b,c,d,e,j,k)

CRACK COMICS No. 1 (5/40, Quality, H)-Debut of Fine's *Black Condor* (the fourth winged hero). *Madame Fatal* begins, a bizarre hero who dresses as a woman to fight crime. A top quality series, lasting 9 years.
(a,b,c,d,e)

CRASH COMICS No. 1 (5/40, Tem/Holyoke, H)-The first Simon & Kirby art team-up, whose loose style of action reached maturity a year later with *Captain America*. Kirby was on his way to becoming one of the most influencial artists in comics. First of a publisher. A short lived mixed anthology series with costumed heroes, lasting 5 issues.
(e,g,k)

DOC SAVAGE COMICS No. 1 (5/40, S&S, H)-The legendary Man of Bronze headlined Street & Smith's second comic title. But it soon became evident that the original 'super man' was out of his depth. His prose adventures, which crackled with vitality in the pulps, seemed bland and derivative in the four-color medium. Outclassed by the characters he inspired, Doc and his title were retired after 3 years of so-so performance.
(c,e)

HYPER MYSTERY COMICS No. 1 (5/40, Hyper, H)-First of a publisher. A costumed hero anthology title which could not compete with the many heroes on the market at this time, lasting 2 issues.
(e,k)

★ **MORE FUN COMICS** No. 55 (5/40, DC, H)-First *Dr. Fate*, DC's second supernatural hero was given immediate cover exposure. Above average art and stories; colorful costume, lasting 3½ years and not achieving his own title.
(a,b,c,d,j)

★★★ **NICKEL COMICS** No. 1 (5/40, Faw, H)-Introduced *Bulletman*, Fawcett's third costumed hero. This book was experimental, selling for 5¢, came out biweekly, and lasting only 8 issues. (After *Bulletman* was moved to ***Master Comics***, he won his own title in 1941.)
(a,c,d,e,j)

WAR COMICS No. 1 (5/40, Dell, W)-The first single theme anthology series devoted to war. The combat genre did not find a significant market until the outbreak of the Korean conflict a decade later.
(e,i,j)

AMAZING ADVENTURE FUNNIES No. 1 (6/40, Centaur, H)-Outstanding collection of Centaur's best characters reprinted from earlier titles. Centaur was increasingly thrown back to all reprint books. Conjecture is that Timely's sudden success pre-empted all of the Everett shop's time.
(c,e)

★★★★ **BATMAN** No. 1 (Spr/40, DC, H)-Has arrival date of 4/25/40. DC's second strongest character achieved stardom and was given his own title. Assembled from ***Detective Comics***' inventory, containing the last solo appearance of *The Batman*. *The Joker* and *The Cat* debut. Title has run uninterrupted over four decades.
(a,b,c,e,j)

BLUE BOLT No. 1 (6/40, Novelty, H)-Second of a publisher. Costumed hero anthology title. Important early Simon & Kirby development began in No. 3. The heroes in this series could not be sustained, with *Dick Cole* eventually taking over, lasting 9 years.
(a,b,c,d,e,j)

CYCLONE COMICS No. 1 (6/40, Bilbara, An)-An anthology title with emphasis on subjects other than costumed hero. First of a publisher, expiring after 5 issues.
(e,j,k)

FUTURE COMICS No. 1 (6/40, McKay, R)-McKay's first new title in about a year. A reprint anthology with a science fiction theme (the fourth ever). This issue is noted for *The Phantom's* origin and science fiction cover. Went down for the count after 4 issues.
(e)

★★★**SPIRIT, THE** No. 1 (6/2/40, Eisner, D)-A weekly comic book (the only in comics) featuring the blockbuster strip distributed through newspapers. Notably, one of the best written and illustrated strips ever. A trend setter. Ingenious themes; capital atmospheric art with movie-like continuity and humorous plotting. Focus on special effects, lighting and unusual angles, lasting 12 years and endlessly revived.
(a,b,c,d,e,f,h,i,j)

STARTLING COMICS No. 1 (6/40, Better, H)-Better's third companion anthology series; *Wonder Man* and *Captain Future* begin. *The Fighting Yank* debuted in No. 10. Schomburg covers began early giving the books more impact. Cover theme changed to science fiction at the end.
(a,b,c,e,j)

SURE-FIRE COMICS No. 1 (6/40, Ace, H)-First of a publisher. A super hero anthology title of average quality lasting 4 issues before a title change.
(e,k)

WHIRLWIND COMICS No. 1 (6/40, Nita, H)-First of a publisher. A Three-issue run of mediocre quality with no sustaining characters.
(e,k)

★★★★ **ALL-AMERICAN COMICS** No. 16 (7/40, DC, H)-DC scored with another winning variation on the mystery man/adventure theme. Origin and first appearance of most enduring of DC's magic oriented heroes. The ancient fable of the magic lamp was transformed into a modern and more accessible, more mysterious form. *The Green Lantern's* chant became a staple of school boy mythology and another great career was launched. Series ended in 1949, although the name continued beyond 4 decades.
(a,b,c,d,j)

★★★ **ALL-STAR COMICS** No. 1 (Sum/40, DC, H)-The first continuous series showcase comic (see ***New York World's Fair***, 1940) for giving more exposure to top characters, who all headlined anthology series but as yet were not strong enough to have titles of their own. (This abundance of popular characters was unique to DC, forcing them to come up with this new format.)
(a,b,c,e)

FLAME, THE No. 1 (Sum/40, Fox, H)-One of Fox's top characters given prominence, reprinted from ***Wonderworld***. Lou Fine art in this issue, but the quality dropped early on, with the title lasting only 1½ years.
(c,e)

GREEN MASK, THE No. 1 (Sum/40, Fox, H)-Fox's emerald mystery man achieved stardom, but was squelched early on due to sub-standard art. An intriguing concept that was resurrected several times over the next 15 years, none of which were successful.
(c,e)

★ **MARVEL MYSTERY COMICS** No. 9 (7/40, Timely, H)-Epic battle issue. The first time in comics that two super heroes appeared together in one story. *Sub-Mariner* and *The Human Torch* each give up their usual space and battle for 22 pages. A coming together of the ancient basic

★ **YOUNG ALLIES** No. 1 (Sum/41, Timely, H)-The first sidekick group in comics. The *Red Skull* guest-starred to give the title a good send-off. Proto-type of the more successful *Teen Titans* of 25 years hence, it managed a respectable run of 5 years.
(e,f,h,i,j)

CAPTAIN FEARLESS No. 1 (8/41, Helnit, H)-Third of a publisher. An interesting mix of super patriots not lasting beyond the second issue.
(e)

★★★★ **MILITARY COMICS** No. 1 (8/41, Qua, Av)-Otherwise predictable war-theme anthology (the third of its kind) sparked by debut of aviation feature of genuine classic proportions. The crack *Blackhawk* team took command of the series and continued at the helm 9 years after a title change (to ***Modern Comics***) indicated the public had grown jaded with war-themes generally. Ace concept (air-borne privateers meet the axis on its own terms) backed by sterling Iger graphics (the shop's piece de resistance) and top-drawer scripting propelled feature into its own title and a phenomenal 40 year run (with interruptions). The introduction of *Blackhawk*, and *Plastic Man* later the same month, lifted Quality into the first rank of comics publishers. A masterpiece of collaborative art.
(a,b,c,d,e,f,h,i,j)

OUR FLAG COMICS No. 1 (8/41, Ace, H)-Ace joined the other publishers with a host of patriotic strongmen debuting in this book. High impact patriotic cover. Series lasted 5 issues.
(e,j)

POCKET COMICS No. 1 (8/41, Harv, H)-An experimental pocket size comic book series featuring Harvey's top characters. Most divergent forms didn't last long and this was no exception, expiring after 4 issues.
(e)

★★★★ **POLICE COMICS** No. 1 (8/41, Quality, H)-Debut of one of the most ingenious super heroes in comics, *Plastic Man*. An original concept, fully exploited by Jack Cole in the ensuing years. Sheer entertainment with the incomparable *Cole* at the top of his form. Shares standard bearer honors with ***Military***, lasting 12 years.
(a,b,c,d,e,f,i,j)

★ **RED RYDER COMICS** No. 3 (8/41, Hawley, Ws)-The first continuous series single theme western comic for newsstand sales. Ties back to a one-shot issue of a year earlier. Title lasted 16 years due to popular movie series.
(a,b,c,e,f,h,i,j)

SPITFIRE COMICS No. 1 (8/41, Harvey, Av)-An experimental aviation pocket size comic book, lasting 2 issues.
(e)

★ **UNCLE SAM QUARTERLY** No. 1 (8/41, Qua, H)-Eisner's version of a patriotic hero, the star of ***National Comics***, is given his own book, lasting 8 issues. Usual Iger shop excellence.
(e)

USA COMICS No. 1 (8/41, Timely, H)-Timely, extending the patriotic theme, created another showcase title for introducing new characters. After five issues, their trend setting *Captain America* was brought in to save the run and it endured 4 years.
(a,c,e)

VICTORY COMICS No. 1 (8/41, Hill, H)-Classic Everett Nazi war cover. Hillman tried their third title, this time with a patriotic costumed hero theme, again unsuccessfully. It lasted only 4 issues.
(e)

BANNER COMICS No. 3 (9/41, Ace, H)-Debut of *Captain Courageous*, a derivative patriotic hero—not prominent enough to survive more than 3 issues.
(e)

CALLING ALL GIRLS No. 1 (9/41, PMI, TR)-Second of a publisher. The true fact anthology, with biographies of famous persons and sketches of historic events (occassionally mixed with magazine-type photo features), was a comics format pioneered by Parent's Magazine Institute. Here the target audience was adolescent girls. Similar titles were cloned later on. Enjoyed a run of 7 years.
(b,e,f,h,i,j)

FOUR FAVORITES No. 1 (9/41, Ace, H)-Ace's first showcase title featuring their top characters together in one book, lasting 6 years.
(e)

REAL HEROES COMICS No. 1 (9/41, PMI, TR)-With the success of ***True Comics***, the publisher attempted another title based on true stories. Their third series, lasting 5 years. ***Heroic Comics*** was later converted to this theme.
(e)

REAL LIFE COMICS No. 1 (9/41, BP, TR)-Inspired by the newsstand success of PMI's ***True Comics***, this publisher came out with their version, lasting 11 years.
(b,e)

STARTLING COMICS No. 10 (9/41, BP, H)-Debut of *The Fighting Yank*, America's super patriot. Interesting variation on the patriotic theme in that he could call up heroes from the American revolution to assist in the modern fight against crime.

Tremendous eye-appeal of character never fully realized due to low standard story art. High impact Schomburg covers sustained the run.
(a,b,c,d,j)

SUPER MAGICIAN COMICS No. 2 (9/41, S&S, Mg)-The first continuous series anthology title on the subject of magic, continuing from ***Super Magic*** and lasting 6 years.
(e,j)

YANKEE COMICS No. 1 (9/41, Chesler, H)-Chesler re-entered the comic market with this patriotic title. Debut of *Yankee Doodle Jones*. Sensational patriotic cover. Despite its visual appeal, it endured only 4 issues.
(e)

★★★★ **CLASSIC COMICS** No. 1 (10/41, Gil, Lit)-First and most enduring of 'educational' theme comics, Gilberton drew on works of great literature for their highly visible newsstand product. One of the few lines that could be endorsed without reservation by parents and educators, its marketing success was not tied to single-theme titles or continuing characters. Variable art quality somewhat diminished the overall impact of the line. The only comic publisher to place each issue into endless reprints while continuing to publish new titles on a monthly basis, lasting 30 years.
(a,b,c,e,f,h,i,j,k)

DOLL MAN No. 1 (Fall/41, Qua, H)-After a successful two-year run in ***Feature***, the mighty mite leaped into his own title, lasting 12 years. The proto-type of the Silver Age Atom.
(a,b,c,e,j)

DYNAMIC COMICS No. 1 (10/41, Chesler, H)-Chesler's second patriotic super hero series. Debut of *Major Victory*. Suspended after three issues and brought back with a format change in 1944, lasting four more years.
(e)

★★★ **GREEN LANTERN** No. 1 (Fall/41, DC, H)-Having headlined ***All-American*** for one year, one of DC's foremost heroes achieved the distinction of his own title. It ran for 8 years and went on to become one of the key revival characters of the Silver Age.
(a,b,c,e)

★★★★ **LOONEY TUNES & MERRY MELODIES** No. 1 (Fall/41, Dell, F)-The companion title to the enormously successful ***WDC&S***. Dell's second funny animal anthology featured *Bugs Bunny*, *Porky Pig* and *Elmer Fudd*. This was the first comic book appearance of Warner Brothers film characters. The series ran for 21 years.
(a,b,c,e,h,j,l)

RANGERS COMICS No. 1(10/41, FH, W)-The publisher's sixth single theme anthology title (war theme). Standard FH style of chessecake art and covers, lasting 11 years.
(a,b,c,e)

SKYMAN No. 1 (Fall/41, CCG, Av)-After a year's successful run in ***Big Shot***, he was given his own title. Second of a publisher, lasting only 4 issues. (He remained the main feature in ***Big Shot*** for 9 years.)
(a,c,e)

★★ **SPYSMASHER** No. 1 (Fall/41, Faw, Av)-Popular war hero graduating from ***Whiz*** into his own title, lasting 2 years. Maiden issue featured unusual logo printed in metallic silver.
(a,c,e)

STAR SPANGLED COMICS No. 1(10/41, DC, H)-DC's first patriotic theme title featuring the *Star Spangled Kid*. Due to the weak contents, the title had a dramatic format change with No. 7 when *The Guardian* and *The Newsboy Legion* were introduced.
(b,e)

WORLD FAMOUS HEROES MAGAZINE No. 1 (10/41, Comic Corp, TR)-Similar theme to PMI's ***Real Heroes***, and Eastern's ***Heroic***, with stories of famous people, lasting 4 issues.
(e)

AIRFIGHTERS COMICS No. 1 (11/41, Hill, Av)-An early attempt at an aviation theme comic (like ***Wings***), lasting only one issue. A year later the title was revived more successfully with a new 'dynamic' character in *Airboy*.
(e)

GREAT COMICS No. 1 (11/41, Great, H)-First of a publisher, featuring super heroes. The third and last issue is a classic: *Futuro* takes *Hitler* to hell.
(e,k)

MAN OF WAR No. 1 (11/41, Centaur, H)-Centaur's third and last patriotic theme title, lasting 2 issues. Conjecture is that Centaur itself expired with this book.
(e)

SCOOP COMICS No. 1 (11/41, Chesler, H)-Chesler's third attempt at a comeback with this anthology of super heroes. Debut of *Rocketman* and *Rocketgirl*, lasting 8 issues.
(e)

U.S. JONES No. 1 (11/41, Fox, H)-Fox's second patriotic theme title, lasting 2 issues.
(e)

★★★★ **ALL-STAR COMICS** No. 8 (11-12/41, DC, H)-*Wonder Woman*, the first super-heroine, created by Charles Moulton and drawn by H.G. Peters, debuted in this issue as an 8 page add-on. Her origin continued in ***Sensation*** No. 1, where

she becomes the lead feature. A trend setter.
(a,b,c,d,f,h,i,j)

BANG-UP COMICS No. 1 (12/41, Progressive, H)-A new publisher entered the field. This series was mediocre in its content only surviving 3 issues.
(e,k)

CAPTAIN AERO COMICS No. 7 (12/41, Hoke, Av)-Cashing in on the popularity of *Spy Smasher* and *Captain Midnight*, this publisher began with another aviation hero. With strong, colorful covers, the series lasted 5 years.
(e)

CHOICE COMICS No. 1 (12/41, Great, H)-The publisher's second title. A mixed anthology, lasting 3 issues.
(e)

MASTER COMICS No. 21 (12/41, Faw, H)-*Captain Marvel* and *Bulletman* team-up to fight *Captain Nazi*. A classic battle sequence, rare in comics at this time. High impact (classic) Raboy cover and story art.
(a,b,c)

PIONEER PICTURE STORIES No. 1 (12/41, S&S, TR)-An anthology of true stories about heroes (ala ***Heroic Comics***), lasting 9 issues.
(e)

★★★★ **PEP COMICS** No. 22 (12/41, MLJ, TA)-The eternal sophomore and his friends began the first of over forty consecutive terms at Riverdale High. Never rose above pat formula, but survived vagaries of shifting market that did in a host of illustrious predecessors and glut of imitators (many of which originated at MLJ itself). Auxillary characters achieved stardom with their own titles. Trend setter, lasting beyond 40 years.
(a,b,c,d,f,h,i,j)

PUNCH COMICS No. 1 (12/41, Chesler, H)-Chesler's fourth attempt to get back into the market. A mixed anthology series with a successful format, lasting 6 years.
(e)

★★★ **WHIZ COMICS** No. 25 (12/12/41, Faw, H)-*Captain Marvel* was cloned for the second time (see *Lt. Marvels*) into a junior size as *Captain Marvel Jr.* . Classic art by Mac Raboy gave the character a slick streamlined 'Raymond' look. He was given immediate headlining in ***Master Comics***. This was the first significant character cloned.
(a,b,c,d,j)

X-MAS COMICS No. 1 (12/41, Faw, H)-A new concept. Earlier in the year, Fawcett began overrunning certain selected comics with indicias, page numbers, etc. removed. These comics were then bound up into a thick book (324 pgs.) to be sold as a special comic for Christmas. This successful format evolved into several other titles and lasted for 11 years.
(a,b,c,e,f,h,j)

CAPTAIN MARVEL THRILL BOOK nn (1941, Faw, H)-A large-size black & white comic reprinting popular *Captain Marvel* stories, lasting one issue. (Half text, half illustration.)
(e)

DICKIE DARE No. 1 (1941, Eastern, R)-Another single theme anthology title of the popular strip, lasting 4 issues.
(e)

DOUBLE UP nn (1941, Elliott, H)-The same idea as ***Double***, except this was a one-shot remarketing of remaindered digest-sized issues of ***Speed***, ***Spitfire*** and ***Pocket***. Probably a special deal to Elliott due to heavy returns?
(e)

FACE, THE No. 1 (1941, CCG, H)-The popular strip from ***Big Shot*** achieved brief stardom, lasting only two issues.
(e)

KEY RING COMICS (1941, Dell, An)-A special formated comic series of 16 pages each to put in a two-ring binder (sold as a set of five).
(e)

TRAIL BLAZERS No. 1 (1941, S&S, TR)-True fact anthology of heroic deeds, lasting 4 issues.
(e)

USA IS READY No. 1 (1941, Dell, W)-Dell's second war title lasting one issue.
(e)

★★★ **ANIMAL COMICS** No. 1 (12-1/41-42, Dell, F)-Debut of Walt Kelly's classic character, *Pogo*, which became syndicated in 1948. Dell's third funny animal single theme anthology title following the success of ***WDC&S*** and ***Looney Tunes***. The first funny animal comic with original characters at Dell.
(a,c,d,e,j)

1942 ■

BIG CHIEF WAHOO No. 1 (Wint/41-42, Eastern, R)-Popular transfer strip debuts in his own comic series, lasting 23 issues.
(c,e)

FOUR MOST No. 1 (Wint/41-42, Novelty, H)-A showcase title featuring Novelty's best characters from ***Target*** and ***Blue Bolt***. Series taken over by *Dick Cole* with No. 3 on. Their third title.
(a,b,c,e)

★ **LEADING COMICS** No. 1 (Wint/41-42, DC,

H)-Like ***All-Star***, this title provided a showcase for DC's secondary heroes (a poor man's ***All-Star***). Series ran 14 issues then changed to a funny animal format for the rest of its 7 year existance.
(e)

★★★★★ **SENSATION COMICS** No. 1 (1/42, DC, H)-*Wonder Woman's* origin continued from ***All-Star*** No. 8 (her first appearance). A very strong character from the onset, achieving stardom instantly as a headline feature of this series. She won her own title within a few months which has run uninterrupted for over 40 years. (One of the few characters to achieve this kind of exposure.)
(a,b,c,e,f,h,j)

SPECIAL COMICS No. 1 (Wint/41-42, MLJ, H)-A one-shot special featuring *The Hangman* from ***Pep Comics***. A hit on the stands, the character was launched into his own series with No. 2.
(c,e)

V...- COMICS No. 1 (1/42, Fox, H)-another short-lived title from Fox. His third patriotic theme comic. Introduced *V-Man*, lasted only two issues.
(e)

AMERICA'S BEST COMICS No. 1 (2/42, BP, H)-A showcase title to give more exposure to their top characters. The high impact covers (many by Schomburg) sustained the run, lasting 7 years.
(a,b,c,e)

CAMP COMICS No. 1 (2/42, Dell, Hm)-A mixed (humorous) anthology title with pretty girl photo covers. An unusual format slanted to the soldier boys at camp.
(e)

★★ **GENE AUTRY COMICS** No. 1 (2/42, Faw, Ws)-The second newsstand continuous series western title devoted to a single character. *Gene* ties with *Roy Rogers* as the most popular cowboy star of the sound era. Title survived 18 years.
(a,b,c,e,h,j,l)

JINGLE JANGLE COMICS No. 1 (2/42, Eastern Color, Hm)-A young children's comic, containing illustrations and script by George Carlson, a children's book heavyweight (*Uncle Wiggily*). Eastern's second anthology title of original material (see ***Heroic***), lasting 7 years.
(a,b,e,j)

TRUE SPORT PICTURE STORIES No. 5 (2/42, S&S, Sp)-Continued from ***Sport Comics***, lasting 7 years.
(e)

CAPTAIN COURAGEOUS COMICS No. 6 (3/42, Ace, H)-Introduced in ***Banner***, the character was given his own title but lasted only one issue.
(e)

TOUGH KID SQUAD No. 1 (3/42, Timely, H)-Timely's second series devoted to sidekicks (see ***Young Allies***). Highly prized due to its rarity.
(e)

★★ **BOY COMICS** No. 3 (4/42, Lev, H)-Gleason's second successful title, introducing *Crimebuster*. This series survived 14 years due to Biro's strong, complex plotting.
(a,b,c,d,e,j)

COMEDY COMICS No. 9 (4/42, Timely, H)-The title is misleading. A super hero anthology title changing to a humorous and funny animal format early on.
(e)

HANGMAN COMICS No. 2 (Spr/42, MLJ, H)-The smash hit of ***Pep Comics*** received his own series, but lasted only 7 issues.
(e)

★ **JOKER COMICS** No. 1 (4/42, Timely, Hm)-First *Powerhouse Pepper* by Wolverton. Wolverton, an original if there ever was one, stood totally aloof from the mainstream of comic art. His effect on later comics ranging from the original ***Mad*** to the sixties undergrounds, is incalculable. (He tried to fit in, but the effect of playing it straight made his work even more bizzarre.)
(a,b,c,d,e,f,g,j)

SHEENA, QUEEN OF THE JUNGLE No. 1 (Spr/42, FH, J)-After three years exposure in ***Jumbo Comics***, *Sheena* finally graduated to her own title, lasting 18 issues spread over 11 years.
(a,b,c,e)

★★ **STAR SPANGLED COMICS** No. 7 (4/42, DC, H)-Debut of *The Guardian* and *The Newsboy Legion* by Simon and Kirby (vintage). Title lasted 11 years.
(a,b,c,d,j)

WAMBI, JUNGLE BOY No. 1 (Spr/42, FH, J)-From ***Jungle Comics***. Not strong enough to carry his own title which had erratic publishing (18 issues in 11 years).
(e)

★★★★ **CRIME DOES NOT PAY** No. 22 (6/42, Lev, C)-Aside from being the first crime comic, this title was the first of any to be deliberately targeted at the adult reader. Inspired by the widely read ***True Detective*** - style magazines of the time. Implicit and unsavory subject matter, in the context of what was popularly understood as publications for children, assured the attention and disapproval of Wertham and others. Established conventions of graphically depicted violence that would be exploited to the extreme in the horror comics of a decade later. Arguably the third most influential comic ever published (after

Action and ***Superman***), ***CDNP*** was a belated trend setter. Gleason had the field all to himself for six years. Then, in 1948 the industry suffered a severe slump in sales. In desperation, publishers turned en masse to the formerly untapped 'crime' market. This move was abetted in part by Gleason himself. In mid-1947 he had begun publishing circulation figures on the covers of ***CDNP***, reporting sales of 5 million - 6 million copies (per issue?), an astounding record for a comics periodical and, an open invitation to imitation.
(a,b,c,e,f,h,i,j)

★ **DETECTIVE COMICS** No. 64 (6/42, DC, H)-Simon and Kirby introduce the *Boy Commandos*. A more timely version of the *Newsboy Legion*, this popular series found the Axis plagued with a platoon of wise-cracking juveniles. An immediate hit, the lads were rewarded with a quarterly of their own within a matter of months.
(a,c,d,j)

FAIRY TALE PARADE No. 1 (6-7/42, Dell, F)-Dell's second continuous series funny animal title with original characters. Its popularity was carried entirely by the imaginative illustrative genius of Walt Kelly.
(c,e)

DIXIE DUGAN No. 1 (7/42, CCG, R)-Popular strip character given own title, lasting 7 years (13 issues).
(e)

KRAZY KOMICS No. 1 (7/42, Timely, F)-With four funny animal anthology titles on the stands (all by Dell), Timely entered this new developing field. This series had a humorous format with no strong characters, lasting 4 years. The second publisher in this genre.
(e)

NEW FUNNIES No. 65 (7/42, Dell, F)-The funny animal fever was catching on as Dell gave stardom to their newly acquired characters, *Andy Panda* and *Woody Woodpecker*. Lantz created these characters who became an instant success for Dell's ***The Funnies***. This was Dell's fifth funny animal series (with only six on the stands).
(a,b,c,e,j)

OAKY DOAKS No. 1 (7/42, Eastern Color, R)-A one-shot strip reprint book which couldn't compete on the stands.
(e)

WAR VICTORY ADVENTURES No. 1 (Sum/42, Harv, W)-A unique super hero title produced to promote purchase of war savings bonds, lasting 3 issues.
(e)

★★★★ **WONDER WOMAN** No. 1 (Sum/42, DC, H)-One of the few characters in comics to make her own title just months from her debut in ***All-Star*** No. 8. The only mythological character to flourish in the comics format, her only concession to the present was adopting a modern costume. The amazing Amazon was a trend setter whose popularity has lasted beyond 40 years.
(a,b,c,e,j)

WAR HEROES No. 1 (7-9/42, Dell, W)-Dell's third war title, lasting 11 issues.
(e)

★ **CAPTAIN MIDNIGHT** No. 1 (9/42, Faw, Av)-This book heralds one of the most changed transfer characters adapted successfully to the comic book format. Fawcett's version of the character is the most memorable (see ***The Funnies*** No. 57), lasting 6 years. Kept alive by the long lasting radio series and a movie serial. A spin-off of *Spy Smasher*.
(a,b,c,e)

FIGHTING YANK No. 1 (9/42, BP, H)-After a year's exposure in ***Startling***, the colonial hero was given his own series. The outstanding Schomburg covers sustained the run, lasting 7 years.
(a,b,c,e,j)

OUR GANG COMICS No. 1 (9-10/42, Dell, F)-A strong early licensed group from MGM films who didn't quite come across as well in the comic medium due to necessary changes in the sterotyping of *Buckwheat* and others. The comic version is mainly collected due to the outstanding art by Walt Kelly and the back-up strips by Carl Barks.
(a,b,c,e,f,j,l)

★ **COO COO COMICS** No. 1 (10/42, BP, F)-Seeing the stands beginning to swell with Dell's funny animal titles (5), Better got on the band wagon. *Super Mouse* debuted, the first funny animal super hero (cloned from *Superman*). (7 funny animal titles now on the stands.)
(a,b,c,d,e,f,h,i,j)

★★★★★ **DONALD DUCK FOUR COLOR** No. 9 (10/42, Dell, F)-Debut of anonymous artist, who breathed life into the character and turned the strip into full-length adventure stories. Carl Barks' successful adaptation won him the position as *Donald Duck's* biographer for almost three decades beginning with ***Walt Disney's Comics and Stories*** No. 31.
(a,b,c,g,h,j)

★ **JUNGLE GIRL** No. 1 (Fall/42, Faw, J)-Inspired by the popular film serial, *Perils of Nyoka*, this one-shot introduced the jungle heroine to comics. The series was picked up again in 1945 (retitled ***Nyoka***, lasting 8 years.
(a,b,c,e,f,j,l)

PICTURE STORIES FROM THE BIBLE No. 1 (Fall/42, DC, TR)-The pilot model of M. C.

Gaines' projected 'educational comics' line was laudable in concept but squelched at the stands by abysmal art, pedantic scripting and the normal resistance of kids to anything even remotely preachy. Sustained primarily by lot sales to educators and church groups. Ironically, the first comic ever to bear the EC seal.
(a,c,e,i,j,l)

SUPERSNIPE COMICS No. 6 (10/42, S&S, H)-Probably the best, and certainly the most original comic book character of this pulp publisher. A super hero parody lasting 7 years.
(a,b,c,e,f,j)

★ **TERRY-TOONS COMICS** No. 1 (10/42, Timely, F)-20th Century Fox's characters enter the comic field with this book. Timely's second funny animal anthology series (8 titles are now on the stands). 20th Century Fox's *Mighty Mouse* appeared in films the following year and entered this run with No. 38.
(a,b,c,e,j,l)

★ **AIR FIGHTERS** No. 2 (11/42, Hill, Av)-First appearance of one ot the top aviation features also marked Hillman's first successful title. Engaging origin featured air-minded monk who designed and built the premier imaginary aircraft in all of comics. At the controls of the unusual bat-winged orinthopter, dubbed *Birdie*, was the youth who would become known as *Airboy*. He managed to make the standard garb of the pilot—goggles, scarf, flight jacket, et al—look as if they were designed expressly for him. Thoughtful scripting and complimentary art (ala Caniff) propelled this feature through the war years and beyond. Duration 11 years. (*The Heap*, one of the most original characters in comics, began in the next issue.)
(a,b,c,d,j)

★★ **CAPTAIN MARVEL JR** No. 1 (11/42, Faw, H)-Fawcett's second most popular hero (from ***Master***) was given his own series. Raboy classic covers/story art sustained the run, lasting 11 years.
(a,b,c,e)

MICKEY FINN No. 1 (11/42, Eastern Color, R)-The popular transfer character tried his wings in a title of his own. Like *Sparky Watts*, only 17 issues came out in a 10 year period.
(a,c,e)

NAPOLEON AND UNCLE ELBY No. 1 (11/42, East-
ern Color, R)-A one-shot single theme anthology title of the popular transfer strip.
(e)

SPARKY WATTS No. 1 (11/42, CCG, R)-Humorous, off-beat character (proven in ***Big Shot***) is given own title, struggling through 10 issues in 7 years.
(a,c,e)

STRICTLY PRIVATE No. 1 (11/42, Eastern Color, R)-A two-issue run of the famous strip, not surviving as a comic book.
(e)

TOPIX No. 1 (11/42, CG, Re)-The first continuous series comic with a religious theme, lasting 10 years. First of a publisher.
(b,e,i,j,k)

★ **CAPTAIN MARVEL ADVENTURES** No. 18 (12/11/42, Faw, H)-*Captain Marvel* is cloned again. Debut of *Mary Marvel* and *The Marvel Family*. *Mary Marvel* was given instant stardom in ***Wow***.
(a,b,c,d,j)

FAWCETT'S FUNNY ANIMAL COMICS No. 1 (12/42, Faw, F)-The first appearance of *Hoppy The Marvel Bunny*, (cloned from *Captain Marvel*), lasting 13 years. The second funny animal super hero (see ***Coo Coo***). Fawcett joined Dell, Timely and Better entering the funny animal market (10 titles now on the stands). (*Captain Marvel* himself introduced *Hoppy* on the cover.)
(a,b,c,d,e,h,j)

FUNNY BOOK No. 1 (12/42, PMI, F)-Another publisher entered the funny animal market with this book. Weak concepts overall, the title lasting 9 issues over 4 years (10 titles now on the stands).
(e)

GIFT COMICS No. 1 (12/42, Faw, H)-Fawcett's second thick-format title containing original comics to be released at Christmas with ***Holiday*** and ***Xmas*** for 50¢.
(a,c,e)

HIT COMICS No. 25 (12/42, Qua, H)-*Kid Eternity* debuts. Recurring war-era theme of life after life was given novel twist in this long running series. Youthful hero, dying ahead of his appointed time, was not only miraculously restored to life but granted the ability to call on all the great heroes of the past for assistance in solving crimes (see *The Fighting Yank*). Intriguing concept was given usual stellar Iger shop treatment.
(a,b,c,d,j)

HOLIDAY COMICS No. 1 (12/42, Faw, H)-Fawcett's third thick-format title of original comics to be released at Christmas with ***Gift*** and ***Xmas*** for 25¢.
(a,c,e)

SANTA CLAUS FUNNIES No. 1 (12/42, Dell, F)-A special Christmas book illustrated by Kelly. A successful concept that was repeated annually for 20 years.

(a,b,c,e)

AMERICA IN ACTION nn (1942, Dell, W)-A one-shot war anthology book.
(e)

FAMOUS STORIES No. 1 (1942, Dell, Lit)-An educational theme comic, similar to ***Classic Comics***, not lasting beyond the 2nd issue.
(e)

JOE PALOOKA No. 1 (1942, CCG, R)-With proven success in ***Big Shot*** (not to mention syndication), the character became a star in his own title. Early issues boast "over 1,000,000 copies sold." The series lasted 19 years.
(a,b,c,e)

WAR STORIES No. 1 (1942, Dell, W)-Dell's fourth war theme anthology title, lasting 8 issues. *Night Devils*, a mysterious costumed war team debuted in No. 3.
(e)

1943 ■

ALL NEW COMICS No. 1 (1/43, Harv, H)-A super hero anthology title of mediocre quality, lasting 15 issues.
(e)

★★★ **ARCHIE COMICS** No. 1 (Wint/42-43, AP, TA)-Early stardom for a non-super hero theme. A successful formula with many spin-off characters, lasting beyond 40 years.
(a,b,c,d,e,h,i,j)

BLACK TERROR No. 1 (Wint/42-43, BP, H)-Fighting his way from ***Exciting***, the character begins his own series. Sterling costume. High impact Schomburg covers mislead the buyer as to the quality of the contents. Lasted 7 years.
(a,b,c,e,j)

BOY COMMANDOS No. 1 (Wint/42-43, DC, W)-After *Captain America*, this was the second title that Simon and Kirby had all to themselves. Pat variation of favorite S&K theme: Kid group with adult mentor. Seldom rose above the expected, but S&K were at their loosest and the strip conveys the sense of fun they probably had doing it. Earlier covers, sans redundant blurbs and intrusive dialogue balloons, are superb poster art.
(a,b,c,e,j)

CAPTAIN BATTLE No. 3 (Wint/42-43, Mag. Press, H)-After a year's delay, the character from ***Silver Streak*** was given another chance, only lasting 3 issues.
(e)

CLUE COMICS No. 1 (1/43, Hill, H)-Hillman's second most successful title. Unusual heroes and bizarre villains sustained run for four years.
(e)

COMIC CAVALCADE No. 1 (Wint/42-43, DC, H)-Following the success of ***World's Finest***, DC launched this companion book in thick format featuring their next tier of top characters, *Wonder Woman, The Flash* and *Green Lantern*.
(a,b,c,e)

COMICS DIGEST No. 1 (Wint/42-43, PMI, TR)-A one-shot war theme reprint anthology (pocket size) from ***True Comics***.
(e)

FLYING CADET No. 1 (1/43, Flying Cadet, Av)-A true theme World War II aviation anthology (with real photos), lasting 4 years.
(e)

GOLDEN ARROW No. 1 (Wint/42-43, Faw, Ws)-Fawcett's original western character from ***Whiz*** finally given own title, lasting 6 issues.
(a,e)

HELLO PAL COMICS No. 1 (1/43, Harv, An)-Unusual format featuring photographic covers of movie stars. *Rocketman* and *Rocketgirl* appear (see ***Scoop***), lasting 3 issues.
(e)

MISS FURY COMICS No. 1 (Wint/42-43, Timely, H)-A strong transfer character by Tarpe Mills. Noteworthy and unique in that she rarely appeared in costume.
(a,c,e,f,j)

MAJOR HOOPLE COMICS No. 1 (1/43, BP, R)-A one-shot comic of the famous strip character, as Better tried to enter the reprint market.
(e)

REAL FUNNIES No. 1 (1/43, Nedor, F)-The publisher's second funny animal title (11 titles now on stands), only lasting 3 issues. First appearance of *The Black Terrier* (cloned from *The Black Terror*), the third funny animal super hero.
(e)

RED DRAGON COMICS No. 5 (1/43, S&S, An)-Pulpy anthology series not strong enough to last over 5 issues.
(e)

DON WINSLOW OF THE NAVY No. 1 (2/43, Faw, W)-His comic book career was launched here with an introduction by *Captain Marvel* himself. Successful adaptation of this popular transfer character, lasting 12 years.
(a,b,c,e,j,l)

HEADLINE COMICS No. 1 (2/43, Prize, TR)-Taking up the "True" theme of PMI's ***True*** and ***Real Heroes*** and Better's ***Real Life***, Prize entered the field with this, their second title, which lasted 13 years.
(b,e)

HOPALONG CASSIDY No. 1 (2/43, Faw, Ws)-A one-shot issue continuing as a series three years later. The third continuous series newsstand western title, lasting 16 years. A transfer character kept alive by William Boyd's strong following in the movies and on TV.
(a,b,c,e)

IBIS, THE INVINCIBLE No. 1 (2/43, Faw, Mg)-As a solid back-up feature in ***Whiz***, he was invincible, but not invincible enough to support a title of his own. The title expired after 6 issues.
(e)

KID KOMICS No. 1 (2/43, Timely, H)-Timely's third series devoted to sidekicks. The Schomburg covers and guest appearances of secondary characters sustained the run through 10 issues.
(e)

ALL HERO COMICS No. 1 (3/43, Faw, H)-Fawcett's second title that showcased their top characters (see ***America's Greatest***). A thick format one-shot.
(a,c,e)

CAPTAIN MARVEL ADVENTURES No. 22 (3/43, Faw, H)-Begins the 25-issue *Mr. Mind* serial which captured nation-wide attention at the time. Tremendous and brilliant marketing strategy by Fawcett. An epic by any standard, unmatched before or since.
(c,d,f,h,i,j)

COMEDY COMICS No. 14 (3/43, Timely, F)-The first *Super Rabbit* (the fourth funny animal super hero) (the 12th title on the stands). Given his own title the following year. (An imitation of *Hoppy The Marvel Bunny*.)
(a,c,d,e,j)

FUNNY FUNNIES No. 1 (4/43, BP, F)-A one-shot funny animal title (their third) (13 titles now on the stands). No enduring characters.
(e)

★★★★ **WALT DISNEY'S COMICS AND STORIES** No. 31 (4/43, Dell, F)-Anonymous staffer who defined what funny animal continuity is all about began this issue (2nd Barks *DD* story; see ***DD Four Color*** No. 9). Cinched long-term success of Disney anthology. One of a half-dozen absolute masters of the form, Carl Barks' achievement on individual stories is exceeded only by remarkable consistency of the series over the length of its run (over 40 years).
(a,b,c,j)

GOOFY COMICS No. 1 (6/43, Nedor, F)-Nedor's fourth funny animal title and one of the most enduring, lasting 10 years. No memorable characters. (13 funny animal titles on the stands.)
(b,e)

JOLLY JINGLES No. 10 (Sum/43, MLJ, F)-A new publisher tried their hand at funny animals, introducing *Super Duck* (the fifth funny animal super hero). (A hybrid of *Superman* and *Donald Duck*.) (14 titles on the stands.)
(a,c,d,e,j)

★★ **PLASTIC MAN** No. 1 (Sum/43, Qua, H)-After a slow start, this title outlasts ***Police Comics***, surviving 13 years. One of the top hero concepts carried by the exciting plotting/art of Jack Cole.
(a,b,c,e)

HAPPY COMICS No. 1 (8/43, Standard, F)-Their fifth funny animal title. No memorable characters, lasting 7 years (14 titles on the stands.)
(b,e)

ALL-SELECT COMICS No. 1 (Fall/43, Timely, H)-Timely's second showcase title featuring their top three characters (see ***All Winners***). Series carried by Schomburg covers (a proven sales feature), lasting 3 years.
(a,c,e)

ALL SURPRISE No. 1 (Fall/43, Timely, F)-Timely's fourth funny animal title, giving more exposure to their leading character, *Super Rabbit*, lasting 4 years. (15 titles on the stands.)
(e)

SUPER RABBIT No. 1 (Fall/43, Timely, F)-After his debut in ***Comedy Comics***, *Super Rabbit* is given his own title, lasting 5 years. (15 titles on the stands.)
(e)

CAPTAIN BATTLE JR No. 1 (Fall/43, Comic House, H)-Clone of *Captain Battle*. The *Claw* vs. *The Ghost*, lasting 2 issues.
(e)

GIGGLE COMICS No. 1 (10/43, ACG, F)-Ties as first title of a new publisher, reinforcing the trend to funny animals. The quality and style of ACG's whole line was heavily influenced by the mastery of the teacher-artist of Ken Hultgren, the series' artist (beginning in 1944). This title lasted 12 years. (17 titles on the stands.)
(a,b,c,e,j,k)

HA HA COMICS No. 1 (10/43, ACG, F)-Ties as first title of a new publisher, reinforcing the trend to funny animals. A double impact-with sister title on the stands. Ingenious plotting and art by Ken Hultgren begins the following year. This series lasted 12 years. (17 titles on the stands.)
(a,b,c,e,j,k)

SUSPENSE COMICS No. 1 (12/43, Continental, D)-Debut of *The Grey Mask* (imitation of *The Spirit*). Atmospheric radio drama in a comic book form, lasting 3 years.
(e)

(Continued on page No. A-66)

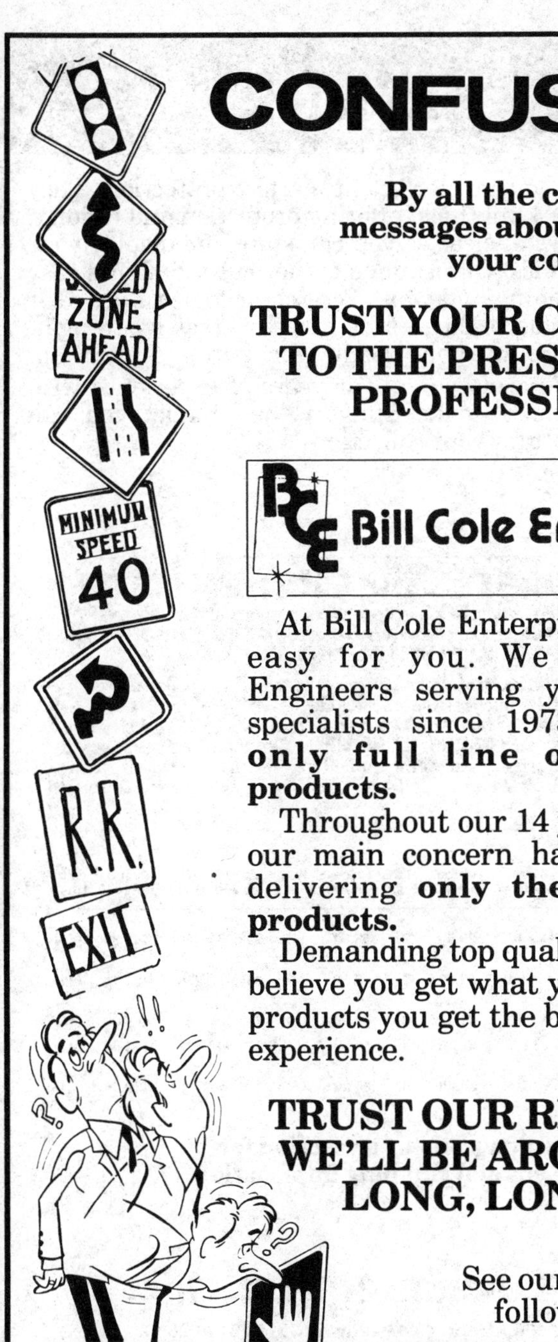

CONFUSED...?

By all the conflicting messages about protecting your comics?

TRUST YOUR COLLECTION TO THE PRESERVATION PROFESSIONALS

BCE Bill Cole Enterprises, Inc.

At Bill Cole Enterprises we can make it easy for you. We are Professsonal Engineers serving you as preservation specialists since 1973. **We supply the only full line of preservation products.**

Throughout our 14 years in the business our main concern has been finding and delivering **only the highest quality products.**

Demanding top quality isn't easy. But we believe you get what you pay for. With our products you get the benefit of our years of experience.

TRUST OUR REPUTATION. WE'LL BE AROUND FOR A LONG, LONG, TIME.

See our products on the following 10 pages.

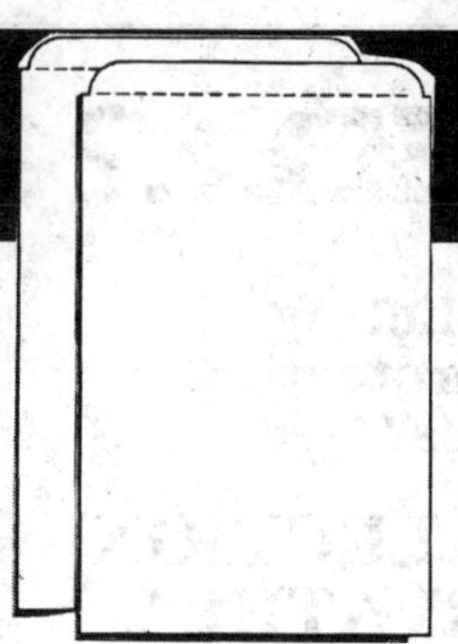

SNUGS™

. . . means perfect fit, perfect protection. They are 4 mil thick, offering protection and rigidity. Crystal clear so you can store and display your comics. Our Unique corner cut tab allows easy opening and won't scratch or tear comics. Our exclusive heat seal process creates stronger, more durable seams for better protection.

And of course, our years of experience with Mylar® make Snugs™ the product you can trust for your collection.

OUR MYLAR® CREDENTIALS

Bill Cole Enterprises has been working with Mylar® since 1979. Other than the company we acquired in 1982, NO ONE ELSE CAN MAKE THAT LEGITIMATE CLAIM.

In these years we've served everyone who finds paper preservation vital. Our customers include THE SMITHSONIAN INSTITUTE, THE LIBRARY OF CONGRESS, AND THE NATIONAL ARCHIVES. These highly regarded institutions will only purchase from well qualified and legitimate organizations. We proudly serve them as we would be equally proud to serve you.

Cat. #	Description	Size (inches)	Price per 50	Wt. (lbs.)	Price per 100	Wt. (lbs.)	Price per 500	Wt. (lbs.)	Price per 1000	Wt. (lbs.)
58	Standard Size late 60's to present	7¼ x 10½	29.50	(2)	53.50	(4)	242.75	(18)	441.50	(40)
61	Silver/Gold Size from 1940's to 1960's	7¾ x 10½	30.85	(2)	56.50	(4)	255.00	(19)	463.75	(42)
62	Super Gold Size larger comics of early 40's	8¼ x 10½	32.50	(2)	59.00	(4)	267.50	(20)	486.00	(42)
63	63 Magazine Size	9 x 11½	36.50	(3)	66.50	(5)	350.00	(22)	546.00	(45)
66B	3-Ring Binder Size	8 x 10½	36.00	(3)	65.50	(5)	296.75	(22)	539.50	(44)

See the last page of our ad section for complete terms and shipping information.

Bill Cole Enterprises, Inc.
P.O. Box 60 • Dept. 47 • Wollaston, MA 02170-0060
(617) 773-2653 • (617) 963-5510

All references to Mylar® refer to uncoated archival quality polyester film such as Mylar® type D by DuPont Co. or, equivalent material such as Melinex® 516 by ICI Corp.

ACID FREE BOXES

Our boxes are made from acid-free, virgin wood cellulose and are of archival quality. Boxes are a tough 52 mils thick. Styles 12, 14 and 10 have metal reinforced edges.

Archives and museums throughout the world use our boxes to store priceless documents and papers. Let them do the job for you, too, acting as an additional preservation material to help retard the aging process.

TRUE ARCHIVAL QUALITY?

Because ordinary cardboard is itself acidic, storage in cardboard may be hazardous to your collection. But so-called "acid-free" materials may not be enough. "Acid-free" means only that cardboard measures no less than pH 7.0. Cardboard of TRUE ARCHIVAL QUALITY must have a minimum pH of 8.5 and a 3% calcium carbonate buffer throughout to provide the best protection. All our acid free products meet this stringent requirement.

Cat. #	Description	Size (inches)	Will Hold (approx.)	Metal Reinf.*	Price per 5	Wt. (lbs.)	Price per 20	Wt. (lbs.)
	Cartons							
17	Comic, Standard Size	7 x 11 x 11	100 comics		27.75	(10)	96.25	(40)
16	Comic, Silver/Gold	8 x 11½ x 11½	85 comics		29.25	(10)	106.25	(40)
18	Magazine, Comic, General Purpose	9 x 12 x 12	75 magazines		37.95	(11)	136.75	(44)
12	Comic Case - library style (open), fits most comics	3 x 8 x 9	25 comics	•	14.75	(5)	51.25	(20)
14	Drop Front Shelf Box fits most comics and magazines	3 x 9½ x 12½	25 comics	•	23.75	(7)	82.00	(28)
10	Flip-Top Box fits most comics	4 x 8 x 11	50 comics	•	29.00	(7)	101.00	(28)

In a hurry? 24 Hour Toll Free Order line for VISA & Mastercard Customers! 1-800-225-8249

Bill Cole Enterprises, Inc.
P.O. Box 60 • Dept. 47 • Wollaston, MA 02170-0060
(617) 773-2653 • (617) 963-5510

See the last page of our ad section for complete ordering and shipping information.

ENCAPSULATION

The Ultimate in Mylar® protection! We can hermetically seal your comic books in crystal clear Mylar® and increase the life expectancy and value of your comics! Available in either #E--4 E-Capsulation™ (4-mil thick) or #N-C7 N-Capsulate™ (7 mil thick).

Bill Cole Enterprises can custom encapsulate any paper collectible. Please write us for a quotation.

All items should be sent with full payment VIA UPS or insured mail. Completed material will be reshipped back to you via UPS C.O.D. (cash only to cover freight charges.) Please allow 4-6 weeks for delivery.

Quantity of Books	#E-C4™ Price (ea.)	#N-C7™ Price (ea.)
1 - 10	2.50	3.00
11 - 25	1.75	2.50
26 - 50	.95	1.50
51 - 100	.89	1.30
101 - 500	.84	1.20

We will custom encapsulate your choice of paper collectible. Please write us for a quotation.

All items for encapsulation should be sent to:

Bill Cole Enterprises, Inc.
121 Liberty Street
S. Quincy, Mass. 02169

Orders sent to our P.O. Box cannot be accepted.

N-Capsulate™ is a trademark of E. Gerber Products with exclusive rights to Bill Cole Enterprises, Inc.
E-Capsulation™ is a trademark of Bill Cole Enterprises, Inc.

ARCHIVAL SUPPLIES

Archival Storage Cabinets

These 100% kiln dried, Maine pine storage cabinets are specifically designed for archival protection of comic books and other paper collectables. They have acrylic sliding doors and are fully modular so they can grow with your collection.

Cat. #	Description	Size (inches)	New Low Price Ea.	Wt. (lbs.)
93	Base Unit	12 x 24 x3	8.25	(5)
94	Full Cabinet	10 x 24 x 11½	18.15	(17)
95	Half Cabinet	10 x 12 x 11½	14.75	(9)

Wei t'o®

Wei t'o® non-aqueous sprays and solutions can safely be used to prevent deterioration of your comics and other paper collectables. One application offers indefinite preservation. And, when used in conjunction with Mylar® and acid-free cardboard, it is the ultimate paper preservation system available.

Cat. #	Description	Size	Price Ea.	Wt (lbs.)
80/12	Aerosol Spray, for thicker paper and boards	1 pt.	18.40	(3)
81/10	Aerosol Spray, for general use	1 pt.	18.40	(3)
82/2	Solution	1 qt.	28.75	(6)

Cat. #	Description	Size	Price Ea.	Wt. (lbs.)
84	Document Repair Tape	1" x 98'	15.35	(½)
92	Archival Double-Faced Tape	¼" x 18'	6.35	(½)
91	Document Cleaning Pad	—	2.60	(½)
77	PH indicator test strips (measures ph of paper)	100/pkg	10.00	(½)

Wei t'o® is a registered trademark of Wei t'o Associates, Inc.

PLASTIC BAGS

Our highest quality, crystal clear 3-mil bags are priced competitively with both the dealer and collector in mind.

These plastic bags are made from the finest quality 3-mil thick polyethylene film available (containing a minimum of plasticizers) and have a single fold flap. The standard of the hobby, our bags are packed flat (no creases or folds). Pre--counted in packages of 100 with outer bag identification for your convenience. These bags are just the thing for short term storage of your collectibles!

Cat. #	Description	Size (inches)	White 1½" flap *	Price per 100	Wt. (lbs.)	Price per 500	Wt. (lbs.)	Price per 1000	Wt. (lbs.)
46	Standard Size	7⅛ x 10½	*	4.50	(3)	17.50	(9)	16.00	(17)
47	Silver/Gold Size	7½ x 10½	*	5.25	(4)	19.00	(10)	22.00	(18)
48	Magazine Size	8½ x 13		5.50	(3)	22.00	(10)	25.00	(20)

Wholesale prices are as follows:

Style #46
Standard Size (7⅛x10½x1½" flap)
Shipping weight: 17 lbs. per case

1,000-9,000 .... $16.00/per 1000
10,000-49,000 .... 15.00/per 1000
50,000-99,000 .... 14.00/per 1000
100,000-249,000 .... 13.00/per 1000
250,000 plus 12.00/per 1000

Style #47
Golden Age Size (7½x10½x1½" flap)
Shipping weight: 18 lbs. per case

1,000-5,000 .... $22.00/per 1000
6,000-9,000 .... 19.50/per 1000
10,000 plus 17.00/per 1000

Style #48
Magazine size (8½x13 without flap)
Shipping weight: 25 lbs. per case

1,000-5,000 .... $25.00/per 1000
6,000-9,000 .... 22.00/per 1000
10,000 plus 19.00/per 1000

• Sold in increments of 1000 only.

Orders over 200 lbs. will be sent via freight collect.
Orders under 200 lbs. please send correct amount to cover shipping.
All above plastic bags may be combined to achieve maximum discounts. Please order in case lots.

See the last page of our ad section for complete ordering and shipping information.

Bill Cole Enterprises, Inc.
P.O. Box 60 • Dept. 47 • Wollaston, MA 02170-0060
(617) 773-2653 • (617) 963-5510

RARE COMIC ART IS MY BAG
. . .and I love to trade bags of money, or other art for items of special interest to me.
I'll pay top dollar for original artwork by Carl Barks, E.C. Segar, and other classic cartoonists, as well as paintings, cartoon movie posters from the '30s and '40s, and other rare comic oriented esoterica.
If you have rare material for sale **contact me first**. If you don't, you may be selling your collection short.
Newton '72
Bruce Hamilton
P. O. Box 1432
Prescott, AZ 86302
(602) 776-1300

THE TWO GREATEST NAMES IN COMICS

GERRY ROSS **ROBERT CRESTOHL**

ROBERT D. CRESTOHL (Price Guide Adviser Since 1974)
and
GERRY ROSS THE COMIC MASTER (World's Rarest Comics)
proudly present OUR COMBINED INVENTORIES TOTALING OVER 2,000,000 MARVELS AT SUPER LOW PRICES:

EARLY MARVEL EXTRAVAGANZA

Thank you for making our last ad a total success. More and more serious collectors are discovering that our combination of high quality comics at very low prices can't be beat. Try us and see for yourself. We want your business!
THE GREATEST BACK ISSUE AD IN MARVEL COMICS HISTORY. Every Marvel comic from the time of **FANTASTIC FOUR #1** onwards is here, in this ad, and in more conditions, and at a cheaper price than **ANY** other dealer in the world. We have 30-300 issues of **EVERY** Marvel published, and we can supply them in more conditions, and at the **WORLD'S CHEAPEST PRICES.** With quality and quantity like this it's hard to take any other so called "big dealers" seriously.
We know how hard it is to find these early issues, and we're sure you'll appreciate them – especially at these prices.
So order now. We expect a large response, so the faster you order, the faster your comics will reach you.

TERMS. **Earliest issues have 3 prices listed.** The first price is for gd/very good condition. The second (in brackets) is for vg/fine condition. The third is for vf/near mint condition. **Later Marvels (1966-75) have 2 prices listed.** vg/fine; and vf/near mint. **Comics after 1975 are listed in one price, and are all nm/mint.** Add prices carefully, minimum order **$10.00. 10% DISCOUNT WITH ALTERNATE CHOICES.** Prices subject to change. Payment MUST be in U.S. funds (cash, check (money order preferred)). Prices are per issue. (Canadian residents add 20% to Canadian funds) Comics shipped quickly! Our complete giant catalog is 50 cents (Free with order).
If you're selling, we're always buying. We pay a firm 70% of current Overstreet Price Guide values by condition in U.S. funds for AVENGERS 1-25, DAREDEVIL 1-17, FANTASTIC FOUR 1-50, HULK 1-6, SPIDERMAN 1-40, X – MEN 1-141.

10% DISCOUNT WITH ALTERNATES

MAIL ALL ORDERS AND CURRENCY TO: Crestohl/Ross,
4732 Circle Rd. Dept.M,
Montreal, Quebec, Canada. H3W 1Z1

10% DISCOUNT WITH ALTERNATES

AVENGERS
1 80.00 (135.00) 260.00
2, 4 30.00 (48.00) 90.00
3 22.50 (33.50) 60.00
5 16.00 (21.50) 37.50
6, 9 14.00 (17.50) 30.00
7, 8, 10, 11 13.50 (22.50)
12-16 8.00 (15.00)
17, 18, 19 6.00 (11.00)
20, 21, 22 5.00 (8.00)
23-30 3.50 (5.25)
31-52, 54-56 2.50 (3.75)
53, 57, 58, 94-99 7.00 (10.50)
59-92 2.50 (3.75)
93, 100 15.00 (22.50)
101-120 2.00 (3.00)
121-140 1.75 (2.50)
141-163, 167-171 2.00
164-166, 181-191 3.00
172-180, 192-199 1.50
201 up 1.00

AMAZING SPIDERMAN
AAF 15 240.00 (400.00) 750.00
1 185.00 (300.00) 550.00
2 75.00 (110.00) 200.00
3 47.50 (67.50) 120.00
4 35.00 (50.00) 90.00
5, 6 25.00 (37.50) 67.50
7-10, 14 20.00 (30.00) 52.50
11-13, 15 16.00 (22.00) 37.50
16-20 18.00 (27.00)
21-25, 121, 122 15.00 (22.50)
26-30, 50, 100 10.00 (15.00)
31-38, 129, 7.00 (10.50)
39, 40, 96-98, 9.00 (13.50)
41-46, 101, 102, 5.00 (7.50)
47-49, 51, 52, 134, 135, 4.00 (6.00)
53-70, 90, 94, 174, 175, 3.50 (5.25)
71-89, 91-93 95, 99 2.75 (4.00)
103-120, 123, 124, 201, 2.50 (3.75)
125-128 130-133 136-150 1.75 (2.50)
151-160, 163-170, 2.00
171-173, 176-188, 191-199 1.50
202-237, 254 up, 1.25
239-251, 253, 3.00
238, 252, 5.00

CONAN
1 50.00 (70.00)
2 25.00 (35.00)
3 37.50 (52.50)
4, 5 18.00 (27.00)

CONAN
6-11 10.00 (15.00)
12-16 8.00 (12.00)
17-24 6.00 (9.00)
26-30 3.00 (4.50)
31-40 2.00 (3.00)
41-57, 100 1.50 (2.25)
58-81 1.50
82-99 1.25
101 up 1.00

DAREDEVIL
1 50.00 (80.00) 150.00
2 21.00 (32.50) 60.00
3 15.00 (22.50) 40.00
4, 5 10.00 (22.50)
6, 7 7.50 (15.00)
8, 9, 10 6.00 (12.00)
11-15 5.00 (7.50)
16, 17 7.00 (11.50)
18-20, 100 3.50 (5.25)
21-30 2.50 (3.75)
31-49, 183, 1.75 (2.50)
54-81 1.50 (2.25)
82-99, 101-105 1.00 (2.00)
106-130, 132-137, 182, 184 up 1.50
139-157, 1.25

FANTASTIC FOUR
1 280.00 (450.00) 825.00
2 110.00 (175.00) 330.00
3 85.00 (140.00) 260.00
4 67.50 (105.00) 195.00
5 50.00 (77.50) 140.00
6-10 30.00 (45.00) 82.50
11, 12 25.00 (37.50) 67.50
13-15 21.00 (30.00) 52.50
16-20 15.00 (22.50) 37.50
21-25, 28, 48 15.00 (22.50)
26, 27, 29, 30, 31 10.00 (15.00)
32-40, 49, 50 8.00 (12.00)
41-47 6.00 (9.00)
51-60, 66, 67 5.00 (7.50)
61-65, 72-77 4.00 (6.00)
68-71, 78-80 3.00 (4.50)
81-99, 121-123 2.50 (3.75)
101-120 1.75 (2.50)
124-150 1.50 (2.25)
151-175 1.50 (2.00)
176-199, 201-208 1.25
209-221 2.00
222 up 1.00

INCREDIBLE HULK
1 165.00 (240.00) 435.00
2 60.00 (90.00) 165.00
3 45.00 (62.50) 112.50
4-6 34.00 (44.00) 75.00
102 7.50 (11.25)
103-105, 162, 172 3.00 (4.50)
106-110 2.50 (3.75)
111-120, 176-178 2.00 (3.00)
121-150 1.50 (2.25)
151-161, 163-171 1.25 (1.75)
173-175, 183-200 1.25
180, 182 10.00
181 30.00
201 up 1.00

PETER PARKER (all nm/m)
1, 69, 70 6.00
2-10, 22, 23 3.00
11-21 2.50
24-26, 29-31 2.00
27, 28, 64, 12.50
32-63, 65-68, 71 up 1.00

SILVER SURFER
1, 4 25.00 (39.50)
2, 3, 5 11.00 (17.50)
6, 7 7.50 (12.50)
8-18, 6.00 (9.00)

TALES OF SUSPENSE
39 87.50 (125.00) 225.00
40 30.00 (42.50) 75.00
41 17.50 (25.00) 45.00
42-45 9.50 (13.50) 20.00
46, 47, 48 7.50 (14.00)
49-59 5.00 (8.00)
60-65 3.50 (5.50)
66-75, 99 2.00 (3.00)
76-98 1.50 (2.50)

TALES TO ASTONISH
27 100.00 (160.00) 300.00
35 37.50 (60.00) 112.50
36 17.50 (25.00) 45.00
37-40, 44 8.50 (12.50) 22.50
41, 42, 43, 49, 59 7.50 (14.00)
45-48, 50, 93 5.00 (9.00)
51-58, 60, 100 4.00 (6.50)
61-65 3.00 (4.50)
66-75, 101 2.00 (3.50)
76-92, 94-99 1.50 (2.50)

THOR & JOURNEY INTO MYSTERY
83 100.00 (160.00) 300.00
84 35.00 (50.00) 90.00
85 24.00 (34.00) 60.00
86 17.50 (25.00) 45.00
87-90 14.00 (18.00) 33.00
91-95, 100 11.00 (15.00) 26.0
96-99, 112 9.00 (12.50) 20.00
101-110 6.00 (9.00)
111, 113-120 4.00 (6.00)
121-140 2.00 (3.00)
141-164 1.50 (2.25)
165, 166, 180, 181 3.00 (4.50)
167-179, 182-192 1.25 (1.75)
193, 200 3.00 (4.50)
194-199, 201-230 1.00 (1.50)
231-336 1.00
337 4.00

X-MEN
1 110.00 (175.00) 350.00
2 47.50 (72.00) 135.00
3 32.50 (45.00) 80.00
4 30.00 (42.00) 70.00
5, 6 20.00 (27.50) 40.00
7-10 18.00 (27.00)
11, 12, 53, 56-65 15.00 (22.50
13-20, 28, 49-51 10.00 (15.00)
21-27, 54, 55, 66 7.00 (10.50)
29-40 6.00 (9.00)
41-48, 52, 67-72 5.00 (7.50)
73-93 3.75 (6.00)

For #s 94 up, two prices ar listed: fine/very fine and nm/mint
94, GS #1 60.00 (100.00)
95, 22.50 (39.50)
96-99, 108, 109 15.00 (28.00)
100, 101 21.00 (35.00)
102-107, 100, 111 12.00 (20.00
112-119 9.00 (15.00)
120, 121 18.00 (29.50)
122, 130 7.50 (12.00)
123-129, 139, 140 6.50 (12.50
131-138 6.00 (9.00)
141-143, 171 4.00 (6.00)
144-150, 165, 166 3.00 (4.50)
151-164, 167-170 2.00 (3.00)
172 up 2.00 mint only

NEW DIMENSIONS
The BIGGEST & THE BEST
IN COMICS
and COMIC
RELATED
MATERIAL

Action Comics No. 23, 1940. © *DC*

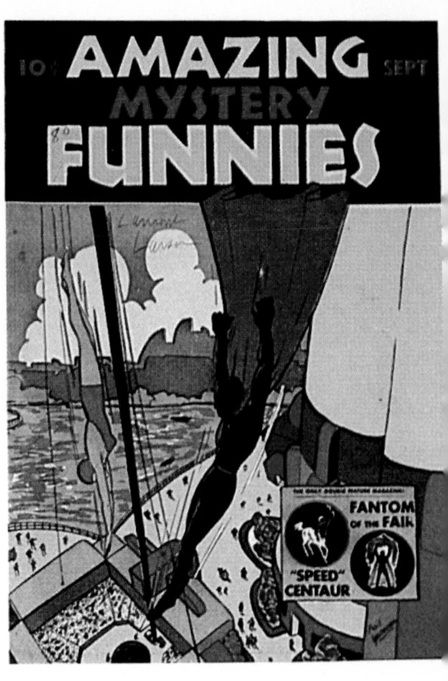

Amazing Mystery Funnies V2/9, 1939. © *Cen*

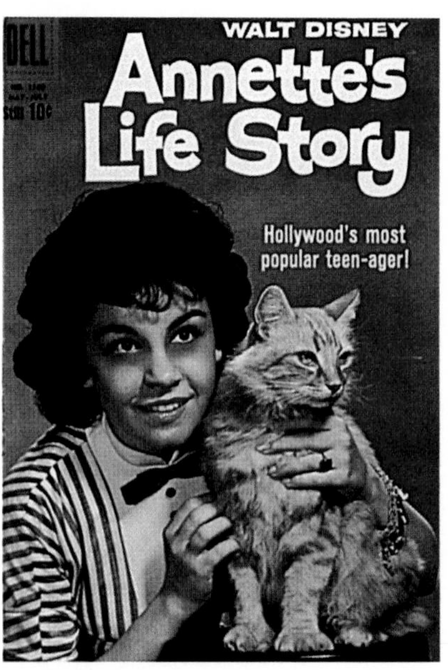

Four Color No. 1100, 1960. ©*WDC*

Archie's Girls Betty and Veronica No. 1, 1950. © *AP*

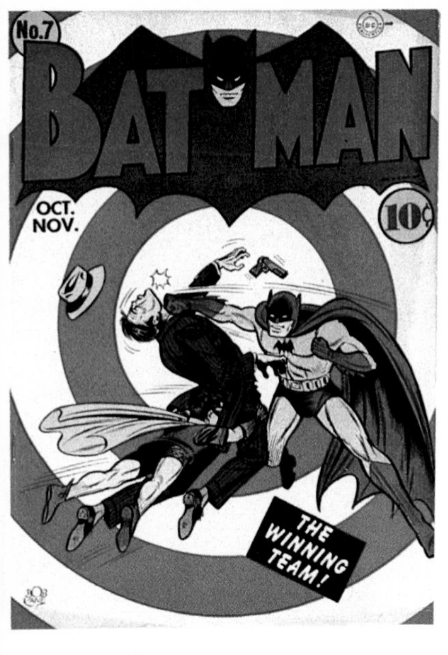

Batman No. 7, 1941. © *DC*

Black Rider No. 8, 1950. © *MCG*

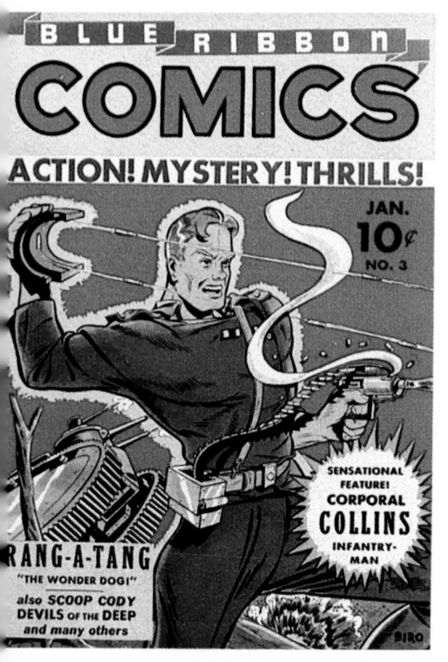

Blue Ribbon Comics No. 3, 1940. © *MLJ*

Four Color No. 448, 1953. © *Bob Clampett*

Bob Steele Western No. 1, 1950. © *Faw*

Bozo No. 4, 1952. © *Capitol Records, Inc.*

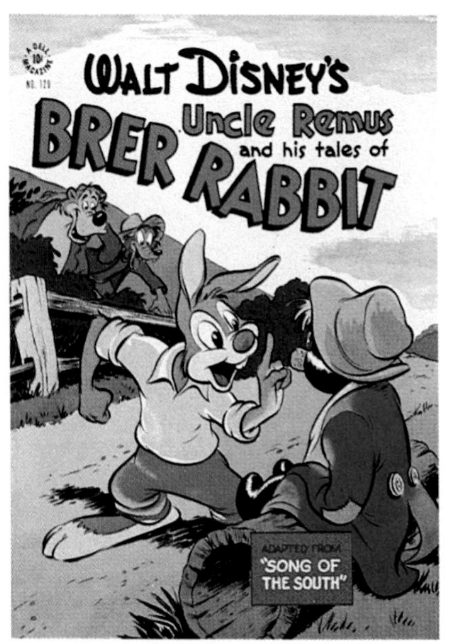

Four Color No. 129, 1946. © *WDC*

Four Color No. 1011, 1959. © *Revue Prod.*

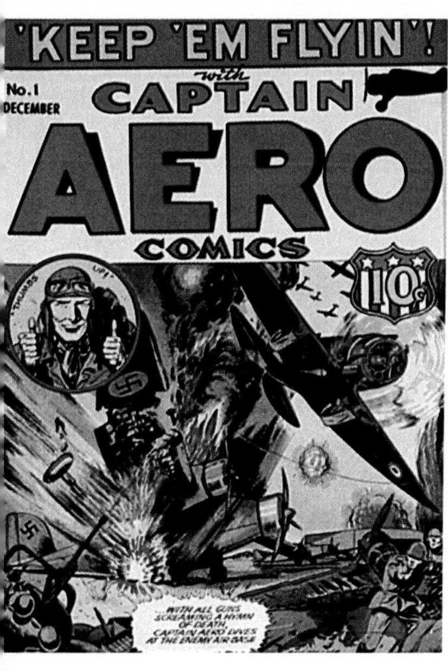

Captain Aero Comics No. 1, 1941. © *Hoke*

Four Color No. 780, 1957. © *Keeshan-Miller*

Captain Marvel No. 16, 1942. © *Faw*

Captain Midnight No. 7, 1943. © *Faw*

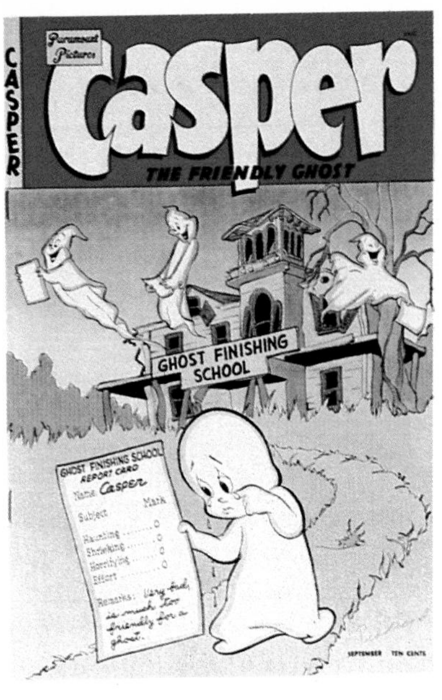

Casper The Friendly Ghost No. 1, 1949. *© Paramount Pictures, Inc.*

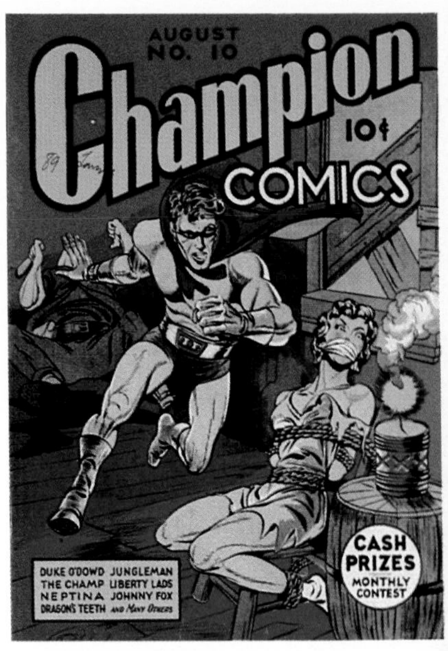

Champion Comics No. 10, 1940. *© Harv*

Four Color No. 785, 1957. *© Norbert Prods. Mickey Dolenz photo-c (Later with the Monkees)*

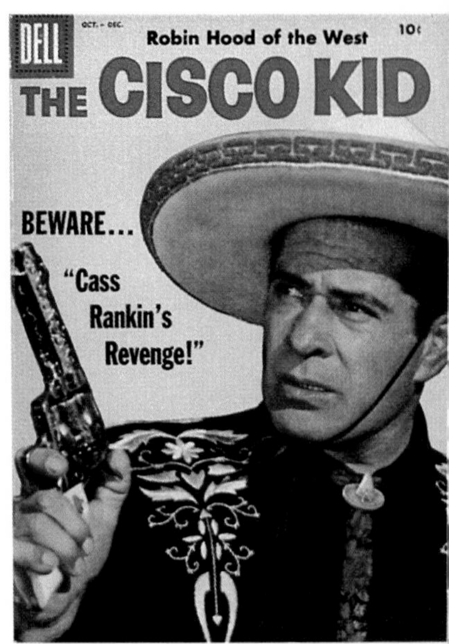

The Cisco Kid No. 37, 1957. *© Cisco Kid Products, Inc.*

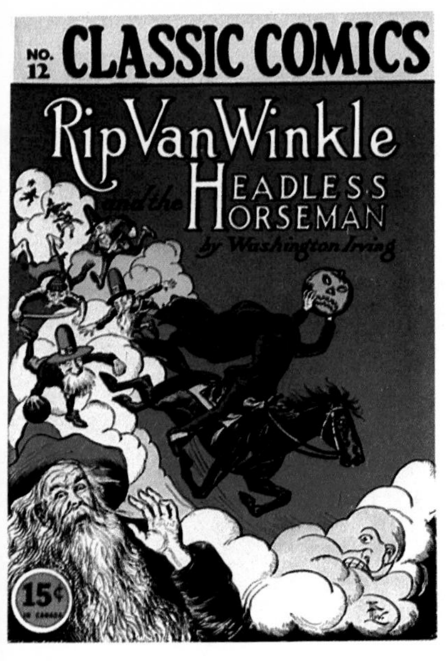

Classic Comics No. 12(HRN 20), 1944. © *Gil*

The Clutching Hand No. 1, 1954. © *ACG*

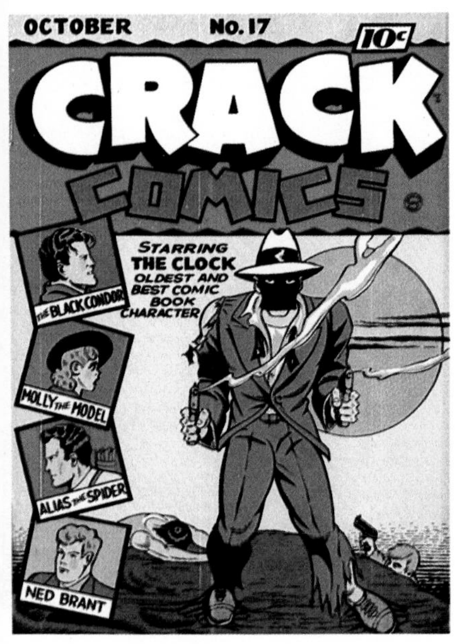

Crack Comics No. 17, 1941. ©*Qua*

Four Color No. 1249, 1962. © *Marterto Ent.*

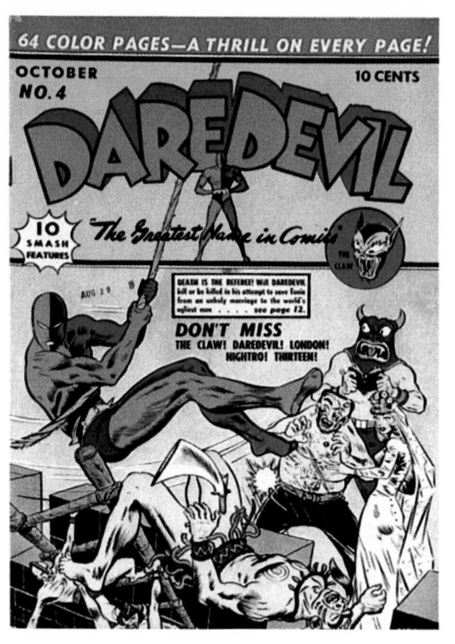

Daredevil No. 4, 1941. © Lev

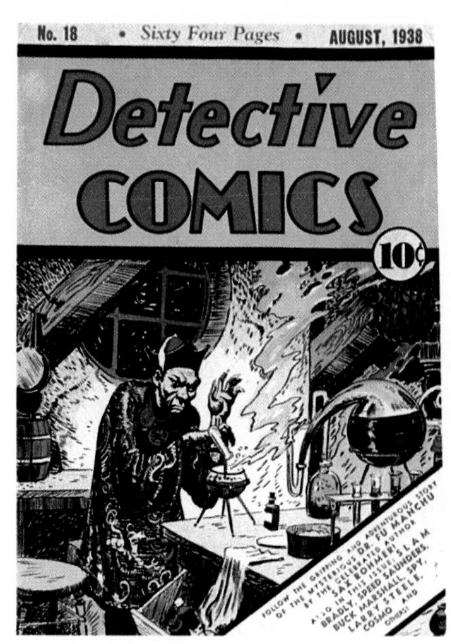

Detective Comics No. 18, 1938. © *DC*

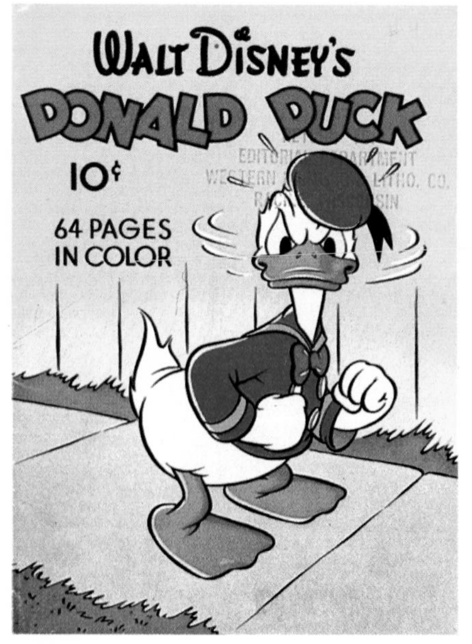

Four Color No. 4, 1940. © *WDC*

Donald Duck Fun Book No. 2, 1954. © *WDC*

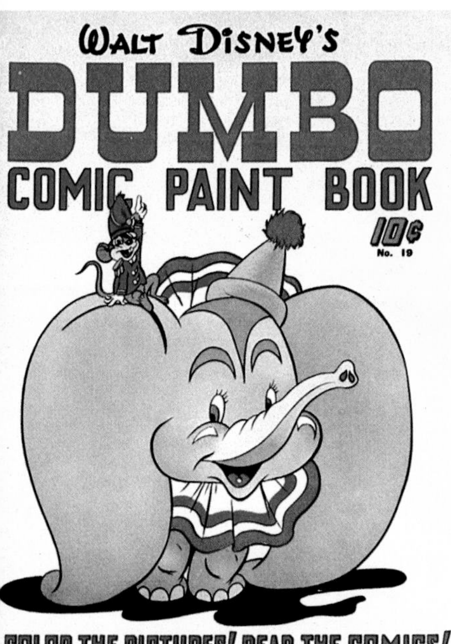

Large Feature Comic No. 19, 1941. © *WDC*

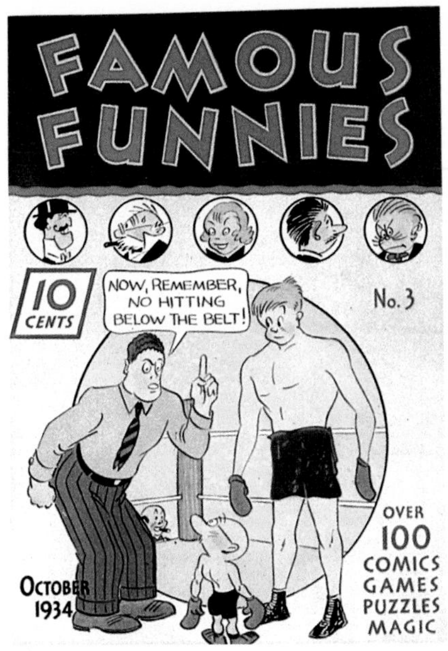

Famous Funnies No. 3, 1934. Buck Rogers strip-r begins. © *EAS*

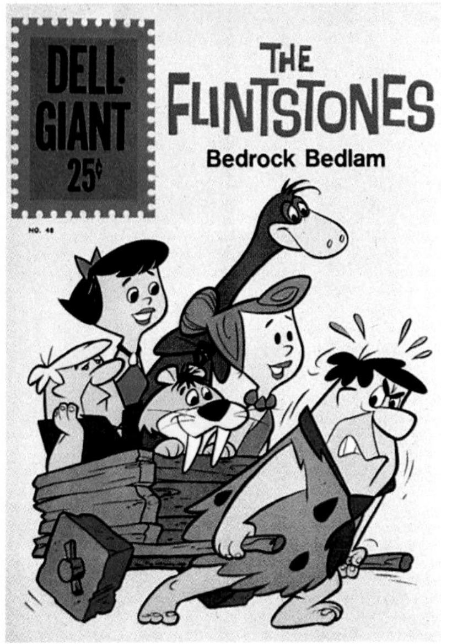

Dell Giant Comics No. 48, 1961. © *Hanna-Barbera Productions*

Flip No. 1, 1954, © *Harv*

Gunsmoke No. 25, 1961. © *Columbia Broadcasting System, Inc.*

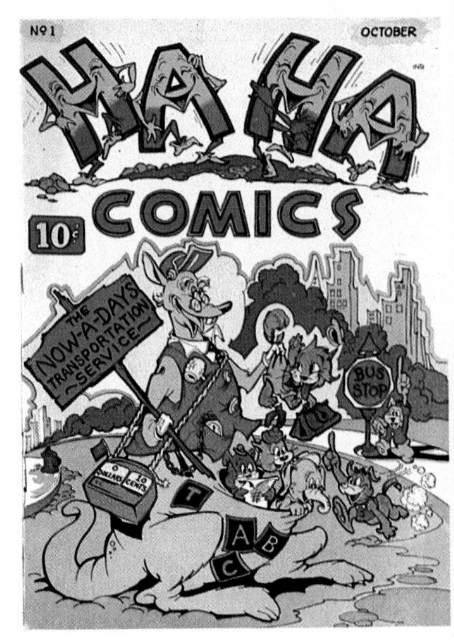

Ha Ha Comics No. 1, 1943. © *ACG*

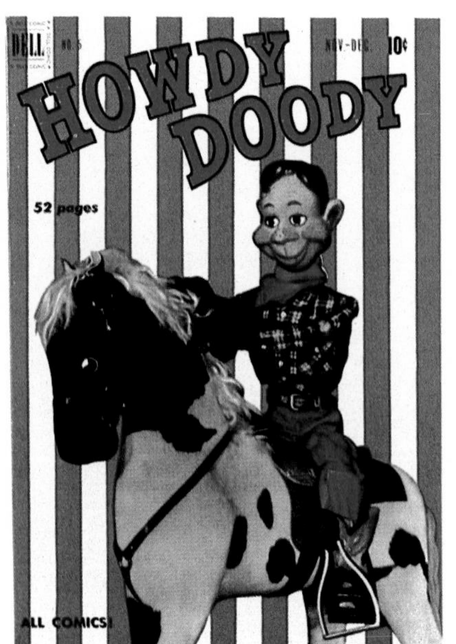

Howdy Doody No. 5, 1950. © *Robert E. Smith*

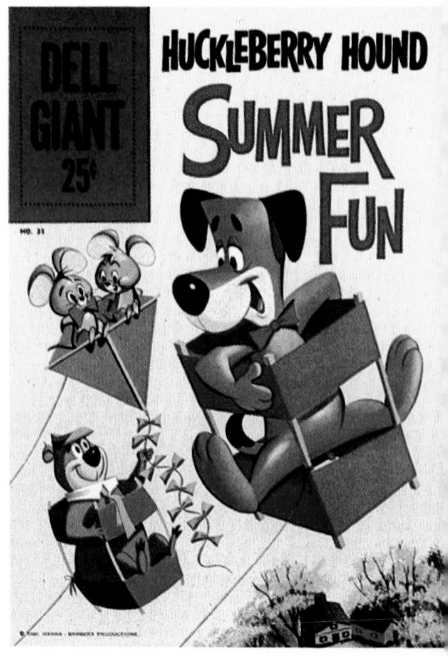

Dell Giant Comics No. 31, 1960. © *Hanna-Barbera Productions*

I Love Lucy Comics No. 3, 1954. © *Desi Arnaz & Lucille Ball*

Jackie Gleason No. 1, 1955. © *VIP Corp.*

Four Color No. 269, 1950. © *Johnny Mack Brown*

Jumbo Comics No. 43, 1942. © *FH*

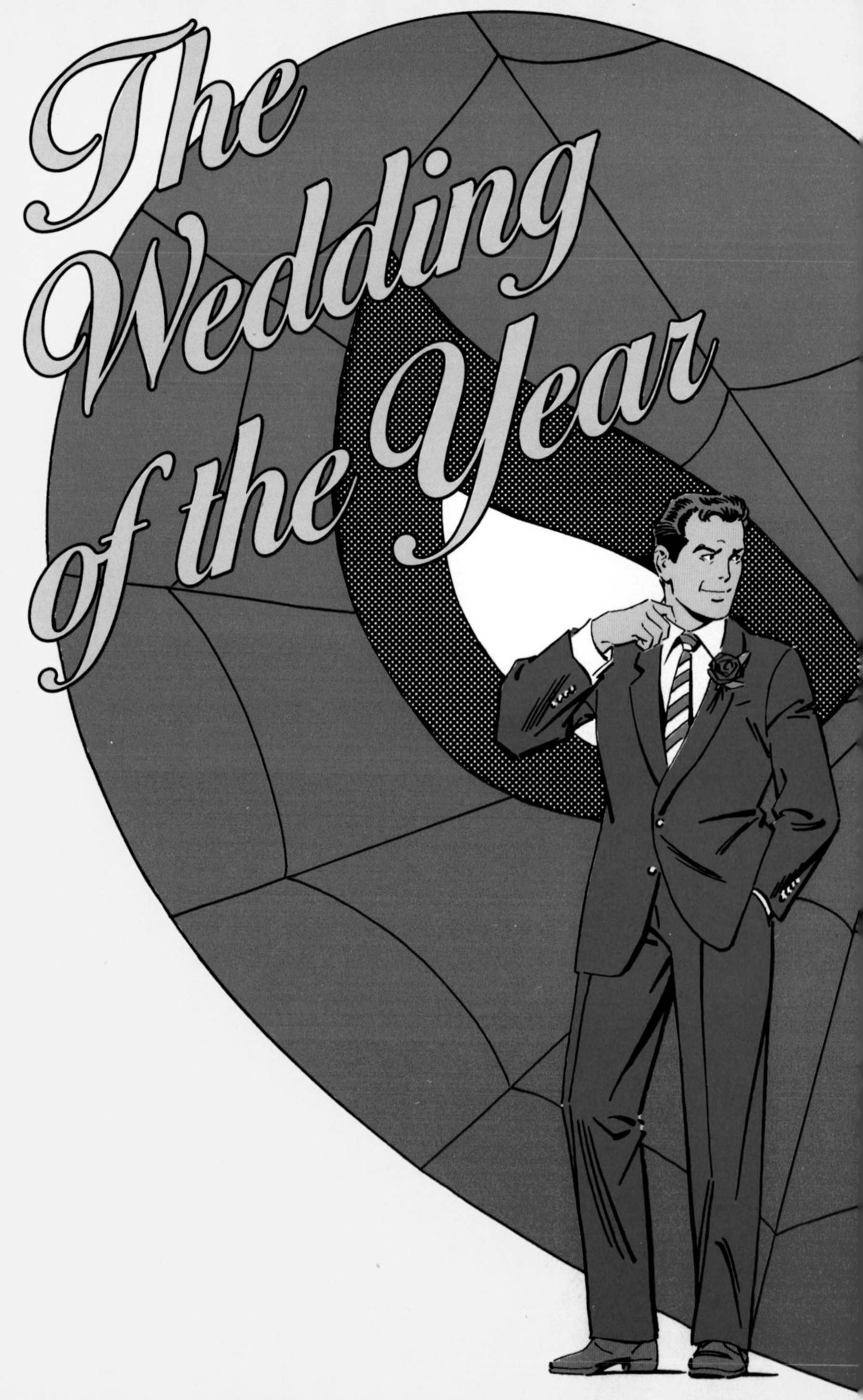

Peter Parker

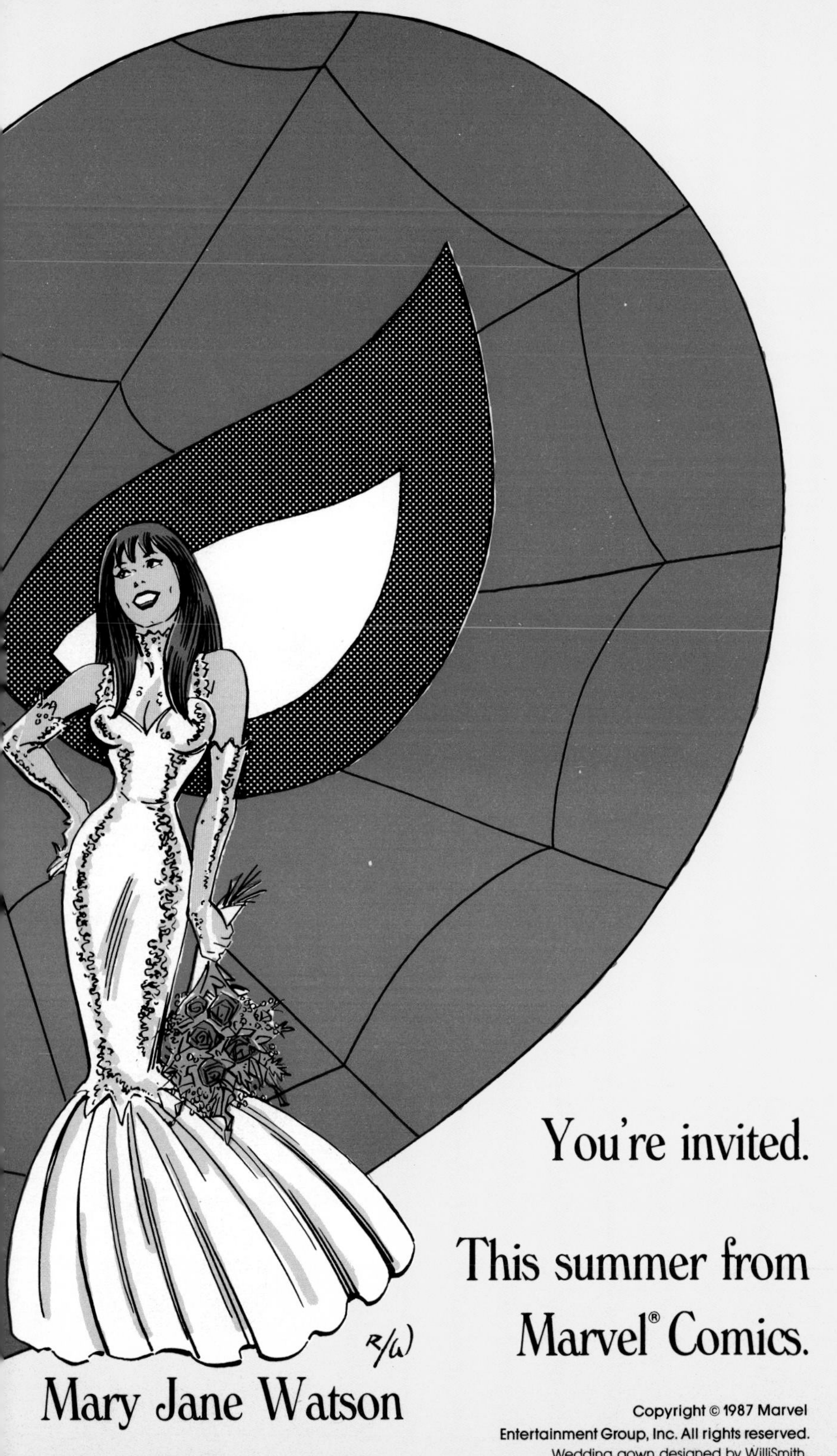
R/W
Mary Jane Watson

NEW FROM
EPIC
1987
On-going Series
VIDEO JACK
POWERLINE
ST GEORGE
DOCTOR ZERO
MARSHAL LAW
Limited Series
BLOOD
HAVOK AND WOLVERINE
Specials
HELLRIDER
BLACK DRAGON
Graphic Novels
MOEBIUS SERIES
SOMEPLACE STRANGE
THE DEATH OF GROO
Copyright © 1987 Marvel Comics Group. All rights reserved. EPIC COMICS is a registered trademark of the Marvel Comics Group.

THE HOTTEST COMIC OF 1987!?!

The first issue of The Adventurers introduces eight new characters ranging from Bladehelm, a greedy and ill-tempered Dwarf from the Iron Reach Mountains, to Nightwind, a female ninja assassin.

"The Adventurers has endless possibilities with its multiple characters. It should become the X-Men of fantasy adventure."

Tom Jones - 8 year veteran of D&D

The Adventurers is one of the hottest new comics on the market. **The Adventurers** is a fantasy adventure teambook which takes place in the mythical world of Anoria; a world of fire-breathing dragons, armored warriors, evil wizards, and deeds of unparallelled bravery and danger.

The art is provided by Canadian talents Peter Hsu and Kent Burles. Hsu has studied under the late Wally Wood, and has been favorably compared to Frank Frazetta. His work is incredible!

The Adventurers has been in the planning stages for over two years. According to writer Scott Behnke, "The Adventurers is written more like a novel than a typical comic book. The first ten issues comprise one story-line, entitled "The Gate of Chaos." The personalities of the characters and the splendor of the world of Anoria will unfold as the Adventurers become embroiled in the affairs of a mad sorcerer."

The first five issues of **The Adventurers** have been instant sellouts! According to Universal Comics, a leading authority in the comic industry, "The Adventurers is one of the best investment comics of 1987. It continues to rise in both price and demand. Highly recommended!"

The Adventurers is available monthly from comic book stores everywhere. Don't miss out on the excitement!

ELF WARRIOR

Elf Warrior spins a tale of a nearly extinct race as they attempt to live in a hostile land ravaged by war.

The story follows the Elves desperate attempt to free their land from the twisted evil of the sorcerer Darkos. From the impenetrable Tower of Blades, to the mass slaughter of battle upon the Weeping Plains, Elf Warrior is rich in action and excitement.

Elf Warrior is Peter Hsu's best work since the Adventurers. Hsu accomplishes a masterpiece of detail and intensity!

NINJA ELITE

Ninja Elite follows the character Nightwind before she joins the Adventurers. Ninja Elite is a story of suspense, political intrigue and treachery, reminiscent of the book, Dune.

The Ninja Elite are the chosen blood guards of powerful aristocratic houses within the city-state of Pandona. Trained in the secret arts of the ninja, they are used to defend their lords, to spy among the other houses, and to assassinate enemies.

Taking his knowledge of a soft-style martial art and his study of both Eastern and Western mysticism, writer Scott Behnke creates a story rich in drama and realism.

For questions or back issue information write to: ADVENTURE PUBLICATION, 3940 Persimmon Dr., Suite 104-G, Fairfax, VA 22031.

AVIATION CADETS nn (1943, S&S, Av)-A World War II aviation anthology one-shot. Navy pre-flight training involving sports.
(e)

COLUMBIA COMICS No. 1 (1943, Wise, R)-More exposure for Columbia's reprint characters, *Joe Palooka, Dixie Duggan*, etc., lasting 3 issues.
(e)

POWERHOUSE PEPPER No. 1 (1943, Timely, Hm)-The protagonist of ***Joker Comics*** of a year earlier, Wolverton's humorous plotting made this character a memorable one. Popular enough to receive his own title.
(a,c,e,j)

TINY TOTS COMICS No. 1 (1943, Dell, F)-A one-shot anthology book of funny animals with Walt Kelly art.
(e)

TREASURE COMICS nn (1943, Prize, H)-Rebinding of coverless copies of ***Prize*** No. 7-11 from 1942. A very rare book with only one copy known to exist.
(e)

UNITED STATES MARINES nn (1943, Wise, W)-A documentary style war anthology series mixed with magazine-type photo features from the front, surviving one year. The title was resurrected for a brief period after the Korean conflict.
(e)

ALL FUNNY COMICS No. 1 (Wint/43-44, DC, Hm)-DC's first all funny anthology title. A popular series with the humorous plotting of *Genius Jones*, lasting 4½ years.
(e,j)

BLACK HOOD COMICS No. 9 (Wint/43-44, MLJ, H)-The Man of Mystery graduates from ***Top-Notch*** into his own title, lasting 11 issues.
(e)

CHRONOLOGICAL LIST OF COMIC BOOK TITLES BY PUBLISHER FOR PERIOD 1933 - 1943

(The indented titles are key books other than No. 1's)

ACE MAGAZINES

Sure-Fire No. 1, 6/40
Super Mystery No. 1, 7/40
Lightning No. 4, 12/40
Our Flag No. 1, 8/41
Banner No. 3, 9/41
Four Favorites No. 1, 9/41
Captain Courageous No. 6, 3/42

AMERICAN COMICS GROUP

Giggle No. 1, 10/43
Ha Ha No. 1, 10/43

BETTER PUBLICATIONS (Standard)

Best No. 1, 11/39
Thrilling No. 1, 2/40
Exciting No. 1, 4/40
  Exciting No. 9, 5/41
Startling No. 1, 6/40
Real Life No. 1, 9/41
  Startling No. 10, 9/41
America's Best No. 1, 2/42
Fighting Yank No. 1, 9/42
Coo Coo No. 1, 10/42
Black Terror No. 1, Wint/42-43
Major Hoople No. 1, 1/43
Real Funnies No. 1, 1/43
Funny Funnies No. 1, 4/43
Goofy No. 1, 6/43
Happy No. 1, 8/43

BILBARA PUBLISHING CO.

Cyclone No. 1, 6/40

CENTAUR PUBLICATIONS

Funny Pages V2/6, 3/38
Funny Pic. Stories V2/6, 3/38
Star Comics No. 10, 3/38
Star Ranger No. 10, 3/38
Cowboy No. 13, 7/38
Keen Detective No. 8, 7/38
Little Giant No. 1, 7/38
Amazing Mystery Funnies No. 1, 8/38
Little Giant Movie No. 1, 8/38
  Funny Pages V2/10, 9/38
Star Ranger Funnies No. 15, 10/38
Little Giant Det. No. 1, 10/38
Keen Komics V2/1, 5/39
  Amazing Mystery Funnies V2/7, 7/39
Comic Pages V3/4, 7/39
  Keen Detective V2/7, 7/39
Amazing Man No. 5, 9/39
Amazing Adventure Funnies No. 1, 6/40
Fantoman No. 2, 8/40
Masked Marvel No. 1, 9/40
Arrow, The No. 1, 10/40
Super Spy No. 1, 10/40
Detective Eye No. 1, 11/40
Wham No. 1, 11/40
Stars and Stripes No. 2, 5/41
Liberty Scouts No. 2, 6/41
World Famous Heroes No. 1, 10/41
Man Of War No. 1, 11/41

CATECHETICAL GUILD

Topix No. 1, 11/42

HARRY 'A' CHESLER

Star No. 1, 2/37
Star Ranger No. 1, 2/37
Feature Funnies No. 1, 10/37
Cocomalt Big Book No. 1, 1938
Yankee No. 1, 9/41
Dynamic No. 1, 10/41
Scoop No. 1, 11/41
Punch No. 1, 12/41

COLUMBIA COMICS GROUP

Big Shot No. 1, 5/40
Skyman No. 1, Fall/41
Face, The No. 1, 1941
Dixie Duggan No. 1, 7/42
Joe Palooka No. 1, 1942
Sparky Watts No. 1, 11/42

COMICS MAGAZINE

Comics Magazine No. 1, 5/36
Funny Pages No. 6, 11/36
Funny Picture Stories No. 1, 11/36
Detective Picture Stories No. 1, 12/36
Western Picture Stories No. 1, 2/37

DC COMICS

New Fun No. 1, 2/35
New Comics No. 1, 12/35
More Fun No. 7, 1/36
Big Book of Fun No. 1, Spr/36
New Book of Comics No. 1, 6-8/36
New Adventure No. 12, 1/37
Detective No. 1, 3/37
Action No. 1, 6/38
  Detective No. 20, 10/38
Adventure No. 32, 11/38
All-American No. 1, 4/39
New York World's Fair 3-5/39
Movie No. 1, 4/39
  Detective No. 27, 5/39
  Adventure No. 40, 7/39
Mutt and Jeff No. 1, Sum/39
Superman No. 1, Sum/39
Double Action No. 2, 1/40
Flash No. 1, 1/40
  More Fun No. 52,53, 2,3/40
  Adventure No. 48, 3/40
Batman No. 1, Spr/40
New York World's Fair 3-5/40

More Fun No. 55, 5/40
All-American No. 16, 7/40
All-Star No. 1, Sum/40
All-American No. 19, 10/40
All-Star No. 3, Wint/40-41
Adventure No. 61, 4/41
World's Best No. 1, Spr/41
All Flash No. 1, Sum/41
World's Finest No. 2, Sum/41
Green Lantern No. 1, Fall/41
Star Spangled No. 1, 10/41
All-Star No. 8, 11-12/41
Leading No. 1, Wint/41-42
Sensation No. 1, 1/42
Star Spangled No. 7, 4/42
Detective No. 64, 6/42
Wonder Woman No. 1, Sum/42
Pic. Stories/Bible No. 1, Fall/42
Boy Commandos No. 1, Wint/42-43
Comic Cavalcade No. 1, Wint/42-43
All Funny No. 1, Wint/43-44

DELL PUBLISHING CO.

Popular No. 1, 2/36
Funnies No. 1, 10/36
Comics No. 1, 3/37
West. Action Thrillers No. 1, 4/37
100 Pages of Comics No. 1, 1937
Super No. 1, 5/38
Crackajack No. 1, 6/38
Nickel No. 1, 1938
Large Feature Comic No. 1, 1939
Four-Color No. 1, 1939
Donald Duck 4-Color No. 4, 3/40?
War No. 1, 5/40
W.D.'s Comics & Stories No. 1, 10/40
Mickey Mouse 4-Color No. 16, 4/41
Funnies No. 57, 7/41
Red Ryder No. 3, 8/41
Looney Tunes No. 1, Fall/41
Key Ring No. 1, 1941
Large Feature No. 1, 1941
USA Is Ready No. 1, 1941
Animal No. 1, 12-1/41-42
Camp No. 1, 2/42
Fairy Tale Parade No. 1, 6-7/42
New Funnies No. 65, 7/42
War Heroes No. 1, 7-9/42
Our Gang No. 1, 9-10/42
Santa Claus Funnies No. 1, 12/42
America In Action No. 1, 1942
Donald Duck 4-Color No. 9, 1942
Famous Stories No. 1, 1942
War Stories No. 1, 1942
W.D. Comics & Stories No. 31, 4/43
Tiny Tots No. 1, 1943

EASTERN COLOR

Funnies On Parade nn, 1933
F. F., A Carnival-- nn, 1933
Century Of Comics nn, 1933
Skippy's Own Book nn, 1934
Famous Funnies Series 1, 1934
Famous Funnies No. 1, 7/34
Heroic No. 1, 8/40
Buck Rogers No. 1, Wint/40-41
Dickie Dare No. 1, 1941
Big Chief Wahoo No. 1, Wint/41-42
Jingle Jangle No. 1, 2/42
Oaky Doaks No. 1, 7/42
Mickey Finn No. 1, 11/42
Napoleon & Uncle Elby No. 1, 11/42
Strictly Private No. 1, 11/42
Tiny Tots No. 1, 1943

WILL EISNER

Spirit No. 1, 6/2/40

ELLIOT PUBLICATIONS

Double 1940
Double Up 1941

FAWCETT PUBLICATIONS

Flash No. 1, 1/40
Whiz No. 2, 2/40
Master No. 1, 3/40
Slam Bang No. 1, 3/40
Nickel No. 1, 5/40
Special Edition No. 1, 8/40
Western Desperado No. 8, 10/40
Wow No. 1, Wint/40-41
Captain Marvel No. 1, 1-2/41
America's Greatest No. 1, 5/41
Bulletman No. 1, 7/41
Minuteman No. 1, 7/41
Capt. Marvel Thrill Book 1941
Gene Autry No. 1, Fall/41
Spysmasher No. 1, Fall/41
Master No. 21, 12/41
Whiz No. 25, 12/12/41
Xmas No. 1, 12/41
Captain Midnight No. 1, 9/42
Jungle Girl No. 1, Fall/42
Captain Marvel Jr. No. 1, 11/42
Captain Marvel No. 18, 12/11/42
Fawcett's Funny Animals No. 1, 12/42
Gift No. 1, 12/42
Holiday No. 1, 12/42
Golden Arrow No. 1, Wint/42-43
Don Winslow No. 1, 2/43
Hopalong Cassidy No. 1, 2/43
Ibis No. 1, 2/43
All Hero No. 1, 3/43
Captain Marvel No. 22, 3/43

FICTION HOUSE

Jumbo No. 1, 9/38
Fight No. 1, 1/40
Jungle No. 1, 1/40
Planet No. 1, 1/40
Wings No. 1, 9/40
Rangers No. 1, 10/41
Sheena No. 1, Spr/42
Wambi No. 1, Spr/42

FLYING CADET

Flying Cadet No. 1, 1/43

FOX FEATURES SYNDICATE

Wonder No. 1, 5/39
Wonderworld No. 3, 7/39
Mysterymen No. 1, 8/39
Fantastic No. 1, 12/39
Blue Beetle No. 1, Wint/39-40
Science No. 1, 2/40
Weird No. 1, 4/40
Flame, The No. 1, Sum/40
Green Mask No. 1, Sum/40
Big 3 No. 1, Fall/40
Rex Dexter No. 1, Fall/40
Samson No. 1, Fall/40
Eagle, The No. 1, 7/41
U.S. Jones No. 1, 11/41
V-Comics No. 1, 1/42

FUNNIES, INC.

Motion Pic. Funn. Weekly No. 1, 5/39?
Green Giant No. 1, 1940

LEV GLEASON

Silver Streak No. 1, 12/39
Silver Streak No. 6, 9/40
Silver Streak No. 7, 1/41
Captain Battle No. 1, Sum/41
Daredevil No. 1, 7/41
Boy No. 3, 4/42
Crime Does Not Pay No. 22, 6/42
Captain Battle No. 3, Wint/42-43
Captain Battle Jr. No. 1, Fall/43

HUGO GERNSBACK

Superworld No. 1, 4/40

GILBERTON PUBLICATIONS

Classic No. 1, 10/41

GLOBE SYNDICATE

Circus No. 1, 6/38

GREAT PUBLICATIONS

Great No. 1, 11/41
Choice No. 1, 12/41

HARVEY PUBLICATIONS (Helnit)

Speed No. 1, 10/39
Champion No. 2, 12/39
Champ No. 11, 10/40
Green Hornet No. 1, 12/40
Pocket No. 1, 8/41
War Victory No. 1, Sum/42
All New No. 1, 1/43
Hello Pal No. 1, 1/43

HAWLEY PUBLICATIONS

Catain Easy nn, 1939
Red Ryder No. 1, 9/40
Sky Blazers No. 1, 9/40
Hi-Spot No. 2, 11/40

HILLMAN PERIODICALS

Miracle No. 1, 2/40
Rocket No. 1, 3/40
Victory No. 1, 8/41
Air Fighters No. 1, 11/41
Air Fighters No. 2, 11/42
Clue No. 1, 1/43

HOLYOKE (Continental)

Crash No. 1, 5/40
Crash No. 4, 9/40
Catman No. 1, 5/41
Captain Fearless No. 1, 8/41
Captain Aero No. 7, 12/41
Suspense No. 1, 12/43

HYPER PUBLICATIONS

Hyper Mystery No. 1, 5/40

K.K. PUBLICATIONS
Mickey Mouse Mag. No. 1, Sum/35
Mickey Mouse Mag. V5/12, 9/40

DAVID MCKAY PUBLICATIONS
King No. 1, 4/36
Wow No. 1, 5/36
Ace No. 1, 4/37
Feature Book nn, 1-4/37
Magic No. 1, 8/39
Future No. 1, 6/40

MLJ MAGAZINES
Blue Ribbon No. 1, 11/39
Top-Notch No. 1, 12/39
Pep No. 1, 1/40
Zip No. 1, 2/40
Shield-Wizard No. 1, Sum/40
  Top-Notch No. 9, 10/40
  Blue Ribbon No. 9, 2/41
Jackpot No. 1, Spr/41
  Pep No. 17, 7/41
  Pep No. 22, 12/41
Special No. 1, Wint/41-42
Hangman No. 2, Spr/42
Archie No. 1, Wint/42-43
Jolly Jingles No. 10, Sum/43
Black Hood No. 9, Wint/43-44

NITA PUBLICATIONS
Whirlwind No. 1, 6/40

NOVELTY PUBLICATIONS
Target No. 1, 2/40
Blue Bolt No. 1, 6/40
Four Most No. 1, Wint/41-42

PARENT'S MAGAZINE INSTITUTE
True No. 1, 4/41
Calling All Girls No. 1, 9/41
Real Heroes No. 1, 9/41
Funny Book No. 1, 12/42
Comics Digest No. 1, Wint/42-43

PRIZE PUBLICATIONS
Prize No. 1, 3/40
  prize No. 7, 9/40
Headline No. 1, 2/43
Treasure nn, 1943

PROGRESSIVE PUBLISHERS
Bang-Up No. 1, 12/41

QUALITY COMICS GROUP
Feature No. 21, 6/39
Smash No. 1, 8/39
  Feature No. 27, 12/39
Crack No. 1, 5/40
Hit No. 1, 7/40
National No. 1, 7/40
Military No. 1, 8/41
Police No. 1, 8/41
Uncle Sam No. 1, 8/41
Doll Man No. 1, Fall/41
  Hit No. 25, 12/42
Plastic Man No. 1, Sum/43

RALSTON-PURINA CO.
Tom Mix No. 1, 9/40

STREET AND SMITH PUBLICATIONS
Shadow No. 1, 3/40
Doc Savage No. 1, 5/40
Bill Barnes No. 1, 10/40
Sport No. 1, 10/40
Army and Navy No. 1, 5/41
Super Magic No. 1, 5/41
Super Magician No. 2, 9/41
Pioneer Pic. Stories No. 1, 12/41
Trail Blazers No. 1, 1941
True Sport Pic. Stories No. 5, 2/42
Supersnipe No. 6, 10/42
Devil Dogs No. 1, 1942
Remember Pearl Harbor nn, 1942
Red Dragon No. 5, 1/43
Aviation Cadets No. 1, 1943

SUN PUBLICATIONS
Colossus No. 1, 3/40
Sun Fun No. 1, 3/40

TIMELY COMICS (Marvel)
Marvel No. 1, 11/39
Marvel Mystery No. 2, 12/39
Daring Mystery No. 1, 1/40
Mystic No. 1, 3/40
  Marvel Mystery No. 9, 7/40
Red Raven No. 1, 8/40
Human Torch No. 2, Fall/40
Captain America No. 1, 3/41
Sub-Mariner No. 1, Spr/41
All-Winners No. 1, Sum/41
Young Allies No. 1, Sum/41
USA No. 1, 8/41
Tough Kid Squad No. 1, 3/42
Comedy No. 9, 4/42
Joker No. 1, 4/42
Krazy No. 1, 7/42
Terry-Toons No. 1, 10/42
Miss Fury No. 1, Wint/42-43
Kid Komics No. 1, 2/43
  Comedy No. 14, 3/43
All-Select No. 1, Fall/43
All-Surprise No. 1, Fall/43
Super Rabbit No. 1, Fall/43
Powerhouse Pepper No. 1, 1943

UNITED FEATURES SYNDICATE
Tip Top No. 1, 4/36
Comics On Parade No. 1, 4/38
Single Series No. 1, 1938
Okay No. 1, 7/40
O.K. No. 1, 7/40
Sparkler No. 1, 7/40
United No. 1, 8/40
Sparkler No. 1, 7/41

WHITMAN PUBLISHING CO.
Mammouth No. 1, 1937
Donald Duck nn, 1938

WILLIAM H. WISE
Columbia Comics No. 1, 1943
United States Marines No. 1, 1943

COMICS WITH LITTLE IF ANY VALUE

There exists in the comic book market, as in all other collector's markets, items, usually of recent origin, that have relatively little if any value. Why even mention it? We wouldn't, except for one thing—this is where you could probably take your worst beating, investment-wise. Since these books are listed by dealers in such profusion, at prices which will vary up to 500 percent from one dealer's price list to another, determining a realistic "market" value is almost impossible. And since the same books are listed repeatedly, list after list, month after month, it is difficult to determine whether or not these books are selling. In some cases, it is doubtful that they are even being collected. Most dealers must get a minimum price for their books; otherwise, it would not be profitable to handle. This will sometimes force a value on an otherwise valueless item. Since new comics are now priced at 65 cents or more each, most dealers who handle them get a minimum price of at least 75 cents. This is the **available** price to obtain a **reading** copy. However, this is not what dealers will pay to restock. Since many of these books are not yet collector's items, their salvage value would be very low. You may not get more than 5 cents to 10 cents per copy selling them back to a dealer. This type of material, from an investment point of view, would be of maximum risk since the salvage value is so low. For this reason, recent comics should be bought for enjoyment as reading copies and if they go up in value, consider it a bonus. On the other hand, you might buy a vastly over-priced golden-age comic and still expect to recover your loss after a reasonable passage of time. This, unfortunately, is not true of so many titles that we are put in a rather awkward position of listing.

THE PRICE GUIDE'S POSITION: We don't want to leave a title out just because it is presently valueless. And at the same time, we don't want to presume to "establish" what is collectible and what isn't. The passage of time and a change in collectors' interests can make almost any comic potentially valuable. Some books, by virtue of their age, will someday obtain a value as a cultural or historical curiosity. Therefore, we feel that all books, regardless of the demand for them, should be listed.

Since speculation in the comic book market began around 1964, most all titles since that time have been saved and are in plentiful supply. These books have been included for your information and can be found listed throughout The Guide with values assigned (under $1.00). The collector would be well advised to compare prices between several dealers' lists before ordering this type of material.

COLLECTING FOREIGN COMICS AND AMERICAN REPRINTS

One extremely interesting source of comics or early vintage—one which does not necessarily have to be expensive—is the foreign market. Many American strips, from both newspapers and magazines, are reprinted abroad (both in English and in other languages) months and even years after they appear in the states. By working out trade agreements with foreign collectors, one can obtain, for practically the cover price, substantial runs of a number of newspaper strips and reprints of American comic books dating back five, ten, or occasionally even twenty or more years. These reprints are often in black and white, and sometimes the reproduction is poor, but this is not always the case. In any event, this is a source of material that every serious collector should look into.

Once the collector discovers comics published in foreign lands, he often becomes fascinated with the original strips produced in these countries. Many are excellent, and have a broader range of appeal than those of American comic books.

CANADIAN REPRINTS

E.C.s: by J. B. Clifford

Several E.C. titles were published in Canada by Superior Comics from 1949 to at least 1953. Canadian editions of the following E.C. titles are known: (Pre-Trend) *Saddle Romances, Moon Girl, A Moon A Girl. . . Romance, Modern Love, Saddle Justice;* (New-Trend) *Crypt of Terror—Tales From the Crypt, Haunt of Fear, Vault of Horror, Weird Science, Weird Fantasy, Two-Fisted Tales, Frontline Combat,* and *Mad. Crime SuspenStories* was also published in Canada under the title *Weird SuspenStories* (Nos. 1-3 known). No reprints of *Shock SuspenStories* by Superior are known, nor have any "New Direction" reprints ever been reported. No reprints later than January 1954 are known. Canadian reprints sometimes exchanged cover and contents with adjacent numbers (e.g., a *Frontline Combat* 12 with a *Frontline Combat* No. 11 cover). They are distinguished both in cover and contents. As the interior pages are always reprinted poorly, these comics are of less value (about ½) than the U.S.

editions; they were printed from asbestos plates made from the original plates. On some reprints, the Superior seal replaces the E.C. seal. Superior publishers took over Dynamic in 1947.

Dells: by Ronald J. Ard

Canadian editions of Dell comics, and presumably other lines, began in March-April, 1948 and lasted until February-March, 1951. They were a response to the great Canadian dollar crisis of 1947. Intensive development of the post-war Canadian economy was financed almost entirely by American capital. This massive import or money reached such a level that Canada was in danger of having grossly disproportionate balance of payments which could drive it into technical bankruptcy in the midst of the biggest boom in its history. The Canadian government responded by banning a long list of imports. Almost 500 separate items were involved. Alas, the consumers of approximately 499 of them were politically more formidable than the consumers of comic books.

Dell responded by publishing its titles in Canada, through an arrangement with Wilson Publishing Company of Toronto. This company had not existed for a number of years and it is reasonable to assume that its sole business was the production and distribution of Dell titles in Canada. There is no doubt that they had a captive market. If you check the publication data on the U. S. editions of the period you will see the sentence "Not for sale in Canada." Canada was thus the only area of the Free World in those days technically beyond the reach of the American comic book industry.

We do not know whether French editions existed of the Dell titles put out by Wilson. The English editions were available nationwide. They were priced at 10 cents and were all 36 pages in length, at a time when their American parents were 52 pages. The covers were made of coarser paper, similar to that used in the Dell Four Color series in 1946 and 1947 and were abandoned as the more glossy cover paper became more economical. There was also a time lag of from six to eight weeks between, say, the date an American comic appeared and the date that the Canadian edition appeared.

Many Dell covers had seasonal themes and by the time the Canadian edition came out (two months later) the season was over. Wilson solved this problem by switching covers around so that the appropriate season would be reflected when the books hit the stands. Most Dell titles were published in Canada during this period including the popular Atom Bomb giveaway, *Walt Disney Comics and Stories* and the *Donald Duck* and *Mickey Mouse* Four Color one-shots. The quality of the Duck one-shots is equal to that of their American counterparts and generally bring about 30 percent less.

By 1951 the Korean War had so stimulated Canadian exports that the restrictions on comic book importation, which in any case were an offense against free trade principle, could be lifted without danger of economic collapse. Since this time Dell, as well as other companies, have been shipping direct into Canada.

DCs: by Doug A. England

Many DC comics were reprinted in Canada by National Comics Publications Limited and Simcoe Publishing and Distributing Co., both of Toronto, for years 1948-1950 at least. Like the Dells, these issues were 36 pages rather than the 52 pages offered in the U.S. editions, and the inscription "Published in Canada" would appear in place of "A 52 Page Magazine" or "52 Big Pages" appearing on U.S. editions. These issues contained no advertisements and some had no issue numbers.

HOW TO START COLLECTING

Most collectors of comic books begin by buying new issues in mint condition directly off the newsstand or from their local comic store. (Subscription copies are available from several mail-order services.) Each week new comics appear on the stands that are destined to become true collectors items. The trick is to locate a store that carries a complete line of comics. In several localities this may be difficult. Most panelologists frequent several magazine stands in order not to miss something they want. Even then, it pays to keep in close contact with collectors in other areas. Sooner or later, nearly every collector has to rely upon a friend in Fandom to obtain for him an item that is unavailable locally.

Before you buy any comic to add to your collection, you should carefully inspect its condition. Unlike stamps and coins, defective comics are generally not highly prized. The cover should be properly cut and printed. Remember that every blemish or sign of wear depreciates the beauty and value of your comics.

The serious panelologist usually purchases extra copies of popular titles. He may trade these multiples for items unavailable locally (for example, foreign comics), or he may store the multiples for resale at some future date. Such speculation is, of course, a gamble, but unless collecting trends change radically in the future, the value of certain comics in mint condition should appreciate greatly, as new generations of readers become interested in collecting.

COLLECTING BACK ISSUES

In addition to current issues, most panelologists want to locate back issues. Some energetic collectors have had great success in running down large hoards of rare comics in their home towns. Occasionally, rare items can be located through agencies that collect old papers and magazines, such as the Salvation Army. The lucky collector can often buy these items for much less than their current market value. Placing advertisements in trade journals, newspapers, etc., can also produce good results. However, don't be discouraged if you are neither energetic nor lucky. Most panelologists build their collections slowly but systematically by placing mail orders with dealers and other collectors.

Comics of early vintage are extremely expensive if they are purchased through a regular dealer or collector, and unless you have unlimited funds to invest in your hobby, you will find it necessary to restrict your collecting in certain ways. However you define your collection, you should be careful to set your goals well within your means.

PROPER HANDLING OF COMIC BOOKS

Before picking up an old rare comic book, caution should be exercised to handle it properly. Old comic books are very fragile and can be easily damaged. Because of this, many dealers hesitate to let customers personally handle their rare comics. They would prefer to remove the comic from its bag and show it to the customer themselves. In this way, if the book is damaged, it would be the dealer's responsibility—not the customer's. Remember, the slightest crease or chip could render an otherwise Mint book to Near Mint or even Very Fine. The following steps are provided to aid the novice in the proper handling of comic books: 1. Remove the comic from its protective sleeve or bag very carefully. 2. Gently lay the comic (un-opened) in the palm of your hand so that it will stay relatively flat and secure. 3. You can now leaf through the book by carefully rolling or flipping the pages with the thumb and forefinger of your other hand. Caution: Be sure the book always remains relatively flat or slightly rolled. Avoid creating stress points on the covers with your fingers and be particularly cautious in bending covers back too far on Mint books. 4. After examining the book, carefully insert it back into the bag or protective sleeve. Watch corners and edges for folds or tears as you replace the book.

HOW TO SELL YOUR COMICS

If you have a collection of comics for sale, large or small, the following steps should be taken. (1) Make a detailed list of the books for sale, being careful to grade them accurately, showing any noticeable defects; i.e., torn or missing pages, centerfolds, etc. (2) Decide whether to sell or trade wholesale to a dealer all in one lump or to go through the long laborious process of advertising and selling piece by piece to collectors. Both have their advantages and disadvantages.

In selling to dealers, you will get the best price by letting everything go at once—the good with the bad—all for one price. Simply select names either from ads in this book or from some of the adzines mentioned below. Send them your list and ask for bids. The bids received will vary depending on the demand, rarity and condition of the books you have. The more in demand, and better the condition, the higher the bids will be.

On the other hand, you could become a "dealer" and sell the books yourself. Order a copy of one or more of the adzines. Take note how most dealers lay out their ads. Type up your ad copy, carefully pricing each book (using the Guide as a reference). Send finished ad copy with payment to adzine editor to be run. You will find that certain books will sell at once while others will not sell at all. The ad will probably have to be retyped, remaining books repriced, and run again. Price books according to how fast you want them to move. If you try to get top dollar, expect a much longer period of time. Otherwise, the better deal you give the collector, the faster they will move. Remember, in being your own dealer, you will have overhead expenses in postage, mailing supplies and advertising cost. Some books might even be returned for refund due to misgrading, etc.

In selling all at once to a dealer, you get instant cash, immediate profit, and eliminate the long process of running several ads to dispose of the books; but if you have patience, and a small amount of business sense, you could realize more profit selling them directly to collectors yourself.

WHERE TO BUY AND SELL

Throughout this book you will find the advertisements of many reputable dealers who sell back-issue comics magazines. If you are an inexperienced collector, be sure to compare prices before you buy. Never send large sums of cash through the mail. Send money orders or checks for your personal protection. Beware of bargains, as the items advertised sometimes do not exist, but are only a fraud to get your money.

The Price Guide is indebted to everyone who placed ads in this volume, whose support has helped in curbing printing costs. Your mentioning this book when dealing with the advertisers would be greatly appreciated.

THE BUYERS GUIDE
Krause Publications
700 E. State St.
Iola, WI 54997
(715) 445-2214

The Price Guide highly recommends the above adzine, which is full of ads buying and selling comics, pulps, radio tapes, premiums, toys and other related items. You can also place ads to buy or sell your comics in the above publication.

COMIC BOOK MAIL ORDER SERVICES

The following offer a mail order service on new comic books. Write for rates and details:

COLLECTOR'S CHOICE, 3405 Keith St., Cleveland, TN 37311

THE COMIC SOURCE, Bruce B. Brittain, P.O. Box 863605, Plano, TX 75086-3605

DOUG SULIPA'S COMIC WORLD, 315 Ellice Ave., Winnipeg, Man., Canada R3B 1X7

FRIENDLY FRANK'S Distribution, Inc., 3990 Broadway, Gary IN 46408-2705 (219)884-5052 or 884-5053

GEPPI'S SUBSCRIPTION SERVICE, 1720 Belmont Ave., Bay-C, Baltimore, MD 21207

HEROES AREN'T HARD TO FIND, 1214 Thomas Ave., Charlotte, NC 28205

PRESIDENTIAL COMIC BOOK SERVICE, P. O. Box 41, Scarsdale, NY 10583

STYX COMIC SERVICE, P. O. Box 3791, Station B, Winnipeg, Manitoba, Can. R2W 3R6

UNIVERSAL COMICS SUBSCRIPTION SERVICE, 235 Main St., Brockton, MA 02401

WESTFIELD COMICS, 8608 University Green, P.O. Box 470, Middleton, WI 53562 (608)836-1945

COMIC BOOK CONVENTIONS

As is the case with most other aspects of comic collecting, comic book conventions, or cons as they are referred to, were originally conceived as the comic-book counterpart to science-fiction fandom conventions. There were many attempts to form successful national cons prior to the time of the first one that materialized, but they were all stillborn. It is interesting that after only three relatively organized years of existence, the first comic con was held. Of course, its magnitude was nowhere near as large as most established cons held today.

What is a comic con? As might be expected, there are comic books to be found at these gatherings. Dealers, collectors, fans, whatever they call themselves can be found trading, selling, and buying the adventures of their favorite characters for hours on end. Additionally if at all possible, cons have guests of honor, usually professionals in the field of comic art, either writers, artists, or editors. The committees put together panels for the con attendees where the assembled pros talk about certain areas of comics, most of the time fielding questions from the assembled audience. At cons one can usually find displays of various and sundry things, usually original art. There might be radio listening rooms; there is most certainly a daily showing of different movies, usually science-fiction or horror type. Of course there is always the chance to get together with friends at cons and just talk about comics; one also has a good opportunity to make new friends who have similar interests and with whom one can correspond after the con.

It is difficult to describe accurately what goes on at a con. The best way to find out is to go to one or more if you can.

The addresses below are those currently available for conventions to be held in the upcoming year. Unfortunately, addresses for certain major conventions are unavailable as this list is being compiled. Once again, the best way to keep abreast of conventions is through the various adzines. Please remember when writing for convention information to include a self-addressed, stamped envelope for reply. Most conventions are non-profit, so they appreciate the help. Here is the list:

NOTE: All convention listings must be submitted to us by December 1.

COMIC BOOK CONVENTIONS FOR 1987

ATLANTA FANTASY FAIR XIII, July 31-Aug., 2, 1987, The Omni Hotel & Georgia World Congress Center, Atlanta, GA., The Atlanta Fantasy Fair, 482 Gardner Rd., Stockbridge, GA 30281. Phone (404) 662-6850

ATLANTA WINTER COMICS FAIR I, Jan., 24-25, 1987, The Omni Hotel & Georgia World Congress Center, Atlanta, GA, 482 Gardner Rd., Stockbridge, GA 30281. Phone (404) 662-6850.

ARIZONA COMIC DEALER NETWORK—P. O. Box 28283, Tempe, AZ 85283. Phone (602) 838-3629. News of conventions in the state.

CAROLINA CON VI—Sept. 12, 1987, Ramada Inn, 1001 S. Church St., Greenville, SC. Send SASE to C.P.F.A. c/o Tom LittleJohn, 460 Patrol Club Rd., Greenville, SC 29609.

CHATTANOOGA COMIC CON, Collector's Choice, 3405 Keith St., Cleveland, TN 37311. Held in Spring and Fall each year.

CHICAGO COMICON—Larry Charet, 1219-A West Devon Ave., Chicago, IL 60660. Phone (312) 274-1832.

CHICAGO-MONTHLY MINI CON—Write Larry Charet, 1219-A West Devon Ave., Chicago, IL 60660.

CHILDHOOD TREASURES SHOW AND CONVENTION, July 11-12, 1987, Dallas, TX. Write: Don Maris, Box 111266, Arlington, TX 76007. Phone (817)261-8745 before 10pm Central Time.

CREATION CON—249-04 Hillside Ave., Bellerose, N.Y. 11426. Phone (718) 343-0202. Holds major conventions in the following cities: Atlanta, Boston, Cincinnati, Cleveland, Detroit, London, Los Angeles, Philadelphia, Rochester, San Francisco, and Washington, D.C. Write or call for details.

EL PASO FANTASY FESTIVAL—c/o Rita's Fantasy Shop, No. 34 Sunrise Center, El Paso, TX 79904. PH: (915) 757-1143. Late July-Early August.

ISLAND NOSTALGIA COMIC BOOK/BASEBALL CARD SHOWS, Colonie Hill, 1717 Motor Pkwy., Hauppauge, L.I., NY., off L.I. E, Exit 57. For info call Dennis (516) 724-7422.

KANSAS CITY MINI-CON—c/o Kansas City Comic Book Club, 136 East Longfellow, Kansas City, MO 64119. Three times a year.

LONG ISLAND COMIC BOOK & COLLECTOR'S MARKET CONVENTION—(Held monthly). Rockville Centre Holiday Inn, 173 Sunrise Hwy., Long Island, NY. For info: Cosmic Comics & Books of Rockville Centre, 139 N. Park Ave., Rockville Centre, NY 11570. (516) 763-1133.

MICHIANA COMICON, April 4 & Oct. 10, 1987. Write Jim Rossow, 53100 Poppy Road, South Bend, IN 46628.

MOBI-CON (Formerly MOBILE COMIC ART AND SCIENCE FICTION FESTIVAL), Howard Johnson's Motor Lodge, 3132 Government Blvd. June, 12-14, 1987. For information: Stephen Barrington, 161 West Grant St., Chickasaw, AL 36611. (205) 456-4514 or 661-4060.

MO-KAN COMIC FESTIVAL—c/o Kansas City Comic Book Club, 136 East Longfellow, Kansas City, MO 64119. Once a year.

NEWCON '87—Don Phelps, P. O. Box 85, Cohasset, MA 02025.

SAN DIEGO COMIC-CON—Box 17066, San Diego, CA 92117. July, 1987.

THE SAN FERNANDO VALLEY COMIC BOOK CONVENTION, held up to 9 times yearly at the Los Angeles Science Fantasy Society, 11513 Burbank Blvd., North Hollywood, CA. Write: Rob Gustavson, 11684 Ventura Bl., No. 335, Studio City, CA 91604. Phone (1-818-792-5667 or 1-213-426-0393).

SEATTLE CENTER CON, Apr, July, 1987, Box 2043, Kirkland, Wash, 98033. Phone (206) 822-5709 or 827-5129.

SEATTLE QUEST NORTHWEST, Seattle, Wash. Write: Ron Church or Steve Sibra, P.O. Box 82676, Kenmore, WA 98028.

THE SUNDAY FUNNIES, Will Murray, 334 E. Squantum St., Quincy, MA 02171. Phone (617) 328-5224.

COMIC BOOK CLUBS

ALABAMA—The Mobile Panelology Assoc. meets 1st Monday of each month at 2301 Airport Blvd. (Mobile Recreation Dept. Bldg.), Mobile, Ala.; 6:30 p.m. to 9:00 p.m. Club business address: 161 West Grant St., Chickasaw, AL 36611. (205) 456-4514. Publishes monthly newsletter. Founded 1973.

ARIZONA—Arizona Comic Dealer Network, P. O. Box 28283, Tempe, AZ 85283. Phone (602) 838-3629. Clearinghouse for dealer and fan activities.

CALIFORNIA—The California Comic Book Collectors Club, c/o Matt Ornbaun, 23601 Hwy. 128, Yorkville, CA 95494. Send 50¢ and SASE for information and enrollment.

GEORGIA—The Defenders of Dreams, Inc., c/o Will Rose, 3121 Shady Grove Rd., Carrollton, GA 30117. (Publishes its own clubzine *Excalibur* bi-monthly and a pulpzine *Real Pulp Adventures*.) Send business size SASE for details.

IDAHO—Mr. O's Comic Book Collectors Club, S. 1200 Agate Rd., Coeur D'Alene, Idaho 83814.

MASSACHUSETTS—The Gloo Club, c/o Ron Holmes, 140 Summit St., New Bedford, Mass. 02740. Write for details and send SASE. (This club is both national and international.)

MISSOURI—The Kansas City Comic Book Club meets the last Sunday of each month at 75th & Quivera (Sun Savings Building), Shawnee, Kansas; 1:30-3:30 p.m. Club business address: 136 East Longfellow, Kansas City, MO 64119. Puts on three conventions a year, publishes monthly newsletter, and gives away free comics to first 20 members that attend meetings. Annual dues $5.00.

OKLAHOMA—T.B.C.F. (Tulsa Believers in Comic Fandom). For information, write to: Annet Hixenbaugh, President, 2962 E. 45th Pl., Tulsa, OK 74105.

TEXAS—The Gulf Coast Comic Collectors' Society (GCCCS). Write to GCCCS Headquarters, c/o Mike Mills, 4318 Iroquois St., Houston, TX 77504.

NOTE: Anyone wanting their clubs listed or re-listed in next year's guide, please send your information in by December 1.

THE HISTORY OF COMICS FANDOM

At this time it is possible to discern two distinct and largely unrelated movements in the history of Comics Fandom. The first of these movements began about 1953 as a response to the then-popular, trend-setting EC lines of comics. The first true comics fanzines of this movement were short-lived. Bhob Stewart's EC FAN BULLETIN was a hectographed newsletter that ran two issues about six months apart; and Jimmy Taurasi's FANTASY COMICS, a newsletter devoted to all science-fiction comics of the period, was a monthly that ran for about six months. These were followed by other newsletters, such as Mike May's EC FAN JOURNAL, and George Jennings' EC WORLD PRESS. EC fanzines of a wider and more critical scope appeared somewhat later. Two of the finest were POTRZEBIE, the product of a number of fans, and Ron Parker's HOOHAH. Gauging from the response that POTRZEBIE received from a plug in an EC letter column, Ted White estimated the average age of EC fans to lie in the range of 9 to 13, while many EC fans were in their mid-teens. This fact was taken as discouraging to many of the faneds, who had hoped to reach an older audience. Consequently, many of them gave up their efforts in behalf of Comics Fandom, especially with the demise of the EC groups, and turned their attention to science-fiction fandom with its longer tradition and older membership. While the flourish of fan activity in response to the EC comics was certainly noteworthy, it is fair to say that it never developed into a full-fledged, independent, and self-sustaining movement.

The second comics fan movement began in 1960. It was largely a response to (though it later became a stimulus for) the Second Heroic Age of Comics. Most fan historians date the Second Heroic Age from the appearance of the new FLASH comics magazine (numbered 105 and dated February 1959). The letter departments of Julius Schwartz (editor at National Periodicals), and later those of Stan Lee (Marvel Group) and Bill Harris (Gold Key) were most influential in bringing comics readers into Fandom. Beyond question, it was the reappearance of the costumed hero that sparked the comics fan movement of the sixties. Sparks were lit among some science-fiction fans first, when experienced fan writers, who were part of an established tradition, produced the first in a series of articles on the comics of the forties—ALL IN COLOR FOR A DIME. The series was introduced in XERO No. 1 (September 1960), a general fanzine for science-fiction fandom edited and published by Dick Lupoff.

Meanwhile, outside science-fiction fandom, Jerry Bails and Roy Thomas, two strictly comics fans of long-standing, conceived the first true comics fanzine in response to the Second Heroic Age. The fanzine, ALTER EGO, appeared in March 1961. The first several issues were widely circulated among comics fans, and were to influence profoundly the comics fan movement to follow. Unlike the earlier EC fan movement, this new movement attracted many fans in their twenties and thirties. A number of these older fans had been active collectors for years but had been largely unknown to each other. Joined by scores of new, younger fans, this group formed the nucleus of a new movement that is still growing and shows every indication of being self-sustaining. Although it has borrowed a few of the more appropriate terms coined by science-fiction fans, Comics Fandom of the Sixties was an independent if fledging movement, without, in most cases, the advantages and disadvantages of a longer tradition. What Comics Fandom did derive from science-fiction fandom it did so thanks largely to the fanzines produced by so-called double fans. The most notable of this type is COMIC ART, edited and published by Don and Maggie Thompson.

HOW TO SELECT FANZINES

In the early 1960s, only a few comic fanzines were being published. A fan could easily afford to subscribe to them all. Today, the situation has radically changed, and it has become something of a problem to decide which fanzines to order.

Fanzines are not all of equal quality or general interest. Even different issues of the same fanzine may vary significantly. To locate issues that will be of interest to you, learn to look for the names of outstanding amateur artists, writers, and editors, and consult fanzine review columns. Although you may not always agree with the judgements of the reviewers, you will find these reviews to be a valuable source of information about the content and quality of the current fanzines.

When ordering a fanzine, remember that print runs are small and the issue you may want may be out of print (OP). Ordinarily in this case, you will receive the next issue. Because of irregular publishing schedules that nearly all fanzines must, of necessity, observe, allow up to 90 days or more for your copy to reach you. It is common courtesy when addressing an inquiry to an ama-publisher to enclose a self-addressed, stamped envelope.

FAN PUBLICATIONS OF INTEREST

NOTE: We must be notified each year by December 1 for listing to be included, due to changes of address, etc. Please send sample copy.

AFTERMATH-Gulf Coast Comics, P.O. Box 310, Winnie, TX 77665. For science fiction fans. $2 cover price plus 50¢ postage.

AMAZING HEROES—4359 Cornell Rd., Agoura, CA 91301. Sample copy $2.50.

THE CLASSICS JOURNAL—Mike Strauss, 26 Madera, San Carlos, CA 94070.

COMIC ART AND FANTASY—Stephen Barrington, 161 West Grant Street, Chickasaw, AL 36611. Published bi-monthly for comics and gaming fans. two issues—$1.00. Official publication of the Mobile Panelology Association.

THE COMIC CORNER—Gulf Coast Comic Collectors' Socity (GCCCS). For sample copy and subscription info, write: The Comic Corner, c/o Mike Mills, 4318 Iroquois St., Pasadena, TX 77504.

THE COMICS FORUM—Kansas City Comic Book Club, 136, East Longfellow, Kansas City, MO 64119. (News, reviews, interviews, and classifieds.)

COMICS INTERVIEW—c/o Fictioneer Books Ltd., #1 Screamer Mtn., Clayton, GA 30525.

THE COMICS JOURNAL—4359 Cornell Rd., Agoura, CA 91301. Sample copy $3.50.

COMIX EMPORIUM NEWSLETTER—Monthly w/Marvel, DC & Independents fan-type news. Sample free. Peter Drizhal, POB 663, Oxon Hill, MD 20745.

THE COMPLETE EC LIBRARY—Russ Cochran, P. O. Box 437, West Plains, MO 65775. (A must for all EC collectors. Reprinting of the complete EC line is planned. Write for details.)

THE DUCKBURG TIMES—400 Valleyview, Selah, WA 98942. A quarterly Disney/Barks fanzine. Send $1.25 for sample, $5.00 for subscription.

FANDOM JOURNAL—Kevin Collier, 18129 136th Ave. Apt. B, Nunica, MI 49448. (Monthly newspaper on small press comics and zines. 25¢ postpaid for sample.)

FANTASY ADVERTISER—Martin Skidmore, 25 Cornleaze, Withywood, Bristol, BS13 7SG, England.

FAWCETT COLLECTORS OF AMERICA NEWSLETTER—Bill & Teresa Harper, 301 E. Buena Vista Ave., North Augusta, SC 29841.

THE GLOO CLUB NEWS—Ron Holmes, 140 Summit St., New Bedford, Mass. 02740. Pub. 6 times/year. Write for details.

HELLFIRE—c/o David & Paul Roach, 36 Lakeside Dr., Lakeside Cardiff, S-Glam Wales, U.K., CF2 6DF. Has articles on American, British, European comics.

KATY KEENE NEWSLETTER—QUARTERLY—Craig Leavitt, 1125 11th St., Modesto, CA 95354. ($6 yr. subscription)

NEMO: THE CLASSIC COMICS LIBRARY—4359 Cornell Rd., Agoura, CA 91301. Reprints classic strips with articles.

COLLECTING STRIPS

Collecting newspaper comic strips is somewhat different than collecting magazines, although it can be equally satisfying.

Obviously, most strip collectors begin by clipping strips from their local paper, but many soon branch out to strips carried in out-of-town papers. Naturally this can become more expensive and it is often frustrating, because it is easy to miss editions of out-of-town papers. Consequently, most strip collectors work out trade agreements with collectors in other cities in order to get an uninterrupted supply of the strips they want. This usually necessitates saving local strips to be used for trade purposes only.

Back issues of strips dating back several decades are also available from time to time from dealers. The prices per panel vary greatly depending on the age, condition, and demand for the strip. When the original strips are unavailable, it is sometimes possible to get photostatic copies from collectors, libraries, or newspaper morgues.

COLLECTING ORIGINAL ART

In addition to magazines and strips, some enthusiasts also collect the original art for the comics. These black and white, inked drawings are usually done on illustration paper at about 30 per cent up (i.e., 30 per cent larger than the original printed panels). Because original art is a one-of-a-kind article, it is highly prized and often difficult to obtain.

Interest in original comic art has increased tremendously in the past several years. Many companies now return the originals to the artists who have in turn offered them for sale, usually at cons but sometimes through agents and dealers. As with any other area of collecting, rarity and demand governs value. Although the masters' works bring fine art prices, most art is available at moderate prices. Comic strips are the most popular facet with collectors, followed by comic book art. Once scarce, current and older comic book art has surfaced within the last few years. In 1974 several original painted covers of vintage comic books and coloring books turned up from Dell, Gold Key, Whitman, and Classic Comics.

The following are sources for original art:

Tony Dispoto
Comic Art Showcase
P. O. Box 425
Lodi, NJ 07644

The Cartoon Museum
Jim Ivey
4310 S. Semoran
Orlando, FL 32807

Graphic Collectibles
Mitch Itkowitz
174 Jewett Ave.
Staten Island, NY 10302

Artman
Bruce Bergstrom
1620 Valley St.
Fort Lee, NJ 07024

Russ Cochran
P. O. Box 437
West Plains, MO 65775

Cartoon Carnival
408 Bickmore Dr.
Wallingford, PA 19086

Museum Graphics
Jerome K. Muller
Box 743
Costa Mesa, CA 92627

Steve Herrington
30 W. 70th St.
New York, NY 10023

The Comic Character Shop
Old Firehouse Antiques
110 Alaskan Way South
Seattle, WA 98104
PH: (206) 283-0532

Collector's Paradise Gallery
Harry Kleiman
P. O. Box 1540
Studio City, CA 91604

San Mateo Comic Books, Baseball
Cards & Original Art
45 N. B Street
San Mateo, CA 94401
PH: (415) 344-1536

Original Artwork
Carsten Lagua
Dillgesstrasse 22
1000 Berlin 46
West Germany

Martin Hilland
AM Josefshaus 6
4040 Neuss 21
West Germany

Richard Halegua
Fantastic Things
110 W. 5th St.
Dayton, Ohio 45402
(513) 222-6242

A Chronology of the Development of THE AMERICAN COMIC BOOK

By
M. Thomas Inge

Precursors: The facsimile newspaper strip reprint collections constitute the earliest "comic books." The first of these was a collection of Richard Outcault's **Yellow Kid** from the Hearst **New York American** in March 1897. Commercial and promotional reprint collections, usually in cardboard covers, appeared through the 1920s and featured such newspaper strips as **Mutt and Jeff, Foxy Grandpa, Buster Brown,** and **Barney Google**. During 1922 a reprint magazine, **Comic Monthly**, appeared with each issue devoted to a separate strip, and in 1929 George Delacorte published 13 issues of **The Funnies** in tabloid format with original comic pages in color, becoming the first four-color comic newsstand publication.

1933: The Ledger syndicate published a small broadside of their Sunday comics on 7" by 9" plates. Employees of Eastern Color Printing Company in New York, sales manager Harry I. Wildenberg and salesman Max C. Gaines, saw it and figured that two such plates would fit a tabloid page, which would produce a book about 7½" x 10" when folded. Thus 10,000 copies of **Funnies on Parade**, containing 32 pages of Sunday newspaper reprints, was published for Proctor and Gamble to be given away as premiums. Some of the strips included were: **Joe Palooka, Mutt and Jeff, Hairbreadth Harry,** and **Reg'lar Fellas**. M. C. Gaines was very impressed with this book and convinced Eastern Color that he could sell a lot of them to such big advertisers as Milk-O-Malt, Wheatena, Kinney Shoe Stores, and others to be used as premiums and radio give-aways. So, Eastern Color printed **Famous Funnies: A Carnival of Comics**, and then **Century of Comics**, both as before, containing Sunday newspaper reprints. Mr. Gaines sold these books in quantities of 100,000 to 250,000.

1934: The give-away comics were so successful that Mr. Gaines believed that youngsters would buy comic books for ten cents like the "Big Little Books" coming out at that time. So, early in 1934, Eastern Color ran off 35,000 copies of **Famous Funnies, Series 1**, 64 pages of reprints for Dell Publishing Company to be sold for ten cents in chain stores. Selling out promptly on the stands, Eastern Color, in May 1934, issued **Famous Funnies** No. 1 (dated July 1934) which became, with issue No. 2 in July, the first monthly comic magazine. The title continued for over 20 years through 218 issues, reaching a circulation peak of nearly one million copies. At the same time, Mr. Gaines went to the sponsors of Percy Crosby's **Skippy**, who was on the radio, and convinced them to put out a Skippy book, advertise it on the air, and give away a free copy to anyone who bought a tube of Phillip's toothpaste. Thus 500,000 copies of **Skippy's Own Book of Comics** was run off and distributed through drug stores everywhere. This was the first four-color comic book of reprints devoted to a single character.

1935: Major Malcolm Wheeler-Nicholson's National Periodical Publications issued in February a tabloid-sized comic publication called **New Fun**, which became **More Fun** after the sixth issue and converted to the normal comic-book size after issue eight. **More Fun** was the first comic book of a standard size to publish original material and continued publication until 1949. **Mickey Mouse Magazine** began in the summer, to become **Walt Disney's Comics and Stories** in 1940, and combined original material with reprinted newspaper strips in most issues.

1936: In the wake of the success of **Famous Funnies**, other publishers, in conjunction with the major newspaper strip syndicates, inaugurated more reprint comic books: **Popular Comics** (News-Tribune, February), **Tip Top Comics** (United Features, April), **King Comics** (King Features, April), and **The Funnies** (new series, NEA, October). Four issues of **Wow Comics**, from David McKay and Henle Publications, appeared, edited by S. M. Iger and including early art by Will Eisner, Bob Kane, and Alex Raymond. The first non-reprint comic book devoted to a single theme was **Detective Picture Stories** issued in December by The Comics Magazine Company.

1937: The second single-theme title, **Western Picture Stories**, came in February from The Comics Magazine Company, and the third was **Detective Comics**, an offshoot of **More Fun**, which began in March to be published to the present. The book's initials, "D.C.," have long served to refer to National Periodical Publications, which was purchased from Major Nicholson by Harry Donenfeld late this year.

1938: "DC" copped a lion's share of the comic book market with the publication of **Action Comics** No. 1 in June which contained the first appearance of Superman by writer Jerry Siegel and artist Joe Shuster, a discovery of Max C. Gaines. The "man of steel" inaugurated the "Golden Era" in comic book history. Fiction House, a pulp publisher, entered the comic book field in September with **Jumbo Comics**, featuring Sheena, Queen of the Jungle, and appearing in over-sized format for the first eight issues.

1939: The continued success of "DC" was assured in May with the publication of **Detective Comics** No. 27 containing the first episode of Batman by artist Bob Kane and writer Bill Finger. **Superman Comics** appeared in the summer. Also, during the summer, a black and white premium comic titled **Motion Picture Funnies Weekly** was published to be given away at motion picture theatres. The plan was to issue it weekly and to have continued stories so that the kids would come back week after week not to miss an episode. Four issues were planned but only one came out. This book contains the first appearance and origin of the Sub-Mariner by Bill Everett (8 pages) which was later reprinted in **Marvel Comics**. In November, the first issue of **Marvel Comics** came out, featuring the Human Torch by Carl Burgos and the Sub-Mariner reprint with color added.

1940: The April issue of **Detective Comics** No. 38 introduced Robin the Boy Wonder as a sidekick to Batman, thus establishing the "Dynamic Duo" and a major precedent for later costume heroes who would also have boy companions. **Batman Comics** began in the spring. Over 60 different comic book titles were being issued, including **Whiz Comics** begun in February by Fawcett Publications. A creation of writer Bill Parker and artist C. C. Beck, **Whiz's** Captain Marvel was the only superhero ever to surpass Superman in comic book sales. Drawing on their own popular pulp magazine heroes, Street and Smith Publications introduced **Shadow Comics** in March and **Doc Savage Comics** in

May. A second trend was established with the summer appearance of the first issue of **All-Star Comics**, which brought several superheroes together in one story and in its third issue that winter would announce the establishment of the Justice Society of America.

1941: Wonder Woman was introduced in the spring issue of **All-Star Comics** No. 8, the creation of psychologist William Moulton Marston and artist Harry Peter. **Captain Marvel Adventures** began this year. By the end of 1941, over 160 titles were being published, including **Captain America** by Jack Kirby and Joe Simon, **Police Comics** with Jack Cole's Plastic Man and later Will Eisner's Spirit, **Military Comics** with Blackhawk by Eisner and Charles Cuidera, **Daredevil Comics** with the original character by Charles Biro, **Air Fighters** with Airboy also by Biro, and **Looney Tunes & Merrie Melodies** with Porky Pig, Bugs Bunny, and Elmer Fudd, reportedly created by Bob Clampett for the Leon Schlesinger Productions animated films and drawn for the comics by Chase Craig. Also, Albert Kanter's Gilberton Company initiated the **Classics Illustrated** series with **The Three Musketeers**.

1942: Crime Does Not Pay by editor Charles Biro and publisher Lev Gleason, devoted to factual accounts of criminals' lives, began a different trend in realistic crime stories. **Wonder Woman** appeared in the summer. John Goldwater's character Archie, drawn by Bob Montana, first published in **Pep Comics**, was given his own magazine **Archie Comics**, which has remained popular over 40 years. The first issue of **Animal Comics** contained Walt Kelly's "Albert Takes the Cake," featuring the new character of Pogo. In mid-1942, the undated Dell Four Color title, No. 9, **Donald Duck Finds Pirate Gold**, appeared with art by Carl Barks and Jack Hannah. Barks, also featured in **Walt Disney's Comics and Stories**, remained the most popular delineator of Donald Duck and later introduced his greatest creation, Uncle Scrooge, in **Christmas on Bear Mountain** (Dell Four Color No. 178). The fantasy work of George Carlson appeared in the first issue of **Jingle Jangle Comics**, one of the most imaginative titles for children ever to be published.

1945: The first issue of **Real Screen Comics** introduced the Fox and the Crow by James F. Davis, and John Stanley began drawing the **Little Lulu** comic book based on a popular feature in the **Saturday Evening Post** by Marjorie Henderson Buell from 1935 to 1944. Bill Woggon's Katy Keene appears in issue No. 5 of **Wilbur Comics** to be followed by appearances in **Laugh, Pep, Suzie** and her own comic book in 1950. The popularity of Dick Briefer's satiric version of the Frankenstein monster, originally drawn for **Prize Comics** in 1941, led to the publication of **Frankenstein** by Prize publications.

1950: The son of Max C. Gaines, William M. Gaines, who earlier had inherited his father's firm Educational Comics (later Entertaining Comics), began publication of a series of well-written and masterfully drawn titles which would establish a "New Trend" in comics magazines: **Crypt of Terror** (later **Tales from the Crypt**, April), **The Vault of Horror** (April), **The Haunt of Fear** (May), **Weird Science** (May), **Weird Fantasy** (May), **Crime SuspenStories** (October), and **Two-Fisted Tales** (November), the latter stunningly edited by Harvey Kurtzman.

1952: In October "E.C." published the first number of **Mad** under Kurtzman's creative editorship.

1953: All Fawcett titles featuring Captain Marvel were ceased after many years of litigation in the courts during which National Periodical Publications claimed that the super-hero was an infringement on the copyrighted Superman.

1954: The appearance of Fredric Wertham's book **Seduction of the Inno-**

cent in the spring was the culmination of a continuing war against comic books fought by those who believed they corrupted youth and debased culture. The U. S. Senate Subcommittee on Juvenile Delinquency investigated comic books and in response the major publishers banded together in October to create the Comics Code Authority and adopted, in their own words, "the most stringent code in existence for any communications media."

1955: In an effort to avoid the Code, "E.C." launched a "New Direction" series of titles, such as **Impact, Valor, Aces High, Extra, M.D.,** and **Psychoanalysis**, none of which lasted beyond the year. **Mad** was changed into a larger magazine format with issue No. 24 in July to escape the Comics Code entirely.

1956: Beginning with the Flash in **Showcase** No. 4, Julius Schwartz began a popular revival of "DC" superheroes which would lead to the "Silver Age" in comic book history.

1960: After several efforts at new satire magazines (**Trump** and **Humbug**), Harvey Kurtzman, no longer with Gaines, issued in August the first number of another abortive effort, **Help!**, where the early work of underground cartoonists Jay Lynch, Skip Williamson, Gilbert Shelton, and Robert Crumb appeared.

1961: Stan Lee edited in November the first **Fantastic Four**, featuring Mr. Fantastic, the Human Torch, the Thing, and the Invisible Girl, and inaugurated an enormously popular line of titles from Marvel Comics featuring a more contemporary style of superhero.

1962: Lee introduced **The Amazing Spider-Man** in August, with art by Steve Ditko, **The Hulk** in May and **Thor** in August, the last two produced by Dick Ayers and Jack Kirby.

1963: Marvel's **The X-Men**, with art by Jack Kirby, began a successful run in November, but the title would experience a revival and have an even more popular reception in the 1980s.

1965: James Warren issued **Creepy**, a larger black and white comic book, outside Comics Code's control, which emulated the "E.C." horror comic line. Warren's **Eerie** began in September and **Vampirella** in September 1969.

1967: Robert Crumb's **Zap** No. 1 appeared, the first popular underground comic book.

1970: Editor Roy Thomas at Marvel begins **Conan the Barbarian** based on fiction by Robert E. Howard with art by Barry Smith.

1972: The Swamp Thing by Berni Wrightson begins in November from "DC."

1973: In February, "DC" revived the original Captain Marvel with new art by C. C. Beck and reprints in the first issue of **Shazam** and in October **The Shadow** with scripts by Denny O'Neil and art by Mike Kaluta.

1974: "DC" began publication in the spring of a series of over-sized facsimile reprints of the most valued comic books of the past under the general title of "Famous First Editions," beginning with a reprint of **Action** No. 1 and including afterwards **Detective Comics** No. 27, **Sensation Comics** No. 1, **Whiz Comics** No. 2, **Batman** No. 1, **Wonder Woman** No. 1, **All-Star Comics** No. 3, and **Flash Comics** No. 1.

1975: In the first collaborative effort between the two major comic book publishers of the previous decade, Marvel and "DC" produced together an over-sized comic-book version of **MGM's Marvelous Wizard of Oz** in the fall, and then the following year in an unprecedented cross-over produced **Superman vs. the Amazing Spider-Man**, written by Gerry Conway, drawn by Ross Andru, and inked by Dick Giordano.

1976: Frank Brunner's Howard the Duck, who had appeared earlier in Marvel's **Fear** and **Man-Thing**, was given his own book in January, which because of distribution problems became an over-night collector's item. After decades of litigation, Jerry Siegel and Joe Shuster were given financial recompense and recognition by National Periodical Publications for their creation of Superman, after several friends of the team made a public issue of the case.

1977: Stan Lee's **Spider-Man** was given a second birth, fifteen years after his first, through a highly successful newspaper comic strip, which began syndication on January 3 with art by John Romita. This invasion of the comic strip by comic book characters continued with the appearance on June 6 of Marvel's **Howard the Duck**, with story by Steve Gerber and visuals by Gene Colan. In an unusually successful collaborative effort, Marvel began publication of the comic book adaption of the George Lucas film **Star Wars**, with script by Roy Thomas and art by Howard Chaykin, at least three months before the film was released nationally on May 25. The demand was so great that all six issues of **Star Wars** were reprinted at least seven times, and the installments were reprinted in two volumes of an over-sized Marvel Special Edition and a single paperback volume for the book trade.

1978: In an effort to halt declining sales, Warner Communications drastically cut back on the number of "DC" titles and overhauled its distribution process in June. The interest of the visual media in comic book characters reached a new high with the Hulk, Spider-Man, and Doctor Strange, the subjects of television shows; with various projects begun to produce film versions of Flash Gordon, Dick Tracy, Popeye, Conan, The Phantom, and Buck Rogers; and with the movement reaching an outlandish peak of publicity with the release of **Superman** in December. Two significant applications of the comic book format to traditional fiction appeared this year: **A Contract with God and Other Tenement Stories** by Will Eisner and **The Silver Surfer** by Stan Lee and Jack Kirby. Eclipse Enterprises published Paul Gulacy's **Sabre**, the first graphic album produced for the direct sales market, and initiated a policy of paying royalties and granting copyrights to comic book creators.

1979: The Micronauts with art by Michael Golden debuted from Marvel in January.

1980: Publication of the November premier issue of **The New Teen Titans**, with art by George Perez and story by Marv Wolfman, brought back to widespread popularity a title originally published by "DC" in 1966.

1981: The distributor Pacific Comics began publishing titles for direct sales through comic shops with the inaugural issue of Jack Kirby's **Captain Victory and the Galactic Rangers** and offered royalties to artists and writers on the basis of sales. "DC" would do the same for regular newsstand comics in November (with payments retroactive to July 1981), and Marvel followed suit by the end of the year.

1982: The first slick format comic book in regular size appeared, **Marvel Fanfare** No. 1, with a March date. The premier March issue of **Captain Carrot and His Amazing Zoo Crew**, with story by Roy Thomas and art by Scott Shaw, revived the concept of funny animal superheroes of the 1940s.

1983: This year saw more comic book publishers, aside from Marvel and DC, issuing more titles than has existed in the past 40 years, most small independent publishers relaying on direct sales, such as Americomics, Capital, Eagle, Eclipse, First, Pacific, and Red Circle, and with Archie, Charlton, and

Whitman publishing on a limited scale. Frank Miller's mini-series **Ronin** demonstrated a striking use of sword-play and martial arts typical of Japanese comic book art, and Howard Chaykin's stylish but controversial **American Flagg** appeared with an October date on its first issue.

1985: Ohio State University's Library of Communication and Graphic Arts hosted the first major exhibition devoted to the comic book May 19 through August 2. In what was billed as an irreversible decision, the silver age superheroine Supergirl was killed in the seventh (October) issue of **Crisis on Infinite Earths**, a limited series intended to reorganize and simplify the DC universe on the occasion of the publisher's 50th anniversary.

1986: In recognition of its twenty-fifth anniversary, Marvel began publication of several new ongoing titles comprising Marvel's "New Universe," a self-contained fictional world. DC attracted extensive publicity and media coverage with its revisions of the character of **Superman** by John Byrne and of **Batman** in the **Dark Knight** series by Frank Miller.

THE MAN BEHIND THE COVER
Ron Dias

Ron busy at work at his studio in Los Angeles.

Ron Dias is one of today's outstanding animation artists, who over the past 30 years, has contributed to almost every animation studio in Los Angeles. His work has appeared on television, in commercials, feature films and educational films.

The cover feature of this year's guide held special significance to Ron. At the age of six, he saw the Disney classic *Snow White and the Seven Dwarfs* and was inspired to become an animation artist. Born in Honolulu, Hawaii, after graduating high school, he persued his childhood dream receiving formal art training at The Honolulu Academy of Art and the Famous Artists Schools in Westport, Conn.

In 1956 Ron won a National contest for his design of a U.S. postage "Children's Friendship" stamp. He was given a jet flight to Washington D.C. and a meeting with President Eisenhower, The First Lady, the acting Postmaster General, and Lady Butterfield, who sponsored the contest.

His first work for Disney was on *Sleeping Beauty* in 1956 & 1957. Columbia Pictures, 20th Century-Fox, Warner Brothers Pictures, and M.G.M. Pictures employed Ron's talents between 1958-60.

Over the next 26 years, Ron's animation background scenes appeared in many films. Some of the more memorable are: Hanna-Barbera's *Hey There, It's Yogi Bear* (1964), *Johnny Quest* (1965) and *Jack And The Beanstalk* (1967); U.P.A. Pictures' *Uncle Sam Magoo* (1970); Bakshi Productions' Tolkien's *Lord Of The Rings* (1977); Ron Campbells' T.V. Special *Treasure Island* (1978); Don Bluth Productions' *The Secret Of Nimh* (1980-83), and *Dragon's Lair* (1984) and Don Bluth's/Ruby-Spears Enterprises' T.V. *Space Ace.*

Ron came to the attention of the comic collecting community when three of his recent paintings (*Pinocchio*), (*Ferdinand The Bull*), and (*Donald Duck*) were sold for a record price at Christie's auction in New York.

He is currently involved in painting a poster for the 1987 re-release of the Disney classic *Snow White and the Seven Dwarfs* For the Walt Disney Studio and One Stop Poster Company.

We were pleased and gratified to have such a high caliber artist doing our cover this year. Special credit should also be given to Karen Storr, who assisted with the inking.

Information courtesy of Don Bluth Studios and Ron Dias.

The Enduring Magic of Disney Comics

by Thomas Andrae
in consultation with Bruce Hamilton

Once the leading purveyor of children's entertainment, The Walt Disney Company seemed to be in decline a few years ago. New animation was so costly it was impossible to duplicate the quality of the great Disney classics, and Disney live-action films—geared towards clean, family entertainment—seemed sadly dated. Then, when Western Publishing—the major publisher of Disney and other funny animal comic books for almost 50 years—decided to discontinue their line of comics, the Disney titles (for many years the most popular of them all) seemed destined for oblivion. Recently, however, there has been a resurgence of activity and interest in all things Disney. The Disney Studio has committed itself to full-scale animation production again, scheduling one completed feature every 18 months, and its ventures into contemporary live-action films have brought the company critical acclaim and box office success. The phenomenal growth of the Disney Channel is adding approximately a million new families yearly to their cable tv subscription service, making it—for its size—the fastest growing in the industry. And the legendary Walt Disney comic books have returned, too, through a new company based in Prescott, Arizona: Gladstone Publishing Ltd.!

Since it assumed the line in mid-1986, Gladstone has featured classic reprints in each issue of its monthly titles as well as in its bi-monthly Comic Digest Magazines, and there seems to be, without doubt, an almost unlimited wealth of reprint material from which they may choose. Besides 50 years of U.S. product, there are 30 to 50 years of stories from European and South American sources representing new product to fandom after translation.

Many collectors deem the better Disney comics to be the best in the field. The first Disney book was published in 1930 by Bibo and Lang. Though more a magazine than a comic book in format and in size, it's actively sought by comic book collectors. Called simply *The Mickey Mouse Book*, it had four very limited print runs and is a rare collectible. It contained a puzzle, games, a Mickey Mouse song and possibly the only "fictionalized" account of Mickey's origin. The story was created by 11-year-old Bobette Bibo, daughter of one of the publishers, and invokes an early Mickey Mouse along the lines established in "Plane Crazy," the first *Mickey* cartoon film short. Mickey Mouse, so Bobette's story goes, was once "angel 13" in mouse fairyland, but was kicked out for pulling the mouse king's beard and lands in Hollywood where Walt Disney makes him a movie star. The story apocraphally reveals that Walt gave him the Irish name Mickey because of the mouse's habit of eating green cheese. To reinforce this theme the book was printed in black and green. The

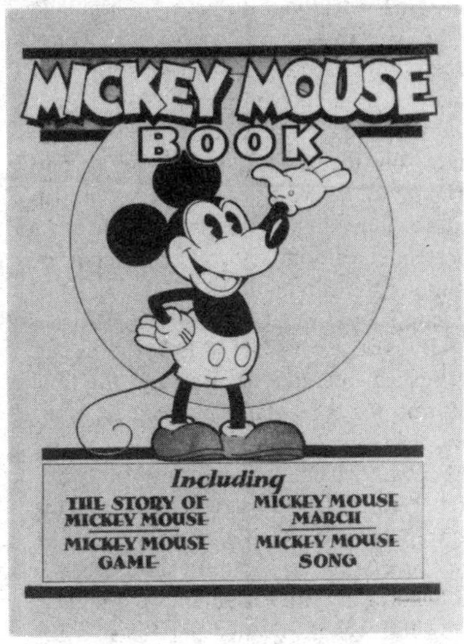

The first Disney book. Circa 1930, published by Bibo and Lang, and highly prized by collectors. © The Walt Disney Company

cover was drawn by Ub Iwerks, one of the greatest and most innovative animators of all time—the man who created Mickey's visual design and singlehandedly animated the first *Mickey* cartoons. He left the Studio in 1930, the same year the Bibo and Lang magazine was released, so this may be the only Disney book to have an originally drawn Iwerks cover. *The Mickey Mouse Book* was printed in four editions, the first and most valuable reprinting a 1930 *Mickey Mouse* newspaper daily comic strip by Win Smith on the back cover. The second through fourth editions omitted the strip and are indistinguishable from each other (these later editions had other differences, including the elimination of "11 year old" Bobette's age).

By the early '30s Mickey was an established international star and the time was ripe for a regularly published Disney periodical. The first was *Mickey Mouse Magazine*, which appeared in three different series before it was converted into the flagship comic book, *Walt Disney's Comics and Stories*. The initial series began publication by Kay Kamen in January, 1933, and was distributed and/or sold for five cents by department stores and at theaters showing Disney cartoons. Small,

Mickey Mouse Magazine No. 9, 1933, dairy giveaway. © The Walt Disney Co.

digest-sized booklets printed in two colors, they consisted of games, puzzles and stories like the ones in the Bibo and Lang book. This first series lasted nine issues, ending in September, 1933. A second series of *Mickey Mouse Magazine* that was a giveaway for various dairy companies started over with a new issue No. 1. It began in November, 1933 and lasted until October, 1935, its twenty fourth issue.

Mickey Mouse Magazine No. 1, 1935. © The Walt Disney Company

The third *Mickey Mouse Magazine*, again starting over with No. 1, was the most attractive and popular, first appearing in Summer, 1935. Though it supported a new, large, 13¼" x 10¼" size, it continued the established format, and was the brainchild of Hal Horne, who had edited the second series and who wanted to publish a magazine he obviously thought had the potential to be sold on newsstands and by subscription. Although the magazine was quite popular (the first issue's sales were 300,000), Horne printed too many copies at the beginning and the publication reportedly floundered in financial troubles until Kamen took over in mid-1936. Despite Horne's excessive print run of the first issue, today it is quite rare—especially in upper grades—and will bring $900 in mint condition. An unknown number of the extra copies of the first issue's overrun were autographed by the editors and given away to new subscribers. This rare, signed edition is easily worth $1,000 or more today in mint. Another special issue desired by collectors is the thick Christmas issue (Volume 2, No. 3), which has three times the number of pages of a regular copy.

The art in *Mickey Mouse Magazine* was often outstanding, even unique. Volume 2, No. 4, for instance, inaugurated a series of *Mickey Mouse* comic strips modeled after newspaper Sunday pages but originally drawn for the magazine and probably appearing nowhere else. A companion *Silly Symphonies* strip began in the next issue. Sometimes artists who became or were already famous for other accomplishments in the comics field drew anonymously for the magazine. John Stanley, artist/writer of the highly acclaimed *Little Lulu* comic books, remembers doing the cover for the first issue of one of the *Mickey Mouse Magazines*. And Otto Messmer, creator for Pat Sullivan of *Felix the Cat* and chief animator on the silent *Felix* cartoons, and who was the principal artist on the *Felix* comic strips and comic books, did one-page illustrations of Mickey and the gang for the magazine (see Volume 1, Nos. 2 and 3, and Volume 2, Nos. 3 and 4). He also did his own strip, *Bobby and Chip*, in Volume 4, Nos. 1 and 2. *Mickey Mouse Magazine* was published during a time when the Disney Studio was expanding, gearing up for the production of feature-length cartoons. As a consequence, many new characters made advance appearances in the magazine to drum up interest in the films. *Snow White and the Seven Dwarfs* appeared in an original, serialized story in the December, 1937 issue (Volume 3, No. 3) more than a month before the film's premiere (magazines are scheduled to go off sale on or before the cover date). Similarly, Pinocchio and Jiminy Cricket make their first appearance in the December, 1939 issue, on sale with an even earlier promotional lead time.

Mickey Mouse Magazine is especially noteworthy for its superb cover illustrations, many of which have been reproduced in recent years on post cards (some of these famous covers are reproduced in the color section in this Price Guide). These covers include not only some of the best and most charming artwork of Mickey and Minnie, but also offer rare glimpses of the early long-billed Donald Duck before he was joined by his nephews, and other characters seldom featured on covers: Pegleg Pete, Ferdinand the Bull and the Big Bad Wolf (the latter the subject of a special Halloween cover for Volume 3, No. 2. By 1941 the editors at Western discovered sales suffered when Mickey, or particularly Donald, weren't featured on a comic cover—a widely observed truism over most of the world to this day). One of the greatest of all Disney covers on a magazine or a comic book appeared on the special July 4th issue

V1/2, 10/35

V1/3, 11/35

V2/4, 1/37

V2/3, 12/36

V3/3, 12/37

V4/8, 5/39

V5/3, 12/39

V4/10, 7/39

of *MMM* (Volume 4, No. 10, in 1939), showing Mickey, Donald and Goofy as American Revolutionary War veterans with Donald playing the fife, Goofy the drum, and Mickey carrying the American flag, a scene loosely adapted from the famous early American painting, "Spirit of '76," ca. 1875 by Archibald M. Willard. During America's bicentennial this Disney cover was reprinted as a puzzle and recreated as a bisque statuette and a figural music box. The latter two items have become valuable collector's items themselves.

With the great success of *Superman* in 1938, comic books became more popular and the demand for a magazine declined. To meet the competition and keep up with the times, *Mickey Mouse Magazine* was gradually transformed into a comic book in the late '30s and 1940, arguably thus making it the longest-running "title" in comic book history. It became smaller in size and was printed in full color, increasingly comprised of comic strip reprints rather than stories and games. The most important of these were the *Mickey Mouse* dailies which were serialized in the magazine as they had been in the newspapers. The late Floyd Gottfredson, one of the all-time Disney greats (referred to in recent years by one top-level Disney executive as one of their two living "men of letters" in publications), plotted the *Mickey* daily in early years and drew the strip for over 45 years. He was the creator of such classic Mouse adventures as "The Phantom Blot," a story about a mysterious thief clad all in black; "Blaggard Castle," a tale of three Boris Karloff-styled mad scientists and their hypnotic ray gun; and "The Seven Ghosts," a suspense thriller about a gang of jewel thieves in ghostly garb, Gottfredson's work was so influential that it has set the standard for Disney comic strip artists ever since and has been so acknowledged, even by the world-renowned Donald Duck artist, Carl Barks.

Mickey Mouse Magazine turned into a full-fledged 68-page comic book with Volume 5, No. 12 (September, 1940). The next issue, which appeared a month later and continuing to fulfill subscriptions to

The legendary transition issue, V5/12, 9/40.

Walt Disney's Comics And Stories No. 31. Barks art begins with this issue. © The Walt Disney Company

the magazine, was the first issue of *Walt Disney's Comics and Stories*, the first regularly published Disney comic book (the numbering system, for the fourth time, started over with No. 1). The Gottfredson "Robinson Crusoe" serial, begun in the magazine, and extended through the transition issue, was concluded in *WDC&S*. *Comics and Stories* followed the format established by its predecessor, consisting chiefly of reprints until No. 31 (April, 1943), in which its first original Donald Duck story was printed. The story was drawn by Carl Barks, later to create Uncle Scrooge and unquestionably the greatest of Disney comic artists. Barks partially rewrote the script for the Donald 10-page story in this issue and because of his proficiency was asked to write the next story himself. For nearly a quarter century after that he was the principal artist/writer for the Donald feature in *WDC&S*. Barks wrote over 500 stories during his career—tales which have become classics and have made him a giant in the field, inspiring artists throughout the world to emulate the subtleties and finesse of his style. He continued to do the Disney ducks until his retirement in 1966, after which he began doing a series of paintings—done in recent years for lithographs—of the characters for which he is famous.

Barks had been an animator and story writer for seven years at the Disney Studio preceding his comic book work, and his early Duck stories show the expertise in drawing and formulating sight gags that he had learned from the film shorts depicting battles between Donald and his nephews. As he developed his own pantheon of auxiliary characters in the late '40s and early '50s, his stories grew more complex, at times even assuming dark and/or ironic tones. It has been attributed to Barks that he portrayed a comedic picture of the breadth of the entire human condition—of life itself and its many vagaries—and in so doing has developed a fiercely loyal and growing cult of readers, most of whom feel he has touched or influenced their personal lives, leaving them at times with the inexplicable feeling that he was writing for each of them alone: this, logically, was one of the keys to his "genius." Comic book publishers circling the globe unanimously agree that all of his stories translate well and are equally "appropriate" for their divergent markets. His following thusly indicates no boundaries of class, age, profession or culture.

Many collectors believe the best of Barks' work appeared in the late '40s to early '50s period. Key issues of *Walt Disney's Comics and Stories* include the introduction of Gladstone Gander, Donald's obnoxious cousin (No. 88) and the first appearance of Uncle Scrooge in this title (No. 98). Other important issues include the debut of the crackpot inventor, Gyro Gearloose (No. 141), the Junior Woodchucks (Barks' parody of the cub scouts, No. 125), and the Beagle Boys (Scrooge's arch nemeses, No. 134). In their precise plotting and wry humor the Donald 10-pagers are arguably Barks' finest work, rivaling the best ever produced in comics. Reprints of the wartime-to-early-'50s Barks material are currently reaching new generations all over the world, kids who disregard dated gags and situations much in the same way school children accept Twain's Tom Sawyer-and-Huckleberry Finn world that portrayed times familiar to our great, great, grandparents.

The covers for *Walt Disney's Comics and Stories* were often contributed by famous Pogo artist Walt Kelly. Before working for Western Publishing on such titles as *Fairy Tale Parade* and *Animal Comics* (in which he first created Pogo), Kelly had been an animator at the Disney Studio, working both on the *Mickey Mouse* cartoons, such as "Clock Cleaners," "The Nifty Nineties," and "The Little Whirlwind," and animated feature films, such as *Pinocchio, Fantasia, Dumbo,* and *The Reluctant Dragon*. His ability to endow Donald and Mickey with charm and expressiveness, the cuteness of his small, naturalistically drawn squirrels and rabbits and his whimsical humor shine through in these covers, some of the best done for any funny animal comic. Kelly began doing covers with *WDC&S* No. 40 and did the bulk of them until No. 118, at which time he was too busy with his *Pogo* comic books and syndicated comic strip to continue. Kelly also did one interior feature in *Comics and Stories*, "The Gremlins" (Nos. 34 to 41), based on an unproduced wartime Disney short for which he did all the storyboards. Barks began doing covers with issue No. 95, becoming the regular cover artist with No. 129.

In the late '40s Gottfredson reprints were dropped from *Comics and Stories* and some of his famous tales redrawn to make the characters look more contemporary and to conform to their current screen appearance. Around 1950 a new crop of Disney comic book artists began to emerge, most of whom had been drawing the Disney newspaper comic strips. Dick Moores, a 1980s Reuben-award winner of *Gasoline Alley* fame, who had drawn the *Uncle Remus* Sunday page as early as 1946, did the first redrawn Gottfredson story, the second retelling of "The Phantom Blot," which began in *WDC&S* No. 107. Bill Wright, who had assisted Gottfredson on the *Mickey* daily strip drew the *Mickey* Sunday pages during World War II while Manuel Gonzales, the regular artist on the strip was in the army (Wright later did the *Uncle Remus* Sundays from 1959-1962). Taking over with *WDC&S* No. 112, Wright redrew Gottfredson's "Monarch of Medioca" story. He also did one of the few *Mickey* Sunday-page full-length adventures in the '40s (as opposed to the usual "gags only" with no continuity from week to week), "The Professor's Experiment," where Mickey encounters very strange creatures after having been shrunk down to a size smaller than a single sodium bicarbonate "atom." The story was reprinted in *WDC&S* Nos. 67 and 68. Later, beginning with Wright's "The Ghost of Maneater Mountain" (No. 129), *Comics and Stories* began publishing originally drawn Mickey serials.

Wright was succeeded as artist on the

WDC&S No. 34 WDC&S No. 40 WDC&S No. 161

Four Color No. 208

Vacation Parade No. 1

WDC&S No. 1

Mouse serials by Paul Murry whose first story. "The Last Resort," appeared in *WDC&S* No. 152 (May, 1953). Murry had been an animator at Disney working on the *Mickey* shorts and numerous features including *Pinocchio, Fantasia, Dumbo,* and *The Reluctant Dragon*. His work on *Saludas Amigos* and *Song of the South* made him a natural choice to adapt those films for comics, and in 1945 he joined the comic strip department penciling the *Jose Carioca, Panchito,* and *Uncle Remus* Sunday pages (all inked by Dick Moores). His first comic book was *Uncle Remus and His Tales of Brer Rabbit* (Dell Four Color No. 129), an adaptation of the feature film, *Song of the South* and *Brer Rabbit Does It Again* (Four Color No. 208). His first Mickey story, "Mickey Mouse and the Monster Whale" appears in a 25¢ Walt Disney giant annual, *Vacation Parade* No. 1 (1950).

Though not widely known among fandom's legions of superhero collectors, *Walt Disney's Comics and Stories* is by far the best-selling comic book of all time in the U.S. and worldwide, both by single issue and cumulative total. Its debut in October, 1940 as a title-change continuation of *Mickey Mouse Magazine* hit the newsstands with a modest quarter million copies, but in 18 months its popularity had boosted sales to one million a month. By 1946 it had passed 2,000,000 and peaked in 1952 at nearly 4,000,000 copies sold per issue. It had become the most popular comic book of all time, a testimony to the greatness of the artists and writers associated with it and its use of a tried-and-true format. Numerous comics have undergone both title and content changes and have still been recognized by collectors as a single, long-running entity. Though *WDC&S* started its numbering system over with No. 1, it was—without question—a continuation of *Mickey Mouse Magazine*; so now, with its resurrection by Gladstone, it could justifiably lay claim to being both the longest-running as well as best-selling comic book of all time!

Western's Dell Giants were another series that adapted the anthology format. The giants were priced at a quarter for, initially, 100 pages rather than 10¢ for what had begun in the 1930s as 68-page comics, but which had gradually shrunk to 36 pages, including covers. The Disney giants most often starred Donald and Mickey, but also contained features from *Comics and Stories*, such as Li'l Bad Wolf and Bucky Bug. Often labeled as "annuals," these story books were usually based on holiday themes and appeared during summer vacation, at Christmas or other special occasions. The most important to collectors is *Vacation Parade* No. 1, which—among other things—contains three Carl Barks stories totaling 55 pages. The lead story, "Vacation Time" by Barks, has both the feel and length of a full-fledged Donald Duck adventure and concerns a careless camper's attempts to blame Donald and the nephews for a forest fire the camper himself has started. The second story, "Camp Counselor," is modeled after the *Comics and Stories* 10 pagers and deals with Donald's misguided efforts to teach his nephews woodcraft, anticipating Barks' Junior Woodchuck stories, which began a year later. "Donald's Cousin Gus," the third *Vacation Parade* feature by Barks, is the first to deal in depth with Grandma Duck and it is also Barks' first comic book use of Gus Goose—Grandma's farm-hand—a character Barks helped create as an animator at the Studio. Two other Dell Giants, *Christmas Parade* No. 1 (1949) and No. 2 (1950), which include hilarious Barks satires on Christmas gift-giving, are also important collector's items.

Of the non-Barks giants the *Peter Pan Treasure Chest* is one of the most valuable and interesting. Issued in 1952 to coincide with the release of the film, it features a Dick Moores reworking of the Barks/Hannah *Donald Duck* epic "Pirate Gold," in which Peter and Captain Hook replace Donald and Pegleg Pete from the original story, although both contain the parrot Yellow Beak. (Ironically, Yellow Beak was the one character that remained constant from the first Disney Studio feature film story outline for the picture that was never produced through to the comics [see the *Carl Barks Library* Set I, published by Another Rainbow].) The *Silly Symphonies* annuals from the '50s are also notable, early issues containing original adaptations from films: "The Sorcerer's Apprentice" from *Fantasia* by Paul Murry or *The Grasshopper and the Ants* by Al Hubbard, as examples. Later issues contain reprints from early *Walt Disney's Comics and Stories*. In the last year all Dell Giants—and especially the Disney's—have become "hot" in the collector's market. Mint condition copies—rare because of the square binding—will often command prices of two or three times "guide" from a year or two ago.

The anthology format established by *Mickey Mouse Magazine* and *Walt Disney's Comics and Stories* was not the only successful one. Books featuring single characters had been popular since the early part of the century when annual reprints of *Mutt and Jeff* and *Bringing Up Father* were sold by the hundreds of thousands. The waning popularity of this format received a new jolt of interest when David McKay published two originally drawn Disney books in the early '30s: *The Adventures of Mickey Mouse* Books I and II. Book I—published in 1931—is significant because it contains the first reference to Donald Duck. The text begins:

> "This story is about Mickey Mouse, who lives in a cozy nest under the floor of an old barn.
>
> "And it is about his friend Minnie Mouse, whose nest is safely hidden, soft and warm, somewhere in the chicken house.

Christmas Parade No. 1

PP Treasure Chest No. 1

Silly Symphonies No. 1

David McKay books No. 1(1931), 2(1932), 3(1933) and 4(1934). Number 3 is in full color and was reissued as Whitman No. 948. © The Walt Disney Company

"Mickey has many friends in the old barnyard, besides Minnie Mouse. There are Henry Horse and Carolyn Cow and Patricia Pig and Donald Duck."

In order to popularize Mickey, Roy O. Disney—Walt's brother—wrote to a number of publishers suggesting a Mickey Mouse book, but he got only negative replies except from David McKay, who had the foresight to want to publish a character who was rapidly becoming world famous. Book I was a best-seller through the 1930s and soon had a concurrent best-selling second volume, Book II. McKay also began in 1931 the first of four soft-cover volumes of Gottfredson *Mickey Mouse* reprints, the first time such collections appeared. It's thought these David McKay editions may have actually been printed by some sort of arrangement with Whitman (Western Publishing), who reissued the third of the three books—the only one in color—under their own imprint. About the same time—in 1935—Whitman published and printed the first book featuring Donald Duck. Consisting of text with accompanying illustrations, this book paved the way for the *Donald Duck* comic books by proving that the foul-tempered fowl was a popular best-selling star. The first *Donald* comic book—published by Whitman in 1938—consisting of reprints of Taliafaro Sunday pages, had an unnumbered cover showing Donald blowing a bubble pipe. Following the exact David McKay Feature Book format (measuring 8½" x 11-3/8" with rough stock color covers and black

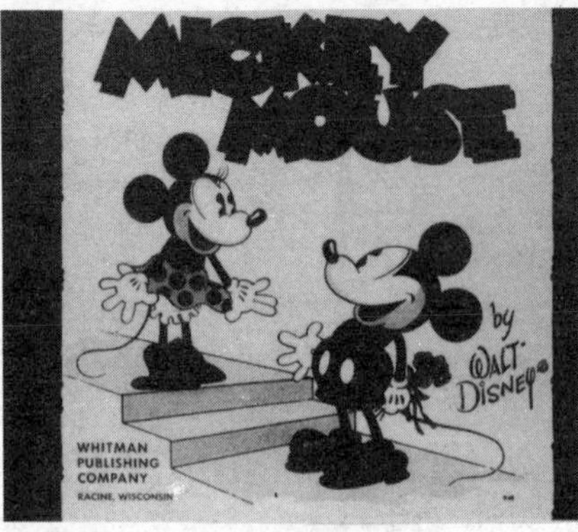

Whitman No. 948 which reprints book number 3 on previous page. © The Walt Disney Company

and white interiors) and also thought to have been printed for McKay by Whitman, it was a predecessor to the Whitman-produced-and-printed Dell Large Feature Comic series that began in 1939.

Besides being the first approximation to a *Donald Duck* comic book, the unnumbered Whitman Feature Book collection is important for another reason: it contains the first appearance of Donald's nephews, Huey, Dewey and Louie. Although it is not widely known, Taliafaro created the nephews in the Sunday Hearst newspaper page which this volume reprints! The strip both predates and inspired their introduction in the cartoon short, *Donald's Nephews*, a fact documented by Walt Disney Studio correspondence in the files of Taliafaro's widow.

Large Feature Comic No. 16, 1941. Has first appearance of Daisy Duck on back cover. © The Walt Disney Company

Whitman book No. 978, 1935. The first *Donald Duck* book. © The Walt Disney Company

Grosset & Dunlap reprint of the No. 978 Whitman book, 1936. © The Walt Disney Company

Next in the series of *Donald* comics was Large Feature Comic No. 16, Series I, a continuation of Western's Dell "feature books" that had, by this time reduced their page count from 76 to 52 pages and had gone to regular, slick comic book covers. LFC No. 16 is another Disney special rarity: it contains a reprint of the first appearance of Daisy Duck from the Sunday newspaper pages.

The first Walt Disney comic to have *all* the features of a modern comic book was

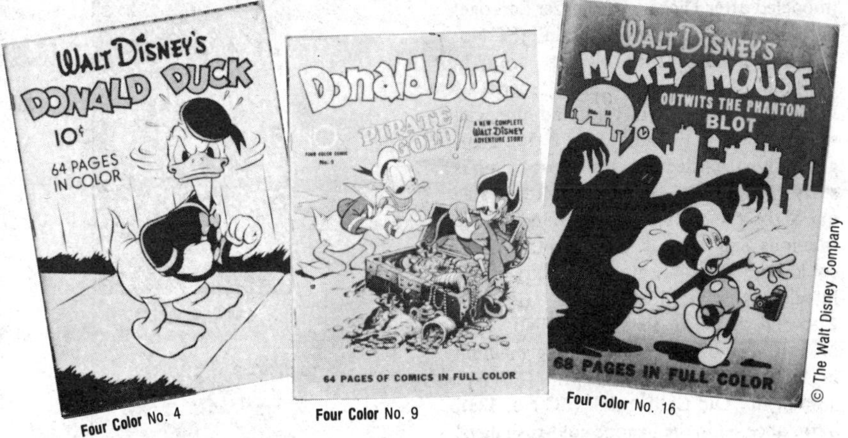

Four Color No. 4 Four Color No. 9 Four Color No. 16

Donald Duck Four Color No. 4 (Series I, 1940), which reprints Al Taliafaro strips in full color. It came out at about the same time or just before *Mickey Mouse Magazine*, Volume 5, No. 9, the first issue of that title reduced to comic book size, but not yet fully converted to comic book format (June, 1940).

Taliafaro created many elements of the Duck saga which Barks and future Duck artists would draw upon and elaborate, including Grandma Duck, Bolivar—Donald's huge St. Bernard—and the duck's famous sport coupe with the 313 license plate.

Whitman—as mentioned before, one of the arms of Western Publishing—first came out with a full-length Disney comic book adventure in 1941 with the appearance of *Mickey Mouse Outwits the Phantom Blot* (Four Color No. 16, Series I, published under a distribution contract using a Dell Comics logo). The book is a nearly complete reprint of a Floyd Gottfredson late-1930s *Mickey* daily strip continuity, though the actual name "Phantom Blot" was never used in the strip (the black, shadow-clad villain was referred to in the newspapers as only "The Blot"), so the first use of the "Phantom" was on the cover of this comic.

Western abandoned reprints the following year for a time in favor of original stories in the *Donald Duck* one-shot comics with the publication of *Donald Duck Finds Pirate Gold* (Four Color No. 9, Series II, 1942: "one shot" is a publisher's term for a title issued only once or on an infrequent or unscheduled basis). Adapted from storyboards to an unproduced feature-length cartoon, *Morgan's Ghost*, the comic book is doubly significant. The first story drawn by Barks and done while he was still working at the Disney Studio, Barks did half of the pages in the story—mostly the outdoor scenes—and the other half was drawn by Jack Hannah, a Disney animator/director/storyman who worked with Barks on the *Donald Duck* cartoons. "Pirate Gold" was also the first originally created and drawn funny animal adventure comic book and set the pattern for stories featuring other film studio characters from the Dell/Whitman/Western line-up.

Barks' next *Donald* adventure comic, "The Mummy's Ring" (FC No. 29, 1943) was written by Western editor Eleanor Packer, but was heavily revised by Barks and begins to show the antiquarianism and use of authentic locales culled from the *National Geographic*, which distinguishes his work from that of other comic book artists.[1] Barks' best work in this series occurs in the late '40s and early '50s, the same period in which he did his best 10 pagers (the *Donald Duck* "one shots" didn't convert to a regularly published frequency until November, 1952). This period includes the introduction of Uncle Scrooge McDuck as a money-hoarding, penny-pinching old miser (modeled after Dickens' Ebenezer Scrooge) in "Christmas on Bear Mountain" (FC No. 178, 1947); Barks' turn towards parody in the take-off of Western films, "Sheriff of Bullet Valley" (FC No. 199); and his social satire, "Lost in the Andes" (FC No. 223), generally regarded as his most famous story, featuring Donald's unforgetable quest for the people and the land of the fabulous square eggs. In contrast, Barks could be both humorous and darkly gothic in tales like "Voodoo Hoodoo" (FC No. 238) and "Ancient Persia" (FC No. 275), or sentimental without becoming maudlin in "Christmas for Shacktown" (FC No. 367) or in "Old California" (FC No. 328), a romance set in the bygone gold-rush days. "Trick or Treat" (*Donald Duck* No. 26, 1952) was the last *Donald* adventure Barks did on a regular basis and marks the waning, we believe, of what is called comics' Golden Age. Hampered by censorship, commercialization, and an increasing workload, Barks' creative vision would become more and more restricted throughout the latter part of his career.

Even under these conditions, however, the Old Duck Man was able to create a new line of *Uncle Scrooge* comics which rival the best of his *Donald* adventures. The first three in the series (FC Nos. 386, 456, and 495) are key stories in the development of Scrooge's mythos, explaining where he got his fortune and what his origins were. Later classics include "Tralla La" (*US* No. 6), a parody of the Shangra-La legend, which shows Barks' continuing fascination with preindustrial cultures; "Land Beneath the Ground" (*US* No. 13), a story of the earthquake-making Terries and Fermies; and "The Peeweegah Indians" (*US* No. 22), an epic tale of a lost race of pygmy Indians. These are among the most polished versions of the motif which Barks originated—and which remain uniquely his—in the *Donald* adventures.

The Disney giveaways are another collecting genre, and among the ones featuring single characters the best have to be the *March of Comics*, given away by various department and shoe stores. Limited in distribution, they are quite rare and are difficult to find in excellent condition because of their pulp covers. The most valuable and

Four Color No. 178

Four Color No. 223

Donald Duck No. 26

Four Color No. 386

March of Comics No. 4 | March of Comics No. 41 | Firestone, 1946

© The Walt Disney Company

desirable issues contain Donald Duck adventures similar to those in the one shots. "Maharajah Donald" (*MOC* No. 4, 1947) is the most valuable Barks comic of them all, selling today for $2,600 in mint. Other important issues are "Race to the South Seas" (*MOC* No. 41, 1949), the first story in which Gladstone's invincible luck appears and "Darkest Africa" (*MOC* No. 20, 1948), Barks' first in a long line of satires on collecting manias. Another series, the *Donald and Mickey Merry Christmas* Firestone giveaways were modeled after the 10 pagers in *Comics and Stories* and were also drawn by Barks. "Donald Duck's Atom Bomb," a pocketsize 1947 *Cheerios* giveaway, portrays Donald as a mad scientist. An eight-page comic book, *Donald Duck Tells About Kites*, is one of the rarest and is *the* most expensive for its page count. It was issued by three known utility companies: Southern California Edison, Florida Power and Light, and Pacific Gas and Electric. The latter has a redrawn page (not by Barks) and is somewhat more common and therefore worth the least of the three. *Donald Duck's Surprise Party*, a 1948 Icy Frost Twins Ice Cream Bars giveaway was a 16-page comic with a Donald Duck story and cover penciled by Walt Kelly and inked by Carl Buettner, an editor at Western during Barks' and Kelly's tenure and an artist on early *Comics and Stories* covers and Li'l Bad Wolf and Bucky Bug features. Although *Surprise Party* is likely one of, if not the rarest Disney giveaway, because it was not drawn by Barks it doesn't command the price that comic books do with his work in them.

The *Mickey Mouse* one shots were still another series which featured a single character and were part of the Dell Four Color comics (until changing to their own numbering system in the early '50s). The first—and most valuable—was FC No. 16 (Series I, 1941), a 68-page reprint of Gottfredson's original "Phantom Blot." With the second *Mickey* comic book release, "The Seven-Colored Terror" (FC No. 27, Series II, 1943) Western shifted to all-original stories, as they had done with two *Donald Duck* one shots already in print. The third all-*Mickey Mouse* comic,

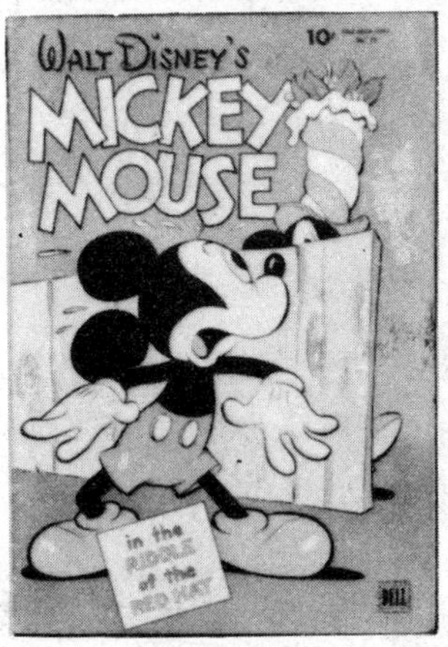

Four Color No. 79. The only Mickey story drawn by Carl Barks. © The Walt Disney Company

however, "The Riddle of the Red Hat" (FC No. 79, 1945), is second only in value and desirability to the "Phantom Blot," as it is the only Mickey story drawn—though not written—by Barks.

Unlike the all-*Donald Duck* adventures, which Barks indelibly stamped with his standout style, no one artist dominated the *Mickey* one shots. Bill Wright wrote and drew excellent stories like "Spook's Island" (FC No. 170), "Jungle Magic" (FC No. 181) and "The Black Sorcerer" (FC No. 258) in the late '40s. Dick Moores continued this tradition of quality with two whimsical stories, "Goofy's Mechanical Man" (FC No. 401) and "The Wonderful Whizzix" (FC No. 427), a 1952 story about a car that comes alive, which was reportedly much loved by Bill Walsh, producer of such Disney hits as *Mary Poppins* and probably inspired his production of *The Love Bug*, about a wayward Volkswagen (this famous comic is scheduled to appear in Gladstone's *Mickey Mouse Digest* No. 5, on sale June 2, 1987). Paul Murry did many late *Mickey* one shots and regular series releases, including "The Mystery of the Double-Cross Ranch" (FC No. 313, 1951).

The Disney animated cartoons—and later live-action films—provided the basis for yet another series of one shots. Disney movie adaptations began with *The Reluctant Dragon* (FC No. 13, Series I, 1941) and *Dumbo, the Flying Elephant* (FC No. 17, Series I), which also reprinted "The Brave Little Tailor," Gottfredson's last syndicate Sunday-page story. Walt Kelly, who helped animate Geppetto in *Pinocchio*, created a comic book based on the film (FC No. 92), which included a backup Donald Duck story. Kelly's best Donald story, however, of the few he did, was his adaptation of *The Three Caballeros* (FC No. 71), retelling Donald's film trip to South America. Another highlight issue was the reprinting of the 1938 *Snow White and the Seven Dwarfs* Sunday pages in Four Color No. 49, written by long-time Gottfredson-*Mickey Mouse*-adventures scripter Merrill de Maris and drawn in an illustrative style by Hank Porter. Also, Al Hubbard, artist for many years on the Mary Jane and Snif-

Four Color No. 71. Cover and story by Walt Kelly.
© The Walt Disney Company

Four Color No. 170

Four Color No. 181

Four Color No. 427

© The Walt Disney Company

Four Color No. 446

Four Color No. 629

Donald Duck No. 250

fles features in the Warner Brothers anthology comic published by Western, *Looney Tunes and Merrie Melodies*—and who succeeded Walt Kelly on the *Peter Wheat* giveaways—had a delicate, fine-line style that lent a storybook quality to his comic adaptations of such Disney films as *Peter Pan* (FC Nos. 442 and 446) and *Lady and the Tramp* (FC Nos. 629 and 634) and its spinoff, *Scamp*, which evolved into its own separate series.

The Disney comics were discontinued in 1984 along with all Western Publishing's other licensed product, as well as their own properties, when they decided to get completely out of comics (they remain the largest publisher of children's books in the world). The Disney titles were the first to rebound with four one shots in 1985 and then with a full complement of regularly released mainstream titles in the summer of 1986, published by Another Rainbow's wholly owned subsidiary, Gladstone Publishing, Ltd., and distributed throughout the United States, Canada, Australia, and New Zealand. On the continent the comics are distributed to newsstands through Curtis, the same company handling the Marvel comics.

Gladstone—a company owned and staffed by collectors—concentrates on bringing back classic stories that have either been out of print for many years or have never been reprinted since their first release, such as Barks' *Donald Duck* comic, "Pirate Gold," which, until its rerelease in late 1986, was a comic few collectors could afford to buy in its original and only previous edition. Gladstone is also making available for the first time in comic book form many of the Gottfredson *Mickey Mouse* adventures that have not been seen by the general public for 40 or 50 years or more. To ensure that the Disney comics heritage will continue to be invigorated with fresh creative energy, Gladstone plans to continue to publish translations of the much-praised European Donald stories which attempt to capture the flavor of Barks' work. It's a fitting continuation of the great Disney comics legacy which began—like Disney's film empire itself—with a muse.

[1]C.F. "The Far Away and Long Ago" by Thomas Andrae and Geoffrey Blum on Barks' use of the *National Geographic* in depicting authentic locales in his stories. *Carl Barks Library*, Set I (Scottsdale, Arizona: Another Rainbow Publishing, 1984), pp. 229-252.

The 2-6-38 Sunday newspaper page, illustrated by Hank Porter. © 1938 The Walt Disney Company

Walt at home on Woking Way, a tiny street tucked into the hillside Los Feliz section of Los Angeles, near Hollywood. Displayed on a library bookcase shelf are Seiberling Latex Products rubber dolls, handpainted Dwarf figurines that were sold individually or in sets. These merchandised items, difficult to find today in prime condition, were also pictured on Walt's desk for the 12-27-37 color cover of *Time* magazine.
© 1987 The Walt Disney Company

Cover of the complete authorized film songbook issued in 1938 by Bourne Inc. of New York, with words and music of all eight tunes used for the soundtrack: *Whistle While You Work, Heigh-Ho* (Dwarfs' Marching Song), *Some Day My Prince Will Come, One Song, With A Smile And A Song, The Dwarfs' Yodel Song, I'm Wishing,* and *Bluddle-Uddle-Um-Dum* (Washing Song). The songbook also included words and music for a ninth tune titled *Snow White*, apparently one of the 17 other numbers that were composed but not used in the picture.

Disney has used since 1960.

Why are Disney collectibles treasured so much? Part of the answer lies in the area of memories evoked. As with numerous other collectibles they were once cast aside and called "trite," accompanied by that old saying "Haven't you grown out of *that* yet?" Both points of view have since proved to be unwise parental and peer pressure cliches. When one loses that small child of wonder in the heart, Peter Pan does fly out your window never to return with imagination and fantasy which keeps all of us young. When one tries to reclaim the treasures of youth, and marvel anew at their timeless qualities, a Disneyana collector is born.

Always a top item is Walt's personal signature to be found on artwork, books, cards, stationery, napkins and other oddments when a fan pressed the object into Walt's hands for an autograph. The demand for his signature on anything has established a great desirability and increased price. Disney's "studio" signature, also very collectible in itself, has become the most recognizable signature in the world, a trademark for the Studio on most merchandise.

Few if any art books on animation or in general can match the Circle Fine Art Press 1978 deluxe edition of *Snow White and the Seven Dwarfs*. This volume, slipcased and limited to 9500 copies worldwide, is a replica of the three-dimensional prop storybook (not animated) used in the picture's opening scene. It warranted a cover of special bonded leather stamped in 22-carat gold and pigment leaf. Its 223 pages bordered in gold ink illustrate over 400 concepts, storyboards, atmospheres and animation drawings used in making the film. Inclusion of four serigraphs created as cel setups from the film's original art are on mylar cels printed with 23 colors, bound in. A truly lavish collectors edition that sold originally for $200, it is still in print and available today from the publisher for $300. Their advertisement can be found elsewhere in this edition.

Other *Snow White* items spanning nearly half a century comprise a lengthy list for Disneyana fans to consider. Here a few more unusual selections that collectors may not be familiar with.

In 1938 toy stores carried the doll line produced by Richard G. Krueger Inc. of New York. The deluxe models made music, fashioning Snow White in an organdy dress and outfitting the Dwarfs in washable sharkskin grain material. Animal helpers completing the ensemble were bluebirds, bunny, chipmunk and fawn.

Knickerbocker Toy Co. manufactured a top doll item: the Dwarfs' forest cottage complete with doe and fawn, various bunnies, chipmunk and squirrels. This set included the evil Queen in her royal robes, a fantastically detailed figure. Knickerbocker also produced musical Dwarfs of a higher quality in character features.

La Mode Studios, creators of Modeware—a plastic and plywood composition material—manufactured nightlights, lamps and bookends. Their top sellers were Dopey with drum leaning over a

OPPOSITE: A page from Kay Kamen's Disney Merchandise Catalog for 1938-39, published by Whitman. *"Every item a feature attraction--cut-out Doll Sets and the popular Walt Disney stories and characters in book form--with illustrations by the staff of the Walt Disney Studios--and written with a wholesomeness characteristic of all Walt Disney film productions."* About half of these offerings were Snow White items, with popular Dopey rating no less than two books compared to his comrades' one each.

The STORY of HAPPY
The STORY of SLEEPY
The STORY of SNEEZY
The STORY of DOC
The STORY BASHFUL
Snow White and the Seven Dwarfs
96 Page Story Book
The STORY of DOPEY
The STORY of SNOW WHITE
STORY GRUMPY
SEVEN DWARFS
Snow White and the Seven Dwarfs
PLUTO THE PUP
Snow White
ANIMALS FROM Snow White and the Seven Dwarfs
DOPEY HE DON'T TALK NONE!
THE WISE LITTLE HEN
WISE LITTLE HEN
TOBY TORTOISE AND THE HARE
DONALD DUCK
MICKEY MOUSE'S FRIENDS WAIT FOR THE COUNTY FAIR
WALT DISNEY SILLY SYMPHONY
MICKEY'S MAGIC HAT
ROBBER KITTEN
THE GOLDEN TOUCH
the TORTOISE and the HARE
the THREE ORPHAN KITTENS
NURSERY STORIES

large kettle drum, and Dopey standing holding drumsticks. These lamps and bookends for children's bedrooms have not survived too well in top conditions because of knockabout use and less-than-durable materials.

The scarcity of Doris Lamp Shades' output is evident by the nature of their relatively fragile product—heavy parchment paper shades, eight inches in diameter, which reproduced scenes from the film. These included "Heigh-Ho," the Dwarfs' marching song going to and from work, the musical dancing sequence, the Dwarfs arriving at their cottage from the diamond mine, and the washing-up scene. Lamps and shades of character design have been a top collectible for many years, and they routinely command high prices when available.

The Lightfoot Schultz Co. produced Castile soap Snow White figurines individually and in special boxed sets carrying some detailed handpainting, presumably non-toxic. It's anybody's guess how many thousands of these were lathered up and washed down the drain day by day.

Marionettes were manufactured by Madame Alexander (number one dollmaker among collectors) featuring Snow White, the Dwarfs, the Prince, a toy wishing well, the Huntsman, the Queen, and the wicked Witch. Great puppets that rarely surface at doll or Disneyana shows.

A 1938 item licensed by a foundation garment company is mainly for Snow White completists and falls into the rare category. Miller Corsets of New York fashioned ten Snow White models in their "Smarties" line, Snow White's likeness being printed or woven into the fabric. One wonders if the dark-haired beauty wore one herself to maintain a girlish figure.

Many companies have produced bisque and ceramics of Snow White and the Dwarfs since 1937, but none can claim the true Disney character as the 1946-47 figurines issued by Evan R. Shaw and

From Harper Bros.' 1938 first edition of *Snow White and the Seven Dwarfs*, containing storybook text and Disney Studio illustrations. "The Lodgemeeting" above and "Bedbuilding" on facing page depict scenes from sequences that were deleted from the film when it was decided they slowed pacing and made the picture too long. *Snow White* was released with a final running time of 83 minutes, and these two sequences would have brought it up to a full hour and a half or more.

American Pottery of Los Angeles. They respectively hold top honors for design, cartoonlike color and quality construction. The sets are in high demand with all Disney collectors since issue, and they grow more popular as years progress.

A very rare Snow White item from the late Thirties has a Yuletide theme. During the Christmas season Walt and selected staff members visited various children's hospitals in the Los Angeles area, bringing gifts of Snow White merchandise. Walt personally signed many Snow White books. The gifts were stuffed in large red and white Christmas stockings, imprinted "Walt Disney's Xmas Surprise Stocking" with two ringing bells and holly on red felt cloth.

Let us not forget the film's musical score which had movie patrons humming and whistling a host of memorable tunes written by Larry Morey (words) and Frank Churchill (music). Twenty-five songs in all were composed during 1934-35, of which eight were chosen for the soundtrack. Of the remaining 17 songs, only two were later released on record. "Music in My Soup" and "You're Never Too Old to Be Young" appeared as a 45rpm children's Story Record in the Fifties.

The complete filmscore of words and music, published by Bourne Inc. of New York and priced at $1.00 (an expensive songbook for the time), featured a wonderful cover of the Dwarfs crossing the tree bridge, Snow White, and the Prince on horseback. Inside were 14 full-page illustrations and a story synopsis.

New Victor Records (RCA) released the 78 rpm album of four discs in 1938, as originally sung in the feature, starting the wave of songsheets, other versions and rerecording of the popular tunes. New Victor's was the first-pressing set of the score.

Another first was Harper Brothers' 1938 hardcover dustjacket edition of *Snow White and the Seven Dwarfs* containing story text and Disney Studio illustrations. This volume included the film's omitted "Bedbuilding" sequence in which the Dwarfs constructed a carved four-poster inlaid with gems from the diamond mine. A second completed sequence, "Soup Concert," was also deleted from the final production due to running time and pacing of action, although detailed color illustrations were done for publishers Harper Brothers, Grosset & Dunlap, and Whitman.

Whitman, who published the majority of quality *Snow White* books (1938-39), had a cover illustration for their linen-like book *Seven Dwarfs* depicting the Dwarfs' discussion of giving Snow White the gift of

an ornate bed. Walt had called this sequence "The Lodgemeeting" at story conferences during production, leading to design of Snow White's bed as seen in the picture.

Disney Studio animators gave the Dwarfs distinct physical attributes and personality traits to match, developing them from a classic fairytale text that was minimal in its description and portrayal of participants. The young maiden known as Snow White, and particularly the Dwarfs, were characterized as little more than quaint, homespun stick figures.

Seven unnamed Dwarfs having no individual personalities appeared in the original Snow White folk tale alternately titled *Snowdrop*, a story brought forth by the Brothers Grimm of Germany when their 1812 *Nursery and Household Tales* collection was initially published. This version had the Queen dressed in a peasant's outfit, giving the girl a poisoned comb (Walt's first choice) and then the near-fatal apple. The simple but engaging fairytale storyline, relating pretty much the same events in both renditions, had its true beginnings in the spoken word, rather than the printed page.

Along about 1806 Jacob and Wilhelm Grimm began their self-appointed task of gathering and transcribing popular Germanic folk tales which had a tradition of being orally passed on from generation to generation. The stories they compiled over the years came from many sources throughout the land, but one of the most valuable contributors turned out to be the Wild family who conveniently enough lived next door to the Grimms. It is known that among the six daughters, Dorothea was an accomplished storyteller. Gretchen, Lisette and Mamma also recorded tales for the brothers, and especially *die alte Marie*, the

Comic Exchange, Inc.
8432 W. Oakland Park Blvd.
Sunrise, FL 33321
PH:305-742-0777 (b,c,e,g,q-s)

Merlin's Books
2562 E. Fowler Ave.
Tampa, FL 33612
PH:813-972-1766 (a-j,p-s)

GEORGIA:

Titan Books & Comics
5436 Riverdale Rd.
College Park, GA 30349
PH:404-996-9129
(a-e,g,m,n,q-s)

Art Moods Cards & Comics
1058 Mistletoe Rd.
Decatur, GA 30033
PH:404-321-1899 (a-c,f,g,m,r,s)

Titan Games & Comics
2585 Spring Rd.
Smyrna, GA 30080
PH:404-433-8226 (a-c,g,m-o,r,s)

Titan Books & Comics II
3377 Lawrenceville Hwy.
Tucker, GA 30084
PH:404-491-8067
(a-c,e,g,m,n,q-s)

HAWAII:

Comic Center
331 Keawe St.
Hilo, HI 96720
PH:808-935-6318 (c,e,m,q,r)

Comic Center
Hilo Shopping Center
1221 Kilauea Ave.
Hilo, HI 96720
PH:808-935-1822 (c,e,m,q,r)

Compleat Comics Company
1728 Kaahumanu Ave.
Wailuku, HI 96793
PH:808-242-5875 (a-c,m,n,q-s)

IDAHO:

King's Komix Kastle
1706 N. 18th St.
Boise, ID 83702 (Appointments)
PH:208-343-7142 (a-i,m,n,q,r)

King's Komix Kastle II
2560 Leadville
Boise, ID 83706 (Drop in)
PH:208-343-7055 (a-i,m,n,q,r)

New Mythology Comics & Science Fiction
1725 Broadway
Boise, ID 83706
PH:208-344-6744 (a-e,n,q,r)

ILLINOIS:

Friendly Frank's Distribution
(Wholesale Whse.—retailers only)
727 Factory Rd.
Addison, IL 60101

Friendly Frank's Comics
11941 S. Cicero
Alsip, IL 60658
PH:312-371-6760
(a-d,f,g,i,j,n,q,r)

Silverspoon
305 N. Illinois
Belleville, IL 62220
PH:618-277-5570 (c,h,s)

Moondog's COMICLAND
Plaza Verde Shopping Center
1231 W. Dundee Rd.
Buffalo Grove, IL 60090
PH:312-259-6060 (a-c,e,m,q-s)

Trackside Hobbies
101 - 8th Street
Cairo, IL 62914
PH:618-734-0125 (a-c,f,g,k,m,r)

Amazing Fantasy Comic Shop
1856 W. Sibley Blvd.
Calumet City, IL 60409
PH:312-891-2260 (a-c,e,m,n,q-s)

Action Video & Comics
501 N. Neil
Champaign, IL 61820
PH:217-356-4773 (a-c,e,i,n,q,r)

Comic Book Collecting World
913 W. Cullom Terrace
Chicago, IL 60613 (appointment)
PH:312-281-2610
(a,b,d,h,m,p,s)

Comics for Heroes
1702 W. Foster
Chicago, IL 60640
PH:312-769-4745 (a-c,m,n,q-s)

Joe Sarno's COMIC KINGDOM
5941 W. Irving Park Rd.
Chicago, IL 60634
PH:312-545-2231 (a-c,j,q-s)

Yesterday
1143 W. Addison St.
Chicago, IL 60613
PH:312-248-8087 (a,b,d-i,k-m,r)

The Paper Escape
318 W. 1st Street
Dixon, IL 61021
PH:815-284-7567
(b,c,e,g,m,q-s)

GEM Comics
156 N. York Rd.
Elmhurst, IL 60126
PH:312-833-8787 (a-c,m,q-s)

Galaxy of Books
Rt. 137 & Sheridan Rd.
Great Lakes Depot
Great Lakes, IL 60064
PH:312-473-1099 (a-c,e,q,r)

Friendly Frank's Comics
3427 Ridge Road
Lansing, IL 60438
PH:312-418-1220
(a-d,f,g,i,j,n,q,r)

Moondog's COMICLAND
139 W. Prospect Ave.
Mt. Prospect, IL 60056
PH:312-398-6060 (a-c,e,m,q-s)

Graham Crackers Comics
5 East Chicago Ave.
Naperville, IL 60540
PH:312-355-4310 (a-d,f,n,q-s)

Tomorrow Is Yesterday
5600 N. 2nd St.
Rockford, IL 61111
PH:815-633-0330 (a-j,m,n,q-s)

Graham Crackers Comics
108 East Main St.
St. Charles, IL 60174
PH:312-584-0610 (a-d,f,j,n,q-s)

Moondog's COMICLAND
1403 W. Schaumburg Rd.
Schaumburg, IL 60194
PH:312-529-6060 (a-c,e,m,q-s)

B.J.'s Comic/Country Corner
260 N. Ardmore Ave.
Villa Park, IL 60181
PH:312-834-0383 (a-r)

Unicorn Comics & Cards
216 S. Villa Ave.
Villa Park, IL 60181
PH:312-279-5777
(a-c,e,g,h,j,l-n,q-s)

The Comic Shop
11110 S. Harlem Ave.
Worth, IL 60482
PH:312-448-2937 (a-c,k,q-s)

Galaxy of Books
1908 Sheridan Road
Zion, IL 60099
PH:312-872-3313 (a-c,e,f,h,l,q,r)

INDIANA:

25th Century Five & Dime
106 E. Kirkwood
Bloomington, IN 47402
PH:812-332-0011
(a-c,e,g-i,n,q-s)

Bookstack
112 W. Lexington Ave.
Elkhart, IN 46516
PH:219-293-3815 (b,e,h)

Spider's Web
51815 State Rd. 19 N.
Elkhart, IN 46514
PH:219-264-9178 (a-c,e,g,l,n)

Books Comics and Things
2212 Maplecrest Rd.
Fort Wayne, IN 46815
PH:219-749-4045 (a-c,e,g,h,q-s)

Broadway Comic Book & Baseball Card Shop
2423 Broadway
Fort Wayne, IN 46807
PH:219-744-1456 (a-g,m,q-s)

Friendly Frank's Distribution, Inc.
(Wholesale by appointment only)
3990 Broadway
Gary, IN 46408
PH:219-884-5052 (c,g,n,r,s)

Friendly Frank's Comics
220 Main Street
Hobart, IN 46342
PH:219-942-6020
(a-d,f,g,i,j,n,q,r)

Comic Carnival & Nostalgia Emporium
6265 N. Carrollton Ave.
Indianapolis, IN 46220
PH:317-253-8882 (a-j,m-p)

Comic Carnival & Nostalgia Emporium
5002 S. Madison Ave.
Indianapolis, IN 46227
PH:317-787-3773 (a-j,m-p)

Comic Carnival & Nostalgia Emporium
982 N. Mitthoeffer Rd.
Indianapolis, IN 46229
PH:317-898-5010 (a-j,m-p)

John's Comic Closet
4610 East 10th St.
Indianapolis, IN 46201
PH:317-357-6611
(b,c,e,g-j,m,n,q-s)

IOWA:

Comiclogue
113 Colorado
Ames, IA 50010
(c,n,q,r)

Comic World & Baseball Cards
1626 Central Ave.
Dubuque, IA 52001
PH:319-557-1897
(a-e,g,m,n,q-s)

Oak Leaf Comics & Records
23 - 5th S.W.
Mason City, IA 50401
PH:515-424-0333
(a-c,e,f,h-n,p-s)

Comiclogue
520 Elm St.
West Des Moines, IA 50265
PH:515-279-9006 (a-c,k,m,n,p-r)

KANSAS:

Comic Corner
2220 Iowa
Lawrence, KS 66046
PH:913-841-4294 (a-j,n,p-s)

Kwality Books, Comics & Games
1111 Massachusetts St.
Lawrence, KS 66044
PH:913-843-7239 (a-c,e,n,q-s)

Air Capital Comics
954 S. Oliver
Wichita, KS 67218
PH:316-681-0219 (a-j,n,p-s)

The Book Nook
7904 E. Harry
Wichita, KS 67207
PH:316-686-3901 (c,e,g,h,r)

Prairie Dog Comics East
Oxford Square Mall
6100 E. 21st St., Suite 190
Wichita, KS 67208
PH:316-688-5576 (a-n,p-s)

Prairie Dog Comics West
Central Heights Mall
7387 West Central
Wichita, KS 67212
PH:316-722-6316 (a-n,p-s)

KENTUCKY:

Book World
7130 Turfway Road
Florence, KY 41042
PH:606-371-9562 (a-c,e,m,q-s)

The Great Escape
2433 Bardstown Rd.
Louisville, KY 40205
PH:502-456-2216 (a-c,i,l-n,q-s)

LOUISIANA:

Comic Book Emporium
Catfish Town
100 St. James St., B305
Baton Rouge, LA 70802
PH:504-381-9619
(a-c,e,g-i,k,n,q-s)

B.T. & W.D. Giles
P. O. Box 271
Keithville, LA 71047
PH:318-925-6654 (a,b,d,f,h)

B S I Comics
5039 Fairfield St.
Metairie, LA 70006
PH:504-889-2665 (a-c,e,g)

The Book Worm
7011 Read Blvd.
New Orleans, LA 70127
PH:504-242-7608 (a-c,e,q-s)

MAINE:

Moonshadow Comics
10 Exchange St.
Portland, ME 04101
PH:207-772-3870
(a-c,e,g,i,j,n,q-s)

MARYLAND:

Universal Comics
5300 East Drive
Arbutus, MD 21227
PH:301-242-4578
(a-c,e,g,k,m,q-s)

Comic Book Kingdom, Inc.
4307 Harford Road
Baltimore, MD 21214
PH:301-426-4529 (a-d,f,g,m,q,r)

Geppi's Comic World
7019 Security Blvd.
Hechinger's Square
at Security Mall
Baltimore, MD 21207
PH:301-298-1758 (a-c,f)

Geppi's Comic World
Harbor Place
Upper Level, Light St. Pavilion
301 Light St.
Baltimore, MD 21202
PH:301-547-0910 (a-c,f)

Big Planet Comics
4865 Cordell Ave. (2nd Floor)
Bethesda, MD 20814
PH:301-654-6856 (c,j,n,q,r)

Bookcom — Book & Comic Outlet
15528 Annapolis Rd.
Freestate Mall
Bowie, MD 20715
PH:301-464-3570 (a-c,e,q,r)

Alternate Worlds
9924 York Road
Cockeysville, MD 21030
PH:301-667-0440
(b,c,e,g,m,n,q-s)

The Closet of Comics
7319 Baltimore Ave.
College Park, MD 20740
PH:301-699-0498 (b,c,e,g,n,q)

Bookcom — E.T. Home Video
Marlboro Pike
Forestville Plaza
Forestville, MD 20747
PH:301-568-6661 (b,c,e,l,r)

Bookcom — Book Exchange
7952 Crain Hwy.
Eastpark Center
Glen Burnie, MD 21061
PH:301-969-2510 (a-c,e,q,r)

Collectors Choice
368 Armstrong Ave.
Laurel, MD 20707
PH:301-725-0887 (a-j,l-n,q,r)

Comic Classics
365 Main Street
Laurel, MD 20707
PH:301-792-4744, 490-9811
(a-c,e,n,q,r)

OREGON:

Pegasus Fantasy Books
4390 S.W. Lloyd
Beaverton, OR 97005
PH:503-643-4222 (a-c,e,i,m)

Pegasus Books of Bend
12 N.W. Greenwood
Bend, OR 97701
PH:503-388-4588 (a-c,e,i,m)

Emerald City Comics
770 East 13th St.
Eugene, OR 97401
PH:503-345-2568 (a-g,i,j,n,q-s)

House of Fantasy
2005 E. Burnside
P. O. Box 472
Gresham, OR 97030
PH:503-661-1815 (a-c,q-s)

Nelscott Books
3412 S.E. Hwy. 101
Lincoln City, OR 97367
PH:503-994-3513 (a,b,d-f,h,r)

More Fun
413 E. Main
Medford, OR 97501
PH:503-776-1200 (b,c,e,m,q-s)

Harti Comics & Cards
Danielson's Hilltop Mall
358 Warner-Milne Rd., G104
Oregon City, OR 97045
PH:503-655-5986 (b,c,m,r)

Future Dreams
1800 East Burnside
Portland, OR 97214
PH:503-231-8311 (b-e,g-j,n,q-s)

Future Dreams Comic Art Reading Library
10506 N.E. Halsey
Portland, OR 97220
PH:503-256-1885 (b,c,n)

Future Dreams Gateway
10508 N.E. Halsey
Portland, OR 97220
PH:503-255-5245 (b,c,e,g,n,q-s)

Pegasus Fantasy Books
5015 N.E. Sandy Blvd.
Portland, OR 97213
PH:503-284-4693 (a-c,e,i,m)

Pegasus Fantasy Books
1401 S.E. Division
Portland, OR
PH:503-284-4693 (a-c,e,i,m)

Serendipity Corner
1401 S.E. Division
Portland, OR 97202
PH:503-233-9884 (a,b,d-f,h,r)

Rackafratz Comics & Cards
3760 Market N.E.
Salem, OR 97301
PH:503-371-1320
(a-c,f,j,k,m,n,p-s)

Lady Jayne's
19060 S.W. Boones Ferry Rd.
Tualatin, OR 97062
PH:503-692-0753 (b,c,e,q-s)

PENNSYLVANIA:

Cap's Comic Cavalcade
1980 Catasauqua Rd.
Allentown, PA 18103
PH:215-264-5540 (a-g,j,n,p-s)

Dreamscape Comics
404 West Broad St.
Bethlehem, PA 18018
PH:215-867-1178 (a-c,e,f,n,q,r)

Mr. Monster's Comic Crypt
347 Ferry Street
Easton, PA 18042
PH:215-250-0659 (a-c,g,i-m,q,r)

Comic Universe
446 MacDade Blvd.
Folsom, PA 19033
PH:215-461-7960 (a-g,i,l,m,q,r)

Golden Unicorn Comics
571 Alter St.
Hazleton, PA 18201
PH:717-455-4645 (a-c,n,q,r)

The Comic Store
The Golden Triangle
1264 Lititz Pike
Lancaster, PA 17601
PH:717-39-SUPER
(a-c,e,g,h,n,q-s)

Comic Relief
Rt. 413 (at I-95 Marketplace)
Levittown, PA 19056
PH:215-757-7494 (a-c,j,n,q,r)

Comicrypt IV—Jonri Ferrero
7598 Haverford Ave.
North Philadelphia, PA 19151
PH:215-473-6333 (b,c,g,q,r)

Comicrypt V
5736 North 5th St.
North Philadelphia, PA 19120
PH:215-924-8210 (b,c,g,q,r)

Comic Investments
8110 Bustleton Ave.
Philadelphia, PA 19152
PH:215-725-7705 (a-c,e-g,m,n)

Fat Jack's Comicrypt—Michael Ferrero
2006 Sansom Street
Philadelphia, PA 19103
PH:215-963-0788 (a-c,e,g,n,q,r)

Sparkle City Comics
Philadelphia, PA
(Philly area by appointment)
PH:609-589-3606 (a,b,d,f)

Eide's Comix & Records
940 Penn Ave.
Pittsburgh, PA 15116
PH:412-261-3666 (a-n,p-s)

Book Swap
110 South Fraser St.
State College, PA 16801
PH:814-234-6005
(a-c,e,g,h,n,q-s)

Comicrypt III
2966 Kensington Ave.
West Philadelphia, PA 19134
PH:215-423-3876 (b,c,g,q,r)

Comic Store West
North Mall
351 Loucks Rd.
York, PA 17404
PH:717-845-9198
(a-c,e,g,h,n,q-s)

RHODE ISLAND:

Starship Excalibur
60 Washington St.
Providence, RI 02903
PH:401-273-8390 (b,c,n,q-s)

Starship Excalibur
834 Hope St.
Providence, RI 02906
PH:401-861-1177 (b,c,n,q,r)

Super Hero Universe #2
#54-56 Arcade Mall
65 Weybossett St.
Providence, RI 02903
PH:401-331-5637 (c,e,g,p-r)

Starship Excalibur
800 Post Rd., Warwick Plaza
Warwick, RI 02888
PH:401-941-8890 (b,c,m,n,q-s)

SOUTH CAROLINA:

Silver City Comics - Science Fiction - Gaming
904 Knox Abbott Drive
Cayce, SC 29033
PH:803-791-4021 (b-e,g,q-s)

Heroes Aren't Hard to Find
1415-A Laurens Rd.
Greenville, SC 29607
PH:803-235-3488 (a-c,i,j,q-s)

Galaxy Book Store
P.O. Box 9612 (appointment only)
Hanahan, SC 29410
PH:803-871-0263 (a-c,j,m)

Captain Lou's Comics
P.O. Box 9612 (appointment only)
Hanahan, SC 29410
PH:803-871-0263 (a-c,j,m)

Super Giant Comics
Suite 30 - West Oak Square
4700 Reidville Rd.
Spartanburg, SC 29301
PH:803-576-4990 (a-c,j,q,r)

TENNESSEE:

Comics and Curios
4272-A Bonny Oaks Drive
Chattanooga, TN 37416
PH:615-698-1710 (a-c,i,j,l,n,q-s)

Enterprise Comics
4154 N. Bonny Oaks Drive
Chattanooga, TN 37406
PH:615-629-6217
(a-e,g,i,l,m,q,r)

White Book Shop
Super Flea Market
4307 Rossville Blvd.
Chattanooga, TN 37407
PH:404-820-1449 (a-e,r)

Collectors Choice
3406 Keith St., Shoney's Plaza
Cleveland, TN 37311
PH:615-472-6649
(a-c,e,g,i,m,q,r)

Clinton Cards, Comics, & Collectibles
Market Place/Market Street
Clinton, TN 37716
PH:615-457-5273 (a-c,m,q-s)

Marnello's
451 E. Elk Avenue
Elizabethton, TN 37643
PH:615-543-6564 (c,e,h,m,q,r)

Bookshelf Comic Shop
2234 N. Roan
Johnson City, TN 37601
PH:615-282-8090 (b,c,e,m,q-s)

Mountain Empire Comics & Collectibles III
1210 N. Roan St.
Johnson City, TN 37602
PH:615-929-8245 (b,c,e,i,q-s)

Mountain Empire Comics & Collectibles II
1451 E. Center St.
Kingsport, TN 37664
PH:615-245-0364 (b,c,e,g,h,q-s)

The Great Escape
139 N. Gallatin Rd.
Madison, TN 37115
PH:615-865-8052 (a-i,l-n,q-s)

Comics & Collectibles
4750 Poplar
Memphis, TN 38117
PH:901-683-7171 (a-i,m,n,q-s)

Memphis Comics, Records
665 S. Highland
Memphis, TN 38111
PH:901-452-1304 (a-i,k-n,p-r)

Memphis Comics & Records
964 June Rd.
Memphis, TN 38119
PH:901-763-1733 (a-i,k-n,p-r)

Book Rack
Hillwood Plaza
Nashville, TN
PH:615-352-3563 (b,c,e,q)

Book Rack
Rivergate Plaza
Nashville, TN
PH:615-859-9814 (b,c,e,q)

The Great Escape
1925 Broadway
Nashville, TN 37203
PH:615-327-0646 (a-i,l-n,q-s)

Walt's Paperback Books
2604 Franklin Rd.
Nashville, TN 37204
PH:615-298-2506 (a-c,e,r)

Collector's Dream World
Rt. 4 Box 155 — Parkway
(just inside Pigeon Forge)
Sevierville, TN 37862
PH:615-428-4261
(a-d,f,i,k,m,p,q)

TEXAS:

Lone Star Comics & Science Fiction
511 East Abram Street
Arlington, TX 76010
PH:817-Metro 265-0491
(b,c,e,g,h,q-s)

Lone Star Comics & Science Fiction
5721 W. I-20 at Green Oaks Blvd.
Arlington, TX 76016
PH:817-478-5405 (b,c,e,g,h,q-s)

Lone Star Comics & Science Fiction
7738 Forest Lane
Dallas, TX 75230
PH:214-373-0934 (a-c,e,h,q-s)

Remember When
2431 Valwood Parkway
Dallas, TX 75234
PH:214-243-3439
(a-c,e,g,i,j,m,o,q-s)

Fantastic Worlds BookStore Fort Worth
3011 Lackland Road
Fort Worth, TX 76116-4121
PH:817-731-6222
(a-c,e,g,h,j,n,q-s)

B & D Trophy Shop
4404 N. Shepherd
Houston, TX 77018
PH:713-694-8436 (a-c,i,r)

A Few Books & Records
11330 Beechnut
Houston, TX 77072
PH:713-933-6629 (c,e,g,h,l,q,r)

Third Planet
2339 Bissonnet
Houston, TX 77005
PH:713-528-1067 (a-s)

Third Planet
10001 Long Point
Houston, TX 77055
PH:713-984-9922 (a-s)
Hot Line: 713-932-1400

Fantastic Worlds BookStore Mid-Cities
807 Melbourne Road
Hurst, TX 76053-4630
PH:(214) or (817) 589-2148
(b,c,e,g,n,q-s)

Lone Star Comics & Science Fiction
2550 N. Beltline Road
Irving, TX 75062
PH:214-659-0317 (b,c,e,g,h,q-s)

Lone Star Comics & Science Fiction
3600 Gus Thomasson, Suite 107
Mesquite, TX 75150
PH:214-681-2040 (b,c,e,q-s)

Fantastic Worlds BookStore Dallas
581 West Campbell Rd. #119
Richardson, TX 75080-3326
PH:214-669-2501 (b,c,e,g,n,q-s)

Ultimate Dreams Comics
3806 South Shaver
South Houston, TX 77587
PH:713-941-1490 (a-c,e-j,l,n,q-s)

Little Shop of Heroes
617 W. Front St.
Tyler, TX 75702
PH:214-597-6533 (b,c,n,q-s)

UTAH:

The Bookshelf
2456 Washington Blvd.
Ogden, UT 84401
PH:801-621-4752
(b,c,e,h,l,m,o,q-s)

The Baseball Card Shop & Comics
141 N. University
Provo, UT 84601
PH:801-373-3482 (a-c,m,n,q-s)

The Baseball Card Shop & Comics Too!
3169 Highland Dr.
Salt Lake City, UT 84106
PH:801-466-3981 (b,c,m,q,r)

Comics Utah
1956 So. 1100 E.
Salt Lake City, UT 84105
PH:801-487-5390 (b,c,e,q-s)

VERMONT:

Earth Prime Comics
127 Bank St.
Burlington, VT 05401
PH:802-863-3666 (a-c,n,q,r)

Comics City, Inc.
329 Main St. (Exit 16, I-89)
Winooski, VT 05404
PH:802-655-7422
(b,c,e,m,n,q-s)

VIRGINIA:

Capital Comics Center & Book Niche, Storyland, U.S.A.
2008 Mt. Vernon Ave.
Alexandria, VA 22301 (D.C. area)
PH:703-548-3466
(a-c,e,f,h,m-o,q,r)

Geppi's Comic World Inc.
8330A Richmond Highway
Alexandria, VA 22309
PH:703-360-0120 (a-c,f)

Geppi's Crystal City Comics
1755 Jefferson Davis Hwy.
Crystal City Underground
Arlington, VA 22202
PH:703-521-4618 (a-c,f)

Mountain Empire Comics & Collectibles I
4 Piedmont Street
Bristol, VA 24201
PH:703-466-6337 (a-e,i,k-m,q-s)

Burke Centre Books
5741 Burke Centre Pkwy.
Burke, VA 22015
PH:703-250-5114 (a-h,m,q-s)

Trilogy Shop #3
3580-F Forest Haven Ln.
Chesapeake, VA 23321
PH:804-483-4173 (b,c,e,m,q-s)

Zeno's Books
1112 Sparrow Road
Chesapeake, VA 23325
PH:804-420-2344 (a-j,m-o,q,r)

Hole in the Wall Books
905 West Broad St.
Falls Church, VA 22046
PH:703-536-2511 (b-e,g,h,l,q-s)

Marie's Books and Things
1701 Princess Anne St.
Fredericksburg, VA 22401
PH:703-373-5196 (a-m)

American Comics
6583 Commerce Court
Gainesville, VA 22110
PH:703-347-7081 (c,q-s)

Bender's
17 East Mellen St.
Hampton, VA 23663
PH:804-723-3741 (a-k,m,n,p-s)

Franklin Farm Books
13320-I Franklin Farm Rd.
Herndon, VA 22070
PH:703-437-9530 (a-h,m,q-s)

Sam's Comics & Collectibles
13770 Warwick Blvd.
Newport News, VA 23602
PH:804-874-5581 (a-c,m,n,q-s)

World's Best Comics & Collectibles
9825 Jefferson Ave.
Newport News, VA 23605
PH:804-595-9005 (a-c,e-i,q-s)

Trilogy Shop #2
340 E. Bayview Blvd.
Norfolk, VA 23503
PH:804-587-2540 (b,c,e,m,q-s)

Ward's Comics
3405 Clifford St.
Portsmouth, VA 23707
No phone (b,c,q-s)

Nostalgia Plus
5610 Patterson Ave.
Richmond, VA 23226
PH:804-282-5532 (a-c,g,n,r)

B&D Comic Shop
3514 Williamson Rd. N.W.
Roanoke, VA 24012
PH:703-563-4161
(a-c,g,m,n,q-s)

Trilogy Shop #1
5773 Princess Anne Rd.
Virginia Beach, VA 23462
PH:804-490-2205 (b,c,e,g,m,r,s)

Zeno's Books
338 Constitution Dr.
Virginia Beach, VA 23462
PH:804-490-1517 (a-j,m-o,q,r)

WASHINGTON:

Paperback Exchange II
Yardbirds
2100 N. National Ave.
Chehalis, WA 98532
PH:206-748-4792 (a-c,e,f,m,q,r)

Comics and Crafts
2934½ Colby Ave.
Everett, WA 98201
PH:206-252-8181 (a-c,m,n,q-s)

Wally's Books and Comics
128 Park Lane
Kirkland, WA 98033
PH:206-822-7333
(a-c,e,g,h,j,n,q,r)

Paperback Exchange I
3944 Pacific Ave. S.E.
Lacey, WA 98503
PH:206-456-8170 (a-c,e,f,m,q,r)

Paperback Exchange III
Yardbirds
506 N. Capital Way
Olympia, WA 98501
PH:206-352-0285 (a-c,e,f,m,q,r)

The Coin House
777 Stevens Dr.
Richland, WA 99352
PH:509-943-6547 (a-c,m,q,r)

The Comic Character Shop
Old Firehouse Antique Mall
110 Alaskan Way South
Seattle, WA 98104
PH:206-283-0532 (a,b,f,h-k,q)

Corner Comics & Book Exchange
6521 N.E. 181st
Seattle, WA 98155
PH:206-486-XMEN (a-c,e,q,s)

Golden Age Collectables
1501 Pike Place Market
401 Lower Level
Seattle, WA 98101
PH:(206)622-9799 (a-d,f,i,j,n,o)

Psycho 5 Comics & Cards
12513 Lake City Way
Seattle, WA 98125
PH:206-367-1620 (a-c,m,q,r)

Rocket Comics
119 N. 85th
Seattle, WA 98103
PH:206-784-7300 (a-d,i,n,q-s)

Wonderworld Books & Gifts
243 S.W. 152nd St.
Seattle, WA 98166
PH:206-433-0279 (a-c,e,j,q-s)

The Book Exchange
K-Mart Center
N. 6504 Division
Spokane, WA 99208
PH:509-489-2053
(a-c,e,g,h,n,q-s)

The Book Exchange
U-City E.
E. 10812 Sprague
Spokane, WA 99206
PH:509-928-4073
(a-c,e,g,h,n,q-s)

Collectors Nook
213 North "I" St.
Tacoma, WA 98403
PH:206-279-9828 (a,b,d-i,m,q)

Pegasus Fantasy Books
813 Grand Blvd.
Vancouver, WA 98661
PH:206-693-1240 (a-c,e,i,m)

Galaxy Comics
1720 - 5th St., Suite D
Wenatchee, WA 98801
PH:509-663-4330 (a-c,g,q-s)

WEST VIRGINIA:

Comic World
613 West Lee St.
Charleston, WV 25302
(a-c,g,q,r)

Comic World
1204 - 4th Avenue
Huntington, WV 25701
PH:304-522-3923 (a-c,g,q,r)

Books and Things
2506 Pike Street
Parkersburg, WV 26101
PH:304-422-0666 (a-c,e,h,q-s)

WISCONSIN:

River City Cards & Comics
115 South 6th Street
Lacrosse, WI 54601
PH:608-782-5540 (b,c,i,m,q-s)

Capital City Comics
1910 Monroe St.
Madison, WI 53711
PH:608-251-8445 (a-c,f,n,q,r)

20th Century Books
108 King Street
Madison, WI 53703
PH:608-251-6226 (b-e,g,h,n,q-s)

Incredible Comics
4429 W. Lisbon Ave.
Milwaukee, WI 53208
PH:414-445-7006
(a-c,f-j,m,n,q,r)

Time Traveler Bookstore
7143 West Burleigh
Milwaukee, WI 53210
PH:414-442-0203 (a-h)

CANADA:

ALBERTA:

Comic Centre
1101 Centre Street N.W.
Calgary, Alberta, Can. T2E 2R1
PH:403-276-6595 (a-c,g,j,n,q,r)

Comic Centre
120 - 8th Avenue S.W.
Calgary, Alberta, Can. T2P 1B3
PH:403-263-8330
(a-c,g,j,m,n,q-s)

BRITISH COLUMBIA:

Funny Pages
382 Tranquille Rd.
Kamloops, B.C., Can. V2B 3G4
PH:604-376-3120 (b,c,e,m,n,q,r)

Page After Page
1763 Harvey Ave.
Kelowna, B.C., Can. V1Y 6G4
PH:604-860-6554 (a,c,e,h,q,r)

Ted's Paperback & Comics
269 Leon Ave.
Kelowna, B.C., Can. V1Y 6J1
PH:604-763-1258 (a-c,e,h,l)

Island Fantasy
50 Commercial St.
Nanaimo, B.C., Can. V9R 5G4
PH:604-753-0011
(a-c,f,g,j,n,q-s)

Bizarre Bazaar Books Ltd.
3211 Dunbar Street
Vancouver, B.C., Can. V6S 2B8
PH:604-224-6212 (a-e,g,h,m,r)

Golden Age Collectables
830 Granville St.
Vancouver, B.C., Can. V3Z 1K3
PH:604-683-2819 (a-d,f,i,j,n,o)

Island Fantasy Comic Service Ltd.
#29 Market Square
560 Johnson St.
Victoria, B.C., Can. V8W 3C6
PH:604-381-1134
(a-c,f,g,j,n,q-s)

MANITOBA:

Calvin Slobodian
859 - 4th Avenue
Rivers, Man., Can. R0K 1X0
PH:204-328-7846 (a-d,f,g,j,r)

Doug Sulipa's Comic World
315 Portage Ave.
Winnipeg, Man., Can. R3B 2B9
PH:204-943-3642

ONTARIO:

Starlite Cleaners & Comic-Book Shop
132 Westminster Drive South
Cambridge (Preston),
Ont., Can. N3H 1S8
PH:519-653-6571 (a-e,h,r)

Bid Time Return
225 Queens Ave.
London, Ont., Can. N6A 1J8
PH:519-679-0295 (a-k,m,n,q-s)

The Comic Book Collector
616 Dundas St.
London, Ont., Can. N5W 2Y8
PH:519-433-6004 (a-c,q,r)

The Comic Connection
2133 Royal Windsor Dr. #37
Mississauga, Ont., Can. L5J 1K5
PH:416-823-9358 (b,c,j,r)

The Cosmic Comic Connection
159 Ross St.
St. Thomas, Ont., Can. N5R 3X9
PH:519-633-0578 (a-d,g,i,m,q,r)

Comics Unlimited
875 Eglinton Ave. W. #11
Toronto, Ont., Can. M6C 3Z9
PH:416-781-5579 (b,c,e,g,m,p-r)

Queen's Comics & Memorabilia
1009 Kingston Rd.
(at Victoria Pk.)
Toronto, Ont., Can. M4E 1T3
PH:416-698-8757 (a-g,l,m,q,r)

The Sports Connection
875 Eglinton Ave. W. #11
Toronto, Ont., Can. M6C 3Z9
PH:416-781-5579 (b,c,e,g,m,p-r)

Ken Mitchell Comics
710 Conacher Drive
Willowdale, Ont., Can. M2M 3N6
(by appointment only)
PH:416-222-5808 (a,b,d,f,g,m)

QUEBEC:

Capitaine Quebec
4305 Blvd. St. Jean
Shakespeare Plaza
Dollard des Ormeaux, Que.,
Can. H9H 2A4
PH:514-620-1866
(a-c,e,g,m,n,q-s)

1,000,000 Comix Inc.
5010 Samson Blvd.
Chomedy, Laval, Que., Can.
PH:514-688-5626
(a-d,f-h,j,m,n,p-s)

Capitaine Quebec
5108 Decarie (at Queen Mary Rd.)
Montreal, Que., Can. H3X 2H9
PH:514-487-0970
(a-c,e,g,m,n,q-s)

Cosmix
11819 Laurentien Blvd.
Montreal, Que., Can. H4J 2M1
PH:514-337-6183 (a-c,e,g,i,q-s)

Komico Books
4210 Decarie Blvd.
Montreal, Que., Can. H4A 3K2
PH:514-489-4009 (a-c,g,j,n,q,r)

Multinational Comic Distribution
5595 Place D'aiguillon
Montreal, Que., Can. H4J 1L8
PH:514-334-2475 (a-c,g,r)

Premiere Issue
54 St. Cyrille W.
Quebec City, Que., Can. G1R 2A4
PH:418-648-8204 (a-c,e,i,q-s)

1,000,000 Comix
7019 Cote St. Luc Rd.
Cote St. Luc, Que., Can. H4U 1J2
PH:514-486-1175
(a-d,f-h,j,m,n,p-s)

AUSTRALIA:

Nostalgia Old Comic Shop
48 Balmoral Rd.
Mortdale Hgts., N.S.W. 2223,
Australia
PH:(02) 57-5332 (a,b)

ENGLAND:

Comic Showcase
76 Neal Street
London WC2, England
PH:01-240-3664 (a-c,j,n,q,r)

Forbidden Planet
23 Denmark St.
London WC2H 8NA, England
PH:01-836-4179 (a-c,e,h-j,n,q-s)

Forbidden Planet Mail Order
P. O. Box 378
London E3 4RD, England
PH:01-980-9711 (c)

Heroes
21, Canonbury Lane,
Islington,
London N1 2SP, England
PH:01-359-8329 (a-e,h,j,k)

DIRECTORY OF ADVERTISERS (Cl=classified, c=color)

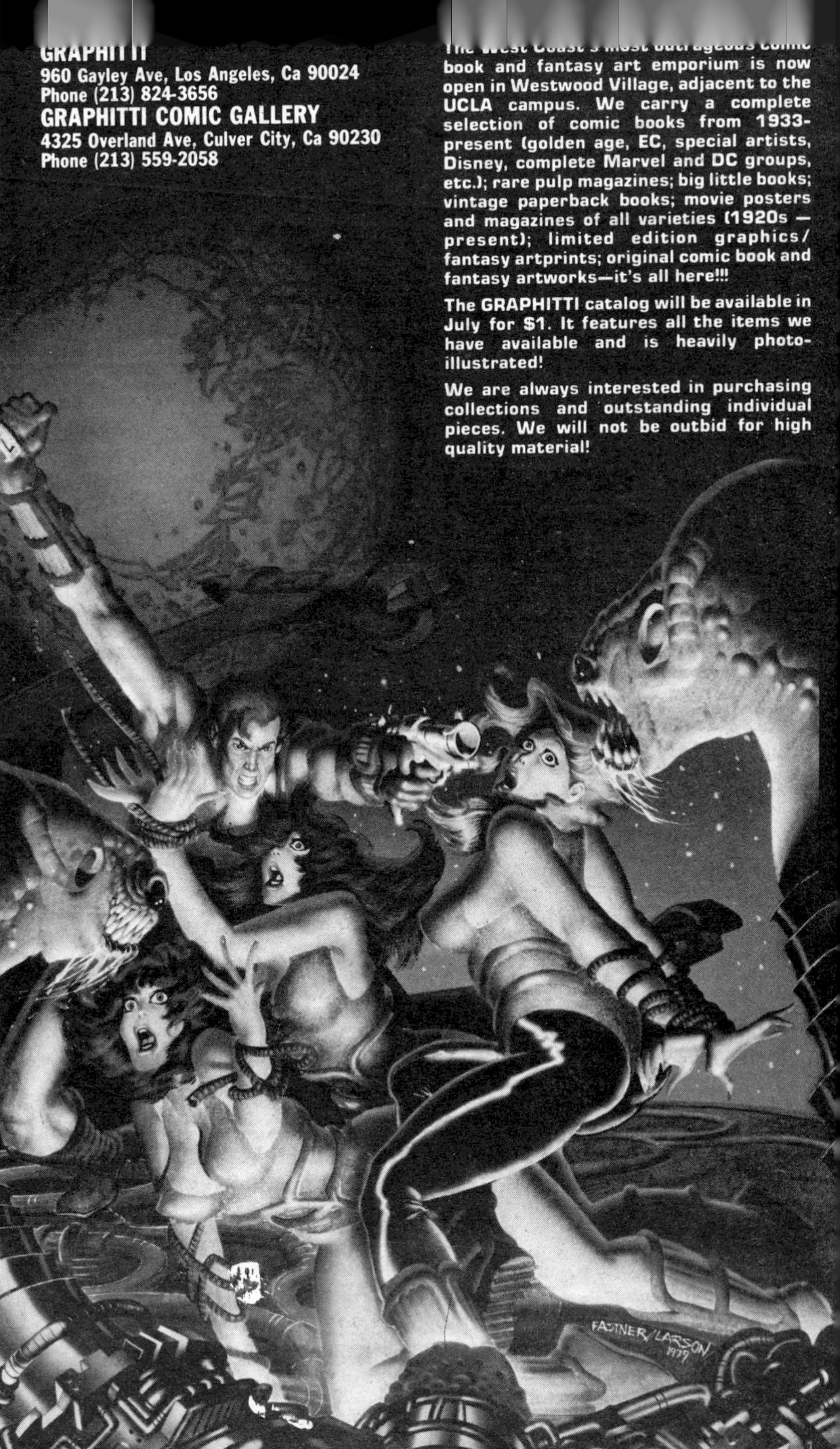
GRAPHITTI
960 Gayley Ave, Los Angeles, Ca 90024
Phone (213) 824-3656
GRAPHITTI COMIC GALLERY
4325 Overland Ave, Culver City, Ca 90230
Phone (213) 559-2058
book and fantasy art emporium is now open in Westwood Village, adjacent to the UCLA campus. We carry a complete selection of comic books from 1933-present (golden age, EC, special artists, Disney, complete Marvel and DC groups, etc.); rare pulp magazines; big little books; vintage paperback books; movie posters and magazines of all varieties (1920s — present); limited edition graphics/fantasy artprints; original comic book and fantasy artworks—it's all here!!!
The GRAPHITTI catalog will be available in July for $1. It features all the items we have available and is heavily photo-illustrated!
We are always interested in purchasing collections and outstanding individual pieces. We will not be outbid for high quality material!
FASTNER/LARSON 1979

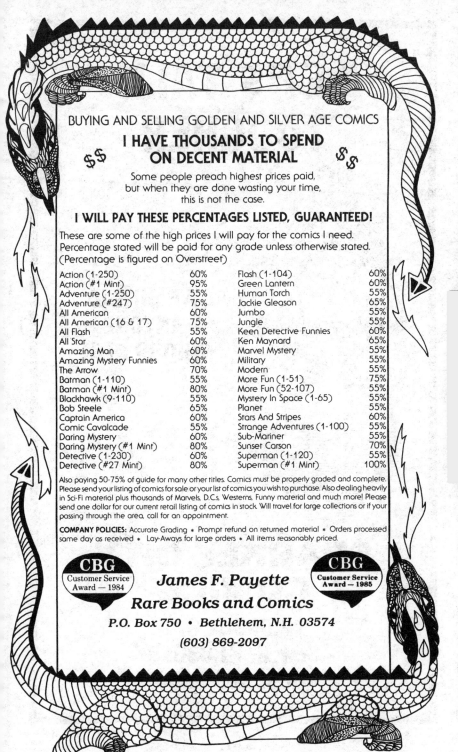

CHICAGO
CHICAGO
CHICAGO
CHICAGO
MOONDOG'S
MOONDOG'S
MOONDOG'S
MOONDOG'S

Since 1978, Moondog's has been the recognized leader in comics retailing in Chicagoland. We sell more new comics, more back issues, more rare high-grade Golden and Silver Age books, and more bags, boxes and supplies than any other stores in Chicago.

Why?

It's simple. We've got the best prices, selection and service.

If you collect comics seriously or just read them, you owe it to yourself to make Moondog's your comic store. If you live too far away from one of our three conveniently located stores to be a regular weekly customer—no problem—we understand. But you've got no excuse not to make it once a month!

Come see why Moondog's Comicland stores are the "Midwest's Finest Shops". We'll be expecting you.

Established 1978

139 W. Prospect Ave. Mt. Prospect, IL 60056 (312) 398-6060	1231 W. Dundee Rd. Buffalo Grove, IL 60090 (312) 259-6060	1403 W. Schaumburg Rd. Schaumburg, IL 60194 (312) 529-6060

EACH STORE OPEN 7 DAYS

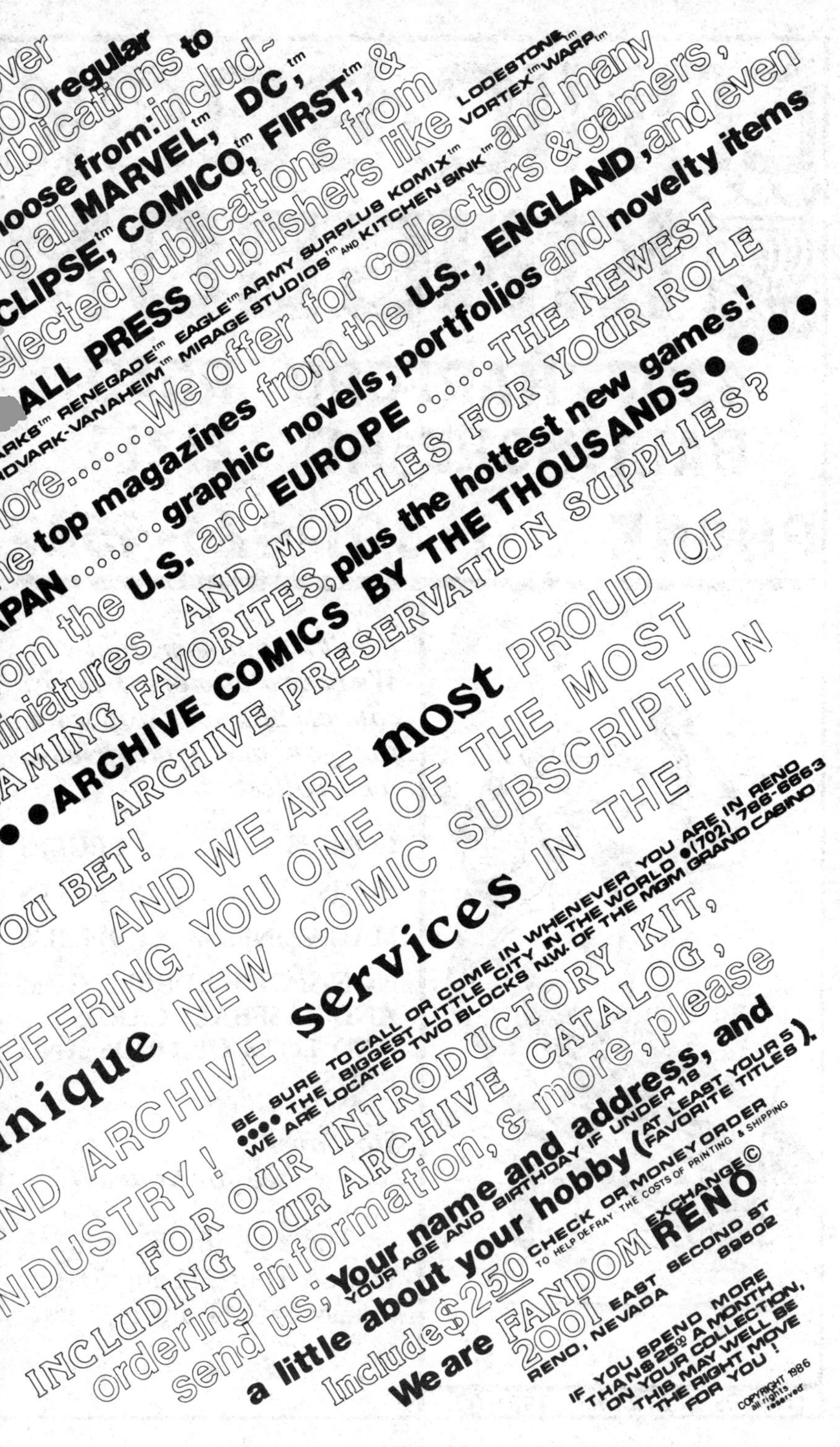

...ver
...00 regular
...ublications to
...hoose from: includ-
...g all MARVEL, DC,
...CLIPSE, COMICO, FIRST, &
...elected publications from
...ALL PRESS publishers like LODESTONE, VORTEX, WARP,
...ARKS RENEGADE EAGLE ARMY SURPLUS KOMIX
...DVARK-VANAHEIM MIRAGE STUDIOS AND KITCHEN SINK and many
...ore.......We offer for collectors & gamers,
...e top magazines from the U.S., ENGLAND, and even
...APAN.......graphic novels, portfolios and novelty items
...om the U.S. and EUROPE......THE NEWEST
...iniatures AND MODULES FOR YOUR ROLE
...AMING FAVORITES, plus the hottest new games!
●●ARCHIVE COMICS BY THE THOUSANDS ●●●
ARCHIVE PRESERVATION SUPPLIES?
...OU BET!
AND WE ARE most PROUD OF
...OFFERING YOU ONE OF THE MOST
...nique services IN THE
...ND ARCHIVE NEW COMIC SUBSCRIPTION
...NDUSTRY!
BE SURE TO CALL OR COME IN WHENEVER YOU ARE IN RENO
●●● THE BIGGEST LITTLE CITY IN THE WORLD ●(702) 786-6863
WE ARE LOCATED TWO BLOCKS N.W. OF THE MGM GRAND CASINO
FOR OUR INTRODUCTORY KIT,
INCLUDING OUR ARCHIVE CATALOG,
ordering information, & more, please
send us; Your name and address, and
YOUR AGE AND BIRTHDAY IF UNDER 18
a little about your hobby (AT LEAST YOUR 5 FAVORITE TITLES).
Include $2.50 CHECK OR MONEY ORDER
TO HELP DEFRAY THE COSTS OF PRINTING & SHIPPING
We are FANDOM EXCHANGE© RENO
2001 EAST SECOND ST
RENO, NEVADA 89502
IF YOU SPEND MORE THAN $25.00 A MONTH ON YOUR COLLECTION, THIS MAY WELL BE THE RIGHT MOVE FOR YOU!
COPYRIGHT 1986 all rights reserved

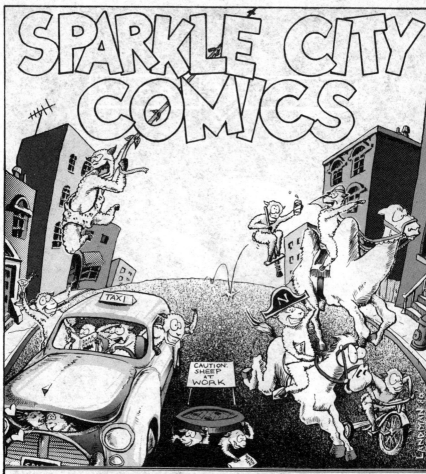

© DC

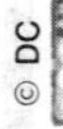

© DC

© DC

WANTED
OLD COMICS!!
$CASH REWARD$

FOR THESE AND MANY OTHER ELUSIVE COMIC BOOKS FROM THE GOLDEN AGE. SEEKING WHITE PAGE COLLECTIBLE COPIES IN VG OR BETTER CONDITION. ALSO GOLDEN AGE **BOUND VOLUMES** WANTED.

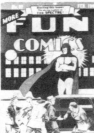

ALL-AMERICAN COMICS
© DC

© MCG

© FH

GREEN LANTERN
NO.1
10¢
© DC

WINTER ISSUE
NO.3
ALL STAR Comics
10¢
© DC

ACTION COMICS
10¢
© DC

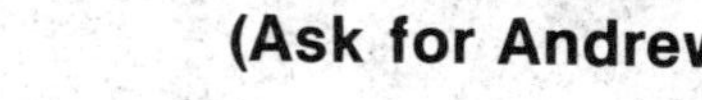

NEW ISSUE

SERVICE

Every month our customers receive a listing of over 600 different items. Our newsletter *Worthy of Note* takes 1000's of pages of advance information, removes the unnecessary and repetitive, adds timely news and market reports from creators, publishers, and retailers, illustrates it with advance covers and art, and creates a concise monthly report on the world of comic books that doesn't take hours of your valuable time to read.

Once you begin to get packages, we enclose flyers, posters, and other freebies with your order. **Our 9th year!**

Items/Month	Discount
10-49	20%*
50-149	30%*
150-249	35%*
250-449	40%
450-749	45%
750-2499	50%
2500-4999	52%
5000-Up	55%

* We pay some shipping

RETAILERS: We pick up comics in Sparta and ship on Thursday unless you pick up at one of our five locations. Service, and responding to customer needs are a specialty. In 1985 we created Chicagoland's first delivery route. In 1986 we were the first to offer top discounts on hot Black & White titles.

REORDERS: Another specialty. Our customers get first choice, but other stores often try us for reorders. If you're not a regular account you can get a courtesy 40% discount. Ask for Dave Whittinghill.

PACKING: We use extra packing at top, bottom and corners. **All orders are double counted for accuracy.**

Write or call for our free mailing.

Grab Bag Box

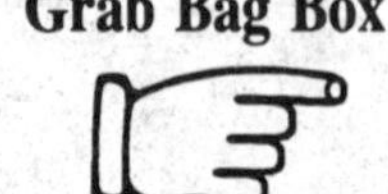

300 different superhero comics in good to mint condition from the last 20 years. Will include Horror, War, Funny type, only if you ask for them.

$50 (33 lbs.)

FRIENDLY FRANK'S

3990 Broadway • Gary, IN 46408-

HIGH CLARITY 3-MIL BAGS

All bags have flaps and are pre-counted in 100's

NEW COMIC (6-7/8x10-1/2") **&**
REGULAR (7-1/8x10-1/2") **SIZE**

100 (2 lbs.) $4.00
200-900 . . . . $2.50/100
1000-1900 . . . . $1.90/100

CASE RATES (24 lbs., 2000 per case)

2000-6000 . . . . $16.00/1000
8000-24,000 . . . . $15.00/1000
26,000-48,000 . . . . $14.50/1000
50,000-up $14.00/1000

GOLDEN AGE (7-3/4x10-1/2") & MAGAZINE BAGS (8-3/4x11")

100 (2 lbs.) $5.00
200-500 . . . . $4.00/100
600-1900 . . . . $2.50/100

G.A. CASE RATE (2500, 40 lbs.) . . $17/1000
MAG CASE RATE (2,000, 31 lbs.) . $20/1000
4 or more cases 10% off

THE STRONGEST STORAGE BOXES IN FANDOM!

Our boxes have become the industry standard. 275 lb. double-walled thickness (twice that on the handles) makes our product strong enough to stand on. Easy fold construction requires no tape or staples.

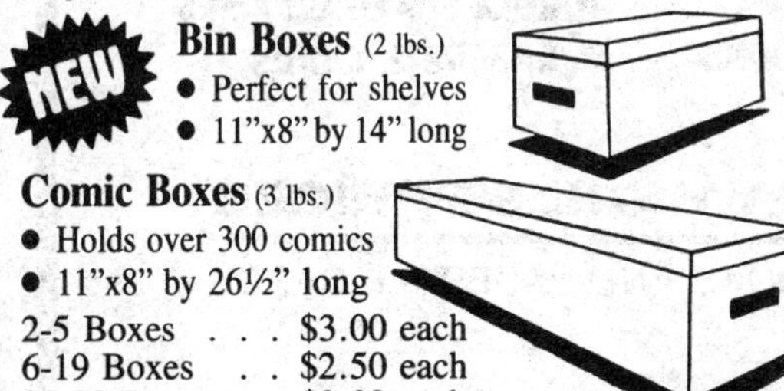

Bin Boxes (2 lbs.)
- Perfect for shelves
- 11"x8" by 14" long

2-29 Boxes . . . $2.50 each
30-90 Boxes . . . $1.50 each
120 or more . . . $1.25 each

Comic Boxes (3 lbs.)
- Holds over 300 comics
- 11"x8" by 26½" long

2-5 Boxes . . . $3.00 each
6-19 Boxes . . $2.50 each
20-39 Boxes . . $2.00 each

Magazine Boxes (2 lbs.)
- Holds 100 Mags
- 9"x12" by 16" long

40-80 Boxes . . $1.75 each
90-470 Boxes . $1.60 each
480-up . . . . $1.40 each

ADVANCED COLLECTING SUPPLIES

Acid-Free Backing Board

White on both sides; lab tested to be Acid- Free. All sizes available at $12 per 100 (5 lbs).

REGULAR: 6-13/16" x 10-1/2"

1000 (45 lbs.) $39.00
5000 or more $35.00/1000

GOLDEN AGE: 7-9/16" x 10-1/2"
MAGAZINE: 8-5/8" x 11"

1000 (45 lbs.) $45.00

Total Weight	If your zip code starts with: 1,2,4 or 6	0,3,5,7 8 or 9
1- 5 lbs.	$ 2.50	$ 3.25
6-12 lbs.	$ 3.75	$ 5.00
13-20	$ 5.00	$ 8.00
21-28 lbs.	$ 6.50	$11.00
29-36	$ 8.00	$13.50
37-50	$10.00	$18.00

Over 50 lbs. — Add weights together, i.e. 60 lbs. to 46408 would be $10.00 & $3.75.

5-MIL MYLAR®

Typical Mylar® bags are 4-mil thick. Now FFD has 20% more protection at less cost than ever! Compare with other (bigger) ads in this edition. (50 - 5 lbs.)

REGULAR (7-1/4x10-1/2")

20-49 bags/70¢ ea. . . . . . 50-250 bags/40¢ ea.
300-950 bags/37¢ ea. . . . 1000-up bags/35¢ ea.

GOLD (7-3/4x10-1/2") or
OLD GOLD (8-1/4x10-1/2")

20-49/75¢ ea. . . . . 50-250/45¢ ea.
300-950/42¢ ea. . . . . 1000-up/37¢ ea.

'MYLAR' is a registered trademark of DuPont Co.

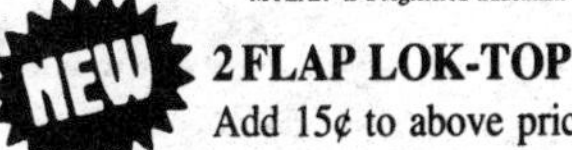

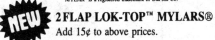

2 FLAP LOK-TOP™ MYLARS®
Add 15¢ to above prices.

SHIPPING: We charge exact costs. UPS COD's cost an extra $1.90 per package.

DISTRIBUTION, INC.

705 • ☎ (219) 884-5052, 884-5053

COMIC COLLECTORS
SF & FANTASY COLLECTORS

15% OFF

ALL NEW COMICS

AND SF/FANTASY ITEMS

Includes: Hard & soft cover books, war games, portfolios, much, much more.

Never miss another issue of your favorite title or the hottest new seller because your local dealer sold out.

Never pay full price again!!!

No minimum order required.

FOR DETAILS AND OUR NEXT LIST, SEND YOUR NAME AND ADDRESS TO:
SCOTT HIPP
P.O. BOX 1413
PLACENTIA, CALIF. 92670

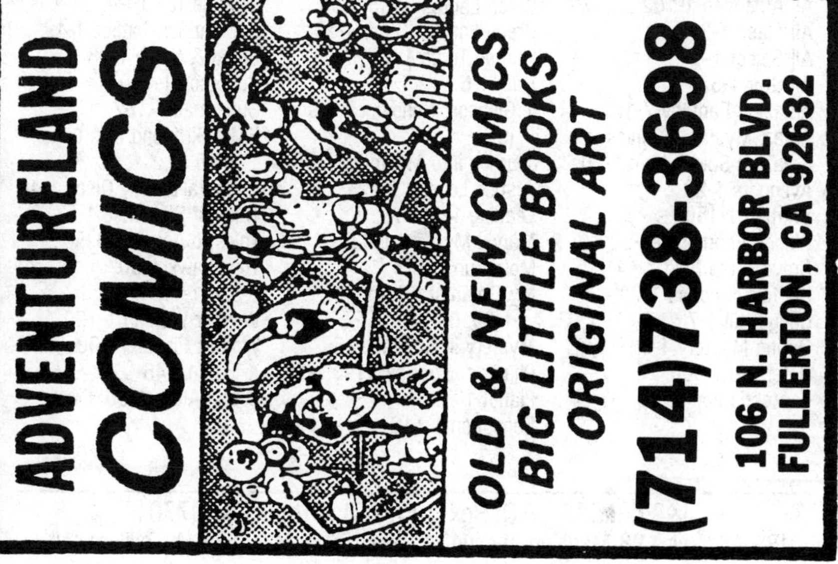

COMIC CARNIVAL

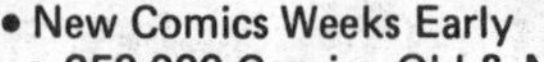

- New Comics Weeks Early
- 250,000 Comics-Old & New Middle Aged Too
- Science Fiction-5,000 Titles, P/B & H/B
- Arkham House, Grant, Other Small Press
- Video Sales & Rentals, Fantasy Games
- Gum Cards, Portfolios, Masks, Memorabilia
- We Pay Premium for old Comics: 1938-65

TM TM

Open Mon - Sat
(317) 898-5010
982 N. Mitthoeffer Rd.
Opp. Washington Sq.
Indianapolis, IN 46229

Open Thurs - Sun
(317) 253-8882
6265 N. Carrollton Av.
In Broad Ripple Vill.
Indianapolis, IN 46220

Open Thur - Sun
(317) 787-3773
5002 S. Madison Av.
At Thompson Rd.
Indianapolis, IN 46227

WE SELL MARVEL COMICS

We've got your new and old MARVEL comics, as well as most other comics in and out of print.

Men's Magazines - Back Issues

Baseball/Sports Cards and other great stuff!

Phone and Mail Orders Accepted

We buy, sell, trade.
Wed. - Sun. 11-6
100 Main St., Nyack, N.Y. 10960
(914) 358-3335

HEROES SUBSCRIPTION SERVICE A HIT!
(because we never miss)

Join HEROES Reserve Subscription Plan and* NEVER *miss another Comic, Magazine or Specialty Item again!!!

When you join HEROES Reserve, you receive FREE your own SOURCE CARD. Joining the Source entitles you to the following:

1. Up to 25% off ALL new comics marked on your reserve list!
2. Up to 25% off ALL posters, graphic novels, mags, t-shirts etc!
3. Always 25% off ALL back issues comics!
4. Always 10% off ALL "Hot" collectors items!
5. 10% off ALL new games and accessories.
6. Lowest prices on supplies!
7. 10% off ALL other new merchandise not on your reserve list.
8. 50% off tickets to EVERY Heroes Convention and Mini-Cons!
9. Monthly specials ONLY for Source Card holders.
10. FREE information packages containing *Marvel Age, DC Releases, Eclipse Extra*, and information on all major upcoming publications. Plus much more!
11. Source Card benefits good at ALL Heroes locations including Convention Booths!!!

1. List the comics you want to collect. Indicate the quantity of copies you want for each title.
2. Send Heroes a security despoit of $10 for 10-49 books per month or $25 for 50 plus books per month. This will be held until you cancel service. There is a 10 book minimum order.
3. All orders of less than 50 books sent monthly. Orders of 50 & up choose shipping frequency.
4. Exact freight charged on all shipments.
5. Books will be shipped after we receive payment for previous shipment.
6. This is a standing order, changes can be made only with written notification.
7. You can use Mastercard/VISA or Choice to make automatic payments. Just fill in the appropriate blanks at the bottom.
8. All books carefully shipped, flat in heavy duty cartons for maximum protection. Never a "bent" or damaged book!!

Chg. Card & No. ______________________

Exp. Date ______________________

Signature ______________________

☐ Please charge my credit card

APPLY FOR YOUR SOURCE CARD TODAY. . .AND NEVER MISS ANOTHER BOOK!!

Please feel free to visit any of our store locations listed below.
For mail order subscription & information, please contact the Charlotte office.

1214 Thomas Ave. Charlotte, NC 28205 704/375-7462	1003 Brookstown Ave. Winston-Salem, NC 27101 919-724-6987	1415-A Laurens Rd. Greenville, SC 29607 803/235-3488

PEREZ
SIENKIEWICZ
GUICE

GRAINGER • POSTON • FRAZEE • VOGEL
(More to be announced)

ART SEMINARS BY THE PROS!!
(You must register in advance-space limited)

ART CONTESTS • AUCTIONS!

Admission - $5 BOTH DAYS - $3 ONE DAY

Saturday 10am - 6 pm • Sunday 11am - 6 pm

ADAM'S MARK HOTEL
555 South McDowell Street • Charlotte, NC

ROOM RATE $55 (single-quad) BEFORE JUNE 17th • REQUEST RESERVATION CARD FROM HEROES

For More Information:
HEROES AREN'T HARD TO FIND
1214 THOMAS AV • CHARLOTTE, NC 28205 • 704-375-7462

JULY 18-19, 1987

★★★★★★★★★★★★★★★★★★★★★★ **Best America**

SUPER HE
UNIVERSE
Stores

#1 1105 Massachusetts Ave.
Cambridge, MA 02138
(617) 354-5344

★

#2 54-56 Arcade Mall
65 Weybossett St.
Providence, RI 02903
(401) 331-5637

★

#3 8 Winter St.
Boston, MA 02108
(617) 423-6676

★

#4 Warehouse
Revere, MA 02151

★

#5 Merrimac Plaza
164 Haverhill St.
Methuen, MA 01844
(617) 688-3980

★

#6 Osceola Mall
3831 Vine St.
Kissimee, FL 32741
Call for Info: 617-354-5344

★

#7 11-A Corinth St.
Roslindale, MA 02131
(617) 327-2400

★

#8 Sycamore Plaza
3064 Cochran St.
Simi Valley, CA 93065
(805) 583-3027

#9 Maingate Mall
7521 West Spacecoast Pkwy
Kissimee, FL 32741
Call for Info: 617-354-5344

SEND ALL INQUIRIES TO STORE #1 DEPT. Q

ics, Inc.
Specializing in New & Old
MARVEL COMICS
nething for
ryone!
MICS
AGAZINES
OKS
STERS
HIRTS
RTFOLIOS
GS & BOXES
TTONS & STICKERS
LE-PLAYING GAMES
DELS
MORE!
Visa &
over Cards
come
Silver Surfer & Galactus
© Marvel Comics Group

Attention Dealers & Store Owners
COMIC INDEX DIVIDERS
INCREASE COMIC BOOK BACK ISSUE SALES!
INDEX MAN
A must for every collector reasonably priced
Over 50% of those who originally placed orders—have already reordered—don't be left out—write:
DIVIDER INDEX SYSTEMS
P.O. Box 917
Marshfield, WI 54449
715-384-4941—Weeday afternoons

Original Cartoon Strip Art
WINDWARD GALLERY
16505 CHAGRIN BLVD.
SHAKER HTS., OH 44120
216·991~2228
Hours:
M-T 12-6
F 11-8
S 10-7

TAKE THE SPARKLE CITY CHALLENGE
We challenge anyone to find a better pre-1964 comic inventory, better service or better value anywhere in the world!! Including all the Balkan states.
AND WHEN WE BUY — WE ARE NEVER OUTBID
SPARKLE CITY COMICS
P.O. Box 67, Sewell, NJ 08080
609-589-3606

The Art Conservatory (Continued)

(6) Deacidification. Of the three types of deacidification processes known (vapor, spray, immersion), we believe that immersion in an alkaline solution to be the best and most effective method. It is also the most expensive as it takes much longer. However, the results speak for themselves.

(7) Fungicide Application. I find that fungus attack is a very serious problem as spores are microscopic, and are present on every piece of paper made. In storage conditions above 70° with high humidity they flourish and cause extensive damage.

(8) Remove Brittleness. In most cases, we have great success in changing dark, cracking, flaking paper into light colored, resilient paper again. The success of this process is determined by the extent of brittleness present in your paper collectable. The worse it is, the less are the chances for complete success. In **all** cases though, the results are **very** satisfying.

(9) Color Retouching. We take great care in matching **all** colors as closely as possible. We are not limited to a specific number of colors as we custom mix all our inks.

SOME OF THE WORK WE WON'T DO IS:

(A) Trim Books. Sorry, but that's not restoration.
(B) Install false Back Covers. It's wrong, so don't even bother asking.
(C) Do quick **Hack Work** in order to make it **look** like a higher grade collectable for the purpose of resale to an unsuspecting collector. Believe me, I have a good reputation and have **no** intention of ruining it. I do things right or **not at all**.

My purpose for this ad is to attract and establish long term relationships with the collector, dealer, and investor who are truly interested in the preservation and proper care of their collectable(s). Anything less is a waste of both my time and yours.

For more information please call or write. All work will be kept confidential between myself and you. Before and after color photos will be provided upon request.

Our rate is $30.00 per hour. Estimates are free. All questions are welcome when you call. **Phone: (415) 471-5434.** References given upon request.

Note: *It is my hope that my wife, our four sons and myself will be moving to the state of Washington this year. If this does come about, I will be sure to leave a forwarding phone number when you call the above number. Thank you.*

ONE PICTURE IS WORTH 400,000 WORDS

FANTAZIA

Just let your imagination run wild. . . then TRIPLE IT!!!

2 So. Central Ave., Hartsdale, NY 10530

(914) 946-3306 Daniel $ Dupcak (914) 946-1236

EVER WONDER WHAT OVER $20,000,000 WORTH OF GOLD & SILVER AGE COMICS, SPORT/NON-SPORT CARDS & MEMORABILIA, & RECORDS WOULD LOOK LIKE ALL UNDER ONE ROOF? Where else in the world can you see Action 1-10's Superman 1-10's, Complete DC, Timely & Marvel Key, Origin, & First Appearance issues in your choice of grade as easily as most dealers can offer you X-Men 170 up? Who else can offer you a complete run of Captain America, Human Torch, Fantastic Four, Miller Daredevils or a plain old X-Men/Micronauts Mini Series with equal facility **at a moments notice?** Who indeed!. . . FANTAZIA. . . The only collector's shop in the universe that deserves the title ''Endless Convention.'' Stop by when in New York, it's worth the trip from anywhere in the country; we guarantee you won't be disappointed. Call for easy access directions from all N.Y. airports & railway systems as well as simple road directions.

If you're selling a collection, sell to us; the company that most dealers earn 90% of their yearly income from. Your books will probably wind up in our hands anyway; why **shouldn't** you be the one to benefit from increased dividends on your collection; eliminate the ''middle-man'' dealer! If you have one of our priority wants, and you're thinking of consignment to one of those services who can't afford to buy your book(s) outright and cons you into believing consignment is the ''best way to go,'' stop & think! We'll take items we want for a full 10% **above** the full projected precentage ''cut of sale price estimate'' you might or might not get 5 years down the road from ''efficient consignment'' services. And of course if you have a Superman 1, Action 1, Detective 1, 27, 29, 33, Marvel 1, All American 16, Flash 1, New Comics 1, New Fun 1-6, More Fun 52, All Star 3 or simply a nice small quality collection give us a call **LAST.** Once you get your **top** offer that's the time to call Fantazia and separate the men from the sheep! We'll go head to herd against any self-appointed ''low-ball grading'' (only when buying **your** books), ''sorry we have too many of these and can only pay 10% of guide this month,'' ''this isn't Mint,'' top prices paid dealers in the world; without the aces and wool up our sleeves. RHETORIC? HARDLY! Rhetoric doesn't sell 17 Superman 1's in a year, produce millions of dollars worth of books at the drop of a hat and manage maintaining a CBG Customer Service Award over thousands of mutual satisfaction transactions. Hard work and truly unlimited cash does; **our own!** Not our stock broker, banker, backers, partners, or loan sharks. That's what gives us the competitive edge on outbiding **anyone** on your collection. We've no one to answer to but ourselves and whether you buy or sell at Fantazia the benifits are yours. We work closer in profit margin than **any** other dealer(s) in the world. We have no ''extra mouths to feed'' when a purchase or sales is made. It's single arithmetic. . . Fantazia. . . you just can't do any better!

EXPENSIVE ITEMS ARE NOT LEFT OVERNIGHT IN STORE

WHOLESALE

NOW AVAILABLE — NEW WHOLESALE LIST

APPROX. 50 PAGES OF THE BEST BUYS IN COMIC-LAND—**COMICS, MONSTER MAGS, FANZINES, PLAYBOY, PENTHOUSE & OTHERS, ETC...**

Send $1.00 To:
PASSAIC BOOK CENTER
594 Main Avenue, Dept. 026
Passaic, New Jersey 07055
PH: (201)778-6646

ALSO AVAILABLE:

- **RETAIL CATALOGUE**—$1.50 postpaid.
- **ADULT CATALOGUE**-Playboys, Penthouse, Etc.—$1.00.
- **ROMANCE CATALOGUE**(Approx. 120 pgs. of Harlequins, Candle Light, Etc.)—$2.00.
- **COMIC GRAB BAGS**—100 diff. Marvel—$27.00; 100 diff. DC—$26.00; 100 diff. Mixed publishers—$22.50. All comics vg-mint. Price includes postage.
- **PLAYBOY PRICE GUIDE**—Latest edition—Very Informative—$10.95 (post free).
- **WANT LISTS ACCEPTED**—for Comics, Monster & Sci Fi Mags, Sci Fi Books, Pulps, Adult Mags & any other items needed.
- **WE BUY**—Comics, Monster Mags, Savage, Sword of Conan, Adult Mags & More—Please Inquire.

Visit our 2nd new location—**The Montclair Book Center**, 221 Glen Ridge Ave., Montclair, NJ 07042. PH: 201-783-3630

WE BUILD OUR REPUTATION THE OLD FASHIONED WAY

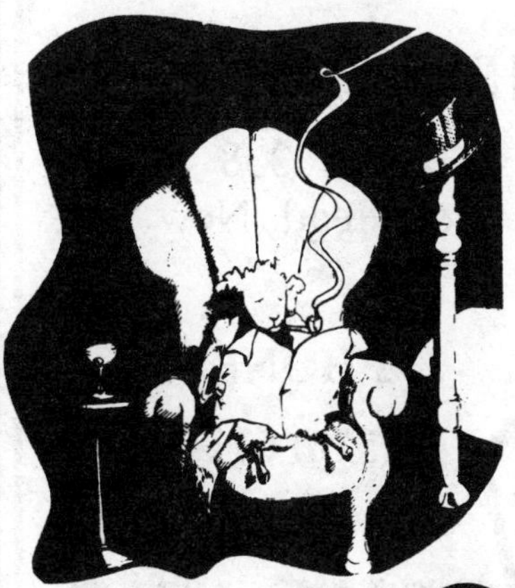

WE EARN IT!

SPARKLE CITY COMICS

P.O. Box 67, Sewell, NJ 08080

609-589-3606

NEW STORE

BID TIME RETURN

225 QUEENS AVE.
LONDON,ONTARIO,CANADA
N6A 1J8
PH:(519)679-0295

LONDON'S LARGEST SELECTION OF OLD AND NEW COMIC BOOKS

LOCATED ONE BLOCK NORTH OF DUNDAS NEAR CLARENCE STREET

-COMIC BOOKS
-MAGAZINES & PULPS
-MOVIE POSTERS
-GUM CARDS
-STAR TREK & STAR WARS ITEMS
-SCIENCE FICTION & FANTASY
-ROLE PLAYING GAMES
-STORAGE SUPPLES & MORE

OPEN

MONDAY TO WEDNESDAY	11:00 - 6:00
THURSDAY & FRIDAY	11:00 - 8:00
SATURDAYS	10:00 - 6:00

SEND .50¢ FOR CATALOG

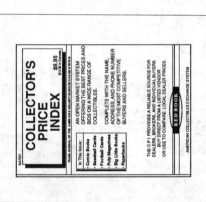

SPECIAL BULLETIN SUPPLEMENT

STOCK MARKET SYSTEM FOR COLLECTIBLES IS INTRODUCED!

Chattanooga, TN.- A new system of buying, selling, and trading collectibles of all types, including comic books and related items, has begun operation here.

The new system is called **American Collectibles Exchange System, Inc.** Based on the trading formats used by the New York Stock Exchange, ACES opened for trading on March 1, 1987. Buyers and sellers may join the exchange as **Collectibles Brokers** and begin trading after their application is accepted by the Review Board. "We are looking for serious collectors and dealers that will be aggressive in using this new system", says founder and CEO Jon R. Warren. "We are making an established market in collectibles for the first time. We purchased almost $50,000 of state-of-the-art main-frame Digital equipment. The computers allow many users to enter data each day. Our system operators are inputting market information such as sell offers, bids, and purchase offers (sent to us by members) ten hours a day, five days a week. The computer is then programmed to sort the database and display the highest bid offer, and the lowest sell offer on every collectible item listed on the Exchange."

The result is **COLLECTOR'S PRICE INDEX™**, the Exchange's monthly trade journal. "We predict that CPI will become the single most useful source for collectibles trading within the next five years. It will be a giant, one-stop catalog."

ACTION COMICS

Issue	Grade	Lo Ask	Hi Bid	Lo Seller	Hi Bidder
23	FR	$25.	XXX.	Boidwell	XXX
24	M	$800.	XXX.	Fantasy Trader	XXX
25	NM	$500.	$480.	Startling Com.	Knoxville Comics
28	VF	$400.	$200.	Smith	Allen
28	VG	$180.	$95.	Jones	Comics Co.
21	VG	$125.	$85.	Jones	Hallis
22	NM	$500.	$450.	Boris	Simpson
23	VF	$300.	$200.	Smith	Jones
23	VG	$100.	$50.	Alop	Lavere
23	FR	$25.	XXX.	Boidwell	XXX
24	M	XXX.	$800.	XXX	Fantasy Trader
25	NM	$500.	$480.	Startling Com.	Knoxville Comics
28	VF	$400.	$200.	Smith	Allen
28	VG	$180.	$95.	Jones	Comics Co.
21	VG	$125.	$85.	Jones	Hallis
22	NM	$500.	$450.	Boris	Simpson
23	VF	$300.	$200.	Smith	Jones
23	VG	$100.	$50.	Alop	Lavere
23	FR	$25.	XXX.	Boidwell	XXX
24	M	XXX.	$800.	XXX	Fantasy Trader

Figure 1.- Exchange members list items either for sale or wanted on the Exchange. The computers then sort the data and produce the publication CPI, sample text shown above.

Members of the Exchange use CPI to transact business. They make purchases, and sell items by either using the Exchange as clearing-house or by directly contacting the members with the best price or bid.

Those members with computers and modems are allowed to tap into the main-frame on a daily basis if desired.

What happens if a member sends a listing that isn't the lowest price for that item? Mr. Warren explains "We have the capability to hold that listing in the database until it becomes the lowest price or it expires unsold. This system encourages competition. If a seller doesn't have the lowest price he makes fewer sales."

Of course on scarcer items it is unlikely that the same item in the same condition will be listed by different sellers in any given month. However, on the more recent collectibles such as recent

Continued On Next Page ...

SPECIAL BULLETIN SUPPLEMENT

comics there will be strong competition and the best seller wins. This also means that the buyers benefit as a result of this competition; buyers get the lowest possible price. The system is very streamlined and simple to use.

COLLECTOR'S PRICE INDEX™ is not a price guide. Mr. Warren warns, "Many users will assume that CPI is a price guide rather than a sales list. This is not the case. Every item listed in CPI is for sale, and all bids are bona-fide offers to buy. This is a unique approach to collectibles dealing and to make comparisons to established formats would be improper."

HOW MUCH DOES MEMBERSHIP COST? Members have a couple of options, their choice determines the type of membership they have. The most common choice is the **Brokerage Account**. This membership allows a member to purchase and sell items through the Exchange. Most collectors choose this membership. The cost is $5.00 per quarter plus a commission paid to the Exchange on each transaction. This membership fee entitles the broker to list an unlimited number of items for sale and make an unlimited number of bids. On anything sold through the Exchange the member pays to the Exchange a 25% commission. On anything purchased through the Exchange the member pays a 5% commission. All transactions under this membership form are handled through the Exchange, acting as a clearinghouse. This membership fee includes a subscription to CPI and a monthly account statement. If the member makes no purchases and sells nothing, he pays nothing more than his $5.00 dues. The second type of membership is called a **Charter Account**. With this arrangement the member pays no commissions to the Exchange. The member is allowed to list an unlimited number of items for sale and to make an unlimited number of offers to buy. The Charter Account membership requires payment of quarterly dues totaling $75. Membership is renewed quarterly. As long as the member keeps his/her account up-to-date all the items listed remain online. Included in this membership is the monthly **COLLECTOR'S PRICE INDEX™** and a monthly account statement.

HOW TO JOIN? Interested parties may request a membership application by calling **American Collectibles Exchange System™** at 1-800-331-4780 or by writing to: P.O. Box 2512, Chattanooga, TN 37409. Members must be over the age of 18 and willing to be governed by the rules and bylaws of **American Collectibles Exchange System™** which pertain to fair trading procedures, accurate grading, timely shipment of goods, and honest dealings in regards to buying and selling collectibles in general. Upon acceptance of the membership application by the Review Board the new member is issued a trading account and trading account number. Thereafter the account remains active as long as the member is in good standing and all dues are paid.

WHAT COLLECTIBLES ARE TRADED ON THE EXCHANGE? During 1987 the Exchange will make available markets in comic books (both Golden Age and Silver Age including recent), baseball and sport cards, big little books, pulp magazines, and vintage paper-backs. Future markets will include rare coins and stamps as well.

WHO SHOULD JOIN? Collectors with a budget over $30 per month, store owners needing an outlet for excess stock, mail-order dealers both large and small, and investors looking for the best price can all benefit from membership in the Exchange.

TO FIND OUT MORE CALL 1-800-331-4780 ...TODAY!

STOCK MARKET SYSTEM FOR COLLECTIBLES IS INTRODUCED

WE'RE BUYING!!!

That's Right

The Greatest "Name"
In Comic Books Is Now
Buying! — And When
WE BUY WE PAY!

We Want All Comics From 1933 to 1958 & Key Books From 1960 to Present. Special Wants & Top Dollar Paid For Action, Superman, Batman, Detective, All Timely's, Early Four Colors, All Mickey Mouse, Donald, March of Comics & ALL Disneys.

We Have Consistantly Paid Guide & Better For Specific Books We Need. These Currently Include All 1930's First Issues Key Golden Age (Action #1 etc.) and Prime Disney, Mickey Mouse Magazine and All Mickey titles.

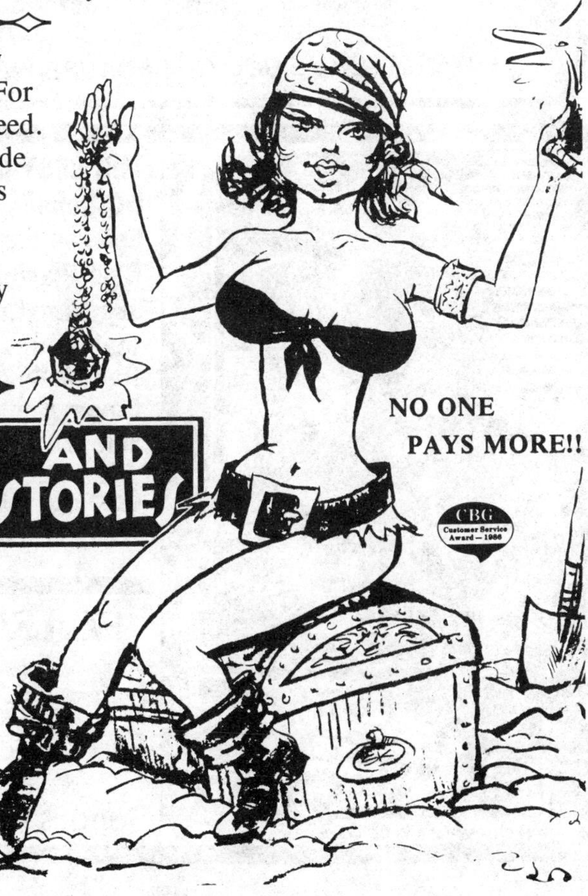

COMICS AND STORIES

NO ONE PAYS MORE!!

CBG Customer Service Award — 1986

Call or Send List,
or Books To:
Comics and Stories
85 Crescent Rd.
Wanaque, N.J.
07465
For Cash Offer
201-839-2192

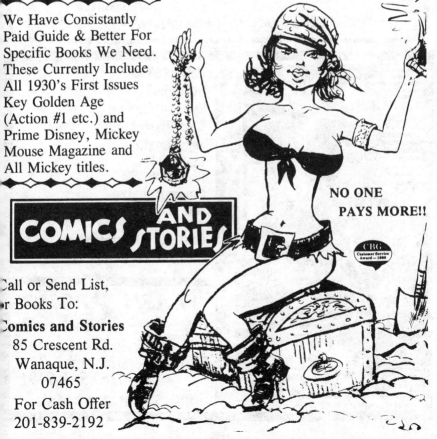

RESTORATIONS™

FREE ESTIMATES!!

FREE ESTIMATES

This advertisement addresses itself to Comic Books primarily. All services and supplies are also available for other paper collectibles such as Sunday Funnies, Daily Newspaper Strips, Baseball Cards, Stamps, Collectible Paper Currency, Books, Magazines, Manuscripts, and other valuable documents. We have worked on Marriage Certificates, Photographs, Stock Certificates, Old Maps, and Ancient Hawaiian Tapa Cloth. Please inquire for the prices of these and other Collectibles.

PRESERVATION

The inevitable fact is that all paper ages, some faster than others. We've all seen brown and even brittle comics. There are ways to slow down the process of aging and there are ways to speed it up (like storing the issues in your hot attic). The key is to preserve your comics BEFORE they turn brown and brittle. It is too easy to ignore those nice white supple pages until the day the sad brown facts stare up at you from the bottom of your plastic bag. The reason paper starts out white is because it is bleached white. The byproducts of acid, oxidation, heat and moisture tend to turn it brown again.

Some of the work we do is:

1. Lighten or whiten your books!! Get rid of that browning.
2. Tape removal...Careful removal of all type of tape!!
3. Old staples replaced with stainless steel staples.
4. Repair rips and tears. We manufacture the same type of cellulose and rebond the fibers, using the original sizing process. The repairs are invisible.
5. Spine damage. Pieces out of the cover. Again we actually remanufacture new paper in the holes. When done, you can't see where the replacement occurred.
6. Dry cleaning. This removes surface stains and dirt.
7. Ink and pencil marks removed.
8. Pressing. Realignment of interior pages and cover. Minimal edge trim to get that extra new appearance.
9. Color retouching. Our Specialty. We'll be glad to touch up any book for anyone. With over 750 seperate colors on our current palette, we can match almost any color. Give it a try!
10. Light glossing for that "Mint" look!!
11. Replace missing covers or interior pages.
12. To get your book restored for the lowest price, if you have any mechanical skills, take the cover off carefully and send it in flat. We'll restore it and return it to you for reassembly - we'll enclose easy to use staples.
13. Start with a book in G or better grade to start. You get a better value for your money by increasing grades from G to VF rather than from P to Fair. The cost would probably be about the same.

★ Restoration by **PROFESSIONALS** ... We have **years** of experience and thousands of invisible restorations.
★ **GUARANTEED RESULTS** ... If you aren't satisfied with our work, we will refund your money or buy your book back at its original grade ... (our choice). **HOW CAN YOU LOSE?**
★ **FREE ESTIMATES ... NO OBLIGATIONS!**
★ **PROMPT SERVICE** ... Standard restorations completed in 30 days.
★ **INVISIBLE REPAIRS** ... YOur restored comics can look new — not restored.
★ **MAKE MONEY** ... There is a huge demand for NM books (many sell for double Overstreet)... We have turned many VG or F books into **N MINT!!!**
★ **YOU KNOW YOUR BOOKS NEED RESTORATIONS™!! GET STARTED NOW ... AND GET IT DONE RIGHT!**

Name ____________________
Address ____________________
City, State, Zip ____________________
Books are for Sale ☐
or Collection ☐
Is This a RUSH ORDER?? ☐ Yes ☐ No
IF YES DATE DUE ____________________
We can ship UPS 2nd day Air or Federal Express.

COMMENTS

"I really appreciate your sending me the Xeroxs on the Action. This was perfect and its just one more indication of why you guys are amongst the best there is!!"
John Kranz, CA

"I want to commend you on the miraculous job you did on my Hulk # 1. It doesn't even look like the same book."
Steve Koons, TX

"Yes there is a "Comic Book God" and he lives in Minden, NV!! Many thanks again! The Detective was a real beauty and the Batman was all we could hope for ... TORCH is just about perfect. Right off the newstand ... I really love your work!!
Larry Cederoth, IA

"Truely this is one of the finest restoration jobs around ... just incredible!! I was truely impressed, so–I am sending along my BATMAN #1 Hope you can work an equal amount of RESTORATION MAGIC with this."
Jim Vacca, CO

"You do an excellent job and your prices are ridiculously lower than many other "so called" pros at restoration who can't do half as good a job."
Joseph Johnson, W VA

"Oh, thanks for the repairs on my MYSTERY IN SPACE#2, it was an EXCELLENT job and I'm very pleased."
John Horn, MI

"I really liked the professional job you did on SUPERMAN #1. I sold it for double guide!"
Cecille del Porto - NV

"Thanks for another masterful performance. You really do great work!!!"
Andrew Laskin, MI

Please pack your issues between 2 pieces of cardboard and ship in a cardboard box surrounded by 2 inches of crumpled newspaper as packing. Insure for the FULL VALUE of your issues for your protection and ours.

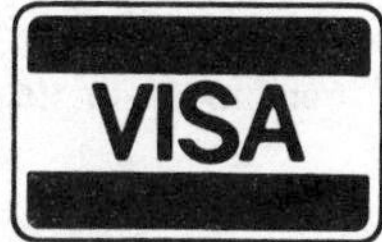

MAIL TO:

RESTORATIONS
563 N. Pine St.
Nevada City, CA 95959
(916) 477-5527

5 Mil MYLAR

MYLAR™ vs PLASTIC BAGS!

What's the difference? Ordinary plastic bags are made of POLYETHYLENE, PVC, or now (the latest attempt at cheap bags) POLYPROPYLENE. These cheap plastics all contain harmful chemical additives or plasticizers that will transfer to the paper. The result: yellowing, browning, staining, or just complete breakdown of the paper!

WANT PROOF? Stack up 25 old plastic bags . . . look through them toward the light . . . I'll bet you'll see brown staining where the comics were centered in the bag!!

MYLAR D is totally inert and offers complete protection for your paper collectables. The US LIBRARY OF CONGRESS USES ONLY MYLAR to preserve its paper documents. *You know they use the very best!!*

WHY BUY FROM NEVADA ???

Unlike another manufacturer of mylar bags, we use ONLY GENUINE **MYLAR D** FROM DUPONT..... NO SUBSTITUTES.

Our Mylars™ are a FULL 5 MILS THICK . . . not 4 or 3½ or 3 mils. This 5 mil thickness (each sheet) will protect your books and other paper collectibles from surface damage, wrinkling, spillage, and careless handling. The stiffness protects the corners from wear or damage.

WITH OUR BAGS, YOU DO NOT NEED A BACKING BOARD!!

We have many years of experience with MYLAR. *Without a doubt, WE ARE THE REAL MYLAR EXPERTS!* Our new, exclusive LAZERWELDER™ allows us to seal a custom bag of any shape or size ... with INTERIOR SEALING or EDGE SEALING or *BOTH!* Do you have a different design? Let us know what you want and we will custom make it for you!!

When was the last time you had service like that!!!

THE CHOICE IS YOURS............CHOOSE MYLARS™

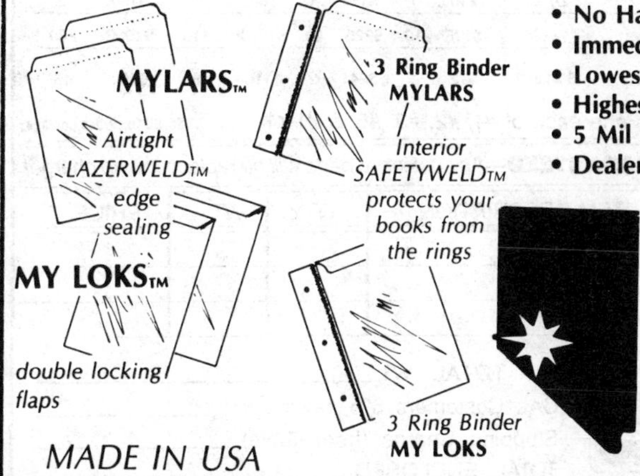

- **No Hassles ... no Delays**
- **Immediate shipments**
- **Lowest Prices**
- **Highest Quality Bags**
- **5 Mil ... Genuine MYLAR D**
- **Dealer Inquiries Invited!**

Mylar Bags
RESTORATIONS
563 N. Pine St.
Nevada City, CA 95959
(916) 477-5527

USE THIS ORDER FORM TO ORDER FROM

RESTORATIONS ••••••••• MYLAR BAGS

SHIPPING INFORMATION

563 N. PINE ST. NEVADA CITY, CA 95959

Date__________________

SHIPPING AND HANDLING CHART

Total Shipping Weight (lbs.)	If your zip code begins with: 9 8,7 or 6 5,4 or 3 0,1 or 2			APO, FPO Alaska-Hawaii	All Foreign Countries
0-2	2.50	2.75	3.25	6.25	8.25
3-5	3.25	3.75	4.50	9.50	13.00
6-10	4.00	5.25	6.50	14.00	19.50
11-15	4.75	6.50	8.50	16.75	25.30
16-20	5.75	7.75	10.75	18.75	32.50
21-25	6.50	9.25	12.75	20.50	39.00
26-30	7.50	10.50	14.75	21.75	45.50
31-35	8.25	12.00	16.75	22.75	51.75
36-40	9.00	13.50	19.00	23.75	58.50
41-45	9.75	14.75	21.00	24.75	64.75
46-50	10.75	16.25	23.25	25.50	71.50

Above 50 lbs. add together additional amounts (Example 60 lbs. in zip 1 would be $10.75 plus $4.00)

Ship To: Name ________________________

Address ________________________

City, State, Zip________________________

If Visa/Master Card are used:

Card # ________________________ Exp.________

Signature ________________________

SHIPPING TABLE

No.	Description	Size (Inches)	Price 50	Ship Wt. lbs.	Price 100	Wt. lbs.	Price 500	Wt. lbs.	Price 1000	Wt. lbs.
#1	Comic-Current size late 60's to present.	7¼x10¾	$20	3	$38	5	$180	24	$340	48
#1-lok	Comics-Current size late 60's to present. 2 pre-folded flaps	7¼x10¾	$30	3	$56	5	$250	24	$450	48
#2	Comic-Silver/Gold 40's to 60's	7¾x10¾	$22	3	$42	5	$200	25	$380	50
#2-lok	Comics-Silver/Gold size 40's-60's. 2 pre-fold flaps	7¾x10¾	$30	3	$56	5	$250	25	$450	50
#3	Comic-Super Gold larger comics of early 40's also 25¢ size 50's-60's	8¼x10¾	$25	3	$45	5	$205	26	$400	52
#3-lok	Comic-Super Gold size 2 pre-folded flaps	8¼x10¾	$33	4	$60	6	$260	26	$490	52
#4	Magazine 8½x11	8 7/8x11 7/8	$30	3	57	6	$250	30	$480	60
#4-lok	Magazine size 8½x11	8 7/8x11 7/8	$36	4	$68	6	$300	30	$550	60
#5b	Comic-3 ring binder Internal seal seperates issue from rings-Top loading	*10¾x10* fits stand. 3ring bind.	$45	3	$70	5	$380	30	$600	60
#5b-lok	Comic-3ring binder, with internal seal-Top loading w/2 pre-fold flaps	10x10¾	$50	4	$90	6	$400	30	$700	60
#6	Baseball Cards	2 7/8x4	$10	1	$17	1	$80	5	$150	8
#8	Newspaper—Original Art	1Ax24	$125	12	$225	24	$1000	110	$1900	220
#7	Postcards Money Photos	3¾x6 1/8	$12	1	$24	2	$110	8	$200	16

#79 Sample Kit contains one each of #1, #2, #3, #6, & #1-lok .... $5.00 (includes postage)

*Highest Quality Bags—***GUARANTEED***—Any defective bags will be replaced at no charge!*

ITEM#	ITEM DESCRIPTION	QTY.	WT.	PRICE

TOTAL WT.________________

VISA MasterCard

CAL Customers 6% sales tax ________________

Shipping Charge (from Table) ________________

TOTAL ENCLOSED ________________

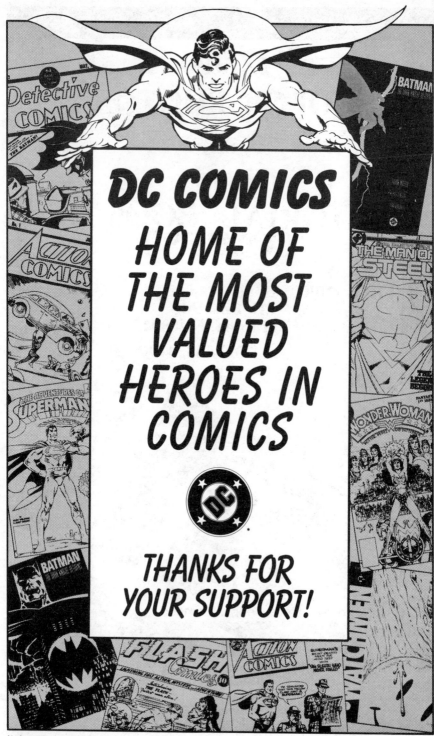

Abbott & Costello #7. © STJ

Ace Comics #65. © DMP

Action Comics #1. © DC

The correct title listing for each comic book can be determined by consulting the indicia (publication data) on the beginning interior pages of the comic. The official title is determined by those words of the title in capital letters only, and not by what is on the cover.

Titles are listed in this book as if they were one word, ignoring spaces, hyphens, and apostrophes, to make finding titles easier.

A-1 (See A-One)

ABBIE AN' SLATS (. . . With Becky No. 1-4) (See Fight for Love, Giant Comics Edition 2, Treasury of Comics, & United Comics)
1940; March, 1948 - No. 4, Aug, 1948 (Reprints)
United Features Syndicate

	Good	Fine	Mint
Single Series 25 ('40)	13.50	40.00	95.00
Single Series 28	11.00	33.00	76.00
1 (1948)	6.00	18.00	42.00
2-4: 3 r-/Sparkler No. 68-72	3.50	10.50	24.00

ABBOTT AND COSTELLO (. . . Comics)
Feb, 1948 - No. 40, Sept?, 1956 (Mort Drucker art in most issues)
St. John Publishing Co.

	Good	Fine	Mint
1	14.50	43.50	100.00
2	7.00	21.00	50.00
3-9 (No.8, 8/49; No. 9, 2/50)	4.50	13.50	31.00
10-Son of Sinbad story by Kubert (new)	11.00	33.00	76.00
11,13-20 (No. 11, 10/50; No. 13, 8/51; No. 15, 12/52)	2.65	8.00	18.00
12-Movie issue	3.50	10.50	24.00
21-30: 28 r-No. 8. 30-Painted-c	2.00	6.00	14.00
31-40	1.75	5.25	12.00
3-D No. 1 (11/53)-Infinity-c	14.50	32.50	100.00

ABBOTT AND COSTELLO (TV)
Feb, 1968 - No. 22, Aug, 1971 (Hanna-Barbera)
Charlton Comics

	Good	Fine	Mint
1	1.00	3.00	7.00
2-10	.55	1.60	3.50
11-22	.35	1.00	2.00

ABC (See America's Best TV Comics)

ABRAHAM LINCOLN LIFE STORY (See Dell Giants)

ABSENT-MINDED PROFESSOR, THE (See 4-Color Comics No. 1199)

ACE COMICS
April, 1937 - No. 151, Oct-Nov, 1949
David McKay Publications

	Good	Fine	Mint
1-Jungle Jim by Alex Raymond, Krazy Kat begin	105.00	315.00	735.00
2	40.00	120.00	280.00
3-5	28.00	84.00	195.00
6-10	19.00	57.00	132.00
11-The Phantom begins(In brown costume, 2/38)	28.00	84.00	195.00
12-20	14.50	44.00	100.00
21-25,27-30	12.00	36.00	84.00
26-Origin Prince Valiant	40.00	120.00	280.00
31-40: 37-Krazy Kat ends	9.35	28.00	65.00
41-60	7.00	21.00	50.00
61-64,66-76-(7/43; last 68pgs.)	6.35	19.00	45.00
65-(8/42; Flag-c)	7.00	21.00	50.00
77-84 (3/44; all 60pgs.)	6.00	18.00	42.00
85-99 (52 pgs.)	5.00	15.00	35.00
100 (7/45; last 52 pgs.)	6.00	18.00	42.00
101-134: 128-11/47; Brick Bradford begins. 134-Last Prince Valiant (All 36 pgs.)	4.25	13.00	30.00
135-151: 135-6/48; Lone Ranger begins	3.35	10.00	24.00

ACE KELLY (See Tops Comics)

ACE KING (See Advs. of the Detective)

ACES HIGH
Mar-Apr, 1955 - No. 5, Nov-Dec, 1955
E.C. Comics

	Good	Fine	Mint
1-Not approved by code	7.00	21.00	50.00
2	6.00	18.00	42.00
3-5	5.00	15.00	35.00

NOTE: *All have stories by* ***Davis, Evans, Krigstein,*** *and* ***Wood; Evans*** *c-1-5.*

ACTION ADVENTURE (War) (Formerly Real Adventure)
June, 1955 - No. 4, Oct, 1955
Gillmor Magazines

	Good	Fine	Mint
V1No.2-4	1.00	3.00	7.00

ACTION COMICS (See Special Edition)
June, 1938 - No. 583, Sept, 1986; No. 584, Jan, 1987 - Present
National Periodical Publ./Detective Comics/DC

1-Origin & 1st app. Superman by Siegel & Shuster, Marco Polo, Tex Thompson, Pep Morgan, Chuck Dawson & Scoop Scanlon; intro. Zatara; Superman story missing 4 pgs. which were included when reprinted in Superman No. 1. Mentioned in **POP**, pg. 86

Good	Fine	VF-NM
4000.00	12000.00	25,000.00

(Only one known copy exists in Mint condition which has not sold)

1-Reprint, Oversize 13½''x10.'' **WARNING:** This comic is an exact reprint of the original except for its size. DC published it in 1974 with a second cover titling it as a **Famous First Edition**. There have been many reported cases of the outer cover being removed and the interior sold as the original edition. The reprint with the new outer cover removed is practically worthless.

	Good	Fine	Mint
1(1976,1983)-Giveaway; paper cover, 16pgs. in color; reprints complete Superman story from No. 1 ('38)	.70	2.00	4.00
2	650.00	1950.00	4550.00
3 (Scarce)	485.00	1455.00	3400.00
4	340.00	1020.00	2380.00
5 (Rare)	400.00	1200.00	2800.00
6-1st Jimmy Olsen (called office boy)	305.00	915.00	2150.00
7,10-Superman covers	350.00	1050.00	2450.00
8,9	270.00	810.00	1890.00
11,12,14: 14-Clip Carson begins, ends No. 41	140.00	420.00	980.00
13-Superman cover; last Scoop Scanlon	165.00	495.00	1155.00
15-Superman cover	170.00	510.00	1190.00
16	110.00	330.00	770.00
17-Superman cover; last Marco Polo	135.00	405.00	945.00
18-Origin 3 Aces	95.00	285.00	665.00
19-Superman covers begin	120.00	360.00	840.00
20-'S' left off Superman's chest-No. 20. 20-Clark Kent works at 'Daily Star'	115.00	345.00	805.00
21,22,24,25: 24-Kent at Daily Planet. 25-Last app. Gargantua T. Potts, Tex Thompson's sidekick	70.00	210.00	490.00
23-1st app. Luthor & Black Pirate; Black Pirate by Moldoff	95.00	285.00	665.00
26-30	50.00	150.00	350.00
31,32	40.00	120.00	280.00
33-Origin Mr. America	48.00	145.00	335.00
34-40: 37-Origin Congo Bill. 40-Intro Star Spangled Kid & Stripsey	40.00	120.00	280.00
41	38.00	115.00	265.00
42-Origin Vigilante; Bob Daley becomes Fat Man; origin Mr. America's magic flying carpet; The Queen Bee & Luthor app; Black Pirate ends; not in No. 41	50.00	150.00	350.00
43-50: 44-Fat Man's i.d. revealed to Mr. America. 45-Intro. Stuff	38.00	115.00	265.00
51-1st app. The Prankster	30.00	90.00	210.00
52-Fat Man & Mr. America become the Ameri-commandos; origin Vigilante retold	35.00	105.00	245.00

ACTION COMICS (continued) Good Fine Mint

53-60: 56-Last Fat Man. 59-Kubert Vigilante begins?, ends No. 70. 60-First app. Lois Lane as Superwoman 28.00 84.00 195.00

61-63,65-70: 63-Last 3 Aces 25.00 75.00 175.00

64-Intro Toyman 28.00 84.00 195.00

71-79: 74-Last Mr. America 21.50 65.00 150.00

80-2nd app. & 1st Mr. Mxyztplk-c (1/45) 32.00 95.00 225.00

81,82,84-90 21.50 65.00 150.00

83-Intro Hocus & Pocus 22.00 66.00 154.00

91-99: 93-X-Mas-c. 99-1st small logo(7/46) 18.50 55.00 130.00

100 33.00 100.00 230.00

101-Nuclear explosion-c 22.00 66.00 154.00

102-120: 105,117-X-Mas-c 18.50 55.00 130.00

121-126,128-140: 135,136,138-Zatara by Kubert 17.00 51.00 120.00

127-Vigilante by Kubert; Tommy Tomorrow begins 28.00 84.00 195.00

141-161: 156-Lois Lane as Super Woman. 161-Last 52 pgs. 17.00 51.00 120.00

162-180: 168,176-Used in **POP**, pg. 90 11.50 35.00 80.00

181-201: 191-Intro. Janu in Congo Bill. 198-Last Vigilante. 201-Last pre-code ish 11.50 35.00 80.00

202-220 8.50 25.50 60.00

221-240: 224-1st Golden Gorilla story 6.00 18.00 42.00

241,243-251: 248-Congo Bill becomes Congorilla. 251-Last Tommy Tomorrow 4.50 13.50 32.00

242-Origin & 1st app. Brainiac (7/58); 1st mention of Shrunken City of Kandor 15.00 45.00 105.00

252-Origin & 1st app. Supergirl and Metallo (5/59) 31.50 95.00 220.00

253-2nd app. Supergirl 4.75 14.00 33.00

254-1st meeting of Bizarro & Superman 3.70 11.00 26.00

255-1st Bizarro Lois & both Bizarros leave Earth to make Bizarro World 3.30 10.00 23.00

256-260: 259-Red Kryptonite used 2.80 8.40 19.50

261-1st X-Kryptonite which gave Streaky his powers; last Congorilla in Action; origin & 1st app. Streaky The Super Cat 2.80 8.40 19.50

262-266,268-270: 263-Origin Bizarro World 2.30 7.00 16.00

267(8/60)-3rd Legion app; 1st app. Chameleon Boy, Colossal Boy, & Invisible Kid 19.00 57.00 132.00

271-275,277-281: 280-Congorilla app. 2.00 6.00 14.00

276(5/61)-6th Legion app; 1st app. Brainiac 5, Phantom Girl, Triplicate Girl, Bouncing Boy, Sun Boy, & Shrinking Violet; Supergirl joins Legion 6.50 20.00 45.00

282-Brainiac 5 cameo (last 10¢ issue) 2.00 6.00 14.00

283(12/61)-Legion of Super-Villains app. 2.15 6.50 15.00

284(1/62)-Mon-el app. 2.15 6.50 15.00

285(2/62)-12th Legion app; Brainiac 5 cameo; Supergirl's existance revealed to world 2.65 8.00 18.00

286(3/62)-Legion of Super Villains app. 1.85 5.50 13.00

287(4/62)-14th Legion app.(cameo) 1.85 5.50 13.00

288-Mon-el app.; r-origin Supergirl 1.85 5.50 13.00

289(6/62)-16th Legion app.(Adult); Lightning Man & Saturn Woman's marriage 1st revealed 1.85 5.50 13.00

290(7/62)-17th Legion app; Phantom Girl app. 1.85 5.50 13.00

291,292,294-299: 292-1st app. Superhorse. 297-Mon-el app; 298-Legion app. 1.10 3.25 6.50

293-Origin Comet(Superhorse) 1.60 4.80 11.00

300 1.50 4.50 10.00

301-303,305-308,310-320: 306-Brainiac 5, Mon-el app. 307-Saturn Girl app. 314-r-origin Supergirl; J.L.A. x-over. 317-Death of Nor-Kan of Kandor. 319-Shrinking Violet app. .90 2.75 5.50

304-Origin & 1st app. Black Flame .90 2.75 5.50

309-Legion app. 1.10 3.25 6.50

321-333,335-340: 336-Origin Akvar(Flamebird). 340-Origin, 1st app. Parasite .70 2.00 4.00

334-Giant G-20; origin Supergirl; Legion-r 1.25 3.75 7.50

Good Fine Mint

341-346,348-359 .55 1.60 3.20

347,360-Gnt. Supergirl G-33,G-45; 360-Legion-r; r-origin Supergirl .90 2.75 5.50

361-372,374-380: 365-Legion app. 370-New facts about Superman's origin. 376-Last Supergirl in Action. 377-Legion begins .35 1.00 2.00

373-Giant Supergirl G-57; Legion-r .65 1.90 3.80

381-392: 392-Last Legion in Action. Saturn Girl gets new costume. .50 1.00

393-402-All Superman issues .50 1.00

403-413: All 52pg. ish; 411-Origin Eclipso-(r). 413-Metamorpho begins; ends No. 418. .50 1.00

414-424: 419-Intro. Human Target. 421-Intro Capt. Strong; Green Arrow begins. 422/423-Origin Human Target .50 1.00

425-Adams-a; Atom begins .35 1.00 2.00

426-436,438-442,444-450 .50 1.00

437,443-100pg. Giants .30 .90 1.80

451-499: 454-Last Atom. 458-Last Green Arrow. 487-488, 44pgs. 487-1st app. Microwave Man; origin Atom retold .50 1.00

500-Infinity-c; Superman life story; $1.00 size; 68 pgs.; shows Legion statues in museum .60 1.20

501-520: 511-514-New Airwave. 513-The Atom begins. 517-Aquaman begins; ends No. 541 .50 1.00

521-534,537-543,545: 521-Intro. & 1st app. The Vixen. 532-New Teen Titans cameo .50 1.00

535,536-Omega Men app.; 536-New Teen Titans cameo. .50 1.00

544: (Mando paper); 68pgs.; Origins New Luthor & Brainiac; Omega Men cameo .50 1.00

546-J.L.A. & New Teen Titans guest .50 1.00

547-559,561,562,564 .50 1.00

560,563,565: Ambush Bug app. .25 .75 1.50

566-583,585-590 .50 1.00

584-Byrne-a begins; New Teen Titans app. .60 1.20

Wheaties Giveaway (1947, 32 pgs., 6½x8¼'', nn)-Vigilante story based on movie serial. NOTE: *All copies were taped to Wheaties boxes and never found in mint condition. The mint grade applies to slight tape residue on book.* 23.00 70.00 160.00

NOTE: ***Supergirl's*** *origin in 262, 280, 285, 291, 305, 309.* **Adams** *c-356, 358, 359, 361-64, 366, 367, 370-74, 377-79i, 398-400, 402, 404-06, 419p, 466, 468, 473i, 485.* **Bailey** *a-24, 25.* **Giffen** *a-560, 563p, 565; c-539p, 560p, 563p.* **Grell** *a-440-442, 444-446, 450-452, 456-458; c-456.* **Guardineer** *a-24, 25; c-8, 11, 12, 14-16, 18, 25.* ***Bob Kane's*** *Clip Carson-14-41.* **Gil Kane** *a-539-541, 544-546, 551-554; c-535p, 540, 541, 544p, 545-49, 551-554.* **Meskin** *a-42-121(most).* **Moldoff** *a-23-25.* **Perez** *c-529p.* **Starlin** *a-509.* **Staton** *a-525p, 526p, 531p, 535p, 536p.* **Toth** *a-406, 407, 413, 418, 419, 425, 431.* **Tuska** *a-486p, 550.*

ACTUAL CONFESSIONS (Formerly Love Adventures)
No. 13, October, 1952 - No. 14, December, 1952
Atlas Comics (MPI)

13,14 1.15 3.50 8.00

ACTUAL ROMANCES
October, 1949 - No. 2, Jan, 1950 (52 pgs.)
Marvel Comics (IPS)

1 2.30 7.00 16.00
2 1.15 3.50 8.00

ADAM AND EVE
1975, 1978 (35-49 cents)
Spire Christian Comics (Fleming H. Revell Co.)

By Al Hartley .25 .50

ADAM AND EVE A.D.
Sept, 1985 - Present ($1.50, B&W)
BAM Productions

1-7 .25 .75 1.50

ADAM-12 (TV)
Dec, 1973 - No. 10, Feb, 1976 (photo covers)

Action Comics #85. © DC

Action Comics #267. © DC

Adam and Eve A.D. #2. © BAM

Adolescent. . . Hamsters #1. © *Eclipse*

Adventure Comics #73, © *DC*

Adventure Comics #168, © *DC*

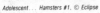

ADAM-12 (continued)
Gold Key

	Good	Fine	Mint
1	.85	2.50	5.00
2-10	.50	1.50	3.00

ADDAMS FAMILY (TV)
Oct, 1974 - No. 3, Apr, 1975 (Hanna-Barbera)
Gold Key

1	1.00	3.00	6.00
2,3	.60	1.80	3.50

ADLAI STEVENSON
December, 1966
Dell Publishing Co.

12-007-612-Life story; photo-c	2.35	7.00	16.00

ADOLESCENT RADIOACTIVE BLACK BELT HAMSTERS (Also see Naive Inter-Dimensional Commando Koalas. . .)
1986 - Present ($1.50, B&W)
Eclipse Comics

1	1.05	3.20	6.40
2-4	.40	1.25	2.50
3-D 1 ($2.50, 7/86), 2,3	.40	1.25	2.50
2-D 1, 2 (100 limited signed & numbered)	.85	2.50	5.00

ADULT TALES OF TERROR ILL. (See Terror Ill.)

ADVENTURE BOUND (See 4-Color Comics No. 239)

ADVENTURE COMICS (Formerly New Adventure)
No. 32, 11/38 - No. 490, 2/82; No. 491, 9/82 - No. 503, 9/83
(The longest continously published comic book title)
National Periodical Publications/DC Comics

	Good	Fine	Mint
32-Anchors Aweigh (ends No. 52), Barry O'Neil (ends No. 60, not in No. 33), Captain Desmo (ends No. 47), Dale Daring (ends No. 47), Federal Men (ends No. 70), The Golden Dragon (ends No. 36), Rusty & His Pals (ends No. 52) by Bob Kane, Todd Hunter (ends No. 38) and Tom Brent (ends No. 39) begin	40.00	120.00	280.00
33-38: 37-c-used on Double Action 2	25.00	75.00	175.00
39(1/39)-Jack Wood begins, ends No. 42: 1st mention of Marijuana in comics	27.00	81.00	190.00
40-Intro. & 1st app. The Sandman. Socko Strong begins, ends No. 54	200.00	600.00	1400.00
41	60.00	180.00	420.00
42-47: 47-Steve Conrad Adventurer begins, ends No. 76	42.00	125.00	295.00
48-Intro. & 1st app. The Hourman by Bernard Baily	190.00	570.00	1330.00
49,50: 50-Cotton Carver by Jack Lehti begins, ends No. 59?	45.00	135.00	315.00
51-60: 53-Intro Jimmy "Minuteman" Martin & the Minutemen of America in Hourman; ends No. 78. 58-Paul Kirk Manhunter begins, ends No. 72	39.00	116.00	272.00
61-Intro/1st app. Starman by Jack Burnley	165.00	495.00	1155.00
62-65,67,68: 67-Origin The Mist	38.00	115.00	265.00
66-Origin Shining Knight	55.00	165.00	385.00
69-Intro. Sandy the Golden Boy (Sandman's sidekick) by Bob Kane; Sandman dons new costume	50.00	150.00	350.00
70-Last Federal Men	38.00	115.00	265.00
71-Jimmy Martin becomes costume aide to the Hourman; intro Hourman's Miracle Ray machine	36.00	108.00	250.00
72-1st Simon & Kirby Sandman	135.00	405.00	945.00
73-Origin Manhunter by Simon & Kirby; begin new series	175.00	525.00	1225.00
74-76: 74-Thorndyke replaces Jimmy, Hourman's assistant	58.00	175.00	405.00
77-Origin Genius Jones; Mist story	58.00	175.00	405.00
78-80-Last Simon & Kirby Manhunter & Burnley Starman	58.00	175.00	405.00
81-90: 83-Last Hourman. 84-Mike Gibbs begins, ends No. 102	36.00	108.00	250.00
91-Last Simon & Kirby Sandman	33.00	100.00	230.00
92-99,101,102-Last Starman, Sandman, & Genius Jones. Most-S&K-c. 92-Last Manhunter	23.00	70.00	160.00
100	34.00	102.00	235.00
103-Aquaman, Green Arrow, Johnny Quick, Superboy begin; 1st small logo (4/46)	67.00	200.00	470.00
104	30.00	90.00	210.00
105-110	26.00	78.00	182.00
111-120: 113-X-Mas-c	22.00	65.00	154.00
121-126,128-130: 128-1st meeting Superboy-Lois Lane	17.00	51.00	120.00
127-Brief origin Shining Knight retold	18.35	55.00	128.00
131-140: 132-Shining Knight 1st return to King Arthur time; origin aide Sir Butch	15.00	45.00	105.00
141,143-149	15.00	45.00	105.00
142-Origin Shining Knight & Johnny Quick retold	16.00	48.00	112.00
150,151,153,155,157,159,161,163-All have 6-pg. Shining Knight stories by Frank Frazetta. 159-Origin Johnny Quick	30.00	90.00	210.00
152,154,156,158,160,162,164-169: 166-Last Shining Knight. 169-Last 52 pgs.	14.35	43.00	100.00
170-180	13.00	40.00	90.00
181-199: 189-B&W and color illo in **POP**	11.35	34.00	80.00
200	14.35	43.00	100.00
201-209: 207-Last Johnny Quick (not in 205). 209-Last Pre-code ish; origin Speedy	11.35	34.00	80.00
210-1st app. Krypto	45.00	135.00	315.00
211-220	8.50	25.00	60.00
221-246: 237-1st Intergalactic Vigilante Squadron (Legion tryout)	8.00	24.00	56.00
247(4/58)-1st Legion of Super Heroes app.; 1st app. Cosmic Boy, Lightning Lad, & Saturn Girl (origin)	188.00	565.00	1320.00
248-255: All Kirby Green Arrow. 253-1st meeting Superboy-Robin. 255-Intro. Red Kryptonite in Superboy (used in No. 252 but with no effect)	5.00	15.00	35.00
256-Origin Green Arrow by Kirby	7.00	21.00	50.00
257-259	5.00	15.00	35.00
260-Origin Aquaman retold	7.00	21.00	50.00
261-266,268,270: 262-Origin Speedy in Green Arrow. 270-Congorilla begins, ends No. 281,283	3.75	11.25	26.00
267(12/59)-2nd Legion of Super Heroes	37.00	110.00	260.00
269-Intro. Aqualad; last Green Arrow (not in No. 206)	5.15	15.50	36.00
271-Origin Luthor	3.75	11.25	26.00
272-280: 275-Origin Superman-Batman team retold (see World's Finest No. 94). 276-Intro Sunboy. 279-Intro White Kryptonite in Superboy. 280-1st meeting Superboy-Lori Lemaris	2.85	8.50	20.00
281,284,287-289: 281-Last Congorilla. 284-Last Aquaman in Adv. 287,288-Intro. Dev-Em, the Knave from Krypton. 287-1st Bizarro Perry White & J. Olsen. 289-Legion cameo (statues)	2.35	7.00	16.00
282(3/61)-5th Legion app; intro & origin Star Boy	7.00	21.00	50.00
283-Intro. The Phantom Zone	3.75	11.25	26.00
285-1st Bizarro World story (ends No. 299) in Adv. (See Action No. 255)	3.35	10.00	23.00
286-1st Bizarro Mxyzptlk	2.85	8.50	20.00
290(11/61)-8th Legion app; origin Sunboy in Legion (last 10¢ issue)	6.00	18.00	42.00

291,292,294-299: 292-1st Bizarro Lana Lang & Lucy Lane. 295-1st

ADVENTURE COMICS (continued) Good Fine Mint

Bizarro Titano. 299-1st Gold Kryptonite (8/62) 2.00 6.00 14.00
293(2/62)-13th Legion app; Mon-el & Legion Super Pets (intro & origin) app. 1st Bizarro Luthor & Kandor 4.65 14.00 32.00
300-Legion series begins; Mon-el leaves Phantom Zone(temporarily), joins Legion 21.00 62.00 145.00
301-Origin Bouncing Boy 6.85 21.00 48.00
302-305: 303-1st app. Matter Eater Lad. 304-Death of Lightning Lad in Legion 3.85 11.50 27.00
306-310: 306-Intro. Legion of Substitute Heroes. 307-Intro. Element Lad in Legion. 308-1st app. Lightning Lass in Legion 2.85 8.50 20.00
311-320: 312-Lightning Lad back in Legion. 315-Last new Superboy story; Colossal Boy app. 316-Origins & powers of Legion given. 317-Intro. Dream Girl in Legion; Lightning Lass becomes Light Lass; Hall of Fame series begins. 320-Dev-Em 2nd app. 2.35 7.00 16.00
321-Intro Time Trapper 1.75 5.25 12.00
322-326,328-330: 329-Intro Legion of Super Bizarros 1.60 4.80 11.00
327-Intro Timber Wolf in Legion 1.60 4.80 11.00
331-340: 337-Chlorophyll Kid & Night Girl app. 340-Intro Computo in Legion 1.50 4.50 10.00
341-Triplicate Girl becomes Duo Damsel 1.25 3.75 7.50
342-345,347,350: 345-Last Hall of Fame; returns in 356,371 1.10 3.25 6.50
346-1st app. Karate Kid, Princess Projectra, Ferro Lad, & Nemesis Kid 1.25 3.75 7.50
348-Origin Sunboy & intro Dr. Regulus in Legion 1.25 3.75 7.50
349-Intro Universo & Rond Vidar 1.25 3.75 7.50
351-1st app. White Witch 1.10 3.25 6.50
352,355-360: 355-Insect Queen joins Legion (4/67) .90 2.75 5.50
353-Death of Ferro Lad in Legion 1.40 4.25 8.50
354(3/67)-Shadow Lass, Chemical King, Reflecto & Quantum Queen app. only as statues 1.10 3.25 6.50
361-364,366,368-370: 369-Intro Mordru in Legion .70 2.10 4.20
365-Intro Shadow Lass; lists origins & powers of L.S.H. .85 2.60 5.20
367-New Legion headquarters .85 2.60 5.20
371-Intro. Chemical King .85 2.60 5.20
372-Timber Wolf & Chemical King join .85 2.60 5.20
373,374,376-380: Last Legion in Adv. .70 2.10 4.20
375-Intro Quantum Queen .85 2.60 5.20
381-389,391-400: 381-Supergirl begins. 399-Unpubbed G.A. Black Canary story. 400-New costume for Supergirl .60 1.20
390-Giant Supergirl G-69 .65 2.00 4.00
401,402,404-410: 409-52pg. issues begin; ends No. 420 .60 1.20
403-68pg. Giant G-81 .65 2.00 4.00
411-415: 412-Animal Man origin reprint/Str. Adv. No. 180. 413-Hawkman by Kubert; G.A. Robotman reprint/Detective 178; Zatanna begins, ends No. 421. .35 .70
416-Giant DC-10. GA-r .60 1.20

417-Morrow Vigilante; Frazetta Shining Knight r-/Adv. No. 161; origin The Enchantress .60 1.20
418,419-New Black Canary by Toth .35 .70
420-424: Last Supergirl in Adv. .30 .60
425-New look, content change to adventure; Toth-a, origin Capt. Fear .25 .75 1.50
426-458: 427-Last Vigilante. 428-430-Black Orchid app. 431-440-Spectre app. 435-Mike Grell's 1st comic work ('74). 440 New Spectre origin. 441-452-Aquaman app. 445-447-The Creeper app. 449-451-Martian Manhunter app. 453-458-Superboy app; intro Mighty Girl No. 453. 457,458-Eclipso app. .25 .50
459-466($1.00 size, 68pgs.): 459-Flash (ends 466), Deadman (ends 466), Wonder Woman (ends 464), Gr. Lantern (ends 460), New Gods begin (ends 460). 460-Aquaman begins; ends 478. 461-Justice Society begins; ends 466; death Earth II Batman (also No. 462) .45 .90
467-490: 467-Starman, Plasticman begin, end 478. 469,470-Origin Starman. 479-Dial 'H' for Hero begins, ends 490 .25 .50
491-499: 491-100pg. Digest size begins; r-Legion of Super Heroes/Adv. 247 & 267; Spectre, Aquaman, Superboy, S&K Sandman, Bl. Canary-r & new Shazam by Newton begin. 493-Challengers of the Unknown begins by Tuska w/brief origin. 492,495,496, 498,499-S&K Sandman-r/Adventure in all; 494-499-Spectre-r/Spectre 1-3, 5-7. 493-495,497-499-G.A. Captain Marvel-r. 498-Plastic Man-r begin; origin Bouncing Boy-r/No. 301 .60 1.20
500-All Legion-r (Digest size, 148 pgs.) .25 .80 1.60
501-503-G.A.-r .60 1.20

NOTE: *Bizarro covers-285, 286, 288, 294, 295. Vigilante app.-420, 426, 427.* ***Adams*** *a(r)-495i-498i; c-365-369, 371-373, 375-379, 381-383.* ***Austin*** *a-449i, 451i.* ***Ditko*** *a-467p-478p; c-467p.* ***Giffen*** *c-491p-494p, 500p.* ***Grell*** *a-435-437, 440.* ***Guardineer*** *c-45.* ***Kaluta*** *c-425.* ***G. Kane*** *a-414r, 425; c-496-499, 537.* ***Kirby*** *a-250-256.* ***Kubert*** *a-413.* ***Meskin*** *a-81, 127.* ***Moldoff*** *a-494i; c-49.* ***Morrow*** *a-413-415, 422, 502r, 503r.* ***Newton*** *a-459-461, 464-466, 491p, 492p.* ***Orlando*** *a-457p, 458p.* ***Perez*** *c-484-486, 490p.* ***Simon/Kirby*** *c-73-97, 101, 102.* ***Starlin*** *c-471.* ***Staton*** *a-445-447i, 456-458p, 459, 460, 461p-465p, 466, 467p-478p, 502p(r); c-458, 461(back).* ***Toth*** *a-431, 495p-497p.* ***Tuska*** *a-494p.*

ADVENTURE COMICS
No date (early 1940s) Paper cover, 32 pgs.
IGA

Two different issues; Super-Mystery reprints from 1941 13.00 40.00 90.00

ADVENTURE INTO FEAR
1951
Superior Publ. Ltd.

1 5.00 15.00 35.00

ADVENTURE INTO MYSTERY
May, 1956 - No. 8, July, 1957
Atlas Comics (BFP No. 1/OPI No. 2-8)

1-Everett-c 5.00 15.00 35.00
2-Everett-c 2.50 7.50 17.50
3,6,8: 3-Everett-c 2.15 6.50 15.00
4-Williamson-a, 4 pgs; Powell-a 5.00 15.00 35.00
5-Everett-c/a, Orlando-a 2.50 7.50 17.50
7-Torres-a; Everett-c 3.00 9.00 21.00

ADVENTURE IS MY CAREER
1945 (44 pgs.)
U.S. Coast Guard Academy/Street & Smith

nn-Simon, Milt Gross-a 4.35 13.00 30.00

ADVENTURERS, THE
August, 1986 - Present ($1.50, B&W)
Aircel Publishing/Adventurer Comics No. 3 on

1 (28 pgs.) 1.00 3.00 6.00
1-cover variant, limited edition; skeleton-c 4.00 12.00 24.00
1-Reprint, new-c .75 1.50
2,3,0,4: 0-Origin .35 1.00 2.00

ADVENTURES (No. 2 Spectacular. . . on cover)
11/49 - No. 2, 2/50 (No. 1 . . . in Romance on cover)
St. John Publishing Co. (Slightly large size)

Adventure Comics #346, © *DC*

Adventure Into Mystery #5, © *MCG*

Adventurers #1, © *Aircel*

Adventures Into the Unknown #8, © ACG

Advs. Into Weird Worlds #1, © MCG

Advs. of Alan Ladd #3, © DC

ADVENTURES (continued)	Good	Fine	Mint
1(Scarce); Bolle, Starr-a(2)	8.35	25.00	58.00
2(Scarce)-Slave Girl; China Bombshell app.; Bolle, L. Starr-a	14.35	43.00	100.00

ADVENTURES FOR BOYS
December, 1954
Bailey Enterprises

	Good	Fine	Mint
Comics, text, & photos	1.50	4.50	10.00

ADVENTURES IN DISNEYLAND (Giveaway)
1955 (12 pgs.) (Dist. by Richfield Oil)
Walt Disney Productions

	Good	Fine	Mint
	3.00	9.00	21.00

ADVENTURES IN PARADISE (See 4-Color No. 1301)

ADVENTURES IN ROMANCE (See Adventures)

ADVENTURES IN SCIENCE (See Classics Special)

ADVENTURES IN THE MYSTWOOD
1986 - Present ($2.00, B&W)
Blackthorne Publ.

	Good	Fine	Mint
1-3	.30	.95	1.90

ADVENTURES IN 3-D
Nov, 1953 - No. 2, Jan, 1954
Harvey Publications

	Good	Fine	Mint
1-Nostrand, Powell-a, 2-Powell-a	6.00	18.00	42.00

ADVENTURES INTO DARKNESS (See Seduction of the Innocent 3-D)
No. 5, Aug, 1952 - No. 14, 1954
Better-Standard Publications/Visual Editions

	Good	Fine	Mint
5-Katz c/a; Toth-a(p)	4.00	12.00	28.00
6-Tuska, Katz-a	3.35	10.00	23.00
7-Katz c/a	3.35	10.00	23.00
8,9-Toth-a(p)	4.35	13.00	30.00
10,11-Jack Katz-a	2.85	8.50	20.00
12-Toth-a?; lingerie panels	3.35	10.00	23.00
13-Toth-a(p); Cannibalism story cited by T. E. Murphy articles	3.85	11.50	27.00
14	2.85	8.50	20.00

NOTE: ***Fawcette*** *a-13.* ***Moriera*** *a-5.* ***Sekowsky*** *a-10, 11, 13(2).*

ADVENTURES INTO TERROR (Formerly Joker Comics)
No. 43, Nov, 1950 - No. 31, May, 1954
Marvel/Atlas Comics (CDS)

	Good	Fine	Mint
43	6.00	18.00	42.00
44(2/51)	4.35	13.00	30.00
3(4/51), 4	2.85	8.50	20.00
5-Wolverton-c panel/Mystic No. 6. Atom Bomb story	3.85	11.50	27.00
6,8: 8-Wolverton text illo r-/Marvel Tales 104	2.50	7.50	17.50
7-Wolverton-a "Where Monsters Dwell", 6 pgs.; Tuska-c	16.00	48.00	112.00
9,10,12-Krigstein-a. 9-Decapitation panels	3.50	10.50	24.50
11,13-20	2.15	6.50	15.00
21-24,26-31	1.85	5.50	13.00
25-Matt Fox-a	3.00	9.00	21.00

NOTE: ***Colan*** *a-3, 5, 14, 24, 25, 29; c-27.* ***Everett*** *c-13, 21, 25.* ***Heath*** *a-43, 44, 4-6, 22, 24, 26; c-43, 9, 11.* ***Lazarus*** *a-7.* ***Maneely*** *a-7, 10, 11.* ***Don Rico*** *a-4, 5.* ***Sekowsky*** *a-43, 3, 4.* ***Sinnott*** *a-8, 9, 11.* ***Tuska*** *a-14.*

ADVENTURES INTO THE UNKNOWN
Fall, 1948 - No. 174, Aug, 1967 (No. 1-33, 52 pgs.)
American Comics Group
(1st continuous series horror comic)

	Good	Fine	Mint
1-Guardineer-a; adapt. of 'Castle of Otranto' by Horace Walpole	27.00	81.00	190.00
2	13.50	40.00	95.00
3-Feldstein-a, 9 pgs.	16.00	48.00	110.00
4,5	9.50	28.50	66.00
6-10	6.50	19.50	45.00
11-16,18-20	4.00	12.00	28.00
17-Story similar to movie 'The Thing'	6.50	19.50	45.00
21-26,28-30	3.50	10.50	24.00
27-Williamson/Krenkel-a, 8 pgs.	14.00	42.00	100.00
31-50	3.00	9.00	21.00
51(1/54) - 59 (3-D effect). 52-E.C. swipe/Haunt Of Fear 14	6.50	19.50	45.00
60-Woodesque-a by Landau	2.15	6.50	15.00
61-Last pre-code ish (1-2/55)	1.85	5.50	13.00
62-70	1.30	4.00	9.00
71-90	.85	2.50	6.00
91,95,96(No. 95 on inside),107,116-All contain Williamson-a	2.65	8.00	18.00
92-94,97-99,101-106,108-115,117-127: 109-113,118-Whitney painted-c	.65	1.90	4.00
100	.80	2.40	4.80
128-Williamson-a(r)/Forbidden Worlds 63	.80	2.40	4.80
129-150	.35	1.00	2.00
151-153: 153-Magic Agent app.		.50	1.00
154-Nemesis series begins (origin), ends No. 170	.40	1.20	2.40
155-167,169-174: 157-Magic Agent app.	.30	.80	1.60
168-Ditko-a(p)	.40	1.20	2.40

NOTE: *"Spirit of Frankenstein" series in 5, 6, 8-10, 12, 16.* ***Buscema*** *a-100, 106, 108-110, 158r, 165r.* ***Craig*** *a-152, 160.* ***Goode*** *a-45, 47, 60.* ***Landau*** *a-59-63.* ***Lazarus*** *a-79.*

ADVENTURES INTO WEIRD WORLDS
Jan, 1952 - No. 30, June, 1954
Marvel/Atlas Comics (ACI)

	Good	Fine	Mint
1-Atom bomb panels	6.50	19.50	45.00
2	3.85	11.50	27.00
3-6,8,9	2.85	8.50	20.00
7-Tongue ripped out	3.70	11.00	26.00
10-Krigstein, Everett-a	3.50	10.50	24.50
11-20	2.15	6.50	15.00
21-23,25,26	1.70	5.00	12.00
24-Man holding hypo and splitting in two	4.80	14.50	33.50
27-Matt Fox end of world story-a; severed head cover	5.00	15.00	35.00
28-30: 28-Atom bomb story; decapitation panels	1.50	4.50	10.50

NOTE: ***Everett*** *c-6, 8, 10-13, 18-20, 22, 24; a-25.* ***Fass*** *a-7.* ***Forte*** *a-24.* ***Heath*** *a-1, 4, 17, 22; c-7.* ***Rico*** *a-13.* ***Maneely*** *a-3, 11, 20, 22, 25; c-3, 25-27, 29.* ***Reinman*** *a-28.* ***Robinson*** *a-13.* ***Sinnott*** *a-25, 30.* ***Tuska*** *a-1, 12, 15.* ***Wildey*** *a-28. Bondage c-22.*

ADVENTURES IN WONDERLAND
April, 1955 - No. 5, Feb, 1956 (Jr. Readers Guild)
Lev Gleason Publications

	Good	Fine	Mint
1-Maurer-a	2.00	6.00	14.00
2-4	1.35	4.00	9.00
5-Christmas issue	1.50	4.50	10.00

ADVENTURES OF ALAN LADD, THE
Oct-Nov, 1949 - No. 9, Feb-Mar, 1951
National Periodical Publications

	Good	Fine	Mint
1-Photo-c	20.00	60.00	140.00
2-Photo-c	12.00	36.00	84.00
3-5: Last photo-c	10.00	30.00	70.00
6-9	9.00	27.00	62.00

NOTE: ***Moreira*** *a-3-7.*

ADVENTURES OF ALICE
1945 (Also see Alice in Wonderland & . . . at Monkey Island)
Civil Service Publ./Pentagon Publishing Co.

	Good	Fine	Mint
1	4.00	12.00	28.00
2-Through the Magic Looking Glass	3.00	9.00	21.00

ADVENTURES OF BOB HOPE, THE
Feb-Mar, 1950 - No. 109, Feb-Mar, 1968
National Periodical Publications

	Good	Fine	Mint
1-Photo-c	30.00	90.00	210.00
2-Photo-c	15.00	45.00	105.00
3,4-Photo-c	10.00	30.00	70.00
5-10	7.00	21.00	50.00
11-20	4.50	13.50	32.00
21-30	3.00	9.00	21.00
31-40	2.15	6.50	15.00
41-50	1.35	4.00	9.50
51-70	1.00	3.00	7.00
71-93,95-105	.70	2.00	4.00
94-Aquaman cameo	.85	2.50	5.00
106-109-Adams c/a	2.50	7.50	15.00

NOTE: *Kitty Karr of Hollywood in No. 17-20,28. Liz in No. 26. Miss Beverly Hills of Hollywood in No. 7, 10, 13, 14. Miss Melody Lane of Broadway in No. 15. Rusty in No. 23, 25. Tommy in No. 24. No 2nd feature in No. 2-4, 6, 8, 11, 12, 28-on.*

ADVENTURES OF CAPTAIN JACK, THE
June, 1986 - Present ($2.00, B&W) (Adults)
Fantagraphics Books

	Good	Fine	Mint
1-6 Funny animal	.35	1.00	2.00

ADVENTURES OF DEAN MARTIN AND JERRY LEWIS, THE
(The Adventures of Jerry Lewis No. 41 on)
July-Aug, 1952 - No. 40, Oct, 1957
National Periodical Publications

	Good	Fine	Mint
1	23.50	70.00	165.00
2	11.00	33.00	77.00
3-10	6.60	20.00	45.00
11-20	3.85	11.50	27.00
21-30	2.65	8.00	18.50
31-40	2.00	6.00	14.00

ADVENTURES OF G. I. JOE
1969 (3¼''x7'') (20 & 16 pgs.)
Giveaways

First Series: 1-Danger of the Depths. 2-Perilous Rescue. 3-Secret Mission to Spy Island. 4-Mysterious Explosion. 5-Fantastic Free Fall. 6-Eight Ropes of Danger. 7-Mouth of Doom. 8-Hidden Missile Discovery. 9-Space Walk Mystery. 10-Fight for Survival. 11-The Shark's Surprise. **Second Series:** 2-Flying Space Adventure. 4-White Tiger Hunt. 7-Capture of the Pygmy Gorilla. 12-Secret of the Mummy's Tomb. **Third Series:** Reprinted surviving titles of First Series. **Fourth Series:** 13-Adventure Team Headquarters. 14-Search For the Stolen Idol. each . . . . .30 .60

ADVENTURES OF HAWKSHAW (See Hawkshaw The Detective)
1917 (9-3/4 x 13½'', 48 pgs., Color & two-tone)
The Saalfield Publishing Co.

	Good	Fine	Mint
By Gus Mager (only 24 pgs. of strips, reverse of each page is blank)	14.00	42.00	100.00

ADVENTURES OF HOMER COBB, THE
September, 1947 (Oversized)
Say/Bart Prod. (Canadian)

	Good	Fine	Mint
1-(Scarce)-Feldstein-a	16.00	48.00	110.00

ADVENTURES OF HOMER GHOST
June, 1957 - No. 2, August, 1957
Atlas Comics

	Good	Fine	Mint
V1No.1, V1No. 2	1.00	3.00	7.00

ADVENTURES OF JERRY LEWIS, THE (Advs. of Dean Martin & Jerry Lewis No. 1-40)(See Super DC Giant)
No. 41, Nov, 1957 - No. 124, May-June, 1971
National Periodical Publications

	Good	Fine	Mint
41-60	1.65	5.00	11.50
61-80: 68,74-Photo-c	1.00	3.00	7.00
81-91,93-96,98-100	.80	2.40	4.80
92-Superman cameo	.90	2.70	5.40
97-Batman/Robin x-over	.90	2.70	5.40
101-104-Adams c/a; 102-Beatles app.	2.50	7.50	15.00
105-Superman x-over	.80	2.40	4.80
106-111,113-116	.35	1.00	2.00
112-Flash x-over	.50	1.50	3.00
117-Wonder Woman x-over	.50	1.50	3.00
118-124		.60	1.20

ADVENTURES OF MARGARET O'BRIEN, THE
1947 (20 pgs. in color; slick cover; regular size) (Premium)
Bambury Fashions (Clothes)

	Good	Fine	Mint
In ''The Big City''-movie adaptation (Scarce)	13.00	40.00	90.00

ADVENTURES OF MIGHTY MOUSE (Mighty Mouse Advs. No. 1)
No. 2, Jan, 1952 - No. 18, May, 1955
St. John Publishing Co.

	Good	Fine	Mint
2	5.50	16.50	38.00
3-5	3.65	11.00	25.00
6-18	2.50	7.50	17.50

ADVENTURES OF MIGHTY MOUSE (2nd Series)
(Two No. 144's; formerly Paul Terry's Comics; No. 129-137 have nn's)(Becomes Mighty Mouse No. 161 on)
No. 126, Aug, 1955 - No. 160, Oct, 1963
St. John/Pines/Dell/Gold Key

	Good	Fine	Mint
126(8/55), 127(10/55), 128(11/55)-St. John	1.75	5.25	12.00
nn(129, 4/56)-144(8/59)-Pines	1.30	4.00	9.00
144(10-12/59)-155(7-9/62) Dell	1.15	3.50	8.00
156(10/62)-160(10/63) Gold Key	1.15	3.50	8.00

NOTE: *Early issues titled ''Paul Terry's Adventures of . . . .''*

ADVENTURES OF MIGHTY MOUSE (Formerly Mighty Mouse)
No. 166, Mar, 1979 - No. 172, Jan, 1980
Gold Key

	Good	Fine	Mint
166-172	.40	1.20	2.40

ADVENTURES OF MR. FROG & MISS MOUSE (See Dell Jr. Treasury No. 4)

ADVENTURES OF OZZIE AND HARRIET, THE (Radio)
Oct-Nov, 1949 - No. 5, June-July, 1950
National Periodical Publications

	Good	Fine	Mint
1-Photo-c	19.00	57.00	132.00
2	13.50	40.00	95.00
3-5	11.50	34.50	80.00

ADVENTURES OF PATORUZU
Aug, 1946 - Winter, 1946
Green Publishing Co.

	Good	Fine	Mint
nn's-Contains Animal Crackers reprints	1.15	3.50	8.00

ADVENTURES OF PINKY LEE, THE (TV)
July, 1955 - No. 5, Dec, 1955
Atlas Comics

	Good	Fine	Mint
1	6.50	19.50	45.00
2-5	4.00	12.00	28.00

ADVENTURES OF PIPSQUEAK, THE (Formerly Pat the Brat)
No. 34, Sept., 1959 - No. 39, July, 1960
Archie Publications (Radio Comics)

	Good	Fine	Mint
34	1.75	5.25	12.00
35-39	1.00	3.00	7.00

Advs. of Bob Hope #1, © *DC*

Advs. of Dean Martin & Jerry Lewis #3, © *DC*

Advs. of Ozzie & Harriet #3, © *DC*

Advs. of Rex the Wonder Dog #7. © DC

Advs. of Rick Raygun #1. © Stop Dragon

Advs. of the Jaguar #14. © AP

ADVENTURES OF QUAKE & QUISP, THE (See Quaker Oats "Plenty of Glutton")

ADVENTURES OF REX THE WONDER DOG, THE (Rex. . No. 1)
Jan-Feb, 1952 - No. 45, May-Jun, 1959; No. 46, Nov-Dec, 1959
National Periodical Publications

	Good	Fine	Mint
1-(Scarce)-Toth-a; Atom bomb-c	40.00	120.00	280.00
2-(Scarce)-Toth-a	20.00	60.00	140.00
3-(Scarce)-Toth-a	16.50	50.00	115.00
4,5	11.00	33.00	75.00
6-10	7.50	22.00	52.00
11-Atom bomb c/story	5.00	15.00	35.00
12-19: Last precode, 1-2/55	4.50	13.50	31.50
20-46	2.85	8.50	20.00

NOTE: ***Infantino, Gil Kane*** *art in most issues.*

ADVENTURES OF RICK RAYGUN, THE
Sept, 1986 - Present ($1.75, B&W)
Stop Dragon Comics

	Good	Fine	Mint
1-4	.35	1.00	2.00

ADVENTURES OF ROBIN HOOD, THE (Formerly Robin Hood)
No. 7, 9/57 - No. 8, 11/57 (Based on Richard Greene TV Show)
Magazine Enterprises (Sussex Publ. Co.)

	Good	Fine	Mint
7,8-Richard Greene photo-c. 7-Powell-a	2.00	6.00	14.00

ADVENTURES OF ROBIN HOOD, THE
March, 1974 - No. 7, Jan, 1975 (Disney Cartoon) (36 pgs.)
Gold Key

	Good	Fine	Mint
1(90291-403)-Part-r of $1.50 editions	.60	1.80	3.60
2-7: 1-7, part-r	.45	1.25	2.50

ADVENTURES OF SLIM AND SPUD, THE
1924 (3¾"x9¾")(104 pg. B&W strip reprints)
Prairie Farmer Publ. Co.

	Good	Fine	Mint
	6.00	18.00	42.00

ADVENTURES OF SPENCER SPOOK, THE (Also see Giggle Comics)
Oct, 1986 - Present ($1.95, B&W, 44pgs.)
Ace Comics (Animated Comics Ent.)

	Good	Fine	Mint
1-3: New & r-material	.35	1.00	2.00

ADVENTURES OF STUBBY, SANTA'S SMALLEST REINDEER, THE
nd (early 1940s) 12 pgs.
W. T. Grant Co. (Giveaway)

	Good	Fine	Mint
nn	2.00	6.00	12.00

ADVENTURES OF SUPERMAN (Formerly Superman)
No. 424, Jan, 1987 - Present
DC comics

	Good	Fine	Mint
424		.70	1.40
425-427		.50	1.00

ADVENTURES OF THE BIG BOY
1956 - 1984 (Giveaway)(East & West editions of early issues)
Timely Comics/Webs Adv. Corp./Illus. Features

	Good	Fine	Mint
1-Everett-a	45.00	135.00	315.00
2-Everett-a	22.00	65.00	154.00
3-5-Everett-a	10.00	30.00	70.00
6,7,9,10: 6-Sci/fic ish.	4.50	13.50	30.00
8-Everett-a	8.00	24.00	56.00
11-20	2.35	7.00	15.00
21-30	1.35	4.00	8.00
31-50	.70	2.00	4.00
51-100	.35	1.00	2.00
101-150		.50	1.00
151-240		.20	.40
241-306: 266-Superman x-over			.10
1-50 ('76-'84,Paragon Prod.)		.10	.20

	Good	Fine	Mint
Summer, 1959 ish, large size	3.35	10.00	20.00

ADVENTURES OF THE DETECTIVE
No date (1930's) 36 pgs.; 9½x12"; B&W (paper cover)
Humor Publ. Co.

	Good	Fine	Mint
Not reprints; Ace King by Martin Nadle	5.00	15.00	35.00
2nd version (printed in red & blue)	5.00	15.00	35.00

ADVENTURES OF THE DOVER BOYS
September, 1950 - No. 2, 1950 (No month given)
Archie Comics (Close-up)

	Good	Fine	Mint
1,2	2.50	7.50	17.50

ADVENTURES OF THE FLY (The Fly, No. 2; Fly Man No. 32-39)
Aug, 1959 - No. 30, Oct, 1964; No. 31, May, 1965
Archie Publications/Radio Comics

	Good	Fine	Mint
1-Shield app.; origin The Fly; S&K-c/a	17.50	52.00	122.00
2-Williamson, S&K, Powell-a	10.00	30.00	70.00
3-Origin retold; Davis, Powell-a	6.50	19.50	45.00
4-Adams-a(p)(1 panel); S&K-c; Powell-a; Shield x-over	4.65	14.00	32.00
5-10: 7-Black Hood app. 8,9-Shield x-over. 9-1st app. Cat Girl. 10-Black Hood app.	2.00	6.00	12.00
11-13,15-20: 20-Origin Flygirl retold	1.35	4.00	8.00
14-Intro. & origin Fly Girl	1.65	5.00	10.00
21-30: 23-Jaguar cameo. 29-Black Hood cameo. 30-Comet x-over in Fly Girl	1.00	3.00	6.00
31-Black Hood, Shield, Comet app.	1.00	3.00	6.00

NOTE: ***Tuska*** *a-1.* ***Simon*** *c-2-4.*

ADVENTURES OF THE JAGUAR, THE
Sept, 1961 - No. 15, Nov, 1963
Archie Publications (Radio Comics)

	Good	Fine	Mint
1-Origin Jaguar	5.00	15.00	35.00
2,3	2.35	7.00	16.00
4,5-Catgirl app.	1.50	4.50	9.00
6-10: 6-Catgirl app.	1.00	3.00	6.00
11-15: 13,14-Catgirl, Black Hood app. in both	.85	2.50	5.00

ADVENTURES OF THE OUTSIDERS, THE (Formerly Batman & The Outsiders)
No. 33, May, 1986 - Present
DC Comics

	Good	Fine	Mint
33-45: 39-The Outsiders (Baxter)-r begin		.35	.70

ADVENTURES OF THEOWN, THE
Oct, 1986 - No. 3, 1986 ($1.70, B&W)(mini-series)
Pyramid Comics

	Good	Fine	Mint
1-3		.75	1.50

ADVENTURES OF TINKER BELL (See 4-Color No. 982)

ADVENTURES OF TOM SAWYER (See Dell Jr. Treasury No. 10)

ADVENTURES OF YOUNG DR. MASTERS, THE
Aug, 1964 - No. 2, Nov, 1964
Archie Comics (Radio Comics)

	Good	Fine	Mint
1,2	.60	1.80	3.60

ADVENTURES ON THE PLANET OF THE APES
Oct, 1975 - No. 11, Dec, 1976
Marvel Comics Group

	Good	Fine	Mint
1-Reprints from Planet of the Apes in color; Starlin-c		.40	.80
2-11		.25	.50

NOTE: ***Alcala*** *a-10r, 11r.* ***Buckler*** *c-2p.* ***Nasser*** *c-7.* ***Ploog*** *a-1-9.* ***Starlin*** *c-6.*

ADVENTURES WITH SANTA CLAUS
No date (early 50's) (24 pgs.; 9¾x6¾"; paper cover) (Giveaway)

ADVS. WITH SANTA CLAUS (continued)
Promotional Publ. Co. (Murphy's Store)

	Good	Fine	Mint
Contains 8 pgs. ads	3.00	9.00	21.00
16 page version	3.00	9.00	21.00

AFRICA
1955
Magazine Enterprises

	Good	Fine	Mint
1(A-1 No. 137)-Cave Girl & Thun'da; Powell-c/a(4)	8.50	25.50	60.00

AFRICAN LION (See 4-Color No. 665)

AFTER DARK
May, 1955 - No. 8, Sept, 1955
Sterling Comics

	Good	Fine	Mint
6-8-Sekowsky-a in all	1.85	5.50	13.00

AGGIE MACK
Jan, 1948 - No. 8, Aug, 1949
Four Star Comics Corp./Superior Comics Ltd.

	Good	Fine	Mint
1-Feldstein-a, "Johnny Prep"	8.00	24.00	56.00
2,3-Kamen-c	4.35	13.00	30.00
4-Feldstein "Johnny Prep"; Kamen-c	5.65	17.00	40.00
5-8-Kamen c/a	4.00	12.00	28.00

AGGIE MACK (See 4-Color Comics No. 1335)

AGAINST BLACKSHARD 3-D
August, 1986 ($2.25)
Sirius Comics

	Good	Fine	Mint
1	.40	1.15	2.30

AIN'T IT A GRAND & GLORIOUS FEELING?
1922 (52 pgs.; 9x9¾"; stiff cardboard cover)
Whitman Publishing Co.

	Good	Fine	Mint
1921 daily strip-r; B&W, color-c; Briggs-a	7.50	22.50	52.00

AIR ACE (Bill Barnes No. 1-12)
V2/1, Jan, 1944 - V3/8(No. 20), Feb-Mar, 1947
Street & Smith Publications

	Good	Fine	Mint
V2/1	4.50	13.50	31.50
V2/2-12: 7-Powell-a	2.50	7.50	17.50
V3/1-6	1.85	5.50	13.00
V3/7-Powell bondage-c/a; all atomic ish.	4.65	14.00	32.00
V3/8 (V5/8 on-c)-Powell c/a	1.85	5.50	13.00

AIRBOY
July, 1986 - Present (No. 1-8, 20pgs., bi-weekly; No. 9-on, 36pgs, monthly)
Eclipse Comics

	Good	Fine	Mint
1	.40	1.25	2.50
2-5: 3-The Heap begins. 5-Valkyrie returns		.65	1.30
6-8		.50	1.00
9-11: 9-Skywolf begins. 11-Origin of Airboy's plane Birdie		.65	1.30

AIRBOY COMICS (Airfighters No. 1-22)
V2/11, Dec, 1945 - V10/4, May, 1953 (No V3/3)
Hillman Periodicals

	Good	Fine	Mint
V2/11	14.00	42.00	100.00
12-Valkyrie app.	10.00	30.00	70.00
V3/1,2(no No. 3)	8.00	24.00	56.00
4-The Heap app. in Skywolf	7.00	21.00	50.00
5-8: 6-Valkyrie app;	6.00	18.00	42.00
9-11: 9-Origin The Heap	6.00	18.00	42.00
12-Skywolf & Airboy x-over; Valkyrie app.	8.00	24.00	56.00
V4/1-Iron Lady app.	7.00	21.00	50.00
2-Rackman begins	4.00	12.00	28.00
3,12	4.00	12.00	28.00
4-Simon & Kirby-c	4.65	14.00	32.00
5-11-All S&K-a	7.00	21.00	50.00
V5/1-9: 4-Infantino Heap. 5-Skull-c	3.00	9.00	21.00
10,11: 10-Origin The Heap	3.00	9.00	21.00
12-Krigstein-a(p)	4.00	12.00	28.00
V6/1-3,5-12: 6,8-Origin The Heap	3.00	9.00	21.00
4-Origin retold	3.50	10.50	24.50
V7/1-12: 7,8,10-Origin The Heap	3.00	9.00	21.00
V8/1-3,6-12	2.50	7.50	17.50
4-Krigstein-a	4.00	12.00	28.00
5(No.100)	3.00	9.00	21.00
V9/1-6,8-12: 2-Valkyrie app.	2.50	7.50	17.50
7-One pg. Frazetta ad	3.00	9.00	21.00
V10/1-4	2.50	7.50	17.50

NOTE: ***Bolle*** *a-V4/12.* ***McWilliams*** *a-V3/7.* ***Powell*** *a-V7/3, V8/1, 6.* ***Starr*** *a-V5/1, 12.* ***Dick Wood*** *a-V4/12. Bondage-c V5/8.*

AIR FIGHTERS COMICS (Airboy No. 23 (V2/11) on)
Nov, 1941; No. 2, Nov, 1942 - V2/10, Fall, 1945
Hillman Periodicals

	Good	Fine	Mint
V1/1-(Produced by Funnies, Inc.); Black Commander only app.	68.00	205.00	475.00
2(11/42)-(Produced by Quality artists & Biro for Hillman); Origin Airboy & Iron Ace; Black Angel, Flying Dutchman & Skywolf begin; Fuje-a; Biro c/a	92.00	275.00	645.00
3-Origin The Heap & Skywolf	50.00	150.00	350.00
4	35.00	105.00	245.00
5,6	24.00	72.00	168.00
7-12	19.50	58.00	136.00
V2/1,3-9: 5-Flag-c; Fuje-a. 7-Valkyrie app.	18.50	55.00	130.00
2-Skywolf by Giunta; Flying Dutchman by Fuje; 1st meeting Valkyrie & Airboy (She worked for the Nazis in beginning).	20.00	60.00	140.00
10-Origin The Heap & Skywolf	20.00	60.00	140.00

AIR FORCES (See American Air Forces)

AIR WAR STORIES
Sept-Nov, 1964 - No. 8, Aug, 1966
Dell Publishing Co.

	Good	Fine	Mint
1-Painted-c; Glanzman c/a begins	.85	2.50	5.00
2-8	.50	1.50	3.00

ALADDIN (See Dell Jr. Treasury No. 2)

ALAN LADD (See Adventures of . . .)

ALARMING ADVENTURES
Oct, 1962 - No. 3, Feb, 1963
Harvey Publications

	Good	Fine	Mint
1	2.50	7.50	17.50
2,3	1.65	5.00	11.50

NOTE: ***Bailey*** *a-1,3.* ***Powell*** *a-2(2).* ***Severin*** *c-1-3.* ***Torres*** *a-2?* ***Tuska*** *a-1.* ***Williamson*** *a-1i, 2, 3.*

ALARMING TALES
Sept, 1957 - No. 6, Nov, 1958
Harvey Publications (Western Tales)

	Good	Fine	Mint
1-Kirby c/a(4)	4.00	12.00	28.00
2-Kirby-a(4)	4.00	12.00	28.00
3,4-Kirby-a	3.00	9.00	21.00
5-Kirby/Williamson-a	3.50	10.50	24.50
6-Torres-a	3.00	9.00	21.00

ALBEDO
April, 1985 - No. 5, 1986
Thoughts And Images

Aggie Mack #1, © SUPR

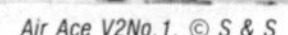
Air Ace V2No.1, © S & S

Airboy Comics V4No.9, © HILL

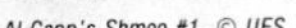
Al Capp's Shmoo #1, © UFS

Algie #1, © Timor

Alien Legion #7, © MCG

ALBEDO (continued)

	Good	Fine	Mint
0-Yellow cover; 50 copies	29.00	87.00	175.00
0-White cover, 450 copies	25.00	75.00	150.00
0-Blue, 1st printing, 500 copies	12.50	37.50	75.00
0-Blue, 2nd printing, 1000 copies	8.35	25.00	50.00
1-Dark red	17.00	50.00	100.00
1-Bright red	12.00	35.00	70.00
2	7.00	20.00	40.00
3	1.20	3.50	7.00
4,6	1.85	5.00	10.00
5	.85	2.50	5.00

(Prices vary widely on this series)

ALBERTO (See The Crusaders)

ALBERT THE ALLIGATOR & POGO POSSUM (See 4-Color Comics No. 105, 148)

ALBUM OF CRIME (See Fox Giants)

ALBUM OF LOVE (See Fox Giants)

AL CAPP'S DOGPATCH (Also see Mammy Yokum)
No. 71, June, 1949 - No. 4, Dec, 1949
Toby Press

	Good	Fine	Mint
71(No. 1)-R-/from Tip Top No. 112-114	8.00	24.00	56.00
2-4: 4-R-/from Li'l Abner No. 73	5.65	17.00	40.00

AL CAPP'S SHMOO (Also see Oxydol-Dreft)
July, 1949 - No. 5, April, 1950 (None by Al Capp)
Toby Press

	Good	Fine	Mint
1	16.00	48.00	110.00
2-5: 3-Sci-fi trip to moon. 4-X-Mas-c; origin/1st app. Super-Shmoo	11.50	34.50	70.00

AL CAPP'S WOLF GAL
1951 - No. 2, 1952
Toby Press

	Good	Fine	Mint
1,2-Edited-r from Li'l Abner No. 63,64	13.00	40.00	90.00

ALEXANDER THE GREAT (See 4-Color No. 688)

ALGIE
Dec, 1953 - No. 3, 1954
Timor Publ. Co.

	Good	Fine	Mint
1	1.25	3.75	9.00
2,3	.85	2.50	6.00
Accepted Reprint No. 2(nd)	.55	1.65	4.00
Super Reprint 15	.40	1.20	2.80

ALICE (New Advs. in Wonderland)
1952
Ziff-Davis Publ. Co.

	Good	Fine	Mint
10-Spanking-c; Berg-a	7.00	21.00	50.00
11-Dave Berg-a	3.50	10.50	24.00
2-Dave Berg-a	3.00	9.00	18.00

ALICE AT MONKEY ISLAND (See The Advs. of Alice)
No. 3, 1946
Pentagon Publ. Co. (Civil Service)

	Good	Fine	Mint
3	3.00	9.00	21.00

ALICE IN BLUNDERLAND
1952 (Paper cover, 16 pages in color)
Industrial Services

	Good	Fine	Mint
nn-Facts about big government waste and inefficiency	10.50	32.00	74.00

ALICE IN WONDERLAND (See Advs. of Alice, 4-Color No. 331,341, Dell Jr. Treasury No. 1, Movie Comics, Single Series No. 24, Walt Disney Showcase No. 22, and World's Greatest Stories)

ALICE IN WONDERLAND
1965; 1982
Western Printing Company/Whitman Publ. Co.

	Good	Fine	Mint
. . . Meets Santa Claus(1950s), nd, 16pgs	2.75	8.00	16.00
Rexall Giveaway(1965, 16 pgs., 5x7¼'') Western Printing (TV-Hanna-Barbera)	2.00	6.00	12.00
Wonder Bakery Giveaway(16 pgs, color, nn, nd) (Continental Baking Co. (1969)	2.00	6.00	12.00
1-(Whitman; 1982)-r/4-Color 331		.40	.80

ALICE IN WONDERLAND MEETS SANTA
nd (16 pgs., 6-5/8x9-11/16'', paper cover)
No publisher (Giveaway)

Good	Fine	Mint
10.00	30.00	60.00

ALIEN DUCKLINGS
Oct, 1987 - Present ($1.75, B&W)
Blackthorne Publ.

	Good	Fine	Mint
1	.30	.90	1.80

ALIEN ENCOUNTERS (Replaces Alien Worlds)
June, 1985 - Present ($1.75; Baxter) (Mature readers)
Eclipse Comics

	Good	Fine	Mint
1-10: Nudity, strong language	.35	1.00	2.00

ALIEN LEGION
April, 1984 - Present
Epic Comics (Marvel)

	Good	Fine	Mint
1-$2.00 cover, high quality paper	.60	1.75	3.50
2-5	.35	1.00	2.00
6-10	.30	.85	1.70
11-18		.75	1.50

NOTE: ***Austin*** *a-1i, 4i; c-3i-5i.*

ALIENS, THE (Captain Johner and . . .)
Sept-Dec, 1967; No. 2, May, 1982
Gold Key

	Good	Fine	Mint
1-Reprints from Magnus No. 1,3,4,6-10, all by Russ Manning	1.00	3.00	6.00
2-Magnus-r/No. 1 by Manning		.50	1.00

ALIEN TERROR (See 3-D Alien Terror)

ALIEN WORLDS
12/82; No. 2, 6/83 - No. 7, 4/84; No. 8, 11/84 - No. 9, 1/85
(Baxter paper, $1.50)
Pacific Comics No. 1-7/Eclipse No. 8, 9

	Good	Fine	Mint
1-Williamson, Redondo-a	.45	1.40	2.80
2-7: 4-Nudity scenes	.35	1.20	2.40
8-Williamson-a	.30	.85	1.70
9-($1.75 cover); Williamson-a	.35	1.00	2.00

NOTE: ***Bolton*** *c-5, 9.* ***Brunner*** *a-6p, 9; c-6.* ***Conrad*** *a-1.* ***Corben*** *a-7.* ***J. Jones*** *a-4p.* ***Krenkel*** *a-6.* ***Morrow*** *a-7.* ***Perez*** *a-7.* ***Stevens*** *a-2, 4i; c-2, 4.* ***Williamson/Frazetta*** *a-4r/Witzend No. 1.*

ALIEN WORLDS 3-D (See 3-Dimensional Alien Worlds)

ALL-AMERICAN COMICS (. . . Western No. 103-126, . . . Men of War No. 127 on)
April, 1939 - No. 102, Oct, 1948
National Periodical Publications/All-American

	Good	Fine	Mint
1-Hop Harrigan, Scribbly, Toonerville Folks, Ben Webster, Spot Savage, Mutt & Jeff, Red White & Blue, Adv. in the Unknown, Tippie, Reg'lar Fellers, Skippy, Bobby Thatcher, Mystery Men of Mars, Daiseybelle, & Wiley of West Point begin	115.00	345.00	805.00
2-Ripley's Believe It or Not begins, ends No. 24	50.00	150.00	350.00

ALL-AMERICAN COMICS (continued)

Issue	Good	Fine	Mint
3-5: 5-The American Way begins, ends No. 10	35.00	105.00	245.00
6,7: 6-Last Spot Savage; Popsicle Pete begins, ends No. 26, 28. 7-Last Bobby Thatcher	25.00	75.00	175.00
8-The Ultra Man begins	40.00	120.00	280.00
9,10: 10-X-Mas-c	32.00	95.00	225.00
11-15: 12-Last Toonerville Folks. 15-Last Tippie & Reg'lar Fellars	25.00	75.00	175.00
16-Origin & 1st app. Green Lantern (Rare), created by Martin Nodell. Inspired by Aladdin's Lamp; the suggested alter ego name Alan Ladd, was never capitalized on. It was changed to Alan Scott before appearance of movie star Alan Ladd	725.00	2175.00	5075.00
(Prices vary widely on this book)			
17-(Scarce)	200.00	600.00	1400.00
18	105.00	315.00	735.00
19-Origin & 1st app. The Atom; Last Ultra Man	155.00	465.00	1085.00
20-Atom dons costume; Hunkle becomes the Red Tornado; Rescue on Mars begins, ends No. 25; 1 pg. origin Green Lantern	90.00	270.00	630.00
21-23: 21-Last Wiley of West Point & Skippy. 23-Last Daiseybelle; 3 Idiots begin, end No. 82	66.00	200.00	460.00
24-Sisty & Dinky become the Cyclone Kids; Ben Webster ends. Origin Dr. Mid-Nite & Sargon, The Sorcerer in text with app.	70.00	210.00	490.00
25-Origin & 1st story app. Dr. Mid-Nite by Stan Asch; Hop Harrigan becomes Guardian Angel; last Adventure in the Unknown	110.00	330.00	770.00
26-Origin & 1st story app. Sargon, the Sorcerer	75.00	225.00	525.00
27: No. 27-32 are misnumbered in indicia with correct No. appearing on cover. Intro. Doiby Dickles, Green Lantern's sidekick	75.00	225.00	525.00
28-Hop Harrigan gives up costumed i.d.	42.00	125.00	295.00
29,30	42.00	125.00	295.00
31-40: 35-Doiby learns Green Lantern's i. d.	32.00	95.00	225.00
41-50: 50-Sargon ends	27.00	80.00	190.00
51-60: 59-Scribbly & The Red Tornado ends	22.00	65.00	154.00
61-Origin Solomon Grundy	54.00	162.00	380.00
62-70: 70-Kubert Sargon; intro Sargon's helper, Maximillian O'Leary	22.00	65.00	154.00
71-Last Red White & Blue	17.00	51.00	120.00
72-Black Pirate begins (not in No. 74-82); last Atom	17.00	51.00	120.00
73-80: 73-Winky, Blinky & Noddy begins, ends No. 82	17.00	51.00	120.00
81-88,90: 90-Origin Icicle	17.00	51.00	120.00
89-Origin Harlequin	22.00	65.00	154.00
91-99-Last Hop Harrigan	17.00	51.00	120.00
100-1st app. Johnny Thunder by Alex Toth	33.00	100.00	230.00
101-Last Mutt & Jeff	22.00	65.00	154.00
102-Last Green Lantern, Black Pirate & Dr. Mid-Nite	22.00	65.00	154.00

NOTE: *No Atom in 47,62-69.* ***Kinstler*** *Black Pirate-89.* ***Stan Aschmeier*** *a-25, 40, 55, 70; c-7.* ***Moldoff*** *c-16-23.* ***Paul Reinman*** *a-55, 70; c-55, 70.* ***Toth*** *a-88, 92, 96, 98-102; c-92, 96-102.*

ALL-AMERICAN MEN OF WAR (Previously All-American Western)
No. 127, Aug-Sept, 1952 - No. 117, Sept-Oct, 1966
National Periodical Publications

Issue	Good	Fine	Mint
127 (1952)	14.00	42.00	100.00
128 (1952)	10.00	30.00	70.00
2(12-1/'52-53)-5	8.00	24.00	55.00
6-10	5.00	15.00	36.00
11-20	3.50	10.50	24.00
21-28	2.65	8.00	18.00
29,30,32-Wood-a	3.50	10.50	24.00
31,33-50	1.50	4.50	9.00
51-66	1.00	3.10	6.20
67-1st Gunner & Sarge by Andru	1.15	3.50	7.00
68-80	.65	2.00	4.00
81-100: 82-Johnny Cloud begins, ends No. 111,114,115	.35	1.00	2.00
101-117: 112-Balloon Buster series begins, ends No. 114,116; 115-Johnny Cloud app.		.60	1.20

NOTE: ***Drucker*** *a-47,65,74,77.* ***Heath*** *a-27, 32, 47, 95; c-95, 100.* ***Krigstein*** *a-128('52), 2, 3, 5.* ***Kirby*** *a-29.* ***Kubert*** *a-29, 36, 38, 41, 43, 47, 49, 50, 52, 53, 55, 56, 60, 63, 65, 69, 71-73, 103; c-41, 77. Tank Killer in 69, 71, 76 by* ***Kubert.***

ALL-AMERICAN SPORTS
October, 1967
Charlton Comics

Issue	Good	Fine	Mint
1		.30	.60

ALL-AMERICAN WESTERN (Formerly All-American Comics; Becomes All-American Men of War)
No. 103, Nov, 1948 - No. 126, June-July, 1952 (52pgs, 103-121)
National Periodical Publications

Issue	Good	Fine	Mint
103-Johnny Thunder & his horse Black Lightning continues by Toth, ends No. 126; Foley of The Fighting 5th, Minstrel Maverick, & Overland Coach begin; Captain Tootsie by Beck; mentioned in ***Love and Death***	12.00	36.00	85.00
104-Kubert-a	8.50	25.50	60.00
105,107-Kubert-a	8.00	24.00	56.00
106,108-110,112: 112-Kurtzman "Pot-Shot Pete," 1 pg.	6.00	18.00	42.00
111,114-116-Kubert-a	6.75	20.00	47.00
113-Intro. Swift Deer, J. Thunder's new sidekick; classic Toth-c; Kubert-a	8.00	24.00	56.00
117-120,122-125	5.50	16.50	38.00
121-Kubert-a	5.50	16.50	38.00
126-Last issue	5.50	16.50	38.00

NOTE: ***Kubert*** *a-103-105, 107, 111, 112(1 pg.), 113-116, 121.* ***Toth*** *c/a 103-126.*

ALL COMICS
1945
Chicago Nite Life News

Issue	Good	Fine	Mint
1	4.00	12.00	28.00

ALLEY OOP (See 4-Color No. 3 and Super Book No. 9)

ALLEY OOP
No. 10, 1947 - No. 18, Oct, 1949
Standard Comics

Issue	Good	Fine	Mint
10	11.00	33.00	76.00
11-18: 17,18-Schomburg-c	8.00	24.00	56.00

ALLEY OOP
Nov, 1955 - No. 3, March, 1956 (Newspaper reprints)
Argo Publ.

Issue	Good	Fine	Mint
1	8.00	24.00	56.00
2,3	5.00	15.00	35.00

ALLEY OOP
12-2/62-63 - No. 2, 9-11/63
Dell Publishing Co.

Issue	Good	Fine	Mint
1,2	4.00	12.00	28.00

ALL-FAMOUS CRIME
1949 - No. 10, Nov, 1951
Star Publications

Issue	Good	Fine	Mint
1	4.35	13.00	30.00
2	2.65	8.00	18.00
3-5	2.35	7.00	16.00

All-American Comics #16, © DC

All-American Western #105, © DC

Alley Oop #17, © NEA Service

All-Flash #1, © DC

All Funny Comics #13, © DC

All Great #13, © FOX

ALL-FAMOUS CRIME (continued) — Good / Fine / Mint

6-8,10 — 2.00 6.00 14.00

9-Used in **SOTI**, illo-''The wish to hurt or kill couples in lovers' lanes is not uncommon perversion;'' L.B. Cole-c/a(r)/Law-Crime No. 3 — 7.00 21.00 50.00

NOTE: *All have* ***L.B. Cole*** *covers.*

ALL FAMOUS CRIME STORIES (See Fox Giants)

ALL-FAMOUS POLICE CASES
Oct, 1951 - No. 16, Sept, 1954
Star Publications

1 — 4.35 13.00 30.00
2 — 2.50 7.50 18.00
3-6,9-16 — 2.35 7.00 16.00
7-Kubert-a — 3.00 9.00 21.00
8-Marijuana story — 3.00 9.00 21.00

NOTE: ***L. B. Cole*** *c-all; a-15, 1pg.* ***Hollingsworth*** *a-15.*

ALL-FLASH (. . . Quarterly No. 1-5)
Summer, 1941 - No. 32, Dec-Jan, 1947-48
National Periodical Publications/All-American

1-Origin The Flash retold by E. E. Hibbard — 175.00 525.00 1225.00
2-Origin recap — 68.00 205.00 475.00
3,4 — 45.00 135.00 315.00
5-Winky, Blinky & Noddy begins, ends No. 32 — 35.00 105.00 245.00
6-10 — 30.00 90.00 210.00
11-13: 12-Origin The Thinker. 13-The King app. — 24.00 72.00 168.00
14-Green Lantern cameo — 27.00 81.00 190.00
15-20: 18-Mutt & Jeff begins, ends No. 22 — 22.00 65.00 154.00
21-31 — 20.00 60.00 140.00
32-Origin The Fiddler; 1st Star Sapphire — 24.00 72.00 168.00

NOTE: *Book length stories in 2-13,16. Bondage c-31, 32.*

ALL FOR LOVE (Young Love V3/5-on)
Apr-May, 1957 - V3No.4, Dec-Jan, 1959-60
Prize Publications

V1No.1 — 2.00 6.00 14.00
2-6: 5-Orlando-c — 1.15 3.50 8.00
V2No.1-6 — .85 2.50 6.00
V3No.1-4: 2-Powell-a — .60 1.80 3.60

ALL FUNNY COMICS
Winter, 1943-44 - No. 23, May-June, 1948
National Periodical Publications (Detective)

1-Genius Jones, Buzzy (ends No. 4) begins; Bailey-a — 15.00 45.00 105.00
2 — 7.50 23.00 52.00
3-10 — 5.00 15.00 35.00
11-13,15,18,19-Genius Jones app. — 4.35 13.00 30.00
14,17,20-23 — 3.00 9.00 21.00
16-DC Super Heroes app. — 7.00 21.00 50.00

ALL GOOD COMICS (See Fox Giants)
Spring, 1946 (36 pgs.)
Fox Features Syndicate

1-Joy Family, Dick Transom, Rick Evans, One Round Hogan — 5.50 16.50 38.00

ALL GOOD
Oct, 1949 (260 pages) (50 cents)
St. John Publishing Co.

(8 St. John comics bound together) — 35.00 105.00 245.00

NOTE: *Also see Li'l Audrey Yearbook & Treasury of Comics.*

ALL GREAT (See Fox Giants)
1946 (36 pgs.)
Fox Features Syndicate — Good / Fine / Mint

1-Crazy House, Bertie Benson Boy Detective, Gussie the Gob — 4.35 13.00 30.00

ALL GREAT
nd (1945?) (132 pgs.)
William H. Wise & Co.

nn-Capt. Jack Terry, Joan Mason, Girl Reporter, Baron Doomsday; Torture scenes — 12.00 36.00 84.00

ALL GREAT (Dagar, Desert Hawk No. 14 on)
No. 14, Oct, 1947 - No. 13, Dec, 1947
Fox Features Syndicate

14-Brenda Starr-r (Scarce) — 12.00 36.00 84.00
13-Origin Dagar, Desert Hawk; Brenda Starr (all-r); Kamen-c — 11.50 34.00 80.00

ALL-GREAT CONFESSIONS (See Fox Giants)

ALL GREAT CRIME STORIES (See Fox Giants)

ALL GREAT JUNGLE ADVENTURES (See Fox Giants)

ALL HERO COMICS
March, 1943 (100 pgs.) (Cardboard cover)
Fawcett Publications

1-Captain Marvel Jr., Capt. Midnight, Golden Arrow, Ibis the Invincible, Spy Smasher, & Lance O'Casey — 55.00 165.00 385.00

ALL HUMOR COMICS
Spring, 1946 - No. 17, December, 1949
Quality Comics Group

1 — 4.50 13.50 31.00
2-Atomic Tot sty; Gustavson-a — 2.25 6.75 16.00
3-9: 5-1st app. Hickory? — 1.65 5.00 11.50
10-17 — 1.15 3.50 8.00

ALL LOVE (. . . Romances No. 26)(Formerly Ernie)
No. 26, May, 1949 - No. 32, May, 1950
Ace Periodicals (Current Books)

26(No. 1)-Ernie, Lily Belle app. — 2.00 6.00 14.00
27-L. B. Cole-a — 2.50 7.50 17.50
28-32 — 1.30 4.00 9.00

ALL-NEGRO COMICS
June, 1947 (15 cents)
All-Negro Comics

1 (Rare) — 60.00 180.00 420.00

NOTE: *Seldom found in fine or mint condition; many copies have brown pages.*

ALL-NEW COLLECTORS' EDITION (Formerly Limited Collectors' Ed.)
Jan, 1978 - No. C-62, 1979 (No. 54-58: 76 pgs.)
DC Comics, Inc.

C-53-Rudolph the Red-Nosed Reindeer — .50 1.00
C-54-Superman Vs. Wonder Woman — .25 .75 1.50
C-55-Superboy & the Legion of Super-Heroes — .70 2.00 4.00
C-56-Superman Vs. Muhammad Ali: story & wraparound Adams-c — .35 1.00 2.00
C-58-Superman Vs. Shazam — .60 1.20
C-60-Rudolph's Summer Fun(8/78) — .60 1.20
C-62-Superman the Movie (68 pgs.; 1979) plus story — .60 1.20

ALL-NEW COMICS (. . . Short Story Comics No. 1-3)
Jan, 1943 - No. 14, Nov, 1946; No. 15, Mar-Apr, 1947
Family Comics (Harvey Publications)

1-Steve Case, Crime Rover, Johnny Rebel, Kayo Kane, The Echo, Night Hawk, Ray O'Light, Detective Shane begin; Red Blazer on cover only; Sultan-a — 40.00 120.00 280.00

ALL-NEW COMICS (continued)

	Good	Fine	Mint
2-Origin Scarlet Phantom by Kubert	20.00	60.00	140.00
3	15.00	45.00	105.00
4,5	13.00	40.00	90.00
6-The Boy Heroes & Red Blazer (text story) begin, end No. 12; Black Cat app.; intro. Sparky in Red Blazer	15.00	45.00	105.00
7-Kubert, Powell-a; Black Cat & Zebra app.	15.00	45.00	105.00
8-Shock Gibson app.; Kubert, Powell-a; Schomburg bondage-c	15.00	45.00	105.00
9-Black Cat app.; Kubert-a	15.00	45.00	105.00
10-The Zebra app.; Kubert-a(3)	13.00	40.00	90.00
11-Girl Commandos, Man In Black app.	13.00	40.00	90.00
12-Kubert-a	13.00	40.00	90.00
13-Stuntman by Simon & Kirby; Green Hornet, Joe Palooka, Flying Fool app.	15.00	45.00	105.00
14-The Green Hornet & The Man in Black Called Fate by Powell, Joe Palooka app.	13.00	40.00	90.00
15-(Rare)-Small size (5½x8½''; B&W; 32 pgs.). Distributed to mail subscribers only. Black Cat and Joe Palooka app. Estimated value....$200-250			

NOTE: Also see Boy Explorers No. 2, Flash Gordon No. 5, and Stuntman No. 3. ***Powell** a-11. **Schomburg** c-7,8,10,11.*

ALL-OUT WAR
Sept-Oct, 1979 - No. 6, Aug, 1980 ($1.00)
DC Comics, Inc.

	Good	Fine	Mint
1-The Viking Commando(origin), Force Three(origin), & Black Eagle Squadron begin		.25	.50
2-6		.25	.50

NOTE: ***Evans** a-1-6. **Kubert** c-1-6.*

ALL PICTURE ADVENTURE MAGAZINE
Oct, 1952 - No. 2, Nov, 1952 (100 pg. Giants)
St. John Publishing Co.

	Good	Fine	Mint
1-War comics	10.50	31.50	74.00
2-Horror-crime comics	13.50	40.00	95.00

NOTE: *Above books contain three St. John comics rebound; variations possible. **Baker** art known in both.*

ALL PICTURE ALL TRUE LOVE STORY
October, 1952 (100 pages)
St. John Publishing Co.

	Good	Fine	Mint
1-Canteen Kate by Matt Baker	20.00	60.00	140.00

ALL-PICTURE COMEDY CARNIVAL
October, 1952 (100 pages)
St. John Publishing Co.

	Good	Fine	Mint
1-(4 rebound comics)-Contents can vary; Baker-a	18.00	54.00	125.00

ALL REAL CONFESSION MAGAZINE (See Fox Giants)

ALL ROMANCES (Mr. Risk No. 7 on)
Aug, 1949 - No. 6, June, 1950
A. A. Wyn (Ace Periodicals)

	Good	Fine	Mint
1	2.50	7.50	17.50
2	1.30	4.00	9.00
3-6	1.15	3.50	8.00

ALL-SELECT COMICS (Blonde Phantom No. 12 on)
Fall, 1943 - No. 11, Fall, 1946
Timely Comics (Daring Comics)

	Good	Fine	Mint
1-Capt. America, Human Torch, Sub-Mariner begin; Black Widow app.	135.00	405.00	945.00
2-Red Skull app.	60.00	180.00	420.00
3-The Whizzer begins	42.00	125.00	295.00
4,5-Last Sub-Mariner	34.50	104.00	240.00
6-The Destroyer app.	26.50	80.00	185.00
7-9: 8-No Whizzer	26.50	80.00	185.00
10-The Destroyer & Sub-Mariner app.; last Capt. America & Human Torch issue	26.50	80.00	185.00
11-1st app. Blonde Phantom; Miss America app.	45.00	135.00	315.00

NOTE: ***Schomburg** c-2,4,9,10. No. 7 & 8 show 1944 in indicia, but should be 1945.*

ALL SPORTS COMICS (Formerly Real Sports Comics; becomes All Time Sports Comics No. 4 on)
No. 2, Dec-Jan, 1948-49, No. 3, Feb-Mar, 1949
Hillman Periodicals

	Good	Fine	Mint
2-Krigstein-a(p), Powell, Starr-a	5.00	15.00	35.00
3-Mort Lawrence-a	4.00	12.00	28.00

ALL STAR COMICS (. . . Western No. 58 on)
Summer, 1940 - No. 57, Feb-Mar, 1951; No. 58, Jan-Feb, 1976 - No. 74, Sept-Oct, 1978
National Periodical Publ./All-American/DC Comics

	Good	Fine	Mint
1-The Flash(No. 1 by Harry Lampert), Hawkman(by Shelly), Hourman, The Sandman, The Spectre, Biff Bronson, Red White & Blue begin; Ultra Man's only app.	400.00	1200.00	2800.00
2-Green Lantern, Johnny Thunder begin	190.00	570.00	1330.00
3-Origin Justice Society of America; Dr. Fate & The Atom begin, Red Tornado cameo; last Red White & Blue; reprinted in Famous First Edition	680.00	2040.00	4760.00
4	180.00	540.00	1260.00
5-Intro. & 1st app. Shiera Sanders as Hawkgirl	150.00	450.00	1050.00
6-Johnny Thunder joins JSA	110.00	330.00	770.00
7-Batman, Superman, Flash cameo; last Hourman; Doiby Dickles app.	110.00	330.00	770.00
8-Origin & 1st app. Wonder Woman(added as 8pgs. making book 76pgs.;origin cont'd in Sensation No. 1); Dr. Fate dons new helmet; Dr.Mid-Nite, Hop Harrigan text stories & Starman begin; Shiera app.; Hop Harrigan JSA guest	250.00	750.00	1750.00
9-Shiera app.	110.00	330.00	770.00
10-Flash, Green Lantern cameo, Sandman new costume	110.00	330.00	770.00
11-Wonder Woman begins; Spectre cameo; Shiera app.	100.00	300.00	700.00
12-Wonder Woman becomes JSA Secretary	100.00	300.00	700.00
13-15: Sandman w/Sandy in No. 14 & 15; 15-Origin Brain Wave; Shiera app.	90.00	270.00	630.00
16-19: 19-Sandman w/Sandy	72.00	215.00	505.00
20-Dr. Fate & Sandman cameo	72.00	215.00	505.00
21-Spectre & Atom cameo; Dr. Fate by Kubert; Dr. Fate, Sandman end	62.00	185.00	435.00
22,23: 22-Last Hop Harrigan; Flag-c. 23-Origin Psycho Pirate; last Spectre & Starman	62.00	185.00	435.00
24-Flash & Green Lantern cameo; Mr. Terrific only app.; Wildcat, JSA guest; Kubert Hawkman begins	62.00	185.00	435.00
25-27: 25-The Flash & Green Lantern start again. 27-Wildcat, JSA guest	57.00	170.00	400.00
28-32	47.00	141.00	330.00
33-Solomon Grundy, Hawkman, Doiby Dickles app.	90.00	270.00	630.00
34,35-Johnny Thunder cameo in both	45.00	135.00	315.00
36-Batman & Superman JSA guests	90.00	270.00	630.00
37-Johnny Thunder cameo; origin Injustice Society; last Kubert Hawkman	47.00	141.00	330.00
38-Black Canary begins; JSA Death issue	54.00	162.00	378.00
39,40: 39-Last Johnny Thunder	38.00	115.00	265.00
41-Black Canary joins JSA; Injustice Society app.	35.00	105.00	245.00
42-Atom & the Hawkman don new costume	35.00	105.00	245.00
43-49	35.00	105.00	245.00
50-Frazetta art, 3 pgs.	45.00	135.00	315.00
51-56	35.00	105.00	245.00

All-New Comics #2, © HARV

All-Select Comics #6, © MCG

All Star Comics #3, © DC

All-Star Squadron #25, © DC

All Star Western #87, © DC

All Top Comics #11, © FOX

ALL STAR COMICS (continued) — Good / Fine / Mint

57-Kubert-a, 6 pgs. (Scarce) 47.00 141.00 330.00
58('76)-Flash, Hawkman, Dr. Mid-Nite, Wildcat, Dr. Fate, Green Lantern, Star Spangled Kid, & Robin app.; intro Power Girl .25 .50
59-74: 69-1st app. Huntress .25 .50

NOTE: *No Atom-27, 36; no Dr. Fate-13; no Flash-8, 9, 11-23; no Green Lantern-8, 9, 11-23; no Johnny Thunder-5, 36; no Wonder Woman-9, 10, 23.* **Baily** *a-1-10, 12, 13, 14i, 15-20.* **Buckler** *c-63, 66p.* **Burnley** *Starman-8-13; c-12, 13.* **Grell** *c-58.* **Kubert** *Hawkman-24-30, 33-37.* **Moldoff** *Hawkman-3-23; c-11.* **Simon & Kirby** *Sandman-14-17, 19.* **Giffen** *a-60p-63p.* **Staton** *a-66-74p; c-71-74.* **Toth** *a-37(2), 38(2), 40, 41; c-38, 41.* **Wood** *a-58i-63i, 64, 65; c-63-65.*

ALL-STAR SQUADRON
Sept, 1981 - No. 67, March, 1987
DC Comics

1-Original Atom, Hawkman, Dr. Mid-Nite, Robotman (origin), Plastic Man, Johnny Quick, Liberty Belle, Shining Knight begin .25 .80 1.60
2 .50 1.00
3-24: 5-Danette Reilly becomes new Firebrand. 12-Origin G.A. Hawkman retold. 23-Intro/origin The Amazing Man .40 .80
25-1st Infinity, Inc. .70 2.10 4.20
26-Origin Infinity, Inc. .50 1.50 3.00
27-49: 31-Origin Freedom Fighters of Earth-X. 41-Origin Starman. 47-Origin Dr. Fate .40 .80
50-Double size; Crisis x-over .25 .70 1.40
51-56-Crisis x-over .45 .90
57-67: 61-Origin Liberty Belle. 62-Origin The Shining Knight. 63-Origin Robotman. 65-Origin Johnny Quick. 66-Origin Tarantula .40 .80
Annual 1(11/82)-Retells origin of G.A. Atom, Guardian & Wildcat .50 1.00
Annual 2(11/83)-Infinity, Inc. app. .50 1.00
Annual 3(9/84) .65 1.30

NOTE: **Kubert** *c-2, 7-18.*

ALL-STAR STORY OF THE DODGERS, THE
April, 1979 (Full Color) ($1.00)
Stadium Communications

1 .50 1.00

ALL STAR WESTERN (All Star No. 1-57)
Apr-May, 1951 - No. 119, June-July, 1961
National Periodical Publications

58-Trigger Twins (end No. 116), Strong Bow, The Roving Ranger & Don Caballero begin 13.00 40.00 90.00
59,60: Last 52 pgs. 6.50 19.50 45.00
61-66: 61,64-Toth-a 5.50 16.50 38.00
67-Johnny Thunder begins; Gil Kane-a 6.50 19.50 45.00
68-81: Last precode, 2-3/55 3.00 9.00 21.00
82-98 2.35 7.00 16.00
99-Frazetta-a r-/Jimmy Wakely No. 4 4.50 13.50 31.50
100 3.00 9.00 21.00
101-107,109-116,118,119 1.85 5.50 13.00
108-Origin Johnny Thunder 3.35 10.00 23.00
117-Origin Super Chief 3.00 9.00 21.00

NOTE: **Infantino** *art in most issues. Madame app.-No. 117-119.*

ALL STAR WESTERN (Weird Western Tales No. 12 on)
Aug-Sept, 1970 - No. 11, Apr-May, 1972
National Periodical Publications

1-Reprints; Infantino-a .35 1.00 2.00
2-Outlaw begins; El Diablo by Morrow begins .30 .80 1.60
3-8: 3-Origin El Diablo. 5-Last Outlaw ish. 6-Billy the Kid begins, ends No. 8 .30 .80 1.60
9-Frazetta-a, 3pgs.(r) .50 1.50 3.00
10-Jonah Hex begins 2.00 6.00 12.00

Good / Fine / Mint

11 .70 2.00 4.00

NOTE: **Adams** *c-1-5;* **Aparo** *a-5.* **G. Kane** *a-3, 4, 6.* **Morrow** *a-2-4, 10, 11. No. 7-11 have 52 pages.*

ALL SURPRISE
Fall, 1943 - No. 12, Winter, 1946-47
Timely/Marvel (CPC)

1-Super Rabbit & Gandy & Sourpuss 7.00 21.00 50.00
2 3.50 10.50 25.00
3-10,12 2.50 7.50 17.00
11-Kurtzman "Pigtales" art 4.35 13.00 30.00

ALL TEEN (Formerly All Winners; Teen Comics No. 21 on)
No. 20, January, 1947
Marvel Comics (WFP)

20 2.35 7.00 16.00

ALL THE FUNNY FOLKS
1926 (hardcover, 112 pgs., 11½x3½") (Full color)
World Press Today, Inc.

nn-Barney Google, Spark Plug, Jiggs & Maggie, Tillie The Toiler, Happy Hooligan, Hans & Fritz, Toots & Casper, etc. 14.00 42.00 95.00

ALL-TIME ROMANCE
1955
Ajax/Farrell Publications

22 1.15 3.50 8.00

ALL-TIME SPORTS COMICS (Formerly All Sports Comics)
No. 4, Apr-May, 1949 - No. 7, Oct-Nov, 1949
Hillman Periodicals

4 3.50 10.50 24.00
5-7: 5-Powell-a. 7-Krigstein-a(p) 2.50 7.50 17.50

ALL TOP
1944 (132 pages)
William H. Wise Co.

Capt. V, Merciless the Sorceress, Red Robbins, One Round Hogan, Mike the M.P., Snooky, Pussy Katnip app. 10.00 30.00 70.00

ALL TOP COMICS (My Experience No. 19 on)
1945; No. 2, Sum, 1946 - No. 18, Mar, 1949; 1957 - 1959
Fox Features Synd./Green Publ./Norlen Mag.

1-Cosmo Cat & Flash Rabbit begin 7.00 21.00 50.00
2 4.00 12.00 28.00
3-7 3.00 9.00 21.00
8-Blue Beetle, Phantom Lady, & Rulah, Jungle Goddess begin (11/47); Kamen-c 45.00 135.00 315.00
9-Kamen-c 26.00 78.00 182.00
10-Kamen bondage-c 26.00 78.00 182.00
11-13,15-17: 15-No Blue Beetle 20.00 60.00 140.00
14-No Blue Beetle; used in **SOTI**, illo-"Corpses of colored people strung up by their wrists." 26.00 78.00 182.00
18-Dagar, Jo-Jo app; no Phantom Lady or Blue Beetle 16.00 48.00 110.00
6(1957-Green Publ.)-Patoruzu the Indian; Cosmo Cat on cover only 1.50 4.50 10.00
6(1958-Literary Ent.)-Muggy Doo; Cosmo Cat on cover only 1.50 4.50 10.00
6(1959-Norlen)-Atomic Mouse; Cosmo Cat on cover only 1.50 4.50 10.00
6(1959)-Little Eva 1.50 4.50 10.00
6(Cornell)-Supermouse on-c 1.50 4.50 10.00

NOTE: *Jo-Jo by* **Kamen**-*12,18.*

ALL TRUE ALL PICTURE POLICE CASES
Oct, 1952 - No. 2, Nov, 1952 (100 pages)

ALL TRUE ALL PICTURE. . . (continued)
St. John Publishing Co.

	Good	Fine	Mint
1-Three rebound St. John crime comics	17.00	51.00	120.00
2-Three comics rebound	15.00	45.00	105.00

NOTE: *Contents may vary.*

ALL-TRUE CRIME (. . . Cases No. 26-35; formerly Official True Crime Cases)
No. 26, Feb, 1948 - No. 52, Sept, 1952
Marvel/Atlas Comics(OFI No. 26,27/CFI No. 28,29/LCC No. 30-46/LMC No. 47-52)

26(No. 1)	3.50	10.50	24.00
27(4/48)-Electric chair-c	3.00	9.00	21.00
28-41,43-48,50-52	1.30	4.00	9.00
42-Krigstein-a	2.55	8.00	18.50
49-Used in **POP**, Pg. 79; Krigstein-a	3.30	10.00	23.00

NOTE: ***Robinson** a-47. **Tuska** a-48(3).*

ALL-TRUE DETECTIVE CASES (Kit Carson No. 5 on)
Feb-Mar, 1954 - No. 4, Aug-Sept, 1954
Avon Periodicals

1	8.00	24.00	56.00
2-Wood-a	8.00	24.00	56.00
3-Kinstler-c	3.50	10.50	24.00
4-Wood(?), Kamen-a	7.00	21.00	50.00
nn(100 pgs.)-7 pg. Kubert-a, Kinstler back-c	19.00	57.00	132.00

ALL TRUE ROMANCE (. . . Illustrated No. 3)
3/51 - No. 34, 3/58; No. 3, 9/57 - No. 4, 11/57
Artful Publ. No. 1-3/Harwell(Comic Media) No. 4-19?/Ajax-Farrell(Excellent Publ.)/Four Star Comic Corp.

1 (3/51)	5.00	15.00	35.00
2	3.35	10.00	23.00
3(12/51)-No. 5(5/52)	2.75	8.25	19.00
6-Wood-a, 9 pgs. (exceptional)	7.00	21.00	50.00
7-10	2.15	6.50	15.00
11-13,16-19 (2/54)	1.60	4.80	11.00
14-Marijuana story	2.50	7.50	17.00
20-27,29-34 (29-34 exist?)	1.50	4.50	10.00
28 (9/56)-L. B. Cole, Disbrow-a	2.50	7.50	17.00
3,4(Farrell, 1957)	.60	1.80	4.00

ALL WESTERN WINNERS (Formerly All Winners; becomes Western Winners with No. 5; see Two-Gun Kid No. 5)
No. 2, Winter, 1948-49 - No. 4, April, 1949
Marvel Comics(CDS)

2-Black Rider (Origin & 1st app.) & his horse Satan, Kid Colt & his horse Steel, & Two-Gun Kid & his horse Cyclone begin	12.00	36.00	84.00
3-Anti-Wertham editorial	8.00	24.00	56.00
4-Black Rider i.d. revealed	8.00	24.00	56.00

ALL WINNERS COMICS (All Teen No. 20; No. 1 adv. as All Aces)
Summer, 1941 - No. 19, Fall, 1946; No. 21, Winter, 1946-47
(no No. 20) (No. 21 continued from Young Allies No. 20)
USA No. 1-7/WFP No. 10-19/YAI No. 21

	Good	Fine	Mint
1-The Angel & Black Marvel only app.; Capt. America by Simon & Kirby, Human Torch & Sub-Mariner begin	230.00	690.00	1610.00
2-The Destroyer & The Whizzer begin; Simon & Kirby Captain America	112.00	335.00	785.00
3,4	88.00	265.00	615.00
5,6: 6-The Black Avenger only app.; no Whizzer story	60.00	180.00	420.00
7-10	50.00	150.00	350.00
11-18: 12-Last Destroyer; no Whizzer story; no Human Torch No. 14-16	30.00	90.00	210.00
19-(Scarce)-1st app. & origin All Winners Squad	73.00	220.00	510.00
21-(Scarce)-All Winners Squad, Miss America app; bondage-c	68.00	205.00	475.00

NOTE: ***Everett** Sub-Mariner-1, 3, 4; **Burgos** Torch-1, 3, 4. **Schomburg** c-12, 14, 15.*

(2nd Series - August, 1948, Marvel Comics (CDS))
(Becomes All Western Winners with No. 2)

1-The Blonde Phantom, Capt. America, Human Torch, & Sub-Mariner app.	58.00	175.00	405.00

ALL YOUR COMICS (See Fox Giants)
Spring, 1946 (36 pages)
Fox Feature Syndicate (R. W. Voight)

1-Red Robbins, Merciless the Sorceress app.	5.50	16.50	38.00

ALMANAC OF CRIME (See Fox Giants)

AL OF FBI (See Little Al of the FBI)

ALONG THE FIRING LINE WITH ROGER BEAN
1916 (Hardcover, B&W) (6x17'') (66 pages)
Chas. B. Jackson

3-by Chic Jackson (1915 daily strips)	6.00	18.00	42.00

ALPHA AND OMEGA
1978 (49 cents)
Spire Christian Comics (Fleming H. Revell)

		.30	.60

ALPHA FLIGHT
Aug, 1983 - Present
Marvel Comics Group

1-Byrne-a (52pgs.)-Wolverine & Nightcrawler cameo	.75	2.30	4.60
2-Vindicator becomes Guardian; origin Marrina & Alpha Flight	.35	1.40	2.80
3-5: 3-Concludes origin Alpha Flight	.40	1.20	2.40
6-11: 6-Origin Shaman. 7-Origin Snowbird. 10,11-Origin Sasquatch	.30	.90	1.80
12-Double size; death of Guardian	.40	1.20	2.40
13-16: 13,16-Wolverine app.		.75	1.50
17-X-Men x-over; Wolverine cameo	.40	1.20	2.40
18-29: 20-New headquarters. 25-Return of Guardian. 29-Last Bryne issue		.75	1.50
30-39		.60	1.20
40-45		.50	1.00
Annual 1 (9/86, $1.25)	.30	.90	1.80

NOTE: ***Austin** c-1i, 2i. **Byrne** a-1-14, 15-17p; c-1p, 2p, 3-17.*

ALPHA TRACK
Feb, 1986 - No. 12, 1987 ($1.75 cover)
Fantasy General Comics

1	.40	1.25	2.50
2-12	.30	.90	1.80

ALPHONSE & GASTON & LEON
1903 (15x10'' Sunday strip reprints in color)
Hearst's New York American & Journal

by Fred Opper	22.00	65.00	154.00

ALTER EGO
May, 1986 - No. 4, Nov, 1986 (mini-series)
First Comics

1	.30	.90	1.80
2-4		.70	1.40

All-True Detective Cases #2, © AVON

All Western Winners #2, © MCG

All Winners Comics #9, © MCG

Amazing Adult Fantasy #11, © MCG

Amazing Detective Cases #11, © MCG

Amazing Ghost Stories #14, © STJ

ALTERNATE HERO
Sept, 1986 ($1.95, B&W)
Prelude Graphics

	Good	Fine	Mint
1	.30	.95	1.90

ALVIN (TV) (See 4-Color Comics No. 1042)
Oct-Dec, 1962 - No. 28, Oct, 1973
Dell Publishing Co.

	Good	Fine	Mint
12-021-212	1.75	5.25	12.00
2	1.15	3.50	8.00
3-10	.85	2.50	6.00
11-28	.75	2.25	5.00
Alvin For President (10/64)	.50	1.50	3.00
. . . & His Pals in Merry Christmas with Clyde Crashcup & Leonardo 1(02-120-402)-12-2/64, reprinted in 1966 (12-023-604)	1.00	3.00	6.00

AMAZING ADULT FANTASY (Amazing Adventures No. 1-6; Amazing Fantasy No. 15)
No. 7, Dec, 1961 - No. 14, July, 1962
Marvel Comics Group (AMI)

	Good	Fine	Mint
7: Ditko-a No. 7-14; c-7-13	8.00	24.00	56.00
8-Last 10¢ issue	6.00	18.00	42.00
9-14: 12-1st app. Mailbag. 13-Anti-communist story	5.85	17.50	40.00

AMAZING ADVENTURE FUNNIES (Fantoman No. 2 on)
June, 1940 - No. 2, Sept. 1940
Centaur Publications

	Good	Fine	Mint
1-The Fantom of the Fair by Gustavson (r-/Amaz. Mystery Funnies V2/7, V2/8), The Arrow, Skyrocket Steele From the Year X by Everett (r-/AMF 2); Burgos-a	75.00	225.00	525.00
2-Reprints. Pub. after Fantoman No. 2	55.00	165.00	385.00

NOTE: ***Burgos** a-1(2). **Everett** a-1(3). **Gustavson** a-1(5), 2(3). **Pinajian** a-2.*

AMAZING ADVENTURES (Also see Science Comics)
1950 - No. 6, Fall, 1952 (Painted covers)
Ziff-Davis Publ. Co.

	Good	Fine	Mint
1950 (no month given) (8½x11") (8 pgs.) Has the front & back cover plus Schomburg story used in Amazing Advs. No. 1 (Sent to subscribers of Z-D s/f magazines & ordered through mail for 10¢. Used to test market) Estimated value....			180.00
1-Wood, Schomburg, Anderson, Whitney-a	26.00	78.00	180.00
2-5-Anderson-a. 3-Starr-a	9.00	27.00	62.00
6-Krigstein-a	13.00	40.00	90.00

AMAZING ADVENTURES (Amazing Adult Fantasy No. 7)
June, 1961 - No. 6, Nov, 1961
Atlas Comics (AMI)/Marvel Comics No. 3 on

	Good	Fine	Mint
1-Origin Dr. Droom (1st Marvel-Age Superhero) by Kirby; Ditko & Kirby-a in all; Kirby c-1-6	13.00	40.00	90.00
2	6.50	20.00	45.00
3-6: Last Dr. Droom	4.50	13.50	31.00

AMAZING ADVENTURES
Aug, 1970 - No. 39, Nov, 1976
Marvel Comics Group

	Good	Fine	Mint
1-Inhumans by Kirby(p) & Black Widow begin; Adams-a(p)	.40	1.20	2.40
2-4: Last Kirby Inhumans	.25	.80	1.60
5-8-Adams-a; 8-Last Black Widow	.50	1.50	3.00
9,10: 10-Last Inhumans (origin-r by Kirby)		.60	1.20
11-New Beast begins(Origin), ends No.17; X-Men cameo	.60	1.75	3.50
12-17	.30	.90	1.80
18-War of the Worlds begins; 1st app. Killraven; Adams-a(p)	.40	1.25	2.50
19-39: 35-Giffen's first art		.30	.60

NOTE: ***Adams** c-6-8. **Buscema** a-1p, 2p. **Colan** a-3-5p, 26p. **Ditko** a-24r. **Everett** inks-3-5, 7, 9. **Giffen** a-35p, 38p. **G. Kane** c-11, 25p, 29p. **Ploog** a-12i. **Starlin** c-15p, 27. **Sutton** a-11-15p.*

AMAZING ADVENTURES
December, 1979 - No. 14, January, 1981
Marvel Comics Group

	Good	Fine	Mint
V2No.1: r-/X-Men No. 1,38		.60	1.20
2-14: 2,4,6-X-Men-r. 7,8-Origin Iceman		.60	1.20

NOTE: ***Byrne** c-6p, 9p. **Kirby** a-1-14r; c-7, 9. **Steranko** a-12r. **Tuska** a-7-9.*

AMAZING ADVENTURES OF CAPTAIN CARVEL AND HIS CARVEL CRUSADERS, THE (See Carvel Comics)

AMAZING CHAN & THE CHAN CLAN, THE (TV)
May, 1973 - No. 4, Feb, 1974 (Hanna-Barbera)
Gold Key

	Good	Fine	Mint
1	.35	1.00	2.00
2-4	.25	.75	1.50

AMAZING COMICS (Complete No. 2)
Fall, 1944
Timely Comics (EPC)

	Good	Fine	Mint
1-The Destroyer, The Whizzer, The Young Allies, Sergeant Dix	60.00	180.00	420.00

AMAZING DETECTIVE CASES (Formerly Suspense No. 2?)
No. 3, Nov, 1950 - No. 14, Sept, 1952
Marvel/Atlas Comics (CCC)

	Good	Fine	Mint
3	3.00	9.00	21.00
4-6	1.60	4.80	11.00
7-10	1.30	4.00	9.00
11,14: 11-(3/52)-change to horror	1.75	5.25	12.00
12-Krigstein-a	2.65	8.00	18.00
13-Everett-a; electrocution-c/story	2.65	8.00	18.00

NOTE: ***Maneely** c-13. **Sekowsky** a-12. **Sinnott** a-13. **Tuska** a-10.*

AMAZING FANTASY (. . . Adult Fantasy No. 7-14)
No. 15, Aug, 1962 (Sept, 1962 shown in indicia)
Marvel Comics Group (AMI)

	Good	Fine	Mint
15-Origin & 1st app. of Spider-Man by Ditko; Kirby/Ditko-c	120.00	500.00	1200.00

AMAZING GHOST STORIES (Formerly Nightmare)
No. 14, Oct, 1954 - No. 16, Feb, 1955
St. John Publishing Co.

	Good	Fine	Mint
14-Pit & the Pendulum story by Kinstler; Baker-c	8.00	24.00	56.00
15-Reprints Weird Thrillers No. 5; Baker-c, Powell-a	5.50	16.50	38.00
16-Kubert reprints of Weird Thrillers No. 4; Baker-c; Roussos, Tuska, Kinstler-a	5.70	17.00	40.00

AMAZING HIGH ADVENTURE
8/84; No. 2, 10/85; No. 3, 10/86 - Present (Baxter No. 3, 4)
Marvel Comics

	Good	Fine	Mint
1-5	.35	1.00	2.00

NOTE: ***Bissette** a-5. **Bolton** c/a-5. **Severin** a-1, 3, 5. **P. Smith** a-2. **Williamson** a-2.*

AMAZING-MAN COMICS (Formerly Motion Pic. Funnies Wkly?)
No. 5, Sept, 1939 - No. 27, Feb, 1942
Centaur Publications

5(No.1)(Rare)-Origin A-Man the Amazing Man by Bill Everett; The Cat-Man by Tarpe Mills (also No. 8), Mighty Man by Filchock,

AMAZING-MAN COMICS (continued) Good Fine Mint

Minimidget & sidekick Ritty, & The Iron Skull by Burgos begins 435.00 1305.00 3050.00

6-Origin The Amazing Man retold; The Shark begins; Ivy Menace by Tarpe Mills app. 140.00 420.00 980.00

7-Magician From Mars begins; ends No.11 82.00 245.00 575.00

8-Cat-Man dresses as woman 65.00 195.00 455.00

9-Magician From Mars battles the 'Elemental Monster,' swiped into The Spectre in More Fun 54 & 55 62.00 185.00 435.00

10,11: 11-Zardi, the Eternal Man begins; ends No. 16; Amazing Man dons costume; last Everett issue 54.00 160.00 380.00

12,13 62.00 185.00 435.00

14-Reef Kinkaid, Rocke Wayburn (ends No. 20), & Dr. Hypno (ends No. 21) begin; no Zardi or Chuck Hardy 40.00 120.00 280.00

15,17-20: 15-Zardi returns; no Rocke Wayburn. 17-Dr. Hypno returns; no zardi 30.00 90.00 210.00

16-Mighty Man's powers of super strength & ability to shrink & grow explained; Rocke Wayburn returns; no Dr. Hypno; Al Avison (a character) begins, ends No. 18 (a tribute to the famed artist) 32.00 95.00 225.00

21-Origin Dash Dartwell (drug-use story); origin & only app. T.N.T. 30.00 90.00 210.00

22-Dash Dartwell, the Human Meteor & The Voice app; last Iron Skull & The Shark; Silver Streak app.. 30.00 90.00 210.00

23-Two Amazing Man stories; intro/origin Tommy the Amazing Kid; The Marksman only app. 32.00 95.00 225.00

24,27: 24-King of Darkness, Nightshade, & Blue Lady begin; end No. 26 30.00 90.00 210.00

25,26 (Scarce)-Meteor Martin by Wolverton in both; 26-Electric Ray app. 68.00 205.00 475.00

NOTE: ***Everett*** *a-5-11; c-5-11.* ***Gilman*** *a-14-20.* ***Giunta/Mirando*** *a-7-10.* ***Sam Glanzman*** *a-14-16, 18-21, 23.* ***Louis Glanzman*** *a-6, 9-11, 14-21; c-14-19, 21.* ***Robert Golden*** *a-9.* ***Gustavson*** *a-6; c-22, 23.* ***Lubbers*** *a-14-21.* ***Simon*** *a-10.* ***Frank Thomas*** *a-6, 9-11, 14, 15, 17-21.*

AMAZING MYSTERIES (Formerly Sub-Mariner No. 31)
No. 32, May, 1949 - No. 35, Jan, 1950
Marvel Comics (CCC)

32-The Witness app; 1st Marvel horror comic 16.00 48.00 110.00

33-Horror format 4.00 12.00 28.00

34,35-Change to Crime 3.00 9.00 21.00

AMAZING MYSTERY FUNNIES
Aug, 1938 - No. 24, Sept, 1940 (All 52 pgs.)
Centaur Publications

V1/1-Everett-c(1st); Dick Kent Adv. story; Skyrocket Steele in the Year X on cover only 125.00 375.00 875.00

2-Everett 1st-a(Skyrocket Steele) 60.00 180.00 420.00

3 37.00 110.00 260.00

3(No. 4, 12/38)-nn on cover, No. 3 on inside; bondage-c 30.00 90.00 210.00

V2/1-4,6: 2-Drug use story. 3-Air-Sub DX begins by Burgos. 4-Dan Hastings, Sand Hog begins (ends No. 5). 6-Last Skyrocket Steele 25.00 75.00 175.00

5-Classic Everett-c 30.00 90.00 210.00

7 (Scarce)-Intro. The Fantom of the Fair; Everett, Gustavson, Burgos-a 132.00 400.00 925.00

8-Origin & 1st app. Speed Centaur 50.00 150.00 350.00

9-11: 11-Self portrait and biog. of Everett; Jon Linton begins 30.00 90.00 210.00

12 (Scarce)-Wolverton Space Patrol-a (12/39) 75.00 225.00 525.00

V3/1(No. 17, 1/40)-Intro. Bullet; Tippy Taylor serial begins, ends No. 24 (cont. in The Arrow 2) 30.00 90.00 210.00

18,20 25.00 75.00 175.00

19,21-24-All have Space Patrol by Wolverton 54.00 162.00 380.00

NOTE: ***Burgos*** *a-V2/3-9.* ***Eisner*** *a-V1/2, 3(2).* ***Everett*** *a-V1/2-4, V2/1, 3-6; c-V1/1-4, V2/3, 5, 18.* ***Filchock*** *a-V2/9.* ***Guardineer*** *a-V1/4, V2/4-6;* ***Gustavson*** *a-V2/4, 5, 9-12, V3/1, 19, 20; c-V2/7, 9, 12, V3/1, 21, 22;* ***McWilliams*** *a-V2/9, 10.* ***Tarpe Mills*** *a-V2/2, 4-6, 9-12, V3/1.* ***Leo Morey****(Pulp artist) c-V2/10; text illo-V2/11.* ***Frank Thomas*** *c-V2/11.* ***Webster*** *a-V2/4.*

AMAZING SAINTS
1974 (39 cents)
Logos International

	Good	Fine	Mint
True story of Phil Saint		.20	.40

AMAZING SPIDER-MAN, THE (See All Detergent Comics, Amazing Fantasy, Aurora, Marvel Tales, Marvel Team-Up, Marvel Treasury Ed., Official Marvel Index To..., Spectacular..., Spider-Man Digest, Spider-Man Vs. Wolverine, Spidey Super Stories, Superman Vs. ..., & Web of Spiderman)

AMAZING SPIDER-MAN, THE
March, 1963 - Present
Marvel Comics Group

1-Retells origin by Steve Ditko; F.F. x-over; intro. John Jameson & The Chameleon; Kirby-c 100.00 335.00 900.00

1-Reprint from the Golden Record Comic set 1.50 4.50 10.00

with record.... 4.35 13.00 30.00

2-Intro. the Vulture & The Terrible Tinkerer 50.00 130.00 350.00

3-Human Torch cameo; intro. & 1st app. Doc Octopus 28.00 75.00 195.00

4-Origin & 1st app. The Sandman; Intro. Betty Brant & Liz Allen 23.00 60.00 160.00

5,6: 5-Dr. Doom app. 6-1st app. Lizard 18.00 45.00 126.00

7-10: 8-Fantastic 4 app. 9-1st app. Electro (origin). 10-1st app. Big Man & Enforcers 14.00 35.00 98.00

11-13,15: 11-1st app. Bennett Brant. 13-1st app. Mysterio. 15-Intro. Kraven the Hunter 8.85 22.00 62.00

14-Intro. Green Goblin; Hulk x-over 10.00 25.00 68.00

16-19: 18-Fant.-4 app; 19-Intro. Ned Leeds 5.00 12.50 35.00

20-Intro & origin The Scorpion 5.50 14.00 40.00

21-30: 22-1st app. Princess Python. 25-1st app. Spencer Smythe. 26-1st app. Crime Master. 28-Origin/1st app. Molten Man 3.00 7.50 20.00

31-38: 31-Intro. Harry Osborn, Gwen Stacy & Prof. Warren. 36-1st app. Looter. 37-Intro. Norman Osborn. 38-Last Ditko issue 1.70 4.25 12.00

39,40-Green Goblin in both; origin No. 40 1.70 4.25 12.00

41-50: 41-1st app. Rhino. 42-1st app. Mary Jane Watson. 46-Intro. Shocker. 50-Intro. Kingpin 1.35 4.00 8.00

51-60: 52-Intro. Joe Robertson. 56-Intro. Capt. George Stacy. 57,58-Ka-Zar app. 59-Intro. Brainwasher (alias Kingpin) .90 2.60 5.20

61-80: 67-Intro. Randy Robertson. 73-Intro. Silvermane. 78-Intro. Prowler .70 2.00 4.00

81-89: 83-Intro. Schemer & Vanessa (Kingpin's wife). .60 1.80 3.60

90-Death of Capt. Stacey 1.00 3.00 6.00

91-93,95,99: 93-Intro. Arthur Stacy .60 1.80 3.60

94-Origin retold .85 2.50 5.00

96-98-Drug books not approved by CCA 1.50 4.50 9.00

100-Anniversary issue 2.00 6.00 12.00

101-Intro. Morbius 1.20 3.50 7.00

102-Origin Morbius (52 pgs.) 1.20 3.50 7.00

103-112: 108-Intro. Sha-Shan. 110-Intro. Gibbon .50 1.50 3.00

113,114-Starlin a(i); 113-Intro. Hammerhead .60 1.80 3.60

115-118 .50 1.50 3.00

119,120 .60 1.80 3.60

121-Death of Gwen Stacy (r-/in Marvel Tales No. 98) 2.50 7.50 15.00

122-Death of Green Goblin 2.50 7.50 15.00

123-128,130-140: 124-Intro. Man Wolf, origin-No. 125. 134-Intro. Tarantula. 139-Intro. Grizzly. 140-Intro. Glory Grant .35 1.00 2.00

129-1st app. The Punisher 2.35 7.00 14.00

Amazing-Man Comics #21, © CEN

Amazing Mystery Funnies #1, © CEN

Amazing Spider-Man #129, © MCG

Amazing Spider-Man Annual #1, © MCG

America in Action #1 ('45), © Mayflower

American Flagg #2, © First

AMAZING SPIDER-MAN (continued) — Good / Fine / Mint

141-160: 143-Intro. Cyclone .25 .75 1.50
161-Nightcrawler app. from X-Men .50 1.50 3.00
162-2nd app. Punisher in Spiderman, Nightcrawler app. 1.00 3.00 6.00
163-173,176-88: 167-1st app. Will O' The Wisp. 171-Nova app. 177-180-Green Goblin app. 181-Origin retold; gives life history of Spider-Man .50 1.00
174,175-Punisher app. .70 2.00 4.00
189,190-Byrne-a(p) .35 1.00 2.00
191-199,201,202,204,205,207-219: 194-1st Black Cat. 196-Death of Aunt May. 210-Intro. & 1st app. Madame Web. 212-Intro. Hydro Man .40 .80
200-Giant origin issue .50 1.50 3.00
203-2nd Dazzler app. .35 1.00 2.00
206-Byrne-a(p) .50 1.00
220-237: 226,227-Black Cat returns. 236-Tarantula dies. 235-Origin Will-'O-The-Wisp .50 1.00
238-1st app. Hobgoblin .40 1.25 2.50
239-251: 241-Origin The Vulture .50 1.00
252-Spider-Man dons new costume (5/84) .85 2.50 5.00
253-255 .25 .75 1.50
256-260: 259-Sp-M back to old costume. 261-Hobgoblin app. .60 1.20
261-274,276-294: 285-Punisher app. .50 1.00
275-Origin-r($1.25) .60 1.25
Annual 1 (1964)-Origin S-M; Intro. Sinister Six 6.50 16.00 45.00
Annual 2 2.00 5.00 14.00
Special 3,4 1.25 3.75 7.50
Special 5-8 (12/71) .70 2.00 4.00
King Size 9 ('73)-Green Goblin app. .35 1.00 2.00
Giant-Size 1(7/74)-Kirby/Ditko-r .50 1.50 3.00
Giant-Size 2(10/74) .25 .75 1.50
Giant-Size 3(1/75), 4(4/75), 5(7/75), 6(9/75) .25 .75 1.50
Annual 10(6/76)-Old Human Fly app. .35 1.00 2.00
Annual 11(9/77), 12(8/78) .30 .80 1.60
Annual 13(11/79)-Byrne-a .35 1.00 2.00
Annual 14(12/80)-Miller c/a(p), 40pgs. .50 1.50 3.00
Annual 15(1981)-Miller c/a(p) .50 1.50 3.00
Annual 16(12/82)-Origin/1st app. new Capt. Marvel (female heroine) .60 1.20
Annual 17(12/83), 18 (1984) .60 1.20
Annual 19(11/85) .65 1.30
Annual 20(11/86)-Origin Iron Man of 2020 .65 1.30
Aim Toothpaste giveaway(36pgs., reg. size)-Green Goblin app. .35 1.00 2.00
Aim Toothpaste giveaway (16pgs., reg. size)-Dr. Octopus app. .50 1.00
All Detergent Giveaway ('79, 36 pgs.), nn-Origin-r .70 2.00 4.00
Giveaway-Acme & Dingo Children's Boots(1980)-Spider-Woman app. .50 1.00
. . .& Power Pack ('84, nn)(Nat'l Committee for Prevention of Child Abuse. (two versions, mail offer & store giveaway)-Mooney-a; Byrne-c .30 .60
. . .& The Hulk (Special Edition)(6/8/80; 20 pgs.; Chicago Tribune giveaway) .70 2.00 4.00
. . .& The Incredible Hulk (1981, 1982; 36 pgs.), Sanger Harris, Dallas Times, Kansas City Star, The Jones Store-giveaway; 16 pgs. (1983) .50 1.50 3.00
. . ., Captain America, The Incredible Hulk, & Spider-Woman ('81) (7-11 Stores giveaway; 36 pgs.) .30 .60
Giveaway-Esquire & Eye Magazines(2/69)-Miniature-Still attached 3.00 9.00 18.00
. . ., Storm & Powerman ('82; 20 pgs.)(American Cancer Society)-giveaway .30 .60

Good / Fine / Mint

. . .Vs. The Hulk (Special Edition; 1979)(Supplement to Columbus Dispatch)-Giveaway .50 1.50 3.00
. . .vs. the Prodigy Giveaway, 16 pgs. in color ('76)-5x6½''-Sex education; (1 million printed;35-50 cents) .25 .50

NOTE: ***Austin*** *a-248i, Annual 13i; c-188i, 241i, 242i, 248i.* ***J. Buscema*** *a(p)-72, 73, 76-81, 84, 85.* ***Byrne*** *a-189p, 190p, 206p, Annual 3r, 6r, 7r, 13p, Gnt-Size 1r, 3-5r; c-189p, 268, Annual 12.* ***Ditko*** *a-1-38, Annual 1, 2, Gnt-Size 4r; c-1-38.* ***Gil Kane*** *a(p)-89-91, 96-105, 120-124, 150, Annual 10, 12i; c-90p, 96, 98, 99, 101-105p, 129p, 131p, 132p, 137-140p, 143p, 148p, 149p, 151p, 153p, 160p, 161p, Annual 10p.* ***Kirby*** *a-8.* ***Miller*** *c-218, 219.* ***Mooney*** *a-65i, 67-82i, 84-88i, 173i, 178i, 189i, 190i, 192i, 193i, 196-202i, 211-219i, 221i, 226i, 227i, 229-233i, Annual 11i, 17i.* ***Nasser*** *c-228p.* ***Pollard*** *a-193-195p, 197p; c-187, 190.* ***Simonson*** *c-222.* ***Starlin*** *a-187p.*

AMAZING WILLIE MAYS, THE
No date (Sept, 1954)
Famous Funnies Publ.

nn 20.00 60.00 140.00

AMBUSH (See 4-Color Comics No. 314)

AMBUSH BUG (Also see Son of. . .)
June, 1985 - No. 4, Sept, 1985 (mini-series)
DC Comics

1-Giffen c/a begins .25 .75 1.50
2-4 .50 1.00
. . .Stocking Stuffer (2/86)-Giffen c/a .65 1.30

AMERICA IN ACTION
1942; Winter, 1945 (36 pages)
Dell(Imp. Publ. Co.)/Mayflower House Publ.

1942-Dell-(68 pages) 6.00 18.00 42.00
1(1945)-Has 3 adaptations from American history; Kiefer, Schrotter & Webb-a 4.00 12.00 28.00

AMERICA MENACED!
1950 (Paper cover)
Vital Publications

Anti-communism. estimated value. . . . 150.00

AMERICAN AIR FORCES, THE (See A-1 Comics)
Sept-Oct, 1944 - 1945; 1951 - 1954
William H. Wise(Flying Cadet Publ. Co./Hasan(No.1)/Life's Romances/Magazine Ent. No. 5 on)

1-Article by Zack Mosley, creator of Smilin' Jack 4.65 14.00 32.00
2-4 3.00 9.00 21.00

NOTE: *All part comic, part magazine. Art by* ***Whitney, Chas. Quinlan, H. C. Kiefer,*** *and* ***Tony Dipreta.***

5(A-1 45)(Formerly Jet Powers), 6(A-1 54),7(A-1 58),8(A-1 65) 9(A-1 67), 10(A-1 74), 11(A-1 79), 12(A-1 91) 2.00 6.00 14.00

NOTE: ***Powell*** *c/a-5-12.*

AMERICAN COMICS
1940's
Theatre Giveaways (Liberty Theatre, Grand Rapids, Mich. known)

Many possible combinations. "Golden Age" superhero comics with new cover added and given away at theaters. Following known: Superman No. 59, Capt. Marvel No. 20, Capt. Marvel Jr. No. 5, Action No. 33, Whiz No. 39. Value would vary with book and should be 70-80 percent of the original.

AMERICAN FLAGG (Also see First Comics Graphic Novel 3)
Oct, 1983 - Present
First Comics

1-Chaykin c/a .85 2.50 5.00
2-4 .45 1.40 2.80
5-10 .40 1.20 2.40
11-20 .30 .90 1.80
21-39: 21-27: Alan Moore scripts. 31-Origin Bob Violence .25 .75 1.50

AMERICAN FLAGG (continued) Good Fine Mint
Special 1 (11/86) .35 1.00 2.00

AMERICAN GRAPHICS
No. 1, 1954; No. 2, 1957 (25 cents)
Henry Stewart

1-The Maid of the Mist, The Last of the Eries (Indian Legends of Niagara) (Sold at Niagara Falls) 2.65 8.00 18.00
2-Victory at Niagara & Laura Secord (Heroine of the War of 1812) 1.65 5.00 11.50

AMERICAN INDIAN, THE (See Picture Progress)

AMERICAN LIBRARY
1944 (68 pages) (15 cents, B&W, text & pictures)
David McKay Publications

3-6: 3-Look to the Mountain. 4-Case of the Crooked Candle (Perry Mason). 5-Duel in the Sun. 6-Wingate's Raiders 5.00 15.00 35.00

NOTE: *Also see Guadalcanal Diary & Thirty Seconds Over Tokyo (part of series?).*

AMERICA'S BEST COMICS
Feb, 1942 - No. 31, July, 1949
Nedor/Better/Standard Publications

1-The Woman in Red, Black Terror, Captain Future, Doc Strange, The Liberator, & Don Davis, Secret Ace begin 45.00 135.00 315.00
2-Origin The American Eagle; The Woman in Red ends 22.00 65.00 154.00
3-Pyroman begins 16.00 48.00 112.00
4 15.00 45.00 105.00
5-Last Captain Future-not in No. 4; Lone Eagle app. 13.00 40.00 90.00
6,7: 6-American Crusader app. 11.00 33.00 76.00
8-Last Liberator 9.30 28.00 65.00
9-The Fighting Yank begins; The Ghost app. 9.30 28.00 65.00
10-14: 10-Flag-c. 14-American Eagle ends 8.00 24.00 56.00
15-20 7.00 21.00 50.00
21-Infinity-c 6.50 19.50 45.00
22-Capt. Future app. 6.50 19.50 45.00
23-Miss Masque begins; last Doc Strange 8.50 25.00 60.00
24-Miss Masque bondage-c 7.00 21.00 50.00
25-Last Fighting Yank; Sea Eagle app. 6.50 19.50 45.00
26-The Phantom Detective & The Silver Knight app.; Frazetta text illo & some panels in Miss Masque 8.00 24.00 56.00
27-31: 27,28-Commando Cubs. 27-Doc Strange. 28-Tuska Bl. Terror. 29-Last Pyroman 6.50 19.50 45.00

NOTE: *American Eagle not in 3, 8, 9, 13. Fighting Yank not in 10, 12. Liberator not in 2, 6, 7. Pyroman not in 9, 11, 14-16, 23, 25-27.* ***Schomburg (Xela)*** *c-5, 7-31. Bondage c-18.*

AMERICA'S BEST TV COMICS (TV)
1967 (Produced by Marvel Comics)
American Broadcasting Company

1-Spider-Man, Fantastic Four, Casper, King Kong, George of the Jungle, Journey to the Center of the Earth app. (Promotes new TV cartoon show) 1.00 3.00 7.00

AMERICA'S BIGGEST COMICS BOOK
1944 (196 pages) (One Shot)
William H. Wise

1-The Grim Reaper, The Silver Knight, Zudo, the Jungle Boy, Commando Cubs, Thunderhoof app. 15.00 45.00 105.00

AMERICA'S FUNNIEST COMICS
1944 (80 pages) (15 cents)
William H. Wise

nn(No.1), 2 7.00 21.00 50.00

AMERICA'S GREATEST COMICS
5?/1941 - No. 8, Summer, 1943 (100 pgs.) (Soft cardboard covers)
Fawcett Publications
Good Fine Mint

1-Bulletman, Spy Smasher, Capt. Marvel, Minute Man & Mr. Scarlet begin; Mac Raboy-c 100.00 300.00 700.00
2 48.00 145.00 335.00
3 32.00 95.00 225.00
4-Commando Yank begins; Golden Arrow, Ibis the Invincible & Spy Smasher cameo in Captain Marvel 27.00 81.00 190.00
5 27.00 81.00 190.00
6 20.00 60.00 140.00
7-Balbo the Boy Magician app.; Captain Marvel, Bulletman cameo in Mr. Scarlet 20.00 60.00 140.00
8-Capt. Marvel Jr. & Golden Arrow app.; Spy Smasher x-over in Capt. Midnight; no Minute Man or Commando Yank 20.00 60.00 140.00

AMERICA'S SWEETHEART SUNNY (See Sunny)

AMERICA VS. THE JUSTICE SOCIETY
Jan, 1985 - No. 4, Apr, 1985 (mini-series)
DC Comics

1-Double size; Alcala-a in all .25 .75 1.50
2-4 .50 1.00

AMERICOMICS
April, 1983 - No. 6, Mar, 1984 (Baxter paper)
Americomics

1-Intro/origin The Shade; The Slayer, & Captain Freedom and The Liberty Corps intro .30 .90 1.80
2-6: 2-Messenger, & Tara on Jungle Island app. 3-New & old Blue Beetle battle. 4-Origin Dragonfly & Shade. 6-Origin The Scarlet Scorpion. .30 .90 1.80
Special 1(8/83, $2.00)-Sentinels of Justice (Blue Beetle, Captain Atom, Nightshade, & The Question) .30 .90 1.80

NOTE: ***Perez*** *c-1.*

AMETHYST
Jan, 1985 - No. 16, Aug, 1986
DC Comics

1 .60 1.20
2-10: 8-Fire Jade's i.d. revealed .50 1.00
11-16 .45 .90
Special 1 (10/86) .65 1.30

AMETHYST, PRINCESS OF GEMWORLD
May, 1983 - No. 12, May, 1984 (12 issue maxi-series)
DC Comics

1-60¢ cover price .25 .75 1.50
1-35¢-tested in Austin & Kansas City 1.35 4.00 8.00
2-35¢-tested in Austin & Kansas City 1.00 3.00 6.00
2-12: Perez-c(p) No. 6-11 .50 1.00
Annual 1(9/84) .65 1.30

ANARCHO DICTATOR OF DEATH (See Comics Novel)

ANCHORS ANDREWS (The Saltwater Daffy)
Jan, 1953 - No. 4, July, 1953 (Anchors the Saltwater... No. 4)
St. John Publishing Co.

1-Canteen Kate by Matt Baker, 9 pgs. 6.00 18.00 42.00
2-4 1.85 5.50 13.00

ANDY & WOODY (See March of Comics No. 40,55,76)

ANDY BURNETT (See 4-Color Comics No. 865)

ANDY COMICS (Formerly Scream Comics; becomes Ernie Comics)
No. 20, June, 1948 - No. 21, Aug?, 1948
Current Publications (Ace Magazines)

20,21-Archie-type comic 1.50 4.50 10.00

America's Best #22, © STD

America's Greatest #7, © FAW

Amethyst #9 (1st series), © DC

Animal Antics #19, © DC

Animal Comics #8, © DELL

Animal Fables #3, © WMG

ANDY DEVINE WESTERN
Dec, 1950 - No. 10, 1952
Fawcett Publications

	Good	Fine	Mint
1	14.00	42.00	95.00
2	7.00	21.00	50.00
3-10 (Exist?)	5.00	15.00	35.00

ANDY GRIFFITH SHOW, THE (See 4-Color No. 1252,1341)

ANDY HARDY COMICS (See Movie Comics No. 3, Fiction House)
April, 1952 - No. 6, Sept-Nov, 1954
Dell Publishing Co.

	Good	Fine	Mint
4-Color 389	1.50	4.50	10.00
4-Color 447,480,515,5,6	1.00	3.00	7.00
...& the New Automatic Gas Clothes Dryer ('52, 16 pgs., 5x7¼'') Bendix Giveaway	2.00	6.00	14.00

ANDY PANDA (Also see Walter Lantz Andy Panda)
1943 - Nov-Jan, 1961-62 (Walter Lantz)
Dell Publishing Co.

	Good	Fine	Mint
4-Color 25('43)	19.00	57.00	132.00
4-Color 54('44)	11.00	33.00	76.00
4-Color 85('45)	6.50	19.50	45.00
4-Color 130('46),154,198	3.50	10.50	24.00
4-Color 216,240,258,280,297	2.00	6.00	14.00
4-Color 326,345,358	1.15	3.50	8.00
4-Color 383,409	1.00	3.00	7.00
16(11-1/52-53) - 30	.70	2.10	5.00
31-56	.55	1.80	4.00

(See March of Comics No. 5,22,79, & Super Book No. 4,15,27.)

ANGEL
Aug, 1954 - No. 16, Nov-Jan, 1958-59
Dell Publishing Co.

	Good	Fine	Mint
4-Color 576(8/54)	1.00	3.00	7.00
2(5-7/55) - 16	.55	1.80	4.00

ANGEL AND THE APE (Meet Angel No. 7) (See Limited Collector's Edition C-34 & Showcase No. 77)
Nov-Dec, 1968 - No. 6, Sept-Oct, 1969
National Periodical Publications

	Good	Fine	Mint
1-Not Wood-a		.35	.70
2-6-Wood inks in all		.35	.70

ANGELIC ANGELINA
1909 (11½x17''; 30 pgs.; 2 colors)
Cupples & Leon Company

	Good	Fine	Mint
By Munson Paddock	8.50	25.00	60.00

ANGEL LOVE
Aug, 1986 - No. 8, Mar, 1987 (mini-series)
DC Comics

	Good	Fine	Mint
1-8		.40	.80

ANGEL OF LIGHT, THE (See The Crusaders)

ANIMAL ADVENTURES
Dec, 1953 - No. 3, Apr?, 1954
Timor Publications/Accepted Publications (reprints)

	Good	Fine	Mint
1	1.30	4.00	9.00
2,3	.85	2.50	6.00
1-3 (reprints, nd)	.70	2.10	5.00

ANIMAL ANTICS (Movie Town... No. 24 on)
Mar-Apr, 1946 - No. 23, Nov-Dec, 1949
National Periodical Publications

	Good	Fine	Mint
1-Raccoon Kids begins by Otto Feur; some-c by Grossman	14.00	42.00	100.00
2	7.00	21.00	50.00
3-10	5.00	15.00	35.00
11-23	3.00	9.00	21.00

NOTE: ***Post** a-10,14,15,19; c-10.*

ANIMAL COMICS
Dec-Jan, 1941-42 - No. 30, Dec-Jan, 1947-48
Dell Publishing Co.

	Good	Fine	Mint
1-1st Pogo app. by Walt Kelly (Dan Noonan art in most issues)	83.00	250.00	580.00
2-Uncle Wiggily begins	34.00	100.00	235.00
3,5	23.00	70.00	160.00
4,6,7-No Pogo	13.00	40.00	90.00
8-10	16.00	48.00	110.00
11-15	10.00	30.00	70.00
16-20	6.50	20.00	45.00
21-30: 25-30-''Jigger'' by John Stanley	4.60	14.00	32.00

NOTE: ***Dan Noonan** a-18-30. **Gollub** art in most later issues.*

ANIMAL CRACKERS (Also see Advs. of Patoruzu)
1946; No. 31, July, 1950; 1959
Green Publ. Co./Norlen/Fox Feat.(Hero Books)

	Good	Fine	Mint
1-Super Cat begins	3.50	10.50	24.00
2	1.75	5.25	12.00
3-10 (Exist?)	1.00	3.00	7.00
31(Fox)-Formerly My Love Secret	2.30	7.00	16.00
9(1959-Norlen)	.70	2.00	5.00
nn, nd ('50s), no publ.; infinity-c	.70	2.00	5.00

ANIMAL FABLES
July-Aug, 1946 - No. 7, Nov-Dec, 1947
E. C. Comics(Fables Publ. Co.)

	Good	Fine	Mint
1-Freddy Firefly (clone of Human Torch), Korky Kangaroo, Petey Pig, Danny Demon begin	20.00	60.00	140.00
2-Aesop Fables begin	12.00	36.00	84.00
3-6	10.00	30.00	70.00
7-Origin Moon Girl	36.00	108.00	250.00

ANIMAL FAIR (Fawcett's...)
March, 1946 - No. 11, Feb, 1947
Fawcett Publications

	Good	Fine	Mint
1	6.00	18.00	42.00
2	3.00	9.00	21.00
3-6	2.35	7.00	16.00
7-11	1.65	5.00	12.00

ANIMAL FUN
1953
Premier Magazines

	Good	Fine	Mint
1-(3-D)	17.00	51.00	120.00

ANIMAL WORLD, THE (See 4-Color Comics No. 713)

ANIMATED COMICS
No date given (Summer, 1947?)
E. C. Comics

	Good	Fine	Mint
1 (Rare)	50.00	150.00	350.00

ANIMATED FUNNY COMIC TUNES (See Funny Tunes)

ANIMATED MOVIE-TUNES (Movie Tunes No. 3)
Fall, 1945 - No. 2, Sum, 1946
Margood Publishing Corp. (Timely)

	Good	Fine	Mint
1,2-Super Rabbit, Ziggy Pig & Silly Seal	6.00	18.00	42.00

ANIMAX
Dec, 1986 - Present
Star Comics (Marvel)

	Good	Fine	Mint
1-4: Based on toys		.40	.80

ANNETTE (See 4-Color Comics No. 905)

ANNETTE'S LIFE STORY (See 4-Color No. 1100)

ANNIE
Oct, 1982 - No. 2, Nov, 1982
Marvel Comics Group

	Good	Fine	Mint
1,2-Movie adaptation		.25	.50
Treasury Edition (Tabloid size)	.35	1.00	2.00

ANNIE OAKLEY (Also see Two-Gun Kid, Wild Western, & Tessie The Typist No. 19)
Spring, 1948 - No. 4, 11/48; No. 5, 6/55 - No. 11, 6/56
Marvel/Atlas Comics(MPI No. 1-4/CDS No. 5 on)

	Good	Fine	Mint
1 (1st Series, '48)-Hedy Devine app.	11.00	33.00	76.00
2 (7/48, 52 pgs.)-Kurtzman-a, "Hey Look," 1pg; Intro. Lana; Hedy Devine app; Captain Tootsie by Beck	8.00	24.00	56.00
3,4	6.00	18.00	42.00
5 (2nd Series)(1955)	4.00	12.00	28.00
6-8: 8-Woodbridge-a	3.00	9.00	21.00
9-Williamson-a, 4 pgs.	3.75	11.25	26.00
10,11: 11-Severin-c	2.65	8.00	18.00

ANNIE OAKLEY AND TAGG (TV)
1953 - No. 18, Jan-Mar, 1959; July, 1965 (all photo-c)
Dell Publishing Co./Gold Key

	Good	Fine	Mint
4-Color 438	4.00	12.00	28.00
4-Color 481,575	2.85	8.50	20.00
4(7-9/55)-10	2.65	8.00	18.00
11-18(1-3/59)	2.00	7.00	14.00
1(7/65-Gold Key)-Photo-c	2.00	6.00	12.00

NOTE: ***Manning** a-13. Photo back c-4, 9, 11.*

ANOTHER WORLD (See Strange Stories From . . .)

ANTHRO (See Showcase)
July-Aug, 1968 - No. 6, July-Aug, 1969
National Periodical Publications

	Good	Fine	Mint
1-Howie Post-a in all	.25	.80	1.60
2-6: 6-Wood inks		.45	.90

ANTONY AND CLEOPATRA (See Ideal, a Classical Comic)

ANYTHING GOES
Oct, 1986 - No. 5, 1987 (mini-series)(Adults, $2.00)
Fantagraphics Books

	Good	Fine	Mint
1-Flaming Carrot app. (1st in color?)	.50	1.50	3.00
2-5: 2-Alan Moore scripts. 3-Capt. Jack, Cerebus app.	.35	1.00	2.00

A-1 COMICS (A-1 appears on covers No. 1-17 only)(See individual title listings. 1st two issues not numbered.)
1944 - No. 139, Sept-Oct, 1955
Life's Romances Publ.-No. 1/Compix/Magazine Ent.

	Good	Fine	Mint
nn-Kerry Drake, Johnny Devildog, Rocky, Streamer Kelly (Slightly large size)	10.00	30.00	70.00
1-Dotty Dripple(1 pg.), Mr. Ex, Bush Berry, Rocky, Lew Loyal (20 pgs.)	4.00	12.00	28.00
2-8,10-Texas Slim & Dirty Dalton, The Corsair, Teddy Rich, Dotty Dripple, Inca Dinca, Tommy Tinker, Little Mexico & Tugboat Tim, The Masquerader & others	1.65	5.00	11.50
9-Texas Slim (all)	1.65	5.00	11.50
11-Teena	2.00	6.00	14.00
12,15-Teena	1.65	5.00	11.50
13-Guns of Fact & Fiction (1948). Used in **SOTI**, pg. 19; narcotics, junkie mentioned; Ingels & J. Craig-a	11.00	33.00	76.00
14-Tim Holt Western Adventures No. 1 (1948)	24.00	70.00	166.00
16-Vacation Comics	1.15	3.50	8.00
17-Tim Holt No. 2. Last issue to carry A-1 on cover (9-10/48)	13.00	40.00	90.00
18-Jimmy Durante-Photo-c	8.00	24.00	56.00
19-Tim Holt No. 3	9.50	28.50	65.00
20-Jimmy Durante-Photo-c	8.00	24.00	56.00
21-Joan of Arc(1949)-Movie adapt.; Ingrid Bergman photo-cvrs & interior photos; Whitney-a	9.50	28.50	65.00
22-Dick Powell(1949)	6.00	18.00	42.00
23-Cowboys 'N' Indians No. 6	1.75	5.25	12.00
24-Trail Colt No. 1-Frazetta, r-in Manhunt No. 13; Ingels-c; L. B. Cole-a	22.00	65.00	154.00
25-Fibber McGee & Molly(1949) (Radio)	2.65	8.00	18.00
26-Trail Colt No. 2-Ingels-c	16.00	48.00	112.00
27-Ghost Rider No. 1(1950)-Origin Ghost Rider	25.00	75.00	175.00
28-Christmas-(Koko & Kola No. 6)(5/47)	1.15	3.50	8.00
29-Ghost Rider No. 2-Frazetta-c (1950)	26.50	80.00	185.00
30-Jet Powers No. 1-Powell-a	12.00	36.00	84.00
31-Ghost Rider No. 3-Frazetta-c & origin (1951)	26.50	80.00	185.00
32-Jet Powers No. 2	8.50	25.50	60.00
33-Muggsy Mouse No. 1(1951)	1.75	5.25	12.00
34-Ghost Rider No. 4-Frazetta-c (1951)	26.50	80.00	185.00
35-Jet Powers No. 3-Williamson/Evans-a	18.00	54.00	125.00
36-Muggsy Mouse No. 2; Racist-c	3.35	10.00	23.00
37-Ghost Rider No. 5-Frazetta-c (1951)	26.50	80.00	185.00
38-Jet Powers No. 4-Williamson & Wood-a	18.00	54.00	125.00
39-Muggsy Mouse No. 3	1.00	3.00	7.00
40-Dogface Dooley No. 1('51)	1.75	5.25	12.00
41-Cowboys 'N' Indians No. 7	1.50	4.50	10.00
42-Best of the West No. 1-Powell-a	15.00	45.00	105.00
43-Dogface Dooley No. 2	1.15	3.50	8.00
44-Ghost Rider No. 6	8.00	24.00	56.00
45-American Air Forces No. 5-Powell-c/a	2.00	6.00	14.00
46-Best of the West No. 2	7.00	21.00	50.00
47-Thun'da, King of the Congo No. 1-Frazetta-c/a('52)	120.00	360.00	840.00
48-Cowboys 'N' Indians No. 8	1.50	4.50	10.00
49-Dogface Dooley No. 3	1.15	3.50	8.00
50-Danger Is Their Business No. 11 (1952)-Powell-a	3.35	10.00	23.00
51-Ghost Rider No. 7 ('52)	8.00	24.00	56.00
52-Best of the West No. 3	6.00	18.00	42.00
53-Dogface Dooley No. 4	1.15	3.50	8.00
54-American Air Forces No. 6(8/52)-Powell-a	2.00	6.00	14.00
55-U.S. Marines No. 5-Powell-a	2.35	7.00	16.00
56-Thun'da No. 2-Powell-c/a	13.50	40.50	95.00
57-Ghost Rider No. 8	6.50	19.50	45.00
58-American Air Forces No. 7-Powell-a	2.00	6.00	14.00
59-Best of the West No. 4	6.00	18.00	42.00
60-The U.S. Marines No. 6-Powell-a	2.35	7.00	16.00
61-Space Ace No. 5(1953)-Guardineer-a	11.50	34.50	80.00
62-Starr Flagg, Undercover Girl No. 5	11.50	34.50	80.00
63-Manhunt No. 13-Frazetta reprinted from A-1 No. 24	13.50	40.50	95.00
64-Dogface Dooley No. 5	1.15	3.50	8.00
65-American Air Forces No. 8-Powell-a	2.00	6.00	14.00
66-Best of the West No. 5	6.00	18.00	42.00
67-American Air Forces No. 9-Powell-a	2.00	6.00	14.00
68-U.S. Marines No. 7-Powell-a	2.35	7.00	16.00
69-Ghost Rider No. 9(10/52)	6.50	19.50	45.00
70-Best of the West No. 6	4.00	12.00	28.00
71-Ghost Rider No. 10(12/52)	6.50	19.50	45.00
72-U.S. Marines No. 8-Powell-a(3)	2.35	7.00	16.00
73-Thun'da No. 3-Powell-c/a	10.00	30.00	70.00
74-American Air Forces No. 10-Powell-a	2.00	6.00	14.00
75-Ghost Rider No. 11(3/52)	5.00	15.00	35.00

Annie Oakley #6, © MCG

A-1 Comics #26, © ME

A-1 Comics #52, © ME

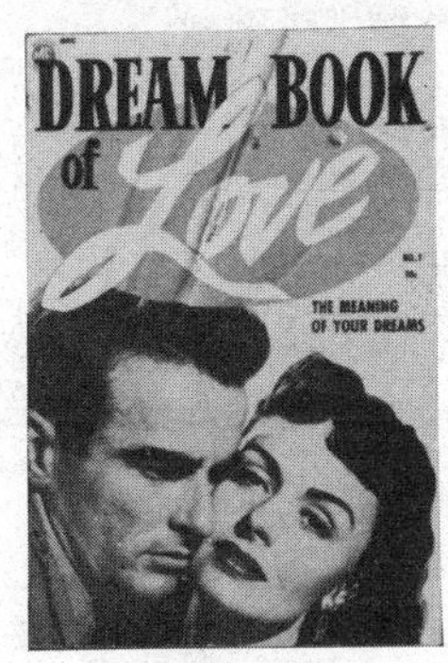

A-1 Comics #106, © ME

Apache Kid #10, © MCG

Approved Comics #6, © STJ

A-1 COMICS (continued)	Good	Fine	Mint
76-Best of the West No. 7	4.00	12.00	28.00
77-Manhunt No. 14 (classic cover)	8.00	24.00	56.00
78-Thun'da No. 4-Powell-c/a	10.00	30.00	70.00
79-American Air Forces No. 11-Powell-a	2.00	6.00	14.00
80-Ghost Rider No. 12(6/52)	5.00	15.00	35.00
81-Best of the West No. 8	4.00	12.00	28.00
82-Cave Girl No. 11(1953)-Powell-c/a; origin	17.00	51.00	120.00
83-Thun'da No. 5-Powell-c/a	8.50	25.50	60.00
84-Ghost Rider No. 13(8/53)	5.00	15.00	35.00
85-Best of the West No. 9	4.00	12.00	28.00
86-Thun'da No. 6-Powell-c/a	8.50	25.50	60.00
87-Best of the West No. 10	4.00	12.00	28.00
88-Bobby Benson's B-Bar-B Riders No. 20	2.65	8.00	18.00
89-Home Run No. 3-Powell-a; Stan Musial photo-c	3.50	10.50	24.00
90-Red Hawk No. 11(1953)-Powell-c/a	3.00	9.00	21.00
91-American Air Forces No. 12-Powell-a	2.00	6.00	14.00
92-Dream Book of Romance No. 5-photo-c; Guardineer-a	2.00	6.00	14.00
93-Great Western No. 8('54)-Origin The Ghost Rider; Powell-a	6.00	18.00	42.00
94-White Indian No. 11-Frazetta-a(r)	18.00	54.00	126.00
95-Muggsy Mouse No. 4	1.00	3.00	7.00
96-Cave Girl No. 12, with Thun'da; Powell-c/a	12.00	36.00	84.00
97-Best of the West No. 11	4.00	12.00	28.00
98-Undercover Girl No. 6-Powell-c	10.00	30.00	70.00
99-Muggsy Mouse No. 5	1.00	3.00	7.00
100-Badmen of the West No. 1-Meskin-a(?)	7.00	21.00	50.00
101-White Indian No. 12-Frazetta-a(r)	18.00	54.00	126.00
101-Dream Book of Romance No. 6; Marlon Brando photo-c; Powell, Bolle, Guardineer-a	4.35	13.00	30.00
103-Best of the West No. 12-Powell-a	4.00	12.00	28.00
104-White Indian No. 13-Frazetta-a(r)('54)	18.00	54.00	126.00
105-Great Western No. 9-Ghost Rider app.; Powell-a, 6 pgs.; Bolle-c	2.65	8.00	18.00
106-Dream Book of Love No. 1 (6-7/54)-Powell, Bolle-a; Montgomery Clift, Donna Reed photo-c	3.00	9.00	21.00
107-Hot Dog No. 1	2.00	6.00	14.00
108-Red Fox No. 15 (1954)-L.B. Cole c/a; Powell-a	6.50	19.50	45.00
109-Dream Book of Romance No. 7 (7-8/54). Powell-a; photo-c	2.00	6.00	14.00
110-Dream Book of Romance No. 8	2.00	6.00	14.00
111-I'm a Cop No. 1 ('54); drug mention story; Powell-a	4.00	12.00	28.00
112-Ghost Rider No. 14 ('54)	5.00	15.00	35.00
113-Great Western No. 10; Powell-a	2.65	8.00	18.00
114-Dream Book of Love No. 2-Guardineer, Bolle-a	2.00	6.00	14.00
115-Hot Dog No. 3	1.15	3.50	8.00
116-Cave Girl No. 13-Powell-c/a	12.00	36.00	84.00
117-White Indian No. 14	6.50	19.50	45.00
118-Undercover Girl No. 7-Powell-c	10.00	30.00	70.00
119-Straight Arrow's Fury No. 1 (origin)	3.65	11.00	25.00
120-Badmen of the West No. 2	4.00	12.00	28.00
121-Mysteries of Scotland Yard No. 1; r-from Manhunt	4.35	13.00	30.00
122-Black Phantom No. 1(11/54)	11.00	33.00	76.00
123-Dream Book of Love No. 3(10-11/54)	2.00	6.00	14.00
124-Dream Book of Romance No. 8(10-11/54)	2.00	6.00	14.00
125-Cave Girl No. 14-Powell-c/a	12.00	36.00	84.00
126-I'm a Cop No. 2-Powell-a	2.00	6.00	14.00
127-Great Western No. 11('54)-Powell-a	2.65	8.00	18.00
128-I'm a Cop No. 3-Powell-a	2.00	6.00	14.00
129-The Avenger No. 1('55)-Powell-c	10.00	30.00	70.00
130-Strongman No. 1-Powell-a	6.65	20.00	46.00
131-The Avenger No. 2('55)-Powell-c/a	5.00	15.00	35.00
132-Strongman No. 2	4.75	14.25	33.00
133-The Avenger No. 3-Powell-c/a	5.00	15.00	35.00
134-Strongman No. 3	4.75	14.25	33.00
135-White Indian No. 15	6.50	19.50	45.00
136-Hot Dog No. 4	1.15	3.50	8.00
137-Africa No. 1-Powell-c/a(4)	8.50	25.50	60.00
138-The Avenger No. 4-Powell-c/a	5.00	15.00	35.00
139-Strongman No. 4-Powell-a	4.75	14.25	33.00

NOTE: ***Bolle*** *a-110. Photo-c-110.*

APACHE
1951
Fiction House Magazines

	Good	Fine	Mint
1-Baker-c	6.00	18.00	42.00
I.W. Reprint No. 1	.70	2.00	4.00

APACHE HUNTER
1954 (18 pgs. in color) (promo copy) (saddle stitched)
Creative Pictorials

	Good	Fine	Mint
Severin, Heath stories	13.00	39.00	90.00

APACHE KID (Formerly Reno Browne; Western Gunfighters No. 20 on)(Also see Two-Gun Western & Wild Western)
No. 53, 12/50 - No. 10, 1/52; No. 11, 12/54 - No. 19, 4/56
Marvel/Atlas Comics(MPC No. 53-10/CPS No. 11 on)

	Good	Fine	Mint
53(No.1)-A. Kid & his horse Nightwind begin	4.35	13.00	30.00
2(2/51)	2.15	6.50	15.00
3-5	1.85	5.50	13.00
6-10 (1951-52)	1.60	4.80	11.00
11-19 (1954-56)	1.15	3.50	8.00

NOTE: ***Heath*** *c-11, 13.* ***Maneely*** *c-12,14-16.* ***Severin*** *c-17.*

APACHE MASSACRE (See Chief Victorio's. . .)

APACHE TRAIL
Sept, 1957 - No. 4, June, 1958
Steinway/America's Best

	Good	Fine	Mint
1	2.35	7.00	16.50
2-4: 2-Tuska-a	1.15	3.50	8.00

APPROVED COMICS
March, 1954 - No. 12, Aug, 1954 (All painted-c)(no c-price)
St. John Publishing Co.

	Good	Fine	Mint
1-The Hawk No. 5-r	2.65	8.00	18.00
2-Invisible Boy-r(3/54)-Origin; Saunders-c	5.00	15.00	35.00
3-Wild Boy of the Congo No. 11-r(4/54); bondage-c	2.65	8.00	18.00
4-Kid Cowboy-r	2.65	8.00	18.00
5-Fly Boy-r	2.65	8.00	18.00
6-Daring Adv.-r(5/54); Krigstein-a(2); Baker-c	4.35	13.00	30.00
7-The Hawk No. 6-r	2.65	8.00	18.00
8-Crime on the Run; Powell-a; Saunders-c	2.65	8.00	18.00
9-Western Bandit Trails No. 3-r, with new-c; Baker c/a	3.70	11.00	26.00
11-Fightin' Marines No. 3-r; Kanteen Kate app; Baker-c/a	4.00	12.00	28.00
12-North West Mounties No. 4-r(8/54); new Baker-c	4.00	12.00	28.00

AQUAMAN (See Showcase, Brave & the Bold, Super DC Giant, Adventure, DC Super-Stars No. 7, Detective, DC Comics Presents No. 5, DC Special Series No. 1, DC Special No. 28, and World's Finest)

AQUAMAN
Jan-Feb, 1962 - No. 56, Mar-Apr, 1971; No. 57, Aug-Sept,

AQUAMAN (continued)
1977 - No. 63, Aug-Sept, 1978
National Periodical Publications/DC Comics

	Good	Fine	Mint
1-Intro. Quisp	7.50	22.00	50.00
2	2.85	7.00	20.00
3-5	2.15	5.35	15.00
6-10	1.85	5.50	11.00
11-20: 11-Intro. Mera. 18-Aquaman weds Mera; JLA cameo	.70	2.00	4.00
21-30: 23-Birth of Aquababy. 26-Huntress app.(3-4/66). 29-Intro. Ocean Master, Aquaman's step-brother	.45	1.40	2.80
31,32,34-40	.35	1.10	2.20
33-Intro. Aqua-Girl	.45	1.30	2.60
41-47,49	.35	1.00	2.00
48-Origin reprinted	.35	1.10	2.20
50-52-Adams Deadman	1.40	4.25	8.50
53-56('71): 56-Intro Crusader		.50	1.00
57('77)-63: 58-Origin retold		.30	.60

NOTE: ***Aparo** a-40-59; c-57-60, 63.* ***Newton** a-60-63.*

AQUAMAN
Feb, 1986 - No. 4, May, 1986 (mini-series)
DC Comics

	Good	Fine	Mint
1	.75	2.25	4.50
2-4	.35	1.00	2.00

AQUANAUTS (See 4-Color No. 1197)

ARABIAN NIGHTS (See Cinema Comics Herald)

ARAK/SON OF THUNDER
Sept, 1981 - No. 50, Nov, 1985
DC Comics

	Good	Fine	Mint
1-Origin; 1st app. Angelica, Princess of White Cathay	.25	.80	1.60
2-4: 3-Intro Valda, The Iron Maiden		.45	.90
5-10: 8-Viking Prince begins, ends No. 11		.35	.70
11-20: 12-Origin Valda. 20-Origin Angelica		.35	.70
21-23,25-27		.35	.70
24-$1.00 size		.45	.90
28-49 (75 cent cover)		.35	.70
50-Double size		.60	1.20
Annual 1(10/84)		.45	.90

NOTE: ***Alcala** a-10i-12i, 13, 14, 15i-26i; c-13-15, 16i-18i, 19, 20i-25i.*

ARCHIE AND BIG ETHEL
1978?
Spire Christian Comics (Fleming H. Revell Co.)

	Good	Fine	Mint
		.30	.60

ARCHIE AND ME
Oct, 1964 - Present
Archie Publications

	Good	Fine	Mint
1	5.75	17.25	40.00
2	2.50	7.50	18.00
3-5	1.70	5.00	12.00
6-10	.85	2.50	5.00
11-20	.35	1.00	2.00
21-42		.50	1.00
43-63-(All Giants)		.50	1.00
64-161-(Regular size)		.30	.60

ARCHIE AND MR. WEATHERBEE
1980 (59¢)
Spire Christian Comics (Fleming H. Revell Co.)

	Good	Fine	Mint
nn		.30	.60

ARCHIE...ARCHIE ANDREWS, WHERE ARE YOU? (...Comics Digest No. 9, 10; ...Comics Digest Mag. No. 11 on)
Feb, 1977 - Present (Digest size, 160-128 pages)
Archie Publications

	Good	Fine	Mint
1	.30	.80	1.60
2,3,5,7-9-Adams-a; 8-r-/origin The Fly by S&K. 9-Steel Sterling-r	.35	1.00	2.00
4,6,10-48 ($1.00-$1.25): 17-Katy Keene sty		.50	1.00

ARCHIE AS PUREHEART THE POWERFUL
Sept, 1966 - No. 6, Nov, 1967
Archie Publications (Radio Comics)

	Good	Fine	Mint
1	2.85	8.50	20.00
2	1.50	4.50	10.00
3-6	.85	2.50	6.00

NOTE: *Evilheart cameos in all. Title: ...As Capt. Pureheart the Powerful-No. 4,6; ...As Capt. Pureheart-No. 5.*

ARCHIE AT RIVERDALE HIGH
Aug, 1972 - Present
Archie Publications

	Good	Fine	Mint
1	1.70	5.00	10.00
2	.85	2.50	5.00
3-5	.45	1.25	2.50
6-10	.25	.75	1.50
11-30		.50	1.00
31-114: 96-Anti-smoking issue		.30	.60

ARCHIE COMICS (Archie No. 158 on)(See Everything's..., Jackpot, Oxydol-Dreft, and Pep)(First Teen-age comic)(Radio)
Winter, 1942-43 - No. 19, 3-4/46; No. 20, 5-6/46 - Present
MLJ Magazines No. 1-19/Archie Publ.No. 20 on

	Good	Fine	Mint
1 (Scarce)-Jughead, Veronica app.	225.00	675.00	1575.00
2	85.00	255.00	600.00
3 (60 pgs.)	60.00	180.00	420.00
4,5	42.00	125.00	295.00
6-10	28.00	84.00	195.00
11-20: 15,17,18-Dotty & Ditto by Woggon	18.00	54.00	125.00
21-30: 23-Betty & Veronica by Woggon	11.50	34.50	80.00
31-40	8.00	24.00	56.00
41-50	5.00	15.00	35.00
51-70 (1954): 65-70-Katy Keene app.	3.00	9.00	21.00
71-99: 72-74-Katy Keene app.	1.70	5.00	12.00
100	2.00	6.00	14.00
101-130 (1962)	1.00	3.00	7.00
131-160	.70	2.00	4.00
161-200	.35	1.00	2.00
201-240		.50	1.00
241-282		.30	.60
283-Cover/story plugs ''International Children's Appeal'' which was a fraudulent charity, according to TV's 20/20 news program broadcast July 20, 1979.		.60	1.25
284-346: 300-Anniversary issue		.25	.50
Annual 1('50)-116 pgs. (Scarce)	60.00	180.00	420.00
Annual 2('51)	30.00	90.00	210.00
Annual 3('52)	15.00	45.00	105.00
Annual 4,5(1953-54)	11.00	33.00	76.00
Annual 6-10(1955-59)	6.00	18.00	42.00
Annual 11-15(1960-65)	2.50	7.50	17.00
Annual 16-20(1966-70)	.70	2.00	4.00
Annual 21-26(1971-75)	.35	1.00	2.00
Annual Digest 27('75)-49('83-'86)(...Magazine No. 35 on)		.40	.80
...All-Star Specials(Winter '75)-$1.25; 6 remaindered Archie comics rebound in each; titles: ''The World of Giant Comics,'' ''Giant Grab Bag of Comics,'' ''Triple Giant Comics,'' and ''Giant Spec. Comics''	.50	1.50	3.00
Mini-Comics (1970-Fairmont Potato Chips Giveaway-Miniature)(8 issues-nn's., 8 pgs. each)	1.00	3.00	6.00

Aquaman #1 (2/86), © DC

Arak/Son of Thunder #26, © DC

Archie Comics #1, © AP

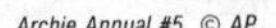
Archie Annual #5, © AP

Archie Giant Series #1, © AP

Archie Giant Series #19, © AP

ARCHIE COMICS (continued)

	Good	Fine	Mint
Official Boy Scout Outfitter(1946)-9½x6½", 16 pgs., B. R. Baker Co.	14.50	43.50	100.00
Shoe Store giveaway (1948, Feb?)	3.00	9.00	21.00

ARCHIE COMICS DIGEST (. . . Magazine No. 37 on)
Aug, 1973 - Present (Small size, 160-128 pages)
Archie Publications

	Good	Fine	Mint
1	1.70	5.00	10.00
2	.85	2.50	5.00
3-5	.40	1.25	2.50
6-10	.25	.75	1.50
11-33: 32-The Fly-r by S&K. 33-The Fly-r		.50	1.00
34-82: 36-Katy Keene story		.30	.60

NOTE: ***Adams*** *a-1,2,4,5,19-21,24,25,27,29,31,33.*

ARCHIE GETS A JOB
1977
Spire Christian Comics (Fleming H. Revell Co.)

	Good	Fine	Mint
		.30	.60

ARCHIE GIANT SERIES MAGAZINE
1954 - Present (No No. 36-135, no No. 252-451)
Archie Publications

	Good	Fine	Mint
1-Archie's Christmas Stocking	32.00	95.00	225.00
2-Archie's Christmas Stocking('55)	16.00	48.00	110.00
3-5-Archie's Christmas Stocking('56-'58)	11.00	33.00	76.00
6-Archie's Christmas Stocking('59)	11.00	33.00	76.00
7-Katy Keene Holiday Fun(9/60)	8.00	24.00	56.00
8-Betty & Veronica Summer Fun (10/60)			
9-The World of Jughead (12/60)			
10-Archie's Christmas Stocking (1/61)			
each. . . .	6.50	20.00	45.00
11-Betty & Veronica Spectacular (6/61)	4.35	13.00	30.00
12-Katy Keene Holiday Fun (9/61)	5.00	15.00	35.00
13-Betty & Veronica Summer Fun (10/61)			
14-The World of Jughead (12/61)			
15-Archie's Christmas Stocking (1/62)			
16-Betty & Veronica Spectacular (6/62)			
17-Archie's Jokes (9/62); Katy Keene app.			
18-Betty & Veronica Summer Fun (10/62)			
19-The World of Jughead (12/62)			
20-Archie's Christmas Stocking (1/63)			
each. . . .	4.35	13.00	30.00
21-Betty & Veronica Spectacular (6/63)			
22-Archie's Jokes (9/63)			
23-Betty & Veronica Summer Fun (10/63)			
24-The World of Jughead (12/63)			
25-Archie's Christmas Stocking (1/64)			
26-Betty & Veronica Spectacular (6/64)			
27-Archie's Jokes (8/64)			
28-Betty & Veronica Summer Fun (9/64)			
29-Around the World with Archie (10/64)			
30-The World of Jughead (12/64)			
each. . . .	3.00	9.00	18.00
31-Archie's Christmas Stocking (1/65)			
32-Betty & Veronica Spectacular (6/65)			
33-Archie's Jokes (8/65)			
34-Betty & Veronica Summer Fun (9/65)			
35-Around the World with Archie (10/65)			
136-The World of Jughead (12/65)			
137-Archie's Christmas Stocking (1/66)			
138-Betty & Veronica Spectacular (6/66)			
139-Archie's Jokes (6/66)			
140-Betty & Veronica Summer Fun (8/66)			
141-Around the World with Archie (9/66)			
each. . . .	2.35	7.00	14.00
142-Archie's Super-Hero Special (10/66)-Origin Capt. Pureheart, Capt. Hero, and Evilheart	2.00	6.00	12.00
143-The World of Jughead (12/66)			
144-Archie's Christmas Stocking (1/67)			
145-Betty & Veronica Spectacular (6/67)			
146-Archie's Jokes (6/67)			
147-Betty & Veronica Summer Fun (8/67)			
148-World of Archie (9/67)			
149-World of Jughead (10/67)			
150-Archie's Christmas Stocking (1/68)			
151-World of Archie (2/68)			
152-World of Jughead (2/68)			
153-Betty & Veronica Spectacular (6/68)			
154-Archie Jokes (6/68)			
155-Betty & Veronica Summer Fun (8/68)			
156-World of Archie (10/68)			
157-World of Jughead (12/68)			
158-Archie's Christmas Stocking (1/69)			
159-Betty & Veronica Christmas Spect. (1/69)			
160-World of Archie (2/69)			
each. . . .	1.20	3.50	7.00
161-World of Jughead (2/69)			
162-Betty & Veronica Spectacular (6/69)			
163-Archie's Jokes (8/69)			
164-Betty & Veronica Summer Fun (9/69)			
165-World of Archie (9/69)			
166-World of Jughead (9/69)			
167-Archie's Christmas Stocking (1/70)			
168-Betty & Veronica Christmas Spect. (1/70)			
169-Archie's Christmas Love-In (1/70)			
170-Jughead's Eat-Out Comic Book Mag. (12/69)			
171-World of Archie (2/70)			
172-World of Jughead (2/70)			
173-Betty & Veronica Spectacular (6/70)			
174-Archie's Jokes (8/70)			
175-Betty & Veronica Summer Fun (9/70)			
176-Li'l Jinx Giant Laugh-Out (8/70)			
177-World of Archie (9/70)			
178-World of Jughead (9/70)			
179-Archie's Christmas Stocking (1/71)			
180-Betty & Veronica Christmas Spect. (1/71)			
181-Archie's Christmas Love-In (1/71)			
182-World of Archie (2/71)			
183-World of Jughead (2/71)			
184-Betty & Veronica Spectacular (6/71)			
185-Li'l Jinx Giant Laugh-Out (6/71)			
186-Archie's Jokes (8/71)			
187-Betty & Veronica Summer Fun (9/71)			
188-World of Archie (9/71)			
189-World of Jughead (9/71)			
190-Archie's Christmas Stocking (12/71)			
191-Betty & Veronica Christmas Spect. (2/72)			
192-Archie's Christmas Love-In (1/72)			
193-World of Archie (3/72)			
194-World of Jughead (4/72)			
195-Li'l Jinx Christmas Bag (1/72)			
196-Sabrina's Christmas Magic (1/72)			
197-Betty & Veronica Spectacular (6/72)			
198-Archie's Jokes (8/72)			
199-Betty & Veronica Summer Fun (9/72)			
200-World of Archie (10/72)			
each. . . .	.45	1.25	2.50
201-Betty & Veronica Spectacular (10/72)			
202-World of Jughead (11/72)			
203-Archie's Christmas Stocking (12/72)			
204-Betty & Veronica Christmas Spect. (2/73)			
205-Archie's Christmas Love-In (1/73)			
206-Li'l Jinx Christmas Bag (12/72)			

ARCHIE GIANT SERIES MAG. (continued)
207-Sabrina's Christmas Magic (12/72)
208-World of Archie (3/73)
209-World of Jughead (4/73)
210-Betty & Veronica Spectacular (6/73)
211-Archie's Jokes (8/73)
212-Betty & Veronica Summer Fun (9/73)
213-World of Archie (10/73)
214-Betty & Veronica Spectacular (10/73)
215-World of Jughead (11/73)
216-Archie's Christmas Stocking (12/73)
217-Betty & Veronica Christmas Spect. (2/74)
218-Archie's Christmas Love-In (1/74)
219-Li'l Jinx Christmas Bag (12/73)
220-Sabrina's Christmas Magic (12/73)
221-Betty & Veronica Spectacular (Advertised as World of Archie) (6/74)
222-Archie's Jokes (Advertised as World of Jughead)(8/74)
223-Li'l Jinx (8/74)
224-Betty & Veronica Summer Fun (9/74)
225-World of Archie (9/74)
226-Betty & Veronica Spectacular (10/74)
227-World of Jughead (10/74)
228-Archie's Christmas Stocking (12/74)
229-Betty & Veronica Christmas Spect. (12/74)
230-Archie's Christmas Love-In (1/75)
231-Sabrina's Christmas Magic (1/75)
232-World of Archie (3/75)
233-World of Jughead (4/75)
234-Betty & Veronica Spectacular (6/75)
235-Archie's Jokes (8/75)
236-Betty & Veronica Summer Fun (9/75)
237-World of Archie (9/75)
238-Betty & Veronica Spectacular (10/75)
239-World of Jughead (10/75)
240-Archie's Christmas Stocking (12/75)
241-Betty & Veronica Christmas Spectacular (12/75)
242-Archie's Christmas Love-In (1/76)
243-Sabrina's Christmas Magic (1/76)
244-World of Archie (3/76)
245-World of Jughead (4/76)
246-Betty & Veronica Spectacular (6/76)
247-Archie's Jokes (8/76)
248-Betty & Veronica Summer Fun (9/76)
249-World of Archie (9/76)
250-Betty & Veronica Spectacular (10/76)

251-World of Jughead (10/76)	Good	Fine	Mint
each....		.40	.80

452-Archie's Christmas Stocking (12/76)
453-Betty & Veronica Christmas Spect. (12/76)
454-Archie's Christmas Love-In (1/77)
455-Sabrina's Christmas Magic (1/77)
456-World of Archie (3/77)
457-World of Jughead (4/77)
458-Betty & Veronica Spectacular (6/77)
459-Archie's Jokes (8/77)-Shows 8/76 in error
460-Betty & Veronica Summer Fun (9/77)
461-World of Archie (9/77)
462-Betty & Veronica Spectacular (10/77)
463-World of Jughead (10/77)
464-Archie's Christmas Stocking (12/77)
465-Betty & Veronica Christmas Spectacular (12/77)
466-Archie's Christmas Love-In (1/78)
467-Sabrina's Christmas Magic (1/78)
468-World of Archie (2/78)
469-World of Jughead (2/78)
470-Betty & Veronica Spectacular (6/78)
471-Archie's Jokes (8/78)
472-Betty & Veronica Summer Fun (9/78)
473-World of Archie (9/78)
474-Betty & Veronica Spectacular (10/78)
475-World of Jughead (10/78)
476-Archie's Christmas Stocking (12/78)
477-Betty & Veronica Christmas Spectacular (12/78)
478-Archie's Christmas Love-In (1/79)
479-Sabrina Christmas Magic (1/79)
480-The World of Archie (3/79)
481-World of Jughead (4/79)
482-Betty & Veronica Spectacular (6/79)
483-Archie's Jokes (8/79)
484-Betty & Veronica Summer Fun (9/79)
485-The World of Archie (9/79)
486-Betty & Veronica Spectacular (10/79)
487-The World of Jughead (10/79)
488-Archie's Christmas Stocking (12/79)
489-Betty & Veronica Christmas Spect. (1/80)
490-Archie's Christmas Love-in (1/80)
491-Sabrina's Christmas Magic (1/80)
492-The World of Archie (2/80)
493-The World of Jughead (4/80)
494-Betty & Veronica Spectacular (6/80)
495-Archie's Jokes (8/80)
496-Betty & Veronica Summer Fun (9/80)
497-The World of Archie (9/80)
498-Betty & Veronica Spectacular (10/80)
499-The World of Jughead (10/80)
500-Archie's Christmas Stocking (12/80)
501-Betty & Veronica Christmas Spect. (12/80)
502-Archie's Christmas Love-in (1/81)
503-Sabrina Christmas Magic (1/81)
504-The World of Archie (3/81)
505-The World of Jughead (4/81)
506-Betty & Veronica Spectacular (6/81)
507-Archie's Jokes (8/81)
508-Betty & Veronica Summer Fun (9/81)
509-The World of Archie (9/81)
510-Betty & Vernonica Spectacular (9/81)
511-The World of Jughead (10/81)
512-Archie's Christmas Stocking (12/81)
513-Betty & Veronica Christmas Spectacular (12/81)
514-Archie's Christmas Love-in (1/82)
515-Sabrina's Christmas Magic (1/82)
516-The World of Archie (3/82)
517-The World of Jughead (4/82)
518-Betty & Veronica Spectacular (6/82)
519-Archie's Jokes (8/82)
520-Betty & Veronica Summer Fun (9/82)
521-The World of Archie (9/82)
522-Betty & Veronica Spectacular (10/82)
523-The World of Jughead (10/82)
524-Archie's Christmas Stocking (1/83)
525-Betty and Veronica Christmas Spectacular (1/83)
526-Betty and Veronica Spectacular (5/83)
527-Little Archie (8/83)
528-Josie and the Pussycats (8/83)
529-Betty and Veronica Summer Fun (8/83)
530-Betty and Veronica Spectacular (9/83)
531-The World of Jughead (9/83)
532-The World of Archie (10/83)
533-Space Pirates by Frank Bolling (10/83)
534-Little Archie (1/84)
535-Archie's Christmas Stocking (1/84)
536-Betty and Veronica Christmas Spectacular (1/84)
537-Betty and Veronica Spectacular (6/84)
538-Little Archie (8/84)
539-Betty and Veronica Summer Fun 8/84)
540-Josie and the Pussycats (8/84)
541-Betty and Veronica Spectacular (9/84)
542-The World of Jughead (9/84)
543-The World of Archie (10/84)
544-Sabrina the Teen-Age Witch (10/84)
545-Little Archie (12/84)
546-Archie's Christmas Stocking (12/84)
547-Betty and Veronica Christmas Spectacular (12/84)
548-
549-Little Archie
550-Betty and Veronica Summer Fun
551-Josie and the Pussycats
552-Betty and Veronica Spectacular
553-The World of Jughead
554-The World of Archie
555-Betty's Diary
556-Little Archie (1/86)
557-Archie's Christmas Stocking (1/86)
558-Betty & Veronica Christmas Spectacular (1/86)
559-Betty & Veronica Spectacular
560-
561-Betty & Veronica Summer Fun
562-Josie and the Pussycats
563-Betty & Veronica Spectacular
564-World Of Jughead
565-World Of Archie
566-Little Archie
567-Archie's Christmas Stocking

568-Betty & Veronica Christmas Spectacular	Good	Fine	Mint
each....		.25	.50

ARCHIE'S ACTIVITY COMICS DIGEST MAGAZINE
1985 (Annual, 128 pgs.; digest size)
Archie Enterprises

1-4		.50	1.00

ARCHIE'S CAR
1979 (49¢)
Spire Christian Comics (Fleming H. Revell Co.)

nn		.30	.60

ARCHIE'S CHRISTMAS LOVE-IN (See Archie Giant Series Mag. No. 169, 181, 192, 205, 218, 230, 242, 454, 466, 478, 490, 502, 514)

ARCHIE'S CHRISTMAS STOCKING (See Archie Giant Series Mag. No. 1-6, 10, 15, 20, 25, 31, 137, 144, 150, 158, 167, 179, 190, 203, 216, 228, 240, 452, 464,

Archie's Girls, Betty & Veronica #1, © AP

Archie's Madhouse #12, © AP

Archie's Mechanics #2, © AP

ARCHIE'S CHRISTMAS STOCKING (cont'd.)
476, 488, 500, 512, 524, 535, 546, 557, 567)

ARCHIE'S CLEAN SLATE
1973 (35-49 cents)
Spire Christian Comics (Fleming H. Revell Co.)

	Good	Fine	Mint
1(Some issues have nn)	.35	1.00	2.00

ARCHIE'S DATE BOOK
1981
Spire Christian Comics (Fleming H. Revell Co.)

	Good	Fine	Mint
		.30	.60

ARCHIE'S DOUBLE DIGEST QUARTERLY MAGAZINE
1981 - Present ($1.95, 256pgs.) (A.D.D. Magazine No. 10 on)
Archie Comics

	Good	Fine	Mint
1-27: 6-Katy Keene sty	.25	.75	1.50

ARCHIE'S FAMILY ALBUM
1978 (36 pages) (39 cents)
Spire Christian Comics (Fleming H. Revell Co.)

	Good	Fine	Mint
		.30	.60

ARCHIE'S FESTIVAL
1980 (49 cents)
Spire Christian Comics (Fleming H. Revell Co.)

	Good	Fine	Mint
		.30	.60

ARCHIE'S GIRLS, BETTY AND VERONICA
1950 - Present
Archie Publications (Close-Up)

	Good	Fine	Mint
1	50.00	150.00	350.00
2	25.00	75.00	175.00
3-5	15.00	45.00	105.00
6-10: 10-2pg. Katy Keene app.	11.50	34.50	80.00
11-20: 11,13,14,17-19-Katy Keene app. 20-Debbie's Diary, 2pgs.	7.00	21.00	50.00
21-30: 27-Katy Keene app.	5.50	16.50	38.00
31-50	3.75	11.25	26.00
51-74	2.35	7.00	16.00
75-Betty & Veronica sell soul to devil	5.00	15.00	35.00
76-99	1.30	4.00	9.00
100	1.70	5.00	12.00
101-140: 118-Origin Superteen. 119-Last Superteen story	.75	2.25	4.50
141-180	.35	1.00	2.00
181-220		.40	.80
221-346: 300-Anniversary issue		.25	.50
Annual 1 (1953)	28.00	85.00	200.00
Annual 2(1954)	13.00	40.00	90.00
Annual 3-5 ('55-'57)	9.00	27.00	60.00
Annual 6-8 ('58-'60)	6.00	18.00	42.00

ARCHIE SHOE-STORE GIVEAWAY
1944-49 (12-15 pgs. of games, puzzles, stories like Superman-Tim books, No nos. - came out monthly)
Archie Publications

	Good	Fine	Mint
(1944-47)-issues	8.35	25.00	55.00
2/48-Peggy Lee photo-c	5.00	15.00	35.00
3/48-Marylee Robb photo-c	5.00	15.00	35.00
4/48-Gloria Dehaven photo-c	5.00	15.00	35.00
5/48,6/48,7/48	5.00	15.00	35.00
8/48-Story on Shirley Temple	5.00	15.00	35.00
10/48-Archie as Wolf on cover	5.00	15.00	35.00
5/49-Kathleen Hughes photo-c	4.00	12.00	28.00
7/49	4.00	12.00	28.00
8/49-Archie photo-c from radio show	5.00	15.00	35.00
10/49-Gloria Mann photo-c from radio show	5.00	15.00	35.00
11/49,12/49	4.00	12.00	28.00

ARCHIE'S JOKEBOOK COMICS DIGEST ANNUAL (See Jokebook. .)

ARCHIE'S JOKE BOOK MAGAZINE (See Joke Book . . .)
1953 - No. 3, Sum, 1954; No. 15, Fall, 1954 - No. 288, 11/82
Archie Publications

	Good	Fine	Mint
1953-One Shot(No.1)	32.00	95.00	225.00
2	17.00	50.00	120.00
3 (nn.4-14)	12.00	35.00	80.00
15-20: 14-17-Katy Keene app.	8.35	25.00	60.00
21-30	6.00	18.00	38.00
31-43	3.00	9.00	18.00
44-1st professional comic work by Neal Adams ('59), 1 pg.	10.00	30.00	70.00
45-47-Adams-a in all, 1-2 pgs.	5.50	16.50	38.00
48-Four pgs. Adams-a	5.50	16.50	38.00
49-60 (1962)	1.70	5.00	10.00
61-80	1.00	3.00	6.00
81-100	.60	1.75	3.50
101-140	.25	.75	1.50
141-200		.40	.80
201-288		.25	.50
Drug Store Giveaway (No. 39 w/new-c)	1.70	5.00	10.00

ARCHIE'S JOKES (See Archie Giant Series Mag. No. 17, 22, 27, 33, 139, 146, 154, 163, 174, 186, 198, 211, 222, 235, 247, 459, 471, 483, 495, 519)

ARCHIE'S LOVE SCENE
1973 (35-49 cents)
Spire Christian Comics (Fleming H. Revell Co.)

	Good	Fine	Mint
1(Some issues have nn)	.35	1.00	2.00

ARCHIE'S MADHOUSE (Madhouse Ma-ad No. 67 on)
Sept, 1959 - No. 66, Feb, 1969
Archie Publications

	Good	Fine	Mint
1-Archie begins	13.00	40.00	90.00
2	6.50	20.00	45.00
3-5	5.00	15.00	35.00
6-10	3.75	11.25	26.00
11-16 (Last w/regular characters)	2.65	8.00	18.00
17-21,23-30 (New format)	1.00	3.00	6.00
22-1st app. Sabrina, the Teen-age Witch (10/62)	3.00	9.00	18.00
31-40	.25	.75	1.50
41-66: 43-Mighty Crusaders cameo		.25	.50
Annual 1 (1962-63)	2.35	7.00	14.00
Annual 2 (1964)	1.20	3.50	7.00
Annual 3 (1965)-Origin Sabrina The Teen-Age Witch	.70	2.00	4.00
Annual 4-6('66-69)(Becomes Madhouse Ma-ad Annual No. 7 on)	.35	1.00	2.00

NOTE: *Cover title to 61-65 is "Madhouse" and to 66 is "Madhouse Ma-ad Jokes."*

ARCHIE'S MECHANICS
Sept, 1954 - 1955
Archie Publications

	Good	Fine	Mint
1-(15 cents; 52 pgs.)	45.00	135.00	315.00
2-(10 cents)	27.00	81.00	190.00
3-(10 cents)	22.00	65.00	154.00

ARCHIE'S ONE WAY
1972 (35 cents, 39 cents, 49 cents) (36 pages)
Spire Christian Comics (Fleming H. Revell Co.)

	Good	Fine	Mint
nn	.35	1.00	2.00

ARCHIE'S PAL, JUGHEAD (Jughead No. 127 on)
1949 - No. 126, Nov, 1965
Archie Publications

	Good	Fine	Mint
1	50.00	150.00	350.00
2	24.00	72.00	170.00

ARCHIE'S PAL, JUGHEAD (continued)

	Good	Fine	Mint
3-5	15.00	45.00	105.00
6-10: 7-Suzie app.	10.00	30.00	70.00
11-20	7.50	22.50	52.00
21-30: 23-25,28-30-Katy Keene app. 28-Debbie's Diary app.	5.00	15.00	35.00
31-50	3.00	9.00	21.00
51-70	2.35	7.00	16.00
71-100	1.35	4.00	8.00
101-126	.85	2.50	5.00
Annual 1 (1953)	21.00	63.00	150.00
Annual 2 (1954)	12.00	36.00	84.00
Annual 3-5 (1955-57)	8.00	24.00	56.00
Annual 6-8 (1958-60)	5.00	15.00	35.00

ARCHIE'S PALS 'N' GALS
1952-53 - No. 6, 1957-58; No. 7, 1958 - Present
Archie Publications

	Good	Fine	Mint
1-(116 pages)	24.00	72.00	170.00
2(Annual)('53-'54)	14.50	43.50	100.00
3-5(Annual, '54-57)	8.50	25.50	60.00
6-10('58-'60)	4.65	14.00	32.00
11-20	2.35	7.00	16.00
21-40: 29-Beatle satire	1.25	3.75	7.50
41-60	.70	2.00	4.00
61-80	.25	.75	1.50
81-110		.50	1.00
111-186		.30	.60

ARCHIE'S PARABLES
1973, 1975 (36 pages, 39-49 cents)
Spire Christian Comics (Fleming H. Revell Co.)

	Good	Fine	Mint
By Al Hartley		.40	.80

ARCHIE'S RIVAL REGGIE (Reggie No. 15 on)
1950 - No. 14, Aug, 1954
Archie Publications

	Good	Fine	Mint
1	37.00	110.00	260.00
2	19.00	58.00	130.00
3-5	12.00	36.00	84.00
6-10	7.50	22.50	52.00
11-14: Katy Keene in No. 10-14, 1-2pgs.	5.35	16.00	36.00

ARCHIE'S ROLLER COASTER
1978?
Spire Christian Comics (Fleming H. Revell Co.)

	Good	Fine	Mint
nn		.40	.80

ARCHIE'S SOMETHING ELSE
1975 (36 pages, 39-49 cents)
Spire Christian Comics (Fleming H. Revell Co.)

	Good	Fine	Mint
nn		.40	.80

ARCHIE'S SONSHINE
1973, 1974 (36 pages, 39-49 cents)
Spire Christian Comics (Fleming H. Revell Co.)

	Good	Fine	Mint
nn	.35	1.00	2.00

ARCHIE'S SPORTS SCENE
1983
Spire Christian Comics (Fleming H. Revell Co.)

	Good	Fine	Mint
nn		.40	.80

ARCHIE'S STORY & GAME COMICS DIGEST MAGAZINE
Nov?, 1986 (Digest size, $1.25, 128 pgs.)
Archie Enterprises

	Good	Fine	Mint
1		.50	1.00

ARCHIE'S SUPER HERO SPECIAL (See Archie Giant Series Magazine No. 142)

ARCHIE'S SUPER HERO SPECIAL (. . . Comics Digest Mag. 2)
Jan, 1979 - No. 2, Aug, 1979 (148 pages, 95 cents)
Archie Publications (Red Circle)

	Good	Fine	Mint
1-Simon & Kirby r-/Double Life of Pvt. Strong No. 1,2; Black Hood, The Fly, Jaguar, The Web app.		.40	.80
2-Contains contents to the never published Black Hood No. 1; origin Black Hood; Adams, Wood, McWilliams, Morrow, S&K(r)-a; Adams-c. The Shield, The Fly, Jaguar, Hangman, Steel Sterling, The Web, The Fox-r		.40	.80

ARCHIE'S TV LAUGH-OUT
Dec, 1969 - No. 106, 1986
Present
Archie Publications

	Good	Fine	Mint
1	3.35	10.00	20.00
2	1.35	4.00	8.00
3-5	.70	2.00	4.00
6-10	.25	.75	1.50
11-20		.40	.80
21-106		.25	.50

ARCHIE'S WORLD
1973, 1976 (39-49 cents)
Spire Christian Comics (Fleming H. Revell Co.)

	Good	Fine	Mint
		.40	.80

ARION, LORD OF ATLANTIS
Nov, 1982 - No. 36, Oct, 1985
DC Comics

	Good	Fine	Mint
1-Story cont'd from Warlord 62		.70	1.40
2-36: 4-Origin		.35	.70
Special No. 1 (11/85)		.55	1.10

ARISTOCATS (See Movie Comics & Walt Disney Showcase No. 16)

ARISTOCRATIC X-TRATERRESTRIAL TIME-TRAVELING THIEVES
August, 1986 (B&W)
Fictioneer Books, Ltd.

	Good	Fine	Mint
1 (28 pgs.)	.35	1.00	2.00
1 (2nd printing)-Southern Knights app.	.30	.90	1.75

ARISTOKITTENS, THE (. . . Meet Jiminy Cricket No. 1)(Disney)
Oct, 1971 - No. 9, Oct, 1975 (No. 6: 52 pages)
Gold Key

	Good	Fine	Mint
1	.50	1.50	3.00
2-9	.25	.75	1.50

ARIZONA KID, THE (Also see Wild Western)
March, 1951 - No. 6, Jan, 1952
Marvel/Atlas Comics(CSI)

	Good	Fine	Mint
1	4.50	13.50	31.50
2-4: 2-Heath-a(3)	2.65	8.00	18.00
5,6	2.15	6.50	15.00

ARK, THE (See The Crusaders)

ARMOR (AND THE SILVER STREAK)
Sept, 1985 - Present
Continuity Comics

	Good	Fine	Mint
1-Intro The Silver Streak; Adams c/a	.35	1.00	2.00
2,3	.30	.90	1.80

ARMY AND NAVY (Supersnipe No. 6 on)
May, 1941 - No. 5, Sept, 1942
Street & Smith Publications

	Good	Fine	Mint
1-Cap Fury & Nick Carter	15.00	45.00	105.00
2-Cap Fury & Nick Carter	7.00	21.00	50.00

Archie's Pal, Jughead #12, © AP

Archie's Rival Reggie #2, © AP

Arion, Lord of Atlantis #10, © DC

Arrowhead #2, © MCG

Astonishing #27, © MCG

Astonishing Tales #9 (12/71), © MCG

ARMY AND NAVY (continued)

	Good	Fine	Mint
3,4	5.00	15.00	35.00
5-Supersnipe app.; see Shadow V2No.3 for 1st app.	15.00	45.00	105.00

ARMY ATTACK
July, 1964 - No. 47, Feb, 1967
Charlton Comics

	Good	Fine	Mint
V1No.1	.30	.80	1.60
2-4(2/65)		.40	.80
V2No.38(7/65)-47 (formerly U.S. Air Force No. 1-37)		.30	.60

NOTE: ***Glanzman** a-1-3. **Montes/Bache** a-44.*

ARMY AT WAR (Also see Our Army at War, Cancelled Comic Cavalcade)
Oct-Nov, 1978
DC Comics

	Good	Fine	Mint
1-Kubert-c		.30	.60

ARMY WAR HEROES
Dec, 1963 - No. 38, June, 1970
Charlton Comics

	Good	Fine	Mint
1	.50	1.50	3.00
2-20		.50	1.00
21-38: 23-Origin & 1st app. Iron Corporal series by Glanzman. 24-Intro. Archer & Corp. Jack series		.40	.80
Modern Comics Reprint 36 ('78)		.30	.60

NOTE: ***Montes/Bache** a-1,16,17,21,23-25,27-30.*

AROUND THE BLOCK WITH DUNC & LOO (See Dunc and Loo)

AROUND THE WORLD IN 80 DAYS (See 4-Color Comics No. 784 and A Golden Picture Classic)

AROUND THE WORLD UNDER THE SEA (See Movie Classics)

AROUND THE WORLD WITH ARCHIE (See Archie Giant Series Mag. No. 29, 35, 141)

AROUND THE WORLD WITH HUCKLEBERRY & HIS FRIENDS (See Dell Giant No. 44)

ARRGH! (Satire)
Dec, 1974 - No. 5, Sept, 1975
Marvel Comics Group

	Good	Fine	Mint
1		.40	.80
2-5		.25	.50

NOTE: ***Alcala** a-2; c-3. **Everett** a-1r, 2r. **Maneely** a-4r. **Sekowsky** a-1p. **Sutton** a-1.*

ARROW, THE (See Funny Pages)
Oct, 1940 - No. 3, Oct, 1941
Centaur Publications

	Good	Fine	Mint
1-The Arrow begins(r/Funny Pages)	65.00	195.00	455.00
2-Tippy Taylor serial cont's/Amaz. Myst. Funnies 24	40.00	120.00	280.00
3-Origin Dash Dartwell, the Human Meteor; origin The Rainbow-r; bondage-c	40.00	120.00	280.00

NOTE: ***Gustavson** a-1,2; c-3.*

ARROWHEAD (See Black Rider, Wild Western)
April, 1954 - No. 4, Nov, 1954
Atlas Comics (CPS)

	Good	Fine	Mint
1-Arrowhead & his horse Eagle begin	3.00	9.00	21.00
2-4	2.00	6.00	14.00

NOTE: ***Maneely** c-2. **Sinnott** a-1-4.*

ASTONISHING (Marvel Boy No. 1,2)
No. 3, April, 1951 - No. 63, Aug, 1957
Marvel/Atlas Comics(20CC)

	Good	Fine	Mint
3-Marvel Boy cont'd.	20.00	60.00	140.00
4-6-Last Marvel Boy; 4-Stan Lee app.	16.00	48.00	110.00
7-10	3.50	10.50	24.00
11,12,15,17,18,20	2.65	8.00	18.00
13,14,16,19-Krigstein-a	3.00	9.00	21.00
21,22,24	2.15	6.50	15.00
23-E.C. swipe-'The Hole In The Wall' from VOH 16	2.75	8.25	19.00
25-Crandall-a	2.75	8.25	19.00
26-29	2.15	6.50	15.00
30-Tentacled eyeball story	3.00	9.00	21.00
31-37-Last pre-code issue	2.00	6.00	14.00
38-43,46,48,49,51,52,56,58,59,61	1.30	4.00	9.00
44-Crandall swipe/Weird Fantasy 22	2.45	7.50	17.00
45,47-Krigstein-a	2.45	7.50	17.00
50-Ditko-a	1.75	5.25	12.00
53-Crandall, Ditko-a	1.75	5.25	12.00
54-Torres-a	1.75	5.25	12.00
55-Crandall, Torres-a	2.35	7.00	16.50
57-Williamson/Krenkel-a, 4 pgs.	3.85	11.50	27.00
60-Williamson/Mayo-a, 4 pgs.	3.85	11.50	27.00
62-Torres, Woodbridge, Powell -a	1.60	4.80	11.00
63-Last issue; Woodbridge-a	1.60	4.80	11.00

NOTE: ***Berg** a-36, 53, 56. **Cameron** a-50. **Gene Colan** a-12, 20, 29, 56. **Ditko** a-50, 53. **Drucker** a-41. **Everett** a-3-5(3), 6, 10, 12, 37, 47, 48, 58, 61; c-3-5, 13, 15, 16, 18, 29, 47, 51, 53-55, 57, 59-62. **Fass** a-34. **Fuje** a-11. **Heath** c/a-8; c-9, 26. **Kirby** a-56. **Lawrence** a-28, 37, 38, 42. **Maneely** c-31, 33, 34, 56. **Moldoff** a-33. **Morrow** a-52, 61. **Orlando** a-47, 58, 61. **Powell** a-43, 44, 48. **Ravielli** a-28. **Reinman** a-34. **Robinson** a-20. **J. Romita** a-7, 24, 43, 57, 61. **Roussos** a-55. **Sekowsky** a-13. **Severin** c-46. **Sinnott** a-30. **Ed Win** a-20. Canadian reprints exist.*

ASTONISHING TALES (See Ka-Zar)
Aug, 1970 - No. 36, July, 1976
Marvel Comics Group

	Good	Fine	Mint
1-Ka-Zar by Kirby(p) & Dr. Doom by Wood begin		.75	1.50
2-Kirby, Wood-a		.50	1.00
3-6: Smith-a(p); Wood-a-No. 3,4. 5-Red Skull app.	.40	1.25	2.50
7-9: 8-Last Dr. Doom. (52 pgs.). 9-Lorna the Jungle Girl-r		.35	.70
10-Smith-a(p)	.40	1.25	2.50
11-Origin Ka-Zar & Zabu		.50	1.00
12-Man Thing by Adams	.40	1.25	2.50
13-20: 14-Jann of the Jungle app. 20-Last Ka-Zar		.35	.70
21-24: 21-It! the Living Colossus begins, ends No. 24		.25	.50
25-Deathlok the Demolisher begins; Perez 1st work, 2pgs. (8/74)	.35	1.20	2.40
26-30: 29-Guardians of the Galaxy app.		.50	1.00
31-36: 31-Wrightson-c(i)		.30	.60

NOTE: ***Buckler** a-13i, 16p, 25, 26p, 27p, 28, 29p-36p; c-13, 25p, 26-30, 32-35p, 36. **John Buscema** a-9, 12p, 13p, 16p; c-4-6p, 12p. **Colan** a-7p, 8p. **Ditko** a-21r. **Everett** a-6i. **G. Kane** a-11p, 15p; c-10p, 11p, 15p, 21p. **McWilliams** a-30i. **Starlin** a-19p; c-16p. **Sutton & Trimpe** a-8. **Tuska** a-5p, 6p. **Wood** a-1-4.*

ASTRO BOY (TV) (Also see March of Comics No. 285)
August, 1965
Gold Key

	Good	Fine	Mint
1(10151-508)	5.00	15.00	35.00

ASTRO COMICS
1969 - 1979 (Giveaway)
American Airlines (Harvey)

	Good	Fine	Mint
nn-Has Harvey's Casper, Spooky, Hot Stuff, Stumbo the Giant, Little Audrey, Little Lotta, & Richie Rich reprints	.70	2.00	4.00

ATARI FORCE
Jan, 1984 - No. 20, Aug, 1985 (Mando paper)
DC Comics

ATARI FORCE (continued)

	Good	Fine	Mint
1-1st app. Tempest, Packrat, Babe, Morphea, & Dart	.25	.75	1.50
2-20		.40	.80
Special 1 (4/86)	.25	.80	1.60

NOTE: ***Byrne*** *c-Special 1i.* ***Giffen*** *a-12p, 13i.* ***Rogers*** *a-18p, Special 1p.*

A-TEAM, THE
March, 1984 - No. 3, May, 1984
Marvel Comics Group

	Good	Fine	Mint
1-3		.30	.60

ATLANTIS, THE LOST CONTINENT (See 4-Color No. 1188)

ATLAS (See First Issue Special)

ATOM, THE (See Action, All-American, Brave & the Bold, D.C. Special Series No. 1, Detective, Showcase, & World's Finest)

ATOM, THE (. . . & the Hawkman No. 39 on)
June-July, 1962 - No. 38, Aug-Sept, 1968
National Periodical Publications

	Good	Fine	Mint
1-Intro Plant-Master	7.50	22.00	50.00
2	3.35	10.00	20.00
3-1st Time Pool story; 1st app. Chronos (origin)	3.00	9.00	18.00
4,5: 4-Snapper Carr x-over	2.50	7.50	15.00
6-10: 7-Hawkman x-over. 8-Justice League, Dr. Light app.	1.85	5.50	11.00
11-20: 19-Zatanna x-over	.70	2.00	4.00
21-30: 29-Golden Age Atom x-over	.45	1.25	2.50
31-38: 31-Hawkman x-over. 36-G.A. Atom x-over. 37-Intro. Major Mynah; Hawkman cameo	.30	.90	1.80

NOTE: ***Anderson*** *a-1-11i, 13i; c-inks-1-25, 31-35, 37.* ***Sid Greene*** *a-8i-38i.* ***Gil Kane*** *a-1p-38p; c-1p-28p, 29, 33p, 34. Pool stories also in 6, 9,12, 17, 21, 27, 35.*

ATOM AGE (See Classics Special)

ATOM-AGE COMBAT
June, 1952 - No. 5, April, 1953
St. John Publishing Co.

	Good	Fine	Mint
1	13.00	40.00	90.00
2	8.50	25.00	60.00
3,5: 3-Mayo-a, 6 pgs.	6.50	20.00	45.00
4 (Scarce)	8.00	24.00	56.00
1(2/58-St. John)	5.00	15.00	35.00

ATOM-AGE COMBAT
Nov, 1958 - No. 3, March, 1959
Fago Magazines

	Good	Fine	Mint
1	6.50	20.00	45.00
2,3	5.00	15.00	35.00

ATOMAN
Feb, 1946 - No. 2, April, 1946
Spark Publications

	Good	Fine	Mint
1-Origin Atoman; Robinson/Meskin-a; Kidcrusaders, Wild Bill Hickok, Marvin the Great app.	16.00	48.00	110.00
2: Robinson/Meskin-a	10.00	30.00	70.00

ATOM & HAWKMAN, THE (Formerly The Atom)
No. 39, Oct-Nov, 1968 - No. 45, Oct-Nov, 1969
National Periodical Publications

	Good	Fine	Mint
39-45: 43-1st app. Gentlemen Ghost, origin-44		.30	.60

NOTE: ***Sid Greene*** *a-40i-45i.* ***Kubert*** *a-40p, 41p; c-39-45.*

ATOM ANT (TV)
January, 1966 (Hanna-Barbera)
Gold Key

	Good	Fine	Mint
1(10170-601)	2.50	7.50	15.00

ATOMIC ATTACK (Formerly Attack, first series)
No. 5, Jan, 1953 - No. 8, Oct, 1953
Youthful Magazines

	Good	Fine	Mint
5-Atomic bomb-c	10.00	30.00	70.00
6-8	5.00	15.00	35.00

ATOMIC BOMB
1945 (36 pgs.)
Jay Burtis Publications

	Good	Fine	Mint
1-Airmale & Stampy	5.50	16.50	38.00

ATOMIC BUNNY (Formerly Atomic Rabbit)
No. 12, Aug, 1958 - No. 19, Dec, 1959
Charlton Comics

	Good	Fine	Mint
12	3.00	9.00	21.00
13-19	1.50	4.50	10.00

ATOMIC COMICS
1946 (Reprints)
Daniels Publications (Canadian)

	Good	Fine	Mint
1-Rocketman, Yankee Boy, Master Key; bondage-c	6.50	19.50	45.00
2-4	4.00	12.00	28.00

ATOMIC COMICS
Jan, 1946 - No. 4, July-Aug, 1946
Green Publishing Co.

	Good	Fine	Mint
1-Radio Squad by Siegel & Shuster; Barry O'Neal app.; Fang Gow cover-r/Det. Comics	16.00	48.00	110.00
2-Inspector Dayton; Kid Kane by Matt Baker; Lucky Wings, Congo King, Prop Powers (only app.) begin	13.00	40.00	90.00
3,4: 3-Zero Ghost Detective app.; Baker-a(2) each; 4-Kamen-c	7.00	21.00	50.00

ATOMIC MOUSE (See Blue Bird & Giant Comics)
3/53 - No. 54, 6/63; No. 1, 12/84; V2/10, 9/85 - No. 13, ?/86
Capitol Stories/Charlton Comics

	Good	Fine	Mint
1-Origin	6.00	18.00	42.00
2	3.00	9.00	21.00
3-10: 5-Timmy The Timid Ghost app.; see Zoo Funnies	2.15	6.50	15.00
11-13,16-25	1.35	4.00	9.00
14,15-Hoppy The Marvel Bunny app.	1.50	4.50	10.00
26-(68 pages)	2.35	7.00	16.00
27-40: 36,37-Atom The Cat app.	1.00	3.00	7.00
41-54	.45	1.35	3.00
1 (1984)		.40	.80
V2/10 (10/85) -13-Fago-r. No.12(1/86)		.40	.75

ATOMIC RABBIT (Atomic Bunny No. 12 on)
August, 1955 - No. 11, March, 1958
Charlton Comics

	Good	Fine	Mint
1-Origin; Al Fago-a	5.50	16.50	38.00
2	2.85	8.50	20.00
3-10-Fago-a in most	2.15	6.50	15.00
11-(68 pages)	2.65	8.00	18.00

ATOMIC SPY CASES
Mar-Apr, 1950
Avon Periodicals

	Good	Fine	Mint
1-Painted-c; No Wood-a	11.50	34.50	80.00

ATOMIC THUNDERBOLT, THE
Feb, 1946 - No. 2, April, 1946
Regor Company

	Good	Fine	Mint
1,2: 1-Intro. Atomic Thunderbolt & Mr. Murdo	6.50	20.00	46.00

The Atom #1, © DC

Atom-Age Combat #1 (6/52), © STJ

Atomic Bunny #17, © CC

Atomic War #1, © ACE

Augie Doggie #1, © Hanna-Barbera

Authentic Police Cases #6, © STJ

ATOMIC WAR!
Nov, 1952 - No. 4, April, 1953
Ace Periodicals (Junior Books)

	Good	Fine	Mint
1-Atomic bomb-c	32.00	95.00	225.00
2,3: 3-Atomic bomb-c	22.00	66.00	154.00
4-Used in **POP**, pg. 96 & illo.	23.00	68.00	160.00

ATOM THE CAT (Formerly Tom Cat)
No. 9, Oct, 1957 - No. 17, Aug, 1959
Charlton Comics

9	2.35	7.00	16.00
10,13-17	1.15	3.50	8.00
11-(64 pages)-Atomic Mouse app., 12(100 pages)	1.75	5.25	12.00

ATTACK
May, 1952 - No. 4, Nov, 1952; No. 5, Jan, 1953 - No. 5, Sept, 1953
Youthful Mag./Trojan No. 5 on

1-(1st series)-Extreme violence	4.35	13.00	30.00
2,3	2.35	7.00	16.00
4-Krenkel-a, 7 pgs, Harrison-a. (Becomes Atomic Attack No. 5 on)	2.65	8.00	18.00
5-(No. 1, Trojan, 2nd series)	2.35	7.00	16.00
6-8 (No. 2-4), 5	1.75	5.25	12.00

ATTACK
No. 54, 1958 - No. 60, Nov, 1959
Charlton Comics

54(100 pages)	2.00	6.00	14.00
55-60	.45	1.35	3.00

ATTACK!
1962 - No. 15, 3/75; No. 16, 8/79 - No. 48, 10/84
Charlton Comics

nn(No. 1)-('62) Special Edition	.35	1.00	2.00
2('63), 3(Fall, '64)		.50	1.00
V4No.3(10/66), 4(10/67)-(Formerly Special War Series No. 2; becomes Attack At Sea V4No.5)		.30	.60
1(9/71)		.50	1.00
2-15(3/75): 4-American Eagle app.		.40	.80
16(8/79) - 47		.30	.60
48(10/84)-Wood-r; S&K-c		.40	.80
Modern Comics 13('78)-r		.20	.40

ATTACK!
1975 (39¢, 49¢) (36 pages)
Spire Christian Comics (Fleming H. Revell Co.)

nn		.40	.80

ATTACK AT SEA (Formerly Attack!, 1967)
October, 1968
Charlton Comics

V4No.5		.30	.60

ATTACK ON PLANET MARS
1951
Avon Periodicals

nn-Infantino, Fawcette, Kubert & Wood-a; adaptation of Tarrano the Conqueror by Ray Cummings	42.00	125.00	294.00

AUDREY & MELVIN (Formerly Little. . .)
No. 62, September, 1974
Harvey Publications

62		.30	.60

AUGIE DOGGIE (TV) (See Whitman Comic Books)
October, 1963 (Hanna-Barbera)
Gold Key

	Good	Fine	Mint
1	2.00	6.00	12.00

AURORA COMIC SCENES INSTRUCTION BOOKLET
1974 (Slick paper, 8 pgs.)(6¼x9¾")(in full color)
(Included with superhero model kits)
Aurora Plastics Co.

181-140-Tarzan; Adams-a	.35	1.00	2.00
182-140-Spider-Man; 183-140-Tonto(Gil Kane art); 184-140-Hulk; 185-140-Superman; 186-140-Superboy; 187-140-Batman; 188-140-The Lone Ranger(1974-by Gil Kane); 192-140-Captain America (1975); 193-140-Robin each. . . .		.50	1.00

AUTHENTIC POLICE CASES
Feb, 1948 - No. 38, Mar, 1955
St. John Publishing Co.

1-Hale the Magician by Tuska begins; bondage-c	9.00	27.00	64.00
2-Lady Satan, Johnny Rebel app.	5.00	15.00	35.00
3-Veiled Avenger app.; blood drainage story plus 2 Lucky Coyne stories; used in **SOTI**, illo. from Red Seal No. 16; bondage-c	19.50	58.00	136.00
4,5: 4-Masked Black Jack app. 5-Late 1930s Jack Cole-a(r); transvestism story	5.00	15.00	35.00
6-Matt Baker-c; used in **SOTI**, illo-"An invitation to learning", r-in Fugitives From Justice No. 3; Jack Cole-a; also used by the N.Y. Legis. Comm.	19.50	58.00	136.00
7,8,10-14: 7-Jack Cole-a; Matt Baker art begins No. 8; Vic Flint in No. 10-14	5.50	16.50	38.00
9-No Vic Flint	4.35	13.00	30.00
15-Drug c/story; Vic Flint app.; Baker-c	6.35	19.00	44.00
16,18,20,21,23	3.00	9.00	21.00
17,19,22-Baker-c	3.35	10.00	23.00
24-28 (All 100 pages): 26-Transvestism story. 27-Junkie mention	9.00	27.00	64.00
29,30	2.15	6.50	15.00
31,32,37-Baker-c	2.50	7.50	17.50
33-Transvestism; Baker-c	3.00	9.00	21.00
34-Drug-c by Baker	3.50	10.50	24.00
35-Baker c/a(2)	3.35	10.00	23.00
36-Vic Flint strip-r; Baker-c	2.50	7.50	17.50
38-Baker c/a	3.35	10.00	23.00

NOTE: ***Matt Baker*** *c-7-16, 22, 36-38; a-13, 16.*

AVENGER, THE (See A-1 Comics)
1955 - No. 4, Aug-Sept, 1955
Magazine Enterprises

1(A-1 129)-Origin	10.00	30.00	70.00
2(A-1 131), 3(A-1 133), 4(A-1 138)	5.00	15.00	35.00
IW Reprint No. 9('64)-Reprints No. 1 (new cover)	1.20	3.50	7.00

NOTE: ***Powell*** *a-2-4; c-1-4.*

AVENGERS, THE (See Kree/Skrull War Starring. .)
Sept, 1963 - Present
Marvel Comics Group

1-Origin The Avengers (Thor, Iron Man, Hulk, Ant-Man, Wasp)	55.00	140.00	440.00
2	20.00	50.00	135.00
3	13.50	34.00	90.00
4-Revival of Captain America who joins the Avengers	22.00	55.00	175.00
4-Reprint from the Golden Record Comic set	1.50	4.50	9.00
With Record. . . .	4.15	12.50	25.00
5-Hulk leaves	7.70	19.50	54.00
6-10: 6-Intro The Masters of Evil. 8-Intro Kang. 9-Intro Wonder Man who dies in same story	6.00	15.00	42.00

THE AVENGERS (continued)	Good	Fine	Mint
11-15: 15-Death of Zemo	4.00	10.00	28.00
16-19: 16-New Avengers line-up (Hawkeye, Quicksilver, Scarlet Witch join; Thor, Iron Man, Giant-Man & Wasp leave.) 19-Intro. Swordsman; origin Hawkeye	2.65	6.75	20.00
20-22: Wood inks	1.75	4.50	12.00
23-30: 28-Giant-Man becomes Goliath	1.25	3.75	7.50
31-40	.75	2.25	4.50
41-50: 48-Intro/Origin new Black Knight	.60	1.80	3.60
51,52,54-56: 52-Black Panther joins; Intro The Grim Reaper. 54-Intro new Masters of Evil	.60	1.80	3.60
53-X-Men app.	1.15	3.50	7.00
57-Intro. The Vision	2.15	6.50	13.00
58-Origin The Vision	1.85	5.50	11.00
59-65,68-70: 59-Intro. Yellowjacket. 60-Wasp & Yellowjacket wed. 63-Goliath becomes Yellowjacket; Hawkeye becomes the new Goliath	.90	2.75	5.50
66,67: Smith-a	1.35	4.00	8.00
71-1st Invaders; Black Knight joins	.85	2.50	5.00
72-80: 80-Intro. Red Wolf	.70	2.00	4.00
81,82,84-91: 87-Origin The Black Panther. 88-Written by Harlan Ellison	.70	2.00	4.00
83-Intro. The Liberators (Wasp, Valkyrie, Scarlet Witch, Medusa & the Black Widow)	.85	2.50	5.00
92-Adams-c	.85	2.50	5.00
93-(52 pgs.)-Adams c/a	5.00	15.00	30.00
94-96-Adams c/a	2.50	7.50	15.00
97-G.A. Capt. America, Sub-Mariner, Human Torch, Patriot, Vision, Blazing Skull, Fin, Angel, & New Capt. Marvel x-over;	1.00	3.00	6.00
98-Goliath becomes Hawkeye; Smith c/a(i)	1.70	5.00	10.00
99-Smith/Sutton-a	1.70	5.00	10.00
100-Smith c/a; featuring everyone who was an Avenger	3.00	9.00	18.00
101-Written by Harlan Ellison	.70	2.00	4.00
102-106,108,109	.70	2.00	4.00
107-Starlin-a(p)	.75	2.20	4.40
110,111-X-Men app.	.95	2.75	5.50
112-1st app. Mantis	.70	2.00	4.00
113-120: 116-118-Defenders/Silver Surfer app.	.50	1.50	3.00
121-130: 123-Origin Mantis	.50	1.50	3.00
131-133,136-140	.40	1.25	2.50
134,135-True origin The Vision	.50	1.50	3.00
141-149: 144-Origin & 1st app. Hellcat	.35	1.10	2.20
150-Kirby-a(r); new line-up begins: Capt. America, Scarlet Witch, Iron Man, Wasp, Yellowjacket, Vision & The Beast	.40	1.20	2.40
151-163: 151-Wonderman returns with new costume	.40	1.10	2.20
164-166-Byrne-a	.65	2.00	4.00
167-170	.35	1.00	2.00
171-180	.25	.75	1.50
181-191-Byrne-a. 181-New line-up: Capt. America, Scarlet Witch, Iron Man, Wasp, Vision, The Beast & The Falcon. 183-Ms Marvel joins. 186-Origin Quicksilver & Scarlet Witch	.40	1.25	2.50
192-199,201,202: Perez-a. 195-1st Taskmaster	.25	.75	1.50
200-Dbl size; Ms. Marvel leaves	.25	.75	1.50
203-220: 211-New line-up: Capt. America, Iron Man, Tigra, Thor, Wasp & Yellowjacket. 213-Yellowjacket leaves. 216-Tigra leaves		.40	.80
221-230: 221-Hawkeye & She-Hulk join. 227-Capt. Marvel (Female) joins; origins of Ant-Man, Wasp, Giant-Man, Goliath, Yellowjacket, & Avengers		.40	.80
231-250: 231-Ironman leaves. 232-Starfox (Eros) joins. 234-Origin Quicksilver, Scarlet Witch. 236-New logo. 238-Origin Blackout. 240-Spider-Woman revived		.40	.80

	Good	Fine	Mint
251-262,264-271,274-280		.40	.80
263-X-Factor tie-in	.30	.85	1.70
272-Alpha Flight guest		.50	1.00
273-Giant size Annual (11/86)		.50	1.00
Annual 6(11/76)	.50	1.50	3.00
Annual 7(11/77)-Starlin c/a; Warlock dies	1.00	3.00	6.00
Annual 8(10/78)	.35	1.00	2.00
Annual 9(10/79)-Newton-a	.25	.75	1.50
Annual 10(10/81)-Golden-p; X-Men cameo	.25	.75	1.50
Annual 11(12/82), 12(1/84), 13(11/84),		.50	1.00
Annual 14(11/85), 15(10/86)		.65	1.30
Special 1(9/67)	2.00	6.00	12.00
Special 2(9/68)	1.00	3.00	6.00
Special 3(9/69)	1.00	3.00	6.00
Special 4(1/71), 5(1/72)	.75	2.20	4.40
Giant Size 1(8/74)	.70	2.00	4.00
Giant Size 2(11/74)(death of the Swordsman), 3(2/75)	.50	1.50	3.00
Giant Size 4(6/75)(Vision marries Scarlet Witch), 5(12/75)	.35	1.00	2.00

NOTE: ***Austin*** *c(i)-157, 167, 168, 170-77, 181, 183-88, 198-201, Annual 8.* ***Buckler*** *a-101p, 102p, 106p, Gnt.-Size 1p; c-101p, 102p, 106-108p.* ***John Buscema*** *a-41-44p, 46p, 47p, 49, 50, 51-62p, 68-71, 74-77, 79-85, 87-91, 97, 105p, 121p, 124p, 125p, 152, 153p; c-41-66, 68-71, 73-91, 97-99, 178.* ***Byrne*** *a-164-66p, 181-191p, 233p, Annual 13; c-186-190p, 233p.* ***Colan*** *c/a(p)-63-65, 111, 206-208, 210.* ***Guice*** *a-Annual 12p.* ***Kane*** *c-37p, 159p.* ***Kane/Everett*** *c-97.* ***Kirby*** *a-1-8p, Special 3, 4p; c-1-30, 148, 151-158; layouts-14-16.* ***Marcos*** *a(i)-154-177, Annual 8; c-163i.* ***Miller*** *c-193p.* ***Mooney*** *a-86i, 179p, 180p.* ***Nebres*** *a-178i; c-179i.* ***Newton*** *a-204p, Annual 9p.* ***Perez*** *a(p)-141, 144, 148, 154p, 155p, 160p, 161, 162, 167, 168, 170, 171, 194, 195, 196p, 198-202, Annual 6(p), 8; c-160-162p, 164-166p, 170-74p, 181p, 183-85p, 191p, 192p, 194-201p, Annual 8.* ***Starlin*** *c-121.* ***Staton*** *a-127-134i.* ***Tuska*** *a-47i, 48i, 51i, 53i, 54i, 106p, 107p, 135p, 137-140p, 163p.*

AVENGERS, THE (TV)
Nov, 1968 (''John Steed & Emma Peel'' cover title) (15¢)
Gold Key

1-Photo-c	7.00	21.00	42.00

AVENGERS VS. THE X-MEN
April, 1987 - Present
Marvel Comics Group

1	.25	.75	1.50

A-V IN 3-D
Dec, 1984 (28 pgs., w/glasses)
Aardvark-Vanaheim

1-Cerebus, Ms. Tree, Normalman	.70	2.00	4.00

AVIATION ADVENTURES AND MODEL BUILDING
Dec, 1946 - No. 17, Feb, 1947 (True Aviation Adv. . . No. 15)
Parents' Magazine Institute

16,17-Half comics and half pictures	2.50	7.50	17.00

AVIATION CADETS
1943
Street & Smith Publications

	4.50	13.50	31.00

AWFUL OSCAR (Formerly & becomes Oscar with No. 13)
No. 11, June, 1949 - No. 12, Aug, 1949
Marvel Comics

11,12	2.15	6.50	15.00

AXEL PRESSBUTTON (Pressbutton No. 5; see Laser Eraser & Pressbutton)
11/84 - No. 6, 7/85 ($1.50-$1.75)
Eclipse Comics

1-r/Warrior (British mag.); Bolland-c; origin Laser Eraser & Pressbutton; Baxter paper	.25	.75	1.50
2-6	.30	.90	1.80

Avengers #57, © MCG

Avengers #1 (GK), © ABC TV

Axel Pressbutton #1, © Eclipse

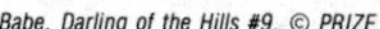

Babe, Darling of the Hills #9, © PRIZE

Badger #2, © First

Baffling Mysteries #22, © ACE

AZ
1984 - No. 2, 1984
Comico

	Good	Fine	Mint
1	.70	2.00	4.00
2	.35	1.10	2.20

AZTEC ACE
3/84 - No. 15, 9/85 (Baxter paper, 36 pgs. No. 2 on)
Eclipse Comics

	Good	Fine	Mint
1-$2.25 cover (52 pgs.)	.50	1.50	3.00
2,3-$1.50 cover	.35	1.00	2.00
4-15-$1.75-$1.50 cover	.35	1.10	2.20

NOTE: ***N. Redondo** a-1i-8i, 10i; c-6-8i.*

BABE (. . . Darling of the Hills, later issues)(Also see Big Shot, Sparky Watts)
June-July, 1948 - No. 11, Apr-May, 1950
Prize/Headline/Feature

	Good	Fine	Mint
1-Boody Rogers-a	6.50	19.50	45.00
2-Boody Rogers-a	4.35	13.00	30.00
3-11-All by Boody Rogers	3.50	10.50	24.50

BABE AMAZON OF OZARKS
No. 5, 1948
Standard Comics

	Good	Fine	Mint
5	3.35	10.00	23.00

BABE RUTH SPORTS COMICS
April, 1949 - No. 11, Feb, 1951
Harvey Publications

	Good	Fine	Mint
1-Powell-a	7.00	21.00	50.00
2-Powell-a	5.00	15.00	35.00
3-11: Powell-a in most	4.00	12.00	28.00

BABES IN TOYLAND (See 4-Color No. 1282 & Golden Pix Story Book ST-3)

BABY HUEY AND PAPA (See Paramount Animated . . .)
May, 1962 - No. 33, Jan, 1968 (Also see Casper The Friendly . .)
Harvey Publications

	Good	Fine	Mint
1	6.75	20.00	40.00
2	3.35	10.00	20.00
3-5	2.00	6.00	12.00
6-10	1.35	4.00	8.00
11-20	.70	2.00	4.00
21-33	.35	1.00	2.00

BABY HUEY DUCKLAND
Nov, 1962 - No. 15, Nov, 1966 (25 cent Giant)
Harvey Publications

	Good	Fine	Mint
1	4.00	12.00	24.00
2-5	1.70	5.00	10.00
6-15	.85	2.50	5.00

BABY HUEY, THE BABY GIANT (Also see Casper, Harvey Hits No. 22, Comics Hits No. 60, & Paramount Animated Comics)
9/56 - No. 97, 10/71; No. 98, 10/72; No. 99, 10/80
Harvey Publications

	Good	Fine	Mint
1-Infinity-c	18.00	56.00	125.00
2	10.00	30.00	70.00
3-Baby Huey takes anti-pep pills	5.35	16.00	38.00
4,5	4.00	12.00	28.00
6-10	2.00	6.00	14.00
11-20	1.35	4.00	9.00
21-40	1.00	3.00	7.00
41-60	.70	2.00	4.00
61-79(12/67)	.35	1.00	2.00
80(12/68) - 98-All Giants	.50	1.50	3.00
99		.50	1.00

BABY SNOOTS (Also see March of Comics No. 359,371,396,401, 419,431,443,450,462,474,485)
Aug, 1970 - No. 22, Nov, 1975
Gold Key

	Good	Fine	Mint
1	.50	1.50	3.00
2-22: 22-Titled Snoots, the Forgetful Elefink		.60	1.20

BACHELOR FATHER (TV)
No. 1332, 4-6/62 - No. 2, 1962
Dell Publishing Co.

	Good	Fine	Mint
4-Color 1332 (No. 1)	3.00	9.00	21.00
2-Written by Stanley	3.00	9.00	21.00

BACHELOR'S DIARY
1949
Avon Periodicals

	Good	Fine	Mint
1(Scarce)-King Features panel cartoons & text-r; pin-up, girl wrestling photos	15.00	45.00	105.00

BADGE OF JUSTICE
No. 22, 1/55 - No. 23, 3/55; 4/55 - No. 4, 10/55
Charlton Comics

	Good	Fine	Mint
22(1/55)	2.00	6.00	14.00
23(3/55), 1	1.35	4.00	9.00
2-4	1.00	3.00	7.00

BADGER, THE
Oct, 1983 - Present (Baxter paper)
Capital Comics/First Comics No. 5 on

	Good	Fine	Mint
1-The Badger, Ham the Weather Wizard begin	.90	2.75	5.50
2-4	.75	2.40	4.80
5(5/85) - 10	.40	1.20	2.40
11-22	.35	1.10	2.20

BADMEN OF THE WEST
1951 (Giant - 132 pages)
Avon Periodicals

	Good	Fine	Mint
1-Contains rebound copies of Jesse James, King of the Bad Men of Deadwood, Badmen of Tombstone; other combinations possible Issues with Kubert-a. . . .	13.50	40.00	95.00

BADMEN OF THE WEST! (See A-1 Comics)
1953 - No. 3, 1954
Magazine Enterprises

	Good	Fine	Mint
1(A-1 100)-Meskin-a?	7.00	21.00	50.00
2(A-1 120), 3: 2-Larsen-a	4.00	12.00	28.00

BADMEN OF TOMBSTONE
1950
Avon Periodicals

	Good	Fine	Mint
nn	5.50	16.50	38.00

BAFFLING MYSTERIES (Formerly Indian Braves No. 1-4; Heroes of the Wild Frontier No. 26-on)
No. 5, Nov, 1951 - No. 26, Oct, 1955
Periodical House (Ace Magazines)

	Good	Fine	Mint
5	5.75	17.00	40.00
6,7,9,10: 10-E.C. Crypt Keeper swipe on-c	3.35	10.00	23.00
8-Woodish-a by Cameron	4.00	12.00	28.00
11-24: 24-Last pre-code ish	3.00	9.00	21.00
25-Reprints; surrealistic-c	3.35	10.00	23.00
26-Reprints	2.35	7.00	16.00

NOTE: ***Cameron** a-8, 16-18, 20-22. **Colan** a-5, 11, 25r/5. **Sekowsky** a-5, 6, 22. Bondage c-20. Reprints in 18(1), 19(1), 24(3).*

BALBO (See Mighty Midget Comics)

BALDER THE BRAVE
Nov, 1985 - No. 4, 1986 (mini-series)

BALDER THE BRAVE (continued)
Marvel Comics Group

	Good	Fine	Mint
1-Simonson c/a begins		.60	1.20
2-4		.50	1.00

BALOO & LITTLE BRITCHES
April, 1968 (Walt Disney)
Gold Key

	Good	Fine	Mint
1-From the Jungle Book	1.35	4.00	8.00

BALTIMORE COLTS
1950 (Giveaway)
American Visuals Corp.

	Good	Fine	Mint
Eisner-c	20.00	60.00	140.00

BAMBI (See 4-Color No. 12,30,186, Movie Classics, Movie Comics, and Walt Disney Showcase No. 31)

BAMBI (Disney)
1941, 1942, 1984
K. K. Publications (Giveaways)/Whitman Publ. Co.

	Good	Fine	Mint
1941-Horlick's Malted Milk & various toy stores - text & pictures; most copies mailed out with store stickers on cover	13.00	40.00	90.00
1942-Same as 4-Color 12, but no price (Same as '41 issue?) (Scarce)	18.00	54.00	125.00
1-(Whitman, 1984; 60¢ cover price)-r/4-Color 186		.30	.60

BAMM BAMM & PEBBLES FLINTSTONE (TV)
Oct, 1964 (Hanna-Barbera)
Gold Key

	Good	Fine	Mint
1	1.70	5.00	10.00

BANANA OIL
1924 (52 pages)(Black & White)
MS Publ. Co.

	Good	Fine	Mint
Milt Gross-a; not reprints	8.00	24.00	56.00

BANANA SPLITS, THE (TV) (See March of Comics No. 364)
June, 1969 - No. 8, Oct, 1971 (Hanna-Barbera)
Gold Key

	Good	Fine	Mint
1	.85	2.50	5.00
2-8	.40	1.20	2.40

BAND WAGON (See Hanna-Barbera . . .)

BANG-UP COMICS
Dec, 1941 - No. 3, June, 1942
Progressive Publishers

	Good	Fine	Mint
1-Cosmo Mann & Lady Fairplay begin; Buzz Balmer by Rick Yager in all (origin No. 1)	28.00	84.00	195.00
2,3	17.00	51.00	120.00

BANNER COMICS (Captain Courageous No. 6)
No. 3, Sept., 1941 - No. 5, Jan, 1942
Ace Magazines

	Good	Fine	Mint
3-Captain Courageous & Lone Warrior & Sidekick Dicky begin	35.00	105.00	245.00
4,5: 4-Flag-c	24.00	72.00	168.00

BARABBAS
1986 - Present ($1.50, B&W)
Slave Labor Graphics

	Good	Fine	Mint
1	.35	1.00	2.00
2	.25	.75	1.50

BARBARIANS, THE
June, 1975
Atlas Comics/Seaboard Periodicals

	Good	Fine	Mint
1-Origin, only app. Andrax; Iron Jaw app.		.50	1.00

BARBARIC TALES
1986 - Present (B&W; mature readers)
Pyramid Comics

	Good	Fine	Mint
1-3,3½	.30	.90	1.70

BARBIE & KEN
May-July, 1962 - No. 5, Nov-Jan, 1963-64
Dell Publishing Co.

	Good	Fine	Mint
01-053-207(No. 1)	3.50	10.50	24.00
2-5	2.15	6.50	15.00

BAREFOOTZ-THE COMIX BOOK STORIES
Mar, 1986 ($1.70, B&W)
Renegade Press

	Good	Fine	Mint
1-Reprints	.30	.85	1.70

BARKER, THE
Autumn, 1946 - No. 15, Dec, 1949
Quality Comics Group/Comic Magazine

	Good	Fine	Mint
1	4.35	13.00	30.00
2	2.15	6.50	15.00
3-10	1.65	5.00	11.50
11-14	1.15	3.50	8.00
15-Jack Cole-a(p)	1.65	5.00	11.50

NOTE: ***Jack Cole** art in some issues.*

BARNEY AND BETTY RUBBLE (TV) (Flintstones' Neighbors)
Jan, 1973 - No. 23, Dec, 1976 (Hanna-Barbera)
Charlton Comics

	Good	Fine	Mint
1	1.00	3.00	6.00
2-10	.60	1.80	3.60
11-23	.40	1.20	2.40

BARNEY BAXTER
1938 - 1956
David McKay/Dell Publishing Co./Argo

	Good	Fine	Mint
Feature Books 15(McKay-1938)	13.50	40.00	95.00
4-Color 20(1942)	11.50	34.50	80.00
4,5	5.50	16.50	38.00
1,2(1956-Argo)	2.15	6.50	15.00

BARNEY BEAR HOME PLATE
1979 (49 cents)
Spire Christian Comics (Fleming H. Revell Co.)

	Good	Fine	Mint
		.30	.60

BARNEY BEAR LOST AND FOUND
1979 (49 cents)
Spire Christian Comics (Fleming H. Revell Co.)

	Good	Fine	Mint
nn		.30	.60

BARNEY BEAR OUT OF THE WOODS
1980 (49 cents)
Spire Christian Comics (Fleming H. Revell Co.)

	Good	Fine	Mint
nn		.30	.60

BARNEY BEAR SUNDAY SCHOOL PICNIC
1981 (69 cents)
Spire Christian Comics (Fleming H. Revell Co.)

	Good	Fine	Mint
nn		.30	.60

BARNEY BEAR THE SWAMP GANG!
1980 (59 cents)
Spire Christian Comics (Fleming H. Revell Co.)

Bambi (1941), © WDC

Banner Comics #5, © ACE

Barbaric Tales #1, © Pyramid

Barnyard Comics #6, © STD

Baseball Thrills #2, © Z-D

Batman #1, © DC

BARNEY BEAR... (continued) — Good / Fine / Mint
nn — .30 .60

BARNEY BEAR WAKES UP
1977 (39 cents)
Spire Christian Comics (Fleming H. Revell Co.)

nn — .30 .60

BARNEY GOOGLE AND SPARK PLUG (See Comic Monthly & Giant Comic Album)
1923 - 1928 (Daily strip reprints; B&W) (52 pages)
Cupples & Leon Co.

	Good	Fine	Mint
1-By Billy DeBeck	13.00	40.00	90.00
2-6	8.50	25.50	60.00

NOTE: *Started in 1918 as newspaper strip; Spark Plug began 1922, 1923.*

BARNEY GOOGLE & SNUFFY SMITH
1942 - April, 1964
Dell Publishing Co./Gold Key

	Good	Fine	Mint
4-Color 19('42)	17.00	51.00	120.00
4-Color 40('43)	9.50	28.50	66.00
Large Feature Comic 11(1943)	9.50	28.50	66.00
1(1950-Dell)-Exist?	2.50	7.50	15.00
1(10113-404)-Gold Key (4/64)	1.50	4.50	9.00

BARNEY GOOGLE & SNUFFY SMITH
June, 1951 - No. 4, Feb, 1952 (Reprints)
Toby Press

	Good	Fine	Mint
1	4.00	12.00	28.00
2,3	2.50	7.50	17.00
4-Kurtzman-a "Pot Shot Pete," 5 pgs.; reprints/John Wayne No. 5	3.35	10.00	23.00

BARNEY GOOGLE AND SNUFFY SMITH
March, 1970 - No. 6, Jan, 1971
Charlton Comics

	Good	Fine	Mint
1	1.00	3.00	6.00
2-6	.70	2.00	4.00

BARNYARD COMICS (Dizzy Duck No. 32 on)
June, 1944 - No. 31, Sept, 1950; 1957
Nedor/Polo Mag./Standard(Animated Cartoons)

	Good	Fine	Mint
1(nn, 52 pgs.)	6.00	18.00	42.00
2	3.00	9.00	21.00
3-5	1.85	5.50	13.00
6-12,16	1.65	5.00	11.50
13-15,17,21,23,26,27,29-All contain Frazetta text illos	3.00	9.00	21.00
18-20,22,24,25-All contain Frazetta-a & text illos	8.00	24.00	56.00
28,30,31	1.00	3.00	7.00
10(1957)(Exist?)	.50	1.50	4.00

BARRY M. GOLDWATER
March, 1965 (Complete life story)
Dell Publishing Co.

12-055-503 — 2.35 7.00 14.00

BASEBALL COMICS
Spring, 1949 (Reprinted later as a Spirit section)
Will Eisner Productions

1-Will Eisner c/a — 25.00 75.00 175.00

BASEBALL HEROES
1952 (One Shot)
Fawcett Publications

nn (Scarce) — 20.00 60.00 140.00

BASEBALL THRILLS
No. 10, Sum, 1951 - No. 3, Sum, 1952 (Saunders painted-c No.1,2)
Ziff-Davis Publ. Co.

	Good	Fine	Mint
10(No. 1)	10.00	30.00	70.00
2-Powell-a(2)(Late Sum, '51)	6.00	18.00	42.00
3-Kinstler c/a	6.00	18.00	42.00

BASICALLY STRANGE (Magazine)
December, 1982 (B&W, $1.95)
JC Comics (Archie Comics Group)

	Good	Fine	Mint
1-(21,000 printed; all but 1,000 destroyed—pages out of sequence)	.30	1.00	2.00
1-Wood, Toth-a; Corben-c. Reprints & new art	.30	1.00	2.00

BASIC HISTORY OF AMERICA ILLUSTRATED
1976 (B&W)
Pendulum Press

07-1999 America Becomes a World Power 1890-1920
07-2251 The Industrial Era 1865-1915
07-226x Before the Civil War 1830-1860
07-2278 Americans Move Westward 1800-1850
07-2286 The Civil War 1850-1876 - Redondo-a
07-2294 The Fight for Freedom 1750-1783
07-2308 The New World 1500-1750
07-2316 Problems of the New Nation 1800-1830
07-2324 Roaring Twenties and the Great Depression 1920-1940
07-2332 The United States Emerges 1783-1800
07-2340 America Today 1945-1976
07-2359 World War II 1940-1945

Softcover — 1.50
Hardcover — 4.50

BASIL (. . . the Royal Cat)
Jan, 1953 - No. 4, Sept, 1953
St. John Publishing Co.

	Good	Fine	Mint
1	1.50	4.50	10.00
2-4	.70	2.10	5.00
I.W. Reprint 1		.50	1.00

BAT LASH (See DC Special Series No. 16, Showcase No. 76)
Oct-Nov, 1968 - No. 7, Oct-Nov, 1969
National Periodical Publications

	Good	Fine	Mint
1	.25	.80	1.60
2-7		.50	1.00

BATMAN (See Aurora, The Best of DC No. 2, The Brave & the Bold, Detective, 80-Page Giants, Limited Coll. Ed., DC 100-Page Super Spec., Shadow of the.., 3-D Batman, Untold Legends of.. & World's Finest)

BATMAN
Spring, 1940 - Present
National Periodical Publ./Detective Comics/DC Comics

	Good	Fine	Mint
1-Origin The Batman retold by Bob Kane; see Detective No. 33 for 1st origin; 1st app. Joker & The Cat (Catwoman); has Batman story without Robin originally planned for Detective No. 38. This book was created entirely from the inventory of Det. Comics	950.00	3000.00	7600.00

(Prices vary widely on this book)

1-Reprint, oversize 13½"x10." **WARNING**: This comic is an exact duplicate reprint of the original except for its size. DC published it in 1974 with a second cover titling it as a **Famous First Edition**. There have been many reported cases of the outer cover being removed and the interior sold as the original edition. The reprint with the new outer cover removed is practically worthless.

	Good	Fine	Mint
2	315.00	945.00	2200.00
3-1st Catwoman in costume; 1st Puppetmaster app.	200.00	600.00	1400.00
4	165.00	500.00	1155.00
5-1st app. of the Batmobile with its bat-head front	120.00	360.00	840.00
6-10: 8-Infinity-c	85.00	255.00	600.00

BATMAN (continued)

	Good	Fine	Mint
11-Classic Joker-c	75.00	225.00	525.00
12-15: 13-Jerry Siegel, creator of Superman appears in a Batman story	70.00	210.00	490.00
16-Intro Alfred	80.00	240.00	560.00
17-20	42.00	125.00	295.00
21-26,28-30: 22-1st Alfred solo. 25-Only Joker/Penguin team-up	35.00	105.00	245.00
27-Christmas-c	38.00	115.00	265.00
31,32,34-40: 32-Origin Robin retold	26.00	78.00	182.00
33-Christmas-c	30.00	90.00	210.00
41-46: 45-Christmas-c	22.00	66.00	154.00
47-1st detailed origin The Batman	62.00	185.00	435.00
48-1000 Secrets of Bat Cave	23.50	70.00	164.00
49,50: 49-1st Vicki Vale & Mad Hatter. 50-Two-Face app.	22.00	66.00	154.00
51-60: 57-Centerfold is a 1950 calendar	20.00	60.00	140.00
61-Origin Batman Plane II	20.00	60.00	140.00
62-Origin Catwoman	25.00	75.00	175.00
63-73: 68-Two-Face app. 73-Last 52 pgs.	16.00	48.00	112.00
74-Used in **POP**, pg. 90	17.00	51.00	120.00
75-77,79,80	16.00	48.00	112.00
78-(9/53)-Ron Kar, The Man Hunter from Mars story-the 1st lawman of Mars to come to Earth (green skinned)	18.50	55.00	130.00
81-89: 84-Two-Face app. 86-Intro Batmarine (Batman's submarine). 89-Last Pre-Code ish.	15.00	45.00	105.00
90-99: 92-1st app. Bat-Hound	10.00	30.00	70.00
100	30.00	90.00	210.00
101-110: 105-1st Batwoman in Batman	6.85	20.00	48.00
111-120: 113-1st app. Fatman	5.50	16.50	38.00
121-130: 127-Superman cameo. 129-Origin Robin retold; Bondage-c	4.65	14.00	32.00
131-143: Last 10¢ issue. 131-Intro 2nd Batman & Robin series. 133-1st Bat-Mite in Batman. 134-Origin The Dummy. 139-Intro old Bat-Girl	3.50	10.50	24.00
144-150	2.65	8.00	18.00
151-170: 164-New Batmobile; New look & Mystery Analysts series begins	1.50	4.50	9.00
171-Riddler app.(5/65), 1st since 12/48	2.00	6.00	12.00
172-175,177-180	.75	2.25	4.50
176-80-Pg. Giant G-17	1.05	3.10	6.20
181,183,184,186,188-190: 181-Batman & Robin poster insert; Intro Poison Ivy	.45	1.40	2.80
182,185,187-80 Pg. Gnt. G-24,G-27,G-30	.60	1.75	3.50
191,192,194-197,199,200: 197-New Bat-Girl app. 200-Retells origin of Batman & Robin	.30	.90	1.80
193-80-Pg. Giant G-37; Batcave blueprints	.40	1.15	2.30
198-80-Pg. Giant G-43; Origin-r	.40	1.15	2.30
201,202,204-207,209,210		.70	1.40
203-80 Pg. Giant G-49	.30	.85	1.70
208-80 Pg. Giant G-55; New origin Batman by Gil Kane	.30	.85	1.70
211,212,214-217: 216-Alfred given a new last name-''Pennyworth.'' (see Det. 96)		.65	1.30
213-80-Pg. Giant G-61; origin Alfred; new origin Robin	.30	.85	1.70
218-80-Pg. Giant G-67	.30	.85	1.70
219-Adams-a	1.00	3.00	6.00
220,221,224-227,229-231		.60	1.20
222-Beatles take-off	.55	1.70	3.40
223,228,233-80-Pg. Giant G-73,G-79,G-85	.25	.80	1.60
232-Adams-a; Intro Ras Al Ghul	1.00	3.00	6.00
234,237: Adams-a. 234-52pg. ish begin, end No. 242. 237-GA Batman-r	1.00	3.00	6.00
235,236,239-242: 241-r-Batman No. 5		.60	1.20
238-DC-8 100 pg. Super Spec.; unpubbed G.A. Atom, Sargon, Plastic Man stories; Doom patrol origin-r; Batman, Legion, Aquaman-r; Adams-c	.35	1.00	2.00
243-245-Adams-a	.70	2.00	4.00
246-250,252,253		.60	1.20
251-Adams-a; Joker app.	.60	1.80	3.60
254-100pg. editions begin	.25	.80	1.60
255-Adams-a; tells of Bruce Wayne's father who wore bat costume & fought crime	.60	1.80	3.60
256-261-Last 100pg. ish; part-r	.25	.80	1.60
262-365,367,369-399: 262-68pgs. 266-Catwoman back to old costume. 311-Batgirl reteams w/Batman. 332-Catwoman's 1st solo. 345-New Dr. Death app.		.60	1.20
366-Jason Todd 1st in Robin costume	.25	.75	1.50
368-1st new Robin in costume (Jason Todd)	.35	1.00	2.00
400 ($1.50, 64pgs.)-Dark Knight special; intro by Steven King	.45	1.30	2.60
401-403,405-410		.60	1.20
404-Miller-a begins	.35	1.00	2.00
Annual 1(8-10/61)-Swan-c	6.50	16.25	45.00
Annual 2	3.15	8.00	22.00
Annual 3(Summer, '62)	2.15	5.50	15.00
Annual 4-7(7/64)	1.60	4.00	11.00
Annual 8(10/82)		.70	1.40
Annual 9(7/85), 10(8/86)	.25	.80	1.60
Pizza Hut giveaway(12/77)-exact reprints of No. 122 & 123		.25	.50
Prell Shampoo giveaway('66)-16 pgs. ''The Joker's Practical Jokes'' (6-7/8''x3-3/8'')	1.00	3.00	6.00
Special 1(4/84)-Golden c/a(p)		.60	1.25

NOTE: ***Adams*** *c-200, 203, 210, 217, 219, 220-22, 224-27, 229, 230, 232, 234, 236-41, 243-46, 251, 255.* ***Aparo*** *c-284, 286, 291-95, 297-99, 301-309, 324-326, 329, 331-338, 340, 341, 348, 352.* ***Buckler*** *a-239-242, 265p, 297p, 329p; c-339p, 346p, 347p.* ***Burnley*** *a-10, 12-18, 20, 25, 27; c-28.* ***Byrne*** *a-401.* ***Colan*** *a-340p, 343p-45p, 348p-51p, 373p, 383p; c-343p, 345p, 350p.* ***J. Cole*** *a-238r.* ***Giffen*** *c-354p.* ***Golden*** *a-295, 303p.* ***Grell*** *a-287, 288p, 289p, 290; c-287-90.* ***Kaluta*** *c-242, 248, 253.* ***Bob Kane*** *a-1, 2; c-1-5, 7.* ***G. Kane*** *a-(R)-254, 255, 259, 261, 353i.* ***Kubert*** *a-238r, 400; c-310,319p, 327, 328, 344.* ***Lopez*** *a-336p, 337p, 353p; c-272, 311, 313, 314, 318, 321, 353.* ***Mooney*** *a-255r.* ***Newton*** *a-305, 306, 328p, 331p, 332p, 337p, 338p, 346p, 352-57p, 360p-72p, 374p-378p; c-374p, 378p.* ***Perez*** *a-400.* ***Robinson/Roussos*** *a-12-17, 20, 22, 24, 25, 27, 28, 31, 33, 37.* ***Robinson*** *a-12, 14, 18, 22-32, 34, 36, 37, 255r, 260r, 261r; c-6, 8-10, 12-15, 18, 21, 24, 26, 27, 30, 37, 39.* ***Simonson*** *a-300p, 312p, 321p; c-300p, 312p, 366.* ***P. Smith*** *a-Annual 9.* ***Starlin*** *a-402.* ***Staton*** *a-334.* ***Wrightson*** *a-265i, 400; c-320r.*

BATMAN (Kellogg's Poptarts comics)

1966 (set of 6) (16 pages)
National Periodical Publications

	Good	Fine	Mint
''The Man in the Iron Mask,'' ''The Penguin's Fowl Play,'' ''The Joker's Happy Victims,'' ''The Catwoman's Catnapping Caper,'' ''The Mad Hatter's Hat Crimes,'' ''The Case of the Batman II'' each....	.70	2.00	4.00

NOTE: All above were folded and placed in Poptarts boxes. ***Infantino*** *art on Catwoman and Joker issues.*

BATMAN AND THE OUTSIDERS (The Advs. of the Outsiders No.33 on)

(Also see The Outsiders)
Aug, 1983 - No. 32, Apr, 1986 (Mando paper No. 5 on)
DC Comics

	Good	Fine	Mint
1-Batman, Halo, Geo-Force, Katana, Metamorpho & Black Lightning begin	.50	1.50	3.00
2-4	.25	.75	1.50
5-(75 cent cover begin)-New Teen Titans app.	.30	.90	1.80
6-10: 9-Halo begins		.60	1.20
11-20: 11,12-Origin Katana. 18-More facts about Metamorpho's origin		.50	1.00
21-32		.45	.90
Annual 1 (9/84)-Miller/Aparo-c; Aparo-a	.25	.75	1.50
Annual 2 (9/85)-Metamorpho & Sapphire Stagg wed; Aparo-c		.65	1.30

NOTE: ***Aparo*** *a-1-9, 11, 12p, 16-20; c-1-4, 5i, 6-21.* ***B. Kane*** *a-3r.* ***Layton*** *a-19i, 20i.* ***Lopez*** *a-3p.* ***Perez*** *c-5p.* ***B. Willingham*** *a-14p.*

Batman #99, © DC

Batman #306, © DC

Batman & the Outsiders #2, © DC

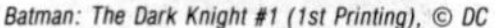
Batman: The Dark Knight #1 (1st Printing), © DC

Bat Masterson #5, © ZIV TV Programs

Battle Cry #11, © Stanmor

BATMAN FAMILY, THE
Sept-Oct, 1975 - No. 20, Oct-Nov, 1978 (No.1-4, 17-on: 68 pages)
(Combined with Detective Comics with No. 481)
National Periodical Publications/DC Comics

	Good	Fine	Mint
1-Origin Batgirl-Robin team-up (The Dynamite Duo); reprints plus one new story begins; Adams-a(r).	.25	.80	1.60
2-5: 3-Batgirl & Robin learn each's i.d.		.40	.80
6-10,14-16: 10-1st revival Batwoman		.30	.60
11-13: Rogers-p. 11-New stories begin; Man-Bat begins	.35	1.00	2.00
17-($1.00 size)-Batman, Huntress begin; Starlin-a		.60	1.20
18-20: Huntress by Staton in all		.40	.80

NOTE: *__Aparo__ a-17; c-11-16. __Austin__ a-12i. __Chaykin__ a-14p. __Michael Golden__ a-15-17, 18-20p. __Grell__ a-1; c-1. __Gil Kane__ a-2r. __Kaluta__ c-17, 19. __Newton__ a-13. __Robinson__ a-1r ,3i(r), 9r. __Russell__ a-18i, 19i. __Starlin__ c-18, 20.*

BATMAN MINIATURE (See Batman Kellogg's)

BATMAN RECORD COMIC
1966 (One Shot)
National Periodical Publications

	Good	Fine	Mint
1-With record	4.00	12.00	24.00
Comic only	1.35	4.00	8.00

BATMAN SPECTACULAR (See DC Special Series No. 15)

BATMAN: THE DARK KNIGHT RETURNS
March, 1986 - No. 4, 1986
DC Comics

	Good	Fine	Mint
1-Miller story & pencils	4.15	12.50	25.00
1-2nd printing	1.00	3.00	6.00
1-3rd printing	.50	1.50	3.00
2	2.00	6.00	12.00
2-2nd printing	.70	2.00	4.00
2-3rd printing	.50	1.50	3.00
3	.70	2.00	4.00
3-2nd printing	.50	1.50	3.00
4	.70	2.00	4.00
Hardcover, signed & numbered edition ($40.00)(4000 copies)	35.00	100.00	200.00
Hardcover, trade edition	7.00	20.00	40.00
Softcover, trade edition	2.50	7.50	15.00

BATMAN VS. THE INCREDIBLE HULK (See DC Special Series No. 27)

BAT MASTERSON (TV)
Aug-Oct, 1959; Feb-Apr, 1960 - No. 9, Nov-Jan, 1961-62
Dell Publishing Co.

	Good	Fine	Mint
4-Color 1013 (8-10/59)-Manning-a	3.00	9.00	21.00
2-9: Gene Barry photo-c on all	2.35	7.00	16.00

BATS (See Tales Calculated to Drive You . . .)

BATTLE
March, 1951 - No. 70, June, 1960
Marvel/Atlas Comics(FPI No. 1-62/Male No. 63 on)

	Good	Fine	Mint
1	4.00	12.00	28.00
2	2.00	6.00	14.00
3-9: 4-1st Buck Pvt. O'Toole	1.50	4.50	10.00
10-Pakula-a	1.70	5.00	12.00
11-20: 11-Check-a	.85	2.50	6.00
21,23-Krigstein-a	1.70	5.00	12.00
22,24-36: 36-Everett-a	.70	2.00	5.00
37-Kubert-a (Last precode, 2/55)	1.35	4.00	9.00
38-40,42-48	.60	1.80	4.20
41-Kubert/Moskowitz-a	1.35	4.00	9.00
49-Davis-a	1.70	5.00	12.00
50-54,56-58	.50	1.50	3.50
55-Williamson-a, 5 pgs.	2.35	7.00	16.00
59-Torres-a	1.20	3.50	8.00
60-62: Combat Kelly app.-No. 60,62; Combat Casey app.-No. 61	.40	1.25	2.80
63-65: 63-Ditko-a. 64,65-Kirby-a	1.20	3.50	8.00
66-Kirby, Davis-a	1.35	4.00	9.00
67-Williamson/Crandall-a, 4 pgs; Kirby, Davis-a	2.35	7.00	16.00
68-Kirby/Williamson-a, 4 pgs; Kirby/Ditko-a	2.35	7.00	16.00
69-Kirby-a	1.00	3.00	7.00
70-Kirby/Ditko-a	1.00	3.00	7.00

NOTE: *__Andru__ a-37. __Berg__ a-8, 14, 60-62. __Colan__ a-33. __Everett__ a-36, 50, 70; c-56, 57. __Heath__ a-6, 9, 13, 31, 69; c-6, 9, 26, 37. __Kirby__ c-64-69. __Maneely__ a-4, 31; c-4, 61. __Orlando__ a-47. __Powell__ a-53, 55. __Reinman__ a-26, 32. __Robinson__ a-9, 39. __Romita__ a-26. __Severin__ a-28, 32-34, 66-68; c-36. __Sinnott__ a-33, 37. __Tuska__ a-32. __Woodbridge__ a-52, 55.*

BATTLE ACTION
Feb, 1952 - No. 12, 5/53; No. 13, 11/54 - No. 30, 8/57
Atlas Comics (NPI)

	Good	Fine	Mint
1-Pakula-a	3.35	10.00	23.00
2	1.35	4.00	9.00
3,4,6,7,9,10: 6-Robinson c/a	1.00	3.00	7.00
5-Used in **POP**, pg. 93,94	1.35	4.00	9.00
8-Krigstein-a	1.70	5.00	12.00
11-15 (Last precode, 2/55)	.85	2.50	6.00
16-26,28,29	.70	2.00	5.00
27,30-Torres-a	1.35	4.00	9.00

NOTE: *Battle Brady app. 5,6,10-12. __Check__ a-11. __Everett__ c-13, 25. __Heath__ a-8; c-21. __Maneely__ a-1. __Reinman__ a-1. __Woodbridge__ a-28,30.*

BATTLE ATTACK
Oct, 1952 - No. 8, Dec, 1955
Stanmor Publications

	Good	Fine	Mint
1	2.50	7.50	18.00
2	1.30	3.85	9.00
3-8: 3-Hollingsworth-a	1.00	3.00	7.00

BATTLE BRADY (Men in Action No. 1-9)
No. 10, Jan, 1953 - No. 14, June, 1953
Atlas Comics (IPC)

	Good	Fine	Mint
10	2.00	6.00	14.00
11-Used in **POP**, pg. 95 plus B&W & color illos.	1.70	5.00	12.00
12-14	1.00	3.00	7.00

BATTLE CLASSICS (See Cancelled Comic Cavalcade)
Sept-Oct, 1978 (44 pages)
DC Comics

	Good	Fine	Mint
1-Kubert-r, new Kubert-c		.40	.80

BATTLE CRY
1952(May) - No. 20, Sept, 1955
Stanmor Publications

	Good	Fine	Mint
1	2.85	8.50	20.00
2	1.50	4.50	10.00
3,5-10: 8-Pvt. Ike begins, ends No. 12,17	1.00	3.00	7.00
4-Classic E.C. swipe	1.50	4.50	10.00
11-Opium-c	1.70	5.00	12.00
12-20	.70	2.00	5.00

NOTE: *__Hollingsworth__ a-9; c-20.*

BATTLEFIELD (War Adventures on the. . .)
April, 1952 - No. 11, May, 1953
Atlas Comics (ACI)

	Good	Fine	Mint
1-Pakula, Reinman-a	2.45	7.40	17.00
2-5	1.15	3.50	8.00
6-11	.70	2.00	5.00

NOTE: *__Colan__ a-11. __Heath__ a-1, 5p; c-2, 9, 11. __Ravielli__ a-11.*

BATTLEFIELD ACTION (Formerly Foreign Intrigues)
No. 16, Nov, 1957 - No. 62, 2-3/66; No. 63, 7/80 - No. 89, 11/84
Charlton Comics

	Good	Fine	Mint
16	.85	2.50	6.00
17,18,20-30	.35	1.00	2.40
19-Check-a	.60	1.80	4.00
31-62(1966)		.30	.60
63-89(1983-'84)		.30	.60

NOTE: ***Montes/Bache** a-43,55,62. **Glanzman** a-87r.*

BATTLE FIRE
April, 1955 -No. 7, 1955
Aragon Magazine/Stanmor Publications

	Good	Fine	Mint
1	1.50	4.50	10.00
2	.70	2.00	5.00
3-7	.60	1.80	4.00

BATTLE FOR A THREE DIMENSIONAL WORLD
May, 1983 (20 pgs., slick paper w/stiff covers, $3.00)
3D Cosmic Publications

	Good	Fine	Mint
nn-Kirby c/a in 3-D; shows history of 3-D	.50	1.50	3.00

BATTLEFRONT
June, 1952 - No. 48, Aug, 1957
Atlas Comics (PPI)

	Good	Fine	Mint
1-Heath-c	3.50	10.50	24.00
2	1.70	5.00	12.00
3-5-Robinson-a(4) in each	1.50	4.50	10.00
6-10: Combat Kelly in No. 6-10	1.20	3.50	8.00
11-28: Last precode (2/55). Battle Brady in No. 14,16	.70	2.00	5.00
29-39	.50	1.50	3.50
40,42-Williamson-a	2.35	7.00	16.00
41,44-47	.40	1.20	2.80
43-Check-a	.70	2.00	5.00
48-Crandall-a	1.20	3.50	8.00

NOTE: ***Ayers** a-19. **Berg** a-44. **Colan** a-21, 22, 33. **Drucker** a-28, 29. **Everett** a-44. **Heath** c-27, 29. **Maneely** c/a-22. **Morisi** a-42. **Morrow** a-41. **Orlando** a-47. **Powell** a-19, 21, 25, 29, 47. **Robinson** a-1, 2, 4, 5; c-4, 5. **Robert Sale** a-19. **Severin** c-40. **Woodbridge** a-45, 46.*

BATTLEFRONT
No. 5, June, 1952
Standard Comics

	Good	Fine	Mint
5-Toth-a	2.75	8.00	18.00

BATTLE GROUND
Sept, 1954 - No. 20, Aug, 1957
Atlas Comics (OMC)

	Good	Fine	Mint
1	2.65	8.00	18.00
2-Jack Katz-a	1.50	4.50	10.00
3,4-Last precode (3/55)	.85	2.50	6.00
5-8,10	.70	2.00	5.00
9-Krigstein-a	1.70	5.00	12.00
11,13,18-Williamson-a in each	2.35	7.00	16.00
12,15-17,19,20	.50	1.50	3.50
14-Kirby-a	.85	2.50	6.00

NOTE: ***Colan** a-11. **Drucker** a-7, 12, 13. **Orlando** a-17. **Pakula** a-11. **Severin** a-5, 12, 19. **Tuska** a-11.*

BATTLE HEROES
Sept, 1966 - No. 2, Nov, 1966 (25 cents)
Stanley Publications

	Good	Fine	Mint
1,2	.30	.80	1.60

BATTLE OF THE BULGE (See Movie Classics)

BATTLE OF THE PLANETS (TV)
6/79 - No. 10, 12/80 (Based on syndicated cartoon by Sandy Frank)
Gold Key/Whitman No. 6 on

	Good	Fine	Mint
1		.40	.80
2-10: Mortimer a-1-4,7-10		.30	.60

BATTLE REPORT
Aug, 1952 - No. 6, June, 1953
Ajax/Farrell Publications

	Good	Fine	Mint
1	1.70	5.00	12.00
2-6	.85	2.50	6.00

BATTLE SQUADRON
April, 1955 - No. 5, Dec, 1955
Stanmor Publications

	Good	Fine	Mint
1	1.50	4.50	10.00
2-5	.70	2.00	5.00

BATTLESTAR GALACTICA (TV)(Also see Marvel Super Spec. No. 8)
March, 1979 - No. 23, January, 1981
Marvel Comics Group

	Good	Fine	Mint
1		.35	.70
2-23: 1-3-Partial-r		.25	.50

NOTE: ***Austin** c-9i, 10i. **Buckler** a-6p, 7p; c-6p-8p. **Simonson** a(p)-4, 5, 11-20, 22, 23; c-4p, 5p, 11p-15p.*

BATTLE STORIES
Jan, 1952 - No. 11, Sept, 1953
Fawcett Publications

	Good	Fine	Mint
1-Evans-a	3.50	10.50	24.00
2	1.70	5.00	12.00
3-11	1.35	4.00	9.00

BATTLE STORIES
1963 - 1964
Super Comics

	Good	Fine	Mint
Reprints No. 10-12,15-18; 15-r-/Amer. Air Forces by Powell	.35	1.00	2.00

BEACH BLANKET BINGO (See Movie Classics)

BEAGLE BOYS, THE (Walt Disney)
11/64; No. 2, 11/65; No. 3, 8/66 - No. 47, 2/79
Gold Key

	Good	Fine	Mint
1	2.00	6.00	12.00
2-5	1.15	3.50	7.00
6-10	.70	2.00	4.00
11-20: 11,14,19-r	.50	1.50	3.00
21-47: 27-r	.25	.75	1.50

BEAGLE BOYS VERSUS UNCLE SCROOGE
March, 1979 - No. 12, Feb, 1980
Gold Key

	Good	Fine	Mint
1	.25	.80	1.60
2-12: 9-r		.40	.80

BEANBAGS
Winter, 1951 - No. 2, Spring, 1952
Ziff-Davis Publ. Co. (Approved Comics)

	Good	Fine	Mint
1,2	2.65	8.00	18.00

BEANIE THE MEANIE
1958 - No. 3, May, 1959
Fago Publications

	Good	Fine	Mint
1-3	.85	2.50	6.00

BEANY AND CECIL (TV) (Bob Clampett's. . .)
Jan, 1952 - 1955; July-Sept, 1962 - No. 5, July-Sept, 1963
Dell Publishing Co.

	Good	Fine	Mint
4-Color 368	6.00	18.00	42.00
4-Color 414,448,477,530,570,635(1/55)	4.65	14.00	32.00

Battlefront #19, © MCG

Battle Ground #12, © MCG

Battlestar Galactica #3, © Univ. City Studios

Bedlam! #1, © Eclipse

Beep Beep, the Road Runner #5, © DELL

Ben Casey Film Story #1, © Bing Crosby Prod.

BEANY AND CECIL (continued)

	Good	Fine	Mint
01-057-209	4.00	12.00	28.00
2-5	3.00	9.00	21.00

BEAR COUNTRY (Disney)(See 4-Color No. 758)

BEATLES, THE (See Strange Tales 130, My Little Margie 54, Jimmy Olsen 79, Marvel Comics Super Special 4, Summer Love)

BEATLES, LIFE STORY, THE
Sept-Nov, 1964 (35 cents)
Dell Publishing Co.

	Good	Fine	Mint
1-(Scarce)-Stories with color photo pin-ups	23.00	70.00	160.00

BEATLES YELLOW SUBMARINE (See Movie Comics under *Yellow...*)

BEAUTY AND THE BEAST, THE
Jan, 1985 - No. 4, Apr, 1985 (Mini-series)
Marvel Comics Group

	Good	Fine	Mint
1-Dazzler & the Beast		.40	.80
2-4		.40	.80

BEAVER VALLEY (See 4-Color No. 625)

BEDKNOBS AND BROOMSTICKS (See Walt Disney Showcase No. 6)

BEDLAM!
9/85 - No. 2, 9/85 (B&W-r in color)
Eclipse Comics

	Good	Fine	Mint
1,2-Bissette-a	.30	.90	1.75

BEDTIME STORY (See Cinema Comics Herald)

BEEP BEEP, THE ROAD RUNNER (TV)(Also see Daffy)
7/58 - No. 14, 8-10/62; 10/66 - No. 105, 1983
Dell Publishing Co./Gold Key No. 1-88/Whitman No. 89 on

	Good	Fine	Mint
4-Color 918	2.00	6.00	14.00
4-Color 1008,1046	1.30	4.00	9.00
4(2-4/60)-14(Dell)	.85	2.50	6.00
1	1.15	3.50	8.00
2-5	.55	1.65	4.00
6-14	.40	1.20	2.80
15-18,20-40	.35	1.00	2.00
19-w/pull-out poster	1.35	4.00	8.00
41-60		.60	1.20
61-105		.40	.80
Florida Power & Light, PG&E Kite Giveaway ('67,'71), 8pgs.	.35	1.00	2.00

(See March of Comics No. 351,353,375,387,397,416,430,442,455)
NOTF: *5,8-10,35,53,59-62,68-r; 96-102, 104 ⅓-r.*

BEETLE BAILEY (Also see Comics Reading Library)
No. 459, 5/53 - No. 38, 5-7/62; No. 39, 11/62 - No. 53, 5/66; No. 54, 8/66 - No. 65, 12/67; No. 67, 2/69 - No. 119, 11/76; No. 120, 4/78 - No. 132, 4/80
Dell Publishing Co./Gold Key No. 39-53/King No. 54-66/Charlton No. 67-119/Gold Key No. 120-131/Whitman No. 132

	Good	Fine	Mint
4-Color 469 (No. 1)-By Mort Walker	2.00	6.00	14.00
4-Color 521,552,622	1.50	4.50	10.00
5(2-4/56)-10(5-7/57)	1.15	3.50	8.00
11-20(4-5/59)	.85	2.50	6.00
21-38(5-7/62)	.55	1.65	4.00
39-53(5/66)	.45	1.35	3.00
54-119 (No. 66 publ. overseas only?)	.50	1.00	1.50
120-132		.50	1.00
Bold Detergent Giveaway('69)-same as regular ish (No. 67) minus price		.40	.80
Cerebral Palsy Assn. Giveaway V2No.71('69)-V2No.73)(No. 1), 1/70, Charlton		.40	.80
Giant Comic Album(1972, 59 cents, 11x14'') Color cover, B&W interior, Modern Promotions (r)		.40	.80
Red Cross Giveaway, 16pp, 5x7'', 1969, paper-c		.40	.80

BEE 29, THE BOMBARDIER
Feb, 1945
Neal Publications

	Good	Fine	Mint
1-(Funny animal)	3.35	10.00	23.00

BEHIND PRISON BARS
1952
Realistic Comics (Avon)

	Good	Fine	Mint
1-Kinstler-c	11.00	33.00	76.00

BEHOLD THE HANDMAID
1954 (Religious) (25 cents with a 20 cent sticker price)
George Pflaum

	Good	Fine	Mint
	4.00	12.00	28.00

NOTE: *Several copies surfaced in 1979 with prices varying widely.*

BELIEVE IT OR NOT (See Ripley's...)

BEN AND ME (See 4-Color No. 539)

BEN BOWIE AND HIS MOUNTAIN MEN
1952 - No. 17, Nov-Jan, 1958-59
Dell Publishing Co.

	Good	Fine	Mint
4-Color 443 (No. 1)	2.15	6.50	15.00
4-Color 513,557,599,626,657	1.50	4.50	10.00
7(5-7/56)-11: 11-Intro/origin Yellow Hair	1.15	3.50	8.00
12-17	.85	2.50	6.00

BEN CASEY (TV)
June-July, 1962 - No. 10, June-Aug, 1965 (Photo-c)
Dell Publishing Co.

	Good	Fine	Mint
12-063-207	1.75	5.25	12.00
2(10/62)-10	1.15	3.50	8.00

BEN CASEY FILM STORY (TV)
November, 1962 (25¢) (Photo-c)
Gold Key

	Good	Fine	Mint
30009-211-All photos	3.50	10.50	24.00

BENEATH THE PLANET OF THE APES (See Movie Comics)

BEN FRANKLIN KITE FUN BOOK
1975, 1977 (16 pages; 5-1/8''x6-5/8'')
Southern Calif. Edison Co./PG&E('77)

	Good	Fine	Mint
	.30	.80	1.60

BEN HUR (See 4-Color No. 1052)

BEN ISRAEL
1974 (39 cents)
Logos International

	Good	Fine	Mint
		.50	1.00

BEOWULF (See First Comics Graphic Novel)
April-May, 1975 - No. 6, Feb-Mar, 1976
National Periodical Publications

	Good	Fine	Mint
1		.45	.90
2-6		.25	.50

BERNI WRIGHTSON, MASTER OF THE MACABRE
July, 1983 - No. 5, Nov, 1984 ($1.50; Baxter paper)
Pacific Comics/Eclipse Comics No. 5

	Good	Fine	Mint
1-Wrightson c/a-r begins	.30	1.00	2.00
2-5	.25	.75	1.50

BERRYS, THE
May, 1956
Argo Publ.

	Good	Fine	Mint
1-Reprints daily & Sunday strips & daily Animal Antics by Ed Nofziger	1.65	5.00	11.50

BEST COMICS
Nov, 1939 - 1940 (large size, reads sideways)
Better Publications

	Good	Fine	Mint
1-(Scarce)-Red Mask begins	22.00	66.00	154.00
2-4: 4-Cannibalism sty	13.00	40.00	90.00

BEST FROM BOY'S LIFE, THE
Oct, 1957 - No. 5, Oct, 1958 (35 cents)
Gilberton Company

1-Space Conquerors & Kam of the Ancient Ones app.; also No. 3	1.75	5.25	12.00
2,3,5	1.00	3.00	7.00
4-L.B. Cole-a	1.30	4.00	9.00

BEST LOVE (Formerly Sub-Mariner No. 32)
No. 33, Aug, 1949 - No. 36, April, 1950 (Photo-c 33-35)
Marvel Comics (MPI)

33-Kubert-a	3.00	9.00	21.00
34	1.65	5.00	11.50
35,36-Everett-a	2.50	7.50	17.00

BEST OF BUGS BUNNY, THE
Oct, 1966 - No. 2, Oct, 1968
Gold Key

1-Giant	1.50	4.50	12.00
2	1.00	3.00	6.00

BEST OF DC, THE (Blue Ribbon Digest) (See Limited Coll. Ed. C-52)
9-10/79 - No. 71, 4/86 (100-148 pgs; all reprints)
DC Comics

1-17,19-34,36-71		.40	.80
18-The New Teen Titans	.25	.80	1.60
35-The Year's Best Comics Stories(148pgs.)		.60	1.20

NOTE: **Adams** *a-36, 51.* **Aparo** *a-9, 14, 26, 30; c-9, 14, 26.* **Austin** *a-51i.* **Buckler** *a-40p; c-22.* **Giffen** *a-50, 52; c-33p.* **Grell** *a-33p.* **Grossman** *a-37.* **Heath** *a-26.* **Kaluta** *a-40.* **G. Kane** *c-40, 44.* **Kubert** *a-21, 26.* **Layton** *a-21.* **S. Mayer** *c-29, 37, 41, 43, 47; a-28, 29, 37, 41, 43, 47, 58, 65, 68.* **Moldoff** *c-64p.* **Morrow** *a-40; c-40.* **W. Mortimer** *a-39p.* **Newton** *a-5, 51.* **Perez** *a-24, 50p; c-18, 21, 23.* **Rogers** *a-14, 51p.* **Spiegle** *a-52.* **Starlin** *a-51.* **Staton** *a-5, 21.* **Tuska** *a-24.* **Wolverton** *a-60.* **Wood** *a-60, 63; c-60, 63.* **Wrightson** *a-60. New art in No. 14, 18, 24.*

BEST OF DENNIS THE MENACE, THE
Summer, 1959 - No. 5, Spring, 1961 (100 pages)
Hallden/Fawcett Publications

1-(all reprints; Wiseman-a)	1.75	5.25	12.00
2-5	1.15	3.50	8.00

BEST OF DONALD DUCK, THE
Nov, 1965 (36 pages)
Gold Key

1-Reprints 4-Color 223 by Barks	5.00	15.00	30.00

BEST OF DONALD DUCK & UNCLE SCROOGE, THE
Nov, 1964 - No. 2, Sept, 1967 (25 cent giant)
Gold Key

1(30022-411)('64)-Reprints 4-Color 189 & 408 by Carl Barks No. 189-c redrawn by Barks	6.00	18.00	36.00
2(30022-709)('67)-Reprints 4-Color 256 & "Seven Cities of Cibola" & U.S. 8 by Barks	5.00	15.00	30.00

BEST OF MARMADUKE, THE
1960 (a dog)
Charlton Comics

1-Brad Anderson's strip reprints	.60	1.80	4.20

BEST OF THE WEST (See A-1 Comics)
1951 - No. 12, April-June, 1954
Magazine Enterprises

	Good	Fine	Mint
1(A-1 42)-Ghost Rider, Durango Kid, Straight Arrow, Bobby Benson begin	15.00	45.00	105.00
2(A-1 46)	7.00	21.00	50.00
3(A-1 52), 4(A-1 59), 5(A-1 66)	6.00	18.00	42.00
6(A-1 70), 7(A-1 76), 8(A-1 81), 9(A-1 85), 10(A-1 87), 11(A-1 97), 12(A-1 103)	4.00	12.00	28.00

NOTE: **Borth** *a-12.* **Guardineer** *a-5, 12.* **Powell** *a-1,12.*

BEST OF UNCLE SCROOGE & DONALD DUCK, THE
November, 1966 (25 cents)
Gold Key

1(30030-611)-Reprints part 4-Color 159 & 456 & Uncle Scrooge 6,7 by Carl Barks	5.00	15.00	30.00

BEST OF WALT DISNEY COMICS, THE
1974 (In color; $1.50; 52 pages) (Walt Disney)
8½x11" cardboard covers; 32,000 printed of each
Western Publishing Co.

96170-Reprints 1st two stories less 1 pg. each from 4-Color 62	1.00	3.00	7.00
96171-Reprints Mickey Mouse and the Bat Bandit of Inferno Gulch from 1934 (strips) by Gottfredson	1.00	3.00	7.00
96172-Reprints Uncle Scrooge 386 & two other stories	1.00	3.00	7.00
96173-Reprints "Ghost of the Grotto" (from 4-Color 159) & "Christmas on Bear Mtn." (from 4-Color 178)	1.00	3.00	7.00

BEST ROMANCE
No. 5, Feb-Mar, 1952 - No. 7, Aug, 1952
Standard Comics (Visual Editions)

5-Toth-a	3.50	10.50	24.00
6,7-Photo-c	1.30	4.00	9.00

BEST SELLER COMICS (See Tailspin Tommy)

BEST WESTERN (Formerly Terry Toons?) (Western Outlaws & Sheriffs No. 60 on)
No. 58, June, 1949 - No. 59, Aug, 1949
Marvel Comics (IPC)

58,59-Black Rider, Kid Colt, Two-Gun Kid app.	3.50	10.50	24.00

BETTY AND HER STEADY (Going Steady with Betty No. 1)
No. 2, Mar-Apr, 1950
Avon Periodicals

2	4.00	12.00	28.00

BETTY AND ME
Aug, 1965 - Present
Archie Publications

1	6.00	18.00	36.00
2	3.00	9.00	18.00
3-5: 3-Origin Superteen. Superteen in new costume No. 4-7; dons new helmet No. 5, ends No. 8	2.00	6.00	12.00
6-10	.85	2.50	5.00
11-30	.35	1.00	2.00
31-55 (52 pages No. 36-55)		.50	1.00
56-154		.30	.60

BETTY AND VERONICA (See Archie's Girls . . .)

BETTY & VERONICA ANNUAL DIGEST (. . . Digest Magazine No. 2-4; . . . Comics Digest Magazine No. 5 on)
November, 1980 - Present ($1.00 - 1.25)
Archie Publications

1, 2(11/81-Katy Keene sty), 3(8/82), 4-6(11/83), 7-20('86)		.40	.80

Best Love #33, © MCG

Best of Dennis the Menace #1, © FAW

Best Western #58, © MCG

Beverly Hillbillies #8, © Filmways TV Prod.

Bewitched #3, © Screen Gems

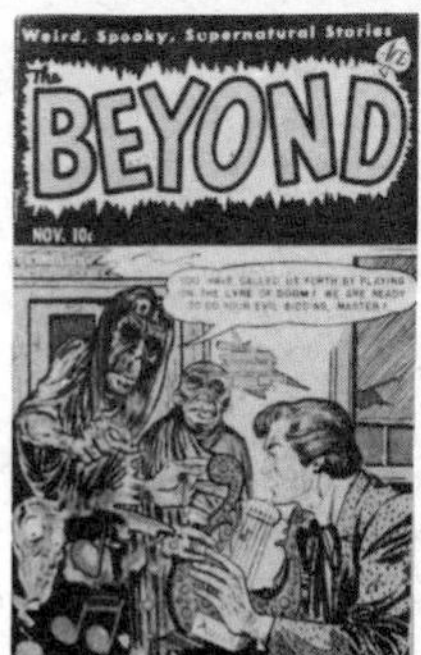

The Beyond #17, © ACE

BETTY & VERONICA CHRISTMAS SPECTACULAR (See Archie Giant Series Mag. No. 159, 168, 180, 191, 204, 217, 229, 241, 453, 465, 477, 489, 501, 513, 525, 536, 547, 558, 568)

BETTY & VERONICA SPECTACULAR (See Archie Giant Series Mag. No.11, 16, 21, 26, 32, 138, 145, 153, 162, 173, 184, 197, 201, 210, 214, 221, 226, 234, 238, 246, 250, 458, 462, 470, 482, 486, 494, 498, 506, 510, 518, 522, 526, 530, 537, 552, 559, 563)

BETTY & VERONICA SUMMER FUN (See Archie Giant Series Mag. No. 8, 13, 18, 23, 28, 34, 140, 147, 155, 164, 175, 187, 199, 212, 224, 236, 248, 460, 484, 496, 508, 520, 529, 539, 550, 561)

BETTY BOOP IN 3-D
Sept, 1986
Blackthorne Publ.

	Good	Fine	Mint
1	.40	1.25	2.50

BETTY'S DIARY (See Archie Giant Series Mag. No. 555)
April, 1986 - Present
Archie Enterprises

	Good	Fine	Mint
1-6		.40	.75

BEVERLY HILLBILLIES (TV)
4-6/63 - No. 18, 8/67; No. 19; No. 20, 10/70; No. 21, Oct, 1971
Dell Publishing Co.

	Good	Fine	Mint
1	4.00	12.00	28.00
2	2.00	6.00	14.00
3-10	1.70	5.00	12.00
11-21	1.35	4.00	8.00

NOTE: *No. 1,2,3,5,8-14,17,18,20,21 are photo covers.*

BEWARE (Formerly Fantastic; Chilling Tales No. 13 on)
No. 10, June, 1952 - No. 12, Oct, 1952
Youthful Magazines

	Good	Fine	Mint
10-Pit & the Pendulum adaptation; Wildey, Harrison-a; atom bomb-c	7.00	21.00	50.00
11-Harrison-a; Ambrose Bierce adapt.	5.00	15.00	35.00
12-Used in **SOTI**, pg. 388; Harrison-a	6.35	19.00	45.00

BEWARE
No. 13, 1/53 - No. 13, 1/55; No. 14, 3/55, No. 15, 5/55
Trojan Magazines No. 13-16,5-13/Merit Publ. No. 14,15

	Good	Fine	Mint
13(No. 1)-Harrison-a	7.00	21.00	50.00
14(No. 2)	5.50	16.50	38.00
15,16(No. 3,4)-Harrison-a	4.50	13.50	31.00
5,9,12,13	4.50	13.50	31.00
6-Ill. in **SOTI**-"Children are first shocked and then desensitized by all this brutality." Corpse on cover swipe/V.O.H. No. 26; girl on cover swipe/Advs. Intro Darkness No. 10	11.00	33.00	76.00
7,8-Check-a	4.65	14.00	32.00
10-Frazetta/Check-c; Disbrow, Check-a	23.50	70.00	165.00
11-Disbrow-a; heart torn out, blood drainage	4.65	14.00	32.00
14-Krenkel/Harrison-c	5.00	15.00	35.00
15-Harrison-a	4.65	14.00	32.00

NOTE: ***Fass*** *a-6; c-6, 11.* ***Hollingsworth*** *a-16(4),9; c-16(4),8,9.* ***Kiefer*** *a-6,10.*

BEWARE! (Tomb of Darkness No. 9 on)
March, 1973 - No. 8, May, 1974
Marvel Comics Group

	Good	Fine	Mint
1		.30	.60
2-8: 6-Tuska-a. 7-Torres r-/Mystical Tales No. 7		.20	.40

BEWARE TERROR TALES
May, 1952 - No. 8, July, 1953
Fawcett Publications

	Good	Fine	Mint
1-E.C. art swipe/Haunt of Fear 5 & Vault of Horror 26	6.00	18.00	42.00
2	3.50	10.50	24.00
3-8: 8-Tothish-a	3.00	9.00	21.00

NOTE: ***Andru*** *a-2.* ***Bernard Bailey*** a-1; c-1-5. ***Powell*** *a-1, 2, 8.* ***Sekowsky*** *a-2.*

BEWARE THE CREEPER (See Adventure, Brave & the Bold, First Issue Special, Showcase, and World's Finest)
May-June, 1968 - No. 6, March-April, 1969
National Periodical Publications

	Good	Fine	Mint
1	.35	1.00	2.00
2-6		.60	1.20

NOTE: ***Ditko*** *a-1-4, 5p; c-1-5.* ***G. Kane*** *c-6.* ***Sparling*** *a-6p.*

BEWITCHED (TV)
4-6/65 - No. 11, 10/67; No. 12 - No. 14, Oct, 1969
Dell Publishing Co.

	Good	Fine	Mint
1	3.00	9.00	21.00
2	1.75	5.25	12.00
3-14: Photo-c No. 3-13	1.15	3.50	8.00

BEYOND, THE
Nov, 1950 - No. 30, Jan, 1955
Ace Magazines

	Good	Fine	Mint
1-Bakerish-a(p)	9.00	27.00	62.00
2-Bakerish-a(p)	5.00	15.00	35.00
3-10: 10-Woodish-a by Cameron	3.65	11.00	25.00
11-17,19,20	2.65	8.00	18.00
18-Used in **POP**, pgs. 81,82	3.00	9.00	21.00
21-26,28-30	2.15	6.50	15.00
27-Used in **SOTI**, pg. 111	2.65	8.00	18.00

NOTE: ***Cameron*** *a-10, 11p, 12p, 15, 20-27, 30; c-20.* ***Colan*** *a-6, 13, 17.* ***Sekowsky*** *a-2, 3, 5, 7, 11, 14, 27r. No. 1 was to appear as Challenge of the Unknown No. 7.*

BEYOND THE GRAVE
7/75 - No. 6, 6/76; No. 7, 1/83 - No. 17, 10/84
Charlton Comics

	Good	Fine	Mint
1-Ditko-a	.30	.80	1.60
2,4-6-Ditko-a		.60	1.20
3-No Ditko-a		.30	.60
7-17: ('83-'84) Reprints		.30	.60
Modern Comics Reprint 2('78)		.20	.40

NOTE: ***Ditko*** *c-2,3,6.* ***Sutton*** *c-15.*

BIBLE TALES FOR YOUNG FOLK (. . . Young People No. 3-5)
Aug, 1953 - No. 5, Mar, 1954
Atlas Comics (OMC)

	Good	Fine	Mint
1	5.00	15.00	35.00
2-Everett, Krigstein-a	4.00	12.00	28.00
3-5	2.65	8.00	18.00

BIG ALL-AMERICAN COMIC BOOK, THE
1944 (One Shot) (132 pages)
All-American/National Periodical Publ.

	Good	Fine	Mint
1-Wonder Woman, Green Lantern, Flash, The Atom, Wildcat, Scribbly, The Whip, Ghost Patrol, Hawkman by Kubert (1st on Hawkman), Hop Harrigan, Johnny Thunder, Little Boy Blue, Mr. Terrific, Mutt & Jeff app.; Sargon on cover only	150.00	450.00	1050.00

BIG BOOK OF FUN COMICS
Spring, 1936 (52 pages, large size) (1st DC Annual)
National Periodical Publications

	Good	Fine	Mint
1 (Very rare)-r-/New Fun No. 1-5	300.00	900.00	2100.00

BIG BOOK ROMANCES
February, 1950(no date given) (148 pages)
Fawcett Publications

1-Contains remaindered Fawcett romance comics - several combina-

BIG BOOK ROMANCES (continued) — Good / Fine / Mint

tions possible 11.00 33.00 76.00

BIG BOY (See Adventures of the. . .)

BIG CHIEF WAHOO
Wint?, 1941-42 No. 23, 1945?
Eastern Color Printing/George Dougherty

	Good	Fine	Mint
1-Newspaper reprints	13.50	40.00	95.00
2-Steve Roper app.	6.85	20.00	48.00
3-5	4.35	13.00	30.00
6-10	3.35	10.00	23.00
11-23	2.65	8.00	18.00

NOTE: *Kerry Drake in some issues.*

BIG CIRCUS, THE (See 4-Color No. 1036)

BIG COUNTRY, THE (See 4-Color No. 946)

BIG DADDY ROTH
Oct-Nov, 1964 - No. 4, Apr-May, 1965 (Magazine; 35 cents)
Millar Publications

	Good	Fine	Mint
1-Toth-a	5.15	15.50	36.00
2-4-Toth-a	4.00	12.00	28.00

BIG HERO ADVENTURES (See Jigsaw)

BIG JIM'S P.A.C.K.
No date (16 pages)
Mattel, Inc. (Marvel Comics)

	Good	Fine	Mint
Giveaway with Big Jim doll		.15	.30

BIG JOHN AND SPARKIE (Formerly Sparkie, Radio Pixie)
1952
Ziff-Davis Publ. Co.

	Good	Fine	Mint
4	4.00	12.00	28.00

BIG LAND, THE (See 4-Color No. 812)

BIG RED (See Movie Comics)

BIG SHOT COMICS
May, 1940 - No. 104, Aug, 1949
Columbia Comics Group

	Good	Fine	Mint
1-Intro. Skyman; The Face (Tony Trent), The Cloak (Spy Master), Marvelo, Monarch of Magicians, Joe Palooka, Charlie Chan, Dixie Dugan, Tom Kerry, Rocky Ryan begin	48.00	145.00	335.00
2	22.00	66.00	154.00
3-The Cloak called Spy Chief; Skyman-c	18.00	54.00	125.00
4,5	15.00	45.00	105.00
6-10	12.00	36.00	84.00
11-14: 14-Origin Sparky Watts	9.50	28.00	66.00
15-Origin The Cloak	10.00	30.00	70.00
16-20	6.50	19.00	45.00
21-30: 29-Intro. Capt. Yank; Bo (a dog) newspaper strip reprints by Frank Beck begins, ends No. 104	4.35	13.00	30.00
31-40: 32-Vic Jordan newspaper strip reprints begin, ends No. 52	3.75	11.25	26.00
41-50: 42-No Skyman. 50-Origin The Face retold	3.35	10.00	23.00
51-60	3.00	9.00	21.00
61-70: 63 on-Tony Trent, the Face	2.65	8.00	18.00
71-80: 73-The Face cameo. 74,80: The Face app. in Tony Trent. 78-Last Charlie Chan strip reprints	2.15	6.50	15.00
81-90: 85-Tony Trent marries Babs Walsh	1.85	5.50	13.00
91-99,101-104: 69-94-Skyman in Outer Space	1.65	5.00	11.50
100	1.85	5.50	13.00

NOTE: ***Mart Bailey*** *art on "The Face"-No. 1-104.* ***Guardineer*** *a-5. Sparky Watts by* ***Boody Rogers****-No. 14-42, 77-104, (by others No. 43-76). Others than Tony Trent wear "The Face" mask in No. 46-63, 93. Skyman by* ***Ogden Whitney****-No. 1, 2, 4, 12-37, 49, 70-101. Skyman covers-No. 1, 6, 10, 11, 14, 16, 20, 27, 89, 95, 100.*

BIG TEX
June, 1953
Toby Press

	Good	Fine	Mint
1-Contains (3) John Wayne stories-r with name changed to Big Tex	2.65	8.00	18.00

BIG-3
Fall, 1940 - No. 7, Jan, 1942
Fox Features Syndicate

	Good	Fine	Mint
1-Blue Beetle, The Flame, & Samson begin	54.00	160.00	375.00
2	25.00	75.00	175.00
3-5	20.00	60.00	140.00
6-Last Samson; bondage-c	17.00	51.00	120.00
7-V-Man app.	17.00	51.00	120.00

BIG TOP COMICS, THE
1951 (no month)
Toby Press

	Good	Fine	Mint
1,2	1.75	5.25	12.00

BIG TOWN (Radio/TV)
Jan, 1951 - No. 50, Mar-Apr, 1958 (No. 1-9, 52pgs.)
National Periodical Publications

	Good	Fine	Mint
1-Dan Barry-a begins	15.00	45.00	105.00
2	7.00	21.00	50.00
3-10	4.00	12.00	28.00
11-20	2.65	8.00	18.00
21-31: Last pre-code (1-2/55)	1.85	5.50	13.00
32-50	1.30	4.00	9.00

BIG VALLEY, THE (TV)
6/66 - No. 5, 10/67; No. 6, 10/69
Dell Publishing Co.

	Good	Fine	Mint
1: Photo-c No. 1-5	2.35	7.00	16.00
2-6: 6 r-/No. 1. 5-Photo-c	1.15	3.50	8.00

BILL BARNES COMICS (. . . America's Air Ace Comics No. 2 on)
(Air Ace V2No.1 on)
Oct, 1940(No. month given) - No. 12, Oct, 1943
Street & Smith Publications

	Good	Fine	Mint
1-23 pgs.-comics; Rocket Rooney begins	23.00	70.00	160.00
2-Barnes as The Phantom Flyer app.; Tuska-a	15.00	45.00	105.00
3-5	12.00	36.00	84.00
6-12	9.00	27.00	62.00

BILL BATTLE, THE ONE MAN ARMY (Also see Master No. 133)
Oct, 1952 - No. 4, Apr, 1953 (All photo-c)
Fawcett Publications

	Good	Fine	Mint
1	2.35	7.00	16.00
2	1.15	3.50	8.00
3,4	1.00	3.00	7.00

BILL BLACK'S FUN COMICS
Dec, 1982 - No. 4, March, 1983 (Baxter paper)
Paragon No. 1-3/Americomics No. 4

	Good	Fine	Mint
1-Intro. Capt. Paragon, Phantom Lady, Commando D	.30	.90	1.80
2,3 (No. 1-3 are fanzines; 8½x11")	.30	.90	1.80
4-First color issue; origin Nightfall (Formerly Phantom Lady) Nightveil app.	.30	.90	1.80

BILL BOYD WESTERN (Movie star; see Hopalong Cassidy & Western Hero)
Feb, 1950 - No. 23, June, 1952 (36pgs., 1-3,7,11,14-on)
Fawcett Publications

Big Chief Wahoo #1, © EAS

Big Shot Comics #95, © CCG

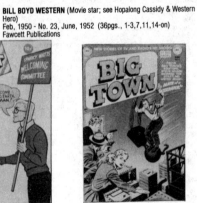

Big Town #6, © DC

Bill Boyd Western #5, © FAW

Bill Stern's Sports Book #10, © Z-D

Billy the Kid #11, © CC

BILL BOYD WESTERN (continued)

	Good	Fine	Mint
1-Bill Boyd & his horse Midnite begin; photo front/back-c	13.00	40.00	90.00
2-Painted-c	9.00	27.00	62.00
3-Photo-c begin, end No. 23; last photo back-c	8.00	24.00	56.00
4-6(52pgs.)	6.50	19.50	45.00
7,11(36pgs.)	5.50	16.50	38.00
8-10,12,13(52pgs.)	6.00	18.00	42.00
14-22	4.50	13.50	32.00
23-Last issue	5.00	15.00	35.00

BILL BUMLIN (See Treasury of Comics No. 3)

BILL ELLIOTT (See Wild Bill Elliott)

BILL STERN'S SPORTS BOOK
Spring-Summer, 1951 - V2No.2, Winter, 1952
Ziff-Davis Publ. Co.(Approved Comics)

	Good	Fine	Mint
V1No.10(1951)	4.00	12.00	28.00
2(Sum'52-reg. size)	3.00	9.00	21.00
V2No.2(1952,96 pgs.)-Krigstein, Kinstler-a	6.50	19.50	45.00

BILLY AND BUGGY BEAR
1958; 1964
I.W. Enterprises/Super

	Good	Fine	Mint
I.W. Reprint No. 1(Early Timely funny animal), No. 7(1958)	.35	1.00	2.00
Super Reprint No. 10(1964)	.35	1.00	2.00

BILLY BUCKSKIN WESTERN (2-Gun Western No. 4)
Nov, 1955 - No. 3, March, 1956
Atlas Comics (IMC No. 1/MgPC No. 2,3)

	Good	Fine	Mint
1-Mort Drucker-a; Maneely-c/a	3.50	10.50	24.00
2-Mort Drucker-a	1.65	5.00	11.50
3-Williamson, Drucker-a	3.65	11.00	25.00

BILLY BUNNY (Black Cobra No. 6 on)
Feb-Mar, 1954 - No. 5, Oct-Nov, 1954
Excellent Publications

	Good	Fine	Mint
1	1.75	5.25	12.00
2	.85	2.50	6.00
3-5	.75	2.25	5.00

BILLY BUNNY'S CHRISTMAS FROLICS
1952 (100 pages)
Farrell Publications

	Good	Fine	Mint
1	4.00	12.00	28.00

BILLY MAKE BELIEVE (See Single Series No. 14)

BILLY THE KID (Formerly Masked Raider)
No. 9, Nov, 1957 - No. 121, Dec, 1976; No. 122, Sept, 1977 - No. 123, Oct, 1977; No. 124, Feb, 1978 - No. 153, Mar, 1983
Charlton Publ. Co.

	Good	Fine	Mint
9	2.35	7.00	16.00
10-12,14,17-19: 11-(68 pages, origin, 1st app. The Ghost Train)	1.50	4.50	10.00
13-Williamson/Torres-a	2.35	7.00	16.00
15-Origin; 2pgs. Williamson-a	2.35	7.00	16.00
16-Two pgs. Williamson	2.35	7.00	16.00
20-22,25-Severin-a(3)	2.35	7.00	16.00
23,24,26-30	.85	2.50	6.00
31-40	.60	1.80	4.20
41-60	.50	1.50	3.00
61-80: 66-Bounty Hunter series begins. Not in No. 79,82,84-86		.40	.80
81-123: 87-Last Bounty Hunter. 111-Origin The Ghost Train; Sutton-a. 117-Gunsmith & Co., The Cheyenne Kid app.		.30	.60
124(2/78)-129		.30	.60
130-153		.30	.60
Modern Comics 109 (1977 reprint)		.15	.30

NOTE: **Severin** a(r)-121-129,134.

BILLY THE KID ADVENTURE MAGAZINE
Oct, 1950 - No. 30, 1955
Toby Press

	Good	Fine	Mint
1-Williamson/Frazetta, 4 pgs.	10.00	30.00	70.00
2	2.65	8.00	18.00
3-Williamson/Frazetta "The Claws of Death," 4 pgs. plus Williamson-a	15.00	45.00	105.00
4,5,7,8,10	1.85	5.50	13.00
6-Frazetta story assist on 'Nightmare;' photo-c	4.50	13.50	31.00
9-Kurtzman Pot-Shot Pete; photo-c	4.00	12.00	28.00
11,12,15-20	1.65	5.00	11.50
13-Kurtzman r-/John Wayne 12 (Genius)	2.15	6.50	15.00
14-Williamson/Frazetta; r-of No. 1, 2 pgs.	4.50	13.50	31.00
21,23-30	1.15	3.50	8.00
22-One pg. Williamson/Frazetta r-/No. 1	1.65	5.00	11.50

BILLY THE KID AND OSCAR
Winter, 1945 - No. 3, Summer, 1946 (funny animal)
Fawcett Publications

	Good	Fine	Mint
1	3.50	10.50	24.00
2,3	1.75	5.25	12.00

BILLY WEST (Bill West No. 9,10)
1949 - No. 9, Feb, 1951; No. 10, Feb, 1952
Standard Comics (Visual Editions)

	Good	Fine	Mint
1	3.75	11.00	26.00
2	1.85	5.50	13.00
3-10: 7,8-Schomburg-c	1.50	4.50	10.00

NOTE: **Celardo** a-1-6,9; c-1-3. **Moreira** a-3. **Roussos** a-2.

BING CROSBY (See Feature Films)

BINGO (. . . Comics) (H. C. Blackerby)
1945 (Reprints National material)
Howard Publ.

	Good	Fine	Mint
1-L. B. Cole opium-c	7.50	22.50	52.00

BINGO, THE MONKEY DOODLE BOY
Aug, 1951; Oct, 1953
St. John Publishing Co.

	Good	Fine	Mint
1(8/51)-by Eric Peters	2.00	6.00	14.00
1(10/53)	1.30	4.00	9.00

BINKY (Formerly Leave It to. . .)
No. 72, 4-5/70 - No. 81, 10-11/71; No. 82, Summer/77
National Periodical Publ./DC Comics

	Good	Fine	Mint
72-81		.50	1.00
82('77)-(One Shot)		.30	.60

BINKY'S BUDDIES
Jan-Feb, 1969 - No. 12, Nov-Dec, 1970
National Periodical Publications

	Good	Fine	Mint
1	.35	1.00	2.00
2-12		.50	1.00

BIONIC WOMAN, THE (TV)
October, 1977 - No. 5, June, 1978
Charlton Publications

	Good	Fine	Mint
1-5		.50	1.00

BIZARRE ADVENTURES (Formerly Marvel Preview)
No. 25, 3/81 - No. 34, 2/83 (Magazine-$1.50, 25-33)

BIZARRE ADVENTURES (continued)
Marvel Comics Group

	Good	Fine	Mint
25-Lethal Ladies. 26-King Kull		.60	1.20
27-Phoenix, Iceman & Nightcrawler app. 28-The Unlikely Heroes; Elektra by Miller; Adams-a	.25	.75	1.50
29-Horror. 30-Tomorrow. 31-After The Violence Stops; new Hangman story; Miller-a. 32-Gods. 33-Horror		.60	1.20
34 ($2.00, Baxter paper, comic size)-Son of Santa; Christmas special; Howard the Duck by P. Smith	.25	.75	1.50

NOTE: ***Alcala*** *a-27i.* ***Austin*** *a-25i, 28i.* ***J. Buscema*** *a-27p, 29, 30p; c-26.* ***Byrne*** *a-31(2pgs.).* ***Golden*** *a-25p, 28p.* ***Gulacy*** *a-25; c-25, 27.* ***Perez*** *a-27p.* ***Reese*** *a-31i.* ***Rogers*** *a-25p.* ***Simonson*** *a-29; c-29.* ***Paul Smith*** *a-34.*

BIZARRE 3-D ZONE (Blackthorne 3-D Series No. 5)
July, 1986 (One shot)($2.25)
Blackthorne Publishing

	Good	Fine	Mint
1-D. Stevens-a	.40	1.25	2.50

BLACK AND WHITE (See Large Feature Comic, Series I)

BLACKBEARD'S GHOST (See Movie Comics)

BLACK BEAUTY (See 4-Color No. 440)

BLACK CAT COMICS (. . West. No. 16-19; . . Mystery No. 30 on)
June-July, 1946 - No. 29, June, 1951
Harvey Publications (Home Comics)

	Good	Fine	Mint
1-Kubert-a	22.00	65.00	154.00
2-Kubert-a	13.00	40.00	90.00
3	9.50	28.50	66.00
4-The Red Demons begin (The Demon No. 4 & 5)	9.50	28.50	66.00
5,6-The Scarlet Arrow app. in ea. by Powell; S&K-a in both. 6-origin Red Demon	11.00	33.00	76.00
7-Vagabond Prince by S&K plus 1 more story	11.00	33.00	76.00
8-S&K-a; Kerry Drake begins, ends No. 13	9.50	28.50	66.00
9-Origin Stuntman (r-/Stuntman No. 1)	13.00	40.00	90.00
10-20: 14,15,17-Mary Worth app. plus Invisible Scarlet O'Neil-No. 15,20,24	6.50	19.50	45.00
21-26	5.50	16.50	38.00
27-Used in **SOTI**, pg. 193; X-Mas-c	6.50	19.50	45.00
28-Intro. Kit, Black Cat's new sidekick	6.50	19.50	45.00
29-Black Cat bondage-c; Black Cat stories	5.00	15.00	35.00

BLACK CAT MYSTERY (Formerly Black Cat; . . . Western Mystery No. 54; . . . Western No. 55,56; . . . Mystery No. 57; . . . Mystic No. 58-62; Black Cat No. 63-65)
No. 30, Aug, 1951 - No. 65, April, 1963
Harvey Publications

	Good	Fine	Mint
30-Black Cat on cover only	4.50	13.50	31.00
31,32,34,37,38,40	3.50	10.50	24.00
33-Used in **POP**, pg. 89; electrocution-c	3.65	11.00	25.00
35-Atomic disaster cover/story	4.35	13.00	30.00
36,39-Used in **SOTI**: No. 36-Pgs. 270,271; No. 39-Pgs. 386, 387,388	8.50	25.50	60.00
41-43	3.00	9.00	21.00
44-Eyes, ears, tongue cut out; Nostrand-a	3.50	10.50	24.00
45-Classic "Colorama" by Powell; Nostrand-a	6.00	18.00	42.00
46-49,51-Nostrand-a in all	3.50	10.50	24.00
50-Check-a; Warren Kremer?-c showing a man's face burning away	6.00	18.00	42.00
52,53 (r-No. 34 & 35)	3.00	9.00	21.00
54-Two Black Cat stories	3.50	10.50	24.00
55,56-Black Cat app.	2.65	8.00	18.00
57(7/56)-Simon?-c	2.50	7.50	17.00
58-60-Kirby-a(4)	3.50	10.50	24.00
61-Nostrand-a; "Colorama" r-/45	3.00	9.00	21.00
62(3/58)-E.C. story swipe	2.35	7.00	16.00
63-Giant(10/62); Reprints; Black Cat app.; origin Black Kitten	3.50	10.50	24.00
64-Giant(1/63); Reprints; Black Cat app.	3.50	10.50	24.00
65-Giant(4/63); Reprints; Black Cat app.; Silhouette nudity, Lingerie panels	3.50	10.50	24.00

NOTE: ***Kremer*** *a-37, 39, 43; c-36, 37, 47.* ***Meskin*** *a-51.* ***Palais*** *a-30, 31(2), 32(2), 33-35, 37-40.* ***Powell*** *a-32-35, 36(2), 40, 41, 43-53, 57.* ***Simon*** *c-63-65.* ***Sparling*** *a-44.* *Bondage-c No. 32, 34, 43.*

BLACK COBRA
No. 1, 10-11/54; No. 6(No. 2), 12-1/54-55; No. 3, 2-3/55
Ajax/Farrell Publications

	Good	Fine	Mint
1	7.00	21.00	50.00
6(No. 2)-Formerly Billy Bunny	4.65	14.00	32.00
3-(pre-code)-Torpedoman app.	4.65	14.00	32.00

BLACK DIAMOND
May, 1983 - No. 5, 1984 (no month) ($2.00-$1.75)(Baxter paper)
Americomics

	Good	Fine	Mint
1-Movie adaptation; Colt back up begins	.30	.90	1.80
2,3-Movie adaptation	.30	.90	1.80
4,5	.25	.75	1.50

NOTE: ***Bill Black*** *a-1i; c-1.* ***Gulacy*** *c-2-5.*

BLACK DIAMOND WESTERN (Desperado No. 1-8)
No. 9, Mar, 1949 - No. 60, Feb, 1956 (No. 9-26, 52 pgs.)
Lev Gleason Publications

	Good	Fine	Mint
9-Origin	5.00	15.00	35.00
10	3.00	9.00	21.00
11-15	2.35	7.00	16.00
16-28-Wolverton's Bing Bang Buster	3.00	9.00	21.00
29,30,32-40	1.50	4.50	10.00
31-One pg. Frazetta-a	1.85	5.50	13.00
41-50,53-59	1.15	3.50	8.00
51-3-D effect c/story	3.00	9.00	21.00
52-3-D effect story	2.65	8.00	18.00
60-Last issue	1.65	5.00	11.50

NOTE: ***Guardineer*** *a-18.* ***Morisi*** *a-55.* ***Tuska*** *a-48.*

BLACK DRAGON, THE
5/85 - No. 6, 10/85 (Baxter paper; mini-series; adults only)
Epic Comics (Marvel)

	Good	Fine	Mint
1: Bolton c/a No. 1-6	.70	2.10	4.20
2	.45	1.30	2.60
3-6	.35	1.10	2.20

BLACK FURY (Wild West No. 58) (See Blue Bird)
May, 1955 - No. 57, Mar-Apr, 1966 (Horse stories)
Charlton Comics Group

	Good	Fine	Mint
1	1.75	5.25	12.00
2	.85	2.50	6.00
3-15	.75	2.25	5.00
16-18-Ditko-a	1.75	5.25	12.00
19-30	.45	1.35	3.00
31-57		.50	1.00

BLACK GOLD
1945? (8 pgs. in color)
Esso Service Station (Giveaway)

	Good	Fine	Mint
Reprints from True Comics	2.50	7.50	18.00

BLACK GOLIATH
Feb, 1976 - No. 5, Nov, 1976
Marvel Comics Group

	Good	Fine	Mint
1		.40	.80
2-5: 1-3-Tuska-a(p)		.30	.60

Bizarre 3-D Zone #1, © Blackthorne

Black Cat Comics #12, © HARV

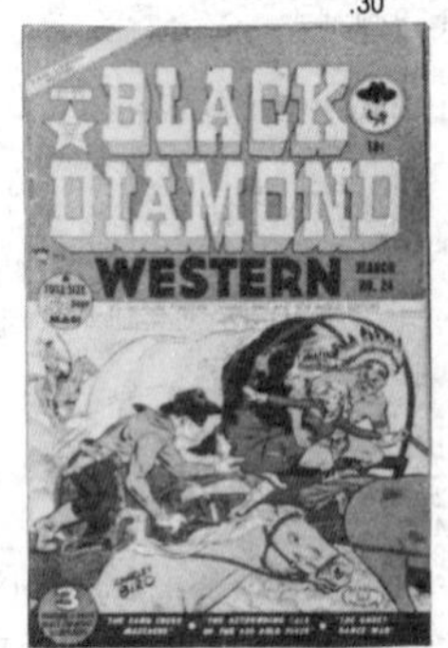

Black Diamond #24, © LEV

Blackhawk #30, © DC

Black Knight #2, © MCG

Black Magic V2No.3, © PRIZE

BLACKHAWK (Formerly Uncle Sam No. 1-8)
No. 9, Winter, 1944 - No. 243, 10-11/68; No. 244, 1-2/76 - No. 250, 1-2/77; No. 251, 10/82 - No. 273, 11/84
Comic Magazines(Quality)No. 9-107(12/56); National Periodical Publ. No. 108(1/57)-250; DC Comics No. 251 on

	Good	Fine	Mint
9 (1944)	70.00	210.00	490.00
10 (1946)	35.00	105.00	245.00
11-15: 14-Ward-a; Fear app.	25.00	75.00	175.00
16-20: 20-Ward Blackhawk	19.00	57.00	132.00
21-30	14.00	42.00	98.00
31-40: 31-Chop Chop by Jack Cole	11.00	33.00	76.00
41-49,51-60	7.00	21.00	50.00
50-1st Killer Shark; origin in text	8.35	25.00	58.00
61-Used in **POP**, pg. 91	7.50	22.50	52.00
62-Used in **POP**, pg. 92 & color illo	7.50	22.50	52.00
63-65,67-70,72-80: 70-Return of Killer Shark. 75-Intro. Blackie the Hawk	6.00	18.00	42.00
66-B&W and color illos in **POP**	7.00	21.00	50.00
71-Origin retold; flying saucer-c; A-Bomb panels	6.50	19.50	45.00
81-86: Last precode, 3/55	5.00	15.00	35.00
87-92,94-99,101-107	4.00	12.00	28.00
93-Origin in text	5.00	15.00	35.00
100	5.00	15.00	35.00
108-Re-intro. Blackie, the Hawk, their mascot; not in No. 115	9.00	27.00	62.00
109-117	2.65	8.00	18.00
118-Frazetta r-/Jimmy Wakely 4, 3 pgs.	5.35	16.00	37.00
119-130	1.50	4.50	10.00
131-142,144-163,165,166: 133-Intro. Lady Blackhawk. 166-Last 10¢ issue	1.00	3.00	7.00
143-Kurtzman r-/Jimmy Wakely 4	1.20	3.50	8.00
164-Origin retold	1.00	3.00	7.00
167-190	.35	1.10	2.20
191-197,199-202,204-210: Combat Diary series begins. 197-New look for Blackhawks	.30	.80	1.60
198-Origin retold	.35	1.00	2.00
203-Origin Chop Chop	.35	1.00	2.00
211-243(1968): 228-Batman, Green Lantern, Superman, The Flash cameos. 230-Blackhawks become superheroes. 242-Return to old costumes	.30	.80	1.60
244 ('76) -250: 250-Chuck dies		.50	1.00
251-Origin retold; Black Knights return		.30	.60
252-264: 252-Intro Domino. 253-Part origin Hendrickson. 258-Blackhawk's Island destroyed. 259-Part origin Chop-Chop		.30	.60
265-273 (75 cent cover price)		.30	.60

NOTE: **Chaykin** a-260; c-257-60, 262. **Cockrum** a-254; c-251-54, 255i, 261i. **Crandall** a-10, 11, 16, 18-20, 22-26, 30-33, 36(2), 37, 39-44, 46-50, 52-58, 60, 63, 64, 66, 67; c-18-20, 22-on(most). **Evans** a-244, 245, 246i, 248-250i. **G. Kane** c-263, 264. **Kubert** c-244, 245. **Newton** a-266p. **Severin** a-257i. **Spiegle** a-261-67, 269-73; c-265-72. **Toth** a-260p. **Ward** a-16-27(Chop Chop, 8pgs. ea.); pencilled stories-No. 17-63(approx.). **Wildey** a-268r.

BLACKHAWK INDIAN TOMAHAWK WAR, THE
1951
Avon Periodicals

	Good	Fine	Mint
nn-Kinstler-c; Kit West story	5.50	16.50	38.00

BLACK HOLE
March, 1980 - No. 4, September, 1980
Whitman Publ. Co.

	Good	Fine	Mint
11295-Photo-c; Spiegle-a		.50	1.00
2,3-Spiegle-a; 3-McWilliams-a; photo-c		.50	1.00
4-Spiegle-a		.40	.80

BLACK HOOD, THE
Jan, 1983 - No. 3, Oct, 1983 (Printed on Mandell paper)
Red Circle Comics

	Good	Fine	Mint
1-Morrow, McWilliams, Wildey-a; Toth-c		.60	1.20
2,3: MLJ's The Fox by Toth, c/a		.50	1.00

BLACK HOOD COMICS (Formerly Hangman No. 2-8; Laugh Comics No. 20 on)
No. 9, Winter, 1943-44 - No. 19, Summer, 1946
MLJ Magazines

	Good	Fine	Mint
9-The Hangman & The Boy Buddies cont'd	22.00	66.00	[illegible].00
10-The Hangman & Dusty, the Boy Detective app.; Fuje-a	11.00	33[illegible]	[illegible]
11-Dusty app.; no Hangman	9.50	28[illegible]	[illegible]
12-18: 17-Bondage-c	9.50	28.[illegible]	[illegible]
19-I.D. exposed	10.00	30.00	[illegible]

(Also see Archie's Super-Hero Special Digest No. 2)

BLACK JACK (Rocky Lane's. . ., formerly Jim Bowie)
No. 20, Nov, 1957 - No. 30, Nov, 1959
Charlton Comics

	Good	Fine	Mint
20	1.75	5.25	1[illegible]0
21,27,29,30	1.00	3.00	7.00
22-(68 pages)	1.50	4.50	10.00
23-Williamson/Torres-a	3.00	9.00	21.00
24-26,28-Ditko-a	1.85	5.50	13.00

BLACK KNIGHT, THE
May, 1953; 1963
Toby Press

	Good	Fine	Mint
1-Bondage-c	4.65	14.00	32.00
Super Reprint No. 11 (1963)	.85	2.50	5.00

BLACK KNIGHT, THE
May, 1955 - No. 5, April, 1956
Atlas Comics (MgPC)

	Good	Fine	Mint
1-Origin Crusader; Maneely c/a	25.00	75.00	175.00
2	19.00	57.00	132.00
3-5: 4-Maneely c/a	16.00	48.00	110.00

BLACK LIGHTNING (See Brave & The Bold, Cancelled Comic Cavalcade, DC Comics Presents No. 16, Detective and World's Finest)
April, 1977 - No. 11, Sept-Oct, 1978
National Periodical Publications/DC Comics

	Good	Fine	Mint
1		.40	.80
2-11: 4-Intro Cyclotronic Man		.25	.50

NOTE: **Buckler** c-1-3p, 6-11p.

BLACK MAGIC (. . . Magazine) (Becomes Cool Cat)
10-11/50 - V4/1, 6-7/53: V4/2, 9-10/53 - V5/3, 11-12/54; V6/1, 9-10/57 - V7/2, 11-12/58: V7/3, 7-8/60 - V8/5, 11-12/61 (V1/1-5, 52pgs.; V1/6-V3/3, 44pgs.)
Crestwood Publ. V1No.1-4,V6No.1-V7No.2/Headline V1No.5-V5No.3,V7No.3-V8No.5

	Good	Fine	Mint
V1/1-S&K-a, 10 pgs.; Meskin-a(2)	11.00	33.00	76.00
2-S&K-a, 17 pgs.; Meskin-a	5.35	16.00	37.00
3-6(8-9/51)-S&K, Roussos, Meskin-a	4.00	12.00	28.00
V2/1(10-11/51),4,5,7(No. 13),9(No. 15),11(No. 17),12(No. 18)-S&K-a	3.00	9.00	21.00
2,3,6,8,10(No. 16)	2.00	6.00	14.00
V3/1(No. 19, 12/52) - 6(No. 24, 5/53)-S&K-a	2.35	7.00	16.00
V4/1(No. 25, 6-7/53), 2(No. 26, 9-10/53)-S&K-a(3-4)	2.65	8.00	18.00
3(No. 27, 11-12/53)-S&K-a; Ditko-a(1st in comics along with Young Romance 36)	7.00	21.00	50.00
4(No. 28)-Eyes ripped out/story-S&K, Ditko-a	6.50	19.50	45.00
5(No. 29, 3-4/54)-S&K, Ditko-a	5.65	17.00	40.00
6(No. 30, 5-6/54)-S&K, Powell?-a	2.35	7.00	17.00

BLACK MAGIC (continued) — Good / Fine / Mint

V5/1(No. 31, 7-8/54 - 3(No. 33, 11-12/54)-S&K-a
 2.35 7.00 17.00
V6/1(No. 34, 9-10/57), 2(No. 35, 11-12/57)
 1.30 4.00 9.00
3(1-2/58) - 6(7-8/58) 1.30 4.00 9.00
V7/1(9-10/58) - 3(7-8/60) 1.00 3.00 7.00
4(9-10/60), 5(11-12/60)-Torres-a 1.50 4.50 10.00
6(1-2/61)-Powell-a(2) 1.00 3.00 7.00
V8/1(3-4/61)-Powell-a 1.00 3.00 7.00
2(5-6/61)-E.C. story swipe/W.F. No. 22; Ditko, Powell-a
 1.50 4.50 10.00
3(7-8/61)-E.C. story swipe/W.F. No. 22; Powell-a(2)
 1.35 4.00 9.00
4(9-10/61)-Powell-a(5) 1.00 3.00 7.00
5-E.C. story swipe/W.S.F. No. 28; Powell-a(3)
 1.35 4.00 9.00

NOTE: ***Bernard Baily*** *a-V4/6?, V5/3(2).* ***Grandenetti*** *a-V2/3, 11.* ***Kirby*** *c-V1/1-6, V2/1-12, V3/1-6, V4/1, 2, 4-6, V5/1-3.* ***McWilliams*** *a-V3/2i.* ***Meskin*** *a-V1/1(2), 2, 3, 4(2), 5(2), 6, V2/1, 2, 3(2), 4(3), 5, 6(2), 7-9, 11, 12i, V3/1(2), 5, 6, V5/1(2), 2.* ***Orlando*** *a-V6/1, 4, V7/2; c-V6/1-6.* ***Powell*** *a-V5/1?.* ***Roussos*** *a-V1/3-5, 6(2), V2/3(2), 4, 5(2), 6, 8, 9, 10(2), 11, 12p, V3/1(2), 2i, 5, V5/2.* ***Simon*** *a-V2/12, V3/2, V7/5? c-V4/3?, V7/3?, 4, 5?, 6?, V8/1-5.* ***Simon & Kirby*** *a-V1/1, 2(2), 3-6, V2/1, 4, 5, 7, 9, 11?, 12, V3/1-6, V4/1(3), 2(4), 3(2), 4(2), 5, 6, V5/1-3; c-V2/1.* ***Leonard Starr*** *a-V1/1.* ***Tuska*** *a-V6/3, 4.* ***Woodbridge*** *a-V7/4.*

BLACK MAGIC
Oct-Nov, 1973 - No. 9, Apr-May, 1975
National Periodical Publications

1-S&K reprints .30 .60
2-9-S&K reprints .20 .40

BLACKMAIL TERROR (See Harvey Comics Library)

BLACKMAN
No Date (1981)
Leader Comics Group

V1No.1 .30 .60

BLACKMOON
1986 - Present ($1.50, B&W)
U.S. Comics

1-3: 1-Origin Blackmoon .25 .75 1.50

BLACKOUTS (See Broadway Hollywood . . .)

BLACK PANTHER, THE (Also see Jungle Action)
1/77 - No. 15, 5/79; 11/84 - No. 4, 2/85
Marvel Comics Group

1 .40 .80
2-15 .25 .50

NOTE: ***J. Buscema*** *c-15p.* ***Kirby*** *c/a 1-12.* ***Layton*** *c-13i.*

1-4('84-'85) .35 .70

BLACK PHANTOM (See Tim Holt & Wisco)
Nov, 1954 - No. 2, Feb?, 1955 (Female outlaw)
Magazine Enterprises

1 (A-1 122)-The Ghost Rider app.; Headlight c/a
 11.00 33.00 76.00
2 (Rare) 16.00 48.00 110.00

BLACK RIDER (Formerly Western Winners; Western Tales of Black Rider No. 28-31; Gunsmoke Western No. 32 on)(Also see All Western Winners, Best Western, Kid Colt, Outlaw Kid, Rex Hart, Two-Gun Kid, Two-Gun Western, Western Winners, Wild Western)
No. 8, 3/50 - No. 18, 1/52; No. 19, 11/53 - No. 27, 3/55
Marvel/Atlas Comics(CDS No. 8-17/CPS No. 19 on)

8 (No. 1)-Black Rider & his horse Satan begin; 52pgs begin, end No. 14; photo-c 10.00 30.00 70.00
9 5.00 15.00 35.00

Good / Fine / Mint

10-Origin Black Rider 6.50 19.50 45.00
11-14(Last 52pgs.) 3.65 11.00 25.00
15-19: 19-Two-Gun Kid app. 3.35 10.00 23.00
20-Classic-c; Two-Gun Kid app. 3.65 11.00 25.00
21-26: 21-23-Two-Gun Kid app. 24,25-Arrowhead app. 26-Kid Colt app. 2.65 8.00 18.00
27-Last issue; Kid Colt app. 3.00 9.00 21.00

NOTE: ***Jack Keller*** *a-15, 27.* ***Maneely*** *a-14; c-16, 17, 25, 27.* ***Syd Shores*** *a-23(3), 24(3), 25; c-19, 23.* ***Sinnott*** *a-24, 25.* ***Tuska*** *a-12, 20, 21.*

BLACK RIDER RIDES AGAIN!, THE
September, 1957
Atlas Comics (CPS)

1-Kirby-a(3); Powell-a; Severin-c 4.50 13.50 31.00

BLACKSTONE (See Wisco Giveaways & Super Magician Comics)

BLACKSTONE, MASTER MAGICIAN COMICS
Mar-Apr, 1946 - No. 3, July-Aug, 1946
Vital Publications/Street & Smith Publ.

1 7.00 21.00 50.00
2,3 5.00 15.00 35.00

BLACKSTONE, THE MAGICIAN
No. 2, May, 1948 - No. 4, Sept, 1948 (no No.1)
Marvel Comics (CnPC)

2-The Blonde Phantom begins 16.00 48.00 110.00
3,4-(. . . Detective on cover only). 3,4-Bondage-c
 13.50 40.00 95.00

BLACKSTONE, THE MAGICIAN DETECTIVE FIGHTS CRIME
Fall, 1947
E. C. Comics

1-1st app. Happy Houlihans 22.00 66.00 154.00

BLACK SWAN COMICS
1945
MLJ Magazines (Pershing Square Publ. Co.)

1-The Black Hood reprints from Black Hood No. 14; Bill Woggon-a; Suzie app. 6.50 19.50 45.00

BLACK TARANTULA (See Feature Presentations No. 5)

BLACK TERROR (See Exciting & America's Best)
Wint, 1942-43 - No. 27, June, 1949
Better Publications/Standard

1-Black Terror, Crime Crusader begin 45.00 135.00 315.00
2 22.00 66.00 154.00
3 16.50 50.00 115.00
4,5 12.00 36.00 84.00
6-10: 7-The Ghost app. 8.50 25.50 60.00
11-19 8.00 24.00 56.00
20-The Scarab app. 8.00 24.00 56.00
21-Miss Masque app. 8.50 25.50 60.00
22-Part Frazetta-a on one Black Terror story 9.35 28.00 65.00
23 8.00 24.00 56.00
24-¼ pg. Frazetta-a 8.50 25.50 60.00
25-27 8.00 24.00 56.00

NOTE: ***Schomburg (Xela)*** *c-2-27; bondage c-2, 17, 24.* ***Meskin*** *a-27.* ***Moreira*** *a-27.* ***Robinson/Meskin*** *a-23, 24(3), 25, 26.* ***Roussos/Mayo*** *a-24.* ***Tuska*** *a-26, 27.*

BLACK ZEPPELIN (See Gene Day's . . .)

BLADERUNNER
Oct, 1982 - No. 2, Nov, 1982
Marvel Comics Group

1-Movie adaptation; Williamson c/a .30 .60
2-Movie adapt. concludes; Williamson a .30 .60

Black Phantom #1, © ME

Black Rider #10, © MCG

Blackstone, Master Magician #3, © Vital

Blaze Carson #5, © MCG

Blazing Comics #4, © RH

Blonde Phantom #14, © MCG

BLAKE HARPER (See City Surgeon . . .)

BLAST (Satire Magazine)
Feb, 1971 - No. 2, May, 1971
G & D Publications

	Good	Fine	Mint
1-Wrightson & Kaluta-a	1.70	5.00	10.00
2-Kaluta-a	1.20	3.50	7.00

BLAST-OFF (Three Rocketeers)
October, 1965
Harvey Publications (Fun Day Funnies)

	Good	Fine	Mint
1-Kirby/Williamson-a(2); Williamson/Crandall-a; Williamson/Torres/Krenkel-a; Kirby/Simon-c	2.00	6.00	12.00

BLAZE CARSON (Rex Hart No. 6 on)
(See Kid Colt, Tex Taylor, Wild Western, Wisco)
Sept, 1948 - No. 5, June, 1949
Marvel Comics (USA)

	Good	Fine	Mint
1	5.00	15.00	35.00
2	3.15	9.50	22.00
3-Used by N.Y. State Legis. Comm.(Injury to eye splash); Tex Morgan app.	4.65	14.00	32.00
4,5: 4-Two-Gun Kid app. 5-Tex Taylor app.	2.85	8.50	20.00

BLAZE THE WONDER COLLIE
No. 2, Oct, 1949 - No. 3, Feb, 1950
Marvel Comics(SePI)

	Good	Fine	Mint
2(No.1), 3-photo-c (Scarce)	7.50	22.50	52.00

BLAZING BATTLE TALES
July, 1975
Seaboard Periodicals (Atlas)

	Good	Fine	Mint
1-Intro. Sgt. Hawk & the Sky Demon by Severin; McWilliams, Sparling-a; Thorne-c		.30	.60

BLAZING COMBAT (Magazine) (35 cents)
Oct, 1965 - No. 4, July, 1966 (Black & White)
Warren Publishing Co.

	Good	Fine	Mint
1-Frazetta-c	6.75	20.00	40.00
2-Frazetta-c	2.50	7.50	15.00
3,4-Frazetta-c; 4-Frazetta ½ pg.	1.70	5.00	10.00
. . . Anthology (reprints from No. 1-4)	.70	2.00	4.00

NOTE: *Above has art by* ***Crandall, Evans, Morrow, Orlando, Severin, Torres, Toth, Williamson,*** *and* ***Wood.***

BLAZING COMICS
June, 1944 - No. 6(V2No.3), 1955?
Enwil Associates/Rural Home

	Good	Fine	Mint
1-The Green Turtle, Red Hawk, Black Buccaneer begin; origin Jun-Gal	13.50	40.00	95.00
2-4: 3-Briefer-a	8.50	25.50	60.00
5(3/55, V2No.2-inside)-Black Buccaneer-c, 6(V2No.3-inside, 1955)-Indian/Jap-c	1.75	5.25	12.00

NOTE: No. 5 & 6 contain remaindered comics rebound and the contents can vary. Cloak & Daggar, Will Rogers, Superman 64, Star Spangled 130, Kaanga known. Value would be half of contents.

BLAZING SIXGUNS
December, 1952
Avon Periodicals

	Good	Fine	Mint
1-Kinstler c/a; Larsen/Alascia-a(2), Tuska?-a; Jesse James, Kit Carson, Wild Bill Hickok app.	6.50	19.50	45.00

BLAZING SIXGUNS
1964
I.W./Super Comics

	Good	Fine	Mint
I.W. Reprint No. 1,8,9: 8-Kinstler-c; 9-Ditko-a	.40	1.20	2.40
Super Reprint No. 10,11,15,16(Buffalo Bill, Swift Deer),17(1964)	.35	1.00	2.00
12-Reprints Bullseye No. 3; S&K-a	2.00	6.00	12.00
18-Powell's Straight Arrow	.85	2.50	5.00

BLAZING SIX-GUNS
Feb, 1971 - No. 2, April, 1971 (52 pages)
Skywald Comics

	Good	Fine	Mint
1-The Red Mask, Sundance Kid begin, Avon's Geronimo reprint by Kinstler		.50	1.00
2-Wild Bill Hickok, Jesse James, Kit Carson-r		.40	.80

BLAZING WEST (Hooded Horseman No. 23 on)
Fall, 1948 - No. 22, Mar-Apr, 1952
American Comics Group(B&I Publ./Michel Publ.)

	Good	Fine	Mint
1-Origin & 1st app. Injun Jones, Tenderfoot & Buffalo Belle; Texas Tim & Ranger begins, ends No. 13	4.65	14.00	32.00
2,3	2.35	7.00	16.00
4-Origin & 1st app. Little Lobo; Starr-a	1.85	5.50	13.00
5-10: 5-Starr-a	1.65	5.00	11.50
11-13	1.30	4.00	9.00
14-Origin & 1st app. The Hooded Horseman; Whitney-c	2.65	8.00	18.00
15-22: 15,16,19-Starr-a	1.30	4.00	9.00

BLAZING WESTERN
Jan, 1954 - No. 5, Sept, 1954
Timor Publications

	Good	Fine	Mint
1-Ditko-a; Text story by Bruce Hamilton	3.50	10.50	24.00
2-4	1.50	4.50	10.00
5-Disbrow-a	1.75	5.25	12.00

BLESSED PIUS X
No date (32 pages; ½ text, ½ comics) (Paper cover)
Catechetical Guild (Giveaway)

	Good	Fine	Mint
	3.00	9.00	21.00

BLITZKRIEG!
Jan-Feb, 1976 - No. 5, Sept-Oct, 1976
National Periodical Publications

	Good	Fine	Mint
1-Kubert-c on all		.25	.50
2-5		.20	.40

BLONDE PHANTOM (Formerly All-Select No. 1-11; Lovers No. 23 on)
(Also see Blackstone, Millie The Model No. 2 and Marvel Mystery)
No. 12, Winter, 1946-47 - No. 22, March, 1949
Marvel Comics (MPC)

	Good	Fine	Mint
12-Miss America begins, ends No. 14	34.00	100.00	238.00
13-Sub-Mariner begins	23.50	70.00	165.00
14,15; 14-Bondage-c. 15-Kurtzman's 'Hey Look'	20.00	60.00	140.00
16-Captain America with Bucky app.; Kurtzman's "Hey Look"	20.00	60.00	140.00
17-22: 22-Anti Wertham editorial	19.00	57.00	132.00

BLONDIE (See Dagwood, Daisy & Her Pups, Eat Right to Work . . ., & Comics Reading Libraries)
1942 - 1946
David McKay Publications

	Good	Fine	Mint
Feature Books 12 (Rare)	33.00	100.00	230.00
Feature Books 27-29,31,34(1940)	6.50	19.50	45.00
Feature Books 36,38,40,42,43,45,47	5.00	15.00	35.00

BLONDIE & DAGWOOD FAMILY
Oct, 1963 - No. 4, Dec, 1965 (68 pages)
Harvey Publications (King Features Synd.)

	Good	Fine	Mint
1	1.00	3.00	6.00

BLONDIE & DAGWOOD FAMILY (continued) Good Fine Mint

2-4 .70 2.00 4.00

BLONDIE COMICS (. . . Monthly No. 16-141)
Spring, 1947 - No. 163, Nov, 1965; No. 164, Aug, 1966 - No. 175, Dec, 1967; No. 177, Feb, 1969 - No. 222, Nov, 1976
David McKay No. 1-15/Harvey No. 16-163/King No. 164-175/ Charlton No. 177 on

1 7.00 21.00 50.00
2 3.50 10.50 24.00
3-5 3.35 10.00 23.00
6-10 2.15 6.50 15.00
11-15 1.65 5.00 11.50
16-(3/50; Harvey) 1.70 5.00 12.00
17-20 1.20 3.50 8.00
21-30 .85 2.50 5.00
31-50 .55 1.60 3.50
51-80 .35 1.00 2.00
81-100 .25 .75 1.50
101-130: 125-80 pg. ish. .60 1.20
131-136,138,139 .50 1.00
137,140-(80 pages) .35 1.00 2.00
141-166(No. 148,155,157-159,161-163 are 68 pgs.) .60 1.20
167-One pg. Williamson ad .40 .80
168-175,177-222(No No. 176) .30 .60
Blondie, Dagwood & Daisy 1(100 pgs., 1953) 6.00 18.00 42.00
1950 Giveaway 1.30 4.00 9.00
1962,1964 Giveaway .40 1.20 2.40
N. Y. State Dept. of Mental Hygiene Giveaway-('50,'56,'61) Regular size (Diff. issues) 16 pages; no No. 1.00 3.00 6.00

BLOOD IS THE HARVEST
1950 (32 pages) (paper cover)
Catechetical Guild

(Scarce)-Anti-communism(13 known copies) 64.00 190.00 450.00
Black & white version (5 known copies), saddle stitched 30.00 90.00 200.00
Untrimmed version (only one known copy); estimated value-$800
NOTE: *In 1979 nine copies of the color version surfaced from the old Guild's files plus the five black & white copies.*

BLOOD OF THE BEAST
Sum, 1986 - No. 4 (mini-series; $2.00, color)
Fantagraphics Books

1-4 .35 1.00 2.00

BLOOD OF THE INNOCENT
1/7/86 - No. 4, 1986 (Weekly mini-series; adults only)
WaRP Graphics

1-4 .35 1.10 2.20

BLOOD RITES (See Americomics Graphic Novel)

BLUE BEETLE, THE (Also see Mystery Men & Weekly Comic Mag.)
Winter, 1939-40 - No. 60, Aug, 1950
Fox Publ. No. 1-11, 31-60; Holyoke No. 12-30

1-Reprints from Mystery Men 1-5; Blue Beetle origin; Yarko the Great-r/from Wonder/Wonderworld 2-5 all by Eisner; Master Magician app.; (Blue Beetle in 4 different costumes) 88.00 265.00 615.00
2-K-51-r by Powell/Wonderworld 8,9 42.00 125.00 295.00
3-Simon-c 30.00 90.00 210.00
4-Marijuana drug mention story 22.00 65.00 154.00
5-Zanzibar The Magician by Tuska 18.00 54.00 125.00
6-Dynamite Thor begins; origin Blue Beetle 16.00 48.00 110.00
7,8-Dynamo app. in both. 8-Last Thor 15.00 45.00 105.00
9,10-The Blackbird & The Gorilla app. in both. 10-Bondage/hypo-c 12.00 36.00 84.00

Good Fine Mint
11(2/42)-The Gladiator app. 12.00 36.00 84.00
12(6/42)-The Black Fury app. 12.00 36.00 84.00
13-V-Man begins, ends No. 18; Kubert-a 15.00 45.00 105.00
14,15-Kubert-a in both. 14-Intro. side-kick (c/text only), Sparky (called Spunky No. 17-19) 14.50 43.50 100.00
16-18 10.00 30.00 70.00
19-Kubert-a 13.00 40.00 90.00
20-Origin/1st app. Tiger Squadron; Arabian Nights begin 13.00 40.00 90.00
21-26: 24-Intro. & only app. The Halo. 26-General Patton sty & photo 8.50 25.50 60.00
27-Tamaa, Jungle Prince app. 7.00 21.00 50.00
28-30(2/44) 6.50 19.50 45.00
31(6/44)-40: "The Threat from Saturn" serial in No. 34-38 5.00 15.00 35.00
41-45 4.00 12.00 28.00
46-The Puppeteer app. 4.50 13.50 31.00
47-Kamen & Baker-a begin 23.50 70.00 165.00
48-50 19.50 58.00 136.00
51,53 17.00 51.00 120.00
52-Kamen bondage-c 23.50 70.00 165.00
54-Used in **SOTI**. Illo-"Children call these 'headlights' comics" 52.00 155.00 365.00
55,57(7/48)-Last Kamen issue 16.50 50.00 115.00
56-Used in **SOTI**, pg. 145 22.00 65.00 154.00
58(4/50)-60-No Kamen-a 3.50 10.50 24.00
NOTE: ***Kamen** a-47-51, 53, 55-57; c-47, 49-52. **Powell** a-4(2). Bondage-c 9, 10, 12, 46, 52.*

BLUE BEETLE (Formerly The Thing; becomes Mr. Muscles No. 22 on) (See Space Adventures)
No. 18, Feb, 1955 - No. 21, Aug, 1955
Charlton Comics

18,19-(Pre-1944-r). 19-Bouncer, Rocket Kelly-r 3.00 9.00 21.00
20-Joan Mason by Kamen 4.65 14.00 32.00
21-New material 3.00 9.00 21.00

BLUE BEETLE (Unusual Tales No. 1-49; becomes Ghostly Tales No. 55 on)
V2No.1, 6/64 - V2No.5, 3-4/65; V3No.50, 7/65 - V3No.54, 2-3/66; No. 1, 6/67 - No. 5, 11/68
Charlton Comics

V2No.1-Origin Dan Garrett-Blue Beetle 1.50 4.50 10.00
2-5, V3No.50-54 1.00 3.00 7.00
1(1967)-Question series begins by Ditko 1.75 5.25 12.00
2-Origin Ted Kord-Blue Beetle; Dan Garrett x-over 1.00 3.00 7.00
3-5 (No. 1-5-Ditko-c/a) .75 2.25 5.00
1,3(Modern Comics-1977)-Reprints .15 .30
NOTE: *No. 6 only appeared in the fanzine 'The Charlton Portfolio.'*

BLUE BEETLE
June, 1986 - Present
DC Comics

1 .25 .75 1.50
2-10: 5,7-The Question app. .45 .90

BLUE BIRD COMICS
Late 1940's - 1964 (Giveaway)
Various Shoe Stores/Charlton Comics

nn(1947-50)(36 pgs.)-Several issues; Human Torch, Sub-Mariner app. in some 3.35 10.00 20.00
1959-Li'l Genius, Timmy the Timid Ghost, Wild Bill Hickok (All No. 1) .70 2.00 4.00

1959-(6 titles; all No. 2) Black Fury No. 1,4,5, Freddy No. 4, Li'l Genius, Timmy the Timid Ghost No. 4, Masked Raider No. 4, Wild

Blondie Comics #5, © KING

Blood of the Innocent #1, © WaRP

Blue Beetle #15, © DC

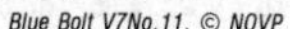
Blue Bolt V7No.11, © NOVP

Blue Bolt #109, © STAR

Blue Ribbon Comics #3, © AP

BLUE BIRD COMICS (continued) Good Fine Mint
Bill Hickok (Charlton) .70 2.00 4.00
1959-(No. 5) Masked Raider No. 21 .70 2.00 4.00
1960-(6 titles)(All No. 4) Black Fury No. 8,9, Masked Raider, Freddy No. 8,9, Timmy the Timid Ghost No. 9, Li'l Genius No. 9 (Charlton) .30 .80 1.60
1961,1962-(All No. 10's) Atomic Mouse No. 12,13,16, Black Fury No. 11,12, Freddy, Li'l Genius, Masked Raider, Six Gun Heroes, Texas Rangers in Action, Timmy the Ghost, Wild Bill Hickok, Wyatt Earp No. 3,11-13,16-18 (Charlton) .50 1.00
1963-Texas Rangers No. 17 (Charlton) .40 .80
1964-Mysteries of Unexplored Worlds No. 18, Teenage Hotrodders No. 18, War Heroes No. 18 (Charlton) .30 .60
1965-War Heroes No. 18 .25 .50
NOTE: *More than one issue of each character could have been published each year. Numbering is sporatic.*

BLUE BIRD CHILDREN'S MAGAZINE, THE
1957 (16 pages; soft cover; regular size)
Graphic Information Service

V1No.2-6: Pat, Pete & Blue Bird app. .40 1.20 2.40

BLUE BOLT
June, 1940 - No. 101 (V10No.2), Sept-Oct, 1949
Funnies, Inc. No. 1/Novelty Press/Premium Group of Comics

V1/1-Origin Blue Bolt by Joe Simon, Sub-Zero, White Rider & Super Horse, Dick Cole, Wonder Boy & Sgt. Spook 83.00 250.00 580.00
2-Simon-a 50.00 150.00 350.00
3-1 pg. Space Hawk by Wolverton; S&K-a 40.00 120.00 280.00
4,5-S&K-a in each; 5-Everett-a begins on Sub-Zero 33.00 100.00 230.00
6,8-10-S&K-a 29.00 87.00 200.00
7-S&K c/a 30.00 90.00 210.00
11,12 13.00 40.00 90.00
V2/1-Origin Dick Cole & The Twister; Twister x-over in Dick Cole, Sub-Zero, & Blue Bolt. Origin Simba Karno who battles Dick Cole through V2/5 & becomes main supporting character V2/6 on; battle-c 9.00 27.00 63.00
2-Origin The Twister retold in text 5.50 16.50 38.00
3-5: 5-Intro. Freezum 4.00 12.00 28.00
6-Origin Sgt. Spook retold 3.00 9.00 21.00
7-12: 7-Lois Blake becomes Blue Bolt's costume aide; last Twister 2.65 8.00 18.00
V3/1-3 2.15 6.50 15.00
4-12: 4-Blue Bolt abandons costume 1.85 5.50 13.00
V4/1-12: 1-Hitler, Tojo, Mussolini-c. 3-Shows V4/3 on-c, V4/4 inside (9-10/43). 8-Last Sub-Zero 1.50 4.50 10.00
V5/1-8, V6/1-3,5-10, V7/1-12 1.15 3.50 8.00
V6/4-Racist cover 1.30 4.00 9.00
V8/1-6,8-12, V9/1-5,7,8 1.00 3.00 7.00
V8/7,V9/6,9-L. B. Cole-c 1.75 5.25 12.00
V10/1(No. 100) 1.50 4.50 10.00
V10/2(No. 101)-Last Dick Cole, Blue Bolt 1.35 4.00 9.00
NOTE: ***Everett** c-V1/4,11, V2/1,2. **Gustavson** a-V1/1-12, V2/1-7. **Rico** a-V6/10, V7/4. Blue Bolt not in V9/8.*

BLUE BOLT (Becomes Ghostly Weird Stories No. 120 on; continuation of Novelty Blue Bolt) (. . Weird Tales No. 112-119)
No. 102, Nov-Dec, 1949 - No. 119, May-June, 1953
Star Publications

102-The Chameleon, & Target app. 7.00 21.00 50.00
103,104-The Chameleon app.; last Target-No. 104 6.50 19.50 45.00
105-Origin Blue Bolt (from No. 1) retold by Simon; Chameleon & Target app.; opium den story 18.50 56.00 130.00
106-Blue Bolt by S&K begins; Spacehawk reprints from Target by Wolverton begins, ends No. 110; Sub-Zero begins; ends No. 109 14.50 43.50 100.00
107-110: 108-Last S&K Blue Bolt reprint. 109-Wolverton-c(r)/inside Spacehawk splash. 110-Target app. 14.50 43.50 100.00
111-Red Rocket & The Mask-r; last Blue Bolt; 1pg. L. B. Cole-a 16.50 50.00 115.00
112-Last Torpedo Man app. 14.50 43.50 100.00
113-Wolverton's Spacehawk r-/Target V3No.7 14.50 43.50 100.00
114,116: 116-Jungle Jo-r 14.50 43.50 100.00
115-Sgt. Spook app. 16.50 50.00 115.00
117-Jo-Jo & Blue Bolt-r 14.50 43.50 100.00
118-"White Spirit" by Wood 16.50 50.00 115.00
119-Disbrow/Cole-c; Jungle Jo-r 14.50 43.50 100.00
Accepted Reprint No. 103(1957?, no date) 3.00 9.00 21.00
NOTE: ***L. B. Cole** c-102-108, 110 on. **Disbrow** a-112(2), 113(3), 114(2), 115(2), 116-118. **Hollingsworth** a-117. **Palais** a-112r.*

BLUE CIRCLE COMICS
June, 1944 - No. 6, April, 1945
Enwil Associates/Rural Home

1-The Blue Circle begins; origin Steel Fist 6.50 19.50 45.00
2 3.65 11.00 25.00
3-5: Last Steel Fist 3.00 9.00 21.00
6-Colossal Features-r 2.65 8.00 18.00

BLUE DEVIL
June, 1984 - No. 31, Dec, 1986
DC Comics

1 .35 1.00 2.00
2-5: 4-Origin Nebiros .60 1.20
6-10: 7-Gil Kane-a .50 1.00
11-16 .45 .90
17-19: Crisis x-over .50 1.00
20-29: 27-Godfrey Goose app. .45 .90
30,31-Double size .65 1.30
Annual 1 (11/85)-Team-ups with Black Orchid, The Creeper, Demon, Madame Xanadu, Man-Bat & Phantom Stranger .25 .70 1.40

BLUE PHANTOM, THE
June-Aug, 1962
Dell Publishing Co.

1(01-066-208)-by Fred Fredericks 1.50 4.50 10.00

BLUE RIBBON COMICS (. . . Mystery Comics No. 9-18)
Nov, 1939 - No. 22, March, 1942 (1st MLJ series)
MLJ Magazines

1-Dan Hastings, Ricky the Amazing Boy, Rang-A-Tang the Wonder Dog begin; Little Nemo app. (not by W. McCay); Jack Cole-a(3) 85.00 255.00 595.00
2-Bob Phantom, Silver Fox (both in No. 3), Rang-A-Tang Club & Cpl. Collins begin; Jack Cole-a 35.00 105.00 245.00
3-J. Cole-a 24.00 72.00 168.00
4-Doc Strong, The Green Falcon, & Hercules begin; origin & 1st app. The Fox & Ty-Gor, Son of the Tiger 25.00 75.00 175.00
5-8: 8-Last Hercules 16.00 48.00 110.00
9-(Scarce)-Origin & 1st app. Mr. Justice 85.00 255.00 595.00
10-12: 12-Last Doc Strong 33.00 100.00 230.00
13-Inferno, the Flame Breather begins, ends No. 19. Devil-c 33.00 100.00 230.00
14,15,17,18: 15-Last Green Falcon 30.00 90.00 210.00
16-Origin & 1st app. Captain Flag 57.00 171.00 400.00
19-22: 20-Last Ty-Gor. 22-Origin Mr. Justice retold 25.00 75.00 175.00

BLUE RIBBON COMICS (Teen-Age Diary Secrets No. 6)
Feb, 1949 - No. 6, Aug, 1949 (See Heckle & Jeckle)
Blue Ribbon (St. John)

	Good	Fine	Mint
1,3-Heckle & Jeckle	2.35	7.00	16.00
2(4/49)-Diary Secrets; Baker-c	4.65	14.00	32.00
4(6/49)-Teen-Age Diary Secrets; Baker c/a(2)	5.50	16.50	38.00
5(8/49)-Teen-Age Diary Secrets; photo-c; Baker-a(2)	5.50	16.50	38.00
6-Dinky Duck(8/49)	1.15	3.50	8.00

BLUE-RIBBON COMICS
Oct, 1983 - No. 14, Dec, 1984
Red Circle Prod./Archie Ent. No. 5 on

	Good	Fine	Mint
1-The Fly No. 1-r		.50	1.00
2-4: 3-Origin Steel Sterling		.50	1.00
5-14: 5-S&K Shield-r. 6,7-The Fox app. 8,11-Black Hood. 12-Thunder Agents. 13-Thunder Bunny. 14-Web & Jaguar		.50	1.00

NOTE: ***Adams** a(r)-8. **Buckler** a-4i. **Nino** a-2i. **McWilliams** a-8. **Morrow** a-8.*

BLUE STREAK (See Holyoke One-Shot No. 8)

BLYTHE (See 4-Color No. 1072)

B-MAN (See Double-Dare Adventures)

B-MOVIE PRESENTS
Mar, 1986 - No. 4, Dec, 1986 ($1.70, B&W, 28pgs.)
B-Movie Comics

	Good	Fine	Mint
1,2-Captain Daring	.30	.90	1.70
3,4-Tasma The Congo Queen	.30	.90	1.70

BO (Also see Big Shot No. 29; Tom Cat No. 4 on)
June, 1955 - No. 3, Oct, 1955
Charlton Comics Group

	Good	Fine	Mint
1-3-(a dog) Newspaper reprints by Frank Beck	3.00	9.00	21.00

BOATNIKS, THE (See Walt Disney Showcase No. 1)

BOB & BETTY & SANTA'S WISHING WELL
1941 (12 pages) (Christmas giveaway)
Sears Roebuck & Co.

	Good	Fine	Mint
	6.00	18.00	42.00

BOBBY BENSON'S B-BAR-B RIDERS (See Best of The West, & Model Fun)
May-June, 1950 - No. 20, May-June, 1953
Magazine Enterprises

	Good	Fine	Mint
1-Powell-a	9.50	28.50	66.00
2	4.75	14.00	33.00
3-5: 4-Lemonade Kid-c	3.85	11.50	27.00
6-8,10	2.85	8.50	20.00
9,11,13-Frazetta-c; Ghost Rider in No. 13-15 (Ayers-a).	13.50	40.50	95.00
12,17-20(A-1 88)	2.65	8.00	18.00
14-Bondage-c	3.35	10.00	23.00
15-Ghost Rider-c	3.35	10.00	23.00
16-Photo-c	3.35	10.00	23.00
...in the Tunnel of Gold-(1936, 5¼x8''; 100 pgs.) Radio giveaway by Hecker-H.O. Company(H.O. Oats); contains 22 color pages of comics, rest in novel form	4.00	12.00	28.00
...And The Lost Herd-same as above	4.00	12.00	28.00

NOTE: ***Ayers** a-13-15, 20. **Powell** a-1-12(4 ea.), 13(3), 14-16(Red Hawk only); c-1-8,10,12. Lemonade Kid in most 1-13.*

BOBBY COMICS
May, 1946
Universal Phoenix Features

	Good	Fine	Mint
1-by S. M. Iger	3.00	9.00	21.00

BOBBY SHELBY COMICS
1949
Shelby Cycle Co./Harvey Publications

	Good	Fine	Mint
	1.65	5.00	11.50

BOBBY SHERMAN (TV)
Feb, 1972 - No. 7, Oct, 1972
Charlton Comics

	Good	Fine	Mint
1-7-Based on TV show ''Getting Together''	1.20	3.50	7.00

BOBBY THATCHER & TREASURE CAVE
1932 (86 pages; B&W; hardcover; 7x9'')
Altemus Co.

	Good	Fine	Mint
Reprints; Storm-a	4.35	13.00	30.00

BOBBY THATCHER'S ROMANCE
1931
The Bell Syndicate/Henry Altemus Co.

	Good	Fine	Mint
nn-By Storm	4.35	13.00	30.00

BOB COLT (Movie star)
Nov, 1950 - No. 10, May, 1952
Fawcett Publications

	Good	Fine	Mint
1-Bob Colt, his horse Buckskin & sidekick Pablo begin; photo front/back-c begin	12.00	36.00	84.00
2	9.50	28.00	66.00
3-5	8.00	24.00	56.00
6-Flying Saucer story	7.00	21.00	50.00
7-10: 9-Last photo back-c	5.75	17.25	40.00

BOB HOPE (See Adventures of...)

BOB SCULLY, TWO-FISTED HICK DETECTIVE
No date (1930's) (36 pages; 9½x12''; B&W; paper cover)
Humor Publ. Co.

	Good	Fine	Mint
By Howard Dell; not reprints	3.65	11.00	25.00

BOB SON OF BATTLE (See 4-Color No. 729)

BOB STEELE WESTERN (Movie star)
Dec, 1950 - No. 10, June, 1952
Fawcett Publications

	Good	Fine	Mint
1-Bob Steele & his horse Bullet begin; photo front/back-c begin	12.00	36.00	84.00
2	9.50	28.00	66.00
3-5: 4-Last photo back-c	8.00	24.00	56.00
6-10: 10-Last photo-c	5.75	17.25	40.00

BOB SWIFT (Boy Sportsman)
May, 1951 - No. 5, Jan, 1952
Fawcett Publications

	Good	Fine	Mint
1	2.00	6.00	14.00
2-5: Saunders painted-c No. 1-5	1.15	3.50	8.00

BOFFO LAFFS
1986 - Present ($2.50-1.95; B&W)
ParaGraphics

	Good	Fine	Mint
1-Hologram-c (1st on a comic)	.50	1.50	3.00
2 (52 pgs.)	.35	1.10	2.20

BOLD ADVENTURES
Oct, 1983 - No. 3, June, 1984
Pacific Comics

	Good	Fine	Mint
1-Time Force, Spitfire, & The Weirdling begin	.30	.90	1.80
2,3	.25	.75	1.50

NOTE: ***Kaluta** c-3. **Nebres** a-3. **Nino** a-2. **Severin** a-3.*

Blue Ribbon Comics #2 (4/49), © STJ

B-Movie Presents #1, © B-Movie

Bob Steele Western #3, © FAW

Bonanza #15, © NBC

Boris Karloff Tales... #61, © Estate of B. K.

Boris the Bear #1, © Dark Horse

BOLD STORIES (Also see Candid Tales, It Rhymes With Lust)
Mar, 1950 - July, 1950 (Digest size; 144 pgs.; full color)
Kirby Publishing Co.

	Good	Fine	Mint
March issue (Very Rare) - Contains "The Ogre of Paris" by Wood	32.00	95.00	225.00
May issue (Very Rare) - Contains "The Cobra's Kiss" by Graham Ingels (21 pgs.)	23.00	70.00	160.00
July issue (Very Rare) - Contains "The Ogre of Paris" by Wood	25.00	75.00	175.00

BOLT & STAR FORCE SIX (See Star Force Six Spec.)
1984 (no month) ($2.00; B&W)
Americomics

	Good	Fine	Mint
1-Origin	.85	2.50	5.00
Bolt Special ('84, no month)	.35	1.00	2.00

BOMBARDIER (See Bee 29, the Bombardier & Cinema Comics Herald)

BOMBA, THE JUNGLE BOY
Sept-Oct, 1967 - No. 7, Sept-Oct, 1968
National Periodical Publications

	Good	Fine	Mint
1-Infantino/Anderson-c		.45	.90
2-7		.30	.60

BOMBER COMICS
March, 1944 - No. 4, Winter, 1944-45
Elliot Publ. Co./Melverne Herald/Farrell/Sunrise Times

	Good	Fine	Mint
1-Wonder Boy, & Kismet, Man of Fate begin	12.00	36.00	84.00
2-4: 2-4-Have Classics Comics ad to HRN 20	8.50	25.50	60.00

BONANZA (TV)
June-Aug, 1960 - No. 37, Aug, 1970 (All Photo-c)
Dell/Gold Key

	Good	Fine	Mint
4-Color 1110	4.00	12.00	28.00
4-Color 1221,1283, also No. 01070-207, 01070-210	3.50	10.50	24.00
1(12/62-Gold Key)	3.50	10.50	24.00
2	2.35	7.00	16.00
3-10	1.75	5.25	12.00
11-20	1.15	3.50	8.00
21-37: 29-r	.85	2.50	6.00

BONGO (See Story Hour Series)

BONGO & LUMPJAW (See 4-Color No. 706,886, and Walt Disney Showcase No. 3)

BON VOYAGE (See Movie Classics)

BOOK OF ALL COMICS
1945 (196 pages)
William H. Wise

	Good	Fine	Mint
Green Mask, Puppeteer	15.00	45.00	105.00

BOOK OF COMICS, THE
No date (1944) (132 pages) (25 cents)
William H. Wise

	Good	Fine	Mint
nn-Captain V app.	15.00	45.00	105.00

BOOK OF LOVE (See Fox Giants)

BOOSTER GOLD
Feb, 1986 - Present
DC comics

	Good	Fine	Mint
1	.30	.90	1.80
2-5		.65	1.30
6-14: 6-Origin		.45	.90

BOOTS AND HER BUDDIES
No. 5, 9/48 - No. 9, 9/49; 12/55 - No. 3, 1956
Standard Comics/Visual Editions/Argo (NEA Service)

	Good	Fine	Mint
5-Strip-r	5.00	15.00	35.00
6,8	3.35	10.00	23.00
7-(Scarce)-Spanking panels(3)	11.50	34.50	80.00
9-(Scarce)-Frazetta-a, 2 pgs.	14.50	43.50	100.00
1-3(Argo-1955-56)-Reprints	1.50	4.50	10.00

BOOTS & SADDLES (See 4-Color No. 919,1029,1116)

BORDER PATROL
May-June, 1951 - No. 3, Sept-Oct, 1951
P. L. Publishing Co.

	Good	Fine	Mint
1	2.65	8.00	18.00
2,3	1.50	4.50	10.00

BORDER WORLDS (Also see Megaton Man)
July, 1986 - Present ($1.95, B&W, Adults)
Kitchen Sink Press

	Good	Fine	Mint
1-3	.35	1.00	2.00

BORIS KARLOFF TALES OF MYSTERY (...Thriller No. 1,2)
No. 3, April, 1963 - No. 97, Feb, 1980 (TV)
Gold Key

	Good	Fine	Mint
3-8,10-(Two No. 5's, 10/63,11/63)	1.00	3.00	6.00
9-Wood-a	1.35	4.00	8.00
11-Williamson-a, Orlando-a, 8 pgs.	1.35	4.00	8.00
12-Torres, McWilliams-a; Orlando-a(2)	1.00	3.00	6.00
13,14,16-20	.70	2.00	4.00
15-Crandall-a	.85	2.50	5.00
21-Jones-a	.85	2.50	5.00
22-50: 23-Reprint	.35	1.00	2.00
51-74: 74-Origin & 1st app. Taurus		.60	1.20
75-79,87-97: 78,81-86,88,90,92,95,97-Reprints		.40	.80
80-86-(52 pages)		.40	.80
Story Digest 1(7/70-Gold Key)-All text	.50	1.50	3.00

(See Mystery Comics Digest No. 2,5,8,11,14,17,20,23,26)
NOTE: ***Bolle*** *a-51-54, 56, 58, 59.* ***McWilliams*** *a-12, 14, 18, 19.* ***Orlando*** *a-11-15, 21.*

BORIS KARLOFF THRILLER (TV) (Becomes Boris Karloff Tales of Mystery No. 3)
Oct, 1962 - No. 2, Jan, 1963 (80 pages)
Gold Key

	Good	Fine	Mint
1-Photo-c	2.00	6.00	16.00
2	1.75	5.25	14.00

BORIS THE BEAR
Aug, 1986 - Present ($1.50, B&W)
Dark Horse Comics

	Good	Fine	Mint
1 (28 pgs.)	2.00	6.00	12.00
2-4	.45	1.25	2.50

BORN AGAIN
1978 (39 cents)
Spire Christian Comics (Fleming H. Revell Co.)

	Good	Fine	Mint
Watergate, Nixon, etc.		.50	1.00

BOUNCER, THE (Formerly Green Mask?)
1944 - No. 14, Jan, 1945
Fox Features Syndicate

	Good	Fine	Mint
nn(1944)-Same as No. 14	5.50	16.50	38.00
11(No.1)(9/44)-Origin	5.50	16.50	38.00
12-14	4.35	13.00	30.00

BOUNTY GUNS (See 4-Color No. 739)

BOY AND THE PIRATES, THE (See 4-Color No. 1117)

BOY COMICS (Captain Battle No. 1&2; Boy Illustories No. 43-108)
(Stories by Charles Biro)
No. 3, April, 1942 - No. 119, March, 1956
Lev Gleason Publications

	Good	Fine	Mint
3(No.1)-Origin Crimebuster, Bombshell & Young Robin Hood; Yankee Longago, Case 1001-1008, Swoop Storm, & Boy Movies begin; intro. Iron Jaw	72.00	215.00	500.00
4-Hitler, Tojo, Mussolini-c	33.00	100.00	230.00
5	28.00	84.00	195.00
6-Origin Iron Jaw; origin & death of Iron Jaw's son; Little Dynamite begins, ends No. 39	57.00	171.00	400.00
7,9: 7-Flag-c	23.00	70.00	160.00
8-Death of Iron Jaw	26.00	78.00	182.00
10-Return of Iron Jaw; classic Biro-c	33.00	100.00	230.00
11-14	15.00	45.00	105.00
15-Death of Iron Jaw	19.50	58.50	136.00
16,18-20	10.00	30.00	70.00
17-Flag-c	11.00	33.00	76.00
21-28: 28-Yankee Longago ends	6.50	19 50	45.00
29-(68 pages)	8.00	24.00	56.00
30-Origin Crimebuster retold	8.50	25.50	60.00
31-40: 32(68pgs.)-Swoop Storm, Young Robin Hood ends. 34-Suicide c/story	3.35	10.00	23.00
41-50	2.15	6.50	15.00
51-59: 57-Dilly Duncan begins, ends No. 71	1.65	5.00	11.50
60-Iron Jaw returns	2.00	6.00	14.00
61-Origin Crimebuster & Iron Jaw retold	2.50	7.50	17.00
62-Death of Iron Jaw explained	2.65	8.00	18.00
63-72	1.50	4.50	10.00
73-Frazetta 1-pg. ad	1.65	5.00	11.50
74-80: 80-1st app. Rocky X of the Rocketeers; becomes "Rocky X" No. 101; Iron Jaw, Sniffer & the Deadly Dozen begins, ends No. 118	1.35	4.00	9.00
81-88	1.35	4.00	9.00
89-92-The Claw serial app. in all	1.65	5.00	11.50
93-Claw cameo; Check-a(Rocky X)	2.15	6.50	15.00
94-97,99	1.35	4.00	9.00
98-Rocky X by Sid Check	2.15	6.50	15.00
100	1.85	5.50	13.00
101-107,109,111,119: 111-Crimebuster becomes Chuck Chandler. 119-Last Crimebuster	1.35	4.00	9.00
108,110,112-118-Kubert-a	1.85	5.50	13.00

(See Giant Boy Book of Comics)

NOTE: *Boy Movies in 3-5,40,41. Iron Jaw app.-3, 4, 6, 8, 10, 11, 13-15; returns-60-62, 68, 69, 72-79, 81-118.* ***Briefer*** *a-18, 19.* ***Fuje*** *a-55, 18 pgs.* ***Palais*** *a-19.*

BOY COMMANDOS (See Detective Comics)
Winter, 1942-43 - No. 36, Nov-Dec, 1949
National Periodical Publications

	Good	Fine	Mint
1-Origin Liberty Belle; The Sandman & The Newsboy Legion x-over in Boy Commandos; S&K-a, 48 pgs.	100.00	300.00	700.00
2-Last Liberty Belle; S&K-a, 46 pgs.	50.00	150.00	350.00
3-S&K-a, 45 pgs.	35.00	105.00	240.00
4,5	20.00	60.00	140.00
6-8,10: 6-S&K-a	13.00	40.00	90.00
9-No S&K-a	9.50	28.50	66.00
11-Infinity-c	11.00	33.00	76.00
12-20	8.00	24.00	56.00
21,22,24-30	4.35	13.00	30.00
23-S&K c/a(all)	5.00	15.00	35.00
31-35: 32-Dale Evans app. on-c. 34-Intro. Wolf, their mascot	3.00	9.00	21.00
36	4.35	13.00	30.00

NOTE: *Most issues signed by* ***Simon & Kirby*** *are not by them.* ***S&K*** *c-1-9.*

BOY COMMANDOS
Sept-Oct, 1973 - No. 2, Nov-Dec, 1973
National Periodical Publications

	Good	Fine	Mint
1,2-G.A. S&K reprints		.30	.60

BOY DETECTIVE
May-June, 1951 - No. 4, May, 1952
Avon Periodicals

	Good	Fine	Mint
1	6.50	19.50	45.00
2,3: 3-Kinstler-c	4.35	13.00	30.00
4-Kinstler c/a	7.00	21.00	50.00

BOY EXPLORERS COMICS (Terry and The Pirates No. 3 on)
May-June, 1946 - No. 2, Sept-Oct, 1946
Family Comics (Harvey Publications)

	Good	Fine	Mint
1-Intro The Explorers, Duke of Broadway, Calamity Jane & Danny Dixon...Cadet; S&K-c/a, 24 pgs	35.00	105.00	245.00
2-(Rare)-Small size (5½x8½"; B&W; 32 pgs.) Distributed to mail subscribers only; S&K-a Estimated value....			$300-$600

(Also see All New No. 15, Flash Gordon No. 5, and Stuntman No. 3)

BOY ILLUSTORIES (See Boy Comics)

BOY LOVES GIRL (Boy Meets Girl No. 1-24)
No. 25, July, 1952 - No. 57, June, 1956
Lev Gleason Publications

	Good	Fine	Mint
25(No.1)	2.00	6.00	14.00
26,27,29-42: 30-33-Serial, 'Loves of My Life.' 39-Lingerie panels	1.35	4.00	9.00
28-Drug propaganda story	2.35	7.00	16.00
43-Toth-a	2.65	8.00	18.00
44-50: 50-Last pre-code (2/55)	1.15	3.50	8.00
51-57: 57-Ann Brewster-a	.70	2.00	6.00

BOY MEETS GIRL (Boy Loves Girl No. 25 on)
Feb, 1950 - No. 24, June, 1952 (No. 1-17, 52 pgs.)
Lev Gleason Publications

	Good	Fine	Mint
1-Guardineer-a	3.00	9.00	21.00
2	1.50	4.50	10.00
3-10	1.35	4.00	9.00
11-24	1.15	3.50	8.00

NOTE: ***Briefer*** *a-24.* ***Fuje*** *c-3,7. Painted-c 1-17. Photo-c 19-21,23.*

BOYS' AND GIRLS' MARCH OF COMICS (See March of Comics)

BOYS' RANCH (Also see Witches' Western Tales)
Oct, 1950 - No. 6, Aug, 1951 (No.1-3, 52 pgs.; No. 4-6, 36 pgs.)
Harvey Publications

	Good	Fine	Mint
1-S&K-a(3)	25.00	75.00	175.00
2-S&K-a(3)	20.00	60.00	140.00
3-S&K-a(2); Meskin-a	17.00	50.00	120.00
4-S&K-c/a, 5pgs.	12.00	35.00	84.00
5,6-S&K splashes & centerspread only; Meskin-a	6.50	20.00	45.00
Shoe Store Giveaway No. 5,6 (Identical to regular issues except S&K centerfold replaced with ad)	5.00	15.00	35.00

NOTE: ***Simon & Kirby*** *c-1-6.*

BOZO THE CLOWN (TV) (Bozo No. 7 on)
July, 1950 - No. 4, Oct-Dec, 1963
Dell Publishing Co.

	Good	Fine	Mint
4-Color 285	4.35	13.00	30.00
2(7-9/51)-7(10-12/52)	2.35	7.00	16.00
4-Color 464,508,551,594(10/54)	2.35	7.00	16.00
1(nn, 5-7/62) - 4(1963)	1.00	3.00	7.00

BOZZ CHRONICLES, THE
Dec, 1985 - Present (Adults only)
Epic Comics (Marvel)

	Good	Fine	Mint
1	.35	1.00	2.00

Boy Comics #11, © LEV

Boy Detective #2, © AVON

Bozo the Clown #4, © Capitol Records

Brain Boy #6, © DELL

Brave & the Bold #28, © DC

Brave & the Bold #54, © DC

BOZZ CHRONICLES (continued)

	Good	Fine	Mint
2-7	.25	.80	1.60

BRADY BUNCH, THE (TV)
Feb, 1970 - No. 2, May, 1970
Dell Publishing Co.

	Good	Fine	Mint
1,2	1.00	3.00	6.00
Kite Fun Book (PG&E, 1976)	.50	1.50	3.00

BRAIN, THE
Sept, 1956 - 1958
Sussex Publ. Co./Magazine Enterprises

	Good	Fine	Mint
1	1.75	5.25	12.00
2,3	.85	2.50	6.00
4-7	.75	2.25	5.00
I.W. Reprints No. 1,3,4,8,9,10('63),14	.30	.80	1.60
I.W. Reprint No. 2-Reprints Sussex No. 2 with new cover added	.30	.80	1.60
Super Reprint No. 17,18(no date)	.30	.80	1.60

BRAIN BOY
April-June, 1962 - No. 6, Sept-Nov, 1963
Dell Publishing Co.

	Good	Fine	Mint
4-Color 1330-Gil Kane-a; origin	3.00	9.00	21.00
2(7-9/62),3-6: 4-origin retold	1.50	4.50	10.00

BRAND ECHH (See Not Brand Echh)

BRAND OF EMPIRE (See 4-Color No. 771)

BRAVADOS, THE (See Wild Western Action)
August, 1971 (52 pages) (One-Shot)
Skywald Publ. Corp.

	Good	Fine	Mint
1-Red Mask, The Durango Kid, Billy Nevada reprints		.30	.60

BRAVE AND THE BOLD, THE (See Super DC Giant)
Aug-Sept, 1955 - No. 200, July, 1983
National Periodical Publications/DC Comics

	Good	Fine	Mint
1-Kubert Viking Prince, Silent Knight, Golden Gladiator begin	72.00	215.00	500.00
2	30.00	90.00	210.00
3,4	16.50	50.00	115.00
5-Robin Hood begins	11.50	35.00	80.00
6-10: 6-Kubert Robin Hood; G. Gladiator last app.; Silent Knight; no V. Prince	12.00	36.00	85.00
11-22: 22-Last Silent Knight	9.35	28.00	65.00
23-Kubert Viking Prince origin	11.50	35.00	80.00
24-Last Kubert Viking Prince	11.50	35.00	80.00
25-27-Suicide Squad	2.50	6.25	17.00
28-Justice League intro.; origin Snapper Carr	63.00	158.00	440.00
29,30-Justice League	22.00	55.00	150.00
31-33-Cave Carson	2.50	6.25	17.00
34-Origin Hawkman & Byth by Kubert	8.50	21.00	60.00
35,36-Kubert Hawkman; origin Shadow Thief No. 36	4.35	11.00	30.00
37-39-Suicide Squad. 38-Last 10¢ issue	1.85	4.60	13.00
40,41-Cave Carson Inside Earth; No. 40 has Kubert art	2.00	5.00	14.00
42,44-Kubert Hawkman	2.75	7.00	19.00
43-Origin Hawkman by Kubert	3.15	8.00	22.00
45-49-Infantino Strange Sports Stories	.70	2.00	4.00
50-The Green Arrow & Manhunter From Mars	.75	2.20	4.40
51-Aquaman & Hawkman	.75	2.20	4.40
52-Kubert Sgt. Rock, Haunted Tank, Johnny Cloud, & Mlle. Marie	1.20	3.50	7.00
53-Toth Atom & The Flash	1.20	3.50	7.00
54-Kid Flash, Robin & Aqualad; 1st app./origin Teen Titans (6-7/64)	6.35	19.00	38.00
55-Metal Men & The Atom	.50	1.40	2.80
56-The Flash & Manhunter From Mars	.50	1.40	2.80
57-Intro & Origin Metamorpho	.50	1.40	2.80
58-Metamorpho by Fradon	.50	1.40	2.80
59-Batman & Green Lantern	.50	1.40	2.80
60-Teen Titans	2.65	8.00	16.00
61,62-Origin Starman & Black Canary by Anderson. 62-Huntress app.	.85	2.50	5.00
63-Supergirl & Wonder Woman	.50	1.40	2.80
64-Batman Versus Eclipso	.50	1.40	2.80
65-Flash & Doom Patrol	.50	1.40	2.80
66-Metamorpho & Metal Men	.50	1.40	2.80
67-Infantino Batman & The Flash	.50	1.50	3.00
68-72	.50	1.40	2.80
73-78	.40	1.20	2.40
79-Batman-Deadman by Adams	1.70	5.00	10.00
80-Batman-Creeper; Adams-a	1.35	4.00	8.00
81-Batman-Flash; Adams-a	1.35	4.00	8.00
82-Batman-Aquaman; Adams-a; origin Ocean Master retold	1.35	4.00	8.00
83-Batman-Teen Titans; Adams-a	2.50	7.50	15.00
84-Batman(GA)-Sgt. Rock; Adams-a	1.35	4.00	8.00
85-Batman-Green Arrow; new costume for Green Arrow by Adams	1.35	4.00	8.00
86-Batman-Deadman; Adams-a	1.35	4.00	8.00
87-92	.35	1.00	2.00
93-Batman-House of Mystery; Adams-a	1.35	4.00	8.00
94-Batman-Teen Titans	.50	1.50	3.00
95-99: 97-Origin Deadman-r	.35	1.00	2.00
100-Batman-Gr. Lantern-Gr. Arrow-Black Canary-Robin; Deadman by Adams	1.00	3.00	6.00
101-Batman-Metamorpho; Kubert Viking Prince	.25	.75	1.50
102-Batman-Teen Titans; Adams-a(p)	.50	1.50	3.00
103-116		.50	1.00
117-148,150		.40	.80
149-Batman-Teen Titans		.60	1.20
151-199: 193-Nemesis dies		.30	.60
200-Double-sized (64 pgs.); printed on Mando paper; Earth One & Earth Two Batman team-up; Intro Batman & The Outsiders	.25	.75	1.50

NOTE: ***Adams** a-79-86, 93, 100r, 102; c-75, 76, 79-86, 88-90, 93, 95, 99, 100r. **Anderson** a-115r; c-72i, 96i. **Aparo** a-98, 100-02, 104-25, 126i, 127-36, 138-45, 147, 148i, 149-52, 154, 155, 157-62, 168-70, 173-78, 180-82, 184, 186i-89i, 191i-93i, 195, 196, 200; c-105-09, 111-36, 137i, 138-75, 177, 180-84, 186-200. **Austin** a-166i. **Buckler** a-185, 186p; c-137, 178p, 185p, 186p. **Giordano** a-143, 144. **Infantino** a-67p, 72p, 97r, 98r, 172p, 183p, 190p, 194p; c-45-49, 67p, 69p, 70p, 72p, 96p, 98r. **Kaluta** c-176. **Kane** a-115r. **Kubert &/or Heath** a-1-24; reprints-101, 113, 115, 117. **Kubert** c-22-24, 34-36, 40, 42-44, 52. **Mooney** a-114r. **Newton** a-153p, 156p, 165p. **Roussos** a-114r. **Staton** 148p. 52 pgs.-97, 100; 64 pgs.-120; 100 pgs.-112-117.*

BRAVE AND THE BOLD SPECIAL, THE (See DC Special Series No. 8)

BRAVE EAGLE (See 4-Color No. 705,770,816,879,929)

BRAVE ONE, THE (See 4-Color No. 773)

BREEZE LAWSON, SKY SHERIFF (See Sky Sheriff)

BRENDA LEE STORY, THE
September, 1962
Dell Publishing Co.

	Good	Fine	Mint
01-078-209	4.00	12.00	28.00

BRENDA STARR (Also see All Great)
No. 13, 9/47; No. 14, 3/48; V2No.3, 6/48 - V2No.12, 12/49
Four Star Comics Corp./Superior Comics Ltd.

	Good	Fine	Mint
V1No.13-By Dale Messick	20.00	60.00	140.00

BRENDA STARR (continued)

	Good	Fine	Mint
14-Kamen bondage-c	22.00	65.00	154.00
V2No.3-Baker-a?	17.00	50.00	120.00
4-Used in **SOTI**, pg. 21; Kamen bondage-c	20.00	60.00	140.00
5-10	15.00	45.00	105.00
11,12 (Scarce)	18.00	54.00	125.00

NOTE: *Newspaper reprints plus original material through No. 6. All original No. 7 on.*

BRENDA STARR (. . . Reporter)(Young Lovers No. 16 on?)
No. 13, June, 1955 - No. 15, Oct, 1955
Charlton Comics

13-15-Newspaper-r	9.00	27.00	62.00

BRENDA STARR REPORTER
October, 1963
Dell Publishing Co.

1	6.00	18.00	42.00

BRER RABBIT (See 4-Color No. 129,208,693, Walt Disney Showcase No. 28, and Wheaties)

BRER RABBIT IN "A KITE TAIL"
1956 (14 pages) (Walt Disney) (Premium)
Pacific Gas & Electric Co.

(Rare)-Kite fun book	13.00	40.00	90.00

BRER RABBIT IN "ICE CREAM FOR THE PARTY"
1955 (14 pages) (Walt Disney) (Premium)
American Dairy Association

(Rare)	7.00	21.00	50.00

BRIAN BOLLAND'S BLACK BOOK
July, 1985
Eclipse Comics

1-British B&W-r	.30	.95	1.90

BRICK BRADFORD
1948 - 1949 (Ritt & Grey reprints)
King Features Syndicate/Standard

5	6.50	19.50	45.00
6-8: 7-Schomburg-c	5.50	16.50	38.00

BRIDE'S DIARY
No. 4, May, 1955 - No. 10, Aug, 1956
Ajax/Farrell Publ.

4 (No. 1)	2.00	6.00	14.00
5-8	1.50	4.50	10.00
9,10-Disbrow-a	1.85	5.50	13.00

BRIDES IN LOVE (Hollywood Romances & Summer Love No. 46 on)
Aug, 1956 - No. 45, Feb, 1965
Charlton Comics

1	2.00	6.00	14.00
2	1.15	3.50	8.00
3-10	.85	2.50	6.00
11-20	.50	1.50	3.00
21-45	.30	.90	1.80

BRIDES ROMANCES
Nov, 1953 - No. 23, Dec, 1956
Quality Comics Group

1	3.65	11.00	25.00
2	1.85	5.50	13.00
3-10	1.50	4.50	10.00
11-14,16,17,19-22	1.15	3.50	8.00
15-Baker-a(p); Colan-a	1.30	4.00	9.00
18-Baker-a	1.65	5.00	11.50
23-Baker c/a	2.50	7.50	17.00

BRIDE'S SECRETS
Apr-May, 1954 - No. 19, May, 1958
Ajax/Farrell(Excellent Publ.)/Four-Star Comic

	Good	Fine	Mint
1	3.65	11.00	25.00
2	1.85	5.50	13.00
3-5	1.50	4.50	10.00
6-19: 12-Disbrow-a. 18-Hollingsworth-a	1.15	3.50	8.00

BRIDE-TO-BE ROMANCES (See True. . .)

BRIGAND, THE (See Fawcett Movie Comics No. 18)

BRINGING UP FATHER (See Large Feature Comic No. 9 & 4-Color No. 37)

BRINGING UP FATHER
1917 (16½x5½"; cardboard cover; 100 pages; B&W)
Star Co. (King Features)

(Rare) Daily strip reprints by George McManus (no price on cover)	22.00	65.00	154.00

BRINGING UP FATHER
1919 - 1934 (by George McManus)
(10x10"; stiff cardboard covers; B&W; daily strip reprints; 52 pgs.)
(No. 22 is 9¼x9½")
Cupples & Leon Co.

1	15.00	45.00	105.00
2-10	7.00	21.00	50.00
11-26 (Scarcer)	11.00	33.00	76.00
The Big Book 1(1926)-Thick book (hardcover); 10¼x10¼", 142pgs.	18.00	54.00	125.00
The Big Book 2(1929)	14.50	43.50	100.00

NOTE: *The Big Books contain 3 regular issues rebound and probably with dust jackets.*

BRINGING UP FATHER, THE TROUBLE OF
1921 (9x15") (Sunday reprints in color)
Embee Publ. Co.

(Rare)	22.00	65.00	154.00

BROADWAY HOLLYWOOD BLACKOUTS
Mar-Apr, 1954 - No. 3, July-Aug, 1954
Stanhall

1	3.50	10.50	24.00
2,3	2.35	7.00	16.00

BROADWAY ROMANCES
January, 1950 - No. 9, 1951
Quality Comics Group

1-Ward c/a, 9pgs.; Gustavson-a	13.00	40.00	90.00
2-Ward-a, 9pgs., photo-c	8.00	24.00	56.00
3-9: 4,5-Photo-c	3.50	10.50	24.00

BROKEN ARROW (See 4-Color No. 855,947)

BROKEN CROSS, THE (See The Crusaders)

BRONCHO BILL
1939 - 1940; No. 5, 1?/48 - No. 16, 8?/50
United Features Syndicate/Standard(Visual Editions) No. 5-on

Single Series 2 ('39)	18.00	54.00	125.00
Single Series 19 ('40)(No.2 on cvr)	14.00	42.00	96.00
5	3.50	10.50	24.00
6(4/48)-10(4/49)	2.00	6.00	14.00
11(6/49)-16	1.65	5.00	11.50

NOTE: ***Schomburg** c-6,7,9-13,16.*

BROTHER POWER, THE GEEK
Sept-Oct, 1968 - No. 2, Nov-Dec, 1968
National Periodical Publications

1,2: 1-Origin; Simon-c(i?)	.35	1.00	2.00

Brenda Starr #6, © SUPR

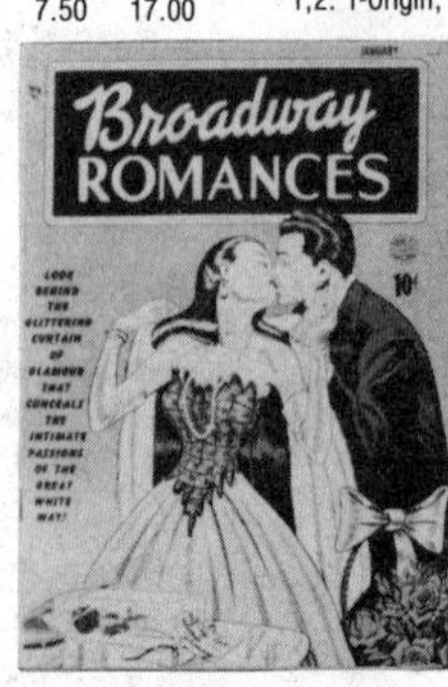

Broadway Romances #1, © QUA

Broncho Bill #7, © UFS

Bruce Gentry #4, © SUPR

Buck Jones #6, © DELL

Buck Rogers #9 (Toby), © KING

BROTHERS, HANG IN THERE, THE
1979 (49 cents)
Spire Christian Comics (Fleming H. Revell Co.)

	Good	Fine	Mint
		.30	.60

BROTHERS OF THE SPEAR (Also see Tarzan)
6/72 - No. 17, 2/76; No. 18, 5/82
Gold Key/Whitman No. 18 on

	Good	Fine	Mint
1	.85	2.50	5.00
2	.50	1.50	3.00
3-10	.35	1.00	2.00
11-17		.40	.80
18-Manning-r/No. 2; Leopard Girl-r		.30	.60

NOTE: *Painted-c No. 2-17.* ***Spiegle*** *a-13-17.*

BROTHERS, THE CULT ESCAPE, THE
1980 (49 Cents)
Spire Christian Comics (Fleming H. Revell Co.)

	Good	Fine	Mint
		.30	.60

BROWNIES (See 4-Color No. 192, 244, 293, 337, 365, 398, 436, 482, 522, 605)

BRUCE GENTRY
Jan, 1948 - No. 2, Nov, 1948; No. 3, Jan, 1949 - No. 8, July, 1949
Better/Standard/Four Star Publ./Superior No. 3

	Good	Fine	Mint
1-Ray Bailey strip reprints begin, end No. 3; E. C. emblem appears as a monogram on stationery in story; negligee panels	15.00	45.00	105.00
2,3	11.00	33.00	76.00
4-8	8.00	24.00	56.00

NOTE: ***Kamenish*** *a-2-4,6,7; c-1-4,6-8.*

BRUTE, THE
Feb, 1975 - No. 3, July, 1975
Seaboard Publ. (Atlas)

	Good	Fine	Mint
1-Origin & 1st app; Sekowsky-a		.40	.80
2,3: 2-Sekowsky-a		.25	.50

BUCCANEER
No date (1963)
I. W. Enterprises

	Good	Fine	Mint
I.W. Reprint No. 1(reprints Quality No. 20), No. 8(reprints No. 23)	1.00	3.00	6.00
Super Reprint No. 12('64, reprints No. 21)-Crandall art	1.00	3.00	6.00

BUCCANEERS (Formerly Kid Eternity)
No. 19, Jan, 1950 - No. 27, May, 1951 (No.24-27: 52 pages)
Quality Comics Group

	Good	Fine	Mint
19-Captain Daring, Black Roger, Eric Falcon & Spanish Main begin; Crandall-a	15.00	45.00	105.00
20,23-Crandall-a	11.50	34.50	80.00
21-Crandall c/a	14.50	43.50	100.00
22-Bondage-c	7.00	21.00	50.00
24,26: 24-Adam Peril, U.S.N. begins; last Spanish Main	6.50	19.50	45.00
25-Origin & 1st app. Corsair Queen	6.50	19.50	45.00
27-Crandall c/a	12.00	36.00	84.00

BUCCANEERS, THE (See 4-Color No. 800)

BUCKAROO BANZAI
Jan, 1985 - No. 2, Feb, 1985
Marvel Comics Group

	Good	Fine	Mint
1,2-r/Marvel Super Special		.40	.80

BUCK DUCK
June, 1953 - No. 4, Dec, 1953
Atlas Comics (ANC)

	Good	Fine	Mint
1-(funny animal)	2.00	6.00	14.00
2-4-(funny animal)	1.30	4.00	9.00

BUCK JONES
No. 299, Oct, 1950 - No. 850, Oct, 1957 (All Painted-c)
Dell Publishing Co.

	Good	Fine	Mint
4-Color 299(No.1)-Buck Jones & his horse Silver-B begin; painted back-c begins, ends No. 5	5.65	17.00	40.00
2(4-6/51)	3.50	10.50	24.00
3-8(10-12/52)	2.65	8.00	18.00
4-Color 460,500,546,589	2.65	8.00	18.00
4-Color 652,733,850	1.75	5.25	12.00

BUCK ROGERS (In the 25th Century)
1933 (36 pages in color) (6x8")
Kelloggs Corn Flakes Giveaway

	Good	Fine	Mint
370A(Rare) by Phil Nowlan & Dick Calkins; 1st Buck Rogers radio premium (tells origin)	24.00	72.00	166.00

BUCK ROGERS (Also see Famous Funnies, Pure Oil Comics, Salerno Carnival of Comics, 24 Pages of Comics, & Vicks Comics)
Winter, 1940-41 - No. 6, Sept, 1943
Famous Funnies

	Good	Fine	Mint
1-Sunday strip reprints by Rick Yager; begins with strip No. 190	85.00	255.00	595.00
2	55.00	165.00	385.00
3,4	45.00	135.00	310.00
5-Story continues with Famous Funnies No. 80; ½ Buck Rogers, ½ Sky Roads	40.00	120.00	280.00
6-Reprints of 1939 dailies; contains B.R. story "Crater of Doom" (2 pgs.) by Calkins not reprinted from Famous Funnies	40.00	120.00	280.00

BUCK ROGERS
No. 100, Jan, 1951 - No. 9, May-June, 1951
Toby Press

	Good	Fine	Mint
100(7)	10.00	30.00	70.00
101(8), 9-All Anderson-a('47-'49-r from dailies)	8.50	25.50	60.00

BUCK ROGERS (. . . in the 25th Century No. 5 on) (TV)
10/64; No. 2, 7/79 - No. 16, 5/82 (no No. 10)
Gold Key/Whitman No. 7 on

	Good	Fine	Mint
1(10128-410)	2.50	7.50	15.00
2(8/79)-Movie adaptation	.35	1.00	2.00
3-9,11-16: 3,4-Movie adaptation; 5-new stories		.50	1.00
Giant Movie Edition 11296(64pp, Whitman, $1.50), reprints GK No. 2-4 minus cover	.35	1.00	2.00
Giant Movie Edition 02489(Western/Marvel, $1.50), reprints GK No. 2-4 minus cover	.35	1.00	2.00

NOTE: ***Bolle*** *a-2p-4p. McWilliams a-2i-4i, 5-11. Painted-c No. 1-13.*

BUCKSKIN (See 4-Color No. 1011,1107 (Movie))

BUDDIES IN THE U.S. ARMY
Nov, 1952 - No. 2, 1953
Avon Periodicals

	Good	Fine	Mint
1	5.50	16.50	38.00
2-Mort Lawrence c/a	4.35	13.00	30.00

BUDDY TUCKER & HIS FRIENDS
1906 (11x17") (In color)
Cupples & Leon Co.

	Good	Fine	Mint
1905 Sunday strip reprints by R. F. Outcault	15.00	45.00	105.00

BUFFALO BEE (See 4-Color No. 957,1002,1061)

BUFFALO BILL (Also see Super Western Comics)
No. 2, Oct., 1950 - No. 9, Dec, 1951

BUFFALO BILL (continued)
Youthful Magazines

	Good	Fine	Mint
2	2.35	7.00	16.00
3-9	1.30	4.00	9.00

BUFFALO BILL CODY (See Cody of the Pony Express)

BUFFALO BILL, JR. (TV) (Also see Western Roundup)
Jan, 1956 - No. 13, Aug-Oct, 1959; 1965 (All photo-c)
Dell Publishing Co./Gold Key

4-Color 673 (No. 1)	2.65	8.00	18.00
4-Color 742,766,798,828,856(11/57)	2.00	6.00	14.00
7(2-4/58)-13	1.75	5.25	12.00
1(6/65-Gold Key)	1.35	4.00	8.00

BUFFALO BILL PICTURE STORIES
June-July, 1949 - No. 2, Aug-Sept, 1949
Street & Smith Publications

1,2-Wildey, Powell-a in each	3.50	10.50	24.00

BUFFALO BILL'S PICTURE STORIES
1909 (Soft cardboard cover)
Street & Smith Publications

	7.00	21.00	50.00

BUGALOOS (TV)
Sept, 1971 - No. 4, Feb, 1972
Charlton Comics

1-4	.35	1.00	2.00

NOTE: *No. 3(1/72) went on sale late in 1972 (after No. 4) with the 1/73 issues.*

BUGHOUSE (Satire)
Mar-Apr, 1954 - No. 4, Sept-Oct, 1954
Ajax/Farrell (Excellent Publ.)

V1No.1	4.00	12.00	28.00
2-4	2.65	8.00	18.00

BUGHOUSE FABLES
1921 (48 pgs.) (4x5½'') (10 cents)
Embee Distributing Co. (King Features)

1-Barney Google	5.00	15.00	35.00

BUG MOVIES
1931 (52 pages) (B&W)
Dell Publishing Co.

Not reprints; Stookie Allen-a	4.00	12.00	28.00

BUGS BUNNY (See Dell Giants for annuals)
1942 - No. 245, 1983
Dell Publishing Co./Gold Key No. 86-218/Whitman No. 219 on

Large Feature Comic 8(1942)-(Rarely found in fine-mint condition)	43.00	130.00	300.00
4-Color 33 ('43)	20.00	60.00	140.00
4-Color 51	14.50	43.50	100.00
4-Color 88	8.00	24.00	56.00
4-Color 123('46),142,164	4.35	13.00	30.00
4-Color 187,200,217,233	3.50	10.50	24.00
4-Color 250-Used in **SOTI**, pg. 309	3.50	10.50	24.00
4-Color 266,274,281,289,298('50)	2.35	7.00	16.00
4-Color 307,317(No.1),327(No.2),338,347,355,366,376,393	1.75	5.25	12.00
4-Color 407,420,432	1.30	4.00	9.00
28(12-1/52-53)-30	1.00	3.00	7.00
31-50	.65	2.00	4.50
51-85(7-9/62)	.50	1.50	3.50
86(10/62)-88-Bugs Bunny's Showtime-(80 pgs.)(25 cents)	1.50	4.50	12.00
89-100	.50	1.50	3.00
101-120	.40	1.25	2.50
121-140	.35	1.00	2.00
141-170		.60	1.20
171-228,230-245		.30	.60
229-Swipe of Barks story/WDC&S 223		.35	.70

NOTE: *Reprints-100, 102, 104, 123, 143, 144, 147, 167, 173, 175-77, 179-85, 187, 190.*

...Comic-Go-Round 11196-(224 pgs.)($1.95)(Golden Press, 1979)	.40	1.20	2.40
Kite Fun Book ('60,'68)-Giveaway	.50	1.50	3.00
Winter Fun 1(12/67-Gold Key)-Giant	1.00	3.00	8.00

BUGS BUNNY (See The Best of...; Camp Comics; Comic Album No. 2, 6, 10, 14; Dell Giant No. 28, 32, 46; Golden Comics Digest No. 1, 3, 5, 6, 8, 10, 14, 15, 17, 21, 26, 30, 34, 39, 42, 47; March of Comics No. 44, 59, 75, 83, 97, 115, 132, 149, 160, 179, 188, 201, 220, 231, 245, 259, 273, 287, 301, 315, 329, 343, 363, 367, 380, 392, 403, 415, 428, 440, 452, 464, 476, 487; Puffed Wheat, Super Book No. 14, 26; and Whitman Comic Books)

BUGS BUNNY (Puffed Rice Giveaway)
1949 (32 pages each, 3-1/8x6-7/8'')
Quaker Cereals

A1-Traps the Counterfeiters, A2-Aboard Mystery Submarine, A3- Rocket to the Moon, A4-Lion Tamer, A5-Rescues the Beautiful Princess, B1-Buried Treasure, B2-Outwits the Smugglers, B3-Joins the Marines, B4-Meets the Dwarf Ghost, B5-Finds Aladdin's Lamp, C1-Lost in the Frozen North, C2-Secret Agent, C3-Captured by Cannibals, C4-Fights the Man from Mars, C5-And the Haunted Cave

each....	1.70	5.00	10.00

BUGS BUNNY (3-D)
1953 (Pocket size) (15 titles)
Cheerios Giveaway

each....	4.30	13.00	30.00

BUGS BUNNY & PORKY PIG
Sept, 1965 (100 pages; paper cover; giant)
Gold Key

1(30025-509)	2.00	6.00	14.00

BUGS BUNNY'S ALBUM (See 4-Color No. 498,585,647,724)

BUGS BUNNY LIFE STORY ALBUM (See 4-Color No. 838)

BUGS BUNNY MERRY CHRISTMAS (See 4-Color No. 1064)

BULLETMAN (See Nickel Comics, Master Comics, Fawcett Miniatures and Mighty Midget Comics)
Sum, 1941 - No. 12, 2/12/43; No. 14, Spr, 1946 - No. 16, Fall, 1946 (nn 13)
Fawcett Publications

1	88.00	265.00	615.00
2	59.00	178.00	410.00
3	40.00	120.00	280.00
4,5	32.00	95.00	225.00
6-10: 7-Ghost Stories as told by the night watchman of the cemetery begins; Eisnerish-a	27.00	81.00	190.00
11,12,14-16 (nn 13)	24.00	72.00	168.00
...Well Known Comics (1942)-Paper cover, glued binding; printed in red (Bestmaid/Samuel Lowe giveaway)	12.00	36.00	72.00

NOTE: ***Mac Raboy** c-1-3,5,10.*

BULLS-EYE (Cody of The Pony Express No. 8 on)
7-8/54 - No. 5, 3-4/55; No. 6, 6/55; No. 7, 8/55
Mainline No. 1-5/Charlton No. 6,7

1-S&K-c, 2 pages	18.50	56.00	130.00
2-S&K c/a	18.50	56.00	130.00
3-5-S&K c/a(2)	11.00	33.00	76.00
6-S&K c/a	9.35	28.00	65.00
7-S&K c/a(3)	11.00	33.00	76.00
Great Scott Shoe Store giveaway-Reprints No. 2 with new cover	7.00	21.00	50.00

Buffalo Bill Jr. #8, © Tie-Ups Co.

Bugs Bunny #88, © L. Schlesinger

Bulletman #15, © FAW

Bullwinkle #01-090-209, © Jay Ward Prod.

Burke's Law #2, © Four Star

Buster Crabbe #3, © FF

BULLS-EYE COMICS
No. 11, 1944
Harry 'A' Chesler

	Good	Fine	Mint
11-Origin K-9, Green Knight's sidekick, Lance; The Green Knight, Lady Satan, Yankee Doodle Jones app.	10.00	30.00	70.00

BULLWHIP GRIFFIN (See Movie Comics)

BULLWINKLE (TV) (. . . and Rocky No. 20 on; See March of Comics No. 233, and Rocky & Bullwinkle)
3-5/62 - No. 11, 4/74; No. 12, 6/76 - No. 19, 3/78; No. 20, 4/79 - No. 25, 2/80 (Jay Ward)
Dell/Gold Key

4-Color 1270 (3-5/62)	3.00	9.00	21.00
01-090-209 (Dell, 7-9/62)	3.00	9.00	21.00
1(11/62, Gold Key)	2.35	7.00	16.00
2(2/63)	1.75	5.25	12.00
3(4/72)-11(4/74-Gold Key)	.70	2.00	4.00
12(6/76)-reprints	.25	.75	1.50
13(9/76), 14-new stories	.35	1.00	2.00
15-25		.60	1.20
Mother Moose Nursery Pomes 01-530-207 (5-7/62-Dell)	3.00	9.00	21.00

NOTE: *Reprints-6,7,20-24*

BULLWINKLE (. . . & Rocky No. 2 on)(TV)
July, 1970 - No. 7, July, 1971
Charlton Comics

1	1.00	3.00	6.00
2-7	.70	2.00	4.00

BUNNY
Dec, 1966 - No. 20, Dec, 1971; No. 21, Nov, 1976
Harvey Publications

1	1.00	3.00	6.00
2-8,10,11,14,17-21	.50	1.50	3.00
9,12,13,15,16-All Giants	1.00	3.00	6.00

BURKE'S LAW (TV)
1-3/64; No. 2, 5-7/64; No. 3, 3-5/65 (Gene Barry photo-c)
Dell Publishing Co.

1-Photo-c	2.00	6.00	12.00
2,3	1.35	4.00	8.00

BURNING ROMANCES (See Fox Giants)

BUSTER BEAR
Dec, 1953 - No. 10, June, 1955
Quality Comics Group (Arnold Publ.)

1	1.75	5.25	12.00
2	1.00	3.00	7.00
3-10	.85	2.50	6.00
I.W. Reprint No. 9,10 (Super on inside)	.30	.80	1.60

BUSTER BROWN
1903 - 1909 (11x17'' strip reprints in color)
Frederick A. Stokes Co.

	Good	Fine	Mint
. . . & His Resolutions (1903) by R. F. Outcault	32.00	96.00	225.00
. . . Abroad (1904)-86 pgs.; hardback; 8x10¼''; B&W; by R. F. Outcault(76pgs.)	25.00	75.00	175.00
. . . His Dog Tige & Their Troubles (1904)	25.00	75.00	175.00
. . . Pranks (1905)	25.00	75.00	175.00
. . . Antics (1906)-11x17'', 30 pages color strip reprints	25.00	75.00	175.00
. . . Mary Jane & Tige (1906)	25.00	75.00	175.00
. . . My Resolutions (1906)-68 pgs.; B&W; hardcover; Sunday panel reprints	25.00	75.00	175.00
Collection of Buster Brown Comics (1908)	25.00	75.00	175.00
Buster Brown Up to Date (1909)	25.00	75.00	175.00
. . . The Little Rogue (1916)(10x15¾,'' 62pp, in color)	18.00	55.00	125.00

NOTE: *Rarely found in fine or mint condition.*

BUSTER BROWN
1906 - 1917 (11x17'' strip reprints in color)
Cupples & Leon Co./N. Y. Herald Co.
(By R. F. Outcault)

. . . His Dog Tige & Their Jolly Times (1906)	23.00	70.00	160.00
. . . Latest Frolics (1906), 58 pgs.	21.00	63.00	146.00
. . . Amusing Capers (1908)	21.00	63.00	146.00
. . . And His Pets (1909)	21.00	63.00	146.00
. . . On His Travels (1910)	21.00	63.00	146.00
. . . Happy Days (1911)	21.00	63.00	146.00
. . . In Foreign Lands (1912)	19.00	57.00	132.00
. . . And the Cat (1917)	17.00	51.00	120.00

NOTE: *Rarely found in fine or mint condition.*

BUSTER BROWN COMICS
1945 - 1959 (No. 5: paper cover)
Brown Shoe Co.

nn, nd (No. 1)	7.00	21.00	50.00
2	3.50	10.50	24.00
3-10	1.85	5.50	13.00
11-20	1.50	4.50	10.00
21-24,26-28	1.15	3.50	8.00
25,31,33-37,40-43-Crandall-a in all	3.65	11.00	25.00
29,30,32-''Interplanetary Police Vs. the Space Siren'' by Crandall	3.65	11.00	25.00
38,39	.85	2.50	6.00
. . . Goes to Mars ('58-Western Printing)	1.00	3.00	7.00
. . . In ''Buster Makes the Team!'' (1959-Custom Comics)	.85	2.50	6.00
. . . In The Jet Age (date?)	1.15	3.50	8.00
. . . Of the Safety Patrol ('60-Custom Comics)	.85	2.50	6.00
. . . Out of This World ('59-Custom Comics)	.85	2.50	6.00
. . . Safety Coloring Book (1958)-Slick paper, 16 pages	.85	2.50	6.00

BUSTER BUNNY
Nov, 1949 - No. 16, Oct, 1953
Standard Comics(Animated Cartoons)/Pines

1-Frazetta 1 pg. text illo.	2.65	8.00	18.00
2	1.30	4.00	9.00
3-16	1.00	3.00	7.00

BUSTER CRABBE
Nov, 1951 - No. 12, 1953
Famous Funnies

1-Frazetta drug pusher back-c	13.00	40.00	90.00
2-Williamson/Evans-c	16.00	48.00	110.00
3-Williamson/Evans c/a	18.00	54.00	126.00
4-Frazetta c/a, 1pg.; bondage-c	21.00	63.00	148.00
5-Frazetta-c; Williamson/Krenkel/Orlando-a, 11pgs. (per Mr. Williamson)	110.00	330.00	770.00
6,8,10-12	3.00	9.00	21.00
7,9-One pg. of Frazetta in each	3.35	10.00	23.00

BUSTER CRABBE (The Amazing Adventures of . .)
Dec, 1953 - No. 4, June, 1954
Lev Gleason Publications

1	5.00	15.00	35.00
2,3-Toth-a	6.85	20.50	48.00
4-Flash Gordon-c	5.00	15.00	35.00

BUTCH CASSIDY
June, 1971 - No. 3, Oct, 1971 (52 pages)
Skywald Comics

	Good	Fine	Mint
1-Red Mask reprint, retitled Maverick; Bolle-a		.40	.80
2-Whip Wilson reprint		.30	.60
3-Dead Canyon Days reprint/Crack Western No. 63; Sundance Kid app.; Crandall-a		.30	.60

BUTCH CASSIDY (. . . & the Wild Bunch)
1951
Avon Periodicals

	Good	Fine	Mint
1-Kinstler c/a	8.00	24.00	56.00

NOTE: *Reinman story; Issue No. on inside spine.*

BUTCH CASSIDY (See Fun-In No. 11)

BUZ SAWYER
June, 1948 - 1949
Standard Comics

	Good	Fine	Mint
1-Roy Crane-a	6.00	18.00	42.00
2	4.00	12.00	28.00
3-5	3.35	10.00	23.00

BUZ SAWYER'S PAL, ROSCOE SWEENEY (See Sweeney)

BUZZY
Winter, 1944-45 - No. 75, 1-2/57; No. 76, 10/57; No. 77, 10/58
National Periodical Publications/Detective Comics

	Good	Fine	Mint
1 (52 pgs. begin)	11.00	33.00	76.00
2	5.35	16.00	37.00
3-5	3.85	11.50	27.00
6-10	2.65	8.00	19.00
11-20	2.00	6.00	14.00
21-30	1.65	5.00	11.50
31,35-38	1.30	4.00	9.00
32-34,39-Last 52 pgs. Scribbly by Mayer in all (These four stories were done for Scribbly No. 14 which was delayed for a year)	1.50	4.50	10.00
40-77	1.00	3.00	7.00

BUZZY THE CROW (See Harvey Hits No. 18)

CADET GRAY OF WEST POINT (See Dell Giants)

CAIN'S HUNDRED (TV)
May-July, 1962 - No. 2, Sept-Nov, 1962
Dell Publishing Co.

	Good	Fine	Mint
nn(01-094-207)	1.30	4.00	9.00
2	.85	2.50	6.00

CALL FROM CHRIST
1952 (36 pages)
Catechetical Educational Society (Giveaway)

	Good	Fine	Mint
	2.30	7.00	16.00

CALLING ALL BOYS (Tex Granger No. 18 on)
Jan, 1946 - No. 17, May, 1948
Parents' Magazine Institute

	Good	Fine	Mint
1	2.65	8.00	18.00
2	1.50	4.50	10.00
3-9,11-17	1.15	3.50	8.00
10-Gary Cooper photo-c	2.35	7.00	16.00

CALLING ALL GIRLS
Sept, 1941 - No. 72, April, 1948 (Part magazine, part comic)
Parents' Magazine Institute

	Good	Fine	Mint
1	4.00	12.00	28.00
2	2.15	6.50	15.00
3-Shirley Temple photo-c	2.65	8.00	18.00
4-10: 9-Flag-c	1.50	4.50	10.00
11-20	1.00	3.00	7.00
21-43(10-11/45)-Last issue with comics	.75	2.25	5.00
44-51(7/46)-Last comic book size issue	.50	1.50	3.00
52-72	.35	1.00	2.00

NOTE: ***Jack Sparling** art in many issues.*

CALLING ALL KIDS
Dec-Jan, 1945-46 - No. 26, Aug, 1949
Parents' Magazine Institute

	Good	Fine	Mint
1	2.35	7.00	16.00
2	1.15	3.50	8.00
3-10	.75	2.25	5.00
11-26	.55	1.65	4.00

CALVIN (See Li'l Kids)

CALVIN & THE COLONEL (TV)
No. 1354, 4-6/62 - No. 2, July-Sept, 1962
Dell Publishing Co.

	Good	Fine	Mint
4-Color 1354	2.00	6.00	14.00
2	1.50	4.50	10.00

CAMELOT 3000
12/82 - No. 11, 7/84; No. 12, 4/85 (Direct Sale; Mando paper)
DC Comics (Maxi-series)

	Good	Fine	Mint
1	.50	1.50	3.00
2,3	.35	1.00	2.00
4-6: 5-Intro Knights of New Camelot	.25	.75	1.50
7-12	.25	.75	1.50

NOTE: ***Austin** a-7i-12i.*

CAMERA COMICS
July, 1944 - No. 9, Summer, 1946
U.S. Camera Publishing Corp./ME

	Good	Fine	Mint
nn (7/44)	6.50	19.50	45.00
nn (9/44)	5.00	15.00	35.00
1(10/44)-The Grey Comet	5.00	15.00	35.00
2	3.50	10.50	24.00
3-Nazi WW II-c; ½ photos	3.00	9.00	21.00
4-9: All ½ photos	2.65	8.00	18.00

CAMP COMICS
Feb, 1942 - No. 3, April, 1942
Dell Publishing Co.

	Good	Fine	Mint
1-"Seaman Sy Wheeler" by Kelly, 7 pgs.; Bugs Bunny app.	27.00	81.00	190.00
2-Kelly-a, 12 pgs.; Bugs Bunny app.	21.00	63.00	150.00
3-(Scarce)-Kelly-a	27.00	81.00	190.00

CAMP RUNAMUCK (TV)
April, 1966
Dell Publishing Co.

	Good	Fine	Mint
1	1.35	4.00	8.00

CAMPUS LOVES
Dec, 1949 - No. 5, Aug, 1950
Quality Comics Group (Comic Magazines)

	Good	Fine	Mint
1-Ward c/a, 9 pgs.	11.50	34.50	80.00
2-Ward c/a	9.50	28.50	66.00
3,4	4.35	13.00	30.00
5-Spanking panels (2)	6.00	18.00	42.00

NOTE: ***Gustavson** a-1-5. Photo-c-3-5.*

CAMPUS ROMANCE (. . . Romances on cover)
Sept-Oct, 1949 - No. 3, Feb-Mar, 1950
Avon Periodicals/Realistic

	Good	Fine	Mint
1-Walter Johnson-a; c-/Avon paperback 348	9.50	28.50	66.00

Buz Sawyer #2, © STD

Camelot 3000 #11, © DC

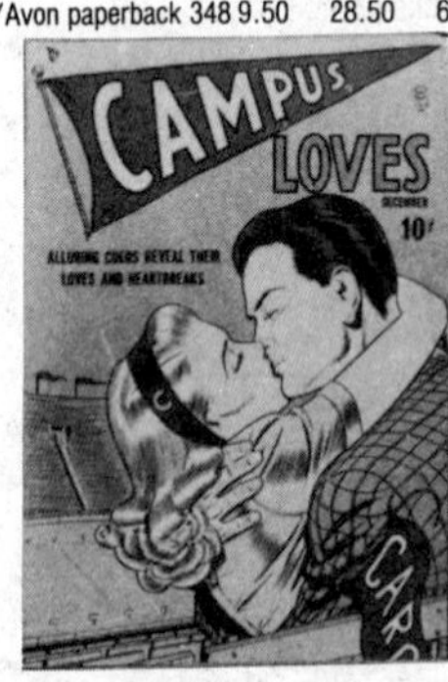

Campus Loves #1, © QUA

Candy #17, © QUA

Cap'n Quick & a Foozle #1, © Eclipse

Captain Aero Comics #14, © HOKE

CAMPUS ROMANCE (continued)

	Good	Fine	Mint
2-Grandenetti-a; c-/Avon paperback 151	8.00	24.00	56.00
3-c-/Avon paperback 201	8.00	24.00	56.00
Realistic reprint	3.50	10.50	24.00

CANADA DRY PREMIUMS (See Swamp Fox, The)

CANCELLED COMIC CAVALCADE
Summer, 1978 - No. 2, Fall, 1978 (8½x11''; B&W)
(Xeroxed pages on one side only w/blue cover and taped spine)
DC Comics, Inc.

1-(412 pages) Contains xeroxed copies of art for: Black Lightning No. 12, cover to No. 13; Claw No. 13,14; The Deserter No. 1; Doorway to Nightmare No. 6; Firestorm No. 6; The Green Team No. 2,3.
2-(532 pages) Contains xeroxed copies of art for: Kamandi No. 60 (including Omac), No. 61; Prez No. 5; Shade No. 9 (including The Odd Man); Showcase No. 105 (Deadman), 106 (The Creeper); The Vixen No. 1; and covers to Army at War No. 2, Battle Classics No. 3, Demand Classics No. 1 & 2, Dynamic Classics No. 3, Mr. Miracle No. 26, Ragman No. 6, Weird Mystery No. 25 & 26, & Western Classics No. 1 & 2. (Rare)
(One set sold in 1980 for $500.00)

NOTE: *In June, 1978, DC cancelled several of their titles. For copyright purposes, the unpublished original art for these titles was xeroxed, bound in the above books, published and distributed. Only 35 copies were made.*

CANDID TALES (Also see Bold Stories & It Rhymes With Lust)
April, 1950, June, 1950 (Digest size) (144 pages) (Full color)
Kirby Publishing Co.

	Good	Fine	Mint
(Scarce) Contains Woodish female pirate story, 15 pgs., and 14 pgs. in June issue	32.00	95.00	220.00

NOTE: *Another version exists with Dr. Kilmore by Wood; no female pirate story.*

CANDY
Fall, 1944 - No. 3, Spring, 1945
William H. Wise & Co.

	Good	Fine	Mint
1-Two Scoop Scuttle stories by Wolverton	10.00	30.00	76.00
2,3-Scoop Scuttle by Wolverton, 2-4 pgs.	8.00	24.00	56.00

CANDY
Fall, 1947 - No. 64, July, 1956
Quality Comics Group

	Good	Fine	Mint
1-Gustavson-a	5.00	15.00	35.00
2-Gustavson-a	3.00	9.00	21.00
3-10	2.00	6.00	14.00
11-30	1.50	4.50	10.00
31-63	1.15	3.50	8.00
64-Ward-c(p)?	1.65	5.00	11.50
Super Reprint No. 2,10,12,16,17,18('63-'64)	.50	1.50	3.00

NOTE: ***Jack Cole** 1-2pg. art in many issues.*

CANNONBALL COMICS
Feb, 1945 - No. 2, Mar, 1945
Rural Home Publishing Co.

	Good	Fine	Mint
1-The Crash Kid, Thunderbrand, The Captive Prince & Crime Crusader begin	15.00	45.00	105.00
2	9.00	27.00	63.00

CANTEEN KATE (Also see All Picture All True Love Story & Fightin' Marines)
June, 1952 - No. 3, Nov, 1952
St. John Publishing Co.

	Good	Fine	Mint
1-Matt Baker c/a	22.00	65.00	154.00
2-Matt Baker c/a	18.50	56.00	130.00
3-(Rare)-Used in **POP**, pg. 75; Baker c/a; transvestism story	23.00	70.00	160.00

CAP'N CRUNCH COMICS (See Quaker Oats)
1963; 1965 (16 pgs.; miniature giveaways; 2½x6½'')
Quaker Oats Co.

	Good	Fine	Mint
(1963 titles)-''The Picture Pirates,'' ''The Fountain of Youth,'' ''I'm Dreaming of a Wide Isthmus.'' (1965 titles)-''Bewitched, Betwitched, & Betweaked,'' Seadog Meets the Witch Doctor''	.75	2.25	5.00

CAP'N QUICK & A FOOZLE
July, 1985 - No. 3, Nov, 1985 ($1.50; Baxter paper)
Eclipse Comics

	Good	Fine	Mint
1-3-Rogers c/a	.25	.75	1.50

CAPTAIN ACTION
Oct-Nov, 1968 - No. 5, June-July, 1969
National Periodical Publications

	Good	Fine	Mint
1-Origin; Wood-a		.40	.80
2-5: 2,3,5-Kane/Wood-a		.30	.60
. . . & Action Boy('67)-Ideal Toy Co. giveaway		.30	.60

CAPTAIN AERO COMICS (Samson No. 1-6)
V1No.7(No.1), Dec, 1941 - V2No.4(No.10), Jan, 1943; V3No.9(No. 11), Sept, 1943 - V4No.3(No.17), Oct, 1944; No. 21, Dec, 1944 - No. 26, Aug, 1946 (no No. 18-20)
Holyoke Publishing Co.

	Good	Fine	Mint
V1No.7(No.1)-Flag-Man & Solar, Master of Magic, Captain Aero, Cap Stone, Adventurer begin	35.00	105.00	245.00
8(No.2)-Pals of Freedom app.	20.00	60.00	140.00
9(No.3)-Alias X begins; Pals of Freedom app.	20.00	60.00	140.00
10(No.4)-Origin The Gargoyle; Kubert-a	20.00	60.00	140.00
11,12(No.5,6)-Kubert-a; Miss Victory app. in No. 6	17.00	51.00	120.00
V2No.1(No.7)	10.00	30.00	70.00
2(No.8)-Origin The Red Cross	10.00	30.00	70.00
3(No.9)-Miss Victory app.	7.00	21.00	50.00
4(No.10)-Miss Victory app.	5.75	17.00	40.00
V3No.9 - V3No.13(No.11-15): 11,15-Miss Victory app.	4.00	12.00	28.00
V4No.2, V4No.3(No.16,17)	3.00	9.00	21.00
21-24,26-L. B. Cole-c	6.35	19.00	44.00
25-L. B. Cole S/F-c	8.00	24.00	56.00

NOTE: ***Hollingsworth** a-23. **Infantino** a-23.*

CAPTAIN AMERICA (See All-Select, All Winners, Aurora, The Invaders, Marvel Super Heroes, Marvel Super-Action, Marvel Team-Up, Marvel Treasury Special, & USA Comics)

CAPTAIN AMERICA (Tales of Suspense No. 1-99; . . . and the Falcon No. 134-223)
No. 100, April, 1968 - Present
Marvel Comics Group

	Good	Fine	Mint
100-Flashback on Cap's revival with Avengers & Sub-Mariner	1.50	4.50	9.00
101-108	.70	2.00	4.00
109-Origin Capt. America	.85	2.50	5.00
110,111,113-Steranko c/a. 110-Rick becomes Cap's partner. 111-Death of Steve Rogers. 113-Cap's funeral	1.40	4.25	8.50
112,114-116,118-120	.30	.90	1.80
117-1st app. The Falcon	.40	1.25	2.50
121-130: 121-Retells origin	.30	.90	1.80
131-139: 133-The Falcon becomes Cap's partner; origin Modok. 137,138-Spider-Man x-over	.35	1.00	2.00
140-Origin Grey Gargoyle retold	.35	1.00	2.00
141-150: 143-(52 pgs.)		.60	1.20
151-171,176-179: 155-Origin; redrawn with Falcon added. 164-1st app. Nightshade. 176-End of Capt. America		.50	1.00
172-175-X-Men x-over	.70	2.00	4.00
180-Intro & origin of Nomad		.50	1.00
181-Intro & origin of new Capt. America		.50	1.00
182,184,185,187-192		.40	.80
183-Death of New Cap; Nomad becomes Cap		.50	1.00

CAPTAIN AMERICA (continued)

	Good	Fine	Mint
186-True origin The Falcon		.60	1.20
193-199,201-246		.30	.60
200	.25	.75	1.50
247-255-Byrne-a. 255-Origin	.25	.75	1.50
256-280: 269-1st Team America		.30	.60
281-330: 281-1950s Bucky returns. 282-Bucky becomes Nomad. 284-Patriot (Jack Mace) app. 285-Death of Patriot. 298-Origin Red Skull		.30	.60
. . . & The Campbell Kids (1980, 36pg. giveaway, Campbell's soup/U.S. Dept. of Energy)	.35	1.00	2.00
Giant Size 1(12/75)	.30	.90	1.80
Special 1(1/71)	.40	1.25	2.50
Special 2(1/72)	.40	1.25	2.50
Annual 3(4/76), 4(8/77)-Kirby c/a, 5(1981), 6(11/82), 7('83), Annual 8(9/86)-Wolverine feat.		.60	1.20

NOTE: ***Austin*** *c-225i, 239i, 246i.* ***Buscema*** *a-115p, 217p; c-136p, 217.* ***Byrne*** *part c-223, 238, 239, 247p-54p, 290, 291; a-247-254p, 255.* ***Colan*** *a(p)-116-137, 256, Annual 5; c(p)-116-123, 126, 129.* ***Everett*** *a-136i, 137i; c-126i.* ***Gil Kane*** *a-145p; c-147p, 149p, 150p, 170p, 172-174, 180, 181p, 183-190p, 215, 216, 220, 221.* ***Kirby*** *a(p)-100-109, 112, 193-214, 216, Giant Size 1, Special 1, 2(layouts), Annual 3,4; c-100-109, 112, 126p, 193-214.* ***Miller*** *c-241p, 244p, 245p, 255p, Annual No. 5.* ***Mooney*** *a-149i.* ***Morrow*** *a-144.* ***Perez*** *c-243p, 246p.* ***Roussos*** *a-140i, 168i.* ***Starlin/Sinnott*** *c-162.* ***Sutton*** *a-244i.* ***Tuska*** *a-112i, 215p, Special 2.* ***Wood*** *a-127i.*

CAPTAIN AMERICA COMICS
Mar, 1941 - No. 75, Jan, 1950; No. 76, 5/54 - No. 78, 9/54
(No. 74 & 75 titled Capt. America's Weird Tales)
Timely/Marvel Comics (TCI 1-20/CmPS 21-68/MjMC 69-75/Atlas Comics (PrPI 76-78)

	Good	Fine	Mint
1-Origin & 1st app. Captain America & Bucky by S&K; Hurricane, Tuk the Caveboy begin by S&K; Red Skull app.	815.00	2445.00	5700.00
(Prices vary widely on this book)			
2-S&K Hurricane; Tuk by Avison (Kirby splash)	357.00	1070.00	2500.00
3-Red Skull app; Stan Lee's 1st text.	250.00	750.00	1750.00
4	165.00	495.00	1155.00
5	150.00	450.00	1050.00
6-Origin Father Time; Tuk the Caveboy ends	125.00	375.00	875.00
7-Red Skull app	125.00	375.00	875.00
8-10-Last S&K issue, (S&K centerfold No. 6-10)	110.00	330.00	770.00
11-Last Hurricane, Headline Hunter; Al Avison Captain America begins, ends No. 20	75.00	225.00	525.00
12-The Imp begins, ends No. 16; Last Father Time	75.00	225.00	525.00
13-Origin The Secret Stamp; classic-c	80.00	240.00	560.00
14,15	75.00	225.00	525.00
16-Red Skull unmasks Cap	80.00	240.00	560.00
17-The Fighting Fool only app.	59.00	177.00	410.00
18,19-Human Torch begins No. 19; not in No. 20	55.00	165.00	385.00
20-Sub-Mariner app.	55.00	165.00	385.00
21-25: 25-Cap drinks liquid opium	50.00	150.00	350.00
26-30: 27-Last Secret Stamp. 30-Last 68 pg. issue	45.00	135.00	315.00
31-36,38-40: 31-60 pg. issues begin	39.00	117.00	272.00
37-Red Skull app.	41.00	122.00	285.00
41-45,47: 41-Last Jap War-c. 47-Last German War-c	35.00	105.00	245.00
46-German Holocaust-c	35.00	105.00	245.00
48-58,60	32.00	96.00	225.00
59-Origin retold	45.00	135.00	310.00
61-Red Skull c/story	40.00	120.00	280.00
62,64,65: 65-''Hey Look'' by Kurtzman	33.00	100.00	230.00
63-Intro/origin Asbestos Lady	35.00	105.00	245.00
66-Bucky is shot; Golden Girl teams up with Captain America & learns his i.d; origin Golden Girl	40.00	120.00	280.00
67-Captain America/Golden Girl team-up; Mxyztplk swipe; last Toro in Human Torch	33.00	100.00	230.00
68,70-Sub-Mariner/Namora, and Captain America/Golden Girl team-up in each. 70-Science fiction c/story	33.00	100.00	230.00
69-Human Torch/Sun Girl team-up	33.00	100.00	230.00
71-Anti Wertham editorial; The Witness, Bucky app.	26.00	78.00	182.00
72,73	26.00	78.00	182.00
74-(Scarce)(1949)-Titled ''C.A.'s Weird Tales;'' Red Skull app.	63.00	190.00	440.00
75(2/50)-Titled ''C.A.'s Weird Tales;'' no C.A. app.; horror cover/stories	40.00	120.00	280.00
76-78(1954); Human Torch/Toro story	24.00	72.00	165.00
132-Pg. Issue (B&W-1942)(Canadian)	100.00	300.00	700.00
Shoestore Giveaway No. 77	14.00	42.00	100.00

NOTE: *Bondage c-3, 7, 15, 16, 34.* ***Crandall*** *a-2i, 3i.* ***Schomburg*** *c-26-29, 31, 33, 37-39, 41-43, 45-54, 58.* ***Shores*** *c-20-25, 30, 32, 34-36, 40, 59, 61-63.* ***S&K*** *c-1, 2, 5-7, 9, 10.*

CAPTAIN AMERICA SPECIAL EDITION
Feb, 1984 - No. 2, Mar, 1984 ($2.00; Baxter paper)
Marvel Comics Group

	Good	Fine	Mint
1,2-Steranko-r, c/a	.35	1.00	2.00

CAPTAIN AND THE KIDS, THE (See Famous Comics Cartoon Books)

CAPTAIN AND THE KIDS, THE (See Comics on Parade and Okay Comics)
1938 - 4-Color No. 881, Feb, 1958
United Features Syndicate/Dell Publ. Co.

	Good	Fine	Mint
Single Series 1('38)	25.00	75.00	175.00
Single Series 1(Reprint)(12/39-''Reprint'' on cover)	15.00	45.00	105.00
1(Summer, 1947-UFS)	4.35	13.00	30.00
2	2.15	6.50	15.00
3-10	1.65	5.00	11.50
11-20	1.35	4.00	9.00
21-32(1955)	1.00	3.00	7.00
50th Anniversary issue('48)-Contains a 2 page history of the strip, including an account of the famous Supreme Court decision allowing both Pulitzer & Hearst to run the same strip under different names.	2.35	7.00	16.00
Special Summer issue, Fall issue (1948)	1.85	5.50	13.00
4-Color 881 (Dell)	1.30	4.00	9.00

CAPTAIN ATOM
1950 - 1951 (5x7¼'') (5 cents, 52 pgs.)
Nationwide Publishers

	Good	Fine	Mint
1-Sci/fic	2.00	6.00	14.00
2-7	1.50	4.50	10.00

CAPTAIN ATOM (Formerly Strange Suspense Stories No. 77)
No. 78, Dec, 1965 - No. 89, Dec, 1967 (Also see Space Advs.)
Charlton Comics

	Good	Fine	Mint
78-Origin retold	1.35	4.00	8.00
79-81	1.20	3.50	7.00
82-Intro. Nightshade	1.20	3.50	7.00
83-86: Ted Kord Blue Beetle in all	1.00	3.00	6.00
87-89-Nightshade by Aparo in all	1.00	3.00	6.00
83-85(Modern Comics-1977)-reprints		.15	.30

NOTE: ***Aparo*** *a-87-89.* ***Ditko*** *c/a(p) 78-87. No. 90 only published in fanzine 'The Charlton Bullseye' No. 1, 2.*

CAPTAIN ATOM
March, 1987 - Present
DC Comics

	Good	Fine	Mint
1		.50	1.00

Captain America Comics #20, © MCG

Captain & the Kids #18, © UFS

Captain Atom #3, © Nationwide

Captain Battle #2, © LEV

Captain Confederacy #1, © SteelDragon

Captain Electron #1, © Brick

CAPTAIN BATTLE (Boy No. 3 on) (See Silver Streak)
Summer, 1941 - No. 2, Fall, 1941
New Friday Publ./Comic House

Good Fine Mint

1-Origin Blackout by Rico; Captain Battle begins 35.00 105.00 245.00
2 22.00 66.00 154.00

CAPTAIN BATTLE (2nd Series)
Wint, 1942-43 - No. 5, Sum, 1943 (No.3: 52pgs., nd)(No.5: 68pgs.)
Magazine Press/Picture Scoop No. 5

3-Origin Silver Streak retold; Simon-a(r) 17.00 51.00 120.00
4 12.00 36.00 84.00
5-Origin Blackout retold 12.00 36.00 84.00

CAPTAIN BATTLE, JR.
Fall, 1943 - No. 2, Winter, 1943-44
Comic House (Lev Gleason)

1-The Claw vs. The Ghost 28.00 84.00 195.00
2-Wolverton's Scoop Scuttle; Don Rico-c/a; The Green Claw story 26.00 78.00 182.00

CAPTAIN BRITAIN (Also see Marvel Team-Up No. 65,66)
Oct. 13, 1976 - No. 39, July 6, 1977 (Weekly)
Marvel Comics International

1-Origin; with Capt. Britain's face mask inside .85 2.50 5.00
2-Origin, conclusion; Britain's Boomerang inside .60 1.80 3.60
3-Vs. Bank Robbers .35 1.00 2.00
4-7-Vs. Hurricane .35 1.00 2.00
8-Vs. Bank Robbers .35 1.00 2.00
9-13-Vs. Dr. Synne .30 .90 1.80
14,15-Vs. Mastermind .30 .90 1.80
16-20-With Capt. America; 17 misprinted & color section reprinted in No. 18 .30 .90 1.80
21-23,25,26-With Capt. America .30 .90 1.80
24-With C.B.'s Jet Plane inside .60 1.80 3.60
27-Origin retold .30 .90 1.80
28-32-Vs. Lord Hawk .25 .75 1.50
33-35-More on origin .30 .90 1.80
36-Star Sceptre .25 .75 1.50
37-39-Vs. Highwayman & Munipulator .25 .75 1.50
Annual(1978,Hardback,64pgs.)-Reprints No. 1-7 with pin-ups of Marvel characters 1.35 4.00 8.00
Summer Special (1980, 52pp)-Reprints .35 1.00 2.00

NOTE: *No. 1,2, & 24 are rarer in mint due to inserts. Distributed in Great Britain only. Nick Fury-r by Steranko in 1-20, 24-31, 35-37. Fantastic Four-r by J. Buscema in all. New Buscema-a in 24-30. Story from No. 39 continues in Super Spider-Man (British weekly) No. 231-247. Following cancellation of his series, new Captain Britain stories appeared in ''Super Spider-Man'' (British weekly) No. 231-247. Captain Britain stories which appear in Super-Spider-Man No. 248-253 are reprints of Marvel Team-Up No. 65&66. Capt. Britain strips also appeared in Hulk Comic (weekly) 1, 3-30, 42-55, 57-60, in Marvel Superheroes (monthly) 377-388, in Daredevils (monthly) 1-11, Mighty World of Marvel (monthly) 7-16 & Captain Britain (monthly) 1-present.*

CAPTAIN CANUCK
7/75 - No. 4, 7/77; No. 4, 7-8/79 - No. 14, 3-4/81
Comely Comix (Canada) (All distr. in U. S.)

1-1st app. Bluefox .40 1.25 2.50
2-1st app. Dr. Walker, Redcoat & Kebec .30 .90 1.80
3(5-7/76)-1st app. Heather .30 .90 1.80
4(1st printing-2/77)-10x14½''; (5.00); B&W; 300 copies serially numbered and signed with one certificate of authenticity. 5.00 15.00 30.00
4(2nd printing-7/77)-11x17'', B&W; only 15 copies printed; signed by creator Richard Comely, serially numbered and two certificates of authenticity inserted; orange cardboard covers (Very Rare) 8.00 25.00 50.00

Good Fine Mint

4(7-8/79)-1st app. Tom Evans & Mr. Gold; origin The Catman .40 .80
5-Origin Capt. Canuck's powers; 1st app. Earth Patrol & Chaos Corps .40 .80
6-14: 8-Jonn 'The Final Chapter'. 9-1st World Beyond. 11-1st 'Chariots of Fire' story. .40 .80
Summer Special 1(7-9/80, 95¢, 64pgs.) .50 1.00

NOTE: *30,000 copies of No. 2 were destroyed in Winnipeg.*

CAPTAIN CARROT AND HIS AMAZING ZOO CREW
March, 1982 - No. 20, Nov, 1983 (Also see New Teen Titans)
DC Comics

1-Superman app. .50 1.00
2-8: 3-Re-intro Dodo & The Frog .35 .70
9-Re-intro Three Mouseketeers, the Terrific Whatzit .35 .70
10,11-Pig Iron reverts back to Peter Porkchops .30 .70
12-20: 20-The Changeling app. .35 .70

CAPTAIN CARVEL AND HIS CARVEL CRUSADERS
(See Carvel Comics)

CAPTAIN CONFEDERACY
1986 - Present ($1.50, B&W)
SteelDragon Press

1 2.85 5.00 10.00
2 .70 2.00 4.00
3,4 .25 .75 1.50

CAPTAIN COURAGEOUS COMICS (Banner No. 3-5)
March, 1942
Periodical House (Ace Magazines)

6-Origin & 1st app. The Sword; Lone Warrior, Capt. Courageous app. 25.00 75.00 175.00

CAPT'N CRUNCH COMICS (See Cap'n. . .)

CAPTAIN DAVY JONES (See 4-Color No. 598)

CAPTAIN EASY
1939 - No. 17, Sept, 1949; April, 1956
Hawley/Dell Publ./Standard(Visual Editions)/Argo

Hawley(1939)-Contains reprints from The Funnies & 1938 Sunday strips by Roy Crane 22.00 66.00 154.00
4-Color 24 (1943) 15.00 45.00 105.00
4-Color 111(6/46) 6.00 18.00 42.00
10(Standard-10/47) 3.00 9.00 21.00
11-17: All contain 1930's & '40's strip-r 2.15 6.50 15.00
Argo 1(4/56)-(r) 1.75 5.25 12.00

NOTE: ***Schomburg** c-13,16.*

CAPTAIN EASY & WASH TUBBS (See Famous Comics Cartoon Books)

CAPTAIN ELECTRON
Aug, 1986 ($2.25, color)
Brick Computer Science Institute

1-Disbrow-a .40 1.15 2.30

CAPTAIN FEARLESS COMICS (Also see Holyoke One-Shot No. 6)
August, 1941 - No. 2, Sept, 1941
Helnit Publishing Co. (Holyoke Publishing Co.)

1-Origin Mr. Miracle, Alias X, Captain Fearless, Citizen Smith Son of the Unknown Soldier; Miss Victory begins 22.00 66.00 154.00
2-Grit Grady, Captain Stone app. 12.00 36.00 84.00

CAPTAIN FLASH
Nov, 1954 - No. 4, July, 1955

CAPTAIN FLASH (continued)
Sterling Comics

	Good	Fine	Mint
1-Origin; Sekowsky-a; Tomboy (female super hero) begins Last pre-code ish	8.00	24.00	56.00
2-4	5.00	15.00	35.00

CAPTAIN FLEET
Fall, 1952
Ziff-Davis Publishing Co.

1	4.50	13.50	31.00

CAPTAIN FLIGHT COMICS
Mar, 1944 - No. 11, Feb-Mar, 1947
Four Star Publications

nn	7.00	21.00	50.00
2	4.35	13.00	30.00
3,4: 4-Rock Raymond begins, ends No. 7	3.50	10.50	24.50
5-Bondage, torture-c; Red Rocket begins; the Grenade app.	5.00	15.00	35.00
6,7	4.00	12.00	28.00
8-Yankee Girl, Black Cobra begin; intro. Cobra Kid	7.00	21.00	50.00
9-Torpedoman app.; last Yankee Girl; Kinstler-a	7.00	21.00	50.00
10-Deep Sea Dawson, Zoom of the Jungle, Rock Raymond, Red Rocket, & Black Cobra app; L. B. Cole bondage-c	7.00	21.00	50.00
11-Torpedoman, Blue Flame app.; last Black Cobra, Red Rocket; L. B. Cole-c	7.00	21.00	50.00

NOTE: ***L. B. Cole*** *c-7-11.*

CAPTAIN FORTUNE PRESENTS
1955 - 1959 (16 pages; 3¼x6-7/8'') (Giveaway)
Vital Publications

''Davy Crockett in Episodes of the Creek War,'' ''Davy Crockett at the Alamo,'' ''In Sherwood Forest Tells Strange Tales of Robin Hood'' ('57), ''Meets Bolivar the Liberator''('59), ''Tells How Buffalo Bill Fights the Dog Soldiers''('57), ''Young Davy Crockett''	.85	2.50	5.00

CAPTAIN GALLANT (. . . of the Foreign Legion) (TV)
(Texas Rangers in Action No. 5 on?)
1955 - No. 4, Sept, 1956
Charlton Comics

1-Buster Crabbe	4.00	12.00	28.00
2-4	2.15	6.50	15.00
Heinz Foods Premium(1955; regular size)-U.S. Pictorial; contains Buster Crabbe photos; Don Heck-a	1.50	4.50	10.00
Non-Heinz version (same as above except pictures of show replaces ads)	1.50	4.50	10.00

CAPTAIN HERO (See Jughead as. . .)

CAPTAIN HERO COMICS DIGEST MAGAZINE
Sept, 1981
Archie Publications

1-Reprints of Jughead as Super-Guy		.30	.60

CAPTAIN HOBBY COMICS
Feb, 1948 (Canadian)
Export Publication Ent. Ltd. (Dist. in U.S. by Kable News Co.)

1	1.75	5.25	12.00

CAPTAIN HOOK & PETER PAN (See 4-Color No. 446 and Peter Pan)

CAPTAIN JET (Fantastic Fears No. 7 on)
May, 1952 - No. 5, Jan, 1953
Four Star Publ./Farrell/Comic Media

	Good	Fine	Mint
1-Bakerish-a	4.50	13.50	31.00
2	3.00	9.00	21.00
3-5,6(?)	2.65	8.00	18.00

CAPTAIN KANGAROO (See 4-Color No. 721,780,872)

CAPTAIN KIDD (Formerly Dagar)
No. 24, June, 1949 - No. 25, Aug?, 1949
Fox Feature Syndicate

24,25	5.00	15.00	35.00

CAPTAIN MARVEL (See All Hero, All-New Coll. Ed., America's Greatest, Fawcett Min., Gift, Limited Coll. Ed., Marvel Family, Master No. 21, Mighty Midget Comics, Shazam, Special Edition Comics, Whiz, Wisco, and X-Mas)

CAPTAIN MARVEL (. . . Presents the Terrible 5 No. 5)
April, 1966 - No. 4, Nov, 1966 (25 cents)
M. F. Enterprises

nn-(No.1 on page 5)-Origin	.35	1.00	2.00
2,4		.60	1.20
3-(No.3 on page 4)-Fights the Bat		.60	1.20

CAPTAIN MARVEL (See Marvel Spotlight & Marvel Super-Heroes 12)
May, 1968 - No. 19, Dec, 1969; No. 20, June, 1970 - No. 21, Aug, 1970; No. 22, Sept, 1972 - No. 62, May, 1979
Marvel Comics Group

1	1.35	4.00	8.00
2-5	.50	1.50	3.00
6-10	.35	1.00	2.00
11-Smith/Trimpe-c; Death of Una	.50	1.50	3.00
12-24: 17-New costume		.60	1.20
25-Starlin c/a	1.35	4.00	8.00
26-Starlin c/a	1.00	3.00	6.00
27-34-Starlin c/a. 29-C.M. gains more powers	.75	2.25	4.50
35,37-40: 39-Origin Watcher		.50	1.00
36-Starlin-a, 3pgs.	.25	.70	1.40
41,43-Wrightson part inks; cover No. 43(inks)		.50	1.00
42,44-48,50		.40	.80
49-Starlin in part		.50	1.00
51-62: 53-Inhumans app.		.30	.60
Giant-Size 1 (12/75)	.40	1.20	2.40

NOTE: ***Alcala*** *a-35.* ***Austin*** *a-46i, 49-53i; c-52i.* ***Buscema*** *a-18p-21p.* ***Colan*** *a(p)-1-4; c(p)-1-4, 8, 9.* ***Heck*** *a-5p-10p, 16p.* ***Gil Kane*** *a-17p-21p, Gnt-Size 1p; c-17p-24p, 37p, 53.* ***McWilliams*** *a-40.*

CAPTAIN MARVEL ADVENTURES (See Special Edition Comics for pre-No. 1)
1941 - No. 150, Nov, 1953
Fawcett Publications

nn(No.1)-Captain Marvel & Sivana by Jack Kirby. The cover was printed on unstable paper stock and is rarely found in Fine or Mint condition; blank inside-c	800.00	2500.00	5700.00
(Prices vary widely on this book)			
2-(Advertised as No. 3, which was counting Special Edition Comics as the real No. 1); Tuska-a	138.00	415.00	965.00
3-Metallic silver-c	65.00	195.00	455.00
4-Three Lt. Marvels app.	45.00	135.00	315.00
5	37.00	110.00	260.00
6-10	30.00	90.00	210.00
11-15: 13-Two-pg. Capt. Marvel pin-up. 15-Comic cards on back cover begin, end No. 26	23.00	70.00	160.00
16,17: 17-Painted-c	21.00	63.00	145.00
18-Origin & 1st app. Mary Marvel & Marvel Family; painted-c (12/11/42)	32.00	95.00	225.00
19-Mary Marvel x-over; Christmas-c	19.00	57.00	132.00

20,21-Attached to the cover, each has a miniature comic just like the Mighty Midget Comics No. 11, except that each has a full color promo ad on the back cover. Most copies were circulated without the miniature comic. These issues with miniatures attached are

Captain Flight #1, © Four Star

Captain Kidd #25, © FOX

Captain Marvel Advs. #2, © FAW

Captain Marvel Advs. #80, © FAW

Captain Marvel Jr. #69, © FAW

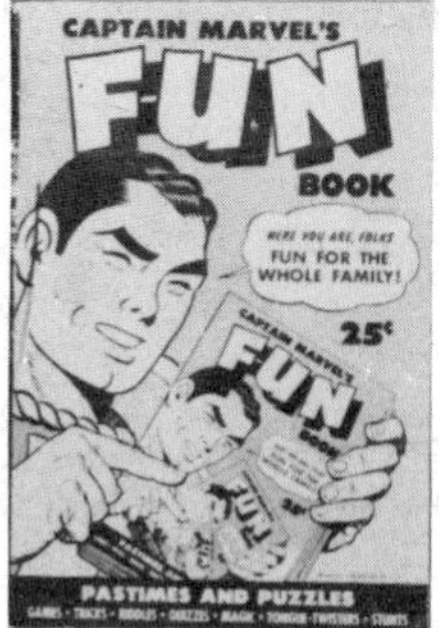

Captain Marvel's Fun Book nn, © FAW

CAPTAIN MARVEL ADVS. (continued)
very rare, and should not be mistaken for copies with the similar Mighty Midget glued in its place. The Mighty Midgets had blank back covers except for a small victory stamp seal. Only the Captain Marvel and Captain Marvel Jr. No. 11 miniatures have been positively documented as having been affixed to these covers. Each miniature was only partially glued by its back cover to the Captain Marvel comic making it easy to see if it's the genuine miniature rather than a Mighty Midget.

	Good	Fine	Mint
with comic attached....	45.00	135.00	315.00
20,21-Without miniature	17.00	51.00	120.00
22-Mr. Mind serial begins	32.00	95.00	225.00
23-25	17.00	50.00	115.00
26-30: 26-Flag-c	14.50	43.50	100.00
31-35: 35-Origin Radar	13.00	40.00	90.00
36-40: 37-Mary Marvel x-over	11.50	34.50	80.00
41-46: 42-Christmas-c. 43-Captain Marvel 1st meets Uncle Marvel; Mary Batson cameo. 46-Mr. Mind serial ends	10.00	30.00	70.00
47-50	8.65	26.00	60.00
51-53,55-60: 52-Origin & 1st app. Sivana Jr.; Capt. Marvel Jr. x-over	6.00	18.00	42.00
54-Special oversize 68-pg. issue	8.00	24.00	56.00
61-The Cult of the Curse serial begins	9.00	27.00	63.00
62-66-Serial ends; Mary Marvel x-over in No. 65	6.00	18.00	42.00
67-77,79: 69-Billy Batson's Christmas; Uncle Marvel, Mary Marvel, Capt. Marvel Jr. x-over. 71-Three Lt. Marvels app. No. 79-Origin Mr. Tawny	5.35	16.00	38.00
78-Origin Mr. Atom	6.00	18.00	42.00
80-Origin Capt. Marvel retold	9.50	28.50	65.00
81-84,86-90: 81,90-Mr. Atom app. 82-Infinity-c. 86-Mr. Tawny app.	6.00	18.00	42.00
85-Freedom Train issue	7.25	21.50	50.00
91-99: 96-Mr. Tawny app.	4.00	12.00	28.00
100-Origin retold	9.00	27.00	63.00
101-120: 116-Flying Saucer ish (1/51)	3.85	11.50	27.00
121-Origin retold	5.35	16.00	38.00
122-141,143-149: 138-Flying Saucer issue (11/52). 141-Pre-code horror story "The Hideous Head-Hunter"	3.50	10.50	24.00
142-Used in **POP**, pgs. 92,96	4.35	13.00	30.00
150-(Low distribution)	9.50	28.50	66.00
Bond Bread Giveaways-(24 pgs.; pocket size-7¼x3½"; paper cover): "...& the Stolen City," "The Boy Who Never Heard of C.M.," "Meets the Weatherman"-(1950)(reprint) each....	13.00	40.00	80.00
...Well Known Comics (1944; 12 pgs.; 8½x10½")-printed in red & in blue; soft-c; glued binding)-Bestmaid/Samuel Lowe Co. giveaway	16.00	48.00	96.00

CAPTAIN MARVEL ADVENTURES (Also see Whiz)
1945 (6x8") (Full color, paper cover)
Fawcett Publications (Wheaties Giveaway)

	Good	Fine	Mint
"Captain Marvel & the Threads of Life" plus 2 other stories (32pgs.)	15.00	45.00	90.00

NOTE: *All copies were taped at each corner to a box of Wheaties and are never found in Fine or Mint condition.*

CAPTAIN MARVEL AND THE GOOD HUMOR MAN
1950
Fawcett Publications

	Good	Fine	Mint
nn	13.00	40.00	90.00

CAPTAIN MARVEL AND THE LTS. OF SAFETY
1950 - 1951 (3 issues - no No.'s)
Fawcett Publications

	Good	Fine	Mint
"Danger Flies a Kite"('50)," "Danger Takes to Climbing"('50), "Danger Smashes Street Lights"('51)	9.20	27.50	65.00

CAPTAIN MARVEL COMIC STORY PAINT BOOK (See Comic Story....)

CAPTAIN MARVEL, JR. (See Fawcett Miniatures, Marvel Family, Master Comics, Mighty Midget Comics, and Shazam)

CAPTAIN MARVEL, JR.
Nov, 1942 - No. 119, June, 1953 (nn 34)
Fawcett Publications

	Good	Fine	Mint
1-Origin Capt. Marvel Jr. retold (Whiz No. 25); Capt. Nazi app.	90.00	270.00	630.00
2-Vs. Capt. Nazi; origin Capt. Nippon	47.00	140.00	330.00
3,4	36.00	108.00	250.00
5-Vs. Capt. Nazi	29.00	87.00	200.00
6-10: 8-Vs. Capt. Nazi. 9-Flag-c	21.00	63.00	146.00
11,12,15-Capt. Nazi app.	18.00	54.00	126.00
13,14,16-20: 16-Capt. Marvel & Sivana x-over. 19-Capt. Nazi & Capt. Nippon app.	12.00	36.00	84.00
21-30: 25-Flag-c	8.00	24.00	56.00
31-33,36-40: 37-Infinity-c	5.00	15.00	35.00
35-No. 34 on inside; the cover shows origin of Sivana Jr. which is not on inside. Evidently the cover to No. 35 was printed out of sequence and bound with contents to No.34	5.00	15.00	35.00
41-50	3.50	10.50	24.00
51-70	3.50	10.50	24.00
71-99,101-103,105-114,116-119	3.00	9.00	21.00
100	3.50	10.50	24.00
104-Used in **POP**, pg. 89	3.50	10.50	24.00
115-Injury to eye-c; Eyeball story w/ injury-to-eye panels	4.00	12.00	28.00
...Well Known Comics (1944; 12 pgs.; 8½x10½")(Printed in blue; paper-c, glued binding)-Bestmaid/Samuel Lowe Co. giveaway	12.00	36.00	72.00

NOTE: ***Mac Raboy** c-1-10,12-14,16,19,25,27,28,30-33,57 among others.*

CAPTAIN MARVEL PRESENTS THE TERRIBLE FIVE
Aug, 1966; V2No.5, Sept, 1967 (no No.2-4) (25 cents)
M. F. Enterprises

	Good	Fine	Mint
1	.35	1.00	1.50
V2No.5-(Formerly Capt. Marvel)	.30	.80	1.20

CAPTAIN MARVEL'S FUN BOOK
1944 (½" thick) (cardboard covers)
Samuel Lowe Co.

	Good	Fine	Mint
Puzzles, games, magic, etc.; infinity-c	6.50	19.50	45.00

CAPTAIN MARVEL SPECIAL EDITION (See Special Edition)

CAPTAIN MARVEL STORY BOOK
Summer, 1946 - No. 4, Summer?, 1948
Fawcett Publications

	Good	Fine	Mint
1-½ text	22.00	66.00	154.00
2-4	15.00	45.00	105.00

CAPTAIN MARVEL THRILL BOOK (Large-Size)
1941 (Black & White; color cover)
Fawcett Publications

	Good	Fine	Mint
1-Reprints from Whiz No. 8,10, & Special Edition No. 1 (Rare)	142.00	425.00	1000.00

NOTE: *Rarely found in Fine or Mint condition.*

CAPTAIN MIDNIGHT (Radio, films, TV) (See The Funnies & Popular Comics) (Becomes Sweethearts No. 68 on)
Sept, 1942 - No. 67, Fall, 1948
Fawcett Publications

	Good	Fine	Mint
1-Origin Captain Midnight; Captain Marvel cameo on cover	65.00	195.00	455.00
2	32.00	96.00	224.00

CAPTAIN MIDNIGHT (continued)

	Good	Fine	Mint
3-5	23.00	70.00	160.00
6-10: 9-Raboy-c. 10-Flag-c	16.00	48.00	110.00
11-20: 11,17-Raboy-c	9.50	28.50	66.00
21-30	6.75	20.00	47.00
31-40	5.00	15.00	35.00
41-59,61-67	3.75	11.00	26.00
60-Flying Saucer ish (2/48)-3rd of this theme; see Shadow Comics V7/10	6.50	19.50	45.00

(See Super Book No. 3)

CAPTAIN NICE (TV)
Nov, 1967 (One Shot)
Gold Key

1(10211-711)-Photo-c	1.70	5.00	10.00

CAPTAIN PARAGON (Also see Bill Black's Fun Comics)
Dec, 1983 - No. 4, 1985?
Americomics

1,2: 1-Ms. Victory begins	.25	.75	1.50
3 (color)	.30	.90	1.80
4 (B&W)	.35	1.00	2.00

CAPTAIN PARAGON AND THE SENTINELS OF JUSTICE
April, 1985 - Present ($1.75; color)
AC Comics

1-Capt. Paragon, Commando D., Nightveil, Scarlet Scorpion, Stardust & Atoman begin	.30	.90	1.75
2-5	.30	.90	1.75

CAPTAIN PUREHEART (See Archie as. . .)

CAPTAIN ROCKET
November, 1951
P. L. Publ. (Canada)

1	12.00	36.00	84.00

CAPTAIN SAVAGE AND HIS LEATHERNECK RAIDERS
Jan, 1968 - No. 19, Mar, 1970 (See Sgt. Fury No. 10)
Marvel Comics Group

1-Sgt. Fury & Howlers cameo		.40	.80
2-19: 2-Origin Hydra		.25	.50

CAPTAIN SCIENCE (Fantastic No. 8 on)
Nov, 1950 - No. 7, Dec, 1951
Youthful Magazines

1-Wood-a; origin	35.00	105.00	245.00
2	13.50	40.50	95.00
3,6,7; 3-Bondage c-swipe/Wings 94. 6,7-Bondage-c	11.50	34.50	80.00
4,5-Wood/Orlando-c/a(2) each	31.00	93.00	218.00

CAPTAIN SILVER'S LOG OF SEA HOUND (See Sea Hound)

CAPTAIN SINDBAD (Movie Adaptation) (See Movie Comics)

CAPTAIN STEVE SAVAGE (. . . & His Jet Fighters, No. 2-13)
1950 - 1952? No. 5, 9-10/54 - No. 13, 5-6/56
Avon Periodicals

	Good	Fine	Mint
nn(1st series)-Wood art, 22 pgs. (titled ". . . Over Korea")	16.00	48.00	110.00
1(4/51)-Reprints nn ish (Canadian)	8.00	24.00	56.00
2-Kamen-a	4.00	12.00	28.00
3-11	2.35	7.00	16.50
12-Wood-a, 6pp	4.50	13.50	31.50
13-Check, Lawrence-a	3.35	10.00	23.00
5(9-10/54-2nd series)(Formerly Sensational Police Cases)	3.00	9.00	21.00
6-Reprints nn ish; Wood-a	5.00	15.00	35.00
7-13	1.30	4.00	9.00

NOTE: ***Kinstler** c-2-5, 7-9, 11. **Lawrence** a-8. **Ravielli** a-5, 9.*

CAPTAIN STONE (See Holyoke One-Shot No. 10)

CAPT. STORM
May-June, 1964 - No. 18, Mar-Apr, 1967
National Periodical Publications

1-Origin		.50	1.00
2-18: 12-Kubert-c		.30	.60

CAPTAIN 3-D
December, 1953
Harvey Publications

1-Kirby/Ditko-a	4.00	12.00	24.00

NOTE: *Many copies surfaced in 1979, causing a set-back in price.*

CAPTAIN TOOTSIE & THE SECRET LEGION (Advs. of. .)
Oct, 1950 - No. 2, 1950
Toby Press

1-Not Beck-a	8.00	24.00	56.00
2-Not Beck-a	5.35	16.00	38.00

CAPTAIN VENTURE & THE LAND BENEATH THE SEA
Oct, 1968 - No. 2, Oct, 1969
Gold Key (See Space Family Robinson)

1,2: 1-r/Space Family Robinson serial; Spiegle-a in both	1.70	5.00	10.00

CAPTAIN VICTORY
Jul, 1981 - No. 13, Jan, 1984 ($1.00) (36-48 pgs.)
Pacific Comics (Sold only through comic shops)

1-1st app. Mr. Mind	.25	.75	1.50
2-13: 3-Adams-a		.50	1.00
Special Issue No. 1(Baxter paper, 10/83)-Kirby c/a(p)		.50	1.00

NOTE: ***Conrad** a-10. **Ditko** a-6. **Kirby** a-1-13p; c-1-13.*

CAPTAIN VIDEO (TV)
Feb, 1951 - No. 6, Dec, 1951 (No. 1,5,6-36pgs.; 2-4, 52pgs.)
Fawcett Publications

1-George Evans-a(2)	24.00	72.00	168.00
2-Used in **SOTI**, pg. 382	18.00	54.00	125.00
3-6-All Evans-a	16.00	48.00	110.00

NOTE: *Minor **Williamson** assist on most issues. Photo c-1, 5, 6; painted c-2-4.*

CAPTAIN WILLIE SCHULTZ
No. 76, Oct, 1985 - No. 77, Jan, 1986
Charlton Comics

76,77		.40	.75

CAPTAIN WIZARD COMICS (Also see Meteor)
1946
Rural Home

1-Capt. Wizard dons new costume; Impossible Man, Race Wilkins app.	5.50	16.50	38.00

CARDINAL MINDSZENTY (The Truth Behind the Trial of. . .)
1949 (24 pages; paper cover, in color)
Catechetical Guild Education Society

nn-Anti-communism	8.35	25.00	50.00
Press Proof-(Very Rare)-(Full color, 7½x11¾", untrimmed) Only two known copies			150.00

Captain Midnight #9, © FAW

Captain Steve Savage #1 (Canadian), © AVON

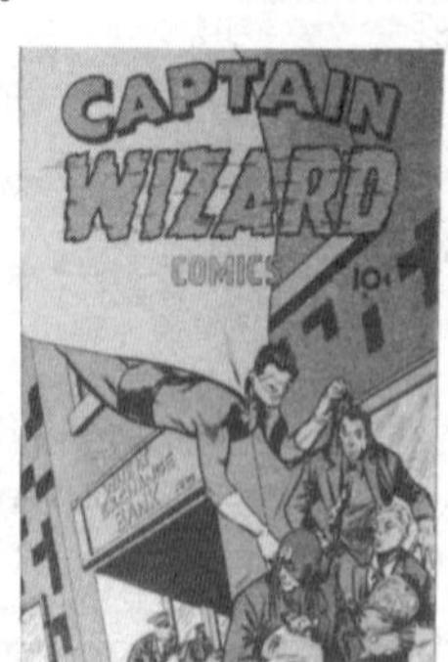

Captain Wizard Comics #1, © RH

Car 54, Where Are You? #2 ('62), © Eupolis Prod.

Cases of Sherlock Holmes #1, © Renegade

Casey—Crime Photographer #1, © MCG

CARDINAL MINDSZENTY (continued) — Good / Fine / Mint

Preview Copy (B&W, stapled), 18 pgs.; contains first 13 pgs. of Cardinal Mindszenty and was sent out as an advance promotion. Only one known copy — $150.00 - $250.00

NOTE: *Regular edition also printed in French.*

CARE BEARS (TV, Movie)
Nov, 1985 - Present
Star Comics

1-9: Post-a — .35 .70

CAREER GIRL ROMANCES (Formerly Three Nurses)
June, 1964 - No. 78, Dec, 1973
Charlton Comics

V4No.24-31,33-78 — .40 .80
32-Presley, Hermans Hermits, Johnny Rivers line drawn-c — .85 2.50 6.00

CAR 54, WHERE ARE YOU? (TV)
Mar-May, 1962 - No. 7, Sept-Nov, 1963; 1964 - 1965 (Photo-c)
Dell Publishing Co.

4-Color 1257(3-5/62) — 1.75 5.25 12.00
2(6-8/62)-7 — 1.00 3.00 7.00
2,3(10-12/64), 4(1-3/65)-Reprints No. 2,3,&4 of 1st series — .75 2.25 5.00

CARNATION MALTED MILK GIVEAWAYS (See Wisco)

CARNIVAL COMICS
1945
Harry 'A' Chesler/Pershing Square Publ. Co.

1 — 3.00 9.00 21.00

CARNIVAL OF COMICS
1954 (Giveaway)
Fleet-Air Shoes

nn-Contains a comic bound with new cover; several combinations possible; Charlton's Eh! known — 1.00 3.00 7.00

CAROLINE KENNEDY
1961 (One Shot)
Charlton Comics

3.35 10.00 23.00

CAROUSEL COMICS
V1No.8, April, 1948
F. E. Howard, Toronto

V1No.8 — 1.30 4.00 9.00

CARTOON KIDS
1957 (no month)
Atlas Comics (CPS)

1-Maneely c/a — 1.15 3.50 8.00

CARVEL COMICS (Amazing Advs. of Capt. Carvel)
1975 (25 cents; No.3-5: 35 cents) (No.4,5: 3¼x5'')
Carvel Corp. (Ice Cream)

1-3 — .15 .30
4,5(1976)-Baseball theme — .85 2.50 5.00

CASE OF THE SHOPLIFTER'S SHOE (Perry Mason) (See Feature Book No. 50 McKay)

CASE OF THE WASTED WATER, THE
1972? (Giveaway)
Rheem Water Heating

Neal Adams-a — 2.00 6.00 14.00

CASE OF THE WINKING BUDDHA, THE
1950 (132 pgs.; 25 cents; B&W; 5½x7-5½x8'')
St. John Publ. Co. — Good / Fine / Mint

Charles Raab-a; reprinted in Authentic Police Cases No. 25 — 10.00 30.00 70.00

CASES OF SHERLOCK HOLMES
May, 1986 - Present (B&W)
Renegade Press

1-4 — .35 1.10 2.20

CASEY-CRIME PHOTOGRAPHER (Two-Gun Western No. 5 on)
Aug, 1949 - No. 4, Feb, 1950 (Radio)
Marvel Comics (BFP)

1: Photo-c — 4.50 13.50 31.00
2-4: Photo-c — 3.00 9.00 21.00

CASEY JONES (See 4-Color No. 915)

CASPER AND NIGHTMARE (See Harvey Hits No. 37, 45, 52, 56, 59, 62, 65, 68, 71, 75)

CASPER AND NIGHTMARE (Nightmare & Casper No. 1-5) (25 cents)
No. 6, 11/64 - No. 44, 10/73; No. 45, 6/74 - No. 46, 8/74
Harvey Publications

6 — 2.00 6.00 12.00
7-10 — 1.00 3.00 6.00
11-20 — .50 1.50 3.00
21-46 — .35 1.00 2.00

CASPER AND SPOOKY (See Harvey Hits No. 20)
Oct, 1972 - No. 7, Oct, 1973
Harvey Publications

1 — .85 2.50 5.00
2-7 — .35 1.00 2.00

CASPER AND THE GHOSTLY TRIO
Nov, 1972 - No. 7, Nov, 1973
Harvey Publications

1 — .85 2.50 5.00
2-7 — .35 1.00 2.00

CASPER AND WENDY
Sept, 1972 - No. 8, Nov, 1973
Harvey Publications

1 — .85 2.50 5.00
2-8 — .35 1.00 2.00

CASPER CAT
1958; 1963
I. W. Enterprises/Super

1,7-Reprint, Super No. 14('63) — .35 1.00 2.00

CASPER DIGEST
Oct, 1986 - Present ($1.25, digest-size)
Harvey Publications

1-4 — .50 1.00

CASPER DIGEST STORIES
2/80 - No. 4, 11/80 (95 cents; 132 pgs.; digest size)
Harvey Publications

1 — .50 1.50 3.00
2-4 — .35 1.00 2.00

CASPER DIGEST WINNERS
April, 1980 - No. 3, Sept, 1980 (95 cents; 132 pgs.; digest size)
Harvey Publications

1 — .35 1.00 2.00
2,3 — .25 .75 1.50

CASPER HALLOWEEN TRICK OR TREAT
January, 1976

CASPER HALLOWEEN. . . (continued)
Harvey Publications

	Good	Fine	Mint
1	.35	1.00	2.00

CASPER IN SPACE (Formerly Casper Spaceship)
No. 6, June, 1973 - No. 8, Oct, 1973
Harvey Publications

	Good	Fine	Mint
6-8	.35	1.00	2.00

CASPER'S GHOSTLAND
Winter, 1958-59 - No. 97, 12/77; No. 98, 12/79 (25 cents)
Harvey Publications

	Good	Fine	Mint
1	6.00	18.00	40.00
2	3.35	10.00	23.00
3-10	2.75	8.00	18.00
11-20: 13-X-Mas-c	1.70	5.00	11.50
21-40	1.00	3.00	7.00
41-60	.75	2.25	5.00
61-80	.50	1.50	3.00
81-97: 94-X-Mas-c	.35	1.00	2.00
98		.50	1.00

CASPER SPACESHIP (Casper in Space No. 6 on)
Aug, 1972 - No. 5, April, 1973
Harvey Publications

	Good	Fine	Mint
1	.85	2.50	5.00
2-5	.35	1.00	2.00

CASPER STRANGE GHOST STORIES
October, 1974 - No. 14, Jan, 1977
Harvey Publications

	Good	Fine	Mint
1	.70	2.00	4.00
2-14	.35	1.00	2.00

CASPER, THE FRIENDLY GHOST (See Famous TV Funday Funnies, The Friendly Ghost. . ., Nightmare &. . ., Richie Rich, & Tastee-Freez)

CASPER, THE FRIENDLY GHOST (Becomes Harvey Comics Hits No. 61 (No. 6), and then continued with Harvey issue No. 7)
9/49 - No. 3, 8/50; 9/50 - No. 5, 5/51
St. John Publishing Co.

	Good	Fine	Mint
1(1949)-Origin & 1st app. Baby Huey	35.00	105.00	245.00
2,3	22.00	65.00	154.00
1(9/50)	25.00	75.00	175.00
2-5	17.00	50.00	120.00

CASPER, THE FRIENDLY GHOST (Paramount Picture Star. . .)
No. 7, Dec, 1952 - No 70, July, 1958
Harvey Publications (Family Comics)

Note: No. 6 is Harvey Comics Hits No. 61 (10/52)

	Good	Fine	Mint
7-Baby Huey begins, ends No. 17?	13.00	40.00	90.00
8-10: 8-Spooky begins, ends No. 70?	6.50	20.00	45.00
11-19: 19-1st app. Nightmare (4/54)	5.00	15.00	35.00
20-Wendy the Witch begins (1st app, 5/54)	6.00	18.00	42.00
21-30: 24-Infinity-c	4.30	13.00	30.00
31-40	3.75	11.25	26.00
41-50	3.00	9.00	21.00
51-70	2.30	7.00	16.00
American Dental Association (Giveaways):			
. . .'s Dental Health Activity Book-1977	.30	.80	1.60
. . .Presents Space Age Dentistry-1972	.40	1.20	2.40
. . ., His Den, & Their Dentist Fight the Tooth Demons-1974	.40	1.20	2.40

CASPER T.V. SHOWTIME
Jan, 1980 - No. 5, Oct, 1980
Harvey Comics

	Good	Fine	Mint
1	.35	1.00	2.00
2-5		.50	1.00

CASTILIAN (See Movie Classics)

CAT, T.H.E. (TV) (See T.H.E. Cat)

CAT, THE (See Movie Classics)

CAT, THE
Nov, 1972 - No. 4, June, 1973
Marvel Comics Group

	Good	Fine	Mint
1-Origin The Cat; Wood, Mooney-a(i)	.40	1.20	2.40
2-Mooney-a(i), 3-Everett inks	.25	.80	1.60
4-Starlin/Weiss-a(p)	.30	.90	1.80

CATHOLIC COMICS (See Heroes All Catholic. . .)
June, 1946 - V3No.10, July, 1949
Catholic Publications

	Good	Fine	Mint
1	6.00	18.00	42.00
2	3.00	9.00	21.00
3-13(7/47)	2.35	7.00	16.00
V2No.1-10	1.50	4.50	10.00
V3No.1-10	1.15	3.50	8.00

CATHOLIC PICTORIAL
1947
Catholic Guild

	Good	Fine	Mint
1-Toth-a(2) (Rare)	14.00	40.00	80.00

CATMAN COMICS (Crash No. 1-5)
5/41 - No. 17, 1/43; No. 18, 7/43 - No. 22, 12/43; No. 23, 3/44 - No. 26, 11/44; No. 27, 4/45 - No. 30, 12/45; No. 31, 6/46 - No. 32, 8/46
Holyoke Publishing Co./Continental Magazines V2No.12, 7/44 on

	Good	Fine	Mint
1(V1No.6)-Origin The Deacon & Sidekick Mickey, Dr. Diamond & Rag-Man; The Black Widow app.; The Catman by Chas. Quinlan & Blaze Baylor begin	45.00	135.00	315.00
2(V1No.7)	23.00	70.00	160.00
3(V1No.8), 4(V1No.9): 3-The Pied Piper begins	18.00	54.00	125.00
5(V2No.10)-Origin Kitten; The Hood begins (c-redated), 6,7(V2No.11,12)	13.00	40.00	90.00
8(V2No.13,3/42)-Origin Little Leaders; Volton by Kubert begins (his 1st comic book work)	20.00	60.00	140.00
9(V2No.14)	11.00	33.00	76.00
10(V2No.15)-Origin Blackout; Phantom Falcon begins	11.00	33.00	76.00
11(V3No.1)-Kubert-a	10.00	30.00	70.00
12(V3No.2) - 18(V3No.8, 7/43)	8.50	25.50	60.00
19(V2No.6) - 23(V2No.10, 3/44): 19-Hitler-c	8.50	25.50	60.00
nn(V3No.13, 5/44)-Rico-a; Schomburg bondage-c	7.00	21.00	50.00
nn(V2No.12, 7/44)	7.00	21.00	50.00
nn(V3No.1, 9/44)-Origin The Golden Archer; Leatherface app.;	6.00	18.00	42.00
nn(V3No.2, 11/44)-L. B. Cole-c	13.50	40.00	95.00
27-Origin Kitten retold; L. B. Cole Flag-c	15.00	45.00	105.00
28-Catman learns Kitten's I.D.; Dr. Macabre, Deacon app.; L. B. Cole-c/a	17.00	51.00	120.00
29-32-L. B. Cole-c; bondage-No. 30	13.50	40.00	95.00

CAUGHT
Aug, 1956 - No. 5, April, 1957
Atlas Comics (VPI)

	Good	Fine	Mint
1	2.35	7.00	16.00
2,4: 4-Severin-c; Maneely-a	1.15	3.50	8.00
3-Torres-a	2.00	6.00	14.00
5-Crandall, Krigstein-a; Severin-c	2.65	8.00	18.00

CAVALIER COMICS
1945; 1952 (Early DC reprints)

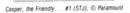

Casper, the Friendly. . . #1 (STJ), © Paramount

Catholic Comics V2No.2, © Catholic Publ.

Catman Comics V2No.12 (7/47), © HOKE

Cerebus the Aardvark #2, © Aardvark-Vanaheim

Challenge of the Unknown #6, © ACE

Challengers of the Unknown #1, © DC

CAVALIER COMICS (continued)
A. W. Nugent Publ. Co.

	Good	Fine	Mint
2(1945)-Speed Saunders, Fang Gow	5.00	15.00	35.00
2(1952)	2.35	7.00	16.00

CAVE GIRL
1953 - 1954
Magazine Enterprises

11(A-1 82)-Origin	17.00	51.00	120.00
12(A-1 96), 13(A-1 116), 14(A-1 125)-Thunda by Powell	12.00	36.00	84.00

NOTE: *Powell c/a in all.*

CAVE KIDS (TV)
Feb, 1963 - No. 16, Mar, 1967 (Hanna-Barbera)
Gold Key

1	1.00	3.00	7.00
2-5	.70	2.00	4.00
6-16	.50	1.50	3.00

CECIL KUNKLE
May, 1986 (One shot, $1.70, B&W)
Renegade Press

1	.30	.85	1.70

CENTURION OF ANCIENT ROME, THE
1958 (no month listed) (36 pages) (B&W)
Zondervan Publishing House

(Rare) All by Jay Disbrow
Estimated Value. . . . 180.00

CENTURY OF COMICS
1933 (100 pages) (Probably the 3rd comic book)
Eastern Color Printing Co.

Bought by Wheatena, Milk-O-Malt, John Wanamaker, Kinney Shoe Stores, & others to be used as premiums and radio giveaways. No publisher listed.

nn-Mutt & Jeff, Joe Palooka, etc. reprints	175.00	525.00	1225.00

CEREBUS JAM
Apr, 1985
Aardvark-Vanaheim

1-Eisner, Austin-a	.75	2.25	4.50

CEREBUS THE AARDVARK
Dec, 1977 - Present
Aardvark-Vanaheim

1-2000 print run; most copies poorly printed	58.00	175.00	350.00

Note: There is a counterfeit version known to exist. It can be distinguished from the original in the following ways: inside cover is glossy instead of flat, black background on the front cover is blotted or spotty. These counterfeits sell for between $20.00 and $30.00.

2,3: 3-Origin Red Sophia	22.35	67.00	135.00
4-Origin Elrod the Albino	11.00	33.00	66.00
5	9.15	27.50	55.00
6-10	5.65	17.00	34.00
11-Origin Moon Roach	5.00	15.00	30.00
12-14: 14-Origin Lord Julius	3.65	11.00	22.00
15-20	2.35	7.00	14.00
21-Scarce	14.00	42.50	85.00
22	2.35	7.00	14.00
23-25	1.35	4.00	8.00
26-30	1.00	3.00	6.00
31	1.35	4.00	8.00
32-40	.85	2.50	5.00
41-52	.70	2.00	4.00
53-Intro. Wolver Roach	1.70	5.00	10.00
54-56-Wolver Roach	.90	2.75	5.50
57-60	.40	1.20	2.40
61-63: Flaming Carrot app.	.60	1.75	3.50
64-80	.35	1.10	2.20
81-92	.30	.90	1.80

CHALLENGE OF THE UNKNOWN (Formerly Love Experiences)
No. 6, Sept, 1950 (See Web Of Mystery No. 19)
Ace Magazines

6-'Villa of the Vampire' used in N.Y. Joint Legislative Comm. Publ; Sekowsky-a	5.50	16.50	38.00

CHALLENGER, THE
1945 - No. 4, Oct-Dec, 1946
Interfaith Publications

nn; nd; 32 pgs.; Origin the Challenger Club; Anti-Fascist with funny animal filler	6.00	18.00	42.00
2-4-Kubert-a; 4-Fuje-a	9.00	27.00	63.00

CHALLENGERS OF THE UNKNOWN (See Showcase, Super DC Giant, and Super Team Family)
4-5/58 - No.77, 12-1/70-71; No.78, 2/73 - No.80, 6-7/73; No.81, 6-7/77 - No.87, 6-7/78
National Periodical Publications/DC Comics

1-Kirby/Stein-a(2)	40.00	120.00	280.00
2-Kirby/Stein-a(2)	20.00	60.00	140.00
3-Kirby/Stein-a(2)	16.00	48.00	110.00
4-8-Kirby/Wood-a plus c-No. 8	12.00	36.00	84.00
9,10	5.00	15.00	30.00
11-22: 14-Origin Multi-Man. 18-Intro. Cosmo, the Challs Spacepet. 22-Last 10¢ issue	2.65	8.00	18.00
23-30	1.35	4.00	8.00
31-40: 31-Retells origin of the Challengers	1.00	3.00	6.00
41-60: 43-New look begins. 48-Doom Patrol app. 49-Intro. Challenger Corps. 51-Sea Devils app. 55-Death of Red Ryan. 60-Red Ryan returns	.40	1.20	2.40
61-63,66-73: 69-Intro. Corinna	.30	.80	1.60
64,65-Kirby origin-r, parts 1 & 2	.35	1.00	2.00
74-Deadman by Tuska/Adams	1.00	3.00	6.00
75-87: 82-Swamp Thing begins		.30	.60

NOTE: ***Adams** c-67, 68, 70, 72, 74i, 81i. **Buckler** c-83-86p. **Giffen** a-83-87p. **Kirby** a-75-80r; c-75, 77, 78. **Kubert** c-64, 66, 69, 76, 79. **Nasser** c/a-81, 82. **Tuska** a-73. **Wood** r-76.*

CHALLENGE TO THE WORLD
1951 (36 pages) (10 cents)
Catechetical Guild

nn	5.00	14.00	28.00

CHAMBER OF CHILLS (. . . of Clues No. 27 on)
No. 21, June, 1951 - No. 26, Dec, 1954
Harvey Publications/Witches Tales

21	8.00	24.00	56.00
22,24	5.50	16.50	38.00
23-Excessive violence; eyes torn out	5.50	16.50	38.00
5(2/52)-Decapitation, acid in face scene	5.50	16.50	38.00
6-Woman melted alive	4.00	12.00	28.00
7-Used in **SOTI**, pg. 389; decapitation/severed head panels	4.00	12.00	28.00
8-10: 8-Decapitation panels	3.50	10.50	24.50
11,12,14	3.35	10.00	23.00
13,15-24-Nostrand-a in all; c-No. 20. 13,21-Decapitation panels. 18-Atom bomb panels	5.50	16.50	38.00
25,26	2.65	8.00	18.00

NOTE: *About half the issues contain bondage, torture, sadism, perversion, gore, cannabalism, eyes ripped out, acid in face, etc. **Kremer** a-12, 17. **Palais** a-21(1), 23. **Nostrand/Powell** a-13, 15, 16. **Powell** a-21, 23, 24('51), 5-8, 11, 13, 18-21, 23-25.*

CHAMBER OF CHILLS (continued)
Bondage-c-21, 24('51), 7. 25 r-No. 5; 26 r-No. 9.

CHAMBER OF CHILLS
Nov, 1972 - No. 25, Nov, 1976
Marvel Comics Group

	Good	Fine	Mint
1		.40	.80
2-25		.20	.40

NOTE: ***Adkins** a-1i, 2i. **Brunner** a-2-4. **Ditko** r-14, 16, 19, 23, 24. **Everett** a-3i, 11r, 21r. **Heath** a-1. **Russell** a-1p, 2p. **Robert E. Howard** horror story adaptation-2, 3.*

CHAMBER OF CLUES (Formerly Chamber of Chills)
Feb, 1955 - No. 28, April, 1955
Harvey Publications

	Good	Fine	Mint
27-Kerry Drake r-/No. 19; Powell-a	4.30	13.00	30.00
28-Kerry Drake	2.30	7.00	16.00

CHAMBER OF DARKNESS (Monsters on the Prowl No. 9)
Oct, 1969 - No. 8, Dec, 1970
Marvel Comics Group

	Good	Fine	Mint
1-Buscema-a(p)		.40	.80
2-Adams script		.40	.80
3-Smith, Gil Kane, Buscema-a		.60	1.20
4-A Conanesque tryout by Smith; reprinted in Conan No. 16	1.25	3.75	7.50
5-8: 5-H.P. Lovecraft adapt.		.30	.60
7-Wrightson c/a, 7pgs. (his 1st work at Marvel); Wrightson draws himself in 1st & last panels	.35	1.00	2.00
1(1/72-25 cent Special)		.40	.80

NOTE: ***Adkins/Everett** a-8. **Craig** a-5. **Ditko** a-6-8r. **Kirby** a(p)-4, 5, 7. **Kirby/Everett** c-5. **Severin/Everett** c-6. **Wrightson** c-7, 8.*

CHAMP COMICS (Champion No. 1-10)
No. 11, Oct, 1940 - No. 29, March, 1944
Worth Publ. Co./Champ Publ./Family Comics(Harvey Publ.)

	Good	Fine	Mint
11-Human Meteor cont'd.	24.00	72.00	168.00
12-18: 14,15-Crandall-c	18.00	54.00	126.00
19-The Wasp app.	18.00	54.00	126.00
20-The Green Ghost app.	18.00	54.00	126.00
21-29: 22-The White Mask app. 23-Flag-c	15.00	45.00	105.00

CHAMPION (See Gene Autry's...)

CHAMPION COMICS (Champ No. 11 on)
No. 2, Dec, 1939 - No. 10, Aug, 1940 (no No.1)
Worth Publ. Co.(Harvey Publications)

	Good	Fine	Mint
2-The Champ, The Blazing Scarab, Neptina, Liberty Lads, Jungleman, Bill Handy, Swingtime Sweetie begin	30.00	90.00	210.00
3-7: 7-The Human Meteor begins?	18.00	54.00	126.00
8-10-Kirbyish-c; bondage No. 10	20.00	60.00	140.00

CHAMPIONS, THE
October, 1975 - No. 17, Jan, 1978
Marvel Comics Group

	Good	Fine	Mint
1-The Angel, Black Widow, Ghost Rider, Hercules, Ice Man (The Champions) begin; Kane/Adkins-c; Venus x-over	.50	1.50	3.00
2-10: 2,3-Venus x-over		.50	1.00
11-15,17-Byrne-a	.50	1.50	3.00
16		.30	.60

NOTE: ***Buckler/Adkins** c-3. **Kane/Layton** c-11. **Layton** a-11i-13i. **Tuska** a-3p, 4p.*

CHAMPIONS
June, 1986 - No. 6, Nov, 1986 (limited series)
Eclipse Comics

	Good	Fine	Mint
1-6: Based on role playing game		.65	1.30

CHAMPIONS
1986? ($2.25, B&W, 52 pgs.)
That Other Comix Co.

	Good	Fine	Mint
1	.35	1.00	2.00

CHAMPION SPORTS
Oct-Nov, 1973 - No. 3, Feb-Mar, 1974
National Periodical Publications

	Good	Fine	Mint
1-3		.30	.60

CHAOS (See The Crusaders)

CHARLIE CHAN (See The New Advs. of...)

CHARLIE CHAN (The Adventures of) (Zaza The Mystic No. 10 on)
6-7/48 - No.5, 2-3/49; No.6, 6/55 - No.9, 3/56
Crestwood(Prize) No.1-5; Charlton No.6(6/55) on

	Good	Fine	Mint
1-S&K-c, 2 pages; Infantino-a	15.00	45.00	105.00
2-S&K-c	9.00	27.00	63.00
3-5-All S&K-c	8.00	24.00	56.00
6(6/55-Charlton)-S&K-c	5.00	15.00	35.00
7-9	3.00	9.00	21.00

CHARLIE CHAN
Oct-Dec, 1965 - No. 2, Mar, 1966
Dell Publishing Co.

	Good	Fine	Mint
1-Springer-a	1.70	5.00	10.00
2	1.00	3.00	6.00

CHARLIE CHAPLIN
1917 (9x16"; large size; softcover; B&W)
Essanay/M. A. Donohue & Co.

	Good	Fine	Mint
Series 1, No. 315-Comic Capers (9¾x15¾")-18pp by Segar, Series 1, No. 316-In the Movies	30.00	90.00	210.00
Series 1, No. 317-Up in the Air. No. 318-In the Army	30.00	90.00	210.00
...Funny Stunts-(12½x16-3/8") in color	20.00	60.00	140.00

NOTE: *All contain **Segar** -a; pre-Thimble Theatre.*

CHARLIE McCARTHY (See Edgar Bergen Presents...)
No. 171, Nov, 1947 - No. 571, July, 1954
Dell Publishing Co.

	Good	Fine	Mint
4-Color 171	4.50	13.50	31.50
4-Color 196-Part photo-c; photo back-c	5.00	15.00	35.00
1(3-5/49)-Part photo-c; photo back-c	5.00	15.00	35.00
2-9(7/52; No. 5,6-52 pgs.)	2.00	6.00	14.00
4-Color 445,478,527,571	1.50	4.50	10.00

CHARLIE THE CAVEMAN
1986?
Fantasy General Comics

	Good	Fine	Mint
1	.25	.75	1.50

CHARLTON BULLSEYE
June, 1981 - No. 10, Dec, 1982; Nov, 1986
Charlton Publications

	Good	Fine	Mint
1-Blue Beetle, The Question		.40	.80
2-10: 2-1st app. Neil The Horse. 6-Origin & 1st app. Thunderbunny		.30	.60
Special 1(11/86)(½-in B&W)	.35	1.00	2.00

CHARLTON CLASSICS
April, 1980 - No. 9, Aug, 1981
Charlton Comics

	Good	Fine	Mint
1		.30	.60
2-9		.25	.50

CHARLTON CLASSICS LIBRARY (1776)
V10No.1, March, 1973 (One Shot)
Charlton Comics

Champ Comics #11, © HARV

Charlie Chan #2, © Crestwood

Charlie McCarthy #6, © Edgar Bergen

Checkmate #2, © Jamco Prod.

Cheerios Premiums, © WDC

Cheyenne #8, © Warner Bros.

CHARLTON CLASSICS LIBRARY (cont'd.) | Good | Fine | Mint

1776 (title) - Adaptation of the film musical "1776"; given away at movie theatres .35 1.00 2.00

CHARLTON PREMIERE (Formerly Marine War Heroes)
V1No.19, July, 1967; V2No.1, Sept, 1967 - No. 4, May, 1968
Charlton Comics

V1No.19-Marine War Heroes, V2No.1-Trio; intro. Shape, Tyro Team, & Spookman, 2-Children of Doom, 3-Sinistro Boy Fiend; Blue Beetle Peacemaker x-over, 4-Unlikely Tales; Ditko-a .40 .80

CHARLTON SPORT LIBRARY - PROFESSIONAL FOOTBALL
Winter, 1969-70 (Jan. on cover) (68 pages)
Charlton Comics

1 .50 1.50 3.00

CHASING THE BLUES
1912 (52 pages) (7½x10"; B&W; hardcover)
Doubleday Page

by Rube Goldberg 16.00 48.00 110.00

CHECKMATE (TV)
Oct, 1962 - No. 2, Dec, 1962
Gold Key

1,2-Photo-c 1.75 5.25 12.00

CHEERIOS PREMIUMS (Disney)
1947 (32 pages) (Pocket size; 16 titles)
Walt Disney Productions

	Good	Fine	Mint
Set "W"-Donald Duck & the Pirates	3.35	10.00	20.00
Pluto Joins the F.B.I.	2.00	6.00	12.00
Bucky Bug & the Cannibal King	2.00	6.00	12.00
Mickey Mouse & the Haunted House	3.00	9.00	18.00
Set "X"-Donald Duck, Counter Spy	2.75	8.00	16.00
Goofy Lost in the Desert	2.00	6.00	12.00
Br'er Rabbit Outwits Br'er Fox	2.00	6.00	12.00
Mickey Mouse at the Rodeo	3.00	9.00	18.00
Set "Y"-Donald Duck's Atom Bomb by Carl Barks	57.00	170.00	380.00
Br'er Rabbit's Secret	2.00	6.00	12.00
Dumbo & the Circus Mystery	2.75	8.00	16.00
Mickey Mouse Meets the Wizard	3.00	9.00	18.00
Set "Z"-Donald Duck Pilots a Jet Plane (not by Barks)	2.75	8.00	16.00
Pluto Turns Sleuth Hound	2.00	6.00	12.00
The Seven Dwarfs & the Enchanted Mtn.	2.75	8.00	16.00
Mickey Mouse's Secret Room	3.00	9.00	18.00

CHEERIOS 3-D GIVEAWAYS (Disney)
1954 (Pocket size) (24 titles)
Walt Disney Productions

(Glasses were cut-outs on boxes)

Glasses only. . . . 3.50 10.50 24.00

(Set 1)
1-Donald Duck & Uncle Scrooge, the Firefighters
2-Mickey Mouse & Goofy, Pirate Plunder
3-Donald Duck's Nephews, the Fabulous Inventors
4-Mickey Mouse, Secret of the Ming Vase
5-Donald Duck with Huey, Dewey, & Louie; . . . the Seafarers (title on 2nd page)
6-Mickey Mouse, Moaning Mountain
7-Donald Duck, Apache Gold
8-Mickey Mouse, Flight to Nowhere
(per book). . . . 5.00 15.00 30.00

(Set 2)
1-Donald Duck, Treasure of Timbuktu
2-Mickey Mouse & Pluto, Operation China
3-Donald Duck in the Magic Cows
4-Mickey Mouse & Goofy, Kid Kokonut
5-Donald Duck, Mystery Ship
6-Mickey Mouse, Phantom Sheriff
7-Donald Duck, Circus Adventures
8-Mickey Mouse, Arctic Explorers | Good | Fine | Mint
(per book). . . . 5.00 15.00 30.00

(Set 3)
1-Donald Duck & Witch Hazel
2-Mickey Mouse in Darkest Africa
3-Donald Duck & Uncle Scrooge, Timber Trouble
4-Mickey Mouse, Rajah's Rescue
5-Donald Duck in Robot Reporter
6-Mickey Mouse, Slumbering Sleuth
7-Donald Duck in the Foreign Legion
8-Mickey Mouse, Airwalking Wonder
(per book). . . . 5.00 15.00 30.00

CHESTY AND COPTIE
1946 (4 pages) (Giveaway) (Disney)
Los Angeles Community Chest

(Very Rare) by Floyd Gottfredson 13.00 40.00 90.00

CHESTY AND HIS HELPERS
1943 (12 pgs., Disney giveaway, 5½x7¼")
Los Angeles War Chest

nn-Chesty & Coptie 14.50 43.50 100.00

CHEYENNE (TV)
No. 734, Oct, 1956 - No. 25, Dec-Jan, 1961-62
Dell Publishing Co.

	Good	Fine	Mint
4-Color 734-Ty Hardin photo-c begin, end No. 12	4.00	12.00	28.00
4-Color 772,803	3.50	10.50	24.00
4(8-10/57) - 12	3.00	9.00	21.00
13-25 (All Clint Walker photo-c)	2.65	8.00	18.00

CHEYENNE AUTUMN (See Movie Classics)

CHEYENNE KID (Wild Frontier No. 1-7)
No. 8, July, 1957 - No. 99, Nov, 1973
Charlton Comics

	Good	Fine	Mint
8 (No. 1)	1.75	5.25	12.00
9,15-17,19	.85	2.50	6.00
10-Williamson/Torres-a(3); Ditko-c	5.00	15.00	35.00
11,12-Williamson/Torres-a(2) each; 11-(68 pgs.)	5.00	15.00	35.00
13-Williamson/Torres-a, 5 pgs.	3.35	10.00	23.00
14,18-Williamson-a, 5 pgs.?	3.35	10.00	23.00
20-22,25-Severin c/a(3) each	1.65	5.00	11.50
23,24,27-29	.75	2.25	5.00
26,30-Severin-a	.85	2.50	6.00
31-59	.35	1.00	2.00
60-99: 66-Wander by Aparo begins, ends No. 87. Apache Red begins No. 88, origin No. 89		.30	.60
Modern Comics Reprint 87,89('78)		.20	.40

CHICAGO MAIL ORDER (See C-M-O Comics)

CHICAGO SUNDAY TRIBUNE COMIC BOOK MAGAZINE
1940 - 1943 (Similar to Spirit Sections)
(7¾x10¾"; full color; 16-24 pages each)
Chicago Tribune

	Good	Fine	Mint
1940 issues	5.00	15.00	35.00
1941, 1942 issues	4.00	12.00	28.00

CHICAGO SUNDAY TRIBUNE. . . (cont'd.) — Good / Fine / Mint

1943 issues — 3.35 — 10.00 — 23.00

NOTE: *Published weekly. Texas Slim, Kit Carson, Spooky, Josie, Nuts & Jolts, Lew Loyal, Brenda Starr, Daniel Boone, Captain Storm, Rocky, Smokey Stover, Tiny Tim, Little Joe, Fu Manchu appear among others. Early issues had photo stories with pictures from the movies; later issues had comic art.*

CHIEF, THE (Indian Chief No. 3 on)
No. 290, Aug, 1950 - No. 2, Apr-June, 1951
Dell Publishing Co.

4-Color 290, 2 — 2.35 — 7.00 — 16.00

CHIEF CRAZY HORSE
1950
Avon Periodicals

nn: Fawcette-c — 9.50 — 28.00 — 66.00

CHIEF VICTORIO'S APACHE MASSACRE
1951
Avon Periodicals

nn-Williamson/Frazetta-a, 7 pgs.; Larsen-a; Kinstler-c — 29.00 — 90.00 — 200.00

CHILDREN'S BIG BOOK
1945 (68 pages; stiff covers) (25 cents)
Dorene Publ. Co.

Comics & fairy tales; David Icove-a — 4.35 — 13.00 — 30.00

CHILI (Millie's Rival)
5/69 - No. 17, 9/70; No. 18, 8/72 - No. 26, 12/73
Marvel Comics Group

	Good	Fine	Mint
1	.50	1.50	3.00
2-5	.30	.80	1.60
6-17		.40	.80
18-26		.25	.50
Special 1(12/71)		.25	.50

CHILLING ADVENTURES IN SORCERY (. . . as Told by Sabrina No. 1, 2) (Red Circle Sorcery No. 6 on)
9/72 - No. 2, 10/72; No. 3, 10/73 - No. 5, 2/74
Archie Publications (Red Circle Prod.)

	Good	Fine	Mint
1,2-Sabrina cameo in both	.50	1.50	3.00
3-Morrow c/a, all	.35	1.00	2.00
4,5-Morrow c/a, 5,6 pgs.	.35	1.00	2.00

CHILLING TALES (Formerly Beware)
No. 13, Dec, 1952 - No. 17, Oct, 1953
Youthful Magazines

	Good	Fine	Mint
13(No.1)-Harrison-a; Matt Fox c/a	8.00	24.00	56.00
14-Harrison-a	5.50	16.50	38.00
15-Has No. 14 on-c; Matt Fox-c; Harrison-a	6.00	18.00	42.00
16-Poe adapt.-'Metzengerstein'; Rudyard Kipling adapt.-'Mark of the Beast,' by Kiefer; bondage-c	5.50	16.50	38.00
17-Matt Fox-c; Sir Walter Scott & Poe adapt.	6.00	18.00	42.00

CHILLING TALES OF HORROR (Magazine)
V1No.1, 6/69 - V1No.7, 12/70; V2No.2, 2/71 - V2No.5, 10/71
(52 pages; black & white) (50 cents)
Stanley Publications

	Good	Fine	Mint
V1No.1	.40	1.25	2.50
2-7: 7-Cameron-a	.30	.90	1.80
V2No.2-Spirit of Frankenstein r-/Adv. into Unknown No. 16; V2No.3,5	.30	.90	1.80
V2No.4-r-9 pg. Feldstein-a from Adv. into Unknown No. 3	.40	1.25	2.50

NOTE: *Two issues of V2No.2 exist, Feb, 1971 and April, 1971.*

CHILLY WILLY (See 4-Color No. 740,852,967,1017,1074,1122,1177,1212,1281)

CHINA BOY (See Wisco)

CHIP 'N' DALE (Walt Disney)
11/53 - No. 30, 6-8/62; 9/67 - No. 83, 1982
Dell Publishing Co./Gold Key/Whitman No. 65 on

	Good	Fine	Mint
4-Color 517	1.30	4.00	9.00
4-Color 581,636	1.00	3.00	7.00
4(12/55-2/56)-10	.75	2.25	5.00
11-30	.55	1.65	4.00
1(Gold Key reprints, 1967)	.50	1.50	3.00
2-10	.25	.75	1.50
11-20		.50	1.00
21-83		.30	.60

NOTE: *All Gold Key/Whitman issues have reprints except No. 32-35, 38-41, 45-47. No. 23-28, 30-42, 45-47, 49 have new covers.*

CHITTY CHITTY BANG BANG (See Movie Comics)

CHOICE COMICS
Dec, 1941 - No. 3, Feb, 1942
Great Publications

	Good	Fine	Mint
1-Origin Secret Circle; Atlas the Mighty app.; Zomba, Jungle Fight, Kangaroo Man, & Fire Eater begin	32.00	96.00	225.00
2	20.00	60.00	140.00
3-Features movie 'The Lost City'' classic cover; continues in Great Comics No. 3	30.00	90.00	210.00

CHOO CHOO CHARLIE
Dec, 1969
Gold Key

1-John Stanley-a — 2.65 — 8.00 — 18.00

CHRISTIAN HEROES OF TODAY
1964 (36 pages)
David C. Cook

.70 — 2.00 — 4.00

CHRISTMAS (See A-1 No. 28)

CHRISTMAS ADVENTURE, A
1969 (25¢ & given away; 4 variations known; slick-c; 28pgs.)
Gilberton (Stacey's & other Dept. Stores)

Some Alex Blum-a; r-/Picture Parade No. 4('53) with new-c; w/& without 'Merry Christmas' on-c — 1.50 — 4.50 — 10.00

CHRISTMAS ADVENTURE, THE
1963 (16 pages)
S. Rose (H. L. Green Giveaway)

.85 — 2.50 — 5.00

CHRISTMAS ALBUM (See March of Comics No. 312)

CHRISTMAS & ARCHIE ($1.00)
Jan, 1975 (68 pages) (10¼x13¼'')
Archie Comics

1 — 1.70 — 5.00 — 10.00

CHRISTMAS AT THE ROTUNDA (Titled Ford Rotunda Christmas Book 1957 on) (Regular size)
Given away every Christmas at one location
1954 - 1961
Ford Motor Co. (Western Printing)

	Good	Fine	Mint
1954-56 issues (nn's)	1.75	5.25	12.00
1957-61 issues (nn's)	1.15	3.50	8.00

CHRISTMAS BELLS (See March of Comics No. 297)

CHRISTMAS CARNIVAL
1952 (100 pages) (One Shot)
Ziff-Davis Publ. Co./St. John Publ. Co. No. 2

	Good	Fine	Mint
nn	5.00	15.00	35.00
2-Reprints Ziff-Davis issue plus-c	4.00	12.00	28.00

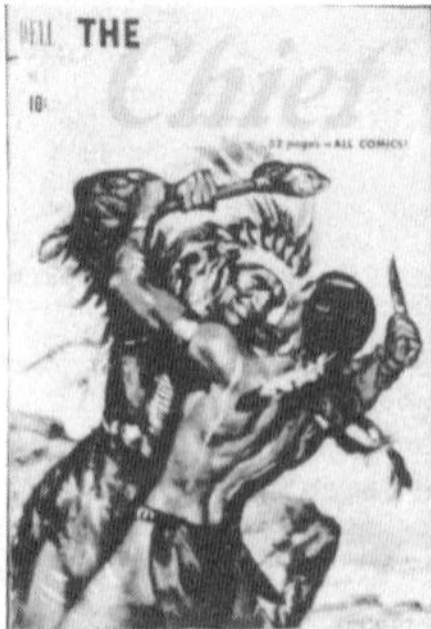

The Chief #2, © DELL

Chilling Tales #15, © YM

Choice Comics #1, © GP

A Christmas Dream, © Promotional Publ.

Christmas Parade #2, © WDC

The Christophers nn, © CG

CHRISTMAS CAROL, A (See March of Comics No. 33)

CHRISTMAS CAROL, A
No date (1942-43) (32 pgs.; 8¼x10¾''; paper cover)
Sears Roebuck & Co. (Giveaway)

	Good	Fine	Mint
nn-Comics & coloring book	5.00	15.00	30.00

CHRISTMAS CAROL, A
1940s ? (20 pgs.)
Sears Roebuck & Co. (Christmas giveaway)

Comic book & animated coloring book	4.00	12.00	24.00

CHRISTMAS CAROLS
1959 ? (16 pgs.)
Hot Shoppes Giveaway

	1.20	3.50	7.00

CHRISTMAS COLORING FUN
1964 (20 pgs.; slick cover; B&W inside)
H. Burnside

	.50	1.50	3.00

CHRISTMAS DREAM, A
1950 (16 pages) (Kinney Shoe Store Giveaway)
Promotional Publishing Co.

nn	1.35	4.00	8.00

CHRISTMAS DREAM, A
1952? (16 pgs.; paper cover)
J. J. Newberry Co. (Giveaway)

	1.35	4.00	8.00

CHRISTMAS DREAM, A
1952 (16 pgs.; paper cover)
Promotional Publ. Co. (Giveaway)

	1.35	4.00	8.00

CHRISTMAS EVE, A (See March of Comics No. 212)

CHRISTMAS FUN AROUND THE WORLD
No date (early 50's) (16 pages; paper cover)
No publisher

	2.00	6.00	12.00

CHRISTMAS IN DISNEYLAND (See Dell Giants)

CHRISTMAS JOURNEY THROUGH SPACE
1960
Promotional Publishing Co.

Reprints 1954 issue Jolly Christmas Book with new slick cover	1.20	3.50	8.00

CHRISTMAS ON THE MOON
1958 (20 pgs.; slick cover)
W. T. Grant Co. (Giveaway)

	1.75	5.25	12.00

CHRISTMAS PARADE (See Dell Giant No. 26, Dell Giants, March of Comics No. 284, & Walt Disney's. . .)

CHRISTMAS PARADE (Walt Disney's)
1/63 (no month) - No. 9, 1/72 (No.1,5: 80pgs.; No.2-4,7-9: 36pgs.)
Gold Key

	Good	Fine	Mint
1 (30018-301)-Giant	3.50	10.50	24.00
2-Reprints 4-Color 367 by Barks	3.75	11.00	26.00
3-Reprints 4-Color 178 by Barks	3.75	11.00	26.00
4-Reprints 4-Color 203 by Barks	3.75	11.00	26.00
5-Reprints Christmas Parade 1(Dell) by Barks; giant	3.75	11.00	26.00
6-Reprints Christmas Parade 2(Dell) by Barks(64pp)-Giant	3.75	11.00	30.00
7,9: 7-Pull-out poster	1.75	5.25	12.00
8-Reprints 4-Color 367 by Barks; pull-out poster	3.75	11.00	26.00

CHRISTMAS PARTY (See March of Comics No. 256)

CHRISTMAS PLAY BOOK
1946 (16 pgs.; paper cover)
Gould-Stoner Co. (Giveaway)

	2.75	8.00	16.00

CHRISTMAS ROUNDUP
1960
Promotional Publishing Co.

Marv Levy c/a	1.00	3.00	7.00

CHRISTMAS STORIES (See 4-Color No. 959,1062)

CHRISTMAS STORY (See March of Comics No. 326)

CHRISTMAS STORY BOOK (See Woolworth's Christmas Book)

CHRISTMAS STORY CUT-OUT BOOK, THE
1951 (36 pages) (15 cents)
Catechetical Guild

393-½ text, ½ comics	2.75	8.00	16.00

CHRISTMAS TREASURY, A (See Dell Giants & March of Comics No. 227)

CHRISTMAS USA (Through 300 Years) (Also see Uncle Sam's. . .)
1956
Promotional Publ. Co. (Giveaway)

Marv Levy c/a	1.00	3.00	6.00

CHRISTMAS WITH ARCHIE
1973, 1974 (52 pages) (49 cents)
Spire Christian Comics (Fleming H. Revell Co.)

nn		.60	1.20

CHRISTMAS WITH MOTHER GOOSE (See 4-Color No. 90,126,172,201,253)

CHRISTMAS WITH SANTA (See March of Comics No. 92)

CHRISTMAS WITH SNOW WHITE AND THE SEVEN DWARFS
1953 (16 pages, paper cover)
Kobackers Giftstore of Buffalo, N.Y.

	3.00	9.00	18.00

CHRISTOPHERS, THE
1951 (36 pages) (Some copies have 15 cent sticker)
Catechetical Guild (Giveaway)

nn-Hammer & sickle dripping blood-c; Stalin as Satan in Hell	25.00	75.00	175.00

CHRONICLES OF CORUM, THE
Jan, 1987 - No. 4, July, 1987 ($1.75, deluxe limited series)
First Comics

1-4: Adapt. M. Moorcock's novel	.30	.90	1.80

CHUCKLE, THE GIGGLY BOOK OF COMIC ANIMALS
1945 (132 pages) (One Shot)
R. B. Leffingwell Co.

1-Funny animal	6.00	18.00	42.00

CHUCK NORRIS AND THE KARATE KOMMANDOS (TV)
Jan, 1987 - Present
Star Comics (Marvel)

1-Ditko-a		.50	1.00

CHUCK NORRIS & THE... (continued)	Good	Fine	Mint
2,3		.40	.80

CHUCK WAGON (See Sheriff Bob Dixon's...)

CICERO'S CAT
July-Aug, 1959 - No. 2, Sept-Oct, 1959
Dell Publishing Co.

1,2	2.00	6.00	14.00

CIMARRON STRIP (TV)
January, 1968
Dell Publishing Co.

1	2.00	6.00	14.00

CINDERELLA (See 4-Color No. 272,786, & Movie Comics)

CINDERELLA
April, 1982
Whitman Publishing Co.

nn-r-/4-Color 272		.30	.60

CINDERELLA IN "FAIREST OF THE FAIR"
1955 (14 pages) (Walt Disney)
American Dairy Association (Premium)

nn	4.35	13.00	26.00

CINDERELLA LOVE
No. 10, 1950; No. 11, 4/51 - No. 12, 9/51; No. 4, 10-11/51 - No. 11, Fall, 1952; No. 12, 10/53 - No. 15, 8/54; No.25, 12/54 -No.29, 10/55 (no No.16-24)
Ziff-Davis/St. John Publ. Co. No. 12 on

10 (1st Series, 1950)	3.35	10.00	23.00
11(4/51), 12(9/51)	1.65	5.00	11.50
4-8: 7-Photo-c	1.50	4.50	10.00
9-Kinstler-a	2.35	7.00	16.00
10-Whitney painted-c	2.00	6.00	14.00
11 (Fall/'52)-Crandall-a; Saunders painted-c	3.00	9.00	21.00
12(St. John-10/53)-No.14	1.35	4.00	9.00
15 (8/54)-Matt Baker-c	2.65	8.00	18.00
25(2nd Series)(Formerly Romantic Marriage)	1.35	4.00	9.00
26-Baker-c; last precode ish	3.00	9.00	21.00
27,28	1.00	3.00	7.00
29-Matt Baker-c	2.65	8.00	18.00

CINDY COMICS (...Smith No. 39,40; Crime Can't Win No. 41 on)(Formerly Krazy Komics)
No. 27, Fall, 1947 - No. 40, July, 1950
Timely Comics

27-Kurtzman-a, 3 pgs: Margie, Oscar begin	5.00	15.00	35.00
28-31-Kurtzman-a	2.65	8.00	18.00
32-40	1.75	5.25	12.00

NOTE: ***Kurtzman's** "Hey Look"-No. 27(3), 29(2), 30(2), 31; "Giggles 'N' Grins"- No. 28.*

CINEMA COMICS HERALD
1941 - 1943 (4-pg. movie "trailers," paper-c, 7½x10½")
Paramount Pictures/Universal/RKO/20th Century Fox/Republic (Giveaway)

	Good	Fine	Mint
"Mr. Bug Goes to Town"-(1941)	3.35	10.00	20.00
"Bedtime Story"	3.35	10.00	20.00
"Lady For A Night," John Wayne, Joan Blondell (1942)	3.35	10.00	20.00
"Reap The Wild Wind"-(1942)	3.35	10.00	20.00
"Thunder Birds"-(1942)	3.35	10.00	20.00
"They All Kissed the Bride"	3.35	10.00	20.00
"Arabian Nights," nd	3.35	10.00	20.00
"Bombardier"-(1943)	3.35	10.00	20.00
"Crash Dive"-(1943)-Tyrone Power	3.35	10.00	20.00

NOTE: *The 1941-42 issues contain line art with color photos. The 1943 issues are line art.*

CIRCUS (...the Comic Riot)
June, 1938 - No. 3, Aug, 1938
Globe Syndicate

1-(Scarce)-Spacehawks (2 pgs.), & Disk Eyes by Wolverton (2 pgs.), Pewee Throttle by Cole (1st comic book work), Beau Gus, Ken Craig & The Lords of Crillon, Jack Hinton by Eisner, Van Bragger by Kane	125.00	375.00	875.00
2,3-(Scarce)-Eisner, Cole, Wolverton, Bob Kane-a in each	65.00	195.00	455.00

CIRCUS BOY (See 4-Color No. 759,785,813)

CIRCUS COMICS
1945 - No. 2, June, 1945; Winter, 1948-49
Farm Women's Publishing Co./D. S. Publ.

1	3.00	9.00	21.00
2	1.75	5.25	12.00
1(1948)-D.S. Publ.; 2 pgs. Frazetta	11.50	34.50	80.00

CIRCUS OF FUN COMICS
1945 - 1947 (a book of games & puzzles)
A. W. Nugent Publishing Co.

1	3.00	9.00	21.00
2,3	1.75	5.25	12.00

CIRCUS WORLD (See Movie Classics)

CISCO KID, THE (TV)
July, 1950 - No. 41, Oct-Dec, 1958
Dell Publishing Co.

4-Color 292(No.1)-Cisco Kid, his horse Diablo, & sidekick Pancho & his horse Loco begin; painted-c begin	6.00	18.00	42.00
2(1/51)-5	3.75	11.25	26.00
6-10	3.35	10.00	23.00
11-20	2.65	8.00	18.00
21-36-Last painted-c	2.35	7.00	16.00
37-41: All photo-c	2.65	8.00	18.00

NOTE: ***Ernest Nordli** painted-c-5-16,20,35.*

CISCO KID COMICS
Winter, 1944 - No. 3, 1945
Bernard Bailey/Swappers Quarterly

1-Illustrated Stories of the Operas: Faust; Funnyman by Giunta; Cisco Kid begins	16.00	48.00	110.00
2,3	12.00	36.00	84.00

CITIZEN SMITH (See Holyoke One-Shot No. 9)

CITY OF THE LIVING DEAD (See Fantastic Tales No. 1)
1952
Avon Periodicals

nn-Hollingsworth c/a	16.00	48.00	110.00

CITY SURGEON (Blake Harper...)
August, 1963
Gold Key

1(10075-308)	1.15	3.50	8.00

CIVIL WAR MUSKET, THE (Kadets of America Handbook)
1960 (36 pages) (Half-size; 25 cents)
Custom Comics, Inc.

nn	1.50	4.50	10.00

Cinderella Love #15, © STJ

Cinema Comics Herald, © Universal

Cisco Kid #37, © Cisco Kid Productions

CLAIRE VOYANT (Also see Keen Teens)
1946 - 1947 (Sparling strip reprints)
Leader Publ./Standard/Pentagon Publ.

	Good	Fine	Mint
nn	24.00	72.00	168.00
2-Kamen-c	18.50	56.00	130.00
3-Kamen bridal-c; contents mentioned in ***Love and Death***, a book by Gershom Legman('49) referenced by Dr. Wertham	30.00	90.00	210.00
4-Kamen bondage-c	19.00	57.00	132.00

CLANCY THE COP
1930 - 1931 (52 pages; B&W) (not reprints) (10''x10'')
Dell Publishing Co. (Soft cover)

1,2-Vep-a	4.50	13.50	31.00

UNDERSTANDING CLASSICS ILLUSTRATED
by Dan Malan

Since 1982, this book has been listing every **Classics** edition. That became possible because of Charles Heffelfinger's 1978 book, **The Classics Handbook**, detailing and illustrating every **Classics** edition. But there are still some areas of confusion, and this revised and expanded introduction will attempt to alleviate those problem areas.

THE HISTORY OF CLASSICS

The **Classics** series was the brainchild of Al Kanter, who sought for a way to introduce children to quality literature. In October 1941 his Gilberton Co. began the series **Classic Comics** with **The Three Musketeers**, with 64 pages of storyline. The early years saw irregular schedules and numerous printers, not to mention some second-class artwork and liberal story adaptations. With No. 13 the page total was dropped to 56 (except for No. 33, originally scheduled to be No. 9), and with No. 15 the next-issue ad on the outside back cover moved indoors. In 1945 the Iger shop began producing Classics, beginning with No. 23. In 1947 the search for a "classier" logo title produced **Classics Illustrated**, beginning with No. 35, **The Last Days Of Pompeii**. With No. 45 the story length dropped again to 48 pages, which was to become the standard.

What was probably the most important development for the success of the **Classics** series began in 1951 with the introduction of painted covers, instead of the old line drawn covers, beginning with No. 81, **The Odyssey**. That served as a good excuse to raise the cover price from 10 to 15 cents and did not hinder the growth of the series. From 1947 to 1953 **Classics** artwork was dominated by H.C. Kiefer and Alex Blum, together accounting for nearly 50 titles. Their distinctive styles gave real personality to the **Classics** series. **Classics** flourished during the fifties, and they diversified with **Juniors**, **Specials**, and **World Around Us** series.

But in the early sixties financial troubles set in. In 1962 the issuing of new titles ended with No. 167, **Faust**. In 1967 the company was sold to the Catholic publisher, Twin Circle. They issued two new titles in 1969 as part of an attempted revival, but succumbed to major distribution problems.

One of the major trademarks of the **Classics** series was the proliferation of reprint variations. Some titles had as many as 25 reprint editions. Reprinting began in 1943. Some of the **Classic Comic** (CC) reprints (r) had the logo format revised to the banner logo, and had the motto added under the banner. Then, reprints of all the CC titles were changed over to the new logo title, **Classics Illustrated** (CI), but still had line drawn covers (LDC). Nos. 13, 18, 29 and 41 received second covers (LDC2), replacing covers considered too violent. During 1948 and 1949, reprints of title Nos. 13 to 44 had pages reduced to 48 (except for No. 26, which had 48 pages to begin with).

Starting in the mid-fifties, 70 of the 80 LDC titles were reissued with new painted covers (PC). Thirty of them also received new interior artwork (A2). The new artwork was generally higher quality with larger art panels and more faithful but abbreviated storylines. There were also 29 second painted covers (PC2) issued, mostly by Twin Circle. The last reprints were issued in 1971. Altogether there were 199 interior artwork variations (169 (0)s plus 30 A2 editions) and 272 different covers (169 (0)s, four LDC2s, 70 new PCs of LDC (0) titles, and 29 PC2s). It is mildly astounding to realize that there were over 1,350 editions in the U.S. **Classics** series.

FOREIGN CLASSICS ILLUSTRATED

If U.S. **Classics** variations are mildly astounding, the veritable plethora of foreign **Classics** variations will boggle your imagination. While research on some countries is ongoing, we have definite information about series in 15 languages, 20 countries of origin (some with two or three series), and 30 distribution countries. There were nearly 200 new **Classics** titles in foreign series and over 300 new foreign covers of U.S. **Classics** titles. Altogether, there were over 4,000 foreign **Classics** editions.

Except for four **Classic Comic** reprints in Canada in 1946, foreign **Classics** began in 1948. But the early series were scattered/isolated and often brief. In the mid-fifties, when the U.S. began developing its PC/A2 editions, that U.S. development was coordinated with multi-European country series utilizing the same editions in nine languages at once. This was the main thrust of foreign **Classics**. And when the U.S. stopped issuing new titles in the early sixties, the European series continued with 80 new European titles, which continued until 1976. There were also 84 new Greek History & Mythology titles. Countries with large numbers of new covers of U.S. titles were Brazil, Mexico, Greece, and the early Australian series.

Here is a chronological list of countries with **Classics** series:

Canada	Japan	Sweden
Australia	Germany	New Zealand
Brazil	Mexico	Finland
Netherlands	Italy	France
Greece	Norway	Singapore
Great Britain	Iceland	Belgium
Argentina	Denmark	

Other listed distribution countries included Austria, Switzerland, Luxemburg, Spain, Morocco, and South Africa.

REFERENCE WORKS ON CLASSICS

The Classics Handbook (3rd edition - 1986) by Charles Heffelfinger. This work identifies and illustrates all U.S. **Classics** editions. It also has illustrations of all **Juniors**, **Specials** & **World Around Us**, plus information on giveaways, artists, etc.

The Classics Index (1986) by Tom Fisher. This comprehensive subject index covers all **Classics** title stories and filler articles, plus all **Juniors**, **Specials** & **World Around Us**.

The Foreign Classics Handbook (preliminary draft - 1986) by Dan Malan. This draft details over 30 series in 20 countries. It also includes a cross-reference index for all U.S. titles/artwork/covers, and a cross-reference comparison chart for all European country series.

All of these works are available through Bob Levy, 2456 East 18 Street, Brooklyn, NY 11235. Write to him for further details.

IDENTIFYING CLASSICS EDITIONS

HRN: This is the highest number on the reorder list. It is crucial to understanding the various **Classics** editions. It is shown in parentheses.

ORIGINALS (0): This is the all-important First Edition. There is one basic rule and two secondary rules (with exceptions) that apply here.

Rule No. 1: All (0)s and only (0)s have an ad for the next title (issue). **Exceptions:** No. 14(15) (reprint) has an ad on the last inside page of the text. No. 14(0) has an ad on the outside back cover and also says 10¢ on the front cover. Nos. 55(75) and 57(75) (reprints) have ads for the next issue. (Rules 2 and 3 apply here.) Nos. 168(0) and 169(0) do not have ads for the next issue. (No. 168 was never reprinted; No. 169(0) has HRN (166), No. 169(169) is the only reprint.)

Rule No. 2: All (0)s and only (0)s (Nos. 1-80) list 10¢ on the front cover. **Exceptions:** Nos. 39(71) and 46(62) (reprints) say 10¢ on the front cover. (Rules 1 and 3 apply here.)

Rule No. 3: All (0)s have HRN very close to the issue No. of that title. **Exceptions:** Many reprints also have HRN very close to the title number. Some CC(r)s, 58(62), 60(62), 149(149), 152(149), 153(149), (r)s of titles in 160's. (Rules 1 and 2 apply here.)

For information on variations of (0)s, see the next section (**TIPS**. . .).

DATES: Many **Classics** editions do not list a date, and others actually list an incorrect date. The dates listed in the price guide are calculated by the HRN. It is safer to go by the HRN to identify an edition. Dates listed in **Classics** are important on editions with HRNs of (167), (166), and (169). By then new titles were no longer being issued, and the date listed in the **Classic** itself does identify the edition (except for '62/63 which were issued in late 1962 to early 1963, but still listed original date).

COVERS: A change from CC to LDC does not indicate a new cover, only a new logo title, while a change from LDC to PC does indicate a new cover. Keep in mind that there are only four new LDC covers—13, 18, 29 and 41. New PCs can be identified by the HRN, and PC2s should be identified by the HRN and the listed date. Remember that many little details can change on a cover and it will still be listed as the same cover.

NOTES: If a front cover states "15¢ in Canada," that does not necessarily mean that it is a Canadian edition. Check the return address to be certain. An HRN listed in the price guide with a "/" in it means that there are two different reorder lists in the front and back covers. Twin Circle editions have a back cover different from regular **Classics**.

TIPS ON LISTING CLASSICS FOR SALE

It may be easy to just list "Edition 17," but **Classics** collectors think of issues in terms of what the HRN is, and whether it is an (0) or an (r), and whether it is a CC, LDC, PC, A2, PC2, stiff cover, etc.

ORIGINALS: The best way to list Originals is to just say (0), unless there are variations of Originals, such as HRN (Nos. 95, 108, 160), printer (Nos. 18-22), color (Nos. 51, 61), etc.

REPRINTS: Just list HRN if it is 165 or below; above that, HRN and date. Also, please list type of logo/cover/art for the convenience of buyers. They will appreciate it.

CLASSIC COMICS (See America in Action, Stories by Famous Authors, Story of the Commandos, & The World Around Us)

CLASSIC COMICS (. . .'s Illustrated No. 35 on)
10/41 - No. 34, 2/47; No. 35, 3/47 - No. 169, Winter/71
(Painted Covers No. 81 on)
Gilberton Publications

Abbreviations:
A—Art; C or c—Cover; CC—Classic Comics; CI—Classics Ill.; Ed—Edition; LDC—Line Drawn Cover; PC—Painted Cover; r—Reprint

CLASSIC COMICS (continued)

1. The Three Musketeers

Ed	HRN	Date	Details	A	C	Good	Fine	Mint
1	—	F/41	Original	1	1	120.00	360.00	840.00
2	10	5/43	10¢ price removed CC-r	1	1	10.00	30.00	70.00
3	15	11/43	Long Isl. Ind. Ed.; CC-r	1	1	7.00	21.00	50.00
4	18/20	6/44	Sunrise Times Ed.; CC-r	1	1	7.00	21.00	50.00
5	21	7/44	Richmond Courier Ed.; CC-r	1	1	5.50	16.50	38.00
6	28	6/46	CC-r	1	1	4.35	13.00	30.00
7	36	4/47	LDC-r	1	1	2.00	6.00	14.00
8	60	6/49	LDC-r	1	1	1.15	3.50	8.00
9	64	10/49	LDC-r	1	1	1.15	3.50	8.00
10	78	12/50	C-price 15¢; LDC-r	1	1	1.15	3.50	8.00
11	93	3/52	LDC-r	1	1	.85	2.50	6.00
12	114	11/53	Last LDC-r	1	1	.85	2.50	6.00
13	134	9/56	New-c; old-a; 64 pg. PC-r	1	2	1.30	4.00	9.00
14	143	3/58	Old-a; PC-r; 64 pg.	1	2	1.15	3.50	8.00
15	150	5/59	New-a; PC-r; Evans/Crandall-a	2	2	1.15	3.50	8.00
16	149	3/61	PC-r	2	2	.70	2.00	4.00
17	167	'62/63	PC-r	2	2	.70	2.00	4.00
18	167	4/64	PC-r	2	2	.70	2.00	4.00
19	167	1/65	PC-r	2	2	.70	2.00	4.00
20	167	3/66	PC-r	2	2	.70	2.00	4.00
21	166	11/67	PC-r	2	2	.70	2.00	4.00
22	166	Spr/69	New 25¢ price; stiff-c; PC-r	2	2	.70	2.00	4.00
23	169	Spr/71	PC-r; stiff-c	2	2	.70	2.00	4.00

2. Ivanhoe

Ed	HRN	Date	Details	A	C	Good	Fine	Mint
1	—	1941	Original	1	1	60.00	180.00	420.00
2	10	5/43	'Presents' removd. from cover; CC-r	1	1	8.00	24.00	56.00
3	15	11/43	Long Isl. Ind. ed.; CC-r	1	1	6.00	18.00	42.00
4	18/20	6/44	Sunrise Times ed.; CC-r	1	1	5.75	17.25	40.00
5	21	7/44	Richmond Courier ed.; CC-r	1	1	5.00	15.00	35.00
6	28	6/46	Last 'Comics'-r	1	1	4.35	13.00	30.00
7	36	4/47	1st LDC-r	1	1	2.00	6.00	14.00
8	60	6/49	LDC-r	1	1	1.15	3.50	8.00
9	64	10/49	LDC-r	1	1	1.15	3.50	8.00
10	78	12/50	C-price 15¢; LDC-r	1	1	1.15	3.50	8.00
11	89	11/51	LDC-r	1	1	.85	2.50	6.00
12	106	4/53	LDC-r	1	1	.85	2.50	6.00
13	121	7/54	Last LDC-r	1	1	.85	2.50	6.00
14	136	1/57	New-c&a; PC-r	2	2	1.50	4.50	10.00
15	142	1/58	PC-r	2	2	.70	2.00	4.00
16	153	11/59	PC-r	2	2	.70	2.00	4.00
17	149	3/61	PC-r	2	2	.70	2.00	4.00
18	167	'62/63	PC-r	2	2	.70	2.00	4.00
19	167	5/64	PC-r	2	2	.70	2.00	4.00
20	167	1/65	PC-r	2	2	.70	2.00	4.00
21	167	3/66	PC-r	2	2	.70	2.00	4.00
22	166	9/67	PC-r	2	2	.70	2.00	4.00
23	166	R/1968	Twin Circle ed.; PC-r	2	2	1.15	3.50	8.00
24	166	R/1968	PC-r	2	2	.70	2.00	4.00
25	169	Win/69	Stiff-c	2	2	.70	2.00	4.00
26	169	Win/71	PC-r; stiff-c	2	2	.70	2.00	4.00

3. The Count of Monte Cristo

Ed	HRN	Date	Details	A	C	Good	Fine	Mint
1	—	3/42	Original	1	1	50.00	150.00	350.00
2	10	5/43	CC-r	1	1	8.00	24.00	56.00
3	15	11/43	Long Isl. Ind. ed.; CC-r	1	1	6.00	18.00	42.00
4	18/20	6/44	Sunrise Times ed.; CC-r	1	1	5.50	16.50	38.00
5	20	6/44	Sunrise Times ed.; CC-r	1	1	5.00	15.00	35.00
6	21	7/44	Richmond Courier ed.; CC-r	1	1	4.50	13.50	32.00
7	28	6/46	CC-r	1	1	4.35	13.00	30.00
8	36	4/47	1st LDC-r	1	1	2.00	6.00	14.00
9	60	6/49	LDC-r	1	1	1.15	3.50	8.00
10	62	8/49	LDC-r	1	1	1.15	3.50	8.00
11	71	5/50	LDC-r	1	1	1.15	3.50	8.00
12	87	9/51	Price 15¢; LDC-r	1	1	.85	2.50	6.00
13	113	11/53	LDC-r	1	1	.85	2.50	6.00
14	135	11/56	New-c&a; PC-r	2	2	1.15	3.50	8.00
15	143	3/58	PC-r	2	2	.70	2.00	4.00
16	153	11/59	PC-r	2	2	.70	2.00	4.00
17	161	3/61	PC-r	2	2	.70	2.00	4.00
18	167	'62/63	PC-r	2	2	.70	2.00	4.00
19	167	7/64	PC-r	2	2	.70	2.00	4.00
20	167	7/65	PC-r	2	2	.70	2.00	4.00
21	167	7/66	PC-r	2	2	.70	2.00	4.00
22	166	R/1968	Price 25¢; PC-r	2	2	.70	2.00	4.00
23	169	Win/69	Stiff-c; PC-r	2	2	.70	2.00	4.00

4. The Last of the Mohicans

Ed	HRN	Date	Details	A	C	Good	Fine	Mint
1	—	8/42	Original	1	1	37.00	110.00	255.00
2	12	6/43	Price balloon deleted; CC-r	1	1	7.00	21.00	50.00
3	15	11/43	Long Isl. Ind. ed.; CC-r	1	1	6.75	20.25	47.00
4	20	6/44	Long Isl. Ind. ed.; CC-r	1	1	6.00	18.00	42.00
5	21	7/44	Queens Home News ed.; CC-r	1	1	4.75	14.00	33.00
6	28	6/46	Last CC-r	1	1	4.35	13.00	30.00
7	36	4/47	1st LDC-r	1	1	1.75	5.25	12.00
8	60	6/49	LDC-r	1	1	1.15	3.50	8.00
9	64	10/49	LDC-r	1	1	1.15	3.50	8.00
10	78	12/50	New price 15¢; LDC-r	1	1	.85	2.50	6.00
11	89	11/51	LDC-r	1	1	.85	2.50	6.00
12	117	3/54	Last LDC-r	1	1	.85	2.50	6.00
13	135	11/56	New-c; PC-r	1	2	1.50	4.50	10.00
14	141	11/57	PC-r	1	2	1.15	3.50	8.00
15	150	5/59	New-a; PC-r; Severin, L.B. Cole-a	2	2	1.15	3.50	8.00
16	161	3/61	PC-r	2	2	.85	2.50	5.00
17	167	'62/63	PC-r	2	2	.70	2.00	4.00
18	167	6/64	PC-r	2	2	.70	2.00	4.00
19	167	8/65	PC-r	2	2	.70	2.00	4.00
20	167	8/66	PC-r	2	2	.70	2.00	4.00
21	166	R/1967	Twin Circle ed.; PC-r	2	2	1.15	3.50	8.00
22	166	R/1967	New price 25¢; PC-r	2	2	.50	1.50	3.00
23	169	Spr/69	Stiff-c; PC-r	2	2	.70	2.00	4.00

5. Moby Dick

Ed	HRN	Date	Details	A	C	Good	Fine	Mint
1	—	9/42	Original	1	1	36.00	108.00	250.00

Classic Comics #1 (Original), © GIL

Classic Comics #2 (HRN 18), © GIL

Classic Comics #3 (HRN 20), © GIL

Classic Comics #5 (HRN 36), © GIL

Classic Comics #8 (HRN 20), © GIL

Classics Illust. #9 (HRN 51), © GIL

CLASSIC COMICS (continued)

Ed	HRN	Date	Details	A C	Good	Fine	Mint
2	10	5/43	C-price removed; CC-r; Conray Products ed.	1 1	8.00	24.00	56.00
3	15	11/43	Long Isl. Ind. ed.; CC-r	1 1	7.00	21.00	50.00
4	18/20	6/44	Sunrise Times ed.; CC-r	1 1	5.00	15.00	35.00
5	20	7/44	Sunrise Times ed.; CC-r	1 1	4.75	14.00	33.00
6	21	7/44	Sunrise Times ed.; CC-r	1 1	4.75	14.00	33.00
7	28	6/46	CC-r	1 1	4.35	13.00	30.00
8	36	4/47	1st LDC-r	1 1	2.00	6.00	14.00
9	60	6/49	LDC-r	1 1	1.15	3.50	8.00
10	62	8/49	LDC-r	1 1	1.15	3.50	8.00
11	71	5/50	LDC-r	1 1	1.15	3.50	8.00
12	87	9/51	New price 15¢; LDC-r	1 1	.85	2.50	6.00
13	118	4/54	LDC-r	1 1	.85	2.50	6.00
14	131	3/56	New c&a; PC-r	2 2	1.15	3.50	8.00
15	138	5/57	PC-r	2 2	.70	2.00	4.00
16	148	1/59	PC-r	2 2	.70	2.00	4.00
17	158	9/60	PC-r	2 2	.70	2.00	4.00
18	167	'62/63	PC-r	2 2	.70	2.00	4.00
19	167	6/64	PC-r	2 2	.70	2.00	4.00
20	167	7/65	PC-r	2 2	.70	2.00	4.00
21	167	3/66	PC-r	2 2	.70	2.00	4.00
22	166	9/67	PC-r	2 2	.70	2.00	4.00
23	166	Win/69	New-c&price 25¢; PC-r	2 3	1.15	3.50	8.00
24	169	Win/71	PC-r	2 3	1.15	3.50	8.00

6. A Tale of Two Cities

Ed	HRN	Date	Details	A C	Good	Fine	Mint
1	—	11/42	Original-Zeckerberg-c/a	1 1	36.00	108.00	250.00
2	14	9/43	C-price deleted; CC-r	1 1	8.00	24.00	56.00
3	18	3/44	Long Isl. Ind. ed.; CC-r	1 1	6.75	20.00	47.00
4	20	6/44	Sunrise Times ed.; CC-r	1 1	6.00	18.00	42.00
5	28	6/46	Last CC-r	1 1	4.35	13.00	30.00
6	51	9/48	1st LDC-r	1 1	1.75	5.25	12.00
7	64	10/49	LDC-r	1 1	1.15	3.50	8.00
8	78	12/50	C-price now 15¢; LDC-r	1 1	.85	2.50	6.00
9	89	11/51	LDC-r	1 1	.85	2.50	6.00
10	117	3/54	LDC-r	1 1	.85	2.50	6.00
11	132	5/56	New-c&a; PC-r; Joe Orlando-a	2 2	1.30	4.00	9.00
12	140	9/57	PC-r	2 2	.60	1.80	3.60
13	147	11/57	PC-r	2 2	.60	1.80	3.60
14	152	9/59	PC-r	2 2	.60	1.80	3.60
15	153	11/59	PC-r	2 2	.60	1.80	3.60
16	149	3/61	PC-r	2 2	.60	1.80	3.60
17	167	'62/63	PC-r	2 2	.60	1.80	3.60
18	167	6/64	PC-r	2 2	.60	1.80	3.60
19	167	8/65	PC-r	2 2	.60	1.80	3.60
20	166	5/67	PC-r	2 2	.60	1.80	3.60
21	166	Fall/68	PC-r(Exist?)	2 2	.60	1.80	3.60
22	166	Fall/68	New-c&price 25¢; PC-r	2 3	1.15	3.50	8.00
23	169	Sum-70	Stiff-c; PC-r	2 3	1.15	3.50	8.00

7. Robin Hood

Ed	HRN	Date	Details	A C	Good	Fine	Mint
1	—	12/42	Original	1 1	30.00	90.00	210.00
2	12	6/43	P.D.C. on cvr. deleted; CC-r	1 1	8.00	24.00	56.00
3	18	3/44	Long Isl. Ind. ed.; CC-r	1 1	6.35	19.00	44.00
4	20	6/44	Nassau Bulletin ed.; CC-r	1 1	5.35	16.00	37.00
5	22	10/44	Queens Cty. Times ed.; CC-r	1 1	5.00	15.00	35.00
6	—	12/44	Saks 34th Ave. X-Mas Giveaway		30.00	90.00	210.00
7	28	6/46	CC-r	1	4.65	14.00	33.00
8	—	—	Robin Hood & His Merry Men, The Ill. Story of (Flour Giveaway)		27.00	81.00	190.00
9	51	9/48	LDC-r	1 1	1.75	5.25	12.00
10	60	6/49	LDC-r	1 1	1.15	3.50	8.00
11	64	10/49	LDC-r	1 1	1.15	3.50	8.00
12	78	12/50	LDC-r	1 1	.85	2.60	6.00
13	97	7/52	LDC-r	1 1	.85	2.60	6.00
14	106	3/53	LDC-r	1 1	.85	2.60	6.00
15	121	7/54	LDC-r	1 1	.85	2.60	6.00
16	129	11/55	New-c; PC-r	1 2	1.15	3.50	8.00
17	136	1/57	New-a; PC-r	2 2	1.15	3.50	8.00
18	143	3/58	PC-r	2 2	.70	2.00	4.00
19	153	11/59	PC-r	2 2	.70	2.00	4.00
20	164	10/61	PC-r	2 2	.70	2.00	4.00
21	167	'62/63	PC-r	2 2	.70	2.00	4.00
22	167	6/64	PC-r	2 2	.70	2.00	4.00
23	167	5/65	PC-r	2 2	.70	2.00	4.00
24	167	7/66	PC-r	2 2	.70	2.00	4.00
25	166	12/67	PC-r	2 2	.70	2.00	4.00
26	169	Sum-69	Stiff-c; PC-r	2 2	.70	2.00	4.00

8. Arabian Nights

Ed	HRN	Date	Details	A C	Good	Fine	Mint
1	—	2/43	Original-Lilian Chestney c/a	1 1	67.00	200.00	470.00
2	14	9/43	CC-r	1 1	30.00	90.00	210.00
3	17	1/44	Long Isl. ed.; CC-r	1 1	20.00	60.00	140.00
4	20	6/44	Nassau Bulletin ed.; 'Three Men Named Smith;' 64 pgs.; CC-r	1 1	19.00	57.00	135.00
5	28	6/46	CC-r	1 1	12.00	36.00	84.00
6	51	9/48	LDC-r	1 1	7.65	23.00	54.00
7	64	10/49	LDC-r	1 1	7.00	21.00	50.00
8	78	12/50	LDC-r	1 1	6.35	19.00	44.00
9	164	10/61	New-c&a; PC-r	2 2	5.35	16.00	37.00

9. Les Miserables

Ed	HRN	Date	Details	A C	Good	Fine	Mint
1	—	3/43	Original	1 1	25.00	75.00	175.00
2	14	9/43	CC-r	1 1	9.00	27.00	62.00
3	18	3/44	Nassau Bulletin ed.; CC-r	1 1	6.35	19.00	44.00
4	20	6/44	Richmond Courier ed.; CC-r	1 1	5.35	16.00	37.00
5	28	6/46	CC-r	1 1	4.35	13.00	30.00
6	51	9/48	LDC-r	1 1	2.00	6.00	14.00
7	71	5/50	LDC-r	1 1	1.75	5.25	12.00
8	87	9/51	New price 15¢; LDC-r	1 1	1.50	4.50	10.00
9	161	3/61	New-c&a; PC-r	2 2	1.15	3.50	8.00
10	167	9/63	PC-r	2 2	.85	2.50	6.00
11	167	12/65	PC-r	2 2	.85	2.50	6.00
12	166	R/1968	New-c&price 25¢; PC-r	2 3	1.50	4.50	10.00

CLASSIC COMICS (continued)

10. Robinson Crusoe (Used in **SOTI**, pg. 142)

Ed	HRN	Date	Details	A	C	Good	Fine	Mint
1	—	4/43	Original-Stanley Zeckerberg c/a	1	1	28.00	84.00	195.00
2	14	9/43	CC-r	1	1	7.65	23.00	54.00
3	18	3/44	Nassau Bulletin ed.; pg.64 has Bill of Rights; CC-r	1	1	6.00	18.00	42.00
4	20	6/44	Queens Home News ed.; CC-r	1	1	5.00	15.00	35.00
5	28	6/46	CC-r	1	1	4.35	13.00	30.00
6	51	9/48	LDC-r	1	1	1.75	5.25	12.00
7	64	10/49	LDC-r	1	1	1.15	3.50	8.00
8	78	12/50	New price 15¢; LDC-r	1	1	1.00	3.00	7.00
9	97	7/52	LDC-r	1	1	1.00	3.00	7.00
10	114	12/53	LDC-r	1	1	1.00	3.00	7.00
11	130	1/56	New-c; PC-r	1	2	1.15	3.50	8.00
12	140	9/57	New-a; PC-r	2	2	1.15	3.50	8.00
13	153	11/59	PC-r	2	2	.55	1.70	3.40
14	164	10/61	PC-r	2	2	.55	1.70	3.40
15	167	'62/63	PC-r	2	2	.55	1.70	3.40
16	167	7/64	PC-r	2	2	.55	1.70	3.40
17	167	5/65	PC-r	2	2	.55	1.70	3.40
18	167	6/66	PC-r	2	2	.55	1.70	3.40
19	166	Fall/68	New price 25¢; PC-r	2	2	.45	1.30	2.60
20	166	R/68	Twin Circle ed.; PC-r	2	2	1.15	3.50	8.00
21	166	R/68	(No Twin Circle ad)	2	2	.45	1.30	2.60
22	169	Sm/70	Stiff-c; PC-r	2	2	.70	2.00	4.00

11. Don Quixote

Ed	HRN	Date	Details	A	C	Good	Fine	Mint
1	—	5/43	Original	1	1	28.00	84.00	195.00
2	18	3/44	Nassau Bulletin ed.; CC-r	1	1	7.00	21.00	50.00
3	21	7/44	Queens Home News ed.; CC-r	1	1	5.35	16.00	37.00
4	28	6/46	CC-r	1	1	4.00	12.00	28.00
5	110	8/53	New-PC; PC-r	1	2	2.35	7.50	16.00
6	156	5/60	Pgs. reduced 64 to 48; PC-r	1	2	.70	2.00	4.00
7	165	1962	PC-r	1	2	.70	2.00	4.00
8	167	1/64	PC-r	1	2	.70	2.00	4.00
9	167	11/65	PC-r	1	2	.70	2.00	4.00
10	166	R/1968	New-c&price 25¢; PC-r	1	3	1.50	4.50	10.00

12. Rip Van Winkle and the Headless Horseman

Ed	HRN	Date	Details	A	C	Good	Fine	Mint
1	—	6/43	Original	1	1	33.00	100.00	230.00
2	15	11/43	Long Isl. Ind. ed.; CC-r	1	1	8.35	25.00	58.00
3	20	6/44	Long Isl. Ind. ed.;	1	1	6.35	19.00	44.00
4	22	10/44	Queens Cty. Times ed.; CC-r	1	1	6.00	18.00	42.00
5	28	6/46	CC-r	1	1	4.65	14.00	32.00
6	60	6/49	1st LDC-r	1	1	1.50	4.50	10.00
7	62	8/49	LDC-r	1	1	1.00	3.00	7.00
8	71	5/50	LDC-r	1	1	1.00	3.00	7.00
	89	11/51	Coward Shoe Give-away (Scarce)	1	1	10.00	30.00	70.00
9	89	11/51	New price 15¢; LDC-r	1	1	.85	2.50	6.00
10	118	4/54	LDC-r	1	1	.85	2.50	6.00
11	132	5/56	New-c; PC-r	1	2	1.15	3.50	8.00
12	150	5/59	New-a; PC-r	2	2	1.15	3.50	8.00
13	158	9/60	PC-r	2	2	.70	2.00	4.00
14	167	'62/63	PC-r	2	2	.70	2.00	4.00
15	167	12/63	PC-r	2	2	.70	2.00	4.00
16	167	4/65	PC-r	2	2	.70	2.00	4.00
17	167	4/66	PC-r	2	2	.70	2.00	4.00
18	166	R/1968	New-c&price 25¢; PC-r; stiff-c	2	3	1.15	3.50	8.00
19	169	Sm/70	PC-r; stiff-c	2	3	1.15	3.50	8.00

13. Dr. Jekyll and Mr. Hyde (Used in **SOTI**, pg. 143)

Ed	HRN	Date	Details	A	C	Good	Fine	Mint
1	—	8/43	Original	1	1	33.00	100.00	230.00
2	15	11/43	Long Isl. Ind. ed.; CC-r	1	1	8.50	25.50	60.00
3	20	6/44	Long Isl. Ind. ed.; CC-r	1	1	6.35	19.00	44.00
4	28	6/46	No c-price; CC-r	1	1	4.35	13.00	30.00
5	60	6/49	New-c; Pgs. reduced from 56 to 48; H.C. Kiefer-c; LDC-r	1	2	1.50	4.50	10.00
6	62	8/49	LDC-r	1	2	1.00	3.00	7.00
7	71	5/50	LDC-r	1	2	1.00	3.00	7.00
8	87	9/51	Date returns (erroneous); LDC-r	1	2	1.00	3.00	7.00
9	112	10/53	New-c&a; PC-r	2	3	1.50	4.50	10.00
10	153	11/59	PC-r	2	3	.70	2.00	4.00
11	161	3/61	PC-r	2	3	.70	2.00	4.00
12	167	'62/63	PC-r	2	3	.70	2.00	4.00
13	167	8/64	PC-r	2	3	.70	2.00	4.00
14	167	11/65	PC-r	2	3	.70	2.00	4.00
15	166	R/1968	New price 25¢; PC-r	2	3	.50	1.50	3.00
16	166	R/1968	Twin Circle ed.; PC-r	2	3	1.15	3.50	8.00
17	169	Wn/69	PC-r; stiff-c	2	3	.70	2.00	4.00

14. Westward Ho!

Ed	HRN	Date	Details	A	C	Good	Fine	Mint
1	—	9/43	Original	1	1	67.00	200.00	470.00
2	15	11/43	Long Isl. Ind. ed.; CC-r	1	1	30.00	90.00	210.00
3	21	7/44	Pg.56 new; CC-r	1	1	22.00	65.00	154.00
4	28	6/46	No c-price; Pg.56 new; CC-r	1	1	18.50	55.00	130.00
5	53	11/48	Pgs. reduced from 56 to 48; LDC-r	1	1	13.00	40.00	90.00

15. Uncle Tom's Cabin (Used in **SOTI**, pgs. 102, 103)

Ed	HRN	Date	Details	A	C	Good	Fine	Mint
1	—	11/43	Original	1	1	25.00	75.00	175.00
2	15	11/43	Price circle blank; Long Isl. Ind. ed; CC-r	1	1	10.00	30.00	70.00
3	21	7/44	Nassau Bulletin ed.; CC-r	1	1	8.50	25.50	60.00
4	28	6/46	No c-price; CC-r	1	1	4.65	14.00	32.00
5	53	11/48	1st pgs. reduced 56 to 48; LDC-r	1	1	3.00	9.00	21.00
6	71	5/50	LDC-r	1	1	2.00	6.00	14.00
7	89	11/51	New price 15¢; LDC-r	1	1	1.75	5.25	12.00
8	117	3/54	New-c/a/lettering changes; PC-r	2	2	1.50	4.50	10.00
9	128	9/55	'Picture Progress' promo; PC-r	2	2	1.20	3.50	8.00

Classic Comics #12 (HRN 20), © GIL

Classics Illust. #13 (HRN 167), © GIL

Classics Illust. #15 (HRN 53), © GIL

Classic Comics #16 (Original), © GIL

Classic Comics #18 (Original), © GIL

Classic Comics #19 (Original), © GIL

CLASSIC COMICS (continued)

Ed	HRN	Date	Details	A	C	Good	Fine	Mint
10	137	3/57	PC-r	2	2	.70	2.00	4.00
11	146	9/58	PC-r	2	2	.70	2.00	4.00
12	154	1/60	PC-r	2	2	.70	2.00	4.00
13	161	3/61	PC-r	2	2	.70	2.00	4.00
14	167	'62/63	PC-r	2	2	.70	2.00	4.00
15	167	6/64	PC-r	2	2	.70	2.00	4.00
16	167	5/65	PC-r	2	2	.70	2.00	4.00
17	166	5/67	PC-r	2	2	.70	2.00	4.00
18	166	Wn/69	New-stiff-c; PC-r	2	3	1.15	3.50	8.00
19	169	Sm/70	PC-r; stiff-c	2	3	1.15	3.50	8.00

16. Gullivers Travels

Ed	HRN	Date	Details	A	C	Good	Fine	Mint
1	—	12/43	Original-Lilian Chestney c/a	1	1	22.00	65.00	154.00
2	18/20	6/44	Price deleted; Queens Home News ed; CC-r	1	1	7.00	21.00	50.00
3	22	10/44	Queens Cty. Times ed.; CC-r	1	1	6.00	18.00	42.00
4	28	6/46	CC-r	1	1	4.35	13.00	30.00
5	60	6/49	Pgs. reduced to 48; LDC-r	1	1	1.00	3.00	7.00
6	62	8/49	LDC-r	1	1	1.00	3.00	7.00
7	64	10/49	LDC-r	1	1	1.00	3.00	7.00
8	78	12/50	New c-price 15¢; LDC-r	1	1	.85	2.50	6.00
9	89	11/51	LDC-r	1	1	.70	2.00	4.00
10	155	3/60	New-c; PC-r	1	2	1.00	3.00	7.00
11	165	1962	PC-r	1	2	.70	2.00	4.00
12	167	5/64	PC-r	1	2	.70	2.00	4.00
13	167	11/65	PC-r	1	2	.70	2.00	4.00
14	166	R/1968	New price 25¢; PC-r	1	2	.50	1.50	3.00
15	166	R/1968	Twin Circle ed.; PC-r	1	2	2.65	8.00	18.50
16	169	Wn/69	PC-r; stiff-c	1	2	.70	2.00	4.00

17. The Deerslayer

Ed	HRN	Date	Details	A	C	Good	Fine	Mint
1	—	1/44	Original	1	1	21.00	62.00	146.00
2	18	3/44	Price removd; CC-r	1	1	5.75	17.25	40.00
3	22	10/44	Queens Cty. Times ed.; CC-r	1	1	4.35	13.00	30.00
4	28	6/46	CC-r	1	1	3.65	11.00	25.00
5	60	6/49	Pgs.reduced to 48; LDC-r	1	1	1.00	3.00	7.00
6	64	10/49	LDC-r	1	1	1.00	3.00	7.00
7	85	7/51	C-price 15¢; LDC-r	1	1	.85	2.50	6.00
8	118	4/54	LDC-r	1	1	.85	2.50	6.00
9	132	5/56	LDC-r	1	1	.70	2.00	4.00
10	167	11/66	Last LDC-r	1	1	.70	2.00	4.00
11	166	R/1968	New-c&price 25¢; PC-r	1	2	1.00	3.00	6.00
12	169	Spr/71	Stiff-c; letters from parents & educators; PC-r	1	2	.70	2.00	4.00

18. The Hunchback of Notre Dame

Ed	HRN	Date	Details	A	C	Good	Fine	Mint
1	—	3/44	Orig.; Gilberton ed.	1	1	28.00	84.00	195.00
2	—	3/44	Orig.; Island Pub. Co. ed.	1	1	24.00	72.00	170.00
3	18/20	6/44	Queens Home News ed.; CC-r	1	1	5.75	17.25	40.00
4	22	10/44	Queens Cty. Times ed.; CC-r	1	1	4.35	13.00	30.00
5	28	6/46	CC-r	1	1	3.65	11.00	25.00
6	60	6/49	New-c; 8pgs. deleted; Kiefer-c; LDC-r	1	2	1.30	4.00	9.00
7	62	8/49	LDC-r	1	2	1.00	3.00	7.00
8	78	12/50	C-price 15¢; LDC-r	1	2	.85	2.50	6.00
9	89	11/51	LDC-r	1	2	.85	2.50	6.00
10	118	4/54	LDC-r	1	2	.85	2.50	6.00
11	140	9/57	New-c; PC-r	1	3	1.70	5.00	12.00
12	146	9/58	PC-r	1	3	1.35	4.00	9.00
13	158	9/60	New-c&a; PC-r; Evans/Crandall-a	2	4	2.00	6.00	14.00
14	165	1962	PC-r	2	4	.50	1.50	3.00
15	167	9/63	PC-r	2	4	.50	1.50	3.00
16	167	10/64	PC-r	2	4	.50	1.50	3.00
17	167	4/66	PC-r	2	4	.50	1.50	3.00
18	166	R/1968	New price 25¢; PC-r	2	4	.50	1.50	3.00
19	169	Sm/70	Stiff-c; PC-r	2	4	.50	1.50	3.00

19. Huckleberry Finn

Ed	HRN	Date	Details	A	C	Good	Fine	Mint
1	—	4/44	Orig.; Gilberton ed.	1	1	16.50	50.00	115.00
2	—	4/44	Orig.; Island Pub. Co. ed.	1	1	15.00	45.00	105.00
3	18	3/44	Nassau Bulletin ed.; CC-r	1	1	5.75	17.25	40.00
4	22	10/44	Queens Cty. Times ed.; CC-r	1	1	4.35	13.00	30.00
5	28	6/46	CC-r	1	1	4.00	12.00	28.00
6	60	6/49	Pgs. reduced to 48; LDC-r	1	1	1.00	3.00	7.00
7	62	8/49	LDC-r	1	1	1.00	3.00	7.00
8	78	12/50	LDC-r	1	1	.85	2.50	6.00
9	89	11/51	LDC-r	1	1	.85	2.50	6.00
10	117	3/54	LDC-r	1	1	.85	2.50	6.00
11	131	3/56	New-c&a; PC-r	2	2	1.20	3.50	8.00
12	140	9/57	PC-r	2	2	.70	2.00	4.00
13	150	5/59	PC-r	2	2	.70	2.00	4.00
14	158	9/60	PC-r	2	2	.70	2.00	4.00
15	165	1962	PC-r	2	2	.70	2.00	4.00
16	167	'62/63	PC-r	2	2	.70	2.00	4.00
17	167	6/64	PC-r	2	2	.70	2.00	4.00
18	167	6/65	PC-r	2	2	.70	2.00	4.00
19	167	10/65	PC-r	2	2	.70	2.00	4.00
20	166	9/67	PC-r	2	2	.70	2.00	4.00
21	166	Win/69	New price 25¢; PC-r; stiff-c	2	2	.50	1.50	3.00
22	169	Sm/70	PC-r; stiff-c	2	2	.70	2.00	4.00

20. The Corsican Brothers

Ed	HRN	Date	Details	A	C	Good	Fine	Mint
1	—	6/44	Orig.; Gilberton ed.	1	1	18.00	54.00	125.00
2	—	6/44	Orig.; Courier ed.	1	1	16.50	50.00	115.00
3	—	6/44	Orig.; Long Island Ind. ed.; CC-r	1	1	16.50	50.00	115.00
4	22	10/44	Queens Cty. Times ed.; CC-r	1	1	7.65	23.00	54.00
5	28	6/46	CC-r	1	1	5.75	17.25	40.00
6	60	6/49	CI logo; no price; 48 pgs.; LDC-r	1	1	4.65	14.00	33.00
7	62	8/49	LDC-r	1	1	4.35	13.00	30.00
8	78	12/50	C-price 15¢; LDC-r	1	1	4.00	12.00	28.00
9	97	7/52	LDC-r	1	1	4.00	12.00	28.00

21. 3 Famous Mysteries (''The Sign of the 4,'' ''The Murders in the Rue Morgue,'' ''The Flayed Hand'')

CLASSIC COMICS (continued)

Ed	HRN	Date	Details	A	C	Good	Fine	Mint
1	—	7/44	Orig.; Gilberton ed.	1	1	32.00	95.00	225.00
2	—	7/44	Orig. Island Pub. Co.; nd or indicia	1	1	30.00	90.00	210.00
3	—	7/44	Original; Richmond Courier Ed.	1	1	30.00	90.00	210.00
4	22	10/44	Nassau Bulletin ed.; CC-r	1	1	14.50	43.50	100.00
5	30	9/46	CC-r	1	1	13.00	40.00	90.00
6	62	8/49	LDC-r	1	1	8.00	24.00	56.00
7	70	4/50	LDC-r	1	1	7.35	22.00	52.00
8	85	7/51	Price 15¢; LDC-r	1	1	7.00	21.00	50.00
9	114	12/53	New-c; PC-r	1	2	7.65	23.00	54.00

22. The Pathfinder

Ed	HRN	Date	Details	A	C	Good	Fine	Mint
1	—	10/44	Orig.; Gilberton ed.	1	1	16.00	48.00	110.00
2	—	10/44	Original; Island Pub. Co. ed.	1	1	15.00	45.00	105.00
3	—	10/44	Original; Queens County Times ed.	1	1	15.00	45.00	105.00
4	30	9/46	C-price removed; CC-r	1	1	7.00	21.00	50.00
5	60	6/49	Pgs. reduced to 48; LDC-r	1	1	1.15	3.50	8.00
6	62	8/49	LDC-r	1	1	.80	2.30	5.60
7	70	4/50	LDC-r	1	1	.80	2.30	5.60
8	85	7/51	15¢ c-price; LDC-r	1	1	.55	1.60	3.80
9	118	4/54	LDC-r	1	1	.55	1.60	3.80
10	132	5/56	LDC-r	1	1	.55	1.60	3.80
11	146	9/58	LDC-r	1	1	.55	1.60	3.80
12	167	11/63	New-c; PC-r	1	2	2.00	6.00	14.00
13	167	12/65	PC-r	1	2	1.15	3.50	8.00
14	166	8/67	PC-r	1	2	1.15	3.50	8.00

23. Oliver Twist (1st Classic produced by the Iger Shop)

Ed	HRN	Date	Details	A	C	Good	Fine	Mint
1	—	7/45	Original	1	1	13.50	40.00	95.00
2	30	9/46	Price circle blank; CC-r	1	1	4.35	13.00	30.00
3	60	6/49	Pgs. reduced to 48; LDC-r	1	1	1.15	3.50	8.00
4	62	8/49	LDC-r	1	1	.85	2.50	6.00
5	71	5/50	LDC-r	1	1	.70	2.00	5.00
6	85	7/51	15¢ c-price; LDC-r	1	1	.55	1.60	3.80
7	94	4/52	LDC-r	1	1	.55	1.60	3.80
8	118	4/54	LDC-r	1	1	.55	1.60	3.80
9	136	1/57	New-PC, old-a; PC-r	1	2	1.20	3.50	8.00
10	150	5/59	Old-a; PC-r	1	2	1.00	3.00	7.00
11	164	1961	Old-a; PC-r	1	2	1.00	3.00	7.00
12	164	1961	New-a; PC-r; Evans/Crandall-a	2	2	1.70	5.00	12.00
13	167	'62/63	PC-r	2	2	.50	1.50	3.00
14	167	8/64	PC-r	2	2	.50	1.50	3.00
15	167	12/65	PC-r	2	2	.50	1.50	3.00
16	166	R/1968	New price 25¢; PC-r	2	2	.50	1.50	3.00
17	169	Win/69	Stiff-c; PC-r	2	2	.70	2.00	4.00

24. A Connecticut Yankee in King Arthur's Court

Ed	HRN	Date	Details	A	C	Good	Fine	Mint
1	—	9/45	Original	1	1	12.00	36.00	84.00
2	30	9/46	Price circle blank; CC-r	1	1	4.35	13.00	30.00
3	60	6/49	8 pgs. deleted; LDC-r	1	1	1.15	3.50	8.00
4	62	8/49	LDC-r	1	1	.85	2.50	6.00
5	71	5/50	LDC-r	1	1	.70	2.00	5.00
6	87	9/51	15¢ c-price; LDC-r	1	1	.70	2.00	5.00
7	121	7/54	LDC-r	1	1	.70	2.00	5.00
8	140	9/57	New-c&a; PC-r	2	2	1.00	3.00	7.00
9	153	11/59	PC-r	2	2	.50	1.50	3.00
10	164	1961	PC-r	2	2	.50	1.50	3.00
11	167	'62/63	PC-r	2	2	.50	1.50	3.00
12	167	7/64	PC-r	2	2	.50	1.50	3.00
13	167	6/66	PC-r	2	2	.50	1.50	3.00
14	166	R/1968	New price 25¢; PC-r	2	2	.50	1.50	3.00
15	169	Spr/71	PC-r; stiff-c	2	2	.50	1.50	3.00

25. Two Years Before the Mast

Ed	HRN	Date	Details	A	C	Good	Fine	Mint
1	—	10/45	Original; Webb/Heames-a&c	1	1	14.00	42.00	98.00
2	30	9/46	Price circle blank; CC-r	1	1	4.35	13.00	30.00
3	60	6/49	8 pgs. deleted; LDC-r	1	1	1.15	3.50	8.00
4	62	8/49	LDC-r	1	1	.85	2.50	6.00
5	71	5/50	LDC-r	1	1	.70	2.00	5.00
6	85	7/51	15¢c-price; LDC-r	1	1	.70	2.00	5.00
7	114	12/53	LDC-r	1	1	.70	2.00	5.00
8	156	5/60	3 pgs. replaced by fillers; new-c; PC-r	1	2	.85	2.50	6.00
9	167	12/63	PC-r	1	2	.50	1.50	3.00
10	167	12/65	PC-r	1	2	.50	1.50	3.00
11	166	9/67	PC-r	1	2	.50	1.50	3.00
12	169	Win/69	New price 25¢; stiff-c; PC-r	1	2	.40	1.20	2.40

26. Frankenstein

Ed	HRN	Date	Details	A	C	Good	Fine	Mint
1	—	12/45	Original; Webb/Brewster a&c	1	1	31.50	95.00	220.00
2	30	9/46	Price circle blank; CC-r	1	1	12.00	36.00	84.00
3	60	6/49	LDC-r	1	1	3.00	9.00	21.00
4	62	8/49	LDC-r	1	1	2.65	8.00	18.00
5	71	5/50	LDC-r	1	1	2.35	7.00	16.00
6	82	4/51	15¢ c-price; LDC-r	1	1	2.00	6.00	14.00
7	117	3/54	LDC-r	1	1	1.75	5.25	12.00
8	146	9/58	New Saunders-c PC-r	1	2	1.75	5.25	12.00
9	153	11/59	PC-r	1	2	.50	1.50	3.00
10	160	1/61	PC-r	1	2	.50	1.50	3.00
11	165	1962	PC-r	1	2	.50	1.50	3.00
12	167	'62/63	PC-r	1	2	.50	1.50	3.00
13	167	6/64	PC-r	1	2	.50	1.50	3.00
14	167	6/65	PC-r	1	2	.50	1.50	3.00
15	167	10/65	PC-r	1	2	.50	1.50	3.00
16	166	9/67	PC-r	1	2	.50	1.50	3.00
17	169	Fall/69	New price 25¢; PC-r; stiff-c	1	2	.50	1.50	3.00
18	169	Spr/71	PC-r; stiff-c	1	2	.50	1.50	3.00

27. The Adventures of Marco Polo

Ed	HRN	Date	Details	A	C	Good	Fine	Mint
1	—	4/46	Original	1	1	14.00	42.00	98.00
2	30	9/46	Last 'Comics' reprint; CC-r	1	1	4.35	13.00	30.00
3	70	4/50	8 pgs. deleted; no c-price; LDC-r	1	1	1.00	3.00	7.00
4	87	9/51	15¢c-price; LDC-r	1	1	.70	2.00	5.00

Classic Comics #21 (Original), © GIL

Classics Illust. #25 (Reprint), © GIL

Classic Comics #27 (Original), © GIL

Classics Illust. #32 (Reprint), © GIL

Classic Comics #33 (Original), © GIL

Classics Illust. #36 (Original), © GIL

CLASSIC COMICS (continued)

Ed	HRN	Date	Details	A	C	Good	Fine	Mint
5	117	3/54	LDC-r	1	1	.70	2.00	5.00
6	154	1/60	New-c; PC-r	1	2	1.15	3.50	8.00
7	165	1962	PC-r	1	2	.50	1.50	3.00
8	167	4/64	PC-r	1	2	.50	1.50	3.00
9	167	6/66	PC-r	1	2	.50	1.50	3.00
10	169	Spr/69	New price 25¢; stiff-c; PC-r	1	2	.50	1.50	3.00

28. Michael Strogoff

Ed	HRN	Date	Details	A	C	Good	Fine	Mint
1	—	6/46	Original	1	1	14.50	43.50	100.00
2	51	9/48	8 pgs. cut; LDC-r	1	1	4.35	13.00	30.00
3	115	1/54	New-c; PC-r	1	2	1.15	3.50	8.00
4	155	3/60	PC-r	1	2	.50	1.50	3.00
5	167	11/63	PC-r	1	2	.50	1.50	3.00
6	167	7/66	PC-r	1	2	.50	1.50	3.00
7	169	Sm/69	PC-r	1	3	.85	2.50	5.00

29. The Prince and the Pauper

Ed	HRN	Date	Details	A	C	Good	Fine	Mint
1	—	7/46	Orig.; ''Horror''-c	1	1	24.00	72.00	170.00
2	60	6/49	8 pgs. cut; new-c; LDC-r	1	2	1.00	3.00	7.00
3	62	8/49	LDC-r	1	2	.85	2.50	6.00
4	71	5/50	LDC-r	1	2	.85	2.50	6.00
5	93	3/52	LDC-r	1	2	.70	2.00	5.00
6	114	12/53	LDC-r	1	2	.70	2.00	5.00
7	128	9/55	New-c; PC-r; H.C. Kiefer-c	1	3	1.00	3.00	7.00
8	138	5/57	PC-r	1	3	.50	1.50	3.00
9	150	5/59	PC-r	1	3	.50	1.50	3.00
10	164	1961	PC-r	1	3	.50	1.50	3.00
11	167	'62/63	PC-r	1	3	.50	1.50	3.00
12	167	7/64	PC-r	1	3	.50	1.50	3.00
13	167	11/65	PC-r	1	3	.50	1.50	3.00
14	166	R/1968	New price 25¢; PC-r	1	3	.40	1.20	2.40
15	169	Sm/70	PC-r; stiff-c	1	3	.50	1.50	3.00

30. The Moonstone

Ed	HRN	Date	Details	A	C	Good	Fine	Mint
1	—	9/46	Original; Rico c/a	1	1	13.00	40.00	90.00
2	60	6/49	LDC-r	1	1	2.50	7.50	17.00
3	70	4/50	LDC-r	1	1	1.75	5.25	12.00
4	155	3/60	New L.B. Cole-c; PC-r	1	2	4.65	14.00	32.00
5	165	1962	PC-r; L.B. Cole-c	1	2	2.00	6.00	12.00
6	167	1/64	PC-r; L.B. Cole-c	1	2	1.35	4.00	8.00
7	167	9/65	PC-r; L.B. Cole-c	1	2	1.00	3.00	6.00
8	166	R/1968	New price 25¢; PC-r	1	2	.70	2.00	4.00

31. The Black Arrow

Ed	HRN	Date	Details	A	C	Good	Fine	Mint
1	—	10/46	Original	1	1	11.00	33.00	76.00
2	51	9/48	CI logo; LDC-r	1	1	1.00	3.00	7.00
3	64	10/49	LDC-r	1	1	1.00	3.00	7.00
4	87	9/51	15¢ c-price; LDC-r	1	1	.70	2.00	5.00
5	108	6/53	LDC-r	1	1	.70	2.00	5.00
6	125	3/55	LDC-r	1	1	.70	2.00	5.00
7	131	3/56	New-c; PC-r	1	2	.85	2.50	6.00
8	140	9/57	PC-r	1	2	.50	1.50	3.00
9	148	1/59	PC-r	1	2	.50	1.50	3.00
10	161	3/61	PC-r	1	2	.50	1.50	3.00
11	167	'62/63	PC-r	1	2	.50	1.50	3.00
12	167	7/64	PC-r	1	2	.50	1.50	3.00
13	167	11/65	PC-r	1	2	.50	1.50	3.00
14	166	R/1968	25¢ new price; PC-r	1	2	.40	1.20	2.40

32. Lorna Doone

Ed	HRN	Date	Details	A	C	Good	Fine	Mint
1	—	12/46	Original; Matt Baker c&a	1	1	11.00	33.00	76.00
2	53/64	10/49	8 pgs. deleted; LDC-r	1	1	3.65	11.00	25.00
3	85	7/51	15¢ price, LDC-r; Baker c&a	1	1	3.00	9.00	21.00
4	118	4/54	LDC-r	1	1	1.35	4.00	9.00
5	138	5/57	New-c; old-c becomes new title pg.; PC-r	1	2	1.35	4.00	9.00
6	150	5/59	PC-r	1	2	.70	2.00	4.00
7	165	1962	PC-r	1	2	.70	2.00	4.00
8	167	'62/63	PC-r	1	2	.70	2.00	4.00
9	167	1/64	PC-r	1	2	.70	2.00	4.00
10	167	11/65	PC-r	1	2	.70	2.00	4.00
11	166	R/1968	New-c; PC-r	1	3	1.15	3.50	8.00

33. The Adventures of Sherlock Holmes

Ed	HRN	Date	Details	A	C	Good	Fine	Mint
1	—	1/47	Original; Kiefer-c	1	1	40.00	120.00	280.00
2	53	11/48	'A Study in Scarlet' (17 pgs.) deleted; LDC-r	1	1	20.00	60.00	140.00
3	71	5/50	LDC-r	1	1	13.00	40.00	90.00
4	89	11/51	15¢ price; LDC-r	1	1	12.00	36.00	84.00

34. Mysterious Island

Ed	HRN	Date	Details	A	C	Good	Fine	Mint
1	—	2/47	Original; Last 'Classic Comic.' Webb/Heames c/a	1	1	12.00	36.00	84.00
2	60	6/49	8 pgs. deleted; LDC-r	1	1	1.20	3.50	8.00
3	62	8/49	LDC-r	1	1	1.00	3.00	7.00
4	71	5/50	LDC-r	1	1	1.00	3.00	7.00
5	78	12/50	15¢ price circle; LDC-r	1	1	.85	2.50	6.00
6	92	2/52	LDC-r	1	1	.85	2.50	6.00
7	117	3/54	LDC-r	1	1	.85	2.50	6.00
8	140	9/57	New-c; PC-r	1	2	.85	2.50	6.00
9	156	5/60	PC-r	1	2	.70	2.00	4.00
10	167	10/63	PC-r	1	2	.70	2.00	4.00
11	167	5/64	PC-r	1	2	.70	2.00	4.00
12	167	6/66	PC-r	1	2	.70	2.00	4.00
13	166	R/1968	New price 25¢; PC-r	1	2	.45	1.30	2.60

35. Last Days of Pompeii

Ed	HRN	Date	Details	A	C	Good	Fine	Mint
1	—	3/47	Original; 1st 'Classics Illus.;'' LDC; Kiefer c/a	1	1	13.00	40.00	90.00
2	161	3/61	New c&a; 15¢; PC-r; Jack Kirby-a	2	2	1.85	5.50	13.00
3	167	1/64	PC-r	2	2	1.00	3.00	6.00
4	167	7/66	PC-r	2	2	1.00	3.00	6.00
5	169	Spr/70	New price 25¢; stiff-c; PC-r	2	2	1.20	3.50	7.00

36. Typee

Ed	HRN	Date	Details	A	C	Good	Fine	Mint
1	—	4/47	Original	1	1	5.75	17.25	40.00

Ed	HRN	Date	Details	A	C	Good	Fine	Mint
2	64	10/49	No c-price; 8 pg. ed.; LDC-r	1	1	2.35	7.00	16.00
3	155	3/60	New-c; PC-r	1	2	1.20	3.50	7.00
4	167	9/63	PC-r	1	2	1.20	3.50	7.00
5	167	7/65	PC-r	1	2	1.20	3.50	7.00
6	169	Sm/69	New price 25¢; stiff-c; PC-r	1	2	.85	2.50	6.00

37. The Pioneers

Ed	HRN	Date	Details	A	C	Good	Fine	Mint
1	37	5/47	Original; Palais-c/a	1	1	6.00	18.00	42.00
2	62	8/49	8 pgs. cut; LDC-r	1	1	2.35	7.00	16.00
3	70	4/50	LDC-r	1	1	.70	2.00	5.00
4	92	2/52	15¢ c-price; LDC-r	1	1	.50	1.50	3.50
5	118	4/54	LDC-r	1	1	.50	1.50	3.50
6	131	3/56	LDC-r	1	1	.50	1.50	3.50
7	132	5/56	LDC-r	1	1	.50	1.50	3.50
8	153	11/59	LDC-r	1	1	.50	1.50	3.50
9	167	5/64	LDC-r	1	1	.50	1.50	3.00
10	167	6/66	LDC-r	1	1	.50	1.50	3.00
11	166	R/1968	New-c&price 25¢; PC-r	1	2	1.15	3.50	8.00

38. Adventures of Cellini

Ed	HRN	Date	Details	A	C	Good	Fine	Mint
1	—	6/47	Original; Froehlich c/a	1	1	11.50	34.50	80.00
2	164	1961	New-c&a; PC-r	2	2	1.15	3.50	8.00
3	167	12/63	PC-r	2	2	1.00	3.00	6.00
4	167	7/66	PC-r	2	2	1.00	3.00	6.00
5	169	Spr/70	Stiff-c; new price 25¢; PC-r	2	2	1.35	4.00	8.00

39. Jane Eyre

Ed	HRN	Date	Details	A	C	Good	Fine	Mint
1	—	7/47	Original	1	1	9.35	28.00	65.00
2	60	6/49	No c-price; 8 pgs. cut; LDC-r	1	1	2.50	7.50	18.00
3	62	8/49	LDC-r	1	1	2.00	6.00	14.00
4	71	5/50	LDC-r	1	1	2.00	6.00	14.00
5	92	2/52	15¢ c-price; LDC-r	1	1	.85	2.50	6.00
6	118	4/54	LDC-r	1	1	.85	2.50	6.00
7	142	1/58	New-c; old-a; PC-r	1	2	1.50	4.50	10.00
8	154	1/60	Old-a; PC-r	1	2	1.35	4.00	9.00
9	165	1962	New-a; PC-r	2	2	1.50	4.50	10.00
10	167	12/63	PC-r	2	2	1.00	3.00	6.00
11	167	4/65	PC-r	2	2	1.00	3.00	6.00
12	167	8/66	PC-r	2	2	1.00	3.00	6.00
13	166	R/1968	New-c; PC-r	2	3	2.65	8.00	18.00

40. Mysteries (''The Pit and the Pendulum,'' ''The Advs. of Hans Pfall,'' ''The Fall of the House of Usher'')

Ed	HRN	Date	Details	A	C	Good	Fine	Mint
1	—	8/47	Original; Kiefer-c/a, Froehlich, Griffiths-a	1	1	32.00	95.00	225.00
2	62	8/49	LDC-r	1	1	10.00	30.00	70.00
3	75	9/50	LDC-r	1	1	7.00	21.00	50.00
4	92	2/52	15¢ c-price; LDC-r	1	1	6.00	18.00	42.00

41. Twenty Years After

Ed	HRN	Date	Details	A	C	Good	Fine	Mint
1	—	9/47	Original; 'horror'-c	1	1	20.00	60.00	140.00
2	62	8/49	New-c; no c-price 8 pgs. cut; LDC-r; Kiefer-c	1	2	1.15	3.50	8.00
3	78	12/50	C-price 15¢; LDC-r	1	2	.70	2.00	5.00
4	156	5/60	New-c; PC-r	1	3	1.00	3.00	7.00
5	167	12/63	PC-r	1	3	.45	1.30	2.60
6	167	11/66	PC-r	1	3	.45	1.30	2.60
7	169	Spr/70	New price 25¢; stiff-c; PC-r	1	3	.70	2.00	4.00

42. Swiss Family Robinson

Ed	HRN	Date	Details	A	C	Good	Fine	Mint
1	42	10/47	Orig.; Kiefer a&c	1	1	5.00	15.00	35.00
2	62	8/49	No c-price; 8 pgs. cut; LDC-r; not all have 'gift box' ad	1	1	1.00	3.00	7.00
3	75	9/50	LDC-r	1	1	.85	2.50	6.00
4	93	3/52	LDC-r	1	1	.85	2.50	6.00
5	117	3/54	LDC-r	1	1	.85	2.50	6.00
6	131	3/56	New-c; old-a; PC-r	1	2	1.35	4.00	9.00
7	137	3/57	Old-a; PC-r	1	2	1.35	4.00	9.00
8	141	11/57	Old-a; PC-r	1	2	1.35	4.00	9.00
9	152	9/59	New-a; PC-r	2	2	.85	2.50	6.00
10	158	9/60	PC-r	2	2	.70	2.00	4.00
11	167	10/47	PC-r	2	2	.70	2.00	4.00
12	165	12/63	PC-r	2	2	.70	2.00	4.00
13	167	12/63	PC-r	2	2	.70	2.00	4.00
14	167	4/65	PC-r	2	2	.70	2.00	4.00
15	166	11/67	PC-r	2	2	.45	1.30	2.60
16	169	Spr/69	PC-r	2	2	.45	1.30	2.60
17	169	Spr/70	New price 25¢; stiff-c; PC-r	2	2	.45	1.30	2.60
18	169	Sm/70	Stiff-c; PC-r	2	2	.50	1.50	3.00

43. Great Expectations (Used in **SOTI**, pg. 311)

Ed	HRN	Date	Details	A	C	Good	Fine	Mint
1	—	11/47	Original; Kiefer-a/c	1	1	36.00	108.00	250.00
2	62	8/49	No c-price; 8 pgs. cut; LDC-r	1	1	26.00	78.00	180.00

44. Mysteries of Paris (Used in **SOTI**, pg. 323)

Ed	HRN	Date	Details	A	C	Good	Fine	Mint
1	44	12/47	Original; 56 pgs.; Kiefer-a/c	1	1	24.00	72.00	168.00
2	62	8/47	No c-price; 8 pgs. cut; LDC-r; not all have 'gift box' ad	1	1	11.00	33.00	76.00
3	78	12/50	C-price 15¢; LDC-r	1	1	8.50	24.50	60.00

45. Tom Brown's School Days

Ed	HRN	Date	Details	A	C	Good	Fine	Mint
1	44	1/48	Original; 1st 48pg. issue	1	1	4.35	13.00	30.00
2	64	10/49	No c-price; LDC-r	1	1	2.35	7.00	16.00
3	161	3/61	New-c&a; PC-r	2	2	1.00	3.00	7.00
4	167	2/64	PC-r	2	2	.85	2.50	6.00
5	167	8/66	PC-r	2	2	.85	2.50	6.00
6	166	R/1968	New price 25¢; PC-r	2	2	.85	2.50	6.00

46. Kidnapped

Ed	HRN	Date	Details	A	C	Good	Fine	Mint
1	47	4/48	Original; Webb-c/a	1	1	4.65	14.00	32.00
2	62	8/49	Red price circle blank or w/10¢ price; LDC-r	1	1	1.15	3.50	8.00
3	78	12/50	15¢ price; LDC-r	1	1	.70	2.00	5.00
4	87	9/51	LDC-r	1	1	.70	2.00	5.00
5	118	4/54	LDC-r	1	1	.60	1.80	4.20
6	131	3/56	New-c; PC-r	1	2	.85	2.50	6.00
7	140	9/57	PC-r	1	2	.60	1.80	4.20

Classics Illust. #38 (Original), © GIL

Classics Illust. #42 (Original), © GIL

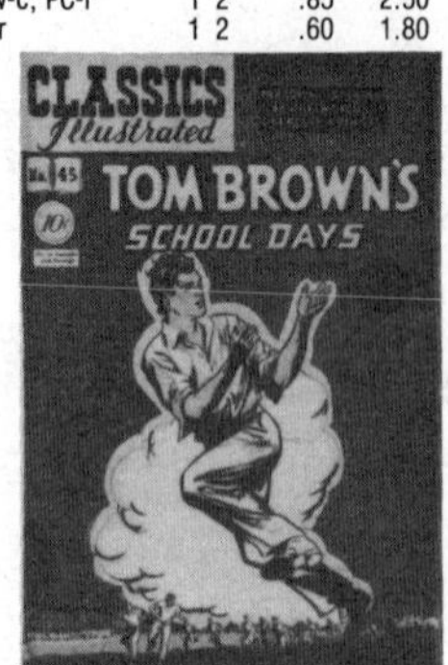

Classics Illust. #45 (Original), © GIL

Classics Illust. #48 (Original), © GIL

CLASSICS Illustrated
FEATURING STORIES BY THE WORLD'S GREATEST AUTHORS
The ADVENTURES of TOM SAWYER
by Mark Twain
No. 50
10¢

Classics Illust. #50 (Original), © GIL

Classics Illust. #54 (Original), © GIL

CLASSICS ILLUSTRATED (continued)

						Good	Fine	Mint
8	150	5/59	PC-r	1	2	.60	1.80	4.20
9	156	5/60	PC-r	1	2	.60	1.80	4.20
10	164	1961	Reduced pg.width; PC-r	1	2	.45	1.40	2.80
11	167	'62/63	PC-r	1	2	.45	1.40	2.80
12	167	3/64	PC-r	1	2	.45	1.40	2.80
13	167	6/65	PC-r	1	2	.45	1.40	2.80
14	167	12/65	PC-r	1	2	.45	1.40	2.80
15	167	9/67	PC-r	1	2	.45	1.40	2.80
16	166	Win/69	New price 25¢; PC-r; stiff-c	1	2	.35	1.00	2.00
17	169	Sm/70	PC-r; stiff-c	1	2	.50	1.50	3.00

47. Twenty Thousand Leagues Under the Sea

Ed	HRN	Date	Details	A	C	Good	Fine	Mint
1	47	5/48	Orig.; Kiefer-a&c	1	1	7.00	21.00	50.00
2	64	10/49	No c-price; LDC-r	1	1	1.20	3.50	8.00
3	78	12/50	15¢ price; LDC-r	1	1	1.00	3.00	7.00
4	94	4/52	LDC-r	1	1	1.00	3.00	7.00
5	118	4/54	LDC-r	1	1	1.00	3.00	7.00
6	128	9/55	New-c; PC-r	1	2	.85	2.50	5.00
7	133	7/56	PC-r	1	2	.85	2.50	5.00
8	140	9/57	PC-r	1	2	.85	2.50	5.00
9	148	1/59	PC-r	1	2	.85	2.50	5.00
10	156	5/60	PC-r	1	2	.85	2.50	5.00
11	165	'62/63	PC-r	1	2	.85	2.50	5.00
12	167	5/48	PC-r	1	2	.85	2.50	5.00
13	167	3/64	PC-r	1	2	.85	2.50	5.00
14	167	8/65	PC-r	1	2	.70	2.10	4.20
15	167	10/66	PC-r	1	2	.85	2.50	5.00
16	166	R/1968	New price 25¢; new-c; PC-r	1	3	1.15	3.50	8.00
17	169	Spr/70	Stiff-c; PC-r	1	3	1.15	3.50	8.00

48. David Copperfield

Ed	HRN	Date	Details	A	C	Good	Fine	Mint
1	47	6/48	Original; Kiefer a/c	1	1	5.50	16.50	38.00
2	64	10/49	Price circle replaced by motif of boy reading; LDC-r	1	1	1.15	3.50	8.00
3	87	9/51	15¢ c-price; LDC-r	1	1	.80	2.30	5.60
4	121	7/54	New-c; PC-r	1	2	.80	2.30	5.60
5	130	1/56	PC-r	1	2	.80	2.30	5.60
6	140	9/57	PC-r	1	2	.80	2.30	5.60
7	148	1/59	PC-r	1	2	.80	2.30	5.60
8	156	5/60	PC-r	1	2	.80	2.30	5.60
9	167	'62/63	PC-r	1	2	.60	1.80	3.60
10	167	4/64	PC-r	1	2	.60	1.80	3.60
11	167	6/65	PC-r	1	2	.60	1.80	3.60
12	166	5/67	PC-r	1	2	.60	1.80	3.60
13	166	R/67	PC-r	1	2	.60	1.80	3.60
14	166	R/1967	Twin Circle ed.; no c-price; PC-r	1	2	1.15	3.50	8.00
15	166	Spr/69	New price 25¢; PC-r; stiff-c	1	2	.35	1.10	2.20
16	169	Win/69	Stiff-c; PC-r	1	2	.50	1.50	3.00

49. Alice in Wonderland

Ed	HRN	Date	Details	A	C	Good	Fine	Mint
1	47	7/48	Original; 1st Blum a & c	1	1	8.50	25.50	60.00
2	64	10/49	No c-price; LDC-r	1	1	1.15	3.50	8.00
3	85	7/51	15¢ c-price; LDC-r	1	1	1.00	3.00	7.00
			w/Coward Shoe ad			2.35	7.00	16.00
4	155	3/60	New PC, similar to orig.; PC-r	1	2	1.15	3.50	8.00
5	165	1962	PC-r	1	2	.70	2.00	4.00
6	167	3/64	PC-r	1	2	.70	2.00	4.00
7	167	6/66	PC-r	1	2	.70	2.00	4.00
8	166	Fall/68	New-c; soft-c; 25¢ price; PC-r	1	3	2.00	6.00	12.00
9	166	Fall/68	Stiff-c; PC-r	1	3	2.35	7.00	16.00

50. Adventures of Tom Sawyer (Used in **SOTI**, pg. 37)

Ed	HRN	Date	Details	A	C	Good	Fine	Mint
1	51	8/48	Original; Aldo Rubano a&c	1	1	4.35	13.00	30.00
2	51	9/48	Original	1	1	4.00	12.00	28.00
3	64	10/49	No c-price; LDC-r	1	1	1.35	4.00	9.00
4	78	12/50	15¢ price; LDC-r	1	1	.85	2.50	6.00
5	94	4/52	LDC-r	1	1	.85	2.50	6.00
6	114	12/53	LDC-r	1	1	.85	2.50	6.00
7	117	3/54	LDC-r	1	1	.85	2.50	6.00
8	132	5/56	LDC-r	1	1	.85	2.50	6.00
9	140	9/57	New-c; PC-r	1	2	1.15	3.50	8.00
10	150	5/59	PC-r	1	2	1.15	3.50	8.00
11	164	1961	New-a; PC-r	2	2	.85	2.50	6.00
12	167	'62/63	PC-r	2	2	.70	2.00	4.00
13	167	1/65	PC-r	2	2	.70	2.00	4.00
14	167	5/66	PC-r	2	2	.70	2.00	4.00
15	166	12/67	PC-r	2	2	.70	2.00	4.00
16	169	Fall/69	New price 25¢; PC-r; stiff-c	2	2	.50	1.50	3.00
17	169	Win/71	PC-r	2	2	.50	1.50	3.00

51. The Spy

Ed	HRN	Date	Details	A	C	Good	Fine	Mint
1	51	9/48	Original; maroon-c	1	1	4.35	13.00	30.00
2	51	9/48	Original; violet-c	1	1	3.65	11.00	25.00
3	89	11/51	New price 15¢; LDC-r	1	1	.85	2.50	6.00
4	121	7/54	LDC-r	1	1	.85	2.50	6.00
5	139	7/57	New-c; PC-r	1	2	.85	2.50	6.00
6	156	5/60	PC-r	1	2	.70	2.00	4.00
7	167	11/63	PC-r	1	2	.70	2.00	4.00
8	167	7/66	PC-r	1	2	.70	2.00	4.00
9	166	Win/69	New price 25¢; Soft & stiff-c; PC-r	1	2	.50	1.50	3.00

52. The House of the Seven Gables

Ed	HRN	Date	Details	A	C	Good	Fine	Mint
1	53	10/48	Orig.; Griffiths a&c	1	1	4.35	13.00	30.00
2	89	11/51	New price 15¢; LDC-r	1	1	.85	2.50	6.00
3	121	7/54	LDC-r	1	1	.85	2.50	6.00
4	142	1/58	New-c&a; PC-r Woodbridge-a	2	2	.85	2.50	6.00
5	156	5/60	PC-r	2	2	.70	2.00	4.00
6	165	1962	PC-r	2	2	.70	2.00	4.00
7	167	5/64	PC-r	2	2	.70	2.00	4.00
8	167	3/66	PC-r	2	2	.70	2.00	4.00
9	166	R/1968	New price 25¢; PC-r	2	2	.50	1.50	3.00
10	169	Spr/70	Stiff-c; PC-r	2	2	.50	1.50	3.00

53. A Christmas Carol

Ed	HRN	Date	Details	A	C	Good	Fine	Mint
1	53	11/48	Original & only ed; Kiefer-a,c	1	1	6.00	18.00	42.00

54. Man in the Iron Mask

Ed	HRN	Date	Details	A	C	Good	Fine	Mint
1	55	12/48	Original; Froehlich-a, Kiefer-c	1	1	4.00	12.00	28.00

CLASSICS ILLUSTRATED (continued)

Ed	HRN	Date	Details	A C	Good	Fine	Mint
2	93	3/52	New price 15¢; LDC-r	1 1	.85	2.50	6.00
3	111	9/53	LDC-r	1 1	.60	1.80	4.20
4	142	1/58	New-c&a; PC-r	2 2	.70	2.00	5.00
5	154	1/60	PC-r	2 2	.50	1.50	3.00
6	165	1962	PC-r	2 2	.50	1.50	3.00
7	167	5/64	PC-r	2 2	.50	1.50	3.00
8	167	4/66	PC-r	2 2	.50	1.50	3.00
9	166	Win/69	New price 25¢; stiff-c; PC-r	2 2	.50	1.50	3.00

55. Silas Marner (Used in **SOTI**, pgs. 311, 312)

Ed	HRN	Date	Details	A C	Good	Fine	Mint
1	55	1/49	Original	1 1	5.50	16.50	38.00
2	75	9/50	Price circle blank; 'Coming Next' ad; LDC-r	1 1	2.00	6.00	14.00
3	97	7/52	LDC-r	1 1	.85	2.50	6.00
4	121	7/54	New-c; PC-r	1 2	.70	2.00	5.00
5	130	1/56	PC-r	1 2	.50	1.50	3.00
6	140	9/57	PC-r	1 2	.50	1.50	3.00
7	154	1/60	PC-r	1 2	.50	1.50	3.00
8	165	1962	PC-r	1 2	.50	1.50	3.00
9	167	2/64	PC-r	1 2	.50	1.50	3.00
10	167	5/64	PC-r	1 2	.50	1.50	3.00
11	167	6/65	PC-r	1 2	.50	1.50	3.00
12	166	5/67	PC-r	1 2	.50	1.50	3.00
13	166	Win/69	New price 25¢; PC-r; stiff-c	1 2	.40	1.20	2.40

56. The Toilers of the Sea

Ed	HRN	Date	Details	A C	Good	Fine	Mint
1	55	2/49	Original; A.M. Froehlich a,c	1 1	7.00	21.00	50.00
2	165	1962	New-c&a; PC-r; Angelo Torres-a	2 2	2.00	6.00	14.00
3	167	3/64	PC-r	2 2	1.75	5.25	12.00
4	167	10/66	PC-r	2 2	1.75	5.25	12.00

57. The Song of Hiawatha

Ed	HRN	Date	Details	A C	Good	Fine	Mint
1	55	3/49	Original; Alex Blum a&c	1 1	3.65	11.00	26.00
2	75	9/50	No c-price; 'Coming Next'ad; LDC-r	1 1	2.00	6.00	14.00
3	94	4/52	15¢ c-price; LDC-r	1 1	.85	2.50	6.00
4	118	4/54	LDC-r	1 1	.60	1.80	4.20
5	134	9/56	New-c; PC-r	1 2	.70	2.00	5.00
6	139	7/57	PC-r	1 2	.50	1.50	3.00
7	154	1/60	PC-r	1 2	.50	1.50	3.00
8	167	'62/63	Has orig.date; PC-r	1 2	.50	1.50	3.00
9	167	9/64	PC-r	1 2	.50	1.50	3.00
10	167	10/65	PC-r	1 2	.50	1.50	3.00
11	166	R/Fall 1968	New price 25¢; PC-r	1 2	.40	1.20	2.40

58. The Prairie

Ed	HRN	Date	Details	A C	Good	Fine	Mint
1	60	4/49	Original; Palais c/a	1 1	3.65	11.00	26.00
2	62	8/49	LDC-r	1 1	2.00	6.00	14.00
3	78	12/50	15¢ price in double circle; LDC-r	1 1	1.50	4.50	10.00
4	114	12/53	LDC-r	1 1	.75	2.20	5.25
5	131	3/56	LDC-r	1 1	.70	2.00	5.00
6	132	5/56	LDC-r	1 1	.70	2.00	5.00
7	146	9/58	New-c; PC-r	1 2	.70	2.00	5.00
8	155	3/60	PC-r	1 2	.50	1.50	3.00
9	167	5/64	PC-r	1 2	.50	1.50	3.00
10	167	4/66	PC-r	1 2	.50	1.50	3.00
11	169	Sm/69	New price 25¢; stiff-c; PC-r	1 2	.50	1.50	3.00

59. Wuthering Heights

Ed	HRN	Date	Details	A C	Good	Fine	Mint
1	60	5/49	Original; Kiefer a/c	1 1	6.00	18.00	42.00
2	85	7/51	15¢ price; LDC-r	1 1	2.00	6.00	14.00
3	156	5/60	New-c; PC-r	1 2	1.20	3.50	8.00
4	167	1/64	PC-r	1 2	.50	1.50	3.00
5	167	10/66	PC-r	1 2	.50	1.50	3.00
6	169	Sm/69	New price 25¢; stiff-c; PC-r	1 2	.50	1.50	3.00

60. Black Beauty

Ed	HRN	Date	Details	A C	Good	Fine	Mint
1	62	6/49	Original; Froehlich c/a	1 1	4.00	12.00	28.00
2	62	8/49	LDC-r	1 1	3.00	9.00	21.00
3	85	7/51	New price 15¢ LDC-r	1 1	2.20	6.50	15.00
4	158	9/60	New L.B. Cole -c&a; PC-r	2 2	2.65	8.00	18.00
5	167	2/64	PC-r	2 2	1.50	4.50	9.00
6	167	3/66	PC-r	2 2	1.20	3.50	7.00
7	167	3/66	'Open book'blank;				
(See Classics Ill. Golden Records)							
8	166	R/1968	New-c&price, 25¢; PC-r	2 3	2.00	6.00	14.00

61. The Woman in White

Ed	HRN	Date	Details	A C	Good	Fine	Mint
1	62	7/49	Original; Blum-c/a Maroon & Violet-c	1 1	4.00	12.00	28.00
2	156	5/60	New-c; PC-r	1 2	1.35	4.00	8.00
3	167	1/64	PC-r	1 2	1.35	4.00	8.00
4	166	R/1968	New price 25¢; PC-r	1 2	1.00	3.00	6.00

62. Western Stories (''The Luck of Roaring Camp'' and ''The Outcasts of Poker Flat'')

Ed	HRN	Date	Details	A C	Good	Fine	Mint
1	62	8/49	Original; Kiefer-a,c	1 1	4.35	13.00	30.00
2	89	11/51	New price 15¢; LDC-r	1 1	1.00	3.00	7.00
3	121	7/54	LDC-r	1 1	.85	2.50	6.00
4	137	3/57	New-c; PC-r	1 2	1.00	3.00	7.00
5	152	9/59	PC-r	1 2	.85	2.50	6.00
6	167	10/63	PC-r	1 2	.85	2.50	6.00
7	167	6/64	PC-r	1 2	.70	2.00	4.00
8	167	11/66	PC-r	1 2	.70	2.00	4.00
9	166	R/1968	New-c&price 25¢; PC-r	1 3	1.70	5.00	10.00

63. The Man Without a Country

Ed	HRN	Date	Details	A C	Good	Fine	Mint
1	62	9/49	Original; Kiefer-a,c	1 1	4.35	13.00	30.00
2	78	12/50	C-price 15¢ in double circle; LDC-r	1 1	1.85	5.50	13.00
3	156	5/60	New-c, old-a; PC-r	1 2	2.35	7.00	16.00
4	165	1962	New-a & text pgs.; PC-r; A. Torres-a	2 2	1.00	3.00	6.00
5	167	3/64	PC-r	2 2	.70	2.00	4.00
6	167	8/66	PC-r	2 2	.70	2.00	4.00
7	169	Sm/69	New price 25¢; stiff-c; PC-r	2 2	.70	2.00	4.00

Classics Illust. #56 (Original), © GIL

Classics Illust. #58 (Original), © GIL

Classics Illust. #61 (Original), © GIL

Classics Illust. #67 (Original), © GIL

Classics Illust. #72 (Original), © GIL

Classics Illust. #74 (Original), © GIL

LASSICS ILLUSTRATED (continued)

64. Treasure Island

Ed	HRN	Date	Details	A	C	Good	Fine	Mint
1	62	10/49	Original; Blum-a,c	1	1	4.35	13.00	30.00
2	82	4/51	New price 15¢; LDC-r	1	1	.75	2.20	5.25
3	117	3/54	LDC-r	1	1	.70	2.00	5.00
4	131	3/56	New-c; PC-r	1	2	.70	2.00	5.00
5	138	5/57	PC-r	1	2	.50	1.50	3.00
6	146	9/58	PC-r	1	2	.50	1.50	3.00
7	158	9/60	PC-r	1	2	.50	1.50	3.00
8	165	1962	PC-r	1	2	.50	1.50	3.00
9	167	'62/63	PC-r	1	2	.50	1.50	3.00
10	167	6/64	PC-r	1	2	.50	1.50	3.00
11	167	12/65	PC-r	1	2	.50	1.50	3.00
12	166	10/67	PC-r	1	2	.50	1.50	3.00
13	166	10/67	w/Grit ad stapled in book	1	2	1.70	5.00	10.00
14	169	Spr/69	New price 25¢; stiff-c; PC-r	1	2	.50	1.50	3.00

65. Benjamin Franklin

Ed	HRN	Date	Details	A	C	Good	Fine	Mint
1	64	11/49	Original; Kiefer-c Iger Shop-a	1	1	3.65	11.00	26.00
2	—	———	Ben Franklin Store Giveaway; diff-c; same interior-a	1		10.00	30.00	70.00
3	—	———	Ben Franklin give-away-Insurance ed	1		13.00	40.00	90.00
4	131	3/56	New-c; PC-r	1	2	.85	2.50	5.00
5	154	1/60	PC-r	1	2	.50	1.50	3.00
6	167	2/64	PC-r	1	2	.50	1.50	3.00
7	167	4/66	PC-r	1	2	.50	1.50	3.00
8	169	Fall/69	New price 25¢; stiff-c; PC-r	1	2	.50	1.50	3.00

66. The Cloister and the Hearth

Ed	HRN	Date	Details	A	C	Good	Fine	Mint
1	67	12/49	Original & only ed; Kiefer-a & c	1	1	9.35	28.00	65.00

67. The Scottish Chiefs

Ed	HRN	Date	Details	A	C	Good	Fine	Mint
1	67	1/50	Original; Blum-a&c	1	1	3.75	11.25	26.00
2	85	7/51	New price 15¢; LDC-r	1	1	.70	2.00	5.00
3	118	4/54	LDC-r	1	1	.70	2.00	5.00
4	136	1/57	New-c; PC-r	1	2	.70	2.00	5.00
5	154	1/60	PC-r	1	2	.50	1.50	3.00
6	167	11/63	PC-r	1	2	.50	1.50	3.00
7	167	8/65	PC-r	1	2	.50	1.50	3.00

68. Julius Caesar (Used in **SOTI**, pgs. 36, 37)

Ed	HRN	Date	Details	A	C	Good	Fine	Mint
1	70	2/50	Original; Kiefer-a,c	1	1	4.65	14.00	32.00
2	85	7/51	New price 15¢; LDC-r	1	1	.75	2.20	5.25
3	108	6/53	LDC-r	1	1	.70	2.00	5.00
4	156	5/60	New L.B. Cole-c; PC-r	1	2	1.70	5.00	12.00
5	165	1962	New-a by Evans, Crandall; PC-r	2	2	1.70	5.00	12.00
6	167	2/64	PC-r	2	2	.70	2.00	4.00
7	167	10/65	Tarzan books inside cover; PC-r	2	2	.50	1.50	3.00
8	166	R/1967	PC-r	2	2	.50	1.50	3.00
9	166	R/1967	Twin Circle ed.; PC-r	2	2	1.15	3.50	8.00
10	169	Win/69	PC-r; stiff-c	2	2	.50	1.50	3.00

69. Around the World in 80 Days

Ed	HRN	Date	Details	A	C	Good	Fine	Mint
1	70	3/50	Original; Kiefer-a/c	1	1	4.35	13.00	30.00
2	87	9/51	New price 15¢; LDC-r	1	1	.85	2.50	6.00
3	125	3/55	LDC-r	1	1	.80	2.30	5.60
4	136	1/57	New-c; PC-r	1	2	.85	2.50	6.00
5	146	9/58	PC-r	1	2	.70	2.00	4.00
6	152	9/59	PC-r	1	2	.70	2.00	4.00
7	164	1961	PC-r	1	2	.70	2.00	4.00
8	167	'62/63	PC-r	1	2	.70	2.00	4.00
9	167	7/64	PC-r	1	2	.70	2.00	4.00
10	167	11/65	PC-r	1	2	.70	2.00	4.00
11	166	7/67	PC-r	1	2	.50	1.50	3.00
12	169	Spr/69	New price 25¢; stiff-c; PC-r	1	2	.50	1.50	3.00

70. The Pilot

Ed	HRN	Date	Details	A	C	Good	Fine	Mint
1	71	4/50	Original; Blum-a,c	1	1	3.00	9.00	21.00
2	75	10/50	New price 15¢ LDC-r	1	1	.85	2.50	6.00
3	92	2/52	LDC-r	1	1	.85	2.50	6.00
4	125	3/55	LDC-r	1	1	.75	2.20	5.25
5	156	5/60	New-c; PC-r	1	2	.85	2.50	6.00
6	167	2/64	PC-r	1	2	.70	2.00	4.00
7	167	5/66	PC-r	1	2	.70	2.00	4.00

71. The Man Who Laughs

Ed	HRN	Date	Details	A	C	Good	Fine	Mint
1	71	5/50	Original; Blum-a,c	1	1	5.35	16.00	37.00
2	165	1962	New-c&a; PC-r	2	2	3.50	10.50	24.00
3	167	4/64	PC-r	2	2	3.00	9.00	18.00

72. The Oregon Trail

Ed	HRN	Date	Details	A	C	Good	Fine	Mint
1	73	6/50	Original; Kiefer-a,c	1	1	3.00	9.00	21.00
2	89	11/51	New price 15¢; LDC-r	1	1	.75	2.20	5.25
3	121	7/54	LDC-r	1	1	.70	2.00	5.00
4	131	3/56	New-c; PC-r	1	2	.85	2.50	6.00
5	140	9/57	PC-r	1	2	.75	2.20	5.25
6	150	5/59	PC-r	1	2	.70	2.00	4.00
7	164	1961	PC-r	1	2	.70	2.00	4.00
8	167	'62/63	PC-r	1	2	.70	2.00	4.00
9	167	8/64	PC-r	1	2	.70	2.00	4.00
10	167	10/65	PC-r	1	2	.70	2.00	4.00
11	166	R/1968	New price 25¢; PC-r	1	2	.50	1.50	3.00

73. The Black Tulip

Ed	HRN	Date	Details	A	C	Good	Fine	Mint
1	75	7/50	1st & only ed.; Alex Blum-a & c	1	1	11.00	33.00	76.00

74. Mr. Midshipman Easy

Ed	HRN	Date	Details	A	C	Good	Fine	Mint
1	75	8/50	1st & only edition	1	1	11.00	33.00	76.00

75. The Lady of the Lake

Ed	HRN	Date	Details	A	C	Good	Fine	Mint
1	75	9/50	Original; Kiefer-a/c	1	1	3.00	9.00	21.00
2	85	7/51	New price 15¢; LDC-r	1	1	1.15	3.50	8.00
3	118	4/54	LDC-r	1	1	.70	2.00	5.00
4	139	7/57	New-c; PC-r	1	2	.70	2.00	5.00

CLASSICS ILLUSTRATED (continued)

Ed	HRN	Date	Details	A	C	Good	Fine	Mint
5	154	1/60	PC-r	1	2	.50	1.50	3.00
6	165	1962	PC-r	1	2	.50	1.50	3.00
7	167	4/64	PC-r	1	2	.50	1.50	3.00
8	167	5/66	PC-r	1	2	.50	1.50	3.00
9	169	Spr/69	New price 25¢; stiff-c; PC-r	1	2	.50	1.50	3.00

76. The Prisoner of Zenda

Ed	HRN	Date	Details	A	C	Good	Fine	Mint
1	75	10/50	Original; Kiefer-a,c	1	1	2.65	8.00	18.00
2	85	7/51	New price 15¢; LDC-r	1	1	1.20	3.50	8.00
3	111	9/53	LDC-r	1	1	.85	2.50	6.00
4	128	9/55	New-c; PC-r	1	2	.60	1.80	4.20
5	152	9/59	PC-r	1	2	.50	1.50	3.00
6	165	1962	PC-r	1	2	.50	1.50	3.00
7	167	4/64	PC-r	1	2	.50	1.50	3.00
8	167	9/66	PC-r	1	2	.50	1.50	3.00
9	169	Fall/69	New price 25¢; stiff-c; PC-r	1	2	.60	1.80	3.60

77. The Iliad

Ed	HRN	Date	Details	A	C	Good	Fine	Mint
1	78	11/50	Original; Blum-a,c	1	1	2.65	8.00	18.00
2	87	9/51	New price 15¢; LDC-r	1	1	1.15	3.50	8.00
3	121	7/54	LDC-r	1	1	.75	2.20	5.25
4	139	7/57	New-c; PC-r	1	2	.85	2.50	6.00
5	150	5/59	PC-r	1	2	.50	1.50	3.00
6	165	1962	PC-r	1	2	.50	1.50	3.00
7	167	10/63	PC-r	1	2	.50	1.50	3.00
8	167	7/64	PC-r	1	2	.50	1.50	3.00
9	167	5/66	PC-r	1	2	.50	1.50	3.00
10	166	R/1968	New price 25¢; PC-r	1	2	.40	1.20	2.40

78. Joan of Arc

Ed	HRN	Date	Details	A	C	Good	Fine	Mint
1	78	12/50	Original; Kiefer-a,c	1	1	2.65	8.00	18.00
2	87	9/51	New price 15¢; LDC-r	1	1	1.15	3.50	8.00
3	113	11/53	LDC-r	1	1	.70	2.00	5.00
4	128	9/55	New-c; PC-r	1	2	.70	2.00	5.00
5	140	9/57	PC-r	1	2	.50	1.50	3.00
6	150	5/59	PC-r	1	2	.50	1.50	3.00
7	159	11/60	PC-r	1	2	.50	1.50	3.00
8	167	'62/63	PC-r	1	2	.50	1.50	3.00
9	167	12/63	PC-r	1	2	.50	1.50	3.00
10	167	6/65	PC-r	1	2	.50	1.50	3.00
11	166	6/67	PC-r	1	2	.50	1.50	3.00
12	166	Win/69	New-c&price, 25¢; PC-r; stiff-c	1	3	1.15	3.50	8.00

79. Cyrano de Bergerac

Ed	HRN	Date	Details	A	C	Good	Fine	Mint
1	78	1/51	Orig.; movie promo inside front-c; Blum-a & c	1	1	2.65	8.00	18.00
2	85	7/51	New price 15¢; LDC-r	1	1	1.15	3.50	8.00
3	118	4/54	LDC-r	1	1	.85	2.50	6.00
4	133	7/56	New-c; PC-r	1	2	1.15	3.50	8.00
5	156	5/60	PC-r	1	2	.85	2.50	6.00
6	167	8/64	PC-r	2	2	.85	2.50	6.00

80. White Fang (Last line drawn cover)

Ed	HRN	Date	Details	A	C	Good	Fine	Mint
1	79	2/51	Orig.; Blum-a&c	1	1	2.65	8.00	18.00
2	87	9/51	LDC-r	1	1	.85	2.50	6.0
3	125	3/55	LDC-r	1	1	.50	1.50	3.5
4	132	5/56	New-c; PC-r	1	2	.50	1.50	3.5
5	140	9/57	PC-r	1	2	.45	1.30	2.6
6	153	11/59	PC-r	1	2	.45	1.30	2.6
7	167	'62/63	PC-r	1	2	.45	1.30	2.6
8	167	9/64	PC-r	1	2	.45	1.30	2.6
9	167	7/65	PC-r	1	2	.45	1.30	2.6
10	166	6/67	PC-r	1	2	.45	1.30	2.6
11	169	Fall/69	New price 25¢; PC-r; stiff-c	1	2	.50	1.50	3.0

81. The Odyssey (1st painted cover)

Ed	HRN	Date	Details	A	C	Good	Fine	Mint
1	82	3/51	Original; Blum-c	1	1	1.75	5.25	12.0
2	167	8/64	PC-r	1	1	.85	2.50	6.0
3	167	10/66	PC-r	1	1	.85	2.50	6.0
4	169	Spr/69	New, stiff-c; PC-r	1	2	1.15	3.50	8.0

82. The Master of Ballantrae

Ed	HRN	Date	Details	A	C	Good	Fine	Mint
1	82	4/51	Original; Blum-c	1	1	1.75	5.25	12.0
2	167	8/64	PC-r	1	1	.85	2.50	6.0
3	166	Fall/68	New, stiff-c; PC-r	1	2	1.15	3.50	8.0

83. The Jungle Book

Ed	HRN	Date	Details	A	C	Good	Fine	Mint
1	85	5/51	Original; Blum-c Bossert/Blum-a	1	1	1.75	5.25	12.0
2	110	8/53	PC-r	1	1	.70	2.00	4.0
3	125	3/55	PC-r	1	1	.35	1.10	2.2
4	134	5/56	PC-r	1	1	.35	1.10	2.2
5	142	1/58	PC-r	1	1	.35	1.10	2.2
6	150	5/59	PC-r	1	1	.35	1.10	2.2
7	159	11/60	PC-r	1	1	.35	1.10	2.2
8	167	'62/63	PC-r	1	1	.35	1.10	2.2
9	167	3/65	PC-r	1	1	.35	1.10	2.2
10	167	11/65	PC-r	1	1	.35	1.10	2.2
11	167	5/66	PC-r	1	1	.35	1.10	2.2
12	166	R/1968	New c&a; stiff-c; PC-r	2	2	1.15	3.50	8.0

84. The Gold Bug and Other Stories (''The Gold Bug,'' ''The Tell-Tale Heart,'' ''The Cask of Amontillado'')

Ed	HRN	Date	Details	A	C	Good	Fine	Mint
1	85	6/51	Original; Blum-c/a Palais, Laverly-a	1	1	5.00	15.00	35.0
2	167	7/64	PC-r	1	1	3.00	9.00	21.0

85. The Sea Wolf

Ed	HRN	Date	Details	A	C	Good	Fine	Mint
1	85	8/51	Original; Blum-a&c	1	1	1.75	5.25	12.0
2	121	7/54	PC-r	1	1	.50	1.50	3.0
3	132	5/56	PC-r	1	1	.50	1.50	3.0
4	141	11/57	PC-r	1	1	.50	1.50	3.0
5	161	3/61	PC-r	1	1	.50	1.50	3.0
6	167	2/64	PC-r	1	1	.50	1.50	3.0
7	167	11/65	PC-r	1	1	.50	1.50	3.0
8	169	Fall/69	New price 25¢; stiff-c; PC-r	1	1	.50	1.50	3.0

86. Under Two Flags

Ed	HRN	Date	Details	A	C	Good	Fine	Mint
1	87	8/51	Original; first delBourgo-a	1	1	1.75	5.25	12.0
2	117	3/54	PC-r	1	1	.40	1.20	2.4
3	139	7/57	PC-r	1	1	.40	1.20	2.4
4	158	9/60	PC-r	1	1	.40	1.20	2.4

Classics Illust. #77 (Original), © GIL

Classics Illust. #79 (Original), © GIL

Classics Illust. #83 (HRN 142), © GIL

Classics Illust. #87 (Original), © GIL

Classics Illust. #95 (Original), © GIL

Classics Illust. #98 (Original), © GIL

CLASSICS ILLUSTRATED (continued)

Ed	HRN	Date	Details	A	C	Good	Fine	Mint
5	167	2/64	PC-r	1	1	.40	1.20	2.40
6	167	8/66	PC-r	1	1	.40	1.20	2.40
7	169	Sm/69	New price 25¢; stiff-c; PC-r	1	1	.50	1.50	3.00

87. A Midsummer Nights Dream

Ed	HRN	Date	Details	A	C	Good	Fine	Mint
1	87	9/51	Original; Blum c/a	1	1	2.00	6.00	14.00
2	161	3/61	PC-r	1	1	.85	2.50	5.00
3	167	4/64	PC-r	1	1	.70	2.00	4.00
4	167	5/66	PC-r	1	1	.70	2.00	4.00
5	169	Sm/69	New price 25¢; stiff-c; PC-r	1	1	.50	1.50	3.00

88. Men of Iron

Ed	HRN	Date	Details	A	C	Good	Fine	Mint
1	89	10/51	Original	1	1	1.75	5.25	12.00
2	154	1/60	PC-r	1	1	.40	1.20	2.40
3	167	1/64	PC-r	1	1	.40	1.20	2.40
4	166	R/1968	New price 25¢; PC-r	1	1	.50	1.50	3.00

89. Crime and Punishment (Cover illo. in **POP**)

Ed	HRN	Date	Details	A	C	Good	Fine	Mint
1	89	11/51	Original; Palais-a	1	1	2.00	6.00	14.00
2	152	9/59	PC-r	1	1	.50	1.50	3.00
3	167	4/64	PC-r	1	1	.50	1.50	3.00
4	167	5/66	PC-r	1	1	.50	1.50	3.00
5	169	Fall/69	New price 25¢ stiff-c; PC-r	1	1	.50	1.50	3.00

90. Green Mansions

Ed	HRN	Date	Details	A	C	Good	Fine	Mint
1	89	12/51	Original; Blum-a&c	1	1	2.35	7.00	16.00
2	148	1/59	New L.B. Cole -c; PC-r	1	2	1.35	4.00	8.00
3	165	1962	PC-r	1	2	.35	1.00	2.00
4	167	4/64	PC-r	1	2	.35	1.00	2.00
5	167	9/66	PC-r	1	2	.35	1.00	2.00
6	169	Sm/69	New price 25¢; stiff-c; PC-r	1	2	.50	1.50	3.00

91. The Call of the Wild

Ed	HRN	Date	Details	A	C	Good	Fine	Mint
1	92	1/52	Orig.; delBourgo-a	1	1	1.75	5.25	12.00
2	112	10/53	PC-r	1	1	.50	1.50	3.00
3	125	3/55	'Picture Progress' on back-c; PC-r	1	1	.70	2.00	4.00
4	134	9/56	PC-r	1	1	.50	1.50	3.00
5	143	3/58	PC-r	1	1	.50	1.50	3.00
6	165	1962	PC-r	1	1	.40	1.20	2.40
7	167	1962	PC-r	1	1	.40	1.20	2.40
8	167	4/65	PC-r	1	1	.40	1.20	2.40
9	167	3/66	PC-r	1	1	.40	1.20	2.40
10	167	3/66	Record ed.; PC-r	1	1	.40	1.20	2.40
11	166	11/67	PC-r	1	1	.40	1.20	2.40
12	169	Spr/70	New price 25¢; stiff-c; PC-r	1	1	.40	1.20	2.40

92. The Courtship of Miles Standish

Ed	HRN	Date	Details	A	C	Good	Fine	Mint
1	92	2/52	Original; Blum-a&c	1	1	1.70	5.00	12.00
2	165	1962	PC-r	1	1	.50	1.50	3.00
3	167	3/64	PC-r	1	1	.50	1.50	3.00
4	166	5/67	PC-r	1	1	.50	1.50	3.00
5	169	Win/69	New price 25¢ stiff-c; PC-r	1	1	.50	1.50	3.00

93. Pudd'nhead Wilson

Ed	HRN	Date	Details	A	C	Good	Fine	Mint
1	94	3/52	Orig.; Kiefer-a&c;	1	1	1.75	5.25	12.00
2	165	1962	New-c; PC-r	1	2	.70	2.00	4.00
3	167	3/64	PC-r	1	2	.70	2.00	4.00
4	166	R/1968	New price 25¢; soft-c; PC-r	1	2	.70	2.00	4.00

94. David Balfour

Ed	HRN	Date	Details	A	C	Good	Fine	Mint
1	94	4/52	Original; Palais-a	1	1	1.75	5.25	12.00
2	167	5/64	PC-r	1	1	.85	2.50	6.00
3	166	R/1968	New price 25¢; PC-r	1	1	.85	2.50	6.00

95. All Quiet on the Western Front

Ed	HRN	Date	Details	A	C	Good	Fine	Mint
1	96	5/52	Orig.; delBourgo-a	1	1	4.35	13.00	30.00
2	99	5/52	Orig.	1	1	4.00	12.00	28.00
3	167	10/64	PC-r	1	1	1.15	3.50	8.00
4	167	11/66	PC-r	1	1	1.15	3.50	8.00

96. Daniel Boone

Ed	HRN	Date	Details	A	C	Good	Fine	Mint
1	97	6/52	Original; Blum-a	1	1	2.00	6.00	14.00
			(Coward Shoe ad)	1	1	4.00	12.00	28.00
2	117	3/54	PC-r	1	1	.50	1.50	3.00
3	128	9/55	PC-r	1	1	.50	1.50	3.00
4	132	5/56	PC-r	1	1	.50	1.50	3.00
5	134	———	'Story of Jesus' on back-c; PC-r	1	1	.50	1.50	3.00
6	158	9/60	PC-r	1	1	.50	1.50	3.00
7	167	1/64	PC-r	1	1	.50	1.50	3.00
8	167	5/65	PC-r	1	1	.50	1.50	3.00
9	167	11/66	PC-r	1	1	.50	1.50	3.00
10	166	Win/69	New-c; price 25¢; PC-r; stiff-c	1	2	1.15	3.50	8.00

97. King Solomon's Mines

Ed	HRN	Date	Details	A	C	Good	Fine	Mint
1	96	7/52	Orig.; Kiefer-a	1	1	2.35	7.00	16.00
2	118	4/54	PC-r	1	1	1.00	3.00	7.00
3	131	3/56	PC-r	1	1	.70	2.00	4.00
4	141	9/51	PC-r	1	1	.70	2.00	4.00
5	158	9/60	PC-r	1	1	.70	2.00	4.00
6	167	2/64	PC-r	1	1	.70	2.00	4.00
7	167	9/65	PC-r	1	1	.70	2.00	4.00
8	169	Sm/69	New price 25¢; stiff-c; PC-r	1	1	.85	2.50	5.00

98. The Red Badge of Courage

Ed	HRN	Date	Details	A	C	Good	Fine	Mint
1	98	8/52	Original	1	1	1.75	5.25	12.00
			(Coward Shoe ad)	1	1	2.50	7.50	17.00
2	118	4/54	PC-r	1	1	.45	1.30	2.60
3	132	5/56	PC-r	1	1	.45	1.30	2.60
4	142	1/58	PC-r	1	1	.45	1.30	2.60
5	152	9/59	PC-r	1	1	.45	1.30	2.60
6	161	3/61	PC-r	1	1	.45	1.30	2.60
7	167	'62/63	Has orig.date; PC-r	1	1	.45	1.30	2.60
8	167	9/64	PC-r	1	1	.45	1.30	2.60
9	167	10/65	PC-r	1	1	.45	1.30	2.60
10	166	R/1968	New-c&price 25¢; PC-r; stiff-c	1	2	1.75	5.25	12.00

99. Hamlet (Used in **POP**, pg. 102)

Ed	HRN	Date	Details	A	C	Good	Fine	Mint
1	98	9/52	Original; Blum-a	1	1	2.35	7.00	16.00

CLASSICS ILLUSTRATED (continued)

Ed	HRN	Date	Details	A	C	Good	Fine	Mint
2	121	7/54	PC-r	1	1	.70	2.00	4.00
3	141	11/57	PC-r	1	1	.70	2.00	4.00
4	158	9/60	PC-r	1	1	.70	2.00	4.00
5	167	'62/63	Has orig.date; PC-r	1	1	.70	2.00	4.00
6	167	7/65	PC-r	1	1	.70	2.00	4.00
7	166	4/67	PC-r	1	1	.70	2.00	4.00
8	169	Spr/69	New-c&price 25¢; PC-r; stiff-c	1	2	1.15	3.50	8.00

100. Mutiny on the Bounty

Ed	HRN	Date	Details	A	C	Good	Fine	Mint
1	100	10/52	Original	1	1	1.50	4.50	10.00
			(Coward Shoe ad)	1	1	2.65	8.00	18.00
2	117	3/54	PC-r	1	1	.50	1.50	3.00
3	132	5/56	PC-r	1	1	.50	1.50	3.00
4	142	1/58	PC-r	1	1	.50	1.50	3.00
5	155	3/60	PC-r	1	1	.50	1.50	3.00
6	167	'62/63	Has orig.date; PC-r	1	1	.50	1.50	3.00
7	167	5/64	PC-r	1	1	.50	1.50	3.00
8	167	3/66	PC-r	1	1	.50	1.50	3.00
9	167	3/66	No # or price; (See Classics Ill. Golden Records)					
10	169	Spr/70	PC-r; stiff-c	1	1	.50	1.50	3.00

101. William Tell

Ed	HRN	Date	Details	A	C	Good	Fine	Mint
1	101	11/52	Original; Kiefer-c delBourgo-a	1	1	1.50	4.50	10.00
			(Coward Shoe ad)	1	1	2.65	8.00	18.00
2	118	4/54	PC-r	1	1	.45	1.30	3.00
3	141	11/57	PC-r	1	1	.35	1.00	2.00
4	158	9/60	PC-r	1	1	.35	1.00	2.00
5	167	'62/63	Has orig.date; PC-r	1	1	.35	1.00	2.00
6	167	11/64	PC-r	1	1	.35	1.00	2.00
7	166	4/67	PC-r	1	1	.35	1.00	2.00
8	169	Win/69	New price 25¢; stiff-c; PC-r	1	1	.50	1.50	3.00

102. The White Company

Ed	HRN	Date	Details	A	C	Good	Fine	Mint
1	101	12/52	Original; Blum-a	1	1	1.75	5.25	12.00
2	165	1962	PC-r	1	1	.85	2.50	6.00
3	167	4/64	PC-r	1	1	.85	2.50	6.00

103. Men Against the Sea (Palais-a)

Ed	HRN	Date	Details	A	C	Good	Fine	Mint
1	104	1/53	Original; Kiefer-c, Palais-a	1	1	1.75	5.25	12.00
			(Coward Shoe ad)	1	1	2.65	8.00	18.00
2	114	12/53	PC-r	1	1	.85	2.50	6.00
3	131	3/56	New-c; PC-r	1	2	.85	2.50	6.00
4	149	3/59	PC-r	1	2	.70	2.00	4.00
5	158	9/60	PC-r	1	2	.70	2.00	4.00
6	167	3/64	PC-r	1	2	.70	2.00	4.00

104. Bring 'Em Back Alive

Ed	HRN	Date	Details	A	C	Good	Fine	Mint
1	105	2/53	Original; Kiefer c/a	1	1	1.85	5.50	13.00
			(Coward Shoe ad)	1	1	3.35	10.00	23.00
2	118	4/54	PC-r	1	1	.50	1.50	3.00
3	133	7/56	PC-r	1	1	.50	1.50	3.00
4	150	5/59	PC-r	1	1	.50	1.50	3.00
5	158	9/60	PC-r	1	1	.50	1.50	3.00
6	167	10/63	PC-r	1	1	.50	1.50	3.00
7	167	9/65	PC-r	1	1	.45	1.40	2.80
8	169	Win/69	New price 25¢; stiff-c; PC-r	1	1	.50	1.50	3.00

105. From the Earth to the Moon

Ed	HRN	Date	Details	A	C	Good	Fine	Mint
1	106	3/53	Original; Blum-a	1	1	1.15	3.50	8.00
			(Coward Shoe ad)	1	1	2.50	7.50	17.50
2	118	4/54	PC-r	1	1	.40	1.20	2.40
3	132	3/56	PC-r	1	1	.40	1.20	2.40
4	141	11/57	PC-r	1	1	.40	1.20	2.40
5	146	9/58	PC-r	1	1	.40	1.20	2.40
6	156	5/60	PC-r	1	1	.40	1.20	2.40
7	167	'62/63	Has orig.date; PC-r	1	1	.40	1.20	2.40
8	167	5/64	PC-r	1	1	.40	1.20	2.40
9	167	5/65	PC-r	1	1	.40	1.20	2.40
10	166	10/67	PC-r	1	1	.40	1.20	2.40
11	169	Sm/69	New price 25¢; stiff-c; PC-r	1	1	.35	1.00	2.00
12	169	Spr/71	PC-r	1	1	.35	1.00	2.00

106. Buffalo Bill

Ed	HRN	Date	Details	A	C	Good	Fine	Mint
1	107	4/53	Orig.; delBourgo-a	1	1	1.20	3.50	8.00
2	118	4/54	PC-r	1	1	.40	1.20	2.40
3	132	3/56	PC-r	1	1	.40	1.20	2.40
4	142	1/58	PC-r	1	1	.40	1.20	2.40
5	161	3/61	PC-r	1	1	.40	1.20	2.40
6	167	3/64	PC-r	1	1	.40	1.20	2.40
7	166	7/67	PC-r	1	1	.40	1.20	2.40
8	169	Fall/69	PC-r; stiff-c	1	1	.40	1.20	2.40

107. King of the Khyber Rifles

Ed	HRN	Date	Details	A	C	Good	Fine	Mint
1	108	5/53	Original	1	1	1.15	3.50	8.00
2	118	4/54	PC-r	1	1	.40	1.20	2.40
3	146	9/58	PC-r	1	1	.40	1.20	2.40
4	158	9/60	PC-r	1	1	.40	1.20	2.40
5	167	'62/63	Has orig.date; PC-r	1	1	.40	1.20	2.40
6	167	'62/63	PC-r	1	1	.35	1.00	2.00
7	167	10/66	PC-r	1	1	.35	1.00	2.00

108. Knights of the Round Table

Ed	HRN	Date	Details	A	C	Good	Fine	Mint
1	108	6/53	Original; Blum-a	1	1	1.70	5.00	12.00
2	109	6/53	Original; Blum-a	1	1	1.75	5.00	12.00
			(Coward Shoe ad)			3.00	9.00	21.00
3	117	3/54	PC-r	1	1	.40	1.20	2.80
4	153	11/59	PC-r	1	1	.35	1.00	2.00
5	165	1962	PC-r	1	1	.35	1.00	2.00
6	167	4/64	PC-r	1	1	.35	1.00	2.00
7	166	4/67	PC-r	1	1	.35	1.00	2.00
8	169	Sm/69	New price 25¢; stiff-c; PC-r	1	1	.50	1.50	3.00

109. Pitcairn's Island

Ed	HRN	Date	Details	A	C	Good	Fine	Mint
1	110	7/53	Original; Palais-a	1	1	2.65	8.00	18.00
2	165	1962	PC-r	1	1	.50	1.50	3.00
3	167	3/64	PC-r	1	1	.50	1.50	3.00
4	166	6/67	PC-r	1	1	.50	1.50	3.00

110. A Study in Scarlet

Ed	HRN	Date	Details	A	C	Good	Fine	Mint
1	111	8/53	Original	1	1	4.65	14.00	32.00
2	165	1962	PC-r	1	1	3.00	9.00	21.00

111. The Talisman

Ed	HRN	Date	Details	A	C	Good	Fine	Mint
1	112	9/53	Original; last H.C. Kiefer-a	1	1	3.65	11.00	25.00
2	165	1962	PC-r	1	1	.50	1.50	3.00

Classics Illust. #100 (Original), © GIL

Classics Illust. #105 (HRN 167), © GIL

Classics Illust. #109 (Original), © GIL

Classics Illust. #115 (Original), © GIL

Classics Illust. #124 (HRN 167), © GIL

Classics Illust. #127 (Original), © GIL

CLASSICS ILLUSTRATED (continued)

Ed	HRN	Date	Details	A C	Good	Fine	Mint
3	167	5/64	PC-r	1 1	.50	1.50	3.00
4	166	Fall/68	New price 25¢; PC-r	1 1	.50	1.40	2.80

112. Adventures of Kit Carson

Ed	HRN	Date	Details	A C	Good	Fine	Mint
1	113	10/53	Original; Palais-a	1 1	2.65	8.00	18.00
			(Coward Shoe ad)	1 1	6.00	18.00	42.00
2	129	11/55	PC-r	1 1	.50	1.40	2.80
3	141	11/57	PC-r	1 1	.50	1.40	2.80
4	152	9/59	PC-r	1 1	.50	1.40	2.80
5	161	3/61	PC-r	1 1	.50	1.40	2.80
6	167	'62/63	PC-r	1 1	.50	1.40	2.80
7	167	2/65	PC-r	1 1	.50	1.40	2.80
8	167	5/66	PC-r	1 1	.50	1.40	2.80
9	166	Win/69	New-c&price 25¢; PC-r; stiff-c	1 2	1.15	3.50	8.00

113. The Forty-Five Guardsmen

Ed	HRN	Date	Details	A C	Good	Fine	Mint
1	114	11/53	Orig.; delBourgo-a	1 1	3.00	9.00	21.00
2	166	7/67	PC-r	1 1	1.15	3.50	8.00

114. The Red Rover

Ed	HRN	Date	Details	A C	Good	Fine	Mint
1	115	12/53	Original	1 1	3.00	9.00	21.00
2	166	7/67	PC-r	1 1	1.15	3.50	8.00

115. How I Found Livingstone

Ed	HRN	Date	Details	A C	Good	Fine	Mint
1	116	1/54	Original	1 1	2.65	8.00	18.00
2	167	1/67	PC-r	1 1	1.15	3.50	8.00

116. The Bottle Imp

Ed	HRN	Date	Details	A C	Good	Fine	Mint
1	117	2/54	Orig.; Cameron-a	1 1	3.50	10.50	24.00
2	167	1/67	PC-r	1 1	1.70	5.00	10.00

117. Captains Courageous

Ed	HRN	Date	Details	A C	Good	Fine	Mint
1	118	3/54	Orig.; Costanza-a	1 1	2.00	6.00	14.00
2	167	2/67	PC-r	1 1	.85	2.50	5.00
3	169	Fall/69	New price 25¢; stiff-c; PC-r	1 1	.70	2.00	4.00

118. Rob Roy

Ed	HRN	Date	Details	A C	Good	Fine	Mint
1	119	4/54	Original; Rudy & Walter Palais-a	1 1	3.00	9.00	21.00
2	167	2/67	PC-r	1 1	1.15	3.50	8.00

119. Soldiers of Fortune

Ed	HRN	Date	Details	A C	Good	Fine	Mint
1	120	5/54	Original Shaffenberger-a	1 1	2.65	8.00	18.00
2	166	3/67	PC-r	1 1	1.00	3.00	6.00
3	169	Spr/70	New price 25¢; stiff-c; PC-r	1 1	.70	2.00	4.00

120. The Hurricane

Ed	HRN	Date	Details	A C	Good	Fine	Mint
1	121	1954	Orig.; Cameron-a	1 1	2.00	6.00	14.00
2	166	3/67	PC-r	1 1	1.15	3.50	8.00

121. Wild Bill Hickok

Ed	HRN	Date	Details	A C	Good	Fine	Mint
1	122	7/54	Original	1 1	1.75	5.25	12.00
2	132	5/56	PC-r	1 1	.40	1.20	2.40
3	141	11/57	PC-r	1 1	.40	1.20	2.40
4	154	1/60	PC-r	1 1	.40	1.20	2.40
5	167	'62/63	PC-r	1 1	.40	1.20	2.40
6	167	8/64	PC-r	1 1	.40	1.20	2.40
7	166	4/67	PC-r	1 1	.35	1.00	2.00
8	169	Win/69	PC-r; stiff-c	1 1	.50	1.50	3.00

122. The Mutineers

Ed	HRN	Date	Details	A C	Good	Fine	Mint
1	123	9/54	Original	1 1	1.15	3.50	8.00
2	136	1/57	PC-r	1 1	.40	1.20	2.40
3	146	9/58	PC-r	1 1	.40	1.20	2.40
4	158	9/60	PC-r	1 1	.40	1.20	2.40
5	167	11/63	PC-r	1 1	.35	1.00	2.00
6	167	3/65	PC-r	1 1	.35	1.00	2.00
7	166	8/67	PC-r	1 1	.35	1.00	2.00

123. Fang and Claw

Ed	HRN	Date	Details	A C	Good	Fine	Mint
1	124	11/54	Original	1 1	1.85	5.50	13.00
2	133	7/56	PC-r	1 1	.45	1.30	2.60
3	143	3/58	PC-r	1 1	.45	1.30	2.60
4	154	1/60	PC-r	1 1	.45	1.30	2.60
5	167	'62/63	Has orig.date; PC-r	1 1	.45	1.30	2.60
6	167	9/65	PC-r	1 1	.45	1.30	2.60

124. The War of the Worlds

Ed	HRN	Date	Details	A C	Good	Fine	Mint
1	125	1/55	Orig.; Cameron c/a	1 1	1.20	3.50	8.00
2	131	3/56	PC-r	1 1	.45	1.30	2.60
3	141	11/57	PC-r	1 1	.45	1.30	2.60
4	148	1/59	PC-r	1 1	.45	1.30	2.60
5	156	5/60	PC-r	1 1	.45	1.30	2.60
6	165	1962	PC-r	1 1	.45	1.30	2.60
7	167	'62/63	PC-r	1 1	.45	1.30	2.60
8	167	11/64	PC-r	1 1	.45	1.30	2.60
9	167	11/65	PC-r	1 1	.45	1.30	2.60
10	166	R/1968	New price 25¢; PC-r	1 1	.35	1.00	2.00
11	169	Sm/70	PC-r; stiff-c	1 1	.50	1.50	3.00

125. The Ox Bow Incident

Ed	HRN	Date	Details	A C	Good	Fine	Mint
1	—	3/55	Original	1 1	1.15	3.50	8.00
2	143	3/58	PC-r	1 1	.40	1.20	2.40
3	152	9/59	PC-r	1 1	.40	1.20	2.40
4	149	3/61	PC-r	1 1	.40	1.20	2.40
5	167	'62/63	PC-r	1 1	.40	1.20	2.40
6	167	11/64	PC-r	1 1	.40	1.20	2.40
7	166	4/67	PC-r	1 1	.40	1.20	2.40
8	169	Win/69	New price 25¢; stiff-c; PC-r	1 1	.35	1.00	2.00

126. The Downfall

Ed	HRN	Date	Details	A C	Good	Fine	Mint
1	—	5/55	Orig.; 'Picture Progress' replaces reorder list; Cameron c/a	1 1	1.20	3.50	8.00
2	167	8/64	PC-r	1 1	.40	1.20	2.40
3	166	1967	PC-r	1 1	.40	1.20	2.40
4		R/1968	New price 25¢; PC-r	1 1	.40	1.20	2.40

127. The King of the Mountains

Ed	HRN	Date	Details	A C	Good	Fine	Mint
1	128	7/55	Original	1 1	1.15	3.50	8.00

CLASSICS ILLUSTRATED (continued)

Ed	HRN	Date	Details	A	C	Good	Fine	Mint
2	167	6/64	PC-r	1	1	.50	1.50	3.00
3	166	F/1968	New price 25¢; PC-r	1	1	.40	1.20	2.40

128. Macbeth (Used in **POP**, pg. 102)

Ed	HRN	Date	Details	A	C	Good	Fine	Mint
1	128	9/55	Orig.; last Blum-a	1	1	2.65	8.00	18.00
2	143	3/58	PC-r	1	1	.45	1.30	2.60
3	158	9/60	PC-r	1	1	.45	1.30	2.60
4	167	'62/63	PC-r	1	1	.45	1.30	2.60
5	167	6/64	PC-r	1	1	.45	1.30	2.60
6	166	4/67	PC-r	1	1	.45	1.30	2.60
7	166	R/1968	New Price 25¢; PC-r	1	1	.35	1.00	2.00
8	166	R/1968	Twin Circle ed.; PC-r	1	1	.35	1.00	2.00
9	169	Spr/70	Stiff-c; PC-r	1	1	.35	1.00	2.00

129. Davy Crockett

Ed	HRN	Date	Details	A	C	Good	Fine	Mint
1	129	11/55	Orig.; Cameron-a	1	1	2.35	7.00	16.00
2	167	9/66	PC-r	1	1	1.75	5.25	12.00

130. Caesar's Conquests

Ed	HRN	Date	Details	A	C	Good	Fine	Mint
1	130	1/56	Original; Orlando-a	1	1	1.20	3.50	8.00
2	142	1/58	PC-r	1	1	.40	1.20	2.40
3	152	9/59	PC-r	1	1	.40	1.20	2.40
4	149	3/61	PC-r	1	1	.40	1.20	2.40
5	167	'62/63	PC-r	1	1	.40	1.20	2.40
6	167	10/64	PC-r	1	1	.40	1.20	2.40
7	167	4/66	PC-r	1	1	.40	1.20	2.40

131. The Covered Wagon

Ed	HRN	Date	Details	A	C	Good	Fine	Mint
1	131	3/56	Original	1	1	1.20	3.50	8.00
2	143	3/58	PC-r	1	1	.40	1.20	2.40
3	152	9/59	PC-r	1	1	.40	1.20	2.40
4	158	9/60	PC-r	1	1	.40	1.20	2.40
5	167	'62/63	PC-r	1	1	.40	1.20	2.40
6	167	11/64	PC-r	1	1	.40	1.20	2.40
7	167	4/66	PC-r	1	1	.40	1.20	2.40
8	169	Win/69	New price 25¢; stiff-c; PC-r	1	1	.35	1.00	2.00

132. The Dark Frigate

Ed	HRN	Date	Details	A	C	Good	Fine	Mint
1	132	5/56	Original	1	1	1.20	3.50	8.00
2	150	5/59	PC-r	1	1	.40	1.20	2.40
3	167	1/64	PC-r	1	1	.40	1.20	2.40
4	166	5/67	PC-r	1	1	.40	1.20	2.40

133. The Time Machine

Ed	HRN	Date	Details	A	C	Good	Fine	Mint
1	132	7/56	Orig.; Cameron-a	1	1	2.00	6.00	14.00
2	142	1/58	PC-r	1	1	.60	1.80	4.20
3	152	9/59	PC-r	1	1	.60	1.80	4.20
4	158	9/60	PC-r	1	1	.60	1.80	4.20
5	167	'62/63	PC-r	1	1	.60	1.80	4.20
6	167	6/64	PC-r	1	1	.60	1.80	4.20
7	167	3/66	PC-r	1	1	.60	1.80	4.20
8	167	3/66	No # or price; (See Classics Ill. Golden Record)					
9	166	12/67	PC-r	1	1	.60	1.80	4.20
10	169	Win/71	New price 25¢; stiff-c; PC-r	1	1	.80	2.40	5.60

134. Romeo and Juliet

Ed	HRN	Date	Details	A	C	Good	Fine	Mint
1	134	9/56	Original; Evans-a	1	1	1.15	3.50	8.00
2	161	3/61	PC-r	1	1	.50	1.50	3.00
3	167	9/63	PC-r	1	1	.50	1.50	3.00
4	167	5/65	PC-r	1	1	.50	1.50	3.00
5	166	6/67	PC-r	1	1	.50	1.50	3.00
6	166	Win/69	New c&price 25¢; stiff-c; PC-r	1	2	1.75	5.25	12.00

135. Waterloo

Ed	HRN	Date	Details	A	C	Good	Fine	Mint
1	135	11/56	Orig.; G. Ingels-a	1	1	1.15	3.50	8.00
2	153	11/59	PC-r	1	1	.50	1.50	3.00
3	167	'62/63	PC-r	1	1	.50	1.50	3.00
4	167	9/64	PC-r	1	1	.50	1.50	3.00
5	166	R/1968	New price 25¢; PC-r	1	1	.50	1.50	3.00

136. Lord Jim

Ed	HRN	Date	Details	A	C	Good	Fine	Mint
1	136	1/57	Original; Evans-a	1	1	1.15	3.50	8.00
2	165	'62/63	PC-r	1	1	.50	1.50	3.00
3	167	3/64	PC-r	1	1	.50	1.50	3.00
4	167	9/66	PC-r	1	1	.50	1.50	3.00
5	169	Sm/69	New price 25¢; stiff-c; PC-r	1	1	.50	1.50	3.00

137. The Little Savage

Ed	HRN	Date	Details	A	C	Good	Fine	Mint
1	136	3/57	Original; Evans-a	1	1	1.20	3.50	8.00
2	148	1/59	PC-r	1	1	.50	1.50	3.00
3	156	5/60	PC-r	1	1	.50	1.50	3.00
4	167	'62/63	PC-r	1	1	.50	1.50	3.00
5	167	10/64	PC-r	1	1	.50	1.50	3.00
6	166	8/67	PC-r	1	1	.50	1.50	3.00
7	169	Spr/70	New price 25¢; stiff-c; PC-r	1	1	.50	1.50	3.00

138. A Journey to the Center of the Earth

Ed	HRN	Date	Details	A	C	Good	Fine	Mint
1	136	5/57	Original	1	1	1.20	3.50	8.00
2	146	9/58	PC-r	1	1	.50	1.50	3.00
3	156	5/60	PC-r	1	1	.50	1.50	3.00
4	158	9/60	PC-r	1	1	.50	1.50	3.00
5	167	'62/63	PC-r	1	1	.50	1.50	3.00
6	167	6/64	PC-r	1	1	.50	1.50	3.00
7	167	4/66	PC-r	1	1	.50	1.50	3.00
8	166	R/1968	New price 25¢; PC-r	1	1	.50	1.50	3.00

139. In the Reign of Terror

Ed	HRN	Date	Details	A	C	Good	Fine	Mint
1	139	7/57	Original; Evans-a	1	1	1.35	4.00	9.00
2	154	1/60	PC-r	1	1	.50	1.50	3.00
3	167	'62/63	Has orig.date; PC-r	1	1	.50	1.50	3.00
4	167	7/64	PC-r	1	1	.50	1.50	3.00
5	166	R/1968	New price 25¢; PC-r	1	1	.40	1.20	2.40

140. On Jungle Trails

Ed	HRN	Date	Details	A	C	Good	Fine	Mint
1	140	9/57	Original	1	1	1.15	3.50	8.00
2	150	5/59	PC-r	1	1	.50	1.50	3.00
3	160	1/61	PC-r	1	1	.50	1.50	3.00
4	167	9/63	PC-r	1	1	.50	1.50	3.00
5	167	9/65	PC-r	1	1	.50	1.50	3.00

Classics Illust. #130 (HRN 167), © GIL

Classics Illust. #133 (HRN 167), © GIL

Classics Illust. #138 (Original), © GIL

Classics Illust. #140 (HRN 160), © GIL

Classics Illust. #148 (Original), © GIL

Classics Illust. #149 (Original), © GIL

CLASSICS ILLUSTRATED (continued)

141. Castle Dangerous

Ed	HRN	Date	Details	A	C	Good	Fine	Mint
1	141	11/57	Original	1	1	1.20	3.50	8.00
2	152	9/59	PC-r	1	1	.50	1.50	3.00
3	167	'62/63	PC-r	1	1	.40	1.20	2.40
4	166	7/67	PC-r	1	1	.40	1.20	2.40

142. Abraham Lincoln

Ed	HRN	Date	Details	A	C	Good	Fine	Mint
1	142	1/58	Original	1	1	1.20	3.50	8.00
2	154	1/60	PC-r	1	1	.40	1.20	2.40
3	158	9/60	PC-r	1	1	.40	1.20	2.40
4	167	10/63	PC-r	1	1	.40	1.20	2.40
5	167	7/65	PC-r	1	1	.40	1.20	2.40
6	166	11/67	PC-r	1	1	.40	1.20	2.40
7	169	Fall/69	New price 25¢; stiff-c; PC-r	1	1	.50	1.50	3.00

143. Kim

Ed	HRN	Date	Details	A	C	Good	Fine	Mint
1	143	3/58	Original; Orlando-a	1	1	1.15	3.50	8.00
2	165	'62/63	PC-r	1	1	.40	1.20	2.40
3	167	11/63	PC-r	1	1	.40	1.20	2.40
4	167	8/65	PC-r	1	1	.40	1.20	2.40
5	169	Win/69	New price 25¢; stiff-c; PC-r	1	1	.50	1.50	3.00

144. The First Men in the Moon

Ed	HRN	Date	Details	A	C	Good	Fine	Mint
1	143	5/58	Original; Woodbridge/Williamson /Torres-a	1	1	2.00	6.00	14.00
2	153	11/59	PC-r	1	1	.50	1.50	3.00
3	161	3/61	PC-r	1	1	.50	1.50	3.00
4	167	'62/63	PC-r	1	1	.50	1.50	3.00
5	167	12/65	PC-r	1	1	.50	1.50	3.00
6	166	Fall/68	New-c&price 25¢; PC-r; stiff-c	1	2	.85	2.50	6.00
7	169	Win/69	Stiff-c; PC-r	1	2	.85	2.50	6.00

145. The Crisis

Ed	HRN	Date	Details	A	C	Good	Fine	Mint
1	143	7/58	Original; Evans-a	1	1	1.15	3.50	8.00
2	156	5/60	PC-r	1	1	.45	1.40	2.80
3	167	10/63	PC-r	1	1	.45	1.40	2.80
4	167	3/65	PC-r	1	1	.45	1.40	2.80
5	166	R/1968	New price 25¢; PC-r	1	1	.45	1.40	2.80

146. With Fire and Sword

Ed	HRN	Date	Details	A	C	Good	Fine	Mint
1	143	9/58	Original; Woodbridge-a	1	1	1.15	3.50	8.00
2	156	5/60	PC-r	1	1	.50	1.50	3.00
3	167	11/63	PC-r	1	1	.50	1.50	3.00
4	167	3/65	PC-r	1	1	.50	1.50	3.00

147. Ben-Hur

Ed	HRN	Date	Details	A	C	Good	Fine	Mint
1	147	11/58	Original; Orlando-a	1	1	1.50	4.50	10.00
2	153	11/59	PC-r	1	1	.50	1.50	3.00
3	158	9/60	PC-r	1	1	.50	1.50	3.00
4	167	'62/63	Orig.date; but PC-r	1	1	.50	1.50	3.00
5	167	———	PC-r	1	1	.50	1.50	3.00
6	167	2/65	PC-r	1	1	.50	1.50	3.00
7	167	9/66	PC-r	1	1	.50	1.50	3.00
8	166	Fall/68	New-c&price 25¢; PC-r; has both hard & soft-c	1	2	1.15	3.50	8.00

148. The Buccaneer

Ed	HRN	Date	Details	A	C	Good	Fine	Mint
1	148	1/59	Orig.; Evans/Jenny-a; Saunders-c	1	1	1.20	3.50	8.00
2	568	———	Juniors list only PC-r	1	1	.50	1.50	3.00
3	167	'62/63	PC-r	1	1	.50	1.50	3.00
4	167	9/65	PC-r	1	1	.50	1.50	3.00
5	169	Sm/69	New price 25¢; PC-r; stiff-c	1	1	.50	1.50	3.00

149. Off on a Comet

Ed	HRN	Date	Details	A	C	Good	Fine	Mint
1	149	3/59	Orig.; G.McCann-a	1	1	1.50	4.50	10.00
2	155	3/60	PC-r	1	1	.50	1.50	3.00
3	149	3/61	PC-r	1	1	.50	1.50	3.00
4	167	12/63	PC-r	1	1	.40	1.20	2.40
5	167	2/65	PC-r	1	1	.40	1.20	2.40
6	167	10/66	PC-r	1	1	.40	1.20	2.40
7	166	Fall/68	New-c&price 25¢; PC-r	1	2	1.15	3.50	8.00

150. The Virginian

Ed	HRN	Date	Details	A	C	Good	Fine	Mint
1	150	5/59	Original	1	1	1.75	5.25	12.00
2	164	1961	PC-r	1	1	.50	1.50	3.00
3	167	'62/63	PC-r	1	1	.50	1.50	3.00
4	167	12/65	PC-r	1	1	.50	1.50	3.00

151. Won By the Sword

Ed	HRN	Date	Details	A	C	Good	Fine	Mint
1	150	7/59	Original	1	1	1.75	5.25	12.00
2	164	1961	PC-r	1	1	.70	2.00	4.00
3	167	10/63	PC-r	1	1	.70	2.00	4.00
4	167	1963	PC-r	1	1	.70	2.00	4.00
5	166	7/67	PC-r	1	1	.70	2.00	4.00

152. Wild Animals I Have Known

Ed	HRN	Date	Details	A	C	Good	Fine	Mint
1	152	9/59	Orig.; L.B. Cole c/a	1	1	1.85	5.50	13.00
2	149	3/61	PC-r	1	1	.70	2.00	4.00
3	167	9/63	PC-r	1	1	.50	1.50	3.00
4	167	8/65	PC-r	1	1	.50	1.50	3.00
5	169	Fall/69	New price 25¢; stiff-c; PC-r	1	1	.50	1.50	3.00

153. The Invisible Man

Ed	HRN	Date	Details	A	C	Good	Fine	Mint
1	153	11/59	Original	1	1	1.15	3.50	8.00
2	149	3/61	PC-r	1	1	.50	1.50	3.00
3	167	'62/63	PC-r	1	1	.50	1.50	3.00
4	167	2/65	PC-r	1	1	.50	1.50	3.00
5	167	9/66	PC-r	1	1	.50	1.50	3.00
6	166	Win/69	New price 25¢; PC-r; stiff-c	1	1	.35	1.00	2.00
7	169	Spr/71	Stiff-c; letters spelling 'Invisible Man' are 'solid' not 'invisible;' PC-r	1	1	.35	1.00	2.00

154. The Conspiracy of Pontiac

Ed	HRN	Date	Details	A	C	Good	Fine	Mint
1	154	1/60	Original	1	1	1.50	4.50	10.00
2	167	11/63	PC-r	1	1	.85	2.50	5.00
3	167	7/64	PC-r	1	1	.85	2.50	5.00
4	166	12/67	PC-r	1	1	.85	2.50	5.00

155. The Lion of the North

Ed	HRN	Date	Details	A	C	Good	Fine	Mint
1	154	3/60	Original	1	1	1.15	3.50	8.00
2	167	1/64	PC-r	1	1	.70	2.00	4.00
3	166	R/1967	New price 25¢; PC-r	1	1	.70	2.00	4.00

156. The Conquest of Mexico

Ed	HRN	Date	Details	A	C	Good	Fine	Mint
1	156	5/60	Orig.; Bruno Premiani-a&c	1	1	1.50	4.50	10.00
2	167	1/64	PC-r	1	1	.50	1.50	3.00
3	166	8/67	PC-r	1	1	.50	1.50	3.00
4	169	Spr/70	New price 25¢; stiff-c; PC-r	1	1	.35	1.00	2.00

157. Lives of the Hunted

Ed	HRN	Date	Details	A	C	Good	Fine	Mint
1	156	7/60	Orig.; L.B. Cole-c	1	1	1.70	5.00	12.00
2	167	2/64	PC-r	1	1	.85	2.50	6.00
3	166	10/67	PC-r	1	1	.85	2.50	6.00

158. The Conspirators

Ed	HRN	Date	Details	A	C	Good	Fine	Mint
1	156	9/60	Original	1	1	1.75	5.25	12.00
2	167	7/64	PC-r	1	1	.85	2.50	6.00
3	166	10/67	PC-r	1	1	.85	2.50	6.00

159. The Octopus

Ed	HRN	Date	Details	A	C	Good	Fine	Mint
1	159	11/60	Orig.; Gray Morrow & Evans-a; L.B. Cole-c	1	1	1.50	4.50	10.00
2	167	2/64	PC-r	1	1	.70	2.00	4.00
3	166	R/1967	New price 25; PC-r	1	1	.50	1.50	3.00

160. The Food of the Gods

Ed	HRN	Date	Details	A	C	Good	Fine	Mint
1	159	1/61	Original	1	1	1.50	4.50	10.00
2	160	1/61	Original; same, except for HRN	1	1	1.50	4.50	10.00
3	167	1/64	PC-r	1	1	.70	2.00	4.00
4	166	6/67	PC-r	1	1	.70	2.00	4.00

161. Cleopatra

Ed	HRN	Date	Details	A	C	Good	Fine	Mint
1	161	3/61	Original	1	1	2.00	6.00	14.00
2	167	1/64	PC-r	1	1	1.15	3.50	8.00
3	166	8/67	PC-r	1	1	1.15	3.50	8.00

162. Robur the Conqueror

Ed	HRN	Date	Details	A	C	Good	Fine	Mint
1	162	5/61	Original	1	1	1.50	4.50	10.00
2	167	7/64	PC-r	1	1	.85	2.50	6.00
3	166	8/67	PC-r	1	1	.85	2.50	6.00

163. Master of the World

Ed	HRN	Date	Details	A	C	Good	Fine	Mint
1	163	7/61	Original; Gray Morrow-a	1	1	1.50	4.50	10.00
2	167	1/65	PC-r	1	1	.70	2.00	4.00
3	166	R/1968	New price 25¢; PC-r	1	1	.70	2.00	4.00

164. The Cossack Chief

Ed	HRN	Date	Details	A	C	Good	Fine	Mint
1	164	(1961)	Original; undated	1	1	1.75	5.25	12.00
2	167	4/65	PC-r	1	1	.85	2.50	6.00
3	166	Fall/68	New price 25¢ PC-r	1	1	.85	2.50	6.00

165. The Queen's Necklace

Ed	HRN	Date	Details	A	C	Good	Fine	Mint
1	164	1/62	Original; Morrow-a	1	1	1.75	5.25	12.00
2	167	4/65	PC-r	1	1	.85	2.50	6.00
3	166	Fall/68	New price 25¢; PC-r	1	1	.85	2.50	6.00

166. Tigers and Traitors

Ed	HRN	Date	Details	A	C	Good	Fine	Mint
1	165	5/62	Original	1	1	2.00	6.00	14.00
2	167	2/64	PC-r	1	1	.85	2.50	6.00
3	166	11/66	PC-r	1	1	.85	2.50	6.00

167. Faust

Ed	HRN	Date	Details	A	C	Good	Fine	Mint
1	165	8/62	Original	1	1	4.65	14.00	32.00
2	167	2/64	PC-r	1	1	2.00	6.00	14.00
3	166	6/67	PC-r	1	1	2.00	6.00	14.00

168. In Freedom's Cause

Ed	HRN	Date	Details	A	C	Good	Fine	Mint
1	169	Win/69	Original; Evans/ Crandall-a; stiff-c	1	1	3.00	9.00	21.00

169. Negro Americans—The Early Years

Ed	HRN	Date	Details	A	C	Good	Fine	Mint
1	166	Spr/69	Orig. & last issue; Stiff-c	1	1	4.65	14.00	32.00
2	169	Spr/69	Stiff-c	1	1	3.50	10.50	24.00

NEWSPAPER CLASSICS—Newspaper Classics are simlar to the Spirit sections and were issued for one year, from 3/30/47 to 3/21/48, and were printed in such newspapers as the New York Post and Chicago Sun. Each section contained 16 reduced comic book pages. These are very rare, and are very significant because they predate the original comic book editions by as much as three years, and contain 64 pages of text of Classics titles that were issued with 48 pages. Though all Classics from No. 45 on were issued with 48 pages, they were originally prepared with more pages. These newspaper sections contain those deleted pages. The newspaper section had a small logo—''Illustrated CLASSIC'' at the top, along with the book title. The only variation was the St. Louis Post-Dispatch edition, which had a large logo ''ACTION and Adventure Series,'' and was arranged in a different strip format (the word ''ACTION'' looks similar to the comic book logo). The last five titles were converted over to a strip format in all the newspapers, differing from the comic book format. These are rarely offered for sale, so the market is still trying to find itself. But here is the basic range I have observed them selling in:

Cl#	Section	Date	Good	Fine	Mint
#46	1 of 4	3/30/47	3.35	10.00	23.00
	2 of 4	4/06/47	3.00	9.00	21.00
	3 of 4	4/13/47	3.00	9.00	21.00
	4 of 4	4/20/47	3.00	9.00	21.00
#47	1 of 4	4/27/47	3.00	9.00	21.00
	2 of 4	5/04/47	3.00	9.00	21.00
	3 of 4	5/11/47	3.00	9.00	21.00
	4 of 4	5/18/47	3.00	9.00	21.00

Classics Illust. #161 (HRN 167), © GIL

Classics Illust. #162 (HRN 167), © GIL

Classics Illust. #166 (HRN 167), © GIL

Classics Illust. Giants, © GIL

Classics Illust. Jr. #507, © GIL

Classics Illust. Jr. #522, © GIL

NEWSPAPER CLASSICS (continued)

			Good	Fine	Mint
#48	1 of 4	5/25/47	3.00	9.00	21.00
	2 of 4	6/01/47	3.00	9.00	21.00
	3 of 4	6/08/47	3.00	9.00	21.00
	4 of 4	6/15/47	3.00	9.00	21.00
#49	1 of 4	6/22/47	3.65	11.00	26.00
	2 of 4	6/29/47	3.65	11.00	26.00
	3 of 4	7/06/47	3.65	11.00	26.00
	4 of 4	7/13/47	3.65	11.00	26.00
#51	1 of 4	7/20/47	3.00	9.00	21.00
	2 of 4	7/27/47	3.00	9.00	21.00
	3 of 4	8/03/47	3.00	9.00	21.00
	4 of 4	8/10/47	3.00	9.00	21.00
#50	1 of 4	8/17/47	3.00	9.00	21.00
	2 of 4	8/24/47	3.00	9.00	21.00
	3 of 4	8/31/47	3.00	9.00	21.00
	4 of 4	9/07/47	3.00	9.00	21.00
#52	1 of 4	9/14/47	3.00	9.00	21.00
	2 of 4	9/21/47	3.00	9.00	21.00
	3 of 4	9/28/47	3.00	9.00	21.00
	4 of 4	10/05/47	3.00	9.00	21.00
#68	1 of 4	10/12/47	3.00	9.00	21.00
	2 of 4	10/19/47	3.00	9.00	21.00
	3 of 4	10/26/47	3.00	9.00	21.00
	4 of 4	11/02/47	3.00	9.00	21.00
#55	1 of 4	11/09/47	3.00	9.00	21.00
	2 of 4	11/16/47	3.00	9.00	21.00
	3 of 4	11/23/47	3.00	9.00	21.00
	4 of 4	11/30/47	3.00	9.00	21.00
#53	1 of 3	12/07/47	4.00	12.00	28.00
	2 of 3	12/14/47	4.00	12.00	28.00
	3 of 3	12/21/47	4.00	12.00	28.00
#75	1 of 4	12/28/47	3.35	10.00	23.00
	2 of 4	1/04/48	3.35	10.00	23.00
	3 of 4	1/11/48	3.35	10.00	23.00
	4 of 4	1/18/48	3.35	10.00	23.00
#54	1 of 4	1/25/48	3.65	11.00	26.00
	2 of 4	2/01/48	3.65	11.00	26.00
	3 of 4	2/08/48	3.65	11.00	26.00
	4 of 4	2/15/48	3.65	11.00	26.00
#56	1 of 4	2/22/48	4.00	12.00	28.00
	2 of 4	2/29/48	4.00	12.00	28.00
	3 of 4	3/07/48	4.00	12.00	28.00
	4 of 4	3/14/48	4.00	12.00	28.00
#92	1 of 1	3/21/48	11.00	33.00	77.00

Note: St. Louis Post-Dispatch sections worth 50% more than above.
* Listing researched and contributed by Dan Malan.

CLASSIC COMICS LIBRARY GIFT BOX (Later boxes titled Classics Illustrated . . .)

These Gift Boxes first appeared in November 1943. They were (at least according to the advertising) designed with the boys in the service in mind. The buyer was told that "the boys relax with Classic Comics." The boxes held five Classics. They began to sell for 50¢ and ceased publication at a price of 79¢. The earlier series is worth more and are more colorful.

Classic Comics boxes:

	Good	Fine	Mint
Box A,B,C,D	40.00	120.00	280.00
1952 Christmas Box: held No. 64,76,82 & 98 (reprints)	35.00	105.00	245.00

NOTE: *These boxes were priced at 50¢. Box A held reprints of No. 1-5; Box B-No. 6-10; Box C-No. 11-15; & Box D-No. 16-20.*

Classics Illustrated boxes:

	Good	Fine	Mint
Boxes with 59¢ price	30.00	90.00	210.00
Boxes with 69¢ price	24.00	72.00	168.00
Boxes with 79¢ price	24.00	72.00	168.00

NOTE: *Condition of box should be graded, also.*

CLASSICS ILLUSTRATED LIBRARY GIFT BOX (See Classics Comics . . .)

CLASSICS ILLUSTRATED EDUCATIONAL SERIES
1951; 1953 (16 pages, giveaway)
Gilberton Corp.

	Good	Fine	Mint
1-Shelter Through the Ages (Ruberoid Co.)(1951; 15 cents) Kiefer-a (with & without Ruberoid ad)	21.00	62.00	145.00
nn-The Westinghouse Story-The Dreams of a Man (Westinghouse Co.-1953) H. C. Kiefer-a (Scarce)	23.00	70.00	160.00

CLASSICS ILLUSTRATED GIANTS
February, 1948 (One-Shots - "OS")
Gilberton Publications

These Giant Editions were on sale for two years, beginning in 1948. They were 50¢ on the newsstand and 60¢ by mail. They are actually four classics in one volume. All the stories are reprints of the Classics Illustrated Series.

	Good	Fine	Mint
"An Illustrated Library of Great Adventure Stories" - reprints of No. 6,7,8,10 (Rare); Kiefer-c	50.00	150.00	350.00
"An Illustrated Library of Exciting Mystery Stories" - reprints of No. 30,21,40,13 (Rare)	55.00	165.00	385.00
"An Illustrated Library of Great Indian Stories" - reprints of No. 4,17, 22,37 (Rare)	47.00	141.00	330.00

CLASSICS ILLUSTRATED "GOLDEN RECORDS GREAT LITERATURE SERIES" ($2.49 retail for comic and record)
Mar, 1966 (All issues) (Record with comic sets)
Gilberton (Comics)/A. A. Records (Records)

SLP-189: Black Beauty, SLP-190: Mutiny on the Bounty, SLP-191: The Time Machine, SLP-192: The Call of the Wild

	Good	Fine	Mint
Comic only	1.35	4.00	8.00
Comic & Record . . . . each			70.00

NOTE: *Comics are all dated 3/66 and the last reorder number on the back is 167.*

CLASSICS ILLUSTRATED JUNIOR
Oct, 1953 - Spring, 1971
Famous Authors Ltd. (Gilberton Publications)

Original editions have ad for the next issue. Reprints are worth 50 per cent less than originals. Prices listed are for originals.

	Good	Fine	Mint
501-Snow White & the Seven Dwarfs; Alex Blum-a	8.00	24.00	56.00
502-The Ugly Duckling	4.50	13.50	31.00
503-Cinderella	1.75	5.25	12.00
504-The Pied Piper	1.15	3.50	8.00
505-The Sleeping Beauty	1.15	3.50	8.00
506-The Three Little Pigs	1.15	3.50	8.00
507-Jack & the Beanstalk	1.50	4.50	10.00
508-Goldilocks & the Three Bears	1.15	3.50	8.00
509-Beauty and the Beast	1.50	4.50	10.00
510-Little Red Riding Hood	1.50	4.50	10.00
511-Puss-N-Boots	1.15	3.50	8.00
512-Rumpel Stiltskin	1.50	4.50	10.00
513-Pinocchio	3.50	10.50	24.00
514-The Steadfast Tin Soldier	4.00	12.00	28.00
515-Johnny Appleseed	1.50	4.50	10.00
516-Aladdin and His Lamp	4.00	12.00	28.00
517-The Emperor's New Clothes	1.50	4.50	10.00
518-The Golden Goose	1.30	4.00	9.00
519-Paul Bunyan	1.15	3.50	8.00
520-Thumbelina	2.00	6.00	14.00
521-King of the Golden River	1.50	4.50	10.00
522-The Nightingale	1.50	4.50	10.00
523-The Gallant Tailor	1.15	3.50	8.00
524-The Wild Swans	1.15	3.50	8.00
525-The Little Mermaid	1.15	3.50	8.00
526-The Frog Prince	1.50	4.50	10.00
527-The Golden-Haired Giant	1.15	3.50	8.00
528-The Penny Prince	1.15	3.50	8.00
529-The Magic Servants	1.15	3.50	8.00
530-The Golden Bird	1.15	3.50	8.00

CLASSICS ILLUSTRATED JR. (cont'd.)

	Good	Fine	Mint
531-Rapunzel	1.50	4.50	10.00
532-The Dancing Princesses	1.15	3.50	8.00
533-The Magic Fountain	1.15	3.50	8.00
534-The Golden Touch	1.15	3.50	8.00
535-The Wizard of Oz	3.35	10.00	24.00
535-Twin Circle edition	7.00	21.00	50.00
536-The Chimney Sweep	1.15	3.50	8.00
537-The Three Fairies	1.15	3.50	8.00
538-Silly Hans	1.15	3.50	8.00
539-The Enchanted Fish	3.00	9.00	21.00
540-The Tinder-Box	5.50	16.50	38.00
541-Snow White & Rose Red	1.30	4.00	9.00
542-The Donkey's Tale	2.65	8.00	18.00
543-The House in the Woods	1.00	3.00	7.00
544-The Golden Fleece	3.50	10.50	24.00
545-The Glass Mountain	1.30	4.00	9.00
546-The Elves & the Shoemaker	2.00	6.00	14.00
547-The Wishing Table	1.00	3.00	7.00
548-The Magic Pitcher	1.00	3.00	7.00
549-Simple Kate	1.00	3.00	7.00
550-The Singing Donkey	1.00	3.00	7.00
551-The Queen Bee	1.00	3.00	7.00
552-The Three Little Dwarfs	2.65	8.00	18.00
553-King Thrushbeard	1.00	3.00	7.00
554-The Enchanted Deer	1.00	3.00	7.00
555-The Three Golden Apples	1.00	3.00	7.00
556-The Elf Mound	1.00	3.00	7.00
557-Silly Willy	.75	2.25	5.00
558-The Magic Dish; L.B. Cole-c	1.00	3.00	7.00
559-The Japanese Lantern; 1 pg. Ingels-a; L.B. Cole-c	3.00	9.00	21.00
560-The Doll Princess; L.B. Cole-c	1.00	3.00	7.00
561-Hans Humdrum; L.B. Cole-c	1.00	3.00	7.00
562-The Enchanted Pony; L.B. Cole-c	2.00	6.00	14.00
563-The Wishing Well; L.B. Cole-c	1.30	4.00	9.00
564-The Salt Mountain; L.B. Cole-c	1.00	3.00	7.00
565-The Silly Princess; L.B. Cole-c	1.30	4.00	9.00
566-Clumsy Hans; L.B. Cole-c	1.00	3.00	7.00
567-The Bearskin Soldier; L.B. Cole-c	1.00	3.00	7.00
568-The Happy Hedgehog; L.B. Cole-c	1.30	4.00	9.00
569-The Three Giants	1.00	3.00	7.00
570-The Pearl Princess	.75	2.25	5.00
571-How Fire Came to the Indians	1.15	3.50	8.00
572-The Drummer Boy	.85	2.50	6.00
573-The Crystal Ball	.75	2.25	5.00
574-Brightboots	.75	2.25	5.00
575-The Fearless Prince	1.00	3.00	7.00
576-The Princess Who Saw Everything	1.50	4.50	10.00
577-The Runaway Dumpling	4.50	13.50	31.00

NOTE: *Last reprint - Spring, 1971.* ***Costanza & Shaffenberger*** *art in many issues.*

CLASSICS ILLUSTRATED SPECIAL ISSUE
Dec, 1955 - July, 1962 (100 pages) (35 cents)
Gilberton Co. (Came out semi-annually)

	Good	Fine	Mint
129-The Story of Jesus (titled ...Special Edition) "Jesus on Mountain" cover	2.35	7.00	16.00
"Three Camels" cover(12/58)	4.35	13.00	30.00
"Mountain" cover (1968 re-issue; has black 50 cent circle)	.75	2.25	5.00
132A-The Story of America (6/56)	2.00	6.00	14.00
135A-The Ten Commandments(12/56)	3.35	10.00	23.00
138A-Adventures in Science(6/57)	2.75	8.00	18.00
141A-The Rough Rider (Teddy Roosevelt)(12/57)	1.15	3.50	8.00
144A-Blazing the Trails West(6/58)- 73 pages of Crandall/Evans plus Severin-a	1.15	3.50	8.00
147A-Crossing the Rockies(12/58)-Crandall/Evans-a	3.00	9.00	21.00
150A-Royal Canadian Police(6/59)-Ingels, Sid Check-a	3.50	10.50	24.00
153A-Men, Guns & Cattle(12/59)-Evans-a, 26 pgs.	3.00	9.00	21.00
156A-The Atomic Age(6/60)-Crandall/Evans, Torres-a	2.00	6.00	14.00
159A-Rockets, Jets and Missiles(12/60)-Evans, Morrow-a	2.35	7.00	16.00
162A-War Between the States(6/61)-Kirby & Crandall/Evans-a	3.00	9.00	21.00
165A-To the Stars(12/61)-Torres, Crandall/Evans, Kirby-a	2.65	8.00	18.00
166A-World War II('62)-Torres, Crandall/Evans, Kirby-a	2.35	7.00	16.00
167A-Prehistoric World(7/62)-Torres & Crandall/Evans-a	3.65	11.00	25.00
nn Special Issue-The United Nations (50 cents); (Scarce)-Not Williamson-a (1960)	13.00	40.00	90.00

NOTE: *158A appeared as DC's Showcase No. 43, "Dr. No" and was only published in Great Britain as 158A with different cover.*

CLASSICS LIBRARY (See King Classics)

CLASSIC X-MEN
Sept, 1986 - Present
Marvel Comics Group

	Good	Fine	Mint
1-Begins-r of New X-Men	.45	1.25	2.50
2-4	.30	.90	1.80
5,6	.25	.75	1.50

CLAW THE UNCONQUERED (See Cancelled Comic Cavalcade)
5-6/75 - No. 9, 9-10/76; No. 10, 4-5/78 - No. 12, 8-9/78
National Periodical Publications/DC Comics

	Good	Fine	Mint
1		.50	1.00
2,3: 3-Nudity panel		.40	.80
4-12: 9-Origin		.25	.50

NOTE: ***Giffen*** *a-8-12p.* ***Kubert*** *c-10-12.* ***Layton*** *a-9i, 12i.*

CLAY CODY, GUNSLINGER
Fall, 1957
Pines Comics

	Good	Fine	Mint
1	1.15	3.50	8.00

CLEAN FUN, STARRING "SHOOGAFOOTS JONES"
1944 (24 pgs.; B&W; oversized covers) (10 cents)
Specialty Book Co.

	Good	Fine	Mint
Humorous situations involving Negroes in the Deep South			
White cover issue....	2.75	8.00	16.00
Dark grey cover issue....	3.00	9.00	18.00

CLEMENTINA THE FLYING PIG (See Dell Jr. Treasury)

CLEOPATRA (See Ideal, a Classical Comic No. 1)

CLIFF MERRITT SETS THE RECORD STRAIGHT
Giveaway (2 different issues)
Brotherhood of Railroad Trainsmen

	Good	Fine	Mint
...and the Very Candid Candidate by Al Williamson	.40	1.20	2.40
...Sets the Record Straight by Al Williamson (2 diff.-c: one by Williamson, the other by McWilliams)	.40	1.20	2.40

CLIFFORD MCBRIDE'S IMMORTAL NAPOLEON AND UNCLE ELBY
1932 (12x17"; softcover cartoon book)
The Castle Press

	Good	Fine	Mint
Intro. by Don Herod	5.00	15.00	35.00

Classics Illust. Jr. #569, © GIL

Classics Ill. Special Issue #150A, © GIL

Classic X-Men #1, © MCG

Cloak and Dagger #4 (1/84), © MCG

Clue #6, © HILL

Code Name: Danger #1, © Lodestone

CLIMAX!
July, 1955 - No. 2, Sept, 1955
Gillmor Magazines

	Good	Fine	Mint
1,2 (Mystery)	3.50	10.50	24.00

CLINT (Also see Adolescent Radioactive. . .)
Sept, 1986 - No. 2, Oct, 1986 ($1.50, B&W)
Eclipse Comics

	Good	Fine	Mint
1,2	.25	.75	1.50

CLINT & MAC (See 4-Color No. 889)

CLOAK AND DAGGER
Fall, 1952
Ziff-Davis Publishing Co.

	Good	Fine	Mint
1-Saunders painted-c	9.50	28.50	66.00

CLOAK AND DAGGER
Oct, 1983 - No. 4, Jan, 1984 (Mini-series)
Marvel Comics Group

	Good	Fine	Mint
1-Austin c/a(i) in all	.25	.75	1.50
2-4: 4-Origin		.50	1.00

CLOAK AND DAGGER
July, 1985 - No. 11, Jan, 1987
Marvel Comics Group

	Good	Fine	Mint
1	.25	.75	1.50
2-10		.50	1.00
11 ($1.25)		.60	1.25

CLOSE SHAVES OF PAULINE PERIL, THE
June, 1970 - No. 4, March, 1971
Gold Key

	Good	Fine	Mint
1	1.00	3.00	6.00
2-4	.70	2.00	4.00

CLOWN COMICS (No. 1 titled Clown Comic Book)
1945 - No. 3, Wint, 1946
Clown Comics/Home Comics/Harvey Publ.

	Good	Fine	Mint
nn	3.00	9.00	21.00
2,3	1.75	5.25	12.00

CLUBHOUSE PRESENTS
June, 1956
Sussex Publ. Co./Magazine Enterprises

	Good	Fine	Mint
1	1.30	4.00	9.00

CLUBHOUSE RASCALS
June, 1956 - No. 2, Oct, 1956
Sussex Publ. Co. (Magazine Enterprises)

	Good	Fine	Mint
1,2: 2-The Brain app.	1.30	4.00	9.00

CLUB "16"
June, 1948 - No. 4, Dec, 1948
Famous Funnies

	Good	Fine	Mint
1	3.50	10.50	24.00
2-4	1.75	5.25	12.00

CLUE COMICS (Real Clue Crime V2No.4 on)
Jan, 1943 - No. 15(V2No.3), May, 1947
Hillman Periodicals

	Good	Fine	Mint
1-Origin The Boy King, Nightmare, Micro-Face, Twilight, & Zippo	30.00	90.00	210.00
2	17.00	51.00	120.00
3	13.00	40.00	90.00
4	10.00	30.00	70.00
5	8.50	25.50	60.00
6,8,9	6.50	19.50	45.00
7-Classic torture-c	8.50	25.50	60.00
10-Origin The Gun Master	6.50	19.50	45.00
11	4.50	13.50	31.00
12-Origin Rackman	6.50	19.50	45.00
V2No.1-Nightro new origin; Iron Lady app.; Simon & Kirby-a	8.00	24.00	56.00
V2No.2-S&K-a(2)-Bondage/torture-c; man attacks & kills people with electric iron. Infantino-a	9.00	28.00	62.00
V2No.3-S&K-a(3)	9.00	28.00	62.00

CLUTCHING HAND, THE
July-Aug, 1954
American Comics Group

	Good	Fine	Mint
1	6.00	18.00	42.00

CLYDE BEATTY
October, 1953 (84 pages)
Commodore Productions

	Good	Fine	Mint
1	7.00	21.00	50.00
. . .African Jungle Book('53)-Richfield Oil Co. giveaway	4.00	12.00	28.00

CLYDE CRASHCUP (TV)
Aug-Oct, 1963 - No. 5, Sept-Nov, 1964
Dell Publishing Co.

	Good	Fine	Mint
1-All written by John Stanley	2.35	7.00	16.00
2-5	1.75	5.25	12.00

C-M-O COMICS
1942
Chicago Mail Order Co.

	Good	Fine	Mint
1-Invisible Terror, Super Ann, & Plymo the Rubber Man app. (All Centaur costume heroes)	5.00	15.00	35.00
2-Invisible Terror, Super Ann app.	4.00	12.00	28.00

COCOMALT BIG BOOK OF COMICS
1938 (Regular size; full color; 52 pgs.)
Harry 'A' Chesler (Cocomalt Premium)

	Good	Fine	Mint
1-(Scarce)-Biro-c/a; Little Nemo by Winsor McCay Jr., Dan Hastings; Guardineer, Jack Cole, Gustavson, Bob Wood-a	40.00	120.00	280.00

CODA
1986 - Present (B&W)
Coda Publishing

	Good	Fine	Mint
1	.35	1.00	2.00

CODE NAME: ASSASSIN (See First Issue Special)

CODENAME: DANGER
Aug, 1985 - No. 2? ($1.50 cover)
Lodestone Publ.

	Good	Fine	Mint
1,2	.25	.75	1.50

CODE NAME: TOMAHAWK
Sept, 1986 - No. 12 (mini-series, color, $1.75)
Fantasy General Comics

	Good	Fine	Mint
1-Sci/fic	.30	.85	1.70

CODY OF THE PONY EXPRESS (See Colossal Features Magazine)
Sept, 1950 - No. 3, Jan, 1951
Fox Features Syndicate

	Good	Fine	Mint
1-3 (actually No. 3-5)	3.50	10.50	24.00

CODY OF THE PONY EXPRESS (Buffalo Bill. . .) (Outlaws of the West No. 11 on; Formerly Bullseye) (See Colossal Features Magazine)
No. 8, Oct, 1955; No. 9, Jan, 1956; No. 10, June, 1956
Charlton Comics

CODY OF THE PONY EXPRESS (continued)

	Good	Fine	Mint
8-Bullseye on splash pg; not S&K-a	2.00	6.00	14.00
9,10	1.30	4.00	9.00

CO-ED ROMANCES
November, 1951
P. L. Publishing Co.

1	2.00	6.00	14.00

COLD-BLOODED CHAMELEON COMMANDOS
Aug, 1986 - Present ($1.50, B&W)
Blackthorne Publ.

1-Origin	.30	.90	1.80
2	.25	.75	1.50

COLLECTORS ITEM CLASSICS (See Marvel Collectors Item Classics)

COLOSSAL FEATURES MAGAZINE (Formerly I Loved) (See Cody of the Pony Express)
No. 33, May, 1950 - No. 34, July, 1950; No. 3, Sept, 1950
Fox Features Syndicate

33,34-Cody of the Pony Express begins (based on serial). 34-Photo-c	4.00	12.00	28.00
3-Authentic criminal cases	3.75	11.25	26.00

COLOSSAL SHOW, THE (TV)
October, 1969
Gold Key

1	1.35	4.00	9.00

COLOSSUS COMICS (Also see Green Giant & Motion Pic. Fun. Wkly)
March, 1940
Sun Publications (Funnies, Inc.?)

1-(Scarce)-Tulpa of Tsang (hero); Colossus app.	70.00	210.00	490.00

NOTE: *Cover by artist that drew Colossus in Green Giant Comics.*

COLT .45 (TV)
No. 924, 8/58 - No. 1058, 11-1/59-60; No. 4, 2-4/60 - No. 9, 5-7/61
Dell Publishing Co.

4-Color 924-Wayde Preston photo-c on all	3.50	10.50	24.00
4-Color 1004,1058; No. 4,5,7-9	2.65	8.00	18.00
6-Toth-a	3.50	10.50	24.00

COLT SPECIAL
Sum, 1985 ($2.00; B&W)
Americomics

1	.35	1.00	2.00

COLUMBIA COMICS
1943
William H. Wise Co.

1-Joe Palooka, Charlie Chan, Capt. Yank, Sparky Watts, Dixie Dugan begin	9.50	28.50	66.00
2-4	5.50	16.50	38.00

COMANCHE (See 4-Color No. 1350)

COMANCHEROS, THE (See 4-Color No. 1300)

COMBAT
June, 1952 - No. 11, April, 1953
Atlas Comics (ANC)

1	2.65	8.00	18.00
2	1.20	3.50	8.00
3,5-9,11	1.00	3.00	7.00
4-Krigstein-a	2.00	6.00	14.00
10-B&W and color illos. in **POP**	2.00	6.00	14.00

NOTE: *Combat Casey in 7,8,10,11.* ***Heath*** *c-1.* ***Maneely*** *a-1.* ***Pakula*** *a-1.* ***Reinman*** *a-1.*

COMBAT
Oct-Nov, 1961 - No. 40, Oct, 1973 (no No.9)
Dell Publishing Co.

	Good	Fine	Mint
1	1.35	4.00	8.00
2-5	.70	2.00	4.00
6,7,8(4-6/63), 8(7-9/63)	.45	1.25	2.50
10-27		.50	1.00
28-40(reprints No. 1-14)		.30	.60

NOTE: ***Glanzman*** *c/a-1-27.*

COMBAT CASEY (Formerly War Combat)
No. 6, Jan, 1953 - No. 34, July, 1957
Atlas Comics (SAI)

6 (Indicia shows 1/52 in error)	2.35	7.00	16.00
7-Spanking panel	2.65	8.00	18.00
8-Used in **POP**, pg. 94	1.70	5.00	12.00
9	1.00	3.00	7.00
10,13-16,18,19-Violent art by R. Q. Sale; Battle Brady x-over No.10	1.35	4.00	9.00
11,12,20-Last Precode (2/55)	.70	2.00	5.00
17-R. Q. Sale-a	1.70	5.00	12.00
21-34	.70	2.00	5.00

NOTE: ***Everett*** *a-6.* ***Heath*** *c-10, 17, 30.* ***Powell*** *a-29(5), 30(5), 34.* ***Severin*** *c-26, 33.*

COMBAT KELLY
Nov, 1951 - No. 44, Aug, 1957
Atlas Comics (SPI)

1-Heath-a	4.35	13.00	30.00
2	2.00	6.00	14.00
3-10	1.35	4.00	9.00
11-Used in **POP**, pages 94,95 plus color illo.	2.00	6.00	14.00
12-Color illo. in **POP**	2.00	6.00	14.00
13-16	.70	2.00	5.00
17-Violent art by R. Q. Sale; Combat Casey app.	2.00	6.00	14.00
18-20,22-44: 18-Battle Brady app. 28-Last precode (1/55). 38-Green Berets story(8/56)	.85	2.50	6.00
21-Transvestite-c	1.50	4.50	10.00

NOTE: ***Berg*** *a-12-14, 16, 17, 19-23, 25, 26, 28, 31-36, 42-44.* ***Colan*** *a-42.* ***Severin*** *c-42.* ***Whitney*** *a-5.*

COMBAT KELLY (and the Deadly Dozen)
June, 1972 - No. 9, Oct, 1973
Marvel Comics Group

1-Intro. Combat Kelly; Mooney-a		.40	.80
2-9		.30	.60

COMBINED OPERATIONS (See The Story of the Commandos)

COMEDY CARNIVAL
no date (1950's) (100 pages)
St. John Publishing Co.

nn-Contains rebound St. John comics	9.00	27.00	62.00

COMEDY COMICS (1st Series) (Daring Mystery No. 1-8) (Margie No. 35 on)
No. 9, April, 1942 - No. 34, Fall, 1946
Timely Comics (TCI 9,10)

9-(Scarce)-The Fin by Everett, Capt. Dash, Citizen V, & The Silver Scorpion app.; Wolverton-a; 1st app. Comedy Kid; satire on Hitler & Stalin	70.00	210.00	490.00
10-(Scarce)-Origin The Fourth Musketeer, Victory Boys; Monstro, the Mighty app.	50.00	150.00	350.00
11-Vagabond, Stuporman app.	16.00	48.00	110.00
12,13	4.00	12.00	28.00
14-Origin & 1st app. Super Rabbit	17.00	51.00	120.00
15-20	4.35	13.00	30.00
21-32	3.00	9.00	21.00
33-Kurtzman-a, 5 pgs.	4.00	12.00	28.00

Colt .45 #4, © Warner Bros.

Combat #7, © DELL

Combat Kelly #22, © MCG

Comedy Comics #1 (5/48), © MCG

Comic Album #7, © KING

Comic Cavalcade #1, © DC

COMEDY COMICS (continued) — Good / Fine / Mint
34-Wolverton-a, 5 pgs. 5.50 16.50 38.00

COMEDY COMICS (2nd Series)
May, 1948 - No. 10, Jan, 1950
Marvel Comics (ACI)

1-Hedy, Tessie, Millie begin; Kurtzman's "Hey Look" (he draws himself) 9.00 27.00 62.00
2 3.50 10.50 24.00
3,4-Kurtzman's "Hey Look"(?&3) 5.50 16.50 38.00
5-10 1.75 5.25 12.00

COMET, THE
Oct, 1983 - No. 2, Dec, 1983
Red Circle Comics

1-Origin The Comet; The American Shield begins .50 1.00
2-Origin continues .50 1.00

COMET MAN, THE
Feb, 1987 - No. 6, July, 1987 (mini-series)
Marvel Comics Group

1-6 .50 1.00

COMIC ALBUM
Mar-May, 1958 - No. 18, June-Aug, 1962
Dell Publishing Co.

1-Donald Duck 2.65 8.00 18.00
2-Bugs Bunny 1.15 3.50 8.00
3-Donald Duck 2.65 8.00 18.00
4-Tom & Jerry 1.15 3.50 8.00
5-Woody Woodpecker 1.15 3.50 8.00
6-Bugs Bunny 1.15 3.50 8.00
7-Popeye (9-11/59) 1.75 5.25 12.00
8-Tom & Jerry 1.15 3.50 8.00
9-Woody Woodpecker 1.15 3.50 8.00
10-Bugs Bunny 1.15 3.50 8.00
11-Popeye (9-11/60) 1.75 5.25 12.00
12-Tom & Jerry 1.15 3.50 8.00
13-Woody Woodpecker 1.15 3.50 8.00
14-Bugs Bunny 1.15 3.50 8.00
15-Popeye 1.75 5.25 12.00
16-Flintstones (12-2/61-62)-3rd app. 1.75 5.25 12.00
17-Space Mouse-3rd app. 1.15 3.50 8.00
18-Three Stooges; photo-c 3.00 9.00 21.00

COMIC BOOK (Also see Comics From Weatherbird)
1954 (Giveaway)
American Juniors Shoe

Contains a comic rebound with new cover. Several combinations possible. Contents determines price.

COMIC BOOKS (Series 1)
1950 (16 pgs.; 5¼x8½"; full color; bound at top; paper cover)
Metropolitan Printing Co. (Giveaway)

1-Boots and Saddles; intro. The Masked Marshal 3.35 10.00 23.00
1-The Green Jet; Green Lama by Raboy 17.00 52.00 120.00
1-My Pal Dizzy (Teen-age) 1.70 5.00 12.00
1-New World; origin Atomaster (costumed hero) 4.65 14.00 32.00
1-Talullah (Teen-age) 1.70 5.00 12.00

COMIC CAPERS
Fall, 1944 - No. 6, Summer, 1946
Red Circle Mag./Marvel Comics

1-Super Rabbit, The Creeper, Silly Seal, Ziggy Pig, Sharpy Fox begin 6.00 18.00 42.00

Good / Fine / Mint
2 3.50 10.50 24.00
3-6 2.35 7.00 16.00

COMIC CAVALCADE
Winter, 1942-43 - No. 63, June-July, 1954
(Contents change with No. 30, Dec-Jan, 1948 on)
All-American/National Periodical Publications

1-The Flash, Green Lantern, Wonder Woman, Wildcat, The Black Pirate by Moldoff (also No. 2), Ghost Patrol, and Red White & Blue begin; Scribbly app., Minute Movies 125.00 375.00 875.00
2-Mutt & Jeff begin; last Ghost Patrol & Black Pirate; Minute Movies 62.00 185.00 435.00
3-Hop Harrigan & Sargon, the Sorcerer begin; The King app. 45.00 135.00 315.00
4-The Gay Ghost, The King, Scribbly, & Red Tornado app. 38.00 115.00 265.00
5-Christmas-c 32.00 96.00 225.00
6-10: 7-Red Tornado & Black Pirate app.; last Scribbly. 9-Christmas-c 27.00 81.00 190.00
11,12,14-20: 12-Last Red White & Blue. 15-Johnny Peril begins, ends No. 29. 19-Christmas-c 24.00 72.00 168.00
13-Solomon Grundy app. 42.00 125.00 295.00
21-23 24.00 72.00 168.00
24-Solomon Grundy x-over in Green Lantern 27.00 81.00 190.00
25-29: 25-Black Canary app.; X-mas-c. 26-28-Johnny Peril app. 28-Last Mutt & Jeff. 29-Last Flash, Wonder Woman, Green Lantern & Johnny Peril 18.00 54.00 125.00
30-The Fox & the Crow, Dodo & the Frog & Nutsy Squirrel begin 13.00 40.00 90.00
31-35 6.00 18.00 42.00
36-49 4.50 13.50 31.00
50-62(Scarce) 6.50 19.50 45.00
63(Rare) 11.00 33.00 76.00
Giveaway (1945, 16 pages, paper-c, in color)-Movie "Tomorrow The World" (Nazi theme) 22.00 65.00 154.00
Giveaway (c. 1944-45; 8 pgs, paper-c, in color)-The Twain Shall Meet-r/C. Cavlacade 12.00 36.00 84.00

NOTE: ***Grossman*** *a-30-63.* ***Sheldon Mayer*** *a(2-3)-40-63.* ***Post*** *a-31, 36.* ***Reinman*** *a-15, 20.* ***Toth*** *a-26-28(Green Lantern); c-23, 27. Atom app.-22, 23.*

COMIC COMICS
April, 1946 - No. 10, Feb, 1947
Fawcett Publications

1-Captain Kidd 4.00 12.00 28.00
2-10-Wolverton-a, 4 pgs. each. 5-Captain Kidd app. 4.65 14.00 32.00

COMIC CUTS (Also see The Funnies)
5/19/34 - 7/28/34 (5 cents; 24 pages) (Tabloid size in full color)
(Not reprints; published weekly; created for newsstand sale)
H. L. Baker Co., Inc.

V1No.1 - V1No.7(6/30/34), V1No.8(7/14/34), V1No.9(7/28/34)-Idle Jack strips 6.00 18.00 42.00

COMIC LAND
March, 1946
Fact and Fiction

1-Sandusky & the Senator, Sam Stuper, Marvin the Great, Sir Passer, Phineas Gruff app.; Irv Tirman & Perry Williams art 2.50 7.50 17.00

COMIC MONTHLY
Jan, 1922 - No. 12, Dec, 1922 (32 pgs.)(8½x9")(10 cents)
(1st monthly newsstand comic publication) (Reprints 1921 B&W dailies)
Embee Dist. Co.

1-Polly & Her Pals 26.00 78.00 180.00

COMIC MONTHLY (continued)

	Good	Fine	Mint
2-Mike & Ike	5.50	16.50	38.00
3-S'Matter, Pop?	5.50	16.50	38.00
4-Barney Google	11.00	33.00	76.00
5-Tillie the Toiler	8.00	24.00	56.00
6-Indoor Sports	4.35	13.00	30.00
7-Little Jimmy	4.35	13.00	30.00
8-Toots and Casper	4.35	13.00	30.00
9,10-Foolish Questions	4.35	13.00	30.00
11-Barney Google & Spark Plug in the Abadaba Handicap	4.35	13.00	30.00
12-Polly & Her Pals	4.35	13.00	30.00

COMICO PRIMER (See Primer)

COMIC PAGES (Formerly Funny Picture Stories)
V3No.4, July, 1939 - V3No.6, Dec, 1939
Centaur Publications

V3No.4-Bob Wood-a	17.00	51.00	120.00
5,6	12.00	36.00	84.00

COMIC PAINTING AND CRAYONING BOOK
1917 (32 pages)(10x13½'')(No price on cover)
Saalfield Publ. Co.

Tidy Teddy by F. M. Follett, Clarence the Cop, Mr. & Mrs. Butt-In. Regular comic stories to read or color	6.00	18.00	42.00

COMICS (See All Good)

COMICS, THE
March, 1937 - No. 11, 1938 (Newspaper strip reprints)
Dell Publishing Co.

1-1st Tom Mix in comics; Wash Tubbs, Tom Beatty, Myra North Arizona Kid, Erik Noble & International Spy w/Doctor Doom begin	36.00	108.00	250.00
2	20.00	60.00	140.00
3-11: 3-Alley Oop begins	15.00	45.00	105.00

COMICS AND STORIES (See Walt Disney's . . .)

COMICS CALENDAR, THE (The 1946 . . .)
1946 (116 pgs.; 25 cents)(Stapled at top)
True Comics Press (ordered through the mail)

(Rare) Has a ''strip'' story for every day of the year in color	14.50	43.50	100.00

COMICS DIGEST (Pocket size)
Winter, 1942-43 (100 pages) (Black & White)
Parents' Magazine Institute

1-Reprints from True Comics (non-fiction World War II stories)	4.35	13.00	30.00

COMIC SELECTIONS (Shoe store giveaway)
1944-46 (Reprints from Calling All Girls, True Comics, True Aviation, & Real Heroes)
Parents' Magazine Press

1	1.35	4.00	9.00
2-5	1.00	3.00	7.00

COMICS FOR KIDS
1945 (no month); No. 2, Sum, 1945 (Funny animal)
London Publishing Co./Timely

1,2-Puffy Pig, Sharpy Fox	4.00	12.00	28.00

COMICS FROM WEATHER BIRD (Also see Comic Book, Free Comics to You, Weather Bird & Edward's Shoes)
1954 - 1957 (Giveaway)
Weather Bird Shoes

Contains a comic bound with new cover. Many combinations possible. Contents would determine price. Some issues do not contain complete comics, but only parts of comics. Value equals 40 to 60 percent of contents.

COMICS HITS (See Harvey Comics Hits)

COMICS MAGAZINE, THE (. . . Funny Pages No. 3)(Funny Pages No. 6 on)
May, 1936 - No. 5, Sept, 1936 (Paper covers)
Comics Magazine Co.

	Good	Fine	Mint
1: Dr. Mystic, The Occult Detective by Siegel & Shuster (1st episode-continues in More Fun No. 14); 1pg. Kelly-a; Sheldon Mayer-a	75.00	225.00	525.00
2: Federal Agent by Siegel & Shuster; 1pg. Kelly-a	45.00	135.00	315.00
3-5	35.00	105.00	245.00

COMICS NOVEL (Anarcho, Dictator of Death)
1947
Fawcett Publications

1-All Radar	14.50	43.50	100.00

COMICS ON PARADE (No. 30 on, continuation of Single Series)
April, 1938 - No. 104, Feb, 1955
United Features Syndicate

1-Tarzan by Foster; Captain & the Kids, Little Mary Mixup, Abbie & Slats, Ella Cinders, Broncho Bill, Li'l Abner begin	75.00	225.00	525.00
2	37.00	110.00	260.00
3	28.00	84.00	195.00
4,5	19.00	57.00	132.00
6-10	16.00	48.00	110.00
11-20	13.00	40.00	90.00
21-29: 22-Son of Tarzan begins. 29-Last Tarzan issue	11.00	33.00	76.00
30-Li'l Abner	8.00	24.00	56.00
31-The Captain & the Kids	6.00	18.00	42.00
32-Nancy & Fritzi Ritz	5.00	15.00	35.00
33-Li'l Abner	8.00	24.00	56.00
34-The Captain & the Kids	5.50	16.50	38.00
35-Nancy & Fritzi Ritz	5.00	15.00	35.00
36-Li'l Abner	8.00	24.00	56.00
37-The Captain & the Kids	5.50	16.50	38.00
38-Nancy & Fritzi Ritz; infinity-c	5.00	15.00	35.00
39-Li'l Abner	8.00	24.00	56.00
40-The Captain & the Kids	5.50	16.50	38.00
41-Nancy & Fritzi Ritz	4.00	12.00	28.00
42-Li'l Abner	7.00	21.00	52.00
43-The Captain & the Kids	5.00	15.00	35.00
44-Nancy & Fritzi Ritz	4.00	12.00	28.00
45-Li'l Abner	6.00	18.00	42.00
46-The Captain & the Kids	5.00	15.00	35.00
47-Nancy & Fritzi Ritz	4.00	12.00	28.00
48-Li'l Abner	6.00	18.00	42.00
49-The Captain & the Kids	5.00	15.00	35.00
50-Nancy & Fritzi Ritz	4.00	12.00	28.00
51-Li'l Abner	5.00	15.00	35.00
52-The Captain & the Kids	3.50	10.50	24.00
53-Nancy & Fritzi Ritz	3.50	10.50	24.00
54-Li'l Abner	5.00	15.00	35.00
55-Nancy & Fritzi Ritz	3.50	10.50	24.00
56-The Captain & the Kids (r-/Sparkler)	3.50	10.50	24.00
57-Nancy & Fritzi Ritz	3.50	10.50	24.00
58-Li'l Abner	5.00	15.00	35.00
59-The Captain & the Kids	3.00	9.00	21.00
60-70-Nancy & Fritzi Ritz	3.00	9.00	21.00
71-76-Nancy only	2.00	6.00	14.00
77-99,101-104-Nancy & Sluggo	2.00	6.00	14.00
100-Nancy & Sluggo	2.50	7.50	17.50

The Comics #2, © DELL

The Comics Magazine #1, © CM

Comics on Parade #51, © UFS

Comics Revue #5, © UFS

Commander Battle & the Atomic Sub #4, © ACG

Commando Adventures #1, © MCG

COMICS ON PARADE (continued) — Good / Fine / Mint

Special Issue, 7/46; Summer, 1948 - The Capt. & the Kids app. 2.00 6.00 14.00

Bound Volume (Very Rare) includes No. 1-12; bound by publisher in pictorial comic boards & distributed at the 1939 World's Fair and through mail order from ads in comic-books (Also see Tip Top) 130.00 390.00 900.00

NOTE: *Li'l Abner reprinted from Tip Top.*

COMICS READING LIBRARIES (Educational Series)
1973, 1977, 1979 (36 pages in color) (Giveaways)
King Features (Charlton Publ.)

	Good	Fine	Mint
R-01-Tiger, Quincy		.15	.30
R-02-Beetle Bailey, Blondie & Popeye		.15	.30
R-03-Blondie, Beetle Bailey		.30	.60
R-04-Tim Tyler's Luck, Felix the Cat		.30	.60
R-05-Quincy, Henry		.15	.30
R-06-The Phantom, Mandrake	.35	1.00	2.00
1977 reprint(R-04)	.20	.60	1.20
R-07-Popeye, Little King	.25	.70	1.40
R-08-Prince Valiant(Foster), Flash Gordon	4.00	12.00	24.00
1977 reprint	1.35	4.00	8.00
R-09-Hagar the Horrible, Boner's Ark		.15	.30
R-10-Redeye, Tiger		.15	.30
R-11-Blondie, Hi & Lois		.25	.50
R-12-Popeye-Swee'pea, Brutus		.30	.60
R-13-Beetle Bailey, Little King		.15	.30
R-14-Quincy-Hamlet		.15	.30
R-15-The Phantom, The Genius	.35	1.00	2.00
R-16-Flash Gordon, Mandrake	4.00	12.00	24.00
1977 reprint	1.35	4.00	8.00
Other 1977 editions. . . .		.15	.30
1979 editions(68pgs.)		.20	.40

NOTE: *Above giveaways available with purchase of $45.00 in merchandise. Used as a reading skills aid for small children.*

COMICS REVUE
June, 1947 - No. 5, Jan, 1948
St. John Publ. Co. (United Features Synd.)

	Good	Fine	Mint
1-Ella Cinders & Blackie	3.50	10.50	24.00
2-Hap Hopper (7/47)	2.35	7.00	16.00
3-Iron Vic (8/47)	2.00	6.00	14.00
4-Ella Cinders (9/47)	2.35	7.00	16.00
5-Gordo No. 1 (1/48)	2.00	6.00	14.00

COMIC STORY PAINT BOOK
1943 (68 pages) (Large size)
Samuel Lowe Co.

1055-Captain Marvel & a Captain Marvel Jr. story to read & color; 3 panels in color per page (reprints) 26.00 78.00 180.00

COMIC TALENT STAR SEARCH
Sept, 1986 ($1.50, B&W)
Solson Productions

1 .25 .75 1.50

COMIX BOOK (B&W Magazine - $1.00)
Oct, 1974 - No. 5, 1976
Marvel Comics Group/Krupp Comics Works No. 4

	Good	Fine	Mint
1-Underground comic artists; 2 pg. Wolverton-a	.70	2.00	4.00
2	.40	1.20	2.40
3-Low distribution (3/75)	.50	1.50	3.00
4(2/76), 4(5/76), 5	.40	1.20	2.40

NOTE: *Print run No. 1-3: 200-250M; No. 4&5: 10M each.*

COMIX INTERNATIONAL
July, 1974 - No. 5, Spring, 1977 (Full color)
Warren Magazines

	Good	Fine	Mint
1-Low distribution; all Corben remainders from Warren	4.00	12.00	24.00
2-Wood, Wrightson-r	1.20	3.50	7.00
3-5	.70	2.00	4.00

NOTE: *No. 4 had two printings with extra **Corben** story in one.*

COMMANDER BATTLE AND THE ATOMIC SUB
July-Aug, 1954 - No. 7, July-Aug, 1955
American Comics Group (Titan Publ. Co.)

	Good	Fine	Mint
1 (3-D effect)	12.00	36.00	84.00
2	5.00	15.00	35.00
3-H-Bomb-c; Atomic Sub becomes Atomic Spaceship	6.00	18.00	42.00
4-7: 6,7-Landau-a	5.00	15.00	35.00

COMMANDMENTS OF GOD
1954, 1958
Catechetical Guild

300-Same contents in both editions; different-c 2.75 8.00 16.00

COMMANDO ADVENTURES
June, 1957 - No. 2, Aug, 1957
Atlas Comics (MMC)

1,2-Severin-c; 2-Drucker-a 1.30 4.00 9.00

COMMANDO YANK (See Mighty Midget Comics)

COMPLETE BOOK OF COMICS AND FUNNIES
1944 (196 pages) (One Shot)
Better Publications

1-Origin Brad Spencer, Wonderman; The Magnet, The Silver Knight by Kinstler, & Zudo the Jungle Boy app. 15.00 45.00 105.00

COMPLETE BOOK OF TRUE CRIME COMICS
No date (Mid 1940's) (132 pages) (25 cents)
William H. Wise & Co.

nn-Contains Crime Does Not Pay rebound (includes No. 22) 38.00 115.00 265.00

COMPLETE COMICS (Formerly Amazing No. 1)
Winter, 1944-45
Timely Comics (EPC)

2-The Destroyer, The Whizzer, The Young Allies & Sergeant Dix 40.00 120.00 280.00

COMPLETE LOVE MAGAZINE (Formerly a pulp with same title)
V26/2, May-June, 1951 - V32/4(No.191), Sept, 1956
Ace Periodicals (Periodical House)

	Good	Fine	Mint
V26/2-Painted-c (52 pgs.)	2.00	6.00	14.00
V26/3-6(2/52), V27/1(4/52)-6(1/53)	1.30	4.00	9.00
V28/1(3/53), V28/2(5/53), V29/3(7/53)-6(12/53)	1.30	4.00	0.00
V30/1(2/54), V30/1(No. 176, 4/54)-6(No.181, 1/55)	1.15	3.50	8.00
V31/1(No.182, 3/55)-Last precode	1.00	3.00	7.00
V31/2(5/55)-6(No.187, 1/56)	.85	2.50	6.00
V32/1(No.188, 3/56)-4(No.191, 9/56)	.80	2.40	5.50

NOTE: *(34 total issues). Photo-c V27/5-on. Painted-c V26/3.*

COMPLETE MYSTERY (True Complete Mystery No. 5 on)
Aug, 1948 - No. 4, Feb, 1949 (Full length stories)
Marvel Comics (PrPI)

	Good	Fine	Mint
1-Seven Dead Men	8.50	25.50	60.00
2-Jigsaw of Doom!	6.00	18.00	42.00
3-Fear in the Night; Burgos-a	6.00	18.00	42.00
4-A Squealer Dies Fast	6.00	18.00	42.00

COMPLETE ROMANCE
1949
Avon Periodicals

	Good	Fine	Mint
1-(Scarce)-Reprinted as Women to Love	20.00	60.00	140.00

COMPLIMENTARY COMICS
No date (1950's)
Sales Promotion Publ. (Giveaway)

	Good	Fine	Mint
1-Strongman by Powell, 3 stories	3.35	10.00	20.00

CONAN (See Chamber of Darkness No. 4, King Conan, Official Handbook of. . . , Robert E. Howard's. . , Savage Sword of Conan, and Savage Tales)

CONAN, THE BARBARIAN
Oct, 1970 - Present
Marvel Comics Group

	Good	Fine	Mint
1-Origin Conan by Barry Smith; Kull app.	12.50	37.50	75.00
2	5.00	15.00	30.00
3-(low distribution in some areas)	8.50	25.00	50.00
4,5	4.25	12.50	25.00
6-10: 8-Hidden panel message, pg. 14. 10-52 pgs.; Black Knight-r; Kull story by Severin	3.00	9.00	18.00
11-13: 11-52 pgs. 12-Wrightson c(i)	2.35	7.00	14.00
14,15-Elric app.	3.00	9.00	18.00
16,19,20: 16-Conan-r/Savage Tales No. 1	1.70	5.00	10.00
17,18-No Smith-a	1.00	3.00	6.00
21,22: 22-has r-from No. 1	1.35	4.00	8.00
23-1st app. Red Sonja	1.70	5.00	10.00
24-1st full story Red Sonja; last Smith-a	1.70	5.00	10.00
25-Buscema-a begins	1.00	3.00	6.00
26-30	.60	1.75	3.50
31-36,38-40	.40	1.20	2.40
37-Adams c/a	.85	2.50	5.00
41-43,46-49	.25	.75	1.50
44,45-Adams inks, c-45; Red Sonja app. No. 43,44,48	.35	1.00	2.00
50-57,60	.25	.80	1.60
58-2nd Belit app.(see Gnt-Size 1)	.50	1.50	3.00
59-Origin Belit	.25	.75	1.50
61-99		.50	1.00
100-(52 pg. Giant)-Death of Belit	.40	1.25	2.50
101-114,117-192		.35	.70
115-double size		.60	1.20
116-Buscema/Adams c/a		.35	.70

NOTE: ***Alcala** a-137. **Austin** a-125, 126; c-125i, 126i. **Brunner** c-17i. **Buckler** a-40p; c-40. **Buscema** a-25-36p, 38, 39, 41-56p, 58-63p, 65-67p, 68, 70-78p, 84-86p, 88-91p, 93-126p, 136p, 140, 141-44p, 146-58p, 159, 161, 162, 163p, 165p-185p, 187p-190p, Annual 2-5p, 7p; c(p)-26, 36, 44, 46, 52, 56, 58, 59, 64, 65, 72, 78-80, 83-91, 93-103, 105-26, 136-51, 155-159, 161, 162, 168, 169, 171, 172, 174, 175, 178-185, 188, 189. **Golden** c-152. **Kaluta** c-167. **Gil Kane** a-12p, 17p, 18p, 127-30, 131-134p, Gnt-Size 1p; c-12p, 17p, 18p, 23, 25, 27-32, 34, 35, 38, 39, 41-43, 45-51, 53-55, 57, 60-63, 65-71, 73p, 76p, 127-34, Gnt-Size 1, 3, 4. **Russell** a-21. **Simonson** c-135. **Smith** a-1p-11p, 12, 13p-15p, 16, 19-21, 23, 24; c-1-11, 13-16, 19-24p. **Sutton** inks-Gnt-Size 1-3. Issues No. 3-5, 7-9, 11, 16-18, 21, 23, 25, 27-30, 35, 37, 38, 42, 45, 52, 57, 58, 65, 69-71, 73, 79-83, 99, 100, 104, 114, Annual 2 have original Robert E. Howard stories adapted. Issues No. 32-34 adapted from Norvell Page's novel **Flame Winds**.*

	Good	Fine	Mint
Giant Size 1(9/74)-Smith r-/No. 3; start adaptation of Howard's ''Hour of the Dragon.'' 1st app. Belit	.70	2.00	4.00
Giant Size 2(12/74)-Smith r-/No. 5; Sutton-a; Buscema-c	.70	2.00	4.00
Giant Size 3(4/75-Smith r-/No. 6; Sutton-a), Giant Size 4(6/75; Smith r-/No. 7), Giant Size 5('75; Smith r-/No. 14,15; Kirby-c)	.30	.90	1.80
King Size 1(9/73-35 cents)-Smith r-/No. 2,4; Smith-c	1.00	3.00	6.00
Annual 2(6/76)-50 cents; new stories	.40	1.20	2.40
Annual 3(2/78)-reprints	.30	.80	1.60
Annual 4(10/78), 5(12/79)-Buscema-a/part-c	.25	.70	1.40
Annual 6(10/81)-Kane c/a	.25	.70	1.40
Annual 7(11/82), 8(2/84)		.60	1.20
Annual 9(12/84), 10(2/87)		.60	1.20

CONAN THE BARBARIAN MOVIE SPECIAL
Oct, 1982 - No. 2, Nov, 1982
Marvel Comics Group

	Good	Fine	Mint
1,2-Movie adapt.; Buscema-a		.25	.50

CONAN THE DESTROYER
Jan, 1985 - No. 2, Mar, 1985 (Movie adaptation)
Marvel Comics Group

	Good	Fine	Mint
1,2-r/Marvel Super Special		.40	.80

CONAN THE KING (Formerly King Conan)
No. 20, Jan, 1984 - Present
Marvel Comics Group

	Good	Fine	Mint
20-40		.60	1.20

NOTE: ***Kaluta** c-20-23, 24i, 26, 27.*

CONCRETE
Sept, 1986 - Present ($1.50, B&W)
Dark Horse Comics

	Good	Fine	Mint
1	.25	.75	1.50

CONDORMAN
Oct, 1981 - No. 3, Jan, 1982
Whitman Publ.

	Good	Fine	Mint
1-3: 1,2-Movie adaptation		.30	.60

CONFESSIONS ILLUSTRATED (Magazine)
Jan-Feb, 1956 - No. 2, Spring, 1956
E. C. Comics

	Good	Fine	Mint
1-Craig, Kamen, Wood, Orlando-a	5.00	15.00	35.00
2-Craig, Crandall, Kamen, Orlando-a	6.00	18.00	42.00

CONFESSIONS OF LOVE
4/50 - No. 2, 7/50 (25 cents; 132 pgs. in color)(7¼x5¼'')
Artful Publ.

	Good	Fine	Mint
1-Bakerish-a	16.50	50.00	115.00
2-Art & text; Bakerish-a	8.00	24.00	56.00

CONFESSIONS OF LOVE (Confessions of Romance No. 7)
No. 11, July, 1952 - No. 6, Aug, 1953
Star Publications

	Good	Fine	Mint
11	3.50	10.50	24.00
12,13-Disbrow-a	3.50	10.50	24.00
14, 6	2.00	6.00	14.00
4-Disbrow-a	2.75	8.00	18.00
5-Wood/?-a	4.00	12.00	28.00

NOTE: *All have **L. B. Cole** covers.*

CONFESSIONS OF ROMANCE (Formerly Confessions of Love)
No. 7, Nov, 1953 - No. 11, Nov, 1954
Star Publications

	Good	Fine	Mint
7	3.50	10.50	24.00
8	2.35	7.00	16.00
9-Wood-a	6.00	18.00	42.00
10,11-Disbrow-a	3.00	9.00	21.00

NOTE: ***L. B. Cole** covers on all.*

CONFESSIONS OF THE LOVELORN (Formerly Lovelorn)
No. 52, Aug, 1954 - No. 114, June-July, 1960
American Comics Group (Regis Publ./Best Synd. Features)

	Good	Fine	Mint
52 (3-D effect)	7.00	21.00	50.00
53,54 (3-D effect)	6.00	18.00	42.00
55	1.50	4.50	10.00

Conan, the Barbarian #12, © MCG

Confessions of Love #4, © STAR

Confessions of Romance #10, © STAR

Conqueror #1, © Harrier

Contact Comics #11, © Aviation Press

Cosmic Boy #1, © DC

CONFESSIONS OF THE LOVELORN (cont'd.)

	Good	Fine	Mint
56-Communist propaganda sty, 10pgs; last pre-code (2/55)	2.00	6.00	14.00
57-90	1.00	3.00	7.00
91-Williamson-a	4.00	12.00	28.00
92-99,101-114	.85	2.50	6.00
100	1.00	3.00	7.00

NOTE: *Whitney a-most issues. 106,107-painted-c.*

CONFIDENTIAL DIARY (Formerly High School Confidential Diary; Three Nurses No. 18 on)
No. 12, May, 1962 - No. 17, March, 1963
Charlton Comics

	Good	Fine	Mint
12-17	.35	1.00	2.00

CONGO BILL (See Action Comics)
Aug-Sept, 1954 - No. 7, Aug-Sept, 1955
National Periodical Publications

	Good	Fine	Mint
1-(Scarce)	20.00	60.00	140.00
2-(Scarce)	17.00	51.00	120.00
3-7 (Scarce), 4-Last precode	15.00	45.00	105.00

CONNECTICUT YANKEE, A (See King Classics)

CONQUEROR (Combined with Swiftsure after No. 9)
Aug, 1984 - No. 9, Dec, 1985 ($1.75, B&W)
Harrier Comics

	Good	Fine	Mint
1-9	.30	.90	1.80
Special Preview Ed. (1984, 16 pgs.)		.50	1.00

CONQUEROR, THE (See 4-Color No. 690)

CONQUEROR COMICS
Winter, 1945
Albrecht Publishing Co.

	Good	Fine	Mint
nn	4.00	12.00	28.00

CONQUEROR OF THE BARREN EARTH
Feb, 1985 - No. 4, May, 1985 (Mini-series)
DC Comics

	Good	Fine	Mint
1-Back-up series from Warlord		.60	1.20
2-4		.50	1.00

CONQUEROR UNIVERSE
Nov, 1985 (One shot)(52 pgs.)
Harrier Comics

	Good	Fine	Mint
1	.45	1.40	2.80

CONQUEST
1953 (6 cents)
Store Comics

	Good	Fine	Mint
1-Richard the Lion Hearted, Beowulf, Swamp Fox	1.50	4.50	10.00

CONQUEST
Spring, 1955
Famous Funnies

	Good	Fine	Mint
1-Crandall-a, 1 pg.; contains contents of 1953 issue	2.00	6.00	14.00

CONTACT COMICS
July, 1944 - No. 12, May, 1946
Aviation Press

	Good	Fine	Mint
nn-Black Venus, Flamingo, Golden Eagle, Tommy Tomahawk begin	10.00	30.00	70.00
2-5: 3-Last Flamingo. 3,4-Black Venus by L. B. Cole. 5-The Phantom Flyer app.	8.00	24.00	56.00
6,11-Kurtzman's Black Venus; 11-Last Golden Eagle, last Tommy Tomahawk; Feldstein-a	11.00	33.00	76.00
7-10,12: 12-Sky Rangers, Air Kids, Ace Diamond app.	6.50	19.50	45.00

NOTE: ***L. B. Cole** a-9; c-1-12. **Giunta** a-3. **Hollingsworth** a-5, 10. **Palais** a-11,12.*

CONTEMPORARY MOTIVATORS
1977 - 1978 (5-3/8x8")(31 pgs., B&W, $1.45)
Pendelum Press

14-3002 The Caine Mutiny; 14-3010 Banner in the Sky; 14-3029 God Is My Co-Pilot; 14-3037 Guadalcanal Diary; 14-3045 Hiroshima; 14-3053 Hot Rod; 14-3061 Just Dial a Number; 14-307x Star Wars; 14-3088 The Diary of Anne Frank; 14-3096 Lost Horizon — 1.50

NOTE: *Also see Now Age III. Above may have been dist. the same.*

CONTEST OF CHAMPIONS (See Marvel Superhero . . .)

COO COO COMICS (. . . the Bird Brain No. 57 on)
Oct, 1942 - No. 62, April, 1952
Nedor Publ. Co./Standard (Animated Cartoons)

	Good	Fine	Mint
1-1st app./origin Super Mouse (cloned from Superman)-The first funny animal super hero	6.00	18.00	42.00
2	3.00	9.00	21.00
3-10	2.00	6.00	14.00
11-33: 33-1pg. Ingels-a	1.30	4.00	9.00
34-40,43-46,48-50-Text illos by Frazetta in all	2.50	7.50	17.00
41-Frazetta-a(2)	8.00	24.00	56.00
42,47-Frazetta-a & text illos.	5.50	16.50	38.00
51-62	1.00	3.00	7.00

"COOKIE"
April, 1946 - No. 55, Aug-Sept, 1955
Michel Publ./American Comics Group(Regis Publ.)

	Good	Fine	Mint
1	5.00	15.00	35.00
2	2.50	7.50	17.50
3-10	1.75	5.25	12.00
11-20	1.30	4.00	9.00
21-30	.85	2.50	6.00
31-34,36-55	.75	2.25	5.00
35-Starlett O'Hara story	.85	2.50	6.00

COOL CAT (Formerly Black Magic)
V8/6, Mar-Apr, 1962 - V9/2, July-Aug, 1962
Prize Publications

	Good	Fine	Mint
V8/6, nn(V9/1), V9/2	.85	2.50	6.00

COPPER CANYON (See Fawcett Movie Comics)

CORBEN SPECIAL, A
May, 1984
Pacific Comics

	Good	Fine	Mint
1	.35	1.00	2.00

CORKY & WHITE SHADOW (See 4-Color No. 707)

CORLISS ARCHER (See Meet . . .)

CORPORAL RUSTY DUGAN (See Rusty Dugan)

CORPSES OF DR. SACOTTI, THE (See Ideal a Classical Comic)

CORSAIR, THE (See A-1 Comics No. 5,7,10)

COSMIC BOY
Dec, 1986 - No. 4, Mar, 1987 (mini-series)
DC Comics

	Good	Fine	Mint
1-Legends tie-in	.25	.75	1.50
2-4		.50	1.00

COSMO CAT
July-Aug, 1946 - No. 10, Oct, 1947; 1957; 1959
Fox Publications/Green Publ. Co./Norlen Mag.

COSMO CAT (continued)

	Good	Fine	Mint
1	5.00	15.00	35.00
2	2.50	7.50	17.50
3-Origin	2.50	7.50	17.50
4-10	1.75	5.25	12.00
2-4(1957-Green Publ. Co.)	.85	2.50	6.00
2-4(1959-Norlen Mag.)	.75	2.25	5.00
I.W. Reprint No. 1	.35	1.00	2.00

COSMO THE MERRY MARTIAN
Sept, 1958 - No. 6, Oct, 1959
Archie Publications (Radio Comics)

	Good	Fine	Mint
1-Bob White-a in all	4.65	14.00	32.00
2-6	3.00	9.00	21.00

COTTON WOODS (See 4-Color No. 837)

COUGAR, THE (Cougar No. 2)
April, 1975 - No. 2, July, 1975
Seaboard Periodicals (Atlas)

	Good	Fine	Mint
1-Adkins-a(p)		.40	.80
2-Origin		.25	.50

COUNTDOWN (See Movie Classics)

COUNT OF MONTE CRISTO, THE (See 4-Color No. 794)

COURAGE COMICS
1945
J. Edward Slavin

	Good	Fine	Mint
1,2,77	2.65	8.00	18.00

COURTSHIP OF EDDIE'S FATHER (TV)
Jan, 1970 - No. 2, May, 1970
Dell Publishing Co.

	Good	Fine	Mint
1,2-Bill Bixby photo-c	1.00	3.00	7.00

COVERED WAGONS, HO (See 4-Color No. 814)

COWBOY ACTION (Western Thrillers No. 1-4; Quick Trigger Western No. 12 on)
No. 5, March, 1955 - No. 11, March, 1956
Atlas Comics (ACI)

	Good	Fine	Mint
5	2.65	8.00	18.00
6-10	1.50	4.50	10.00
11-Williamson-a, 4 pgs., Baker-a	3.65	11.00	25.00

NOTE: ***Maneely*** *c/a-5.* ***Severin*** *c-10.*

COWBOY COMICS (. . Stories No. 14, formerly Star Ranger)
(Star Ranger Funnies No. 15 on)
No. 13, July, 1938 - No. 14, Aug, 1938
Centaur Publishing Co.

	Good	Fine	Mint
13-(Rare)-Ace and Deuce, Lyin Lou, Air Patrol, Aces High, Lee Trent, Trouble Hunters begin	32.00	96.00	225.00
14	22.00	66.00	154.00

NOTE: ***Guardineer*** *a-13, 14.* ***Gustavson*** *a-13, 14.*

COWBOY IN AFRICA (TV)
March, 1968
Gold Key

	Good	Fine	Mint
1(10219-803)-Chuck Connors photo-c	1.50	4.50	10.00

COWBOY LOVE (Becomes Range Busters?)
7/49 - V2/10, 6/50; No. 11, 1951; No. 28, 2/55 - No. 31, 8/55
Fawcett Publications/Charlton Comics No. 28 on

	Good	Fine	Mint
V1/1-Rocky Lane photo back-c	3.50	10.50	24.00
2	1.65	5.00	11.50
V1/3,4,6 (12/49)	1.30	4.00	9.00
5-Bill Boyd photo back-c (11/49)	2.15	6.50	15.00
V2/7-Williamson/Evans-a	3.65	11.00	25.00
V2/8-11	1.15	3.50	8.00
V1/28-31(1955-Charlton)(Formerly Romantic Story?; becomes Sweetheart Love Story?)	.85	2.50	6.00

NOTE: ***Powell*** *a-10. Photo c-1-11 No. 1-10, 52 pgs.*

COWBOY ROMANCES (Young Men No. 4 on)
Oct, 1949 - No. 3, Mar, 1950
Marvel Comics (IPC)

	Good	Fine	Mint
1-Photo-c	5.50	16.50	38.00
2-William Holden, Mona Freeman 'Streets of Laredo' photo-c	4.00	12.00	28.00
3	3.50	10.50	24.00

COWBOYS 'N' INJUNS (. . . 'N' Indians No. 6 on)
1946 - No. 5, 1947; No. 6, 1949 - No. 8, 1952
Compix No. 1-5/Magazine Enterprises No. 6 on

	Good	Fine	Mint
1	2.35	7.00	16.00
2-5-All funny animal western	1.50	4.50	10.00
6(A-1 23)-half violent, half funny	1.75	5.25	12.00
7(A-1 41, 1950), 8(A-1 48)-All funny	1.50	4.50	10.00
I.W. Reprint No. 1,7 (reprinted in Canada by Superior, No. 7)	.35	1.00	2.00
Super Reprint No. 10 (1963)	.35	1.00	2.00

COWBOY WESTERN COMICS (Formerly Jack In The Box; Becomes Space Western No. 40-45 & Wild Bill Hickok & Jingles No. 68 on; title: . . . Heroes No. 47 & 48; Cowboy Western No. 49 on (TV))
No. 17, 7/48 - No. 39, 8/52; No. 46, 10/53; No. 47, 12/53; No. 48 Spr, '54; No. 49, 5-6/54 - No. 67, 3/58 (nn 40-45)
Charlton(Capitol Stories)

	Good	Fine	Mint
17	3.75	11.25	26.00
18,19-Orlando c/a	2.65	8.00	18.00
20-25	1.75	5.25	12.00
26-Photo-c	2.65	8.00	18.00
27,30-Sunset Carson photo-c	7.00	21.00	50.00
28,29-Sunset Carson app.	4.00	12.00	28.00
31-39,47-50 (no No.40-45)	1.15	3.50	8.00
46-(Formerly Space Western)-space western story	4.00	12.00	28.00
51-66	1.00	3.00	7.00
67-Williamson/Torres-a, 5 pgs.	4.75	14.00	33.00

NOTE: Many issues trimmed 1'' shorter.

COWGIRL ROMANCES (Formerly Jeanie)
No. 28, Jan, 1950
Marvel Comics (CCC)

	Good	Fine	Mint
28(No.1)-Photo-c	6.50	19.50	45.00

COWGIRL ROMANCES
1950 - No. 12, Winter, 1952-53 (No. 1-3, 52 pgs.)
Fiction House Magazines

	Good	Fine	Mint
1-Kamen-a	11.00	33.00	76.00
2	5.50	16.50	38.00
3-5	4.50	13.50	30.00
6-9,11,12	3.65	11.00	25.00
10-Frazetta?/Williamson-a; Kamen/Baker-a	15.00	45.00	105.00

COW PUNCHER (. . . Comics)
Jan, 1947; No. 2, Sept, 1947 - No. 7, 1949
Avon Periodicals

	Good	Fine	Mint
1-Clint Cortland, Texas Ranger, Kit West, Pioneer Queen begin; Kubert-a; Alabam stories begin	16.00	48.00	110.00
2-Kubert, Kamen/Feldstein-a; Kamen bondage-c	12.00	36.00	84.00
3-5,7: 3-Kiefer story	9.00	27.00	63.00
6-Opium drug mention story; bondage, headlight-c; Reinman-a	11.00	33.00	76.00

Courtship of Eddie's Father #2, © M.G.M.

Cowboys 'n' Injuns #4, © ME

Cowboy Western Comics #17, © CC

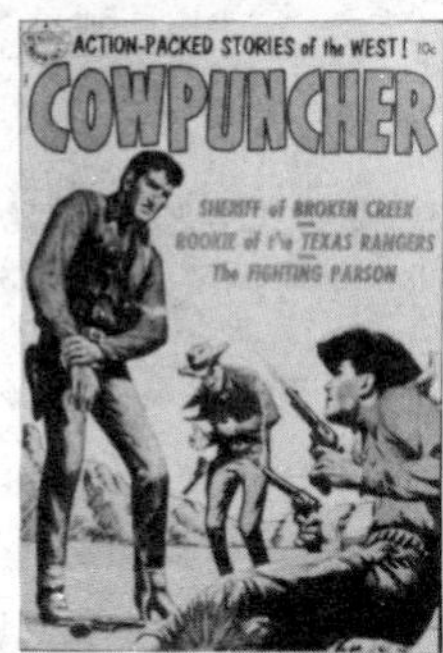

Cowpuncher nn, © REAL

Crackajack Funnies #9, © DELL

Crack Comics #31, © QUA

COWPUNCHER
1953 (nn) (Reprints Avon's No. 2)
Realistic Publications

	Good	Fine	Mint
Kubert-a	4.50	13.50	31.00

COWSILLS, THE (See Harvey Pop Comics)

COYOTE
June, 1983 - No. 16, Mar, 1986 (Adults only) ($1.50)
Epic Comics (Marvel)

	Good	Fine	Mint
1-Origin	.25	.75	1.50
2-5: 2-Origin concludes	.25	.75	1.50
6-16: 7,9-Ditko-p. 14-Badger x-over from First Comics	.25	.75	1.50

CRACKAJACK FUNNIES (Giveaway)
1937 (32 pgs.; full size; soft cover; full color)(Before No. 1?)
Malto-Meal

	Good	Fine	Mint
Features Dan Dunn, G-Man, Speed Bolton, Freckles, Buck Jones, Clyde Beatty, The Nebbs, Major Hoople, Wash Tubbs	35.00	105.00	245.00

CRACKAJACK FUNNIES
June, 1938 - No. 43, Jan, 1942
Dell Publishing Co.

	Good	Fine	Mint
1-Dan Dunn, Freckles, Myra North, Wash Tubbs, Apple Mary, The Nebbs, Don Winslow, Tom Mix, Buck Jones, Major Hoople, Clyde Beatty, Boots begin	55.00	165.00	385.00
2	26.00	78.00	182.00
3	20.00	60.00	140.00
4,5	16.00	48.00	110.00
6-8,10	12.00	36.00	84.00
9-Red Ryder strip-r begin by Harman; 1st app. in comics & 1st cover	17.00	51.00	120.00
11-14	10.00	30.00	70.00
15-Tarzan text feature begins by Burroughs; not in No. 26,35	11.00	33.00	76.00
16-24	9.00	27.00	62.00
25-The Owl begins; in new costume No. 26 by Frank Thomas	21.00	64.00	148.00
26-30: 28-Owl-c	15.00	45.00	105.00
31-Owl covers begin	13.00	40.00	90.00
32-Origin Owl Girl	15.00	45.00	105.00
33-38: 36-Last Tarzan ish	9.50	28.50	67.00
39-Andy Panda begins (intro/1st app.)	10.00	30.00	70.00
40-43: 42-Last Owl cover	9.00	27.00	62.00

NOTE: *McWilliams art in most issues.*

CRACK COMICS (. . .Western No. 63 on)
May, 1940 - No. 62, Sept, 1949
Quality Comics Group

	Good	Fine	Mint
1-Origin The Black Condor by Lou Fine, Madame Fatal, Red Torpedo, Rock Bradden & The Space Legion; The Clock, Alias the Spider, Wizard Wells, & Ned Bryant begin; Powell-a; Note: Madame Fatal is a man dressed up as a woman	155.00	465.00	1085.00
2	75.00	225.00	585.00
3	60.00	180.00	420.00
4	52.00	156.00	364.00
5-10: 10-Tor, the Magic Master begins	40.00	120.00	280.00
11-20	35.00	105.00	245.00
21-24-Last Fine Black Condor	27.00	81.00	190.00
25,26	18.00	54.00	125.00
27-Intro & Origin Captain Triumph by Alfred Andriola (Kerry Drake artist)	33.00	100.00	230.00
28-30	15.00	45.00	105.00
31-39: 31-Last Black Condor	9.00	27.00	62.00
40-46	6.00	18.00	42.00
47-57,59,60-Capt. Triumph by Crandall	6.50	19.50	45.00
58,61,62-Last Captain Triumph	4.75	14.00	33.00

NOTE: *Black Condor by* ***Fine****: No. 1, 2, 4-6, 8, 10-24; by* ***Sultan****: No. 3, 7; by* ***Fugitani****: No. 9.* ***Crandall*** *c-55, 59.* ***Guardineer*** *a-17.* ***Gustavson*** *a-17.* ***McWilliams*** *art-No. 15-21, 23-27.*

CRACKED (Magazine) (Satire)
Feb-Mar, 1958 - Present
Major Magazines

	Good	Fine	Mint
1-One pg. Williamson	5.00	15.00	35.00
2-1st Shut-Ups & Bonus Cut-Outs	2.50	7.50	17.50
3-6	1.15	3.50	8.00
7-10: 7-R/1st 6 covers on-c	.85	2.50	6.00
11-12, 13(nn,3/60), 14-17, 18(nn,2/61), 19,20	.75	2.25	4.50
21-27(11/62), 27(No.28, 2/63; misnumbered), 29(5/63)	.45	1.25	2.50
31-60		.60	1.20
61-100: 99-Alfred E. Neuman on-c		.50	1.00
101-227		.40	.80
Biggest. . .(Winter, 1977)		.60	1.20
Biggest, Greatest. . .nn('65)	.50	1.50	3.00
Biggest, Greatest. . .2('66)-No.12('76)	.25	.75	1.50
. . .Digest 1(Fall, '86)-No. 2; 148pgs.	.35	1.00	2.00
. . .Collectors' Edition ('73; formerly . . .Special) 4	.35	1.00	2.00
5-70		.60	1.25
. . .Shut-Ups (2/72-'72; Cracked Special No. 3) 1,2	.35	1.00	2.00
. . .Special 3('73; formerly Cracked Shut-Ups; . . .Collectors' Edition No. 4 on)	.35	1.00	2.00
Extra Special. . .1('76), 2('76)		.60	1.20
Giant. . .nn('65)	.50	1.50	3.00
Giant. . .2('66)-12('76), nn(9/77)-48('87)		.60	1.20
King Sized. . .1('67)	.50	1.50	3.00
King Sized. . .2('68)-11('77)	.35	1.00	2.00
King Sized. . .12-22 (Sum/'86)		.60	1.20
Super. . .1('68)	.50	1.50	3.00
Super. . .2('69)-34('87): 2-Spoof on Beatles movie by Severin	.35	1.00	2.00

NOTE: ***Burgos*** *a-1-10.* ***Davis*** *a-5, 11-18, 24, 80; c-12-14, 16.* ***Elder*** *a-5, 6, 10-13; c-10.* ***Everett*** *a-1-10, 23-25, 61; c-1.* ***Heath*** *a-1-3, 6, 13, 14, 17, 110; c-6.* ***Jaffee*** *a-5, 6.* ***Morrow*** *a-8-10.* ***Reinman*** *a-1-4.* ***Severin*** *a-in most all issues.* ***Shores*** *a-3-7.* ***Torres*** *a-7-10.* ***Ward*** *a-143, 144, 156.* ***Williamson*** *a-1 (1 pg.).* ***Wolverton*** *a-10 (2 pgs.), Giant nn('65).*

CRACK WESTERN (Formerly Crack; Jonesy No. 85 on)
No. 63, Nov, 1949 - No. 84, May, 1953 (36pgs., 63-68,74-on)
Quality Comics Group

	Good	Fine	Mint
63(No.1)-Two-Gun Lil (Origin & 1st app.)(ends No. 84), Arizona Ames, his horse Thunder (sidekick Spurs & his horse Calico), Frontier Marshal (ends No. 70), & Dead Canyon Days (ends No. 69) begin; Crandall-a	6.50	19.50	45.00
64,65-Crandall-a	4.35	13.00	30.00
66,68-Photo-c. 66-Arizona Ames becomes A. Raines (ends No. 84)	4.35	13.00	30.00
67-Randolph Scott Photo-c; Crandall-a	5.00	15.00	35.00
69(52pgs.)-Crandall-a	4.35	13.00	30.00
70(52pgs.)-The Whip (Origin & 1st app.) & his horse Diablo begin (ends No. 84); Crandall-a	4.35	13.00	30.00
71(52pgs.)-Frontier Marshal becomes Bob Allen F. Marshal (ends No. 84); Crandall-c/a	5.00	15.00	35.00
72(52pgs.)-Tim Holt Photo-c	4.35	13.00	30.00
73(52pgs.)-Photo-c	3.00	9.00	21.00
74,77,79,80,82	2.35	7.00	16.00
75,76,78,81,83-Crandall-c	3.00	9.00	21.00
84-Crandall c/a	4.35	13.00	30.00

CRASH COMICS (Catman No. 6 on)
May, 1940 - No. 5, Nov, 1940

CRASH COMICS (continued)
Tem Publishing Co.

	Good	Fine	Mint
1-The Blue Streak, Strongman (origin), The Perfect Human, Shangra begin; Simon & Kirby-a(1st team-up)	60.00	180.00	420.00
2-Simon & Kirby-a	30.00	90.00	210.00
3-Simon & Kirby-a	24.00	72.00	168.00
4-Origin & 1st app. The Catman; S&K-a	40.00	120.00	280.00
5-S&K-a	24.00	72.00	168.00

NOTE: *Solar Legion by* ***Kirby*** *No. 1-5 (5 pgs. each).*

CRASH DIVE (See Cinema Comics Herald)

CRASH RYAN
Oct, 1984 - No. 4, Jan, 1985 (Baxter paper, limited series)
Epic Comics (Marvel)

	Good	Fine	Mint
1	.35	1.00	2.00
2-4	.25	.75	1.50

CRAZY
Dec, 1953 - No. 7, July, 1954
Atlas Comics (CSI)

	Good	Fine	Mint
1-Everett c/a	5.00	15.00	35.00
2	3.50	10.50	24.00
3-7	2.75	8.25	19.00

NOTE: ***Berg*** *a-1, 2.* ***Burgos*** *c-5.* ***Drucker*** *a-6.* ***Everett*** *a-1-4.* ***Heath*** *a-3.* ***Maneely*** *a-1-7; c-3.* ***Post*** *a-3, 5, 6.*

CRAZY (People Who Buy This Magazine Is . . .) (Formerly This Magazine Is . . .)
V3No.3, Nov, 1957 - V4No.8, Feb, 1959 (Magazine) (Satire)
Charlton Publications

	Good	Fine	Mint
V3No.3 - V4No.7	.50	1.50	3.00
V4No.8-Davis-a, 8 pgs.	1.00	3.00	6.00

CRAZY (Satire)
Feb, 1973 - No. 3, June, 1973
Marvel Comics Group

	Good	Fine	Mint
1-3-Not Brand Echh-r		.30	.60

CRAZY (Magazine) (Satire)
Oct, 1973 - No. 94, Mar, 1983 (40 cents) (Black & White)
Marvel Comics Group

	Good	Fine	Mint
1-Wolverton(1 pg.), Ploog, Bode-a; 3 pg. photo story of Adams & Giordano	.35	1.00	2.00
2-Adams-a; Kurtzman's "Hey Look" reprint, 2 pgs.; Buscema-a		.60	1.20
3,5,6,8: 3-Drucker-a		.40	.80
4,7-Ploog-a		.40	.80
9-16-Eisner-a		.40	.80
17-81,83-94: 43-E.C. swipe from Mad 131. 76-Best of. . Super Special		.30	.60
82-Super Special ish; X-Men on-c	.30	.60	1.20
Super Special 1(Summer,'75, 100pgs.)-Ploog, Adams-r	.30	.80	1.60

NOTE: ***Austin*** *a-82i.* ***Buscema*** *a-82.* ***Byrne*** *c-82p.* ***Cardy*** *c-7,8.* ***Freas*** *c-1,2,4,6; a-7.* ***Rogers*** *a-82.*

CRAZY, MAN, CRAZY (Magazine) (Satire)
June, 1956
Humor Magazines

	Good	Fine	Mint
V2No.2-Wolverton-a, 3pgs.	3.00	9.00	21.00

CREATURE, THE (See Movie Classics)

CREATURES ON THE LOOSE (Tower of Shadows No. 1-9)
No. 10, March, 1971 - No. 37, Sept, 1975
Marvel Comics Group

	Good	Fine	Mint
10-First King Kull story; Wrightson-a	1.35	4.00	8.00
11-15: 13-Crandall-a		.40	.80
16-Origin Warrior of Mars		.50	1.00
17-20		.30	.60
21,22: Steranko-c; Thongor begins No. 22, ends No. 29		.25	.50
23-37: 30-Manwolf begins		.25	.50

NOTE: ***Ditko*** *r-15, 17, 18, 20, 22, 24, 27, 28.* ***Everett*** *a-16i(r).* ***Gil Kane*** *a-16p(r); c-16, 20, 25, 29, 33p, 35p, 36p.* ***Morrow*** *a-20, 21.* ***Perez*** *a-33-37; c-34p.* ***Tuska*** *a-32p.*

CREEPER, THE (See Beware. . . & First Issue Special)

CREEPY (Magazine)
1964 - No. 145, Feb, 1983
Warren Publishing Co.

	Good	Fine	Mint
1-Frazetta-a	.85	2.50	5.00
2	.50	1.50	3.00
3-13	.35	1.00	2.00
14-Adams 1st Warren work	.60	1.75	3.50
15-25	.35	1.00	2.00
26-40: 32-Harlan Ellison story	.25	.75	1.50
41-47,49-54,56-61: 61-Wertham parody		.60	1.20
48,55-(1973, 1974 Annuals)	.35	1.00	2.00
62-64,66-145		.50	1.00
65-(1975 Annual)	.25	.75	1.50
Year Book 1968, 1969	.50	1.50	3.00
Year Book 1970-Adams, Ditko-a(r)	.50	1.50	3.00
Annual 1971,1972	.35	1.00	2.00

NOTE: *Above books contain many good artists works:* ***Adams, Brunner, Corben, Craig (Taycee), Crandall, Ditko, Evans, Frazetta, Heath, Jeff Jones, Krenkel, McWilliams, Morrow, Nino, Orlando, Ploog, Severin, Torres, Toth, Williamson, Wood,*** *&* ***Wrightson;*** *covers by* ***Crandall, Davis, Frazetta, Morrow, SanJulian, Todd/Bode;*** *Otto Binder's "Adam Link" stories in No. 2, 4, 6, 8, 9, 12, 13, 15 with* ***Orlando*** *art.*

CREEPY THINGS
July, 1975 - No. 6, June, 1976
Charlton Comics

	Good	Fine	Mint
1		.50	1.00
2-6		.40	.80
Modern Comics Reprint 2-6('77)		.25	.50

NOTE: ***Ditko*** *a-3,5.* ***Sutton*** *c-3,4.*

CRIME AND JUSTICE (Rookie Cop? No. 27 on)
March, 1951 - No. 26, Sept, 1955
Capitol Stories/Charlton Comics

	Good	Fine	Mint
1-Spanking panel	8.00	24.00	56.00
2	2.00	6.00	14.00
3-8,10,13: 6-Negligee panels	1.75	5.25	12.00
9-Classic story "Comics Vs. Crime"	4.50	13.50	31.00
11-Narcotics story; bra & panties panel	3.50	10.50	24.00
12-Bondage-c	3.50	10.50	24.00
14-Color illos in **POP**; gory story of man who beheads women	5.50	16.50	38.00
15-17,19-26	1.30	4.00	9.00
18-Ditko-a	8.00	24.00	56.00

NOTE: ***Ayers*** *a-17.* ***Shuster*** *a-19-21; c-19. Bondage c-11.*

CRIME AND PUNISHMENT (Title inspired by 1935 film)
April, 1948 - No. 74, Aug, 1955
Lev Gleason Publications

	Good	Fine	Mint
1	6.00	18.00	42.00
2	3.00	9.00	21.00
3-Used in **SOTI**, pg. 112; injury-to-eye panel; Fuje-a	5.00	15.00	35.00
4,5	2.35	7.00	16.00
6-10	1.85	5.50	13.00
11-20	1.50	4.50	10.00
21-30	1.15	3.50	8.00
31-38,40-44	1.00	3.00	7.00
39-Drug mention story "The 5 Dopes"	3.50	10.50	24.00
45-"Hophead Killer" drug story	3.25	9.75	22.00

Crash Ryan #1, © MCG

Crime & Justice #12, © CC

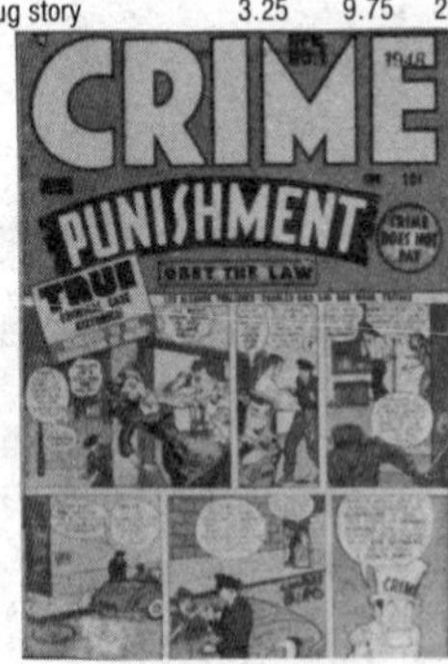

Crime & Punishment #1, © LEV

Crime Clinic #5, © Z-D

Crime Does Not Pay #41, © LEV

Crime Exposed #4, © MCG

CRIME AND PUNISHMENT (continued)	Good	Fine	Mint
46-One page Frazetta	1.85	5.50	13.00
47-57,60-65,70-74	1.00	3.00	7.00
58-Used in **POP**, pg. 79	2.50	7.50	17.00
59-Used in **SOTI**, illo-''What comic-book America stands for''	8.50	25.50	60.00
66-Toth c/a(4); 3-D effect ish(3/54)	11.00	33.00	75.00
67-''Monkey on His Back''-heroin story; 3-D effect ish.	8.00	24.00	56.00
68-3-D effect ish; Toth-c (7/54).	6.00	18.00	42.00
69-''The Hot Rod Gang''-dope crazy kids	4.35	13.00	30.00

NOTE: ***Everett*** *a-31.* ***Fuje*** *a-3, 12, 13, 17, 18, 26, 27.* ***Guardineer*** *a-2, 3, 10, 14, 17, 18, 26-28, 40-44.* ***Kinstler*** *c-69.* ***McWilliams*** *a-41, 48, 49.* ***Tuska*** *a-28, 30.*

CRIME CAN'T WIN (Formerly Cindy Smith)
No. 41, 9/50 - No. 43, 2/51; No. 4, 4/51 - No. 12, 9/53
Marvel/Atlas Comics (TCI 41/CCC 42,43,4-12)

41	3.50	10.50	24.00
42	2.00	6.00	14.00
43-Horror story	2.35	7.00	16.00
4(4/51), 5-9,11,12	1.75	5.25	12.00
10-Possible use in **SOTI**, pg. 161	2.15	6.50	15.00

NOTE: ***Robinson*** *a-9-11.* ***Tuska*** *a-43.*

CRIME CASES COMICS (Formerly Willie Comics)
No. 24, 8/50 - No. 27, 3/51; No. 5, 5/51 - No. 12, 7/52
Marvel/Atlas Comics(CnPC No.24-8/MJMC No.9-12)

24 (52 pgs.)	2.65	8.00	18.00
25,26	1.75	5.25	12.00
27-Morisi-a	1.70	5.00	12.00
5-12: 11-Robinson-a	1.50	4.50	10.00

CRIME CLINIC
No. 10, July-Aug, 1951 - No. 5, Summer, 1952
Ziff-Davis Publishing Co.

10-Painted-c	6.00	18.00	42.00
11,4,5-Painted-c	4.00	12.00	28.00
3-Used in **SOTI**, pg. 18	5.50	16.50	38.00

NOTE: *Painted covers by* ***Saunders.***

CRIME DETECTIVE COMICS
Mar-Apr, 1948 - V3/8, May-June, 1953
Hillman Periodicals

V1/1-The Invisible 6, costumed villains app; Fuje-c	4.00	12.00	28.00
2	2.00	6.00	14.00
3,4,7,10-12	1.50	4.50	10.00
5-Krigstein-a	2.65	8.00	18.00
6-McWilliams-a	1.50	4.50	10.00
8-Kirbyish-a by McCann	2.20	6.50	15.00
9-Used in **SOTI**, pg. 16 & ''Caricature of the author in a position comic book publishers wish he were in permanently'' illo.	16.00	48.00	110.00
V2/1,4,7-Krigstein-a	2.00	6.00	14.00
2,3,5,6,8-12 (1-2/52)	1.15	3.50	8.00
V3/1-Drug use-c	1.50	4.50	10.00
2-8	1.00	3.00	7.00

NOTE: ***Briefer*** *a-V3/1.* ***Kinstlerish*** *-a by McCann-V2/7, V3/2.* ***Powell*** *a-11.*

CRIME DETECTOR
Jan, 1954 - No. 5, Sept, 1954
Timor Publications

1	3.75	11.25	26.00
2	1.85	5.50	13.00
3,4	1.65	5.00	11.50
5-Disbrow-a (classic)	4.75	14.25	33.00

CRIME DOES NOT PAY (Formerly Silver Streak No. 1-21)
No. 22, June, 1942 - No. 147, July, 1955 (1st crime comic)
Comic House/Lev Gleason/Golfing (Title inspired by film)

	Good	Fine	Mint
22(23 on cover, 22 on indicia)-Origin The War Eagle & only app.; Chip Gardner begins; No. 22 rebound in True Crime, Complete Book of (Scarce)	62.00	185.00	435.00
23 (Scarce)	35.00	105.00	245.00
24-Intro. & 1st app. Mr. Crime (Scarce)	30.00	90.00	210.00
25-30	15.00	45.00	105.00
31-40	9.00	27.00	62.00
41-Origin & 1st app. Officer Common Sense	5.50	16.50	38.00
42-Electrocution-c	6.50	19.50	45.00
43-46,48-50	4.75	14.25	33.00
47-Electric chair-c	6.50	19.50	45.00
51-62,65-70	2.50	7.50	17.00
63,64-Possible use in **SOTI**, pg. 306. No. 63-Contains Biro-Gleason's self censorship code of 12 listed restrictions (5/48)	2.50	7.50	17.00
71-99: 87-Chip Gardner begins, ends No. 99,102.	1.50	4.50	10.00
100	1.85	5.50	13.00
101-104,107-110	1.15	3.50	8.00
105-Used in **POP**, pg. 84	2.50	7.50	17.00
106,114-Frazetta, 1 pg.	1.85	5.50	13.00
111-Used in **POP**, pgs. 80,81 & Injury to eye story illo	2.50	7.50	17.00
112,113,115-130	1.00	3.00	7.00
131-140	.85	2.50	6.00
141,142-Last pre-code ish; Kubert-a(1)	2.00	6.00	14.00
143,147-Kubert-a, one each	2.00	6.00	14.00
144-146	.85	2.50	6.00
1(Golfing-1945)	1.15	3.50	8.00
The Best of...(1944)-128 pgs.; Series contains 4 rebound issues	20.00	60.00	140.00
...1945 issue	16.00	48.00	110.00
...1946-48 issues	13.50	40.50	95.00
...1949-50 issues	11.00	33.00	75.00
...1951-53 issues	8.50	25.50	60.00

NOTE: *Many issues contain violent covers and stories. Whodunnit by* ***Guardineer****-39-105, 108-110; Chip Gardner by* ***Bob Fujitani (Fuje)****-88-103; c-103.* ***Alderman*** *a-41-43.* ***Kubert*** *c-143.* ***Landau****-a-118.* ***Maurer*** *a-41, 42.* ***McWilliams*** *a-91, 93, 95, 100-103.* ***Palais*** *a-41-43.* ***Powell*** *a-146, 147.* ***Tuska*** *a-51, 52, 56, 61, 63, 64, 66, 67. Bondage c-62,98.*

CRIME EXPOSED
June, 1948; Dec, 1950 - No. 14, June, 1952
Marvel Comics (PPI)/Marvel Atlas Comics (PrPI)

1(6/48)	5.00	15.00	35.00
1(12/50)	2.85	8.50	20.00
2	1.75	5.25	12.00
3-9,11,14	1.50	4.50	10.00
10-Used in **POP**, pg. 81	2.00	6.00	14.00
12-Krigstein & Robinson-a	2.00	6.00	14.00
13-Used in **POP**, pg. 81; Krigstein-a	2.65	8.00	18.00

NOTE: ***Maneely*** *c-8.* ***Robinson*** *a-11,12.* ***Tuska*** *a-4.*

CRIMEFIGHTERS
April, 1948 - No. 10, Nov, 1949
Marvel Comics (CmPS 1-3/CCC 4-10)

1-Some copies are undated & could be reprints	4.00	12.00	28.00
2	2.00	6.00	14.00
3-Morphine addict story	3.00	9.00	21.00
4-10: 6-Anti-Wertham editorial. 9,10-Photo-c	1.50	4.50	10.00

CRIME FIGHTERS (...Always Win)
No. 11, Sept, 1954 - No. 13, Jan, 1955
Atlas Comics (CnPC)

11,12: 11-Maneely-a	1.65	5.00	11.00

CRIME FIGHTERS (continued)

	Good	Fine	Mint
13-Pakula, Reinman, Severin-a	1.85	5.50	13.00

CRIME FIGHTING DETECTIVE (Shock Detective Cases No. 20 on; formerly Criminals on the Run?)
No. 11, Apr-May, 1950 - No. 19, June, 1952
Star Publications

	Good	Fine	Mint
11-L. B. Cole c/a, 2pgs.	3.00	9.00	21.00
12,13,15-19: 17-Young King Cole & Dr. Doom app.; L. B. Cole-c on all	2.35	7.00	16.00
14-L. B. Cole-c/a, r-/Law-Crime No. 2	3.00	9.00	21.00

CRIME FILES
No. 5, Sept, 1952 - No. 6, Nov, 1952
Standard Comics

	Good	Fine	Mint
5-Alex Toth-a; used in **SOTI**, pg. 4 (text)	6.50	19.50	45.00
6-Sekowsky-a	2.50	7.50	17.00

CRIME ILLUSTRATED (Magazine)
Nov-Dec, 1955 - No. 2, Spring, 1956
E. C. Comics

	Good	Fine	Mint
1-Ingels & Crandall-a	6.75	20.00	46.00
2-Ingels & Crandall-a	5.35	16.00	36.00

NOTE: ***Craig** a-2. **Crandall** a-1, 2; c-2. **Evans** a-1. **Davis** a-2. **Ingels** a-1, 2. **Krigstein/Crandall** a-1. **Orlando** a-1, 2; c-1.*

CRIME INCORPORATED (Formerly Crimes Incorporated)
No. 2, Aug, 1950; No. 3, Aug, 1951
Fox Features Syndicate

	Good	Fine	Mint
2	5.00	15.00	35.00
3(1951)-Hollingsworth-a	3.50	10.50	24.00

CRIME MACHINE (Magazine)
Feb, 1971 - No. 2, May, 1971 (B&W)
Skywald Publications

	Good	Fine	Mint
1-Kubert-a(2)(r)(Avon)	.85	2.50	5.00
2-Torres, Wildey-a; Violent c/a	.60	1.80	3.60

CRIME MUST LOSE! (Formerly Sports Action?)
No. 4, Oct, 1950 - No. 12, April, 1952
Sports Action (Atlas Comics)

	Good	Fine	Mint
4-Ann Brewster-a in all; c-used in N.Y. Legis. Comm. documents	3.00	9.00	21.00
5-10,12	1.65	5.00	11.00
11-Used in **POP**, pg. 89	2.15	6.50	15.00

NOTE: ***Robinson** a-9.*

CRIME MUST PAY THE PENALTY (Formerly Four Favorites; Penalty No. 47,48)
No. 33, Feb, 1948 - No. 48, Jan, 1956
Ace Magazines (Current Books)

	Good	Fine	Mint
33(2/48)-Becomes Four Teeners No. 34?	5.75	17.25	40.00
2(6/48)-Extreme violence; Palais-a?	3.75	11.25	26.00
3-'Frisco Mary' story used in Senate Investigation report, pg. 7	1.65	5.00	11.50
4,8-Transvestism story	3.50	10.50	24.00
5-7,9,10	1.50	4.50	10.00
11-20: 18-2pg. text on cocaine	1.15	3.50	8.00
21-32,34-40,42-48	1.00	3.00	7.00
33(7/53)-''Dell Fabry-Junk King''-drug story; mentioned in **Love and Death**	2.50	7.50	18.00
41-Drug story-''Dealers in White Death''	2.50	7.50	18.00

NOTE: ***Cameron** a-30-32,34,39-41. **Colan** a-20, 31. **Kremer** a-3, 37r. **Palais** a-2?, 5?.*

CRIME MUST STOP
October, 1952
Hillman Periodicals

	Good	Fine	Mint
V1No.1(Scarce)-Similar to Monster Crime; Mort Lawrence-a	22.00	66.00	154.00

CRIME MYSTERIES (Secret Mysteries No. 16 on; combined with Crime Smashers No. 12? on)
May, 1952 - No. 15, Sept, 1954
Ribage Publishing Corp. (Trojan Magazines)

	Good	Fine	Mint
1-Transvestism story	14.50	43.50	100.00
2-Marijuana story (7/52)	11.00	33.00	75.00
3-One pg. Frazetta	6.50	19.50	45.00
4-Cover shows girl in bondage having her blood drained; 1 pg. Frazetta	14.50	43.50	100.00
5-10	5.75	17.25	40.00
11-14	4.75	14.25	33.00
15-Acid in face-c	9.00	27.00	62.00

NOTE: ***Hollingsworth** a-10-12, 15; c-12, 15. **Woodbridge** a-13. Bondage-c-1, 8, 12.*

CRIME ON THE RUN (See Approved Comics)
1949
St. John Publishing Co.

	Good	Fine	Mint
8 (Exist?)	2.15	6.50	15.00

CRIME ON THE WATERFRONT (Formerly Famous Gangsters)
No. 4, May, 1952 (Painted cover)
Realistic Publications

	Good	Fine	Mint
4	9.35	28.00	65.00

CRIME PATROL (International No. 1-5; International Crime Patrol No. 6, becomes Crypt of Terror No. 17 on)
No. 7, Summer, 1948 - No. 16, Feb-Mar, 1950
E. C. Comics

	Good	Fine	Mint
7-Intro. Captain Crime	26.00	78.00	182.00
8-14: 12-Ingels-a	24.00	72.00	168.00
15-Intro. of Crypt Keeper & Crypt of Terror; used by N.Y. Legis. Comm.-last pg. Feldstein-a	57.00	170.00	400.00
16-2nd Crypt Keeper app.	47.00	140.00	330.00

NOTE: ***Craig** c/a in most.*

CRIME PHOTOGRAPHER (See Casey. . .)

CRIME REPORTER
Aug, 1948 - No. 3, Dec, 1948 (Shows Oct.)
St. John Publ. Co.

	Good	Fine	Mint
1-Drug club story	13.50	40.00	95.00
2-Used in **SOTI**: illo-''Children told me what the man was going to do with the red-hot poker;'' r-/Dynamic No. 17 with editing; Baker-c; Tuska-a	29.00	87.00	200.00
3-Baker-c; Tuska-a	10.00	30.00	70.00

CRIMES BY WOMEN
June, 1948 - No. 15, Aug, 1951; 1954
Fox Features Syndicate

	Good	Fine	Mint
1	28.00	84.00	195.00
2	14.50	43.50	100.00
3-Used in **SOTI**, pg. 234	16.50	50.00	115.00
4,5,7,9,11-15	13.00	40.00	90.00
6-Classic girl fight-c; acid-in-face panel	16.50	50.00	115.00
8-Used in **POP**	14.50	43.50	100.00
10-Used in **SOTI**, pg. 72	14.50	43.50	100.00
54(M.S. Publ.-'54)-Reprint; (formerly My Love Secret)	6.50	19.50	45.00

CRIMES INCORPORATED (Formerly My Past)
No. 12, June, 1950 (Crime Incorporated No. 2 on)
Fox Features Syndicate

	Good	Fine	Mint
12	3.35	10.00	23.00

CRIMES INCORPORATED (See Fox Giants)

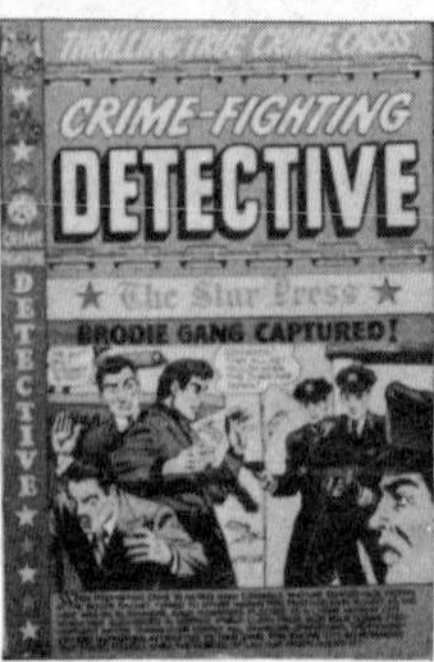

Crime Fighting Detective #11, © STAR

Crime Mysteries #14, © TM

Crimes Incorporated #12, © FOX

Crime Suspenstories #1, © WMG

Crisis on Infinite Earths #1, © DC

Crossfire #7, © Evanier, Meugniot, & Spiegle

CRIME SMASHER
Summer, 1948 (One Shot)
Fawcett Publications

	Good	Fine	Mint
1 (Spy Smasher)	11.00	33.00	76.00

CRIME SMASHERS (Secret Mysteries No. 16 on)
Oct, 1950 - No. 15, Mar, 1953
Ribage Publishing Corp.(Trojan Magazines)

	Good	Fine	Mint
1-Used in **SOTI**, pg. 19,20, & illo-''A girl raped and murdered;'' Sally the Sleuth begins	22.00	66.00	154.00
2-Kubert-c	10.00	30.00	70.00
3,4	8.00	24.00	56.00
5-Wood-a	13.00	40.00	90.00
6,8-11	6.50	19.50	45.00
7-Female heroin junkie sty	6.50	19.50	45.00
12-Injury to eye panel; 1pg. Frazetta	8.00	24.00	56.00
13-Used in **POP**, pgs. 79,80; 1pg. Frazetta	8.00	24.00	56.00
14,15	6.50	19.50	45.00

NOTE: ***Hollingsworth** a-14. **Kiefer** a-15. Bondage c-7,9.*

CRIME SUSPENSTORIES (Formerly Vault of Horror No. 12-14)
No. 15, Oct-Nov, 1950 - No. 27, Feb-Mar, 1955
E. C. Comics

15-Identical to No. 1 in content; No. 1 printed on outside front cover. No. 15 (formerly ''The Vault of Horror'') printed and blackened out on inside front cover with Vol. 1, No. 1 printed over it. Evidently, several of No. 15 were printed before a decision was made not to drop the Vault of Horror and Haunt of Fear series. The print run was stopped on No. 15 and continued on No. 1. All of No. 15 were changed as described above.

	Good	Fine	Mint
	56.00	168.00	390.00
1	47.00	140.00	335.00
2	28.00	84.00	195.00
3-5	20.00	60.00	140.00
6-10	15.00	45.00	105.00
11,12,14,15	11.00	33.00	75.00
13,16-Williamson-a	15.00	45.00	105.00
17-Williamson/Frazetta-a, 6 pgs.	17.00	52.00	120.00
18	8.00	24.00	55.00
19-Used in **SOTI**, pg. 235	10.00	30.00	70.00
20-Cover used in **SOTI**, illo-''Cover of a children's comic book''	12.00	36.00	86.00
21,25-27	6.50	19.50	45.00
22,23-Used in Senate investigation on juvenile delinquency. 22-Ax decapitation-c	10.00	30.00	70.00
24-'Food For Thought' similar to 'Cave In' in Amaz. Det. No. 13 (1952)	6.50	19.50	45.00

NOTE: ***Craig** a-1-21; c-1-18,20-22. **Crandall** a-18-26. **Davis** a-4, 5, 7, 9-12, 20. **Elder** a-17, 18. **Evans** a-15, 19, 21, 23, 25, 27; c-23, 24. **Feldstein** c-19. **Ingels** a-1-12, 14, 15, 27. **Kamen** a-2, 4-18, 20-27; c-25-27. **Krigstein** a-22, 24, 25, 27. **Kurtzman** a-1, 3. **Orlando** a-16, 22, 24, 26. **Wood** a-1, 3. Issues No. 11-15 have E. C. ''quickie'' stories. No. 25 contains the famous ''Are You a Red Dupe?'' editorial.*

CRIMINALS ON THE RUN (Formerly Young King Cole)
(Crime Fighting Detective No. 11 on?)
Aug-Sept, 1948 - No. 10, Dec-Jan, 1949-50
Premium Group (Novelty Press)

	Good	Fine	Mint
V4No.1-Young King Cole begins	5.00	15.00	35.00
2-6: 6-Dr. Doom app.	4.00	12.00	28.00
7-Classic ''Fish in the Face'' cover by L. B. Cole	9.00	27.00	62.00
V5No.1,2	4.00	12.00	28.00
10-L. B. Cole-c	4.00	12.00	28.00

NOTE: *Most issues have **L. B. Cole** covers. **McWilliams** a-V4No.6,7, V5No.2; c-V4No.5*

CRISIS ON INFINITE EARTHS (See Official . . . Index)
Apr, 1985 - No. 12, Mar, 1986 (12 issue maxi-series)
DC Comics

	Good	Fine	Mint
1-Perez-c on all	.60	1.75	3.50
2	.40	1.20	2.40
3	.35	1.10	2.20
4-6	.35	1.00	2.00
7-Double size; death of Supergirl	.40	1.25	2.50
8-11		.75	1.50
12-Double size; deaths of Dove, Kole, Lori Lemaris, Sunburst, G.A. Robin & Huntress	.35	1.10	2.20

CRITTERS (Also see Usagi Yojimbo Summer Special)
1986 - Present ($1.70-$2.00, B&W)
Fantagraphics Books

	Good	Fine	Mint
1-Funny animal	1.15	3.50	7.00
2	.60	1.75	3.50
3-5	.40	1.25	2.50
6-10	.35	1.00	2.00

CROSLEY'S HOUSE OF FUN
1950 (32 pgs.; full color; paper cover)
Crosley Div. AVCO Mfg. Corp. (Giveaway)

	Good	Fine	Mint
Strips revolve around Crosley appliances	1.70	5.00	10.00

CROSS AND THE SWITCHBLADE, THE
1972 (35-49 cents)
Spire Christian Comics/Fleming H. Revell Co.

	Good	Fine	Mint
1(Some issues have nn)		.40	.80

CROSSFIRE
1973 (39,49 cents)
Spire Christian Comics (Fleming H. Revell Co.)

	Good	Fine	Mint
nn		.40	.80

CROSSFIRE
May, 1984 - No. 17, Mar, 1986 (Baxter paper)
Eclipse Comics

	Good	Fine	Mint
1-DNAgents x-over; Spiegle c/a begins	.30	.90	1.80
2-17: 12,13-Death of Marilyn Monroe	.25	.75	1.50

CROSSFIRE AND RAINBOW
June, 1986 - No. 4, Sept, 1986 (mini-series)
Eclipse Comics

	Good	Fine	Mint
1-4: Spiegle-a		.65	1.30

CROSSING THE ROCKIES (See Classics Special)

CROWN COMICS
Winter, 1944-45 - No. 19, July, 1949
Golfing/McCombs Publ.

	Good	Fine	Mint
1-''The Oblong Box''-Poe adaptation	12.00	36.00	84.00
2,3-Baker-a	8.00	24.00	56.00
4-6-Baker c/a; Voodah app. No. 4,5	8.00	24.00	56.00
7-Feldstein, Baker, Kamen-a; Baker-c	6.50	19.50	45.00
8-Baker-a; Voodah app.	6.50	19.50	45.00
9-11,13-19: Voodah in No. 10-19	3.75	11.25	26.00
12-Feldstein?, Starr-a	4.75	14.25	33.00

NOTE: ***Bolle** a-13, 15, 18, 19; c-15. **Powell** a-19. **Starr** a-12, 13.*

CROW OF THE BEARCLAN
Sept, 1986 - Present ($1.50, B&W)
Blackthorne Publ.

	Good	Fine	Mint
1	.40	1.25	2.50
2		.75	1.50

CRUSADER FROM MARS (See Tops in Adventure)
Jan-Mar, 1952 - No. 2, Fall, 1952
Ziff-Davis Publ. Co.

	Good	Fine	Mint
1	23.00	70.00	160.00
2-Bondage-c	18.50	56.00	130.00

CRUSADER RABBIT (See 4-Color No. 735,805)

CRUSADERS, THE
1974 - Vol. 15, 1983 (36 pgs.) (39-69¢) (Religious)
Chick Publications

	Good	Fine	Mint
Vol. 1-Operation Bucharest('74). Vol. 2-The Broken Cross('74). Vol. 3-Scarface('74). Vol. 4-Exorcists('75). Vol. 5-Chaos('75). each....		.40	.80
Vol. 6-Primal Man?('76)-(Disputes evolution theory). Vol. 7-The Ark-(Claims proof of existence, destroyed by Bolsheviks). Vol. 8-The Gift-(Life story of Christ). Vol. 9-Angel of Light-(Story of the Devil). Vol. 10-Spellbound?-(Tells how rock music is Satanical & produced by witches). 11-Sabotage?. 12-Alberto. 13-Double-Cross. 14-The Godfathers. (No. 6-14 low in distribution; Loaded in religious propaganda.). 15-The Force		.40	.80

CRUSADERS, THE (Southern Knights No. 2 on)
1982?
Guild Publs.

	Good	Fine	Mint
1	3.35	10.00	20.00

CRYIN' LION, THE
Fall, 1944 - No. 3, Spring, 1945
William H. Wise Co.

	Good	Fine	Mint
1	3.75	11.25	26.00
2,3	2.35	7.00	16.00

CRYPT OF SHADOWS
Jan, 1973 - No. 21, Nov, 1975
Marvel Comics Group

	Good	Fine	Mint
1-Wolverton-a r-/Advs. Into Terror No. 7		.30	.60
2-21		.25	.50

NOTE: *Briefer a-2r. Ditko a-13r, 18-20r. Everett a-6, 14r. Heath a-1r. Mort Lawrence a-1r. Maneely a-2r. Moldoff a-8. Powell a-12r, 14r.*

CRYPT OF TERROR (Tales From the Crypt No. 20 on; formerly Crime Patrol)
No. 17, Apr-May, 1950 - No. 19, Aug-Sept, 1950
E. C. Comics

	Good	Fine	Mint
17	67.00	200.00	470.00
18,19	50.00	150.00	350.00

NOTE: *Craig c/a-17-19. Feldstein a-17-19. Ingels a-19. Kurtzman a-18. Wood a-18. Canadian reprints known; see Table of Contents.*

CUPID
Dec, 1949 - No. 2, Mar, 1950
Marvel Comics (U.S.A.)

	Good	Fine	Mint
1,2: 1-Photo-c	3.00	9.00	21.00

CURIO
1930's(?) (Tabloid size, 16-20 pages)
Harry 'A' Chesler

	Good	Fine	Mint
	4.50	13.50	31.00

CURLY KAYOE COMICS
1946 - 1948; 1948 - 1950; Jan, 1958
United Features Syndicate/Dell Publ. Co.

	Good	Fine	Mint
1 (1946)	4.00	12.00	28.00
2	2.15	6.50	15.00
3-8	1.65	5.00	11.00
United Presents...(Fall, 1948)	1.65	5.00	11.00
4-Color 871 (Dell, 1/58)	1.50	4.50	10.00

CUSTER'S LAST FIGHT
1950
Avon Periodicals

	Good	Fine	Mint
nn-Partial reprint of Cowpuncher No. 1	8.00	24.00	56.00

CUTEY BUNNY
1985 - Present
Joshua Quagmire Prod./Eclipse No. 5 on (distributed)

	Good	Fine	Mint
1-6	.25	.80	1.60

CUTIE PIE
May, 1955 - No. 5, Aug, 1956
Junior Reader's Guild/Lev Gleason

	Good	Fine	Mint
1	1.65	5.00	11.00
2-5	.85	2.50	6.00

CYCLONE COMICS
June, 1940 - No. 5, Nov, 1940
Bilbara Publishing Co.

	Good	Fine	Mint
1-Origin Tornado Tom; Volton begins, Mister Q app.	30.00	90.00	210.00
2	15.00	45.00	105.00
3-5	12.00	36.00	84.00

CYNTHIA DOYLE, NURSE IN LOVE (Formerly and becomes Sweetheart Diary No. 75 on)
No. 66, Oct, 1962 - No. 74, Feb, 1964
Charlton Publications

	Good	Fine	Mint
66-74 (No. 74, exist?)	.30	.80	1.60

DAFFY (...Duck No. 18 on)
No. 457, 3/53 - No. 30, 7-9/62; No. 31, 10-12/62 - No. 145, 1983 (no No. 132,133)
Dell Publishing Co./Gold Key No. 31-127/Whitman No. 128 on

	Good	Fine	Mint
4-Color 457-Elmer Fudd x-overs begin	1.50	4.50	10.00
4-Color 536,615('55)	1.15	3.50	8.00
4(1-3/56)-11('57)	.85	2.50	6.00
12-19(1958-59)	.75	2.25	5.00
20-40(1960-64)	.60	1.75	3.50
41-60(1964-68)	.35	1.00	2.00
61-90(1969-73)-Road Runner in most		.60	1.20
91-131,134-145(1974-83)		.40	.80
Mini-Comic 1 (1976; 3¼x6½'')		.25	.50

NOTE: *Reprint issues-No.41-46, 48, 50, 53-55, 58, 59, 67, 69, 73, 81, 96, 103-08; 136-142, 144, 145(⅓-⅔-r). (See March of Comics No. 277, 288, 313, 331, 347, 357, 375, 387, 397, 402, 413, 425, 437, 460)*

DAFFYDILS
1911 (52 pgs.; 6x8''; B&W; hardcover)
Cupples & Leon Co.

	Good	Fine	Mint
by Tad	6.00	18.00	42.00

DAFFY QADDAFI
1986 (One shot, B&W)
Comics Unlimited Limited

	Good	Fine	Mint
1	.30	.90	1.80

DAFFY TUNES COMICS
June, 1947 - No. 2, Aug, 1947
Four Star Publications

	Good	Fine	Mint
nn	2.00	6.00	14.00
2-Al Fago c/a	2.35	7.00	16.00

DAGAR, DESERT HAWK (Capt. Kidd No. 24-on; formerly All Great)
No. 14, Feb, 1948 - No. 23, Apr, 1949 (No No.17,18)
Fox Features Syndicate

	Good	Fine	Mint
14-Tangi & Safari Cary begin; Edmond Good bondage-c/a	20.00	60.00	140.00
15,16-E. Good-a; 15-Bondage-c	13.00	40.00	90.00
19,20,22	10.00	30.00	70.00
21-'Bombs & Bums Away' panel in 'Flood of Death' story used in SOTI	13.00	40.00	90.00
23-Bondage-c	13.00	40.00	90.00

NOTE: *Tangi by Kamen-14-16, 19; c-21.*

Crypt of Terror #18, © WMG

Daffy #14, © Warner Bros.

Daffy Qaddafi nn, © Comics Unlimited Ltd.

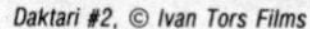
Daktari #2, © Ivan Tors Films

Dale Evans Comics #12, © Roy Rogers

Dalgoda #1, © Fantagraphics

DAGAR THE INVINCIBLE (Tales of Sword & Sorcery...)
10/72 - No. 18, 12/76; No. 19, 4/82 (See Dan Curtis)
Gold Key

	Good	Fine	Mint
1-Origin; intro. Villains Olstellon & Scorpio	1.00	3.00	6.00
2-5: 3-Intro. Graylin, Dagar's woman; Jarn x-over	.50	1.50	3.00
6-1st Dark Gods story	.35	1.00	2.00
7-10: 9-Intro. Torgus. 10-1st Three Witches story	.35	1.00	2.00
11-18: 13-Durak & Torgus x-over; story continues in Dr. Spektor No. 15. 14-Dagar's origin retold. 18-Origin retold		.60	1.20
19-Origin-r/No. 18		.40	.80

NOTE: *Durak app.-7,12,13. Tragg app.-5,11.*

DAGWOOD (Chic Young's) (Also see Blondie)
Sept, 1950 - No. 140, Nov, 1965
Harvey Publications

	Good	Fine	Mint
1	6.00	18.00	42.00
2	3.00	9.00	21.00
3-10	2.50	7.50	17.50
11-30	1.50	4.50	10.00
31-70	.85	2.50	6.00
71-100	.55	1.60	4.00
101-128,130,135	.45	1.35	3.00
129,131-134,136-140-All are 68-pg. issues	.75	2.25	5.00

NOTE: *Popeye and other one page strips appeared in early issues.*

DAGWOOD SPLITS THE ATOM (Also see Topix V8No.4)
1949 (Science comic with King Features characters) (Giveaway)
King Features Syndicate

	Good	Fine	Mint
nn-½ comic, ½ text; Popeye, Olive Oyl, Henry, Mandrake, Little King, Katzenjammer Kids app.	2.65	8.00	18.00

DAISY AND DONALD (See Walt Disney Showcase No. 8)
May, 1973 - No. 59, 1984 (no No. 48)
Gold Key/Whitman No. 42 on

	Good	Fine	Mint
1-Barks r-/WDC&S 280,308	.50	1.50	3.00
2-5: 4-Barks r-/WDC&S 224	.35	1.00	2.00
6-10	.25	.75	1.50
11-20		.50	1.00
21-47,49,50: 32-r-/WDC&S 308. 50-r-/No. 3		.40	.80
51-Barks r-/4-Color 1150		.50	1.00
52-59: 52-r-/No. 2. 55-r-/No. 5		.35	.70

DAISY & HER PUPS (Blondie's Dogs)
No. 21, 7/51 - No. 27, 7/52; No. 8, 9/52 - No. 25, 7/55
Harvey Publications

	Good	Fine	Mint
21-27: 26,27 have No. 6 & 7 on cover but No. 26 & 27 on inside	1.00	3.00	6.00
8-25: 19-25-Exist?	.85	2.50	5.00

DAISY COMICS
Dec, 1936 (Small size: 5¼x7½")
Eastern Color Printing Co.

	Good	Fine	Mint
Joe Palooka, Buck Rogers (2 pgs. from Famous Funnies No. 18), Napoleon Flying to Fame, Butty & Fally	12.00	36.00	84.00

DAISY DUCK & UNCLE SCROOGE PICNIC TIME (See Dell Giant No.33)

DAISY DUCK & UNCLE SCROOGE SHOW BOAT (See Dell Giant No.55)

DAISY DUCK'S DIARY (See 4-Color No. 600,659,743,858,948,1055,1150,1247)

DAISY HANDBOOK
1946 - 1948 (132 pgs.)(10 cents)(Pocket-size)
Daisy Manufacturing Co.

	Good	Fine	Mint
1-Buck Rogers, Red Ryder	11.00	33.00	76.00
2-Captain Marvel & Ibis the Invincible, Red Ryder, Boy Commandos, & Robotman; 2 pgs. Wolverton-a; contains 8pg. color catalog.	11.00	33.00	76.00

DAISY LOW OF THE GIRL SCOUTS
1954, 1965 (16 pgs.; paper cover)
Girl Scouts of America

	Good	Fine	Mint
1954-Story of Juliette Gordon Low	2.00	6.00	14.00
1965	.50	1.50	3.00

DAISY MAE (See Oxydol-Dreft)

DAISY'S RED RYDER GUN BOOK
1955 (132 pages)(25 cents)(Pocket-size)
Daisy Manufacturing Co.

	Good	Fine	Mint
Boy Commandos, Red Ryder, 1 pg. Wolverton-a	8.00	24.00	56.00

DAKOTA LIL (See Fawcett Movie Comics)

DAKOTA NORTH
1986 - Present
Marvel Comics Group

	Good	Fine	Mint
1-5		.40	.80

DAKTARI (Ivan Tors) (TV)
7/67 - No. 3, 10/68; No. 4, 9/69 (Photo-c)
Dell Publishing Co.

	Good	Fine	Mint
1	1.15	3.50	8.00
2-4	.85	2.50	6.00

DALE EVANS COMICS (Also see Queen of the West...)
Sept-Oct, 1948 - No. 24, July-Aug, 1952 (No. 1-19, 52 pgs.)
National Periodical Publications

	Good	Fine	Mint
1-Dale Evans & her horse Buttermilk begin; Sierra Smith begins by Alex Toth	14.50	43.50	100.00
2-Alex Toth-a	10.00	30.00	70.00
3-11-Alex Toth-a	9.00	27.00	62.00
12-24	4.35	13.00	30.00

NOTE: *Photo-c, 1,2,4-14.*

DALGODA
Aug, 1984 - No. 8, Feb?, 1986
Fantagraphics Books

	Good	Fine	Mint
1-Full color, high quality paper ($2.25 cover price). Fujitake a/c	.50	1.50	3.00
2-8-($1.50 cover price). 2,3-Debut Grimwood's Daughter	.35	1.00	2.00

DALTON BOYS, THE
1951
Avon Periodicals

	Good	Fine	Mint
1-(No. on spine)-Kinstler-c	8.00	24.00	56.00

DAN CURTIS GIVEAWAYS
1974 (24 pages) (3x6") (in color, all reprints)
Western Publishing Co.

	Good	Fine	Mint
1-Dark Shadows, 2-Star Trek, 3-The Twilight Zone, 4-Ripley's Believe It or Not!, 5-Turok, Son of Stone, 6-Star Trek, 7-The Occult Files of Dr. Spektor, 8-Dagar the Invincible, 9-Grimm's Ghost Stories Set...	.50	1.50	3.00

DANDEE
1947
Four Star Publications

	Good	Fine	Mint
	2.00	6.00	14.00

DAN DUNN (See Detective Dan & Super Book nn)

DANDY COMICS (Also see Happy Jack Howard)
Spring, 1947 - No. 7, Spring, 1948

DANDY COMICS (continued)
E. C. Comics

	Good	Fine	Mint
1-Vince Fago-a in all	13.50	40.00	95.00
2	10.00	30.00	70.00
3-7	9.00	27.00	62.00

DANGER
January, 1953 - No. 11, Aug, 1954
Comic Media/Allen Hardy Assoc.

	Good	Fine	Mint
1-Heck-a	3.50	10.50	24.00
2,3,5-7,9-11	1.65	5.00	11.00
4-Marijuana cover/story	4.65	14.00	32.00
8-Bondage/torture/headlights panels	4.00	12.00	28.00

NOTE: *Morisi a-2,5,6(3); c-2. Contains some-r from Danger & Dynamite.*

DANGER (Jim Bowie No. 15 on; formerly Comic Media title)
No. 12, June, 1955 - No. 14, Oct, 1955
Charlton Comics Group

	Good	Fine	Mint
12(No.1)	2.65	8.00	18.00
13,14: 14 r-/No. 12	1.65	5.00	11.00

DANGER
1964
Super Comics

	Good	Fine	Mint
Super Reprint No. 10-12 (Black Dwarf; No. 11-r-/from Johnny Danger), No. 15,16 (Yankee Girl & Johnny Rebel), No. 17 (Capt. Courage & Enchanted Dagger), No. 18(nd) (Gun-Master, Annie Oakley, The Chameleon; L.B. Cole-a)	.70	2.00	4.00

DANGER AND ADVENTURE (Formerly This Magazine Is Haunted; Robin Hood and His Merry Men No. 28 on)
No. 22, Feb, 1955 - No. 27, Feb, 1956
Charlton Comics

	Good	Fine	Mint
22-Ibis the Invincible app.	2.65	8.00	18.00
23-Nyoka, Lance O'Casey app.	2.65	8.00	18.00
24-27: 24-Mike Danger & Johnny Adventure begin	1.75	5.25	12.00

DANGER IS OUR BUSINESS!
1953(Dec.) - No. 10, June, 1955
Toby Press

	Good	Fine	Mint
1-Captain Comet by Williamson/Frazetta-a, 6 pgs. (Science Fiction)	23.50	70.00	165.00
2	3.00	9.00	21.00
3-10	2.65	8.00	18.00
I.W. Reprint No. 9('64)-Williamson/Frazetta-a r-/No. 1; Kinstler-c	7.00	21.00	40.00

DANGER IS THEIR BUSINESS (See A-1 Comics No. 50)

DANGER MAN (See 4-Color No. 1231)

DANGER TRAIL
July-Aug, 1950 - No. 5, Mar-Apr, 1951
National Periodical Publications

	Good	Fine	Mint
1-King Farrady begins, ends No. 4; Toth-a	23.50	70.00	165.00
2-Toth-a	19.00	57.00	132.00
3-5-Toth-a in all; Johnny Peril app. No. 5	16.50	50.00	115.00

DANIEL BOONE (See The Exploits of..., 4-Color No. 1163, The Legends of..., Frontier Scout..., Fighting..., & March of Comics No. 306)

DAN'L BOONE
Sept, 1955 - No. 8, Sept, 1957
Magazine Enterprises/Sussex Publ. Co. No. 2 on

	Good	Fine	Mint
1	2.65	8.00	18.00
2	1.50	4.50	10.00
3-8	1.30	4.00	9.00

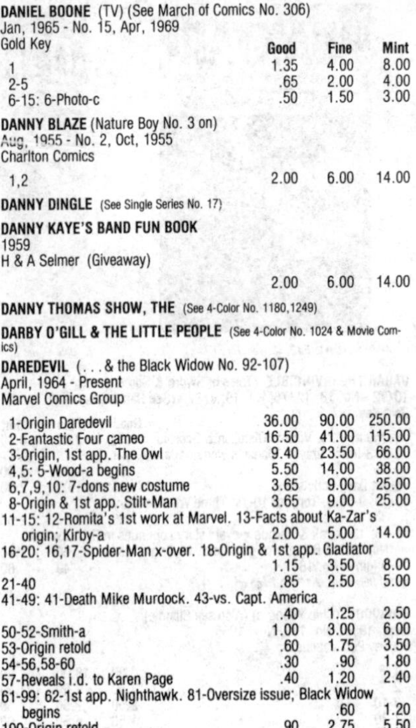

DANIEL BOONE (TV) (See March of Comics No. 306)
Jan, 1965 - No. 15, Apr, 1969
Gold Key

	Good	Fine	Mint
1	1.35	4.00	8.00
2-5	.65	2.00	4.00
6-15: 6-Photo-c	.50	1.50	3.00

DANNY BLAZE (Nature Boy No. 3 on)
Aug, 1955 - No. 2, Oct, 1955
Charlton Comics

	Good	Fine	Mint
1,2	2.00	6.00	14.00

DANNY DINGLE (See Single Series No. 17)

DANNY KAYE'S BAND FUN BOOK
1959
H & A Selmer (Giveaway)

	Good	Fine	Mint
	2.00	6.00	14.00

DANNY THOMAS SHOW, THE (See 4-Color No. 1180,1249)

DARBY O'GILL & THE LITTLE PEOPLE (See 4-Color No. 1024 & Movie Comics)

DAREDEVIL (. . . & the Black Widow No. 92-107)
April, 1964 - Present
Marvel Comics Group

	Good	Fine	Mint
1-Origin Daredevil	36.00	90.00	250.00
2-Fantastic Four cameo	16.50	41.00	115.00
3-Origin, 1st app. The Owl	9.40	23.50	66.00
4,5: 5-Wood-a begins	5.50	14.00	38.00
6,7,9,10: 7-dons new costume	3.65	9.00	25.00
8-Origin & 1st app. Stilt-Man	3.65	9.00	25.00
11-15: 12-Romita's 1st work at Marvel. 13-Facts about Ka-Zar's origin; Kirby-a	2.00	5.00	14.00
16-20: 16,17-Spider-Man x-over. 18-Origin & 1st app. Gladiator	1.15	3.50	8.00
21-40	.85	2.50	5.00
41-49: 41-Death Mike Murdock. 43-vs. Capt. America	.40	1.25	2.50
50-52-Smith-a	1.00	3.00	6.00
53-Origin retold	.60	1.75	3.50
54-56,58-60	.30	.90	1.80
57-Reveals i.d. to Karen Page	.40	1.20	2.40
61-99: 62-1st app. Nighthawk. 81-Oversize issue; Black Widow begins		.60	1.20
100-Origin retold	.90	2.75	5.50
101-106,108-113		.60	1.20
107-Starlin-c	.30	.90	1.80
114-1st app. Deathstalker	.30	.90	1.80
115-130,132-137,139,140: 124-1st app. Copperhead; Black Widow leaves. 126-1st New Torpedo. 131-1st app. & origin Bullseye		.60	1.20
131-Origin & 1st app. Bullseye	.75	2.25	4.50
138-Byrne-a	.45	1.40	2.80
141-150: 142-Nova cameo. 148-30 & 35¢ issues exist. 150-1st app. Paladin		.60	1.20
151-Reveals i.d. to Heather Glenn		.60	1.20
152-157		.50	1.00
158-Frank Miller art begins (5/79); origin & death of Deathstalker	4.15	16.50	33.00
159	2.00	6.00	12.00
160,161	1.70	5.00	10.00
162	.35	1.00	2.00
163,164: 163-Hulk cameo. 164-Origin	1.35	4.00	8.00
165-167,170	1.05	3.20	6.40
168-Intro/origin Elektra	2.65	8.00	16.00
169-Elektra app.	1.35	4.00	8.00
171-175: 174,175-Elektra app.	.70	2.10	4.20

Dan'l Boone #5, © Sussex

Daredevil #17, © MCG

Daredevil #161, © MCG

Daredevil #227, © MCG

Daredevil Battles Hitler #1, © LEV

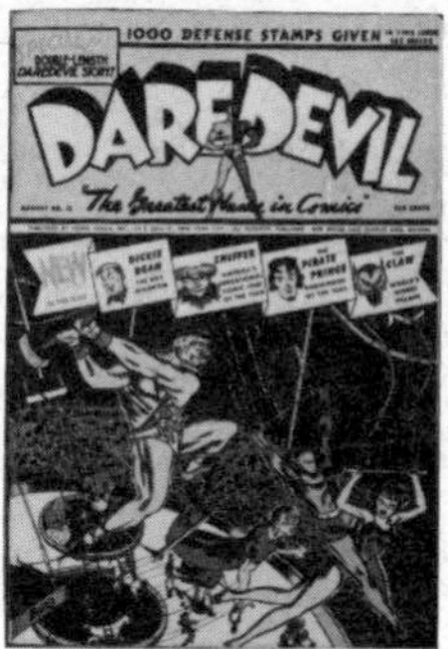

Daredevil Comics #12, © LEV

DAREDEVIL (continued) — Good / Fine / Mint

176-180-Elektra app. 179-Anti-smoking issue mentioned in the Congressional Record .40 1.25 2.50
181-Double size; death of Elektra .45 1.40 2.80
182-189: 183,184-Angel dust story. 187-New Black Widow. 189-Death of Stick .70 1.40
190-Double size; return of Elektra, part origin .70 1.40
191-Last Miller Daredevil .60 1.20
192-210: 196-Wolverine app. 208-Harlan Ellison scripts .60 1.20
211-225 .50 1.00
226-Frank Miller plots begin .60 1.20
227-Miller story & art begin .70 2.00 4.00
228-233-Last Miller script/art .35 1.00 2.00
234-241 .50 1.00
Giant Size 1 ('75) .35 1.10 2.20
Special 1(9/67)-new art .60 1.75 3.50
Special 2(2/71)(Wood-r), 3(1/72)-r .35 1.10 2.20
Annual 4(10/76) .35 1.10 2.20

NOTE: **Art Adams** *c-238p, 239.* **Austin** *a-191i; c-151i, 200i.* **John Buscema** *a-136, 137p, 234p, 235p; c-86p, 136i, 137p, 142, 219.* **Byrne** *c-200p, 201, 203, 223.* **Colan** *a(p)-20-49, 53-82, 84-98, 100, 110, 112, 124, 153, 154, 156, 157, Spec. 1p; c(p)-20-42, 44-49, 53-60, 71, 92, 98, 138, 153, 154, 156, 157, Annual 1.* **Craig** *a-50i, 52i.* **Ditko** *c/a-162.* **Everett** *a/c-1; inks-21, 81, 83.* **Gil Kane** *a-141p, 146-48p, 151p; c(p)-85, 90, 91, 93, 94, 115, 116, 119, 120, 125-28, 133, 139, 147, 152.* **Kirby** *c-2-4, 5p, 12p, 13p, 136p.* **Layton** *c-202.* **Miller** *script-168-182, 183(part), 184-191; a-158-161p, 163-184p, 191p; c-158-161p, 163-184p, 185-189, 190p, 191.* **Orlando** *a-2-4p.* **Powell** *a-9p, 11p, Special 1r, 2r.* **B. Smith** *a-236p.* **Smith** *c-51p, 52p.* **Simonson** *c-199.* **Starlin** *a-105p.* **Tuska** *a-39i, 145p.* **Williamson** *a-237i, 239i.* **Wood** *a-5-9i, 10, 11i, Spec. 2i; c-5i, 6-11, 164i.*

DAREDEVIL COMICS (See Silver Streak)
July, 1941 - No. 134, Sept, 1956 (Charles Biro stories)
Lev Gleason Publications (Funnies, Inc. No. 1)
(No. 1 titled "Daredevil Battles Hitler")

1-The Silver Streak, Lance Hale, Dickey Dean, Pirate Prince & Cloud Curtis team up with Daredevil and battle Hitler; Daredevil battles the Claw; Origin of Hitler feature story 190.00 570.00 1330.00
2-London, Pat Patriot, Nightro, Real American No. 1, Dickie Dean, Pirate Prince, & Times Square begin; intro. & only app. The Pioneer, Champion of America 110.00 330.00 770.00
3-Origin of 13 60.00 180.00 420.00
4 49.00 148.00 345.00
5-Intro. Sniffer & Jinx; Ghost vs. Claw begins by Bob Wood, ends No. 20 47.00 140.00 330.00
6-(No. 7 on indicia) 37.00 110.00 260.00
7-10: 8-Nightro ends 33.00 100.00 230.00
11-London, Pat Patriot end; bondage/torture-c 30.00 90.00 210.00
12-Origin of The Claw; Scoop Scuttle by Wolverton begins (2-4 pgs.), ends No. 22, not in No. 21 40.00 120.00 280.00
13-Intro. of Little Wise Guys 40.00 120.00 280.00
14 22.00 66.00 154.00
15-Death of Meatball 33.00 100.00 230.00
16,17 19.50 59.00 136.00
18-New origin of Daredevil-Not same as Silver Streak No. 6 42.00 125.00 295.00
19,20 17.50 52.00 122.00
21-Reprints cover of Silver Streak No. 6(on inside) plus intro. of The Claw from Silver Streak No. 1 25.00 75.00 175.00
22-30 10.00 30.00 70.00
31-Death of The Claw 15.50 46.00 110.00
32-37: 34-Two Daredevil stories begin, end No. 68 7.00 21.00 50.00
38-Origin Daredevil retold from No. 18 14.50 43.00 100.00
39,40 7.00 21.00 50.00
41-50: 42-Intro. Kilroy in Daredevil 4.35 13.00 30.00
51-69-Last Daredevil ish. 3.00 9.00 21.00
70-Little Wise Guys take over book; McWilliams-a; Hot Rock Flanagan begins, ends No. 80 2.00 6.00 14.00

Good / Fine / Mint

71-79,81: 79-Daredevil returns 1.50 4.50 10.00
80-Daredevil x-over 1.50 4.50 10.00
82,90-One page Frazetta ad in both (No. 82 is an anti-drug ad) 1.85 5.50 13.00
83-89,91-99,101-134 1.30 4.00 9.00
100 2.00 6.00 14.00

NOTE: **Wolverton's** *Scoop Scuttle-12-20, 22.* **Bolle** *a-125.* **Maurer** *a-75.* **McWilliams** *a-73, 75, 79, 80.*

DARING ADVENTURES (Also see Approved Comics)
Nov, 1953 (3-D)
St. John Publishing Co.

1 (3-D)-Reprints lead story/Son of Sinbad No. 1 by Kubert 16.50 50.00 115.00

DARING ADVENTURES
1963 - 1964
I.W. Enterprises/Super Comics

I.W. Reprint No. 9-Disbrow-a(3) 2.00 6.00 12.00
Super Reprint No. 10,11('63)-r/Dynamic No. 24,16; 11-Marijuana story; Yankee Boy app. 1.00 3.00 6.00
Super Reprint No. 12('64)-Phantom Lady from Fox(r/No. 14,15) 6.00 18.00 40.00
Super Reprint No. 15('64)-Hooded Menace 5.00 15.00 35.00
Super Reprint No. 16('64)-r/Dynamic No. 12 1.00 3.00 6.00
Super Reprint No. 17('64)-Green Lama by Raboy from Green Lama No. 3 2.00 6.00 12.00
Super Reprint No. 18-Origin Atlas 1.00 3.00 6.00

DARING COMICS (Formerly Daring Mystery) (Jeanie No. 13 on)
No. 9, Fall, 1944 - No. 12, Fall, 1945
Timely Comics (HPC)

9-Human Torch & Sub-Mariner begin 30.00 90.00 210.00
10-The Angel only app. 26.00 78.00 182.00
11,12-The Destroyer app. 26.00 78.00 182.00

DARING CONFESSIONS (Formerly Youthful Hearts)
No. 4, 10/52 - No. 7, 5/53; No. 8, 10/53
Youthful Magazines

4-Doug Wildey-a 3.50 10.50 24.00
5-8: 6,8-Wildey-a 2.35 7.00 16.00

DARING LOVE (Radiant Love No. 2 on)
Sept-Oct, 1953
Gillmor Magazines

1 2.85 8.50 20.00

DARING LOVE
No. 15, Dec, 1952; No. 17, Apr, 1953 (No. 16(2/53) on-c; No. 17(4/53) in indicia) (no No. 16)
Ribage/Pix

15-(Formerly & becomes Youthful Romances) 2.85 8.50 20.00
17: Photo-c; (Formerly & becomes Youthful Romances) 2.00 6.00 14.00

NOTE: **Colletta** *a-15.* **Wildey** *a-17.*

DARING LOVE STORIES (See Fox Giants)

DARING MYSTERY COMICS (Comedy No. 9 on; title changed to Daring with No. 9)
Jan, 1940 - No. 8, Jan, 1942
Timely Comics (TPI 1-6/TCI 7,8)

1-Origin The Fiery Mask by Joe Simon; Monako, Prince of Magic, John Steele, Soldier of Fortune, Doc Doyle begin; Flash Foster & Barney Mullen, Sea Rover only app; bondage-c 395.00 1185.00 2765.00
2-(Rare)-Origin The Phantom Bullet & only app.; The Laughing Mask

DARING MYSTERY COMICS (continued)

	Good	Fine	Mint
& Mr. E only app.; Trojak the Tiger Man begins, ends No. 6; Zephyr Jones & K-4 & His Sky Devils app., also No. 4	195.00	585.00	1365.00
3-The Phantom Reporter, Dale of FBI, Breeze Barton, Captain Strong & Marvex the Super-Robot only app.; The Purple Mask begins	140.00	420.00	980.00
4-Last Purple Mask; Whirlwind Carter begins; Dan Gorman, G-Man app.	100.00	300.00	700.00
5-The Falcon begins; The Fiery Mask, Little Hercules app. by Sagendorf in the Segar style; bondage-c	95.00	285.00	665.00
6-Origin & only app. Marvel Boy by S&K; Flying Flame, Dynaman, & Stuporman only app.; The Fiery Mask by S&K; S&K bondage-c	120.00	360.00	840.00
7-Origin The Blue Diamond, Captain Daring by S&K, The Challenger, The Fin by Everett, The Silver Scorpion & The Thunderer by Burgos; Mr. Millions app.	120.00	360.00	840.00
8-Origin Citizen V; Last Fin, Silver Scorpion, Capt. Daring by Borth, Blue Diamond & The Thunderer; S&K-c; Rudy the Robot only app.	90.00	270.00	630.00

NOTE: ***Schomburg*** *c-1-4.* ***Simon*** *a-2,3,5.*

DARING NEW ADVENTURES OF SUPERGIRL, THE
Nov, 1982 - No. 13, Nov, 1983 (Supergirl No. 14-on)
DC Comics

	Good	Fine	Mint
1-Origin retold		.40	.80
2-13: 13-New costume; flag-c		.25	.50

NOTE: ***Giffen*** *c-3p, 4p.* ***Buckler*** *c-1p, 2p.* ***Gil Kane*** *c-6, 8, 9, 11-13.*

DARK CRYSTAL, THE
April, 1983 - No. 2, May, 1983
Marvel Comics Group

	Good	Fine	Mint
1,2-Movie adaptation, part 1&2		.25	.50

DARK HORSE PRESENTS
July, 1986 - Present ($1.50, B&W)
Dark Horse Comics

	Good	Fine	Mint
1-Black Cross app.	.35	1.00	2.00
2,3-Black Cross app.		.75	1.50

DARK KNIGHT (See Batman: The Dark Knight Returns)

DARKLON THE MYSTIC
Oct, 1983 (One shot)
Pacific Comics

	Good	Fine	Mint
1-Starlin c/a(r)	.25	.75	1.50

DARK MANSION OF FORBIDDEN LOVE, THE (Becomes Forbidden Tales of Dark Mansion No. 5 on)
Sept-Oct, 1971 - No. 4, Mar-Apr, 1972
National Periodical Publications

	Good	Fine	Mint
1-4: 2-Adams-c. 3-Jeff Jones-c		.40	.80

DARK MYSTERIES
June-July, 1951 - No. 25, 1955
''Master''-''Merit'' Publications

	Good	Fine	Mint
1-Wood c/a, 8 pgs.	20.00	60.00	140.00
2-Wood/Harrison c/a, 8 pgs.	15.50	46.00	110.00
3-9	4.35	13.00	30.00
10-Cannibalism story; bondage-c	5.50	16.50	38.00
11-13,15-18: 11-Severed head panels. 18-Bondage-c	3.75	11.25	26.00
14-Several E.C. Craig swipes	4.35	13.00	30.00
19-Injury to eye panel; bondage-c	5.50	16.50	38.00
20-Female bondage, blood drainage story	4.35	13.00	30.00
21,22-Last pre-code ish, mis-dated 3/54 instead of 3/55	3.35	10.00	23.00
23-25	2.35	7.00	16.00

NOTE: ***Cameron*** *a-1, 2.* ***Harrison*** *a-3, 7; c-3.* ***Hollingsworth*** *a-7-17, 20, 21, 23.* ***Woodish*** *art by Fleishman-9.*

DARK SHADOWS
October, 1957 - 1958
Steinway Comic Publications (Ajax)

	Good	Fine	Mint
1	3.00	9.00	21.00
2,3	1.75	5.25	12.00

DARK SHADOWS (TV) (See Dan Curtis)
March, 1969 - No. 35, Feb, 1976 (Photo-c, 1-7)
Gold Key

	Good	Fine	Mint
1(30039-903)-with pull-out poster	4.00	12.00	24.00
2	2.00	6.00	12.00
3-with pull-out poster	2.65	8.00	16.00
4-7: Last photo-c	1.70	5.00	10.00
8-10	1.35	4.00	8.00
11-20	1.00	3.00	6.00
21-35: 30-last painted-c	.70	2.00	4.00
Story Digest 1 (6/70)	.70	2.00	4.00

DARLING LOVE
Oct-Nov, 1949 - No. 11, 1952 (no month)
Close Up/Archie Publ. (A Darling Magazine)

	Good	Fine	Mint
1	4.00	12.00	28.00
2	2.35	7.00	16.00
3-8,10,11: 5,6-photo-c	2.00	6.00	14.00
9-Krigstein-a	3.35	10.00	23.00

DARLING ROMANCE
Sept-Oct, 1949 - No. 7, 1951
Close Up (MLJ Publications)

	Good	Fine	Mint
1	4.00	12.00	28.00
2	2.35	7.00	16.00
3-7	2.00	6.00	14.00

DASTARDLY & MUTTLEY IN THEIR FLYING MACHINES (See Fun-In No. 1-4,6)

DASTARDLY & MUTTLEY KITE FUN BOOK (Giveaway)
1969 (16 pages) (5x7'') (Hanna-Barbera's)
Florida Power & Light Co./Sou. Calif. Edison/Pacific Gas & Electric

	Good	Fine	Mint
	.75	2.25	5.00

DATE WITH DANGER
No. 5, Dec, 1952 - No. 6, Feb, 1953
Standard Comics

	Good	Fine	Mint
5,6	2.35	7.00	16.00

DATE WITH DEBBI
1-2/69 - No. 17, 9-10/71; No. 18, 10-11/72
National Periodical Publications

	Good	Fine	Mint
1	.85	2.50	5.00
2-18	.50	1.50	3.00

DATE WITH JUDY, A (Radio/TV)
Oct-Nov, 1947 - No. 79, Oct-Nov, 1960 (No. 1-24, 52 pgs.)
National Periodical Publications

	Good	Fine	Mint
1	9.00	27.00	62.00
2	4.50	13.50	31.00
3-10	3.35	10.00	23.00
11-20	2.35	7.00	16.00
21-40	1.65	5.00	11.00
41-45: 45-Last pre-code (2-3/55)	1.15	3.50	8.00
46-79: 79-Drucker c/a	1.00	3.00	7.00

DATE WITH MILLIE, A (Life With Millie No. 8 on)
Oct, 1956 - No. 7, Aug, 1957; Oct, 1959 - No. 7, Oct, 1960
Atlas/Marvel Comics (MPC)

	Good	Fine	Mint
1(10/56)-(1st Series)	4.35	13.00	30.00

Daring Mystery Comics #4, © MCG

Dark Mysteries #11, © Master

Dark Shadows #26 (GK), © Dan Curtis

Date With Patsy #1, © MCG

DC Challenge #1, © DC

DC Comics Presents #59, © DC

A DATE WITH MILLIE (continued)

	Good	Fine	Mint
2	2.15	6.50	15.00
3-7	1.85	5.50	13.00
1(10/59)-(2nd Series)	2.85	8.50	20.00
2-7	1.50	4.50	10.00

DATE WITH PATSY, A
September, 1957
Atlas Comics

	Good	Fine	Mint
1	2.35	7.00	16.00

DAVID AND GOLIATH (See 4-Color No. 1205)

DAVID CASSIDY
Feb, 1972 - No. 14, Sept, 1973
Charlton Comics

	Good	Fine	Mint
1	1.00	3.00	6.00
2-14	.70	2.00	4.00

DAVID LADD'S LIFE STORY (See Movie Classics)

DAVY CROCKETT (See Dell Giants, Fightin..., Frontier Fighters, It's Game Time, & Western Tales)

DAVY CROCKETT
1951
Avon Periodicals

	Good	Fine	Mint
nn-Tuska?, Reinman-a; Fawcette-c	7.00	20.00	50.00

DAVY CROCKETT (...King of the Wild Frontier No. 1,2)(TV)
5/55 - No. 671, 12/55; No. 1, 12/63; No. 2, 11/69 (Walt Disney)
Dell Publishing Co./Gold Key

	Good	Fine	Mint
4-Color 631-Fess Parker photo-c	2.35	7.00	16.00
4-Color 639-Photo-c	2.00	6.00	14.00
4-Color 664,671(Marsh-a)-Photo-c	2.65	8.00	18.00
1(12/63-Gold Key)-r	1.50	4.50	10.00
2(11/69)-r	1.00	3.00	6.00
..Christmas Book (no date, 16pgs, paper-c) Sears giveaway	1.50	4.50	10.00
..In the Raid at Piney Creek (1955, 16pgs, 5x7¼'')American Motors giveaway	2.85	8.50	20.00
..Safety Trails (1955, 16pgs, 3¼x7'') Cities Service giveaway	2.15	6.50	15.00

DAVY CROCKETT (...Frontier Fighter No. 1,2; Kid Montana No. 9 on)
Aug, 1955 - No. 8, Jan, 1957
Charlton Comics

	Good	Fine	Mint
1	2.35	7.00	16.00
2	1.15	3.50	8.00
3-8	.85	2.50	6.00
Hunting With...('55, 16 pgs.)-Ben Franklin Store giveaway (Publ.-S. Rose)	.85	2.50	6.00

DAYS OF THE MOB (See In the Days of the Mob)

DAZEY'S DIARY
June-Aug, 1962
Dell Publishing Co.

	Good	Fine	Mint
01-174-208: Bill Woggon-a?	2.00	6.00	14.00

DAZZLER, THE (Also see X-Men No. 130)
March, 1981 - No. 42, Mar, 1986
Marvel Comics Group

	Good	Fine	Mint
1-X-Men app; Alcala art	.25	.75	1.50
2-X-Men app.		.50	1.00
3-20: 23,24-Power Man & Iron Fist app. 32-The Inhumans app.		.40	.80
21-Double size; photo-c; many cameos		.50	1.00
22-35		.35	.70

	Good	Fine	Mint
36-42: 38-X-Men app.		.40	.80

NOTE: *No. 1 distributed only through comic shops.* ***Alcala*** *a-1i, 2i.* ***Guice*** *a-42.*

DC CHALLENGE
11/85 - No. 12, 10/86 ($1.25-$2.00; 12 issue maxi-series)
DC Comics

	Good	Fine	Mint
1	.25	.75	1.50
2-11		.65	1.30
12($2.00)-Perez/Austin-c	.35	1.00	2.00

DC COMICS PRESENTS
July-Aug, 1978 - No. 97, Sept, 1986
DC Comics

(Superman team-ups with No. 1-on)

	Good	Fine	Mint
1	.40	1.25	2.50
2-10	.25	.75	1.50
11,12,14-20		.60	1.20
13-Legion of Super Heroes	.45	1.25	2.50
21-25		.50	1.00
26-(10/80)-Green Lantern; intro Cyborg, Starfire, Raven, New Teen Titans; Starlin-c/a; Sargon the Sorcerer back-up; 16 pgs. preview of the New Teen Titans	2.00	6.00	12.00
27-51: 41-16 pg. W. Woman insert; 1st app. in new costume. 43-Legion app.		.30	.60
52-1st app. Ambush Bug	.25	.75	1.50
53-58,60-80		.40	.80
59,81-Ambush Bug app.		.50	1.00
82-85		.40	.80
86,88-Crisis x-over		.50	1.00
87-Double size; Crisis x-over		.65	1.30
89-96: 90-Origin Capt. Atom retold		.45	.90
97-Double size		.65	1.30
Annual 1(9/82)-G.A. Superman		.60	1.20
Annual 2(7/83)-Intro/origin Superwoman		.60	1.20
Annual 3(9/84)-Shazam; intro Capt. Thunder		.60	1.20
Annual 4(10/85)-Superwoman		.65	1.30

NOTE: ***Adkins*** *a-2, 54; c-2.* ***Alcala*** *a-48.* ***Buckler*** *a-12p, 33p, 34p, 45p, 49p, Annual 1p; c-30p, 33p, 34p, 49p, 50p, Annual 1p.* ***Giffen*** *a/c-52p, 59p, 81p.* ***Gil Kane*** *a-28, 35, Annual 3; c-48p, 56, 58, 60, 62, 64, 68, Annual 2, 3.* ***Kubert*** *c/a-66.* ***Morrow*** *c/a-65.* ***Newton*** *a/c-54p.* ***Orlando*** *c-53i.* ***Perez*** *a-26p, 61p; c-38, 61, 94.* ***Starlin*** *a-26-29p, 36p, 37p; c-26-29, 36, 37, 93.* ***Staton*** *a(p)-9-11, 15, 16, 19, 21, 23, 39, 96p; c-15p.* ***Williamson*** *i-79, 85, 87.*

DC GRAPHIC NOVEL (Also see DC Science Fiction...)
Nov, 1983 - Present ($5.95, 68 pgs.)
DC Comics

	Good	Fine	Mint
1-Star Raiders	1.00	3.00	6.00
2-Warlords; not from the regular Warlord series	1.00	3.00	6.00
3-The Medusa Chain; Ernie Colon story/a	1.00	3.00	6.00
4-The Hunger Dogs; Kirby-a	1.00	3.00	6.00
5-Me And Joe Priest	1.00	3.00	6.00
6-Metalzoic	1.20	3.50	7.00
7-Space Clusters	1.00	3.00	6.00

DC 100 PAGE SUPER SPECTACULAR (50 cents)
(Title is 100 Page...No. 14 on)(Square bound)
1971 - No. 13, 6/72; No. 14, 2/73 - No. 22, 11/73 (No No.1-3)
National Periodical Publications

	Good	Fine	Mint
4-Weird Mystery Tales-Johnny Peril & Phantom Stranger; cover & splashes by Wrightson; origin Jungle Boy of Jupiter		.60	1.20
5-Love stories; Wood Inks, 7pgs.		.60	1.20
6-''World's Greatest Super-Heroes''-JLA, JSA, Spectre, Johnny Quick, Vigilante, Wildcat & Hawkman; Adams wrap-around-c	.25	.75	1.50

DC 100 PAGE SUPER SPEC. (continued)
7-(See Superman No. 245),8-(See Batman No. 238)
9-(See Our Army at War No. 242),10-(See Adventure No. 416)
11-(See Flash No. 214),12-(See Superboy No. 185)
13-(See Superman No. 252) **Good Fine Mint**
14-22: 22-r/All Flash 13 .40 .80

NOTE: ***Anderson*** *a-11, 14, 18i, 22.* ***B. Baily*** *a-18r, 20r.* ***Burnley*** *a-20r.* ***Crandall*** *a-14p(r).* ***Drucker*** *a-4r.* ***Infantino*** *a-17, 20, 22.* ***G. Kane*** *a-18.* ***Kubert*** *a-6, 7, 16, 17; c-16,19.* ***Meskin*** *a-4, 22.* ***Mooney*** *a-15r, 21r.* ***Toth*** *a-17, 20.*

DC SCIENCE FICTION GRAPHIC NOVEL
1985 - Present ($5.95)
DC Comics

SF1-Hell on Earth by Robert Bloch, SF2-Nightwings by Robert Silverberg, SF3-Frost & Fire by Bradbury 1.00 3.00 5.95
SF4-Merchants of Venus .85 2.50 4.95
SF5-Demon With A Glass Hand by Ellison; M. Rogers-a 1.00 3.00 5.95
SF6-The Magic Goes Away by Niven 1.00 3.00 5.95

DC SPECIAL (Also see Super DC . . .)
10-12/68 - No. 15, 11-12/71; No. 16, Spr/75 - No. 29, 8-9/77
National Periodical Publications

1-All Infantino ish; Flash, Batman, Adam Strange-r (68 pgs.) begin .60 1.20
2-4,6-11,13,14 .30 .60
5-All Kubert ish. Viking Prince, Sgt. Rock-r .50 1.00
12-Viking Prince; Kubert-c .50 1.00
15-G.A. Plastic Man origin r/Police No. 1; origin Woozy by Cole Last 68 pg. ish .60 1.20
16-27: 16-Super Heroes Battle Super Gorillas .30 .60
28-Earth Shattering Disaster Stories; Legion of Super-Heroes story .30 .60
29-Secret Origin of the Justice Society .30 .60

NOTE: ***Adams*** *c-3, 4, 6, 11, 29.* ***Buckler*** *a-27p; c-27p.* ***Grell*** *a-20; c-17.* ***Heath*** *a-12r.* ***G. Kane*** *a-6p, 17r, 19-21r.* ***Kubert*** *a-6r, 12r, 22.* ***Staton*** *a-29p.* ***Toth*** *a-13.*

DC SPECIAL BLUE-RIBBON DIGEST
Mar-Apr, 1980 - No. 24, Aug, 1982
DC Comics

1-24 .50 1.00

NOTE: ***Adams*** *a-16(6)r, 17r, 23r; c-16.* ***Aparo*** *a-6r, 24r; c-23.* ***Grell*** *a-8, 10; c-10.* ***Heath*** *a-14.* ***Kaluta*** *a-17r.* ***Gil Kane*** *a-22r.* ***Kirby*** *a-23r.* ***Kubert*** *a-3, 18r, 21r; c-7, 12, 14, 17, 18, 21, 24.* ***Morrow*** *a-24r.* ***Orlando*** *a-17r, 20r, 22r; c-1, 20.* ***Perez*** *c-19p.* ***Wood*** *a-3, 17r, 24r.* ***Toth*** *a-21r, 24r.* ***Wrightson*** *a-16r, 17r, 24r.*

DC SPECIAL SERIES
9/77 - No. 16, Fall, 1978; No. 17, 8/79 - No. 27, Fall, 1981
(No. 23 & 24 - digest size; No. 25-27 - over-sized)
National Periodical Publications/DC Comics

1-Five-Star Super-Hero Spectacular; Atom, Flash, Green Lantern, Aquaman, Batman, Kobra app.; Adams-c; Staton, Nasser-a .50 1.00
2(No.1)-Original Swamp Thing Saga, The(9-10/77)-reprints Swamp Thing No. 1&2 by Wrightson; Wrightson wrap-around-c .50 1.00
3-20,22-24: 10-Origin Dr. Fate, Lightray & Black Canary .25 .50
21-Miller-a .35 1.00 2.00
25-Superman II The Adventure Continues (Sum '81); photos from movie($2.95) (Same as All-New Coll. Ed. C-64?) .35 1.00 2.00
26-Superman and His Incredible Fortress of Solitude (Sum '81) ($2.50) (Same as All-New Co.. Ed. C-63?) .35 1.00 2.00
27-Batman vs. The Incredible Hulk($2.50) .35 1.00 2.00

DC SPOTLIGHT
1985 (50th anniversary special)
DC Comics (giveaway)

Good Fine Mint
1 .40 .80

DC SUPER-STARS
March, 1976 - No. 18, Winter, 1978 (No.3-18: 52 pgs.)
National Periodical Publications/DC Comics

1-Teen Titans (68 pgs.) .60 1.20
2-16,18 .30 .60
17-Secret Origins of Super-Heroes(1st app. & origin of The Huntress) Legion app. .60 1.20

NOTE: ***Aparo*** *c-7, 14, 17, 18.* ***Austin*** *a-11i.* ***Buckler*** *a-14p; c-10.* ***Grell*** *a-17.* ***G. Kane*** *a-1r, 10r.* ***Kubert*** *c-15.* ***Layton*** *c/a-16i, 17i.* ***Mooney*** *a-4r, 6r.* ***Morrow*** *c/a-11r.* ***Nasser*** *a-11.* ***Newton*** *c/a-16p.* ***Staton*** *a-17; c-17. No. 10, 12-18 contain all new material; the rest are reprints.*

D-DAY (Also see Special War Series)
Sum/63; No. 2, Fall/64; No. 4, 9/66; No. 5, 10/67; No. 6, 11/68
Charlton Comics (no No. 3)

1(1963)-Montes/Bache-c .35 1.00 2.00
2(Fall,'64)-Wood-a(3) 1.00 3.00 6.00
4-6('66-'68)-Montes/Bache-a No. 5 .25 .75 1.50

DEAD END CRIME STORIES
April, 1949 (52 pages)
Kirby Publishing Co.

nn-(Scarce)-Powell, Roussos-a 17.00 51.00 120.00

DEAD-EYE WESTERN COMICS
Nov-Dec, 1948 - V3No.1, Apr-May, 1953
Hillman Periodicals

V1No.1(52 pgs.)-Krigstein, Roussos-a 4.65 14.00 32.00
V1No.2,3(52 pgs.) 2.35 7.00 16.00
V1No.4-12 1.35 4.00 9.00
V2No.1,2,5-8,10-12 1.00 3.00 7.00
3,4-Krigstein-a 2.00 6.00 14.00
9-One pg. Frazetta ad 1.50 4.50 10.00
V3No.1 .85 2.50 6.00

NOTE: ***Briefer*** *a-V1No.8. Kinstleresque stories by* ***McCann****-12, V2No.1,2, V3No.1.*

DEADLIEST HEROES OF KUNG FU
Summer, 1975 (Magazine)
Marvel Comics Group

1 .30 .90 1.80

DEADLY HANDS OF KUNG FU, THE
April, 1974 - No. 33, Feb, 1977 (75 cents) (B&W - Magazine)
Marvel Comics Group

1(V1No.4 listed in error)-Origin Sons of the Tiger; Shang-Chi, Master of Kung Fu begins; Bruce Lee photo pin-up .40 1.25 2.50
2,3,5 .30 .90 1.80
4-Bruce Lee painted-c by Adams; 8 pg. biog of B. Lee .40 1.25 2.50
6-14 .30 .90 1.80
15-(Annual 1, Summer '75) .30 .90 1.80
16-19,21-27,29-33: 19-1st White Tiger .60 1.20
20-Origin The White Tiger; Perez-a .30 .90 1.80
28-Origin Jack of Hearts; Bruce Lee life story .40 1.25 2.50
Special Album Edition 1(Summer, '74)-Adams-i .30 .90 1.80

NOTE: ***Adams*** *c-1, 2-4, 11, 12, 14, 17.* ***Giffen*** *a-22p, 24p.* ***G. Kane*** *a-23p.* ***Kirby*** *a-5r.* ***Perez*** *a(p)-6-14, 16, 17, 19.* ***Rogers*** *a-32, 33.* ***Starlin*** *a-1, 2r, 15r.* ***Staton*** *a-28p, 31, 32. Sons of the Tiger in 1, 3, 4, 6-14, 16-19.*

DEADMAN
May, 1985 - No. 7, Nov, 1985
DC Comics

1-Deadman-r by Infantino, Adams .35 1.00 2.00
2-7 .30 .90 1.80

DC Special Series #20, © DC

DC Super-Stars #4, © DC

Dead-Eye Western V2No.3, © HILL

Deadman #1 (3/86), © DC

Dear Nancy Parker #1, © K.K. Publ.

Death Rattle V2No.1, © Kitchen Sink

DEADMAN
Mar, 1986 - No. 4, June, 1986 (mini-series)
DC Comics

	Good	Fine	Mint
1-4-Lopez-c/a		.45	.90

DEAD OF NIGHT
Dec, 1973 - No. 11, Aug, 1975
Marvel Comics Group

	Good	Fine	Mint
1-Reprints		.30	.60
2-11: 11-Kane/Wrightson-c		.25	.50

NOTE: *Ditko a-7r, 10r.*

DEAD WHO WALK, THE
1952 (One Shot)
Realistic Comics

	Good	Fine	Mint
nn	18.50	56.00	130.00

DEADWOOD GULCH
1931 (52 pages) (B&W)
Dell Publishing Co.

	Good	Fine	Mint
By Gordon Rogers	5.00	15.00	35.00

DEADWORLD
Dec, 1986 - Present ($1.50, B&W)
Arrow Comics

	Good	Fine	Mint
1		.75	1.50

DEAN MARTIN & JERRY LEWIS (See Adventures of. . .)

DEAR BEATRICE FAIRFAX
Nov, 1949 - No. 9, Sept, 1951 (Vern Greene art)
Best/Standard Comics(King Features)

	Good	Fine	Mint
1	2.65	8.00	18.00
2	1.65	5.00	11.00
3-9	1.35	4.00	9.00

NOTE: *Schomburg air brush-c-1-9.*

DEAR HEART (Formerly Lonely Heart)
No. 15, July, 1956 - No. 16, Sept, 1956
Ajax

	Good	Fine	Mint
15,16	1.65	5.00	11.00

DEAR LONELY HEART (. . . Illustrated No. 1-6)
Mar, 1951; No. 3, Dec, 1951 - No. 8, Oct, 1952
Artful Publications

	Good	Fine	Mint
1	7.00	21.00	50.00
2	3.65	11.00	25.00
3-Matt Baker Jungle Girl story	8.00	24.00	56.00
4-8	3.35	10.00	23.00

DEAR LONELY HEARTS
Aug, 1953 - No. 8, Oct, 1954
Harwell Publ./Mystery Publ. Co.

	Good	Fine	Mint
1	2.85	8.50	20.00
2-8	1.65	5.00	11.00

DEARLY BELOVED
Fall, 1952
Ziff-Davis Publishing Co.

	Good	Fine	Mint
1-Photo-c	6.00	18.00	42.00

DEAR NANCY PARKER
June, 1963 - No. 2, Sept, 1963
Gold Key

	Good	Fine	Mint
1,2	1.50	4.50	10.00

DEATH CRAZED TEENAGE SUPERHEROES
1986 ($1.50, B&W)
Arf! Arf!

	Good	Fine	Mint
1	.35	1.00	2.00

DEATH RATTLE (Formerly an Underground)
V2/1, 10/85 - Present ($1.95, Baxter paper)(Mature readers)
Kitchen Sink Press

	Good	Fine	Mint
V2/1-Corben-c	.35	1.00	2.00
2-5: 2-Unpubbed Spirit sty by Eisner. 5-Robot Woman by Wolverton-r	.35	1.00	2.00
6,7: 6-B&W issues begin	.35	1.00	2.00

DEATH VALLEY
Oct, 1953 - No. 6, Aug, 1954?
Comic Media

	Good	Fine	Mint
1-Old Scout	3.00	9.00	21.00
2	1.75	5.25	12.00
3-6	1.15	3.50	8.00

DEATH VALLEY (Becomes Frontier Scout, Daniel Boone No.10-13)
No. 7, 6/55 - No. 9, 10/55 (Cont. from Comic Media series)
Charlton Comics

	Good	Fine	Mint
7-9	1.15	3.50	8.00

DEBBIE DEAN, CAREER GIRL
April, 1945 - No. 2, 1945
Civil Service Publ.

	Good	Fine	Mint
1,2-Newspaper reprints by Bert Whitman	5.50	16.50	38.00

DEBBI'S DATES
Apr-May, 1969 - No. 11, Dec-Jan, 1970-71
National Periodical Publications

	Good	Fine	Mint
1-11: 4-Adams text illo.	.25	.75	1.50

DEEP, THE (Movie)
November, 1977
Marvel Comics Group

	Good	Fine	Mint
1-Infantino c/a		.40	.80

DEFENDERS, THE (TV)
Sept-Nov, 1962 - No. 2, Feb-Apr, 1963
Dell Publishing Co.

	Good	Fine	Mint
12-176-211(No.1), 304(No.2)	1.15	3.50	8.00

DEFENDERS, THE (Also see Marvel Feature; The New. . . No. 140-on)
Aug, 1972 - No. 152, Feb, 1986
Marvel Comics Group

	Good	Fine	Mint
1-The Hulk, Doc Strange, & Sub-Mariner begin	1.70	5.00	10.00
2	.85	2.50	5.00
3-5: 4-Valkyrie joins	.70	2.00	4.00
6-10: 9,10-Avengers app. 10-Thor-Hulk battle	.40	1.25	2.50
11-20: 12-Xemnu, The Titan app. 13,14-Squadron Sinister app.; Sub-Mariner leaves, Nighthawk joins. 15,16-Magneto app. 17-19-Powerman, Wrecking Crew app.	.25	.80	1.60
21-30: 25-Powerman app. 26-29-Guardians of the Galaxy app. 27-1st app. Starhawk (cameo). 28-Starhawk app.		.50	1.00
31-46: 31,32-Origin Nighthawk. 35-Intro. New Red Guardian. 44-Hellcat joins. 45-Dr. Strange leaves		.40	.80
47-51-Giffen-a; Moon Knight x-over; 47-Wonderman app.	.25	.75	1.50
52-Giffen-a(p)		.50	1.00
53,54-Golden/Giffen-a		.50	1.00
55-99: 55-Origin Red Guardian. 57-Ms. Marvel app. 62-64-Nova & others cameo. 77-Origin Omega. 99-Silver Surfer app.		.40	.80
100-Double size; Silver Surfer app.		.50	1.00

THE DEFENDERS (continued)	Good	Fine	Mint
101-124: 101,107,123-Silver Surfer app. 106-Death of Nighthawk		.40	.80
125-($1.25)Double size; 1st app. Mad Dog; Hellcat & Son of Satan wed; intro. new Defenders		.60	1.20
126-149,151: 140-Moondragon new costume		.30	.60
150-Double size; origin Cloud		.65	1.30
152-Double size; ties in with X-Factor & Secret Wars II		.75	1.50

NOTE: ***Austin*** *a-53i; c-65i, 119i, 145i.* ***Frank Bolle*** *a-7i, 10i, 11i.* ***Buckler*** *c(p)-34, 38, 76, 77, 79-86, 90, 91.* ***J. Buscema*** *c-66.* ***Ditko*** *a-Gnt-Size 1-4r.* ***Everett*** *r-Gnt-Size 4.* ***Giffen*** *a-42-49p, 50, 51p, 52p, 53i, 54p.* ***Golden*** *a-53p, 54i; c-94, 96.* ***Guice*** *c-129.* ***G. Kane*** *c(p)-13, 16, 18, 19, 21-26, 31-33, 35-37, 40, 41, 52, 55, Gnt-Size 2, 4.* ***Kirby*** *c-42-45.* ***Mooney*** *a-3i, 31-34i, 62i, 63i, 85i.* ***Nasser*** *c-88p.* ***Perez*** *c(p)-51, 53, 54.* ***Rogers*** *c-98.* ***Starlin*** *c-110.* ***Tuska*** *a-57p. Silver Surfer in No. 2, 3, 6, 8-11.*

	Good	Fine	Mint
Annual 1(11/76)	.35	1.00	2.00
Giant Size 1(7/74)-Silver Surfer app.; Starlin-a; Everett, Ditko, & Kirby-r	.50	1.50	3.00
Giant Size 2(10/74)-G. Kane-a; Everett, Ditko-r		.50	1.00
Giant Size 3(1/75)-Starlin, Newton, Everett-a		.50	1.00
Giant Size 4(4/75), 5(7/75)-Guardians app.		.50	1.00

DEFENDERS OF THE EARTH (TV)
Jan, 1987 - Present
Star Comics (Marvel)

	Good	Fine	Mint
1-The Phantom, Mandrake The Magician, Flash Gordon		.40	.80

THE DEFINITIVE DIRECTORY OF THE DC UNIVERSE (See Who's Who . . .)

DELECTA OF THE PLANETS (See Fawcett Miniatures & Don Fortune)

DELLA VISION
April, 1955 - No. 3, Aug, 1955
Atlas Comics

	Good	Fine	Mint
1	4.65	14.00	32.00
2,3	3.50	10.50	24.00

DELL GIANT COMICS
No. 21, Sept, 1959 - No. 55, Sept, 1961 (Most 84 pages, 25 cents)
Dell Publishing Co.

	Good	Fine	Mint
21-M.G.M.'s Tom & Jerry Picnic Time (84pp, stapled binding)	2.50	7.50	20.00
22-Huey, Dewey & Louie Back to School(10/59, 84pp, square binding begins)	2.50	10.00	25.00
23-Marge's Little Lulu & Tubby Halloween Fun (10/59)-Stanley-a	5.00	20.00	50.00
24-Woody Woodpeckers Family Fun (11/59)	1.60	6.40	16.00
25-Tarzan's Jungle World(11/59)-Marsh-a	3.00	12.00	30.00
26-Christmas Parade-Barks-a, 16pgs.(Disney; 12/59)-Barks draws himself on wanted poster pg. 13	7.00	28.00	70.00
27-Man in Space r-/4-Color 716,866, & 954 (100 pages, 35 cents) (Disney)(TV)	2.50	10.00	25.00
28-Bugs Bunny's Winter Fun (2/60)	1.60	6.40	16.00
29-Marge's Little Lulu & Tubby in Hawaii (4/60)-Stanley-a	5.00	20.00	50.00
30-Disneyland USA(6/60)-Reprinted in Vacation in Disneyland	3.00	12.00	30.00
31-Huckleberry Hound Summer Fun (7/60)(TV)	2.00	8.00	20.00
32-Bugs Bunny Beach Party	1.60	6.40	16.00
33-Daisy Duck & Uncle Scrooge Picnic Time (9/60)	3.00	12.00	30.00
34-Nancy & Sluggo Summer Camp (8/60)	2.00	8.00	20.00
35-Huey, Dewey & Louie Back to School (10/60)	2.50	10.00	25.00
36-Marge's Little Lulu & Witch Hazel Halloween Fun(10/60)-Stanley-a	5.00	20.00	50.00
37-Tarzan, King of the Jungle(11/60)-Marsh-a	2.50	10.00	25.00
38-Uncle Donald & His Nephews Family Fun (11/60)	2.50	10.00	25.00
39-Walt Disney's Merry Christmas(12/60)	2.50	10.00	25.00
40-Woody Woodpecker Christmas Parade(12/60)	1.60	6.40	16.00
41-Yogi Bear's Winter Sports (12/60)(TV)	2.00	8.00	20.00
42-Marge's Little Lulu & Tubby in Australia (4/61)	5.00	20.00	50.00
43-Mighty Mouse in Outer Space (5/61)	5.00	20.00	50.00
44-Around the World with Huckleberry & His Friends (7/61)(TV)	2.00	8.00	20.00
45-Nancy & Sluggo Summer Camp (8/61)	2.00	8.00	20.00
46-Bugs Bunny Beach Party (8/61)	1.60	6.40	16.00
47-Mickey & Donald in Vacationland (8/61)	2.50	10.00	25.00
48-The Flintstones (No. 1)(Bedrock Bedlam)(7/61)(TV)	3.00	12.00	30.00
49-Huey, Dewey & Louie Back to School (9/61)	2.50	10.00	25.00
50-Marge's Little Lulu & Witch Hazel Trick 'N' Treat (10/61)	5.00	20.00	50.00
51-Tarzan, King of the Jungle by Jesse Marsh (11/61)	2.50	10.00	25.00
52-Uncle Donald & His Nephews Dude Ranch (11/61)	2.50	10.00	25.00
53-Donald Duck Merry Christmas(12/61)-Not by Barks	2.50	10.00	25.00
54-Woody Woodpecker Christmas Party(12/61)-issued after No. 55	2.00	8.00	20.00
55-Daisy Duck & Uncle Scrooge Showboat (9/61)-1st app. Daisy Duck's nieces, April, May & June	3.50	14.00	35.00

NOTE: *All issues printed with & without ad on back cover.*

(OTHER DELL GIANT EDITIONS)

	Good	Fine	Mint
Abraham Lincoln Life Story 1(3/58, 100p)	2.00	8.00	20.00
Bugs Bunny Christmas Funnies 1(11/50, 116p)	5.00	20.00	50.00
. . .**Christmas Funnies** 2(11/51, 116p)	3.50	14.00	35.00
. . .**Christmas Funnies** 3-5(11/52-11/54, 100p)-Becomes Christmas Party No. 6	2.50	10.00	25.00
. . .**Christmas Funnies** 7-9(12/56-12/58, 100p)	2.00	8.00	20.00
. . .**Christmas Party** 6(11/55, 100p)-Formerly B.B. Christmas Funnies No. 5	2.50	10.00	25.00
. . .**County Fair** 1(9/57, 100p)	2.75	11.00	27.50
. . .**Halloween Parade** 1(10/53, 100p)	4.50	18.00	45.00
. . .**Halloween Parade** 2(10/54, 100p)-Trick 'N' Treat Halloween Fun No. 3-on	3.00	12.00	30.00
. . .**Trick 'N' Treat Halloween Fun** 3,4(10/55-10/56, 100p)-Formerly Halloween Parade 2	2.50	10.00	25.00
. . .**Vacation Funnies** 1(7/51, 112p)	5.00	20.00	50.00
. . .**Vacation Funnies** 2('52, 100p)	3.50	14.00	35.00
. . .**Vacation Funnies** 3-5('53-'55, 100p)	2.50	10.00	25.00
. . .**Vacation Funnies** 6-9('54-6/59, 100p)	2.00	8.00	20.00
Cadet Gray of West Point 1(4/58, 100p)-Williamson-a, 10pgs.	3.00	12.00	30.00
Christmas In Disneyland 1(12/57, 100p)-Barks-a, 18pgs.	6.00	24.00	60.00
Christmas Parade 1(11/49)-Barks-a, 25pgs; r-in G.K. Christmas Parade 5	27.00	108.00	270.00
Christmas Parade 2('50)-Barks-a, 25pgs; r-in G.K. Christmas Parade 6	16.00	64.00	160.00
Christmas Parade 3-7('51-'55, 100p)	3.00	12.00	30.00
Christmas Parade 8(12/56, 100p)-Barks-a, 8pgs.	6.00	24.00	60.00
Christmas Parade 9(12/58, 100p)-Barks-a, 20pgs.	8.00	32.00	80.00
Christmas Treasury, A 1(11/54, 100p)	4.00	16.00	40.00

The Defenders #125, © MCG

Dell Giant Comics #37, © ERB

Christmas Parade #8, © WDC

Lone Ranger Western Treasury #1, © Lone Ranger

Mickey Mouse in Frontier Land #1, © WDC

Tom & Jerry Winter Carnival #1, © M.G.M.

DELL GIANT COMICS (continued) — Good / Fine / Mint

Davy Crockett, King Of The Wild Frontier 1(9/55, 100p)-Photo-c; Marsh-a 6.00 24.00 60.00

Disneyland Birthday Party 1(10/58, 100p)-Barks-a, 16pgs. 5.50 22.00 55.00

Donald and Mickey In Disneyland 1(5/58, 100p) 2.75 11.00 27.50

Donald Duck Beach Party 1(7/54, 100p) 4.00 16.00 40.00

. . . **Beach Party** 2('55, 100p) 3.00 12.00 30.00

. . . **Beach Party** 3-5('56-'58, 100p) 2.50 10.00 25.00

. . . **Beach Party** 6(8/59, 84p)-Stapled 2.00 8.00 20.00

Donald Duck Fun Book 1,2('53-10/54, 100p)-Games, puzzles, comics & cut-outs (Rare) 6.00 24.00 60.00

Donald Duck In Disneyland 1(9/55, 100p) 2.75 11.00 27.50

Golden West Rodeo Treasury 1(10/57, 100p) 3.00 12.00 30.00

Huey, Dewey and Louie Back To School 1(9/58, 100p) 3.00 12.00 30.00

Lady and The Tramp 1(6/55, 100p) 3.00 12.00 30.00

Life Stories of American Presidents 1(11/57, 100p)-Buscema-a 2.00 8.00 20.00

Lone Ranger Golden West 3(8/55, 100p)-Formerly West. Treasury 3.50 14.00 35.00

. . . **Movie Story** nn(3/56, 100p)-Origin Lone Ranger in text; Clayton Moore photo-c 10.00 40.00 100.00

. . . **Western Treasury** 1(9/53, 100p)-Origin L. Ranger, Silver, & Tonto 8.00 32.00 80.00

. . . **Western Treasury** 2(8/54, 100p)-Becomes Golden West No. 3 4.50 18.00 45.00

Marge's Little Lulu & Alvin Story Telling Time 1(3/59)-r/No.2,5,3, 11,30,10,21,17,8,14,16; Stanley-a 6.00 24.00 60.00

. . . **& Her Friends** 4(3/56, 100p)-Stanley-a 5.00 20.00 50.00

. . . **& Her Special Friends** 3(3/55, 100p)-Stanley-a 5.00 20.00 50.00

. . . **& Tubby At Summer Camp** 5(10/57, 100p)-Stanley-a 5.00 20.00 50.00

. . . **& Tubby At Summer Camp** 2(10/58, 100p)-Stanley-a 5.00 20.00 50.00

. . . **& Tubby Halloween Fun** 6(10/57, 100p)-Stanley-a 5.00 20.00 50.00

. . . **& Tubby Halloween Fun** 2(10/58, 100p)-Stanley-a 5.00 20.00 50.00

. . . **& Tubby In Alaska** 1(7/59, 100p)-Stanley-a 5.00 20.00 50.00

. . . **On Vacation** 1(7/54, 100p)-r/4C-110,14,4C-146,5,4C-97,4, 4C-158,3,1; Stanley-a 8.00 32.00 80.00

. . . **& Tubby Annual** 1(3/53, 100p)-r/4C-165,4C-74,4C-146,4C-97, 4C-158,4C-139,4C-131; Stanley-a 13.00 52.00 130.00

. . . **& Tubby Annual** 2('54, 100p)-r/4C-139,6,4C-115,4C-74,5, 4C-97,3,4C-146,18; Stanley-a 12.00 48.00 120.00

Marge's Tubby & His Clubhouse Pals 1(10/56, 100p)-1st app. Gran'pa Feeb, written by Stanley; Tripp-a 7.00 28.00 70.00

Mickey Mouse Almanac 1(12/57, 100p)-Barks-a, 8pgs. 7.00 28.00 70.00

. . . **Birthday Party** 1(9/53, 100p)-r-/entire 48pgs. of Gottfredson's "M.M. in Love Trouble" from WDC&S 36-39. Quality equal to original. Also reprints one story each from 4-Color 27, 29, & 181 plus 6 panels of highlights in the career of Mickey Mouse 12.00 48.00 120.00

. . . **Club Parade** 1(12/55, 100p)-R-/4-Color 16 with some art redrawn by Paul Murry & recolored with night scenes turned into day; quality much poorer than original 9.00 36.00 90.00

. . . **In Fantasy Land** 1(5/57, 100p) 4.00 16.00 40.00

. . . **In Frontier Land** 1(5/56, 100p)-M.M. Club issue 4.00 16.00 40.00

. . . **Summer Fun** 1(8/58, 100p)-Mobile cut-outs on back-c; becomes Summer Fun No. 2 3.50 14.00 35.00

Moses & The Ten Commandments 1(8/57, 100p)-Not based on movie; Dell's adapt; Sekowsky-a 2.50 10.00 25.00

Good / Fine / Mint

Nancy & Sluggo Travel Time 1(9/58, 100p) 2.50 10.00 25.00

Peter Pan Treasure Chest 1(1/53, 212p)-Disney; contains movie adapt. plus other stories 15.00 60.00 150.00

Picnic Party 6,7(7/55-6/56, 100p)(Formerly Vacation Parade)-Uncle Scrooge 2.50 10.00 25.00

Picnic Party 8(7/57, 100p)-Barks-a, 6pgs. 4.50 18.00 45.00

Pogo Parade 1(9/53, 100p)-Kelly-a(r-/Pogo from Animal Comics in this order: No. 11,13,21,14,27,16,23,9,18,15,17) 13.00 52.00 130.00

Raggedy Ann & Andy 1(2/55, 100p) 4.00 16.00 40.00

Santa Claus Funnies 1(11/52, 100p)-Dan Noonan -**A Christmas Carol** adaptation 3.50 14.00 35.00

Silly Symphonies 1(9/52, 100p)-r/Chicken Little, M. Mouse "The Brave Little Tailor," Mother Pluto, Three Little Pigs, Lady, Bucky Bug, Wise Little Hen, Little Hiawatha, Pedro, The Grasshopper & The Ants 7.00 28.00 70.00

Silly Symphonies 2(9/53, 100p)-r/M. Mouse-"The Sorcerer's Apprentice," Little Hiawatha, Peculiar Penguins, Lambert The Sheepish Lion, Pluto, Spotty Pig, The Golden Touch, Elmer Elephant, The Pelican & The Snipe 5.00 20.00 50.00

Silly Symphonies 3(2/54, 100p)-r/Mickey & The Beanstalk (4-Color 157), Little Minnehaha, Pablo, The Flying Gauchito, Pluto, & Bongo 5.00 20.00 50.00

Silly Symphonies 4(8/54, 100p)-r/Dumbo (4-Color 234), Morris The Midget Moose, The Country Cousin, Bongo, & Clara Cluck 4.00 16.00 40.00

Silly Symphonies 5(2/55, 100p)-r/Cinderella (4-Color 272), Bucky Bug, Pluto, Little Hiawatha, The 7 Dwarfs & Dumbo, Pinocchio 4.00 16.00 40.00

Silly Symphonies 6(8/55, 100p)-r/Pinocchio(WDC&S 63), The 7 Dwarfs & Thumper (WDC&S 45), M. Mouse-"Adventures With Robin Hood," Johnny Appleseed, Pluto & Peter Pan, & Bucky Bug; Cut-out on back-c 4.00 16.00 40.00

Silly Symphonies 7(2/57, 100p)-r/Reluctant Dragon (4-Color 13), Ugly Duckling, M. Mouse & Peter Pan, Jiminy Cricket, Peter & The Wolf, Brer Rabbit, Bucky Bug; Cut-out on back-c 5.00 20.00 50.00

Silly Symphonies 8(2/58, 100p)-r/Thumper Meets The 7 Dwarfs (4-Color 19), Jiminy Cricket, Niok, Brer Rabbit; Cut-out on back-c 4.00 16.00 40.00

Silly Symphonies 9(2/59, 100p)-r/Paul Bunyan, Humphrey Bear, Jiminy Cricket, The Social Lion, Goliath II; Cut-out on back-c 4.00 16.00 40.00

Sleeping Beauty 1(4/59, 100p) 6.00 24.00 60.00

Summer Fun 2(8/59, 100p)(Formerly M. Mouse. . .)-Barks-a(2), 24 pgs. 5.00 20.00 50.00

Tales From The Tomb (See Tales From The Tomb)

Tarzan's Jungle Annual 1(8/52, 100p) 4.00 16.00 40.00

. . . **Annual** 2(8/53, 100p) 3.00 12.00 30.00

. . . **Annual** 3-7('54-9/58, 100p)(two No. 5s)-Manning-a-No. 3,5-7; Marsh-a in No. 1-7 2.00 8.00 20.00

Tom And Jerry Back To School 1(9/56, 100p) 2.50 10.00 25.00

. . . **Picnic Time** 1(7/58, 100p) 2.00 8.00 20.00

. . . **Summer Fun** 1(7/54, 100p)-Droopy written by Barks 4.50 18.00 45.00

. . . **Summer Fun** 2-4(7/55-7/57, 100p) 2.00 8.00 20.00

. . . **Toy Fair** 1(6/58, 100p) 2.50 10.00 25.00

. . . **Winter Carnival** 1(12/52, 100p)-Droopy written by Barks 6.00 24.00 60.00

. . . **Winter Carnival** 2(12/53, 100p)-Droopy written by Barks 3.50 14.00 35.00

. . . **Winter Fun** 3(12/54, 100p) 2.50 10.00 25.00

. . . **Winter Fun** 4-7(12/55-11/58, 100p) 2.00 8.00 20.00

Treasury of Dogs, A 1(10/56, 100p) 2.00 8.00 20.00

Treasury of Horses, A 1(9/55, 100p) 2.00 8.00 20.00

Uncle Scrooge Goes To Disneyland 1(8/57, 100p)-Barks-a, 20pgs. 6.00 24.00 60.00

DELL GIANT COMICS (continued) Good Fine Mint

Universal Presents-Dracula-The Mummy & Other Stories 02-530-311 (9-11/63, 84p)-R-/Dracula 12-231-212, The Mummy 12-437-211 & part of Ghost Stories No. 1 2.00 8.00 20.00

Vacation In Disneyland 1(8/58, 100p) 3.00 12.00 30.00

Vacation Parade 1(7/50, 130p)-Donald Duck & M. Mouse; Barks-a, 55 pgs. 45.00 180.00 450.00

Vacation Parade 2(7/51, 100p) 6.00 24.00 60.00

Vacation Parade 3-5(7/52-7/54, 100p)-Picnic Party No. 6 on 3.00 12.00 30.00

Western Roundup 1(6/52, 100p)-Photo-c; Gene Autry, Roy Rogers, Johnny Mack Brown, Rex Allen, & Bill Elliott begin; photo back-c begin, end No. 14,16,18 6.00 24.00 60.00

Western Roundup 2(2/53, 100p)-Photo-c 4.00 16.00 40.00

Western Roundup 3-5(7-9/53 - 1-3/54)-Photo-c 3.50 14.00 35.00

Western Roundup 6-10(4-6/54 - 4-6/55)-Photo-c 3.00 12.00 30.00

Western Roundup 11-13,16,17(100p)-Photo-c; Manning-a. 11-Flying A's Range Rider, Dale Evans begin 2.75 11.00 27.50

Western Roundup 14,15,25(1-3/59; 100p)-Photo-c 2.50 10.00 25.00

Western Roundup 18(100p)-Toth-a; last photo-c; Gene Autry ends 3.50 14.00 35.00

Western Roundup 19-24(100p)-Manning-a; 19-Buffalo Bill Jr. begins. 21-Rex Allen, Johnny Mack Brown end. 22-Jace Pearson's Texas Rangers, Rin Tin Tin, Tales of Wells Fargo & Wagon Train begin 2.50 10.00 25.00

Woody Woodpecker Back To School 1(10/52, 100p) 2.50 10.00 25.00

. . . **Back To School** 2-4,6('53-10/57, 100p)-County Fair No. 5 2.00 8.00 20.00

. . . **County Fair** 5(9/56, 100p)-Formerly Back To School 2.00 8.00 20.00

. . . **County Fair** 2(11/58, 100p) 2.00 8.00 20.00

DELL JUNIOR TREASURY (15 cents)
June, 1955 - No. 10, Oct, 1957
Dell Publishing Co.

1-Alice in Wonderland-Reprints 4-Color 331 (52 pgs.) 4.00 12.00 28.00
2-Aladdin & the Wonderful Lamp 3.50 10.50 24.00
3-Gulliver's Travels(1/56) 3.00 9.00 21.00
4-Advs. of Mr. Frog & Miss Mouse 4.00 12.00 28.00
5-The Wizard of Oz(7/56) 3.50 10.50 24.00
6-Heidi (10/56) 3.00 9.00 21.00
7-Santa and the Angel 3.00 9.00 21.00
8-Raggedy Ann and the Camel with the Wrinkled Knees 3.00 9.00 21.00
9-Clementina the Flying Pig 3.50 10.50 24.00
10-Adventures of Tom Sawyer 4.00 12.00 28.00

DEMON, THE (See Detective No. 482-485)
8-9/72 - No. 16, 1/74; 1/87 - No. 4, 4/87 (mini series)
National Periodical Publications

1-Origin; Kirby-c/a in 1-16 .50 1.00
2-16 .30 .60
1-4('87) .40 .80

DEMON DREAMS
Feb, 1984 - No. 2, May, 1984
Pacific Comics

1,2-Mostly r-/Heavy Metal .25 .75 1.50

DEMON-HUNTER
September, 1975
Seaboard Periodicals (Atlas)

1-Origin; Buckler c/a .30 .60

DENNIS THE MENACE (See The Best of . . . & The Very Best of . . .)
8/53 - No. 14, 1/56; No. 15, 3/56 - No. 31, 11/58; No. 32, 1/59 - No. 166, 11/79 Good Fine Mint
Standard Comics/Pines No.15-31/Hallden (Fawcett) No.32 on

1-1st app. Mr. & Mrs. Wilson, Ruff & Dennis' mom & dad; Wiseman-a, written by Fred Toole-most all issues 16.00 48.00 110.00
2 8.00 24.00 56.00
3-10 4.00 12.00 28.00
11-20 2.35 7.00 16.00
21-40: 22-1st app. Margaret w/blonde hair. 31-1st Joey app. 1.15 3.50 8.00
41-60 .75 2.25 5.00
61-90 .50 1.50 3.00
91-166 .30 .80 1.60
. . . & Dirt('59,'68)-Soil Conservation giveaway; r-No. 36; Wiseman c/a .25 .70 1.40
. . . Away We Go('70)-Caladayl giveaway .25 .70 1.40
. . . Coping with Family Stress-giveaway .30 .60
. . . Takes a Poke at Poison('61)-Food & Drug Assn. giveaway; Wiseman c/a .35 1.00 2.00
. . . Takes a Poke at Poison-Revised 1/66, 11/70, 1972, 1974, 1977, 1981 .30 .60

NOTE: *Wiseman c/a-1-46,53,68,69.*

DENNIS THE MENACE (Giants) (No. 1 titled Giant Vacation Special; becomes Bonus Magazine No. 76 on)
(No. 1-8,18,23,25,30,38: 100 pgs.; rest to No. 41: 84 pgs.; No. 42-75: 68 pgs.)
Summer, 1955 - No. 75, Dec, 1969
Standard/Pines/Hallden(Fawcett)

nn-Giant Vacation Special(Summer '55-Standard) 4.00 12.00 32.00
nn-Christmas issue (Winter '55) 3.00 9.00 24.00
2-Giant Vacation Special (Summer '56-Pines)
3-Giant Christmas issue (Winter '56-Pines)
4-Giant Vacation Special (Summer '57-Pines)
5-Giant Christmas issue (Winter '57-Pines)
6-In Hawaii (Giant Vacation Special)(Summer '58-Pines)-Reprinted Summer '59 plus 3 more times
6-Giant Christmas issue (Winter '58)
each. . . . 2.15 6.50 18.00
7-In Hollywood (Winter '59-Hallden)
8-In Mexico (Winter '60, 100 pgs.-Hallden/Fawcett)
8-In Mexico (Summer '62, 2nd printing)
9-Goes to Camp (Summer '61, 84 pgs., 2nd printing-Summer '62)-1st CCA approved ish.
10-X-Mas issue (Winter '61)
11-Giant Christmas issue (Winter '62)
12-Triple Feature (Winter '62)
each. . . . 1.75 5.25 14.00
13-Best of Dennis the Menace (Spring '63)-Reprints
14-And His Dog Ruff (Summer '63)
15-In Washington, D.C. (Summer '63)
16-Goes to Camp (Summer '63)-Reprints No. 9
17-& His Pal Joey (Winter '63)
18-In Hawaii (Reprints No. 6)
19-Giant Christmas issue (Winter '63)
20-Spring Special (Spring '64)
each. . . . 1.25 3.75 10.00
21-40 1.00 3.00 6.00
41-75 .50 1.50 3.00

NOTE: *Wiseman c/a-1-8,12,14,15,17,20,22,27,28,31,35,36,41,49.*

DENNIS THE MENACE
Nov, 1981 - No. 13, Nov, 1982
Marvel Comics Group

1,2-New art .25 .50

Universal Presents #02-530-311, © Universal

Woody Woodpecker's County Fair #5, © W. Lantz

Dell Junior Treasury #7, © DELL

Dennis the Menace & His Pal Joey #1, © FAW

Desperado #1, © LEV

Destroyer Duck #7, © Eclipse

DENNIS THE MENACE (continued)

	Good	Fine	Mint
3-13: 3-Part-r. 4,5-r		.25	.50

NOTE: ***Hank Ketcham*** *c-most; a-3,12.* ***Wiseman*** *a-4,5.*

DENNIS THE MENACE AND HIS DOG RUFF
Summer, 1961
Hallden/Fawcett

	Good	Fine	Mint
1-Wiseman c/a	2.00	6.00	16.00

DENNIS THE MENACE AND HIS FRIENDS
1969; No. 5, Jan, 1970 - No. 46, April, 1980 (All reprints)
Fawcett Publications

	Good	Fine	Mint
Dennis T.M. & Joey No. 2 (7/69)	1.35	4.00	8.00
Dennis T.M. & Ruff No. 2 (9/69)	1.00	3.00	6.00
Dennis T.M. & Mr. Wilson No. 1 (10/69)	1.00	3.00	6.00
Dennis & Margaret No. 1 (Winter '69)	.50	1.50	3.00
5-10: No. 5-Dennis T.M. & Margaret. No. 6-& Joey. No. 7-& Ruff. No. 8-& Mr. Wilson	.25	.70	1.40
11-20	.25	.70	1.40
21-37		.60	1.20
38(begin digest size, 148 pgs., 4/78, 95 cents) - 46		.60	1.20

NOTE: *Titles rotate every four issues, beginning with No. 5.*

DENNIS THE MENACE AND HIS PAL JOEY
Summer, 1961 (10 cents) (See Dennis the Menace Giants No. 45)
Fawcett Publications

	Good	Fine	Mint
1-Wiseman c/a	2.00	6.00	14.00

DENNIS THE MENACE AND THE BIBLE KIDS
1977 (36 pages)
Word Books

	Good	Fine	Mint
1-Jesus. 2-Joseph. 3-David. 4-The Bible Girls. 5-Moses. 6-More About Jesus. 7-The Lord's Prayer. 8-Stories Jesus told. 9-Paul, God's Traveller. 10-In the Beginning each....		.25	.50

NOTE: ***Ketcham*** *c/a in all.*

DENNIS THE MENACE BONUS MAGAZINE (Formerly Dennis the Menace Giants Nos. 1-75)
No. 76, 1/70 - No. 194, 10/79; (No. 76-124: 68 pgs.; No. 125-163: 52 pgs.; No. 164 on: 36 pgs.)
Fawcett Publications

	Good	Fine	Mint
76-90	.30	.90	1.80
91-110		.60	1.20
111-140		.40	.80
141-194		.30	.60

DENNIS THE MENACE BIG BONUS SERIES
No. 10, 1980 - No. 11, 1980
Fawcett Publications

	Good	Fine	Mint
10,11		.50	1.00

DENNIS THE MENACE COMICS DIGEST
April, 1982 - No. 3, Aug, 1982 (Digest Size, $1.25)
Marvel Comics Group

	Good	Fine	Mint
1-3-Reprints	.20	.60	1.25

NOTE: ***Hank Ketcham*** *c-all.* ***Wiseman*** *a-all. A few thousand No. 1's were published with a DC emblem on cover.*

DENNIS THE MENACE FUN BOOK
1960 (100 pages)
Fawcett Publications/Standard Comics

	Good	Fine	Mint
1-Part Wiseman-a	2.00	6.00	16.00

DENNIS THE MENACE POCKET FULL OF FUN!
Spring, 1969 - No. 50, March, 1980 (196 pages) (Digest size)
Fawcett Publications (Hallden)

	Good	Fine	Mint
1-Reprints in all issues	.70	2.00	4.00
2-10	.35	1.00	2.00
11-28		.50	1.00
29-50: 35,40,46-Sunday strip-r		.40	.80

NOTE: *No. 1-28 are 196 pgs.; No. 29-36: 164 pgs.; No. 37: 148 pgs.; No. 38 on: 132 pgs. No. 8, 11, 15, 21, 25, 29 all contain strip reprints.*

DENNIS THE MENACE TELEVISION SPECIAL
Summer, 1961 - No. 2, Spring, 1962 (Giant)
Fawcett Publications (Hallden Div.)

	Good	Fine	Mint
1	1.75	5.25	14.00
2	1.15	3.50	9.20

DENNIS THE MENACE TRIPLE FEATURE
Winter, 1961 (Giant)
Fawcett Publications

	Good	Fine	Mint
1-Wiseman c/a	1.50	4.50	12.00

DEPUTY, THE (See 4-Color No. 1077,1130,1225)

DEPUTY DAWG (TV) (Also see New Terrytoons)
Oct-Dec, 1961 - No. 1, Aug, 1965
Dell Publishing Co./Gold Key

	Good	Fine	Mint
4-Color 1238,1299	3.00	9.00	21.00
1(10164-508)	2.35	7.00	16.00

DEPUTY DAWG PRESENTS DINKY DUCK AND HASHIMOTO-SAN (TV)
August, 1965
Gold Key

	Good	Fine	Mint
1(10159-508)	2.35	7.00	16.00

DESIGN FOR SURVIVAL (Gen. Thomas S. Power's. . .)
1968 (36 pages in color) (25 cents)
American Security Council Press

	Good	Fine	Mint
nn-Propaganda against the Threat of Communism-Aircraft cover	3.00	9.00	18.00
Twin Circle edition-cover shows panels from inside	1.70	5.00	10.00

DESPERADO (Black Diamond Western No. 9 on)
June, 1948 - No. 8, Feb, 1949
Lev Gleason Publications

	Good	Fine	Mint
1-Biro-c	4.00	12.00	28.00
2	2.00	6.00	14.00
3-8	1.65	5.00	11.00

NOTE: ***Barry*** *a-2.* ***Kida*** *a-3-7.* ***Fuje*** *a-4, 8.* ***Guardineer*** *a-6, 7.* ***Ed Moore*** *a-4, 6.*

DESTINATION MOON (See Fawcett Movie Comics & Strange Adventures No. 1)

DESTROYER DUCK
1982 (no month) - No. 7, 5/84 (2-7: Baxter paper) ($1.50)
Eclipse Comics

	Good	Fine	Mint
1-Origin D. Duck & Groo	.25	.75	1.50
2-7: 2-Starling back-up begins	.25	.75	1.50

NOTE: ***Adams*** *c-1i.* ***Kirby*** *a-1-5p; c-1-5p.* ***Miller*** *c-7.*

DESTRUCTOR, THE
February, 1975 - No. 4, Aug, 1975
Atlas/Seaboard

	Good	Fine	Mint
1-Origin; Ditko/Wood-a; Wood-c(i)		.60	1.20
2-4: 2-Ditko/Wood-a. 3,4-Ditko-a(p)		.40	.80

DETECTIVE COMICS (See Special Edition)
March, 1937 - Present
National Periodical Publications/DC Comics

1-(Scarce)-Slam Bradley & Spy by Siegel & Shuster, Speed Saunders by Guardineer, Flat Foot Flannigan by Gustavson, Cosmo, the

DETECTIVE COMICS (continued)

Phantom of Disguise, Buck Marshall, Bruce Nelson begin; Chin Lung-c from 'Claws of the Red Dragon' serial; Flessel-c(1st?)

	Good	Fine	VF-NM
	1300.00	4000.00	7500.00

(No copy is known to exist beyond VF condition)

	Good	Fine	Mint
2 (Rare)	343.00	1030.00	2400.00
3 (Rare)	270.00	810.00	1890.00
4,5: 5-Larry Steele begins	130.00	390.00	900.00
6,7,9,10	90.00	270.00	630.00
8-Mister Chang-c	110.00	330.00	770.00
11-17,19: 17-1st app. Fu Manchu	75.00	225.00	525.00
18-Fu Manchu-c	105.00	315.00	735.00
20-The Crimson Avenger begins (intro. & 1st app.)	105.00	315.00	735.00
21,23-25	53.00	160.00	370.00
22-1st Crimson Avenger-c (12/38)	70.00	210.00	490.00
26	57.00	170.00	400.00

27-1st app. The Batman & Commissioner Gordon by Bob Kane

	Good	Fine	VF-NM
	2800.00	8400.00	17,500

(No copy known to exist beyond VF-NM condition)
Prices vary widely on this book)

27-Reprint, Oversize 13½''x10.'' **WARNING:** This comic is an exact duplicate reprint of the original except for its size. DC published it in 1974 with a second cover titling it as Famous First Edition. There have been many reported cases of the outer cover being removed and the interior sold as the original edition. The reprint with the new outer cover removed is practically worthless.

	Good	Fine	Mint
27(1984)-Oreo Cookies giveaway (32 pgs., paper-c, r-/Det. 27, 38 & Batman No. 1 (1st Joker)	2.65	8.00	16.00
28	600.00	1800.00	4200.00
29-Batman-c; Doctor Death app.	343.00	1030.00	2400.00
30,32: 30-Dr. Death app. 32-Batman uses gun	185.00	555.00	1300.00
31-Classic Batman-c; 1st Julie Madison, Bat Plane (Bat-Gyro) & Batarang	310.00	930.00	2170.00
33-Origin The Batman; Batman gunholster-c	535.00	1605.00	3745.00
34-Steve Malone begins; 2nd Crimson Avenger-c	150.00	450.00	1050.00
35-37: Batman-c. 35-Hypo-c. 36-Origin Hugo Strange. 37-Cliff Crosby begins	162.00	485.00	1135.00
38-Origin/1st app. Robin the Boy Wonder	535.00	1605.00	3745.00
39	135.00	405.00	945.00
40-Origin & 1st app. Clay Face; 1st Joker cover app.	112.00	335.00	785.00
41-Robin's 1st solo	92.00	275.00	645.00
42-45: 44-Crimson Avenger dons new costume. 45-1st Joker story in Det. (3rd app.)	60.00	180.00	420.00
46-50: 48-1st time car called Batmobile; Gotham City 1st mention. 49-Last Clay Face	57.00	170.00	400.00
51-57,59: 59-Last Steve Malone; 2nd Penguin; Wing becomes Crimson Avenger's aide	46.00	138.00	320.00
58-1st Penguin app.; last Speed Saunders	75.00	225.00	525.00
60-Intro. Air Wave	47.00	140.00	330.00
61-63: 63-Last Cliff Crosby; 1st app. Mr. Baffle	45.00	135.00	315.00
64-Origin & 1st app. Boy Commandos by Simon & Kirby	122.00	365.00	854.00
65-Boy Commandos-c	60.00	180.00	420.00
66-Origin & 1st app. Two-Face	65.00	195.00	455.00
67,69,70	38.00	115.00	265.00
68-Two-Face app.	43.00	130.00	300.00
71-75: 74-1st Tweedledum & Tweedledee; S&K-a	32.00	95.00	224.00
76-Newsboy Legion & The Sandman x-over in Boy Commandos; S&K-a	40.00	120.00	280.00
77-79: All S&K-a	32.00	95.00	224.00
80-Two-Face app.; S&K-a	33.00	100.00	230.00
81,82,84-90: 81-1st Cavalier app. 85-Last Spy. 89-Last Crimson Avenger	30.00	90.00	210.00
83-1st ''Skinny'' Alfred; last S&K Boy Commandos? Note: most issues No. 84 on signed S&K are not by them	32.00	95.00	224.00
91-99: 96-Alfred's last name 'Beagle' revealed, later changed to 'Pennyworth'-Batman 214	26.50	80.00	185.00
100	42.00	125.00	295.00
101-120: 114-1st small logo(7/46)	24.50	73.00	170.00
121-130: 126-Electrocution-c	23.00	70.00	160.00
131-137,139: 137-Last Air Wave	21.50	64.00	150.00
138-Origin Robotman (See Star Spangled No. 7, 1st app.); series ends No. 202	35.00	105.00	245.00
140-1st app. The Riddler	48.00	145.00	335.00
141,143-150: 150-Last Boy Commandos	21.50	64.00	150.00
142-2nd Riddler app.	25.00	75.00	175.00
151-Origin & 1st app. Pow Wow Smith	23.00	70.00	160.00
152,154,155,157-160: 152-Last Slam Bradley	21.50	64.00	150.00
153-1st Roy Raymond app.; origin The Human Fly	22.00	65.00	154.00
156(2/50)-The new classic Batmobile	22.00	65.00	154.00
161-167,169-176: Last 52 pgs.	21.50	64.00	150.00
168-Origin the Joker	48.00	145.00	335.00
177-189,191-199,201-204,206-212,214-216: 187-Two-Face app. 202-Last Robotman & Pow Wow Smith. 216-Last precode (2/55)	16.00	48.00	110.00
190-Origin Batman retold	19.00	57.00	132.00
200	22.00	65.00	154.00
205-Origin Batcave	21.00	62.00	145.00
213-Origin Mirror Man	21.00	62.00	145.00
217-224	14.50	44.00	100.00
225-(11/55)-Intro. & 1st app. Martian Manhunter-John Jones, later changed to J'onn J'onzz (1st National Silver Age hero); also see Batman 78	75.00	225.00	525.00
226	19.50	59.00	136.00
227-229	13.50	40.50	95.00
230-Mad Hatter app.	16.00	48.00	110.00
231-Origin Martian Manhunter retold	10.00	30.00	70.00
232,234-240	8.00	24.00	56.00
233-Origin & 1st app. Batwoman	13.00	40.00	90.00
241-260: 246-Intro. Diane Meade, J. Jones' girl. 257-Intro. & 1st app. Whirly Bats	6.50	19.50	45.00
261-264,266,268-270: 261-1st app. Dr. Double X. 262-Origin Jackal	4.00	12.00	28.00
265-Batman's origin retold	5.00	15.00	35.00
267-Origin & 1st app. Bat-Mite	5.00	15.00	35.00
271-280: 276-2nd Bat-Mite	3.35	10.00	23.00
281-297: 287-Origin J'onn J'onzz retold. 292-Last Roy Raymond. 293-Aquaman begins, ends No. 300. 297-Last 10¢ issue(11/61)	2.35	7.00	15.00
298-1st modern Clayface	3.00	9.00	21.00
299-327,329,330: 311-Intro. Zook in John Jones; 1st app. Catman. 322-Batgirl's only app. in Detective. 326-Last J'onn J'onzz; intro. Idol-Head of Diabolu. 327-Elongated Man begins; new Batman costume	1.25	3.75	7.50
328-Death of Alfred	1.25	3.75	7.50
331-368,370: 345-Intro The Block Buster. 351-Elongated Man new costume. 355-Zatanna x-over in Elongated Man. 356-Alfred brought back in Batman. 359-Intro/origin new Batgirl	.75	2.25	4.50
369-Adams-a	1.70	5.00	10.00

371-390: 383-Elongated Man series ends. 387-r/1st Batman story

Detective Comics #1, © DC

Detective Comics #27, © DC

Detective Comics #156, © DC

Detective Eye #2, © CEN

Devil-Dog Dugan #1, © MCG

Devil Kids Starring Hot Stuff #12, © HARV

DETECTIVE COMICS (continued) — Good / Fine / Mint

from No. 27 .60 1.75 3.50
391-394,396,398,399,401,403,405,406,409: 392-1st app. Jason Bard. 400,401-1st Batgirl/Robin team-up .45 1.40 2.80
395,397,400,402,404,407,408,410-Adams-a. 400-Origin & 1st app. Man-Bat 1.20 3.50 7.00
411-420: 414-52 pgs. begin, end No. 424. 418-Creeper x-over .40 1.20 2.40
421-436: 424-Last Batgirl; 1st She-Bat. 426-Elongated Man begins, ends No. 436. 428,434-Hawkman begins, ends No. 467 .30 .90 1.80
437-New Manhunter begins by Simonson, ends No. 443 .40 1.20 2.40
438-439(100 pgs.): 439-Origin Manhunter .50 1.50 3.00
440(100 pgs.)-G.A. Manhunter, Hawkman, Dollman, Gr. Lantern; Toth-a .45 1.30 2.60
441(100 pgs.)-G.A. Plastic Man, Batman, Ibis-r .45 1.30 2.60
442(100 pgs.)-G.A. Newsboy Legion, Bl. Canary, Elongated Man, Dr. Fate-r .45 1.30 2.60
443(100 pgs.)-Origin The Creeper-r; death of Manhunter; G.A. Gr. Lantern, Spectre-r .45 1.30 2.60
444,445(100 pgs.): 444-G.A. Kid Eternity-r. 445-G.A. Dr. Midnite-r .65 1.30
446-460: 457-Origin retold & updated .65 1.30
461-465,469,470,480 .65 1.30
466-468,471-476,478,479-Rogers-a .75 2.30 4.60
477-Adams-a(r); Rogers-a, 3pgs. .60 1.75 3.50
481-(Combined with Batman Family, 12/78-1/79)(Begin $1.00 issues) .60 1.75 3.50
482-Starlin/Russell, Golden-a .35 1.00 2.00
483-40th Anniversary ish.; origin retold; Newton Batman begins .65 1.30
484-495: 487-The Odd Man by Ditko. 490-Black Lightning begins. 491(492 on inside) .65 1.30
496-499,501-520: 519-Last Batgirl .60 1.20
500-($1.50)-Batman/Deadman team-up .45 1.25 2.50
521-525: 521-Green Arrow series begins .60 1.20
526-Batman's 500th app. in Det. Comics (68 pgs., $1.50) .40 1.20 2.40
527-550: 535-Intro. new Robin (Jason Todd) .60 1.20
551-565: 554-1st app. new Bl. Canary .65 1.30
566-575: 567-H. Ellison scripts .50 1.00

NOTE: **Adams** *c-369, 370, 372, 383, 385, 389, 391, 392, 394-422, 439.* **Aparo** *a-437, 438, 444-46, 500; c-430, 437, 440-46, 448, 468-70, 480, 484(back), 492-9, 500-02, 508, 509, 515, 518-22.* **Austin** *a-450i, 451i, 463i-68i, 471i-76i; c-474-76i, 478i.* **Baily** *a-443r.* **Buckler** *a-434, 446p, 479p; c-467p, 482p, 505p, 506p, 511p, 513-16p, 518p.* **Colan** *a(p)-510, 512, 517, 523, 528-38, 540-46, 555-64; c(p)-510, 512, 528, 530-35, 537, 538, 540, 541, 543-45, 556-58, 560-64.* **J. Craig** *a-488.* **Ditko** *a-443r, 483-85, 487.* **Golden** *a-482p.* **Grell** *a-445, 455, 463p, 464p; c-455.* **Gustavson** *a-441r.* **Kaluta** *c-423, 424, 426-28, 431, 434, 438, 484, 486, 572.* **Bob Kane** *a-Most early ish. No. 27 on, 297r, 438-40r, 442r, 443r.* **Gil Kane** *a(p)-368, 370-74, 384, 385, 388-407, 438r, 439r, 520.* **Kubert** *a-438r, 439r, 500; c-348-500.* **Meskin** *a-420r.* **Mooney** *a-444r.* **Moreira** *a-153-300, 419r, 444r, 445r.* **Newton** *a(p)-480, 481, 483-99, 501-09, 511, 513-16, 518-20, 524, 526, 539; c-526p.* **Robinson** *a-part: 66, 68, 71-73; all: 74-76, 79, 80; c-62, 64, 66, 68-74, 76, 79, 82, 86, 88, 442r, 443r.* **Rogers** *a-467, 478p, 479p, 481p; c-471p, 472p, 473, 474-479p.* **Roussos** *Airwave-76-105(most).* **Russell** *a-481i, 482i.* **Simon/Kirby** *a-440r, 442r.* **Simonson** *a-437-43, 450, 469, 470, 500.* **Starlin** *a-481p, 482p; c-503, 504.* **Starr** *a-444r.* **Toth** *a-414r, 416r, 418r, 424r, 440-44r, 527.* **Tuska** *a-486p, 490p.* **Wrightson** *c-425.*

DETECTIVE DAN, SECRET OP. 48
1933 (36 pgs.; 9½x12") (B&W; Softcover)
Humor Publ. Co.

By Norman Marsh; forerunner of Dan Dunn 5.00 15.00 35.00

DETECTIVE EYE (See Keen Detective Funnies)
Nov, 1940 - No. 2, Dec, 1940
Centaur Publications

1-Air Man & The Eye Sees begins; The Masked Marvel app. 60.00 180.00 420.00
2-Opium smuggling story 48.00 145.00 335.00

DETECTIVE PICTURE STORIES (Keen Det. Funnies No. 8 on?)
Dec, 1936 - No. 7, 1937
Comics Magazine Company

1 60.00 180.00 420.00
2-The Clock app. 30.00 90.00 210.00
3,4: 4-Eisner-a 27.00 81.00 190.00
5-7: 5-Kane-a 23.50 70.00 165.00

DETECTIVES, THE (See 4-Color No. 1168,1219,1240)

DETECTIVES, INC.
April, 1985 - No. 2, April, 1985 (Both have April dates)
Eclipse Comics

1,2: 2-Nudity .35 1.00 2.00
...Graphic Album (5/80) 1.35 4.00 7.95

DEVIL DINOSAUR
April, 1978 - No. 9, Dec, 1978
Marvel Comics Group

1-9 .25 .50

NOTE: **Byrne** *a(i)-4-8. All* **Kirby** *c/a.* **Kirby/Byrne** *c-9.*

DEVIL-DOG DUGAN (Tales of the Marines No. 4 on)
July, 1956 - No. 3, Nov, 1956
Atlas Comics (OPI)

1-Severin-c 2.65 8.00 18.00
2-Iron Mike McGraw x-over; Severin-c 1.35 4.00 9.00
3 1.35 4.00 9.00

DEVIL DOGS
1942
Street & Smith Publishers

1-Boy Rangers 6.50 19.50 45.00

DEVILINA
Feb, 1975 - No. 2, May, 1975 (Magazine) (B&W)
Atlas/Seaboard

1,2 .50 1.50 3.00

DEVIL KIDS STARRING HOT STUFF
July, 1962 - No. 107, Oct, 1981 (Giant-Size No. 45? on)
Harvey Publications (Illustrated Humor)

1 6.75 20.00 45.00
2 3.35 10.00 21.00
3-10 (1/64) 2.35 7.00 14.00
11-20 1.35 4.00 8.00
21-30 1.00 3.00 6.00
31-50 ('71) .70 2.00 4.00
51-70 .40 1.20 2.40
71-90 .30 .80 1.60
91-107 .30 .60

DEXTER COMICS
Summer, 1948 - No. 5, July, 1949
Dearfield Publ.

1 2.35 7.00 16.00
2 1.50 4.50 10.00
3-5 1.15 3.50 8.00

DEXTER THE DEMON (Formerly Melvin The Monster)
No. 7, Sept, 1957
Atlas Comics (HPC)

7 .85 2.50 6.00

DIARY CONFESSIONS (Formerly Ideal Romance)
May, 1955 - 1956

DIARY CONFESSIONS (continued)
Stanmor/Key Publ.

	Good	Fine	Mint
9	1.85	5.50	15.00
10-14	1.30	4.00	9.00

DIARY LOVES (G. I. Sweethearts No. 32 on)
Nov, 1949 - No. 31, April, 1953
Quality Comics Group

	Good	Fine	Mint
1-Crandall, Colan-a	8.00	24.00	56.00
2-Ward c/a, 9 pgs.	8.50	25.00	60.00
3,5-7,10	2.00	6.00	14.00
4-Crandall-a	4.65	14.00	32.00
8,9-Ward-a 6,8 pgs. plus Gustavson-No. 8	5.50	16.50	38.00
11,13,14,17-20	1.65	5.00	11.50
12,15,16-Ward-a 9,7,8 pgs.	4.65	14.00	32.00
21-Ward-a, 7 pgs.	3.85	11.50	27.00
22-31: 31-Whitney-a	1.30	4.00	9.00

NOTE: *Photo c-13-27.*

DIARY OF HORROR
December, 1952
Avon Periodicals

	Good	Fine	Mint
1-Hollingsworth c/a; bondage-c	13.00	40.00	90.00

DIARY SECRETS (Formerly Teen-Age Diary Secrets)
No. 10, June, 1950 - No. 30, Sept, 1955
St. John Publishing Co.

	Good	Fine	Mint
10	6.00	18.00	42.00
11-Spanking panel	8.00	24.00	56.00
12-16,18,19	4.65	14.00	32.00
17,20-Kubert-a	5.50	16.50	38.00
21-30	2.85	8.50	20.00
Annual (nn)(25 cents)	12.00	36.00	84.00

NOTE: ***Baker** c/a most issues.*

DICK COLE (Sport Thrills No. 11 on)
Dec-Jan, 1948-49 - No. 10, June-July, 1950
Curtis Publ./Star Publications

	Good	Fine	Mint
1-Sgt. Spook; L. B. Cole-c; McWilliams-a; Curt Swan's 1st work	5.75	17.25	40.00
2	3.75	11.25	26.00
3-10	3.35	10.00	23.00
Accepted Reprint No. 7(V1No.6 on-c)(1950's)-Reprints No. 7 L.B. Cole-c	2.00	6.00	14.00
Accepted Reprint No. 9(nd)-(Reprints No. 9 & cover to No. 8)	2.00	6.00	14.00

NOTE: ***L. B. Cole** a-all; c 1,3,4,6-10. Dick Cole in 1-9.*

DICKIE DARE
1941 - No. 4, 1942
Eastern Color Printing Co.

	Good	Fine	Mint
1-Caniff-a, Everett-c	13.50	40.00	95.00
2	8.50	25.00	60.00
3,4-Half Scorchy Smith by Noel Sickles who was very influential in Milton Caniff's development	9.50	28.00	65.00

DICK POWELL (See A-1 Comics No. 22)

DICK QUICK, ACE REPORTER (See Picture News)

DICK'S ADVENTURES IN DREAMLAND (See 4-Color No. 245)

DICK TRACY (See Merry Christmas, Popular Comics, Super Comics, Tastee-Freez, Limited Coll. Ed., Harvey Comics Library, & Super Book No. 1, 7, 13, 25, nn)

DICK TRACY
1939 - No. 24, Dec, 1949
Dell Publishing Co.

	Good	Fine	Mint
Large Feat. Comic 1(1939)	70.00	210.00	490.00
Large Feat. Comic 4	42.00	125.00	294.00
Large Feat. Comic 8,11,13,15	36.00	108.00	252.00
4-Color 1(1939)('35-r)	95.00	285.00	665.00
4-Color 6(1940)('37-r)-(Scarce)	58.00	174.00	405.00
4-Color 8(1940)('38-'39-r)	36.00	108.00	252.00
Large Feature Comics 3(1941)	32.00	95.00	225.00
4-Color 21('41)('38-r)	34.00	100.00	238.00
4-Color 34('43)('39-'40-r)	25.00	75.00	175.00
4-Color 56('44)('40-r)	17.00	51.00	120.00
4-Color 96('46)('40-r)	14.00	42.00	98.00
4-Color 133('47)('40-'41-r)	11.00	33.00	76.00
4-Color 163('47)('41-r)	9.00	27.00	62.00
4-Color 215('48)-Titled "Sparkle Plenty," Tracy-r	6.50	19.50	45.00
Buster Brown Shoes giveaway-36 pgs. in color (1938-r)	22.00	65.00	154.00
Gillmore Giveaway-(See Super Book)			
...Hatful of Fun(no date, 1950-52)-32 pgs.; 8½x10"-Dick Tracy hat promotion; D. Tracy games, magic tricks. Miller Bros. premium	5.50	16.50	38.00
Motorola Giveaway('53)-Reprints Harvey Comics Library No. 2	3.00	9.00	21.00
Popped Wheat Giveaway('47)-'40-r; 16 pgs. in color; Sig Feuchtwanger publ.; Gould-a	.85	2.50	5.00
...Presents the Family Fun Book-Tip Top Bread Giveaway, no date, number (1940); 16 pgs. in color; Spy Smasher, Ibis, Lance O'Casey app. Fawcett Publ.	22.00	65.00	154.00
Same as above but without app. of heroes & Dick Tracy on cover only	7.50	22.50	45.00
Service Station giveaway(1958)-16 pgs. in color, regular size; Harvey Info. Press(slick cover)	1.65	5.00	11.50
1(1/48)('34-r)	30.00	90.00	210.00
2,3	15.00	45.00	105.00
4-10	13.00	40.00	90.00
11-18: 13-Bondage-c	9.00	27.00	62.00
19-1st app. Sparkle Plenty, B.O. Plenty & Gravel Gertie in a 3-pg. strip not by Gould	6.00	18.00	42.00
20-1st app. Sam Catchem c/a not by Gould	5.00	15.00	35.00
21-24-Only 2 pg. Gould-a in each	5.00	15.00	35.00

NOTE: No. 19-24 have a 2 pg. biography of a famous villain illustrated by Gould: 19-Little Face; 20-Flattop; 21-Breathless Mahoney; 22-Measles; 23-Itchy; 24-The Brow.

DICK TRACY (Cont'd. from Dell series)
No. 25, Mar, 1950 - No. 145, April, 1961
Harvey Publications

	Good	Fine	Mint
25	13.00	40.00	90.00
26-28,30: 28-Bondage-c	11.00	33.00	76.00
29-1st app. Gravel Gertie in a Gould-r	13.00	40.00	90.00
31,32,34,35,37-40	9.00	27.00	62.00
33-"Measles the Teen-Age Dope Pusher"	11.00	33.00	76.00
36-1st app. B.O. Plenty in a Gould-r	11.00	33.00	76.00
41-50	8.00	24.00	56.00
51-56,58-80: 51-2pgs Powell-a	7.00	21.00	50.00
57-1st app. Sam Catchem	9.00	27.00	62.00
81-99,101-140	5.50	16.50	38.00
100	5.75	17.25	40.00
141-145 (25 cents)	5.00	15.00	35.00

NOTE: ***Powell** a(1-2pgs.)-43,44,104,145. No. 110-120, 141-145 are all reprints from earlier issues.*

DICK TRACY
May, 1937 - Jan, 1938
David McKay Publications

	Good	Fine	Mint
Feature Books nn - 100 pgs., part reprinted as 4-Color No. 1 (appeared before Large Feat. Comics, 1st Dick Tracy comic book) (Very Rare-three known copies) Estimated Value....	400.00	1200.00	2800.00
Feature Books 4 - Reprints nn issue but with new cover added	70.00	210.00	490.00

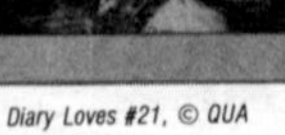

Diary Loves #21, © QUA

Dick Cole #6, © STAR

Dick Tracy #20, © N.Y. News Synd.

Dick Tracy & D.T. Jr. & How... #1, © N.Y. News

Ditko's World #1, © Renegade

Dixie Dugan #3 ('40s), © McNaught Synd.

DICK TRACY (continued)	Good	Fine	Mint
Feature Books 6,9	55.00	165.00	385.00

DICK TRACY & DICK TRACY JR. CAUGHT THE RACKETEERS, HOW
1933 (88 pages) (7x8½") (Hardcover)
Cupples & Leon Co.

	Good	Fine	Mint
2-(numbered on pg. 84)-Continuation of Stooge Viller book (daily strip reprints from 8/3/33 thru 11/8/33) (Rarer than No. 1)	32.00	95.00	225.00
with dust jacket....	50.00	150.00	350.00
Book 2 (32 pgs.; soft-c; has strips 9/18/33-11/8/33)	15.00	45.00	105.00

DICK TRACY & DICK TRACY JR. AND HOW THEY CAPTURED "STOOGE" VILLER (See Treasure Box of Famous Comics)
1933 (7x8½") (Hard cover; One Shot; 100 pgs.)
Reprints 1932 & 1933 Dick Tracy daily strips
Cupples & Leon Co.

	Good	Fine	Mint
nn(No.1)-1st app. of "Stooge" Viller	22.00	65.00	154.00
with dust jacket....	36.00	105.00	250.00

DICK TRACY, EXPLOITS OF
1946 (Strip reprints) (Hardcover) ($1.00)
Rosdon Books, Inc.

	Good	Fine	Mint
1-Reprints the complete case of "The Brow" from early 1940's	17.00	51.00	120.00
with dust jacket....	29.00	87.00	200.00

DICK TRACY MONTHLY
May, 1986 - Present ($2.00, B&W)
Blackthorne Publ.

	Good	Fine	Mint
1-7: Gould-r	.35	1.00	2.00
3-D Special 1('86)('58-r)	.60	1.75	3.50

DICK TRACY SHEDS LIGHT ON THE MOLE
1949 (16 pgs.) (Ray-O-Vac Flashlights giveaway)
Western Printing Co.

	Good	Fine	Mint
Not by Gould	4.35	13.00	30.00

DICK TURPIN (See Legend of Young...)

DICK WINGATE OF THE U.S. NAVY
1951; 1953 (no month)
Superior Publ./Toby Press

	Good	Fine	Mint
nn-U.S. Navy giveaway	1.15	3.50	8.00
1(1953, Toby)	1.65	5.00	11.00

DIE, MONSTER, DIE (See Movie Classics)

DIG 'EM
1973 (16 pgs.) (2-3/8x6")
Kellogg's Sugar Smacks Giveaway

	Good	Fine	Mint
4 different		.50	1.00

DILLY (From Daredevil Comics)
May, 1953 - No. 3, Sept, 1953
Lev Gleason Publications

	Good	Fine	Mint
1-Biro-c	1.75	5.25	12.00
2,3-Biro-c	1.00	3.00	7.00

DIME COMICS
1945; 1951
Newsbook Publ. Corp.

	Good	Fine	Mint
1-Silver Streak app.; L. B. Cole-c	13.00	40.00	90.00
1(1951), 5	1.65	5.00	11.00

DINGBATS (See First Issue Special)

DING DONG
1946
Compix/Magazine Enterprises

	Good	Fine	Mint
1	2.35	7.00	16.00
2	1.15	3.50	8.00
3-5	.85	2.50	6.00

DINKY DUCK (Paul Terry's...) (See Blue Ribbon Comics)
11/51 - No. 16, 9/55; No. 16, Fall/'56; No. 17, 5/57 - No. 19, Summer/'58
St. John Publishing Co./Pines No. 16 on

	Good	Fine	Mint
1	2.35	7.00	16.00
2	1.15	3.50	8.00
3-10	.85	2.50	6.00
11-16(9/55)	.75	2.25	5.00
16(Fall,'56) - 19	.55	1.65	4.00

DINKY DUCK & HASHIMOTO-SAN (See Deputy Dawg Presents...)

DINO (TV)(The Flintstones)
Aug, 1973 - No. 20, Jan, 1977
Charlton Publications

	Good	Fine	Mint
1	.50	1.50	3.00
2-20		.50	1.00

DINOSAUR REX
Sum, 1986 - No. 3, 1986 (mini-series; $2.00)
Upshot Graphics (Fantagraphics Books)

	Good	Fine	Mint
1-3	.35	1.00	2.00

DINOSAURUS (See 4-Color No. 1120)

DIPPY DUCK
October, 1957
Atlas Comics (OPI)

	Good	Fine	Mint
1-Maneely-a	1.30	4.00	9.00

DIRTY DOZEN (See Movie Classics)

DISNEYLAND BIRTHDAY PARTY (Also see Dell Giants)
Aug, 1985 ($2.50)
Gladstone Publishing Co.

	Good	Fine	Mint
1-R-/Dell Giant with new-c	.40	1.25	2.50

DISNEYLAND, USA (See Dell Giant No. 30)

DISTANT SOIL, A (Magazine size)
Dec, 1983 - Present ($1.50, B&W)
WaRP Graphics

	Good	Fine	Mint
1	.35	1.00	2.00
2-10	.25	.75	1.50

DITKO'S WORLD (Featuring Static)
May, 1986 - No. 3, July, 1986 (mini-series; $1.70, B&W)
Renegade Press

	Good	Fine	Mint
1-3: Ditko c/a	.30	.85	1.70

DIVER DAN (TV)
Feb-Apr, 1962 - No. 2, June-Aug, 1962
Dell Publishing Co.

	Good	Fine	Mint
4-Color 1254, 2	1.75	5.25	12.00

DIXIE DUGAN
July, 1942 - No. 13, 1949
McNaught Syndicate/Columbia/Publication Ent.

	Good	Fine	Mint
1-Joe Palooka x-over by Ham Fisher	9.00	27.00	62.00
2	5.00	15.00	35.00
3	4.00	12.00	28.00
4,5(1945-46)	2.35	7.00	16.00
6-13(1948-49)	1.75	5.25	12.00

DIXIE DUGAN
Nov, 1951 - V4/4, Feb, 1954

DIXIE DUGAN (continued)
Prize Publications (Headline)

	Good	Fine	Mint
V3No.1	2.15	6.50	15.00
2-4	1.50	4.50	10.00
V4No.1-4(No.5-8)	1.15	3.50	8.00

DIZZY DAMES
Sept-Oct, 1952 - No. 6, July-Aug, 1953
American Comics Group (B&M Distr. Co.)

1	3.00	9.00	21.00
2	2.00	6.00	14.00
3-6	1.30	4.00	9.00

DIZZY DON COMICS
1942 - No. 22, Oct, 1946 (B&W)
F. E. Howard Publications/Dizzy Don Ent. Ltd (Canada)

1	2.00	6.00	12.00
2	1.15	3.50	8.00
3-21	1.00	3.00	7.00
22-Full color, 52pgs.	1.65	5.00	11.00

DIZZY DUCK (Formerly Barnyard Comics)
No. 32, Nov, 1950 - No. 39, Mar, 1952
Standard Comics

32	2.35	7.00	16.00
33-39	1.15	3.50	8.00

DNAGENTS (The New DNAgents V2/1 on)
March, 1983 - No. 24, July, 1985 ($1.50, Baxter paper)
Eclipse Comics

1-Origin	.55	1.65	3.30
2-10: 4-Amber app.	.45	1.40	2.80
11-24: 18-Infinity-c	.35	1.00	2.00

NOTE: ***Spiegle** a-9. **Dave Stevens** c-24.*

DOBERMAN (See Sgt. Bilko's Private. . .)

DOBIE GILLIS (See The Many Loves of. . .)

DOC CARTER VD COMICS
1949 (16 pages in color) (Paper cover)
Health Publications Institute, Raleigh, N. C. (Giveaway)

	16.00	48.00	110.00

DOC SAVAGE
November, 1966
Gold Key

1-Adaptation of the Thousand-Headed Man; James Bama-c r-/'64 Doc Savage paperback	1.75	5.25	12.00

DOC SAVAGE
Oct, 1972 - No. 8, Jan, 1974
Marvel Comics Group

1		.40	.80
2-8: 2,3-Steranko-c		.25	.50
Giant-Size 1(1975)-Reprints No. 1 & 2		.30	.60

NOTE: ***Mooney** a-1i, Gnt-Size 1r. No. 1,2 adapts pulp story "The Man of Bronze," No. 3,4 adapts "Death in Silver," No. 5,6 adapts "The Monsters," No. 7,8 adapts "The Brand of The Werewolf."*

DOC SAVAGE (Magazine)
Aug, 1975 - No. 8, Spr, 1977 (Black & White)
Marvel Comics Group

1-Cover from movie poster	.25	.75	1.50
2-8		.50	1.00

NOTE: ***John Buscema** a-1,3.*

DOC SAVAGE COMICS (Also see Shadow Comics)
May, 1940 - No. 20, Oct, 1943
Street & Smith Publications

	Good	Fine	Mint
1-Doc Savage, Cap Fury, Danny Garrett, Mark Mallory, The Whisperer, Captain Death, Billy the Kid, Sheriff Pete & Treasure Island begin; Norgil, the Magician app.	80.00	240.00	560.00
2-Origin & 1st app. Ajax, the Sun Man; Danny Garrett, The Whisperer end	40.00	120.00	280.00
3	31.00	93.00	215.00
4-Treasure Island ends; Tuska-a	22.00	65.00	154.00
5-Origin & 1st app. Astron, the Crocodile Queen, not in No. 9 & 11; Norgil the Magician app.	19.50	58.00	135.00
6-9: 6-Cap Fury ends; origin & only app. Red Falcon in Astron story. 8-Mark Mallory ends. 9-Supersnipe app.	16.00	48.00	110.00
10-Origin & only app. The Thunderbolt	16.00	48.00	110.00
11,12	13.00	40.00	90.00
V2No.1-8(No.13-20): 16-The Pulp Hero, The Avenger app. 17-Sun Man ends; Nick Carter begins	13.00	40.00	90.00

DR. ANTHONY KING, HOLLYWOOD LOVE DOCTOR
1952(Jan.) - No. 3, May, 1953; No. 4, May, 1954
Minoan Publishing Corp./Harvey Publications No. 4

1	3.50	10.50	24.00
2-4: 4-Powell-a	2.35	7.00	16.00

DR. ANTHONY'S LOVE CLINIC (See Mr. Anthony's. . .)

DR. BOBBS (See 4-Color No. 212)

DR. FATE (See First Issue Special, The Immortal. . ., Justice League, More Fun, & Showcase)

DR. FU MANCHU (See The Mask of. . .)
1964
I.W. Enterprises

1-Reprints Avon's "Mask of Dr. Fu Manchu;" Wood-a	6.75	20.00	45.00

DOCTOR GRAVES (Formerly The Many Ghosts of. . .)
No. 73, Sept, 1985 - No. 75, Jan, 1986
Charlton Comics

73-75		.40	.75

DR. JEKYLL AND MR. HYDE (See A Star Presentation)

DR. KILDARE (TV)
No. 1337, 4-6/62 - No. 9, 4-6/65 (All photo-c)
Dell Publishing Co.

4-Color 1337('62)	2.35	7.00	16.00
2-9	1.30	4.00	9.00

DR. MASTERS (See The Adventures of Young. . .)

DOCTOR SOLAR, MAN OF THE ATOM
10/62 - No. 27, 4/69; No. 28, 4/81 - No. 31, 3/82
Gold Key/Whitman No. 28 on (Painted-c No. 1-27)

1-Origin Dr. Solar (1st Gold Key comic-No. 10000-210)	3.00	9.00	21.00
2-Prof. Harbinger begins	1.50	4.50	10.00
3-5: 5-Intro. Man of the Atom in costume	1.15	3.50	8.00
6-10	.85	2.50	6.00
11-14,16-20	.55	1.65	4.00
15-Origin retold	.75	2.25	5.00
21-27	.45	1.35	3.00
28-31: 29-Magnus Robot Fighter begins. 31-The Sentinel app.		.40	.80

NOTE: ***Frank Bolle** a-6-19, 29-31; c-29i, 30i. **Bob Fugitani** a-1-5. **Spiegle** a-29-31. **Al McWilliams** a-20-23.*

DOCTOR SPEKTOR (See The Occult Files of. . .)

DOCTOR STRANGE (Strange Tales No. 1-168) (Also see Marvel Premiere and Strange Tales, 2nd Series)
No. 169, 6/68 - No. 183, 11/69; 6/74 - No. 81, 2/87

Doc Savage Comics V2No.3, © S&S

Dr. Kildare #6, © M.G.M.

Doctor Solar #11, © GK

Doctor Strange #28, © MCG

Doctor Who #1, © BBC

Doll Man #28, © QUA

DOCTOR STRANGE (continued)
Marvel Comics Group

	Good	Fine	Mint
169(No.1)-Origin; panel swipe/M.D. No. 1-c	.85	2.50	5.00
170-183: 177-New costume	.35	1.00	2.00
1(6/74)-Brunner c/a	1.00	3.00	6.00
2-5	.35	1.00	2.00
6-26: 21-Origin/Str. Tales 169		.50	1.00
27,30-32,34-47,49-54		.40	.80
28,29,33-Brunner-c		.50	1.00
48-Rogers-a		.50	1.00
55-Double size		.50	1.00
56-81: 56-Origin retold		.40	.80

NOTE: ***Adkins*** *a-169, 170, 171i; c-169-71, 172i, 173.* ***Austin*** *a-48-60i, 66i, 68i, 70i; c-38i, 47-53i, 55i, 58-60i, 70i.* ***Brunner*** *a-1-5p; c-1-6, 22, 28-30, 33.* ***Colan*** *a(p)-172-78, 180-83, 6-18, 36-45, 47; c(p)-172, 174-83, 11-21, 23, 27, 35, 36, 47.* ***Ditko*** *a-179r, 3r.* ***Everett*** *c-183i.* ***Golden*** *a-55p; c-42-44, 46, 55p.* ***G. Kane*** *c(p)-8-10.* ***Miller*** *c-46p.* ***Nebres*** *a-20, 22, 23, 24i, 26i, 32i; c-32i, 34.* ***Rogers*** *a-48-53p; c-47p-53p.* ***Russell*** *a-34i, 46i, Annual 1.* ***B. Smith*** *c-179.* ***Paul Smith*** *a-54p, 56p, 65, 66p, 68p, 69, 71, 72; c-56, 65, 66, 68, 71.* ***Starlin*** *a-23p, 24-26; c-25, 26.* ***Sutton*** *a-27-29p, 34p.*

	Good	Fine	Mint
Annual 1(1976)-Russell-a	.35	1.00	2.00
Giant Size 1(11/75)-Str. Tales-r	.35	1.00	2.00
. . . /Silver Dagger (Special Edition)(2/83)($2.50, Baxter paper)-r-/ Dr. Strange 1 & Strange Tales 127; Wrightson-c	.35	1.00	2.00

DOCTOR STRANGE CLASSICS
Mar, 1984 - No. 4, June, 1984 ($1.50 cover price; Baxter paper)
Marvel Comics Group

	Good	Fine	Mint
1-4: Ditko reprints	.25	.75	1.50

DOCTOR STRANGE SPECIAL EDITION
June, 1983
Marvel Comics Group

	Good	Fine	Mint
1	.35	1.00	2.00

DR. TOM BRENT, YOUNG INTERN
Feb, 1963 - No. 5, Oct, 1963
Charlton Publications

	Good	Fine	Mint
1	.30	.80	1.60
2-5		.50	1.00

DR. VOLTZ (See Mighty Midget Comics)

DOCTOR WHO
Oct, 1984 - No. 23, Aug, 1986 (Direct sales, Baxter paper, $1.50)
Marvel Comics Group

	Good	Fine	Mint
1-($1.50 cover)-British-r	.40	1.25	2.50
2-23	.30	.90	1.80

DR. WHO & THE DALEKS (See Movie Classics)

DO-DO
1950 - 1951 (5x7¼'' Miniature) (5 cents)
Nation Wide Publishers

	Good	Fine	Mint
1-(52 pgs.); funny animal	.85	2.50	6.00
2-7	.70	2.00	4.00

DODO & THE FROG, THE (Formerly Funny Stuff)
9-10/54 - No. 88, 1-2/56; No. 89, 8-9/56; No. 90, 10-11/56; No. 91, 9/57; No. 92, 11/57 (See Comic Cavalcade)
National Periodical Publications

	Good	Fine	Mint
80-Doodles Duck by Sheldon Mayer	2.85	8.50	20.00
81-91: Doodles Duck by Sheldon Mayer in No. 81,83-90	2.00	6.00	12.00
92-(Scarce)-Doodles Duck by S. Mayer	3.00	9.00	21.00

DOGFACE DOOLEY
1951 - 1953
Magazine Enterprises

	Good	Fine	Mint
1(A-1 40)	1.75	5.25	12.00
2(A-1 43), 3(A-1 49), 4(A-1 53), 5(A-1 64)	1.15	3.50	8.00
I.W. Reprint No.1('64), Super Reprint No.17	.60	1.80	3.60

DOG OF FLANDERS, A (See 4-Color No. 1088)

DOGPATCH (See Al Capp's. . . & Mammy Yokum)

DOINGS OF THE DOO DADS, THE
1922 (34 pgs.; 7¾x7¾''; B&W) (50 cents)
(Red & White cover; square binding)
Detroit News (Universal Feat. & Specialty Co.)

	Good	Fine	Mint
Reprints 1921 newspaper strip ''Text & Pictures'' given away as prize in the Detroit News Doo Dads contest; by Arch Dale	5.00	15.00	35.00

DOLLFACE & HER GANG (See 4-Color No. 309)

DOLL MAN
Fall, 1941 - No. 7, Fall, '43; No. 8, Spring, '46 - No. 47, Oct, 1953
Quality Comics Group

	Good	Fine	Mint
1-Dollman (by Cassone) & Justin Wright begin	78.00	235.00	545.00
2-The Dragon begins; Crandall-a(5)	44.00	130.00	305.00
3	29.00	86.00	200.00
4	22.00	65.00	154.00
5-Crandall-a	19.00	57.00	132.00
6,7(1943)	14.50	43.50	100.00
8(1946)-1st app. Torchy by Bill Ward	17.00	51.00	120.00
9	13.00	40.00	90.00
10-20	10.00	30.00	70.00
21-30	9.00	27.00	62.00
31-36,38,40: Jeb Rivers app. No. 32-34	7.00	21.00	48.00
37-Origin Dollgirl; Dollgirl bondage-c	9.00	27.00	62.00
39-''Narcotics. . . the Death Drug''-cover/story; bondage-c	7.00	21.00	48.00
41-47	5.50	16.50	38.00
Super Reprint No. 11('64, r-No. 20),15(r-No.23),17(r-No.28): Torchy app.-No.15,17	1.35	4.00	8.00

NOTE: ***Ward*** *Torchy in 8, 9, 11, 12, 14-24, 27; by* ***Fox****-No. 30, 35-47.* ***Crandall*** *a-2,5,10,13 & Super No. 11,17,18.*

DOLLY
1951 (Funny animal)
Ziff-Davis Publ. Co.

	Good	Fine	Mint
10	1.15	3.50	8.00

DOLLY DILL
1945
Marvel Comics/Newsstand Publ.

	Good	Fine	Mint
1	5.00	15.00	35.00

DOLLY DIMPLES & BOBBY BOONCE'
1933
Cupples & Leon Co.

	Good	Fine	Mint
	4.35	13.00	30.00

DOMINO CHANCE
May, 1984 - No. 9, May, 1985
Chance Ent.

	Good	Fine	Mint
1	1.00	3.00	6.00
1-Reprint, May 1985	.45	1.25	2.50
2-6	.70	2.00	4.00
7-1st app. Gizmo, 2 pgs.	1.35	4.00	8.00
8-1st full Gizmo story	1.70	5.00	10.00

DONALD AND MICKEY IN DISNEYLAND (See Dell Giants)

DONALD AND MICKEY MERRY CHRISTMAS (Formerly Famous Gang)
1943 - 1949 (20 pgs.)(Giveaway) Put out each Christmas; 1943 iss-

DONALD & MICKEY MERRY XMAS (cont'd.)
ue titled "Firestone Presents Comics" (Disney)
K. K. Publ./Firestone Tire & Rubber Co.

	Good	Fine	Mint
1943-Donald Duck reprint from WDC&S No. 32 by Carl Barks	50.00	150.00	350.00
1944-Donald Duck reprint from WDC&S No. 35 by Barks	46.00	138.00	320.00
1945-"Donald Duck's Best Christmas," 8 pgs. Carl Barks; intro. & 1st app. Grandma Duck in comic books	61.00	185.00	430.00
1946-Donald Duck in "Santa's Stormy Visit," 8 pgs. Carl Barks	44.00	130.00	310.00
1947-Donald Duck in "Three Good Little Ducks," 8 pgs. Carl Barks	37.00	110.00	260.00
1948-Donald Duck in "Toyland," 8 pgs. Carl Barks	34.00	100.00	240.00
1949-Donald Duck in "New Toys," 8 pgs. Carl Barks	44.00	130.00	310.00

DONALD AND THE WHEEL (See 4-Color No. 1190)

DONALD DUCK (See Cheerios, Uncle Scrooge, Walt Disney Comics & Stories, Whitman Comic Books)

DONALD DUCK (Also see The Wise Little Hen)
1935, 1936 (Linen-like text & color pictures; 1st Donald Duck book ever) (9½x13")
Whitman Publishing Co./Grosset & Dunlap/K.K.

	Good	Fine	Mint
978(1935)-16 pgs.; story book	43.00	130.00	300.00
nn(1936)-36 pgs.; reprints '35 edition with expanded ill. & text	34.00	100.00	240.00
with dust jacket....	47.00	140.00	330.00

DONALD DUCK (Walt Disney's) (10 cents)
1938 (B&W) (8½x11½") (Cardboard covers)
Whitman/K.K. Publications

(Has Donald Duck with bubble pipe on front cover)

	Good	Fine	Mint
nn-The first Donald Duck & Walt Disney comic book; 1936 & 1937 Sunday strip-r(in B&W); same format as the Feature Books; 1st strips with Huey, Dewey & Louie	85.00	255.00	600.00

(Prices vary widely on this book)

DONALD DUCK (See 4-Color listings for titles & 4-Color No. 1109 for origin story)
1940 - No. 84, 9-11/62; No. 85, 12/62 - No. 245, 1984; No. 246, 10/86 - Present
Dell Publishing Co./Gold Key No. 85-216/Whitman No. 217-245/ Gladstone No. 246 on

	Good	Fine	Mint
4-Color 4(1940)-Daily 1939 strip-r by Al Taliaferro	243.00	730.00	1700.00
Large Feat. Comic 16(1/41?)-1940 Sunday strips-r in B&W	142.00	425.00	1000.00
Large Feat. Comic 20('41)-Comic Paint Book, r-single panels from Large Feat. 16 at top of each page to color; daily strip-r across bottom of each page	200.00	600.00	1400.00
4-Color 9('42)-"Finds Pirate Gold;"-64 pgs. by Carl Barks & Jack Hannah (pgs. 1,2,5,12-40 are by Barks, his 1st comic book work; © 8/17/42)	285.00	855.00	2000.00
4-Color 29(9/43)-"Mummy's Ring" by Carl Barks; reprinted in Uncle Scrooge & Donald Duck No. 1('65) & W.D. Comics Digest No. 44('73)	214.00	642.00	1500.00

(Prices vary widely on all above books)

	Good	Fine	Mint
4-Color 62(1/45)-"Frozen Gold;" 52 pgs. by Carl Barks, reprinted in The Best of W.D. Comics	118.00	354.00	825.00
4-Color 108(1946)-"Terror of the River;" 52 pgs. by Carl Barks	85.00	255.00	595.00
4-Color 147(5/47)-in "Volcano Valley" by Carl Barks	60.00	180.00	420.00
4-Color 159(8/47)-in "The Ghost of the Grotto;" 52 pgs. by Carl Barks-reprinted in Best of Uncle Scrooge & Donald Duck No. 1 ('66) & The Best of W.D. Comics; two Barks stories	52.00	156.00	364.00
4-Color 178(12/47)-1st Uncle Scrooge by Carl Barks; reprinted in Gold Key Christmas Parade No. 3 & The Best of W.D. Comics	54.00	162.00	378.00
4-Color 189(6/48)-by Carl Barks; reprinted in Best of Donald Duck & Uncle Scrooge No. 1('64)	52.00	156.00	364.00
4-Color 199(10/48)-by Carl Barks; mentioned in **Love and Death**	52.00	156.00	364.00
4-Color 203(12/48)-by Barks; reprinted as Gold Key Christmas Parade No. 4	36.00	108.00	250.00
4-Color 223(4/49)-by Barks; reprinted as Best of Donald Duck No. 1('65)	47.00	140.00	330.00
4-Color 238(8/49), 256(12/49)-by Barks; No. 256-reprinted in Best of Donald Duck & Uncle Scrooge No. 2('67) & W.D. Comics Digest No. 44('73)	26.00	78.00	182.00
4-Color 263(2/50)-Two Barks stories	26.00	78.00	182.00
4-Color 275(5/50), 282(7/50), 291(9/50), 300(11/50)-All by Carl Barks; No. 275,282 reprinted in W.D. Comics Digest No. 44('73)	24.00	72.00	168.00
4-Color 308(1/51), 318(3/51)-by Barks; No. 318-reprinted in W.D. Comics Digest No. 34	20.00	60.00	140.00
4-Color 328(5/51)-by Carl Barks (drug issue)	22.00	65.00	154.00
4-Color 339(7-8/51), 379-not by Barks	4.00	12.00	28.00
4-Color 348(9-10/51), 356,394-Barks-c only	5.00	15.00	35.00
4-Color 367(1-2/52)-by Barks; reprinted as Gold Key Christmas Parade No. 2 & again as No. 8	18.50	55.00	130.00
4-Color 408(7-8/52), 422(9-10/52)-All by Carl Barks. No. 408-reprinted in Best of Donald Duck & Uncle Scrooge No. 1('64)	18.50	55.00	130.00
26(11-12/52)-In "Trick or Treat"(Barks-a, 36pgs.) 1st story r-/Walt Disney Digest No. 16	18.50	55.00	130.00
27-30-Barks-c only	3.50	10.50	24.00
31-40	2.00	6.00	14.00
41-44,47-50	1.50	4.50	10.00
45-Barks-a, 6 pgs.	6.00	18.00	42.00
46-"Secret of Hondorica" by Barks, 24 pgs.; reprinted in Donald Duck No. 98 & 154	7.00	21.00	50.00
51-Barks, ½ pg.	1.50	4.50	10.00
52-"Lost Peg-Leg Mine" by Barks, 10 pgs.	6.00	18.00	42.00
53,55-59	1.30	4.00	9.00
54-"Forbidden Valley" by Barks, 26 pgs.	7.00	21.00	50.00
60-"D.D. & the Titanic Ants" by Barks, 20 pgs. plus 6 more pgs.	6.00	18.00	42.00
61-67,69,70	1.00	3.00	7.00
68-Barks-a, 5 pgs.	3.50	10.50	24.00
71-Barks-r, ½ pg.	1.30	4.00	9.00
72-78,80,82-97,100: 96-Donald Duck Album	.85	2.50	6.00
79,81-Barks-a, 1pg.	1.30	4.00	9.00
98-Reprints No. 46 (Barks)	2.00	6.00	14.00
99-Xmas Album	1.00	3.00	7.00
101-133: 112-1st Moby Duck	.75	2.25	5.00
134-Barks-r/No. 52 & WDC&S 194	.85	2.50	6.00
135-Barks-r/WDC&S 198, 19 pgs.	.70	2.00	4.00
136-153	.35	1.00	2.00
154-Barks-r(No.46)	.70	2.00	4.00
155,156,158	.35	1.00	2.00
157-Barks-r(No.45)	.40	1.25	2.50
159-Reprints/WDC&S No. 192	.40	1.25	2.50
160-Barks-r(No.26)	.40	1.25	2.50
161-163,165-170		.60	1.20
164-Barks-r(No.79)	.40	1.25	2.50
171-173,175-187,189-191		.50	1.00
174-Reprints 4-Color 394	.35	1.00	2.00
188-Barks-r/No. 68	.35	1.00	2.00

Donald & Mickey Merry Christmas (1947), © WDC

Donald Duck #978, © WDC

Donald Duck 4-Color #147, © WDC

Donald Duck's Surprise Party (1948), © WDC

Donatello #1, © Mirage

Don Fortune #2, © Don Fortune

DONALD DUCK (continued) — Good / Fine / Mint

192-Barks-r(40 pgs.) from Donald Duck No. 60 & WDC&S No. 226,234(52 pgs.) — .40 1.25 2.50
193-200,202-207,209-211,213-218: 217 has 216 on-c — .50 1.00
201-Barks-r/Christ. Parade 26, 16pgs. — .35 1.00 2.00
208-Barks-r/No. 60 — .35 1.00 2.00
212-Barks-r/WDC&S 130 — .35 1.00 2.00
219-Barks-r/WDC&S 106,107, 2 pgs. ea. — .60 1.20
220-227,231-245 — .35 .70
228-Barks-r/F.C. 275 — .25 .75 1.50
229-Barks-r/F.C. 282 — .25 .75 1.50
230-Barks-r/No. 52 & WDC&S 194 — .25 .75 1.50
246-249,251-253: 246-Barks-r/FC 422. 248-Barks-r/DD 54. 249-Barks-r/DD 26. 251-Barks-r/'45 Firestone — .40 .75
250-Barks r/4-Color 9, 64 pgs. — .35 1.00 2.00
Mini-Comic No. 1(1976)-(3¼x6½''); Reprints/Donald Duck No. 150 — .10

NOTE: ***Carl Barks*** *wrote all issues he illustrated, but No. 117, 126, 138 contain his script only. Issues 4-Color No.189, 199, 203, 223, 238, 256, 263, 275, 282, 308, 348, 356, 367, 394, 408, 422, 26-30, 35, 44, 46, 52, 55, 57, 60, 65, 70-73, 77-80, 83, 101, 103, 105, 106, 111, 126 all have* ***Barks*** *covers. No. 96 titled ''Comic Album,'' No. 99-''Christmas Album.'' New art issues-106-46, 148-63, 167, 169, 170, 172, 173, 175, 178, 179, 196, 209, 223, 225, 236.*

DONALD DUCK
1944 (16 pg. Christmas giveaway)(paper cover)(2 versions)
K. K. Publications

Kelly cover reprint — 35.00 105.00 250.00

DONALD DUCK ALBUM (See Duck Album & Comic Album No. 1,3)
May-July, 1959 - Oct, 1963
Dell Publishing Co./Gold Key

4-Color 995,1182, 01204-207 (1962-Dell) — 1.50 4.50 10.00
4-Color 1099,1140,1239-Barks-c — 1.75 5.25 12.00
1(8/63-Gold Key)-Barks-c — 1.75 5.25 12.00
2(10/63) — .75 2.25 5.00

DONALD DUCK AND THE BOYS (Also see Story Hour Series)
1948 (Hardcover book; 5¼x5½'') 100pgs., ½art, ½text
Whitman Publishing Co.

845-Partial r-/WDC&S No. 74 by Barks — 16.00 48.00 110.00
(Prices vary widely on this book)

DONALD DUCK AND THE RED FEATHER
1948 (4 pages) (8½x11'') (Black & White)
Red Feather Giveaway

4.00 12.00 28.00

DONALD DUCK BEACH PARTY (See Dell Giants)
Sept, 1965 (25¢)
Gold Key

1(No. 10158-509)-Barks-r/WDC&S No. 45 — 3.00 9.00 21.00

DONALD DUCK BOOK (See Story Hour Series)

DONALD DUCK COMIC PAINT BOOK (See Large Feat. Comic No. 20)

DONALD DUCK COMICS DIGEST
1986 - Present ($1.25, 96 pgs.)
Gladstone Publishing

1-Barks c/a-r — .60 1.25

DONALD DUCK FUN BOOK (See Dell Giants)

DONALD DUCK IN DISNEYLAND (See Dell Giants)

DONALD DUCK IN ''THE LITTERBUG''
1963 (15 pages) (Disney giveaway)

Keep America Beautiful — Good / Fine / Mint — 1.50 4.50 10.00

DONALD DUCK MARCH OF COMICS
1947 - 1951 (Giveaway) (Disney)
K. K. Publications

nn(No.4)-''Maharajah Donald;'' 30 pgs. by Carl Barks-(1947) — 416.00 1250.00 2600.00
20-''Darkest Africa'' by Carl Barks-(1948); 22 pgs. — 250.00 750.00 1600.00
41-''Race to South Seas'' by Carl Barks-(1949); 22 pgs. — 180.00 550.00 1200.00
56-(1950)-Barks-a on back-c — 20.00 60.00 135.00
69-(1951)-Not Barks — 17.00 52.00 115.00
263 — 5.35 16.00 32.00

DONALD DUCK MERRY XMAS (See Dell Giant No. 53)

DONALD DUCK PICNIC PARTY (See Picnic Party under Dell Giant)

DONALD DUCK ''PLOTTING PICNICKERS''
1962 (14 pages) (Disney)
Fritos Giveaway

1.70 5.00 10.00

DONALD DUCK'S SURPRISE PARTY
1948 (16 pgs.) (Giveaway for Icy Frost Twins Ice Cream Bars)
Walt Disney Productions

(Rare)Kelly c/a — 100.00 300.00 650.00

DONALD DUCK TELLS ABOUT KITES
11/54 (Giveaway) (8 pgs. - no cover) (Disney)
Southern California Edison Co./Pacific Gas & Electric Co./Florida Power & Light Co.

Fla. Power, S.C.E. & version with blank label issues-Barks pencils-8 pgs.; inks-7 pgs. (Rare) — 285.00 850.00 1800.00
P.G.&E. issue-7th page redrawn changing middle 3 panels to show P.G.&E. in story line; (All Barks; last page Barks pencils only) (Scarce) — 250.00 750.00 1600.00
(Prices vary widely on above books)

NOTE: *These books appeared one month apart in the fall and were distributed on the West and East Coasts.*

DONALD DUCK, THIS IS YOUR LIFE (See 4-Color No. 1109)

DONALD DUCK XMAS ALBUM (See regular Donald Duck No. 99)

DONALD IN MATHMAGIC LAND (See 4-Color No. 1051, 1198)

DONATELLO, TEENAGE MUTANT NINJA TURTLE
Aug, 1986 (One-shot, $1.50, B&W, 44 pgs.)
Mirage Studios

1 — .50 1.50 3.00

DONDI (See 4-Color No. 1176,1276)

DON FORTUNE MAGAZINE
Aug, 1946 - No. 6, Feb, 1947
Don Fortune Publishing Co.

1-Delecta of the Planets by C. C. Beck in all — 6.00 18.00 42.00
2 — 3.75 11.25 26.00
3-6: 3-Bondage-c — 3.00 9.00 21.00

DON NEWCOMBE
1950 (Baseball)
Fawcett Publications

nn — 10.00 30.00 70.00

DON'T GIVE UP THE SHIP (See 4-Color No. 1049)

DON WINSLOW OF THE NAVY (See 4-Color No. 2,22, & Super Book No. 5,6)

DON WINSLOW OF THE NAVY (See TV Teens; Movie, Radio, TV)
Feb, 1943 - No. 73, Sept, 1955 (Fightin' Navy No. 74 on)
Fawcett Publications/Charlton No. 70 on

	Good	Fine	Mint
1-Captain Marvel on cover	30.00	90.00	210.00
2	15.00	45.00	105.00
3	10.00	30.00	70.00
4,5	8.00	24.00	56.00
6-Flag-c	6.00	18.00	42.00
7-10	5.00	15.00	35.00
11-20	3.50	10.50	24.00
21-40	2.50	7.50	17.50
41-63	2.15	6.50	15.00
64(12/48)-Matt Baker-a	2.50	7.50	17.50
65(1/51)-69(9/51): All photo-c. 65-Flying Saucer attack	3.00	9.00	21.00
70(3/55)-73: 70-73 r-/No. 26,58 & 59	1.75	5.25	12.00

DOOM PATROL, THE (My Greatest Adv. No. 1-85; see DC Spec. Bl. Ribbon Digest 19, Official. . . Index & Showcase No. 94-96)
3/64 - No. 121, 9-10/68; 2/73 - No. 124, 6-7/73
National Periodical Publications

	Good	Fine	Mint
86-1pg. origin	2.35	7.00	14.00
87-99: 88-Origin The Chief. 91-Intro. Mento. 99-Intro. Beast Boy who later became the Changeling in the New Teen Titans	1.15	4.50	9.00
100-Origin Beast Boy; Robot-Maniac series begins	2.15	6.50	13.00
101-110: 102-Challengers/Unknown app. 105-Robot-Maniac series ends. 106-Negative Man begins (origin)	.75	2.25	4.50
111-120	.65	1.90	3.80
121-Death of Doom Patrol; Orlando-c	.45	1.30	2.60
122-124(reprints)		.40	.80

DOOMSDAY + 1
7/75 - No. 6, 5/76; No. 7, 6/68 - No. 12, 5/79
Charlton Comics

	Good	Fine	Mint
1	1.00	3.00	6.00
2	.75	2.25	4.50
3-6: 4-Intro Lor	.70	2.00	4.00
V3No.7-12 (reprints No. 1-6)	.30	.80	1.60
5 (Modern Comics reprint, 1977)		.20	.40

NOTE: ***Byrne** c/a-1-12; Painted covers-2-7. **Ditko** a-5, 11r.*

DOOMSDAY SQUAD, THE
Aug, 1986 - No. 7, Feb, 1987 ($2.00)
Fantagraphics Books

	Good	Fine	Mint
1-Byrne-a	.35	1.00	2.00
2,4-7	.35	1.00	2.00
3-Usagi Yojimbo app.	.50	1.50	3.00

DOORWAY TO NIGHTMARE (See Cancelled Comic Cavalcade)
Jan-Feb, 1978 - No. 5, Sept-Oct, 1978
DC Comics

	Good	Fine	Mint
1-5-Madame Xanadu in all. 4-Craig-a		.30	.60

NOTE: ***Kaluta** covers on all. Merged into The Unexpected with No. 190.*

DOPEY DUCK COMICS (Wacky Duck No. 3) (See Super Funnies)
Fall, 1945 - No. 2, April, 1946
Timely Comics (NPP)

	Good	Fine	Mint
1,2-Casper Cat, Krazy Krow	6.50	19.50	45.00

DOROTHY LAMOUR (Formerly Jungle Lil)
No. 2, June, 1950 - No. 3, Aug, 1950
Fox Features Syndicate

	Good	Fine	Mint
2,3-Wood-a(3) each, photo-c	6.50	19.50	45.00

DOT AND DASH AND THE LUCKY JINGLE PIGGIE
1942 (12 pages)
Sears Roebuck Christmas giveaway

	Good	Fine	Mint
Contains a war stamp album and a punch out Jingle Piggie bank	3.50	10.50	24.00

DOT DOTLAND (Formerly Little Dot. . .)
No. 62, Sept, 1974 - No. 63, November, 1974
Harvey Publications

	Good	Fine	Mint
62,63		.60	1.20

DOTTY (. . . & Her Boy Friends) (Formerly Four Teeners; Glamorous Romances No. 41 on)
No. 35, July, 1948 - No. 40, May, 1949
Ace Magazines (A. A. Wyn)

	Good	Fine	Mint
35	3.00	9.00	21.00
36,38-40	1.75	5.25	12.00
37-Transvestite story	1.85	5.50	13.00

DOTTY DRIPPLE (Horace & Dotty Dripple No. 25 on)
1946 - No. 24, June, 1952 (See A-1 No. 1-8, 10)
Magazine Ent.(Life's Romances)/Harvey No. 3 on

	Good	Fine	Mint
nn (nd) (10¢)	2.35	7.00	16.00
2	1.15	3.50	8.00
3-10: 3,4-Powell-a	.85	2.50	6.00
11-24	.75	2.25	5.00

DOTTY DRIPPLE AND TAFFY
No. 646, Sept, 1955 - No. 903, May, 1958
Dell Publishing Co.

	Good	Fine	Mint
4-Color 646	1.50	4.50	10.00
4-Color 691,718,746,801,903	1.15	3.50	8.00

DOUBLE ACTION COMICS
No. 2, Jan, 1940 (Regular size; 68 pgs.; B&W, color cover)
National Periodical Publications

2-Contains original stories(?); pre-hero DC contents; same cover as Adventure No. 37. (Five known copies) (not an ashcan)
Estimated value. . . . 5800.00

NOTE: *The cover to this book was probably reprinted from Adventure No. 37. No. 1 exists as an ash can copy with B&W cover; contains a coverless comic on inside with 1st & last page missing.*

DOUBLE COMICS
1940 - 1944 (132 pages)
Elliot Publications

	Good	Fine	Mint
1940 issues	60.00	180.00	420.00
1941 issues	46.00	138.00	320.00
1942 issues	30.00	90.00	210.00
1943,44 issues	25.00	75.00	175.00

NOTE: Double Comics consisted of an almost endless combination of pairs of remaindered, unsold issues of comics representing most publishers and usually mixed publishers in the same book; e.g., a Captain America with a Silver Streak, or a Feature with a Detective, etc., could appear inside the same cover. The actual contents would have to determine its price. Prices listed are for average contents. Any containing rare origin or first issues are worth much more. Covers also vary in same year. Value would be approximately 50 percent of contents.

DOUBLE-CROSS (See The Crusaders)

DOUBLE-DARE ADVENTURES
Dec, 1966 - No. 2, March, 1967 (35-25 cents, 68 pgs.)
Harvey Publications

	Good	Fine	Mint
1-Origin Bee-Man, Glowing Gladiator, & Magic-Master; Simon/Kirby-a	.70	2.00	4.00
2-Williamson/Crandall-a; r-/Alarming Adv. No. 3('63)	1.00	3.00	6.00

NOTE: ***Powell** a-1. **Wildey** a-1r. **Simon/Sparling** c-1,2.*

DOUBLE LIFE OF PRIVATE STRONG, THE
June, 1959 - No. 2, Aug, 1959
Archie Publications/Radio Comics

Don Winslow of the Navy #13, © FAW

Doom Patrol #101, © DC

Doomsday Squad #1, © Fantagraphics

D.P. 7 #1, © MCG

Dracula #2, © DELL

Dreadstar #6, © MCG

DOUBLE LIFE OF PVT. STRONG (cont'd.)

	Good	Fine	Mint
1-Origin The Shield; Simon & Kirby c/a; The Fly app.	12.00	36.00	84.00
2-S&K c/a; Tuska-a; The Fly app.	8.00	24.00	56.00

DOUBLE TALK (Also see Two-Faces)
No date (1962?) (32 pgs.; full color; slick cover)
Christian Anti-Communism Crusade (Giveaway)
Feature Publications

	Good	Fine	Mint
	15.00	45.00	90.00

DOUBLE TROUBLE
Nov, 1957 - No. 2, Jan, 1958?
St. John Publishing Co.

	Good	Fine	Mint
1,2	1.15	3.50	8.00

DOUBLE TROUBLE WITH GOOBER
No. 417, Aug, 1952 - No. 556, May, 1954
Dell Publishing Co.

	Good	Fine	Mint
4-Color 417	1.15	3.50	8.00
4-Color 471,516,556	.85	2.50	6.00

DOUBLE UP
1941 (200 pages) (Pocket size)
Elliott Publications

	Good	Fine	Mint
1-Contains rebound copies of digest sized issues of Pocket Comics, Speed Comics, & Spitfire Comics	33.00	100.00	230.00

DOVER BOYS (See Adventures of the . . .)

DOVER THE BIRD
Spring, 1955
Famous Funnies Publishing Co.

	Good	Fine	Mint
1	1.15	3.50	8.00

DOWN WITH CRIME
Nov, 1952 - No. 7, Nov, 1953
Fawcett Publications

	Good	Fine	Mint
1	5.75	17.25	40.00
2,4-Powell-a each	3.35	10.00	23.00
3-Used in **POP**, pg. 106; heroin drug cover/story	5.50	16.50	38.00
5-Bondage-c	3.75	11.25	26.00
6-Used in **POP**, pg. 80	3.35	10.00	23.00
7	2.65	8.00	18.00

DO YOU BELIEVE IN NIGHTMARES?
Nov, 1957 - No. 2, Jan, 1958
St. John Publishing Co.

	Good	Fine	Mint
1-Ditko c/a(most)	8.00	24.00	56.00
2-Ayers-a	3.35	10.00	23.00

D.P. 7
Nov, 1986 - Present
Marvel Comics Group

	Good	Fine	Mint
1	.30	.90	1.80
2-5		.60	1.20

DRACULA (See Tomb of . . . & Movie Classics under Universal Presents as well as Dracula)

DRACULA (See Movie Classics for No. 1)
11/66 - No. 4, 3/67; No. 6, 7/72 - No. 8, 7/73 (No No.5)
Dell Publishing Co.

	Good	Fine	Mint
2-Origin Dracula (11/66)	.35	1.00	2.00
3,4-Intro. Fleeta No. 4('67)	.25	.75	1.50
6-('72)-r-/No. 2 w/origin		.50	1.00
7,8: 7 r-/No.3, 8-r/No.4		.40	.80

DRACULA (Magazine)
1979 (120 pages) (full color)
Warren Publishing Co.

	Good	Fine	Mint
Book 1-Maroto art; Spanish material translated into English	1.00	3.00	6.00

DRACULA LIVES! (Magazine)
1973(no month) - No. 13, July, 1975 (B&W) (75 cents)
Marvel Comics Group

	Good	Fine	Mint
1-Boris-c	.50	1.50	3.00
2-Origin; Adams c/a; Starlin-a	.50	1.50	3.00
3-Adams-a(i)	.50	1.50	3.00
4-Ploog-a	.45	1.25	2.50
5(V2No.1)-13: 5-Dracula series begins	.35	1.00	2.00
Annual 1('75)-Adams-a(r)	.35	1.00	2.00

NOTE: ***Alcala*** *a-9.* ***Buscema*** *a-6p.* ***Buckler*** *a-1p.* ***Colan*** *a(p)-1, 5, 6, 8.* ***Evans*** *a-7.* ***Heath*** *a-1r, 13.* ***Pakula*** *a-6r.*

DRAG 'N' WHEELS (Formerly Top Eliminator)
No. 30, Sept, 1968 - No. 59, May, 1973
Charlton Comics

	Good	Fine	Mint
30-59-Scot Jackson feat.		.40	.80
Modern Comics Reprint 58('78)		.20	.40

DRAGONFLY
Sum, 1985 - Present ($1.75)(No. 1&3, color)
Americomics

	Good	Fine	Mint
1-5	.30	.90	1.75

DRAGONRING
1986 - Present ($1.70, B&W)
Aircel Publ.

	Good	Fine	Mint
1	.60	1.75	3.50
2-6	.35	1.10	2.20
V2/1 ($2.00, color)	.35	1.00	2.00

DRAGONSLAYER
October, 1981 - No. 2, Nov, 1981
Marvel Comics Group

	Good	Fine	Mint
1,2-Paramount Disney movie adaptation		.25	.50

DRAGOON WELLS MASSACRE (See 4-Color No. 815)

DRAGSTRIP HOTRODDERS (World of Wheels No. 17 on)
Sum, 1963; No. 2, Jan, 1965 - No. 16, Aug, 1967
Charlton Comics

	Good	Fine	Mint
1		.50	1.00
2-16		.40	.80

DRAMA OF AMERICA, THE
1973 (224 pages) ($1.95)
Action Text

	Good	Fine	Mint
1-"Students' Supplement to History"	.50	1.50	3.00

DREADSTAR ($1.50)
Nov, 1982 - Present (Direct sale, Baxter paper)
Epic Comics (Marvel)/First Comics No. 27 on

	Good	Fine	Mint
1	.70	2.00	4.00
2	.50	1.50	3.00
3-5	.40	1.25	2.50
6-10	.30	.90	1.80
11-26: 12-New costume. 16-New powers	.25	.75	1.50
27-29: New look	.30	.90	1.80
Annual 1 (12/83)-Reprints The Price	.30	1.00	2.00

NOTE: ***Starlin*** *c/a-1-19, Annual 1.* ***Wrightson*** *a-6, 7.*

DREADSTAR AND COMPANY
July, 1985 - No. 6, Dec, 1985

DREADSTAR AND COMPANY (continued)
Epic Comics (Marvel)

	Good	Fine	Mint
1-Reprints of Dreadstar series		.55	1.10
2-6		.40	.80

DREAM BOOK OF LOVE (See A-1 Comics No. 106,114,123)

DREAM BOOK OF ROMANCE (See A-1 No. 92,101,109,110,124)

DREAM OF LOVE
1958 (Reprints)
I. W. Enterprises

1,2,8,9: 1-Powell-a. 8-Kinstler-c	.50	1.50	3.00

DREAMS OF THE RAREBIT FIEND
1905
Doffield & Co.?

By Winsor McCay (Very Rare) (Three copies known to exist)
Estimated value. . . . $500.00—$900.00

DRIFT MARLO
May-July, 1962 - No. 2, Oct-Dec, 1962
Dell Publishing Co.

01-232-207, 2(12-232-212)	1.00	3.00	7.00

DRISCOLL'S BOOK OF PIRATES
1934 (124 pgs.) (B&W; hardcover; 7x9")
David McKay Publ. (Not reprints)

By Montford Amory	5.00	15.00	35.00

DROIDS
April, 1986 - Present (Based on Sat. morning cartoon)
Star Comics (Marvel)

1-R2D2, C-3PO from Star Wars		.35	.70
2-6: 3-Romita/Williamson-a		.35	.70

DRUM BEAT (See 4-Color No. 610)

DUCK ALBUM (See Donald Duck Album)
Oct, 1951 - Sept, 1957
Dell Publishing Co.

4-Color 353-Barks-c	2.35	7.00	16.00
4-Color 450-Barks-c	2.00	6.00	14.00
4-Color 492,531,560,586,611,649,686	1.50	4.50	10.00
4-Color 726,782,840	1.15	3.50	8.00

DUDLEY (Teen-age)
Nov-Dec, 1949 - No. 3, Mar-Apr, 1950
Feature/Prize Publications

1-By Boody Rogers	4.00	12.00	28.00
2,3	2.00	6.00	14.00

DUDLEY DO-RIGHT (TV)
Aug, 1970 - No. 7, Aug, 1971 (Jay Ward)
Charlton Comics

1	.85	2.50	6.00
2-7	.50	1.50	3.00

DUKE OF THE K-9 PATROL
April, 1963
Gold Key

1 (10052-304)	1.75	5.25	12.00

DUMBO (See 4-Color No. 17,234,668, Movie Comics, & Walt Disney Showcase No. 12)

DUMBO (Walt Disney's. . .)
1941 (K.K. Publ. Giveaway)
Weatherbird Shoes/Ernest Kern Co.(Detroit)

	Good	Fine	Mint
16 pgs., 9x10" (Rare)	20.00	60.00	140.00
52 pgs., 5½x8½", slick cover in color; B&W interior; half text, half reprints/4-Color No. 17	12.00	35.00	80.00

DUMBO COMIC PAINT BOOK (See Large Feat. Comic No. 19)

DUMBO WEEKLY
1942 (Premium supplied by Diamond D-X Gas Stations)
Walt Disney Productions

1	10.00	30.00	60.00
2-16	5.00	15.00	30.00

NOTE: *A cover and binder came separate at gas stations. Came with membership card.*

DUNC AND LOO (1-3 titled "Around the Block with Dunc and Loo")
Oct-Dec, 1961 - No. 8, Oct-Dec, 1963
Dell Publishing Co.

1	3.50	10.50	24.00
2	2.35	7.00	16.00
3-8	1.50	4.50	10.00

NOTE: *Written by **John Stanley**; **Bill Williams** art.*

DUNE
April, 1985 - No. 3, June, 1985
Marvel Comics

1-3-r/Marvel Super Special; movie adaptation		.40	.80

DURANGO KID, THE (Also see Best of the West, White Indian, & Great Western; Charles Starrett starred in Columbia's Durango Kid movies)
Oct-Nov, 1949 - No. 41, Oct-Nov, 1955 (All 36pgs.)
Magazine Enterprises

1-Charles Starrett Photo-c; Durango Kid & his horse Raider begin; Dan Brand & Tipi (Origin) begin by Frazetta & continue through No. 16	30.00	90.00	210.00
2(Starrett Photo-c)	19.00	57.00	132.00
3-5(All-Starrett Photo-c)	17.00	51.00	120.00
6-10	13.50	40.50	94.00
11-16-Last Frazetta ish.	12.00	36.00	84.00
17-Origin Durango Kid	8.00	24.00	56.00
18-Fred Meagher-a on Dan Brand begins	3.50	10.50	24.00
19-30: 19-Guardineer c/a(3) begin, end No. 41. 23-Intro. The Red Scorpion	4.00	12.00	28.00
31-Red Scorpion returns	3.50	10.50	24.00
32-41-Bolle/Frazetta-a (Dan Brand)	4.65	14.00	32.00

NOTE: *No. 6,8,14,15 contain **Frazetta** art not reprinted in White Indian. **Guardineer** a(3)-19-41; c-19-41. **Fred Meagher** a-18-29 at least.*

DWIGHT D. EISENHOWER
December, 1969
Dell Publishing Co.

01-237-912 - Life story	2.00	6.00	12.00

DYNABRITE COMICS
1978 - 1979 (69 cents; 48 pgs.)(10x7-1/8"; cardboard covers)
(Blank inside covers)
Whitman Publishing Co.

11350 - Walt Disney's Mickey Mouse & the Beanstalk (4-C 157)
11350-1 - Mickey Mouse Album (4-C 1057,1151,1246)
11351 - Mickey Mouse & His Sky Adventure (4-C 214,343)
11352 - Donald Duck (4-C 408, Donald Duck 45,52)-Barks
11352-1 - Donald Duck (4-C 318, 10 pg. Barks/WDC&S 125,128)-Barks-c(r)
11353 - Daisy Ducks Diary (4-C 1055,1150) - Barks-a
11354 - Goofy: A Gaggle of Giggles
11354-1 - Super Goof Meets Super Thief
11355 - Uncle Scrooge (Barks-a/U.S. 12,33)
11355-1 - Uncle Scrooge (Barks-a/U.S. 13,16) - Barks-c(r)
11356 - Bugs Bunny(?)
11357 - Star Trek (r-Star Trek 33 & 41)
11358 - Star Trek (r-Star Trek 34,36)
11359 - Bugs Bunny-r

Duck Album #450, © WDC

Dumbo Weekly #9, © WDC

Durango Kid #16, © ME

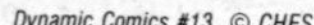
Dynamic Comics #13, © CHES

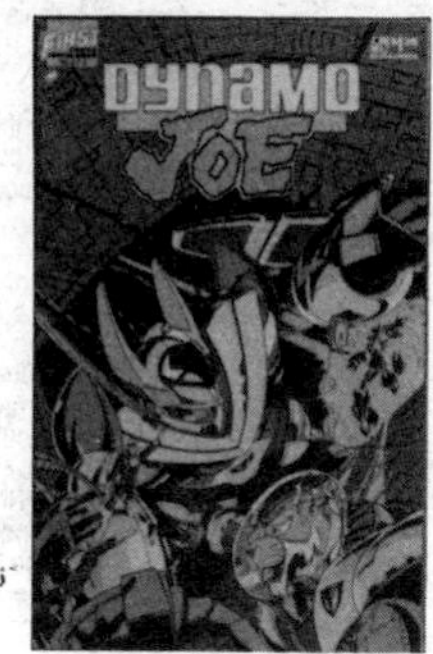

Dynamo Joe #2, © First

Eb'nn the Raven #3, © Now

DYNABRITE COMICS (continued)

	Good	Fine	Mint
11360 - Winnie the Pooh Fun and Fantasy (Disney-r)			
11361 - Gyro Gearloose & the Disney Ducks (4-C 1047,1184)-Barks-c(r)			
each....		.40	.80

DYNAMIC ADVENTURES
No. 8,9, 1964
I. W. Enterprises

	Good	Fine	Mint
8	1.20	3.50	7.00
9-Reprints Avon's "Escape From Devil's Island"	1.35	4.00	8.00
nn(no date)-Reprints Risks Unlimited with Rip Carson, Senorita Rio	1.20	3.50	7.00

DYNAMIC CLASSICS (See Cancelled Comic Cavalcade)
Sept-Oct, 1978
DC Comics

	Good	Fine	Mint
1-Adams Batman, Simonson Manhunter-r		.30	.60

DYNAMIC COMICS (No No.4-7)
Oct, 1941 - No. 3, Feb, 1942; No. 8, 1944 - No. 25, May, 1948
Harry 'A' Chesler

	Good	Fine	Mint
1-Origin Major Victory by Charles Sultan (reprinted in Major Victory No. 1), Dynamic Man & Hale the Magician; The Black Cobra only app.	45.00	135.00	315.00
2-Origin Dynamic Boy & Lady Satan; intro. The Green Knight & side-kick Lance Cooper	22.00	66.00	154.00
3	18.00	54.00	125.00
8-Dan Hastings, The Echo, The Master Key, Yankee Boy begin; Yankee Doodle Jones app.; hypo story	18.00	54.00	125.00
9-Mr. E begins; Mac Raboy-c	19.00	57.00	133.00
10-Drug story	15.00	45.00	105.00
11-14	11.00	33.00	76.00
15-Morphine drug dealing story; The Sky Chief app.	12.00	36.00	84.00
16-Marijuana story; bondage-c	13.50	40.50	95.00
17(1/46)-Illustrated in **SOTI**, "The children told me what the man was going to do with the hot poker," but Wertham saw this in Crime Reporter No. 2 (this is a morphine drug story)	16.00	48.00	110.00
18,19,21,22,24,25	8.00	24.00	56.00
20-Bare-breasted woman-c	8.50	25.50	60.00
23-Yankee Girl app.	8.00	24.00	56.00
I.W. Reprint No. 1,8('64): 1-r/No. 23	.70	2.00	4.00

NOTE: ***Kinstler** c-IW No. 1. **Tuska** art in many issues, No. 3, 9, 11, 12, 16, 19.*

DYNAMITE (Johnny Dynamite No. 10 on)
May, 1953 - No. 9, Sept, 1954
Comic Media/Allen Hardy Publ.

	Good	Fine	Mint
1-Pete Morisi-a; r-as Danger No. 6	5.00	15.00	35.00
2	2.50	7.50	17.50
3-Marijuana story; Johnny Dynamite begins by Pete Morisi	3.35	10.00	23.00
4-Injury-to-eye, prostitution; Morisi-a	4.35	13.00	30.00
5-9-Morisi-a in all	2.00	6.00	14.00

DYNAMO
Aug, 1966 - No. 4, June, 1967 (25 cents)
Tower Comics

	Good	Fine	Mint
1-Crandall/Wood, Ditko/Wood-a; Weed series begins; NoMan & Lightning cameos; Wood c/a	1.50	4.50	10.00
2-4: Wood c/a in all	1.00	3.00	7.00

NOTE: ***Adkins/Wood** a-2. **Ditko** a-4. **Tuska** a-2,3.*

DYNAMO JOE (Also see Mars & First Advs.)
May, 1986 - Present
First Comics

	Good	Fine	Mint
1	.25	.80	1.60
2-4: 4-Cargonauts begin		.65	1.30
Special 1(1/87)-Mostly-r/Mars	.25	.75	1.50

DYNOMUTT (TV)
Nov, 1977 - No. 6, Sept, 1978
Marvel Comics Group

	Good	Fine	Mint
1-6		.50	1.00

EAGLE, THE (1st Series)
July, 1941 - No. 4, Jan, 1942
Fox Features Syndicate

	Good	Fine	Mint
1-The Eagle begins; Rex Dexter of Mars app. by Briefer	45.00	135.00	315.00
2-The Spider Queen begins (origin)	22.00	65.00	154.00
3,4: 3-Joe Spook begins (origin)	18.00	54.00	125.00

EAGLE (2nd Series)
Feb-Mar, 1945 - No. 2, Apr-May, 1945
Rural Home Publ.

	Good	Fine	Mint
1-Aviation stories	6.00	18.00	42.00
2-Lucky Aces	5.00	15.00	35.00

NOTE: ***L. B. Cole** c/a.*

EAGLE
Sept, 1986 - Present ($1.50, B&W)
Crystal

	Good	Fine	Mint
1	.40	1.25	2.50
1-Limited edition signed/numbered	.85	2.50	5.00
2	.25	.75	1.50

EARTHLORE: THE LEGEND OF BEK LARSON
1986 - Present ($1.50, B&W)
Eternity Comics

	Good	Fine	Mint
1	.25	.75	1.50

EARTHLORE: THE REIGN OF THE DRAGONLORD
1986 - Present ($1.80, B&W)
Eternity Comics

	Good	Fine	Mint
1-3	.30	.90	1.80

EARTH MAN ON VENUS (An . . .) (Also see Strange Planets)
1951
Avon Periodicals

	Good	Fine	Mint
nn-Wood-a, 26 pgs.	75.00	225.00	520.00

EASTER BONNET SHOP (See March of Comics No. 29)

EASTER WITH MOTHER GOOSE (See 4-Color No. 103,140,185,220)

EAT RIGHT TO WORK AND WIN
1942 (16 pages) (Giveaway)
Swift & Company

	Good	Fine	Mint
Blondie, Henry, Flash Gordon by Alex Raymond, Toots & Casper, Thimble Theatre (Popeye), Tillie the Toiler, The Phantom, The Little King, & Bringing Up Father - original strips just for this book - (in daily strip form which shows what foods we should eat and why)	18.00	54.00	125.00

EB'NN THE RAVEN
Oct, 1985 - Present (B&W)
Crowquill/Now Comics No. 3-on

	Good	Fine	Mint
1	.85	2.50	5.00
2-6: 2-1st app. Silverwing	.35	1.00	2.00

E. C. CLASSIC REPRINTS
May, 1973 - No. 12, 1976 (E. C. Comics reprinted in full color minus ads)
East Coast Comix Co.

E.C. CLASSIC REPRINTS (continued)

	Good	Fine	Mint
1-The Crypt of Terror No. 1 (Tales From the Crypt No. 46)	.70	2.00	4.00
2-Weird Science No. 15('52)	.50	1.50	3.00
3-Shock SuspenStories No. 12	.35	1.00	2.00
4-12: 4-Haunt of Fear No. 12. 5-Weird Fantasy No. 13('52). 6-Crime SuspenStories No. 25. 7-Vault of Horror No. 26. 8-Shock SuspenStories No. 6. 9-Two-Fisted Tales No. 34. 10-Haunt of Fear No. 23. 11-Weird Science No. 12(No.1). 12-Shock SuspenStories No. 2	.35	1.00	2.00

EC CLASSICS
1985 - Present (High quality paper; r-/8 stories in color)
Russ Cochran

	Good	Fine	Mint
(All No. 1)-Shock Suspenstories, Two-Fisted Tales, Vault of Horror, Weird Fantasy	.85	2.50	4.95

ECHO OF FUTUREPAST
May, 1984 - Present (52 pgs., $2.95)
Pacific Comics/Continuity Comics

	Good	Fine	Mint
1-Adams c/a begins	.60	1.80	3.50
2-11	.50	1.50	3.00

NOTE: ***Adams** a-1-6; c-1-3, 5p, 8. **Golden** a-1-6; c-6. **Toth** a-6, 7.*

ECLIPSE GRAPHIC ALBUM
1987 - Present (8½x11")
Eclipse Comics

	Good	Fine	Mint
8-Somerset Holmes (128 pgs.); soft-c	2.50	7.50	14.95
8-hard-c	4.15	12.50	24.95
9-Zorro, Vol. 1, 64pgs; soft-c.	1.15	3.50	6.95
9-hard-c	2.00	6.00	11.95

ECLIPSE MONTHLY
8/83 - No. 10, 7/84 (Baxter paper; 1-3: 52 pgs., $2.00)
Eclipse Comics

	Good	Fine	Mint
1-3: ($2.00)-Cap'n Quick and a Foozle by Rogers, Static by Ditko, Dope by Trina Robbins, Rio by Doug Wildey, The Masked Man by Boyer begin. 3-Ragamuffins begins	.35	1.00	2.00
4-8 ($1.50 cover)	.25	.75	1.50
9,10-($1.75 cover)	.30	.90	1.80

NOTE: ***Boyer** c-6. **Ditko** a-3. **Rogers** a-3-5; c-2, 4. **Wildey** a-1, 2, 5, 6, 9; c-5, 10.*

E. C. 3-D CLASSICS (See Three Dimensional. . .)

EDDIE STANKY (Baseball Hero)
1951 (New York Giants)
Fawcett Publications

	Good	Fine	Mint
nn	5.00	15.00	30.00

EDGAR BERGEN PRESENTS CHARLIE McCARTHY
1938 (36 pgs.; 15x10½"; in color)
Whitman Publishing Co. (Charlie McCarthy Co.)

	Good	Fine	Mint
764 (Scarce)	32.00	95.00	224.00

EDGE OF CHAOS
July, 1983 - No. 3, Jan, 1984
Pacific Comics

	Good	Fine	Mint
1-3-Morrow c/a; all contain nudity		.50	1.00

EDWARD'S SHOES GIVEAWAY
1954 (Has clown on cover)
Edward's Shoe Store

Contains comic with new cover. Many combinations possible. Contents determines price, 50-60 percent of original. (Similar to Comics From Weatherbird & Free Comics to You)

ED WHEELAN'S JOKE BOOK STARRING FAT & SLAT (See Fat & Slat)

EERIE (Strange Worlds No. 18 on)
No. 1, Jan, 1947; No. 1, May-June, 1951 - No. 17, Aug-Sept, 1954
Avon Periodicals

	Good	Fine	Mint
1(1947)-1st horror comic; Kubert, Fugitani-a; bondage-c	28.00	84.00	195.00
1(1951)-Reprints story/'47 No. 1	17.00	51.00	115.00
2-Wood c/a; bondage-c	19.00	57.00	132.00
3-Wood-c, Kubert, Wood/Orlando-a	19.00	57.00	132.00
4,5-Wood-c	17.00	51.00	120.00
6,13,14	6.00	18.00	42.00
7-Wood/Orlando-c; Kubert-a	11.00	33.00	76.00
8-Kinstler-a; bondage-c; Phantom Witch Doctor story	6.50	19.50	45.00
9-Kubert-a; Check-c	8.00	24.00	56.00
10,11-Kinstler-a	6.50	19.50	45.00
12-25-pg. Dracula story from novel	9.00	27.00	62.00
15-Reprints No. 1('51)minus-c(bondage)	4.00	12.00	28.00
16-Wood-a r-/No. 2	5.75	17.25	40.00
17-Wood/Orlando & Kubert-a; reprints No. 3 minus inside & outside Wood-c	8.00	24.00	56.00

NOTE: ***Hollingsworth** a-9-11; c-10,11.*

EERIE
1964
I. W. Enterprises

	Good	Fine	Mint
I.W. Reprint No. 1(1964)-Wood-c(r)	1.20	3.50	7.00
I.W. Reprint No. 2,6,8: 8-Dr. Drew by Grandenetti from Ghost No. 9	.85	2.50	5.00
I.W. Reprint No. 9-From Eerie No. 2(Avon); Wood-c	1.35	4.00	8.00

EERIE (Magazine)
No. 1, Sept, 1965; No. 2, Mar, 1966 - No. 139, Feb, 1983
Warren Publishing Co.

1-24 pgs., black & white, small size (5¼x7¼"), low distribution; cover from inside back cover of Creepy No. 2; stories reprinted from Creepy No. 7, 8. At least three different versions exist.

First Printing - B&W, 5¼" wide x 7¼" high, evenly trimmed. On page 18, panel 5, in the upper left-hand corner, the large rear view of a bald headed man blends into solid black and is unrecognizable. Overall printing quality is poor.

Good	Fine	Mint
13.00	40.00	90.00

Second Printing - B&W, 5¼x7¼", with uneven, untrimmed edges (if one of these were trimmed evenly, the size would be less than as indicated). The figure of the bald headed man on page 18, panel 5 is cleared and discernible. The staples have a ¼" blue stripe.

Good	Fine	Mint
7.00	20.00	40.00

Other unauthorized reproductions for comparison's sake would be practically worthless. One known version was probably shot off a first printing copy with some loss of detail; the finer lines tend to disappear in this version which can be determined by looking at the lower right-hand corner of page one, first story. The roof of the house is shaded with straight lines. These lines are sharp and distinct on original, but broken on this version.

Good	Fine	Mint
1.35	4.00	8.00

NOTE: ***The Comic Book Price Guide** recommends that, before buying, you consult an expert.*

	Good	Fine	Mint
2-Frazetta-c	1.00	3.00	6.00
3-Frazetta-c, 1 pg.	.70	2.00	4.00
4-10: 4-Frazetta ½ page	.50	1.50	3.00
11-25	.45	1.25	2.50
26-41,43-45	.35	1.00	2.00
42-(1973 Annual)	.50	1.50	3.00
46-50,52,53,56-78: 78-The Mummy-r		.75	1.50
51-(1974 Annual)	.50	1.50	3.00
54,55-Color Spirit story by Eisner, 12/21/47 & 6/16/46	.35	1.00	2.00
79,80-Origin Darklon the Mystic by Starlin		.75	1.50
81-139		.60	1.20
Year Book 1970-Reprints	.85	2.50	5.00
Year Book 1971-Reprints	.85	2.50	5.00
Year Book 1972-Reprints	.70	2.00	4.00

NOTE: *The above books contain art by many good artists: **Adams, Brunner, Corben, Craig (Taycee), Crandall, Ditko, Eisner, Evans, Jeff Jones, Kinstler, Krenkel, McWilliams, Morrow, Orlando, Ploog, Severin, Starlin, Torres, Toth, Williamson, Wood,** and **Wrightson;** covers by **Bode', Corben, Davis, Frazetta, Morrow,** and **Orlando. An-***

Eddie Stanky nn, © FAW

Eerie #1 ('47), © AVON

Eerie #60, © WP

Egbert #12, © QUA

80 Page Giant #1, © DC

Electric Warrior #1, © DC

EERIE (continued)
nuals from 1973-on are included in regular numbering. 1970-74 Annuals are complete reprints. Annuals from 1975-on are in the format of the regular issues.

EERIE ADVENTURES
Winter, 1951
Ziff-Davis Publ. Co.

	Good	Fine	Mint
1-Powell-a(2), Kinstler-a; used in **SOTI**; bondage-c; Krigstein back-c	6.00	18.00	42.00

NOTE: *Title dropped due to similarity to Avon's Eerie & legal action.*

EERIE TALES (Magazine)
1959 (Black & White)
Hastings Associates

1-Williamson, Torres, Powell(2), & Morrow(2)-a	3.50	10.50	24.00

EERIE TALES
1964
Super Comics

Super Reprint No. 10,11,12,18: Purple Claw in No. 11,12; No. 12 r-Avon Eerie No. 1('51)	.70	2.00	4.00
15-Wolverton-a, Spacehawk-r/Blue Bolt Weird Tales No. 113; Disbrow-a	2.00	6.00	12.00

EGBERT
Spring, 1946 - No. 20, 1950
Arnold Publications/Quality Comics Group

1-Funny animal	6.00	18.00	42.00
2	3.00	9.00	21.00
3-10	1.75	5.25	12.00
11-20	1.30	4.00	9.00

EH! (. . . Dig This Crazy Comic) (From Here to Insanity No. 8 on)
Dec, 1953 - No. 7, Nov-Dec, 1954 (Satire)
Charlton Comics

1-Davisish-a by Ayers, Woodish-a by Giordano; Atomic Mouse app.	6.00	18.00	42.00
2	4.00	12.00	28.00
3-7: 4,6-Sexual innuendo-c	3.50	10.50	24.00

80 PAGE GIANT (. . . Magazine No. 1-15) (25 cents)
8/64 - No. 15, 10/65; No. 16, 11/65 - No. 89, 7/71 (All-r)
National Periodical Publications (No.57-89: 68 pages)

1-Superman	3.35	10.00	27.00
2-Jimmy Olsen	1.25	3.75	10.00
3-Lois Lane	.75	2.25	6.00
4-Flash-G.A.-r; Infantino-a	.75	2.25	6.00
5-Batman; has Sunday newspaper strip	.75	2.25	6.00
6-Superman	.75	2.25	6.00
7-Sgt. Rock's Prize Battle Tales; Kubert c/a	.75	2.25	6.00
8-More Secret Origins-origins of JLA, Aquaman, Robin, Atom, & Superman; Infantino-a	2.50	7.50	20.00
9-Flash(reprints Flash No. 123)-Infantino-a	.75	2.25	6.00
10-Superboy	.75	2.25	6.00
11-Superman-All Luthor issue	.50	1.50	4.00
12-Batman; has Sunday newspaper strip	.50	1.50	4.00
13-Jimmy Olsen	.50	1.50	4.00
14-Lois Lane	.50	1.50	4.00
15-Superman and Batman	.50	1.50	4.00

Continued as part of regular series under each title in which that particular book came out, a Giant being published instead of the regular size. Issues No. 16 to No. 89 are listed for your information. See individual titles for prices.

16-JLA No. 39 (11/65)
17-Batman No. 176
18-Superman No. 183
19-Our Army at War No. 164
20-Action No. 334
21-Flash No. 160
22-Superboy No. 129
23-Superman No. 187
24-Batman No. 182
25-Jimmy Olsen No. 95
26-Lois Lane No. 68
27-Batman No. 185
28-World's Finest No. 161
29-JLA No. 48
30-Batman No. 187
31-Superman No. 193
32-Our Army at War No. 177
33-Action No. 347
34-Flash No. 169
35-Superboy No. 138
36-Superman No. 197
37-Batman No. 193
38-Jimmy Olsen No. 104
39-Lois Lane No. 77
40-World's Finest No. 170
41-JLA No. 58
42-Superman No. 202
43-Batman No. 198
44-Our Army at War No. 190
45-Action No. 360
46-Flash No. 178
47-Superboy No. 147
48-Superman No. 207
49-Batman No. 203
50-Jimmy Olsen No. 113
51-Lois Lane No. 86
52-World's Finest No. 179
53-JLA No. 67
54-Superman No. 212
55-Batman No. 208
56-Our Army at War No. 203
57-Action No. 373
58-Flash No. 187
59-Superboy No. 156
60-Superman No. 217
61-Batman No. 213
62-Jimmy Olsen No. 122
63-Lois Lane No. 95
64-World's Finest No. 188
65-JLA No. 76
66-Superman No. 222
67-Batman No. 218
68-Our Army at War No. 216
69-Adventure No. 390
70-Flash No. 196
71-Superboy No. 165
72-Superman No. 227
73-Batman No. 223
74-Jimmy Olsen No. 131
75-Lois Lane No. 104
76-World's Finest No. 197
77-JLA No. 85
78-Superman No. 232
79-Batman No. 228
80-Our Army at War No. 229
81-Adventure No. 403
82-Flash No. 205
83-Superboy No. 174
84-Superman No. 239
85-Batman No. 233
86-Jimmy Olsen No. 140
87-Lois Lane No. 113
88-World's Finest No. 206
89-JLA No. 93

87TH PRECINCT (TV)
Apr-June, 1962 - No. 2, July-Sept, 1962
Dell Publishing Co.

	Good	Fine	Mint
4-Color 1309; Krigstein-a	5.00	15.00	35.00
2	4.00	12.00	28.00

EL BOMBO COMICS
1946
Standard Comics/Frances M. McQueeny

nn(1946)	3.35	10.00	23.00
1(no date)	3.35	10.00	23.00

EL CID (See 4-Color No. 1259)

EL DORADO (See Movie Classics)

ELECTRIC WARRIOR
May, 1986 - Present (Baxter paper)
DC Comics

1	.45	1.40	2.80
2-5	.35	1.00	2.00
6-11	.30	.85	1.70

ELEKTRA: ASSASSIN
Aug, 1986 - No. 8, Mar, 1987 (limited series)(Adults)
Epic Comics (Marvel)

1-Miller-a(p) begins	.35	1.10	2.20
2-6	.30	.85	1.70

ELEKTRA SAGA, THE
Feb, 1984 - No. 4, June, 1984 ($2.00 cover; Baxter paper)
Marvel Comics Group

1-4-r/Daredevil 168-190; Miller a/c	.70	2.00	4.00

ELEMENTALS, THE (Also see The Justice Machine)
Jan, 1984 - Present ($1.50; Baxter paper)
Comico The Comic Co.

THE ELEMENTALS (continued)

	Good	Fine	Mint
1-Willingham c/a, 1-8	2.50	7.50	15.00
2	1.10	3.25	6.50
3	.75	2.25	4.50
4-7	.55	1.60	3.20
8-10: 9-Bissette-a(p)	.35	1.00	2.00
Special 1 (3/86)-Willingham-a(p)	.35	1.00	2.00

ELFLORD
1986 - Present ($1.70, B&W)($2.00, color)
Aircel Publishing

	Good	Fine	Mint
1	1.70	5.00	10.00
1-2nd printing	.35	1.00	2.00
2	.85	2.50	5.00
2-2nd printing	.30	.85	1.70
3-6: Last B&W issue	.35	1.00	2.00
V2/1-4: 1-Begin color series	.35	1.00	2.00

ELFQUEST (Also see Fantasy Quarterly)
No. 2, Aug, 1978 - No. 21, Feb, 1985
No. 1, April, 1979
WaRP Graphics, Inc.

Note: *Elfquest* was originally published as one of the stories in *Fantasy Quarterly* No. 1. When the publisher went out of business, the creative team, Wendy and Richard Pini, formed WaRP Graphics and continued the series, beginning with *Elfquest* No. 2. *Elfquest* No. 1, which reprinted the story from *Fantasy Quarterly*, was published about the same time *Elfquest* No. 4 was released. Thereafter, most issues were reprinted as demand warranted, until Marvel announced it would reprint the entire series under its Epic imprint (Aug., 1985).

	Good	Fine	Mint
1(4/79)-Reprints Elfquest story from Fantasy Quarterly No. 1			
1st printing ($1.00 cover)	.70	2.00	4.00
2nd printing ($1.25 cover)	.25	.75	1.50
3rd printing ($1.50 cover)	.25	.75	1.50
2(8/78)-5: 1st printing ($1.00 cover)	.50	1.50	3.00
2nd printing ($1.25 cover)	.25	.75	1.50
3rd printing ($1.50 cover)	.25	.75	1.50
6-9: 1st printing ($1.25 cover)	.45	1.40	2.80
2nd printing ($1.50 cover)	.25	.75	1.50
10-21: ($1.50 cover); 16-8pg. preview of A Distant Soil	.30	.90	1.80

ELFQUEST
Aug, 1985 - Present
Epic Comics (Marvel)

	Good	Fine	Mint
1-Reprints in color the Elfquest epic by WaRP Graphics	.30	.90	1.80
2-5		.60	1.20
6-10		.50	1.00
11-20		.40	.80

ELFQUEST: SIEGE AT BLUE MOUNTAIN
Dec, 1986 - No. 8, 1987 (mini-series)
Apple/WaRp Graphics

	Good	Fine	Mint
1	.30	.90	1.75

ELFTREK
July, 1986 ($1.75, B&W)
Dimension Graphics

	Good	Fine	Mint
1-Star Trek parody	.30	.90	1.80

ELLA CINDERS (See Famous Comics Cartoon Book)

ELLA CINDERS
1938 - 1940
United Features Syndicate

	Good	Fine	Mint
Single Series 3(1938)	16.00	48.00	110.00
Single Series 21(No.2 on cover, No.21 on inside), 28('40)	12.00	36.00	84.00

ELLA CINDERS (See Comics Revue No. 1,4)
March, 1948 - No. 5, 1949
United Features Syndicate

	Good	Fine	Mint
1	5.00	15.00	35.00
2	2.65	8.00	18.00
3-5	2.15	6.50	15.00

ELLERY QUEEN
May, 1949 - No. 4, Nov, 1949
Superior Comics Ltd.

	Good	Fine	Mint
1-Kamen c; L.B. Cole-a	15.00	45.00	105.00
2,4	9.35	28.00	65.00
3-Drug use stories(2)	10.00	30.00	70.00

NOTE: *Iger shop art-all issues.*

ELLERY QUEEN (TV)
1-3/52 - No. 2, Summer/52 (Saunders painted covers)
Ziff-Davis Publishing Co.

	Good	Fine	Mint
1-Saunders-c	13.50	40.50	95.00
2-Saunders bondage, torture-c	13.50	40.50	95.00

ELLERY QUEEN (See 4-Color No. 1165,1243,1289)

ELMER FUDD (Also see Camp Comics & Daffy)
May, 1953 - No. 1293, Mar-May, 1962
Dell Publishing Co.

	Good	Fine	Mint
4-Color 470,558,628,689('56)	1.15	3.50	8.00
4-Color 725,783,841,888,938,977,1032,1081,1131,1171,1222, 1293('61)	.85	2.50	6.00

(See Super Book No. 10,22, & No No.)

ELMO COMICS
January, 1948 (Daily strip-r)
St. John Publishing Co.

	Good	Fine	Mint
1-By Cecil Jensen	3.50	10.50	24.00

ELRIC OF MELNIBONE (See First Comics Graphic Novel)
Apr, 1983 - No. 6, Apr, 1984 ($1.50, Baxter paper)
Pacific Comics

	Good	Fine	Mint
1-Russell c/a(i) in all	.35	1.10	2.20
2-6	.35	1.00	2.00

ELRIC: SAILOR ON THE SEAS OF FATE
Aug, 1985 - No. 7, June, 1986 (Limited series; $1.75 cover)
First Comics

	Good	Fine	Mint
1-Adapts M. Moorcock's novel	.40	1.25	2.50
2-7	.30	.90	1.80

ELRIC: WEIRD OF THE WHITE WOLF
Oct, 1986 - No. 5, 1987 (limited series)
First Comics

	Good	Fine	Mint
1-3: Adapts M. Moorcock's novel	.30	.90	1.80

ELSIE THE COW
Oct-Nov, 1949 - No. 3, July-Aug, 1950
D. S. Publishing Co.

	Good	Fine	Mint
1-(36 pages)	9.50	28.50	66.00
2,3	6.50	19.50	45.00
Borden Milk Giveaway-(16 pgs., nn) (3 issues, 1957)	3.00	9.00	21.00
Elsie's Fun Book(1950; Borden Milk)	4.50	13.50	31.00
Everyday Birthday Fun With. . .(1957; 20 pgs.)(100th Anniversary); Kubert-a	3.50	10.50	24.00

ELVIRA'S HAUNTED HOLIDAYS
Mar, 1987
DC Comics

	Good	Fine	Mint
1-Colan-a		.60	1.25

The Elementals #3, © Comico

Elflord #2, © Aircel

Ellery Queen #3, © SUPR

Elvira's House of Mystery #1, © DC

Epsilon Wave #1, © Elite

Eradicators #1, © Silverwolf

ELVIRA'S HOUSE OF MYSTERY
Jan, 1986 - No. 12, Dec, 1986 (maxi-series)
DC Comics

	Good	Fine	Mint
1 ($1.50, 68pgs.)-Photo back-c	.30	.90	1.80
2-10,12: 6-Reads sideways. 7-Sci/fic ish. 9-Photo-c		.40	.80
11-Double-size Halloween ish		.60	1.25

NOTE: ***Ayers/DeZuniga*** *a-5.* ***Bolland*** *c-1.* ***Spiegel*** *a-1.* ***D. Stevens*** *c-11.*

ELVIS PRESLEY (See Career Girl Romances 32, I Love You 60 & Young Lovers 18)

E-MAN
Oct, 1973 - No. 10, Sept, 1975 (Painted-c No. 7-10)
Charlton Comics

	Good	Fine	Mint
1-Origin E-Man; Staton c/a in all	1.20	3.50	7.00
2-Ditko-a	.70	2.00	4.00
3,4: 3-Howard-a. 4-Ditko-a	.70	2.00	4.00
5-Miss Liberty Belle app. by Ditko	.50	1.50	3.00
6,7,9,10-Byrne-a in all	.70	2.00	4.00
8-Full-length story; Nova begins as E-Man's partner	.85	2.50	5.00
1-4,9,10(Modern Comics reprints, '77)		.15	.30

NOTE: *Killjoy app.-No. 2,4. Liberty Belle app.-No. 5. Rog 2000 app.-No. 6, 7, 9, 10. Travis app.-No. 3.* ***Tom Sutton*** *a-1.*

E-MAN (Also see The Original. . . & Michael Mauser)
Apr, 1983 - No. 25, Aug, 1985 (Direct Sale only, $1.00-$1.25)
First Comics

	Good	Fine	Mint
1		.50	1.00
2-10: 2-X-Men satire. 3-X-Men/Phoenix satire. 6-Origin retold. 10-Origin Nova Kane		.50	1.00
11-25: 13-Chaos x-over from Warp		.50	1.00

NOTE: ***Staton*** *a-1-5, 6-25p; c-1-25.*

EMERGENCY (Magazine)
June, 1976 - No. 4, Jan, 1977 (B&W)
Charlton Comics

	Good	Fine	Mint
1-Adams c/a, Heath, Austin-a	.50	1.50	3.00
2-Adams-c	.30	.80	1.60
3-Adams c/a	.35	1.00	2.00
4-Alcala-a	.30	.80	1.60

EMERGENCY (TV)
June, 1976 - No. 4, Dec, 1976
Charlton Comics

	Good	Fine	Mint
1-Staton-c, Byrne-a	.50	1.50	3.00
2-4: 2-Staton-c	.25	.75	1.50

EMERGENCY DOCTOR
Summer, 1963 (One Shot)
Charlton Comics

	Good	Fine	Mint
1	.30	.80	1.60

EMIL & THE DETECTIVES (See Movie Comics)

EMMA PEEL & JOHN STEED (See The Avengers)

EMPIRE STRIKES BACK, THE (See Marvel Comics Super Special 16)

ENCHANTED APPLES OF OZ, THE (See First Comics Graphic Novel)

ENCHANTING LOVE
Oct, 1949 - No. 6, July, 1950
Kirby Publishing Co.

	Good	Fine	Mint
1-Photo-c	4.00	12.00	28.00
2-Photo-c; Powell-a	2.35	7.00	16.00
3,4,6	2.00	6.00	14.00
5-Ingels-a, 9 pgs.; photo-c	8.00	24.00	56.00

ENCHANTMENT VISUALETTES (Magazine)
Dec, 1949 - No. 5, April, 1950
World Editions

	Good	Fine	Mint
1-Contains two romance comic strips each; painted-c	7.00	21.00	50.00
2	6.00	18.00	42.00
3-5	5.00	15.00	35.00

ENEMY ACE (See Star-Spangled War Stories)

ENSIGN O'TOOLE (TV)
Aug-Oct, 1963 - No. 2, 1964
Dell Publishing Co.

	Good	Fine	Mint
1,2	1.15	3.50	8.00

ENSIGN PULVER (See Movie Classics)

ENTROPY TALES
1986 ($1.50, B&W)
Entropy Ent.

	Good	Fine	Mint
1	.25	.75	1.50

EPIC ILLUSTRATED (Magazine)
Spring, 1980 - No. 34, Mar, 1986 (B&W/Color) ($2.00-$2.50)
Marvel Comics Group

	Good	Fine	Mint
1	.35	1.00	2.00
2-10	.25	.75	1.50
11,13-15: 14-Revenge of the Jedi preview. 15-Vallejo-c & interview; ties into Dreadstar No. 1	.25	.75	1.50
12-Wolverton Spacehawk-r edited & recolored with article on him	.25	.75	1.50
16-B. Smith c/a(2)	.25	.75	1.50
17-26: 26-Galactus series begins, ends No. 34; Cerebus the Aardvark story by Dave Sim	.25	.75	1.50
27-34: ($2.50): 28-Cerebus app.	.40	1.25	2.50

NOTE: ***Adams*** *a-7; c-6.* ***Austin*** *a-15-20i.* ***Bode*** *a-19, 23, 27.* ***Bolton*** *a-7, 10-12, 15, 18, 22-25; c-10, 18, 22, 23.* ***Boris*** *c/a-15.* ***Brunner*** *c-12.* ***Buscema*** *a-1p, 9p, 11p-13p.* ***Byrne/Austin*** *a-26-32.* ***Chaykin*** *a-2; c-8.* ***Conrad*** *a-2-5, 7-9, 25-34.* ***Corbin*** *a-15; c-2.* ***Frazetta*** *c-1.* ***Golden*** *a-3.* ***Gulacy*** *c-3.* ***Jeff Jones*** *c-25.* ***Kaluta*** *a-17, 21, 26; c-4, 28.* ***Nebres*** *a-1.* ***Reese*** *a-12.* ***Russell*** *a-2-4, 9, 14.* ***Smith*** *a-7, 16; c-7, 16.* ***Starlin*** *a-1-9, 14, 15.* ***Steranko*** *c-19.* ***Williamson*** *a-27.* ***Wrightson*** *a-13p, 22, 25, 27; c-30.*

EPSILON WAVE
Oct, 1985 - Present
Elite Comics

	Good	Fine	Mint
1-Seadragon app.	.35	1.00	2.00
2-4: 2,3-Seadragon app.	.25	.80	1.60
5-10: 6-Seadragon app.	.30	.90	1.75
V2/1 (B&W)	.30	.80	1.60

EQUINE THE UNCIVILIZED
1985 ($2.00, B&W)
GraphXpress

	Good	Fine	Mint
1	.35	1.00	2.00

ERADICATORS, THE
May, 1986 - Present ($1.50, B&W)
Silverwolf Comics

	Good	Fine	Mint
1	.50	1.50	3.00
2-4	.25	.75	1.50

ERNIE COMICS (Formerly Andy Comics No. 21; All Love Romances No. 26 on)
Sept, 1948 - No. 25, Mar, 1949
Current Books/Ace Periodicals

	Good	Fine	Mint
nn(9/48,11/48; No. 22,23)	2.35	7.00	16.00
24,25	1.30	4.00	9.00

ESCAPADE IN FLORENCE (See Movie Comics)

ESCAPE FROM DEVIL'S ISLAND
1952
Avon Periodicals

ESCAPE FROM DEVIL'S ISLAND (cont'd.)	Good	Fine	Mint
1-Kinstler-c; r/as Dynamic Adv. No. 9	13.50	40.00	95.00

ESCAPE FROM FEAR
1956, 1962, 1969 (8 pages full color) (On birth control)
Planned Parenthood of America (Giveaway)

	Good	Fine	Mint
1956 edition	13.00	40.00	80.00
1962 edition	10.00	30.00	60.00
1969 edition	5.00	15.00	30.00

ESCAPE TO THE STARS
1986 - Present ($1.25, B&W)
Visionary Graphics/Solson Prod.

	Good	Fine	Mint
1-5		.65	1.30
Reprint 1-5 (Solson)		.65	1.30

ESCAPE TO WITCH MOUNTAIN (See Walt Disney Showcase No. 29)

ESPERS
July, 1986 - No. 6, 1987 (mini-series, mando paper)
Eclipse Comics

	Good	Fine	Mint
1	.25	.75	1.50
2,3		.65	1.30

ESPIONAGE (TV)
May-July, 1964 - No. 2, Aug-Oct, 1964
Dell Publishing Co.

	Good	Fine	Mint
1,2	1.15	3.50	8.00

ETERNAL BIBLE, THE
1946 (Large size) (16 pages in color)
Authentic Publications

	Good	Fine	Mint
1	4.50	13.50	31.00

ETERNALS, THE
July, 1976 - No. 19, Jan, 1978
Marvel Comics Group

	Good	Fine	Mint
1-Origin		.40	.80
2-19: 2-1st app. Ajak & The Celestials		.25	.50
Annual 1(10/77)		.25	.50

NOTE: ***Kirby** c/a(p) in all. Price changed from 25 cents to 30 cents during run of No. 1.*

ETERNALS, THE
10/85 - No. 12, 9/86 (12 issue maxi-series, mando paper)
Marvel Comics Group

	Good	Fine	Mint
1 ($1.25 cover)	.25	.75	1.50
2-11 (75¢ cover)		.45	.90
12-Double size ($1.25)-Simonson-a		.65	1.30

ETERNITY SMITH
Sept, 1986 - Present
Renegade Press

	Good	Fine	Mint
1		.65	1.30
2	.25	.75	1.50
3	.35	1.00	2.00

ETTA KETT
No. 11, Dec, 1948 - No. 14, Sept, 1949
King Features Syndicate/Standard

	Good	Fine	Mint
11	3.50	10.50	24.00
12-14	2.15	6.50	15.00

EVANGELINE (Also see Primer)
1/84 - No. 2, 1984 ($1.50; full color; Baxter paper)
Comico

	Good	Fine	Mint
1	.85	2.50	5.00
2	.45	1.25	2.50

EVA THE IMP
1957 - No. 2, Nov, 1957
Red Top Comic/Decker

	Good	Fine	Mint
1,2	1.00	3.00	7.00

EVEL KNIEVEL
1974 (20 pages) (Giveaway)
Marvel Comics Group (Ideal Toy Corp.)

	Good	Fine	Mint
nn		.40	.80

EVERYBODY'S COMICS (See Fox Giants)

EVERYTHING HAPPENS TO HARVEY
Sept-Oct, 1953 - No. 7, Sept-Oct, 1954
National Periodical Publications

	Good	Fine	Mint
1	7.00	21.00	50.00
2	5.00	15.00	35.00
3-7	4.00	12.00	28.00

EVERYTHING'S ARCHIE
May, 1969 - Present (Giant issues No. 1-20)
Archie Publications

	Good	Fine	Mint
1	4.00	12.00	24.00
2	2.00	6.00	12.00
3-5	1.20	3.50	7.00
6-10	.70	2.00	4.00
11-20	.35	1.00	2.00
21-40		.50	1.00
41-128		.30	.60

EVERYTHING'S DUCKY (See 4-Color No. 1251)

EWOKS
June, 1985 - Present
Star Comics (Marvel)

	Good	Fine	Mint
1-12: 10-Williamson-a		.35	.70

EXCITING COMICS
April, 1940 - No. 69, Sept, 1949
Nedor/Better Publications/Standard Comics

	Good	Fine	Mint
1-Origin The Mask, Jim Hatfield, Sgt. Bill King, Dan Williams begin	52.00	156.00	364.00
2-The Sphinx begins; The Masked Rider app.	22.00	65.00	154.00
3	18.50	55.00	130.00
4	14.50	43.50	100.00
5	11.00	33.00	76.00
6-8	8.50	25.50	60.00
9-Origin/1st app. of The Black Terror & sidekick Tim; bondage-c	52.00	156.00	364.00
10-13	21.00	62.00	145.00
14-Last Sphinx, Dan Williams	13.00	40.00	90.00
15-Origin The Liberator	16.00	48.00	110.00
16-20: 20-The Mask ends	9.00	27.00	62.00
21,23-30: 28-Crime Crusader begins, ends No. 58	9.00	27.00	62.00
22-Origin The Eaglet; The American Eagle begins	9.00	27.00	62.00
31-38: 35-Liberator ends, not in 31-33	8.50	25.50	60.00
39-Origin Kara, Jungle Princess	11.00	33.00	76.00
40-50: 42-The Scarab begins. 49-Last Kara, Jungle Princess. 50-Last American Eagle	10.00	30.00	70.00
51-Miss Masque begins	13.50	40.00	95.00
52-54: Miss Masque ends	10.00	30.00	70.00
55-Judy of the Jungle begins(origin), ends No. 69; 1 pg. Ingels-a	14.50	43.50	100.00
56-58: All airbrush-c	11.50	34.50	80.00

Escape to the Stars #5, © Visionary Graphics

Evangeline #1, © Comico

Exciting Comics #1, © BP

Exciting Romances #7, © FAW

Ex-Mutants #1, © Eternity

Fairy Tale Parade #4, © DELL

EXCITING COMICS (continued)

	Good	Fine	Mint
59-Frazetta art in Caniff style; signed Frank Frazeta (one t), 9 pgs.	17.00	51.00	120.00
60-65: 60-Rick Howard, the Mystery Rider begins	11.50	34.50	80.00
66-Cocaine drug story; Robinson/Meskin-a	11.50	34.50	80.00
67-69	6.50	19.50	45.00

NOTE: ***Schomburg (Xela)*** *c-28-68; airbrush c-57-66. Black Terror by* ***R. Moreira****-No. 65.* ***Roussos*** *a-62. Bondage-c 13, 20, 23, 25, 30, 59.*

EXCITING ROMANCES
1949; No. 4, 1951(no month); No. 5, 9/51 - No. 12, 1/53
Fawcett Publications

	Good	Fine	Mint
1(1949)-Photo-c	3.00	9.00	21.00
4(1951)-Photo-c	2.50	7.50	18.00
5-12: 6-Photo-c	1.50	4.50	10.00

NOTE: ***Powell*** *a-8-10. Photo-c, 1,4,5,6,11 at least.*

EXCITING ROMANCE STORIES (See Fox Giants)

EXCITING WAR
No. 5, Sept, 1952 - No. 8, May, 1953; No. 9, Nov, 1953
Standard Comics (Better Publ.)

	Good	Fine	Mint
5	2.35	7.00	16.00
6,7,9	1.35	4.00	9.00
8-Toth-a	2.85	8.50	20.00

EX-MUTANTS
Aug, 1986 - Present ($1.80, B&W)
Eternity Comics/Amazing Comics

	Good	Fine	Mint
1	.60	1.75	3.50
2-5	.35	1.00	2.00

EXORCISTS (See The Crusaders)

EXOTIC ROMANCES (Formerly True War Romances)
No. 22, Oct, 1955 - No. 31, Nov, 1956
Quality Comics Group (Comic Magazines)

	Good	Fine	Mint
22	3.00	9.00	21.00
23-26,29	1.65	5.00	11.00
27,31-Baker c/a	3.85	11.50	27.00
28,30-Baker-a	3.35	10.00	23.00

EXPLOITS OF DANIEL BOONE
Nov, 1955 - No. 6, Sept, 1956
Quality Comics Group

	Good	Fine	Mint
1	4.65	14.00	32.00
2	2.65	8.00	18.00
3-6	2.35	7.00	16.00

EXPLOITS OF DICK TRACY (See Dick Tracy)

EXPLORER JOE
Winter, 1951 - No. 2, Oct-Nov, 1952
Ziff-Davis Comic Group (Approved Comics)

	Good	Fine	Mint
1-Saunders painted-c	4.35	13.00	30.00
2-Krigstein-a	5.00	15.00	35.00

EXPOSED (. . . True Crime Cases)
Mar-Apr, 1948 - No. 9, July-Aug, 1949
D. S. Publishing Co.

	Good	Fine	Mint
1	4.65	14.00	32.00
2-Giggling killer story with excessive blood; two eye injury panels	5.50	16.50	38.00
3,8,9	2.15	6.50	15.00
4-Orlando-a	3.35	10.00	23.00
5-Breeze Lawson, Sky Sheriff by E. Good	2.15	6.50	15.00
6-Ingels-a; used in **SOTI**, illo.-"How to prepare an alibi."	13.00	40.00	90.00
7-Illo. in **SOTI**, "Diagram for housebreakers"; used by N.Y. Legis. Comm.	11.00	33.00	76.00

EXTRA
1948
Magazine Enterprises

	Good	Fine	Mint
1-Giant; consisting of rebound ME comics. Two versions known: (1)-Funny Man by Siegel & Shuster, Space Ace, Undercover Girl, & (2)-All Funnyman	17.00	51.00	120.00

EXTRA!
Mar-Apr, 1955 - No. 5, Nov-Dec, 1955
E. C. Comics

	Good	Fine	Mint
1	6.00	18.00	42.00
2-5	4.00	12.00	28.00

NOTE: ***Craig, Crandall, Severin*** *art in all.*

EXTREMELY SILLY COMICS
April, 1986 - Present (B&W)
Antarctic Press

	Good	Fine	Mint
1 (B&W-c)		.50	1.00
V2/1 (10/86)(color-c)		.60	1.20

FACE, THE (Tony Trent, the Face No. 3 on)
1941 (See Big Shot Comics)
Columbia Comics Group

	Good	Fine	Mint
1-The Face	23.00	70.00	160.00
2	13.50	40.50	95.00

FACE, THE
Sept, 1986 - Present ($1.95, B&W)
ACE Comics

	Good	Fine	Mint
1-Ditko-a	.35	1.00	2.00

FAIRY TALE PARADE (See Famous Fairy Tales)
June-July, 1942 - No. 121, Oct, 1946 (Most all by Walt Kelly)
Dell Publishing Co.

	Good	Fine	Mint
1-Kelly-a begins	78.00	234.00	545.00
2(1943)	44.00	132.00	305.00
3-5	28.00	84.00	195.00
6-9(1943)	22.00	65.00	155.00
4-Color 50('44)	21.00	63.00	145.00
4-Color 69('45)	18.00	54.00	125.00
4-Color 87('45)	16.00	48.00	110.00
4-Color 104,114('46)-Last Kelly ish.	12.00	36.00	84.00
4-Color 121('46)-Not Kelly	8.00	24.00	56.00

NOTE: *No. 1-9, 4-Color No. 50,69 have* ***Kelly*** *c/a; 4-Color No. 87, 104, 114-****Kelly*** *art only. No. 9 has a redrawn version of The Reluctant Dragon.*

FAIRY TALES
No. 10, 1951 - No. 11, June-July, 1951
Ziff-Davis Publ. Co. (Approved Comics)

	Good	Fine	Mint
10,11	4.00	12.00	28.00

FAITHFUL
November, 1949 - No. 2, Feb, 1950
Marvel Comics/Lovers' Magazine

	Good	Fine	Mint
1,2-Photo-c	2.35	7.00	16.00

FALCON
Nov, 1983 - No. 4, Feb, 1984 (mini-series)
Marvel Comics Group

	Good	Fine	Mint
1-Paul Smith c/a(p)		.50	1.00
2-4: 2-Smith-c		.50	1.00

FALLEN ANGELS
April, 1987 - No. 8, 1987 (mini-series)

FALLEN ANGELS (continued)
Marvel Comics Group

	Good	Fine	Mint
1		.40	.80

FALLING IN LOVE
Sept-Oct, 1955 - No. 143, Oct-Nov, 1973
Arleigh Publ. Co./National Periodical Publications

	Good	Fine	Mint
1	8.00	24.00	56.00
2	3.75	11.25	26.00
3-10	2.85	8.50	20.00
11-20	1.65	5.00	11.00
21-40	1.15	3.50	8.00
41-50	.85	2.50	6.00
51-100	.50	1.50	3.00
101-107,109-143		.60	1.20
108-Wood-a, 4pgs. (7/69)	.35	1.00	2.00

FALL OF THE HOUSE OF USHER, THE
May, 1984 (One-shot; E. A. Poe adaptation)
Pacific Comics

	Good	Fine	Mint
1-Corben c/a	.25	.75	1.50

FALL OF THE ROMAN EMPIRE (See Movie Comics)

FAMILY AFFAIR (TV)
Feb, 1970 - No. 4, Oct, 1970 (25 cents)
Gold Key

	Good	Fine	Mint
1-Pull-out poster; photo-c	2.00	6.00	12.00
2-4: 3,4-Photo-c	1.15	3.50	7.00

FAMILY FUNNIES
No. 9, Aug-Sept, 1946
Parents' Magazine Institute

	Good	Fine	Mint
9	1.75	5.25	12.00

FAMILY FUNNIES (Tiny Tot Funnies No. 9 on)
Sept, 1950 - No. 8, April?, 1951
Harvey Publications

	Good	Fine	Mint
1-Mandrake	3.00	9.00	21.00
2-Flash Gordon, 1 pg.	2.35	7.00	16.00
3-8: 4,5,7-Flash Gordon, 1 pg.	2.00	6.00	14.00
1(black & white)	1.20	3.50	8.00

FAMOUS AUTHORS ILL. (See Stories by . . .)

FAMOUS COMICS (Also see Favorite Comics)
No date; Mid 1930's (24 pages) (paper cover)
Zain-Eppy/United Features Syndicate

	Good	Fine	Mint
Reprinted from 1934 newspaper strips in color; Joe Palooka, Hairbreadth Harry, Napoleon, The Nebbs, etc.	16.00	48.00	110.00

FAMOUS COMICS
1934 (100 pgs., daily newspaper reprints)
(3½x8½''; paper cover) (came in a box)
King Features Syndicate (Whitman Publ. Co.)

	Good	Fine	Mint
684(No.1)-Little Jimmy, Katzenjammer Kids, & Barney Google	12.00	36.00	84.00
684(No.2)-Polly, Little Jimmy, Katzenjammer Kids	12.00	36.00	84.00
684(No.3)-Little Annie Rooney, Polly, Katzenjammer Kids	12.00	36.00	84.00
. . . . Box price	4.50	13.50	31.00

FAMOUS COMICS CARTOON BOOKS
1934 (72 pgs.; 8x7¼''; daily strip reprints)
Whitman Publishing Co. (B&W; hardbacks)

	Good	Fine	Mint
1200-The Captain & the Kids; Dirks reprints credited to Bernard Dibble	9.00	27.00	62.00
1202-Captain Easy & Wash Tubbs by Roy Crane	13.00	40.00	90.00
1203-Ella Cinders	8.50	25.50	60.00
1204-Freckles & His Friends	7.00	21.00	50.00

NOTE: *Called Famous Funnies Cartoon Books inside.*

FAMOUS CRIMES
June, 1948 - No. 19, Sept, 1950; No. 20, Aug, 1951
Fox Features Syndicate/M.S. Dist. No. 51,52

	Good	Fine	Mint
1-Blue Beetle app. & crime story r-/Phantom Lady No. 16	10.00	30.00	70.00
2-Shows woman dissolved in acid; lingerie-c/panels	7.00	21.00	50.00
3-Injury-to-eye story used in **SOTI**, pg. 112; has two electrocution stories	10.00	30.00	70.00
4-6	4.50	13.50	31.00
7-''Tarzan, the Wyoming Killer'' used in **SOTI**, pg. 44; drug trial/possession story	8.50	25.50	60.00
8-20: 17-Morisi-a	3.50	10.50	24.00
51(nd, 1953)	4.00	12.00	28.00
52	2.35	7.00	16.00

FAMOUS FAIRY TALES
1943 (32 pgs.); 1944 (16 pgs.) (Soft covers)
K. K. Publ. Co. (Giveaway)

	Good	Fine	Mint
1943-Reprints from Fairy Tale Parade No. 2,3; Kelly inside art	40.00	120.00	260.00
1944-Kelly inside art	28.00	85.00	180.00

FAMOUS FEATURE STORIES
1938 (68 pgs., 7½x11'')
Dell Publishing Co.

	Good	Fine	Mint
1-Tarzan, Terry & the Pirates, King of the Royal Mtd., Buck Jones, Dick Tracy, Smilin' Jack, Dan Dunn, Don Winslow, G-Man, Tailspin Tommy, Mutt & Jeff, & Little Orphan Annie reprints - all illustrated text	30.00	90.00	210.00

FAMOUS FIRST EDITION (See Limited Collectors Edition)
($1.00; 10x13½''-Giant Size)(72pgs.; No.6-8, 68 pgs.)
1974 - No. 8, Aug-Sept, 1975; C-61, Sept, 1978
National Periodical Publications/DC Comics

	Good	Fine	Mint
C-26-Action No. 1	1.15	3.50	8.00
C-28-Detective No. 27	1.15	3.50	8.00
C-30-Sensation No. 1(1974)	1.15	3.50	8.00
F-4-Whiz No. 2(No.1)(10-11/74)-Cover not identical to original	1.15	3.50	8.00
F-5-Batman No. 1(F-6 on inside)	1.15	3.50	8.00
F-6-Wonder Woman No. 1	.85	2.50	6.00
F-7-All-Star Comics No. 3	1.15	3.50	8.00
F-8-Flash No. 1(8-9/75)	.85	2.50	6.00
C-61-Superman No. 1(9/78)	1.15	3.50	8.00
Hardbound editions w/dust jackets ($5.00) (Lyle Stuart, Inc.) C-26,C-28,C-30,F-4,F-6 known	1.75	5.25	12.00

Warning: The above books are almost **exact** reprints of the originals that they represent except for the Giant-Size format. None of the originals are Giant-Size. The first five issues and C-61 were printed with two covers. Reprint information can be found on the outside cover, but not on the inside cover which was reprinted exactly like the original (inside and out).

FAMOUS FUNNIES
1933 - No. 218, July, 1955
Eastern Color

	Good	Fine	Mint
A Carnival of Comics (probably the second comic book), 36 pgs., no date given, no publisher, no number; contains strip reprints of The Bungle Family, Dixie Dugan, Hairbreadth Harry, Joe Palooka, Keeping Up With the Jones, Mutt & Jeff, Reg'lar Fellers, S'Matter Pop, Strange As It Seems, and others. This book was sold by M. C. Gaines to Wheatena, Milk-O-Malt, John Wanamaker, Kinney Shoe Stores, & others to be given away as premiums and radio giveaways (1933).	145.00	435.00	1015.00

Series 1-(Very rare)(nd-early 1934)(68 pgs.) No publisher given (Eastern Color Printing

Famous Crimes #2, © FOX

Famous First Edition #C-26, © DC

Famous Funnies (A Carnival of Comics), # EAS

Famous Funnies #2, © EAS

Famous Funnies #213, © EAS

Famous Gangsters #1, © AVON

FAMOUS FUNNIES (continued) — Good / Fine / Mint

Co.); sold in chain stores for 10 cents. 35,000 print run. Contains Sunday strip reprints of Mutt & Jeff, Reg'lar Fellers, Nipper, Hairbreadth Harry, Strange As It Seems, Joe Palooka, Dixie Dugan, The Nebbs, Keeping Up With the Jones, and others. Inside front and back covers and pages 1-16 of Famous Funnies Series 1, Nos. 49-64 reprinted from **Famous Funnies, A Carnival of Comics,** and most of pages 17-48 reprinted from **Funnies on Parade.** This was the first comic book sold. 200.00 600.00 1400.00

No. 1 (Rare)(7/34-on stands 5/34) - Eastern Color Printing Co. First monthly newsstand comic book. Contains Sunday strip reprints of Toonerville Folks, Mutt & Jeff, Hairbreadth Harry, S'Matter Pop, Nipper, Dixie Dugan, The Bungle Family, Connie, Ben Webster, Tailspin Tommy, The Nebbs, Joe Palooka, & others. 175.00 525.00 1225.00

2 (Rare) 60.00 180.00 420.00
3-Buck Rogers Sunday strip reprints by Rick Yager begins, ends No. 218; not in No. 191-208; the number of the 1st strip reprinted is pg. 190, Series No. 1 80.00 240.00 560.00
4 40.00 120.00 280.00
5 30.00 90.00 210.00
6-10 25.00 75.00 175.00
11,12,18-Four pgs. of Buck Rogers in each issue, completes stories in Buck Rogers No. 1 which lacks these pages; No. 18-Two pgs. of Buck Rogers reprinted in Daisy Comics No. 1 22.00 65.00 154.00
13-17,19,20: 14-Has two Buck Rogers panels missing. 17-1st Christmas-c on a newsstand comic 17.00 51.00 120.00
21,23-30: 27-War on Crime begins 12.00 36.00 84.00
22-Four pgs. of Buck Rogers needed to complete stories in Buck Rogers No. 1 13.50 40.00 95.00
31,32,34,36,37,39,40 9.50 28.50 66.00
33-Careers of Baby Face Nelson & John Dillinger traced 9.50 28.50 66.00
35-Two pgs. Buck Rogers omitted in Buck Rogers No. 2 12.00 36.00 84.00
38-Full color portrait of Buck Rogers 10.00 30.00 70.00
41-60: 55-Last bottom panel, pg. 4 in Buck Rogers redrawn in Buck Rogers No. 3 8.00 24.00 56.00
61-64,66,67,69,70 7.00 21.00 50.00
65,68-Two pgs. Kirby-a-''Lightnin & the Lone Rider'' 7.50 22.50 53.00
71,73,77-80: 80-Buck Rogers story continues from B. R. No. 5 5.50 16.50 38.00
72-Speed Spaulding begins by Marvin Bradley (artist), ends No. 88. This series was written by Edwin Balmer & Philip Wylie and later appeared as film & book ''When Worlds Collide.'' 7.00 21.00 50.00
74-76-Two pgs. Kirby-a in all 5.50 16.50 38.00
81-Origin Invisible Scarlet O'Neil; strip begins No. 82, ends No. 167 4.35 13.00 30.00
82-Buck Rogers-c 5.50 16.50 38.00
83-87,90: 87 has last Buck Rogers full page-r. 90-Bondage-c 4.35 13.00 30.00
88-Buck Rogers in ''Moon's End'' by Calkins, 2 pgs.(not reprints). Beginning with No. 88, all Buck Rogers pages have rearranged panels 5.00 15.00 35.00
89-Origin Fearless Flint, the Flint Man 5.00 15.00 35.00
91-93,95,96,98-99,101-110: 105-Series 2 begins (Strip Page No. 1) 3.75 11.25 26.00
94-Buck Rogers in ''Solar Holocaust'' by Calkins, 3 pgs.(not reprints) 4.35 13.00 30.00
97-War Bond promotion, Buck Rogers by Calkins, 2 pgs.(not reprints) 4.35 13.00 30.00
100 4.35 13.00 30.00
111-130 3.00 9.00 21.00
131-150: 137-Strip page No. 110½ omitted 2.15 6.50 15.00
151-162,164-168 1.85 5.50 13.00
163-St. Valentine's Day-c 2.35 7.00 16.00
169,170-Two text illos. by Williamson, his 1st comic book work 4.35 13.00 30.00
171-180: 171-Strip pgs. 227,229,230, Series 2 omitted. 172-Strip Pg. 232 omitted 1.85 5.50 13.00

Good / Fine / Mint

181-190: Buck Rogers ends with start of strip pg. 302, Series 2 1.50 4.50 10.00
191-197,199,201,203,206-208: No Buck Rogers 1.30 4.00 9.00
198,202,205-One pg. Frazetta ads; no Buck Rogers 1.65 5.00 11.50
200-Frazetta 1 pg. ad 1.85 5.50 13.00
204-Used in **POP**, pgs. 79,99 2.15 6.50 15.00
209-Buck Rogers begins with strip pg. 480, Series 2; Frazetta-c 22.00 65.00 154.00
210-216: Frazetta-c. 211-Buck Rogers ads by Anderson begins, ends No. 217. No. 215-Contains Buck Rogers strip pg. 515-518, Series 2 followed by pgs. 179-181, Series 3 22.00 65.00 154.00
217,218-Buck Rogers ends with pg. 199, Series 3 1.50 4.50 10.00

NOTE: ***Rick Yager*** *did the Buck Rogers Sunday strips reprinted in Famous Funnies. The Sundays were formerly done by Russ Keaton and Lt. Dick Calkins did the dailies, but would sometimes assist Yager on a panel or two from time to time. Strip No. 169 is Yager's first full Buck Rogers page. Yager did the strip until 1958 when* ***Murphy Anderson*** *took over.* ***Tuska*** *art from 4/26/59 - 1965. Virtually every panel was rewritten for Famous Funnies. Not identical to the original Sunday page. The Buck Rogers reprints run continuously through Famous Funnies issue No. 190 (Strip No. 302) with no break in story line. The story line has no continuity after No. 190. The Buck Rogers newspaper strips came out in four series: Series 1, 3/30/30 - 9/21/41 (No. 1 - 600); Series 2, 9/28/41 -10/21/51 (No. 1 -525)(Strip No. 110½ (½ pg.) published in only a few newspapers); Series 3, 10/28/51 -2/9/58 (No. 100-428)(No No. 1-99); Series 4, 2/16/58 - 6/13/65 (No numbers, dates only).* ***Everett*** *c-86.* ***Moulton*** *a-100.*

FAMOUS FUNNIES
1964
Super Comics

Reprint No. 15-18 .40 1.20 2.40

FAMOUS GANG BOOK OF COMICS (Donald & Mickey Merry Christmas 1943 on)
1942 (32 pgs.; paper cover) (Christmas giveaway)
Firestone Tire & Rubber Co.

(Rare)-Porky Pig, Bugs Bunny; r-/Looney Tunes 67.00 200.00 500.00

FAMOUS GANGSTERS (Crime on the Waterfront No. 4)
April, 1951 - No. 3, Feb, 1952
Avon Periodicals/Realistic

1-Narcotics mentioned; Capone, Dillinger; c-/Avon paperback No. 329 12.00 36.00 84.00
2-Wood-c/a (1 pg.); r-/Saint No. 7 & retitled ''Mike Strong'' 13.00 40.00 90.00
3-Lucky Luciano & Murder, Inc; c-/Avon paperback 66 13.00 40.00 90.00

FAMOUS INDIAN TRIBES
July-Sept, 1962; July, 1972
Dell Publishing Co.

12-264-209 (The Sioux) .85 2.50 6.00
2(7/72)-Reprints above .25 .75 1.50

FAMOUS STARS
Nov-Dec, 1950 - No. 6, Spring, 1952 (All photo covers)
Ziff-Davis Publ. Co.

1-Shelley Winters, Susan Peters, Ava Gardner, Shirley Temple 10.00 30.00 70.00
2-Betty Hutton, Bing Crosby, Colleen Townsend, Gloria Swanson; Everett-a(2) 8.00 24.00 56.00
3-Farley Granger, Judy Garland's ordeal, Alan Ladd 7.00 21.00 50.00
4-Al Jolson, Bob Mitchum, Ella Raines, Richard Conte, Vic Damone; Crandall-a, 6pgs. 6.50 19.50 45.00

FAMOUS STARS (continued) | Good | Fine | Mint
5-Liz Taylor, Betty Grable, Esther Williams, George Brent; Krigstein-a
9.50 28.50 66.00
6-Gene Kelly, Hedy Lamarr, June Allyson, William Boyd, Janet Leigh, Gary Cooper 6.50 19.50 45.00
NOTE: ***Whitney*** *a-1,3.*

FAMOUS STORIES (. . . Book No. 2)
1942
Dell Publishing Co.

1-Treasure Island 9.00 27.00 62.00
2-Tom Sawyer 9.00 27.00 62.00

FAMOUS TV FUNDAY FUNNIES
Sept, 1961
Harvey Publications

1-Casper the Ghost 3.00 9.00 21.00

FAMOUS WESTERN BADMEN (Formerly Redskin)
No. 13, Dec, 1952 - No. 15, 1953
Youthful Magazines

13 3.00 9.00 21.00
14,15 2.00 6.00 14.00

FANTASCI
Oct, 1986 - Present ($1.50, B&W)
WaRP Graphics

1-Captain Obese by Don Lomax .35 1.00 2.00
2-5 .30 .90 1.80

FANTASTIC (Formerly Capt. Science; Beware No. 10 on)
No. 8, Feb, 1952 - No. 9, April, 1952
Youthful Magazines

8-Capt. Science by Harrison 8.50 25.50 60.00
9-Harrison-a 5.00 15.00 35.00

FANTASTIC (Fantastic Fears No. 1-9)
No. 10, Nov-Dec, 1954 - No. 11, Jan-Feb, 1955
Ajax/Farrell Publ.

10,11 3.00 9.00 21.00

FANTASTIC ADVENTURES
1963 - 1964 (Reprints)
Super Comics

9,10,12,15,16,18: 16-Briefer-a. 18-r/Superior Stories No. 1
1.00 3.00 6.00
11-Wood-a; r/Blue Bolt No. 118 1.70 5.00 10.00
17-Baker-a(2) r-/Seven Seas 6 1.35 4.00 8.00

FANTASTIC COMICS
Dec, 1939 - No. 23, Nov, 1941
Fox Features Syndicate

1-Intro/Origin Samson; Stardust, The Super Wizard, Space Smith, Sub Saunders, Capt. Kidd begin 90.00 270.00 630.00
2-Powell text illos 45.00 135.00 315.00
3-5: 3-Powell text illos 37.00 110.00 260.00
6-9: 6,7-Simon-c 30.00 90.00 210.00
10-Intro/origin David, Samson's aide 23.00 70.00 160.00
11-17: 16-Stardust ends 17.00 51.00 120.00
18-Intro. Black Fury & sidekick Chuck; ends No. 23
20.00 60.00 140.00
19,20 17.00 51.00 120.00
21-The Banshee begins(origin); ends No. 23 20.00 60.00 140.00
22 17.00 51.00 120.00
23-Origin The Gladiator 20.00 60.00 140.00
NOTE: ***Lou Fine*** *c-1-5.* ***Tuska*** *a-3-5, 8. Bondage c-6, 8, 9.*

FANTASTIC FEARS (Formerly Captain Jet) (Fantastic No. 10 on)
No. 7, May, 1953 - No. 9, Sept-Oct, 1954
Ajax/Farrell Publ.

| | Good | Fine | Mint
7(5/53) 6.00 18.00 42.00
8(7/53) 4.00 12.00 28.00
3,4 3.00 9.00 21.00
5-1st Ditko story is written by Bruce Hamilton reprinted in Weird V2No.8 15.00 45.00 105.00
6-Decapitation of girl's head with paper cutter (classic)
8.00 24.00 56.00
7(5-6/54), 9(9-10/54) 3.00 9.00 21.00
8(7-8/54)-Contains story intended for Jo-Jo; name changed to Kaza; decapitation story 4.35 13.00 30.00

FANTASTIC FOUR (See Official Marvel Index to. . .)
Nov, 1961 - Present
Marvel Comics Group

1-Origin & 1st app. The Fantastic Four (Reed Richards: Mr. Fantastic, Johnny Storm: The Human Torch, Sue Storm: The Invisible Girl, & Ben Grimm: The Thing); origin The Mole Man
130.00 500.00 1250.00
1-Reprint from the Golden Record Comic Set 1.50 4.50 9.00
with record. . . . 4.35 13.00 30.00
2-Vs. The Skrulls (last 10¢ issue) 71.00 180.00 500.00
3-Fantastic Four don costumes & establish Headquarters
57.00 145.00 400.00
4-1st Silver Age Sub-Mariner app. 44.00 110.00 305.00
5-Origin & 1st app. Doctor Doom 32.00 80.00 225.00
6-10: 6-Sub-Mariner, Dr. Doom team up. 7-1st app. Kurrgo. 8-1st app. Puppet-Master & Alicia Masters 20.00 50.00 137.00
11-Origin The Impossible Man 14.00 35.00 100.00
12-Fantastic Four Vs. The Hulk 14.00 35.00 100.00
13-15: 13-Intro. The Watcher; 1st app. The Red Ghost
13.00 33.00 80.00
16-20: 18-Origin The Super Skrull. 19-Intro. Rama-Tut. 20-Origin The Molecule Man 7.00 18.00 50.00
21-30: 21-Intro. The Hate Monger. 25,26-The Thing Vs. the Hulk. 28-X-Men app. 30-Intro. Diablo 4.35 11.00 30.00
31-40: 31-Avengers x-over. 33-1st app. Attuma. 35-Intro/1st app. Dragon Man. 36-Intro/1st app. Madam Medusa & the Frightful Four (Sandman, Wizard, Paste Pot Pete). 39-Wood inks on Daredevil 2.35 6.00 16.00
41-47: 41-43-Frightful Four app. 44-Intro. Gorgan. 45-Intro. The Inhumans 1.70 5.00 10.00
48-Intro/1st app. The Silver Surfer, & Galactus (3/66)
5.00 15.00 30.00
49,50-Silver Surfer x-over 2.50 7.50 15.00
51-60: 52-Intro. The Black Panther; origin-No. 53. Silver Surfer x-over in No. 55-60,61(cameo). 54,59,60-Inhumans cameo
1.35 4.00 8.00
61-65,68-70 1.00 3.00 6.00
66,67-1st app. & origin Him (Warlock) 1.35 4.00 8.00
71,73,78-80 .70 2.00 4.00
72,74-77: Silver Surfer app. 1.35 4.00 8.00
81-90: 81-Crystal joins & dons costume. 82,83-Inhumans app. 84-87-Dr. Doom app. .65 1.90 3.80
91-99,101,102: 94-Intro. Agatha Harkness. Last Kirby issue No. 102,108 .65 1.90 3.80
100 2.00 6.00 12.00
103-111 .45 1.35 2.70
112-Hulk Vs. Thing .70 2.00 4.00
113-120: 116-(52 pgs.) .45 1.25 2.50
121-123-Silver Surfer x-over .70 2.00 4.00
124-127,129-140: 126-Origin F.F. retold. 129-Intro. Thundra. 130-Sue leaves F.F. 132-Medusa joins. 133-Thundra Vs. Thing
.35 1.00 2.00

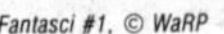
Fantasci #1, © WaRP

Fantastic Comics #6, © FOX

Fantastic Four #50, © MCG

Fantastic Four #250, © MCG

Fantastic Worlds #5, © STD

Fantasy Masterpieces #10, © MCG

FANTASTIC FOUR (continued)

	Good	Fine	Mint
128-Four pg. glossy insert of F.F. Friends & Fiends	.50	1.50	3.00
141-149,151-154,158-160: 142-Kirbyish art by Buckler begins. 151-Origin Thundra. 159-Medusa leaves, Sue rejoins	.30	.80	1.60
150-Crystal & Quicksilver's wedding	.40	1.20	2.40
155-157: Silver Surfer in all	.35	1.00	2.00
161-180: 164-The Crusader (old Marvel Boy) revived; origin No. 165. 176-Re-intro Impossible Man; Marvel artists app.		.60	1.20
181-199: 190-191-F.F. breaks up		.50	1.00
200-Giant size-FF re-united	.50	1.50	3.00
201-208,219		.50	1.00
209-216,218,220,221-Byrne-a. 209-1st Herbie the Robot. 220-Brief origin	.25	.75	1.50
217-Dazzler app. by Byrne	.40	1.25	2.50
222-231		.50	1.00
232-Byrne-a begins	.35	1.15	2.30
233-235,237-249: Byrne-a. 238-Origin Frankie Ray	.25	.80	1.60
236-20th Anniversary issue(11/81, 64pgs., $1.00)-Brief origin F.F.	.40	1.20	2.40
250-Double size; Byrne-a; Skrulls impersonate New X-Men	.40	1.20	2.40
251-259: Byrne c/a. 252-Reads sideways; Annihilus app.	.25	.80	1.60
260-Alpha Flight app.	.35	1.10	2.20
261-285: 261-Silver Surfer. 262-Origin Galactus		.60	1.20
286-Ties in w/X-Factor		.70	1.40
287-295		.50	1.00
296-Barry Smith c/a; Thing rejoins	.30	.90	1.80
297-300		.45	.90
Giant-Size 2(8/74) - 4: Formerly G-S Super-Stars	.50	1.50	3.00
Giant-Size 5(5/75), 6(8/75)	.30	.80	1.60
Annual 1('63)-Origin F.F.; Ditko-i	8.50	21.50	60.00
Annual 2('64)-Dr. Doom origin & x-over	4.00	10.00	28.00
Annual 3('65)-Reed & Sue wed	1.75	4.50	12.00
Special 4(11/66)-G.A. Torch x-over & origin retold	.90	2.75	5.50
Special 5(11/67)-New art; Intro. Psycho-Man; Silver Surfer, Black Panther, Inhumans app.	.70	2.00	4.00
Special 6(11/68)-Intro. Annihilus; no reprints; birth of Franklin Richards	.55	1.70	3.40
Special 7(11/69), 8(12/70), 9(12/71), 10('73)	.40	1.20	2.40
Annual 11(6/76), 12(2/78)	.25	.75	1.50
Annual 13(10/78), 14(1/80)		.65	1.30
Annual 15(10/80), 16(10/81), 17(9/83)		.55	1.10
Annual 18(11/84), 19(11/85)		.70	1.40
Special Edition 1 (5/84)-r/Annual No. 1; Byrne c/a		.50	1.00
Giveaway (nn, 1981, 32pgs., Young Model Builders Club)		.50	1.00

NOTE: ***Austin*** *c(i)-232-236, 238, 240-42, 250i, 286i.* ***Buckler*** *a-142-163p, 168, 169; c-140-49p, 151-59p, 161-63pp, 165, 166p, 169, 170p, 216.* ***John Buscema*** *a(p)-107, 108(w/****Kirby & Romita****),109-130, 132, 134-141, 160, 173-175, 202, 297, 298, Annual 11, 13, Gnt-Size 1-4; c(p)-107-122, 124-129, 133-139, 202, Annual 12p, Special 10.* ***Byrne*** *a-209-218p, 220p, 221p, 232-65, 266i, 267-73, 274-80p; c-211-14p, 220p, 232-236p, 237, 238p, 239, 240-42p, 243-49, 250p, 251-67, 269-73.* ***Ditko*** *a-13i, Gnt Size 2r, Annual 16.* ***G. Kane*** *c-150p, 160p.* ***Kirby*** *a-1-102p, 108, 180r, 189r, 236p(r), Special 1-10, Giant-Size 5, 6r; c-1-101, 164, 167, 171-177, 180, 181, 190, 200, Annual 11, Giant-Size 5, Special 1-7, 9.* ***Marcos*** *a-Annual 14i.* ***Mooney*** *a-118i, 152i.* ***Perez*** *a-164-167; 170-172, 176-178, 184-188, 191p, 192p. Annual 14p, 15p; c(p)-183-88, 191, 192, 194-197.* ***Simonson*** *c-212.* ***B. Smith*** *a-296.* ***Steranko*** *c-130-132p.*

FANTASTIC FOUR INDEX (See Official . . .)

FANTASTIC FOUR ROAST
May, 1982 (One Shot, Direct Sale)
Marvel Comics Group

	Good	Fine	Mint
1-Celebrates 20th anniversary of Fantastic Four No. 1; Golden, Miller, Byrne, Anderson, Austin-a; Austin-c(i)		.50	1.00

FANTASTIC FOUR VERSUS THE X-MEN
Feb, 1987 - No. 4, May, 1987 (mini-series)
Marvel Comics Group

	Good	Fine	Mint
1-4	.25	.75	1.50

FANTASTIC GIANTS (Konga No. 1-23)
September, 1966 (25 cents, 68 pgs.)
Charlton Comics

	Good	Fine	Mint
V2No.24-Origin Konga & Gorgo reprinted; two new Ditko stories	2.00	6.00	12.00

FANTASTIC TALES
1958 (no date) (Reprint)
I. W. Enterprises

	Good	Fine	Mint
1-Reprints Avon's "City of the Living Dead"	1.35	4.00	8.00

FANTASTIC VOYAGE (See Movie Comics)
Aug, 1969 - No. 2, Dec, 1969
Gold Key

	Good	Fine	Mint
1,2 (TV)	1.70	5.00	10.00

FANTASTIC VOYAGES OF SINDBAD, THE
Oct, 1965 - No. 2, June, 1967
Gold Key

	Good	Fine	Mint
1,2	2.15	6.50	15.00

FANTASTIC WORLDS
No. 5, Sept, 1952 - No. 7, Jan, 1953
Standard Comics

	Good	Fine	Mint
5-Toth, Anderson-a	8.50	25.50	60.00
6-Toth story	6.50	19.50	45.00
7	4.35	13.00	30.00

FANTASY MASTERPIECES (Marvel Super Heroes No. 12 on)
Feb, 1966 - No. 11, Oct, 1967; Dec, 1979 - No. 14, Jan, 1981
Marvel Comics Group

	Good	Fine	Mint
1-Photo of Stan Lee	.40	1.25	2.50
2		.60	1.20
3-G.A. Captain America-r begin; 1st 25 cent ish.		.60	1.20
4-6-Capt. America-r		.60	1.20
7-Begin G.A. Sub-Mariner, Torch-r		.50	1.00
8-Torch battles the Sub-Mariner r-/Marvel Mystery No. 9		.50	1.00
9-Origin Human Torch r-/Marvel Comics No.1		.50	1.00
10-All Winners-r		.50	1.00
11-Reprint of origin Toro & Black Knight		.50	1.00
V2No.1(12/79)-52 pgs.; 75 cents; reprints origin Silver Surfer from Silver Surfer No. 1 with editing; J. Buscema-a		.65	1.30
2-4-Silver Surfer-r		.50	1.00
5-14-Silver Surfer-r		.30	.60

NOTE: ***Buscema*** *c-V2No.7-9(in part).* ***Ditko*** *a-1-3r, 7r, 9r.* ***Everett*** *a-9r.* ***Matt Fox*** *a-9i(r).* ***Kirby*** *a-2-4r, 8r, 11r.* ***Starlin*** *a-8-13r. Some direct sale V2No14's had a 50 cent cover price.*

FANTASY QUARTERLY (Also see Elfquest)
Spring, 1978
Independent Publishers Syndicate

	Good	Fine	Mint
1-1st app. Elfquest (2nd printing exist?)	6.00	18.00	36.00

FANTOMAN (Formerly Amazing Adv. Funnies)
No. 2, Aug, 1940 - No. 4, Dec, 1940
Centaur Publications

FANTOMAN (continued)

	Good	Fine	Mint
2-The Fantom of the Fair, The Arrow, Little Dynamite-r begin; Burgos J. Cole, Ernst, Gustavson-a	50.00	150.00	350.00
3,4: Gustavson-a(r). 4-Bondage-c	33.00	100.00	230.00

FARGO KID (Formerly Justice Traps the Guilty)
V11No.3(No.1), June-July, 1958 - V11No.5, Oct-Nov, 1958
Prize Publications

V11No.3(No.1)-Origin Fargo Kid, Severin-c/a; Williamson-a(2)	6.00	18.00	42.00
V11No.4,5-Severin c/a	3.50	10.50	24.00

FARMER'S DAUGHTER, THE
2-3/54 - No. 3, 6-7/54; No. 4, 2-3/55
Stanhall Publ./Trojan Magazines/Merit No. 4

1-Lingerie, nudity panel	6.00	18.00	42.00
2,3('54)(Stanhall)	3.35	10.00	23.00
4(Merit, 2-3/55)(Exist?)	1.75	5.25	12.00

FASHION IN ACTION SUMMER SPECIAL
Aug, 1986 ($1.75, Baxter)
Eclipse Comics

1	.30	.85	1.70

FASTEST GUN ALIVE, THE (See 4-Color No. 741)

FAST FICTION (. . . Action) (Stories by Famous Authors Illustrated No. 6 on)
Oct, 1949 - No. 5, Mar, 1950 (All have Kiefer-c)
Seaboard Publ./Famous Authors Ill.

1-Scarlet Pimpernel; Jim Lavery-a	14.50	43.50	100.00
2-Captain Blood; H. C. Kiefer-a	11.50	34.50	80.00
3-She, by Rider Haggard; Vincent Napoli-a	20.00	60.00	140.00
4-(52pgs, 1/50)-The 39 Steps; Lavery-a	8.50	25.50	60.00
5-Beau Geste; Kiefer-a	8.50	25.50	60.00

NOTE: ***Kiefer** a-2, 5; c-2, 3, 5. **Lavery** a-1, 4; c-1, 4. **Napoli** a-3.*

FAST WILLIE JACKSON
October, 1976 - No. 7, 1977
Fitzgerald Periodicals, Inc.

1		.50	1.00
2-7		.40	.80

FAT ALBERT (. . . & the Cosby Kids) (TV)
March, 1974 - No. 29, Feb, 1979
Gold Key

1	.35	1.00	2.00
2-29		.40	.80

FAT AND SLAT (Ed Wheelan) (Gunfighter No. 5 on)
Summer, 1947 - No. 4, Spring, 1948
E. C. Comics

1	13.00	40.00	90.00
2	10.00	30.00	70.00
3,4	9.50	28.50	66.00

FAT AND SLAT JOKE BOOK
Summer, 1944 (One Shot, 52 pages)
All-American Comics (William H. Wise)

by Ed Wheelan	9.50	28.50	66.00

FATE (See Hand of Fate, & Thrill-O-Rama)

FATHER OF CHARITY
No date (32 pgs.; paper cover)
Catechetical Guild Giveaway

	2.00	6.00	12.00

FATIMA...CHALLENGE TO THE WORLD
1951, 36 pgs. (15¢ cover)
Catechetical Guild

	Good	Fine	Mint
nn (not same as 'Challenge to the World')	3.00	9.00	18.00

FATMAN, THE HUMAN FLYING SAUCER
April, 1967 - No. 3, Aug-Sept, 1967 (68 pgs.)
Lightning Comics(Milson Publ. Co.) (Written by Otto Binder)

1-Origin Fatman & Tinman by C. C. Beck	2.00	6.00	14.00
2-Beck-a	1.75	5.25	12.00
3-(Scarce)-Beck-a	3.50	10.50	24.00

FAUNTLEROY COMICS (Superduck Presents . . .)
1950 - No. 3, 1952
Close-Up/Archie Publications

1	3.50	10.50	24.00
2,3	1.75	5.25	12.00

FAVORITE COMICS (Also see Famous Comics)
1934 (36 pgs.)
Grocery Store Giveaway (Dif Corp.) (detergent)

Book No. 1-The Nebbs, Strange As It Seems, Napoleon, Joe Palooka, S'Matter Pop, Dixie Dugan, Hairbreadth Harry, etc. reprints	16.00	48.00	110.00
Book No. 2,3	13.00	40.00	90.00

FAWCETT MINIATURES (See Mighty Midget)
1946 (12-24 pgs.; 3¾x5") (Wheaties giveaways)
Fawcett Publications

Captain Marvel-"And the Horn of Plenty;" Bulletman story	2.35	7.00	16.00
Captain Marvel-"& the Raiders From Space;" Golden Arrow story	2.35	7.00	16.00
Captain Marvel Jr.-"The Case of the Poison Press!" Bulletman story	2.35	7.00	16.00
Delecta of the Planets-C. C. Beck art; B&W inside; 12 pgs.; 3 printing variations (coloring) exist. Only 6 known copies exist	8.00	24.00	56.00

FAWCETT MOTION PICTURE COMICS (See Motion Picture Comics)

FAWCETT MOVIE COMIC
1949 - No. 20, Dec, 1952
Fawcett Publications

nn-"Dakota Lil"-George Montgomery & Rod Cameron('49)	17.00	51.00	120.00
nn-"Copper Canyon"-Ray Milland & Hedy Lamarr('50)	12.00	36.00	84.00
nn-"Destination Moon"-(1950)	40.00	120.00	280.00
nn-"Montana"-Errol Flynn & Alexis Smith('50)	12.00	36.00	84.00
nn-"Pioneer Marshal"-Monte Hale(1950)	12.00	36.00	84.00
nn-"Powder River Rustlers"-Rocky Lane(1950)	13.00	40.00	90.00
nn-"Singing Guns"-Vaughn Monroe & Ella Raines(1950)	12.00	36.00	84.00
7-"Gunmen of Abilene"-Rocky Lane; Bob Powell-a(1950)	13.00	40.00	90.00
8-"King of the Bullwhip"-Lash LaRue; Bob Powell-a(1950)	17.00	51.00	120.00
9-"The Old Frontier"-Monte Hale; Bob Powell-a(2/51; mis-dated 2/50)	12.00	36.00	84.00
10-"The Missourians"-Monte Hale(4/51)	12.00	36.00	84.00
11-"The Thundering Trail"-Lash LaRue(6/51)	17.00	51.00	120.00
12-"Rustlers on Horseback"-Rocky Lane(8/51)	13.00	40.00	90.00

Fargo Kid V11No.5, © PRIZE

Fatman, the Human . . . #1, © Lightning

Fawcett Movie Comic nn, © Republic Pictures

Fawcett's Funny Animals #1, © FAW

The F.B.I. #1, © DELL

Feature Books #56, © KING

FAWCETT MOVIE COMIC (continued) — Good / Fine / Mint

13-"Warpath"-Edmond O'Brien & Forrest Tucker(10/51) 12.00 36.00 84.00
14-"Last Outpost"-Ronald Reagan(12/51) 30.00 90.00 210.00
15-(Scarce)-"The Man From Planet X"-Robert Clark; Shaffenberger-a (2/52) 145.00 435.00 1015.00
16-"10 Tall Men"-Burt Lancaster 9.00 27.00 62.00
17-"Rose of Cimarron"-Jack Buetel & Mala Powers 6.50 19.50 45.00
18-"The Brigand"-Anthony Dexter; Shaffenberger-a 6.50 19.50 45.00
19-"Carbine Williams"-James Stewart; Costanza-a 8.00 24.00 56.00
20-"Ivanhoe"-Liz Taylor 10.00 30.00 70.00

FAWCETT'S FUNNY ANIMALS (No. 1-26, 80-on titled "Funny Animals;" Li'l Tomboy No. 92 on?)
12/42 - No. 79, 4/53; No. 80, 6/53 - No. 83, 12?/53; No. 84, 4/54 - No. 91, Feb, 1956
Fawcett Publications/Charlton Comics No. 84 on

1-Capt. Marvel on cover; Intro. Hoppy The Marvel Bunny, cloned from Capt. Marvel 18.50 55.50 130.00
2 9.00 27.00 62.00
3-5 6.50 19.50 45.00
6-10: 8-Flag-c 4.35 13.00 30.00
11-20 2.65 8.00 18.00
21-40 1.65 5.00 11.50
41-88,90,91 1.30 4.00 9.00
89-Merry Mailman ish 1.65 5.00 11.50

NOTE: *Marvel Bunny in all issues to at least No. 68 (not in 49-54).*

FAZE ONE FAZERS
1986 - No. 4, Sept, 1986 (mini-series)
Americomics (AC Comics)

1-4 .40 1.25 2.50

F.B.I., THE
April-June, 1965
Dell Publishing Co.

1-Sinnott-a 1.00 3.00 7.00

F.B.I. STORY, THE (See 4-Color No. 1069)

FEAR (Adventure into...)
Nov, 1970 - No. 31, Dec, 1975 (No.1-6 - Giant Size)
Marvel Comics Group

1-Reprints Fantasy & Sci-Fi stories .60 1.20
2-9: 9-Everett-a .30 .60
10-Man-Thing begins; Morrow c/a(p) .70 2.00 4.00
11-Adams-c .25 .75 1.50
12-Starlin/Buckler-a .25 .75 1.50
13-18 .30 .60
19-Intro. Howard the Duck; Val Mayerick-a 1.70 5.00 10.00
20-Morbius, the Living Vampire begins, ends No. 31; Gulacy-a(p) .30 .60
21-31: 30-Evans-a .30 .60

NOTE: ***Bolle** a-13i. **Brunner** c-15-17. **Buckler** a-11p, 22p; c-13p, 22p. **Chaykin** a-10i. **Colan** a-23r. **Ditko** a-6-8r. **Everett** a-21r. **Gil Kane** a-21p; c(p)-20, 21, 23-28, 31. **Kirby** a-8r, 9r. **Maneely** a-24r. **Mooney** a-11i, 26r. **Paul Reinman** a-14r. **Russell** a-23p, 24p. **Severin** c-8. **Starlin** c-12p.*

FEAR BOOK
April, 1986 (One shot) ($1.75, adults)
Eclipse Comics

1-Scholastic Mag.-r; Bissette-a .30 .90 1.80

FEAR IN THE NIGHT (See Complete Mystery No. 3)

FEARLESS FAGAN (See 4-Color No. 441)

FEATURE BOOK (Dell) (See Large Feature Comic)

FEATURE BOOKS (Newspaper-r, early issues)
May, 1937 - No. 57, 1948
David McKay Publications — Good / Fine / Mint

nn-Popeye & the Jeep (No.1, 100 pgs.); reprinted as Feature Books No. 3 (Very Rare; only 3 known copies, 1-vf, 2-in low grade)
Estimated value.... 385.00 1155.00 2700.00
nn-Dick Tracy (No.1)-Reprinted as Feature Book No. 4 (100 pgs.) & in part as 4-Color No. 1 (Rare, less than 10 known copies)
Estimated Value.... 400.00 1200.00 2800.00

NOTE: *Above books were advertised together with different covers from Feature Books No. 3 & 4.*

1-King of the Royal Mtd. (No.1) 33.00 100.00 230.00
2-Popeye(6/37) by Segar 45.00 135.00 315.00
3-Popeye(7/37) by Segar; same as nn issue but a new cover added 38.50 115.00 270.00
4-Dick Tracy(8/37)-Same as nn issue but a new cover added 70.00 210.00 490.00
5-Popeye(9/37) by Segar 30.00 90.00 210.00
6-Dick Tracy(10/37) 55.00 165.00 385.00
7-Little Orphan Annie (No. 1) (Rare) 68.00 205.00 475.00
8-Secret Agent X-9-Not by Raymond 19.00 57.00 132.00
9-Dick Tracy(1/38) 55.00 165.00 385.00
10-Popeye(2/38) 30.00 90.00 210.00
11-Little Annie Rooney (No. 1) 15.00 45.00 105.00
12-Blondie (No.1) (4/38) (Rare) 33.00 100.00 230.00
13-Inspector Wade 9.50 28.50 65.00
14-Popeye(6/38) by Segar (Scarce) 44.50 134.00 310.00
15-Barney Baxter (No.1) (7/38) 13.50 40.00 95.00
16-Red Eagle 8.00 24.00 56.00
17-Gangbusters (No.1) 19.00 57.00 132.00
18,19-Mandrake 19.00 57.00 132.00
20-Phantom (No. 1) 36.00 105.00 245.00
21-Lone Ranger 35.00 105.00 245.00
22-Phantom 30.00 90.00 210.00
23-Mandrake 19.00 57.00 132.00
24-Lone Ranger(1941) 35.00 105.00 245.00
25-Flash Gordon (No.1)-Reprints not by Raymond 46.00 138.00 322.00
26-Prince Valiant(1941)-Harold Foster-a; newspaper strips reprinted, pgs. 1-28,30-63 66.00 200.00 462.00
27-29,31,34-Blondie 6.50 19.50 45.00
30-Katzenjammer Kids (No.1) 7.00 21.00 50.00
32,35,41,44-Katzenjammer Kids 5.50 16.50 38.00
33(nn)-Romance of Flying-World War II photos 4.65 14.00 32.00
36,38,40,42,43,45,47-Blondie 5.00 15.00 35.00
37-Katzenjammer Kids; has photo & biog of Harold H. Knerr(1883-1949) who took over strip from Rudolph Dirks in 1914 6.50 19.50 45.00
39-Phantom 20.00 60.00 140.00
46-Mandrake in the Fire World-(58 pgs.) 14.50 43.50 100.00
48-Maltese Falcon('46) 30.00 90.00 210.00
49,50-Perry Mason 9.50 28.50 65.00
51,54-Rip Kirby by Raymond; origin-No. 51 14.50 43.50 100.00
52,55-Mandrake 13.00 40.00 90.00
53,56,57-Phantom 15.00 45.00 105.00

NOTE: *All Feature Books through No. 25 are over-sized 8½x11-3/8" comics with color covers and black and white interiors. The covers are rough, heavy stock. The page counts, including covers, are as follows: nn, No.3,4-100 pgs.; No.1,2-52 pgs.; No.5-25 are all 76 pgs. No. 33 was found in bound set from publisher.*

FEATURE COMICS (Formerly Feature Funnies)
No. 21, June, 1939 - No. 144, May, 1950
Quality Comics Group

21 15.00 45.00 105.00
22-26: 23-Charlie Chan begins 11.00 33.00 76.00

FEATURE COMICS (continued) — Good / Fine / Mint

26-(nn, nd)-c-in one color, (10 cents, 36pgs.; issue No. blanked out. 2 variations exist, each contain half of the regular No. 26) 4.35 13.00 30.00
27-Origin & 1st app. of Dollman by Eisner 125.00 375.00 875.00
28-1st Fine Dollman 58.00 174.00 400.00
29,30 36.00 108.00 250.00
31-Last Clock & Charlie Chan issue 30.00 90.00 210.00
32-37: 32-Rusty Ryan & Samar begin. 37-Last Fine Dollman 23.00 70.00 160.00
38-41: 38-Origin the Ace of Space. 39-Origin The Destroying Demon, ends No. 40. 40-Bruce Blackburn in costume 16.50 50.00 115.00
42-USA, the Spirit of Old Glory begins 9.50 28.50 65.00
43,45-50: 46-Intro. Boyville Brigadiers in Rusty Ryan. 48-USA ends 9.50 28.50 65.00
44-Dollman by Crandall begins, ends No. 63; Crandall-a(2) 14.50 43.50 100.00
51-55 8.00 24.00 56.00
56-Marijuana story in ''Swing Session'' 8.50 25.50 60.00
57-Spider Widow begins 8.00 24.00 56.00
58-60: 60-Raven begins, ends No. 71 8.00 24.00 56.00
61-68 (5/43) 7.00 21.00 50.00
69,70-Phantom Lady x-over in Spider Widow 8.00 24.00 56.00
71-80: 71-Phantom Lady x-over. 72-Spider Widow ends 5.00 15.00 35.00
81-99 4.00 12.00 28.00
100 5.00 15.00 35.00
101-144: 139-Last Dollman. 140-Intro. Stuntman Stetson 4.00 12.00 28.00

NOTE: ***Celardo** a-37-43. **Crandall** a-44-60, 62, 63-on(most). **Gustavson** a-(Rusty Ryan)-32-47. **Powell** a-34, 64-73.*

FEATURE FILMS
Mar-Apr, 1950 - No. 4, Sept-Oct, 1950 (Photo-c 2,3)
National Periodical Publications

1-''Captain China'' with John Payne & Gail Russell 21.00 63.00 146.00
2-''Riding High'' with Bing Crosby 16.00 48.00 110.00
3-''The Eagle & the Hawk'' with John Payne, Rhonda Fleming & D. O'Keefe 16.00 48.00 110.00
4-''Fancy Pants''-Bob Hope & Lucille Ball 17.00 51.00 120.00

FEATURE FUNNIES (Feature Comics No. 21 on)
Oct, 1937 - No. 20, May, 1939
Harry 'A' Chesler

1(V9/1-indicia)-Joe Palooka, Mickey Finn, The Bungles, Jane Arden, Dixie Dugan, Big Top, Ned Bryant, Strange As It Seems, & Off the Record strip reprints begin 70.00 210.00 490.00
2-The Hawk app. (11/37) 35.00 105.00 245.00
3-Hawks of Seas begins by Eisner, ends No. 12; The Clock begins; Christmas-c 23.00 70.00 160.00
4,5 18.00 54.00 125.00
6-12: 11-Archie O'Toole by Bud Thomas begins, ends No. 22 15.00 45.00 105.00
13-Espionage, Starring Black X begins by Eisner, ends No. 20 17.00 51.00 120.00
14-20 12.00 36.00 84.00

FEATURE PRESENTATION, A (Feature Presentations Mag. No. 6) (Formerly Women in Love) (Also see Startling Terror Tales No. 11)
No. 5, April, 1950
Fox Features Syndicate

5-Black Tarantula 12.00 36.00 84.00

FEATURE PRESENTATIONS MAGAZINE (Formerly A Feature Presentation No. 5; becomes Feature Stories Mag. No. 3 on)
No. 6, July, 1950
Fox Features Syndicate

Good / Fine / Mint
6-Moby Dick; Wood-c 10.00 30.00 70.00

FEATURE STORIES MAGAZINE (Formerly Feat. Present. Mag. No.6)
No. 3, Aug, 1950 - No. 4, Oct, 1950
Fox Features Syndicate

3-Jungle Lil, Zegra stories; bondage-c 9.50 28.50 66.00
4 6.50 19.50 45.00

FEDERAL MEN COMICS
1945 (DC reprints from 1930's)
Gerard Publ. Co.

2-Siegel & Shuster-a; cover redrawn from Detective No. 9; spanking panel 7.00 21.00 50.00

FELIX'S NEPHEWS INKY & DINKY
Sept, 1957 - No. 7, Oct, 1958
Harvey Publications

1-Cover shows Inky's left eye with 2 pupils 3.50 10.50 24.00
2-7 1.75 5.25 12.00

NOTE: *Contains no **Messmer** art.*

FELIX THE CAT
1927 - 1931 (24 pgs.; 8x10¼'')(1926,'27 color strip reprints)
McLoughlin Bros.

260-(Rare)-by Otto Messmer 52.00 156.00 365.00

FELIX THE CAT (See March of Comics)
1943 - No. 12, July-Sept, 1965
Dell Publ. No.1-19/Toby No.20-61/Harvey No.62-118/Dell

4-Color 15 33.00 100.00 230.00
4-Color 46('44) 22.00 65.00 154.00
4-Color 77('45) 18.00 54.00 125.00
4-Color 119('46) 12.00 36.00 84.00
4-Color 135('46) 10.00 30.00 70.00
4-Color 162(9/47) 8.00 24.00 56.00
1(2-3/48)(Dell) 10.00 30.00 70.00
2 5.00 15.00 35.00
3-5 4.00 12.00 28.00
6-19(2-3/51-Dell) 3.00 9.00 21.00
20-30(Toby): 28-2/52 some copies have No. 29 on cover, No. 28 on inside 2.35 7.00 16.00
31,34,35-No Messmer-a 1.30 4.00 9.00
32,33,36-61(6/55-Toby)-Last Messmer ish. 1.85 5.50 13.00
62(8/55)-100 (Harvey) .85 2.50 6.00
101-118(11/61) .75 2.25 5.00
12-269-211(9-11/62)(Dell) 1.50 4.50 10.00
2-12(7-9/65)(Dell, TV) .75 2.25 5.00
. . .& His Friends 1(12/53-Toby) 3.00 9.00 21.00
. . .& His Friends 2-4 2.00 6.00 14.00
3-D Comic Book 1(1953-One Shot) 16.00 48.00 110.00
Summer Annual 2('52)-Early 1930s Sunday strip-r (Exist?) 16.00 48.00 110.00
Summer Annual nn('53, 100 pgs., Toby)-1930s daily & Sunday-r 11.00 33.00 76.00
Winter Annual 2('54, 100 pgs., Toby)-1930s daily & Sunday-r 8.00 24.00 56.00
Summer Annual 3('55) (Exist?) 6.00 18.00 42.00

(See March of Comics No. 24,36,51)

NOTE: *4-Color No. 15, 46, 77 and the Toby Annuals are all daily or Sunday newspaper reprints from the 1930's drawn by Otto Messmer, who created Felix in 1915 for the Sullivan animation studio. He drew Felix from the beginning under contract to Pat Sullivan. In 1946 he went to work for Dell and wrote and pencilled most of the stories and inked some of them through the Toby Press issues. No. 107 reprints No. 71 interior; No. 110 reprints No. 56 interior.*

FEMFORCE
Apr, 1985 - No. 6, 1985 ($1.75 cover; in color)
Americomics

Feature Comics #81, © QUA

Feature Funnies #1, © CHES

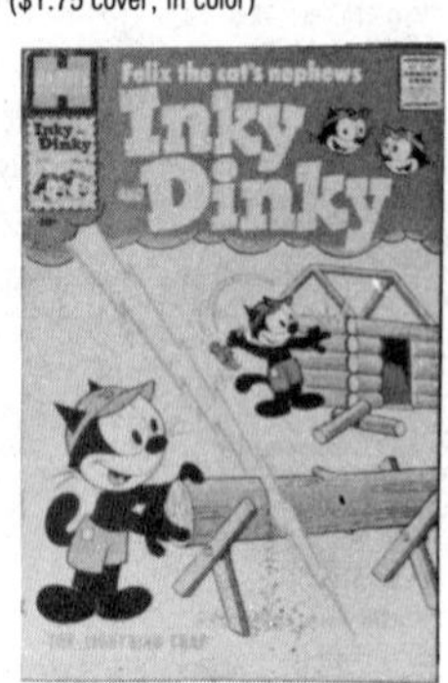

Felix's Nephews #6, © KING

Fight Against Crime #3, © Story

Fight Comics #19, © FH

Fightin' Air Force #9, © CC

FEMFORCE (continued)

	Good	Fine	Mint
1-6: Black-a	.30	.90	1.80
Special 1 (Fall, '84)(B&W, 52pgs.)	.25	.75	1.50

FERDINAND THE BULL
1938 (10 cents)(Large size; some color, rest B&W)
Dell Publishing Co.

	Good	Fine	Mint
nn	6.00	18.00	42.00

FIBBER McGEE & MOLLY (See A-1 Comics No. 25)

55 DAYS AT PEKING (See Movie Comics)

FIGHT AGAINST CRIME (Fight Against the Guilty No. 22)
May, 1951 - No. 21, Sept, 1954
Story Comics

	Good	Fine	Mint
1	5.00	15.00	35.00
2	2.50	7.50	17.50
3	2.00	6.00	14.00
4-Drug story-''Hopped Up Killers''	4.65	14.00	32.00
5-Frazetta, 1 pg.	2.00	6.00	14.00
6-Used in **POP**, pgs. 83,84	3.00	9.00	21.00
7	3.00	9.00	21.00
8-Last crime format issue	2.00	6.00	14.00

NOTE: *No. 9-21 contain violent, gruesome stories with blood, dismemberment, decapitation, E.C. style plot twists and several E.C. swipes.*

	Good	Fine	Mint
9-11,13	5.00	15.00	35.00
12-Morphine drug story-''The Big Dope''	6.50	19.50	45.00
14-Tothish art by Ross Andru	5.00	15.00	35.00
15-B&W & color illos in **POP**	6.00	18.00	42.00
16-E.C. story swipe/Haunt of Fear No. 19; Tothish-a by Ross Andru; bondage-c	6.00	18.00	42.00
17-Wildey E.C. swipe/Shock SuspenStories No. 9; knife through neck-c (1/54)	6.00	18.00	42.00
18,19	5.00	15.00	35.00
20-Decapitation cover; contains hanging, ax murder, blood & violence	14.50	43.50	100.00
21-E.C. swipe	6.00	18.00	42.00

NOTE: ***Cameron** a-5. **Hollingsworth** a-3, 9, 10, 13. **Wildey** a-15, 16.*

FIGHT AGAINST THE GUILTY (Formerly Fight Against Crime)
No. 22, Dec, 1954 - No. 23, Mar, 1955
Story Comics

	Good	Fine	Mint
22-Tothish-a by Ross Andru; Ditko-a; E.C. story swipe	5.00	15.00	35.00
23-Hollingsworth-a	3.50	10.50	24.00

FIGHT COMICS
Jan, 1940 - No. 86, Summer, 1953
Fiction House Magazines

	Good	Fine	Mint
1-Origin Spy Fighter, Starring Saber; Fine/Eisner-c; Eisner-a	60.00	180.00	420.00
2	30.00	90.00	210.00
3-Rip Regan, the Power Man begins	25.00	75.00	175.00
4,5: 4-Fine-c	20.00	60.00	140.00
6-10	16.00	48.00	110.00
11-14: Rip Regan ends	14.50	43.50	100.00
15-1st Super American	20.00	60.00	140.00
16-Captain Fight begins; Spy Fighter ends	20.00	60.00	140.00
17,18: Super American ends	17.00	51.00	120.00
19-Captain Fight ends; origin & 1st app. Senorita Rio; Rip Carson, Chute Trooper begins	17.00	51.00	120.00
20	13.00	40.00	90.00
21-30	9.50	28.50	65.00
31,33-35: 31-Decapitation-c	8.50	25.50	60.00
32-Tiger Girl begins	9.50	28.50	65.00
36-47,49,50: 44-Capt. Fight returns	8.00	24.00	56.00
48-Used in **Love and Death** by Legman	9.50	28.50	65.00
51-Origin Tiger Girl	12.00	36.00	84.00
52-60	6.00	18.00	42.00
61-Origin Tiger Girl retold	7.00	21.00	50.00
62-65-Last Baker issue	6.00	18.00	42.00
66-77	5.00	15.00	35.00
78-Used in **POP**, pg. 99	5.75	17.25	40.00
79-The Space Rangers app.	5.00	15.00	35.00
80-85	4.00	12.00	28.00
86-Two Tigerman stories by Evans; Moreira-a	5.00	15.00	35.00

NOTE: *Bondage c-No. 20, 21, 30, 32, 40, 41, 43, 44, 52. Lingerie, headlights panels are common. Tiger Girl by **Baker**-No. 36-60,62-65; Kayo Kirby by **Baker**-No. 52-64, 67. **Eisner** c-1-3, 5, 10, 11. **Kamen** a-54?, 57?. **Tuska** a-1, 5, 8, 10.*

FIGHT FOR FREEDOM
1949, 1951 (16 pgs.) (Giveaway)
National Association of Mfgrs./General Comics

	Good	Fine	Mint
Dan Barry-a; used in **POP**, pg. 102	5.00	15.00	30.00

FIGHT FOR LOVE
1952 (no month)
United Features Syndicate

	Good	Fine	Mint
nn-Abbie & Slats newspaper-r	6.00	18.00	42.00

FIGHTING AIR FORCE (See United States Fighting Air Force)

FIGHTIN' AIR FORCE (Formerly Sherlock Holmes?; War and Attack No. 54 on)
No. 3, Feb, 1956 - No. 53, Feb-Mar, 1966
Charlton Comics

	Good	Fine	Mint
V1No.3	1.15	3.50	8.00
4-10	.60	1.80	4.20
11(68 pgs.)(3/58)	.85	2.50	6.00
12 (100 pgs.)	1.15	3.50	8.00
13-30	.30	.90	2.00
31-50: 50-American Eagle begins		.40	.80
51-53		.30	.60

***Glanzman** a-13,24; c-24.*

FIGHTING AMERICAN
Apr-May, 1954 - No. 7, Apr-May, 1955
Headline Publications/Prize

	Good	Fine	Mint
1-Origin Fighting American & Speedboy; S&K c/a(3)	60.00	180.00	420.00
2-S&K-a(3)	30.00	90.00	210.00
3,4-S&K-a(3)	25.00	75.00	175.00
5-S&K-a(2), Kirby/?-a	25.00	75.00	175.00
6-Four pg. reprint of origin, plus 2 pgs. by S&K	22.00	65.00	154.00
7-Kirby-a	21.00	62.00	145.00

NOTE: ***Simon & Kirby** covers on all.*

FIGHTING AMERICAN
October, 1966 (25 cents)
Harvey Publications

	Good	Fine	Mint
1-Origin Fighting American & Speedboy by S&K-r; S&K-c/a(3); 1 pg. Adams ad	2.00	6.00	12.00

FIGHTIN' ARMY (Formerly Soldier and Marine Comics)
No. 16, 1/56 - No. 127, 12/76; No. 128, 9/77 - No. 172, 11/84
Charlton Comics

	Good	Fine	Mint
16	.75	2.25	5.00
17-19,21-30	.35	1.00	2.50
20-Ditko-a	.85	2.50	6.00
31-45	.25	.75	1.50
46-60		.40	.80
61-80: 75-The Lonely War of Willy Schultz begins, ends No. 92		.30	.60
81-172: 89,90,92-Ditko-a; Devil Brigade in No. 79,82,83		.30	.60

FIGHTIN' ARMY (continued)

	Good	Fine	Mint
108(Modern Comics-1977)-Reprint		.15	.30

NOTE: *Aparo c-154. **Montes/Bache** a-48,49,51,69,75,76, 170r.*

FIGHTING DANIEL BOONE
1953
Avon Periodicals

	Good	Fine	Mint
nn-Kinstler c/a, 22 pgs.	7.00	21.00	50.00
I.W. Reprint No. 1-Kinstler c/a; Lawrence/Alascia-a	1.00	3.00	6.00

FIGHTING DAVY CROCKETT (Formerly Kit Carson)
No. 9, Oct-Nov, 1955
Avon Periodicals

	Good	Fine	Mint
9-Kinstler-c	3.00	9.00	21.00

FIGHTIN' 5, THE (Formerly Space War; also see The Peacemaker)
7/64 - No. 41, 1/67; No. 42, 10/81 - No. 49, 12/82
Charlton Comics

	Good	Fine	Mint
V2No.28-Origin Fightin' Five	.35	1.00	2.00
29-39,41		.50	1.00
40-Peacemaker begins	.35	1.00	2.00
42-49: Reprints		.30	.60

FIGHTING FRONTS!
Aug, 1952 - No. 5, Jan, 1953
Harvey Publications

	Good	Fine	Mint
1	1.70	5.00	12.00
2-Extreme violence; Nostrand/Powell-a	2.00	6.00	14.00
3-5: 3-Powell-a	1.20	3.50	8.00

FIGHTING INDIAN STORIES (See Midget Comics)

FIGHTING INDIANS OF THE WILD WEST!
Mar, 1952 - No. 2, Nov, 1952
Avon Periodicals

	Good	Fine	Mint
1-Kinstler, Larsen-a	6.50	19.50	45.00
2-Kinstler-a	4.00	12.00	28.00
100 Pg. Annual(1952, 25 cents)-Contains three comics rebound	13.50	40.50	95.00

FIGHTING LEATHERNECKS
Feb, 1952 - No. 6, Dec, 1952
Toby Press

	Good	Fine	Mint
1-"Duke's Diary"-full pg. pin-ups by Sparling	4.00	12.00	28.00
2-"Duke's Diary"	3.00	9.00	21.00
3-5-"Gil's Gals"-full pg. pin-ups	3.00	9.00	21.00
6-(Same as No. 3-5?)	2.00	6.00	14.00

FIGHTING MAN, THE (War)
May, 1952 - No. 8, July, 1953
Ajax/Farrell Publications(Excellent Publ.)

	Good	Fine	Mint
1	2.00	6.00	14.00
2	1.00	3.00	7.00
3-8	.85	2.50	6.00
Annual 1 (100 pgs, 1952)	10.00	30.00	70.00

FIGHTIN' MARINES (Formerly The Texan; see Approved Comics)
No. 15, 8/51 - No. 10, 12/52; No. 14, 5/55 - No. 132, 11/76;
No. 133, 10/77 - No. 176, 9/84 (no No. 11-13)
St. John(Approved Comics)/Charlton Comics No. 14 on

	Good	Fine	Mint
15(No.1)-Matt Baker c/a "Leatherneck Jack;" slightly large size; Fightin' Texan No. 16 & 17?	8.00	24.00	56.00
2-1st Canteen Kate by Baker; slightly large size	10.00	30.00	70.00
3-9-Canteen Kate by Matt Baker; Baker c-No. 2,3,5-9	5.50	16.50	38.00
10 (12/52; last St. John issue; see Approved Comics)-Baker-c	1.50	4.50	10.00
14 (5/55; 1st Charlton issue; formerly?)-Canteen Kate by Baker	4.00	12.00	28.00
15-Baker-c	1.50	4.50	10.00
16,18-20-Not Baker-c	.85	2.50	6.00
17-Canteen Kate by Baker	4.00	12.00	28.00
21-24	.50	1.50	3.50
25-(68 pgs.)(3/58)	1.15	3.50	8.00
26-(100 pgs.)(8/58)	2.00	6.00	14.00
27-50		.60	1.20
51-81,83-100: 78-Shotgun Harker & the Chicken series begin		.40	.80
82-(100 pgs.)	.50	1.50	3.00
101-121		.30	.60
122-Pilot issue for "War" title (Fightin' Marines Presents War)		.30	.60
123-176		.30	.60
120(Modern Comics reprint, 1977)		.20	.40

NOTE: *No. 14 & 16 (CC) reprints St. John issue; No. 16 reprints St. John insignia on cover. **Colan** a-3, 7. **Glanzman** c/a-92, 94. **Montes/Bache** a-48, 53, 55, 64, 65, 72-74, 77-83, 176r.*

FIGHTING MARSHAL OF THE WILD WEST (See The Hawk)

FIGHTIN' NAVY (Formerly Don Winslow)
No. 74, 1/56 - No. 125, 4-5/66; No. 126, 8/83 - No. 133, 10/84
Charlton Comics

	Good	Fine	Mint
74	.70	2.00	5.00
75-81	.35	1.10	2.50
82-Sam Glanzman-a	.35	1.10	2.50
83-99,101-105	.25	.75	1.50
100	.35	1.00	2.00
106-125 ('66), 126-133('84)		.30	.60

NOTE: ***Montes/Bache** a-109. **Glanzman** a-131r.*

FIGHTING PRINCE OF DONEGAL, THE (See Movie Comics)

FIGHTIN' TEXAN (Formerly The Texan & Fightin' Marines No. 15?)
No. 16, Oct, 1952 - No. 17, Dec, 1952
St. John Publishing Co.

	Good	Fine	Mint
16,17-Tuska-a each. 17-Cameron-c/a	2.00	6.00	14.00

FIGHTING UNDERSEA COMMANDOS
1952 - No. 5, April, 1953
Avon Periodicals

	Good	Fine	Mint
1	4.00	12.00	28.00
2	2.65	8.00	18.00
3-5: 4-Kinstler-c	2.35	7.00	16.00

FIGHTING WAR STORIES
Aug, 1952 - 1953
Men's Publications/Story Comics

	Good	Fine	Mint
1	1.75	5.25	12.00
2	.90	2.75	6.00
3-5	.60	1.80	4.00

FIGHTING YANK (See Startling & America's Best)
Sept, 1942 - No. 29, Aug, 1949
Nedor/Better Publ./Standard

	Good	Fine	Mint
1-The Fighting Yank begins; Mystico, the Wonder Man app; bondage-c	45.00	135.00	315.00
2	22.00	65.00	154.00
3	14.50	43.50	100.00
4	11.00	33.00	76.00
5-10: 7-The Grim Reaper app.	9.50	28.50	65.00
11-The Oracle app.	8.00	24.00	56.00
12-17: 12-Hirohito bondage-c	8.00	24.00	56.00

Fighting Fronts #1, © HARV

Fighting Man #8, © AJAX

Fighting Yank #10, © BP

Film Funnies #1, © MCG

First Issue Special #5, © DC

First Love #17, © HARV

FIGHTING YANK (continued) — Good / Fine / Mint

18-The American Eagle app. 5.75 17.25 40.00
19,20 5.75 17.25 40.00
21,23,24: 21-Kara, Jungle Princess app. 24-Miss Masque app. 9.00 27.00 62.00
22-Miss Masque-c/story 10.00 30.00 70.00
25-Robinson/Meskin-a; strangulation, lingerie panel; The Cavalier app. 10.00 30.00 70.00
26-29: All-Robinson/Meskin-a. 28-One pg. Williamson-a 9.50 28.50 65.00

NOTE: ***Schomburg (Xela)*** *c-4-29; airbrush-c 28, 29. Bondage c-4, 8, 11, 15, 17.*

FIGHT THE ENEMY
Aug, 1966 - No. 3, Mar, 1967 (25 cents)
Tower Comics

1-Lucky 7 & Mike Manly begin; Grandenetti-a .40 1.20 2.40
2-Boris Vallejo, McWilliams-a 1.00 3.00 6.00
3-Wood-a ½pg; McWilliams, Bolle-a .30 .80 1.60

FILM FUNNIES
Nov, 1949 - No. 2, Feb, 1950
Marvel Comics (CPC)

1 5.00 15.00 35.00
2 3.50 10.50 24.00

FILM STARS ROMANCES
Jan-Feb, 1950 - No. 3, May-June, 1950
Star Publications

1-Rudy Valentino story; L. B. Cole-c; lingerie panels 11.50 34.50 80.00
2-Liz Taylor/Robert Taylor photo-c 13.00 40.00 90.00
3-Photo-c 10.00 30.00 70.00

FIRE AND BLAST
1952 (16 pgs.; paper cover) (Giveaway)
National Fire Protection Assoc.

Mart Baily A-Bomb cover; about fire prevention 12.00 35.00 70.00

FIRE BALL XL5 (See Steve Zodiac)

FIRE CHIEF AND THE SAFE OL' FIREFLY, THE
1952 (16 pgs.) (Safety brochure given away at schools)
National Board of Fire Underwriters (produced by American Visuals Corp.) (Eisner)

(Rare) Eisner c/a 20.00 60.00 140.00

FIREHAIR COMICS (Pioneer West Romances No. 3-6)
Winter/48-49 - No. 2, Spr/49; No. 7, Spr/51 - No. 11, Spr/52
Fiction House Magazines (Flying Stories)

1 13.00 40.00 90.00
2 6.50 19.50 46.00
7-11 5.50 16.50 38.00
I.W. Reprint 8-Kinstler-c; reprints Rangers No. 57; Dr. Drew story by Grandenetti (nd) .85 2.50 5.00

FIRESTAR
March, 1986 - No. 4, June, 1986 (From TV Spider-Man series)
Marvel Comics Group

1-X-men & New Mutants app. .30 .90 1.80
2-4 .25 .70 1.40

FIRESTONE (See Donald & Mickey)

FIRESTORM (See Cancelled Comic Cavalcade & DC Comics Presents)
March, 1978 - No. 5, Oct-Nov, 1978 (See The Fury of. . .)
DC Comics

1-Origin & 1st app. .40 1.25 2.50

Good / Fine / Mint

2-5: 2-Origin Multiplex. 3-Origin Killer Frost. 4-1st app. Hyena .25 .75 1.50

FIRST ADVENTURES
Dec, 1985 - No. 5, Apr, 1986
First Comics

1-5: 1-Blaze Barlow, Whisper & Dynamo Joe begin .65 1.30

FIRST AMERICANS, THE (See 4-Color No. 843)

FIRST CHRISTMAS, THE (3-D)
1953 (25 cents) (Oversized - 8¼x10¼")
Fiction House Magazines (Real Adv. Publ. Co.)

nn-(Scarce)-Kelly Freas-c 20.00 60.00 140.00

FIRST COMICS GRAPHIC NOVEL
Jan, 1984 - Present (52-176 pgs, high quality paper)
First Comics

1-Beowulf ($5.95) 1.00 3.00 6.00
2-Time Beavers ($5.95) 1.00 3.00 6.00
3($11.95, 100 pgs.)-Hard Times; American Flagg-r 2.00 6.00 11.95
4-Nexus ($6.95)-r/B&W 1-3 1.30 4.00 8.00
5-The Enchanted Apples of Oz ($7.95, 52pp)-Intro by Harlan Ellison (1986) 1.35 4.00 7.95
6-Elric of Melnibone ($14.95, 176pp)-r with new color 2.50 7.50 14.95
7-The Secret Island Of Oz ($7.95) 1.35 4.00 7.95
8-Teenage Mutant Ninja Turtles (132 pgs., r-/TMNT No. 1-3 in color w/12 pgs. new-a ($9.95) 1.70 5.00 9.95
9-Time 2: The Epiphany by Chaykin, 52 pgs. ($7.95) 1.35 4.00 7.95

FIRST ISSUE SPECIAL
April, 1975 - No. 13, April, 1976
National Periodical Publications

1-Intro. Atlas; Kirby c/a .50 1.00
2-7: 2-Green Team (See Cancelled Comic Cavalcade). 3-Metamorpho. 4-Lady Cop. 5-Manhunter; Kirby c/a. 6-Dingbats; Kirby c/a, 7-The Creeper .25 .50
8-The Warlord (origin); Grell c/a 2.00 6.00 12.00
9-Dr. Fate; Kubert-c; Simonson-a .25 .50
10-13: 10-The Outsiders. 11-Code Name: Assassin; Redondo-a. 12-Origin/1st app. new Starman. 13-Return of the New Gods .25 .50

FIRST KISS
Dec, 1957 - No. 40, Jan, 1965
Charlton Comics

V1No.1 .85 2.50 6.00
V1No.2-10 .50 1.50 3.00
11-40 .50 1.00

FIRST LOVE ILLUSTRATED
2/49 - No. 86, 3/58; No. 87, 9/58 - No. 88, 11/58; No. 89, 11/62, No. 90, 2/63
Harvey Publications(Home Comics)(True Love)

1-Powell-a(2) 3.50 10.50 24.00
2-Powell-a 2.00 6.00 14.00
3-"Was I Too Fat To Be Loved" story 2.50 7.50 17.00
4-10 1.70 5.00 12.00
11-30: 30-Lingerie panel 1.00 3.00 7.00
31-34,37,39-49: 49-Last pre-code (2/55) .85 2.50 6.00
35-Used in **SOTI**, illo-"The title of this comic book is First Love;" 7.00 21.00 50.00
36-Communism story, "Love Slaves" 1.15 3.50 8.00

FIRST LOVE ILLUSTRATED (continued)

	Good	Fine	Mint
38-Nostrand-a	2.00	6.00	14.00
50-90	.50	1.50	3.50

NOTE: *Disbrow a-13. Orlando c-87. Powell a-1, 3-5, 7, 10, 11, 13-17, 19-24, 26-29, 33, 35-41, 43, 45, 46, 50, 54, 55, 57, 58, 61-63, 65, 71-73, 76, 79r, 82, 84, 88.*

FIRST MEN IN THE MOON (See Movie Comics)

FIRST ROMANCE MAGAZINE
8/49 - No. 6, 6/50; No. 7, 6/51 - No. 50, 2/58; No. 51, 9/58 - No. 52, 11/58
Home Comics(Harvey Publ.)/True Love

	Good	Fine	Mint
1	3.50	10.50	24.00
2	2.00	6.00	14.00
3-5	1.70	5.00	12.00
6-10	1.35	4.00	9.00
11-20	1.00	3.00	7.00
21-27,29-32: 32-Last pre-code (2/55)	.70	2.00	5.00
28-Nostrand-a(Powell swipe)	1.70	5.00	12.00
33-52	.50	1.50	3.50

NOTE: *Powell a-1-5,8-10,14,18,20-22,24,25,28,36,46,48,51.*

FIRST TRIP TO THE MOON (See Space Advs. No. 20)

FISH POLICE, THE
Dec, 1985 - Present
Fishwrap Productions

	Good	Fine	Mint
1	4.65	14.00	28.00
1-2nd printing (5/86)	.25	.75	1.50
2	1.30	4.00	8.00
2-2nd printing	.25	.75	1.50
3-6	.25	.75	1.50

5-STAR SUPER-HERO SPEC. (See DC Special Series No. 1)

FLAME, THE
Summer, 1940 - No. 8, Jan, 1942
Fox Features Syndicate

	Good	Fine	Mint
1-Flame stories from Wonderworld No. 5-9; origin The Flame; Lou Fine-a, 36 pgs., r-/Wonderworld 3,10	90.00	270.00	630.00
2-Fine-a(2); Wing Turner by Tuska	45.00	135.00	315.00
3-8: 3-Powell-a	22.00	65.00	154.00

FLAME, THE (Formerly Lone Eagle)
No. 5, Dec-Jan, 1954-55 - No. 4, June-July, 1955
Ajax/Farrell Publications (Excellent Publ.)

	Good	Fine	Mint
5(No.1)	8.00	24.00	56.00
2-4	5.00	15.00	35.00

FLAMING CARROT
Summer-Fall, 1981 (One Shot)
Kilian Barracks Press

	Good	Fine	Mint
1 (Large size, 8½x11)	12.50	37.50	75.00

FLAMING CARROT
5/84 - No. 5, 1/85; No. 6, 3/85 - Present (B&W)
Aardvark-Vanaheim/Renegade Press No. 6 on

	Good	Fine	Mint
1	3.00	9.00	18.00
2	2.35	7.00	14.00
3,4	2.00	6.00	12.00
5,6	1.10	3.25	6.50
7-10	.55	1.65	3.30
11-15	.35	1.00	2.00

FLAMING LOVE
Dec, 1949 - No. 6, Oct, 1950 (Photo covers No. 2-6)
Quality Comics Group (Comic Magazines)

	Good	Fine	Mint
1-Ward-c, 9 pgs.	13.00	40.00	90.00
2	5.50	16.50	38.00
3-Ward-a, 9 pgs.; Crandall-a	10.00	30.00	70.00
4-6: 4-Gustavson-a	4.75	14.25	33.00

FLAMING WESTERN ROMANCES
Nov-Dec, 1949 - No. 3, Mar-Apr, 1950
Star Publications

	Good	Fine	Mint
1-L. B. Cole-c	11.00	33.00	75.00
2-L. B. Cole-c	7.00	21.00	50.00
3-Robert Taylor, Arlene Dahl photo-c with biographies inside; L. B. Cole-c; spanking panel	15.00	45.00	105.00

FLASH, THE (Formerly Flash Comics)(See Adventure, The Brave & the Bold, DC Comics Presents, DC Special Series, DC Super-Stars, Green Lantern, Showcase, Super Team Family, & World's Finest)
No. 105, Feb-Mar, 1959 - No. 350, Oct, 1985
National Periodical Publications/DC Comics

	Good	Fine	Mint
105-Origin Flash(retold), & Mirror Master	60.00	180.00	420.00
106-Origin Grodd & Pied Piper	27.00	68.00	190.00
107-109	10.00	25.00	70.00
110-Intro/origin Kid Flash & The Weather Wizard	13.00	33.00	90.00
111,115	5.00	13.00	35.00
112-Intro & Origin Elongated Man	5.75	15.00	40.00
113-Origin Trickster	4.65	12.00	32.00
114-Origin Captain Cold	4.65	12.00	32.00
116-120: 117-Origin Capt. Boomerang. 119-Elongated Man marries Sue Dearborn	4.00	9.00	28.00
121	2.65	7.00	20.00
122-Origin & 1st app. The Top	2.65	7.00	20.00
123-Re-intro. Golden Age Flash; origins of both Flashes; 1st mention of an Earth II where DC Golden Age heroes live	14.00	35.00	100.00
124-Last 10¢ issue	2.00	5.00	14.00
125-128,130: 128-Origin Abra Kadabra	1.05	3.20	6.40
129-G.A. Flash x-over; J.S.A. cameo (1st since 2-3/51)	3.00	9.00	18.00
131-136,138-140: 136-1st Dexter Miles. 139-Origin Prof. Zoom. 140-Origin & 1st app. Heat Wave	1.05	3.20	6.40
137-G.A. Flash x-over; J.S.A. cameo; 1st Silver Age app. Vandall Savage	1.35	4.00	8.00
141-150	.70	2.00	4.00
151-159: 151-G.A. Flash x-over	.50	1.50	3.00
160-80-Pg. Giant G-21-G.A.-r Flash & Johnny Quick	.70	2.00	4.00
161-168,170: 165-Silver Age Flash weds Iris West. 167-New facts about Flash's origin. 170-Dr. Mid-Nite, Dr. Fate, G.A. Flash x-over	.35	1.00	2.00
169-80-Pg. Giant G-34	.40	1.20	2.40
171-177,179,180: 171-JLA, Green Lantern, Atom flashbacks. 173-G.A. Flash x-over. 174-Barry Allen reveals I.D. to wife. 175-2nd Superman/Flash race; JLA cameo	.25	.70	1.40
178-80-Pg. Giant G-46	.35	1.00	2.00
181-186,188-190: 186-Re-intro. Sargon		.50	1.00
187-68-Pg. Giant G-58	.30	.80	1.60
191-195,197-200		.50	1.00
196-68-Pg. Giant G-70	.30	.80	1.60
201-204,206-210: 201-New G.A. Flash story. 208-52 pg. begin, end No. 213,215,216. 206-Elongated Man begins		.40	.80
205-68-Pg. Giant G-82	.30	.80	1.60
211-213,216: 211-G.A. Flash origin (No.104). 213-All-r.		.40	.80
214-Giant DC-11; origin Metal Men-r; 1st pubbed G.A. Flash story	.30	.80	1.60
215 (52 pgs.)-Flash-r/Showcase 4; G.A. Flash x-over, r-in No. 216		.40	.80

The Fish Police #1 (1st printing), © Fishwrap Prod.

Flaming Carrot #12, © B. Burden

The Flash #123, © DC

The Flash #306, © DC

Flash Comics #1, © DC

Flash Comics #92, © DC

THE FLASH (continued)

	Good	Fine	Mint
217-219: Adams-a in all. 217-Green Lantern/Green Arrow series begins. 219-Last Green Arrow	.85	2.50	5.00
220-222,224,225,227,228,230,231		.40	.80
223,226-Adams-a	.50	1.50	3.00
229,232,233-(100 pgs. each)	.30	.80	1.60
234-270: 243-Death of The Top. 246-Last Green Lantern. 256-Death of The Top retold. 267-Origin of Flash's uniform. 270-Intro The Clown		.35	.70
271-274,277-288,290: 286-Intro/origin Rainbow Raider		.35	.70
275,276-Iris West Allen dies	.30	.80	1.60
289-Perez 1st DC art; new Firestorm series begins, ends No. 304		.50	1.00
291-299,301-305: 291-Intro/origin Colonel Computron. 298-Intro/origin Shade. 301-Atomic Bomb-c. 303-The Top returns. 305-G.A. Flash x-over		.35	.70
300-52pgs.; origin Flash retold	.30	.80	1.60
306-Dr. Fate by Giffen begins, ends 313	.35	1.00	2.00
307-313-Giffen-a. 309-Origin Flash retold	.25	.70	1.40
314-330: 318-23-The Creeper app. 324-Death of Reverse Flash (Prof. Zoom). 328-Iris West Allen's death retold		.35	.70
331-349: 344-Origin Kid Flash		.35	.70
350-Double size ($1.25)	.35	1.00	2.00
Annual 1(10-12/63, 84pgs.)-Origin Elongated Man & Kid Flash-r; origin Grodd, G.A. Flash-r	2.85	7.00	20.00

NOTE: ***Adams*** *c-194, 195, 203, 204, 206-208, 211, 213, 215, 246.* ***Aparo*** *c-311.* ***Austin*** *a-233i, 234i.* ***Buckler*** *a-271p, 272p; c(p)-247-50, 252, 253p, 255, 256p, 258, 262, 265-67, 269-71.* ***Giffen*** *a-306p-313p; c-310p, 315.* ***Sid Greene*** *a-167-74i, 229i(r).* ***Grell*** *a-237p, 238p, 240-43p; c-236.* ***G. Kane*** *a-195p, 197-99p, 229r, 232r; c-197-99, 312p.* ***Kubert*** *a-108p, 215i(r); c-189-191.* ***Lopez*** *c-272.* ***Meskin*** *a-229r, 232r.* ***Perez*** *a-289-293p; c-293.* ***Starlin*** *a-294-296p.* ***Staton*** *c-263p, 264p. Green Lantern x-over-131, 143, 168, 171, 191.*

FLASH COMICS (Whiz Comics No. 2 on)
Jan, 1940 (12 pgs., B&W, regular size)
(Not distributed to newsstands; printed for in-house use)
Fawcett Publications

NOTE: **Whiz Comics** No. 2 was preceded by two books, **Flash Comics** and **Thrill Comics**, both dated Jan, 1940, (12 pgs, B&W, regular size) and were not distributed. These two books are identical except for the title. It is believed that the complete 68 page issue of Fawcett's **Flash** and **Thrill Comics** No. 1 was finished and ready for publication with the January date. Since D.C. Comics was also about to publish a book with the same date and title, Fawcett hurriedly printed up the black and white version of **Flash Comics** to secure copyright before D.C. The inside covers are blank, with the covers and inside pages printed on a high quality uncoated paper stock. The eight page origin story of *Captain Thunder* is composed of pages 1-7 and 13 of the *Captain Marvel* story essentially as they appeared in the first issue of **Whiz Comics**. The balloon dialogue on page thirteen was relettered to tie the story into the end of page seven in **Flash** and **Thrill Comics** to produce a shorter version of the origin story for copyright purposes. Obviously, D.C. acquired the copyright and Fawcett dropped **Flash** as well as **Thrill** and came out with **Whiz Comics** a month later. Fawcett never used the cover to **Flash** and **Thrill** No. 1, designing a new cover for **Whiz Comics**. Fawcett also must have discovered that *Captain Thunder* had already been used by another publisher. All references to *Captain Thunder* were relettered to *Captain Marvel* before appearing in **Whiz**.

1 (nn on-c, No. 1 on inside)-Origin & 1st app. Captain Thunder.
Eight copies of **Flash** and three copies of **Thrill** exist. All 3 copies of Thrill sold in 1986 for between $4,000-$10,000 each. All available copies of Flash sold in 1986 for between $3,000-$8,400.

FLASH COMICS (The Flash No. 105 on) (Also see All-Flash)
Jan, 1940 - No. 104, Feb, 1949
National Periodical Publications/All-American

	Good	Fine	Mint
1-Origin The Flash by Harry Lampert, Hawkman by Gardner Fox, The Whip, & Johnny Thunder by Stan Asch; Cliff Cornwall by Moldoff, Minute Movies begin; Moldoff (Shelly) cover; 1st app. Shiera Sanders who later becomes Hawkgirl, No. 24; reprinted in Famous First Edition	550.00	1650.00	3850.00
2-Rod Rian begins, ends No. 11	180.00	540.00	1260.00
3-The King begins, ends No. 41	130.00	390.00	910.00
4-Moldoff (Shelly) Hawkman begins	112.00	335.00	785.00
5	97.00	290.00	675.00
6,7	78.00	234.00	545.00
8-10: 8-Male bondage-c	63.00	190.00	440.00
11-20: 12-Les Watts begins; "Sparks" No. 16 on. 17-Last Cliff Cornwall	46.00	138.00	320.00
21-23	35.00	105.00	245.00
24-Shiera becomes Hawkgirl	45.00	135.00	315.00
25-30: 28-Last Les Sparks. 29-Ghost Patrol begins(origin, 1st app.), ends No. 104	32.00	96.00	225.00
31-40: 35-Origin Shade	26.00	78.00	180.00
41-50	23.00	70.00	160.00
51-61: 59-Last Minute Movies. 61-Last Moldoff Hawkman	18.00	54.00	125.00
62-Hawkman by Kubert begins	25.00	75.00	175.00
63-70: 66-68-Hop Harrigan in all	21.00	63.00	145.00
71-80: 80-Atom begins, ends No. 104	21.00	63.00	145.00
81-85	21.00	63.00	145.00
86-Intro. The Black Canary in Johnny Thunder; rare in Mint due to black ink smearing on white cover	58.00	175.00	405.00
87-90: 88-Origin Ghost	26.00	78.00	182.00
91,93-99: 98-Atom dons new costume	34.00	102.00	238.00
92-1st solo Black Canary	56.00	168.00	390.00
100,103(Scarce)	64.00	192.00	450.00
101,102(Scarce)	53.00	160.00	370.00
104-Origin The Flash retold (Scarce)	130.00	390.00	910.00
Wheaties Giveaway (1946, 32 pgs., 6½x8¼")-Johnny Thunder, Ghost Patrol, The Flash & Kubert Hawkman app. NOTE: *All known copies were taped to Wheaties boxes and are never found in mint condition. Copies with light tape residue bring the listed prices in all grades*	24.00	70.00	150.00

NOTE: ***Infantino*** *a-86p, 90, 93-95, 99-104.* ***Kinstler*** *a-87, 89(Hawkman).* ***Chet Kozlak*** *c-77, 79, 81.* ***Krigstein*** *a-94.* ***Kubert*** *a-62-76, 83, 85, 86, 88-104; c-63, 65, 67, 70, 71, 73, 75, 83, 85, 86, 88, 89, 91, 94, 96, 98, 100, 104.* ***Moldoff*** *c/a-3.*

FLASH DIGEST, THE (See DC Spec. Series 24)

FLASH GORDON (See Eat Right to Work. . . , Feature Book No. 25 (McKay), King Classics, King Comics, March of Comics No. 118, 133, 142, and Street Comix)

FLASH GORDON
No. 10, 1943 - No. 512, Nov, 1953
Dell Publishing Co.

	Good	Fine	Mint
4-Color 10(1943)-by Alex Raymond; reprints/"The Ice Kingdom"	47.00	141.00	330.00
4-Color 84(1945)-by Alex Raymond; reprints/"The Fiery Desert"	29.00	87.00	200.00
4-Color 173,190: 190-Bondage-c	9.00	27.00	63.00
4-Color 204,247	7.00	21.00	50.00
4-Color 424	5.00	15.00	35.00
2(5-7/53-Dell)-Evans-a	3.50	10.50	24.00
4-Color 512	3.00	9.00	21.00
Macy's Giveaway(1943)-(Rare)-20 pgs.; not by Raymond	60.00	160.00	320.00

FLASH GORDON
Oct, 1950 - No. 4, April, 1951
Harvey Publications

	Good	Fine	Mint
1-Alex Raymond-a; bondage-c	17.00	51.00	120.00
2-Alex Raymond-a	13.00	40.00	90.00
3,4-Alex Raymond	12.00	36.00	80.00
5-(Rare)-Small size-5½x8½"; B&W; 32 pgs.; Distributed to some mail subscribers only Estimated value. . . .			$200.00—$300.00

(Also see All-New No. 15, Boy Explorers No. 2, and Stuntman No. 3)

FLASH GORDON
1951 (Paper cover; 16 pgs. in color; regular size)
Harvey Comics (Gordon Bread giveaway)

	Good	Fine	Mint
1 (1938), 2(1941?)-Reprints by Raymond each. . . .	10.00	30.00	60.00

NOTE: *Most copies have brittle edges.*

FLASH GORDON
June, 1965
Gold Key

	Good	Fine	Mint
1 (1947 reprint)	1.75	5.25	12.00

FLASH GORDON (Also see Comics Reading Libraries)
9/66 - No. 18, 1/70; No. 19, 10-11/78 - No. 37, 3/82
(Painted covers No. 19-30,34)
King, No.1-11(12/67)/Charlton, No.12(2/69)-18/Gold Key, No.19-27/Whitman No. 28 on

	Good	Fine	Mint
1-Army giveaway(1968)(''Complimentary'' on cover)(Same as regular No. 1 minus Mandrake story & back cover)	1.20	3.50	7.00
1-Williamson c/a(2); E.C. swipe/Incred. S.F. 32. Mandrake sty	1.50	4.50	9.00
2-Bolle, Gil Kane-c/a; Mandrake sty	1.15	3.50	7.00
3-Williamson-c	1.30	4.00	8.00
4-Secret Agent X-9 begins, Williamson-c/a(3)	1.30	4.00	8.00
5-Williamson c/a(2)	1.30	4.00	8.00
6,8-Crandall-a. 8-Secret Agent X-9-r	1.30	4.00	8.00
7-Raboy-a	1.00	3.00	6.00
9,10-Raymond-r	1.30	4.00	8.00
11-Crandall-a	.85	2.50	5.00
12-Crandall c/a	1.00	3.00	6.00
13-Jeff Jones-a	1.00	3.00	6.00
14-17: 17-Brick Bradford sty	.50	1.50	3.00
18-Kaluta-a	.70	2.00	4.00
19(9/78, G.K.), 20-30(10/80)	.35	1.00	2.00
30 (7/81; re-issue)		.30	.60
31-33: Movie adapt; Williamson-a		.50	1.00
34-37: Movie adapt		.40	.80

NOTE: *Aparo a-8. **Bolle** a-21, 22. **Buckler** a-9, 10. **Crandall** c-6. **Estrada** a-3. **Gene Fawcette** a-29, 30, 34, 37. **McWilliams** a-36.*

FLASH GORDON GIANT COMIC ALBUM
1972 (11x14''; cardboard covers; 48 pgs.; B&W; 59 cents)
Modern Promotions, N. Y.

	Good	Fine	Mint
Reprints 1968, 1969 dailies by Dan Barry	.25	.70	1.40

FLASH SPECTACULAR, THE (See DC Special Series No. 11)

FLAT TOP
11/53 - No. 3, 5/54; No. 4, 3/55 - No. 6, 7/55
Mazie Comics/Harvey Publ.(Magazine Publ.) No. 4 on

	Good	Fine	Mint
1	1.15	3.50	8.00
2,3	.70	2.00	4.00
4-6	.50	1.50	3.00

FLESH AND BONES
June, 1986 - No. 4, Dec, 1986 (mini-series)
Upshot Graphics (Fantagraphics Books)

	Good	Fine	Mint
1-4: Dalgoda by Fujitake-r	.35	1.00	2.00

FLINTSTONES, THE (TV)(See Dell Giant No.48 for No. 1)
No. 2, Nov-Dec, 1961 - No. 60, Sept, 1970 (Hanna-Barbera)
Dell Publ. Co./Gold Key No. 7 (10/62) on

	Good	Fine	Mint
2	2.15	6.50	15.00
3-6(7-8/62)	1.30	4.00	9.00
7 (10/62; 1st GK)	1.30	4.00	9.00
8-10: Mr. & Mrs. J. Evil Scientist begin?	1.15	3.50	8.00
11-1st app. Pebbles (6/63)	1.50	4.50	10.00
12-15,17-20	1.00	3.00	7.00
16-1st app. Bamm-Bamm (1/64)	1.30	4.00	9.00
21-30: 26,27-The Grusomes app.	.85	2.50	5.00
31-33,35-40: 31-Xmas-c. 33-Meet Frankenstein & Dracula. 39-Reprints	.70	2.00	4.00
34-1st app. The Great Gazoo	.85	2.50	5.00
41-60	.60	1.75	3.50
At N. Y. World's Fair('64)-J.W. Books(25 cents)-1st printing; no date on-c	1.75	5.25	12.00
At N. Y. World's Fair (1965 on-c; re-issue). NOTE: Warehouse find in 1984	.35	1.00	2.00
Bigger & Boulder 1(30013-211)G.K. Giant(25 cents); 84 pgs.	2.00	6.00	16.00
Bigger & Boulder 2-(25 cents)(1966)-reprints B&B No. 1	1.75	5.25	14.00
. . . With Pebbles & Bamm Bamm(100 pgs., G.K.)-30028-511 (paper-c, 25 cents)(11/65)	2.00	6.00	14.00

(See Comic Album No. 16, Bamm-Bamm & Pebbles Flintstone, Dell Giant 48, March of Comics No. 229, 243, 271, 289, 299, 317, 327, 341, Pebbles Flintstone, and Whitman Comic Books.)

FLINTSTONES, THE (TV)(. . . & Pebbles)
Nov, 1970 - No. 50, Feb, 1977 (Hanna-Barbera)
Charlton Comics

	Good	Fine	Mint
1	1.15	3.50	8.00
2	.70	2.00	4.00
3-7,9,10	.50	1.50	3.00
8-''Flintstones Summer Vacation,'' 52 pgs. (Summer, 1971)	.70	2.00	4.00
11-20	.35	1.00	2.00
21-50: 42-Byrne-a, 2pgs.	.25	.75	1.50

(Also see Barney & Betty Rubble, Dino, The Great Gazoo, and Pebbles & Bamm-Bamm)

FLINTSTONES, THE (TV)(See Yogi Bear, 3rd series)
October, 1977 - No. 9, Feb, 1979 (Hanna-Barbera)
Marvel Comics Group

	Good	Fine	Mint
1-9: 1-Yogi Bear begins		.25	.50

FLINTSTONES CHRISTMAS PARTY, THE (See The Funtastic World of Hanna-Barbera No. 1)

FLIP
April, 1954 - No. 2, June, 1954 (Satire)
Harvey Publications

	Good	Fine	Mint
1,2-Nostrand-a each. 2-Powell-a	5.00	15.00	35.00

FLIPPER (TV)
April, 1966 - No. 3, Nov, 1967
Gold Key

	Good	Fine	Mint
1-Photo-c	1.75	5.25	12.00
2,3	1.00	3.00	7.00

FLIPPITY & FLOP
12-1/51-52 - No. 46, 8-10/59; No. 47, 9-11/60
National Periodical Publ. (Signal Publ. Co.)

	Good	Fine	Mint
1	8.00	24.00	56.00
2	4.00	12.00	28.00
3-5	3.50	10.50	24.00
6-10	3.00	9.00	21.00
11-20	2.15	6.50	15.00
21-47	1.50	4.50	10.00

FLY, THE
May, 1983 - No. 9, Oct, 1984 (See The Advs. of. . .)
Archie Enterprises, Inc.

	Good	Fine	Mint
1-Mr. Justice app; origin Shield.		.50	1.00
2-9: 2-Flygirl app.		.40	.80

NOTE: ***Ditko** a-2-8; c-5p, 7p. **Buckler** a-1, 2. **Nebres** c-4, 5i, 6, 7i. **Steranko** c-1-3.*

FLY BOY (Also see Approved Comics)
Spring, 1952 - No. 4, 1953
Ziff-Davis Publ. Co. (Approved)

	Good	Fine	Mint
1-Saunders painted-c	4.00	12.00	28.00
2-Saunders painted-c	2.65	8.00	18.00
3,4-Saunders painted-c	2.35	7.00	16.00

Flash Gordon #2, © KING

Flintstones #11 (GK), © Hanna-Barbera

The Fly #3, © AP

Flying A's Range Rider #10, © Tie-Ups

Follow the Fun #2, © 20th Century Fox

Forbidden Worlds #3, © ACG

FLYING ACES
July, 1955 - No. 5, March, 1956
Key Publications

	Good	Fine	Mint
1	1.50	4.50	10.00
2-5: 2-Trapani-a	.85	2.50	6.00

FLYING A'S RANGE RIDER, THE (TV) (See 4-Color No. 404 for No. 1) (See Western Roundup)
No. 2, June-Aug, 1953 - No. 24, Aug, 1959 (All photo-c)
Dell Publishing Co.

2	3.00	9.00	21.00
3-10	2.65	8.00	18.00
11-16,18-24	2.35	7.00	16.00
17-Toth-a	3.00	9.00	21.00

FLYING CADET (WW II Plane Photos)
Jan, 1943 - 1947 (½ photos, ½ comics)
Flying Cadet Publishing Co.

V1No.1	4.00	12.00	28.00
2	2.00	6.00	14.00
3-9 (Two No. 6's, Sept. & Oct.)	1.65	5.00	11.50
V2No.1-7(No.10-16)	1.30	4.00	9.00
8(No.17)-Bare-breasted woman-c	3.00	9.00	21.00

FLYIN' JENNY
1946 - 1947 (1945 strip reprints)
Pentagon Publ. Co.

nn	4.35	13.00	30.00
2-Baker-c	5.50	16.50	38.00

FLYING MODELS
May, 1954 (16 pgs.) (5 cents)
H-K Publ. (Health-Knowledge Publs.)

V61No.3 (Rare)	3.00	9.00	21.00

FLYING NUN (TV)
Feb, 1968 - No. 4, Nov, 1968
Dell Publishing Co.

1	1.35	4.00	8.00
2-4	.85	2.50	5.00

FLYING NURSES (See Sue & Sally Smith . . .)

FLYING SAUCERS
1950 - 1953
Avon Periodicals/Realistic

1(1950)-Wood-a, 21 pgs.	33.00	100.00	230.00
nn(1952)-Cover altered plus 2 pgs. of Wood-a not in original	30.00	90.00	210.00
nn(1953)-Reprints above	17.00	50.00	120.00

FLYING SAUCERS (Comics)
April, 1967 - No. 4, Nov, 1967; No. 5, Oct, 1969
Dell Publishing Co.

1	.85	2.50	5.00
2-5	.50	1.50	3.00

FLY MAN (Formerly Adv. of The Fly; Mighty Comics . . . No. 40 on)
No. 32, July, 1965 - No. 39, Sept, 1966
Mighty Comics Group (Radio Comics) (Archie)

32,33-Comet, Shield, Black Hood, The Fly & Flygirl x-over; re-intro. Wizard, Hangman No. 33	.70	2.00	4.00
34-Shield begins	.70	2.00	4.00
35-Origin Black Hood	.70	2.00	4.00
36-Hangman x-over in Shield; re-intro. & origin of Web	.70	2.00	4.00
37-Hangman, Wizard x-over in Flyman; last Shield issue	.70	2.00	4.00
38-Web story	.70	2.00	4.00
39-Steel Sterling story	.70	2.00	4.00

FOLLOW THE SUN (TV)
May-July, 1962 - No. 2, Sept-Nov, 1962 (Photo-c)
Dell Publishing Co.

01-280-207(No.1), 12-280-211(No.2)	1.75	5.25	12.00

FOODINI (TV)(The Great . . . ; also see Pinhead & . . . , & Jingle Dingle)
March, 1950 - No. 5, 1950
Continental Publications (Holyoke)

1	4.00	12.00	28.00
2	2.00	6.00	14.00
3-5	1.50	4.50	10.00

FOOEY (Magazine) (Satire)
Feb, 1961 - No. 4, May, 1961
Scoff Publishing Co.

1	1.20	3.50	7.00
2-4	.70	2.00	4.00

FOOTBALL THRILLS
Fall-Winter, 1951-52 - No. 2, 1952
Ziff-Davis Publ. Co.

1-Powell a(2); Saunders painted-c	6.00	18.00	42.00
2-Saunders painted-c	4.00	12.00	28.00

FOR A NIGHT OF LOVE
1951
Avon Periodicals

nn-Two stories adapted from the works of Emile Zola; Astarita, Ravielli-a; Kinstler-c	15.00	45.00	105.00

FORBIDDEN LOVE
Mar, 1950 - No. 4, Sept, 1950
Quality Comics Group

1-(Scarce)Classic photo-c; Crandall-a	50.00	150.00	350.00
2,3(Scarce)-Photo-c	22.00	65.00	150.00
4-(Scarce)Ward/Cuidera-a; photo-c	24.00	72.00	170.00

FORBIDDEN LOVE (See Dark Mansion of . . .)

FORBIDDEN TALES OF DARK MANSION (Dark Mansion of Forbidden Love No. 1-4)
No. 5, May-June, 1972 - No. 15, Feb-Mar, 1974
National Periodical Publications

5-15: 13-Kane/Howard-a		.25	.50

NOTE: **Alcala** a-9-11, 13. **Chaykin** a-7-15. **Evans** a-14. **Kaluta** c-7-11, 13. **G. Kane** a-13. **Kirby** a-6. **Nino** a-8, 12, 15. **Redondo** a-14.

FORBIDDEN WORLDS
7-8/51 - No. 34, 10-11/54; No. 35, 8/55 - No. 145, 8/67
(No.1-5: 52 pgs.; No.6-8: 44 pgs.)
American Comics Group

1-Williamson/Frazetta-a, 10pgs.	40.00	120.00	280.00
2	16.00	48.00	110.00
3-Williamson/Wood/Orlando-a, 7pgs.	19.00	57.00	132.00
4	8.00	24.00	56.00
5-Williamson/Krenkel-a, 8pgs.	16.00	48.00	110.00
6-Harrison/Williamson-a, 8pgs.	13.50	40.50	95.00
7,8,10	4.65	14.00	32.00
9-A-Bomb explosion story	5.00	15.00	35.00
11-20	3.50	10.50	24.00
21-33: 24-E.C. swipe by Landau	2.35	7.00	16.00
34(10-11/54)(Becomes Young Heroes No. 35 on)-Last pre-code ish; A-Bomb explosion story	2.65	8.00	18.00
35(8/55)-62	1.15	3.50	8.00

FORBIDDEN WORLDS (continued) — Good — Fine — Mint

63,69,76,78-Williamson-a in all; w/Krenkel No. 69 — 3.00 — 9.00 — 21.00
64,66-68,70-72,74,75,77,79-90 — .85 — 2.50 — 6.00
65-''There's a New Moon Tonight'' listed in No. 114 as holding 1st record fan mail response — 1.00 — 3.00 — 7.00
73-Intro., 1st app. Herbie by Whitney — 12.50 — 37.50 — 75.00
91-93,95,97-100 — .70 — 2.00 — 4.00
94-Herbie app. — 4.00 — 12.00 — 24.00
96-Williamson-a — 2.35 — 7.00 — 14.00
101-109,111-113,115,117-120 — .50 — 1.50 — 3.00
110,114,116-Herbie app. 114 contains list of editor's top 20 ACG stories — 2.00 — 6.00 — 12.00
121-124: 124-Magic Agent app. — .40 — 1.20 — 2.40
125-Magic Agent app.; intro. & origin Magicman series, ends No. 141 — .50 — 1.50 — 3.00
126-130 — .40 — 1.10 — 2.20
131,132,134-141: 136-Nemesis x-over in Magicman. 140-Mark Midnight app. by Ditko — .30 — .90 — 1.80
133-Origin & 1st app. Dragonia in Magicman (1-2/66); returns No. 138 — .30 — .90 — 1.80
142-145 — .25 — .70 — 1.40

NOTE: ***Buscema** a-75, 79, 81, 82, 140r. **Disbrow** a-10. **Ditko** a-137p, 138, 140. **Landau** a-24, 28, 31-34, 48, 86r, 96, 143-45. **Lazarus** a-23. **Moldoff** a-31, 139r. **Whitney** a-115, 116, 137; c-129.*

FORCE, THE (See The Crusaders)

FORCE AND THE HERO NETWORK
Nov, 1986 - Present ($1.25, B&W)
Charlton Comics

1 — .60 — 1.25

FORD ROTUNDA CHRISTMAS BOOK (See Christmas at the Rotunda)

FOREIGN INTRIGUES (Formerly Johnny Dynamite; Battlefield Action No. 16 on)
No. 13, 1956 - No. 15, Aug, 1956
Charlton Comics

13-15-Johnny Dynamite continues — 1.65 — 5.50 — 11.50

FOREMOST BOYS (See Four Most)

FOREST FIRE (Also see Smokey The Bear)
1949 (dated-1950) (16 pgs., paper-c)
American Forestry Assn.(Commerical Comics)

nn-Intro/1st app. Smokey The Forest Fire Preventing Bear; created by Rudy Wendelein; Wendelein/Sparling-a; 'Carter Oil Co.' on back-c of original — 10.00 — 30.00 — 60.00

FOREVER, DARLING (See 4-Color No. 681)

FOREVER PEOPLE
Feb-Mar, 1971 - No. 11, Oct-Nov, 1972
National Periodical Publications

1-Superman x-over; Kirby-c/a begins — .50 — 1.50 — 3.00
2-11: 4-G.A.-r begin, end No. 9 — .60 — 1.20

NOTE: ***Kirby** c/a(p)-1-11; No. 4-9 contain Sandman reprints from Adventure No. 85, 84, 75, 80, 77, 74 in that order. No. 1-3, 10-11 are 36pgs; No. 4-9 are 52pgs.*

FOR GIRLS ONLY
Nov, 1953 (Digest size, 100 pgs.)
Bernard Bailey Enterprises

1-½ comic book, ½ magazine — 5.00 — 15.00 — 35.00

FORGOTTEN STORY BEHIND NORTH BEACH, THE
No date (8 pgs.; paper cover)
Catechetical Guild

— 3.00 — 9.00 — 18.00

FOR LOVERS ONLY (Formerly Hollywood Romances)
No. 60, Aug, 1971 - No. 87, Nov, 1976
Charlton Comics — Good — Fine — Mint

60-87 — .25 — .50

40 BIG PAGES OF MICKEY MOUSE
1936 (44 pgs.; 10¼x12½''; cardboard cover)
Whitman Publishing Co.

945-Reprints Mickey Mouse Magazine No. 1, but with a different cover. Ads were eliminated and some illustrated stories had expanded text. The book is ¾'' shorter than Mickey Mouse Mag. No. 1, but the reprints are the same size. (Rare) — 36.00 — 108.00 — 252.00

48 FAMOUS AMERICANS
1947 (Giveaway) (Half-size in color)
J. C. Penney Co. (Cpr. Edwin H. Stroh)

Simon & Kirby-a — 6.75 — 20.00 — 40.00

FOR YOUR EYES ONLY
October, 1981 - No. 2, Nov., 1981
Marvel Comics Group

1,2-James Bond movie adaptation — .30 — .60

NOTE: ***Chaykin** c/a(p)-1, 2.*

FOUR COLOR
1939 - No. 1354, Apr-June, 1962
Dell Publishing Co.

NOTE: *Four Color only appears on issues No. 19-25, 1-99,101. Dell Publishing Co. filed these as Series I, No. 1-25, and Series II, No. 1-1354. Issues beginning with No. 710? were printed with and without ads on back cover. Issues without ads are worth more.*

SERIES I:

1(nn)-Dick Tracy — 95.00 — 285.00 — 665.00
2(nn)-Don Winslow of the Navy (No.1) (Rare) — 55.00 — 165.00 — 385.00
3(nn)-Myra North — 17.00 — 51.00 — 120.00
4-Donald Duck by Al Taliaferro('40)(Disney) — 243.00 — 730.00 — 1700.00
(Prices vary widely on this book)
5-Smilin' Jack (No.1) — 32.00 — 100.00 — 230.00
6-Dick Tracy (Scarce) — 58.00 — 174.00 — 405.00
7-Gang Busters — 15.00 — 45.00 — 105.00
8-Dick Tracy — 36.00 — 108.00 — 252.00
9-Terry and the Pirates-r/Super 9-29 — 35.00 — 105.00 — 245.00
10-Smilin' Jack — 29.00 — 85.00 — 200.00
11-Smitty (No.1) — 17.00 — 51.00 — 120.00
12-Little Orphan Annie — 25.00 — 75.00 — 175.00
13-Walt Disney's Reluctant Dragon('41)-Contains 2 pages of photos from film; 2 pg. foreword to Fantasia by Leopold Stokowski; Donald Duck, Goofy, Baby Weems & Mickey Mouse (as the Sorcerer's Apprentice) app. (Disney) — 58.00 — 174.00 — 405.00
14-Moon Mullins (No.1) — 15.00 — 45.00 — 105.00
15-Tillie the Toiler (No.1) — 15.00 — 45.00 — 105.00
16-Mickey Mouse (No.1) (Disney) by Gottfredson — 235.00 — 700.00 — 1600.00
(Prices vary widely on this book)
17-Walt Disney's Dumbo, the Flying Elephant (No.1)(1941)-Mickey Mouse, Donald Duck, & Pluto app. (Disney) — 63.00 — 190.00 — 440.00
18-Jiggs and Maggie (No.1)(1936-'38-r) — 15.00 — 45.00 — 105.00
19-Barney Google and Snuffy Smith (No.1)-(1st issue with Four Color on the cover) — 17.00 — 51.00 — 120.00
20-Tiny Tim — 15.00 — 45.00 — 105.00
21-Dick Tracy — 34.00 — 100.00 — 238.00
22-Don Winslow — 12.00 — 36.00 — 84.00
23-Gang Busters — 11.00 — 33.00 — 76.00
24-Captain Easy — 15.00 — 45.00 — 105.00

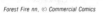

Forest Fire nn, © Commercial Comics

Four Color #8 (1st Series), © N.Y. News Synd.

Four Color #13 (1st Series), © WDC

Four Color #9 (2nd Series), © WDC

Four Color #49, © WDC

Four Color #95, © Roy Rogers

FOUR COLOR (continued)

	Good	Fine	Mint
25-Popeye	33.00	100.00	230.00
SERIES II:			
1-Little Joe	19.00	57.00	132.00
2-Harold Teen	12.00	36.00	84.00
3-Alley Oop (No.1)	26.00	78.00	180.00
4-Smilin' Jack	24.00	72.00	165.00
5-Raggedy Ann and Andy (No.1)	25.00	75.00	175.00
6-Smitty	10.00	30.00	70.00
7-Smokey Stover (No.1)	16.50	50.00	115.00
8-Tillie the Toiler	9.50	28.50	65.00
9-Donald Duck Finds Pirate Gold, by Carl Barks & Jack Hannah (Disney) (c. 8/17/42)	285.00	855.00	2000.00
(Prices vary widely on this book)			
10-Flash Gordon by Alex Raymond-Reprints from "The Ice Kingdom"	47.00	141.00	330.00
11-Wash Tubbs	15.00	45.00	105.00
12-Walt Disney's Bambi (No.1)	27.00	81.00	190.00
13-Mr. District Attorney (No.1)	11.00	33.00	76.00
14-Smilin' Jack	19.00	57.00	132.00
15-Felix the Cat (No.1)	33.00	100.00	230.00
16-Porky Pig (No.1)(1942)-"Secret of the Haunted House"	30.00	90.00	210.00
17-Popeye	26.00	78.00	180.00
18-Little Orphan Annie's Junior Commandos; Flag-c	19.00	57.00	132.00
19-Walt Disney's Thumper Meets the Seven Dwarfs (Disney); r-in Silly Symphonies	27.00	81.00	190.00
20-Barney Baxter	11.50	34.50	80.00
21-Oswald the Rabbit (No.1)(1943)	16.50	49.50	115.00
22-Tillie the Toiler	7.00	21.00	50.00
23-Raggedy Ann and Andy	18.00	54.00	125.00
24-Gang Busters	11.00	33.00	76.00
25-Andy Panda (No.1) (Walter Lantz)	19.00	57.00	132.00
26-Popeye	24.00	72.00	170.00
27-Walt Disney's Mickey Mouse and the Seven Colored Terror	42.00	125.00	295.00
28-Wash Tubbs	11.00	33.00	76.00
29-Donald Duck and the Mummy's Ring, by Carl Barks (Disney) (9/43)	214.00	642.00	1500.00
(Prices vary widely on this book)			
30-Bambi's Children(1943)-Disney	25.00	75.00	175.00
31-Moon Mullins	9.50	28.50	65.00
32-Smitty	8.00	24.00	56.00
33-Bugs Bunny "Public Nuisance No. 1"	20.00	60.00	140.00
34-Dick Tracy	25.00	75.00	175.00
35-Smokey Stover	9.50	28.50	65.00
36-Smilin' Jack	11.00	33.00	76.00
37-Bringing Up Father	9.50	28.50	65.00
38-Roy Rogers (No.1, c. 4/44)-1st western comic with photo-c	38.00	114.00	265.00
39-Oswald the Rabbit('44)	11.50	34.50	80.00
40-Barney Google and Snuffy Smith	9.50	28.50	66.00
41-Mother Goose and Nursery Rhyme Comics (No.1)-All by Kelly	16.00	48.00	110.00
42-Tiny Tim (1934-r)	8.50	25.50	60.00
43-Popeye (1938-'42-r)	15.00	45.00	105.00
44-Terry and the Pirates	20.00	60.00	140.00
45-Raggedy Ann	13.50	40.50	95.00
46-Felix the Cat and the Haunted Castle	22.00	65.00	154.00
47-Gene Autry (© 6/16/44)	24.50	73.50	170.00
48-Porky Pig of the Mounties by Carl Barks (7/44)	60.00	180.00	420.00
49-Snow White and the Seven Dwarfs (Disney)	22.00	65.00	154.00
50-Fairy Tale Parade-Walt Kelly art (1944)	21.00	63.00	145.00
51-Bugs Bunny Finds the Lost Treasure	14.50	43.50	100.00

	Good	Fine	Mint
52-Little Orphan Annie	13.00	40.00	90.00
53-Wash Tubbs	7.00	21.00	50.00
54-Andy Panda	11.00	33.00	76.00
55-Tillie the Toiler	5.75	17.25	40.00
56-Dick Tracy	17.00	51.00	120.00
57-Gene Autry	21.00	62.00	145.00
58-Smilin' Jack	11.00	33.00	76.00
59-Mother Goose and Nursery Rhyme Comics-Kelly c/a	13.50	40.50	95.00
60-Tiny Folks Funnies	8.00	24.00	56.00
61-Santa Claus Funnies(11/44)-Kelly art	18.00	54.00	125.00
62-Donald Duck in Frozen Gold, by Carl Barks (Disney) (1/45)	118.00	354.00	825.00
63-Roy Rogers-Photo-c	24.00	72.00	166.00
64-Smokey Stover	6.50	19.50	45.00
65-Smitty	6.50	19.50	45.00
66-Gene Autry	21.00	62.00	145.00
67-Oswald the Rabbit	8.00	24.00	56.00
68-Mother Goose and Nursery Rhyme Comics, by Walt Kelly	13.50	40.50	95.00
69-Fairy Tale Parade, by Walt Kelly	18.00	54.00	125.00
70-Popeye and Wimpy	13.00	40.00	90.00
71-Walt Disney's Three Caballeros, by Walt Kelly(c. 4/45)-(Disney)	53.00	160.00	370.00
72-Raggedy Ann	11.50	34.50	80.00
73-The Gumps (No.1)	5.00	15.00	35.00
74-Marge's Little Lulu (No.1)	80.00	240.00	560.00
75-Gene Autry and the Wildcat	19.00	57.00	132.00
76-Little Orphan Annie	11.00	33.00	76.00
77-Felix the Cat	18.00	54.00	125.00
78-Porky Pig and the Bandit Twins	10.00	30.00	70.00
79-Walt Disney's Mickey Mouse in The Riddle of the Red Hat by Carl Barks(8/45)	56.00	168.00	390.00
80-Smilin' Jack	9.50	28.50	65.00
81-Moon Mullins	5.00	15.00	35.00
82-Lone Ranger	22.00	65.00	154.00
83-Gene Autry in Outlaw Trail	19.00	57.00	132.00
84-Flash Gordon by Alex Raymond-Reprints from "The Fiery Desert"	29.00	87.00	200.00
85-Andy Panda and the Mad Dog Mystery	6.50	19.50	45.00
86-Roy Rogers-Photo-c	19.00	57.00	132.00
87-Fairy Tale Parade by Walt Kelly; Dan Noonan cover	16.00	48.00	110.00
88-Bugs Bunny's Great Adventure	8.00	24.00	56.00
89-Tillie the Toiler	5.00	15.00	35.00
90-Christmas with Mother Goose by Walt Kelly (11/45)	13.50	40.50	95.00
91-Santa Claus Funnies by Walt Kelly (11/45)	13.50	40.50	95.00
92-Walt Disney's The Wonderful Adventures Of Pinocchio(1945); Donald Duck by Kelly, 16 pgs. (Disney)	22.00	65.00	154.00
93-Gene Autry in The Bandit of Black Rock	15.00	45.00	105.00
94-Winnie Winkle (1945)	6.50	19.50	45.00
95-Roy Rogers Comics-Photo-c	19.00	57.00	132.00
96-Dick Tracy	14.00	42.00	98.00
97-Marge's Little Lulu (1946)	43.00	130.00	300.00
98-Lone Ranger, The	19.00	57.00	132.00
99-Smitty	5.50	16.50	38.00
100-Gene Autry Comics-Photo-c	15.00	45.00	105.00
101-Terry and the Pirates	13.00	40.00	90.00

NOTE: *No. 101 is last issue to carry "Four Color" logo on cover; all issues beginning with No. 100 are marked ". . . O. S." (One Shot) which can be found in the bottom left-hand panel on the first page; the numbers following "O. S." relate to the year/month issued.*

	Good	Fine	Mint
102-Oswald the Rabbit-Walt Kelly art, 1 pg.	8.00	24.00	56.00
103-Easter with Mother Goose by Walt Kelly	13.00	40.00	90.00
104-Fairy Tale Parade by Walt Kelly	12.00	36.00	84.00

FOUR COLOR (continued)

	Good	Fine	Mint
105-Albert the Alligator and Pogo Possum (No.1) by Kelly (4/46)	52.00	156.00	365.00
106-Tillie the Toiler	4.35	13.00	30.00
107-Little Orphan Annie	9.50	28.50	66.00
108-Donald Duck in The Terror of the River, by Carl Barks (Disney) (c. 4/16/46)	85.00	255.00	595.00
109-Roy Rogers Comics	15.00	45.00	105.00
110-Marge's Little Lulu	30.00	90.00	210.00
111-Captain Easy	6.00	18.00	42.00
112-Porky Pig's Adventure in Gopher Gulch	6.00	18.00	42.00
113-Popeye	7.00	21.00	50.00
114-Fairy Tale Parade by Walt Kelly	12.00	36.00	84.00
115-Marge's Little Lulu	30.00	90.00	210.00
116-Mickey Mouse and the House of Many Mysteries (Disney)	13.00	40.00	90.00
117-Roy Rogers Comics-Photo-c	11.00	33.00	76.00
118-Lone Ranger, The	19.00	57.00	132.00
119-Felix the Cat	12.00	36.00	84.00
120-Marge's Little Lulu	27.00	81.00	190.00
121-Fairy Tale Parade-(not Kelly)	8.00	24.00	56.00
122-Henry (No.1)(10/46)	4.35	13.00	30.00
123-Bugs Bunny's Dangerous Venture	4.35	13.00	30.00
124-Roy Rogers Comics-Photo-c	11.00	33.00	76.00
125-Lone Ranger, The	13.00	40.00	90.00
126-Christmas with Mother Goose by Walt Kelly (1946)	11.50	34.50	80.00
127-Popeye	7.00	21.00	50.00
128-Santa Claus Funnies-''Santa & the Angel'' by Gollub; ''A Mouse in the House'' by Kelly	11.50	34.50	80.00
129-Walt Disney's Uncle Remus and His Tales of Brer Rabbit (No.1) (1946)	11.00	33.00	76.00
130-Andy Panda (Walter Lantz)	3.50	10.50	24.00
131-Marge's Little Lulu	27.00	81.00	190.00
132-Tillie the Toiler('47)	4.35	13.00	30.00
133-Dick Tracy	11.00	33.00	76.00
134-Tarzan and the Devil Ogre	30.00	90.00	210.00
135-Felix the Cat	10.00	30.00	70.00
136-Lone Ranger, The	13.00	40.00	90.00
137-Roy Rogers Comics-Photo-c	11.00	33.00	76.00
138-Smitty	4.65	14.00	32.00
139-Marge's Little Lulu (1947)	25.00	75.00	175.00
140-Easter with Mother Goose by Walt Kelly	11.50	34.50	80.00
141-Mickey Mouse and the Submarine Pirates (Disney)	12.00	36.00	84.00
142-Bugs Bunny and the Haunted Mountain	4.35	13.00	30.00
143-Oswald the Rabbit and the Prehistoric Egg	3.35	10.00	23.00
144-Roy Rogers Comics ('47)-Photo-c	11.00	33.00	76.00
145-Popeye	7.00	21.00	50.00
146-Marge's Little Lulu	25.00	75.00	175.00
147-Donald Duck in Volcano Valley, by Carl Barks (Disney)(5/47)	60.00	180.00	420.00
148-Albert the Alligator and Pogo Possum by Walt Kelly (5/47)	40.00	120.00	280.00
149-Smilin' Jack	6.50	19.50	45.00
150-Tillie the Toiler (6/47)	3.00	9.00	21.00
151-Lone Ranger, The	11.00	33.00	76.00
152-Little Orphan Annie	7.00	21.00	50.00
153-Roy Rogers Comics-Photo-c	8.00	24.00	56.00
154-Walter Lantz Andy Panda	3.50	10.50	24.00
155-Henry (7/47)	3.50	10.50	24.00
156-Porky Pig and the Phantom	4.00	12.00	28.00
157-Mickey Mouse and the Beanstalk (Disney)	12.00	36.00	84.00
158-Marge's Little Lulu	25.00	75.00	175.00
159-Donald Duck in the Ghost of the Grotto, by Carl Barks (Disney) (8/47)	52.00	156.00	364.00
160-Roy Rogers Comics-Photo-c	8.00	24.00	56.00
161-Tarzan and the Fires Of Tohr	26.00	78.00	182.00
162-Felix the Cat (9/47)	8.00	24.00	56.00
163-Dick Tracy	9.00	27.00	62.00
164-Bugs Bunny Finds the Frozen Kingdom	4.35	13.00	30.00
165-Marge's Little Lulu	25.00	75.00	175.00
166-Roy Rogers Comics-52 pgs.,Photo-c	8.00	24.00	56.00
167-Lone Ranger, The	11.00	33.00	76.00
168-Popeye (10/47)	7.00	21.00	50.00
169-Woody Woodpecker (No.1)-''Manhunter in the North''; drug use story	4.65	14.00	32.00
170-Mickey Mouse on Spook's Island (11/47)(Disney)-reprinted in M. M. No. 103	11.00	33.00	76.00
171-Charlie McCarthy (No.1) and the Twenty Thieves	4.50	13.50	31.50
172-Christmas with Mother Goose by Walt Kelly (11/47)	11.50	34.50	80.00
173-Flash Gordon	9.00	27.00	63.00
174-Winnie Winkle	3.50	10.50	24.00
175-Santa Claus Funnies by Walt Kelly ('47)	11.50	34.50	80.00
176-Tillie the Toiler (12/47)	3.00	9.00	21.00
177-Roy Rogers Comics-36 pgs, Photo-c	8.00	24.00	56.00
178-Donald Duck ''Christmas on Bear Mountain'' by Carl Barks; 1st app. Uncle Scrooge (Disney)(12/47)	54.00	162.00	378.00
179-Uncle Wiggily (No.1)-Walt Kelly-c	7.00	21.00	50.00
180-Ozark Ike (No.1)	5.75	17.25	40.00
181-Walt Disney's Mickey Mouse in Jungle Magic	11.00	33.00	76.00
182-Porky Pig in Never-Never Land (2/48)	4.00	12.00	28.00
183-Oswald the Rabbit (Lantz)	3.35	10.00	23.00
184-Tillie the Toiler	3.00	9.00	21.00
185-Easter with Mother Goose by Walt Kelly (1948)	11.00	33.00	76.00
186-Walt Disney's Bambi (4/48)-Reprinted as Bambi No. 3('56)	6.50	19.50	45.00
187-Bugs Bunny and the Dreadful Dragon	3.50	10.50	24.00
188-Woody Woodpecker (Lantz, 5/48)	3.65	11.00	25.00
189-Donald Duck in The Old Castle's Secret, by Carl Barks (Disney) (6/48)	52.00	156.00	364.00
190-Flash Gordon ('48)	9.00	27.00	63.00
191-Porky Pig to the Rescue	4.00	12.00	28.00
192-The Brownies (No.1)-by Walt Kelly (7/48)	11.00	33.00	76.00
193-M.G.M. Presents Tom and Jerry (No.1)(1948)	5.50	16.50	38.00
194-Mickey Mouse in The World Under the Sea (Disney)-Reprinted in M.M. No. 101	11.00	33.00	76.00
195-Tillie the Toiler	2.65	8.00	18.00
196-Charlie McCarthy in The Haunted Hide-Out	5.00	15.00	35.00
197-Spirit of the Border (No.1) (Zane Grey) (1948)	4.00	12.00	28.00
198-Andy Panda	3.50	10.50	24.00
199-Donald Duck in Sheriff of Bullet Valley, by Carl Barks; Barks draws himself on wanted poster, last page; used in ***Love & Death*** (Disney) (10/48)	52.00	156.00	364.00
200-Bugs Bunny, Super Sleuth (10/48)	3.50	10.50	24.00
201-Christmas with Mother Goose by Walt Kelly	8.50	25.50	60.00
202-Woody Woodpecker	2.00	6.00	14.00
203-Donald Duck in the Golden Christmas Tree, by Carl Barks (Disney) (12/48)	36.00	108.00	250.00
204-Flash Gordon (1948)	7.00	21.00	50.00
205-Santa Claus Funnies by Walt Kelly	10.00	30.00	70.00
206-Little Orphan Annie	5.00	15.00	35.00
207-King of the Royal Mounted	10.00	30.00	70.00
208-Brer Rabbit Does It Again (Disney)(1/49)	6.50	19.50	45.00

Four Color #116, © WDC

Four Color #135, © KING

Four Color #185, © DELL

Four Color #217, © L. Schlesinger

Four Color #260, © Warner Bros.

Four Color #293, © DELL

FOUR COLOR (continued)	Good	Fine	Mint
209-Harold Teen	2.00	6.00	14.00
210-Tippie and Cap Stubbs	2.00	6.00	14.00
211-Little Beaver (No.1)	2.65	8.00	18.00
212-Dr. Bobbs	2.00	6.00	14.00
213-Tillie the Toiler	2.65	8.00	18.00
214-Mickey Mouse and His Sky Adventure (2/49)(Disney)-Reprinted in M.M. No. 105	7.00	21.00	50.00
215-Sparkle Plenty (Dick Tracy reprints by Gould)	6.50	19.50	45.00
216-Andy Panda and the Police Pup (Lantz)	2.00	6.00	14.00
217-Bugs Bunny in Court Jester	3.50	10.50	24.00
218-3 Little Pigs and the Wonderful Magic Lamp (Disney)(3/49)	6.00	18.00	42.00
219-Swee'pea	6.00	18.00	42.00
220-Easter with Mother Goose by Walt Kelly	10.00	30.00	70.00
221-Uncle Wiggily-Walt Kelly cover in part	6.00	18.00	42.00
222-West of the Pecos (Zane Grey)	3.50	10.50	24.00
223-Donald Duck ''Lost in the Andes'' by Carl Barks (Disney-4/49) (square egg story)	47.00	140.00	330.00
224-Little Iodine (No.1), by Hatlo (4/49)	3.75	11.25	26.00
225-Oswald the Rabbit (Lantz)	2.15	6.50	15.00
226-Porky Pig and Spoofy, the Spook	2.85	8.50	20.00
227-Seven Dwarfs (Disney)	6.00	18.00	42.00
228-Mark of Zorro, The (No.1) ('49)	12.00	36.00	84.00
229-Smokey Stover	2.35	7.00	16.00
230-Sunset Pass (Zane Grey)	3.50	10.50	24.00
231-Mickey Mouse and the Rajah's Treasure (Disney)	7.00	21.00	50.00
232-Woody Woodpecker (Lantz, 6/49)	2.00	6.00	14.00
233-Bugs Bunny, Sleepwalking Sleuth	3.50	10.50	24.00
234-Dumbo in Sky Voyage (Disney)	5.00	15.00	35.00
235-Tiny Tim	2.65	8.00	18.00
236-Heritage of the Desert (Zane Grey)('49)	3.50	10.50	24.00
237-Tillie the Toiler	2.65	8.00	18.00
238-Donald Duck in Voodoo Hoodoo, by Carl Barks (Disney) (8/49)	26.00	78.00	182.00
239-Adventure Bound (8/49)	2.00	6.00	14.00
240-Andy Panda (Lantz)	2.00	6.00	14.00
241-Porky Pig, Mighty Hunter	2.85	8.50	20.00
242-Tippie and Cap Stubbs	1.75	5.25	12.00
243-Thumper Follows His Nose (Disney)	5.00	15.00	35.00
244-The Brownies by Walt Kelly	9.00	27.00	63.00
245-Dick's Adventures in Dreamland (9/49)	2.65	8.00	18.00
246-Thunder Mountain (Zane Grey)	2.65	8.00	18.00
247-Flash Gordon	7.00	21.00	50.00
248-Mickey Mouse and the Black Sorcerer (Disney)	7.00	21.00	50.00
249-Woody Woodpecker in the Globetrotter'' (10/49)	2.00	6.00	14.00
250-Bugs Bunny in Diamond Daze-Used in **SOTI**, pg. 309	3.50	10.50	24.00
251-Hubert at Camp Moonbeam	2.00	6.00	14.00
252-Pinocchio(Disney)-not Kelly; origin	6.00	18.00	42.00
253-Christmas with Mother Goose by Walt Kelly	8.50	25.50	60.00
254-Santa Claus Funnies by Walt Kelly; Pogo & Albert story by Kelly (11/49)	10.00	30.00	70.00
255-The Ranger (Zane Grey) (1949)	2.65	8.00	18.00
256-Donald Duck in ''Luck of the North'' by Carl Barks (Disney) (12/49)-Shows No. 257 on inside	26.00	78.00	182.00
257-Little Iodine	2.85	8.50	20.00
258-Andy Panda and the Balloon Race (Lantz)	2.00	6.00	14.00
259-Santa and the Angel (Gollub art-condensed from No. 128) & Santa at the Zoo (12/49)-two books in one	3.00	9.00	21.00
260-Porky Pig, Hero of the Wild West(12/49)	2.85	8.50	20.00
261-Mickey Mouse and the Missing Key (Disney)	7.00	21.00	50.00

	Good	Fine	Mint
262-Raggedy Ann and Andy	3.50	10.50	24.00
263-Donald Duck in ''Land of the Totem Poles'' by Carl Barks (Disney)(2/50)-has two Barks stories	26.00	78.00	182.00
264-Woody Woodpecker in the Magic Lantern (Lantz)	2.00	6.00	14.00
265-King of the Royal Mounted (Zane Grey)	6.00	18.00	42.00
266-Bugs Bunny on the Isle of Hercules''(2/50)-Reprinted in Best of B.B. No. 1	2.35	7.00	16.00
267-Little Beaver-Harmon c/a	1.75	5.25	12.00
268-Mickey Mouse's Surprise Visitor (1950) (Disney)	7.00	21.00	50.00
269-Johnny Mack Brown (No.1)-Photo-c	6.50	19.50	45.00
270-Drift Fence (Zane Grey) (3/50)	2.65	8.00	18.00
271-Porky Pig in Phantom of the Plains	2.85	8.50	20.00
272-Cinderella (Disney)(4/50)	4.65	14.00	32.00
273-Oswald the Rabbit (Lantz)	2.15	6.50	15.00
274-Bugs Bunny, Hare-brained Reporter	2.35	7.00	16.00
275-Donald Duck in ''Ancient Persia'' by Carl Barks (Disney) (5/50)	24.00	72.00	168.00
276-Uncle Wiggily	3.50	10.50	24.00
277-Porky Pig in Desert Adventure (5/50)	2.85	8.50	20.00
278-Bill Elliott Comics (No.1)-Photo-c	5.75	17.25	40.00
279-Mickey Mouse and Pluto Battle the Giant Ants (Disney)-Reprinted in M.M. No. 102	5.50	16.50	40.00
280-Andy Panda in The Isle Of Mechanical Men (Lantz)	2.00	6.00	14.00
281-Bugs Bunny in The Great Circus Mystery	2.35	7.00	16.00
282-Donald Duck and the Pixilated Parrot by Carl Barks (Disney) (c. 5/23/50)	24.00	72.00	168.00
283-King of the Royal Mounted (7/50)	6.00	18.00	42.00
284-Porky Pig in The Kingdom of Nowhere	2.85	8.50	20.00
285-Bozo the Clown and His Minikin Circus (No.1)(TV)	4.35	13.00	30.00
286-Mickey Mouse in The Uninvited Guest (Disney)	5.50	16.50	40.00
287-Gene Autry's Champion in The Ghost Of Black Mountain (No.1)-Photo-c	3.50	10.50	24.00
288-Woody Woodpecker in Klondike Gold (Lantz)	2.00	6.00	14.00
289-Bugs Bunny in ''Indian Trouble''	2.35	7.00	16.00
290-The Chief	2.35	7.00	16.00
291-Donald Duck in ''The Magic Hourglass'' by Carl Barks (Disney) (9/50)	24.00	72.00	168.00
292-The Cisco Kid Comics (No.1)	6.00	18.00	42.00
293-The Brownies-Kelly c/a	9.00	27.00	63.00
294-Little Beaver	1.75	5.25	12.00
295-Porky Pig in President Porky (9/50)	2.85	8.50	20.00
296-Mickey Mouse in Private Eye for Hire (Disney)	5.50	16.50	40.00
297-Andy Panda in The Haunted Inn (Lantz, 10/50)	2.00	6.00	14.00
298-Bugs Bunny in Sheik for a Day	2.35	7.00	16.00
299-Buck Jones and the Iron Horse Trail (No.1)	5.65	17.00	40.00
300-Donald Duck in ''Big-Top Bedlam'' by Carl Barks (Disney) (11/50)	24.00	72.00	168.00
301-The Mysterious Rider (Zane Grey)	2.65	8.00	18.00
302-Santa Claus Funnies (11/50)	2.00	6.00	14.00
303-Porky Pig in The Land of the Monstrous Flies	2.00	6.00	14.00
304-Mickey Mouse in Tom-Tom Island (Disney) (12/50)	4.35	13.00	30.00
305-Woody Woodpecker (Lantz)	1.50	4.50	10.00
306-Raggedy Ann	3.00	9.00	21.00
307-Bugs Bunny in Lumber Jack Rabbit	1.75	5.25	12.00
308-Donald Duck in ''Dangerous Disguise'' by Carl Barks (Disney) (1/51)	20.00	60.00	140.00

FOUR COLOR (continued)	Good	Fine	Mint
309-Betty Betz' Dollface and Her Gang ('51)	2.00	6.00	14.00
310-King of the Royal Mounted (1/51)	4.00	12.00	28.00
311-Porky Pig in Midget Horses of Hidden Valley	2.00	6.00	14.00
312-Tonto (No.1)	6.00	18.00	42.00
313-Mickey Mouse in The Mystery of the Double-Cross Ranch (No. 1)(Disney)	4.35	13.00	30.00
314-Ambush (Zane Grey)	2.65	8.00	18.00
315-Oswald the Rabbit (Lantz)	1.30	4.00	9.00
316-Rex Allen (No.1)-Photo-c; Marsh-a	7.00	21.00	50.00
317-Bugs Bunny in Hair Today Gone Tomorrow (No.1)	1.75	5.25	12.00
318-Donald Duck in "No Such Varmint" by Carl Barks (No. 1) (Disney, c. 1/23/51)	19.00	58.00	135.00
319-Gene Autry's Champion	2.35	7.00	16.00
320-Uncle Wiggily (No. 1)	2.65	8.00	18.00
321-Little Scouts (No.1)	1.70	4.00	9.00
322-Porky Pig in Roaring Rockets (No.1)	2.00	6.00	14.00
323-Susie Q. Smith (3/51)	1.50	4.50	10.00
324-I Met a Handsome Cowboy (3/51)	3.65	11.00	25.00
325-Mickey Mouse in The Haunted Castle (No. 2)(Disney)(4/51)	4.35	13.00	30.00
326-Andy Panda (No. 1, Lantz)	1.15	3.50	8.00
327-Bugs Bunny and the Rajah's Treasure (No. 2)	1.75	5.25	12.00
328-Donald Duck in Old California (No.2) by Carl Barks-Peyote drug use issue (Disney) (5/51)	22.00	65.00	154.00
329-Roy Roger's Trigger (No.1)(5/51)-Photo-c	4.00	12.00	28.00
330-Porky Pig Meets the Bristled Bruiser (No.2)	2.00	6.00	14.00
331-Alice in Wonderland (Disney) (1951)	5.00	15.00	35.00
332-Little Beaver	1.75	5.25	12.00
333-Wilderness Trek (Zane Grey) (5/51)	2.65	8.00	18.00
334-Mickey Mouse and Yukon Gold (Disney) (6/51)	4.35	13.00	30.00
335-Francis the Famous Talking Mule (No.1)	1.50	4.50	10.00
336-Woody Woodpecker (Lantz)	1.50	4.50	10.00
337-The Brownies-not by Walt Kelly	2.35	7.00	16.00
338-Bugs Bunny and the Rocking Horse Thieves	1.75	5.25	12.00
339-Donald Duck and the Magic Fountain-not by Carl Barks (Disney) (7-8/51)	4.00	12.00	28.00
340-King of the Royal Mounted (7/51)	4.00	12.00	28.00
341-Unbirthday Party with Alice in Wonderland (Disney) (7/51)	5.00	15.00	35.00
342-Porky Pig the Lucky Peppermint Mine	1.50	4.50	10.00
343-Mickey Mouse in The Ruby Eye of Homar-Guy-Am (Disney)-Reprinted in M.M. No. 104	3.50	10.50	24.00
344-Sergeant Preston from Challenge of The Yukon (No.1)(TV)	3.50	10.50	24.00
345-Andy Panda in Scotland Yard (8-10/51)(Lantz)	1.15	3.50	8.00
346-Hideout (Zane Grey)	2.65	8.00	18.00
347-Bugs Bunny the Frigid Hare (8-9/51)	1.75	5.25	12.00
348-Donald Duck "The Crocodile Collector"-Barks-c only (Disney) (9-10/51)	5.00	15.00	35.00
349-Uncle Wiggily	2.65	8.00	18.00
350-Woody Woodpecker (Lantz)	1.50	4.50	10.00
351-Porky Pig and the Grand Canyon Giant (9-10/51)	1.50	4.50	10.00
352-Mickey Mouse in The Mystery of Painted Valley (Disney)	3.50	10.50	24.00
353-Duck Album (No.1)-Barks-c (Disney)	2.35	7.00	16.00
354-Raggedy Ann & Andy	3.00	9.00	21.00
355-Bugs Bunny Hot-Rod Hare	1.75	5.25	12.00

	Good	Fine	Mint
356-Donald Duck in "Rags to Riches"-Barks-c only (Disney)	5.00	15.00	35.00
357-Comeback (Zane Grey)	2.00	6.00	14.00
358-Andy Panda (Lantz)(11-1/52)	1.15	3.50	8.00
359-Frosty the Snowman (No.1)	2.00	6.00	14.00
360-Porky Pig in Tree of Fortune (11-12/51)	1.50	4.50	10.00
361-Santa Claus Funnies	2.00	6.00	14.00
362-Mickey Mouse and the Smuggled Diamonds (Disney)	3.50	10.50	24.00
363-King of the Royal Mounted	3.50	10.50	24.00
364-Woody Woodpecker (Lantz)	1.30	4.00	9.00
365-The Brownies-not by Kelly	2.35	7.00	16.00
366-Bugs Bunny Uncle Buckskin Comes to Town (12-1/52)	1.75	5.25	12.00
367-Donald Duck in "A Christmas for Shacktown" by Carl Barks (Disney) (1-2/52)	18.50	55.00	130.00
368-Bob Clampett's Beany and Cecil (No.1)	6.00	18.00	42.00
369-The Lone Ranger's Famous Horse Hi-Yo Silver (No.1); Silver's origin	3.75	11.25	26.00
370-Porky Pig in Trouble in the Big Trees	1.50	4.50	10.00
371-Mickey Mouse in The Inca Idol Case ('52) (Disney)	3.50	10.50	24.00
372-Riders of the Purple Sage (Zane Grey)	2.00	6.00	14.00
373-Sergeant Preston (TV)	3.00	9.00	21.00
374-Woody Woodpecker (Lantz)	1.30	4.00	9.00
375-John Carter of Mars (E. R. Burroughs)-Jesse Marsh-a; origin	9.50	28.50	65.00
376-Bugs Bunny, "The Magic Sneeze"	1.75	5.25	12.00
377-Susie Q. Smith	1.50	4.50	10.00
378-Tom Corbett, Space Cadet (No.1)(TV)-McWilliams-a	4.65	14.00	32.00
379-Donald Duck in "Southern Hospitality"-not by Barks (Disney)	4.00	12.00	28.00
380-Raggedy Ann & Andy	3.00	9.00	21.00
381-Marge's Tubby (No.1)	11.00	33.00	76.00
382-Snow White and the Seven Dwarfs (Disney)-origin; partial reprint of 4-Color No. 49 (Movie)	5.00	15.00	35.00
383-Andy Panda (Lantz)	1.00	3.00	7.00
384-King of the Royal Mounted (3/52)(Zane Grey)	3.50	10.50	24.00
385-Porky Pig in The Isle of Missing Ships (3-4/52)	1.50	4.50	10.00
386-Uncle Scrooge No. 1 by Carl Barks (Disney) in "Only a Poor Old Man" (3/52)	56.00	168.00	390.00
387-Mickey Mouse in High Tibet (Disney) (4-5/52)	3.50	10.50	24.00
388-Oswald the Rabbit (Lantz)	1.30	4.00	9.00
389-Andy Hardy Comics (No.1)	1.50	4.50	10.00
390-Woody Woodpecker (Lantz)	1.30	4.00	9.00
391-Uncle Wiggily	2.35	7.00	16.00
392-Hi-Yo Silver	2.35	7.00	16.00
393-Bugs Bunny	1.75	5.25	12.00
394-Donald Duck in Malayalaya-Barks-c only (Disney)	5.00	15.00	35.00
395-Forlorn River (Zane Grey) (1952)-First Nevada (5/52)	2.00	6.00	14.00
396-Tales of the Texas Rangers (No.1)(TV)-Photo-c	3.50	10.50	24.00
397-Sergeant Preston of the Yukon (TV)(5/52)	3.00	9.00	21.00
398-The Brownies-not by Kelly	2.35	7.00	16.00
399-Porky Pig in The Lost Gold Mine	1.50	4.50	10.00
400-Tom Corbett, Space Cadet (TV)-McWilliams c/a	3.75	11.25	26.00
401-Mickey Mouse and Goofy's Mechanical Wizard (Disney) (6-7/52)	3.00	9.00	21.00

Four Color #335, © DELL

Four Color #368, © Bob Clampett

Four Color #397, © Sgt. Preston

AFTER 45 YEARS
R
HAPPY
BIRTHDAY
Dan DeCarlo

The Greatest Stars in Comics!
STAR comics
TM
INHUMANOIDS: TM & © 1987 Hasbro, Inc.
THUNDERCATS is a trademark of Telepictures Corporation.
SILVERHAWKS is a trademark of Lorimar-Telepictures Corporation. HE-MAN AND THE MASTERS OF THE UNIVERSE: TM & © 1987 Mattel Ir
CHUCK NORRIS AND THE KARATE KOMMANDOS: TM & © 1987 Ruby-Spears Enterprises, Inc. DEFENDERS OF THE EARTH: TM & © 1987 King
Features Entertainment, Inc./King Features Syndicate, Inc. STAR Comics is a trademark of the Marvel Entertainment Group, Inc. All rights
reserved.

new universe™

FROM MARVEL® COMICS

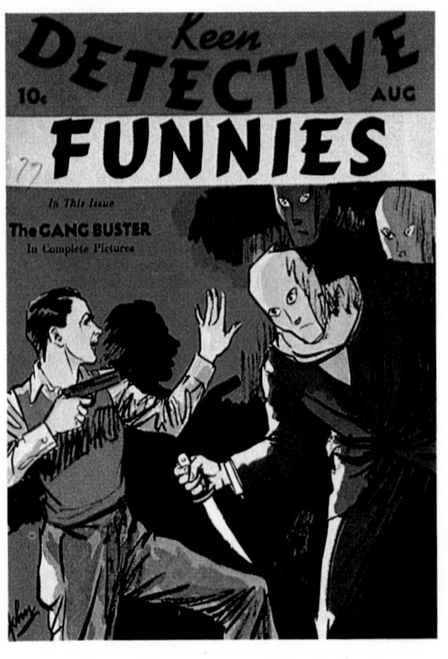

Keen Detective Funnies V1/9, 1938. © *Cen*

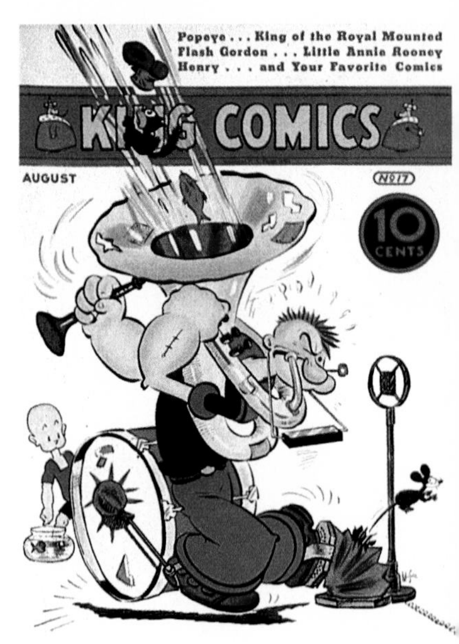

King Comics No. 17, 1937. © *King Features Syndicate*

Four Color No. 1103, 1960. © *Gomalco Prod.*

Four Color No. 913, 1958. © *Warner Bros.*

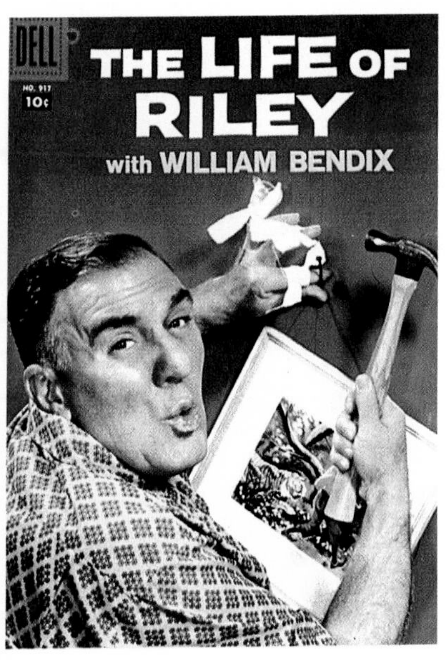

Four Color No. 917, 1958. © *Calif. National Productions*

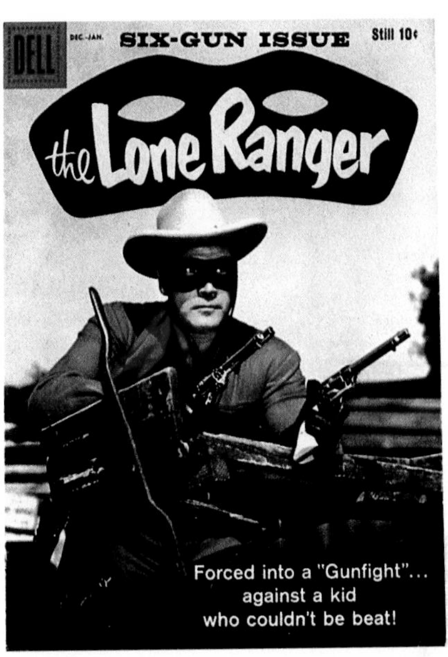

The Lone Ranger No. 125, 1959. © *The Lone Ranger, Inc.*

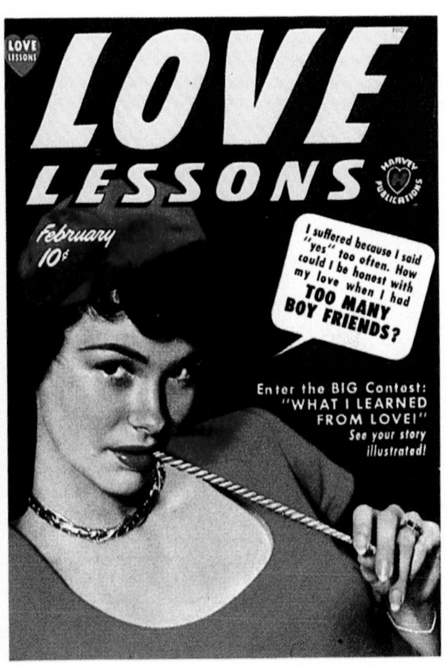

Love Lessons No. 3, 1950. © *Harv*

Four Color No. 962, 1959. © *Warner Bros.*

Four Color No. 27, 1943. © *WDC*

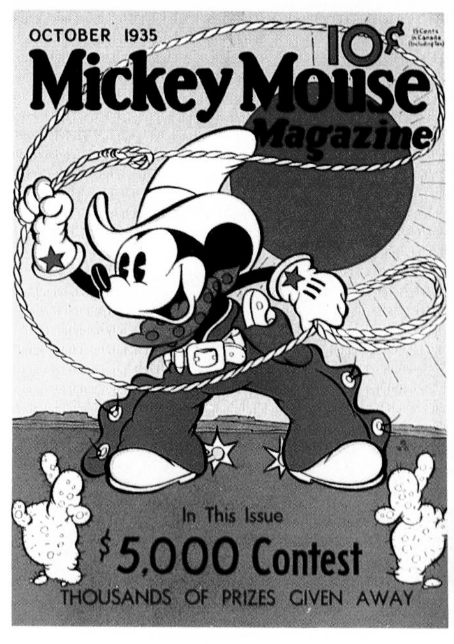

Mickey Mouse Magazine No. 2, 1935. © *WDC*

Mickey Mouse Magazine No. 5, 1936. © *WDC*

Mickey Mouse Magazine V2/3, 1936. Rare Special Christmas issue. © *WDC*

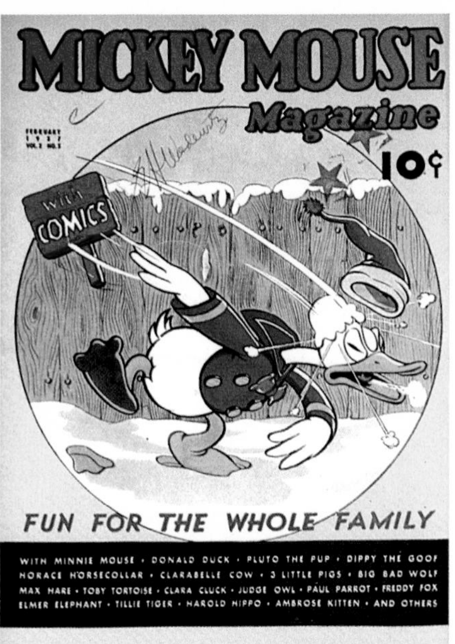

Mickey Mouse Magazine V2/5, 1937.
© *WDC*

Mickey Mouse Magazine V2/11, 1937.
© *WDC*

Mickey Mouse Magazine V3/3, 1937.
1st app. Snow White & the Seven Dwarfs by Disney. © *WDC*

Mickey Mouse Magazine V3/5, 1938.
1st Snow White cover. © *WDC*

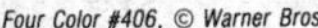
Four Color #406, © Warner Bros.

Four Color #438, © DELL

Four Color #497, © DELL

FOUR COLOR (continued)	**Good**	**Fine**	**Mint**
402-Mary Jane and Sniffles	5.00	15.00	35.00
403-Li'l Bad Wolf (Disney) (6/52)	1.75	5.25	12.00
404-The Range Rider (No.1)(TV)-Photo-c	3.50	10.50	24.00
405-Woody Woodpecker (Lantz)	1.30	4.00	9.00
406-Tweety and Sylvester (No.1)	1.30	4.00	9.00
407-Bugs Bunny, Foreign-Legion Hare	1.30	4.00	9.00
408-Donald Duck and the Golden Helmet by Carl Barks (Disney) (7-8/52)	18.50	55.00	130.00
409-Andy Panda (7-9/52)	1.00	3.00	7.00
410-Porky Pig in The Water Wizard	1.50	4.50	10.00
411-Mickey Mouse and the Old Sea Dog (Disney) (8-9/52)	3.00	9.00	21.00
412-Nevada (Zane Grey)	2.00	6.00	14.00
413-Robin Hood (Disney-Movie) (8/52)-Photo-c	2.00	6.00	14.00
414-Bob Clampett's Beany and Cecil (TV)	4.65	14.00	32.00
415-Rootie Kazootie (No.1)(TV)	2.35	7.00	16.00
416-Woody Woodpecker (Lantz)	1.30	4.00	9.00
417-Double Trouble with Goober (No.1)	1.15	3.50	8.00
418-Rusty Riley, a Boy, a Horse, and a Dog (No.1)-Frank Godwin-a (strip reprints) (8/52)	2.00	6.00	14.00
419-Sergeant Preston (TV)	3.00	9.00	21.00
420-Bugs Bunny in The Mysterious Buckaroo (8-9/52)	1.30	4.00	9.00
421-Tom Corbett, Space Cadet (TV)-McWilliams-a	3.75	11.25	26.00
422-Donald Duck and the Gilded Man, by Carl Barks (Disney) (9-10/52) (No.423 on inside)	18.50	55.00	130.00
423-Rhubarb, Owner of the Brooklyn Ball Club (The Millionaire Cat) (No.1)	1.15	3.50	8.00
424-Flash Gordon-Test Flight in Space (9/52)	5.00	15.00	35.00
425-Zorro, the Return of	5.75	17.25	40.00
426-Porky Pig in The Scalawag Leprechaun	1.50	4.50	10.00
427-Mickey Mouse and the Wonderful Whizzix (Disney) (10-11/52)-reprinted in M.M. No. 100	3.00	9.00	21.00
428-Uncle Wiggily	2.00	6.00	14.00
429-Pluto in ''Why Dogs Leave Home'' (Disney)(10/52)	1.50	4.50	10.00
430-Marge's Tubby, the Shadow of a Man-Eater	6.00	18.00	42.00
431-Woody Woodpecker (10/52)(Lantz)	1.30	4.00	9.00
432-Bugs Bunny and the Rabbit Olympics	1.30	4.00	9.00
433-Wildfire (Zane Grey)	2.00	6.00	14.00
434-Rin Tin Tin-''In Dark Danger'' (No.1)(TV)(11/52)-Photo-c	3.50	10.50	24.00
435-Frosty the Snowman	1.50	4.50	10.00
436-The Brownies-not by Kelly (11/52)	2.00	6.00	14.00
437-John Carter of Mars (E. R. Burroughs)-Marsh-a	8.00	24.00	56.00
438-Annie Oakley (No.1) (TV)	4.00	12.00	28.00
439-Little Hiawatha (Disney) (12/52)	1.75	5.25	12.00
440-Black Beauty (12/52)	1.75	5.25	12.00
441-Fearless Fagan	1.15	3.50	8.00
442-Peter Pan (Disney) (Movie)	4.65	14.00	32.00
443-Ben Bowie and His Mountain Men (No.1)	2.15	6.50	15.00
444-Marge's Tubby	6.00	18.00	42.00
445-Charlie McCarthy	1.50	4.50	10.00
446-Captain Hook and Peter Pan (Disney) (Movie) (1/53)	4.65	14.00	32.00
447-Andy Hardy Comics	1.00	3.00	7.00
448-Bob Clampett's Beany and Cecil (TV)	4.65	14.00	32.00
449-Tappan's Burro (Zane Grey) (2-4/53)	2.00	6.00	14.00
450-Duck Album-Barks-c (Disney)	2.00	6.00	14.00
451-Rusty Riley-Frank Godwin-a (strip reprints) (2/53)	1.75	5.25	12.00
452-Raggedy Ann & Andy ('53)	3.00	9.00	21.00
453-Susie Q. Smith (2/53)	1.30	4.00	9.00

	Good	**Fine**	**Mint**
454-Krazy Kat Comics-not by Herriman	1.75	5.25	12.00
455-Johnny Mack Brown Comics(3/53)-Photo-c	2.65	8.00	18.00
456-Uncle Scrooge Back to the Klondike (No.2) by Barks (3/53) (Disney)	26.00	78.00	180.00
457-Daffy (No.1)	1.50	4.50	10.00
458-Oswald the Rabbit (Lantz)	.85	2.50	6.00
459-Rootie Kazootie (TV)	2.00	6.00	14.00
460-Buck Jones (4/53)	2.65	8.00	18.00
461-Marge's Tubby	6.00	18.00	42.00
462-Little Scouts	.85	2.50	6.00
463-Petunia (4/53)	1.15	3.50	8.00
464-Bozo (4/53)	2.35	7.00	16.00
465-Francis the Famous Talking Mule	.85	2.50	6.00
466-Rhubarb, the Millionaire Cat	.85	2.50	6.00
467-Desert Gold (Zane Grey) (5-7/53)	2.00	6.00	14.00
468-Goofy (No.1) (Disney)	2.65	8.00	18.00
469-Beetle Bailey (No.1)(5/53)	2.00	6.00	14.00
470-Elmer Fudd	1.15	3.50	8.00
471-Double Trouble with Goober	.85	2.50	6.00
472-Wild Bill Elliott (6/53)-Photo-c	2.85	8.50	20.00
473-Li'l Bad Wolf (Disney)	1.30	4.00	9.00
474-Mary Jane and Sniffles	4.00	12.00	28.00
475-M.G.M.'s The Two Mouseketeers (No.1)	1.50	4.50	10.00
476-Rin Tin Tin (TV)-Photo-c	2.65	8.00	18.00
477-Bob Clampett's Beany and Cecil (TV)	4.65	14.00	32.00
478-Charlie McCarthy	1.50	4.50	10.00
479-Queen of the West Dale Evans (No.1)	4.50	13.50	30.00
480-Andy Hardy Comics	1.00	3.00	7.00
481-Annie Oakley And Tagg (TV)	2.85	8.50	20.00
482-Brownies-not by Kelly	2.00	6.00	14.00
483-Little Beaver (7/53)	1.50	4.50	10.00
484-River Feud (Zane Grey) (8-10/53)	2.00	6.00	14.00
485-The Little People-Walt Scott (No.1)	1.75	5.25	12.00
486-Rusty Riley-Frank Godwin strip-r	1.75	5.25	12.00
487-Mowgli, the Jungle Book (Rudyard Kipling's)	1.75	5.25	12.00
488-John Carter of Mars (Burroughs)-Marsh-a	7.00	21.00	50.00
489-Tweety and Sylvester	1.00	3.00	7.00
490-Jungle Jim (No.1)	2.35	7.00	16.00
491-Silvertip (No.1) (Max Brand)-Kinstler-a (8/53)	3.00	9.00	21.00
492-Duck Album (Disney)	1.50	4.50	10.00
493-Johnny Mack Brown-Photo-c	2.65	8.00	18.00
494-The Little King (No.1)	2.00	6.00	14.00
495-Uncle Scrooge (No.3)(Disney)-by Carl Barks (9/53)	23.00	70.00	160.00
496-The Green Hornet	6.50	19.50	45.00
497-Zorro (Sword of. . .)	5.75	17.25	40.00
498-Bugs Bunny's Album (9/53)	1.15	3.50	8.00
499-M.G.M.'s Spike and Tyke (No.1)(9/53)	1.30	4.00	9.00
500-Buck Jones	2.65	8.00	18.00
501-Francis the Famous Talking Mule	.85	2.50	6.00
502-Rootie Kazootie (TV)	2.00	6.00	14.00
503-Uncle Wiggily (10/53)	2.00	6.00	14.00
504-Krazy Kat-not by Herriman	1.75	5.25	12.00
505-The Sword and the Rose (Disney) (10/53) (TV)-Photo-c	2.65	8.00	18.00
506-The Little Scouts	.85	2.50	6.00
507-Oswald the Rabbit (Lantz)	.85	2.50	6.00
508-Bozo (10/53)	2.35	7.00	16.00
509-Pluto (Disney) (10/53)	1.50	4.50	10.00
510-Son of Black Beauty	1.50	4.50	10.00
511-Outlaw Trail (Zane Grey)-Kinstler-a	2.35	7.00	16.00
512-Flash Gordon (11/53)	3.00	9.00	21.00
513-Ben Bowie and His Mountain Men	1.50	4.50	10.00
514-Frosty the Snowman	1.30	4.00	9.00

FOUR COLOR (continued)

	Good	Fine	Mint
515-Andy Hardy	1.00	3.00	7.00
516-Double Trouble With Goober	.85	2.50	6.00
517-Chip 'N' Dale (No.1)(Disney)	1.30	4.00	9.00
518-Rivets (11/53)	1.00	3.00	7.00
519-Steve Canyon (No.1)-not by Milton Caniff	3.50	10.50	24.00
520-Wild Bill Elliott-Photo-c	2.85	8.50	20.00
521-Beetle Bailey (12/53)	1.50	4.50	10.00
522-The Brownies	2.00	6.00	14.00
523-Rin Tin Tin (TV)-Photo-c	2.65	8.00	18.00
524-Tweety and Sylvester	1.00	3.00	7.00
525-Santa Claus Funnies	1.15	3.50	8.00
526-Napoleon	1.15	3.50	8.00
527-Charlie McCarthy	1.50	4.50	10.00
528-Queen of the West Dale Evans-Photo-c	3.50	10.50	24.00
529-Little Beaver	1.50	4.50	10.00
530-Bob Clampett's Beany and Cecil (TV) (1/54)	4.65	14.00	32.00
531-Duck Album (Disney)	1.50	4.50	10.00
532-The Rustlers (Zane Grey) (2-4/54)	2.00	6.00	14.00
533-Raggedy Ann and Andy	3.00	9.00	21.00
534-Western Marshal (Ernest Haycox's)-Kinstler-a	2.65	8.00	18.00
535-I Love Lucy (No. 1)(TV) (2/54)-Photo-c	6.00	18.00	42.00
536-Daffy (3/54)	1.15	3.50	8.00
537-Stormy, the Thoroughbred . . . (Disney-Movie) on top ⅔ of each page; Pluto story on bottom ⅓ of each page (2/54)	2.00	6.00	14.00
538-The Mask of Zorro-Kinstler-a	6.50	19.50	45.00
539-Ben and Me (Disney) (3/54)	1.50	4.50	10.00
540-Knights of the Round Table (3/54) (Movie)-Photo-c	3.00	9.00	21.00
541-Johnny Mack Brown-Photo-c	2.65	8.00	18.00
542-Super Circus Featuring Mary Hartline (TV) (3/54)	2.00	6.00	14.00
543-Uncle Wiggily (3/54)	2.00	6.00	14.00
544-Rob Roy (Disney-Movie)-Manning-a; photo-c	3.00	9.00	21.00
545-The Wonderful Adventures of Pinocchio-Partial reprint of 4-Color 92 (Disney-Movie)	2.35	7.00	16.00
546-Buck Jones	2.65	8.00	18.00
547-Francis the Famous Talking Mule	.85	2.50	6.00
548-Krazy Kat-not by Herriman (4/54)	1.50	4.50	10.00
549-Oswald the Rabbit (Lantz)	.85	2.50	6.00
550-The Little Scouts	.85	2.50	6.00
551-Bozo (4/54)	2.35	7.00	16.00
552-Beetle Bailey	1.50	4.50	10.00
553-Susie Q. Smith	1.30	4.00	9.00
554-Rusty Riley (Frank Godwin strip-r)	1.75	5.25	12.00
555-Range War (Zane Grey)	2.00	6.00	14.00
556-Double Trouble With Goober (5/54)	.85	2.50	6.00
557-Ben Bowie and His Mountain Men	1.50	4.50	10.00
558-Elmer Fudd (5/54)	1.15	3.50	8.00
559-I Love Lucy (No. 2)(TV)-Photo-c	4.35	13.00	30.00
560-Duck Album (Disney)	1.50	4.50	10.00
561-Mr. Magoo (5/54)	3.00	9.00	21.00
562-Goofy (Disney)	2.00	6.00	14.00
563-Rhubarb, the Millionaire Cat (6/54)	.85	2.50	6.00
564-Li'l Bad Wolf (Disney)	1.30	4.00	9.00
565-Jungle Jim	1.75	5.25	12.00
566-Son of Black Beauty	1.75	5.25	12.00
567-Prince Valiant (No.1)-by Bob Fuje (Movie)-Photo-c	5.00	15.00	35.00
568-Gypsy Colt (Movie)	2.00	6.00	14.00
569-Priscilla's Pop	1.15	3.50	8.00
570-Bob Clampett's Beany and Cecil (TV)	4.65	14.00	32.00
571-Charlie McCarthy	1.50	4.50	10.00
572-Silvertip (Max Brand)(7/54); Kinstler-a	2.65	8.00	18.00

	Good	Fine	Mint
573-The Little People by Walt Scott	1.30	4.00	9.00
574-The Hand of Zorro	5.75	17.25	40.00
575-Annie Oakley and Tagg(TV)-Photo-c	2.85	8.50	20.00
576-Angel (No.1) (8/54)	1.00	3.00	7.00
577-M.G.M.'s Spike and Tyke	1.00	3.00	7.00
578-Steve Canyon (8/54)	3.00	9.00	21.00
579-Francis the Famous Talking Mule	.85	2.50	6.00
580-Six Gun Ranch (Luke Short-8/54)	1.75	5.25	12.00
581-Chip 'N' Dale (Disney)	1.00	3.00	7.00
582-Mowgli Jungle Book (Kipling)	1.50	4.50	10.00
583-The Lost Wagon Train (Zane Grey)	2.00	6.00	14.00
584-Johnny Mack Brown-Photo-c	2.65	8.00	18.00
585-Bugs Bunny's Album	1.15	3.50	8.00
586-Duck Album (Disney)	1.50	4.50	10.00
587-The Little Scouts	.85	2.50	6.00
588-King Richard and the Crusaders (Movie) (10/54) Matt Baker-a; photo-c	6.00	18.00	42.00
589-Buck Jones	2.65	8.00	18.00
590-Hansel and Gretel	2.65	8.00	18.00
591-Western Marshal (Ernest Haycox's)-Kinstler-a	2.65	8.00	18.00
592-Super Circus (TV)	2.00	6.00	14.00
593-Oswald the Rabbit (Lantz)	.85	2.50	6.00
594-Bozo (10/54)	2.35	7.00	16.00
595-Pluto (Disney)	1.15	3.50	8.00
596-Turok, Son of Stone (No.1)	17.00	51.00	120.00
597-The Little King	1.50	4.50	10.00
598-Captain Davy Jones	1.15	3.50	8.00
599-Ben Bowie and His Mountain Men	1.50	4.50	10.00
600-Daisy Duck's Diary (No.1)(Disney)(11/54)	1.50	4.50	10.00
601-Frosty the Snowman	1.30	4.00	9.00
602-Mr. Magoo and Gerald McBoing-Boing	3.00	9.00	21.00
603-M.G.M.'s The Two Mouseketeers	1.00	3.00	7.00
604-Shadow on the Trail (Zane Grey)	2.00	6.00	14.00
605-The Brownies-not by Kelly (12/54)	2.00	6.00	14.00
606-Sir Lancelot (not TV)	4.00	12.00	28.00
607-Santa Claus Funnies	1.15	3.50	8.00
608-Silvertip-''Valley of Vanishing Men'' (Max Brand)-Kinstler-a	2.65	8.00	18.00
609-The Littlest Outlaw (Disney-Movie) (1/55)-Photo-c	2.35	7.00	16.00
610-Drum Beat (Movie); Alan Ladd photo-c	4.00	12.00	28.00
611-Duck Album (Disney)	1.50	4.50	10.00
612-Little Beaver (1/55)	1.15	3.50	8.00
613-Western Marshal (Ernest Haycox's) (2/55)-Kinstler-a	2.65	8.00	18.00
614-20,000 Leagues Under the Sea (Disney) (Movie) (2/55)	2.35	7.00	16.00
615-Daffy	1.15	3.50	8.00
616-To the Last Man (Zane Grey)	2.00	6.00	14.00
617-The Quest of Zorro	5.75	17.25	40.00
618-Johnny Mack Brown-Photo-c	2.65	8.00	18.00
619-Krazy Kat-not by Herriman	1.50	4.50	10.00
620-Mowgli Jungle Book (Kipling)	1.50	4.50	10.00
621-Francis the Famous Talking Mule	.85	2.50	6.00
622-Beetle Bailey	1.50	4.50	10.00
623-Oswald the Rabbit (Lantz)	.75	2.25	5.00
624-Treasure Island (Disney-Movie) (4/55)-Photo-c	2.00	6.00	14.00
625-Beaver Valley (Disney-Movie)	1.30	4.00	9.00
626-Ben Bowie and His Mountain Men	1.50	4.50	10.00
627-Goofy (Disney) (5/55)	2.00	6.00	14.00
628-Elmer Fudd	1.15	3.50	8.00
629-Lady and the Tramp with Jock (Disney)	1.75	5.25	12.00
630-Priscilla's Pop	1.00	3.00	7.00
631-Davy Crockett, Indian Fighter (No.1)(Disney)(5/55)(TV)-Fess Parker photo-c	2.35	7.00	16.00

Four Color #517, © WDC

Four Color #535, © Lucille Ball & Desi Arnaz

Four Color #608, © DELL

Four Color #649, © WDC

Four Color #670, © M.G.M.

Four Color #714, © WDC

FOUR COLOR (continued)	Good	Fine	Mint
632-Fighting Caravans (Zane Grey)	2.00	6.00	14.00
633-The Little People by Walt Scott	1.30	4.00	9.00
634-Lady and the Tramp Album (Disney) (6/55)	1.50	4.50	10.00
635-Bob Clampett's Beany and Cecil (TV)	4.65	14.00	32.00
636-Chip 'N' Dale (Disney)	1.00	3.00	7.00
637-Silvertip (Max Brand)-Kinstler-a	2.65	8.00	18.00
638-M.G.M.'s Spike and Tyke (8/55)	1.00	3.00	7.00
639-Davy Crockett at the Alamo (Disney) (7/55)(TV)-Fess Parker photo-c	2.00	6.00	14.00
640-Western Marshal (Ernest Haycox's)-Kinstler-a	2.65	8.00	18.00
641-Steve Canyon ('55)-by Caniff	3.00	9.00	21.00
642-M.G.M.'s The Two Mouseketeers	1.00	3.00	7.00
643-Wild Bill Elliott-Photo-c	2.65	8.00	18.00
644-Sir Walter Raleigh (5/55)-Based on movie "The Virgin Queen"-Photo-c	2.65	8.00	18.00
645-Johnny Mack Brown-Photo-c	2.65	8.00	18.00
646-Dotty Dripple and Taffy (No.1)	1.50	4.50	10.00
647-Bugs Bunny's Album (9/55)	1.15	3.50	8.00
648-Jace Pearson of the Texas Rangers (TV)-Photo-c	2.65	8.00	18.00
649-Duck Album (Disney)	1.50	4.50	10.00
650-Prince Valiant - by Bob Fuje	3.00	9.00	21.00
651-King Colt (Luke Short)(9/55)-Kinstler-a	2.35	7.00	16.00
652-Buck Jones	1.75	5.25	12.00
653-Smokey the Bear (No.1) (10/55)	1.75	5.25	12.00
654-Pluto (Disney)	1.15	3.50	8.00
655-Francis the Famous Talking Mule	.85	2.50	6.00
656-Turok, Son of Stone (No.2) (10/55)	12.00	36.00	84.00
657-Ben Bowie and His Mountain Men	1.50	4.50	10.00
658-Goofy (Disney)	2.00	6.00	14.00
659-Daisy Duck's Diary (Disney)	1.30	4.00	9.00
660-Little Beaver	1.15	3.50	8.00
661-Frosty the Snowman	1.30	4.00	9.00
662-Zoo Parade (TV)-Marlin Perkins (11/55)-Photo-c	1.75	5.25	12.00
663-Winky Dink (TV)	2.15	6.50	15.00
664-Davy Crockett in the Great Keelboat Race (TV) (Disney)(11/55)-Fess Parker photo-c	2.65	8.00	18.00
665-The African Lion (Disney-Movie) (11/55)	1.75	5.25	12.00
666-Santa Claus Funnies	1.15	3.50	8.00
667-Silvertip and the Stolen Stallion (Max Brand) (12/55)-Kinstler-a	2.65	8.00	18.00
668-Dumbo (Disney) (12/55)	3.00	9.00	21.00
668-Dumbo (Disney) (1/58) different cover, same contents	3.00	9.00	21.00
669-Robin Hood (Disney-Movie) (12/55)-reprint of No. 413-Photo-c	1.75	5.25	12.00
670-M.G.M's Mouse Musketeers (No.1)(1/56)-Formerly the Two Mouseketeers	1.00	3.00	7.00
671-Davy Crockett and the River Pirates (TV) (Disney) (12/55)-Jesse Marsh-a; Fess Parker photo-c	2.65	8.00	18.00
672-Quentin Durward (1/56)(Movie)-Photo-c	2.65	8.00	18.00
673-Buffalo Bill, Jr. (No.1)(TV)-Photo-c	2.65	8.00	18.00
674-The Little Rascals (No.1) (TV)	1.75	5.25	12.00
675-Steve Donovan, Western Marshal (No.1)(TV)-Kinstler-a; photo-c	3.00	9.00	21.00
676-Will-Yum!	1.00	3.00	7.00
677-Little King	1.50	4.50	10.00
678-The Last Hunt (Movie)-Photo-c	2.65	8.00	18.00
679-Gunsmoke (No.1) (TV)	4.00	12.00	28.00
680-Out Our Way with the Worry Wart (2/56)	1.15	3.50	8.00
681-Forever, Darling (Movie) with Lucille Ball & Desi Arnaz (2/56)-Photo-c	3.50	10.50	24.00
682-When Knighthood Was in Flower (Disney-Movie)-Reprint of No. 505-Photo-c	2.15	6.50	15.00

	Good	Fine	Mint
683-Hi and Lois (3/56)	.85	2.50	6.00
684-Helen of Troy (Movie)-Buscema-a; photo-c	5.00	15.00	35.00
685-Johnny Mack Brown-Photo-c	2.65	8.00	18.00
686-Duck Album (Disney)	1.50	4.50	10.00
687-The Indian Fighter (Movie)-Kirk Douglas Photo-c	2.35	7.00	16.00
688-Alexander the Great (Movie) (5/56) Buscema-a; photo-c	3.00	9.00	21.00
689-Elmer Fudd (3/56)	1.15	3.50	8.00
690-The Conqueror (Movie) - John Wayne-Photo-c	6.00	18.00	42.00
691-Dotty Dripple and Taffy	1.15	3.50	8.00
692-The Little People-Walt Scott	1.30	4.00	9.00
693-Song of the South (Disney)(1956)-Partial reprint of No. 129	1.75	5.25	12.00
694-Super Circus (TV)-Photo-c	2.00	6.00	14.00
695-Little Beaver	1.15	3.50	8.00
696-Krazy Kat-not by Herriman (4/56)	1.50	4.50	10.00
697-Oswald the Rabbit (Lantz)	.75	2.25	5.00
698-Francis the Famous Talking Mule	.85	2.50	6.00
699-Prince Valiant-by Bob Fuje	3.00	9.00	21.00
700-Water Birds and the Olympic Elk (Disney-Movie)(4/56)	2.00	6.00	14.00
701-Jiminy Crickett (No.1)(Disney)(5/56)	2.00	6.00	14.00
702-The Goofy Success Story (Disney)	1.75	5.25	12.00
703-Scamp (No.1) (Disney)	1.30	4.00	9.00
704-Priscilla's Pop (5/56)	1.00	3.00	7.00
705-Brave Eagle (No.1) (TV)-Photo-c	1.75	5.25	12.00
706-Bongo and Lumpjaw (Disney)(6/56)	1.30	4.00	9.00
707-Corky and White Shadow (Disney)(5/56)-Mickey Mouse Club (TV)-Photo-c	2.00	6.00	14.00
708-Smokey the Bear	1.30	4.00	9.00
709-The Searchers (Movie) - John Wayne photo-c	9.50	28.50	65.00
710-Francis the Famous Talking Mule	.85	2.50	6.00
711-M.G.M's Mouse Musketeers	.85	2.50	6.00
712-The Great Locomotive Chase (Disney-Movie) (9/56)-Photo-c	2.35	7.00	16.00
713-The Animal World (Movie) (8/56)	2.00	6.00	14.00
714-Spin and Marty (No.1)(TV)(Disney)-Mickey Mouse Club (6/56)-Photo-c	3.00	9.00	21.00
715-Timmy (8/56)	1.15	3.50	8.00
716-Man in Space (Disney-Movie)	1.75	5.25	12.00
717-Moby Dick (Movie)-Photo-c	4.00	12.00	28.00
718-Dotty Dripple and Taffy	1.15	3.50	8.00
719-Prince Valiant - by Bob Fuje	3.00	9.00	21.00
720-Gunsmoke (TV)-Photo-c	3.00	9.00	21.00
721-Captain Kangaroo (TV)-Photo-c	4.00	12.00	28.00
722-Johnny Mack Brown-Photo-c	2.65	8.00	18.00
723-Santiago (Movie)-Kinstler-a(9/56); Alan Ladd photo-c	4.00	12.00	28.00
724-Bugs Bunny's Album	1.15	3.50	8.00
725-Elmer Fudd (9/56)	.85	2.50	6.00
726-Duck Album (Disney)	1.15	3.50	8.00
727-The Nature of Things (TV) (Disney)-Jesse Marsh-a	1.75	5.25	12.00
728-M.G.M's Mouse Musketeers	.85	2.50	6.00
729-Bob Son of Battle (11/56)	1.50	4.50	10.00
730-Smokey Stover	1.50	4.50	10.00
731-Silvertip and The Fighting Four (Max Brand)-Kinstler-a	2.65	8.00	18.00
732-Zorro, the Challenge of (10/56)	5.75	17.25	40.00
733-Buck Jones	1.75	5.25	12.00
734-Cheyenne (No.1)(TV)(10/56)-Photo-c	4.00	12.00	28.00
735-Crusader Rabbit (No. 1) (TV)	3.00	9.00	21.00
736-Pluto (Disney)	1.00	3.00	7.00

FOUR COLOR (continued)	Good	Fine	Mint
737-Steve Canyon-Caniff-a	3.00	9.00	21.00
738-Westward Ho, the Wagons (Disney-Movie)-Photo-c	1.75	5.25	12.00
739-Bounty Guns (Luke Short)-Drucker-a	1.75	5.25	12.00
740-Chilly Willy (No.1)(Walter Lantz)	1.15	3.50	8.00
741-The Fastest Gun Alive (Movie) (9/56)-Photo-c	2.65	8.00	18.00
742-Buffalo Bill, Jr. (TV)-Photo-c	2.00	6.00	14.00
743-Daisy Duck's Diary (Disney) (11/56)	1.30	4.00	9.00
744-Little Beaver	1.15	3.50	8.00
745-Francis the Famous Talking Mule	.85	2.50	6.00
746-Dotty Dripple and Taffy	1.15	3.50	8.00
747-Goofy (Disney)	1.75	5.25	12.00
748-Frosty the Snowman (11/56)	1.15	3.50	8.00
749-Secrets of Life (Disney-Movie)-Photo-c	1.75	5.25	12.00
750-The Great Cat Family (Disney-Movie)	2.00	6.00	14.00
751-Our Miss Brooks (TV)-Photo-c	2.65	8.00	18.00
752-Mandrake, the Magician	3.50	10.50	24.00
753-Walt Scott's Little People (11/56)	1.30	4.00	9.00
754-Smokey the Bear	1.30	4.00	9.00
755-The Littlest Snowman (12/56)	1.50	4.50	10.00
756-Santa Claus Funnies	1.15	3.50	8.00
757-The True Story of Jesse James (Movie)-Photo-c	3.50	10.50	24.00
758-Bear Country (Disney-Movie)	1.75	5.25	12.00
759-Circus Boy (TV)-The Monkees' Mickey Dolenz photo-c	3.00	9.00	21.00
760-The Hardy Boys (No. 1) (TV) (Disney)-Mickey Mouse Club-Photo-c	3.00	9.00	21.00
761-Howdy Doody (TV) (1/57)	3.00	9.00	21.00
762-The Sharkfighters (Movie)(1/57)(Scarce); Buscema-a; photo-c	5.00	15.00	35.00
763-Grandma Duck's Farm Friends (No. 1) (Disney)	1.75	5.25	12.00
764-M.G.M's Mouse Musketeers	.85	2.50	6.00
765-Will-Yum!	.85	2.50	6.00
766-Buffalo Bill, Jr. (TV)-Photo-c	2.00	6.00	14.00
767-Spin and Marty (TV)(Disney)-Mickey Mouse Club (2/57)	2.65	8.00	18.00
768-Steve Donovan, Western Marshal (TV)-Kinstler-a; photo-c	2.65	8.00	18.00
769-Gunsmoke (TV)	3.00	9.00	21.00
770-Brave Eagle (TV)-Photo-c	1.30	4.00	9.00
771-Brand of Empire (Luke Short)(3/57)-Drucker-a	1.75	5.25	12.00
772-Cheyenne (TV)-Photo-c	3.50	10.50	24.00
773-The Brave One (Movie)-Photo-c	1.75	5.25	12.00
774-Hi and Lois (3/57)	.85	2.50	6.00
775-Sir Lancelot and Brian (TV)-Buscema-a; photo-c	4.00	12.00	28.00
776-Johnny Mack Brown-Photo-c	2.65	8.00	18.00
777-Scamp (Disney)	1.00	3.00	7.00
778-The Little Rascals (TV)	1.30	4.00	9.00
779-Lee Hunter, Indian Fighter (3/57)	1.75	5.25	12.00
780-Captain Kangaroo (TV)-Photo-c	4.00	12.00	28.00
781-Fury (No.1)(TV)(3/57)-Photo-c	3.50	10.50	24.00
782-Duck Album (Disney)	1.15	3.50	8.00
783-Elmer Fudd	.85	2.50	6.00
784-Around the World in 80 Days (Movie) (2/57)-Photo-c	2.65	8.00	18.00
785-Circus Boy (TV) (4/57)-The Monkees' Mickey Dolenz photo-c	3.00	9.00	21.00
786-Cinderella (Disney) (3/57)-Partial reprint of No. 272	1.75	5.25	12.00
787-Little Hiawatha (Disney) (4/57)	1.30	4.00	9.00
788-Prince Valiant - by Bob Fuje	3.00	9.00	21.00

	Good	Fine	Mint
789-Silvertip-Valley Thieves (Max Brand) (4/57)-Kinstler-a	2.65	8.00	18.00
790-The Wings of Eagles (Movie) (John Wayne)-Toth-a; photo-c	6.50	19.50	45.00
791-The 77th Bengal Lancers (TV)-Photo-c	3.00	9.00	21.00
792-Oswald the Rabbit (Lantz)	.75	2.25	5.00
793-Morty Meekle	1.30	4.00	9.00
794-The Count of Monte Cristo (5/57) (Movie)-Buscema-a	5.00	15.00	35.00
795-Jiminy Cricket (Disney)	1.50	4.50	10.00
796-Ludwig Bemelman's Madeleine and Genevieve	1.75	5.25	12.00
797-Gunsmoke (TV)-Photo-c	3.00	9.00	21.00
798-Buffalo Bill, Jr. (TV)-Photo-c	2.00	6.00	14.00
799-Priscilla's Pop	1.00	3.00	7.00
800-The Buccaneers (TV)-Photo-c	3.65	11.00	25.00
801-Dotty Dripple and Taffy	1.15	3.50	8.00
802-Goofy (Disney) (5/57)	1.75	5.25	12.00
803-Cheyenne (TV)-Photo-c	3.50	10.50	24.00
804-Steve Canyon-Caniff-a (1957)	3.00	9.00	21.00
805-Crusader Rabbit (TV)	3.00	9.00	21.00
806-Scamp (Disney) (6/57)	1.00	3.00	7.00
807-Savage Range (Luke Short)-Drucker-a	1.75	5.25	12.00
808-Spin and Marty (TV)(Disney)-Mickey Mouse Club-Photo-c	2.65	8.00	18.00
809-The Little People-Walt Scott	1.30	4.00	9.00
810-Francis the Famous Talking Mule	.85	2.50	6.00
811-Howdy Doody (TV) (7/57)	3.00	9.00	21.00
812-The Big Land(Movie); Alan Ladd photo-c	4.00	12.00	28.00
813-Circus Boy (TV)-The Monkees' Mickey Dolenz photo-c	3.00	9.00	21.00
814-Covered Wagons, Ho! (Disney)-Donald Duck (TV)(6/57)	1.75	5.25	12.00
815-Dragoon Wells Massacre (Movie)-Photo-c	3.65	11.00	25.00
816-Brave Eagle (TV)-Photo-c	1.30	4.00	9.00
817-Little Beaver	1.15	3.50	8.00
818-Smokey the Bear (6/57)	1.30	4.00	9.00
819-Mickey Mouse in Magicland (Disney) (7/57)	1.75	5.25	12.00
820-The Oklahoman (Movie)-Photo-c	3.65	11.00	25.00
821-Wringle Wrangle (Disney)-Based on movie "Westward Ho, the Wagons"-Marsh-a; Fess Parker photo-c	2.65	8.00	18.00
822-Paul Revere's Ride with Johnny Tremain (TV)(Disney)-Toth-a	5.00	15.00	35.00
823-Timmy	1.00	3.00	7.00
824-The Pride and the Passion (Movie)(8/57)-Frank Sinatra photo-c	3.00	9.00	21.00
825-The Little Rascals (TV)	1.30	4.00	9.00
826-Spin and Marty and Annette (TV)(Disney)-Mickey Mouse Club-Annette photo-c	5.00	15.00	35.00
827-Smokey Stover (8/57)	1.50	4.50	10.00
828-Buffalo Bill, Jr. (TV)-Photo-c	2.00	6.00	14.00
829-Tales of the Pony Express (TV) (8/57)-Painted-c	1.75	5.25	12.00
830-The Hardy Boys (TV)(Disney)-Mickey Mouse Club (8/57)-Photo-c	2.65	8.00	18.00
831-No Sleep 'Til Dawn (Movie)-Photo-c	2.65	8.00	18.00
832-Lolly and Pepper (No.1)	1.50	4.50	10.00
833-Scamp (Disney) (9/57)	1.00	3.00	7.00
834-Johnny Mack Brown-Photo-c	2.65	8.00	18.00
835-Silvertip-The Fake Rider (Max Brand)	2.00	6.00	14.00
836-Man in Flight (Disney) (TV)(9/57)	1.75	5.25	12.00
837-All-American Athlete Cotton Woods	1.75	5.25	12.00
838-Bugs Bunny's Life Story Album (9/57)	1.50	4.50	10.00
839-The Vigilantes (Movie)	3.00	9.00	21.00
840-Duck Album (Disney)	1.15	3.50	8.00

Four Color #747, © WDC

Four Color #785, © Norbert Prod.

Four Color #820, © DELL

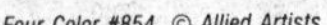
Four Color #854, © Allied Artists

Four Color #897, © WDC

Four Color #913, © DELL

FOUR COLOR (continued)	Good	Fine	Mint
841-Elmer Fudd	.85	2.50	6.00
842-The Nature of Things (Disney-Movie)('57)-Jesse Marsh-a (TV series)	2.00	6.00	14.00
843-The First Americans (Disney)(TV)-Marsh-a	2.00	6.00	14.00
844-Gunsmoke (TV)-Photo-c	3.00	9.00	21.00
845-The Land Unknown (Movie)-Alex Toth-a	6.50	19.50	45.00
846-Gun Glory (Movie)-by Alex Toth-Photo-c	6.00	18.00	42.00
847-Perri (squirrels) (Disney-Movie)-Two different covers published	1.30	4.00	9.00
848-Marauder's Moon	2.35	7.00	16.00
849-Prince Valiant-by Bob Fuje	3.00	9.00	21.00
850-Buck Jones	1.75	5.25	12.00
851-The Story of Mankind (Movie) (1/58)-Photo-c	2.65	8.00	18.00
852-Chilly Willy (2/58)(Lantz)	.75	2.25	5.00
853-Pluto (Disney) (10/57)	1.00	3.00	7.00
854-The Hunchback of Notre Dame (Movie)-Photo-c	6.00	18.00	42.00
855-Broken Arrow (TV)-Photo-c	2.35	7.00	16.00
856-Buffalo Bill, Jr. (TV)-Photo-c	2.00	6.00	14.00
857-The Goofy Adventure Story (Disney) (11/57)	1.75	5.25	12.00
858-Daisy Duck's Diary (Disney) (11/57)	1.30	4.00	9.00
859-Topper and Neil (TV)(11/57)	1.00	3.00	7.00
860-Wyatt Earp (No.1)(TV)-Manning-a; photo-c	4.00	12.00	28.00
861-Frosty the Snowman	1.15	3.50	8.00
862-The Truth About Mother Goose (Disney-Movie) (11/57)	3.00	9.00	21.00
863-Francis the Famous Talking Mule	.85	2.50	6.00
864-The Littlest Snowman	1.50	4.50	10.00
865-Andy Burnett (TV) (Disney) (12/57)-Photo-c	2.65	8.00	18.00
866-Mars and Beyond (Disney-Movie)	1.75	5.25	12.00
867-Santa Claus Funnies	1.15	3.50	8.00
868-The Little People (12/57)	1.30	4.00	9.00
869-Old Yeller (Disney-Movie)-Photo-c	2.35	7.00	16.00
870-Little Beaver (1/58)	1.15	3.50	8.00
871-Curly Kayoe	1.50	4.50	10.00
872-Captain Kangaroo (TV)-Photo-c	4.00	12.00	28.00
873-Grandma Duck's Farm Friends (Disney)	1.30	4.00	9.00
874-Old Ironsides (Disney-Movie with Johnny Tremain) (1/58)	2.00	6.00	14.00
875-Trumpets West (Luke Short) (2/58)	1.75	5.25	12.00
876-Tales of Wells Fargo (No.1) (TV) (2/58)-Photo-c	3.00	9.00	21.00
877-Frontier Doctor with Rex Allen (TV)-Alex Toth-a; photo-c	5.00	15.00	35.00
878-Peanuts (No.1)-Schulz-c only (2/58)	3.50	10.50	24.00
879-Brave Eagle (TV)(2/58)-Photo-c	1.30	4.00	9.00
880-Steve Donovan, Western Marshal-Drucker-a (TV)-Photo-c	1.75	5.25	12.00
881-The Captain and the Kids	1.30	4.00	9.00
882-Zorro (Disney)-1st Disney issue by Alex Toth (TV) (2/58)-Photo-c	4.35	13.00	30.00
883-The Little Rascals (TV)	1.70	4.00	9.00
884-Hawkeye and the Last of the Mohicans (TV)-Photo-c	2.00	6.00	14.00
885-Fury (TV) (3/58)-Photo-c	2.65	8.00	18.00
886-Bongo and Lumpjaw (Disney, 3/58)	1.15	3.50	8.00
887-The Hardy Boys (Disney)(TV)-Mickey Mouse Club (1/58)-Photo-c	2.65	8.00	18.00
888-Elmer Fudd (3/58)	.85	2.50	6.00
889-Clint and Mac (Disney)(TV)-Alex Toth-a (3/58)-Photo-c	5.00	15.00	35.00

	Good	Fine	Mint
890-Wyatt Earp (TV)-by Russ Manning; photo-c	3.00	9.00	21.00
891-Light in the Forest (Disney-Movie) (3/58)-Photo-c	2.00	6.00	14.00
892-Maverick (No.1) (TV) (4/58)	4.00	12.00	28.00
893-Jim Bowie (TV)-Photo-c	2.00	6.00	14.00
894-Oswald the Rabbit (Lantz)	.75	2.25	5.00
895-Wagon Train (No.1)(TV)(3/58)-Photo-c	3.50	10.50	24.00
896-The Adventures of Tinker Bell (Disney)	2.65	8.00	18.00
897-Jiminy Cricket (Disney)	1.30	4.00	9.00
898-Silvertip (Max Brand)-Kinstler-a (5/58)	2.65	8.00	18.00
899-Goofy (Disney)	1.75	5.25	12.00
900-Prince Valiant-by Bob Fuje	3.00	9.00	21.00
901-Little Hiawatha (Disney)	1.30	4.00	9.00
902-Will-Yum!	.85	2.50	6.00
903-Dotty Dripple and Taffy	1.15	3.50	8.00
904-Lee Hunter, Indian Fighter	1.50	4.50	10.00
905-Annette (Disney,TV, 5/58)-Mickey Mouse Club-Photo-c	8.00	24.00	56.00
906-Francis the Famous Talking Mule	.85	2.50	6.00
907-Sugarfoot (No.1)(TV)Toth-a; photo-c	6.50	19.50	45.00
908-The Little People and the Giant-Walt Scott (5/58)	1.30	4.00	9.00
909-Smitty	1.15	3.50	8.00
910-The Vikings (Movie)-Buscema-a; photo-c	3.65	11.00	25.00
911-The Gray Ghost (TV)(Movie)-Photo-c	3.00	9.00	21.00
912-Leave It to Beaver (No.1)(TV)-Photo-c	7.00	21.00	42.00
913-The Left-Handed Gun (Movie) (7/58); Paul Newman photo-c	3.65	11.00	25.00
914-No Time for Sergeants (Movie)-Photo-c; Toth-a	5.00	15.00	35.00
915-Casey Jones (TV)-Photo-c	2.00	6.00	14.00
916-Red Ryder Ranch Comics	1.50	4.50	10.00
917-The Life of Riley (TV)-Photo-c	4.00	12.00	28.00
918-Beep Beep, the Roadrunner (No.1)(7/58)-Two different back covers published	2.00	6.00	14.00
919-Boots and Saddles (No.1)(TV)-Photo-c	3.00	9.00	21.00
920-Zorro (Disney-TV)(6/58)Toth-a; photo-c	4.35	13.00	30.00
921-Wyatt Earp (TV)-Manning-a; photo-c	3.00	9.00	21.00
922-Johnny Mack Brown by Russ Manning-Photo-c	3.00	9.00	21.00
923-Timmy	1.00	3.00	7.00
924-Colt .45 (No.1)(TV)(8/58)-Photo-c	3.50	10.50	24.00
925-Last of the Fast Guns (Movie) (8/58)-Photo-c	2.65	8.00	18.00
926-Peter Pan (Disney)-Reprint of No. 442	1.75	5.25	12.00
927-Top Gun (Luke Short) Buscema-a	1.75	5.25	12.00
928-Sea Hunt (No.1) (TV)-Lloyd Bridges photo-c	3.50	10.50	24.00
929-Brave Eagle (TV)-Photo-c	1.30	4.00	9.00
930-Maverick (TV) (7/58)-James Garner photo-c	3.50	10.50	24.00
931-Have Gun, Will Travel (No.1) (TV)-Photo-c	3.50	10.50	24.00
932-Smokey the Bear (His Life Story)	1.30	4.00	9.00
933-Zorro (Disney)-by Alex Toth (TV)(9/58)	4.35	13.00	30.00
934-Restless Gun (No.1)(TV)-Photo-c	3.75	11.25	26.00
935-King of the Royal Mounted	2.65	8.00	18.00
936-The Little Rascals (TV)	1.30	4.00	9.00
937-Ruff and Reddy (No.1)(TV)(Hanna-Barbera)	1.50	4.50	10.00
938-Elmer Fudd (9/58)	.85	2.50	6.00
939-Steve Canyon - not by Caniff	2.65	8.00	18.00
940-Lolly and Pepper	1.15	3.50	8.00
941-Pluto (Disney) (10/58)	1.00	3.00	7.00
942-Pony Express (TV)	1.75	5.25	12.00

FOUR COLOR (continued)	Good	Fine	Mint
943-White Wilderness (Disney-Movie) (10/58)	2.00	6.00	14.00
944-The 7th Voyage of Sindbad (Movie) (9/58)-Buscema-a	7.00	21.00	50.00
945-Maverick (TV)-James Garner photo-c	3.50	10.50	24.00
946-The Big Country (Movie)-Photo-c	2.65	8.00	18.00
947-Broken Arrow (TV)-Photo-c	2.35	7.00	16.00
948-Daisy Duck's Diary (Disney) (11/58)	1.30	4.00	9.00
949-High Adventure (Lowell Thomas')(TV)-Photo-c	1.75	5.25	12.00
950-Frosty the Snowman	1.15	3.50	8.00
951-The Lennon Sisters Life Story (TV)-Toth-a, 32pgs.-Photo-c	6.00	18.00	42.00
952-Goofy (Disney) (11/58)	1.75	5.25	12.00
953-Francis the Famous Talking Mule	.85	2.50	6.00
954-Man in Space-Satellites (Disney-Movie)	1.75	5.25	12.00
955-Hi and Lois (11/58)	.85	2.50	6.00
956-Ricky Nelson (No.1)(TV)-Photo-c	7.00	21.00	50.00
957-Buffalo Bee (No.1)(TV)	1.75	5.25	12.00
958-Santa Claus Funnies	1.00	3.00	7.00
959-Christmas Stories-(Walt Scott's Little People)(1951-56 strip reprints)	1.30	4.00	9.00
960-Zorro (Disney)(TV)(12/58)-Toth art	4.35	13.00	30.00
961-Jace Pearson's Tales of the Texas Rangers (TV)-Spiegle-a; photo-c	2.65	8.00	18.00
962-Maverick (TV) (1/59)-James Garner photo-c	3.50	10.50	24.00
963-Johnny Mack Brown-Photo-c	2.65	8.00	18.00
964-The Hardy Boys (TV)(Disney)-Mickey Mouse Club (1/59)-Photo-c	2.65	8.00	18.00
965-Grandma Duck's Farm Friends (Disney) (1/59)	1.30	4.00	9.00
966-Tonka (starring Sal Mineo; Disney-Movie)-Photo-c	2.65	8.00	18.00
967-Chilly Willy (2/59)(Lantz)	.75	2.25	5.00
968-Tales of Wells Fargo (TV)-Photo-c	2.35	7.00	16.00
969-Peanuts (2/59)	3.00	9.00	21.00
970-Lawman (No.1)(TV)-Photo-c	4.00	12.00	28.00
971-Wagon Train (TV)-Photo-c	2.65	8.00	18.00
972-Tom Thumb (Movie)-George Pal	3.65	11.00	25.00
973-Sleeping Beauty and the Prince (Disney) (5/59)	3.00	9.00	21.00
974-The Little Rascals (TV)(3/59)	1.30	4.00	9.00
975-Fury (TV)-Photo-c	2.65	8.00	18.00
976-Zorro (Disney)(TV)-Toth-a; photo-c	4.35	13.00	30.00
977-Elmer Fudd	.85	2.50	6.00
978-Lolly and Pepper	1.15	3.50	8.00
979-Oswald the Rabbit (Lantz)	.75	2.25	5.00
980-Maverick (TV) (4-6/59)-James Garner & Jack Kelly photo-c	3.50	10.50	24.00
981-Ruff and Reddy (TV)(Hanna-Barbera)	1.15	3.50	8.00
982-The New Adventures of Tinker Bell (TV-Disney)	2.65	8.00	18.00
983-Have Gun, Will Travel (TV) (4-6/59)-Photo-c	3.00	9.00	21.00
984-Sleeping Beauty's Fairy Godmothers (Disney)	3.00	9.00	21.00
985-Shaggy Dog (Disney-Movie)-Photo-c	2.00	6.00	14.00
986-Restless Gun (TV)-Photo-c	3.00	9.00	21.00
987-Goofy (Disney) (7/59)	1.75	5.25	12.00
988-Little Hiawatha (Disney)	1.30	4.00	9.00
989-Jiminy Cricket (Disney) (5-7/59)	1.30	4.00	9.00
990-Huckleberry Hound (No.1)(TV)(Hanna-Barbera)	2.00	6.00	14.00
991-Francis the Famous Talking Mule	.85	2.50	6.00
992-Sugarfoot (TV)-Toth-a; photo-c	6.00	18.00	42.00
993-Jim Bowie (TV)-Photo-c	2.00	6.00	14.00
994-Sea Hunt (TV)-Lloyd Bridges photo-c	3.00	9.00	21.00

	Good	Fine	Mint
995-Donald Duck Album (Disney) (5-7/59)	1.50	4.50	10.00
996-Nevada (Zane Grey)	2.00	6.00	14.00
997-Walt Disney Presents-Tales of Texas John Slaughter (TV-Disney)-Photo-c	2.35	7.00	16.00
998-Ricky Nelson (TV)-Photo-c	7.00	21.00	50.00
999-Leave It to Beaver (TV)-Photo-c	6.00	18.00	42.00
1000-The Gray Ghost (Movie) (6-8/59)-Photo-c	3.00	9.00	21.00
1001-Lowell Thomas' High Adventure (TV) (8-10/59)-Photo-c	1.75	5.25	12.00
1002-Buffalo Bee (TV)	1.50	4.50	10.00
1003-Zorro (TV) (Disney)-Photo-c	3.50	10.50	24.00
1004-Colt .45 (TV) (6-8/59)-Photo-c	2.65	8.00	18.00
1005-Maverick (TV)-James Garner photo-c	3.50	10.50	24.00
1006-Hercules (Movie)-Buscema-a	6.00	18.00	42.00
1007-John Paul Jones (Movie)-Photo-c	2.00	6.00	14.00
1008-Beep Beep, the Road Runner (7-9/59)	1.30	4.00	9.00
1009-The Rifleman (No.1) (TV)-Photo-c	5.00	15.00	35.00
1010-Grandma Duck's Farm Friends (Disney)-by Carl Barks	5.00	15.00	35.00
1011-Buckskin (No.1)(TV)-Photo-c	2.65	8.00	18.00
1012-Last Train from Gun Hill (Movie) (7/59)-Photo-c	3.00	9.00	21.00
1013-Bat Masterson (No.1) (TV) (8/59)-Manning-a; Gene Barry photo-c	3.00	9.00	21.00
1014-The Lennon Sisters (TV)-Toth-a; photo-c	5.00	15.00	35.00
1015-Peanuts-Schulz-c	3.00	9.00	21.00
1016-Smokey the Bear Nature Stories	1.00	3.00	7.00
1017-Chilly Willy (Lantz)	.75	2.25	5.00
1018-Rio Bravo (Movie)(6/59)-John Wayne; Toth-a; John Wayne, Dean Martin & Ricky Nelson photo-c	8.00	24.00	56.00
1019-Wagon Train (TV)-Photo-c	2.65	8.00	18.00
1020-Jungle Jim-McWilliams-a	1.50	4.50	10.00
1021-Jace Pearson's Tales of the Texas Rangers (TV)-Photo-c	2.35	7.00	16.00
1022-Timmy	1.00	3.00	7.00
1023-Tales of Wells Fargo (TV)-Photo-c	2.35	7.00	16.00
1024-Darby O'Gill and the Little People (Disney-Movie)-Toth-a; Photo-c	5.00	15.00	35.00
1025-Vacation in Disneyland (8-10/59)-Carl Barks-a (Disney)	5.35	16.00	37.00
1026-Spin and Marty (TV)(Disney)-Mickey Mouse Club (9-11/59)-Photo-c	2.35	7.00	16.00
1027-The Texan (TV)-Photo-c	2.35	7.00	16.00
1028-Rawhide (No.1)(TV)-Clint Eastwood photo-c	7.00	21.00	48.00
1029-Boots and Saddles (9/59, TV)-Photo-c	2.35	7.00	16.00
1030-Spanky and Alfalfa, the Little Rascals (TV)	1.30	4.00	9.00
1031-Fury (TV)-Photo-c	2.65	8.00	18.00
1032-Elmer Fudd	.85	2.50	6.00
1033-Steve Canyon-not by Caniff; photo-c	2.65	8.00	18.00
1034-Nancy and Sluggo Summer Camp (9-11/59)	1.15	3.50	8.00
1035-Lawman (TV)-Photo-c	3.00	9.00	21.00
1036-The Big Circus (Movie)-Photo-c	1.75	5.25	12.00
1037-Zorro (Disney)(TV)-Tufts-a; Annette Funicello photo-c	5.00	15.00	35.00
1038-Ruff and Reddy (TV)(Hanna-Barbera)('59)	1.15	3.50	8.00
1039-Pluto (Disney) (11-1/60)	1.00	3.00	7.00
1040-Quick Draw McGraw (No.1)(TV)(Hanna-Barbera)(12-2/60)	2.00	6.00	14.00
1041-Sea Hunt (TV)-Toth-a; Lloyd Bridges photo-c	4.00	12.00	28.00
1042-The Three Chipmunks (Alvin, Simon & Theodore) (No.1)(TV)			

Four Color #962, © Warner Bros.

Four Color #1000, © DELL

Four Color #1040, © Hanna-Barbera

Four Color #1043, © Norman Maurer Prod.

Four Color #1084, © Warner Bros.

Four Color #1100, © WDC

FOUR COLOR (continued)	Good	Fine	Mint
(10-12/59)	.75	2.25	5.00
1043-The Three Stooges (No.1)-Photo-c	3.50	10.50	24.00
1044-Have Gun, Will Travel (TV)-Photo-c	3.00	9.00	21.00
1045-Restless Gun (TV)-Photo-c	3.00	9.00	21.00
1046-Beep Beep, the Road Runner (11-1/60)	1.30	4.00	9.00
1047-Gyro Gearloose (No.1)(Disney)-Barks c/a	5.75	17.25	40.00
1048-The Horse Soldiers (Movie) (John Wayne)-Sekowsky-a	7.00	21.00	50.00
1049-Don't Give Up the Ship (Movie) (8/59)-Jerry Lewis photo-c	2.35	7.00	16.00
1050-Huckleberry Hound (TV)(Hanna-Barbera)(10-12/59)	1.50	4.50	10.00
1051-Donald in Mathmagic Land (Disney-Movie)	1.75	5.25	12.00
1052-Ben-Hur (Movie) (11/59)-Manning-a	5.00	15.00	35.00
1053-Goofy (Disney) (11-1/60)	1.75	5.25	12.00
1054-Huckleberry Hound Winter Fun (TV)(Hanna-Barbera)(12/59)	1.50	4.50	10.00
1055-Daisy Duck's Diary (Disney)-by Carl Barks (11-1/60)	4.65	14.00	32.00
1056-Yellowstone Kelly (Movie)-Photo-c	2.00	6.00	14.00
1057-Mickey Mouse Album (Disney)	1.50	4.50	10.00
1058-Colt .45 (TV)-Photo-c	2.65	8.00	18.00
1059-Sugarfoot (TV)-Photo-c	3.65	11.00	25.00
1060-Journey to the Center of the Earth (Movie)-Photo-c	5.00	15.00	35.00
1061-Buffalo Bee (TV)	1.50	4.50	10.00
1062-Christmas Stories-(Walt Scott's Little People strip-r)	1.30	4.00	9.00
1063-Santa Claus Funnies	1.00	3.00	7.00
1064-Bugs Bunny's Merry Christmas (12/59)	1.15	3.50	8.00
1065-Frosty the Snowman	1.15	3.50	8.00
1066-77 Sunset Strip (No.1)(TV)-Toth-a (1-3/60)-Photo-c	4.35	13.00	30.00
1067-Yogi Bear (No.1)(TV)(Hanna-Barbera)	1.75	5.25	12.00
1068-Francis the Famous Talking Mule	.85	2.50	6.00
1069-The FBI Story (Movie)-Toth-a; photo-c	5.00	15.00	35.00
1070-Solomon and Sheba (Movie)-Sekowsky-a; photo-c	4.00	12.00	28.00
1071-The Real McCoys (No.1)(TV)-Photo-c	4.00	12.00	28.00
1072-Blythe (Marge's)	1.75	5.25	12.00
1073-Grandma Duck's Farm Friends-Barks c/a (Disney)	5.00	15.00	35.00
1074-Chilly Willy (Lantz)	.75	2.25	5.00
1075-Tales of Wells Fargo (TV)-Photo-c	2.35	7.00	16.00
1076-The Rebel (No.1)(TV)-Sekowsky-a; photo-c	4.00	12.00	28.00
1077-The Deputy (No.1)(TV)-Buscema-a; Henry Fonda photo-c	4.00	12.00	28.00
1078-The Three Stooges (2-4/60)-Photo-c	3.00	9.00	21.00
1079-The Little Rascals (TV)(Spanky & Alfalfa)	1.70	4.00	9.00
1080-Fury (TV) (2-4/60)-Photo-c	2.65	8.00	18.00
1081-Elmer Fudd	.85	2.50	6.00
1082-Spin and Marty (Disney)(TV)-Photo-c	2.35	7.00	16.00
1083-Men into Space (TV)-Anderson-a; photo-c	2.00	6.00	14.00
1084-Speedy Gonzales	1.15	3.50	8.00
1085-The Time Machine (H.G. Wells) (Movie) (3/60)-Alex Toth-a	6.00	18.00	42.00
1086-Lolly and Pepper	1.15	3.50	8.00
1087-Peter Gunn (TV)-Photo-c	3.00	9.00	21.00
1088-A Dog of Flanders (Movie)-Photo-c	1.75	5.25	12.00
1089-Restless Gun (TV)-Photo-c	3.00	9.00	21.00
1090-Francis the Famous Talking Mule	.85	2.50	6.00
1091-Jacky's Diary (4-6/60)	2.00	6.00	14.00

	Good	Fine	Mint
1092-Toby Tyler (Disney-Movie)-Photo-c	1.75	5.25	12.00
1093-MacKenzie's Raiders (Movie)-Photo-c	3.00	9.00	21.00
1094-Goofy (Disney)	1.75	5.25	12.00
1095-Gyro Gearloose (Disney)-Barks-c/a	4.65	14.00	32.00
1096-The Texan (TV)-Photo-c	2.35	7.00	16.00
1097-Rawhide (TV)-Manning-a; Clint Eastwood photo-c	5.00	15.00	35.00
1098-Sugarfoot (TV)-Photo-c	3.65	11.00	25.00
1099-Donald Duck Album (Disney) (5-7/60) - Barks-c	1.75	5.25	12.00
1100-Annette's Life Story (Disney-Movie)(5/60)-Photo-c	9.00	27.00	62.00
1101-Robert Louis Stevenson's Kidnapped (Disney-Movie) (5/60); photo-c	2.00	6.00	14.00
1102-Wanted: Dead or Alive (No.1)(TV) (5-7/60); Steve McQueen photo-c	4.00	12.00	28.00
1103-Leave It to Beaver (TV)-Photo-c	6.00	18.00	42.00
1104-Yogi Bear Goes to College (TV)(Hanna-Barbera)(6-8/60)	1.30	4.00	9.00
1105-Gale Storm (Oh! Susanna) (TV)-Toth-a; photo-c	5.00	15.00	35.00
1106-77 Sunset Strip (TV)(6-8/60)-Toth-a; photo-c	3.75	11.25	26.00
1107-Buckskin (TV)-Photo-c	2.65	8.00	18.00
1108-The Troubleshooters (TV)-Photo-c	2.00	6.00	14.00
1109-This Is Your Life, Donald Duck (Disney)(TV)(8-10/60)-Gyro flash-back to WDC&S 141. Origin Donald Duck (1st told)	4.00	12.00	28.00
1110-Bonanza (No.1) (TV) (6-8/60)-Photo-c	4.00	12.00	28.00
1111-Shotgun Slade (TV)	2.65	8.00	18.00
1112-Pixie and Dixie and Mr. Jinks (No.1)(TV)(Hanna-Barbera) (7-9/60)	1.75	5.25	12.00
1113-Tales of Wells Fargo (TV)-Photo-c	2.35	7.00	16.00
1114-Huckleberry Finn (Movie) (7/60)-Photo-c	2.00	6.00	14.00
1115-Ricky Nelson (TV)-Manning-a; photo-c	7.00	21.00	50.00
1116-Boots and Saddles (TV)(8/60)-Photo-c	2.35	7.00	16.00
1117-The Boy and the Pirates (Movie)-Photo-c	2.65	8.00	18.00
1118-The Sword and the Dragon (Movie) (6/60)-Photo-c	3.00	9.00	21.00
1119-Smokey the Bear Nature Stories	1.00	3.00	7.00
1120-Dinosaurus (Movie)-Painted-c	2.35	7.00	16.00
1121-Hercules Unchained (Movie)(8/60)-Crandall/Evans-a	4.00	12.00	28.00
1122-Chilly Willy (Lantz)	.75	2.25	5.00
1123-Tombstone Territory (TV)-Photo-c	3.00	9.00	21.00
1124-Whirlybirds (No.1) (TV)-Photo-c	3.00	9.00	21.00
1125-Laramie (No.1)(TV)-Photo-c	3.50	10.50	24.00
1126-Sundance (TV) (8-10/60)-Photo-c	3.50	10.50	24.00
1127-The Three Stooges-Photo-c	3.00	9.00	21.00
1128-Rocky and His Friends (No.1)(TV) (Jay Ward) (8-10/60)	4.00	12.00	28.00
1129-Pollyanna (Disney-Movie)-Photo-c	4.65	14.00	32.00
1130-The Deputy (TV)-Buscema-a; photo-c	3.50	10.50	24.00
1131-Elmer Fudd (9-11/60)	.85	2.50	6.00
1132-Space Mouse (Lantz)(8-10/60)	1.15	3.50	8.00
1133-Fury (TV)-Photo-c	2.65	8.00	18.00
1134-Real McCoys (TV)-Toth-a; photo-c	4.35	13.00	30.00
1135-M.G.M.'s Mouse Musketeers	.85	2.50	6.00
1136-Jungle Cat (Disney-Movie) (9-11/60)-Photo-c	2.65	8.00	18.00
1137-The Little Rascals (TV)	1.30	4.00	9.00
1138-The Rebel (TV)-Photo-c	3.50	10.50	24.00
1139-Spartacus (Movie) (11/60)-Buscema-a; photo-c	4.65	14.00	32.00
1140-Donald Duck Album (Disney)	1.75	5.25	12.00

FOUR COLOR (continued)

	Good	Fine	Mint
1141-Huckleberry Hound for President (TV)(Hanna-Barbera)(10/60)	1.50	4.50	10.00
1142-Johnny Ringo (TV)-Photo-c	3.00	9.00	21.00
1143-Pluto (Disney) (11-1/61)	1.00	3.00	7.00
1144-The Story of Ruth (Movie)-Photo-c	4.00	12.00	28.00
1145-The Lost World (Movie)-Gil Kane-a; photo-c	4.00	12.00	28.00
1146-Restless Gun (TV)-Photo-c	3.00	9.00	21.00
1147-Sugarfoot (TV)-Photo-c	3.65	11.00	25.00
1148-I Aim at the Stars-the Wernher Von Braun Story (Movie) (11-1/61)-Photo-c	1.75	5.25	12.00
1149-Goofy (Disney) (11-1/61)	1.75	5.25	12.00
1150-Daisy Duck's Diary (Disney) (12-1/61) by Carl Barks	4.65	14.00	32.00
1151-Mickey Mouse Album (Disney) (11-1/61)	1.50	4.50	10.00
1152-Rocky and His Friends (Jay Ward) (TV) (12-2/61)	3.65	11.00	25.00
1153-Frosty the Snowman	1.00	3.00	7.00
1154-Santa Claus Funnies	1.00	3.00	7.00
1155-North to Alaska (Movie) - J. Wayne-Photo-c	6.50	19.50	45.00
1156-Walt Disney Swiss Family Robinson (Movie) (12/60)-Photo-c	2.65	8.00	18.00
1157-Master of the World (Movie) (7/61)	2.65	8.00	18.00
1158-Three Worlds of Gulliver (2 issues with different covers) (Movie)-Photo-c	2.65	8.00	18.00
1159-77 Sunset Strip (TV)-Toth-a; photo-c	3.75	11.25	26.00
1160-Rawhide (TV)-Clint Eastwood photo-c	5.00	15.00	35.00
1161-Grandma Duck's Farm Friends (Disney) by Carl Barks (2-4/61)	5.00	15.00	35.00
1162-Yogi Bear Joins the Marines (TV)(Hanna-Barbera)(5-7/61)	1.30	4.00	9.00
1163-Daniel Boone (3-5/61); Marsh-a	2.00	6.00	14.00
1164-Wanted: Dead or Alive (TV); Steve McQueen photo-c	3.65	11.00	25.00
1165-Ellery Queen (No.1)(3-5/61)	3.50	10.50	24.00
1166-Rocky and His Friends (Jay Ward) (TV)	3.65	11.00	25.00
1167-Tales of Wells Fargo (TV)-Photo-c	2.35	7.00	16.00
1168-The Detectives (TV)-Photo-c	2.65	8.00	18.00
1169-New Adventures of Sherlock Holmes	6.85	20.50	48.00
1170-The Three Stooges-Photo-c	3.00	9.00	21.00
1171-Elmer Fudd	.85	2.50	6.00
1172-Fury (TV)-Photo-c	2.65	8.00	18.00
1173-The Twilight Zone (No.1) by Reed Crandall (TV) (5/61)	3.75	11.25	26.00
1174-The Little Rascals (TV)	1.30	4.00	9.00
1175-M.G.M.'s Mouse Musketeers (3-5/61)	.85	2.50	6.00
1176-Dondi (Movie)-Origin; photo-c	1.50	4.50	10.00
1177-Chilly Willy (Lantz)(4-6/61)	.75	2.25	5.00
1178-Ten Who Dared (Disney-Movie) (12/60)	2.00	6.00	14.00
1179-The Swamp Fox (TV)(Disney)-Photo-c	2.35	7.00	16.00
1180-The Danny Thomas Show (TV)-Toth-a; photo-c	5.00	15.00	35.00
1181-Texas John Slaughter (TV)(Disney)(4-6/61)-Photo-c	1.75	5.26	12.00
1182-Donald Duck Album (Disney) (5-7/61)	1.50	4.50	10.00
1183-101 Dalmatians (Disney-Movie) (3/61)	2.00	6.00	14.00
1184-Gyro Gearloose; Barks c/a (Disney) (5-7/61) Two variations exist	4.65	14.00	32.00
1185-Sweetie Pie	1.50	4.50	10.00
1186-Yak Yak (No.1) by Jack Davis (2 versions - one minus 3-pg. Davis-c/a)	3.50	10.50	24.00
1187-The Three Stooges (6-8/61)-Photo-c	3.00	9.00	21.00
1188-Atlantis, the Lost Continent (Movie) (5/61)-Photo-c	4.00	12.00	28.00

	Good	Fine	Mint
1189-Greyfriars Bobby (Disney-Movie, 11/61)-Photo-c	2.00	6.00	14.00
1190-Donald and the Wheel (Disney-Movie) (11/61); Barks-c	2.35	7.00	16.00
1191-Leave It to Beaver (TV)-Photo-c	6.00	18.00	42.00
1192-Ricky Nelson (TV)-Manning-a; photo-c	7.00	21.00	50.00
1193-The Real McCoys (TV)(6-8/61)-Photo-c	3.50	10.50	24.00
1194-Pepe (Movie) (4/61)-Photo-c	1.50	4.50	10.00
1195-National Velvet (No.1)(TV)-Photo-c	2.00	6.00	14.00
1196-Pixie and Dixie and Mr. Jinks (TV)(Hanna-Barbera)(7-9/61)	1.50	4.50	10.00
1197-The Aquanauts (TV)(5-7/61)-Photo-c	2.65	8.00	18.00
1198-Donald in Mathmagic Land - reprint of No. 1051 (Disney-Movie)	1.50	4.50	10.00
1199-The Absent-Minded Professor (Disney-Movie) (4/61)-Photo-c	2.00	6.00	14.00
1200-Hennessey (TV) (8-10/61)-Gil Kane-a; photo-c	2.65	8.00	18.00
1201-Goofy (Disney) (8-10/61)	1.75	5.25	12.00
1202-Rawhide (TV)-Clint Eastwood photo-c	5.00	15.00	35.00
1203-Pinocchio (Disney) (3/62)	1.75	5.25	12.00
1204-Scamp (Disney)	.75	2.25	5.00
1205-David and Goliath (Movie) (7/61)-Photo-c	2.35	7.00	16.00
1206-Lolly and Pepper (9-11/61)	1.15	3.50	8.00
1207-The Rebel (TV)-Sekowsky-a; photo-c	3.50	10.50	24.00
1208-Rocky and His Friends (Jay Ward) (TV)	3.65	11.00	25.00
1209-Sugarfoot (TV)-Photo-c	3.65	11.00	25.00
1210-The Parent Trap (Disney-Movie)(8/61)(Haley Mills photo-c)	4.65	14.00	32.00
1211-77 Sunset Strip (TV)-Manning-a; photo-c	3.00	9.00	21.00
1212-Chilly Willy (Lantz)(7-9/61)	.75	2.25	5.00
1213-Mysterious Island (Movie)-Photo-c	3.00	9.00	21.00
1214-Smokey the Bear	1.00	3.00	7.00
1215-Tales of Wells Fargo (TV) (10-12/61)-Photo-c	2.35	7.00	16.00
1216-Whirlybirds (TV)-Photo-c	2.65	8.00	18.00
1218-Fury (TV)-Photo-c	2.65	8.00	18.00
1219-The Detectives (TV)-Photo-c	2.35	7.00	16.00
1220-Gunslinger (TV)-Photo-c	2.35	7.00	16.00
1221-Bonanza (TV) (9-11/61)-Photo-c	3.50	10.50	24.00
1222-Elmer Fudd (9-11/61)	.85	2.50	6.00
1223-Laramie (TV)-Gil Kane-a; photo-c	3.00	9.00	21.00
1224-The Little Rascals (TV)(10-12/61)	1.30	4.00	9.00
1225-The Deputy (TV)-Photo-c	3.50	10.50	24.00
1226-Nikki, Wild Dog of the North (Disney-Movie) (9/61)-Photo-c	1.75	5.25	12.00
1227-Morgan the Pirate (Movie)-Photo-c	4.00	12.00	28.00
1229-Thief of Baghdad (Movie)-Evans-a; photo-c	6.00	18.00	42.00
1230-Voyage to the Bottom of the Sea (No.1)(Movie)-Photo-c	2.65	8.00	18.00
1231-Danger Man (TV)(9-11/61); Patrick McGoohan photo-c	3.50	10.50	24.00
1232-On the Double (Movie)	1.75	5.25	12.00
1233-Tammy Tell Me True (Movie) (1961)	3.00	9.00	21.00
1234-The Phantom Planet (Movie) (1961)	2.65	8.00	18.00
1235-Mister Magoo (12-2/62)	2.65	8.00	18.00
1235-Mister Magoo (3-5/65) 2nd printing - reprints of '61 issue	2.35	7.00	12.00
1236-King of Kings (Movie)-Photo-c	3.50	10.50	24.00
1237-The Untouchables (No.1)(TV)-not by Toth; photo-c	3.00	9.00	21.00
1238-Deputy Dawg (TV)	3.00	9.00	21.00

Four Color #1166, © Jay Ward Prod.

Four Color #1191, © Gomalco Prod.

Four Color #1211, © Warner Bros.

Four Color #1269, © CBS

Four Color #1295, © The Mr. Ed Co.

Four Favorites #15, © ACE

FOUR COLOR (continued)	Good	Fine	Mint
1239-Donald Duck Album (Disney) (10-12/61)-Barks-c	1.75	5.25	12.00
1240-The Detectives (TV)-Tufts-a; photo-c	2.35	7.00	16.00
1241-Sweetie Pie	1.50	4.50	10.00
1242-King Leonardo and His Short Subjects (No.1)(TV)(11-1/62)	2.65	8.00	18.00
1243-Ellery Queen	3.00	9.00	21.00
1244-Space Mouse (Lantz)(11-1/62)	1.15	3.50	8.00
1245-New Adventures of Sherlock Holmes	6.85	20.50	48.00
1246-Mickey Mouse Album (Disney)	1.50	4.50	10.00
1247-Daisy Duck's Diary (Disney) (12-2/62)	1.30	4.00	9.00
1248-Pluto (Disney)	1.00	3.00	7.00
1249-The Danny Thomas Show (TV)-Manning-a; photo-c	4.65	14.00	32.00
1250-The Four Horsemen of the Apocalypse (Movie)-Photo-c	3.50	10.50	24.00
1251-Everything's Ducky (Movie) (1961)	2.00	6.00	14.00
1252-The Andy Griffith Show (TV)-Photo-c; 1st show aired 10/3/60	4.50	13.50	31.50
1253-Space Man (No.1) (1-3/62)	2.35	7.00	16.00
1254-"Diver Dan" (TV) (2-4/62)-Photo-c	1.75	5.25	12.00
1255-The Wonders of Aladdin (Movie) (1961)	2.65	8.00	18.00
1256-Kona, Monarch of Monster Isle (No.1)(2-4/62)-Glanzman-a	2.00	6.00	14.00
1257-Car 54, Where Are You? (No.1) (TV) (3-5/62)-Photo-c	1.75	5.25	12.00
1258-The Frogmen (No.1)-Evans-a	2.65	8.00	18.00
1259-El Cid (Movie) (1961)-Photo-c	2.65	8.00	18.00
1260-The Horsemasters (TV, Movie - Disney) (12-2/62)-Annette Funicello photo-c	3.50	10.50	24.00
1261-Rawhide (TV)-Clint Eastwood photo-c	5.00	15.00	35.00
1262-The Rebel (TV)-Photo-c	3.50	10.50	24.00
1263-77 Sunset Strip (TV) (12-2/62)-Manning-a; photo-c	3.00	9.00	21.00
1264-Pixie and Dixie and Mr. Jinks (TV)(Hanna-Barbera)	1.50	4.50	10.00
1265-The Real McCoys (TV)-Photo-c	3.50	10.50	24.00
1266-M.G.M.'s Spike and Tyke (12-2/62)	.85	2.50	6.00
1267-Gyro Gearloose; Barks c/a, 4 pgs. (Disney) (12-2/62)	3.50	10.50	24.00
1268-Oswald the Rabbit (Lantz)	.75	2.25	5.00
1269-Rawhide (TV)-Clint Eastwood photo-c	5.00	15.00	35.00
1270-Bullwinkle and Rocky (No.1)(Jay Ward)(TV)(3-5/62)	3.00	9.00	21.00
1271-Yogi Bear Birthday Party (TV)(Hanna-Barbera)(11/61)	1.00	3.00	7.00
1272-Frosty the Snowman	1.00	3.00	7.00
1273-Hans Brinker (Disney-Movie)-Photo-c	2.00	6.00	14.00
1274-Santa Claus Funnies	1.00	3.00	7.00
1275-Rocky and His Friends (Jay Ward) (TV)	3.65	11.00	25.00
1276-Dondi	1.50	4.50	10.00
1278-King Leonardo and His Short Subjects (TV)	2.65	8.00	18.00
1279-Grandma Duck's Farm Friends (Disney)	1.30	4.00	9.00
1280-Hennessey (TV)-Photo-c	2.35	7.00	16.00
1281-Chilly Willy (Lantz)(4-6/62)	.75	2.25	5.00
1282-Babes in Toyland (Disney-Movie) (1/62); Annette Funicello photo-c	4.00	12.00	28.00
1283-Bonanza (TV) (2-4/62)-Photo-c	3.50	10.50	24.00
1284-Laramie (TV)-Heath-a; photo-c	3.00	9.00	21.00
1285-Leave It to Beaver (TV)-Photo-c	6.00	18.00	42.00
1286-The Untouchables (TV)-Photo-c	2.65	8.00	18.00
1287-Man from Wells Fargo (TV)-Photo-c	2.65	8.00	18.00
1288-The Twilight Zone (TV) (4/62)-Crandall/Evans c/a	3.15	9.50	22.00
1289-Ellery Queen	3.00	9.00	21.00
1290-M.G.M.'s Mouse Musketeers	.85	2.50	6.00
1291-77 Sunset Strip (TV)-Manning-a; photo-c	3.00	9.00	21.00
1293-Elmer Fudd (3-5/62)	.85	2.50	6.00
1294-Ripcord (TV)-Photo-c	2.35	7.00	16.00
1295-Mister Ed, the Talking Horse (No.1)(TV)(3-5/62)-Photo-c	2.00	6.00	14.00
1296-Fury (TV) (3-5/62)-Photo-c	2.65	8.00	18.00
1297-Spanky, Alfalfa and the Little Rascals (TV)	1.30	4.00	9.00
1298-The Hathaways (TV)-Photo-c	2.00	6.00	14.00
1299-Deputy Dawg (TV)	3.00	9.00	21.00
1300-The Comancheros (Movie) (1961)-John Wayne	7.00	21.00	50.00
1301-Adventures in Paradise (TV) (2-4/62)	1.75	5.25	12.00
1302-Johnny Jason, Teen Reporter (2-4/62)	1.00	3.00	7.00
1303-Lad: A Dog (Movie)-Photo-c	2.00	6.00	14.00
1304-Nellie the Nurse (3-5/62)-Stanley-a	4.65	14.00	32.00
1305-Mister Magoo (3-5/62)	2.65	8.00	18.00
1306-Target: the Corrupters (TV) (3-5/62)	2.15	6.50	15.00
1307-Margie (TV) (3-5/62)	2.00	6.00	14.00
1308-Tales of the Wizard of Oz (TV) (3-5/62)	4.00	12.00	28.00
1309-87th Precinct (TV) (4-6/62)-Krigstein-a; photo-c	5.00	15.00	35.00
1310-Huck and Yogi Winter Sports (TV)(Hanna-Barbera)(3/62)	1.30	4.00	9.00
1311-Rocky and His Friends (Jay Ward) (TV)	3.65	11.00	25.00
1312-National Velvet (TV)-Photo-c	1.75	5.25	12.00
1313-Moon Pilot (Disney-Movie)-Photo-c	2.00	6.00	14.00
1328-The Underwater City (Movie)-Evans-a (1961)-Photo-c	3.00	9.00	21.00
1330-Brain Boy (No.1)-Gil Kane-a	3.00	9.00	21.00
1332-Bachelor Father (TV)	3.00	9.00	21.00
1333-Short Ribs (4-6/62)	2.00	6.00	14.00
1335-Aggie Mack (4-6/62)	1.50	4.50	10.00
1336-On Stage - not by Leonard Starr	2.00	6.00	14.00
1337-Dr. Kildare (No.1) (TV)-Photo-c	2.35	7.00	16.00
1341-The Andy Griffith Show (TV) (4-6/62)-Photo-c	4.50	13.50	31.50
1348-Yak Yak (No.2)-Jack Davis c/a	3.00	9.00	21.00
1349-Yogi Bear Visits the U.N. (TV)(Hanna-Barbera)(1/62)	1.15	3.50	8.00
1350-Comanche (Disney-Movie)(1962)-Reprints 4-Color 966 (title change from "Tonka" to "Comanche")(4-6/62)-Sal Mineo photo-c	1.50	4.50	10.00
1354-Calvin & the Colonel (TV)(4-6/62)	2.00	6.00	14.00

NOTE: *Missing numbers probably do not exist.*

FOUR FAVORITES (Crime Must Pay the Penalty No. 33 on)
Sept, 1941 - No. 32, Dec, 1947
Ace Magazines

	Good	Fine	Mint
1-Vulcan, Lash Lightning, Magno the Magnetic Man & The Raven begin; Flag-c	31.00	92.00	215.00
2-The Black Ace only app.	15.00	45.00	105.00
3-Last Vulcan	13.50	40.50	95.00
4,5: 4-The Raven & Vulcan end; Unknown Soldier begins, ends No. 28. 5-Captain Courageous begins, ends No. 28; not in No. 6	12.00	36.00	84.00
6-8: 6-The Flag app.; Mr. Risk begins	9.50	28.50	66.00
9,11-Kurtzman-a; 11-L.B. Cole-a	13.00	40.00	90.00
10-Classic Kurtzman c/a	15.00	45.00	105.00
12-L.B. Cole-a	8.00	24.00	56.00
13-20: 18-Palais c/a	6.50	19.50	45.00
21-No Unknown Soldier; The Unknown app.	5.00	15.00	35.00
22-Captain Courageous drops costume	5.00	15.00	35.00
23-26: 23-Unknown Soldier drops costume. 26-Last Magno	5.00	15.00	35.00
27-32	4.00	12.00	28.00

FOUR HORSEMEN OF THE APOCALYPSE, THE (See 4-Color No. 1250)

FOUR MOST (. . . Boys No. 32-41)
Winter, 1941-42 - V8No.5(No. 36), 9-10/49; No. 37, 11-12/49 - No. 41, 6-7/50
Novelty Publications/Star Publications No. 37-on

	Good	Fine	Mint
V1No.1-The Target by Sid Greene, The Cadet & Dick Cole begin w/origins retold; produced by Funnies Inc.	30.00	90.00	210.00
2-Last Target	15.00	45.00	105.00
3-Flag-c	13.50	40.50	95.00
4-1pg. Dr. Seuss(signed)	11.00	33.00	76.00
V2No.1-4, V3No.1-4	2.15	6.50	15.00
V4No.1-4	1.75	5.25	12.00
V5No.1-The Target & Targeteers app.	1.50	4.50	10.00
2-5	1.50	4.50	10.00
V6No.1-White Rider & Super Horse begins	1.50	4.50	10.00
2-4,6	1.50	4.50	10.00
5-L. B. Cole-c	3.00	9.00	21.00
V7No.1,3,5, V8No.1	1.50	4.50	10.00
2,4,6-L. B. Cole-c. 6-Last Dick Cole	3.00	9.00	21.00
V8No.2,3,5-L. B. Cole c/a	4.00	12.00	28.00
4-L. B. Cole-a	2.35	7.00	16.00
37-41: 38,39-L.B. Cole-c. 38-J. Weismuller life story	2.35	7.00	16.00
Accepted Reprint 38-40 (nd); L.B. Cole-c	1.50	4.50	10.00

FOUR STAR BATTLE TALES
Feb-Mar, 1973 - No. 5, Nov-Dec, 1973
National Periodical Publications

	Good	Fine	Mint
1-All reprints		.30	.60
2-5: 5-Krigstein-a(r)		.25	.50

NOTE: ***Drucker** a-1,3-5r. **Heath** a-2r. **Kubert** a-4r; c-2.*

FOUR STAR SPECTACULAR
Mar-Apr, 1976 - No. 6, Jan-Feb, 1977
National Periodical Publications

	Good	Fine	Mint
1-Superboy, Wonder Woman reprints begin		.30	.60
2-6: 2-Infinity cover		.25	.50

NOTE: *All contain DC Superhero reprints. No. 1 has 68 pages; No. 2-6, 52 pages. No. 1,4-Hawkman app.; No. 2-Flash app.; No. 3-Green Lantern app; No. 4-Wonder Woman, Superboy app; No. 5-Gr. Arrow, Vigilante app; No. 6-Blackhawk G.A.-r.*

FOUR TEENERS (Formerly Crime Must Pay The Penalty?; Dotty No. 35 on)
April, 1948 (Teen-age comic)
A. A. Wyn

	Good	Fine	Mint
34	1.65	5.00	11.50

FOX AND THE CROW (Stanley & His Monster No. 109 on)
(See Comic Cavalcade & Real Screen Comics)
Dec-Jan, 1951-52 - No. 108, Feb-Mar, 1968
National Periodical Publications

	Good	Fine	Mint
1	37.00	110.00	260.00
2(Scarce)	18.50	55.00	130.00
3-5	12.00	36.00	84.00
6-10	8.00	24.00	56.00
11-20	5.00	15.00	35.00
21-40	3.50	10.50	24.00
41-60	2.00	6.00	14.00
61-80	1.30	4.00	9.00
81-94	1.00	3.00	6.00
95-Stanley & His Monster begins(origin)	1.15	3.50	8.00
96-99,101-108	.85	2.50	5.00
100	1.15	3.50	8.00

NOTE: *Many covers by **Mort Drucker**.*

FOX AND THE HOUND, THE (Disney)
Aug, 1981 - No. 3, Oct, 1981
Whitman Publishing Co.

	Good	Fine	Mint
11292 ('81)-Based on animated movie		.30	.60
2,3		.30	.60

FOX GIANTS
1944 - 1950 (132 - 196 pgs.)
Fox Features Syndicate

	Good	Fine	Mint
Album of Crime nn(1949, 132p)	20.00	60.00	140.00
Album of Love nn(1949, 132p)	15.00	45.00	105.00
All Famous Crime Stories nn('49, 132p)	20.00	60.00	140.00
All Good Comics 1(1944, 132p)(R.W. Voigt)-The Bouncer, Purple Tigress, Puppeteer, Green Mask; Infinity-c	15.00	45.00	105.00
All Great nn(1944, 132p)-Capt. Jack Terry, Rick Evans, Jaguar Man	15.00	45.00	105.00
All Great nn(1945, 132p)-Green Mask, Bouncer, Puppeteer, Rick Evans, Rocket Kelly	18.00	54.00	126.00
All-Great Confessions nn(1949, 132p)	15.00	45.00	105.00
All Great Crime Stories nn('49, 132p)	20.00	60.00	140.00
All Great Jungle Adventures nn('49, 132p)	20.00	60.00	140.00
All Real Confession Mag. 3 (3/49, 132p)	15.00	45.00	105.00
All Real Confession Mag. 4 (4/49, 132p)	15.00	45.00	105.00
All Your Comics 1(1944, 132p)-The Puppeteer, Red Robbins, & Merciless the Sorcerer	15.00	45.00	105.00
Almanac Of Crime nn(1948, 148p)	22.00	66.00	155.00
Almanac Of Crime 1(1950, 132p)	22.00	66.00	155.00
Book Of Love nn(1950, 132p)	15.00	45.00	105.00
Burning Romances 1(1949, 132p)	18.00	54.00	126.00
Crimes Incorporated nn(1950, 132p)	20.00	60.00	140.00
Daring Love Stories nn(1950, 132p)	15.00	45.00	105.00
Everybody's Comics 1(1944, 196p)-The Green Mask, The Puppeteer, The Bouncer ; (50¢)	18.00	54.00	126.00
Everybody's Comics 1(1946, 196p)-Green Lama, The Puppeteer	15.00	45.00	105.00
Everybody's Comics 1(1946, 196p)-Same as '45 Ribtickler	12.00	36.00	84.00
Everybody's Comics nn(1947, 132p)-Jo-Jo, Purple Tigress, Cosmo Cat, Bronze Man	15.00	45.00	105.00
Exciting Romance Stories nn('49, 132p)	15.00	45.00	105.00
Intimate Confessions nn(1950, 132p)	15.00	45.00	105.00
Journal Of Crime nn(1949, 132p)	20.00	60.00	140.00
Love Problems nn(1949, 132p)	15.00	45.00	105.00
Love Thrills nn(1950, 132p)	15.00	45.00	105.00
Revealing Love Stories nn(1950, 132p)	15.00	45.00	105.00
Ribtickler nn(1945, 196p, 50¢)-Chicago Nite Life News; Marvel Mutt, Cosmo Cat, Flash Rabbit, The Nebbs app.	15.00	45.00	105.00
Romantic Thrills nn(1950, 132p)	15.00	45.00	105.00
Secret Love nn(1949, 132p)	15.00	45.00	105.00
Secret Love Stories nn(1949, 132p)	15.00	45.00	105.00
Strange Love nn(1950, 132p)-Photo-c	20.00	60.00	140.00
Sweetheart Scandals nn(1950, 132p)	15.00	45.00	105.00
Teen-Age Love nn(1950, 132p)	15.00	45.00	105.00
Throbbing Love nn(1950, 132p)-Photo-c	20.00	60.00	140.00
Truth About Crime nn(1949, 132p)	20.00	60.00	140.00
Variety Comics 1(1946, 132p)-Blue Beetle, Jungle Jo	15.00	45.00	105.00
Variety Comics nn(1950, 132p)	15.00	45.00	105.00
Western Roundup nn(1950, 132p)-Hoot Gibson	15.00	45.00	105.00

Note: Each of the above usually contain four remaindered Fox books minus covers. Since these missing covers often had the first page of the first story, most Giants therefore are incomplete. Approximate

Four Most #4, © NOVP

Fox & the Crow #1, © DC

Fox Giants (Crimes Inc.) nn, © FOX

Foxy Fagan #4, © Dearfield

Fractured Fairy Tales #1, © Jay Ward Prod.

Frankenstein Comics #3, © PRIZE

FOX GIANTS (continued)
values are listed. Books with appearances of Phantom Lady, Rulah, Jo-Jo, etc. could bring more.

FOXHOLE
9-10/54 - No. 4, 3-4/55; No. 5, 7/55 - No. 7, 3/56
Mainline/Charlton Comics No. 5 on

	Good	Fine	Mint
1-Kirby-c	4.35	13.00	30.00
2-Kirby c/a(2)	4.35	13.00	30.00
3,5-Kirby-c only	2.00	6.00	14.00
4,7	.85	2.50	6.00
6-Kirby c/a(2)	3.85	11.50	27.00
Super Reprints No. 10-12,15-18	.30	.80	1.60

NOTE: ***Kirby*** *a(r)-Super No. 11,12,18.* ***Powell*** *a(r)-Super No. 15,16.*

FOXY FAGAN
Dec, 1946 - No. 7, Summer, 1948
Dearfield Publishing Co.

	Good	Fine	Mint
1-Foxy Fagan & Little Buck begin	4.00	12.00	28.00
2	2.00	6.00	14.00
3-7	1.65	5.00	11.50

FOXY GRANDPA
1901 - 1916 (Hardcover; strip reprints)
N. Y. Herald/Frederick A. Stokes Co./M. A. Donahue & Co./Bunny Publ.(L. R. Hammersly Co.)

	Good	Fine	Mint
1901-9x15" in color-N. Y. Herald	23.00	70.00	164.00
1902-"Latest Larks of. . . ," 32 pgs. in color, 9½x15½"	23.00	70.00	160.00
1902-"The Many Advs. of. . . , 9x15", 148pgs. in color (Hammersly)	30.00	90.00	210.00
1903-"Latest Advs.," 9x15", 24 pgs. in color, Hammersly Co.	23.00	70.00	160.00
1903-". . . 's New Advs.," 10x15, 32 pgs. in color, Stokes	23.00	70.00	160.00
1904-"Up to Date," 10x15", 28 pgs. in color, Stokes	23.00	70.00	160.00
1905-"& Flip Flaps," 9½x15½", 52 pgs., in color	23.00	70.00	160.00
1905-"The Latest Advs. of," 9x15", 28 pgs., in color, M.A. Donohue Co.; re-issue of 1902 ish	13.00	40.00	90.00
1905-"Merry Pranks of," 9½x15½", 52 pgs. in color, Donahue	13.00	40.00	90.00
1905-"Latest Larks of," 9½x15½", 52 pgs. in color, Donahue; re-issue of 1902 ish	13.00	40.00	90.00
1906-"Frolics," 10x15", 30 pgs. in color, Stokes	13.00	40.00	90.00
1907	11.00	33.00	76.00
1908?-"Triumphs," 10x15"	11.00	33.00	76.00
1908?-"& Little Brother," 10x15"	11.00	33.00	76.00
1911-"Latest Tricks," r-1910,1911 Sundays in color-Stokes Co.	12.00	36.00	84.00
1914-9½x15½", 24 pgs., 6 color cartoons/page, Bunny Publ.	8.00	24.00	56.00
1916-"Merry Book," 10x15", 30 pgs. in color, Stokes	8.00	24.00	56.00

FOXY GRANDPA SPARKLETS SERIES
1908 (6½x7¾"; 24 pgs. in color)
M. A. Donahue & Co.

	Good	Fine	Mint
". . . Rides the Goat," ". . . & His Boys," ". . . Playing Ball," ". . . Fun on the Farm," ". . . Fancy Shooting," ". . . Show the Boys Up Sports," ". . . Plays Santa Claus" each. . . .	13.00	40.00	90.00
900-. . . Playing Ball; Bunny illos; 8 pgs., linen like pgs., no date	6.00	18.00	42.00

FRACTURED FAIRY TALES (TV)
October, 1962
Gold Key

	Good	Fine	Mint
1 (10022-210)	3.00	9.00	21.00

FRAGGLE ROCK
April, 1985 - No. 8, Sept, 1986
Star Comics (Marvel)

	Good	Fine	Mint
1		.40	.80
2-8		.35	.70

FRANCIS, BROTHER OF THE UNIVERSE
1980 (75 cents) (52 pgs.) (One Shot)
Marvel Comics Group

	Good	Fine	Mint
Buscema/Marie Severin-a; story of Francis Bernadone celebrating his 800th birthday in 1982		.30	.60

FRANCIS THE FAMOUS TALKING MULE (All based on movie) (See 4-Color No. 335, 465, 501, 547, 579, 621, 655, 698, 710, 745, 810, 863, 906, 953, 991, 1068, 1090)

FRANK BUCK (Formerly My True Love)
No. 70, May, 1950 - No. 3, Sept, 1950
Fox Features Syndicate

	Good	Fine	Mint
70-Wood a(p)(3)	7.00	21.00	50.00
71-Wood a? (9 pgs.), 3	4.00	12.00	28.00

FRANKENSTEIN (See Movie Classics)
Aug-Oct, 1964; No. 2, Sept, 1966 - No. 4, Mar, 1967
Dell Publishing Co.

	Good	Fine	Mint
1(12-283-410)(1964)	.70	2.00	4.00
2-Intro. & origin super-hero character (9/66)	.35	1.00	2.00
3,4		.50	1.00

FRANKENSTEIN (The Monster of. . .)
Jan, 1973 - No. 18, Sept, 1975
Marvel Comics Group

	Good	Fine	Mint
1-Ploog-a begins		.30	.60
2-18: 8,9-Dracula app.		.25	.50
Power Record giveaway-(12¼x12¼"; 16 pgs.); Adams, Ploog-a		.60	1.20

NOTE: ***Adkins*** *c-17i.* ***Buscema*** *a-7-10p.* ***Ditko*** *a-12r.* ***G. Kane*** *c-15p.* ***Orlando*** *a-8r.* ***Ploog*** *a-1-3, 4p, 5p, 6; c-1-6.* ***Wrightson*** *c-18i.*

FRANKENSTEIN COMICS (Also See Prize Comics)
Sum, 1945 - V5/5(No.33), Oct-Nov, 1954
Prize Publications (Crestwood/Feature)

	Good	Fine	Mint
1-Frankenstein begins by Dick Briefer (origin); Frank Sinatra parody	22.00	65.00	154.00
2	11.00	33.00	76.00
3-5	9.50	28.50	65.00
6-10: 7-S&K a(r)/Headline Comics. 8(7-8/47)-Superman satire	8.00	24.00	56.00
11-17(1-2/49)-11-Boris Karloff parody c/story. 17-Last humor issue	5.50	16.50	38.00
18(3/52)-New origin, horror series begins	7.00	21.00	50.00
19,20(V3No.4, 8-9/52)	5.00	15.00	35.00
21(V3/5), 22(V3/6)	5.00	15.00	35.00
23(V4/1)-No.28(V4/6)	4.35	13.00	30.00
29(V5/1)-No.33(V5/5)	4.35	13.00	30.00

NOTE: ***Meskin*** *a-21, 29.*

FRANKENSTEIN, JR. (. . . & the Impossibles) (TV)
January, 1967 (Hanna-Barbera)
Gold Key

	Good	Fine	Mint
1	1.35	4.00	8.00

FRANKIE COMICS (. . . & Lana No. 13-15) (Formerly Movie Tunes; becomes Frankie Fuddle No. 16 on)
No. 4, Wint, 1946-47 - No. 15, June, 1949
Marvel Comics (MgPC)

FRANKIE COMICS (continued)	Good	Fine	Mint
4-Mitzi, Margie, Daisy app.	3.50	10.50	24.00
5-8	1.85	5.50	13.00
9-Transvestite story	2.50	7.50	17.00
10-15: 13-Anti-Wertham editorial	1.50	4.50	10.00

FRANKIE DOODLE (See Single Series No. 7 and Sparkler No. 2)

FRANKIE FUDDLE (Formerly Frankie & Lana)
No. 16, Aug, 1949 - No. 17, Nov, 1949
Marvel Comics

	Good	Fine	Mint
16,17	1.50	4.50	10.00

FRANK LUTHER'S SILLY PILLY COMICS (See Jingle Dingle. . .)
1950 (10 cents)
Children's Comics

	Good	Fine	Mint
1-Characters from radio, records, & TV	2.15	6.50	15.00

FRANK MERRIWELL AT YALE (Speed Demons No. 5 on?)
June, 1955 - No. 4, Jan, 1956
Charlton Comics

	Good	Fine	Mint
1	1.65	5.00	11.50
2-4	.85	2.50	6.00

FRANTIC (Magazine) (See Zany & Ratfink)
Oct, 1958 - V2No.2, April, 1959 (Satire)
Pierce Publishing Co.

	Good	Fine	Mint
V1No.1,2	.70	2.00	4.00
V2No.1,2	.35	1.00	2.00

FRECKLES AND HIS FRIENDS (See Famous Comics Cartoon Book & Honeybee Birdwhistle. . .)

FRECKLES AND HIS FRIENDS
No. 5, 11/47 - No. 12, 8/49; 11/55 - No. 4, 6/56
Standard Comics/Argo

	Good	Fine	Mint
5-Reprints	3.50	10.50	24.00
6-12-Reprints; 11-Lingerie panels	1.85	5.50	13.00

NOTE: *Some copies of No. 8 & 9 contain a printing oddity. The negatives were elongated in the engraving process, probably to conform to page dimensions on the filler pages. Those pages only look normal when viewed at a 45 degree angle.*

	Good	Fine	Mint
1(Argo,'55)-Reprints	2.15	6.50	15.00
2-4	1.30	4.00	9.00

FREDDY (Formerly My Little Margie's Boy Friends)
June, 1958 - No. 47, Feb, 1965 (Also see Blue Bird)
Charlton Comics

	Good	Fine	Mint
V2No.12	.85	2.50	5.00
13-15	.40	1.25	2.50
16-47	.30	.80	1.60
Schiff's Shoes Presents. . . No. 1(1959)-Giveaway		.60	1.20

FREDDY
May-July, 1963 - No. 3, Oct-Dec, 1964
Dell Publishing Co.

	Good	Fine	Mint
1-3	.55	1.65	4.00

FREE COMICS TO YOU FROM. . . (name of shoe store) (Has clown on cover & another with a rabbit) (Like comics from Weather Bird & Edward's Shoes)
Circa 1956, 1960-61
Shoe Store Giveaway

Contains a comic bound with new cover - several combinations possible; Some Harvey titles known. contents determines price.

FREEDOM AGENT (Also see John Steele)
April, 1963
Gold Key

	Good	Fine	Mint
1 (10054-304)	1.00	3.00	7.00

FREEDOM FIGHTERS (See Justice League No. 107,108)
Mar-Apr, 1976 - No. 15, July-Aug, 1978
National Periodical Publications/DC Comics

	Good	Fine	Mint
1-Uncle Sam, The Ray, Black Condor, Doll Man, Human Bomb, & Phantom Lady begin		.35	.70
2-15: 7-1st app. Crusaders. 10-Origin Doll Man. 11-Origin The Ray. 12-Origin Firebrand. 13-Origin Black Condor. 15-Origin Phantom Lady		.25	.50

NOTE: ***Buckler** c-5-11p, 13p, 14p.*

FREEDOM TRAIN
1948 (Giveaway)
Street & Smith Publ.

	Good	Fine	Mint
Powell-c	1.70	5.00	10.00

FRENZY (Magazine) (Satire)
April, 1958 - No. 6, March, 1959
Picture Magazine

	Good	Fine	Mint
1	.70	2.00	4.00
2-6	.35	1.00	2.00

FRIDAY FOSTER
October, 1972
Dell Publishing Co.

	Good	Fine	Mint
1	.85	2.50	5.00

FRIENDLY GHOST, CASPER, THE (See Casper. . .)
8/58 - No. 224, 10/82; No. 225, 10/86 - Present
Harvey Publications

	Good	Fine	Mint
1-Infinity-c	13.00	40.00	90.00
2	6.45	20.00	45.00
3-10: 6-X-Mas-c	4.00	12.00	28.00
11-20: 18-X-Mas-c	2.65	8.00	18.00
21-30	1.20	3.50	8.00
31-50	.70	2.00	5.00
51-100: 54-X-Mas-c	.55	1.60	3.20
101-150		.60	1.20
151-230: 173,179,185-Cub Scout Specials		.35	.70
American Dental Assoc. giveaway-Small size (1967, 16 pgs.)	.50	1.50	3.00

FRIGHT
June, 1975 (August on inside)
Atlas/Seaboard Periodicals

	Good	Fine	Mint
1-Origin The Son of Dracula; Frank Thorne c/a		.40	.80

FRISKY ANIMALS (Formerly Frisky Fables)
No. 44, Jan, 1951 - No. 58, 1954
Star Publications

	Good	Fine	Mint
44-Super Cat	5.00	15.00	35.00
45-Classic L. B. Cole-c	8.00	24.00	56.00
46-51,53-58-Super Cat	4.35	13.00	30.00
52-L. B. Cole c/a, 3pgs.	5.00	15.00	35.00

NOTE: *All have **L. B. Cole**-c. No. 47-No Super Cat. **Disbrow** a-49,52. **Fago** a-51.*

FRISKY ANIMALS ON PARADE (Formerly Parade; becomes Superspook)
Sept, 1957 - No. 3, Dec/Jan, 1957-1958
Ajax-Farrell Publ. (Four Star Comic Corp.)

	Good	Fine	Mint
1-L. B. Cole-c	3.75	11.25	26.00
2-No L. B. Cole-c	1.85	5.50	13.00
3-L. B. Cole-c	2.65	8.00	18.00

Freedom Agent #1, © GK

Friendly Ghost, Casper #3, © Paramount

Frisky Animals #50, © STAR

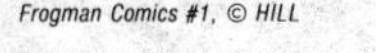
Frogman Comics #1, © HILL

Frontier Romances #1, © AVON

Frontline Combat #9, © WMG

FRISKY FABLES (Frisky Animals No. 44 on)
Spring, 1945 - No. 44, Oct-Nov, 1949
Premium Group/Novelty Publ.

	Good	Fine	Mint
V1/1-Al Fago c/a	4.00	12.00	28.00
2,3(1945)	2.00	6.00	14.00
4-7(1946)	1.30	4.00	9.00
V2/1-9,11,12(1947)	1.00	3.00	7.00
10-Christmas-c	1.15	3.50	8.00
V3/1-12(1948): 4-Flag-c. 9-Infinity-c	.85	2.50	6.00
V4/1-7	.85	2.50	6.00
36-44(V4/8-12, V5/1-4)-L. B. Cole-c; 40-X-mas-c	4.65	14.00	32.00
Accepted Reprint No. 43 (nd); L.B. Cole-c	1.70	5.00	12.00

FRITZI RITZ (See Single Series No. 5,1(reprint), United Comics and Comics on Parade)

FRITZI RITZ
Fall/48 - No. 42, 1/55; No. 43, 1955 - No. 55, 9-11/57; No. 56, 12-2/57-58 - No. 59, 9-11/58
United Features Synd./St. John No. 43-55/Dell No. 56 on

	Good	Fine	Mint
nn(1948)-Special Fall ish.	4.00	12.00	28.00
2	2.00	6.00	14.00
3-5	1.65	5.00	11.50
6-10: 6-Abbie & Slats app. 7-Lingerie panel	1.30	4.00	9.00
11-19,21-28	1.15	3.50	8.00
20-Strange As It Seems; Russell Patterson Cheesecake-a; negligee panel	1.50	4.50	10.00
29-Five pg. Abbie & Slats; 1 pg. Mamie by Russell Patterson	1.15	3.50	8.00
30-59: 36-1 pg. Mamie by Patterson. 43-Peanuts by Schulz	.85	2.50	6.00

NOTE: *Abbie & Slats in No. 7, 8, 11, 18, 20, 27, 29. Li'l Abner in No. 35, 36.*

FROGMAN COMICS
Jan-Feb, 1952 - No. 11, May, 1953
Hillman Periodicals

	Good	Fine	Mint
1	3.00	9.00	21.00
2	1.65	5.00	11.50
3,4,6-11: 4-Meskin-a	1.30	4.00	9.00
5-Krigstein, Torres-a	3.00	9.00	21.00

FROGMEN, THE
No. 1258, Feb-Apr, 1962 - No. 11, Nov-Jan/1964-65
Dell Publishing Co.

	Good	Fine	Mint
4-Color 1258-Evans-a	2.65	8.00	18.00
2,3-Evans-a; part Frazetta inks in No. 2,3	3.50	10.50	24.00
4,6-11	1.00	3.00	7.00
5-Toth-a	2.00	6.00	14.00

FROM BEYOND THE UNKNOWN
10-11/69 - No.25, 11-12/73 (No.7-11: 64 pgs.; No.12-17: 52 pgs.)
National Periodical Publications

	Good	Fine	Mint
1		.30	.60
2-10: 7-Intro. Col. Glenn Merrit		.25	.50
11-25: Star Rovers reprints begin No. 18,19. Space Museum in No. 23-25		.25	.50

NOTE: ***Adams** c-3, 6, 8, 9. **Anderson** c-2, 4, 5, 10, 11i, 15-17, 22; reprints-3, 4, 6-8, 10, 11, 13-16, 24, 25. **Infantino** reprints-1-5, 7-19, 23-25; c-11p. **Kaluta** c-18,19. **Kubert** c-1,7, 12-14. **Toth** a-2r. **Wood** a-13i.*

FROM HERE TO INSANITY (Satire) (Eh No. 1-7)
(See Frantic & Frenzy)
No. 8, Feb, 1955 - V3No.1, 1956
Charlton Comics

	Good	Fine	Mint
8	2.65	8.00	18.00
9	1.85	5.50	13.00
10-Ditko-c/a, 3 pgs.	5.00	15.00	35.00
11,12-All Kirby except 4 pgs.	6.00	18.00	42.00
V3No.1(1956)-Ward-c/a(2)(signed McCartney); 5 pgs. Wolverton; 3 pgs. Ditko; magazine format	13.50	40.50	95.00

FRONTIER DAYS
1956 (Giveaway)
Robin Hood Shoe Store (Brown Shoe)

	Good	Fine	Mint
1	1.35	4.00	8.00

FRONTIER DOCTOR (See 4-Color No. 877)

FRONTIER FIGHTERS
Sept-Oct, 1955 - No. 8, Nov-Dec, 1956
National Periodical Publications

	Good	Fine	Mint
1-Davy Crockett, Buffalo Bill by Kubert, Kit Carson begin (Scarce)	16.00	48.00	110.00
2	9.00	27.00	62.00
3-8	7.00	21.00	50.00

NOTE: *Buffalo Bill by **Kubert** in all.*

FRONTIER ROMANCES
Nov-Dec, 1949 - No. 2, Jan-Feb, 1950
Avon Periodicals/I. W.

	Good	Fine	Mint
1-Used in **SOTI**, pg. 180(General reference) & illo. ''Erotic spanking in a western comic book;''	33.00	100.00	230.00
2 (Scarce)	16.00	48.00	110.00
1-I.W.(reprints Avon's No. 1)	2.75	8.00	16.00
I.W. Reprint No. 9	1.35	4.00	8.00

FRONTIER SCOUT: DAN'L BOONE (Formerly Death Valley; The Masked Raider No. 14 on)
No. 10, Jan, 1956 - No. 13, Aug, 1956; No. 14, March, 1965
Charlton Comics

	Good	Fine	Mint
10	1.75	5.25	12.00
11-13(1956)	1.00	3.00	7.00
V2No.14(3/65)	.35	1.00	2.00

FRONTIER TRAIL (The Rider No. 1-5)
No. 6, May, 1958
Ajax/Farrell Publ.

	Good	Fine	Mint
6	1.00	3.00	7.00

FRONTIER WESTERN
Feb, 1956 - No. 10, Aug, 1957
Atlas Comics (PrPl)

	Good	Fine	Mint
1	4.00	12.00	28.00
2,3,6-Williamson-a, 4 pgs. each	4.35	13.00	30.00
4,7,9,10: 10-Check-a	1.65	5.00	11.50
5-Crandall, Baker, Wildey, Davis-a; Williamson text illos	3.35	10.00	23.00
8-Crandall, Morrow, & Wildey-a	1.85	5.50	13.00

NOTE: ***Drucker** a-3,4. **Heath** c-5. **Severin** c-6,8,10. Ringo Kid in No. 4.*

FRONTLINE COMBAT
July-Aug, 1951 - No. 15, Jan, 1954
E. C. Comics

	Good	Fine	Mint
1	33.00	100.00	230.00
2	22.00	65.00	155.00
3	16.00	48.00	110.00
4-Used in **SOTI**, pg. 257; contains ''Airburst'' by Kurtzman which is his personal all-time favorite story	13.00	40.00	90.00
5	12.00	36.00	80.00
6-10	9.00	27.00	60.00
11-15	7.00	21.00	48.00

NOTE: ***Davis** a-in all; c-11,12. **Evans** a-10-15. **Heath** a-1. **Kubert** a-14. **Kurtzman** a-1-5; c-1-9. **Severin** a-5-7, 9, 13, 15. **Severin/Elder** a-2-11; c-10. **Toth** a-8, 12. **Wood** a-1-4, 6-10, 12-15; c-13-15. Special issues: No. 7 (Iwo Jima), No. 9 (Civil War), No. 12 (Air Force). (Canadian reprints known; see Table of Contents.)*

FRONT PAGE COMIC BOOK
1945
Front Page Comics (Harvey)

FRONT PAGE COMIC BOOK (continued) — Good / Fine / Mint

1-Kubert-a; intro. & 1st app. Man in Black by Powell; Fuje-c — 11.50 34.50 80.00

FROST AND FIRE (See DC Science Fic. Graphic Novel)

FROSTY THE SNOWMAN
No. 359, Nov, 1951 - No. 1272, Dec-Feb?/1961-62
Dell Publishing Co.

4-Color 359 — 2.00 6.00 14.00
4-Color 435 — 1.50 4.50 10.00
4-Color 514,601,661 — 1.30 4.00 9.00
4-Color 748,861,950,1065 — 1.15 3.50 8.00
4-Color 1153,1272 — 1.00 3.00 7.00

FRUITMAN SPECIAL
Dec, 1969 (68 pages)
Harvey Publications

1-Funny super hero — 1.00 3.00 6.00

F-TROOP (TV)
Aug, 1966 - No. 7, Aug, 1967 (All have photo-c)
Dell Publishing Co.

1 — 2.00 6.00 14.00
2-7 — 1.15 3.50 8.00

FUGITIVES FROM JUSTICE
Feb, 1952 - No. 5, Oct, 1952
St. John Publishing Co.

1 — 4.35 13.00 30.00
2-Matt Baker-a; Vic Flint strip reprints begin, end No. 5 — 4.35 13.00 30.00
3-Reprints panel from Authentic Police Cases that was used in **SOTI** with changes; Tuska-a — 8.00 24.00 56.00
4 — 2.35 7.00 16.00
5-Bondage-c — 3.35 10.00 23.00

FUGITOID
Jan, 1986 (40 pg. One Shot; B&W)
Mirage Studios

1-Ties into Teenage Mutant Ninja Turtles No. 5 — .50 1.50 3.00

FULL COLOR COMICS
1946
Fox Features Syndicate

nn — 4.00 12.00 28.00

FULL OF FUN
Aug, 1957 - No. 2, Nov, 1957; 1964
Red Top (Decker Publ.)(Farrell)/I. W. Enterprises

1(1957)-Dave Berg-a — 1.50 4.50 10.00
2-Reprints Bingo, the Monkey Doodle Boy — .85 2.50 6.00
8-I.W. Reprint('64) — .30 .80 1.60

FUN AT CHRISTMAS (See March of Comics No. 138)

FUN CLUB COMICS (See Interstate Theatres. . .)

FUN COMICS (Mighty Bear No. 13 on)
Jan, 1953 - No. 12, Oct, 1953
Star Publications

9(Giant)-L. B. Cole-c — 5.00 15.00 35.00
10-12-L. B. Cole-c — 3.35 10.00 23.00

FUN COMICS (See Bill Black's. . .)

FUNDAY FUNNIES (See Famous TV. . ., and Harvey Hits No. 35,40)

FUN-IN (TV)(Hanna-Barbera)
Feb, 1970 - No. 10, Jan, 1972; No. 11, 4/74 - No. 15, 12/74
Gold Key — Good / Fine / Mint

1-Dastardly & Muttley in Their Flying Machines; Perils of Penelope Pitstop in 1-4; It's the Wolf in all — .85 2.50 5.00
2-4,6-Cattanooga Cats in 2-4 — .50 1.50 3.00
5,7-Motormouse & Autocat, Dastardly & Muttley in both; It's the Wolf in No. 7 — .40 1.20 2.40
8,10-The Harlem Globetrotters, Dastardly & Muttley in No. 10 — .40 1.20 2.40
9-Where's Huddles?, Dastardly & Muttley, Motormouse & Autocat app. — .40 1.20 2.40
11-15: 11-Butch Cassidy. 12,15-Speed Buggy. 13-Hair Bear Bunch. 14-Inch High Private Eye — .25 .75 1.50

FUNKY PHANTOM, THE (TV)
Mar, 1972 - No. 13, Mar, 1975 (Hanna-Barbera)
Gold Key

1 — .85 2.50 5.00
2-13 — .40 1.20 2.40

FUNLAND
No date (25 cents)
Ziff-Davis (Approved Comics)

Contains games, puzzles, etc. — 4.00 12.00 28.00

FUNLAND COMICS
1945
Croyden Publishers

1 — 3.00 9.00 21.00

FUNNIES, THE (Also see Comic Cuts)
1929 - No. 36, 10/18/30 (10 cents; 5 cents No.22 on) (16 pgs.)
Full tabloid size in color; not reprints; published every Saturday
Dell Publishing Co.

1-My Big Brudder, Johnathan, Jazzbo & Jim, Foxy Grandpa, Sniffy, Jimmy Jams & other strips begin; first four-color comic newsstand publication; also contains magic, puzzles & stories — 24.00 72.00 168.00
2-21 (1930, 30 cents) — 8.50 25.50 60.00
22(nn-7/12/30-5 cents) — 6.50 19.50 45.00
23(nn-7/19/30-5 cents), 24(nn-7/26/30-5 cents), 25(nn-8/2/30), 26(nn-8/9/30), 27(nn-8/16/30), 28(nn-8/23/30), 29(nn-8/30/30), 30(nn-9/6/30), 31(nn-9/13/30), 32(nn-9/20/30), 33(nn-9/27/30), 34(nn-10/4/30), 35(nn-10/11/30), 36(nn, no date-10/18/30) each. . . . — 6.50 19.50 45.00

FUNNIES, THE (New Funnies No. 65 on)
Oct, 1936 - No. 64, May, 1942
Dell Publishing Co.

1-Tailspin Tommy, Mutt & Jeff, Alley Oop, Capt. Easy, Don Dixon begin — 52.00 156.00 364.00
2-Scribbly by Mayer begins — 26.00 78.00 182.00
3 — 22.00 65.00 154.00
4,5: 4-Christmas-c — 19.00 57.00 132.00
6-10 — 14.50 43.50 100.00
11-29: 16-Christmas-c — 12.00 36.00 84.00
30-John Carter of Mars (origin) begins by Edgar Rice Burroughs — 35.00 105.00 245.00
31-44: 33-John Coleman Burroughs art begins on John Carter — 20.00 60.00 140.00
45-Origin Phantasmo, the Master of the World & intro. his sidekick Whizzer McGee — 16.00 48.00 112.00
46-50: 46-The Black Knight begins, ends No. 62 — 13.50 40.50 95.00

Fugitives From Justice #1, © STJ

Fun Comics #10, © STAR

The Funnies #7 (4/37), © DELL

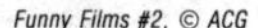
Funny Films #2, © ACG

Funnyman #4, © ME

Funny Pages V3No.9, © CEN

THE FUNNIES (continued)

	Good	Fine	Mint
51-56-Last ERB John Carter of Mars	13.50	40.50	95.00
57-Intro. & origin Captain Midnight	35.00	105.00	245.00
58-60	15.00	45.00	105.00
61-Andy Panda begins by Walter Lantz	16.00	48.00	110.00
62,63-Last Captain Midnight cover	13.50	40.50	95.00
64-Format change; Oswald the Rabbit, Felix the Cat, Li'l Eight Ball app.; origin & 1st app. Woody Woodpecker in Andy Panda; last Capt. Midnight & Phantasmo	27.00	81.00	190.00

NOTE: ***Mayer*** *c-26.* ***McWilliams*** *art in many issues on "Rex King of the Deep."*

FUNNIES ANNUAL, THE
1959 ($1.00)(B&W; tabloid-size, approx. 7x10")
Avon Periodicals

	Good	Fine	Mint
1-(Rare)-Features the best newspaper comic strips of the year: Archie, Snuffy Smith, Beetle Bailey, Henry, Blondie, Steve Canyon, Buz Sawyer, The Little King, Hi & Lois, Popeye, & others. Also has a chronological history of the comics from 2000 B.C. to 1959.	22.00	65.00	154.00

FUNNIES ON PARADE (Premium)
1933 (Probably the 1st comic book) (36 pgs.; slick cover)
No date or publisher listed
Eastern Color Printing Co.

	Good	Fine	Mint
nn-Contains Sunday page reprints of Mutt & Jeff, Joe Palooka, Hairbreadth Harry, Reg'lar Fellers, Skippy, & others (10,000 print run). This book was printed for Proctor & Gamble to be given away & came out before Famous Funnies or Century of Comics.	150.00	450.00	1050.00

FUNNY ANIMALS (See Fawcett's Funny Animals)
Sept, 1984 - No. 2, Nov, 1984
Charlton Comics

	Good	Fine	Mint
1,2-Atomic Mouse-r		.30	.60

FUNNYBONE
1944 (132 pages)
La Salle Publishing Co.

	Good	Fine	Mint
	6.00	18.00	42.00

FUNNY BOOK (. . . Magazine) (Hocus Pocus No. 9)
Dec, 1942 - No. 8, June-July?, 1946
Parents' Magazine Press

	Good	Fine	Mint
1-Funny animal	5.00	15.00	35.00
2	2.65	8.00	18.00
3-8	1.75	5.25	12.00

FUNNY COMICS (7 cents)
1955 (36 pgs.; 5x7"; in color)
Modern Store Publ.

	Good	Fine	Mint
1-Funny animal	.50	1.50	3.50

FUNNY COMIC TUNES (See Funny Tunes)

FUNNY FABLES
Aug, 1957 - V2No. 2, Nov, 1957
Decker Publications (Red Top Comics)

	Good	Fine	Mint
V1No.1	1.15	3.50	8.00
V2No.1,2	.55	1.65	4.00

FUNNY FILMS
Sept-Oct, 1949 - No. 29, May-June, 1954 (No. 1-4, 52 pgs.)
American Comics Group(Michel Publ./Titan Publ.)

	Good	Fine	Mint
1-Puss An' Boots, Blunderbunny begin	5.00	15.00	35.00
2	2.35	7.00	16.00
3-10	1.65	5.00	12.00
11-20	1.30	4.00	9.00
21-29	1.00	3.00	7.00

FUNNY FOLKS (Hollywood. . . on cover only No. 17-26; becomes Hollywood Funny Folks No. 27 on)
April-May, 1946 - No. 26, June-July, 1950
National Periodical Publications

	Good	Fine	Mint
1-1st app. Nutsy Squirrel by Rube Grossman	12.00	36.00	84.00
2	6.00	18.00	42.00
3-5	5.00	15.00	35.00
6-10	3.50	10.50	24.00
11-26	2.35	7.00	16.00

NOTE: ***Sheldon Mayer*** *a-in some issues.*

FUNNY FROLICS
Summer, 1945 - No. 5, Dec, 1946
Timely/Marvel Comics (SPI)

	Good	Fine	Mint
1-Sharpy Fox, Puffy Pig, Krazy Krow	5.00	15.00	35.00
2	3.00	9.00	21.00
3,4	2.35	7.00	16.00
5-Kurtzman-a	3.50	10.50	24.00

FUNNY FUNNIES
April, 1943 (68 pages)
Nedor Publishing Co.

	Good	Fine	Mint
1 (Funny animals)	7.00	21.00	50.00

FUNNYMAN
Dec, 1947; No. 1, Jan, 1948 - No. 5, 1948
Magazine Enterprises

	Good	Fine	Mint
nn(12/47)-Prepublication B&W undistributed copy by Siegel & Shuster-(5¾x8"), 16 pgs.; Sold in San Francisco in 1976 for $300.00			
1-Siegel & Shuster in all	11.50	34.50	80.00
2	8.00	24.00	56.00
3-5	6.50	19.50	45.00

FUNNY MOVIES (See 3-D Funny Movies)

FUNNY PAGES (Formerly The Comics Magazine)
No. 6, Nov, 1936 - No. 42, Oct, 1940
Comics Magazine Co./Ultem Publ.(Chesler)/Centaur Publications

	Good	Fine	Mint
V1/6 (nn, nd)-The Clock begins (2 pgs.), ends No. 11 (1st app.)	28.00	84.00	195.00
7-11	19.00	57.00	132.00
V2/1 (9/37)(V2/2 on-c; V2/1 in indicia)	15.00	45.00	105.00
V2/2 (10/37)(V2/3 on-c; V2/2 in indicia)	15.00	45.00	105.00
3(11/37)-5	15.00	45.00	105.00
6(1st Centaur, 3/38)	22.00	65.00	154.00
7-9	17.00	51.00	120.00
10(Scarce)-1st app. of The Arrow by Gustavson (Blue costume)	65.00	195.00	455.00
11,12	35.00	105.00	245.00
V3/1-6	35.00	105.00	245.00
7-1st Arrow-c; 9/39	42.00	125.00	295.00
8	35.00	105.00	245.00
9-Tarpe Mills Jungle-c	35.00	105.00	245.00
10-2nd Arrow-c	38.00	115.00	265.00
V4/1(1/40, Arrow-c)-(Rare)-The Owl & The Phantom Rider app.; origin Mantoka, Maker of Magic by Jack Cole. Tarpe Mills-a	45.00	135.00	315.00
35-Arrow-c	32.00	95.00	225.00
36-38-Mad Ming-c. 36-Mad Ming begins, ends No. 42	32.00	95.00	225.00
39-42-Arrow-c. 42-Last Arrow	32.00	95.00	225.00

NOTE: ***Burgos*** *c-V3/10.* ***Jack Cole*** *a-V2/3, 7, 8, 10, 11, V3/2, 6, 9, 10, V4/1, 37.* ***Eisner*** *a-V1/7, 8, 10.* ***Everett*** *a-V2/11 (illos).* ***Gill Fox*** *a-V2/11.* ***Sid Greene*** *a-39.* ***Guardineer*** *a-V2/2, 3, 5.* ***Gustavson*** *a-V2/5, 11, 12, V3/1-10, 35, 38-42; c-V3/7, 35, 39-42.* ***Bob Kane*** *a-V3/1.* ***McWilliams*** *a-V2/12, V3/1, 3-6.* ***Tarpe Mills*** *a-V3/8-10, V4/1; c-V3/9.* ***Ed Moore Jr.*** *a-V2/12.* ***Bob Wood*** *a-V2/2, 3, 8, 11, V3/6, 9, 10; c-V2/6, 7.*

FUNNY PICTURE STORIES (Comic Pages V3/4 on)
Nov, 1936 - V3/3, May, 1939
Comics Magazine Co./Centaur Publications

FUNNY PICTURE STORIES (continued)

	Good	Fine	Mint
V1/1-The Clock begins (c-feature)(See Funny Pages for 1st app.)	50.00	150.00	350.00
2	25.00	75.00	175.00
3-9: 4-Eisner-a; Christmas-c	18.00	54.00	125.00
V2/1 (9/37; V1/10 on-c; V2/1 in indicia)-Jack Strand begins	15.00	45.00	105.00
2 (10/37; V1/11 on-c; V2/2 in indicia)	15.00	45.00	105.00
3-5: 4-Xmas-c	12.00	36.00	84.00
6-(1st Centaur, 3/38)	21.00	65.00	145.00
7-11	15.00	45.00	105.00
V3/1-3	12.00	36.00	84.00

NOTE: ***Guardineer*** *a-V1/11.* ***Bob Wood*** *a/c-V1/11.*

FUNNY STUFF (Becomes The Dodo & the Frog No. 80)
Summer, 1944 - No. 79, July-Aug, 1954
All-American/National Periodical Publications No. 7 on

	Good	Fine	Mint
1-The Three Mouseketeers & The "Terrific Whatzit" begin-Sheldon Mayer-a	30.00	90.00	210.00
2-Sheldon Mayer-a	15.00	45.00	105.00
3-5	9.00	27.00	63.00
6-10	6.00	18.00	42.00
11-20: 18-Dodo & the Frog begin?	4.50	13.50	31.50
21,23-30: 24-Infinity-c	3.00	9.00	21.00
22-Superman cameo	9.00	27.00	62.00
31-79: 75-Bo Bunny by Mayer	2.00	6.00	14.00
Wheaties Giveaway(1946, 6½x8¼") (Scarce)	7.00	21.00	50.00

NOTE: ***Mayer*** *a-1-8, 55, ,57, 58, 61, 62, 64, 65, 68, 70, 72, 74-79; c-6.*

FUNNY STUFF STOCKING STUFFER
March, 1985 (52 pgs.)
DC Comics

	Good	Fine	Mint
1-Almost every DC funny animal		.60	1.25

FUNNY 3-D
December, 1953
Harvey Publications

	Good	Fine	Mint
1	6.00	18.00	42.00

FUNNY TUNES (Animated Funny Comic Tunes No. 16-22; Funny Comic Tunes No. 23, on covers only; formerly Human Torch; Oscar No. 24 on)
No. 16, Summer, 1944 - No. 23, Fall, 1946
U.S.A. Comics Magazine Corp. (Timely)

	Good	Fine	Mint
16-Silly, Ziggy, Krazy Krow begin	4.00	12.00	28.00
17-22	2.35	7.00	16.00
23-Kurtzman-a	3.50	10.50	24.00

FUNNY TUNES
July, 1953 - No. 3, Dec-Jan, 1953-54
Avon Periodicals

	Good	Fine	Mint
1-Space Mouse begins	2.35	7.00	16.00
2,3	1.50	4.50	10.00

FUNNY WORLD
1947 - 1948
Marbak Press

	Good	Fine	Mint
1-Newspaper strip reprints in all	3.00	9.00	21.00
2,3	2.00	6.00	14.00

FUNTASTIC WORLD OF HANNA-BARBERA, THE (TV)
Dec, 1977 - No. 3, June, 1978 ($1.25) (Oversized)
Marvel Comics Group

	Good	Fine	Mint
1-The Flintstones Christmas Party(12/77); 2-Yogi Bear's Easter Parade(3/78); 3-Laff-a-lympics(6/78) each....	.35	1.00	2.00

FUN TIME
1953 - No. 4, Winter, 1953-54
Ace Periodicals

	Good	Fine	Mint
1,2	1.30	4.00	9.00
3,4 (100 pgs. each)	3.50	10.50	24.00

FUN WITH SANTA CLAUS (See March of Comics No. 11,108,325)

FURTHER ADVENTURES OF INDIANA JONES, THE
Jan, 1983 - No. 34, Mar, 1986
Marvel Comics Group

	Good	Fine	Mint
1-Byrne/Austin-a		.60	1.20
2-Byrne/Austin-c/a		.40	.80
3-34		.35	.70

NOTE: ***Austin*** *a-6i, 9i; c-1i, 2i, 6i, 9i.* ***Chaykin*** *a-6p; c-9p, 10p.* ***Ditko*** *a-21p, 25, 26, 34.* ***Golden*** *c-26.* ***Simonson*** *c-9.*

FURY (Straight Arrow's Horse...) (See A-1 No. 119)

FURY (TV)
No. 781, Mar, 1957 - Nov, 1962 (All photo-c)
Dell Publishing Co./Gold Key

	Good	Fine	Mint
4-Color 781	3.50	10.50	24.00
4-Color 885,975	2.65	8.00	18.00
4-Color 1031,1080,1133,1172,1218,1296, 01292-208(No.1-'62)	2.65	8.00	18.00
10020-211(11/62-G.K.)-Crandall-a	2.65	8.00	18.00

(See March of Comics No. 200)

FURY OF FIRESTORM, THE (Also see Firestorm)
June, 1982 - Present (No. 19-on: 75¢)
DC Comics

	Good	Fine	Mint
1-Intro The Black Bison; brief origin	.40	1.20	2.40
2	.25	.75	1.50
3-18: 17-1st app. Firehawk		.60	1.20
19-40: 22-Origin. 24-1st app. Blue Devil. 39-Weasel's i.d. revealed.		.50	1.00
41,42-Crisis x-over		.50	1.00
43-49: 48-Intro. Moonbow		.45	.90
50-58: 53-Origin/1st app. Silver Shade. 55,56-Legends x-over		.40	.80
Annual 1(11/83), 2(11/84), 3(11/85)		.65	1.30
Annual 4(10/86)		.60	1.25

NOTE: ***Colan*** *a-19p, Annual 4p.* ***Giffen*** *a-Annual 4p.* ***Tuska*** *a-17p, 18p, 32p, 45p.*

FUTURE BEAT
July, 1986 - Present ($1.50, B&W)
Oasis Comics

	Good	Fine	Mint
1 (28 pgs.)	.25	.75	1.50

FUTURE COMICS
June, 1940 - No. 4, Sept, 1940
David McKay Publications

	Good	Fine	Mint
1-Origin The Phantom; The Lone Ranger, & Saturn Against the Earth begin	105.00	315.00	735.00
2	45.00	135.00	315.00
3,4	35.00	105.00	245.00

FUTURE WORLD COMICS
Summer, 1946 - No. 2, Fall, 1946
George W. Dougherty

	Good	Fine	Mint
1,2	7.00	21.00	50.00

FUTURE WORLD COMIX (Warren Presents... on cover)
September, 1978
Warren Publications

	Good	Fine	Mint
1		.50	1.00

Funny Picture Stories V1No.7, © CEN

Funny Stuff #1, © DC

Fury of Firestorm #17, © DC

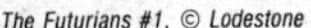
The Futurians #1, © Lodestone

Gabby Hayes Western #1, © FAW

Garrison's Gorillas #5, © Belmur Prod.

FUTURIANS, THE
Oct, 1985 - Present ($1.50 cover)
Lodestone Publ.

	Good	Fine	Mint
1-Cockrum c/a	.50	1.50	3.00
2	.35	1.00	2.00
3	.25	.75	1.50

G-8 (See G-Eight)

GABBY (Formerly Ken Shannon)
No. 11, July, 1953; No. 2, Sept, 1953 - No. 9, Sept, 1954
Quality Comics Group

	Good	Fine	Mint
11(No.1)(7/53)	2.15	6.50	15.00
2	1.15	3.50	8.00
3-9	1.00	3.00	7.00

GABBY GOB (See Harvey Hits No. 85,90,94,97,100,103,106,109)

GABBY HAYES WESTERN (Movie star) (See Monte Hale, & Western Hero)
Nov, 1948 - No. 50, Jan, 1953; Dec, 1954 - No. 59, Jan, 1957
Fawcett/Toby Press/Charlton Comics No. 51 on

	Good	Fine	Mint
1-Gabby & his horse Corker begin; Photo front/back-c begin	17.00	51.00	120.00
2	8.50	25.50	60.00
3-5	6.00	18.00	42.00
6-10	5.00	15.00	35.00
11-20: 19-Last photo back-c?	4.00	12.00	28.00
21-49	2.50	7.50	17.50
50-(1/53)-Last Fawcett issue; last photo-c?	3.00	9.00	21.00
51-(12/54)-1st Charlton issue; photo-c	3.00	9.00	21.00
52-59(Charlton '54-57): 53,55-Photo-c	1.75	5.25	12.00
1(Toby)(12/53)-Photo-c	4.35	13.00	30.00
Quaker Oats Giveaway nn(No. 1-5, 1951) (Dell?)	2.50	7.50	17.00

GAGS
July, 1937 - V3No.10, Oct, 1944 (13¾x10¾'')
United Features Synd./Triangle Publ. No. 9 on

	Good	Fine	Mint
1(7/37)-52 pgs.; 20 pgs. Grin & Bear It, Fellow Citizen	3.00	9.00	21.00
V1No.9 (36 pgs.; 15¢) (7/42)	2.00	6.00	14.00
V3No.10	1.50	4.50	10.00

GALACTIC WAR COMIX (Warren Presents . . . on cover)
December, 1978
Warren Publications

	Good	Fine	Mint
nn		.50	1.00

GALLANT MEN, THE (TV)
October, 1963 (Photo-c)
Gold Key

	Good	Fine	Mint
1(10085-310)-Manning-a	1.15	3.50	8.00

GALLEGHER, BOY REPORTER (TV)
May, 1965 (Disney) (Photo-c)
Gold Key

	Good	Fine	Mint
1(10149-505)	1.15	3.50	8.00

GAMBIT
Sept, 1986 - Present ($1.50, B&W)
Oracle Comics

	Good	Fine	Mint
1-sci/fic	.25	.75	1.50

GANDY GOOSE (See Paul Terry's & Terry-Toons Comics)
Mar, 1953 - No. 5, Nov, 1953; No. 5, Fall, 1956 - No. 6, Sum/58
St. John Publ. Co./Pines No. 5,6

	Good	Fine	Mint
1	2.15	6.50	15.00
2	1.15	3.50	8.00
3-5(1953)(St. John)	.85	2.50	6.00
5,6(1956-58)(Pines)	.75	2.25	5.00

GANG BUSTERS
1938 - 1943
David McKay/Dell Publishing Co.

	Good	Fine	Mint
Feature Books 17(McKay)('38)	19.00	57.00	132.00
Large Feat. Comic 10('39)-(Scarce)	23.00	70.00	160.00
Large Feat. Comic 17('41)	15.00	45.00	105.00
4-Color 7(1940)	15.00	45.00	105.00
4-Color 23,24('42-43)	11.00	33.00	76.00

GANG BUSTERS (Radio/TV)
Dec-Jan, 1947-48 - No. 67, Dec-Jan, 1958-59 (No. 1-23, 52 pgs.)
National Periodical Publications

	Good	Fine	Mint
1	21.00	62.00	145.00
2	9.50	28.50	66.00
3-8	6.00	18.00	42.00
9,10-Photo-c	6.50	19.50	45.00
11-13-Photo-c	5.00	15.00	35.00
14,17-Frazetta-a, 8 pgs. each. 14-Photo-c	16.00	48.00	112.00
15,16,18-20	3.75	11.25	26.00
21-30	2.65	8.00	18.00
31-44: 44-Last Pre-code (2-3/55)	2.00	6.00	14.00
45-67	1.30	4.00	9.00

NOTE: ***Barry*** *a-6, 8, 10.* ***Drucker*** *a-51.* ***Roussos*** *a-8.*

GANGSTERS AND GUN MOLLS
Sept, 1951 - No. 4, June, 1952
Avon Periodical/Realistic Comics

	Good	Fine	Mint
1-Wood-a, 1 pg; c-/Avon paperback 292	15.00	45.00	105.00
2-Check-a, 8 pgs.; Kamen-a	11.00	33.00	76.00
3-Marijuana mention story; used in **POP**, pg. 84-85	11.00	33.00	76.00
4	8.50	25.50	60.00

GANGSTERS CAN'T WIN
Feb-Mar, 1948 - No. 9, June-July, 1949
D. S. Publishing Co.

	Good	Fine	Mint
1	7.00	21.00	50.00
2	3.50	10.50	24.00
3-Two bra & panties panels	5.00	15.00	35.00
4-Narcotics mentioned; acid in face story	5.00	15.00	35.00
5,6-Ingels-a. 5-McWilliams-a	5.75	17.25	40.00
7-McWilliams-a	2.65	8.00	18.00
8-9	2.65	8.00	18.00

GANG WORLD
No. 5, Nov, 1952 - No. 6, Jan, 1953
Standard Comics

	Good	Fine	Mint
5-Bondage-c	6.00	18.00	42.00
6-Opium story	3.50	10.50	24.00

GARGOYLE
June, 1985 - No. 4, Sept, 1985 (Limited series)
Marvel Comics Group

	Good	Fine	Mint
1- Character from The Defenders; Wrightson-c	.25	.75	1.50
2-4		.50	1.00

GARRISON'S GORILLAS (TV)
Jan, 1968 - No. 4, Oct, 1968; No. 5, Oct, 1969 (Photo-c)
Dell Publishing Co.

	Good	Fine	Mint
1	1.50	4.50	10.00
2-5: 5-Reprints No. 1	1.00	3.00	7.00

GASOLINE ALLEY (Also see Super Comics 117)
1929 (B&W daily strip reprints)(7x8¾''; hardcover)

GASOLINE ALLEY (continued)
Reilly & Lee Publishers

	Good	Fine	Mint
By King (96 pgs.)	7.00	21.00	50.00

GASOLINE ALLEY
Oct, 1950 - No. 2, 1950 (Newspaper reprints)
Star Publications

	Good	Fine	Mint
1-Contains 1 pg. intro. history of the strip (The Life of Skeezix); reprints 15 scenes of highlights from 1921-1935, plus an adventure from 1935 and 1936 strips; a 2-pg. filler is included on the life of the creator Frank King, with photo of the cartoonist.	8.00	24.00	56.00
2-(1936-37 reprints)-L. B. Cole-c	8.50	25.50	60.00

(See Super Book No. 21)

GASP!
March, 1967 - No. 4, Aug, 1967
American Comics Group

	Good	Fine	Mint
1-L.S.D. drug mention	1.00	3.00	6.00
2-4	.70	2.00	4.00

GAY COMICS (Honeymoon No. 41)
Mar, 1944 (no month); No. 18, Fall, 1944 - No. 40, Oct, 1949
Timely Comics/USA Comic Mag. Co. No. 18-24

	Good	Fine	Mint
1-Wolverton's Powerhouse Pepper; Tessie the Typist begins (One Shot)	15.00	45.00	105.00
18-Wolverton-a	8.00	24.00	56.00
19-29-Wolverton-a in all; Kurtzman in No. 24, 29	6.50	19.50	45.00
30,33,36,37-Kurtzman's "Hey Look"	2.15	6.50	15.00
31-Kurtzman's "Hey Look"(1), Giggles 'N' Grins (1½)	2.15	6.50	15.00
32,35,38-40	1.65	5.00	11.50
34-Three Kurtzman's "Hey Look"	3.00	9.00	21.00

GAY COMICS (Also see Tickle, Smile, & Whee Comics)
1955 (52 pgs.; 5x7¼"; 7 cents)
Modern Store Publ.

	Good	Fine	Mint
1	.50	1.50	3.00

GAY PURR-EE (See Movie Comics)

GEEK, THE (See Brother Power...)

G-8 AND HIS BATTLE ACES
October, 1966
Gold Key

	Good	Fine	Mint
1 (10184-610)-Painted-c	1.75	5.25	12.00

GEM COMICS
April, 1945 (52 pgs.) (Bondage-c)
Spotlight Publishers

	Good	Fine	Mint
1-Little Mohee, Steve Strong app.	5.00	15.00	35.00

GENE AUTRY (See March of Comics No. 25,28,39,54,78,90,104,120,135,150, & Western Roundup)

GENE AUTRY COMICS (Movie, Radio star; singing cowboy)
(Dell takes over with No. 11)
1941 (On sale 12/31/41) - No. 10, 1943 (68 pgs.)
Fawcett Publications

	Good	Fine	Mint
1 (Rare)-Gene Autry & his horse Champion begin	88.00	265.00	610.00
2	38.00	115.00	265.00
3-5	28.00	84.00	195.00
6-10	25.00	75.00	175.00

GENE AUTRY COMICS (...& Champion No. 102 on)
No. 11, 1943 - No. 121, Jan-Mar, 1959 (TV)-later issues
Dell Publishing Co.

	Good	Fine	Mint
11,12(1943-2/44)-Continuation of Fawcett series (60pgs. each); No. 11-photo back-c	24.50	73.50	170.00
4-Color 47(1944, 60 pgs.)	24.50	73.50	170.00
4-Color 57(11/44),66('45)(52 pgs. each)	21.00	62.00	145.00
4-Color 75,83('45, 36 pgs. each)	19.00	57.00	132.00
4-Color 93,100('45-46, 36 pgs. each)	15.00	45.00	105.00
1(5-6/46, 52 pgs.)	25.00	75.00	175.00
2(7-8/46)-Photo-c begin, end No. 111	13.00	40.00	90.00
3-5: 4-Intro Flapjack Hobbs	9.00	27.00	62.00
6-10	7.00	20.00	50.00
11-20: 20-Panhandle pete begins	4.65	14.00	32.00
21-29(36pgs.)	3.50	10.50	24.00
30-40(52pgs.)	3.50	10.50	24.00
41-56(52pgs.)	2.85	8.50	20.00
57-66(36pgs.): 58-X-mas-c	2.00	6.00	14.00
67-80(52pgs.)	2.35	7.00	16.00
81-90(52pgs.): 82-X-mas-c. 87-Blank inside-c	1.75	5.25	12.00
91-99(36pgs. No. 91-on). 94-X-mas-c	1.50	4.50	10.00
100	1.75	5.25	12.00
101-111-Last Gene Autry photo-c	1.30	4.00	9.00
112-121-All Champion painted-c	1.15	3.50	8.00
...Adventure Comics And Play-Fun Book ('40s)-36 pgs., 8x6½"; games, comics, magic	8.00	24.00	56.00
Pillsbury Premium('47)-36 pgs., 6½x7½"; games, comics, puzzles	8.00	24.00	56.00
Quaker Oats Giveaway(1950)-2½x6¾"; 5 different versions; "Death Card Gang, Phantoms of the Cave, Riddle of Laughing Mtn., Secret of Lost Valley." each....	4.00	12.00	28.00
3-D Giveaway(1953)-Pocket-size; 5 different	4.00	12.00	28.00

NOTE: *Photo back-c, 4-18,20-45,48-65.* ***Manning*** *a-118.* ***Jesse Marsh*** *art: 4-Color No. 66, 75, 93, 100, No. 1-25, 27-37, 39, 40.*

GENE AUTRY'S CHAMPION (TV)
No. 287, 8/50; No. 319, 2/51; No. 3, 8-10/51 - No. 19, 8-10/55
Dell Publishing Co.

	Good	Fine	Mint
4-Color 287('50, 52pgs.)-Photo-c	3.50	10.50	24.00
4-Color 319('51), 3-(Painted-c begin)	2.35	7.00	16.00
4-19: 19-Last painted-c	1.30	4.00	9.00

GENE AUTRY TIM (Formerly Tim) (Becomes Tim in Space)
1950 (Half-size) (Black & White Giveaway)
Tim Stores

	Good	Fine	Mint
Several issues (All Scarce)	5.00	15.00	35.00

GENE DAY'S BLACK ZEPPELIN
April, 1985 - No. 6, 1986 ($1.70, B&W)
Renegade Press

	Good	Fine	Mint
1	.35	1.00	2.00
2-6	.30	.90	1.80

GENERAL DOUGLAS MACARTHUR
1951
Fox Features Syndicate

	Good	Fine	Mint
nn	8.00	24.00	56.00

GENERIC COMIC BOOK, THE
April, 1984 (One-shot)
Marvel Comics Group

	Good	Fine	Mint
1		.30	.60

GENTLE BEN (TV)
Feb, 1968 - No. 5, Oct, 1969 (All photo-c)
Dell Publishing Co.

	Good	Fine	Mint
1	1.15	3.50	8.00
2-5: 5-Reprints No. 1	.75	2.25	5.00

Gay Comics #1 (3/44), © MCG

Gene Autry Comics #58, © Gene Autry

Gene Autry's Champion #10, © Gene Autry

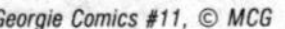

Georgie Comics #11, © MCG

Gerald McBoing-Boing. . . #4, © UPA

Ghost #1, © FH

GEORGE OF THE JUNGLE (TV)
Feb, 1969 - No. 2, Oct, 1969 (Jay Ward)
Gold Key

	Good	Fine	Mint
1,2	1.70	5.00	10.00

GEORGE PAL'S PUPPETOONS
Dec, 1945 - No. 18, Dec, 1947; No. 19, 1950
Fawcett Publications

	Good	Fine	Mint
1-Captain Marvel on cover	13.00	40.00	90.00
2	6.50	19.50	45.00
3-10	4.75	14.25	33.00
11-19	3.00	9.00	21.00

GEORGIE COMICS (. . . & Judy Comics No. 20-35?)
Spring, 1945 - No. 39, Oct, 1952
Timely Comics/GPI No. 1-34

	Good	Fine	Mint
1-Dave Berg-a	6.00	18.00	42.00
2	3.35	10.00	23.00
3-5,7,8	2.15	6.50	15.00
6-Georgie visits Timely Comics	2.50	7.50	17.50
9,10-Kurtzman's "Hey Look" (1 & ?); Margie app.	3.35	10.00	23.00
11,12: 11-Margie, Millie app.	1.65	5.00	11.50
13-Kurtzman's "Hey Look," 3 pgs.	2.85	8.50	20.00
14-Wolverton art, 1 pg. & Kurtzman's "Hey Look"	3.00	9.00	21.00
15,16,18-20	1.30	4.00	9.00
17,29-Kurtzman's "Hey Look," 1 pg.	2.15	6.50	15.00
21-24,27,28,30-39: 21-Anti-Wertham editorial	1.00	3.00	7.00
25-Painted cover by classic pin-up artist Peter Driben	2.15	6.50	15.00
26-Logo design swipe from Archie Comics	1.00	3.00	7.00

GERALD McBOING-BOING AND THE NEARSIGHTED MR. MAGOO
(Mr. Magoo No. 6)
Aug-Oct, 1952 - No. 5, Aug-Oct, 1953
Dell Publishing Co.

	Good	Fine	Mint
1	4.00	12.00	28.00
2-5	3.00	9.00	21.00

GERIATRIC GANGRENE JUJITSU GERBILS
Aug, 1986 - No. 4, 1987 ($1.50, B&W)
Planet X Productions

	Good	Fine	Mint
1	.35	1.00	2.00
2-4	.25	.75	1.50

GERONIMO
1950 - No. 4, Feb, 1952
Avon Periodicals

	Good	Fine	Mint
1-Indian Fighter; Maneely-a; Texas Rangers r-/Cowpuncher No. 1; Fawcette-c	8.00	24.00	56.00
2-On the Warpath; Kit West app.; Kinstler c/a	4.65	14.00	32.00
3-And His Apache Murderers; Kinstler c/a(2); Kit West, drug story r-Cowpuncher No. 6	4.65	14.00	32.00
4-Savage Raids of; Kinstler c/a(3)	3.85	11.50	27.00

GERONIMO JONES
Sept, 1971 - No. 9, Jan, 1973
Charlton Comics

	Good	Fine	Mint
1		.50	1.00
2-9		.30	.60
Modern Comics Reprint 7		.20	.40

GETALONG GANG, THE
May, 1985 - Present
Star Comics (Marvel)

	Good	Fine	Mint
1-8: Saturday morning TV stars		.35	.70

GET LOST
Feb-Mar, 1954 - No. 3, June-July, 1954 (Satire)
Mikeross Publications

	Good	Fine	Mint
1	5.00	15.00	35.00
2-Has 4 pg. E.C. parody featuring "the Sewer Keeper"	3.50	10.50	24.00
3	2.35	7.00	16.00

GET SMART (TV)
June, 1966 - No. 8, Sept, 1967 (All have photo-c)
Dell Publishing Co.

	Good	Fine	Mint
1	2.35	7.00	16.00
2-Ditko-a	2.35	7.00	16.00
3-8	1.50	4.50	10.00

GHOST
1951(Winter) - No. 11, Summer, 1954
Fiction House Magazines

	Good	Fine	Mint
1	20.00	60.00	140.00
2	11.00	33.00	76.00
3-9: 3,6,7,9-Bondage-c	8.00	24.00	56.00
10,11-Dr. Drew by Grandenetti in each, reprinted from Rangers; Evans-a-No. 11	9.50	28.50	65.00

GHOST BREAKERS (Also see (CC) Sherlock Holmes Comics, Racket Squad in Action & Red Dragon)
Sept, 1948 - No. 2, Dec, 1948 (52 pages)
Street & Smith Publications

	Good	Fine	Mint
1-Powell-c/a(3); Dr. Neff (magician) app.	10.00	30.00	70.00
2-Powell-c/a(2); Maneely-a	8.00	24.00	56.00

GHOSTBUSTERS
Feb, 1987 - Present
First Comics

	Good	Fine	Mint
1-Based on new animated TV series	.25	.75	1.50
2,3		.65	1.30

GHOST CASTLE (See Tales of. . .)

GHOSTLY HAUNTS (Formerly Ghost Manor)
No. 20, 9/71 - No. 53, 12/76; No. 54, 9/77 - No. 55, 10/77; No. 56, 1/78 - No. 58, 4/78
Charlton Comics

	Good	Fine	Mint
20,21		.40	.80
22-41,43-58: 27-Dr. Graves x-over. 39-Origin & 1st app. Destiny Fox		.40	.80
42-Newton c/a		.40	.80
40,41(Modern Comics-r, 1977)		.15	.30

NOTE: ***Ditko*** *a-22-28, 30-34, 36-41, 43-48, 50, 52, 54, 56r; c-22-27, 30, 33-38, 47, 54, 56.* ***Glanzman*** *a-20.* ***Howard*** *a-27, 42.* ***Staton*** *a-35; c-46.* ***Sutton*** *c-33, 39.*

GHOSTLY TALES (Blue Beetle No. 50-54)
No. 55, 4-5/66 - No. 124, 12/76; No. 125, 9/77 - No. 169, 10/84
Charlton Comics

	Good	Fine	Mint
55-Intro. & origin Dr. Graves		.60	1.20
56-70-Dr. Graves ends		.40	.80
71-106,108-113,115-169		.30	.60
107-Sutton, Wood-a		.40	.80
114-Newton-a		.40	.80

NOTE: ***Ditko*** *a-55, 57, 58, 60, 61, 67, 69-73, 75-90, 92-97, 99-118, 120-122, 125r, 126r, 131-33r, 136-41r, 143r, 144r, 152, 155, 161, 163; c-67, 69, 73, 77, 78, 83, 84, 86-90, 92-97, 99, 102, 107, 109, 111, 118, 120-22, 125, 131-33, 163.* ***Glanzman*** *a-167.* ***Howard*** *a-95, 98, 99, 117; c-98, 107, 120, 121, 161.* ***Newton*** *c-115.* ***Staton*** *a-161; c-117.* ***Sutton*** *a-112-114.*

GHOSTLY WEIRD STORIES (Formerly Blue Bolt Weird)
No. 120, Sept, 1953 - No. 124, Sept, 1954
Star Publications

GHOSTLY WEIRD STORIES (continued)

	Good	Fine	Mint
120-Jo-Jo-r	8.50	25.50	60.00
121-Jo-Jo-r	6.50	19.50	45.00
122-The Mask-r/Capt. Flight 5; Rulah-r; has 1pg. story 'Death and the Devil Pills'-r/Western Outlaws 17	6.50	19.50	45.00
123-Jo-Jo; Disbrow-a(2)	6.50	19.50	45.00
124-Torpedo Man	6.50	19.50	45.00

NOTE: ***Disbrow** a-120-124. **L. B. Cole** covers-all issues.*

GHOST MANOR (Ghostly Haunts No. 20 on)
July, 1968 - No. 19, July, 1971
Charlton Comics

	Good	Fine	Mint
1		.50	1.00
2-12,17		.40	.80
13-16,18,19-Ditko-a; c-15,18,19		.60	1.20

GHOST MANOR (2nd Series)
Oct, 1971 - No. 32, Dec, 1976; No. 33, Sept, 1977 - No. 77, 11/84
Charlton Comics

	Good	Fine	Mint
1		.50	1.00
2-7,9,10		.40	.80
8-Wood-a		.50	1.00
11-17,19		.30	.60
18,20-22: 18,20-Newton-a. 22-Newton c/a. 21-E-Man, Blue Beetle, Capt. Atom cameos		.30	.60
23-39,4l-56,58-77: 28-Nudity panels		.30	.60
40-Torture & drug use		.30	.60
57-Wood, Ditko, Howard-a		.40	.80
19(Modern Comics reprint, 1977)		.20	.40

NOTE: ***Ditko** a-4, 8, 10, 18, 20-22, 24-26, 28, 29, 31, 37r, 38r, 40r, 42-44r, 46r, 51r, 52r, 57, 62, 71; c-2-7, 9-11, 14-16, 28, 31, 37, 38, 42, 43, 46, 51, 52, 62. **Howard** a-4, 8, 19-21, 57. **Sutton** a-19; c-8.*

GHOST RIDER (See A-1 Comics, Best of the West, Black Phantom, Bobby Benson, Great Western, Red Mask & Tim Holt)
1950 - 1954
Magazine Enterprises

NOTE: The character was inspired by Vaughn Monroe's "Ghost Riders in the Sky," and Disney's movie "The Headless Horseman."

	Good	Fine	Mint
1(A-1 27)-Origin Ghost Rider	25.00	75.00	175.00
2(A-1 29), 3(A-1 31), 4(A-1 34), 5(A-1 37)-All Frazetta-c only	26.50	80.00	185.00
6(A-1 44), 7(A-1 51)	8.00	24.00	56.00
8(A-1 57)-Drug use story, 9(A-1 69)-L.S.D. story	6.50	19.50	45.00
10(A-1 71)-vs. Frankenstein	6.50	19.50	45.00
11(A-1 75), 12(A-1 80, bondage-c), 13(A-1 84), 14(A-1 112)	5.00	15.00	35.00

NOTE: ***Dick Ayers** art in all.*

GHOST RIDER, THE (See Night Rider)
Feb, 1967 - No. 7, Nov, 1967
Marvel Comics Group

	Good	Fine	Mint
1-Origin Ghost Rider; Kid Colt-r begin		.50	1.00
2-7: 6-Last Kid Colt-r		.30	.60

GHOST RIDER (See Marvel Spotlight)
Sept, 1973 - No. 81, June, 1983 (Super-hero)
Marvel Comics Group

	Good	Fine	Mint
1	1.25	3.75	7.50
2-10: 10-Ploog-a; origin-r/M. Spotlight 5	.50	1.50	3.00
11-19	.35	1.00	2.00
20-Byrne-a	.70	2.00	4.00
21-50: 50-Double size; Night Rider app.		.60	1.20
51-81: 68-Origin		.40	.80

NOTE: ***Anderson** c-64p. **Infantino** a(p)-43, 44, 51. **G. Kane** a-21p; c(p)-1, 2, 4, 5, 8, 9, 11-13, 19, 20, 24, 25. **Kirby** c-21-23. **Mooney** a-2-9p, 30i. **Nebres** c-26i. **Newton** a-23i. **Perez** c-26p. **J. Sparling** a-62p, 64p, 65p. **Starlin** a(p)-35. **Sutton** a-1p, 44i, 64i, 65i, 66, 67i. **Tuska** a-13p, 14p, 16p.*

GHOSTS (Ghost No. 1)
Sept-Oct, 1971 - No. 112, May, 1982 (No. 1-5: 52 pgs.)
National Periodical Publications/DC Comics

	Good	Fine	Mint
1,2: 2-Wood-a		.40	.80
3-112: 97-99-The Spectre app. 100-Infinity-c		.25	.50

NOTE: ***B. Baily** a-77. **Buscema** a-101. **J. Craig** a-108. **Ditko** a-77, 111. **Giffen** a-104p, 106p, 111p. **Golden** a-88. **Kaluta** c-7, 93, 101. **Kubert** c-89, 105-08, 111. **Sheldon Mayer** a-111. **McWilliams** a-99. **Win Mortimer** a-89, 91, 94. **Newton** a-92p, 94p. **Nino** a-35, 37, 57. **Orlando** a-74i; c-80. **Redondo** a-8, 13, 45. **Sparling** a-90p, 93p, 94p.*

GHOSTS SPECIAL (See DC Special Series No. 7)

GHOST STORIES (See Amazing Ghost Stories)

GHOST STORIES
Sept-Nov, 1962; No. 2, Apr-June, 1963 - No. 37, Oct, 1973
Dell Publishing Co.

	Good	Fine	Mint
12-295-211-Written by John Stanley	1.75	5.25	12.00
2	.85	2.50	6.00
3-10: Two No. 6's exist with diff. c/a(12-295-406,12-295-503)	.50	1.50	3.00
11-37		.50	1.00

NOTE: *No. 21-34,36,37 all reprint earlier issues.*

GHOUL TALES (Magazine)
Nov, 1970 - No. 5, July, 1971 (52 pages) (B&W)
Stanley Publications

	Good	Fine	Mint
1-Aragon pre-code reprints; Mr. Mystery as host; bondage-c	.40	1.20	2.40
2-(1/71)Reprint/Climax No. 1		.60	1.20
3-(3/71)		.60	1.20
4-(5/71)Reprints story "The Way to a Man's Heart" used in **SOTI**	1.00	3.00	7.00
5-ACG reprints		.60	1.20

NOTE: *No. 1-4 contain pre-code Aragon reprints.*

GIANT BOY BOOK OF COMICS (See Boy)
1945 (Hardcover) (240 pages)
Newsbook Publications (Gleason)

	Good	Fine	Mint
1-Crimebuster & Young Robin Hood	35.00	105.00	245.00

GIANT COMIC ALBUM
1972 (52 pgs.; 11x14"; B&W; 59 cents)
King Features Syndicate

	Good	Fine	Mint
Newspaper reprints: Little Iodine, Katzenjammer Kids, Henry, Mandrake the Magician ('59 Falk), Popeye, Beetle Bailey, Barney Google, Blondie, Flash Gordon ('68-69 Dan Barry), & Snuffy Smith each...	1.00	3.00	6.00

GIANT COMICS
Summer, 1957 - No. 3, Winter, 1957 (100 pgs.) (25 cents)
Charlton Comics

	Good	Fine	Mint
1-Atomic Mouse, Hoppy app.	5.00	15.00	35.00
2,3-Atomic Mouse, Rabbit, Christmas Book, Romance stories known	4.00	12.00	28.00

NOTE: *The above may be rebound comics; contents could vary.*

GIANT COMICS (See Wham-O Giant Comics)

GIANT COMICS EDITION (See Terry-Toons)
1947 - No. 17, 1950 (All 100-164 pgs.) (25 cents)
St. John Publishing Co.

	Good	Fine	Mint
1-Mighty Mouse	15.00	45.00	105.00
2-Abbie & Slats	7.00	21.00	50.00
3-Terry-Toons Album; 100 pgs.	10.00	30.00	70.00
4-Crime comics; contains Red Seal No. 16, used & illo. in **SOTI**	19.00	57.00	132.00

Ghostly Weird Stories #120 © STAR

Ghost Rider #10, © ME

Ghosts #99, © DC

Giant Comics Edition #8, © STJ

Giant-Size Mini Comics #1, © Eclipse

G.I. Combat #1, © QUA

GIANT COMICS EDITION (continued)

	Good	Fine	Mint
5-Police Case Book(4/49)-Contents varies; contains remaindered St. John books - some volumes contain 5 copies rather than 4, with 160 pages; Matt Baker-c	17.00	51.00	120.00
5A-Terry-Toons Album, 132 pgs.	10.00	30.00	70.00
6-Western Picture Stories; Baker-c/a(3); The Sky Chief, Blue Monk, Ventrilo app.; Tuska-a	16.00	48.00	110.00
7-Contains a teen-age romance plus 3 Mopsy comics	12.00	36.00	84.00
8-The Advs. of Mighty Mouse (10/49)	12.00	36.00	84.00
9-Romance and Confession Stories; Kubert-a(4); Baker-a; photo-c	16.00	48.00	110.00
10-Terry-Toons	10.00	30.00	70.00
11-Western Picture Stories-Baker c/a(4); The Sky Chief, Desperado, & Blue Monk app.; another version with Son of Sinbad by Kubert	15.00	45.00	105.00
12-Diary Secrets; Baker prostitute-c; 4 St. John romance comics; Baker-a	38.00	115.00	265.00
13-Romances; Baker, Kubert-a	16.00	48.00	110.00
14-Mighty Mouse Album	9.00	27.00	62.00
15-Romances (4 love comics)-Baker-c	16.00	48.00	110.00
16-Little Audrey, Abbott & Costello, Casper	9.00	27.00	62.00
17(nn)-Mighty Mouse Album (nn, no date, but did follow No. 16); 100 pgs. on cover but has 148 pgs.	9.00	27.00	62.00

NOTE: *The above books contain remaindered comics and contents could vary with each issue. No. 11,12 have part photo mag. insides.*

GIANT COMICS EDITIONS
1940's (132 pages)
United Features Syndicate

	Good	Fine	Mint
1-Abbie & Slats, Abbott & Costello, Jim Hardy, Ella Cinders, Iron Vic	15.00	45.00	105.00
2-Jim Hardy & Gordo	10.00	30.00	70.00

NOTE: *Above books contain rebound copies; contents can vary.*

GIANT GRAB BAG OF COMICS (See Archie All-Star Specials under Archie Comics)

GIANTS (See Thrilling True Stories of . . .)

GIANT-SIZE (Avengers, Captain America, Captain Marvel, Conan, Daredevil, Defenders, Fantastic Four, Hulk, Invaders, Iron Man, Kid Colt, Man-Thing, Master of Kung Fu, Power Man, Spider-Man, Super-Villain Team-Up, Thor, Werewolf, and X-Men are listed under their own titles.)

GIANT-SIZE CHILLERS (Giant-Size Dracula No. 2)
June, 1974; Feb, 1975 - No. 3, Aug, 1975 (35 cents)
Marvel Comics Group

	Good	Fine	Mint
1-(6/74)-Tomb of Dracula (52 pgs.); Origin & 1st app. Lilith, Dracula's daughter; Heath-a(r)		.50	1.00
1-(2/75)(50 cents)(68 pgs.)-Alcala-a		.40	.80
2-(5/75)-All-r		.30	.60
3-(8/75)-Wrightson c/a; Smith-a(r)		.50	1.00

NOTE: ***Everett** reprint-No. 2/Advs. Into Weird Worlds No. 10.*

GIANT SIZE CREATURES (Giant-Size Werewolf No. 2)
July, 1974 (52 pgs.) (35 cents)
Marvel Comics Group

	Good	Fine	Mint
1-Werewolf, Tigra app.; Crandall-a(r)		.30	.60

GIANT-SIZE DRACULA (Formerly Giant-Size Chillers)
No. 2, Sept, 1974 - No. 5, June, 1975 (50 cents)
Marvel Comics Group

	Good	Fine	Mint
2		.50	1.00
3-Fox-a/Uncanny Tales No. 6		.40	.80
4-Ditko-a(2)(r)		.30	.60
5-1st Byrne-a at Marvel	.70	2.00	4.00

GIANT-SIZE MINI COMICS (Regular size)
Aug, 1986 - Present ($1.50, B&W)
Eclipse Comics

	Good	Fine	Mint
1-3	.25	.75	1.50

GIANT-SIZE SUPER HEROES
June, 1974 (35 cents) (52 pgs.)
Marvel Comics Group

	Good	Fine	Mint
1-Spider-Man vs. Man-Wolf; Morbius, The Living Vampire app. Ditko-a(r); G. Kane-a(p)	.50	1.50	3.00

GIANT-SIZE SUPER-STARS (Giant-Size Fantastic Four No. 2)
May, 1974 (35 cents) (52 pgs.)
Marvel Comics Group

	Good	Fine	Mint
1-Fantastic Four, Thing, Hulk by Buckler (p); Kirbyish-a		.50	1.00

GIANT SPECTACULAR COMICS (See Archie All-Star Special under Archie Comics)

GIANT SUMMER FUN BOOK (See Terry-Toons . . .)

G. I. COMBAT
Oct, 1952 - No. 43, Dec, 1956
Quality Comics Group

	Good	Fine	Mint
1-Crandall-c	9.50	28.50	65.00
2	4.50	13.50	31.00
3-5,10-Crandall c/a	4.65	14.00	32.00
6-Crandall-a	4.00	12.00	28.00
7-9	3.35	10.00	23.00
11-20	1.85	5.50	13.00
21-31,33,35-43	1.70	5.00	12.00
32-Nuclear attack-c	3.35	10.00	23.00
34-Crandall-a	3.35	10.00	23.00

NOTE: ***Everett** c-29.*

G. I. COMBAT
No. 44, Jan, 1957 - No. 288, Mar, 1987
National Periodical Publications/DC Comics

	Good	Fine	Mint
44	9.50	28.50	65.00
45	4.50	13.50	31.00
46-50	2.65	8.00	18.00
51-60	1.35	4.00	9.00
61-66,68-80	1.00	3.00	7.00
67-1st Tank Killer	2.65	8.00	18.00
81,82,84-86,88-90: Last 10¢ issue	.50	1.50	3.00
83-1st Big Al, Little Al, & Charlie Cigar	1.35	4.00	9.00
87-1st Haunted Tank	2.65	8.00	18.00
91-113,115-120	.35	1.00	2.00
114-Origin Haunted Tank	1.00	3.00	6.00
121-137,139,140		.50	1.00
138-Intro. The Losers (Capt. Storm, Gunner/Sarge, Johnny Cloud) in Haunted Tank	.25	.80	1.60
141-150,152,154		.40	.80
151,153-Medal of Honor series by Maurer		.40	.80
155-200,207,208		.35	.70
201-206,209-245,247-259 ($1.00 size). 232-Origin Kana the Ninja. 244-Death of Slim Stryker; 1st app. The Mercenaries. 257-Intro. Stuart's Raiders		.50	1.00
246-(72 pgs.)30th Anniversary issue		.50	1.00
260-281 ($1.25 size). 264-Intro Sgt. Bullet and the Bravos of Vietnam; origin Kana		.60	1.20
282-288 (75¢ size)		.40	.80

NOTE: ***Adams** c-168, 201, 202. **Check** a-168, 173. **Drucker** a-48, 61, 63, 66, 71, 72, 76, 134, 140, 141, 144, 147, 148, 153. **Evans** a-135, 138, 158, 164, 166, 202, 204, 205, 215, 256. **Giffen** a-267. **Glanzman** a-most issues. **Kubert/Heath** a-most issues; **Kubert** covers most issues. **Morrow** a-159-161(2 pgs.). **Redondo** a-189, 240i, 243i. **Sekowsky** a-162p. **Severin** a-152. **Simonson** c-169. **Thorne** a-152, 156. **Wildey** a-153. Johnny Cloud app.-No. 112, 115, 120. Mlle. Marie app.-No. 123, 132, 200. Sgt. Rock app.-No. 111-113, 115, 120, 125, 141, 146, 147, 149, 200. USS Stevens by **Glanzman**-No. 145, 150-153, 157.*

G. I. COMICS (Also see Jeep & Overseas Comics)
1945 (distributed to U. S. armed forces)
Giveaways

33-49-Contains Prince Valiant by Foster, Blondie, Smilin' Jack, Mick-

G.I. COMICS (continued)

	Good	Fine	Mint
ey Finn, Terry & the Pirates, Donald Duck, Alley Oop, Moon Mullins, & Capt. Easy strip reprints	4.00	12.00	28.00

GIDGET (TV)
April, 1966 - No. 2, Dec, 1966
Dell Publishing Co.

	Good	Fine	Mint
1,2	1.50	4.50	10.00

GIFT (See The Crusaders)

GIFT COMICS (50 cents)
1942 - No. 4, 1949 (No.1-3: 324 pgs.; No. 4: 152 pgs.)
Fawcett Publications

	Good	Fine	Mint
1-Captain Marvel, Bulletman, Golden Arrow, Ibis the Invincible, Mr. Scarlet, & Spy Smasher app. Not rebound, remaindered comics, printed at same time as originals	100.00	300.00	700.00
2	75.00	225.00	525.00
3	55.00	165.00	385.00
4-The Marvel Family, Captain Marvel, etc.; each issue can vary in contents	35.00	105.00	245.00

GIFTS FROM SANTA (See March of Comics No. 137)

GIGGLE COMICS (Spencer Spook No. 100) (Also see Ha Ha)
Oct, 1943 - No. 99, Jan-Feb, 1955
Creston No.1-63/American Comics Group No. 64 on

	Good	Fine	Mint
1	9.00	27.00	62.00
2	4.50	13.50	31.00
3-5: Ken Hultgren-a begins?	3.00	9.00	21.00
6-10: 9-1st Superkatt	2.00	6.00	14.00
11-20	1.50	4.50	10.00
21-40	1.15	3.50	8.00
41-54,56-59,61-99: 95-Spencer Spook app.	.85	2.50	6.00
55,60-Milt Gross-a	1.30	4.00	9.00

G-I IN BATTLE (G-I No. 1 only)
Aug, 1952 - No. 9, July, 1953; Mar, 1957 - No. 6, May, 1958
Ajax-Farrell Publ./Four Star

	Good	Fine	Mint
1	2.35	7.00	16.00
2	1.15	3.50	8.00
3-9	.85	2.50	6.00
Annual 1(1952, 100 pgs.)	10.00	30.00	70.00
1(1957-Ajax)	1.50	4.50	10.00
2-6	.70	2.00	5.00

G. I. JANE
May, 1953 - No. 11, Mar, 1955 (Misdated 3/54)
Stanhall/Merit No. 11

	Good	Fine	Mint
1	3.50	10.50	24.00
2-7(5/54)	1.75	5.25	12.00
10(12/54, Stanhall)	1.50	4.50	10.00
11 (3/55, Merit)	1.35	4.00	9.00

G. I. JOE (Also see Advs. of . . . & Showcase No. 53,54)
No. 10, 1950; No. 11, 4-5/51 - No. 51, 6/57 (52pgs., 10-14,6-17?)
Ziff-Davis Publ. Co.

	Good	Fine	Mint
10(No.1, 1950)-Saunders painted-c begin	3.50	10.50	24.00
11-14(10/51)	2.00	6.00	14.00
V2No.6(12/51)-17-(Last 52pgs.?)	1.75	5.25	12.00
18-(100 pg. Giant-'52)	6.00	18.00	42.00
19-30	1.50	4.50	10.00
31-47,49-51	1.15	3.50	8.00
48-Atom bomb story	1.50	4.50	10.00

NOTE: ***Powell*** *a-V2/7, 8, 11.* ***Norman Saunders*** *painted c-10-14, 6-14, 26, 30, 31, 35, 38, 39. Bondage c-29,35,38.* ***Tuska*** *a-7.*

G. I. JOE (America's Movable Fighting Man)
1967 (36 pages) (5-1/8''x8-3/8'')
Custom Comics

	Good	Fine	Mint
Schaffenberger-a		.40	.80

G. I. JOE AND THE TRANSFORMERS
Jan, 1987 - No. 4, Apr, 1987 (mini-series)
Marvel Comics Group

	Good	Fine	Mint
1		.60	1.20
2-4		.50	1.00

G. I. JOE, A REAL AMERICAN HERO (See Official Handbook . . .)
June, 1982 - Present
Marvel Comics Group

	Good	Fine	Mint
1-Printed on Baxter paper	3.00	9.00	18.00
2-Printed on reg. paper	6.00	18.00	36.00
2 (2nd printing)	.50	1.50	3.00
3-5	1.70	5.00	10.00
3-5 (2nd printing)	.45	1.25	2.50
6,8	1.85	5.50	11.00
6,8 (2nd printing)	.40	1.25	2.50
7,9,10	1.30	4.00	8.00
7,9,10 (2nd printing)	.35	1.00	2.00
11-Intro Airborne	1.15	3.50	7.00
12	1.50	4.50	9.00
13-15	.95	2.90	5.80
14 (2nd printing)	.35	1.00	2.00
16-20	.85	2.50	5.00
17-19 (2nd printing)	.25	.75	1.50
21-25	.75	2.25	4.50
21,23,25 (2nd printing)	.35	1.00	2.00
26-Origin Snake-Eyes; ends No. 27	1.15	3.50	7.00
27	1.00	3.00	6.00
26,27 (2nd printing)		.60	1.20
28-30	.50	1.50	3.00
29,30 (2nd printing)	.25	.75	1.50
31-40: 33-New headquarters	.50	1.50	3.00
34,35,36 (2nd printing)		.60	1.20
41-49	.30	.90	1.80
50-Double size; intro Special Missions	.35	1.00	2.00
51-60		.60	1.20
61		.45	.90
Special Treasury Edition (1982)-r/No. 1	.85	2.50	5.00
. . . Yearbook 1 ('84)-r/No. 1	.75	2.25	4.50
. . . Yearbook 2 ('85)	.50	1.50	3.00
. . . Yearbook 3 ('86, 68pgs.)	.25	.75	1.50

NOTE: ***Golden*** *c-23.* ***Heath*** *a-24. 2nd printings exist.*

G. I. JOE DIGEST
Dec, 1986 - Present ($1.50, digest-size)
Marvel Comics Group

	Good	Fine	Mint
1,2: 1-r/G.I. Joe 1	.25	.75	1.50

G. I. JOE ORDER OF BATTLE, THE
Dec, 1986 - No. 4, Mar, 1987 (mini-series)
Marvel Comics Group

	Good	Fine	Mint
1	.25	.75	1.50
2-4		.65	1.30

G. I. JOE SPECIAL MISSIONS
Oct, 1986 - Present
Marvel Comics Group

	Good	Fine	Mint
1	.25	.75	1.50
2-4		.50	1.00

G. I. JUNIORS (See Harvey Hits No. 86, 91, 95, 98, 101, 104, 107, 110, 112, 114, 116, 118, 120, 122)

GIL THORP
May-July, 1963

G-I in Battle #2, © AJAX

G.I. Joe V1No.14, © Z-D

G.I. Joe Order of Battle #1, © MCG

Girls in Love #56, © QUA

Girls' Romances #13, © DC

Gizmo #1, © Mirage

GIL THORP (continued)
Dell Publishing Co.

	Good	Fine	Mint
1-Caniffish-a	1.75	5.25	12.00

GINGER (Li'l Jinx No. 11 on?)
1951 - No. 10, Summer, 1954
Archie Publications

1	5.00	15.00	35.00
2	3.00	9.00	21.00
3-6	2.35	7.00	16.00
7-10-Katy Keene app.	3.50	10.50	24.00

GIRL COMICS (Girl Confessions No. 13 on)
Nov, 1949 - No. 12, Jan, 1952 (Photo-c 1-4)
Marvel/Atlas Comics(CnPC)

1	5.50	16.50	38.00
2-Kubert-a	3.00	9.00	21.00
3-Everett-a; Liz Taylor photo-c	3.75	11.25	26.00
4-11	1.65	5.00	11.50
12-Krigstein-a	3.00	9.00	21.00

GIRL CONFESSIONS (Formerly Girl Comics)
No. 13, Mar, 1952 - No. 35, Aug, 1954
Atlas Comics (CnPC/ZPC)

13-Everett-a	3.00	9.00	21.00
14,15,19,20	1.50	4.50	10.00
16-18-Everett-a	2.15	6.50	15.00
21-35	1.30	4.00	9.00

GIRL FROM U.N.C.L.E., THE (TV)
Jan, 1967 - No. 5, Oct, 1967
Gold Key

1-McWilliams-a; photo-c	2.35	7.00	16.00
2-5-Leonard Swift-Courier No. 5	1.50	4.50	10.00

GIRLS' FUN & FASHION MAGAZINE (Formerly Polly Pigtails)
V5No.44, Jan, 1950 - V5No.47, July, 1950
Parents' Magazine Institute

V5No.44	1.75	5.25	12.00
45-47	.85	2.50	6.00

GIRLS IN LOVE
May, 1950 - No. 2, July, 1950
Fawcett Publications

1,2-Photo-c	4.00	12.00	28.00

GIRLS IN LOVE (Formerly G. I. Sweethearts No. 45)
No. 46, Sept, 1955 - No. 57, Dec, 1956
Quality Comics Group

46	2.35	7.00	16.00
47-56: 54-'Commie' story	1.15	3.50	8.00
57-Matt Baker c/a	3.35	10.00	23.00

GIRLS IN WHITE (See Harvey Comics Hits No. 58)

GIRLS' LIFE
Jan, 1954 - No. 6, Nov, 1954
Atlas Comics (BFP)

1-Patsy Walker	3.00	9.00	21.00
2	1.50	4.50	10.00
3-6	1.15	3.50	8.00

GIRLS' LOVE STORIES
Aug-Sept, 1949 - No. 180, Nov-Dec, 1973 (No. 1-13, 52 pgs.)
National Comics(Signal Publ. No.9-65/Arleigh No.83-117)

	Good	Fine	Mint
1-Toth, Kinstler-a, 8 pgs. each; photo-c	14.50	43.50	100.00
2-Kinstler-a?	6.50	19.50	45.00
3-10: 1-9-Photo-c	4.35	13.00	30.00
11-20	2.85	8.50	20.00
21-33: 21-Kinstler-a. 33-Last pre-code (1-2/55)	1.85	5.50	13.00
34-50	1.50	4.50	10.00
51-99	.85	2.50	6.00
100	.85	2.50	6.00
101-146: 113-117-April O'Day app.	.40	1.25	2.50
147-151-''Confessions'' serial		.50	1.00
152-180: 161-170, 52 pgs.		.30	.60

GIRLS' ROMANCES
Feb-Mar, 1950 - No. 160, Oct, 1971 (No. 1-11, 52 pgs.)
National Per. Publ.(Signal Publ. No.7-79/Arleigh No.84)

1-Photo-c	14.50	43.50	100.00
2-Photo-c; Toth-a	8.00	24.00	56.00
3-10: 3-6-Photo-c	4.35	13.00	30.00
11,12,14-20	2.85	8.50	20.00
13-Toth-c	3.35	10.00	23.00
21-31: 31-Last pre-code (2-3/55)	1.85	5.50	13.00
32-50	1.50	4.50	10.00
51-99	.85	2.50	6.00
100	1.00	3.00	7.00
101-108,110-133,135-160	.45	1.35	3.00
109-Beatles c/story	1.75	5.25	12.00
134-Adams-c	.55	1.65	4.00

G. I. SWEETHEARTS (Formerly Diary Loves; Girls In Love No. 46 on)
No. 32, June, 1953 - No. 45, May, 1955
Quality Comics Group

32	2.15	6.50	15.00
33-45: 43-Last pre-code? (1/55)	1.30	4.00	9.00

G. I. TALES (Sgt. Barney Barker No. 1-3)
No. 4, Feb, 1957 - No. 6, July, 1957
Atlas Comics (MCI)

4-Severin-a(4)	1.70	5.00	12.00
5	.85	2.50	6.00
6-Orlando, Powell, & Woodbridge-a	1.35	4.00	9.00

G. I. WAR BRIDES
April, 1954 - No. 8, June, 1955
Superior Publishers Ltd.

1	2.15	6.50	15.00
2	1.20	3.50	8.00
3-8: 4-Kamenesque-a; lingerie panels	1.00	3.00	7.00

G. I. WAR TALES
Mar-Apr, 1973 - No. 4, Oct-Nov, 1973
National Periodical Publications

1,3-Reprints		.15	.30
2-Adams-a(r), 4-Krigstein-a(r)		.15	.30

NOTE: ***Drucker** a-3r,4r. **Heath** a-4r. **Kubert** a-2,3; c-4r.*

GIZMO
May/June, 1985 (One shot)
Chance Enterprises

1	2.50	7.50	15.00

GIZMO
1986 - Present
Mirage Studios

1	1.00	3.00	6.00
2-4	.35	1.00	2.00

GLAMOROUS ROMANCES (Formerly Dotty)
No. 41, Sept, 1949 - No. 90, Oct, 1956 (Photo-c 68-90)
Ace Magazines (A. A. Wyn)

41-Dotty app.	2.15	6.50	15.00

GLAMOROUS ROMANCES (continued) | Good | Fine | Mint
42-72,74-80: 50-61-Painted-c. 80-Last pre-code (2/55)
 1.15 3.50 8.00
73-L.B. Cole-a 1.65 5.00 11.50
81-90 1.00 3.00 7.00

GNATRAT: THE DARK GNAT RETURNS
July, 1986 ($1.95, B&W)
Prelude Graphics

1-Dark Knight parody .50 1.50 3.00

GNOME MOBILE, THE (See Movie Comics)

GOBLIN, THE
June, 1982 - No. 4, Dec, 1982 (Magazine, $2.25)
Warren Publishing Co.

1-The Gremlin app; Golden-a(p) .35 1.10 2.25
2-4: 2-1st Hobgoblin .35 1.10 2.25

GODFATHERS, THE (See The Crusaders)

GOD IS
1973, 1975 (35-49 Cents)
Spire Christian Comics (Fleming H. Revell Co.)

By Al Hartley .40 .80

GOD'S HEROES IN AMERICA
1956 (nn) (68 pgs.) (25¢; 35¢)
Catechetical Guild Educational Society

307 1.70 5.00 10.00
NOTE: *Warehouse find in 1979.*

GOD'S SMUGGLER (Religious)
1972 (39¢, 49¢)
Spire Christian Comics/Fleming H. Revell Co.

1-Two variations exist .40 .80

GODZILLA
August, 1977 - No. 24, July, 1979
Marvel Comics Group

1-Mooney-i .50 1.00
2-24: 3-Champions x-over; 4,5-Sutton-a .30 .60

GO-GO
June, 1966 - No. 9, Oct, 1967
Charlton Comics

1-Miss Bikini Luv begins; Rolling Stones, Beatles, Elvis, Sonny & Cher, Sinatra, Bob Dylan parody; Herman's Hermits pin-ups
 2.00 6.00 14.00
2-Ringo Starr, David McCallum, Beatles photo cover; Beatles story and photos 2.00 6.00 14.00
3-Blooperman begins, ends No. 6 .85 2.50 5.00
4 .85 2.50 5.00
5-Super Hero & TV satire by J. Aparo & Grass Green begin
 1.20 3.50 7.00
6-9: 6,8-Aparo-a .85 2.50 5.00

GO-GO AND ANIMAL (See Tippy's Friends. . .)

GOING STEADY (Formerly Teen-Age Temptations)
No. 10, 1954 - No. 13, June, 1955; No. 14, Oct, 1955; V3No.3, Jan-Feb, 1960; V3No.4, Sept-Oct, 1960 - No. 6, Jan-Feb, 1961
St. John Publishing Co./Prize (Headline)

10(1954)-Matt Baker c/a 6.00 18.00 42.00
11(2/55), 12(4/55)-Baker-c 3.00 9.00 21.00
13(6/55)-Baker c/a 4.35 13.00 30.00
14(10/55)-Matt Baker-c/a, 25 pgs. 4.65 14.00 33.00
V3No.3-6(1960-61) .35 1.00 2.00

GOING STEADY WITH BETTY (Betty & Her Steady No. 2)
Nov-Dec, 1949
Avon Periodicals

| | Good | Fine | Mint
1 5.75 17.25 40.00

GOLDEN ARROW (See Fawcett Miniatures & Mighty Midget Comics)

GOLDEN ARROW (. . . Western No. 6)
Wint, 1942-43 - No. 6, Spring, 1947
Fawcett Publications

1-Golden Arrow begins 11.00 33.00 76.00
2 5.50 16.50 38.00
3-5 3.65 11.00 25.00
6-Krigstein-a 4.35 13.00 30.00
Well Known Comics (1944; 12 pgs.; 8½x10½''; paper-c; glued binding)-Bestmaid/Samuel Lowe giveaway; printed in green
 6.00 18.00 42.00

GOLDEN COMICS DIGEST
May, 1969 - No. 48, Jan, 1976
Gold Key

NOTE: *Whitman editions exist of many titles and are generally valued less.*

1-Tom & Jerry, Woody Woodpecker, Bugs Bunny
 1.00 3.00 6.00
2-Hanna-Barbera TV Fun Favorites .50 1.50 3.00
3-Tom & Jerry, Woody Woodpecker .50 1.50 3.00
4-Tarzan; Manning & Marsh-a 1.50 4.50 10.00
5,8-Tom & Jerry, Woody Woodpecker, Bugs Bunny
 .35 1.00 2.00
6-Bugs Bunny .35 1.00 2.00
7-Hanna-Barbera TV Fun Favorites .35 1.00 2.00
9-Tarzan 1.20 3.50 8.00
10-Bugs Bunny .35 1.00 2.00
11-Hanna-Barbera TV Fun Favorites .25 .75 1.50
12-Tom & Jerry, Bugs Bunny, Woody Woodpecker Journey to the Sun
 .25 .75 1.50
13-Tom & Jerry .25 .75 1.50
14-Bugs Bunny Fun Packed Funnies .25 .75 1.50
15-Tom & Jerry, Woody Woodpecker, Bugs Bunny
 .25 .75 1.50
16-Woody Woodpecker Cartoon Special .25 .75 1.50
17-Bugs Bunny .25 .75 1.50
18-Tom & Jerry; Barney Bear-r by Barks .60 1.75 3.50
19-Little Lulu 1.50 4.50 10.00
20-Woody Woodpecker Falltime Funtime .25 .75 1.50
21-Bugs Bunny Showtime .25 .75 1.50
22-Tom & Jerry Winter Wingding .25 .75 1.50
23-Little Lulu & Tubby Fun Fling 1.50 4.50 10.00
24-Woody Woodpecker Fun Festival .25 .75 1.50
25,28-Tom & Jerry .25 .75 1.50
26-Bugs Bunny Halloween Hulla-Boo-Loo; Dr. Spektor article, also No. 25 .25 .75 1.50
27-Little Lulu & Tubby in Hawaii 1.35 4.00 9.00
29-Little Lulu & Tubby 1.35 4.00 9.00
30-Bugs Bunny Vacation Funnies .25 .75 1.50
31-Turok, Son of Stone; reprints 4-Color No. 596,656
 .85 2.50 6.00
32-Woody Woodpecker Summer Fun .25 .75 1.50
33-Little Lulu & Tubby Halloween Fun; Dr. Spektor app.
 1.50 4.50 10.00
34-Bugs Bunny Winter Funnies .25 .75 1.50
35-Tom & Jerry Snowtime Funtime .25 .75 1.50
36-Little Lulu & Her Friends 1.50 4.50 10.00
37-Woody Woodpecker County Fair .25 .75 1.50
38-The Pink Panther .25 .75 1.50
39-Bugs Bunny Summer Fun .25 .75 1.50

Glamorous Romances #61, © ACE

Going Steady With Betty #1, © AVON

Golden Arrow #1, © FAW

Golden Lad #2, © Spark

Golden West Love #3, © Kirby Publ.

Goldyn in 3-D #1, © Blackthorne

GOLDEN COMICS DIGEST (continued)

	Good	Fine	Mint
40-Little Lulu & Tubby Trick or Treat; all by Stanley	1.50	4.50	10.00
41-Tom & Jerry Winter Carnival		.50	1.00
42-Bugs Bunny		.50	1.00
43-Little Lulu in Paris	1.50	4.50	10.00
44-Woody Woodpecker Family Fun Festival		.50	1.00
45-The Pink Panther		.60	1.20
46-Little Lulu & Tubby	1.35	4.00	9.00
47-Bugs Bunny		.50	1.00
48-The Lone Ranger	.35	1.00	2.00

NOTE: *No. 1-30, 164 pages; No. 31 on, 132 pages.*

GOLDEN LAD
July, 1945 - No. 5, June, 1946
Spark Publications

	Good	Fine	Mint
1-Origin Golden Lad & Swift Arrow	22.00	65.00	154.00
2-Mort Meskin-a	11.00	33.00	76.00
3,4: 3-Mort Meskin-a	10.00	30.00	70.00
5-Origin Golden Girl; Shaman & Flame app.	11.00	33.00	76.00

NOTE: *All **Robinson, Meskin,** and **Roussos** art.*

GOLDEN LEGACY
1966 - 1972 (Black History) (25 cents)
Fitzgerald Publishing Co.

1-Toussaint L'Ouverture (1966), 2-Harriet Tubman (1967), 3-Crispus Attucks & the Minutemen (1967), 4-Benjamin Banneker (1968), 5-Matthew Henson (1969), 6-Alexander Dumas & Family (1969), 7-Frederick Douglass, Part 1 (1969), 8-Frederick Douglass, Part 2 (1970), 9-Robert Smalls (1970), 10-J. Cinque & the Amistad Mutiny (1970), 11-Men in Action: White, Marshall J. Wilkins (1970), 12-Black Cowboys (1972), 13-The Life of Martin Luther King, Jr. (1972), 14-The Life of Alexander Pushkin (1971), 15-Ancient African Kingdoms (1972), 16-Black Inventors (1972)

	Good	Fine	Mint
each....		.50	1.00
1-10,12,13,15,16(1976)-Reprints		.15	.30

GOLDEN LOVE STORIES (Formerly Golden West Love)
No. 4, April, 1950
Kirby Publishing Co.

	Good	Fine	Mint
4-Powell-a; Glenn Ford & Janet Leigh photo-c	6.00	18.00	42.00

GOLDEN PICTURE CLASSIC, A
1956, 1957 (Text stories w/illustrations in color; 100 pgs. each)
(1956 softcover 49¢; hardcover 69¢; 1957 softcover 50¢, hard-$1.00)
Western Printing Co. (Simon & Shuster)

CL-401: Treasure Island; CL-402: Tom Sawyer; CL-403: Black Beauty; CL-404: Little Women; CL-405: Heidi; CL-406: Ben Hur; CL-407: Around the World in 80 Days; CL-408: Sherlock Holmes; CL-409: The Three Musketeers; CL-410: The Merry Advs. of Robin Hood; CL-411: Hans Brinker; CL-412: The Count of Monte Cristo

	Good	Fine	Mint
Softcover editions....	1.35	4.00	8.00
Hardcover editions....	2.65	8.00	16.00

NOTE: *Issues CL-401 to CL-412 were issued in 1956 with numbers CL-1-49 to CL-12-49. The 1957 hardcover editions were numbered CL-101 to CL-112.*

GOLDEN PICTURE STORY BOOK
Dec, 1961 (52 pgs.; 50 cents; large size)
Racine Press (Western)

	Good	Fine	Mint
ST-1-Huckleberry Hound (TV)	3.00	9.00	21.00
ST-2-Yogi Bear (TV)	3.00	9.00	21.00
ST-3-Babes in Toyland (Walt Disney's...)-Annette Funicello photo-c	3.00	9.00	21.00
ST-4-(...of Disney Ducks)-Walt Disney's Wonderful World of Ducks (Donald Duck, Uncle Scrooge, Donald's Nephews, Grandma Duck, Ludwig Von Drake, & Gyro Gearloose stories)	4.00	12.00	28.00

GOLDEN WEST LOVE (Golden Love Stories No. 4)
Sept-Oct, 1949 - No. 3, Feb, 1950 (No. 1, 52 pgs.)
Kirby Publishing Co.

	Good	Fine	Mint
1-Powell-a in all; Roussos-a	6.00	18.00	42.00
2,3: 3-Photo-c	4.35	13.00	30.00

GOLDEN WEST RODEO TREASURY (See Dell Giants)

GOLDILOCKS (See March of Comics No. 1)

GOLDILOCKS & THE THREE BEARS
1943 (Giveaway)
K. K. Publications

	Good	Fine	Mint
	6.75	20.00	40.00

GOLD KEY CHAMPION
Mar, 1978 - No. 2, May, 1978 (52 pages) (50 cents)
Gold Key

	Good	Fine	Mint
1-Space Family Robinson; ½-r		.40	.80
2-Mighty Samson; ½-r		.40	.80

GOLD KEY SPOTLIGHT
May, 1976 - No. 11, Feb, 1978
Gold Key

	Good	Fine	Mint
1-Tom, Dick & Harriet		.60	1.20
2-Wacky Advs. of Cracky		.50	1.00
3-Wacky Witch		.50	1.00
4-Tom, Dick & Harriet		.50	1.00
5-Wacky Advs. of Cracky		.50	1.00
6-Dagar the Invincible; Santos-a; origin Demonomicon	.50	1.50	3.00
7-Wacky Witch & Greta Ghost		.50	1.00
8-The Occult Files of Dr. Spektor, Simbar, Lu-sai; Santos-a	.50	1.50	3.00
9-Tragg	.50	1.50	3.00
10-O. G. Whiz		.50	1.00
11-Tom, Dick & Harriet		.50	1.00

GOLD MEDAL COMICS
1945 (132 pages)
Cambridge House

	Good	Fine	Mint
nn-Captain Truth by Fugitani, Crime Detector, The Witch of Salem, Luckyman, others app.	7.00	21.00	50.00
2	4.75	14.25	33.00
3-5	4.00	12.00	28.00

GOLDYN IN 3-D (Blackthorne 3-D Series No. 4)
June, 1986 ($2.25)
Blackthorne Publishing, Inc.

	Good	Fine	Mint
1	.35	1.15	2.30

GOMER PYLE (TV)
July, 1966 - No. 3, Jan, 1967
Gold Key

	Good	Fine	Mint
1-Photo front/back-c	2.15	6.50	15.00
2,3	1.50	4.50	10.00

GOODBYE, MR. CHIPS (See Movie Comics)

GOOFY (Disney)
No. 468, May, 1953 - Sept-Nov, 1962
Dell Publishing Co.

	Good	Fine	Mint
4-Color 468	2.65	8.00	18.00
4-Color 562,627,658	2.00	6.00	14.00
4-Color 747,802,899,952,987,1053,1094,1149,1201	1.75	5.25	12.00
12-308-211(Dell, 9-11/62)	1.75	5.25	12.00

GOOFY ADVENTURE STORY (See 4-Color No. 857)

GOOFY COMICS
June, 1943 - No. 48, 1953
Nedor Publ. Co. No. 1-14/Standard No. 14-48(Animated Cartoons)

	Good	Fine	Mint
1	7.00	21.00	50.00

GOOFY COMICS (continued)

	Good	Fine	Mint
2	3.50	10.50	24.00
3-10	2.50	7.50	17.50
11-19	1.75	5.25	12.00
20-35-Frazetta text illos in all	3.00	9.00	21.00
36-48	1.15	3.50	8.00

GOOFY SUCCESS STORY (See 4-Color No. 702)

GOOSE (Humor magazine)
Sept, 1976 - No. 3, 1976 (52 pgs.) (75 cents)
Cousins Publ. (Fawcett)

	Good	Fine	Mint
1-3		.50	1.00

GORDO (See Comics Revue No. 5)

GORE SHRIEK
Sept, 1986 - Present ($1.50, B&W)
Fantaco Enterprises

	Good	Fine	Mint
1-Bissette-a	.25	.75	1.50

GORGO (Based on movie) (See Return of. . .)
May, 1961 - No. 23, Sept, 1965
Charlton Comics

	Good	Fine	Mint
1-Ditko-a, 22 pgs.	10.00	30.00	70.00
2,3-Ditko c/a	5.00	15.00	35.00
4-10: 4-Ditko-c	3.50	10.50	24.00
11,13-16-Ditko-a	2.50	7.50	17.00
12,17-23: 12-Reptisaurus x-over; Montes/Bache-a-No. 17-23. 20-Giordano-c	1.00	3.00	6.00
Gorgo's Revenge('62)-Becomes Return of Gorgo	2.00	6.00	14.00

GOSPEL BLIMP, THE
1973, 1974 (36 pgs.) (35, 39 cents)
Spire Christian Comics (Fleming H. Revell Co.)

	Good	Fine	Mint
nn		.50	1.00

GOTHIC ROMANCES
January, 1975 (B&W Magazine) (75 cents)
Atlas/Seaboard Publ.

	Good	Fine	Mint
1-Adams-a	.30	.90	1.80

GOVERNOR & J. J., THE (TV)
Feb, 1970 - No. 3, Aug, 1970 (Photo-c)
Gold Key

	Good	Fine	Mint
1	1.50	4.50	9.00
2,3	1.00	3.00	6.00

GRANDMA DUCK'S FARM FRIENDS (See 4-Color No. 763, 873, 965, 1010, 1073, 1161, 1279)

GRAND PRIX (Formerly Hot Rod Racers)
No. 16, Sept, 1967 - No. 31, May, 1970
Charlton Comics

	Good	Fine	Mint
16-31: Features Rick Roberts		.25	.50

GRAY GHOST, THE (See 4-Color No. 911,1000)

GREAT ACTION COMICS
1958 (Reprints)
I. W. Enterprises

	Good	Fine	Mint
1-Captain Truth	1.00	3.00	6.00
8,9-Phantom Lady No. 15 & 23	5.00	15.00	35.00

GREAT AMERICAN COMICS PRESENTS - THE SECRET VOICE
1945 (10 cents)
Peter George 4-Star Publ./American Features Syndicate

	Good	Fine	Mint
1-All anti-Nazi	5.50	16.50	38.00

GREAT CAT FAMILY, THE (See 4-Color No. 750)

GREAT COMICS
Nov, 1941 - No. 3, Jan, 1942
Great Comics Publications

	Good	Fine	Mint
1-Origin The Great Zarro; Madame Strange begins	30.00	90.00	210.00
2	19.00	57.00	132.00
3-Futuro Takes Hitler to Hell; movie story cont'd./Choice No. 3	35.00	105.00	245.00

GREAT COMICS
1945
Novack Publishing Co./Jubilee Comics

	Good	Fine	Mint
1-The Defenders, Capt. Power app.; L. B. Cole-c	5.50	16.50	38.00
1-Same cover; Boogey Man, Satanas, & The Sorcerer & His Apprentice	3.50	10.50	24.00

GREAT DOGPATCH MYSTERY (See Mammy Yokum & the. . .)

GREAT EXPLOITS
October, 1957
Decker Publ./Red Top

	Good	Fine	Mint
1-Krigstein-a(2) (re-issue on cover); reprints/Daring Advs. No. 6	3.00	9.00	21.00

GREAT FOODINI, THE (See Foodini)

GREAT GAZOO, THE (The Flintstones)(TV)
Aug, 1973 - No. 20, Jan, 1977 (Hanna-Barbera)
Charlton Comics

	Good	Fine	Mint
1		.60	1.20
2-20		.30	.60

GREAT GRAPE APE, THE (TV)
Sept, 1976 - No. 2, Nov, 1976 (Hanna-Barbera)
Charlton Comics

	Good	Fine	Mint
1,2		.50	1.00

GREAT LOCOMOTIVE CHASE, THE (See 4-Color No. 712)

GREAT LOVER ROMANCES (Young Lover Romances No. 4,5?)
March, 1951 - No. 22, May, 1955 (Photo-c 1-3,13,17)
Toby Press

	Good	Fine	Mint
1-Jon Juan-r/J.J. No. 1 by Schomburg; Dr. Anthony King app.	4.35	13.00	30.00
2-Jon Juan, Dr. Anthony King app.	2.00	6.00	14.00
3,7,9-14,16-22 (no No. 4,5)	1.15	3.50	8.00
6-Kurtzman-a	2.65	8.00	18.00
8-Five pgs. of "Pin-Up Pete" by Sparling	3.50	10.50	24.00
15-Liz Taylor photo-c	1.75	5.25	12.00

GREAT PEOPLE OF GENESIS, THE
No date (64 pgs.) (Religious giveaway)
David C. Cook Publ. Co.

	Good	Fine	Mint
Reprint/Sunday Pix Weekly	1.50	4.50	10.00

GREAT RACE, THE (See Movie Classics)

GREAT SACRAMENT, THE
1953 (36 pages)
Catechetical Guild giveaway

	Good	Fine	Mint
	2.00	6.00	14.00

GREAT SCOTT SHOE STORE (See Bulls-Eye)

GREAT WEST (Magazine)
1969 (52 pages) (Black & White)
M. F. Enterprises

Goofy Comics #9, © BP

Governor and J.J. #1, © CBS

Great Lover Romances #2, © TOBY

Green Hornet Comics #6, © HARV

Green Lantern #30 (1st Series), © DC

Green Lantern #40 (2nd Series), © DC

GREAT WEST (continued) — Good / Fine / Mint

V1No.1 — .40 .80

GREAT WESTERN
Jan-Mar, 1954 - No. 11, Oct-Dec, 1954
Magazine Enterprises

8(A-1 93)-Origin The Ghost Rider-r/Tim Holt No. 11; Powell Red Hawk-r/Straight Arrow begins, ends No. 11 — 6.00 18.00 42.00
9(A-1 105), 11(A-1 127)-Ghost Rider, Durango Kid app. — 2.65 8.00 18.00
10(A-1 113)-The Calico Kid by Guardineer-r/Tim Holt No. 8; Straight Arrow, Durango Kid app. — 2.65 8.00 18.00
I.W. Reprint No. 1,2 9: Straight Arrow app. in No. 1,2 — .70 2.00 4.00
I.W. Reprint No. 8-Origin Ghost Rider(Tim Holt No.11); Tim Holt app.; Bolle-a — 1.20 3.50 7.00

NOTE: ***Powell** a(r)-8-11 (from Straight Arrow.)*

GREEN ARROW (See Adventure, Action, Brave & the Bold, Flash, Green Lantern, Leading, More Fun, and World's Finest)

GREEN ARROW
May, 1983 - No. 4, Aug, 1983 (Mini-series)
DC Comics

1-Origin; Speedy cameo — .50 1.00
2-4 — .40 .80

GREEN BERET, THE (See Tales of. . .)

GREEN GIANT COMICS (Also see Colossus Comics)
1940 (no price on cover)
Pelican Publications (Funnies, Inc.)

1-Dr. Nerod, Green Giant, Black Arrow, Mundoo & Master Mystic app; origin Colossus. (Rare, currently only 5 copies known) — 270.00 810.00 1890.00

NOTE: *The idea for this book came about by a stroll through a grocery store. Printed by Moreau Publ. of Orange, N.J. as an experiment to see if they could profitably use the idle time of their 40-page Hoe color press. The experiment failed due to the difficulty of obtaining good quality color registration and Mr. Moreau believes the book never reached the stands. The book has no price or date which lends credence to this. Contains five pages reprinted from Motion Picture Funnies Weekly.*

GREEN HORNET, THE (TV)(See Four Color 496)
Feb, 1967 - No. 3, Aug, 1967 (All have photo-c)
Gold Key

1 — 3.50 10.50 24.00
2,3 — 2.65 8.00 18.00

GREEN HORNET COMICS (. . .Racket Buster No. 44)
Dec, 1940 - No. 47, Sept, 1949
Helnit Publ. Co.(Holyoke) No. 1-6/Family Comics No. 7-on(Harvey)

1-Green Hornet begins — 80.00 240.00 560.00
2 — 40.00 120.00 280.00
3 — 32.00 95.00 225.00
4-6 (8/41) — 24.00 72.00 165.00
7 (6/42)-Origin The Zebra; Robin Hood & Spirit of 76 begin — 22.00 65.00 154.00
8-10 — 17.00 51.00 120.00
11,12-Mr. Q in both — 14.50 43.50 100.00
13-20 — 13.00 40.00 90.00
21-30: 24-Sci-Fi-c — 11.50 34.50 80.00
31-The Man in Black Called Fate begins — 12.00 36.00 84.00
32-36: 36-Spanking panel — 10.00 30.00 70.00
37-Shock Gibson app. by Powell; S&K Kid Adonis reprinted from Stuntman No. 3 — 11.00 33.00 76.00
38-Shock Gibson, Kid Adonis app. — 10.00 30.00 70.00
39-Stuntman story by S&K — 13.50 40.50 95.00
40,41 — 7.00 21.00 50.00
42-45,47-Kerry Drake in all. 45-Boy Explorers on cover only — 7.00 21.00 50.00

Good / Fine / Mint

46-"Case of the Marijuana Racket" cover/story; Kerry Drake app. — 8.00 24.00 56.00

NOTE: ***Fuje** a-23, 24, 26. **Kubert** a-20, 30. **Powell** a-7-10, 12, 14, 16-21, 30, 31(2), 32(3), 33, 34(3), 35, 36, 37(2), 38. **Robinson** a-27. **Schomburg** c-15, 17-23. Kirbyish c-7, 9, 15. Bondage c-8, 14, 18, 26, 36.*

GREEN JET COMICS, THE (See Comic Books, Series 1)

GREEN LAMA (Also see Comic Books, Series 1 & Prize Comics)
Dec, 1944 - No. 8, March, 1946
Spark Publications/Prize No. 7 on

1-Intro. The Green Lama, Lt. Hercules & The Boy Champions; Mac Raboy-a No. 1-8 — 40.00 120.00 280.00
2-Lt. Hercules borrows the Human Torch's powers for one panel — 28.00 84.00 195.00
3,6-8: 7-Christmas-c — 20.00 60.00 140.00
4-Dick Tracy take-off in Lt. Hercules story by H. L. Gold (sci-fiction writer) — 20.00 60.00 140.00
5-Lt. Hercules story; Little Orphan Annie, Smilin' Jack & Snuffy Smith take-off — 20.00 60.00 140.00

NOTE: ***Robinson** a-3-5.*

GREEN LANTERN (1st Series) (See All-American, All Flash Quarterly, All Star Comics, The Big All-American & Comic Cavalcade)
Fall, 1941 - No. 38, May-June, 1949
National Periodical Publications/All-American

1-Origin retold — 300.00 900.00 2100.00
2-1st book-length story — 140.00 420.00 980.00
3 — 105.00 315.00 735.00
4 — 72.00 215.00 500.00
5 — 60.00 180.00 420.00
6-8: 8-Hop Harrigan begins — 50.00 150.00 350.00
9,10: 10-Origin Vandal Savage — 43.00 130.00 300.00
11-17,19,20: 12-Origin Gambler — 35.00 105.00 245.00
18-Christmas-c — 40.00 120.00 280.00
21-29: 27-Origin Sky Pirate — 32.00 95.00 225.00
30-Origin/1st app. Streak the Wonder Dog by Toth — 32.00 95.00 225.00
31-35 — 28.00 84.00 195.00
36-38: 37-Sargon the Sorcerer app. — 32.00 95.00 225.00

NOTE: *Book-length stories No. 2-8. **Toth** a-28, 30, 31, 34-38; c-28, 30, 34, 36-38.*

GREEN LANTERN (2nd Series) (See Adventure, DC Spec., DC Spec. Series, Flash, and Showcase; Gr. Lant. Corps No. 206 on)
7-8/60 - No. 89, 4-5/72; No. 90, 8-9/76 - Present
National Periodical Publications/DC Comics

1-Origin retold; Gil Kane-a begins — 50.00 130.00 350.00
2-1st Pieface — 19.00 50.00 135.00
3 — 11.50 30.00 80.00
4,5: 5-Origin & 1st app. Hector Hammond; 1st 5700 A.D. story — 9.50 25.00 66.00
6-10: 6-Intro Tomar-re the alien G.L. 7-Origin Sinestro. 9-1st Jordan Brothers; last 10¢ issue — 5.00 12.50 35.00
11-15: 13-Flash x-over. 14-Origin Sonar — 3.65 9.00 25.00
16-20: 16-Origin Star Sapphire. 20-Flash x-over — 3.00 9.00 18.00
21-30: 21-Origin Dr. Polaris. 23-1st Tattooed Man. 24-Origin Shark. 29-JLA cameo; 1st Blackhand — 2.00 6.00 12.00
31-39 — 1.15 3.50 7.00
40-1st app. Crisis; 1st G.A. Green Lantern in Silver Age; origin The Guardians — 4.65 14.00 28.00
41-50: 42-Zatanna x-over. 43-Flash x-over. No. 45-G.A. Green Lantern x-over — .75 2.20 4.40
51-75: 52,61-G.A. Green Lantern x-over. 69-Wood inks — .55 1.65 3.30
76-Begin Green Lantern/Green Arrow series by Neal Adams — 7.00 21.00 42.00
77 — 3.00 9.00 18.00

GREEN LANTERN (continued)

	Good	Fine	Mint
78-80	2.50	7.50	15.00
81,82: 82-One pg. Wrightson inks	1.85	5.50	11.00
83-G.L. reveals i.d. to Carol Ferris	1.85	5.50	11.00
84-Adams/Wrightson-a, 22 pgs.	1.85	5.50	11.00
85,86(52 pgs.)-Drug propaganda books. 86-G.A. Gr. Lant.-r; Toth-a	2.50	7.50	15.00
87,89(52 pgs.): 89-G.A. Green Lantern-r	1.50	4.50	9.00
88(52 pgs., '72)-Unpubbed G.A. Gr. Lantern story; Gr. Lant.-r/Showcase 23. Adams-a(1 pg.)	.35	1.00	2.00
90('76)-99		.50	1.00
100-(Giant)-1st app. new Air Wave	.40	1.10	2.20
101-107,113-119		.40	.80
108-110(44 pgs.)-G.A. Gr. Lant. stories		.40	.80
111-Origin retold; G.A. Gr. Lant. app.		.40	.80
112-G.A. Gr. Lant. origin retold		.40	.80
120-130		.35	.70
131-135,138-140,145-149: 131,132-Tales of the G.L. Corps. 132-Adam Strange begins new series, ends 147. 148-Tales of the G.L. Corps begins, ends No. 173; not in 149,150		.35	.70
136,137-1st app. Citadel	.30	1.00	2.00
141-1st app. Omega Men	1.25	3.75	7.50
142,143-The Omega Men app.; Perez-c	.90	2.75	5.50
144-Omega Men app. (2 pgs.)	.35	1.00	2.00
150-Anniversary ish., 52 pgs.		.50	1.00
151-159,162-170: 159-Origin Evil Star		.40	.80
160,161-Omega Men app.	.25	.75	1.50
171-193,196,197: (75¢ cover). 174-Book-length stories begin		.40	.80
194,195-Crisis x-over. 195-Guy Gardner becomes Gr. Lantern		.50	1.00
198,200 ($1.25): 198-Crisis x-over		.60	1.25
199,201-210		.40	.80
Annual 2 (12/86)-Moore scripts		.60	1.25

NOTE: ***Adams*** *a-76, 77p-87p, 89; c-63, 76-89.* ***Austin*** *a-93i, 94i, 171i.* ***Buckler*** *c-136p.* ***Greene*** *a-39-49i, 58-63i; c-54-58i.* ***Grell*** *a-90, 91, 92-100p, 106p, 108-110p; c-90, 93-100, 101p, 102-106, 108-112.* ***Gil Kane*** *a-1-49p, 50-57, 58-61p, 68-75p, 85p(r), 87p(r), 88p(r), 156, 177, 184p; c-1-52, 54-61p, 67-75, 123, 154, 156, 165-71, 177, 184.* ***Newton*** *a-148p, 149p, 181.* ***Perez*** *c-132p, 141-144.* ***Sekowsky*** *a-65p, 170p.* ***Sparling*** *a-63p.* ***Starlin*** *c-129, 133.* ***Staton*** *a-117p, 123-127p, 128, 129-31p, 132-39, 140p, 141-46, 147p, 148-50, 151-55p; c-107p, 117p, 135(i), 136p, 145p, 146, 147, 148-152p, 155p.* ***Toth*** *a-86r, 171p.* ***Tuska*** *a-166-68p, 170p.* ***Willingham*** *a-Annual 2.*

GREEN LANTERN/GREEN ARROW
Oct, 1983 - No. 7, April, 1984
DC Comics

	Good	Fine	Mint
1-Reprints begin	.45	1.25	2.50
2-6 (52 pgs.)	.45	1.25	2.50
7 (60 pgs.; $2.50)	.45	1.25	2.50

NOTE: ***Adams*** *a-1-7; c-1-4.* ***Wrightson*** *a-4, 5.*

GREEN MASK, THE (The Bouncer No. 11 on? See Mystery Men)
Summer, 1940 - No. 9, 2/42; No. 10, 8/44 - No. 11, 11/44;
V2/1, Spr, 1945 - No. 6, 10-11/46
Fox Features Syndicate

	Good	Fine	Mint
V1/1-Origin The Green Mask & Domino; reprints/Mystery Men No. 1-3,5-7; Lou Fine-c	65.00	195.00	455.00
2-Zanzibar The Magician by Tuska	32.00	96.00	224.00
3-Powell-a; Marijuana story	20.00	60.00	140.00
4-Navy Jones begins, ends No. 6	16.00	48.00	110.00
5	13.50	40.50	95.00
6-The Nightbird begins, ends No. 9; bondage/torture-c	12.00	36.00	84.00
7-9	10.00	30.00	70.00
10,11: 10-Origin One Round Hogan & Rocket Kelly	9.50	28.50	65.00
V2/1	6.50	19.50	45.00
2-6	5.00	15.00	35.00

GREEN PLANET, THE
1962 (One Shot)
Charlton Comics

	Good	Fine	Mint
nn	1.75	5.25	12.00

GREEN TEAM (See First Issue Special)

GREETINGS FROM SANTA (See March of Comics No. 48)

GRENDEL (Also see Primer No. 2 and Mage)
Dec, 1985 - No. 3, 1986
Comico

	Good	Fine	Mint
1	5.50	16.50	33.00
2,3	4.25	12.50	25.00

GRENDEL
Oct, 1986 - Present ($1.50, color)
Comico

	Good	Fine	Mint
1	.35	1.00	2.00
2,3	.25	.75	1.50

GREYFRIARS BOBBY (See 4-Color No. 1189)

GREYLORE
12/85 - No. 6, 9/86 ($1.50-$1.75, full color, high quality paper)
Sirius Comics

	Good	Fine	Mint
1	.35	1.00	2.00
2-6	.30	.90	1.80

GRIM GHOST, THE
Jan, 1975 - No. 3, July, 1975
Atlas/Seaboard Publ.

	Good	Fine	Mint
1-Origin		.40	.80
2,3-Heath-c		.30	.60

GRIMJACK
Aug, 1984 - Present
First Comics

	Good	Fine	Mint
1	.40	1.20	2.40
2-5	.35	1.00	2.00
6-10	.25	.80	1.60
11-25: 20-Sutton c/a begins		.70	1.40
26-1st color Teenage Mutant Ninja Turtles	.60	1.75	3.50
27-33: 30-Dynamo Joe x-over		.65	1.30

GRIMM'S GHOST STORIES (See Dan Curtis)
Jan, 1972 - No. 60, June, 1982 (Painted-c No. 1-56)
Gold Key/Whitman No. 55 on

	Good	Fine	Mint
1	.50	1.50	3.00
2-4,6,7,9,10	.25	.75	1.50
5,8-Williamson-a	.40	1.25	2.50
11-16,18-20		.50	1.00
17-Crandall-a	.35	1.00	2.00
21-35: No. 32,34-reprints		.50	1.00
36-55,57-60: 43,44-(52 pgs.)		.40	.80
56-Williamson-a		.50	1.00
Mini-Comic No. 1 (3¼x6½'', 1976)		.30	.60

NOTE: *Reprints-No. 32?, 34?, 39, 43, 44, 47?, 53; 56-60(⅓).* ***Bolle*** *a-23-25, 27, 29(2), 33, 35, 43r, 45(2), 48(2), 50, 52.* ***Lopez*** *a-24, 25.* ***McWilliams*** *a-33, 44r, 48, 58.* ***Win Mortimer*** *a-31, 33, 49, 51, 55, 56, 58(2), 59, 60.* ***Roussos*** *a-25, 30.* ***Sparling*** *a-23, 24, 28, 30, 31, 33, 43r, 45, 51(2), 52, 56, 58, 59(2), 60.*

GRIN (The American Funny Book) (Magazine)
Nov, 1972 - No. 3, April, 1973 (52 pgs.) (Satire)
APAG House Pubs

	Good	Fine	Mint
1		.60	1.20

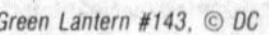

Green Lantern #143, © DC

Green Mask #10, © FOX

Grimjack #26, © First

Groo the Wanderer #1 (12/82), © Aragones

Gunfighter #6, © WMG

The Gunhawk #12, © MCG

GRIN (continued) — Good / Fine / Mint
2,3 — .40 .80

GRIN & BEAR IT (See Large Feature Comic No. 28)

GRIT GRADY (See Holyoke One-Shot No. 1)

GROO SPECIAL
Oct, 1984 (52 pgs.; $2.00; Baxter paper)
Eclipse Comics

	Good	Fine	Mint
1	.70	2.00	4.00

GROO THE WANDERER
Dec, 1982 - No. 8, March, 1984
Pacific Comics

	Good	Fine	Mint
1-Aragones c/a(p)	.70	2.00	4.00
2-8: Aragones c/a(p)	.40	1.25	2.50

GROO THE WANDERER
March, 1985 - Present
Epic Comics (Marvel)

	Good	Fine	Mint
1-Aragones-c/a	.60	1.75	3.50
2	.40	1.20	2.40
3-5	.35	1.00	2.00
6-10	.30	.85	1.70
11-20		.65	1.30
21-26		.50	1.00

GROOVY (Cartoon Comics - not CCA approved)
March, 1968 - No. 3, July, 1968
Marvel Comics Group

	Good	Fine	Mint
1-3	.70	2.00	4.00

GUADALCANAL DIARY (Also see American Library)
1945 (One Shot) (See Thirty Seconds Over Tokyo)
David McKay Publishing Co.

	Good	Fine	Mint
nn-B&W text & pictures; painted-c	10.00	30.00	70.00

GUARDIAN
Mar, 1984 - No. 2, June, 1984
Spectrum Comics

	Good	Fine	Mint
1,2		.50	1.00

GUERRILLA WAR (Formerly Jungle War Stories)
No. 12, July-Sept, 1965 - No. 14, Mar, 1966
Dell Publishing Co.

	Good	Fine	Mint
12-14	.50	1.50	3.00

GUILTY (See Justice Traps the Guilty)

GULF FUNNY WEEKLY (Gulf Comic Weekly No. 1-4)
1933 - No. 422, 5/23/41 (in full color; 4 pgs.; tabloid size to 2/3/39; 2/10/39 on, regular comic book size)(early issues undated)
Gulf Oil Company (Giveaway)

	Good	Fine	Mint
1	10.00	30.00	60.00
2-30	4.00	12.00	24.00
31-100	3.00	9.00	18.00
101-196	2.00	6.00	12.00
197-Wings Winfair begins(1/29/37); by Fred Meagher beginning in 1938	15.00	45.00	90.00
198-300 (Last tabloid size)	7.00	20.00	40.00
301-350 (Regular size)	3.35	10.00	20.00
351-422	2.35	7.00	14.00

GULLIVER'S TRAVELS (See Dell Jr. Treasury No. 3)
Sept-Nov, 1965 - No. 3, May, 1966
Dell Publishing Co.

	Good	Fine	Mint
1	1.15	3.50	8.00
2,3	.85	2.50	6.00

GUMBY 3-D
Oct, 1986 - Present ($2.50)
Blackthorne Publishing

	Good	Fine	Mint
1,2	.40	1.25	2.50

GUMPS, THE
1918 - No. 8, 1931 (10x10'')(52 pgs.; black & white)
Landfield-Kupfer/Cupples & Leon No. 2

	Good	Fine	Mint
Book No.2(1918)-(Rare); 5¼x13⅓''; paper cover; 36 pgs. daily strip reprints by Sidney Smith	12.00	36.00	84.00
nn(1924)-by Sidney Smith	8.00	24.00	56.00
2,3	7.00	21.00	50.00
4-7	6.00	18.00	42.00
8-(10x14''); 36 pgs.; B&W; National Arts Co.	6.00	18.00	42.00

GUMPS, THE (. . . in Radioland)
1937 (95 pgs.) (Mostly text)
Pebco Tooth Paste Premium

	Good	Fine	Mint
	6.00	18.00	42.00

GUMPS, THE (Also see Merry Christmas. . .)
1945 - No. 5, Nov-Dec, 1947
Dell Publ. Co./Bridgeport Herald Corp.

	Good	Fine	Mint
4-Color 73 (Dell)(1945)	5.00	15.00	35.00
1 (3-4/47)	5.00	15.00	35.00
2-5	3.50	10.50	24.00

GUNFIGHTER (Fat & Slat No. 1-4) (Becomes Haunt of Fear No.15 on)
No. 5, Summer, 1948 - No. 14, Mar-Apr, 1950
E. C. Comics

	Good	Fine	Mint
5,6-Moon Girl in each	30.00	90.00	210.00
7-14: 14-Bondage-c	22.00	65.00	154.00

NOTE: ***Craig & H. C. Kiefer*** *art in most issues.* ***Feldstein/Craig*** *a-10.* ***Feldstein*** *a-7-11.* ***Harrison/Wood*** *a-13, 14.* ***Ingels*** *a-5-14; c-7-12.*

GUNFIGHTERS, THE
1963 - 1964
Super Comics (Reprints)

	Good	Fine	Mint
10,11(Billy the Kid), 12(Swift Arrow), 15(Straight Arrow-Powell-a), 16,18-All reprints	.50	1.50	3.00

GUNFIGHTERS, THE (Formerly Kid Montana)
No. 51, 10/66 - No. 52, 10/67; No. 53, 6/79 - No. 85, 7/84
Charlton Comics

	Good	Fine	Mint
51,52	.30	.80	1.60
53,54-Williamson a(r)/Wild Bill Hickok		.40	.80
55,57-85		.30	.60
56-Williamson/Severin-c/a; r-Sheriff of Tombstone		.40	.80
85-S&K-r/1955 Bullseye		.40	.80

GUN GLORY (See 4-Color No. 846)

GUNHAWK, THE (Formerly Whip Wilson)(See Wild Western)
No. 12, Nov, 1950 - No. 18, Dec, 1951
Marvel Comics/Atlas (MCI)

	Good	Fine	Mint
12	3.65	11.00	25.00
13-18: 13-Tuska-a	2.65	8.00	18.00

GUNHAWKS (Gunhawk No. 7)
October, 1972 - No. 7, October, 1973
Marvel Comics Group

	Good	Fine	Mint
1-Reno Jones, Kid Cassidy		.40	.80
2-7: 6-Kid Cassidy dies. 7-Reno Jones solo		.25	.50

GUNMASTER (Judo Master No. 89 on; formerly Six-Gun Heroes)
9/64 - No. 4, 1965; No. 84, 7/65 - No. 88, 3-4/66; No. 89, 10/67

GUNMASTER (continued)
Charlton Comics

	Good	Fine	Mint
V1No.1	.35	1.00	2.00
2-4,V5No.84-86: 4-Blank inside-c		.60	1.20
V5No.87-89		.50	1.00

NOTE: *Vol. 5 was originally cancelled with No. 88 (3-4/66). No. 89 on, became Judo Master, then later in 1967, Charlton issued No. 89 as a Gunmaster one-shot.*

GUNS AGAINST GANGSTERS
Sept-Oct, 1948 - V2No.2, 1949
Curtis Publications/Novelty Press

	Good	Fine	Mint
1-Toni Gayle begins by Schomburg	8.00	24.00	56.00
2	5.65	17.00	40.00
3-6, V2/1,2: 6-Toni Gayle-c	5.35	16.00	37.00

NOTE: ***L. B. Cole** c-1-6; a-1,2,3(2),4-6.*

GUNSLINGER (See 4-Color No. 1220)

GUNSLINGER (Formerly Tex Dawson. . .)
No. 2, April, 1973 - No. 3, June, 1973
Marvel Comics Group

	Good	Fine	Mint
2,3		.30	.60

GUNSMOKE
Apr-May, 1949 - No. 16, Jan, 1952
Youthful Magazines

	Good	Fine	Mint
1-Gunsmoke & Masked Marvel begin by Ingels; Ingels bondage-c	14.50	43.50	100.00
2-Ingels c/a(2)	8.00	24.00	56.00
3-Ingels bondage-c/a	6.50	19.50	45.00
4-6: Ingels-c	4.35	13.00	30.00
7-10	3.35	10.00	23.00
11-16	2.15	6.50	15.00

GUNSMOKE (TV)
No. 679, 2/56 - No. 27, 6-7/61; 2/69 - No. 6, 2/70
Dell Publishing Co./Gold Key (All have photo-c)

	Good	Fine	Mint
4-Color 679	4.00	12.00	28.00
4-Color 720,769,797,844	3.00	9.00	21.00
6(11-1/57-58), 7	3.00	9.00	21.00
8,9,11,12-Williamson-a in all, 4 pgs. each	3.50	10.50	24.00
10-Williamson/Crandall-a, 4 pgs.	3.50	10.50	24.00
13-27	2.65	8.00	18.00
Gunsmoke Film Story (11/62-G.K. Giant) No. 30008-211	3.00	9.00	21.00
1 (G.K.)	1.70	5.00	10.00
2-6('69-70)	1.00	3.00	6.00

GUNSMOKE TRAIL
June, 1957 - No. 4, Dec, 1957
Ajax-Farrell Publ./Four Star Comic Corp.

	Good	Fine	Mint
1	2.35	7.00	16.00
2-4	1.30	4.00	9.00

GUNSMOKE WESTERN (Formerly Western Tales of Black Rider)
Dec, 1955 - No. 77, July, 1963
Atlas Comics No. 32-35(CPS/NPI); Marvel No. 36 on

	Good	Fine	Mint
32	3.00	9.00	21.00
33,35,36-Williamson-a in each: 5,6 & 4 pgs. plus Drucker No. 33	3.65	11.00	25.00
34-Baker-a, 3pgs.	1.65	5.00	11.50
37-Davis-a(2); Williamson text illo	2.00	6.00	14.00
38,39	1.15	3.50	8.00
40-Williamson/Mayo-a, 4 pgs.	3.65	11.00	25.00
41,42,45-49,51-55,57-59: 49,52-Kid From Texas story. 57-1st Two Gun Kid by Severin. 60-Sam Hawk app. in Kid Colt	1.00	3.00	7.00
43,44-Torres-a	1.50	4.50	10.00
50,60,61-Crandall-a	1.50	4.50	10.00
56-Matt Baker-a	1.50	4.50	10.00
62-77: 72-Origin Kid Colt	.85	2.50	6.00

NOTE: ***Colan** a-37. **Davis** a-37, 52, 54, 55; c-50, 54. **Ditko** a-56, 66. **Jack Keller** a-40, 72; c-72. **Kirby** a-47, 50, 51, 59, 62(3), 63, 65-67, 69, 71, 73, 77; c-56(w/**Ditko**),57, 58, 61(w/**Ayers**), 62, 63, 66, 68, 69, 71-77. **Severin** c-43. **Wildey** a-10, 37, 42, 57. Kid Colt in all. Two-Gun Kid in No. 57, 59, 60-63. Wyatt Earp in No. 45, 48, 49, 52, 54, 55, 58.*

GUNS OF FACT & FICTION (See A-1 Comics No. 13)

GUN THAT WON THE WEST, THE
1956 (24 pgs.; regular size) (Giveaway)
Winchester-Western Division & Olin Mathieson Chemical Corp.

	Good	Fine	Mint
nn-Painted-c	2.00	6.00	14.00

GYPSY COLT (See 4-Color No. 568)

GYRO GEARLOOSE (See Walt Disney Showcase No. 18)
No. 1047, Nov-Jan/1959-60 - May-July, 1962 (Disney)
Dell Publishing Co.

	Good	Fine	Mint
4-Color 1047 (No. 1)-Barks c/a	5.75	17.25	40.00
4-Color 1095,1184-All by Carl Barks	4.65	14.00	32.00
4-Color 1267-Barks c/a, 4 pgs.	3.50	10.50	24.00
No. 01-329-207 (5-7/62)-Barks-c only	2.35	7.00	16.00

HAGAR THE HORRIBLE (See Comics Reading Libraries)

HA HA COMICS (Teepee Tim No. 100 on) (Also see Giggle)
Oct, 1943 - No. 99, Jan, 1955
Scope Mag.(Creston Publ.) No. 1-80/American Comics Group

	Good	Fine	Mint
1	9.00	27.00	62.00
2	4.50	13.50	31.00
3-5: Ken Hultgren-a begins?	3.00	9.00	21.00
6-10	2.00	6.00	14.00
11-20: 14-Infinity-c	1.50	4.50	10.00
21-40	1.15	3.50	8.00
41-94,96-99	.85	2.50	6.00
95-3-D effect-c	3.00	9.00	21.00

HAIR BEAR BUNCH, THE (TV) (See Fun-In No. 13)
Feb, 1972 - No. 9, Feb, 1974 (Hanna-Barbera)
Gold Key

	Good	Fine	Mint
1	.35	1.00	2.00
2-9		.50	1.00

HALLELUJAH TRAIL, THE (See Movie Classics)

HALL OF FAME
May, 1983 - No. 3, Dec, 1983
JC Productions(Archie Comics Group)

	Good	Fine	Mint
1-3: T.H.U.N.D.E.R. Agents-r		.45	.90

HAMSTER VICE
June, 1986 - Present ($1.50, B&W)
Blackthorne Publishing

	Good	Fine	Mint
1	.70	2.00	4.00
2-4: 3-Intro Alpo Flight	.30	.90	1.80
3-D 1(10/86)	.40	1.25	2.50

HAND OF FATE (Formerly Men Against Crime)
No. 8, Dec, 1951 - No. 26, March, 1955
Ace Magazines

	Good	Fine	Mint
8: Surrealistic text story	7.00	21.00	50.00
9,10	4.00	12.00	28.00
11-18,20,22,23	2.65	8.00	18.00
19-Bondage, hypo needle scenes	3.75	11.25	26.00

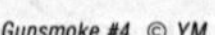
Gunsmoke #4, © YM

Gunsmoke #20, © CBS

Hamster Vice #1, © Blackthorne

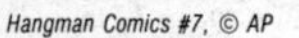
Hangman Comics #7, © AP

Hanna-Barbera Band Wagon #1, © Hanna-Barbera

Happy Comics #15, © STD

HAND OF FATE (continued) — Good / Fine / Mint

21-Necronomicon story; drug belladonna used 4.35 13.00 30.00
24-Electric Chair-c 5.00 15.00 35.00
25(11/54), 25(12/54) 3.65 11.00 25.00
26-Nostrand-a 4.35 13.00 30.00

NOTE: *Cameron art-No. 9, 10, 18-25; c-13. Sekowsky a-8, 9, 13, 14.*

HANDSHADOWS
Nov, 1985 ($1.50, B&W)
Doyan Productions

1 .25 .75 1.50

HANDS OF THE DRAGON
June, 1975
Seaboard Periodicals (Atlas)

1-Origin; Mooney inks .50 1.00

HANGMAN COMICS (Special No. 1; Black Hood No. 9 on)
No. 2, Spring, 1942 - No. 8, Fall, 1943 (See Pep Comics)
MLJ Magazines

2-The Hangman, Boy Buddies begin 52.00 155.00 365.00
3-8 28.00 84.00 195.00

NOTE: *Fuje a-7(3), 8(3); c-3.*

HANK
1946
Pentagon Publications

nn-Coulton Waugh's newspaper reprint 3.00 9.00 21.00

HANNA-BARBERA (See Golden Comics Digest No. 2,7,11)

HANNA-BARBERA BAND WAGON (TV)
Oct, 1962 - No. 3, April, 1963
Gold Key

1,2-Giants, 84 pgs. 2.25 6.75 18.00
3-Regular size 1.15 3.50 8.00

HANNA-BARBERA HI-ADVENTURE HEROES (See Hi-Adventure. . .)

HANNA-BARBERA PARADE (TV)
Sept, 1971 - No. 10, Dec, 1972
Charlton Comics

1 1.20 3.50 7.00
2-6,8-10 .70 2.00 4.00
7-''Summer Picnic''-52 pgs. .85 2.50 5.00

NOTE: *No. 4 (1/72) went on sale late in 1972 with the January 1973 issues.*

HANNA-BARBERA SPOTLIGHT (See Spotlight)

HANNA-BARBERA SUPER TV HEROES (TV)
April, 1968 - No. 7, Oct, 1969 (Hanna-Barbera)
Gold Key

1-The Birdman, The Herculoids, Moby Dick, Young Samson & Goliath, and The Mighty Mightor begin; Spiegle-a in all
2.35 7.00 16.00
2-The Galaxy Trio only app.; Shazzan begins; no Samson & Goliath
1.75 5.25 12.00
3-7: 3-The Space Ghost app.; also No. 3,6,7, no Herculoids; no Samson & Goliath in No. 4-7 1.30 4.00 9.00

HANNA-BARBERA (TV STARS) (See TV Stars)

HANS AND FRITZ
1929 (28 pgs.; 10x13½''; B&W Sunday strip reprints)
The Saalfield Publishing Co.

193-(Very Rare)-By R. Dirks; contains B&W Sunday strip reprints of Katzenjammer Kids & Hawkshaw the Detective from 1916
20.00 60.00 140.00
. . .The Funny Larks Of 2(1929) 20.00 60.00 140.00

HANS BRINKER (See 4-Color No. 1273)

HANS CHRISTIAN ANDERSEN
1953 (100 pgs. - Special Issue)
Ziff-Davis Publ. Co.

Good / Fine / Mint
nn-Danny Kaye (movie)-Photo-c 7.00 21.00 50.00

HANSEL & GRETEL (See 4-Color No. 590)

HANSI, THE GIRL WHO LOVED THE SWASTIKA
1973, 1976 (39-49 cents)
Spire Christian Comics (Fleming H. Revell Co.)

.50 1.00

HAP HAZARD COMICS (Real Love No. 25 on)
1944 - No. 24, Feb, 1949
Ace Magazines (Readers' Research)

1 4.00 12.00 28.00
2 2.00 6.00 14.00
3-10 1.50 4.50 10.00
11-13,15-24 1.15 3.50 8.00
14-Feldstein-c (4/47) 3.35 10.00 23.00

HAP HOPPER (See Comics Revue No. 2)

HAPPIEST MILLIONAIRE, THE (See Movie Comics)

HAPPINESS AND HEALING FOR YOU (Also see Oral Roberts' . . .)
1955 (36 pgs.; slick cover) (Oral Roberts Giveaway)
Commercial Comics

7.00 20.00 40.00

NOTE: *The success of this book prompted Oral Roberts to go into the publishing business himself to produce his own material.*

HAPPI TIM (See March of Comics No. 182)

HAPPY COMICS (Happy Rabbit No. 41 on)
Aug, 1943 - No. 40, Dec, 1950
Nedor Publ./Standard Comics (Animated Cartoons)

1 7.00 21.00 50.00
2 4.00 12.00 28.00
3-10 2.65 8.00 18.00
11-19 1.50 4.50 10.00
20-31,34-37-Frazetta text illos in all; 2 in No. 34, 3 in No. 27,28,30
2.65 8.00 18.00
32-Frazetta-a, 7 pgs. plus two text illos; Roussos-a
8.00 24.00 56.00
33-Frazetta-a(2), 6 pgs. each (Scarce) 15.00 45.00 105.00
38-40 1.00 3.00 7.00

NOTE: *Al Fago a-27.*

HAPPY DAYS (TV)
March, 1979 - No. 6, Feb, 1980
Gold Key

1 .35 1.00 2.00
2-6 .50 1.00
. . .With the Fonz Kite Fun Book(6¾x5¼'','78)-PG&E
.35 1.00 2.00

HAPPY HOLIDAY (See March of Comics No. 181)

HAPPY HOOLIGAN (See Alphonse. . .)
1903 (18 pgs.) (Sunday strip reprints in color)
Hearst's New York American-Journal

Book 1-by Fred Opper 22.00 65.00 154.00
50 Pg. Edition(1903)-10x15'' in color 26.00 78.00 182.00

HAPPY HOOLIGAN (Handy. . .) (See The Travels of. . .)
1908 (32 pgs. in color) (10x15''; cardboard covers)
Frederick A. Stokes Co.

18.00 54.00 125.00

HAPPY HOOLIGAN (Story of. . .)
1932 (16 pgs.; 9½x12''; softcover)

HAPPY HOOLIGAN (continued)
McLoughlin Bros.

	Good	Fine	Mint
281-Three-color text, pictures on heavy paper	5.50	16.50	38.00

HAPPY HOULIHANS (Saddle Justice No. 3 on)
Fall, 1947 - No. 2, Winter, 1947-48
E. C. Comics

1-Origin Moon Girl	22.00	65.00	154.00
2	10.00	30.00	70.00

HAPPY JACK
August, 1957 - No. 2, Nov, 1957
Red Top (Decker)

V1No.,1,2	1.00	3.00	7.00

HAPPY JACK HOWARD
1957
Red Top (Farrell)/Decker

nn-Reprints Handy Andy story from E. C. Dandy Comics No. 5, renamed "Happy Jack"	1.50	4.50	10.00

HAPPY RABBIT (Formerly Happy Comics)
No. 41, Feb, 1951 - No. 48, April, 1952
Standard Comics (Animated Cartoons)

41	2.15	6.50	15.00
42-48	1.15	3.50	8.00

HARDY BOYS, THE (See 4-Color No. 760,830,887,964-Disney)

HARDY BOYS, THE (TV)
April, 1970 - No. 4, Jan, 1971
Gold Key

1	.85	2.50	5.00
2-4	.40	1.25	2.50

HARLEM GLOBETROTTERS (TV) (See Fun-In No. 8,10)
April, 1972 - No. 12, Jan, 1975 (Hanna-Barbera)
Gold Key

1	.50	1.50	3.00
2-12	.25	.75	1.50

NOTE: *No. 4, 8, and 12 contain 16 extra pages of advertising.*

HAROLD TEEN (See 4-Color No. 2, 209, & Treasure Box of Famous Comics)

HAROLD TEEN (Adv. of. . .)
1929-31 (36-52 pgs.) (Paper covers)
Cupples & Leon Co.

B&W daily strip reprints by Carl Ed	7.00	21.00	50.00

HARVEY
Oct, 1970; No. 2, 12/70; No. 3, 6/72 - No. 6, 12/72
Marvel Comics Group

1	.50	1.50	3.00
2-6	.25	.75	1.50

HARVEY COLLECTORS COMICS (Richie Rich Collectors Comics No. 10 on, cover title only)
9/75 - No. 15, 1/78; No. 16, 10/79 (52 pgs.)
Harvey Publications

1-Reprints Richie Rich No. 1,2	.70	2.00	4.00
2-10	.40	1.20	2.40
11-16: 16-Sad Sack-r		.50	1.00

NOTE: *All reprints: Casper-No. 2, 7, Richie Rich-No. 1, 3, 5, 6, 8-15, Wendy-No. 4. No. 6 titled 'Richie Rich. . . on inside.*

HARVEY COMICS HITS
No. 51, Oct, 1951 - No. 62, Dec, 1952
Harvey Publications

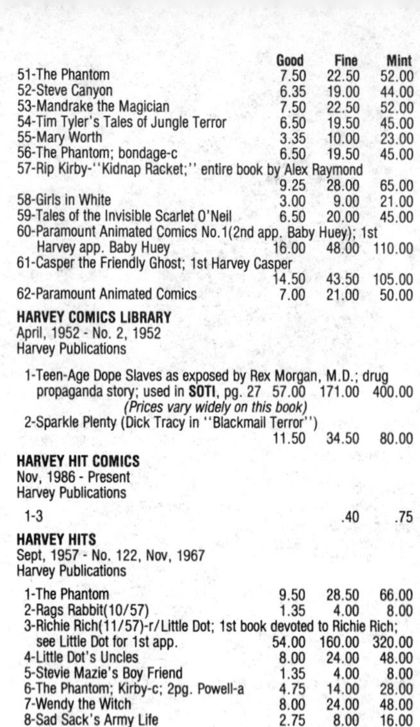

	Good	Fine	Mint
51-The Phantom	7.50	22.50	52.00
52-Steve Canyon	6.35	19.00	44.00
53-Mandrake the Magician	7.50	22.50	52.00
54-Tim Tyler's Tales of Jungle Terror	6.50	19.50	45.00
55-Mary Worth	3.35	10.00	23.00
56-The Phantom; bondage-c	6.50	19.50	45.00
57-Rip Kirby-"Kidnap Racket;" entire book by Alex Raymond	9.25	28.00	65.00
58-Girls in White	3.00	9.00	21.00
59-Tales of the Invisible Scarlet O'Neil	6.50	20.00	45.00
60-Paramount Animated Comics No.1(2nd app. Baby Huey); 1st Harvey app. Baby Huey	16.00	48.00	110.00
61-Casper the Friendly Ghost; 1st Harvey Casper	14.50	43.50	105.00
62-Paramount Animated Comics	7.00	21.00	50.00

HARVEY COMICS LIBRARY
April, 1952 - No. 2, 1952
Harvey Publications

1-Teen-Age Dope Slaves as exposed by Rex Morgan, M.D.; drug propaganda story; used in **SOTI**, pg. 27	57.00	171.00	400.00
(Prices vary widely on this book)			
2-Sparkle Plenty (Dick Tracy in "Blackmail Terror")	11.50	34.50	80.00

HARVEY HIT COMICS
Nov, 1986 - Present
Harvey Publications

1-3		.40	.75

HARVEY HITS
Sept, 1957 - No. 122, Nov, 1967
Harvey Publications

1-The Phantom	9.50	28.50	66.00
2-Rags Rabbit(10/57)	1.35	4.00	8.00
3-Richie Rich(11/57)-r/Little Dot; 1st book devoted to Richie Rich; see Little Dot for 1st app.	54.00	160.00	320.00
4-Little Dot's Uncles	8.00	24.00	48.00
5-Stevie Mazie's Boy Friend	1.35	4.00	8.00
6-The Phantom; Kirby-c; 2pg. Powell-a	4.75	14.00	28.00
7-Wendy the Witch	8.00	24.00	48.00
8-Sad Sack's Army Life	2.75	8.00	16.00
9-Richie Rich's Golden Deeds-r (2nd book devoted to Richie Rich)	25.00	75.00	150.00
10-Little Lotta	6.00	18.00	36.00
11-Little Audrey Summer Fun (7/58)	4.35	13.00	26.00
12-The Phantom; Kirby-c; 2pg. Powell-a	4.00	12.00	24.00
13-Little Dot's Uncles (9/58); Richie Rich 1pg.	5.35	16.00	32.00
14-Herman & Katnip (10/58)	1.35	4.00	8.00
15-The Phantom (1958)-1 pg. origin	3.00	9.00	18.00
16-Wendy the Witch (1/59)	4.00	12.00	24.00
17-Sad Sack's Army Life (2/59)	1.35	4.00	8.00
18-Buzzy & the Crow	1.35	4.00	8.00
19-Little Audrey	2.75	8.00	16.00
20-Casper & Spooky	4.00	12.00	24.00
21-Wendy the Witch	3.00	9.00	18.00
22-Sad Sack's Army Life	1.00	3.00	6.00
23-Wendy the Witch	3.00	9.00	18.00
24-Little Dot's Uncles (9/59); Richie Rich 1pg.	4.00	12.00	24.00
25-Herman & Katnip (10/59)	1.00	3.00	6.00
26-The Phantom (11/59)	3.00	9.00	18.00
27-Wendy the Good Little Witch	3.00	9.00	18.00
28-Sad Sack's Army Life	.50	1.50	3.00

Happy Houlihans #1, © WMG

Harvey Comics Hits #54, © HARV

Harvey Hits #12, © HARV

Harvey Hits #50, © HARV

Haunted #21, © CC

Haunted Thrills #4, © AJAX

HARVEY HITS (continued)	Good	Fine	Mint
29-Harvey-Toon (No.1)('60); Casper, Buzzy	2.00	6.00	12.00
30-Wendy the Witch (3/60)	2.75	8.00	16.00
31-Herman & Katnip (4/60)	.70	2.00	4.00
32-Sad Sack's Army Life (5/60)	.50	1.50	3.00
33-Wendy the Witch (6/60)	2.75	8.00	16.00
34-Harvey-Toon (7/60)	1.00	3.00	6.00
35-Funday Funnies (8/60)	.70	2.00	4.00
36-The Phantom (1960)	2.00	6.00	12.00
37-Casper & Nightmare	2.00	6.00	12.00
38-Harvey-Toon	1.35	4.00	8.00
39-Sad Sack's Army Life (12/60)	.50	1.50	3.00
40-Funday Funnies	.50	1.50	3.00
41-Herman & Katnip	.50	1.50	3.00
42-Harvey-Toon (3/61)	.80	2.30	4.60
43-Sad Sack's Army Life (4/61)	.35	1.00	2.00
44-The Phantom	2.00	6.00	12.00
45-Casper & Nightmare	2.00	5.00	10.00
46-Harvey-Toon	.80	2.30	4.60
47-Sad Sack's Army Life (8/61)	.40	1.20	2.40
48-The Phantom (1961)	2.00	6.00	12.00
49-Stumbo the Giant (See Hot Stuff for 1st app.)	5.00	15.00	30.00
50-Harvey-Toon (11/61)	.80	2.30	4.60
51-Sad Sack's Army Life (12/61)	.40	1.20	2.40
52-Casper & Nightmare	1.70	5.00	10.00
53-Harvey-Toons (2/62)	.70	2.00	4.00
54-Stumbo the Giant	2.75	8.00	16.00
55-Sad Sack's Army Life (4/62)	.40	1.20	2.40
56-Casper & Nightmare	1.70	5.00	10.00
57-Stumbo the Giant	2.75	8.00	16.00
58-Sad Sack's Army Life	.40	1.20	2.40
59-Casper & Nightmare (7/62)	1.70	5.00	10.00
60-Stumbo the Giant (9/62)	2.75	8.00	16.00
61-Sad Sack's Army Life	.40	1.20	2.40
62-Casper & Nightmare	1.35	4.00	8.00
63-Stumbo the Giant	2.75	8.00	16.00
64-Sad Sack's Army Life (1/63)	.40	1.20	2.40
65-Casper & Nightmare	1.35	4.00	8.00
66-Stumbo The Giant	2.75	8.00	16.00
67-Sad Sack's Army Life (4/63)	.40	1.20	2.40
68-Casper & Nightmare	1.35	4.00	8.00
69-Stumbo the Giant (6/63)	2.75	8.00	16.00
70-Sad Sack's Army Life (7/63)	.40	1.20	2.40
71-Casper & Nightmare (8/63)	.40	1.20	2.40
72-Stumbo the Giant	2.75	8.00	16.00
73-Little Sad Sack (10/63)	.40	1.20	2.40
74-Sad Sack's Muttsy... (11/63)	.40	1.20	2.40
75-Casper & Nightmare	1.00	3.00	6.00
76-Little Sad Sack	.40	1.20	2.40
77-Sad Sack's Muttsy...	.40	1.20	2.40
78-Stumbo the Giant	2.75	8.00	16.00
79-Little Sad Sack (4/64)	.40	1.20	2.40
80-Sad Sack's Muttsy... (5/64)	.40	1.20	2.40
81-Little Sad Sack	.40	1.20	2.40
82-Sad Sack's Muttsy...	.40	1.20	2.40
83-Little Sad Sack (8/64)	.40	1.20	2.40
84-Sad Sack's Muttsy...	.40	1.20	2.40
85-Gabby Gob (No.1)(10/64)	.40	1.20	2.40
86-G. I. Juniors (No.1)	.40	1.20	2.40
87-Sad Sack's Muttsy...	.40	1.20	2.40
88-Stumbo the Giant (1/65)	2.75	8.00	16.00
89-Sad Sack's Muttsy...	.40	1.20	2.40
90-Gabby Gob	.35	1.00	2.00
91-G. I. Juniors	.35	1.00	2.00
92-Sad Sack's Muttsy... (5/65)	.35	1.00	2.00
93-Sadie Sack (6/65)	.35	1.00	2.00
94-Gabby Gob	.35	1.00	2.00
95-G. I. Juniors	.35	1.00	2.00
96-Sad Sack's Muttsy... (9/65)	.35	1.00	2.00
97-Gabby Gob	.35	1.00	2.00
98-G. I. Juniors (9/65)	.35	1.00	2.00
99-Sad Sack's Muttsy... (12/65)	.35	1.00	2.00
100-Gabby Gob	.35	1.00	2.00
101-G. I. Juniors (2/66)	.35	1.00	2.00
102-Sad Sack's Muttsy... (3/66)	.35	1.00	2.00
103-Gabby Gob	.35	1.00	2.00
104-G. I. Juniors	.35	1.00	2.00
105-Sad Sack's Muttsy...	.35	1.00	2.00
106-Gabby Gob (7/66)	.35	1.00	2.00
107-G. I. Juniors (8/66)	.35	1.00	2.00
108-Sad Sack's Muttsy...	.35	1.00	2.00
109-Gabby Gob	.35	1.00	2.00
110-G. I. Juniors (11/66)	.35	1.00	2.00
111-Sad Sack's Muttsy... (12/66)	.35	1.00	2.00
112-G. I. Juniors	.35	1.00	2.00
113-Sad Sack's Muttsy...	.35	1.00	2.00
114-G. I. Juniors	.35	1.00	2.00
115-Sad Sack's Muttsy...	.35	1.00	2.00
116-G. I. Juniors	.35	1.00	2.00
117-Sad Sack's Muttsy...	.35	1.00	2.00
118-G. I. Juniors	.35	1.00	2.00
119-Sad Sack's Muttsy... (8/67)	.35	1.00	2.00
120-G. I. Juniors (9/67)	.35	1.00	2.00
121-Sad Sack's Muttsy... (10/67)	.35	1.00	2.00
122-G. I. Juniors	.35	1.00	2.00

HARVEY POP COMICS (Teen Humor)
Oct, 1968 - No. 2, Nov, 1969
Harvey Publications

	Good	Fine	Mint
1,2-The Cowsills	1.00	3.00	6.00

HARVEY 3-D HITS (See Sad Sack)

HARVEY-TOON (. . . S) (See Harvey Hits No. 29,34,38,42,46,50,53)

HATARI (See Movie Classics)

HATHAWAYS, THE (See 4-Color No. 1298)

HAUNTED (See This Magazine Is Haunted)

HAUNTED
9/71 - No. 30, 11/76; No. 31, 9/77 - No. 75, 9/84
Charlton Comics

	Good	Fine	Mint
1		.60	1.20
2-5		.50	1.00
6-21		.40	.80
22-75: 64,75-r		.30	.60

NOTE: ***Aparo*** *c-45.* ***Ditko*** *a-1-8, 11-16, 18, 23, 24, 28, 30, 34r, 36r, 39-42r, 47r, 49-51r, 60. c-1-7, 11, 13, 14, 16, 30, 41, 47, 49-51.* ***Howard*** *a-18, 22, 32.* ***Morisi*** *a-13.* ***Newton*** *a-17, 21; c-21,22(painted).* ***Staton*** *a-18, 21, 22, 30, 33; c-18, 33.* ***Sutton*** *a-21, 22, 38; c-17, 64r. No. 51 reprints No. 1; No. 49 reprints Tales/Myst. Traveler No. 4.*

HAUNTED LOVE
April, 1973 - No. 11, Sept, 1975
Charlton Comics

	Good	Fine	Mint
1-Tom Sutton-a, 16 pgs.		.50	1.00
2,3,6-11		.30	.60
4,5-Ditko-a		.40	.80
Modern Comics No. 1(1978)		.20	.40

NOTE: ***Howard*** *a-8i.* ***Newton*** *c-8,9.* ***Staton*** *a-5.*

HAUNTED THRILLS
June, 1952 - No. 18, Nov-Dec, 1954
Ajax/Farrell Publications

	Good	Fine	Mint
1: r-/Ellery Queen 1	7.00	21.00	50.00
2-L. B. Cole-a r-/Ellery Queen 1	5.50	16.50	38.00
3-5: 3-Drug use story	3.75	11.25	25.00

HAUNTED THRILLS (continued)

	Good	Fine	Mint
6-12: 12-Webb-a	2.85	8.50	20.00
13,16,17	2.15	6.50	15.00
14-Jesus Christ apps. in story by Webb	2.15	6.50	15.00
15-Jo-Jo-r	3.75	11.25	25.00
18-Lingerie panels	2.15	6.50	15.00

NOTE: *Kamenish art in most issues.*

HAUNT OF FEAR (Formerly Gunfighter)
No. 15, May-June, 1950 - No. 28, Nov-Dec, 1954
E. C. Comics

	Good	Fine	Mint
15(1950)	92.00	276.00	645.00
16	50.00	150.00	350.00
17-Origin of Crypt of Terror, Vault of Horror, & Haunt of Fear; used in **SOTI**, pg. 43; last pg. Ingels-a used by N.Y. Legis. Comm.	50.00	150.00	350.00
4	38.00	115.00	265.00
5-Injury-to-eye panel, pg. 4	28.00	84.00	195.00
6-10	20.00	60.00	140.00
11-13,15-18	13.50	41.00	95.00
14-Origin Old Witch by Ingels	20.00	60.00	140.00
19-Used in **SOTI**, ill.-"A comic book baseball game" & Senate investigation on juvenile delinq. bondage/decapitation-c	20.00	60.00	140.00
20-Feldstein r-/Vault of Horror No. 12	12.00	36.00	80.00
21,22,25,27	8.00	24.00	55.00
23-Used in **SOTI**, pg. 241	10.00	30.00	70.00
24-Used in Senate Investigative Report, pg. 8	9.00	27.00	60.00
26-Contains anti-censorship editorial, 'Are you a Red Dupe?'	9.00	27.00	60.00
28-Low distribution	9.00	27.00	60.00

(Canadian reprints known; see Table of Contents.)
NOTE: ***Craig** a-15-17, 5, 7, 10, 12, 13; c-15-17, 5-7. **Crandall** a-20, 21, 26, 27. **Davis** a-4-26, 28. **Evans** a-15-19, 22-25, 27. **Feldstein** a-15-17, 20; c-4, 8-10. **Ingels** a-16, 17, 4-28; c-11-28. **Kamen** a-16, 4, 6, 7, 9-11, 13-19, 21-28. **Krigstein** a-28. **Kurtzman** a-15/1, 17/3. **Orlando** a-9, 12. **Wood** a-15, 16, 4-6.*

HAUNT OF HORROR, THE (Magazine)
5/74 - No. 5, 1/75 (75 cents) (B&W)
Cadence Comics Publ. (Marvel)

	Good	Fine	Mint
1-Alcala-a	.85	2.50	5.00
2-Origin & 1st app. Gabriel the Devil Hunter; Satana begins	.70	2.00	4.00
3	.50	1.50	3.00
4-Adams-a	.70	2.00	4.00
5-Evans-a(2)	.50	1.50	3.00

NOTE: ***Alcala** a-2. **Colan** a-2p. **Heath** r-1. **Krigstein** r-3. **Reese** a-1.*

HAVE GUN, WILL TRAVEL (TV)
No. 931, 8/58 - No. 14, 7-9/62 (All Richard Boone photo-c)
Dell Publishing Co.

	Good	Fine	Mint
4-Color 931	3.50	10.50	24.00
4-Color 983,1044	3.00	9.00	21.00
4 (1-3/60) - 14	2.65	8.00	18.00

HAWAIIAN EYE (TV)
July, 1963 (Troy Donahue, Connie Stevens photo-c)
Gold Key

	Good	Fine	Mint
1 (10073-307)	1.75	5.25	12.00

HAWAIIAN ILLUSTRATED LEGENDS SERIES
1975 (B&W)(Cover printed w/blue, yellow, and green)
Hogarth Press

	Good	Fine	Mint
1-Kalelealuaka, the Mysterious Warrior		.60	1.20
2,3(Exist?)		.40	.80

HAWK, THE (Also see Approved Comics)
Wint/51 - No. 3, 11-12/52; No. 4, 1953 - No. 12, 5/55
Ziff-Davis/St. John Publ. Co. No. 4 on

	Good	Fine	Mint
1-Anderson-a	6.00	18.00	42.00
2-Kubert, Infantino-a; painted-c	3.50	10.50	24.00
3-8,10-11: 8-Reprints No. 3 with diff.-c. 10-Reprints one story/No. 2. 11-Buckskin Belle & The Texan app.	2.65	8.00	18.00
9-Baker c/a; Kubert-a(r)/No. 2	3.35	10.00	23.00
12-Baker c/a	3.35	10.00	23.00
3-D 1(11/53)-Baker-c	13.50	40.50	95.00

NOTE: ***Baker** c-8,9,11. **Tuska** a-9.*

HAWK AND THE DOVE, THE (See Showcase)
Aug-Sept, 1968 - No. 6, June-July, 1969
National Periodical Publications

	Good	Fine	Mint
1-Ditko c/a		.50	1.00
2-6: 5-Teen Titans cameo		.40	.80

NOTE: ***Ditko** c/a-2. **Gil Kane** a-3p, 4p, 5, 6p; c-3-6.*

HAWKEYE
Sept, 1983 - No. 4, Dec, 1983 (Mini-series)
Marvel Comics Group

	Good	Fine	Mint
1-Origin		.50	1.00
2-4: 3-Origin Mockingbird		.40	.80

HAWKEYE & THE LAST OF THE MOHICANS (See 4-Color No. 884)

HAWKMAN (See Atom & Hawkman, The Brave & the Bold, DC Comics Presents, Detective, Mystery in Space, Shadow War Of. . ., Showcase, & World's Finest)
Apr-May, 1964 - No. 27, Aug-Sept, 1968; Mar, 1986
National Periodical Publications

	Good	Fine	Mint
1	6.00	18.00	36.00
2	3.00	9.00	18.00
3-5: 4-Zatanna x-over(origin-1st app.)	1.35	4.00	8.00
6-10: 9-Atom cameo; Hawkman & Atom learn each other's I.D.; 2nd app. Shadow Thief	1.15	3.40	6.80
11-15	.70	2.00	4.00
16-27: Adam Strange x-over No. 18, cameo No. 19. 25-G.A. Hawkman-r	.45	1.40	2.80
. . . Special 1 (3/86)		.60	1.25

NOTE: ***Anderson** a-1-21; c-1-21. **Kubert** c-27. **Moldoff** a-25r.*

HAWKMAN
Aug, 1986 - Present
DC Comics

	Good	Fine	Mint
1		.50	1.00
2-8		.40	.80

HAWKMOON: THE JEWEL IN THE SKULL
May, 1986 - No. 4, Nov, 1986 (Limited series, Baxter)
First Comics

	Good	Fine	Mint
1-4: Adapts novel by Michael Moorcock	.35	1.00	2.00

HAWKMOON: THE MAD GOD'S AMULET
Jan, 1987 - No. 4, July, 1987 (Limited series)
First Comics

	Good	Fine	Mint
1-4: Adapts novel by Michael Moorcock	.30	.90	1.80

HAWKSHAW THE DETECTIVE (See Advs. of. . ., Hans & Fritz & Okay)
1917 (24 pgs.; B&W; 10½x13½") (Sunday strip reprints)
The Saalfield Publishing Co.

	Good	Fine	Mint
By Gus Mager	6.00	18.00	42.00

Haunt of Fear #4, © WMG

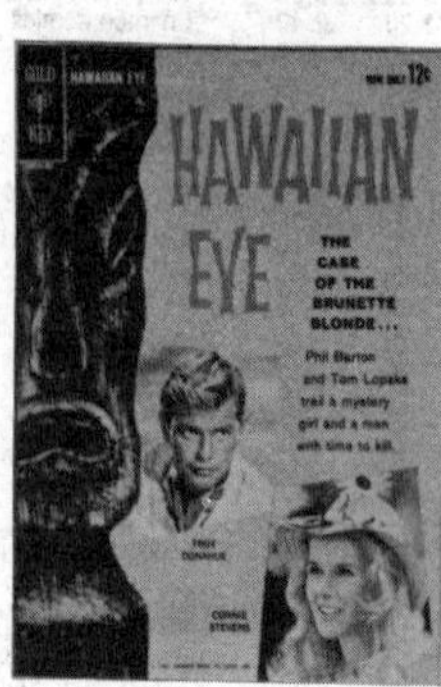

Hawaiian Eye #1, © Warner Bros.

Hawkman #1 (4-5/64), © DC

Headline Comics #12, © PRIZE

Heavy Armor #1, © Fantasy General

Heckle & Jeckle #2 (GK 2/63), © MGM

HAWTHORN-MELODY FARMS DAIRY COMICS
No date (1950's) (Giveaway)
Everybody's Publishing Co.

	Good	Fine	Mint
Cheerie Chick, Tuffy Turtle, Robin Koo Koo, Donald & Longhorn Legends	.70	2.50	5.00

HEADLINE COMICS (. . . Crime No. 32-39)
Feb, 1943 - No. 22, Nov-Dec, 1946; 1947 - No. 77, Oct, 1956
Prize Publications

	Good	Fine	Mint
1-Yank & Doodle x-over in Junior Rangers	12.00	36.00	84.00
2	5.50	16.50	38.00
3-Used in **POP**, pg. 84	6.00	18.00	42.00
4-7,9,10: 4,10-Hitler story	4.00	12.00	28.00
8-Classic Hitler-c	5.75	17.25	40.00
11,12	2.65	8.00	18.00
13-15-Blue Streak in all	3.00	9.00	21.00
16-Origin Atomic Man	6.00	18.00	42.00
17,18,20,21: 21-Atomic Man ends	3.75	11.25	26.00
19-S&K-a	9.35	28.00	65.00
22-Kiefer-c	1.85	5.50	13.00
23-(All S&K-a)	9.35	28.00	65.00
24-(All S&K-a); dope-crazy killer story	9.35	28.00	65.00
25-35-S&K c/a. 25-Powell-a	5.00	15.00	35.00
36-S&K-a	3.35	10.00	23.00
37-One pg. S&K, Severin-a	2.35	7.00	16.00
38,40-Meskin-a	1.65	5.00	11.50
39,41-43,45-48,50-55: 51-Kirby-c	1.00	3.00	7.00
44-S&K-c; Severin/Elder, Meskin-a	3.15	9.50	22.00
49-Meskin-a	1.30	4.00	9.00
56,57-S&K-a	2.35	7.00	16.00
58-77: 72-Meskin c/a(i)	1.00	3.00	7.00

HEAP, THE
Sept, 1971 (52 pages)
Skywald Publications

	Good	Fine	Mint
1-Kinstler-a, r-/Strange Worlds No. 8	.50	1.50	3.00

HEART AND SOUL
April-May, 1954 - No. 2, June-July, 1954
Mikeross Publications

	Good	Fine	Mint
1,2	2.15	6.50	15.00

HEART THROBS (Love Stories No. 147 on)
8/49 - No. 8, 10/50; No. 9, 3/51 - No. 146, Oct, 1972
Quality/National No. 47(4-5/57) on (Arleigh No. 48-101)

	Good	Fine	Mint
1-Classic Ward-c, Gustavson-a, 9pgs.	17.00	51.00	120.00
2-Ward c/a, 9 pgs; Gustavson-a	10.00	30.00	70.00
3-Gustavson-a	4.00	12.00	28.00
4,6,8-Ward-a, 8-9 pgs.	6.50	19.50	45.00
5,7	2.15	6.50	15.00
9-Robert Mitchum, Jane Russell photo-c	2.50	7.50	17.50
10,15-Ward-a	4.65	14.00	32.00
11-14,16-20: 12 (7/52)	1.50	4.50	10.00
21-Ward-c	3.65	11.00	25.00
22,23-Ward-a(p)	2.65	8.00	18.00
24-32: 24-Lingerie panels. 32-Last pre-code?	1.15	3.50	8.00
33-39,41-46 (12/56; last Quality)	1.00	3.00	7.00
40-Ward-a; r-7 pgs./No. 21	2.00	6.00	14.00
47-(4-5/57; 1st DC)	2.35	7.00	16.00
48-60	.85	2.50	6.00
61-70	.55	1.65	4.00
71-100	.50	1.50	3.00
101-The Beatles app. on-c	1.50	4.50	10.00
102-119,121-146: 102-123-(Serial)-Three Girls, Their Lives, Their Loves	.25	.75	1.50
120-Adams-c	.35	1.00	2.00

NOTE: ***Gustavson** a-8. Photo-c 8, 9, 17.*

HEATHCLIFF
Apr, 1985 - Present
Star Comics (Marvel)

	Good	Fine	Mint
1-15		.35	.70

HEATHCLIFF'S FUNHOUSE
March, 1987 - Present
Star Comics (Marvel)

	Good	Fine	Mint
1		.40	.75

HEAVY ARMOR
1985 - No. 3, 1985 ($1.70, B&W) (mini-series)
Fantasy General Comics

	Good	Fine	Mint
1-3	.30	.90	1.70

HECKLE AND JECKLE (See Blue Ribbon, Paul Terry's & Terry-Toons Comics)
10/51 - No. 24, 10/55; No. 25, Fall/56 - No. 34, 6/59
St. John Publ. Co. No. 1-24/Pines No. 25 on

	Good	Fine	Mint
1	11.50	34.50	80.00
2	5.50	16.50	38.00
3-5	4.00	12.00	28.00
6-10	3.15	9.50	22.00
11-20	2.00	6.00	14.00
21-34	1.15	3.50	8.00

HECKLE AND JECKLE (TV) (See New Terrytoons)
11/62 - No. 4, 8/63; 5/66; No. 2, 10/66 - No. 3, 8/67
Gold Key/Dell Publishing Co.

	Good	Fine	Mint
1 (11/62; Gold Key)	1.15	3.50	8.00
2-4	.75	2.25	5.00
1 (5/66; Dell)	.85	2.50	6.00
2,3	.70	2.00	4.00

(See March of Comics No. 379,472,484)

HECTOR COMICS
Nov, 1953 - 1954
Key Publications

	Good	Fine	Mint
1	1.75	5.25	12.00
2,3	1.00	3.00	7.00

HECTOR HEATHCOTE (TV)
March, 1964
Gold Key

	Good	Fine	Mint
1 (10111-403)	1.50	4.50	10.00

HEDY DEVINE COMICS (Formerly All Winners No. 21?; Hedy of Hollywood No. 36 on; also see Annie Oakley & Venus)
No. 22, Aug, 1947 - No. 50, Sept, 1952
Marvel Comics (RCM)

	Good	Fine	Mint
22	3.15	9.50	22.00
23,24,27-30: 23-Wolverton-a, 1 pg; Kurtzman's ''Hey Look,'' 2 pgs. 24,27-30-''Hey Look'' by Kurtzman, 1-3 pgs.	4.35	13.00	30.00
25-Classic ''Hey Look'' by Kurtzman-''Optical Illusion''	5.00	15.00	35.00
26-''Giggles & Grins'' by Kurtzman	3.35	10.00	23.00
31-34,36-50: 32-Anti-Wertham editorial	1.50	4.50	10.00
35-Four pgs. ''Rusty'' by Kurtzman	3.35	10.00	23.00

HEDY-MILLIE-TESSIE COMEDY (See Comedy)

HEDY WOLFE
August, 1957
Atlas Publishing Co. (Emgee)

	Good	Fine	Mint
1	2.00	6.00	14.00

HEE HAW (TV)
July, 1970 - No. 7, Aug, 1971

HEE HAW (continued)
Charlton Press

	Good	Fine	Mint
1-7	.50	1.50	3.00

HEIDI (See Dell Jr. Treasury No. 6)

HELEN OF TROY (See 4-Color No. 684)

HELLO, I'M JOHNNY CASH
1976 (39-49 cents)
Spire Christian Comics (Fleming H. Revell Co.)

	Good	Fine	Mint
nn		.40	.80

HELL ON EARTH (See DC Science Fic. Graphic Novel)

HELLO PAL COMICS (Short Story Comics)
Jan, 1943 - No. 3, May, 1943 (Photo-c)
Harvey Publications

	Good	Fine	Mint
1-Rocketman & Rocketgirl begin; Yankee Doodle Jones app.; Mickey Rooney cover	20.00	60.00	140.00
2-Charlie McCarthy cover	13.50	40.50	95.00
3-Bob Hope cover	14.50	43.50	100.00

HELL-RIDER (Magazine)
Aug, 1971 - No. 2, Oct, 1971 (B&W)
Skywald Publications

	Good	Fine	Mint
1-Origin & 1st app.; Butterfly & Wildbunch begins; heroin drug story	.80	2.40	3.60
2	.70	2.00	3.00

NOTE: *No. 3 advertised in Psycho No. 5 but did not come out.* ***Buckler*** *a-1,2.* ***Morrow*** *c-3.*

HE-MAN (See Masters Of The Universe)

HE-MAN
Fall, 1952
Ziff-Davis Publ. Co. (Approved Comics)

	Good	Fine	Mint
1-Kinstler-c; Powell-a	4.35	13.00	30.00

HE-MAN
May, 1954 - No. 2, July, 1954
Toby Press

	Good	Fine	Mint
1	4.00	12.00	28.00
2	2.65	8.00	18.00

HENNESSEY (See 4-Color No. 1200,1280)

HENRY
1935 (52 pages) (Daily B&W strip reprints)
David McKay Publications

	Good	Fine	Mint
1-by Carl Anderson	5.00	15.00	35.00

HENRY
No. 122, Oct, 1946 - No. 65, Apr-June, 1961
Dell Publishing Co.

	Good	Fine	Mint
4-Color 122	4.35	13.00	30.00
4-Color 155 (7/47)	3.50	10.50	24.00
1 (1-3/48)	3.50	10.50	24.00
2	1.75	5.25	12.00
3-10	1.30	4.00	9.00
11-20: 20-Infinity-c	1.00	3.00	7.00
21-30	.75	2.25	5.00
31-40	.55	1.65	4.00
41-65	.40	1.25	3.00

HENRY (See March of Comics No. 43, 58, 84, 101, 112, 129, 147, 162, 178, 189 and Giant Comic Album)

HENRY ALDRICH COMICS (TV)
Aug-Sept, 1950 - No. 22, Sept-Nov, 1954
Dell Publishing Co.

	Good	Fine	Mint
1-Part series written by John Stanley; Bill Williams-a	3.50	10.50	24.00
2	2.00	6.00	14.00
3-5	1.70	5.00	12.00
6-10	1.50	4.50	10.00
11-22	1.15	3.50	8.00

HENRY BREWSTER
Feb, 1966 - V2No.7, Sept, 1967 (All Giants)
Country Wide (M.F. Ent.)

	Good	Fine	Mint
1-6(12/66)-Powell-a in most		.40	.80
V2No.7		.30	.60

HERBIE (See Forbidden Worlds)
April-May, 1964 - No. 23, Feb, 1967
American Comics Group

	Good	Fine	Mint
1	6.75	20.00	47.00
2-4	3.35	10.00	23.00
5-Beatles, Dean Martin, F. Sinatra app.	4.00	12.00	28.00
6,7,9,10	2.00	6.00	14.00
8-Origin The Fat Fury	3.00	9.00	21.00
11-22: 14-Nemesis & MagicMan app. 17-R-1st Herbie/F.W. No. 73	1.35	4.00	9.00
23-R-2nd Herbie/F.W. No.94	1.35	4.00	9.00

NOTE: *Most have* ***Whitney*** *c/a.*

HERBIE GOES TO MONTE CARLO, HERBIE RIDES AGAIN (See Walt Disney Showcase No. 24, 41)

HERCULES
Oct, 1967 - No. 13, Sept, 1969; Dec, 1968
Charlton Comics

	Good	Fine	Mint
1-Thane of Bagarth series begins; Glanzman-a	.55	1.65	4.00
2-13: 10-Aparo-a	.35	1.00	2.00
8-(Low distribution)(12/68)-35¢; magazine format; B&W; reprints	2.35	7.00	16.00
Modern Comics reprint 10('77), 11('78)		.20	.40

HERCULES (See The Mighty . . .)

HERCULES, PRINCE OF POWER
9/82 - No. 4, 12/82; 3/84 - No. 4, 6/84
Marvel Comics Group

	Good	Fine	Mint
1	.25	.75	1.50
2-4		.50	1.00
V2/1 (Mini-series)	.25	.75	1.50
2-4		.50	1.00

NOTE: ***Layton*** *a-1, 2, 3p, 4p, V2/1-4; c-1-4, V2/1-4.*

HERCULES UNBOUND
Oct-Nov, 1975 - No. 12, Aug-Sept, 1977
National Periodical Publications

	Good	Fine	Mint
1-Wood inks begin		.40	.80
2-5		.30	.60
6-12: 10-Atomic Knights x-over		.25	.50

NOTE: ***Buckler*** *c-7p.* ***Layton*** *inks-No. 9, 10.* ***Simonson*** *a-7-10p, 11, 12; c- 8p, 9-12.* ***Wood*** *inks-1-8; c-7i, 8i.*

HERCULES UNCHAINED (See 4-Color No. 1006,1121)

HERE COMES SANTA (See March of Comics No. 30,213,340)

HERE IS SANTA CLAUS
1930s (16 pgs., 8 in color) (stiff paper covers)
Goldsmith Publishing Co. (Kann's in Washington, D.C.)

	Good	Fine	Mint
nn	3.50	10.50	24.00

He-Man #1, © TOBY

Herbie #2, © ACG

Hercules, Prince of Power #3 (11/82), © MCG

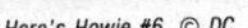
Here's Howie #6, © DC

Heroes, Inc. #1, © Wally Wood

Heroic Comics #62, © EAS

HERE'S HOW AMERICA'S CARTOONISTS HELP TO SELL U.S. SAVINGS BONDS
1950? (16 pgs.; paper cover)
Harvey Comics giveaway

	Good	Fine	Mint
Contains: Joe Palooka, Donald Duck, Archie, Kerry Drake, Red Ryder, Blondie & Steve Canyon	12.00	35.00	70.00

HERE'S HOWIE COMICS
Jan-Feb, 1952 - No. 18, Nov-Dec, 1954
National Periodical Publications

1	8.50	25.50	60.00
2	3.85	11.50	27.00
3-5	3.65	11.00	25.00
6-10	2.85	8.50	20.00
11-18	2.15	6.50	15.00

HERMAN & KATNIP (See Harvey Hits No. 14,25,31,41)

HERO ALLIANCE, THE
Dec, 1985; No. 2, Sept, 1986 - Present (No. 2, $1.50)
Sirius Comics

1		.65	1.30
2	.25	.75	1.50
The Special Edition 1 (7/86)-Full color	.25	.75	1.50

HEROES
1986 - Present (B&W) (No. 1-3, mag.-size)
Blackbird Comics

1	1.00	3.00	6.00
2,3	.65	1.90	3.80
4,5: Begin comic book size	.40	1.25	2.50

HEROES AGAINST HUNGER
1986 (One shot)
DC Comics

1-Superman, Batman app.; Adams-c(p)	.30	.90	1.80

HEROES ALL CATHOLIC ACTION ILLUSTRATED
1943 - V6No.5, March 10, 1948 (paper covers)
Heroes All Co.

V1No.1,2-(16 pgs., 8x11")	4.00	12.00	28.00
V2No.1(1/44)-3(3/44)-(16 pgs., 8x11")	2.50	7.50	17.50
V3No.1(1/45)-10(10/45)-(16 pgs., 8x11")	2.00	6.00	14.00
V4No.1-35 (12/20/46)-(16 pgs.)	1.50	4.50	10.00
V5No.1(1/10/47)-8(2/28/47)-(16 pgs.)	1.15	3.50	8.00
V5No.9(3/7/47)-20(11/25/47)-(32 pgs.)	1.15	3.50	8.00
V6No.1(1/10/48)-5(3/10/48)-(32 pgs.)	1.15	3.50	8.00

HEROES FOR HOPE STARRING THE X-MEN
Dec, 1985 ($1.50, One Shot, 52 pgs.)
Marvel Comics Group

1-Proceeds donated to famine relief; scripts by Harlan Ellison, Stephen King; Wrightson, Corben-a	.35	1.10	2.20

HEROES, INC. PRESENTS CANNON
1969 - No. 2, 1976 (Sold at Army PX's)
Wally Wood/CPL/Gang Publ. No. 2

nn-Wood/Ditko-a	1.35	4.00	8.00
2-Wood-c; Ditko, Byrne, Wood-a; 8½x10½"; B&W; $2.00	.70	2.00	4.00

NOTE: *First issue not distributed by publisher; 1,800 copies were stored and 900 copies were stolen from warehouse. Many copies have surfaced in recent years.*

HEROES OF THE WILD FRONTIER (Formerly Baffling Mysteries)
No. 26, 3/55; No. 27, 1/56 - No. 2, 4/56
Ace Periodicals

26(No.1)	1.75	5.25	12.00
27,28,2	1.00	3.00	7.00

HERO FOR HIRE (Power Man No. 17 on)
June, 1972 - No. 16, Dec, 1973
Marvel Comics Group

	Good	Fine	Mint
1-Origin Luke Cage retold; marijuana mention: Tuska-a(p)	.50	1.50	3.00
2-10: 3-1st pp. Mace. 4-1st app. Phil Fox of the Bugle; 2,3-Tuska-a(p)		.50	1.00
11-16: 14-Origin retold. 15-Everett Subby-r('53). 16-Origin Stilletto; death of Rackham		.50	1.00

HEROIC ADVENTURES (See Adventures)

HEROIC COMICS (Reg'lar Fellas No. 1-15; New Heroic No. 41 on)
Aug, 1940 - No. 97, June, 1955
Eastern Color Printing Co./Famous Funnies(Funnies, Inc. No. 1)

1-Hydroman(origin) by Bill Everett, The Purple Zombie(origin) & Mann of India by Tarpe Mills begins	35.00	105.00	245.00
2	18.00	54.00	125.00
3,4	15.00	45.00	105.00
5,6	11.00	33.00	76.00
7-Origin Man O'Metal, 1 pg.	13.50	40.50	95.00
8-10: 10-Lingerie panels	8.00	24.00	56.00
11,13: 13-Crandall/Fine-a	6.50	19.50	45.00
12-Music Master(origin) begins by Everett, ends No. 31; last Purple Zombie & Mann of India	8.50	25.50	60.00
14-Hydroman x-over in Rainbow Boy; also in No. 15; origin Rainbow Boy	8.50	25.50	60.00
15-Intro. Downbeat	8.00	24.00	56.00
16-20: 17-Rainbow Boy x-over in Hydroman. 19-Rainbow Boy x-over in Hydroman & vice versa	5.50	16.50	38.00
21-30: No. 25-Rainbow Boy x-over in Hydroman. 28-Last Man O'Metal. 29-Last Hydroman	3.35	10.00	23.00
31,34,38	1.20	3.50	8.00
32,36,37-Toth-a, 3-4 pgs.	2.00	6.00	14.00
33,35-Toth-a, 8 & 9 pgs.	2.35	7.00	16.00
39-42-Toth, Ingels-a	2.35	7.00	16.00
43,46,47,49-Toth-a, 2-4 pgs. 47-Ingels-a	1.50	4.50	10.00
44,45,50-Toth-a, 6-9 pgs.	1.70	5.00	12.00
48,52-54	.85	2.50	6.00
51-Williamson-a	3.35	10.00	23.00
55-Toth c/a	1.50	4.50	10.00
56-60-Toth-c. 60-Everett-a	1.20	3.50	8.00
61-Everett-a	.85	2.50	6.00
62,64-Everett-c/a	1.00	3.00	7.00
63-Everett-c	.70	2.00	5.00
65-Williamson/Frazetta-a; Evans-a, 2 pgs.	4.35	13.00	30.00
66,75,94-Frazetta-a, 2 pgs. each	1.50	4.50	10.00
67,73-Frazetta-a, 4 pgs. each	2.50	7.50	17.00
68,74,76-80,84,85,88-93,95-97	.60	1.80	4.00
69,72-Frazetta-a (6 & 8 pgs. each)	4.35	13.00	30.00
70,71,86,87-Frazetta, 3-4 pgs. each; 1 pg. drug mention by Frazetta in No. 70	2.50	7.50	17.00
81,82-One pg. Frazetta art	1.00	3.00	7.00
83-Frazetta-a, ½ pg.	1.00	3.00	7.00

NOTE: ***Evans** a-64, 65. **Everett** a-(Hydroman-c/a-No. 1-9), 44, 60-64; c-1-9, 62-64. **Sid Greene** a-38-43, 46. **Guardineer** a-42(3), 43, 44, 45(2), 49(3), 50, 60, 61(2), 65, 67(2), 70-72. **Ingels** c-41. **Kiefer** a-46, 48; c-19-22, 24, 44, 46, 48, 51-53, 65, 67-69, 71-74, 76, 77, 79, 80, 82, 85, 88, 89. **Mort Lawrence** a-45. **Tarpe Mills** a-2(2), 3(2), 10. **Ed Moore** a-49, 52-54, 56-63, 65-69, 72-74, 76, 77. **H.G. Peter** a-58-74, 76, 77, 87. **Paul Reinman** a-49. **Rico** a-31. Captain Tootsie by Beck-31, 32.*

HERO MAN
1986 - Present ($1.75, B&W)
Dimension Graphics

1	.30	.90	1.75

HEX (Replaces Jonah Hex)
Sept, 1985 - No. 18, Feb, 1987
DC Comics

1-Hex in post-atomic war world; origin		.65	1.30

HEX (continued) — Good | Fine | Mint

	Good	Fine	Mint
2-5		.45	.90
6-18: 6-Origin Stiletta. 13-Intro The Dogs of War (Origin No. 15)		.40	.80

HEY THERE, IT'S YOGI BEAR (See Movie Comics)

HI-ADVENTURE HEROES (Hanna-Barbera)(TV)
May, 1969 - No. 2, Aug, 1969
Gold Key

	Good	Fine	Mint
1-Three Musketeers, Gulliver, Arabian Knights stories	.55	1.65	4.00
2-Three Musketeers, Micro-Venture, Arabian Knights	.30	.90	2.00

HI AND LOIS (See 4-Color No. 683,774,955)

HI AND LOIS
Nov, 1969 - No. 11, July, 1971
Charlton Comics

	Good	Fine	Mint
1	.50	1.50	3.00
2-11	.35	1.00	2.00

HICKORY
Oct, 1949 - No. 6, Aug, 1950
Quality Comics Group

	Good	Fine	Mint
1-Sahl c/a; Feldstein?-a	5.00	15.00	35.00
2	2.65	8.00	18.00
3-6	2.35	7.00	16.00

HIDDEN CREW, THE (See The United States A. F.)

HIDE-OUT (See 4-Color No. 346)

HIDING PLACE, THE
1973 (35-49 cents)
Spire Christian Comics/Fleming H. Revell Co.

	Good	Fine	Mint
nn		.40	.80

HIGH ADVENTURE
October, 1957
Red Top(Decker) Comics (Farrell)

	Good	Fine	Mint
1-Krigstein-r from Explorer Joe (re-issue on cover)	1.65	5.00	11.50

HIGH ADVENTURE (See 4-Color No. 949,1001)

HIGH CHAPPARAL (TV)
August, 1968
Gold Key

	Good	Fine	Mint
1 (10226-808)-Tufts-a	2.15	6.50	15.00

HIGH SCHOOL CONFIDENTIAL DIARY (Confidential Diary No. 12 on)
June, 1960 - No. 11, March, 1962
Charlton Comics

	Good	Fine	Mint
1	.75	2.25	5.00
2-11	.35	1.00	2.00

HI-HO COMICS
nd (2/46?) - No. 3, 1946
Four Star Publications

	Good	Fine	Mint
1-Funny Animal; L. B. Cole-c	5.75	17.25	40.00
2,3: 2-L. B. Cole-c	3.35	10.00	23.00

HI-JINX
July-Aug, 1947 - 1949
B&I Publ. Co.(American Comics Group)/Creston/LaSalle

	Good	Fine	Mint
1	4.00	12.00	28.00
2,3	2.00	6.00	14.00
4-7-Milt Gross	3.15	9.50	22.00
132 Pg. issue, nn, no date (LaSalle)	5.75	17.25	40.00

HI-LITE COMICS
Fall, 1945
E. R. Ross Publishing Co.

	Good	Fine	Mint
1-Miss Shady	4.50	13.50	31.00

HILLBILLY COMICS
Aug, 1955 - No. 4, July, 1956 (Satire)
Charlton Comics

	Good	Fine	Mint
1	2.15	6.50	15.00
2-4	1.15	3.50	8.00

HIP-IT-TY HOP (See March of Comics No. 15)

HI-SCHOOL ROMANCE (. . .Romances No. 41 on)
Oct, 1949 - No. 5, June, 1950; No. 6, Dec, 1950 - No. 73, Mar, 1958; No. 74, Sept, 1958 - No. 75, Nov, 1958
Harvey Publications/True Love(Home Comics)

	Good	Fine	Mint
1	3.00	9.00	21.00
2	1.70	5.00	12.00
3-9: 5-Photo-c	1.35	4.00	9.00
10-Rape story	1.70	5.00	12.00
11-20	1.00	3.00	7.00
21-31	.85	2.50	6.00
32-''Unholy passion'' story	1.35	4.00	9.00
33-36: 36-Last pre-code (2/55)	.70	2.00	5.00
37-75	.60	1.80	4.00

NOTE: ***Powell*** *a-1-3, 5, 8, 12-14, 16, 18, 21-23, 25-27, 30-34, 36, 37, 39, 45-48, 50-52, 57, 58, 60, 64, 65, 67, 69.*

HI-SCHOOL ROMANCE DATE BOOK
Nov, 1962 - No. 3, Mar, 1963 (25¢ Giant)
Harvey Publications

	Good	Fine	Mint
1-Powell, Baker-a	2.35	7.00	14.00
2,3	1.00	3.00	6.00

HIS NAME IS SAVAGE (Magazine format)
No. 1, June, 1968 (One Shot)
Adventure House Press

	Good	Fine	Mint
1-Gil Kane-a	1.75	5.25	12.00

HI-SPOT COMICS (Red Ryder No. 1 & No. 3 on)
No. 2, Nov, 1940
Hawley Publications

	Good	Fine	Mint
2-David Innes of Pellucidar; art by J. C. Burroughs; written by Edgar R. Burroughs	45.00	135.00	315.00

HISTORY OF THE DC UNIVERSE
9/86 - No. 3, 11/86; 1/87 - No. 2, 2/87
DC Comics

	Good	Fine	Mint
1-3 (1st Series)-Perez c/a	.70	2.00	4.00
2,3	.80	1.75	3.50
1,2 (2nd Series)	.50	1.50	3.00

HIT COMICS
July, 1940 - No. 65, July, 1950
Quality Comics Group

	Good	Fine	Mint
1-Origin Neon, the Unknown & Hercules; intro. The Red Bee; Blaze Barton, the Strange Twins, X-5 Super Agent, Casey Jones, Jack & Jill (ends No.7), & Bob & Swab begin	155.00	465.00	1085.00
2-The Old Witch begins, ends No. 14	75.00	225.00	525.00
3-Casey Jones ends; transvestite story-'Jack & Jill'	60.00	180.00	420.00

Hex #2, © DC

Hickory #1, © QUA

Hi-School Romance #5, © HARV

Hit Comics #31, © QUA

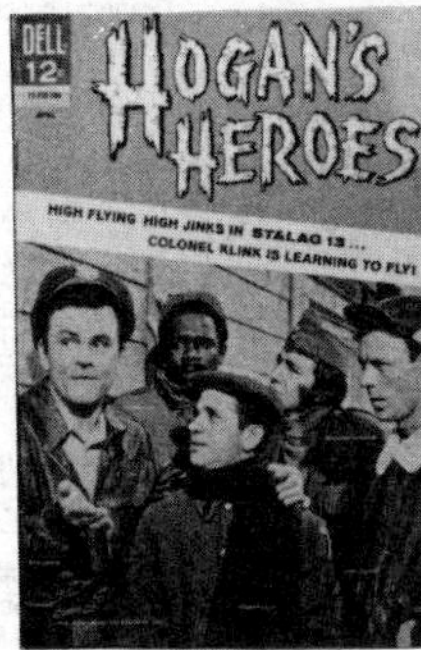

Hogan's Heroes #5, © Bing Crosby

Hollywood Secrets #5, © QUA

HIT COMICS (continued)

	Good	Fine	Mint
4-Super Agent (ends No. 17), & Betty Bates (ends No. 65) begin; X-5 ends	50.00	150.00	350.00
5-Classic cover	75.00	225.00	525.00
6-10: 10-Old Witch by Crandall, 4 pgs.-1st work in comics	42.00	125.00	295.00
11-17: 13-Blaze Barton ends. 17-Last Neon; Crandall Hercules in all	40.00	120.00	280.00
18-Origin Stormy Foster, the Great Defender; The Ghost of Flanders begins; Crandall-c	43.00	130.00	300.00
19,20	40.00	120.00	280.00
21-24: 21-Last Hercules. 24-Last Red Bee & Strange Twins	34.00	102.00	236.00
25-Origin Kid Eternity by Moldoff	43.00	130.00	300.00
26-Blackhawk x-over in Kid Eternity	30.00	90.00	210.00
27-29	18.00	54.00	126.00
30,31-''Bill the Magnificent'' by Kurtzman, 11 pgs. in each	16.00	48.00	110.00
32-40: 32-Plastic Man x-over. 34-Last Stormy Foster	8.50	25.50	60.00
41-50	5.85	17.50	40.00
51-60-Last Kid Eternity	5.00	15.00	35.00
61,63-Crandall c/a; Jeb Rivers begins No. 61	5.85	17.50	40.00
62	4.35	13.00	30.00
64,65-Crandall-a	5.35	16.00	37.00

NOTE: ***Crandall** a-11-17(Hercules), 23, 24(Stormy Foster); c-18-20, 23, 24. **Fine** c-1-14, 16, 17(most). **Ward** c-33. Bondage c-64.*

HI-YO SILVER (See Lone Ranger's Famous Horse . . ., March of Comics No. 215, and The Lone Ranger)

HOCUS POCUS (Formerly Funny Book)
No. 9, Aug-Sept, 1946
Parents' Magazine Press

9	1.75	5.25	12.00

HOGAN'S HEROES (TV) (No. 1-7 have photo-c)
June, 1966 - No. 8, Sept, 1967; No. 9, Oct, 1969
Dell Publishing Co.

1	2.00	6.00	14.00
2,4-9: No. 9-Reprints No. 1	1.15	3.50	8.00
3-Ditko-a(p)	1.50	4.50	10.00

HOLIDAY COMICS
1942 (196 pages) (25 cents)
Fawcett Publications

1-Contains three Fawcett comics; Capt. Marvel, Nyoka No. 1, & Whiz. Not rebound, remaindered comics—printed at the same time as originals	62.00	185.00	435.00

HOLIDAY COMICS
January, 1951 - No. 8, Oct, 1952
Star Publications

1-Funny animal contents (Frisky Fables) in all; L. B. Cole-c.	8.00	24.00	56.00
2-Classic L. B. Cole-c	8.50	25.50	60.00
3-8: 5,8-X-Mas-c; all L.B. Cole-c	6.50	19.50	45.00
Accepted Reprint 4 (nd)-L.B. Cole-c	3.00	9.00	21.00

HOLI-DAY SURPRISE (Formerly Summer Fun)
No. 55, Mar, 1967 (25 cents)
Charlton Comics

V2No.55-Giant		.40	.80

HOLLYWOOD COMICS
Winter, 1944
New Age Publications

1	4.35	13.00	30.00

HOLLYWOOD CONFESSIONS
Oct, 1949 - No. 2, Dec, 1949
St. John Publishing Co.

	Good	Fine	Mint
1-Kubert c/a-entire book	11.00	33.00	76.00
2-Kubert c/a(2) (Scarce)	17.00	51.00	120.00

HOLLYWOOD DIARY
Dec, 1949 - No. 5, July-Aug, 1950
Quality Comics Group

1	6.75	20.00	47.00
2-Photo-c	4.35	13.00	30.00
3-5: 3-Photo-c	3.85	11.50	27.00

HOLLYWOOD FILM STORIES
April, 1950 - No. 4, Oct, 1950
Feature Publications/Prize

1	6.75	20.00	47.00
2,4	4.35	13.00	30.00
3-A movie magazine; no comics	4.35	13.00	30.00

HOLLYWOOD FUNNY FOLKS (Formerly Funny Folks; Nutsy Squirrel No. 61 on)
No. 27, Aug-Sept, 1950 - No. 60, July-Aug, 1954
National Periodical Publications

27	3.00	9.00	21.00
28-40	1.75	5.25	12.00
41-60	1.30	4.00	9.00

NOTE: ***Sheldon Mayer** a-27-35, 37-40, 43-46, 48-51, 53, 56, 57, 60.*

HOLLYWOOD LOVE DOCTOR (See Doctor Anthony King . . .)

HOLLYWOOD PICTORIAL (. . . Romances on cover)
No. 3, January, 1950
St. John Publishing Co.

3-Matt Baker-a; photo-c	7.00	21.00	50.00

(Becomes a movie magazine - Hollywood Pictorial West. with No. 4.)

HOLLYWOOD ROMANCES (Formerly Brides In Love)
No. 46, 11/66; No. 47, 10/67; No. 48, 11/68; No. 49, 11/69 - No. 59, 6/71 (Becomes For Lovers Only No. 60-on)
Charlton Comics

V2No. 46-Rolling Stones c/story	.50	1.50	3.00
V2No. 47-59: 56-''Born to Heart Break'' begins		.30	.60

HOLLYWOOD SECRETS
Nov, 1949 - No. 6, Sept, 1950
Quality Comics Group

1-Ward-c/a, 9pgs.	16.00	48.00	110.00
2-Crandall-a, Ward c/a, 9 pgs.	9.50	28.50	65.00
3-6: All photo-c	4.00	12.00	28.00
. . . of Romance, I.W. Reprint No. 9	.85	2.50	5.00

HOLYOKE ONE-SHOT
1944 - 1945 (All reprints)
Holyoke Publishing Co. (Tem Publ.)

1-Grit Grady (on cover only), Miss Victory, Alias X (origin)-All reprints from Captain Fearless	4.35	13.00	30.00
2-Rusty Dugan (Corporal); Capt. Fearless (origin), Mr. Miracle (origin), app.	4.35	13.00	30.00
3-Miss Victory-Crash No. 4 reprints; Cat Man (origin), Solar Legion by Kirby app.; Miss Victory on cover only (1945)	11.00	33.00	75.00
4-Mr. Miracle-The Blue Streak app.	4.35	13.00	30.00
5-U.S. Border Patrol Comics (Sgt. Dick Carter of the . . .), Miss Victory (story matches cover No. 3), Citizen Smith, & Mr. Miracle app.	4.85	14.50	34.00

6-Capt. Fearless, Alias X, Capt. Stone (splash used as cover-No.10);

HOLYOKE ONE-SHOT (continued) — Good / Fine / Mint

Diamond Jim & Rusty Dugan (splash from cover-No.2) 4.35 13.00 30.00
7-Z-2, Strong Man, Blue Streak (story matches cover-No.8)-Reprints from Crash No. 2 5.50 16.50 38.00
8-Blue Streak, Strong Man (story matches cover-No.7)-Crash reprints 4.35 13.00 30.00
9-Citizen Smith, The Blue Streak, Solar Legion by Kirby & Strongman, the Perfect Human app.; reprints from Crash No. 4 & 5; Citizen Smith on cover only-from story in No. 5(1944-before No.3) 6.50 19.50 45.00
10-Captain Stone (Crash reprints); Solar Legion by S&K 6.50 19.50 45.00

HOMER COBB (See Adventures of. . .)

HOMER HOOPER
July, 1953 - No. 4, Dec., 1953
Atlas Comics

1 2.00 6.00 14.00
2-4 1.15 3.50 8.00

HOMER, THE HAPPY GHOST (See Adventures of. . .)
3/55 - No. 22, 11/58; V2No.1, 11/69 - V2No.5, 7/70
Atlas(ACI/PPI/WPI)/Marvel Comics

V1No.1 2.65 8.00 18.00
2 1.30 4.00 9.00
3-10 1.15 3.50 8.00
11-22 1.00 3.00 7.00
V2No.1 - V2No.5 (1969-70) .50 1.50 3.00

HOME RUN (See A-1 Comics No. 89)

HOME, SWEET HOME
1925 (10¼x10")
M.S. Publishing Co.

nn-By Tuthill 7.00 21.00 50.00

HONEYBEE BIRDWHISTLE AND HER PET PEPI (Introducing)
1969 (24 pgs.; B&W; slick cover)
Newspaper Enterprise Association (Giveaway)

nn-Contains Freckles newspaper strips with a short biography of Henry Fornhals (artist) & Fred Fox (writer) of the strip. 2.75 8.00 16.00

HONEYMOON (Formerly Gay Comics)
No. 41, January, 1950
A Lover's Magazine(USA) (Marvel)

41 2.15 6.50 15.00

HONEYMOONERS, THE
Oct, 1986 - Present ($1.50, in color)
Lodestone Publishing

1-Photo-c .30 .90 1.80
2 .25 .75 1.50

HONEYMOON ROMANCE
April, 1950 - No. 2, July, 1950 (25 cents) (digest size)
Artful Publications(Canadian)

1,2-(Rare) 17.00 51.00 120.00

HONEY WEST (TV)
September, 1966 (Photo-c)
Gold Key

1 (10186-609) 3.50 10.50 24.00

HONG KONG PHOOEY (Hanna-Barbera)(TV)
June, 1975 - No. 9, Nov, 1976
Charlton Comics

Good / Fine / Mint
1-9 — .40 .80

HOODED HORSEMAN, THE (Formerly Blazing West)
No.23, 5-6/52 - No.27, 1-2/53; No.18, 12-1/54-55 - No.27, 6-7/56
American Comics Group (Michel Publ.)

23(5-6/52)-Hooded Horseman, Injun Jones continues 4.35 13.00 30.00
24,25,27(1-2/53) 2.15 6.50 15.00
26-Origin/1st app. Cowboy Sahib 2.65 8.00 18.00
18(11-12/54)(Formerly Out of the Night) 2.15 6.50 15.00
19-3-D effect-c; last precode, 1-2/55 4.35 13.00 30.00
20-Origin Johnny Injun 2.15 6.50 15.00
21-24,26,27(6-7/56) 1.85 5.50 13.00
25-Cowboy Sahib on cover only; Hooded Horseman i.d. revealed 2.15 6.50 15.00

NOTE: ***Whitney*** *c/a-20-22.*

HOODED MENACE, THE (Also see Daring Advs.)
1951 (One Shot)
Realistic/Avon Periodicals

nn-Based on a band of hooded outlaws in the Pacific Northwest, 1900-1906; reprinted in Daring Advs. No. 15 32.00 95.00 225.00

HOODS UP
1953 (16 pgs.; 15 cents)
Fram Corp. (Dist. to service station owners)

1-(Very Rare; only 2 known)-Eisner-c/a 30.00 90.00 210.00
2-6-(Very Rare; only 1 known of each)-Eisner-c/a 30.00 90.00 210.00

NOTE: *Convertible Connie gives tips for service stations, selling Fram oil filters.*

HOOT GIBSON WESTERN (Formerly My Love Story; see Fox Giants)
No. 5, May, 1950 - No. 3, Sept, 1950
Fox Features Syndicate

5,6(No. 1,2) 6.00 18.00 42.00
3-Wood-a 10.00 30.00 70.00

HOPALONG CASSIDY (Also see Bill Boyd Western, Master Comics, Real Western Hero, & Western Hero; Bill Boyd starred as H. Cassidy in the movies; H. Cassidy in movies, radio & TV)
Feb, 1943; No. 2, Summer, 1946 - No. 85, Jan, 1954
Fawcett Publications

1 (1943, 68pgs.)-H. Cassidy & his horse Topper begin (On sale 1/8/43) 75.00 225.00 525.00
2-(Sum, '46) 27.00 80.00 190.00
3,4: 3-(Fall, '46, 52pgs. begin) 13.00 40.00 90.00
5-"Mad Barber" story mentioned in **SOTI**, pgs. 308,309 13.00 40.00 90.00
6-10 11.00 33.00 76.00
11-19: 11,13-19-Photo-c 8.00 24.00 56.00
20-29 (52pgs.)-Painted/photo-c 6.00 18.00 42.00
30,31,33,34,37-39,41 (52pgs.)-Painted-c 4.50 13.50 31.00
32,40 (36pgs.)-Painted-c 3.75 11.25 26.00
35,42,43,45 (52pgs.)-Photo-c 4.50 13.50 31.00
36,44,48 (36pgs.)-Photo-c 3.75 11.25 26.00
46,47,49-51,53,54,56 (52pgs.)-Photo-c 4.00 12.00 28.00
52,55,57-70 (36pgs.)-Photo-c 3.00 9.00 21.00
71-84-Photo-c 2.50 7.50 17.50
85-Last Fawcett issue; photo-c 2.75 8.25 19.00

NOTE: *Line-drawn c-1-10, 12*

Grape Nuts Flakes giveaway(1950,9x6") 6.00 18.00 42.00
. . .& the Mad Barber(1951 Bond Bread giveaway)-7x5"; used in **SOTI**, pgs. 308,309 15.00 45.00 105.00
. . .& The Stampede(1950,5x5")52 pgs.; Color; Samuel Lowe Co.

Hooded Menace nn, © AVON

Hoot Gibson Western #5, © FOX

Hopalong Cassidy #85, © FAW

Hoppy the Marvel Bunny #4, © FAW

Horace & Dotty Dripple #25, © HARV

Horrific #7, © Artful

HOPALONG CASSIDY (continued)

	Good	Fine	Mint
No. 511-5, ½ art/½ text	6.00	18.00	42.00
. . . & The Stolen Treasure(1950,5x5")52 pgs.; Color; Samuel Lowe Co. No. 511-5, ½ art/½ text	4.00	12.00	28.00
. . . in the Strange Legacy	6.00	18.00	42.00
. . . Gives a Helping Hand(1951)-52 pgs.; B&W; Samuel Lowe Co. No. 517-5	6.00	18.00	42.00
. . . Meets the Brend Brothers Bandits	6.00	18.00	42.00
White Tower Giveaway (1946, 16pgs., paper-c)	6.00	18.00	42.00

HOPALONG CASSIDY (TV)
No. 86, Feb, 1954 - No. 135, May-June, 1959 (All-36pgs.)
National Periodical Publications

	Good	Fine	Mint
86-Photo-c continues	8.00	24.00	56.00
87	4.00	12.00	28.00
88-90	3.00	9.00	21.00
91-99 (98 has No. 93 on-c & is last precode ish, 2/55)	2.65	8.00	18.00
100	3.35	10.00	24.00
101-108-Last photo-c	2.50	7.50	17.50
109-123,125-134	2.35	7.00	16.00
124-Painted-c	2.50	7.50	17.00
135-Last issue	2.50	7.50	17.00

NOTE: ***Gil Kane** art-1956 up.*

HOPE SHIP
June-Aug, 1963
Dell Publishing Co.

	Good	Fine	Mint
1	1.35	4.00	8.00

HOPPY THE MARVEL BUNNY (See Fawcett's Funny Animals)
Dec, 1945 - No. 15, Sept, 1947
Fawcett Publications

	Good	Fine	Mint
1	8.00	24.00	56.00
2	3.75	11.25	26.00
3-15	3.35	10.00	23.00
. . . Well Known Comics (1944,8½x10½",paper-c) Bestmaid/Samuel Lowe (Printed in red or blue)	6.75	20.00	40.00

HORACE & DOTTY DRIPPLE (Dotty Dripple No. 1-24)
No. 25, Aug, 1952 - No. 43, Oct, 1955
Harvey Publications

	Good	Fine	Mint
25-43	.70	2.00	5.00

HORIZONTAL LIEUTENANT, THE (See Movie Classics)

HORRIFIC (Terrific No. 14 on)
Sept, 1952 - No. 13, Sept, 1954
Artful/Comic Media/Harwell/Mystery

	Good	Fine	Mint
1	6.50	19.50	45.00
2	3.35	10.00	23.00
3-Bullet in head-c	5.75	17.25	40.00
4,5,7,9,10	2.50	7.50	17.50
6-Jack The Ripper story	2.75	8.25	19.00
8-Origin & 1st app. The Teller(E.C. parody)	3.35	10.00	23.00
11-Swipe/Witches Tales No. 6,27	2.15	6.50	15.00
12,13	2.15	6.50	15.00

NOTE: ***Don Heck** a-8; c-3-13. **Hollingsworth** a-4. **Morisi** a-8. **Palais** a-5, 8, 11.*

HORROR FROM THE TOMB (Mysterious Stories No. 2)
Sept, 1954
Premier Magazine Co.

	Good	Fine	Mint
1-Woodbridge/Torres, Check-a	6.50	19.50	45.00

HORRORS, THE
No. 11, Jan, 1953 - No. 15, Apr, 1954
Star Publications

	Good	Fine	Mint
11-Horrors of War; Disbrow-a(2)	6.00	18.00	42.00
12-Horrors of War; color illo in **POP**	6.00	18.00	42.00
13-Horrors of Mystery; crime stories	5.50	16.50	38.00
14,15-Horrors of the Underworld	5.50	16.50	38.00

NOTE: *All have **L. B. Cole** covers. **Hollingsworth** a-13. **Palais** a-13r.*

HORROR TALES (Magazine)
V1No.7, 6/69 - V6No.6, 12/74; V7No.1, 2/75; V7No.2, 5/76 - V8No.5, 1977; (V1-V6, 52 pgs.; V7, V8No.2, 112 pgs.; V8No.4 on, 68 pgs.) (No V5No.3, V8No.1,3)
Eerie Publications

	Good	Fine	Mint
V1No.7-9		.60	1.20
V2No.1-6('70), V3No.1-6('71)		.40	.80
V4No.1-3,5-7('72)		.40	.80
V4No.4-LSD story reprint/Weird V3No.5	.70	2.00	4.00
V5No.1,2,4,5(6/73),5(10/73),6(12/73)		.40	.80
V6No.1-6('74),V7No.1,2,4('76)		.40	.80
V7No.3('76)-Giant issue		.50	1.00
V8No.2,4,5('77)		.40	.80

NOTE: *Bondage-c-V6No.1,3, V7No.2.*

HORSE FEATHERS COMICS
Nov, 1945 - No. 4, 1946
Lev Gleason Publications

	Good	Fine	Mint
1-Wolverton's Scoop Scuttle, 2 pgs.	8.00	24.00	56.00
2	2.65	8.00	18.00
3,4	2.00	6.00	14.00

HORSEMASTERS, THE (See 4-Color No. 1260)

HORSE SOLDIERS, THE (See 4-Color No. 1048)

HORSE WITHOUT A HEAD, THE (See Movie Comics)

HOT DOG
June-July, 1954 - No. 4, Dec-Jan, 1954-55
Magazine Enterprises

	Good	Fine	Mint
1(A-1 107)	2.00	6.00	14.00
2,3(A-1 115),4(A-1 136)	1.15	3.50	8.00

HOTEL DEPAREE - SUNDANCE (See 4-Color No. 1126)

HOT ROD AND SPEEDWAY COMICS
Feb-Mar, 1952 - No. 5, Apr-May, 1953
Hillman Periodicals

	Good	Fine	Mint
1	3.65	11.00	25.00
2-Krigstein-a	3.65	11.00	25.00
3-5	1.30	4.00	9.00

HOT ROD COMICS
Nov, 1951 (no month given) - V2No.7, Feb, 1953
Fawcett Publications

	Good	Fine	Mint
nn (V1No.1)-Powell-c/a in all	5.00	15.00	35.00
2	2.65	8.00	18.00
3-6, V2No.7	1.65	5.00	11.50

HOT ROD KING
Fall, 1952
Ziff-Davis Publ. Co.

	Good	Fine	Mint
1-Giacoia-a; painted-c	5.00	15.00	35.00

HOT ROD RACERS (Grand Prix No. 16 on)
Dec, 1964 - No. 15, July, 1967
Charlton Comics

	Good	Fine	Mint
1	.50	1.50	3.00
2-5	.35	1.00	2.00
6-15		.50	1.00

HOT RODS AND RACING CARS
Nov, 1951 - No. 120, June, 1973
Charlton Comics (Motor Mag. No. 1)

HOT RODS AND RACING CARS (continued)

	Good	Fine	Mint
1	3.50	10.50	24.00
2	2.00	6.00	12.00
3-10	1.15	3.50	8.00
11-20	.85	2.50	6.00
21-40	.55	1.65	4.00
41-60	.35	1.00	2.50
61-80		.50	1.00
81-120		.30	.60

HOT SHOT CHARLIE
1947 (Lee Elias)
Hillman Periodicals

	Good	Fine	Mint
1	2.00	6.00	14.00

HOT STUFF CREEPY CAVES
Nov, 1974 - No. 7, Nov, 1975
Harvey Publications

	Good	Fine	Mint
1	.55	1.60	3.20
2-5	.30	.80	1.60
6,7		.40	.80

HOT STUFF SIZZLERS
July, 1960 - No. 59, March, 1974
Harvey Publications

	Good	Fine	Mint
1	4.00	12.00	24.00
2-5	1.35	4.00	8.00
6-10: 8-Giant size	1.00	3.00	6.00
11-20	.70	2.00	4.00
21-59	.35	1.00	2.00

HOT STUFF, THE LITTLE DEVIL (Also see Harvey Hits)
10/57 - No. 141, 7/77; No. 142, 2/78 - No. 164, 8/82; No. 165, 10/86 - Present
Harvey Publications (Illustrated Humor)

	Good	Fine	Mint
1	12.00	35.00	70.00
2-1st app. Stumbo the Giant	6.75	20.00	40.00
3-5	5.75	17.00	34.00
6-10	3.00	9.00	18.00
11-20	1.35	4.00	8.00
21-40	.70	2.00	4.00
41-60	.55	1.60	3.20
61-100	.30	.80	1.60
101-168		.40	.80
Shoestore Giveaway('63)	.35	1.00	2.00

HOT WHEELS (TV)
Mar-Apr, 1970 - No. 6, Jan-Feb, 1971
National Periodical Publications

	Good	Fine	Mint
1	1.50	4.50	9.00
2,4,5	.85	2.50	5.00
3-Adams-c	2.00	6.00	12.00
6-Adams c/a	2.50	7.50	15.00

NOTE: ***Toth*** *a-1p, 2-5; c-1p, 4, 5.*

HOUSE OF MYSTERY (See Limited Collectors' Edition & Super DC Giant)

HOUSE OF MYSTERY, THE (Also see Elvira's. . .)
Dec-Jan, 1951-52 - No. 321, Oct, 1983 (No. 199-203: 52 pgs.)
National Periodical Publications/DC Comics

	Good	Fine	Mint
1	30.00	90.00	210.00
2	13.00	40.00	90.00
3	11.50	34.50	80.00
4,5	10.00	30.00	70.00
6-10	8.00	24.00	56.00
11-15	7.00	21.00	50.00
16(7/53)-35(2/55)-Last pre-code ish; No. 30-Woodish-a	3.85	11.50	27.00
36-49	2.15	6.50	15.00
50-Text story of Orson Welles' War of the Worlds broadcast	1.15	3.50	8.00
51-60	1.00	3.00	7.00
61,63,65,66,70,72-Kirby-a	1.00	3.00	7.00
62,64,67-69,71,73-75	.75	2.25	5.00
76,84,85-Kirby-a	1.00	3.00	7.00
77-83,86-99	.65	2.00	4.50
100	.80	2.40	5.50
101-108,110-116: Last 10¢ ish.	.55	1.65	4.00
109,120-Toth-a; Kubert No. 109	.65	2.00	4.50
117-119,121-130	.35	1.00	2.00
131-142,144-150: 149-Toth-a		.50	1.00
143-J'onn J'onzz, Manhunter begins, ends No. 173 (6/64); story continues/Detective No. 326	.35	1.00	2.50
151-155,157-177: 158-Origin/last app. Diabolu Idol-Head in J'onn J'onzz. 160-Intro Marco Xavier (Martian Manhunter) & Vulture Crime Organization; ends No. 173. 169-Origin/1st app. Gem Girl. 174-Mystery format begins		.30	.60
156-Robby Reed begins (Origin), ends 173		.60	1.20
178-Adams-a	.50	1.50	3.00
179-Adams/Orlando, Wrightson-a (1st pro work, 3 pgs.)	.85	2.50	5.00
180,181,183: Wrightson-a(3, 10, & 3 pgs.). 180,183-Wood-a	.30	1.00	2.00
182-Toth-a(r)		.40	.80
184-Kane/Wood, Toth-a	.25	.75	1.50
185-Williamson/Kaluta-a; 3 pgs. Wood-a	.50	1.50	3.00
186-Adams-a; Wrightson-a, 10 pgs.	.50	1.50	3.00
187		.30	.60
188-Wrightson-a, 8 pgs.	.50	1.50	3.00
189-Wood-a, Toth-a(r)	.25	.75	1.50
190,196-Toth-a(r)		.40	.80
191,195-Wrightson-a, 3 & 10 pgs.	.50	1.50	3.00
192,193,197,198		.30	.60
194-Toth, Kirby-a; 48pg. ish. begin, end No. 198		.60	1.20
199-Wood, Kirby-a; 52pgs. begin, end 203	.30	1.00	2.00
200-203,205,206,208-220		.30	.60
204-Wrightson-a, 9 pgs.	.30	1.00	2.00
207-Wrightson, Starlin-a	.25	.75	1.50
221-Wrightson/Kaluta-a, 8 pgs.	.25	.75	1.50
222,223,225		.30	.60
224-Adams/Wrightson-a(r); begin 100 pg. issues; Phantom Stranger-r	.40	1.20	2.40
226-Wrightson-r; Phantom Stranger-r		.60	1.20
227,230-250: 230-68 pgs.		.30	.60
228-Adams inks; Wrightson-r	.30	1.00	2.00
229-Wrightson-a(r); Toth-r; last 100 pg. issue		.60	1.20
251-($1.00 size)-Wood-a, 8 pgs.		.50	1.00
252,253,255,256,258		.40	.80
254,274,277-Rogers-a		.50	1.00
257,259-Golden-a; last $1.00 size		.50	1.00
260-273,275,276,278-282		.40	.80
283-321: 290-I, Vampire begins, ends No. 319		.60	1.20

NOTE: ***Adams*** *c-175-192, 197, 199, 251-254.* ***Aragones*** *a-186, 251.* ***Baily*** *a-279p.* ***Buckler*** *a-199.* ***Colan*** *a-202r.* ***Craig*** *a-263, 275, 295, 300.* ***Ditko*** *a-236, 247, 254, 258, 276; c-277.* ***Drucker*** *a-37.* ***Giffen*** *a-284p, 301.* ***Heath*** *a-194r; c-203.* ***Howard*** *a-182, 187, 196, 229r, 247i, 254, 279i.* ***Kaluta*** *a-200, 250; c-200-202, 210, 212, 233, 260, 261, 263, 265, 267, 268, 273, 276, 284, 287, 288, 293-295, 300, 302, 304, 305, 309-319, 321.* ***Bob Kane*** *a-84.* ***Gil Kane*** *a-196p, 253p, 300p.* ***Kirby*** *a-194r, 199r; c-65, 76, 78, 79, 85.* ***Kubert*** *c-282, 283, 285, 286, 289-292, 297-99, 301, 303, 306-308.* ***Mayer*** *a-317p.* ***Meskin*** *a-52-144 (most), 224r, 229r; c-63, 66, 124, 127.* ***Mooney*** *a-160.* ***Moreira*** *a-3, 20-50, 58, 59, 62, 68, 77, 79, 90, 201r, 228; c-44, 47, 50, 54,*

Hot Rods & Racing Cars #1, © CC

House of Mystery #16, © DC

House of Mystery #185, © DC

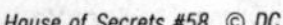

House of Secrets #58, © DC

Howard the Duck #5, © MCG

Howdy Doody #17, © Kagran Corp.

HOUSE OF MYSTERY (continued)

*59, 62, 64, 68, 70, 73. **Morrow** a-192, 196, 255, 320. **Mortimer** a-204. **Nasser** a-276. **Newton** a-259, 272. **Nino** a-204, 212, 213, 220, 224, 225, 245, 250, 252-256, 283. **Orlando** a-175(2 pgs.), 178; c-240, 258p, 262, 264p, 270p, 271, 272, 274, 275, 278, 296i. **Redondo** a-194, 195, 197, 202, 203, 207, 211, 214, 217, 219, 226, 227, 229, 235, 241, 287(layout), 302p, 303i, 308; c-229. **Reese** a-195, 200, 205i. **Roussos** a-65, 84, 224i. **Sekowsky** a-282p. **Sparling** a-203. **Starlin** a-207(2 pgs.), 282p; c-281. **Leonard Starr** a-9. **Staton** a-300p. **Sutton** a-271, 290, 291, 293, 295, 297-99, 302, 303, 306-09, 310-13i, 314. **Tuska** a-293p, 294p, 316p. **Wrightson** c-193-195, 204, 207, 209, 211, 213, 214, 217, 221, 231, 236, 255, 256.*

HOUSE OF SECRETS
11-12/56 - No. 80, 9-10/66; No. 81, 8-9/69 - No. 140, 2-3/76; No. 141, 8-9/76 - No. 154, 10-11/78
National Periodical Publications/DC Comics

	Good	Fine	Mint
1-Drucker-a; Moreira-c	18.50	56.00	130.00
2-Moreira-a	9.50	29.00	68.00
3-Kirby c/a	8.00	24.00	56.00
4,8-Kirby-a	3.65	11.00	25.00
5-7,9-11	2.50	7.50	17.50
12-Kirby c/a	3.65	11.00	25.00
13-20	1.85	5.50	13.00
21,22,24-47,49,50: Last 10¢ ish.	1.00	3.00	7.00
23-Origin Mark Merlin	1.50	4.50	10.00
48-Toth-a	1.30	4.00	9.00
51-60,62: 58-Origin Mark Merlin retold	.50	1.50	3.00
61-First Eclipso	.70	2.00	4.00
63-67-Toth-a	.70	2.00	4.00
68-80: 73-Mark Merlin ends, Prince Ra-Man begins. 80-Eclipso, Prince Ra-Man end		.40	.80
81,84,86,88,89: 81-Mystery format begins		.30	.60
82-Adams-c(i)	.50	1.50	3.00
83-Toth-a	.40	1.20	2.40
85-Adams-a(i)	.50	1.50	3.00
87-Wrightson & Kaluta-a	.50	1.50	3.00
90-Buckler-a (1st comic art)/Adams-a	.50	1.50	3.00
91-Wood-i	.40	1.20	2.40
92-Intro. Swamp Thing; Wrightson-a (6-7/71); J. Jones part inks	4.00	12.00	24.00
93,96,98-Toth-a(r). 96-Wood-a		.60	1.20
94-Wrightson inks; Toth-a(r)	.50	1.50	3.00
95,97,99,100		.30	.60
101-154: 140-Origin The Patchworkman		.30	.60

NOTE: ***Adams** c-81, 82, 84-88, 90, 91. **Colan** a-63. **Ditko** a-139p, 148. **Evans** a-118. **Finlay** a-7. **Glanzman** a-91. **Golden** a-151. **Kaluta** a-87, 98, 99; c-98, 99, 101, 102, 151, 154. **Bob Kane** a-18, 21. **G. Kane** a-85p. **Kirby** c-11. **Kubert** a-39. **Meskin** a-2-68 (most); c-55-60. **Moreira** a-7, 8, 102-104, 106, 108, 113, 116, 118, 121, 123, 127; c-2, 7-9. **Morrow** a-86, 89, 90; c-89, 147, 148. **Nino** a-101, 103, 106, 109, 115, 117, 126, 128, 131, 147, 153. **Redondo** a-95, 99, 102, 104p, 113, 116, 134, 139, 140. **Reese** a-85. **Starlin** c-150. **Sutton** a-154. **Toth** a-63-67, 123. **Tuska** a-90, 104. **Wrightson** c-92-94, 96, 100, 103, 106, 107, 135, 139.*

HOUSE OF TERROR (3-D)
October, 1953 (1st 3D horror comic)
St. John Publishing Co.

	Good	Fine	Mint
1-Kubert, Baker-a	13.00	40.00	90.00

HOUSE OF YANG, THE (See Yang)
July, 1975 - No. 6, June, 1976; 1978
Charlton Comics

	Good	Fine	Mint
1-Opium propaganda story		.40	.80
2-6		.30	.60
Modern Comics No. 1,2(1978)		.30	.60

HOWARD THE DUCK (See Fear, Man-Thing, & Marvel Treasury Ed.)
1/76 - No. 31, 5/79; No. 32, 1/86; No. 33, 9/86 - Present
Marvel Comics Group

	Good	Fine	Mint
1-Brunner c/a; Spider-Man x-over (low distribution)	1.15	3.50	7.00
2-Brunner c/a (low distr.)	.40	1.25	2.50
3-Buscema-a	.25	.80	1.60
4-10		.60	1.20
11-31: 12-1st app. Kiss. 16-Album issue; all text; 3pg. comics		.35	.70
32-P. Smith-a(p)		.40	.80
33-(Direct sale, Baxter)	.25	.75	1.50
Annual 1(9/77)		.40	.80

NOTE: ***Austin** c-29i. **Bolland** c-33. **Brunner** a-1p, 2p; c-1, 2. **Buckler** c-3p. **Buscema** a-3p. **Colan** a(p)-4-15, 17-20, 24-27, 30, 31; c(p)-4-31, Annual 1. **Leialoha** a-1-13i; c(i)-3-5, 8-11. **Mayerik** a-22, 23, 33.*

HOWARD THE DUCK MAGAZINE
October, 1979 - No. 9, March, 1981
Marvel Comics Group

	Good	Fine	Mint
1		.50	1.00
2,3,5-9: 7-Has poster by Byrne		.30	.60
4-Beatles, John Lennon, Elvis, Kiss & Devo cameos; Hitler app.		.40	.80

NOTE: ***Buscema** a-4. **Colan** a-1-5p, 7-9p. **Davis** c-3. **Golden** a-1, 5p, 6p(51pgs.). **Rogers** a-7, 8. **Simonson** a-7.*

HOWARD THE DUCK: THE MOVIE
Dec, 1986 - No. 3, Feb, 1987 (mini-series)
Marvel Comics Group

	Good	Fine	Mint
1-3		.40	.80

HOW BOYS AND GIRLS CAN HELP WIN THE WAR
1942 (One Shot) (10 cents)
The Parents' Magazine Institute

	Good	Fine	Mint
1	8.00	24.00	56.00

HOWDY DOODY (TV)(See Poll Parrot)
1/50 - No. 38, 7-9/56; No. 761, 1/57; No. 811, 7/57
Dell Publishing Co.

	Good	Fine	Mint
1-Photo-c; 1st TV comic?	10.00	30.00	70.00
2-Photo-c	5.00	15.00	35.00
3-5: 3,5-Photo-c	3.75	11.25	26.00
6-Used in **SOTI**, pg. 309	3.75	11.25	26.00
7-10	2.36	8.00	18.00
11-20	2.00	6.00	14.00
21-38	1.50	4.50	10.00
4-Color 761,811	3.00	9.00	21.00

HOW IT BEGAN (See Single Series No. 15)

HOW SANTA GOT HIS RED SUIT (See March of Comics No. 2)

HOW STALIN HOPES WE WILL DESTROY AMERICA
1951 (16 pgs.) (Giveaway)
Joe Lowe Co. (Pictorial News)

	Good	Fine	Mint
	47.00	140.00	280.00

(Prices vary widely on this book)

HOW THE WEST WAS WON (See Movie Comics)

HOW TO DRAW FOR THE COMICS
No date (1942?) (64 pgs.; B&W & color) (10 Cents) (No ads)
Street and Smith

	Good	Fine	Mint
nn-Art by Winsor McCay, George Marcoux(Supersnipe artist), Vernon Greene(The Shadow artist), Jack Binder(with biog), Thorton Fisher, Jon Small, & Jack Farr. Has biographies of each artist	9.50	28.50	65.00

H. R. PUFNSTUF (TV) (See March of Comics 360)
Oct, 1970 - No. 8, July, 1972
Gold Key

	Good	Fine	Mint
1	.50	1.50	3.00
2-8	.25	.75	1.50

HUBERT (See 4-Color No. 251)

HUCK & YOGI JAMBOREE (TV)
March, 1961 (116 pgs.; $1.00) (B&W original material)
(6¼x9"; cardboard cover; high quality paper)
Dell Publishing Co.

	Good	Fine	Mint
	1.50	4.50	10.00

HUCK & YOGI WINTER SPORTS (See 4-Color No. 1310)

HUCK FINN (See New Advs. of. . .)

HUCKLEBERRY FINN (See 4-Color No. 1114)

HUCKLEBERRY HOUND (See Dell Giant No. 31,44, Spotlight No. 1, March of Comics No. 199,214,235, Whitman Comic Books & Golden Picture Story Book)

HUCKLEBERRY HOUND (TV)
No. 990, 5-7/59 - No. 43, 10/70 (Hanna-Barbera)
Dell/Gold Key No. 18 (10/62) on

	Good	Fine	Mint
4-Color 990	2.00	6.00	14.00
4-Color 1050,1054 (12/59)	1.50	4.50	10.00
3(1-2/60) - 7 (9-10/60)	1.50	4.50	10.00
4-Color 1141 (10/60)	1.50	4.50	10.00
8-10	1.15	3.50	8.00
11-17 (6-8/62)	.85	2.50	6.00
18,19 (84pgs.; 18-20 titled . . . Chuckleberry Tales)	2.00	6.00	16.00
20-30: 20-Titled Chuckleberry Tales	.75	2.25	4.50
31-43: 37-reprints	.50	1.50	3.00
. . . Kite Fun Book(1961)-16 pgs.; small size	1.50	4.50	10.00

HUCKLEBERRY HOUND (TV)
Nov, 1970 - No. 8, Jan, 1972 (Hanna-Barbera)
Charlton Comics

	Good	Fine	Mint
1	.35	1.00	2.00
2-8		.50	1.00

HUEY, DEWEY, & LOUIE (See Donald Duck, 1938 for 1st app.)

HUEY, DEWEY, & LOUIE BACK TO SCHOOL (See Dell Giant No. 22,35,49 & Dell Giants)

HUEY, DEWEY AND LOUIE JUNIOR WOODCHUCKS
Aug, 1966 - No. 81, 1984 (Disney)
Gold Key No. 1-61/Whitman No. 62 on

	Good	Fine	Mint
1	2.15	6.50	15.00
2,3(12/68)	1.50	4.50	10.00
4,5(4/70)-Barks-r	1.50	4.50	10.00
6-17-Written by Barks	1.00	3.00	7.00
18,27-30	.70	2.00	4.00
19-23,25-Written by Barks. 22,23,25-Barks-r	.85	2.50	5.00
24,26-Barks-r	.85	2.50	5.00
31-57,60-81: 41,70,80-Reprints	.25	.75	1.50
58,59-Barks-r	.35	1.00	2.00

NOTE: ***Barks** story reprints-No. 22-26,35,42,45,51.*

HUGGA BUNCH
Oct, 1986 - Present
Star Comics (Marvel)

	Good	Fine	Mint
1-4		.35	.70

HULK, THE (See The Incredible Hulk)

HULK, THE (Formerly The Rampaging Hulk)
No. 10, 8/78 - No. 27, June, 1981 (Magazine)($1.50)(in color)
Marvel Comics Group

	Good	Fine	Mint
10-12: 12-Moon Knight begins		.60	1.20
13-27: 13-Color issues begin. 23-Anti-Gay issue		.60	1.20

NOTE: ***Alcala** a(i)-15, 18-20, 22, 24-27. **Buscema** a-23; c-26. **Chaykin** a-21-25. **Colan** a(p)-11, 17, 19, 24-27. **Simonson** a-27; c-23.*

HUMAN FLY
1963 - 1964 (Reprints)
I.W. Enterprises/Super

	Good	Fine	Mint
I.W. Reprint No. 1-Reprints Blue Beetle No. 44('46)	.70	2.00	4.00
Super Reprint No. 10-Reprints Blue Beetle No. 46('47)	.70	2.00	4.00

HUMAN FLY, THE
Sept, 1977 - No. 19, Mar, 1979
Marvel Comics Group

	Good	Fine	Mint
1-Origin; Spider-Man x-over		.40	.80
2-19: 9-Daredevil x-over; Byrne/Austin-c		.25	.50

NOTE: ***Austin** c-4i. **Elias** a-1, 3p, 4p, 7p, 10-12p, 15p, 18p, 19p. **Layton** c-19.*

HUMAN TORCH, THE (Red Raven No. 1) (See Marvel Mystery)
No. 2, Fall, 1940 - No. 15, Spring, 1944 (becomes Funny Tunes);
No. 16, Fall, 1944 - No. 35, Mar, 1949 (becomes Love Tales);
No. 36, April, 1954 - No. 38, Aug, 1954
Timely/Marvel Comics (TP 2,3/TCI 4-9/SePI 10/SnPC 11-25/CnPC 26-35/Atlas Comics (CPC 36-38))

	Good	Fine	Mint
2(No.1)-Intro & Origin Toro; The Falcon, The Fiery Mask, Mantor the Magician, & Microman only app.; Human Torch by Burgos, Sub-Mariner by Everett begin (origin of each in text)	415.00	1245.00	3000.00
(Prices vary widely on this book)			
3(No.2)-40pg. H.T. story; H.T. & S.M. battle over who is best artist in text-Everett or Burgos	180.00	540.00	1260.00
4(No.3)-Origin The Patriot in text; last Everett Sub-Mariner; Sid Greene-a	137.00	410.00	960.00
5(No.4)-The Patriot app; Angel x-over in Sub-Mariner. (Summer, 1941)	95.00	285.00	665.00
5-Human Torch battles Sub-Mariner (Fall,'41)	155.00	465.00	1085.00
6,7,9	63.00	190.00	440.00
8-Human Torch battles Sub-Mariner; Wolverton-a, 1 pg.	95.00	285.00	665.00
10-Human Torch battles Sub-Mariner; Wolverton-a, 1 pg.	77.00	230.00	540.00
11-15	49.00	147.00	340.00
16-20: 20-Last War issue	38.00	115.00	265.00
21-30	31.50	94.00	220.00
31-Namora x-over in Sub-Mariner (also No. 30); last Toro	24.00	72.00	168.00
32-Sungirl, Namora app.; Sungirl-c	24.00	72.00	168.00
33-Capt. America x-over	24.00	72.00	168.00
34-Sungirl solo	24.00	72.00	168.00
35-Captain America & Sungirl app. (1949)	24.00	72.00	168.00
36-38(1954)-Sub-Mariner in all	19.00	57.00	132.00

NOTE: ***Burgos** c-36. **Everett** a-1-3, 27, 28, 30, 37, 38. **Powell** a-36. **Schomburg** c-5, 7, 12, 14, 15, 16, 19. **Mickey Spillane** text 4-6. Bondage-c No. 2, 12, 19. Since there is a six month delay between No. 15 & 16, it is believed that Funny Tunes No. 16 continued after Human Torch No. 15.*

HUMAN TORCH, THE
Sept, 1974 - No. 8, Nov, 1975
Marvel Comics Group

	Good	Fine	Mint
1		.40	.80
2-8		.25	.50

NOTE: *Golden age Torch-r No. 1-8. **Kirby/Ayers** a-1-5,8r.*

HUMBUG (Satire by Harvey Kurtzman)
8/57 - No. 9, 5/58; No. 10, 6/58; No. 11, 10/58
Humbug Publications

	Good	Fine	Mint
1	5.50	16.50	38.00
2	2.50	7.50	17.50
3-9: 8-Elvis in Jailbreak Rock	2.00	6.00	14.00

Huckleberry Hound #3, © Hanna-Barbera

The Human Fly #7, © MCG

Human Torch #22 (1st Series), © MCG

Humdinger V2No.2, © NOVP

Ibis, the Invincible #4, © FAW

Ideal #1 (7/48), © MCG

HUMBUG (continued)

	Good	Fine	Mint
10,11-Magazine format	2.00	6.00	14.00
Bound Volume(No.1-6)-Sold by publisher	14.50	43.50	100.00
Bound Volume(No.1-9)	18.50	55.00	130.00

NOTE: ***Davis** a-1-11. **Elder** a-2-4, 6-9, 11. **Heath** a-2, 4-8, 10. **Jaffee** a-2, 4-9. **Kurtzman** a-11. **Wood** a-1.*

HUMDINGER
May-June, 1946 - V2/2, July-Aug, 1947
Novelty Press/Premium Group

	Good	Fine	Mint
1-Jerkwater Line, Mickey Starlight by Don Rico, Dink begin	3.00	9.00	21.00
2	1.75	5.25	12.00
3-6,V2No.1,2	1.30	4.00	9.00

HUMOR (See All Humor Comics)

HUMPHREY COMICS
October, 1948 - No. 21, Feb, 1952
Harvey Publications

	Good	Fine	Mint
1-Joe Palooka's pal (r); Powell-a	4.65	14.00	32.00
2,3: Powell-a	2.35	7.00	16.00
4-Boy Heroes app.; Powell-a	3.35	10.00	23.00
5-8,10: 7-Little Dot app.	1.70	5.00	12.00
9-Origin Humphrey	2.50	7.50	17.00
11-21	1.50	4.50	10.00

HUNCHBACK OF NOTRE DAME, THE (See 4-Color No. 854)

HUNK
August, 1961 - No. 11, 1963
Charlton Comics

	Good	Fine	Mint
1	.50	1.50	3.00
2-11	.25	.75	1.50

HUNTED (Formerly My Love Memoirs)
No. 13, July, 1950 - No. 2, Sept, 1950
Fox Features Syndicate

	Good	Fine	Mint
13(No.1)-Used in **SOTI**, pg. 42 & illo.-''Treating police contemptuously'' (lower left); Hollingsworth bondage-c	13.00	40.00	90.00
2	5.00	15.00	35.00

HURRICANE COMICS
1945 (52 pgs.)
Cambridge House

	Good	Fine	Mint
1-(Humor, funny animal)	2.65	8.00	18.00

HYPER MYSTERY COMICS
May, 1940 - No. 2, June, 1940
Hyper Publications

	Good	Fine	Mint
1-Hyper, the Phenomenal begins	35.00	105.00	235.00
2	26.00	78.00	180.00

I AIM AT THE STARS (See 4-Color No. 1148)

I AM COYOTE (Graphic Novel)
Nov, 1984 (76 pgs.) ($7.95)
Eclipse Comics

	Good	Fine	Mint
1-r-/Eclipse Monthly; Rogers c/a	1.35	4.00	8.00

IBIS, THE INVINCIBLE (See Fawcett Min., Mighty Midget & Whiz)
1943 (Feb) - No. 2, 1943; No. 3, Wint, 1945 - No. 6, Spring, 1948
Fawcett Publications

	Good	Fine	Mint
1-Origin Ibis; Raboy-c; on sale 1/2/43	57.00	170.00	400.00
2-Bondage-c	30.00	90.00	210.00
3-Wolverton-a No. 3-6 (4 pgs. each)	23.00	70.00	160.00
4-6: 5-Bondage-c. 6-Beck-c	19.00	57.00	132.00

ICEMAN
Dec, 1984 - No. 4, June, 1985 (Limited series)
Marvel Comics Group

	Good	Fine	Mint
1	.30	.90	1.80
2-4		.50	1.00

IDAHO
June-Aug, 1963 - No. 8, July-Sept, 1965
Dell Publishing Co.

	Good	Fine	Mint
1	1.00	3.00	7.00
2-8	.75	2.25	5.00

IDEAL (. . . a Classical Comic) (2nd Series) (Love Romances No. 6?)
July, 1948 - No. 5, March, 1949 (Feature length stories)
Timely Comics

	Good	Fine	Mint
1-Antony & Cleopatra	11.00	33.00	76.00
2-The Corpses of Dr. Sacotti	8.50	25.50	60.00
3-Joan of Arc; used in **SOTI**, pg. 308-'Boer War'	8.00	24.00	56.00
4-Richard the Lion-hearted; titled ''. . . the World's Greatest Comics;'' The Witness app.	9.50	28.50	65.00
5-Ideal Love & Romance; photo-c	5.00	15.00	35.00

IDEAL COMICS (1st Series) (Willie No. 5 on)
Fall, 1944 - No. 4, Spring, 1946
Timely Comics (MgPC)

	Good	Fine	Mint
1	5.00	15.00	35.00
2-Super Rabbit	3.50	10.50	24.00
3,4-Super Rabbit	2.65	8.00	18.00

IDEAL LOVE & ROMANCE (See Ideal, A Classical Comic)

IDEAL ROMANCE (Formerly Tender Romance)
April, 1954 - No. 8, Feb, 1955 (Diary Confessions No. 9 on)
Key Publications

	Good	Fine	Mint
3	2.65	8.00	18.00
4-8	1.30	4.00	9.00

IDEAL ROMANCES
1950
Stanmor

	Good	Fine	Mint
6	1.65	5.00	11.50

I DREAM OF JEANNIE (TV)
April, 1965 - No. 2, Dec, 1966 (Photo-c)
Dell Publishing Co.

	Good	Fine	Mint
1,2	2.00	6.00	14.00

IF THE DEVIL WOULD TALK
1950; 1958 (32 pgs.; paper cover; in full color)
Roman Catholic Catechetical Guild/Impact Publ.

	Good	Fine	Mint
nn-(Scarce)-About secularism (20-30 copies known to exist); very low distribution	50.00	150.00	350.00
1958 Edition-(Rare)-(Impact Publ.); art & script changed to meet church criticism of earlier edition; only 6 known copies exist	50.00	150.00	350.00
Black & White version of nn edition; small size; only 4 known copies exist	30.00	90.00	200.00

NOTE: *The original edition of this book was printed and killed by the Guild's board of directors. It is believed that a very limited number of copies were distributed. The 1958 version was a complete bomb with very limited, if any, circulation. In 1979, 11 original, 4 1958 reprints, and 4 B&W's surfaced from the Guild's old files in St. Paul, Minnesota.*

ILLUSTRATED GAGS (See Single Series No. 16)

ILLUSTRATED LIBRARY OF . . ., AN (See Classics Illustrated Giants)

ILLUSTRATED STORIES OF THE OPERAS
1943 (16 pgs.; B&W) (25 cents) (cover-B&W & red)
Baily (Bernard) Publ. Co.

	Good	Fine	Mint
nn-(Rare)-Faust (part reprinted in Cisco Kid No. 1)	13.00	40.00	90.00

ILL. STORIES OF THE OPERAS (continued)

	Good	Fine	Mint
nn-(Rare)-Aida	13.00	40.00	90.00
nn-(Rare)-Carmen; Baily-a	13.00	40.00	90.00
nn-(Rare)-Rigoleito	13.00	40.00	90.00

ILLUSTRATED STORY OF ROBIN HOOD & HIS MERRY MEN, THE
(See Robin Hood)

ILLUSTRATED TARZAN BOOK, THE (See Tarzan Book)

I LOVED (Formerly Rulah; Colossal Feature Mag. No. 33 on)
No. 28, July, 1949 - No. 32, Mar, 1950
Fox Features Syndicate

	Good	Fine	Mint
28	3.50	10.50	24.00
29-32	2.35	7.00	16.00

I LOVE LUCY COMICS (TV) (Also see The Lucy Show)
No. 535, Feb, 1954 - No. 35, Apr-June, 1962 (All photo-c)
Dell Publishing Co.

	Good	Fine	Mint
4-Color 535	6.00	18.00	42.00
4-Color 559 (5/54)	4.35	13.00	30.00
3 (8-10/54) - 5	4.00	12.00	28.00
6-10	3.65	11.00	25.00
11-20	3.00	9.00	21.00
21-35	2.35	7.00	16.00

I LOVE YOU
June, 1950 - No. 6, 1951
Fawcett Publications

	Good	Fine	Mint
1	5.00	15.00	35.00
2	2.65	8.00	18.00
3-6	2.35	7.00	16.00

I LOVE YOU (Formerly In Love)
No. 7, 9/55 - No. 121, 12/76; No. 122, 3/79 - No. 130, 5/80
Charlton Comics

	Good	Fine	Mint
7-Kirby-c, Powell-a	3.65	11.00	25.00
8-10	1.15	3.50	8.00
11-16,18-20	1.00	3.00	7.00
17-68 pg. Giant	1.30	4.00	9.00
21-25,27-50	.55	1.65	4.00
26-Torres-a	1.00	3.00	7.00
51-59	.35	1.00	2.00
60(1/66)-Elvis Presley drawn c/story	4.00	12.00	28.00
61-130		.40	.80

I'M A COP
1954
Magazine Enterprises

	Good	Fine	Mint
1(A-1 111)	4.00	12.00	28.00
2(A-1 126), 3(A-1 128)	2.00	6.00	14.00

NOTE: ***Powell*** *c/a-1-3.*

I'M DICKENS - HE'S FENSTER (TV)
May-July, 1963 - No. 2, Aug-Oct, 1963
Dell Publishing Co.

	Good	Fine	Mint
1,2	1.50	4.50	10.00

I MET A HANDSOME COWBOY (See 4-Color No. 324)

IMMORTAL DOCTOR FATE, THE
Jan, 1985 - No. 3, Mar, 1985 (Mini-series)
DC Comics

	Good	Fine	Mint
1-Simonson c/a		.65	1.30
2,3: 2-Giffen c/a(p)		.65	1.30

IMPACT
Mar-Apr, 1955 - No. 5, Nov-Dec, 1955
E. C. Comics

	Good	Fine	Mint
1	7.00	21.00	50.00
2	5.00	15.00	35.00
3-5: 4-Crandall-a	4.50	13.50	32.00

NOTE: ***Crandall*** *a-1-4.* ***Davis*** *a-2-4; c-1-5.* ***Evans*** *a-1, 4, 5.* ***Ingels*** *a-in all.* ***Kamen*** *a-3.* ***Krigstein*** *a-1, 5.* ***Orlando*** *a-2, 5.*

INCREDIBLE HULK, THE (See Aurora and Rampaging Hulk)
May, 1962 - No. 6, Mar, 1963; No. 102, Apr, 1968 - Present
Marvel Comics Group

	Good	Fine	Mint
1-Origin	90.00	260.00	630.00
2	33.00	90.00	230.00
3-Origin retold	24.00	68.00	165.00
4-6: 4-Brief origin retold. 6-Intro. Teen Brigade	17.00	45.00	120.00
102-(Formerly Tales to Astonish)-Origin retold	2.00	6.00	12.00
103-110: 105-1st Missing Link	.75	2.25	4.50
111-115	.40	1.25	2.50
116-125	.30	.90	1.80
126-139: 126-1st Barbara Norriss (Valkyrie). 131-1st Jim Wilson, Hulk's new sidekick. 136-1st Xeron, The Star-Slayer	.25	.75	1.50
140-Written by Harlan Ellison; 1st Jarella, Hulk's love	.25	.75	1.50
141-1st app. Doc Samson	.40	1.20	2.40
142-160: 145-52 pgs. 149-1st The Inheritor. 155-1st app. Shaper	.25	.75	1.50
161,163-175,179: 161-The Mimic dies. 163-1st app. The Gremlin. 164-1st app. Capt. Omen & Colonel John D. Armbruster. 166-1st Zzzax. 168-1st The Harpy. 169-1st Bi-Beast. 172-X-Men cameo; origin Juggernaut retold		.50	1.00
162-1st app. The Wendigo	.50	1.50	3.00
176-178-Warlock app.	.50	1.50	3.00
180-1st app. Wolverine(cameo)	1.30	4.00	8.00
181-Wolverine app.	5.35	16.00	32.00
182-Wolverine cameo; 1st Crackajack Jackson	1.35	4.00	8.00
183-199: 185-Death of Col. Armbruster.		.50	1.00
200-Silver Surfer app.	.40	1.20	2.40
201-240: 212-1st The Constrictor		.50	1.00
241-249,251-271: 271-Rocket Raccoon app.		.35	.70
250-Giant size; Silver Surfer app.		.60	1.20
272-Alpha Flight app.	.35	1.00	2.00
273-299,301-313: 279-X-men & Alpha Flight cameos		.35	.70
300-Double size		.50	1.00
314-320: 314-Byrne c/a begins		.45	.90
321-330		.40	.75
Giant-Size 1 ('75)	.40	1.10	2.20
Special 1 (10/68)-New material; Steranko-c	1.20	3.50	7.00
Special 2 (10/69)-Origin retold	.70	2.00	4.00
Special 3(1/71)	.50	1.50	3.00
Annual 4 (1/72),5(10/76)		.60	1.20
Annual 6 (11/77)		.50	1.00
Annual 7(8/78)-Byrne/Layton-c/a; Iceman & Angel app.	.50	1.50	3.00
8(11/79), 9(9/80), 10('81)		.50	1.00
Annual 11(10/82)-Miller, Buckler-a(p)		.50	1.00
Annual 12(8/83), 13(11/84)		.50	1.00
Annual 14(12/85), 15(10/86)		.65	1.30
Special 1(. . . Versus Quasimodo,3/83)-Based on Sat. morning cartoon		.25	.50

NOTE: ***Adkins*** *a-111-16i.* ***Austin*** *c-302i.* ***J. Buscema*** *c-202p.* ***Byrne*** *a-314p-319p; c-314-316, 318, 319.* ***Ditko*** *a-2, 6, 249, Annual 2r(3), 3r, 9p; c-2i, 6, 235, 249.* ***Everett*** *c-133i.* ***Golden*** *c-248, 251.* ***Kane*** *c(p)-193, 194, 196, 198.* ***Kirby*** *a-1-5, Special 2, 3p, Annual 5p; c-1-5, Annual 5.* ***Miller*** *c-258p, 261, 264, 268.* ***Mooney*** *a-230p, 287i, 288i.* ***Powell*** *a-Special 3r(2).* ***Severin*** *a(i)-108-110, 131-33, 141-51, 153-55; c(i)-109, 110,*

I Love Lucy #14, © Lucille Ball & Desi Arnaz

Immortal Doctor Fate #1, © DC

Incredible Hulk #105, © MCG

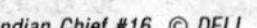
Indian Chief #16, © DELL

Infinity, Inc. #1, © DC

The Informer #2, © Feat. TV Prod.

THE INCREDIBLE HULK (continued)
132, 142, 144-55. ***Simonson*** *c-283.* ***Starlin*** *a-222p; c-217.* ***Staton*** *a(i)-187-89, 191-209.* ***Tuska*** *a-102i, 105i, 106i, 218p.* ***Williamson*** *a-310i; c-310i, 311i.* ***Wrightson*** *c-197.*

INCREDIBLE HULK AND WOLVERINE, THE
Oct, 1986 (One shot)
Marvel Comics Group

	Good	Fine	Mint
1-r-/1st app. Wolverine	.35	1.00	2.00

INCREDIBLE MR. LIMPET, THE (See Movie Classics)

INCREDIBLE SCIENCE FICTION (Formerly Weird Science-Fantasy)
July-Aug, 1955 - No. 33, Jan-Feb, 1956
E. C. Comics

30,33: 33-Story-r/W.F. No. 18	18.00	54.00	125.00
31-Williamson/Krenkel-a, Wood-a(2)	22.00	65.00	154.00
32-Williamson/Krenkel-a	22.00	65.00	154.00

NOTE: ***Davis*** *a-30, 32, 33; c-30-32.* ***Krigstein*** *a-in all.* ***Orlando*** *a-30, 32, 33(''Judgement Day'' reprint).* ***Wood*** *a-30, 31, 33; c-33.*

INDIANA JONES (See Further Adventures of. . .)

INDIANA JONES AND THE TEMPLE OF DOOM
Sept, 1984 - No. 3, Nov, 1984
Marvel Comics Group

1-3-r/Marvel Super Special; movie adaptation by Guice		.30	.60

INDIAN BRAVES (Baffling Mysteries No. 5 on)
March, 1951 - No. 4, Sept, 1951
Ace Magazines

1	2.65	8.00	18.00
2	1.30	4.00	9.00
3,4	1.15	3.50	8.00
I.W. Reprint No. 1 (no date)	.50	1.50	3.00

INDIAN CHIEF (White Eagle. . .) (Formerly The Chief)
No. 3, July-Sept, 1951 - No. 33, Jan-Mar, 1959
Dell Publishing Co.

3	1.75	5.25	12.00
4-11: 6-White Eagle app.	1.15	3.50	8.00
12-1st White Eagle(10-12/53)-Not same as earlier character	1.50	4.50	10.00
13-29	1.00	3.00	7.00
30-33-Buscema-a	1.15	3.50	8.00

INDIAN CHIEF (See March of Comics No. 94,110,127,140,159,170,187)

INDIAN FIGHTER, THE (See 4-Color No. 687)

INDIAN FIGHTER
May, 1950 - No. 11, Jan, 1952
Youthful Magazines

1	2.65	8.00	18.00
2-Wildey-a/c(bondage)	1.30	4.00	9.00
3-11: 3,4-Wildey-a	1.15	3.50	8.00

INDIAN LEGENDS OF THE NIAGARA (See American Graphics)

INDIANS
Spring, 1950 - No. 17, Spring, 1953
Fiction House Magazines (Wings Publ. Co.)

1-Manzar, White Indian, Long Bow & Orphan of the Storm begin	6.00	18.00	42.00
2-Starlight begins	3.50	10.50	24.00
3-5	3.00	9.00	21.00
6-10	2.00	6.00	14.00
11-17	1.75	5.25	12.00

INDIANS OF THE WILD WEST
Circa 1958? (no date)
I. W. Enterprises

	Good	Fine	Mint
9-Reprints	.50	1.50	3.00

INDIANS ON THE WARPATH
No date (Late 40s, early 50s) (132 pages)
St. John Publishing Co.

nn-Matt Baker-c; contains St. John comics rebound. Many combinations possible	12.00	36.00	84.00

INDIAN TRIBES (See Famous Indian Tribes)

INDIAN WARRIORS (Formerly White Rider. . .)
No. 7, June, 1951 - No. 11, 1952
Star Publications

7	3.50	10.50	24.00
8-11: 11-White Rider & Superhorse app.; L. B. Cole-c	2.35	7.00	16.00
3-D 1(12/53)-L. B. Cole-c	15.00	45.00	105.00
Accepted Reprint(nn)(inside cover shows White Rider & Superhorse No. 11)-Reprints cover/No. 7; origin White Rider &. . .;	1.70	5.00	12.00
Accepted Reprint No. 8 (nd); L.B. Cole-c	1.70	5.00	12.00

INDOORS-OUTDOORS (See Wisco)

INDOOR SPORTS
nd (64 pgs.; 6x9''; B&W reprints; hardcover)
National Specials Co.

By Tad	3.35	10.00	20.00

INFERIOR FIVE, THE (. . .5 No. 11,12) (See Showcase)
3-4/67 - No. 10, 9-10/68; No. 11, 8-9/72 - No. 12, 10-11/72
National Periodical Publications

1-Sekowsky-a(p)		.60	1.20
2-Plastic Man app.; Sekowsky-a(p)		.40	.80
3-10: 10-Superman x-over		.25	.50
11,12-Orlando c/a; both r-/Showcase No. 62,63		.25	.50

INFINITY, INC.
March, 1984 - Present ($1.25; Baxter paper; 36 pgs.)
DC Comics

1-Brainwave, Jr., Fury, The Huntress, Jade, Northwind, Nuklon, Obsidian, Power Girl, Silver Scarab & Star Spangled Kid begin	.55	1.70	3.40
2-5: 2-Dr. Midnite, G.A. Flash, W. Woman, Dr. Fate, Hourman, G.A. Gr. Lantern, Wildcat app. 5-Nudity panels	.35	1.10	2.20
6-10	.30	.95	1.90
11-17		.70	1.40
18-24-Crisis x-over. 21-Intro new Hourman & Dr. Midnight	.25	.80	1.60
25-30: 26-New Wildcat app.		.70	1.40
31-35: 31-Star-Spangled Kid becomes Skyman. 33-Origin Obsidian		.65	1.30
Annual 1 (12/85)-Crisis x-over	.35	1.00	2.00

NOTE: ***Kubert*** *r-4.* ***Newton*** *a-12p, 13p(last work 4/85).* ***Tuska*** *a-11p. JSA app. 3-10.*

INFORMER, THE
April, 1954 - No. 5, Dec, 1954
Feature Television Productions

1-Sekowsky-a begins	3.00	9.00	21.00
2	2.00	6.00	14.00
3-5	1.50	4.50	10.00

IN HIS STEPS
1973, 1977 (39, 49 cents)
Spire Christian Comics (Fleming H. Revell Co.)

nn		.40	.80

INHUMANS, THE (See Amazing Advs.)
Oct, 1975 - No. 12, Aug, 1977

THE INHUMANS (continued)
Marvel Comics Group

	Good	Fine	Mint
1		.50	1.00
2-12: 9-Reprints		.30	.60

NOTE: ***Buckler** c-2p-4p, 5. **Gil Kane** a-5-7p; c-1p, 7p, 8p. **Kirby** a-9r. **Mooney** a-11i. **Perez** a-1-4p, 8p.*

INHUMANOIDS, THE (TV)
Jan, 1987 - Present
Star Comics (Marvel)

	Good	Fine	Mint
1-Earth Corps begin; based on Hasbro toys & tv show		.50	1.00
2,3		.40	.80

INKY & DINKY (See Felix's Nephews . . .)

IN LOVE (I Love You No. 7 on)
Aug-Sept, 1954 - No. 6, July, 1955
Mainline/Charlton No. 5 (5/55)-on

	Good	Fine	Mint
1-Simon & Kirby-a	6.75	20.00	47.00
2-S&K-a	3.35	10.00	23.00
3,4-S&K-a	2.65	8.00	18.00
5-S&K-c only	1.65	5.00	11.50
6-No S&K-a	1.15	3.50	8.00

IN LOVE WITH JESUS
1952 (36 pages) (Giveaway)
Catechetical Educational Society

	Good	Fine	Mint
	4.00	12.00	28.00

IN SEARCH OF THE CASTAWAYS (See Movie Comics)

INSIDE CRIME (Formerly My Intimate Affair)
No. 3, July, 1950 - No. 2, Sept, 1950
Fox Features Syndicate (Hero Books)

	Good	Fine	Mint
3-Wood-a, 10 pgs.; L. B. Cole-c	9.50	28.50	65.00
2(9/50)-Used in **SOTI**, pg. 182-3; Lingerie panel; r-/Spook No. 24	8.00	24.00	56.00
nn(no publ. listed, nd)	3.00	9.00	21.00

INSPECTOR, THE (Also see The Pink Panther)
July, 1974 - No. 19, Feb, 1978
Gold Key

	Good	Fine	Mint
1	.60	1.75	3.50
2-5	.30	.90	1.80
6-19: 11-Reprints		.50	1.00

INSPECTOR WADE (See Feature Books No. 13, McKay)

INTERNATIONAL COMICS (. . . Crime Patrol No. 6)
Spring, 1947 - No. 5, Nov-Dec, 1947
E. C. Comics

	Good	Fine	Mint
1	28.00	84.00	195.00
2	22.00	65.00	154.00
3-5	19.00	57.00	132.00

INTERNATIONAL CRIME PATROL (Formerly International Comics No. 1-5; becomes Crime Patrol No. 7 on)
Spring, 1948
E. C. Comics

	Good	Fine	Mint
6-Moon Girl app.	27.00	81.00	190.00

INTERSTATE THEATRES' FUN CLUB COMICS
Mid 1940's (10 cents on cover) (B&W cover) (Premium)
Interstate Theatres

Cover features MLJ characters looking at a copy of Top-Notch Comics, but contains an early Detective Comic on inside; many combinations possible

	Good	Fine	Mint
	5.35	16.00	24.00

IN THE DAYS OF THE MOB (Magazine)
Fall, 1971 (Black & White)
Hampshire Dist. Ltd. (National)

	Good	Fine	Mint
1-Kirby-a; has John Dillinger wanted poster inside	.80	2.40	3.60

IN THE PRESENCE OF MINE ENEMIES
1973 (35-49 cents)
Spire Christian Comics/Fleming H. Revell Co.

	Good	Fine	Mint
		.50	1.00

INTIMATE (Teen-Age Love No. 4 on?)
December, 1957 - No. 3, May, 1958
Charlton Comics

	Good	Fine	Mint
1-3	1.00	3.00	7.00

INTIMATE CONFESSIONS (See Fox Giants)

INTIMATE CONFESSIONS
July-Aug, 1951 - No. 8, Mar, 1953
Realistic Comics

	Good	Fine	Mint
1-Kinstler-c/a; c/Avon paperback 222	50.00	150.00	350.00
2	9.00	27.00	60.00
3-c/Avon paperback 250; Kinstler-c/a	12.00	36.00	80.00
4-c/Avon paperback 304; Kinstler-c	9.00	27.00	60.00
5	9.00	27.00	60.00
6-c/Avon paperback 120	9.00	27.00	60.00
7-Spanking panel	10.00	30.00	70.00
8-c/Avon paperback 375; Kinstler-a	9.00	27.00	60.00

INTIMATE CONFESSIONS
1964
I. W. Enterprises/Super Comics

	Good	Fine	Mint
I.W. Reprint No. 9,10	.70	2.00	4.00
Super Reprint No. 12,18	.70	2.00	4.00

INTIMATE LOVE
1950 - No. 28, Aug, 1954
Standard Comics

	Good	Fine	Mint
5	2.00	6.00	14.00
6-8-Severin/Elder-a	2.65	8.00	18.00
9	1.15	3.50	8.00
10-Jane Russell, Robert Mitchum photo-c	1.85	5.50	13.00
11-18,20,23,25,27,28	1.00	3.00	7.00
19,21,22,24,26-Toth-a	3.35	10.00	23.00

NOTE: ***Celardo** a-8, 10. **Colletta** a-23. **Moreira** a-13(2). Photo-c-7, 14, 18, 20, 24.*

INTIMATE ROMANCES
1950 - 1954
Standard Comics

	Good	Fine	Mint
1	2.85	8.50	20.00
2	1.85	5.50	13.00
3-19	1.50	4.50	10.00

INTIMATE SECRETS OF ROMANCE
Sept, 1953 - No. 2, April, 1954
Star Publications

	Good	Fine	Mint
1,2-L. B. Cole-c	4.35	13.00	30.00

INTRIGUE
January, 1955
Quality Comics Group

	Good	Fine	Mint
1-Horror; Jack Cole reprt/Web of Evil	6.50	19.50	45.00

INVADERS, THE (TV)
Oct, 1967 - No. 4, Oct, 1968 (All have photo-c)
Gold Key

Inside Crime #2, © FOX

Intimate Love #14, © STD

Intrigue #1, © QUA

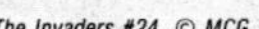
The Invaders #24, © MCG

Invisible Scarlet O'Neil #1, © HARV

Iron Man #6, © MCG

THE INVADERS (continued)	Good	Fine	Mint
1-Spiegle-a in all	2.35	7.00	16.00
2-4	1.75	5.25	12.00

INVADERS, THE (Also see Avengers No. 71)
August, 1975 - No. 41, Sept, 1979
Marvel Comics Group

	Good	Fine	Mint
1-Captain America, Sub-Mariner & Human Torch begin	.40	1.20	2.40
2-1st app. Mailbag & Brain-Drain		.60	1.20
3-5: 3-Intro U-Man		.35	.70
6-Liberty Legion app; intro/1st app. Union Jack. Two cover prices, 25¢ & 30¢		.35	.70
7-10: 7-Intro Baron Blood; Human Torch origin retold. 9-Origin Baron Blood. 10-G.A. C. Amer.-r		.35	.70
11-Origin Spitfire; intro The Blue Bullet		.25	.50
12-19: 14-1st app. The Crusaders. 16-Re-intro The Destroyer. 17-Intro Warrior Woman. 18-Re-intro The Destroyer w/new origin.		.25	.50
20-Reprints Sub-Mariner story/Motion Picture Funnies Weekly with color added & brief write-up about MPFW		.25	.50
21-r-/Marvel Mystery No. 10		.25	.50
22-30: 22-New origin Toro. 24-Reprint/Marvel Mystery No. 17. 28-Intro new Human Top & Golden Girl. 29-Intro Teutonic Knight		.25	.50
31-40(5/79): 34-Mighty Destroyer joins		.25	.50
41-Double size		.25	.50
Giant Size... 1(6/75)-50 cents; origin; GA Sub-Mariner r-/Sub-Mariner 1; intro Master-Man		.50	1.00
Annual 1(9/77)-Schomburg, Rico stories; Schomburg-c; Avengers app; re-intro The Shark & The Hyena.		.35	.70

NOTE: **Buckler** *a-5.* **Everett** *a-21r(1940), 24r, Annual 1r.* **Gil Kane** *c(p)-13, 17, 18, 20-27.* **Kirby** *c(p)-3-12, 14-16, 32, 33.* **Mooney** *a-5, 16, 22.*

INVISIBLE BOY (See Approved Comics)

INVISIBLE MAN, THE (See Superior Stories No. 1)

INVISIBLE SCARLET O'NEIL (Also see Harvey Comics Hits 59)
Dec, 1950 - No. 3, April, 1951
Famous Funnies (Harvey)

	Good	Fine	Mint
1	9.00	27.00	60.00
2,3	6.00	18.00	42.00

IRON CORPORAL, THE
No. 23, Oct, 1985 - No. 25, Feb, 1986
Charlton Comics

	Good	Fine	Mint
23-25: Glanzman-a(r)		.40	.75

IRON FIST (Also see Marvel Premiere & Powerman & Iron Fist)
Nov, 1975 - No. 15, Sept, 1977
Marvel Comics Group

	Good	Fine	Mint
1-McWilliams-a(i); Iron Man app.	1.50	4.50	9.00
2	.85	2.50	5.00
3-5	.70	2.00	4.00
6-10: 8-Origin retold	.50	1.50	3.00
11-14: 12-Capt. America app.	.45	1.25	2.50
15-New X-Men app.	3.35	10.00	20.00

NOTE: **Adkins** *a-8p, 13i; c-8i.* **Byrne** *a-1-15p; c-8p.* **G. Kane** *c-4-6p.*

IRON HORSE (TV)
March, 1967 - No. 2, June, 1967
Dell Publishing Co.

	Good	Fine	Mint
1,2	1.00	3.00	7.00

IRON JAW (Also see The Barbarians)
Jan, 1975 - No. 4, July, 1975
Atlas/Seaboard Publ.

	Good	Fine	Mint
1-Adams-c; Sekowsky-a(p)	.25	.75	1.50
2-Adams-c		.50	1.00
3,4: 4-Origin		.30	.60

IRON MAN (Also see Tales of Suspense)
May, 1968 - Present
Marvel Comics Group

	Good	Fine	Mint
1-Origin	8.00	24.00	48.00
2	2.35	7.00	14.00
3-5	1.35	4.00	8.00
6-10	.85	2.50	5.00
11-15	.55	1.70	3.40
16-20	.45	1.40	2.80
21-40: 22-Death of Janice Cord. 27-Intro Fire Brand. 33-Intro Spymaster	.35	1.10	2.20
41-46,48-50: 43-Intro The Guardsman. 46-The Guardsman dies. 50-Princess Python app.	.35	1.10	2.20
47-Origin retold; Smith-a(p)	.85	2.50	5.00
51,52	.35	1.00	2.00
53-Starlin-p(part)	.40	1.25	2.50
54-Everett Sub-Mariner in part	.35	1.00	2.00
55,56-Starlin-a; 55-Starlin-c	.70	2.00	4.00
57-67,69,70: 65-Origin Dr. Spectrum	.30	1.00	2.00
68-Starlin-c; origin retold	.35	1.10	2.20
71-85,88-90: 76 r-/No. 9		.60	1.20
86-1st app. Blizzard	.35	1.00	2.00
87-Origin Blizzard	.35	1.00	2.00
91-99	.25	.75	1.50
100-Starlin-c	.60	1.80	3.60
101-117: 101-Intro DreadKnight. 109-1st app. new Crimson Dynamo. 110-Origin Jack of Hearts retold	.25	.75	1.50
118-Byrne-a(p)	.70	2.00	4.00
119,120,123-128-Tony Stark recovers from alcohol problem	.45	1.25	2.50
121,122,129-140: 122-Origin		.50	1.00
141-149: 142-Intro deep space armor		.50	1.00
150-Double size		.60	1.20
151-158,160: 152-New armor		.45	.90
159-Paul Smith-c/a(p); (6/82)	.35	1.10	2.20
161-Moon Knight app.		.50	1.00
162-168: 167-Tony Stark alcohol problem starts again		.45	.90
169,170-New Iron Man (Jim Rhodes replaces Tony Stark)	.35	1.10	2.20
171-199: 186-Intro Vibro. 191-Tony Stark new armor		.45	.90
200-Double size ($1.25)	.25	.70	1.40
201-216: 213-Intro new Dominic Fortune		.45	.90
Giant Size 1('75)-Ditko-a(r)	.35	1.00	2.00
Special 1(8/70)-Everett-c	.70	2.00	4.00
Special 2(11/71)	.35	1.00	2.00
Annual 3(6/76)-Man-Thing app.	.30	.80	1.60
Annual 5(12/82), 6(11/83), 7(10/84)		.65	1.30
Annual 8(10/86)-X-Factor app.		.65	1.30
King Size 4(8/77)-Newton-a(i)	.25	.80	1.60

NOTE: **Austin** *c-105i, 109-11i, 151i.* **Byrne** *a-118p; c-109p.* **Colan** *a-Special 1p(3).* **Craig** *a-1i, 2-4, 5-13i, 14, 15-19i, 24p, 25p, 26-28i; c-2-4.* **Ditko** *a-160p.* **Giffen** *a-114p.* **G. Kane** *c(p)-52-54, 63, 67, 72-75, 77, 78, 88, 98.* **Kirby** *a-Special 1p; c-80p, 90, 92-95.* **Layton** *a-116-128i, 130, 131-135i, 137-139, 140-154i; c-116i, 118, 119i, 120, 121, 122i, 123, 124i, 125, 126i, 127-48, 149i, 150i, 151p, 152p, 153, 154i, 155, 156i, 157i, 158, 213.* **Mooney** *a-40i, 47i.* **Perez** *c-103p.* **Starlin** *a-53p, 55p, 56p; c-55p, 160, 163.* **Tuska** *a-5-13p, 15-23p, 24i, 32p, 38-46p, 48-54p, 57-69p, 70-72p, 78p, 86-92p, 95-106p, Annual 4p.* **Wood** *a-Special 1i.*

IRON MAN & SUB-MARINER
April, 1968 (One Shot)
Marvel Comics Group

	Good	Fine	Mint
1-Colan/Craig-a-Iron Man; Colan-c	1.00	3.00	7.00

IRON VIC (See Comics Revue No. 3)
1940; Aug, 1947 - No. 3, 1947
United Features Syndicate/St. John Publ. Co.

IRON VIC (continued) — Good / Fine / Mint
Single Series 22 11.00 33.00 76.00
2,3(St. John) 1.75 5.25 12.00

ISIS (TV) (Also see Shazam)
Oct-Nov, 1976 - No. 8, Dec-Jan, 1977-78
National Periodical Publications/DC Comics

1-Wood inks .40 .80
2-8: 5-Isis new look. 7-Origin .25 .50

ISLAND AT THE TOP OF THE WORLD (See Walt Disney Showcase 27)

ISLAND OF DR. MOREAU, THE (Movie)
October, 1977 (52 pgs.)
Marvel Comics Group

1 .50 1.00

I SPY (TV)
Aug, 1966 - No. 6, Sept, 1968 (Photo-c)
Gold Key

1 3.00 9.00 21.00
2-6: 3,4-McWilliams-a 1.75 5.25 12.00

IS THIS TOMORROW?
1947 (One Shot) (3 editions) (52 pages)
Catechetical Guild

1-Theme of communists taking over the USA; (no price on cover) Used in **POP**, pg. 102 12.00 36.00 80.00
1-(10 cents on cover) 17.00 51.00 120.00
1-Has blank circle with no price on cover 17.00 51.00 120.00
Black & White advance copy titled "Confidential"-(52 pgs.)-Contains script and art edited out of the color edition, including one page of extreme violence showing mob nailing a Cardinal to a door; (only two known copies) 50.00 150.00 320.00

NOTE: *The original color version first sold for 10 cents. Since sales were good, it was later printed as a giveaway. Approximately four million in total were printed. The two black and white copies listed plus two other versions as well as a full color untrimmed version surfaced in 1979 from the Guild's old files in St. Paul, Minnesota.*

IT! (See Supernatural Thrillers No.1 & Astonishing Tales No.21-24)

IT HAPPENS IN THE BEST FAMILIES
1920 (52 pages) (B&W Sundays)
Powers Photo Engraving Co.

By Briggs 5.00 15.00 35.00
Special Railroad Edition(30 cents)-r-/strips from 1914-1920 4.35 13.00 30.00

IT REALLY HAPPENED
1944 - No. 11, Oct, 1947
William H. Wise No. 1,2/Standard (Visual Editions)

1 5.00 15.00 35.00
2 3.00 9.00 21.00
3-7,9 2.65 8.00 18.00
8-Story of Roy Rogers 4.35 13.00 30.00
10-Honus Wagner story 3.00 9.00 21.00
11-Baker-a 4.00 12.00 28.00

NOTE: ***Guardineer** a-7(2), 8(2), 11. **Schomburg** c-1-7, 9-11.*

IT RHYMES WITH LUST (Also see Bold Stories, Candid Tales)
1950 (Digest size) (128 pages)
St. John Publishing Co.

(Rare)-Matt Baker & Ray Osrin-a 26.00 78.00 180.00

IT'S ABOUT TIME (TV)
January, 1967
Gold Key

1 (10195-701)-Photo-c 2.00 6.00 14.00

IT'S A DUCK'S LIFE
Feb, 1950 - No. 11, Feb, 1952
Marvel Comics/Atlas(MMC) — Good / Fine / Mint

1-Buck Duck, Super Rabbit begin 4.00 12.00 28.00
2 2.00 6.00 14.00
3-11 1.30 4.00 9.00

IT'S FUN TO STAY ALIVE (Giveaway)
1948 (16 pgs.) (heavy stock paper)
National Automobile Dealers Association

Featuring: Bugs Bunny, The Berrys, Dixie Dugan, Elmer, Tim Tyler, Bruce Gentry, Abbie & Slats, Joe Jinks, The Toodles, & Cokey; all art copyright 1946-48 drawn especially for this book. 9.00 27.00 62.00

IT'S GAMETIME
Sept-Oct, 1955 - No. 4, Mar-Apr, 1956
National Periodical Publications

1-(Scarce)-Infinity-c; Davy Crockett app. in puzzle 18.00 54.00 125.00
2-4(Scarce): 2-Dodo & The Frog 14.50 43.50 90.00

IT'S LOVE, LOVE, LOVE
November, 1957 - No. 2, Jan, 1958 (10 cents)
St. John Publishing Co.

1,2 2.00 6.00 14.00

IT'S SCIENCE WITH DR. RADIUM
Nov, 1986 - Present ($1.50)
Slave Labor Graphics

1 .25 .75 1.50

IVANHOE (See Fawcett Movie Comics No. 20)

IVANHOE
July-Sept, 1963
Dell Publishing Co.

1 (12-373-309) 1.75 5.25 12.00

IWO JIMA (See Spectacular Features Magazine)

JACE PEARSON OF THE TEXAS RANGERS (Tales of the Texas Rangers 4-Color 396; . . . 's Tales of . . . No. 11-on)(See Western Roundup)
No. 396, 5/52 - No. 1021, 8-10/59 (No No. 10) (All-Photo-c)
Dell Publishing Co.

4-Color 396 (No. 1) 3.50 10.50 24.00
2(5-7/53) 2.65 8.00 18.00
3-9(2-4/55) 2.65 8.00 18.00
4-Color 648(9/55) 2.65 8.00 18.00
11(11-2/55/56) - 14,17-20(6-8/58) 2.35 7.00 16.00
15,16-Toth-a 3.50 10.50 24.00
4-Color 961-Spiegle-a 2.65 8.00 18.00
4-Color 1021 2.35 7.00 16.00

JACK & JILL VISIT TOYTOWN WITH ELMER THE ELF
1949 (16 pgs.) (paper cover)
Butler Brothers (Toytown Stores Giveaway)

1.70 5.00 10.00

JACK ARMSTRONG
11/47 - No. 9, 9/48; No. 10, 3/49 - No. 13, Sept, 1949
Parents' Institute

1 8.00 24.00 56.00
2 4.35 13.00 30.00
3-5 3.75 11.25 26.00
6-13 2.85 8.50 20.00
12-Premium version(distr. in Chicago only); Free printed on upper right-c; no price (Rare) 9.00 27.00 62.00

I Spy #3, © Three F Prod.

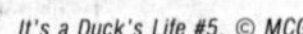
It's a Duck's Life #5, © MCG

Jace Pearson #11, © DELL

Jackpot #6, © AP

Jack the Giant Killer #1, © Bimfort

Jeanie Comics #17, © MCG

JACKIE GLEASON
1948; Sept, 1955 - No. 5, Dec, 1955
St. John Publishing Co.

	Good	Fine	Mint
1(1948)	22.00	65.00	154.00
2(1948)	12.00	36.00	84.00
1(1955)(TV)-Photo-c	13.00	40.00	90.00
2-5	9.00	27.00	62.00

JACKIE GLEASON AND THE HONEYMOONERS (TV)
June-July, 1956 - No. 12, Apr-May, 1958
National Periodical Publications

	Good	Fine	Mint
1	25.00	75.00	175.00
2	16.00	48.00	110.00
3-11	12.00	36.00	84.00
12 (Scarce)	14.50	43.50	100.00

JACKIE JOKERS (Also see Richie Rich &. . .)
March, 1973 - No. 4, Sept, 1973
Harvey Publications

	Good	Fine	Mint
1-4; 2-President Nixon app.		.20	.40

JACKIE ROBINSON (Famous Plays of. . .)
May, 1950 - No. 6, 1952 (Baseball hero)
Fawcett Publications

	Good	Fine	Mint
nn	17.00	51.00	120.00
2	12.00	36.00	84.00
3-6	11.00	33.00	76.00

JACK IN THE BOX (Formerly Yellowjacket No. 1-10)
(Cowboy Western Comics No. 17 on)
Feb, 1946; No. 11, Oct, 1946 - No. 16, Nov-Dec, 1947
Frank Comunale/Charlton Comics No. 11 on

	Good	Fine	Mint
1-Stitches, Marty Mouse & Nutsy McKrow	3.35	10.00	23.00
11-Yellowjacket	4.00	12.00	28.00
12,14-16	1.50	4.50	10.00
13-Wolverton-a	8.00	24.00	56.00

JACK OF HEARTS
Jan, 1984 - No. 4, April, 1984 (Mini-series)
Marvel Comics Group

	Good	Fine	Mint
1		.60	1.20
2-4		.45	.90

JACKPOT COMICS (Jolly Jingles No. 10 on)
Spring, 1941 - No. 9, Spring, 1943
MLJ Magazines

	Good	Fine	Mint
1-The Black Hood, Mr. Justice, Steel Sterling & Sgt. Boyle begin; Biro-c	77.00	230.00	540.00
2	35.00	105.00	245.00
3	31.00	92.00	215.00
4-Archie begins (on sale 12/41)-(Also see Pep Comics No. 22); Montana-c	88.00	264.00	615.00
5	38.00	115.00	265.00
6-9: 6,7-Bondage-c	32.00	95.00	224.00

JACK Q FROST (See Unearthly Spectaculars)

JACK THE GIANT KILLER (See Movie Classics)

JACK THE GIANT KILLER (New Advs. of. . .)
Aug-Sept, 1953
Bimfort & Co.

	Good	Fine	Mint
V1No.1-H. C. Kiefer-a	6.50	19.50	45.00

JACKY'S DIARY (See 4-Color No. 1091)

JAGUAR, THE (See The Advs. of. . .)

JAMBOREE
Feb, 1946(no mo. given) - No. 3, April, 1946
Round Publishing Co.

	Good	Fine	Mint
1	3.00	9.00	21.00
2,3	1.50	4.50	10.00

JANE ARDEN (See Pageant of Comics)
March, 1948 - No. 2, June, 1948
St. John (United Features Syndicate)

	Good	Fine	Mint
1-Newspaper reprints	7.00	21.00	50.00
2	4.00	12.00	28.00

JANN OF THE JUNGLE (Jungle Tales No. 1-7)
No. 8, Nov, 1955 - No. 17, June, 1957
Atlas Comics (CSI)

	Good	Fine	Mint
8(No.1)	6.50	19.50	45.00
9,11-15	4.00	12.00	28.00
10-Williamson/Colleta-c	5.00	15.00	35.00
16,17-Williamson/Mayo-a(3), 5 pgs. each	8.00	24.00	56.00

NOTE: ***Everett*** *c-15-17.* ***Heck*** *a-8, 15, 17.* ***Shores*** *a-8.*

JASON & THE ARGONAUTS (See Movie Classics)

JAWS 2 (See Marvel Super Special, A)

JCP FEATURES
Feb, 1982-c; Dec, 1981-indicia (One-shot)
J.C. Productions (Archie)

	Good	Fine	Mint
1-T.H.U.N.D.E.R. Agents		.50	1.00

JEANIE COMICS (Cowgirl Romances No. 28) (Formerly Daring)
No. 13, April, 1947 - No. 27, Oct, 1949
Marvel Comics/Atlas(CPC)

	Good	Fine	Mint
13-Mitzi, Willie begin	5.00	15.00	35.00
14,15	3.00	9.00	21.00
16-Used in **Love and Death** by Legman; Kurtzman's "Hey Look"	5.00	15.00	35.00
17-19,22-Kurtzman's "Hey Look," 1-3 pgs. each	3.00	9.00	21.00
20,21,23-27	1.70	5.00	12.00

JEEP COMICS (Also see G.I. and Overseas Comics)
Winter, 1944 - No. 3, Mar-Apr, 1948
R. B. Leffingwell & Co.

	Good	Fine	Mint
1-Capt. Power, Criss Cross & Jeep & Peep (costumed)	6.00	18.00	42.00
2,3-Capt. Power in No. 2; Criss Cross & Jeep & Peep (costumed)	3.75	11.25	26.00
1-29(Giveaway)-Strip reprints in all; Tarzan, Flash Gordon, Blondie, The Nebbs, Little Iodine, Red Ryder, Don Winslow, The Phantom, Johnny Hazard, Katzenjammer Kids; distributed to U.S. Armed Forces in mid 1940's	3.35	10.00	20.00

NOTE: ***L. B. Cole*** *c-3.*

JEFF JORDAN, U.S. AGENT
Dec, 1947 - Jan, 1948
D. S. Publishing Co.

	Good	Fine	Mint
1	3.75	11.25	26.00

JEMM, SON OF SATURN
9/84 - No. 12, 8/85 (12 part maxi-series; mando paper)
DC Comics

	Good	Fine	Mint
1-Colan p-all; c-1-5p,7-12p	.25	.75	1.50
2-12: 3-Origin		.45	.90

JERRY DRUMMER (Formerly Soldier & Marine V2No.9)
No. 10, Apr, 1957 - No. 12, Oct, 1957
Charlton Comics

	Good	Fine	Mint
V2No.10, V3No.11,12	1.00	3.00	7.00

JERRY IGER'S CLASSIC SHEENA (Also see Sheena 3-D Special)
April, 1985 (One-shot)

JERRY IGER'S CLASSIC SHEENA (cont'd.)
Blackthorne Publishing

	Good	Fine	Mint
1	.25	.75	1.50

JERRY IGER'S FAMOUS FEATURES
July, 1984 (One-shot)
Pacific Comics

1-Unpub. Flamingo & Wonder Boy by Baker	.25	.75	1.50

JERRY IGER'S GOLDEN FEATURES
1986 - No. 6, 1987 ($2.00, B&W)
Blackthorne Publ.

1-6	.30	.90	1.80

JERRY LEWIS (See Adventures of. . .)

JESSE JAMES (See 4-Color No. 757 & The Legend of. . .)

JESSE JAMES (See Badmen of the West & Blazing Sixguns)
Aug, 1950 - No. 29, Aug-Sept, 1956
Avon Periodicals

1-Kubert Alabam r-/Cowpuncher No. 1	10.00	30.00	70.00
2-Kubert-a(3)	8.00	24.00	56.00
3-Kubert Alabam r-/Cowpuncher No. 2	6.50	19.50	45.00
4-No Kubert	2.65	8.00	18.00
5,6-Kubert Jesse James-a(3); one pg. Wood-a, No. 5	6.50	19.50	45.00
7-Kubert Jesse James-a(2)	5.75	17.25	40.00
8-Kinstler-a(3)	3.85	11.50	27.00
9,10-No Kubert	2.65	8.00	18.00
11-14 (Exist?)	2.00	6.00	14.00
15-Kinstler r-/No. 3	2.00	6.00	14.00
16-Kinstler r-/No. 3 & Sheriff Bob Dixon's Chuck Wagon No. 1 with name changed to Sheriff Tom Wilson	2.35	7.00	16.00
17-Jesse James r-/No. 4; Kinstler-c idea from Kubert splash in No. 6	1.65	5.00	11.50
18-Kubert Jesse James r-/No. 5	1.65	5.00	11.50
19-Kubert Jesse James-r	1.65	5.00	11.50
20-Williamson/Frazetta-a; r-Chief Vic. Apache Massacre; Kubert Jesse James r-/No. 6	8.00	24.00	56.00
21-Two Jesse James r-/No. 4, Kinstler r-/No. 4	1.65	5.00	11.50
22,23-No Kubert	1.50	4.50	10.00
24-New McCarty strip by Kinstler plus Kinstler r-/No. 9	1.50	4.50	10.00
25-New McCarty Jesse James strip by Kinstler; Kinstler J. James r-/No. 7,9	1.50	4.50	10.00
26,27-New McCarty J. James strip plus a Kinstler/McCann Jesse James-r	1.50	4.50	10.00
28-Reprints most of Red Mountain, Featuring Quantrells Raiders	1.50	4.50	10.00
29	1.50	4.50	10.00
Annual(nn; 1952; 25 cents)-". . . Brings Six-Gun Justice to the West"(100 pgs.)-3 earlier issues rebound; Kubert, Kinstler-a(3)	16.00	48.00	110.00

NOTE: *Mostly reprints No. 10 on.* ***Kinstler*** *a-3, 4, 7-9, 15r, 16(2), 21-27; c-3, 4, 9, 17, 18, 20-27.*

JESSE JAMES
July, 1953
Realistic Publications

nn-Reprints Avon's No. 1, same cover, colors different	4.00	12.00	28.00

JEST (Kayo No. 12) (Formerly Snap)
1944
Harry 'A' Chesler

	Good	Fine	Mint
10-Johnny Rebel & Yankee Boy app. in text	3.75	11.25	26.00
11-Little Nemo in Adventure Land	4.35	13.00	30.00

JESTER
1945
Harry 'A' Chesler

10	3.35	10.00	23.00

JESUS
1979 (49 cents)
Spire Christian Comics (Fleming H. Revell Co.)

		.30	.60

JET (See Jet Powers)

JET ACES
1952 - 1953
Fiction House Magazines

1	4.35	13.00	30.00
2	3.00	9.00	21.00
3,4	2.50	7.50	17.00

JET DREAM (. . . & Her Stuntgirl Counterspies)
June, 1968
Gold Key

1	1.50	4.50	10.00

JET FIGHTERS
No. 5, Nov, 1952 - No. 7, Mar, 1953
Standard Magazines

5,7-Toth-a	4.35	13.00	30.00
6-Celardo-a	1.85	5.50	13.00

JET POWERS (American Air Forces No. 5 on)
1950 - 1951
Magazine Enterprises

1(A-1 30)-Powell-a begins	12.00	36.00	84.00
2(A-1 32)	8.50	25.50	60.00
3(A-1 35)-Williamson/Evans-a	18.00	54.00	125.00
4(A-1 38)-Williamson/Wood-a; "The Rain of Sleep" drug story	18.00	54.00	125.00
I.W. Reprint 1,2(1963)-r-/No. 1,2	1.00	3.00	6.00

JET PUP (See 3-D Features)

JETSONS, THE (TV)(See March of Comics 276,330,348)
Jan, 1963 - No. 36, Oct, 1970 (Hanna-Barbera)
Gold Key

1	3.50	10.50	24.00
2	2.35	7.00	16.00
3-10	1.75	5.25	12.00
11-20	1.15	3.50	8.00
21-36	.85	2.50	6.00

JETSONS, THE (TV) (Hanna-Barbera)
Nov, 1970 - No. 20, Dec, 1973
Charlton Comics

1	2.00	6.00	14.00
2	1.00	3.00	7.00
3-10	.85	2.50	6.00
11-20	.75	2.25	5.00

JETTA OF THE 21ST CENTURY
No. 5, 1952 - No. 7, Mar, 1953 (Teen-age Archie type)
Standard Comics

5	5.00	15.00	35.00

Jerry Iger's Famous Features #1, © Pacific

Jessie James #20, © AVON

The Jetsons #1 (GK), © Hanna-Barbera

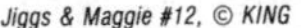
Jiggs & Maggie #12, © KING

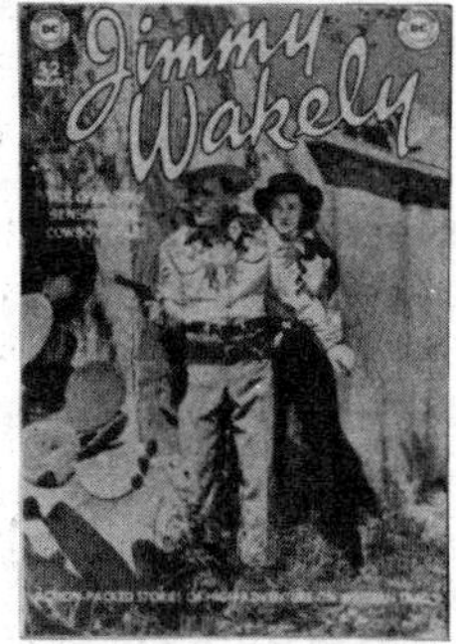

Jimmy Wakely #4, © DC

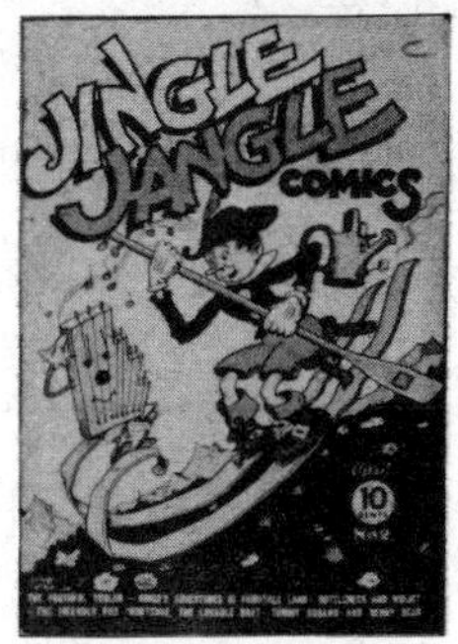

Jingle Jangle Comics #2, © EAS

JETTA OF THE 21ST CENTURY (continued) — Good / Fine / Mint
6,7 — 2.85 — 8.50 — 20.00

JIGGS & MAGGIE (See 4-Color No. 18)

JIGGS & MAGGIE
No. 11, 1949(Aug.) - No. 21, 2/53; No. 22, 4/53 - No. 27, 2-3/54
Standard Comics/Harvey Publications No. 22 on

11 — 5.00 — 15.00 — 35.00
12-15,17-21 — 2.65 — 8.00 — 18.00
16-Wood text illos. — 3.75 — 11.25 — 26.00
22-25,27: 22-24-Little Dot app. — 2.00 — 6.00 — 14.00
26-Four pgs. partially in 3-D — 8.00 — 24.00 — 56.00

NOTE: *Sunday page reprints by* ***McManus*** *loosely blended into story continuity. Advertised on covers as "All New."*

JIGSAW (Big Hero Adventures)
Sept, 1966 - No. 2, Dec, 1966 (36 pgs.)
Harvey Publications (Funday Funnies)

1-Origin; Crandall-a, 5pgs. — .70 — 2.00 — 4.00
2-Man From S.R.A.M. — .35 — 1.00 — 2.00

JIGSAW OF DOOM (See Complete Mystery No. 2)

JIM BOWIE (Formerly Danger; Black Jack No. 20 on)
No. 15, 1955? - No. 19, April, 1957
Charlton Comics

15 — 1.75 — 5.25 — 12.00
16-19 — 1.00 — 3.00 — 7.00

JIM BOWIE (See 4-Color No. 893,993, & Western Tales)

JIM DANDY
May, 1956 - No. 3, Sept, 1956 (Charles Biro)
Dandy Magazine (Lev Gleason)

1 — 2.00 — 6.00 — 14.00
2,3 — 1.00 — 3.00 — 7.00

JIM HARDY (Also see Treasury of Comics No. 2&5 & Sparkler)
1939 - 1940; 1947
United Features Syndicate/Spotlight Publ.

Single Series 6 — 15.00 — 45.00 — 105.00
Single Series 27('40) — 11.00 — 33.00 — 76.00
1('47)-Spotlight Publ. — 3.75 — 11.25 — 26.00
2 — 2.00 — 6.00 — 14.00

JIM HARDY
1944 (132 pages, 25 cents) (Tip Top, Sparkler-r)
Spotlight/United Features Syndicate

(1944)-Origin Mirror Man; Triple Terror app. — 13.00 — 40.00 — 90.00

JIMINY CRICKET (See 4-Color No. 701,795,897,989 & Walt Disney Showcase No. 37)

JIMMY (James Swinnerton)
1905 (10x15") (40 pages in color)
N. Y. American & Journal

13.50 — 40.50 — 95.00

JIMMY DURANTE (See A-1 Comics No. 18,20)

JIMMY OLSEN (See Superman's Pal . . .)

JIMMY WAKELY (Cowboy movie star)
Sept-Oct, 1949 - No. 18, July-Aug, 1952 (52pgs., 1-13)
National Periodical Publications

1-Photo-c, 52pgs. begin; Alex Toth-a; Kit Colby Girl Sheriff begins — 20.00 — 60.00 — 140.00
2-Toth-a — 13.50 — 40.50 — 95.00
3,6,7-Frazetta-a in all, 3 pgs. each; Toth-a in all. 7-Last photo-c? — 16.50 — 50.00 — 115.00
4-Frazetta-a, 3pgs.; Kurtzman "Pot-Shot Pete," 1pg; Toth-a — 16.50 — 50.00 — 115.00

Good / Fine / Mint
5,8-15,18-Toth-a; 12,14-Kubert-a, 3 & 2 pgs. — 11.00 — 33.00 — 76.00
16,17 — 8.00 — 24.00 — 56.00

JIM RAY'S AVIATION SKETCH BOOK
Feb, 1946 - No. 2, May-June, 1946
Vital Publishers

1,2-Picture stories about planes and pilots — 11.00 — 33.00 — 76.00

JIM SOLAR (See Wisco/Klarer)

JINGLE BELLS (See March of Comics No. 65)

JINGLE BELLS CHRISTMAS BOOK
1971 (20 pgs.; B&W inside; slick cover)
Montgomery Ward (Giveaway)

— .40 — .80

JINGLE DINGLE CHRISTMAS STOCKING COMICS
V2No.1, 1951 (no date listed) (100 pgs.; giant-size)(25 cents)
Stanhall Publications (Publ.-annually)

V2No.1-Foodini & Pinhead, Silly Pilly plus games & puzzles — 5.00 — 15.00 — 35.00

JINGLE JANGLE COMICS (Also see Puzzle Fun)
Feb, 1942 - No. 42, Dec, 1949
Eastern Color Printing Co.

1-Pie-Face Prince of Old Pretzleburg, & Jingle Jangle Tales by George Carlson, Hortense, & Benny Bear begin — 18.00 — 55.00 — 125.00
2,3-No Pie-Face Prince — 8.35 — 25.00 — 58.00
4-Pie-Face Prince cover — 8.35 — 25.00 — 58.00
5 — 7.35 — 22.00 — 51.00
6-10: 8-No Pie-Face Prince — 6.00 — 18.00 — 42.00
11-15 — 3.65 — 11.00 — 25.00
16-30: 17,18-No Pie-Face Prince — 3.00 — 9.00 — 21.00
31-42 — 2.20 — 6.50 — 15.00

NOTE: ***George Carlson*** *a-(2) in all except No. 2, 3, 8, 17, 18; c-1-6.* ***Carlson*** *1 pg. puzzles in 9, 10, 12-15, 18, 20.* ***Carlson*** *illustrated a series of Uncle Wiggily books in 1930's.*

JING PALS
Feb, 1946 - No. 4, Aug?, 1946 (Funny animal)
Victory Publishing Corporation

1-Wishing Willie, Puggy Panda & Johnny Rabbit begin — 3.50 — 10.50 — 24.00
2-4 — 2.00 — 6.00 — 14.00

JINKS, PIXIE, AND DIXIE (See Whitman Comic . . .)
1965 (Giveaway) (Hanna-Barbera)
Florida Power & Light

.35 — 1.00 — 2.00

JOAN OF ARC (See A-1 Comics No. 21 & Ideal a Classical Comic)

JOAN OF ARC
No date (28 pages)
Catechetical Guild (Topix) (Giveaway)

7.00 — 21.00 — 50.00

NOTE: *Unpublished version exists which came from the Guild's files.*

JOE COLLEGE
Fall, 1949 - No. 2, Winter, 1950
Hillman Periodicals

1,2-Powell-a; 1-Briefer-a — 2.35 — 7.00 — 16.00

JOE JINKS (See Single Series No. 12)

JOE LOUIS
Sept, 1950 - No. 2, Nov, 1950 (Photo-c)
Fawcett Publications

JOE LOUIS (continued) — Good / Fine / Mint
1 — 16.00 50.00 115.00
2 — 12.00 36.00 84.00

JOE PALOOKA
1933 (B&W daily strip reprints) (52 pages)
Cupples & Leon Co.

nn-(Scarce)-by Fisher — 35.00 105.00 245.00

JOE PALOOKA (1st Series)(Also see Big Shot)
1942 - 1944
Columbia Comic Corp. (Publication Enterprises)

1 — 22.00 65.00 154.00
2 (1943)-Hitler-c — 11.50 34.50 80.00
3,4 — 8.50 25.50 60.00

JOE PALOOKA (2nd Series) (Battle Adv. No. 68-74; . . . Advs. No. 75-87; Champ of the Comics No. 89-93)
Nov, 1945 - No. 118, Mar, 1961
Harvey Publications

1 — 17.00 51.00 120.00
2 — 8.50 25.50 60.00
3,4,6 — 5.50 16.50 38.00
5-Boy Explorers by S&K (7-8/46) — 8.00 24.00 56.00
7-1st Powell Flyin' Fool, ends No. 25 — 5.00 15.00 35.00
8-Lingerie panel — 5.00 15.00 35.00
9,10 — 3.50 10.50 24.00
11-14,16-20: 19-Freedom Train-c — 3.50 10.50 24.00
15-Origin Humphrey; Super heroine Atoma app. by Powell — 5.00 15.00 35.00
21-30: 30-Nude female painting — 2.50 7.50 17.50
31-61: 35-1st app. Little Max? 44-Joe Palooka marries Ann Howe. 50-Bondage-c — 2.00 6.00 14.00
62-S&K Boy Explorers-r — 2.50 7.50 17.50
63-80: 66,67-'commie' torture story — 1.50 4.50 10.00
81-99,101-115 — 1.30 4.00 9.00
100 — 1.75 5.25 12.00
116-S&K Boy Explorers (r) (Giant, '60) — 2.85 8.50 20.00
117,118-Giants — 2.65 8.00 18.00
. . . Body Building Instruction Book (1958 Sports Toy giveaway, 16 pgs, 5¼x7'')-Origin — 4.00 12.00 28.00
. . . Fights His Way Back (1945 Giveaway, 24 pgs.) Family Comics — 13.00 40.00 90.00
. . . in Hi There! (1949 Red Cross giveaway, 12 pgs., 4¾x6'') — 3.50 10.50 24.00
. . . in It's All in the Family (1945 Red Cross giveaway, 16 pgs., regular size) — 6.00 18.00 42.00
. . . Visits the Lost City(1945)(One Shot)(nn)(50 cents)-164 page continuous story strip reprint. Has biography & photo of Ham Fisher; possibly the single longest comic book story published (159 pgs.?) — 35.00 105.00 245.00

NOTE: ***Nostrand/Powell*** *a-73.* ***Powell*** *a-7, 8, 10, 12, 17, 19, 26-45, 47-53, 70, 73 at least. Black Cat text stories No. 8, 12, 13, 19.*

JOE YANK
March, 1952 - 1954
Standard Comics (Visual Editions)

5-Celardo, Tuska-a — 2.00 6.00 14.00
6-Toth, Severin/Elder-a — 3.35 10.00 23.00
7 — 1.30 4.00 9.00
8-Toth-c — 2.50 7.50 17.00
9-16: 12-Andru-a — 1.00 3.00 7.00

JOHN BOLTON'S HALLS OF HORROR
June, 1985 - No. 2, June, 1985 ($1.75 cover)
Eclipse Comics

1,2-British-r — .30 .90 1.80

JOHN CARTER OF MARS (See 4-Color No. 375,437,488)

JOHN CARTER OF MARS
April, 1964 - No. 3, Oct, 1964
Gold Key — Good / Fine / Mint

1(10104-404)-Reprints 4-Color 375; Jesse Marsh-a — 2.50 7.50 17.50
2(407), 3(410)-Reprints 4-Color 437 & 488; Marsh-a — 2.00 6.00 14.00

JOHN CARTER OF MARS
1970 (72 pgs.; paper cover; 10½x16½''; B&W)
House of Greystroke

1941-42 Sunday strip reprints; John Coleman Burroughs-a — 2.35 7.00 16.00

JOHN CARTER, WARLORD OF MARS
June, 1977 - No. 28, Oct, 1979
Marvel Comics Group

1-Origin by Gil Kane — .50 1.00
2-10-Last Kane issue — .30 .60
11-17,19-28: 11-Origin Dejah Thoris — .25 .50
18-Miller-a(p) — .35 1.00 2.00
Annual 1(10/77), 2(9/78), 3(10/79) — .40 .80

NOTE: ***Austin*** *c-24i.* ***Gil Kane*** *a-1-10p; c-1p, 2p, 3, 4-9p, 10, 15p, Annual 1p.* ***Layton*** *a-17i.* ***Miller*** *c-25, 26p.* ***Nebres*** *a-2-4i, 8-16i; c(i)-6-9, 11-22, 25, Annual 1.* ***Perez*** *c-24p.* ***Simonson*** *a-15p.* ***Sutton*** *a-7i.*

JOHN F. KENNEDY, CHAMPION OF FREEDOM
1964 (no month) (25 cents)
Worden & Childs

nn-Photo-c — 2.65 8.00 18.00

JOHN F. KENNEDY LIFE STORY
Aug-Oct, 1964; Nov, 1965; June, 1966 (12 cents)
Dell Publishing Co.

12-378-410 — 2.00 6.00 14.00
12-378-511 (reprint) — 1.35 4.00 9.00
12-378-606 (reprint) — 1.00 3.00 7.00

JOHN FORCE (See Magic Agent)

JOHN HIX SCRAP BOOK, THE
Late 1930's (no date) (68 pgs.; reg. size; 10 cents)
Eastern Color Printing Co. (McNaught Synd.)

1-Strange As It Seems (resembles Single Series books) — 8.00 24.00 56.00
2-Strange As It Seems — 6.00 18.00 42.00

JOHN LAW DETECTIVE
April, 1983 ($1.50; Baxter paper)
Eclipse Comics

1-Three Eisner stories originally drawn in 1948 for the never published John Law No. 1; original cover pencilled in 1948 & inked in 1982 by Eisner — .25 .75 1.50

JOHNNY CASH (See Hello, I'm. . .)

JOHNNY DANGER
1950
Toby Press

1 — 5.00 15.00 35.00

JOHNNY DANGER PRIVATE DETECTIVE
1954 (Reprinted in Danger No. 11 (Super))
Toby Press

1-Opium den story — 4.00 12.00 28.00

Joe Louis #1, © FAW

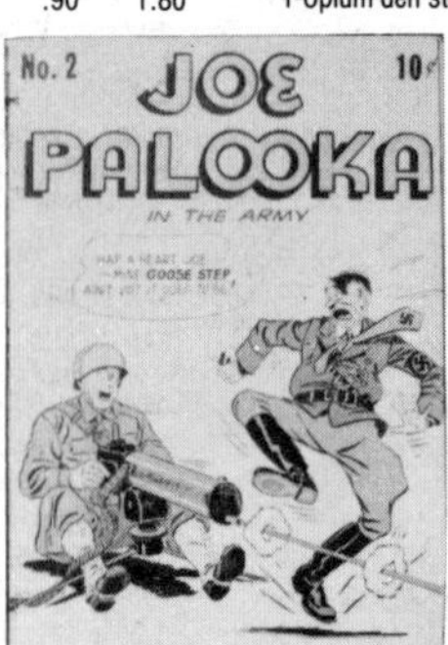

Joe Palooka #2, © CCG

John Carter, Warlord of Mars #3, © MCG

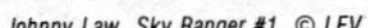
Johnny Law, Sky Ranger #1, © LEV

John Wayne Adv. Comics #11, © TOBY

Jo-Jo Comics #22, © FOX

JOHNNY DYNAMITE (Formerly Dynamite No. 1-9)
No. 10, 6/55 - No. 12, 10/55 (Foreign Intrigues No. 13 on)
Charlton Comics

	Good	Fine	Mint
10-12	1.65	5.00	11.50

JOHNNY HAZARD
No. 5, Aug, 1948 - No. 8, May, 1949
Best Books (Standard Comics)

5-Strip reprints by Frank Robbins	7.00	21.00	50.00
6,8-Strip reprints by Frank Robbins	5.00	15.00	35.00
7-New art, not Robbins	3.75	11.25	26.00
35	3.75	11.25	26.00

JOHNNY JASON (. . . Teen Reporter)
Feb-Apr, 1962 - No. 2, June-Aug, 1962
Dell Publishing Co.

4-Color 1302, 2(01380-208)	1.00	3.00	7.00

JOHNNY JINGLE'S LUCKY DAY
1956 (16 pgs.; 7¼x5-1/8") (Giveaway) (Disney)
American Dairy Association

	2.35	7.00	14.00

JOHNNY LAW, SKY RANGER
Apr, 1955 - No. 3, Aug, 1955; No. 4, Nov, 1955
Good Comics (Lev Gleason)

1-Edmond Good-a	2.85	8.50	20.00
2-4	1.65	5.00	11.50

JOHNNY MACK BROWN (TV western star; see Western Roundup)
No. 269, Mar, 1950 - No. 963, Feb, 1959 (All Photo-c)
Dell Publishing Co.

4-Color 269(3/50, 52pgs.)-J. Mack Brown & his horse Rebel begin; photo front/back-c begin; Marsh-a begins, ends No. 9	6.50	19.50	45.00
2(10-12/50, 52pgs.)	4.00	12.00	28.00
3(1-3/51, 52pgs.)	3.00	9.00	21.00
4-10 (9-11/52)(36pgs.)	2.65	8.00	18.00
4-Color 455,493	2.65	8.00	18.00
4-Color 541,584,618,645,685,722,776,834,963	2.65	8.00	18.00
4-Color 922-Manning-a	3.00	9.00	21.00

JOHNNY NEMO
Sept, 1985 - No. 3, Feb, 1986 (Mini-series)
Eclipse Comics

1,2 ($1.75 cover)	.30	.90	1.75
3 ($2.00 cover)	.35	1.00	2.00

JOHNNY RINGO (See 4-Color No. 1142)

JOHNNY STARBOARD (See Wisco)

JOHNNY THUNDER
Feb-Mar, 1973 - No. 3, July-Aug, 1973
National Periodical Publications

1-Johnny Thunder & Nighthawk-r begin	.25	.75	1.50
2,3: 2-Trigger Twins app.		.50	1.00

NOTE: *__Drucker__ a-2r, 3r. __G. Kane__ a-2r, 3r. __Nino__ c-1. __Toth__ a-1r, 3r; c-3r. Also see All-American, All-Star Western and Western Comics.*

JOHN PAUL JONES (See Four Color No. 1007)

JOHN STEED & EMMA PEEL (See The Avengers)

JOHN STEELE SECRET AGENT
December, 1964 (Freedom Agent)
Gold Key

1	1.50	4.50	10.00

JOHN WAYNE ADVENTURE COMICS (Movie star; See Big Tex, & Oxydol-Dreft)
Winter, 1949 - No. 31, May, 1955 (Photo-c, 1-12,17,25-on)
Toby Press

	Good	Fine	Mint
1 (36pgs.)-Photo-c begin	26.00	78.00	182.00
2 (36pgs.)-Williamson/Frazetta-a(2) (one r-/Billy the Kid No. 1), 6 & 2 pgs; photo back-c	28.00	84.00	195.00
3 (36pgs.)-Williamson/Frazetta-a(2), 16 pgs. total; photo back-c	27.00	81.00	190.00
4 (52pgs.)-Williamson/Frazetta-a(2), 16pgs total	27.00	81.00	190.00
5 (52pgs.)-Kurtzman-a-(Alfred "L" Newman in Potshot Pete)	17.00	51.00	120.00
6 (52pgs.)-Williamson/Frazetta-a, 10pgs; Kurtzman a-"Pot-Shot Pete," 5pg. story; & "Genius Jones," 1pg.	25.00	75.00	175.00
7 (52pgs.)-Williamson/Frazetta-a, 10pgs.	22.00	65.00	154.00
8 (36pgs.)-Williamson/Frazetta-a(2), 12 & 9 pgs.	25.00	75.00	175.00
9-11: Photo western-c	11.00	33.00	76.00
12-Photo war-c; Kurtzman-a, 2pgs. "Genius"	11.50	34.50	80.00
13-15: 13-Line-drawn-c begin, end No. 24	10.00	30.00	70.00
16-Williamson/Frazetta r-from Billy the Kid No. 1	13.50	40.50	90.00
17-Photo-c	11.00	33.00	76.00
18-Williamson/Frazetta-a r-/No. 4 & 8, 19pgs.	18.00	54.00	125.00
19-24: 23-Evans-a?	9.00	27.00	62.00
25-Photo-c return; end No. 31; Williamson/Frazetta-a r-/Billy the Kid No. 3	17.00	51.00	120.00
26-28,30-Photo-c	11.00	33.00	76.00
29-Williamson/Frazetta-a r-/No. 4	17.00	51.00	120.00
31-Williamson/Frazetta-a r-/No. 2	17.00	51.00	120.00

NOTE: *Williamsonish art in later issues by __Gerald McCann__.*

JO-JO COMICS (. . . Congo King No. 7-29; My Desire No. 30 on)
(Also see Fantastic Fear and Jungle Jo)
1945 - No. 29, July, 1949 (two No.7's; no No. 13)
Fox Features Syndicate

nn(1945)-Funny animal	3.50	10.50	24.00
2(Sum,'46)-6: Funny animal; 2-Ten pg. Electro story	2.00	6.00	14.00
7(7/47)-Jo-Jo, Congo King begins	20.00	60.00	140.00
7(No.8) (9/47)	14.50	43.50	100.00
8-10(No.9-11): 8-Tanee begins	11.50	34.50	80.00
11,12(No.12,13),14,16	10.00	30.00	70.00
15-Cited by Dr. Wertham in 5/47 Saturday Review of Literature	11.50	34.50	80.00
17-Kamen bondage-c	11.50	34.50	80.00
18-20	10.00	30.00	70.00
21-29	8.50	25.50	60.00

NOTE: *Many bondage-c/a by __Baker/Kamen/Feldstein/Good__. No. 7's have Princesses Gwenna, Geesa, Yolda, & Safra before settling down on Tanee.*

JO-JOY (Adventures of. . .)
1945 - 1953 (Christmas gift comic)
W. T. Grant Dept. Stores

1945-53 issues	1.50	4.50	10.00

JOKEBOOK COMICS DIGEST ANNUAL (. . . Mag. No. 5 on)
10/77 - No. 13, 10/83 (Digest Size)
Archie Publications

1(10/77)-Reprints; Adams-a		.60	1.20
2(4/78)-13		.60	1.20

JOKER, THE (See Batman, Brave & the Bold, and Detective)
May, 1975 - No. 9, Sept-Oct, 1976

THE JOKER (continued)
National Periodical Publications

	Good	Fine	Mint
1-Two-Face app.		.30	.60
2-4, V2/5-9		.25	.50

JOKER COMICS (Adventures Into Terror No. 43 on)
April, 1942 - No. 42, August, 1950
Timely/Marvel Comics No. 36 on (TCI/CDS)

	Good	Fine	Mint
1-(Rare)-1st app. Powerhouse Pepper by Wolverton; Stuporman app. from Daring	68.00	204.00	475.00
2-Wolverton-a continued; 1st app. Tessie the Typist	29.00	87.00	200.00
3-5-Wolverton-a	20.00	60.00	140.00
6-10-Wolverton-a	13.00	40.00	90.00
11-20-Wolverton-a	11.00	33.00	76.00
21,22,24-27,29,30-Wolverton cont'd. & Kurtzman's "Hey Look" in No. 24-27	8.50	25.50	60.00
23-1st "Hey Look" by Kurtzman; Wolverton-a	10.00	30.00	70.00
28,32,34,37-41	1.65	5.00	11.50
31-Last Powerhouse Pepper; not in No. 28	6.50	19.50	45.00
33,35,36-Kurtzman's "Hey Look"	2.85	8.50	20.00
42-Only app. 'Patty Pinup,' a clone of Millie the Model	1.85	5.50	13.00

JOLLY CHRISTMAS, A (See March of Comics No. 269)

JOLLY CHRISTMAS BOOK (See Christmas Journey Through Space)
1951; 1954; 1955 (36 pgs.; 24 pgs.)
Promotional Publ. Co.

	Good	Fine	Mint
1951-(Woolworth giveaway)-slightly oversized; no slick cover; Marv Levy c/a	2.00	6.00	14.00
1954-(Hot Shoppes giveaway)-regular size-reprints 1951 issue; slick cover added; 24 pgs.; no ads	2.00	6.00	14.00
1955-(J. M. McDonald Co. giveaway)-regular size	1.50	4.50	10.00

JOLLY COMICS
1947
Four Star Publishing Co.

	Good	Fine	Mint
1	2.65	8.00	18.00

JOLLY JINGLES (Formerly Jackpot)
No. 10, Sum, 1943 - No. 16, Wint, 1944/45
MLJ Magazines

	Good	Fine	Mint
10-Super Duck begins (origin & 1st app.)	12.00	36.00	84.00
11	5.50	16.50	38.00
12-16	2.85	8.50	20.00

JONAH HEX (See All-Star Western, Hex and Weird Western Tales)
Mar-Apr, 1977 - No. 92, Aug, 1985
National Periodical Publications/DC Comics

	Good	Fine	Mint
1	.50	1.50	3.00
2-6,8-10: 9-Wrightson-c		.50	1.00
7-Explains Hex's face disfigurement	.25	.75	1.50
11-20: 12-Starlin-c		.40	.80
21-78: 31,32-Origin retold		.25	.50
79-92 (75¢ cover)		.25	.50

NOTE: ***Aparo** c-76p. **Ayers** a(p)-35-37, 41,44-53, 56, 58-82. **Kubert** c-43-46. **Morrow** c-10. **Spiegle**(Tothish) a-34, 38, 40, 49, 52.*

JONAH HEX AND OTHER WESTERN TALES (Blue Ribbon Digest)
Sept-Oct, 1979 - No. 3, Jan-Feb, 1980 (100 pgs.)
DC Comics

	Good	Fine	Mint
1-Origin Scalphunter-r; painted-c		.40	.80
2-Reprints from Weird Western Tales; Adams, Toth, Aragones, Gil Kane-a		.40	.80
3		.40	.80

JONAH HEX SPECTACULAR (See DC Special Series No. 16)

JONESY (Formerly Crack Western)
No. 85, Aug, 1953; No. 2, Oct, 1953 - No. 8, Oct, 1954
Comic Favorite/Quality Comics Group

	Good	Fine	Mint
85(No.1)	2.15	6.50	15.00
2	1.15	3.50	8.00
3-8	.85	2.50	6.00

JON JUAN (Also see Great Lover Romances)
Spring, 1950
Toby Press

	Good	Fine	Mint
1-All Schomburg-a (signed Al Reid on-c); written by Siegel; used in **SOTI**, pg. 38	10.00	30.00	70.00

JONNI THUNDER
Feb, 1985 - No. 4, Aug, 1985 (Mini-series)
DC Comics

	Good	Fine	Mint
1-Origin		.50	1.00
2-4		.45	.90

JONNY QUEST (TV)
December, 1964 (Hanna-Barbera)
Gold Key

	Good	Fine	Mint
1 (10139-412)	3.50	10.50	24.00

JONNY QUEST
June, 1986 - Present
Comico

	Good	Fine	Mint
1	.60	1.75	3.50
2-6	.30	.90	1.80

NOTE: ***Pini** a-2. **Rude** a-1. **Stevens** c-3, 5. **Wildey** a-1, c-1. **Williamson** a-4; c-4i.*

JON SABLE, FREELANCE
June, 1983 - Present
First Comics

	Good	Fine	Mint
1-Created, story/a&c by Mike Grell	.60	1.75	3.50
2-5: 3-5-Origin, parts 1-3	.30	.90	1.80
6-10: 6-Origin, part 4	.35	1.10	2.20
11-20: 14-Mando paper begins	.35	1.00	2.00
21-33: 25-30-Shatter app.	.25	.75	1.50
34-45: 34-Deluxe format begins ($1.75)	.30	.90	1.80

JOSEPH & HIS BRETHREN (See The Living Bible)

JOSIE (She's... No. 1-16) (... & the Pussycats No. 45 on)
2/63 - No. 106, 10/82 (See Archie Giant Series 528,540,551,562)
Archie Publications/Radio Comics

	Good	Fine	Mint
1	7.00	21.00	50.00
2	3.50	10.50	24.00
3-5	2.65	8.00	18.00
6-10	1.70	5.00	12.00
11-20	1.15	3.50	8.00
21,23-30	.75	2.25	5.00
22-Mighty Man & Mighty (Josie Girl) app.	.75	2.25	5.00
31-54	.45	1.35	3.00
55-74(52pg. ish.)		.50	1.00
75-106		.35	.70

JOURNAL OF CRIME (See Fox Giants)

JOURNEY
1983 - No. 14, 9/84; No. 15, 4/85 - No. 27, 1986 (B&W)
Aardvark-Vanaheim 1-14/Fantagraphics Books No. 15-on

	Good	Fine	Mint
1	1.70	5.00	10.00

Joker Comics #1, © MCG

Jonesy #6, © QUA

Jonny Quest #1, © Comico

Journey Into Fear #1, © SUPR

Journey Into Mystery #50, © MCG

Journey Into Unknown Worlds #32, © MCG

JOURNEY (continued)

	Good	Fine	Mint
2-25	.30	.90	1.80
26,27	.35	1.00	2.00

JOURNEY INTO FEAR
May, 1951 - No. 21, Sept, 1954
Superior-Dynamic Publications

	Good	Fine	Mint
1-Baker-a(2)-r	11.50	34.50	80.00
2	6.50	19.50	45.00
3,4	5.50	16.50	38.00
5-10	4.35	13.00	30.00
11-14,16-21	3.85	11.50	27.00
15-Used in **SOTI**, pg. 389	6.50	19.50	45.00

NOTE: *Kamenish, 'headlight'-a most issues.* ***Robinson*** *a-10.*

JOURNEY INTO MYSTERY (1st Series) (Thor No. 126 on)
6/52 - No. 48, 8/57; No. 49, 11/58 - No. 125, 2/66
Atlas(CPS No.1-48/AMI No.49-68/Marvel No.69(6/61) on)

	Good	Fine	Mint
1	40.00	120.00	280.00
2	21.00	62.00	145.00
3,4	16.00	48.00	110.00
5-11	10.00	30.00	70.00
12-20,22: 22-Davisesque-a; last pre-code issue (2/55)	6.50	19.50	45.00
21-Kubert-a; Tothish-a by Andru	7.00	21.00	50.00
23-32,35-38,40: 24-Torres?-a	3.35	10.00	23.00
33-Williamson-a	7.00	21.00	50.00
34-Krigstein-a	6.00	18.00	42.00
39-Wood-a	6.00	18.00	42.00
41-Crandall-a; Frazettaesque-a by Morrow	3.85	11.50	27.00
42,48-Torres-a	3.35	10.00	23.00
43,44-Williamson/Mayo-a in both	3.85	11.50	27.00
45,47,49,52,53: 49-Check-a	2.35	7.00	16.00
46-Torres & Krigstein-a	3.85	11.50	27.00
50-Davis-a	2.50	7.50	17.00
51-Kirby/Wood-a	2.50	7.50	17.00
54-Williamson-a	2.50	7.50	17.00
55-61,63-73: 66-Return of Xemnu	1.85	5.50	13.00
62-1st app. Xemnu (Titan) called "The Hulk"	3.65	11.00	25.00
74-82-Fantasy content No. 74 on. 75-Last 10¢ issue. 80-Anti-communist propaganda story by Ditko	1.30	4.00	9.00
83-Reprint from the Golden Record Comic Set	1.15	3.50	8.00
with the record....	3.65	11.00	25.00
83-Origin & 1st app. The Mighty Thor by Kirby (8/62)	55.00	175.00	450.00
84	13.50	34.00	95.00
85-1st app. Loki & Heimdall	11.00	28.00	75.00
86-1st app. Odin	8.00	20.00	55.00
87,88	6.50	16.00	45.00
89-Origin Thor reprint/No. 83	6.50	16.00	45.00
90-No Kirby-a; Aunt May proto-type	4.50	12.00	30.00
91,92,94-96-Sinnott-a	3.65	9.00	25.00
93,97-Kirby-a; Tales of Asgard series begins No. 97(Origin which concludes No. 99)	4.00	10.00	28.00
98-100-Kirby/Heck-a. 99-1st app. Surtur & Mr. Hyde	3.25	8.00	22.00
101-104,110: 102-Intro Sif	1.85	5.50	11.00
105-109-Ten extra pages Kirby-a. 107-1st app. Grey Gargoyle	1.85	5.50	11.00
111,113,114,116-125: 119-Intro Hogun, Fandrall, Volstagg	1.15	3.50	7.00
112-Thor Vs. Hulk; origin Loki begins; ends No. 113	1.70	5.00	10.00
115-Detailed origin Loki	1.70	5.00	10.00
Annual 1('65)-1st app. Hercules; Kirby c/a	2.50	7.50	15.00

NOTE: ***Ayers*** *a-14.* ***Bailey*** *a-43.* ***Briefer*** *a-5, 12.* ***Check*** *a-17.* ***Colan*** *a-23, 81.* ***Ditko*** *a-33, 38, 50-96; c-71, 88i.* ***Ditko/Kirby*** *a-38, 50-83.* ***Everett*** *a-20, 40, 42, 48; c-4-7, 9, 37, 39, 40, 41, 44, 45.* ***Forte*** *a-19.* ***Heath*** *a-4, 5, 11, 14; c-1, 11, 15, 51.* ***Kirby*** *a(p)-60, 66, 76, 80, 83-89, 93, 97, 98, 100(w/Heck), 101-125; c-50-82(w/****Ditko****), 83-152p.* ***Leiber/Fox*** *a-93, 98-102.* ***Morrow*** *a-41, 42.* ***Orlando*** *a-30, 45, 57.* ***Mac Pakula****(Tothish) a-9.* ***Powell*** *a-20, 27, 34.* ***Reinman*** *a-87, 92, 96i.* ***Robinson*** *a-9.* ***Robert Sale*** *a-14.* ***Severin*** *a-27.* ***Tuska*** *a-11.* ***Wildey*** *a-16.*

JOURNEY INTO MYSTERY (2nd Series)
Oct, 1972 - No. 19, Oct, 1975
Marvel Comics Group

	Good	Fine	Mint
1-Robert Howard adaptation; Starlin/Ploog-a		.40	.80
2,3,5-Bloch adaptation; 5-Last new story		.30	.60
4-H. P. Lovecraft adaptation		.30	.60
6-19		.30	.60

NOTE: ***Adams*** *a-2i.* ***Ditko*** *a(r)-7, 10, 12, 14, 15, 19; c-10.* ***Everett*** *a-9r.* ***G. Kane*** *a-1p, 2p; c-1-3p.* ***Kirby*** *a-7r, 13r, 18r, 19r; c-7.* ***Mort Lawrence*** *a-2r.* ***Maneely*** *a-3r.* ***Orlando*** *a-16r.* ***Reese*** *a-1, 2i.* ***Starlin*** *a-3p.* ***Wildey*** *a-9r, 14r.*

JOURNEY INTO UNKNOWN WORLDS (Formerly Teen)
No. 36, 9/50 - No. 38, 2/51; No. 4, 4/51 - No. 59, 8/57
Atlas Comics (WFP)

	Good	Fine	Mint
36(No.1)-Science fiction/weird	23.00	70.00	160.00
37(No.2)-Science fiction; Everett-c/a	18.00	54.00	125.00
38(No.3)-Science fiction	13.50	40.50	95.00
4-6,8,10-Science fiction/weird	8.50	25.50	60.00
7-Wolverton-a-"Planet of Terror," 6 pgs; electric chair c-inset/story	18.50	55.00	130.00
9-Giant eyeball story	9.50	28.50	66.00
11,12-Krigstein-a	7.00	21.00	50.00
13,16,17,20	4.00	12.00	28.00
14-Wolverton-a-"One of Our Graveyards Is Missing," 4 pgs; Tuska-a	18.50	55.00	130.00
15-Wolverton-a-"They Crawl By Night," 5 pgs.	18.50	55.00	130.00
18,19-Matt Fox-a	4.85	14.50	34.00
21-26,28-33-Last pre-code (2/55). 21-Decapitation-c. 24-Sci/fic story. 26-Atom bomb panel	2.15	6.50	15.00
27-Sid Check-a	2.50	7.50	17.00
34-Kubert, Torres-a	3.65	11.00	25.00
35-Torres-a	2.65	8.00	18.00
36-42	1.85	5.50	13.00
43-Krigstein-a	3.35	10.00	23.00
44-Davis-a	3.35	10.00	23.00
45,55,59-Williamson-a in all with Mayo No. 55,59 plus Crandall-a, No. 55,59	5.00	15.00	35.00
46,47,49,52,56-58	1.50	4.50	10.00
48,53-Crandall-a; Check-a, No. 48	4.45	13.00	30.00
50-Davis, Crandall-a	4.00	12.00	28.00
51-Ditko, Wood-a	3.65	11.00	25.00
54-Torres-a	2.85	8.50	20.00

NOTE: ***Ayers*** *a-24, 43.* ***Berg*** *a-38(No.3), 43.* ***Lou Cameron*** *a-33.* ***Colan*** *a-37(No.2), 6, 17, 20, 39.* ***Ditko*** *a-51.* ***Evans*** *a-20.* ***Everett*** *a-37(No.2), 11, 14, 41, 47, 55, 56; c-11, 13, 14, 17, 22, 24, 28, 47, 48p, 50, 51, 53-55, 59.* ***Fox*** *a-21i.* ***Heath*** *a-36(No.1), 4, 6-8, 17, 20, 22, 36i.* ***Mort Lawrence*** *a-38, 39.* ***Maneely*** *a-7, 8, 15, 16, 22, 49; c-25, 52.* ***Morrow*** *a-48.* ***Orlando*** *a-44, 57.* ***Powell*** *a-42, 53, 54.* ***Rico*** *a-21.* ***Reinman*** *a-8.* ***Robert Sale*** *a-24.* ***Sekowsky*** *a-4, 5, 9.* ***Severin*** *a-38, 51; c-38, 48i, 56.* ***Sinnott*** *a-9, 21.* ***Tuska*** *a-38(No.3).* ***Wildey*** *a-25, 44.*

JOURNEY OF DISCOVERY WITH MARK STEEL (See Mark Steel)

JOURNEY TO THE CENTER OF THE EARTH (See 4-Color No. 1060)

JUDE, THE FORGOTTEN SAINT
1954 (16 pgs.; 8x11"; full color; paper cover)
Catechetical Guild Education Society

	Good	Fine	Mint
nn	2.00	6.00	12.00

JUDGE COLT
Oct, 1969 - No. 4, Sept, 1970
Gold Key

	Good	Fine	Mint
1	.85	2.50	6.00
2-4	.70	2.00	4.00

JUDGE DREDD
Nov, 1983 - No. 35, 1986; Oct, 1986 - Present

JUDGE DREDD (continued)
Eagle Comics/IPC Magazines Ltd./Quality Comics No. 34 on

	Good	Fine	Mint
1-Bolland c/a begins	.70	2.00	4.00
2,3	.45	1.30	2.60
4-10	.35	1.00	2.00
11-20	.25	.75	1.50
21-35		.60	1.20
V2/1-6 ('86)		.40	.75
7		.50	.95

JUDGE DREDD'S CRIME FILE
Aug, 1985 - No. 6, Feb, 1986 (Mini-series)
Eagle Comics

	Good	Fine	Mint
1-6: 1-Byrne-a	.30	.85	1.70

JUDGE DREDD: THE EARLY CASES
Feb, 1986 - No. 6, July, 1986 (Mega-series, Mando paper)
Eagle Comics

	Good	Fine	Mint
1-6: 2000 A.D.-r	.30	.85	1.70

JUDGE DREDD: THE JUDGE CHILD QUEST
Aug, 1984 - No. 5, Oct, 1984 (Limited series, Baxter paper)
Eagle Comics

	Good	Fine	Mint
1-5: 2000 A.D.-r; Bolland c/a	.30	.85	1.70

JUDGE PARKER
Feb, 1956
Argo

	Good	Fine	Mint
1	2.15	6.50	15.00
2	1.30	4.00	9.00

JUDO JOE
Aug, 1953 - No. 3, Dec, 1953
Jay-Jay Corp.

	Good	Fine	Mint
1-Drug ring story	3.35	10.00	23.00
2,3: 3-Hypo needle story	1.75	5.25	12.00

JUDOMASTER (Gun Master No. 84-89) (See Special War Series)
No. 89, May-June, 1966 - No. 98, Dec, 1967 (two No. 89's)
Charlton Comics

	Good	Fine	Mint
89-98: 91-Sarge Steel begins. 93-Intro. Tiger	.50	1.50	3.00
93,94,96,98(Modern Comics reprint, 1977)		.15	.30

NOTE: *Morisi Thunderbolt No. 90.*

JUDY CANOVA (Formerly My Experience)
May, 1950 - No. 3, Sept, 1950
Fox Features Syndicate

	Good	Fine	Mint
23(No.1)-Wood-c,a(p)?	6.50	19.50	45.00
24-Wood-a(p)	6.50	19.50	45.00
3-Wood-c; Wood/Orlando-a	9.00	27.00	62.00

JUDY GARLAND (See Famous Stars)

JUDY JOINS THE WAVES
1951 (For U.S. Navy)
Toby Press

	Good	Fine	Mint
nn	2.00	6.00	14.00

JUGHEAD (Formerly Archie's Pal . . .)
No. 127, Dec, 1965 - Present
Archie Publications

	Good	Fine	Mint
127-130	.85	2.50	5.00
131,133,135-160	.60	1.75	3.50
132-Shield-c; The Fly & Black Hood app.; Shield cameo	.60	1.75	3.50
134-Shield-c	.60	1.75	3.50
161-200	.35	1.00	2.00
201-240		.50	1.00
241-351: 300-Anniversary issue		.30	.60

JUGHEAD AS CAPTAIN HERO
Oct, 1966 - No. 7, Nov, 1967
Archie Publications

	Good	Fine	Mint
1	2.50	7.50	15.00
2	1.35	4.00	8.00
3-7	.85	2.50	5.00

JUGHEAD JONES COMICS DIGEST, THE (. . . Magazine No. 10-on)
June, 1977 - Present (Digest-size)
Archie Publications

	Good	Fine	Mint
1-Adams-a; Capt. Hero-r	.70	2.00	4.00
2(9/77)-Adams-a	.35	1.00	2.00
3-43: 7-Origin Jaguar-r; Adams-a. 13-r-/1957 Jughead's Folly		.50	1.00

JUGHEAD'S EAT-OUT COMIC BOOK MAGAZINE (See Archie Giant Series Mag. No. 170)

JUGHEAD'S FANTASY
Aug, 1960 - No. 3, Dec, 1960
Archie Publications

	Good	Fine	Mint
1	9.00	27.00	63.00
2	6.00	18.00	42.00
3	4.65	14.00	32.00

JUGHEAD'S FOLLY
1957
Archie Publications (Close-Up)

	Good	Fine	Mint
1-Jughead a la Elvis (Rare)	23.00	70.00	160.00

JUGHEAD'S JOKES
Aug, 1967 - No. 78, Sept, 1982
(No. 1-8, 38 on: reg. size; No. 9-23: 68 pgs.; No. 24-37: 52 pgs.)
Archie Publications

	Good	Fine	Mint
1	3.50	10.50	21.00
2	1.70	5.00	10.00
3-5	1.00	3.00	6.00
6-10	.70	2.00	4.00
11-30	.25	.75	1.50
31-50		.45	.90
51-78		.30	.60

JUGHEAD'S SOUL FOOD
1979 (49 cents)
Spire Christian Comics (Fleming H. Revell Co.)

	Good	Fine	Mint
		.30	.60

JUGHEAD WITH ARCHIE DIGEST (. . . Plus Betty & Veronica & Reggie Too No. 1,2; . . . Magazine No. 33 on)
March, 1974 - Present (Digest Size; $1.00-$1.25)
Archie Publications

	Good	Fine	Mint
1	1.00	3.00	6.00
2	.45	1.25	2.50
3-10	.25	.75	1.50
11-20: Capt. Hero r-in No. 14-16; Pureheart the Powerful No. 18,21,22; Capt. Pureheart No. 17,19		.50	1.00
21-79: 29-The Shield-r. 30-The Fly-r		.50	1.00

JUKE BOX COMICS
March, 1948 - No. 6, 1949
Famous Funnies

	Good	Fine	Mint
1-Toth c/a; Hollingsworth-a	15.00	45.00	105.00

Judge Dredd #1 (11/83), © Eagle

Judy Canova #23, © FOX

Juke Box Comics #1, © FF

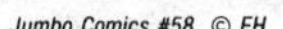
Jumbo Comics #58, © FH

Jumbo Comics #114, © FH

Jungle Comics #49, © FH

JUKE BOX COMICS (continued)	**Good**	**Fine**	**Mint**
2-Transvestism story	7.00	21.00	50.00
3-6	6.50	19.50	45.00

JUMBO COMICS (Created by S.M. Iger)
Sept, 1938 - No. 167, Apr, 1953 (No.1-3: 68 pgs.; No.4-8: 52 pgs.)
(No. 1-8 oversized-10½x14½''; black & white)
Fiction House Magazines (Real Adv. Publ. Co.)

	Good	Fine	Mint
1-(Rare)-Sheena Queen of the Jungle by Meskin, The Hawk by Eisner, The Hunchback by Dick Briefer(ends No.8) begin; 1st comic art by Jack Kirby (Count of Monte Cristo & Wilton of the West); Mickey Mouse appears (1 panel) with brief biography of Walt Disney. ***Note:*** Sheena was created by Iger for publication in England as a newspaper strip. The early issues of Jumbo contain Sheena strip-r	250.00	750.00	1750.00
2-(Rare)-Origin Sheena. Diary of Dr. Hayward by Kirby (also No.3) plus 2 other stories; contains strip from Universal Film featuring Edgar Bergen & Charlie McCarthy	125.00	375.00	875.00
3-Last Kirby issue	80.00	240.00	560.00
4-(Scarce)-Origin The Hawk by Eisner; Wilton of the West by Fine (ends No.14)(1st comic work); Count of Monte Cristo by Fine (ends No.15); The Diary of Dr. Hayward by Fine (cont'd. No. 8,9)	85.00	255.00	600.00
5	60.00	180.00	420.00
6-8-Last B&W issue. No. 8 was a N. Y. World's Fair Special Edition	50.00	150.00	350.00
9-Stuart Taylor begins by Fine; Fine-c; 1st color issue(8-9/39)-8¼x10¼''(oversized in width only)	55.00	165.00	385.00
10-14: 10-Regular size 68 pg. issues begin; Sheena dons new costume No. 10	30.00	90.00	210.00
15-Lightning begins	25.00	75.00	175.00
16-20	20.00	60.00	140.00
21-30: 22-1st Tom, Dick & Harry; origin The Hawk retold	18.00	54.00	125.00
31-40: 35 shows V2No.11 (correct number does not appear)	17.00	51.00	120.00
41-50	15.00	45.00	105.00
51-60: 52-Last Tom, Dick & Harry	13.00	40.00	90.00
61-70: 68-Sky Girl begins, ends No. 130; not in No. 79	10.00	30.00	70.00
71-80	9.00	27.00	62.00
81-93,95-99: 89-ZX5 becomes a private eye	9.00	27.00	62.00
94-Used in **Love and Death** by Legman	9.50	28.50	66.00
100	10.00	30.00	70.00
101-110: 103-Lingerie panel	7.00	21.00	50.00
111-140	6.00	18.00	42.00
141-149-Two Sheena stories. 141-Long Bow, Indian Boy begins, ends No. 160	7.00	21.00	50.00
150-154,156-158	6.00	18.00	42.00
155-Used in **POP**, pg. 98	6.50	19.50	45.00
159-163: Space Scouts serial in all; 163-Suicide Smith app.	6.00	18.00	42.00
164-The Star Pirate begins, ends No. 165	6.00	18.00	42.00
165-167: 165,167-Space Rangers app.	6.00	18.00	42.00

NOTE: *Bondage covers, negligee panels, torture, etc. are common in this series. Hawks of the Seas, Inspector Dayton, Spies in Action, Sports Shorts, & Uncle Otto by* ***Eisner****, No. 1-7. Hawk by* ***Eisner****-No. 10-15;* ***Eisner*** *c-1, 3-6, 12, 13, 15. 1pg. Patsy pin-ups in 92-97, 99-101. Sheena by* ***Meskin****-No. 1, 4; by* ***Powell****-No. 2, 3, 5-28. Sky Girl by* ***Matt Baker****-No. 69-78, 80-124.* ***Bailey*** *a-3-8.* ***Briefer*** *a-1-8, 10.* ***Fine*** *c-8-11.* ***Kamen*** *a-101, 105, 123, 132; c-105.* ***Bob Kane*** *a-1-8.*

JUMPING JACKS PRESENTS THE WHIZ KIDS
1978 (In 3-D) with glasses (4 pages)
Jumping Jacks Stores giveaway

	Good	Fine	Mint
nn		.40	.80

JUNGLE ACTION
Oct, 1954 - No. 6, Aug, 1955
Atlas Comics (IPC)

	Good	Fine	Mint
1-Leopard Girl begins; Maneely c/a-all	7.00	21.00	50.00
2-(3-D effect cover)	8.50	25.50	60.00
3-6: 3-Last precode (2/55)	5.00	15.00	35.00

JUNGLE ACTION
Oct, 1972 - No. 24, Nov, 1976
Marvel Comics Group

	Good	Fine	Mint
1-Lorna, Jann-r		.40	.80
2-5: 5-Black Panther begins (new-a)		.30	.60
6-18-All new stories. 8-Origin Black Panther		.30	.60
19-23-KKK x-over. 23-r-/No. 22		.30	.60
24-1st Wind Eagle		.30	.60

NOTE: ***Buckler*** *a-6-9pp, 22; c-8p, 12p.* ***Buscema*** *a-5p; c-22.* ***Byrne*** *c-23.* ***Gil Kane*** *c-2, 4, 10p, 11p, 13-17, 19, 24.* ***G. Kane*** *a-8p.* ***Kirby*** *c-18.* ***Russell*** *a-13i.* ***Starlin*** *c-3p.*

JUNGLE ADVENTURES
1963 - 1964 (Reprints)
Super Comics

	Good	Fine	Mint
10,12(Rulah), 15(Kaanga/Jungle No. 152)	1.35	4.00	9.00
17(Jo-Jo)	1.35	4.00	9.00
18-Reprints/White Princess of the Jungle No. 1; no Kinstler-a; origin of both White Princess & Cap'n Courage	1.75	5.25	12.00

JUNGLE ADVENTURES
March, 1971 - No. 3, June, 1971
Skywald Comics

	Good	Fine	Mint
1-Zangar origin; reprints of Jo-Jo, Blue Gorilla(origin)/White Princess No. 3, Kinstler-a/White Princess No. 2	.50	1.50	3.00
2-Zangar, Sheena/Sheena No. 17 & Jumbo No. 162, Jo-Jo, origin Slave Girl Princess-r	.50	1.50	3.00
3-Zangar, Jo-Jo, White Princess-r	.50	1.50	3.00

JUNGLE BOOK, THE (See Movie Comics)

JUNGLE CAT (See 4-Color No. 1136)

JUNGLE COMICS
Jan, 1940 - No. 163, Summer, 1954
Fiction House Magazines

	Good	Fine	Mint
1-Origin The White Panther, Kaanga, Lord of the Jungle, Tabu, Wizard of the Jungle; Wambi, the Jungle Boy & Camilla begin	95.00	285.00	665.00
2-Fantomah, Mystery Woman of the Jungle begins	45.00	135.00	315.00
3,4	36.00	108.00	250.00
5	30.00	90.00	210.00
6-10	24.00	72.00	168.00
11-20	18.00	54.00	125.00
21-30: 25 shows V2No.1 (correct number does not appear). No. 27-New origin Fantomah, Daughter of the Pharoahs; Camilla dons new costume	15.00	45.00	105.00
31-40	13.00	40.00	90.00
41,43-50	10.00	30.00	70.00
42-Kaanga by Crandall, 12 pgs.	12.00	36.00	84.00
51-60	9.00	27.00	62.00
61-70	8.00	24.00	56.00
71-80: 79-New origin Tabu; part nudity panel	7.00	21.00	50.00
81-97,99,101-110	6.00	18.00	42.00
98-Used in **SOTI**, pg. 185 & illo-''In ordinary comic books, there are pictures within pictures for children who know how to look''; used by N.Y. Legis. Comm.	13.00	40.00	90.00
100	7.00	21.00	50.00
111-142,144,146-150: 135-Desert Panther begins in Terry Thunder (origin), not in No. 137; ends (dies) No. 138	6.00	18.00	42.00
143,145-Used in **POP**, pg. 99	6.50	19.50	45.00
151-157,159-163: 152-Tiger Girl begins	6.00	18.00	42.00
158-Sheena app.	7.00	21.00	50.00
I.W. Reprint No. 1,9: 9-r-/No. 151	1.00	3.00	6.00

NOTE: *Bondage covers, negligee panels, torture, etc. are common to this series. Camilla*

JUNGLE COMICS (continued)

by Fran Hopper-No. 73, 78, 80-90; by Baker-No. 101, 103, 106, 107, 109, 111-13. Kaanga by John Celardo-No. 80-110; by Maurice Whitman-No. 124-163. Tabu by Whitman-No. 93-110. Celardo a-78; c-98, 99, 106, 109, 112. Eisner c-2, 5, 6. Fine c-1. Larsen a-65, 66, 72, 74, 75, 79, 83, 84, 87-90.

JUNGLE GIRL (See Lorna, . . .)

JUNGLE GIRL (Nyoka, Jungle Girl No. 2 on)
Fall, 1942 (No month listed) (Based on film character)
Fawcett Publications

	Good	Fine	Mint
1-Bondage-c	40.00	120.00	280.00

JUNGLE JIM
Jan, 1949 - No. 20, Apr, 1951
Standard Comics (Best Books)

11	3.00	9.00	21.00
12-20	1.75	5.25	12.00

JUNGLE JIM
No. 490, 8/53 - No. 1020, 8-10/59
Dell Publishing Co.

4-Color 490	2.35	7.00	16.00
4-Color 565(6/54)	1.75	5.25	12.00
3(10-12/54)-5	1.50	4.50	10.00
6-19(1-3/59)	1.15	3.50	8.00
4-Color 1020(No.20)	1.50	4.50	10.00

JUNGLE JIM
December, 1967
King Features Syndicate

5-Reprints Dell No. 5; Wood-c	.55	1.65	4.00

JUNGLE JIM (Continued from Dell)
No. 22, Feb, 1969 - No. 28, Feb, 1970 (No. 21 was an overseas edition only)
Charlton Comics

22-Dan Flagg begins, ends No. 23; Wood & Ditko-a	1.15	3.50	8.00
23-28: 23-Howard-c. 24-Jungle People begin. 27-Howard, Ditko-a. 28-Ditko-a	.55	1.65	4.00

JUNGLE JO
Mar, 1950 - No. 6, Mar, 1951
Fox Feature Syndicate (Hero Books)

nn-Jo-Jo blanked out, leaving Congo King; came out after Jo-Jo No. 29 (intended as Jo-Jo No. 30?)	9.50	28.50	65.00
1-Tangi begins; part Wood-a	11.00	33.00	76.00
2	8.00	24.00	56.00
3-6	7.00	21.00	50.00

JUNGLE LIL (Dorothy Lamour No. 2 on) (Also see Feature Stories Magazine)
April, 1950
Fox Feature Syndicate (Hero Books)

1	10.00	30.00	70.00

JUNGLE TALES (Jann of the Jungle No. 8 on)
Sept, 1954 - No. 7, Sept, 1955
Atlas Comics (CSI)

1-Jann of the Jungle	7.00	21.00	50.00
2-7: 3-Last precode (1/55)	5.00	15.00	35.00

NOTE: *Heck a-6, 7. Maneely a-2; c-1, 3. Shores a-5-7. Tuska a-2.*

JUNGLE TALES OF TARZAN
Dec, 1964 - No. 4, July, 1965
Charlton Comics

	Good	Fine	Mint
1	1.35	4.00	9.00
2-4	1.00	3.00	7.00

NOTE: *Giordano c-3p. Glanzman a-1-3. Montes/Bache a-4.*

JUNGLE TERROR (See Comics Hits No. 54)

JUNGLE THRILLS (Terrors of the Jungle No. 17)
No. 16, February, 1952
Star Publications

16-Phantom Lady & Rulah story-reprint/All Top No. 15; used in **POP**, pg. 98,99; L. B. Cole-c	13.50	40.50	95.00
3-D 1(12/53)-Jungle Lil & Jungle Jo appear; L. B. Cole-c	19.00	57.00	132.00
7-Titled 'Picture Scope Jungle Adventures;'(1954, 36 pgs, 15¢)-3-D effect c/stories; story & coloring book; Disbrow-a/script; L.B. Cole-c	10.00	30.00	70.00

JUNGLE TWINS, THE (Tono & Kono)
4/72 - No. 17, 11/75; No. 18, 5/82
Gold Key/Whitman No. 18 on

1	.30	.90	1.80
2-5		.60	1.20
6-18: 18-r		.40	.80

NOTE: *UFO c/story No. 13. Painted-c No. 1-17. Spiegle c-18.*

JUNGLE WAR STORIES (Guerrilla War No. 12 on)
July-Sept, 1962 - No. 11, Apr-June, 1965
Dell Publishing Co.

01-384-209	.55	1.60	4.00
2-11	.40	1.20	2.40

JUNIE PROM
Winter, 1947-48 - No. 7, Aug, 1949
Dearfield Publishing Co.

1-Teen-age	3.75	11.25	26.00
2	1.85	5.50	13.00
3-7	1.50	4.50	10.00

JUNIOR COMICS
No. 9, Sept, 1947 - No. 16, July, 1948
Fox Feature Syndicate

9-Feldstein c/a	30.00	90.00	210.00
10-16-Feldstein c/a	27.00	81.00	190.00

JUNIOR FUNNIES (Formerly Tiny Tot Funnies No. 9)
No. 10, Aug, 1951 - No. 13, Feb, 1952
Harvey Publications (King Features Synd.)

10-Partial reprints in all-Blondie, Popeye, Felix, Katzenjammer Kids	1.50	4.50	10.00
11-13	1.20	3.50	8.00

JUNIOR HOPP COMICS
Feb, 1952 - No. 3, July, 1952
Stanmor Publ.

1	3.00	9.00	21.00
2,3: 3-Dave Berg-a	1.65	5.00	11.50

JUNIOR MEDICS OF AMERICA, THE
1957 (15 cents)
E. R. Squire & Sons

1359	1.15	3.50	8.00

JUNIOR MISS
Winter, 1944; No. 24, April, 1947 - No. 39, Aug, 1950
Timely/Marvel Comics (CnPC)

1-Frank Sinatra & June Allyson life story	6.00	18.00	42.00
24	3.00	9.00	21.00

Jungle Jim #4, © KING

Jungle Tales of Tarzan #3, © ERB

Junie Prom #1, © Dearfield

Justice #1, © MCG

Justice Comics #15, © MCG

Justice League of America #22, © DC

JUNIOR MISS (continued)

	Good	Fine	Mint
25-38	1.65	5.00	11.50
39-Kurtzman-a	2.15	6.50	15.00

NOTE: *Painted-c 35-37. 37-all romance. 35,36,38-mostly teen humor.*

JUNIOR PARTNERS (Formerly Oral Roberts' True Stories)
No. 120, Aug, 1959 - V3No.12, Dec, 1961
Oral Roberts Evangelistic Assn.

	Good	Fine	Mint
120(No.1)	1.50	4.50	10.00
2(9/59)	1.00	3.00	7.00
3-12(7/60)	.45	1.20	3.00
V2No.1(8/60)-5(12/60)	.35	1.00	2.00
V3No.1(1/61)-12		.50	1.00

JUNIOR TREASURY (See Dell Junior . . .)

JUNIOR WOODCHUCKS (See Huey, Dewey & Louie . . .)

JUSTICE
Nov, 1986 - Present
Marvel Comics Group

	Good	Fine	Mint
1		.50	1.00
2-5		.40	.80

JUSTICE COMICS (Tales of Justice No. 53 on; formerly Wacky Duck)
No. 7, Fall/47 - No. 9, 6/48; No. 4, 8/48 - No. 52, 3/55
Marvel/Atlas comics (NPP 7-9,4-19/CnPC 20-23/MjMC 24-38/Male 39-52

	Good	Fine	Mint
7('47)	3.50	10.50	24.00
8-Kurtzman-a-"Giggles 'N' Grins," (3)	3.35	10.00	23.00
9('48)	2.50	7.50	17.00
4	2.15	6.50	15.00
5-9: 8-Anti-Wertham editorial	1.50	4.50	10.00
10-15-Photo-c	1.70	5.00	11.50
16-30	1.15	3.50	8.00
31-40,42-47,49-52-Last precode	1.00	3.00	7.00
41-Electrocution-c	3.35	10.00	23.00
48-Pakula & Tuska-a	1.30	4.00	9.00

NOTE: ***Pakula*** *a-43, 45.* ***Louis Ravielli*** *a-39.* ***Robinson*** *a-22, 25, 41.* ***Wildey*** *a-52.*

JUSTICE, INC. (The Avenger)
May-June, 1975 - No. 4, Nov-Dec, 1975
National Periodical Publications

	Good	Fine	Mint
1-McWilliams-a; origin		.40	.80
2-4		.25	.50

NOTE: ***Kirby*** *c-2, 3p; a-2-4p.* ***Kubert*** *c-1, 4.*

JUSTICE LEAGUE OF AMERICA (See Brave & the Bold)
(See Official . . . Index)
10-11/60 - No. 261, 4/87 (52pgs.-91-99,139-157)
National Periodical Publications/DC Comics

	Good	Fine	Mint
1-Origin Despero	62.00	190.00	490.00
2	23.00	58.00	160.00
3-Origin/1st app. Kanjar Ro	16.00	40.00	110.00
4,5: 4-Green Arrow joins JLA. 5-Origin Dr. Destiny	9.50	24.00	66.00
6-8,10: 6-Origin Prof. Amos Fortune. 7-Last 10¢ issue. 10-Origin Felix Faust; 1st app. Time Lord	6.35	16.00	44.00
9-Origin J.L.A.	9.65	24.00	68.00
11-15: 12-Origin & 1st app. Dr. Light. 13-Speedy app. 14-Atom joins JLA	4.15	12.50	25.00
16-20: 17-Adam Strange flashback	2.65	8.00	16.00
21,22: 21-Re-intro. of JSA. 22-JSA x-over	5.00	15.00	30.00
23-28: 24-Adam Strange app. 28-Robin app.	1.50	4.50	9.00
29,30-JSA x-over	1.50	4.50	9.00
31-Hawkman joins JLA, Hawkgirl cameo	1.15	3.40	6.80
32-Intro & Origin Brain Storm	1.15	3.40	6.80
33-36,40	.95	2.80	5.60
37,38-JSA x-over	1.15	3.40	6.80
39-25¢ Giant G-16	1.50	4.50	9.00
41-Intro & Origin The Key	.95	2.80	5.60
42-45: 42-Metamorpho app.	.70	2.00	4.00
46,47-JSA x-over	.90	2.70	5.40
48-25¢ Giant G-29	1.10	3.25	6.50
49-57,59,60: 55-Intro. Earth 2 Robin	.70	2.00	4.00
58-25¢ Giant G-41	.90	2.70	5.40
61-66,68-70: 64-Intro/origin Red Tornado. 69-Wonder Woman quits	.50	1.50	3.00
67-25¢ Giant G-53	.60	1.80	3.60
71-75,77-80: 71-Manhunter leaves JLA. 74-Black Canary joins. 78-Re-intro Vigilante	.35	1.10	2.20
76-25¢ Giant G-65	.45	1.40	2.80
81-84,86-92: 83-Death of Spectre	.35	1.10	2.20
85,93-(Giant G-77,G-89; 68 pgs.)	.45	1.40	2.80
94-Origin Sandman (Adv. No. 40) & Starman (Adv. No. 61); Deadman x-over; Adams-a	1.70	5.00	10.00
95-Origin Dr. Fate & Dr. Midnight reprint (More Fun No. 67, All-American No. 25)	.45	1.25	2.50
96-Origin Hourman (Adv. No. 48); Wildcat-r	.45	1.25	2.50
97-Origin JLA retold; Sargon, Starman-r	.50	1.50	3.00
98,99: 98-G.A. Sargon, Starman-r. 99-G.A. Sandman, Starman, Atom-r	.35	1.00	2.00
100	.60	1.80	3.60
101,102: 102-Red Tornado dies	.45	1.35	2.70
103-106: 103-Phantom Stranger joins. 105-Elongated Man joins. 106-New Red Tornado joins	.30	.90	1.80
107,108-G.A. Uncle Sam, Black Condor, The Ray, Dollman, Phantom Lady, & The Human Bomb x-over	.45	1.35	2.70
109-Hawkman resigns	.25	.75	1.50
110-116: All 100 pg. issues; 111-Shining Knight, Green Arrow-r. 112-Crimson Avenger, Vigilante, origin Starman-r	.30	.80	1.60
117-190: 117-Hawkman rejoins. 128-Wonder Woman rejoins. 129-Death of Red Tornado. 135-37-G.A. Bulletman, Bulletgirl, Spy Smasher, Mr. Scarlet, Pinky & Ibis x-over. 137-Superman battles G.A. Capt. Marvel. 144-Origin retold; origin J'onn J'onnz. 145-Red Tornado resurrected. 161-Zatanna joins & new costume. 171-Mr. Terrific murdered. 179-Firestorm joins. 181-Gr. Arrow leaves		.60	1.20
191,194-199		.50	1.00
192-Real origin Red Tornado, ends No. 193		.50	1.00
193-Free 16pg. insert-All-Star Squadron (1st app.)	.35	1.00	2.00
200-Anniversary ish. (76pgs., $1.50); origin retold; Green Arrow rejoins	.35	1.00	2.00
201-220: 203-Intro/origin new Royal Flush Gang. 208-All-Star Squadron app. 219,220-Origin Black Canary		.40	.80
221-249,251-261 (75¢): 228-Re-intro Martian Manhunter. 233-New J.L.A. begins. 243-Aquaman leaves. 244,245-Crisis x-over. 253-Origin Despero. 258-Death of Vibe		.45	.90
250-Batman rejoins		.60	1.25
Annual 1(7/83)	.35	1.00	2.00
Annual 2(10/84)-Intro new J.L.A.		.50	1.00
Annual 3(11/85)-Crisis x-over		.65	1.30

NOTE: ***Adams*** *c-63, 66, 67, 70, 74, 79, 81, 82, 86-89, 91, 92, 94, 96-98, 138, 139.* ***Aparo*** *a-200.* ***Austin*** *a-200i.* ***Baily*** *a-96r.* ***Burnley*** *a-94r, 98r, 99r.* ***Greene*** *a-46-61i, 64-73i, 110i(r).* ***Grell*** *c-117, 122.* ***Kaluta*** *c-154p.* ***Gil Kane*** *a-200.* ***Krigstein*** *a-96(r-Sensation No. 84.)* ***Kubert*** *a-200; c-72, 73.* ***Nino*** *a-228i, 230i.* ***Orlando*** *c-151i.* ***Perez*** *a-184-86p, 192-97p, 200p; c-184p, 186, 192-195, 196p, 197p, 199, 200, 201p, 202, 203-05p, 207-09, 212-15, 217-20.* ***Reinman*** *a-97r.* ***Roussos*** *a-62i.* ***Sekowsky*** *a-44-63p, 110-12p(r); c-46-48p, 51p.* ***Smith*** *c-185i.* ***Starlin*** *c-178-80, 183, 185p.* ***Staton*** *a-244p; c-157p, 244p.* ***Toth*** *a-110r.* ***Tuska*** *a-153, 228p, 241-243p. JSA x-over-55, 56, 64, 65, 73, 74, 82, 83, 91, 92, 101, 102, 107, 108, 110, 113, 115, 123, 124, 135-37, 147, 148, 159, 160, 171, 172, 183-85, 195-97, 207, 208, 209, 219, 220, 231, 232.*

JUSTICE MACHINE, THE
June, 1981 - No. 5, Nov, 1983 ($2.00, No. 1-3, Magazine size)
Noble Comics

JUSTICE MACHINE (continued)

	Good	Fine	Mint
1-Byrne-c(p)	4.50	13.50	27.00
2-Austin-c(i)	2.00	6.00	12.00
3	1.70	5.00	10.00
4,5	1.00	3.00	6.00
Annual 1 (1/84, 68 pgs.)(published by Texas Comics); 1st app. The Elementals	3.00	9.00	18.00

JUSTICE MACHINE FEATURING THE ELEMENTALS
May, 1986 - No. 4, Aug, 1986 (mini-series)
Comico

	Good	Fine	Mint
1	.45	1.30	2.60
2-4	.30	.90	1.80

JUSTICE TRAPS THE GUILTY (Fargo Kid V11No.3 on)
Oct-Nov, 1947 - V11No.2(No.92), Apr-May, 1958
Prize/Headline Publications

	Good	Fine	Mint
V2No.1-S&K c/a; electrocution-c	10.00	30.00	70.00
2-S&K-c/a	5.50	16.50	38.00
3-5-S&K c/a	4.75	14.25	33.00
6-S&K c/a; Feldstein-a	5.50	16.50	38.00
7,9-S&K c/a	3.35	10.00	23.00
8,10-Krigstein-a; S&K-c. 10-S&K-a	4.35	13.00	30.00
11,19-S&K-c	1.85	5.50	13.00
12,14-17,20-No S&K	1.30	4.00	9.00
13-Used in **SOTI**, pg. 110-111	3.35	10.00	23.00
18-S&K-c, Elder-a	1.85	5.50	13.00
21-S&K c/a	1.85	5.50	13.00
22,23,27-S&K-c	1.70	5.00	11.50
24-26,28-50	1.00	3.00	7.00
51-57,59-70	.85	2.50	6.00
58-Illo. in **SOTI**, ''Treating police contemptuously''(top left); text on heroin	8.00	24.00	56.00
71-75,77-92	.85	2.50	6.00
76-Orlando-a	1.00	3.00	7.00

NOTE: ***Bailey*** *a-12, 13.* ***Elder*** *a-8.* ***Kirby*** *a-19p.* ***Meskin*** *a-22, 27, 63, 64.* ***Robinson/Meskin*** *a-5, 19.* ***Severin*** *a-8, 11p. Photo-c No. 15, 16.*

JUST IMAGINE COMICS AND STORIES
1986 - Present ($1.50, B&W)
Just Imagine

	Good	Fine	Mint
1-12	.35	1.00	2.00
. . .Special 1 (7/86)	.25	.75	1.50

JUST KIDS
1932 (16 pages; 9½x12''; paper cover)
McLoughlin Bros.

	Good	Fine	Mint
283-Three-color text, pictures on heavy paper	4.35	13.00	30.00

JUST MARRIED
January, 1958 - No. 114, Dec, 1976
Charlton Comics

	Good	Fine	Mint
1	1.30	4.00	9.00
2	.75	2.25	5.00
3-10	.45	1.35	3.00
11-30	.25	.75	1.50
31-50		.30	.60
51-114		.20	.40

KA'A'NGA COMICS (. . .Jungle King)(See Jungle Comics)
Spring, 1949 - No. 20, Summer, 1954
Fiction House Magazines (Glen-Kel Publ. Co.)

	Good	Fine	Mint
1-Ka'a'nga, Lord of the Jungle begins	17.00	51.00	120.00
2	9.50	28.50	65.00
3,4	8.00	24.00	56.00
5-Camilla app.	5.00	15.00	35.00
6-9: 7-Tuska-a. 9-Tabu, Wizard of the Jungle app.	3.75	11.25	26.00
10-Used in **POP**, pg. 99	4.35	13.00	30.00
11-15	2.85	8.50	20.00
16-Sheena app.	3.35	10.00	23.00
17-20	2.65	8.00	18.00
I.W. Reprint No. 1 (r-/No. 18) Kinstler-c	.70	2.00	4.00
I.W. Reprint No. 8 (reprints No. 10)	.70	2.00	4.00

KAMANDI, THE LAST BOY ON EARTH (Also see Cancelled Comic Cavalcade and Brave & the Bold No. 120)
Oct-Nov, 1972 - No. 59, Sept-Oct, 1978
National Periodical Publications/DC Comics

	Good	Fine	Mint
1-Origin	.35	1.00	2.00
2-10: 4-Intro. Prince Tuftan of the Tigers		.50	1.00
11-31: 29-Superman x-over. 31-Intro Pyra		.30	.60
32-68 pg. Giant; origin from No. 1		.50	1.00
33-40-Last Kirby issue		.30	.60
41-58: 43-46-Tales of the Great Disaster		.20	.40
59-Starlin c(p)/a(p)		.50	1.00

NOTE: ***Ayers*** *a(p)-48-59 (most).* ***Giffen*** *a-44-47p.* ***Kirby*** *a-1-40p; c-1-33.* ***Kubert*** *c-34-41.* ***Nasser*** *a-45p, 46p.* ***Starlin*** *c-57, 59p.*

KARATE KID (See Action, Adventure, Legion of Super-Heroes, & Superboy)
Mar-Apr, 1976 - No. 15, July-Aug, 1978
National Periodical Publications/DC Comics

	Good	Fine	Mint
1-Meets Iris Jacobs; Estrada/Staton-a		.40	.80
2-15: 2-Major Disaster app. 15-Continued into Kamandi No. 58		.30	.60

NOTE: ***Grell*** *c-1-5, 6p, 7-15.* ***Staton*** *a-1-9i. Legion x-over-No. 1, 2, 4, 6, 10, 12, 13. Princess Projectra x-over-No. 8, 9*

KASCO KOMICS
1945; 1949 (regular size; paper cover)
Kasko Grainfeed (Giveaway)

	Good	Fine	Mint
1(1945)-Similar to Katy Keene; Bill Woggon-a; 28 pgs.; 6-7/8''x9-7/8''	9.35	28.00	65.00
2(1949)	8.00	24.00	55.00

KATHY
September, 1949 - 1953
Standard Comics

	Good	Fine	Mint
1	2.85	8.50	20.00
2	1.65	5.00	11.50
3-5	1.15	3.50	8.00
6-16	.85	2.50	6.00

KATHY
Oct, 1959 - No. 27, Feb, 1964
Atlas Comics/Marvel (ZPC)

	Good	Fine	Mint
1	2.00	6.00	14.00
2	1.00	3.00	7.00
3-15	.75	2.25	5.00
16-27	.45	1.25	2.50

KAT KARSON
No date (Reprint)
I. W. Enterprises

	Good	Fine	Mint
1-Funny animals	.50	1.50	3.00

KATY AND KEN VISIT SANTA WITH MISTER WISH
1948 (16 pgs.; paper cover)
S. S. Kresge Co. (Giveaway)

	Good	Fine	Mint
	2.35	7.00	14.00

Justice Machine #1 (5/86), © Comico

Justice Traps the Guilty #5, © PRIZE

Ka'a'nga Comics #13, © FH

Katy Keene Spectacular #1, © AP

Katzenjammer Kids #13, © KING

Keen Detective Funnies #20, © CEN

KATY KEENE (Also see Kasco Komics, Laugh, Pep, Suzie, & Wilbur)
1949 - No. 4, 1951; No. 5, 3/52 - No. 62, Oct, 1961
Archie Publ./Close-Up/Radio Comics

	Good	Fine	Mint
1-Bill Woggon-a begins	55.00	165.00	385.00
2	27.00	81.00	190.00
3-5	24.00	72.00	165.00
6-10	19.00	57.00	132.00
11,13-20	16.00	48.00	110.00
12-(Scarce)	17.00	51.00	120.00
21-40	11.00	33.00	76.00
41-62	7.00	21.00	50.00
Annual 1('54)	29.00	86.00	200.00
Annual 2-6('55-59)	13.50	40.50	95.00
3-D 1(1953-Large size)	25.00	75.00	175.00
Charm 1(9/58)	13.00	40.00	90.00
Glamour 1(1957)	13.00	40.00	90.00
Spectacular 1('56)	13.00	40.00	90.00

KATY KEENE FASHION BOOK MAGAZINE
1955 - No. 13, Sum, '56 - No. 23, Wint, '58-59 (nn 3-10)
Radio Comics/Archie Publications

	Good	Fine	Mint
1	27.00	81.00	190.00
2	15.00	45.00	105.00
11-18: 18-Photo Bill Woggon	11.50	34.50	80.00
19-23	8.50	25.50	60.00

KATY KEENE HOLIDAY FUN (See Archie Giant Series Mag. No. 7,12)

KATY KEENE PINUP PARADE
1955 - No. 15, Summer, 1961 (25 cents)
Radio Comics/Archie Publications

	Good	Fine	Mint
1	27.00	81.00	190.00
2	15.00	45.00	105.00
3-5	12.00	36.00	84.00
6-10,12-14: 8-Mad parody. 10-Photo Bill Woggon	10.00	30.00	70.00
11-Story of how comics get CCA approved, narrated by Katy	12.00	36.00	84.00
15(Rare)-Photo artist & family	27.00	81.00	190.00

KATY KEENE SPECIAL (Katy Keene No. 7 on)
Sept, 1983 - Present
Archie Enterprises

	Good	Fine	Mint
1-Woggon-r; new Woggon-c		.50	1.00
2-20: 3-Woggon-r		.30	.60

KATZENJAMMER KIDS, THE
1903 (50 pgs.; 10x15¼''; in color)
New York American & Journal

(by Rudolph Dirks, strip 1st appeared in 1898)

	Good	Fine	Mint
1903 (Rare)	21.00	62.00	145.00
1905-Tricks of...(10x15)	16.00	48.00	110.00
1906-Stokes-10x16'', 32 pgs. in color	16.00	48.00	110.00
1910-The Komical...(10x15)	16.00	48.00	110.00
1921-Embee Dist. Co., 10x16'', 20 pgs. in color	13.50	40.50	95.00

KATZENJAMMER KIDS, THE (See Giant Comic Album)
1945-1946; Summer, 1947 - No. 27, Feb-Mar, 1954
David McKay Publ./Standard No.12-21(Spring/'50 - 53)/Harvey No. 22, 4/53 on

	Good	Fine	Mint
Feature Books 30	7.00	21.00	50.00
Feature Books 32,35('45),41,44('46)	5.50	16.50	38.00
Feature Book 37-Has photos & biog. of Harold Knerr	6.50	19.50	45.00
1(1947)	6.50	19.50	45.00
2	3.35	10.00	23.00
3-11	2.65	8.00	18.00
12-14(Standard)	1.75	5.25	12.00
15-21(Standard)	1.30	4.00	9.00
22-25,27(Harvey): 22-24-Henry app.	1.00	3.00	7.00
26-½ in 3-D	11.00	33.00	76.00

KAYO (Formerly Jest?)
March, 1945
Harry 'A' Chesler

	Good	Fine	Mint
12-Green Knight, Capt. Glory, Little Nemo (not by McCay)	4.00	12.00	28.00

KA-ZAR
Aug, 1970 - No. 3, Mar, 1971 (Giant-Size, 68 pgs.)
Marvel Comics Group

	Good	Fine	Mint
1-Reprints earlier Ka-Zar stories; Avengers x-over in Hercules; Daredevil, X-Men app; hidden profanity-c	.25	.75	1.50
2,3-Daredevil app., Ka-Zar origin No. 2; Angel in both		.50	1.00

NOTE: ***Kirby** c/a-all. **Colan** a-1p(r).*

KA-ZAR
Jan, 1974 - No. 20, Feb, 1977 (Regular Size)
Marvel Comics Group

	Good	Fine	Mint
1		.60	1.20
2-10: 4-Brunner-c		.40	.80
11-20		.30	.60

NOTE: ***Alcala** a-6i, 8i. **J. Buscema** a-6-10p; c-1, 5, 7. **Heath** a-12. **Gil Kane** c(p)-3, 5, 8-11, 15, 20. **Kirby** c-12p. **Reinman** a-1p.*

KA-ZAR THE SAVAGE
4/81 - No. 34, 10/84 (Regular size) (Mando paper No. 10 on)
Marvel Comics Group

	Good	Fine	Mint
1	.25	.75	1.50
2-9		.50	1.00
10-First direct sale	.35	1.00	2.00
11-Origin Zabu		.50	1.00
12-Two versions: With & without panel missing (1600 printed with panel)		.50	1.00
13-28,30-34: 21-26-Spider-Man x-over		.40	.80
29-Double size; Ka-Zar & Shanna wed		.40	.80

NOTE: ***B. Anderson** a-1p-15p, 18, 19; c-1-17, 18p, 20(back-c). **Gil Kane** a-11, 12, 14. Photo-c No. 26.*

KEEN DETECTIVE FUNNIES (Formerly Det. Picture Stories?)
No. 8, July, 1938 - No. 24, Sept, 1940
Centaur Publications

	Good	Fine	Mint
8-The Clock continues-r/Funny Pic. Stories 1	45.00	135.00	315.00
9-Tex Martin by Eisner	30.00	90.00	210.00
10,11	25.00	75.00	175.00
V2No.1,2-The Eye Sees by Frank Thomas begins; ends No. 23(Not in V2No.3). 2-Jack Cole-a	22.00	65.00	154.00
3-TNT Todd begins	22.00	65.00	154.00
4,5	22.00	65.00	154.00
6,9-11: 11-Dean Denton begins	22.00	65.00	154.00
7-The Masked Marvel by Ben Thompson begins	43.00	130.00	300.00
8-Nudist ranch panel w/four girls	25.00	75.00	175.00
12(12/39)-Origin The Eye Sees by Frank Thomas; death of Masked Marvel's sidekick 2L	30.00	90.00	210.00
V3No.1,2	25.00	75.00	175.00
18,19,21,22: 18-Bondage/torture-c	25.00	75.00	175.00
20-Classic Eye Sees-c by Thomas	30.00	90.00	210.00
23-Air Man begins (intro)	30.00	90.00	210.00
24-Air Man-c	30.00	90.00	210.00

NOTE: ***Burgos** a-V2/2. **Jack Cole** a-V2/2. **Eisner** a-V2/6r. **Ken Ernst** a-V2/4-7, 9, 10, 19, 21. **Everett** a-V2/6, 7, 9, 11, 12, 20. **Guardineer** a-V2/5, 66. **Gustavson** a-V2/4-6. **Simon** c-V3/1.*

KEEN KOMICS
V2No.1, May, 1939 - V2No.3, Nov, 1939
Centaur Publications

	Good	Fine	Mint
V2No.1(Large size)-Dan Hastings (s/f), The Big Top, Bob Phantom the Magician, The Mad Goddess app.	25.00	75.00	175.00
V2No.2(Reg. size)-The Forbidden Idol of Machu Picchu; Cut Carson by Burgos begins	18.00	56.00	125.00
V2No.3-Saddle Sniffl by Jack Cole, Circus Pays, Kings Revenge app.	18.00	56.00	125.00

NOTE: *Binder a-V2/2. Burgos a-V2/2,3. Ken Ernst a-V2/3. Gustavson a-V2/2. Jack Cole a-V2/3.*

KEEN TEENS
1945 - No. 6, Sept, 1947
Life's Romances Publ./Leader/Magazine Enterprises

nn-14 pgs. Claire Voyant (cont'd. in other nn issue) movie photos, Dotty Dripple, Gertie O'Grady & Sissy	8.00	24.00	56.00
nn-16 pgs. Claire Voyant & 16 pgs. movie photos	8.00	24.00	56.00
3-6: 4-Glenn Ford-c. 5-Perry Como-c	2.35	7.00	16.00

KEEPING UP WITH THE JONESES
1920 - No. 2, 1921 (52 pgs.; 9¼x9¼''; B&W daily strip reprints)
Cupples & Leon Co.

1,2-By Pop Momand	5.00	15.00	35.00

KELLYS, THE (Formerly Rusty; Spy Cases No. 26 on)
No. 23, Jan, 1950 - No. 25, June, 1950
Marvel Comics (HPC)

23	3.50	10.50	24.00
24,25: 24-Margie app.	2.00	6.00	14.00

KELVIN MACE
1986 - Present
Vortex Publs.

1-Super-hero parody	.85	2.50	5.00
1 (2nd printing)	.25	.75	1.50
2-4	.40	1.25	2.50

KEN MAYNARD WESTERN (Movie star)
Sept, 1950 - No. 8, Feb, 1952 (All-36pgs; photo front/back-c)
Fawcett Publications

1-K. Maynard & his horse Tarzan begin	15.00	45.00	105.00
2	10.00	30.00	70.00
3-8	8.50	25.50	60.00

KEN SHANNON (Gabby No. 11)
Oct, 1951 - No. 15, 1953 (a private eye)
Quality Comics Group

1-Crandall-a	8.50	25.50	60.00
2-Crandall c/a(2); text on narcotics	8.00	24.00	56.00
3-5-Crandall-a	4.65	14.00	32.00
6	3.35	10.00	23.00
7,9,10-Crandall-a	4.00	12.00	28.00
8-Opium den drug use story	4.65	14.00	32.00
11-15 (Exist?)	2.15	6.50	15.00

NOTE: *Jack Cole a-1-9. No. 11-15 published after title change to Gabby.*

KEN STUART
Jan, 1949 (Sea Adventures)
Publication Enterprises

1-Frank Borth-c/a	2.65	8.00	18.00

KENT BLAKE OF THE SECRET SERVICE (Spy)
May, 1951 - No. 14, July, 1953
Marvel/Atlas Comics(20CC)

	Good	Fine	Mint
1-Injury to eye, bondage, torture	4.00	12.00	28.00
2-Drug use w/hypo scenes	2.15	6.50	15.00
3-14	1.30	4.00	9.00

NOTE: *Heath c-5, 7. Infantino c-12. Sinnott a-2(3).*

KERRY DRAKE (Also see Green Hornet)
Jan, 1956 - No. 2, March, 1956
Argo

1,2-Newspaper-r	2.15	6.50	15.00

KERRY DRAKE DETECTIVE CASES (. . . Racket Buster No. 32,33)
(Also see Chamber of Clues)
1944; No. 6, Jan, 1948 - No. 33, Aug, 1952
Life's Romances/Compix/Magazine Ent. No.1-5/Harvey No.6 on

nn(1944)(A-1 Comics)(slightly over-size)	10.00	30.00	70.00
2	6.50	19.50	45.00
3-5(1944)	5.75	17.25	40.00
6,8(1948); 8-Bondage-c	3.35	10.00	23.00
7-Kubert-a; biog of Andriola	4.00	12.00	28.00
9,10-Two-part marijuana story; Kerry smokes marijuana-No. 10	6.75	20.00	47.00
11-15	3.00	9.00	21.00
16-33	2.35	7.00	16.00
. . . in the Case of the Sleeping City-(1951-Publishers Synd.)-16 pg. giveaway for armed forces; paper cover	2.35	7.00	16.00

NOTE: *Berg a-5. Powell a-10-13, 23.*

KEWPIES
Spring, 1949
Will Eisner Publications

1-Feiffer-a; used in **SOTI** in a non-seductive context, pg. 35	15.00	45.00	105.00

KEY COMICS
Jan, 1944 - No. 5, Aug, 1946
Consolidated Magazines

1-The Key, Will-O-The-Wisp begin	6.00	18.00	42.00
2	3.50	10.50	24.00
3-5	3.00	9.00	21.00

KEY COMICS
1951 - 1956 (32 pages) (Giveaway)
Key Clothing Co./Peterson Clothing

Contains a comic from different publishers bound with new cover. Cover changed each year. Many combinations possible. Distributed in Nebraska, Iowa, & Kansas. Contents would determine price, 40-60 percent of original.

KEY RING COMICS
1941 (16 pgs.; two colors) (sold 5 for 10 cents)
Dell Publishing Co.

1-Sky Hawk	2.00	6.00	12.00
1-Viking Carter	2.00	6.00	12.00
1-Features Sleepy Samson	2.00	6.00	12.00
1-Origin Greg Gilday r-/War Comics No. 2	2.35	7.00	14.00
1-Radior(Super hero)	2.35	7.00	14.00

NOTE: *Each book has two holes in spine to put in binder.*

KICKERS, INC.
Nov, 1986 - Present
Marvel Comics Group

1		.50	1.00
2-6		.40	.80

KID CARROTS
September, 1953
St. John Publishing Co.

Ken Maynard Western #7, © FAW

Kent Blake of the. . . #6, © MCG

Kerry Drake Detective Cases #6. © HARV

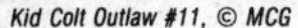
Kid Colt Outlaw #11, © MCG

Kid From Dodge City #1, © MCG

Kid Komics #5, © MCG

KID CARROTS (continued)

	Good	Fine	Mint
1	1.15	3.50	8.00

KID COLT OUTLAW (Kid Colt No. 1-4; . . . Outlaw No. 5-on)(Also see All Western Winners, Best Western, Black Rider, Two-Gun Kid, Two-Gun Western, Western Winners, Wild Western, & Wisco)
8/48 - No. 139, 3/68; No. 140, 11/69 - No. 229, 4/79
Marvel Comics(LCC) 1-16; Atlas(LMC) 17-102; Marvel 103-on

	Good	Fine	Mint
1-Kid Colt & his horse Steel begin; Two-Gun Kid app.	20.00	60.00	140.00
2	10.00	30.00	70.00
3-5: 4-Anti-Wertham editorial; Tex Taylor app. 5-Blaze Carson app.	6.00	18.00	42.00
6-8: 6-Tex Taylor app; 7-Nimo the Lion begins, ends No. 10	4.00	12.00	28.00
9,10 (52pgs.)	4.65	14.00	32.00
11-Origin	4.65	14.00	32.00
12-20	2.65	8.00	18.00
21-32	2.15	6.50	15.00
33-45: Black Rider in all	1.85	5.50	13.00
46,47,49,50	1.50	4.50	10.00
48-Kubert-a	2.15	6.50	15.00
51-53,55,56	1.30	4.00	9.00
54-Williamson/Maneely-c	2.50	7.50	17.00
57-60,66: 4-pg. Williamson-a in all. 59-Reprint Rawhide Kid No. 79	3.65	11.00	25.00
61-63,67-78,80-85	.85	2.50	6.00
64,65-Crandall-a	1.15	3.50	8.00
79-Origin retold	1.15	3.50	8.00
86-Kirby-a(r)	.85	2.50	6.00
87-Davis-a(r)	1.15	3.50	8.00
88,89-Williamson-a in both (4 pgs.). 89-Redrawn Matt Slade No. 2	2.15	6.50	15.00
90-99	.45	1.25	3.00
100-Last 10¢ ish.	.55	1.65	4.00
101-120	.25	.75	1.50
121-140: 121-Rawhide Kid x-over. 125-Two-Gun Kid x-over. 130-132 -68pg. issues with one new story each; 130-Origin. 140-Reprints begin		.30	.60
141-160: 156-Giant; reprints		.30	.60
161-229: 170-Origin retold		.25	.50
. . . Album (no date; 1950's; Atlas Comics)-132 pgs.; random binding, cardboard cover, B&W stories; contents can vary	7.00	21.00	50.00
Giant Size 1(1/75), 2(4/75), 3(7/75)		.40	.80

NOTE: ***Ayers*** *a-many.* ***Colan*** *a-52, 53; c(p)-223, 228, 229.* ***Crandall*** *a-140r, 167r.* ***Everett*** *a-137i, 225i(r).* ***Heath*** *c-34, 35, 39, 46, 48, 49, 57.* ***Jack Keller*** *a-25(2), 26-68(3-4), 78, 94p, 98, 99, 108, 110, 132.* ***Kirby*** *a-86r, 93, 96, 119, 176(part); c-87, 92-95, 97, 99-112, 114-117, 121-123, 197r.* ***Maneely*** *a-12, 68, 81; c-41-43, 52, 53, 62, 65, 68, 78, 81.* ***Morrow*** *a-173r.* ***Rico*** *a-13, 18.* ***Severin*** *c-58.* ***Shores*** *a-39, 41-43; c-24.* ***Sutton*** *a-137p, 225p(r).* ***Wildey*** *a-82.* ***Williamson*** *a-147r, 170r, 172r.* ***Woodbridge*** *a-64, 81. Black Rider in No. 33-45, 74, 86. Iron Mask in No. 110, 114, 121, 127. Sam Hawk in No. 84, 101, 111, 121, 146, 174, 181, 188.*

KID COWBOY (Also see Approved Comics No. 4)
1950 - 1954 (painted covers)
Ziff-Davis Publ./St. John (Approved Comics)

	Good	Fine	Mint
1-Lucy Belle begins	3.50	10.50	24.00
2	2.00	6.00	14.00
3-14: 11-Bondage-c	1.35	5.00	11.50

NOTE: ***Berg*** *a-5.* ***Maneely*** *c-2.*

KIDDIE KAPERS
1945?(nd); Oct, 1957; 1963 - 1964
Decker Publ. (Red Top-Farrell)

	Good	Fine	Mint
1(nd, 1945-46?)-Infinity-c	2.00	6.00	14.00
1(10/57)(Decker)-Little Bit reprints from Kiddie Karnival	.75	2.25	5.00
Super Reprint No. 7, 10('63), 12, 14('63), 15,17('64), 18('64)	.35	1.00	2.00

KIDDIE KARNIVAL
1952 (100 pgs.) (One Shot)
Ziff-Davis Publ. Co. (Approved Comics)

	Good	Fine	Mint
nn-Rebound Little Bit No. 1,2	4.00	12.00	28.00

KID ETERNITY (Becomes Buccaneers) (See Hit)
Spring, 1946 - No. 18, Nov, 1949
Quality Comics Group

	Good	Fine	Mint
1	27.00	81.00	190.00
2	13.50	40.50	95.00
3-Mac Raboy-a	14.50	43.50	100.00
4-10	8.00	24.00	56.00
11-18	5.00	15.00	35.00

KID FROM DODGE CITY, THE
July, 1957 - No. 2, Sept, 1957
Atlas Comics (MMC)

	Good	Fine	Mint
1	2.00	6.00	14.00
2-Everett-c	1.15	3.50	7.00

KID FROM TEXAS, THE (A Texas Ranger)
June, 1957 - No. 2, Aug, 1957
Atlas Comics (CSI)

	Good	Fine	Mint
1-Powell-a	2.35	7.00	16.00
2	1.15	3.50	8.00

KID KOKO
1958
I. W. Enterprises

	Good	Fine	Mint
Reprint No. 1,2-(reprints M.E.'s Koko & Kola No. 4, 1947)	.50	1.50	3.00

KID KOMICS (. . . Movie Komics No. 11)
Feb, 1943 - No. 10, Spring, 1946
Timely Comics (USA 1,2/FCI 3-10)

	Good	Fine	Mint
1-Origin Captain Wonder & sidekick Tim Mullrooney, & Subbie; intro the Sea-Going Lad, Pinto Pete, & Trixy Trouble; Knuckles & White-wash Jones only app.; Wolverton art, 7 pgs.	100.00	300.00	700.00
2-The Young Allies, Red Hawk, & Tommy Tyme begin; last Captain Wonder & Subbie	56.00	168.00	390.00
3-The Vision & Daredevils app.	38.00	115.00	265.00
4-The Destroyer begins; Sub-Mariner app.; Red Hawk & Tommy Tyme end	32.00	96.00	224.00
5,6	23.00	70.00	160.00
7-10: The Whizzer app. 7; Destroyer not in No. 7,8; 10-Last Destroyer, Young Allies & Whizzer	19.00	57.00	132.00

KID MONTANA (Formerly Davy Crockett Frontier Fighter; The Gunfighters No. 51 on)
V2No.9, Nov, 1957 - No. 50, Mar, 1965
Charlton Comics

	Good	Fine	Mint
V2No.9	1.75	5.25	12.00
10	.85	2.50	6.00
11,12,14-20	.55	1.65	4.00
13-Williamson-a	1.70	5.00	11.50
21-35	.45	1.35	3.00
36-50		.40	.80

NOTE: *Title change to Montana Kid on cover only on No. 44; remained Kid Montana on inside.*

KID MOVIE KOMICS (Formerly Kid Komics; Rusty No. 12 on)
No. 11, Summer, 1946
Timely Comics

	Good	Fine	Mint
11-Silly Seal & Ziggy Pig; 2 pgs. Kurtzman "Hey Look" plus 6 pg. story	7.00	21.00	50.00

KIDNAPPED (See 4-Color No. 1101 & Movie Comics)

KIDNAP RACKET (See Comics Hits No. 57)

KID SLADE GUNFIGHTER (Formerly Matt Slade. . .)
No. 5, Jan, 1957 - No. 8, July, 1957
Atlas Comics (SPI)

	Good	Fine	Mint
5-Severin-a; Maneely-c	2.35	7.00	16.00
6,8	1.15	3.50	8.00
7-Williamson/Mayo-a, 4 pgs.	3.35	10.00	23.00

KID ZOO COMICS
July, 1948 (52 pgs.)
Street & Smith Publications

	Good	Fine	Mint
1-Funny Animal	3.00	9.00	21.00

KILLER
March, 1985 (One-shot)(Baxter paper)
Eclipse Comics

	Good	Fine	Mint
1	.30	.90	1.80

KILLERS, THE
1947 - 1948 (No month)
Magazine Enterprises

	Good	Fine	Mint
1-Mr. Zin, the Hatchet Killer; mentioned in **SOTI**, pgs. 179,180; Used by N.Y. Legis. Comm. L. B. Cole-c	48.00	145.00	335.00
2-(Scarce)-Hashish smoking story; "Dying, Dying, Dead" drug story; Whitney, Ingels-a; Whitney hanging-c	48.00	145.00	335.00

KILROYS, THE
June-July, 1947 - No. 54, June-July, 1955
B&I Publ. Co. No. 1-19/American Comics Group

	Good	Fine	Mint
1	5.00	15.00	35.00
2	2.65	8.00	18.00
3-5: 5-Gross-a	2.15	6.50	15.00
6-10: 8-Milt Gross's Moronica	1.75	5.25	12.00
11-20: 14-Gross-a	1.30	4.00	9.00
21-30	1.00	3.00	7.00
31-47,50-54	.75	2.25	5.00
48,49-(3-D effect)	5.00	15.00	35.00

KING CLASSICS
1977 (85 cents each) (36 pages, cardboard covers)
King Features (Printed in Spain for U.S. distr.)

1-Connecticut Yankee, 2-Last of the Mohicans, 3-Moby Dick, 4-Robin Hood, 5-Swiss Family Robinson, 6-Robinson Crusoe, 7-Treasure Island, 8-20,000 Leagues, 9-Christmas Carol, 10-Huck Finn, 11-Around the World in 80 Days, 12-Davy Crockett, 13-Don Quixote, 14-Gold Bug, 15-Ivanhoe, 16-Three Musketeers, 17-Baron Munchausen, 18-Alice in Wonderland, 19-Black Arrow, 20-Five Weeks in a Balloon, 21-Great Expectations, 22-Gulliver's Travels, 23-Prince & Pauper, 24-Lawrence of Arabia

	Good	Fine	Mint
(Originals, 1977-78) each. . . .	.85	2.50	6.00
(Reprints, 1979; HRN-24)	.70	2.00	4.00

NOTE: *The first eight issues were not numbered. Issues No. 25-32 were advertised but not published. The 1977 originals have HRN 32a; the 1978 originals have HRN 32b.*

KING COLT (See 4-Color No. 651)

KING COMICS (Strip reprints)
Apr, 1936 - No. 159, Feb, 1952 (Winter on cover)
David McKay Publications/Standard No. 156-on

	Good	Fine	Mint
1-Flash Gordon by Alex Raymond; Brick Bradford, Mandrake the Magician & Popeye begin	190.00	570.00	1330.00
2	90.00	270.00	630.00
3	65.00	195.00	455.00
4	40.00	120.00	280.00
5	30.00	90.00	210.00
6-10: 9-X-Mas-c	20.00	60.00	140.00
11-20	18.00	54.00	125.00
21-30	15.00	48.00	105.00
31-40: 33-Last Segar Popeye	13.00	40.00	90.00
41-50: 46-Little Lulu, Alvin & Tubby app. as text illos by Marge Buell			
50-The Lone Ranger begins	11.00	33.00	76.00
51-60: 52-Barney Baxter begins?	9.00	27.00	62.00
61-The Phantom begins	8.00	24.00	56.00
62-99	6.65	20.00	46.00
100	8.00	24.00	56.00
101-115-Last Raymond issue	5.50	16.50	38.00
116-145: 117-Phantom origin retold	4.35	13.00	30.00
146,147-Prince Valiant in both	3.50	10.50	24.00
148-155-Flash Gordon ends	3.50	10.50	24.00
156-159	2.75	8.25	19.00

NOTE: ***Marge Buell*** *text illos in No. 24-46 at least.*

KING CONAN (Conan The King No. 20 on)
March, 1980 - No. 19, Nov, 1983 (52 pgs.)
Marvel Comics Group

	Good	Fine	Mint
1	.50	1.50	3.00
2-6: 4-Death of Thoth Amon	.30	.90	1.80
7-1st Paul Smith-a, 2 pgs. (9/81)	.35	1.00	2.00
8-10		.60	1.20
11-19		.50	1.00

NOTE: ***Buscema*** *a-1p-9p, 17p; c(p)-1-5, 7-9, 14, 17.* ***Kaluta*** *c-19.* ***Nebres*** *a-17i, 18, 19i.* ***Severin*** *c-18.* ***Simonson*** *c-6.*

KING KONG (See Movie Comics)

KING LEONARDO & HIS SHORT SUBJECTS (TV)
Nov-Jan, 1961-62 - No. 4, Sept, 1963
Dell Publishing Co./Gold Key

	Good	Fine	Mint
4-Color 1242,1278	2.65	8.00	18.00
01390-207(5-7/62)(Dell)	2.35	7.00	16.00
1 (10/62)	2.35	7.00	16.00
2-4	1.50	4.50	10.00

KING LOUIE & MOWGLI
May, 1968 (Disney)
Gold Key

	Good	Fine	Mint
1 (10223-805)	1.15	3.50	8.00

KING OF DIAMONDS (TV)
July-Sept, 1962
Dell Publishing Co.

	Good	Fine	Mint
01-391-209-Photo-c	1.75	5.25	12.00

KING OF KINGS (See 4-Color No. 1236)

KING OF THE BAD MEN OF DEADWOOD
1950
Avon Periodicals

	Good	Fine	Mint
nn-Kinstler-c; Kamen/Feldstein-a r-/Cowpuncher 2	9.00	27.00	62.00

KING OF THE ROYAL MOUNTED (See Large Feat. Comic No. 9, Feature Books No. 1 (McKay), & Super Book No. 2,6)

KING OF THE ROYAL MOUNTED (Zane Grey's)
No. 207, Dec, 1948 - No. 935, Sept-Nov, 1958
Dell Publishing Co.

	Good	Fine	Mint
4-Color 207('48)	10.00	30.00	70.00
4-Color 265,283	6.00	18.00	42.00
4-Color 310,340	4.00	12.00	28.00
4-Color 363,384	3.50	10.50	24.00
8(6-8/52)-10	3.50	10.50	24.00
11-20	3.00	9.00	21.00
21-28 (3-5/58)	2.65	8.00	18.00
4-Color 935(9-11/58)	2.65	8.00	18.00

NOTE: *4-Color No. 207,265,283,310,340,363,384 are all newspaper reprints with* ***Jim Gary*** *art. No. 8 on are all Dell originals.* ***Painted*** *c-No. 9-on.*

KING RICHARD & THE CRUSADERS (See 4-Color No. 588)

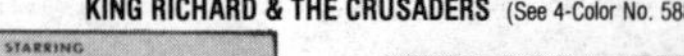

Kid Slade Gunfighter #5, © MCG

King Comics #46, © DMP

King Leonardo #01390-207, © Leonardo TV Prod.

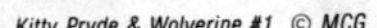
Kitty Pryde & Wolverine #1, © MCG

Koko & Kola #3, © ME

Konga #16, © CC

KING SOLOMON'S MINES
1951 (Movie)
Avon Periodicals

	Good	Fine	Mint
nn(No.1 on 1st page)	19.50	58.00	135.00

KISS (See Marvel Comics Super Special & Howard the Duck No. 12)

KIT CARSON (See Frontier Fighters)

KIT CARSON (Formerly All True Detective Cases No. 4; Fighting Davy Crockett No. 9; see Blazing Sixguns)
1950; No. 2, 8/51 - No. 3, 12/51; No. 5, 11-12/54 - No. 8, 9/55
Avon Periodicals

nn(No.1) (1950)	5.50	16.50	38.00
2(8/51)	3.35	10.00	23.00
3(12/51)	2.65	8.00	18.00
5-6,8('54-'55)	2.35	7.00	16.00
7-Kinstler-a(2)	2.65	8.00	18.00
I.W. Reprint No. 10('63)	.85	2.50	5.00

NOTE: *Kinstler c-1-3,5-8.*

KIT CARSON & THE BLACKFEET WARRIORS
1953
Realistic

nn-Reprint; Kinstler-c	4.00	12.00	28.00

KIT KARTER
May-July, 1962
Dell Publishing Co.

1	1.15	3.50	8.00

KITTY
October, 1948
St. John Publishing Co.

1-Lily Renee-a	2.35	7.00	16.00

KITTY PRYDE AND WOLVERINE
Nov, 1984 - No. 6, April, 1985 (6 issue mini-series)
Marvel Comics Group

1	.35	1.00	2.00
2-6	.25	.75	1.50

KITZ 'N' KATZ KOMIKS
1985 - Present ($1.50-$2.00; B&W)
Eclipse Comics No. 2 on

1-3	.25	.75	1.50
4 ($2.00)	.35	1.00	2.00

KLARER GIVEAWAYS (See Wisco)

KNIGHTS OF THE ROUND TABLE (See 4-Color No. 540)

KNIGHTS OF THE ROUND TABLE
No. 10, April, 1957
Pines Comics

10	1.15	3.50	8.00

KNIGHTS OF THE ROUND TABLE
Nov-Jan, 1963/64
Dell Publishing Co.

1 (12-397-401)	2.00	6.00	14.00

KNOCK KNOCK
1936 (32 pages) (B&W)
Gerona Publications

1-Bob Dunn-a	5.00	15.00	35.00

KNOCKOUT ADVENTURES
Winter, 1953-54
Fiction House Magazines

	Good	Fine	Mint
1-Reprints/Fight Comics No. 53	3.50	10.50	24.00

KNOW YOUR MASS
1958 (100 Pg. Giant) (35 cents) (square binding)
Catechetical Guild

303-In color	4.00	12.00	28.00

KOBRA (See DC Special Series No. 1)
Feb-Mar, 1976 - No. 7, Mar-Apr, 1977
National Periodical Publications

1-Art plotted by Kirby		.40	.80
2-7: 3-1st Giffen pro art		.25	.50

NOTE: *Austin a-3i. Buckler a-5p; c-5p. Kubert c-4. Nasser a-6p, 7.*

KOKEY KOALA
May, 1952
Toby Press

1	1.75	5.25	12.00

KOKO AND KOLA
Fall, 1946 - No. 5, May, 1947; No. 6, 1950
Compix/Magazine Enterprises

1-Funny animal	2.65	8.00	18.00
2	1.30	4.00	9.00
3-5,6(A-1 28)	1.15	3.50	8.00

KO KOMICS
October, 1945
Gerona Publications

1-The Duke of Darkness & The Menace (hero)	6.00	18.00	42.00

KOMIC KARTOONS
Fall, 1945 - No. 2, Winter, 1945
Timely Comics (EPC)

1,2-Andy Wolf, Bertie Mouse	4.65	14.00	32.00

KOMIK PAGES
April, 1945
Harry 'A' Chesler, Jr. (Our Army, Inc.)

10(No.1 on inside)-Land O' Nod by Rick Yager (2 pgs.), Animal Crackers, Foxy GrandPa, Tom, Dick & Mary, Cheerio Minstrels, Red Starr plus other 1-2 pg. strips; Cole-a; all-r	5.75	17.25	40.00

KONA (. . . Monarch of Monster Isle)
Feb-Apr, 1962 - No. 21, Jan-Mar, 1967
Dell Publishing Co.

4-Color 1256	2.00	6.00	14.00
2-10: 4-Anak begins	1.00	3.00	7.00
11-21	.75	2.25	4.50

NOTE: *Glanzman a-all issues.*

KONGA (Fantastic Giants No. 24) (See Return of. . .)
1960; No. 2, Aug, 1961 - No. 23, Nov, 1965
Charlton Comics

1(1960)-Based on movie	10.00	30.00	70.00
2	5.00	15.00	35.00
3-5	4.00	12.00	28.00
6-15	2.65	8.00	18.00
16-23	1.50	4.50	10.00

NOTE: *Ditko a-1, 3-15; c-4, 6-9. Glanzman a-12. Montes & Bache a-16-23.*

KONGA'S REVENGE (Formerly Return of. . .)
No. 2, Summer, 1963 - No. 3, Fall, 1964; Dec, 1968
Charlton Comics

2,3: 2-Ditko c/a	2.00	6.00	14.00
1('68)-Reprints Konga's Revenge No. 3	1.00	3.00	7.00

KONG THE UNTAMED
June-July, 1975 - No. 5, Feb-Mar, 1976
National Periodical Publications

	Good	Fine	Mint
1		.40	.80
2-5		.25	.50

NOTE: ***Alcala** a-1-3. **Wrightson** c-1,2.*

KOOKIE
Feb-Apr, 1962 - No. 2, May-July, 1962
Dell Publishing Co.

1,2-Written by John Stanley; Bill Williams-a	3.00	9.00	21.00

K. O. PUNCH, THE (Also see Lucky Fights It Through)
1948 (Educational giveaway)
E. C. Comics

Feldstein-splash; Kamen-a	117.00	340.00	700.00

KORAK, SON OF TARZAN (Edgar Rice Burroughs)
Jan, 1964 - No. 45, Jan, 1972 (Painted-c No. 1-?)
Gold Key

1-Russ Manning-a	2.50	7.50	17.00
2-11-Russ Manning-a	1.15	3.50	8.00
12-21: 14-Jon of the Kalahari ends. 15-Mabu, Jungle Boy begins; Manning-a No. 21	.75	2.25	5.00
22-30	.60	1.75	3.50
31-45	.45	1.25	2.50

NOTE: ***Warren Tufts** a-12, 13.*

KORAK, SON OF TARZAN (Tarzan Family No. 60 on)
No. 46, May-June, 1972 - No. 56, Feb-Mar, 1974; No. 57, May-June, 1975 - No. 59, Sept-Oct, 1975 (Edgar Rice Burroughs)
National Periodical Publications

46-(52 pgs.)-Carson of Venus begins (origin); Pellucidar feature		.50	1.00
47-50: 49-Origin Korak retold		.35	.70
51-59: 56-Last Carson of Venus		.25	.50

NOTE: ***Kaluta** a-46-56. All have covers by **Joe Kubert**. **Manning** strip reprints-No. 57-59. **Frank Thorn** a-46-51.*

KOREA MY HOME (Also see Yalta to Korea)
nd (1950s)
Johnstone and Cushing

nn-Anti-communist; Korean War	15.00	45.00	90.00

KORG: 70,000 B. C. (TV)
May, 1975 - No. 9, Nov, 1976 (Hanna-Barbera)
Charlton Publications

1	.25	.75	1.50
2-9		.50	1.00

KORNER KID COMICS
1947
Four Star Publications

1	2.65	8.00	18.00

KRAZY KAT
1946 (Hardcover)
Holt

Reprints daily & Sunday strips by Herriman	25.00	75.00	160.00
with dust jacket (Rare)....	53.00	160.00	370.00

KRAZY KAT (See Ace Comics & March of Comics No. 72,87)

KRAZY KAT COMICS (... & Ignatz the Mouse early issues)
May-June, 1951 - Jan, 1964 (None by Herriman)
Dell Publishing Co./Gold Key

	Good	Fine	Mint
1(1951)	3.50	10.50	24.00
2-5 (No. 5, 8-10/52)	2.15	6.50	15.00
4-Color 454,504	1.75	5.25	12.00
4-Color 548,619,696 (4/56)	1.50	4.50	10.00
1(10098-401)(1/64-Gold Key)(TV)	1.50	4.50	10.00

KRAZY KOMICS (1st Series) (Cindy No. 27 on)
July, 1942 - No. 26, Spr, 1947 (Also see Ziggy Pig)
Timely Comics (USA No. 1-21/JPC No. 22-26)

1-Ziggy Pig begins	13.00	40.00	90.00
2	6.50	19.50	45.00
3-10	4.35	13.00	30.00
11,13,14	3.35	10.00	23.00
12-Timely's entire art staff drew themselves into a Creeper story	4.35	13.00	30.00
15-Has "Super Soldier" by Pfc. Stan Lee	3.35	19.00	23.00
16-24,26	2.15	6.50	15.00
25-Kurtzman-a, 6 pgs.	3.75	11.25	26.00

KRAZY KOMICS (2nd Series)
Aug, 1948 - No. 2, Nov, 1948
Timely/Marvel Comics

1-Wolverton (10 pgs.) & Kurtzman (8 pgs.)-a; Eustice Hayseed begins, Li'l Abner swipe	15.00	45.00	105.00
2-Wolverton-a, 10 pgs.; Powerhouse Pepper cameo	9.00	27.00	62.00

KRAZY KROW
Summer, 1945 - No. 3, Wint, 1945/46
Marvel Comics (ZPC)

1	4.00	12.00	28.00
2,3	2.15	6.50	15.00
I.W. Reprint No. 1('57), 2('58), 7	.30	.80	1.60

KRAZYLIFE
1945 (no month)
Fox Features Syndicate

1-Funny animal	4.00	12.00	28.00

KREE/SKRULL WAR STARRING THE AVENGERS, THE
Sept, 1983 - No. 2, Oct, 1983 ($2.50; Baxter paper)
Marvel Comics Group

1,2	.45	1.25	2.50

NOTE: ***Adams** a-1r, 2. **Buscema** a-1r, 2r. **Simonson** c(p)/a(p)-1.*

KRIM-KO COMICS
1936 - 1939 (4 pg. giveaway) (weekly)
Krim-ko Chocolate Drink

Lola, Secret Agent; 184 issues - all original stories each....	1.35	4.00	8.00

KROFFT SUPERSHOW (TV)
April, 1978 - No. 6, Jan, 1979
Gold Key

1		.60	1.20
2-6		.35	.70

KRULL
Nov, 1983 - No. 2, Dec, 1983
Marvel Comics Group

1,2-Film adapt. r/Marvel Super Spec.		.25	.50

KRYPTON CHRONICLES
Sept, 1981 - No. 3, Nov, 1981
DC Comics

1-Buckler-c(p)		.40	.80
2,3		.30	.60

Korak, Son of Tarzan #5, © ERB

Krazy Kat Comics #1 (5-6/51), © Herriman

Krazy Komics #23, © MCG

Lady Luck #90, © QUA

Laffin' Gas #1, © Blackthorne

Lance O'Casey #3, © FAW

KULL & THE BARBARIANS (Magazine)
May, 1975 - No. 3, Sept, 1975 (B&W) ($1.00)
Marvel Comics Group

	Good	Fine	Mint
1-Andru/Wood-r/Kull No. 1; 2 pgs. Adams; Gil Kane, Severin-a	.40	1.25	2.50
2-Red Sonja by Chaykin begins; Adams-i; Gil Kane-a	.30	.90	1.80
3-Origin Red Sonja by Chaykin; Adams-a; Solomon Kane app.	.30	.90	1.80

KULL THE CONQUEROR (. . . the Destroyer No. 11 on)
June, 1971 - No. 2, Sept, 1971; No. 3, July, 1972 - No. 15, Aug, 1974; No. 16, Aug, 1976 - No. 29, Oct, 1978
Marvel Comics Group

1-Andru/Wood-a; origin Kull	.70	2.00	4.00
2-5	.25	.75	1.50
6-10		.60	1.20
11-15-Ploog-a		.40	.80
16-29		.30	.60

NOTE: *No. 1,2,7-9,11 are based on Robert E. Howard stories.* ***Alcala*** *a-17p, 18-20i; c-24.* ***Ditko*** *a-12r, 15r.* ***Gil Kane*** *c-15p, 21.* ***Nebres*** *a-22i-27i; c-25i, 27i.* ***Ploog*** *c-11, 12p, 13.* ***Severin*** *a-2-9i, 10p; c-2-10i, 19.* ***Starlin*** *c-14.*

KULL THE CONQUEROR
Dec, 1982 - No. 2, Mar, 1983 (52 pgs., printed on Baxter paper)
Marvel Comics Group

1-Buscema-a(p)	.45	1.25	2.50
2	.35	1.00	2.00

KULL THE CONQUEROR (No. 9,10 titled 'Kull')
5/83 - No. 10, 6/85 (52 pgs.; $1.25-60¢; Mando paper)
Marvel Comics Group

V3No.1,2($1.25)		.65	1.30
3,4($1.00)		.50	1.00
5-10(60-65¢)		.30	.60

KUNG FU (See Deadly Hands of. . ., & Master of. . .)

KUNG FU FIGHTER (See Richard Dragon. . .)

K-Z COMICS PRESENTS
June, 1985 ($1.50, B&W, 44 pgs.)
K-Z Comics

1-Colt	.25	.75	1.50

LABOR FORCE
Sept, 1986 - Present ($1.50, B&W)
Blackthorne Publ.

1,2	.25	.75	1.50

LABOR IS A PARTNER
1949 (32 pgs. in color; paper cover)
Catechetical Guild Educational Society

nn-Anti-communism	30.00	80.00	160.00
Confidential Preview-(B&W, 8½x11'', saddle stitched)-only one known copy; text varies from color version, advertises next book on secularism (If the Devil Would Talk)	35.00	100.00	200.00

LABYRINTH
Nov, 1986 - No. 3, Jan, 1987 (mini-series)
Marvel Comics Group

1-3: Reprints		.40	.80

LAD: A DOG
1961 - No. 2, July-Sept, 1962
Dell Publishing Co.

4-Color 1303 (movie), 2	2.00	6.00	14.00

LADY AND THE TRAMP (See Dell Giants, 4-Color No. 629,634, & Movie Comics)

LADY AND THE TRAMP IN ''BUTTER LATE THAN NEVER''
1955 (14 pgs.) (Walt Disney)
American Dairy Association (Premium)

	Good	Fine	Mint
	2.00	6.00	14.00

LADY BOUNTIFUL
1917 (10¼x13½''; 24 pgs.; B&W; cardboard cover)
Saalfield Publ. Co./Press Publ. Co.

by Gene Carr; 2 panels per page	5.00	15.00	35.00

LADY COP (See First Issue Special)

LADY FOR A NIGHT (See Cinema Comics Herald)

LADY LUCK (Formerly Smash No. 1-85)
Dec, 1949 - No. 90, Aug, 1950
Quality Comics Group

86(No.1)	27.00	81.00	190.00
87-90	21.00	63.00	146.00

LAFF-A-LYMPICS (TV)(See The Funtastic World of Hanna-Barbera)
Mar, 1978 - No. 13, Mar, 1979
Marvel Comics Group

1		.30	.60
2-13		.25	.50

LAFFIN' GAS (Also see Adolescent Radioactive. . . & Pre-Teen Dirty-Gene. . .)
June, 1986 - Present ($2.00, B&W)
Blackthorne Publ.

1	.40	1.20	2.40
2,3	.35	1.00	2.00

LAFFY-DAFFY COMICS
Feb, 1945 - No. 2, March, 1945
Rural Home Publ. Co.

1,2	2.00	6.00	14.00

LANA (Little Lana & True Life Tales No. 8 on?)
Aug, 1948 - No. 7, Aug, 1949 (Also see Annie Oakley)
Marvel Comics (MjMC)

1-Rusty, Millie begin	3.75	11.25	26.00
2-Kurtzman's ''Hey Look'' (1); last Rusty	3.35	10.00	23.00
3-7: 3-Nellie begins	1.65	5.00	11.50

LANCELOT & GUINEVERE (See Movie Classics)

LANCELOT LINK, SECRET CHIMP (TV)
April, 1971 - No. 8, Feb, 1973
Gold Key

1-Photo-c	1.35	4.00	8.00
2-8	.85	2.50	5.00

LANCELOT STRONG (See The Shield)

LANCE O'CASEY (See Mighty Midget Comics)
Spring, 1946 - No. 3, Fall, 1946; No. 4, Summer, 1948
Fawcett Publications

1	7.00	21.00	50.00
2	4.35	13.00	30.00
3,4	3.75	11.25	26.00

LANCER (TV)(Western)
Feb, 1969 - No. 3, Sept, 1969
Gold Key

1-Photo-c	2.00	6.00	14.00
2,3	1.50	4.50	10.00

LAND OF THE GIANTS (TV)
Nov, 1968 - No. 5, Sept, 1969

LAND OF THE GIANTS (continued)
Gold Key

	Good	Fine	Mint
1-Bondage photo-c	1.35	4.00	9.00
2-5	1.00	3.00	7.00

LAND OF THE LOST COMICS (Radio)
July-Aug, 1946 - No. 9, Spring, 1948
E. C. Comics

1	15.00	45.00	105.00
2	10.00	30.00	70.00
3-9	9.00	27.00	62.00

LAND UNKNOWN, THE (See 4-Color No. 845)

LARAMIE (TV)
Aug, 1960 - July, 1962 (All photo-c)
Dell Publishing Co.

4-Color 1125	3.50	10.50	24.00
4-Color 1223,1284	3.00	9.00	21.00
01-418-207	3.00	9.00	21.00

LAREDO (TV)
June, 1966
Gold Key

1 (10179-606)	2.00	6.00	14.00

LARGE FEATURE COMIC (Formerly called Black & White)
1939 - No. 12, 1943
Dell Publishing Co.

1 **(Series I)**-Dick Tracy Meets the Blank	70.00	210.00	490.00
2-Terry & the Pirates (No. 1)	36.00	108.00	252.00
3-Heigh-Yo Silver! The Lone Ranger (text & ill.)(76 pgs.)	36.00	108.00	252.00
4-Dick Tracy Gets His Man	42.00	125.00	294.00
5-Tarzan (No. 1) by Harold Foster (origin); reprints 1st dailies from '29	76.00	228.00	532.00
6-Terry & the Pirates & The Dragon Lady; reprints dailies from 1936	35.00	105.00	245.00
7-(Scarce)-52 pgs.; The Lone Ranger-Hi-Yo Silver the Lone Ranger to the Rescue	47.00	141.00	330.00
8-Dick Tracy Racket Buster	36.00	108.00	252.00
9-King of the Royal Mounted	14.50	43.50	100.00
10-(Scarce)-Gang Busters (No. appears on inside front cover); first slick cover	23.00	70.00	160.00
11-Dick Tracy Foils the Mad Doc Hump	36.00	108.00	252.00
12-Smilin' Jack	20.00	60.00	140.00
13-Dick Tracy & Scotty	36.00	108.00	252.00
14-Smilin' Jack	20.00	60.00	140.00
15-Dick Tracy & the Kidnapped Princess	36.00	108.00	252.00
16-Donald Duck-1st app. Daisy Duck on back cover (6/41-Disney)	142.00	435.00	1000.00
(Prices vary widely on this book)			
17-Gang Busters (1941)	15.00	45.00	105.00
18-Phantasmo	13.50	40.50	95.00
19-Dumbo Comic Paint Book (Disney); partial-r 4-Color 17	96.00	288.00	672.00
20-Donald Duck Comic Paint Book (Rarer than No. 16) (Disney)	200.00	600.00	1400.00
(Prices vary widely on this book)			
21-Private Buck	5.75	17.25	40.00
22-Nuts & Jolts	5.75	17.25	40.00
23-The Nebbs	6.50	19.50	45.00
24-Popeye (Thimble Theatre) ½ by Segar	30.00	90.00	210.00
25-Smilin' Jack	20.00	60.00	140.00
26-Smitty	11.50	34.50	80.00
27-Terry & the Pirates	24.00	72.00	166.00
28-Grin & Bear It	5.50	16.50	38.00
29-Moon Mullins	11.00	33.00	76.00
30-Tillie the Toiler	9.50	28.50	65.00
1 **(Series II)**-Peter Rabbit by Cady	25.00	75.00	175.00
2-Winnie Winkle (No. 1)	8.00	24.00	56.00
3-Dick Tracy	32.00	95.00	225.00
4-Tiny Tim (No. 1)	15.00	45.00	105.00
5-Toots & Casper	5.50	16.50	38.00
6-Terry & the Pirates	24.00	72.00	166.00
7-Pluto Saves the Ship (No. 1)(Disney) written by Carl Barks, Jack Hannah, & Nick George. (Possibly Barks' 2nd comic book work)	52.00	156.00	364.00
8-Bugs Bunny (No. 1)('42)	43.00	130.00	300.00
9-Bringing Up Father	6.50	19.50	45.00
10-Popeye (Thimble Theatre)	24.00	72.00	170.00
11-Barney Google & Snuffy Smith	9.50	28.50	66.00
12-Private Buck	5.50	16.50	38.00
13-(nn)-1001 Hours Of Fun; puzzles & games; by A. W. Nugent. This book was bound as No. 13 with Large Feat. Comics in Publishers files	5.50	16.50	38.00

NOTE: *The Black & White Feature Books are oversized 8½x11-3/8" comics with color covers and black and white interiors. The first nine issues all have rough, heavy stock covers and, except for No. 7, all have 76 pages, including covers. No. 7 and No. 10-on all have 52 pages. Beginning with No. 10 the covers are slick and thin and, because of their size, are difficult to handle without damaging. For this reason, they are seldom found in fine to mint condition. The paper stock, unlike Wow No. 1 and Capt. Marvel No. 1, is itself not unstable . . . just thin.*

LARRY DOBY, BASEBALL HERO
1950 (Cleveland Indians)
Fawcett Publications

nn-Bill Ward-a	19.50	58.50	135.00

LARRY HARMON'S LAUREL AND HARDY (. . . Comics)
July-Aug, 1972 (Regular size)
National Periodical Publications

1	.35	1.00	2.00

LARS OF MARS
Apr-May, 1951 - No. 11, July-Aug, 1951
Ziff-Davis Publishing Co.

10-Origin; Anderson-a(3) in each	22.00	65.00	154.00
11-Painted-c	19.50	58.50	135.00

LASER ERASER & PRESSBUTTON (See Axel Pressbutton & Miracleman 9)
11/85 - No. 12, 1987 (12 issue series)
Eclipse Comics

1-4		.40	.80
5-10		.50	1.00
. . . In 3D 1 (8/86, $2.50)	.40	1.25	2.50
2-D 1 (B&W, limited to 100 copies signed & numbered)	.85	2.50	5.00

LASH LARUE WESTERN (Movie star; king of the bullwhip)
Sum, 1949 - No. 46, Jan, 1954 (36pgs., 1-7,9,13,16-on)
Fawcett Publications

1-Lash & his horse Black Diamond begin; photo front/back-c begin	25.00	75.00	175.00
2(11/49)	18.00	54.00	125.00
3-5	16.00	48.00	110.00
6,7,9: 6-Last photo back-c; intro. Frontier Phantom (Lash's twin brother)	10.00	30.00	70.00
8,10 (52pgs.)	11.00	33.00	76.00
11,12,14,15 (52pgs.)	7.00	21.00	50.00
13,16-20 (36pgs.)	6.00	18.00	42.00

Laramie #01-418-207, © Revue Studios

Large Feature Comic #9, © KING

Laser Eraser & Pressbotton #1, © Eclipse

Lash LaRue Western #47, © CC

Lassie #20, © MGM

Laugh Comics #43, © AP

LASH LARUE WESTERN (continued)

	Good	Fine	Mint
21-30: 21-The Frontier Phantom app.	5.00	15.00	35.00
31-45	4.00	12.00	28.00
46-Last Fawcett issue & photo-c	5.00	15.00	35.00

LASH LARUE WESTERN (Continues from Fawcett)
No. 47, Mar-Apr, 1954 - No. 84, June, 1961
Charlton Comics

	Good	Fine	Mint
47-Photo-c	4.00	12.00	28.00
48	2.75	8.25	19.00
49-60	2.35	7.00	16.00
61-66,69,70: 52-r/No.8; 53-r/No.22	1.85	5.50	13.00
67,68-(68 pgs.). 68-Check-a	2.65	8.00	18.00
71-83	1.50	4.50	10.00
84-Last issue	1.85	5.50	13.00

LASSIE (TV)(M-G-M's. . . No. 1-36)
Oct-Dec, 1950 - No. 70, July, 1969
Dell Publishing Co./Gold Key No. 59 (10/62) on

	Good	Fine	Mint
1	3.50	10.50	24.00
2	2.00	6.00	14.00
3-10	1.50	4.50	10.00
11-19: 12-Rocky Langford (Lassie's master) marries Gerry Lawrence. 15-1st app. Timbu	1.15	3.50	8.00
20-22-Matt Baker-a	1.75	5.25	12.00
23-40: 33-Robinson-a. 39-1st app. Timmy as Lassie picks up her TV family	.75	2.25	5.00
41-70: 63-Last Timmy. 64-r/No. 19. 65-Forest Ranger Corey Stuart begins, ends No. 69. 70-Forest Rangers Bob Ericson & Scott Turner app. (Lassie's new masters)	.45	1.35	3.00
11193(1978-Golden Press)-224 pgs.; $1.95; Baker-a(r), 92 pgs.	.55	1.65	4.00
The Adventures of. . .(Red Heart Dog Food giveaway, 1949)	3.00	9.00	21.00
Kite Fun Book('73)-Pacific Gas & Elect. Co., Sou. Calif. Edison & Florida Power & Light(16 pgs.; 5x7")	2.00	6.00	14.00

NOTE: Photo c-57. (See March of Comics No. 210, 217, 230, 254, 266, 278, 296, 308, 324, 334, 346, 358, 370, 381, 394, 411, 432)

LAST DAYS OF THE JUSTICE SOCIETY SPECIAL
1986 (One shot, 68 pgs.)
DC Comics

	Good	Fine	Mint
1	.45	1.25	2.50

LAST HUNT, THE (See 4-Color No. 678)

LAST OF THE COMANCHES
1953 (Movie)
Avon Periodicals

	Good	Fine	Mint
nn-Kinstler c/a, 21pgs.; Ravielli-a	8.00	24.00	56.00

LAST OF THE ERIES, THE (See American Graphics)

LAST OF THE FAST GUNS, THE (See 4-Color No. 925)

LAST OF THE MOHICANS (See King Classics)

LAST STARFIGHTER, THE
Oct, 1984 - No. 3, Dec, 1984
Marvel Comics Group

	Good	Fine	Mint
1-3: Movie adaptation-r/Marvel Super Special; Guice-c		.30	.60

LAST TRAIN FROM GUN HILL (See 4-Color No. 1012)

LATEST ADVENTURES OF FOXY GRANDPA (See Foxy. . .)

LATEST COMICS (Super Duper No. 3?)
March, 1945
Spotlight Publ./Palace Promotions (Jubilee)

	Good	Fine	Mint
1-Super Duper	3.00	9.00	21.00
2-Bee-29 (nd)	2.00	6.00	14.00

LAUGH COMICS (Formerly Black Hood No. 1-19) (Laugh No. 226 on)
No. 20, Fall, 1946 - Present
Archie Publications (Close-Up)

	Good	Fine	Mint
20-Archie & Katy Keene begin	37.00	110.00	250.00
21-23,25: 21-1st app. Taffy	17.00	52.00	115.00
24-"Pipsy" by Kirby, 6 pgs.	18.00	55.00	125.00
26-30	10.00	30.00	70.00
31-40	8.00	24.00	50.00
41-60: 41,54-Debbi by Woggon	4.50	13.50	30.00
61-80: 67-Debbi by Woggon. 76-Katy Keene app.	2.85	8.50	20.00
81-99	2.00	6.00	14.00
100	2.65	8.00	18.00
101-126: 125-Debbi app.	1.35	4.00	9.00
127,130,131,133,135,140-142,144-Jaguar app.	1.35	4.00	9.00
128,129,132,134,138,139-Fly app.	1.35	4.00	9.00
136,143-Flygirl app.	1.35	4.00	9.00
137-Flyman & Flygirl app.	1.35	4.00	9.00
145-160: 157-Josie app.	.75	2.25	4.50
161-165,167-200	.50	1.50	3.00
166-Beatles-c	.85	2.50	5.00
201-240	.25	.75	1.50
241-280		.40	.80
281-400: 381-384-Katy Keene app.; by Woggon-381,382		.30	.60

NOTE: *Josie app.-No. 145, 160, 164. Katy Keene app.-No. 20-125, 129, 130, 133.*

LAUGH COMICS DIGEST (. . . Mag. No. 23 on)
8/74; No. 2, 9/75; No. 3, 3/76 - Present (Digest-size)
Archie Publications (Close-Up No. 1, 3 on)

	Good	Fine	Mint
1-Adams-a	.70	2.00	4.00
2,7,8,19-Adams-a	.35	1.00	2.00
3-6,9,10		.50	1.00
11-18,20-70		.50	1.00

NOTE: ***Katy Keene** in 23, 25, 27, 32-38, 40, 45-48, 50. **The Fly**-r in 19, 20. **The Jaguar**-r in 25, 27. **Mr. Justice**-r in 21. **The Web**-r in 23.*

LAUGH COMIX (Formerly Top Notch Laugh; Suzie No. 49 on)
No. 46, Summer, 1944 - No. 48, Winter, 1944-45
MLJ Magazines

	Good	Fine	Mint
46-Wilbur & Suzie in all	6.00	18.00	42.00
47,48	4.50	13.50	31.00

LAUGH-IN MAGAZINE (Magazine)
Oct, 1968 - No. 12, Oct, 1969 (50 cents) (Satire)
Laufer Publ. Co.

	Good	Fine	Mint
V1No.1	.85	2.50	5.00
2-12	.50	1.50	3.00

LAUREL & HARDY (See Larry Harmon's. . . & March of Comics No. 302,314)

LAUREL AND HARDY (. . . Comics)
March, 1949 - No. 28, 1951
St. John Publishing Co.

	Good	Fine	Mint
1	22.00	65.00	154.00
2	11.00	33.00	76.00
3,4	8.00	24.00	56.00
5-10	6.50	19.50	45.00
11-28	5.00	15.00	35.00

LAUREL AND HARDY (TV)
Oct, 1962 - No. 4, Sept-Nov, 1963
Dell Publishing Co.

	Good	Fine	Mint
12-423-210 (8-10/62)	1.75	5.25	12.00
2-4 (Dell)	1.30	4.00	9.00

LAUREL AND HARDY
Jan, 1967 - No. 2, Oct, 1967 (Larry Harmon's)
Gold Key

LAUREL AND HARDY (continued)

	Good	Fine	Mint
1,2: 1-Photo back-c	1.15	3.50	8.00

LAW AGAINST CRIME (Law-Crime on cover)
April, 1948 - No. 3, Aug, 1948
Essenkay Publishing Co.

	Good	Fine	Mint
1-(No.1-3: ½ funny animal, ½ crime)-L. B. Cole electrocution-c/a	21.00	62.00	146.00
2-L. B. Cole c/a	14.50	43.50	100.00
3-L. B. Cole c/a; used in **SOTI**, pg. 180,181 & illo-''The wish to hurt or kill couples in lovers' lanes;'' reprinted in All-Famous Crime No. 9	22.00	65.00	154.00

LAWBREAKERS (. . . Suspense Stories No. 10 on)
Mar, 1951 - No. 9, Oct-Nov, 1952
Law and Order Magazines (Charlton Comics)

	Good	Fine	Mint
1	5.00	15.00	35.00
2	2.50	7.50	17.50
3,5,6,8,9	2.00	6.00	14.00
4-''White Death'' junkie story	4.00	12.00	28.00
7-''The Deadly Dopesters'' drug story	3.65	11.00	25.00

LAWBREAKERS ALWAYS LOSE!
Spring, 1948 - No. 10, Oct, 1949
Marvel Comics (CBS)

	Good	Fine	Mint
1-2pg. Kurtzman-a, 'Giggles 'n Grins'	6.50	20.00	45.00
2	3.15	9.50	22.00
3-5: 4-Vampire story	2.65	8.00	18.00
6(2/49)-Has editorial defense against charges of Dr. Wertham	3.65	11.00	25.00
7-Used in **SOTI**, illo-''Comic-book philosophy;''	8.00	24.00	56.00
8-10: 9,10-Photo-c	1.75	5.25	12.00

LAWBREAKERS SUSPENSE STORIES (Formerly Lawbreakers; Strange Suspense Stories No. 16 on)
No. 10, Jan, 1953 - No. 15, Nov, 1953
Capitol Stories/Charlton Comics

	Good	Fine	Mint
10	3.50	10.50	24.00
11 (3/53)-Severed tongues c/story & woman negligee scene	18.00	54.00	125.00
12-14	2.65	8.00	18.00
15-Acid-in-face c/story; hands dissolved in acid story	8.50	25.50	60.00

LAW-CRIME (See Law Against Crime)

LAWMAN (TV)
No. 970, Feb, 1959 - No. 11, Apr-June, 1962 (All photo-c)
Dell Publishing Co.

	Good	Fine	Mint
4-Color 970	4.00	12.00	28.00
4-Color 1035('60)	3.00	9.00	21.00
3(2-4/60)-Toth-a	4.00	12.00	28.00
4-11	2.65	8.00	18.00

LAWRENCE (See Movie Classics)

LEADING COMICS (. . . Screen Comics No. 42 on)
Winter, 1941-42 - No. 41, Feb-Mar, 1950
National Periodical Publications

	Good	Fine	Mint
1-Origin The Seven Soldiers of Victory; Crimson Avenger, Green Arrow & Speedy, Shining Knight, The Vigilante, Star Spangled Kid & Stripsey begin. The Dummy (Vigilante villain) app.	110.00	330.00	770.00
2-Meskin-a	48.00	145.00	335.00
3	40.00	120.00	280.00
4,5	34.00	102.00	236.00
6-10	28.00	84.00	195.00
11-14(Spring, 1945)	20.00	60.00	140.00
15-Content change to funny animal	6.00	18.00	42.00
16-22,24-30	3.00	9.00	21.00
23-1st app. Peter Porkchops by Otto Feur	6.50	19.50	45.00
31,32,34-41	2.35	7.00	16.00
33-(Scarce)	4.35	13.00	30.00

NOTE: ***Rube Grossman**-a(Peter Porkchops)-most No. 15-on; c-15-41. **Post** a-23-37, 39, 41.*

LEADING SCREEN COMICS (Formerly Leading Comics)
No. 42, Apr-May, 1950 - No. 77, Aug-Sept, 1955
National Periodical Publications

	Good	Fine	Mint
42	3.50	10.50	24.00
43-77	2.00	6.00	14.00

NOTE: ***Grossman** a-most. **Mayer** a-45-48, 50, 54-57, 60, 62-74, 75(3), 76, 77.*

LEATHERNECK THE MARINE (See Mighty Midget Comics)

LEAVE IT TO BEAVER (TV)
No. 912, June, 1958 - May-July, 1962 (All photo-c)
Dell Publishing Co.

	Good	Fine	Mint
4-Color 912	7.00	21.00	50.00
4-Color 999,1103,1191,1285, 01-428-207	6.00	18.00	42.00

LEAVE IT TO BINKY (Binky No. 72 on) (See Super DC Giant and Showcase) (No. 1-22, 52 pgs.)
2-3/48 - No. 60, 10/58; No. 61, 6-7/68 - No. 71, 2-3/70
National Periodical Publications

	Good	Fine	Mint
1	11.00	33.00	76.00
2	5.50	16.50	38.00
3-5	4.35	13.00	30.00
6-10	3.65	11.00	25.00
11-20	2.50	7.50	17.00
21-28,30-45: 45-Last pre-code (2/55)	1.50	4.50	10.00
29-Used in **POP**, pg. 78	2.35	7.00	16.00
46-60	1.00	3.00	7.00
61-71	.70	2.00	4.00

NOTE: ***Drucker** a-28. **Mayer** a-1, 2, 15.*

LEE HUNTER, INDIAN FIGHTER (See 4-Color No. 779,904)

LEFT-HANDED GUN, THE (See 4-Color No. 913)

LEGEND OF CUSTER, THE (TV)
January, 1968
Dell Publishing Co.

	Good	Fine	Mint
1	1.15	3.50	8.00

LEGEND OF JESSE JAMES, THE (TV)
February, 1966
Gold Key

	Good	Fine	Mint
10172-602	1.75	5.25	12.00

LEGEND OF LOBO, THE (See Movie Comics)

LEGEND OF WONDER WOMAN, THE
May, 1986 - No. 4, Aug, 1986 (mini-series)
DC Comics

	Good	Fine	Mint
1		.50	1.00
2-4		.40	.80

LEGEND OF YOUNG DICK TURPIN, THE (TV)
May, 1966 (Disney TV episode)
Gold Key

	Good	Fine	Mint
1 (10176-605)-Photo/painted-c	1.15	3.50	8.00

LEGENDS
Nov, 1986 - No. 6, Apr, 1987 (mini-series)
DC Comics

Lawman #11, © Warner Bros.

Leading Comics #9, © DC

Leave It to Beaver #01-428-207, © Gomalco Prod.

Legends #1, © DC

Legion of Super-Heroes #291, © DC

Leroy #1, © STD

LEGENDS (continued)

	Good	Fine	Mint
1-Byrne c/a(p) begins		.50	1.00
2-6: 2-Intro Suicide Squad		.45	.90

LEGENDS OF DANIEL BOONE, THE
Oct-Nov, 1955 - No. 8, Dec-Jan, 1956-57
National Periodical Publications

	Good	Fine	Mint
1 (Scarce)	13.00	40.00	90.00
2 (Scarce)	8.50	25.50	60.00
3-8 (Scarce)	8.00	24.00	56.00

LEGIONNAIRES THREE
Jan, 1986 - No. 4, May, 1986 (Mini-series)
DC comics

	Good	Fine	Mint
1-4		.40	.80

LEGION OF MONSTERS (Magazine)
September, 1975 (black & white)
Marvel Comics Group

	Good	Fine	Mint
1-Origin & 1st app. Legion of Monsters; Adams-c; Morrow-a; origin & only app. The Manphibian	.35	1.00	2.00

LEGION OF SUBSTITUTE HEROES SPECIAL
July, 1985 (One Shot)
DC Comics

	Good	Fine	Mint
1-Giffen c/a(p)	.25	.75	1.50

LEGION OF SUPER-HEROES (See Action, Adventure, All New Collectors Ed., Limited Collectors Ed., Superboy, & Superman)
Feb, 1973 - No. 4, July-Aug, 1973
National Periodical Publications

	Good	Fine	Mint
1-Legion & Tommy Tomorrow reprints begin	.70	2.00	4.00
2-4: 3-r/Adv. 340, Action 240. 4-r/Adv. 341, Action 233	.35	1.00	2.00

LEGION OF SUPER-HEROES, THE (Formerly Superboy; Tales of The Legion No. 314 on)(See Secrets of. . .)
No. 259, Jan, 1980 - No. 313, July, 1984
DC Comics

	Good	Fine	Mint
259(No.1)-Superboy leaves Legion	.45	1.25	2.50
260-264,266-270	.35	1.00	2.00
265-Contains 28pg. insert 'Superman & the TR5-80 Computer;' origin Tyroc; Tyroc leaves Legion	.35	1.00	2.00
271-284: 272-Blok joins; origin; 20pg. insert-Dial 'H' For Hero. 277-Intro Reflecto. 280-Superboy re-joins legion. 282-Origin Reflecto	.25	.75	1.50
285,286-Giffen back up story	.70	2.00	4.00
287-Giffen-a on Legion begins	1.10	3.25	6.50
288-290: 290-Great Darkness saga begins, ends No. 294	.40	1.25	2.50
291-293	.25	.75	1.50
294-Double size (52 pgs.); Giffen-a(p)	.30	.90	1.80
295-299: 297-Origin retold		.60	1.20
300-Double size, 64 pgs., Mando paper; c/a by almost everyone at D.C.	.35	1.00	2.00
301-305: 304-Karate Kid & Princess Projectra resign		.50	1.00
306-313 (75 cent cover price): 306-Brief origin Star Boy		.45	.90
Annual 1(1982)-Giffen c/a; 1st app./origin new Invisible Kid who joins Legion	.35	1.00	2.00
Annual 2(10/83)-Giffen-c/a; Karate Kid & Princess Projectra wed	.25	.75	1.50
Annual 3('84)		.60	1.25

NOTE: ***Aparo*** *c-282, 283.* ***Austin*** *c-268i.* ***Buckler*** *c-273p, 274p, 276p.* ***Colan*** *a-311p.* ***Ditko*** *a(p)-267, 268, 272, 274, 276, 281.* ***Giffen*** *a-285p-313p, Annual No. 1p, 2p; c-287p, 288p, 289, 290p, 291p, 292, 293, 294-299p, 300, 301p-313p, Annual 1p, 2p.* ***Perez*** *c-268p, 277-80, 281p.* ***Starlin*** *a-265.* ***Staton*** *a-259p, 260p, 280.* ***Tuska*** *a-308p.*

LEGION OF SUPER-HEROES
Aug, 1984 - Present ($1.25-$1.50, deluxe format)
DC Comics

	Good	Fine	Mint
1	.40	1.25	2.50
2-5: 4-Death of Karate Kid. 5-Death of Nemesis Kid	.35	1.00	2.00
6-10	.30	.90	1.80
11-17: 12-Cosmic Boy, Lightning Lad, & Saturn Girl resign. 14-Intro new members: Tellus, Sensor Girl, Quislet	.25	.75	1.50
18-Crisis x-over	.30	.90	1.80
19-32: 25-Sensor Girl i.d. revealed as Princess Projectra	.25	.75	1.50
Annual 1 (10/85)-Crisis x-over	.35	1.10	2.20
Annual 2 (10/86)	.35	1.00	2.00

NOTE: ***Giffen*** *a(p)-1, 2, Annual 1, 2; c-1-5p, Annual 1.* ***Orlando*** *a-6p.*

LENNON SISTERS LIFE STORY, THE (See 4-Color No. 951,1014)

LEO THE LION
No date (10 cents)
I. W. Enterprises

	Good	Fine	Mint
1-Reprint	.50	1.50	3.00

LEROY
Nov, 1949 - No. 6, Nov, 1950
Standard Comics

	Good	Fine	Mint
1	2.00	6.00	14.00
2-Frazetta text illo.	2.15	6.50	15.00
3-6: 3-Lubbers-a	1.15	3.50	8.00

LET'S PRETEND
May-June, 1950 - No. 3, Sept-Oct, 1950
D. S. Publishing Co.

	Good	Fine	Mint
1	5.00	15.00	35.00
2,3	2.65	8.00	18.00

LET'S READ THE NEWSPAPER
1974
Charlton Press

	Good	Fine	Mint
Features Quincy by Ted Sheares		.30	.60

LET'S TAKE A TRIP (TV) (CBS TV Presents)
Spring, 1958
Pines

	Good	Fine	Mint
1-Marv Levy c/a	1.00	3.00	7.00

LETTERS TO SANTA (See March of Comics No. 228)

LIBERTY COMICS (Miss Liberty No. 1)
1945 - 1946 (MLJ & other reprints)
Green Publishing Co.

	Good	Fine	Mint
4	6.50	19.50	45.00
5 (5/46)-The Prankster app; Starr-a	4.35	13.00	30.00
10-Hangman & Boy Buddies app.; Suzie & Wilbur begin; reprint of Hangman No. 8	5.75	17.25	40.00
11(V2/2, 1/46)-Wilbur in women's clothes	9.20	27.50	64.00
12-Black Hood & Suzie app.	5.50	16.50	38.00
14,15-Patty of Airliner; Starr-a in both	2.85	8.50	20.00

LIBERTY GUARDS
No date (1946?)
Chicago Mail Order

	Good	Fine	Mint
nn-Reprints Man of War No. 1 with cover of Liberty Scouts No. 1; Gustavson-c	11.00	33.00	75.00

LIBERTY SCOUTS (See Man of War & Liberty Guards)
June, 1941 - No. 3, Aug, 1941
Centaur Publications

2(No.1)-Origin The Fire-Man, Man of War; Vapo-Man & Liberty

LIBERTY SCOUTS (continued)

	Good	Fine	Mint
Scouts begin; Gustavson-c/a	55.00	165.00	385.00
3(No.2)-Origin & 1st app. The Sentinel; Gustavson-c/a	40.00	120.00	280.00

LIDSVILLE (TV)
Oct, 1972 - No. 5, Oct, 1973
Gold Key

	Good	Fine	Mint
1	1.15	3.50	7.00
2-5	.70	2.00	4.00

LIEUTENANT, THE (TV)
April-June, 1964
Dell Publishing Co.

	Good	Fine	Mint
1	1.15	3.50	8.00

LT. ROBIN CRUSOE, U.S.N. (See Movie Comics and Walt Disney Showcase 26)

L.I.F.E. BRIGADE, THE
1986 - Present ($1.80, B&W)
Blue Comet Comics

	Good	Fine	Mint
1-Last Individuals Fighting Evil	.50	1.50	3.00

LIFE OF CAPTAIN MARVEL, THE
Aug, 1985 - No. 5, Dec, 1985 ($2.00 cover; Baxter paper)
Marvel Comics Group

	Good	Fine	Mint
1-5: r-/Starlin issues of Capt. Marvel	.35	1.00	2.00

LIFE OF CHRIST, THE
1949 (100 pages) (35 cents)
Catechetical Guild Educational Society

	Good	Fine	Mint
301-Reprints from Topix(1949)-V5No.11,12	4.00	12.00	28.00

LIFE OF CHRIST VISUALIZED
1942 - 1943
Standard Publishers

	Good	Fine	Mint
1-3: All came in cardboard case	2.75	8.00	16.00

LIFE OF CHRIST VISUALIZED
1946? (48 pgs. in color)
The Standard Publ. Co.

	Good	Fine	Mint
	1.00	3.00	6.00

LIFE OF ESTHER VISUALIZED
1947 (48 pgs. in color)
The Standard Publ. Co.

	Good	Fine	Mint
2062	1.00	3.00	6.00

LIFE OF JOSEPH VISUALIZED
1946 (48 pgs. in color)
The Standard Publ. Co.

	Good	Fine	Mint
1054	1.00	3.00	6.00

LIFE OF PAUL (See The Living Bible)

LIFE OF POPE JOHN PAUL II, THE
Jan, 1983
Marvel Comics Group

	Good	Fine	Mint
1	.25	.75	1.50

LIFE OF RILEY, THE (See 4-Color No. 917)

LIFE OF THE BLESSED VIRGIN
1950 (68 pages) (square binding)
Catechetical Guild (Giveaway)

	Good	Fine	Mint
nn-Contains "The Woman of the Promise" & "Mother of Us All" rebound	4.00	12.00	24.00

LIFE'S LIKE THAT
1945 (68 pgs.; B&W; 25 cents)
Croyden Publ. Co.

	Good	Fine	Mint
nn-Newspaper Sunday strip reprints by Neher	1.75	5.25	12.00

LIFE'S LITTLE JOKES
No date (1924) (52 pgs.; B&W)
M.S. Publ. Co.

	Good	Fine	Mint
By Rube Goldberg	11.00	33.00	75.00

LIFE STORIES OF AMERICAN PRESIDENTS (See Dell Giants)

LIFE STORY
4/49 - V8/46, 1/53; V8/47, 4/53 (All have photo-c?)
Fawcett Publications

	Good	Fine	Mint
V1/1	3.65	11.00	25.00
2	1.75	5.25	12.00
3-6	1.50	4.50	10.00
V2/7-12	1.30	4.00	9.00
V3/13-Wood-a	6.50	19.50	45.00
V3/14-18, V4/19-21,23,24	1.15	3.50	8.00
V4/22-Drug use story	1.50	4.50	10.00
V5/25-30, V6/31-36	1.00	3.00	7.00
V7/37,40-42, V8/44,45	.85	2.50	6.00
V7/38, V8/43-Evans-a	1.70	5.00	11.50
V7/39-Drug Smuggling & Junkie sty	1.00	3.00	7.00
V8/46,47 (Scarce)	1.15	3.50	8.00

NOTE: ***Powell** a-13,23,26,28,30,32,39.*

LIFE WITH ARCHIE
Sept, 1958 - Present
Archie Publications

	Good	Fine	Mint
1	18.00	54.00	125.00
2	9.00	27.00	62.00
3-5	7.00	20.00	50.00
6-10	3.50	10.50	24.00
11-20	1.70	5.00	12.00
21-30	1.25	3.75	8.50
31-41	.85	2.50	6.00
42-45: 42-Pureheart begins	.70	2.00	4.00
46-Origin Pureheart	.70	2.00	4.00
47-50: 50-United Three begin; Superteen, Capt. Hero app.	.50	1.50	3.00
51-59-Pureheart ends	.50	1.50	3.00
60-100: 60-Archie band begins	.35	1.00	2.00
101-150		.50	1.00
151-259		.30	.60

LIFE WITH MILLIE (Formerly A Date With Millie) (Modeling With Millie No. 21 on)
No. 8, Dec, 1960 - No. 20, Dec, 1962
Atlas/Marvel Comics Group

	Good	Fine	Mint
8	1.70	5.00	10.00
9-11	1.20	3.50	7.00
12-20	.85	2.50	5.00

LIFE WITH SNARKY PARKER (TV)
August, 1950
Fox Feature Syndicate

	Good	Fine	Mint
1	6.00	18.00	42.00

LIGHT IN THE FOREST (See 4-Color No. 891)

LIGHTNING COMICS (Formerly Sure-Fire No. 1-3)
No. 4, Dec, 1940 - No. 13(V3No.1), June, 1942
Ace Magazines

	Good	Fine	Mint
4	25.00	75.00	175.00

L.I.F.E. Brigade #1, © Blue Comet

Life Story #5, © FAW

Life With Archie #13, © AP

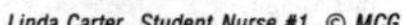
Linda Carter, Student Nurse #1, © MCG

Lippy the Lion... #1, © Hanna-Barbera

Li'l Abner #76, © UFS

LIGHTNING COMICS (continued)

	Good	Fine	Mint
5,6: 6-Dr. Nemesis begins	17.00	51.00	120.00
V2No.1-6: 2-''Flash Lightning'' becomes ''Lash. . .''	15.00	45.00	105.00
V3No.1-Intro. Lightning Girl & The Sword	15.00	45.00	105.00

NOTE: ***Anderson*** *a-V2No.6. Bondage-c V2No.6.*

LI'L (See Little)

LILY OF THE ALLEY IN THE FUNNIES
No date (1920's?) (10¼x15½''; 28 pgs. in color)
Whitman Publishers

	Good	Fine	Mint
W936 - by T. Burke	5.00	15.00	35.00

LIMITED COLLECTORS' EDITION (See Famous 1st Edition & Rudolph the Red Nosed Reindeer; becomes All-New Collectors' Edition)
(No.21-34,51-59: 84 pgs.; No.35-41: 68 pgs.; No.42-50: 60 pgs.)
C-21, Summer, 1973 - No. C-59, 1978 ($1.00) (10x13½'')
National Periodical Publications/DC Comics

	Good	Fine	Mint
nn(C-20)-Rudolph	.70	2.00	4.00
C-21: Shazam (TV); Captain Marvel Jr. reprint by Raboy	.50	1.50	3.00
C-22: Tarzan; complete origin reprinted from No. 207-210; all Kubert	.50	1.50	3.00
C-23: House of Mystery; Wrightson, Adams, Wood, Toth, Orlando-a	.35	1.00	2.00
C-24: Rudolph The Red-nosed Reindeer	.35	1.00	2.00
C-25: Batman; Adams-c/a	.50	1.50	3.00
C-27: Shazam (TV)	.35	1.00	2.00
C-29: Tarzan; reprints ''Return of Tarzan'' from No. 219-223 by Kubert	.50	1.50	3.00
C-31: Superman; origin-r; Adams-a	.50	1.50	3.00
C-32: Ghosts (new-a)	.35	1.00	2.00
C-33: Rudolph The Red-nosed Reindeer (new-a)	.35	1.00	2.00
C-34: Xmas with the Super-Heroes; unpublished Angel & Ape story by Oksner & Wood	.50	1.50	3.00
C-35: Shazam; cover features TV's Captain Marvel, Jackson Bostwick (TV)	.35	1.00	2.00
C-36: The Bible; all new adaptation beginning with Genesis by Kubert, Redondo & Mayer	.50	1.50	3.00
C-37: Batman; r-1946 Sundays	.35	1.00	2.00
C-38: Superman; 1 pg. Adams	.35	1.00	2.00
C-39: Secret Origins/Super Villains; Adams-a(r)	.35	1.00	2.00
C-40: Dick Tracy by Gould featuring Flattop; newspaper-r from 12/21/43 - 5/17/44	.50	1.50	3.00
C-41: Super Friends; Toth-c/a	.35	1.00	2.00
C-42: Rudolph	.35	1.00	2.00
C-43: Christmas with the Super-Heroes; Wrightson, S&K, Adams-a	.50	1.50	3.00
C-44: Batman; Adams-r; painted-c	.35	1.00	2.00
C-45: Secret Origins/Super Villains; Flash-r/105	.35	1.00	2.00
C-46: Justice League of America; 3 pg. Toth-a	.50	1.50	3.00
C-47: Superman Salutes the Bicentennial (Tomahawk interior); 2 pgs. new-a	.25	.75	1.50
C-48: The Superman-Flash Race; 6 pgs. Adams-a	.35	1.00	2.00
C-49: Superboy & the Legion of Super-Heroes	.35	1.00	2.00
C-50: Rudolph The Red-nosed Reindeer	.25	.75	1.50
C-51: Batman; Adams-c/a	.50	1.50	3.00
C-52: The Best of DC; Adams-c/a; Toth, Kubert-a	.35	1.00	2.00
C-57: Welcome Back, Kotter-r(TV)(5/78)	.25	.75	1.50
C-59: Batman's Strangest Cases; Adams, Wrightson-r; Adams/Wrightson-c	.35	1.00	2.00

NOTE: *All-r with exception of some special features and covers.* ***Aparo*** *a-52r; c-37.* ***Giordano*** *a-39, 45.* ***Grell*** *c-49.* ***Infantino*** *a-25, 39, 44, 45, 52.*

LINDA (Phantom Lady No. 5 on)
Apr-May, 1954 - No. 4, Oct-Nov, 1954
Ajax-Farrell Publ. Co.

	Good	Fine	Mint
1-Kamenish-a	5.75	17.25	40.00
2-Lingerie panel	3.85	11.50	27.00
3,4	3.65	11.00	25.00

LINDA CARTER, STUDENT NURSE
Sept, 1961 - No. 9, Jan, 1963
Atlas Comics (AMI)

	Good	Fine	Mint
1	1.00	3.00	7.00
2-9	.55	1.65	4.00

LINDA LARK
Oct-Dec, 1961 - No. 8, Aug-Oct, 1963
Dell Publishing Co.

	Good	Fine	Mint
1	1.00	3.00	7.00
2-8	.55	1.65	4.00

LINUS, THE LIONHEARTED (TV)
September, 1965
Gold Key

	Good	Fine	Mint
1 (10155-509)	1.50	4.50	10.00

LION, THE (See Movie Comics)

LION OF SPARTA (See Movie Classics)

LIPPY THE LION AND HARDY HAR HAR (TV)
March, 1963 (Hanna-Barbera)
Gold Key

	Good	Fine	Mint
1 (10049-303)	1.75	5.25	12.00

LI'L ABNER (See Comics on Parade)
1939 - 1940
United Features Syndicate

	Good	Fine	Mint
Single Series 4 ('39)	25.00	75.00	175.00
Single Series 18 ('40) (No. 18 on inside, No. 2 on cover)	20.00	60.00	140.00

LI'L ABNER (Al Capp's) (See Oxydol-Dreft)
No. 61, Dec, 1947 - No. 97, Jan, 1955
Harvey Publ. No. 61-69 (2/49)/Toby Press No. 70 on

	Good	Fine	Mint
61(No.1)-Wolverton-a	10.00	30.00	70.00
62-65	7.00	21.00	50.00
66,67,69,70	6.00	18.00	42.00
68-Full length Fearless Fosdick story	7.00	21.00	50.00
71-74,76,80	4.35	13.00	30.00
75,77-79,86,91-All with Kurtzman art; 91 reprints No. 77	5.50	16.50	38.00
81-85,87-90,92-94,96,97: 93-reprints No. 71	3.75	11.25	26.00
95-Full length Fearless Fosdick story	5.50	16.50	38.00
. . .& the Creatures from Drop-Outer Space-nn (Job Corps giveaway; 36pgs., in color	4.35	13.00	30.00
. . .Joins the Navy (1950) (Toby Press Premium)	4.35	13.00	30.00
. . .by Al Capp Giveaway (Circa 1955, nd)	4.35	13.00	30.00

NOTE: ***Powell*** *a-61, 65.*

LI'L ABNER
1951
Toby Press

	Good	Fine	Mint
1	5.00	15.00	35.00

LI'L ABNER'S DOGPATCH (See Al Capp's. . .)

LITTLE AL OF THE F.B.I.
No. 10, 1950 (no month) - No. 11, Apr-May, 1951

LITTLE AL OF THE F.B.I. (continued)
Ziff-Davis Publications (Saunders painted-c)

	Good	Fine	Mint
10(1950)	4.00	12.00	28.00
11(1951)	3.35	10.00	23.00

LITTLE AL OF THE SECRET SERVICE
No. 10, 7-8/51; No. 2, 9-10/51; No. 3, Wint., 1951
Ziff-Davis Publications (Saunders painted-c)

	Good	Fine	Mint
10(No.1)-Spanking panel	5.75	17.25	40.00
2,3	3.35	10.00	23.00

LITTLE AMBROSE
September, 1958
Archie Publications

	Good	Fine	Mint
1	6.50	19.50	45.00

LITTLE ANGEL
No. 5, Sept, 1954; No. 6, Sept, 1955 - No. 16, Sept, 1959
Standard (Visual Editions)/Pines

	Good	Fine	Mint
5	2.00	6.00	14.00
6-16	1.00	3.00	7.00

LITTLE ANNIE ROONEY
1935 (48 pgs.; B&W dailies) (25 cents)
David McKay Publications

	Good	Fine	Mint
Book 1-Daily strip-r by Darrell McClure	7.00	21.00	50.00

LITTLE ANNIE ROONEY
1938; Aug, 1948 - No. 3, Oct, 1948
David McKay/St. John/Standard

	Good	Fine	Mint
Feature Books 11 (McKay, 1938)	15.00	45.00	105.00
1 (St. John)	5.00	15.00	35.00
2,3	2.65	8.00	18.00

LITTLE ARCHIE (The Adventures of. . . No.13-on) (Also see Archie Giant Series No. 527,534,538,545,549,556,566)
1956 - No. 180, 2/83 (Giants No. 3-84)
Archie Publications

	Good	Fine	Mint
1-(Scarce)	21.00	62.00	145.00
2	11.00	33.00	75.00
3-5	7.00	21.00	50.00
6-10	5.00	15.00	35.00
11-20	3.35	10.00	23.00
21-30	2.00	6.00	14.00
31-40: Little Pureheart begins No. 40, ends No. 42,44	1.00	3.00	7.00
41-60: 42-Intro. The Little Archies. 59-Little Sabrina begins	.50	1.50	3.00
61-80	.35	1.00	2.00
81-100		.50	1.00
101-180		.40	.80
. . . In Animal Land 1('57)	9.20	27.50	64.00
. . . In Animal Land 17(Winter, 1957-58)-19(Summer,'58)-Formerly Li'l Jinx	4.50	13.50	31.00

LITTLE ARCHIE COMICS DIGEST ANNUAL (. . . Mag. No. 5 on)
Oct, 1977 - Present (Digest-size)
Archie Publications

	Good	Fine	Mint
1(10/77)-Reprints	.35	1.00	2.00
2(4/78)-Adams-a		.50	1.00
3(11/78)-The Fly-r by S&K; Adams-a		.50	1.00
4(4/79) - 23('86)		.50	1.00

LITTLE ARCHIE MYSTERY
Aug, 1963 - No. 2, Oct, 1963
Archie Publications

	Good	Fine	Mint
1	7.50	22.50	45.00
2	3.35	10.00	20.00

LITTLE ASPIRIN (See Wisco)
July, 1949 - No. 3, Dec, 1949 (52 pages)
Marvel Comics (CnPC)

	Good	Fine	Mint
1-Kurtzman-a, 4 pgs.	4.65	14.00	32.00
2-Kurtzman-a, 4 pgs.	2.65	8.00	18.00
3-No Kurtzman	1.30	4.00	9.00

LITTLE AUDREY
April, 1948 - No. 24, June, 1952
St. John Publ.

	Good	Fine	Mint
1	16.00	48.00	110.00
2	8.00	24.00	56.00
3-5	7.00	21.00	50.00
6-10	4.00	12.00	28.00
11-20	2.00	6.00	14.00
21-24	1.30	4.00	9.00

LITTLE AUDREY (See Harvey Hits No. 11,19)
No. 25, Aug, 1952 - No. 53, April, 1957
Harvey Publications

	Good	Fine	Mint
25	4.00	12.00	28.00
26-30: 26-28-Casper app.	2.00	6.00	14.00
31-40: 32-35-Casper app.	1.50	4.50	10.00
41-53	1.00	3.00	7.00

LITTLE AUDREY (. . . Yearbook)
1950 (260 pages) (50 cents)
St. John Publishing Co.

	Good	Fine	Mint
Contains 8 complete 1949 comics rebound; Casper, Alice in Wonderland, Little Audrey, Abbott & Costello, Pinocchio, Moon Mullins, Three Stooges (from Jubilee), Little Annie Rooney app. (Rare)	42.00	125.00	295.00

(Also see All Good & Treasury of Comics)
NOTE: *This book contains remaindered St. John comics; many variations possible.*

LITTLE AUDREY (See Playful. . .)

LITTLE AUDREY & MELVIN (Audrey &. . . No. 62)
May, 1962 - No. 61, Dec, 1973
Harvey Publications

	Good	Fine	Mint
1	5.35	16.00	32.00
2-5	2.75	8.00	16.00
6-10	1.70	5.00	10.00
11-20	1.00	3.00	6.00
21-40	.70	2.00	4.00
41-61	.50	1.50	3.00

LITTLE AUDREY TV FUNTIME
Sept, 1962 - No. 33, Oct, 1971
Harvey Publications

	Good	Fine	Mint
1-Richie Rich app.	3.35	10.00	20.00
2,3: Richie Rich app.	2.00	6.00	12.00
4,5	1.70	5.00	10.00
6-10: 6,10-Giant size	.85	2.50	5.00
11-20: 20-Giant size	.70	2.00	4.00
21-33: 24-Giant size	.50	1.50	3.00

LITTLE BAD WOLF (See 4-Color No. 403,473,564, Walt Disney Showcase No. 21 and Wheaties)

LITTLE BEAVER
No. 211, Jan, 1949 - No. 870, Jan, 1958 (All painted-c)
Dell Publishing Co.

	Good	Fine	Mint
4-Color 211('49)-All Harman-a	2.65	8.00	18.00
4-Color 267,294,332(5/51)	1.75	5.25	12.00

Little Al of the Secret Service #2, © Z-D

Little Annie Rooney #1, © STJ

Little Audrey #21, © HARV

Little Beaver #6, © DELL

Little Dot Dotland #1, © HARV

Little Iodine #7, © DELL

LITTLE BEAVER (continued)

	Good	Fine	Mint
3(10-12/51)-8(1-3/53)	1.50	4.50	10.00
4-Color 483(8-10/53),529	1.50	4.50	10.00
4-Color 612,660,695,744,817,870	1.15	3.50	8.00

LITTLE BIT
March, 1949 - No. 2, 1949
Jubilee/St. John Publishing Co.

1,2	1.30	4.00	9.00

LITTLE DOT (See Tastee-Freez Comics, Li'l Max, Humphrey, and Sad Sack)
Sept, 1953 - No. 164, April, 1976
Harvey Publications

1-Intro. & 1st app. Richie Rich & Little Lotta	50.00	150.00	280.00
2	27.00	80.00	140.00
3	15.00	45.00	90.00
4	11.00	32.50	65.00
5-Origin dots on Little Dot's Dress	12.50	37.50	75.00
6-Richie Rich, Little Lotta, & Little Dot all on cover; 1st Richie Rich cover featured	12.50	37.50	75.00
7-10	5.35	16.00	32.00
11-20	4.35	13.00	26.00
21-40	2.35	7.00	14.00
41-60	1.20	3.50	7.00
61-80	.70	2.00	4.00
81-100	.50	1.50	3.00
101-130	.35	1.00	2.00
131-164		.50	1.00

NOTE: *Richie Rich & Little Lotta in all.*

LITTLE DOT DOTLAND (Dot Dotland No. 62,63)
July, 1962 - No. 61, Dec, 1973
Harvey Publications

1-Richie Rich begins	4.00	12.00	24.00
2,3	2.00	6.00	12.00
4,5	1.70	5.00	10.00
6-10	1.35	4.00	8.00
11-20	1.00	3.00	6.00
21-30	.50	1.50	3.00
31-61	.35	1.00	2.00

LITTLE DOT'S UNCLES & AUNTS (See Harvey Hits No. 4,13,24)
May, 1962 - No. 52, April, 1974
Harvey Publications

1-Richie Rich begins	4.00	12.00	24.00
2,3	2.00	6.00	12.00
4,5	1.70	5.00	10.00
6-10	1.35	4.00	8.00
11-20	1.00	3.00	6.00
21-30: 24,25-Giant size	.50	1.50	3.00
31-52	.35	1.00	2.00

LITTLE EVA
May, 1952 - No. 31, Nov, 1956
St. John Publishing Co.

1	5.00	15.00	35.00
2	2.35	7.00	16.00
3-5	2.00	6.00	14.00
6-10	1.30	4.00	9.00
11-31	1.15	3.50	8.00
3-D 1,2(10/53-11/53); 1-Infinity-c	11.00	33.00	75.00
I.W. Reprint No. 1-3,6-8	.30	.90	1.80
Super Reprint No. 10,12('63),14,16,18('64)	.30	.90	1.80

LITTLE FIR TREE, THE
1942 (8½x11'') (12 pgs. with cover)
W. T. Grant Co. (Christmas giveaway)

8 pg. Kelly-a reprint/Santa Claus Funnies not signed.
(One copy in M sold for $1750.00 in 1986)

LI'L GENIUS (Summer Fun No. 54) (See Blue Bird)
1954 - No. 52, 1/65; No. 53, 10/65; No. 54, 10/85 - No. 55, 1/86
Charlton Comics

	Good	Fine	Mint
1	2.15	6.50	15.00
2	1.15	3.50	8.00
3-16,19,20	1.00	3.00	7.00
17-(68 pgs.)	1.15	3.50	8.00
18-(100 pgs., 10/58)	1.70	5.00	11.50
21-35	.75	2.25	5.00
36-53	.50	1.50	3.00
54,55	.25	.75	1.50

LI'L GHOST
Feb, 1958 - No. 3, Mar, 1959
St. John Publishing Co./Fago No. 1 on

1(St. John)	2.15	6.50	15.00
1(Fago)	1.75	5.25	12.00
2,3	1.00	3.00	7.00

LITTLE GIANT COMICS
7/38 - No. 3, 10/38; No. 4, 2/39 (132 pgs.) (6¾x4½'')
Centaur Publications

1-B&W with color-c	18.00	54.00	125.00
2,3-B&W with color-c	15.00	45.00	105.00
4 (6-5/8x9-3/8'')(68 pgs., B&W inside)	12.00	36.00	84.00

NOTE: ***Gustavson** a-1. **Pinajian** a-4. **Bob Wood** a-1.*

LITTLE GIANT DETECTIVE FUNNIES
Oct, 1938 - No. 4, Jan, 1939 (132 pgs., B&W) (6¾x4½'')
Centaur Publications

1-B&W with color-c	18.00	54.00	125.00
2,3	15.00	45.00	105.00
4(1/39)-B&W; color-c; 68 pgs., 6½x9½''; Eisner-r	15.00	45.00	105.00

LITTLE GIANT MOVIE FUNNIES
Aug, 1938 - No. 2, Oct, 1938 (132 pgs., B&W) (6¾x4½'')
Centaur Publications

1-Ed Wheelan's ''Minute Movies''-r	18.00	54.00	125.00
2-Ed Wheelan's ''Minute Movies''-r	13.00	40.00	90.00

LITTLE GROUCHO (. . . Grouchy No. 2) (See Tippy Terry)
Feb-Mar, 1955 - No. 2, June-July, 1955
Reston Publ. Co.

16, 1	1.75	5.25	12.00
2(6-7/55)	1.00	3.00	7.00

LITTLE HIAWATHA (See 4-Color No. 439,787,901,988)

LITTLE IKE
April, 1953 - No. 4, Oct, 1953
St. John Publishing Co.

1	2.65	8.00	18.00
2	1.35	4.00	9.00
3,4	1.15	3.50	8.00

LITTLE IODINE (See Giant Comic Album)
April, 1949 - No. 56, Apr-June, 1962 (52pgs., 1-4)
Dell Publishing Co.

4-Color 224-By Jimmy Hatlo	3.75	11.25	26.00
4-Color 257	2.85	8.50	20.00
1(3-5/50)	2.85	8.50	20.00
2-5	1.75	5.25	12.00
6-10	1.15	3.50	8.00
11-20	1.00	3.00	7.00

LITTLE IODINE (continued)

	Good	Fine	Mint
21-30	.85	2.50	6.00
31-40	.55	1.65	4.00
41-56	.45	1.35	3.00

LITTLE JACK FROST
1951
Avon Periodicals

	Good	Fine	Mint
1	3.35	10.00	23.00

LI'L JINX (Formerly Ginger?) (Little Archie in Animal Land No. 17)
No. 1(No.11), Nov, 1956 - No. 16, Sept, 1957
Archie Publications

	Good	Fine	Mint
11 (No. 1)	4.00	12.00	28.00
12-16	2.65	8.00	18.00

LI'L JINX (See Archie Giant Series Magazine No. 223)

LI'L JINX CHRISTMAS BAG (See Archie Giant Series Mag. No. 195,206,219)

LI'L JINX GIANT LAUGH-OUT
No. 33, Sept, 1971 - No. 43, Nov, 1973 (52 pgs.)
Archie Publications

	Good	Fine	Mint
33-43	.35	1.00	2.00

(See Archie Giant Series Mag. No. 176,185)

LITTLE JOE (See 4-Color No. 1)

LITTLE JOE
April, 1953
St. John Publishing Co.

	Good	Fine	Mint
1	1.15	3.50	8.00

LITTLE JOHNNY & THE TEDDY BEARS
1907 (10x14") (32 pgs. in color)
Reilly & Britton Co.

	Good	Fine	Mint
By J. R. Bray	13.00	40.00	90.00

LI'L KIDS
8/70 - No. 2, 10/70; No. 3, 11/71 - No. 12, 6/73
Marvel Comics Group

	Good	Fine	Mint
1	.50	1.50	3.00
2-12: 10,11-Calvin app.	.25	.75	1.50

LITTLE KING (See 4-Color No. 494,597,677)

LITTLE KLINKER
1960 (20 pgs.) (slick cover)
Little Klinker Ventures (Montgomery Ward Giveaway)

	Good	Fine	Mint
		1.00	2.00

LITTLE LANA (Formerly Lana)
No. 8, Nov, 1949 - No. 9, Mar, 1950
Marvel Comics (MjMC)

	Good	Fine	Mint
8,9	1.50	4.50	10.00

LITTLE LENNY
June, 1949 - No. 3, Nov, 1949
Marvel Comics (CDS)

	Good	Fine	Mint
1	2.35	7.00	16.00
2,3	1.15	3.50	8.00

LITTLE LIZZIE
6/49 - No. 5, 4/50; 9/53 - No. 3, Jan, 1954
Marvel Comics (PrPI)/Atlas (OMC)

	Good	Fine	Mint
1	2.35	7.00	16.00
2-5	1.15	3.50	8.00
1 (1953)	1.75	5.25	12.00
2,3	.85	2.50	6.00

LITTLE LOTTA (See Harvey Hits No. 10)
11/55 - No. 110, 11/73; No. 111, 9/74 - No. 121, 5/76
Harvey Publications

	Good	Fine	Mint
1-Richie Rich & Little Dot begin	17.00	50.00	100.00
2,3	8.35	25.00	50.00
4,5	5.00	15.00	30.00
6-10	3.35	10.00	20.00
11-20	2.00	6.00	12.00
21-40	1.35	4.00	8.00
41-60	1.00	3.00	6.00
61-80	.50	1.50	3.00
81-100	.35	1.00	2.00
101-121	.25	.75	1.50

LITTLE LOTTA FOODLAND
9/63 - No. 14, 10/67; No. 15, 10/68 - No. 29, Oct, 1972
Harvey Publications

	Good	Fine	Mint
1	4.00	12.00	24.00
2,3	2.35	7.00	14.00
4,5	2.00	6.00	12.00
6-10	1.50	4.50	9.00
11-20	1.00	3.00	6.00
21-29	.70	2.00	4.00

LITTLE LULU (Formerly Marge's. . .)
No. 207, Sept., 1972 - No. 268, April, 1984
Gold Key 207-257/Whitman 258 on

	Good	Fine	Mint
207,209,220-Stanley-r	.50	1.50	3.00
208,210-219	.35	1.00	2.00
221-240,242-253	.25	.75	1.50
241,254,255,263,265,268-Stanley-r	.25	.75	1.50
256-262,264,266-267		.50	1.00

LITTLE MARY MIXUP (See Single Series No. 10,26)

LITTLE MAX COMICS (Joe Palooka's Pal; see Joe Palooka)
Oct, 1949 - No. 73, Nov, 1961
Harvey Publications

	Good	Fine	Mint
1-Infinity-c; Little Dot begins	7.00	21.00	50.00
2-Little Dot app.	3.50	10.50	24.00
3-Little Dot app.	2.75	8.00	19.00
4-10: 5-Little Dot app., 1pg.	1.50	4.50	10.00
11-20	1.00	3.00	7.00
21-68,70-72: 23-Little Dot app. 38-r/20	.75	2.25	5.00
69,73-Richie Rich app.	.85	2.50	6.00

LI'L MENACE
Dec, 1958 - No. 3, May, 1959
Fago Magazine Co.

	Good	Fine	Mint
1-Peter Rabbit app.	1.75	5.25	12.00
2-Peter Rabbit (Vincent Fago's)	1.00	3.00	7.00
3	.85	2.50	6.00

LITTLE MISS MUFFET
Dec, 1948 - No. 13, March, 1949
Standard Comics/King Features Synd.

	Good	Fine	Mint
11-Strip reprints; Fanny Cory-a	3.00	9.00	21.00
12,13-Strip reprints; Fanny Cory-a	1.70	5.00	11.50

LITTLE MISS SUNBEAM COMICS
June-July, 1950 - No. 4, Dec-Jan, 1950-51
Magazine Enterprises/Quality Bakers of America

	Good	Fine	Mint
1	4.00	12.00	28.00
2	2.65	8.00	18.00
3,4	2.35	7.00	16.00
. . .Advs. In Space ('55)	1.30	4.00	9.00

Little Jack Frost #1, © AVON

Little Lizzie #2, © MCG

Little Lotta #21, © HARV

Little Miss Sunbeam 1957 Bread Giveaway

Little Orphan Annie #2 ('27 C&L), © News Synd.

Little Scouts #4, © DELL

LITTLE MISS SUNBEAM COMICS (cont'd.)

	Good	Fine	Mint
Bread Giveaway 1-4(Quality Bakers, 1949-50)-14 pgs. each	1.30	4.00	9.00
Bread Giveaway (1957,61; 16 pgs, reg. size)	1.00	3.00	7.00

LITTLE MONSTERS, THE (See March of Comics No. 423 & Three Stooges No. 17)
Nov, 1964 - No. 44, Feb, 1978
Gold Key

	Good	Fine	Mint
1	1.00	3.00	6.00
2-10	.50	1.50	3.00
11-20	.30	.80	1.60
21-44: 20,34-39,43-reprints		.40	.80

LITTLE NEMO (See Cocomalt, Future Comics, Help, Jest, Kayo, Punch, Red Seal, & Superworld; most by Winsor McCay Jr., son of famous artist) (Other McCay books: see Little Sammy Sneeze & Dreams of the Rarebit Fiend)

LITTLE NEMO (. . . in Slumberland)
1906, 1909 (Sunday strip reprints in color) (cardboard covers)
Doffield & Co.(1906)/Cupples & Leon Co.(1909)

	Good	Fine	Mint
1906-11x16½'' in color by Winsor McCay; 30 pgs. (Very Rare)	120.00	300.00	700.00
1909-10x14'' in color by Winsor McCay (Very Rare)	100.00	250.00	600.00

LITTLE NEMO (. . . in Slumberland)
1945 (28 pgs.; 11x7¼''; B&W)
McCay Features/Nostalgia Press('69)

	Good	Fine	Mint
1905 & 1911 reprints by Winsor McCay	2.65	8.00	18.00
1969-70 (exact reprint)	1.50	4.00	8.00

LITTLE ORPHAN ANNIE (See Annie, Marvel Super Special, Merry Christmas. . ., & Super Book No. 7, 11, 23)

LITTLE ORPHAN ANNIE (See Treasury Box of. . .)
1926 - 1934 (Daily strip reprints) (7x8¾'') (B&W)
Cupples & Leon Co.

(Hardcover Editions, 100 pages)

	Good	Fine	Mint
1(1926)-Little Orphan Annie	13.50	40.50	95.00
2('27)-In the Circus	11.00	33.00	75.00
3('28)-The Haunted House	11.00	33.00	75.00
4('29)-Bucking the World	11.00	33.00	75.00
5('30)-Never Say Die	11.00	33.00	75.00
6('31)-Shipwrecked	11.00	33.00	75.00
7('32)-A Willing Helper	8.00	24.00	56.00
8('33)-In Cosmic City	8.00	24.00	56.00
9('34)-Uncle Dan	11.00	33.00	75.00

NOTE: *Hardcovers with dust jackets are worth 20-50 percent more; the earlier the book, the higher the percentage. Each book reprints dailies from the previous year.*

LITTLE ORPHAN ANNIE
No. 7, 1937 - No. 3, Sept-Nov, 1948
David McKay Publ./Dell Publishing Co.

	Good	Fine	Mint
Feature Books(McKay) 7-('37) (Very Rare)	68.00	205.00	475.00
4-Color 12(1941)	25.00	75.00	175.00
4-Color 18('43)-Flag-c	19.00	57.00	132.00
4-Color 52('44)	13.00	40.00	90.00
4-Color 76('45)	11.00	33.00	76.00
4-Color 107('46)	9.50	28.50	66.00
4-Color 152('47)	7.00	21.00	50.00
4-Color 206(12/48)	5.00	15.00	35.00
1(3-5/48)	12.00	36.00	84.00
2,3	7.00	21.00	50.00
Junior Commandos Giveaway(same cover as 4-Color No. 18, K.K. Publ.(Big Shoe Store); same back cover as '47 Popped Wheat giveaway; 16 pgs.	14.50	43.50	100.00
Popped Wheat Giveaway('47)-16 pgs. full color; '40 reprints	.85	2.50	6.00
Quaker Giveaway(1940)	6.00	18.00	42.00
Quaker Giveaway(Full color-20 pgs., 1941); ''LOA and the Rescue,'' ''LOA and the Kidnappers,'' '' Advs. of LOA'' each. . . .	5.00	15.00	35.00
Sparkies Giveaway(Full color-20 pgs., 1942); ''LOA and Mr. Grudge'' and ''LOA and the Great Am''	3.35	10.00	23.00

LI'L PALS
Sept, 1972 - No. 5, May, 1973
Marvel Comics Group

	Good	Fine	Mint
1-5		.40	.80

LI'L PAN
No. 6, Dec-Jan, 1947 - No. 8, Apr-May, 1947
Fox Features Syndicate

	Good	Fine	Mint
6	2.00	6.00	14.00
7,8	1.50	4.50	10.00

LITTLE PEOPLE (See 4-Color No. 485, 573, 633, 692, 753, 809, 868, 908, 959, 1024, 1062)

LITTLE RASCALS (See 4-Color No. 674, 778, 825, 883, 936, 974, 1030, 1079, 1137, 1174, 1224, 1297)

LI'L RASCAL TWINS (Formerly Nature Boy)
1957 - No. 18, Jan, 1960
Charlton Comics

	Good	Fine	Mint
6-Li'l Genius & Tomboy in all	1.30	4.00	9.00
7-18	.75	2.25	5.00

LITTLE ROQUEFORT
June, 1952 - No. 9, Oct, 1953; No. 10, Summer, 1958
St. John Publishing Co./Pines No. 10

	Good	Fine	Mint
1	2.65	8.00	18.00
2	1.30	4.00	9.00
3-10	1.15	3.50	8.00

LITTLE SAD SACK (See Harvey Hits No. 73,76,79,81,83)
Oct, 1964 - No. 19, Nov, 1967
Harvey Publications

	Good	Fine	Mint
1-Richie Rich app. cover only	1.35	4.00	8.00
2-19	.35	1.00	2.00

LITTLE SAMMY SNEEZE
1905 (28 pgs. in color; 11x16½'')
New York Herald Co.

	Good	Fine	Mint
By Winsor McCay (Rare)	150.00	400.00	750.00

NOTE: *Rarely found in fine to mint condition.*

LITTLE SCOUTS
No. 321, Mar, 1951 - No. 587, Oct, 1954
Dell Publishing Co.

	Good	Fine	Mint
4-Color No. 321 ('51)	1.30	4.00	9.00
2(10-12/51) - 6(10-12/52)	.85	2.50	6.00
4-Color No. 462,506,550,587	.85	2.50	6.00

LITTLE SHOP OF HORRORS SPECIAL
Feb, 1987
DC Comics

	Good	Fine	Mint
1-Colan-a	.25	.75	1.50

LITTLE SPUNKY
No date (1963?) (10 cents)
I. W. Enterprises

	Good	Fine	Mint
1-Reprint	.30	.80	1.60

LITTLE STOOGES, THE (The Three Stooges' Sons)
Sept, 1972 - No. 7, Mar, 1974
Gold Key

	Good	Fine	Mint
1-Norman Maurer cover/stories in all	.70	2.00	4.00
2-7	.35	1.00	2.00

LITTLEST OUTLAW (See 4-Color No. 609)

LITTLEST SNOWMAN, THE
No. 755, 12/56; No. 864, 12/57; 12-2/1963-64
Dell Publishing Co.

	Good	Fine	Mint
4-Color No. 755,864, 1(1964)	1.50	4.50	10.00

LI'L TOMBOY (Formerly Fawcett's Funny Animals)
V14No.92, 10/56; No. 93, 3/57 - No. 107, 2/60
Charlton Comics

	Good	Fine	Mint
V14No.92	1.75	5.25	12.00
93-107: 97-Atomic Bunny app.	.85	2.50	6.00

LI'L WILLIE COMICS (Formerly & becomes Willie Comics No. 22 on)
July, 1949 - No. 21, Sept, 1949
Marvel Comics (MgPC)

	Good	Fine	Mint
20,21: 20-Little Aspirin app.	1.30	4.00	9.00

LIVE IT UP
1973, 1976 (39-49 cents)
Spire Christian Comics (Fleming H. Revell Co.)

	Good	Fine	Mint
nn		.40	.80

LIVING BIBLE, THE
Fall, 1945 - No. 3, Spring, 1946
Living Bible Corp.

	Good	Fine	Mint
1-Life of Paul	6.50	19.50	45.00
2-Joseph & His Brethren	4.35	13.00	30.00
3-Chaplains of War (classic-c)	9.00	27.00	62.00

NOTE: *All have L. B. Cole -c.*

LLOYD LLEWELLYN
1986 - Present
Fantagraphics Books

	Good	Fine	Mint
1	.45	1.25	2.50
2-5	.35	1.00	2.00

LOBO
Dec, 1965 - No. 2, Oct, 1966
Dell Publishing Co.

	Good	Fine	Mint
1,2	.85	2.50	6.00

LOCO (Magazine) (Satire)
Aug, 1958 - V1No.3, Jan, 1959
Satire Publications

	Good	Fine	Mint
V1No.1-Chic Stone-a	.85	2.50	5.00
V1No.2,3-Severin-a, 2 pgs. Davis; 3-Heath-a	.50	1.50	3.00

LOGAN'S RUN
Jan, 1977 - No. 7, July, 1977
Marvel Comics Group

	Good	Fine	Mint
1		.40	.80
2-7		.25	.50

NOTE: *Austin a-6i. Gulacy c-6. Kane c-7p. Perez a-1-5p; c-1-5p. Sutton a-6p, 7p.*

LOIS LANE (Also see Superman's Girlfriend . . .)
Aug, 1986 - No. 2, Sept, 1986 (52 pgs.)
DC Comics

	Good	Fine	Mint
1,2-Morrow c/a	.25	.75	1.50

LOLLY AND PEPPER
No. 832, Sept, 1957 - July, 1962
Dell Publishing Co.

	Good	Fine	Mint
4-Color 832	1.50	4.50	10.00
4-Color 940,978,1086,1206	1.15	3.50	8.00
01-459-207	1.15	3.50	8.00

LOMAX (See Police Action)

LONE EAGLE (The Flame No. 5 on)
Apr-May, 1954 - No. 4, Oct-Nov, 1954
Ajax/Farrell Publications

	Good	Fine	Mint
1	3.00	9.00	21.00
2-4: 2,3-Bondage-c	1.75	5.25	12.00

LONELY HEART (Dear Heart No. 15 on)
No. 9, March, 1955 - No. 14, Feb, 1956
Ajax/Farrell Publ. (Excellent Publ.)

	Good	Fine	Mint
9-Kamenesque-a; lingerie panel	2.65	8.00	18.00
10-14	1.30	4.00	9.00

LONE RANGER, THE (See Aurora, Dell Giants, Feature Books No. 21, 24(McKay), Future Comics, & March of Comics No. 165, 174, 193, 208, 225, 238, 310, 322, 338, 350)

LONE RANGER, THE
No. 3, 1939 - No. 167, Feb, 1947
Dell Publishing Co.

	Good	Fine	Mint
Large Feat. Comic 3('39)-Heigh-Yo Silver; text with ill. by Robert Weisman	35.00	105.00	245.00
Large Feat. Comic 7('39)-Ill. by Henry Valleley; Hi-Yo Silver the Lone Ranger to the Rescue	47.00	141.00	330.00
4-Color 82('45)	22.00	65.00	154.00
4-Color 98('45),118('46)	19.00	57.00	132.00
4-Color 125('46),136('47)	13.00	40.00	90.00
4-Color 151,167('47)	11.00	33.00	75.00

LONE RANGER COMICS, THE (10 cents)
1939 (inside) (shows 1938 on cover) (68 pgs. in color; regular size)
Lone Ranger, Inc. (Ice cream mail order)

	Good	Fine	Mint
(Scarce)-not by Valleley	45.00	135.00	315.00

LONE RANGER, THE (Movie, radio & TV; Clayton Moore starred as L. Ranger in the movies; No. 1-37: strip reprints)(See Dell Giants)
Jan-Feb, 1948 - No. 145, May-July, 1962
Dell Publishing Co.

	Good	Fine	Mint
1 (36pgs.)-The L. Ranger, his horse Silver, companion Tonto & his horse Scout begin	35.00	105.00	245.00
2 (52pgs. begin, end No. 41)	18.00	54.00	125.00
3-5	15.00	45.00	105.00
6,7,9,10	13.00	40.00	90.00
8-Origin retold; indian back-c begin, end No. 35	14.50	43.50	100.00
11-20: 11-"Young Hawk" Indian boy serial begins, ends 145	8.00	24.00	56.00
21,22,24-31: 21-Reprint. 31-1st Mask logo	6.50	19.50	45.00
23-Origin retold	9.00	27.00	62.00
32-37: 32-Painted-c begin. 36-Animal photo back-c begin, end No. 49. 37-Last newspaper-r issue; new outfit	5.00	15.00	35.00
38-41 (All 52pgs.)	3.50	10.50	24.00
42-50 (36pgs.)	2.65	8.00	18.00
51-74 (52pgs.): 71-Blank inside-c	2.85	8.50	20.00
75-99: 76-Flag-c. 79-X-mas-c	2.35	7.00	16.00
100	2.85	8.50	20.00
101-111: Last painted-c	2.00	6.00	14.00
112-Clayton Moore photo-c begin, end No. 145	9.00	27.00	62.00
113-117	5.00	15.00	35.00
118-Origin Lone Ranger, Tonto, & Silver retold; Special anniversary issue	8.00	24.00	56.00
119-145: 139-Last issue by Fran Striker	4.00	12.00	28.00
Cheerios Giveaways 1-"The Lone Ranger, His Mask & How He Met Tonto." 2-"The Lone Ranger & the Story of Silver" (1954) each. . . .	4.00	12.00	28.00

Doll Giveaways (Gabriel Ind.)(1973, 3¼x5")-"The Story of The L.R."

The Living Bible #2, © Living Bible

Lone Eagle #4, © AJAX

The Lone Ranger #1, © Lone Ranger

Lone Ranger's Famous Horse... #3, © L. Ranger

Long Bow #2, © FH

Looney Tunes #15 (1st Series), © L. Schlesinger

THE LONE RANGER (continued) — Good / Fine / Mint
& The Carson City Bank Robbery.'' .75 2.25 5.00
How the L. R. Captured Silver Book(1936)-Silvercup Bread giveaway 25.00 75.00 175.00
...In Milk for Big Mike(1955, Dairy Association giveaway) 6.00 18.00 42.00
Merita Bread giveaway('54; 16 pgs.; 5x7¼'')-''How to Be a L. R. Health & Safety Scout'' 6.00 18.00 42.00
9.00 27.00 63.00

NOTE: ***Hank Hartman*** *painted c(signed)-65, 66, 70, 75, 82; unsigned-64?, 67-69?, 71, 72, 73?, 74?, 76-78, 80, 81, 83-91, 92?, 93-111.* ***Ernest Nordli*** *painted c(signed)-42, 50, 52, 53, 56, 59, 60; unsigned-39-41, 44-49, 51, 54, 55, 57, 58, 61-63?*

LONE RANGER, THE
9/64 - No. 16, 12/69; No. 17, 11/72; No. 18, 9/74 - No. 28, 3/77
Gold Key (Reprints No. 13-20)

1-Retells origin 2.15 6.50 15.00
2 1.30 4.00 9.00
3-10: Small Bear-r in No. 6-10 1.00 3.00 7.00
11-17: Small Bear-r in No. 11,12 .85 2.50 6.00
18-28 .55 1.65 4.00
Golden West 1(30029-610)-Giant, 10/66-r most Golden West No. 3-including Clayton Moore photo front/back-c 3.50 10.50 24.00

LONE RANGER'S COMPANION TONTO, THE (TV)
No. 312, Jan, 1951 - No. 33, Nov-Jan/58-59 (All painted-c)
Dell Publishing Co.

4-Color 312(1951) 6.00 18.00 42.00
2(8-10/51),3: (No. 2 titled 'Tonto') 3.50 10.50 24.00
4-10 2.00 6.00 14.00
11-20 1.75 5.25 12.00
21-33 1.30 4.00 9.00

NOTE: ***Ernest Nordli*** *painted c(signed)-2, 7; unsigned-3-6, 8-11, 12?, 13, 14, 18?, 22-24? See Aurora Comic Booklets.*

LONE RANGER'S FAMOUS HORSE HI-YO SILVER, THE (TV)
No. 369, Jan, 1952 - No. 36, Oct-Dec, 1960 (All painted-c)
Dell Publishing Co.

4-Color 369-Silver's origin as told by The L.R. 3.75 11.25 26.00
4-Color 392(4/52) 2.35 7.00 16.00
3(7-9/52)-10(4-6/52) 1.50 4.50 10.00
11-36 1.15 3.50 8.00

LONE RIDER
April, 1951 - No. 26, July, 1955 (36pgs., 3-on)
Superior Comics(Farrell Publications)

1 (52pgs.)-The Lone Rider & his horse Lightnin begin; Kamenish-a begins 5.00 15.00 35.00
2 (52pgs.)-The Golden Arrow begins (origin) 3.00 9.00 21.00
3-6: 6-Last Golden Arrow 2.35 7.00 16.00
7-Swift Arrow begins; origin of his shield 2.65 8.00 18.00
8-Origin Swift Arrow 3.50 10.50 24.00
9,10 1.85 5.50 13.00
11-14 1.50 4.50 10.00
15-Reprints origin Golden Arrow from No. 2, changing name to Swift Arrow 1.85 5.50 13.00
16-20,22-26: 23-Apache Kid app. 1.15 3.50 8.00
21-3-D effect-c 3.35 10.00 23.00

LONG BOW (...Indian Boy)
1951 - No. 9, Wint, 1952/53
Fiction House Magazines (Real Adventures Publ.)

1 4.00 12.00 28.00
2 2.65 8.00 18.00
3-9 2.00 6.00 14.00

LONGEST DAY (See Movie Classics)

LONG JOHN SILVER & THE PIRATES (Formerly Terry & the Pirates)
No. 30, Aug, 1956 - No. 32, March, 1957 (TV)
Charlton Comics — Good / Fine / Mint
30-32: Whitman-c 2.00 6.00 14.00

LONGSHOT
Sept, 1985 - No. 6, Feb, 1986 (Limited-series)
Marvel Comics Group

1-Arthur Adams-a .60 1.80 3.60
2-5 .40 1.20 2.40
6-Double size .50 1.50 3.00

LOONEY TUNES AND MERRIE MELODIES COMICS (''Looney Tunes'' No. 166 (8/55) on)
1941 - No. 246, July-Sept, 1962
Dell Publishing Co.

1-Porky Pig, Bugs Bunny, Elmer Fudd, Mary Jane & Sniffles, Pat, Patsy and Pete begin (1st comic book app.). Bugs Bunny story by Win Smith (early Mickey Mouse artist) 85.00 255.00 595.00
2 (11/41) 45.00 135.00 315.00
3-Kandi the Cave Kid begins by Walt Kelly; also in No. 4-6,8,11,15 40.00 120.00 280.00
4-Kelly-a 35.00 105.00 245.00
5-Bugs Bunny The Super Rabbit app. (1st funny animal super hero?) Kelly-a 25.00 75.00 175.00
6,8-Kelly-a 18.00 54.00 125.00
7,9,10 13.00 40.00 90.00
11,15-Kelly-a; 15-X-Mas-c 13.00 40.00 90.00
12-14,16-19 11.00 33.00 75.00
20-25: Pat, Patsy & Pete by Kelly in all 11.00 33.00 75.00
26-30 7.75 23.00 54.00
31-40 5.75 17.00 40.00
41-50 3.50 10.50 24.00
51-60 2.65 8.00 18.00
61-80 1.75 5.25 12.00
81-99: 87-X-Mas-c 1.50 4.50 10.00
100 1.75 5.25 12.00
101-120 1.30 4.00 9.00
121-150 1.00 3.00 7.00
151-200 .75 2.25 5.00
201-246 .45 1.35 3.00

LOONEY TUNES (2nd Series)
April, 1975 - No. 47, July, 1984
Gold Key/Whitman

1 .50 1.00
2-47: Reprints-No. 1-4,16; 38-46(⅓r) .30 .60

LOONY SPORTS (Magazine)
Spring, 1975 (68 pages)
3-Strikes Publishing Co.

1-Sports satire .30 .80 1.60

LOOY DOT DOPE (See Single Series No. 13)

LORD JIM (See Movie Comics)

LORDS OF THE ULTRA-REALM
June, 1986 - No. 6, Nov, 1986 (mini-series)
DC Comics

1 .55 1.65 3.30
2-6 .30 .85 1.70

LORNA THE JUNGLE GIRL (...Jungle Queen No. 1-5)
July, 1953 - No. 26, Aug, 1957
Atlas Comics (NPI 1/OMC 2-11/NPI 12-26)

1-Origin 8.00 24.00 56.00
2-Intro. & 1st app. Greg Knight 4.65 14.00 32.00
3-5 3.85 11.50 27.00
6-11: 11-Last pre-code (1/55) 3.35 10.00 23.00
12-16,17,19-26 2.50 7.50 17.00

LORNA THE JUNGLE GIRL (continued)

	Good	Fine	Mint
18-Williamson/Colleta-c	3.85	11.50	27.00

NOTE: ***Everett*** *a-24, 25; c-23, 24, 26.* ***Heath*** *c-6, 7.* ***Maneely*** *c-12, 15.* ***Romita*** *a-20, 22.* ***Shores*** *a-16; c-13, 16.* ***Tuska*** *a-6.*

LOSERS SPECIAL
Sept, 1985 ($1.25 cover) (One Shot)
DC Comics

	Good	Fine	Mint
1-Capt. Storm, Gunner & Sarge; Crisis x-over		.65	1.30

LOST IN SPACE (Space Family Robinson . . ., on Space Station One)
(Formerly Space Family Robinson, see Gold Key Champion)
No. 37, 10/73 - No. 54, 11/78; No. 55, 3/81 - No. 59, 5/82
Gold Key

	Good	Fine	Mint
37-48	.35	1.00	2.00
49-59: Reprints-No. 49,50,55-59		.50	1.00

NOTE: ***Spiegle*** *a-37-59. All have painted-c.*

LOST WORLD, THE (See 4-Color No. 1145)

LOST WORLDS
No. 5, Oct, 1952 - No. 6, Dec, 1952
Standard Comics

	Good	Fine	Mint
5-''Alice in Terrorland'' by Toth; J. Katz-a	10.00	30.00	70.00
6-Toth-a	6.50	19.50	45.00

LOTS 'O' FUN COMICS
1940's? (5 cents) (heavy stock; blue covers)
Robert Allen Co.

nn-Contents can vary; Felix, Planet Comics known; contents would determine value. Similar to Up-To-Date Comics. Remainders - re-packaged.

LOU GEHRIG (See The Pride of the Yankees)

LOVE ADVENTURES (Actual Confessions No. 13)
10/49; No. 2, 1/50; No. 3, 2/51 - No. 12, 8/52
Marvel (IPS)/Atlas Comics (MPI)

	Good	Fine	Mint
1	2.85	8.50	20.00
2-Powell-a; Tyrone Power, Gene Tierney photo-c	2.85	8.50	20.00
3-8,10-12: 8-Robinson-a	1.30	4.00	9.00
9-Everett-a	1.85	5.50	13.00

LOVE AND MARRIAGE
March, 1952 - No. 16, Sept, 1954
Superior Comics Ltd.

	Good	Fine	Mint
1	3.75	11.25	26.00
2	1.85	5.50	13.00
3-10	1.30	4.00	9.00
11-16	1.15	3.50	8.00
I.W. Reprint No. 1,2,8,11,14	.30	.80	1.60
Super Reprint No. 10('63),15,17('64)	.30	.80	1.60

NOTE: *All issues have Kamenish art.*

LOVE AND ROCKETS
July, 1982 - Present (Adults only)
Fantagraphics Books

	Good	Fine	Mint
1-B&W-c ($2.95)	33.00	100.00	200.00
1 (Fall, '82; 2nd printing; color-c)	18.00	55.00	110.00
2	7.00	21.00	42.00
3-5	4.15	12.50	25.00
6-10	1.30	4.00	8.00
11-15	.50	1.50	3.00
16-20	.40	1.25	2.50

LOVE AND ROMANCE
Sept, 1971 - No. 24, Sept, 1975
Charlton Comics

	Good	Fine	Mint
1		.30	.60
2-24		.15	.30

LOVE AT FIRST SIGHT
Oct, 1949 - No. 42, Aug, 1956 (Photo-c 21-42)
Ace Magazines (RAR Publ. Co./Periodical House)

	Good	Fine	Mint
1-Painted-c	3.75	11.25	26.00
2-Painted-c	1.85	5.50	13.00
3-10: 4-Painted-c	1.30	4.00	9.00
11-20	1.15	3.50	8.00
21-33: 33-Last pre-code	1.00	3.00	7.00
34-42: 36,37-Photo-c	.85	2.50	6.00

LOVE BUG, THE (See Movie Comics)

LOVE CLASSICS
Nov, 1949 - No. 2, Feb, 1950
A Lover's Magazine/Marvel Comics

	Good	Fine	Mint
1,2: 2-Virginia Mayo photo-c; 30 pg. story 'I Was a Small Town Flirt'	3.75	11.25	26.00

LOVE CONFESSIONS
Oct, 1949 - No. 54, Dec, 1956 (Photo-c 6,11-18,21)
Quality Comics Group

	Good	Fine	Mint
1-Ward c/a, 9 pgs; Gustavson-a	13.50	40.50	95.00
2-Gustavson-a	4.65	14.00	32.00
3	3.35	10.00	23.00
4-Crandall-a	4.65	14.00	32.00
5-Ward-a, 7 pgs.	5.50	16.50	38.00
6,7,9	1.70	5.00	11.50
8-Ward-a	4.65	14.00	32.00
10-Ward-a(2)	4.65	14.00	32.00
11-13,15,16,18	1.70	5.00	11.50
14,17,19,22-Ward-a; 17-Faith Domerque photo-c	3.85	11.50	27.00
20-Baker-a, Ward-a(2)	4.65	14.00	32.00
21,23-28,30-38,40,41: Last precode, 2/55	1.15	3.50	8.00
29-Ward-a	3.65	11.00	25.00
39-Matt Baker-a	1.70	5.00	11.50
42-44,46-48,50-54: 47-Ward-c?	1.00	3.00	7.00
45-Ward-a	2.15	6.50	15.00
49-Baker c/a	2.65	8.00	18.00

LOVE DIARY
July, 1949 - No. 48, Oct, 1955 (Photo-c 1-24,27,29)
Our Publishing Co./Toytown/Patches

	Good	Fine	Mint
1-Krigstein-a	5.75	17.25	40.00
2,3-Krigstein & Mort Leav-a in each	3.75	11.25	26.00
4-8	1.70	5.00	11.50
9,10-Everett-a	1.85	5.50	13.00
11-20	1.30	4.00	9.00
21-30,32-48	1.00	3.00	7.00
31-J. Buscema headlights-c	1.15	3.50	8.00

LOVE DIARY
September, 1949
Quality Comics Group

	Good	Fine	Mint
1-Ward-c, 9 pgs.	11.00	33.00	76.00

LOVE DIARY
July, 1958 - No. 102, Dec, 1976
Charlton Comics

	Good	Fine	Mint
1	1.75	5.25	12.00
2	.85	2.50	6.00
3-5,7-10	.55	1.65	4.00
6-Torres-a	1.15	3.50	8.00

Love Adventures #11, © MCG

Love at First Sight #21, © ACE

Love Confessions #16, © QUA

Love Experiences #1, © ACE

Love Lessons #3, © HARV

Love Problems & Advice Ill. #3, © HARV

LOVE DIARY (continued)

	Good	Fine	Mint
11-20: 16,20-Leav-a	.35	1.00	2.50
21-40		.50	1.00
41-102: 45-Leav-a		.20	.40

NOTE: *Photo c-10, 20.*

LOVE DOCTOR (See Dr. Anthony King. . .)

LOVE DRAMAS (True Secrets No. 3 on?)
Oct, 1949 - No. 2, Jan, 1950
Marvel Comics (IPS)

	Good	Fine	Mint
1-Jack Kamen-a	5.00	15.00	35.00
2	2.65	8.00	18.00

LOVE EXPERIENCES (Challenge of the Unknown No. 6)
10/49 - No. 5, 1950; No. 6, 4/51 - No. 38, 6/56
Ace Periodicals (A.A. Wyn/Periodical House)

	Good	Fine	Mint
1	3.00	9.00	21.00
2	1.65	5.00	11.50
3-5	1.30	4.00	9.00
6-10	1.00	3.00	7.00
11-30: 30-Last pre-code (2/55)	.85	2.50	6.00
31-38: 38-Indicia date-6/56; c-date-8/56	.75	2.25	5.00

NOTE: ***Anne Brewster** a-15. Photo c-4,15-35,38.*

LOVE EXPRESSIONS
1949?
Ace Magazines

	Good	Fine	Mint
1	3.00	9.00	21.00

LOVE JOURNAL
No. 10, Oct, 1951 - No. 25, July, 1954
Our Publishing Co.

	Good	Fine	Mint
10	2.50	7.50	17.00
11-25	1.30	4.00	9.00

LOVELAND
Nov, 1949 - No. 2, Feb, 1950
Mutual Mag./Eye Publ. (Marvel)

	Good	Fine	Mint
1,2-Photo-c	2.35	7.00	16.00

LOVE LESSONS
Oct, 1949 - No. 5, June, 1950
Harvey Comics/Key Publ. No. 5

	Good	Fine	Mint
1-Metallic silver-c printed over extra covers of Love Letters No. 1; indicia title is 'Love Letters'	3.50	10.50	24.00
2-Powell-a	1.50	4.50	10.00
3-5: 3-Photo-c	1.15	3.50	8.00

LOVE LETTERS
Oct, 1949
Harvey Comics

	Good	Fine	Mint
1-Cover-r as Love Lessons 1	3.00	9.00	21.00

LOVE LETTERS (Love Secrets No. 32 on)
11/49 - No. 31, 6/53; No. 32, 2/54 - No. 51, Dec, 1956
Quality Comics Group

	Good	Fine	Mint
1-Ward-c, Gustavson-a	8.50	25.50	60.00
2-Ward-c, Gustavson-a	8.00	24.00	56.00
3-Gustavson-a	4.75	14.25	33.00
4-Ward-a, 9 pgs.	8.00	24.00	56.00
5-8,10	1.70	5.00	11.50
9-One pg. Ward-''Be Popular with the Opposite Sex''; Robert Mitchum photo-c	3.35	10.00	23.00
11-Ward-r/Broadway Romances 2 & retitled	3.35	10.00	23.00
12-15,18-20	1.30	4.00	9.00
16,17-Ward-a; 16-Anthony Quinn photo-c. 17-Jane Russell photo-c	4.35	13.00	30.00
21-29	1.15	3.50	8.00
30,31(6/53)-Ward-a	2.65	8.00	18.00
32(2/54) - 38: Last precode, 2/55	1.00	3.00	7.00
39-48	.70	2.00	5.00
49,50-Baker-a	2.65	8.00	18.00
51-Baker-c	2.15	6.50	15.00

NOTE: *Photo-c on most 3-28.*

LOVE LIFE
1951
P. L. Publishing Co.

	Good	Fine	Mint
1	2.65	8.00	18.00

LOVELORN (Confessions of the Lovelorn No. 52 on)
Aug-Sept, 1949 - No. 51, July, 1954 (No. 1-26, 52 pgs.)
American Comics Group (Michel Publ./Regis Publ.)

	Good	Fine	Mint
1	2.85	8.50	20.00
2	1.50	4.50	10.00
3-10	1.30	4.00	9.00
11-20,22-48: 18-Drucker-a, 2pgs.	.85	2.50	6.00
21-Prostitution story	1.65	5.00	11.50
49-51-Has 3-D effect	5.00	15.00	35.00

LOVE MEMORIES
1949 (no month) - No. 4, July, 1950 (Photo-c all)
Fawcett Publications

	Good	Fine	Mint
1	3.35	10.00	23.00
2-4	1.65	5.00	11.50

LOVE MYSTERY
June, 1950 - No. 3, Oct, 1950
Fawcett Publications

	Good	Fine	Mint
1-Photo-c; George Evans-a	7.00	21.00	50.00
2,3-Evans-a. 3-Powell-a; photo-c	5.00	15.00	35.00

LOVE PROBLEMS (See Fox Giants)

LOVE PROBLEMS AND ADVICE ILLUSTRATED (Becomes Romance Stories of True Love No. 45 on)
June, 1949 - No. 6, Apr, 1950; No. 7, Jan, 1951 - No. 44, Mar, 1957
McCombs/Harvey Publ./Home Comics

	Good	Fine	Mint
V1No.1	3.00	9.00	21.00
2	1.50	4.50	10.00
3-10	1.15	3.50	8.00
11-13,15-23,25-31: 31-Last pre-code (1/55)	.70	2.00	5.00
14,24-Rape scene	.85	2.50	6.00
32-37,39-44	.60	1.80	4.00
38-S&K-c	1.35	4.00	9.00

NOTE: ***Powell** a-1,2,7-14,17-25,28,29,33,40,41. No. 3 has True Love. . on inside.*

LOVE ROMANCES (Formerly Ideal No. 5?)
No. 6, May, 1949 - No. 106, July, 1963
Timely/Marvel/Atlas(TCI No. 7-71/Male No. 72-106)

	Good	Fine	Mint
6-Photo-c	2.65	8.00	18.00
7-Kamen-a	1.70	5.00	12.00
8-Kubert-a; photo-c	3.15	9.50	22.00
9-20: 9-12-Photo-c	1.30	4.00	9.00
21,24-Krigstein-a	2.50	7.50	17.00
22,23,25-35,37,39,40	1.00	3.00	7.00
36,38-Krigstein-a	2.00	6.00	14.00
41-43,46-48,50-52,54-56,58-74	.85	2.50	6.00
44-lingerie panel	.85	2.50	6.00
45,57-Matt Baker-a	1.65	5.00	11.50
49,53-Toth-a, 6 & ? pgs.	2.00	6.00	14.00
75,77,82-Matt Baker-a	1.65	5.00	11.50
76,78-81,84,86-95: Last 10¢ ish.?	.55	1.65	4.00
83-Kirby-c, Severin-a	1.30	4.00	9.00
85,96-Kirby c/a	1.30	4.00	9.00

LOVE ROMANCES (continued)

	Good	Fine	Mint
97,100-104	.35	1.00	2.40
98-Kirby-a(4)	2.35	7.00	16.00
99,105,106-Kirby-a	1.00	3.00	7.00

NOTE: *Anne Brewster a-67, 72. Colletta a-37, 40, 42, 44, 67(2); c-42, 44, 49, 80. Everett c-70. Kirby c-80, 85, 88. Robinson a-29.*

LOVERS (Formerly Blonde Phantom)
No. 23, May, 1949 - No. 86, Aug?, 1957
Marvel Comics No. 23,24/Atlas No. 25 on (ANC)

	Good	Fine	Mint
23-Photo-c	2.65	8.00	18.00
24-Tothish plus Robinson-a; photo-c	1.50	4.50	10.00
25,30-Kubert-a; 7, 10 pgs.	2.65	8.00	18.00
26-29,31-36,39,40: 26,27-photo-c	1.15	3.50	8.00
37,38-Krigstein-a	2.65	8.00	18.00
41-Everett-a(2)	1.65	5.00	11.50
42,44-65: 65-Last pre-code (1/55)	.85	2.50	6.00
43-1pg. Frazetta ad	1.30	4.00	9.00
66,68-86	.75	2.25	5.00
67-Toth-a	2.00	6.00	14.00

NOTE: *Anne Brewster a-86. Colletta a-59, 62, 64, 69; c-64. Powell a-27, 30. Robinson a-56.*

LOVERS' LANE
Oct, 1949 - No. 41, June, 1954 (No. 1-18, 52 pgs.)
Lev Gleason Publications

	Good	Fine	Mint
1	2.85	8.50	20.00
2	1.50	4.50	10.00
3-10	1.15	3.50	8.00
11-19	.85	2.50	6.00
20-Frazetta 1 pg. ad	1.30	4.00	9.00
21-38,40,41	.85	2.50	6.00
39-Story narrated by Frank Sinatra	1.65	5.00	11.50

NOTE: *Briefer a-6, 21. Fuje a-4, 16; c-many. Guardineer a-1. Kinstler c-41. Tuska a-6. Painted-c 1-18. Photo-c 19-21, 22, 26, 28.*

LOVE SCANDALS
Feb, 1950 - No. 5, Oct, 1950 (No. 3-5 - photo covers)
Quality Comics Group

	Good	Fine	Mint
1-Ward c/a, 9 pgs.	11.00	33.00	76.00
2,3: 2-Gustavson-a	3.65	11.00	25.00
4-Ward c/a, 18 pgs; Gil Fox-a	10.00	30.00	70.00
5-C. Cuidera-a; tomboy story 'I Hated Being a Woman'	3.65	11.00	25.00

LOVE SECRETS (Formerly Love Letters No. 31)
Nov, 1949; No. 32, Aug, 1953 - No. 56, Dec, 1956
Quality Comics Group

	Good	Fine	Mint
1-Photo-c (11/49)	2.85	8.50	20.00
32	2.35	7.00	16.00
33,35-39	1.30	4.00	9.00
34-Ward-a	3.75	11.25	26.00
40-Matt Baker-c	2.50	7.50	17.00
41-44,47-50,53,54	1.15	3.50	8.00
45-Ward-a	2.85	8.50	20.00
46-Baker, Ward-a	2.85	8.50	20.00
51,52-Ward(r). 52-r/Love Confessions No. 17	1.65	5.00	11.50
55,56-Baker-a; cover-No. 56	1.65	5.00	11.50

LOVE SECRETS
No. 2, Jan, 1950
Marvel Comics(IPC)

	Good	Fine	Mint
2	2.35	7.00	16.00

LOVE STORIES
No. 6, 1950 - No. 18, Aug, 1954
Fox Feature Syndicate/Star Publ. No. 13 on

	Good	Fine	Mint
6,8-Wood-a	8.00	24.00	56.00
7,9-12	2.85	8.50	20.00
13-18-L. B. Cole-a	3.35	10.00	23.00

LOVE STORIES (Formerly Heart Throbs)
No. 147, Nov, 1972 - No. 152, Oct-Nov, 1973
National Periodical Publications

	Good	Fine	Mint
147-152		.20	.40

LOVE STORIES OF MARY WORTH (See Harvey Comics Hits No. 55 & Mary Worth)
Sept, 1949 - No. 5, May, 1950
Harvey Publications

	Good	Fine	Mint
1-1940's newspaper reprints-No. 1-4	3.50	10.50	24.00
2	2.50	7.50	17.00
3-5: 3-Kamen/Baker-a?	2.35	7.00	16.00

LOVE TALES (Formerly The Human Torch No. 35)
No. 36, May, 1949 - No. 75, Sept, 1957
Marvel/Atlas Comics (ZPC No. 36-50/MMC No. 67-75)

	Good	Fine	Mint
36-Photo-c	2.65	8.00	18.00
37	1.30	4.00	9.00
38-44,46-50: 40,41-Photo-c	1.00	3.00	7.00
45-Powell-a	1.20	3.50	8.00
51,69-Everett-a	1.65	5.00	11.50
52-Krigstein-a	2.15	6.50	15.00
53-60: 60-Last pre-code (2/55)	.85	2.50	6.00
61-68,70-75	.55	1.65	4.00

LOVE, 10 STORIES
July, 1955
Charlton Comics

	Good	Fine	Mint
6	.85	2.50	6.00

LOVE THRILLS (See Fox Giants)

LOVE TRAILS
Dec, 1949 - No. 2, Mar, 1950 (52 pgs.)
A Lover's Magazine (CDS)(Marvel)

	Good	Fine	Mint
1,2: Photo-c, No. 1	2.85	8.50	20.00

LOWELL THOMAS' HIGH ADVENTURE (See 4-Color No. 949,1001)

LT. (See Lieutenant)

LUCKY COMICS
Jan, 1944; No. 2, Summer, 1945 - No. 5, Summer, 1946
Consolidated Magazines

	Good	Fine	Mint
1-Lucky Starr, Bobbie	3.75	11.25	26.00
2-5	1.85	5.50	13.00

LUCKY DUCK
No. 5, Jan, 1953 - No. 8, Sept, 1953
Standard Comics (Literary Ent.)

	Good	Fine	Mint
5-Irving Spector-a	2.35	7.00	16.00
6-8-Irving Spector-a	1.50	4.50	10.00

LUCKY FIGHTS IT THROUGH (Also see The K. O. Punch)
1949 (16 pgs. in color; paper cover) (Giveaway)
Educational Comics

	Good	Fine	Mint
(Very Rare)-1st Kurtzman work for E. C.; V.D. prevention	140.00	420.00	800.00

(Prices vary widely on this book)

NOTE: *Subtitled "The Story of That Ignorant, Ignorant Cowboy." Prepared for Communications Materials Center, Columbia University.*

LUCKY "7" COMICS
1944 (No date listed)

Lovers' Lane #6, © LEV

Love Stories of Mary Worth #1, © HARV

Lucky Comics #5, © Consolidated Mag.

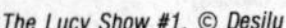
The Lucy Show #1, © Desilu

Macross #1, © Comico

Mad #3, © EC

LUCKY '7' COMICS (continued)
Howard Publishers Ltd.

	Good	Fine	Mint
1-Congo Raider, Punch Powers; bondage-c	8.50	25.50	60.00

LUCKY STAR (Western)
1950 - No. 7, 1951; No. 8, 1953 - No. 14, 1955 (5x7¼''; full color)
Nation Wide Publ. Co.

	Good	Fine	Mint
1-Jack Davis-a	4.00	12.00	28.00
2,3-(52 pgs.)-Davis-a	2.65	8.00	18.00
4-7-(52 pgs.)-Davis-a	2.00	6.00	14.00
8-14-(36 pgs.)	1.50	4.50	10.00
Given away with Lucky Star Western Wear by the Juvenile Mfg. Co.	1.50	4.50	10.00

LUCY SHOW, THE (TV) (Also see I Love Lucy)
June, 1963 - No. 5, June, 1964 (Photo-c, 1,2)
Gold Key

	Good	Fine	Mint
1	3.50	10.50	24.00
2	2.65	8.00	18.00
3-5: Photo back-c,1,2,4,5	2.15	6.50	15.00

LUCY, THE REAL GONE GAL (Meet Miss Pepper No. 5 on)
June, 1953 - No. 4, Dec, 1953
St. John Publishing Co.

	Good	Fine	Mint
1-Negligee panels	3.15	9.50	22.00
2	1.65	5.00	11.50
3,4: 3-Drucker-a	1.30	4.00	9.00

LUDWIG BEMELMAN'S MADELEINE & GENEVIEVE (See 4-Color No. 796)

LUDWIG VON DRAKE (TV)(Walt Disney)
Nov-Dec, 1961 - No. 4, June-Aug, 1962
Dell Publishing Co.

	Good	Fine	Mint
1	1.50	4.50	10.00
2-4	1.00	3.00	7.00
...Fish Stampede (15 pgs.; 1962; Fritos giveaway)	1.00	3.00	7.00

LUKE CAGE (See Hero for Hire)

LUKE SHORT'S WESTERN STORIES
No. 580, Aug, 1954 - No. 927, Aug, 1958
Dell Publishing Co.

	Good	Fine	Mint
4-Color 580(8/54)	1.75	5.25	12.00
4-Color 651(9/55)-Kinstler-a	2.35	7.00	16.00
4-Color 739,771,807,875,927	1.75	5.25	12.00
4-Color 848	2.35	7.00	16.00

LUNATICKLE (Magazine) (Satire)
Feb, 1956 - No. 2, Apr, 1956
Whitstone Publ.

	Good	Fine	Mint
1,2-Kubert-a	1.50	4.50	9.00

LYNDON B. JOHNSON
March, 1965
Dell Publishing Co.

	Good	Fine	Mint
12-445-503	1.50	4.50	10.00

MACHINE MAN (Also see 2001...)
4/78 - No. 9, 12/78; No. 10, 8/79 - No.19, 2/81
Marvel Comics Group

	Good	Fine	Mint
1		.60	1.20
2-17,19: 19-Intro Jack O'Lantern		.30	.60
18-Wendigo, Alpha Flight-ties into X-Men No. 140	.85	2.50	5.00

NOTE: ***Austin*** *c-7i, 19i.* ***Buckler*** *c-17p, 18p.* ***Byrne*** *c-14p, 16p.* ***Ditko*** *a-10-19; c-10-13, 14i, 15, 16.* ***Kirby*** *a-1-9p; c-1-5, 7-9p.* ***Layton*** *c-7i.* ***Miller*** *c-19p.* ***Simonson*** *c-6.*

MACHINE MAN
Oct, 1984 - No. 4, Jan, 1985 (Limited-series)
Marvel Comics Group

	Good	Fine	Mint
1-Barry Smith-a(i)	.25	.75	1.50
2-4: Smith-a, 1-3i, 4-c/a		.60	1.20

MACKENZIE'S RAIDERS (See 4-Color No. 1093)

MACO TOYS COMIC
1959 (36 pages; full color) (Giveaway)
Maco Toys/Charlton Comics

	Good	Fine	Mint
1-All military stories featuring Maco Toys	1.00	3.00	6.00

MACROSS (Robotech: The Macross Saga No. 2 on)
Jan, 1984 ($1.50)
Comico

	Good	Fine	Mint
1	2.50	7.50	15.00

MAD
Oct-Nov, 1952 - Present (No. 24 on, magazine format)
(Kurtzman editor No. 1-28, Feldstein No. 29 on)
E. C. Comics

	Good	Fine	Mint
1-Wood, Davis, Elder start as regulars	72.00	215.00	500.00
2-Davis-c	35.00	105.00	245.00
3	22.00	65.00	154.00
4-Reefer mention story ''Flob Was a Slob'' by Davis	22.00	65.00	154.00
5-Low distribution; Elder-c	47.00	141.00	330.00
6-10	15.00	45.00	105.00
11-Wolverton-a	15.00	45.00	105.00
12-15	13.00	40.00	90.00
16-23(5/55): 21-1st app. Alfred E. Neuman on-c in fake ad. 22-all by Elder. 23-Special cancel announcement	10.00	30.00	70.00
24(7/55)-1st magazine issue (25 cents); Kurtzman logo & border on-c	20.00	60.00	140.00
25-Jaffee starts as regular writer	11.00	33.00	76.00
26	7.00	21.00	50.00
27-Davis-c; Jaffee starts as story artist; new logo	7.00	21.00	50.00
28-Elder-c; Heath back-c; last issue edited by Kurtzman; (three cover variations exist with different wording on contents banner on lower right of cover; value of each the same)	6.00	18.00	42.00
29-Wood-c; Kamen-a; Don Martin starts as regular; Feldstein editing begins	6.00	18.00	42.00
30-1st A. E. Neuman cover by Mingo; Crandall inside-c; last Elder art; Bob Clarke starts as regular	7.00	21.00	50.00
31-Freas starts as regular; last Davis art until No. 99	5.00	15.00	35.00
32-Orlando, Drucker, Woodbridge start as regulars; Wood back-c	4.75	14.25	33.00
33-Orlando back-c	4.75	14.25	33.00
34-Berg starts as regular	4.00	12.00	28.00
35-Mingo wraparound-c; Crandall-a	4.00	12.00	28.00
36-40	3.00	9.00	21.00
41-50	2.15	6.50	15.00
51-60: 60-Two Clarke-c; Prohias starts as regular	1.15	3.50	8.00
61-70: 64-Rickard starts as regular. 68-Martin-c	1.00	3.00	7.00
71-80: 76-Aragones starts as regular	.85	2.50	6.00
81-90: 86-1st Fold-in. 89-One strip by Walt Kelly. 90-Frazetta back-c	.75	2.25	5.00
91-100: 91-Jaffee starts as story artist. 99-Davis-a resumes	.50	1.50	3.50
101-120: 101-Infinity-c. 105-Batman TV show take-off. 106-Frazetta back-c	.40	1.25	2.50
121-140: 130-Torres starts as regular. 122-Drucker & Mingo-c. 128-Last Orlando. 135,139-Davis-c	.35	1.00	2.00

MAD (continued) — Good / Fine / Mint
141-170: 165-Martin-c. 169-Drucker-c .25 .75 1.50
171-200: 173,178-Davis-c. 176-Drucker-c. 182-Bob Jones starts as regular. 186-Star Trek take-off. 187-Harry North starts as regular. 196-Star Wars take-off .25 .75 1.50
201-270: 203-Star Wars take-off. 204-Hulk TV show take-off. 208-Superman movie take-off .50 1.00

NOTE: ***Jules Feiffer** a(r)-42. **Freas**-most-c and back covers-40-74. **Heath** a-14, 27. **Kamen** a-29. **Krigstein** a-12, 17, 24, 26. **Kurtzman** c-1, 3, 4, 6-10, 13, 14, 16, 18. **Mingo** c-30-37, 75-111. **John Severin** a-1-6, 9, 10. **Wolverton** c-11; a-11, 17, 29, 31, 36, 40, 82, 137. **Wood** a-24-45, 59; c-26, 29.*

MAD (See . . . Follies, . . . Special, More Trash from . . ., and The Worst from . . .)

MAD ABOUT MILLIE
April, 1969 - No. 17, Dec, 1970
Marvel Comics Group

1-Giant issue .35 1.00 2.00
2-17: 16,17-r .50 1.00
Annual 1(11/71) .40 .80

MADAME XANADU
July, 1981 (No ads; $1.00; 32 pgs.)
DC Comics

1-Marshall Rogers-a(25 pgs.); Kaluta-c/a(2 pgs.); pin-up of Madame Xanadu .50 1.00

MADBALLS
Sept, 1986 - No. 3, Nov, 1986 (Limited series)
Star Comics (Marvel)

1-3: Based on toys .40 .80

MAD FOLLIES (Special)
1963 - No. 7, 1969
E. C. Comics

nn(1963)-Paperback book covers 5.75 17.25 40.00
2(1964)-Calendar 3.75 11.25 26.00
3(1965)-Mischief Stickers 2.65 8.00 18.00
4(1966)-Mobile; reprints Frazetta back-c/Mad No. 90 3.50 10.50 24.00
5(1967)-Stencils 2.65 8.00 18.00
6(1968)-Mischief Stickers 1.75 5.25 12.00
7(1969)-Nasty Cards 1.75 5.25 12.00

NOTE: ***Clarke** c-4. **Mingo** c-1-3. **Orlando** a-5.*

MAD HATTER, THE (Costume Hero)
Jan-Feb, 1946 - No. 2, Sept-Oct, 1946
O. W. Comics Corp.

1-Freddy the Firefly begins; Giunta-a 16.00 48.00 110.00
2-Has ad for E.C.'s Animal Fables No. 1 11.00 33.00 76.00

MADHOUSE
3-4/54 - No. 4, 9-10/54; 6/57 - No. 4, Dec?, 1957
Ajax/Farrell Publ. (Excellent Publ./4-Star)

1(1954) 6.50 19.50 45.00
2,3 3.00 9.00 21.00
4-Surrealistic-c 5.00 15.00 35.00
1(1957) 2.65 8.00 18.00
2-4 1.50 4.50 10.00

MADHOUSE (Formerly Madhouse Glads; . . . Comics No. 104? on)
No. 95, 9/74 - No. 97, 1/75; No. 98, 8/75 - No. 130, 10/82
Red Circle Productions/Archie Publications

95-Horror stories through No. 97 .60 1.20
96 .60 1.20
97-Intro. Henry Hobson; Morrow, Thorne-a .40 .80
98-130-Satire/humor stories .30 .60
Annual 8(1970-71)- 12(1974-75)-Formerly Madhouse Ma-ad Annual. 11-Wood-a(r) .40 .80
. . . Comics Digest 1(1975-76)- 8(8/82)(. . . Mag. No. 5 on) .50 1.00

NOTE: ***McWilliams** a-97. **Morrow** a-96; c-95-97. See Archie Comics Digest No. 1, 13.*

MADHOUSE GLADS (Formerly Madhouse Ma-ad; Madhouse No. 95 on)
No. 73, May, 1970 - No. 94, Aug, 1974 (No. 78-92: 52 pgs.)
Archie Publications

73 .25 .50
74-94 .20 .40

MADHOUSE MA-AD (. . . Jokes No. 67-70; . . . Freak-Out No. 71-74) (Formerly Archie's Madhouse) (Becomes Madhouse Glads No. 75 on)
No. 67, April, 1969 - No. 72, Jan, 1970
Archie Publications

67-72 .25 .50
. . . Annual 7(1969-70)-Formerly Archie's Madhouse Annual; becomes Madhouse Annual .30 .60

MAD MONSTER PARTY (See Movie Classics)

MAD SPECIAL (. . . Super Special)
Fall, 1970 - Present (84 - 116 pages)
E. C. Publications, Inc.

Fall 1970(No.1)-Bonus-Voodoo Doll; contains 17 pgs. new material 2.65 8.00 18.00
Spring 1971(No.2)-Wall Nuts; 17 pgs. new material 1.75 5.25 12.00
3-Protest Stickers 1.75 5.25 12.00
4-8: 4-Mini Posters. 5-Mad Flag. 7-Presidential candidate posters, Wild Shocking Message posters. 8-TV Guise 1.30 4.00 9.00
9(1972)-Contains Nostalgic Mad No. 1 (28 pgs.) 1.15 3.50 8.00
10,11,13: 10-Nonsense Stickers (Don Martin). 11-33⅓ RPM record. 13-Sickie Stickers; 3 pgs. new Wolverton 1.15 3.50 8.00
12-Contains Nostalgic Mad No. 2 (36 pgs.); Davis, Wolverton-a 1.15 3.50 8.00
14-Vital Message posters & Art Depreciation paintings .85 2.50 6.00
15-Contains Nostalgic Mad No. 3 (28 pgs.) 1.15 3.50 8.00
16,17,19,20: 16-Mad-hesive Stickers. 17-Don Martin posters. 20-Martin Stickers .75 2.25 5.00
18-Contains Nostalgic Mad No. 4 (36 pgs.) .85 2.50 6.00
21,24-Contains Nostalgic Mad No. 5 (28 pgs.) & No. 6 (28 pgs.) .85 2.50 6.00
22,23,25-27,29,30: 22-Diplomas. 23-Martin Stickers. 25-Martin Posters. 26-33⅓ RPM record. 27-Mad Shock-Sticks. 29-Mad Collectable-Correctables Posters. 30-The Movies .55 1.65 4.00
28-Contains Nostalgic Mad No. 7 (36 pgs.) .75 2.25 5.00
31-40 .55 1.65 4.00

NOTE: *No. 28-30: no number on cover. **Mingo** c-9, 11, 15, 19, 23.*

MAGE (The Hero Discovered . . .)
1984 (no month) - No. 15, 10/86 ($1.50; 36 pgs; Mando paper)
Comico

1-Violence 1.00 3.00 6.00
2 .60 1.75 3.50
3-5: 3-Intro Edsel .50 1.50 3.00
6-Grendel begins (1st in color) 2.00 6.00 12.00
7-1st new Grendel story .85 2.50 5.00
8-14: 14-Grendel ends .40 1.20 2.40
15-Dbl. size, photo-c .50 1.50 3.00

Madballs #1, © MCG

Madhouse #2 (5-6/54), © AJAX

Mage #1, © Comico

Magic Comics #28, © DMP

Magnus, Robot Fighter #14, © GK

Man Comics #3, © MCG

MAGIC AGENT (See Unknown Worlds)
Jan-Feb, 1962 - No. 3, May-June, 1962
American Comics Group

	Good	Fine	Mint
1-Origin & 1st app. John Force	.40	1.20	2.40
2,3	.30	.80	1.60

MAGIC COMICS
Aug, 1939 - No. 123, Nov-Dec, 1949
David McKay Publications

	Good	Fine	Mint
1-Mandrake the Magician, Henry, Popeye (not by Segar), Blondie, Barney Baxter, Secret Agent X-9 (not by Raymond), Bunky by Billy DeBeck & Thornton Burgess text stories illustrated by Harrison Cady begin	60.00	180.00	420.00
2	30.00	90.00	210.00
3	22.00	65.00	154.00
4	18.00	54.00	125.00
5	15.00	45.00	105.00
6-10	12.00	36.00	84.00
11-16,18-20	10.00	30.00	70.00
17-The Lone Ranger begins	11.00	33.00	76.00
21-30	8.00	24.00	56.00
31-40	6.00	18.00	42.00
41-50	5.00	15.00	35.00
51-60	4.00	12.00	28.00
61-70	3.00	9.00	21.00
71-99	2.50	7.50	17.50
100	3.00	9.00	21.00
101-106,109-123	2.00	6.00	14.00
107,108-Flash Gordon in each, not by Raymond	3.75	11.25	26.00

MAGICA DE SPELL (See Walt Disney Showcase No. 30)

MAGIC OF CHRISTMAS AT NEWBERRYS, THE
1967 (20 pgs.; slick cover; B&W inside)
E. S. London (Giveaway)

	Good	Fine	Mint
		.60	1.20

MAGIC SWORD, THE (See Movie Classics)

MAGIK
Dec, 1983 - No. 4, Mar, 1984 (mini-series)
Marvel Comics Group

	Good	Fine	Mint
1-Illyana & Storm series from X-Men	.25	.75	1.50
2-4		.60	1.20

NOTE: ***Buscema** a-1p,2p; c-1p.*

MAGILLA GORILLA (TV) (Hanna-Barbera)
May, 1964 - No. 10, Dec, 1968
Gold Key

	Good	Fine	Mint
1	1.50	4.50	10.00
2-10: 3-Vs. Yogi Bear for President	.85	2.50	6.00

MAGILLA GORILLA (TV)
Nov, 1970 - No. 5, July, 1971 (Hanna-Barbera)
Charlton Comics

	Good	Fine	Mint
1-5	.70	2.00	4.00

MAGNUS, ROBOT FIGHTER (. . . 4000 A.D.)
Feb, 1963 - No. 46, Jan, 1977 (Painted-covers)
Gold Key

	Good	Fine	Mint
1-Origin Magnus; Aliens series begins	7.00	21.00	50.00
2,3	3.50	10.50	24.00
4-10	2.00	6.00	14.00
11-20	1.50	4.50	10.00
21,22,24-28: 22-Origin-r/No. 1. 28-Aliens series ends	.85	2.50	6.00
23-Exists with two different prices, 12 cents and 15 cents	.85	2.50	6.00
29-46-Reprints	.50	1.50	3.00

NOTE: ***Manning** a-1-22, 29-43(r). **Spiegle** a-23, 44r.*

MAID OF THE MIST (See American Graphics)

MAJOR HOOPLE COMICS
nd (Jan, 1943)
Nedor Publications

	Good	Fine	Mint
1-Mary Worth, Phantom Soldier by Moldoff app.	12.00	36.00	84.00

MAJOR INAPAK THE SPACE ACE
1951 (20 pages) (Giveaway)
Magazine Enterprises (Inapac Foods)

	Good	Fine	Mint
1-Bob Powell-a	.30	.80	1.60

NOTE: *Many warehouse copies surfaced in 1973.*

MAJOR VICTORY COMICS
1944 - No. 3, Summer, 1945
H. Clay Glover/Service Publ./Harry 'A' Chesler

	Good	Fine	Mint
1-Origin Major Victory by C. Sultan (reprint from Dynamic No. 1); Spider Woman 1st app.	20.00	60.00	140.00
2-Dynamic Boy app.	12.00	36.00	84.00
3-Rocket Boy app.	10.00	30.00	70.00

MALTESE FALCON (See Feature Books No. 48 (McKay))

MALU IN THE LAND OF ADVENTURE
1964
I. W. Enterprises

	Good	Fine	Mint
1-Reprints Avon's Slave Girl Comics No. 1; Severin-c	4.75	14.00	28.00

MAMMOTH COMICS
1938 (84 pages) (Black & White, 8½x11½")
Whitman Publishing Co.(K. K. Publications)

	Good	Fine	Mint
1-Terry & the Pirates, Dick Tracy, Little Orphan Annie, Wash Tubbs, & other reprints	45.00	135.00	315.00

MAMMY YOKUM & THE GREAT DOGPATCH MYSTERY
1951 (Giveaway)
Toby Press

	Good	Fine	Mint
Li'l Abner	8.50	25.50	60.00

MAN-BAT (Also see Detective No. 400, Brave & the Bold, and Batman Family)
Dec-Jan, 1975-76 - No. 2, Feb-Mar, 1976; Dec, 1984
National Periodical Publications/DC Comics

	Good	Fine	Mint
1-Ditko-a(p); Aparo-c; She-Bat app.		.30	.60
2-Aparo-c		.30	.60
. . .Vs. Batman 1 (12/84)-Adams-a(r)	.45	1.25	2.50

MAN COMICS
Dec, 1949 - No. 28, Sept, 1953 (52 pgs., No. 1-4)
Marvel/Atlas Comics (NPI)

	Good	Fine	Mint
1-Tuska-a	2.85	8.50	20.00
2-Tuska-a	1.50	4.50	10.00
3-5	1.30	4.00	9.00
6-8	1.15	3.50	8.00
9-13,15: 9-Format changes to war	.85	2.50	6.00
14-Krenkel (3pgs.), Pakula-a	1.70	5.00	12.00
16-21,23-28: 28-Crime ish.	.70	2.00	5.00
22-Krigstein-a, 5 pgs.	2.65	8.00	18.00

NOTE: ***Berg** a-14, 15. **Colan** a-21. **Everett** a-8, 22; c-22, 25. **Heath** a-11, 17. Kubertish a-by **Bob Brown**-3. **Maneely** c-10, 11. **Robinson** a-10, 14.*

MANDRAKE THE MAGICIAN (See Feature Books No. 18,19,23,46,52,55)

MANDRAKE THE MAGICIAN (See Harvey Comics Hits No. 53)
No. 752, Nov, 1956; Sept, 1966 - No. 10, Nov, 1967

MANDRAKE THE MAGICIAN (continued)
Dell Publishing Co./King Comics

	Good	Fine	Mint
4-Color 752('56)	3.50	10.50	24.00
1(King)-Begin S.O.S. Phantom series, ends No. 3	.75	2.25	5.00
2-5: 4-Girl Phantom app. 5-Brick Bradford app., also No. 6	.55	1.65	4.00
6,7,9: 7-Origin Lothar. 9-Brick Bradford app.	.50	1.50	3.00
8-Jeff Jones-a	.85	2.50	6.00
10-Rip Kirby app.; 14 pgs. art by Raymond	1.50	4.50	10.00

MANDRAKE THE MAGICIAN GIANT COMIC ALBUM
1972 (48 pgs.; 11x14''; B&W; cardboard covers)
Modern Promotions

	Good	Fine	Mint
nn-Strip reprints by Lee Falk	1.70	5.00	10.00

MAN FROM ATLANTIS (TV)
Feb, 1978 - No. 7, Aug, 1978
Marvel Comics Group

	Good	Fine	Mint
1-(84 pgs.; $1.00)-Sutton-a(p), Buscema-c; origin		.30	.60
2-7		.25	.50

MAN FROM U.N.C.L.E., THE (TV)
Feb, 1965 - No. 22, April, 1969 (All photo covers)
Gold Key

	Good	Fine	Mint
1	3.50	10.50	24.00
2-Photo back c-2-8	2.35	7.00	16.00
3-10: 7-Jet Dream begins	1.50	4.50	10.00
11-22: 21,22-Reprints	1.15	3.50	8.00

MAN FROM WELLS FARGO (TV)
No. 1287, Feb-Apr, 1962 - May-July, 1962 (Photo-c)
Dell Publishing Co.

	Good	Fine	Mint
4-Color 1287, 01-495-207	2.65	8.00	18.00

MANGAZINE
Aug, 1985 - Present ($1.25-$1.50)
Antarctic Press

	Good	Fine	Mint
1-Paper-c	.70	2.00	4.00
1 (2nd printing)-Slick-c	.25	.75	1.50
2,3	.35	1.00	2.00
4,5	.25	.75	1.50

MANHUNT! (Becomes Red Fox No. 15 on)
Oct, 1947 - No. 14, 1953
Magazine Enterprises

	Good	Fine	Mint
1-Red Fox by L. B. Cole, Undercover Girl by Whitney, Space Ace begin; negligee panels	16.00	48.00	110.00
2-Electrocution-c	11.50	34.50	80.00
3-5	10.00	30.00	70.00
6-Bondage-c by Whitney	10.00	30.00	70.00
7-9: 7-Space ace ends. 8-Trail Colt begins	8.00	24.00	56.00
10-G. Ingels-a	8.00	24.00	56.00
11(8/48)-Frazetta-a, 7 pgs.; The Duke, Scotland Yard begin	16.50	50.00	115.00
12	5.50	16.50	38.00
13(A-1 63)-Frazetta, r-/Trail Colt No. 1, 7 pgs.	13.50	40.50	95.00
14(A-1 77)-Classic bondage-c; last L. B. Cole Red Fox; Ingels-a	8.00	24.00	56.00

NOTE: ***Guardineer** a-1-5; c-8. **Whitney** a-2-14; c-1-6, 10. Red Fox by **L. B. Cole**-No. 1-14. No. 15 was advertised but came out as Red Fox No. 15.*

MANHUNTER (See First Issue Special)
May, 1984 (76 pgs; high quality paper)
DC Comics

	Good	Fine	Mint
1-Simonson c/a(r)/Detective	.45	1.25	2.50

MANIMAL
Jan, 1986 (B&W)(Adults only)
Renegade Press

	Good	Fine	Mint
1	.30	.85	1.70

MAN IN BLACK (See Thrill-O-Rama) (Also see Front Page and Strange Story Comics)
Sept, 1957 - No. 4, Mar, 1958
Harvey Publications

	Good	Fine	Mint
1-Bob Powell c/a	6.00	18.00	42.00
2-4: Powell c/a	5.00	15.00	35.00

MAN IN FLIGHT (See 4-Color No. 836)

MAN IN SPACE (See Dell Giant No. 27 & 4-Color No. 716,954)

MAN OF PEACE, POPE PIUS XII
1950 (See Pope Pius XII. . . & Topix V2No.8)
Catechetical Guild

	Good	Fine	Mint
All Powell-a	5.35	16.00	32.00

MAN OF STEEL, THE
June, 1986 - No. 6, 1986 (mini-series)
DC Comics

	Good	Fine	Mint
1-Byrne story & art begins; origin	.25	.75	1.50
1-Alternate-c for newsstand sales		.60	1.20
2-6: 2-Intro. Lois Lane. 4-Intro. Lex Luthor		.50	1.00

MAN OF WAR (See Liberty Scouts & Liberty Guards)
Nov, 1941 - No. 2, Jan, 1942
Centaur Publications

	Good	Fine	Mint
1-The Fire-Man, Man of War, The Sentinel, Liberty Guards, & Vapo-Man begin; Gustavson-c/a; Flag-c	60.00	180.00	420.00
2-The Ferret app.; Gustavson-c/a	47.00	141.00	330.00

MAN O' MARS
1953; 1964
Fiction House Magazines

	Good	Fine	Mint
1-Space Rangers	11.50	34.50	80.00
I.W. Reprint No. 1/Man O'Mars No. 1; Murphy Anderson-a	2.75	8.00	16.00

MANTECH ROBOT WARRIORS
Sept, 1984 - No. 4, May, 1985
Archie Enterprises, Inc.

	Good	Fine	Mint
1-4		.40	.80

MAN-THING (See Fear)
Jan, 1974 - No. 22, Oct, 1975; Nov, 1979 - V2No. 11, July, 1981
Marvel Comics Group

	Good	Fine	Mint
1-Howard the Duck cont./Fear 19.(2nd app.)	.85	2.50	5.00
2-4	.25	.70	1.40
5-11-Ploog-a		.50	1.00
12-22: 19-1st app. Scavenger. 21-Origin Scavenger & Man-Thing. 22-Howard the Duck cameo		.30	.60
V2No.1(1979)		.40	.80
2-11: 6-Golden-c		.25	.50
Giant Size 1(8/74)-Ploog c/a		.60	1.20
Giant Size 2,3		.50	1.00
Giant Size 4(5/75)-Howard the Duck by Brunner; Ditko-a(r)	.85	2.50	5.00
Giant Size 5(8/75)-Howard the Duck by Brunner (p)	.85	2.50	5.00

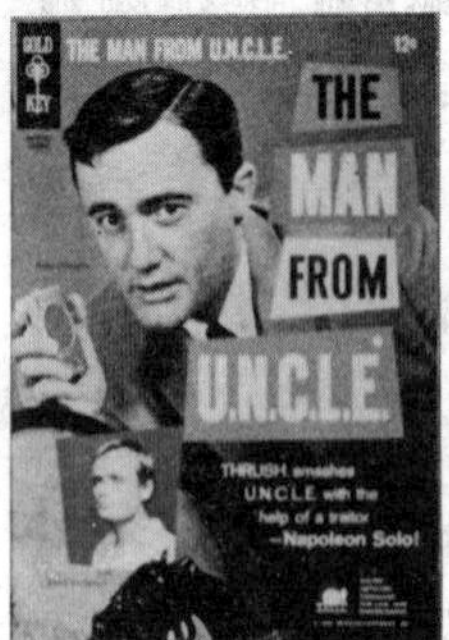

Man From U.N.C.L.E. #4, © MGM

Mangazine #1 (1st printing), © Antarctic Press

Man of Steel #1 (direct sale), © DC

Many Loves of Dobie Gillis #25, © DC

March of Comics #8, © WDC

March of Comics #39, © Gene Autry

MAN-THING (continued)

NOTE: ***Alcala*** *a-14, Gnt Size 3.* ***Brunner*** *c-1, Gnt Size 4.* ***J. Buscema*** *a-12p, 13p, 16p, Gnt Size 2p, 5p; c-Gnt Size 2.* ***Ditko*** *a-Gnt Size 1r, 3r, 4r.* ***Gil Kane*** *c-4p, 10p, 12-20p, 21, Gnt-Size 3p, 5p.* ***Kirby*** *a-Gnt Size 1-3r.* ***Mooney*** *a-17, 18, 19p, 20-22, V2No.1-3p.* ***Ploog*** *Man-Thing-5p, 6p, 7, 8, 9-11p, Gnt Size 1p; c-5, 6, 8, 9, 11.* ***Powell*** *a-Gnt Size 2r.* ***Sutton*** *a-13i, Gnt-Size 3r, 5i.*

MAN WITH THE X-RAY EYES, THE (See X,. . . under Movie Comics)

MANY GHOSTS OF DR. GRAVES, THE (Doctor Graves No. 73 on)
5/67 - No. 60, 12/76; No. 61, 9/77 - No. 62, 10/77; No. 63, 2/78 - No. 65, 4/78; No. 66, 6/81 - No. 72, 5/82
Charlton Comics

	Good	Fine	Mint
1	.40	1.20	2.40
2-10		.50	1.00
11-20		.40	.80
21-44,46,48,50-72		.30	.60
45-1st Newton comic book work, 8pgs.	.35	1.00	2.00
47,49-Newton-a		.40	.80
Modern Comics Reprint 12,25		.20	.40

NOTE: ***Aparo*** *a-66r, 69r; c-66, 67.* ***Byrne*** *c-54.* ***Ditko*** *a-1, 7, 9, 11-13, 15-18, 20-22, 24, 26, 35, 37, 38, 40-44, 47, 48, 51-54, 58, 60r-65r, 72; c-11-13, 16-18, 22, 24, 26-35, 38, 40, 55, 58, 62-65.* ***Newton*** *a-45, 47p, 49p; c-49, 52.* ***Sutton*** *c/a-42, 49.*

MANY LOVES OF DOBIE GILLIS (TV)
May-June, 1960 - No. 26, Oct, 1964
National Periodical Publications

	Good	Fine	Mint
1	7.00	21.00	50.00
2-5	3.50	10.50	24.00
6-10	3.00	9.00	21.00
11-26	2.50	7.50	17.50

MARAUDER'S MOON (See 4-Color No. 848)

MARCH HARE, THE
Aug, 1986 ($1.50, B&W)
Lodestone Publ.

	Good	Fine	Mint
1-Giffen c/a(p)	.25	.75	1.50

MARCH OF COMICS (Boys' and Girls'. . . No. 1-353)
1946 - No. 488, Apr, 1982 (No. 1-4: No No.'s)
(K.K. Giveaway) (Founded by Sig Feuchtwanger)
K. K. Publications/Western Publishing Co.

Early issues were full size, 32 pages, and were printed with and without an extra cover of slick stock, just for the advertiser. The binding was stapled if the slick cover was added; otherwise, the pages were glued together at the spine. Most 1948 - 1951 issues were full size, 24 pages, pulp covers. Starting in 1952 they were half-size and 32 pages with slick covers. 1959 and later issues had only 16 pages plus covers. 1952 -1959 issues read oblong; 1960 and later issues read upright.

	Good	Fine	Mint
1(nn)(1946)-Goldilocks; Kelly back-c; 16pgs., stapled	22.00	65.00	154.00
2(nn)(1946)-How Santa Got His Red Suit; Kelly-a(11 pgs., r-/4-Color 61)('44); 16pgs., stapled	22.00	65.00	154.00
3(nn)(1947)-Our Gang (Walt Kelly)	40.00	110.00	235.00
4(nn)Donald Duck by Carl Barks, ''Maharajah Donald,'' 28 pgs.; Kelly-c?	416.00	1250.00	2600.00
5-Andy Panda	13.00	40.00	80.00
6-Popular Fairy Tales; Kelly-c; Noonan-a(2)	17.00	50.00	100.00
7-Oswald the Rabbit	17.00	50.00	100.00
8-Mickey Mouse, 32 pgs.	60.00	150.00	320.00
9(nn)-The Story of the Gloomy Bunny	8.00	24.00	48.00
10-Out of Santa's Bag	6.75	20.00	40.00
11-Fun With Santa Claus	5.35	16.00	32.00
12-Santa's Toys	5.35	16.00	32.00
13-Santa's Surprise	5.35	16.00	32.00
14-Santa's Candy Kitchen	5.35	16.00	32.00
15-Hip-It-Ty Hop & the Big Bass Viol	5.35	16.00	32.00
16-Woody Woodpecker (1947)	8.35	25.00	50.00
17-Roy Rogers (1948)	18.00	54.00	125.00
18-Popular Fairy Tales	10.00	30.00	60.00
19-Uncle Wiggily	7.50	22.50	45.00
20-Donald Duck by Carl Barks, ''Darkest Africa,'' 22 pgs.; Kelly-c	250.00	750.00	1600.00
21-Tom and Jerry	7.50	22.50	45.00
22-Andy Panda	7.50	22.50	45.00
23-Raggedy Ann; Kerr-a	12.00	35.00	70.00
24-Felix the Cat, 1932 daily strip reprints by Otto Messmer	17.00	52.00	115.00
25-Gene Autry	18.00	54.00	125.00
26-Our Gang; Walt Kelly	20.00	60.00	120.00
27-Mickey Mouse	34.00	100.00	225.00
28-Gene Autry	18.00	54.00	125.00
29-Easter Bonnet Shop	4.00	12.00	24.00
30-Here Comes Santa	3.35	10.00	20.00
31-Santa's Busy Corner	3.35	10.00	20.00
32-No book produced			
33-A Christmas Carol	3.35	10.00	20.00
34-Woody Woodpecker	5.85	17.50	35.00
35-Roy Rogers (1948)	18.00	54.00	125.00
36-Felix the Cat(1949)-by Messmer; '34 daily strip-r	15.00	45.00	90.00
37-Popeye	12.50	37.50	80.00
38-Oswald the Rabbit	5.85	17.50	35.00
39-Gene Autry	18.00	54.00	125.00
40-Andy and Woody	5.85	17.50	35.00
41-Donald Duck by Carl Barks, ''Race to the South Seas,'' 22 pgs.; Kelly-c	180.00	550.00	1200.00
42-Porky Pig	5.85	17.50	35.00
43-Henry	3.75	11.00	22.00
44-Bugs Bunny	5.85	17.50	35.00
45-Mickey Mouse	27.00	80.00	170.00
46-Tom and Jerry	5.85	17.50	35.00
47-Roy Rogers	15.00	45.00	100.00
48-Greetings from Santa	2.75	8.00	16.00
49-Santa Is Here	2.75	8.00	16.00
50-Santa Claus' Workshop (1949)	2.75	8.00	16.00
51-Felix the Cat (1950) by Messmer	12.50	37.50	75.00
52-Popeye	10.00	30.00	65.00
53-Oswald the Rabbit	5.85	17.50	35.00
54-Gene Autry	14.00	42.50	90.00
55-Andy and Woody	5.00	15.00	30.00
56-Donald Duck-not by Barks; Barks art on back-c	20.00	60.00	135.00
57-Porky Pig	5.00	15.00	30.00
58-Henry	3.00	9.00	18.00
59-Bugs Bunny	5.00	15.00	30.00
60-Mickey Mouse	18.00	55.00	125.00
61-Tom and Jerry	4.35	13.00	26.00
62-Roy Rogers	14.00	42.50	90.00
63-Welcome Santa; ½-size, oblong	2.75	8.00	16.00
64(nn)-Santa's Helpers; ½-size, oblong	2.75	8.00	16.00
65(nn)-Jingle Bells (1950)-½-size, oblong	2.75	8.00	16.00
66-Popeye (1951)	8.35	25.00	55.00
67-Oswald the Rabbit	4.00	12.00	24.00
68-Roy Rogers	13.00	40.00	85.00
69-Donald Duck; Barks-a on back-c	17.00	52.00	115.00
70-Tom and Jerry	4.00	12.00	24.00
71-Porky Pig	4.00	12.00	24.00
72-Krazy Kat	6.00	18.00	36.00
73-Roy Rogers	12.00	35.00	75.00
74-Mickey Mouse (1951)	14.00	42.50	85.00
75-Bugs Bunny	4.00	12.00	24.00
76-Andy and Woody	4.00	12.00	24.00
77-Roy Rogers	12.00	35.00	75.00
78-Gene Autry(1951)-Last regular size issue	12.00	35.00	75.00
79-Andy Panda (1952)-5x7'' size	2.75	8.00	16.00
80-Popeye	7.50	22.50	50.00
81-Oswald the Rabbit	3.00	9.00	18.00

MARCH OF COMICS (continued)

	Good	Fine	Mint
82-Tarzan	13.00	40.00	85.00
83-Bugs Bunny	3.00	9.00	18.00
84-Henry	2.35	7.00	14.00
85-Woody Woodpecker	2.35	7.00	14.00
86-Roy Rogers	8.50	25.50	60.00
87-Krazy Kat	4.75	14.00	30.00
88-Tom and Jerry	2.35	7.00	14.00
89-Porky Pig	2.35	7.00	14.00
90-Gene Autry	8.50	25.50	60.00
91-Roy Rogers & Santa	8.50	25.50	60.00
92-Christmas with Santa	2.00	6.00	12.00
93-Woody Woodpecker (1953)	2.35	7.00	14.00
94-Indian Chief	5.35	16.00	35.00
95-Oswald the Rabbit	2.35	7.00	14.00
96-Popeye	7.00	20.00	45.00
97-Bugs Bunny	2.35	7.00	14.00
98-Tarzan-Photo-c	13.00	40.00	85.00
99-Porky Pig	2.35	7.00	14.00
100-Roy Rogers	7.00	20.00	45.00
101-Henry	2.00	6.00	12.00
102-Tom Corbett (TV)	8.50	25.50	60.00
103-Tom and Jerry	2.00	6.00	12.00
104-Gene Autry	7.00	20.00	45.00
105-Roy Rogers	7.00	20.00	45.00
106-Santa's Helpers	2.00	6.00	12.00
107-Santa's Christmas Book - not published			
108-Fun with Santa (1953)	2.00	6.00	12.00
109-Woody Woodpecker (1954)	2.00	6.00	12.00
110-Indian Chief	3.00	9.00	20.00
111-Oswald the Rabbit	2.00	6.00	12.00
112-Henry	1.70	5.00	10.00
113-Porky Pig	2.00	6.00	12.00
114-Tarzan (Russ Manning)	13.00	40.00	85.00
115-Bugs Bunny	2.00	6.00	12.00
116-Roy Rogers	7.00	20.00	45.00
117-Popeye	7.00	20.00	45.00
118-Flash Gordon	10.00	30.00	70.00
119-Tom and Jerry	2.00	6.00	12.00
120-Gene Autry	7.00	20.00	45.00
121-Roy Rogers	7.00	20.00	45.00
122-Santa's Surprise (1954)	1.50	4.50	9.00
123-Santa's Christmas Book	1.50	4.50	9.00
124-Woody Woodpecker (1955)	1.70	5.00	10.00
125-Tarzan-Photo-c	12.00	35.00	75.00
126-Oswald the Rabbit	1.70	5.00	10.00
127-Indian Chief	2.35	7.00	16.00
128-Tom and Jerry	1.70	5.00	10.00
129-Henry	1.50	4.50	9.00
130-Porky Pig	1.70	5.00	10.00
131-Roy Rogers	7.00	20.00	45.00
132-Bugs Bunny	1.70	5.00	10.00
133-Flash Gordon	8.50	25.50	60.00
134-Popeye	4.00	12.00	28.00
135-Gene Autry	5.85	17.50	40.00
136-Roy Rogers	5.85	17.50	40.00
137-Gifts from Santa	1.35	4.00	8.00
138-Fun at Christmas (1955)	1.35	4.00	8.00
139-Woody Woodpecker (1956)	1.70	5.00	10.00
140-Indian Chief	2.65	8.00	16.00
141-Oswald the Rabbit	1.70	5.00	10.00
142-Flash Gordon	8.50	25.50	60.00
143-Porky Pig	1.70	5.00	10.00
144-Tarzan (Russ Manning)	10.00	30.00	65.00
145-Tom and Jerry	1.70	5.00	10.00
146-Roy Rogers-Photo-c	7.00	20.00	45.00

	Good	Fine	Mint
147-Henry	1.35	4.00	8.00
148-Popeye	4.00	12.00	28.00
149-Bugs Bunny	1.70	5.00	10.00
150-Gene Autry	5.85	17.50	40.00
151-Roy Rogers	5.85	17.50	40.00
152-The Night Before Christmas	1.35	4.00	8.00
153-Merry Christmas (1956)	1.35	4.00	8.00
154-Tom and Jerry (1957)	1.70	5.00	10.00
155-Tarzan-Photo-c	10.00	30.00	65.00
156-Oswald the Rabbit	1.70	5.00	10.00
157-Popeye	3.00	9.00	21.00
158-Woody Woodpecker	1.70	5.00	10.00
159-Indian Chief	2.65	8.00	16.00
160-Bugs Bunny	1.70	5.00	10.00
161-Roy Rogers	4.65	14.00	32.00
162-Henry	1.35	4.00	8.00
163-Rin Tin Tin (TV)	2.65	8.00	16.00
164-Porky Pig	1.70	5.00	10.00
165-The Lone Ranger	5.75	17.25	40.00
166-Santa and His Reindeer	1.35	4.00	8.00
167-Roy Rogers and Santa	4.65	14.00	32.00
168-Santa Claus' Workshop (1957)	1.35	4.00	8.00
169-Popeye (1958)	3.00	9.00	21.00
170-Indian Chief	2.65	8.00	16.00
171-Oswald the Rabbit	1.50	4.50	9.00
172-Tarzan	8.00	24.00	55.00
173-Tom and Jerry	1.50	4.50	9.00
174-The Lone Ranger	5.65	17.00	40.00
175-Porky Pig	1.50	4.50	9.00
176-Roy Rogers	4.65	14.00	32.00
177-Woody Woodpecker	1.50	4.50	9.00
178-Henry	1.35	4.00	8.00
179-Bugs Bunny	1.50	4.50	9.00
180-Rin Tin Tin (TV)	2.65	8.00	16.00
181-Happy Holiday	1.20	3.50	7.00
182-Happi Tim	1.50	4.50	9.00
183-Welcome Santa (1958)	1.20	3.50	7.00
184-Woody Woodpecker (1959)	1.50	4.50	9.00
185-Tarzan-Photo-c	8.00	24.00	55.00
186-Oswald the Rabbit	1.50	4.50	9.00
187-Indian Chief	2.65	8.00	16.00
188-Bugs Bunny	1.50	4.50	9.00
189-Henry	1.20	3.50	7.00
190-Tom and Jerry	1.50	4.50	9.00
191-Roy Rogers	4.65	14.00	32.00
192-Porky Pig	1.50	4.50	9.00
193-The Lone Ranger	5.75	17.25	40.00
194-Popeye	3.00	9.00	21.00
195-Rin Tin Tin (TV)	2.65	8.00	16.00
196-Sears Special - not published			
197-Santa Is Coming	1.20	3.50	7.00
198-Santa's Helpers (1959)	1.20	3.50	7.00
199-Huckleberry Hound (TV)(1960)	1.70	5.00	10.00
200-Fury (TV)	3.00	9.00	18.00
201-Bugs Bunny	1.35	4.00	8.00
202-Space Explorer	4.00	12.00	28.00
203-Woody Woodpecker	1.35	4.00	8.00
204-Tarzan	5.75	17.25	40.00
205-Mighty Mouse	2.50	7.50	15.00
206-Roy Rogers-Photo-c	5.00	15.00	35.00
207-Tom and Jerry	1.35	4.00	8.00
208-The Lone Ranger-Clayton Moore photo-c	6.50	19.50	45.00
209-Porky Pig	1.35	4.00	8.00
210-Lassie (TV)	2.65	8.00	16.00
211-Sears Special - not published			

March of Comics #118, © KING

March of Comics #155, © ERB

March of Comics #190, © MGM

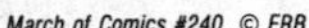
March of Comics #240, © ERB

March of Comics #287, © L. Schlesinger

March of Comics #310, © Lone Ranger

MARCH OF COMICS (continued)	Good	Fine	Mint
212-Christmas Eve	1.20	3.50	7.00
213-Here Comes Santa (1960)	1.20	3.50	7.00
214-Huckleberry Hound (TV)(1961)	1.70	5.00	10.00
215-Hi Yo Silver	4.00	12.00	24.00
216-Rocky & His Friends (TV)	2.85	8.50	20.00
217-Lassie (TV)	2.35	7.00	14.00
218-Porky Pig	1.35	4.00	8.00
219-Journey to the Sun	3.00	9.00	21.00
220-Bugs Bunny	1.35	4.00	8.00
221-Roy and Dale-Photo-c	4.35	13.00	30.00
222-Woody Woodpecker	1.35	4.00	8.00
223-Tarzan	6.00	18.00	40.00
224-Tom and Jerry	1.35	4.00	8.00
225-The Lone Ranger	4.35	13.00	30.00
226-Christmas Treasury (1961)	1.20	3.50	7.00
227-Sears Special - not published?			
228-Letters to Santa (1961)	1.20	3.50	7.00
229-The Flintstones (TV)(1962)	2.85	8.50	20.00
230-Lassie (TV)	2.35	7.00	14.00
231-Bugs Bunny	1.20	3.50	7.00
232-The Three Stooges	4.35	13.00	30.00
233-Bullwinkle (TV)	3.65	11.00	25.00
234-Smokey the Bear	1.35	4.00	8.00
235-Huckleberry Hound (TV)	1.70	5.00	10.00
236-Roy and Dale	3.65	11.00	25.00
237-Mighty Mouse	2.00	6.00	12.00
238-The Lone Ranger	4.35	13.00	30.00
239-Woody Woodpecker	1.35	4.00	8.00
240-Tarzan	5.00	15.00	35.00
241-Santa Claus Around the World	1.20	3.50	7.00
242-Santa's Toyland (1962)	1.20	3.50	7.00
243-The Flintstones (TV)(1963)	2.50	7.50	15.00
244-Mister Ed (TV)-Photo-c	2.00	6.00	12.00
245-Bugs Bunny	1.35	4.00	8.00
246-Popeye	2.50	7.50	15.00
247-Mighty Mouse	2.00	6.00	12.00
248-The Three Stooges	4.35	13.00	30.00
249-Woody Woodpecker	1.35	4.00	8.00
250-Roy and Dale	3.65	11.00	25.00
251-Little Lulu	13.00	40.00	85.00
252-Tarzan	5.00	15.00	35.00
253-Yogi Bear (TV)	2.00	6.00	12.00
254-Lassie (TV)	2.35	7.00	14.00
255-Santa's Christmas List	1.20	3.50	7.00
256-Christmas Party (1963)	1.20	3.50	7.00
257-Mighty Mouse	2.00	6.00	12.00
258-The Sword in the Stone (Disney)	5.00	15.00	35.00
259-Bugs Bunny	1.35	4.00	8.00
260-Mister Ed (TV)	1.70	5.00	10.00
261-Woody Woodpecker	1.35	4.00	8.00
262-Tarzan	5.00	15.00	35.00
263-Donald Duck-not Barks	5.35	16.00	32.00
264-Popeye	2.50	7.50	15.00
265-Yogi Bear (TV)	1.70	5.00	10.00
266-Lassie (TV)	2.00	6.00	12.00
267-Little Lulu; Irving Tripp-a	11.00	32.50	70.00
268-The Three Stooges	3.65	11.00	25.00
269-A Jolly Christmas	1.20	3.50	7.00
270-Santa's Little Helpers	1.20	3.50	7.00
271-The Flintstones (TV)(1965)	2.50	7.50	15.00
272-Tarzan	5.00	15.00	35.00
273-Bugs Bunny	1.35	4.00	8.00
274-Popeye	2.50	7.50	15.00
275-Little Lulu-Irving Tripp-a	8.35	25.00	55.00
276-The Jetsons (TV)	3.65	11.00	25.00
277-Daffy Duck	1.35	4.00	8.00
278-Lassie (TV)	2.00	6.00	12.00
279-Yogi Bear (TV)	1.70	5.00	10.00

	Good	Fine	Mint
280-The Three Stooges-Photo-c	3.65	11.00	25.00
281-Tom and Jerry	1.00	3.00	6.00
282-Mister Ed (TV)	1.70	5.00	10.00
283-Santa's Visit	1.20	3.50	7.00
284-Christmas Parade (1965)	1.20	3.50	7.00
285-Astro Boy (TV)	20.00	60.00	120.00
286-Tarzan	5.00	15.00	35.00
287-Bugs Bunny	1.00	3.00	6.00
288-Daffy Duck	1.00	3.00	6.00
289-The Flintstones (TV)	2.00	6.00	12.00
290-Mister Ed (TV)-Photo-c	1.30	4.00	8.00
291-Yogi Bear (TV)	1.30	4.00	8.00
292-The Three Stooges-Photo-c	3.65	11.00	25.00
293-Little Lulu; Irving Tripp-a	5.75	17.25	40.00
294-Popeye	2.50	7.50	15.00
295-Tom and Jerry	.85	2.50	5.00
296-Lassie (TV)-Photo-c	1.70	5.00	10.00
297-Christmas Bells	1.20	3.50	7.00
298-Santa's Sleigh (1966)	1.20	3.50	7.00
299-The Flintstones (TV)(1967)	2.00	6.00	12.00
300-Tarzan	5.00	15.00	35.00
301-Bugs Bunny	.85	2.50	5.00
302-Laurel and Hardy (TV)-Photo-c	2.35	7.00	14.00
303-Daffy Duck	.70	2.00	4.00
304-The Three Stooges-Photo-c	3.00	9.00	21.00
305-Tom and Jerry	.70	2.00	4.00
306-Daniel Boone (TV)-Photo-c	2.35	7.00	14.00
307-Little Lulu; Irving Tripp-a	5.35	16.00	35.00
308-Lassie (TV)-Photo-c	1.50	4.50	9.00
309-Yogi Bear (TV)	1.00	3.00	6.00
310-The Lone Ranger-Clayton Moore photo-c	4.35	13.00	30.00
311-Santa's Show	1.00	3.00	6.00
312-Christmas Album (1967)	1.00	3.00	6.00
313-Daffy Duck (1968)	.70	2.00	4.00
314-Laurel and Hardy (TV)	2.35	7.00	14.00
315-Bugs Bunny	.85	2.50	5.00
316-The Three Stooges	3.00	9.00	21.00
317-The Flintstones (TV)	1.70	5.00	10.00
318-Tarzan	4.65	13.00	32.00
319-Yogi Bear (TV)	1.00	3.00	6.00
320-Space Family Robinson (TV); Spiegle-a	5.35	16.00	35.00
321-Tom and Jerry	.70	2.00	4.00
322-The Lone Ranger	4.35	13.00	30.00
323-Little Lulu-not Stanley	3.35	10.00	20.00
324-Lassie (TV)-Photo-c	1.50	4.50	9.00
325-Fun with Santa	1.00	3.00	6.00
326-Christmas Story (1968)	1.00	3.00	6.00
327-The Flintstones (TV)(1969)	1.70	5.00	10.00
328-Space Family Robinson (TV); Spiegle-a	5.35	16.00	35.00
329-Bugs Bunny	.85	2.50	5.00
330-The Jetsons (TV)	2.85	8.50	20.00
331-Daffy Duck	.70	2.00	4.00
332-Tarzan	3.65	11.00	25.00
333-Tom and Jerry	.70	2.00	4.00
334-Lassie (TV)	1.15	3.50	7.00
335-Little Lulu	3.35	10.00	20.00
336-The Three Stooges	3.00	9.00	21.00
337-Yogi Bear (TV)	.85	2.50	5.00
338-The Lone Ranger	4.35	13.00	30.00
339-(Did not come out)			
340-Here Comes Santa (1969)	1.00	3.00	6.00
341-The Flintstones (TV)	1.30	4.00	8.00
342-Tarzan	3.65	11.00	25.00
343-Bugs Bunny	.70	2.00	4.00
344-Yogi Bear (TV)	.85	2.50	5.00
345-Tom and Jerry	.70	2.00	4.00
346-Lassie (TV)	1.15	3.50	7.00
347-Daffy Duck	.70	2.00	4.00

MARCH OF COMICS (continued)	Good	Fine	Mint
348-The Jetsons (TV)	2.50	7.50	15.00
349-Little Lulu-not Stanley	2.50	7.50	15.00
350-The Lone Ranger	3.65	11.00	25.00
351-Beep-Beep, the Road Runner	1.35	4.00	8.00
352-Space Family Robinson (TV)-Spiegle-a	5.35	16.00	35.00
353-Beep-Beep, the Road Runner (1971)	1.35	4.00	8.00
354-Tarzan (1971)	3.00	9.00	21.00
355-Little Lulu-not Stanley	2.50	7.50	15.00
356-Scooby Doo, Where Are You? (TV)	1.70	5.00	10.00
357-Daffy Duck & Porky Pig	.70	2.00	4.00
358-Lassie (TV)	1.15	3.50	7.00
359-Baby Snoots	1.35	4.00	8.00
360-H. R. Pufnstuf (TV)-Photo-c	1.00	3.00	6.00
361-Tom and Jerry	.70	2.00	4.00
362-Smokey the Bear (TV)	.70	2.00	4.00
363-Bugs Bunny & Yosemite Sam	.70	2.00	4.00
364-The Banana Splits (TV)-Photo-c	.85	2.50	5.00
365-Tom and Jerry (1972)	.70	2.00	4.00
366-Tarzan	3.00	9.00	21.00
367-Bugs Bunny & Porky Pig	.70	2.00	4.00
368-Scooby Doo (TV)(4/72)	1.50	4.50	10.00
369-Little Lulu-not Stanley	2.00	6.00	12.00
370-Lassie (TV)-Photo-c	1.15	3.50	7.00
371-Baby Snoots	1.00	3.00	6.00
372-Smokey the Bear (TV)	.70	2.00	4.00
373-The Three Stooges	3.00	9.00	18.00
374-Wacky Witch	.70	2.00	4.00
375-Beep-Beep & Daffy Duck	.70	2.00	4.00
376-The Pink Panther (1972)	1.35	4.00	8.00
377-Baby Snoots (1973)	1.00	3.00	6.00
378-Turok, Son of Stone	5.75	17.25	40.00
379-Heckle & Jeckle New Terrytoons	.50	1.50	3.00
380-Bugs Bunny & Yosemite Sam	.50	1.50	3.00
381-Lassie (TV)	.85	2.50	5.00
382-Scooby Doo, Where Are You? (TV)	1.30	4.00	8.00
383-Smokey the Bear (TV)	.50	1.50	3.00
384-Pink Panther	1.00	3.00	6.00
385-Little Lulu	2.50	7.50	15.00
386-Wacky Witch	.50	1.50	3.00
387-Beep-Beep & Daffy Duck	.50	1.50	3.00
388-Tom and Jerry (1973)	.50	1.50	3.00
389-Little Lulu-not Stanley	2.00	6.00	12.00
390-Pink Panther	.70	2.00	4.00
391-Scooby Doo (TV)	1.30	4.00	8.00
392-Bugs Bunny & Yosemite Sam	.50	1.50	3.00
393-New Terrytoons (Heckle & Jeckle)	.50	1.50	3.00
394-Lassie (TV)	.70	2.00	4.00
395-Woodsy Owl	.50	1.50	3.00
396-Baby Snoots	.70	2.00	4.00
397-Beep-Beep & Daffy Duck	.50	1.50	3.00
398-Wacky Witch	.50	1.50	3.00
399-Turok, Son of Stone	5.00	15.00	35.00
400-Tom and Jerry	.50	1.50	3.00
401-Baby Snoots (1975) (r-/No. 371)	.70	2.00	4.00
402-Daffy Duck (r-/No. 313)	.50	1.50	3.00
403-Bugs Bunny (r-/No. 343)	.50	1.50	3.00
404-Space Family Robinson (TV)(r-/No. 328)	4.00	12.00	28.00
405-Cracky	.50	1.50	3.00
406-Little Lulu (r-/No. 355)	2.00	6.00	12.00
407-Smokey the Bear (TV)(r-/No. 362)	.50	1.50	3.00
408-Turok, Son of Stone	4.35	13.00	30.00
409-Pink Panther	.50	1.50	3.00
410-Wacky Witch	.35	1.00	2.00
411-Lassie (TV)(r-/No. 324)	.70	2.00	4.00
412-New Terrytoons (1975)	.35	1.00	2.00

	Good	Fine	Mint
413-Daffy Duck (1976)(r-/No. 331)	.35	1.00	2.00
414-Space Family Robinson (r-/No. 328)	3.00	9.00	18.00
415-Bugs Bunny (r-/No. 329)	.35	1.00	2.00
416-Beep-Beep, the Road Runner (r-/No. 353)	.35	1.00	2.00
417-Little Lulu (r-/No. 323)	1.70	5.00	10.00
418-Pink Panther (r-/No. 384)	.35	1.00	2.00
419-Baby Snoots (r-/No. 377)	.50	1.50	3.00
420-Woody Woodpecker	.35	1.00	2.00
421-Tweety & Sylvester	.35	1.00	2.00
422-Wacky Witch (r-/No. 386)	.35	1.00	2.00
423-Little Monsters	.35	1.00	2.00
424-Cracky (12/76)	.35	1.00	2.00
425-Daffy Duck	.35	1.00	2.00
426-Underdog (TV)	.70	2.00	4.00
427-Little Lulu (r/No. 335)	1.50	4.50	9.00
428-Bugs Bunny	.35	1.00	2.00
429-The Pink Panther	.35	1.00	2.00
430-Beep-Beep, the Road Runner	.35	1.00	2.00
431-Baby Snoots	.50	1.50	3.00
432-Lassie (TV)	.50	1.50	3.00
433-Tweety & Sylvester	.35	1.00	2.00
434-Wacky Witch	.35	1.00	2.00
435-New Terrytoons	.35	1.00	2.00
436-Wacky Advs. of Cracky	.35	1.00	2.00
437-Daffy Duck	.35	1.00	2.00
438-Underdog (TV)	.70	2.00	4.00
439-Little Lulu (r/No. 349)	1.35	4.00	8.00
440-Bugs Bunny	.35	1.00	2.00
441-The Pink Panther	.35	1.00	2.00
442-Beep-Beep, the Road Runner	.35	1.00	2.00
443-Baby Snoots	.50	1.50	3.00
444-Tom and Jerry	.35	1.00	2.00
445-Tweety and Sylvester	.35	1.00	2.00
446-Wacky Witch	.35	1.00	2.00
447-Mighty Mouse	.50	1.50	3.00
448-Cracky	.35	1.00	2.00
449-Pink Panther	.35	1.00	2.00
450-Baby Snoots	.35	1.00	2.00
451-Tom and Jerry	.35	1.00	2.00
452-Bugs Bunny	.35	1.00	2.00
453-Popeye	.35	1.00	2.00
454-Woody Woodpecker	.35	1.00	2.00
455-Beep-Beep, the Road Runner	.35	1.00	2.00
456-Little Lulu (r/No. 369)	1.00	3.00	6.00
457-Tweety & Sylvester	.35	1.00	2.00
458-Wacky Witch	.35	1.00	2.00
459-Mighty Mouse	.50	1.50	3.00
460-Daffy Duck	.35	1.00	2.00
461-The Pink Panther	.35	1.00	2.00
462-Baby Snoots	.35	1.00	2.00
463-Tom and Jerry	.35	1.00	2.00
464-Bugs Bunny	.35	1.00	2.00
465-Popeye	.35	1.00	2.00
466-Woody Woodpecker	.35	1.00	2.00
467-Underdog (TV)	.35	1.00	2.00
468-Little Lulu (r/No. 385)	.70	2.00	4.00
469-Tweety & Sylvester	.35	1.00	2.00
470-Wacky Witch	.35	1.00	2.00
471-Mighty Mouse	.50	1.50	3.00
472-Heckle & Jeckle(12/80)	.35	1.00	2.00
473-Pink Panther(1/81)	.35	1.00	2.00
474-Baby Snoots	.35	1.00	2.00
475-Little Lulu (r/No. 323)	.50	1.50	3.00
476-Bugs Bunny	.35	1.00	2.00
477-Popeye	.35	1.00	2.00

March of Comics #360, © Krofft Prod.

March of Comics #402, © Warner Bros.

March of Comics #465, © KING

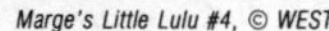
Marge's Little Lulu #4, © WEST

Tubby & the Little Men From Mars #410, © WEST

Margie #2 (Dell), © 20th Century-Fox

MARCH OF COMICS (continued)

	Good	Fine	Mint
478-Woody Woodpecker	.35	1.00	2.00
479-Underdog (TV)	.35	1.00	2.00
480-Tom and Jerry	.35	1.00	2.00
481-Tweety and Sylvester	.35	1.00	2.00
482-Wacky Witch	.35	1.00	2.00
483-Mighty Mouse	.50	1.50	3.00
484-Heckle & Jeckle	.35	1.00	2.00
485-Baby Snoots	.35	1.00	2.00
486-The Pink Panther	.35	1.00	2.00
487-Bugs Bunny	.35	1.00	2.00
488-Little Lulu (r/No. 335)	.50	1.50	3.00

MARCH OF CRIME (My Love Affair No. 1-6) (See Fox Giants)
No. 7, July, 1950 - No. 2, Sept, 1950; No. 3, Sept, 1951
Fox Features Syndicate

	Good	Fine	Mint
7(No.1)(7/50)-Wood-a	11.00	33.00	76.00
2(9/50)-Wood-a (exceptional)	10.00	30.00	70.00
3(9/51)	4.00	12.00	28.00

MARCO POLO
1962 (Movie classic)
Charlton Comics Group

	Good	Fine	Mint
nn (Scarce)	8.00	24.00	56.00

MARGARET O'BRIEN (See The Adventures of. . .)

MARGE'S LITTLE LULU (Little Lulu No. 207 on)
No. 74, 6/45 - No. 164, 7-9/62; No. 165, 10/62 - No. 206, 8/72
Dell Publishing Co./Gold Key 165-206

Marjorie Henderson Buell, born in Philadelphia, Pa., in 1904, created Little Lulu, a cartoon character that appeared weekly in the Saturday Evening Post from Feb. 23, 1935 through Dec. 30, 1944. She was not responsible for any of the comic books. **John Stanley** did pencils only on all Little Lulu Comics through at least No. 175. He did pencils and inks on Four Color 74,97 only. He did storyboards (layouts), pencils, and scripts in all cases and inking only on covers. His word balloons were written in cursive. The Whitman artists in Poughkeepsie, N.Y. blew up the pencilled pages, inked the blowups, and lettered them. The earlier issues had to be approved by Buell prior to publication.

	Good	Fine	Mint
4-Color 74('45)-Intro Luly, Tubby & Alvin	80.00	240.00	560.00
4-Color 97(2/46)	43.00	130.00	300.00
(Above two books done entirely by John Stanley - cover, pencils, and inks.)			
4-Color 110('46)-1st Alvin Story Telling Time; 1st app. Willy	30.00	90.00	210.00
4-Color 115-1st app. Boys' Clubhouse	30.00	90.00	210.00
4-Color 120, 131: 120-1st app. Eddie	27.00	81.00	190.00
4-Color 139('47),146,158	25.00	75.00	175.00
4-Color 165 (10/47)-Smokes doll hair & has wild hallucinations	25.00	75.00	175.00
1(1-2/48)-Lulu's Diary feat. begins	52.00	156.00	365.00
2-1st app. Gloria; 1st Tubby story in a L.L. comic	26.00	78.00	182.00
3-5	23.00	70.00	160.00
6-10: 7-1st app. Annie	16.50	50.00	115.00
11-20	13.50	40.50	95.00
21-30: 26-r/F.C. 110. 30-Xmas-c	10.00	30.00	70.00
31-38,40	8.50	25.50	60.00
39-Intro. Witch Hazel in "That Awful Witch Hazel"	10.00	30.00	70.00
41-60: 45-2nd Witch Hazel app. 49-Gives Stanley & others credit	8.00	24.00	56.00
61-80: 63-1st app. Chubby (Tubby's cousin). 80-Intro. Little Itch (2/55)	5.00	15.00	35.00
81-99	3.75	11.25	26.00
100	4.00	12.00	28.00
101-130	3.00	9.00	21.00
131-164	2.35	7.00	16.00
165-Giant; . . . In Paris ('62)	3.75	11.25	30.00
166-Giant; . . . Christmas Diary ('62-'63)	3.75	11.25	30.00
167-169	2.00	6.00	14.00
170,172,175,176,178-196,198-200-Stanley-r	1.30	4.00	9.00
171,173,174,177,197	.85	2.50	6.00
201,203,206-Last issue to carry Marge's name	.55	1.65	4.00
202,204,205-Stanley-r	1.00	3.00	7.00
. . . & Tubby in Japan (12 cents)(5-7/62) 01476-207	4.50	13.50	31.50
. . . Summer Camp 1(8/67-G.K.-Giant) '57-58-r	3.00	9.00	24.00
. . . Trick 'N' Treat 1(12¢)(12/62-Gold Key)	3.65	11.00	25.00

NOTE: *See* **Dell Giant Comics** No. 23, 29, 36, 42, 50, & **Dell Giants** for annuals. All Giants not by **Stanley** from L.L. & Tubby in Alaska (7/59)-on.

MARGE'S LITTLE LULU (See Golden Comics Digest No. 19, 23, 27, 29, 33, 36, 40, 43, 46 & March of Comics No. 251, 267, 275, 293, 307, 323, 335, 349, 355, 369, 385, 406, 417, 427, 439, 456, 468, 475, 488)

MARGE'S TUBBY (Little Lulu)(See Dell Giants)
No. 381, Aug, 1952 - No. 49, Dec-Feb, 1961-62
Dell Publishing Co./Gold Key

	Good	Fine	Mint
4-Color 381-Stanley script; Irving Tripp-a	11.00	33.00	76.00
4-Color 430,444-Stanley-a	6.00	18.00	42.00
4-Color 461 (4/53)-1st Tubby & Men From Mars story; Stanley-a	6.00	18.00	42.00
5 (7-9/53)-Stanley-a	5.00	15.00	35.00
6-10	3.50	10.50	24.00
11-20	2.85	8.50	20.00
21-30	2.35	7.00	16.00
31-49	2.00	6.00	14.00
. . . & the Little Men From Mars No. 30020-410(10/64-G.K.)-25 cents; 68 pgs.	5.00	15.00	40.00

NOTE: ***Lloyd White*** *did all art except F.C. 430, 444, 461, 5.*

MARGIE (See My Little. . .)

MARGIE (TV)
No. 1307, Mar-May, 1962 - No. 2, July-Sept, 1962 (Photo-c)
Dell Publishing Co.

	Good	Fine	Mint
4-Color 1307, 2	2.00	6.00	14.00

MARGIE COMICS (Formerly Comedy) (Reno Browne No. 50 on)
No. 35, Winter, 1946-47 - No. 49, Dec, 1949
Marvel Comics (ACI)

	Good	Fine	Mint
35	3.35	10.00	23.00
36-38,42,45,47-49	1.65	5.00	11.50
39,41,43(2),44,46-Kurtzman's "Hey Look"	2.50	7.50	17.50
40-Three "Hey Looks," three "Giggles & Grins" by Kurtzman	3.75	11.25	26.00

MARINES (See Tell It to the. . .)

MARINES ATTACK
Aug, 1964 - No. 9, Feb-Mar, 1966
Charlton Comics

	Good	Fine	Mint
1		.40	.80
2-9		.30	.60

MARINES AT WAR (Tales of the Marines No. 4)
No. 5, April, 1957 - No. 7, Aug, 1957
Atlas Comics (OPI)

	Good	Fine	Mint
5-7	.50	1.50	3.50

NOTE: ***Colan*** *a-5.* ***Drucker*** *a-5.* ***Maneely*** *a-5.* ***Orlando*** *a-7.* ***Severin*** *c-5.*

MARINES IN ACTION
June, 1955 - No. 14, Sept, 1957
Atlas News Co.

	Good	Fine	Mint
1-Rock Murdock, Boot Camp Brady begin	1.50	4.50	10.00
2-14	.70	2.00	5.00

NOTE: ***Berg*** *a-2, 8, 9, 11, 14.* ***Heath*** *c-2, 9.* ***Severin*** *a-4; c-7-11, 14.*

MARINES IN BATTLE
Aug, 1954 - No. 25, Sept, 1958
Atlas Comics (ACI No. 1-12/WPI No. 13-25)

	Good	Fine	Mint
1-Heath-c; Iron Mike McGraw by Heath; history of U.S. Marine Corps. begins	2.35	7.00	16.00
2	1.20	3.50	8.00
3-6,8-10: 4-Last precode (2/55)	1.00	3.00	7.00
7-Six pg. Kubert/Moskowitz-a	1.70	5.00	12.00
11-16,18-22,24	.70	2.00	5.00
17-Williamson-a, 3 pgs.	3.00	9.00	21.00
23-Crandall-a; Mark Murdock app.	1.70	5.00	12.00
25-Torres-a	1.70	5.00	12.00

NOTE: ***Berg*** *a-22.* ***Drucker*** *a-6.* ***Everett*** *a-4, 15; c-21.* ***Maneely*** *c-24.* ***Orlando*** *a-14.* ***Pakula*** *a-6.* ***Powell*** *a-16.*

MARINE WAR HEROES (Charlton Premiere No. 19)
Jan, 1964 - No. 18, Mar, 1967
Charlton Comics

	Good	Fine	Mint
1		.40	.80
2-18		.30	.60

NOTE: ***Montes/Bache*** *a-1,14,18; c-1.*

MARK HAZZARD: MERC
Nov, 1986 - Present
Marvel Comics Group

	Good	Fine	Mint
1-Morrow-a begins		.60	1.20
2-6		.45	.90

MARK OF ZORRO (See 4-Color No. 228)

MARK STEEL
1967, 1968, 1972 (24 pgs.) (Color)
American Iron & Steel Institute (Giveaway)

	Good	Fine	Mint
1967,1968-"Journey of Discovery with. . ."; Neal Adams art	2.35	7.00	16.00
1972-". . . Fights Pollution;" Adams-a	1.35	4.00	8.00

MARK TRAIL
Oct, 1955 - No. 5, Summer, 1959
Standard Magazines (Hall Syndicate)/Fawcett Publ. No. 5

	Good	Fine	Mint
1-Sunday strip-r	3.35	10.00	23.00
2-5	1.65	5.00	11.50
. . . Adventure Book of Nature 1(Summer, 1958; Pines)-100 pg. Giant; contains 78 Sunday strip-r	4.00	12.00	28.00

MARMADUKE MONK
No date; 1963 (10 cents)
I. W. Enterprises/Super Comics

	Good	Fine	Mint
1-I.W. Reprint, 14-(Super Reprint)('63)		.60	1.20

MARMADUKE MOUSE
Spring, 1946 - No. 65, Dec, 1956
Quality Comics Group (Arnold Publ.)

	Good	Fine	Mint
1	4.35	13.00	30.00
2	2.15	6.50	15.00
3-10	1.65	5.00	11.50
11-30	1.30	4.00	9.00
31-65	1.00	3.00	7.00
Super Reprint No. 14(1963)		.60	1.20

MARS
Jan, 1984 - No. 12, Mar, 1985 (Mando paper)
First Comics

	Good	Fine	Mint
1-12: 2-The Black Flame begins. 10-Dynamo Joe begins		.50	1.00

MARS & BEYOND (See 4-Color No. 866)

M.A.R.S. PATROL TOTAL WAR (Total War No. 1,2)
No. 3, Sept, 1966 - No. 10, Aug, 1969 (All-Painted-c)
Gold Key

	Good	Fine	Mint
3-Wood-a	1.15	3.50	8.00
4-10	.55	1.65	4.00

MARTHA WAYNE (See The Story of. . .)

MARTIN KANE (Formerly My Secret Affair)
No. 4, June, 1950 - No. 2, Aug, 1950
Fox Features Syndicate (Hero Books)

	Good	Fine	Mint
4(No.1)-Wood-c/a(2); used in **SOTI**, pg. 160	13.00	40.00	90.00
2-Orlando-a, 5pgs; Wood-a(2)	8.00	24.00	56.00

MARTY MOUSE
No date (1958?) (10 cents)
I. W. Enterprises

	Good	Fine	Mint
1-Reprint		.60	1.20

MARVEL ADVENTURES (. . . Adventure No. 4 on)
Dec, 1975 - No. 6, Oct, 1976
Marvel Comics Group

	Good	Fine	Mint
1-No. 1-6 r-/Daredevil 22-27		.25	.50
2-6		.20	.40

MARVEL AND DC PRESENT (Featuring the Uncanny X-Men and the New Teen titans)
Nov, 1982 (One Shot, 68pgs, $2.00 cover, printed on Baxter paper)
Marvel Comics Group/DC Comics

	Good	Fine	Mint
1-Simonson/Austin c/a; Perez-a(p)	.60	1.75	3.50

MARVEL BOY (Astonishing No. 3 on)
Dec, 1950 - No. 2, Feb, 1951
Marvel Comics (MPC)

	Good	Fine	Mint
1-Origin Marvel Boy by Russ Heath	23.50	70.00	165.00
2-Everett-a	19.50	58.00	135.00

MARVEL CHILLERS
Oct, 1975 - No. 7, Oct, 1976
Marvel Comics Group

	Good	Fine	Mint
1-Intro. Modred the Mystic; Kane-c(p)		.30	.60
2-5,7: 3-Tigra, the Were-Woman begins (origin), ends No. 7. 7-Kirby-c, Tuska-p		.25	.50
6-Byrne-a(p); Buckler-c(p)		.50	1.00

MARVEL CLASSICS COMICS (Also see Pendulum Ill. Class.)
1976 - No. 36, Dec, 1978 (52 pgs., no ads)
Marvel Comics Group

	Good	Fine	Mint
1-36: 1-Dr. Jekyll and Mr. Hyde, 2-Time Machine, 3-Hunchback of Notre Dame, 4-20,000 Leagues Under the Sea, 5-Black Beauty, 6-Gulliver's Travels, 7-Tom Sawyer, 8-Moby Dick, 9-Dracula, 10-Red Badge of Courage, 11-Mysterious Island, 12-The Three Musketeers, 13-Last of the Mohicans, 14-War of the Worlds, 15-Treasure Island, 16-Ivanhoe, 17-The Count of Monte Cristo, 18-The Odyssey, 19-Robinson Crusoe, 20-Frankenstein, 21-Master of the World, 22-Food of the Gods, 23-The Moonstone, 24-She, 25-The Invisible Man, 26-The Illiad, 27-Kidnapped, 28-The Pit and the Pendulum, 29-Prisoner of Zenda, 30-Arabian Nights, 31-First Man in the Moon, 32-White Fang, 33-The Prince and the Pauper, 34-Robin Hood, 35-Alice in Wonderland, 36-A Christmas Carol each. . . .		.30	.60

NOTE: ***Alcala*** *a-34i; c-34.* ***Bolle*** *a-35.* ***Buscema*** *c-17p.* ***Golden*** *a-28.* ***Gil Kane*** *c-1-4p, 7p, 12p, 21p, 24p.* ***Nebres*** *a-5; c-24i.* ***Nino*** *a-2, 8, 12.* ***Redondo*** *a-1, 9. No. 1-12 were reprinted from Pendulum Ill. Classics.*

MARVEL COLLECTORS ITEM CLASSICS
1965 - No. 22, Aug, 1969 (Marvel's Greatest No. 23 on)

Mark Hazzard: Merc #1, © MCG

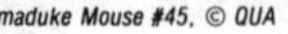

Marmaduke Mouse #45, © QUA

Mars #1, © First

Marvel Comics #1, © MCG

Marvel Comics Super Special #10, © MCG

Marvel Family #19, © FAW

MARVEL COLLECTORS ITEM... (cont'd.)
Marvel Comics Group

	Good	Fine	Mint
1-Fantastic Four & other-r begin	.85	2.50	5.00
2 (4/66) - 4	.35	1.00	2.00
5-22		.60	1.20

NOTE: *All reprints;* ***Ditko, Kirby*** *art in all.*

MARVEL COMICS (Marvel Mystery No. 2 on)
October, November, 1939
Timely Comics (Funnies, Inc.)

NOTE: The first issue was originally dated October 1939. Most copies have a black circle stamped over the date (on cover and inside) with "November" printed over it. However, some copies do not have the November overprint and could have a higher value. Most No. 1's have printing defects, i.e., tilted pages which caused trimming into the panels usually on right side and bottom.

	Good	Fine	VF-NM
1-Origin Sub-Mariner by Bill Everett(1st newsstand app.); 1st 8 pgs. reprinted from Motion Picture Funnies Weekly No. 1; Human Torch by Carl Burgos, Kazar the Great, & Jungle Terror (only app.); intro. The Angel by Gustavson, The Masked Raider (ends No. 12); cover by sci/fi pulp illustrator Frank R. Paul	4200.00	12,600.00	26,000.00

(Only one known copy exists in Mint condition which traded twice in 1986 for $69,000 & later for $80,000. Two other copies are known in NM-M condition & their value would vary beyond the VF-NM price)

MARVEL COMICS SUPER SPECIAL (Marvel Super Special No. 5 on; also see Howard the Duck No. 12) (Magazine) ($1.50)
September, 1977 - Present (nn 7)
Marvel Comics Group

	Good	Fine	Mint
1-Kiss, 40 pgs. comics plus photos & features; Simonson-a(p)	.85	2.50	5.00
2-Conan (3/78)	.50	1.50	3.00
3-Close Encounters of the Third Kind (6/78); Simonson-a	.35	1.00	2.00
4-The Beatles Story (8/78)-Perez/Janson-a	.50	1.50	3.00
5-Kiss (12/78)	.30	.90	1.80
6-Jaws II (12/78)	.25	.75	1.50
7-Published in Britain only-Sgt. Pepper's Lonely Hearts Club Band			
8-Battlestar Galactica-tabloid size	.35	1.00	2.00
8-Battlestar Galactica publ. in reg. magazine format; low distribution ($1.50)8½x11"	.85	2.50	5.00
9-Conan	.35	1.00	2.00
10-Star Lord	.35	1.00	2.00
11-13-Weirdworld begins No. 11; 25 copy special press run of each with gold seal and signed by artists (Proof quality), Spring-June, 1979	10.00	30.00	60.00
11-Weirdworld (regular issue)	.70	2.00	4.00
12-Weirdworld (regular issue)	.40	1.25	2.50
13-Weirdworld (regular issue)	.30	.90	1.80
14-Adapts movie 'Meteor'		.60	1.20
15-Star Trek with photos & pin-ups($1.50)		.60	1.20
15-with $2.00 price(scarce); the price was changed at tail end of a 200,000 press run	.70	2.00	4.00
16-20: 16-'Empire Strikes Back'-Williamson-a, 17-Xanadu, 18-Raiders of the Lost Ark, 19-For Your Eyes Only (James Bond), 20-Dragon Slayer each....	.30	.90	1.80
21-40 (Movie adaptations): 21-Conan, 22-Bladerunner; Williamson-a; Steranko-c, 23-Annie, 24-The Dark Crystal, 25-Rock and Rule-w/photos, 26-Octopussy (James Bond), 27-Fire and Ice (Return of the Jedi), 28-Krull, 29-Tarzan of the Apes (Greystoke movie), 30-Indiana Jones and the Temple of Doom, 31-The Last Star Fighter, 32-The Muppets Take Manhattan, 33-Buckaroo Bonzai, 34-Sheena, 35-Conan The Destroyer, 36-Dune, 37-2010, 38-Red Sonja-movie adapt. 39-Santa Claus: The Movie. 40-Labyrinth each....	.35	1.00	2.00
41-Howard The Duck-movie adapt.(11/86)	.45	1.25	2.50

NOTE: ***J. Buscema*** *a-1, 2, 9, 11-13, 18p, 21, 40; c-11(part), 12.* ***Chaykin*** *a-9, 19p; c-18, 19.* ***Colan*** *a(p)-6, 10, 14.* ***Spiegle*** *a-29.*

MARVEL DOUBLE FEATURE
Dec, 1973 - No. 21, Mar, 1977
Marvel Comics Group

	Good	Fine	Mint
1-Captain America & Iron Man-r begin		.30	.60
2-21: 17-r/Iron Man & Sub-Mariner No. 1		.25	.50

NOTE: ***Colan*** *a-1-19p(r).* ***Gil Kane*** *a-15p(r).* ***Kirby*** *a-1r, 2-8p(r), 17p(r); c-17-20.*

MARVEL FAMILY (Also see Captain Marvel No. 18)
Dec, 1945 - No. 89, Jan, 1954
Fawcett Publications

	Good	Fine	Mint
1-Origin Captain Marvel, Captain Marvel Jr., Mary Marvel, & Uncle Marvel retold; Black Adam origin & 1st app.	52.00	156.00	365.00
2	28.00	84.00	195.00
3	20.00	60.00	140.00
4,5	14.50	43.50	100.00
6-10: 7-Shazam app.	11.50	34.50	80.00
11-20	8.00	24.00	56.00
21-30	6.00	18.00	42.00
31-40	5.50	16.50	38.00
41-46,48-50	4.35	13.00	30.00
47-Flying Saucer c/stry	5.00	15.00	35.00
51-76,79,80,82-89	3.65	11.00	25.00
77-Communist Threat-c	5.50	16.50	38.00
78,81-Used in **POP**, pgs. 92,93	4.35	13.00	30.00

MARVEL FANFARE
March, 1982 - Present ($1.25-$1.50, slick paper) (Direct Sale only)
Marvel Comics Group

	Good	Fine	Mint
1-Spider-Man/Angel team-up; 1st Paul Smith story	1.50	4.50	9.00
2-Spider-Man, Ka-Zar, The Angel. F.F. origin retold	1.65	5.00	10.00
3-X-Men & Ka-Zar	.75	2.30	4.60
4-X-Men & Ka-Zar	.90	2.75	5.50
5-Dr. Strange, Capt. America	.50	1.50	3.00
6-Spider-Man, Scarlet Witch	.35	1.10	2.20
7-Incredible Hulk; Daredevil backup	.35	1.10	2.20
8-Dr. Strange; Wolf Boy begins	.35	1.10	2.20
9-Man-Thing by Morrow	.35	1.10	2.20
10-13-Black Widow	.35	1.10	2.20
14-The Vision	.35	1.00	2.00
15-The Thing by Barry Smith, c/a	.35	1.00	2.00
16,17-Skywolf	.35	1.00	2.00
18-Capt. America; Miller c/a	.25	.75	1.50
19-Cloak and Dagger	.25	.75	1.50
20,21-The Thing/Incredible Hulk	.25	.75	1.50
22,23-Iron Man vs. Dr. Octopus	.25	.75	1.50
24-26-Weirdworld-Ploog/Russell-a	.25	.75	1.50
27-31: 27-Daredevil/Spider-Man. 28-Alpha Flight. 29-Hulk. 30-Moon Knight. 31-Capt. America	.25	.75	1.50

NOTE: ***Austin*** *a-1i, 4i; c-8i.* ***Byrne*** *a-1p, 29; c-29. .* ***Golden*** *a-1p, 2p, 4p; c-1, 2.* ***Infantino*** *c/a(p)-8.* ***Gil Kane*** *a-8-11p.* ***Miller*** *c-1(Back-c).* ***Perez*** *a-10, 11p, 12, 13p; c-10p-13p.* ***Rogers*** *a-5p; c-5p.* ***Russell*** *a-5i, 6i, 8-11i; c-5i, 6.* ***Paul Smith*** *a-1p, 4p; c-4p.* ***Williamson*** *a-30.*

MARVEL FEATURE (See Marvel Two-In-One)
Dec, 1971 - No. 12, Nov, 1973 (No. 1,2: 25 cents)
Marvel Comics Group

	Good	Fine	Mint
1-Origin The Defenders; Sub-Mariner, The Hulk & Dr. Strange; G.A. Sub-Mariner-r, Adams-c	1.35	4.00	8.00
2-G.A. 1950s Sub-Mariner-r	.70	2.00	4.00
3-Defender series ends	.70	2.00	4.00
4-7: 4-Begin Ant-Man series; brief origin		.40	.80
8-Origin Antman & The Wasp		.50	1.00
9,10-Last Ant-Man. 9-Iron Man app.		.40	.80
11,12-Thing team-ups. 11-Origin Fantastic-4 retold		.40	.80

NOTE: ***Bolle*** *a-9i.* ***Everett*** *a-1i, 3i.* ***Kane*** *c-3p, 7p.* ***Russell*** *a-7-10p.* ***Starlin*** *a-8, 11, 12.*

MARVEL FEATURE (Also see Red Sonja)
Nov, 1975 - No. 7, Nov, 1976

MARVEL FEATURE (continued)
Marvel Comics Group

	Good	Fine	Mint
1-Red Sonja begins; Adams r/Savage Sword of Conan No. 1	.25	.80	1.60
2-7		.50	1.00

NOTE: ***Thorne** c/a-2-7.*

MARVEL FUMETTI BOOK
April, 1984 (One shot) ($1.00 cover price)
Marvel Comics Group

	Good	Fine	Mint
1		.40	.80

MARVEL GRAPHIC NOVEL
1982 - Present ($5.95-$6.95)
Marvel Comics Group (Epic Comics)

	Good	Fine	Mint
1 (First Printing)-Death of Captain Marvel	3.00	9.00	18.00
1 (2nd & 3rd Printing)	1.00	3.00	6.00
2-Elric: The Dreaming City	.85	2.50	5.00
3-Dreadstar; Starlin-a, 48pgs.	1.00	3.00	6.00
4-The New Mutants-Origin	1.35	4.00	8.00
5-X-Men; book-length story	1.35	4.00	8.00

6-The Star Slammers, 7-Killraven, 8-Super Boxers, 9-The Futurians, 10-Heartburst, 11-Void Indigo, 12-The Dazzler, 13-Starstruck, 14-The Swords Of The Swashbucklers, 15-The Raven Banner (Asgard), 16-The Aladdin Effect, 17-Revenge Of The Living Monolith

	Good	Fine	Mint
18-She Hulk	1.00	3.00	6.00
19-The Witch Queen of Acheron (Conan)	1.20	3.50	7.00
20-Greenberg the Vampire; Wrightson c/a	1.70	5.00	10.00
21-Marada The She-Wolf	1.20	3.50	7.00
22-Amaz. Spider-Man in Hooky by Wrightson	1.70	5.00	10.00
23-Dr. Strange. 24-Love And War by Miller. 26-Silver Surfer	1.00	3.00	6.00
25-Dracula	1.20	3.50	7.00

NOTE: ***Byrne** c/a-18. **Kaluta** c/a-13. **Miller** a-23p. **Russell** c/a-2. **Simonson** a-5, 6; c-6. **Starlin** c/a-1,3. **Wrightson** c/a(painted)-20.*

MARVEL MINI-BOOKS
1966 (50 pgs., B&W; 5/8''x7/8'') (6 different issues)
Marvel Comics Group (Smallest comics ever published)

	Good	Fine	Mint
Captain America, Spider-Man, Sgt. Fury, Hulk, Thor	.50	1.50	3.00
Millie the Model	.35	1.00	2.00

NOTE: *Each came in six different color covers, usually one color: Pink, yellow, green, etc.*

MARVEL MOVIE PREMIERE (Magazine)
Sept, 1975 (One Shot) (Black & White)
Marvel Comics Group

	Good	Fine	Mint
1-Burroughs "The Land That Time Forgot" adaptation	.35	1.00	2.00

MARVEL MOVIE SHOWCASE
Nov, 1982 - No. 2, Dec, 1982 (68 pgs.)
Marvel Comics Group

	Good	Fine	Mint
1,2-Star Wars movie adaptation r/Star Wars No. 1-6		.60	1.20

MARVEL MOVIE SPOTLIGHT
Nov, 1982 (68 pgs.)
Marvel Comics Group

	Good	Fine	Mint
1-Edited r/Raiders of the Lost Ark No. 1-3; Buscema-c/a(p)		.40	.80

MARVEL MYSTERY COMICS (Formerly Marvel Comics) (Marvel Tales No. 93 on)
No. 2, Dec, 1939 - No. 92, June, 1949
Timely /Marvel Comics (TP 2-17/TCI 18-54/MCI 55-92)

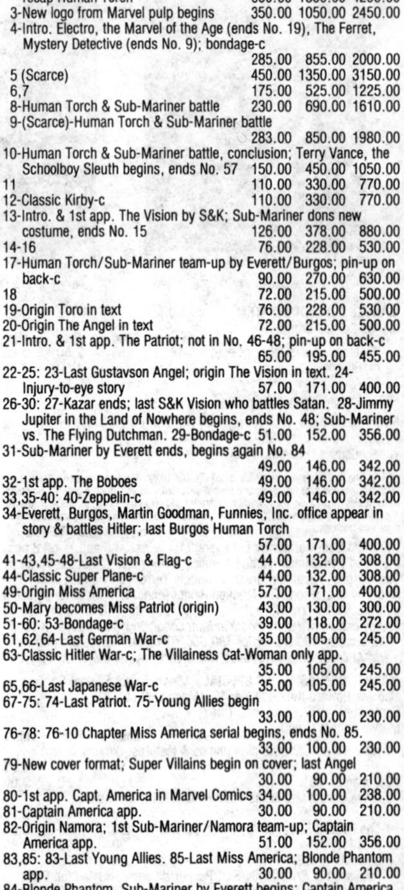

	Good	Fine	Mint
2-American Ace begins, ends No. 3; Human Torch (blue costume) by Burgos, Sub- Mariner by Everett continues; 2pg. origin recap Human Torch	600.00	1800.00	4200.00
3-New logo from Marvel pulp begins	350.00	1050.00	2450.00
4-Intro. Electro, the Marvel of the Age (ends No. 19), The Ferret, Mystery Detective (ends No. 9); bondage-c	285.00	855.00	2000.00
5 (Scarce)	450.00	1350.00	3150.00
6,7	175.00	525.00	1225.00
8-Human Torch & Sub-Mariner battle	230.00	690.00	1610.00
9-(Scarce)-Human Torch & Sub-Mariner battle	283.00	850.00	1980.00
10-Human Torch & Sub-Mariner battle, conclusion; Terry Vance, the Schoolboy Sleuth begins, ends No. 57	150.00	450.00	1050.00
11	110.00	330.00	770.00
12-Classic Kirby-c	110.00	330.00	770.00
13-Intro. & 1st app. The Vision by S&K; Sub-Mariner dons new costume, ends No. 15	126.00	378.00	880.00
14-16	76.00	228.00	530.00
17-Human Torch/Sub-Mariner team-up by Everett/Burgos; pin-up on back-c	90.00	270.00	630.00
18	72.00	215.00	500.00
19-Origin Toro in text	76.00	228.00	530.00
20-Origin The Angel in text	72.00	215.00	500.00
21-Intro. & 1st app. The Patriot; not in No. 46-48; pin-up on back-c	65.00	195.00	455.00
22-25: 23-Last Gustavson Angel; origin The Vision in text. 24-Injury-to-eye story	57.00	171.00	400.00
26-30: 27-Kazar ends; last S&K Vision who battles Satan. 28-Jimmy Jupiter in the Land of Nowhere begins, ends No. 48; Sub-Mariner vs. The Flying Dutchman. 29-Bondage-c	51.00	152.00	356.00
31-Sub-Mariner by Everett ends, begins again No. 84	49.00	146.00	342.00
32-1st app. The Boboes	49.00	146.00	342.00
33,35-40: 40-Zeppelin-c	49.00	146.00	342.00
34-Everett, Burgos, Martin Goodman, Funnies, Inc. office appear in story & battles Hitler; last Burgos Human Torch	57.00	171.00	400.00
41-43,45-48-Last Vision & Flag-c	44.00	132.00	308.00
44-Classic Super Plane-c	44.00	132.00	308.00
49-Origin Miss America	57.00	171.00	400.00
50-Mary becomes Miss Patriot (origin)	43.00	130.00	300.00
51-60: 53-Bondage-c	39.00	118.00	272.00
61,62,64-Last German War-c	35.00	105.00	245.00
63-Classic Hitler War-c; The Villainess Cat-Woman only app.	35.00	105.00	245.00
65,66-Last Japanese War-c	35.00	105.00	245.00
67-75: 74-Last Patriot. 75-Young Allies begin	33.00	100.00	230.00
76-78: 76-10 Chapter Miss America serial begins, ends No. 85.	33.00	100.00	230.00
79-New cover format; Super Villains begin on cover; last Angel	30.00	90.00	210.00
80-1st app. Capt. America in Marvel Comics	34.00	100.00	238.00
81-Captain America app.	30.00	90.00	210.00
82-Origin Namora; 1st Sub-Mariner/Namora team-up; Captain America app.	51.00	152.00	356.00
83,85: 83-Last Young Allies. 85-Last Miss America; Blonde Phantom app.	30.00	90.00	210.00
84-Blonde Phantom, Sub-Mariner by Everett begins; Captain America app.	34.00	100.00	238.00
86-Blonde Phantom i.d. revealed; Captain America app.; last Bucky app.	34.00	100.00	238.00
87-1st Capt. America/Golden Girl team-up	36.00	108.00	252.00

88-Golden Girl, Namora, & Sungirl (1st in Marvel Comics) x-over;

Marvel Feature #1 (11/75), © MCG

Marvel Mystery Comics #9, © MCG

Marvel Mystery Comics #55, © MCG

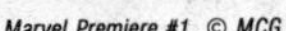
Marvel Premiere #1, © MCG

Marvels of Science #1, © CC

Marvel Spotlight #6, © MCG

MARVEL MYSTERY COMICS (continued) Good Fine Mint
Captain America, Blonde Phantom, Sun Girl app.; last Toro
34.00 100.00 238.00
89-1st Human Torch/Sun Girl team-up; 1st Captain America solo; Blonde Phantom app. 36.00 108.00 252.00
90-Blonde Phantom un-masked; Captain America app.
32.00 95.00 225.00
91-Capt. America app.; intro Venus; Blonde Phantom & Sub-Mariner end 32.00 95.00 225.00
92-Feature story on the birth of the Human Torch and the death of professor Horton (his creator); 1st app. The Witness in Marvel Comics; Captain America app. 60.00 180.00 420.00
(Very rare) 132 Pg. issue, B&W, 25 cents (1943-44)-printed in N. Y.; square binding, blank inside covers; has Marvel No. 33-c in color; contains 2 Capt. America & 2 Marvel Mystery Comics-r (Two known copies) 235.00 705.00 1645.00

NOTE: ***Everett*** *c-7-9, 27.* ***Schomburg*** *c-3-11, 13-15, 18, 19, 22-29, 33, 35, 36, 39-48, 50-57, 59, 63-66. Bondage covers-3, 7, 12, 28, 49, 50, 52, 56, 57, 65.*

MARVEL NO-PRIZE BOOK, THE
Jan, 1983 (One Shot, Direct Sale only)
Marvel Comics Group

1-Golden-c .50 1.00

MARVEL PREMIERE
April, 1972 - No. 61, Aug, 1981
Marvel Comics Group

1-Origin Warlock by Gil Kane/Adkins; origin Counter-Earth
1.00 3.00 6.00
2-Warlock ends; Kirby Yellow Claw-r .85 2.50 5.00
3-Dr. Strange series begins, Smith-a(p) 1.25 3.75 7.50
4-Smith/Brunner-a .70 2.00 4.00
5-10: 10-Death of the Ancient One .35 1.00 2.00
11-14: 11-Origin-r by Ditko. 14-Intro. God; last Dr. Strange
.30 .80 1.60
15-Iron Fist begins (origin), ends 25 .85 2.50 5.00
16-20 .35 1.00 2.00
21-24,26-28: 26-Hercules. 27-Satana. 28-Legion of Monsters
.25 .80 1.60
25-Byrne's 1st Iron Fist .85 2.50 5.00
29-56: 35-Origin/1st app. 3-D Man. 47-Origin new Ant-Man
.40 .80
57-Dr. Who (1st U.S. app.) .35 1.00 2.00
58-60-Dr. Who .25 .75 1.50
61-Star Lord .50 1.00

NOTE: ***Austin*** *a-50i, 56i; c-46i, 50i, 56i, 58.* ***Brunner*** *a-4i, 6p, 9-14p; c-9-14.* ***Byrne*** *a-47p, 48p.* ***Giffen*** *a-31p, 44p; c-44.* ***Gil Kane*** *a-1p, 2p, 15p; c-1p, 22-24p, 27p, 36p, 37p.* ***Kirby*** *c-26, 29-31, 35.* ***Layton*** *a-47i, 48i; c-47.* ***McWilliams*** *a-25i.* ***Miller*** *c-49p, 53p, 58p.* ***Nebres*** *a-44i; c-38i.* ***Nino*** *a-38i.* ***Perez*** *c/a-38p, 45p, 46p.* ***Ploog*** *c-5-7.* ***Russell*** *a-7p.* ***Simonson*** *a-60; c-57.* ***Starlin*** *a-8p; c-8.* ***Sutton*** *a-41, 43, 50p, 61; c-50p, 61. No. 57-60 were published with two different prices on cover.*

MARVEL PRESENTS
October, 1975 - No. 12, Aug, 1977
Marvel Comics Group

1-Bloodstone app. .40 .80
2-Origin Bloodstone; Kirby-c .30 .60
3-Guardians of the Galaxy .50 1.00
4-7,9,11,12-Guardians of the Galaxy .40 .80
8-Reprints Silver Surfer No. 2 .40 .80
10-Starlin-a(p) .40 .80

NOTE: ***Austin*** *a-6i.* ***Kane*** *c-1p.*

MARVEL PREVIEW (Magazine) (Bizarre Advs. No. 25 on)
Feb, 1975 - No. 24, Winter, 1980 (B&W) ($1.00)
Marvel Comics Group

1-Man Gods From Beyond the Stars; Adams-a(i) & cover; Nino-a
.70 2.00 4.00
2-Origin The Punisher (see Amaz. Spider-Man 129); 1st app. Dominic Fortune; Morrow-c 2.00 6.00 12.00

Good Fine Mint
3-Blade the Vampire Slayer .30 .90 1.80
4-Star-Lord & Sword in the Star (origins & 1st app.)
1.20 3.50 7.00
5,6-Sherlock Holmes .50 1.50 3.00
7-9: 7-Satana, Sword in the Star app., 8-Legion of Monsters, 9-Man-God; origin Star Hawk, ends No.20 .35 1.00 2.00
10-Thor the Mighty; Starlin-a .40 1.25 2.50
11-Star-Lord; Byrne-a .40 1.25 2.50
12-20: 12-Haunt of Horror, 16-Detectives, 17-Black Mark by G. Kane, 18-Star-Lord, 19-Kull, 20-Bizarre Advs. .50 1.00
21,22,24: 21-Moon Knight; Ditko-a, 22-King Arthur. 24-Debut Paradox .50 1.00
23-Miller-a; Bizarre Advs. .35 1.00 2.00

NOTE: ***Buscema*** *a-22, 23.* ***Byrne*** *a-10, 11.* ***Colan*** *a-16p, 18p, 23p; c-16p.* ***Giffen*** *a-7.* ***Infantino*** *a-14.* ***Kaluta*** *a-12.* ***Miller*** *a-23.* ***Morrow*** *c-2-4.* ***Perez*** *a-20.* ***Ploog*** *a-8.* ***Starlin*** *c-13, 14.*

MARVEL SAGA, THE
Dec, 1985 - Present
Marvel Comics Group

1 .35 1.00 2.00
2,3 .25 .75 1.50
4-16 .55 1.10

MARVEL'S GREATEST COMICS (Marvel Coll. Item Classics No. 1-22)
No. 23, Oct, 1969 - No. 96, Jan, 1981
Marvel Comics Group

23-34,38-96 .25 .50
35-37-Silver Surfer-r/Fantastic Four No. 48-50 .40 .80

NOTE: *Dr. Strange, Fantastic-4, Iron Man, Watcher-No. 23,24. Capt. America, Dr. Strange, Iron Man, Fantastic-4-No. 25-28. Fantastic Four-No. 38-60.* ***Buscema*** *a-85-92r; c-87-92r.* ***Ditko*** *a-23-28r.* ***Kirby*** *a(r)-1-82; c-75, 77p, 80p.*

MARVELS OF SCIENCE
March, 1946 - No. 4, June, 1946
Charlton Comics

1-(1st Charlton comic)-A-Bomb sty 5.00 15.00 35.00
2-4 2.65 8.00 18.00

MARVEL SPECIAL EDITION (Also see Special Collectors' Edition)
1975 - 1978 (84 pgs.) (Oversized)
Marvel Comics Group

1-Spider-Man(r); Ditko-a(r) .25 .75 1.50
1-Star Wars ('77); r-Star Wars No. 1-3 .25 .75 1.50
2-Star Wars ('78); r-Star Wars No. 4-6 .50 1.00
3-Star Wars ('78, 116 pgs.); r-Star Wars No. 1-6
.50 1.00
3-Close Encounters ('78, 56 pgs., movie) .50 1.00
V2No.2(Spr. '80, $2.00, oversized)-"Star Wars: The Empire Strikes Back;" r-/Marvel Comics S. Special 16 .50 1.00

NOTE: ***Chaykin*** *c/a-1(1977), 2, 3.*

MARVEL SPECTACULAR
Aug, 1973 - No. 19, Nov, 1975
Marvel Comics Group

1-Thor-r begin by Kirby .30 .60
2-19 .25 .50

MARVEL SPOTLIGHT
11/71 - No. 33, 4/77; 7/79 - V2No. 11, 3/81
Marvel Comics Group

1-Origin Red Wolf; Wood inks, Adams-c .45 1.30 2.60
2-(Giant, 52pgs.)-Venus-r by Everett; origin Werewolf by Ploog; Adams-c .30 .90 1.80
3,4-Werewolf ends No. 4 .60 1.20
5-Origin/1st app. Ghost Rider 1.35 4.00 8.00
6-8-Last Ploog issue .50 1.50 3.00
9-11-Last Ghost Rider .25 .75 1.50
12-20: 12-The Son of Satan begins (Origin) .40 .80

MARVEL SPOTLIGHT (continued)

	Good	Fine	Mint
21-27: 25-Sinbad. 26-Scarecrow. 27-Sub-Mariner		.30	.60
28,29-Moon Knight	.50	1.50	3.00
30-The Warriors Three, 31-Nick Fury		.30	.60
32-Intro/partial origin Spider-Woman		.50	1.00
33-Deathlok		.40	.80
V2No.1-7,9-11: Capt. Marvel No. 1-4. 5-Dragon Lord. 6,7-Star-Lord; origin No. 6. 9-11-Capt. Universe app.		.30	.60
8-Capt. Marvel; Miller a(p)	.35	1.00	2.00

NOTE: ***Austin*** *c-V2/2i, 8.* ***J. Buscema*** *c/a-30p.* ***Ditko*** *a-V2/4, 5, 9-11; c-V2/4, 9-11.* ***Kane*** *c-21p, 32p.* ***Kirby*** *c-29.* ***McWilliams*** *a-20i.* ***Miller*** *a-V2/8p; c-V2/2, 5p, 7p, 8p.* ***Mooney*** *a-8i, 10i, 14-17p, 24p, 27, 32i.* ***Nasser*** *a-33p.* ***Ploog*** *a-2-5, 6-8p; c-3-9.* ***Sutton*** *a-9-11p, V2/6, 7. No. 29-25 cent & 30 cent issues exist.*

MARVEL SUPER ACTION (Magazine)
January, 1976 (One Shot) (76 pgs.; black & white)
Marvel Comics Group

	Good	Fine	Mint
1-Origin & 2nd app. Dominic Fortune; The Punisher app., Weird World & The Huntress; Evans & Ploog-a	.70	2.00	4.00

MARVEL SUPER-ACTION
May, 1977 - No. 37, Nov, 1981
Marvel Comics Group

	Good	Fine	Mint
1-Capt. America-r by Kirby begin		.30	.60
2-5: 4-Marvel Boy-r(origin)/M. Boy No. 1		.25	.50
6-37: 11-C.A. Origin-r. 14-37-Avengers-r		.25	.50

NOTE: ***Buscema*** *a(r)-14p, 15p; c-18-20, 22, 35r-37.* ***Evans*** *a-1.* ***Everett*** *a-4.* ***Heath*** *a-4.* ***Ploog*** *a-1.* ***Smith*** *a-27r, 28r.* ***Steranko*** *a(r)-12p, 13p; c-12, 13.*

MARVEL SUPER-HERO CONTEST OF CHAMPIONS
June, 1982 - No. 3, Aug, 1982 (Mini-Series)
Marvel Comics Group

	Good	Fine	Mint
1-Features nearly all Marvel characters currently appearing in comics	.85	2.50	5.00
2,3	.70	2.00	4.00

MARVEL SUPER HEROES
October, 1966
Marvel Comics Group

	Good	Fine	Mint
1-r-origin Daredevil; Avengers-r; G.A. Sub-Mariner & H. Torch-r/M. Mystery No. 8	.60	1.75	3.50

MARVEL SUPER-HEROES (Fantasy Masterpieces No. 1-11)
(Also see Giant Size Super Heroes)
No. 12, 12/67 - No. 31, 11/71; No. 32, 9/72 - No. 105, 1/82
Marvel Comics Group

	Good	Fine	Mint
12-Origin & 1st app. Capt. Marvel of the Kree; G.A. H. Torch, Destroyer, Capt. America, Black Knight, Sub-Mariner-r	.60	1.75	3.50
13-G.A. Black Knight, Torch, Vision, Capt. America, Sub-Mariner-r; Capt. Marvel app.	.25	.75	1.50
14-G.A. Sub-Mariner, Torch, Mercury, Black Knight, Capt. America reprints; Spider-Man app.	.25	.75	1.50
15-Black Bolt cameo in Medusa; G.A. Black Knight, Sub-Mariner, Black Marvel, Capt. America-r	.25	.75	1.50
16-Origin & 1st app. Phantom Eagle; G.A. Torch, Capt. America, Black Knight, Patriot, Sub-Mariner-r		.40	.80
17-Origin Black Knight; G.A. Torch, Sub-Mariner, All-Winners Squad reprints		.40	.80
18-Origin Guardians of the Galaxy; G.A. Sub-Mariner, All-Winners Squad-r	.40	1.20	2.40
19-G.A. Torch, Marvel Boy, Black Knight, Sub-Mariner-r; Smith-c(p) Tuska-a(r)		.40	.80
20-Reprints Young Men No. 24 w/-c		.40	.80
21-105: All-r ish. 31-Last Giant ish.		.25	.50

NOTE: ***Austin*** *a-104.* ***Colan*** *a-12p, 13p, 15p, 18p; c-12, 13, 15, 18.* ***Everett*** *a-14i, 15i(r), 33(r); c-85(r). New* ***Kirby*** *c-22, 27.* ***Maneely*** *a-15(r), 19(r).* ***Severin*** *a-83-85i(r), 100-102(r); c-100-102(r).* ***Starlin*** *c-47.* ***Tuska*** *a-19p.*

MARVEL SUPER-HEROES SECRET WARS (Also see Secret Wars II)
May, 1984 - No. 12, Apr, 1985 (Limited series)
Marvel Comics Group

	Good	Fine	Mint
1	.60	1.75	3.50
2-4	.35	1.10	2.20
5-7: 6-The Wasp dies. 7-Intro. new Spider-Woman	.35	1.00	2.00
8-Spider-Man's new costume explained	.40	1.25	2.50
9-12	.35	1.00	2.00

MARVEL SUPER SPECIAL (See Marvel Comics Super . . .)

MARVEL TAILS STARRING PETER PORKER THE SPECTACULAR SPIDER-HAM
Nov, 1983 (One Shot)
Marvel Comics Group

	Good	Fine	Mint
1-Peter Porker, The Spectacular Spider-Ham, Captain Americat, Goose Rider, Hulk Bunny app.		.30	.60

MARVEL TALES (Marvel Mystery No. 1-92)
No. 93, Aug, 1949 - No. 159, Aug, 1957
Marvel/Atlas Comics (MCI)

	Good	Fine	Mint
93	24.00	72.00	166.00
94-Everett-a	18.00	54.00	125.00
95,96,99,101,103,105: 96-Bondage-c	9.00	27.00	62.00
97-Sun Girl, 2 pgs; Kirbyish-a; one story used in N.Y. State Legislative document	14.50	43.50	100.00
98-Krigstein-a	10.00	30.00	70.00
100	10.00	30.00	70.00
102-Wolverton-a "The End of the World," 6 pgs.	23.00	70.00	160.00
104-Wolverton-a "Gateway to Horror," 6 pgs; Heath-c	20.00	60.00	140.00
106,107-Krigstein-a. 106-Decapitation story	9.50	28.50	65.00
108-120: 120-Jack Katz-a	4.65	14.00	32.00
121,123-131-Last precode (2/55)	4.00	12.00	28.00
122-Kubert-a	5.50	16.50	38.00
132,133,135-141,143,145	2.65	8.00	18.00
134-Krigstein, Kubert-a; flying saucer-c	4.00	12.00	28.00
142-Krigstein-a	3.65	11.00	25.00
144-Williamson/Krenkel-a, 3 pgs.	4.00	12.00	28.00
146,148-151,154,155,158	1.85	5.50	13.00
147-Ditko-a	3.00	9.00	21.00
152-Wood, Morrow-a	3.35	10.00	23.00
153-Everett End of World c/story	3.00	9.00	21.00
156-Torres-a	2.65	8.00	18.00
157,159-Krigstein-a	3.65	11.00	25.00

NOTE: ***Andru*** *a-103.* ***Briefer*** *a-118.* ***Colan*** *a-105, 107, 118, 120, 121, 127, 131.* ***Sid Check*** *a-147.* ***Drucker*** *a-127, 135, 141, 146, 150.* ***Everett*** *a-98, 104, 106(2), 108(2), 131, 148, 151, 153, 155; c-111, 114, 117, 127, 143, 148-151, 153, 155.* ***Forte*** *a-125, 130.* ***Heath*** *a-118, 119; c-104-106, 130.* ***Gil Kane*** *a-117.* ***Lawrence*** *a-130.* ***Maneely*** *a-111, 126, 129; c-108, 116, 120, 129, 152.* ***Mooney*** *a-114.* ***Morrow*** *a-150, 152, 156.* ***Orlando*** *a-149, 151, 157.* ***Pakula*** *a-121, 144, 150, 152, 156.* ***Powell*** *a-136, 137, 150, 154.* ***Rico*** *a-97, 99.* ***Romita*** *a-108.* ***Sekowsky*** *a-96-98.* ***Sinnott*** *a-105.* ***Tuska*** *a-114* ***Whitney*** *a-107.* ***Wildey*** *a-126, 138.*

MARVEL TALES (. . .Annual No. 1,2: . . .Starring Spider-Man No. 123 on)
1964 - Present (No. 1-32, 72 pgs.)
Marvel Comics Group

	Good	Fine	Mint
1-Origin Spider-Man, Hulk, Ant/Giant Man, Iron Man, Thor, & Sgt. Fury; all-r	7.50	22.50	45.00
2 ('65)-r-X-Men No. 1(origin), Avengers No. 1(origin) & origin Dr. Strange/Str. Tales 115	2.00	6.00	12.00
3 (7/66)-Spider-Man-r begin	.85	2.50	5.00
4,5	.45	1.25	2.50
6-15: 13-Origin Marvel Boy-r/M. Boy No. 1	.25	.80	1.60

Marvel Super Action #4, © MCG

Marvel Super-Heroes #19, © MCG

Marvel Tales #110 (1st Series), © MCG

Marvel Tales #138 (2nd Series), © MCG

Marvel Team-Up #53, © MCG

Marvel Treasury Edition #1, © MCG

MARVEL TALES (continued) — Good / Fine / Mint

16-30: 30-New Angel story .40 .80
31-74,76,80-97 .30 .60
75-Origin Spider-Man-r .40 .80
77-79-Drug issues-r/Spider-Man No. 96-98 .50 1.00
98-Death of Gwen Stacy-r/Amazing Spider-Man No. 121 .60 1.20
99-Death Green Goblin .60 1.20
100-(52 pgs.)-New Hawkeye/Two Gun Kid sty .40 .80
101-133-All Spider-Man-r .35 .70
134-136-Dr. Strange-r begin; SpM stories continue. 134-Dr. Strange r/Strange Tales 110 .35 .70
137-Origin-r Dr. Strange; shows original unprinted-c & origin Spider-Man/Amazing Fantasy 15 .50 1.00
137-Nabisco giveaway .50 1.00
138-Reprints all Amazing Spider-Man No. 1 .50 1.00
139-144: r-/Amazing Spider-Man No. 2-7 with original covers .40 .80
145-190: Spider-Man-r .40 .80
191 (68 pgs., $1.50)-r-Spider-Man 96-98 .25 .75 1.50
192 (52 pgs., $1.25)-r-Spider-Man 121,122 .60 1.25
193-197 .40 .80

NOTE: *All are reprints.* ***Austin*** *a-100i.* ***Byrne*** *a-194.* ***Ditko*** *a-1-30, 83, 100, 137-55.* ***G. Kane*** *a-71, 81, 98-101p; c-125-127p, 130p, 137-55.* ***Mooney*** *a-63, 95-97i, 103(i).* ***Nasser*** *a-100p.*

MARVEL TEAM-UP (See Official Marvel Index To. . .)
March, 1972 - No. 150, Feb, 1985
Marvel Comics Group

NOTE: *Spider-Man team-ups in all but Nos. 18,23,26,29,32,35,97,104,105,137.*

1-H-T 3.35 10.00 20.00
2,3-H-T 1.50 4.50 9.00
4-X-Men 1.65 5.00 10.00
5-10: 5-Vision. 6-Thing. 7-Thor. 8-The Cat. 9-Iron Man. 10-H-T .75 2.25 4.50
11-20: 11-Inhumans. 12-Werewolf. 13-Capt. America. 14-Sub-Mariner. 15-Ghost Rider (new.). 16-Capt. Marvel. 17-Mr. Fantastic. 18-H-T/Hulk. 19-Ka-Zar. 20-Black Panther .50 1.50 3.00
21-30: 21-Dr. Strange. 22-Hawkeye. 23-H-T/Iceman. 24-Brother Voodoo. 25-Daredevil. 26-H-T/Thor. 27-Hulk. 28-Hercules. 29-H-T/Iron Man. 30-Falcon .35 1.00 2.00
31-40: 31-Iron Fist. 32-H-T/Son of Satan. 33-Nighthawk. 34-Valkyrie. 35-H-T/Dr. Strange. 36-Frankenstein. 37-Man-Wolf. 38-Beast. 39-H-T. 40-Sons of the Tiger/H-T .25 .75 1.50
41-50: 41-Scarlet Witch. 42-The Vision. 43-Dr. Doom; retells origin. 44-Moondragon. 45-Killraven. 46-Deathlok. 47-Thing. 48-Iron Man. 49,50-Dr. Strange/Iron Man .60 1.20
51,52,56-58: 51-Dr. Strange/Iron Man. 52-Capt. America. 56-Daredevil. 57-Black Widow. 58-Ghost Rider .50 1.00
53-Woodgod/Hulk; new X-Men app., 1st by Byrne 1.20 3.50 7.00
54-Hulk/Woodgod; Byrne-a(p) .70 2.00 4.00
55,59,60: 55-Warlock. 59-Yellowjacket/The Wasp. 60-The Wasp-All Byrne-a .70 2.00 4.00
61-70: 61-H-T. 62-Ms. Marvel. 63-Iron Fist. 64-Daughters of the Dragon. 65-Capt. Britain (1st U.S. app.). 66-Capt. Britain; 1st app. Arcade. 67-Tigra. 68-Man-Thing. 69-Havock. 70-Thor-All Bryne-a .45 1.25 2.50
71,72,76: 71-Falcon. 72-Iron Man. 76-Dr. Strange. Byrne-c .50 1.00
73,77,78,80: 73-Daredevil. 77-Ms. Marvel. 78-Wonder Man. 80-Dr. Strange/Clea .40 .80
74-Not Ready for Prime Time Players (Belushi) .40 .80
75,79: 75-Power Man. 79-Mary Jane Watson as Red Sonja. Both Byrne-a(p) .45 1.25 2.50
81-88,90: 81-Satana. 82-Black Widow. 83-Nick Fury. 84-Shang-Chi. 85-Shang-Chi/Black Widow/Nick Fury. 86-Guardians of the Galaxy. 87-Black Panther. 88-The Invisible Girl. 90-Beast .40 .80
89-Nightcrawler .25 .75 1.50
91-99: 91-Ghost Rider. 92-Hawkeye. 93-Werewolf by Night. 94-SpM vs. The Shroud. 95-Nick Fury/Shield; intro. Mockingbird. 96-Howard The Duck. 97-Spider-Woman/Hulk. 98-Black Widow. 99-Machine Man .40 .80
100-Fantastic-4(Double size); origin/1st app. Karma, one of the New Mutants; origin Storm; X-Men x-over; Miller-a/c(p); Byrne-a .85 2.50 5.00
101-116: 101-Nighthawk(Ditko-a). 102-Doc Samson. 103-Ant-Man. 104-Hulk/Ka-Zar. 105-Hulk/Powerman/Iron Fist. 106-Capt. America. 107-She-Hulk. 108-Paladin; Dazzler cameo. 109-Paladin/Dazzler. 110-Iron Man. 111-Devil-Slayer. 112-King Kull. 113-Quasar. 114-Falcon. 115-Thor. 116-Valkyrie .40 .80
117-Wolverine .35 1.00 2.00
118-Professor X .25 .75 1.50
119-149: 118-Professor X. 119-Gargoyle. 120-Dominic Fortune. 121-Human Torch. 122-Man-Thing. 123-Daredevil. 124-The Beast. 125-Tigra. 126-Hulk & Powerman/Son of Satan. 127-The Watcher. 128-Capt. America. 129-The Vision. 130-Scarlet Witch. 131-Frogman. 132-Mr. Fantastic. 133-Fantastic-4. 134-Jack of Hearts. 135-Kitty Pryde; X-Men cameo. 136-Wonder Man. 137-Aunt May/Franklin Richards. 138-Sandman. 139-Nick Fury, 140-Black Widow. 141-Daredevil; new SpM/Black Widow app. 142-Captain Marvel. 143-Starfox. 144-Moon Knight. 145-Iron Man. 146-Nomad. 147-Human Torch; SpM old costume. 148-Thor. 149-Cannonball .40 .80
150-X-Men .35 1.00 2.00
Annual 1(1976)-New X-Men app. 1.50 4.50 9.00
Annual 2(12/79)-SpM/Hulk .25 .75 1.50
Annual 3(11/80)-Hulk/Power Man/Machine Man/Iron Fist; Miller-c(p) .60 1.20
Annual 4(10/81)-SpM/Daredevil/Moon Knight/Power Man/Iron Fist; brief origins of each; Miller-c(p)/a .35 1.00 2.00
Annual 5(1982)-SpM/The Thing/Scarlet Witch/Dr. Strange/Quasar .50 1.00
Annual 6(10/83)-New Mutants, Cloak & Dagger app. .25 .75 1.50
Annual 7(10/84)-Alpha Flight; Byrne-c(i) .50 1.00

NOTE: ***Adams*** *c-141p.* ***Austin*** *a-79i; c-76i, 79i, 96i, 101i, 112i, 130i.* ***Bolle*** *a-9i.* ***Byrne*** *a(p)-53-55, 59-70, 75, 79, 100; c-68p, 70p, 72p, 75, 76p, 79p, 129i, 133i.* ***Colan*** *a-87p.* ***Ditko*** *a-101.* ***Kane*** *a(p)-4-6, 13, 14, 16-19, 23; c(p)-4, 13, 14, 17-19, 23, 25, 26, 32-35, 37, 41, 44, 45, 47, 53, 54.* ***Miller*** *c-95p, 99p, 102p, 106.* ***Mooney*** *a-2i, 7i, 8, 10p, 11p, 16i, 24p, 29p, 72, 93i, Annual 5i.* ***Nasser*** *a-89p; c-101p.* ***Simonson*** *c-99i, 148.* ***Paul Smith*** *c-131, 132.* ***Starlin*** *c-27.* ***Sutton*** *a-93p. "H-T" means Human Torch; "SpM" means Spider-Man; "S-M" means Sub-Mariner.*

MARVEL TREASURY EDITION ($1.50-$2.50)
Sept, 1974 - No. 28, 1981 (100 pgs.; oversized, reprints)
Marvel Comics Group

1-Spider-Man .35 1.00 2.00
2-Fantastic Four, Silver Surfer .50 1.00
3-The Mighty Thor .50 1.00
4-Conan; Smith-c/a .25 .75 1.50
5-14,16,17: 5-The Hulk (origin), 6-Doctor Strange, 7-Avengers, 8-Christmas stories; Spider-Man, Hulk, Nick Fury, 9-Giant; Super-hero Team-up, 10-Thor, 11-Fantastic Four, 12-Howard the Duck, 13-Giant Super-hero Holiday Grab-Bag, 14-Spider-Man, 16-Super-hero Team-up; The Defenders (origin) & Valkyrie, 17-The Hulk .50 1.00
15-Conan; Smith, Adams-a .35 1.00 2.00
18-Marvel Team-up; Spider-Man's 1st team-ups with the X-Men .25 .75 1.50
19-28: 19-Conan the Barbarian, 20-Hulk, 21-Fantastic Four, 22-Spider-Man, 23-Conan, 24-Rampaging Hulk, 25-Spider-Man vs. The Hulk, 26-The Hulk; Wolverine app., 27-Spider-Man, 28-Spider-

MARVEL TREASURY EDITION (continued)

	Good	Fine	Mint
Man/Superman; (origin of each)		.50	1.00

NOTE: *Reprints-2,3,5,7-9,13,14,16,17.* ***Adams*** *a-6(i), 15.* ***Brunner*** *c/a-6.* ***Buscema*** *a-15, 19, 28; c-28.* ***Colan*** *c-12p.* ***Ditko*** *a-1, 6.* ***Kirby*** *a-2, 10, 11; c-7.* ***Smith*** *c/a-4.*

MARVEL TREASURY OF OZ (See MGM's Marvelous. . .)
1975 (oversized) ($1.50)
Marvel Comics Group

	Good	Fine	Mint
1-The Marvelous Land of Oz; Buscema-a		.60	1.20

MARVEL TREASURY SPECIAL (Also see 2001: A Space Odyssey)
1974; 1976 (84 pgs.; oversized) ($1.50)
Marvel Comics Group

	Good	Fine	Mint
Vol. 1-Spider-Man, Torch, Sub-Mariner, Avengers "Giant Superhero Holiday Grab-Bag;" Smith-a		.50	1.00
Vol. 1-Capt. America's Bicentennial Battles (6/76)-Kirby-a; Smith inks, 11 pgs.		.50	1.00

MARVEL TRIPLE ACTION
2/72 - No. 24, 3/75; No. 25, 8/75 - No. 47, 4/79
Marvel Comics Group

	Good	Fine	Mint
1-Giant (52 pgs.)		.40	.80
2-4		.30	.60
5-47: 7-Starlin-c. 45,46-X-Men-r		.25	.50
Giant-Size 1(5/75), 2(7/75)		.25	.50

NOTE: *Fantastic Four reprints-No. 1-4; Avengers reprints-No. 5 on.* ***Buscema*** *a(r)-35p, 36p, 38p, 39p, 41, 42, 43p, 44p, 46p, 47p.* ***Ditko*** *a-2r; c-47.* ***Kirby*** *a(r)-1-4p.* ***Tuska*** *a(r)-40p, 43i, 46i, 47i.*

MARVEL TWO-IN-ONE (See The Thing)
January, 1974 - No. 100, June, 1983
Marvel Comics Group

	Good	Fine	Mint
1-Thing team-ups begin	1.20	3.50	7.00
2-4: 3-Daredevil app.	.60	1.75	3.50
5-Guardians of the Galaxy	.70	2.00	4.00
6-10	.50	1.50	3.00
11-20	.35	1.10	2.20
21-40	.25	.70	1.40
41,42,44-49		.50	1.00
43,50,53-55-Byrne-a. 54-Death of Deathlok	.45	1.25	2.50
51-Miller-a(p)	.50	1.50	3.00
52-Moon Knight app.	.35	1.00	2.00
56-82: 60-Intro. Impossible Woman. 61-63-Warlock app.		.40	.80
83,84-Alpha Flight app.	.50	1.50	3.00
85-99: 93-Jocasta dies. 96-X-Men cameo		.30	.60
100-Double size, Byrne scripts	.25	.75	1.50
Annual 1(6/76)-Liberty Legion x-over	.30	.80	1.60
Annual 2(2/77)-Starlin c/a; Thanos dies	1.25	3.75	7.50
Annual 3(7/78), 4(9/79)		.50	1.00
Annual 5(9/80), 6(10/81)		.40	.80
Annual 7(10/82)-The Thing/Champion; Sasquatch, Colossus app.		.50	1.00

NOTE: ***Austin*** *c-42i, 54i, 56i, 58i, 61i, 63i, 66i.* ***John Buscema*** *a-30p, 45; c-30p.* ***Byrne*** *a-43p, 50p, 53-55p; c-43, 53p, 56p, 98i, 99i.* ***Gil Kane*** *a-1p, 2p; c(p)-1-3, 9, 11, 14, 28.* ***Kirby*** *c-10, 12, 19p, 20, 25, 27.* ***Mooney*** *a-18i, 38i, 90i.* ***Nasser*** *a-70p.* ***Perez*** *a-56-58p, 60p, 64p, 65p; c-32p, 33p, 42p, 50-52p, 54p, 55p, 57p, 58p, 61-66p, 70p.* ***Roussos*** *a-Annual 1i.* ***Simonson*** *c-43i; Annual 6i.* ***Starlin*** *c-6, Annual 1.* ***Tuska*** *a-6p.*

MARVEL UNIVERSE (See Official Handbook. . .)

MARVIN MOUSE
September, 1957
Atlas Comics (BPC)

	Good	Fine	Mint
1-Everett c/a; Maneely-a	2.00	6.00	14.00

MARY JANE & SNIFFLES (See 4-Color No. 402,474)

MARY MARVEL COMICS (Monte Hale No. 29 on) (Also see Captain Marvel No. 18, Marvel Family, Shazam, & Wow)
Dec, 1945 - No. 28, Sept, 1948
Fawcett Publications

	Good	Fine	Mint
1-Intro/origin Georgia Sivana	47.00	141.00	330.00
2	22.00	65.00	154.00
3	16.50	50.00	115.00
4	13.00	40.00	90.00
5-8: 8-Bulletgirl x-over in Mary Marvel	11.00	33.00	76.00
9,10	8.00	24.00	56.00
11-20	6.00	18.00	42.00
21-28	5.50	16.50	38.00

MARY POPPINS (See Walt Disney Showcase No. 17 & Movie Comics)

MARY'S GREATEST APOSTLE (St. Louis Grignion de Montfort)
No date (16 pages; paper cover)
Catechetical Guild (Topix) (Giveaway)

	Good	Fine	Mint
	2.35	7.00	16.00

MARY WORTH (See Love Stories of. . . & Harvey Comic Hits No. 55)
March, 1956
Argo

	Good	Fine	Mint
1	3.00	9.00	21.00

MASK
Dec, 1985 - No. 4, Mar, 1986 (mini-series)
DC Comics

	Good	Fine	Mint
1-(Sat. morning TV show)	.35	1.00	2.00
2-4	.25	.70	1.40

MASK
Feb, 1987 - Present
DC Comics

	Good	Fine	Mint
1,2		.40	.75

MASK COMICS
Feb-Mar, 1945 - No. 2, Apr-May, 1945; No. 2, Fall, 1945
Rural Home Publications

	Good	Fine	Mint
1-Classic L. B. Cole Satan-c/a; Palais-a	70.00	210.00	490.00
2-(Scarce)Classic L. B. Cole Satan-c; Black Rider, The Boy Magician, & The Collector app.	35.00	105.00	245.00
2(Fall, 1945)-No publ.-same as regular No. 2; L. B. Cole-c	25.00	75.00	175.00

MASKED BANDIT, THE
1952
Avon Periodicals

	Good	Fine	Mint
nn-Kinstler-a	8.00	24.00	56.00

MASKED MAN, THE
12/84 - No. 10, 4/86 ($1.75-$2.00; 32 pgs.; Baxter paper)
Eclipse Comics

	Good	Fine	Mint
1-Origin retold	.35	1.00	2.00
2-8: 3-Origin Aphid-Man	.30	.90	1.80
9,10 ($2.00)	.35	1.00	2.00

MASKED MARVEL (See Keen Det. Funnies)
Sept, 1940 - No. 3, Dec, 1940
Centaur Publications

	Good	Fine	Mint
1-The Masked Marvel begins	60.00	180.00	420.00
2,3: 2-Gustavson, Tarpe Mills-a	38.00	115.00	265.00

MASKED RAIDER, THE (Billy The Kid No. 9 on; Frontier Scout, Daniel Boone No. 10-13; also see Blue Bird)
6/55 - No. 8, 7/57; No. 14, 8/58 - No. 30, 6/61
Charlton Comics

	Good	Fine	Mint
1-Painted-c	3.00	9.00	21.00
2	1.75	5.25	12.00

Marvel Two-In-One #52, © MCG

Mary Marvel Comics #24, © FAW

Masked Raider #2, © CC

Masked Ranger #2, © PG

Master Comics #2, © FAW

Master of Kung-Fu #19, © MCG

MASKED RAIDER (continued) — Good / Fine / Mint

3-8: 8-Billy The Kid app. 1.30 4.00 9.00
14,16-30: 22-Rocky Lane app. 1.00 3.00 7.00
15-Williamson-a, 7 pgs. 2.35 7.00 16.00

MASKED RANGER
April, 1954 - No. 9, Aug, 1955
Premier Magazines

1-The M. Ranger, his horse Streak, & The Crimson Avenger (origin) begin, end No.9; Woodbridge-a; Check-a 6.00 18.00 42.00
2,3 3.00 9.00 21.00
4-8-All Woodbridge-a. 5-Jesse James by Woodbridge. 6-Billy The Kid by Woodbridge. 7-Wild Bill Hickok by Woodbridge. 8-Jim Bowie's Life Story 3.50 10.50 24.00
9-Torres-a; Wyatt Earp by Woodbridge 4.00 12.00 28.00

NOTE: ***Woodbridge*** *c/a-1,4-9.*

MASK OF DR. FU MANCHU, THE (See Dr. Fu Manchu)
1951
Avon Periodicals

1-Sax Rohmer adapt.; Wood c/a, 26 pgs., Hollingsworth-a 85.00 255.00 595.00

MASQUE OF THE RED DEATH (See Movie Classics)

MASTER COMICS
Mar, 1940 - No. 133, Apr, 1953 (No. 1-6: oversized issues)
(No. 1-3, 15¢, 52pgs.; No. 4-6, 10¢, 36pgs.)
Fawcett Publications

1-Origin Masterman; The Devil's Dagger, El Carim, Master of Magic, Rick O'Say, Morton Murch, White Rajah, Shipwreck Roberts, Frontier Marshall, Streak Sloan, Mr. Clue begin (all features end No. 6) 125.00 375.00 875.00
2 60.00 180.00 420.00
3-5 35.00 105.00 245.00
6-Last Masterman 30.00 90.00 210.00

NOTE: *Issues 1-6 are rarely found in near mint to mint condition due to large-size format.*

7-(10/40)-Bulletman, Zorro, the Mystery Man (ends No. 22), Lee Granger, Jungle King, & Buck Jones begin; only app. The War Bird & Mark Swift & the Time Retarder 75.00 225.00 525.00
8-The Red Gaucho (ends No. 13), Captain Venture (ends No. 22) & The Planet Princess begin 35.00 105.00 245.00
9,10: 10-Lee Granger ends 31.00 92.00 216.00
11-Origin Minute-Man 60.00 180.00 420.00
12 40.00 120.00 280.00
13-Origin Bulletgirl 55.00 165.00 385.00
14-16: 14-Companions Three begins, ends No. 31 33.00 100.00 230.00
17-20: 17-Raboy-a on Bulletman begins. 20-Captain Marvel cameo app. in Bulletman 38.00 115.00 265.00
21-(Scarce)-Captain Marvel x-over in Bulletman; Capt. Nazi origin 157.00 471.00 1100.00
22-Captain Marvel Jr. x-over in Bulletman; Capt. Nazi app; bondage-c 126.00 378.00 880.00
23-Capt. Marvel Jr. begins, vs. Capt. Nazi 98.00 295.00 685.00
24,25,29 35.00 105.00 245.00
26-28,30-Captain Marvel Jr. vs. Capt. Nazi. 30-Flag-c 35.00 105.00 245.00
31,32: 32-Last El Carim & Buck Jones; Balbo, the Boy Magician intro. in El Carim 25.00 75.00 175.00
33-Balbo, the Boy Magician (ends No. 47), Hopalong Cassidy (ends No. 49) begins 25.00 75.00 175.00
34-Capt. Marvel Jr. vs. Capt. Nazi 25.00 75.00 175.00
35 25.00 75.00 175.00
36-40: 40-Flag-c 23.00 70.00 160.00
41-Bulletman, Capt. Marvel Jr. & Bulletgirl x-over in Minute-Man; only app. Crime Crusaders Club (Capt. Marvel Jr., Minute-Man, Bulletman & Bulletgirl)-only team in Fawcett Comics 25.00 75.00 175.00

Good / Fine / Mint

42-47,49: 47-Hitler becomes Corpl. Hitler Jr. 49-Last Minute-Man 14.50 43.50 100.00
48-Intro. Bulletboy; Capt. Marvel cameo in Minute-Man 15.00 45.00 105.00
50-Radar, Nyoka the Jungle Girl begin; Capt. Marvel x-over in Radar; origin Radar 10.00 30.00 70.00
51-58 6.50 19.50 45.00
59-62: Nyoka serial ''Terrible Tiara'' in all; 61-Capt. Marvel Jr. 1st meets Uncle Marvel 8.00 24.00 56.00
63-80 5.50 16.50 38.00
81-92,94-99: 88-Hopalong Cassidy begins (ends No. 94). 95-Tom Mix begins (ends No. 133) 4.65 14.00 32.00
93-Krigstein-a 5.00 15.00 35.00
100 5.50 16.50 38.00
101-106-Last Bulletman 3.65 11.00 25.00
107-131 3.35 10.00 23.00
132-B&W and color illos in **POP** 4.65 14.00 32.00
133-Bill Battle app. 5.50 16.50 38.00

NOTE: ***Mac Raboy*** *a-15-39, 40 in part, 42, 58; c-21-49, 51, 52, 54, 56, 58, 59.*

MASTER DETECTIVE
1964 (Reprint)
Super Comics

10,17,18: 17-Young King Cole; McWilliams-a .40 1.20 2.40

MASTER OF KUNG FU (Formerly Special Marvel Edition)
No. 17, April, 1974 - No. 125, June, 1983
Marvel Comics Group

17-Starlin-a; intro Black Jack Tarr .40 1.20 2.40
18-20: 19-Man-Thing app. .35 1.00 2.00
21-23,25-30 .60 1.20
24-Starlin, Simonson-a .25 .75 1.50
31-40: 33-1st Leiko Wu .40 .80
41-99 .30 .60
100-(Double size) .60 1.20
101-117,119-124: 104-Cerebus cameo .30 .60
118,125-(Double size) .50 1.00
Giant Size 1(9/74)-Russell-a; Yellow Claw-r .25 .75 1.50
Giant Size 2-r/Yellow Claw No. 1 .60 1.20
Giant Size 3,4(6/75)-r-/2 Kirby stories/Yellow Claw .60 1.20
Annual 1(4/76)-Iron Fist .60 1.20

NOTE: ***Austin*** *c-63i, 74i.* ***Buscema*** *c-44p.* ***Gulacy*** *a(p)-18-20, 22, 25, 29-31, 33-35, 38, 39, 40(p&i), 42-50, Giant Size No. 1, 2; c-51, 55, 64, 67.* ***Gil Kane*** *c(p)-20, 38, 39, 42, 45, 59, 63.* ***Nebres*** *c-73i.* ***Starlin*** *a-17p; c-54.* ***Sutton*** *a-42i.*

MASTER OF THE WORLD (See 4-Color No. 1157)

MASTERS OF TERROR (Magazine)
July, 1975 - No. 2, Sept, 1975 (Black & White) (All Reprints)
Marvel Comics Group

1-Brunner, Smith-a; Morrow-c; Adams-a(i)(r); Starlin-a(p) Gil Kane-a .30 .90 1.80
2-Reese, Kane, Mayerik-a; Steranko-c .60 1.20

MASTERS OF THE UNIVERSE
Dec, 1982 - No. 3, Feb, 1983
DC Comics

1 .60 1.20
2,3: 2-Origin He-Man & Ceril .50 1.00

NOTE: ***Alcala*** *a-1i, 2i.* ***Tuska*** *a-1-3p; c-1-3p. No. 2 has 75¢ & 95¢ cover price.*

MASTERS OF THE UNIVERSE (Comic Album)
1984 (8½x11''; $2.95; 64 pgs.)
Western Publishing Co.

11362-Based on Mattel toy & cartoon .50 1.50 2.95

MASTERS OF THE UNIVERSE (TV)
May, 1986 - Present

MASTERS OF THE UNIVERSE (continued)
Star Comics (Marvel)

	Good	Fine	Mint
1		.55	1.10
2-6		.40	.80

MASTERWORKS SERIES OF GREAT COMIC BOOK ARTISTS, THE
May, 1983 - No. 3, Dec, 1983 (Baxter paper)
Sea Gate Distributors/DC Comics

	Good	Fine	Mint
1,2-Shining Knight by Frazetta r-/Adventure. 2-Tomahawk by Frazetta-r	.25	.75	1.50
3-Wrightson-r	.25	.75	1.50

NOTE: ***Frazetta** c/a(r)-1,2. **Simon & Kirby** a(r)-1(5), 2, 3. **Wrightson** c/a(r)-3.*

MATT SLADE GUNFIGHTER (Stories of Romance & Kid Slade Gunfighter No. 5 on?)
May, 1956 - No. 4, Nov, 1956
Atlas Comics (SPI)

	Good	Fine	Mint
1-Williamson/Torres-a	5.00	15.00	35.00
2-Williamson-a	3.85	11.50	27.00
3,4	2.00	6.00	14.00

MAUD
1906 (32 pgs. in color; 10x15½'') (cardboard covers)
Frederick A. Stokes Co.

	Good	Fine	Mint
By Fred Opper	11.00	33.00	76.00

MAVERICK (TV)
No. 892, 4/58 - No. 19, 4-6/62 (All have photo-c)
Dell Publishing Co.

	Good	Fine	Mint
4-Color 892 (No.1): James Garner/Jack Kelly photo-c begin	4.00	12.00	28.00
4-Color 930,945,962,980,1005 (6-8/59)	3.50	10.50	24.00
7 (10-12/59) - 14: Last Garner/Kelly-c	3.00	9.00	21.00
15-19: Jack Kelly/Roger Moore photo-c	3.00	9.00	21.00

MAVERICK MARSHAL
Nov, 1958 - No. 7, May, 1960
Charlton Comics

	Good	Fine	Mint
1	1.15	3.50	8.00
2-7	.55	1.65	4.00

MAX BRAND (See Silvertip)

MAX OF THE REGULATORS
1985 - Present? ($1.75, B&W)
Atlantic Comics

	Good	Fine	Mint
1-3: 1-Atomic explosion-c	.30	.90	1.80

MAXWELL MOUSE FOLLIES
Feb, 1986 - Present ($1.70-$2.00, B&W)
Renegade Press

	Good	Fine	Mint
1-3	.30	.85	1.70
4,5	.35	1.00	2.00

MAYA (See Movie Classics)
March, 1968
Gold Key

	Good	Fine	Mint
1 (10218-803)(TV)	1.15	3.50	8.00

MAZIE (. . . & Her Friends) (See Tastee-Freez)
1953 - No. 12, 1954; No. 13, 12/54 - No. 22, 9/56; No. 23, 9/57 - No. 28, 8/58
Mazie Comics(Magazine Publ.)/Harvey Publ. No. 13-on

	Good	Fine	Mint
1	1.15	3.50	8.00
2	.70	2.00	4.00
3-10	.50	1.50	3.00
11-28		.50	1.00

MAZIE
1950 - 1951 (5 cents) (5x7¼''-miniature)(52 pgs.)
Nation Wide Publishers

	Good	Fine	Mint
1-Teen-age	1.00	3.00	7.00
2-7	.50	1.50	3.50

MAZING MAN
Jan, 1986 - No. 12, Dec, 1986
DC Comics

	Good	Fine	Mint
1		.50	1.00
2-12: 7,8-Hembeck-a		.40	.80

McCRORY'S CHRISTMAS BOOK
1955 (36 pgs.; slick cover)
Western Printing Co. (McCrory Stores Corp. giveaway)

	Good	Fine	Mint
	1.35	4.00	8.00

McCRORY'S TOYLAND BRINGS YOU SANTA'S PRIVATE EYES
1956 (16 pgs.)
Promotional Publ. Co. (Giveaway)

	Good	Fine	Mint
Has 9 pg. story plus 7 pg. toy ads	1.00	3.00	6.00

McCRORY'S WONDERFUL CHRISTMAS
1954 (20 pgs.; slick cover)
Promotional Publ. Co. (Giveaway)

	Good	Fine	Mint
	1.35	4.00	8.00

McHALE'S NAVY (TV) (See Movie Classics)
May-July, 1963 - No. 3, Nov-Jan, 1963-64 (Photo-c)
Dell Publishing Co.

	Good	Fine	Mint
1	1.50	4.50	10.00
2,3	1.00	3.00	7.00

McKEEVER & THE COLONEL (TV)
Feb-Apr, 1963 - No. 3, Aug-Oct, 1963
Dell Publishing Co.

	Good	Fine	Mint
1	2.00	6.00	14.00
2,3	1.50	4.50	10.00

McLINTOCK (See Movie Comics)

MD
Apr-May, 1955 - No. 5, Dec-Jan, 1955-56
E. C. Comics

	Good	Fine	Mint
1-Not approved by code	5.75	17.50	40.00
2-5	4.35	13.00	30.00

NOTE: ***Crandall, Evans, Ingels, Orlando** art in all issues; **Craig** c-1-5.*

MECHANICS
Oct, 1985 - No. 3, Dec, 1985 ($2.00 cover; adults only)
Fantagraphics Books

	Good	Fine	Mint
1-Love & Rockets in all	.40	1.25	2.50
2,3	.35	1.00	2.00

MEDAL FOR BOWZER, A
No date (1948-50?)
Will Eisner Giveaway

	Good	Fine	Mint
Eisner-c/script	13.00	40.00	90.00

MEDAL OF HONOR COMICS
Spring, 1946
A. S. Curtis

	Good	Fine	Mint
1	3.50	10.50	24.00

MEET ANGEL (Formerly Angel & the Ape)
No. 7, Nov-Dec, 1969
National Periodical Publications

Masters of the Universe #1 (5/86), © MCG

Maverick #11, © Warner Bros.

McKeever & the Colonel #1, © Four Star-Harlen

Meet Merton #3, © TOBY

Menace #5, © MCG

Men Against Crime #5, © ACE

MEET ANGEL (continued)

	Good	Fine	Mint
7-Wood-a(i)		.40	.80

MEET CORLISS ARCHER (My Life No. 4 on)(Radio/Movie)
March, 1948 - No. 3, July, 1948
Fox Features Syndicate

	Good	Fine	Mint
1-Feldstein c/a	22.00	65.00	154.00
2-Feldstein-c only	16.50	50.00	115.00
3-Part Feldstein-c only	12.00	36.00	84.00

NOTE: *No. 1-3 used in* ***Seduction of the Innocent****, pg. 39.*

MEET HERCULES (See Three Stooges)

MEET HIYA A FRIEND OF SANTA CLAUS
1949 (18 pgs.?) (paper cover)
Julian J. Proskauer (Giveaway)

	Good	Fine	Mint
	3.00	9.00	18.00

MEET MERTON
Dec, 1953 - No. 4, June, 1954
Toby Press

	Good	Fine	Mint
1-Dave Berg-a	2.00	6.00	14.00
2-Dave Berg-a	1.00	3.00	7.00
3,4-Dave Berg-a	.85	2.50	6.00
I.W. Reprint No. 9		.50	1.00
Super Reprint No. 11('63), 18		.40	.80

MEET MISS BLISS
May, 1955 - No. 4, Nov., 1955
Atlas Comics (LMC)

	Good	Fine	Mint
1	3.00	9.00	21.00
2-4	1.50	4.50	10.00

MEET MISS PEPPER (Formerly Lucy . . .)
No. 5, April, 1954 - No. 6, June, 1954
St. John Publishing Co.

	Good	Fine	Mint
5-Kubert/Maurer-a	10.00	30.00	70.00
6-Kubert/Maurer-a; Kubert-c; opium mention	8.00	24.00	56.00

MEET THE NEW POST GAZETTE SUNDAY FUNNIES
3/12/49 (16 pgs.; paper covers) (7¼x10¼'')
Commercial comics (insert in newspaper)
Pittsburgh Post Gazette

Dick Tracy by Gould, Gasoline Alley, Terry & the Pirates, Brenda Starr, Buck Rogers by Yager, The Gumps, Peter Rabbit by Fago, Superman, Funnyman by Siegel & Shuster, The Saint, Archie, & others done especially for this book. A fine copy sold at auction in 1985 for $276.00.

Estimated value. . . . $150—$300

MEGATON
11/83; No. 2, 10/85 - Present (B&W)
Megaton Publ.

	Good	Fine	Mint
1,2 ($2.00 cover)	.35	1.00	2.00
3-7 ($1.50 cover)	.25	.75	1.50

MEGATON MAN (Also see Border Worlds)
Dec, 1984 - No. 10, 1986 ($2.00; Baxter paper)
Kitchen Sink Enterprises

	Good	Fine	Mint
1-Silver-Age heroes parody	1.25	3.75	7.50
2	.45	1.25	2.50
3-10: 6-Border Worlds begins	.35	1.00	2.00

MEL ALLEN SPORTS COMICS
No. 5, Nov, 1949 - No. 6, Jan, 1950?
Standard Comics

	Good	Fine	Mint
5(No. 1 on inside)-Tuska-a	3.50	10.50	24.00
6	1.85	5.50	13.00

MELVIN MONSTER
Apr-June, 1965 - No. 10, Oct, 1969
Dell Publishing Co.

	Good	Fine	Mint
1-by John Stanley	5.00	15.00	35.00
2-10-All by Stanley. No. 10 r-/No. 1	3.00	9.00	21.00

MELVIN THE MONSTER (Dexter The Demon No. 7)
July, 1956 - No. 6, July, 1957
Atlas Comics (HPC)

	Good	Fine	Mint
1	2.35	7.00	16.00
2-6: 4-Maneely c/a	1.15	3.50	8.00

MENACE
March, 1953 - No. 11, May, 1954
Atlas Comics (HPC)

	Good	Fine	Mint
1-Everett-a	7.00	21.00	50.00
2-Post-atom bomb disaster by Everett; anti-Communist propaganda/torture scenes	4.00	12.00	28.00
3,4,6-Everett-a	3.50	10.50	24.00
5-Origin & 1st app. The Zombie by Everett (reprinted in Tales of the Zombie No. 1)(7/53)	6.00	18.00	42.00
7,10,11: 7-Frankenstein story. 10-H-Bomb panels	2.65	8.00	18.00
8-End of world story	2.65	8.00	18.00
9-Everett-a r-in Vampire Tales No. 1	3.50	10.50	24.00

NOTE: ***Colan*** *a-6.* ***Everett*** *a-1-6, 9; c-1-3, 5, 6.* ***Heath*** *a-1-8; c-10.* ***Katz*** *a-11.* ***Maneely*** *a-3.* ***Powell*** *a-11.* ***Romita*** *a-3, 6, 11.* ***Shelly*** *a-10.* ***Sinnott*** *a-2.* ***Tuska*** *a-1, 2, 5.*

MEN AGAINST CRIME (Formerly Mr. Risk)
No. 3, Feb, 1951 - No. 7, Oct, 1951 (Hand of Fate No. 8 on)
Ace Magazines

	Good	Fine	Mint
3-Mr. Risk app.	3.00	9.00	21.00
4-7: 4-Colan-a; entire book reprinted as Trapped! No. 4	1.75	5.25	12.00

MEN, GUNS, & CATTLE (See Classics Special)

MEN IN ACTION (Battle Brady No. 10 on)
April, 1952 - No. 9, Dec, 1952
Atlas Comics (IPS)

	Good	Fine	Mint
1	2.65	8.00	18.00
2	1.20	3.50	8.00
3-6,8,9: 3-Heath c/a	1.00	3.00	7.00
7-Krigstein-a	2.75	8.00	18.00

MEN IN ACTION
April, 1957 - No. 9, 1958
Ajax/Farrell Publications

	Good	Fine	Mint
1	1.70	5.00	12.00
2	1.00	3.00	7.00
3-9	.85	2.50	6.00

MEN INTO SPACE (See 4-Color No. 1083)

MEN OF BATTLE (See New. . .)

MEN OF COURAGE
1949
Catechetical Guild

	Good	Fine	Mint
Contains bound Topix comics-V7No.2,4,6,8,10,16,18,20	3.00	9.00	18.00

MEN OF WAR
August, 1977 - No. 26, March, 1980
DC Comics, Inc.

	Good	Fine	Mint
1-Origin Gravedigger, cont'd. in No. 2		.30	.60
2-26		.25	.50

NOTE: ***Chaykin*** *a-9, 10, 12-14, 19, 20.* ***Evans*** *c-25.* ***Kubert*** *c-2-23, 24p, 26.*

MEN'S ADVENTURES (Formerly True Adventures)
No. 4, Aug, 1950 - No. 28, July, 1954
Marvel/Atlas Comics (CCC)

MEN'S ADVENTURES (continued) Good Fine Mint
4(No.1) 4.00 12.00 28.00
5-Flying Saucer story 2.00 6.00 14.00
6-8: 8-Sci/fic story 1.70 5.00 11.50
9-20: All war format 1.15 3.50 8.00
21,22,24-26: All horror format 1.15 3.50 8.00
23-Crandall-a; Fox-a(i) 2.65 8.00 18.00
27,28-Captain America, Human Torch, & Sub-Mariner app. in each 17.00 51.00 120.00

NOTE: ***Berg*** *a-16.* ***Burgos*** *c-27.* ***Everett*** *a-10, 22, 25, 28; c-21-23.* ***Heath*** *a-8, 24.* ***Lawrence*** *a-23.* ***Mac Pakula*** *a-25.* ***Post*** *a-23.* ***Powell*** *a-27.* ***Reinman*** *a-12.* ***Robinson*** *c-19.* ***Romita*** *a-22.* ***Sinnott*** *a-21. Adventure-No. 4-8; War-No. 9-20; Horror-No. 21-26.*

MEN WHO MOVE THE NATION
(Giveaway) (Black & White)

Neal Adams-a 2.65 8.00 16.00

MERC (See Mark Hazzard: Merc)

MERLIN JONES AS THE MONKEY'S UNCLE (See Movie Comics and The Misadventures of. . . under Movie Comics)

MERLINREALM 3-D (Blackthorne 3-D series No. 2)
Oct, 1985 ($2.25)
Blackthorne Publ., Inc.

1-1st printing .35 1.15 2.30

MERRILL'S MARAUDERS (See Movie Classics)

MERRY CHRISTMAS (See A Christmas Adv., Donald Duck. . ., Dell Giant No. 39, & March of Comics No. 153)

MERRY CHRISTMAS, A
1948 (nn) (Giveaway)
K. K. Publications (Child Life Shoes)

2.75 8.00 16.00

MERRY CHRISTMAS
1956 (7¼x5¼")
K. K. Publications (Blue Bird Shoes Giveaway)

1.00 3.00 6.00

MERRY CHRISTMAS FROM MICKEY MOUSE
1939 (16 pgs.) (Color & B&W)
K. K. Publications (Shoe store giveaway)

Donald Duck & Pluto app.; text with art (Rare); c-reprint/ Mickey Mouse Mag. V3/3 (12/37) 70.00 200.00 400.00

MERRY CHRISTMAS FROM SEARS TOYLAND
1939 (16 pgs.) (In color)
Sears Roebuck Giveaway

Dick Tracy, Little Orphan Annie, The Gumps, Terry & the Pirates 15.00 45.00 90.00

MERRY COMICS
December, 1945 (No cover price)
Carlton Publishing Co.

nn-Boogeyman app. 3.50 10.50 24.00

MERRY COMICS
1947
Four Star Publications

1 3.00 9.00 21.00

MERRY-GO-ROUND COMICS
1944 (132 pgs.; 25 cents); 1946; 9-10/47 - No. 2, 1948
LaSalle Publ. Co./Croyden Publ./Rotary Litho.

nn(1944)(LaSalle) 5.75 17.25 40.00
21 1.50 4.50 10.00

Good Fine Mint
1(1946)(Croyden) 2.65 8.00 18.00
V1No.1,2(9-10/47, 1948; 52 pgs.)(Rotary Litho. Co. Ltd., Canada); Ken Hultgren-a 1.75 5.25 12.00

MERRY MAILMAN (See Funny Animals)

MERRY MOUSE
June, 1953 - No. 4, Jan-Feb, 1954
Avon Periodicals

1 2.65 8.00 18.00
2-4 1.50 4.50 10.00

MESSIAH
Aug, 1986 ($1.50, B&W)
Pinnacle Comics

1 .25 .75 1.50

METAL MEN (See Brave & the Bold, DC Comics Presents, and Showcase)
4-5/63 - No. 41, 12-1/69-70; No. 42, 2-3/73 - No. 44, 7-8/73; No. 45, 4-5/76 - No. 56, 2-3/78
National Periodical Publications/DC Comics

1 2.65 8.00 16.00
2 1.35 4.00 8.00
3-5 1.00 3.00 6.00
6-10 .70 2.20 4.00
11-26 .55 1.60 3.20
27-Origin Metal Men .55 1.60 3.20
28-41(1968-70) .60 1.20
42-44(1973)-Reprints .40 .80
45('76)-49-Simonson-a in all .40 .80
50-56: 50-Part-r. 54,55-Green Lantern x-over .30 .60

NOTE: ***Aparo*** *c-53-56.* ***Giordano*** *c-45, 46.* ***Kane*** *a-30, 31p; c-31.* ***Simonson*** *a-45-49; c-47-52.* ***Staton*** *a-50-56.*

METAMORPHO (See Action, Brave & the Bold, First Issue Special, & World's Finest)
July-Aug, 1965 - No. 17, Mar-Apr, 1968
National Periodical Publications

1 1.35 4.00 8.00
2-5 .70 2.00 4.00
6-9 .35 1.10 2.20
10-Origin & 1st app. Element Girl (1-2/67) .35 1.10 2.20
11-17 .65 1.30

NOTE: ***Ramona Fraden*** *a-1-4.* ***Orlando*** *a-5, 6; c-5-9, 11.* ***Sal Trapani*** *a-7-16.*

METEOR COMICS
November, 1945
L. L. Baird (Croyden)

1-Captain Wizard, Impossible Man, Race Wilkins app.; origin Baldy Bean, Capt. Wizard's sidekick; Bare-breasted mermaids story 9.50 28.50 65.00

MGM'S MARVELOUS WIZARD OF OZ
November, 1975 (84 pgs.; oversize) ($1.50)
Marvel Comics Group/National Periodical Publications

1-Adaptation of MGM's movie (See Marvel Treasury of. . .) .70 2.00 4.00

M.G.M'S MOUSE MUSKETEERS (Formerly M.G.M.'s The Two Mouseketeers)
No. 670, Jan, 1956 - No. 1290, Mar-May, 1962
Dell Publishing Co.

4-Color 670 1.00 3.00 7.00
4-Color 711,728,764 .85 2.50 6.00
8 (4-6/57) - 21 (3-5/60) .75 2.25 5.00
4-Color 1135,1175,1290 .85 2.50 6.00

Men's Adventures #6, © MCG

Merlinrealm 3-D #1, © Blackthorne

Metal Men #17, © DC

Miami Mice #1 (3rd Printing), © Rip Off

Mickey Finn #10, © McNaught Synd.

Mickey Mouse, 4-Color #181, © WDC

M.G.M.'S SPIKE AND TYKE
No. 499, Sept, 1953 - No. 1266, Dec-Feb, 1961-62
Dell Publishing Co.

	Good	Fine	Mint
4-Color 499	1.30	4.00	9.00
4-Color 577,638	1.00	3.00	7.00
4(12-2/55-56)-10	.85	2.50	6.00
11-24(12-2/60-61)	.75	2.25	5.00
4-Color 1266	.85	2.50	6.00

M.G.M.'S THE TWO MOUSKETEERS (See 4-Color 475,603,642)

MIAMI MICE
1986 - Present ($2.00-$1.50, B&W)
Rip Off Press

	Good	Fine	Mint
1	1.50	4.50	9.00
1-2nd & 3rd printing	.25	.75	1.50
2,3	.35	1.00	2.00
3-Bound with sheet recording of The Miami Mice theme song	1.70	5.00	9.95

NOTE: *Fire in Rip Off Press warehouse reportedly destroyed 20,000 copies.*

MICHAELANGELO, TEENAGE MUTANT NINJA TURTLE
1986 (One shot) ($1.50)
Mirage Studios

	Good	Fine	Mint
1	.60	1.75	3.50

MICKEY AND DONALD IN VACATIONLAND (See Dell Giant No. 47)

MICKEY & THE BEANSTALK (See Story Hour Series)

MICKEY & THE SLEUTH (See Walt Disney Showcase No. 38,39)

MICKEY FINN
Nov?, 1942 - V3No. 2, May, 1952
Eastern Color 1-4/McNaught Synd. No. 5 on (Columbia)/Headline V3No.2

	Good	Fine	Mint
1	10.00	30.00	70.00
2	5.00	15.00	35.00
3-Charlie Chan app.	3.50	10.50	24.50
4	2.35	7.00	16.00
5-10	1.50	4.50	10.00
11-15(1949): 12-Sparky Watts app.	1.30	4.00	9.00
V3No.1,2(1952)	1.15	3.50	8.00

MICKEY MOUSE
1931 - 1934 (52 pgs.; 10x9¾''; cardboard covers)
David McKay Publications

	Good	Fine	Mint
1(1931)	80.00	240.00	430.00
2(1932)	60.00	180.00	315.00
3(1933)-All color Sunday reprints; page No.'s 5-17, 32-48 reissued in Whitman No. 948	120.00	350.00	600.00
4(1934)	50.00	150.00	290.00

NOTE: *Each book reprints strips from previous year - dailies in black and white in No. 1,2,4; Sundays in color in No. 3. Later reprints exist; i.e., No. 2 (1934).*

MICKEY MOUSE
1933 (Copyright date, printing date unknown)
(30 pages; 10x8¾''; cardboard covers)
Whitman Publishing Co.

	Good	Fine	Mint
948-(1932 Sunday strips in color)	80.00	240.00	400.00

NOTE: *Some copies were bound with a second front cover upside-down instead of the regular back cover; both covers have the same art, but different right and left margins. The above book is an exact, but abbreviated reissue of David McKay No. 3 but with ½-inch of border trimmed from the top and bottom.*

MICKEY MOUSE (See The Best of Walt Disney Comics, Cheerios giveaways, 40 Big Pages..., Merry Christmas From..., The New..., and Wheaties)

MICKEY MOUSE (...Secret Agent No. 107-109; Walt Disney's... No. 148-205?) (See Dell Giants for annuals)
No. 16, 1941 - No. 84, 7-9/62; No. 85, 11/62 - No. 218, 7/84; No. 219, 10/86-on
Dell Publ. Co./Gold Key No. 85-204/Whitman No. 205-218/ Gladstone No. 219 on

	Good	Fine	Mint
4-Color 16(1941)-1st M.M. comic book-''vs. the Phantom Blot'' by Gottfredson	235.00	700.00	1600.00
(Prices vary widely on this book)			
4-Color 27(1943)-''7 Colored Terror''	42.00	125.00	295.00
4-Color 79(1945)-By Carl Barks (1 story)	56.00	168.00	390.00
4-Color 116(1946)	13.00	40.00	90.00
4-Color 141,157(1947)	12.00	36.00	84.00
4-Color 170,181,194('48)	11.00	33.00	76.00
4-Color 214('49),231,248,261	7.00	21.00	50.00
4-Color 268-Reprints/WDC&S No. 22-24 by Gottfredson (''Surprise Visitor'')	7.00	21.00	50.00
4-Color 279,286,296	5.50	16.50	40.00
4-Color 304,313(No.1),325(No.2),334	4.35	13.00	30.00
4-Color 343,352,362,371,387	3.50	10.50	24.00
4-Color 401,411,427(10-11/52)	3.00	9.00	21.00
4-Color 819-M.M. in Magicland	1.75	5.25	12.00
4-Color 1057,1151,1246(1959-61)-Album	1.50	4.50	10.00
28(12-1/52-53)-32,34	1.50	4.50	10.00
33-(Exists with 2 dates, 10-11/53 & 12-1/54)	1.50	4.50	10.00
35-50	1.15	3.50	8.00
51-73,75-80	.85	2.50	6.00
74-Story swipe-'The Rare Stamp Search'/4-Color 422-'The Gilded Man	1.15	3.50	8.00
81-99: 93,95-titled ''Mickey Mouse Club Album''	.85	2.50	6.00
100-105: Reprints 4-Color 427,194,279,170,343,214 in that order	1.00	3.00	7.00
106-120	.75	2.25	5.00
121-130	.45	1.35	3.00
131-146	.35	1.00	2.00
147-Reprints ''The Phantom Fires'' from WDC&S 200-202	.85	2.50	5.00
148-Reprints ''The Mystery of Lonely Valley'' from WDC&S 208-210	.85	3.50	5.00
149-158	.25	.75	1.50
159-Reprints ''The Sunken City'' from WDC&S 205-207	.70	2.00	4.00
160-170: 162-170-r	.25	.75	1.50
171-178,180-199		.50	1.00
179-(52 pgs.)		.40	.80
200-r-Four Color 371		.40	.80
201-218		.40	.80
219-225: 219-The Seven Ghosts serial-r begins by Gottfredson. 222-Editor-in Grief strip-r		.40	.80

NOTE: *Reprints No. 195-97, 198(⅔), 199(⅓), 200-208, 211(½), 212, 213, 215(⅓), 216-218.*

	Good	Fine	Mint
Album 01-518-210(Dell), 1(10082-309)(9/63-Gold Key)	.85	2.50	6.00
...& Goofy ''Bicep Bungle''(1952, 14 pgs.) Fritos giveaway	2.35	7.00	14.00
...& Goofy Explore Business(1978)		.40	.80
...& Goofy Explore Energy(1976-1978) 36 pgs.; Exxon giveaway in color; regular size		.40	.80
...& Goofy Explore Energy Conservation(1976-1978)-Exxon		.40	.80
...& Goofy Explore The Universe of Energy(1985) 20pgs.; Exxon giveaway in color; regular size		.40	.80
Club 1(1/64-G.K.)(TV)	1.75	5.25	12.00
Mini Comic 1(1976)(3¼x6½'')-Reprints 158			.15
New Mickey Mouse Club Fun Book 11190 (Golden Press, $1.95; 224pgs, 1977)	.40	1.20	2.40
Surprise Party 1(30037-901, G.K.)(1/69)-40th Anniversary	2.35	7.00	16.00
Surprise Party 1(1979)-r-/'69 ish	.35	1.00	2.00

MICKEY MOUSE BOOK
1930 (4 printings, 20pgs., magazine size, paperbound)
Bibo & Lang

MICKEY MOUSE BOOK (continued)

nn-Very first Disney book with games, cartoons & songs; only Disney book to offer the origin of Mickey (based on a story originated by 11 yr. old Bobette Bibo). First app. Mickey & Minnie Mouse. Clarabelle Cow & Horace Horsecollar app. on back cover. Walt Disney, so the story goes, named him 'Mickey Mouse' after the green color of Ireland because he ate old green cheese. The book was printed in black & green to reinforce the Irish theme.

NOTE: The 1st printing has a daily Win Smith M. Mouse strip at bottom of back-c; the reprints are blank in this area. Most copies are missing pages 9 & 10 which contain a puzzle to be cut out.

	Good	Fine	Mint
First Printing (complete)	150.00	400.00	850.00
First Printing (Pgs. 9&10 missing)	24.00	70.00	155.00
2nd-4th Printings (complete)	94.00	280.00	620.00
2nd-4th Printings (pgs. 9&10 missing)	18.00	55.00	125.00

MICKEY MOUSE CLUB MAGAZINE (See Walt Disney...)

MICKEY MOUSE CLUB SPECIAL (See The New Mickey Mouse...)

MICKEY MOUSE COMICS DIGEST
1986 - Present ($1.25, 96 pgs.)
Gladstone Publishing

	Good	Fine	Mint
1,2		.60	1.25

MICKEY MOUSE MAGAZINE
V1No.1, Jan, 1933 - V1No.9, Sept, 1933 (5¼x7¼")
No. 1-3 published by Kamen-Blair (Kay Kamen, Inc.)
Walt Disney Productions

(Scarce)-Distributed by leading stores through their local theatres. First few issues had 5 cents listed on cover, later ones had no price.

	Good	Fine	Mint
V1No.1	120.00	300.00	600.00
2-9	60.00	150.00	300.00

MICKEY MOUSE MAGAZINE
V1No.1, Nov, 1933 - V2No.12, Oct, 1935
Mills giveaways issued by different dairies
Walt Disney Productions

	Good	Fine	Mint
V1No.1	25.00	75.00	160.00
2-12	15.00	45.00	90.00
V2No.1-12	10.00	30.00	60.00

MICKEY MOUSE MAGAZINE (Becomes Walt Disney's Comics & Stories) (No V3/1, V4/6)
Summer, 1935 (June-Aug, indicia) - V5/12, Sept, 1940
V1/1-5, V3/11,12, V4/1-3 are 44 pgs; V2/3-100 pgs; V5/12-68 pgs; rest are 36 pgs.
K. K. Publications

	Good	Fine	Mint
V1/1 (Large size, 13¼x10¼"; 25¢)-Contains puzzles, games, cels, stories and comics of Disney characters. Promotional magazine for Disney cartoon movies and paraphernalia	120.00	360.00	840.00
1 (As above, but autographed by the editors; given away with all early one year subscriptions)	125.00	375.00	875.00
2 (Size change, 11½x8½"; 10/35; 10¢)-High quality paper begins; Messmer-a	70.00	210.00	490.00
3,4: 3-Messmer-a	40.00	120.00	280.00
5-1st Donald Duck solo-c; last 44pg. & high quality paper issue	40.00	120.00	280.00
6-9: 6-36 pg. issues begin; Donald becomes editor. 8-2nd Donald solo-c. 9-1st Mickey/Minnie-c	30.00	90.00	200.00
10-12, V2/1,2: 11-1st Pluto/Mickey-c; Donald fires himself and appoints Mickey as editor	25.00	75.00	175.00
V2/3-Special 100 pg. Christmas issue (25¢); Messmer-a; Donald becomes editor of Wise Quacks	50.00	150.00	350.00
4-Mickey Mouse Comics & Roy Ranger (adventure strip) begin; both end V2/9; Messmer-a	23.00	70.00	160.00
5-Ted True (adventure strip, ends V2/9) & Silly Symphony Comics (ends V3/3) begin	20.00	60.00	140.00
6-9: 6-1st solo Minnie-c. 6-9-Mickey Mouse Movies cut-out in each	20.00	60.00	140.00
10-1st full color issue; Mickey Mouse (by Gottfredson; ends V3/12) & Silly Symphony (ends V3/3) full color Sunday-r, Peter The Farm Detective (ends V5/8) & Ole Of The North (ends V3/3) begins	25.00	75.00	175.00
11-13: 12-Hiawatha-c & feat. sty	20.00	60.00	140.00
V3/2-Big Bad Wolf Halloween-c	20.00	60.00	140.00
3 (12/37)-1st app. Snow White & The Seven Dwarfs (before release of movie); Mickey Christmas-c	25.00	75.00	175.00
4 (1/38)-Snow White & The Seven Dwarfs serial & Ducky Symphony (ends V3/11) begin	22.00	65.00	154.00
5-1st Snow White & Seven Dwarfs-c (St. Valentine's Day)	20.00	60.00	140.00
6-Snow White serial ends	18.50	55.00	130.00
7-Seven Dwarfs Easter-c	17.00	51.00	120.00
8-10: 9-Dopey-c. 10-1st solo Goofy-c	17.00	51.00	120.00
11,12 (44 pgs; 8 more pages color added). 11-Mickey The Sheriff serial (ends V4/3) & Donald Duck strip-r (ends V3/12) begin	20.00	60.00	140.00
V4/1 (10/38; 44 pgs.)-Brave Little Tailor-c/feature story, nominated for Academy Award; Bobby & Chip by Otto Messmer (ends V4/2) & The Practical Pig (ends V4/2) begin	20.00	60.00	140.00
2 (44 pgs.)-1st Huey, Dewey & Louie-c	18.50	55.00	130.00
3 (12/38, 44 pgs.)-Ferdinand The Bull-c/feature story, Academy Award winner; Mickey Mouse & The Whalers serial begins, ends V4/12	20.00	60.00	140.00
4,5: 5-St. Valentine's day-c. 4-Spotty, Mother Pluto strip-r begin, end V4/8. 5-1st Pluto solo-c	17.00	51.00	120.00
7 (3/39)-The Ugly Ducklin-c/feature story, Academy Award winner; The Hockey Champ feature with gags created by Carl Barks	18.50	55.00	130.00
7 (4/39)-Goofy & Wilbur The Grasshopper classic-c/feature story from 1st Goofy cartoon movie; Donald's Cousin Gus feature with gags created by Carl Barks; Timid Elmer begins, ends V5/5	18.50	55.00	130.00
8-Big Bad Wolf-c from Practical Pig movie poster; Practical Pig feature story	18.50	55.00	130.00
9-Donald Duck & Mickey Mouse Sunday-r begin; The Pointer feature story, nominated for Academy Award & Sea Scouts feature story app.	18.50	55.00	130.00
10-Classic July 4th drum & fife-c; last Donald Sunday-r	23.00	70.00	160.00
11-1st slick-c; last over-sized ish	17.00	51.00	120.00
12 (9/39; format change, 10¼x8¼")-1st full color, cover to cover issue. Donald's Penguin-c/feature story with gags created by Carl Barks	21.50	64.00	150.00
V5/1-Black Pete-c; Officer Duck-c/feature story; Autograph Hound feature story; Robinson Crusoe serial begins	21.50	64.00	150.00
2-Goofy-c	21.50	64.00	150.00
3 (12/39)-Pinocchio Christmas-c (1st app; before movie release). Pinocchio serial begins; 1st app. Jimminy Crickett	27.00	81.00	190.00
4,5: 5-Jimminy Crickett-c; Pinocchio serial ends; Donald's Dog Laundry feature story	23.00	70.00	160.00
6-Tugboat Mickey feature story; Rip Van Winkle feature begins, ends V5/8	21.50	64.00	150.00
7-2nd Huey, Dewey & Louie-c	21.50	64.00	150.00
8-Last magazine size issue; 2nd solo Pluto-c; Figaro & Cleo feature story	21.50	64.00	150.00
9 (6/40; change to comic book size)-Jimminy Crickett feature story; Donald-c & Sunday-r begin	35.00	100.00	245.00

Mickey Mouse Magazine #11, © WDC

Mickey Mouse Magazine V2No.10, © WDC

Mickey Mouse Magazine V3No.7, © WDC

Micronauts #40, © MCG

Midnight Mystery #1, © ACG

Mighty Bear #13, © STAR

MICKEY MOUSE MAGAZINE (continued)

	Good	Fine	Mint
10-Special Independence Day issue	35.00	100.00	245.00
11-Hawaiian Holiday & Mickey's Trailor feature stories; last 36 pg. issue	35.00	100.00	245.00
12 (Format change)-The transition issue (68 pgs.) becoming a comic book. With only a title change to follow, becomes Walt Disney's Comics & Stories No. 1 with the next issue	130.00	390.00	910.00
V4/1 (Giveaway)	18.50	55.00	130.00

MICKEY MOUSE MARCH OF COMICS
1947 - 1951 (Giveaway) (See March of Comics No. 447)
K. K. Publications

8(1947)-32 pgs.	60.00	150.00	320.00
27(1948)	34.00	100.00	225.00
45(1949)	27.00	80.00	170.00
60(1950)	18.00	55.00	125.00
74(1951)	14.00	42.50	85.00

MICKEY MOUSE SUMMER FUN (See Dell Giants)

MICKEY MOUSE'S SUMMER VACATION (See Story Hour Series)

MICRA
Sept, 1986 - No. 12, 1987 ($1.75, B&W, mini-series)
Comics Interview (Fictioneer Books)

1-Mind Controlled Remote Automation	.35	1.00	2.00
2	.30	.90	1.80

MICROBOTS, THE
December, 1971 (One Shot)
Gold Key

1 (10271-112)	.85	2.50	5.00

MICRONAUTS
Jan, 1979 - No. 59, Aug, 1984 (Mando paper No. 53 on)
Marvel Comics Group

1-Intro/1st app. Baron Karza	.75	2.25	4.50
2-5	.35	1.10	2.20
6-10: 7-Man-Thing app. 8-1st app. Capt. Universe. 9-1st app. Cilicia	.30	.90	1.80
11-20: 13-1st app. Jasmine. 15-Death of Microtron. 15-17-Fantastic-4 app. 17-Death of Jasmine. 20 Ant-Man app.	.25	.75	1.50
21-30: 21-Microverse series begins. 25-Origin Baron Karza. 25-29-Nick Fury app. 27-Death of Biotron		.60	1.20
31-34: Dr. Strange app. No. 34,35		.40	.80
35-Double size; origin Microverse; intro Death Squad	.25	.70	1.40
36-Giffen-a(p)		.65	1.30
37-New X-Men app.; Giffen-a(p)	.40	1.20	2.40
38-First direct sale	.45	1.40	2.80
39,40: 40-Fantastic-4 app.		.65	1.30
41-59: 57-Double size		.40	.80
nn-Reprints No.1-3; blank UPC; diamond on top		.20	.40
Annual 1(12/79)-Ditko c/a	.30	.90	1.80
Annual 2(10/80)-Ditko c/a		.50	1.00

NOTE: *No. 38-on distributed only through comic shops.* ***Adams*** *c-7i.* ***Chaykin*** *a-13-18p.* ***Ditko*** *a-39p.* ***Giffen*** *a-36p, 37p.* ***Golden*** *a-1-12p; c-2-6p, 7-23, 24p, 38-40.* ***Guice*** *a-48-58p; c-49-58.* ***Gil Kane*** *a-38i, 40p-45p; c-40-45.* ***Layton*** *c-33-37.* ***Miller*** *c-31.*

MICRONAUTS
Oct, 1984 - No. 20, May, 1986
Marvel Comics Group

V2/1		.45	.90
2-20		.35	.70

NOTE: ***Golden*** *a-1; c-1, 6.* ***Guice*** *a-4p; c-2p.*

MICRONAUTS SPECIAL EDITION
Dec, 1983 - No. 5, Apr, 1984 ($2.00; mini-series; Baxter paper)
Marvel Comics Group

	Good	Fine	Mint
1: 1-5 r-/original series 1-12	.25	.80	1.60
2-5: Guice-c(p)-all	.25	.70	1.40

MIDGET COMICS (Fighting Indian Stories)
Feb, 1950 - No. 2, Apr, 1950 (5-3/8''x7-3/8'')
St. John Publishng Co.

1-Matt Baker-c	3.50	10.50	24.00
2-Tex West, Cowboy Marshal	1.75	5.25	12.00

MIDNIGHT
April, 1957 - No. 6, June, 1958
Ajax/Farrell Publ. (Four Star Comic Corp.)

1-Reprints from Voodoo & Strange Fantasy with some changes	2.65	8.00	18.00
2-5	1.30	4.00	9.00
6-Baker-r/Phantom Lady	2.65	8.00	18.00

MIDNIGHT MYSTERY
Jan-Feb, 1961 - No. 7, Oct, 1961
American Comics Group

1-Sci/Fic story	2.00	6.00	14.00
2-7: 7-Reinman-a	1.00	3.00	7.00

MIDNIGHT TALES
Dec, 1972 - No. 18, May, 1976
Charlton Press

V1No.1		.60	1.20
2-10,15-18		.40	.80
11-14-Newton-a		.40	.80
12,17(Modern Comics reprint, 1977)		.15	.30

NOTE: ***Adkins*** *a-12i, 13i.* ***Ditko*** *a-12.* ***Howard*** *(Wood imitator) a-1-15, 17, 18; c-1-18.* ***Staton*** *a-6, 8, 9, 13.* ***Sutton*** *a-8, 9.*

MIDNITE SKULKER, THE
1986 - Present? ($1.75, B&W)
E. Larry Dobias/Target Comics No. 2 on

1,2: 1-Capt. Airhead. 2-Duck Knight	.35	1.00	2.00
Special Edition 1 (6/86, $1.75)	.35	1.00	2.00

MIGHTY ATOM, THE (. . . & the Pixies No. 6)
(Formerly The Pixies No. 1-5)
No. 6, 1949; 11/57 - No. 6, 8-9/58
Magazine Enterprises

6(1949-M.E.)-no month (1st Series)	2.00	6.00	14.00
1-6(2nd Series)-Pixies-r	1.00	3.00	7.00
I.W. Reprint No. 1(nd)	.30	.90	1.80
Giveaway(1959, Whitman)-Evans-a	1.35	4.00	8.00
Giveaway (1967r, 1968r, 1973r, 1976r)		.50	1.00

MIGHTY BEAR (Formerly Fun Comics, Mighty Ghost No. 4)
No. 13, Jan, 1954 - No. 14, Mar, 1954; 9/57 - No. 3, 2/58
Star Publ. No. 13,14/Ajax-Farrell (Four Star)

13,14-L. B. Cole-c	3.00	9.00	21.00
1-3('57-'58)Four Star (Ajax)	1.00	3.00	7.00

MIGHTY COMICS (. . . Presents) (Formerly Flyman)
No. 40, Nov, 1966 - No. 50, Oct, 1967
Radio Comics (Archie)

40-Web	.85	2.50	5.00
41-Shield, Black Hood	.70	2.00	4.00
42-Black Hood	.70	2.00	4.00
43-Shield, Web & Black Hood	.70	2.00	4.00
44-Black Hood, Steel Sterling & The Shield	.70	2.00	4.00
45-Shield & Hangman; origin Web retold	.70	2.00	4.00
46-Steel Sterling, Web & Black Hood	.70	2.00	4.00
47-Black Hood & Mr. Justice	.70	2.00	4.00
48-Shield & Hangman; Wizard x-over in Shield	.70	2.00	4.00

MIGHTY COMICS (continued) — Good / Fine / Mint

49-Steel Sterling & Fox; Black Hood x-over in Steel Sterling — .70 2.00 4.00
50-Black Hood & Web; Inferno x-over in Web — .70 2.00 4.00

NOTE: ***Paul Reinman** a-40-50.*

MIGHTY CRUSADERS, THE (Also see Fly Man, Advs. of the Fly)
Nov, 1965 - No. 7, Oct, 1966
Mighty Comics Group (Radio Comics)

1-Origin The Shield — 1.35 4.00 8.00
2-Origin Comet — 1.00 3.00 6.00
3-Origin Fly-Man — .70 2.00 4.00
4-Fireball, Inferno, Firefly, Web, Fox, Bob Phantom, Blackjack, Hangman, Zambini, Kardak, Steel Sterling, Mr. Justice, Wizard, Capt. Flag, Jaguar x-over — .85 2.50 5.00
5-Intro. Ultra-Men (Fox, Web, Capt. Flag) & Terrific Three (Jaguar, Mr. Justice, Steel Sterling) — .70 2.00 4.00
6,7: 7-Steel Sterling feature; origin Fly-Girl — .70 2.00 4.00

NOTE: ***Reinman** a-6.*

MIGHTY CRUSADERS, THE (All New Advs. of. . . No. 2)
3/83 - No. 13, 9/85 ($1.00, 36 pgs, Mando paper)
Red Circle Prod./Archie Ent. No. 6 on

1-Origin Black Hood, The Fly, Fly Girl, The Shield, The Wizard, The Jaguar, Pvt. Strong & The Web — .45 .90
2-13: 2-Mister Midnight begins. 4-Darkling replaces Shield. 5-Origin Jaguar, Shield begins. 7-Untold origin Jaguar — .45 .90

NOTE: ***Buckler** a-1-3, 4i, 5p, 7p, 8i, 9i; c-1-10p.*

MIGHTY GHOST (Formerly Mighty Bear)
No. 4, June, 1958
Ajax/Farrell Publ.

4 — .85 2.50 6.00

MIGHTY HERCULES, THE (TV)
July, 1963 - No. 2, Nov, 1963
Gold Key

1,2(10072-307,311) — 1.50 4.50 10.00

MIGHTY HEROES, THE (TV) (Funny)
Mar, 1967 - No. 4, July, 1967
Dell Publishing Co.

1-1957 Heckle & Jeckle-r — .45 1.35 3.00
2,3 — .35 1.00 2.00
4-Two 1958 Mighty Mouse-r — .40 1.25 2.50

MIGHTY MARVEL WESTERN, THE
10/68 - No. 46, 9/76 (No. 1-14: 68 pgs.; No. 15,16: 52 pgs.)
Marvel Comics Group

1-Begin Kid Colt, Rawhide Kid, Two-Gun Kid-r — .40 .80
2-10 — .30 .60
11-20 — .30 .60
21-30: 24-Kid Colt-r end. 25-Matt Slade-r begin — .30 .60
31,33-36,38-46: 31-Baker-r — .30 .60
32-Origin-r/Ringo Kid No. 23; Williamson-r/Kid Slade No.7 — .30 .60
37-Williamson, Kirby-r/Two-Gun Kid 51 — .30 .60

NOTE: ***Jack Davis** a(r)-21-24. **Kirby** a(r)-1-3, 6, 9, 12, 14, 16, 26, 29, 32, 36, 41, 43, 44; c-29. **Maneely** a(r)-22. No Matt Slade-No. 43.*

MIGHTY MIDGET COMICS, THE (Miniature)
No date; circa 1942-1943 (36 pages) (Approx. 5x4'')
(Black & White & Red) (Sold 2 for 5 cents)
Samuel E. Lowe & Co.

Good / Fine / Mint

Bulletman No. 11(1943)-Reprints cover/Bulletman No. 3 — 3.00 9.00 21.00
Captain Marvel No. 11 — 3.00 9.00 21.00
Captain Marvel No. 11 (Same as above except for full color ad on back cover; this issue was glued to cover of Captain Marvel No. 20 and is not found in fine-mint condition) — 3.00 9.00 21.00
Captain Marvel Jr. No. 11 — 3.00 9.00 21.00
Captain Marvel Jr. No. 11 (Same as above except for full color ad on back-c; this issue was glued to cover of Captain Marvel No. 21 and is not found in fine-mint condition) — 3.00 9.00 21.00
Golden Arrow No. 11 — 2.00 6.00 14.00
Ibis the Invincible No. 11(1942)-Origin; r-/cover/Ibis No. 1 — 3.00 9.00 21.00
Spy Smasher No. 11(1942) — 3.00 9.00 21.00

NOTE: *The above books came in a box called ''box full of books'' and was distributed with other Samuel Lowe puzzles, paper dolls, coloring books, etc. They are not titled Mighty Midget Comics. All have a war bond seal on back cover which is otherwise blank. These books came in a ''Mighty Midget'' counter display rack.*

Balbo, the Boy Magician No. 12 — 1.50 4.50 10.00
Bulletman No. 12 — 3.00 9.00 21.00
Commando Yank No. 12 — 2.00 6.00 14.00
Dr. Voltz the Human Generator — 1.50 4.50 10.00
Lance O'Casey No. 12 — 1.50 4.50 10.00
Leatherneck the Marine — 1.50 4.50 10.00
Minute Man No. 12 — 3.00 9.00 21.00
Mister Q — 1.50 4.50 10.00
Mr. Scarlet & Pinky No. 12 — 3.00 9.00 21.00
Pat Wilton & His Flying Fortress — 1.50 4.50 10.00
The Phantom Eagle No. 12 — 2.00 6.00 14.00
State Trooper Stops Crime — 1.50 4.50 10.00
Tornado Tom; reprints from Cyclone No. 1-3; origin — 2.00 6.00 12.00

MIGHTY MOUSE (See Adventures of. . ., Dell Giant No. 43, Giant Comics Edition, March of Comics No. 205, 237, 247, 257, 459, 471, 483, Oxydol-Dreft, Paul Terry's, & Terry-Toons Comics)

MIGHTY MOUSE (1st Series)
Fall, 1946 - No. 4, Summer, 1947
Timely/Marvel Comics (20th Century Fox)

1 — 35.00 105.00 245.00
2 — 17.00 51.00 120.00
3,4 — 13.00 40.00 90.00

MIGHTY MOUSE (2nd Series) (Paul Terry's. . . No. 62-71)
Aug, 1947 - No. 67, 11/55; No. 68, 3/56 - No. 83, 6/59
St. John Publishing Co./Pines No. 68 (3/56) on

5(No.1) — 11.50 34.50 80.00
6-10 — 5.50 16.50 38.00
11-19 — 3.35 10.00 23.00
20-25-(52 pgs.) — 3.00 9.00 21.00
20-25-(36 pg. editions) — 2.35 7.00 16.00
26-37 — 2.00 6.00 14.00
38-45-(100 pgs.) — 4.50 13.50 30.00
46-83: 62-Painted-c. 82-Infinity-c — 1.30 4.00 9.00
Album 1(10/52)-100 pgs. — 9.00 27.00 62.00
Album 2(11/52-St. John) - 3(12/52) (100 pgs.) — 7.00 21.00 50.00
Fun Club Magazine 1(Fall, 1957-Pines) (TV-Tom Terrific) — 5.00 15.00 35.00
Fun Club Magazine 2-6(Winter, 1958-Pines) — 3.00 9.00 21.00
3-D 1-(1st printing-9/53)(St. John)-stiff covers — 17.00 51.00 120.00
3-D 1-(2nd printing-10/53)-slick, glossy covers, slightly smaller — 13.50 40.50 95.00
3-D 2(11/53), 3(12/53)-(St. John) — 13.00 40.00 90.00

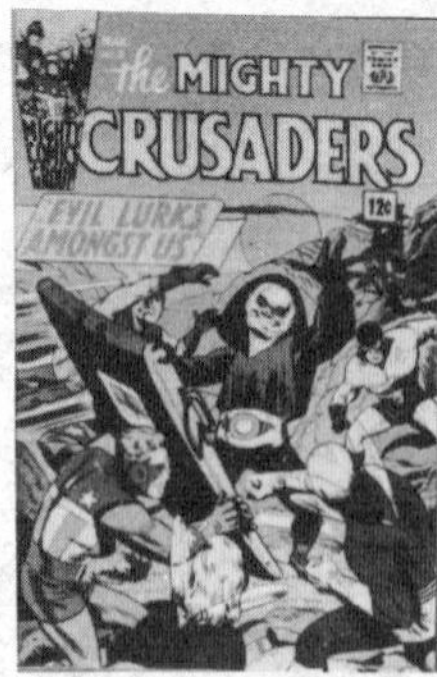

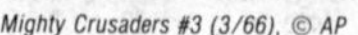
Mighty Crusaders #3 (3/66), © AP

Mighty Midget (Mr. Scarlet & Pinky), © FAW

Mighty Mouse #20 (52 pgs.), © MGM

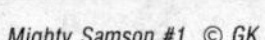

Mighty Samson #1, © GK

Military Comics #5, © QUA

Millie the Model #10, © MCG

MIGHTY MOUSE (TV)(3rd Series)(Formerly Advs. of Mighty Mouse)
No. 161, Oct, 1964 - No. 172, Oct, 1968
Gold Key/Dell Publishing Co. No. 166-on

	Good	Fine	Mint
161(10/64)-165(9/65)-(Becomes Advs. of... No. 166 on)	1.50	4.50	10.00
166(3/66), 167(6/66)-172	1.15	3.50	8.00

MIGHTY MOUSE ADVENTURES (Advs. of... No. 2 on)
November, 1951
St. John Publishing Co.

1	13.00	40.00	90.00

MIGHTY MOUSE ADVENTURE STORIES
1953 (384 pgs.) (50 Cents)
St. John Publishing Co.

Rebound issues	22.00	65.00	154.00

MIGHTY SAMSON (Also see Gold Key Champion)
7/64 - No.20, 11/69?; No.21, 8/72; No.22, 12/73 - No.31, 3/76; No. 32, 8/82 (Painted-c No. 1-31)
Gold Key

1-Origin; Thorne-a begins	1.15	3.50	8.00
2-5	.75	2.25	5.00
6-10: 7-Tom Morrow begins, ends No. 20	.50	1.50	3.00
11-20	.35	1.00	2.00
21-32: 21,22,32-r		.50	1.00

MIGHTY THOR (See Thor)

MIKE BARNETT, MAN AGAINST CRIME (TV)
Dec, 1951 - No. 6, 1952
Fawcett Publications

1	3.75	11.25	26.00
2	2.35	7.00	16.00
3,4,6	2.00	6.00	14.00
5-"Market for Morphine" cover/story	3.75	11.25	26.00

MIKE MIST MINUTE MIST-ERIES
1986 (B&W)
Eclipse Comics

1	.35	1.00	2.00

MIKE SHAYNE PRIVATE EYE
Nov-Jan, 1962 - No. 3, Sept-Nov, 1962
Dell Publishing Co.

1	1.30	4.00	9.00
2,3	1.00	3.00	7.00

MILITARY COMICS (Becomes Modern No. 44 on)
Aug, 1941 - No. 43, Oct, 1945
Quality Comics Group

	Good	Fine	Mint
1-Origin Blackhawk by C. Cuidera, Miss America, The Death Patrol by Jack Cole (also No. 2-7,27-30), & The Blue Tracer by Guardineer; X of the Underground, The Yankee Eagle, Q-Boat & Shot & Shell, Archie Atkins, Loops & Banks by Bud Ernest (Bob Powell) (ends No. 13) begin	192.00	575.00	1345.00
2-Secret War News begins (by McWilliams No. 2-16); Cole-a	92.00	275.00	645.00
3-Origin/1st app. Chop Chop	70.00	210.00	490.00
4	60.00	180.00	420.00
5-The Sniper begins; Miss America in costume No. 4-7	50.00	150.00	350.00
6-9: 8-X of the Underground begins (ends No. 13). 9-The Phantom Clipper begins (ends No. 16)	40.00	120.00	280.00
10-Classic Eisner-c	45.00	135.00	315.00
11-Flag-c	33.00	100.00	230.00
12-Blackhawk by Crandall begins, ends No. 22	45.00	135.00	315.00
13-15: 14-Private Dogtag begins (ends No. 83)	32.00	95.00	225.00
16-20: 16-Blue Tracer ends. 17-P.T. Boat begins	25.00	75.00	175.00
21-31: 22-Last Crandall Blackhawk. 27-Death Patrol revived	22.00	65.00	154.00
32-43	19.50	58.00	135.00

NOTE: ***Berg** a-6. **J. Cole** a-1-3, 27-32. **Crandall** a-12-22; c-13-22. **Eisner** c-1, 9, 10. **McWilliams** a-2-16. **Powell** a-1-13. **Ward** Blackhawk-30, 31(15 pgs. each); c-29, 30.*

MILITARY WILLY
1907 (14 pgs.; ½ in color (every other page)) (regular comic book format)(7x9½")(stapled)
J. I. Austen Co.

By F. R. Morgan	9.00	27.00	62.00

MILLIE, THE LOVABLE MONSTER
Sept-Nov, 1962 - No. 6, Jan, 1973
Dell Publishing Co.

12-523,211, 2(8-10/63)	1.00	3.00	7.00
3(8-10/64)	.85	2.50	6.00
4(7/72), 5(10/72), 6(1/73)	.70	2.00	4.00

NOTE: ***Woggon** a-3-6; c-3-6. 4 reprints 1; 5 reprints 2; 6 reprints 3.*

MILLIE THE MODEL (See Modeling With..., A Date With..., and Life With...)
1945 - No. 207, December, 1973
Marvel/Atlas/Marvel Comics (SPI/Male/VPI)

1	15.00	45.00	105.00
2 (10/46)-Millie becomes The Blonde Phantom to sell Blonde Phantom perfume; a pre-Blonde Phantom app. (see All-Select No. 11, Fall, '46)	9.00	27.00	62.00
3-7: 7-Willie smokes extra strong tobacco	4.00	12.00	28.00
8,10-Kurtzman's "Hey Look"	4.35	13.00	30.00
9-Powerhouse Pepper by Wolverton, 4 pgs.	8.00	24.00	56.00
11-Kurtzman-a	3.35	10.00	23.00
12,15,17-20	1.85	5.50	13.00
13,14,16-Kurtzman's "Hey Look"	2.50	7.50	17.50
21-30	1.50	4.50	10.00
31-60	.85	2.50	6.00
61-99	.45	1.35	3.00
100	.75	2.25	5.00
101-106,108-207: 192-(52 pgs.)	.25	.75	1.50
107-Jack Kirby app. in story	.25	.75	1.50
Annual 1(1962)	2.00	6.00	14.00
Annual 2-10(1963-11/71)	1.00	3.00	7.00
Queen-Size 11(9/74), 12(1975)	.50	1.50	3.00

MILLION DOLLAR DIGEST
Aug, 1986 - Present ($1.25, digest size)
Harvey Publications

1,2		.60	1.25

MILT GROSS FUNNIES
Aug, 1947 - No. 2, Sept, 1947
Milt Gross, Inc. (ACG?)

1,2	3.50	10.50	24.00

MILTON THE MONSTER & FEARLESS FLY (TV)
May, 1966
Gold Key

1 (10175-605)	1.50	4.50	10.00

MINUTE MAN (See Master & Mighty Midget Comics)
Sum, 1941 - No. 3, Spring, 1942
Fawcett Publications

1	55.00	165.00	385.00
2,3	40.00	120.00	280.00

MINUTE MAN
No date (B&W; 16 pgs.; paper cover blue & red)
Sovereign Service Station giveaway

	Good	Fine	Mint
American history	1.00	3.00	6.00

MINUTE MAN ANSWERS THE CALL, THE
1942 (4 pages)
By M. C. Gaines (War Bonds giveaway)

	Good	Fine	Mint
Sheldon Moldoff-a	4.00	12.00	24.00

MIRACLE COMICS
Feb, 1940 - No. 4, March, 1941
Hillman Periodicals

	Good	Fine	Mint
1-Sky Wizard, Master of Space, Dash Dixon, Man of Might, Dusty Doyle, Pinkie Parker, The Kid Cop, K-7, Secret Agent, The Scorpion, & Blandu, Jungle Queen begin; Masked Angel only app.	38.00	115.00	265.00
2	25.00	75.00	175.00
3,4: 3-Bill Colt, the Ghost Rider begins. 4-The Veiled Prophet & Bullet Bob app.	22.00	65.00	154.00

MIRACLEMAN
Aug, 1985 - Present (Mando paper, 7-10)
Eclipse Comics

	Good	Fine	Mint
1-r-/of British Marvelman series; Alan Moore scripts in all	.35	1.00	2.00
1-Gold edition	8.35	25.00	50.00
1-Silver edition	3.35	10.00	20.00
2-5		.50	1.00
6-11: 9,10-Origin Miracleman. 9-Shows graphic scenes of childbirth		.50	1.00
3-D 1 (12/85)	.40	1.25	2.50
2-D 1 (B&W, 100 copy limited signed & numbered edition)	.85	2.50	5.00

NOTE: ***Miller** c-9.*

MIRACLE OF THE WHITE STALLIONS, THE (See Movie Comics)

MIRACLE SQUAD, THE
Aug, 1986 - No. 4 ($2.00, color, mini-series)
Upshot Graphics (Fantagraphics Books)

	Good	Fine	Mint
1-4	.35	1.00	2.00

MISADVENTURES OF MERLIN JONES, THE (See Movie Comics & Merlin Jones as the Monkey's Uncle under Movie Comics)

MISCHIEVOUS MONKS OF CROCODILE ISLE, THE
1908 (8½x11½''; 4 pgs. in color; 12 pgs.)
J. I. Austen Co., Chicago

	Good	Fine	Mint
By F. R. Morgan; reads longwise	5.00	15.00	35.00

MISS AMERICA COMICS (Miss America Mag. No. 2 on)
1944 (One Shot)
Marvel Comics (20CC)

	Good	Fine	Mint
1-2 pgs. pin-ups	45.00	135.00	315.00

MISS AMERICA MAGAZINE (Formerly Miss America) (Miss America No. 51 on)
V1/2, Nov, 1944 - No. 93, Nov, 1958
Miss America Publ. Corp./Marvel/Atlas (MAP)

	Good	Fine	Mint
V1/2: Photo cover of teenage girl in Miss America costume; Miss America, Patsy Walker (intro.) comic stories plus movie reviews & stories; intro. Buzz Baxter & Hedy Wolfe	40.00	120.00	280.00
3-5-Miss America & Patsy Walker stories	13.50	40.50	95.00
6-Patsy Walker only	3.35	10.00	23.00
V2/1(4/45)-6(9/45)-Patsy Walker continues	1.85	5.50	13.00
V3/1(10/45)-6(4/46)	1.85	5.50	13.00
V4/1(5/46)-3(7/46), V5/1(11/46)-6(4/47), V6/1(5/47)-3(7/47)	1.50	4.50	10.00
V4/4 (8/46; 68pgs.)	1.50	4.50	10.00
V4/5 (9/46)-Liz Taylor photo-c	3.00	9.00	21.00
V4/6 (10/46; 92pgs.)	1.50	4.50	10.00
V7/1(8/47)-14,16-23(6/49)	1.15	3.50	8.00
V7/15-All comics	1.50	4.50	10.00
V7/24(7/49)-Kamen-a	1.35	4.00	9.00
V7/25(8/49), 27-44(3/52), VII,nn(5/52)	1.15	3.50	8.00
V7/26(9/49)-All comics	1.50	4.50	10.00
V1,nn(7/52)-V1,nn(1/53)(No.46-49)	1.15	3.50	8.00
V7/50(Spring '53), V1/51-V7?/54(7/53)	1.00	3.00	7.00
55-93	1.00	3.00	7.00

NOTE: Photo-c 1, V2/4, V3/5, V4/4,6, V7/15, 24, 26, 34, 37, 38.

MISS BEVERLY HILLS OF HOLLYWOOD
Mar-Apr, 1949 - No. 9, July-Aug, 1950
National Periodical Publications

	Good	Fine	Mint
1	15.00	45.00	105.00
2-William Holden photo-c	11.50	34.50	80.00
3-5: 3-Photo-c	9.50	28.50	66.00
6,7,9	8.00	24.00	56.00
8-Reagan photo on-c	11.00	33.00	76.00

MISS CAIRO JONES
1945
Croyden Publishers

	Good	Fine	Mint
1-Bob Oksner daily newspaper-r (1st strip story); lingerie panels	10.00	30.00	70.00

MISS FURY COMICS (Newspaper strip reprints)
Winter, 1942-43 - No. 8, Winter, 1946
Timely Comics (NPI 1/CmPI 2/MPC 3-8)

	Good	Fine	Mint
1-Origin Miss Fury by Tarpe' Mills (68 pgs.) in costume w/pin-ups	125.00	375.00	875.00
2-(60 pgs.)-In costume w/pin-ups	55.00	165.00	385.00
3-(60 pgs.)-In costume w/pin-ups	45.00	135.00	315.00
4-(52 pgs.)-Costume, 2 pgs. w/pin-ups	38.00	115.00	265.00
5-(52 pgs.)-In costume w/pin-ups	34.00	100.00	235.00
6-(52 pgs.)-Not in costume in inside stories, w/pin-ups	30.00	90.00	210.00
7,8-(36 pgs.)-In costume 1 pg. each, no pin-ups	30.00	90.00	210.00

MISSION IMPOSSIBLE (TV)
5/67 - No. 4, 10/68; No. 5, 10/69 (No. 1-5 have photo-c)
Dell Publishing Co.

	Good	Fine	Mint
1	3.50	10.50	24.00
2-5	2.65	8.00	18.00

MISS LIBERTY (Becomes Liberty)
1945 (MLJ reprints)
Burten Publishing Co.

	Good	Fine	Mint
1-The Shield & Dusty, The Wizard, & Roy, the Super Boy app.; r-/Shield-Wizard No. 13	11.00	33.00	76.00

MISS MELODY LANE OF BROADWAY
Feb-Mar, 1950 - No. 3, June-July, 1950
National Periodical Publications

	Good	Fine	Mint
1	15.00	45.00	105.00
2,3	11.50	34.50	80.00

MISS PEACH
Oct-Dec, 1963; 1969

Miracle Squad #1, © Fantagraphics

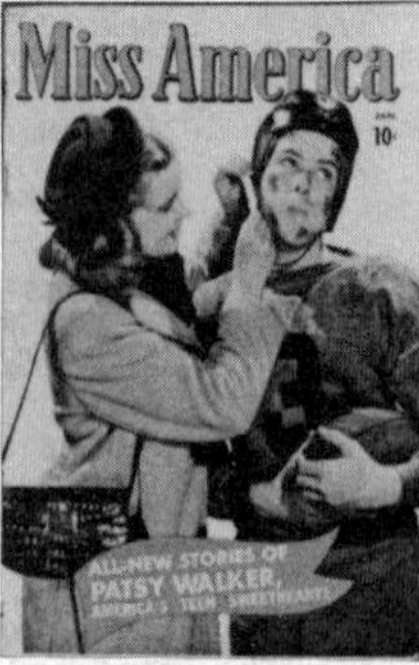

Miss America Magazine #37, © MCG

Mission Impossible #4, © Paramount Pictures

Mr. & Mrs. J. Evil Scientist #1, © Hanna-Barbera

Mr. District Attorney #10, © DC

Mr. Monster's Three-Dimensional... #1, © Eclipse

MISS PEACH (continued)
Dell Publishing Co.

	Good	Fine	Mint
1-Jack Mendelsohn-a/script	3.50	10.50	24.00
...Tells You How to Grow(1969; 25 cents)-Mell Lazarus-a; also given away (36 pgs.)	2.65	8.00	16.00

MISS PEPPER (See Meet Miss Pepper)

MISS SUNBEAM (See Little Miss...)

MISS VICTORY (See Holyoke One-Shot No. 3)
1945
Holyoke Publishing Co. (Tem)

	Good	Fine	Mint
1	11.50	34.50	80.00
2	9.50	28.50	65.00

MR. & MRS.
1922 (52, 28 pgs.) (9x9½'', cardboard-c)
Whitman Publishing Co.

	Good	Fine	Mint
By Briggs (B&W, 52pgs.)	5.00	15.00	35.00
28 page edition-(9x9½'')-Reprints Sunday strips in full color	11.00	33.00	76.00

MR. & MRS. BEANS (See Single Series No. 11)

MR. & MRS. J. EVIL SCIENTIST (TV)(See The Flintstones)
Nov, 1963 - No. 4, Sept, 1966 (Hanna-Barbera)
Gold Key

	Good	Fine	Mint
1-From The Flintstones	1.30	4.00	9.00
2-4	.85	2.50	6.00

MR. ANTHONY'S LOVE CLINIC
Nov, 1949 - No. 5, Apr-May, 1950
Hillman Periodicals

	Good	Fine	Mint
1-Photo-c	3.50	10.50	24.00
2	1.75	5.25	12.00
3-5: 5-Photo-c	1.50	4.50	10.00

MR. BUG GOES TO TOWN (See Cinema Comics Herald)

MR. DISTRICT ATTORNEY (Radio/TV)
Jan-Feb, 1948 - No. 67, Jan-Feb, 1959 (52 pgs. 1-23)
National Periodical Publications

	Good	Fine	Mint
1	16.00	48.00	110.00
2	8.00	24.00	56.00
3-5	6.50	19.50	45.00
6-10	5.00	15.00	35.00
11-20	4.00	12.00	28.00
21-43: 43-Last pre-code (1-2/55)	3.00	9.00	21.00
44-67	2.00	6.00	14.00

MR. DISTRICT ATTORNEY (See 4-Color No. 13)

MISTER ED, THE TALKING HORSE (TV)
Mar-May, 1962 - No. 6, Feb, 1964 (All photo-c; photo back-c, 1-6)
Dell Publishing Co./Gold Key

	Good	Fine	Mint
4-Color 1295	2.00	6.00	14.00
1(11/62)-6 (Gold Key)-Photo-c	1.30	4.00	9.00

(See March of Comics No. 244,260,282,290)

MR. MAGOO (TV) (The Nearsighted..., ...& Gerald McBoing Boing 1954 issues; formerly Gerald...)
No. 6, Nov-Jan, 1953-54; 1963 - 1965
Dell Publishing Co.

	Good	Fine	Mint
6	3.00	9.00	21.00
4-Color 561(5/54),602(11/54)	3.00	9.00	21.00
4-Color 1235,1305('61)	2.65	8.00	18.00
3(9-11/63) - 5	2.65	8.00	16.00
4-Color 1235(12-536-505)(3-5/65)-2nd Printing	1.75	4.25	12.00

MISTER MIRACLE (See Brave & the Bold & Cancelled Comic Caval.)
3-4/71 - No. 18, 2-3/74; No. 19, 9/77 - No. 25, 8-9/78
National Periodical Publications/DC Comics (No. 7,8-52 pgs.)

	Good	Fine	Mint
1	.35	1.00	2.00
2	.25	.75	1.50
3-10: 4-Boy Commando-r begin. 9-Origin Mr. Miracle		.60	1.20
11-17: 15-Intro/1st app. Shilo Norman		.40	.80
18-Barda & Scott Free wed; New Gods app.		.40	.80
19-22-Rogers-a(p)		.40	.80
23-25-Golden-a(p)		.25	.50

NOTE: ***Austin*** *a-19i.* ***Ditko*** *a-6r.* ***Golden*** *c-25p.* ***Heath*** *a-24i, 25i; c-25i.* ***Kirby*** *a(p)/c-1-18.* ***Nasser*** *a-19i.* ***Rogers*** *c-19, 20p, 21p, 22-24.* ***Wolverton*** *a-6r. 4-8 contain* ***Simon & Kirby*** *Boy Commando reprints from Detective 82,76, Boy Commandos 1,3, Detective 64 in that order.*

MR. MIRACLE (See Holyoke One-Shot No. 4)

MR. MONSTER
1/85 - Present ($1.75; Baxter paper)
Eclipse Comics

	Good	Fine	Mint
1	.50	1.50	3.00
2-Dave Stevens-c	.35	1.00	2.00
3-5: 3-Alan Moore scripts	.30	.90	1.80
...In 3-D	.35	1.00	2.00

MR. MONSTER'S HIGH-OCTANE HORROR
Aug, 1986 ($1.75)
Eclipse Comics

	Good	Fine	Mint
1-Bissette, Evans, Wolverton-r	.30	.85	1.70
...Three Dimensional High-Octane Horror (5/86)-Powell, Kubert Gilbert-a(r)	.40	1.25	2.50
...in 2-D: 100 copies signed & numbered (B&W)	1.00	3.00	6.00

MR. MONSTER'S TRUE CRIME
Sept, 1986 - Present ($1.75)
Eclipse Comics

	Good	Fine	Mint
1,2-r-/True Crime	.30	.90	1.80

MR. MUSCLES (Formerly Blue Beetle No. 18-21)
No. 22, Mar, 1956 - No. 23, Aug, 1956
Charlton Comics

	Good	Fine	Mint
22,23	1.50	4.50	10.00

MISTER MYSTERY
Sept, 1951 - No. 19, Oct, 1954
Mr. Publ. (Media Publ.) No. 1-3/SPM Publ./Stanmore (Aragon)

	Good	Fine	Mint
1-Kurtzmanesque horror story	13.00	40.00	90.00
2,3-Kurtzmanesque story	9.50	28.50	65.00
4,6: Bondage-c; 6-Torture	9.50	28.50	65.00
5,8,10	8.00	24.00	56.00
7-''The Brain Bats of Venus'' by Wolverton; partially re-used in Weird Tales of the Future No. 7	37.00	110.00	260.00
9-Nostrand-a	8.00	24.00	56.00
11-Wolverton ''Robot Woman'' story/Weird Mysteries No. 2, cut up, rewritten & partially redrawn	18.00	54.00	125.00
12-Classic injury to eye-c	24.00	72.00	165.00
13,14,17,19	5.00	15.00	35.00
15-''Living Dead'' junkie story	8.00	24.00	56.00
16-Bondage-c; drug story	8.00	24.00	56.00
18-''Robot Woman'' by Wolverton reprinted from Weird Mysteries No. 2; bondage-c	16.00	48.00	110.00

NOTE: ***Andru*** *c/a-1, 2.* ***Bailey*** *c-10-19(most). Bondage c-7.*

MISTER Q (See Mighty Midget Comics)

MR. RISK (Formerly All Romances; Men Against Crime No. 3 on)
No. 7, Oct, 1950 - No. 2, Dec, 1950
Ace Magazines

MR. RISK (continued)

	Good	Fine	Mint
7,2	1.75	5.25	12.00

MR. SCARLET & PINKY (See Mighty Midget Comics)

MISTER UNIVERSE (Professional wrestler)
July, 1951 - No. 5, 1952?
Mr. Publications Media Publ. (Stanmor, Aragon)

	Good	Fine	Mint
1	6.00	18.00	42.00
2-'Jungle That Time Forgot', 24pg. story	4.35	13.00	30.00
3-Marijuana story	4.35	13.00	30.00
4,5-''Goes to War''	2.15	6.50	15.00

MR. X
June, 1984 - Present ($1.50-$1.75; direct sales; Baxter paper)
Mr. Publications/Vortex Comics

	Good	Fine	Mint
1	.70	2.00	4.00
2	.45	1.40	2.80
3-9	.35	1.10	2.20

MISTY
Dec, 1985 - No. 6, May, 1986 (mini-series)
Star Comics (Marvel)

	Good	Fine	Mint
1-Millie The Model's niece		.35	.70
2-6		.40	.80

MITES
1986 - Present ($1.80, B&W)
Eternity Comics

	Good	Fine	Mint
1-The X-Mites parody	.30	.90	1.80
2A,2B-Dark Knight parody	.30	.90	1.80

MITZI COMICS (. . . Boy Friend No. 2 on)
Spring, 1948 (One Shot)
Timely Comics

	Good	Fine	Mint
1-Kurtzman's ''Hey Look'' plus 3 pgs. ''Giggles 'n' Grins''	4.35	13.00	30.00

MITZI'S BOY FRIEND (Formerly Mitzi; becomes Mitzi's Romances)
No. 2, June, 1948 - No. 7, April, 1949
Marvel Comics

	Good	Fine	Mint
2	2.00	6.00	14.00
3-7	1.30	4.00	9.00

MITZI'S ROMANCES (Formerly Mitzi's Boy Friend)
No. 8, June, 1949 - No. 10, Dec, 1949
Timely/Marvel Comics

	Good	Fine	Mint
8	2.00	6.00	14.00
9,10: 10-Painted-c	1.30	4.00	9.00

MOBY DICK (See 4-Color No. 717, Feature Presentations No. 6, and King Classics)

MOBY DUCK (See W. D. Showcase No. 2,11, Donald Duck No. 112)
10/67 - No. 11, 10/70; No. 12, 1/74 - No. 30, 2/78
Gold Key (Disney)

	Good	Fine	Mint
1	.85	2.50	6.00
2-5	.70	2.00	4.00
6-11	.35	1.00	2.00
12-30: 21,30-r		.60	1.20

MODEL FUN (With Bobby Benson)
No. 3, Winter, 1954-55 - No. 5, July, 1955
Harle Publications

	Good	Fine	Mint
3-Bobby Benson	2.00	6.00	14.00
4,5-Bobby Benson	1.30	4.00	9.00

MODELING WITH MILLIE (Formerly Life With Millie)
No. 21, Feb, 1963 - No. 54, June, 1967
Atlas/Marvel Comics Group (Male Publ.)

	Good	Fine	Mint
21	.85	2.50	5.00
22-30	.50	1.50	3.00
31-54	.25	.75	1.50

MODERN COMICS (Military No. 1-43)
No. 44, Nov, 1945 - No. 102, Oct, 1950
Quality Comics Group

	Good	Fine	Mint
44	17.00	51.00	120.00
45-52: 49-1st app. Fear, Lady Adventuress	11.50	34.50	80.00
53-Torchy by Ward begins (9/46)	16.50	49.50	115.00
54-60: 55-J. Cole-a	11.00	33.00	76.00
61-77,79,80: 73-J. Cole-a	10.00	30.00	70.00
78-1st app. Madame Butterfly	11.00	33.00	76.00
81-99,101: 82,83-One pg. J. Cole-a	9.50	28.50	65.00
100	10.00	30.00	70.00
102-(Scarce)-J. Cole-a; some issues have Spirit by Eisner	13.00	40.00	90.00

NOTE: ***Crandall*** *Blackhawk-No. 46-51, 54, 56, 58-60, 64, 67-70, 73, 82, 83.* ***Gustavson*** *a-47.* ***Jack Cole*** *a-73.* ***Ward*** *Blackhawk-No. 52, 53, 55 (15 pgs. each). Torchy in No. 53-102; by* ***Ward*** *only in No. 53-89(9/49); by* ***Gil Fox*** *No. 93, 102.*

MODERN LOVE
June-July, 1949 - No. 8, Aug-Sept, 1950
E. C. Comics

	Good	Fine	Mint
1	38.00	115.00	265.00
2-Craig/Feldstein-c	30.00	90.00	210.00
3-Spanking panels	25.00	75.00	175.00
4-6 (Scarce): 4-Bra/panties panels	35.00	105.00	245.00
7,8	26.00	78.00	180.00

NOTE: ***Feldstein*** *a-in most issues.* ***Ingels*** *a-1, 2, 4-7.* ***Wood*** *a-7. (Canadian reprints known; see Table of Contents.)*

MOD LOVE
1967 (36 pages) (50 cents)
Western Publishing Co.

	Good	Fine	Mint
1	1.50	4.50	10.00

MODNIKS, THE
Aug, 1967 - No. 2, Aug, 1970
Gold Key

	Good	Fine	Mint
10206-708(No.1), 2	.75	2.25	5.00

MOD SQUAD (TV)
Jan, 1969 - No. 3, Oct, 1969 - No. 8, April, 1971
Dell Publishing Co.

	Good	Fine	Mint
1	1.50	4.50	10.00
2-8: 8 reprints No. 2	1.00	3.00	7.00

MOD WHEELS
March, 1971 - No. 19, Jan, 1976
Gold Key

	Good	Fine	Mint
1	1.00	3.00	6.00
2-19: 11,15-Extra 16pgs. ads	.50	1.50	3.00

MOE & SHMOE COMICS
Spring, 1948 - No. 2, Summer, 1948
O. S. Publ. Co.

	Good	Fine	Mint
1	2.65	8.00	18.00
2	1.75	5.25	12.00

MOLLY MANTON'S ROMANCES (My Love No. 3)
Sept, 1949 - No. 2, Dec, 1949 (52 pgs.)
Marvel Comics (SePI)

	Good	Fine	Mint
1-Photo-c	3.50	10.50	24.00
2-Titled 'Romances of. . .'; photo-c	2.35	7.00	16.00

Mr. X #6, © Vortex

Modern Comics #45, © QUA

Modern Love #2, © WMG

The Monkees #10, © DELL

The Monroes #1, © 20th Century-Fox

Monte Hale Western #32, © FAW

MOLLY O'DAY (Super Sleuth)
February, 1945 (1st Avon comic)
Avon Periodicals

	Good	Fine	Mint
1-Molly O'Day, The Enchanted Dagger by Tuska (reprint/Yankee No. 1), Capt'n Courage, Corporal Grant app.	28.00	84.00	195.00

MONKEES, THE (TV)(Also see Circus Boy)
March, 1967 - No. 17, Oct, 1969 (No. 1-4,6,7 have photo-c)
Dell Publishing Co.

	Good	Fine	Mint
1	2.35	7.00	16.00
2-17: 17 reprints No. 1	1.30	4.00	9.00

MONKEY & THE BEAR, THE
Sept, 1953 - No. 3, Jan, 1954
Atlas Comics (ZPC)

	Good	Fine	Mint
1-Howie Post-a	1.75	5.25	12.00
2,3	1.00	3.00	7.00

MONKEYSHINES COMICS (Ernie No. 24? on)
Summer, 1944 - No. 26, May, 1949
Ace Periodicals/Publishers Specialists/Current Books/Unity Publ.

	Good	Fine	Mint
1	3.00	9.00	21.00
2	1.50	4.50	10.00
3-10	1.15	3.50	8.00
11-26: 23-Fago c/a	1.00	3.00	7.00

MONKEY SHINES OF MARSELEEN
1909 (11½x17") (28 pages in two colors)
Cupples & Leon Co.

	Good	Fine	Mint
By Norman E. Jennett	8.00	24.00	56.00

MONKEY'S UNCLE, THE (See Merlin Jones As. . . under Movie Comics)

MONROES, THE (TV)
April, 1967
Dell Publishing Co.

	Good	Fine	Mint
1-Photo-c	1.75	5.25	12.00

MONSTER
1953
Fiction House Magazines

	Good	Fine	Mint
1-Dr. Drew by Grandenetti; reprint from Rangers Comics	12.00	36.00	84.00
2	10.00	30.00	70.00

MONSTER CRIME COMICS (Also see Crime Must Stop)
October, 1952 (52 pgs., 15¢)
Hillman Periodicals

	Good	Fine	Mint
1 (Scarce)	30.00	90.00	210.00

MONSTER HOWLS (Magazine)
December, 1966 (Satire) (35 cents) (68 pgs.)
Humor-Vision

	Good	Fine	Mint
1	.85	2.50	5.00

MONSTER HUNTERS
8/75 - No. 9, 1/77; No. 10, 10/77 - No. 18, 2/79
Charlton Comics

	Good	Fine	Mint
1-Howard-a, Newton-c		.40	.80
2-Ditko-a		.40	.80
3-11		.30	.60
12,13,15-18-All reprints		.25	.50
14-Special all-Ditko issue		.50	1.00
1,2(Modern Comics reprints, 1977)		.15	.30

NOTE: **Ditko** a-6, 8, 10, 13-15r, 18r; c-13-15, 18. **Morisi** a-1. **Staton** a-1,13. **Sutton** a-2, 4; c-2, 4.

MONSTER OF FRANKENSTEIN (See Frankenstein)

MONSTERS ON THE PROWL (Chamber of Darkness No. 1-8)
No. 9, 2/71 - No. 27, 11/73; No. 28, 6/74 - No. 30, 10/74
Marvel Comics Group (No. 13,14: 52 pgs.)

	Good	Fine	Mint
9-Smith inks		.50	1.00
10-30		.30	.60

NOTE: **Ditko** a-9r, 14r, 16r. **Kirby** r-10-17, 21, 23, 25, 27, 28, 30; c-9, 25. **Kirby/Ditko** r-14, 17-20, 22, 24, 26, 29. **Marie/John Severin** a-16(Kull). 9-13, 15-contain one new story. Woodish art by **Reese**-11.

MONSTERS UNLEASHED (Magazine)
July, 1973 - No. 11, April, 1975; Summer, 1975 (B&W)
Marvel Comics Group

	Good	Fine	Mint
1	.35	1.00	2.00
2-The Frankenstein Monster begins		.60	1.20
3-Adams-c; The Man-Thing begins (origin-r)-Adams-a	.25	.75	1.50
4-Intro. Satana, the Devil's daughter; Krigstein-r	.25	.75	1.50
5-7: 7-Williamson-a(r)		.60	1.20
8,10,11: 8-Adams-r. 10-Origin Tigra		.50	1.00
9-Wendigo app.	.40	1.25	2.50
Annual 1(Summer,'75)-Kane-a		.50	1.00

NOTE: **Boris** c-2, 6. **Brunner** a-2; c-11. **J. Buscema** a-2p, 4p, 5p. **Colan** a-1, 4r. **Davis** a-3r. **Everett** a-2r. **G. Kane** a-3. **Morrow** a-3; c-1. **Perez** a-8. **Reese** a-1, 2. **Tuska** a-3p. **Wildey** a-1r.

MONTANA KID, THE (See Kid Montana)

MONTE HALE WESTERN (Movie star; Formerly Mary Marvel No. 1-28; also see Western Hero and Picture News No. 8)
No. 29, Oct, 1948 - No. 88, Jan, 1956
Fawcett Publications/Charlton No. 83 on

	Good	Fine	Mint
29-(No.1, 52pgs.)-Photo-c begin, end No. 82; Monte Hale & his horse Pardner begin	15.00	45.00	105.00
30-(52 pgs.)-Big Bow and Little Arrow begin, end No. 34; Captain Tootsie by Beck	8.00	24.00	56.00
31-36,38-40-(52 pgs.): 34-Gabby Hayes begins, ends No. 80. 39-Captain Tootsie by Beck	6.50	19.50	45.00
37,41,45,49-(36 pgs.)	4.50	13.50	31.00
42-44,46-48,50-(52 pgs.): 47-Big Bow & Little Arrow app.	5.00	15.00	35.00
51,52,54-56,58,59-(52 pgs.)	3.65	11.00	25.00
53,57-(36 pgs.): 53-Slim Pickens app.	3.35	10.00	23.00
60-81: 36pgs. No. 60-on. 80-Gabby Hayes ends	3.35	10.00	23.00
82-Last Fawcett issue (6/53)	4.00	12.00	28.00
83-1st Charlton issue (2/55); B&W photo back-c begin. Gabby Hayes returns, ends No. 86	4.00	12.00	28.00
84 (4/55)	3.65	11.00	25.00
85-86	3.35	10.00	23.00
87-Wolverton-r, ½pg.	3.65	11.00	25.00
88-Last issue	3.65	11.00	25.00

NOTE: **Gil Kane** a-33?, 34? **Rocky Lane** ½-1 pg. (Carnation ad)-38, 40, 41, 43, 44, 46, 55.

MONTY HALL OF THE U.S. MARINES (See With the Marines. . .)
Aug, 1951 - No. 11, 1953
Toby Press

	Good	Fine	Mint
1	3.65	11.00	25.00
2	2.85	8.50	20.00
3-5	2.50	7.50	17.00
6-11	1.85	5.50	13.00

NOTE: 3-5 full page pin-ups (Pin-Up Pete) by **Jack Sparling** in all.

A MOON, A GIRL. . .ROMANCE (Becomes Weird Fantasy No. 13 on; formerly Moon Girl No. 1-8)
No. 9, Sept-Oct, 1949 - No. 12, Mar-Apr, 1950
E. C. Comics

	Good	Fine	Mint
9-Moon Girl cameo; spanking/lingerie panels	49.00	146.00	342.00

A MOON, A GIRL...ROMANCE (continued) — Good / Fine / Mint
10,11 — 38.00 115.00 265.00
12-(Scarce) — 53.00 160.00 370.00
NOTE: *Feldstein, Ingels art in all. Canadian reprints known; see Table of Contents.*

MOON GIRL AND THE PRINCE (No. 1) (Moon Girl No. 2-6; Moon Girl Fights Crime No. 7,8; becomes A Moon, A Girl, Romance No. 9 on)
Fall, 1947 - No. 8, Summer, 1949
E. C. Comics (Also see Happy Houlihans)

1-Origin Moon Girl — 55.00 165.00 385.00
2 — 32.00 95.00 225.00
3,4: 4-Moon Girl vs. a vampire — 27.00 81.00 190.00
5-E.C.'s 1st horror story, "Zombie Terror" — 60.00 180.00 420.00
6-8 (Scarce): 7-Origin Star (Moongirl's sidekick) — 32.00 95.00 225.00
NOTE: *No. 2 & No. 3 are 52 pgs., No. 4 on, 36 pgs. Canadian reprints known; (see Table of Contents.)*

MOON KNIGHT (Also see Werewolf by Night No. 32)
November, 1980 - No. 38, July, 1984 (Mando paper No. 33 on)
Marvel Comics Group

1-Origin resumed in No. 4 — .45 1.35 2.70
2-5: 4-Intro Midnight Man — .25 .80 1.60
6-14 — .60 1.20
15-First direct sale; Miller c(p) — .55 1.60 3.20
16 — .30 .90 1.80
17-24 — .25 .70 1.40
25-Double size — .25 .75 1.50
26-34,36-38 — .45 .90
35-(52 pgs., $1.00)-X-men app. — .60 1.20
NOTE: ***Austin** c-27i, 31i. **Miller** c-9, 12p, 13p, 15p, 27p.*

MOON KNIGHT
June, 1985 - No. 6, Dec, 1985
Marvel Comics Group

1(V2/1)-Double size; new costume — .60 1.20
2-6 — .35 .70

MOON KNIGHT SPECIAL EDITION
Nov, 1983 - No. 3, Jan, 1984 (mini-series) (Baxter paper)
Marvel Comics Group

1-3: 1-Hulk-r — .25 .80 1.60

MOON MULLINS
1927 - 1933 (52 pgs.) (daily B&W strip reprints)
Cupples & Leon Co.

Series 1('27)-By Willard — 10.00 30.00 70.00
Series 2('28), Series 3('29), Series 4('30) — 7.00 21.00 50.00
Series 5('31), 6('32), 7('33) — 5.50 16.50 38.00
Big Book 1('30)-B&W — 13.00 40.00 90.00

MOON MULLINS (See Superbook No. 3)
1941 - 1945
Dell Publishing Co.

4-Color 14(1941) — 15.00 45.00 105.00
Large Feature Comic 29(1941) — 11.00 33.00 76.00
4-Color 31(1943) — 9.50 28.50 65.00
4-Color 81(1945) — 5.00 15.00 35.00

MOON MULLINS
Dec-Jan, 1947-48 - No. 8, 1949 (52 pgs.)
Michel Publ. (American Comics Group)

1-Alternating Sunday & daily strip-r — 6.00 18.00 42.00
2 — 3.50 10.50 24.00
3-8 — 3.00 9.00 21.00
NOTE: ***Milt Gross** a-2, 4-6, 8. **Willard** r-all.*

MOON PILOT (See 4-Color No. 1313)

MOONSHADOW
5/85 - No. 12, 2/87 ($1.50-$1.75)(Adults only)
Epic Comics (Marvel) — Good / Fine / Mint

1-Origin — .40 1.20 2.40
2-12: 11-Origin — .30 .90 1.80

MOON-SPINNERS, THE (See Movie Comics)

MOPSY (See TV Teens & Pageant of Comics)
Feb, 1948 - No. 19, Sept, 1953
St. John Publ. Co.

1-Part-r; r-/"Some Punkins" by Neher — 7.00 21.00 50.00
2 — 4.00 12.00 28.00
3-10(1953): 8-Lingerie panels — 3.50 10.50 24.00
11-19: 19-Lingerie-c — 3.00 9.00 21.00
NOTE: No. 1, 4-6, 8, 13, 19 have paper dolls.

MORE FUN COMICS (Formerly New Fun No. 1-6)
No. 7, Jan, 1936 - No. 127, Nov-Dec, 1947 (No. 7,9-11 paper-c)
National Periodical Publications

7(1/36)-Oversized, paper-c; 1 pg. Kelly-a — 150.00 450.00 1050.00
8(2/36)-Oversized (10x12"), slick-c; 1 pg. Kelly-a — 100.00 300.00 700.00
9(3-4/36)(Very Rare)-Last Henri Duval by Siegel & Shuster — 130.00 390.00 910.00
10,11(7/36): 11-1st 'Calling All Cars' by Siegel & Shuster — 85.00 255.00 595.00
12(8/36)-Slick-c begin — 75.00 225.00 525.00
V2No.1(9/36, No.13) — 75.00 225.00 525.00
2(10/36, No.14)-Dr. Occult in costume (Superman prototype) begins, ends No. 17; see The Comics Magazine — 80.00 240.00 560.00
V2No.3(11/36, No.15), 16(V2No.4), 17(V2No.5)-Cover numbering begins No. 16 — 50.00 150.00 350.00
18-20(V2No.8, 5/37) — 35.00 105.00 245.00
21(V2No.9)-24(V2No.12, 9/37) — 30.00 90.00 210.00
25(V3No.1, 10/37)-27(V3No.3, 12/37) — 30.00 90.00 210.00
28-30: 30-1st non-funny cover — 30.00 90.00 210.00
31-35: 32-Last Dr. Occult — 27.00 81.00 190.00
36-40: 36-The Masked Ranger begins, ends No. 41 — 25.00 75.00 175.00
41-50 — 23.50 70.00 165.00
51-1st app. The Spectre (in costume) in one panel ad at end of Buccaneer story — 45.00 135.00 315.00
52-Origin The Spectre (out of costume), Part 1 by Bernard Baily; last Wing Brady (Rare) — 1000.00 3000.00 7000.00
53-Origin The Spectre (out of costume), Part 2; Capt. Desmo begins (Scarce) — 685.00 2055.00 4800.00
(Prices vary widely on above two books)
54-The Spectre in costume; last King Carter — 250.00 750.00 1705.00
55-(Scarce)-Dr. Fate begins (Intro & 1st app.); last Bulldog Martin — 230.00 690.00 1600.00
56-60: 56-Congo Bill begins — 115.00 345.00 805.00
61-66: 63-Last St. Bob Neal. 64-Lance Larkin begins — 85.00 255.00 595.00
67-(Scarce)-Origin Dr. Fate; last Congo Bill & Biff Bronson — 117.00 351.00 820.00
68-70: 68-Clip Carson begins. 70-Last Lance Larkin — 70.00 210.00 490.00
71-(Scarce)-Origin & 1st app. Johnny Quick by Mort Wysinger — 115.00 345.00 805.00
72-Dr. Fate's new helmet; last Sgt. Carey, Sgt. O'Malley & Captain Desmo — 60.00 180.00 420.00
73-(Rare)-Origin & 1st app. Aquaman; intro. Green Arrow & Speedy — 175.00 525.00 1225.00

Moon Girl & the Prince #4, © WMG

Moon Knight #27, © MCG

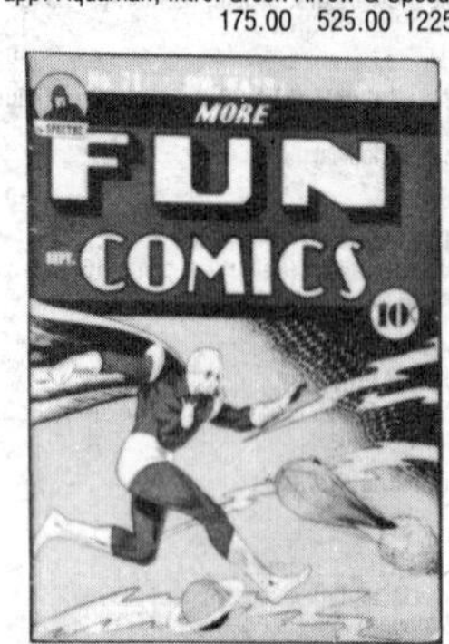

More Fun Comics #71, © DC

More Fun Comics #103, © DC

Morlock 2001 #1, © Seaboard

Motion Picture Comics #112, © Columbia Pictures

MORE FUN COMICS (continued)

	Good	Fine	Mint
74-2nd Aquaman	65.00	195.00	455.00
75-80: 76-Last Clip Carson; Johnny Quick by Meskin begins, ends No. 97. 80-1st small logo	60.00	180.00	420.00
81-88: 87-Last Radio Squad	45.00	135.00	315.00
89-Origin Green Arrow & Speedy Team-up	53.00	160.00	370.00
90-99: 93-Dover & Clover begin. 97-Kubert-a. 98-Last Dr. Fate	28.00	84.00	195.00
100	40.00	120.00	280.00
101-Origin & 1st app. Superboy (not by Siegel & Shuster); last Spectre issue	215.00	645.00	1500.00
102-2nd Superboy	53.00	160.00	370.00
103-3rd Superboy	40.00	120.00	280.00
104-107: 107-Last Johnny Quick & Superboy	33.00	100.00	230.00
108-120: 108-Genius Jones begins	5.50	16.50	38.00
121-124,126: 121-123-Kellyish-c by Post	4.50	13.50	30.00
125-Superman on cover	22.00	65.00	154.00
127-(Scarce)-Post c/a	13.00	40.00	90.00

NOTE: *Cover features: The Spectre-No. 52-55, 57-60, 62-67. Dr. Fate-No. 55, 56, 61, 68-76. The Green Arrow & Speedy-No. 77-85, 88-97, 99, 101; w/Dover & Clover-No. 98, 103. Johnny Quick-No. 86, 87, 100. Superboy-No. 101-107; w/Dover & Clover-No. 102-107. Genius Jones-No. 108-127.* ***Bailey*** *a-45.* ***Al Capp*** *a-45(signed Koppy).* ***Kiefer*** *a-20.* ***Moldoff*** *c-51.*

MORE SEYMOUR (See Seymour My Son)
October, 1963
Archie Publications

	Good	Fine	Mint
1	1.35	4.00	8.00

MORE TRASH FROM MAD (Annual)
1958 - No. 12, 1969
E. C. Comics

	Good	Fine	Mint
nn(1958)-8 pgs. color Mad reprint from No. 20	7.00	21.00	50.00
2(1959)-Market Product Labels	5.00	15.00	35.00
3(1960)-Text book covers	4.00	12.00	28.00
4(1961)-Sing Along with Mad booklet	4.00	12.00	28.00
5(1962)-Window Stickers; reprint from Mad No. 39	3.00	9.00	18.00
6(1963)-TV Guise booklet	3.35	10.00	20.00
7(1964)-Alfred E. Neuman commemorative stamps	2.00	6.00	12.00
8(1965)-Life size poster-A. E. Neuman	2.00	6.00	12.00
9,10(1966-67)-Mischief Sticker	1.50	4.50	9.00
11(1968)-Campaign poster & bumper sticker	1.50	4.50	9.00
12(1969)-Pocket medals	1.50	4.50	9.00

NOTE: ***Kelly Freas*** *c-1, 2, 4.* ***Mingo*** *c-3, 5-9, 12.*

MORGAN THE PIRATE (See 4-Color No. 1227)

MORLOCK 2001 (. . . & the Midnight Men No. 3)
Feb, 1975 - No. 3, July, 1975
Atlas/Seaboard Publ.

	Good	Fine	Mint
1-Origin & 1st app.		.50	1.00
2		.30	.60
3-Ditko/Wrightson-a; origin The Midnight Man & The Midnight Men		.60	1.20

MORTIE (Mazie's Friend)
Dec, 1952 - No. 4, June, 1953?
Magazine Publishers

	Good	Fine	Mint
1	2.00	6.00	14.00
2	1.00	3.00	7.00
3,4	.85	2.50	6.00

MORTY MEEKLE (See 4-Color No. 793)

MOSES & THE TEN COMMANDMENTS (See Dell Giants)

MOTHER GOOSE (See Christmas With Mother Goose & 4-Color No. 41, 59, 68, 862)

MOTHER OF US ALL
1950? (32 pgs.)
Catechetical Guild Giveaway

	Good	Fine	Mint
	2.00	6.00	12.00

MOTHER TERESA OF CALCUTTA
1984
Marvel Comics Group

	Good	Fine	Mint
1		.60	1.25

MOTION PICTURE COMICS (See Fawcett Movie Comics)
1950 - No. 114, Jan, 1953
Fawcett Publications

	Good	Fine	Mint
101-"Vanishing Westerner"-Monte Hale (1950)	18.00	54.00	125.00
102-"Code of the Silver Sage"-Rocky Lane (1/51)	16.00	48.00	110.00
103-"Covered Wagon Raid"-Rocky Lane (3/51)	16.00	48.00	110.00
104-"Vigilante Hideout"-Rocky Lane (5/51)-book length Powell-a	16.00	48.00	110.00
105-"Red Badge of Courage"-Audie Murphy; Bob Powell-a (7/51)	22.00	65.00	154.00
106-"The Texas Rangers"-George Montgomery (9/51)	19.00	57.00	132.00
107-"Frisco Tornado"-Rocky Lane (11/51)	14.50	43.50	100.00
108-"Mask of the Avenger"-John Derek	11.50	34.50	80.00
109-"Rough Rider of Durango"-Rocky Lane	14.50	43.50	100.00
110-"When Worlds Collide"-George Evans-a (1951); Williamson & Evans drew themselves in story; (Also see Famous Funnies No. 72-88)	62.00	185.00	435.00
111-"The Vanishing Outpost"-Lash LaRue	17.00	51.00	120.00
112-"Brave Warrior"-Jon Hall & Jay Silverheels	11.00	33.00	76.00
113-"Walk East on Beacon"-George Murphy; Shaffenberger-a	8.00	24.00	56.00
114-"Cripple Creek"-George Montgomery (1/53)	9.00	27.00	62.00

MOTION PICTURE FUNNIES WEEKLY (Amazing Man No. 5 on?)
1939 (36 pgs.)(Giveaway)(Black & White)
No month given; last panel in Sub-Mariner story dated 4/39
(Also see Colossus, Green Giant & Invaders No. 20)
First Funnies, Inc.

	Good	Fine	Mint
1-Origin & 1st printed app. Sub-Mariner by Bill Everett (8 pgs.); Fred Schwab-c; reprinted in Marvel Mystery No. 1 with color added over the craft tint which was used to shade the black & white version; Spy Ring, American Ace (reprinted in Marvel Mystery No. 3) app. (Rare)-only seven (7) known copies, all with brown pages.	2500.00	5000.00	———
Covers only to No. 2-4 (set)			600.00

NOTE: The only seven known copies (with an eighth suspected) were discovered in 1974 in the estate of the deceased publisher. Covers only to issues No. 2-4 were also found which evidently were printed in advance along with No. 1. No. 1 was to be distributed only through motion picture movie houses. However, it is believed that only advanced copies were sent out and the motion picture houses not going for the idea. Possible distribution at local theaters in Boston suspected. The last panel of Sub-Mariner contains a rectangular box with "Continued Next Week" printed in it. When reprinted in Marvel Mystery, the box was left in with lettering omitted.

MOUNTAIN MEN (See Ben Bowie)

MOUSE MUSKETEERS (See M.G.M.'s . . .)

MOUSE ON THE MOON, THE (See Movie Classics)

MOVIE CLASSICS
Jan, 1953 - Dec, 1969
Dell Publishing Co.

(Before 1962, most movie adaptations were part of the 4-Color Series)

MOVIE CLASSICS (continued)	Good	Fine	Mint
Around the World Under the Sea 12-030-612 (12/66)	1.30	4.00	9.00
Bambi 3(4/56)-Disney; r-/4-Color 186	1.30	4.00	9.00
Battle of the Bulge 12-056-606 (6/66)	1.30	4.00	9.00
Beach Blanket Bingo 12-058-509	4.00	12.00	28.00
Bon Voyage 01-068-212 (12/62)-Disney	1.30	4.00	9.00
Castilian, The 12-110-401	1.75	5.25	12.00
Cat, The 12-109-612 (12/66)	1.00	3.00	7.00
Cheyenne Autumn 12-112-506 (4-6/65)	3.35	10.00	23.00
Circus World, Samuel Bronston's 12-115-411; John Wayne app. Photo-c	3.35	10.00	23.00
Countdown 12-150-710 (10/67); James Caan photo-c	1.30	4.00	9.00
Creature, The 1 (12-142-302) (12-2/62-63)	2.00	6.00	14.00
Creature, The 12-142-410 (10/64)	1.30	4.00	9.00
David Ladd's Life Story 12-173-212 (10-12/62)	4.65	14.00	32.00
Die, Monster, Die 12-175-603 (3/66)-Photo-c	1.75	5.25	12.00
Dirty Dozen 12-180-710 (10/67)	2.00	6.00	14.00
Dr. Who & the Daleks 12-190-612 (12/66)-Photo-c	11.00	33.00	75.00
Dracula 12-231-212 (10-12/62)	1.50	4.50	10.00
El Dorado 12-240-710 (10/67)-John Wayne; photo-c	6.00	18.00	42.00
Ensign Pulver 12-257-410 (8-10/64)	1.30	4.00	9.00
Frankenstein 12-283-305 (3-5/63)	1.75	5.25	12.00
Great Race, The 12-299-603 (3/66)-Photo-c	2.00	6.00	14.00
Hallelujah Trail, The 12-307-602 (2/66) (Shows 1/66 inside); Photo-c	3.35	10.00	23.00
Hatari 12-340-301 (1/63)-John Wayne	3.00	9.00	21.00
Horizontal Lieutenant, The 01-348-210 (10/62)	1.30	4.00	9.00
Incredible Mr. Limpet, The 12-370-408; Don Knotts photo-c	1.30	4.00	9.00
Jack the Giant Killer 12-374-301 (1/63)	4.00	12.00	28.00
Jason & the Argonauts 12-376-310 (8-10/63)	4.65	14.00	32.00
Lancelot & Guinevere 12-416-310 (10/63)	4.00	12.00	28.00
Lawrence 12-426-308 (8/63)-Story of Lawrence of Arabia; movie ad on back-c; not exactly like movie	3.00	9.00	21.00
Lion of Sparta 12-439-301 (1/63)	1.30	4.00	9.00
Longest Day, The ('62)	2.00	6.00	14.00
Mad Monster Party 12-460-801 (9/67)	4.35	13.00	30.00
Magic Sword, The 01-496-209 (9/62)	3.00	9.00	21.00
Masque of the Red Death 12-490-410 (8-10/64)-Photo-c	2.00	6.00	14.00
Maya 12-495-612 (12/66)-Photo-c	2.00	6.00	14.00
McHale's Navy 12-500-412 (10-12/64)	1.50	4.50	10.00
Merrill's Marauders 12-510-301 (1/63)-Photo-c	1.30	4.00	9.00
Mouse on the Moon, The 12-530-312 (10/12/63)	1.50	4.50	10.00
Mummy, The 12-537-211 (9-11/62) 2 different back-c issues	2.00	6.00	14.00
Music Man, The 12-538-301 (1/63)	1.30	4.00	9.00
Naked Prey, The 12-545-612 (12/66)-Photo-c	3.00	9.00	21.00
Night of the Grizzly, The 12-558-612 (12/66)-Photo-c	1.75	5.25	12.00
None But the Brave 12-565-506 (4-6/65)	2.00	6.00	14.00
Operation Bikini 12-597-310 (10/63)-Photo-c	1.75	5.25	12.00
Operation Crossbow 12-590-512 (10-12/65)	1.75	5.25	12.00
Prince & the Pauper, The 01-654-207 (5-7/62)-Disney	1.75	5.25	12.00
Raven, The 12-680-309 (9/63)-Photo-c	2.00	6.00	14.00
Ring of Bright Water 01-701-910 (10/69) (inside shows No. 12-701-909)	1.50	4.50	10.00

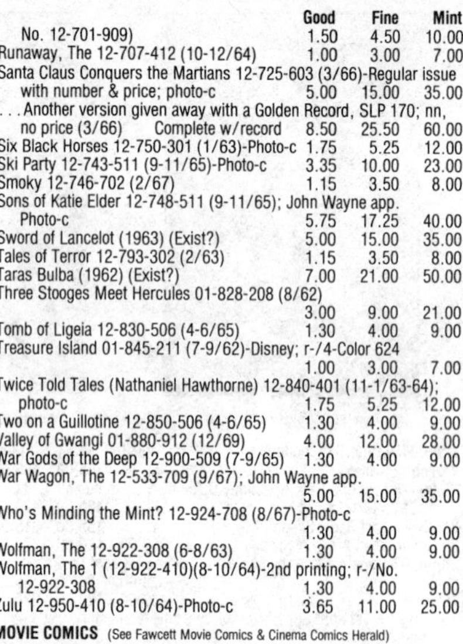

	Good	Fine	Mint
Runaway, The 12-707-412 (10-12/64)	1.00	3.00	7.00
Santa Claus Conquers the Martians 12-725-603 (3/66)-Regular issue with number & price; photo-c	5.00	15.00	35.00
. . . Another version given away with a Golden Record, SLP 170; nn, no price (3/66) Complete w/record	8.50	25.50	60.00
Six Black Horses 12-750-301 (1/63)-Photo-c	1.75	5.25	12.00
Ski Party 12-743-511 (9-11/65)-Photo-c	3.35	10.00	23.00
Smoky 12-746-702 (2/67)	1.15	3.50	8.00
Sons of Katie Elder 12-748-511 (9-11/65); John Wayne app. Photo-c	5.75	17.25	40.00
Sword of Lancelot (1963) (Exist?)	5.00	15.00	35.00
Tales of Terror 12-793-302 (2/63)	1.15	3.50	8.00
Taras Bulba (1962) (Exist?)	7.00	21.00	50.00
Three Stooges Meet Hercules 01-828-208 (8/62)	3.00	9.00	21.00
Tomb of Ligeia 12-830-506 (4-6/65)	1.30	4.00	9.00
Treasure Island 01-845-211 (7-9/62)-Disney; r-/4-Color 624	1.00	3.00	7.00
Twice Told Tales (Nathaniel Hawthorne) 12-840-401 (11-1/63-64); photo-c	1.75	5.25	12.00
Two on a Guillotine 12-850-506 (4-6/65)	1.30	4.00	9.00
Valley of Gwangi 01-880-912 (12/69)	4.00	12.00	28.00
War Gods of the Deep 12-900-509 (7-9/65)	1.30	4.00	9.00
War Wagon, The 12-533-709 (9/67); John Wayne app.	5.00	15.00	35.00
Who's Minding the Mint? 12-924-708 (8/67)-Photo-c	1.30	4.00	9.00
Wolfman, The 12-922-308 (6-8/63)	1.30	4.00	9.00
Wolfman, The 1 (12-922-410)(8-10/64)-2nd printing; r-/No. 12-922-308	1.30	4.00	9.00
Zulu 12-950-410 (8-10/64)-Photo-c	3.65	11.00	25.00

MOVIE COMICS (See Fawcett Movie Comics & Cinema Comics Herald)

MOVIE COMICS
April, 1939 - No. 6, Sept, 1939 (Most all photo-c)
National Periodical Publications/Picture Comics

	Good	Fine	Mint
1-"Gunga Din," "Son of Frankenstein," "The Great Man Votes," "Fisherman's Wharf," & "Scouts to the Rescue" part 1; Wheelan "Minute Movies" begin	130.00	390.00	910.00
2-"Stagecoach," "The Saint Strikes Back," "King of the Turf," "Scouts to the Rescue" part 2, "Arizona Legion"	75.00	225.00	525.00
3-"East Side of Heaven," "Mystery in the White Room," "Four Feathers," "Mexican Rose" with Gene Autry, "Spirit of Culver," "Many Secrets," "The Mikado"	65.00	195.00	455.00
4-"Captain Fury," Gene Autry in "Blue Montana Skies," "Streets of N. Y." with Jackie Cooper, "Oregon Trail" part 1 with Johnny Mack Brown, "Big Town Czar" with Barton MacLane, & "Star Reporter" with Warren Hull	58.00	174.00	405.00
5-"Man in the Iron Mask," "Five Came Back," Wolf Call," "The Girl & the Gambler," "The House of Fear," "The Family Next Door," "Oregon Trail" part 2	58.00	174.00	405.00
6-"The Phantom Creeps," "Chumps at Oxford," & "The Oregon Trail" part 3	78.00	235.00	545.00

NOTE: *Above books contain many original movie stills with dialogue from movie scripts.*

MOVIE COMICS
Dec, 1946 - 1947
Fiction House Magazines

	Good	Fine	Mint
1-Big Town & Johnny Danger begin; Celardo-a	20.00	60.00	140.00
2-"White Tie & Tails" with William Bendix; Mitzi of the Movies begins by Matt Baker, ends No. 4	13.50	40.50	95.00
3-Andy Hardy	13.50	40.50	95.00

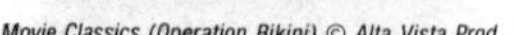

Movie Classics (Operation Bikini) © Alta Vista Prod.

Movie Classics (Zulu), © Embassy Pictures

Movie Comics #2, © FH

Movie Comics (Capt. Sindbad), © King Bros. Prod.

Movie Comics (Gay Purr-ee), © UPA Pictures

Movie Comics (Misadvs. of Merlin Jones), © WDC

MOVIE COMICS (continued) — Good / Fine / Mint

4-Mitzi In Hollywood by Matt Baker 17.00 51.00 120.00

MOVIE COMICS
Oct, 1962 - March, 1972
Gold Key/Whitman

Alice in Wonderland 10144-503 (3/65)-Disney; partial reprint of 4-Color 331 1.75 5.25 12.00
Aristocats, The 1 (30045-103)(3/71)-Disney; with pull-out poster (25 cents) 2.65 8.00 18.00
Bambi 1 (10087-309)(9/63)-Disney; reprints 4-Color 186 1.75 5.25 12.00
Bambi 2 (10087-607)(7/66)-Disney; reprints 4-Color 186 1.50 4.50 10.00
Beneath the Planet of the Apes 30044-012 (12/70)-with pull-out poster; photo-c 2.65 8.00 18.00
Big Red 10026-211 (11/62)-Disney 1.15 3.50 8.00
Big Red 10026-503 (3/65)-Disney; reprints 10026-211 1.15 3.50 8.00
Blackbeard's Ghost 10222-806 (6/68)-Disney 1.50 4.50 10.00
Buck Rogers Giant Movie Edition 11296 (Whitman), 02489 (Marvel)-2 formats; 1979; tabloid size; $1.50; adaptation of movie; Bolle, McWilliams-a .30 .80 1.60
Bullwhip Griffin 10181-706 (6/67)-Disney; Manning-a 2.35 7.00 16.00
Captain Sindbad 10077-309 (9/63)-Manning-a 3.50 10.50 24.00
Chitty Chitty Bang Bang 1 (30038-902)(2/69)-with pull-out poster; Disney 2.65 8.00 18.00
Cinderella 10152-508 (8/65)-Disney; reprints 4-Color 786 1.50 4.50 10.00
Darby O'Gill & the Little People 10251-001(1/70)-Disney; reprints 4-Color 1024 (Toth) 2.65 8.00 18.00
Dumbo 1 (10090-310)(10/63)-Disney; reprints 4-Color 668 1.50 4.50 10.00
Emil & the Detectives 10120-502 (2/65)-Disney 2.35 7.00 16.00
Escapade in Florence 1 (10043-301)(1/63)-Disney; starring Annette 4.00 12.00 28.00
Fall of the Roman Empire 10118-407 (7/64); Sophia Loren photo-c 1.75 5.25 12.00
Fantastic Voyage 10178-702 (2/67)-Wood/Adkins-a; photo-c 2.35 7.00 16.00
55 Days at Peking 10081-309 (9/63) 2.00 6.00 14.00
Fighting Prince of Donegal, The 10193-701 (1/67)-Disney 1.50 4.50 10.00
First Men in the Moon 10132-503 (3/65)-Fred Fredericks-a 2.00 6.00 14.00
Gay Purr-ee 30017-301(1/63, 84pgs.) 2.85 8.50 20.00
Gnome Mobile, The 10207-710 (10/67)-Disney 2.00 6.00 14.00
Goodbye, Mr. Chips 10246-006 (6/70) 1.75 5.25 12.00
Happiest Millionaire, The 10221-804 (4/68)-Disney 1.15 3.50 8.00
Hey There, It's Yogi Bear 10122-409 (9/64)-Hanna-Barbera 1.75 5.25 12.00
Horse Without a Head, The 10109-401 (1/64)-Disney 1.50 4.50 10.00
How the West Was Won 10074-307 (7/63)-Tufts-a 3.00 9.00 21.00
In Search of the Castaways 10048-303 (3/63)-Disney; Haley Mills; photo-c 3.50 10.50 24.00
Jungle Book, The 1 (6022-801)(1/68-Whitman)-Disney; large size (10x13½''); 59 cents 1.50 4.50 10.00
Jungle Book, The 1 (30033-803)(3/68, 68 pgs.)-Disney; same contents as Whitman No. 1 1.15 3.50 8.00
Jungle Book, The 1 (6/78, $1.00 tabloid) .60 1.20
Jungle Book ('84)-r-/Giant .40 .80

Kidnapped 10080-306 (6/63)-Disney; reprints 4-Color 1101; photo-c 1.15 3.50 8.00
King Kong 30036-809(9/68-68 pgs.)-painted-c 2.35 7.00 16.00
King Kong nn-Whitman Treasury($1.00,68pgs.,1968), same cover as Gold Key issue .50 1.50 3.00
King Kong 11299(No. 1-786, 10x13¼'', 68pgs., $1.00, 1978) .50 1.00
Lady and the Tramp 10042-301 (1/63)-Disney; r-4-Color 629 1.50 4.50 10.00
Lady and the Tramp 1 (1967-Giant; 25 cents)-Disney; r-part of Dell No. 1 2.50 7.50 20.00
Lady and the Tramp 2 (10042-203)(3/72)-Disney; r-4-Color 629 1.15 3.50 8.00
Legend of Lobo, The 1 (10059-303)(3/63)-Disney; photo-c 1.15 3.50 8.00
Lt. Robin Crusoe, U.S.N. 10191-610 (10/66)-Disney 1.50 4.50 10.00
Lion, The 10035-301 (1/63)-Photo-c 1.15 3.50 8.00
Lord Jim 10156-509 (9/65) 1.75 5.25 12.00
Love Bug, The 10237-906 (6/69)-Disney 1.50 4.50 10.00
Mary Poppins 10136-501 (1/65)-Disney; photo-c 2.65 8.00 18.00
Mary Poppins 30023-501 (1/65-68 pgs.)-Disney; photo-c 3.00 9.00 24.00
McLintock 10110-403 (3/64); John Wayne app.; photo-c 5.75 17.25 40.00
Merlin Jones as the Monkey's Uncle 10115-510 (10/65)-Disney 1.50 4.50 10.00
Miracle of the White Stallions, The 10065-306 (6/63)-Disney 1.75 5.25 12.00
Misadventures of Merlin Jones, The 10115-405 (5/64)-Disney Annette Funicello photo front/back-c 2.50 7.50 15.00
Moon-Spinners, The 10124-410 (10/64)-Disney; Haley Mills 3.50 10.50 24.00
Mutiny on the Bounty 1 (10040-302)(2/63) 1.75 5.25 12.00
Nikki, Wild Dog of the North 10141-412 (12/64)-Disney; reprints 4-Color 1226 1.15 3.50 8.00
Old Yeller 10168-601 (1/66)-Disney; reprints 4-Color 869 1.15 3.50 8.00
One Hundred & One Dalmations 1 (10247-002) (2/70)-Disney; reprints 4-Color 1183 1.50 4.50 10.00
Peter Pan 1 (10086-309)(9/63)-Disney; reprints 4-Color 442 2.00 6.00 12.00
Peter Pan 2 (10086-909)(9/69)-Disney; reprints 4-Color 442 1.15 3.50 8.00
Peter Pan 1 ('83)-r/4-Color 442 .40 .80
P.T. 109 10123-409 (9/64)-John F. Kennedy 2.65 8.00 18.00
Rio Conchos 10143-503(3/65) 2.35 7.00 16.00
Robin Hood 10163-506 (6/65)-Disney; reprints 4-Color 413 1.50 4.50 10.00
Shaggy Dog & the Absent-Minded Professor 30032-708 (8/67-Giant, 68 pgs.)-Disney; reprints 4-Color 985,1199 2.50 7.50 20.00
Sleeping Beauty 1 (30042-009)(9/70)-Disney; reprints 4-Color 973; with pull-out poster 2.65 8.00 18.00
Snow White & the Seven Dwarfs 1 (10091-310)(10/63)-Disney; reprints 4-Color 382 1.75 5.25 12.00
Snow White & the Seven Dwarfs 10091-709 (9/67)-Disney; reprints 4-Color 382 1.50 4.50 10.00
Snow White & the Seven Dwarfs nn(2/84)-r-/4-Color 382 .40 .80
Son of Flubber 1 (10057-304)(4/63)-Disney; sequel to "The Absent-Minded Professor" 1.75 5.25 12.00
Summer Magic 10076-309 (9/63)-Disney; Haley Mills; Manning-a 4.00 12.00 28.00
Swiss Family Robinson 10236-904 (4/69)-Disney; reprints

MOVIE COMICS (continued)

	Good	Fine	Mint
4-Color 1156	1.75	5.25	12.00
Sword in the Stone, The 30019-402 (2/64-Giant, 84 pgs.)-Disney	2.50	7.50	20.00
That Darn Cat 10171-602 (2/66)-Disney; Haley Mills photo-c	3.50	10.50	24.00
Those Magnificent Men in Their Flying Machines 10162-510 (10/65)	1.75	5.25	12.00
Three Stooges in Orbit 30016-211 (11/62-Giant, 32 pgs.)-All photos from movie; stiff-c	4.00	12.00	28.00
Tiger Walks, A 10117-406 (6/64)-Disney; Torres, Tufts-a; photo-c	2.35	7.00	16.00
Toby Tyler 10142-502 (2/65)-Disney; reprints 4-Color 1092	1.50	4.50	10.00
Treasure Island 1 (10200-703)(3/67)-Disney; reprints 4-Color 624	1.15	3.50	8.00
20,000 Leagues Under the Sea 1 (10095-312)(12/63)-Disney; reprints 4-Color 614	1.15	3.50	8.00
Wonderful Adventures of Pinocchio, The 1 (10089-310)(10/63)-Disney; reprints 4-Color 545	1.15	3.50	8.00
Wonderful Adventures of Pinocchio, The 10089-109 (9/71)-Disney; reprints 4-Color 545	1.15	3.50	8.00
Wonderful World of the Brothers Grimm 1 (10008-210)(10/62)	2.65	8.00	18.00
X, the Man with the X-Ray Eyes 10083-309 (9/63)	3.00	9.00	21.00
Yellow Submarine 35000-902 (2/69-Giant, 68 pgs.)-with pull-out poster; The Beatles cartoon movie	5.35	16.00	37.00

MOVIE LOVE (See Personal Love)
Feb, 1950 - No. 22, Aug, 1953
Famous Funnies

	Good	Fine	Mint
1	4.00	12.00	28.00
2	2.35	7.00	16.00
3-7,9	2.00	6.00	14.00
8-Williamson/Frazetta-a, 6 pgs.	26.00	78.00	180.00
10-Frazetta-a, 6 pgs.	32.00	95.00	225.00
11,12,14-16	2.00	6.00	14.00
13-Ronald Reagan photo-c with 1 pg. biography	8.00	24.00	56.00
17-One pg. Frazetta ad	3.00	9.00	21.00
18-22	1.85	5.50	13.00

NOTE: *Each issue has a full-length movie adaptation with photo covers.*

MOVIE THRILLERS
1949 (Movie adaptation; photo-c)
Magazine Enterprises

	Good	Fine	Mint
1-"Rope of Sand" with Burt Lancaster	16.00	48.00	110.00

MOVIE TOWN ANIMAL ANTICS (Formerly Animal Antics; Raccoon Kids No. 52 on)
No. 24, Jan-Feb, 1950 - No. 51, July-Aug, 1954
National Periodical Publications

	Good	Fine	Mint
24-Raccoon Kids continue	3.50	10.50	24.00
25-51	2.65	8.00	18.00

NOTE: ***Sheldon Mayer** a-28-33, 35, 37-41, 43, 44, 47, 49-51.*

MOVIE TUNES COMICS (Formerly Animated . . .; Frankie No. 4 on)
No. 3, Fall, 1946
Marvel Comics (MgPC)

	Good	Fine	Mint
3-Super Rabbit, Krazy Krow, Silly Seal & Ziggy Pig	3.35	10.00	23.00

MOWGLI JUNGLE BOOK (See 4-Color No. 487,582,620)

MR. (See Mister)

MS. MARVEL
Jan, 1977 - No. 23, Apr, 1979
Marvel Comics Group

	Good	Fine	Mint
1-Buscema-a		.50	1.00
2-Origin		.30	.60
3-23: 5-Vision app. 20-New costume		.25	.50

NOTE: ***Austin** c-14i, 16i, 17i, 22i. **Buscema** a-1-3p; c(p)-2, 4, 6, 7, 15. **Infantino** a-14p, 19p. **Gil Kane** c-8. **Mooney** a-4-8p, 13p, 15-18p. **Starlin** c-12.*

MS. MYSTIC (Also see Captain Victory . . .)
10/82 - No. 2, 2/84
Pacific Comics/Continuity Comics No. 3

	Good	Fine	Mint
1-Origin; intro Erth, Ayre, Fyre & Watr; Adams script/a/c		.50	1.00
2 ($1.50)-Adams c/a & script	.25	.75	1.50

MS. TREE'S THRILLING DETECTIVE ADVENTURES (Ms. Tree No. 4 on) (Baxter paper No. 4-9)
2/83 - No. 9, 7/84; No. 10, 8/84 - No. 18, 5/85; No. 19, 6/85 -Present
Eclipse Comics/Aardvark-Vanaheim 10-18/Renegade Press 19 on

	Good	Fine	Mint
1		.50	1.00
2-8: 2-Scythe begins	.25	.75	1.50
9-Last Eclipse & last color issue		.50	1.00
10,11 (Aardvark-Vanaheim) B&W		.50	1.00
12-33 ($1.70)	.30	.85	1.70
34,35 ($2.00)	.35	1.00	2.00
Summer Special 1(8/86)	.35	1.00	2.00

NOTE: ***Miller** pin-up-1-4,6.*

MS. TREE/MIKE MIST IN 3-D
Aug, 1985 (One Shot)
Renegade Press

	Good	Fine	Mint
1-With glasses	.40	1.25	2.50

MS. VICTORY SPECIAL
Jan, 1985
Americomics

	Good	Fine	Mint
1	.30	.85	1.70

MUGGSY MOUSE
1951 - 1953; 1963
Magazine Enterprises

	Good	Fine	Mint
1(A-1 33)	1.75	5.25	12.00
2(A-1 36)-Racist-c	3.35	10.00	23.00
3(A-1 39), 4(A-1 95), 5(A-1 99)	1.00	3.00	7.00
Super Reprint No. 14(1963)	.30	.80	1.60
I.W. Reprint No. 1,2 (no date)	.30	.80	1.60

MUGGY-DOO, BOY CAT
July, 1953 - No. 4, Jan, 1954
Stanhall

	Good	Fine	Mint
1-Irving Spector-a	2.00	6.00	14.00
2-4	1.15	3.50	8.00
Super Reprint No. 12('63), 16('64)		.50	1.00

MUMMY, THE (See Movie Classics)

MUNSTERS, THE (TV)
Jan, 1965 - No. 16, Jan, 1968
Gold Key

	Good	Fine	Mint
1 (10134-501)-Photo-c	4.00	12.00	28.00
2	1.65	8.00	18.00
3-5	2.35	7.00	16.00
6-16	1.75	5.25	12.00

Movie Comics (X, the Man With . . .), © Alta Vista

Ms. Marvel #1, © MCG

The Munsters #4, © Kayro-Vue Prod.

Murderous Gangsters #4, © REAL

Mutt & Jeff #100, © Ball Synd.

My Date Comics #4, © HILL

MUPPET BABIES, THE (TV)
May, 1985 - Present (Children's book)
Star Comics (Marvel)

	Good	Fine	Mint
1-12		.35	.70

MUPPETS TAKE MANHATTAN, THE
Nov, 1984 - No. 3, Jan, 1985
Marvel Comics Group

	Good	Fine	Mint
1-3-Movie adapt. r-/Marvel Super Special		.30	.60

MURDER
8/86 - No. 3, 10/86 ($1.70-$2.00, B&W, mini-series)
Renegade Press

	Good	Fine	Mint
1	.30	.85	1.70
2,3	.35	1.00	2.00

NOTE: *Ditko a-1, 3. Toth a-1; c-3. Edgar Allan Poe adapt. in each.*

MURDER, INCORPORATED (My Private Life No. 16 on)
1/48 - No. 15, 12/49; (2 No.9's); 6/50 - No. 3, 8/51
Fox Feature Syndicate

	Good	Fine	Mint
1 (1st Series)	12.00	36.00	84.00
2-Transvestite, electrocution story	8.00	24.00	56.00
3-7,9(4/49),10(5/49),11-15	5.00	15.00	35.00
8-Used in **SOTI**, pg. 160	8.00	24.00	56.00
9(3/49)-Possible use in **SOTI**, pg. 145; r-Blue Beetle No. 56('48)	8.00	24.00	56.00
5(6/50)(2nd Series)-Formerly My Desire	4.00	12.00	28.00
2(8/50)-Morisi-a	2.65	8.00	18.00
3(8/51)-Used in **POP**, pg. 81; Rico-a; lingerie-c/panels	4.75	14.25	33.00

MURDEROUS GANGSTERS
July, 1951; No. 2, Dec, 1951 - No. 4, June, 1952
Avon Periodicals/Realistic No. 3 on

	Good	Fine	Mint
1-Pretty Boy Floyd, Leggs Diamond; 1 pg. Wood	15.00	45.00	105.00
2-Baby-Face Nelson; 1 pg. Wood	9.50	28.50	65.00
3	8.00	24.00	56.00
4-"Murder by Needle" drug story; Mort Lawrence-a; Kinstler-c	9.50	28.50	65.00

MURDER TALES (Magazine)
V1No.10, Nov, 1970 - V1No.11, Jan, 1971 (52 pages)
World Famous Publications

	Good	Fine	Mint
V1No.10-One pg. Frazetta ad	.50	1.50	3.00
11-Guardineer-r; bondage-c	.25	.75	1.50

MUSHMOUSE AND PUNKIN PUSS (TV)
September, 1965 (Hanna-Barbera)
Gold Key

	Good	Fine	Mint
1 (10153-509)	2.35	7.00	16.00

MUSIC MAN, THE (See Movie Classics)

MUTINY (Stormy Tales of Seven Seas)
Oct, 1954 - No. 3, Feb, 1955
Aragon Magazines

	Good	Fine	Mint
1	4.00	12.00	28.00
2,3: 2-Capt. Mutiny. 3-Bondage-c	2.00	6.00	14.00

MUTINY ON THE BOUNTY (See Classics Ill. 100 & Movie Comics)

MUTT & JEFF (. . .Cartoon, The) (See Xmas Comics)
1910 - 1916 (5¾x15½'') (Hardcover-B&W)
Ball Publications

	Good	Fine	Mint
1(1910)	20.00	60.00	140.00
2(1911), 3(1912)	15.00	45.00	105.00
4(1915) (Scarce)	18.00	54.00	125.00
5(1916) (Rare)	22.00	65.00	154.00

NOTE: *Cover variations exist showing Mutt & Jeff reading various newspapers; i.e., The Oregon Journal, The American, and The Detroit News. Reprinting of each issue began soon after publication. No. 5 may not have been reprinted. Values listed include the reprints.*

MUTT & JEFF
1916 - 1933? (B&W dailies) (9½x9½''; stiff cover; 52 pgs.)
Cupples & Leon Co.

	Good	Fine	Mint
6-22-By Bud Fisher	10.00	30.00	70.00

NOTE: *Later issues are somewhat rarer.*

	Good	Fine	Mint
nn(1920)-(Advs. of. . .) 16x11''; 20 pgs.; reprints 1919 Sunday strips	20.00	60.00	140.00
Big Book nn(1926, 144pgs., hardcovers)	15.00	45.00	105.00
w/dust jacket. . . .	25.00	75.00	175.00
Big Book 1(1928)-Thick book (hardcovers)	15.00	45.00	105.00
w/dust jacket. . . .	25.00	75.00	175.00
Big Book 2(1929)-Thick book (hardcovers)	15.00	45.00	105.00
w/dust jacket. . . .	25.00	75.00	175.00

NOTE: *The Big Books contain three previous issues rebound.*

MUTT & JEFF
1921 (9x15'')
Embee Publ. Co.

	Good	Fine	Mint
Sunday strips in color (Rare)	35.00	105.00	245.00

MUTT AND JEFF
Summer, 1939 (nd) - No. 148, Nov, 1965
All American/National 1-103(6/58)/Dell 104(10/58)-115(10-12/59)/Harvey 116(2/60)-148

	Good	Fine	Mint
1(nn)-Lost Wheels	55.00	165.00	385.00
2(nn)-Charging Bull (Summer 1940, nd)	30.00	90.00	210.00
3(nn)-Bucking Broncos (Summer 1941, nd)	20.00	60.00	140.00
4(Winter,'41), 5(Summer,'42)	15.00	45.00	105.00
6-10	9.00	27.00	62.00
11-20	5.00	15.00	35.00
21-30	4.00	12.00	28.00
31-50	2.65	8.00	18.00
51-75-Last Fisher issue. 53-Last 52pgs.	1.75	5.25	12.00
76-99,101-103	1.30	4.00	9.00
100	1.75	5.25	12.00
104-148: 117,118,120-131-Richie Rich app.	.85	2.50	6.00
. . .Jokes 1-3(8/60-61, Harvey)-84 pgs.; Richie Rich in all; Little Dot in No. 2,3	1.50	4.50	10.00
. . .New Jokes 1-4(10/63-11/65, Harvey)-68 pgs.; Richie Rich in 1-3; Stumbo in No. 1	.75	2.25	5.00

NOTE: *Issues 1-74 by **Bud Fisher**. 86 on by **Al Smith**. Issues from 1963 on have **Fisher** reprints. Clarification: early issues signed by Fisher are mostly drawn by Smith.*

MY BROTHERS' KEEPER
1973 (36 pages) (35-49 cents)
Spire Christian Comics (Fleming H. Revell Co.)

	Good	Fine	Mint
nn		.50	1.00

MY CONFESSIONS (My Confession No. 7; formerly Western True Crime; A Spectacular Feature Magazine No. 11)
No. 7, Aug, 1949 - No. 10, Jan-Feb, 1950
Fox Feature Syndicate

	Good	Fine	Mint
7-Wood-a, 10 pgs.	9.50	28.50	65.00
8-Wood-a, 18 pgs.	8.00	24.00	56.00
9,10	3.50	10.50	24.00

MY DATE COMICS
July, 1947 - V1No.4, Jan, 1948 (1st Romance comic)
Hillman Periodicals

	Good	Fine	Mint
1-S&K-c/a	9.50	28.50	65.00
2-4-S&K, Dan Barry-a	5.50	16.50	38.00

MY DESIRE (Formerly Jo-Jo) (Murder, Inc. No. 5 on)
No. 30, Aug, 1949 - No. 4, April, 1950
Fox Feature Syndicate

MY DESIRE (continued)

	Good	Fine	Mint
30(No.1)	4.00	12.00	28.00
31(No.2), 3, 4	2.85	8.50	20.00
31 (Canadian edition)	1.50	4.50	10.00
32(12/49)-Wood-a	8.00	24.00	56.00

MY DIARY
Dec, 1949 - No. 2, Mar, 1950
Marvel Comics (A Lovers Mag.)

	Good	Fine	Mint
1,2	3.00	9.00	21.00

MY DOG TIGE (Buster Brown's Dog)
1957 (Giveaway)
Buster Brown Shoes

	Good	Fine	Mint
	1.70	5.00	10.00

MY EXPERIENCE (Formerly All Top; Judy Canova No. 23 on)
No. 19, Sept, 1949 - No. 22, Mar, 1950
Fox Feature Syndicate

	Good	Fine	Mint
19-Wood-a	9.50	28.50	65.00
20	2.85	8.50	20.00
21-Wood-a(2)	11.00	33.00	76.00
22-Wood-a, 9 pgs.	8.00	24.00	56.00

MY FAVORITE MARTIAN (TV)
1/64; No.2, 7/64 - No. 9, 10/66 (No. 1,3-9 have photo-c)
Gold Key

	Good	Fine	Mint
1-Russ Manning-a	3.00	9.00	21.00
2	1.75	5.25	12.00
3-9	1.50	4.50	10.00

MY FRIEND IRMA (Radio/TV) (Formerly Western Life Romances)
No. 3, June, 1950 - No. 47, Dec, 1954; No. 48, Feb, 1955
Marvel/Atlas Comics (BFP)

	Good	Fine	Mint
3	4.00	12.00	28.00
4-Kurtzman-a, 10 pgs.	5.75	17.25	40.00
5-"Egghead Doodle" by Kurtzman, 4 pgs.	4.00	12.00	28.00
6,8-10: 9-paper dolls, 1pg; Millie app.	1.85	5.50	13.00
7-One pg. Kurtzman	2.50	7.50	17.00
11,13-22	1.30	4.00	9.00
12-Silhoutted nudity	1.75	5.25	12.00
23-One pg. Frazetta	1.50	4.50	10.00
24-48	1.00	3.00	7.00

MY GIRL PEARL
4/55 - No. 4, 10/55; No. 5, 7/57 - No. 6, 9/57; No. 7, 8/60 - No. 11, ?/61
Atlas Comics

	Good	Fine	Mint
1	2.65	8.00	18.00
2	1.30	4.00	9.00
3-6	1.00	3.00	7.00
7-11	.55	1.65	4.00

MY GREATEST ADVENTURE (Doom Patrol No. 86 on)
Jan-Feb, 1955 - No. 85, Feb, 1964
National Periodical Publications

	Good	Fine	Mint
1-Before CCA	28.00	84.00	195.00
2	13.50	40.50	95.00
3-5	11.00	33.00	76.00
6-10	5.50	16.50	38.00
11-15,19	3.35	10.00	23.00
16,20,21,28-Kirby-a	3.65	11.00	25.00
17,18-Kirby-a; 18-Kirby-c	4.35	13.00	30.00
22-27,29,30	2.50	7.50	17.00
31-57,59	1.00	3.00	7.00
58,60,61-Toth-a; Last 10¢ ish	1.50	4.50	10.00
62-76,78,79	.50	1.50	3.00
77-Toth-a	.85	2.50	6.00
80-(6/63)-Intro/origin Doom Patrol; origin Robotman, Negative Man, & Elasti-Girl	5.00	15.00	35.00
81,85-Toth-a	2.50	7.50	17.50
82-84	1.00	3.00	7.00

NOTE: ***Anderson** a-42. **Colan** a-77. **Meskin** a-25, 26, 32, 39, 45, 50, 56, 57, 61, 64, 70, 73, 74, 76, 79; c-76. **Moreira** a-17, 20, 23, 25, 27, 37, 40-42, 46, 48, 55-57, 59, 60, 62-65, 67, 69, 70. **Roussos** c/a-71-73.*

MY GREATEST THRILLS IN BASEBALL
(16 pg. Giveaway)
Mission of California

	Good	Fine	Mint
By Mickey Mantle	20.00	60.00	120.00

MY GREAT LOVE
Oct, 1949 - No. 4, Apr, 1950
Fox Feature Syndicate

	Good	Fine	Mint
1	4.65	14.00	32.00
2-4	2.85	8.50	20.00

MY INTIMATE AFFAIR (Inside Crime No. 3)
Mar, 1950 - No. 2, May, 1950
Fox Feature Syndicate

	Good	Fine	Mint
1	4.65	14.00	32.00
2	2.85	8.50	20.00

MY LIFE (Formerly Meet Corliss Archer)
No. 4, Sept, 1948 - No. 15, July, 1950
Fox Feature Syndicate

	Good	Fine	Mint
4-Used in **SOTI**, pg. 39; Kamen/Feldstein-a	14.50	43.50	100.00
5-Kamen-a	7.50	22.50	52.00
6-Kamen/Feldstein-a	7.50	22.50	52.00
7-Wash cover	4.65	14.00	32.00
8,9,11-15	2.85	8.50	20.00
10-Wood-a	8.00	24.00	56.00

MY LITTLE MARGIE (TV)
July, 1954 - No. 54, Nov, 1964
Charlton Comics

	Good	Fine	Mint
1-Photo-c	6.00	18.00	42.00
2	2.50	7.50	17.50
3-7,10	1.75	5.25	12.00
8,9-Infinity-c	2.00	6.00	14.00
11,12,14-19	1.15	3.50	8.00
13-Photo-c (8/56)	1.50	4.50	10.00
20-(100 page ish)	2.35	7.00	16.00
21-35-Last 10¢ ish?	.75	2.25	5.00
36-53	.45	1.35	3.00
54-Beatles on cover; lead story spoofs the Beatle haircut craze of the 1960's	4.65	14.00	32.00

NOTE: *Doll cut-outs in 32,33,40,45,50.*

MY LITTLE MARGIE'S BOY FRIENDS (TV)(Freddy V2/12 on)
Aug, 1955 - No. 11, Apr?, 1958
Charlton Comics

	Good	Fine	Mint
1-Has several Archie swipes	3.00	9.00	21.00
2	1.50	4.50	10.00
3-11	1.00	3.00	7.00

MY LITTLE MARGIE'S FASHIONS (TV)
Feb, 1959 - No. 5, Nov, 1959
Charlton Comics

	Good	Fine	Mint
1	2.35	7.00	16.00
2-5	1.15	3.50	8.00

My Favorite Martian #4, © Jack Chertok TV

My Greatest Adventure #1, © DC

My Little Margie #1, © CC

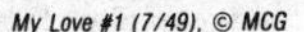
My Love #1 (7/49), © MCG

My Romance #1, © MCG

My Secret Affair #1, © FOX

MY LOVE (Formerly Molly Manton's Romances No. 1 & 2)
July, 1949 - No. 4, Apr, 1950 (All photo-c)
Marvel Comics (CLDS)

	Good	Fine	Mint
1	2.35	7.00	16.00
2-4	1.15	3.50	8.00

MY LOVE
Sept, 1969 - No. 39, Mar, 1976
Marvel Comics Group

	Good	Fine	Mint
1-9		.30	.60
10-Williamson-r/My Own Romance No. 71; Kirby-a		.60	1.20
11-20: 14-Morrow-a		.20	.40
21,22,24-39: 38,39-Reprints		.20	.40
23-Steranko-r/Our Love Story No. 5	.35	1.00	2.00
Special(12/71)		.30	.60

MY LOVE AFFAIR (March of Crime No. 7)
July, 1949 - No. 6, May, 1950
Fox Feature Syndicate

	Good	Fine	Mint
1	5.00	15.00	35.00
2	2.85	8.50	20.00
3-6-Wood-a	8.00	24.00	56.00

MY LOVE LIFE (Formerly Zegra)
No. 6, June, 1949 - No. 13, Aug, 1950; No. 13, Sept, 1951
Fox Feature Syndicate

	Good	Fine	Mint
6-Kamenish-a	6.00	18.00	42.00
7-13	2.85	8.50	20.00
13 (9/51)	2.15	6.50	15.00

MY LOVE MEMOIRS (Formerly Women Outlaws; Hunted No. 13 on)
No. 9, Nov, 1949 - No. 12, May, 1950
Fox Feature Syndicate

	Good	Fine	Mint
9,11,12-Wood-a	8.00	24.00	56.00
10	2.85	8.50	20.00

MY LOVE SECRET (Formerly Phantom Lady) (Animal Crackers No.31)
No. 24, June, 1949 - No. 30, June, 1950; 1954
Fox Feature Syndicate/M. S. Distr.

	Good	Fine	Mint
24-Kamen/Feldstein-a	6.75	20.00	46.00
25-Possible caricature of Wood on the cover?	3.35	10.00	23.00
26,28-Wood-a	8.00	24.00	56.00
27,29,30: 30-photo-c	2.65	8.00	18.00
53-(Reprint, M.S. Distr.) 1954? no date given; formerly Western Thrillers No. 52 (Crimes by Women No. 54). Photo-c	1.70	5.00	11.50

MY LOVE STORY (Hoot Gibson Western No. 5 on)
Sept, 1949 - No. 4, Mar, 1950
Fox Feature Syndicate

	Good	Fine	Mint
1	5.00	15.00	35.00
2	2.85	8.50	20.00
3,4-Wood-a	8.00	24.00	56.00

MY LOVE STORY
April, 1956 - No. 9, Aug, 1957
Atlas Comics (GPS)

	Good	Fine	Mint
1	2.00	6.00	14.00
2	1.00	3.00	7.00
3-Matt Baker-a	2.00	6.00	14.00
4-9	.85	2.50	6.00

NOTE: ***Colletta** a 1(2), 4(2), 5.*

MY ONLY LOVE
July, 1975 - No. 9, Nov, 1976
Charlton Comics

	Good	Fine	Mint
1,2,4-9		.20	.40
3-Toth-a	.35	1.00	2.00

MY OWN ROMANCE (Formerly My Romance; Teen-Age Romance No. 77 on)
No. 4, Mar, 1949 - No. 76, July, 1960
Marvel/Atlas (MjPC/RCM No. 4-59/ZPC No. 60-76)

	Good	Fine	Mint
4-Photo-c	3.00	9.00	21.00
5-10	1.65	5.00	11.50
11-20: 14-Powell-a	1.30	4.00	9.00
21-42: 42-Last pre-code	1.00	3.00	7.00
43-54,56-60	.75	2.25	5.00
55-Toth-a	2.15	6.50	15.00
61-70,72-76	.55	1.65	4.00
71-Williamson-a	3.75	11.25	26.00

NOTE: ***Colletta** a-45(2), 48, 50, 55; c-50i. **Everett** a-25; c-50p. **Romita** a-36.*

MY PAST (. . . Confessions) (Formerly Western Thrillers)
No. 7, Aug, 1949 - No. 11, April, 1950 (Crimes Inc. No. 12)
Fox Feature Syndicate

	Good	Fine	Mint
7	4.00	12.00	28.00
8-10	2.85	8.50	20.00
11-Wood-a	8.00	24.00	56.00

MY PERSONAL PROBLEM
Nov, 1955 - No. 4, Nov, 1956; Oct, 1957 - No. 3, May, 1958
Ajax/Farrell/Steinway Comic

	Good	Fine	Mint
1	2.50	7.50	17.00
2-4	1.50	4.50	10.00
1(10/57)-3('58)-Steinway	1.00	3.00	7.00

MY PRIVATE LIFE (Formerly Murder, Inc.)
No. 16, Feb, 1950 - No. 17, April, 1950
Fox Feature Syndicate

	Good	Fine	Mint
16,17	3.35	10.00	23.00

MYRA NORTH (See 4-Color No. 3)

MY REAL LOVE
No. 5, June, 1952
Standard Comics

	Good	Fine	Mint
5-Toth-a, 3 pgs.; Tuska, Cardy, Vern Greene-a; photo-c	3.85	11.50	27.00

MY ROMANCE (My Own Romance No. 4 on)
Sept, 1948 - No. 3, Jan, 1949
Marvel Comics (RCM)

	Good	Fine	Mint
1	3.35	10.00	23.00
2,3	1.65	5.00	11.50

MY ROMANTIC ADVENTURES (Formerly Romantic Adventures)
No. 68, Aug, 1956 - No. 138, Mar, 1964
American Comics Group

	Good	Fine	Mint
68	1.75	5.25	12.00
69-85	1.00	3.00	7.00
86-Three pg. Williamson-a (2/58)	2.85	8.50	20.00
87-100	.50	1.50	3.50
101-138	.35	1.00	2.00

NOTE: ***Whitney** art in most.*

MY SECRET (Our Secret No. 4 on)
Aug, 1949 - No. 3, Oct, 1949
Superior Comics, Ltd.

	Good	Fine	Mint
1	3.50	10.50	24.00
2,3	2.35	7.00	16.00

MY SECRET AFFAIR (Martin Kane No. 4)
Dec, 1949 - No. 3, April, 1950
Hero Book (Fox Feature Syndicate)

	Good	Fine	Mint
1-Harrison/Wood-a, 10 pgs.	9.50	28.50	65.00
2-Wood-a (poor)	5.50	16.50	38.00
3-Wood-a	8.00	24.00	56.00

MY SECRET CONFESSION
September, 1955
Sterling Comics

	Good	Fine	Mint
1-Sekowsky-a	1.85	5.50	13.00

MY SECRET LIFE (Formerly Western Outlaws; Romeo Tubbs No. 26 on)
No. 22, July, 1949 - No. 27, May, 1950
Fox Feature Syndicate

	Good	Fine	Mint
22	3.50	10.50	24.00
23,26-Wood-a, 6 pgs.	8.00	24.00	56.00
24,25,27	2.15	6.50	15.00

NOTE: *The title was changed to Romeo Tubbs after No. 25 even though No. 26 & 27 did come out.*

MY SECRET LIFE (Formerly Young Lovers; Sue and Sally Smith No. 48 on)
No. 19, Aug, 1957 - No. 47, Sept, 1962
Charlton Comics

	Good	Fine	Mint
19	.75	2.25	5.00
20-35	.45	1.35	2.50
36-47: 44-Last 10¢ ish.		.50	1.00

MY SECRET MARRIAGE
May, 1953 - No. 24, July, 1956
Superior Comics, Ltd.

	Good	Fine	Mint
1	3.35	10.00	23.00
2	1.65	5.00	11.50
3-24	1.30	4.00	9.00
I.W. Reprint No. 9	.30	.90	1.80

NOTE: *Many issues contain Kamenish art.*

MY SECRET ROMANCE (A Star Presentation No. 3)
Jan, 1950 - No. 2, March, 1950
Hero Book (Fox Feature Syndicate)

	Good	Fine	Mint
1-Wood-a	9.00	27.00	62.00
2-Wood-a	8.00	24.00	56.00

MY SECRET STORY (Sabu No. 30 on)
No. 26, Oct, 1949 - No. 29, April, 1950
Fox Feature Syndicate

	Good	Fine	Mint
26	3.85	11.50	27.00
27-29	2.85	8.50	20.00

MYSTERIES (. . . Weird & Strange)
May, 1953 - No. 11, Jan, 1955
Superior/Dynamic Publ. (Randall Publ. Ltd.)

	Good	Fine	Mint
1	6.50	19.50	45.00
2-A-Bomb blast story	3.75	11.25	26.00
3-9,11	2.65	8.00	18.00
10-Kamenish c/a r-/Strange Mysteries No. 2; cover from a panel in S.M. No. 2	3.50	10.50	24.00

MYSTERIES OF SCOTLAND YARD (See A-1 Comics No. 121)

MYSTERIES OF UNEXPLORED WORLDS (See Blue Bird) (Son of Vulcan V2No.49 on)
Aug, 1956 - No. 48, Sept, 1965
Charlton Comics

	Good	Fine	Mint
1	8.00	24.00	56.00
2-No Ditko	2.35	7.00	16.00
3,4,6,8,9-Ditko-a	5.00	15.00	35.00
5-Ditko c/a (all)	5.50	16.50	38.00
7-(68 pg. ish); Ditko-a	6.50	19.50	45.00
10-Ditko-c/a(4)	5.50	16.50	38.00
11-Ditko-c/a(3)-signed J. Kotdi	5.00	15.00	35.00
12,19,21-24,26-Ditko-a	3.50	10.50	24.00
13-18,20	1.15	3.50	8.00
25,27-30	1.00	3.00	7.00
31-45	.45	1.35	3.00
46(5/65)-Son of Vulcan begins (origin)	.70	2.00	4.00
47,48	.50	1.50	3.00

NOTE: ***Ditko** c-3-6, 10, 11, 19, 21-24.*

MYSTERIOUS ADVENTURES
March, 1951 - No. 24, Mar, 1955; No. 25, Aug, 1955
Story Comics

	Good	Fine	Mint
1	10.00	30.00	70.00
2	5.00	15.00	35.00
3,4,6,9,10	3.85	11.50	27.00
5-Bondage-c	4.75	14.25	33.00
7-Daggar in eye panel; dismemberment	8.00	24.00	56.00
8-Eyeball story	6.00	18.00	42.00
11(12/52)-Used in **SOTI**, pg. 84.	8.00	24.00	56.00
12-Dismemberment, eyes ripped out	9.00	27.00	62.00
13-Eye injury panel	8.00	24.00	56.00
14,19	4.00	12.00	28.00
15-Violence; beheading, acid in face, face carved with knife	8.50	25.50	60.00
16-Violence, dismemberment, injury to eye	8.50	25.50	60.00
17-Violence, dismemberment	8.50	25.50	60.00
18-Used in Sentate Investigative report, pgs. 5,6; E.C. swipe/ T.F.T.C. 35	8.50	25.50	60.00
20-Violence, head split open, fried body organs-used by Wertham in the Senate hearings	8.50	25.50	60.00
21-Blood drainage story, hanging panels, intestines pulled out; bondage/beheading-c	8.50	25.50	60.00
22-'Cinderella' parody	4.00	12.00	28.00
23-Disbrow-a	4.85	14.50	34.00
24,25	3.50	10.50	24.00

NOTE: *Tothish art by **Ross Andru**-No. 22, 23. **Bache** a-8. **Cameron** a-6, 7. **Hollingsworth** a-3-8, 12. **Schaffenberger** a-24, 25. **Wildey** a-17.*

MYSTERIOUS ISLAND (See 4-Color No. 1213)

MYSTERIOUS ISLE
Nov-Jan, 1963/64 (Jules Verne)
Dell Publishing Co.

	Good	Fine	Mint
1	1.00	3.00	7.00

MYSTERIOUS STORIES (Horror From the Tomb No. 1)
Dec-Jan, 1954-1955 - No. 7, Dec, 1955
Premier Magazines

	Good	Fine	Mint
2-Woodbridge-c	6.00	18.00	42.00
3-Woodbridge c/a	5.00	15.00	35.00
4-7: 5-Cinderella parody. 6-Woodbridge-c	4.00	12.00	28.00

NOTE: ***Hollingsworth** a-2,4.*

MYSTERIOUS SUSPENSE
October, 1968
Charlton Comics

	Good	Fine	Mint
1-The Question app. by Ditko-c/a	1.75	5.25	12.00

MYSTERIOUS TRAVELER (See Tales of the. . .)

MYSTERIOUS TRAVELER COMICS (Radio)
Nov, 1948 - No. 4, 1949
Trans-World Publications

	Good	Fine	Mint
1-Powell-c/a(2); Poe adaptation, 'Tell Tale Heart'	14.50	43.50	100.00
2-4	10.00	30.00	70.00

MYSTERY COMICS
1944 - No. 4, 1944 (No month given)

Mysteries #7, © SUPR

Mysteries of Unexplored Worlds #1, © CC

Mysterious Adventures #22, © Story

Mystery in Space #5, © DC

Mystery Men Comics #14, © FOX

Mystery Tales #8, © MCG

MYSTERY COMICS (continued)
William H. Wise & Co.

	Good	Fine	Mint
1-The Magnet, The Silver Knight, Brad Spencer, Wonderman, Dick Devins, King of Futuria, & Zudo the Jungle Boy begin	26.00	78.00	182.00
2-Bondage-c	17.00	51.00	120.00
3-Lance Lewis, Space Detective begins	16.00	48.00	110.00
4(V2No.1 inside)	16.00	48.00	110.00

NOTE: ***Schomburg** c-1-4.*

MYSTERY COMICS DIGEST
March, 1972 - No. 26, Oct, 1975
Gold Key

	Good	Fine	Mint
1-Ripley's; reprint of Ripley's No. 1; origin Ra-Ka-Tep the Mummy; Wood-a	.85	2.50	5.00
2-Boris Karloff; Wood-a; 1st app. Werewolf Count Wulfstein	.40	1.25	2.50
3-Twilight Zone (TV); Crandall, Toth & George Evans-a; 1st app. Tragg & Simbar the Lion Lord; 2 Crandall/Frazetta-a r-Twilight Zone No. 1	.40	1.25	2.50
4-Ripley's Believe It or Not; 1st app. Baron Tibor, the Vampire	.35	1.00	2.00
5-Boris Karloff Tales of Mystery; 1st app. Dr. Spektor	.35	1.00	2.00
6-Twilight Zone (TV); 1st app. U.S. Marshal Reid & Sir Duane	.35	1.00	2.00
7-Ripley's Believe It or Not; origin The Lurker in the Swamp; 1st app. Duroc		.60	1.20
8-Boris Karloff Tales of Mystery		.60	1.20
9-Twilight Zone (TV); Williamson, Crandall, McWilliams-a; 2nd Tragg app.	.40	1.25	2.50
10,13-Ripley's Believe It or Not		.50	1.00
11,14-Boris Karloff Tales of Mystery. 14-1st app. Xorkon		.40	.80
12,15-Twilight Zone (TV)		.40	.80
16,19,22,25-Ripley's Believe It or Not		.40	.80
17-Boris Karloff Tales of Mystery; Williamson-r	.25	.75	1.50
18,21,24-Twilight Zone (TV)		.40	.80
20,23,26-Boris Karloff Tales of Mystery		.40	.80

NOTE: *Dr. Spektor app.-No. 5,10-12,21. Durak app.-No. 15. Duroc app.-No. 14 (later called Durak). King George 1st app.-No. 8.*

MYSTERY IN SPACE
Apr-May, 1951 - No. 110, Sept, 1966; (No. 1-3: 52 pgs.)
No. 111, Sept, 1980 - No. 117, March, 1981
National Periodical Publications

	Good	Fine	Mint
1-Frazetta-a, 8 pgs.; Knights of the Galaxy begins, ends No. 8	105.00	315.00	735.00
2	43.00	130.00	300.00
3	35.00	105.00	245.00
4,5	23.00	70.00	160.00
6-10: 7-Toth-a	17.00	51.00	120.00
11-15: 13-Toth-a	12.00	36.00	84.00
16-18,20-25: Interplanetary Insurance feature by Infantino in all. 24-Last precode issue	11.00	33.00	76.00
19-Virgil Finlay-a	13.50	40.50	95.00
26-34,36-40: 26-Space Cabbie begins	7.00	21.00	50.00
35-Kubert-a	8.00	24.00	56.00
41-52: 47-Space Cabbie feature ends	4.00	12.00	28.00
53-Adam Strange begins (1st app. in Showcase)	27.00	81.00	190.00
54	12.00	36.00	84.00
55	8.50	25.50	60.00
56-60	6.00	18.00	42.00
61-71: 61-1st app. Adam Strange foe Ulthoon. 62-1st app. A.S. foe Mortan. 63-Origin Vandor. 66-Star Rovers begin. 68-Dust Devils app. 71-Last 10¢ ish.	3.50	10.50	24.00
72-80: 75-JLA x-over in Adam Strange	2.65	8.00	18.00
81-86	1.50	4.50	10.00
87-90-Hawkman in all	1.00	3.00	7.00
91-102: 91-End Infantino art on Adam Strange. 92-Space Ranger begins. 94,98-Adam Strange/Space Ranger team-up. 102-Adam Strange ends	.55	1.65	4.00
103-Origin Ultra, the Multi-Alien; Space Ranger ends	.55	1.65	4.00
104-110(9/66)	.35	1.00	2.00
111(9/80)-117		.50	1.00

NOTE: ***Anderson** a-2, 4, 8-10, 12-17, 19, 45-48, 51, 57, 61-64, 70, 76, 87-98; c-9, 10, 15-25, 87, 89, 105-108, 110. **Aparo** a-111. **Austin** a-112i. **Craig** a-114, 116. **Ditko** a-111, 114-116. **Drucker** a-13, 14. **Golden** a-113p. **Sid Greene** a-78, 91. **Infantino** a-1-8, 11, 14-25, 27-46, 48, 49, 51, 53-91, 103, 117; c-60-86, 88, 90, 91, 105, 107. **Gil Kane** a-18, 100-102; c-52, 101. **Kubert** a-113; c-111-15. **Newton** a-117p. **Rogers** a-111. **Sekowsky** a-52. **Simon & Kirby** a-4(2 pgs.). **Spiegle** a-111, 114. **Starlin** c-116. **Sutton** a-112. **Tuska** a-115p, 117p.*

MYSTERY MEN COMICS
Aug, 1939 - No. 31, Feb, 1942
Fox Features Syndicate

	Good	Fine	Mint
1-Intro. & 1st app. The Blue Beetle, The Green Mask, Rex Dexter of Mars by Briefer, Zanzibar by Tuska, Lt. Drake, D-13-Secret Agent by Powell, Chen Chang, Wing Turner, & Captain Denny Scott	100.00	300.00	700.00
2-Opium story	50.00	150.00	350.00
3	40.00	120.00	280.00
4-Capt. Savage begins	35.00	105.00	245.00
5	28.00	84.00	195.00
6-8	25.00	75.00	175.00
9-The Moth begins	21.00	62.00	146.00
10-Wing Turner by Kirby	20.00	60.00	140.00
11-Intro. Domino	17.00	51.00	120.00
12,14-18	14.50	43.50	100.00
13-Intro. Lynx & sidekick Blackie	17.00	51.00	120.00
19-Intro. & 1st app. Miss X (ends No. 21)	17.00	51.00	120.00
20-25,27-31	13.50	40.50	95.00
26-The Wraith begins	13.50	40.50	95.00

NOTE: ***Briefer** a-1, 5, 24. **Cuidera** a-22. **Lou Fine** c-1-9. **Powell** a-1-9, 24. **Simon** c-10-12. **Tuska** a-1-9, 22, 24. Bondage-c 1, 3, 7, 8, 25, 27-29, 31.*

MYSTERY TALES
March, 1952 - No. 54, Aug, 1957
Atlas Comics (20CC)

	Good	Fine	Mint
1	11.00	33.00	76.00
2-Krigstein-a	5.75	17.25	40.00
3-9: 6-A-Bomb panel	3.50	10.50	24.00
10-Story similar to 'The Assassin' from Shock SuspenStories	4.00	12.00	28.00
11,13-20	2.15	6.50	15.00
12-Matt Fox-a	3.00	9.00	21.00
21-Decapitation story	3.00	9.00	21.00
22-Forte/Matt Fox c; a(i)	4.00	12.00	28.00
23-26 (2/55)-Last precode issue	2.00	6.00	14.00
27,29-32,34,35,37,38,41-43,48,49	1.50	4.50	10.00
28-Jack Katz-a	2.35	7.00	16.00
33-Crandall-a	3.65	11.00	25.00
36,39-Krigstein-a	3.65	11.00	25.00
40,45-Ditko-a	2.85	8.50	20.00
44,51-Williamson/Mayo-a	4.65	14.00	32.00
46-Williamson/Krenkel-a	4.65	14.00	32.00
47-Crandall, Ditko, Powell-a	3.35	10.00	23.00
50-Torres, Morrow-a	3.35	10.00	23.00
52,53	1.50	4.50	10.00
54-Crandall, Check-a	2.65	8.00	18.00

NOTE: ***Berg** a-17, 51. **Colan** a-1, 3, 18, 35, 43. **Everett** a-2, 29, 33, 35, 41, 43?; c-8-11, 14, 16, 38, 39, 41, 43, 44, 46, 48-51, 53?. **Fass** a-16. **Forte** a-21, 22. **Matt Fox** a-12?, 22; c-22. **Heath** a-3; c-3, 15, 17, 26. **Heck** a-25. **Kinstler** a-15. **Mort Lawrence** a-26, 32, 34. **Maneely** a-1, 9, 14, 22; c-12, 23, 24, 27. **Mooney** a-3, 40. **Morisi** a-43, 49, 52. **Morrow** a-50. **Pakula** a-16. **Powell** a-21, 29, 37, 38, 47. **Robinson** a-7p, 42. **Roussos** a-44. **Severin** c-52. **Torres** c-20? **Tuska** a-10, 12, 14. **Whitney** a-2.*

MYSTERY TALES
1964
Super Comics

	Good	Fine	Mint
Super Reprint No. 16,17('64)	.50	1.50	3.00
Super Reprint No. 18-Kubert art/Strange Terrors No. 4	.50	1.50	3.00

MYSTIC (3rd Series)
March, 1951 - No. 61, Aug, 1957
Marvel/Atlas Comics (CLDS 1/CSI 2-21/OMC 22-35/CSI 35-61)

	Good	Fine	Mint
1-Atom bomb panels	12.00	36.00	84.00
2	6.00	18.00	42.00
3-Eyes torn out	4.00	12.00	28.00
4-"The Devil Birds" by Wolverton, 6 pgs.	18.00	54.00	125.00
5,7,9,10	3.50	10.50	24.00
6-"The Eye of Doom" by Wolverton, 7 pgs.	18.00	54.00	125.00
11-20: 16-Bondage/torture c/story	3.00	9.00	21.00
21-25,27-30,32-36-Last precode (3/55)	2.50	7.50	17.50
26-Atomic War, severed head stories	2.85	8.50	20.00
31-Sid Check-a	2.15	6.50	15.00
37-51,53-57,61	1.50	4.50	10.00
52-Wood, Crandall-a	4.35	13.00	30.00
58,59-Krigstein-a	3.35	10.00	23.00
60-Williamson/Mayo-a, 4 pgs.	3.85	11.50	27.00

NOTE: ***Andru*** *a-23, 25.* ***Check*** *a-60.* ***Colan*** *a-3, 7, 12, 21, 37.* ***Drucker*** *a-46, 52, 56.* ***Everett*** *a-8, 9, 17, 40, 44, 57; c-18, 21, 42, 47, 49, 52-55, 58, 59, 61.* ***Fox*** *a-24i.* ***Heath*** *a-10; c-10, 22, 23, 25, 30.* ***Infantino*** *a-12.* ***Kane*** *a-8, 24p.* ***Jack Katz*** *a-31, 33.* ***Mort Lawrence*** *a-37.* ***Maneely*** *a-22, 24, 58; c-28, 29, 31.* ***Moldoff*** *a-29.* ***Morrow*** *a-51.* ***Orlando*** *a-57, 61.* ***Powell*** *a-52, 55, 56.* ***Robinson*** *a-5.* ***Romita*** *a-11.* ***Sekowsky*** *a-1, 2, 4, 5.* ***Severin*** *c-56.* ***Whitney*** *a-33.* ***Wildey*** *a-28, 30. Canadian reprints known-title 'Startling'.*

MYSTICAL TALES
June, 1956 - No. 8, Aug, 1957
Atlas Comics (CCC 1/EPI 2-8)

	Good	Fine	Mint
1-Everett c/a	7.00	21.00	50.00
2,4: 2-Berg-a	3.50	10.50	24.00
3-Crandall-a	4.35	13.00	30.00
5-Williamson-a, 4 pgs.	5.00	15.00	35.00
6-Torres, Krigstein-a	4.35	13.00	30.00
7-Torres, Orlando, Crandall, Everett-a	3.65	11.00	25.00
8-Krigstein, Check-a	4.35	13.00	30.00

NOTE: ***Everett*** *a-1, 7; c-2, 4, 6, 7.* ***Orlando*** *a-1, 2.* ***Powell*** *a-1, 4.*

MYSTIC COMICS (1st Series)
March, 1940 - No. 10, Aug, 1942
Timely Comics (TPI 1-5/TCI 8-10)

	Good	Fine	Mint
1-Origin The Blue Blaze, The Dynamic Man, & Flexo the Rubber Man; Zephyr Jones, 3X's & Deep Sea Demon app.; The Magician begins; bondage-c	345.00	1035.00	2415.00
2-The Invisible Man & Master Mind Excello begin; Space Rangers, Zara of the Jungle, Taxi Taylor app; bondage-c	140.00	420.00	980.00
3-Origin Hercules, who last appears in No. 4	112.00	336.00	785.00
4-Origin The Thin Man & The Black Widow; Merzak the Mystic app.; last Flexo, Dynamic Man, Invisible Man & Blue Blaze. (Some issues have date sticker on cover; others have July w/August overprint in silver color); Roosevelt assassination-c	132.00	395.00	925.00
5-Origin The Black Marvel, The Blazing Skull, The Sub-Earth Man, Super Slave & The Terror; The Moon Man & Black Widow app.	125.00	375.00	875.00
6-Origin The Challenger & The Destroyer	105.00	315.00	735.00
7-The Witness begins (origin); origin Davey & the Demon; last Black Widow; Simon & Kirby-c	87.00	261.00	610.00
8	74.00	221.00	515.00
9-Gary Gaunt app.; last Black Marvel, Mystic & Blazing Skull; bondage-c	74.00	221.00	515.00
10-Father Time, World of Wonder, & Red Skeleton app.; last Challenger & Terror	74.00	221.00	515.00

NOTE: ***Schomburg*** *a-1-4.*

MYSTIC COMICS (2nd Series)
Oct, 1944 - No. 4, Winter, 1944-45
Timely Comics (ANC)

	Good	Fine	Mint
1-The Angel, The Destroyer, The Human Torch, Terry Vance the Schoolboy Sleuth, & Tommy Tyme begin	59.00	178.00	410.00
2-Last Human Torch & Terry Vance; bondage-hypo-c	37.00	110.00	260.00
3-Last Angel (two stories) & Tommy Tyme	35.00	105.00	245.00
4-The Young Allies app.	30.00	90.00	210.00

MY STORY (. . . True Romances in Pictures No. 5,6) (Formerly Zago)
No. 5, May, 1949 - No. 12, Aug, 1950
Hero Books (Fox Features Syndicate)

	Good	Fine	Mint
5-Kamen/Feldstein-a	6.50	19.50	45.00
6-8,11,12	2.85	8.50	20.00
9,10-Wood-a	8.00	24.00	56.00

MYTHADVENTURES (Magazine size)
March, 1984 - Present (B&W)
WaRP Graphics/Apple Press No. 10 on

	Good	Fine	Mint
1-12: Early ishs. mag. size	.30	.90	1.80

MY TRUE LOVE (Frank Buck No. 70 on)
No. 65, July, 1949 - No. 69, March, 1950
Fox Features Syndicate

	Good	Fine	Mint
65	4.00	12.00	28.00
66-69: 69-Morisi-a	2.65	8.00	18.00

NAIVE INTER-DIMENSIONAL COMMANDO KOALAS
Aug, 1986 - Present ($1.50, B&W)
Eclipse Comics

	Good	Fine	Mint
1	.30	.90	1.80

NAKED PREY, THE (See Movie Classics)

NAM, THE
Dec, 1986 - Present
Marvel Comics Group

	Good	Fine	Mint
1-Golden a(p)/c begins	.50	1.50	3.00
1 (2nd printing)		.40	.80
2-4	.25	.75	1.50

NAMORA
Fall, 1948 - No. 3, Dec, 1948
Marvel Comics (PrPI)

	Good	Fine	Mint
1-Sub-Mariner x-over in Namora; Everett-a	55.00	165.00	385.00
2-The Blonde Phantom app. in Sub-Mariner story; Everett-a	45.00	135.00	315.00
3-(Scarce)-Sub-Mariner app.; Everett-a	40.00	120.00	280.00

NANCY AND SLUGGO
No. 16, 1949 - No. 23, 1954
United Features Syndicate

	Good	Fine	Mint
16(No.1)	2.65	8.00	18.00
17-23	1.75	5.25	12.00

NANCY & SLUGGO (Nancy No. 146-173; formerly Sparkler Comics)
No. 121, Apr, 1955 - No. 192, Oct, 1963
St. John/Dell No. 146-187/Gold Key No. 188 on

	Good	Fine	Mint
121(4/55)(St. John)	2.15	6.50	15.00
122-145(7/57)(St. John)	1.75	5.25	12.00

Mystic Comics #1 (2nd Series), © MCG

Mythadventures #1, © WaRP

Namora #1, © MCG

Nanny & the Professor #1, © 20th Century-Fox *National Comics #39, © QUA* *National Velvet #1 (GK), © MGM*

NANCY & SLUGGO (continued) — Good / Fine / Mint

146(9/57)-Peanuts begins, ends No. 192 (Dell) 1.50 4.50 10.00
147-161 (Dell) 1.30 4.00 9.00
162-165,177-180-John Stanley-a 2.85 8.50 20.00
166-176-Oona & Her Haunted House series; Stanley-a 3.00 9.00 21.00
181-187(3-5/62)(Dell) 1.15 3.50 8.00
188(10/62)-192 (G.Key) 1.15 3.50 8.00
4-Color 1034(9-11/59)-Summer Camp 1.15 3.50 8.00
(See Dell Giant No. 34,45 & Dell Giants)

NANNY AND THE PROFESSOR (TV)
Aug, 1970 - No. 2, Oct, 1970 (Photo-c)
Dell Publishing Co.

1(01-546-008), 2 1.70 5.00 10.00

NAPOLEON (See 4-Color No. 526)

NAPOLEON & SAMANTHA (See Walt Disney Showcase No. 10)

NAPOLEON & UNCLE ELBY (See Clifford McBride's...)
Nov?, 1942 (68 pages) (One Shot)
Eastern Color Printing Co.

1 11.00 33.00 76.00
1945-American Book-Strafford Press (128 pgs.) (8x10½''-B&W reprints; hardcover) 5.75 17.25 40.00

NATHANIEL DUSK
Feb, 1984 - No. 4, May, 1984 (mini-series; Baxter paper)
DC Comics (Direct Sale only)

1-Intro/origin .60 1.25
2-4 ($1.25): Colan c/a .60 1.25

NATHANIEL DUSK II
Oct, 1985 - No. 4, Jan, 1986 (mini-series; Baxter paper)
DC Comics

1 ($2.00 cover); Colan c/a .30 .90 1.80
2-4 .55 1.10

NATIONAL COMICS
July, 1940 - No. 75, Nov, 1949
Quality Comics Group

1-Uncle Sam begins; Origin sidekick Buddy by Eisner; origin Wonder Boy & Kid Dixon; Merlin the Magician (ends No. 45); Cyclone, Kid Patrol, Sally O'Neal Policewoman, Pen Miller (ends No. 22), Prop Powers (ends No. 26), & Paul Bunyan (ends No. 22) begin 145.00 435.00 1015.00
2 70.00 210.00 490.00
3-Last Eisner Uncle Sam 56.00 168.00 392.00
4-Last Cyclone 40.00 120.00 280.00
5-Quick Silver begins (3rd w/lightning speed?); origin Uncle Sam; bondage-c 52.00 156.00 364.00
6-11: 8-Jack & Jill begins (ends No. 22). 9-Flag-c 38.00 115.00 265.00
12 28.00 84.00 195.00
13-16-Lou Fine-a 35.00 105.00 245.00
17,19-22 25.00 75.00 175.00
18-(12/41)-Shows orientals attacking Pearl Harbor; on stands one month before actual event 30.00 90.00 210.00
23-The Unknown & Destroyer 171 begin 28.00 84.00 195.00
24-26,28,30: 26-Wonder Boy ends 19.50 58.50 135.00
27-G-2 the Unknown begins (ends No. 46) 19.50 58.50 135.00
29-Origin The Unknown 19.50 58.50 135.00
31-33: 33-Chic Carter begins (ends No. 47) 17.00 51.00 120.00
34-40: 35-Last Kid Patrol 10.00 30.00 70.00
41-47,49,50: 42-The Barker begins 8.00 24.00 56.00
48-Origin The Whistler 8.00 24.00 56.00
51-Sally O'Neil by Ward, 8 pgs. (12/45) 11.50 34.50 80.00

Good / Fine / Mint

52-60 6.50 19.50 45.00
61-67: 67-Format change; Quicksilver app. 4.65 14.00 32.00
68-75: The Barker ends 2.85 8.50 20.00

NOTE: ***Cole*** *Quicksilver-13; Barker-43; c-46.* ***Crandall*** *Uncle Sam-11-13 (with* ***Fine****), 25, 26; c-24-26, 30-33, 43.* ***Crandall*** *Paul Bunyan-10-13.* ***Fine*** *Uncle Sam-13 (w/****Crandall****), 17, 18; c-1-14, 16, 18, 21.* ***Guardineer*** *Quicksilver-27.* ***Gustavson*** *Quicksilver-14-26.* ***McWilliams*** *a-23-28, 55, 57. Uncle Sam-c No. 1-41.*

NATIONAL CRUMB, THE (Magazine-Size)
August, 1975 (52 pages) (Satire)
Mayfair Publications

1 .50 1.50 3.00

NATIONAL VELVET (TV)
May-July, 1961 - March, 1963 (All photo-c)
Dell Publishing Co./Gold Key

4-Color 1195 2.00 6.00 14.00
4-Color 1312 1.75 5.25 12.00
01-556-207,12-556-210 1.50 4.50 10.00
1(12/62), 2(3/63)-Gold Key 1.50 4.50 10.00

NATURE BOY (Formerly Danny Blaze; Li'l Rascal Twins No. 6 on)
No. 3, March, 1956 - No. 5, Feb, 1957
Charlton Comics

3-Origin; Blue Beetle story; Buscema-a 8.50 25.50 60.00
4,5 5.50 16.50 38.00

NOTE: ***Buscema*** *a-3, 4p, 5.* ***Powell*** *a-4.*

NATURE OF THINGS (See 4-Color No. 727,842)

NAVY ACTION (Sailor Sweeney No. 12-14)
Aug, 1954 - No. 11, Apr, 1956; No. 15, 1/57 - No. 18, 8/57
Atlas Comics (CDS)

1-Powell-a 2.65 8.00 18.00
2 1.35 4.00 9.00
3-11: 4-Last precode (2/55) 1.20 3.50 8.00
15-18 .85 2.50 6.00

NOTE: ***Berg*** *a-9.* ***Colan*** *a-8.* ***Drucker*** *a-7, 17.* ***Everett*** *a-3, 7, 16; c-16, 17.* ***Maneely*** *a-8.* ***Reinman*** *a-17.*

NAVY COMBAT
June, 1955 - No. 20, Oct, 1958
Atlas Comics (MPI)

1-Torpedo Taylor begins by D. Heck 2.65 8.00 18.00
2 1.20 3.50 8.00
3-10 1.00 3.00 7.00
11-13,15,16,18-20 .85 2.50 6.00
14-Torres-a 2.00 6.00 14.00
17-Williamson-a, 4 pgs. 2.75 8.00 18.00

NOTE: ***Berg*** *a-10,11.* ***Drucker*** *a-7, 11.* ***Everett*** *a-3, 8 & 9 w/****Tuska****, 20; c-10, 14-16.* ***Pakula*** *a-7.* ***Powell*** *a-20.*

NAVY HEROES
1945
Almanac Publishing Co.

1-Heavy in propaganda 3.00 9.00 21.00

NAVY: HISTORY & TRADITION
1958 - 1961 (nn) (Giveaway)
Stokes Walesby Co./Dept. of Navy

1772-1778, 1778-1782, 1782-1817, 1817-1865, 1865-1936, 1940-1945 2.00 6.00 14.00
1861: Naval Actions of the Civil War: 1865 2.00 6.00 14.00

NAVY PATROL
May, 1955 - No. 4, Nov, 1955
Key Publications

1 2.00 6.00 14.00
2-4 1.00 3.00 7.00

NAVY TALES
Jan, 1957 - No. 4, July, 1957
Atlas Comics (CDS)

	Good	Fine	Mint
1-Everett-c; Berg, Powell-a	2.65	8.00	18.00
2-Williamson/Mayo-a, 5 pgs; Crandall-a	3.50	10.50	24.00
3,4-Krigstein-a; Severin-c	2.00	6.00	14.00

NAVY TASK FORCE
Feb, 1954 - No. 8, April, 1956
Stanmor Publications/Aragon Mag. No. 4-8

	Good	Fine	Mint
1	2.00	6.00	14.00
2	1.00	3.00	7.00
3-8	.85	2.50	6.00

NAVY WAR HEROES
Jan, 1964 - No. 7, Mar-Apr, 1965
Charlton Comics

	Good	Fine	Mint
1		.40	.80
2-7		.30	.60

NAZA (Stone Age Warrior)
Nov-Jan, 1963/64 - No. 9, March, 1966
Dell Publishing Co.

	Good	Fine	Mint
1 (12-555-401)-Painted-c	.85	2.50	6.00
2-9: 2,3-Painted-c	.55	1.65	4.00

NEAT STUFF
1986 - Present ($2.25)(Mature readers)
Fantagraphics Books

	Good	Fine	Mint
1	.45	1.25	2.50
2-6	.35	1.10	2.25

NEBBS, THE
1928 (Daily B&W strip reprints; 52 pages)
Cupples & Leon Co.

	Good	Fine	Mint
By Sol Hess; Carlson-a	4.00	12.00	28.00

NEBBS, THE
1941 - 1945
Dell Publishing Co./Croydon Publishing Co.

	Good	Fine	Mint
Large Feat. Comic 23(1941)	6.50	19.50	45.00
1(1945, 36 pgs.)-Reprints	3.50	10.50	24.00

NEGRO (See All-Negro)

NEGRO HEROES (Reprints from True, Real Heroes, & Calling All Girls)
Spring, 1947 - No. 2, Summer, 1948
Parents' Magazine Institute

	Good	Fine	Mint
1	22.00	65.00	154.00
2 (Scarce)	33.00	100.00	230.00

NEGRO ROMANCE (Negro Romances No. 4?)
June, 1950 - No. 3, Oct, 1950
Fawcett Publications

	Good	Fine	Mint
1-Evans-a	57.00	171.00	400.00
2,3	44.50	134.00	310.00

NEGRO ROMANCES (Formerly Negro Romance?)
No. 4, May, 1955 (Romantic Secrets No. 5 on?)
Charlton Comics

	Good	Fine	Mint
4-Reprints Fawcett No. 2	30.00	90.00	210.00

NEIL THE HORSE (Arn Saba's. . .)
2/83 - No. 10, 12/84; No. 11, 4/85 - No. 14, 1986
Aardvark-Vanaheim No. 1-10/Renegade Press No. 11 on

	Good	Fine	Mint
1	.65	1.90	3.80
2	.45	1.25	2.50
3-12,14: 11-Vicki Valentine app; w/paper dolls	.35	1.00	2.00
13-Double size; w/paper dolls	.35	1.00	2.00

NELLIE THE NURSE
1945 - No. 36, Oct, 1952; 1957
Marvel/Atlas Comics (SPI/LMC)

	Good	Fine	Mint
1	7.00	21.00	50.00
2	3.75	11.25	26.00
3,4	3.15	9.50	22.00
5-Kurtzman's "Hey Look"	3.75	11.25	26.00
6-8,10: 7,8-Georgie app. 10-Millie app.	2.15	6.50	15.00
9-Wolverton-a, 1 pg.	2.50	7.50	17.50
11,14-16,18-Kurtzman's "Hey Look"	3.35	10.00	23.00
12-"Giggles 'n' Grins" by Kurtzman	2.50	7.50	17.50
13,17,19,20: 17-Annie Oakley app.	1.85	5.50	13.00
21-27,29,30	1.70	5.00	11.50
28-Kurtzman's Rusty reprint	1.85	5.50	13.00
31-36	1.30	4.00	9.00
1('57)-Leading Mag. (Atlas)	1.15	3.50	8.00

NELLIE THE NURSE (See 4-Color No. 1304)

NEMESIS THE WARLOCK
Sept, 1984 - No. 7, Mar, 1985 (Limited series; 36 pgs.)
Eagle Comics (Baxter paper)

	Good	Fine	Mint
1-2000 A.D. reprints	.25	.75	1.50
2-7	.25	.75	1.50

NERVOUS REX
Sept, 1985 - Present
Blackthorne Publ.

	Good	Fine	Mint
1-8	.35	1.00	2.00
1 (2nd printing)	.35	1.00	2.00

NEUTRO
January, 1967
Dell Publishing Co.

	Good	Fine	Mint
1-Jack Sparling c/a	.75	2.25	5.00

NEVADA (See Zane Grey's Stories of the West No. 1)

NEVER AGAIN (War stories; becomes Soldier & Marine V2No.9)
Aug, 1955 - No. 2, Oct?, 1955; No. 8, July, 1956 (no No. 3-7)
Charlton Comics

	Good	Fine	Mint
1	2.65	8.00	18.00
2,8	1.50	4.50	10.00

NEW ADVENTURE COMICS (Formerly New Comics; becomes Adventure Comics No. 32 on)
V1No.12, Jan, 1937 - No. 31, Oct, 1938
National Periodical Publications

	Good	Fine	Mint
V1No.12-Federal Men by Siegel & Shuster continues; Jor-L mentioned	58.00	174.00	405.00
V2No.1(2/37, No.13)	45.00	135.00	315.00
14(V2No.2)-20(V2No.8): 15-1st Adventure logo. 16-1st Shuster-c; 1st non-funny cover. 17-Nadir, Master of Magic begins, ends No. 30	45.00	135.00	315.00
21(V2No.9),22(V2No.10, 2/37)	35.00	105.00	245.00
23-31	30.00	90.00	210.00

NEW ADVENTURE OF WALT DISNEY'S SNOW WHITE AND THE SEVEN DWARFS, A (See Snow White Bendix Giveaway)

NEW ADVENTURES OF CHARLIE CHAN, THE (TV)
May-June, 1958 - No. 6, Mar-Apr, 1959
National Periodical Publications

Nellie the Nurse #11, © MCG

Nervous Rex #1, © Blackthorne

Never Again #1, © CC

New Advs. of Huck Finn #1, © Hanna-Barbera

New Comics #2, © DC

New Funnies #76, © DELL

NEW ADVS. OF CHARLIE CHAN (continued) — Good / Fine / Mint
1 (Scarce) 13.00 40.00 90.00
2 (Scarce) 7.00 21.00 50.00
3-6 (Scarce) 6.00 18.00 42.00
NOTE: ***Sid Greene** a-1-6i. **Gil Kane** a-1-6p.*

NEW ADVENTURES OF HUCK FINN, THE (TV)
December, 1968 (Hanna-Barbera)
Gold Key
1-"The Curse of Thut" 1.00 3.00 7.00

NEW ADVENTURES OF PETER PAN (Disney)
1953 (36 pgs.; 5x7¼") (Admiral giveaway)
Western Publishing Co.
4.65 14.00 32.00

NEW ADVENTURES OF PINOCCHIO (TV)
Oct-Dec, 1962 - No. 3, Sept-Nov, 1963
Dell Publishing Co.
12-562-212 3.50 10.50 24.00
2,3 2.65 8.00 18.00

NEW ADVENTURES OF ROBIN HOOD (See Robin Hood)

NEW ADVENTURES OF SHERLOCK HOLMES (See 4-Color No. 1169, 1245)

NEW ADVENTURES OF SUPERBOY, THE
Jan, 1980 - No. 54, June, 1984
DC Comics
1 .60 1.20
2-5 .50 1.00
6-10 .40 .80
11-47: 11-Superboy gets new power. 15-Superboy gets new parents. 28-Dial "H" For Hero begins, ends No. 49. 45-47-1st app. Sunburst .30 .60
48,49,51-54 (75¢-c) .40 .80
50 ($1.25, 52 pgs.) .60 1.25
NOTE: ***Buckler** a-9p; c-36p. **Giffen** a-50; c-50. 40i. **Gil Kane** c-32p, 33p, 35, 39, 41-49. **Miller** c-51. **Starlin** a-7.*

NEW ADVENTURES OF THE PHANTOM BLOT, THE (See Phantom Blot, The)

NEW BOOK OF COMICS
1936; Spring, 1938 (100 pgs. each) (Reprints)
National Periodical Publications
1(Rare)-Contains r-/New Comics No. 1-4 & More Fun No. 9; r-Federal Men (8pgs.), Henri Duval (1pg.), & Dr. Occult in costume (1pg.) by Siegel & Shuster; Moldoff, Sheldon Mayer (15pgs.)-a 190.00 570.00 1330.00
2-Contains r-/More Fun No. 15 & 16; r-/Dr. Occult in costume (a Superman proto-type), & Calling All Cars (4pgs.) by Siegel & Shuster 125.00 375.00 875.00

NEW COMICS (New Adventure No. 12 on)
12/35 - No. 11, 12/36 (No. 1-6, paper cover) (No. 1-5, 84 pgs.)
National Periodical Publications
V1No.1-Billy the Kid, Sagebrush 'n' Cactus, Jibby Jones, Needles, The Vikings, Sir Loin of Beef, Now-When I Was a Boy, & other 1-2 pg. strips; 2 pgs. Kelly art(1st)-(Gulliver's Travels); Sheldon Mayer-a(1st) 215.00 645.00 1500.00
2-Federal Men by Siegel & Shuster begins (Also see The Comics Magazine No.2); Sheldon Mayer, Kelly-a 120.00 360.00 840.00
3-6: 3,4-Sheldon Mayer-a which continues in The Comics Magazine No. 1; 5-Kiefer-a 75.00 225.00 525.00
7-11 60.00 180.00 420.00
NOTE: *No. 1-6 rarely occur in mint condition.*

NEW DEFENDERS (See Defenders)

NEW DNAGENTS, THE (Formerly DNAgents)
Oct, 1985 - Present
Eclipse Comics — Good / Fine / Mint
V2/1-Origin recap .50 1.00
2-6 .40 .80
7-16 (95¢): Mando paper .60 1.25
3-D 1 (1/86) .35 1.15 2.30
2-D 1 (1/86)-Limited ed. (100 copies) .85 2.50 5.00

NEW FUN COMICS (More Fun No. 7 on)
Feb, 1935 - No. 6, Oct, 1935 (10x15", No. 1-4,6-slick covers) (No. 1-5, 84 pgs; 68 pgs. No. 6-on)
National Periodical Publications
V1No.1 (1st DC comic); 1st app. Oswald The Rabbit 500.00 1500.00 3500.00
2(3/35)-(Very Rare) 400.00 1200.00 2800.00
3-5(8/35): 5-Soft-c 180.00 540.00 1260.00
6(10/35)-1st Dr. Occult by Siegel & Shuster(Leger & Reuths); last "New Fun" title. "New Comics" No. 1 begins in Dec. which is reason for title change to More Fun; Henri Duval (ends No. 9) by Siegel & Shuster begins; Paper-c 220.00 660.00 1540.00

NEW FUNNIES (The Funnies, No. 1-64; Walter Lantz. . ., No. 109 on; No. 259,260,272,273-New TV. . .; No. 261-271-TV Funnies)
No. 65, July, 1942 - No. 288, Mar-Apr, 1962
Dell Publishing Co.
65(No.1)-Andy Panda, Raggedy Ann, Oswald the Rabbit, & Li'l Eight Ball begin 30.75 92.00 215.00
66-70: 67-Billy & Bonnie Bee by Frank Thomas begins. 69-2pg. Kelly-a 13.50 40.50 95.00
71-73,75: 72-Kelly illos; W. Woodpecker app.; Brownies sty, 1st? 8.50 25.50 60.00
74-Brownies by Kelly 10.75 32.25 75.00
76-Andy Panda (Carl Barks & Pabian art); Brownies by Kelly; Woody Woodpecker app. in Oswald story 57.00 171.00 400.00
77-Brownies by Kelly 8.50 25.50 60.00
78,79-Andy Panda in a World of Real People ends, becomes all funny animal 7.00 21.00 50.00
80-82 7.00 21.00 50.00
83-Kelly text illos; X-mas-c 7.00 21.00 50.00
84,85-Kelly text illos 6.50 19.50 45.00
86-90 3.00 9.00 21.00
91-99 2.00 6.00 14.00
100 2.35 7.00 16.00
101-110 1.50 4.50 10.00
111-120: 119-X-mas-c 1.70 4.00 9.00
121-150: 143-X-mas-c 1.00 3.00 7.00
151-200: 155-X-mas-c. 168-X-mas-c. 182-Origin & 1st app. Knothead & Splinter. 191-X-mas-c .75 2.25 5.00
201-240 .55 1.65 4.00
241-288: 270-Walter Lantz c-app. 281-1st story swipe/WDC&S No.100 .45 1.35 3.00
NOTE: *Early issues written by **John Stanley**.*

NEW GODS, THE (New Gods No. 12 on) (See Adventure, First Issue Spec., & Super-Team Family)
2-3/71 - No. 11, 10-11/72; No. 12, 7/77 - No. 19, 7-8/78
National Periodical Publications/DC Comics
1-Intro/1st app. Orion .40 1.25 2.50
2 .35 1.00 2.00
3,4: 4-Origin Manhunter-r .25 .75 1.50
5-11: 5-Young Gods feature. 7-Origin Orion. 7,8-Young Gods app. 9-1st app. Bug .60 1.20
12-19 .30 .60
NOTE: *No. 4-9 (52 pgs.) contain Manhunter-r by **Simon & Kirby** from Adventure No. 73, 74, 75, 76, 77, 78 with covers in that order. **Adkins** i-12-14, 17-19. **Buckler** a-15p; c-14p, 15p. **Kirby** c/a-1-11p. **Newton** p-12-14, 16-19. **Starlin** c-17. **Staton** c-19p.*

NEW GODS, THE
5/84 - No. 6, 11/84 ($2.00; direct sale; Baxter paper)
DC Comics

	Good	Fine	Mint
1-New Kirby-c begin; r-/New Gods 1&2	.35	1.00	2.00
2-6: 6-Original art by Kirby	.35	1.00	2.00

NEW HEROIC (See Heroic)

NEWLYWEDS
1907; 1917 (cardboard covers)
Saalfield Publ. Co.

	Good	Fine	Mint
...'& Their Baby' by McManus; Saalfield, 1907, 13x10'', 57pgs. daily strips in full color	22.00	65.00	154.00
...'& Their Baby's Comic Pictures, The', by McManus, Saalfield, 1917, 14x10'', 22pgs, oblong, cardboard covers. Reprints 'Newlyweds' (Baby Snookums strips) mainly from 1916; blue cover; says for painting and crayoning, but some pages in color. (Scarce)	16.00	48.00	110.00

NEW MEN OF BATTLE, THE
1949 (nn) (Cardboard covers)
Catechetical Guild

	Good	Fine	Mint
nn(V8No.1-V8No.6)-192 pgs.; contains 6 issues of Topix rebound	2.00	6.00	14.00
nn(V8No.7-V8No.11)-160 pgs.; contains 5 issues of Topix	2.00	6.00	14.00

NEW MUTANTS, THE
March, 1983 - Present
Marvel Comics Group

	Good	Fine	Mint
1	.70	2.00	4.00
2,3	.40	1.25	2.50
4-10: 10-1st app. Magma	.35	1.00	2.00
11-20: 18-Intro. Warlock	.30	.90	1.80
21-Double size; new Warlock origin	.35	1.00	2.00
22-30: 23-25-Cloak & Dagger app.	.25	.75	1.50
31-40		.60	1.20
41-49		.50	1.00
50 ($1.25)		.60	1.25
Annual 1 (1984)		.60	1.20
Annual 2 (10/86; $1.25)	.25	.75	1.50
Special 1-Special Edition ('85; 64 pgs.)-ties in with X-Men Alpha Flight mini-series; A. Adams/Austin-a	.40	1.25	2.50

NOTE: ***Sienkowitz** a-18-25. **Simonson** c-11p. **B. Smith** c-46. **W. Smith** c-43.*

NEW PEOPLE, THE (TV)
Jan, 1970 - No. 2, May, 1970
Dell Publishing Co.

	Good	Fine	Mint
1,2	1.00	3.00	6.00

NEW ROMANCES
No. 5, May, 1951 - No. 21, Apr?, 1954
Standard Comics

	Good	Fine	Mint
5	3.00	9.00	21.00
6-9: 6-Barbara Bel Geddes, Richard Basehart ''Fourteen Hours;''	1.70	5.00	11.50
10,14,16,17-Toth-a	3.75	11.25	26.00
11-Toth-a; Liz Taylor, Montgomery Cliff photo-c	4.35	13.50	30.00
12,13,15,18-21	1.15	3.50	8.00

NOTE: ***Celardo** a-9. **Moreira** a-6. **Tuska** a-7, 20. Photo c-6, 8, 9, 11, 13.*

NEW TALENT SHOWCASE (Talent Showcase No. 16 on)
Jan, 1984 - No. 19, Oct, 1985 (Direct sales only)
DC Comics

	Good	Fine	Mint
1-10: Features new strips & artists		.35	.70
11-19 ($1.25): 18-Williamson c(i)		.35	.70

NEW TEEN TITANS, THE (See DC Comics Presents 26, Marvel and DC Present & Teen Titans; Tales of the Teen Titans No. 41 on)
November, 1980 - No. 40, March, 1984
DC Comics

	Good	Fine	Mint
1-Robin, Kid Flash, Wonder Girl, The Changeling, Starfire, The Raven, Cyborg begin; partial origin	3.00	9.00	18.00
2	1.70	5.00	10.00
3-Origin Starfire; Intro The Fearsome 5	1.35	4.00	8.00
4-Origin continues; J.L.A. app.	1.35	4.00	8.00
5,6: 6-Raven origin	.85	2.50	5.00
7-10: 7-Cyborg origin. 8-Origin Kid Flash retold. 10-Origin Changeling retold	.70	2.00	4.00
11,12	.50	1.50	3.00
13-15: 13-Return of Madame Rouge & Capt. Zahl; Robotman revived. 14-Return of Mento; origin Doom Patrol. 15-Death of Madame Rouge & Capt. Zahl	.35	1.00	2.00
16-1st app. Capt. Carrot (free 16 pg. preview)	.25	.75	1.50
17-19: 18-Return of Starfire. 19-Hawkman teams-up	.25	.75	1.50
20-Marv Wolfman & George Perez kidnapped in story	.25	.75	1.50
21-23: 21-Intro Night Force in free 16 pg. insert; intro Brother Blood. 23-1st app. Vigilante (not in costume), & Blackfire	.35	1.00	2.00
24-Omega Men app.	.35	1.00	2.00
25-30: 25-Omega Men cameo. 26-1st Terra. 29-The New Brotherhood of Evil & Speedy app. 30-Terra joins the Titans	.35	1.00	2.00
31-40: 38-Origin Wonder Girl. 39-Kid Flash quits		.50	1.00
Annual 1(11/82)-Omega Men app.	.25	.75	1.50
Annual 2(9/83)-1st app. Vigilante in costume		.50	1.00
Annual 3(1984)-Death of Terra		.50	1.00
nn(11/83-Keebler Co. Giveaway)-In cooperation with ''The President's Drug Awareness Campaign.''		.60	1.20
nn-(re-issue of above on Mando paper for direct sales market); America Soft Drink Ind. version; I.B.M. Corp. version		.50	1.00

NOTE: ***Perez** a-1-4p, 6-40p, Annual 1p, 2p; c-1-12, 13-17p, 18-21, 22p, 23p, 24-37, 38,39(painted), 40, Annual 1, 2.*

NEW TEEN TITANS, THE
Aug, 1984 - Present ($1.25; deluxe format)
DC Comics

	Good	Fine	Mint
1-New storyline; Perez c/a	1.00	3.00	6.00
2,3	.60	1.75	3.50
4-10: 5-Death of Trigon. 7-9-Origin Lilith. 8-Intro Kole. 10-Kole joins	.35	1.10	2.20
11-29: 13,14-Crisis x-over. 20-Original T. Titans return	.25	.80	1.60
Annual 1 (9/85)-Intro. Vanguard	.35	1.10	2.30
Annual 2 (8/86; $2.50): Byrne c/a; origin Brother Blood; intro new Dr. Light	.50	1.50	3.00

NOTE: ***Perez** c/a 1-6; c-20, 22, 23.*

NEW TERRYTOONS (TV)
6-8/60 - No. 8, 3-5/62; 10/62 - No. 54, 1/79
Dell Publishing Co./Gold Key

	Good	Fine	Mint
1('60-Dell)-Deputy Dawg begins	1.50	4.50	10.00
2-8('62)	.85	2.50	6.00
1(30010-210)(10/62-G.Key, 84 pgs.)-Heckle & Jeckle begins	2.50	7.50	20.00
2(30010-301)-84 pgs.	2.00	6.00	16.00
3-10	.75	2.25	5.00
11-20	.50	1.50	3.00
21-30	.25	.75	1.50

New Mutants #1, © MCG

New Romances #8, © STD

New Teen Titans #5 (3/81), © DC

Nexus #2, © First Comics

Nickel Comics #4, © FAW

Nick Fury #1, © MCG

NEW TERRYTOONS (continued) — Good Fine Mint

31-54 .40 .80

NOTE: *Reprints: No. 4-12, 38, 40, 47. (See March of Comics No. 393, 412, 435)*

NEW TESTAMENT STORIES VISUALIZED
1946 - 1947
Standard Publishing Co.

''New Testament Heroes—Acts of Apostles Visualized, Book I''
''New Testament Heroes—Acts of Apostles Visualized, Book II''
''Parables Jesus Told'' Set.... 10.00 30.00 60.00

NOTE: *All three are contained in a cardboard case, illustrated on front and info about the set.*

NEW TRIUMPH (FEATURING NORTHGUARD)
1986 - Present ($1.75, B&W)
Matrix Graphics

1-4 .30 .90 1.75

NEW TV FUNNIES (See New Funnies)

NEW WAVE, THE
6/10/86 - Present (No. 1-8, bi-weekly, 20 pgs; No. 9-on, monthly)
DC Comics

1-Origin .30 .60
2-8: 6-Origin Megabyte .30 .60
9,10 ($1.50) .25 .75 1.50

NEW YORK CITY OUTLAWS, THE
1986 - Present ($2.00, B&W)
Outlaw Comics

1-3 .35 1.00 2.00

NEW YORK GIANTS (See Thrilling True Story of the Baseball Giants)

NEW YORK STATE JOINT LEGISLATIVE COMMITTEE TO STUDY THE PUBLICATION OF COMICS, THE
1951, 1955
N. Y. State Legislative Document

This document was referenced by Wertham for **Seduction of the Innocent**. Contains numerous repros from comics showing violence, sadism, torture, and sex.
1955 version (196p, No. 37, 2/23/55)-Sold for $180 in 1986

NEW YORK WORLD'S FAIR
1939, 1940 (100 pgs.) (Cardboard covers)
National Periodical Publications

1939-Scoop Scanlon, Superman, Sandman, Zatara, Slam Bradley, Ginger Snap by Bob Kane begin 215.00 645.00 1500.00
1940-Batman, Hourman, Johnny Thunderbolt app. 125.00 375.00 875.00

NOTE: The 1939 edition was published at 25 cents. Since all other comics were 10 cents, it didn't sell. Remaining copies were repriced with 15 cents stickers placed over the 25 cents price. Four variations on the 15 cents stickers known. It was advertised in other DC comics at 25 cents. Everyone who sent a quarter through the mail for it received a free Superman No. 1 or No. 2 to make up the dime difference. The 1940 edition was priced at 15 cents.

NEXT MAN
Feb, 1985 - No. 5, Oct, 1985 ($1.50 cover; Baxter paper)
Comico

1 .50 1.50 3.00
2-5 .30 .90 1.80

NEXUS (Also see First Comics Graphic Novel)
6/81 - No. 6, 3/84; No. 7, 4/85 - Present
(Direct sale only, 36 pgs.; V2/1('83)-printed on Baxter paper)
Capital Comics/First Comics No. 7 on

1-B&W version; magazine size 6.00 18.00 36.00
1-B&W 1981 limited edition; 500 copies printed and signed; same as above except this version has a 2-pg. poster and a pencil sketch on paperboard by Rude 8.00 24.00 48.00
2 (B&W; magazine size) 2.65 8.00 16.00
3 (B&W; magazine size)-Contains 33⅓ rpm record ($2.95 price) 1.10 3.30 6.60
V2/1,2-Color version. 2-Nexus' origin begins .30 1.00 2.00
3-31 .30 1.00 2.00

NOTE: ***Bissette** c-29. **Rude** c-3(B&W), V2/1-22, 24-27; a-1-3, V2/1-7, 8p-16p, 18p-22p, 24p-27p.*

NICKEL COMICS
1938 (Pocket size - 7½x5½'') (132 pages)
Dell Publishing Co.

1-''Bobby & Chip'' by Otto Messmer, Felix the Cat artist. Contains some English reprints 17.00 51.00 120.00

NICKEL COMICS
May, 1940 - No. 8, Aug, 1940 (36 pgs.) (Bi-Weekly) (5 cents)
Fawcett Publications

1-Origin/1st app. Bulletman 70.00 210.00 490.00
2 36.00 108.00 252.00
3 30.00 90.00 210.00
4-The Red Gaucho begins 27.00 81.00 190.00
5-7: 5-Bondage-c 23.00 70.00 160.00
8-World's Fair-c; Bulletman moved to Master Comics No. 7 in Oct. 23.00 70.00 160.00

NOTE: ***Beck** c-5-8. **Jack Binder** c-1-4.*

NICK FURY, AGENT OF SHIELD (See Shield)
6/68 - No. 15, 11/69; No. 16, 11/70 - No. 18, 3/71
Marvel Comics Group

1 1.00 3.00 6.00
2-7; 4-Origin retold .70 2.00 4.00
8-11: 9-Hate Monger begins (ends No. 11). 11-Smith-c .50 1.00
12-Smith c/a .35 1.00 2.00
13-15 .40 .80
16-18-All reprints; 52 pgs. .30 .60

NOTE: ***Adkins** a-3i. **Craig** a-10i. **Sid Greene** a-12i. **Kirby** a-16-18r. **Springer** a-4, 6, 7, 8p, 9, 10p, 11; c-8, 9. **Steranko** a(p)-1-3, 5; c-1-7.*

NICK FURY, AGENT OF SHIELD
Dec, 1983 - No. 2, Jan, 1984 ($2.00; 52 pgs.; Baxter paper)
Marvel Comics Group

1,2-Nick Fury-r; Steranko-c/a .60 1.20

NICK HALIDAY
May, 1956
Argo

1-Daily & Sunday strip-r by Petree 3.00 9.00 21.00

NIGHT BEFORE CHRISTMAS, THE (See March of Comics No. 152)

NIGHTCRAWLER
Nov, 1985 - No. 4, Feb, 1986 (mini-series)(from X-Men)
Marvel Comics Group

1-Cockrum c/a .35 1.00 2.00
2-4 .25 .70 1.40

NIGHT FORCE, THE
Aug, 1982 - No. 14, Sept, 1983
DC Comics

1 .40 .80
2-14: 13-Origin The Baron. 14-Nudity panels .30 .60

NOTE: ***Colan** c/a-1-14p. **Giordano** c-1i, 2i, 4i, 5i, 7i, 12i.*

NIGHTINGALE, THE
1948 (14pgs., 7¼x10¼'', ½B&W) (10 cents)
Henry H. Stansbury Once-A-Time Press, Inc.

(Very Rare)-low distribution; distributed to Westchester County & Bronx, N.Y. only; used in **Seduction of the Innocent**, pg. 312,313 as the 1st and only ''good'' comic book ever

THE NIGHTINGALE (continued) — Good / Fine / Mint

published; ill. by Dong Kingman; 1,500 words of text, printed on high quality paper & no word balloons. Copyright registered 10/22/48, distributed week of 12/5/48. (by Hans Christian Andersen) Estimated value. . . 125.00

NIGHTMARE
Summer, 1952 - No. 2, Fall, 1952; No. 3,4, 1953 (Painted-c)
Ziff-Davis (Approved Comics)/St. John No. 3,4

	Good	Fine	Mint
1-1pg. Kinstler-a; Tuska-a(2)	11.50	34.50	80.00
2-Kinstler-a-Poe's "Pit & the Pendulum"	8.50	25.50	60.00
3-Kinstler-a	8.00	24.00	56.00
4	6.50	19.50	45.00

NIGHTMARE (Formerly Weird Horrors No. 1-9) (Amazing Ghost Stories No. 14 on)
No. 10, Dec, 1953 - No. 13, Aug, 1954
St. John Publishing Co.

	Good	Fine	Mint
10-Reprints Ziff-Davis Weird Thrillers No. 2 with new Kubert-c plus 2 pgs. Kinstler, & Toth-a	14.50	43.50	100.00
11-Krigstein-a; Poe adapt., "Hop Frog"	10.00	30.00	70.00
12-Kubert bondage-c; adaptation of Poe's 'The Black Cat;' Cannibalism story	8.00	24.00	56.00
13-Reprints Z-D Weird Thrillers No. 3 with new cover; Powell-a(2), Tuska-a; Baker-c	5.60	16.50	38.00

NOTE: ***Anderson** a-10. **Colan** a-10.*

NIGHTMARE (Magazine)
Dec, 1970 - No. 23, Feb, 1975 (B&W) (68 pages)
Skywald Publishing Corp.

	Good	Fine	Mint
1-Everett-a	1.00	3.00	6.00
2-5: 4-Decapitation story	.70	2.00	4.00
6-Kaluta-a	.70	2.00	4.00
7,9,10	.50	1.50	3.00
8-Features E. C. movie "Tales From the Crypt;" reprints some E. C. comics panels	1.15	3.50	7.00
11-20: 12-Excessive gore, severed heads. 20-Severed head-c	.35	1.00	2.00
21-(1974 Summer Special)-Kaluta-a	.35	1.00	2.00
22-Tomb of Horror issue	.35	1.00	2.00
23-(1975 Winter Special)	.35	1.00	2.00
Annual 1(1972)	.35	1.00	2.00
Winter Special 1(1973)	.35	1.00	2.00
Yearbook-nn(1974)	.35	1.00	2.00

NOTE: ***Adkins** a-5. **Boris** c-2, 4, 5. **Byrne** a-20p. **Everett** a-4, 5. **Jones** a-6, 21; c-6. **Katz** a-5. **Wildey** a-5, 6,'74 Yearbook. **Wrightson** a-9.*

NIGHTMARE & CASPER (See Harvey Hits No. 71) (Casper & Nightmare No. 6 on)
Aug, 1963 - No. 5, Aug, 1964 (25 cents)
Harvey Publications

	Good	Fine	Mint
1	5.35	16.00	32.00
2-5	2.35	7.00	14.00

NIGHTMARES (See Do You Believe in . . .)

NIGHTMARES
May, 1985 - No. 2, May, 1985 (Baxter paper)
Eclipse Comics

	Good	Fine	Mint
1,2	.30	.90	1.80

NIGHTMASK
Nov, 1986 - Present
Marvel Comics Group

	Good	Fine	Mint
1		.45	.90
2-6		.40	.80

NIGHT MASTERS, THE
1985 - Present ($1.50, B&W)
Custom Pic Comics

	Good	Fine	Mint
1-5	.25	.75	1.50

NIGHT MUSIC
Dec, 1984 - Present ($1.75, Baxter paper)
Eclipse Comics

	Good	Fine	Mint
1-3: 3-Russell's Jungle Book adapt.	.30	.90	1.80
4,5-Pelleas And Melisande (dbl. titled)	.30	.90	1.80
6-Salome' (dbl. titled)	.30	.90	1.80
. . . Graphic Album 1(11/79)	1.35	4.00	8.00

NIGHT NURSE
Nov, 1972 - No. 4, May, 1973
Marvel Comics Group

	Good	Fine	Mint
1-4		.40	.80

NIGHT OF MYSTERY
1953 (no month) (One Shot)
Avon Periodicals

	Good	Fine	Mint
nn-1pg. Kinstler-a, Hollingsworth-c	11.00	33.00	76.00

NIGHT OF THE GRIZZLY, THE (See Movie Classics)

NIGHT RIDER
Oct, 1974 - No. 6, Aug, 1975
Marvel Comics Group

	Good	Fine	Mint
1		.50	1.00
2-6		.30	.60

NOTE: *No. 1-6 reprints Ghost Rider No. 1-6.*

NIGHT STREETS
July, 1986 - Present ($1.50, B&W)
Arrow Comics

	Good	Fine	Mint
1	.35	1.00	2.00
2-Intro Black Dahlia	.25	.75	1.50

NIGHTVEIL (Also see Bill Blacks's Fun Comics)
Nov, 1984 - Present ($1.75 cover)
Americomics

	Good	Fine	Mint
1-6: Bill Black c/a. 4-The Scarlet Scorpion begins	.30	.90	1.80

NIGHTWINGS (See DC Science Fic. Graphic Novel)

NIKKI, WILD DOG OF THE NORTH (See 4-Color No. 1226 & Movie Comics)

1984 (Magazine) (1994 No. 11 on)
June, 1978 - No. 10, Jan, 1980 ($1.50)
Warren Publishing Co.

	Good	Fine	Mint
1	.50	1.50	3.00
2-10	.30	.90	1.80

NOTE: ***Alacla** a-1-3. 5i. **Corben** a-1-8; c-1,2. **Nino** a-1-10, 20(2). **Thorne** a-7-10. **Wood** a-1, 2, 5i.*

1994 (Formerly 1984) (Magazine)
No. 11, Feb, 1980 - No. 29, Feb, 1983
Warren Publishing Co.

	Good	Fine	Mint
11-29: 27-The Warhawks return	.35	1.00	2.00

NOTE: ***Corben** c-26. **Nino** a-11-21, 25, 26, 28; c-21. **Redondo** c-20. **Thorne** a-11-14, 17-21, 25, 26, 28, 29.*

NINJA
Oct, 1986 - Present ($1.80, B&W)
Eternity Comics

	Good	Fine	Mint
1-3	.30	.90	1.80

NINJA FUNNIES
Oct, 1986 - Present ($1.40, B&W, 28 pgs.)
Eternity Comics

Nightmare #11, © STJ

Night Music #4, © Eclipse

Nightveil #4, © AC

Normalman #7, © Renegade Press

Northwest Mounties #3, © STJ

The Nurses #1, © CBS

NINJA FUNNIES (continued)

	Good	Fine	Mint
1,2	.25	.75	1.50

NIPPY'S POP
1917 (Sunday strip reprints-B&W) (10½x13½")
The Saalfield Publishing Co.

32 pages	4.35	13.00	30.00

NOAH'S ARK
1973 (35-49 Cents)
Spire Christian Comics/Fleming H. Revell Co.

By Al Hartley		.40	.80

NOMAN
Nov, 1966 - No. 2, March, 1967 (68 pgs.)
Tower Comics

1-Wood/Williamson-c; Lightning begins; Dynamo cameo; Kane-a(p)	1.50	4.50	10.00
2-Wood-c only; Dynamo x-over; Whitney-a-No. 1,2	.85	2.50	6.00

NONE BUT THE BRAVE (See Movie Classics)

NOODNIK COMICS (See Pinky the Egghead)
1953; No. 2, Feb, 1954 - No. 5, Aug, 1954
Comic Media/Mystery/Biltmore

3-D(1953-Comic Media)(No.1)	17.00	50.00	120.00
2-5	1.75	5.25	12.00

NORMALMAN
1/84 - No. 8, 1985; No. 9, 6/85 - Present
Aardvark-Vanaheim/Renegade Press No. 9 on

1-5 ($1.70)	.35	1.10	2.20
6-12 ($2.00): 8-Star Wars parody	.40	1.20	2.40
Annual 1-(3-D)	.40	1.25	2.50

NORTH TO ALASKA (See 4-Color No. 1155)

NORTHWEST MOUNTIES (Also see Approved Comics)
Oct, 1948 - No. 4, July, 1949
Jubilee Publications/St. John

1-Rose of the Yukon by Matt Baker; Walter Johnson-a; Lubbers-c	14.50	43.50	100.00
2-Baker-a; Lubbers-c. Ventrilo app.	11.00	33.00	76.00
3-Bondage-c, Baker-a; Sky Chief, K-9 app.	11.50	34.50	80.00
4-Baker-c, 2 pgs.; Blue Monk app.	11.50	34.50	80.00

NO SLEEP 'TIL DAWN (See 4-Color No. 831)

NOT BRAND ECHH (Brand Echh No. 1-4)
Aug, 1967 - No. 13, May, 1969 (No. 9-13: 68 pages)
Marvel Comics Group

1	1.25	3.75	7.50
2-4: 3-Origin Thor, Hulk & Capt. America; Monkees, Alfred E. Neuman cameo. 4-X-Men app.	.75	2.25	4.50
5-Origin & intro. Forbush Man	.65	1.90	3.80
6-8: 7-Origin Fantastical-4 & Stuporman. 8-Beatles cameo; X-Men satire	.65	1.90	3.80
9-13-All Giants. 9-Beatles cameo. 10-All-r; The Old Witch, Crypt Keeper & Vault Keeper cameos. 12,13-Beatles cameo, Avengers satire No. 12	.45	1.40	2.80

NOTE: ***Colan** a-4p, 5p, 8p. **Everett** a-1i. **Kirby** a(p)-1,3,5-7,10; c-1. **Severin** a-1; c-3, 7, 8. **Sutton** a-4, 5i, 7i, 8; c-5. Archie satire-No. 9.*

NO TIME FOR SERGEANTS (TV)
No. 914, July, 1958 - No. 3, Aug-Oct, 1965
Dell Publishing Co.

4-Color 914 (Movie)-Toth-a	5.00	15.00	35.00
1(2-4/65)-3 (TV)	1.50	4.50	10.00

NOVA (The Man Called. . . No. 22-25)
Sept, 1976 - No. 25, May, 1979
Marvel Comics Group

	Good	Fine	Mint
1-Origin	.45	1.40	2.80
2,3		.60	1.20
4-10		.35	.70
11-20: Nick Fury & Shield app. No. 15-18		.25	.50
21-25: 21,22-The Comet (MLJ) app.		.25	.50

NOTE: ***Austin** c-21i, 23i. **John Buscema** a(p)-1, 2, 3p, 8p, 21; c-1p, 2, 15. **Infantino** a(p)-15-20, 22-25; c-17-20, 21p, 23p, 24p. **Kirby** c-4p, 5, 7. **Nebres** c-25i. **Simonson** a-23i.*

NOW AGE ILLUSTRATED (See Pendulum Ill. Classics)

NUKLA
Oct-Dec, 1965 - No. 4, Sept, 1966
Dell Publishing Co.

1-Origin Nukla	1.15	3.50	8.00
2,3	.75	2.25	5.00
4-Ditko-a, c(p)	.85	2.50	6.00

NURSE BETSY CRANE (Formerly Teen Secret Diary)
Aug, 1961 - No. 27, Mar, 1964
Charlton Comics

V2No.12-27		.60	1.20

NURSE HELEN GRANT (See The Romances of. . .)

NURSE LINDA LARK (See Linda Lark)

NURSERY RHYMES
1950 - No. 10, July-Aug, 1951
Ziff-Davis Publ. Co. (Approved Comics)

2	4.50	13.50	31.00
3-10: 10-Howie Post-a	2.65	8.00	18.00

NURSES, THE (TV)
April, 1963 - No. 3, Oct, 1963 (All photo-c)
Gold Key

1	1.50	4.50	10.00
2,3	.85	2.50	6.00

NUTS! (Satire)
March, 1954 - No. 5, Nov, 1954
Premiere Comics Group

1-Hollingsworth-a	5.00	15.00	35.00
2,4,5: 5-Capt. Marvel parody	3.50	10.50	24.00
3-Drug "reefers" mentioned	4.35	13.00	30.00

NUTS (Magazine) (Satire)
Feb, 1958 - No. 2, April, 1958
Health Knowledge

1	2.00	6.00	14.00
2	1.35	4.00	9.00

NUTS & JOLTS (See Large Feat. Comic No. 22)

NUTSY SQUIRREL (Formerly Hollywood Funny Folks)
(Also see Comic Cavalcade)
No. 61, 9-10/54 - No. 69, 1-2/56; No. 70, 8-9/56 - No. 71, 10-11/56; No. 72, 11/57
National Periodical Publications

61-Mayer-a; Grossman-a in all	2.35	7.00	16.00
62-72: Mayer a-62,65,67-72	1.15	3.50	8.00

NUTTY COMICS
Winter, 1946
Fawcett Publications

1-Capt. Kidd story; 1pg. Wolverton-a	5.75	17.25	40.00

NUTTY COMICS
1945 - No. 8, June-July, 1947
Home Comics (Harvey Publications)

	Good	Fine	Mint
nn-Helpful Hank, Bozo Bear & others	3.00	9.00	21.00
2-4	2.00	6.00	14.00
5-8: 5-Rags Rabbit begins; infinity-c	1.50	4.50	10.00

NUTTY LIFE
No. 2, Summer, 1946
Fox Features Syndicate

2	2.65	8.00	18.00

NYOKA, THE JUNGLE GIRL (Formerly Jungle Girl; see Master)
No. 2, Winter, 1945 - No. 77, June, 1953 (Movie serial)
Fawcett Publications

2	28.00	84.00	195.00
3	16.50	50.00	115.00
4,5	13.00	40.00	90.00
6-10	9.50	28.50	66.00
11,13,14,16-18-Krigstein-a	10.00	30.00	70.00
12,15,19,20	8.00	24.00	56.00
21-30	5.00	15.00	35.00
31-40	3.65	11.00	25.00
41-50	2.85	8.50	20.00
51-60	2.15	6.50	15.00
61-77	1.70	5.00	11.50

NOTE: *Photo-c from movies 25-70. Bondage c-4, 5, 8.*

NYOKA, THE JUNGLE GIRL (Formerly Zoo Funnies; Space Adventures No. 23 on)
No. 14, Nov, 1955 - No. 22, Nov, 1957
Charlton Comics

14	2.35	7.00	16.00
15-22	1.70	5.00	11.50

OAKY DOAKS
July, 1942 (One Shot)
Eastern Color Printing Co.

1	11.00	33.00	76.00

OAKLAND PRESS FUNNYBOOK, THE
9/17/78 - 4/13/80 (16 pgs.) (Weekly)
Full color in comic book form; changes to tabloid size 4/20/80-on
The Oakland Press

Contains Tarzan by Manning, Marmaduke, Bugs Bunny, etc. (low distribution); 9/23/79 - 4/13/80 contain Buck Rogers by Gray Morrow & Jim Lawrence	.30	.80	1.60

OBIE
1953 (6 cents)
Store Comics

1	.70	2.00	4.00

OBNOXIO THE CLOWN
April, 1983 (One Shot) (From Crazy Magazine)
Marvel Comics Group

1-Vs. the X-Men		.30	.60

OCCULT FILES OF DR. SPEKTOR, THE
4/73 - No. 24, 2/77; No. 25, 5/82 (Painted-c No. 1-24)
Gold Key/Whitman No. 25 on

1-1st app. Lakota; Baron Tibor begins	.70	2.00	4.00
2-5	.35	1.00	2.00
6-10	.25	.75	1.50
11-13: 11-1st app. Spektor as Werewolf		.50	1.00
14-Dr. Solar app.		.50	1.00

	Good	Fine	Mint
15-25: 25-Reprints		.50	1.00
9(Modern Comics reprint, 1977)		.15	.30

NOTE: *Also see Dan Curtis, Golden Comics Digest 33, Mystery Comics Digest 5, & Spine Tingling Tales.*

OCTOBERFEST
Fall, 1976 (One shot)
Now & Then Publs.

1-Print run 3000, pre-Cerebus Dave Sims	1.00	3.00	6.00

ODELL'S ADVENTURES IN 3-D (See Adventures in . . .)

OFFICIAL CRISIS INDEX, THE
March, 1986
Independent Comics Group (Eclipse)

1	.30	.90	1.80

OFFICIAL CRISIS ON INFINITE EARTHS CROSSOVER INDEX, THE
July, 1986
Independent Comics Group (Eclipse)

1	.30	.90	1.80

OFFICIAL DOOM PATROL INDEX, THE
Feb, 1986 - No. 2, Mar, 1986 (2 part series)
Independent Comics Group (Eclipse)

1,2	.25	.75	1.50

OFFICIAL HANDBOOK OF THE CONAN UNIVERSE, THE
June, 1985 (One Shot)
Marvel Comics Group

1		.65	1.30

OFFICIAL HANDBOOK OF THE MARVEL UNIVERSE, THE
Jan, 1983 - No. 15, May, 1984
Marvel Comics Group

1-Lists Marvel heroes & villains (letter A)	1.00	3.00	6.00
2 (B-C)	.75	2.25	4.50
3-5: 3-(C-D). 4-(D-G). 5-(H-J).	.60	1.75	3.50
6-9: 6-(K-L). 7-(M). 8-(N-P). 9-(Q-S)	.45	1.40	2.80
10-12: 10-(S). 11-(S-U). 12-(U-Z)	.40	1.20	2.40
13-15: 13,14-Book of the Dead. 15-Weaponry catalogue	.35	1.00	2.00

NOTE: ***Byrne** c/a(p)-1-14; c-15p. **Grell** a-9. **Layton** a-2, 5, 7. **Miller** a-2, 3. **Nebres** a-3, 4, 8. **Simonson** a-11. **Paul Smith** a-1-3, 6, 7, 9, 10, 12. **Starlin** a-7. **Steranko** a-8p.*

OFFICIAL HANDBOOK OF THE MARVEL UNIVERSE, THE
Dec, 1985 - Present ($1.50 cover; maxi-series)
Marvel Comics Group

1(V2/1)	.40	1.25	2.50
2-5	.35	1.00	2.00
6-10	.30	.90	1.80
11-18	.25	.80	1.60

OFFICIAL JUSTICE LEAGUE OF AMERICA INDEX, THE
April, 1986 - No. 7, 1987 ($2.00, Baxter)
Independent Comics Group (Eclipse)

1-7	.30	.90	1.80

OFFICIAL MARVEL INDEX TO MARVEL TEAM-UP
Jan, 1986 - Present
Marvel Comics Group

1-3		.65	1.30

OFFICIAL MARVEL INDEX TO THE AMAZING SPIDER-MAN
Apr, 1985 - No. 9, Dec, 1985
Marvel Comics Group

Nyoka, the Jungle Girl #25, © FAW

Occult Files of Dr. Spektor #14, © GK

Official Doom Patrol Index #1, © Eclipse

Official True Crime Cases #25, © MCG

Okay Comics #1 (7/40), © UFS

Omega Men #11, © DC

OFFICIAL MARVEL INDEX. . . (continued)

	Good	Fine	Mint
1	.25	.75	1.50
2-9		.65	1.30

OFFICIAL MARVEL INDEX TO THE FANTASTIC FOUR
Dec, 1985 - No. 12, Dec?, 1986
Marvel Comics Group

	Good	Fine	Mint
1-12		.65	1.30

OFFICIAL MARVEL INDEX TO THE X-MEN
Mar, 1987 - Present
Marvel Comics Group

	Good	Fine	Mint
1	.50	1.50	2.95

OFFICIAL SOUPY SALES COMIC (See Soupy Sales)

OFFICIAL TEEN TITANS INDEX, THE
Aug, 1985 - No. 5, 1986 ($1.50 cover)
Independent Comics Group (Eclipse)

	Good	Fine	Mint
1-5	.25	.75	1.50

OFFICIAL TRUE CRIME CASES (Formerly Sub-Mariner No. 23; All-True Crime Cases No. 26 on)
No. 24, Fall, 1947 - No. 25, Winter, 1947-48
Marvel Comics (OCI)

	Good	Fine	Mint
24(No.1)-Burgos-a	4.00	12.00	28.00
25-Kurtzman's "Hey Look"	3.50	10.50	24.00

OF SUCH IS THE KINGDOM
1955 (36 pgs., 15¢)
George A. Pflaum

	Good	Fine	Mint
nn-R-/1951 Treasure Chest	1.00	3.00	7.00

O.G. WHIZ
2/71 - No. 6, 5/72; No. 7, 5/78 - No. 11, 1/79 (No. 7-52 pgs.)
Gold Key

	Good	Fine	Mint
1,2-John Stanley scripts	3.65	11.00	25.00
3-6(1972)	1.50	4.50	10.00
7-11('78-'79)-Part-r: 9-Tubby app.	.60	1.75	3.50

OH, BROTHER! (Teen Comedy)
Jan, 1953 - No. 5, Oct, 1953
Stanhall Publ.

	Good	Fine	Mint
1	1.75	5.25	12.00
2-5	1.00	3.00	7.00

OH SKIN-NAY!
1913
P.F. Volland & Co.

	Good	Fine	Mint
nn-The Days Of Real Sport by Briggs	7.00	21.00	50.00

OH SUSANNA (See 4-Color No. 1105)

OKAY COMICS
July, 1940
United Features Syndicate

	Good	Fine	Mint
1-Captain & the Kids & Hawkshaw the Detective reprints	13.50	40.50	95.00

OK COMICS
July, 1940 - No. 2, Oct, 1940
United Features Syndicate

	Good	Fine	Mint
1-Little Giant, Phantom Knight, Sunset Smith, & The Teller Twins begin	23.00	70.00	160.00
2 (Rare)-Origin Mister Mist	23.00	70.00	160.00

OKLAHOMA KID
June, 1957 - No. 4, 1958
Ajax/Farrell Publ.

	Good	Fine	Mint
1	2.35	7.00	16.00
2-4	1.15	3.50	8.00

OKLAHOMAN, THE (See 4-Color No. 820)

OLD GLORY COMICS
1944 (Giveaway)
Chesapeake & Ohio Railway

	Good	Fine	Mint
Capt. Fearless reprint	2.35	7.00	16.00

OLD IRONSIDES (See 4-Color No. 874)

OLD YELLER (See 4-Color No. 869, Movie Comics, and Walt Disney Showcase No. 25)

OMAC (One Man Army, . . . Corps. No. 4 on)
Sept-Oct, 1974 - No. 8, Nov-Dec, 1975
National Periodical Publications

	Good	Fine	Mint
1-Origin		.40	.80
2-8: 8-2pg. Adams ad		.25	.50

NOTE: ***Kirby*** *a-1-8p; c-1-7p.* ***Kubert*** *c-8. See Kamandi No. 59 & Cancelled Comic Cavalcade.*

O'MALLEY AND THE ALLEY CATS
April, 1971 - No. 9, Jan, 1974 (Disney)
Gold Key

	Good	Fine	Mint
1	1.00	3.00	6.00
2-9	.50	1.50	3.00

OMEGA MEN, THE
Dec, 1982 - No. 38, May, 1986 ($1.00-$1.50; Baxter paper)
DC Comics

	Good	Fine	Mint
1	.35	1.10	2.20
2-Origin Broot	.30	.90	1.80
3-30: 7-Origin The Citadel. 26,27-Alan Moore scripts. 30-Intro new Primus	.25	.70	1.40
31-38: 31-Crisis x-over. 34,35-Teen Titans x-over		.50	1.00
Annual 1(11/84, 52 pgs.)	.30	.90	1.80
Annual 2(11/85, 52 pgs.)	.30	.90	1.80

NOTE: ***Giffen*** *c/a-1-6p.* ***Morrow*** *a-24r.* ***Nino*** *a-16, 21; c-16.*

OMEGA THE UNKNOWN
March, 1976 - No. 10, Oct, 1977
Marvel Comics Group

	Good	Fine	Mint
1		.40	.80
2-10: 2-Hulk app. 3-Electro app.		.30	.60

NOTE: ***Kane*** *c(p)-3, 5, 8, 9.* ***Mooney*** *a-1-3, 4p, 5, 6p, 7, 8i, 9, 10.*

ONE, THE
July, 1985 - No. 6, Feb, 1986 (mini-series; adults only)
Epic Comics (Marvel)

	Good	Fine	Mint
1-Post nuclear holocaust super-hero	.35	1.00	2.00
2-6: 2-Intro. The Other	.25	.75	1.50

ONE HUNDRED AND ONE DALMATIANS (See 4-Color No. 1183, Movie Comics, and Walt Disney Showcase No. 9,51)

100 PAGES OF COMICS
1937 (Stiff covers; square binding)
Dell Publishing Co.

	Good	Fine	Mint
101(Found on back cover)-Alley Oop, Wash Tubbs, Capt. Easy, Og Son of Fire, Apple Mary, Tom Mix, Dan Dunn, Tailspin Tommy, Doctor Doom	40.00	120.00	250.00

100-PAGE SUPER SPECTACULAR (See DC. . .)

$1,000,000 DUCK (See Walt Disney Showcase No. 5)

ONE MILLION YEARS AGO (Tor No. 2 on)
September, 1953

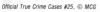

ONE MILLION YEARS AGO (continued)
St. John Publishing Co.

	Good	Fine	Mint
1-Origin; Kubert-a	15.00	45.00	105.00

ONE SHOT (See 4-Color. . .)

1001 HOURS OF FUN (See Large Feature Comic No. 13)

ON STAGE (See 4-Color No. 1336)

ON THE AIR
1947 (Giveaway) (paper cover)
NBC Network Comic

(Rare)	8.00	24.00	56.00

ON THE DOUBLE (See 4-Color No. 1232)

ON THE LINKS
December, 1926 (48 pages) (9x10'')
Associated Feature Service

Daily strip-r	5.00	15.00	35.00

ON THE ROAD WITH ANDRAE CROUCH
1973, 1977 (39 cents)
Spire Christian Comics (Fleming H. Revell)

nn		.50	1.00

ON THE SPOT (Pretty Boy Floyd. . .)
Fall, 1948
Fawcett Publications

nn-Bondage-c	9.00	27.00	62.00

OPERATION BIKINI (See Movie Classics)

OPERATION BUCHAREST (See The Crusaders)

OPERATION CROSSBOW (See Movie Classics)

OPERATION PERIL
Oct-Nov, 1950 - No. 16, Apr-May, 1953
American Comics Group (Michel Publ.)

1-Time Travelers, Danny Danger (by Leonard Starr) & Typhoon Tyler (by Ogden Whitney) begin	6.50	19.50	45.00
2	4.00	12.00	28.00
3-5: 3-Horror story	3.65	11.00	25.00
6-12-Last Time Travelers	3.15	9.50	22.00
13-16: All war format	1.35	4.00	9.00

NOTE: ***Starr*** *a-2.* ***Whitney*** *a-1,2,6,8-10; c-1,8,9.*

ORACLE PRESENTS
Sum?, 1986 - Present (B&W)
Oracle Comics

1 (8¼x10¾'')-Topaz app.		.50	1.00
2 (Reg. size)-The Critter Corps app.		.50	1.00

ORAL ROBERTS' TRUE STORIES (Junior Partners No. 120 on)
1956 (no month) - No. 119, 7/59 (15¢)(No No., 102: 25¢)
TelePix Publ. (Oral Roberts' Evangelistic Assoc./Healing Waters)

V1No.1(1956)-(Not code approved)-''The Miracle Touch''	5.00	15.00	35.00
102-(only issue approved by code)(10/56)	3.00	9.00	21.00
103-119: 115-(114 on inside)	2.00	6.00	14.00

NOTE: *Also see Happiness & Healing For You.*

ORANGE BIRD, THE
No date (1980) (36 pgs.; in color; slick cover)
Walt Disney Educational Media Co.

Included with educational kit on foods		.30	.60

ORIGINAL E-MAN AND MICHAEL MAUSER, THE
Oct, 1985 - No. 7, April, 1986 ($1.75 cover; Baxter paper)
First Comics

	Good	Fine	Mint
1-Has r-/Charlton's E-Man & Vengeance Squad	.35	1.00	2.00
2-6	.30	.90	1.80
7 ($2.00; 44 pgs.)-Staton-a	.35	1.00	2.00

ORIGINAL SHIELD, THE
April, 1984 - No. 4, Oct, 1984
Archie Enterprises, Inc.

1-Origin Shield		.35	.70
2-4		.35	.70

ORIGINAL SWAMP THING SAGA, THE (See DC Spec. Series No.2,14)

OSCAR COMICS (Formerly Funny Tunes; Awful. . . No. 11 & 12)
No. 24, Spring, 1947 - No. 10, Apr, 1949; No. 13, Oct, 1949
Marvel Comics

24(1947)	3.00	9.00	21.00
25(Sum, '47)-Wolverton-a plus Kurtzman's ''Hey Look''	5.50	16.50	38.00
3-9,13: 8-Margie app.	2.15	6.50	15.00
10-Kurtzman's ''Hey Look''	3.35	10.00	23.00

OSWALD THE RABBIT (Also see New Fun Comics No. 1)
No. 21, 1943 - No. 1268, 12-2/61-62 (Walter Lantz)
Dell Publishing Co.

4-Color 21(1943)	16.50	49.50	115.00
4-Color 39(1943)	11.50	34.50	80.00
4-Color 67(1944)	8.00	24.00	56.00
4-Color 102(1946)-Kelly-a, 1 pg.	8.00	24.00	56.00
4-Color 143,183	3.35	10.00	23.00
4-Color 225,273	2.15	6.50	15.00
4-Color 315,388	1.30	4.00	9.00
4-Color 458,507,549,593	.85	2.50	6.00
4-Color 623,697,792,894,979,1268	.75	2.25	5.00

OSWALD THE RABBIT (See March of Comics No. 7, 38, 53, 67, 81, 95, 111, 126, 141, 156, 171, 186, & Super Book No. 8, 20)

OUR ARMY AT WAR (Sgt. Rock No. 302 on)
Aug, 1952 - No. 301, Feb, 1977
National Periodical Publications

1	26.00	78.00	182.00
2	13.00	40.00	90.00
3	12.00	35.00	84.00
4-Krigstein-a	12.00	35.00	84.00
5-7	5.85	17.50	40.00
8-11,14-Krigstein-a	6.75	20.00	47.00
12,15-20	4.35	13.00	30.00
13-Krigstein c/a	7.00	21.00	50.00
21-30	3.35	10.00	23.00
31-40	2.35	7.00	16.00
41-60	2.00	6.00	14.00
61-70	1.20	3.50	8.00
71-80	1.00	3.00	7.00
81-1st Sgt. Rock app. by Andru & Esposito in Easy Co. story	12.00	35.00	75.00
82-Sgt. Rock cameo in Easy Co. story (6 panels)	4.20	12.50	25.00
83-1st Kubert Sgt. Rock	7.00	21.00	42.00
84,86-90	2.50	7.50	15.00
85-1st app. & origin Ice Cream Soldier	2.75	8.00	20.00
91-All Sgt. Rock issue	3.50	10.00	20.00
92-100: 92-1st app. Bulldozer. 95-1st app. Zack	1.00	3.00	6.00

Operation Peril #3, © ACG

Oscar Comics #9, © MCG

Our Army at War #1, © DC

Our Fighting Forces #27, © DC

Our Flag Comics #1, © ACE

Our Gang Comics #11, © DELL

OUR ARMY AT WAR (continued)	Good	Fine	Mint
101-120: 101-1st app. Buster. 111-1st app. Wee Willie & Sunny. 113-1st app. Jackie Johnson. 118-Sunny dies. 120-1st app. Wildman	.85	2.50	5.00
121-127,129-150: 126-1st app. Canary. 139-1st app. Little Sure Shot	.70	2.00	4.00
128-Training & origin Sgt. Rock	.85	2.50	5.00
151-Intro. Enemy Ace by Kubert	.85	2.50	5.00
152-157,159-163,165-170: 153,155-Enemy Ace stories. 157-Two pg. pin-up. 162,163-Viking Prince x-over in Sgt. Rock	.70	2.00	4.00
158-1st app. & origin Iron Major(1965), formerly Iron Captain	.85	2.50	5.00
164-Giant G-19	.85	2.50	5.00
171-176,178-181	.25	.75	1.50
177-(80 pg. Giant G-32)	.35	1.00	2.00
182,183,186-Adams-a; 186-Origin retold	.70	2.00	4.00
184,185,187-189,191-199: 184-Wee Willie dies. 189-Intro. The Teen-age Underground Fighters of Unit 3		.50	1.00
190-(80 pg. Giant G-44)	.25	.75	1.50
200-12 pg. Rock story told in verse; Evans-a		.50	1.00
201-Krigstein-r/No. 14		.50	1.00
202,206-215		.35	.70
203-(80 pg. Giant G-56)-All-r, no Sgt. Rock		.50	1.00
204,205-All-r, no Sgt. Rock		.35	.70
216-(80 pg. Giant G-68)		.50	1.00
217-228		.35	.70
229-(80 pg. Giant G-80)		.50	1.00
230-239,241		.30	.60
240-Adams-a		.60	1.20
242-(50¢ ish. DC-9)-Kubert-c		.50	1.00
243-248,250-301		.30	.60
249-Wood-a		.50	1.00

NOTE: ***Alcala*** *a-251.* ***Drucker*** *a-27, 67, 68, 79, 82, 83, 96, 164, 177, 203, 212, 243r, 244, 269r, 275r, 280r.* ***Evans*** *a-165-175, 200, 266, 269, 270, 274, 276, 278, 280.* ***Glanzman*** *a-218, 220, 222, 223, 225, 227, 230-32, 238, 240, 241, 244, 247, 248, 256-59, 261, 265-67, 271, 282, 283, 298.* ***Grell*** *a-287.* ***Heath*** *a-50, & most 176-271.* ***Kubert*** *a-38,59, 67, 68 & most issues from 83-165.* ***Maurer*** *a-233, 237, 239, 240, 280, 284, 288, 290, 291, 295.* ***Severin*** *a-251-53, 260, 261, 265-67, 269r, 272.* ***Toth*** *a-235, 241, 254.* ***Wildey*** *a-283-85, 287p.*

OUR FIGHTING FORCES
Oct-Nov, 1954 - No. 181, Sept-Oct, 1978
National Periodical Publications/DC Comics

Issue	Good	Fine	Mint
1-Grandenetti c/a	20.00	60.00	140.00
2	10.00	30.00	70.00
3-Kubert c	8.35	25.00	58.00
4,5	6.00	18.00	42.00
6-9	4.35	13.00	30.00
10-Wood-a	6.75	20.00	47.00
11-20	2.75	8.00	19.00
21-30	2.00	6.00	14.00
31-40	1.50	4.50	10.00
41-44: 41-Unknown Soldier tryout	1.20	3.50	8.00
45-Gunner & Sarge begin (ends No. 94)	5.00	15.00	30.00
46-58: 58-Last 10¢ issue	.70	2.00	4.00
59-90	.55	1.60	3.20
91-100: 95-Devil-Dog begins, ends No. 98. 99-Capt. Hunter begins, ends No. 106	.35	1.00	2.00
101-122: 106-Hunters Hellcats begin. 116-Mlle. Marie app. 121-Intro. Heller		.50	1.00
123-Losers (Capt. Storm, Gunner/Sarge, Johnny Cloud) begin		.40	.80
124-132,138-145,147-181		.30	.60
133,135-137 (48-52 pgs.)		.30	.60
134,146-Toth-a		.30	.60

NOTE: ***Adams*** *c-147.* ***Drucker*** *a-28, 37, 39, 42-44, 49, 133r.* ***Evans*** *a-149, 164-73, 177-81.* ***Glanzman*** *a-125-28, 132, 134, 138-41, 143, 144.* ***Heath*** *a-2, 16, 18, 28, 41, 44, 49, 114, 135r, 138r.* ***Kirby*** *a-151-162p; c-152-159.* ***Kubert*** *c/a in many issues.* ***Maurer*** *a-135.* ***Redondo*** *a-166.* ***Severin*** *a-123-30, 131i, 132-50.*

OUR FIGHTING MEN IN ACTION (See Men In Action)

OUR FLAG COMICS
Aug, 1941 - No. 5, April, 1942
Ace Magazines

Issue	Good	Fine	Mint
1-Captain Victory, The Unknown Soldier & The Three Cheers begin	75.00	225.00	525.00
2-Origin The Flag	33.00	100.00	230.00
3-5: 5-Intro & 1st app. Mr. Risk	28.50	85.00	200.00

NOTE: ***Anderson*** *a-1, 4.* ***Mooney*** *a-1, 2.*

OUR GANG COMICS (With Tom & Jerry No. 39-59; becomes Tom & Jerry No. 60 on; based on film characters)
Sept-Oct, 1942 - No. 59, June, 1949
Dell Publishing Co.

Issue	Good	Fine	Mint
1-Our Gang & Barney Bear by Kelly, Tom & Jerry, Pete Smith, Flip & Dip, The Milky Way begin	54.00	162.00	380.00
2	26.00	78.00	180.00
3-5	17.00	51.00	120.00
6-Bumbazine & Albert only app. by Kelly	31.00	92.00	220.00
7-No Kelly story	13.00	40.00	90.00
8-Benny Burro begins by Barks	30.00	90.00	200.00
9-Barks-a(2): Benny Burro & Happy Hound; no Kelly story	24.00	70.00	160.00
10-Benny Burro by Barks	20.00	60.00	130.00
11-1st Barney Bear & Benny Burro by Barks; Happy Hound by Barks	20.00	60.00	130.00
12-20	12.00	36.00	80.00
21-30	9.00	27.00	60.00
31-36-Last Barks issue	6.50	19.50	45.00
37-40	2.65	8.00	18.00
41-50	2.00	6.00	14.00
51-57	1.75	5.25	12.00
58,59-No Kelly art or Our Gang story	1.50	4.50	12.00

NOTE: ***Barks*** *art in part only.* ***Barks*** *did not write Barney Bear stories No. 30-34. (See March of Comics No. 3,26)*

OUR LADY OF FATIMA
3/11/55 (15 cents) (36 pages)
Catechetical Guild Educational Society

Issue	Good	Fine	Mint
395	3.00	9.00	18.00

OUR LOVE (Romantic Affairs No. 3)
Sept, 1949 - No. 2, Jan, 1950
Marvel Comics (SPC)

Issue	Good	Fine	Mint
1	3.35	10.00	23.00
2-Photo-c	1.70	5.00	11.50

OUR LOVE STORY
Oct, 1969 - No. 38, Feb, 1976
Marvel Comics Group

Issue	Good	Fine	Mint
1	.55	1.65	4.00
2-4,6-13: 9-J. Buscema-a	.35	1.00	2.00
5-Steranko-a	1.30	4.00	9.00
14-New story by Gary Fredrich & Tarpe' Mills	.55	1.65	4.00
15-38		.40	.80

OUR MISS BROOKS (See 4-Color No. 751)

OUR SECRET (Formerly My Secret)
No. 4, Dec, 1949 - No. 8, Aug, 1950
Superior Comics Ltd.

Issue	Good	Fine	Mint
4-Kamen-a; spanking scene	3.00	9.00	21.00
5,6,8	2.00	6.00	14.00
7-Contains 9 pg. story intended for unpublished Ellery Queen No. 5	2.85	8.50	20.00

OUTBURSTS OF EVERETT TRUE
1921 (32 pages) (B&W)
Saalfield Publ. Co.

OUTBURSTS OF EVERETT TRUE (continued)

	Good	Fine	Mint
1907 (2-panel strips reprint)	6.50	19.50	45.00

OUTER LIMITS, THE (TV)
Jan-Mar, 1964 - No. 18, Oct, 1969
Dell Publishing Co.

	Good	Fine	Mint
1	2.35	7.00	16.00
2	1.30	4.00	9.00
3-10	.85	2.50	6.00
11-18: 17 reprints No. 1; 18-No. 2	.55	1.65	4.00

OUTER SPACE (Formerly This Mag. Is Haunted, 2nd Series)
May, 1958 - No. 25, Dec, 1959; Nov, 1968
Charlton Comics

	Good	Fine	Mint
17-Williamson/Wood style art; not by them (Sid Check?)	3.00	9.00	21.00
18-20-Ditko-a	4.00	12.00	28.00
21-25: 21-Ditko-c	2.35	7.00	16.00
V2No.1(11/68)-Boyette-c	1.00	3.00	7.00

OUTLAW (See Return of the . . .)

OUTLAW FIGHTERS
Aug, 1954 - No. 5, April, 1955
Atlas Comics (IPC)

	Good	Fine	Mint
1-Tuska-a	3.00	9.00	21.00
2-5: 5-Heath-a, 7pgs.	1.70	5.00	11.50

OUTLAW KID, THE (1st Series; see Wild Western)
Sept, 1954 - No. 19, Sept, 1957
Atlas Comics (CCC No. 1-11/EPI No. 12-29)

	Good	Fine	Mint
1-Origin; The Outlaw Kid & his horse Thunder begin; Black Rider app.	4.65	14.00	32.00
2-Black Rider app.	2.35	7.00	16.00
3-7,9	1.70	5.00	11.50
8-Williamson/Woodbridge-a, 4 pgs.	3.85	11.50	27.00
10-Williamson-a	3.85	11.50	27.00
11-17,19	1.50	4.50	10.00
18-Williamson-a	3.35	10.00	23.00

NOTE: ***Berg*** *a-7, 13.* ***Maneely*** *c-1, 5-8, 11, 12, 18.* ***Severin*** *c-10.* ***Shores*** *a-1.* ***Wildey*** *a-1(3), 4-8, 10-18; c-4.*

OUTLAW KID, THE (2nd Series)
Aug, 1970 - No. 30, Oct, 1975
Marvel Comics Group

	Good	Fine	Mint
1,2-Reprints; Wildey-a		.40	.80
3,9-Williamson-a(r)		.40	.80
4-8		.30	.60
10-Origin Outlaw Kid; new material begins		.25	.50
11-30: 27-Origin r-/No. 10		.25	.50

NOTE: ***Berg*** *a-7.* ***Gil Kane*** *c-10, 11, 15.* ***Roussos*** *a-10i, 27i(r).* ***Severin*** *c-1.* ***Wildey*** *a-1r, 3r, 6r, 7r, 19, 21, 22, 26.* ***Williamson*** *a-28r.*

OUTLAWS
Feb-Mar, 1948 - No. 9, June-July, 1949
D. S. Publishing Co.

	Good	Fine	Mint
1	8.50	25.50	60.00
2-Ingels-a	8.50	25.50	60.00
3,5,6: 3-Not Frazetta	3.35	10.00	23.00
4-Orlando-a	5.50	16.50	38.00
7,8-Ingels-a in each	8.00	24.00	56.00
9-(Scarce)-Frazetta-a, 7 pgs.	26.00	78.00	182.00

NOTE: *No. 3 was printed in Canada with* ***Frazetta*** *art ''Prairie Jinx,'' 7 pgs.* ***McWilliams*** *a-6.*

OUTLAWS, THE (Formerly Western Crime Cases?)
No. 10, May, 1952 - No. 13, Sept, 1953; No. 14, April, 1954
Star Publishing Co.

	Good	Fine	Mint
10-L. B. Cole-c	3.35	10.00	23.00
11-14-L. B. Cole-c. 14-Kamen, Feldstein-a	2.35	7.00	16.00

OUTLAWS OF THE WEST (Formerly Cody of the Pony Express No. 10)
No. 11, 7/57 - No. 81, 5/70; No. 82, 7/79 - No. 88, 4/80
Charlton Comics

	Good	Fine	Mint
11	2.35	7.00	16.00
12,13,15-17,19,20	1.15	3.50	8.00
14-(68 pgs.)(15¢)	1.50	4.50	10.00
18-Ditko-a	3.15	9.50	22.00
21-30	.75	2.25	5.00
31-50	.45	1.35	3.00
51-70: 54-Kid Montana app. 64-Captain Doom begins (1st app.)		.40	.80
71-81: 73-Origin & 1st app. The Sharp Shooter, last app. No. 74. 75-Last Capt. Doom. 80,81-Ditko-a		.40	.80
82-88		.30	.60
64,79(Modern Comics reprint, 1977)		.15	.30

OUTLAWS OF THE WILD WEST
1952 (132 pages) (25¢)
Avon Periodicals

	Good	Fine	Mint
1-Wood back-c; Kubert-a (3 Jesse James-r)	13.50	40.50	95.00

OUT OF SANTA'S BAG (March of Comics No. 10)

OUT OF THE NIGHT (The Hooded Horseman No. 18 on)
Feb-Mar, 1952 - No. 17, Oct-Nov, 1954
American Comics Group (Creston/Scope)

	Good	Fine	Mint
1-Williamson/LeDoux-a, 9 pgs	15.00	45.00	105.00
2-Williamson-a, 5 pgs.	12.00	36.00	84.00
3,5-10: 9-Sci/Fic sty	3.50	10.50	24.00
4-Williamson-a, 7 pgs.	12.00	36.00	84.00
11,12,14-16	2.65	8.00	18.00
13-Nostrand-a	3.35	10.00	23.00
17-E.C. Wood swipe; lingerie panels	2.85	8.50	20.00

NOTE: ***Landau*** *a-14, 16, 17.* ***Shelly*** *a-12.*

OUT OF THE PAST A CLUE TO THE FUTURE
1946? (16 pages) (paper cover)
E. C. Comics (Public Affairs Comm.)

	Good	Fine	Mint
Based on public affairs pamphlet-''What Foreign Trade Means to You''	9.00	27.00	62.00

OUT OF THE SHADOWS
No. 5, July, 1952 - No. 14, Aug, 1954
Standard Comics/Visual Editions

	Good	Fine	Mint
5-Toth-p; Moreira, Tuska-a	6.00	18.00	42.00
6-Toth/Celardo-a	5.00	15.00	35.00
7-Jack Katz-a(2)	3.50	10.50	24.00
8,10	2.65	8.00	18.00
9-Crandall-a(2)	4.65	14.00	32.00
11-Toth-a, 2 pgs.	3.00	9.00	21.00
12-Toth/Peppe-a(2)	6.00	18.00	42.00
13-Cannabalism story	3.75	11.25	26.00
14-Toth-a	4.50	13.50	31.00

NOTE: ***Katz*** *a-6(2), 7(2), 11, 12.* ***Sekowsky*** *a-10, 13.*

OUT OF THIS WORLD
June, 1950 (One Shot)
Avon Periodicals

	Good	Fine	Mint
1-Kubert-a(2) (one reprint/Eerie No. 1-'47) plus Crom the Barbarian by Giunta (origin)	33.00	100.00	230.00

OUT OF THIS WORLD
Aug, 1956 - No. 16, Dec, 1959

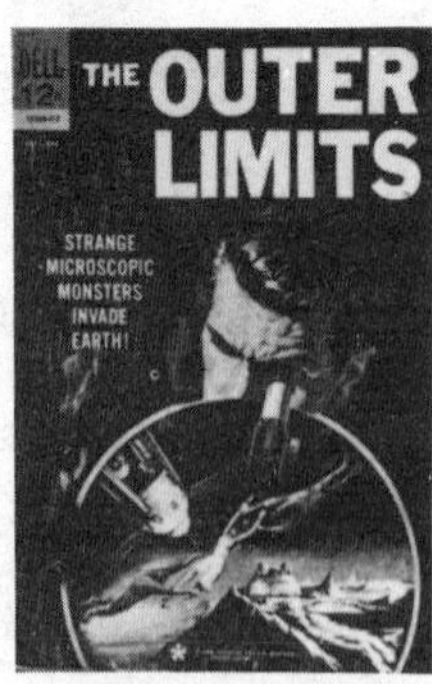

Outer Limits #4, © U. A.

Outlaw Kid #4 (3/55), © MCG

Out of the Night #1, © ACG

The Outsiders #1, © DC

Ozark Ike #18, © STD

Panic #4, © WMG

OUT OF THIS WORLD (continued)
Charlton Comics

	Good	Fine	Mint
1	4.35	13.00	30.00
2	2.15	6.50	15.00
3-6-Ditko-a(4) each	6.50	19.50	45.00
7-(68 pgs.; 15¢)-Ditko-c/a(4)	7.00	21.00	50.00
8-(68 pgs.)-Ditko-a(2)	5.00	15.00	35.00
9-12,16-Ditko-a	4.35	13.00	30.00
13-15	1.30	4.00	9.00

NOTE: ***Ditko*** *c-3-7,11,16.* ***Reinman*** *a-10.*

OUT OUR WAY WITH WORRY WART (See 4-Color No. 680)

OUTSIDERS, THE (Also see Batman & the. . .)
Nov, 1985 - Present
DC Comics

	Good	Fine	Mint
1	.35	1.00	2.00
2-18	.25	.75	1.50
Annual 1 (12/86; $2.50)	.40	1.25	2.50

OUTSTANDING AMERICAN WAR HEROES
1944 (16 pgs.) (paper cover)
The Parents' Institute

	Good	Fine	Mint
nn-Reprints from True Comics	2.35	7.00	14.00

OVERSEAS COMICS (Also see G.I. & Jeep Comics)
1944 (7¼x10¼''; 16 pgs. in color)
Giveaway (Distributed to U.S. armed forces)

	Good	Fine	Mint
23-65-Bringing Up Father, Popeye, Joe Palooka, Dick Tracy, Superman, Gasoline Alley, Buz Sawyer, Li'l Abner, Blondie, Terry & the Pirates, Out Our Way	3.00	9.00	21.00

OWL, THE
April, 1967; No. 2, April, 1968
Gold Key

	Good	Fine	Mint
1,2-Written by Jerry Siegel	.85	2.50	6.00

OXYDOL-DREFT
1950 (Set of 6 pocket-size giveaways; distributed through the mail as a set) (Scarce)
Oxydol-Dreft

	Good	Fine	Mint
1-Li'l Abner, 2-Daisy Mae, 3-Shmoo	6.00	18.00	36.00
4-John Wayne; Williamson/Frazetta-c from John Wayne No. 3	8.00	24.00	48.00
5-Archie	5.00	15.00	30.00
6-Terrytoons Mighty Mouse	4.00	12.00	24.00

NOTE: *Set is worth more with original envelope.*

OZ (See MGM's Marvelous. . ., Marvel Treasury. . ., & First Comics Graphic Novel)

OZARK IKE
Feb, 1948; Nov, 1948 - No. 24, Dec, 1951; No. 25, Sept, 1952
Dell Publishing Co./Standard Comics

	Good	Fine	Mint
4-Color 180(1948-Dell)	5.75	17.25	40.00
B11, B12, 13-15	4.00	12.00	28.00
16-25	3.50	10.50	24.00

OZ-WONDERLAND WAR
Jan, 1986 - No. 3, March, 1986 (mini-series)
DC Comics

	Good	Fine	Mint
1-3	.35	1.00	2.00

OZZIE & BABS (TV Teens No. 14 on)
1947 - No. 13, Fall, 1949
Fawcett Publications

	Good	Fine	Mint
1	3.50	10.50	24.00
2	1.75	5.25	12.00
3-13	1.50	4.50	10.00

OZZIE & HARRIET (See The Adventures of. . .)

PACIFIC COMICS GRAPHIC NOVEL
Sept, 1984
Pacific Comics

	Good	Fine	Mint
1-The Seven Samuroid; Brunner-a	1.00	3.00	6.00

PACIFIC PRESENTS
10/82 - No. 2, 4/83; No. 3, 3/84 - No. 4, 6/84
Pacific Comics

	Good	Fine	Mint
1-The Rocketeer by Stevens app.	.50	1.50	3.00
2-4: 2-Nudity panels. 3-1st Vanity	.25	.75	1.50

NOTE: ***Conard*** *a-3, 4; c-3.* ***Ditko*** *a-1-3.* ***Stevens*** *c/a-1, 2.*

PADRE OF THE POOR
nd (Giveaway) (16 pgs.; paper cover)
Catechetical Guild

	Good	Fine	Mint
	2.35	7.00	14.00

PAGEANT OF COMICS (See Jane Arden & Mopsy)
Sept, 1947 - No. 2, Oct, 1947
Archer St. John

	Good	Fine	Mint
1-Mopsy strip-r	4.00	12.00	28.00
2-Jane Arden strip-r	4.00	12.00	28.00

PANCHO VILLA
1950
Avon Periodicals

	Good	Fine	Mint
nn-Kinstler-c	11.00	33.00	76.00

PANHANDLE PETE AND JENNIFER (TV)
July, 1951 - No. 3, Nov, 1951
J. Charles Laue Publishing Co.

	Good	Fine	Mint
1	2.65	8.00	18.00
2,3	1.75	5.25	12.00

PANIC (Companion to Mad)
Feb-Mar, 1954 - No. 12, Dec-Jan, 1955-56
E. C. Comics

	Good	Fine	Mint
1-Used in Senate Investigation hearings; Elder draws entire E. C. staff	6.00	18.00	42.00
2	5.00	15.00	35.00
3-Senate Subcommittee parody; Davis draws Gaines, Feldstein & Kelly, 1 pg.	3.50	10.50	24.00
4-Infinity-c	3.50	10.50	24.00
5-11	3.00	9.00	21.00
12 (Low distribution; many thousand were destroyed)	4.00	12.00	28.00

NOTE: ***Davis*** *a-1-12; c-12.* ***Elder*** *a-1-12.* ***Feldstein*** *c-1-3,5.* ***Kamen*** *a-1.* ***Orlando*** *a-1-9.* ***Wolverton*** *c-4, panel-3.* ***Wood*** *a-2-9, 11, 12.*

PANIC (Magazine) (Satire)
7/58 - No. 6, 7/59; V2No.10, 12/65 - V2No.12, 1966
Panic Publications

	Good	Fine	Mint
1	1.70	5.00	10.00
2-6	1.20	3.50	7.00
V2No.10-12: Reprints earlier issues	.50	1.50	3.00

NOTE: ***Davis*** *a-3(2 pgs.), 4, 5, 10; c-10.* ***Elder*** *a-5.* ***Powell*** *a-V2No.10.* ***Torres*** *a-1-5.*

PARADAX (Also see Strange Days)
1986 (One Shot)
Eclipse Comics

	Good	Fine	Mint
1	.35	1.00	2.00

PARADE (See Hanna-Barbera. . .)

PARADE COMICS (Frisky Animals on Parade No. 2 on)
Sept, 1957
Ajax/Farrell Publ. (World Famous Publ.)

	Good	Fine	Mint
1	1.15	3.50	8.00

NOTE: *Cover title: Frisky Animals on Parade.*

PARADE OF PLEASURE
1954 (192 pgs.) (Hardback book)
Derric Verschoyle Ltd., London, England

	Good	Fine	Mint
By Geoffrey Wagner. Contains section devoted to the censorship of American comic books with illustrations in color and black and white. (Also see **Seduction of the Innocent**). Distributed in USA by Library Publishers, N. Y.	27.00	80.00	170.00
with dust jacket....	50.00	150.00	340.00

PARAMOUNT ANIMATED COMICS (Also see Harvey Comics Hits No. 60,62)
Feb, 1953 - No. 22, July, 1956
Harvey Publications

	Good	Fine	Mint
1-Baby Huey, Herman & Katnip, Buzzy the Crow begin	9.00	27.00	62.00
2	6.00	18.00	42.00
3-6	5.00	15.00	35.00
7-Baby Huey becomes permanent cover feature; cover title becomes Baby Huey with No. 9	9.00	27.00	62.00
8-10: 9-Infinity-c	4.00	12.00	28.00
11-22	2.65	8.50	18.00

PARENT TRAP, THE (See 4-Color No. 1210)

PAROLE BREAKERS
Dec, 1951 - No. 3, July, 1952
Avon Periodicals/Realistic

	Good	Fine	Mint
1(No.2 on inside)-c-/Avon paperback 283	13.00	40.00	90.00
2-Kubert-a; c-/Avon paperback 114	11.00	33.00	76.00
3-Kinstler-c	9.00	27.00	62.00

PARTRIDGE FAMILY, THE (TV)
March, 1971 - No. 21, Dec, 1973
Charlton Comics

	Good	Fine	Mint
1	1.15	3.50	7.00
2-4,6-21	.70	2.00	4.00
5-Partridge Family Summer Special (52 pgs.); The Shadow, Lone Ranger, Charlie McCarthy, Flash Gordon, Hopalong Cassidy, Gene Autry & others app.	1.00	3.00	6.00

PASSION, THE
1955
Catechetical Guild

	Good	Fine	Mint
394	3.35	10.00	20.00

PAT BOONE (TV)(Also see Superman's Girlfriend Lois Lane No. 9)
Sept-Oct, 1959 - No. 5, May-Jun, 1960
National Periodical Publications

	Good	Fine	Mint
1-Photo-c	12.00	36.00	84.00
2-5: 4-Previews 'Journey To The Center Of The Earth'. 5-Photo-c	9.00	27.00	62.00

PATCHES
Mar-Apr, 1945 - No. 11, Nov, 1947
Rural Home/Patches Publ. (Orbit)

	Good	Fine	Mint
1-L. B. Cole-c	8.00	24.00	56.00
2	4.00	12.00	28.00
3-8,10,11: 5-L.B. Cole-c	3.65	11.00	25.00
9-Leav/Krigstein-a, 16 pgs.	4.35	13.00	30.00

PATHWAYS TO FANTASY
July, 1984
Pacific Comics

	Good	Fine	Mint
1-Barry Smith-c/a; J. Jones-a	.25	.75	1.50

PATORUZU (See Adventures of...)

PATSY & HEDY
Feb, 1952 - No. 110, Feb, 1967
Atlas Comics/Marvel (GPI/Male)

	Good	Fine	Mint
1	4.65	14.00	32.00
2	2.35	7.00	16.00
3-10	2.00	6.00	14.00
11-20	1.30	4.00	9.00
21-40	1.00	3.00	7.00
41-60	.55	1.65	4.00
61-110: 88-Lingerie panel	.30	.80	1.60
Annual 1('63)	1.70	5.00	10.00

PATSY & HER PALS
May, 1953 - No. 29, Aug, 1957
Atlas Comics (PPI)

	Good	Fine	Mint
1	4.00	12.00	28.00
2	2.00	6.00	14.00
3-10	1.70	5.00	11.50
11-29: 24-Everett-c	1.15	3.50	8.00

PATSY WALKER (Also see Girls' Life & Miss America Magazine)
1945 (no month) - No. 124, Dec, 1965
Marvel/Atlas Comics (BPC)

	Good	Fine	Mint
1	13.50	40.50	95.00
2	6.50	19.50	45.00
3-10: 5-Injury-to-eye-c	4.65	14.00	32.00
11,12,15,16,18	2.50	7.50	17.50
13,14,17,19-22-Kurtzman's "Hey Look"	3.75	11.25	26.00
23,24	2.15	6.50	15.00
25-Rusty by Kurtzman; painted-c	3.85	11.50	27.00
26-29,31: 28-31-52 pgs.	1.85	5.50	13.00
30-Egghead Doodle by Kurtzman, 1pg. (52 pgs.)	3.35	10.00	23.00
32-50	1.15	3.50	8.00
51-80	.80	2.40	5.50
81-99	.45	1.35	3.00
100	.50	1.50	3.50
101-124		.60	1.20
Fashion Parade 1('66)-68 pgs.	1.15	3.50	8.00

NOTE: *Lingerie panel-9, 11. Painted c-25-28. 21-Anti-Wertham editorial.*

PAT THE BRAT (Adventures of Pipsqueak No. 34 on)
June, 1953; Summer, 1955 - No. 33, July, 1959
Archie Publications (Radio)

	Good	Fine	Mint
nn(6/53)	5.00	15.00	35.00
1(Summer, 1955)	3.35	10.00	23.00
2-4-(5/56) (No. 5-14 not published)	1.70	5.00	11.50
15-(7/56)-33	1.15	3.50	8.00

PAT THE BRAT COMICS DIGEST MAGAZINE
October, 1980
Archie Publications

	Good	Fine	Mint
1		.50	1.00

PATTY POWERS
No. 4, Oct, 1955 - No. 7, Oct, 1956
Atlas Comics

	Good	Fine	Mint
4	1.75	5.25	12.00
5-7	1.15	3.50	8.00

PAT WILTON (See Mighty Midget Comics)

PAUL
1978 (49 cents)
Spire Christian Comics (Fleming H. Revell Co.)

	Good	Fine	Mint
		.40	.80

Patches #10, © RH

Patsy & Her Pals #2, © MCG

Patsy Walker #20, © MCG

Paul Terry's Comics #113, © MGM

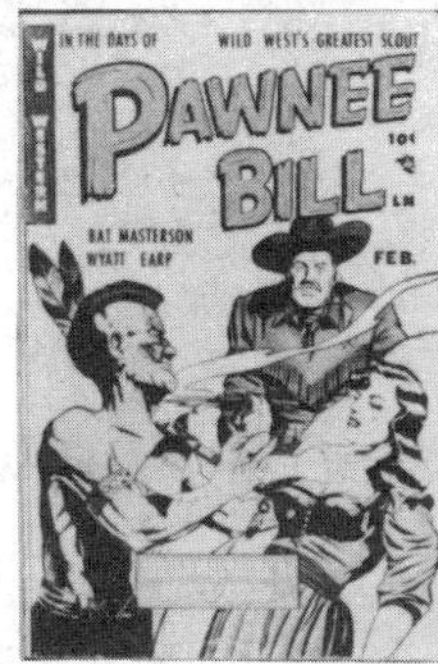

Pawnee Bill #1, © Story

Pebbles Flintstone #1, © Hanna-Barbera

PAULINE PERIL (See The Close Shaves of. . .)

PAUL REVERE'S RIDE (See 4-Color No. 822)

PAUL TERRY'S ADVENTURES OF MIGHTY MOUSE (See Adventures of. . .)

PAUL TERRY'S COMICS (Formerly Terry-Toons Comics; becomes Adventures of Mighty Mouse No. 126 on)
No. 85, Mar, 1951 - No. 125, May, 1955
St. John Publishing Co.

	Good	Fine	Mint
85,86-Same as Terry-Toons No. 85, & 86 with only a title change	3.00	9.00	21.00
87-99	2.00	6.00	14.00
100	2.35	7.00	16.00
101-104,107-125-Mighty Mouse	1.50	4.50	10.00
105,106-Giant Comics Edition, 100pgs. (9/53, ?)	4.65	14.00	32.00

PAUL TERRY'S HOW TO DRAW FUNNY CARTOONS
1940's (14 pages) (Black & White)
Terrytoons, Inc. (Giveaway)

Heckle & Jeckle, Mighty Mouse, etc.	5.00	15.00	30.00

PAUL TERRY'S MIGHTY MOUSE (See Mighty Mouse)

PAUL TERRY'S MIGHTY MOUSE ADVENTURE STORIES
1953 (384 pgs.) (50 cents) (cardboard covers)
St. John Publishing Co.

nn	25.00	75.00	175.00

PAWNEE BILL
Feb, 1951 - No. 3, July, 1951
Story Comics

1-Bat Masterson, Wyatt Earp app.	3.50	10.50	24.00
2,3: 3-Origin Golden Warrior; Cameron-a	1.75	5.25	12.00

PAY-OFF (This Is the. . ., . . . Crime, . . . Detective Stories)
July-Aug, 1948 - No. 5, Mar-Apr, 1949 (52 pages)
D. S. Publishing Co.

1	4.00	12.00	28.00
2	2.65	8.00	18.00
3-5	2.00	6.00	14.00

PEACEMAKER, THE (Also see Fightin' 5)
Mar, 1967 - No. 5, Nov, 1967
Charlton Comics

1-Fightin' Five begins	.30	.90	1.80
2,3,5		.60	1.20
4-Origin The Peacemaker	.30	.80	1.60
1,2(Modern Comics reprint, 1978)		.15	.30

PEANUTS (Charlie Brown) (See Nancy & Sluggo & Fritzi Ritz)
No. 878, 2/58 - No. 13, 5-7/62; 5/63 - No. 4, 2/64
Dell Publishing Co./Gold Key

4-Color 878	3.50	10.50	24.00
4-Color 969,1015('59)	3.00	9.00	21.00
4(2-4/60)	2.35	7.00	16.00
5-13	1.50	4.50	10.00
1(G.Key)	1.75	5.25	12.00
2-4	1.30	4.00	9.00
1(1953-54)-Reprints United Features' Strange As It Seems, Willie, Fernand	4.00	12.00	28.00

PEBBLES & BAMM BAMM (TV)
Jan, 1972 - No. 36, Dec, 1976 (Hanna-Barbera)
Charlton Comics

1	1.30	4.00	8.00
2-10	.70	2.00	4.00
11-36	.50	1.50	3.00

PEBBLES FLINTSTONE (TV)
Sept, 1963 (Hanna-Barbera)
Gold Key

	Good	Fine	Mint
1 (10088-309)	1.75	5.25	12.00

PECKS BAD BOY
1906 - 1908 (Strip reprints) (11¼x15¾'')
Thompson of Chicago (by Walt McDougal)

. . .& Cousin Cynthia(1907)-In color	13.00	40.00	90.00
. . .& His Chums(1908)-Hardcover; in full color; 16 pgs.	13.00	40.00	90.00
Advs. of. . .And His Country Cousins (1906)-In color, 18 pgs., oblong	13.00	40.00	90.00
Advs. of. . .in Pictures(1908)-In color; Stanton & Van V. Liet Co.	13.00	40.00	90.00

PEDRO (Also see Romeo Tubbs)
No. 18, June, 1950 - No. 2, Aug, 1950?
Fox Features Syndicate

18(No.1)-Wood c/a(p)	9.50	28.50	65.00
2-Wood-a?	8.00	24.00	56.00

PEE-WEE PIXIES (See The Pixies)

PELLEAS AND MELISANDE (See Night Music No. 4,5)

PENALTY (See Crime Must Pay the. . .)

PENDULUM ILLUSTRATED BIOGRAPHIES
1979 (B&W)
Pendulum Press

19-355x-George Washington/Thomas Jefferson, 19-3495-Charles Lindbergh/Amelia Earhart, 19-3509-Harry Houdini/Walt Disney, 19-3517-Davy Crockett/Daniel Boone-Redondo-a, 19-3525-Elvis Presley/Beatles, 19-3533-Benjamin Franklin/Martin Luther King Jr, 19-3541-Abraham Lincoln/Franklin D. Roosevelt, 19-3568-Marie Curie/Albert Einstein-Redondo-a, 19-3576-Thomas Edison/Alexander Graham Bell-Redondo-a, 19-3584-Vince Lombardi/Pele, 19-3592-Babe Ruth/Jackie Robinson, 19-3606-Jim Thorpe/Althea Gibson

Softback	1.50
Hardback	4.50

NOTE: *Above books still available from publisher.*

PENDULUM ILLUSTRATED CLASSICS (Now Age Illustrated)
1973 - 1978 (62pp, B&W, 5-3/8x8'') (Also see Marvel Classics)
Pendulum Press

64-100x(1973)-Dracula-Redondo art, 64-131x-The Invisible Man-Nino art, 64-0968-Dr Jekyll and Mr Hyde-Redondo art, 64-1005-Black Beauty, 64-1010-Call of the Wild, 64-1020-Frankenstein, 64-1025-Hucklebury Finn, 64-1030-Moby Dick-Nino-a, 64-1040-Red Badge of Courage, 64-1045-The Time Machine-Nino-a, 64-1050-Tom Sawyer, 64-1055-Twenty Thousand Leagues Under the Sea, 64-1069-Treasure Island, 64-1328(1974)-Kidnapped, 64-1336-Three Musketeers-Nino art, 64-1344-A Tale of Two Cities, 64-1352-Journey to the Center of the Earth, 64-1360-The War of the Worlds-Nino-a, 64-1379-The Greatest Advs of Sherlock Holmes-Redondo art, 64-1387-Mysterious Island, 64-1395-Hunchback of Notre Dame, 64-1409-Helen Keller-story of my life, 64-1417-Scarlet Letter, 64-1425-Gulliver's Travels, 64-2618(1977)-Around the World in Eighty Days, 64-2626-Captains Courageous, 64-2634-Connecticut Yankee, 64-2642-The Hound of the Baskervilles, 64-2650-The House of Seven Gables, 64-2669-Jane Eyre, 64-2677-The Last of the Mohicans, 64-2685-The Best of O'Henry, 64-2693-The Best of Poe-Redondo-a, 64-2707-Two Years Before the Mast, 64-2715-White Fang, 64-2723-Wuthering Heights, 64-3126(1978)-Ben Hur-Redondo art, 64-3134-A Christmas Carol, 64-3142-The Food of the Gods, 64-3150-Ivanhoe, 64-3169-The Man in the Iron Mask, 64-3177-The Prince and the Pauper, 64-3185-The Prisoner of Zenda, 64-3193-The Return of the Native, 64-3207-Robinson Crusoe, 64-3215-The Scarlet Pimpernal, 64-3223-The Sea Wolf, 64-3231-The Swiss Family Robinson, 64-3851-Billy Budd, 64-386x-Crime and Punishment, 64-3878-Don Quixote, 64-3886-Great Expectations, 64-3894-Heidi, 64-3908-The Iliad, 64-3916-Lord Jim, 64-3924-The Mutiny on Board H.M.S. Bounty, 64-3932-The Odyssey, 64-3940-Oliver Twist, 64-3959-Pride and Prejudice, 64-3967-The Turn of the Screw

Softback	1.45
Hardback	4.50

NOTE: *All of the above books can be ordered from the publisher; some were reprinted as Marvel Classic Comics No. 1-12.*

PENDULUM ILLUSTRATED ORIGINALS
1979 (in color)
Pendulum Press

PENDULUM ILL. ORIGINALS (continued)

	Good	Fine	Mint
94-4254-Solarman: The Beginning	.30	.80	1.60

PENNY
1947 - No. 6, 9-10/49 (Newspaper reprints)
Avon Comics

	Good	Fine	Mint
1-Photo & biography of creator	4.00	12.00	28.00
2-5	2.00	6.00	14.00
6-Perry Como photo-c	2.65	8.00	18.00

PEP COMICS
Jan, 1940 - Present
MLJ Magazines/Archie Publications No. 56 (3/46) on

	Good	Fine	Mint
1-Intro. The Shield by Irving Novick (1st patriotic hero); origin The Comet by Jack Cole, The Queen of Diamonds & Kayo Ward; The Rocket, The Press Guardian (The Falcon No. 1 only), Sergeant Boyle, Fu Chang, & Bentley of Scotland Yard	135.00	405.00	945.00
2-Origin The Rocket	60.00	180.00	420.00
3	45.00	135.00	315.00
4-Wizard cameo	40.00	120.00	280.00
5-Wizard cameo in Shield story	40.00	120.00	280.00
6-10: 6-Transvestite story in Sgt. Boyle. 8-Last Cole Comet, no Cole art in No. 6,7	30.00	90.00	210.00
11-Dusty, Shield's sidekick begins; last Press Guardian, Fu Chang	28.50	85.00	200.00
12-Origin Fireball; last Rocket & Queen of Diamonds; bondage-c	40.00	120.00	280.00
13-15: 14-Lingerie panels. 15-Bondage-c	28.00	84.00	195.00
16-Origin Madam Satan; blood drainage-c	40.00	120.00	280.00
17-Origin The Hangman; death of The Comet	85.00	255.00	595.00
18-20-Last Fireball	25.00	75.00	175.00
21-Last Madam Satan	25.00	75.00	175.00
22-Intro. & 1st app. Archie, Betty, & Jughead(12/41); (also see Jackpot)	170.00	510.00	1190.00
(Prices vary widely on this book.)			
23	50.00	150.00	350.00
24,25	43.00	130.00	300.00
26-1st app. Veronica Lodge	48.00	145.00	335.00
27-30: 30-Capt. Commando begins	35.00	105.00	245.00
31-35: 31-Bondage-c. 34-Bondage/Hypo-c	25.00	75.00	175.00
36-1st Archie-c	40.00	120.00	280.00
37-40	20.00	60.00	140.00
41-50: 41-Archie-c begin. 47-Last Hangman issue. 48-Black Hood begins (5/44); ends No. 51,59,60	14.50	43.50	100.00
51-60: 52-Suzie begins. 56-Last Capt. Commando; lingerie panel. 59-Black Hood not in costume; spanking & lingerie panels; Archie dresses as his aunt; Suzie ends. 60-Katy Keene begins, ends No. 154	11.00	33.00	76.00
61-65-Last Shield. 62-1st app. Li'l Jinx	8.00	24.00	56.00
66-80: 66-G-Man Club becomes Archie Club (2/48)	6.00	18.00	42.00
81-99	4.00	12.00	28.00
100	4.65	14.00	32.00
101-130	2.00	6.00	14.00
131-149	1.00	3.00	7.00
150,152,157,159-Jaguar stories in all	.65	2.00	4.50
151,154,160-The Fly stories in all	.65	2.00	4.50
153,155,156,158-Flygirl stories in all	.65	2.00	4.50
161-167,169-200	.35	1.00	2.50
168-Jaguar app.	.55	1.65	4.00
201-260		.50	1.00
261-411: 383-Marvelous Maureen begins (Sci/fi). 393-Thunderbunny begins		.35	.70

NOTE: ***Biro*** *a-2, 4, 5.* ***Jack Cole*** *a-1-5, 8.* ***Fuje*** *a-39, 47.* ***Meskin*** *a-2, 4, 5, 11(2).* ***Schomburg*** *c-38.* ***Bob Wood*** *a-2, 4-6, 11. Katy Keene by* ***Bill Woggon*** *in many later issues. Bondage c-7, 18, 21, 32.*

PEPE (See 4-Color No. 1194)

PERCY & FERDIE
1921 (52 pages) (B&W dailies, 10x10'', cardboard-c)
Cupples & Leon Co.

	Good	Fine	Mint
By H. A. MacGill	5.00	15.00	35.00

PERFECT CRIME, THE
Oct, 1949 - No. 33, Feb?, 1953 (No. 5-12, 52 pgs.)
Cross Publications

	Good	Fine	Mint
1-Powell-a(2)	4.65	14.00	32.00
2	3.35	10.00	23.00
3-7,9,10: 7-Steve Duncan begins, ends No. 30	2.85	8.50	20.00
8-Heroin drug story	5.50	16.50	38.00
11-Used in **SOTI**, pg. 159; bondage-c	5.50	16.50	38.00
12-14	1.85	5.50	13.00
15-''The Most Terrible Menace''-2 pg. drug editorial	3.85	11.50	27.00
16,17,19-25,27-29,31-33	1.50	4.50	10.00
18-Drug cover, heroin drug propaganda story, plus 2 pg. drug editorial	6.50	19.50	45.00
26-Drug-c with hypodermic; drug propaganda story	7.00	21.00	50.00
30-Strangulation cover	5.50	16.50	38.00

NOTE: ***Powell*** *a-No. 1,2,4.* ***Wildey*** *a-1,5.*

PERFECT LOVE
No. 10, 8-9/51 (cover date; 5-6/51 indicia date); No. 2, 10-11/51 -No. 10, 12/53
Ziff-Davis(Approved Comics)/St. John No. 9 on

	Good	Fine	Mint
10(8-9/51)	4.65	13.00	32.00
2(10-11/51)	2.85	8.50	20.00
3,6,7,9,10: 3-Painted-c	2.15	6.50	15.00
4,8-Kinstler-a	2.50	7.50	17.50
5-Woodbridge-a?	2.15	6.50	15.00

PERRI (See 4-Color No. 847)

PERRY MASON (See Feature Books No. 49,50 (McKay))

PERRY MASON MYSTERY MAGAZINE (TV)
June-Aug, 1964 - No. 2, Oct-Dec, 1964
Dell Publishing Co.

	Good	Fine	Mint
1,2	1.30	4.00	9.00

PERSONAL LOVE (Also see Movie Love)
Jan, 1950 - No. 33, June, 1955
Famous Funnies

	Good	Fine	Mint
1	5.00	15.00	35.00
2	3.35	10.00	23.00
3-7,10	2.85	8.50	20.00
8,9-Kinstler-a	3.35	10.00	23.00
11-Toth-a	5.00	15.00	35.00
12,16,17-One pg. Frazetta	3.15	9.50	22.00
13-15,18-23	2.00	6.00	14.00
24,25,27,28-Frazetta-a in all-8,7,8&6 pgs.	24.50	74.00	170.00
26,29-31,33: 31-Last pre-code	1.70	5.00	11.50
32-Classic Frazetta-a, 8 pgs.	43.00	130.00	300.00

NOTE: *All have photo-c.* ***Everett*** *a-5, 24.*

PERSONAL LOVE
V1No.1, Sept, 1957 - V3No.2, Nov-Dec, 1959
Prize Publ. (Headline)

	Good	Fine	Mint
V1No.1	1.75	5.25	12.00
2	1.00	3.00	7.00
3-6(7-8/58)	.85	2.50	6.00
V2No.1(9-10/58)-V2No.6(7-8/59)	.75	2.25	5.00

Penny #6, © AVON

Pep Comics #5, © AP

Perfect Crime #28, © Cross Publ.

Peter Penny nn, © American Bankers

Peter Porkchops #3, © DC

Peter Rabbit #1, © AVON

PERSONAL LOVE (continued)

	Good	Fine	Mint
V3No.1-Wood/Orlando-a	1.50	4.50	10.00
2	.55	1.65	4.00

NOTE: *Photo covers on most issues.*

PETER COTTONTAIL
Jan, 1954; Feb, 1954 - No. 2, Mar, 1954
Key Publications

1(1/54)-Not 3-D	3.00	9.00	21.00
1(2/54)-(3-D); written by Bruce Hamilton	12.00	36.00	84.00
2-Reprints 3-D No. 1 but not in 3-D	2.00	6.00	14.00

PETER GUNN (See 4-Color No. 1087)

PETER PAN (See New Adventures of. . ., 4-Color No. 442,446,926, and Movie Classics & Comics)

PETER PANDA
Aug-Sept, 1953 - No. 31, Aug-Sept, 1958
National Periodical Publications

1-Grossman-c/a in all	10.00	30.00	70.00
2	5.00	15.00	35.00
3-10	3.85	11.50	27.00
11-31	1.85	5.50	13.00

PETER PAN TREASURE CHEST (See Dell Giants)

PETER PARKER (See The Spectacular Spider-Man)

PETER PAT (See Single Series No. 8)

PETER PAUL'S 4 IN 1 JUMBO COMIC BOOK
No date (1953)
Capitol Stories

1-Contains 4 comics bound; Space Adventures, Space Western, Crime & Justice, Racket Squad in Action	13.50	40.50	95.00

PETER PENNY AND HIS MAGIC DOLLAR
1947 (16 pgs.; paper cover; regular size)
American Bankers Association, N. Y. (Giveaway)

nn-(Scarce)-Used in **SOTI**, pg. 310, 311	6.00	18.00	42.00
Another version (7¼x11'')-redrawn, 16 pgs., paper-c	5.00	15.00	35.00

PETER PIG
No. 5, May, 1953 - No. 6, Aug, 1953
Standard Comics

5,6	1.15	3.50	8.00

PETER PORKCHOPS
Nov-Dec, 1949 - No. 61, Sept-Nov, 1959; No. 62, Oct-Dec, 1960
National Periodical Publications

1	11.50	34.50	80.00
2	5.50	16.50	38.00
3-10	4.00	12.00	28.00
11-30	2.65	8.00	18.00
31-62	1.50	4.50	10.00

NOTE: ***Otto Feur** a-all. **Sheldon Mayer** a-30-38, 40-44, 46-52, 61.*

PETER PORKER, THE SPECTACULAR SPIDER-HAM
May, 1985 - Present
Star Comics (Marvel)

1		.50	1.00
2-6		.40	.80
7-14: 13-Halloween ish.		.35	.70

PETER POTAMUS (TV)
January, 1965 (Hanna-Barbera)
Gold Key

1	1.50	4.50	10.00

PETER RABBIT (See Large Feature Comic No. 1)

PETER RABBIT
1922 - 1923 (9¼x6¼'') (paper cover)
John H. Eggers Co. The House of Little Books Publishers

	Good	Fine	Mint
B1-B4-(Rare)-(Set of 4 books which came in a cardboard box)-Each book reprints ½ of a Sunday page per page and contains 8 B&W and 2 color pages; by Harrison Cady each. . . .	18.00	54.00	125.00

PETER RABBIT (Adventures of. . .)
1947 - No. 34, Aug-Sept, 1956
Avon Periodicals

1(1947)-Reprints 1943-44 Sunday strips; contains a biography & drawing of Cady	22.00	65.00	154.00
2	18.00	54.00	125.00
3-6(1949)-Last Cady issue	16.50	50.00	115.00
7-10(1950-8/51)	2.85	8.50	20.00
11(11/51)-34('56)-Avon's character	1.85	5.50	13.00
. . .Easter Parade (132 pgs.; 1952)	8.50	25.50	60.00
. . .Jumbo Book(1954-Giant Size, 25 cents)-6 pgs.; Jesse James by Kinstler	13.00	40.00	90.00

PETER RABBIT
1958
Fago Magazine Co.

1	2.35	7.00	16.00

PETER, THE LITTLE PEST (No. 4 titled Petey)
Nov, 1969 - No. 4, May, 1970
Marvel Comics Group

1	.50	1.50	3.00
2-4-Reprints Dexter the Demon & Melvin the Monster	.35	1.00	2.00

PETER WHEAT (The Adventures of. . .)
1948 - 1956? (16 pgs. in color) (paper covers)
Bakers Associates Giveaway

nn(No.1)-States on last page, end of 1st Adventure of. . .; Kelly-a	22.00	65.00	140.00
nn(4 issues)-Kelly-a	17.00	50.00	100.00
6-10-All Kelly-a	12.00	36.00	72.00
11-20-All Kelly-a	10.00	30.00	60.00
21-35-All Kelly-a	8.00	24.00	48.00
36-66	5.00	15.00	30.00
. . .Artist's Workbook ('54, digest size)	4.50	13.50	27.00
. . .Four-In-One Fun Pack (Vol. 2, '54), oblong, comics w/puzzles	5.00	15.00	30.00
. . .Fun Book ('52, 32pgs., paper-c, B&W & color, 8¼''x10¾''), contains cut-outs, puzzles, games, magic & pages to color	7.00	21.00	50.00

NOTE: ***Al Hubbard** art No. 36 on; written by Del Connell.*

PETER WHEAT NEWS
1948 - No. 30, 1950 (4 pgs. in color)
Bakers Associates

Vol. 1-All have 2 pgs. Peter Wheat by Kelly	18.00	55.00	120.00
2-10	13.00	40.00	80.00
11-20	6.75	20.00	40.00
21-30	4.00	12.00	24.00

NOTE: *Early issues have no date & Kelly art.*

PETE THE PANIC
November, 1955? (mid 1950s)
Stanmor Publications

nn	1.00	3.00	7.00

PETEY (See Peter, the Little Pest)

PETTICOAT JUNCTION (TV)
Oct-Dec, 1964 - No. 5, Oct-Dec, 1965 (Photo-c)
Dell Publishing Co.

PETTICOAT JUNCTION (continued)

	Good	Fine	Mint
1	2.65	8.00	18.00
2-5	1.50	4.50	10.00

PETUNIA (See 4-Color No. 463)

PHANTASMO (See Large Feat. Comic No. 18)

PHANTOM, THE
1939 - 1949
David McKay Publishing Co.

Feature Books 20	35.00	105.00	245.00
Feature Books 22	30.00	90.00	210.00
Feature Books 39	20.00	60.00	140.00
Feature Books 53,56,57	15.00	45.00	105.00

PHANTOM, THE (See Ace Comics, Eat Right to Work. . ., Future Comics, Harvey Comics Hits No.51,56 & Harvey Hits No. 1, 6, 12, 15, 26, 36, 44, 48)

PHANTOM, THE (nn 29-Published overseas only) (Also see Comics Reading Library)
Nov, 1962 - No. 17, July, 1966; No. 18, Sept, 1966 - No. 28, Dec, 1967; No. 30, Feb, 1969 - No. 74, Jan, 1977
Gold Key (No.1-17)/King (No.18-28)/Charlton (No.30 on)

1-Manning-a	2.65	8.00	18.00
2-King, Queen & Jack begins, ends No. 11	1.15	3.50	8.00
3-10	.85	2.50	6.00
11-17: 12-Track Hunter begins	.55	1.65	4.00
18-Flash Gordon begins; Wood-a	.85	2.50	6.00
19,20-Flash Gordon ends	.55	1.65	4.00
21-24,26,27: 21-Mandrake begins. 21,24-Girl Phantom app. 26-Brick Bradford app.	.50	1.50	3.00
25-Jeff Jones-a; 1 pg. Williamson ad	.75	2.25	5.00
28(nn)-Brick Bradford app.	.55	1.65	4.00
30-40: 36,39-Ditko-a	.50	1.50	3.00
41-66: 46-Intro. The Piranha. 62-Bolle-c	.35	1.00	2.00
67-71,73-Newton c/a; 67-Origin retold	.35	1.00	2.00
72	.25	.75	1.50
74-Newton Flag-c; Newton-a	.35	1.00	2.00

NOTE: ***Aparo** a-36-38; c-35-38, 60, 61. Painted-c No. 1-17.*

PHANTOM BLOT, THE (No. 1 titled New Adventures of. . .)
Oct, 1964 - No. 7, Nov, 1966 (Disney)
Gold Key

1	2.00	6.00	14.00
2-1st Super Goof	1.50	4.50	10.00
3-7	1.15	3.50	8.00

PHANTOM EAGLE (See Mighty Midget Comics & Marvel Super Heroes No. 16)

PHANTOM LADY (1st Series) (My Love Secret No. 24 on) (Also see All Top, Daring Adventures, Jungle Thrills, and Wonder Boy)
Aug, 1947 - No. 23 April, 1949
Fox Features Syndicate

13(No.1)-Phantom Lady by Matt Baker begins; The Blue Beetle app.	100.00	300.00	700.00
14(No.2)	62.00	185.00	435.00
15-P.L. injected with experimental drug	53.00	160.00	370.00
16-Negligee-c, panels	53.00	160.00	370.00
17-Classic bondage cover; used in **SOTI**, illo-''Sexual stimulation by combining 'headlights' with the sadist's dream of tying up a woman''	140.00	420.00	980.00
18,19	47.00	141.00	330.00
20-23: 23-Bondage-c	40.00	120.00	280.00

NOTE: ***Matt Baker** a-in all; c-13, 15-21. **Kamen** a-22, 23.*

PHANTOM LADY (2nd Series) (See Terrific Comics) (Formerly Linda)
Dec-Jan, 1955 - No. 4, June, 1955
Ajax/Farrell Publ.

	Good	Fine	Mint
V1/5(No.1)-by Matt Baker	22.00	65.00	154.00
V1/2-Last pre-code	18.00	54.00	125.00
3,4-Red Rocket	15.00	45.00	105.00

PHANTOM PLANET, THE (See 4-Color No. 1234)

PHANTOM STRANGER, THE (1st Series)
Aug-Sept, 1952 - No. 6, June-July, 1953
National Periodical Publications

1 (Scarce)	40.00	120.00	280.00
2 (Scarce)	30.00	90.00	210.00
3-6 (Scarce)	25.00	75.00	175.00

PHANTOM STRANGER, THE (2nd Series) (See Showcase)
May-June, 1969 - No. 41, Feb-Mar, 1976
National Periodical Publications

1	.70	2.00	4.00
2,3,6-10		.60	1.20
4,5-Adams-a	.70	2.00	4.00
11-22: 22-Dark Circle begins		.40	.80
23-Spawn of Frankenstein begins by Kaluta; series ends No. 30	.25	.75	1.50
24,25		.50	1.00
26-31: 31-The Black Orchid begins		.40	.80
32,35,36-Black Orchid by Redondo		.40	.80
33,34,37,38-41: 33, 39-41-Deadman app.		.30	.60

NOTE: ***Adams** a-4, 5i; c-3-19. **Aparo** a-7-26; c-20-24, 33-41. **Dezuniga** a-14-16, 19-22, 31, 34. **Grell** a-33. **Kaluta** a-23-25; c-26. **Meskin** r-15, 16, 18. **Sparling** a-20. **Starr** a-17. **Toth** a-15r. **Wrightson** a-14. Black Orchid by **Carrilo**-38-41. Dr. 13 solo in-13, 18, 20. Frankenstein by **Kaluta**-23-25; by **Baily**-27-30. No Black Orchid-33, 34, 37.*

PHANTOM WITCH DOCTOR
1952 (Also see Eerie No. 8)
Avon Periodicals

1-Kinstler-c, 7 pgs.	18.00	54.00	125.00

PHANTOM ZONE, THE
January, 1982 - No. 4, April, 1982
DC Comics

1-Superman app. in all		.40	.80
2-4: Batman, Gr. Lantern app.		.30	.60

NOTE: ***Colan** a-1-4p; c-1-4p. **Giordano** c-1-4i.*

PHASE ONE
Mar, 1986 - Present ($1.80, B&W)
Victory Productions

1-3	.25	.75	1.50

PHIGMENTS
Oct, 1986 - Present ($1.80, B&W)
Amazing Comics

1,2-Super hero team	.30	.90	1.80

PHIL RIZZUTO (Baseball Hero)
1951 (New York Yankees)
Fawcett Publications

nn	15.00	45.00	105.00

PHOENIX
Jan, 1975 - No. 4, Oct, 1975
Atlas/Seaboard Publ.

1-Origin		.30	.60
2,3: 3-Origin & only app. The Dark Avenger		.25	.50
4-New origin/costume The Protector (formerly Phoenix)		.25	.50

NOTE: ***Infantino** appears in No. 1,2. **Austin** a-3i. **Thorne** c-3.*

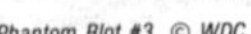
Phantom Blot #3, © WDC

Phantom Lady #19, © FOX

Phase One #1, © Victory

Pictorial Confessions #2, © STJ

Picture Parade #1, © GIL

Pinhead & Foodini #1, © FAW

PHOENIX-THE UNTOLD STORY
April, 1984 (One shot; $2.00)
Marvel Comics Group

	Good	Fine	Mint
1-Byrne/Austin-r/X-Men 137 with original unpubbed ending	.55	1.60	3.20

PHONEY PAGES
Apr, 1986 - No. 2, May, 1986 ($1.70, B&W)
Renegade Press

1,2-Reprints from CBG strips	.35	1.00	2.00

PICNIC PARTY (See Dell Giants)

PICTORIAL CONFESSIONS (Pictorial Romances No. 4 on)
Sept, 1949 - No. 3, Dec, 1949
St. John Publishing Co.

1-Baker-c/a(3)	11.00	33.00	76.00
2-Baker-a; photo-c	5.50	16.50	38.00
3-Kubert, Baker-a; part Kubert-c	8.00	24.00	56.00

PICTORIAL LOVE STORIES (Formerly Tim McCoy)
No. 22, Oct, 1949 - No. 26, July, 1950
Charlton Comics

22-26-''Me-Dan Cupid'' in all	4.65	14.00	32.00

PICTORIAL LOVE STORIES
October, 1952
St. John Publishing Co.

1-Baker c/a	9.50	28.50	65.00

PICTORIAL ROMANCES (Formerly Pictorial Confessions)
No. 4, Jan, 1950 - No. 24, Mar, 1954
St. John Publishing Co.

4-All Baker	8.50	25.50	60.00
5,10-All Matt Baker issues	7.00	21.00	50.00
6-9,12,13,15,16-Baker-c, 2-3 stories	5.00	15.00	35.00
11-Baker c/a(3); Kubert-a	6.00	18.00	42.00
14,21-24-Baker-c/a each	3.65	11.00	25.00
17-20(7/53)-100 pgs. each; Baker-c/a	8.50	25.50	60.00

NOTE: ***Matt Baker*** *art in most issues.* ***Estrada*** *a-19(2).*

PICTURE NEWS
Jan, 1946 - No. 10, Jan-Feb, 1947
Lafayette Street Corp.

1-Milt Gross begins, ends No. 6; 4 pg. Kirby-a; A-Bomb-c/story	8.00	24.00	56.00
2-Atomic explosion panels; Frank Sinatra, Perry Como stories	3.65	11.00	25.00
3-Atomic explosion panels; Frank Sinatra, June Allyson stories	2.85	8.50	20.00
4-Atomic explosion panels; ''Caesar and Cleopatra'' movie adaptation; Jackie Robinson story	2.85	8.50	20.00
5-7: 5-Hank Greenberg story. 6-Joe Louis c/story	2.00	6.00	14.00
8-Monte Hale story(9-10/46; 1st?)	3.00	9.00	21.00
9-A-Bomb story; ''Crooked Mile'' movie adaptation; Joe DiMaggio story	3.35	10.00	23.00
10-A-Bomb story; Krigstein, Gross-a	3.65	11.00	25.00

PICTURE PARADE (Picture Progress No. 5 on)
Sept, 1953 - V1/4, Dec, 1953 (28 pages)
Gilberton Company (Also see A Christmas Adventure)

V1/1-Andy's Atomic Adventures-A-bomb blast-c; (Teachers version distr. to schools exists	4.00	12.00	28.00
2-Around the World with the United Nations	3.00	9.00	21.00
3-Adventures of the Lost One(The Amer. Indian), 4-A Christmas Adventure (r-under same title in '69)	3.00	9.00	21.00

PICTURE PROGRESS (Formerly Picture Parade)
V1No.5, Jan, 1954 - V3No.2, Oct, 1955 (28-36 pgs.)
Gilberton Corp.

	Good	Fine	Mint
V1No.5-News in Review 1953, 6-The Birth of America, 7-The Four Seasons, 8-Paul Revere's Ride, 9-The Hawaiian Islands(5/54), V2No.1-The Story of Flight(9/54), 2-Vote for Crazy River(The Meaning of Elections), 3-Louis Pasteur, 4-The Star Spangled Banner, 5-News in Review 1954, 6-Alaska: The Great Land, 7-Life in the Circus, 8-The Time of the Cave Man, 9-Summer Fun(5/55) each....	1.50	4.50	10.00
V3No.1-The Man Who Discovered America, 2-The Lewis & Clark Expedition each....	1.50	4.50	10.00

PICTURE SCOPE JUNGLE ADVENTURES (See Jungle Thrills)

PICTURE STORIES FROM AMERICAN HISTORY
1945 - 1947 (68 - 52 pages)
National/All-American/E. C. Comics

1	5.50	16.50	38.00
2-4	3.85	11.50	27.00

PICTURE STORIES FROM SCIENCE
Spring, 1947 - No. 2, Fall, 1947
E. C. Comics

1,2	6.65	20.00	46.00

PICTURE STORIES FROM THE BIBLE
Fall, 1942-43 & 1944-46
National/All-American/E. C. Comics

1-4('42-Fall,'43)-Old Testament (DC)	6.65	20.00	46.00
Complete Old Testament Edition, 232 pgs. (1943-DC); contains No. 1-4	8.50	25.50	60.00
Complete Old Testament Edition (1945-publ. by Bible Pictures Ltd.)-232 pgs., hardbound, in color with dust jacket	8.50	25.50	60.00

NOTE: *Both Old and New Testaments published in England by Bible Pictures Ltd. in hardback, 1943, in color, 376 pages, and were also published by Scarf Press in 1979 (Old Test., $9.95) and in 1980 (New Test., $7.95).*

1-3(New Testament)(1944-46-DC)-52 pgs. each	5.50	16.50	38.00
The Complete Life of Christ Edition(1945)-96 pgs.; contains No. 1 & 2 of the New Testament Edition	6.65	20.00	46.00
1,2(Old Testament-r in comic book form)(E.C., 1946)-52 pgs.	5.50	16.50	38.00
1-3(New Testament-r in comic book form)(E.C., 1946)-52 pgs.	5.50	16.50	38.00
Complete New Testament Edition(1946-E.C.)-144 pgs.; contains No. 1-3	7.00	21.00	50.00

PICTURE STORIES FROM WORLD HISTORY
Spring, 1947 - No. 2, Summer, 1947 (52, 48 pgs.)
E. C. Comics

1,2	5.00	15.00	35.00

PINHEAD & FOODINI (TV) (Also see Foodini)
July, 1951 - No. 4, Jan, 1952
Fawcett Publications

1-Photo-c	5.00	15.00	35.00
2-Photo-c	3.50	10.50	24.00
3,4: 3-Photo-c	2.35	7.00	16.00

PINK LAFFIN
1922 (9x12'') (strip reprints)
Whitman Publishing Co.

...the Lighter Side of Life, ...He Tells 'Em, ...and His Family, ...Knockouts — art by Ray Gleason (All Rare) each....	6.00	18.00	42.00

PINK PANTHER, THE (TV)
April, 1971 - No. 87, 1984
Gold Key

	Good	Fine	Mint
1-The Inspector begins	1.20	3.50	7.00
2-10	.70	2.00	4.00
11-30: Warren Tufts-a No. 16 on	.40	1.25	2.50
31-60	.25	.75	1.50
61-87		.50	1.00
Kite Fun Book(1972)-16 pgs.; Sou. Calif. Edison Co. giveaway	.70	2.00	4.00
Mini-Comic No. 1(1976)(3¼x6½'')		.50	1.00

NOTE: *Pink Panther began as a movie cartoon. (See Golden Comics Digest No. 38, 45 and March of Comics No. 376, 384, 390, 409, 418, 429, 441, 449, 461, 473, 486). No. 37, 72, 80-85 contain reprints.*

PINKY LEE (See The Adventures of. . .)

PINKY THE EGGHEAD
1963 (Reprints from Noodnik)
I. W./Super Comics

	Good	Fine	Mint
I.W. Reprint No. 1,2 (no date)		.60	1.20
Super Reprint No. 14		.60	1.20

PINOCCHIO (See 4-Color No. 92,252,545,1203, Movie Comics under Wonderful Advs. of. . ., Mickey Mouse Mag, Wonderful Advs. of. . ., World's Greatest Stories No. 2 & New Advs. of. . .)

PINOCCHIO
1940 (10 pages) (linen-like paper)
Montgomery Ward Co. (Giveaway)

	Good	Fine	Mint
	12.00	35.00	70.00

PINOCCHIO LEARNS ABOUT KITES (Also see Donald Duck & Brer Rabbit) (Disney)
1954 (8 pages) (Premium)
Pacific Gas & Electric Co./Florida Power & Light

	Good	Fine	Mint
	20.00	60.00	120.00

PIN-UP PETE (Also see Monty Hall. . . & Great Lover Romances)
1952
Toby Press

	Good	Fine	Mint
1-Jack Sparling pin-ups	8.00	24.00	56.00

PIONEER MARSHAL (See Fawcett Movie Comics)

PIONEER PICTURE STORIES
Dec, 1941 - No. 9, Dec, 1943
Street & Smith Publications

	Good	Fine	Mint
1	7.00	21.00	50.00
2	4.35	13.00	30.00
3-9	3.35	10.00	23.00

PIONEER WEST ROMANCES (Firehair No. 1,2,7-11)
No. 3, Summer, 1949 - No. 6, Winter, 1949-50
Fiction House Magazines

	Good	Fine	Mint
3-Firehair continues	6.85	20.50	46.00
4-6	5.00	15.00	35.00

PIPSQUEAK (See The Adventures of. . .)

PIRACY
Oct-Nov, 1954 - No. 7, Oct-Nov, 1955
E. C. Comics

	Good	Fine	Mint
1-Williamson/Torres-a	12.00	36.00	85.00
2-Williamson/Torres-a	9.00	27.00	62.00
3-7	7.00	21.00	50.00

NOTE: ***Crandall** a-in all; c-2-4. **Davis** a-1, 2, 6. **Evans** a-3-7; c-7. **Ingels** a-3-7. **Krigstein** a-3-5, 7; c-5, 6. **Wood** a-1, 2; c-1.*

PIRANA (See Thrill-O-Rama No. 2,3)

PIRATE OF THE GULF, THE (See Superior Stories No. 2)

PIRATES COMICS
Feb-Mar, 1950 - No. 4, Aug-Sept, 1950 (All 52 pgs.)
Hillman Periodicals

	Good	Fine	Mint
1	5.00	15.00	35.00
2-Berg-a	2.85	8.50	20.00
3,4-Berg-a	2.50	7.50	17.00

P.I.'S: MICHAEL MAUSER AND MS. TREE, THE
Jan, 1985 - No. 3, May, 1985 (mini-series)
First Comics

	Good	Fine	Mint
1-3: Staton c/a(p)		.65	1.30

PIUS XII MAN OF PEACE
No date (12 pgs.; 5½x8½'') (B&W)
Catechetical Guild Giveaway

	Good	Fine	Mint
	4.00	12.00	24.00

PIXIE & DIXIE & MR. JINKS (TV)
July-Sept, 1960 - Feb, 1963 (Hanna-Barbera)
Dell Publishing Co./Gold Key

	Good	Fine	Mint
4-Color 1112	1.75	5.25	12.00
4-Color 1196,1264	1.50	4.50	10.00
01-631-207 (Dell)	1.50	4.50	10.00
1(2/63-G.K.)	1.50	4.50	10.00

PIXIE PUZZLE ROCKET TO ADVENTURELAND
November, 1952
Avon Periodicals

	Good	Fine	Mint
1	4.65	14.00	32.00

PIXIES, THE (Advs. of. . .) (Mighty Atom No. 6 on)
Winter, 1946 - No. 4, Fall?, 1947; No. 5, 1948
Magazine Enterprises

	Good	Fine	Mint
1-Mighty Atom	2.65	8.00	18.00
2-5-Mighty Atom	1.50	4.50	10.00
I.W. Reprint No. 1(1958), 8-(Pee-Wee Pixies), 10-I.W. on cover, Super on inside	.40	1.20	2.40

PLANET COMICS
Jan, 1940 - No. 73, Winter, 1953
Fiction House Magazines

	Good	Fine	Mint
1-Origin Auro, Lord of Jupiter; Flint Baker & The Red Comet begin; Eisner/Fine-c	270.00	810.00	1890.00
2-(Scarce)	140.00	420.00	980.00
3-Eisner-c	112.00	336.00	784.00
4-Gale Allen and the Girl Squadron begins	95.00	285.00	665.00
5,6-(Scarce)	86.00	258.00	600.00
7-11	72.00	215.00	500.00
12-The Star Pirate begins	72.00	215.00	500.00
13-15: 13-Reff Ryan begins. 15-Mars, God of War begins	54.00	162.00	380.00
16-20,22	50.00	150.00	350.00
21-The Lost World & Hunt Bowman begin	54.00	162.00	380.00
23-26: 26-The Space Rangers begin	50.00	150.00	350.00
27-30	41.00	123.00	285.00
31-35: 33-Origin Star Pirates Wonder Boots, reprinted in No. 52. 35-Mysta of the Moon begins	32.00	95.00	225.00
36-45: 41-New origin of ''Auro, Lord of Jupiter.'' 42-Last Gale Allen. 43-Futura begins	28.50	85.00	200.00
46-52,54-60	22.00	65.00	154.00
53-Used in **SOTI**, pg. 32; bondage-c	23.00	70.00	160.00
61-64	15.00	45.00	105.00
65-68,70: 65-70-All partial-r of earlier issues	14.50	43.50	100.00
69-Used in **POP**, pgs. 101,102	15.00	45.00	105.00
71-73-No series stories	12.00	36.00	84.00

Piracy #7, © WMG

Pixie & Dixie. . . #01-631-207, © Hanna-Barbera

Planet Comics #6, © FH

Plastic Man #2, © QUA

Pogo Possum #13, © Walt Kelly

Police Action #2, © MCG

PLANET COMICS (continued)

	Good	Fine	Mint
I.W. Reprint No. 1(nd)-r-/No. 70; c-from Attack on Planet Mars	2.75	8.00	16.00
I.W. Reprint No. 8 (r-/No. 72), 9-r-/No. 73	2.75	8.00	16.00

NOTE: No. 33-38, 40-51-Star Pirate by **Anderson**. **Fine** *c-2, 5.* **Evans** *a-50-64 (Lost World).* **Ingels** *a-24-31, 56-61 (Auro, Lord of Jupiter). Mysta of the Moon by* **Maurice Whitman**-*51, 52; by* **Matt Baker**-*53-59. Star Pirate by* **Tuska**-*30; by* **M. Whitman**-*54-56.* **Starr** *a-59.*

PLANET OF THE APES (Magazine) (Also see Advs. on the. . .)
Aug, 1974 - No. 29, Feb, 1977 (B&W) (Based on movies)
Marvel Comics Group

	Good	Fine	Mint
1-Ploog-a	.40	1.25	2.50
2-Ploog-a	.35	1.00	2.00
3-10	.25	.70	1.40
11-20		.50	1.00
21-29		.40	.80

NOTE: **Alcala** *a-7-11, 17-22, 24.* **Ploog** *a-1-8, 11, 13, 14, 19.* **Sutton** *a-11, 12, 15, 17, 19, 20, 23, 24, 29.*

PLANET OF VAMPIRES
Feb, 1975 - No. 3, July, 1975
Seaboard Publications (Atlas)

	Good	Fine	Mint
1-Adams-c(i); 1st Broderick c/a(p)		.40	.80
2-Adams-c, 3-Heath-c/a		.30	.60

PLANET TERRY
April, 1985 - No. 12, 1986 (children's comic)
Star Comics (Marvel)

	Good	Fine	Mint
1-12		.35	.70

PLASTIC MAN (Also see Police & Smash 17)
Sum, 1943 - No. 64, Nov, 1956
Vital Publ. No. 1,2/Quality Comics No. 3 on

	Good	Fine	Mint
nn(No.1)-'In The Game of Death;' Jack Cole-a begins; ends-No. 64?	95.00	285.00	665.00
2(nn, 2/44)-'The Gay Nineties Nightmare'	62.00	185.00	432.00
3 (Spr, '46)	40.00	120.00	280.00
4 (Sum, '46)	35.00	105.00	245.00
5 (Aut, '46)	30.00	90.00	210.00
6-10: 8-Extreme violence	21.00	62.00	145.00
11-20	18.50	55.50	130.00
21-30: 26-Last non-r issue?	14.50	43.50	100.00
31-39	11.00	34.50	80.00
40-Used in **POP**, pg. 91	12.00	36.00	84.00
41-64: 53-Last precode issue	8.50	25.50	60.00
Super Reprint 11('63, r-/No.16), 16 (r-No.21, Cole-a), 18('64-Spirit app. by Eisner/Police 95)	2.00	6.00	12.00

NOTE: **Cole** *r-44,49,56,58,59 at least.*

PLASTIC MAN (See Brave & the Bold and DC Special No. 15)
11-12/66 - No. 10, 5-6/68; No. 11, 2-3/76 - No. 20, 10-11/77
National Periodical Publications/DC Comics

	Good	Fine	Mint
1	.40	1.25	2.50
2-5: 4-Infantino-c		.60	1.20
6-10('68)		.40	.80
11('76)-20: 17-Origin retold		.25	.50

NOTE: **Gil Kane** *c/a-1.* **Mortimer** *a-4.* **Sparling** *a-10.*

PLAYFUL LITTLE AUDREY (Also see Little Audrey No. 25)
6/57 - No. 110, 11/73; No. 111, 8/74 - No. 121, 4/76
Harvey Publications

	Good	Fine	Mint
1	11.50	34.50	80.00
2	5.70	17.00	40.00
3-5	5.00	15.00	35.00
6-10	3.35	10.00	23.00
11-20	1.70	5.00	12.00
21-40	1.35	4.00	9.00
41-60	.85	2.50	5.00
61-80	.50	1.50	3.00
81-99	.40	1.25	2.50
100	.70	2.00	4.00
101-121	.35	1.00	2.00
Clubhouse 1(10/61)	1.15	3.50	8.00

PLOP!
Sept-Oct, 1973 - No. 24, Nov-Dec, 1976
National Periodical Publications

	Good	Fine	Mint
1,5-Wrightson-a		.40	.80
2-4,6-10		.30	.60
11-24: 21-24-Giant size, 52 pgs.		.25	.50

NOTE: **Alcala** *a-1-3.* **Anderson** *a-5.* **Aragones** *a-1-22, 24.* **Ditko** *a-16p.* **Evans** *a-1.* **Orlando** *a-21, 22; c-21.* **Sekowsky** *a-5, 6p.* **Toth** *a-11.* **Wolverton** *a-4, 22, 23(1 pg.); c-1-12, 14, 17, 18.* **Wood** *a-14, 16i, 18-24; c-13, 15, 16, 19.*

PLUTO (See Cheerios Premiums, Four Color 537, Mickey Mouse Mag. & Walt Disney Showcase No. 4,7,13,20,23)
No. 7, 1942; No. 429, 10/52 - No. 1248, 11-1/61-62 (Walt Disney)
Dell Publishing Co.

	Good	Fine	Mint
Large Feature Comic 7(1942)	52.00	156.00	364.00
4-Color 429,509	1.50	4.50	10.00
4-Color 595,654	1.15	3.50	8.00
4-Color 736,853,941,1039,1143,1248	1.00	3.00	7.00

POCAHONTAS
1941 - No. 2, 1942
Pocahontas Fuel Company

	Good	Fine	Mint
nn(No.1), 2	4.00	12.00	28.00

POCKET COMICS
Aug, 1941 - No. 4, Jan, 1942 (Pocket size; 100 pgs.)
Harvey Publications

	Good	Fine	Mint
1-Origin The Black Cat, Cadet Blakey the Spirit of '76, The Phantom Sphinx, The Red Blazer, & The Zebra; Phantom Ranger, British Agent No. 99, Spin Hawkins, Satan, Lord of Evil begin	32.00	95.00	225.00
2	20.00	60.00	140.00
3,4	16.00	48.00	110.00

POGO PARADE (See Dell Giants)

POGO POSSUM (Also see Animal Comics & Special Delivery)
April, 1946 - No. 16, April-June, 1954
Dell Publishing Co.

	Good	Fine	Mint
4-Color 105(1946)-Kelly-a	52.00	156.00	365.00
4-Color 148-Kelly-a	40.00	120.00	280.00
1-(10-12/49)-Kelly art in all	35.00	105.00	245.00
2	17.00	51.00	120.00
3-5	13.00	40.00	90.00
6-10: 10-Infinity-c	11.00	33.00	76.00
11-16: 11-X-mas-c	8.50	25.50	60.00

NOTE: *No. 1-4,9-13: 52 pgs.; No. 5-8,14-16: 36 pgs.*

POLICE ACTION
Jan, 1954 - No. 7, Nov, 1954
Atlas News Co.

	Good	Fine	Mint
1	3.15	9.50	22.00
2	1.85	5.50	13.00
3-7: 7-Powell-a	1.70	5.00	11.50

NOTE: **Ayers** *a-4.* **Maneely** *a-3.*

POLICE ACTION
Feb, 1975 - No. 3, June, 1975
Atlas/Seaboard Publ.

	Good	Fine	Mint
1-Lomax, N.Y.P.D., Luke Malone begin; McWilliams-a; bondage-c		.40	.80
2,3: 2-Origin Luke Malone, Manhunter		.30	.60

NOTE: **Ploog** *art in all.* **Sekowsky/McWilliams** *a-1-3.* **Thorne** *c-3.*

POLICE AGAINST CRIME
April, 1954 - No. 9, Aug, 1955
Premiere Magazines

	Good	Fine	Mint
1-Disbrow-a; extreme violence - man's face slashed with knife; Hollingsworth-a	5.00	15.00	35.00
2-Hollingsworth-a	2.85	8.50	20.00
3-9	1.85	5.50	13.00

POLICE BADGE #479 (Spy Thrillers No. 1-4)
No. 5, Sept, 1955
Atlas Comics (PrPI)

	Good	Fine	Mint
5-Maneely-c	1.75	5.25	12.00

POLICE CASE BOOK (See Giant Comics Editions)

POLICE CASES (See Authentic . . . & Record Book of . . .)

POLICE COMICS
Aug, 1941 - No. 127, Oct, 1953
Quality Comics Group (Comic Magazines)

	Good	Fine	Mint
1-Origin Plastic Man by Jack Cole, The Human Bomb by Gustavson, & No. 711; intro. Chic Carter by Eisner, The Firebrand by R. Crandall, The Mouthpiece, Phantom Lady, & The Sword	220.00	660.00	1540.00
2-Plastic Man smuggles opium	118.00	354.00	825.00
3	95.00	285.00	665.00
4	82.00	245.00	575.00
5-Plastic Man forced to smoke marijuana	82.00	245.00	575.00
6,7	75.00	225.00	525.00
8-Origin Manhunter	86.00	255.00	600.00
9,10	70.00	210.00	490.00
11-The Spirit strip-r begin by Eisner(Origin-strip No. 1)	114.00	345.00	800.00
12-Intro. Ebony	75.00	225.00	525.00
13-Intro. Woozy Winks; last Firebrand	75.00	225.00	525.00
14-19: 15-Last No. 711; Destiny begins	47.00	141.00	330.00
20-The Raven x-over in Phantom Lady; features Jack Cole himself	47.00	141.00	330.00
21,22-Raven & Spider Widow x-over in Phantom Lady No. 21, cameo in Phantom Lady No. 22	33.00	100.00	230.00
23-30: 23-Last Phantom Lady. 24-Chic Carter becomes The Sword, only issue. 24-26-Flatfoot Burns by Kurtzman in all	30.00	90.00	210.00
31-41-Last Spirit-r by Eisner	21.00	62.00	145.00
42,43-Spirit-r by Eisner/Fine	19.00	57.00	132.00
44-Fine Spirit-r begin, end No. 88,90,92	15.00	45.00	105.00
45-50-(No.50 on-c, No.49 on inside)(1/46)	15.00	45.00	105.00
51-60: 58-Last Human Bomb	11.00	33.00	76.00
61,62,64-88	10.00	30.00	70.00
63-(Some issues have No.65 printed on cover, but No.63 on inside) Kurtzman-a, 6pgs.	10.00	30.00	70.00
89,91,93-No Spirit	9.50	28.50	65.00
90,92-Spirit by Fine	10.00	30.00	70.00
94-99,101,102: Spirit by Eisner in all; 101-Last Manhunter. 102-Last Spirit & Plastic Man by Jack Cole	13.00	40.00	90.00
100	14.50	43.50	100.00
103-Content change to crime - Ken Shannon	6.50	19.50	45.00
104-111,114-127-Crandall-a most issues	5.00	15.00	35.00
112-Crandall-a	5.00	15.00	35.00
113-Crandall-c/a(2), 9 pgs. each	5.50	16.50	38.00

NOTE: *Most Spirit stories signed by **Eisner** are not by him; all are reprints. **Cole** c-20, 24-26, 28, 29, 31, 36-38, 40, 46, 68, 69, 73. **Crandall** Firebrand-1-8. Spirit by **Eisner** 1-41, 94-102; by **Eisner/Fine**-42, 43; by **Fine**-44-88, 90, 92. 103, 109, 125-Bondage-c.*

POLICE LINE-UP
Aug, 1951 - No. 4, July, 1952
Realistic Comics/Avon Periodicals

	Good	Fine	Mint
1-Wood-a, 1 pg. plus part-c; spanking panel-r/Saint No. 5	12.00	36.00	84.00
2-Classic story "The Religious Murder Cult," drugs, perversion r-/Saint No. 5; c-/Avon paperback 329	11.00	33.00	76.00
3-Kubert-a(r)/part-c, Kinstler-a; drug mention story	6.50	19.50	45.00
4-Kinstler-a	6.50	19.50	45.00

POLICE THRILLS
1954
Ajax/Farrell Publications

	Good	Fine	Mint
1	2.35	7.00	16.00

POLICE TRAP (Public Defender In Action No. 7 on)
8-9/54 - No. 4, 2-3/55; No. 5, 7/55 - No. 6, 9/55
Mainline No. 1-4/Charlton No. 5,6

	Good	Fine	Mint
1-S&K covers-all issues	4.65	14.00	32.00
2-4	2.35	7.00	16.00
5,6-S&K-c/a	4.35	13.00	30.00

POLICE TRAP
No. 11, 1963; No. 16-18, 1964
Super Comics

	Good	Fine	Mint
Reprint No. 11,16-18	.50	1.50	3.00

POLL PARROT
Poll Parrot Shoe Store/International Shoe
1950 - 1951; 1959 - 1962
K. K. Publications (Giveaway)

	Good	Fine	Mint
1 ('50)-Howdy Doody; small size	2.00	6.00	14.00
2-4('50)-Howdy Doody	1.15	3.50	8.00
2('59)-16('61): 2-The Secret of Crumbley Castle. 5-Bandit Busters. 7-The Make-Believe Mummy. 8-Mixed Up Mission('60). 10-The Frightful Flight. 11-Showdown at Sunup. 13-. . . and the Runaway Genie. 14-Bully for You. 16-. . . & the Rajah's Ruby('62)	.50	1.50	3.00

POLLY & HER PALS (See Comic Monthly No. 1)

POLLYANNA (See 4-Color No. 1129)

POLLY PIGTAILS (Girls' Fun & Fashion Mag. No. 44 on)
Jan, 1946 - V4No.43, Oct-Nov, 1949
Parents' Magazine Institute/Polly Pigtails

	Good	Fine	Mint
1-Infinity-c	4.00	12.00	28.00
2	2.00	6.00	14.00
3-5	1.75	5.25	12.00
6-10	1.35	4.00	9.00
11-30	1.15	3.50	8.00
31-43	1.00	3.00	7.00

PONY EXPRESS (See Four Color No. 942)

PONYTAIL
7-9/62 - No. 12, 10-12/65; No. 13, 11/69 - No. 20, 1/71
Dell Publishing Co./Charlton No. 13 on

	Good	Fine	Mint
12-641-209(No.1)	.75	2.25	5.00
2-12	.50	1.50	3.00
13-20	.35	1.00	2.00

POP COMICS (7 cents)
1955 (36 pgs.; 5x7"; in color)
Modern Store Publ.

	Good	Fine	Mint
1-Funny animal	.50	1.50	3.00

POPEYE (See Comic Album No. 7,11,15, Comics Reading Libraries, Eat Right to Work. . ., Giant Comic Album & March of Comics No. 37, 52, 66, 80, 96, 117, 134, 148, 157, 169, 194, 246, 264, 274, 294, 453, 465, 477)

Police Badge #479, #5, © MCG

Police Comics #45, © QUA

Police Line-Up #1, © AVON

Popeye #8, © KING

Popeye #66 (GK Giant), © KING

Popular Comics #12, © DELL

POPEYE (See Thimble Theatre)
1935 (25 cents; 52 pgs.; B&W) (By Segar)
David McKay Publications

	Good	Fine	Mint
1-Daily strip serial reprints-''The Gold Mine Thieves''	40.00	120.00	280.00
2-Daily strip-r	32.00	95.00	225.00

NOTE: *Popeye first entered Thimble Theatre in 1929.*

POPEYE
1937 (8-3/8''x9-3/8'') (cardboard covers)
(All color drawings plus text taken from Segar; probably not by him)
Whitman Publishing Co.

	Good	Fine	Mint
. . . Borrows a Baby Nurse (72 pgs.)			
. . . & His Jungle Pet (72 pgs.)			
each. . . .	19.00	57.00	132.00
. . . Goes Duck Hunting (28 pgs.)			
Wimpy Tricks Popeye & Rough-House (28 pgs.)			
. . . Plays Nursemaid to Sweet Pea (28 pgs.)			
. . . Calls on Olive Oyl (28 pgs.)			
each. . . .	16.00	48.00	110.00

POPEYE
1937 - 1939 (All by Segar)
David McKay Publications

	Good	Fine	Mint
Feature Books nn (100 pgs.) (Very Rare)	385.00	1155.00	2700.00
Feature Books 2 (52 pgs.)	45.00	135.00	315.00
Feature Books 3 (100 pgs.)-r-/nn issue with a new-c	38.50	115.00	270.00
Feature Books 5,10 (76 pgs.)	30.00	90.00	210.00
Feature Books 14 (76 pgs.) (Scarce)	44.50	134.00	310.00

POPEYE (Strip reprints through 4-Color No. 70)
1941 - 1947; No. 1, 2-4/48 - No. 65, 7-9/62; No. 66, 10/62 - No. 80, 5/66; No. 81, 8/66 - No. 92, 12/67; No. 94, 2/69 - No. 138, 1/77; No. 139, 5/78 - No. 171, 7/84 (no No.93,160,161)
Dell No. 1-65/Gold Key No. 66-80/King No. 81-92/Charlton No. 94-138/Gold Key No. 139-155/Whitman No. 156 on

	Good	Fine	Mint
Large Feat. Comic 24('41)-½ by Segar	30.00	90.00	210.00
4-Color 25('41)-by Segar	33.00	100.00	230.00
Large Feature Comic 10('43)	24.00	72.00	170.00
4-Color 17('43)-by Segar	26.00	78.00	180.00
4-Color 26('43)-by Segar	24.00	72.00	170.00
4-Color 43('44)	15.00	45.00	105.00
4-Color 70('45)-Title: . . . & Wimpy	13.00	40.00	90.00
4-Color 113('46-original strips begin),127,145('47),168	7.00	21.00	50.00
1(2-4/48)(Dell)	17.00	51.00	120.00
2	8.50	25.50	60.00
3-10	7.00	21.00	50.00
11-20	5.00	15.00	35.00
21-40	3.65	11.00	25.00
41-45,47-50	2.65	8.00	18.00
46-Origin Swee' Pee	3.65	11.00	25.00
51-60	1.75	5.25	12.00
61-65 (Last Dell ish.)	1.30	4.00	9.00
66,67-both 84 pgs. (G. Key)	2.50	7.50	20.00
68-80	1.30	4.00	9.00
81-92,94-100	.75	2.25	5.00
101-130	.50	1.50	3.50
131-143,145-159,162-171	.45	1.35	3.00
144-50th Anniversary issue	.45	1.35	3.00

NOTE: *Reprints-No. 145, 147, 149, 151, 153, 155, 157, 163-68(⅓), 170.*

	Good	Fine	Mint
Bold Detergent giveaway (Same as regular issue No. 94)	.35	1.00	2.00
. . . Kite Fun Book (PG&E, 1977)	1.00	3.00	6.00

POPEYE
1972 - 1974 (36 pgs. in color)
Charlton (King Features) (Giveaway)

	Good	Fine	Mint
E-1 to E-15 (Educational comics)		.50	1.00
nn-Popeye Gettin' Better Grades-4 pgs. used as intro. to above giveaways (in color)		.50	1.00

POPEYE CARTOON BOOK
1934 (40 pgs. plus cover)(8½x13'')(cardboard covers)
The Saalfield Publ. Co.

	Good	Fine	Mint
2095-(Rare)-1933 strip reprints in color by Segar; each page contains a vertical half of a Sunday strip, so the continuity reads row by row completely across each double page spread. If each page is read by itself, the continuity makes no sense. Each double page spread reprints one complete Sunday page (from 1933).	75.00	225.00	525.00
12 Page Version	40.00	120.00	280.00

POPPLES (TV, Movie)
Dec, 1986 - Present
Star Comics (Marvel)

	Good	Fine	Mint
1,2-Based on toys		.35	.70

POPPO OF THE POPCORN THEATRE
10/29/55 - 1956 (published weekly)
Fuller Publishing Co. (Publishers Weekly)

	Good	Fine	Mint
1	1.75	5.25	12.00
2-13	1.00	3.00	7.00

NOTE: *By **Charles Biro**. 10¢ cover price, given away by supermarkets such as IGA.*

POP-POP COMICS
No date (Circa 1945) (52 pgs.)
R. B. Leffingwell Co.

	Good	Fine	Mint
1-Funny animal	3.50	10.50	24.00

POPSICLE PETE FUN BOOK
1947, 1948
Joe Lowe Corp.

	Good	Fine	Mint
nn-36 pgs. in color; Sammy 'n' Claras, The King Who Couldn't Sleep & Popsicle Pete stories, games, cut-outs	4.00	12.00	28.00
Adventure Book ('48)	3.35	10.00	23.00

POPULAR COMICS
Feb, 1936 - No. 145, July-Sept, 1948
Dell Publishing Co.

	Good	Fine	Mint
1-Dick Tracy, Little Orphan Annie, Terry & the Pirates, Gasoline Alley, Moon Mullins, The Gumps begin (all strip-r)	85.00	255.00	600.00
2	40.00	120.00	280.00
3	35.00	105.00	245.00
4,5	25.00	75.00	175.00
6-10: 8-Scribbly app.	20.00	60.00	140.00
11-20	16.00	48.00	110.00
21-27-Last Terry & the Pirates, Little Orphan Annie, & Dick Tracy	14.00	42.00	95.00
28-37: 35-Christmas-c	12.00	36.00	84.00
38-43-Tarzan in text only	13.50	40.50	95.00
44,45	9.00	27.00	62.00
46-Origin Martan, the Marvel Man	13.00	40.00	90.00
47-50	9.00	27.00	62.00
51-Origin The Voice (The Invisible Detective) strip begins	10.00	30.00	70.00
52-59: 55-End of World sty	8.00	24.00	56.00
60-Origin Professor Supermind and Son	9.00	27.00	62.00
61-71: 63-Smilin' Jack begins	8.00	24.00	56.00
72-The Owl & Terry & the Pirates begin; Smokey Stover reprints begin	10.00	30.00	70.00
73-75	8.00	24.00	56.00
76-78-Capt. Midnight in all	10.00	30.00	70.00
79-85-Last Owl	7.00	21.00	50.00

POPULAR COMICS (continued)

	Good	Fine	Mint
86-99: 98-Felix the Cat, Smokey Stover-r begin	5.75	17.25	40.00
100	7.00	21.00	50.00
101-130: 115-Last Dick Tracy-r	4.00	12.00	28.00
131-145	3.50	10.50	24.00

POPULAR FAIRY TALES (See March of Comics No. 6,18)

POPULAR ROMANCE
No. 5, Dec, 1949 - No. 29, 1954
Better-Standard Publications

	Good	Fine	Mint
5	3.15	9.50	22.00
6-9	2.00	6.00	14.00
10-Wood-a, 2 pgs.	3.65	11.00	25.00
11,12,14-21,28,29	1.70	5.00	11.50
13-Severin/Elder-a, 3 pgs.	1.85	5.50	13.00
22-27-Toth-a	4.00	12.00	28.00

NOTE: *All have photo-c.* ***Tuska*** *art in most issues.*

POPULAR TEEN-AGERS (Secrets of Love) (Formerly School Day Romances)
Sept, 1950 - No. 23, Nov, 1954
Star Publications

	Good	Fine	Mint
5-Toni Gay, Honey Bunn, etc.; L. B. Cole-c	10.00	30.00	70.00
6-8-Toni Gay, Honey Bunn, etc.; all have L. B. Cole-c; 6-Negligee panels	9.00	27.00	62.00
9-(. . . Romances; change to romance format)	3.50	10.50	24.00
10-(. . . Secrets of Love)	3.50	10.50	24.00
11,16,18,19,22,23	2.85	8.50	20.00
12,13,17,20,21-Disbrow-a	3.50	10.50	24.00
14-Harrison/Wood-a; 2 spanking scenes	11.50	34.50	80.00
15-Wood?, Disbrow-a	8.00	24.00	55.00
Accepted Reprint 5,6 (nd); L.B. Cole-c	2.00	6.00	14.00

NOTE: *All have* ***L. B. Cole*** *covers.*

PORE LI'L MOSE
1902 (30 pgs.; 10½x15''; in full color)
New York Herald Publ. by Grand Union Tea
Cupples & Leon Co.

	Good	Fine	Mint
By R. F. Outcault; 1 pg. strips about early Negroes	27.00	81.00	190.00

PORKY PIG (. . & Bugs Bunny No. 40-69)
No. 16, 1942 - No. 109, July, 1984
Dell Publishing Co./Gold Key No. 1-93/Whitman No. 94 on

	Good	Fine	Mint
4-Color 16(1942)	30.00	90.00	210.00
4-Color 48(1944)-Carl Barks-a	60.00	180.00	420.00
4-Color 78(1945)	10.00	30.00	70.00
4-Color 112(7/46)	6.00	18.00	42.00
4-Color 156,182,191('49)	4.00	12.00	28.00
4-Color 226,241('49),260,271,277,284,295('50)	2.85	8.50	20.00
4-Color 303,311,322,330	2.00	6.00	14.00
4-Color 342,351,360,370,385,399('52),410,426	1.50	4.50	10.00
25 (11-12/52)-30	1.00	3.00	7.00
31-50	.55	1.65	4.00
51-81(3-4/62)	.45	1.35	3.00
1(1/65-G.K.)(2nd Series)	.75	2.25	5.00
2,4,5-Reprints 4-Color 226,284 & 271 in that order	.45	1.35	3.00
3,6-10	.35	1.00	2.00
11-50		.50	1.00
51-109		.30	.60

NOTE: *Reprints-No. 1-8, 9-35(2/3); 36-46,58,67,69-74,76,78,102-109(1/3-1/2).*

PORKY PIG (See March of Comics No. 42, 57, 71, 89, 99, 113, 130, 143, 164, 175, 192, 209, 218, 367, and Super Book No. 6, 18, 30)

PORKY'S BOOK OF TRICKS
1942 (48 pages) (8½x5½'')
K. K. Publications (Giveaway)

	Good	Fine	Mint
7 pg. comic story, text stories, plus games & puzzles	24.00	70.00	150.00

POST GAZETTE (See Meet the New. . .)

POWDER RIVER RUSTLERS (See Fawcett Movie Comics)

POWER COMICS
1944 - 1945
Holyoke Publ. Co./Narrative Publ.

	Good	Fine	Mint
1-L. B. Cole-c	13.50	40.50	95.00
2-4: 2-Dr. Mephisto begins. 3,4-L. B. Cole-c; Miss Espionage app. each	12.00	36.00	84.00

POWERHOUSE PEPPER COMICS (See Gay & Joker Comics)
No. 1, 1943; No. 2, May, 1948 - No. 5, Nov, 1948
Marvel Comics (20CC)

	Good	Fine	Mint
1-(60 pgs.)-Wolverton-a	50.00	150.00	350.00
2-Wolverton-a	30.00	90.00	210.00
3,4-Both by Wolverton	28.00	84.00	195.00
5-(Scarce)-Wolverton-a	34.00	102.00	236.00

POWER LORDS
Dec, 1983 - No. 3, Feb, 1984 (Mando paper)
DC Comics

	Good	Fine	Mint
1-Based on Revell toys		.40	.80
2,3		.40	.80

POWER MAN (Formerly Hero for Hire; . . & Iron Fist No. 68 on)
No. 17, Feb, 1974 - No. 125, Sept, 1986
Marvel Comics Group

	Good	Fine	Mint
17-20: 17-Iron Man app.	.40	1.20	2.40
21-31: 31-Part adams inks		.60	1.20
32-47: 36-Reprint. 45-Starlin-c		.50	1.00
48-Byrne-a; Powerman/Iron Fist 1st meet	.50	1.50	3.00
49,50-Byrne-a(p); 50-Iron Fist joins Cage	.50	1.50	3.00
51-56,58-60: 58-Intro El Aguila		.40	.80
57-New X-Men app.	.85	2.50	5.00
61-74: 68-Miller c/a		.30	.60
75-Double size; Larkin painted-c	.25	.75	1.50
76,77-Miller Daredevil (2 pgs. ea.)		.40	.80
78-99,101-124: 87-Moon Knight app. 90-Unus app. 109-The Reaper app.		.30	.60
100-Double size; painted-c; origin K'un L'un		.50	1.00
125-Double size		.60	1.20
Giant-Size 1('75)	.30	.80	1.60
Annual 1(11/76)		.50	1.00

NOTE: ***Austin*** *c-102i.* ***Byrne*** *a-48-50; c-102, 104, 106, 107.* ***Kane*** *c(p)-24, 25, 28, 48.* ***Layton*** *c-55p, 56-59, 60p, 61, 62i, 124i.* ***Leialoha*** *a-60i.* ***Miller*** *c-66, 67, 70-74, 80i.* ***Mooney*** *a-53i, 55i.* ***Nebres*** *a-76p.* ***Nino*** *a-42i, 43i.* ***Perez*** *a-27.* ***Tuska*** *a-17p.*

POWERMOWERMAN AND POWER MOWER SAFETY
1966 (16 pgs.) (Giveaway)
Frank Burgmeier Co. (Outdoor Power Equipment Inst.)

	Good	Fine	Mint
nn-Vaughn Bode'-a	22.00	65.00	130.00

POWER PACK
Aug, 1984 - Present
Marvel Comics Group

	Good	Fine	Mint
1-($1.00)	.50	1.50	3.00
2-5	.35	1.10	2.20
6-8-Cloak & Dagger app.	.30	.90	1.80
9-18		.60	1.20

Popular Teen-Agers #11, © STAR

Powerhouse Pepper Comics #5, © MCG

Power Man #49, © MCG

Primer #2, © Comico

Prime Slime Tales #1, © Mirage

Prison Break! #2, © AVON

POWER PACK (continued)

	Good	Fine	Mint
19-Dbl. size; Cloak & Dagger, Wolverine app.	.35	1.00	2.00
20-24		.50	1.00
25-Double size	.25	.75	1.50
26-Direct sale; Cloak & Dagger app.		.50	1.00
27-30		.50	1.00

POWER PLAYS
Sum, 1985 - Present ($1.75, B&W, 52 pgs.)
Americomics

	Good	Fine	Mint
1,2: 1-Reprint	.30	.90	1.75

POW MAGAZINE (Bob Sproul's) (Satire Magazine)
Aug, 1966 - No. 3, Feb, 1967 (30 cents)
Humor-Vision

	Good	Fine	Mint
1-3: 2-Jones-a. 3-Wrightson-a	.85	2.50	5.00

PREHISTORIC WORLD (See Classics Special)

PREMIERE (See Charlton Premiere)

PRESSBUTTON (See Axel Pressbutton)

PRESTO KID, THE (See Red Mask)

PRE-TEEN DIRTY-GENE KUNG-FU KANGAROOS (Also see Laffin' Gas No. 1)
Aug, 1986 - Present ($1.50, B&W)
Blackthorne Publ.

	Good	Fine	Mint
1,2	.25	.75	1.50

PRETTY BOY FLOYD (See On the Spot)

PREZ (See Cancelled Comic Cavalcade & Supergirl No. 10)
Aug-Sept, 1973 - No. 4, Feb-Mar, 1974
National Periodical Publications

	Good	Fine	Mint
1-Origin		.30	.60
2-4		.25	.50

PRICE, THE
Oct, 1981 (Graphic Album, $7.95)
Eclipse Comics

	Good	Fine	Mint
1-Starlin-a	1.35	4.00	7.95

PRIDE AND THE PASSION, THE (See 4-Color No. 824)

PRIDE OF THE YANKEES, THE
1949 (The Life of Lou Gehrig)
Magazine Enterprises

	Good	Fine	Mint
nn-Ogden Whitney-a	18.00	54.00	125.00

PRIMAL MAN (See The Crusaders)

PRIMER (Comico. . .)
1982 - No. 6, 1985 (B&W)
Comico

	Good	Fine	Mint
1 (52 pgs.)	.70	2.00	4.00
2-1st app. Grendel by Wagner	6.00	18.00	36.00
3-5	.45	1.40	2.80
6-Intro Evangeline	1.50	4.50	9.00

PRIME SLIME TALES
1986 - Present ($1.50, B&W)
Mirage Studios/Now Comics No. 3 on

	Good	Fine	Mint
1	.45	1.30	2.60
2,3	.35	1.10	2.20

PRIMUS (TV)
Feb, 1972 - No. 7, Oct, 1972
Charlton Comics

	Good	Fine	Mint
1-5,7-Staton-a in all	.35	1.00	2.00
6-Drug propaganda story	.35	1.00	2.00

PRINCE & THE PAUPER, THE (See Movie Classics)

PRINCE NAMOR, THE SUB-MARINER
Sept, 1984 - No. 4, Dec, 1984 (mini-series)
Marvel Comics Group

	Good	Fine	Mint
1		.60	1.20
2-4		.45	.90

PRINCE VALIANT (See Comics Reading Libraries, Feature Books No. 26, McKay, and 4-Color No. 567, 650, 699, 719, 788, 849, 900)

PRISCILLA'S POP (See 4-Color No. 569,630,704,799)

PRISON BARS (See Behind. . .)

PRISON BREAK!
1951 (Sept) - No. 5, Sept, 1952
Avon Periodicals/Realistic No. 4 on

	Good	Fine	Mint
1-Wood-c & 1 pg.; has r-/Saint No. 7 retitled Michael Strong Private Eye	15.00	45.00	105.00
2-Wood-c/Kubert-a plus 2 pgs. Wood-a	10.00	30.00	70.00
3-Orlando, Check-a; c-/Avon paperback 179	9.00	27.00	62.00
4,5: Kinstler-c. 5-Infantino-a	8.00	24.00	56.00

PRISON RIOT
1952
Avon Periodicals

	Good	Fine	Mint
1-Marijuana Murders-1 pg. text; Kinstler-c	12.00	36.00	84.00

PRISON TO PRAISE
1974 (35 ¢)
Logos International

	Good	Fine	Mint
True Story of Merlin R. Carothers		.30	.60

PRIVATE BUCK (See Large Feature Comic No. 12 & 21)

PRIVATE EYE (Rocky Jordan. . . No. 6-8)
Jan, 1951 - No. 8, March, 1952
Atlas Comics (MCI)

	Good	Fine	Mint
1	3.65	11.00	25.00
2,3-Tuska c/a(3)	2.35	7.00	16.00
4-8	2.00	6.00	14.00

NOTE: ***Henkel** a-6(3), 7; c-7. **Sinnott** a-6.*

PRIVATE EYE (See Mike Shayne. . .)

PRIVATE SECRETARY
Dec-Feb, 1962-63 - No. 2, Mar-May, 1963
Dell Publishing Co.

	Good	Fine	Mint
1,2	1.00	3.00	7.00

PRIVATE STRONG (See The Double Life of. . .)

PRIZE COMICS (. . . Western No. 69 on) (Also see Treasure Comics)
March, 1940 - No. 68, Feb-Mar, 1948
Prize Publications

	Good	Fine	Mint
1-Origin Power Nelson, The Futureman & Jupiter, Master Magician; Ted O'Neil, Secret Agent M-11, Jaxon of the Jungle, Bucky Brady & Storm Curtis begin	57.00	171.00	400.00
2-The Black Owl begins	28.00	84.00	195.00
3,4	22.00	65.00	154.00
5,6: Dr. Dekkar, Master of Monsters app. in each	20.00	60.00	140.00
7-Black Owl by S&K; origin/1st app. Dr. Frost & Frankenstein; The Green Lama, Capt. Gallant, The Great Voodini & Twist Turner begin; Kirby-c	45.00	135.00	315.00
8,9-Black Owl & Ted O'Neil by S&K	23.00	70.00	160.00
10-12,14-20: 11-Origin Bulldog Denny. 16-Spike Mason begins	20.00	60.00	140.00
13-Origin Yank & Doodle	25.00	75.00	175.00
21-24	11.00	33.00	76.00

PRIZE COMICS (continued) — Good / Fine / Mint

25-30 8.50 25.50 60.00
31-33 6.50 19.50 45.00
34-Origin Airmale, & Yank & Doodle; The Black Owl joins army, Yank & Doodle's father assumes Black Owl's role
7.00 21.00 50.00
35-40: 35-Flying Fist & Bingo begin. 37-Intro. Stampy, Airmale's sidekick 5.50 16.50 38.00
41-50: 45-Yank & Doodle learn Black Owl's I.D. (their father). 48-Prince Ra begins 4.35 13.00 30.00
51-62,64-68: 53-Transvestism sty. 55-No Frankenstein. 64-Black Owl retires 3.75 11.25 26.00
63-Simon & Kirby c/a 5.50 16.50 38.00

NOTE: *Briefer a 7-on.* ***J. Binder*** *a-16.*

PRIZE COMICS WESTERN (Prize No. 1-68)
No. 69(V7No.2), Apr-May, 1948 - No. 119, Nov-Dec, 1956
Prize Publications (Feature) (No. 69-84, 52 pgs.)

69(V7No.2) 5.00 15.00 35.00
70-75 3.75 11.25 26.00
76-Randolph Scott photo-c; "Canadian Pacific" movie adapt.
5.00 15.00 35.00
77-Photo-c; Severin, Mart Bailey-a; 'Streets of Laredo' movie adapt.
4.35 13.00 30.00
78-Photo-c; Kurtzman-a, 10 pgs.; Severin, Mart Bailey-a; 'Bullet Code,' & 'Roughshod' movie adapt. 6.50 19.50 45.00
79-Photo-c; Kurtzman-a, 8 pgs.; Severin & Elder, Severin, Mart Bailey-a; 'Stage To Chino' movie adapt. 6.50 19.50 45.00
80,81-Photo-c; Severin/Elder-a(2) 4.00 12.00 28.00
82-Photo-c; 1st app. The Preacher by Mart Bailey; Severin/Elder-a(3)
4.00 12.00 28.00
83,84 3.50 10.50 24.00
85-American Eagle by John Severin begins (1-2/50)
7.00 21.00 50.00
86,92,95,101-105 3.35 10.00 23.00
87-91,93,94,96-99,110,111-Severin/Elder a(2-3) each
3.65 11.00 25.00
100 5.00 15.00 35.00
106-108,112 2.85 8.50 20.00
109-Severin/Williamson-a 4.75 14.25 33.00
113-Williamson/Severin-a(2) 5.50 16.50 38.00
114-119: Drifter series in all; by Mort Meskin 114-118
2.35 7.00 16.00

NOTE: ***Fass*** *a-81.* ***Severin & Elder*** *c-88, 92, 94-96, 98.* ***Severin*** *a-72, 75, 77-79, 83-86, 96, 97, 100-105; c-most 85-109.* ***Simon & Kirby*** *c-75, 83.*

PRIZE MYSTERY
May, 1955 - No. 3, Sept, 1955
Key Publications

1 2.15 6.50 15.00
2,3 1.50 4.50 10.00

PROFESSIONAL FOOTBALL (See Charlton Sport Library)

PROFESSOR COFFIN
No. 19, Oct, 1985 - No. 21, Feb, 1986
Charlton Comics

19-21: Wayne Howard-a(r) .40 .80

PSI FORCE
Nov, 1986 - Present
Marvel Comics Group

1 .60 1.20
2-6 .50 1.00

PSYCHO (Magazine)
Jan, 1971 - No. 24, Mar, 1975 (68 pgs.; B&W) (no No.22?)
Skywald Publishing Corp.

Good / Fine / Mint

1-All reprints .35 1.10 2.20
2-Origin & 1st app. The Heap, & Frankenstein series by Adkins
.30 .90 1.80
3-10 .30 .80 1.60
11-21,23: 13-Cannabalism. 18-Injury to eye-c. 20-Severed Head-c
.50 1.00
24-1975 Winter Special .60 1.20
Annual 1('72) .30 .80 1.60
Fall Special('74) .60 1.20
Yearbook(1974-nn) .60 1.20

NOTE: ***Boris*** *c-3, 5.* ***Buckler*** *a-4 ,5.* ***Everett*** *a-3-6.* ***Jones*** *a-7; c-12.* ***Kaluta*** *a-13.* ***Katz/Buckler*** *a-3.* ***Morrow*** *a-1.* ***Reese*** *a-5.* ***Sutton*** *a-3.* ***Wildey*** *a-5.*

PSYCHOANALYSIS
Mar-Apr, 1955 - No. 4, Sept-Oct, 1955
E. C. Comics

1-All Kamen; not approved by code 6.00 18.00 38.00
2-4-Kamen-a in all 4.75 14.00 30.00

P.T. 109 (See Movie Comics)

PUBLIC DEFENDER IN ACTION (Formerly Police Trap)
No. 7, Mar, 1956 - No. 12, Oct, 1957
Charlton Comics

7 2.15 6.50 15.00
8-12 1.30 4.00 9.00

PUBLIC ENEMIES
1948 - No. 9, June-July, 1949
D. S. Publishing Co.

1 4.65 14.00 32.00
2-Used in **SOTI**, pg. 95 6.50 19.50 45.00
3-5 2.75 8.25 19.00
6,8,9 2.50 7.50 17.50
7-McWilliams-a; injury to eye panel 3.75 11.25 26.00

PUDGY PIG
Sept, 1958 - No. 2, Nov, 1958
Charlton Comics

1,2 .75 2.25 5.00

PUNCH & JUDY COMICS
1944 - V3No.9, Dec, 1951
Hillman Periodicals

V1No.1-(60 pgs.) 4.65 14.00 32.00
2 2.35 7.00 16.00
3-12(7/46) 1.70 5.00 11.50
V2No.1,3-9 1.30 4.00 9.00
V2No.2,10-12, V3No.1-Kirby-a(2) each 6.50 19.50 45.00
V3No.2-Kirby-a 5.50 16.50 38.00
3-9 1.15 3.50 8.00

PUNCH COMICS
Dec, 1941 - No. 26, Dec, 1947
Harry 'A' Chesler

1-Mr. E, The Sky Chief, Hale the Magician, Kitty Kelly begin
32.00 95.00 225.00
2-Captain Glory app. 16.00 48.00 110.00
3 13.50 40.50 95.00
4 11.50 34.50 80.00
5 9.50 28.50 65.00
6-8 8.50 25.50 60.00
9-Rocketman & Rocket Girl & The Master Key begin
9.50 28.50 65.00
10-Sky Chief app.; J. Cole-a; Master Key r-/Scoop 3
8.50 25.50 60.00

Prize Comics #31, © PRIZE

Prize Comics Western #92, © PRIZE

Public Enemies #6, © DS

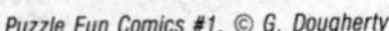
Puzzle Fun Comics #1, © G. Dougherty

Queen of the West, Dale Evans #4, © Roy Rogers

Quick-Draw McGraw #12, © Hanna-Barbera

PUNCH COMICS (continued)

	Good	Fine	Mint
11-Origin Master Key-r/Scoop 1; Sky Chief, Little Nemo app.; Jack Cole-a; Fineish art by Sultan	8.50	25.50	60.00
12-Rocket Boy & Capt. Glory app; Skull-c	7.00	21.00	50.00
13-17,19: 13-Cover has list of 4 Chesler artists' names on tombstone	7.00	21.00	50.00
18-Bondage-c; hypodermic panels	8.50	25.50	60.00
20-Unique cover with bare-breasted women	13.50	40.50	95.00
21-Hypo needle story	7.00	21.00	50.00
22-26: 22,23-Little Nemo-not by McCay	6.50	19.50	45.00

PUNCHY AND THE BLACK CROW
No. 10, Oct, 1985 - No. 12, Feb, 1986
Charlton Comics

10-12: Al Fago funny animal-r .40 .80

PUNISHER (Also see Amaz. Spider-Man, Marvel Preview 2 & Marvel Super Action)
Jan, 1986 - No. 5, May, 1986 (mini-series)
Marvel Comics Group

1-Double size	.90	2.75	5.50
2	.55	1.70	3.40
3	.45	1.40	2.80
4,5	.35	1.10	2.20

PUPPET COMICS
Spring, 1946 - No. 2, Summer, 1946
George W. Dougherty Co.

1,2 2.65 8.00 18.00

PUPPETOONS (See George Pal's . . .)

PURE OIL COMICS (Also see Salerno Carnival of Comics, 24 Pages of Comics, & Vicks Comics)
Late 1930's (24 pgs.; regular size) (paper cover)
Pure Oil Giveaway

nn-Contains 1-2 pg. strips; i.e., Hairbreadth Harry, Skyroads, Buck Rogers by Calkins & Yager, Olly of the Movies, Napoleon, S'Matter Pop, etc.	24.00	70.00	150.00
Also a 16 pg. 1938 giveaway with Buck Rogers	18.50	55.00	120.00

PURPLE CLAW, THE (Also see Tales of Horror)
Jan, 1953 - No. 3, May, 1953
Minoan Publishing Co./Toby Press

1-Origin	6.50	19.50	45.00
2,3: 1-3 r-in Tales of Horror No. 9-11	4.50	13.50	30.00
I.W. Reprint No. 8-Reprints No. 1	.80	2.40	4.80

PUSSYCAT (Magazine)
Oct, 1968 (B&W reprints from Men's magazines)
Marvel Comics Group

1-(Scarce)-Ward, Everett, Wood-a; Everett-c 12.00 36.00 84.00

PUZZLE FUN COMICS (Also see Jingle Jangle)
Spring, 1946 - No. 2, Summer, 1946 (52 pgs.)
George W. Dougherty Co.

1(1946)-Gustavson-a	6.50	19.50	45.00
2	5,00	15.00	35.00

NOTE: *No. 1,2('46) each contain a **George Carlson** cover plus a 6 pg. story "Alec in Fumbleland;" also many puzzles in each.*

QUAKER OATS (Also see Cap'n Crunch)
1965 (Giveaway) (2½x5½") (16 pages)
Quaker Oats Co.

"Plenty of Glutton," "Lava Come-Back," "Kite Tale," "A Witch in Time" .50 1.00

QUEEN OF THE WEST, DALE EVANS (TV)(See Western Roundup)
No. 479, 7/53 - No. 22, 1-3/59 (All photo-c; photo back c-4-8, 15)
Dell Publishing Co.

	Good	Fine	Mint
4-Color 479('53)	4.50	13.50	30.00
4-Color 528('54)	3.50	10.50	24.00
3(4-6/54)-Toth-a	4.00	12.00	28.00
4-Toth, Manning-a	4.00	12.00	28.00
5-10-Manning-a. 5-Marsh-a?	2.85	8.50	20.00
11,19,21-No Manning 21-Tufts-a	2.00	6.00	14.00
12-18,20,22-Manning-a	2.65	8.00	18.00

QUENTIN DURWARD (See 4-Color No. 672)

QUESTAR ILLUSTRATED SCIENCE FICTION CLASSICS
1977 (224 pgs.) ($1.95)
Golden Press

11197-Stories by Asimov, Sturgeon, Silverberg & Niven; Star-stream-r .50 1.50 3.00

QUESTION, THE (See Mysterious Suspense)

QUESTION, THE
Feb, 1987 - Present
DC Comics

1,2 .25 .75 1.50

QUEST PRESENTS
July, 1983 - No. 3, Nov, 1983
Quest Publications

1,2 (B&W)-Lance Carrigan of the Galactic Legion begins by Disbrow		.50	1.00
3 ($1.50, color)	.25	.75	1.50

QUESTPROBE
8/84; (One-shot) 9/85 - No. 4, 12/85 (limited series)
Marvel Comics Group

1 (8/84)		.40	.80
1-4		.40	.80

QUICK-DRAW McGRAW (TV) (Hanna-Barbera)
No. 1040, 12-2/59-60 - No. 11, 7-9/62; No. 12, 11/62; No. 13, 2/63; No. 14, 4/63; No. 15, 6/69
Dell Publishing Co./Gold Key No. 12 on

4-Color 1040	2.00	6.00	14.00
2(4-6/60)-6	1.15	3.50	8.00
7-11	.85	2.50	6.00
12,13-Title change to . . . Fun-Type Roundup (84 pgs.)	2.50	7.50	20.00
14,15	.85	2.50	6.00

(See Whitman Comic Books)

QUICK-DRAW McGRAW (TV)
Nov, 1970 - No. 8, Jan, 1972 (Hanna-Barbera)
Charlton Comics

1	.85	2.50	5.00
2-8	.50	1.50	3.00

QUICK-TRIGGER WESTERN (. . . Action No. 12; formerly Cowboy Action)
No. 12, May, 1956 - No. 19, Sept, 1957
Atlas Comics (ACI No. 12/WPI No. 13-19)

12-Baker-a	3.15	9.50	22.00
13-Williamson-a, 5 pgs.	3.85	11.50	27.00
14-Everett, Crandall, Torres-a; Heath-c	3.35	10.00	23.00
15-Torres, Crandall-a	2.50	7.60	17.50
16-Orlando, Kirby-a	2.15	6.50	15.00
17-Crandall-a	1.85	5.50	13.00
18-Baker-a	1.85	5.50	13.00

QUICK-TRIGGER WESTERN (continued)

	Good	Fine	Mint
19	1.15	3.50	8.00

NOTE: ***Morrow*** *a-18.* ***Powell*** *a-14.* ***Severin*** *c-13,16,17,19.*

QUINCY (See Comics Reading Libraries)

RACCOON KIDS, THE (Formerly Movietown Animal Antics)
No. 52, Sept-Oct, 1954 - No. 64, Nov, 1957
National Periodical Publications (Arleigh No. 63,64)

	Good	Fine	Mint
52-Doodles Duck by Mayer	3.15	9.50	22.00
53-64: 53-62-Doodles Duck by Mayer	1.85	5.50	13.00

RACE FOR THE MOON
March, 1958 - No. 3, Nov, 1958
Harvey Publications

	Good	Fine	Mint
1-Powell-a(5); ½-pg. S&K-a; c-redrawn from Galaxy Science Fiction pulp (5/53)	5.00	15.00	35.00
2-Kirby/Williamson c(r)/a(3)	13.50	40.50	95.00
3-Kirby/Williamson c/a(4)	14.50	43.50	100.00

RACKET SQUAD IN ACTION
May-June, 1952 - No. 29, March, 1958
Capitol Stories/Charlton Comics

	Good	Fine	Mint
1	5.00	15.00	35.00
2-4	2.00	6.00	14.00
5-Dr. Neff, Ghost Breaker app; headlights-c	2.65	8.00	18.00
6-Dr. Neff, Ghost Breaker app.	2.35	7.00	16.00
7-10: 10-Explosion-c	2.00	6.00	14.00
11-Ditko c/a	6.00	18.00	42.00
12-Ditko explosion-c (classic); Shuster-a(2)	13.50	40.50	95.00
13-Shuster c/a; Ditko-a; acid in woman's face shown	6.00	18.00	42.00
14-"Shakedown"-marijuana story	4.65	14.00	32.00
15-28	1.70	5.00	11.50
29-(68 pgs.)(15¢)	1.85	5.50	13.00

RADIANT LOVE (Formerly Daring Love No. 1)
No. 2, Dec, 1953 - No. 6, Aug, 1954
Gilmor Magazines

	Good	Fine	Mint
2	2.50	7.50	17.50
3-6	1.70	5.00	11.50

RADIUM AND HIS INTERGALACTIC ODDSQUAD
1986 ($1.70, B&W)
Fantasy General Comics

	Good	Fine	Mint
1	.30	.90	1.70

RAGAMUFFINS
Jan, 1985 (One Shot)
Eclipse Comics

	Good	Fine	Mint
1-Eclipse Magazine-r, w/color	.30	.90	1.80

RAGGEDY ANN AND ANDY (See Dell Giants & March of Comics 23)
No. 5, 1942 - No. 533, 2/54; 10-12/64 - No. 4, 3/66
Dell Publishing Co.

	Good	Fine	Mint
4-Color 5(1942)	25.00	75.00	175.00
4-Color 23(1943)	18.00	54.00	125.00
4-Color 45(1943)	13.50	40.50	95.00
4-Color 72(1945)	11.50	34.50	80.00
1(6/46)-Billy & Bonnie Bee by Frank Thomas	13.00	40.00	90.00
2,3: 3-Egbert Elephant by Dan Noonan begins	7.00	21.00	50.00
4-Kelly-a, 16 pgs.	8.00	24.00	56.00
5-10: 7-Little Black Sambo, Black Mumbo & Black Jumbo only app; Christmas-c	6.00	18.00	42.00
11-20	4.65	14.00	32.00
21-Alice In Wonderland cover/story	4.65	14.00	32.00
22-39(8/49), 4-Color 262(1/50)	3.50	10.50	24.00
4-Color 306,354,380,452,533	3.00	9.00	21.00
1(10-12/64-Dell)	1.15	3.50	8.00
2,3(10-12/65), 4(3/66)	.75	2.25	5.00

NOTE: ***Kelly*** *art ("Animal Mother Goose")-No. 1-34, 36, 37; c-28. Peterkin Pottle by* ***John Stanley*** *in 32-38.*

RAGGEDY ANN AND ANDY
Dec, 1971 - No. 6, Sept, 1973
Gold Key

	Good	Fine	Mint
1	.70	2.00	4.00
2-6	.35	1.00	2.00

RAGGEDY ANN & THE CAMEL WITH THE WRINKLED KNEES (See Dell Jr. Treasury No. 8)

RAGMAN (See Batman Family No. 20 & Cancelled Comic Cavalcade)
Aug-Sept, 1976 - No. 5, June-July, 1977
National Periodical Publications

	Good	Fine	Mint
1-Origin		.40	.80
2-Origin concludes; Kubert-c		.30	.60
3-5: 4-Drug use story		.25	.50

NOTE: ***Kubert*** *a-4 ,5; c-1-5.* ***Redondo*** *studios a-1-4.*

RAGS RABBIT (See Harvey Hits No. 2 & Tastee Freez)
No. 11, June, 1951 - No. 18, March, 1954
Harvey Publications

	Good	Fine	Mint
11	1.00	3.00	7.00
12-18	.85	2.50	6.00

RAIDERS OF THE LOST ARK
Sept, 1981 - No. 3, Nov, 1981 (Movie adaptation)
Marvel Comics Group

	Good	Fine	Mint
1		.40	.80
2,3: 3-Final chapter of movie adapt.		.30	.60

NOTE: ***Buscema*** *a(p)-1-3; c(p)-1.* ***Simonson*** *a-2i, 3i.*

RAINBOW BRITE AND THE STAR STEALER
1985
DC Comics

	Good	Fine	Mint
nn-Movie adapt.		.40	.80

RALPH KINER, HOME RUN KING
1950 (Pittsburgh Pirates)
Fawcett Publications

	Good	Fine	Mint
nn	15.00	45.00	105.00

RALPH SNART ADVENTURES
June, 1986 - Present
Now Comics

	Good	Fine	Mint
1	.35	1.00	2.00
2,3	.25	.75	1.50
V2/1,2 (28 pgs.): 1-Origin Rodent Ralph	.25	.75	1.50

RAMAR OF THE JUNGLE (TV)
1954 (no month); No. 2, 9/55 - No. 5, 9/56
Toby Press No. 1/Charlton No. 2 on

	Good	Fine	Mint
1-Jon Hall photo-c	5.00	15.00	35.00
2-5	3.65	11.00	25.00

RAMPAGING HULK, THE (Magazine) (The Hulk No. 10 on)
Jan, 1977 - No. 9, June, 1978
Marvel Comics Group

	Good	Fine	Mint
1-Bloodstone featured	.50	1.50	3.00
2-Old X-Men app; origin old & new X-Men in text	.35	1.00	2.00

Racket Squad in Action #5, © CC

Raggedy Ann & Andy #8, © DELL

Ralph Snart Advs. #1 (6/86), © Now Comics

Range Romances #2, © QUA

Rat Patrol #5, © Mirisch-Rich TV Prod.

Rawhide #2, © CBS

RAMPAGING HULK (continued)

	Good	Fine	Mint
3-9		.50	1.00

NOTE: ***Alcala** a-1-3i, 5i, 8i. **Buscema** a-1. **Giffen** a-4. **Nino** a-4i. **Simonson** a-1-3p. **Starlin** a-4(w/Nino), 7; c-4, 5, 7.*

RANGE BUSTERS
Sept, 1950 - No. 8, 1951
Fox Features Syndicate

1	5.00	15.00	35.00
2	2.65	8.00	18.00
3-8	2.35	7.00	16.00

RANGE BUSTERS (Formerly Cowboy Love?; Wyatt Earp, Frontier Marshall No. 11 on)
No. 8, May, 1955 - No. 10, Sept, 1955
Charlton Comics

8	2.15	6.50	15.00
9,10	1.15	3.50	8.00

RANGELAND LOVE
Dec, 1949 - No. 2, Mar, 1950
Atlas Comics (CDS)

1,2	3.35	10.00	23.00

RANGER, THE (See 4-Color No. 255)

RANGE RIDER (See Flying A's. . .)

RANGE RIDER, THE (See 4-Color No. 404)

RANGE ROMANCES
Dec, 1949 - No. 5, Aug, 1950
Comic Magazines (Quality Comics)

1-Gustavson-c/a	11.00	33.00	76.00
2-Crandall-c/a; ''spanking'' scene	14.50	43.50	100.00
3-Crandall, Gustavson-a; photo-c	8.00	24.00	56.00
4-Crandall-a; photo-c	6.00	18.00	42.00
5-Gustavson-a; Crandall-a(p)	7.00	21.00	50.00

RANGERS COMICS (. . . of Freedom No. 1-7)
Oct, 1941 - No. 69, Winter, 1952-53
Fiction House Magazines (Flying stories)

1-Intro. Ranger Girl & The Rangers of Freedom; ends No. 7, cover app. only-No. 5	58.00	174.00	405.00
2	28.00	84.00	195.00
3	23.00	70.00	160.00
4,5	20.00	60.00	140.00
6-10: 8-U.S. Rangers begin	17.00	51.00	120.00
11,12-Commando Rangers app.	15.00	45.00	105.00
13-Commando Ranger begins-not same as Comm. Rangers	15.00	45.00	105.00
14-20	11.00	33.00	76.00
21-Firehair begins	13.50	40.50	95.00
22-30: 23-Kazanda begins, ends No. 28. 28-Origin Tiger Man. 30-Crusoe Island begins, ends No. 40	10.00	30.00	70.00
31-40: 33-Hypodermic panels	9.00	27.00	62.00
41-46	7.00	21.00	50.00
47-56-''Eisnerish'' Dr. Drew by Grandenetti	8.00	24.00	56.00
57-60-Straight Dr. Drew by Grandenetti	6.00	18.00	42.00
61,62,64-66: 64-Suicide Smith begins	5.00	15.00	35.00
63-Used in **POP**, pgs. 85, 99	5.50	16.50	38.50
67-69: 67-The Space Rangers begin, end No. 69	5.00	15.00	35.00

NOTE: *Bondage, discipline covers, lingerie panels are common. **Baker** a-36-38. **John Celardo** a-36-39. **Lee Elias** a-21-28. **Evans** a-19, 38-45, 47-52. **Ingels** a-13-16. **Larsen** a-34. **Bob Lubbers** a-30-38. **Moreira** a-45. **Tuska** a-16, 17, 19, 22.*

RANGO (TV)
August, 1967
Dell Publishing Co.

1	1.75	5.25	12.00

RAPHAEL
1985 (One Shot)
Mirage Studios

	Good	Fine	Mint
1	.50	1.50	3.00

RATFINK (See Frantic & Zany)
October, 1964
Canrom, Inc.

1-Woodbridge-a	2.35	7.00	14.00

RAT PATROL, THE (TV)
March, 1967 - No. 5, Nov, 1967; No. 6, Oct, 1969
Dell Publishing Co.

1	3.00	9.00	21.00
2	2.00	6.00	14.00
3-6: 3-6-Photo-c	1.50	4.50	10.00

RAVEN, THE (See Movie Classics)

RAVENS AND RAINBOWS
Dec, 1983 (Baxter paper)
Pacific Comics

1-Jeff Jones-c/a(r); nudity scenes	.25	.75	1.50

RAWHIDE (TV)
Sept-Nov, 1959 - June-Aug, 1962; July, 1963 - No. 2, Jan, 1964
Dell Publishing Co./Gold Key

4-Color 1028	7.00	21.00	48.00
4-Color 1097,1160,1202,1261,1269	5.00	15.00	35.00
01-684-208(8/62-Dell)	5.00	15.00	35.00
1(10071-307, G.K.), 2	4.35	13.00	30.00

NOTE: *All have Clint Eastwood photo-c. **Tufts** a-1028.*

RAWHIDE KID
3/55 - No. 16, 9/57; No. 17, 8/60 - No. 151, 5/79
Atlas/Marvel Comics (CnPC No. 1-16/AMI No. 17-30)

1-Rawhide Kid, his horse Apache & sidekick Randy begin; Wyatt Earp app.	10.00	30.00	70.00
2	5.00	15.00	35.00
3-5	3.00	9.00	21.00
6,8-10	2.00	6.00	14.00
7-Williamson-a, 4 pgs.	3.00	9.00	21.00
11-15	1.50	4.50	10.00
16-Torres-a	1.85	5.50	13.00
17-Origin by J. Kirby	2.65	8.00	18.00
18-22,24-30	.85	2.50	6.00
23-Origin by J. Kirby	2.15	6.50	15.00
31,32,36-44: 40-Two-Gun Kid x-over. 42-1st Larry Lieber issue	.75	2.25	5.00
33-35-Davis-a. 35-Intro & death of The Raven	1.00	3.00	7.00
45-Origin retold	1.30	4.00	9.00
46-Toth-a	1.15	3.50	8.00
47-70: 50-Kid Colt x-over. 64-Kid Colt story. 66-Two-Gun Kid story. 67-Kid Colt story	.50	1.50	3.00
71-85: 79-Williamson-a(r)		.60	1.20
86-Origin-r; Williamson-a r-/Ringo Kid No. 13, 4 pgs.	.35	1.00	2.00
87-99,101-115: Last new story		.60	1.20
100-Origin retold & expanded	.25	.75	1.50
116-151		.60	1.20
Special 1(9/71)-Reprints		.50	1.00

NOTE: ***Ayers** a-16. **Colan** c-145p, 148p. **Davis** a-125r. **Everett** a-54i, 65, 66, 88, 96i, 148i(r). **Gulacy** c-147. **Heath** c-4. **G. Kane** c-101, 144. **Keller** a-5. **Kirby** a-17-32, 34, 42, 43, 84, 86, 92, 109r, 112r, 137r, Spec. 1; c-17-35, 40, 41, 43-47, 137. **Maneely** c-1, 2. **McWilliams** a-41. **Severin** a-16; c-8. **Torres** a-99r. **Williamson** a-95r, 111r.*

RAWHIDE KID
Aug, 1985 - No. 4, Nov, 1985 (mini-series)
Marvel Comics Group

RAWHIDE KID (continued)

	Good	Fine	Mint
1	.25	.70	1.40
2-4		.50	1.00

REAGAN'S RAIDERS
Aug, 1986 - Present ($1.95, B&W)
Solson Publications

	Good	Fine	Mint
1-Ayers-a	.50	1.50	3.00
2	.40	1.20	2.40

REAL ADVENTURE COMICS (Action Adventure No. 2 on)
April, 1955
Gillmor Magazines

	Good	Fine	Mint
1	1.30	4.00	9.00

REAL CLUE CRIME STORIES (Formerly Clue)
June, 1947 - V8No.3, May, 1953
Hillman Periodicals

	Good	Fine	Mint
V2No.4(No.1)-S&K c/a(3); Dan Barry-a	8.50	25.50	60.00
5-7-S&K c/a(3-4); 7-Iron Lady app.	7.00	21.00	50.00
8-12	1.70	5.00	11.50
V3No.1-8,10-12, V4No.1-8,11,12	1.50	4.50	10.00
9-Used in **SOTI**, pg. 102	3.85	11.50	27.00
V4No.9,10-Krigstein-a	2.85	8.50	20.00
V5No.1-5,7,8,10,12	1.00	3.00	7.00
6,9,11-Krigstein-a	2.35	7.00	16.00
V6No.1-5,8,9,11	1.00	3.00	7.00
6,7,10,12-Krigstein-a. 10-Bondage-c	2.00	6.00	14.00
V7No.1-3,5,7-11, V8No.1-3	1.00	3.00	7.00
4,12-Krigstein-a	2.00	6.00	14.00
6-1 pg. Frazetta ad	1.15	3.50	8.00

NOTE: *Barry a-9, 10.* ***Briefer*** *a-V6/6.* ***Fuje*** *a- V2/11.* ***Infantino*** *a-V2/8.* ***Lawrence*** *a-V5/7.* ***Powell*** *a-V4/11, 12. V5/4,7 are 68 pgs.*

REAL EXPERIENCES (Formerly Tiny Tessie)
No. 25, January, 1950
Atlas Comics (20CC)

	Good	Fine	Mint
25	1.50	4.50	10.00

REAL FACT COMICS
Mar-Apr, 1946 - No. 21, July-Aug, 1949
National Periodical Publications

	Good	Fine	Mint
1-S&K-a; Harry Houdini sty; Just Imagine begins (not by Finlay)	15.00	45.00	105.00
2-S&K-a; Rin-Tin-Tin sty	8.50	25.50	60.00
3-H.G. Wells, Lon Chaney sty	4.35	13.00	30.00
4-Virgil Finlay-a on 'Just Imagine' begins, ends No. 12 (2 pgs. ea.); Jimmy Stewart sty	8.00	24.00	56.00
5-Batman/Robin-c; 5pg. story about creation of Batman & Robin	25.00	75.00	175.00
6-Origin & 1st app. Tommy Tomorrow by Finlay; Flag-c; 1st writing by Harlan Ellison (letter column, non-professional)	30.00	90.00	210.00
7-(No. 6 on inside)-Roussos-a	3.65	11.00	25.00
8-2nd app. Tommy Tomorrow by Finlay	17.00	51.00	120.00
9-S&K-a; Glenn Miller sty	6.00	18.00	42.00
10-Vigilante by Meskin	6.00	18.00	42.00
11,12: 11-Kinstler-a	3.65	11.00	25.00
13-Tommy Tomorrow cover/story	15.00	45.00	105.00
14,17,18	3.35	10.00	23.00
15-Nuclear Explosion part-c	3.65	11.00	25.00
16-Tommy Tomorrow app.; 1st Planeteers app.?	15.00	45.00	105.00
19-Sir Arthur Conan Doyle sty	3.65	11.00	25.00
20-Kubert-a, 4 pgs.	7.00	21.00	50.00
21-Kubert-a, 2 pgs.	3.65	11.00	25.00

NOTE: ***Roussos*** *a-1-4.*

REAL FUN OF DRIVING!!, THE
1965, 1967 (Regular size)
Chrysler Corp.

	Good	Fine	Mint
Shaffenberger-a, 12pgs.	.70	2.00	4.00

REAL FUNNIES
Jan, 1943 - No. 3, June, 1943
Nedor Publishing Co.

	Good	Fine	Mint
1-Funny animal, humor; Black Terrier app. (clone of The Black Terror)	7.00	21.00	50.00
2,3	4.00	12.00	28.00

REAL HEROES COMICS
Sept, 1941 - No. 16, Oct, 1946
Parents' Magazine Institute

	Good	Fine	Mint
1	6.50	19.50	45.00
2	3.00	9.00	21.00
3-5,7-10	2.35	7.00	16.00
6-Lou Gehrig c/sty	2.65	8.00	18.00
11-16: 13-Kiefer-a	1.75	5.25	12.00

REAL HIT
1944 (Savings Bond premium)
Fox Features Publications

	Good	Fine	Mint
1-Blue Beetle-r	7.00	21.00	50.00

NOTE: Two versions exist, with and without covers. The coverless version has the title, No. 1 and price printed at top of splash page.

REALISTIC ROMANCES
July-Aug, 1951 - No. 17, Aug-Sept, 1954 (no No. 9-14)
Realistic Comics/Avon Periodicals

	Good	Fine	Mint
1-Kinstler-a; c-/Avon paperback 211	8.00	24.00	56.00
2	3.65	11.00	25.00
3,4	3.35	10.00	23.00
5,8-Kinstler-a	3.65	11.00	25.00
6-c-Diversey Prize Novels 6; Kinstler-a	4.00	12.00	28.00
7-Evans-a?; c-/Avon paperback 360	4.00	12.00	28.00
15,17	2.65	8.00	18.00
16-Kinstler marijuana story-r/Romantic Love No. 6	5.00	15.00	35.00
I.W. Reprint No. 1,8,9	.45	.90	1.80

NOTE: ***Astarita*** *a-2-4,7,8.*

REAL LIFE COMICS
Sept, 1941 - No. 59, Sept, 1952
Nedor/Better/Standard Publ./Pictorial Magazine No. 13

	Good	Fine	Mint
1	9.50	28.50	65.00
2	4.65	14.00	32.00
3-Hitler cover	6.00	18.00	42.00
4,5: 4-Story of American flag "Old Glory"	3.00	9.00	21.00
6-10	2.65	8.00	18.00
11-20: 17-Albert Einstein sty.	2.15	6.50	15.00
21-23,25,26,28-30	1.65	5.00	11.50
24-Story of Baseball	2.00	6.00	14.00
27-Schomburg A-Bomb-c; sty. of A-Bomb	3.00	9.00	21.00
31-33,35,36,42-44,48,49	1.30	4.00	9.00
34,37-41,45-47: 34-Jimmy Stewart sty. 37-Sty. of motion pictures; Bing Crosby sty. 38-Jane Froman sty. 39-"1,000,000 A.D." sty. 40-Bob Feller sty. 41-Jimmie Foxx sty.; "Home Run" Baker sty. 45-Sty. of Olympic games; Burl Ives sty. 46-Douglas Fairbanks Jr. & Sr. sty. 47-George Gershwin sty.	1.50	4.50	10.00
50-Frazetta-a, 5 pgs.	10.00	30.00	70.00
51-Jules Verne "Journey to the Moon" by Evans	4.35	13.00	30.00
52-Frazetta-a, 4 pgs.; Severin/Elder-a(2); Evans-a	11.00	33.00	76.00
53-57-Severin/Elder-a	2.65	8.00	18.00

Real Clue Crime Stories V2No.10, © HILL

Real Fact Comics #16, © DC

Real Life Comics #17, © BP

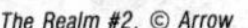
The Realm #2, © Arrow

Real McCoys #01-689-207, © Brennan-Westgate

Real West Romances #2, © PRIZE

REAL LIFE COMICS (continued)	Good	Fine	Mint
58-Severin/Elder-a(2)	3.00	9.00	21.00
59-1pg. Frazetta; Severin/Elder-a	3.00	9.00	21.00

NOTE: *Some issues had two titles.* ***Guardineer*** *a-40(2), 44.* ***Schomburg*** *c-1, 2, 4, 5, 7, 11, 13-21, 23, 24, 26, 28, 30-32, 34-40, 42, 44-47.*

REAL LIFE SECRETS (Real Secrets No. 3 on)
Sept, 1949 - No. 2, Nov?, 1949
Ace Periodicals

	Good	Fine	Mint
1-Painted-c	2.65	8.00	18.00
2	1.30	4.00	9.00

REAL LIFE STORY OF FESS PARKER (Magazine)
1955
Dell Publishing Co.

	Good	Fine	Mint
1	4.00	12.00	28.00

REAL LIFE TALES OF SUSPENSE (See Suspense)

REAL LOVE (Formerly Hap Hazard)
No. 25, April, 1949 - No. 76, Nov, 1956
Ace Periodicals (A. A. Wyn)

	Good	Fine	Mint
25	3.00	9.00	21.00
26	1.70	5.00	11.50
27-L. B. Cole-a	3.00	9.00	21.00
28-35	1.15	3.50	8.00
36-66: 66-Last pre-code (2/55)	1.00	3.00	7.00
67-76	.75	2.25	5.00

NOTE: *Photo-c No. 50-76. Painted-c No. 46.*

REALM, THE
Feb, 1986 - Present ($1.50, B&W)
Arrow Comics

	Good	Fine	Mint
1	3.00	9.00	18.00
2	.45	1.40	2.80
3-5	.35	1.00	2.00

REAL McCOYS, THE (TV)
No. 1071, 1-3/60 - 5-7/1962 (Photo-c)
Dell Publishing Co.

	Good	Fine	Mint
4-Color 1071	4.00	12.00	28.00
4-Color 1193,1265	3.50	10.50	24.00
4-Color 1134-Toth-a	4.35	13.00	30.00
01-689-207 (5-7/62)	3.00	9.00	21.00

REAL SCREEN COMICS (No. 1 titled Real Screen Funnies; TV Screen Cartoons No. 129-138)
Spring, 1945 - No. 128, May-June, 1959
National Periodical Publications

	Good	Fine	Mint
1-The Fox & the Crow, Flippity & Flop begin	44.00	132.00	305.00
2	22.00	65.00	154.00
3-5	12.00	36.00	84.00
6-10	8.50	25.50	60.00
11-20	6.50	19.50	45.00
21-30	4.35	13.00	30.00
31-50	3.35	10.00	23.00
51-99	2.35	7.00	16.00
100	2.65	8.00	18.00
101-128	1.70	5.00	11.50

REAL SECRETS (Formerly Real Life Secrets)
No. 3, Jan?, 1950 - No. 5, May, 1950
Ace Periodicals

	Good	Fine	Mint
3-Photo-c	2.50	7.50	17.50
4,5	1.50	4.50	10.00

REAL SPORTS COMICS (All Sports Comics No. 2 on)
Oct-Nov, 1948
Hillman Periodicals

	Good	Fine	Mint
1-12 pg. Powell-a	9.00	27.00	62.00

REAL WESTERN HERO (Formerly Wow No. 1-69; becomes Western Hero No. 76 on)
No. 70, Sept, 1948 - No. 75, Feb, 1949 (All 52 pgs.)
Fawcett Publications

	Good	Fine	Mint
70(No.1)-Tom Mix, Monte Hale, Hopalong Cassidy, Young Falcon begin	12.00	36.00	84.00
71-Gabby Hayes begins; Captain Tootsie by Beck	8.00	24.00	56.00
72-75: 72-Captain Tootsie by Beck. 75-Big Bow and Little Arrow app.	6.50	19.50	45.00

NOTE: *Painted/photo c-70-73; painted c-74,75.*

REAL WEST ROMANCES
Apr-May, 1949 - V2/1, Apr-May, 1950 (No. 1-5, 52 pgs.)
Crestwood Publishing Co./Prize Publ.

	Good	Fine	Mint
V1/1-S&K-a(p)	6.75	20.25	48.00
2-Spanking panel; photo-c	6.00	18.00	42.00
3-Kirby-a(p) only	2.85	8.50	20.00
4-S&K-a; Whip Wilson, Reno Browne photo-c	3.50	10.50	24.00
5-Audie Murphy, Gale Storm photo-c; S&K-a	3.50	10.50	24.00
6,7-S&K-a	3.50	10.50	24.00
V2/1-Kirby-a(p)	2.85	8.50	20.00

NOTE: ***Meskin*** *a-V1/5.* ***Severin & Elder*** *a-V1/3-6, V2/1.* ***Leonard Starr*** *a-1-3. Photo-c V1/2-5, V2/1.*

REAP THE WILD WIND (See Cinema Comics Herald)

REBEL, THE (See 4-Color No. 1076,1138,1207,1262)

RECORD BOOK OF FAMOUS POLICE CASES
1949 (132 pages) (25 cents)
St. John Publishing Co.

	Good	Fine	Mint
nn-Kubert-a(3) r-/Son of Sinbad; Matt Baker-c	15.00	45.00	105.00

RED ARROW
May, 1951 - No. 3, Oct, 1951
P. L. Publishing Co.

	Good	Fine	Mint
1	2.35	7.00	16.00
2,3	1.15	3.50	8.00

RED BALL COMIC BOOK
1947 (Red Ball Shoes giveaway)
Parents' Magazine Institute

	Good	Fine	Mint
Reprints from True Comics	1.15	3.50	8.00

RED BAND COMICS
Feb, 1945 - No. 4, May, 1945
Enwil Associates

	Good	Fine	Mint
1	7.00	21.00	50.00
2-Origin Boogeyman & Santanas	5.75	17.25	40.00
3,4-Captain Wizard app. in both; identical contents in each	5.75	17.25	40.00

RED CIRCLE COMICS
Jan, 1945 - No. 4, April, 1945
Rural Home Publications (Enwil)

	Good	Fine	Mint
1-The Prankster & Red Riot begin	7.00	21.00	50.00
2-Starr-a; The Judge (costumed hero) app.	5.75	17.25	40.00
3,4-Starr-a. 3-The Prankster not in costume; Starr-c	4.00	12.00	28.00
4-Variations exist; Woman Outlaws, Dorothy Lamour, Crime Does Not Pay, Sabu & Young Love V3/3 known ('50s-r)	3.65	11.00	25.00

RED CIRCLE SORCERY (Chilling Advs. in Sorcery No. 1-5)
No. 6, Apr, 1974 - No. 11, Feb, 1975
Red Circle Productions (Archie)

	Good	Fine	Mint
6-11		.40	.80

NOTE: ***Chaykin** a-6, 10. **B. Jones** a-7. **McWilliams** a-10. **Morrow** a-5-11; c-6-11. **Thorne** a-8, 10. **Toth** a-8, 9. **Wood** a-10.*

RED DRAGON COMICS (1st Series) (Trail Blazers No. 1-4)
No. 5, Jan, 1943 - No. 9, Jan, 1944
Street & Smith Publications

	Good	Fine	Mint
5-Origin Red Rover, the Crimson Crimebuster; Rex King, Man of Adventure, Captain Jack Commando, & The Minute Man begin; text origin Red Dragon	24.50	73.50	170.00
6-Origin The Black Crusader & Red Dragon (3/43)	17.00	51.00	120.00
7	14.50	43.50	100.00
8-The Red Knight app.	14.50	43.50	100.00
9-Origin Chuck Magnon, Immortal Man	14.50	43.50	100.00

RED DRAGON COMICS (2nd Series)
Nov, 1947 - No. 6, Jan, 1949; No. 7, July, 1949
Street & Smith Publications

	Good	Fine	Mint
1-Red Dragon begins; Elliman, Nigel app.; Ed Cartier-c/a	22.00	65.00	154.00
2-Cartier-c	17.00	51.00	120.00
3-1st app. Dr. Neff by Powell; Elliman, Nigel app.	14.50	43.50	100.00
4-Cartier c/a	16.00	48.00	110.00
5-7	11.00	33.00	76.00

NOTE: ***Maneely** a-5,7. **Powell** a-2-7; c-3,5,7.*

REDDY GOOSE
No. 2, Jan, 1959 - No. 16, July, 1962 (Giveaway)
International Shoe Co. (Western Printing)

	Good	Fine	Mint
2-16	.30	.80	1.60

REDDY KILOWATT (5 cents) (Also see Story of Edison)
1946 - No. 2, 1947; 1956 - 1960 (no month) (16 pgs.; paper cover)
Educational Comics (E. C.)

	Good	Fine	Mint
nn-Reddy Made Magic	12.00	35.00	70.00
nn-Reddy Made Magic (1958)	5.35	16.00	32.00
2-Edison, the Man Who Changed the World (¾'' smaller than No. 1)	12.00	35.00	70.00
...Comic Book 2 (1954)-''Light's Diamond Jubilee''	6.75	20.00	40.00
...Comic Book 2 (1958)-''Wizard of Light,'' 16 pgs.	5.35	16.00	32.00
...Comic Book 3 (1956)-''The Space Kite,'' 8 pgs.; Orlando story; regular size	5.35	16.00	32.00
...Comic Book 3 (1960)-''The Space Kite,'' 8 pgs.; Orlando story; regular size	4.75	14.00	28.00

NOTE: *Several copies surfaced in 1979.*

REDDY MADE MAGIC
1956, 1958 (16 pages) (paper cover)
Educational Comics (E. C.)

	Good	Fine	Mint
1-Reddy Kilowatt-r (splash panel changed)	8.00	24.00	48.00
1 (1958 edition)	5.00	15.00	30.00

RED EAGLE (See Feature Books No. 16, McKay)

REDEYE (See Comics Reading Libraries)

RED FOX (Manhunt No. 1-14)
1954
Magazine Enterprises

	Good	Fine	Mint
15(A-1 108)-Undercover Girl app.; L.B. Cole c/a (Red Fox); r-from Manhunt; Powell-a	6.50	19.50	45.00

REDFOX
Jan, 1986 - Present ($1.75, B&W)
Harrier Comics

	Good	Fine	Mint
1	2.50	7.50	15.00
1 (2nd printing)	.30	.90	1.75
2	1.50	4.50	9.00
3	.40	1.25	2.50
4-7	.30	.90	1.80

RED GOOSE COMIC SELECTIONS (See Comic Selections)

RED HAWK (See A-1 Comics No. 90)

RED ICEBERG, THE
1960 (10 cents) (16 pgs.) (Communist propaganda)
Impact Publ. (Catechetical Guild)

	Good	Fine	Mint
(Rare)-'We The People'-back-c	37.00	110.00	240.00
2nd version-'Impact Press'-back-c	43.00	130.00	280.00

NOTE: *This book was the Guild's last anti-communist propaganda book and had very limited circulation. 3 - 4 copies surfaced in 1979 from the defunct publisher's files.*

RED MASK (Formerly Tim Holt)
No. 42, 6-7/1954 - No. 53, 5/56; No. 54, 9/57
Magazine Enterprises No. 42-53/Sussex No. 54

	Good	Fine	Mint
42-Ghost Rider by Ayers continues, ends No. 50; Black Phantom continues; 3-D effect c/stories begin	9.00	27.00	62.00
43-3-D effect-c/stories	7.00	21.00	50.00
44-50-3-D effect stories only. 50-Last Ghost Rider	6.00	18.00	42.00
51-The Presto Kid begins by Ayers (1st app.); Presto Kid-c begins, ends No. 54; last 3-D effect story	6.00	18.00	42.00
52-Origin The Presto Kid	6.00	18.00	42.00
53,54-Last Black Phantom	4.00	12.00	28.00
I.W. Reprint No. 1 (r-/No.52), 2,3 (r-/No.51), 8 (no date; Kinstler-c)	.80	2.40	4.80

NOTE: ***Ayers** art on Ghost Rider & Presto Kid. **Bolle** art in all (Red Mask). **Guardineer** a-52. **Black Phantom** in No. 42-44, 47-50, 53, 54.*

RED MOUNTAIN FEATURING QUANTRELL'S RAIDERS
1952 (Movie) (Also see Jesse James No. 28)
Avon Periodicals

	Good	Fine	Mint
Alan Ladd; Kinstler c/a	13.00	40.00	90.00

''RED'' RABBIT COMICS
Jan, 1947 - No. 22, Aug-Sept, 1951
Dearfield Comic/J. Charles Laue Publ. Co.

	Good	Fine	Mint
1	3.65	11.00	25.00
2	1.85	5.50	13.00
3-10	1.70	5.00	11.50
11-22	1.15	3.50	8.00

RED RAVEN COMICS (Human Torch No. 2 on)
August, 1940 (Also see Sub-Mariner No. 26, 2nd series)
Timely Comics

	Good	Fine	Mint
1-Origin Red Raven; Comet Pierce & Mercury by Kirby, The Human Top & The Eternal Brain; intro. Magar, the Mystic & only app.; Kirby-c	385.00	1155.00	2700.00

(Prices vary widely on this book)

RED RYDER COMICS (Hi Spot No. 2)(Movies, radio)
(Also see Crackajack Funnies)
9/40; No. 3, 8/41 - No. 5, 12/41; No. 6, 4/42 - No. 151, 4-6/57
Hawley Publ. No. 1-5/Dell Publishing Co.(K.K.) No. 6 on

	Good	Fine	Mint
1-Red Ryder, his horse Thunder, Little Beaver & his horse Papoose strip reprints begin by Fred Harman; 1st meeting of Red & Little Beaver; Harman line-drawn-c No. 1-85	67.00	200.00	470.00
3-(Scarce)-Alley Oop, Freckles & His Friends, Dan Dunn, Capt. Easy, King of the Royal Mtd. strip-r begin	40.00	120.00	280.00

Red Dragon Comics #9 (1/44), © S&S

Redfox #1 (1st Printing), © Harrier

''Red'' Rabbit Comics #18, © Dearfield

Red Ryder Comics #30, © DELL

Red Ryder Victory Patrol nn, © DELL

Redskin #1, © YM

RED RYDER COMICS (continued)

	Good	Fine	Mint
4,5	22.00	65.00	154.00
6-1st Dell issue	22.00	65.00	154.00
7-10	17.00	51.00	120.00
11-20	11.50	34.50	80.00
21-32-Last Alley Oop, Dan Dunn, Capt. Easy, Freckles	8.00	24.00	56.00
33-41 (52 pgs.)	5.00	15.00	35.00
42 (52 pgs.)-Rocky Lane photo back-c; photo back-c begin, end No. 57	5.00	15.00	35.00
43-46 (52 pgs.). 46-Last Red Ryder strip-r	4.00	12.00	28.00
47-53 (52 pgs.). 47-New stories on Red Ryder begin	3.65	11.00	25.00
54-60 (36 pgs.)	3.00	9.00	21.00
61-73 (36 pgs.). 73-Last King of the Royal Mtd. strip-r by Jim Gary	2.65	8.00	18.00
74-85,93 (52 pgs.)-Harman line-drawn-c	2.85	8.50	20.00
86-92 (52 pgs.)-Harman painted-c	2.85	8.50	20.00
94-96 (36 pgs.)-Harman painted-c	2.00	6.00	14.00
97,98,107,108 (36 pgs.)-Harman line-drawn-c	2.00	6.00	14.00
99,101-106 (36 pgs.)-Jim Bannon Photo-c	2.00	6.00	14.00
100 (36 pgs.)-Bannon Photo-c	2.35	7.00	16.00
109-118 (52 pgs.)-Harman line-drawn-c	1.75	5.25	12.00
119-129 (52 pgs.). 119-Painted-c begin, not by Harman, end No. 151	1.50	4.50	10.00
130-144 (36 pgs., No. 130-on)	1.30	4.00	9.00
145-148: 145-Title change to Red Ryder Ranch Magazine with photos	1.15	3.50	8.00
149-151: 149-Title changed to Red Ryder Ranch Comics	1.15	3.50	8.00
4-Color 916 (7/58)	1.50	4.50	10.00
Red Ryder Super Book Of Comics 10 (1944; paper-c; 32 pgs.; blank back-c)-Magic Morro app.	17.00	52.00	120.00
Red Ryder Victory Patrol-nn(1944, 32 pgs.)-r-/No. 43,44; comic has a paper-c & is stapled inside a triple cardboard fold-out-c; contains membership card, decoder, map of R.R. home range, etc. Herky app. (Langendorf Bread giveaway; sub-titled 'Super Book Of Comics')	25.00	75.00	175.00
Wells Lamont Corp. giveaway (1950)-16 pgs. in color; regular size; paper-c; 1941-r	17.00	52.00	120.00

NOTE: ***Fred Harman*** *a-1-99; c-1-98, 107-118. Don Red Barry, Allan Rocky Lane, Wild Bill Elliott & Jim Bannon starred as Red Ryder in the movies. Robert Blake starred as Little Beaver.*

RED RYDER PAINT BOOK
1941 (148 pages) (8½x11½'')
Whitman Publishing Co.

	Good	Fine	Mint
Reprints 1940 daily strips	12.00	35.00	84.00

RED SEAL COMICS
10/45 - No. 18, 10/46; No. 19, 6/47 - No. 22, 12/47
Harry 'A' Chesler/Superior Publ. No. 19 on

	Good	Fine	Mint
14-The Black Dwarf begins; Little Nemo app; bondage/hypo-c; Tuska-a	13.50	40.50	95.00
15-Drug mention, torture story	11.00	33.00	76.00
16-Used in **SOTI**, pg. 181, illo-''Outside the forbidden pages of de Sade, you find draining a girl's blood only in children's comics;'' drug club story r-later in Crime Reporter No. 1; Veiled Avenger & Barry Kuda app; Tuska-a	17.00	51.00	120.00
17-Lady Satan, Yankee Girl & Sky Chief app; Tuska-a	10.00	30.00	70.00
18,20-Lady Satan & Sky Chief app.	10.00	30.00	70.00
19-No Black Dwarf-on cover only; Zor, El Tigre app.	8.50	25.50	60.00
21-Lady Satan & Black Dwarf app.	8.50	25.50	60.00
22-Zor, Rocketman app.	8.50	25.50	60.00

REDSKIN (Famous Western Badmen No. 13 on)
Sept, 1950 - No. 12, Oct, 1952
Youthful Magazines

	Good	Fine	Mint
1	3.15	9.50	22.00
2	1.85	5.50	13.00
3-12: 6,12-Bondage-c	1.70	5.00	11.50

RED SONJA (Also see Conan No. 23 & Marvel Feature)
1/77 - No. 15, 5/79; V1/1, 2/83 - V2/2, 3/83;
V3/1, 8/83 - V3/4, 2/84; V3/5, 1/85 - V3/13, 1986
Marvel Comics Group

	Good	Fine	Mint
1	.35	1.10	2.20
2-5	.30	.80	1.60
6-10		.40	.80
11-15, V1/1,V2/2		.30	.60
V3/1,2 ($1.00)		.50	1.00
V3/3-13 (65-75¢)		.35	.70

NOTE: ***Brunner*** *c-12-14.* ***J. Buscema*** *a(p)-12, 13, 15; c-V1No.1.* ***Nebres*** *a-V3/3i.* ***N. Redondo*** *a-8i, V3/2i, 3i.* ***Simonson*** *a-V3No.1.* ***Thorne*** *a-1-11; c-1-11.*

RED SONJA: THE MOVIE
Nov, 1985 - No. 2, Dec, 1985 (limited-series)
Marvel Comics Group

	Good	Fine	Mint
1,2-Movie adapt-r		.40	.80

RED TORNADO
July, 1985 - No. 4, Oct, 1985 (mini-series)
DC Comics

	Good	Fine	Mint
1-4		.40	.80

RED WARRIOR
Jan, 1951 - No. 6, Dec, 1951
Marvel/Atlas Comics (TCI)

	Good	Fine	Mint
1-Tuska-a	3.15	9.50	22.00
2	1.85	5.50	13.00
3-6	1.70	5.00	11.50

RED WOLF
May, 1972 - No. 9, Sept, 1973
Marvel Comics Group

	Good	Fine	Mint
1-Kane/Severin-c		.30	.60
2-9: 9-Origin sidekick, Lobo (wolf)		.25	.50

NOTE: ***G. Kane*** *c-1p, 2.*

REESE'S PIECES
Oct, 1985 - No. 2, Oct, 1985
Eclipse Comics

	Good	Fine	Mint
1,2-B&W-r in color	.30	.90	1.80

REFORM SCHOOL GIRL!
1951
Realistic Comics

	Good	Fine	Mint
nn-Used in **SOTI**, pg. 358, & cover ill. with caption ''Comic books are supposed to be like fairy tales''	107.00	321.00	750.00

(Prices vary widely on this book)

NOTE: *The cover and title originated from a digest-sized book published by Diversey Publishing Co. of Chicago in 1948. The original book ''House of Fury,'' Doubleday, came out in 1941. The girl's real name which appears on the cover of the digest and comic is Marty Collins, Canadian model and ice skating star who posed for this special color photograph for the Diversey novel.*

REGGIE (Formerly Archie's Rival . . .; Reggie & Me No. 19 on)
No. 15, Sept, 1963 - No. 18, Nov, 1965
Archie Publications

	Good	Fine	Mint
15(9/63), 16(10/64)	3.35	10.00	20.00
17(8/65), 18(11/65)	3.35	10.00	20.00

NOTE: *Cover title No. 15,16 is Archie's Rival. . . .*

REGGIE AND ME (Formerly Reggie)
No. 19, 8/66 - No. 126, 9/80 (No. 50-68: 52 pgs.)
Archie Publications

REGGIE AND ME (continued)

	Good	Fine	Mint
19-Evilheart app.	1.70	5.00	10.00
20-23-Evilheart app.; with Pureheart No. 22	.85	2.50	5.00
24-40	.35	1.00	2.00
41-60		.40	.80
61-126		.25	.50

REGGIE'S JOKES (See Reggie's Wise Guy Jokes)

REGGIE'S WISE GUY JOKES
Aug, 1968 - No. 60, Jan, 1982 (No. 5 on are Giants)
Archie Publications

1	1.70	5.00	10.00
2-4	.75	2.25	4.50
5-10	.25	.75	1.50
11-28		.40	.80
29-60		.25	.50

REGISTERED NURSE
Summer, 1963
Charlton Comics

1-Reprints Nurse Betsy Crane & Cynthia Doyle	.35	1.00	2.00

REG'LAR FELLERS (See Treasure Box of. . .)
1921 - 1929
Cupples & Leon Co./MS Publishng Co.

1(1921)-52 pgs. B&W dailies (Cupples & Leon, 10x10'')	7.00	21.00	50.00
1925, 48 pgs. B&W dailies (MS Publ.)	7.00	21.00	50.00
Softcover (1929, nn, 36 pgs.)	7.00	21.00	50.00
Hardcover (1929)-B&W reprints, 96 pgs.	8.00	24.00	56.00

REG'LAR FELLERS
No. 5, Nov, 1947 - No. 6, Mar, 1948
Visual Editions (Standard)

5,6	2.50	7.50	17.00

REG'LAR FELLERS HEROIC (See Heroic)

REID FLEMING, WORLD'S TOUGHEST MILKMAN
Aug, 1986 ($2.50, B&W); Dec, 1986 - Present
Eclipse Comics

1 (3rd printing; large size)	.40	1.25	2.50
1 (12/86)	.35	1.00	2.00

RELUCTANT DRAGON, THE (See 4-Color No. 13)

REMEMBER PEARL HARBOR
1942 (68 pages)
Street & Smith Publications

nn	14.50	43.50	100.00

RENEGADE RABBIT
Nov, 1986 ($1.75, B&W)
Printed Matter Comics

1	.30	.90	1.75

RENO BROWNE, HOLLYWOOD'S GREATEST COWGIRL (Formerly Margie; Apache Kid No. 53 on)
No. 50, April, 1950 - No. 52, Sept, 1950
Marvel Comics (MPC)

50	6.00	18.00	42.00
51,52	5.00	15.00	35.00

REPTILICUS (Reptisaurus No. 3 on)
Aug, 1961 - No. 2, Oct, 1961
Charlton Comics

	Good	Fine	Mint
1 (Movie)	3.15	9.50	22.00
2	2.15	6.50	15.00

REPTISAURUS (Reptilicus No. 1,2)
Jan, 1962 - No. 8, Dec, 1962; Summer, 1963
Charlton Comics

V2No.3-8: 8-Montes/Bache c/a	1.35	4.00	8.00
Special Edition 1 (1963)	1.35	4.00	8.00

RESCUERS, THE (See Walt Disney Showcase No. 40)

RESTLESS GUN (See 4-Color No. 934,986,1045,1089,1146)

RETURN OF GORGO, THE (Formerly Gorgo's Revenge)
No. 2, Summer, 1963 - No. 3, Fall, 1964
Charlton Comics

2,3-Ditko-a	2.50	7.50	15.00

RETURN OF KONGA, THE (Konga's Revenge No. 2 on)
1962
Charlton Comics

nn	1.75	5.25	12.00

RETURN OF THE OUTLAW
Feb, 1953 - No. 11, 1955
Toby Press (Minoan)

1-Billy the Kid	2.65	8.00	18.00
2	1.30	4.00	9.00
3-11	1.15	3.50	8.00

REVEALING LOVE STORIES (See Fox Giants)

REVEALING ROMANCES
Sept, 1949 - No. 6, Aug, 1950
Ace Magazines

1	2.65	8.00	18.00
2	1.30	4.00	9.00
3-6	1.15	3.50	8.00

REVENGERS, THE (Featuring Armor And Silverstreak)
Sept, 1985 ($2.00)
Continuity Comics

1-Origin; Adams c/a	.35	1.00	2.00

REVENGERS STARRING MEGALITH
Sept, 1985 - Present
Continuity Comics

1-3-Adams c/a, scripts	.35	1.00	2.00

REVOLVER (Also see Ditko's World & Murder)
Nov, 1985 - No. 6, Apr, 1986 (B&W)
Renegade Press

1-Ditko c/a	.30	.85	1.70
2-6	.30	.85	1.70
Annual 1 (11/86)-Toth-c	.35	1.00	2.00

NOTE: ***Bissette** c/a-6. **Ditko** a-1,2,4,5; c-1,4.*

REVOLVING DOORS
Oct, 1986 - Present ($1.75, B&W)
Blackthorne Publishing

1	.30	.90	1.75

REX ALLEN COMICS (Movie star)(Also see 4-Color No. 877 & Western Roundup)
No. 316, Feb, 1951 - No. 31, Dec-Feb, 1958-59 (All-photo-c)
Dell Publishing Co.

4-Color 316(No.1)(52 pgs.)-Rex Allen & his horse Koko begin; Marsh-a	7.00	21.00	50.00

Remember Pearl Harbor nn, © S&S

Revealing Romances #1, © ACE

Revengers, Featuring Armor &. . . #1, © Continuity

Rex Allen Comics #24, © DELL

Rex Hart #7, © MCG

Richie Rich #4, © HARV

REX ALLEN COMICS (continued)

	Good	Fine	Mint
2 (9-11/51, 36 pgs.)	4.00	12.00	28.00
3-10	3.65	11.00	25.00
11-20	3.00	9.00	21.00
21-23,25-31	2.35	7.00	16.00
24-Toth-a	3.15	9.50	22.00

NOTE: *Manning a-20,27-30. Photo back-c 316,2-12,20,21.*

REX DEXTER OF MARS (See Mystery Men Comics)
Fall, 1940
Fox Features Syndicate

1-Rex Dexter, Patty O'Day, & Zanzibar (Tuska-a) app.; Briefer-c/a 55.00 165.00 385.00

REX HART (Formerly Blaze Carson; Whip Wilson No. 9 on)
No. 6, Aug, 1949 - No. 8, Feb, 1950 (All photo-c)
Timely/Marvel Comics (USA)

6-Rex Hart & his horse Warrior begin; Black Rider app; Captain Tootsie by Beck 5.00 15.00 35.00
7,8: 18pg. Thriller in each. 8-Blaze the Wonder Collie app. in text 4.00 12.00 28.00

REX MORGAN, M.D. (Also see Harvey Comics Library)
Dec, 1955 - No. 3, 1956
Argo Publ.

1-Reprints Rex Morgan daily newspaper strips & daily panel reprints of "These Women" by D'Alessio & "Timeout" by Jeff Keate 4.00 12.00 28.00
2,3 2.35 7.00 16.00

REX THE WONDER DOG (See The Adventures of . . .)

RHUBARB, THE MILLIONAIRE CAT (See 4-Color No. 423,466,563)

RIBTICKLER (Also see Fox Giants)
1945 - No. 9, Aug, 1947; 1957 - 1959
Fox Features Synd./Green Publ. (1957)/Norlen (1959)

	Good	Fine	Mint
1	2.65	8.00	18.00
2	1.30	4.00	9.00
3-9: 7-Cosmo Cat app.	1.00	3.00	7.00
3,7,8 (Green Publ.-1957)	.75	2.25	5.00
3,7,8 (Norlen Mag.-1959)	.75	2.25	5.00

RICHARD DRAGON, KUNG-FU FIGHTER (See Brave & the Bold)
Apr-May, 1975 - No. 18, Nov-Dec, 1977
National Periodical Publications/DC Comics

	Good	Fine	Mint
1,2: 2-Starlin-a(p). 3-Kirby-c; a(p).		.45	.90
3-18: 4-8-Wood inks		.30	.60

RICHARD THE LION-HEARTED (See Ideal a Classic . . .)

RICHIE RICH (See Harvey Collectors Comics, Harvey Hits, Little Dot, Little Lotta, Little Sad Sack, Mutt & Jeff, Super Richie, and 3-D Dolly)

RICHIE RICH (. . . the Poor Little Rich Boy) (See Harvey Hits No. 3,9)
11/60 - No. 218, 10/82; No. 219, 10/86 - Present
Harvey Publications

	Good	Fine	Mint
1-(See Little Dot for 1st app.)	90.00	250.00	440.00
2	40.00	100.00	180.00
3-5	20.00	60.00	120.00
6-10: 8-Christmas-c	12.50	37.50	75.00
11-20	5.35	16.00	32.00
21-40	3.00	9.00	18.00
41-60	2.00	6.00	12.00
61-80: 65-1st app. Dollar the Dog	1.20	3.50	7.00
81-100	.70	2.00	4.00
101-120	.50	1.50	3.00
121-140	.40	1.25	2.50
141-160: 145,149-Infinity-c	.35	1.00	2.00
161-180	.25	.75	1.50
181-200		.50	1.00
201-224		.40	.75

RICHIE RICH AND BILLY BELLHOPS
October, 1977 (One Shot) (52pgs.)
Harvey Publications

	Good	Fine	Mint
1	.50	1.50	3.00

RICHIE RICH AND CADBURY
10/77; No. 2, 9/78 - No. 23, 7/82 (No. 1-10, 52pgs.)
Harvey Publications

	Good	Fine	Mint
1	.70	2.00	4.00
2-5	.35	1.00	2.00
6-10		.50	1.00
11-23		.40	.80

RICHIE RICH AND CASPER
Aug, 1974 - No. 45, Sept, 1982
Harvey Publications

	Good	Fine	Mint
1	1.15	3.50	7.00
2-5	.50	1.50	3.00
6-10: 10-X-Mas-c	.35	1.00	2.00
11-20		.50	1.00
21-40		.40	.80
41-45		.30	.60

RICHIE RICH AND DOLLAR THE DOG
9/77 - No. 24, 8/82 (No. 1-10, 52pgs.)
Harvey Publications

	Good	Fine	Mint
1	.70	2.00	4.00
2-5	.35	1.00	2.00
6-24		.50	1.00

RICHIE RICH AND DOT
October, 1974 (One Shot)
Harvey Publications

	Good	Fine	Mint
1	1.00	3.00	6.00

RICHIE RICH AND GLORIA
Sept, 1977 - No. 25, Sept, 1982 (No. 1-11, 52pgs.)
Harvey Publications

	Good	Fine	Mint
1	.70	2.00	4.00
2-5	.35	1.00	2.00
6-25		.40	.80

RICHIE RICH AND HIS GIRLFRIENDS
April, 1979 - No. 16, Dec, 1982
Harvey Publications

	Good	Fine	Mint
1	.50	1.50	3.00
2-10	.35	1.00	2.00
11-16		.40	.80

RICHIE RICH AND HIS MEAN COUSIN REGGIE
April, 1979 - No. 4, Apr?, 1980 (50 cents) (No. 1,2-52pgs.)
Harvey Publications

	Good	Fine	Mint
1	.35	1.00	2.00
2-4	.25	.75	1.50

RICHIE RICH AND JACKIE JOKERS
Nov, 1973 - No. 48, Dec, 1982
Harvey Publications

	Good	Fine	Mint
1	1.70	5.00	10.00
2-5	.85	2.50	5.00
6-10	.50	1.50	3.00
11-20	.35	1.00	2.00
21-40		.50	1.00
41-48		.40	.80

RICHIE RICH AND TIMMY TIME
Sept, 1977 (50 Cents) (One Shot) (52 pages)
Harvey Publications

	Good	Fine	Mint
1	.50	1.50	3.00

RICHIE RICH BANK BOOKS
Oct, 1972 - No. 59, Sept, 1982
Harvey Publications

	Good	Fine	Mint
1	2.00	6.00	12.00
2-5	1.00	3.00	6.00
6-10	.70	2.00	4.00
11-20	.50	1.50	3.00
21-30	.35	1.00	2.00
31-40		.50	1.00
41-59		.40	.80

RICHIE RICH BEST OF THE YEARS
Oct, 1977 - No. 6, June, 1980 (Digest) (128 pages)
Harvey Publications

	Good	Fine	Mint
1(10/77)-Reprints, No. 2(10/78)-Reprints, No. 3(6/79-75 cents)	.35	1.00	2.00
4-6(11/79-6/80-95 cents)		.50	1.00

RICHIE RICH BILLIONS
10/74 - No. 48, 10/82 (No. 1-33, 52pgs.)
Harvey Publications

	Good	Fine	Mint
1	1.70	5.00	10.00
2-5	.85	2.50	5.00
6-10	.70	2.00	4.00
11-20	.35	1.00	2.00
21-30		.50	1.00
31-48		.40	.80

RICHIE RICH CASH
Sept, 1974 - No. 47, Aug, 1982
Harvey Publications

	Good	Fine	Mint
1	1.70	5.00	10.00
2-5	.85	2.50	5.00
6-10	.50	1.50	3.00
11-20	.35	1.00	2.00
21-30		.50	1.00
31-47		.40	.80

RICHIE RICH, CASPER & WENDY NATIONAL LEAGUE
June, 1976 (52 pages)
Harvey Publications

	Good	Fine	Mint
1	.70	2.00	3.00

RICHIE RICH COLLECTORS COMICS (See Harvey Coll. Comics)

RICHIE RICH DIAMONDS
8/72 - No. 59, 8/82 (No. 1-12,23-45, 52pgs.)
Harvey Publications

	Good	Fine	Mint
1	2.35	7.00	14.00
2-5	1.00	3.00	6.00
6-10	.70	2.00	4.00
11-20	.50	1.50	3.00
21-30	.35	1.00	2.00
31-40: 39-Origin Little Dot		.50	1.00
41-50		.40	.80
51-59		.30	.60

RICHIE RICH DIGEST
Oct, 1986 - Present ($1.25, digest-size)
Harvey Publications

	Good	Fine	Mint
1-5		.60	1.25

RICHIE RICH DIGEST STORIES (. . . Magazine No. ?-on)
10/77 - No. 17, 10/82 (Digest) (132 pages) (75-95 cents)
Harvey Publications

	Good	Fine	Mint
1-Reprints	.30	.80	1.60
2-17: 4-Infinity-c		.40	.80

RICHIE RICH DIGEST WINNERS
12/77 - No. 16, 9/82 (Digest) (132 pages) (75-95 Cents)
Harvey Publications

	Good	Fine	Mint
1	.30	.80	1.60
2-16		.40	.80

RICHIE RICH DOLLARS & CENTS
8/63 - No. 109, 8/82 (No. 1-61,72-94, 52pgs.)
Harvey Publications

	Good	Fine	Mint
1	8.00	24.00	48.00
2	4.00	12.00	24.00
3-5	2.35	7.00	14.00
6-10	1.70	5.00	10.00
11-20: No. 11-68 pgs.	1.35	4.00	8.00
21-30	.85	2.50	5.00
31-50	.50	1.50	3.00
51-70	.35	1.00	2.00
71-90 (Early issues are reprints)		.50	1.00
91-99,101-109		.40	.80
100-Anniversary issue		.40	.80

RICHIE RICH FORTUNES
Sept, 1971 - No. 63, July, 1982 (No. 1-17, 52pgs.)
Harvey Publications

	Good	Fine	Mint
1	2.35	7.00	14.00
2-5	1.15	3.50	7.00
6-10	.85	2.50	5.00
11-20	.70	2.00	4.00
21-30	.35	1.00	2.00
31-40		.50	1.00
41-63		.40	.80

RICHIE RICH GEMS
Sept, 1974 - No. 43, Sept, 1982
Harvey Publications

	Good	Fine	Mint
1	1.70	5.00	10.00
2-5	.85	2.50	5.00
6-10	.50	1.50	3.00
11-20	.35	1.00	2.00
21-30		.50	1.00
31-43		.40	.80

RICHIE RICH GOLD AND SILVER
Sept, 1975 - No. 42, Oct, 1982 (No. 1-27, 52pgs.)
Harvey Publications

	Good	Fine	Mint
1	1.35	4.00	8.00
2-5	.70	2.00	4.00
6-10	.35	1.00	2.00
11-20		.50	1.00
21-42		.40	.80

RICHIE RICH HOLIDAY DIGEST MAGAZINE
January, 1980 - No. 3, Jan, 1982
Harvey Publications

	Good	Fine	Mint
1-3: All X-Mas-c		.50	1.00

RICHIE RICH INVENTIONS
Oct, 1977 - No. 26, Oct, 1982 (No. 1-11, 52pgs.)
Harvey Publications

	Good	Fine	Mint
1	.70	2.00	4.00

Richie Rich #40, © HARV

Richie Rich Dollars & Cents #11, © HARV

Richie Rich Millions #45, © HARV

RICHIE RICH INVENTIONS (continued)

	Good	Fine	Mint
2-5	.35	1.00	2.00
6-10		.50	1.00
11-26		.40	.80

RICHIE RICH JACKPOTS
Oct, 1972 - No. 58, Aug, 1982 (No. 41-43, 52pgs.)
Harvey Publications

	Good	Fine	Mint
1	2.00	6.00	12.00
2-5	1.00	3.00	6.00
6-10	.70	2.00	4.00
11-20	.35	1.00	2.00
21-30	.25	.75	1.50
31-50		.50	1.00
51-58		.40	.80

RICHIE RICH MILLION DOLLAR DIGEST (. . . Magazine No. ?-on)
October, 1980 - No. 10, Oct, 1982
Harvey Publications

	Good	Fine	Mint
1-10		.50	1.00

RICHIE RICH MILLIONS
9/61; No. 2, 9/62 - No. 113, 10/82 (No. 1-66,52-68pgs.; 85-97, 52pgs.)
Harvey Publications

	Good	Fine	Mint
1	9.00	27.00	62.00
2	4.75	14.00	32.00
3-10	3.35	10.00	23.00
11-20	1.70	5.00	12.00
21-30	1.00	3.00	6.00
31-40	.80	2.30	4.60
41-50	.50	1.50	3.00
51-70	.35	1.00	2.00
71-90	.30	.80	1.60
91-100 (Early issues are reprints)		.50	1.00
101-113		.40	.80

RICHIE RICH MONEY WORLD
Sept, 1972 - No. 59, Sept, 1982
Harvey Publications

	Good	Fine	Mint
1	2.35	7.00	14.00
2-5	1.00	3.00	6.00
6-10: 9,10-R. Rich mistakenly named Little Lotta on covers	.50	1.50	3.00
11-20	.35	1.10	2.20
21-30	.25	.75	1.50
31-50		.50	1.00
51-59		.40	.80

RICHIE RICH PROFITS
Oct, 1974 - No. 47, Sept, 1982
Harvey Publications

	Good	Fine	Mint
1	2.00	6.00	12.00
2-5	1.00	3.00	6.00
6-10	.50	1.50	3.00
11-20	.35	1.00	2.00
21-30		.50	1.00
31-47		.40	.80

RICHIE RICH RICHES
7/72 - No. 59, 8/82 (No. 1-13, 41-45, 52pgs.)
Harvey Publications

	Good	Fine	Mint
1	2.00	6.00	12.00
2-5	1.00	3.00	6.00
6-10	.50	1.50	3.00
11-20	.35	1.00	2.00
21-40		.50	1.00
41-59		.40	.80

RICHIE RICH SUCCESS STORIES
11/64 - No. 105, 9/82 (No. 1-16,18-56, 67-90, 52pgs; 17-68pgs..)
Harvey Publications

	Good	Fine	Mint
1	6.75	20.00	47.00
2-5	3.00	9.00	21.00
6-10	2.00	6.00	12.00
11-30: 27-1st Penny Van Dough (8/69)	1.00	3.00	6.00
31-50	.50	1.50	3.00
51-70	.35	1.00	2.00
71-90 (Early issues are reprints)		.50	1.00
91-105		.40	.80

RICHIE RICH TREASURE CHEST DIGEST (. . . Mag. No. 3)
4/82 - No. 3, 8/82 (95 Cents, Digest Magazine)
Harvey Publications

	Good	Fine	Mint
1-3		.50	1.00

RICHIE RICH VACATIONS DIGEST
11/77; No. 2, 10/78 - No. 7, 10/81; No. 8, 8/82 (Digest, 132 pgs.)
Harvey Publications

	Good	Fine	Mint
1-Reprints	.30	.80	1.60
2-8		.50	1.00

RICHIE RICH VAULTS OF MYSTERY
Nov, 1974 - No. 47, Sept, 1982
Harvey Publications

	Good	Fine	Mint
1	1.50	4.50	9.00
2-10	.70	2.00	4.00
11-20	.35	1.00	2.00
21-30	.25	.75	1.50
31-47		.40	.80

RICHIE RICH ZILLIONZ
10/76 - No. 33, 9/82 (No. 1-4, 68pgs.; No. 5-18, 52pgs.)
Harvey Publications

	Good	Fine	Mint
1	1.35	4.00	8.00
2-5	.70	2.00	4.00
6-10	.35	1.00	2.00
11-20		.50	1.00
21-33		.40	.80

RICKY
September, 1953
Standard Comics (Visual Editions)

	Good	Fine	Mint
5	1.00	3.00	7.00

RICKY NELSON (TV)
No. 956, 12/58 - No. 1192, 6/61 (All photo-c)
Dell Publishing Co.

	Good	Fine	Mint
4-Color 956,998	7.00	21.00	50.00
4-Color 1115,1192-Manning-a	7.00	21.00	50.00

RIDER, THE (Frontier Trail No. 6)
March, 1957 - No. 5, 1958
Ajax/Farrell Publ. (Four Star Comic Corp.)

	Good	Fine	Mint
1	2.15	6.50	15.00
2-5	1.15	3.50	8.00

The Rifleman #3, © Four Star

RIFLEMAN, THE (TV)
No. 1009, 7-9/59 - No. 12, 7-9/62; No. 13, 11/62 - No. 20, 10/64
Dell Publ. Co./Gold Key No. 13 on

	Good	Fine	Mint
4-Color 1009	5.00	15.00	35.00
2 (1-3/60)	4.00	12.00	28.00
3-Toth-a, 4 pgs.	4.65	14.00	32.00
4,5,7-10	3.00	9.00	21.00
6-Toth-a	3.50	10.50	24.00
11-20	2.35	7.00	16.00

NOTE: ***Warren Tufts*** *a-2-9. All have photo-c. Photo back-c, No. 13-15.*

RIMA, THE JUNGLE GIRL
Apr-May, 1974 - No. 7, Apr-May, 1975
National Periodical Publications

	Good	Fine	Mint
1-Origin, part 1		.60	1.20
2-4-Origin, part 2,3,&4		.40	.80
5-7: 7-Origin & only app. Space Marshal		.30	.60

NOTE: ***Kubert*** *c-1-7.* ***Nino*** *a-1-5.* ***Redondo*** *a-1-6.*

RING OF BRIGHT WATER (See Movie Classics)

RINGO KID, THE (2nd Series)
1/70 - No. 23, 11/73; No. 24, 11/75 - No. 30, 11/76
Marvel Comics Group

	Good	Fine	Mint
1(1970)-Williamson-a r-from No. 10, 1956		.40	.80
2-30: 20-Williamson-r/No. 1		.25	.50

NOTE: ***Wildey*** *a-13r.*

RINGO KID WESTERN, THE (1st Series)(See Wild Western)
Aug, 1954 - No. 21, Sept, 1957
Atlas Comics (HPC)/Marvel Comics

	Good	Fine	Mint
1-Origin; The Ringo Kid & his horse Arab begin	4.65	14.00	32.00

RINGO KID WESTERN (continued)

	Good	Fine	Mint
2-Black Rider app.	2.35	7.00	16.00
3-5	1.70	5.00	11.50
6-8-Severin-c/a(3) each	2.50	7.50	17.50
9,11,14-21	1.30	4.00	9.00
10,13-Williamson-a, 4 pgs.	3.35	10.00	23.00
12-Orlando-a, 4 pgs.	1.70	5.00	11.50

NOTE: ***Berg*** *a-8.* ***Maneely*** *a-1, 4, 5, 15, 18, 20, 21; c-1, 6, 15, 16, 18, 20.* ***J. Severin*** *c-10, 11.* ***Sinnott*** *a-1.* ***Wildey*** *a-16-18.*

RIN TIN TIN (See March of Comics No. 163,180,195)

RIN TIN TIN (TV) (. . & Rusty No. 21 on; see Western Roundup)
Nov, 1952 - No. 38, May-July, 1961; 1963 (All Photo-c)
Dell Publishing Co./Gold Key

	Good	Fine	Mint
4-Color 434 (No.1)	3.50	10.50	24.00
4-Color 476,523	2.65	8.00	18.00
4(3-5/54)-10	2.35	7.00	16.00
11-20	1.75	5.25	12.00
21-38	1.50	4.50	10.00
1(11/63-G.K.) . . . & Rusty	1.50	4.50	10.00

RIO BRAVO (See 4-Color No. 1018)

RIO CONCHOS (See Movie Comics)

RION 2990
Summer, 1986 - No. 4 ($1.50, B&W)(mini-series)
Rion Procustions

	Good	Fine	Mint
1-Signed & numbered	.85	2.50	5.00
1	.40	1.25	2.50
2-4	.25	.75	1.50

RIOT (Satire)
Apr, 1954 - No. 3, Aug, 1954; No. 4, Feb, 1956 - No. 6, June, 1956
Atlas Comics (ACI No. 1-5/WPI No. 6)

	Good	Fine	Mint
1-Russ Heath-a	4.00	12.00	28.00
2-Li'l Abner satire by Post	2.85	8.50	20.00
3-Last precode (8/54)	2.65	8.00	18.00
4-Infinity-c; Marilyn Monroe '7 Year Itch' movie satire; Mad Rip-off ads	3.35	10.00	23.00
5-Marilyn Monroe, John Wayne parody	3.65	11.00	25.00
6-Lorna of the Jungle satire by Everett; Dennis the Menace satire cover/story	2.65	8.00	18.00

NOTE: ***Everett*** *a-1, 4, 6.* ***Maneely*** *a-1, 2, 4-6; c-6.* ***Severin*** *a-1, 4-6.*

RIPCORD (See 4-Color No. 1294)

RIP HUNTER TIME MASTER (See Showcase)
Mar-Apr, 1961 - No. 29, Nov-Dec, 1965
National Periodical Publications

	Good	Fine	Mint
1	5.50	16.50	35.00
2	2.65	8.00	18.00
3-5: 5-Last 10¢ issue	1.75	5.25	12.00
6,7-Toth-a in each	2.00	6.00	14.00
8-15	1.15	3.50	8.00
16-29: 29-G. Kane-c	.55	1.65	4.00

RIP IN TIME
Aug, 1986 - No. 5, 1987 ($1.50, B&W)
Fantagor Press

	Good	Fine	Mint
1-5: B. Jones-a; Corben-c/a	.25	.75	1.50

RIP KIRBY (See Feat. Books No. 51,54, Harvey Comics Hits No.57, & Street Comix)

RIPLEY'S BELIEVE IT OR NOT!
Sept, 1953 - No. 4, March, 1954
Harvey Publications

	Good	Fine	Mint
1-Powell-a	5.00	15.00	35.00
2-4	2.65	8.00	18.00
J. C. Penney giveaway (1948)	3.00	9.00	21.00

RIPLEY'S BELIEVE IT OR NOT! (Formerly. . . True War Stories)
No. 4, April, 1967 - No. 94, Feb, 1980
Gold Key

	Good	Fine	Mint
4-McWilliams-a	1.15	3.50	8.00
5-Subtitled "True War Stories;" Evans-a	.75	2.25	5.00
6-9: 6-McWilliams-a. 8-Orlando-a	.75	2.25	5.00
10-Evans-a(2)	.75	2.25	5.00
11-14,16-20	.55	1.65	4.00
15-Evans-a	.55	1.65	4.00
21-30	.50	1.50	3.00
31-38,40-60	.35	1.00	2.00
39-Crandall-a	.40	1.25	2.50
61-94: 74,77-83 (52 pgs.)	.25	.75	1.50
Story Digest Mag. 1(6/70)-4¾x6½"	.50	1.50	3.00

NOTE: ***Evanish*** *art by* ***Luiz Dominguez*** *No. 22-25, 27, 30, 31, 40.* ***Sparling*** *c-68. Reprints-No. 74,77-84,87 (part); 91,93 (all).*

RIPLEY'S BELIEVE IT OR NOT! (See Ace Comics, All-American Comics, Mystery Comics Digest No. 1, 4, 7, 10, 13, 16, 19, 22, 25)

RIPLEY'S BELIEVE IT OR NOT TRUE GHOST STORIES (Becomes . . . True War Stories) (See Dan Curtis)
June, 1965 - No. 2, Oct, 1966
Gold Key

	Good	Fine	Mint
1-Williamson, Wood & Evans-a; photo-c	2.00	6.00	14.00
2-Orlando, McWilliams-a	1.15	3.50	8.00
Mini-Comic 1(1976-3¼x6½")		.30	.60
11186(1977)-Golden Press; 224 pgs. ($1.95)-Reprints	.50	1.50	3.00
11401(3/79)-Golden Press; 96 pgs. ($1.00)-Reprints		.60	1.20

RIPLEY'S BELIEVE IT OR NOT TRUE WAR STORIES (Formerly . . . True Ghost Stories; becomes Ripley's Believe It or Not No. 4 on)
Nov, 1966
Gold Key

	Good	Fine	Mint
1(No.3)-Williamson-a	1.50	4.50	10.00

RIPLEY'S BELIEVE IT OR NOT! TRUE WEIRD
June, 1966 - No. 2, Aug, 1966 (B&W Magazine)
Ripley Enterprises

	Good	Fine	Mint
1,2-Comic stories & text	.40	1.20	2.40

RIVETS (See 4-Color No. 518)

RIVETS (A dog)
Jan, 1956 - No. 3, May, 1956
Argo Publ.

	Good	Fine	Mint
1-Reprints Sunday & daily newspaper strips	2.15	6.50	15.00
2,3	1.15	3.50	8.00

ROAD RUNNER, THE (See Beep Beep. . .)

ROBERT E. HOWARD'S CONAN THE BARBARIAN
1983 (No month) ($2.50, printed on Baxter paper)
Marvel Comics Group

	Good	Fine	Mint
1-r-/Savage Tales No. 2,3 by Smith; c-r/Conan No. 21 by Smith	.45	1.25	2.50

ROBIN (See Aurora)

ROBIN HOOD (See 4-Color No. 413,669, King Classics, Movie Comics, & The Advs. of. . .)

ROBIN HOOD (. . . & His Merry Men, The Illustrated Story of. . .) (See Classic Comics No. 7)

Rin Tin Tin #5, © Screen Gems

Rion 2990 #1, © Rion Prod.

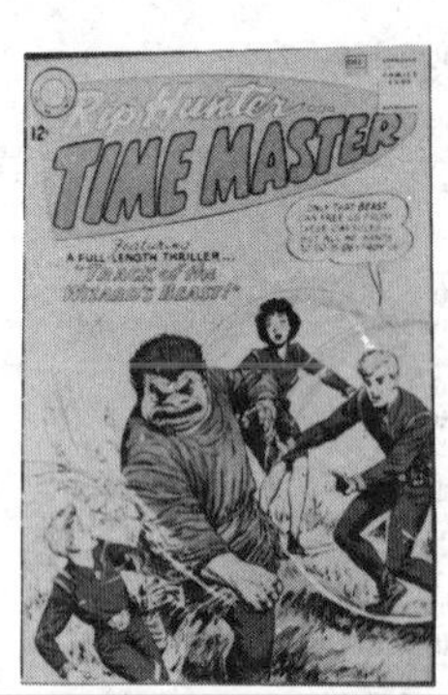

Rip Hunter Time Master #17, © DC

Robin Hood & His Merry Men #32, © CC

Robo-Hunter #4, © Eagle

Robotech: The New Generation #1, © Comico

ROBIN HOOD (New Adventures of. . .)
1952 (36 pages) (5x7¼'')
Walt Disney Productions (Flour giveaways) — Good Fine Mint

''New Adventures of Robin Hood,'' ''Ghosts of Waylea Castle,'' & ''The Miller's Ransom'' each. . . . 1.35 4.00 8.00

ROBIN HOOD (Adventures of. . . No. 7, 8)
No. 52, Nov, 1955 - No. 6, June, 1957
Magazine Enterprises (Sussex Publ. Co.)

52-Origin Robin Hood & Sir Gallant of the Round Table 3.00 9.00 21.00
53, 3-6 2.00 6.00 14.00
I.W. Reprint No. 1,2 (r-No. 4), 9 (r-No. 52)(1963) .40 1.20 2.40
Super Reprint No. 10 (r-No. 53 or 3), 11,15 (r-No. 5), 17(1964) .40 1.20 2.40
NOTE: ***Bolle*** *a-in all.* ***Powell*** *a-6.*

ROBIN HOOD (. . . Western Tales)
No date (Circa 1955) 20 pages
Shoe Store Giveaway (Robin Hood Stores)

1-7-Reed Crandall-a 2.65 8.00 16.00

ROBIN HOOD (Not Disney)
May-July, 1963 (One shot)
Dell Publishing Co.

1 .75 2.25 5.00

ROBIN HOOD ($1.50)
1973 (Disney) (8½x11''; cardboard covers) (52 pages)
Western Publishing Co.

96151-''Robin Hood,'' based on movie, 96152-''The Mystery of Sherwood Forest,'' 96153-''In King Richard's Service,'' 96154-''The Wizard's Ring'' each. 70 2.00 4.00

ROBIN HOOD AND HIS MERRY MEN (Formerly Danger & Adv.)
No. 28, April, 1956 - No. 38, Aug, 1958
Charlton Comics

28 1.75 5.25 12.00
29-37 1.00 3.00 7.00
38-Ditko-a, 5 pgs. 2.65 8.00 18.00

ROBIN HOOD TALES (National Periodical No. 7 on)
Feb, 1956 - No. 6, Nov-Dec, 1956
Quality Comics Group (Comic Magazines)

1 3.15 9.50 22.00
2-5-Matt Baker-a 3.65 11.00 25.00
6 1.65 5.00 11.50
Frontier Days giveaway (1956) 1.30 4.00 9.00

ROBIN HOOD TALES (Continued from Quality)
No. 7, Jan-Feb, 1957 - No. 14, Mar-Apr, 1958
National Periodical Publications

7 6.00 18.00 42.00
8-14 5.00 15.00 35.00

ROBINSON CRUSOE (Also see King Classics)
Nov-Jan, 1963-64
Dell Publishing Co.

1 .85 2.50 6.00

ROBO-HUNTER
April, 1984 - Present
Eagle Comics

1-6-2000 A.D.-r .50 1.00
7 ($1.25) .60 1.25

ROBOTECH DEFENDERS
Mar, 1985 - No. 2, Apr, 1985 (mini-series)
DC Comics — Good Fine Mint

1,2 .30 .90 1.80

ROBOTECH MASTERS (TV)
July, 1985 - Present
Comico

1 .40 1.25 2.50
2-4 .35 1.00 2.00
5-12 .25 .75 1.50

ROBOTECH THE GRAPHIC NOVEL
Oct, 1986 ($5.95, 8½x11'', 52 pgs.)
Comico

1-Origin SDF-1; intro T.R. Edwards 1.00 3.00 5.95

ROBOTECH: THE MACROSS SAGA (Formerly Macross)(TV)
No. 2, Dec, 1984 - Present
Comico

2 .75 2.25 4.50
3-5 .50 1.50 3.00
6-10 .35 1.00 2.00
11-15 .25 .75 1.50

ROBOTECH: THE NEW GENERATION (TV)
July, 1985 - Present
Comico

1 .40 1.25 2.50
2-4 .35 1.00 2.00
5-12 .25 .75 1.50

ROBOTIX
Feb, 1986 (One Shot)
Marvel Comics Group

1-Based on toy .50 1.00

ROBOTMEN OF THE LOST PLANET (Also see Space Thrillers)
1952
Avon Periodicals

1-3pg. Kinstler-a 54.00 170.00 380.00

ROB ROY (See 4-Color No. 544)

ROCK AND ROLLO (Formerly T.V. Teens)
V2No.14, Oct, 1957 - No. 19, Sept, 1958
Charlton Comics

14-19 .60 1.80 4.20

ROCKET COMICS
Mar, 1940 - No. 3, May, 1940
Hillman Periodicals

1-Rocket Riley, Red Roberts the Electro Man(Origin), The Phantom Ranger, The Steel Shark, The Defender, Buzzard Barnes, Lefty Larson, & Man With a Thousand Faces begin 50.00 150.00 350.00
2,3 30.00 90.00 210.00

ROCKETEER, THE
Sept, 1985 (Graphic Novel; $7.95 cover)
Eclipse Books

1-R-/Rocketeer saga in one volume by Dave Stevens 1.35 4.00 8.00

ROCKETEER SPECIAL EDITION, THE
Nov, 1984 ($1.50; Baxter paper)
Eclipse Comics

1-Dave Stevens-c/a .50 1.50 3.00

ROCKET KELLY
1944; Fall, 1945 - No. 5, 10-11/46
Fox Features Syndicate

ROCKET KELLY (continued)

	Good	Fine	Mint
nn (1944)	6.00	18.00	42.00
1	6.00	18.00	42.00
2-The Puppeteer app. (costumed hero)	4.00	12.00	28.00
3-5: 5-(No. 5 on cover, No. 4 inside)	3.65	11.00	25.00

ROCKETMAN (See Hello Pal & Scoop Comics)
June, 1952
Ajax/Farrell Publications

	Good	Fine	Mint
1-Rocketman & Cosmo	10.00	30.00	70.00

ROCKET RACCOON
May, 1985 - No. 4, Aug, 1985 (mini-series)
Marvel Comics Group

	Good	Fine	Mint
1	.25	.75	1.50
2-4		.50	1.00

ROCKETS AND RANGE RIDERS
1957 (16 pages) (Giveaway)
Richfield Oil Corp.

	Good	Fine	Mint
Toth-a	8.50	25.50	60.00

ROCKET SHIP X
September, 1951; 1952
Fox Features Syndicate

	Good	Fine	Mint
1	30.00	90.00	210.00
1952 (nn, nd, no publ.)-Edited '51-c	22.00	65.00	154.00

ROCKET TO ADVENTURE LAND (See Pixie Puzzle. . .)

ROCKET TO THE MOON
1951
Avon Periodicals

	Good	Fine	Mint
nn-Orlando c/a; adapts Otis Aldebert Kline's "Maza of the Moon"	53.00	160.00	370.00

ROCK HAPPENING (Harvey Pop Comics:)
Sept, 1969 - No. 2, Nov, 1969
Harvey Publications

	Good	Fine	Mint
1,2	1.00	3.00	6.00

ROCKY AND BULLWINKLE KITE FUN BOOK
1963; 1970 (8 pgs.; 16 pgs.) (soft cover) (Giveaway)
Pacific Gas & Electric Co./Southern Calif. Edison

	Good	Fine	Mint
nn(1963)(PG&E)-8 pgs.	3.50	10.50	24.00
nn(1970)(SCEC)-16 pgs.	2.15	6.50	15.00

ROCKY AND HIS FIENDISH FRIENDS (TV)
Oct, 1962 - No. 5, Sept, 1963 (Jay Ward)
Gold Key

	Good	Fine	Mint
1 (84 pgs.)	4.00	12.00	32.00
2,3 (84 pgs.)	3.00	9.00	24.00
4,5 (Regular size)	2.35	7.00	16.00

ROCKY AND HIS FRIENDS (See 4-Color No. 1128, 1152, 1166, 1208, 1275, 1311 and March of Comics No. 216)

ROCKY JONES SPACE RANGER (See Space Adventures No. 15-18)

ROCKY LANE WESTERN (Rocky Allan Lane starred in Republic movies (for a short time as Red Ryder) & TV)(See Black Jack)
May, 1949 - No. 87, Nov, 1959
Fawcett Publications/Charlton No. 56 on

	Good	Fine	Mint
1 (36 pgs.)-Rocky, his stallion Black Jack, & Slim Pickens begin; photo-c begin, end No. 57; photo back-c	20.00	60.00	140.00
2 (36 pgs.)-Last photo back-c	10.00	30.00	70.00
3-5 (52 pgs.). 4-Captain Tootsie by Beck	8.00	24.00	56.00
6,10 (36 pgs.)	6.50	19.50	45.00
7-9 (52 pgs.)	7.00	21.00	50.00
11-13,15-17 (52 pgs.): 15-Black Jack's Hitching Post begins, ends No. 25	5.00	15.00	35.00
14,18 (36 pgs.)	4.65	14.00	32.00
19-21,23,24 (52 pgs.): 20-Last Slim Pickens. 21-Dee Dickens begins, ends No. 55,57,65-68	4.65	14.00	32.00
22,25-28,30 (36 pgs. begin)	4.35	13.00	30.00
29-Classic complete novel "The Land of Missing Men,"-hidden land of ancient temple ruins (r-in No. 65)	5.00	15.00	35.00
31-40	3.65	11.00	25.00
41-54	3.00	9.00	21.00
55-Last Fawcett issue (1/54)	4.00	12.00	28.00
56-1st Charlton issue (2/54)-Photo-c	4.00	12.00	28.00
57-Photo-c	3.00	9.00	21.00
58-64: 59-61-Young Falcon app. 64-Slim Pickens app.	2.65	8.00	18.00
65-R-/No. 29, "The Land of Missing Men"	3.00	9.00	21.00
66-68: Reprints No. 30,31,32	2.15	6.50	15.00
69-78,80-86	2.15	6.50	15.00
79-Giant Edition, 68 pgs.	3.00	9.00	21.00
87-Last issue	2.65	8.00	18.00

NOTE: ***Complete novels** in No. 10, 14, 18, 22, 25, 30-32, 36, 38, 39, 49. **Captain Tootsie** in No. 4, 12, 20. **Big Bow and Little Arrow** in No. 11, 28, 63. **Black Jack's Hitching Post** in No. 15-25, 64, 73.*

ROD CAMERON WESTERN (Movie star)
Feb, 1950 - No. 20, April, 1953
Fawcett Publications

	Good	Fine	Mint
1-Rod Cameron, his horse War Paint, & Sam The Sheriff begin; photo front/back-c begin	18.00	54.00	125.00
2	9.50	28.50	65.00
3-Novel length story "The Mystery of the Seven Cities of Cibola"	7.00	21.00	50.00
4-10: 9-Last photo back-c	6.00	18.00	42.00
11-19	5.00	15.00	35.00
20-Last issue & photo-c	5.50	16.50	38.00

NOTE: ***Novel length stories** in No. 1-8,12-14.*

RODEO RYAN (See A-1 Comics No. 8)

ROGER BEAN, R. G. (Regular Guy)
1915 - 1917 (34 pgs.; B&W; 4¾x16"; cardboard covers)
(No. 1 & 4 bound on side, No. 3 bound at top)
The Indiana News Co.

	Good	Fine	Mint
1-By Chic Jackson (48 pgs.)	5.00	15.00	35.00
2-4	4.00	12.00	28.00

ROGER DODGER (Also in Exciting No. 57 on)
No. 5, Aug, 1952
Standard Comics

	Good	Fine	Mint
5	1.00	3.00	7.00

ROG 2000
June, 1982 ($2.95)
Pacific Comics

	Good	Fine	Mint
nn-Byrne c/a-r	.50	1.50	3.00

ROGUE TROOPER
Oct, 1986 - Present
Quality Comics

	Good	Fine	Mint
1-5		.40	.80
6-Double size ($1.50)	.25	.75	1.50

ROLY POLY COMIC BOOK
1945 - 1946 (MLJ reprints)
Green Publishing Co.

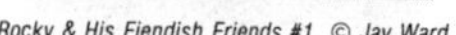

Rocky & His Fiendish Friends #1, © Jay Ward

Rocky Lane Western #4, © FAW

Rod Cameron Western #6, © FAW

Roly Poly Comic Book #15, © Green Publ.

Rom #56, © MCG

Romantic Hearts #1 (3/51), © Story

ROLY POLY COMIC BOOK (continued)

	Good	Fine	Mint
1-Red Rube & Steel Sterling begin	8.50	25.50	60.00
6-The Blue Circle & The Steel Fist app.	4.65	14.00	32.00
10-Origin Red Rube retold; Steel Sterling story (Zip No. 41)	5.00	15.00	35.00
11,12,14-The Black Hood in all	5.00	15.00	35.00
15-The Blue Circle & The Steel Fist app.; cover exact swipe from Fox Blue Beetle No. 1	13.50	41.00	95.00

ROM
December, 1979 - No. 75, Feb, 1986
Marvel Comics Group

	Good	Fine	Mint
1-Based on a Parker Bros. toy-origin	.65	1.90	3.80
2	.35	1.10	2.20
3-5: 3-Miller-c	.30	.90	1.80
6-10	.25	.70	1.40
11-16: 13-Saga of the Space Knights begins		.55	1.10
17,18-X-Men app.	.45	1.40	2.80
19-24,26-30: 19-X-Men cameo		.45	.90
25-Double size		.60	1.20
31,33-49		.35	.70
32-X-Men cameo		.40	.80
50-Double size		.50	1.00
51-55		.35	.70
56,57-Alpha Flight app.	.25	.75	1.50
58-75: 65-X-Men & Beta Ray Bill app.		.40	.80
Annual 1(11/82)		.60	1.20
Annual 2(11/83), 3(1984)		.50	1.00
Annual 4(1985)		.60	1.20

NOTE: **Austin** c-3i, 18i, 61i. **Byrne** c-56, 57. **Ditko** a-59-64p. **Golden** c-7-12, 19. **Guice** a-61i; c-55, 58, 60p. **Layton** a-59i; c-15, 59i. **Miller** c-3p, 17p, 18p. **Russell** a(i)-64, 65, 67, 69; c-64, 65i, 66. **P. Smith** c-59p **Starlin** c-67.

ROMANCE (See True Stories of. . .)

ROMANCE AND CONFESSION STORIES (Also See Giant Comics Edition)
No date (1949) (100pgs.)
St. John Publishing Co.

	Good	Fine	Mint
1-Baker c/a; remaindered St. John love comics	19.00	57.00	132.00

ROMANCE DIARY
December, 1949 - No. 2, March, 1950
Marvel Comics (CDS)(CLDS)

	Good	Fine	Mint
1,2	3.15	9.50	22.00

ROMANCE OF FLYING, THE (See Feature Books No. 33)

ROMANCES OF MOLLY MANTON (See Molly Manton)

ROMANCES OF NURSE HELEN GRANT, THE
August, 1957
Atlas Comics (VPI)

	Good	Fine	Mint
1	1.15	3.50	8.00

ROMANCES OF THE WEST
Nov, 1949 - No. 2, Mar, 1950
Marvel Comics (SPC)

	Good	Fine	Mint
1-Movie photo of Calamity Jane & Sam Bass	5.00	15.00	35.00
2	3.50	10.50	24.00

ROMANCE STORIES OF TRUE LOVE (Formerly Love Problems & Advice)
No. 45, 5/57 - No. 50, 3/58; No. 51, 9/58 - No. 52, 11/58
Harvey Publications

	Good	Fine	Mint
45-51	1.00	3.00	7.00
52-Matt Baker-a	2.35	7.00	16.00

NOTE: **Powell** a-45,46,48-50.

ROMANCE TALES
No. 7, Oct, 1949 - No. 9, March, 1950 (No. 7,8-photo-c)
Marvel Comics (CDS)

	Good	Fine	Mint
7	2.35	7.00	16.00
8,9: 8-Everett-a	1.70	5.00	11.50

ROMANCE TRAIL
July-Aug, 1949 - No. 6, May-June, 1950
National Periodical Publications

	Good	Fine	Mint
1-Kinstler, Toth-a; Photo-c	12.00	36.00	84.00
2-Kinstler-a; photo-c	6.00	18.00	42.00
3-Photo-c; Kinstler, Toth-a	6.00	18.00	42.00
4-Photo-c; Toth-a	5.50	16.50	38.00
5,6: 5-Photo-c	4.65	14.00	32.00

ROMAN HOLIDAYS, THE (TV)
Feb, 1973 - No. 4, Nov, 1973 (Hanna-Barbera)
Gold Key

	Good	Fine	Mint
1	1.35	4.00	8.00
2-4	1.00	3.00	6.00

ROMANTIC ADVENTURES (My. . . No. 49-67, covers only)
Mar-Apr, 1949 - No. 67, July, 1956 (My. . . No. 68 on)
American Comics Group (B&I Publ. Co.)

	Good	Fine	Mint
1	3.35	10.00	23.00
2	1.70	5.00	11.50
3-10	1.15	3.50	8.00
11-20 (4/52)	.85	2.50	6.00
21-52: 52-Last Pre-code (2/55)	.65	2.00	4.50
53-67	.50	1.50	3.50

NOTE: No. 1-22, 52 pgs. **Shelly** a-40. **Whitney** art in many issues.

ROMANTIC AFFAIRS (Formerly Our Love?)
No. 3, March, 1950
Marvel Comics (Select Publications)

	Good	Fine	Mint
3-Photo-c	1.70	5.00	11.50

ROMANTIC CONFESSIONS
Oct, 1949 - V3No.1, April-May, 1953
Hillman Periodicals

	Good	Fine	Mint
V1No.1-McWilliams-a	3.65	11.00	25.00
2-Briefer-a; negligee panels	2.00	6.00	14.00
3-12	1.50	4.50	10.00
V2No.1,2,4-8,10-12	1.15	3.50	8.00
3-Krigstein-a	2.65	8.00	18.00
9-One pg. Frazetta ad	1.50	4.50	10.00
V3No.1	1.00	3.00	7.00

NOTE: **McWilliams** a-V2No.2.

ROMANTIC HEARTS
Mar, 1951 - No. 9, Aug, 1952; July, 1953 - No. 12, July, 1955
Story Comics/Master/Merit Pubs.

	Good	Fine	Mint
1(3/51) (1st Series)	3.35	10.00	23.00
2	1.70	5.00	11.50
3-9	1.50	4.50	10.00
1(7/53) (2nd Series)	2.00	6.00	14.00
2	1.30	4.00	9.00
3-12	1.00	3.00	7.00

ROMANTIC LOVE
No. 4, June, 1950
Quality Comics Group

	Good	Fine	Mint
4 (6/50)(Exist?)	1.70	5.00	11.50
I.W. Reprint No. 2,3,8		.60	1.20

ROMANTIC LOVE
Sept-Oct, 1949 - No. 23, Sept-Oct, 1954 (no No. 14-19)
Avon Periodicals/Realistic

ROMANTIC LOVE (continued)

	Good	Fine	Mint
1-c-/Avon paperback 252	8.50	25.50	60.00
2	4.35	13.00	30.00
3-c-/paperback Novel Library 12	5.00	15.00	35.00
4-c-/paperback Diversey Prize Novel 5	5.00	15.00	35.00
5-c-/paperback Novel Library 34	5.00	15.00	35.00
6-''Thrill Crazy''-marijuana story; c-/Avon paperback 207; Kinstler-a	7.00	21.00	50.00
7,8: 8-Astarita-a(2)	4.35	13.00	30.00
9-c-/paperback/Novel Library 41; Kinstler-a	5.00	15.00	35.00
10-c-/Avon paperback 212	5.00	15.00	35.00
11-c-/paperback Novel Library 17; Kinstler-a	5.00	15.00	35.00
12-c-/paperback Novel Library 13	5.00	15.00	35.00
13,21,22	4.35	13.00	30.00
20-Kinstler-c/a	4.35	13.00	30.00
23-Kinstler-c	3.65	11.00	25.00
nn(1-3/53)(Realistic-r)	2.85	8.50	20.00

NOTE: ***Astarita** a-7,10,11,21.*

ROMANTIC MARRIAGE (Cinderella Love No. 25 on)
No. 1-3 (1950, no month); No. 4, 5-6/51 - No. 17, 9/52; No. 18, 9/53 - No. 24, Sept, 1954
Ziff-Davis/St. John No. 18 on

	Good	Fine	Mint
1-Photo-c	5.00	15.00	35.00
2	2.65	8.00	18.00
3-9: 3,8,9-Painted-c; 5,7-Photo-c	2.15	6.50	15.00
10-Unusual format; front-c is a painted-c; back-c is a photo-c complete with logo, price, etc.	3.35	10.00	23.00
11-17 (9/52; last Z-D ish.): 13-Photo-c	1.85	5.50	13.00
18-22,24: 13-Photo-c	1.85	5.50	13.00
23-Baker-c	2.15	6.50	15.00

ROMANTIC PICTURE NOVELETTES
1946
Magazine Enterprises

	Good	Fine	Mint
1-Mary Worth-r	6.50	19.50	45.00

ROMANTIC SECRETS (Becomes Time For Love)
Sept, 1949 - No. 39, 4/53; No. 5, 10/55 - No. 52, 11/64
Fawcett/Charlton Comics No. 5 (10/55) on

	Good	Fine	Mint
1	3.35	10.00	23.00
2,3	1.65	5.00	11.50
4,9-Evans-a	2.15	6.50	15.00
5-8,10	1.50	4.50	10.00
11-23	1.15	3.50	8.00
24-Evans-a	2.00	6.00	14.00
25-39	.85	2.50	6.00
5 (Charlton)(10/55, formerly Negro Romances No. 4?)	1.75	5.25	12.00
6-10	.85	2.50	6.00
11-20	.45	1.35	3.00
21-35: Last 10¢ ish?	.35	1.00	2.50
36-52('64)		.40	.80

NOTE: ***Bailey** a-20. **Powell** a(1st series)-5,7,10,12,16,17,20,26,29,33,34,36,37. Photo c(1st series)-1-5, 25, 27, 33. **Sekowsky** a-26.*

ROMANTIC STORY
11/49 - No. 22, Sum, 1953; No. 23, 5/54 - No. 130, 11/73
Fawcett/Charlton Comics No. 23 on

	Good	Fine	Mint
1	4.00	12.00	28.00
2	2.00	6.00	14.00
3-5	1.65	5.00	11.50
6-14	1.50	4.50	10.00
15-Evans-a	2.00	6.00	14.00
16-22(Sum, '53; last Fawcett ish.). 21-Toth-a?	1.15	3.50	8.00
23-39,41-50: 29-Wood swipes	1.15	3.50	8.00
40-(100 pgs.)	2.85	8.50	20.00
51-56,58-80	.45	1.35	3.00
57-Hypo needle story	.70	2.00	4.00
81-130		.40	.80

NOTE: ***Powell** a-7,8,16,20,30. Photo c-8,10,11,13,19,24.*

ROMANTIC THRILLS (See Fox Giants)

ROMANTIC WESTERN
Winter, 1949 - No. 3, June, 1950 (Photo-c all)
Fawcett Publications

	Good	Fine	Mint
1	5.00	15.00	35.00
2-Williamson, McWilliams-a	8.00	24.00	56.00
3	3.35	10.00	23.00

ROMEO TUBBS (Formerly My Secret Life)
No. 26, 5/50 - No. 28, 7/50; No. 1, 1950; No. 27, 12/52
Fox Feature Syndicate/Green Publ. Co. No. 27

	Good	Fine	Mint
26	4.35	13.00	30.00
27-Contains Pedro on inside; Wood-a	6.50	19.50	45.00
28, 1	3.35	10.00	23.00

RONALD McDONALD (TV)
Sept, 1970 - No. 4, March, 1971
Charlton Press (King Features Synd.)

	Good	Fine	Mint
1		.50	1.00
2-4		.25	.50

RONIN
July, 1983 - No. 6, Apr, 1984 (mini-series) (52 pgs., $2.50)
DC Comics

	Good	Fine	Mint
1-Miller script, c/a in all	.55	1.60	3.20
2	.50	1.50	3.00
3-5	.45	1.40	2.80
6	.55	1.60	3.20

ROOK
November, 1979 - No. 14, April, 1982
Warren Publications

	Good	Fine	Mint
1-Nino-a		.40	.80
2-14: 3,4-Toth-a		.30	.60

ROOKIE COP (Formerly Crime and Justice?)
Nov, 1955 - No. 33, Aug, 1957
Charlton Comics

	Good	Fine	Mint
27	2.00	6.00	14.00
28-33	1.15	3.50	8.00

ROOM 222 (TV)
Jan, 1970; No. 2, May, 1970 - No. 4, Jan, 1971
Dell Publishing Co.

	Good	Fine	Mint
1,2,4: 2-Photo-c. 4 r-/No. 1	1.75	5.25	12.00
3-Marijuana story	1.50	4.50	10.00

ROOTIE KAZOOTIE (TV)(See 3-D-ell)
No. 415, Aug, 1952 - No. 6, Oct-Dec, 1954
Dell Publishing Co.

	Good	Fine	Mint
4-Color 415	2.35	7.00	16.00
4-Color 459,502	2.00	6.00	14.00
4(4-6/54)-6	1.75	5.25	12.00

ROOTS OF THE SWAMPTHING
July, 1986 - No. 5, Nov, 1986 ($2.00, Baxter)
DC Comics

	Good	Fine	Mint
1-5: All Wrightson-r	.35	1.00	2.00

Romantic Love #22, © AVON

Romantic Secrets #2, © FAW

Room 222 #2, © 20th Century-Fox

Roy Campanella nn, © FAW

Roy Rogers Comics #20, © Roy Rogers

Ruff & Reddy #4, © DELL

ROUND THE WORLD GIFT
No date (mid 1940's) (4 pages)
National War Fund (Giveaway)

	Good	Fine	Mint
	10.00	30.00	60.00

ROUNDUP (Western Crime)
July-Aug, 1948 - No. 5, Mar-Apr, 1949 (52 pgs.)
D. S. Publishing Co.

	Good	Fine	Mint
1-1pg. Frazetta on 'Mystery of the Hunting Lodge'?; Ingels-a?	4.65	14.00	32.00
2-Marijuana drug mention story	3.85	11.50	27.00
3-5	2.50	7.50	17.00

ROYAL ROY
May, 1985 - Present (Children's book)
Star Comics (Marvel)

	Good	Fine	Mint
1-7		.35	.70

ROY CAMPANELLA, BASEBALL HERO
1950
Fawcett Publications

	Good	Fine	Mint
nn	15.00	45.00	105.00

ROY ROGERS (See March of Comics No. 17, 35, 47, 62, 68, 73, 77, 86, 91, 100, 105, 116, 121, 131, 136, 146, 151, 161, 167, 176, 191, 206, 221, 236, 250)

ROY ROGERS AND TRIGGER
April, 1967
Gold Key

	Good	Fine	Mint
1-Photo-c; reprints	1.75	5.25	12.00

ROY ROGERS COMICS (See Western Roundup)
No. 38, 4/44 - No. 177, 12/47 (52 pgs.-No. 38-166)
Dell Publishing Co.

	Good	Fine	Mint
4-Color 38 (1944)-49pg. story; photo front/back/inside-c on all 4-Color issues	38.00	114.00	265.00
4-Color 63 (1945)	24.00	72.00	166.00
4-Color 86,95 (1945)	19.00	57.00	132.00
4-Color 109 (1946)	15.00	45.00	105.00
4-Color 117,124,137,144	11.00	33.00	76.00
4-Color 153,160,166: 166-48pg. story	8.00	24.00	56.00
4-Color 177 (36 pgs.)-32pg. story	8.00	24.00	56.00

ROY ROGERS COMICS (. . . & Trigger No. 92(8/55)-on)(Roy starred in Republic movies, radio & TV) (Singing cowboy) (Also see Dale Evans, Queen of the West. . ., & Roy Roger's Trigger)
Jan, 1948 - No. 145, Sept-Oct, 1961 (36pgs. No. 1-19)
Dell Publishing Co.

	Good	Fine	Mint
1-Roy, his horse Trigger, & Chuck Wagon Charley's Tales begin; photo-c begin, end No. 145	28.00	84.00	195.00
2	15.00	45.00	105.00
3-5	12.00	36.00	84.00
6-10	9.00	27.00	62.00
11-19: 19-. . .Charley's Tales ends	6.50	19.50	45.00
20 (52 pgs.)-Trigger feature begins, ends No. 46	6.50	19.50	45.00
21-30 (52 pgs.)	5.50	16.50	38.00
31-46 (52 pgs.)	4.75	14.25	33.00
47-56 (36 pgs.): 47-Chuck Wagon Charley's Tales returns, ends No. 133? 49-X-mas-c. 55-Last photo back-c	3.65	11.00	25.00
57 (52 pgs.)-Heroin drug propaganda story	4.35	13.00	30.00
58-70 (52 pgs.): 61-X-mas-c	3.15	9.50	22.00
71-80 (52 pgs.): 73-X-mas-c	2.65	8.00	18.00
81-91 (36 pgs. No. 81-on): 85-X-mas-c	2.35	7.00	16.00
92-Title changed to Roy Rogers and Trigger (8/55)	2.35	7.00	16.00
93-99,101-110,112-118	2.35	7.00	16.00
100-Trigger feature returns, ends No. 133?	3.50	10.50	24.00
111,119-124-Toth-a	4.00	12.00	28.00
125-131	2.35	7.00	16.00
132-144-Manning-a. 144-Dale Evans feat.	2.65	8.00	18.00
145-Last issue	2.65	8.00	18.00
. . .& the Man From Dodge City (Dodge giveaway, 16 pgs., 1954)-Frontier, Inc. (5x7¼'')	8.00	24.00	56.00
. . .Riders Club Comics (1952; 16 pgs., reg. size, paper-c)	9.00	27.00	62.00

NOTE: ***Buscema** a-2 each-74-108. **Manning** a-123, 124, 132-144. **Marsh** a-110. Photo back-c No. 1-9, 11-35, 38-55.*

ROY ROGERS' TRIGGER (TV)
No. 329, May, 1951 - No. 17, June-Aug, 1955
Dell Publishing Co.

	Good	Fine	Mint
4-Color 329-Painted-c	4.00	12.00	28.00
2 (9-11/51)-Photo-c	3.50	10.50	24.00
3-5: Painted-c No. 3-on	1.70	5.00	12.00
6-17	1.15	3.50	8.00

RUDOLPH, THE RED NOSED REINDEER (See Limited Collectors Edition No. 20,24,33,42,50)

RUDOLPH, THE RED NOSED REINDEER
1939 (2,400,000 copies printed); Dec, 1951
Montgomery Ward (Giveaway)

	Good	Fine	Mint
Paper cover - 1st app. in print; written by Robert May; ill. by Denver Gillen	8.35	25.00	50.00
Hardcover version	10.00	30.00	70.00
1951 version (Has 1939 date)-36 pgs., illos in three colors; red-c	3.00	9.00	21.00

RUDOLPH, THE RED-NOSED REINDEER
1950 - No. 13?, Winter, 1962-63
(Issues are not numbered) (15 different issues known)
National Periodical Publications

	Good	Fine	Mint
1950 issue; Grossman-c/a begins	3.65	11.00	25.00
1951-54 issues (4 total)	2.65	8.00	18.00
1955-62 issues (8 total)	1.50	4.50	10.00

NOTE: *The 1962-63 issue is 84 pages. 13 total issues published.*

RUFF & REDDY (TV)
No. 937, 9/58 - No. 12, 1-3/62 (Hanna-Barbera)
Dell Publishing Co./Gold Key

	Good	Fine	Mint
4-Color 937	1.50	4.50	10.00
4-Color 981,1038	1.15	3.50	8.00
4(1-3/60)-12	.85	2.50	6.00

RUGGED ACTION (Strange Stories of Suspense No. 5 on)
Dec, 1954 - No. 4, June, 1955
Atlas Comics (CSI)

	Good	Fine	Mint
1	2.65	8.00	18.00
2-4: 2-Last precode (2/55)	1.30	4.00	9.00

RULAH JUNGLE GODDESS (Formerly Zoot; I Loved No. 28 on) (Also see Terrors of the Jungle)
No. 17, Aug, 1948 - No. 27, June, 1949
Fox Features Syndicate

	Good	Fine	Mint
17	23.00	70.00	160.00
18-Classic girl-fight interior splash	20.00	60.00	140.00
19,20	18.00	54.00	125.00
21-Used in **SOTI**, pg. 388,389	20.00	60.00	140.00
22-Used in **SOTI**, pg. 22,23	18.00	54.00	125.00
23-27	13.50	40.50	95.00

NOTE: ***Kamen** c-17-19,21,22.*

RUNAWAY, THE (See Movie Classics)

RUN BABY RUN
1974 (39 cents)
Logos International

RUN BABY RUN (continued)

	Good	Fine	Mint
By Tony Tallarico from Nicky Cruz's book		.30	.60

RUN, BUDDY, RUN (TV)
June, 1967 (Photo-c)
Gold Key

	Good	Fine	Mint
1 (10204-706)	1.15	3.50	8.00

RUSTY, BOY DETECTIVE
Mar-April, 1955 - No. 5, Nov, 1955
Good Comics/Lev Gleason

	Good	Fine	Mint
1-Bob Wood, Carl Hubbell-a begins	2.15	6.50	15.00
2-5	1.30	4.00	9.00

RUSTY COMICS (Formerly Kid Movie Comics; Rusty and Her Family No. 21, 22; The Kelleys No. 23 on)
No. 12, Apr, 1947 - No. 22, Sept, 1949
Marvel Comics (HPC)

	Good	Fine	Mint
12-Mitzi app.	5.00	15.00	35.00
13	2.50	7.50	17.00
14-Wolverton's Powerhouse Pepper (4 pgs.) plus Kurtzman's "Hey Look"	5.50	16.50	38.00
15-17-Kurtzman's "Hey Look"	4.35	13.00	30.00
18,19	1.85	5.50	13.00
20-Kurtzman, 5 pgs.	4.65	14.00	32.00
21,22-Kurtzman, 17 & 22 pgs.	8.00	24.00	56.00

RUSTY DUGAN (See Holyoke One-Shot No. 2)

RUSTY RILEY (See 4-Color No. 418,451,486,554)

SAARI (The Jungle Goddess)
November, 1951
P. L. Publishing Co.

	Good	Fine	Mint
1	14.50	43.50	100.00

SABOTAGE (See The Crusaders)

SABRE
10/78; 1/79; 8/82 - No. 14, 8/85; (Baxter paper No. 4 on)
Eclipse Comics

	Good	Fine	Mint
1-($1.00)-Sabre & Morrigan Tales begin	.25	.75	1.50
2,3-($1.00)		.50	1.00
4-10: ($1.50); 4-6-Origin Incredible Seven	.25	.75	1.50
11,12	.30	.90	1.80
13,14 ($2.00 cover)	.35	1.00	2.00
Graphic Album (10/78)	1.35	4.00	7.95
Graphic Album (1/79; 2nd edition)	1.35	4.00	7.95

NOTE: ***Colan** c-11p. **Gulacy** c/a-1, 2.*

SABRINA'S CHRISTMAS MAGIC (See Archie Giant Series Mag. No. 196, 207, 220, 231, 243, 455, 467, 479, 491, 503, 515)

SABRINA, THE TEEN-AGE WITCH (TV) (See Archie's TV Laugh-Out, Archie Madhouse & Archie Giant Series No. 544)
April, 1971 - No. 77, Jan, 1983 (Giants No. 1-17)
Archie Publications

	Good	Fine	Mint
1	2.00	6.00	12.00
2	1.00	3.00	6.00
3-5: 3,4-Archie's Group x-over	.50	1.50	3.00
6-10	.25	.75	1.50
11-20		.40	.80
21-77		.25	.50

SABU, "ELEPHANT BOY" (Movie; formerly My Secret Story)
No. 30, June, 1950 - No. 2, Aug, 1950
Fox Features Syndicate

	Good	Fine	Mint
30(No.1)-Wood-a; photo-c	8.00	24.00	56.00
2-Photo-c; Kamen-a	5.50	16.50	38.00

SACRAMENTS, THE
October, 1955 (25 cents)
Catechetical Guild Educational Society

	Good	Fine	Mint
304	2.00	6.00	12.00

SAD CASE OF WAITING ROOM WILLIE, THE
1950? (nd) (14 pgs. in color; paper covers; regular size)
American Visuals Corp. (For Baltimore Medical Society)

	Good	Fine	Mint
By Will Eisner (Rare)	25.00	75.00	175.00

SADDLE JUSTICE (Happy Houlihans No. 1,2; becomes Saddle Romances No. 9 on)
No. 3, Spring, 1948 - No. 8, Sept-Oct, 1949
E. C. Comics

	Good	Fine	Mint
3-The first E. C. by Bill Gaines to break away from M. C. Gaines' old Educational Comics format. Craig, Feldstein, H. C. Kiefer, & Stan Asch-a. Mentioned in **Love and Death**	28.00	84.00	195.00
4-1st Graham Ingels E. C.-a	28.00	84.00	195.00
5-8-Ingels-a in all	24.00	72.00	166.00

NOTE: ***Craig** and **Feldstein** art in most issues. Canadian reprints known; see Table of Contents.*

SADDLE ROMANCES (Saddle Justice No. 3-8; continued as Weird Science No. 12 on)
No. 9, Nov-Dec, 1949 - No. 11, Mar-Apr, 1950
E. C. Comics

	Good	Fine	Mint
9-Ingels-a	28.00	84.00	195.00
10-Wood's 1st work at E. C.; Ingels-a	30.00	90.00	210.00
11-Ingels-a	28.00	84.00	195.00

NOTE: *Canadian reprints known; see Table of Contents.*

SADIE SACK (See Harvey Hits No. 93)

SAD SACK AND THE SARGE
Sept, 1957 - No. 155, June, 1982
Harvey Publications

	Good	Fine	Mint
1	5.00	15.00	35.00
2	2.00	6.00	14.00
3-10	1.70	5.00	12.00
11-20	1.00	3.00	6.00
21-50	.40	1.20	2.40
51-100		.50	1.00
101-155		.25	.50

SAD SACK COMICS (See Harvey Collector's Comics 16, Little Sad Sack, Tastee Freez Comics 4 & True Comics No. 55)
Sept, 1949 - No. 287, Oct, 1982
Harvey Publications

	Good	Fine	Mint
1-Infinity-c; Little Dot begins (1st app.); civilian issues begin, end No. 21	17.00	51.00	120.00
2-Flying Fool by Powell	8.50	25.50	60.00
3	5.50	16.50	38.00
4-10	3.50	10.50	24.00
11-21	2.35	7.00	16.00
22-("Back In The Army Again" on covers No. 22-36). "The Specialist" story about Sad Sack's return to Army	1.35	4.00	8.00
23-50	.85	2.50	5.00
51-100	.40	1.20	2.40
101-150		.50	1.00
151-222		.25	.50
223-228 (25¢ Giants, 52 pgs.)		.40	.80
229-287: 286,287 had limited distribution		.25	.50
3-D 1 (1/54-titled "Harvey 3-D Hits")	9.00	27.00	60.00
Armed Forces Complimentary copies, HD No. 2-40 ('57-'62)	.40	1.20	2.40

Sabu, Elephant Boy #30, © FOX

Saddle Romances #9, © WMG

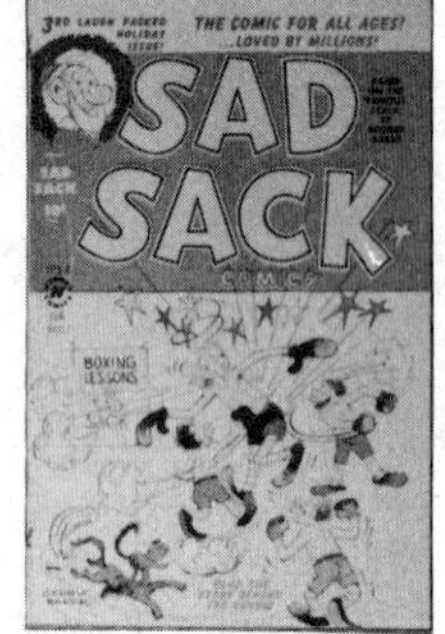

Sad Sack Comics #3, © HARV

Sad Sack Laugh Special #6, © HARV

Saga of Swamp Thing #20, © DC

The Saint #5, © AVON

SAD SACK COMICS (continued)

NOTE: *The **Sad Sack Comics** comic book was a spin-off from a Sunday Newspaper strip launched through John Wheeler's Bell Syndicate. The previous Sunday page and the first 21 comics depicted the Sad Sack in civvies. Unpopularity caused the Sunday page to be discontinued in the early '50s. Meanwhile Sad Sack returned to the Army, by popular demand, in issue No. 22, remaining there ever since. Incidentally, relatively few of the first 21 issues were ever collected and remain scarce due to this.*

SAD SACK FUN AROUND THE WORLD
1974 (no month)
Harvey Publications

	Good	Fine	Mint
1-About Great Britain		.40	.80

SAD SACK GOES HOME
1951 (16 pgs. in color)
Harvey Publications

	Good	Fine	Mint
nn-by George Baker	3.35	10.00	20.00

SAD SACK LAUGH SPECIAL
Winter, 1958-59 - No. 93, Feb, 1977
Harvey Publications

	Good	Fine	Mint
1	2.75	8.00	16.00
2-10	1.35	4.00	8.00
11-30	.70	2.00	4.00
31-50	.40	1.20	2.40
51-93		.50	1.00

SAD SACK NAVY, GOBS 'N' GALS
Aug, 1972 - No. 8, Oct, 1973
Harvey Publications

	Good	Fine	Mint
1		.50	1.00
2-8		.30	.60

SAD SACK'S ARMY LIFE (See Harvey Hits No. 8, 17, 22, 28, 32, 39, 43, 47, 51, 55, 58, 61, 64, 67, 70)

SAD SACK'S ARMY LIFE (. . . Parade No. 1-57, . . . Today No. 58 on)
Oct, 1963 - No. 60, Nov, 1975; No. 61, May, 1976
Harvey Publications

	Good	Fine	Mint
1	2.00	6.00	12.00
2-10	1.00	3.00	6.00
11-20	.40	1.20	2.40
21-40		.50	1.00
41-61		.30	.60

SAD SACK'S FUNNY FRIENDS (See Harvey Hits No. 75)
Dec, 1955 - No. 75, Oct, 1969
Harvey Publications

	Good	Fine	Mint
1	3.35	10.00	20.00
2-10	1.70	5.00	10.00
11-20	.85	2.50	5.00
21-30	.40	1.20	2.40
31-50		.50	1.00
51-75		.30	.60

SAD SACK'S MUTTSY (See Harvey Hits No. 74, 77, 80, 82, 84, 87, 89, 92, 96, 99, 102, 105, 108, 111, 113, 115, 117, 119, 121)

SAD SACK USA (. . . Vacation No. 8)
Nov, 1972 - No. 7, Nov, 1973; No. 8, Oct, 1974
Harvey Publications

	Good	Fine	Mint
1		.50	1.00
2-8		.25	.50

SAD SACK WITH SARGE & SADIE
Sept, 1972 - No. 8, Nov, 1973
Harvey Publications

	Good	Fine	Mint
1		.50	1.00
2-8		.25	.50

SAD SAD SACK WORLD
Oct, 1964 - No. 46, Dec, 1973
Harvey Publications

	Good	Fine	Mint
1	.85	2.50	5.00
2-10	.40	1.20	2.40
11-46		.50	1.00

SAGA OF BIG RED, THE
Sept, 1976 ($1.25) (In color)
Omaha World-Herald

	Good	Fine	Mint
nn-by Win Mumma; story of the Nebraska Cornhuskers (sports)	.30	.80	1.60

SAGA OF CRYSTAR, CRYSTAL WARRIOR, THE
May, 1983 - No. 11, Feb, 1985
Marvel Comics Group

	Good	Fine	Mint
1-($2.00; Baxter paper)	.35	1.00	2.00
2-9: Golden-c No. 6-9,11		.30	.60
10,11 ($1.00, 52 pgs.)-11-Alpha Flight app.		.50	1.00

SAGA OF ELF FACE, THE
1986 - Present ($1.50, B&W)
Exeter Entrance Studios

	Good	Fine	Mint
1,2	.25	.75	1.50

SAGA OF SWAMP THING, THE (Swamp Thing No. 39-41,46 on)
May, 1982 - Present
DC Comics

	Good	Fine	Mint
1-Origin retold; Phantom Stranger series begins; ends No. 13; movie adapt.		.50	1.00
2-15: 2-Photo-c		.35	.70
16-19: Bissette-a	.25	.75	1.50
20-1st Alan Moore issue	2.50	7.50	15.00
21-New origin	3.00	9.00	18.00
22-25	.85	2.50	5.00
26-30	.65	2.00	4.00
31-35	.40	1.25	2.50
36-40	.35	1.00	2.00
41-45	.25	.75	1.50
46-52: 46-Crisis x-over		.60	1.20
53-Double size ($1.25)	.25	.75	1.50
54-60		.45	.90
Annual 1(11/82)-Movie Adaptation		.50	1.00
Annual 2(1/85)		.50	1.00

NOTE: ***Bissette** a(p)-16-19, 21-27, 29, 30, 34-36, 39-42, 44, 46, 50; c-17i, 24p-32p, 35p-37p, 40p, 44p, 46p-50p. **Spiegle** a-1-3, 6. **Totleben** a(i)-10, 16-27, 29, 31, 34-40, 42, 44, 46, 48, 50; c-25-32i, 33, 35-40i, 42i, 44i, 46-50i, 53, 55i. **Wrightson** a-18i(r).*

SAILOR SWEENEY (Navy Action No. 1-11, 15 on)
No. 12, July, 1956 - No. 14, Nov, 1956
Atlas Comics (CDS)

	Good	Fine	Mint
12-14: 12-Shores-a. 13-Severin-c	1.30	4.00	9.00

SAINT, THE
Aug, 1947 - No. 12, Mar, 1952
Avon Periodicals

	Good	Fine	Mint
1-Kamen bondage c/a	26.00	78.00	182.00
2	13.50	40.50	98.00
3,4: 4-Lingerie panels	11.50	34.50	80.00
5-Spanking panel	17.00	51.00	120.00
6-Miss Fury app., 14 pgs.	19.00	57.00	132.00
7-c-/Avon paperback 118	10.00	30.00	70.00
8,9(12/50): Saint strip-r in No. 8-12; 9-Kinstler-c	8.50	25.50	60.00
10-Wood-a, 1 pg; c-/Avon paperback 289	8.50	25.50	60.00
11	6.00	18.00	42.00
12-c-/Avon paperback 123	8.00	24.00	56.00

NOTE: *Lucky Dale, Girl Detective in No. 1,4,6. **Hollingsworth** a-4.*

SALERNO CARNIVAL OF COMICS (Also see Pure Oil Comics, 24 Pages of Comics, & Vicks Comics)

SALERNO CARNIVAL OF COMICS (cont'd.)
Late 1930s (16 pgs.) (paper cover) (Giveaway)
Salerno Cookie Co.

	Good	Fine	Mint
nn-Color reprints of Calkins' Buck Rogers & Skyroads, plus other strips from Famous Funnies	22.00	65.00	154.00

SALIMBA (3-D)
1986 - No. 2, Sept, 1986
Blackthorne Publ.

	Good	Fine	Mint
1,2-Jungle girl stories	.35	1.10	2.25

SALOME' (See Night Music No. 6)

SAM HILL PRIVATE EYE
1950 - No. 7, 1951
Close-Up

	Good	Fine	Mint
1-Negligee panel	3.75	11.25	26.00
2	1.85	5.50	13.00
3-7	1.70	5.00	11.50

SAM SLADE ROBOHUNTER
Oct, 1986 - Present
Quality Comics

	Good	Fine	Mint
1-5		.40	.75
6 ($1.25)-Origin Ro-Busters		.60	1.25

SAMSON (1st Series) (Capt. Aero No. 7 on)
Fall, 1940 - No. 6, Sept, 1941 (See Fantastic Comics)
Fox Features Syndicate

	Good	Fine	Mint
1-Powell-a, signed 'Rensie;' Wing Turner by Tuska app.	45.00	135.00	315.00
2-Dr. Fung by Powell	22.00	65.00	154.00
3-Navy Jones app.; Simon-c	17.00	51.00	120.00
4-Yarko the Great, Master Magician by Eisner begins; Fine-c?	15.00	45.00	105.00
5,6: 6-Origin The Topper	15.00	45.00	105.00

SAMSON (2nd Series) (See Spectacular Features Magazine)
No. 12, April, 1955 - No. 14, Aug, 1955
Ajax/Farrell Publications (Four Star)

	Good	Fine	Mint
12-Wonder Boy	5.50	16.50	40.00
13,14: 13-Wonder Boy, Rocket Man	3.85	11.50	27.00

SAMSON (See Mighty Samson)

SAMSON & DELILAH (See A Spectacular Feature Magazine)

SAMUEL BRONSTON'S CIRCUS WORLD (See Circus World under Movie Comics)

SAMURAI
1985 - Present ($1.70, B&W)
Aircel Publ.

	Good	Fine	Mint
1	4.20	12.50	25.00
1 (2nd printing)	.50	1.50	3.00
1 (3rd printing)	.30	.85	1.70
2	1.00	3.00	6.00
2 (2nd printing)	.30	.85	1.70
3-5	.50	1.50	3.00
6-12	.35	1.00	2.00

SAMURAI PENGUIN
1986 - Present ($1.50, B&W)
Slave Labor Graphics

	Good	Fine	Mint
1	.50	1.50	3.00
2	.35	1.00	2.00
3	.25	.75	1.50

SAMURAI SQUIRREL
1986 - Present ($1.75, B&W)
Spotlight Comics

	Good	Fine	Mint
1	.30	.85	1.70

SANDMAN, THE
Winter, 1974; No. 2, Apr-May, 1975 - No. 6, Dec-Jan, 1975-76
National Periodical Publications

	Good	Fine	Mint
1-Kirby-a		.30	.60
2-6: 6-Kirby/Wood c/a		.25	.50

NOTE: *Kirby a-1p, 4-6p; c-1-5.*

SANDS OF THE SOUTH PACIFIC
January, 1953
Toby Press

	Good	Fine	Mint
1	8.00	24.00	56.00

SANTA AND HIS REINDEER (See March of Comics No. 166)

SANTA AND POLLYANNA PLAY THE GLAD GAME
1960 (15 pages) (Disney giveaway)
Sales Promotion

	Good	Fine	Mint
	1.00	3.00	6.00

SANTA AND THE ANGEL (See 4-Color No. 259 & Dell Jr. Treasury No. 7)

SANTA & THE BUCCANEERS
1959
Promotional Publ. Co. (Giveaway)

	Good	Fine	Mint
Reprints 1952 Santa & the Pirates	.50	1.50	3.00

SANTA & THE CHRISTMAS CHICKADEE
1974 (20 pgs.)
Murphy's (Giveaway)

	Good	Fine	Mint
		.50	1.00

SANTA & THE PIRATES
1952
Promotional Publ. Co. (Giveaway)

	Good	Fine	Mint
Marv Levy c/a	.85	2.50	5.00

SANTA AT THE ZOO (See 4-Color No. 259)

SANTA CLAUS
Apr, 1986 - No. 3, June, 1986 (mini-series)
Star Comics (Marvel)

	Good	Fine	Mint
1-3: r-/Marvel Super Sp. 39		.40	.80

SANTA CLAUS AROUND THE WORLD (See March of Comics No. 241)

SANTA CLAUS CONQUERS THE MARTIANS (See Movie Classics)

SANTA CLAUS FUNNIES
No date (1940s) (Color & B&W; 8x10''; 12pgs., heavy paper)
W. T. Grant Co. (Giveaway)

	Good	Fine	Mint
March Of Comics-r?	6.75	20.00	40.00

SANTA CLAUS FUNNIES (Also see Dell Giants)
Dec?, 1942 - No. 1274, Dec, 1961
Dell Publishing Co.

	Good	Fine	Mint
nn(No.1)(1942)-Kelly-a	25.00	75.00	175.00
2(12/43)-Kelly-a	18.00	54.00	125.00
4-Color 61(1944)-Kelly-a	18.00	54.00	125.00
4-Color 91(1945)-Kelly-a	13.50	40.50	95.00
4-Color 128('46),175('47)-Kelly-a	11.50	34.50	80.00
4-Color 205,254-Kelly-a	10.00	30.00	70.00
4-Color 302,361	2.00	6.00	14.00
4-Color 525,607,666,756,867	1.15	3.50	8.00

Sam Hill Private Eye #1, © Close-Up

Samson #3, © FOX

Samurai #1 (1st Printing), © Aircel

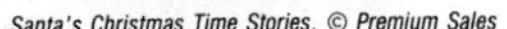
Santa's Christmas Time Stories, © Premium Sales

Santa's Gift Book

Sarge Steel #1, © CC

SANTA CLAUS FUNNIES (continued) — Good / Fine / Mint
4-Color 958,1063,1154,1274 — 1.00 / 3.00 / 7.00
NOTE: *Most issues contain only one **Kelly** story.*

SANTA CLAUS PARADE
1951; 1952; 1955 (25 cents)
Ziff-Davis (Approved Comics)/St. John Publishing Co.

nn(1951-Ziff-Davis)-116 pgs. (Xmas Special) 5.00 15.00 35.00
2(12/52-Ziff-Davis)-100 pgs.; Dave Berg-a 4.00 12.00 28.00
V1No.3(1/55-St. John)-100 pgs. 3.50 10.50 24.00

SANTA CLAUS' WORKSHOP (See March of Comics No. 50,168)

SANTA IS COMING (See March of Comics No. 197)

SANTA IS HERE (See March of Comics No. 49)

SANTA ON THE JOLLY ROGER
1965
Promotional Publ. Co. (Giveaway)

Marv Levy c/a .50 1.50 3.00

SANTA! SANTA!
1974 (20 pgs.)
R. Jackson (Montgomery Ward giveaway)

.50 1.00

SANTA'S BUSY CORNER (See March of Comics No. 31)

SANTA'S CANDY KITCHEN (See March of Comics No. 14)

SANTA'S CHRISTMAS BOOK (See March of Comics No. 123)

SANTA'S CHRISTMAS COMICS
December, 1952 (100 pages)
Standard Comics (Best Books)

nn-Supermouse, Dizzy Duck, Happy Rabbit, etc.
4.00 12.00 28.00

SANTA'S CHRISTMAS COMIC VARIETY SHOW
1943 (24 pages)
Sears Roebuck & Co.

Contains puzzles & new comics of Dick Tracy, Little Orphan Annie, Moon Mullins, Terry & the Pirates, etc. 7.50 22.50 52.00

SANTA'S CHRISTMAS LIST (See March of Comics No. 255)

SANTA'S CHRISTMAS TIME STORIES
nd (late 1940s) (16 pgs.; paper cover)
Premium Sales, Inc. (Giveaway)

2.00 6.00 12.00

SANTA'S CIRCUS
1964 (half-size)
Promotional Publ. Co. (Giveaway)

Marv Levy c/a .50 1.50 3.00

SANTA'S FUN BOOK
1951, 1952 (regular size, 16 pages, paper-c)
Promotional Publ. Co. (Murphy's giveaway)

1.70 5.00 10.00

SANTA'S GIFT BOOK
No date (16 pgs.)
No Publisher

Puzzles, games only .70 2.00 4.00

SANTA'S HELPERS (See March of Comics No. 64,106,198)

SANTA'S LITTLE HELPERS (See March of Comics No. 270)

SANTA'S NEW STORY BOOK
1949 (16 pgs.; paper cover)
Wallace Hamilton Campbell (Giveaway) — Good / Fine / Mint
2.75 8.00 16.00

SANTA'S REAL STORY BOOK
1948, 1952 (16 pgs.)
Wallace Hamilton Campbell/W. W. Orris (Giveaway)
2.00 6.00 12.00

SANTA'S RIDE
1959
W. T. Grant Co. (Giveaway)

1.35 4.00 8.00

SANTA'S RODEO
1964 (half-size)
Promotional Publ. Co. (Giveaway)

Marv Levy-a .70 2.00 4.00

SANTA'S SECRETS
1951, 1952? (16 pgs.; paper cover)
Sam B. Anson Christmas giveaway

2.00 6.00 12.00

SANTA'S SHOW (See March of Comics No. 311)

SANTA'S SLEIGH (See March of Comics No. 298)

SANTA'S STORIES
1953 (regular size; paper cover)
K. K. Publications (Klines Dept. Store)

Kelly-a 10.00 30.00 70.00

SANTA'S SURPRISE (See March of Comics No. 13)

SANTA'S SURPRISE
1947 (36 pgs.; slick cover)
K. K. Publications (Giveaway)

2.75 8.00 16.00

SANTA'S TINKER TOTS
1958
Charlton Comics

1-Based on "The Tinker Tots Keep Christmas"
1.00 3.00 6.00

SANTA'S TOYLAND (See March of Comics No. 242)

SANTA'S TOYS (See March of Comics No. 12)

SANTA'S TOYTOWN FUN BOOK
1952, 1953?
Promotional Publ. Co. (Giveaway)

Marv Levy-c 1.00 3.00 6.00

SANTA'S VISIT (See March of Comics No. 283)

SANTIAGO (See 4-Color No. 723)

SARGE SNORKEL (Beetle Bailey)
Oct, 1973 - No. 17, Dec, 1976
Charlton Comics

1-17 .30 .60

SARGE STEEL (Becomes Secret Agent No. 9 on)
Dec, 1964 - No. 8, Mar-Apr, 1966
Charlton Comics

1-Origin .30 .80 1.60
2-8: 6-Judo Master app. .50 1.00

SAVAGE COMBAT TALES
Feb, 1975 - No. 3, July, 1975
Atlas/Seaboard Publ.

SAVAGE COMBAT TALES (continued) Good Fine Mint
1-3: 1-Sgt. Stryker's Death Squad begins (origin). 2-Only app. Warhawk .30 .60
NOTE: ***McWilliams*** *a-1, 2; c-1.* ***Sparling*** *a-1.* ***Toth*** *a-2.*

SAVAGE RAIDS OF GERONIMO (See Geronimo No. 4)

SAVAGE RANGE (See 4-Color No. 807)

SAVAGE SHE-HULK, THE
Feb, 1980 - No. 25, Feb, 1982
Marvel Comics Group

1-Origin & 1st app. .50 1.00
2-5 .30 .60
6-25: 25-52 pgs. .25 .50
NOTE: ***Austin*** *a-25i; c-23i-25i.* ***J. Buscema*** *a-1p; c-1, 2p.* ***Golden*** *c-8-11.*

SAVAGE SWORD OF CONAN, THE (Magazine)
Aug, 1974 - Present (B&W)(Mature readers)
Marvel Comics Group

1-Smith-r; Buscema/Adams/Krenkel-a; origin Blackmark by Gil Kane(part 1) & Red Sonja (3rd app.) 2.50 7.50 15.00
2-Adams-c; Chaykin/Adams-a 1.25 3.75 7.50
3-Severin/Smith-a; Adams-a 1.00 3.00 6.00
4-Adams/Kane-a(r) .85 2.50 5.00
5-10 .70 2.00 4.00
11-20 .60 1.75 3.50
21-30 .50 1.50 3.00
31-50 .35 1.00 2.00
51-134: 70-Article on movie. 83-Red Sonja-r by Adams from No. 1 .25 .75 1.50
Annual 1('75)-B&W, Smith-r (Conan No. 10,13) .50 1.50 3.00
NOTE: ***Adams*** *a-14p, 60, 83p(r).* ***Alcala*** *a-2 ,4, 7, 12, 15-20, 23, 24, 28, 59, 67, 69, 75, 76i, 80i, 82i, 83i, 89.* ***Austin*** *a-78i.* ***Boris*** *c-1, 4, 5, 7, 9, 10, 12, 15.* ***Brunner*** *a-30; c-8, 30.* ***Buscema*** *a-1-5, 7, 10-12, 15-24, 26-28, 31, 32, 36-43, 45, 47-58p, 60-67p, 70, 71-74p, 76-81p, 87-96p, 98, 99p-101p; c-40.* ***Corbin*** *a-4, 16, 29.* ***Finlay*** *a-16.* ***Golden*** *a-98, 101.* ***Kaluta*** *a-11, 18; c-3, 91, 93.* ***Gil Kane*** *a-2, 3, 8, 13r, 29, 47, 64, 65, 67, 85p, 86p.* ***Krenkel*** *a-9, 11, 14, 16, 24.* ***Morrow*** *a-7.* ***Nebres*** *a-93i, 101i, 107, 114.* ***Newton*** *a-6.* ***Nino*** *a/c-6.* ***Redondo*** *c-48, 50, 52, 56, 57, 85i, 90, 96i.* ***Simonson*** *a-7, 8, 12, 15-17.* ***Smith*** *a-7, 16, 24, 82r.* ***Starlin*** *c-26. No. 8 & 10 contain a Robert E. Howard Conan adaptation.*

SAVAGE TALES (Magazine) (B&W)
May, 1971; No. 2, 10/73; No. 3, 2/74 - No. 12, Summer, 1975
Marvel Comics Group

1-Origin & 1st app. The Man-Thing by Morrow; Conan the Barbarian by Barry Smith, Femizons by Romita begin; Ka-Zar app. 7.00 20.00 40.00
2-Smith, Brunner, Morrow, Williamson, Wrightson-a (reprint/Creatures on the Loose No. 10); King Kull app. 2.50 7.50 15.00
3-Smith, Brunner, Steranko, Williamson-a 1.70 5.00 10.00
4,5-Adams-c; last Conan (Smith-r/No. 4) plus Kane/Adams-a. 5-Brak the Barbarian begins, ends No. 8 1.00 3.00 6.00
6-Ka-Zar begins; Williamson-r; Adams-c .50 1.50 3.00
7-Buscema/Adams-a .50 1.50 3.00
8-Shanna, the She-Devil begins, ends No. 10; Williamson-r .50 1.50 3.00
9,11 .40 1.20 2.40
10-Adams-a(i) .50 1.50 3.00
Annual 1(Summer'75)(No.12 on inside)-Ka-Zar origin by G. Kane; B&W; Smith-r/Astonishing Tales .40 1.20 2.40
NOTE: ***Boris*** *c-7,10.* ***Buscema*** *a-5r, 6p, 8p; c-2.* ***Fabian*** *c-8.* ***Heath*** *a-10p, 11p.* ***Kaluta*** *c-9.* ***Maneely*** *a-2r.* ***Starlin*** *a-5. Robert E. Howard adaptations-1-4.*

SAVAGE TALES (Magazine size)
Nov, 1985 - Present (B&W) ($1.50) (Mature readers)
Marvel Comics Group

1-9 .25 .75 1.50

SCAMP (Walt Disney)
No. 703, 5/56 - No. 1204, 8-10/61; 11/67 - No. 45, 1/79
Dell Publishing Co./Gold Key

	Good	Fine	Mint
4-Color 703	1.30	4.00	9.00
4-Color 777,806('57),833	1.00	3.00	7.00
5(3-5/58)-10(6-8/59)	.75	2.25	5.00
11-16(12-2/60-61)	.55	1.65	4.00
4-Color 1204(1961)	.75	2.25	5.00
1(12/67-G.K.)-Reprints begin	.55	1.65	4.00
2(3/69)-10	.35	1.00	2.00
11-20	.25	.75	1.50
21-45		.40	.80

NOTE: *New stories-No. 20(in part), 22-25, 27, 29-31, 34, 36-40, 42-45. New covers-No. 11, 12, 14, 15, 17-25, 27, 29-31, 34, 36-38.*

SCAR FACE (See The Crusaders)

SCARECROW OF ROMNEY MARSH, THE
April, 1964 - No. 3, Oct, 1965 (Disney TV Show)
Gold Key

10112-404 (No.1) 2.00 6.00 14.00
2,3 1.50 4.50 10.00

SCARLET O'NEIL (See Harvey Comics Hits No. 59)

SCARY TALES
8/75 - No. 9, 1/77; No. 10, 9/77 - No. 20, 6/79; No. 21, 8/80 - No. 46, 10/84
Charlton Comics

1-Origin & 1st app. Countess Von Bludd, not in No. 2 .40 .80
2-11 .30 .60
12-36,39,46-All reprints .30 .60
37,38,40-45-New-a. 38-Mr. Jigsaw app. .30 .60
1(Modern Comics reprint, 1977) .15 .30
NOTE: ***Adkins*** *a-31i; c-31i.* ***Ditko*** *a-3, 5, 7, 8(2), 11,,12, 14-16r, 18(3)r, 19r, 21r, 32, 39r; c-5, 11, 14, 18, 32.* ***Newton*** *a-31p; c-31p.* ***Powell*** *a-18r.* ***Staton*** *a-1(2 pgs.), 4, 20r; c-1, 20.* ***Sutton*** *a-9; c-4, 9.*

SCHOOL DAY ROMANCES (. . . of Teen-Agers No. 4) (Popular Teen-Agers No. 5 on)
Nov-Dec, 1949 - No. 4, May-June, 1950
Star Publications

1-Tony Gayle (later Gay), Gingersnapp begin 6.50 19.50 45.00
2,3 4.00 12.00 28.00
4-Ronald Reagan photo-c 10.00 30.00 70.00
NOTE: *All have* ***L. B. Cole*** *covers.*

SCHWINN BICYCLE BOOK (. . . Bike Thrills, 1959)
1949; 1952; 1959 (10¢)
Schwinn Bicycle Co.

1949 2.35 7.00 14.00
1952-Believe It or Not type facts; comic format; 36 pgs. 1.35 4.00 8.00
1959 1.00 3.00 6.00

SCIENCE COMICS (1st Series)
Feb, 1940 - No. 8, Sept, 1940
Fox Features Syndicate

1-Origin Dynamo (called Electro in No. 1), The Eagle, & Navy Jones; Marga, The Panther Woman, Cosmic Carson & Perisphere Payne, Dr. Doom begin; bondage/hypo-c 85.00 255.00 595.00
2 50.00 150.00 350.00
3,4: 4-Kirby-a 40.00 120.00 280.00
5-8 28.00 84.00 195.00
NOTE: *Cosmic Carson by* ***Tuska****-No. 1-3; by* ***Kirby****-No. 4.* ***Lou Fine*** *c-1-3 only.*

Savage She-Hulk #3, © MCG

Scamp #16, © WDC

Science Comics #5 (6/40), © FOX

Scout #9, © Eclipse

Scream #1 (Fall, '44), © ACE

Sea Devils #19, © DC

SCIENCE COMICS (2nd Series)
January, 1946 - No. 5, 1946
Humor Publications (Ace Magazines?)

	Good	Fine	Mint
1-Palais c/a in No. 1-3; A-Bomb-c	3.15	9.50	22.00
2	1.85	5.50	13.00
3-Feldstein-a, 6 pgs.	4.35	13.00	30.00
4,5	1.65	5.00	11.50

SCIENCE COMICS
May, 1947 (8 pgs. in color)
Ziff-Davis Publ. Co.

	Good	Fine	Mint
nn-Could be ordered by mail for 10¢; like the nn Amazing Advs. (1950)-used to test the market	20.00	60.00	130.00

SCIENCE COMICS
March, 1951
Export Publication Ent., Toronto, Canada
Distr. in U.S. by Kable News Co.

	Good	Fine	Mint
1-Science Adventure stories plus some true science features	1.65	5.00	11.50

SCIENCE FICTION SPACE ADVENTURES (See Space Adventures)

SCOOBY DOO (. . .Where are you? No. 1-16,26; . . . Mystery Comics No. 17-25,27 on) (TV)
March, 1970 - No. 30, Feb, 1975
Gold Key

	Good	Fine	Mint
1	2.65	8.00	16.00
2-5	1.30	4.00	8.00
6-10	.85	2.50	5.00
11-20: 11-Tufts-a	.50	1.50	3.00
21-30	.35	1.00	2.00

(See March of Comics No. 356,368,382,391)

SCOOBY DOO (TV)
April, 1975 - No. 11, Dec, 1976 (Hanna Barbera)
Charlton Comics

	Good	Fine	Mint
1	1.00	3.00	6.00
2-5	.50	1.50	3.00
6-11	.35	1.00	2.00

SCOOBY-DOO (TV)
Oct, 1977 - No. 9, Feb, 1979
Marvel Comics Group

	Good	Fine	Mint
1-Dyno-Mutt begins	.25	.75	1.50
2-9		.40	.80

SCOOP COMICS
November, 1941 - No. 8, 1946
Harry 'A' Chesler (Holyoke)

	Good	Fine	Mint
1-Intro. Rocketman & Rocketgirl; origin The Master Key; Dan Hastings begins; Charles Sultan c/a	25.00	75.00	175.00
2-Rocket Boy app; Injury to eye story (Same as Spotlight No. 3)	15.00	45.00	105.00
3-Injury to eye story-r from No. 2	12.00	36.00	84.00
4-8	9.00	27.00	62.00

SCOOTER (See Swing with. . .)

SCOOTER
April, 1946
Rucker Publ. Ltd. (Canadian)

	Good	Fine	Mint
1	1.75	5.25	12.00

SCORPION
Feb, 1975 - No. 3, July, 1975
Atlas/Seaboard Publ.

	Good	Fine	Mint
1-Intro.; bondage-c by Chaykin		.40	.80
2-Wrightson, Kaluta, Simonson-a(i)		.30	.60
3-Mooney-a(i)		.25	.50

NOTE: ***Chaykin*** *a-1,2.*

SCORPIO ROSE
Jan, 1983; No. 2, Oct, 1983 (Baxter paper)
Eclipse Comics

	Good	Fine	Mint
1-Dr. Orient back-up story begins	.25	.75	1.50
2-Origin	.25	.75	1.50

NOTE: ***Rogers*** *c/a 1,2.*

SCOTLAND YARD (Inspector Farnsworth of. . .)
(Texas Rangers In Action No. 5 on?)
June, 1955 - No. 4, March, 1956
Charlton Comics Group

	Good	Fine	Mint
1-Tothish-a	4.00	12.00	28.00
2-4: 2-Tothish-a	2.35	7.00	16.00

SCOUT
9/85 - Present ($1.75 - $1.25; Baxter, Mando paper)
Eclipse Comics

	Good	Fine	Mint
1	.35	1.00	2.00
2-8,11: 11-Monday: The Eliminator begins	.30	.90	1.80
9,10: 9-Airboy app. 10-Bissette-a		.60	1.25
12-14	.30	.90	1.80

SCRATCH
1986 - Present ($1.75, B&W)
Outside Comics

	Good	Fine	Mint
1,2	.30	.90	1.80

SCREAM (. . .Comics) (Andy Comics No. 20 on)
Fall, 1944 - No. 19, April, 1948
Humor Publications/Current Books(Ace Magazines)

	Good	Fine	Mint
1	4.00	12.00	28.00
2	2.00	6.00	14.00
3-15: 11-Racist humor (Indians)	1.65	5.00	11.50
16-Intro. Lily-Belle	1.65	5.00	11.50
17,19	1.30	4.00	9.00
18-Transvestite, Hypo needle story	2.65	8.00	18.00

SCREAM (Magazine)
Aug, 1973 - No. 11, Feb, 1975 (68 pgs.) (B&W)
Skywald Publishing Corp.

	Good	Fine	Mint
1	.50	1.50	3.00
2-5: 2-Origin Lady Satan. 3 (12/73)-No. 3 found on pg. 22	.30	.80	1.60
6-11: 6-Origin The Victims. 9-Severed head-c		.50	1.00

SCRIBBLY (See All-American, Buzzy, The Funnies & Popular Comics)
8-9/48 - No. 13, 8-9/50; No. 14, 10-11/51 - No. 15, 12-1/51-52
National Periodical Publications

	Good	Fine	Mint
1	36.00	108.00	252.00
2	20.00	60.00	140.00
3-5	18.00	54.00	125.00
6-10	12.00	36.00	84.00
11-15	9.00	27.00	62.00

NOTE: ***Sheldon Mayer*** *art in all.*

SEA DEVILS (See DC Special No. 10,19, DC Super-Stars No. 14,17, Limited Collectors Ed. No. 39,45, & Showcase)
Sept-Oct, 1961 - No. 35, May-June, 1967
National Periodical Publications

	Good	Fine	Mint
1	4.75	14.25	33.00
2-Last 10¢ issue	2.35	7.00	16.00
3-5	1.35	4.00	9.00
6-10	1.00	3.00	6.00
11,12,14-20	.70	2.00	4.00

SEA DEVILS (continued)

	Good	Fine	Mint
13-Kubert, Colan-a	.85	2.50	5.00
21,23-35	.50	1.50	3.00
22-Intro. International Sea Devils; origin & 1st app. Capt. X & Man Fish	.50	1.50	3.00

NOTE: *Heath a-1-10; c-1-10,14-16.*

SEADRAGON (Also see The Epsilon Wave)
May, 1986 - Present ($1.75, color)
Elite Comics

	Good	Fine	Mint
1	.35	1.00	2.00
1 (2nd printing)	.30	.90	1.75
2-6	.30	.90	1.75

SEA HOUND, THE (Capt. Silver's Log of. . .)
1945 (no month) - No. 4, Jan-Feb, 1946
Avon Periodicals

	Good	Fine	Mint
nn	4.00	12.00	28.00
2-4	2.65	8.00	18.00

SEA HOUND, THE (Radio)
No. 3, July, 1949 - No. 4, Sept, 1949
Capt. Silver Syndicate

	Good	Fine	Mint
3,4	2.35	7.00	16.00

SEA HUNT (TV)
No. 928, 8/58; No. 994, 10-12/59; No. 4, 1-3/60 - No. 13, 4-6/62
Dell Publishing Co. (All have Lloyd Bridges photo-c)

	Good	Fine	Mint
4-Color 928	3.50	10.50	24.00
4-Color 994, 4-13: Manning-a No. 4-6,8-11,13	3.00	9.00	21.00
4-Color 1041-Toth-a	4.00	12.00	28.00

SEARCH FOR LOVE
Feb-Mar, 1950 - No. 2, Apr-May, 1950 (52 pgs.)
American Comics Group

	Good	Fine	Mint
1	3.15	9.50	22.00
2	1.65	5.00	11.50

SEARCHERS (See 4-Color No. 709)

SEARS (See Merry Christmas From. . .)

SEASON'S GREETINGS
1935 (6¼x5¼") (32 pgs. in color)
Hallmark (King Features)

Cover features Mickey Mouse, Popeye, Jiggs & Skippy. "The Night Before Christmas" told one panel per page, each panel by a famous artist featuring their character. Art by Alex Raymond, Gottfredson, Swinnerton, Segar, Chic Young, Milt Gross, Sullivan (Messmer), Herriman, McManus, Percy Crosby & others (22 artists in all)
Estimated value. . . . $200.00—$400.00

SECOND CITY
Nov, 1986 - Present ($1.95, B&W)
Harrier Publishing

	Good	Fine	Mint
1	.35	1.00	1.95

SECRET AGENT (Formerly Sarge Steel)
Oct, 1966 - V2No.10, Oct, 1967
Charlton Comics

	Good	Fine	Mint
V2No.9-Sarge Steel part-r begins	.30	.80	1.60
10-Tiffany Sinn, CIA app. (from Career Girl Romances No. 39); Aparo-a		.40	.80

SECRET AGENT (TV)
Nov, 1966 - No. 2, Jan, 1968
Gold Key

	Good	Fine	Mint
1,2-Photo-c	1.50	4.50	10.00

SECRET AGENT X-9
1934 (Book 1: 84 pgs.; Book 2: 124 pgs.) (8x7½")
David McKay Publications

	Good	Fine	Mint
Book 1-Contains reprints of the first 13 weeks of the strip by Alex Raymond; complete except for 2 dailies	32.00	95.00	224.00
Book 2-Contains reprints immediately following contents of Book 1, for 20 weeks by Alex Raymond; complete except for two dailies. Note: Raymond mis-dated the last five strips from June, 1934, and while the dating sequence is confusing, the continuity is correct.	25.00	75.00	175.00

SECRET AGENT X-9 (See Feature Books No. 8, McKay)

SECRET AGENT Z-2 (See Holyoke One-Shot No. 7)

SECRET DIARY OF EERIE ADVENTURES
1953 (One Shot) (Giant-100 pgs.)
Avon Periodicals

	Good	Fine	Mint
(Rare) Kubert-a; Hollingsworth-c; Check back-c	82.00	246.00	575.00

SECRET HEARTS
9-10/49 - No. 6, 7-8/50; No. 7, 12-1/51-52 - No. 153, 7/71
(No. 1-6, photo-c; all 52 pgs.)
National Periodical Publications (Beverly)(Arleigh No. 50-113)

	Good	Fine	Mint
1	11.00	33.00	76.00
2	5.50	16.50	38.00
3,6 (1950)	4.35	13.00	30.00
4,5-Toth-a	5.50	16.50	38.00
7(12-1/51-52) (Rare)	5.00	15.00	35.00
8-10 (1952)	2.85	8.50	20.00
11-20	2.35	7.00	16.00
21-26: 26-Last pre-code (2-3/55)	1.85	5.50	13.00
27-40	1.65	5.00	11.50
41-50	.95	2.85	6.50
51-60	.55	1.65	4.00
61-75: Last 10¢ ish?	.35	1.00	2.00
76-109		.60	1.20
110-"Reach for Happiness" serial begins, ends No. 138		.50	1.00
111-119,121-133,135-138		.40	.80
120,134-Adams-c	.30	.80	1.60
139,140		.25	.50
141,142-"20 Miles to Heartbreak," Chapter 2 & 3 (See Young Love for Chapter 1 & 4); Toth, Colletta-a		.40	.80
143-148,150-153: 144-Morrow-a		.25	.50
149-Toth-a		.30	.60

SECRET ISLAND OF OZ, THE (See First Comics Graphic Novel)

SECRET LOVE (See Fox Giants)

SECRET LOVE
12/55 - No. 3, 8/56; 4/57 - No. 5, 2/58; No. 6, 6/58
Ajax-Farrell/Four Star Comic Corp. No. 2 on

	Good	Fine	Mint
1(12/55-Ajax)	2.00	6.00	14.00
2,3	1.30	4.00	9.00
1(4/57-Ajax)	1.65	5.00	11.50
2-6: 5-Bakerish-a	1.15	3.50	8.00

SECRET LOVE (See Sinister House of. . .)

SECRET LOVES
Nov, 1949 - No. 6, Sept, 1950
Comic Magazines/Quality Comics Group

	Good	Fine	Mint
1-Ward-c	8.50	25.50	60.00

Seadragon #1 (1st Printing), © Elite

Sea Hunt #4, © DELL

Secret Agent #1, © GK

Secret Loves #2, © QUA

Secret Origins #3 (6/86), © DC

Secrets of Haunted House #35, © DC

SECRET LOVES (continued)

	Good	Fine	Mint
2-Ward-c	8.00	24.00	56.00
3-Crandall-a	5.50	16.50	38.00
4,6	2.85	8.50	20.00
5-Suggestive art-''Boom Town Babe''	3.85	11.50	27.00

SECRET LOVE STORIES (See Fox Giants)

SECRET MISSIONS
February, 1950
St. John Publishing Co.

1-Kubert-c	6.50	19.50	45.00

SECRET MYSTERIES (Formerly Crime Mysteries & Crime Smashers)
No. 16, Nov, 1954 - No. 19, July, 1955
Ribage/Merit Publications No. 17 on

16-Horror, Palais-a	3.50	10.50	24.00
17-19-Horror; No. 17-mis-dated 3/54?	2.50	7.50	17.50

SECRET ORIGINS (See 80 Page Giant No. 8)
Aug-Oct, 1961 (Annual) (Reprints)
National Periodical Publications

1('61)-Origin Adam Strange (Showcase No. 17), Green Lantern (G. L. No. 1), Challs (partial/Showcase No. 6, 6 pgs. Kirby-a). J'onn J'onzz (Detective No. 225), New Flash (Showcase No. 4). Green Arrow (1 pg. text). Superman-Batman team (W. Finest 94). Wonder Woman (W. Woman 105)	8.00	24.00	56.00

SECRET ORIGINS
Feb-Mar, 1973 - No. 6, Jan-Feb, 1974; No. 7, Oct-Nov, 1974
National Periodical Publications (All reprints)

1-Origin Superman, Batman, The Ghost, The Flash (Showcase No. 4); Infantino & Kubert-a	.25	.75	1.50
2-Origin new Green Lantern, the new Atom, & Supergirl; Kane-a		.50	1.00
3-Origin Wonder Woman, Wildcat		.50	1.00
4-Origin Vigilante by Meskin, Kid Eternity		.50	1.00
5-Origin The Spectre; Colan-c(p)		.45	.90
6-Origin Blackhawk & Legion of Super Heroes		.45	.90
7-Origin Robin, Aquaman		.45	.90

SECRET ORIGINS
April, 1986 - Present (All origins)
DC Comics

1-Origin Superman	.25	.75	1.50
2-4: 2-Blue Beetle. 3-Capt. Marvel. 4-Firestorm		.50	1.00
5-8: 5-Crimson Avenger. 6-Batman. 7-Green Lantern, Sandman 8-Doll Man		.45	.90
9-12: 9-Flash, Skyman. 10-Phantom Stranger. 11-Hawkman, Power Girl		.40	.80

SECRET ORIGINS OF SUPER-HEROES (See DC Special Series No. 10,19)

SECRET ROMANCE
10/68 - No. 41, 11/76; No. 42, 3/79 - No. 48, 2/80
Charlton Comics

1		.40	.80
2-48: 9-Reese-a		.20	.40

NOTE: *Beyond the Stars app.-No. 9,11,12,14.*

SECRET ROMANCES
April 1951 - No. 27, July, 1955
Superior Publications Ltd.

1	4.35	13.00	30.00
2	2.65	8.00	18.00
3-10	2.35	7.00	16.00
11-13,15-18,20-27	1.65	5.00	11.50
14,19-Lingerie panels	2.65	8.00	18.00

SECRET SERVICE (See Kent Blake of the. . .)

SECRET SIX
Apr-May, 1968 - No. 7, Apr-May, 1969
National Periodical Publications

	Good	Fine	Mint
1-Origin		.50	1.00
2-7		.30	.60

SECRET SOCIETY OF SUPER-VILLAINS
May-June, 1976 - No. 15, June-July, 1978
National Periodical Publications/DC Comics

1-Origin; JLA cameo		.65	1.30
2-5: 2-Re-intro/origin Capt. Comet; Gr. Lantern x-over		.30	.60
6-15: 9,10-Creeper x-over. 15-G.A. Atom, Dr. Midnite, & JSA app.		.25	.50

NOTE: ***Jones** a-'77 Special. **Orlando** a-11i.*

SECRET SOCIETY OF SUPER-VILLAINS SPECIAL (See DC Special Series No. 6)

SECRETS OF HAUNTED HOUSE
4-5/75 - No. 5, 12-1/75-76; No. 6, 6-7/77 - No. 14, 10-11/78; No. 15, 8/79 - No. 46, 3/82
National Periodical Publications/DC Comics

1		.50	1.00
2-46: 31-Mr. E series begins, ends No. 41		.25	.50

NOTE: ***Buckler** c-32-40p. **Ditko** a-9, 12, 41, 45. **Golden** a-10. **Howard** a-13i. **Kaluta** c-10, 11, 14, 16, 29. **Kubert** c-41, 42. **Sheldon Mayer** a-43p. **Newton** a-30p. **Nino** a-1, 13, 19. **Orlando** c-13, 30, 43, 45i. **Redondo** a-4, 29. **Rogers** c-26. **Spiegle** a-31-41. **Wrightson** c-5, 44.*

SECRETS OF HAUNTED HOUSE SPECIAL (See DC Spec. Ser. No. 12)

SECRETS OF LIFE (See 4-Color No. 749)

SECRETS OF LOVE (See Popular Teen-Agers. . .)

SECRETS OF LOVE AND MARRIAGE
Aug, 1956 - V2No.25, June, 1961
Charlton Comics

V2No.1	1.15	3.50	8.00
V2No.2-6	.55	1.65	4.00
V2No.7-9(All 68 pgs.)	.45	1.35	3.00
10-25	.35	1.00	2.00

SECRETS OF MAGIC (See Wisco)

SECRETS OF SINISTER HOUSE (S.H. of Secret Love No. 1-4)
No. 5, June-July, 1972 - No. 18, June-July, 1974
National Periodical Publications

5-9: 7-Redondo-a		.30	.60
10-Adams-a(i)	.50	1.50	3.00
11-18: 17-Toth-r?		.25	.50

NOTE: ***Alcala** a-6, 13, 14. **Kaluta** c-7, 11. **Nino** a-8, 11-13. **Wrightson** c-6. Ambrose Bierce adaptation-No. 14.*

SECRETS OF THE LEGION OF SUPER-HEROES
Jan, 1981 - No. 3, March, 1981 (mini-series)
DC Comics

1-Origin of the Legion		.50	1.00
2-Retells origins of Brainiac 5, Shrinking Violet, Sun-Boy, Bouncing Boy, Ultra-Boy, Matter-Eater Lad, Mon-El, Karate Kid, & Dream Girl		.40	.80
3		.40	.80

SECRETS OF TRUE LOVE
February, 1958
St. John Publishing Co.

1	1.30	4.00	9.00

SECRETS OF YOUNG BRIDES
No. 5, 9/57 - No. 44, 10/64; 7/75 - No. 9, 11/76

SECRETS OF YOUNG BRIDES (continued)
Charlton Comics

	Good	Fine	Mint
5	1.15	3.50	8.00
6-10: 8-Negligee panel	.55	1.65	4.00
11-20	.45	1.35	3.00
21-30: Last 10¢ ish?	.35	1.00	2.00
31-44		.50	1.00
1-9		.25	.50

SECRET SQUIRREL (TV)
October, 1966 (Hanna-Barbera)
Gold Key

	Good	Fine	Mint
1	1.75	5.25	12.00
Florida Power & Light giveaway (1966)	1.75	5.25	12.00

SECRET STORY ROMANCES (Becomes True Tales of Love?)
Nov, 1953 - No. 21, Mar, 1956
Atlas Comics (TCI)

	Good	Fine	Mint
1-Everett-a	2.65	8.00	18.00
2	1.30	4.00	9.00
3-11: 11-Last pre-code (2/55)	1.15	3.50	8.00
12-21	1.00	3.00	7.00

NOTE: ***Colletta** a-10,14,15,17,21; c-10,14,17.*

SECRET VOICE, THE (See Great American Comics)

SECRET WARS II (Also see Marvel Super Heroes . . .)
July, 1985 - No. 9, Mar, 1986 (maxi-series)
Marvel Comics Group

	Good	Fine	Mint
1-Byrne/Austin-c	.25	.75	1.50
2-9: 9-Double sized (75¢)		.50	1.00

SECTAURS
June, 1985 - Present
Marvel Comics Group

	Good	Fine	Mint
1-Based on Coleco Toys		.50	1.00
2-8		.45	.90

SEDUCTION OF THE INNOCENT (Also see N. Y. State Joint Legis. Committee to Study . . .)
1953, 1954 (399 pages) (Hardback)
Rinehart & Co., Inc., N. Y. (Also printed in Canada by Clarke, Irwin & Co. Ltd., Toronto)

Written by Dr. Fredric Wertham

	Good	Fine	Mint
(1st Version)-with bibliographical note intact (several copies got out before the comic publishers forced the removal of this page)		65.00	145.00
with dust jacket. . . .		100.00	235.00
(2nd Version)-		40.00	85.00
with dust jacket. . . .		60.00	125.00
(3rd Version)-Published in England by Kennikat Press, 1954, 399pgs. has bibliographical page		27.50	55.00
1972 r-/of 3rd version; 400pgs w/bibliography page; Kennikat Press		7.50	15.00

NOTE: *Material from this book appeared in the November, 1953(Vol.70, pp50-53,214) issue of the **Ladies' Home Journal** under the title "What Parents Don't Know About Comic Books." With the release of this book, Dr. Wertham reveals seven years of research attempting to link juvenile delinquency to comic books. Many illustrations showing excessive violence, sex, sadism, and torture are shown. This book was used at the Kefauver Senate hearings which led to the Comics Code Authority. Because of the influence this book had on the comic industry and the collector's interest in it, we feel this listing is justified. Also see **Parade of Pleasure.***

SEDUCTION OF THE INNOCENT!
Nov, 1985 - No. 6, Apr, 1986 ($1.75 cover)
Eclipse Comics

	Good	Fine	Mint
1-6	.30	.90	1.80
. . . 3-D 1(10/85; $2.25 cover)-Contains unpub. Advs. Into Darkness No. 15 (pre-code) (36 pgs.)	.40	1.15	2.30
2-D 1 (100 copy limited signed & numbered edition)(B&W)	.85	2.50	5.00
. . . 3-D 2 (4/86)-Baker, Toth-a	.40	1.25	2.50
2-D 2 (100 copy limited signed & numbered edition)(B&W)	.85	2.50	5.00

SELECT DETECTIVE
Aug-Sept, 1948 - No. 3, Dec-Jan, 1948-49
D. S. Publishing Co.

	Good	Fine	Mint
1-Matt Baker-a	5.50	16.50	38.00
2-Baker, McWilliams-a	3.85	11.50	27.00
3	3.35	10.00	23.00

SENSATIONAL POLICE CASES (Becomes Captain Steve Savage, 2nd series)
1952; 1954
Avon Periodicals

	Good	Fine	Mint
nn-100 pg. issue (1952, 25 cents)-Kubert & Kinstler-a	15.00	45.00	105.00
1 (1954)	5.00	15.00	35.00
2,3: 2-Kirbyish-a	3.85	11.50	27.00
4-Reprint/Saint No. 5	3.85	11.50	27.00

SENSATIONAL POLICE CASES
No date (1963?)
I. W. Enterprises

	Good	Fine	Mint
Reprint No. 5-Reprints Prison Break No. 5(1952-Avon); Infantino-a	.80	2.40	4.80

SENSATION COMICS (. . . Mystery No. 110 on)
Jan, 1942 - No. 109, May-June, 1952
National Periodical Publ./All-American

	Good	Fine	Mint
1-Origin Mr. Terrific, Wildcat, The Gay Ghost, & Little Boy Blue; Wonder Woman(cont'd from All Star No. 8), The Black Pirate begin; intro. Justice & Fair Play Club	243.00	730.00	1700.00

1-Reprint, Oversize 13½"x10." **WARNING:** This comic is an exact duplicate reprint of the original except for its size. DC published it in 1974 with a second cover titling it as a Famous First Edition. There have been many reported cases of the outer cover being removed and the interior sold as the original edition. The reprint with the new outer cover removed is practically worthless.

	Good	Fine	Mint
2	115.00	345.00	800.00
3-W. Woman gets secretary's job	67.00	200.00	470.00
4-1st app. Stretch Skinner in Wildcat	59.00	177.00	410.00
5-Intro. Justin, Black Pirate's son	43.00	130.00	300.00
6-Origin/1st app. Wonder Woman's magic lasso	37.00	110.00	260.00
7-10	35.00	105.00	245.00
11-20: 13-Hitler, Tojo, Mussolini-c	28.00	84.00	195.00
21-30	20.00	60.00	140.00
31-33	16.50	50.00	115.00
34-Sargon, the Sorcerer begins, ends No. 36; begins again No. 52	16.50	50.00	115.00
35-40: 38-X-Mas-c	13.50	40.50	95.00
41-50: 43-The Whip app.	11.50	34.50	80.00
51-60: 56,57-Sargon by Kubert	11.00	33.00	76.00
61-80: 63-Last Mr. Terrific. 65,66-Wildcat by Kubert. 68-Origin Huntress. 73-Bondage-c	10.00	30.00	70.00
81-Used in **SOTI**, pg. 33,34; Krigstein-a	13.00	40.00	90.00
82-90: 83-Last Sargon. 86-The Atom app. 90-Last Wildcat	8.50	25.50	60.00
91-Streak begins by Alex Toth	8.50	25.50	60.00
92,93: 92-Toth-a, 2 pgs.	8.00	24.00	56.00
94-1st all girl issue	10.00	30.00	70.00
95-99,101-106: Wonder Woman ends. 99-1st app. Astra, Girl of the Future, ends No. 106. 105-Last 52 pgs.	10.00	30.00	70.00

Seduction of the Innocent 3-D #1, © Eclipse

Select Detective #2, © DS

Sensation Comics #7, © DC

Sergeant Bilko #7, © CBS

Sgt. Preston #19, © Sgt. Preston of the Yukon

77 Sunset Strip #01-742-209, © Warner Bros.

SENSATION COMICS (continued)

	Good	Fine	Mint
100	11.50	34.50	80.00
107-(Scarce)-1st mystery issue; Toth-a	15.00	45.00	105.00
108-(Scarce)-J. Peril by Toth(p)	11.00	33.00	76.00
109-(Scarce)-J. Peril by Toth(p)	15.00	45.00	105.00

NOTE: ***Krigstein*** *a-(Wildcat)-81, 83, 84.* ***Moldoff*** *Black Pirate-1-25. Wonder Woman by* ***H. C. Peter****, all issues except No. 8, 17-19, 21.*

SENSATION MYSTERY (Sensation No. 1-109)
No. 110, July-Aug, 1952 - No. 116, July-Aug, 1953
National Periodical Publications

110-Johnny Peril	8.50	25.50	60.00
111-116-Johnny Peril in all	8.00	24.00	56.00

NOTE: ***Colan*** *a-114p.* ***Giunta*** *a-112.* ***G. Kane*** *c-112, 113, 115.*

SENTINELS OF JUSTICE, THE (See Captain Paragon &. . .)

SERGEANT BARNEY BARKER (G. I. Tales No. 4 on)
Aug, 1956 - No. 3, Dec, 1956
Atlas Comics (MCI)

1-Severin-a(4)	4.00	12.00	28.00
2,3-Severin-a(4)	2.15	6.50	15.00

SERGEANT BILKO (Phil Silvers) (TV)
May-June, 1957 - No. 18, Mar-Apr, 1960
National Periodical Publications

1	10.00	30.00	70.00
2	7.00	21.00	50.00
3-5	5.50	16.50	40.00
6-18: 11,15-Photo-c	4.35	13.00	30.00

SGT. BILKO'S PVT. DOBERMAN (TV)
June-July, 1958 - No. 11, Feb-Mar, 1960
National Periodical Publications

1	8.50	25.50	60.00
2	5.50	16.50	40.00
3-5	4.35	13.00	30.00
6-11: 9-Photo-c	3.50	10.50	24.00

SGT. DICK CARTER OF THE U.S. BORDER PATROL (See Holyoke One-Shot)

SGT. FURY (& His Howling Commandos)
May, 1963 - No. 167, Dec, 1981
Marvel Comics Group

1-1st app. Sgt. Fury; Kirby/Ayers c/a	13.00	32.50	90.00
2-Kirby-a	4.00	10.00	28.00
3-5: 3-Reed Richards x-over. 4-Death of Junior Juniper. 5-1st Baron Strucker app.; Kirby-a	1.00	3.00	7.00
6-10: 8-Baron Zemo, 1st Percival Pinkerton app. 10-1st app. Capt. Savage (the Skipper)	.60	1.80	3.60
11,12,14-20: 14-1st Blitz Squad. 18-Death of Pamela Hawley	.25	.75	1.50
13-Captain America app.; Kirby-a	.25	.75	1.50
21-30: 25-Red Skull app. 27-1st Eric Koenig app., origin Fury's eye patch		.50	1.00
31-40: 34-Origin Howling Commandos. 35-Eric Koeing joins Howlers		.50	1.00
41-60: 43-Bob Hope, Glen Miller app. 44-Flashback-Howlers 1st mission. 51-Roosevelt, Churchill, Stalin app.		.50	1.00
61-100: 64-Capt. Savage & Raiders x-over. 76-Fury's Father app. in WWI story. 98-Deadly Dozen x-over. 100-Captain America, Fantastic Four cameos; Stan Lee, Martin Goodman & others app.		.40	.80
101-Origin retold		.40	.80
102-166: 113,121-166-r		.35	.70
167-Reprints No. 1		.35	.70
Annual 1('65)	.70	2.00	4.00
Special 2-7('66-11/71)-Eisenhower app.		.50	1.00

NOTE: ***Ditko*** *a-15i.* ***Gil Kane*** *c-37, 96.* ***Kirby*** *a-1-8, 13p, 167p. Special 5; c-1-20, 25, 167p.* ***Severin*** *a-44, 48, 162, 164; inks-49-79; c-149i, 155i, 162-166.* ***Sutton*** *a-57p. Reprints in No. 80, 82, 85, 87, 89, 91, 93, 95, 99, 101, 103, 105, 107, 109, 111, 145.*

SGT. FURY AND HIS HOWLING DEFENDERS (See The Defenders)

SERGEANT PRESTON OF THE YUKON (TV)
No. 344, Aug, 1951 - No. 29, Nov-Jan, 1958-59
Dell Publishing Co.

	Good	Fine	Mint
4-Color 344(No.1)-Sergeant Preston & his dog Yukon King begin; painted-c begin, end No. 18	3.50	10.50	24.00
4-Color 373,397,419('52)	3.00	9.00	21.00
5(11-1/52-53)-10(2-4/54)	2.65	8.00	18.00
11,12,14-17	2.00	6.00	14.00
13-Origin S. Preston	2.65	8.00	18.00
18-Origin Yukon King; last painted-c	2.65	8.00	18.00
19-29: All photo-c	2.65	8.00	18.00

SERGEANT PRESTON OF THE YUKON
1956 (4 comic booklets) (7x2½'' & 5x2½'')
Giveaways with Quaker Cereals

'How He Found Yukon King;' each. . .	3.35	10.00	23.00

SGT. ROCK (Formerly Our Army at War)
No. 302, March, 1977 - Present
National Periodical Publications/DC Comics

302-414: 318-Reprints		.25	.50
Annual 2(9/82), 3(8/83), 4(8/84)		.50	1.00

NOTE: ***Estrada*** *a-322, 327, 331, 336, 337, 341, 342i.* ***Glanzman*** *a-384.* ***Kubert*** *a-328, 356, 368, 373; c-317, 318r, 319-323, 325-333-on, Annual 2, 3.* ***Spiegle*** *a-382, Annual 2, 3.* ***Thorne*** *a-384.* ***Toth*** *a-385r.*

SGT. ROCK SPECIAL (See DC Special Series No. 3)

SGT. ROCK SPECTACULAR (See DC Special Series No. 13)

SGT. ROCK'S PRIZE BATTLE TALES (See DC Spec. Series No. 18)
Winter, 1964 (One Shot) (Giant - 80 pgs.)
National Periodical Publications

1-Kubert, Heath-r; new Kubert-c	.70	2.00	4.00

SERGIO ARAGONES GROO THE WANDERER (See Groo. . .)

SEVEN DEAD MEN (See Complete Mystery No. 1)

SEVEN DWARFS (See 4-Color No. 227,382)

SEVEN SEAS COMICS
Apr, 1946 - No. 6, 1947 (no month)
Universal Phoenix Features/Leader No. 6

1-South Sea Girl by Matt Baker, Capt. Cutlass begin; Tugboat Tessie by Baker app.	23.00	70.00	160.00
2	20.00	60.00	140.00
3-6: 3-Six pg. Feldstein-a	18.00	54.00	125.00

NOTE: ***Baker*** *a-1-6; c-3-6.*

1776 (See Charlton Classic Library)

7TH VOYAGE OF SINBAD, THE (See 4-Color No. 944)

77 SUNSET STRIP (TV)
No. 1066, 1-3/60 - No. 2, 2/63 (All photo-c)
Dell Publ. Co./Gold Key

4-Color 1066-Toth-a	4.35	13.00	30.00
4-Color 1106,1159-Toth-a	3.75	11.25	26.00
4-Color 1211,1263,1291, 01742-209(7-9/62)-Manning-a in all	3.00	9.00	21.00
1(11/62-G.K.), 2-Manning-a in each	2.65	8.00	18.00

77TH BENGAL LANCERS, THE (See 4-Color No. 791)

SEYMOUR, MY SON (See More Seymour)
September, 1963
Archie Publications (Radio Comics)

1	2.75	8.00	16.00

SHADE SPECIAL
Fall, 1984
AC Comics

	Good	Fine	Mint
1	.25	.75	1.50

SHADE, THE CHANGING MAN (See Cancelled Comic Cavalcade)
June-July, 1977 - No. 8, Aug-Sept, 1978
National Periodical Publications/DC Comics

	Good	Fine	Mint
1-Ditko c/a in all		.40	.80
2-8		.30	.60

SHADOW, THE
Aug, 1964 - No. 8, Sept, 1965
Archie Comics (Radio Comics)

	Good	Fine	Mint
1	.85	2.50	6.00
2-8-The Fly app. in some issues	.55	1.65	4.00

SHADOW, THE
Oct-Nov, 1973 - No. 12, Aug-Sept, 1975
National Periodical Publications

	Good	Fine	Mint
1-Kaluta-a begins		.65	1.30
2		.50	1.00
3-Kaluta/Wrightson-a		.60	1.20
4,6-Kaluta-a ends		.50	1.00
5,7-12: 11-The Avenger (pulp character) x-over		.30	.60

NOTE: ***Craig*** *a-10.* ***Cruz*** *a-10-12.* ***Kaluta*** *a-1, 2, 3p, 4, 6; c-1-4, 6, 10-12.* ***Kubert*** *c-9.* ***Robbins*** *a-5, 7-9; c-5, 7.*

SHADOW, THE
May, 1986 - No. 4, Aug, 1986 (mini-series) (mature readers)
DC Comics

	Good	Fine	Mint
1	1.00	3.00	6.00
2	.70	2.00	4.00
3,4	.50	1.50	3.00

SHADOW COMICS (Pulp, radio)
March, 1940 - V9No.5, Aug, 1949
Street & Smith Publications

NOTE: *The Shadow first appeared in Fame & Fortune Magazine, 1929, began on radio the same year, and was featured in pulps beginning in 1931.*

	Good	Fine	Mint
V1No.1-Shadow, Doc Savage, Bill Barnes, Nick Carter, Frank Merriwell, Iron Munro, the Astonishing Man begin	92.00	275.00	645.00
2-The Avenger begins, ends No. 6; Capt. Fury only app.	41.00	123.00	286.00
3(nn-5/40)-Norgil the Magician app. (also No. 9)	33.00	100.00	230.00
4,5: 4-The Three Musketeers begins, ends No. 8. 5-Doc Savage ends	27.00	81.00	190.00
6,8,9	20.00	60.00	140.00
7-Origin & 1st app. Hooded Wasp & Wasplet; series ends V3No.8	22.00	65.00	154.00
10-Origin The Iron Ghost, ends No. 11; The Dead End Kids begins, ends No. 14	20.00	60.00	140.00
11-Origin The Hooded Wasp & Wasplet retold	20.00	60.00	140.00
12-Dead End Kids app.	17.00	51.00	120.00
V2No.1,2(11/41): 2-Dead End Kid story	16.00	48.00	110.00
3-Origin & 1st app. Supersnipe; series begins	20.00	60.00	140.00
4,5: 4-Little Nemo story	11.50	34.50	80.00
6-9: 6-Blackstone the Magician app.	11.00	33.00	76.00
10-Supersnipe app.	11.00	33.00	76.00
11,12	11.00	33.00	76.00
V3No.1-12: 10-Doc Savage begins, not in V5No.5, V6No.10-12, V8No.4	8.50	25.50	60.00
V4No.1-12	8.00	24.00	56.00
V5No.1-12	6.50	19.50	45.00
V6No.1-11: 9-Intro. Shadow, Jr.	5.75	17.25	40.00
12-Powell-c/a; atom bomb panels	10.00	30.00	70.00
V7No.1,2,5,7-9,12: 2,5-Shadow, Jr. app.; Powell-a	10.00	30.00	70.00
3,6,11-Powell c/a	11.50	34.50	80.00
4-Powell c/a; Atom bomb panels	13.00	40.00	90.00
10(1/48)-Flying Saucer issue; Powell c/a (2nd of this theme; see The Spirit 9/28/47)	14.50	43.50	100.00
V8No.1-12-Powell-a	11.00	33.00	76.00
V9No.1,5-Powell-a	10.00	30.00	70.00
2-4-Powell c/a	11.00	33.00	76.00

NOTE: ***Powell*** *art in most issues beginning V6No.12.*

SHADOW OF THE BATMAN
Dec, 1985 - No. 5, Apr, 1986 ($1.75 cover; mini-series)
DC Comics

	Good	Fine	Mint
1	.35	1.00	2.00
2-5: Detective-r	.30	.90	1.80

NOTE: ***Austin*** *a-2-4i.* ***Rogers*** *c/a 1-5.*

SHADOW PLAY
June, 1982
Whitman Publications

	Good	Fine	Mint
1		.30	.60

SHADOWS FROM BEYOND (Formerly Unusual Tales)
October, 1966
Charlton Comics

	Good	Fine	Mint
V2No.50-Ditko-c	.35	1.00	2.00

SHADOWSTAR
1986 - Present ($1.50, B&W)
Savage Graphics/Slave Labor Graphics No. 3 on

	Good	Fine	Mint
1-4	.25	.75	1.50

SHADOW WAR OF HAWKMAN
May, 1985 - No. 4, Aug, 1985 (mini-series)
DC Comics

	Good	Fine	Mint
1-Alcala inks		.40	.80
2-4		.40	.80

SHAGGY DOG & THE ABSENT-MINDED PROFESSOR (See 4-Color No. 985 and Movie Comics)

SHANNA, THE SHE-DEVIL
Dec, 1972 - No. 5, Aug, 1973
Marvel Comics Group

	Good	Fine	Mint
1-Steranko-c; Tuska-a		.40	.80
2-5: 2-Steranko-c		.30	.60

SHARK FIGHTERS, THE (See 4-Color No. 762)

SHARP COMICS (Slightly large size)
Winter, 1945-46 - V1No.2, Spring, 1946 (52 pgs.)
H. C. Blackerby

	Good	Fine	Mint
V1No.1-Origin Dick Royce Planetarian	9.50	28.50	65.00
2-Origin The Pioneer; Michael Morgan, Dick Royce, Sir Gallagher, Planetarian, Steve Hagen, Weeny and Pop app.	6.85	20.50	48.00

SHARPY FOX
1958; 1963
I. W. Enterprises/Super Comics

	Good	Fine	Mint
1,2-I.W. Reprint (1958)	.30	.80	1.60
14-Super Reprint (1963)	.30	.80	1.60

The Shadow #1 (5/86), © DC

Shadow Comics V3No.10, © S&S

Shadow of the Batman #4, © DC

Sheena, Queen of the Jungle #12, © FH

Sherlock Holmes #1 (10/55), © CC

Shield Wizard Comics #4, © AP

SHATTER
June, 1985 (One Shot; Baxter paper)
First Comics

	Good	Fine	Mint
1-1st computer-generated artwork in a comic book	1.10	3.25	6.50
1-2nd printing	.35	1.00	2.00

NOTE: *1st printings have the number "1" included in the row of numbers at the bottom of the indicia.*

SHATTER
Dec, 1985 - Present ($1.75 cover; deluxe paper)
First Comics

1-Continues computer-generated art and lettering	.40	1.25	2.50
2-7	.30	.90	1.80

SHAZAM (See Giant Comics to Color & Limited Collector's Edition)

SHAZAM! (TV)(See World's Finest)
Feb, 1973 - No. 35, May-June, 1978
National Periodical Publications/DC Comics

1-1st revival of original Captain Marvel(origin retold), by C. C. Beck; Captain Marvel Jr. & Mary Marvel x-over		.30	.60
2-7,9,10: 2-Infinity-c; re-intro Mr. Mind & Tawney. 4-Origin retold. 10-Last Beck ish.		.25	.50
8-100 pgs.; reprints Capt. Marvel Jr. by Raboy; origin/C.M. No. 80; origin Mary Marvel/C.M. No. 18		.30	.60
11-Shaffenberger-a begins		.25	.50
12-17-All 100 pgs.; 15-Lex Luthor x-over		.30	.60
18-35: 25-1st app. Isis. 34-Origin Capt. Nazi & Capt. Marvel Jr. retold		.25	.50

NOTE: *Reprints in No. 1-8,10,12-17,21-24.* ***Beck*** *a-1-10, 12-17r, 21-24r; c-1, 3-9.* ***Nasser*** *c-35p.* ***Newton*** *a-35p.* ***Shaffenberger*** *a-11, 14-20, 25, 26, 27p, 28, 29-31p, 33i, 35i; c-20, 22, 23, 25, 26i, 27i, 28-33.*

SHEA THEATRE COMICS
No date (1940's) (32 pgs.)
Shea Theatre

Contains Rocket Comics; MLJ cover in mono color	10.00	20.00	30.00

SHEENA, QUEEN OF THE JUNGLE (See Jumbo Comics, Jerry Iger's Classic. . ., & 3-D. . .)
Spring, 1942 - No. 18, Winter, 1952-53
Fiction House Magazines

1-Sheena begins	80.00	240.00	560.00
2 (Winter, 1942/43)	40.00	120.00	280.00
3 (Spring, 1943)	30.00	90.00	210.00
4 (Fall, 1948)	17.00	51.00	120.00
5(Summer'49)-10(Fall,'50)	14.50	43.50	100.00
11-17	11.50	34.50	80.00
18-Used in **POP**, pg. 98	12.00	36.00	84.00
I.W. Reprint No. 9-Reprints No. 17	2.50	7.50	15.00

SHEENA, QUEEN OF THE JUNGLE
Dec, 1984 - No. 2, Feb, 1985 (Limited series)
Marvel Comics Group

1,2-r-/Marvel Super Special; movie adaption		.40	.80

SHEENA 3-D SPECIAL
May, 1985 ($2.00)
Blackthorne Publishing

1-r-/1953 3-D Sheena	.35	1.00	2.00

SHE-HULK (See The Savage She-Hulk)

SHERIFF BOB DIXON'S CHUCK WAGON (TV)
November, 1950
Avon Periodicals

1-Kinstler c/a(3)	5.50	16.50	38.00

SHERIFF OF COCHISE, THE
1957 (16 pages) (TV Show)
Mobil Giveaway

	Good	Fine	Mint
Shaffenberger-a	1.00	3.00	7.00

SHERIFF OF TOMBSTONE
Nov, 1958 - No. 17, Sept, 1961
Charlton Comics

V1No.1-Williamson/Severin-c	2.85	8.50	20.00
2	1.30	4.00	9.00
3-17	.95	2.85	6.50

SHERLOCK HOLMES (See Cases Of. . ., 4-Color No. 1169,1245 & Spect. Stories)

SHERLOCK HOLMES (All New Baffling Advs. of)
(Young Eagle No. 3 on?)
Oct, 1955 - No. 2, Mar, 1956
Charlton Comics

1-Dr. Neff, Ghost Breaker app. (No. 1 only - 36 pgs.)	17.00	51.00	120.00
2	15.00	45.00	105.00

SHERLOCK HOLMES (Also see The Joker)
Sept-Oct, 1975
National Periodical Publications

1-Cruz-a; Simonson-c		.50	1.00

SHERRY THE SHOWGIRL (Showgirls No. 4)
7/56 - No. 3, 12/56; No. 5, 4/57 - No. 7, 8/57
Atlas Comics

1	2.85	8.50	20.00
2	1.50	4.50	10.00
3,5-7	1.30	4.00	9.00

SHIELD (Nick Fury & His Agents of. . .) (See Nick Fury)
Feb, 1973 - No. 5, Oct, 1973
Marvel Comics Group

1-Steranko-c		.50	1.00
2-Steranko-c		.30	.60
3-5: 1-5 all contain-r from Strange Tales No. 146-155. 3-5-Cover-r		.30	.60

NOTE: ***Buscema*** *a-3p(r).* ***Kirby*** *layouts 1-5.* ***Steranko*** *a-4r.*

SHIELD, THE (Becomes Shield-Steel Sterling No. 3; No. 1 titled 'Lancelot Strong;' also see Advs. of the Fly, Double Life of Private Strong, Fly Man, Mighty Comics, & The Mighty Crusaders)
June, 1983 - No. 2, Aug, 1983
Archie Enterprises, Inc.

1,2: Steel Sterling app.		.45	.90

SHIELD-STEEL STERLING (Formerly The Shield)
No. 3, Dec, 1983 (Becomes Steel Sterling No. 4)
Archie Enterprises, Inc.

3-Nino-a		.45	.90

SHIELD WIZARD COMICS (Also see Pep & Top-Notch Comics)
Summer, 1940 - No. 13, Spring, 1944
MLJ Magazines

1-(V1No.5 on inside)-Origin The Shield by Irving Novick & The Wizard by Ed Ashe, Jr; Flag-c	90.00	270.00	630.00
2-Origin The Shield retold; intro. Wizard's sidekick, Roy	45.00	135.00	315.00
3,4	29.00	87.00	200.00
5-Dusty, the Boy Detective begins	25.00	75.00	175.00
6-8: 6-Roy the Super Boy begins	21.00	62.00	146.00
9,10	19.00	57.00	132.00
11-13: 13-Bondage-c	17.00	51.00	120.00

SHIP AHOY
November, 1944 (52 pgs.)

SHIP AHOY (continued)
Spotlight Publishers

	Good	Fine	Mint
1-L. B. Cole-c	4.65	14.00	32.00

SHMOO (See Al Capp's. . . & Washable Jones &. . .)

SHOCK (Magazine)
(Reprints from horror comics) (Black & White)
May, 1969 - V3No.4, Sept, 1971
Stanley Publications

	Good	Fine	Mint
V1No.1-Cover-r/Weird Tales of the Future No. 7 by Bernard Baily	.50	1.50	3.00
2-Wolverton-r/Weird Mysteries 5; r-Weird Mysteries 7 used in **SOTI**; cover r-/Weird Chills No. 1	.50	1.50	3.00
3,5,6	.25	.75	1.50
4-Harrison/Williamson-r/Forbidden Worlds No. 6	.50	1.50	3.00
V2No.2, V1No.8, V2No.4-6, V3No.1-4	.25	.75	1.50

NOTE: ***Disbrow*** *r-V2No.4; bondage covers-V1No.4, V2No.6, V3No.1.*

SHOCK DETECTIVE CASES (Formerly Crime Fighting Detective)
(Becomes Spook Detective Cases No. 22)
No. 20, Sept, 1952 - No. 21, Nov, 1952
Star Publications

	Good	Fine	Mint
20,21-L.B. Cole-c	4.00	12.00	28.00

NOTE: ***Palais*** *a-20. No. 21-Fox-r.*

SHOCK ILLUSTRATED (Magazine format)
Sept-Oct, 1955 - No. 3, Spring, 1956
E. C. Comics

	Good	Fine	Mint
1-All by Kamen; drugs, prostitution, wife swapping	3.00	9.00	21.00
2-Williamson-a redrawn from Crime SuspenStories No. 13 plus Ingels, Crandall, & Evans	3.50	10.50	24.00
3-Only 100 known copies bound & given away at E.C. office; Crandall, Evans-a	100.00	300.00	700.00

(Prices vary widely on this book)

SHOCKING MYSTERY CASES (Formerly Thrilling Crime Cases)
No. 50, Sept, 1952 - No. 60, Oct, 1954
Star Publications

	Good	Fine	Mint
50-Disbrow ''Frankenstein'' story	10.00	30.00	70.00
51-Disbrow-a	4.75	14.00	33.00
52-55,57-60	4.00	12.00	28.00
56-Drug use story	4.75	14.00	33.00

NOTE: ***L. B. Cole*** *covers on all; a-60(2 pgs.).* ***Hollingsworth*** *a-52.* ***Morisi*** *a-55.*

SHOCKING TALES DIGEST MAGAZINE
Oct, 1981 (95 cents)
Harvey Publications

	Good	Fine	Mint
1-1957-58-r; Powell, Kirby, Nostrand-a		.50	1.00

SHOCK SUSPENSTORIES
Feb-Mar, 1952 - No. 18, Dec-Jan, 1954-55
E. C. Comics

	Good	Fine	Mint
1-Classic Feldstein electrocution-c. Bradbury adaptation	43.00	130.00	300.00
2	26.00	78.00	180.00
3	17.00	51.00	120.00
4-Used in **SOTI**, pg. 387,388	19.00	58.00	130.00
5	17.00	51.00	115.00
6,7: 6-Classic bondage-c. 7-Classic face melting-c	20.00	60.00	140.00
8-Williamson-a	18.00	55.00	120.00
9-11: 10-Junkie story	13.00	40.00	90.00
12-''The Monkey''-classic junkie cover/story; drug propaganda ish.	18.00	54.00	125.00
13-Frazetta's only solo story for E.C., 7 pgs.	23.00	70.00	160.00
14-Used in Senate Investigation hearings	10.00	30.00	70.00
15-Used in 1954 Reader's Digest article, ''For the Kiddies to Read''	10.00	30.00	70.00
16-''Red Dupe'' editorial; rape story	10.00	30.00	70.00
17,18	10.00	30.00	70.00

NOTE: ***Craig*** *a-11; c-11.* ***Crandall*** *a-9-13, 15-18.* ***Davis*** *a-1-5.* ***Evans*** *a-7, 8, 14-18; c-16-18.* ***Feldstein*** *c-1, 7-9, 12.* ***Ingels*** *a-1, 2, 6.* ***Kamen*** *a-in all.* ***Krigstein*** *a-14, 18.* ***Orlando*** *a-1, 3-7, 9, 10, 12, 16, 17.* ***Wood*** *a-2-15; c-2-6, 14.*

SHOCK THERAPY
Dec, 1986 - Present ($1.95, B&W)
Harrier Publishing

	Good	Fine	Mint
1	.35	1.00	1.95

SHOGUN WARRIORS
Feb, 1979 - No. 20, Sept, 1980
Marvel Comics Group

	Good	Fine	Mint
1-Raydeen, Combatra, & Dangard Ace begin		.40	.80
2-20		.25	.50

SHOOK UP (Magazine) (Satire)
November, 1958
Dodsworth Publ. Co.

	Good	Fine	Mint
V1No.1	1.00	3.00	6.00

SHORT RIBS (See 4-Color No. 1333)

SHORT STORY COMICS (See Hello Pal,. . .)

SHORTY SHINER
June, 1956 - No. 3, Oct, 1956
Dandy Magazine (Charles Biro)

	Good	Fine	Mint
1	1.75	6.25	12.00
2,3	1.00	3.00	7.00

SHOTGUN SLADE (See 4-Color No. 1111)

SHOWCASE (See Cancelled Comic Cavalcade & New Talent. . .)
3-4/56 - No. 93, 9/70; No. 94, 8-9/77 - No. 104, 9/78
National Periodical Publications/DC Comics

	Good	Fine	Mint
1-Fire Fighters	60.00	180.00	420.00
2-King of the Wild; Kubert-a	22.00	65.00	155.00
3-The Frogmen	19.00	57.00	132.00
4-Origin The Flash (Silver Age) & The Turtle; Kubert-a	170.00	510.00	1250.00
5-Manhunters	16.00	48.00	115.00
6-Origin Challengers by Kirby, partly r-/in Secret Origins No. 1 & Challengers of the Unknown No. 64,65	47.00	141.00	330.00
7-Challengers by Kirby r-in/Challengers of the Unknown No. 75	26.00	78.00	185.00
8-The Flash; intro/origin Capt. Cold	61.00	182.00	425.00
9,10-Lois Lane	25.00	75.00	175.00
11,12-Challengers by Kirby	21.00	62.00	150.00
13-The Flash; origin Mr. Element	44.00	132.00	310.00
14-The Flash; origin Dr. Alchemy, former Mr. Element	44.00	132.00	310.00
15,16-Space Ranger	13.00	40.00	90.00
17-Adam Strange-Origin & 1st app.	32.00	95.00	225.00
18,19-Adam Strange	20.00	60.00	140.00
20-1st app/origin Rip Hunter; Moriera-a	6.50	20.00	45.00
21-Rip Hunter; Sekowsky c/a	6.50	20.00	45.00
22-Origin & 1st app. Silver Age Green Lantern by Gil Kane	59.00	176.00	415.00
23,24-Green Lantern. 23-Nuclear explosion-c	24.00	72.00	165.00
25,26-Rip Hunter by Kubert	3.50	11.00	24.00
27-29-Sea Devils by Heath, c/a	2.85	8.50	20.00

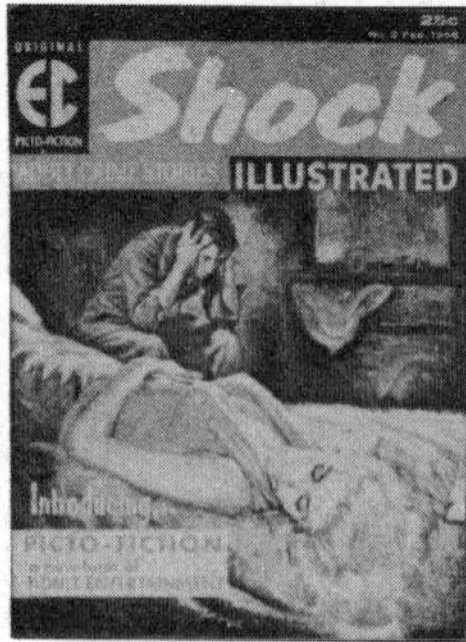

Shock Illustrated #2, © WMG

Shocking Mystery Cases #58, © STAR

Showcase #10, © DC

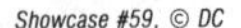

Showcase #59, © DC

Shuriken #3, © Victory

Silent Invasion #1, © Renegade Press

SHOWCASE (continued)

	Good	Fine	Mint
30-Origin Aquaman	4.00	12.00	28.00
31-33-Aquaman	2.00	6.00	14.00
34-Origin & 1st app. Silver Age Atom by Kane & Anderson	4.65	14.00	34.00
35-The Atom by Gil Kane; last 10¢ ish.	3.50	10.50	24.00
36-The Atom by Gil Kane	3.00	9.00	21.00
37-1st app. Metal Men	2.00	6.00	14.00
38-40-Metal Men	1.70	5.00	10.00
41,42-Tommy Tomorrow	1.00	3.00	6.00
43-Dr. No (James Bond); Nodel-a; originally done for Classics Ill. Series (appeared as British Classics Ill. No. 158A)	14.00	42.00	95.00
44-Tommy Tomorrow	.85	2.50	5.00
45-Sgt. Rock; origin retold; Heath-c	1.35	4.00	8.00
46,47-Tommy Tomorrow	.85	2.50	5.00
48,49-Cave Carson	.85	2.50	5.00
50,51-I Spy (Danger Trail-r by Infantino), King Farady story (not reprint-No. 50)	.85	2.50	5.00
52-Cave Carson	.85	2.50	5.00
53,54-G.I. Joe; Heath-a	.85	2.50	5.00
55,56-Dr. Fate & Hourman	.85	2.50	5.00
57,58-Enemy Ace by Kubert	.85	2.50	5.00
59-Teen Titans	2.50	7.50	15.00
60-The Spectre by Anderson	.80	2.40	4.80
61,64-The Spectre by Anderson	.70	2.00	4.00
62-Origin/1st app. Inferior Five	.25	.75	1.50
63,65-Inferior Five	.25	.75	1.50
66,67-B'wana Beast		.50	1.00
68,69,71-Maniaks		.40	.80
70-Binky		.40	.80
72-Top Gun (Johnny Thunder-r)-Toth-a		.60	1.20
73-Creeper; Ditko c/a	.85	2.50	5.00
74-Anthro; Post c/a	.30	.80	1.60
75-Hawk & the Dove; Ditko c/a	.60	1.80	3.60
76-Bat Lash	.40	1.20	2.40
77-Angel & Ape		.60	1.20
78-Jonny Double		.60	1.20
79-Dolphin; Aqualad origin-r	.30	.90	1.80
80-Phantom Stranger-r; Adams-c	.50	1.50	3.00
81-Windy & Willy	.30	.90	1.80
82-Nightmaster by Grandenetti & Giordano; Kubert-c	.30	.90	1.80
83,84-Nightmaster by Wrightson/Jones/Kaluta in each; Kubert-c. 84-Origin retold	1.35	4.00	8.00
85-87-Firehair; Kubert-a	.50	1.50	3.00
88-90-Jason's Quest: 90-Manhunter 2070 app.		.50	1.00
91-93-Manhunter 2070; origin-92		.50	1.00
94-Intro/origin new Doom Patrol & Robotman		.80	1.60
95,96-The Doom Patrol. 95-Origin Celsius		.50	1.00
97-99-Power Girl; origin-97,98; JSA cameos		.40	.80
100-(52 pgs.)-Features most Showcase characters		.50	1.00
101-103-Hawkman; Adam Strange x-over		.40	.80
104-(52 pgs.)-O.S.S. Spies at War		.40	.80

NOTE: ***Anderson** a-22-24i, 34-36i, 55, 56, 60, 61, 64, 101-03i; c-50i, 51i, 55, 56, 60, 61, 64. **Aparo** c-94-96. **Estrada** a-104. **Infantino** a/c-4, 8, 13, 14; c-50p, 51p. **Gil Kane** a-22-24p, 34-36p; c-17-19, 22-24, 31, 34-36. **Kirby** c-6, 7, 11, 12. **Kubert** a-2, 4i, 25, 26, 45, 53, 54, 72; c-25, 26, 53, 54, 57, 58, 82-87, 101-04. **Orlando** a-62p, 63p, 97i; c-62, 63, 97i. **Sekowsky** a-65p. **Sparling** a-78. **Staton** a-94, 95-99p, 100; c-97-100p.*

SHROUD OF MYSTERY
June, 1982
Whitman Publications

	Good	Fine	Mint
1		.30	.60

SHOWGIRLS (Formerly Sherry the Showgirl No. 3)
No. 4, 1-2/57?; June, 1957 - No. 2, Aug, 1957
Atlas Comics (MPC No. 2)

	Good	Fine	Mint
4	1.50	4.50	10.00
1-Millie, Sherry, Chili, Pearl & Hazel begin	3.00	9.00	21.00
2	1.75	5.25	12.00

SHURIKEN
Summer, 1985 - Present (1.50, B&W)
Victory Productions

	Good	Fine	Mint
1	1.50	4.50	9.00
1-Reprint, Winter, 1985	.25	.75	1.50
2	.35	1.00	2.00
3-5	.25	.75	1.50

SICK (Magazine) (Satire)
Aug, 1960 - No. 140?, 1980?
Feature Publ./Headline Publ./Crestwood Publ. Co./Hewfred Publ./Pyramid Comm./Charlton Publ. No. 109 (4/76) on

	Good	Fine	Mint
V1No.1-Torres-a	4.35	13.00	30.00
2-5-Torres-a in all	2.00	6.00	14.00
6	1.20	3.50	8.00
V2No.1-8(No.7-14)	1.00	3.00	7.00
V3No.1-8(No.15-22)	.75	2.25	5.00
V4No.1-5(No.23-27)	.70	2.00	4.00
28-40	.50	1.50	3.00
41-140: 45 has No. 44 on cover & No. 45 on inside	.35	1.00	2.00
Annual 1969, 1970, 1971	.70	2.00	4.00
Annual 2-4('80)	.50	1.50	3.00
Special 2 ('78)	.35	1.00	2.00

NOTE: ***Davis** c/a in most issues of No. 16-27, 30-32, 34, 35. **Simon** a-1-3. **Torres** a-V2No.7, V4No.2. Civil War Blackouts-23, 24.*

SIDESHOW
1949 (One Shot)
Avon Periodicals

	Good	Fine	Mint
1-(Rare)-Similar to Bachelor's Diary	15.00	45.00	105.00

SIEGEL AND SHUSTER: DATELINE 1930s
11/84 - No. 2, 9/85 (Baxter paper No. 1; $1.50)
Eclipse Comics

	Good	Fine	Mint
1-Unpubbed samples of strips from 1935; includes 'Interplanetary Police;' Shuster-c	.25	.75	1.50
2 (B&W)-Unpubbed strips	.25	.75	1.50

SILENT INVASION, THE
April, 1986 - No. 12, 1987 ($1.70-$2.00, B&W)
Renegade Press

	Good	Fine	Mint
1-UFO sightings of '50s	.35	1.00	2.00
2-12	.35	1.00	2.00

SILK HAT HARRY'S DIVORCE SUIT
1912 (5¾x15½'') (B&W)
M. A. Donoghue & Co.

	Good	Fine	Mint
Newspaper reprints by Tad (Thomas Dorgan)	6.00	18.00	42.00

SILLY PILLY (See Frank Luther's. . .)

SILLY SYMPHONIES (See Dell Giants)

SILLY TUNES
Fall, 1945 - No. 7, June, 1947
Timely Comics

	Good	Fine	Mint
1	4.65	14.00	32.00
2	2.35	7.00	16.00
3-7	1.85	5.50	13.00

SILVER (See Lone Ranger's Famous Horse. . .)

SILVERHEELS
Dec, 1983 - No. 3, May, 1984
Pacific Comics

	Good	Fine	Mint
1-3	.25	.75	1.50

SILVER KID WESTERN
Oct, 1954 - No. 5, 1955
Key/Stanmor Publications

	Good	Fine	Mint
1	2.65	8.00	18.00
2	1.30	4.00	9.00
3-5	1.15	3.50	8.00
I.W. Reprint No. 1,2	.50	1.50	3.00

SILVER STAR
Feb, 1983 - No. 6, Jan, 1984
Pacific Comics

	Good	Fine	Mint
1-Kirby/Royer-a		.60	1.20
2-6		.50	1.00

NOTE: ***Kirby** a-1-5p; c-1-5p.*

SILVER STREAK COMICS (Crime Does Not Pay No. 22 on)
Dec, 1939 - May, 1942; 1946 (Silver logo-No. 1-5)
Your Guide Publs. No. 1-7/New Friday Publs. No. 8-17/Comic House Publ./Newsbook Publ.

	Good	Fine	Mint
1-Intro. The Claw by Cole (r-/in Daredevil No. 21), Red Reeves, Boy Magician, & Captain Fearless; The Wasp, Mister Midnight begin; Spirit Man app. Silver metallic-c begin, end No. 5 (Scarce)	260.00	780.00	1820.00
2-The Claw by Cole; Simon c/a	115.00	345.00	805.00
3-1st app. & origin Silver Streak (2nd with lightning speed); Dickie Dean the Boy Inventor, Lance Hale, Ace Powers, Bill Wayne, & The Planet Patrol begin	102.00	305.00	715.00
4-Sky Wolf begins; Silver Streak by Jack Cole (new costume); intro. Jackie, Lance Hale's sidekick	55.00	165.00	385.00
5-Jack Cole c/a(2)	62.00	185.00	435.00
6-(Scarce)-Origin & 1st app. Daredevil (blue & yellow costume) by Jack Binder; The Claw returns; classic Cole Claw-c	235.00	705.00	1645.00
(Prices vary widely on this book)			
7-Claw vs. Daredevil (new costume-blue & red) by Jack Cole & 3 other Cole stories (38 pgs.)	143.00	430.00	1000.00
8-Claw vs. Daredevil by Cole; last Cole Silver Streak	85.00	255.00	595.00
9-Claw vs. Daredevil by Cole	62.00	185.00	435.00
10-Origin Captain Battle; Claw vs. Daredevil by Cole	58.00	175.00	405.00
11-Intro. Mercury by Bob Wood, Silver Streak's sidekick; conclusion Claw vs. Daredevil by Rico; in 'Presto Martin,' 2nd pg., news paper says 'Roussos does it again.'	40.00	120.00	280.00
12-14: 13-Origin Thun-Dohr	32.00	95.00	224.00
15-17-Last Daredevil issue	28.00	84.00	195.00
18-The Saint begins; by Leslie Charteris (See Movie Comics 2, DC)	24.00	72.00	166.00
19-21(1942): 20,21 have Wolverton's Scoop Scuttle	15.00	45.00	105.00
22,24(1946)-Reprints	10.00	30.00	70.00
23-Reprints?; bondage-c	10.00	30.00	70.00
nn(11/46)(Newsbook Publ.)-Reprints S.S. story from No. 4-7 plus 2 Captain Fearless stories, all in color; bondage/torture-c	20.00	60.00	140.00

NOTE: ***Jack Cole** a-(Daredevil)-6-10, (Dickie Dean)-3-10, (Pirate Prince)-7, (Silver Streak)-4-8, nn, (Silver Streak-c)-5. **Everett** Red Reed begins No. 20. **Guardineer** a-8-13. **Don Rico** Daredevil-11-17. **Simon** Silver Streak-3. **Bob Wood** Silver Streak-9. Claw c-1, 2, 6-8: by **Cole**-6-8.*

SILVER SURFER, THE (See Fantastic Four)
Aug, 1968 - No. 18, Sept, 1970; June, 1982 (No. 1-7: 68 pgs.)
Marvel Comics Group

	Good	Fine	Mint
1-Origin by John Buscema (p); Watcher begins (origin), ends No. 7	7.00	20.00	40.00
2	2.65	8.00	16.00
3-1st app. Mephisto	2.50	7.50	15.00
4-Low distribution; Thor app.	5.35	16.00	32.00
5-7-Last giant size. 5-The Stranger app. 6-Brunner inks. 7-Brunner-c	1.60	4.75	9.50
8-10	1.15	3.50	7.00
11-18: 14-Spider-Man x-over. 18-Kirby c/a	.60	1.75	3.50
V2No.1 (6/82, 52 pgs.)-Byrne-c/a	.40	1.25	2.50

NOTE: ***Adkins** a-8-15i. **Brunner** a-6i; c-7. **J. Buscema** a-1-17p. **Colan** a-1-3p. **Reinman** a-1-4i.*

SILVERTIP (Max Brand)
No. 491, Aug, 1953 - No. 898, May, 1958
Dell Publishing Co.

	Good	Fine	Mint
4-Color 491	3.00	9.00	21.00
4-Color 572,608,637,667,731,789,898-Kinstler-a; all painted-c	2.65	8.00	18.00
4-Color 835	2.00	6.00	14.00

SINBAD, JR (TV Cartoon)
Sept-Nov, 1965 - No. 3, May, 1966
Dell Publishing Co.

	Good	Fine	Mint
1	1.30	4.00	9.00
2,3	.75	2.25	5.00

SINDBAD (See Movie Comics: Capt. Sindbad, and Fantastic Voyages of Sindbad)

SINGING GUNS (See Fawcett Movie Comics)

SINGLE SERIES (Comics on Parade No. 30 on)(Also see John Hix. . .)
1938 - 1940
United Features Syndicate

	Good	Fine	Mint
1-Captain and the Kids (No.1)	25.00	75.00	175.00
2-Broncho Bill (1939) (No.1)	18.00	54.00	125.00
3-Ella Cinders (No.1)	16.00	48.00	110.00
4-Li'l Abner (1939) (No.1)	25.00	75.00	175.00
5-Fritzi Ritz (No.1)	11.00	33.00	76.00
6-Jim Hardy by Dick Moores (No.1)	15.00	45.00	105.00
7-Frankie Doodle	10.00	30.00	70.00
8-Peter Pat (On sale 7/14/39)	10.00	30.00	70.00
9-Strange As It Seems	10.00	30.00	70.00
10-Little Mary Mixup	10.00	30.00	70.00
11-Mr. and Mrs. Beans	9.50	28.50	65.00
12-Joe Jinks	10.00	30.00	70.00
13-Looy Dot Dope	9.50	28.50	65.00
14-Billy Make Believe	9.50	28.50	65.00
15-How It Began (1939)	10.00	30.00	70.00
16-Illustrated Gags (1940)	5.50	16.50	38.00
17-Danny Dingle	8.00	24.00	56.00
18-Li'l Abner	20.00	60.00	140.00
19-Broncho Bill (No. 2 on cover)	14.00	42.00	96.00
20-Tarzan by Hal Foster	67.00	200.00	470.00
21-Ella Cinders (No. 2 on cover)	12.00	36.00	84.00
22-Iron Vic	11.00	33.00	76.00
23-Tailspin Tommy by Hal Forrest (No.1)	12.00	36.00	84.00
24-Alice in Wonderland (No.1)	15.00	45.00	105.00
25-Abbie and Slats (No.1)	13.50	40.00	95.00
26-Little Mary Mixup	11.00	33.00	76.00
27-Jim Hardy by Dick Moores	11.00	33.00	76.00
28-Ella Cinders and Abbie and Slats	11.00	33.00	76.00
1-Captain and the Kids (1939 reprint)	15.00	45.00	105.00
1-Fritzi Ritz (1939 reprint)-2nd edition	9.50	28.50	65.00

NOTE: *Some issues given away at the 1939-40 New York World's Fair (No. 6).*

SINISTER HOUSE OF SECRET LOVE, THE (Secrets of Sinister House No. 5 on)
Oct-Nov, 1971 - No. 4, Apr-May, 1972
National Periodical Publications

	Good	Fine	Mint
1		.50	1.00

Silver Streak Comics #10, © LEV

Silver Surfer #6, © MCG

Single Series #8, © UFS

Six-Gun Heroes #34, © CC

Skeleton Hand #1, © ACG

Skellon Empire #1, © Fantasy General

SINISTER HOUSE OF SECRET... (cont'd.)

	Good	Fine	Mint
2-4: 3-Toth-a, 36 pgs.		.35	.70

SIR LANCELOT (See 4-Color No. 606,775)

SIR WALTER RALEIGH (See 4-Color No. 644)

SISTERHOOD OF STEEL, THE
12/84 - No. 8, 4/86 ($1.50; Baxter paper) (Adults only)
Epic Comics (Marvel)

	Good	Fine	Mint
1-(Women mercenaries)	.35	1.10	2.20
2-8	.25	.75	1.80

6 BLACK HORSES (See Movie Classics)

SIX FROM SIRIUS
July, 1984 - No. 4, Oct, 1984 (mini-series; $1.50)
Epic Comics (Marvel)

	Good	Fine	Mint
1-Gulacy c/a in all	.35	1.00	2.00
2-4	.30	.90	1.80

SIX FROM SIRIUS II
Dec, 1985 - No. 4, May, 1986 (Adults only)
Epic Comics (Marvel)

	Good	Fine	Mint
1-4	.25	.75	1.50

SIX-GUN HEROES
March, 1950 - No. 23, Nov, 1953 (Photo-c No. 1-23)
Fawcett Publications

	Good	Fine	Mint
1-Rocky Lane, Hopalong Cassidy, Smiley Burnette begin	16.00	48.00	110.00
2	10.00	30.00	70.00
3-5	7.00	21.00	50.00
6-15: 6-Lash LaRue begins	5.00	15.00	35.00
16-22: 17-Last Smiley Burnette. 18-Monte Hale begins	4.35	13.00	30.00
23-Last Fawcett issue	5.00	15.00	35.00

SIX-GUN HEROES (Cont'd from Fawcett)
(Becomes Gunmasters No. 84 on)
Jan, 1954 - No. 83, Mar-Apr, 1965 (All Vol. 4)
Charlton Comics

	Good	Fine	Mint
24-Tom Mix, Lash Larue	3.50	10.50	24.00
25	2.35	7.00	16.00
26-30	2.00	6.00	14.00
31-40-Tom Mix, Lash Larue, Rocky Lane, Tex Ritter	1.50	4.50	10.00
41-46,48,50	1.15	3.50	8.00
47-Williamson-a, 2 pgs; Torres-a	2.85	8.50	20.00
49-Williamson-a, 5 pgs.	2.85	8.50	20.00
51-61,63-75,82: 58-Gunmaster app.	.70	2.00	4.00
62-Origin, Gunmaster	1.00	3.00	6.00
76-81,83-Gunmaster in all	.35	1.00	2.00
1962 Shoe Store giveaway		.50	1.00

SIXGUN RANCH (See 4-Color No. 580)

SIX-GUN WESTERN
Jan, 1957 - No. 4, July, 1957
Atlas Comics (CDS)

	Good	Fine	Mint
1-Crandall-a; two Williamson text illos	4.00	12.00	28.00
2,3-Williamson-a in both	4.00	12.00	28.00
4-Woodbridge-a	1.75	5.25	12.00

NOTE: ***Maneely*** *c-2.* ***Orlando*** *a-2.* ***Pakula*** *a-2.* ***Powell*** *a-3.* ***Severin*** *c-1.*

SIX MILLION DOLLAR MAN (TV)(Magazine)
June, 1976 - No. 7, Nov, 1977 (B&W)
Charlton Comics

	Good	Fine	Mint
1-Adams c/a	.50	1.50	3.00
2-Adams-c	.30	.80	1.60
3-7		.60	1.20

SIX MILLION DOLLAR MAN (TV)
6/76 - No. 4, 1/77; No. 5, 10/77; No. 6, 2/78 - No. 9, 6/78
Charlton Comics

	Good	Fine	Mint
1-Staton c/a	.30	.80	1.60
2-Adams-c; Staton-a		.50	1.00
3-9		.30	.60

SKATEMAN
Dec, 1983 (One Shot) (Baxter paper)
Pacific Comics

	Good	Fine	Mint
1-Adams c/a	.25	.75	1.50

SKATING SKILLS
1957 (36 & 12 pages; 5x7'', two versions) (10 cents)
Custom Comics, Inc.
Chicago Roller Skates

	Good	Fine	Mint
Resembles old ACG cover plus interior art	.40	1.20	2.40

SKEEZIX
1925 - 1928 (Strip reprints) (soft covers) (pictures & text)
Reilly & Lee Co.

	Good	Fine	Mint
...and Uncle Walt (1924)-Origin	7.00	21.00	50.00
...and Pal (1925)	5.50	16.50	38.00
...at the Circus (1926)	5.50	16.50	38.00
...& Uncle Walt (1927)	5.50	16.50	38.00
...Out West (1928)	5.50	16.50	38.00
Hardback Editions...	8.00	24.00	56.00

SKELETON HAND (...In Secrets of the Supernatural)
Sept-Oct, 1952 - No. 6, July-Aug, 1953
American Comics Group (B&M Dist. Co.)

	Good	Fine	Mint
1	5.75	17.25	45.00
2	4.35	13.00	30.00
3-6	3.50	10.50	24.00

SKELLON EMPIRE
1985 - No. 12 (12 part series)($1.75, B&W)
Fantasy General Comics

	Good	Fine	Mint
1-6	.30	.90	1.80

SKI PARTY (See Movie Classics)

SKIPPY'S OWN BOOK OF COMICS
1934 (52 pages) (Giveaway)
No publisher listed

	Good	Fine	Mint
nn-(Rare)-Strip-r by Percy Crosby	175.00	525.00	1225.00

Published by Max C. Gaines for Phillip's Dental Magnesia to be advertised on the Skippy Radio Show and given away with the purchase of a tube of Phillip's Tooth Paste. This is the first four-color comic book of reprints about one character.

SKROG
1984
Comico

	Good	Fine	Mint
1	.40	1.20	2.40

SKULL, THE SLAYER
August, 1975 - No. 8, Nov, 1976
Marvel Comics Group

	Good	Fine	Mint
1-Origin; Gil Kane-c		.40	.80
2-8: 2-Gil Kane-c. 8-Kirby-c		.30	.60

SKY BLAZERS (Radio)
Sept, 1940 - No. 2, Nov, 1940
Hawley Publications

	Good	Fine	Mint
1-Sky Pirates, Ace Archer, Flying Aces begin	12.00	36.00	84.00
2	9.50	28.50	65.00

SKY KING "RUNAWAY TRAIN" (TV)
1964 (16 pages) (regular size)

SKY KING. . . (continued)
National Biscuit Co.

	Good	Fine	Mint
	1.00	3.00	7.00

SKYMAN (See Big Shot)
Fall?, 1941 - No. 2, 1941; No. 3, 1948 - No. 4, 1948
Columbia Comics Group

	Good	Fine	Mint
1-Origin Skyman, The Face, Sparky Watts app.; Whitney-a; 3rd story r-/Big Shot No. 1	23.00	70.00	160.00
2 (1941)-Yankee Doodle	13.00	40.00	90.00
3,4 (1948)	8.00	24.00	56.00

SKY PILOT
1950 - No. 11, Apr-May, 1951 (Norman Saunders painted-c)
Ziff-Davis Publ. Co.

	Good	Fine	Mint
10,11-Frank Borth-a	3.50	10.50	24.00

SKY RANGER (See Johnny Law. . .)

SKYROCKET
1944
Harry 'A' Chesler

	Good	Fine	Mint
nn-Alias the Dragon, Dr. Vampire, Skyrocket app.	6.00	18.00	42.00

SKY SHERIFF (Breeze Lawson. . .) (Also see Exposed)
Summer, 1948
D. S. Publishing Co.

	Good	Fine	Mint
1-Edmond Good-a	4.35	13.00	30.00

SLAM BANG COMICS (Western Desperado No. 8)
March, 1940 - No. 7, Sept, 1940
Fawcett Publications

	Good	Fine	Mint
1-Diamond Jack, Mark Swift & The Time Retarder, Lee Granger, Jungle King begin	40.00	120.00	280.00
2	20.00	60.00	140.00
3	17.00	51.00	120.00
4-7: 7-Bondage-c	15.00	45.00	105.00

SLAM BANG COMICS
nd
Post Cereal Giveaway

	Good	Fine	Mint
9-Dynamic Man, Echo, Mr. E, Yankee Boy app.	1.35	4.00	9.00

SLAPSTICK COMICS
nd (1946?) (36 pages)
Comic Magazines Distributors

	Good	Fine	Mint
nn-Firetop feature; Post-a(2)	4.65	14.00	32.00

SLASH-D DOUBLECROSS
1950 (132 pgs.) (pocket size)
St. John Publishing Co.

	Good	Fine	Mint
Western comics	5.50	16.50	38.00

SLAUGHTERMAN
1986
Comico

	Good	Fine	Mint
1,2	.40	1.20	2.40

SLAVE GIRL COMICS (See Malu. . .)
Feb, 1949 - No. 2, Apr, 1949
Avon Periodicals

	Good	Fine	Mint
1-Larsen c/a	45.00	135.00	315.00
2	33.00	100.00	230.00

SLEEPING BEAUTY (See Dell Giants, 4-Color No. 973,984, Movie Comics)

SLICK CHICK COMICS
1947
Leader Enterprises

	Good	Fine	Mint
1	4.00	12.00	28.00
2,3	2.65	8.00	18.00

SLIM MORGAN (See Wisco)

SLUGGER (of the Little Wise Guys)
April, 1956
Lev Gleason Publications

	Good	Fine	Mint
1	1.30	4.00	9.00

SMASH COMICS (Lady Luck No. 86 on)
Aug, 1939 - No. 85, Oct, 1949
Quality Comics Group

	Good	Fine	Mint
1-Origin Hugh Hazard & His Iron Man, Bozo the Robot, Espionage, Starring Black X by Eisner, & Invisible Justice; Chic Carter & Wings Wendell begin	55.00	165.00	385.00
2-The Lone Star Rider app; Invisible Hood gains power of invisibility	25.00	75.00	175.00
3-Captain Cook & John Law begin	17.00	51.00	120.00
4,5: 4-Flash Fulton begins	15.00	45.00	105.00
6-12: 12-One pg. Fine-a	12.00	36.00	84.00
13-Magno begins; last Eisner issue; The Ray app. in full page ad; The Purple Trio begins	12.00	36.00	84.00
14-Intro. The Ray by Lou Fine & others	100.00	300.00	700.00
15,16	50.00	150.00	350.00
17-Wun Cloo becomes plastic super-hero by Jack Cole (9-months before Plastic Man)	50.00	150.00	350.00
18-Origin Midnight by Jack Cole	60.00	180.00	420.00
19-22: Last Fine Ray; The Jester begins-No. 22	34.00	102.00	236.00
23,24: 24-The Sword app.; last Chic Carter; Wings Wendall dons new costume No. 24,25	26.50	80.00	185.00
25-Origin Wildfire	30.00	90.00	210.00
26-30	23.00	70.00	160.00
31,32,34: Ray by Rudy Palais; also No. 33	18.00	54.00	125.00
33-Origin The Marksman	20.00	60.00	140.00
35-37	18.00	54.00	125.00
38-The Yankee Eagle begins; last Midnight by Jack Cole	18.00	54.00	125.00
39,40-Last Ray issue	14.50	43.50	100.00
41,43-50	6.65	20.00	46.00
42-Lady Luck begins by Klaus Nordling	9.50	28.50	65.00
51-60	5.50	16.50	38.00
61-70	4.35	13.00	30.00
71-85	4.00	12.00	28.00

NOTE: ***Cole*** *a-17-38, 68, 69, 72, 73, 78, 80, 83, 85; c-38, 60-62, 75, 80.* ***Crandall*** *a-(Ray)-23-29, 35-38; c-36, 39, 40, 43, 44, 46.* ***Fine*** *a(Ray)-14, 15, 16(w/****Tuska****), 17-22.* ***Fuje*** *Ray-30.* ***Gil Fox*** *a-6-7, 9, 11-13.* ***Guardineer*** *a-(The Marksman)-39-?, 49, 52.* ***Gustavson*** *a-4-7, 9, 11-13 (The Jester)-22-46; (Magno)-13-21; (Midnight)-39(****Cole*** *inks), 49, 52, 63-65.* ***Kotzky*** *a-(Espionage)-33-38; c-45, 47.* ***Nordling*** *a-49, 52, 63-65.* ***Powell*** *a-11,12, (Abdul the Arab)-13-24.*

SMASH HIT SPORTS COMICS
Jan, 1949
Essankay Publications

	Good	Fine	Mint
V2No.1-L.B. Cole c/a	4.00	12.00	28.00

S'MATTER POP?
1917 (44 pgs.; B&W; 10x14''; cardboard covers)
Saalfield Publ. Co.

	Good	Fine	Mint
By Charlie Payne; ½ in full color; pages printed on one side	5.50	16.50	38.00

SMILE COMICS (Also see Gay Comics, Tickle, & Whee)
1955 (52 pages; 5x7¼'') (7 cents)

Slam Bang Comics #5, © FAW

Slave Girl Comics #2, © AVON

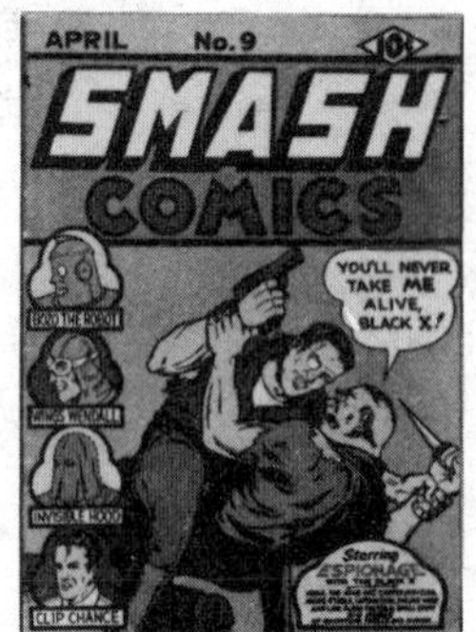

Smash Comics #9, © QUA

Smilin' Jack #4, © N.Y. News Synd.

Snagglepuss #2, © Hanna-Barbera

Snooper & Blabber #1, © Hanna-Barbera

SMILE COMICS (continued)
Modern Store Publ.

	Good	Fine	Mint
1	.50	1.50	3.00

SMILEY BURNETTE WESTERN
March, 1950 - No. 4, Oct, 1950
Fawcett Publications

	Good	Fine	Mint
1	10.00	30.00	70.00
2-4	7.00	21.00	50.00

SMILIN' JACK (See Super Book No. 1,2,7,19)
No. 5, 1940 - No. 8, Oct-Dec, 1949
Dell Publishing Co.

	Good	Fine	Mint
4-Color 5	33.00	100.00	230.00
4-Color 10 (1940)	29.00	85.00	200.00
Large Feature Comic 12,14,25 (1941)	20.00	60.00	140.00
4-Color 4 (1942)	24.00	72.00	165.00
4-Color 14 (1943)	19.00	57.00	132.00
4-Color 36,58 (1943-44)	11.00	33.00	76.00
4-Color 80 (1945)	9.50	28.50	65.00
4-Color 149 (1947)	6.50	19.50	45.00
1 (1-3/48)	6.50	19.50	45.00
2	3.50	10.50	24.00
3-8 (10-12/49)	2.85	8.50	20.00
Popped Wheat Giveaway(1947)-1938 reprints; 16 pgs. in full color	.80	2.40	4.80
Shoe Store Giveaway-1936 reprints; 16 pgs.	2.75	8.00	16.00
Sparked Wheat Giveaway(1942)-16 pgs. in full color	2.00	6.00	12.00

SMILING SPOOK SPUNKY (See Spunky)

SMITTY (See Treasure Box of Famous Comics)
1928 - 1933 (B&W newspaper strip reprints)
(cardboard covers; 9½x9½'', 52 pgs.; 7x8¼'', 36 pgs.)
Cupples & Leon Co.

	Good	Fine	Mint
1928-(96pgs. 7x8¾'')	8.50	25.50	60.00
1928-(Softcover, 36pgs., nn)	10.00	30.00	70.00
1929-At the Ball Game, 1930-The Flying Office Boy, 1931-The Jockey, 1932-In the North Woods....each....	7.00	21.00	50.00
1933-At Military School	7.00	21.00	50.00
Mid 1930's issue (reprint of 1928 Treasure Box issue)-36 pgs.; 7x8¾''	5.50	16.50	38.00
Hardback Editions (100 pgs., 7x8¼'') with dust jacket each....	11.00	33.00	76.00

SMITTY (See Super Book No. 2, 4)
No. 11, 1940 - No. 7, Aug-Oct, 1949; Apr, 1958
Dell Publishing Co.

	Good	Fine	Mint
4-Color 11 (1940)	17.00	51.00	120.00
Large Feature Comic 26 (1941)	11.50	34.50	80.00
4-Color 6 (1942)	10.00	30.00	70.00
4-Color 32 (1943)	8.00	24.00	56.00
4-Color 65 (1945)	6.50	19.50	45.00
4-Color 99 (1946)	5.50	16.50	38.00
4-Color 138 (1947)	4.65	14.00	32.00
1 (11-1/47-48)	4.65	14.00	32.00
2	2.85	8.50	20.00
3,4 (1949)	1.75	5.25	12.00
5-7	1.50	4.50	10.00
4-Color 909	1.15	3.50	8.00

SMOKEY BEAR (TV)
Feb, 1970 - No. 13, Mar, 1973
Gold Key

	Good	Fine	Mint
1	.70	2.00	4.00
2-13	.45	1.25	2.50

(See March of Comics No. 362,372,383,407)

SMOKEY STOVER (See Super Book 5,17,29 & Super Comics 116,118)

SMOKEY STOVER
No. 7, 1942 - No. 827, Aug, 1957
Dell Publishing Co.

	Good	Fine	Mint
4-Color 7 (1942)-Reprints	16.50	50.00	115.00
4-Color 35 (1943)	9.50	28.50	65.00
4-Color 64 (1944)	6.50	19.50	45.00
4-Color 229 (1949)	2.35	7.00	16.00
4-Color 730,827	1.50	4.50	10.00
General Motors giveaway (1953)	3.00	9.00	21.00
National Fire Protection giveaway('53 & '54)-16 pgs., paper-c	3.00	9.00	21.00

SMOKEY THE BEAR (See Forest Fire for 1st app.)
No. 653, Oct, 1955 - No. 1214, Aug, 1961
Dell Publishing Co.

	Good	Fine	Mint
4-Color 653	1.75	5.25	12.00
4-Color 708,754,818,932	1.30	4.00	9.00
4-Color 1016,1119,1214	1.00	3.00	7.00
True Story of..., The('60)-U.S. Forest Service giveaway-Publ. by Western Printing Co. (reprinted in '64 & '69)-Reprints 1st 16 pgs. of 4-Color 932	.85	2.50	6.00

(See March of Comics No. 234)

SMOKY (See Movie Classics)

SMURFS (TV)
Dec, 1982 (No month given) - No. 3, Feb, 1983
Marvel Comics Group

	Good	Fine	Mint
1-3		.30	.60
...Treasury Edition 1(64pgs.)-r/No. 1-3	.40	1.25	2.50

SNAFU (Magazine)
Nov, 1955 - V2/2, Mar, 1956 (B&W)
Atlas Comics (RCM)

	Good	Fine	Mint
V1/1-Heath/Severin-a	3.50	10.50	24.00
V2/1,2-Severin-a	2.35	7.00	16.00

SNAGGLEPUSS (TV)
Oct, 1962 - No. 4, Sept, 1963 (Hanna-Barbera)
Gold Key

	Good	Fine	Mint
1	1.50	4.50	10.00
2-4	1.00	3.00	7.00

SNAP (Jest No. 10?)
1944
Harry 'A' Chesler

	Good	Fine	Mint
9-Manhunter, The Voice	4.00	12.00	28.00

SNAPPY COMICS
1945
Cima Publ. Co. (Prize Publ.)

	Good	Fine	Mint
1-Airmale app.	2.65	8.00	18.00

SNARKY PARKER (See Life with...)

SNIFFY THE PUP
No. 5, Nov, 1949 - No. 18, Sept, 1953
Standard Publications (Animated Cartoons)

	Good	Fine	Mint
5-Two Frazetta text illos	2.65	8.00	18.00
6-10	.85	2.50	6.00
11-18	.55	1.65	4.00

SNOOPER AND BLABBER DETECTIVES (TV) (See Whitman Comic Books)
Nov, 1962 - No. 3, May, 1963 (Hanna-Barbera)
Gold Key

	Good	Fine	Mint
1	1.50	4.50	10.00
2,3	1.15	3.50	8.00

SNOW FOR CHRISTMAS
1957 (16 pages) (Giveaway)
W. T. Grant Co.

	Good	Fine	Mint
	1.20	3.50	7.00

SNOW WHITE (See 4-Color 49,227,382, Mickey Mouse Mag., & Movie Comics)

SNOW WHITE AND THE SEVEN DWARFS
1952 (32 pgs.; 5x7¼'') (Disney)
Bendix Washing Machines

5.00 15.00 35.00

SNOW WHITE AND THE SEVEN DWARFS
April, 1982 (60¢ cover price)
Whitman Publications

nn-r/4-Color No. 49 .30 .60

SNOW WHITE AND THE 7 DWARFS IN ''MILKY WAY''
1955 (16 pgs.) (Disney premium)
American Dairy Association

5.00 15.00 35.00

SNOW WHITE AND THE SEVEN DWARFS
1957 (small size)
Promotional Publ. Co.

2.75 8.00 19.00

SNOW WHITE AND THE SEVEN DWARFS
1958 (16 pages) (Disney premium)
Western Printing Co.

''Mystery of the Missing Magic'' 3.50 10.50 24.00

SOAP OPERA LOVE
Feb, 1983 - No. 3, June, 1983
Charlton Comics

1-3 .25 .50

SOAP OPERA ROMANCES
July, 1982 - No. 5, March, 1983
Charlton Comics

1-5-Nurse Betsy Crane-r .25 .50

SOJOURN ($1.50)
9/77 - No. 2, 1978 (Full tabloid size) (Color & B&W)
White Cliffs Publ. Co.

1-Tor by Kubert, Eagle by Severin, E. V. Race, Private Investigator by Doug Wildey, T. C. Mars by S. Aragones begin plus other strips .30 .80 1.60
2 .30 .80 1.60

SOLARMAN
Dec, 1986 (One-shot)($1.50, B&W)
Star Comics (Marvel)

1-Mooney-a .50 1.00

SOLDIER & MARINE COMICS (Fightin' Army No. 16 on)
No. 11, 12/54 - No. 15, 8/55; V2No.9, 12/56
Charlton Comics (Toby Press of Conn. V1No.11)

V1No.11 (12/54) 1.00 3.00 7.00
V1No.12(2/55)-15 .50 1.50 3.50
V2No.9(Formerly Never Again; Jerry Drummer V2No.10 on) .50 1.50 3.50

NOTE: *Bob Powell a-11.*

SOLDIER COMICS
Jan, 1952 - No. 11, Sept, 1953
Fawcett Publications

	Good	Fine	Mint
1	3.00	9.00	21.00
2	1.50	4.50	10.00
3-5	1.35	4.00	9.00
6,7,9-11	.85	2.50	6.00
8-Illo. in **POP**	2.00	6.00	14.00

SOLDIERS OF FORTUNE
Feb-Mar, 1951 - No. 13, Feb-Mar, 1953
American Comics Group (Creston Publ. Corp.)

1-Capt. Crossbones by Shelly, Ace Carter, Lance Larson begin 4.65 14.00 32.00
2 3.50 10.50 24.00
3-10: 6-Bondage-c 2.85 8.50 20.00
11-13 (War format) 1.00 3.00 7.00

NOTE: *Shelly a-1-3, 5. Whitney a-6, 8-13; c-1-3, 6. Most issues are 52 pages.*

SOLD OUT
Oct, 1986 - No. 2, 1986 ($1.50, B&W)
FantaCo Enterprises

1,2: Satire .25 .75 1.50

SOLOMON AND SHEBA (See 4-Color No. 1070)

SOLOMON KANE
Sept, 1985 - No. 6, Mar, 1986 (mini-series)
Marvel Comics Group

1 .50 1.00
2-6: 3,4-Williamson-a .45 .90

SOMERSET HOLMES
9/83 - No. 4, 4/84; No. 5, 11/84 - No. 6, 12/84 ($1.50; Baxter)
Pacific Comics/Eclipse Comics No. 5, 6

1-B. Anderson c/a; Cliff Hanger by Williamson begins, ends No. 6 .30 1.00 2.00
2-6 .25 .75 1.50

SONG OF PAIN AND SORROW
1986 (Proceeds donated to famine relief)
DC Comics

1-Top artist line-up .40 .80

SONG OF THE SOUTH (See 4-Color No. 693 & Brer Rabbit)

SON OF AMBUSH BUG (Also see Ambush Bug)
July, 1986 - No. 6, Dec, 1986
DC Comics

1 .50 1.00
2-6 .40 .80

SON OF BLACK BEAUTY (See 4-Color No. 510,566)

SON OF FLUBBER (See Movie Comics)

SON OF SATAN
Dec, 1975 - No. 8, Feb, 1977
Marvel Comics Group

1-Mooney-a .40 .80
2-Origin The Possessor .25 .50
3-8: 4,5-Russell-a(p). 8-Heath-a .20 .40

SON OF SINBAD (Also see Daring Adventures, Abbott & Costello)
February, 1950
St. John Publishing Co.

1-Kubert c/a 25.00 75.00 175.00

SON OF TOMAHAWK (See Tomahawk)

SON OF VULCAN (Mysteries of Unexplored Worlds No. 1-48; Thunderbolt, V3No.51 on)

Snow White... (Bendix Giveaway), © WDC

Soldier Comics #11, © FAW

Soldiers of Fortune #8, © ACG

Southern Knights #10, © Fictioneer Books

Space Adventures #10, © CC

Space Family Robinson #13, © GK

SON OF VULCAN (continued)
Nov, 1965 - V2No.50, Jan, 1966
Charlton Comics

	Good	Fine	Mint
49,50	.30	.90	1.80

SONS OF KATIE ELDER (See Movie Classics)

SORCERY (See Chilling Adventures in... & Red Circle...)

SORORITY SECRETS
July, 1954
Toby Press

	Good	Fine	Mint
1	2.00	6.00	14.00

SOUPY SALES COMIC BOOK (TV)(The Official...)
1965
Archie Publications

	Good	Fine	Mint
1	4.00	12.00	28.00

SOUTHERN KNIGHTS, THE (Formerly Crusaders No. 1)
No. 2, 1983 - No. 7, 9/84; No. 8, 1984 - Present ($1.75)
Guild/Fictioneer Books (Comics Interview) No. 8 on

	Good	Fine	Mint
2	.85	2.50	5.00
3	.70	2.00	4.00
4,5	.55	1.70	3.40
6-10	.45	1.35	2.70
11-18	.35	1.10	2.20
Annual 1 ('86)	.45	1.35	2.70
Graphic Novel 1,2 (5/86, 9/86)	.85	2.50	5.00

SPACE ACE
1952
Magazine Enterprises

	Good	Fine	Mint
5(A-1 61)-Guardineer-a	11.50	34.50	80.00

SPACE ACTION
June, 1952 - No. 3, Oct, 1952
Ace Magazines (Junior Books)

	Good	Fine	Mint
1	18.50	56.00	130.00
2,3	14.50	43.50	100.00

SPACE ADVENTURES (War At Sea No. 22 on)
7/52 - No. 21, 5/56; No. 23, 5/58 - No. 59, 11/64; V3/60, 10/67; V1/2, 7/68 - V1No.8, 7/69; No. 9, 5/78 - No. 13, 3/79
Capitol Stories/Charlton Comics

	Good	Fine	Mint
1	9.50	28.50	65.00
2	5.00	15.00	35.00
3-5	4.35	13.00	30.00
6,8,9	3.85	11.50	27.00
7-Transvestite story	5.75	17.25	40.00
10-Ditko c/a	15.00	45.00	105.00
11-Ditko c/a(2)	15.00	45.00	105.00
12-Ditko-c (Classic)	17.00	51.00	120.00
13-(Fox-r, 10-11/54); Blue Beetle story	4.65	14.00	32.00
14-Blue Beetle story (Fox-r, 12-1/54-55)	3.85	11.50	27.00
15,17-19: 15-18-Rocky Jones app.(TV)	3.15	9.50	22.00
16-Krigstein, Ditko-a	8.00	24.00	56.00
20-Reprints Fawcett's "Destination Moon"	9.50	28.50	65.00
21-(8/56) (no No. 22)-Ditko-a	4.65	14.00	32.00
23-(5/58; formerly Nyoka, The Jungle Girl)-Reprints Fawcett's "Destination Moon"	8.00	24.00	56.00
24,25,29,31,32-Ditko-a	4.65	14.00	32.00
26,27-Ditko-a(4) each	6.50	19.50	46.00
28,30	1.70	5.00	11.50
33-1st app./origin Captin Atom by Ditko (3/60)	11.00	33.00	76.00
34-40,42-All Captain Atom by Ditko	4.65	14.00	32.00
41,43,46-59	.50	1.50	3.00
44,45-Mercury Man in each	.50	1.50	3.00
V3No.60(10/67)-Origin Paul Mann & The Saucers From the Future		.40	.80
2-8('68-'69)-All Ditko-a; Aparo-a No. 2		.30	.60
9-13('78-'79)-Capt. Atom-r/Space Advs. by Ditko; 9-Origin-r		.30	.60

NOTE: *Aparo a-V3No.60. Ditko c-12, 31, 33-42. Shuster a-11.*

SPACE ARK
June, 1985 - Present
Americomics (AC Comics)/WaRp No. 3 on

	Good	Fine	Mint
1-3-Funny animal	.30	.90	1.80

SPACE BEAVER
Oct, 1986 - Present ($1.50, B&W)
Ten-Buck Comics

	Good	Fine	Mint
1	.25	.75	1.50

SPACE BUSTERS
Spring/52 - No. 3, Fall/52 (Painted covers by Norman Saunders)
Ziff-Davis Publ. Co.

	Good	Fine	Mint
1-Krigstein-a	26.00	78.00	182.00
2,3: 2-Two pgs. Kinstler-a; bondage-c	19.50	58.50	136.00

NOTE: *Anderson a-2.*

SPACE CADET (See Tom Corbett,...)

SPACE COMICS
No. 4, Mar-Apr, 1954 - No. 5, May-June, 1954
Avon Periodicals

	Good	Fine	Mint
4,5-Space Mouse, Peter Rabbit, Super Pup, & Merry Mouse app.	2.15	6.50	15.00
I.W. Reprint No. 8 (nd)-Space Mouse-r	.50	1.50	2.25

SPACE DETECTIVE
July, 1951 - No. 4, July, 1952
Avon Periodicals

	Good	Fine	Mint
1-Red Hathway, Space Det. begins, ends No. 4; Wood c/a(3)-23 pgs.; "Opium Smugglers of Venus" drug story; Lucky Dale-r/Saint No. 4	60.00	180.00	420.00
2-Tales from the Shadow Squad story; Wood/Orlando-c; Wood inside layouts	29.00	85.50	200.00
3-Kinstler-c	18.00	54.00	126.00
4-Kinstler-a	18.00	54.00	126.00
I.W. Reprint No. 1(Reprints No. 2), 8(Reprints cover No. 1 & part Famous Funnies No. 191)	1.35	4.00	8.00
I.W. Reprint No. 9	1.35	4.00	8.00

SPACE EXPLORER (See March of Comics No. 202)

SPACE FAMILY ROBINSON (TV)(...Lost in Space No. 15 on)(Lost in Space No. 37 on)
Dec, 1962 - No. 36, Oct, 1969 (All painted covers)
Gold Key

	Good	Fine	Mint
1-(low distr.); Spiegle-a in all	5.75	17.25	40.00
2(3/63)-Became Lost in Space	2.85	8.50	20.00
3-10: 6-Captain Venture begins	1.50	4.50	10.00
11-20	.85	2.50	6.00
21-36	.55	1.65	4.00

SPACE FAMILY ROBINSON (See March of Comics No. 320,328,352,404, 414)

SPACE GHOST (TV)
March, 1967 (Hanna-Barbera) (TV debut was 9/66)
Gold Key

	Good	Fine	Mint
1 (10199-703)-Spiegle-a	4.35	13.00	30.00

SPACE KAT-ETS (in 3-D)
Dec, 1953 (25 cents)
Power Publishing Co.

SPACE KAT-ETS (continued)

	Good	Fine	Mint
1	16.00	48.00	110.00

SPACEMAN (Speed Carter. . .)
Sept, 1953 - No. 6, July, 1954
Atlas Comics (CnPC)

	Good	Fine	Mint
1	11.50	34.50	80.00
2	7.00	21.00	50.00
3-6	6.00	18.00	42.00

NOTE: ***Everett*** *c-1, 3.* ***Maneely*** *a-1-8?; c-6.* ***Tuska*** *a-5(3).*

SPACE MAN
No. 1253, 1-3/62 - No. 8, 3-5/64; No. 9, 7/72 - No. 10, 10/72
Dell Publishing Co.

	Good	Fine	Mint
4-Color 1253 (1-3/62)	2.35	7.00	16.00
2,3	1.30	4.00	9.00
4-8	.85	2.50	6.00
9-Reprints No. 1253	.40	1.25	2.80
10-Reprints No. 2	.35	1.00	2.00

SPACE MOUSE (Also see Space Comics)
April, 1953 - No. 5, Apr-May, 1954
Avon Periodicals

	Good	Fine	Mint
1	3.50	10.50	24.00
2	2.00	6.00	14.00
3-5	1.50	4.50	10.00

SPACE MOUSE (Walter Lantz. . .No. 1; see Comic Album No. 17)
No. 1132, 8-10/60 - No. 5, 11/63 (Walter Lantz)
Dell Publishing Co./Gold Key

	Good	Fine	Mint
4-Color 1132,1244	1.15	3.50	8.00
1(11/62)(G.K.)	1.15	3.50	8.00
2-5	.85	2.50	6.00

SPACE MYSTERIES
1964 (Reprints)
I.W. Enterprises

	Good	Fine	Mint
1-r-/Journey Into Unknown Worlds No. 4 w/new-c	.50	1.50	3.00
8,9	.50	1.50	3.00

SPACE: 1999 (TV)
Nov, 1975 - No. 7, Nov, 1976
Charlton Comics

	Good	Fine	Mint
1-Staton-c/a; origin Moonbase Alpha		.60	1.20
2-Staton-a		.50	1.00
3-6: All byrne-a; c-5	.50	1.50	3.00
7		.50	1.00

SPACE: 1999 (TV)(Magazine)
Nov, 1975 - No. 8, Nov, 1976
Charlton Comics

	Good	Fine	Mint
1-Origin Moonbase Alpha; Morrow c/a	.50	1.50	3.00
2,3-Morrow c/a	.30	.90	1.80
4-8 (No. 7 shows No. 6 on inside)	.30	.80	1.60

SPACE PATROL (TV)
Summer/52 - No. 2, Oct-Nov/52 (Painted-c by Norman Saunders)
Ziff-Davis Publishing Co. (Approved Comics)

	Good	Fine	Mint
1-Krigstein-a	30.00	90.00	210.00
2-Krigstein-a	25.00	75.00	175.00
. . .'s Special Mission (8 pgs., B&W, Giveaway)	50.00	150.00	300.00

SPACE PIRATES (See Archie Giant Series No. 533)

SPACE SQUADRON (Space Worlds No. 6)
June, 1951 - No. 5, Feb, 1952
Marvel/Atlas Comics (ACI)

	Good	Fine	Mint
1	14.50	43.50	100.00
2	11.00	33.00	76.00
3-5	9.00	27.00	62.00

SPACE THRILLERS
1954 (Giant) (25 cents)
Avon Periodicals

	Good	Fine	Mint
nn-(Scarce)-Robotmen of the Lost Planet; contains 3 rebound comics of The Saint & Strange Worlds. Contents could vary	67.00	200.00	470.00

SPACE TRIP TO THE MOON (See Space Adventures No. 23)

SPACE WAR (Fightin' Five No. 28 on)
Oct, 1959 - No. 27, Mar, 1964; No. 28, Mar, 1978 - No. 34, 3/79
Charlton Comics

	Good	Fine	Mint
V1No.1	3.15	9.50	22.00
2,3	1.75	5.00	11.50
4,5,8,10-Ditko c/a	5.50	16.50	38.00
6-Ditko-a	4.00	12.00	28.00
7,9,11-15: Last 10¢ ish?	1.15	3.50	8.00
16-27	.85	2.50	6.00
28,29,33,34-Ditko c/a(r)	1.50	4.50	10.00
30-Ditko c/a(r); Staton, Sutton/Wood-a	1.85	5.50	13.00
31-Ditko c/a; atom-blast-c	1.85	5.50	13.00
32-r-/Charlton Premiere V2/2	.30	.90	1.80

NOTE: ***Everett*** *a-34.* ***Sutton*** *a-30, 33.*

SPACE WESTERN (Formerly Cowboy Western Comics; becomes Cowboy Western Comics No. 46 on)
No. 40, Oct, 1952 - No. 45, Aug, 1953
Charlton Comics (Capitol Stories)

	Good	Fine	Mint
40	20.00	60.00	140.00
41,43-45	14.50	43.50	100.00
42-Atom bomb explosion-c	16.50	50.00	115.00

SPACE WORLDS (Space Squadron No. 1-5)
No. 6, April, 1952
Atlas Comics (Male)

	Good	Fine	Mint
6	6.50	19.50	45.00

SPANKY & ALFALFA AND THE LITTLE RASCALS (See The Little Rascals)

SPANNER'S GALAXY
Dec, 1984 - No. 6, May, 1985 (mini-series)
DC Comics

	Good	Fine	Mint
1-Mandrake c/a begins		.50	1.00
2-6: 2-Intro sidekick Gadg		.40	.80

SPARKIE, RADIO PIXIE (Big John & Sparkie No. 4)
Winter, 1951 - No. 3, 1952
Ziff-Davis Publ. Co.

	Good	Fine	Mint
1	5.00	15.00	35.00
2,3	4.00	12.00	28.00

SPARKLE COMICS
Oct-Nov, 1948 - No. 33, Dec-Jan, 1953-54
United Features Syndicate

	Good	Fine	Mint
1-Li'l Abner, Nancy, Captain & the Kids	4.65	14.00	32.00
2	2.35	7.00	16.00
3-10	2.00	6.00	14.00
11-20	1.50	4.50	10.00
21-33	1.15	3.50	8.00

SPARKLE PLENTY (See 4-Color No. 215 & Harvey Com. Libr. No. 2)

SPARKLER COMICS (1st Series)
July, 1940 - No. 2, 1940

Space Patrol #2, © Z-D

Space War #1, © CC

Space Western #43, © CC

Sparkler Comics #18, © UFS

Special Agent #7, © PMI

Special Edition #2, © DC

SPARKLER COMICS (continued)
United Feature Comic Group

	Good	Fine	Mint
1-Jim Hardy	13.50	40.50	95.00
2-Frankie Doodle	10.00	30.00	70.00

SPARKLER COMICS (2nd Series)(Nancy & Sluggo No. 121 on)
July, 1941 - No. 120, Jan, 1955
United Features Syndicate

	Good	Fine	Mint
1-Origin Sparkman; Tarzan (by Hogarth in all issues), Captain & the Kids, Ella Cinders, Danny Dingle, Dynamite Dunn, Nancy, Abbie & Slats, Frankie Doodle, Broncho Bill begin	47.00	141.00	330.00
2	23.00	70.00	160.00
3,4	20.00	60.00	140.00
5-10: 9-Sparkman's new costume	15.00	45.00	105.00
11-13,15-20: 12-Sparkman new costume-color change. 19-1st Race Riley?	13.50	40.50	95.00
14-Hogarth Tarzan-c	16.00	48.00	110.00
21-24,26,27,29,30: 22-Race Riley & the Commandos strips begin, ends No. 44	10.00	30.00	70.00
25,28,31,34,37,39-Tarzan-c by Hogarth	13.50	40.50	95.00
32,33,35,36,38,40	6.50	19.50	45.00
41,43,45,46,48,49	4.65	14.00	32.00
42,44,47,50-Tarzan-c	8.00	24.00	56.00
51,52,54-70: 57-Li'l Abner begins (not in No. 58); Fearless Fosdick app.-No. 58	3.50	10.50	24.00
53-Tarzan-c	6.85	20.50	48.00
71-80	2.65	8.00	18.00
81,82,84-90: 85-Li'l Abner ends. 86-Lingerie panels	2.00	6.00	14.00
83-Tarzan-c	3.65	11.00	25.00
91-96,98-99	1.85	5.50	13.00
97-Origin Casey Ruggles by Warren Tufts	3.65	11.00	25.00
100	2.65	8.00	18.00
101-107,109-112,114-120	1.50	4.50	10.00
108,113-Toth-a	3.35	10.00	23.00

SPARKLING LOVE
June, 1950; 1953
Avon Periodicals/Realistic (1953)

	Good	Fine	Mint
1(Avon)-Kubert-a	11.00	33.00	76.00
nn(1953)-Reprint; Kubert-a	4.65	14.00	32.00

SPARKLING STARS
June, 1944 - No. 33, March, 1948
Holyoke Publishing Co.

	Good	Fine	Mint
1-Hell's Angels, FBI, Boxie Weaver & Ali Baba begin	5.00	15.00	35.00
2	3.00	9.00	21.00
3-Actual FBI case photos & war photos	2.00	6.00	14.00
4-10: 7-X-mas-c	1.70	5.00	12.00
11-19,21-29,32,33: 29-Bondage-c	1.50	4.50	10.00
20,30-Fangs the Wolf Boy app.	1.70	5.00	12.00
31-Spanking panel; Sid Greene-a	1.70	5.00	12.00

SPARK MAN
1945 (One Shot) (36 pages)
Frances M. McQueeny

	Good	Fine	Mint
1-Origin Spark Man; female torture story; cover redrawn from Sparkler No. 1	10.00	30.00	70.00

SPARKY WATTS
Nov?, 1942 - No. 10, 1949
Columbia Comic Corp.

	Good	Fine	Mint
1(1942)-Skyman & The Face app.	10.00	30.00	70.00
2(1943)	5.00	15.00	35.00
3(1944)	4.75	14.25	33.00
4(1944)-Origin	3.85	11.50	27.00
5(1947)-Skyman app.	3.35	10.00	23.00
6('47),7,8('48),9,10('49)	2.15	6.50	15.00

SPARTACUS (See 4-Color No. 1139)

SPECIAL AGENT (Steve Saunders . . .)
Dec, 1947 - No. 8, Sept, 1949
Parents' Magazine Institute (Commended Comics No. 2)

	Good	Fine	Mint
1	3.35	10.00	23.00
2	1.70	5.00	11.50
3-8	1.15	3.50	8.00

SPECIAL COLLECTORS' EDITION
Dec, 1975 (No month given) (10¼x13½'')
Marvel Comics Group

	Good	Fine	Mint
1-Kung Fu, Iron Fist & Sons of the Tiger	.30	.90	1.80

SPECIAL COMICS (Hangman No. 2 on)
Winter, 1941-42
MLJ Magazines

	Good	Fine	Mint
1-Origin The Boy Buddies (Shield & Wizard x-over); death of The Comet; origin The Hangman retold	77.00	231.00	540.00

SPECIAL DELIVERY
1951 (32 pgs.; B&W)
Post Hall Synd. (Giveaway)

Origin of Pogo, Swamp, etc.; 2 pg. biog. on Walt Kelly
(Sold in 1980 for $150.00)

SPECIAL EDITION (See Gorgo, Reptisaurus)

SPECIAL EDITION (U. S. Navy Giveaways)
1944 - 1945 (Regular comic format with wording simplified, 52pgs.)
National Periodical Publications

	Good	Fine	Mint
1-Action (1944)-reprints Action 80	65.00	195.00	455.00
2-Action (1944)-reprints Action 81	65.00	195.00	455.00
3-Superman (1944)-reprints Superman 33	65.00	195.00	455.00
4-Detective (1944)-reprints Det. 97	65.00	195.00	455.00
5-Superman (1945)-reprints Superman 34	70.00	210.00	490.00
6-Action (1945)-reprints Action 84	70.00	210.00	490.00

SPECIAL EDITION COMICS
1940 (Aug.) (One Shot, 68pgs.)
Fawcett Publications

	Good	Fine	Mint
1-1st book devoted entirely to Captain Marvel; C.C. Beck c/a; only app. of C. Marvel with belt buckle; C. Marvel appears with button-down flap, 1st story (came out before Captain Marvel No. 1)	210.00	630.00	1680.00

NOTE: *Prices vary widely on this book. Since this book is all Captain Marvel stories, it is actually a pre-Captain Marvel No. 1. There is speculation that this book almost became **Captain Marvel** No. 1. After **Special Edition** was published, there was an editor change at Fawcett. The new editor commissioned Kirby to do a nn **Captain Marvel** book early in 1941. This book was followed by a 2nd book several months later. This 2nd book was advertised as a No. 3 (making Special Edition the No. 1, & the nn issue the No. 2). However, the 2nd book did come out as a No. 2.*

SPECIAL EDITION X-MEN
Feb, 1983 (One Shot) (Baxter paper, $2.00)
Marvel Comics Group

	Good	Fine	Mint
1-r-/Giant-Size X-Men plus one new story	.70	2.00	4.00

SPECIAL MARVEL EDITION (Master of Kung Fu No. 17 on)
Jan, 1971 - No. 16, Feb, 1974
Marvel Comics Group

	Good	Fine	Mint
1-Thor begins (r)		.35	.70
2-4-Last Thor (r); all Giants		.30	.60
5-14: Sgt. Fury-r; 11 r-/Sgt. Fury No. 13 (Captain America)		.30	.60
15-Master of Kung Fu begins; Starlin-a; origin & 1st app. Nayland Smith & Dr. Petric		.60	1.20
16-1st app. Midnight; Starlin-a		.60	1.20

SPECIAL MISSIONS (See G.I. Joe. . .)

SPECIAL WAR SERIES (Attack V4/3 on?)
Aug, 1965 - No. 4, Nov, 1965
Charlton Comics

	Good	Fine	Mint
V4No.1-D-Day (See D-Day listing)		.50	1.00
2-Attack!		.40	.80
3-War & Attack		.40	.80
4-Judomaster	.85	2.50	5.00

SPECTACULAR ADVENTURES (See Adventures)

SPECTACULAR FEATURE MAGAZINE, A (Formerly My Confessions)
(Spectacular Features Magazine No. 12)
No. 11, April, 1950
Fox Feature Syndicate

	Good	Fine	Mint
11-Samson & Delilah	10.00	30.00	70.00

SPECTACULAR FEATURES MAGAZINE (Formerly A Spectacular Feature Magazine)
No. 12, June, 1950 - No. 3, Aug, 1950
Fox Feature Syndicate

	Good	Fine	Mint
12-Iwo Jima; photo flag-c	10.00	30.00	70.00
3-Drugs/prostitution story	8.00	24.00	56.00

SPECTACULAR SPIDER-MAN, THE (See Marvel Treasury Edition and Marvel Special Edition)

SPECTACULAR SPIDER-MAN, THE (Magazine)
July, 1968 - No. 2, Nov, 1968 (35 cents)
Marvel Comics Group

	Good	Fine	Mint
1-(Black & White)	1.20	3.50	7.00
2-(Color)-Green Goblin app.	1.00	3.00	6.00

SPECTACULAR SPIDER-MAN, THE (Peter Parker. . No. 54 on)
Dec, 1976 - Present
Marvel Comics Group

	Good	Fine	Mint
1	1.00	3.00	6.00
2-5	.45	1.40	2.80
6-10	.40	1.25	2.50
11-20	.35	1.00	2.00
21,24-26	.30	.85	1.70
22,23-Moon Knight app.	.40	1.25	2.50
27-Miller's 1st Daredevil	1.40	4.25	8.50
28-Miller Daredevil (p)	1.10	3.25	6.50
29-40; 33-Origin Iguana	.25	.75	1.50
41-57,59	.25	.75	1.50
58-Byrne a(p)	.40	1.25	2.50
60-Double size; origin retold with new facts revealed	.25	.75	1.50
61-63,65-68,71-74,76-80		.50	1.00
64-1st Cloak & Dagger app.	1.35	4.00	8.00
69,70-Cloak & Dagger app.	.70	2.00	4.00
75-Double size	.25	.75	1.50
81-83-Punisher app.	.50	1.50	3.00
84-93,97-99: 98-Intro The Spot		.50	1.00
94-96-Cloak & Dagger app.		.50	1.00
100-Double size		.50	1.00
101-124: 111-Secret Wars II tie-in		.50	1.00
Annual 1 (12/79)	.25	.75	1.50
Annual 2 (8/80)-1st app. & origin Rapier	.25	.75	1.50
Annual 3 (11/81)-Last Manwolf	.25	.75	1.50
Annual 4 (11/84)-Black Cat app.	.25	.75	1.50
Annual 5 (10/85)($1.25)	.25	.75	1.50

NOTE: ***Austin*** *c-21i.* ***Buckler*** *a-Annual 1p; c-Annual 1.* ***Byrne*** *c(p)-17, 43, 58.* ***Gulacy*** *c-8.* ***Layton*** *c-32, 65p.* ***Miller*** *c-46p, 48p, 50, 51p, 52p, 54p, 55, 56p, 57, 60.* ***Mooney*** *a-7i, 11i, 21p, 23p, 25p, 26p, 29-34p, 36p, 37p, 39i, 41, 42i, 49p, 50i, 51i, 53p, 54-57i, 59-66i, 68i, 71i, 73-79i, 81-83i, 85i, 87-96i, Annual 1i, 2p.* ***Nasser*** *c-37p.* ***Perez*** *c-10.* ***Simonson*** *c-54i.*

SPECTACULAR STORIES MAGAZINE (Formerly A Star Presentation)
No. 4, July, 1950 - No. 3, Sept, 1950
Fox Feature Sydicate (Hero Books)

	Good	Fine	Mint
4-Sherlock Holmes	15.00	45.00	105.00
3-The St. Valentine's Day Massacre	9.00	27.00	62.00

SPECTRE, THE (See Adventure, Showcase, & More Fun)
Nov-Dec, 1967 - No. 10, May-June, 1969
National Periodical Publications

	Good	Fine	Mint
1-Anderson c/a	.85	2.50	5.00
2-5-Adams c/a; 3-Wildcat x-over	.75	2.25	4.50
6-8,10: 7-Hourman app.	.35	1.00	2.00
9-Wrightson-a	.60	1.75	3.50

NOTE: ***Anderson*** *inks-No. 6-8.*

SPEED BUGGY (TV)(Also see Fun-In No. 12,15)
July, 1975 - No. 9, Nov, 1976 (Hanna-Barbera)
Charlton Comics

	Good	Fine	Mint
1-9		.25	.50

SPEED CARTER SPACEMAN (See Spaceman)

SPEED COMICS (New Speed)
Oct, 1939 - No. 44, 1-2/47 (No.14-16: pocket size, 100 pgs.)
Brookwood Publ./Speed Publ./Harvey Publications No. 12 on

	Good	Fine	Mint
1-Origin Shock Gibson; Ted Parrish, the Man with 1000 Faces begins; Powell-a	60.00	180.00	420.00
2-Powell-a	30.00	90.00	210.00
3	18.00	54.00	125.00
4-Powell-a	16.00	48.00	110.00
5	14.50	43.50	100.00
6-12 (3/41): 7-Mars Mason begins, ends No. 11. 12-The Wasp begins; Major Colt app. (Capt. Colt No. 12)	12.00	36.00	84.00
13-Intro. Captain Freedom & Young Defenders; Girl Commandos, Pat Parker, War Nurse begins; Major Colt app.	17.00	51.00	120.00
14-16 (100 pg. pocket size, 1941): 15-Pat Parker dons costume, last in costume No. 23; no Girl Commandos	13.00	40.00	90.00
17-Black Cat begins (origin), r-/Pocket No. 1; not in No. 40,41	22.00	65.00	154.00
18-20	12.00	36.00	84.00
21,22,25-30	10.00	30.00	70.00
23-Origin Girl Commandos	15.00	45.00	105.00
24-Pat Parker team-up with Girl Commandos	10.00	30.00	70.00
31-44: 35-Bondage-c. 38-Flag-c	8.00	24.00	56.00

NOTE: ***Kubert*** *a-7-11(Mars Mason), 37, 38, 42-44.* ***Powell*** *a-1, 2, 4-7, 28, 31, 44.* ***Schomburg*** *c-31, 32, 34-36.* ***Tuska*** *a-3, 7. Bondage c-18.*

SPEED DEMONS (Formerly Frank Merriwell at Yale?; Submarine Attack No. 11 on)
No. 5, Feb, 1957 - No. 10, 1958
Charlton Comics

	Good	Fine	Mint
5-10	.30	.80	1.60

SPEED SMITH THE HOT ROD KING
Spring, 1952
Ziff-Davis Publishing Co.

	Good	Fine	Mint
1-Saunders painted-c	4.65	14.00	32.00

SPEEDY GONZALES (See 4-Color No. 1084)

SPEEDY RABBIT
nd (1953); 1963
Realistic/I. W. Enterprises/Super Comics

	Good	Fine	Mint
nn (1953)	.70	2.00	4.00
I.W. Reprint No. 1 (2 versions w/diff. c/stories exist)	.30	.80	1.60

A Spectacular Feat. Mag. #11, © FOX

Spectacular Spider-Man #81, © MCG

Speed Comics #13, © HARV

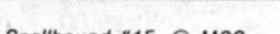
Spellbound #15, © MCG

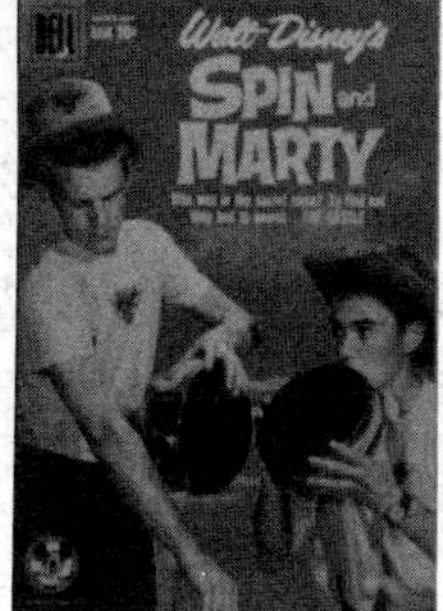

Spin & Marty #9, © WDC

The Spirit, 1/12/41, © Will Eisner

SPEEDY RABBIT (continued)

	Good	Fine	Mint
Super Reprint No. 14(1963)	.30	.80	1.60

SPELLBINDERS
Nov, 1986 - Present (52 pgs.)
Quality Comics

	Good	Fine	Mint
1-3: Nemesis The Warlock, Amadeus Wolf		.60	1.25

SPELLBOUND (See The Crusaders)

SPELLBOUND (Tales to Hold You... No. 1, Stories...)
3/52 - No. 23, 6/54; No. 24, 10/55 - No. 34, 6/57
Atlas Comics (ACI 1-15/Male 16-23/BPC 24-34)

	Good	Fine	Mint
1	10.00	30.00	70.00
2-Edgar A. Poe app.	5.00	15.00	35.00
3-5: 3-Cannibalism story	4.00	12.00	28.00
6-Krigstein-a	4.65	14.00	32.00
7-10	3.00	9.00	21.00
11-16,18-20	2.65	8.00	18.00
17-Krigstein-a	4.35	13.00	30.00
21-23-Last precode (6/54)	2.15	6.50	15.00
24,26,27,30,31,34	1.70	5.00	11.50
25-Orlando-a	1.85	5.50	13.00
28,29-Ditko-a	2.35	7.00	16.00
32,33-Torres-a	3.85	11.50	27.00

NOTE: ***Colan** a-17. **Ditko** a-28, 29. **Everett** a-2, 5, 7, 10, 16, 28, 31; c-2, 8, 14, 17-19, 28, 30. **Forte/Fox** a-16. **Heath** a-2, 4, 8,.9, 12, 14, 16; c-3, 4, 12, 16, 20, 21. **Infantino** a-15. **Maneely** a-7, 14, 27; c-24, 31. **Mooney** a-5, 13, 18. **Mac Pakula** a-22, 32. **Post** a-8. **Powell** a-19, 20, 32. **Robinson** a-1. **Romita** a-24, 26, 27. **Severin** c-29. **Sinnott** a-8, 16.*

SPENCER SPOOK (Formerly Giggle; see Advs. of...)
No. 100, Mar-Apr, 1955 - No. 101, May-June, 1955
American Comics Group

	Good	Fine	Mint
100,101	.85	2.50	6.00

SPIDER-MAN (See Amazing... & Spectacular...)

SPIDER-MAN AND DAREDEVIL
March, 1984 (One-Shot; $2.00; deluxe paper)
Marvel Comics Group

	Good	Fine	Mint
1-r-/Spectacular Spider-Man Nos. 26-28 by Frank Miller	.25	.80	1.60

SPIDER-MAN AND HIS AMAZING FRIENDS
Dec, 1981 (One shot)
Marvel Comics Group

	Good	Fine	Mint
1-Adapted from TV cartoon show; Green Goblin app.; Spiegle-a(p)		.30	.60

SPIDER-MAN COMICS MAGAZINE
Jan, 1987 - Present ($1.50, Digest-size)
Marvel Comics Group

	Good	Fine	Mint
1,2-Reprints	.25	.75	1.50

SPIDER-MAN VERSUS WOLVERINE
Feb, 1987 (One-shot, 68 pgs.)
Marvel Comics Group

	Good	Fine	Mint
1-Williamson-i; intro Charlemagne	.40	1.25	2.50

SPIDER-WOMAN (Also see Marvel Spotlight No. 32)
April, 1978 - No. 50, June, 1983 (See Marvel Two-In-One)
Marvel Comics Group

	Good	Fine	Mint
1-New origin & mask added		.50	1.00
2-20: 20-Spider-Man app.		.35	.70
21-36,39-49: 37-Photo-c; 47-New look		.25	.50
37,38-New X-Men x-over; 37-1st Siryn; origin retold	.35	1.10	2.20
50-Double size; photo-c; Death of S-W		.40	.80

NOTE: ***Austin** a-37i. **Byrne** c-26p. **Layton** c-19. **Miller** c-32p.*

SPIDEY SUPER STORIES (Spider-Man)
Oct, 1974 - No. 57, Mar, 1982 (35 cents) (no ads)
Marvel/Children's TV Workshop

	Good	Fine	Mint
1-(Stories simplified)		.30	.60
2-57		.25	.50

SPIKE AND TYKE (See M.G.M.'s...)

SPIN & MARTY (TV) (Walt Disney's)
No. 714, June, 1956 - No. 1082, Mar-May, 1960 (All photo-c)
Dell Publishing Co. (Mickey Mouse Club)

	Good	Fine	Mint
4-Color 714	3.00	9.00	21.00
4-Color 767,808	2.65	8.00	18.00
4-Color 826-Annette Funicello photo-c	5.00	15.00	35.00
5(3-5/58) - 9(6-8/59)	2.35	7.00	16.00
4-Color 1026,1082	2.35	7.00	16.00

SPINE-TINGLING TALES (Doctor Spektor Presents...)
May, 1975 - No. 4, Jan, 1976
Gold Key

	Good	Fine	Mint
1-1st Tragg r-/Mystery Comics Digest No. 3		.40	.80
2-Origin Ra-Ka-Tep r-/Mystery Comics Digest No. 1; Dr. Spektor/No. 12		.40	.80
3-All Durak issue; (r)		.40	.80
4-Baron Tibor's 1st app. r-/Mystery Comics Digest No. 4		.40	.80

SPIRAL PATH, THE
July, 1986 - No. 2, 1986 ($1.75, Baxter, color)
Eclipse Comics

	Good	Fine	Mint
1,2	.30	.90	1.80

SPIRIT, THE (Weekly Comic Book)
6/2/40 - 10/5/52 (16 pgs.; 8 pgs.) (no cover) (in color)
(Distributed through various newspapers and other sources)
Will Eisner

NOTE: ***Eisner** script, pencils/inks for the most part from 6/2/40-4/26/42; a few stories assisted by Jack Cole, Fine, Powell and Kotsky.*

	Good	Fine	Mint
6/2/40(No.1)-Origin; reprinted in Police No. 11; Lady Luck (Brenda Banks) by Chuck Mazoujian & Mr. Mystic by S. R. (Bob) Powell begin	75.00	220.00	485.00
6/9/40(No.2)	30.00	90.00	200.00
6/16/40(No.3)-Black Queen app. in Spirit	20.00	60.00	125.00
6/23/40(No.4)-Mr. Mystic receives magical necklace	17.00	50.00	105.00
6/30/40(No.5)	17.00	50.00	105.00
7/7/40(No.6)-Black Queen app. in Spirit	17.00	50.00	105.00
7/14/40(No.7)-8/4/40(No.10)	12.50	37.50	75.00
8/11/40-9/22/40	12.00	35.00	70.00
9/29/40-Ellen drops engagement with Homer Creep	10.00	30.00	60.00
10/6/40-11/3/40	10.00	30.00	60.00
11/10/40-The Black Queen app.	10.00	30.00	60.00
11/17/40, 11/24/40	10.00	30.00	60.00
12/1/40-Ellen spanking by Spirit on cover & inside; Eisner-1st 3 pgs., J. Cole rest	15.00	45.00	90.00
12/8/40-3/9/41	7.75	23.00	46.00
3/16/41-Intro. & 1st app. Silk Satin	13.00	40.00	80.00
3/23/41-6/1/41: 5/11/41-Last Lady Luck by Mazoujian; 5/18/41-Lady Luck by Nick Viscardi begins, ends 2/22/42	7.75	23.00	46.00
6/8/41-2nd app. Satin; Spirit learns Satin is also a British agent	12.00	35.00	70.00
6/15/41-1st app. Twilight	9.20	27.50	55.00
6/22/41-Hitler app. in Spirit	7.00	21.00	42.00
6/29/41-1/25/42,2/8/42	7.00	21.00	42.00
2/1/42-1st app. Duchess	9.20	27.50	55.00
2/15/42-4/26/42-Lady Luck by Klaus Nordling begins 3/1/42	7.00	21.00	42.00

THE SPIRIT (continued)

	Good	Fine	Mint
5/3/42-8/16/42-Eisner/Fine/Quality staff assists on Spirit	4.00	12.00	24.00
8/23/42-Satin cover splash; Spirit by Eisner/Fine although signed by Fine	10.00	30.00	60.00
8/30/42,9/27/42-10/11/42,10/25/42-11/8/42-Eisner/Fine/Quality staff assists on Spirit	4.00	12.00	24.00
9/6/42-9/20/42,10/18/42-Fine/Belfi art on Spirit; scripts by Manly Wade Wellman	2.75	8.00	16.00
11/15/42-12/6/42,12/20/42,12/27/42,1/17/43-4/18/43, 5/9/43-8/8/43-Wellman/Woolfolk scripts, Fine pencils, Quality staff inks	2.75	8.00	16.00
12/13/42,1/3/43,1/10/43,4/25/43,5/2/43-Eisner scripts/layouts; Fine pencils, Quality staff inks	3.35	10.00	20.00
8/15/43-Eisner script/layout; pencils/inks by Quality staff; Jack Cole-a	2.00	6.00	12.00
8/22/43-12/12/43-Wellman/Woolfolk scripts, Fine pencils, Quality staff inks; Mr. Mystic by Guardineer-10/10/43-10/24/43	2.00	6.00	12.00
12/19/43-8/13/44-Wellman/Woolfolk/Jack Cole scripts; art by Cole, Fine & Robin King; Last Mr. Mystic-5/14/44	1.70	5.00	10.00
8/22/44-12/16/45-Wellman/Woolfolk scripts; Fine art with unknown staff assists	1.70	5.00	10.00

NOTE: *Scripts/layouts by Eisner, or Eisner/Nordling, Eisner/Mercer or Spranger/Eisner; inks by Eisner or Eisner/Spranger in issues 12/23/45-2/2/47.*

	Good	Fine	Mint
12/23/45-1/6/46	5.35	16.00	32.00
1/13/46-Origin Spirit retold	8.50	25.00	50.00
1/20/46-1st postwar Satin app.	7.50	22.50	45.00
1/27/46-3/10/46: 3/3/46-Last Lady Luck by Nordling	5.35	16.00	32.00
3/17/46-Intro. & 1st app. Nylon	7.50	22.50	45.00
3/24/46,3/31/46,4/14/46	5.35	16.00	32.00
4/7/46-2nd app. Nylon	7.00	20.00	40.00
4/21/46-Intro. & 1st app. Mr. Carrion & His Buzzard Pet Julia	9.20	27.50	55.00
4/28/46-5/12/46,5/26/46-6/30/46: Lady Luck by Fred Schwab in issues 5/5/46-11/3/46	5.35	16.00	32.00
5/19/46-2nd app. Mr. Carrion	6.75	20.00	40.00
7/7/46-Intro. & 1st app. Dulcet Tone & Skinny	8.35	25.00	50.00
7/14/46-9/29/46	5.35	16.00	32.00
10/6/46-Intro. & 1st app. P'Gell	10.00	30.00	60.00
10/13/46-11/3/46,11/16/46-11/24/46	5.35	16.00	32.00
11/10/46-2nd app. P'Gell	7.00	21.00	42.00
12/1/46-3rd app. P'Gell	6.00	18.00	36.00
12/8/46-2/2/47	5.00	15.00	30.00

NOTE: *Scripts, pencils/inks by Eisner except where noted in issues 2/9/47-12/19/48.*

	Good	Fine	Mint
2/9/47-7/6/47: 6/8/47-Eisner self satire	5.00	15.00	30.00
7/13/47-"Hansel & Gretel" fairy tales	7.50	22.50	45.00
7/20/47-Li'L Abner, Daddy Warbucks, Dick Tracy, Fearless Fosdick parody; A-Bomb blast-c	7.50	22.50	45.00
7/27/47-9/14/47	5.00	15.00	30.00
9/21/47-Pearl Harbor flashback	5.00	15.00	30.00
9/28/47-1st mention of Flying Saucers in comics-3 months after 1st sighting in Idaho on 6/25/47	11.00	32.00	64.00
10/5/47-"Cinderella" fairy tales	7.50	22.50	45.00
10/12/47-11/30/47	5.00	15.00	30.00
12/7/47-Intro. & 1st app. Powder Pouf	8.50	25.50	50.00
12/14/47-12/28/47	5.00	15.00	30.00
1/4/48-2nd app. Powder Pouf	6.75	20.00	40.00
1/11/48-1st app. Sparrow Fallon; Powder Pouf app.	6.75	20.00	40.00
1/18/48-He-Man ad cover; satire issue	6.75	20.00	40.00
1/25/48-Intro. & 1st app. Castanet	7.50	22.50	45.00
2/1/48-2nd app. Castanet	5.35	16.00	32.00
2/8/48-3/7/48	5.00	15.00	30.00
3/14/48-Only app. Kretchma	5.35	16.00	32.00
3/21/48,3/28/48,4/11/48-4/25/48	5.00	15.00	30.00
4/4/48-Only app. Wild Rice	5.35	16.00	32.00
5/2/48-2nd app. Sparrow	5.00	15.00	30.00
5/9/48-6/27/48,7/11/48,7/18/48	5.00	15.00	30.00
7/4/48-Spirit by Andre Le Blanc	2.75	8.00	16.00
7/25/48-Ambrose Bierce's "The Thing" adaptation classic by Eisner/Grandenetti	11.00	32.00	64.00
8/1/48-8/15/48,8/29/48-9/12/48	5.00	15.00	30.00
8/22/48-Poe's "Fall of the House of Usher" classic by Eisner/Grandenetti	11.00	32.00	64.00
9/19/48-Only app. Lorelei	6.00	18.00	36.00
9/26/48-10/31/48	5.00	15.00	30.00
11/7/48-Only app. Plaster of Paris	6.75	20.00	40.00
11/14/48-12/19/48	5.00	15.00	30.00

NOTE: *Scripts by Eisner or Feiffer or Eisner/Feiffer or Nordling. Art by Eisner with backgrounds by Eisner, Grandenetti, Le Blanc, Stallman, Nordling, Dixon and/or others in issues 12/26/48-4/1/51 except where noted.*

	Good	Fine	Mint
12/26/48-Reprints some covers of 1948 with flashbacks	5.00	15.00	30.00
1/2/49-1/16/49	5.00	15.00	30.00
1/23/49,1/30/49-1st & 2nd app. Thorne	6.75	20.00	40.00
2/6/49-8/14/49	5.00	15.00	30.00
8/21/49,8/28/49-1st & 2nd app. Monica Veto	6.75	20.00	40.00
9/4/49,9/11/49	5.00	15.00	30.00
9/18/49-Love comic cover; has gag love comic ads on inside	7.35	22.00	44.00
9/25/49-Only app. Ice	6.35	19.00	38.00
10/2/49,10/9/49-Autumn News appears & dies in 10/9 ish.	6.35	19.00	38.00
10/16/49-11/27/49,12/18/49,12/25/49	5.00	15.00	30.00
12/4/49,12/11/49-1st & 2nd app. Flaxen	6.00	18.00	36.00
1/1/50-Flashbacks to all of the Spirit girls-Thorne, Ellen, Satin, & Monica	9.00	27.00	54.00
1/8/50-Intro. & 1st app. Sand Saref	12.00	36.00	72.00
1/15/50-2nd app. Saref	9.20	27.50	55.00
1/22/50-2/5/50	5.00	15.00	30.00
2/12/50-Roller Derby ish.	5.75	17.00	34.00
2/19/50-Half Dead Mr. Lox - Classic horror	6.35	19.00	38.00
2/26/50-4/23/50,5/14/50,5/28/50,7/23/50-9/3/50	5.00	15.00	30.00
4/30/50-Script/art by Le Blanc with Eisner framing	1.70	5.00	10.00
5/7/50,6/4/50-7/16/50-Abe Kanegson-a	1.70	5.00	10.00
5/21/50-Script by Feiffer/Eisner, art by Blaisdell, Eisner framing	1.70	5.00	10.00
9/10/50-P'Gell returns	6.75	20.00	40.00
9/17/50-1/7/51	5.00	15.00	30.00
1/14/51-Life Magazine cover; brief biography of Comm. Dolan, Sand Saref, Silk Satin, P'Gell, Sammy & Willum, Darling O'Shea, & Mr. Carrion & His Pet Buzzard Julia, with pin-ups by Eisner	6.35	19.00	38.00
1/21/51,2/4/51-4/1/51	5.00	15.00	30.00
1/28/51-"The Meanest Man in the World" classic by Eisner	6.35	19.00	38.00
4/8/51-7/29/51,8/12/51-Last Eisner issue	5.00	15.00	30.00
8/5/51,8/19/51-7/20/52-Not Eisner	1.70	5.00	10.00
7/27/52-(Rare)-Denny Colt in Outer Space by Wally Wood; 7 pg. S/F story of E.C. vintage	70.00	200.00	350.00
8/3/52-(Rare)-"Mission. . . The Moon" by Wood	70.00	200.00	350.00
8/10/52-(Rare)-"A DP On The Moon" by Wood	70.00	200.00	350.00
8/17/52-(Rare)-"Heart" by Wood/Eisner	55.00	160.00	285.00
8/24/52-(Rare)-"Rescue" by Wood	70.00	200.00	350.00

The Spirit, 5/25/47, © Will Eisner

The Spirit, 4/3/49, © Will Eisner

The Spirit, 8/3/52, © Will Eisner

The Spirit #22 (Quality), © Will Eisner

The Spirit #4 (FH), © Will Eisner

Spitfire #133, © EP

THE SPIRIT (continued) — Good / Fine / Mint

8/31/52-(Rare)-''The Last Man'' by Wood 70.00 200.00 350.00
9/7/52-(Rare)-''The Man in The Moon'' by Wood
70.00 200.00 350.00
9/14/52-(Rare)-Eisner/Wenzel-a 10.00 30.00 60.00
9/21/52-(Rare)-''Denny Colt, Alias The Spirit/Space Report'' by Eisner/Wenzel 20.00 60.00 125.00
9/28/52-(Rare)-''Return From The Moon'' by Wood
70.00 200.00 350.00
10/5/52-(Rare)-''The Last Story'' by Eisner 20.00 60.00 125.00
Large Tabloid pages from 1946 on (Eisner) - Price 30 percent over listed prices.

NOTE: *Spirit sections came out in both large and small format. Some newspapers went to the 8-pg. format months before others. Some printed the pages so they cannot be folded into a small comic book section; these are worth less. (Also see Three Comics & Spiritman).*

SPIRIT, THE (Section)
January 9, 1966
N. Y. Sunday Herald Tribune

New 5-pg. Spirit story by Eisner; 2 pg. article on super-heroes; 2 pgs. color strips (BC, Miss Peach, Peanuts, Wizard of Id)
13.00 40.00 80.00

SPIRIT, THE (1st Series)
1944 - No. 22, Aug, 1950
Quality Comics Group (Vital)

nn(No.1)-''Wanted Dead or Alive'' 37.00 110.00 260.00
nn(No.2)-''Crime Doesn't Pay'' 23.00 70.00 160.00
nn(No.3)-''Murder Runs Wild'' 17.00 51.00 120.00
4,5 13.00 40.00 90.00
6-10 11.50 34.50 80.00
11 10.00 30.00 70.00
12-17-Eisner-c 18.00 54.00 125.00
18-21-Strip-r by Eisner; Eisner-c 26.00 78.00 180.00
22-Used by N.Y. Legis. Comm; Classic Eisner-c
40.00 120.00 280.00
Super Reprint No. 11-Reprints Quality Spirit No. 19 by Eisner; Crandall-c 1.35 4.00 8.00
Super Reprint No. 12-Reprints Quality Spirit No. 17 by Fine
1.00 3.00 6.00

SPIRIT, THE (2nd Series)
Spring, 1952 - 1954
Fiction House Magazines

1-Not Eisner 16.00 48.00 110.00
2-Eisner c/a(2) 19.00 57.00 132.00
3-Eisner/Grandenetti-c 13.00 40.00 90.00
4-Eisner/Grandenetti-c; Eisner-a 16.00 48.00 110.00
5-Eisner c/a(4) 19.00 57.00 132.00

SPIRIT, THE
Oct, 1966 - No. 2, Mar, 1967 (Giant Size, 68 pgs.)
Harvey Publications

1-Eisner-r plus 9 new pgs.(Origin Denny Colt, Take 3, plus 2 filler pages) 4.00 12.00 24.00
2-Eisner-r plus 9 new pgs.(Origin of the Octopus)
4.00 12.00 24.00

SPIRIT, THE (Underground)
Jan, 1973 - No. 2, Sept, 1973 (Black & White)
Kitchen Sink Enterprises (Krupp Comics)

1-New Eisner-c, 4 pgs. new Eisner-a plus-r (titled Crime Convention) 1.00 3.00 6.00
2-New Eisner-c, 4 pgs. new Eisner-a plus-r(titled Meets P'Gell)
1.35 4.00 8.00

SPIRIT, THE
Oct, 1983 - Present (Baxter paper)
Kitchen Sink Enterprises

Good / Fine / Mint

1-Origin; r/12/23/45 Spirit Section .30 .90 1.80
2-r/sections 1/20/46-2/10/46 .30 .90 1.80
3-r/sections 2/17/46-3/10/46 .30 .90 1.80
4-r/sections 3/17/46-4/7/46 .30 .90 1.80
5-11 ($2.95 cover) .50 1.50 3.00
12-26 ($1.95 cover, B&W) .35 1.00 2.00
. . . In 3-D (11/85)-Eisner-r; new Eisner-c .35 1.00 2.00

SPIRIT, THE (Magazine)
4/74 - No. 16, 10/76; No. 17, Winter, 1977 - No. 41, 6/83
Warren Publ. Co./Krupp Comic Works No. 17 on

1-Eisner-r begin .80 2.40 4.80
2-5 .50 1.50 3.00
6-9,11-16: 7-All Ebony ish. 8-Female Foes ish. 12-X-Mas ish.
.40 1.20 2.40
10-Origin .50 1.40 2.80
17,18(8/78) .60 1.20
19-21-New Eisner-a plus Wood No. 20,21 .60 1.20
22,23-Wood-r .60 1.20
24-35: 28-r-last story (10/5/52) .60 1.20
36-Begin Spirit Section-r; r-1st story (6/2/40) in color; new Eisner c/a (18 pgs.)($2.95) .50 1.50 3.00
37-r-2nd story in color plus 18 pgs. new Eisner-a
.50 1.50 3.00
38-41: r-3rd-6th story in color .50 1.50 3.00
Special 1('75)-All Eisner-a .30 .90 1.80

NOTE: *Covers pencilled/inked by* **Eisner** *only No. 1-9,12-16; painted by Eisner & Ken Kelly No. 10 & 11; painted by Eisner No. 17-up; one color story reprinted in No. 1-10.* **Austin** *a-30i.* **Byrne** *a-30p.* **Miller** *a-30p.*

SPIRITMAN (Also see Three Comics)
No date (1944) (10 cents)
(Triangle Sales Co. ad on back cover)
No publisher listed

1-Three 16pg. Spirit sections bound together, (1944, 48 pgs., 10 cents) 12.00 35.00 84.00
2-Two Spirit sections (3/26/44, 4/2/44) bound together; by Lou Fine 9.20 27.50 64.00

SPIRIT WORLD (Magazine)
Fall, 1971 (Black & White)
National Periodical Publications

1-Kirby-a/Adams-c .70 2.00 4.00

SPITFIRE
1944 (Aug) - 1945 (Female undercover agent)
Malverne Herald (Elliot)(J. R. Mahon)

132,133: Both have Classics Gift Box ads on b/c with checklist to No. 20 5.00 15.00 35.00

SPITFIRE AND THE TROUBLESHOOTERS
Oct, 1986 - Present
Marvel Comics Group

1 .50 1.00
2-6 .40 .80

SPITFIRE COMICS (Also see Double Up)
Aug, 1941 - No. 2, Oct, 1941 (Pocket size; 100 pgs.)
Harvey Publications

1-Origin The Clown, The Fly-Man, The Spitfire & The Magician From Bagdad 19.00 57.00 132.00
2 16.00 48.00 110.00

SPOOF!
Oct, 1970 - No. 2, Nov, 1972 - No. 5, May, 1973
Marvel Comics Group

1-Infinity-c .30 .60
2-5 .25 .50

SPOOK (Formerly Shock Detective Cases)
No. 22, Jan, 1953 - No. 30, Oct, 1954
Star Publications

	Good	Fine	Mint
22-Sgt. Spook-r; acid in face story	7.00	21.00	50.00
23,25,27: 27-two Sgt. Spook-r	5.00	15.00	35.00
24-Used in **SOTI**, pg. 182,183-r/Inside Crime 2; Transvestite story	7.50	22.50	52.00
26-Disbrow-a	5.75	17.00	40.00
28,29-Rulah app.; Jo-Jo in No. 29	5.75	17.00	40.00
30-Disbrow c/a(2); only Star-c	5.75	17.00	40.00

NOTE: ***L. B. Cole*** *covers-all issues; a-28(1pg.).* ***Disbrow*** *a-26(2), 28, 29(2), 30(2); No. 30 r-/Blue Bolt Weird Tales No. 114.*

SPOOK COMICS
1946
Baily Publications/Star

1-Mr. Lucifer app.	7.00	21.00	50.00

SPOOKY (The Tuff Little Ghost)
11/55 - 139, 11/73; No. 140, 7/74 - No. 155, 3/77; No. 156, 12/77 - No. 158, 4/78; No. 159, 9/78; No. 160, 10/79; No. 161, 9/80
Harvey Publications

1-Nightmare begins (See Casper 19)	12.00	36.00	84.00
2	6.00	18.00	42.00
3-10(1956-57)	3.00	9.00	21.00
11-20(1957-58)	1.50	4.50	10.00
21-40(1958-59)	.70	2.00	5.00
41-60	.50	1.50	3.00
61-80	.35	1.10	2.20
81-100	.30	.90	1.80
101-120	.25	.70	1.40
121-140		.60	1.20
141-161		.40	.80

SPOOKY HAUNTED HOUSE
Oct, 1972 - No. 15, Feb, 1975
Harvey Publications

1	1.00	3.00	6.00
2-5	.50	1.50	3.00
6-10	.30	.80	1.60
11-15		.60	1.20

SPOOKY MYSTERIES
No date (1946) (10 cents)
Your Guide Publ. Co.

1-Mr. Spooky, Super Snooper, Pinky, Girl Detective app.	3.35	10.00	23.00

SPOOKY SPOOKTOWN
6/62 - No. 52, 12/73; No. 53, 10/74 - No. 66, Dec, 1976
Harvey Publications

1-Casper, Spooky	5.85	17.50	35.00
2	3.00	9.00	18.00
3-5	2.75	8.00	16.00
6-10	1.35	4.00	8.00
11-20	1.00	3.00	6.00
21-40	.50	1.50	3.00
41-66	.30	.80	1.60

SPORT COMICS (True Sport Picture Stories No. 4 on?)
Oct, 1940(No mo.) - No. 4, Nov, 1941
Street & Smith Publications

1-Life story of Lou Gehrig	11.50	34.50	80.00
2	5.50	16.50	40.00
3,4	5.00	15.00	35.00

SPORT LIBRARY (See Charlton Sport . . .)

SPORTS ACTION (Formerly Sport Stars)
No. 2, Feb, 1950 - No. 14, Sept, 1952
Marvel/Atlas Comics (ACI No. 2,3/SAI No. 4-14)

	Good	Fine	Mint
2	4.00	12.00	28.00
3-Everett-a	3.35	10.00	23.00
4-11,14: Weiss-a. 9,10-Maneely-c	2.85	8.50	20.00
12-Everett-c	3.35	10.00	23.00
13-Krigstein-a	3.65	11.00	25.00

NOTE: *Title may have changed after No. 3, to Crime Must Lose No. 4 on, due to publisher change.*

SPORT STARS
2-3/46 - No. 4, 8-9/46 (½ comic, ½ photo magazine)
Parents' Magazine Institute (Sport Stars)

1-"How Tarzan Got That Way" story of Johnny Weissmuller	7.00	21.00	50.00
2-Baseball greats	5.00	15.00	35.00
3,4	3.50	10.50	24.00

SPORT STARS (Sports Action No. 2)
Nov, 1949
Marvel Comics (ACI)

1-Knute Rockne; painted-c	7.00	21.00	50.00

SPORT THRILLS (Formerly Dick Cole)
No. 11, Nov, 1950 - No. 15, Nov, 1951
Star Publications

11-Dick Cole app.	4.00	12.00	28.00
12-L. B. Cole c/a	3.35	10.00	23.00
13-15-All L. B. Cole-c; 13-Dick Cole app.	3.35	10.00	23.00
Accepted Reprint No. 11 (No. 15 on-c, nd); L.B. Cole-c	1.70	5.00	12.00
Accepted Reprint No. 12 (nd); L.B. Cole-c	1.70	5.00	12.00

SPOTLIGHT (TV)
Sept, 1978 - No. 4, Mar, 1979 (Hanna-Barbera)
Marvel Comics Group

1-Huckleberry Hound, 2-Quick Draw McGraw, 3-The Jetsons, 4-Magilla Gorilla		.25	.50

SPOTLIGHT COMICS
Nov, 1944 - No. 3, 1945
Harry 'A' Chesler (Our Army, Inc.)

1-The Black Dwarf, The Veiled Avenger, & Barry Kuda begin; Tuska-c	16.00	48.00	110.00
2	13.50	40.50	95.00
3-Injury to eye story(Same as Scoop No. 3)	13.50	40.50	95.00

SPOTTY THE PUP
No. 2, Oct-Nov?, 1953 - No. 3, Dec-Jan, 1953-54
Avon Periodicals

2,3	1.30	4.00	9.00

SPUNKY (. . .Junior Cowboy)(. . .Comics No. 2 on)
April, 1949 - No. 7, Nov, 1951
Standard Comics

1,2-Text illos by Frazetta	3.00	9.00	21.00
3-7	1.15	3.50	8.00

SPUNKY THE SMILING SPOOK
Aug, 1957 - No. 4, May, 1958
Ajax/Farrell (World Famous Comics/Four Star Comic Corp.)

1-Reprints from Frisky Fables	1.75	5.25	12.00
2-4	1.00	3.00	7.00

SPY AND COUNTERSPY (Spy Hunters No. 3 on)
Aug-Sept, 1949 - No. 2, Oct-Nov, 1949

Spooky Mysteries #1, © Your Guide

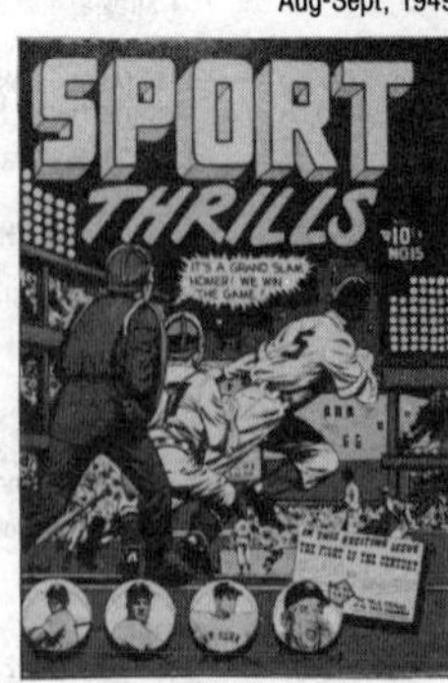

Sport Thrills #15, © STAR

Spotlight Comics #1, © CHES

Spy Cases #28, © MCG

Spy Smasher #6, © FAW

Star Comics #5, © CEN

SPY AND COUNTERSPY (continued)
American Comics Group

	Good	Fine	Mint
1-Origin, 1st app. Jonathan Kent, Counterspy	4.00	12.00	28.00
2	2.85	8.50	20.00

SPY CASES (Formerly The Kellys)
No. 26, Sept, 1950 - No. 19, Oct, 1953
Marvel/Atlas Comics (Hercules Publ.)

	Good	Fine	Mint
26	3.75	11.25	26.00
27,28(2/51): 27-Everett-a; bondage-c	2.85	8.50	20.00
4(4/51)-6,7,9,10: 7-Tuska-a	1.65	5.00	11.50
8-A-Bomb-c/story	1.85	5.50	13.00
11-19: 13-War format	1.50	4.50	10.00

SPY FIGHTERS
March, 1951 - No. 15, July, 1953
Marvel/Atlas Comics (CSI)

	Good	Fine	Mint
1	3.75	11.25	26.00
2	1.85	5.50	13.00
3-13	1.50	4.50	10.00
14,15-Pakula-a(3), Ed Win-a	1.70	5.00	12.00

SPY-HUNTERS (Formerly Spy & Counterspy)
No. 3, Dec-Jan, 1949-50 - No. 24, June-July, 1953
American Comics Group

	Good	Fine	Mint
3-Jonathan Kent begins, ends No. 10	4.00	12.00	28.00
4-10: 8-Starr-a	2.65	8.00	18.00
11-15,17-22,24	1.70	5.00	11.50
16-Williamson-a (9 pgs.)	5.50	16.50	38.00
23-Graphic torture, injury to eye panel	5.50	16.50	38.00

NOTE: ***Whitney** a-many issues; c-8, 10, 11, 16.*

SPYMAN (Top Secret Adventures on cover)
Sept, 1966 - No. 3, Feb, 1967
Harvey Publications

	Good	Fine	Mint
1-Steranko-a(p)-1st pro work; 1pg. Adams ad; Tuska c/a, Crandall-a(i)	.50	1.50	3.00
2,3: Simon-c. 2-Steranko-a(p)	.35	1.00	2.00

SPY SMASHER (See Mighty Midget Comics)
Fall, 1941 - No. 11, Feb, 1943
Fawcett Publications

	Good	Fine	Mint
1-Spy Smasher begins; silver metallic-c	82.00	245.00	575.00
2-Raboy-c	42.00	126.00	294.00
3,4: 3-Bondage-c	35.00	105.00	245.00
5-7: Raboy-a; 6-Raboy c/a	30.00	90.00	210.00
8-11: 10-Hitler-c	26.00	78.00	182.00
Well Known Comics (1944, 12 pgs., 8½x10½'', paper-c, glued binding, printed in green; Bestmaid/Samuel Lowe giveaway	15.00	45.00	90.00

SPY THRILLERS (Police Badge No. 479 No. 5)
Nov, 1954 - No. 4, May, 1955
Atlas Comics (PrPI)

	Good	Fine	Mint
1	2.85	8.50	20.00
2-Last precode (1/55)	1.50	4.50	10.00
3,4	1.30	4.00	9.00

SQUADRON SUPREME
Sept, 1985 - No. 12, Aug, 1986 (maxi-series)
Marvel Comics Group

	Good	Fine	Mint
1	.30	.90	1.80
2-11		.50	1.00
12-Double size ($1.25)	.25	.75	1.50

SQUEEKS
Oct, 1953 - No. 5, June, 1954
Lev Gleason Publications

	Good	Fine	Mint
1-Biro-c	2.15	6.50	15.00
2-Biro-c	1.15	3.50	8.00
3-5: 3-Biro-c	1.00	3.00	7.00

STAINLESS STEEL RAT
Oct, 1985 - No. 6, Mar, 1986 (limited-series)
Eagle Comics

	Good	Fine	Mint
1 (52 pgs.; $2.25 cover)	.35	1.10	2.20
2-6 (36 pgs.)	.25	.75	1.50

STALKER
June-July, 1975 - No. 4, Dec-Jan, 1975-76
National Periodical Publications

	Good	Fine	Mint
1-Origin & 1st app; Ditko/Wood c/a		.40	.80
2-4-Ditko/Wood c/a		.30	.60

STAMP COMICS (Stamps. . . on-c; Thrilling Advs. In. . No. 8)
Oct, 1951 - No. 7, Oct, 1952 (No. 1: 15 cents)
Youthful Magazines/Stamp Comics, Inc.

	Good	Fine	Mint
1('Stamps' on indicia No. 1)	7.00	21.00	50.00
2	4.35	13.00	30.00
3-6: 3,4-Kiefer, Wildey-a	3.65	11.00	25.00
7-Roy Krenkel, 4 pgs.	7.00	21.00	50.00

NOTE: *Promotes stamp collecting; gives stories behind various commemorative stamps. No. 2, 10 cents printed over 15 cents c-price. **Kiefer** a-1-7. **Kirkel** a-1-6. **Napoli** a-2-7. **Palais** a-2-4, 7.*

STANLEY & HIS MONSTER (Formerly The Fox & the Crow)
No. 109, Apr-May, 1968 - No. 112, Oct-Nov, 1968
National Periodical Publications

	Good	Fine	Mint
109-112	.70	2.00	4.00

STAR BRAND
Oct, 1986 - Present
Marvel Comics Group

	Good	Fine	Mint
1	.25	.75	1.50
2		.45	.90
3-6: 3-Williamson-i		.40	.80

STAR COMICS
Feb, 1937 - V2No.7 (No. 23), Aug, 1939 (No. 1-6: large size)
Ultem Publ. (Harry 'A' Chesler)/Centaur Publications

	Good	Fine	Mint
V1No.1-Dan Hastings (s/f) begins	45.00	135.00	315.00
2	22.00	65.00	154.00
3-6 (No. 6, 9/37): 5-Little Nemo	20.00	60.00	140.00
7-9: 8-Severed head centerspread; Impy & Little Nemo by Windsor McKay Jr, Popeye app. by Bob Wood; Mickey Mouse-c app.	18.00	54.00	125.00
10 (1st Centaur; 3/38)-Impy by Winsor McCay Jr; Don Marlow by Guardineer begins	27.00	81.00	190.00
11-15: 12-Riders of the Golden West begins; Little Nemo app. 15-Speed Silvers by Gustavson & The Last Pirate by Burgos begins	17.00	51.00	120.00
16 (12/38)-The Phantom Rider begins, ends V2/6	17.00	51.00	120.00
V2No.1(No. 17, 2/39)	17.00	51.00	120.00
2-7(No. 18-23): 2-Diana Deane by Tarpe Mills app. 3-Drama of Hollywood by Mills begins. 7-Jungle Queen app.	15.00	45.00	105.00

NOTE: ***Biro** c-9, 10. **Burgos** a-15, 16, V2/1-7. **Ken Ernst** a-10, 12, 14. **Gill Fox** c-V2/2. **Guardineer** a-6, 8-10, 12-14. **Gustavson** a-13-16, V2/1-7. **Tarpe Mills** a-15, V2/1-7. **Bob Wood** a-10, 12, 13; c-8.*

STAR COMICS DIGEST
Dec, 1986 - Present ($1.50, Digest-size)
Star Comics (Marvel)

	Good	Fine	Mint
1-Heathcliff, Muppet Babies, Ewoks, Carebears, Top Dog app.	.25	.75	1.50

STAR FEATURE COMICS
1963
I. W. Enterprises

	Good	Fine	Mint
Reprint No. 9-Stunt-Man Stetson app.	.50	1.50	3.00

STARFIRE
Aug-Sept, 1976 - No. 8, Oct-Nov, 1977
National Periodical Publications/DC Comics

1-Origin & 1st app; (CCA stamp fell off cover art; so it **was** approved by code)		.50	1.00
2-8		.30	.60

STAR FORCE SIX SPECIAL
Nov?, 1984 (B&W)
Americomics

1	.35	1.00	2.00

STAR HUNTERS (See DC Super Stars No. 16)
Oct-Nov, 1977 - No. 7, Oct-Nov, 1978
National Periodical Publications/DC Comics

1-Newton-a(p)		.30	.60
2-6		.25	.50
7-Giant		.30	.60

NOTE: ***Buckler*** *a-4p-7p; c-1p-7p.* ***Layton*** *a-1i-5i; c-1i-6i.* ***Nasser*** *a-3p.* ***Sutton*** *a-6i.*

STARK: FUTURE
Aug, 1986 - Present ($1.70, B&W)
Aircel Publishing

1	.40	1.25	2.50
2,3	.35	1.00	2.00
4-6	.30	.85	1.70

STARK TERROR (Magazine)
Dec, 1970 - No. 5, Aug, 1971 (52 pages) (B&W)
Stanley Publications

1-Bondage, torture-c	.50	1.50	3.00
2-4 (Gillmor/Aragon-r)	.30	.80	1.60
5 (ACG-r)		.60	1.20

STARLET O'HARA IN HOLLYWOOD
Dec, 1948 - No. 4, Sept, 1949
Standard Comics

1-Owen Fitzgerald-a in all	5.75	17.25	40.00
2	3.65	11.00	25.00
3,4	3.35	10.00	23.00

STAR-LORD (Also see Marvel Spotlight V2/6,7)
Feb, 1982 (One Shot) (Direct sale, Baxter paper)
Marvel Comics Group

1-Byrne/Austin-a; Austin-c, Golden-a(p)	.40	1.25	2.50

STARMAN (See Adventure, First Issue Special, Showcase, & Justice League)

STARMASTERS
Mar, 1984
Americomics

1-The Women of W.O.S.P. & Breed begin	.25	.75	1.50

STAR PRESENTATION, A (Formerly My Secret Romance No. 1,2; Spectacular Stories No. 4) (Also see This Is Suspense)
No. 3, May, 1950
Fox Features Syndicate (Hero Books)

3-Dr. Jekyll & Mr. Hyde by Wood & Harrison (reprinted in Startling Terror Tales No. 10); 'The Repulsing Dwarf' by Wood; Wood-c	43.00	130.00	300.00

STAR QUEST COMIX (Warren Presents . . . on cover)
October, 1978
Warren Publications

	Good	Fine	Mint
1		.50	1.00

STAR RAIDERS (See DC Graphic Novel No. 1)

STAR RANGER (Cowboy Comics No. 13 on)
Feb, 1937 - No. 12, May, 1938 (Large size: No. 1-6)
Ultem Publ./Centaur Publications

1-(1st Western comic)-Ace & Deuce, Air Plunder	45.00	135.00	315.00
2	22.00	65.00	154.00
3-6	20.00	60.00	140.00
7-9: 8-Christmas-c	18.00	54.00	125.00
V2No.10 (1st Centaur; 3/38)	27.00	81.00	190.00
11,12	17.00	51.00	120.00

NOTE: ***J. Cole*** *a-10, 12; c-12.* ***Ken Ernst*** *a-11.* ***Gill Fox*** *a-8(illo), 9, 10.* ***Guardineer*** *a-3, 6, 7, 8(illos), 9, 10, 12.* ***Gustavson*** *a-8-10, 12.* ***Bob Wood*** *a-8-10.*

STAR RANGER FUNNIES (Formerly Cowboy Comics?)
V1No.15, Oct, 1938 - V2No.5, Oct, 1939
Centaur Publications

V1No.15-Eisner, Gustavson-a	28.00	84.00	195.00
V2No.1 (1/39)	20.00	60.00	140.00
2-5: 2-Night Hawk by Gustavson. 4-Kit Carson app.	18.00	54.00	125.00

NOTE: ***Jack Cole*** *a-V2/1,3; c-V2/1.* ***Guardineer*** *a-V2/3.* ***Gustavson*** *a-V2/2.* ***Pinajian*** *c/a-V2/5.*

STAR REACH CLASSICS
Mar, 1984 - No. 6, Aug, 1984 ($1.50; color; Baxter paper)
Eclipse Comics

1-Adams-r/Star Reach No. 1	.25	.75	1.50
2-6	.25	.75	1.50

NOTE: ***Brunner*** *c/a-4r.* ***Nino*** *a-3r.* ***Russell*** *c/a-3r.*

STARR FLAGG, UNDERCOVER GIRL (See Undercover . . .)

STARRIORS
Nov, 1984 - No. 4, Feb, 1985 (limited-series)
Marvel Comics Group

1-Based on Tomy Toy robots		.50	1.00
2-4		.45	.90

STARS AND STRIPES COMICS
May, 1941 - No. 6, Dec, 1941
Centaur Publications

2(No.1)-The Shark, The Iron Skull, Aman, The Amazing Man, Mighty Man, Minimidget begin; The Voice & Dash Dartwell, the Human Meteor, Reef Kinkaid app.; Gustavson Flag-c	72.00	215.00	505.00
3-Origin Dr. Synthe; The Black Panther app.	50.00	150.00	350.00
4-Origin/1st app. The Stars and Stripes; injury to eye-c	42.00	125.00	295.00
5(No.5 on cover & inside)	28.00	84.00	195.00
5(No.6)-(No.5 on cover, No.6 on inside)	28.00	84.00	195.00

NOTE: ***Gustavson*** *c/a-3.*

STARSLAYER
2/82 - No. 6, 4/83; No. 7, 8/83 - No. 34, 11/85
Pacific Comics/First Comics No. 7 on

1-Origin; excessive blood & gore	.45	1.40	2.80
2-Intro & origin the Rocketeer by Dave Stevens	.85	2.50	5.00
3-Rocketeer continues	.70	2.20	4.40
4-7: 5-Preview of Groo the Wanderer by Aragones	.25	.75	1.50

8-21: 10-Intro Grimjack (ends No. 17). 19-Starslayer meets Grim-

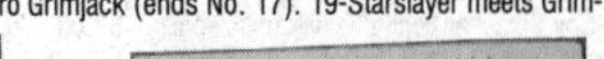

Stark: Future #1, © Aircel

Starlet O'Hara in Hollywood #1, © STD

Star Ranger #6 (9/37), © CEN

Star Spangled Comics #7, © DC

Star Spangled War Stories #39, © DC

Startling Comics #11, © BP

STARSLAYER (continued) — Good / Fine / Mint

jack; book length story. 20-The Black Flame begins, ends No. 33 — .50 1.00
22-34 ($1.25) — .65 1.30

NOTE: ***Grell*** *a-1-7; c-1-8.* ***Sutton*** *a-17p, 20-22p.*

STAR SPANGLED COMICS (. . . War Stories No. 131 on)
Oct, 1941 - No. 130, July, 1952
National Periodical Publications

	Good	Fine	Mint
1-Origin Tarantula; Captain X of the R.A.F., Star Spangled Kid(See Action No. 40) & Armstrong of the Army begin	93.00	280.00	650.00
2	46.00	138.00	322.00
3-5	30.00	90.00	210.00
6-Last Armstrong/Army	20.00	60.00	140.00
7-Origin/1st app. The Guardian by S&K, & Robotman by Paul Cassidy; The Newsboy Legion & TNT begin; last Captain X	122.00	366.00	854.00
8-Origin TNT & Dan the Dyna-Mite	60.00	180.00	420.00
9,10	54.00	162.00	375.00
11-17	42.00	125.00	294.00
18-Origin Star Spangled Kid	54.00	162.00	375.00
19-Last Tarantula	42.00	125.00	294.00
20-Liberty Belle begins	42.00	125.00	294.00
21-29-Last S&K issue; 23-Last TNT. 25-Robotman by Jimmy Thompson begins	30.00	90.00	210.00
30-40	15.00	45.00	105.00
41-50	12.00	36.00	84.00
51-64: Last Newsboy Legion & The Guardian; 53 by S&K	11.50	34.50	80.00
65-Robin begins	13.50	40.50	95.00
66-68,70-80	8.50	25.50	60.00
69-Origin Tomahawk	12.00	36.00	84.00
81-Origin Merry, Girl of 1000 Gimmicks	8.50	25.50	60.00
82-Last Star Spangled Kid	8.50	25.50	60.00
83-Capt. Compass begins, ends No. 130	8.50	25.50	60.00
84,87 (Rare)	10.00	30.00	70.00
85,86,88,95-99	7.00	21.00	50.00
89-94: Batman-c/stories in all. 91-Federal Men begin, end No. 93. 94-Manhunters Around the World begin, end No. 121	9.00	27.00	62.00
100	9.50	28.50	65.00
101-112,114,115,117-121: 114-Retells Robin's origin. 121-Last 52 pgs.	6.00	18.00	42.00
113-Frazetta-a, 10 pgs.	20.00	60.00	140.00
116-Flag-c	7.00	21.00	50.00
122-Ghost Breaker begins (origin), ends No. 130	6.00	18.00	42.00
123-129	5.75	17.25	40.00
130	6.85	20.50	48.00

NOTE: *Most all issues after No. 29 signed by* ***Simon & Kirby*** *are* ***not*** *by them.* ***Batman*** *c/stories-89-94.*

STAR SPANGLED WAR STORIES (Star Spangled Comics No. 1-130; The Unknown Soldier No. 205 on) (See Showcase)
No. 131, 8/52 - No. 133, 10/52; No. 3, 11/52 - No. 204, 2-3/77
National Periodical Publications

	Good	Fine	Mint
131(No.1)	19.00	57.00	132.00
132	11.50	34.50	80.00
133-Used in **POP**, Pg. 94	11.50	34.50	80.00
3-5: 4-Devil Dog Dugan app.	8.50	25.50	60.00
6-Evans-a	6.85	20.50	48.00
7-10	5.00	15.00	35.00
11-20	4.00	12.00	28.00
21-30	3.00	9.00	21.00
31-33,35-40	2.35	7.00	16.00
34-Krigstein-a	4.00	12.00	28.00
41-50	2.00	6.00	14.00
51-83: 67-Easy Co. story w/o Sgt. Rock	1.75	5.25	12.00
84-Origin Mlle. Marie	3.50	10.50	24.00
85-89-Mlle. Marie in all	2.00	6.00	14.00
90-1st Dinosaur issue	5.75	17.25	40.00
91-100	1.30	4.00	9.00
101-120	.75	2.25	5.00
121-133,135-137-Last dinosaur story; Heath Birdman-No. 129,131	.50	1.50	3.00
134,144-Adams-a plus Kubert No. 144	.85	2.50	5.00
138-Enemy Ace begins by Joe Kubert	.70	2.00	4.00
139-143,145-148,152,153,155	.45	1.25	2.50
149,150-Viking Prince by Kubert	.50	1.50	3.00
151-1st Unknown Soldier	.35	1.00	2.00
154-Origin Unknown Soldier	.35	1.00	2.00
156-1st Battle Album		.50	1.00
157-161-Last Enemy Ace		.50	1.00
162-204: 181-183-Enemy Ace vs. Balloon Buster serial app.		.40	.80

NOTE: ***Drucker*** *a-59, 61, 64, 66, 67, 73-84.* ***Estrada*** *a-149.* ***John Giunta*** *a-72.* ***Glanzman*** *a-167, 171, 172, 174.* ***Heath*** *c-67.* ***Kaluta*** *a-197i; c-167.* ***Kubert*** *a-6-138(most later issues), 200.* ***Maurer*** *a-160.* ***Severin*** *a-65.* ***Simonson*** *a-170, 172, 174, 180.* ***Sutton*** *a-168.* ***Thorne*** *a-183.* ***Toth*** *a-164.* ***Wildey*** *a-161. Suicide Squad in 110, 116-118, 120, 121, 127.*

STARSTREAM (Adventures in Science Fiction)
1976 (68 pgs.; cardboard covers) (79 cents)
Whitman/Western Publishing Co.

	Good	Fine	Mint
1-Bolle-a	.30	.80	1.60
2-4-McWilliams & Bolle-a		.60	1.20

STARSTRUCK
Feb, 1985 - No. 6, Feb, 1986 ($1.50; adults only)
Epic Comics (Marvel)

	Good	Fine	Mint
1-Nudity & strong language	.30	.85	1.70
2-6	.25	.70	1.40

NOTE: ***Kaluta*** *a-1-6; c-1-6.*

STAR STUDDED
1945 (25 cents; 132 pgs.); 1945 (196 pgs.)
Cambridge House/Superior Publishers

	Good	Fine	Mint
1-Captain Combat by Giunta, Ghost Woman, Commandette, & Red Rogue app.	10.00	30.00	70.00
nn-The Cadet, Edison Bell, Hoot Gibson, Jungle Lil (196 pgs.); copies vary - Blue Beetle in some	8.00	24.00	56.00

STAR TEAM
1977 (20 pgs.) (6½x5'')
Marvel Comics Group (Ideal Toy Giveaway)

	Good	Fine	Mint
nn		.15	.30

STARTLING COMICS
June, 1940 - No. 53, May, 1948
Better Publications (Nedor)

	Good	Fine	Mint
1-Origin Captain Future, Mystico (By Eisner/Fine), the Wonder Man; The Masked Rider begins; drug use story	52.00	156.00	362.00
2	23.00	70.00	160.00
3	17.00	51.00	120.00
4	12.00	36.00	84.00
5-9	10.00	30.00	70.00
10-Origin & 1st app. The Fighting Yank	40.00	120.00	280.00
11-15	11.00	33.00	76.00
16-Origin The Four Comrades; not in No. 32,35; bondage-c	13.50	40.50	95.00
17-Last Masked Rider & Mystico	8.50	25.50	60.00
18-Origin Pyroman	21.00	62.00	146.00
19	9.50	28.50	65.00
20-The Oracle begins; not in No. 26,28,33,34	9.50	28.50	65.00

STARTLING COMICS (continued)

	Good	Fine	Mint
21-Origin The Ape, Oracle's enemy	8.00	24.00	56.00
22-33	8.00	24.00	56.00
34-Origin The Scarab & only app.	8.50	25.50	60.00
35-Hypodermic syringe attacks Fighting Yank in drug story	8.50	25.50	60.00
36-43: 36-Last Four Comrades. 40-Last Capt. Future & Oracle. 41-Front Page Peggy begins. 43-Last Pyroman	8.00	24.00	56.00
44-Lance Lewis, Space Detective begins; Ingels-c	13.50	40.50	95.00
45-Tygra begins (origin)	11.50	34.50	80.00
46-Ingels c/a	11.50	34.50	80.00
47-53: 49-Last Fighting Yank. 50,51-Sea-Eagle app.	9.50	28.50	65.00

NOTE: ***Ingels*** *c-44, 46(Wash).* ***Schomburg (Xela)*** *c-21-43; 47-53 (airbrush).* ***Tuska*** *c-45? Bondage c-21, 46-49.*

STARTLING TERROR TALES
5/52 - No. 14, 2/53; No. 4, 4/53 - No. 11, 1954
Star Publications

	Good	Fine	Mint
10-(1st Series)-Wood/Harrison-a (r-A Star Presentation No. 3) Disbrow/Cole-c	17.00	51.00	120.00
11-L. B. Cole Spider-c; r-Fox's "A Feat. Presentation No. 5"	8.50	25.50	60.00
12,14	3.65	11.00	25.00
13-Jo-Jo-r; Disbrow-a	4.00	12.00	28.00
4-7,9,11('53-54) (2nd Series)	3.00	9.00	21.00
8-Spanking scene; Palais-a(r)	4.65	14.00	32.00
10-Disbrow-a	4.00	12.00	28.00

NOTE: ***L. B. Cole*** *covers-all issues.* ***Palais*** *a-V2No.11r.*

STAR TREK (TV) (See Dan Curtis)
7/67; No. 2, 6/68; No. 3, 12/68; No. 4, 6/69 - No. 61, 3/79
Gold Key

	Good	Fine	Mint
1	5.75	17.25	40.00
2-5	2.85	8.50	20.00
6-10: 1-9-Photo-c	1.75	5.25	12.00
11-20	1.15	3.50	8.00
21-30	.85	2.50	6.00
31-40	.55	1.65	4.00
41-61: 52-Drug propaganda story	.35	1.00	2.00
...the Enterprise Logs nn(8/76)-Golden Press, 224 pgs. ($1.95)-Reprints No. 1-8 plus 7 pgs. by McWilliams (No. 11185)	1.00	3.00	6.00
...the Enterprise Logs Vol.2('76)-Reprints No. 9-17 (No. 11187)	.85	2.50	5.00
...the Enterprise Logs Vol.3('77)-Reprints No. 18-26 (No. 11188); McWilliams-a (4 pgs.)	.70	2.00	4.00
Star Trek Vol.4(Winter'77)-Reprints No. 27,28,30-36,38 (No. 11189) plus 3 pgs. new art	.70	2.00	4.00

NOTE: ***McWilliams*** *a-38, 40-44, 46-61. No. 29 reprints No. 1; No. 35 reprints No. 4; No. 37 reprints No. 5; No. 45 reprints No. 7. The tabloids all have photo covers and blank inside covers. Painted covers No. 10-44, 46-59.*

STAR TREK
April, 1980 - No. 18, Feb, 1982
Marvel Comics Group

	Good	Fine	Mint
1-r/Marvel Super Special; movie adapt.		.40	.80
2-18		.30	.60

NOTE: ***Austin*** *c-18i.* ***Buscema*** *a-13.* ***Chaykin*** *a-15.* ***Gil Kane*** *a-15.* ***Miller*** *c-5.* ***Nasser*** *c/a-7.* ***Simonson*** *c-17.*

STAR TREK
Feb, 1984 - Present (Mando paper)
DC Comics

	Good	Fine	Mint
1-Sutton-a(p)	.40	1.25	2.50
2-5	.25	.75	1.50
6-10 (75¢ cover price)		.60	1.20
11-20		.50	1.00
21-32,34-36		.45	.90
33 ($1.25)		.60	1.25
Annual 1 (10/85), 2 (9/86)	.25	.75	1.50

NOTE: ***Orlando*** *c-8i.* ***Perez*** *c-1-3.* ***Sutton*** *a-1-6p, 8p, 9p; c-4-6p, 8p, 9p.*

STAR TREK III MOVIE SPECIAL
June, 1984 (One-Shot) (68pgs; $1.50)
DC Comics

	Good	Fine	Mint
1-Adapts movie; Sutton-a(p)	.25	.75	1.50

STAR TREK IV MOVIE SPECIAL
1987
DC Comics

	Good	Fine	Mint
1-Sutton-a; adapts movie	.35	1.00	2.00

STAR WARS (Movie) (Also see Contemporary Motivators & Marvel Special Edition)
July, 1977 - No. 107, Sept, 1986
Marvel Comics Group

	Good	Fine	Mint
1-(Regular 30¢ edition)-Price in square w/UPC code	1.35	4.00	8.00
1-(35¢ cover price; limited distribution - 1500 copies?)- Price in square w/UPC code	18.50	55.00	130.00
2-4	.70	2.00	4.00
5-10	.50	1.50	3.00
11-20	.35	1.00	2.00
21-37	.25	.75	1.50
38-Golden c/a	.35	1.00	2.00
39-The Empire Strikes Back r-begin, ends No. 44; Williamson c/a	.35	1.00	2.00
40-44-Williamson c/a	.35	1.00	2.00
45-49,51-99: 81-Painted-c		.40	.80
50-(75 cents, 52pgs.) Williamson-a		.50	1.00
100-Double size		.65	1.30
101-107		.35	.70
1-9-Reprints; has "reprint" in upper lefthand corner of cover or on inside or price and number inside a diamond with no date or UPC on cover; 30 cents and 35 cents issues published		.25	.50
Annual 1 (12/79)	.35	1.00	2.00
Annual 2 (11/82), 3(12/83)		.60	1.20

NOTE: ***Austin*** *c-11-15i, 21i, 38; c-12-15i, 21i.* ***Byrne*** *c-13p.* ***Chaykin*** *a-1-10p; c-1.* ***Leialoha*** *inks-2-5.* ***Miller*** *c-47p.* ***Nebres*** *c/a-Annual 2i.* ***Simonson*** *a-16p, 49p, 51-63p, 65p, 66p; c-16, 49-51, 52p, 53-62, Annual 1.* ***Williamson*** *a-39-44p, 50p; c-39, 40, 41-44p, 98.*

STAR WARS: RETURN OF THE JEDI
Oct, 1983 - No. 4, Jan, 1984 (Mini-series)
Marvel Comics Group

	Good	Fine	Mint
1-4-Williamson-a(p) in all		.30	.60
Oversized issue ('83; 10¾x8¼"; 68 pgs.; cardboard-c)-Reprints above 4 issues	.50	1.50	2.95

STATIC
No. 11, Oct, 1985 - No. 12, Dec, 1985
Charlton Comics

	Good	Fine	Mint
11,12: Ditko c/a		.40	.80

STEEL CLAW, THE
Nov, 1986 - No. 4, June, 1987 (mini-series)
Quality Comics

	Good	Fine	Mint
1-3		.40	.75
4 ($1.50)	.25	.75	1.50

Startling Terror Tales #9, © STAR

Star Trek #11, © Paramount

Star Wars #3, © Lucasfilms

Steelgrip Starkey #1, © MCG

Stony Craig nn, © Pentagon Publ.

Stories by Famous Authors #9, © Seaboard

STEELGRIP STARKEY
July, 1986 - No. 6, Feb, 1987 (mini-series)($1.50, Baxter)
Epic Comics (Marvel)

	Good	Fine	Mint
1-6	.25	.75	1.50

STEEL STERLING (Formerly Shield-Steel Sterling)
No. 4, Jan, 1984 - No. 7, July, 1984
Archie Enterprises, Inc.

4-7: 6-McWilliams-a		.40	.80

STEEL, THE INDESTRUCTIBLE MAN
March, 1978 - No. 5, Oct-Nov, 1978
DC Comics, Inc.

1		.30	.60
2-5: 5-Giant		.25	.50

STEVE CANYON (See 4-Color No. 519, 578, 641, 737, 804, 939, 1033, and Harvey Comics Hits No. 52)

STEVE CANYON
1959 (96 pgs.; no text; 6¾x9''; hardcover)(B&W inside)
Grosset & Dunlap

100100-Reprints 2 stories from strip (1953, 1957)	3.00	9.00	21.00
100100 (softcover edition)	2.50	7.50	17.00

STEVE CANYON COMICS
Feb, 1948 - No. 6, Dec, 1948 (Strip reprints) No. 4,5-52pgs.
Harvey Publications

1-Origin; has biog of Milton Caniff; Powell-a, 2pgs.; Caniff-a	13.50	40.50	95.00
2-Caniff, Powell-a	10.00	30.00	70.00
3-6: Caniff, Powell-a in all	8.50	25.50	60.00
Dept. Store giveaway No. 3(6/48, 36pp)	8.50	25.50	60.00
. . .'s Secret Mission (1951, 16 pgs., Armed Forces giveaway) -Caniff-a	8.00	24.00	48.00
Strictly for the Smart Birds-16 pgs., 1951; Information Comics Div. (Harvey) Premium	8.00	24.00	48.00

STEVE CANYON IN 3-D
June, 1986 (One shot, $2.25)
Kitchen Sink Press

1	.35	1.15	2.30

STEVE DONOVAN, WESTERN MARSHAL (TV)
No. 675, Feb, 1956 - No. 880, Feb, 1958 (All photo-c)
Dell Publishing Co.

4-Color 675-Kinstler-a	3.00	9.00	21.00
4-Color 768-Kinstler-a	2.65	8.00	18.00
4-Color 880	1.75	5.25	12.00

STEVE ROPER
April, 1948 - No. 5, Dec, 1948
Famous Funnies

1-Contains 1944 daily newspaper-r	3.65	11.00	25.00
2	1.85	5.50	13.00
3-5	1.65	5.00	11.50

STEVE SAUNDERS SPECIAL AGENT (See Special Agent)

STEVE SAVAGE (See Captain. . .)

STEVE ZODIAC & THE FIRE BALL XL-5 (TV)
January, 1964
Gold Key

1 (10108-401)	3.50	10.50	24.00

STEVIE
Nov, 1952 - No. 6, April, 1954
Mazie (Magazine Publ.)

	Good	Fine	Mint
1	1.00	3.00	7.00
2-6	.85	2.50	6.00

STEVIE MAZIE'S BOY FRIEND (See Harvey Hits No. 5)

STEWART THE RAT
1980 (Graphic Album, $7.95)
Eclipse Comics

1	1.35	4.00	7.95

STIGG'S INFERNO
1985 - Present
Vortex Publs.

1	.50	1.50	3.00
2-4	.35	1.00	2.00
5	.30	.90	1.80

STONEY BURKE (TV)
June-Aug, 1963 - No. 2, Sept-Nov, 1963
Dell Publishing Co.

1,2	1.15	3.50	8.00

STONY CRAIG
1946 (No No.)
Pentagon Publishing Co.

Reprints Bell Syndicate's ''Sgt. Stony Craig'' newspaper strips	2.65	8.00	18.00

STORIES BY FAMOUS AUTHORS ILLUSTRATED (Fast Fiction No.1-5)
Fall, 1950 - No. 13, May, 1951
Seaboard Publ./Famous Authors Ill.

1-Scarlet Pimpernel-Baroness Orczy	11.50	34.50	80.00
2-Capt. Blood-Rafael Sabatini	11.00	33.00	76.00
3-She, by Haggard	14.50	43.50	100.00
4-The 39 Steps-John Buchan	7.00	21.00	50.00
5-Beau Geste-P. C. Wren	7.00	21.00	50.00

NOTE: The above five issues are exact reprints of Fast Fiction No. 1-5 except for the title change and new Kiefer covers on No. 1 and 2. The above 5 issues were released before Famous Authors No. 6.

6-Macbeth, by Shakespeare; Kiefer art (8/50); used in **SOTI**, pg. 22,143. Kiefer-c	10.00	30.00	70.00
7-The Window; Kiefer-c/a	7.00	21.00	50.00
8-Hamlet, by Shakespeare; Kiefer-c/a	10.00	30.00	70.00
9-Nicholas Nickleby, by Dickens; G. Schrotter-a	7.00	21.00	50.00
10-Romeo & Juliet, by Shakespeare; Kiefer-c/a	7.00	21.00	50.00
11-Ben-Hur; Schrotter-a	8.50	25.50	60.00
12-La Svengali; Schrotter-a	8.50	25.50	60.00
13-Scaramouche; Kiefer-c/a	8.50	25.50	60.00

STORIES OF CHRISTMAS
1942 (32 pages; paper cover) (Giveaway)
K. K. Publications

Adaptation of ''A Christmas Carol;'' Kelly story-''The Fir Tree'' Infinity-c	40.00	100.00	200.00

STORIES OF ROMANCE (Formerly Matt Slade Gunfighter?)
No. 5, Mar, 1956 - No. 13, Aug, 1957
Atlas Comics (LMC)

5-Baker-a?	2.00	6.00	14.00
6-13	1.15	3.50	8.00

NOTE: ***Colletta** a-9(2); c-5.* ***Ann Brewster** a-13.*

STORMY (See 4-Color No. 537)

STORY HOUR SERIES (Disney)
1948, 1949; 1951-1953 (36 pgs.) (4½x6¼'')
Given away with subscription to Walt Disney's Comics & Stories

STORY HOUR SERIES (continued)
Whitman Publishing Co.

	Good	Fine	Mint
nn(1949)-Johnny Appleseed(B&W & color)	2.35	7.00	16.00
nn(1949)-The Three Orphan Kittens(B&W & color)	2.35	7.00	16.00
nn(1949)-Danny-The Little Black Lamb	2.35	7.00	16.00
nn-Donald Duck in "Bringing Up the Boys"			
1948 Paper Cover	8.00	24.00	56.00
1953	4.00	12.00	28.00
801-Mickey Mouse's Summer Vacation			
1948 Paper Cover	4.00	12.00	28.00
1951, 1952 edition	2.00	6.00	14.00
803-Bongo			
1948 Paper Cover	3.35	8.00	18.00
804-Mickey and the Beanstalk			
1948 Paper Cover	3.35	10.00	23.00
808-15(1949)-Johnny Appleseed	2.75	8.00	18.00

1948 Hard Cover Edition of each. . . . $2.00 - $3.00 more

STORY OF CHECKS, THE
1972 (5th edition)
Federal Reserve Bank of New York

	Good	Fine	Mint
Severin-a	.40	1.25	2.50

STORY OF EDISON, THE
1956 (16 pgs.) (Reddy Killowatt)
Educational Comics

	Good	Fine	Mint
Reprint of Reddy Killowatt No. 2(1947)	4.75	14.00	28.00

STORY OF HARRY S. TRUMAN, THE
1948 (16 pgs.) (in color, regular size)(Soft-c)
Democratic National Committee (Giveaway)

	Good	Fine	Mint
Gives biography on career of Truman; used in **SOTI**, pg. 311	18.00	54.00	110.00

STORY OF JESUS (See Classics Special)

STORY OF MANKIND, THE (See 4-Color No. 851)

STORY OF MARTHA WAYNE, THE
April, 1956
Argo Publ.

	Good	Fine	Mint
1-Newspaper-r	1.50	4.50	10.00

STORY OF RUTH, THE (See 4-Color No. 1144)

STORY OF THE COMMANDOS, THE (Combined Operations)
1943 (68 pgs..; B&W) (15 cents)
Long Island Independent (Distr. by Gilberton)

	Good	Fine	Mint
nn-All text (no comics); photos & illustrations; ads for Classic Comics on back cover (Rare)	9.00	27.00	62.00

STORY OF THE GLOOMY BUNNY, THE (See March of Comics No. 9)

STRAIGHT ARROW (Radio)(See Best of the West, Great Western)
Feb-Mar, 1950 - No. 55, Mar, 1956 (all 36 pgs.)
Magazine Enterprises

	Good	Fine	Mint
1-Straight Arrow (alias Steve Adams) & his palomino Fury begin; 1st mention of Sundown Valley & the Secret Cave; Whitney-a	15.00	45.00	105.00
2-Red Hawk begins by Powell (Origin), ends No. 55	7.00	21.00	50.00
3-Frazetta-c	14.50	43.50	100.00
4,5: 4-Secret Cave-c	4.35	13.00	30.00
6-10	3.65	11.00	25.00
11-Classic story "The Valley of Time," with an ancient civilization made of gold	3.65	11.00	25.00
12-19	2.65	8.00	18.00
20-Origin S. Arrow's Shield	3.50	10.50	24.00
21-Origin Fury	4.00	12.00	28.00
22-Frazetta-c	11.00	33.00	76.00
23,25-30: 25-Secret Cave-c. 28-Red Hawk meets The Vikings	2.15	6.50	15.00
24-Classic story "The Dragons of Doom!" with prehistoric pteradactyls	3.35	10.00	23.00
31-38	1.85	5.50	13.00
39-Classic story "The Canyon Beast," with a dinosaur egg hatching a Tyranosaurus Rex	2.65	8.00	18.00
40-Classic story "Secret of The Spanish Specters," with Conquistadors lost treasure	2.65	8.00	18.00
41,42,44-54: 45-Secret Cave-c	1.65	5.00	11.50
43-Intro & 1st app. Blaze, S. Arrow's Warrior dog	1.85	5.50	13.00
55-Last issue	2.15	6.50	15.00

NOTE: ***Fred Meagher*** *a 1-55; c-1,2,4-21,23-55.* ***Powell*** *a 2-55. Many issues advertise the radio premiums associated with Straight Arrow.*

STRAIGHT ARROW'S FURY (See A-1 Comics No. 119)

STRANGE
March, 1957 - No. 6, May, 1958
Ajax-Farrell Publ. (Four Star Comic Corp.)

	Good	Fine	Mint
1	3.15	9.50	22.00
2	1.70	5.00	11.50
3-6	1.50	4.50	10.00

STRANGE ADVENTURES
Aug-Sept, 1950 - No. 244, Oct-Nov, 1973 (No. 1-12: 52 pgs.)
National Periodical Publications

	Good	Fine	Mint
1-Adaptation of "Destination Moon;" Kris KL-99 & Darwin Jones begin	71.00	215.00	500.00
2	37.00	110.00	260.00
3,4	23.00	70.00	160.00
5-8,10: 7-Origin Kris KL-99	21.00	62.00	146.00
9-Intro. & origin Captain Comet (6/51)	57.00	171.00	400.00
11,14,15	15.00	45.00	105.00
12,13,17-Toth-a	17.00	51.00	120.00
16,18-20	11.00	33.00	76.00
21-30	10.00	30.00	70.00
31,34-38	8.00	24.00	56.00
32,33-Krigstein-a	9.00	27.00	62.00
39-Ill. in **SOTI**-"Treating police contemptuously" (top right)	15.00	45.00	105.00
40-49-Last Capt. Comet; not in 45,47,48	6.85	20.50	48.00
50-53-Last pre-code issue	4.65	14.00	32.00
54-70	2.65	8.00	18.00
71-99	2.00	6.00	14.00
100	2.65	8.00	18.00
101-110: 104-Space Museum begins by Sekowsky	1.50	4.50	10.00
111-116,118-120: 114-Star Hawkins begins, ends No. 185; Heath -a in Wood E.C. style	1.15	3.50	8.00
117-Origin Atomic Knights	6.00	18.00	42.00
121-134: 124-Origin Faceless Creature. 134-Last 10¢ issue	.85	2.50	6.00
135-160: 159-Star Rovers app. 160-Last Atomic Knights	.35	1.00	2.00
161-179: 161-Last Space Museum. 163-Star Rovers app. 170-Infinity-c. 177-Origin Immortal Man	.30	.90	1.80
180-Origin Animal Man	.35	1.00	2.00
181-186,188-204: 201-Last Animal Man		.50	1.00
187-Origin The Enchantress		.50	1.00
205-Intro & origin Deadman by Infantino	3.00	9.00	18.00
206-Adams-a begins	1.70	5.00	10.00

Story of Martha Wayne #1, © Argo

Straight Arrow #11, © ME

Strange Adventures #1, © DC

Strange Fantasy #12, © AJAX

Strange Mysteries #15, © SUPR

Strange Planets #1, © I.W.

STRANGE ADVENTURES (continued)

	Good	Fine	Mint
207-210	1.30	4.00	8.00
211-216-Last Deadman	1.25	3.75	7.50
217-Adam Strange & Atomic Knights-r begin		.40	.80
218-225: 222-New Adam Strange story by Gil Kane		.25	.50
226-231(All 68 pgs.): 226-Atomic blast-c. 231-Last Atomic Knights-r		.25	.50
232-236(All 52 pgs.): Star Rovers app.-No. 232-234,236		.25	.50
237-244		.25	.50

NOTE: ***Adams** a-206-216, 228, 235; c-207-216. **Anderson** a-8-52, 94, 96, 97, 99, 115, 117, 119-163, 217r, 218r, 222-25r, 222, 226, 242i(r); c/r-157i, 190i, 217-224, 228-31, 233, 235-39, 241-43. **Ditko** a-188, 189. **Drucker** a-42, 43, 45. **Finlay** a-2, 3, 6, 7, 210r, 229r. **Infantino** a-10-101, 106-151, 154, 157-163, 180, 190, 223-25p(r), 242p(r); c/r-190p, 197, 199-211, 218-221, 223-244. **Kaluta** c-238, 240. **Gil Kane** a-8-116, 124, 125, 130, 138, 146-157, 173-186, 204r, 222r, 227-231r; c-154p, 157p. **Kubert** a-55(2 pgs.), 226; c-219, 220, 225-227, 232, 234. **Moriera** c-71. **Morrow** c-230. **Powell** a-4. **Mike Sekowsky** a-71p, 97-162p, 217p(r), 218p(r); c-206, 217-219r. **Simon & Kirby** a-2r (2 pg.) **Sparling** a-201. **Toth** a-8, 12, 13, 17-19. **Wood** a-154i. **Chris KL99** in 1-3, 5, 7, 9, 11, 15. **Capt. Comet** covers-9-14, 17-19, 24, 26, 27, 32-44.*

STRANGE AS IT SEEMS (See Famous Funnies, A Carnival of Comics, Feature Funnies No. 1, The John Hix Scrap Book & Peanuts)

STRANGE AS IT SEEMS
1932 (64 pgs.; B&W; square binding)
Blue-Star Publishing Co.

	Good	Fine	Mint
1-Newspaper-r	11.00	33.00	76.00

NOTE: *Published with and without No. 1 and price on cover.*

	Good	Fine	Mint
Ex-Lax giveaway(1936,24pgs,5x7'',B&W)-McNaught Synd.	2.00	6.00	14.00

STRANGE AS IT SEEMS
1939
United Features Syndicate

	Good	Fine	Mint
Single Series 9, 1,2	10.00	30.00	70.00

STRANGE BREW
1986
Aardvark-Vanaheim

	Good	Fine	Mint
1	.35	1.00	2.00

STRANGE CONFESSIONS
Jan-Mar, 1952 - No. 4, Fall, 1952
Ziff-Davis Publ. Co. (Approved)

	Good	Fine	Mint
1(Scarce)-Photo-c; Kinstler-a	17.00	51.00	120.00
2(Scarce)	11.00	33.00	76.00
3(Scarce)-No. 3 on-c, No. 2 on inside	10.00	30.00	70.00
4(Scarce)-Reformatory girl story	10.00	30.00	70.00

STRANGE DAYS
Oct, 1984 - No. 3, Apr, 1985 ($1.75; Baxter paper)
Eclipse Comics

	Good	Fine	Mint
1-3-Freakwave & Johnny Nemo & Paradax from Vanguard Ill.; nudity, violence, strong language	.25	.75	1.50

STRANGE FANTASY
Aug, 1952 - No. 14, Oct-Nov, 1954
Harvey Publ./Ajax-Farrell No. 2 on

	Good	Fine	Mint
2(8/52)-Jungle Princess story; no Black Cat; Kamenish-a; r-/Ellery Queen No. 1	5.75	17.25	40.00
2(10/52)-No Black Cat or Rulah; Bakerish, Kamenish-a; hypo/meat-hook-c	5.50	16.50	38.00
3-Rulah story, called Pulah	5.50	16.50	38.00
4-Rocket Man app.	4.35	13.00	30.00
5,6,8,10,12,14	3.15	9.50	22.00
7-Madam Satan/Slave story	3.75	11.25	26.00
9(w/Black Cat), 9(w/Boy's Ranch; S&K-a)	5.50	16.50	38.00
9-Regular issue	3.50	10.50	24.00
11-Jungle story	3.75	11.25	26.00
13-Bondage-c; Rulah (Kolah) story	5.50	16.50	38.00

STRANGE GALAXY (Magazine)
V1No.8, Feb, 1971 - No. 11, Aug, 1971 (B&W)
Eerie Publications

	Good	Fine	Mint
V1No.8-Cover reprinted from Fantastic V19No.3 (2/70) (a pulp)		.60	1.20
9-11		.60	1.20

STRANGE JOURNEY
Sept, 1957 - No. 4, June, 1958 (Farrell reprints)
America's Best (Steinway Publ.) (Ajax/Farrell)

	Good	Fine	Mint
1	4.00	12.00	28.00
2-4	2.65	8.00	18.00

STRANGE LOVE (See Fox Giants)

STRANGE MYSTERIES
Sept, 1951 - No. 21, Jan, 1955
Superior/Dynamic Publications

	Good	Fine	Mint
1-Kamenish-a begins	11.00	33.00	76.00
2	5.50	16.50	38.00
3-5	4.35	13.00	30.00
6-8	3.15	9.50	22.00
9-Bondage 3-D effect-c	4.65	14.00	32.00
10-Used in **SOTI**, pg. 181	4.65	14.00	32.00
11-18	2.65	8.00	18.00
19-r-/Journey Into Fear No. 1; cover is a splash from one story; Baker-a(2)(r)	5.75	17.25	40.00
20,21-Reprints; 20-r-/No. 1 with new-c	2.65	8.00	18.00

STRANGE MYSTERIES
1963 - 1964
I. W. Enterprises/Super Comics

	Good	Fine	Mint
I.W. Reprint No. 9; Rulah-r	.60	1.80	3.60
Super Reprint No. 10-12,15-17('63-'64): No. 12-reprints Tales of Horror No. 5 (3/53) less cover. No. 15,16-reprints The Dead Who Walk	.60	1.80	3.60
Super Reprint No. 18-Reprint of Witchcraft No. 1; Kubert-a	.60	1.80	3.60

STRANGE PLANETS
1958; 1963-64
I. W. Enterprises/Super Comics

	Good	Fine	Mint
I.W. Reprint No. 1(no date)-E. C. Incredible S/F No. 30 plus-c/Strange Worlds No. 3	5.00	15.00	35.00
I.W. Reprint No. 8	1.35	4.00	9.00
I.W. Reprint No. 9-Orlando/Wood-a (Strange Worlds No. 4); c-from Flying Saucers No. 1	6.00	18.00	42.00
Super Reprint No. 10-22 pg. Wood-a from Space Detective No. 1; c-/Attack on Planet Mars	6.00	18.00	42.00
Super Reprint No. 11-25 pg. Wood-a from An Earthman on Venus	9.20	27.50	64.00
Super Reprint No. 12-Orlando-a from Rocket to the Moon	5.85	17.50	40.00
Super Reprint No. 15-Reprints Atlas stories; Heath, Colan-a	1.35	4.00	9.00
Super Reprint No. 16-Avon's Strange Worlds No. 6; Kinstler, Check art	2.00	6.00	14.00
Super Reprint No. 17	1.35	4.00	9.00
Super Reprint No. 18-Reprints Daring Adventures; Space Busters, Explorer Joe, The Son of Robin Hood; Krigstein-a	2.00	6.00	14.00

STRANGE SPORTS STORIES (See Brave & the Bold, DC Special, and DC Super Stars No. 10)
Sept-Oct, 1973 - No. 6, July-Aug, 1974
National Periodical Publications

STRANGE SPORTS STORIES (continued)

	Good	Fine	Mint
1		.30	.60
2-6: 3-Swan/Anderson-a		.25	.50

STRANGE STORIES FROM ANOTHER WORLD (Unknown World No. 1)
No. 2, Aug, 1952 - No. 5, Feb, 1953
Fawcett Publications

	Good	Fine	Mint
2-Saunders painted-c	8.50	25.50	60.00
3-5-Saunders painted-c	5.75	17.25	40.00

STRANGE STORIES OF SUSPENSE (Rugged Action No. 1-4)
No. 5, Oct, 1955 - No. 16, Aug, 1957
Atlas Comics (CSI)

	Good	Fine	Mint
5(No.1)	4.65	14.00	32.00
6,9	2.65	8.00	18.00
7-E. C. swipe cover/Vault of Horror No. 32	2.85	8.50	20.00
8-Williamson/Mayo-a; Pakula-a	3.85	11.50	27.00
10-Crandall, Torres, Meskin-a	3.85	11.50	27.00
11,13	1.70	5.00	11.50
12-Torres, Pakula-a	2.65	8.00	18.00
14-Williamson-a	3.65	11.00	25.00
15-Krigstein-a	2.85	8.50	20.00
16-Fox, Powell-a	2.85	8.50	20.00

NOTE: ***Everett** a-6, 7, 13; c-9, 11-14. **Heath** a-5. **Maneely** c-5. **Morrow** a-13. **Powell** a-8. **Severin** c-7.*

STRANGE STORY (Also see Front Page)
June-July, 1946 (52 pages)
Harvey Publications

	Good	Fine	Mint
1-The Man in Black Called Fate by Powell	7.00	21.00	50.00

STRANGE SUSPENSE STORIES (Lawbreakers Suspense Stories No. 10-15; This Is Suspense No. 23-26; Captain Atom V1No.78 on)
6/52 - No. 5, 2/53; No. 16, 1/54 - No. 22, 11/54; No. 27, 10/55 - No. 77, 10/65; V3No. 1, 10/67 - V1No.9, 9/69
Fawcett Publications/Charlton Comics No. 16 on

	Good	Fine	Mint
1-(Fawcett)-Powell, Sekowsky-a	12.00	36.00	84.00
2-George Evans horror story	7.00	21.00	50.00
3-5 (2/53)-George Evans horror stories	5.75	17.25	40.00
16(1-2/54)	4.35	13.00	30.00
17,21	3.35	10.00	23.00
18-E.C. swipe/HOF 7; Ditko c/a(2)	8.50	25.50	60.00
19-Ditko electric chair-c; Ditko-a	10.00	30.00	70.00
20-Ditko c/a(2)	8.50	25.50	60.00
22(11/54)-Ditko-c, Shuster-a; last pre-code issue; becomes This Is Suspense	5.75	17.25	40.00
27(10/55)-(Formerly This Is Suspense No. 26?)	1.75	5.25	12.00
28-30,38	1.50	4.50	10.00
31-Ditko-c	2.00	6.00	14.00
32,35,37,40-Ditko c/a(2-3)	3.85	11.50	27.00
33,39,41,51-53-Ditko-a	3.50	10.50	24.00
34-Story of ruthless business man-Wm. B. Gaines; Ditko-c/a	5.50	16.50	38.00
36-(68 pgs.); Ditko-a	5.50	16.50	38.00
42-44,46,49,54-60	1.15	3.50	8.00
45,47,48,50-Ditko c/a	3.00	9.00	21.00
61-74	.50	1.50	3.00
75(6/65)-Origin Captain Atom by Ditko-r/Space Advs.	5.35	16.00	32.00
76,77-Ditko Captain Atom-r/Space Advs.	2.00	6.00	12.00
V3No.1(10/67)-4		.40	.80
V1No.2-9: 2-Ditko-a, atom bomb-c		.30	.60

NOTE: ***Alascia** a-19. **Aparo** a-V3/1. **Bailey** a-1-3; c-5. **Evans** c-4. **Powell** a-4. **Shuster** a-19, 21.*

STRANGE TALES (Dr. Strange No. 169 on)
6/51 - No. 168, 5/68; No. 169, 9/73 - No. 188, 11/76
Atlas (CCPC No. 1-67/ZPC No. 68-79/VPI No. 80-85)/Marvel No. 86(7/61) on

	Good	Fine	Mint
1	55.00	165.00	385.00
2	26.00	78.00	182.00
3,5: 3-Atom bomb panels	18.50	55.50	130.00
4-"The Evil Eye," cosmic eyeball sty	20.00	60.00	140.00
6-9	13.00	40.00	90.00
10-Krigstein-a	14.50	43.50	100.00
11-14,16-20	5.50	16.50	38.00
15-Krigstein-a	6.50	19.50	45.00
21,23-27,29-32,34-Last precode ish(2/55): 27-Atom bomb panels	4.65	14.00	32.00
22-Krigstein, Forte/Fox-a	4.85	14.50	34.00
28-Jack Katz story used in Senate Investigation report, pgs. 7 & 169	4.85	14.50	34.00
33-Davis-a	4.85	14.50	34.00
35-41,43,44	2.50	7.50	17.50
42,45,59,61-Krigstein-a; No. 61 (2/58)	3.65	11.00	25.00
46-52,54,55,57,60: 60 (8/57)	2.15	6.50	15.00
53-Torres, Crandall-a	3.85	11.50	27.00
56-Crandall-a	3.65	11.00	25.00
58,64-Williamson-a in each, with Mayo-No. 58	3.85	11.50	27.00
62-Torres-a	2.50	7.50	17.50
63,65	2.15	6.50	15.00
66-Crandall-a	2.50	7.50	17.50
67-80-Ditko/Kirby-a. 79-Dr. Strange proto-type app.	2.15	6.50	15.00
81-92-Last 10¢ ish. Ditko/Kirby-a	1.85	5.50	13.00
93-100-Kirby-a	1.50	4.50	10.00
101-Human Torch begins by Kirby (10/62)	15.00	38.00	105.00
102	7.50	19.00	53.00
103-105	6.00	15.00	42.00
106,108,109	4.35	11.00	30.00
107-Human Torch/Sub-Mariner battle	5.00	12.00	35.00
110-Intro Dr. Strange, Ancient One & Wong by Ditko	11.00	28.00	75.00
111-2nd Dr. Strange	3.00	7.50	21.00
112,113	1.75	4.35	12.00
114-Acrobat disguised as Captain America, 1st app. since the G.A.; intro. & 1st app. Victoria Bentley	2.15	5.50	15.00
115-Origin Dr. Strange; Sandman (villain) app.	5.15	13.00	36.00
116-120: 116-Thing/Torch battle	.85	2.50	5.00
121-125: 123-Thor app.	.50	1.50	3.00
126-129,131-133: Thing/Torch team-up in all; 126-Intro Clea	.50	1.50	3.00
130-The Beatles cameo	1.00	3.00	6.00
134-Last Human Torch; Wood-a(i)	.50	1.50	3.00
135-Origin Nick Fury, Agent of Shield by Kirby	1.00	3.00	6.00
136-147,149: 146-Last Ditko Dr. Strange who is in consecutive stories since No. 113	.35	1.00	2.00
148-Origin Ancient One	.45	1.25	2.50
150(11/66)-J. Buscema 1st work at Marvel	.30	1.00	2.00
151-1st Marvel work by Steranko (w/Kirby)	.50	1.50	3.00
152,153-Kirby/Steranko-a	.35	1.00	2.00
154-158-Steranko-a/script	.35	1.00	2.00
159-Origin Nick Fury; Intro Val; Captain America app; Steranko-a	.45	1.25	2.50
160-162-Steranko-a/scripts; Capt. America app.	.35	1.00	2.00
163-166,168-Steranko-a(p)	.35	1.00	2.00
167-Steranko pen/script; classic flag-c	.50	1.50	3.00

Strange Stories of Suspense #9, © MCG

Strange Suspense Stories #22, © CC

Strange Tales #4, © MCG

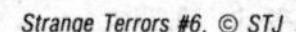
Strange Terrors #6, © STJ

Strange Worlds #1, © AVON

Strata #1, © Renegade Press

STRANGE TALES (continued)

	Good	Fine	Mint
169,170-Brother Voodoo origin in each; series ends No. 173		.30	.60
171-177: 174-Origin Golem. 177-Brunner-c		.30	.60
178-Warlock by Starlin with covers; origin Warlock & Him	1.00	3.00	6.00
179-181-Warlock by Starlin with covers. 179-Intro/1st app. Pip the Troll. 180-Intro Gamora	.60	1.75	3.50
182-188		.25	.50
Annual 1(1962)-Reprints from Str. Tales No. 73,76,78, Tales of Suspense No. 7,9, Tales to Astonish No. 1,6,7, & Journey Into Mystery No. 53,55,59	6.50	16.00	45.00
Annual 2(1963)-Reprints from Str. Tales No. 67, Str. Worlds (Atlas) No. 1-3, World of Fantasy No. 16, Human Torch vs. Spider-Man by Kirby/Ditko; Kirby-c	5.50	14.00	38.00

NOTE: ***Briefer*** *a-17.* ***Burgos*** *a-123p.* ***J. Buscema*** *a-174p.* ***Colan*** *a-11, 20, 169-73p, 188p.* ***Davis*** *c-71.* ***Ditko*** *a-46, 50, 67-122, 123-25p, 126-146, 175r, 182-88r; c-93, 115, 121, 146.* ***Everett*** *a-4, 21, 40-42, 73, 147-52, 164i; c-10, 11, 13, 24, 45, 50, 51, 53, 60, 61, 63, 148, 150, 152, 158i.* ***Forte*** *a-27, 43, 50, 53, 60.* ***Heath*** *c-20.* ***Kamen*** *a-45.* ***G. Kane*** *c-170-72-, 173, 182p.* ***Kirby*** *Human Torch-101-105, 108, 109, 114, 120; Nick Fury-135p, 141-43p; (Layouts)-135-153; other* ***Kirby*** *a-73, 79p, 84p, 97-99p; c-68-70, 72-92, 94, 95, 101-114, 116-123, 125-130, 132-135, 136p, 138-145, 147, 149, 151p.* ***Lawrence*** *a-29.* ***Leiber/Fox*** *a-110, 111, 113.* ***Maneely*** *a-3, 42.* ***Moldoff*** *a-20.* ***Mooney*** *a-174i.* ***Morisi*** *a-53.* ***Orlando*** *a-41, 44, 46, 49, 52.* ***Powell*** *a-42, 44, 49, 54, 130-34p; c-131p.* ***Reinman*** *a-50, 74, 88, 95, 104, 106, 112i, 124-127i.* ***Robinson*** *a-17.* ***Sekowski*** *a-3, 11.* ***Starlin*** *a-178, 179, 180p, 181p; c-178-80, 181p.* ***Steranko*** *a-151-61, 162-68p; c-151i, 153, 155, 157, 159, 161, 163, 165, 167.* ***Tuska*** *a-14, 166p.* ***Wildey*** *a-42.* ***Woodbridge*** *a-59. Fantastic Four cameo-101-134. Jack Katz app.-26.*

STRANGE TALES
Apr, 1987 - Present
Marvel Comics Group

	Good	Fine	Mint
1		.40	.75

STRANGE TALES OF THE UNUSUAL
Dec, 1955 - No. 11, Aug, 1957
Atlas Comics (ACI No. 1-4/WPI No. 5-11)

	Good	Fine	Mint
1-Powell-a	5.75	17.25	40.00
2	2.85	8.50	20.00
3-Williamson-a, 4 pgs.	4.65	14.00	32.00
4,6,8,11	1.50	4.50	10.00
5-Crandall, Ditko-a	3.50	10.50	24.00
7-Kirby, Orlando-a	2.65	8.00	18.00
9-Krigstein-a	2.85	8.50	20.00
10-Torres, Morrow-a	2.65	8.00	18.00

NOTE: ***Baily*** *a-6.* ***Everett*** *a-2, 6; c-6, 11.* ***Heck*** *a-1.* ***Maneely*** *c-1.* ***Orlando*** *a-7.* ***Romita*** *a-1.*

STRANGE TERRORS
June, 1952 - No. 7, Mar, 1953
St. John Publishing Co.

	Good	Fine	Mint
1-Bondage-c; Zombies spelled Zoombies on-c; Finesque-a	8.50	25.50	60.00
2	3.85	11.50	27.00
3-Kubert-a; painted-c	8.00	24.00	56.00
4-Kubert-a(r-/in Mystery Tales No. 18); Ekgren-c; Fineesque-a; Jerry Iger caricature	16.00	48.00	110.00
5-Kubert-a; painted-c	8.00	24.00	56.00
6-Giant, 100 pgs.(1/53); bondage-c	11.50	34.50	80.00
7-Giant, 100 pgs.; Kubert c/a	16.00	48.00	110.00

NOTE: ***Cameron*** *a-6, 7.* ***Morisi*** *a-6.*

STRANGE WORLD OF YOUR DREAMS
Aug, 1952 - No. 4, Jan-Feb, 1953
Prize Publications

	Good	Fine	Mint
1-Simon & Kirby-a	16.00	48.00	110.00
2,3-Simon & Kirby-a. 2-Meskin-a	11.50	34.50	80.00
4-S&K-c; Meskin-a	11.00	33.00	76.00

STRANGE WORLDS (No. 18 continued from Avon's Eerie No. 1-17)
Nov, 1950 - No. 22, Sept-Oct, 1955 (no No. 11-17)
Avon Periodicals

	Good	Fine	Mint
1-Kenton of the Star Patrol by Kubert (r-/Eerie No. 1-'47); Crom the Barbarian by John Giunta	36.00	108.00	250.00
2-Wood-a; Crom the Barbarian by Giunta; Dara of the Vikings app.; used in **SOTI**, pg. 112; injury to eye panel	31.00	92.00	215.00
3-Wood/Orlando-a(Kenton), Wood/Williamson/Frazetta/Krenkel/Orlando-a (7 pgs.); Malu Slave Girl Princess app.; Kinstler-c	75.00	225.00	525.00
4-Wood c/a (Kenton); Orlando-a; origin The Enchanted Daggar; Sultan-a	31.00	92.00	215.00
5-Orlando/Wood-a (Kenton); Wood-c	26.00	78.00	182.00
6-Kinstler-a(2); Orlando/Wood-c, Check-a	16.00	48.00	110.00
7-Kinstler, Fawcette & Becker/Alascia-a	12.00	36.00	84.00
8-Kubert, Kinstler, Hollingsworth & Lazarus-a; Lazarus-c	13.50	40.50	95.00
9-Kinstler, Fawcette, Alascia-a	12.00	36.00	84.00
10	11.50	34.50	80.00
18-Reprints "Attack on Planet Mars" by Kubert	13.00	40.00	90.00
19-Reprints Avon's Robotmen of the Lost Planet	13.00	40.00	90.00
20-War stories; Wood-c(r)/U.S. Paratroops No. 1	3.65	11.00	25.00
21,22-War stories	3.35	10.00	23.00
I.W. Reprint No. 5-Kinstler-a(r)/Avon's No. 9	1.35	4.00	8.00

STRANGE WORLDS
Dec, 1958 - No. 5, Aug, 1959
Marvel Comics (MPI No. 1,2/Male No. 3,5)

	Good	Fine	Mint
1-Kirby & Ditko-a; flying saucer ish.	11.00	32.00	75.00
2-Ditko c/a	5.75	17.25	40.00
3-Kirby-a(2)	5.00	15.00	35.00
4-Williamson-a	8.00	24.00	56.00
5-Ditko-a	5.00	15.00	35.00

NOTE: ***Buscema*** *a-3.* ***Ditko*** *a-1-5; c-2.* ***Kirby*** *a-1, 3; c-1, 3-5.*

STRATA
Jan, 1986 - Present ($2.00-$1.70, B&W)
Renegade Press

	Good	Fine	Mint
1,4	.35	1.00	2.00
2,3	.30	.85	1.70

STRAWBERRY SHORTCAKE
Apr, 1985 - Present (Children's comic)
Star Comics (Marvel)

	Good	Fine	Mint
1-Howie Post-a		.40	.80
2-6		.35	.70

STREET COMIX (50 cents)
1973 (36 pgs.; B&W) (20,000 print run)
Street Enterprises/King Features

	Good	Fine	Mint
1-Rip Kirby		.40	.80
2-Flash Gordon		.60	1.20

STREET FIGHTER
Aug, 1986 - No. 4, 1986 ($1.75, B&W)(mini-series)
Ocean Comics

	Good	Fine	Mint
1,2: 2-Origin begins	.25	.85	1.70

STREET WOLF
July, 1986 - No. 3, Sept, 1986 ($2.00, B&W, Adults)
Blackthorne Publ.

	Good	Fine	Mint
1-3	.30	.95	1.90

STRICTLY PRIVATE
Nov?, 1942
Eastern Color Printing Co.

	Good	Fine	Mint
1,2	8.00	24.00	56.00

STRIKEFORCE: MORITURI
Dec, 1986 - Present
Marvel Comics Group

	Good	Fine	Mint
1	.25	.75	1.50
2-5		.50	1.00

STRONG MAN (Also see Complimentary Comics)
Mar-Apr, 1955 - No. 4, Sept-Oct, 1955
Magazine Enterprises

	Good	Fine	Mint
1(A-1 130)-Powell-a	6.65	20.00	46.00
2(A-1 132), 3(A-1 134), 4(A-1 139)-Powell-a	4.75	14.25	33.00

STRONTIUM DOG
Dec, 1985 - No. 4, Mar, 1986 (mutie series. $1.25 cover)
Eagle Comics

	Good	Fine	Mint
1-4		.65	1.30
Special 1 ('86)-Moore scripts	.25	.75	1.50

STUMBO THE GIANT (See Harvey Hits No. 49,54,57,60,63,66,69,72,78,88)

STUMBO TINYTOWN
Oct, 1963 - No. 13, Nov, 1966
Harvey Publications

	Good	Fine	Mint
1	8.50	25.50	60.00
2	4.30	13.00	30.00
3-5	3.00	9.00	21.00
6-13	2.00	6.00	14.00

STUNTMAN COMICS
Apr-May, 1946 - No. 2, June-July, 1946; No. 3, Oct-Nov, 1946
Harvey Publications

	Good	Fine	Mint
1-Origin Stuntman by S&K reprinted in Black Cat No. 9	46.00	138.00	325.00
2-S&K-a	30.00	90.00	200.00

3-Small size (5½x8½''; B&W; 32 pgs.); distributed to mail subscribers only; S&K-a; Kid Adonis by S&K reprinted in Green Hornet No. 37. Estimated value. . . $300.00-$500.00

(Also see All-New No. 15, Boy Explorers No. 2, & Flash Gordon No. 5)

SUBMARINE ATTACK (Formerly Speed Demons)
No. 11, May, 1958 - No. 54, Feb-Mar, 1966
Charlton Comics

	Good	Fine	Mint
11	.70	2.00	4.00
12-20	.35	1.00	2.00
21-54		.60	1.20

NOTE: ***Glanzman** c/a-25. **Montes/Bache** a-38, 40, 41.*

SUB-MARINER (See All-Winners, Blonde Phantom, Daring, Human Torch, Marvel Mystery, Motion Picture Funnies Weekly, Prince Namor, The. . ., & Namora)

SUB-MARINER, THE (2nd Series) (Sub-Mariner No. 31 on)
May, 1968 - No. 72, Sept, 1974 (No. 43: 52 pgs.)
Marvel Comics Group

	Good	Fine	Mint
1-Origin Sub-Mariner	1.35	4.00	8.00
2-Triton app.	.50	1.50	3.00
3-10: 5-1st Tiger Shark	.35	1.00	2.00
11-13,15-20: 19-1st Sting Ray		.60	1.20
14-Sub-Mariner vs. G.A. Human Torch; death of Toro	.30	.90	1.80
21-33,36,37,39,40: 37-Death of Lady Dorma		.40	.80
34-Silver Surfer, Hulk app.		.50	1.00
35-Ties into 1st Defenders story; Avengers, Silver Surfer, Hulk app.		.50	1.00
38-Origin		.60	1.20
41-49: 44,45-Sub-Mariner vs. H. Torch		.40	.80
50-60: 50-1st app. Nita, Namor's niece. 57-Venus app.		.30	.60
61-Last artwork by Everett; 1st 4 pgs. completed by Mortimer; pgs. 5-20 by Mooney		.25	.50
62-72: 62-1st Tales of Atlantis, ends No. 66		.25	.50
Special 1(1/71)		.50	1.00
Special 2(1/72)-Everett-a		.40	.80

NOTE: ***Bolle** a-67i. **Buscema** a(p)-1-8, 20, 24. **Colan** a-10p, 11p, 40p, 43p, 46-49p, Spec. 1p, 2; c(p)-10, 11, 40. **Craig** a-19-23i. **Everett** a-45r, 50-55, 57, 58, 59-61(plot), 63(plot); c-47, 55, 57-59i, 61, Spec. 2. **G. Kane** c(p)-42-52, 58, 66, 70, 71. **Mooney** a-24i, 25i, 32-35i, 39i, 42i, 44i, 45i, 60i, 61i, 65p, 66p, 68i. **Severin** c/a-38i. **Starlin** c-59p. **Tuska** a-41p, 42p, 69-71p. **Wrightson** a-36i.*

SUB-MARINER COMICS (1st Series) (The Sub-Mariner No. 1,2 33-42) (Official True Crime Cases No. 24 on; Amazing Mysteries No. 32 on; Best Love No. 33 on)
Spring, 1941 - No. 23, Sum, '47; No. 24, Wint, '47 - No. 31, 4/49; No. 32, 7/49; No. 33, 4/54 - No. 42, 10/55
Timely/Marvel Comics (TCI 1-7/SePI 8/MPI 9-32/Atlas Comics (CCC 33-42))

	Good	Fine	Mint
1-The Sub-Mariner by Everett & The Angel begin	343.00	1030.00	2400.00
2-Everett-a	171.00	513.00	1200.00
3-Churchill assassination-c; 40 pg. S-M story	120.00	360.00	840.00
4-Everett-a, 40 pgs.; 1 pg. Wolverton-a	105.00	315.00	735.00
5	77.00	231.00	540.00
6-10: 9-Wolverton-a, 3 pgs.; flag-c	57.00	181.00	400.00
11-15	40.00	120.00	280.00
16-20	36.00	108.00	252.00
21-Last Angel; Everett-a	27.00	81.00	190.00
22-Young Allies app.	27.00	81.00	190.00
23-The Human Torch, Namora x-over	27.00	81.00	190.00
24-Namora x-over	27.00	81.00	190.00
25-The Blonde Phantom begins, ends No. 31; Kurtzman-a; Namora x-over	33.50	100.00	235.00
26,27	30.00	90.00	210.00
28-Namora cover; Everett-a	30.00	90.00	210.00
29-31 (4/49): 29-The Human Torch app. 31-Capt. America app.	30.00	90.00	210.00
32 (7/49, Scarce)-Origin Sub-Mariner	48.00	145.00	335.00
33 (4/54)-Origin Sub-Mariner; The Human Torch app.; Namora x-over in Sub-Mariner, No. 33-42	28.00	84.00	195.00
34,35-Human Torch in each	19.00	57.00	132.00
36,37,39-41: 36,39-41-Namora app.	19.00	57.00	132.00
38-Origin Sub-Mariner's wings; Namora app.	24.50	73.00	170.00
42-Last issue	22.00	65.00	154.00

NOTE: *Angel by **Gustavson**-No. 1. **Everett** a-1-4, 24, 26-42; c-2, 32, 33, 40. **Maneely** c-37, 39, 41. **Schomburg** c-1-4, 6, 8-14, 16-18, 20. Bondage c-13, 22, 24, 25, 34.*

SUE & SALLY SMITH (Formerly My Secret Life)
No. 48, 11/62 - No. 54, 11/63 (Flying Nurses)
Charlton Comics

	Good	Fine	Mint
V2No.48-54		.20	.40

SUGAR & SPIKE (Also see The Best of DC)
Apr-May, 1956 - No. 98, Oct-Nov, 1971
National Periodical Publications

	Good	Fine	Mint
1 (Scarce)	45.00	135.00	315.00
2	23.00	70.00	160.00
3-5	20.00	60.00	140.00
6-10	13.00	40.00	90.00
11-20	10.00	30.00	70.00
21-29,31-40	5.00	15.00	35.00
30-Scribbly x-over	6.50	19.50	45.00
41-60	2.50	7.50	17.00
61-80: 72-Origin & 1st app. Bernie the Brain	1.70	5.00	10.00

Sub-Mariner #7, © MCG

Sub-Mariner Comics #25, © MCG

Sugar & Spike #21, © DC

Sun Girl #2, © MCG

Sunny, America's Sweetheart #14, © FOX

Super Book #2 (Smitty), © N.Y. News Synd.

SUGAR & SPIKE (continued)

	Good	Fine	Mint
81-98: 85-68 pgs.; r-No. 72. No. 96-68 pgs. No. 97,98-52 pgs.	1.35	4.00	8.00

NOTE: *All written and drawn by **Sheldon Mayer**.*

SUGAR BEAR
No date (16 pages) (2½x4½'')
Post Cereal Giveaway

	Good	Fine	Mint
''The Almost Take Over of the Post Office,'' ''The Race Across the Atlantic,'' ''The Zoo Goes Wild'' each...		.40	.80

SUGAR BOWL COMICS
May, 1948 - 1949
Famous Funnies

	Good	Fine	Mint
1-Toth-c/a	5.50	16.50	38.00
2,4,5	2.15	6.50	15.00
3-Toth-a	3.75	11.25	26.00

SUGARFOOT (See 4-Color No. 907,992,1059,1098,1147,1209)

SUMMER FUN (See Dell Giants)

SUMMER FUN (Formerly Li'l Genius; Holiday Surprise No. 55)
No. 54, Oct, 1966 (Giant)
Charlton Comics

	Good	Fine	Mint
54		.40	.80

SUMMER LOVE (Formerly Brides in Love?)
V2/46, 10/65; V2/47, 10/66; V2/48, 11/68
Charlton Comics

	Good	Fine	Mint
V2No.46-Beatle c/sty	2.00	6.00	14.00
47-Beatle story	2.00	6.00	14.00
48	.35	1.00	2.00

SUMMER MAGIC (See Movie Comics)

SUNDANCE (See 4-Color No. 1126)

SUNDANCE KID
June, 1971 - No. 3, Sept, 1971 (52 pages)
Skywald Publications

	Good	Fine	Mint
1-Durango Kid; 2 Kirby Bullseye-r		.60	1.20
2-Swift Arrow, Durango Kid, Bullseye by S&K; Meskin plus 1 pg. origin		.40	.80
3-Durango Kid, Billy the Kid, Red Hawk-r		.30	.60

SUNDAY FUNNIES
1950
Harvey Publications

	Good	Fine	Mint
1	1.50	4.50	10.50

SUN DEVILS
July, 1984 - No. 12, June, 1985 (12-issue series; $1.25)
DC Comics

	Good	Fine	Mint
1-12: 6-Death of Sun Devil		.60	1.20

SUN FUN KOMIKS
1939 (15¢; black, white & red)
Sun Publications

	Good	Fine	Mint
1-Satire on comics	11.00	33.00	76.00

SUN GIRL
Aug, 1948 - No. 3, Dec, 1948
Marvel Comics (CCC)

	Good	Fine	Mint
1-Sun Girl begins; Miss America app.	46.00	138.00	320.00
2,3: 2-The Blonde Phantom begins	33.00	100.00	230.00

SUNNY, AMERICA'S SWEETHEART
No. 11, Dec, 1947 - No. 14, June, 1948
Fox Features Syndicate

	Good	Fine	Mint
11-Feldstein c/a	23.00	70.00	160.00
12-14-Feldstein c/a; 14-Lingerie panels	20.00	60.00	140.00
I.W. Reprint No. 8-Feldstein-a; r-Fox issue	3.50	10.50	24.00

SUN-RUNNERS (Also see Tales of the...)
2/84 - No. 3, 5/84; No. 4, 11/84 - No. 6, '86 (Baxter paper)
Pacific Comics/Eclipse Comics No. 4 on

	Good	Fine	Mint
1-6: P. Smith-a	.25	.80	1.60

SUNSET CARSON (Also see Cowboy Western)
Feb, 1951 - No. 4, 1951
Charlton Comics

	Good	Fine	Mint
1-Photo-c	25.00	75.00	175.00
2	16.00	48.00	110.00
3,4	14.50	43.50	100.00

SUPER ANIMALS PRESENTS PIDGY & THE MAGIC GLASSES
Dec, 1953
Star Publications

	Good	Fine	Mint
3-D 1-L. B. Cole-c	17.00	51.00	120.00

SUPER BOOK OF COMICS
(Omar Bread & Hancock Oil Co. giveaways)
1943 - 1946 (32 pgs.; later issues-16 pgs.) (some No.'s repeated)
Dell Publishing Co.

	Good	Fine	Mint
1-Smilin' Jack (Omar)	4.35	13.00	26.00
1-Dick Tracy	12.00	35.00	70.00
2-Bugs Bunny	3.65	11.00	22.00
2-King of the Royal Mtd.	5.00	15.00	30.00
2-Smitty	2.65	8.00	16.00
2-Smilin' Jack (Omar)	3.65	11.00	22.00
3-Captain Midnight	10.00	30.00	60.00
3-Terry & the Pirates	9.00	27.00	54.00
3-Moon Mullins	2.35	7.00	14.00
4-Smitty	2.35	7.00	14.00
4-Andy Panda	3.00	9.00	18.00
5-Don Winslow	3.00	9.00	18.00
5-Smokey Stover (Omar)	2.35	7.00	14.00
5-Terry & the Pirates	9.00	27.00	54.00
6-Don Winslow; McWilliams-a	3.65	11.00	22.00
6-King of the Royal Mtd.	5.35	16.00	32.00
6-Porky Pig	3.00	9.00	18.00
7-Dick Tracy	9.00	27.00	54.00
7-Little Orphan Annie	4.35	13.00	26.00
7-Smilin' Jack (Omar)	3.00	9.00	18.00
8-Oswald the Rabbit	2.35	7.00	14.00
9-Alley Oop	7.00	21.00	42.00
9-Terry & the Pirates	6.00	18.00	36.00
10-Elmer Fudd (Omar)	2.00	6.00	12.00
11-Little Orphan Annie	4.35	13.00	26.00
12-Woody Woodpecker	2.35	7.00	14.00
13-Dick Tracy (16 pgs.) (Omar)	9.00	27.00	54.00
14-Bugs Bunny (Omar)	3.00	9.00	18.00
15-Andy Panda	2.00	6.00	12.00
16-Terry & the Pirates	7.00	21.00	42.00
17-Smokey Stover	3.00	9.00	18.00
18-Porky Pig (Omar)	2.35	7.00	14.00
19-Smilin' Jack (Omar)	3.00	9.00	18.00
20-Oswald the Rabbit (Omar)	2.35	7.00	14.00
21-Gasoline Alley (Omar)	4.35	13.00	26.00
22-Elmer Fudd	2.00	6.00	12.00
23-Little Orphan Annie (Omar)	3.65	11.00	22.00
24-Woody Woodpecker (Omar)	1.70	5.00	10.00
25-Dick Tracy	7.00	21.00	42.00
26-Bugs Bunny (Omar)	1.70	5.00	10.00
27-Andy Panda	1.70	5.00	10.00
28-Terry & the Pirates (1946)(Omar)	7.00	21.00	42.00
29-Smokey Stover	2.00	6.00	12.00
30-Porky Pig (Omar)	1.70	5.00	10.00

SUPER BOOK OF COMICS (continued)

	Good	Fine	Mint
nn-Bugs Bunny ('48)	1.70	5.00	10.00
nn-Dan Dunn ('39 reprint)	3.00	9.00	18.00
nn-Dick Tracy	6.00	18.00	36.00
nn-Elmer Fudd ('46)	1.70	5.00	10.00
nn-Gasoline Alley	2.35	7.00	14.00
nn-Oswald the Rabbit	1.70	5.00	10.00
nn-Smilin' Jack	2.35	7.00	14.00
nn-Woody Woodpecker	1.70	5.00	10.00

SUPERBOY (See Adventure, Aurora, DC Comics Presents, DC Super Stars, 80 page Giant No. 10, More Fun, and The New Advs. of..)

SUPERBOY (...& the Legion of Super Heroes with No. 231)
(Becomes The Legion of Super Heroes No. 259 on)
Mar-Apr, 1949 - No. 258, Dec, 1979 (No. 1-16, 52 pgs.)
National Periodical Publications/DC Comics

	Good	Fine	Mint
1	210.00	630.00	1470.00
2-Used in **SOTI**, pg. 35-36,226	80.00	240.00	560.00
3	57.00	171.00	400.00
4,5: 5-Pre-Supergirl tryout	47.00	141.00	330.00
6-10: 8-1st Superbaby. 10-1st app. Lana Lang	34.00	102.00	238.00
11-15	27.00	81.00	190.00
16-20	19.00	57.00	132.00
21-26,28-30	13.50	40.50	95.00
27-Low distribution	14.50	43.50	100.00
31-38: 38-Last pre-code ish.	10.00	30.00	70.00
39-50 (7/56)	7.00	21.00	50.00
51-60: 55-Spanking-c	5.00	15.00	35.00
61-67	4.00	12.00	28.00
68-Origin & 1st app. original Bizarro (10-11/58)	6.00	18.00	42.00
69-77,79: 75-Spanking-c. 76-1st Supermonkey. 77-Pre-Pete Ross tryout	2.65	8.00	18.00
78-Origin Mr. Mxyzptlk & Superboy's costume	3.50	10.50	24.00
80-1st meeting Superboy/Supergirl (4/60)	2.65	8.00	18.00
81,84,85,87,88,90-92: 90-Pete Ross learns Superboy's I.D. 92-Last 10¢ issue	2.00	6.00	14.00
82-1st Bizarro Krypto	2.00	6.00	14.00
83-Origin & 1st app. Kryptonite Kid	2.00	6.00	14.00
86(1/61)-4th Legion app; Intro Pete Ross	7.00	21.00	50.00
89(6/61)-Mon-el 1st app.	5.75	17.25	40.00
93(12/61)-10th Legion app; Chameleon Boy app.	3.00	9.00	21.00
94-97,99	1.50	4.50	10.00
98(7/62)-19th Legion app; Origin & intro. Ultra Boy; Pete Ross joins Legion	2.50	7.50	17.00
100-Ultra Boy app; 1st app. Phantom Zone villains, Dr. Xadu & Erndine. 2 pg. map of Krypton; origin Superboy retold; r-cover of Superman 1; Pete Ross joins Legion	3.00	9.00	21.00
101-103,105-116,118-120: 111-1st app. Mental Emperor(Pa Kent) 115-Atomic bomb-c	1.00	3.00	6.00
104-Origin Phantom Zone	1.00	3.00	6.00
117-Legion app.	1.00	3.00	6.00
121-123,127,128	.50	1.50	3.00
124(10/65)-1st app. Insect Queen (Lana Lang)	.50	1.50	3.00
125-Only app./origin Kid Psycho; Legion cameo	.50	1.50	3.00
126-Origin Krypto the Super Dog retold with new facts	.50	1.50	3.00
129,138 (80-pg. Giant G-22,35)	.60	1.75	3.50
130-137,139,140: 131-Legion cameo (statues). 132-1st app. Supremo	.40	1.25	2.50
141-146,149-155,157-164,166-173,175,176: 145-Superboy's parents regain their youth. 172,173,176-Legion app.; 172-Origin Yango (Super Ape)	.35	1.00	2.00
147(6/68)-Giant G-47; origin Saturn Girl, Lightning Lad, & Cosmic Boy	.85	2.50	5.00
148-Polar Boy app.	.35	1.00	2.00
156,165,174 (Giants G-59,71,83)	.50	1.50	3.00
177-184,186,187 (All 52 pgs.): 184-Origin Dial H for Hero-r		.50	1.00
185-100 pg. Super Spec. No. 12; Legion app.-c, story; Teen Titans, Kid Eternity, Star Spangled Kid-r	.25	.75	1.50
188-190: 188-Origin Karkan		.50	1.00
191-Origin Sunboy retold; Legion app.		.50	1.00
192-196,198,199: 193-Chameleon Boy & Shrinking Violet get new costumes. 195-1st app. Erg/Wildfire; Phantom Girl gets new costume. 196-Last Superboy solo story		.50	1.00
197-Legion begins; Lightning Lad's new costume	.75	2.25	4.50
198,199: 198-Element Lad & Princess Projectra get new costumes	.35	1.00	2.00
200-Bouncing Boy & Duo Damsel marry; Jonn' Jonzz' cameo	.75	2.25	4.50
201,204,206,207,209: 201-Re-intro Erg as Wildfire. 204-Supergirl resigns from Legion. 206-Ferro Lad & Invisible Kid app. 209-Karate Kid new costume	.35	1.00	2.00
202,205-(100 pgs.): 202-Light Lass gets new costume	.45	1.25	2.50
203-Invisible Kid dies	.50	1.50	3.00
208-(68 pgs.)	.45	1.25	2.50
210-Origin Karate Kid	.45	1.25	2.50
211-215,217-220: 212-Matter-Eater Lad resigns	.30	.90	1.80
216-1st app. Tyroc who joins Legion in No. 218	.30	.90	1.80
221-249: 226-Intro. Dawnstar. 228-Death of Chemical King. 240-Origin Dawnstar		.60	1.20
250-258: 253-Intro Blok		.50	1.00
Annual 1 (Sum/64)-Origin Krypto-r	1.50	4.50	10.00

NOTE: **Adams** *c-143, 145, 146, 148-155, 157-161, 163, 164, 166-168, 172, 173, 175, 176, 178.* **Ditko** *a-257p.* **Grell** *a-202i, 203-219, 220-24p, 235p; c-207-232, 235, 236p, 237, 239p, 240p, 243p, 246, 258.* **Nasser** *a(p)-222, 225, 226, 230, 231, 233, 236.* **Simonson** *a-237p.* **Starlin** *a(p)-239, 250, 251; c-238.* **Staton** *a-227p, 243-249p, 252-258p; c-247-51p.* **Tuska** *a-172, 173, 176, 235p.* **Wood** *inks-152-155, 157-161. Legion app.-172, 173, 176, 177, 183, 184, 188, 190, 191, 193, 195.*

SUPERBOY SPECTACULAR
1980 (Giant)
DC Comics

	Good	Fine	Mint
1-Distributed only through comic shops; mostly reprints		.50	1.00

SUPER BRAT
January, 1954 - No. 4, July, 1954
Toby Press

	Good	Fine	Mint
1(1954)	1.50	4.50	10.00
2-4: 4-Li'l Teevy by Mel Lazarus	.75	2.25	5.00
I.W. Reprint No. 1,2,3,7,8('58)		.40	.80
I.W. (Super) Reprint No. 10('63)		.40	.80

SUPERCAR (TV)
Nov, 1962 - No. 4, Aug, 1963 (All painted covers)
Gold Key

	Good	Fine	Mint
1	2.85	8.50	20.00
2-4	2.00	6.00	12.00

SUPER CAT (Also see Frisky Animals)
Sept, 1957 - No. 4, May, 1958
Ajax/Farrell Publ. (Four Star Comic Corp.)

	Good	Fine	Mint
1('57-Ajax)	1.30	4.00	9.00
2-4	.75	2.25	5.00

Superboy #10, © DC

Superboy #121, © DC

Super Cat #2, © AJAX

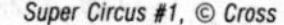
Super Circus #1, © Cross

Super Comics #2, © DELL

Supergear Comics nn, © Jacobs Corp.

SUPER CIRCUS
January, 1951 - No. 5, 1951
Cross Publishing Co.

	Good	Fine	Mint
1	2.35	7.00	16.00
2	1.65	5.00	12.00
3-5	1.35	4.00	9.00

SUPER CIRCUS (TV)
No. 542, March, 1954 - No. 694, Mar, 1956
Dell Publishing Co.

	Good	Fine	Mint
4-Color 542,592,694	2.00	6.00	14.00

SUPER COMICS
May, 1938 - No. 121, Feb-Mar, 1949
Dell Publishing Co.

	Good	Fine	Mint
1-Terry & The Pirates, The Gumps, Dick Tracy, Little Orphan Annie, Gasoline Alley, Little Joe, Smilin' Jack, Smokey Stover, Smitty, Tiny Tim, Moon Mullins, Harold Teen, Winnie Winkle begin	60.00	180.00	420.00
2	30.00	90.00	210.00
3	25.00	75.00	175.00
4,5	20.00	60.00	140.00
6-10	16.00	48.00	110.00
11-20	14.50	43.50	100.00
21-29: 21-Origin Magic Morro	11.50	34.50	80.00
30-''Sea Hawk'' movie adaptation-c/story with Errol Flynn	11.50	34.50	80.00
31-40	9.00	27.00	62.00
41-50: 43-Terry & The Pirates ends	7.00	21.00	50.00
51-60	5.50	16.50	38.00
61-70: 67-X-mas-c	4.35	13.00	30.00
71-80	3.75	11.25	26.00
81-99	3.35	10.00	23.00
100	4.35	13.00	30.00
101-115-Last Dick Tracy (graduates to own title)	3.00	9.00	21.00
116,118-All Smokey Stover	2.65	8.00	18.00
117-All Gasoline Alley	2.65	8.00	18.00
119-121: 119-121-Terry & The Pirates app.	2.65	8.00	18.00

SUPER COPS, THE
July, 1974 (One Shot)
Red Circle Productions (Archie)

	Good	Fine	Mint
1-Morrow-c/a		.30	.60

SUPER CRACKED (See Cracked)

SUPER DC GIANT (25 cents) (No No. 1-12)
No. 13, 9-10/70 - No. 26, 7-8/71; No. 27, Summer, 1976
National Periodical Publications

	Good	Fine	Mint
S-13-Binky		.40	.80
S-14-Top Guns of the West; Kubert-c; Trigger Twins, Johnny Thunder, Wyoming Kid-r		.30	.60
S-15-Western Comics; Kubert-c; Pow Wow Smith, Vigilante, Buffalo Bill-r		.30	.60
S-16-Best of the Brave & the Bold; Kubert-a		.40	.80
S-17-Love 1970		.40	.80
S-18-Three Mouseketeers; Dizzy Dog, Doodles Duck, Bo Bunny-r; Sheldon Mayer-a		.40	.80
S-19-Jerry Lewis; no Adams-a		.40	.80
S-20-House of Mystery; Adams-c; Kirby-a(3)(r)		.40	.80
S-21-Love 1971		.30	.60
S-22-Top Guns of the West		.30	.60
S-23-The Unexpected		.30	.60
S-24-Supergirl		.40	.80
S-25-Challengers of the Unknown; all Kirby/Wood-r		.40	.80
S-26-Aquaman (1971)		.40	.80
27-Strange Flying Saucers Adventures (Fall, '76)		.30	.60

NOTE: ***Sid Greene*** *a-27p(r),* ***Heath*** *a-27r.* ***G. Kane*** *a-14r, 15r, 27p(r).*

SUPER-DOOPER COMICS
1946 (10 cents)(32 pages)(paper cover)
Able Manufacturing Co.

	Good	Fine	Mint
1-The Clock, Gangbuster app.	4.00	12.00	28.00
2	2.00	6.00	14.00
3,4,6	1.75	5.25	12.00
5,7-Capt. Freedom & Shock Gibson	2.65	8.00	18.00
8-Shock Gibson, Sam Hill	2.65	8.00	18.00

SUPER DUCK COMICS (The Cockeyed Wonder) (See Jolly Jingles)
Fall, 1944 - No. 94, Dec, 1960
MLJ Mag. No. 1-4(9/45)/Close-Up No. 5 on (Archie)

	Good	Fine	Mint
1-Origin	14.50	43.50	100.00
2	6.50	20.00	45.00
3-5: 3-1st Mr. Monster	5.50	16.50	38.00
6-10	3.35	10.00	23.00
11-20	2.15	6.50	15.00
21,23-40	1.65	5.00	11.50
22-Used in **SOTI**, pg. 35,307,308	3.15	9.50	22.00
41-60	1.15	3.50	8.00
61-94	1.00	3.00	7.00

SUPER DUPER
1941
Harvey Publications

	Good	Fine	Mint
5-Captain Freedom & Shock Gibson app.	8.50	25.50	60.00
8,11	4.65	14.00	32.00

SUPER DUPER COMICS (Formerly Latest Comics?)
May-June, 1947
F. E. Howard Publ.

	Good	Fine	Mint
3-Mr. Monster app.	2.65	8.00	18.00

SUPER FRIENDS (TV) (Also see Best of DC & Limited Coll. Ed.)
Nov, 1976 - No. 47, Aug, 1981
National Periodical Publications/DC Comics

	Good	Fine	Mint
1-Superman, Batman, Wonder Woman, Aquaman, Atom, Robin, Wendy, Marvin & Wonder Dog begin		.30	.60
2-10: 7-1st app. Wonder Twins, & The Seraph. 8-1st app. Jack O'Lantern		.25	.50
11-47: 13-1st app. Dr. Mist. 14-Origin Wonder Twins. 25-1st app. Green Fury. 31-Black Orchid app. 47-Origin Green Fury		.25	.50

NOTE: ***Estrada*** *a-1p, 2p.* ***Orlando*** *a-1p.* ***Staton*** *a-43, 45.*

SUPER FRIENDS SPECIAL, THE
1981 (Giveaway) (no code or price) (no ads)
DC Comics

	Good	Fine	Mint
1		.30	.60

SUPER FUN
January, 1956 (By A.W. Nugent)
Gillmor Magazines

	Good	Fine	Mint
1-Comics, puzzles, cut-outs	1.00	3.00	7.00

SUPER FUNNIES (. . . Western Funnies No. 3,4)
Dec, 1953 - No. 4, June, 1954
Superior Comics Publishers Ltd. (Canada)

	Good	Fine	Mint
1-(3-D)-Dopey Duck; make your own 3-D glasses cut-out inside front-c; did not come w/glasses	20.00	60.00	140.00
2-Horror & crime satire	1.75	5.25	12.00
3-Geronimo, Billy The Kid app.	1.30	4.00	9.00
4-(Western-Phantom Ranger)	1.30	4.00	9.00

SUPERGEAR COMICS
1976 (4 pages in color) (slick paper)
Jacobs Corp. (Giveaway)

	Good	Fine	Mint
(Rare)-Superman, Lois Lane; Steve Lombard app.		.40	.80

NOTE: *500 copies printed, over half destroyed?*

SUPERGIRL (See Action, Adv., Brave & the Bold, Daring New Advs. of. . ., Super DC Giant, Superman Family, & Super-Team Family)
11/72 - No. 9, 12-1/73-74; No. 10, 9-10/74
National Periodical Publications

	Good	Fine	Mint
1-Zatanna begins; ends No. 5		.50	1.00
2-5: 5-Zatanna origin-r		.40	.80
6-10: 8-JLA x-over		.30	.60

NOTE: Zatanna in No. 1-5,7(Guest); Prez-No. 10.

SUPERGIRL (Formerly Daring New Advs. of. . .)
No. 14, Dec, 1983 - No. 23, Sept, 1984
DC Comics

	Good	Fine	Mint
14,15,17-23: 20-New Teen Titans app.		.40	.80
16-Ambush Bug app.		.60	1.20
Movie Special (1985)-Adapts movie		.60	1.20
Giveaway ('84, Baxter, nn)(American Honda)-Torres-a		.60	1.20

SUPER GOOF (Walt Disney)
Oct, 1965 - No. 74, 1982
Gold Key No. 1-57/Whitman No. 58 on

	Good	Fine	Mint
1	1.15	3.50	8.00
2-10	.55	1.65	4.00
11-20	.45	1.35	3.00
21-30	.35	1.00	2.00
31-50		.50	1.00
51-74		.30	.60

NOTE: *Reprints in No. 16,24,28,29,37,38,43,45,46,54(½),56-58,65(½),72(r-No.2).*

SUPER GREEN BERET (Tod Holton. . .)
April, 1967 - No. 2, June, 1967 (68 pages)
Lightning Comics (Milson Publ. Co.)

	Good	Fine	Mint
1,2	.70	2.00	4.00

SUPER HEROES (See Marvel. . . & Giant-Size. . .)

SUPER HEROES
Jan, 1967 - No. 4, June, 1967
Dell Publishing Co.

	Good	Fine	Mint
1-Origin & 1st app. Fab 4	1.15	3.50	8.00
2-4	.85	2.50	6.00

SUPER-HEROES BATTLE SUPER-GORILLAS (See DC Special No. 16)
Winter, 1976-77 (One Shot)
National Periodical Publications

	Good	Fine	Mint
1-Superman, Batman, Flash stories; Infantino-a(p); all-r		.30	.60

SUPER HEROES PUZZLES AND GAMES
1979 (32 pgs.) (regular size)
General Mills Giveaway (Marvel Comics Group)

	Good	Fine	Mint
Four 2-pg. origin stories of Spider-Man, Captain America, The Hulk, Spider-Woman	.50	1.50	3.00

SUPERHEROES VERSUS SUPERVILLAINS
July, 1966 (no month given)
Archie Publications

	Good	Fine	Mint
1-Flyman, Black Hood, The Web, Shield-r; Reinman-a	1.15	3.50	8.00

SUPERICHIE (Formerly Super Richie)
No. 5, Oct, 1976 - No. 18, Jan, 1979
Harvey Publications

	Good	Fine	Mint
5-18		.25	.50

SUPERIOR STORIES
May-June, 1955 - No. 4, Nov-Dec, 1955
Nesbit Publishing Co.

	Good	Fine	Mint
1-Invisible Man app.	5.00	15.00	35.00
2-The Pirate of the Gulf by J.H. Ingrahams	2.85	8.50	20.00
3-Wreck of the Grosvenor	2.85	8.50	20.00
4-O'Henry's "The Texas Rangers"	3.50	10.50	24.00

NOTE: *Morisi c/a in all.*

SUPER MAGIC (Super Magician No. 2 on)
May, 1941
Street & Smith Publications

	Good	Fine	Mint
V1No.1-Blackstone the Magician app.; origin & 1st app. Rex King (Black Fury); not Eisner-c	26.00	78.00	182.00

SUPER MAGICIAN COMICS (Super Magic No. 1)
No. 2, Sept, 1941 - V5No.8, Feb-Mar, 1947
Street & Smith Publications

	Good	Fine	Mint
V1No.2-Rex King, Man of Adventure app.	8.50	25.50	60.00
3-Tao-Anwar, Boy Magician begins	6.00	18.00	42.00
4-Origin Transo	5.00	15.00	35.00
5-12: 8-Abbott & Costello sty. 11-Supersnipe app.	5.00	15.00	35.00
V2No.1-The Shadow app.	4.00	12.00	28.00
2-12: 5-Origin Tigerman. 8-Red Dragon begins	3.35	10.00	23.00
V3No.1-12: 5-Origin Mr. Twilight	3.35	10.00	23.00
V4No.1-12: 11-Nigel Elliman begins	3.00	9.00	21.00
V5No.1-6	3.00	9.00	21.00
7,8-Red Dragon by Cartier	8.50	25.50	60.00

SUPERMAN (See Action Comics, Advs. of. . ., All-New Coll. Ed., All-Star Comics, Best of DC, Brave & the Bold, DC Comics Presents, Limited Coll. Ed., Man of Steel, Special Edition, Taylor's Christmas Tabloid, Three-Dimension Advs., World's Finest Comics & World of Krypton)

SUPERMAN (Adventures Of. . . No. 424 on)
Summer, 1939 - No. 423, Sept, 1986
National Periodical Publications/DC Comics

	Good	Fine	VF-NM
1(nn)-1st four Action stories reprinted; origin Superman by Siegel & Shuster; has a new 2 pg. origin plus 4 pgs. omitted in Action story	2900.00	8700.00	18,000.00

(No known copy exists beyond Vf-NM condition)

1-Reprint, Oversize 13½"x10." **WARNING:** This comic is an exact duplicate reprint of the original except for its size. DC published it in 1978 with a second cover titling it as a Famous First Edition. There have been many reported cases of the outer cover being removed and the interior sold as the original edition. The reprint with the new outer cover removed is practically worthless.

	Good	Fine	Mint
2-All daily strip-r	420.00	1260.00	2940.00
3-2nd story-r from Action No. 5; 3rd story-r from Action No. 6	290.00	870.00	2025.00
4-1st mention of Daily Planet	207.00	620.00	1450.00
5	173.00	520.00	1210.00
6,7: 7-1st Perry White?	130.00	390.00	910.00
8-10: 10-1st bald Luthor	103.00	310.00	720.00
11-13,15: 13-Jimmy Olsen app.	74.00	220.00	515.00
14-Patriotic Shield-c	87.00	260.00	610.00
16-20	63.00	190.00	440.00
21-23,25	49.00	147.00	342.00
24-Flag-c	60.00	180.00	420.00
26-29: 28-Lois Lane Girl Reporter series begins, ends No. 40,42	45.00	135.00	315.00
28-Overseas edition for Armed Forces; same as reg. No. 28	44.00	135.00	315.00
30-Origin & 1st app. Mr. Mxyztplk (pronounced "Mix-it-plk"); name later became Mxyzptlk ("Mix-yez-pit-l-ick"); the character was inspired by a combination of the name of Al Capp's Joe Blyfstyk (the little man with the black cloud over his head) & the devilish antics of Bugs Bunny	82.00	245.00	575.00

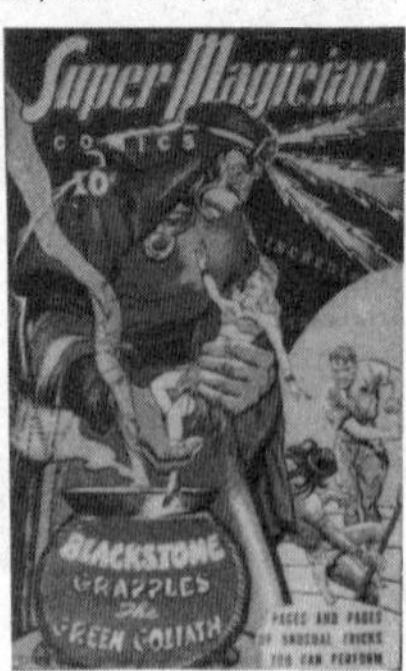

Super Magician V3No.11, © S&S

Superman #1, © DC

Superman #23, © DC

Superman #53, © DC

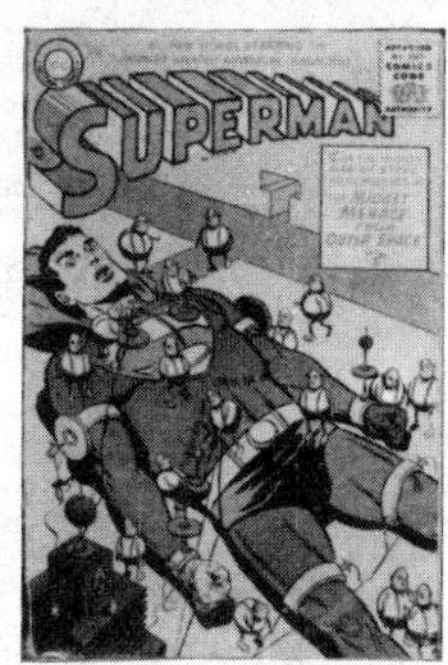

Superman #102, © DC

Superman #190, © DC

SUPERMAN (continued)

	Good	Fine	Mint
31,32,34-40	35.00	105.00	245.00
33-(3-4/45)-3rd app. Mxyztplk	40.00	120.00	280.00
41-50: 45-Lois Lane as Superwoman (see Action 60 for 1st app.)	26.00	78.00	180.00
51,52	23.00	70.00	160.00
53-Origin Superman retold	52.00	155.00	365.00
54,56-60	23.00	70.00	160.00
55-Used in **SOTI**, pg. 33	25.00	75.00	175.00
61-Origin Superman retold; origin Green Kryptonite (1st Kryptonite story)	40.00	120.00	280.00
62-65,67-70: 62-Orson Wells app. 65-1st Krypton Foes: Mala, K120, & U-Ban	23.00	70.00	160.00
66-2nd Superbaby story	24.00	72.00	166.00
71-75: 75-Some have No. 74 on-c	22.00	65.00	154.00
72-Giveaway(9-10/51)-(Rare)-Price blackened out; came with banner wrapped around book	27.00	81.00	190.00
76-Batman x-over; Superman & Batman learn each other's I.D.	50.00	150.00	350.00
77-80: 78-Last 52 pgs.	19.00	57.00	132.00
81-Used in **POP**, pg. 88	19.50	58.50	136.00
82-90	17.00	51.00	120.00
91-95: 95-Last pre-code ish.	16.50	50.00	115.00
96-99	11.50	34.50	80.00
100 (11/55)	30.00	90.00	210.00
101-110	9.00	27.00	62.00
111-120	7.00	21.00	50.00
121-130: 123-Pre-Supergirl tryout. 127-Origin/1st app. Titano. 128-Red Kryptonite used (4/59). 129-Intro/origin Lori Lemaris, The Mermaid	5.75	17.25	40.00
131-139: 139-Lori Lemaris app.	4.35	13.00	30.00
140-1st Blue Kryptonite & Bizarro Supergirl; origin Bizarro Jr. No. 1	3.85	11.50	27.00
141-145,148,150: 142-2nd Batman x-over	2.65	8.00	18.00
146-Superman's life story	3.85	11.50	27.00
147(8/61)-7th Legion app; 1st app. Legion of Super-Villains; intro. Adult Legion	4.75	14.25	33.00
149(11/61)-9th Legion app.-cameo; last 10¢ issue	4.75	14.25	33.00
151,153-154,158-160: 158-1st app. Flamebird & Nightwing & Nor-Kan of Kandor	2.15	6.50	13.00
152(4/62)-15th Legion app.	2.15	6.50	13.00
155(8/62)-20th Legion app; Lightning Man & Cosmic Man, & Adult Legion app.	2.15	6.50	13.00
156,162-Legion app.	2.15	6.50	13.00
157-Gold Kryptonite used (see Adv. 299); Mon-el app.; Lightning Lad cameo (11/62)	2.15	6.50	13.00
161-1st told death of Ma and Pa Kent	2.15	6.50	13.00
163-166,168-180: 169-Last Sally Selwyn. 172,173-Legion cameo	1.00	3.00	7.00
167-New origin Brainiac & Brainiac 5; intro Tixarla (Later Luthor's wife)	1.50	4.50	10.00
181,182,184-186,188-192,194-196,198,200: 181-1st 2965 story/series. 189-Origin/destruction of Krypton II	.90	2.75	5.50
183,187,193,197 (Giants G-18,G-23,G-31,G-36)	1.00	3.00	7.00
199-1st Superman/Flash race	.90	2.75	5.50
201,203-206,208-211,213-216,218-221,223-226,228-231,234-238: 213-Brainiac-5 app.	.60	1.75	3.50
202,207,212,217,222,227,239 (Giants G-42,G-48,G-54,G-60,G-66, G-72,G-84). 207-Legion app.	.75	2.25	4.50
232(Giant, G-78)-All Krypton issue	.75	2.25	4.50
233-1st app. Morgan Edge, Clark Kent switch from newspaper reporter to TV newscaster	.60	1.75	3.50
240-Kaluta-a	.25	.75	1.50
241-244 (52 pgs.). 243-G.A.-r/No. 38	.30	.90	1.80
245-DC 100 pg. Super Spec. No. 7; Air Wave, Kid Eternity, Hawkman, Atom-r	.40	1.25	2.50
246-248,250,251,253 (All 52 pgs.): 246-G.A.-r/No. 40. 248-World of Krypton story. 251-G.A.-r/No. 45. 253-Finlay-a, 2pgs., G.A.-r/No. 13		.50	1.00
249,254-Adams-a. 249-(52 pgs.); origin & 1st app. Terra-Man by Adams (inks)	.85	2.50	5.00
252-DC 100 pg. Super Spec. No. 13; Ray, Black Condor, Starman, Hawkman, Dr. Fate, Spectre app.; Adams-c	.70	2.00	4.00
255-263: 263-Photo-c		.50	1.00
264-1st app. Steve Lombard	.25	.75	1.50
265-271,273-277,279-283,285-299: 292-Origin Lex Luthor retold		.50	1.00
272,278,284-All 100 pgs. G.A.-r in all	.25	.70	1.40
300-Retells origin	.30	.85	1.70
301-330: 301,320-Solomon Grundy app. 323-Intro. Atomic Skull. 327-329-(44 pgs.). 330-More facts revealed about I. D.		.40	.80
331-389: 338-The bottled city of Kandor enlarged. 372-Superman 2021 app. 376-Free 16 pg. preview of Daring, New Advs. of Supergirl		.40	.80
390-399 (75¢ cover)		.50	1.00
400 (10/84, $1.50, 68 pgs.)-Many top artists featured		.70	1.40
401-423: 415-Crisis x-over		.45	.90
Annual 1(10/60)-Reprints 1st Supergirl/Action No. 252; r-/Lois Lane No. 1	11.50	34.50	80.00
Annual 2(1960)-Brainiac, Titano, Metallo, Bizarro origin-r	8.00	24.00	55.00
Annual 3(1961)	5.00	15.00	35.00
Annual 4(1961)-11th Legion app; 1st Legion origins-text & pictures	4.00	12.00	28.00
Annual 5(Sum, '62)-All Krypton issue	2.65	8.00	18.00
Annual 6(Wint, '62-'63)-Legion-r/Adv. No. 247	2.00	6.00	14.00
Annual 7(Sum/'63)-Origin-r/Superman-Batman team/Adv. 275; r-1955 Superman dailies	1.75	5.25	12.00
Annual 8(Wint, '63-'64)	1.30	4.00	9.00
Annual 9(9/83)-Toth/Austin-a		.50	1.00
Annual 10(11/84; $1.25)		.60	1.25
Annual 11(9/85)-Moore scripts		.60	1.25
Annual 12 (8/86)		.60	1.25
Special 1(3/83)-G. Kane c/a; r-that appeared in Germany		.50	1.00
Special 2(3/84, 48pgs.)		.60	1.25
Special 3(4/85; $1.25)		.60	1.25
The Amazing World of Superman "Official Metropolis Edition" ($2.00; 1973, 14x10½")-Origin retold	1.35	4.00	8.00
Kelloggs Giveaway-(⅔ normal size, 1954)-r-two stories/Superman No. 55	30.00	90.00	200.00
. . . Movie Special-(9/83)-Adaptation of Superman III		.50	1.00
Pizza Hut Giveaway(12/77)-Exact-r of No. 97,113	.25	.75	1.50
Radio Shack Giveaway-36pgs. (7/80) 'The Computers That Saved Metropolis;' Starlin/Giordano-a; advertising insert in Action 509, New Advs. of Superboy 7, Legion of Super-Heroes 265, & House of Mystery 282. (All comics were 64 pgs. & 40 cents; all dated 7/80.) Cover of inserts printed on newsprint. Giveaway contains 4 extra pgs. of Radio Shack advertising that inserts do not.	.25	.75	1.50
Radio Shack Giveaway-(7/81) 'Victory by Computer;' Super-Girl guest stars; also the TRS-80 Computer Whiz Kids	.25	.75	1.50
Radio Shack Giveaway-(7/82) 'Computer Masters of Metropolis'		.50	1.00
11195(2/79,224pp,$1.95)-Golden Press	.40	1.20	2.40

NOTE: ***Adams*** *a-249i, 254p; c-204-208, 210, 212-215, 219, 231, 233-237, 240-243, 249-252, 254, 263, 307, 308, 313, 314, 317.* ***Adkins*** *a-323i.* ***Austin*** *c-368i.* ***Wayne Boring*** *art-late 1940's to early 1960's.* ***Buckler*** *a-352p, 363p, 364p, 369p; c-324-327p,*

SUPERMAN (continued)
356p, 363p, 368p, 369p, 373p, 376p, 378p. ***Burnley*** *a-252r.* ***Fine*** *a-252r.* ***Gil Kane*** *a-272r, 367, 372, 375; c-374p, 375p, 377, 381, 382, 384-90, 392, Annual 9.* ***Kubert*** *c-216.* ***Morrow*** *a-238.* ***Perez*** *c-364p.* ***Starlin*** *c-355.* ***Staton*** *a-354i, 355i.* ***Williamson*** *a-408-410i, 412i, 416i; c-408i, 409i.* ***Wrightson*** *a-416.*

SUPERMAN
Jan, 1987 - Present
DC Comics

	Good	Fine	Mint
1-Byrne c/a; intro Metallo	.25	.75	1.50
2,3		.45	.90

SUPERMAN & THE GREAT CLEVELAND FIRE (Giveaway)
1948 (4 pages, no cover) (Hospital Fund)
National Periodical Publications

In full color	42.00	125.00	285.00

SUPERMAN FAMILY, THE (Formerly Superman's Pal Jimmy Olsen)
No. 164, Apr-May, 1974 - No. 222, Sept, 1982
National Periodical Publications/DC Comics

164-Jimmy Olsen, Supergirl, Lois Lane begin		.60	1.20
165-176 (100 - 68 pgs.)		.45	.90
177-181 (52 pgs.)		.40	.80
182-$1.00 ish. begin; Marshall Rogers-a; Krypto begins, ends No. 192	.25	.75	1.50
183-193,195-222: 183-Nightwing-Flamebird begins, ends No. 194. 189-Brainiac 5, Mon-el app. 191-Superboy begins, ends No. 198. 200-Book length story		.40	.80
194-Rogers-a	.25	.75	1.50

NOTE: ***Adams*** *c-182-185.* ***Anderson*** *a-186i.* ***Buckler*** *c-190p, 191p, 209p, 210p, 215p, 217p, 220p.* ***Jones*** *a-191-193.* ***Gil Kane*** *c-221p, 222p.* ***Mortimer*** *a-191-93p, 199p, 201-22p.* ***Orlando*** *a-186i, 187i.* ***Rogers*** *a-182, 194.* ***Staton*** *a-191-194, 196p.* ***Tuska*** *a-203p, 207-209p.*

SUPERMAN (Miniature)
1942; 1955 - 1956 (3 issues) (No No.'s) (32 pgs.)
The pages are numbered in the 1st issue: 1-32; 2nd: 1A-32A, and 3rd: 1B-32B
National Periodical Publications

No date-Py-Co-Pay Tooth Powder giveaway (8 pgs.; circa 1942)	40.00	120.00	280.00
1-The Superman Time Capsule (Kellogg's Sugar Smacks)(1955)	17.00	51.00	120.00
1A-Duel in Space	13.00	40.00	90.00
1B-The Super Show of Metropolis (also No. 1-32, no B)	13.00	40.00	90.00

NOTE: *Numbering variations exist. Each title could have any combination-No. 1, 1A, or 1B.*

SUPERMAN RECORD COMIC
1966 (Golden Records)
National Periodical Publications

(with record)-Record reads origin of Superman from comic; came with iron-on patch, decoder, membership card & button; comic r-/Superman 125, 146	3.65	11.00	25.00
Comic only	1.50	4.50	10.00

SUPERMAN'S BUDDY (Costume Comic)
1954 (4 pgs.) (One Shot) (Came in box w/costume; slick-paper/c)
National Periodical Publications

1-(Rare)-w/box & costume	55.00	165.00	385.00
Comic only	30.00	90.00	210.00

SUPERMAN'S CHRISTMAS ADVENTURE
1940, 1944 (16 pgs.) (Giveaway)
Distr. by Nehi drinks, Bailey Store, Ivey-Keith Co., Kennedy's Boys Shop, Macy's Store
National Periodical Publications

	Good	Fine	Mint
1(1940)-by Burnley	70.00	200.00	425.00
nn(1944)	54.00	160.00	350.00

SUPERMAN SCRAPBOOK (Has blank pages; contains no comics)

SUPERMAN'S GIRLFRIEND LOIS LANE (See 80 Pg. Giants No. 3,14, Showcase, & Superman Family)

SUPERMAN'S GIRLFRIEND LOIS LANE (Also see Lois Lane)
3-4/58 - No. 136, 1-2/74; No. 137, 9-10/74
National Periodical Publications

1	40.00	120.00	280.00
2	18.00	54.00	125.00
3	13.50	40.50	95.00
4,5	11.00	33.00	76.00
6-10: 9-Pat Boone app.	6.50	19.50	45.00
11-20: 14-Supergirl x-over	3.35	10.00	23.00
21-29: 23-1st app. Lena Thorul, Lex Luthor's sister. 29-Aquaman, Batman, Green Arrow cameo; last 10¢ issue	1.50	4.50	10.00
30-32,34-49: 47-Legion app.	.85	2.50	5.00
33(5/62)-Mon-el app.	1.50	4.50	9.00
50-Triplicate Girl, Phantom Girl & Shrinking Violet app.	.70	2.00	4.00
51-55,57-67,69,70	.25	.75	1.50
56-Saturn Girl app.	.35	1.00	2.00
68-(Giant G-26)	.35	1.00	2.00
71-76,78: 74-1st Bizarro Flash		.50	1.00
77-(Giant G-39)		.60	1.20
79-Adams-c begin, end No. 95,108		.50	1.00
80-85,87-94: 89-Batman x-over; all Adams-c		.40	.80
86-(Giant G-51)-Adams-c		.60	1.20
95-(Giant G-63)-Wonder Woman x-over; Adams-c		.60	1.20
96-103,106,107,109-111		.25	.50
104-(Giant G-75)		.50	1.00
105-Origin & 1st app. The Rose & the Thorn		.25	.50
108-Adams-c		.25	.50
112,114-123 (52 pgs.): 111-Morrow-a. 122-G.A.-r/Superman No. 30. 123-G.A. Batman-r		.25	.50
113-(Giant G-87)		.40	.80
124-137: 130-Last Rose & the Thorn. 132-New Zatanna story. 136-Wonder Woman x-over		.25	.50
Annual 1(Sum,'62)	1.30	4.00	9.00
Annual 2(Sum,'63)	.75	2.25	5.00

NOTE: ***Buckler*** *a-117-121p.* ***Curt Swan*** *a-1-50(most).*

SUPERMAN'S PAL JIMMY OLSEN (Superman Family No. 164 on)
(See 80 Page Giants)
Sept-Oct, 1954 - No. 163, Feb-Mar, 1974
National Periodical Publications

1	68.00	205.00	476.00
2	29.00	85.00	200.00
3-Last pre-code ish.	19.50	58.50	135.00
4,5	13.00	40.00	90.00
6-10	8.50	25.50	60.00
11-20	5.50	16.50	38.00
21-30: 29-1st app. Krypto in J.O.	2.65	8.00	18.00
31-40: 31-Origin Elastic Lad. 33-One pg. biography of Jack Larson (TV Jimmy Olsen). 36-Intro Lucy Lane	1.65	5.00	11.50
41-47,49,50: 41-1st J.O. Robot	1.00	3.00	7.00
48-Intro/origin Superman Emergency Squad	1.15	3.50	8.00
51-56: 56-Last 10¢ issue	.75	2.25	5.00
57-61,64-69: 57-Olsen marries Supergirl	.55	1.60	3.20
62(7/62)-18th Legion app.; Mon-el, Elastic Lad app.	1.35	4.00	8.00
63(9/62)-Legion of Super-Villains app.	.60	1.80	3.60

Superman Record Comic (1966), © DC

Superman's Girlfriend Lois Lane #28, © DC

Superman's Pal Jimmy Olsen #2, © DC

Superman-Tim, 9/44, © DC

Supermouse #1, © STD

Super-Mystery Comics #6, © ACE

SUPERMAN'S PAL... (continued) — Good / Fine / Mint

70-Element Lad app. .55 1.60 3.20
71,74,75,78,80-84,86,89,90: 86-J.O. Robot becomes Congorilla .35 1.00 2.00
72(10/63)-Legion app; Elastic Lad (Olsen) joins .50 1.50 3.00
73-Ultra Boy app. .40 1.25 2.50
76,85-Legion app. .50 1.50 3.00
77-Olsen with Colossal Boy's powers & costume; origin Titano retold .40 1.25 2.50
79(9/64)-Titled The Red-headed Beatle of 1000 B.C. .40 1.25 2.50
87-Legion of Super-Villains app. .50 1.50 3.00
88-Star Boy app. .35 1.00 2.00
91-94,96-98,101-103,105,107-110 .50 1.00
95,104 (Giants G-25,G-38). 95-Transvestite story .60 1.20
99-Legion app; Olsen with powers/costumes of Lightning Lad, Sun Boy, & Star Boy .30 1.00 2.00
100-Legion cameo app. .30 1.00 2.00
106-Legion app. .60 1.20
111,112,114-121,123-130,132 .25 .50
113,122,131 (Giants G-50,G-62,G-74) .50 1.00
133-Newsboy Legion by Kirby begins .30 1.00 2.00
134-139: 135-G.A. Guardian app. 136-Origin new Guardian .50 1.00
140-(Giant G-86) .50 1.00
141-Newsboy Legion reprints by S&K begin (52 pg. issues begin) .40 .80
142-148-Newsboy Legion-r .40 .80
149,150-G.A. Plastic Man reprint in both; last 52 pg. ish. 150-Newsboy Legion app. .25 .50
151-163 .25 .50

NOTE: *Issues No. 141-148 contain* ***Simon & Kirby*** *Newsboy Legion reprints from Star Spangled No. 7, 8, 9, 10, 11, 12, 13, 14 in that order.* ***Adams*** *c-109-112, 115, 117, 118, 120, 121, 132, 134-136, 147, 148.* ***Kirby*** *a-133-139p, 141-148p; c-133, 139, 145p.* ***Kirby/Adams*** *c-137, 138, 141-144, 146.*

SUPERMAN SPECTACULAR (Also see DC Special Series No. 5)
1982 (Magazine size)(Square binding)
DC Comics

1 .35 1.00 2.00

SUPERMAN: THE SECRET YEARS
Feb, 1985 - No. 4, May, 1985 (mini-series)
DC Comics

1-Miller-c on all .25 .75 1.50
2-4 .50 1.00

SUPERMAN 3-D (See Three-Dimension Adventures)

SUPERMAN-TIM (Becomes Tim)
1942 - May, 1950 (½-size) (B&W Giveaway)
Superman-Tim Stores/National Periodical Publications

2/43, 3/43, 6/43, 8/43, 9/43, 3/44, 11/49 issues-Two pg. Superman illos 8.00 24.00 56.00
10/43, 12/43, 2/44, 4/44-1/45, 3/45, 4/45, 4/46 issues-No Superman 5.50 16.50 40.00
2/45, 6/46, 8/46, 11/46, 3/47, 5/47-8/47, 10/47 issues-Superman story 13.00 40.00 90.00
2/48, 6/48, 8/48-11/48, 2/49-4/49, 12/49-5/50 issues-No Superman 4.65 14.00 32.00

SUPERMAN VS. THE AMAZING SPIDER-MAN
(Also see Marvel Treasury Edition No. 28)
April, 1976 (100 pgs.) ($2.00) (Over-sized)
National Periodical Publications/Marvel Comics Group

1 .50 1.50 3.00
1-2nd printing; 5000 numbered copies signed by Stan Lee & Carmine Infantino on front cover & sold through mail .85 2.50 5.00

SUPERMAN WORKBOOK
1945 (One Shot) (68 pgs; reprints) (B&W)
National Periodical Publ./Juvenile Group Foundation

c-r/Superman No. 14 55.00 165.00 385.00

SUPERMOUSE (...the Big Cheese; see Coo Coo Comics)
12/48 - No. 34, 9/55; No. 35, 4/56 - No. 45, Fall, 1958
Standard Comics/Pines No. 35 on (Literary Ent.)

1-Frazetta text illos (3) 11.50 34.50 80.00
2-Frazetta text illos 5.50 16.50 38.00
3,5,6-Text illos by Frazetta in all 4.35 13.00 30.00
4-Two pg. text illos by Frazetta 4.65 14.00 32.00
7-10 1.70 5.00 11.50
11-20: 13-Racist humor (Indians) 1.00 3.00 7.00
21-45 .75 2.25 5.00
1-Summer Holiday issue (Summer,'56-Pines)-100 pgs. 2.65 8.00 18.00
2-Giant Summer issue (Summer,'58-Pines)-100 pgs. 2.00 6.00 14.00

SUPER-MYSTERY COMICS
July, 1940 - V8No.6, July, 1949
Ace Magazines (Periodical House)

V1No.1-Magno, the Magnetic Man & Vulcan begin 54.00 162.00 375.00
2 25.00 75.00 175.00
3-The Black Spider begins 20.00 60.00 140.00
4-Origin Davy 19.00 57.00 132.00
5-Intro. The Clown 19.00 57.00 132.00
6(2/41) 16.00 48.00 110.00
V2No.1(4/41)-Origin Buckskin 16.00 48.00 110.00
2-6(2/42): 3-The Clown app. 5,6-Bondage-c 13.50 40.50 95.00
V3No.1(4/42),2: 1-Vulcan & Black Ace begin. 2-Bondage-c 11.50 34.50 80.00
3-Intro. The Lancer; Dr. Nemesis & The Sword begin; Kurtzman c/a(2) (Mr. Risk & Paul Revere Jr.) 17.00 51.00 120.00
4-Kurtzman-a 13.50 40.50 95.00
5-Kurtzman-a(2); L.B. Cole-a; Mr. Risk app; bondage-c 14.50 43.50 100.00
6(10/43)-Mr. Risk app.; Kurtzman's Paul Revere Jr.; L.B. Cole-a 14.50 43.50 100.00
V4No.1(1/44)-L.B. Cole-a 10.00 30.00 70.00
2-6(4/45): 2,6-Mr. Risk app. 8.50 25.50 60.00
V5No.1(7/45)-6 7.00 21.00 50.00
V6No.1-6: 3-Torture story. 4-Last Magno. Mr. Risk app. in No. 2,4-6 6.00 18.00 42.00
V7No.1-6, V8No.1-4,6 6.00 18.00 42.00
V8No.5-Meskin, Tuska, Sid Greene-a 7.00 21.00 50.00

NOTE: ***Mooney*** *c-V2/5, 6.* ***Palais*** *c/a-V5/3,4.*

SUPERNATURAL THRILLERS
12/72 - No. 6, 11/73; No. 7, 7/74 - No. 15, 10/75
Marvel Comics Group

1-It!-Sturgeon adaptation, 2-The Invisible Man, 3-The Valley of the Worm .40 .80
4-Dr. Jekyll & Mr. Hyde, 5-The Living Mummy, 6-The Headless Horseman .25 .50
7-15: 7-The Living Mummy begins .25 .50

NOTE: ***Brunner*** *c-11.* ***Buckler*** *a-5p.* ***Ditko*** *a-8r, 9r.* ***G. Kane*** *a-3p; c-3, 9p, 15p.* ***Mayerik*** *a-2p, 7, 8, 9p, 10p, 11.* ***McWilliams*** *a-14i.* ***Mortimer*** *a-4.* ***Steranko*** *c-1, 2.* ***Sutton*** *a-15.* ***Tuska*** *a-6p. Robert E. Howard story-No. 3.*

SUPER POWERS
7/84 - No. 5, 11/84; 9/85 - No. 6, 2/86; 9/86 - No. 4, 12/86

SUPER POWERS (continued)
DC Comics

	Good	Fine	Mint
1-Kirby-c		.60	1.20
2-5		.45	.90
1-('85)Kirby c/a in all; 1st app Samurai from Super Friends TV show; Capt. Marvel, Dr. Fate join		.50	1.00
2-6		.45	.90
1-4 ('86)		.40	.80

SUPER PUP
No. 4, Mar-Apr, 1954 - No. 5, 1954
Avon Periodicals

	Good	Fine	Mint
4,5	1.15	3.50	8.00

SUPER RABBIT (See Animated Movie Tunes, Comedy Comics, Comic Capers, Ideal Comics, Movie Tunes & Wisco)
Fall, 1943 - No. 14, Nov, 1948
Timely Comics (CmPI)

	Good	Fine	Mint
1	22.00	65.00	154.00
2	11.00	33.00	76.00
3-5	6.50	19.50	45.00
6-Origin	5.00	15.00	35.00
7-10; 9-Infinity-c	3.85	11.50	27.00
11-Kurtzman's "Hey Look"	5.00	15.00	35.00
12-14	3.15	9.50	22.00
I.W. Reprint No. 1,2('58),7,10('63)	.70	2.00	4.00

SUPER RICHIE (Superichie No. 5 on)
Sept, 1975 - No. 4, Mar, 1976 (52 pages)
Harvey Publications

	Good	Fine	Mint
1	.35	1.00	2.00
2-4		.50	1.00

SUPERSNIPE COMICS (Army & Navy No. 1-5)
Oct, 1942 - V5No.1, Aug-Sept, 1949 (Also see Shadow Comics)
Street & Smith Publications

	Good	Fine	Mint
V1No.6-Rex King Man of Adventure(costumed hero) by Jack Binder begins; Supersnipe by George Marcoux continues from Army & Navy No. 5; Bill Ward-a	22.00	65.00	154.00
7-12: 9-Doc Savage x-over in Supersnipe. 11-Little Nemo app.	14.50	43.50	100.00
V2No.1-12: 1-Huck Finn by Clare Dwiggins begins, ends V3/5	10.00	30.00	70.00
V3No.1-12: 8-Bobby Crusoe by Dwiggins begins, ends V3/12	8.00	24.00	56.00
V4No.1-12, V5No.1	5.75	17.25	40.00

NOTE: *Doc Savage in some issues.*

SUPERSPOOK (Formerly Frisky Animals on Parade)
No. 4, June, 1958
Ajax/Farrell Publications

	Good	Fine	Mint
4	1.20	3.50	8.00

SUPER SPY (See Wham)
Oct, 1940 - No. 2, Nov, 1940 (Reprints)
Centaur Publications

	Good	Fine	Mint
1-Origin The Sparkler	50.00	150.00	350.00
2-The Inner Circle, Dean Denton, Tim Blain, The Drew Ghost, The Night Hawk by Gustavson, & S.S. Swanson by Glanz app.	35.00	105.00	245.00

SUPER STAR HOLIDAY SPECIAL (See DC Special Series No. 21)

SUPER-TEAM FAMILY
10-11/75 - No. 15, 3-4/78 (No.1-4: 68 pgs.; No.5 on: 52 pgs.)
National Periodical Publications/DC Comics

	Good	Fine	Mint
1-Reprints; Adams, Kane/Wood		.40	.80
2-7: 4-7-Reprints		.25	.50
8-15-New stys; Chall. of the Unknown in 8-10		.25	.50

NOTE: ***Adams** a-1r-3r. **Brunner** c-3. **Buckler** c-8p. **Estrada** a-2. **Tuska** a-7r. **Wood** a-1i(r), 3.*

SUPER TV HEROES (See Hanna-Barbera. . .)

SUPER-VILLAIN CLASSICS
May, 1983 (One Shot)
Marvel Comics Group

	Good	Fine	Mint
1-"Galactus the Origin"		.50	1.00

SUPER-VILLAIN TEAM-UP
8/75 - No. 14, 10/77; No. 15, 11/78; No. 16, 5/79; No. 17, 6/80
Marvel Comics Group

	Good	Fine	Mint
1-Sub-Mariner app.		.60	1.20
2-5: 4-Mooney-a		.30	.60
6-17: 5-1st app. The Shroud. 7-Origin The Shroud		.30	.60
Giant-Size 1(3/75, 68 pgs.)-Craig inks-r		.50	1.00
Giant-Size 2(6/75, 68 pgs.)-Dr. Doom, Sub-Mariner app.		.40	.80

NOTE: ***Buscema** c-1. **Byrne/Austin** c-14. **Buckler** c-4p, 5p, 7p. **Ditko** a-Gnt-Size 2r. **Evans** a-1p, 3p. **Everett** a-1p. **Giffen** a-8p, 13p; c-13p. **Kane** c-2p, 9p. **Mooney** a-4i. **Sekowsky** a-Gnt-size 2p. **Starlin** c-6. **Tuska** a-1p, 15p(r). **Wood** a-15p(r).*

SUPER WESTERN COMICS (Also see Buffalo Bill)
Aug, 1950 - No. 4, Mar, 1951
Youthful Magazines

	Good	Fine	Mint
1-Buffalo Bill begins; Powell-a	3.15	9.50	22.00
2-4	1.70	5.00	11.50

SUPER WESTERN FUNNIES (See Super Funnies)

SUPERWORLD COMICS
April, 1940 - No. 3, Aug, 1940
Hugo Gernsback (Komos Publ.)

	Good	Fine	Mint
1-Origin Hip Knox, Super Hypnotist; Mitey Powers & Buzz Allen, the Invisible Avenger, Little Nemo begin; cover by Frank R. Paul	65.00	195.00	455.00
2-Marvo 1,2 Go+, the Super Boy of the Year 2680	40.00	120.00	280.00
3	35.00	105.00	245.00

SURE-FIRE COMICS (Lightning Comics No. 4 on)
June, 1940 - No. 4, Oct, 1940 (Two No. 3's)
Ace Magazines

	Good	Fine	Mint
V1No.1-Origin Flash Lightning; X-The Phantom Fed, Ace McCoy, Buck Steele, Marvo the Magician, The Raven, Whiz Wilson (Time Traveler) begin	43.00	130.00	300.00
2	27.00	81.00	190.00
3(9/40)	22.00	65.00	154.00
3(No.4)(10/40)-nn on cover, No. 3 on inside	22.00	65.00	154.00

SURF 'N' WHEELS
Nov, 1969 - No. 6, Sept, 1970
Charlton Comics

	Good	Fine	Mint
1		.40	.80
2-6		.25	.50

SURGE
July, 1984 - No. 4, Jan, 1985 (mini-series) ($1.50; Baxter paper)
Eclipse Comics

	Good	Fine	Mint
1-4-Ties into DNAgents series	.30	.90	1.80

Supersnipe Comics V3No.7, © S&S

Superworld Comics #3, © H. Gernsback

Surge #2, © Evanier & Meugniot

Suspense Comics #8, © Continental

Suspense Detective #3, © FAW

Swamp Thing #7, © DC

SURPRISE ADVENTURES (Formerly Tormented)
Mar, 1955 - No. 5, July, 1955
Sterling Comic Group

	Good	Fine	Mint
3-5: 3,5-Sekowsky-a	1.15	3.50	8.00

SURVIVORS, THE (They were Chosen To Be. . .)
Jan, 1985 - No. 5, 1985 ($1.50; B&W)
Spectrum Comics

1-5	.25	.75	1.50

SUSIE Q. SMITH (See Four Color 323,377,453,553)

SUSPENSE (Radio/TV; Real Life Tales of. . . No. 1-4) (Amazing Detective Cases No. 3 on?. . . change to horror)
Dec, 1949 - No. 29, Apr, 1953 (No. 1-8,17-23: 52 pgs.)
Marvel/Atlas Comics (CnPC No. 1-10/BFP No. 11-29)

1-Powell-a; Peter Lorre, Sidney Greenstreet photo-c from Hammett's 'The Maltese Falcon'	11.50	34.50	80.00
2-Crime stories; photo-c	5.50	16.50	38.00
3-Change to horror	5.50	16.50	38.00
4,7-10	3.75	11.25	26.00
5-Krigstein, Tuska, Everett-a	4.85	14.50	34.00
6-Tuska, Everett, Morisi-a	4.00	12.00	28.00
11-17,19,20: 14-Hypo-c; A-Bomb panels	3.35	10.00	23.00
18,22-Krigstein-a	4.00	12.00	28.00
21,23,26-29	2.65	8.00	18.00
24-Tuska-a	2.85	8.50	20.00
25-Electric chair c/a	5.75	17.25	40.00

NOTE: ***Briefer** a-5, 7, 27. **Colan** a-8(2), 9. **Everett** a-5, 6(2), 19, 23, 28; c-21-23, 26. **Fuje** a-29. **Heath** a-5, 6, 8, 10, 12, 14; c-14, 19, 24. **Maneely** a-29; c-10. **Morisi** a-6. **Palais** a-10. **Rico** a-7-9. **Robinson** a-29. **Romita** a-25. **Sekowsky** a-11, 13, 14. **Sinnott** a-23, 25. **Tuska** a-5, 6, 12; c-12. **Whitney** a-15, 16, 22.*

SUSPENSE COMICS
Dec, 1943 - No. 12, Dec?, 1946
Continental Magazines

1-The Grey Mask begins; bondage/torture-c; L. B. Cole-a, 7pgs.	25.00	75.00	175.00
2-Intro. The Mask; Rico, Giunta, L. B. Cole-a, 7pgs.	16.50	50.00	115.00
3-L.B. Cole-a; Schomburg-c	16.50	50.00	115.00
4-6: 5-Schomburg-c	15.00	45.00	105.00
7,9,10	14.50	43.50	100.00
8-Classic L. B. Cole spider-c	33.50	100.00	235.00
11-Classic Devil-c	22.00	65.00	154.00
12-r-No.7-c	14.50	43.50	100.00

NOTE: ***L. B. Cole** c-6-12. **Larsen** a-11. **Palais** a-10,11.*

SUSPENSE DETECTIVE
June, 1952 - No. 5, Mar, 1953
Fawcett Publications

1-Evans-a, 11 pgs; Baily c/a	7.00	21.00	50.00
2-Evans-a, 10 pgs.	4.35	13.00	30.00
3,5	3.15	9.50	22.00
4-Bondage-c	3.75	11.25	26.00

NOTE: ***Baily** a-4, 5. **Sekowsky** a-2, 4, 5; c-5.*

SUSPENSE STORIES (See Strange Suspense Stories)

SUZIE COMICS (Formerly Laugh Comix)
No. 49, Spring, 1945 - No. 100, Aug, 1954
Close-Up No. 49,50/MLJ Mag./Archie No. 51 on

	Good	Fine	Mint
49-Ginger begins	10.00	30.00	70.00
50-55: 54-Transvestite story	7.00	21.00	50.00
56-Katy Keene begins by Woggon	6.00	18.00	42.00
57-65	4.35	13.00	30.00
66-80	3.65	11.00	25.00
81-87,89-99	3.35	10.00	23.00
88-Used in **POP**, pg. 76,77; Bill Woggon draws himself in story	4.35	13.00	30.00
100-Last Katy Keene	3.65	11.00	25.00

NOTE: ***Katy Keene** in 53-82,85-100.*

SWAMP FOX, THE (See 4-Color No. 1179)

SWAMP FOX, THE
1960 (14 pgs, small size) (Canada Dry Premiums)
Walt Disney Productions

Titles: (A)-Tory Masquerade, (B)-Rindau Rampage, (C)-Turnabout Tactics; each came in paper sleeve, books 1,2 & 3;

Set with sleeves	3.00	9.00	21.00
Comic only	1.00	3.00	6.00

SWAMP THING (See Brave & Bold, DC Comics Presents 8, DC Spec. Series 2, 14, House of Sec. 92, Roots of the. . ., & The Saga of. . .)
Oct-Nov, 1972 - No. 24, Aug-Sept, 1976
National Periodical Publications/DC Comics

1-c/a by Wrightson begin	.85	2.50	5.00
2	.40	1.20	2.40
3-Intro. Patchworkman	.30	.90	1.80
4-10: 7-Batman app. 10-Last Wrightson issue		.60	1.20
11-23-Redondo-a; 23-Swamp Thing reverts back to Dr. Holland		.40	.80
24		.25	.50

NOTE: ***J. Jones** a-9i. **Kaluta** a-9i. **Redondo** c-12-19, 21.*

SWAT MALONE
Sept, 1955
Swat Malone Enterprises

V1No.1-Hy Fleishman-a	2.85	8.50	20.00

SWEENEY (Buz Sawyer's Pal, Roscoe. . .)
1949
Standard Comics

4,5-Crane-a No. 5	2.50	7.50	17.50

SWEE'PEA (See 4-Color No. 219)

SWEETHEART DIARY (Cynthia Doyle No. 66-on)
Wint, 1949 - No. 14, 1/53; No. 33, 4/56 - No. 65, 8/62
(No. 1-14, photo-c)
Fawcett Publications/Charlton Comics No. 33 on

1	5.00	15.00	35.00
2	2.65	8.00	18.00
3,4-Wood-a	8.00	24.00	56.00
5-10: 8-Bailey-a	2.35	7.00	16.00
11-14-Last Fawcett issue	1.30	4.00	9.00
33 (4/56; 1st Charlton ish.)(Formerly Sweetheart Love Story?)	1.15	3.50	8.00
34-40	.85	2.50	6.00
41-60	.35	1.00	2.00
61-65		.40	.80

SWEETHEART LOVE STORY (Formerly Cowboy Love No. 28-31? Sweetheart Diary No. 33-on?)
No. 32, Oct, 1955
Charlton Comics

32	.55	1.65	4.00

SWEETHEARTS (Formerly Captain Midnight)
No. 68, 10/48 - No. 121, 5/53; No. 122, 3/54 - No. 137, 12/73
Fawcett Publications/Charlton No. 122 on

68-Robert Mitchum photo-c	4.00	12.00	28.00
69-80: 72-Baker-a?	2.00	6.00	14.00
81-84,86-93,95-99	1.50	4.50	10.00
85,94,103,105,110,117-George Evans-a	2.35	7.00	16.00
100	1.85	5.50	13.00
101-Powell-a	1.65	5.00	11.50

SWEETHEARTS (continued)

	Good	Fine	Mint
102,104,106-109,112-116,118,121	1.15	3.50	8.00
111-1 pg. Ronald Reagan biog	2.65	8.00	18.00
119-Marilyn Monroe photo-c; also appears in story; part Wood-a	5.75	17.25	40.00
120-Atom Bomb story	2.35	7.00	16.00
122-(1st Charlton?)-Marijuana story	2.00	6.00	14.00
123-125 (Exist?)	1.00	3.00	7.00
V2/26 (?/54)-28: Last Pre-code ish	.85	2.50	6.00
29-39,41,43-45,47-50	.60	1.80	4.00
40-Photo-c; Tommy Sands story	.85	2.50	6.00
42-Ricky Nelson photo-c/sty	1.00	3.00	7.00
46-Jimmy Rodgers photo-c/sty	.85	2.50	6.00
51-60	.55	1.65	4.00
61-80	.30	1.00	2.00
81-100		.50	1.00
101-137		.25	.50

NOTE: *Photo c-68-121.*

SWEETHEART SCANDALS (See Fox Giants)

SWEETIE PIE (See 4-Color No. 1185,1241)

SWEETIE PIE
Dec, 1955 - No. 15, Fall, 1957
Ajax-Farrell/Pines (Literary Ent.)

	Good	Fine	Mint
1-By Napine Seltzer	2.35	7.00	16.00
2 (5/56; last Ajax?)	1.15	3.50	8.00
3-15 (No. 3-10, exist?)	.85	2.50	6.00

SWEET LOVE
Sept, 1949 - No. 5, May, 1950
Home Comics (Harvey)

	Good	Fine	Mint
1-Photo-c	2.00	6.00	14.00
2	1.50	4.50	10.00
3,4: 3-Powell-a	1.35	4.00	9.00
5-Kamen, Powell-a; photo-c	2.75	8.00	18.00

SWEET ROMANCE
October, 1968
Charlton Comics

	Good	Fine	Mint
1		.40	.80

SWEET SIXTEEN
Aug-Sept, 1946 - No. 13, Jan, 1948
Parents' Magazine Institute

	Good	Fine	Mint
1-Van Johnson's life story; Dorothy Dare, Queen of Hollywood Stunt Artists begins (in all issues)	4.00	12.00	28.00
2-Jane Powell, Roddy McDowall ''Holiday in Mexico'' photo-c	2.65	8.00	18.00
3-6,8-11: 6-Dick Haymes story	2.35	7.00	16.00
7-Ronald Reagan's life story	9.50	28.50	65.00
12-Bob Cummings, Vic Damone story	3.15	9.50	22.00
13-Robert Mitchum's life story	3.85	11.50	27.00

SWIFT ARROW (Also see Lone Rider)
2-4/54 - No. 5, 10-11/54; 4/57 - No. 3, 9/57
Ajax/Farrell Publications

	Good	Fine	Mint
1(1954) (1st Series)	3.15	9.50	22.00
2	1.65	5.00	11.50
3-5: 5-Lone Rider sty	1.50	4.50	10.00
1 (2nd Series) (Swift Arrow's Gunfighters No. 4)	1.50	4.50	10.00
2,3: 2-Lone Rider begins	1.15	3.50	8.00

SWIFT ARROW'S GUNFIGHTERS (Formerly Swift Arrow)
No. 4, Nov, 1957
Ajax/Farrell Publ. (Four Star Comic Corp.)

	Good	Fine	Mint
4	1.15	3.50	8.00

SWIFTSURE
May, 1985 - Present
Harrier Comics

	Good	Fine	Mint
1-8,10	.30	.90	1.80
9-Intro/1st app. Red Fox	1.35	4.00	8.00
11-13	.35	1.00	1.95

SWING WITH SCOOTER
6-7/66 - No. 35, 8-9/71; No. 36, 10-11/72
National Periodical Publications

	Good	Fine	Mint
1	.75	2.25	5.00
2-10	.50	1.50	3.00
11-32,35,36	.25	.75	1.50
33-Interview with David Cassidy	.25	.75	1.50
34-Interview with Ron Ely (Doc Savage)	.25	.75	1.50

NOTE: ***Orlando** a-1-11; c-1-11, 13. No. 20, 33, 34: 68 pgs.; No. 35: 52 pgs.*

SWISS FAMILY ROBINSON (See 4-Color No. 1156, King Classics, & Movie Comics)

SWORD & THE DRAGON, THE (See 4-Color No. 1118)

SWORD & THE ROSE, THE (See 4-Color No. 505,682)

SWORD IN THE STONE, THE (See March of Comics No. 258 & Movie Comics)

SWORD OF LANCELOT (See Movie Classics)

SWORD OF SORCERY
Feb-Mar, 1973 - No. 5, Nov-Dec, 1973
National Periodical Publications

	Good	Fine	Mint
1-Leiber Fafhrd & The Gray Mouser; Adams/Bunkers inks; also No. 2; Kaluta-c	.25	.75	1.50
2-Wrightson-c(i); Adams-a(i)	.25	.75	1.50
3-5: 5-Starlin-a; Conan cameo		.60	1.20

NOTE: ***Chaykin** a-1p, 2-4; c-2p, 3-5. **Kaluta** a-3i. **Simonson** a-1i, 3p, 4, 5p; c-5. **Starlin** a-5p.*

SWORD OF THE ATOM
Sept, 1983 - No. 4, Dec, 1983 (Mini-series)
DC Comics

	Good	Fine	Mint
1-Kane c/a begins		.50	1.00
2-4		.40	.80
Special 1(7/84), 2(7/85): Kane c/a each		.65	1.30

SWORDS OF THE SWASHBUCKLERS
Mar, 1985 - Present ($1.50) (Mature readers)
Epic Comics (Marvel)

	Good	Fine	Mint
1-Butch Guice-c/a cont'd from Marvel Graphic Novel	.35	1.00	2.00
2-8	.25	.80	1.60

SYPHONS
July, 1986 - Present ($1.50, color)
Now Comics

	Good	Fine	Mint
1-4	.25	.75	1.50

TAFFY
Mar-Apr, 1945 - No. 12, 1948
Rural Home/Orbit Publ.

	Good	Fine	Mint
1-L. B. Cole-c; origin of Wonderworm plus 7 chapter WWII Funny Animal Adv.	4.65	14.00	32.00
2-L. B. Cole-c	3.35	10.00	23.00
3,4,6-12: 6-Perry Como c/story. 7-Duke Ellington, 2 pgs.	2.35	7.00	16.00
5-L.B. Cole-c; Van Johnson story	3.35	10.00	23.00

Sweethearts #120, © FAW

Swift Arrow #1 (1st Series), © AJAX

Syphons #1, © Now Comics

Tales From the Aniverse #1, © Arrow

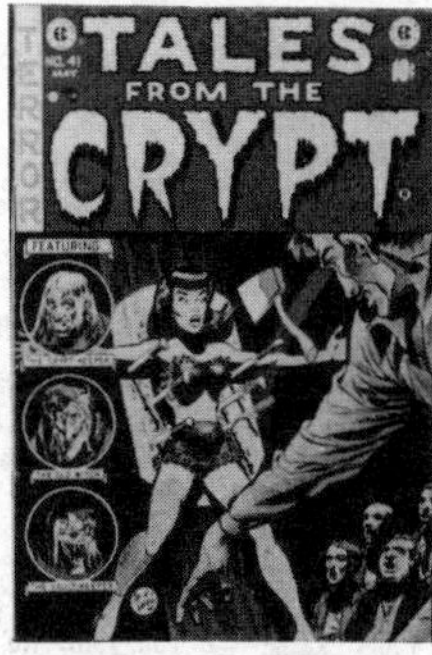

Tales From the Crypt #41, © WMG

Tales of Horror #4, © TOBY

TAILSPIN
November, 1944
Spotlight Publishers

	Good	Fine	Mint
nn-Firebird app.; L. B. Cole-c	4.65	14.00	32.00

TAILSPIN TOMMY STORY & PICTURE BOOK
1931? (no date) (Color strip reprints) (10½x10'')
McLoughlin Bros.

266-by Forrest	11.00	33.00	76.00

TAILSPIN TOMMY
1932 (100 pages) (hardcover)
Cupples & Leon Co.

(Rare)-B&W strip reprints from 1930 by Hal Forrest & Glenn Claffin	13.50	40.50	95.00

TAILSPIN TOMMY
1940; 1946
United Features Syndicate/Service Publ. Co.

Single Series 23('40)	11.50	34.50	80.00
Best Seller 1(nd, '46)-Service Publ. Co.	6.65	20.00	46.00

TALENT SHOWCASE (See New Talent Showcase)

TALES CALCULATED TO DRIVE YOU BATS
Nov, 1961 - No. 7, Nov, 1962; 1966
Archie Publications

1	3.00	9.00	18.00
2	1.50	4.50	9.00
3-6	1.20	3.50	7.00
7-Story line change	.70	2.00	4.00
1('66)-25 cents; r-No. 1,2	.80	2.40	4.80

TALES FROM THE ANIVERSE
1985 (no month) - Present ($1.50, B&W)
Arrow Comics

1-(Animal universe)-sci/fi	1.35	4.00	8.00
2-4	.35	1.00	2.00

TALES FROM THE CRYPT (Formerly The Crypt of Terror No. 17-19)
No. 20, Oct-Nov, 1950 - No. 46, Feb-Mar, 1955
E. C. Comics

20	41.00	123.00	285.00
21-Kurtzman-r/Haunt of Fear No.15/(1)	34.00	102.00	235.00
22-Moon Girl costume at costume party, one panel	27.00	80.00	190.00
23-25	20.00	60.00	140.00
26-30	16.00	48.00	110.00
31-Williamson-a (1st at EC); B&W and color illos. in **POP**; Kamen draws himself, Gaines & Feldstein; Ingels, Craig & Davis draw themselves in his story	20.00	60.00	140.00
32,35-39	12.00	36.00	84.00
33-Origin The Crypt Keeper	20.00	60.00	140.00
34-Used in **POP**, pg. 83; lingerie panels	12.00	36.00	84.00
40-Used in Senate hearings & in Hartford Cournat anti-comics editorials-1954	12.00	36.00	84.00
41-45: 45-2pgs. showing E.C. staff	11.00	33.00	75.00
46-Low distribution; pre-advertised cover for unpublished 4th horror title 'Crypt of Terror' used on this book	12.00	36.00	84.00

NOTE: ***Craig** a-20, 22-24; c-20. **Crandall** a-38, 44. **Davis** a-23, 24-46; c-29-46. **Elder** a-37, 38. **Evans** a-32-34, 36, 40, 41, 43, 46. **Feldstein** a-20-23; c-21-25, 28. **Ingels** a-in all. **Kamen** a-20, 22, 25, 27-31, 33-36, 39, 41-45. **Krigstein** a-40, 42, 45. **Kurtzman** a-21. **Orlando** a-27-30, 35, 37, 39, 46. **Wood** a-21, 24, 25; c-26, 27. Canadian reprints known; see Table of Contents.*

TALES FROM THE CRYPT (Magazine)
No. 10, July, 1968 (35 cents) (B&W)
Eerie Publications

10-Contains Farrell reprints from 1950's	.40	1.25	2.50

TALES FROM THE GREAT BOOK
Feb, 1955 - No. 4, Jan, 1956
Famous Funnies

	Good	Fine	Mint
1	2.85	8.50	20.00
2-4-Lehti-a in all	1.50	4.50	10.00

TALES FROM THE TOMB
Oct, 1962 - No. 2, Dec, 1962
Dell Publishing Co.

1(02-810-210)(Giant)-All stories written by John Stanley	1.35	5.25	12.00
2	1.35	4.00	9.00

TALES FROM THE TOMB (Magazine)
V1No.6, July, 1969 - V6No.6, Dec, 1974 (52 pgs.)
Eerie Publications

V1No.6-8	.50	1.50	3.00
V2No.1-3,5,6: 6-Rulah-r	.35	1.00	2.00
4-LSD story-r/Weird V3No.5	.70	2.00	4.00
V3No.1-Rulah-r	.50	1.50	3.00
2-6('70), V4No.1-6('72), V5No.1-6('73), V6No.1-6('74)	.35	1.00	2.00

TALES OF ASGARD
Oct, 1968 (68 pages); Feb, 1984 ($1.25, 52 pgs.)
Marvel Comics Group

1-Thor r-/from Journey into Mystery No. 97-106; new Kirby-c	.25	.75	1.50
V2/1 (2/84)-Thor-r; Simonson-c		.40	.80

TALES OF DEMON DICK & BUNKER BILL
1934 (78 pgs; 5x10½''; B&W) (hardcover)
Whitman Publishing Co.

793-by Dick Spencer	6.00	18.00	42.00

TALES OF EVIL
Feb, 1975 - No. 3, July, 1975
Atlas/Seaboard Publ.

1		.30	.60
2-Intro. The Bog Beast		.25	.50
3-Origin The Man-Monster		.25	.50

NOTE: ***Lieber** c-1. **Sekowsky** a-1. **Sparling** a-2. **Sutton** a-2. **Thorne** c-2.*

TALES OF GHOST CASTLE
May-June, 1975 - No. 3, Sept-Oct, 1975
National Periodical Publications

1-3: 1,3-Redondo-a. 2-Nino-a		.25	.50

TALES OF HORROR
June, 1952 - No. 13, Oct, 1954
Toby Press/Minoan Publ. Corp.

1	6.00	18.00	42.00
2-Torture scenes	4.35	13.00	30.00
3-8,13	3.15	9.50	22.00
9-11-Reprints Purple Claw No. 1-3	4.35	13.00	30.00
12-Myron Fass c/a; torture scenes	3.50	10.50	24.00

NOTE: ***Andru** a-5. **Bailey** a-5. **Myron Fass** a-2, 3, 12; c-1-3, 12. **Hollingsworth** a-2. **Sparling** a-6, 9; c-9.*

TALES OF JUSTICE (Formerly Justice Comics)
No. 53, May, 1955 - No. 67, Aug, 1957
Atlas Comics (MjMC No. 53-66/Male No. 67)

53	2.85	8.50	20.00
54-57	2.00	6.00	14.00
58,59-Krigstein-a	2.85	8.50	20.00
60-63,65	1.15	3.50	8.00
64,67-Crandall-a	2.00	6.00	14.00
66-Torres, Orlando-a	2.00	6.00	14.00

NOTE: ***Everett** a-53, 60. **Orlando** a-65,66. **Powell** a-54. **Severin** c-58, 65.*

TALES OF SUSPENSE (Captain America No. 100 on)
Jan, 1959 - No. 99, March, 1968
Atlas (WPI No. 1,2/Male No. 3-12/VPI No. 13-18)/Marvel No. 19 on

	Good	Fine	Mint
1-Williamson-a, 5 pgs.	30.00	90.00	210.00
2,3	12.00	36.00	84.00
4-Williamson-a, 4 pgs; Kirby/Everett c/a	13.00	40.00	90.00
5-10	6.75	20.00	47.00
11,13-20: 14-Intro. Colossus . 16-Intro Metallo (Pre-Iron Man proto-type)	5.00	15.00	35.00
12-Crandall-a	5.75	17.25	40.00
21-25: 25-Last 10¢ ish.	3.00	9.00	21.00
26-38: 32-Sazzik The Sorcerer app. (Dr. Strange proto-type)	2.35	7.00	16.00
39-Origin & 1st app. Iron Man; 1st Iron Man story-Kirby layouts	50.00	125.00	365.00
40-Iron Man in new armor	18.00	45.00	128.00
41	10.00	25.00	70.00
42-45: 45-Intro. & 1st app. Happy & Pepper	3.65	9.00	25.00
46,47	1.85	4.65	13.00
48-New Iron Man armor	2.30	6.00	16.00
49-51: 50-1st app. Mandarin	1.15	3.00	8.00
52-1st app. The Black Widow	1.50	4.00	10.00
53-Origin The Watcher (5/64); Black Widow app.	1.15	3.00	8.00
54-56	.85	2.50	5.00
57-1st app./Origin Hawkeye (9/64)	.85	2.50	5.00
58-Captain America begins (10/64)	.85	2.50	5.00
59-Iron Man plus Captain America features begin; intro Jarvis, Avenger's butler	.60	1.80	3.60
60,61,64	.30	1.00	2.00
62-Origin Mandarin (2/65)	.40	1.20	2.40
63-Origin Captain America (3/65)	.60	1.80	3.60
65-1st Silver-Age Red Skull (6/65)	.30	1.00	2.00
66-Origin Red Skull	.30	1.00	2.00
67-94,96-99: 69-1st app. Titanium Man. 75-Intro/1st app. Agent 13 later named Sharon Carter. 76-Intro Batroc & Sharon Carter, Agent 13 of Shield. 79-Intro Cosmic Cube. 94-Intro Modok	.30	1.00	2.00
95-Capt. America's i.d. revealed	.30	1.00	2.00

NOTE: ***Colan*** *a-39, 73-99p; c(p)-73, 75, 77, 79, 81, 83, 85-87, 89, 91, 93, 95, 97, 99.* ***Craig*** *a-99i.* ***Crandall*** *a-12.* ***Davis*** *a-38.* ***Ditko/Kirby*** *art in most issues No. 1-15, 17-49.* ***Everett*** *a-8.* ***Forte*** *a-5, 9.* ***Gil Kane*** *a-88p, 89-91; c-88, 89-91p.* ***Kirby*** *a(p)40, 41, 43, 59-75, 77-86, 92-99; layouts-69-75, 77; c(p)29-56, 58-72, 74, 76, 78, 80, 82, 84, 86, 92, 94, 96, 98.* ***Leiber/Fox*** *a-42, 43, 45, 51.* ***Reinman*** *a-26, 44i, 49i, 52i, 53i.* ***Tuska*** *a-58, 70-74.* ***Wood*** *c/a-71i.*

TALES OF SWORD & SORCERY (See Dagar)

TALES OF TERROR
1952 (no month)
Toby Press Publications

	Good	Fine	Mint
1-Fawcette-c; Ravielli-a	3.50	10.50	24.00

NOTE: *This title was cancelled due to similarity to the E.C. title.*

TALES OF TERROR (See Movie Classics)

TALES OF TERROR (Magazine)
Summer, 1964
Eerie Publications

	Good	Fine	Mint
1	1.00	3.00	6.00

TALES OF TERROR
July, 1985 - Present ($1.75; Baxter paper; mature readers)
Eclipse Comics

	Good	Fine	Mint
1	.40	1.25	2.50
2-9: 3-Morrow-a. 7-Bissette, Bolton-a	.35	1.00	2.00

TALES OF TERROR ANNUAL
1951 - 1953 (25 cents)
E. C. Comics

	Good	Fine	Mint
nn(1951)(Scarce)-Infinity-c	200.00	600.00	1400.00
2(1952)	100.00	300.00	700.00
3(1953)	70.00	210.00	490.00

No. 1 contains three horror and one science fiction comic which came out in 1950. No. 2 contains a horror, crime, and science fiction book which generally had cover dates in 1951, and No. 3 had horror, crime, and shock books that generally appeared in 1952. All E. C. annuals contain four complete books that did not sell on the stands which were rebound in the annual format, minus the covers, and sold from the E. C. office and on the stands in key cities. The contents of each annual may vary in the same year.

TALES OF TERROR ILLUSTRATED (See Terror Ill.)

TALES OF TEXAS JOHN SLAUGHTER (See 4-Color No. 997)

TALES OF THE BEANWORLD
Feb, 1985 - Present ($1.50; B&W)
Eclipse Comics

	Good	Fine	Mint
1	.50	1.50	3.00
2-5	.25	.75	1.50

TALES OF THE GREEN BERET
Jan, 1967 - No. 5, Oct, 1969
Dell Publishing Co.

	Good	Fine	Mint
1	1.00	3.00	7.00
2-5: 5 reprints No. 1	.75	2.25	5.00

NOTE: ***Glanzman*** *a-1-4.*

TALES OF THE GREEN LANTERN CORPS
May, 1981 - No. 3, July, 1981
DC Comics

	Good	Fine	Mint
1-Origin of G.L. & the Guardians; Staton-a(p)		.45	.90
2,3-Staton-a(p)		.30	.60
Annual 1 (1/85)-G. Kane c/a		.65	1.30

TALES OF THE INVISIBLE SCARLET O'NEIL (See Harv. Comics Hits No. 59)

TALES OF THE JACKALOPE
Feb, 1986 - Present ($2.00, B&W)
Blackthorne Publ.

	Good	Fine	Mint
1-5	.35	1.00	2.00

TALES OF THE KILLERS (Magazine)
V1No.10, Dec, 1970 - V1No.11, Feb, 1971 (52 pgs.) (B&W)
World Famous Periodicals

	Good	Fine	Mint
V1No.10-One pg. Frazetta	.80	2.40	4.80
11	.50	1.50	3.00

TALES OF THE LEGION (Formerly The Legion of Super-Heroes)
No. 314, Aug, 1984 - Present
DC Comics

	Good	Fine	Mint
314-325: 314-Origin The White Witch		.40	.80
326-345: r-/Legion S.H. (Baxter series)		.45	.90
Annual 4 ('86)		.65	1.30

NOTE: ***Tuska*** *a-314-317p.*

TALES OF THE MARINES (Devil-Dog Dugan No. 3; Marines at War No. 5 on)
February, 1957
Atlas Comics (OPI)

	Good	Fine	Mint
4-Powell-a	1.20	3.50	8.00

TALES OF THE MYSTERIOUS TRAVELER (See Mysterious. . .)
8/56 - No. 13, 6/59; V2/14, 10/85 - No. 15, 12/85
Charlton Comics

	Good	Fine	Mint
1-No Ditko-a	10.00	30.00	70.00
2-Ditko-a(1)	8.50	25.50	60.00
3-Ditko c/a(1)	7.00	21.00	50.00
4-6-Ditko c/a(3-4)	10.00	30.00	70.00

Tales of Suspense #39, © MCG

Tales of Terror Annual #1, © WMG

Tales of the Jackalope #1, © Blackthorne

Tales of the Sun Runners #1, © Sirius Comics

Tales of the Unexpected #41, © DC

Tales to Astonish #46, © MCG

TALES OF THE MYSTERIOUS... (cont'd.) — Good / Fine / Mint

7-9-Ditko-a(1-2) 6.00 18.00 42.00
10,11-Ditko-c/a(3-4) 8.00 24.00 56.00
12,13 3.15 9.50 22.00
14,15 (1985)-Ditko c/a .40 .80

TALES OF THE NEW TEEN TITANS
June, 1982 - No. 4, Sept, 1982 (mini-series)
DC Comics

1-Origin Cyborg-book length story .30 .90 1.80
2-Origin Raven-book length story .25 .75 1.50
3-Origin Changeling .25 .75 1.50
4-Origin Starfire .25 .75 1.50

NOTE: ***Perez*** *a-1-4p; c-1-4.*

TALES OF THE PONY EXPRESS (See 4-Color No. 829,942)

TALES OF THE SUN RUNNERS
July, 1986 - Present ($1.50, color)
Sirius Comics/Amazing Comics No. 3 on

V2/1-3 .25 .75 1.50
Christmas Special 1(12/86) .25 .75 1.50

TALES OF THE TEEN TITANS (Formerly The New...)
No. 41, April, 1984 - Present
DC Comics

41-49,51-59: 44-1st app/origin Terminator; Jericho & Nightwing join. 46-Aqualad & Aquagirl join. 53-Intro Azreal. 56-Intro Jinx. 57-Neutron app. 59-r/DC Comics Presents 26 .45 .90
50-Double size .60 1.20
60-76: r/New Teen Titans Baxter series. 69-Origin Kole .40 .80
Annual 3('84; $1.25)-Death of Terra .60 1.20
Annual 4(11/86)-r .60 1.20

NOTE: ***Buckler*** *a-51p, 52p.* ***Perez*** *a-41-49p, 50; c-41-50.*

TALES OF THE TEXAS RANGERS (See Jace Pearson...)

TALES OF THE UNEXPECTED (The Unexpected No. 105 on) (See Super DC Giant)
Feb-Mar, 1956 - No. 104, Dec-Jan, 1967-68
National Periodical Publications

1 22.00 65.00 155.00
2 9.50 28.50 65.00
3-5 5.75 17.25 40.00
6-10 4.35 13.00 30.00
11,12,14 2.35 7.00 16.00
13,15-18,21-23: Kirby-a. 16-Character named 'Thor' with a magic hammer - not like later Thor 3.50 10.50 24.00
19,20,24-39: 24-Cameron-c/a 1.50 4.50 10.00
40-Space Ranger begins, ends No. 82 7.00 21.00 50.00
41-50 1.00 3.00 7.00
51-67: 67-Last 10¢ issue .75 2.25 5.00
68-100: 91-1st Automan (also in No. 94,97) .35 1.00 2.00
101-104 .50 1.00

NOTE: ***Adams*** *c-104.* ***Anderson*** *a-50.* ***Heath*** *a-31, 49.* ***Bob Kane*** *a-48.* ***Kirby*** *a-12, 24; c-22.* ***Brown*** *a-50-82(Space Ranger).* ***Meskin*** *a-15, 18, 26, 27, 35, 66.* ***Moreira*** *a-16, 29, 38, 44, 62; c-38.*

TALES OF THE WEST (See 3-D...)

TALES OF THE WIZARD OF OZ (See 4-Color No. 1308)

TALES OF THE ZOMBIE (Magazine)
Aug, 1973 - No. 10, Mar, 1975 (75 cents) (B&W)
Marvel Comics Group

V1No.1-Reprint/Menace No. 5; origin .85 2.50 5.00
2-Everett biography & memorial .50 1.50 3.00
3 .50 1.50 3.00

Good / Fine / Mint

V2No.1(No.4)-Photos, text of Bond movie 'Live & Let Die' .50 1.50 3.00
5-10: 8-Kaluta-a .50 1.50 3.00
Annual 1(Summer,'75)(No.11)-B&W; Everett, Buscema-a .50 1.50 3.00

NOTE: ***Alcala*** *a-7-9.* ***Boris*** *c-1-4.* ***Colan*** *a-2r, 6.* ***Heath*** *a-5r.* ***Reese*** *a-2.* ***Tuska*** *a-2r.*

TALES OF THUNDER
March, 1985
Deluxe Comics

1-Dynamo, Iron Maiden & Menthor app.; Giffen-a .35 1.00 2.00

TALES OF VOODOO (Magazine)
V1No.11, Nov, 1968 - V7No.6, Nov, 1974
Eerie Publications

V1No.11 .70 2.00 4.00
V2No.1(3/69)-V2No.4(9/69) .35 1.00 2.00
V3No.1-6('70): 4-'Claws of the Cat' redrawn from Climax No. 1 .35 1.00 2.00
V4No.1-6('71), V5No.1-6('72), V6No.1-6('73), V7No.1-6('74) .35 1.00 2.00
Annual 1 .50 1.50 3.00

NOTE: *Bondage-c-V1No.10, V2No.4, V3No.4.*

TALES OF WELLS FARGO (See 4-Color No. 876, 968, 1023, 1075, 1113, 1167, 1215, & Western Roundup)

TALES TO ASTONISH (The Incredible Hulk No. 102 on)
Jan, 1959 - No. 101, March, 1968
Atlas (MAP No. 1/ZPC No. 2-14/VPI No. 15-21)/Marvel No. 22 on

1-Jack Davis-a 31.00 92.00 215.00
2-Ditko-c 14.50 43.50 100.00
3 11.00 33.00 76.00
4 7.00 21.00 50.00
5-Williamson-a, 4 pgs. 9.50 28.50 65.00
6-10 5.50 16.50 38.00
11-20 3.65 11.00 25.00
21-26 2.15 6.50 15.00
27-1st Antman app. (1/62); last 10¢ ish 65.00 165.00 460.00
28-34 1.70 5.00 12.00
35-2nd Antman, 1st in costume; begins series 25.00 63.00 175.00
36 9.25 23.00 65.00
37-40 4.50 11.25 31.00
41-43 1.70 4.25 12.00
44-Origin & 1st app. The Wasp 2.00 5.00 14.00
45-48: 46-1st Crimson Dynamo 1.50 3.75 10.00
49-Antman becomes Giant Man 1.70 4.25 12.00
50-60: 52-Origin & 1st app. Black Knight. 59-Giant Man vs. Hulk feat. story. 60-Giant Man & Hulk double feature begins .85 2.50 5.00
61-70: 62-1st app./origin The Leader; new Wasp costume. 65-New Giant Man costume. 68-New Human Top costume. 69-Last Giant Man. 70-Sub-Mariner begins .40 1.30 2.60
71-80 .30 1.00 2.00
81-91: 90-1st app. The Abomination .25 .80 1.60
92,93-Silver Surfer app. .70 2.00 4.00
94-99 .25 .75 1.50
100,101: 100: Hulk battles Sub-Mariner .30 1.00 2.00

NOTE: ***Berg*** *a-1.* ***Burgos*** *a-62-64p.* ***Buscema*** *a-85-87p.* ***Colan*** *a(p)-70-76, 78-82, 84, 85, 101; c(p)-71-76, 78, 80, 82, 84, 86, 88, 90.* ***Ditko*** *a-most issues-1-48, 50i, 60-67.* ***Everett*** *a-78, 79i, 80-84, 85-90i, 94i, 95, 96; c(i)-79-81, 83, 86, 88.* ***Forte*** *a-6.* ***Kane*** *a-76, 88-91; c-89, 91.* ***Kirby*** *a(p)-1-34(most), 35-40, 44, 49-51, 68-70, 82, 83; layouts-71-84; c(p)-1, 5, 27, 35-48, 50-70, 72, 73, 75, 77, 78, 79, 81, 85, 90.* ***Leiber/Fox*** *a-47, 48, 50, 51.* ***Powell*** *a-65-69p, 73, 74.* ***Reinman*** *a-6, 36, 45, 46, 54i, 56-60i.*

TALES TO ASTONISH (2nd Series)
Dec, 1979 - No. 14, Jan, 1981

TALES TO ASTONISH (continued)
Marvel Comics Group

	Good	Fine	Mint
V2No.1-Buscema-r from Sub-Mariner No. 1		.30	.60
2-14: Reprints Sub-Mariner 2-14		.25	.50

TALES TO HOLD YOU SPELLBOUND (See Spellbound)

TALKING KOMICS
1957 (20 pages) (Slick covers)
Belda Record & Publ. Co.

Each comic contained a record that followed the story - much like the Golden Record sets. Known titles: Chirpy Cricket, Lonesome Octopus, Sleepy Santa, Grumpy Shark, Flying Turtle, Happy Grasshopper

	Good	Fine	Mint
with records....	.80	2.40	4.80

TALLY-HO COMICS
December, 1944
Swappers Quarterly (Baily Publ. Co.)

	Good	Fine	Mint
nn-Frazetta's 1st work as Giunta's assistant; Man In Black story; violence	18.00	54.00	126.00

TAMMY, TELL ME TRUE (See 4-Color No. 1233)

TARANTULA (See Weird Suspense)

TARAS BULBA (See Movie Classics)

TARGET COMICS (...Western Romances No. 106 on)
Feb, 1940 - V10/3(No. 105), Aug-Sept, 1949
Funnies, Inc./Novelty Publications/Star Publications

	Good	Fine	Mint
V1/1-Origin & 1st app. Manowar, The White Streak by Burgos; & Bulls-Eye Bill by Everett; City Editor (ends No. 5), High Grass Twins by Jack Cole (ends No. 4), T-Men by Joe Simon (ends No. 9), Rip Rory (ends No. 4), Fantastic Feature Films by Tarpe Mills (ends No. 39), & Calling 2-R (ends No. 14) begin; Marijuana use story	130.00	390.00	910.00
2	65.00	195.00	455.00
3,4	47.00	141.00	330.00
5-Origin The White Streak in text; Space Hawk by Wolverton begins (See Circus)	105.00	315.00	735.00
6-The Chameleon by Everett begins; White Streak origin cont'd. in text	60.00	180.00	420.00
7-Wolverton-c (Scarce)	140.00	420.00	980.00
8,9,12	45.00	135.00	315.00
10-Intro. & 1st app. The Target; Kirby-c	60.00	180.00	420.00
11-Origin The Target & The Targeteers	53.00	160.00	370.00
V2/1,2: 1-Target by Bob Wood	32.00	95.00	224.00
3-5: 4-The Cadet begins	20.00	60.00	140.00
6-9-Red Seal with White Streak in 6-10	20.00	60.00	140.00
10-Classic-c	23.00	70.00	160.00
11,12	20.00	60.00	140.00
V3/1-10-Last Wolverton issue	20.00	60.00	140.00
11,12	3.00	9.00	21.00
V4/1-5,7-12	1.85	5.50	13.00
6-Targetoons by Wolverton, 1 pg.	2.00	6.00	14.00
V5/1-8	1.65	5.00	11.50
V6/1-10, V7/1-12	1.15	3.50	8.00
V8/1,3-5,8,9,11,12	1.15	3.50	8.00
V8/2,6,7-Krigstein-a	1.65	5.00	11.50
10-L. B. Cole-c	4.35	13.00	30.00
V9/1,3,6,8,10,12, V10/2-L.B. Cole-c	4.35	13.00	30.00
V9/2,4,5,7,9,11, V10/1,3	1.15	3.50	8.00

NOTE: *Jack Cole a-1-8. Everett c-1-9. Rico a-V7/4,10, V8/5,6, V9/3. Simon a-1, 2. Tarpe Mills a-1-4, 6, 8, 11, V2/1.*

TARGET: THE CORRUPTORS (TV)
No. 1306, Mar-May, 1962 - No. 3, Oct-Dec, 1962 (Photo-c)
Dell Publishing Co.

	Good	Fine	Mint
4-Color 1306, No. 2,3	2.15	6.50	15.00

TARGET WESTERN ROMANCES (Formerly Target)
No. 106, Oct-Nov, 1949 - No. 107, Dec-Jan, 1949-50
Star Publications

	Good	Fine	Mint
106-Silhouette nudity panel; L. B. Cole-c	7.00	21.00	50.00
107-L. B. Cole-c; lingerie panels	5.00	15.00	35.00

TARGITT
March, 1975 - No. 3, July, 1975
Atlas/Seaboard Publ.

	Good	Fine	Mint
1-Origin; Nostrand-a in all		.30	.60
2,3: 2-1st in costume		.25	.50

TARZAN (See Aurora, Comics on Parade, Crackajack Comics, DC 100-Page Super Spec., Famous Feat. Stories 1, Golden Comics Digest No. 4,9, Jeep Comics 1-29, Jungle Tales of..., Limited Collectors Edition, Popular Comics, Sparkler, Sport Stars 1, Tip Top, & Top Comics)

TARZAN
No. 5, 1939 - No. 161, Aug, 1947
Dell Publishing Co./United Features Syndicate

	Good	Fine	Mint
Large Feat. Comic 5('39)-(Scarce)-by Hal Foster; r-1st dailies from 1929	76.00	228.00	532.00
Single Series 20('40)-by Hal Foster	67.00	200.00	470.00
4-Color 134(2/47)-Marsh-a	30.00	90.00	210.00
4-Color 161(8/47)-Marsh-a	26.00	78.00	182.00

TARZAN (...of the Apes No. 138 on)
1-2/48 - No. 131, 7-8/62; No. 132, 11/62 - No. 206, 2/72
Dell Publishing Co./Gold Key No. 132 on

	Good	Fine	Mint
1-Jesse Marsh-a begins	50.00	150.00	350.00
2	30.00	90.00	180.00
3-5	21.50	64.50	150.00
6-10: 6-1st Tantor the Elephant. 7-1st Valley of the Monsters	17.00	51.00	120.00
11-15: 11-Two Against the Jungle begins, ends No. 24. 13-Lex Barker photo-c begin	14.50	43.50	100.00
16-20	11.00	33.00	76.00
21-24,26-30	8.00	24.00	56.00
25-1st "Brothers of the Spear" episode; series ends No. 156,160, 161,196-206	9.50	28.50	65.00
31-40	4.65	14.00	32.00
41-54: Last Barker photo-c	3.50	10.50	24.00
55-60: 56-Eight pg. Boy story	2.85	8.50	20.00
61,62,64-70	2.00	6.00	14.00
63-Two Tarzan stories, 1 by Manning	2.35	7.00	16.00
71-79	1.75	5.25	12.00
80-99: 80-Photo-c begin	2.00	6.00	14.00
100	2.35	7.00	16.00
101-109	1.50	4.50	10.00
110 (Scarce)-Last photo-c	1.70	5.00	12.00
111-120	1.15	3.50	8.00
121-131: Last Dell issue	.85	2.50	6.00
132-154: Gold Key issues	.75	2.25	5.00
155-Origin Tarzan	.85	2.50	6.00
156-161,166-170: 157-Bantu, Dog of the Arande begins, ends No. 159, 195. 169-Leopard Girl app.	.55	1.65	4.00
162-165: Ron Ely photo-c	.75	2.25	5.00
171-199,201-206: 178-Tarzan origin r-/No. 155; Leopard Girl app, also in No. 179,190-193	.40	1.25	2.50
200 (Scarce)	.75	2.25	5.00
Story Digest 1(6/70-G.K.)	.75	2.25	5.00

NOTE: *No. 162, 165, 168, 171 are TV issues. No. 1-153-all have **Marsh** art on Tarzan. No. 154-161, 163, 164, 166, 167, 172-177 all have **Manning** art on Tarzan. No. 178, 202 have **Manning** Tarzan reprints. No "Brothers of the Spear" in No. 1-24, 157-159, 162-195. No. 39-126, 128-156 all have **Russ Manning** art on "Brothers of the Spear;"*

Target Comics #4, © NOVP

Target: The Corruptors #2, © Four Star

Tarzan #25, © ERB

Tasmanian Devil & His... #1, © Warner Bros.

Tastee-Freez Comics #6, © N.Y. News Synd.

Team America #3, © MCG

TARZAN (continued)
*No. 196-201, 203-205 all have **Manning** B.O.T.S. reprints; No. 25-38, 127 all have **Jesse Marsh** art on B.O.T.S. No. 206 has a **Marsh** B.O.T.S. reprint. **Doug Wildey** art-No. 179-187. Many issues have front and back photo covers.*

TARZAN (Continuation of Gold Key series)
No. 207, April, 1972 - No. 258, Feb, 1977
National Periodical Publications

	Good	Fine	Mint
207-Origin Tarzan by Joe Kubert, part 1; John Carter begins (origin); 52 pg. issues thru No. 209	.40	1.20	2.40
208-210: Origin, parts 2-4. 209-Last John Carter. 210-Kubert-a		.60	1.20
211-Hogarth, Kubert-a		.50	1.00
212-214: Adaptations from "Jungle Tales of Tarzan." 213-Beyond the Farthest Star begins, ends No. 218		.50	1.00
215-218,224,225-All by Kubert. 215-part Foster-r		.50	1.00
219-223: Adapts "The Return of Tarzan" by Kubert		.50	1.00
226-229: 226-Manning-a		.40	.80
230-100 pgs.; Kubert, Kaluta-a(p); Korak begins, ends No. 234; Carson of Venus app.	.35	1.00	2.00
231-234: Adapts "Tarzan and the Lion Man;" all 100 pgs.; Rex, the Wonder Dog r-No. 232,233	.25	.75	1.50
235-Last Kubert issue; 100 pgs.	.25	.75	1.50
236,237,239,244-249,257,258		.50	1.00
238-(68 pgs.)		.50	1.00
240-243: Adapts "Tarzan & the Castaways"		.50	1.00
250-256: Adapts "Tarzan the Untamed;" 252,253-r/No. 213		.50	1.00
Comic Digest 1(Fall,'72)(DC)-50 cents; 160 pgs.; digest size; Kubert-c, Manning-a	.55	1.65	4.00

*NOTE: **Anderson** a-207, 209, 217, 218. **Chaykin** a-216. **Finlay** a(r)-212. **Foster** strip-r No. 208, 209, 211, 221. **Heath** a-230i. **G. Kane** a-232p, 233p. **Kubert** a-207-25, 227-35, 257r, 258r; c-207-249, 253. **Lopez** a-250-55p; c-250p, 251, 252, 254. **Manning** strip-r 230-235, 238. **Morrow** a-208. **Nino** a-231-234. **Sparling** a-230. **Starr** a-233r.*

TARZAN
June, 1977 - No. 29, Oct, 1979
Marvel Comics Group

	Good	Fine	Mint
1		.35	.70
2-29: 2-Origin by J. Buscema		.25	.50
Annual 1 (10/77)		.35	.70
Annual 2 (11/78), Annual 3 (10/79)		.25	.50

*NOTE: **Adams** c-11i, 12i. **Alcala** a-9i, 10i; c-8i, 9i. **Buckler** c-25-27p, Annual 3p. **John Buscema** a-1-3, 4-18p; c-1-7, 8p, 9p, 10, 11p, 12p, 13, 14p-19p, 21p, 22, 23p, 24p, 28p. **Buscema** c/a-Annual 1. **Mooney** a-22i. **Nebres** a-21i. **Russell** a-29i.*

TARZAN BOOK (The Illustrated...)
1929 (80 pages) (7x9")
Grosset & Dunlap

	Good	Fine	Mint
1-(Rare)-Contains 1st B&W Tarzan newspaper comics from 1929. Cloth reinforced spine & dust jacket (50 cents)			
with dust jacket....	45.00	135.00	315.00
without dust jacket....	19.00	57.00	132.00
2nd Printing(1934)-76 pgs.; 25 cents; 4 Foster pages dropped; paper spine, circle in lower right cover with 25 cents price. The 25 cents is barely visible on some copies.	13.50	41.00	95.00
1967-House of Greystoke reprint-7x10"; using the complete 300 illustrations/text from the 1929 edition minus the original indicia, foreword, etc. Initial version bound in gold paper & sold for $5.00. Officially titled **Burroughs Biblophile No. 2.** A very few additional copies were bound in heavier blue paper.			
Gold binding....	2.15	6.50	15.00
Blue binding....	3.00	9.00	21.00

TARZAN FAMILY, THE (Formerly Korak)
No. 60, Nov-Dec, 1975 - No. 66, Nov-Dec, 1976
(No. 60-62: 68 pgs.; No. 63 on: 52 pgs.)
National Periodical Publications

	Good	Fine	Mint
60-Korak begins; Kaluta-r		.30	.60
61-66		.25	.50

*NOTE: Carson of Venus-r 60-65. New John Carter-62-64, 65r, 66r. New Korak-60-66. Pellucidar feature-66. **Foster** Sunday r-60('32)-63. **Kaluta** Carson of Venus-60-65. **Kubert** c-60-64. **Manning** strip-r 60-62, 64. **Morrow** a-66r.*

TARZAN KING OF THE JUNGLE (See Dell Giant No. 37,51)

TARZAN, LORD OF THE JUNGLE
Sept, 1965 (Giant) (soft paper cover) (25 cents)
Gold Key

	Good	Fine	Mint
1-Marsh-r	2.00	6.00	14.00

TARZAN MARCH OF COMICS (See March of Comics No. 82, 98, 114, 125, 144, 155, 172, 185, 204, 223, 240, 252, 262, 272, 286, 300, 318, 332, 342, 354, 366)

TARZAN OF THE APES
July, 1984 - No. 2, Aug, 1984
Marvel Comics Group

	Good	Fine	Mint
1,2: origin-r/Marvel Super Spec.		.30	.60

TARZAN OF THE APES TO COLOR
1933 (24 pages) (10¾x15¼") (Coloring book)
Saalfield Publishing Co.

	Good	Fine	Mint
988-(Very Rare)-Contains 1929 daily reprints with some new art by Hal Foster. Two panels blown up large on each page; 25 percent in color; believed to be the only time these panels ever appeared in color.	70.00	210.00	490.00

TARZAN'S JUNGLE ANNUAL (See Dell Giants)

TARZAN'S JUNGLE WORLD (See Dell Giant No. 25)

TASMANIAN DEVIL & HIS TASTY FRIENDS
November, 1962
Gold Key

	Good	Fine	Mint
1-Bugs Bunny & Elmer Fudd x-over	3.50	10.50	24.00

TASTEE-FREEZ COMICS
1957 (36 pages) (10 cents) (6 different issues)
Harvey Comics

	Good	Fine	Mint
1-Little Dot, 3-Casper	3.35	10.00	23.00
2-Rags Rabbit, 5-Mazie	2.00	6.00	14.00
4-Sad Sack	2.00	6.00	14.00
6-Dick Tracy	4.00	12.00	28.00

TAYLOR'S CHRISTMAS TABLOID
Mid 1930's, Cleveland, Ohio
Dept. Store Giveaway (Tabloid size; in color)

nn-(Very Rare)-Among the earliest pro work of Siegel & Shuster; one full color page called "The Battle in the Stratosphere," with a pre-Superman look; Shuster art throughout. (Only 1 known copy)
Estimated value.... $600.00

TEACH YE ALL NATIONS
No date (16 pages) (paper cover)
Catechetical Guild giveaway

	Good	Fine	Mint
	2.75	8.00	16.00

NOTE: B&W editor's version(5½x8½") exists; only one known copy.

TEAM AMERICA (See Capt. America 269)
June, 1982 - No. 12, May, 1983
Marvel Comics Group

	Good	Fine	Mint
1-Origin; Ideal Toy motorcycle characters		.40	.80
2-12: 11-Ghost Rider app. 12-Double size		.30	.60

TEDDY ROOSEVELT & HIS ROUGH RIDERS
1950
Avon Periodicals

TEDDY ROOSEVELT. . . (continued)

	Good	Fine	Mint
1-Kinstler-c; Palais-a; Flag-c	9.50	28.50	65.00

TEDDY ROOSEVELT ROUGH RIDER (See Classics Special)

TEE AND VEE CROSLEY IN TELEVISION LAND COMICS
1951 (52 pgs.; 8x11''; paper cover; in color)
Crosley Division, Avco Mfg. Corp. (Giveaway)

Many stories, puzzles, cut-outs, games, etc.	2.00	6.00	12.00

TEENA
1948 - No. 22, Oct, 1950
Magazine Enterprises/Standard Comics

A-1 No. 11	2.00	6.00	14.00
A-1 No. 12,15	1.65	5.00	11.50
20-22 (Standard)	1.15	3.50	8.00

TEEN-AGE BRIDES (True Bride's Experiences No. 8)
Aug, 1953 - No. 7, Aug, 1954
Harvey/Home Comics

1-Powell-a	2.00	6.00	14.00
2-Powell-a	1.50	4.50	10.00
3-7: 3,6-Powell-a	1.35	4.00	9.00

TEEN-AGE CONFESSIONS (See Teen Confessions)

TEEN-AGE CONFIDENTIAL CONFESSIONS
July, 1960 - No. 22, 1964
Charlton Comics

1	.55	1.65	4.00
2-10	.35	1.00	2.00
11-22		.50	1.00

TEEN-AGE DIARY SECRETS (Formerly Blue Ribbon Comics) (Becomes Diary Secrets No. 10 on)
Sept, 1949 - No. 9, Aug, 1950
St. John Publishing Co.

nn(9/49)-oversized issue; Baker-a	8.50	25.50	60.00
6-8-Photo-c; Baker-a (2-3) in each	6.00	18.00	42.00
9-Pocket size	7.00	21.00	50.00

TEEN-AGE DOPE SLAVES (See Harvey Comics Library No. 1)

TEENAGE HOTRODDERS (Top Eliminator No. 25 on)
April, 1963 - No. 24, July, 1967
Charlton Comics

1	.50	1.50	3.00
2-24	.30	.80	1.60

TEEN-AGE LOVE (See Fox Giants)

TEEN-AGE LOVE (Formerly Intimate?)
V2No.4, July, 1958 - No. 96, Dec, 1973
Charlton Comics

V2No.4	.85	2.50	6.00
5-9	.45	1.35	3.00
10(9/59)-35		1.00	2.00
36-96: 61&62-Origin Jonnie Love & begin series		.20	.40

TEENAGE MUTANT NINJA TURTLES (Also see Donatello, First Comics Graphic Novel, Grimjack No. 26, Michaelangelo & Raphael)
1984 - Present (B&W)
Mirage Studios

	Good	Fine	Mint
1-1st printing	23.00	70.00	140.00
1-2nd printing	4.15	12.50	25.00
1-3rd printing	1.15	3.50	7.00
1-4th,5th printing; new-c	.50	1.50	3.00
2-1st printing	5.00	15.00	30.00
2-2nd printing	1.15	3.50	7.00
2-3rd printing; new Corbin-c & story	.45	1.25	2.50
3	2.00	6.00	12.00
4	1.35	4.00	8.00
5	1.00	3.00	6.00
6	.70	2.00	4.00
7-4pg. color insert by Corbin. 8-Rion 2990 begins	.50	1.50	3.00
8,9	.35	1.10	2.20
Book 1,2 ($1.50, B&W): 2-Corben-c	.25	.75	1.50

TEEN-AGE ROMANCE (Formerly My Own Romance)
No. 77, Sept, 1960 - No. 86, March, 1962
Marvel Comics (ZPC)

77-86	.60	1.80	3.60

TEEN-AGE ROMANCES
Jan, 1949 - No. 45, Dec, 1955
St. John Publ. Co. (Approved Comics)

1-Baker c/a(1)	11.50	34.50	80.00
2-Baker c/a	7.00	21.00	50.00
3-Baker c/a(3); spanking panel	8.00	24.00	56.00
4,5,7,8-Photo-c; Baker-a(2-3) each	5.50	16.50	38.00
6-Slightly large size; photo-c; part magazine; Baker-a (10/49)	5.50	16.50	38.00
9-Baker c/a; Kubert-a	8.00	24.00	56.00
10-12,20-Baker c/a(2-3) each	5.50	16.50	38.00
13-19,21,22-Complete issues by Baker	8.00	24.00	56.00
23-25-Baker c/a(2-3) each	4.75	14.25	33.00
26,27,33,34,36-42-Last Precode, 3/55; Baker-a. 38-Suggestive-c	3.35	10.00	23.00
28-30-No Baker-a	1.65	5.00	11.50
31-Baker-c	2.15	6.50	15.00
32-Baker c/a, 1pg.	2.15	6.50	15.00
35-Baker c/a, 16pgs.	3.65	11.00	25.00
43-45-Baker-a	2.50	7.50	17.00

TEEN-AGE TALK
1964
I. W. Enterprises

Reprint No. 5,8,9	.30	.80	1.60

TEEN-AGE TEMPTATIONS (Going Steady No. 10 on) (See True Love Pictorial)
Oct, 1952 - No. 9, Aug, 1954
St. John Publishing Co.

1-Baker c/a; has story ''Reform School Girl'' by Estrada	13.00	40.00	90.00
2-Baker-c	4.75	14.25	33.00
3-7,9-Baker c/a	8.00	24.00	56.00
8-Teenagers smoke reefers; Baker c/a	8.50	25.50	60.00

NOTE: *Estrada a-1, 4, 5.*

TEEN BEAM (Teen Beat No. 1)
No. 2, Jan-Feb, 1968 (Monkees photo-c)
National Periodical Publications

2-Orlando, Drucker-a(r)	.75	2.25	5.00

TEEN BEAT (Teen Beam No. 2)
Nov-Dec, 1967
National Periodical Publications

1-Photos & text only	1.00	3.00	7.00

TEEN COMICS (Formerly All Teen; Journey Into Unknown Worlds No. 36 on)

Teen-Age Diary Secrets #8, © STJ

Teenage Mutant. . . #1 (3rd Printing), © Mirage

Teen-Age Romances #6, © STJ

Teen Confessions #90, © CC

Teen Titans #8, © DC

Tell It to the Marines #6, © TOBY

TEEN COMICS (continued)
No. 21, April, 1947 - No. 35, May, 1950
Marvel Comics (WFP)

	Good	Fine	Mint
21-Kurtzman's "Hey Look"; Patsy Walker, Cindy, Georgie, Margie app.	3.50	10.50	24.00
22,23,25,27,29,31-35	1.75	5.25	12.00
24,26,28,30-Kurtzman's "Hey Look"	2.85	8.50	20.00

TEEN CONFESSIONS
Aug, 1959 - No. 97, Nov, 1976
Charlton Comics

	Good	Fine	Mint
1	2.50	7.50	17.50
2	1.15	3.50	8.00
3-10	.95	2.80	6.50
11-30	.40	1.20	2.80
31-36,38-97: 89,90-Newton-c		.50	1.00
37 (1/66)-Beatles Fan Club story; Beatles-c	1.15	3.50	8.00

TEENIE WEENIES, THE
1950 - 1951 (Newspaper reprints)
Ziff-Davis Publishing Co.

	Good	Fine	Mint
10,11	4.35	13.00	30.00

TEEN-IN (Tippy Teen)
Summer, 1968 - No. 4, Fall, 1969
Tower Comics

	Good	Fine	Mint
nn(Summer,'68), nn(Spring,'69), 3,4	.70	2.00	4.00

TEEN LIFE (Formerly Young Life)
No. 3, Winter, 1945 - No. 5, Fall, 1945
New Age/Quality Comics Group

	Good	Fine	Mint
3-June Allyson photo-c	2.65	8.00	18.00
4-Duke Ellington story	1.85	5.50	13.00
5-Van Johnson, Woody Herman & Jackie Robinson articles	2.65	8.00	18.00

TEEN ROMANCES
1964
Super Comics

	Good	Fine	Mint
10,11,15-17-Reprints		.30	.60

TEEN SECRET DIARY (Nurse Betsy Crane No. 12 on)
Oct, 1959 - No. 11, June, 1961; No. 1, 1972
Charlton Comics

	Good	Fine	Mint
1	1.15	3.50	8.00
2	.55	1.65	4.00
3-11	.35	1.00	2.50
1(1972)		.30	.60

TEEN TALK (See Teen)

TEEN TITANS (See Brave & the Bold, DC Super-Stars No. 1, Marvel and DC Present, New Teen Titans, Official . . . Index and Showcase)
1-2/66 - No. 43, 1-2/73; No. 44, 11/76 - No. 53, 2/78
National Periodical Publications/DC Comics

	Good	Fine	Mint
1-Titans join peace corps; Batman, Flash, Aquaman, Wonder Woman cameos	5.85	17.50	35.00
2	2.00	6.00	12.00
3-5: 4-Speedy app.	1.20	3.50	7.00
6-10	.85	2.50	5.00
11-18: 11-Speedy app.	.50	1.50	3.00
19-Wood-i; Speedy begins as regular	.50	1.50	3.00
20-22: All Adams-a; 21-Hawk & Dove app. 22-Origin Wonder Girl	1.00	3.00	6.00
23-Wonder Girl dons new costume	.50	1.50	3.00
24	.50	1.50	3.00
25-Flash, Aquaman, Batman, Green Arrow, Green Lantern, Superman, & Hawk & Dove guests	.50	1.50	3.00
26-30: 29-Hawk & Dove & Ocean Master app. 30-Aquagirl app.	.50	1.50	3.00
31-43: 31-Hawk & Dove app. 36,37-Superboy-r. 38-Green Arrow/Speedy-r; Aquaman/Aqualad story. 39-Hawk & Dove-r. (36-39, 52 pgs.)	.35	1.00	2.00
44-47,49-52: 44-Mal becomes the Guardian. 46-Joker's Daughter begins. 50-Intro. Teen Titans West; 1st revival original Bat-Girl	.25	.75	1.50
48-Intro Bumblebee; Joker's Daughter becomes Harlequin	.25	.75	1.50
53-Origin retold	.25	.75	1.50

NOTE: ***Aparo** a-36. **Buckler** c-46-53. **Kane** a(p)-19, 22-24, 39r. **Tuska** a(p)-31, 36, 38, 39.*

TEEN TITANS SPOTLIGHT
Aug, 1986 - Present
DC Comics

	Good	Fine	Mint
1-3		.40	.80
4-8: 7-Guice's 1st work at DC		.35	.70

TEEPEE TIM (Formerly Ha Ha Comics)
No. 100, Feb-Mar, 1955 - No. 102, June-July, 1955
American Comics Group

	Good	Fine	Mint
100-102	.55	1.65	4.00

TEGRA JUNGLE EMPRESS (Zegra No. 2 on)
August, 1948
Fox Features Syndicate

	Good	Fine	Mint
1-Blue Beetle, Rocket Kelly app.; used in **SOTI**, pg. 31	17.00	51.00	120.00

TELEVISION (See TV)

TELEVISION COMICS
No. 5, Feb, 1950 - No. 8, Nov, 1950
Standard Comics (Animated Cartoons)

	Good	Fine	Mint
5-1st app. Willy Nilly	1.65	5.00	11.50
6-8: 6 has No. 2 on outside	1.00	3.00	7.00

TELEVISION PUPPET SHOW
1950 - No. 2, Nov, 1950
Avon Periodicals

	Good	Fine	Mint
1,2	3.75	11.25	26.00

TELEVISION TEENS MOPSY (See TV Teens)

TELL IT TO THE MARINES
Mar, 1952 - No. 15, July, 1955
Toby Press Publications

	Good	Fine	Mint
1-Lover O'Leary and His Liberty Belles (with pin-ups), ends No. 6	4.65	14.00	32.00
2-Madame Cobra app. c/story	3.15	9.50	22.00
3,5	2.65	8.00	18.00
4-Transvestism story	4.35	13.00	30.00
6-15: 7-9,14-Photo-c	1.50	4.50	10.00
I.W. Reprint No. 1,9	.30	.90	1.80
Super Reprint No. 16('64)	.30	.90	1.80

TEN COMMANDMENTS (See Moses & the . . . and Classics Special)

TENDER LOVE STORIES
Feb, 1971 - No. 4, July, 1971 (All 52 pgs.) (25 cents)
Skywald Publ. Corp.

	Good	Fine	Mint
1-4	.30	.80	1.60

TENDER ROMANCE (Ideal Romance No. 3 on)
December, 1953 - No. 2, Feb, 1954
Key Publications (Gilmour Magazines)

	Good	Fine	Mint
1-Headlight & lingerie panels	4.65	14.00	32.00

TENDER ROMANCE (continued)

	Good	Fine	Mint
2	2.50	7.50	17.50

TENNESSEE JED (Radio)
No date (1945) (16 pgs.; paper cover; regular size) (Giveaway)
Fox Syndicate? (Wm. C. Popper & Co.)

	Good	Fine	Mint
	7.00	20.00	40.00

TENNIS (For Speed, Stamina, Strength, Skill)
1956 (16 pgs.) (soft cover) (10 cents)
Tennis Educational Foundation
Derus Productions

	Good	Fine	Mint
Book 1-Endorsed by Gene Tunney, Ralph Kiner, etc. showing how tennis has helped them	1.35	4.00	8.00

TENSE SUSPENSE
Dec, 1958 - No. 2, Feb, 1959
Fago Publications

	Good	Fine	Mint
1,2	1.30	4.00	9.00

TEN STORY LOVE (Formerly a pulp magazine with same title)
V29/3, 6-7/51 - V36/5(No. 209), 9/56 (No. 3-6, 52 pgs.)
Ace Periodicals

	Good	Fine	Mint
V29/3(No.177)-Part comic, part text	2.65	8.00	18.00
4-6(1/52)	1.30	4.00	9.00
V30/1(3/52)-6(1/53)	1.00	3.00	7.00
V31/1(2/53), V32/2(4/53)-6(12/53)	.85	2.50	6.00
V33/1(1/54)-3(5/54, No. 195), V34/4(7/54, No. 196)-6 (10/54, No. 198)	.80	2.40	5.50
V35/1(12/54, No. 199)-3(4/55, No. 201)-Last precode	.75	2.25	5.00
V35/4-6(9/55, No. 201-204), V36/1(11/55, No. 205)-3, 5(9/56, No. 209)	.55	1.65	4.00
V36/4-L. B. Cole-a	1.15	3.50	8.00

NOTE: *33 issues total. Photo-c V31/1-on.*

TEN WHO DARED (See 4-Color No. 1178)

TERRANAUTS
Aug, 1986 - Present ($1.75, color)
Fantasy General Comics

	Good	Fine	Mint
1,2	.30	.85	1.70

TERRIFIC COMICS
Jan, 1944 - No. 6, Nov, 1944
Continental Magazines

	Good	Fine	Mint
1-Kid Terrific; opium story	22.00	65.00	154.00
2-The Boomerang by L. B. Cole & Ed Wheelan's "Comics" McCormick, called the world's No. 1 comic book fan begins; Schomburg-c	18.50	56.00	130.00
3,4: 3-Diana becomes Boomerang's costumed aide	17.00	51.00	120.00
5-The Reckoner begins; Boomerang & Diana by L. B. Cole; Schomburg bondage-c	18.50	56.00	130.00
6-L.B. Cole c/a	19.50	58.50	135.00

NOTE: ***L. B. Cole** a-1, 2(2), 3-6. **Fuje** a-5, 6. **Rico** a-2.*

TERRIFIC COMICS (Formerly Horrific, Wonder Boy No. 17 on)
No. 14, Dec, 1954 - No. 16, Mar, 1955
Mystery Publ.(Comic Media)/(Ajax/Farrell)

	Good	Fine	Mint
14-Art swipe/Advs. Into Unknown 37; injury-to-eye-c; page-2, panel 5 swiped from Phantom Stranger No. 4; surrealistic Palais-a; Human Cross story	4.00	12.00	28.00
15,16-No Phantom Lady. 16-Wonder Boy app. (pre-code)	3.50	10.50	24.00

TERRIFYING TALES
No. 11, Jan, 1953 - No. 15, Apr, 1954
Star Publications

	Good	Fine	Mint
11-Used in **POP**, pgs. 99,100; all Jo-Jo-r	12.00	36.00	84.00
12-All Jo-Jo-r; L. B. Cole splash	10.00	30.00	70.00
13-All Rulah-r; classic devil-c	14.50	43.50	100.00
14-All Rulah reprints	10.00	30.00	70.00
15-Rulah, Zago-r; used in **SOTI**-r/Rulah No. 22	10.00	30.00	70.00

NOTE: *All issues have **L. B. Cole** covers; bondage covers-No. 12-14.*

TERROR ILLUSTRATED (Adult Tales of . . .)
Nov-Dec, 1955 - No. 2, Spring, 1956 (Magazine)
E. C. Comics

	Good	Fine	Mint
1	5.70	17.00	40.00
2	5.00	15.00	35.00

NOTE: ***Craig** a-1. **Crandall** a-1,2; c-1,2. **Evans** a-1, 2. **Ingels** a-1, 2.*

TERRORS OF THE JUNGLE (Formerly Jungle Thrills)
No. 17, May, 1952 - No. 10, Sept, 1954
Star Publications

	Good	Fine	Mint
17-Reprints Rulah No. 21, used in **SOTI**; L. B. Cole bondage-c	11.50	34.50	80.00
18-Jo-Jo-r	8.00	24.00	55.00
19,20(1952)-Jo-Jo-r; Disbrow-a	7.00	21.00	50.00
21-Jungle Jo, Tangi-r; used in **POP**, pg. 100 & color illos.	9.00	27.00	60.00
4,6,7-Disbrow-a	7.00	21.00	50.00
5,8,10: All Disbrow-a. 5-Jo-Jo-r. 8-Rulah, Jo-Jo-r. 10-Rulah-r	7.00	21.00	50.00
9-Jo-Jo-r; Disbrow-a; Tangi by Orlando	7.00	21.00	50.00

NOTE: ***L. B. Cole** c-all; bondage c-17, 19, 21, 5, 7.*

TERROR TALES (See Beware Terror Tales)

TERROR TALES (Magazine)
V1/7, 1969 - V6/6, 12/74; V7/1, 4/76 - V/10, 1979?
(V1-V6, 52 pgs.; V7 on, 68 pgs.)
Eerie Publications

	Good	Fine	Mint
V1No.7	.50	1.50	3.00
V1No.8-11('69): 9-Bondage-c	.35	1.00	2.00
V2No.1-6('70), V3No.1-6('71), V4No.1-6('72), V5No.1-6('73), V6No.1-6('74)	.35	1.00	2.00
V7No.1,4(no V7No.2), V8No.1-3('77), V9, V10	.35	1.00	2.00
V7No.3-LSD story-r/Weird V3No.5	.35	1.00	2.00

TERRY AND THE PIRATES (See Merry Christmas . . ., Superbook No. 3,5,9,16,28, & Super Comics)

TERRY AND THE PIRATES
1939 - 1953 (By Milton Caniff)
Dell Publishing Co.

	Good	Fine	Mint
Large Feat. Comic 2('39)	36.00	108.00	252.00
Large Feat. Comic 6('39)-1936 dailies	35.00	105.00	245.00
4-Color 9(1940)	35.00	105.00	245.00
Large Feature Comic 27('41), 6('42)	24.00	72.00	166.00
4-Color 44('43)	20.00	60.00	140.00
4-Color 101('45)	13.00	40.00	90.00
Buster Brown Shoes giveaway(1938)-32 pgs.; in color	20.00	60.00	140.00
Canada Dry Premiums-Books No. 1-3(1953-Harvey)-2x5"; 36 pgs.	5.00	15.00	35.00
Family Album(1942)	8.50	25.50	60.00
Gambles Giveaway ('38)-16 pgs.	4.00	12.00	24.00
Gillmore Giveaway('38)-24 pgs.	4.75	14.00	28.00
Popped Wheat Giveaway('38)-Reprints in full color; Caniff-a	.85	2.50	5.00
Shoe Store giveaway('38, 14pp)	2.00	6.00	12.00
Sparked Wheat Giveaway('42)-16 pgs. in full color	4.00	12.00	28.00

Terranauts #1, © Fantasy Gen.

Terrific Comics #5, © Continental

Terrifying Tales #14, © STAR

Terry-Toons Comics #47, © MGM

Tessie the Typist #12, © MCG

The Texan #15, © STJ

TERRY AND THE PIRATES
1941 (16 pgs.; regular size)
Libby's Radio Premium

	Good	Fine	Mint
"Adventure of the Ruby of Genghis Khan" - Each pg. is a puzzle that must be completed to read the story	8.50	25.50	60.00

TERRY AND THE PIRATES (Formerly Boy Explorers; Long John Silver & the Pirates No. 30 on) (Daily strip-r) (Two No. 26's)
No. 3, 4/47 - No. 26, 4/51; No. 26, 6/55 - No. 28, 10/55
Harvey Publications/Charlton No. 26-28

	Good	Fine	Mint
3(No.1)-Boy Explorers by S&K; Terry & the Pirates begin by Caniff	20.00	60.00	140.00
4-S&K Boy Explorers	13.00	40.00	90.00
5-10	7.00	21.00	50.00
11-Man in Black app. by Powell	7.00	21.00	50.00
12-20: 16-Girl threatened with red hot poker	5.35	16.00	37.00
21-26(4/51)-Last Caniff issue	4.75	14.00	33.00
26-28('55)(Formerly This Is Suspense)-Not by Caniff	3.35	10.00	23.00

NOTE: ***Powell** a (Tommy Tween)-5-10,12,14; 15-17(½-2 pgs.).*

TERRY BEARS COMICS (TerryToons, The... No. 4)
June, 1952 - No. 3, Oct, 1952
St. John Publishing Co.

	Good	Fine	Mint
1-3	1.50	4.50	10.00

TERRY-TOONS COMICS (1st Series) (Becomes Paul Terry's Comics No.85 on; later issues titled "Paul Terry's...) (See Giant Comics Ed.)
Oct, 1942 - No. 86, Feb?, 1951
Timely/Marvel No. 1-60 (8/47)(Becomes Best Western No. 58 on?, Marvel)/St. John No. 60 (9/47) on

	Good	Fine	Mint
1 (Scarce)	36.00	108.00	252.00
2	18.00	54.00	125.00
3-5	11.00	33.00	76.00
6-10	8.00	24.00	56.00
11-20	5.00	15.00	35.00
21-37	3.50	10.50	24.00
38-Mighty Mouse begins (1st app.)(11/45)	30.00	90.00	210.00
39	10.00	30.00	70.00
40-49: 43-Infinity-c	4.00	12.00	28.00
50-1st app. Heckle & Jeckle	9.50	28.50	65.00
51-60(8/47): 55-Infinity-c. 60-Atomic explosion panel (9/47)	3.35	10.00	23.00
61-84	2.00	6.00	14.00
85,86-Same book as Paul Terry's Comics No. 85,86 with only a title change	2.00	6.00	14.00

TERRY-TOONS COMICS (2nd Series)
June, 1952 - No. 9, Nov, 1953
St. John Publishing Co./Pines

	Good	Fine	Mint
1	3.50	10.50	24.00
2	2.15	6.50	15.00
3-9	1.65	5.00	11.50
Giant Summer Fun Book 101,102(Summer,'57-Summer,'58)(TV, Tom Terrific app.)	1.65	5.00	11.50

TERRYTOONS, THE TERRY BEARS (Formerly Terry Bears)
No. 4, Summer, 1958
Pines Comics

	Good	Fine	Mint
4	1.00	3.00	7.00

TESSIE THE TYPIST (Tiny Tessie No. 24; see Gay & Joker Comics)
Summer, 1944 - No. 23, Aug, 1949
Timely/Marvel Comics (20CC)

	Good	Fine	Mint
1-Doc Rockblock & others by Wolverton	17.00	51.00	120.00
2-Wolverton's Powerhouse Pepper	10.00	30.00	70.00
3-No Wolverton	3.35	10.00	23.00
4,5,7,8-Wolverton-a	6.50	20.00	45.00
6-Kurtzman's "Hey Look," 2 pgs. Wolverton	7.00	21.00	50.00
9-Wolverton's Powerhouse Pepper (8 pgs.) & Kurtzman's "Hey Look" (1)	8.00	24.00	56.00
10-4 pgs. Wolverton's Powerhouse Pepper	6.50	20.00	45.00
11-8 pgs. Wolverton's Powerhouse Pepper	8.00	24.00	56.00
12-4 pgs. Wolverton's Powerhouse Pepper & 1 pg. Kurtzman's "Hey Look"	6.50	20.00	45.00
13-4 pgs. Wolverton's Powerhouse Pepper	6.00	18.00	42.00
14-1 pg. Wolverton's Dr. Whackyhack, 1½ pgs. Kurtzman's "Hey Look"	4.35	13.00	30.00
15-3 pgs. Kurtzman's "Hey Look" & 3 pgs. Giggles 'n' Grins	4.35	13.00	30.00
16-18-Kurtzman's "Hey Look" (?, 2 & 1)	3.35	10.00	23.00
19-Eight pg. Annie Oakley	2.15	6.50	15.00
20-23: 20-Anti-Wertham editorial (2/49)	1.70	5.00	11.50

NOTE: *Lana app.-21. Millie The Model app.-13, 15, 17, 21. Rusty app.-10, 11, 13, 15, 17.*

TEXAN, THE (Fightin' Marines No. 15 on; Fightin' Texan No. 16 on)
Aug, 1948 - No. 15, Oct, 1951
St. John Publishing Co.

	Good	Fine	Mint
1-Buckskin Belle	5.00	15.00	35.00
2	2.65	8.00	18.00
3,5,10: 10-Over-sized issue	2.35	7.00	16.00
4,7,15-Baker c/a	4.85	14.50	33.00
6,9-Baker-c	2.75	8.25	19.00
8,11,13,14-Baker c/a(2-3) each	4.85	14.50	33.00
12-All Matt Baker; Peyote story	5.50	16.50	38.00

NOTE: ***Matt Baker** c-6-15. **Larsen** a-6, 8. **Tuska** a-1, 2, 8.*

TEXAN, THE (See 4-Color No. 1027,1096)

TEXAS JOHN SLAUGHTER (See 4-Color No. 997,1181)

TEXAS KID (See Two-Gun Western, Wild Western)
Jan, 1951 - No. 10, July, 1952
Marvel/Atlas Comics (LMC)

	Good	Fine	Mint
1-Origin; Texas Kid (alias Lance Temple) & his horse Thunder begin; Tuska-a	4.00	12.00	28.00
2	2.00	6.00	14.00
3-10	1.65	5.00	11.50

NOTE: ***Maneely** a-1-3; c-3, 5-10.*

TEXAS RANGERS, THE (See Superior Stories No. 4 and Jace Pearson of...)

TEXAS RANGERS IN ACTION (Formerly Captain Gallant or Scotland Yard?) (See Blue Bird Comics)
No. 5, July, 1956 - No. 79, Aug, 1970
Charlton Comics

	Good	Fine	Mint
5	1.75	5.25	12.00
6-10	.85	2.50	6.00
11-Williamson-a(5,5,&8 pgs.); Torres-a	4.35	13.00	30.00
12,14-20	.55	1.65	4.00
13-Williamson-a, 5 pgs; Torres-a	3.35	10.00	23.00
21-30: 30-Last 10¢ ish?	.45	1.35	3.00
31-59	.25	.80	1.60
60-Rileys Rangers begin		.40	.80
61-70: 65-1st app. The Man Called Loco, origin-No. 67		.30	.60
71-79		.25	.50
76(Modern Comics-r, 1977)		.15	.30

TEXAS SLIM (See A-1 Comics No. 2-8,10)

TEX BENSON
Oct?, 1986 - No. 4, 1987 (mini-series)($2.00, B&W)
Metro Comics

	Good	Fine	Mint
1-4	.35	1.00	2.00

TEX DAWSON, GUN-SLINGER (Gunslinger No. 2 on)
January, 1973
Marvel Comics Group

	Good	Fine	Mint
1-Steranko-c; Williamson-a(r); Tex Dawson-r		.30	.60

TEX FARNUM (See Wisco)

TEX FARRELL
Mar-Apr, 1948
D. S. Publishing Co.

	Good	Fine	Mint
1-Tex Farrell & his horse Lightning begin; Shelly-c	4.00	12.00	28.00

TEX GRANGER (Formerly Calling All Boys)
No. 18, June, 1948 - No. 24, Sept, 1949
Parents' Magazine Institute/Commended

	Good	Fine	Mint
18-Tex Granger & his horse Bullet begin	3.00	9.00	21.00
19	2.15	6.50	15.00
20-24	1.50	4.50	10.00

TEX MORGAN (See Blaze Carson, Wild Western)
Aug, 1948 - No. 9, Feb, 1950
Marvel Comics (CCC)

	Good	Fine	Mint
1-Tex Morgan, his horse Lightning & sidekick Lobo begin	6.50	19.50	45.00
2	4.35	13.00	30.00
3-6: 4-Arizona Annie app.	3.00	9.00	21.00
7-9: All photo-c. 7-Captain Tootsie by Beck. 8-18pg. story "The Terror of Rimrock Valley;" Diablo app.	4.35	13.00	30.00

NOTE: ***Tex Taylor** app.-6,7,9.*

TEX RITTER WESTERN (Movie star; singing cowboy; see Six-Gun Heroes, Western Hero)
Oct, 1950 - No. 46, May, 1959 (Photo-c, 1-21)
Fawcett No. 1-20 (1/54)/Charlton No. 21 on

	Good	Fine	Mint
1-Tex Ritter, his stallion White Flash & dog Fury begin; photo front/back-c begin	18.00	54.00	125.00
2	10.00	30.00	70.00
3-5: 5-Last photo back-c	8.50	25.50	60.00
6-10	7.00	21.00	50.00
11-19	4.35	13.00	30.00
20-Last Fawcett issue (1/54)	4.65	14.00	32.00
21-1st Charlton issue; photo-c (3/54)	4.65	14.00	32.00
22	2.85	8.50	20.00
23-30: 23-25-Young Falcon app.	2.15	6.50	15.00
31-38,40-45	1.85	5.50	13.00
39-Williamson-c/a (1/58)	4.35	13.00	30.00
46-Last issue	2.15	6.50	15.00

NOTE: *B&W photo back-c No. 23-32.*

TEX TAYLOR (See Blaze Carson, Kid Colt, Tex Morgan, Wild West, Wild Western, & Wisco)
Sept, 1948 - No. 9, March, 1950
Marvel Comics (HPC)

	Good	Fine	Mint
1-Tex Taylor & his horse Fury begin	6.50	19.50	45.00
2	4.35	13.00	30.00
3	3.00	9.00	21.00
4-6: All photo-c. 4-Anti-Wertham editorial. 5,6-Blaze Carson app.	3.50	10.50	24.00
7-Photo-c; 18pg. Movie-Length Thriller "Trapped in Time's Lost Land!" with sabre toothed tigers, dinosaurs; Diablo app.	4.35	13.00	30.00
8-Photo-c; 18pg. Movie-Length Thriller "The Mystery of Devil-Tree Plateau!" with dwarf horses, dwarf people & a lost miniature Inca type village; Diablo app.	4.35	13.00	30.00
9-Photo-c; 18pg. Movie-Length Thriller "Guns Along the Border!" Captain Tootsie by Schreiber; Nimo The Mountain Lion app.	4.35	13.00	30.00

THANE OF BAGARTH
No. 24, Oct, 1985 - No. 25, Dec, 1985
Charlton Comics

	Good	Fine	Mint
24,25		.40	.80

THAT'S MY POP! GOES NUTS FOR FAIR
1939 (76 pages) (B&W)
Bystander Press

	Good	Fine	Mint
nn-by Milt Gross	5.50	16.50	38.00

THAT DARN CAT (See Movie Comics & Walt Disney Showcase No.19)

THAT THE WORLD MAY BELIEVE
No date (16 pgs.) (Graymoor Friars distr.)
Catechetical Guild Giveaway

	Good	Fine	Mint
	1.70	5.00	10.00

THAT WILKIN BOY (Meet Bingo. . .)
Jan, 1969 - No. 52, Oct, 1982
Archie Publications

	Good	Fine	Mint
1	1.35	4.00	8.00
2-10	.70	2.00	4.00
11-26 (last Giant issue)	.35	1.00	2.00
27-52		.50	1.00

T.H.E. CAT (TV)
Mar, 1967 - No. 4, Oct, 1967 (All have photo-c)
Dell Publishing Co.

	Good	Fine	Mint
1	1.50	4.50	10.00
2-4	1.00	3.00	7.00

THERE'S A NEW WORLD COMING
1973 (35-49 Cents)
Spire Christian Comics/Fleming H. Revell Co.

	Good	Fine	Mint
		.50	1.00

THEY ALL KISSED THE BRIDE (See Cinema Comics Herald)

THEY RING THE BELL
1946
Fox Feature Syndicate

	Good	Fine	Mint
1	4.75	14.25	33.00

THIEF OF BAGHDAD (See 4-Color No. 1229)

THIMBLE THEATRE STARRING POPEYE
1931, 1932 (52 pgs.; 25 cents; B&W)
Sonnet Publishing Co.

	Good	Fine	Mint
1-Daily strip serial reprints in both by Segar	42.00	125.00	295.00
2	37.00	110.00	260.00

NOTE: *Probably the first Popeye reprint book. Popeye first entered Thimble Theatre in 1929.*

THIMK (Magazine) (Satire)
May, 1958 - No. 6, May, 1959
Counterpart

	Good	Fine	Mint
1	1.70	5.00	10.00
2-6	1.00	3.00	6.00

THING!, THE (Blue Beetle No. 18 on)
Feb, 1952 - No. 17, Nov, 1954
Song Hits No. 1,2/Capitol Stories/Charlton

	Good	Fine	Mint
1	14.50	43.50	100.00
2,3	11.00	33.00	76.00

Tex Morgan #4, © MCG

Tex Ritter Western #21, © FAW

Tex Taylor #4, © MCG

The Thing! #14, © CC

This Magazine Is Haunted #17, © CC

Thor #339, © MCG

THE THING! (continued)

	Good	Fine	Mint
4-6,8,10	8.50	25.50	60.00
7-Injury to eye-c & inside panel. E.C. swipes from VOH No. 28	17.00	51.00	120.00
9-Used in **SOTI**, pg. 388 & illo-''Stomping on the face is a form of brutality which modern children learn early''	20.00	60.00	140.00
11-Necronomicon story; Hansel & Gretel parody; Injury-to-eye panel; Check-a	14.50	43.50	100.00
12-''Cinderella'' parody; Ditko-c/a; lingerie panels	26.00	78.00	182.00
13,15-Ditko c/a(3 & 5); 13-Ditko E.C. swipe/HOF No. 15/1-''House of Horror''	26.00	78.00	182.00
14-Extreme violence/torture; Rumpelstiltskin story; Ditko c/a(4)	26.00	78.00	182.00
16-Injury to eye panel	14.50	43.50	100.00
17-Ditko-c; classic parody-''Through the Looking Glass;'' Powell-a(r)	20.00	60.00	140.00

NOTE: Excessive violence, severed heads, injury to eye are common No. 5 on.

THING, THE (Also see Marvel Two-In-One)
July, 1983 - No. 36, June, 1986
Marvel Comics Group

	Good	Fine	Mint
1-Byrne scripts 1-13,18 on; life story of Ben Grimm		.60	1.20
2-10		.45	.90
11-36		.40	.80

NOTE: ***Byrne** a-2i, 7; c-1, 7.*

THIRTEEN (. . . Going on 18)
11-1/61-62 - No. 25, 12/67; No. 26, 7/69 - No. 29, 1/71
Dell Publishing Co.

	Good	Fine	Mint
1	3.00	9.00	21.00
2-10	2.35	7.00	16.00
11-29: 26-29-r	1.75	5.25	12.00

NOTE: ***John Stanley** script-No. 3-29; art?*

39 SCREAMS, THE
1986 - Present (B&W; high quality paper)
Thunder Baas Press

	Good	Fine	Mint
1-3	.30	.90	1.70

THIRTY SECONDS OVER TOKYO (Also see Guadacanal Diary)
1943 (Movie) (Also see American Library)
David McKay Co.

	Good	Fine	Mint
nn(B&W, text & pictures)	11.50	34.50	80.00

THIS IS SUSPENSE! (Formerly Strange Suspense Stories; Strange Suspense Stories No. 27 on)
No. 23, Feb, 1955 - No. 26, Aug, 1955
Charlton Comics

	Good	Fine	Mint
23-Wood-a(r)/A Star Presentation No. 3-''Dr. Jekyll & Mr. Hyde''	8.50	25.50	60.00
24-Evans-a	3.00	9.00	21.00
25,26	1.65	5.00	11.50

THIS IS THE PAYOFF (See Pay-Off)

THIS IS WAR
No. 5, July, 1952 - No. 9, May, 1953
Standard Comics

	Good	Fine	Mint
5-Toth-a	4.35	13.00	30.00
6,9-Toth-a	3.35	10.00	23.00
7,8	1.20	3.50	8.00

THIS IS YOUR LIFE, DONALD DUCK (See 4-Color No. 1109)

THIS MAGAZINE IS CRAZY (Crazy V3No.3 on)
V3No.2, July, 1957 (68 pgs.) (25 cents) (Satire)
Charlton Publ. (Humor Magazines)

	Good	Fine	Mint
V3No.2	.80	2.40	4.80

THIS MAGAZINE IS HAUNTED (Danger and Adventure No. 22 on)
Oct, 1951 - No. 14, 12/53; No. 15, 2/54 - V3/21, Nov, 1954
Fawcett Publications/Charlton No. 15(2/54) on

	Good	Fine	Mint
1-Evans-a(i?)	11.50	34.50	80.00
2,5-Evans-a	8.00	24.00	56.00
3,4	4.35	13.00	30.00
6-9,11,12,14	3.65	11.00	25.00
10-Severed head-c	5.00	15.00	35.00
13-Severed head story	4.65	14.00	32.00
15,20	3.15	9.50	22.00
16,19-Ditko-c. 19-Injury-to-eye panel; story r-/No. 1	7.00	21.00	50.00
17-Ditko-c/a(3); blood drainage story	11.50	34.50	80.00
18-Ditko-c/a; E.C. swipe/Haunt of Fear 5; injury-to-eye panel	9.50	28.50	65.00
21-Ditko-c, Evans-a	7.00	21.00	50.00

NOTE: ***Bailey** a-1, 3, 4, 21r/No.1. **Powell** a-3-5, 11, 12, 17. **Shuster** a-18-20.*

THIS MAGAZINE IS HAUNTED (2nd Series) (Formerly Zaza the Mystic; Outer Space No. 17 on)
V2No.12, July, 1957 - V2No.16, April, 1958
Charlton Comics

	Good	Fine	Mint
V2No.12-14-Ditko c/a in all	7.00	21.00	50.00
15-No Ditko-c/a	1.30	4.00	9.00
16-Ditko-a	5.00	15.00	35.00

THIS MAGAZINE IS WILD (See Wild)

THIS WAS YOUR LIFE (Religious)
1964 (3½x5½'') (40 pgs.) (Black, white & red)
Jack T. Chick Publ.

	Good	Fine	Mint
		.40	.80
Another version (5x2¾'', 26pgs.)		.60	1.20

THOR (Formerly Journey Into Mystery)
March, 1966 - Present
Marvel Comics Group

	Good	Fine	Mint
126	.85	2.50	5.00
127-133,135-140	.50	1.50	3.00
134-Intro High Evolutionary	.85	2.50	5.00
141-145,150: 146-Inhumans begin, end No. 151	.35	1.00	2.00
146,147-Origin The Inhumans	.40	1.20	2.40
148,149-Origin Black Bolt in each; 149-Origin Medusa, Crystal, Maximus, Gorgon, Kornak	.35	1.00	2.00
151-157,159,160	.35	1.00	2.00
158-Origin-r/No. 83; origin Dr. Blake, concludes No. 159	.50	1.50	3.00
161,163,164,167,170-179-Last Kirby issue	.35	1.00	2.00
162,168,169-Origin Galactus	.35	1.10	2.20
165,166-Warlock(Him) app.	.50	1.50	3.00
180,181-Adams-a	.70	2.00	4.00
182-192,194-199	.25	.75	1.50
193-(52 pgs.); Silver Surfer x-over	.85	2.50	5.00
200	.45	1.25	2.50
201-226: 225-Intro. Firelord		.50	1.00
227-299: 294-Origin Asgard & Odin		.40	.80
300-End of Asgard; origin of Odin & The Destroyer	.25	.75	1.50
301-336		.40	.80
337-Simonson-a; Beta Ray Bill becomes new Thor	1.00	3.00	6.00
338	.35	1.00	2.00
339,340: 340-Donald Blake returns as Thor	.25	.75	1.50
341-350		.50	1.00
351-377: 373-X-Factor tie-in		.40	.80

THOR (continued)

	Good	Fine	Mint
Giant-Size 1('75)		.50	1.00
Special 2(9/66)-See Journey Into Myst. for 1st annual	.35	1.00	2.00
Special 3,4('67-12/71)	.35	1.00	2.00
Annual 5(11/76)		.50	1.00
Annual 6(10/77), 7(9/78), 8(11/79)		.40	.80
Annual 9(11/81), 10(11/82), 11(11/83)		.40	.80
Annual 12(11/84)		.40	.80
Annual 13(12/85)		.65	1.30

NOTE: ***Adams** c-179-181. **Austin** a-342i, 346i; c-312i. **Buscema** a(p)-178, 182-213, 215-226, 231-238, 241-253, 254r, 256-259, 272-278, 283-285, Annual 6, 8; c(p)-175, 182-196, 198-200, 202-204, 206, 211, 212, 215, 219, 221, 226, 256, 259, 261, 262, 272-278, 283, 289, Annual 6. **Everett** a(i)-143, 170-175; c(i)-171, 172, 174, 176, 241. **Gil Kane** a-318p; c(p)-201, 205, 207-10, 216, 220, 222, 223, 231, 233-40, 242, 243, 318. **Kirby** a(p)-126-177, 179, 194, 254r; c(p)-126-169, 171-174, 176, 177, 178, 249-253, 255, 257, 258, Annual 5, Special 1-4. **Layton** c-285i, 287i, 288i, 290-93i, 316i, 334, 336, Annual 8i. **Mooney** a(i)-201, 204, 214-16, 218, 322i, 324i, 325i, 327i. **Simonson** a-260-71p, 337-50, Annual 7p; c-260, 263-71, 337-50, Annual 7. **Starlin** c-213.*

THOSE MAGNIFICENT MEN IN THEIR FLYING MACHINES (See Movie Comics)

THREAT!
June, 1986 - Present (Magazine size, B&W, high quality paper)
Fantagraphics Books ($2.25)

1	.50	1.50	3.00
2-10	.35	1.00	2.00

THREE CABALLEROS (See 4-Color No. 71)

THREE CHIPMUNKS, THE (See 4-Color No. 1042)

THREE COMICS (Also see Spiritman)
1944 (10 cents, 48pgs.) (2 different covers exist)
The Penny King Co.

1,3,4-Lady Luck, Mr. Mystic, The Spirit app. (3 Spirit sections bound together)-Lou Fine-a	13.00	40.00	90.00

NOTE: *No. 1 contains Spirit Sections 4/9/44 - 4/23/44, and No. 4 is also from April, 1944.*

3-D (NOTE: *The prices of all the 3-D comics listed include glasses. Deduct 40-50 percent if glasses are missing, and reduce slightly if glasses are loose.)*

3-D ACTION
Jan, 1954 (Oversized) (15 cents)
Atlas Comics (ACI)

1-Battle Brady	17.00	51.00	120.00

3-D ALIEN TERROR
June, 1986
Eclipse Comics

1-Morrow-a; Old Witch, Crypt-Keeper, Vault Keeper cameo	.45	1.25	2.50
. . . in 2-D: 100 copies signed & numbered (B&W)	.85	2.50	5.00

3-D ANIMAL FUN (See Animal Fun)

3-D BATMAN
1953, Reprinted in 1966
National Periodical Publications

1953-Reprints Batman No. 42 & 48; Tommy Tomorrow app.	43.00	130.00	300.00
1966-Tommy Tomorrow app.	9.00	27.00	62.00

3-D CIRCUS
1953 (25 cents)
Fiction House Magazines

1	17.00	51.00	120.00

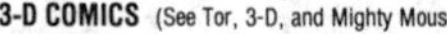

3-D COMICS (See Tor, 3-D, and Mighty Mouse)

3-D DOLLY
December, 1953
Harvey Publications

	Good	Fine	Mint
1-Richie Rich story redrawn from his 1st app. in Little Dot No. 1	11.50	34.50	80.00

3-D-ELL
1953 (3-D comics) (25¢)
Dell Publishing Co.

1,2-Rootie Kazootie	16.00	48.00	110.00
3-Flukey Luke	15.00	45.00	105.00

3-D FEATURES PRESENT JET PUP
Oct-Dec, 1953
Dimensions Public

1-Irving Spector-a(2)	17.00	51.00	120.00

3-D FUNNY MOVIES
1953 (25¢)
Comic Media

1	16.00	48.00	110.00

3-D HEROES (Blackthorne 3-D Series No. 3)
Feb, 1986 ($2.25)
Blackthorne Publishing, Inc.

1		1.25	2.50

THREE-DIMENSION ADVENTURES (Superman)
1953 (Large size)
National Periodical Publications

Origin Superman (new art)	50.00	150.00	350.00

THREE DIMENSIONAL ALIEN WORLDS
July, 1984 (One-Shot)
Pacific Comics

1-Bolton/Stevens-a	.65	1.90	3.80

THREE DIMENSIONAL DNAGENTS (See New DNAgents)

THREE DIMENSIONAL E. C. CLASSICS (Three Dimensional Tales From the Crypt No. 2)
Spring, 1954 (Prices include glasses)
E. C. Comics

1-Reprints: Wood (Mad No. 3), Krigstein (W.S. No. 7), Evans (F.C. No. 13), & Ingels (CSS No. 5); Kurtzman-c	30.00	90.00	210.00

NOTE: *Stories redrawn to 3-D format. Original stories not necessarily by artists listed. CSS: Crime SuspenStories; F.C.: Frontline Combat; W.S.: Weird Science.*

THREE DIMENSIONAL TALES FROM THE CRYPT (Formerly Three Dimensional E. C. Classics)
Spring, 1954 (Prices include glasses)
E. C. Comics

2-Davis (TFTC No.25), Elder (VOH No.14), Craig (TFTC No.24), & Orlando (TFTC No.22) stories; Feldstein-c	32.00	95.00	225.00

NOTE: *Stories redrawn to 3-D format. Original stories not necessarily by artists listed. TFTC: Tales From the Crypt; VOH: Vault of Horror.*

3-D LOVE
December, 1953 (25 cents)
Steriographic Publ. (Mikeross Publ.)

1	17.00	51.00	120.00

3-D NOODNICK (See Noodnick)

Threat! #1, © Fantagraphics

3-D Batman, 1953, © DC

3-D Heroes #1, © Blackthorne

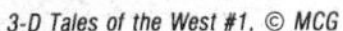
3-D Tales of the West #1, © MCG

Three Stooges #15, © GK

Thrilling Comics #10, © BP

3-D ROMANCE
January, 1954 (25 cents)
Steriographic Publ. (Mikeross Publ.)

Good Fine Mint
1 17.00 51.00 120.00

3-D SHEENA, JUNGLE QUEEN
1953
Fiction House Magazines

1 28.00 84.00 195.00

3-D TALES OF THE WEST
Jan, 1954 (Oversized) (15 cents)
Atlas Comics (CPS)

1 (3-D) 17.00 51.00 120.00

3-D THREE STOOGES (See Three Stooges)

3-D WHACK (See Whack)

3 FUNMAKERS, THE
1908 (64 pgs.) (10x15")
Stokes and Company

Maude, Katzenjammer Kids, Happy Hooligan (1904-06 Sunday strip reprints in color) 22.00 65.00 154.00

3 LITTLE PIGS (See 4-Color No. 218)

3 LITTLE PIGS, THE (See Walt Disney Showcase No. 15,21)
May, 1964 - No. 2, Sept, 1968 (Walt Disney)
Gold Key

1-Reprints 4-Color 218 1.00 3.00 7.00
2 .75 2.25 5.00

THREE MOUSEKETEERS, THE (1st Series)
3-4/56 - No. 24, 9-10/59; No. 25, 8-9/60 - No. 26, 10-12/60
National Periodical Publications

1 5.00 15.00 35.00
2 3.00 9.00 21.00
3-10 2.35 7.00 16.00
11-26 1.50 4.50 10.00

NOTE: ***Rube Grossman** a-1-26. **Sheldon Mayer** a-1-8; c-1,3,4,6,7.*

THREE MOUSEKETEERS, THE (2nd Series) (See Super DC Giant)
May-June, 1970 - No. 7, May-June, 1971
National Periodical Publications

1-Mayer-a .25 .75 1.50
2-7-Mayer-a (68 pgs. No. 5-7) .30 .60

THREE NURSES (Formerly Confidential Diary; Career Girl Romances No. 24 on)V3No.18, May, 1963 - V3No.23, Mar, 1964
Charlton Comics

V3No.18-23 .50 1.00

THREE RASCALS
1958; 1963
I. W. Enterprises

I.W. Reprint No. 1 (Says Super Comics on inside)-(M.E.'s Clubhouse Rascals), No. 2('58) .30 .80 1.60
10('63)-Reprints No. 1 .30 .80 1.60

THREE RING COMICS
March, 1945
Spotlight Publishers

1 2.35 7.00 16.00

THREE ROCKETEERS (See Blast-Off)

THREE STOOGES (See Comic Album No. 18, The Little Stooges, March of Comics No. 232, 248, 268, 280, 292, 304, 316, 336, 373, & Movie Classics & Comics)

THREE STOOGES
Feb, 1949 - No. 2, May, 1949; Sept, 1953 - No. 7, Oct, 1954
Jubilee No. 1,2/St. John No. 1 (9/53) on

Good Fine Mint
1-(Scarce, 1949)-Kubert-a; infinity-c 33.50 100.00 235.00
2-(Scarce)-Kubert, Maurer-a 27.00 81.00 190.00
1(9/53)-Hollywood Stunt Girl by Kubert, 7 pgs. 26.00 78.00 180.00
2(3-D, 10/53)-Stunt Girl story by Kubert 17.00 51.00 120.00
3(3-D, 11/53) 15.00 45.00 105.00
4(3/54)-7(10/54) 7.00 21.00 50.00

NOTE: *All issues have **Kubert-Maurer** art.*

THREE STOOGES
No. 1043, Oct-Dec, 1959 - No. 55, June, 1972
Dell Publishing Co./Gold Key No. 10 (10/62) on

4-Color 1043 3.50 10.50 24.00
4-Color 1078,1127,1170,1187 3.00 9.00 21.00
6(9-11/61) - 10: 6-Professor Putter begins; ends No. 16 2.00 6.00 14.00
11-14,16-20: 17-The Little Monsters begin (5/64)(1st app.?) 2.35 7.00 16.00
15-Go Around the World in a Daze (movie scenes) 2.85 8.50 20.00
21,23-30 1.50 4.50 10.00
22-Movie scenes/'The Outlaws Is Coming' 2.65 8.00 18.00
31-55 .85 3.50 7.00

NOTE: *All Four Colors, 6-50,52-55 have photo-c.*

THREE STOOGES 3-D
1986
Eclipse Comics

1,2-Gulacy-c; 1-r/No.1 from '53 1.25 2.50

3 WORLDS OF GULLIVER (See 4-Color No. 1158)

THRILL COMICS (See Flash Comics, Fawcett)

THRILLER
Nov, 1983 - No. 12, Nov, 1984 ($1.25; Baxter paper)
DC Comics

1-Intro Seven Seconds .50 1.00
2-10: 2-Origin. 5,6-Elvis satire .50 1.00
11,12 ($2.00; 52 pgs.) .50 1.00

THRILLING ADVENTURES IN STAMPS COMICS (Formerly Stamp Comics)
Jan, 1953 (25 cents) (100 pages)
Stamp Comics, Inc.

V1No.8-Harrison, Wildey, Kiefer, Napoli-a 7.00 21.00 50.00

THRILLING ADVENTURE STORIES
Feb, 1975 - No. 2, July-Aug, 1975 (B&W) (68 pgs.)
Atlas/Seaboard Publ.

1-Tigerman, Kromag the Killer begin; Heath, Thorne-a .40 1.20 2.40
2-Toth, Severin, Simonson-a; Adams-c .40 1.20 2.40

THRILLING COMICS
Feb, 1940 - No. 80, April, 1951
Better Publ./Nedor/Standard Comics

1-Origin Doc Strange (37 pgs.); Nickie Norton of the Secret Service begins 48.00 145.00 335.00
2-The Rio Kid, The Woman in Red, Pinocchio begins 22.00 65.00 154.00
3-The Ghost & Lone Eagle begin 19.50 58.50 135.00
4-10 13.00 40.00 90.00
11-18,20 10.00 30.00 70.00
19-Origin The American Crusader, ends No. 39,41 14.50 43.50 100.00
21-30: 24-Intro. Mike, Doc Strange's sidekick. 29-Last Rio Kid 8.00 24.00 56.00

THRILLING COMICS (continued) — Good / Fine / Mint

31-40: 36-Commando Cubs begin 6.50 20.00 45.00
41-52: 41-Hitler bondage-c. 52-The Ghost ends 5.00 15.00 35.00
53-The Phantom Detective begins; The Cavalier app.; no Commando Cubs 5.00 15.00 35.00
54-The Cavalier app.; no Commando Cubs 5.00 15.00 35.00
55-Lone Eagle ends 5.00 15.00 35.00
56-Princess Pantha begins 11.00 33.00 76.00
57-60: 61-The Lone Eagle app. 10.00 30.00 70.00
61-65: 61-Ingels-a; The Lone Eagle app. 65-Last Phantom Detective & Commando Cubs 11.00 33.00 76.00
66-Frazetta text illo 9.50 28.50 65.00
67,70-73: Frazetta-a(5-7 pgs.) in each. 72-Sea Eagle app. 14.50 43.50 100.00
68,69-Frazetta-a(2), 8 & 6 pgs.; 9 & 7 pgs. 16.00 48.00 110.00
74-Last Princess Pantha; Tara app. 5.00 15.00 35.00
75-78: 75-Western format begins 2.85 8.50 20.00
79-Krigstein-a 4.35 13.00 30.00
80-Severin & Elder, Celardo, Moreira-a 4.35 13.00 30.00

NOTE: *Bondage c-5, 9, 13, 22, 27-29, 38, 41, 52, 54.* ***Kinstler*** *a-45, 48.* ***Leo Morey*** *a-7.* ***Schomburg (Xela)*** *c-No. 36-71; airbrush 62-71. Woman in Red not in No. 19, 23, 31-33, 39-45. No. 72 exists as a Canadian reprint with no Frazetta story.*

THRILLING CRIME CASES (Shocking Mystery Cases No. 50 on)
No. 41, June-July, 1950 - No. 49, 1952
Star Publications

41 4.75 14.25 33.00
42-44-Chameleon story-Fox-r 4.35 13.00 30.00
45-48: 47-Used in **POP**, pg. 84 4.00 12.00 28.00
49-Classic L. B. Cole-c 10.00 30.00 70.00

NOTE: *All have* ***L. B. Cole****-c; a-43p, 45p, 46p, 49(2pgs.).* ***Disbrow*** *a-48.* ***Hollingsworth*** *a-48.*

THRILLING ROMANCES
No. 5, Dec, 1949 - No. 26, June, 1954
Standard Comics

5 3.15 9.50 22.00
6,8 1.65 5.00 11.50
7-Severin/Elder-a, 7 pgs. 3.00 9.00 21.00
9,10-Severin/Elder-a 2.35 7.00 16.00
11,14-21,26 1.15 3.50 8.00
12-Wood-a, 2 pgs.; photo-c 4.35 13.00 30.00
13-Severin-a 2.00 6.00 14.00
22-25-Toth-a 3.50 10.50 24.00

NOTE: *All photo-c.* ***Celardo*** *a-9,16.* ***Colletta*** *a-23, 24(2).* ***Tuska*** *a-9.*

THRILLING TRUE STORY OF THE BASEBALL GIANTS
1952 (2nd issue titled . . . Baseball Yankees)
Fawcett Publications

Each. . . . 17.00 51.00 120.00

THRILLOGY
Jan, 1984 (One-shot)
Pacific Comics

1-Conrad c/a .50 1.00

THRILL-O-RAMA
Oct, 1965 - No. 3, Dec, 1966
Harvey Publications (Fun Films)

1-Fate (Man in Black) by Powell app.; Doug Wildey-a; Simon-c .70 2.00 4.00
2-Pirana begins; Williamson 2 pgs.; Fate (Man in Black) app.; Tuska/Simon-c .70 2.00 4.00
3-Fate (Man in Black) app.; Sparling-c .35 1.00 2.00

THRILLS OF TOMORROW (Formerly Tomb of Terror)
No. 17, Oct, 1954 - No. 20, April, 1955
Harvey Publications — Good / Fine / Mint

17-Powell-a (horror); r/Witches Tales No. 7. 2.35 7.00 16.00
18-Powell-a (horror); r/Tomb of Terror No. 1 2.00 6.00 14.00
19,20-Stuntman by S&K (r/from Stuntman 1 & 2); 19 has origin & is last pre-code (2/55) 13.50 40.50 95.00

NOTE: ***Palais*** *a-17.*

THROBBING LOVE (See Fox Giants)

THROUGH GATES OF SPLENDOR
1973, 1974 (36 pages) (39-49 cents)
Spire Christian Comics (Fleming H. Revell Co.)

nn .40 .80

THUMPER (See 4-Color No. 19 & 243)

THUN'DA
1952 - 1953
Magazine Enterprises

1(A-1 47)-Origin; Frazetta c/a; only comic done entirely by Frazetta; Cave Girl app. 120.00 360.00 840.00
2(A-1 56) 13.50 40.50 95.00
3(A-1 73), 4(A-1 78) 10.00 30.00 70.00
5(A-1 83), 6(A-1 86) 8.50 25.50 60.00

NOTE: ***Powell*** *c/a-2-6.*

THUNDER AGENTS
11/65 - No. 17, 12/67; No. 18, 9/68, No. 19, 11/68, No. 20, 11/69 (No. 1-16: 68 pgs.; No. 17 on: 52 pgs.)
Tower Comics

1-Origin & 1st app. Dynamo, Noman, Menthor, & The Thunder Squad; 1st app. The Iron Maiden 4.00 12.00 24.00
2-Death of Egghead 1.70 5.00 10.00
3-5: 4-Guy Gilbert becomes Lightning who joins Thunder Squad; Iron Maiden app. 1.35 4.00 8.00
6-10: 7-Death of Menthor. 8-Origin & 1st app. The Raven .85 2.50 5.00
11-15: 13-Undersea Agent app.; no Raven story .70 2.00 4.00
16-19 .50 1.50 3.00
20-All reprints .35 1.00 2.00

NOTE: ***Crandall*** *a-1, 4p, 5p, 18, 20r; c-18.* ***Ditko*** *a-6, 7p, 12p, 13, 14p, 16, 18.* ***Kane*** *a-1, 5p, 6p, 14, 16p; c-14, 15.* ***Tuska*** *a-1p, 7, 8, 10, 13-17, 19.* ***Whitney*** *a-9p, 10, 13, 15, 17, 18; c-17.* ***Wood*** *a-1-11,(w/****Ditko****-12,18), (inks-No. 9, 13, 14, 16, 17), 19i, 20r; c-1-8, 9i, 10-13(No. 10 w/****Williamson****(p)), 16.*

T.H.U.N.D.E.R. AGENTS (See Wally Wood's. . . & JCP Features)
May, 1983 - No. 2, Jan, 1984
JC Comics (Archie Publications)

1,2-New material .50 1.00

THUNDER BIRDS (See Cinema Comics Herald)

THUNDERBOLT (See The Atomic. . .)

THUNDERBOLT (Peter Cannon. . .) (Formerly Son of Vulcan No. 50)
Jan, 1966; No. 51, Mar-Apr, 1966 - No. 60, Nov, 1967
Charlton Comics

1-Origin .50 1.50 3.00
51 .30 .80 1.60
52-58: 54-Sentinels begin. 58-Last Thunderbolt & Sentinels .60 1.20
59,60: 60-Prankster app. .50 1.00
Modern Comics-r. 57,58('77) .15 .30

NOTE: ***Aparo*** *a-60.* ***Morisi*** *a-1, 51-56, 58; c-1, 51-56, 58, 59.*

THUNDERBUNNY (Also see Pep No. 393)
Jan, 1984 (Direct sale only)
Red Circle Comics

Thrilling Romances #25, © STD

Thrilling True Story of Baseball Yankees, © FAW

T.H.U.N.D.E.R. Agents #12, © TC

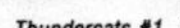
Thundercats #1, © MCG

Thundermace Comics #1 (2-color), © WEST

Tiger Girl #1, © GK

THUNDERBUNNY (continued)

	Good	Fine	Mint
1-Origin		.60	1.20

THUNDERBUNNY
June, 1985 - Present (B&W, magazine format)
WaRP Graphics/Apple Press No. 6 on

	Good	Fine	Mint
1 (Red logo and yellow logo)-Both versions printed at same time & are identical except for color variation; equal quantities of each printed; origin retold	.25	.75	1.50
2-7	.25	.75	1.50
8,9	.30	.90	1.75

THUNDERCATS (TV)
Dec, 1985 - Present
Star Comics (Marvel)

	Good	Fine	Mint
1-Mooney c/a begins	1.00	3.00	6.00
2-(65¢&75¢ cover exist)	.45	1.25	2.50
3-10		.50	1.00

THUNDERMACE COMICS
March, 1986 - Present ($1.50; B&W; 28pgs.)
R.A.K. Graphics

	Good	Fine	Mint
1-two color cover	7.00	20.00	40.00
1 (2nd printing)	.35	1.00	2.00

THUNDER MOUNTAIN (See 4-Color No. 246)

TICKLE COMICS (Also see Gay, Smile, & Whee Comics)
1955 (52 pages) (5x7¼'') (7 cents)
Modern Store Publ.

	Good	Fine	Mint
1	.40	1.20	2.40

TICK TOCK TALES
Jan, 1946 - No.34, 1951
Magazine Enterprises

	Good	Fine	Mint
1	3.75	11.25	26.00
2	1.85	5.50	13.00
3-10	1.50	4.50	10.00
11-34: 19-Flag-c	1.00	3.00	7.00

TIGER (Also see Comics Reading Libraries)
March, 1970 - No. 6, Jan, 1971 (15 cents)
Charlton Press (King Features)

	Good	Fine	Mint
1	.30	.80	1.60
2-6		.50	1.00

TIGER BOY (See Unearthly Spectaculars)

TIGER GIRL
September, 1968
Gold Key

	Good	Fine	Mint
1 (10227-809)	1.75	5.25	12.00

NOTE: *Sparling c/a; written by Jerry Siegel.*

TIGERMAN
April, 1975 - No. 3, Sept, 1975
Seaboard Periodicals (Atlas)

	Good	Fine	Mint
1		.40	.80
2,3-Ditko-p in each		.30	.60

TIGER WALKS, A (See Movie Comics)

TILLIE THE TOILER
1925 - 1933 (52 pgs.) (B&W daily strip reprints)
Cupples & Leon Co.

	Good	Fine	Mint
nn (No. 1)	7.00	21.00	50.00
2-8	5.00	15.00	35.00

NOTE: *First strip app. was January, 1921.*

TILLIE THE TOILER (See Comic Monthly)
No. 15, 1941 - No. 237, July, 1949
Dell Publishing Co.

	Good	Fine	Mint
4-Color 15(1941)	15.00	45.00	105.00
Large Feature Comic 30(1941)	9.50	28.50	65.00
4-Color 8(1942)	9.50	28.50	65.00
4-Color 22(1943)	7.00	21.00	50.00
4-Color 55(1944)	5.75	17.25	40.00
4-Color 89(1945)	5.00	15.00	35.00
4-Color 106('45),132('46)	4.35	13.00	30.00
4-Color 150,176,184	3.00	9.00	21.00
4-Color 195,213,237	2.65	8.00	18.00

TILLY AND TED-TINKERTOTLAND
1945 (Giveaway) (20 pgs.)
W. T. Grant Co.

	Good	Fine	Mint
nn-Christmas comic	1.70	5.00	12.00

TIM (Formerly Superman-Tim; becomes Gene Autry-Tim)
June, 1950 (Half-size, B&W)
Tim Stores

	Good	Fine	Mint
4 issues	2.50	7.50	15.00

TIME BANDITS
Feb, 1982 (One shot)
Marvel Comics Group

	Good	Fine	Mint
1-Movie adaptation		.50	1.00

TIME BEAVERS (See First Comics Graphic Novel)

TIME FOR LOVE (Formerly Romantic Secrets)
V2/53, Oct, 1966 - No. 47, May, 1976
Charlton Comics

	Good	Fine	Mint
V2/53(10/66), 1(10/67), 2(12/67)		.40	.80
3-47		.15	.30

TIMELESS TOPIX (See Topix)

TIME MACHINE, THE (See 4-Color No. 1085)

TIMESPIRITS
Dec, 1984 - No. 8, Mar, 1986 ($1.50, Baxter paper; adults only)
Epic Comics (Marvel)

	Good	Fine	Mint
1	.30	.90	1.80
2-8: 4-Williamson-a	.25	.75	1.50

TIME TO RUN
1973 (39, 49 cents)
Spire Christian Comics (Fleming H. Revell Co.)

	Good	Fine	Mint
nn-by Al Hartley (from Billy Graham movie)		.40	.80

TIME TUNNEL, THE (TV)
Feb, 1967 - No. 2, July, 1967
Gold Key

	Good	Fine	Mint
1,2-Photo back-c	1.75	5.25	12.00

TIME 2: THE EPIPHANY (See First Comics Graphic Novel)

TIME WARP
Oct-Nov, 1979 - No. 5, July, 1980 ($1.00)
DC Comics, Inc.

	Good	Fine	Mint
1		.40	.80
2-5		.30	.60

NOTE: ***Aparo** a-1. **Buckler** a-1p. **Chaykin** a-2. **Ditko** a-1-4. **Kaluta** c-1-5. **G. Kane** a-2. **Nasser** a-4. **Newton** a-1-5p. **Orlando** a-2. **Sutton** a-1-3.*

TIME WARRIORS THE BEGINNING
1986 (Aug) - Present (color)
Fantasy General Comics

	Good	Fine	Mint
1-Alpha Track/Skellon Empire	.25	.75	1.50
2		.40	.75

TIM HOLT (Movie star) (Becomes Red Mask No. 42 on; also see Crack Western No. 72, & Great Western)

TIM HOLT (continued)
1948 - No. 41, April-May, 1954 (All 36 pgs.)
Magazine Enterprises

	Good	Fine	Mint
1(A-1 14)-Photo-c begin, end No. 18, 29; Tim Holt, His horse Lightning & sidekick Chito begin	24.00	70.00	165.00
2(A-1 17)(9-10/48)	13.00	40.00	90.00
3(A-1 19)-Photo back-c	9.50	28.50	65.00
4(1-2/49),5: 5-Photo back-c	8.00	24.00	56.00
6-1st app. The Calico Kid (alias Rex Fury), his horse Ebony & Sidekick Sing-Song (begin series); photo back-c	9.50	28.50	65.00
7-10: 7-Calico Kid by Ayers. 8-Calico Kid by Guardineer (r-/in Great Western 10). 9-Map of Tim's Home Range	6.50	20.00	45.00
11-The Calico Kid becomes The Ghost Rider (Origin & 1st app.) by Dick Ayers (r-/in Great Western 8); his horse Spectre & sidekick Sing-Song begin series	20.00	60.00	140.00
12-16,18-Last photo-c	4.75	14.25	33.00
17-Frazetta Ghost Rider-c	19.50	58.00	135.00
19,22,24: 19-Last Tim Holt-c; Bolle line-drawn-c begin	3.65	11.00	25.00
20-Tim Holt becomes Redmask (Origin); begin series; Redmask-c No. 20-on	7.00	21.00	50.00
21-Frazetta Ghost Rider/Redmask-c	17.00	51.00	120.00
23-Frazetta Redmask-c	15.00	45.00	105.00
25-1st app. Black Phantom	7.00	21.00	50.00
26-30: 28-Wild Bill Hickok, Bat Masterson team up with Redmask. 29-B&W photo-c	3.35	10.00	23.00
31-33-Ghost Rider ends	3.00	9.00	21.00
34-Tales of the Ghost Rider begins (horror)-Classic "The Flower Women" & "Hard Boiled Harry!"	3.75	11.25	26.00
35-Last Tales of the Ghost Rider	3.00	9.00	21.00
36-The Ghost Rider returns, ends No. 41; liquid hallucinogenic drug story	4.00	12.00	28.00
37-Ghost Rider classic "To Touch Is to Die!," about Inca treasure	4.00	12.00	28.00
38-The Black Phantom begins; classic Ghost Rider "The Phantom Guns of Feather Gap!"	4.00	12.00	28.00
39-41: All 3-D effect c/stories	9.50	28.50	65.00

NOTE: ***Dick Ayers** a-7, 9-41. **Bolle** a-1-41; c-19,20,22,24-28,30-41.*

TIM IN SPACE (Formerly Gene Autry Tim; becomes Tim Tomorrow)
1950 (½-size giveaway) (B&W)
Tim Stores

	Good	Fine	Mint
	1.70	5.00	10.00

TIM McCOY (Formerly Zoo Funnies; Pictorial Love Stories No. 22 on)
No. 16, Oct, 1948 - No. 21, Aug-Sept, 1949
Charlton Comics

	Good	Fine	Mint
16	10.00	30.00	70.00
17-21	8.50	25.50	60.00

TIM McCOY, POLICE CAR 17
1934 (32 pgs.) (11x14¾") (B&W) (Like Feature Books)
Whitman Publishing Co.

	Good	Fine	Mint
674-1933 movie ill.	7.00	21.00	50.00

TIMMY (See 4-Color No. 715,823,923,1022)

TIMMY THE TIMID GHOST (Formerly Win-A-Prize?; see Blue Bird)
No. 3, 2/56 - No. 44, 10/64; No. 45, 9/66; 10/67 - No. 23, 7/71; V4/24, 9/85 - No. 26, 1/86
Charlton Comics

	Good	Fine	Mint
3(1956) (1st Series)	2.00	6.00	14.00
4,5	1.00	3.00	7.00
6-10	.50	1.50	3.50
11,12(4/58,10/58)(100pgs.)	.90	2.70	6.50
13-20	.45	1.35	3.00
21-45('66)		.50	1.00
1(10/67)		.30	.60
2-23		.25	.50
24-26 (1985): Fago-r		.40	.80
Shoe Store Giveaway		.40	.80

TIM TOMORROW (Formerly Tim In Space)
8/51, 9/51, 10/51, Christmas, 1951 (5x7¾")
Tim Stores

	Good	Fine	Mint
Features Prof. Fumble & Captain Kit Comet in all	1.35	4.00	8.00

TIM TYLER (See Harvey Comics Hits No. 54)

TIM TYLER (Also see Comics Reading Libraries)
1942
Better Publications

	Good	Fine	Mint
1	4.65	14.00	32.00

TIM TYLER COWBOY
No. 11, Nov, 1948 - No. 18, 1950
Standard Comics

	Good	Fine	Mint
11	3.15	9.50	22.00
12-18	2.00	6.00	14.00

TINKER BELL (See 4-Color No. 896,982, & Walt Disney Showcase No. 37)

TINY FOLKS FUNNIES (See 4-Color No. 60)

TINY TESSIE (Tessie No. 1-23; Real Experiences No. 25)
No. 24, Oct, 1949
Marvel Comics (20CC)

	Good	Fine	Mint
24	1.30	4.00	9.00

TINY TIM
No. 4, 1941 - No. 235, July, 1949
Dell Publishing Co.

	Good	Fine	Mint
Large Feature Comic 4('41)	15.00	45.00	105.00
4-Color 20(1941)	15.00	45.00	105.00
4-Color 42(1943)	8.50	25.50	60.00
4-Color 235	2.65	8.00	18.00

TINY TOT COMICS
Mar, 1946 - No. 10, Nov-Dec, 1947 (For younger readers)
E. C. Comics

	Good	Fine	Mint
1(nn)	11.50	34.50	80.00
2 (5/46)	9.50	28.50	65.00
3-10: 10-Christmas-c	8.00	24.00	56.00

TINY TOT FUNNIES (Formerly Family Funnies)
June, 1951 (Becomes Junior Funnies)
Harvey Publ. (King Features Synd.)

	Good	Fine	Mint
9-Flash Gordon, Mandrake	2.50	7.50	17.00

TINY TOTS COMICS
1943 (Not reprints)
Dell Publishing Co.

	Good	Fine	Mint
1-Kelly-a(2)	30.00	90.00	210.00

TIPPY & CAP STUBBS (See 4-Color No. 210,242)

TIPPY'S FRIENDS GO-GO & ANIMAL
July, 1966 - No. 15, Oct, 1969 (25 cents)
Tower Comics

	Good	Fine	Mint
1	.75	2.25	5.00
2-7,9-15: 12-15 titled "Tippy's Friend Go-Go"	.50	1.50	3.50
8-Beatles on front/back-c	2.00	6.00	14.00

Tim Holt #6, © ME

Tim Tyler Cowboy #14, © STD

Tiny Tots Comics #1, © DELL

Tip Top Comics #8, © UFS

T-Man #1, © QUA

Tomahawk #53, © DC

TIPPY TEEN
Nov, 1965 - No. 27, Feb, 1970 (25 cents)
Tower Comics

	Good	Fine	Mint
1	.70	2.00	4.00
2-27: 5-1pg. Beatle pin-up	.35	1.00	2.00
Special Collectors' Editions(1969-nn)(25¢)	.35	1.00	2.00

TIPPY TERRY
1963
Super/I. W. Enterprises

	Good	Fine	Mint
Super Reprint No. 14('63)-Little Grouchy reprints		.60	1.20
I.W. Reprint No. 1 (no date)		.60	1.20

TIP TOP COMICS
4/36 - No. 210, 1957; No. 211, 11-1/57-58 - No. 225, 5-7/61
United Features No. 1-187/St. John No. 188-210/Dell Publishing Co. No. 211 on

	Good	Fine	Mint
1-Tarzan by Hal Foster, Li'l Abner begin; strip-r	95.00	285.00	665.00
2	47.00	141.00	330.00
3	36.00	108.00	250.00
4	29.00	86.00	200.00
5-10: 7-Photo & biography of Edgar Rice Burroughs. 8-Christmas-c	23.00	70.00	160.00
11-20	17.00	51.00	120.00
21-40: 36-Kurtzman panel (1st published comic work)	15.00	45.00	105.00
41-Has 1st Tarzan Sunday	15.00	45.00	105.00
42-50: 43-Mort Walker panel	13.50	40.50	95.00
51-53	10.00	30.00	70.00
54-Origin Mirror Man & Triple Terror, also featured on cover	15.00	45.00	105.00
55,56,58,60: Last Tarzan by Foster	10.00	30.00	70.00
57,59,61,62-Tarzan by Hogarth	13.50	40.50	95.00
63-80: 65,67-70,72,73,77,78-No Tarzan	7.00	21.00	50.00
81-90	6.50	19.50	45.00
91-99	4.35	13.00	30.00
100	5.00	15.00	35.00
101-140: 110-Gordo story. 111-Li'l Abner app. 118, 132-no Tarzan	3.35	10.00	23.00
141-170: 145,151-Gordo story. 157-Last Li'l Abner; lingerie panels	2.35	7.00	16.00
171-188-Tarzan reprints by B. Lubbers in all. No. 177?-Peanuts by Shulz begins; no Peanuts in No. 178,179,181-183	2.65	8.00	18.00
189-225	1.50	4.50	10.00
Bound Volumes (Very Rare) sold at 1939 World's Fair; bound by publ. in pictorial comic boards. (Also see Comics on Parade)			
Bound issues 1-12	135.00	405.00	945.00
Bound issues 13-24	80.00	240.00	560.00
Bound issues 25-36	60.00	180.00	420.00

NOTE: *Tarzan covers-No. 3, 9, 11, 13, 16, 18, 21, 24, 27, 30, 32-34, 36, 37, 39, 41, 43, 45, 47, 50, 52 (all worth 10-20 percent more). Tarzan by* ***Foster****-No. 1-40, 44-50; by* ***Rex Maxon****-No. 41-43; by* ***Byrne Hogarth****-No. 57, 59, 62.*

TIP TOPPER COMICS
1949 - 1954
United Features Syndicate

	Good	Fine	Mint
1-Li'l Abner, Abbie & Slats	3.15	9.50	22.00
2	1.85	5.50	13.00
3-5	1.65	5.00	11.50
6-25: 17-22,24,26-Peanuts app. (2 pgs.)	1.50	4.50	10.00
26-28-Twin Earths	3.35	10.00	23.00

NOTE: *Many lingerie panels in Fritzi Ritz stories.*

T-MAN
Sept, 1951 - No. 38, Dec, 1956
Quality Comics Group

	Good	Fine	Mint
1-Jack Cole-a	8.00	24.00	56.00
2-Crandall-c	5.35	16.00	37.00
3,6-8: Crandall-c	4.35	13.00	30.00
4,5-Crandall c/a each; 5-Drug test	4.85	14.50	34.00
9-Crandall-c	3.50	10.50	24.00
10,12	2.50	7.50	17.50
11-Used in **POP**, pg. 95 & color illo.	5.00	15.00	35.00
13-19,21-24,26	2.15	6.50	15.00
20-Nuclear explosion-c	4.65	14.00	32.00
25-All Crandall-a	3.85	11.50	27.00
27-38	1.65	5.00	11.50

NOTE: *Anti-communist stories are common. Bondage c-15.*

TNT COMICS
Feb, 1946 (36 pgs.)
Charles Publishing Co.

	Good	Fine	Mint
1-Yellowjacket app.	5.50	16.50	40.00

TOBY TYLER (See Movie Comics & 4-Color No. 1092)

TODAY'S BRIDES
Nov, 1955 - No. 4, Nov, 1956
Ajax/Farrell Publishing Co.

	Good	Fine	Mint
1	2.65	8.00	18.00
2-4	1.30	4.00	9.00

TODAY'S ROMANCE
No. 5, March, 1952 - No. 8, Sept, 1952
Standard Comics

	Good	Fine	Mint
5	2.35	7.00	16.00
6-Toth-a	3.15	9.50	22.00
7,8	1.30	4.00	9.00

TOKA (Jungle King)
Aug-Oct, 1964 - No. 10, Jan, 1967
Dell Publishing Co.

	Good	Fine	Mint
1	.50	1.50	3.00
2	.35	1.00	2.00
3-10	.25	.70	1.40

TOMAHAWK (Son of . . . No. 131-140 on cover) (See Star Spangled Comics)
Sept-Oct, 1950 - No. 140, May-June, 1972
National Periodical Publications

	Good	Fine	Mint
1	30.00	90.00	210.00
2-Frazetta/Williamson-a, 4 pgs.	19.00	57.00	132.00
3-5	9.50	28.50	65.00
6-10: 7-Last 52 pgs.	6.50	19.50	45.00
11-20	4.00	12.00	28.00
21-27,30	2.85	8.50	20.00
28-1st app. Lord Shilling (arch-foe)	3.75	11.25	26.00
29-Frazetta-r/Jimmy Wakely No. 3, 3 pgs.	11.00	33.00	76.00
31-40	2.35	7.00	16.00
41-50	1.85	5.50	13.00
51-56,58-60	1.30	4.00	9.00
57-Frazetta-r/Jimmy Wakely No. 6, 3 pgs.	6.00	18.00	42.00
61-77: 77-Last 10¢ ish.	.75	2.25	5.00
78-85: 81-1st app. Miss Liberty. 83-Origin Tomahawk's Rangers	.35	1.00	2.00
86-100: 96-Origin/1st app. The Hood, alias Lady Shilling		.50	1.00
101-130,132-138,140: 107-Origin/1st app. Thunder-Man		.30	.60
131-Frazetta-r/Jimmy Wakely No. 7, 3 pgs.; origin Firehair retold	.35	1.00	2.00
139-Frazetta-r/Star Spangled No. 113		.50	1.00

NOTE: ***Adams*** *c-116-119, 121, 123-130. Firehair by* ***Kubert****-131-134, 136.* ***Maurer*** *a-138.* ***Severin*** *a-135.*

TOM AND JERRY (See Comic Album No. 4, 8, 12, Dell Giant No. 21, Dell Giants, Golden Comics Digest No. 1, 5, 8, 13, 15, 18, 22, 25, 28, 35, & March of Comics No. 21, 46, 61, 70, 88, 103, 119, 128, 145, 154, 173, 190, 207, 224, 281, 295, 305, 321, 333, 345, 361, 365, 388, 400, 444, 451, 463, 480)

TOM AND JERRY (. . Comics, early issues) (M.G.M.)
(Formerly Our Gang No. 1-59) (See Dell Giants for annuals)
No. 193, 6/48; No. 60, 7/49 - No. 212, 7-9/62; No. 213, 11/62 - No. 291, 2/75; No. 292, 3/77 - No. 342, 5/82 - No. 344, 1982?
Dell Publishing Co./Gold Key No. 213-327/Whitman No. 328 on

	Good	Fine	Mint
4-Color 193 (No. 1)	5.50	16.50	38.00
60	3.50	10.50	24.00
61	2.85	8.50	20.00
62-70: 66-X-mas-c	2.35	7.00	16.00
71-80	1.75	5.25	12.00
81-99: 90-X-mas-c	1.50	4.50	10.00
100	1.75	5.25	12.00
101-120	1.15	3.50	8.00
121-140: 126-X-mas-c	.85	2.50	6.00
141-160	.75	2.25	5.00
161-200	.55	1.65	4.00
201-212(7-9/62)(Last Dell ish.)	.45	1.35	3.00
213,214-(84 pgs.)-titled ". . . Funhouse"	1.50	4.50	12.00
215-240: 215-titled ". . . Funhouse"	.45	1.35	3.00
241-270	.35	1.00	2.00
271-300: 286 "Tom & Jerry"	.25	.75	1.50
301-344		.40	.80
Mouse From T.R.A.P. 1(7/66)-Giant, G. K.	1.50	4.50	12.00
Summer Fun 1(7/67, 68pgs.)(Gold Key)-R-/Barks' Droopy/Summer Fun No. 1	1.50	4.50	12.00
. . . Tells About Kites(1959, PG&E giveaway)	.85	2.50	5.00

NOTE: *No. 60-87, 98-121, 268, 277, 289, 302 are 52 pages. Reprints-No. 225, 241, 245, 247, 252, 254, 266, 268, 270, 292-327, 329-342, 344.*

TOMB OF DARKNESS (Formerly Beware)
No. 9, July, 1974 - No. 23, Nov, 1976
Marvel Comics Group

	Good	Fine	Mint
9-19: 17-Woodbridge-r/Astonishing No. 62		.25	.50
20-Everett Venus r-/Venus No. 19		.25	.50
21-23: 23-Everett-a(r)		.25	.50

NOTE: ***Ditko*** *a-15r, 19r.*

TOMB OF DRACULA (See Giant-Size Dracula & Dracula Lives)
April, 1972 - No. 70, Aug, 1979
Marvel Comics Group

	Good	Fine	Mint
1-Colan-p in all	.85	2.50	5.00
2-9: 3-Intro. Dr. Rachel Van Helsing & Inspector Chelm. 6-Adams-c	.30	.90	1.80
10-1st app. Blade the Vampire Slayer	.35	1.00	2.00
11,12,14-20: 12-Brunner-c(p)		.60	1.20
13-Origin Blade the Vampire Slayer	.25	.70	1.40
21-40		.45	.90
41-70: 43-Wrightson-c. 70-Double size		.35	.70

NOTE: ***Colan*** *a-1-70p; c(p)-8, 38-42, 44-56, 58-70.*

TOMB OF DRACULA (Magazine)
Nov, 1979 - No. 6, Sept, 1980 (B&W)
Marvel Comics Group

	Good	Fine	Mint
1		.60	1.20
2,4-6: 2-Ditko-a (36 pgs.)	.35	1.00	2.00
3-Miller-a	.35	1.00	2.00

NOTE: ***Buscema*** *a-4p, 5p.* ***Chaykin*** *c-5, 6.* ***Colan*** *a(p)-1, 3-6.* ***Miller*** *a-3.*

TOMB OF LIGEIA (See Movie Classics)

TOMB OF TERROR (Thrills of Tomorrow No. 17 on)
June, 1952 - No. 16, July, 1954
Harvey Publications

	Good	Fine	Mint
1	6.50	19.50	45.00
2	4.35	13.00	30.00
3-Bondage-c; atomic disaster story	5.00	15.00	35.00
4-7: 4-Heart ripped out	4.35	13.00	30.00
8-12-Nostrand-a	4.35	13.00	30.00
13-Special S/F ish	6.00	18.00	42.00
14-Check-a; special S/F ish	6.00	18.00	42.00
15-S/F ish.; c-shows head exploding; Nostrand-a(r)	8.00	24.00	55.00
16-Special S/F ish; Nostrand-a	6.00	18.00	42.00

NOTE: ***Kremer*** *a-1, 7; c-1.* ***Palais*** *a-2, 3, 5-7.* ***Powell*** *a-1, 3, 5, 9-16.* ***Sparling*** *a-12, 13, 15.*

TOMBSTONE TERRITORY (See 4-Color No. 1123)

TOM CAT (Formerly Bo, Atom The Cat No. 9 on)
No. 4, Apr, 1956 - No. 8, July, 1957
Charlton Comics

	Good	Fine	Mint
4	1.30	4.00	9.00
5-8	.75	2.25	5.00

TOM CORBETT, SPACE CADET (TV)
No. 378, 1-2/52 - No. 11, 9-11/54 (All painted covers)
Dell Publishing Co.

	Good	Fine	Mint
4-Color 378-McWilliams-a	4.65	14.00	32.00
4-Color 400,421-McWilliams-a	3.75	11.25	26.00
4(11-1/53) - 11	2.35	7.00	16.00

TOM CORBETT SPACE CADET (See March of Comics No. 102)

TOM CORBETT SPACE CADET (TV)
May-June, 1955 - V2No.3, Sept-Oct, 1955
Prize Publications

	Good	Fine	Mint
V2No.1	6.00	18.00	42.00
2,3	5.00	15.00	35.00

TOM LANDRY AND THE DALLAS COWBOYS
1973 (35-49 cents)
Spire Christian Comics/Fleming H. Revell Co.

	Good	Fine	Mint
nn	.25	.75	1.50

TOM MIX (. . . Commandos Comics No. 10-12)
Sept, 1940 - No. 12, Nov, 1942 (36 pages); 1983 (One-shot)
Given away for two Ralston box-tops; in cereal box, 1983
Ralston-Purina Co.

	Good	Fine	Mint
1-Origin (life) Tom Mix; Fred Meagher-a	50.00	150.00	350.00
2	30.00	90.00	210.00
3-9	27.00	81.00	190.00
10-12: 10-Origin Tom Mix Commando Unit; Speed O'Dare begins. 12-Sci/fi-c	20.00	60.00	140.00
1983-'Taking of Grizzly Grebb,' Toth-a; 16 pg. miniature	1.00	3.00	6.00

TOM MIX WESTERN (Movie, radio star) (Also see The Comics, Crackajack Funnies, Master Comics, 100 Pages Of Comics, Real Western Hero, Six Gun Heroes, & Western Hero)
Jan, 1948 - No. 61, May, 1953 (52pgs., 1-17)
Fawcett Publications

	Good	Fine	Mint
1 (Photo-c, 52 pgs.)-Tom Mix & his horse Tony begin; Tumbleweed Jr begins, ends No. 52,54,55	30.00	90.00	210.00
2 (Photo-c)	16.50	50.00	115.00
3-5 (Painted/photo-c): 5-Billy the Kid & Oscar app.	13.00	40.00	90.00
6,7 (Painted/photo-c)	11.00	33.00	76.00
8-Kinstler tempera-c	11.00	33.00	76.00
9,10 (Painted/photo-c)-Used in **SOTI**, pgs. 323-325	11.00	33.00	76.00

Tom & Jerry The Mouse From TRAP #1, © MGM

Tomb of Terror #14, © HARV

Tom Corbett Space Cadet #9, © DELL

Tom Mix Western #24, © FAW

Tom-Tom the Jungle Boy #1 (1957), © ME

Top Cat #2, © Hanna-Barbera

TOM MIX WESTERN (continued)

	Good	Fine	Mint
11-Kinstler oil-c	9.00	27.00	62.00
12 (Painted/photo-c)	8.00	24.00	56.00
13-17 (Painted-c, 52 pgs.)	8.00	24.00	56.00
18,22 (Painted-c, 36 pgs.)	6.00	18.00	42.00
19 (Photo-c, 52 pgs.)	8.00	24.00	56.00
20,21,23 (Painted-c, 52 pgs.)	6.50	19.50	45.00
24,25,27-29 (52 pgs.): 24-Photo-c begin, end No. 61. 29-Slim Pickens app.	6.50	19.50	45.00
26,30 (36 pgs.)	5.75	17.25	40.00
31-33,35-37,39,40,42 (52 pgs.): 39-Red Eagle app.	5.00	15.00	35.00
34,38 (36 pgs. begin)	4.00	12.00	28.00
41,43-60	3.00	9.00	21.00
61-Last issue	4.00	12.00	28.00

NOTE: *Photo-c from 1930s Tom Mix movies (he died in 1940). Many issues contain ads for Tom Mix, Rocky Lane, Space Patrol and other premiums.* ***Captain Tootsie*** *by C.C. Beck in No. 6-11, 20.*

TOMMY OF THE BIG TOP
No. 10, Sept, 1948 - No. 12, Mar, 1949
King Features Syndicate/Standard Comics

	Good	Fine	Mint
10	2.35	7.00	16.00
11,12	1.30	4.00	9.00

TOM SAWYER (See Famous Stories & Advs. of . . .)

TOM SAWYER & HUCK FINN
1925 (52 pgs.) (10¾x10'') (stiff covers)
Stoll & Edwards Co.

	Good	Fine	Mint
By Dwiggins; reprints 1923, 1924 Sunday strips in color	7.00	21.00	50.00

TOM SAWYER COMICS
1951? (paper cover)
Giveaway

	Good	Fine	Mint
Contains a coverless Hopalong Cassidy from 1951; other combinations possible.	1.00	3.00	6.00

TOM SKINNER-UP FROM HARLEM (See Up From Harlem)

TOM TERRIFIC! (TV)
Summer, 1957 - No. 6, Fall, 1958
Pines Comics

	Good	Fine	Mint
1	6.00	18.00	42.00
2-6	4.00	12.00	28.00

TOM THUMB (See 4-Color No. 972)

TOM-TOM, THE JUNGLE BOY
1947; Nov, 1957 - No. 3, Mar, 1958
Magazine Enterprises

	Good	Fine	Mint
1-Funny animal	2.65	8.00	18.00
2,3(1947)	1.65	5.00	11.50
1(1957)(& Itchi the Monk), 2,3('58)	.85	2.50	6.00
I.W. Reprint No. 1,2,8,10		.40	.80

TONKA (See 4-Color No. 966)

TONTO (See The Lone Ranger's Companion . . .)

TONY TRENT (The Face No. 1,2)
1948 - 1949
Big Shot/Columbia Comics Group

	Good	Fine	Mint
3,4: 3-The Face app.	4.00	12.00	28.00

TOODLE TWINS, THE
1-2/51 - No. 10, 7-8/51; 1956 (Newspaper reprints)
Ziff-Davis (Approved Comics)/Argo

	Good	Fine	Mint
1	2.65	8.00	18.00
2	1.85	5.50	13.00
3-9	1.65	5.00	11.50
10-Painted-c, some newspaper-r	1.65	5.00	11.50
1(Argo, 3/56)	1.50	4.50	10.00

TOONERVILLE TROLLEY
1921 (Daily strip reprints) (B&W) (52 pgs.)
Cupples & Leon Co.

	Good	Fine	Mint
1-By Fontaine Fox	11.00	33.00	76.00

TOOTS & CASPER (See Large Feature Comic No. 5)

TOP ADVENTURE COMICS
1964 (Reprints)
I. W. Enterprises

	Good	Fine	Mint
1-Reprints/Explorer Joe No. 2; Krigstein-a	.70	2.00	4.00
2-Black Dwarf	.80	2.40	4.80

TOP CAT (TV) (Hanna-Barbera)
12-2/61-62 - No. 3, 6-8/62; No. 4, 10/62 - No. 31, 9/70
Dell Publishing Co./Gold Key No. 4 on

	Good	Fine	Mint
1	1.75	5.25	12.00
2-5	1.15	3.50	8.00
6-10	.85	2.50	6.00
11-20	.55	1.65	4.00
21-31: 21,24,25,29-Reprints	.35	1.00	2.00

TOP CAT (TV) (Hanna-Barbera)
Nov, 1970 - No. 20, Nov, 1973
Charlton Comics

	Good	Fine	Mint
1	.60	1.75	3.50
2-20	.25	.75	1.50

NOTE: *No. 8 (1/72) went on sale late in 1972 between No. 14 and No. 15 with the January 1973 issues.*

TOP COMICS
July, 1967 (All rebound issues)
K. K. Publications/Gold Key

	Good	Fine	Mint
nn-The Gnome-Mobile (Disney-movie)	.50	1.50	3.00
1-Beagle Boys (No.7), Bugs Bunny, Chip 'n' Dale, Daffy Duck (No. 50), Flintstones, Flipper, Huckleberry Hound, Huey, Dewey & Louie, Junior Woodchucks, The Jetsons, Lassie, The Little Monsters (No.71), Moby Duck, Porky Pig (has Gold Key label - says Top Comics on inside), Scamp, Super Goof, Tarzan of the Apes (No.169), Three Stooges (No.35), Tom & Jerry, Top Cat (No.21), Tweety & Sylvester (No.7), Walt Disney Comics & Stories (No. 322), Woody Woodpecker, Yogi Bear, Zorro known; each character given own book.	.30	.90	1.80
1-Uncle Scrooge (No.70)	1.00	3.00	6.00
1-Donald Duck (not Barks), Mickey Mouse	.70	2.00	4.00
2-Bugs Bunny, Daffy Duck, Donald Duck (not Barks), Mickey Mouse (No.114), Porky Pig, Super Goof, Three Stooges, Tom & Jerry, Tweety & Sylvester, Uncle Scrooge (No. 71)-Barks-c, Walt Disney's C&S (r-/No.325), Woody Woodpecker, Yogi Bear (No. 30), Zorro (r-No. 8; Toth-a)	.30	.90	1.80
2-Snow White & 7 Dwarfs(6/67)(1944-r)	.80	2.40	4.80
3-Donald Duck	.50	1.50	3.00
3-Uncle Scrooge (No.72)	1.00	3.00	6.00
3-The Flintstones, Mickey Mouse (reprints No.115), Tom & Jerry, Woody Woodpecker, Yogi Bear		.50	1.00
4-The Flintstones, Mickey Mouse, Woody Woodpecker		.50	1.00

NOTE: *Each book in this series is identical to its counterpart except for cover, and came out at same time. The number in parentheses is the original issue it contains.*

TOP DETECTIVE COMICS
1964 (Reprints)
I. W. Enterprises

	Good	Fine	Mint
9-Young King Cole & Dr. Drew (not Grandenetti)	.40	1.20	2.40

TOP DOG
Apr, 1985 - Present (Children's book)
Star Comics (Marvel)

	Good	Fine	Mint
1-12		.35	.70

TOP ELIMINATOR (Formerly Teenage Hotrodders; Drag 'n' Wheels No. 30 on)
No. 25, Sept, 1967 - No. 29, July, 1968
Charlton Comics

25-29		.40	.80

TOP FLIGHT COMICS
1947; July, 1949
Four Star Publications/St. John Publishing Co.

1	2.85	8.50	20.00
1(7/49)-Hector the Inspector	1.85	5.50	13.00

TOP GUN (See 4-Color No. 927)

TOP GUNS (See Super DC Giant & Showcase No. 72)

TOPIX (. . . Comics) (Timeless Topix-early issues) (Also see Men of Courage & Treasure Chest)(V1-V5/1,V7/1-20-paper-c)
11/42 - V10No.15, 1/28/52 (Weekly - later issues)
Catechetical Guild Educational Society

V1No.1(8pgs.,8x11")	6.00	18.00	36.00
2,3(8pgs.,8x11")	3.35	10.00	20.00
4-8(16pgs.,8x11")	2.50	7.50	15.00
V2No.1-10(16pgs.,8x11"): V2No.8-Pope Pius XII	2.50	7.50	15.00
V3No.1-10(16pgs.,8x11")	2.00	6.00	12.00
V4No.1-10	2.00	6.00	12.00
V5No.1(10/46,52pgs.)-9,12-15(12/47)-No.13 shows V5No.4	1.00	3.00	6.00
10,11-Life of Christ eds.	2.35	7.00	14.00
V6No.1-14	.70	2.00	4.00
V7No.1(9/1/48)-20(6/15/49), 32pgs.	.70	2.00	4.00
V8No.1(9/19/49)-3,5-11,13-30(5/15/50)	.70	2.00	4.00
4-Dagwood Splits the Atom(10/10/49)-Magazine format	1.35	4.00	8.00
12-Ingels-a	2.75	8.00	16.00
V9No.1(9/25/50)-11,13-30(5/14/51)	.50	1.50	3.00
12-Special 36pg. Xmas ish., text illos format	.85	2.50	5.00
V10No.1(10/1/51)-15	.50	1.50	3.00

NOTE: ***Hollingsworth** a-V10No.14.*

TOP JUNGLE COMICS
1964 (Reprint)
I. W. Enterprises

1(no date)-Reprints White Princess of the Jungle No. 3, minus cover	.80	2.40	4.80

TOP LOVE STORIES
No. 3, May, 1951 - No. 19, Mar, 1954
Star Publications

3	3.85	11.50	27.00
4,5,7-9	3.00	9.00	21.00
6-Wood-a	6.35	19.00	44.00
10-16,18,19-Disbrow-a	3.35	10.00	23.00
17-Wood art (Fox-r)	5.00	15.00	35.00

NOTE: *All have **L. B. Cole** covers.*

TOP-NOTCH COMICS (. . . Laugh No. 28-45; Laugh No. 46 on)
Dec, 1939 - No. 45, June, 1944
MLJ Magazines

	Good	Fine	Mint
1-Origin The Wizard; Kardak the Mystic Magician, Swift of the Secret Service (ends No. 3), Air Patrol, The Westpointer, Manhunters (by J. Cole), Mystic (ends No. 2) & Scott Rand (ends No. 3) begin	72.00	215.00	500.00
2-Dick Storm (ends No. 8), Stacy Knight M.D. (ends No. 4) begin; Jack Cole-a	36.00	108.00	250.00
3-Bob Phantom, Scott Rand on Mars begin; J. Cole-a	30.00	90.00	210.00
4-Origin/1st app. Streak Chandler on Mars; Moore of the Mounted only app.; J. Cole-a	25.00	75.00	175.00
5-Flag-c; origin/1st app. Galahad; Shanghai Sheridan begins (ends No. 8); Shield cameo	20.00	60.00	140.00
6-The Shield app.	17.00	51.00	120.00
7-Balthar, the Giant Man x-over in Kardak; The Shield x-over in Wizard; The Wizard dons new costume	31.00	92.00	218.00
8-Origin The Firefly & Roy, the Super Boy	33.00	100.00	230.00
9-Origin & 1st app. The Black Hood; Fran Frazier begins	72.00	215.00	500.00
10	32.00	95.00	224.00
11-20	20.00	60.00	140.00
21-30: 23,24-No Wizard, Roy app. in each. 25-Last Bob Phantom, Roy app. 26-Roy app. 27-Last Firefly. 28-Suzie begins. 29-Last Kardak	17.00	51.00	120.00
31-44: 33-Dotty & Ditto by Woggon begins. 44-Black Hood series ends	9.50	28.50	65.00
45-Last issue	5.50	16.50	38.00

NOTE: ***J. Binder** a-1-3. **Meskin** a-2,3, 15. **Woggon** a-33-40, 42. Bondage c-17, 19.*

TOPPER & NEIL (See 4-Color No. 859)

TOPPS COMICS
1947
Four Star Publications

1-L. B. Cole-c	3.65	11.00	25.00

TOPS
July, 1949 - No. 2, Sept, 1949 (68 pgs, 25¢) (10¼x13¼")
(Large size-magazine format; for the adult reader)
Tops Magazine, Inc. (Lev Gleason)

1 (Rare)-Story by Dashiell Hammett; Crandall/Lubbers, Tuska, Dan Barry, Fuje-a; Biro painted-c	50.00	150.00	350.00
2 (Rare)-Crandall/Lubbers, Biro, Kida, Fuje, Guardineer-a	43.00	130.00	300.00

TOPS COMICS (See Tops in Humor)
1944 (Small size, 32 pgs.) (7¼x5")
Consolidated Book (Lev Gleason)

2001-The Jack of Spades	8.00	24.00	56.00
2002-Rip Raider	3.65	11.00	25.00
2003-Red Birch (gag cartoons)	1.00	3.00	7.00

TOPS COMICS
1944 (132 pages) (10 cents)
Consolidated Book Publishers

nn(Color-c, inside in red shade & some in full color)-Ace Kelly by Rick Yager, Black Orchid, Don on the Farm, Dinky Dinkerton (Rare)	11.50	34.50	80.00

NOTE: *This book is printed in such a way that when the staple is removed, the strips on the left side of the book correspond with the same strips on the right side. Therefore, if strips are removed from the book, each strip can be folded into a complete comic section of its own.*

TOP SECRET
January, 1952
Hillman Publ.

1	5.75	17.25	40.00

TOP SECRET ADVENTURES (See Spyman)

Topix V5No.9, © CG

Top Love Stories #4, © STAR

Top-Notch Comics #4, © AP

Tor 3-D #2 (10/53), © STJ

Torchy #2, © QUA

Total War #1, © GK

TOP SECRETS (. . . of the F.B.I.)
Nov, 1947 - No. 10, July-Aug, 1949
Street & Smith Publications

	Good	Fine	Mint
1-Powell c/a	8.00	24.00	56.00
2-Powell-c/a	5.75	17.25	40.00
3-6,8-10-Powell-a	5.00	15.00	35.00
7-Used in **SOTI**, pg. 90 & illo.-''How to hurt people;'' used by N.Y. Legis. Comm.; Powell c/a	9.50	28.50	65.00

NOTE: *Powell c-1-3,5-10.*

TOPS IN ADVENTURE
Fall, 1952 (132 pages)
Ziff-Davis Publishing Co.

1-Crusader from Mars & The Hawk; Powell-a	19.00	57.00	132.00

TOPS IN HUMOR (See Tops Comics?)
1944 (Small size) (7¼x5'')
Consolidated Book Publ. (Lev Gleason)

2001(No.1)-Origin The Jack of Spades, Ace Kelly by Rick Yager, Black Orchid (female crime fighter) app.	8.50	25.50	60.00
2	4.35	13.00	30.00

TOP SPOT COMICS
1945
Top Spot Publ. Co.

1-The Menace, Duke of Darkness app.	6.50	19.50	45.00

TOPSY-TURVY
April, 1945
R. B. Leffingwell Publ.

1	2.00	6.00	14.00

TOR (Formerly One Million Years Ago)
No. 2, Oct, 1953 - No. 3, May, 1954 - No. 5, Oct, 1954
St. John Publishing Co.

3-D 2(10/53)-Kubert-a	10.00	30.00	70.00
3-D 2(10/53)-Oversized, otherwise same contents	9.00	27.00	62.00
3-D 2(11/53)-Kubert-a	9.00	27.00	62.00
3-5-Kubert-a; 3-Danny Dreams by Toth	10.00	30.00	70.00

NOTE: *The two October 3-D's have same contents and **Powell** art; the Nov. issue is titled 3-D Comics.*

TOR (See Sojourn)
May-June, 1975 - No. 6, Mar-Apr, 1976
National Periodical Publications

1-New origin by Kubert		.30	.60
2-6: 2-Origin-r/St. John No. 1		.25	.50

NOTE: ***Kubert** a-1; 2-6r; c-1-6. **Toth** a(p)-3r.*

TOR 3-D
July, 1986 - No. 2, Aug, 1986
Eclipse Comics

1-r-/One Million Years Ago	.40	1.25	2.50
2-D 1-Limited signed & numbered edition	.85	2.50	5.00
2-r-/Tor 3-D No. 2	.40	1.25	2.50

TORCHY (. . . Blonde Bombshell) (See Dollman, Military, & Modern)
Nov, 1949 - No. 6, Sept, 1950
Quality Comics Group

1-Bill Ward-c, Gil Fox-a	75.00	225.00	525.00
2,3-Fox c/a	32.00	95.00	225.00
4-Fox c/a(3), Ward-a, 9pgs.	42.00	125.00	295.00
5,6-Ward c/a, 9 pgs; Fox-a(3) each	52.00	155.00	365.00
Super Reprint No. 16('64)-Reprints No. 4 with new cover	6.00	18.00	36.00

TORMENTED, THE (Surprise Adventure No. 3)
July, 1954 - No. 2, Sept, 1954
Sterling Comics

	Good	Fine	Mint
1,2	3.50	10.00	24.00

TORNADO TOM (See Mighty Midget Comics)

TOTAL WAR (M.A.R.S. Patrol No. 3 on)
July, 1965 - No. 2, Oct, 1965 (Painted covers)
Gold Key

1,2-Wood-a	1.50	4.50	10.00

TOUGH KID SQUAD COMICS
March, 1942
Timely Comics (TCI)

1-(Scarce)-Origin The Human Top & The Tough Kid Squad; The Flying Flame app.	230.00	690.00	1610.00

TOWER OF SHADOWS (Creatures on the Loose No. 10 on)
Sept, 1969 - No. 9, Jan, 1971
Marvel Comics Group

1-Steranko, Craig-a		.50	1.00
2-Neal Adams-a		.40	.80
3-Smith, Tuska-a		.40	.80
4-Kirby/Everett-c		.25	.50
5,7-Smith(p), Wood-a (Wood draws himself-1st pg., 1st panel -No. 5)	.25	.75	1.50
6,8: Wood-a; 8-Wrightson-c		.40	.80
9-Wrightson-c; Roy Thomas app.		.25	.50
Special 1(12/71)-Adams-a		.25	.50

NOTE: ***J. Buscema** a-1p, 2p. **Colan** a-3p, 6p. **J. Craig** a-1. **Ditko** a-6, 8, 9r, Special 1. **Everett** a-9(i)r; c-5i. **Kirby** a-9(p)r. **Severin** c-5p, 6. **Steranko** a-1. **Wood** a-5-8. Issues 1-9 contain new stories with some pre-Marvel age reprints in 6-9. H. P. Lovecraft adaptation-9.*

TOWN & COUNTRY
May, 1940

Origin The Falcon	17.00	51.00	120.00

TOWN THAT FORGOT SANTA, THE
1961 (24 pages) (Giveaway)
W. T. Grant Co.

nn	1.35	4.00	8.00

TOYLAND COMICS
Jan, 1947 - No. 4, July?, 1947
Fiction House Magazines

1	6.50	19.50	45.00
2-4: 3-Tuska-a	4.00	12.00	28.00
148 pg. issue	8.50	25.50	60.00

NOTE: *All above contain strips by **Al Walker**.*

TOY TOWN COMICS
1945 - No. 7, May, 1947
Toytown/Orbit Publ./B. Antin/Swapper Quarterly

1-Mertie Mouse; L. B. Cole-c/a	6.00	18.00	42.00
2-L. B. Cole-a	3.50	10.50	24.00
3-7-L. B. Cole-a	2.85	8.50	20.00

TRAGG AND THE SKY GODS (See Mystery Comics Digest No. 3 & Spine Tingling Tales) (Painted-c No. 3-8)
June, 1975 - No. 8, Feb, 1977; No. 9, May, 1982
Gold Key/Whitman No. 9

1-Origin		.60	1.20
2-9: 4-Sabre-Fang app. 8-Ostellon app.; 9-r No. 1		.40	.80

NOTE: ***Santos** a-1,2,9r; c-3-7. **Spiegel** a-3-8.*

TRAIL BLAZERS (Red Dragon No. 5 on)
1941 - 1942

TRAIL BLAZERS (continued)
Street & Smith Publications

	Good	Fine	Mint
1-True stories of American heroes	9.50	28.50	65.00
2	6.50	19.50	45.00
3,4	5.50	16.50	38.00

TRAIL COLT
1949
Magazine Enterprises

	Good	Fine	Mint
nn(A-1 24)-7 pg. Frazetta-a r-in Manhunt No.13; Undercover Girl app.; The Red Fox by L. B. Cole; Ingels-c; (Scarce)	22.00	65.00	154.00
2(A-1 26)-Undercover Girl; Ingels-c; L. B. Cole-a, 6pgs.	16.00	48.00	112.00

TRANSFORMERS, THE
Sept, 1984 - Present
Marvel Comics Group

	Good	Fine	Mint
1-Based on Hasbro toy	1.10	3.25	6.50
2,3	.50	1.50	3.00
4-10	.35	1.10	2.20
11-15		.65	1.30
16-26: 21-Intro The Aerialbots		.45	.90

NOTE: Second and third printings of all issues exist.

TRANSFORMERS COMICS MAGAZINE, THE
Oct, 1986 - Present ($1.50, Digest-size)
Marvel Comics Group

	Good	Fine	Mint
1	.25	.75	1.50

TRANSFORMERS, THE MOVIE
Dec, 1986 - No. 3, Feb, 1987 (mini-series)
Marvel Comics Group

	Good	Fine	Mint
1-Adapts animated movie		.60	1.20
2,3		.50	1.00

TRANSFORMERS UNIVERSE, THE
Dec, 1986 - No. 4, March, 1987 ($1.25, mini-series)
Marvel Comics Group

	Good	Fine	Mint
1-A guide to all characters	.25	.75	1.50
2-4		.65	1.30

TRAPPED
1951 (Giveaway) (16 pages) (soft cover)
Harvey Publications (Columbia University Press)

	Good	Fine	Mint
Drug education comic (30,000 printed?) distributed to schools. Mentioned in **SOTI**, pgs. 256,350	2.00	6.00	12.00

NOTE: *Many copies surfaced in 1979 causing a setback in price; beware of trimmed edges, because many copies have a brittle edge.*

TRAPPED!
Oct, 1954 - No. 5, June?, 1955
Periodical House Magazines (Ace)

	Good	Fine	Mint
1 (All-r)	3.15	9.50	22.00
2-5: 4-r-entire Men Against Crime 4	1.75	5.25	12.00

NOTE: ***Colan** a-1, 4. **Sekowsky** a-1.*

TRAVELS OF HAPPY HOOLIGAN, THE
1906 (10¼"x15¾", 32 pgs., cardboard covers)
Frederick A. Stokes Co.

	Good	Fine	Mint
1905-r	17.00	51.00	120.00

TRAVELS OF JAIMIE McPHEETERS,THE (TV)
December, 1963
Gold Key

	Good	Fine	Mint
1-Kurt Russell	1.50	4.50	10.00

TREASURE BOX OF FAMOUS COMICS
Mid 1930's (36 pgs.) (6-7/8"x8½") (paper covers)
Cupples & Leon Co.

	Good	Fine	Mint
Box plus 5 titles: Reg'lar Fellers(1928), Little Orphan Annie(1926), Smitty(1928), Harold Teen(1931), How D. Tracy & D. Tracy Jr. Caught The Racketeers (1933) (These are abbreviated versions of hardcover editions) (Set)....	70.00	200.00	400.00

NOTE: *Dates shown are copyright dates; all books actually came out in 1934 or later.*

TREASURE CHEST (Catholic Guild; also see Topix)
3/12/46 - V27No.8, July, 1972 (Educational comics)
George A. Pflaum (not publ. during summer)

	Good	Fine	Mint
V1/1	6.00	18.00	36.00
2-6 (5/21/46): 5-Dr. Styx app. by Baily	2.50	7.50	15.00
V2/1 (9/3/46) - 6	1.35	4.00	8.00
V3/1-5,7-20 (1st slick cover)	1.35	4.00	8.00
V3/6-Jules Verne's "Voyage to the Moon"	3.35	10.00	20.00
V4/1-20 (9/9/48-5/31/49)	1.35	4.00	8.00
V5/1-20 (9/6/49-5/31/50)	1.00	3.00	6.00
V6/1-20 (9/14/50-5/31/51)	1.00	3.00	6.00
V7/1-20 (9/13/51-6/5/52)	.70	2.00	4.00
V8/1-20 (9/11/52-6/4/53)	.70	2.00	4.00
V9/1-20 ('53-'54)	.50	1.50	3.00
V10/1-20 ('54-'55)	.50	1.50	3.00
V11('55-'56), V12('56-'57)	.50	1.50	3.00
V13/1,3-5,7,9,10,12-V17/1 ('57-'63)	.35	1.00	2.00
V13/2,6,8,11-Ingels-a	1.70	5.00	10.00
V17/2-'This Godless Communism' series begins (Not in V17/3, 7,11) Cover shows hammer & sickle over Statue of Liberty; 8pg. Crandall-a of family life under communism	7.50	22.50	45.00
V17/3-7,9,11,13-15,17,19	.30	.80	1.60
V17/8-Shows red octopus encompassing Earth, firing squad; 8pg. Crandall-a	6.00	18.00	36.00
V17/10-'This Godless Communism'-how Stalin came to power, part I; Crandall-a	6.00	18.00	36.00
V17/12-Stalin in WWII, forced labor, death by exhaustion; Crandall-a	6.00	18.00	36.00
V17/16-Kruschev takes over; de-Stalinization	6.00	18.00	36.00
V17/18-Kruschev's control; murder of revolters, brainwash, space race by Crandall	6.00	18.00	36.00
V17/20-End of series; Kruschev-people are puppets, firing squads hammer & sickle over Statue of Liberty, snake around communist manifesto by Crandall	6.00	18.00	36.00
V18,V19/5,11-20,V20('64-'65)		.40	.80
V18/ 5-'What About Red China?'-describes how communists took over China	2.75	8.00	16.00
V19/1-4,6-10-'Red Victim' anti-communist series in all	2.75	8.00	16.00
V21-V25('65-'70)-(two V24/5's 11/7/68 & 11/21/68) (no V24/6)		.30	.60
V26, V27/1-8 (V26,27-68 pgs.)		.30	.60
Summer Edition V1/1-6('66), V2/1-6('67)		.20	.40

NOTE: ***Anderson** a-V18/13. **Borth** a-V7/10-19 (serial), V8/8-17 (serial), V9/1-10 (serial), V13/2, 6, 11, V15/2, V18/1, V19/4, 11, 19, V20/10, 15, 16, 18, V21/5, V22/7, 9, 14, V24/7, Summer Ed. V1/3, 5. **Crandall** a-V7/20, V16/7, 9, 12, 14, 17, 20; V17/1, 2, 4, 5, 14, 16-18, 20; V18/1, 7, 9, 10, 15, 17, 19; V19/4, 11, 13, 16, 19; V20/1, 2, 6, 9, 10, 12, 14-16, 18, 20; V21/1-3, 5, 8, 9, 11, 13, 16, 17; V22/3, 7, 9-11, 14, 16, 20; V23/3, 6, 9, 13, 16; V24/7, 8, 10; V25/16; V27/1, 3-5r, 6r, 8(2 pg.), Summer Ed. V1/3, 5; c-V16/7, V18/10, V19/4, V21/5, 9, V22/7, 11, V23/9, 16 at least. **Powell** a-V10/11. V19/11, 15, V10/13, V13/6, 8 all have wraparound covers. All the above Crandall issues should be priced by condition from $4-8.00 unless already priced.*

TREASURE CHEST OF THE WORLD'S BEST COMICS
1945 (500 pgs.) (hardcover)
Superior, Toronto, Canada

Contains Blue Beetle, Captain Combat, John Wayne, Dynamic Man,

Trail Blazers #1, © S&S

Transformers #4, © MCG

Treasure Box of... (Dick Tracy), © N.Y. News

Treasure Comics #1 (6-7/45), © PRIZE

Trollords #1 (1st Printing), © Tru Studios

True Aviation Pic. Stories #1, © PMI

TREASURE CHEST OF... (continued) — Good / Fine / Mint

Nemo, Li'l Abner; contents can vary - represents random binding of extra books; Capt. America on-c — 29.00 87.00 200.00

TREASURE COMICS
No date (1943) (324 pgs.; cardboard covers) (50 cents)
Prize Publications? (no publisher listed)

nn-(Rare)-Contains Prize Comics No. 7-11 from 1942 (blank inside covers) — 125.00 375.00 875.00

TREASURE COMICS
June-July, 1945 - No. 12, Fall, 1947
Prize Publications (American Boys' Comics)

1-Paul Bunyan & Marco Polo begin; Highwayman & Carrot Topp only app.; Kiefer-a — 7.00 21.00 50.00
2-Arabian Knight, Gorilla King, Dr. Styx begin — 3.65 11.00 25.00
3,4,9,12 — 2.65 8.00 18.00
5-Marco Polo-c; Kirby a(p); Krigstein-a — 5.50 16.50 38.00
6,11-Krigstein-a; c-No. 11 — 5.00 15.00 35.00
7,8-Frazetta, 5 pgs. each — 19.00 57.00 132.00
10-Jr. Rangers by Kirby; Kirby-c — 6.50 19.50 45.00

TREASURE ISLAND (See 4-Color No. 624, King Classics, & Movie Classics & Comics)

TREASURY OF COMICS
1947; No. 2, July, 1947 - No. 4, Sept, 1947; No. 5, Jan, 1948
St. John Publishing Co.

nn(No.1)-Abbie 'n' Slats (nn on cover, No. 1 on inside) — 6.50 19.50 45.00
2-Jim Hardy — 4.65 14.00 32.00
3-Bill Bumlin — 3.85 11.50 27.00
4-Abbie 'n' Slats — 4.65 14.00 32.00
5-Jim Hardy Comics No. 1 — 4.65 14.00 32.00

TREASURY OF COMICS
Mar, 1948 - No. 5, 1948; 1948-1950-(Over 500 pgs., $1.00)
St. John Publishing Co.

1 — 9.50 28.50 65.00
2(No. 2 on cover, No. 1 on inside) — 5.50 16.50 38.00
3-5 — 5.00 15.00 35.00
1-(1948, 500 pgs., hardcover)-Abbie & Slats, Abbott & Costello, Casper, Little Annie Rooney, Little Audrey, Jim Hardy, Ella Cinders (16 books bound together) (Rare) — 85.00 255.00 595.00
1(1949, 500pgs.)-Same format as above — 85.00 255.00 595.00
1(1950, 500pgs.)-Same format as above; different-c; (Also see Little Audrey Yearbook) (Rare) — 85.00 255.00 595.00

TREASURY OF DOGS, A (See Dell Giants)

TREASURY OF HORSES, A (See Dell Giants)

TRIALS OF LULU AND LEANDER, THE
1906 (32 pgs. in color) (10x16")
William A. Stokes Co.

By F. M. Howarth — 11.00 33.00 76.00

TRIGGER (See Roy Rogers...)

TRIGGER TWINS
Mar-Apr, 1973 (One Shot)
National Periodical Publications

1-Trigger Twins & Pow Wow Smith-r; Infantino-a(p) — .40 .80

TRIPLE GIANT COMICS (See Archie All-Star Spec. under Archie Comics)

TRIPLE THREAT
Winter, 1945
Special Action/Holyoke/Gerona Publ.

1-Duke of Darkness, King O'Leary — 4.65 14.00 32.00

TRIP WITH SANTA ON CHRISTMAS EVE, A
No date (early 50's) (16 pgs.; full color; paper cover)
Rockford Dry Goods Co. (Giveaway) — Good / Fine / Mint
2.00 6.00 12.00

TROLLORDS
Feb, 1986 - Present ($1.50, B&W)
Tru Studios

1-1st printing — 3.35 10.00 20.00
1-2nd printing — .25 .75 1.50
2 — .45 1.25 2.50
3-6 — .25 .75 1.50
Special Edition 1('86) — .25 .75 1.50

TROUBLE SHOOTERS, THE (See 4-Color No. 1108)

TRUE ADVENTURES (Formerly True Western)(Men's Advs. No. 4 on)
No. 3, May, 1950
Marvel Comics (CCC)

3-Powell, Sekowsky-a — 4.00 12.00 28.00

TRUE ANIMAL PICTURE STORIES
Winter, 1947 - No. 2, Spr-Summer, 1947
True Comics Press

1,2 — 2.35 7.00 16.00

TRUE AVIATION PICTURE STORIES (Aviation Adventures & Model Building No. 16)
1942 - No. 15, Sept-Oct, 1946
Parents' Magazine Institute

1-(No. 1 & 2 titled ...Aviation Comics Digest)(not digest size) — 5.00 15.00 35.00
2 — 3.00 9.00 21.00
3-14 — 2.50 7.50 17.50
15-(titled "True Aviation Advs. & Model Building") — 2.50 7.50 17.50

TRUE BRIDE'S EXPERIENCES (Formerly Teen-Age Brides)
(True Bride-To-Be Romances No. 17 on)
No. 8, Oct, 1954 - No. 16, Feb, 1956
True Love (Harvey Publications)

8 — 1.70 5.00 12.00
9,10: 10-Last pre-code (2/55) — 1.35 4.00 9.00
11-15 — 1.00 3.00 7.00
16-Spanking issue — 5.00 15.00 35.00

NOTE: *Powell a-8-10, 12, 13.*

TRUE BRIDE-TO-BE ROMANCES (Formerly True Bride's Experiences)
No. 17, Apr, 1956 - No. 30, Nov, 1958
Home Comics/True Love (Harvey)

17-S&K-c, Powell-a — 2.00 6.00 14.00
18-20,22,25-28,30 — 1.00 3.00 7.00
21,23,24-Powell-a — 1.20 3.50 8.00
29-Powell, 1 pg. Baker-a — 1.35 4.00 9.00

TRUE COMICS (Also see Outstanding American War Heroes)
April, 1941 - No. 84, Aug, 1950
True Comics/Parents' Magazine Press

1-Marathon run story — 10.00 30.00 70.00
2-Everett-a — 5.50 16.50 38.00
3-5: 3-Baseball Hall of Fame sty. 4-Sty. of American flag "Old Glory." 5-Life story of Joe Louis — 4.75 14.25 33.00
6-Baseball World Series sty. — 3.65 11.00 25.00
7-10 — 3.35 10.00 23.00
11-20: 13-Harry Houdini sty. 14-Charlie McCarthy sty. 15-Flag-c; Bob Feller sty. 17-Brooklyn Dodgers sty. 18-Story of America begins, ends No. 26 — 2.85 8.50 20.00
21-30 — 2.50 7.50 17.50

TRUE COMICS (continued)

	Good	Fine	Mint
31-Red Grange story	1.85	5.50	13.00
32-45	1.65	5.00	11.50
46-George Gershwin sty.	1.70	5.00	12.00
47-Atomic bomb issue	3.15	9.50	22.00
48-67: 55(12/46)-1st app. Sad Sack by Baker, ½ pg. 58-Jim Jeffries (boxer) sty.; Harry Houdini sty. 59-Bob Hope sty. 66-Will Rogers story	1.30	4.00	9.00
68-1st oversized ish?; Steve Saunders, Special Agent begins	2.00	6.00	14.00
69-72,74-79: 69-Jack Benny sty.	1.15	3.50	8.00
73-Walt Disney's life story	2.00	6.00	14.00
80-84 (Rare)-All distr. to subscribers through mail only; paper-c	18.00	54.00	125.00

(Prices vary widely on these books)

NOTE: ***Bob Kane** a-7. **Palais** a-80. **Powell** c/a-80. No. 80-84 have soft covers and combined with Tex Granger, Jack Armstrong, and Calling All Kids. No. 68-78 featured true FBI adventures.*

TRUE COMICS AND ADVENTURE STORIES
1965 (Giant) (25 cents)
Parents' Magazine Institute

	Good	Fine	Mint
1,2-Fighting Hero of Viet Nam; LBJ on-c	.50	1.50	3.00

TRUE COMPLETE MYSTERY (Formerly Complete Mystery)
No. 5, April, 1949 - No. 8, Oct, 1949
Marvel Comics (PrPl)

	Good	Fine	Mint
5	5.00	15.00	35.00
6-8: 6,8-Photo-c	3.75	11.25	26.00

TRUE CONFESSIONS
1949
Fawcett Publications

	Good	Fine	Mint
1	4.65	14.00	32.00

TRUE CONFIDENCES
1949 (Fall) - No. 4, June, 1950 (All photo-c)
Fawcett Publications

	Good	Fine	Mint
1-Has ad for Fawcett Love Adventures No. 1, but publ. as Love Memoirs No. 1 as Marvel publ. the title first	4.65	14.00	32.00
2-4: 4-Powell-a	2.15	6.50	15.00

TRUE CRIME CASES
1944; V1No.6, June-July 1949 - V2No.1, Aug-Oct, 1949
St. John Publishing Co.

	Good	Fine	Mint
1944-(100 pgs.)	16.00	48.00	112.00
V1No.6, V2No.1	3.15	9.50	22.00

TRUE CRIME COMICS (Also see Complete Book of...)
No. 2, May, 1947; No. 3, Jul-Aug, 1948 - No. 6, June-Jul, 1949; V2No.1, Aug-Sept, 1949
Magazine Village

	Good	Fine	Mint
2-Jack Cole c/a; used in **SOTI**, pg. 81,82 plus illo.-"A sample of the injury-to-eye motif" & illo.-"Dragging living people to death;" used in **POP**, pg. 105; "Murder, Morphine and Me" classic drug propaganda story used by N.Y. Legis. Comm.	87.00	261.00	610.00
3-Classic Cole c/a; drug sty with hypo, opium den & withdrawing addict	56.00	168.00	390.00
4-Jack Cole-c/a; c-taken from a story panel in No. 3; r-(2) **SOTI** & **POP** stories/No. 2	50.00	150.00	350.00
5-Jack Cole-c; Marijuana racket story	25.00	75.00	175.00
6	10.00	30.00	70.00
V2No.1-Used in **SOTI**, pgs. 81,82 & illo.-"Dragging living people to death;" Toth, Wood (3 pgs.), Roussos-a; Cole-r from No. 2	36.00	108.00	252.00

NOTE: *V2/1 was reprinted in Canada as V2/9 (12/49); same cover & contents minus Wood-a.*

TRUE GHOST STORIES (See Ripley's...)

TRUE LIFE ROMANCES (...Romance on cover)
Dec, 1955 - No. 3, Aug, 1956
Ajax/Farrell Publications

	Good	Fine	Mint
1	3.00	9.00	21.00
2	1.65	5.00	11.50
3-Disbrow-a	2.50	7.50	17.50

TRUE LIFE SECRETS
Mar-April, 1951 - No. 28, Sept, 1955; No. 29, Jan, 1956
Romantic Love Stories/Charlton

	Good	Fine	Mint
1	4.00	12.00	28.00
2	2.65	8.00	18.00
3-12,15-19	2.00	6.00	14.00
13-Headlight-a	5.35	16.00	37.00
14-Drug mention story(marijuana)	3.15	9.50	22.00
20-22,24-29	1.50	4.50	10.00
23-Suggestive-c	2.50	7.50	17.50

TRUE LIFE TALES (Formerly Lana?)
No. 8, Oct, 1949 - No. 2, Jan, 1950
Marvel Comics (CCC)

	Good	Fine	Mint
8(10/49), 2(1/50)-Photo-c	2.50	7.50	17.50

TRUE LOVE
Jan, 1986 - No. 2, Jan, 1986 ($2.00, Baxter paper)
Eclipse Comics

	Good	Fine	Mint
1,2-Love stories-r from pre-code Standard Comics; Toth-a	.35	1.00	2.00

TRUE LOVE CONFESSIONS
May, 1954 - No. 11, Jan, 1956
Premier Magazines

	Good	Fine	Mint
1-Marijuana story	3.75	11.25	26.00
2	1.65	5.00	11.50
3-11	1.30	4.00	9.00

TRUE LOVE PICTORIAL
1952 - No. 11, Aug, 1954
St. John Publishing Co.

	Good	Fine	Mint
1	5.00	15.00	35.00
2	2.35	7.00	16.00
3-5(All 100 pgs.): 5-Formerly Teen-Age Temptations (4/53); Kubert-a-No. 3,5; Baker-a-No. 3-5	13.50	40.50	95.00
6,7-Baker c/a	5.50	16.50	38.00
8,10,11-Baker c/a	4.65	14.00	32.00
9-Baker-c	3.65	11.00	25.00

TRUE MOVIE AND TELEVISION (Part magazine)
No. 1, Aug, 1950 - No. 3, Nov, 1950 (52 pgs.) (10 cents)
Toby Press

	Good	Fine	Mint
1-Liz Taylor photo-c; Gene Autry, Shirley Temple, Li'l Abner app.	17.00	51.00	120.00
2-Frazetta John Wayne illo	11.00	33.00	76.00
3-June Allyson-c; lingerie scene; Montgomery Cliff, Esther Williams Andrews Sisters app; Li'l Abner feat.	11.00	33.00	76.00

NOTE: *16 pages in color, rest movie material in black & white.*

TRUE SECRETS (Formerly Love Dramas?)
No. 3, Mar, 1950; No. 4, Feb, 1951 - No. 40, Sept, 1956

True Comics #39, © PMI

True Life Secrets #11, © CC

True Love #1, © Eclipse

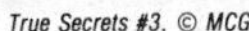
True Secrets #3, © MCG

True-To-Life Romances #21, © STAR

Trufan Advs. Theatre #1, © Paragraphix

TRUE SECRETS (continued)
Marvel (IPS)/Atlas Comics (MPI)

	Good	Fine	Mint
3 (52 pgs.)	3.15	9.50	22.00
4,5,7-10	1.65	5.00	11.50
6,22-Everett-a	2.15	6.50	15.00
11-20	1.30	4.00	9.00
21,23-28: 28-Last pre-code (2/55)	1.00	3.00	7.00
29-40	.85	2.50	6.00

NOTE: ***Colletta*** *a-34, 36; c-24.*

TRUE SPORT PICTURE STORIES (Formerly Sport Comics)
Feb, 1942? - V5/2, July-Aug, 1949
Street & Smith Publications

	Good	Fine	Mint
V1/5	7.00	21.00	50.00
6-12 (1942-43)	4.35	13.00	30.00
V2/1-12 (1944-45)	3.35	10.00	23.00
V3/1-12 (1946-47)	2.75	8.25	19.00
V4/1-12 (1948-49), V5/1,2	2.00	6.00	14.00

NOTE: ***Powell*** *a-V3/10, V4/1-4, 6-8, 10-12; V5/1, 2; c-V4/5, 6, 9, 10.*

TRUE STORIES OF ROMANCE
Jan, 1950 - No. 3, May, 1950 (All photo-c)
Fawcett Publications

	Good	Fine	Mint
1	4.00	12.00	28.00
2,3	2.50	7.50	17.50

TRUE STORY OF JESSE JAMES, THE (See 4-Color No. 757)

TRUE SWEETHEART SECRETS
May, 1950 - No. 11, Jan, 1953 (All photo-c?)
Fawcett Publications

	Good	Fine	Mint
1-Photo-c; Debbie Reynolds?	4.00	12.00	28.00
2-Wood-a, 11 pgs.	8.00	24.00	56.00
3-11: 4,5-Powell-a	2.35	7.00	16.00

TRUE TALES OF LOVE (Formerly Secret Story Romances)
No. 22, April, 1956 - No. 31, Sept, 1957
Atlas Comics (TCI)

	Good	Fine	Mint
22	1.50	4.50	10.00
23-31-Colletta-a in most	.85	2.50	6.00

TRUE TALES OF ROMANCE
No. 4, June, 1950
Fawcett Publications

	Good	Fine	Mint
4	2.50	7.50	17.50

TRUE 3-D
Dec, 1953 - No. 2, Feb, 1954
Harvey Publications

	Good	Fine	Mint
1-Nostrand, Powell-a	5.70	17.00	40.00
2-Powell-a	10.00	30.00	70.00

NOTE: *Many copies of No. 1 surfaced in 1984.*

TRUE-TO-LIFE ROMANCES
No. 9, 1-2/50; No. 3, 4/50 - No. 23, 10/54
Star Publications

	Good	Fine	Mint
9(1950)	5.00	15.00	35.00
3-10	4.35	13.00	30.00
11,22,23	4.00	12.00	28.00
12-14,17-21-Disbrow-a	6.00	16.00	37.00
15,16-Wood & Disbrow-a in each	8.35	25.00	58.00

NOTE: ***Kamen*** *a-13.* ***Kamen/Feldstein*** *a-14. All have* ***L.B. Cole*** *covers.*

TRUE WAR EXPERIENCES
Aug, 1952 - No. 4, Dec, 1952
Harvey Publications

	Good	Fine	Mint
1	2.35	7.00	16.00
2-4	1.35	4.00	9.00

TRUE WAR ROMANCES
Sept, 1952 - No. 21, June, 1955
Quality Comics Group

	Good	Fine	Mint
1-Photo-c	4.35	13.00	30.00
2	2.20	6.50	15.00
3-10: 9-Whitney-a	1.85	5.50	13.00
11-21: 14-Whitney-a	1.50	4.50	10.00

TRUE WAR STORIES (See Ripley's...)

TRUE WESTERN (True Adventures No. 3)
Dec, 1949 - No. 2, March, 1950
Marvel Comics (MMC)

	Good	Fine	Mint
1-Photo-c	4.35	13.00	30.00
2: Alan Ladd photo-c	4.35	13.00	30.00

TRUE WEST ROMANCE
1952
Quality Comics Group

	Good	Fine	Mint
21 (Exist?)	2.50	7.50	17.50

TRUFAN ADVENTURES THEATRE
1985 - Present ($1.95, B&W)(magazine-size)
Paragraphix

	Good	Fine	Mint
1 (52 pgs.)	.70	2.00	4.00
2-Contains 4 pgs. 3-D	.40	1.25	2.50

TRUMP (Magazine format)
Jan, 1957 - No. 2, Mar, 1957
HMH Publishing Co.

	Good	Fine	Mint
1-Harvey Kurtzman satire	8.50	25.50	60.00
2-Harvey Kurtzman satire	6.50	19.50	45.00

NOTE: ***Davis, Elder, Heath, Jaffee*** *art-No. 1, 2;* ***Wood****-No. 1. No. 2-article by Mel Brooks.*

TRUMPETS WEST (See 4-Color No. 875)

TRUTH ABOUT CRIME (See Fox Giants)

TRUTH ABOUT MOTHER GOOSE (See 4-Color No. 862)

TRUTH BEHIND THE TRIAL OF CARDINAL MINDSZENTY, THE (See Cardinal...)

TRUTHFUL LOVE (Formerly Youthful Love)
No. 2, July, 1950
Youthful Magazines

	Good	Fine	Mint
2	2.15	6.50	15.00

TUBBY (See Marge's...)

TUFF GHOSTS STARRING SPOOKY
7/62 - No. 39, 11/70; No. 40, 9/71 - No. 43, 10/72
Harvey Publications

	Good	Fine	Mint
1	4.00	12.00	24.00
2-5	2.00	6.00	12.00
6-10	1.35	4.00	8.00
11-20	.70	2.00	4.00
21-30	.50	1.50	3.00
31-43		.50	1.00

TUFFY
1949 - 1950
Standard Comics

	Good	Fine	Mint
1-All by Sid Hoff	2.50	7.50	17.50
2	1.30	4.00	9.00
3-10	1.15	3.50	8.00

TUFFY TURTLE
No date
I. W. Enterprises

	Good	Fine	Mint
1-Reprint	.30	.80	1.60

TUROK, SON OF STONE (See Golden Comics Digest No. 31, March of Comics No. 378,399,408, and Dan Curtis)
No. 596, 12/54 - No. 29, 6-8/62; No. 30, 12/62 - No. 125, 1/80; No. 126, 3/81 - No. 130, 4/82
Dell Publ. Co. No. 1-29/Gold Key No. 30-125/Whitman No. 126 on

	Good	Fine	Mint
4-Color 596 (12/54)(No.1)	17.00	51.00	120.00
4-Color 656 (10/55)	12.00	36.00	84.00
3(3-5/56)-5	9.00	27.00	62.00
6-10	5.50	16.50	38.00
11-20	3.00	9.00	21.00
21-30	1.50	4.50	10.00
31-50: 31-Drug use story	.85	2.50	6.00
51-60	.70	2.00	4.00
61-83: 63-Only line drawn-c	.35	1.00	2.00
84-Origin & 1st app. Hutec	.35	1.00	2.00
85-130: 114-(52 pgs.)		.50	1.00
Giant 1(30031-611) (11/66)	3.50	10.50	28.00

NOTE: ***Alberto Gioletti*** *painted-c No. 30-129.* ***Sparling*** *a-126-30. Reprints-No. 36, 54, 57, 75, 112, 118, 125, 127-130(⅓).*

TV CASPER & COMPANY
Aug, 1963 - No. 46, April, 1974 (25 cent Giants)
Harvey Publications

	Good	Fine	Mint
1	4.00	12.00	24.00
2-5	2.00	6.00	12.00
6-10	1.35	4.00	8.00
11-20	.70	2.00	4.00
21-30	.50	1.50	3.00
31-46		.50	1.00

TV FUNDAY FUNNIES (See Famous TV. . .)

TV FUNNIES (See New Funnies)

TV FUNTIME (See Little Audrey)

TV LAUGHOUT (See Archie's. . .)

TV SCREEN CARTOONS (Formerly Real Screen)
No. 129, July-Aug, 1959 - No. 138, Jan-Feb, 1961
National Periodical Publications

	Good	Fine	Mint
129-138 (Scarce)	1.50	4.50	10.00

TV STARS (TV)(Hanna-Barbera)
Aug, 1978 - No. 4, Feb, 1979
Marvel Comics Group

	Good	Fine	Mint
1-Sparling-a		.50	1.00
2,4		.40	.80
3-Toth-c/a	.50	1.50	3.00

TV TEENS (Formerly Ozzie & Babs; Rock and Rollo No. 14 on)
Feb, 1954 - V2No.13, July, 1956
Charlton Comics

	Good	Fine	Mint
V1No.14-Ozzie & Babs	2.50	7.50	17.50
15	1.65	5.00	11.50
V2No.3(6/54) - 7-Don Winslow	2.00	6.00	14.00
8(7/55)-13-Mopsy	1.65	5.00	11.50

TWEETY AND SYLVESTER (1st Series)
No. 406, June, 1952 - No. 37, June-Aug, 1962
Dell Publishing Co.

	Good	Fine	Mint
4-Color 406	1.30	4.00	9.00
4-Color 489,524	1.00	3.00	7.00
4 (3-5/54) - 20	.85	2.50	6.00
21-37	.55	1.65	4.00

(See March of Comics No. 421,433,445,457,469,481)

TWEETY AND SYLVESTER (2nd Series)
Nov, 1963; No. 2, Nov, 1965 - No. 121, July, 1984
Gold Key No. 1-102/Whitman No. 103 on

	Good	Fine	Mint
1	.85	2.50	6.00
2-10	.45	1.35	3.00
11-30	.25	.75	1.50
31-70		.50	1.00
71-121: 99,119-r(⅓)		.30	.60
Mini Comic No. 1(1976)-3¼x6½''		.30	.60

12 O'CLOCK HIGH (TV)
Jan-Mar, 1965 - No. 2, Apr-June, 1965 (Photo-c)
Dell Publishing Co.

	Good	Fine	Mint
1,2	2.00	6.00	14.00

24 PAGES OF COMICS (No title) (Also see Pure Oil Comics, Salerno Carnival of Comics, & Vicks Comics)
Late 1930s
Giveaway by various outlets including Sears

	Good	Fine	Mint
Contains strip reprints-Buck Rogers, Napoleon, Sky Roads, War on Crime	20.00	60.00	120.00

20,000 LEAGUES UNDER THE SEA (See 4-Color No. 614, King Classics, and Movie Comics)

TWICE TOLD TALES (See Movie Classics)

TWILIGHT AVENGER, THE
July, 1986 - No. 4, Jan, 1987 ($1.75, color, mini-series)
Elite Comics

	Good	Fine	Mint
1-4	.35	1.00	2.00

TWILIGHT ZONE, THE (TV) (See Dan Curtis)
No. 1173, 3-5/61 - No. 91, 4/79; No. 92, 5/82
Dell Publishing Co./Gold Key/Whitman No. 92

	Good	Fine	Mint
4-Color 1173-Crandall/Evans-c/a	3.75	11.25	26.00
4-Color 1288-Crandall/Evans c/a	3.15	9.50	22.00
01-860-207 (5-7/62-Dell)	2.65	8.00	18.00
12-860-210 on-c; 01-860-210 on inside(8-10/62-Dell)-Evans c/a; Crandall/Frazetta-a(2)	2.65	8.00	18.00
1(11/62-Gold Key)-Crandall,Evans-a	2.85	8.50	20.00
2,5-11	1.15	3.50	8.00
3,4-Toth-a, 11 & 10 pgs.	1.75	5.25	12.00
12-Williamson-a	1.65	5.00	10.00
13,15-Crandall-a	1.65	5.00	10.00
14-Williamson/Orlando/Crandall/Torres-a	2.00	6.00	12.00
16-20	.85	2.50	6.00
21-Crandall-a(r)	.70	2.00	4.00
22-24	.50	1.50	3.00
25-Evans/Crandall-a(r)	.50	1.50	3.00
26-Crandall, Evans-a(r)	.50	1.50	3.00
27-Evans-a(2)(r)	.50	1.50	3.00
28-32: 32-Evans-a(r)	.35	1.00	2.00
33-42,44-50,52-70	.25	.75	1.50
43-Crandall-a	.30	.90	1.80
51-Williamson-a	.30	.90	1.80
71-92: 71-Reprint. 83,84-(52 pgs.)		.50	1.00
Mini Comic No. 1(1976-3¼x6½'')		.30	.60

NOTE: ***Bolle*** *a-13(w/****McWilliams****), 50, 57, 59.* ***McWilliams*** *a-59.* ***Orlando*** *a-19, 20, 22, 23.* ***Sekowsky*** *a-3. (See Mystery Comics Digest 3, 6, 9, 12, 15, 18, 21, 24). Reprints-26(⅓), 71, 73, 79, 83, 84, 86, 92. Painted-c 1-91.*

TWINKLE COMICS
May, 1945
Spotlight Publishers

	Good	Fine	Mint
1	4.65	14.00	32.00

Turok, Son of Stone #33, © GK

Twilight Avenger #1, © Elite

Twilight Zone #18, © DELL

The Twist #01-864-209, © DELL

Two-Fisted Tales #26, © WMG

Two-Gun Kid #3, © MCG

TWIST, THE
July-September, 1962
Dell Publishing Co.

	Good	Fine	Mint
01-864-209-painted-c	3.00	9.00	21.00

TWISTED TALES
11/82 - No. 8, 5/84; No. 9, 11/84; No. 10, 12/84 (Baxter paper)
Pacific Comics/Independent Comics Group No. 9, 10/Blackthorne

	Good	Fine	Mint
1-Nudity/Violence in all	.35	1.00	2.00
2-10	.25	.75	1.50
3-D 1-r/earlier issues in 3-D	.45	1.25	2.50

NOTE: ***Alcala*** *a-1.* ***John Bolton*** *painted c-4, 6, 7; a-7.* ***Conrad*** *a-1.* ***Corben*** *a-1, 3, 5; c-1, 3, 5.* ***Guice*** *a-8.* ***Morrow*** *a-10.* ***Ploog*** *a-2.* ***Wildey*** *a-3.* ***Wrightson*** *a(Painted)-10; c-2.*

TWISTED TALES OF BRUCE JONES, THE
Feb, 1986 - No. 4, Mar, 1986 ($1.75, Baxter)
Eclipse Comics

	Good	Fine	Mint
1-4	.30	.90	1.80

TWISTED TANTRUMS OF THE PURPLE SNIT, THE
Oct, 1986 - Present ($1.75, B&W)
Blackthorne Publishing

	Good	Fine	Mint
1	.30	.90	1.75

TWO BIT THE WACKY WOODPECKER (See Wacky. . .)
1951 - No. 3, May, 1953
Toby Press

	Good	Fine	Mint
1	2.00	6.00	14.00
2,3	1.15	3.50	8.00

TWO FACES OF COMMUNISM (Also see Double Talk)
1961 (36 pgs.; paper cover) (Giveaway)
Christian Anti-Communism Crusade, Houston, Texas

	Good	Fine	Mint
	10.00	30.00	60.00

TWO-FISTED TALES (Formerly Haunt of Fear No. 15-17)
No. 18, Nov-Dec, 1950 - No. 41, Feb-Mar, 1955
E. C. Comics

	Good	Fine	Mint
18(No.1)-Kurtzman-c	61.00	182.00	430.00
19-Kurtzman-c	45.00	135.00	315.00
20-Kurtzman-c	27.00	81.00	190.00
21,22-Kurtzman-c	21.00	62.00	145.00
23-25-Kurtzman-c	15.00	45.00	105.00
26-35: 33-''Atom Bomb'' by Wood	12.00	36.00	80.00
36-41	7.35	22.00	50.00
Two-Fisted Annual, 1952	61.00	182.00	430.00
Two-Fisted Annual, 1953	45.00	135.00	315.00

NOTE: ***Berg*** *a-29.* ***Craig*** *a-18, 19, 32.* ***Crandall*** *a-35, 36.* ***Davis*** *a-20-36, 40; c-30, 34, 35, 41, Annual 2.* ***Evans*** *a-34, 40, 41; c-40.* ***Feldstein*** *a-18.* ***Krigstein*** *a-41.* ***Kubert*** *a-32, 33.* ***Kurtzman*** *a-18-25; c-18-29, 31, Annual 1.* ***Severin*** *a-26, 28, 29, 31, 34-41 (No.37-39 are* ***all-Severin*** *issues); c-36-39.* ***Severin/Elder*** *a-19-29, 31, 33, 36.* ***Wood*** *a-18-28, 30-35, 41; c-32, 33. Special issues: No. 26 (ChanJin Reservoir), 31 (Civil War), 35 (Civil War). Canadian reprints known; see Table of Contents.*

TWO-GUN KID (Also see All Western Winners, Best Western, Black Rider, Blaze Carson, Kid Colt, Western Winners, Wild West, & Wild Western
3/48(No mo.) - No. 10, 11/49; No. 11, 12/53 - No. 59, 4/61; No. 60, 11/62 - No. 92, 3/68; No. 93, 7/70 - No. 136, 4/77
Marvel/Atlas (MCI No. 1-10/HPC No. 11-59/Marvel No. 60 on)

	Good	Fine	Mint
1-Two-Gun Kid & his horse Cyclone begin; The Sheriff begins	20.00	60.00	140.00
2	9.50	28.50	65.00
3,4: 3-Annie Oakley app.	6.50	19.50	45.00
5-Pre-Black Rider app. (Wint. 48/49); Spanking panel. Anti-Wertham editorial (1st?)	8.50	25.50	60.00
6-10 (11/49)	4.65	14.00	32.00
11 (12/53)-Black Rider app.	3.65	11.00	25.00
12-Black Rider app.	3.65	11.00	25.00
13-20	3.35	10.00	23.00
21-24,26-29	2.50	7.50	17.50
25,30-Williamson-a in both, 5 & 4 pgs.	3.65	11.00	25.00
31-33,35,37-40	1.65	5.00	11.50
34-Crandall-a	2.35	7.00	16.00
36,41,42,48-Origin in all	2.00	6.00	14.00
43,44,47	1.10	3.25	7.50
45,46-Davis-a	2.15	6.50	15.00
49,50,52,55,57-Severin-a(3) in each	1.15	3.50	8.00
51-Williamson-a, 5pgs.	2.75	8.25	19.00
53,54,56	.50	1.50	3.50
58,60-New origin. 58-Last 10¢ ish.	.50	1.50	3.50
59,61-80: 64-Intro. Boom-Boom		.50	1.00
81-92: 92-Last new story		.30	.60
93-100,102-136		.25	.50
101-Origin retold/No. 58		.30	.60

NOTE: ***Ayers*** *a-26, 27.* ***Davis*** *c-45-47.* ***Everett*** *a-82, 91.* ***Fuje*** *a-13.* ***Heath*** *c-13, 21, 23.* ***Keller*** *a-16, 19, 28.* ***Kirby*** *a-54, 55, 57-62, 75-77, 90, 95, 101, 119, 120, 129; c-10, 52, 54-65, 67-72, 74-76, 116.* ***Maneely*** *a-20; c-16, 19, 20, 25-28, 49.* ***Powell*** *a-38, 102, 104.* ***Severin*** *a-29, 51.* ***Whitney*** *a-87, 89-91, 98-113, 124, 129; c-87, 89, 91, 113.* ***Wildey*** *a-21.* ***Williamson*** *a-110r. Kid Colt in No. 13, 14, 16-19, 21.*

TWO GUN WESTERN (1st Series) (Formerly Casey Crime Photographer)
No. 5, Nov, 1950 - No. 14, June, 1952
Marvel/Atlas Comics (MPC)

	Good	Fine	Mint
5-The Apache Kid (Intro & origin) & his horse Nightwind begin by Buscema	5.00	15.00	35.00
6-10: 8-Kid Colt, The Texas Kid & his horse Thunder begin?	2.50	7.50	17.50
11-14: 13-Black Rider app.	2.15	6.50	15.00

NOTE: ***Maneely*** *a-9; c-11-13.* ***Wildey*** *a-8.*

2-GUN WESTERN (2nd Series) (Formerly Billy Buckskin; Two-Gun Western No. 5 on)
No. 4, May, 1956
Atlas Comics (MgPC)

	Good	Fine	Mint
4-Apache Kid; Ditko-a	4.65	14.00	32.00

TWO-GUN WESTERN (Formerly 2-Gun Western)
No. 5, July, 1956 - No. 12, Sept, 1957
Atlas Comics (MgPC)

	Good	Fine	Mint
5-Apache Kid, Kid Colt Outlaw, Doc Holiday begin	2.35	7.00	16.00
6,7,12	1.50	4.50	10.00
8,10-Crandall-a	2.50	7.50	17.50
9,11-Williamson-a in both, 5 pgs. each	3.65	11.00	25.00

NOTE: ***Morrow*** *a-9,10.* ***Powell*** *a-7, 11.* ***Severin*** *c-10.*

TWO MOUSEKETEERS, THE (See 4-Color No. 475,603,642 under M.G.M.'s. . . ; becomes M.G.M.'s Mouse Musketeers)

TWO ON A GUILLOTINE (See Movie Classics)

2000 A.D. MONTHLY
Apr, 1985 - Present (Mando paper)
Eagle Comics/Quality Comics No. 5 on

	Good	Fine	Mint
1-4-r/British series featuring Judge Dredd; Alan Moore scripts begin		.50	1.00
5-11-New look		.60	1.30

2001: A SPACE ODYSSEY (Marvel Treasury Special)
Oct, 1976 (One Shot) (Over-sized)
Marvel Comics Group

	Good	Fine	Mint
1-Kirby, Giacoia-a	.35	1.00	2.00

2001, A SPACE ODYSSEY
Dec, 1976 - No. 10, Sept, 1977 (Regular size)
Marvel Comics Group

2001, A SPACE ODYSSEY (continued)

	Good	Fine	Mint
1-Kirby c/a in all		.30	.60
2-10: 8-Origin/1st app. Machine Man (called Mr. Machine)		.25	.50
Howard Johnson giveaway(1968, 8pp); 6pg. movie adaptation, 2pg. games, puzzles		.25	.50

2010
Apr, 1985 - No. 2, May, 1985
Marvel Comics Group

	Good	Fine	Mint
1,2-r/Marvel Super Special		.40	.80

UFO & ALIEN COMIX
Jan, 1978 (One Shot)
Warren Publishing Co.

	Good	Fine	Mint
Toth, Severin-a(r)	.30	.80	1.60

UFO & OUTER SPACE (Formerly UFO Flying Saucers)
No. 14, June, 1978 - No. 25, Feb, 1980 (all painted covers)
Gold Key

	Good	Fine	Mint
14-Reprints UFO Flying Saucers No. 3	.35	1.00	2.00
15,16-Reprints		.60	1.20
17-20-New material	.25	.75	1.50
21-25: 23-McWilliams-a. 24-3 pg.-r. 25-r-UFO Flying Saucers No. 2 w/cover		.50	1.00

UFO ENCOUNTERS
May, 1978 (228 pages) ($1.95)
Western Publishing Co.

	Good	Fine	Mint
11192-Reprints UFO Flying Saucers	.70	2.00	4.00
11404-Vol.1 (128 pgs.)-See UFO Mysteries for Vol.2	.35	1.00	2.00

UFO FLYING SAUCERS (UFO & Outer Space No. 14 on)
Oct, 1968 - No. 13, Jan, 1977 (No. 2 on, 36 pgs.)
Gold Key

	Good	Fine	Mint
1(30035-810) (68 pgs.)	1.15	3.50	8.00
2(11/70), 3(11/72), 4(11/74)	1.00	3.00	6.00
5(2/75)-13: Bolle-a No. 4 on	.70	2.00	4.00

UFO MYSTERIES
1978 (96 pages) ($1.00) (Reprints)
Western Publishing Co.

	Good	Fine	Mint
11400(96 pgs., $1.00)	.25	.75	1.50
11404(Vol.2)-Cont'd from UFO Encounters, pgs. 129-224	.25	.75	1.50

ULTRA KLUTZ
1981; June, 1986 - Present
Onward Comics

	Good	Fine	Mint
1 (1981)	.25	.75	1.50
1 (6/86)	.50	1.50	3.00
2-5	.25	.75	1.50

UNBIRTHDAY PARTY WITH ALICE IN WONDERLAND (See 4-Color No. 341)

UNCANNY TALES
June, 1952 - No. 56, Sept, 1957
Atlas Comics (PrPI/PPI)

	Good	Fine	Mint
1-Heath-a	11.50	34.50	80.00
2	5.50	16.50	38.00
3-5	4.65	14.00	32.00
6-Wolvertonish-a by Matt Fox	5.50	16.50	38.00
7,8,10: 8-Tothish-a	4.35	13.00	30.00
9-Crandall-a	5.00	15.00	35.00
11-20: 17-Atom bomb panels; anti-communist story. 19-Krenkel-a	3.35	10.00	23.00
21-27: 25-Nostrand-a?	2.85	8.50	20.00
28-Last precode ish (1/55); Kubert-a; No. 1-28 contain 2-3 sci/fic stories each	3.85	11.50	27.00
29-41,43-49,52	1.50	4.50	10.00
42,54,56-Krigstein-a	2.85	8.50	20.00
50,53,55-Torres-a	2.85	8.50	20.00
51,57-Williamson-a (No. 57, exist?)	3.85	11.50	27.00

NOTE: ***Bailey** a-51. **Briefer** a-19, 20. **Colan** a-11, 16, 17. **Drucker** a-37, 42, 45. **Everett** a-2, 12, 32, 36, 39, 47, 48; c-7, 11, 17, 39, 41, 50, 52, 53. **Forte** a-27. **Heath** a-13, 14; c-10. **Keller** a-3. **Lawrence** a-14, 17, 19, 23, 27, 28, 35. **Maneely** a-4, 8, 10, 16, 29, 35; c-33, 38. **Moldoff** a-23. **Morrow** a-46, 51. **Orlando** a-49, 50, 53. **Powell** a-12, 18, 38, 43, 50, 53, 56. **Robinson** a-3, 13. **Roussos** a-8. **Sekowsky** a-25. **Tothish**-a by Andru-27. **Wildey** a-48.*

UNCANNY TALES
Dec, 1973 - No. 12, Oct, 1975
Marvel Comics Group

	Good	Fine	Mint
1-Crandall-a(r-'50s No. 9)		.30	.60
2-12		.25	.50

NOTE: ***Ditko** reprints-No. 4, 6-8, 10-12.*

UNCANNY X-MEN, THE (See X-Men)

UNCANNY X-MEN AND THE NEW TEEN TITANS (See Marvel and DC Present)

UNCANNY X-MEN AT THE STATE FAIR OF TEXAS, THE
1983 (36 pgs.)(One-Shot)
Marvel Comics Group

	Good	Fine	Mint
nn	1.00	3.00	6.00

UNCLE CHARLIE'S FABLES
Jan, 1952 - No. 5, Sept, 1952
Lev Gleason Publications

	Good	Fine	Mint
1-Norman Maurer-a; has Biro's picture	3.50	10.50	24.00
2-Fuje-a; Biro photo; painted-c	2.35	7.00	16.00
3-5	1.85	5.50	13.00

UNCLE DONALD & HIS NEPHEWS DUDE RANCH (See Dell Giant No. 52)

UNCLE DONALD & HIS NEPHEWS FAMILY FUN (See Dell Giant No. 38)

UNCLE JOE'S FUNNIES
1938
Centaur Publications

	Good	Fine	Mint
1-Games/puzzles, some interior art; Bill Everett-c	17.00	51.00	120.00

UNCLE MILTY (TV)
Dec, 1950 - No. 4, July, 1951
Victoria Publications/True Cross

	Good	Fine	Mint
1-Milton Berle	12.00	36.00	84.00
2	6.00	18.00	42.00
3,4	5.00	15.00	35.00

UNCLE REMUS & HIS TALES OF BRER RABBIT (See 4-Color No. 129, 208, 693)

UNCLE SAM QUARTERLY (Blackhawk No. 9 on)
Autumn, 1941 - No. 8, Fall, 1943 (Also see National Comics)
Quality Comics Group

	Good	Fine	Mint
1-Origin Uncle Sam; Fine/Eisner-c, chapter headings, 2 pgs. by Eisner. (2 versions: dark cover, no price; light cover with price); Jack Cole-a	85.00	255.00	595.00
2-Cameos by The Ray, Black Condor, Quicksilver, The Red Bee, Alias the Spider, Hercules & Neon the Unknown; Eisner, Fine c/a	42.00	125.00	295.00

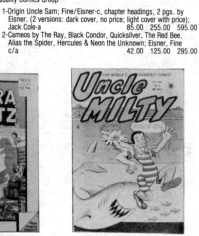

UFO Flying Saucers #2, © GK

Ultra Klutz #1, © Onward

Uncle Milty #4, © Victoria Publ.

Uncle Scrooge #45, © WDC

Undersea Agent #1, © TC

Underworld #2, © DS

UNCLE SAM QUARTERLY (continued)

	Good	Fine	Mint
3-Tuska-a	29.00	86.00	200.00
4	25.00	75.00	175.00
5-8	20.00	60.00	140.00

NOTE: ***Kotzky*** *or* ***Tuska*** *a-4-8.*

UNCLE SAM'S CHRISTMAS STORY
1958
Promotional Publ. Co. (Giveaway)

	Good	Fine	Mint
Reprints 1956 Christmas USA	1.00	3.00	6.00

UNCLE SCROOGE (Walt Disney)(See Dell Giants 33,55 & WDC&S)
3/52 - No. 39, 8-10/62; No. 40, 12/62 - No. 209, 1984; No. 210, 10/86 - Present
Dell No. 1-39/Gold Key No. 40-173/Whitman No. 174-209/Gladstone No. 210-on

	Good	Fine	Mint
4-Color 386(No.1)-in "Only a Poor Old Man" by Carl Barks; r-in Uncle Scrooge & Donald Duck No. 1('65) & The Best of Walt Disney Comics('74)	56.00	168.00	390.00
4-Color 456(No.2)-in "Back to the Klondike" by Carl Barks; r-in Best of U.S. & D.D. No. 1('66)	26.00	78.00	180.00
4-Color 495(No.3)-r-in No. 105	23.00	70.00	160.00
4(12-2/53-54)	18.00	54.00	125.00
5-r-in W.D. Digest No. 1	14.00	42.00	100.00
6-r-in U.S. No. 106,165 & Best of U.S. & D.D. No. 1('66)	13.00	40.00	90.00
7-r-in Best of D.D. & U.S. No. 2('67)	10.00	30.00	70.00
8-10: 8-r-in No. 111. 9-r-in No. 104. 10-r-in No. 67	7.35	22.00	50.00
11-20	6.00	18.00	42.00
21-30	5.00	15.00	35.00
31-40	4.35	13.00	30.00
41-50	3.35	10.00	20.00
51-60	3.00	9.00	18.00
61-66,68-70: 70-Last Barks issue with original story	2.35	7.00	14.00
67,72,73-Barks-r	1.50	4.50	9.00
71-Written by Barks only	1.70	5.00	9.00
74-One pg. Barks-r	1.00	3.00	6.00
75-81,83-Not by Barks	1.00	3.00	6.00
82,84-Barks-r begin	1.00	3.00	6.00
85-100	.85	2.50	5.00
101-110	.75	2.25	4.50
111-120	.60	1.75	3.50
121-141,143-152,154-157	.50	1.50	3.00
142-Reprints 4-Color 456 with-c	.60	1.75	3.50
153,158,162-164,166,168-170,178,180,182,186,191-194,197-202, 204-206: No Barks		.40	.80
159-160,165,167,172-176-Barks-a		.60	1.20
184,185,187,188-Barks-a		.50	1.00
161(r-No.14), 171(r-No.11), 177(r-No.16), 179(r-No.9), 183(r-No.6), 189(r-No.5), 190(r-No.4), 196(r-No.13), 203(r-No.12), 207(r-93,92), 208(r-U.S. 18), 209(r-U.S. 21)		.60	1.20
181(r-4-Color 495), 195(r-4-Color 386)	.25	.70	1.40
210-216		.40	.75
Uncle Scrooge & Money(G.K.)-Barks reprint from WDC&S No. 130 (3/67)	4.00	12.00	24.00
Mini Comic No. 1(1976)(3¼x6½")-Reprint/U.S. No. 115; Barks-c			.20

NOTE: ***Barks*** *c-4-Color 386, 456, 495, No. 4-37, 39, 40, 43-71.*

UNCLE SCROOGE & DONALD DUCK
June, 1965 (25 cents) (Paper cover)
Gold Key

	Good	Fine	Mint
1-Reprint of 4-Color 386(No.1) & lead story from 4-Color 29	8.35	25.00	50.00

UNCLE SCROOGE COMICS DIGEST
1986 - Present ($1.25, Digest-size)
Gladstone Publishing

	Good	Fine	Mint
1,2		.60	1.25

UNCLE SCROOGE GOES TO DISNEYLAND (See Dell Giants)
Aug, 1985 ($2.50)
Gladstone Publishing Ltd.

	Good	Fine	Mint
1-r/Dell Giant w/new-c by Mel Crawford, based on old cover	.40	1.25	2.50

UNCLE WIGGILY (See 4-Color No. 179, 221, 276, 320, 349, 391, 428, 503, 543, & March of Comics No. 19)

UNDERCOVER GIRL (Starr Flagg)
1952 - 1954
Magazine Enterprises

	Good	Fine	Mint
5(No.1)(A-1 62)	11.50	34.50	80.00
6(A-1 98), 7(A-1 118)-All have Starr Flagg	10.00	30.00	70.00

NOTE: ***Powell*** *c-6,7.* ***Whitney*** *a-5-7.*

UNDERDOG (TV) (See March of Comics 426,438,467,479)
July, 1970 - No. 10, Jan, 1972; Mar, 1975 - No. 23, Feb, 1979
Charlton Comics/Gold Key

	Good	Fine	Mint
1	1.30	4.00	8.00
2-10	.70	2.00	4.00
1 (G.K.)	1.00	3.00	6.00
2-10	.50	1.50	3.00
11-23: 13-1st app. Shack of Solitude	.25	.75	1.50
Kite Fun Book('74)-5x7"; 16 pgs. Sou. Calif. Edison	.35	1.00	2.00

UNDERSEA AGENT
Jan, 1966 - No. 6, Mar, 1967 (68 pages)
Tower Comics

	Good	Fine	Mint
1-Davy Jones, Undersea Agent begins	.50	1.50	3.00
2-6: 2-Jones gains magnetic powers. 5-Origin & 1st app. of Merman. 6-Kane?/Wood-c(r)	.40	1.20	2.40

NOTE: ***Gil Kane*** *a-3-6; c-4, 5.* ***Moldoff*** *a-2i.*

UNDERSEA FIGHTING COMMANDOS
May, 1952 - No. 5, Jan, 1953; 1964
Avon Periodicals

	Good	Fine	Mint
1	4.00	12.00	28.00
2	2.50	7.50	17.50
3-5	2.15	6.50	15.00
I.W. Reprint No. 1,2('64)	.85	2.00	4.00

UNDERWATER CITY, THE (See 4-Color No. 1328)

UNDERWORLD (True Crime Stories)
Feb-Mar, 1948 - No. 9, June-July, 1949 (52 pgs.)
D. S. Publishing Co.

	Good	Fine	Mint
1-Moldoff-c; excessive violence	10.00	30.00	70.00
2-Moldoff-c; Ma Barker story used in **SOTI**, pg. 95; female electrocution panel; lingerie art	11.00	33.00	76.00
3-McWilliams c/a; extreme violence, mutilation	8.50	25.50	60.00
4-Used in **Love and Death** by Legman; Ingels-a	5.75	17.25	40.00
5-Ingels-a	4.35	13.00	30.00
6-9: 8-Ravielli-a	3.35	10.00	23.00

UNDERWORLD CRIME
June, 1952 - No. 9, Oct, 1953
Fawcett Publications

	Good	Fine	Mint
1	6.85	20.50	48.00
2	3.50	10.50	24.00
3-6,8,9 (8,9-exist?)	2.85	8.50	20.00
7-Bondage/torture-c	8.00	24.00	56.00

UNDERWORLD STORY, THE
1950 (Movie)
Avon Periodicals

	Good	Fine	Mint
nn-(Scarce)	11.50	34.50	80.00

UNEARTHLY SPECTACULARS
Oct, 1965 - No. 3, Mar, 1967
Harvey Publications

	Good	Fine	Mint
1-Tiger Boy; Simon-c	.50	1.50	3.00
2-Jack Q. Frost app.; Wood, Williamson, Kane art; r-1 story/ Thrill-O-Rama No. 2	1.70	5.00	10.00
3-Jack Q. Frost app.; Williamson/Crandall-a; r-from Alarming Advs. No. 1, 1962	1.70	5.00	10.00

NOTE: ***Crandall** a-3r. **G. Kane** a-2. **Orlando** a-3. **Simon, Sparling, Wood** c-2. **Simon/Kirby** a-3r. **Torres** a-1. **Wildey** a-1(3). **Williamson** a-2, 3r. **Wood** a-2(2).*

UNEXPECTED, THE (Formerly Tales of the . . .)
No. 105, Feb-Mar, 1968 - No. 222, May, 1982
National Periodical Publications/DC Comics

	Good	Fine	Mint
105-115,117,118,120,122-127		.30	.60
116,119,121,128-Wrightson-a		.50	1.00
129-156: 132-136-(52 pgs.)		.30	.60
157-162-(All 100 pgs.)		.30	.60
163-188		.25	.50
189,190,192-195 ($1.00 size)		.40	.80
191-Rogers-a(p) ($1.00 size)		.50	1.00
196-218,220,221: 205-213-Johnny Peril app. 210-Time Warp app.		.25	.50
219,222-Giffen-a		.30	.60

NOTE: ***Adams** c-110, 112-118, 121, 124. **J. Craig** a-195. **Ditko** a-189, 221p, 222p; c-222. **Drucker** a-107. **Kaluta** c-203, 212. **Kirby** a-127, 162. **Kubert** c-204, 214-16, 219-21. **Mayer** a-217p, 220, 221p. **Moldoff** a-136r. **Moreira** a-133. **Mortimer** a-212p. **Newton** a-204p. **Orlando** a-202; c-191. **Perez** a-217p. **Redondo** a-155, 195. **Reese** a-145. **Sparling** a-107, 205-09p, 212p. **Spiegle** a-217. **Starlin** c-198. **Toth** a-126r, 127r. **Tuska** a-132, 136, 139, 152, 180, 200p. **Wildey** a-193. **Wood** a-122i, 133i, 137i, 138i. **Wrightson** a-161r(2 pgs.). Johnny Peril in No. 107-117.*

UNEXPECTED ANNUAL, THE (See DC Spec. Series No. 4)

UNICORN ISLE
1986 - Present
WaRP Graphics

	Good	Fine	Mint
1-5	.25	.75	1.50

UNITED COMICS
Aug, 1940 - No. 26, Jan-Feb, 1953
United Features Syndicate

	Good	Fine	Mint
1-Fritzi Ritz & Phil Fumble	8.50	25.50	60.00
2-Fritzi Ritz, Abbie & Slats	4.35	13.00	30.00
3-9-Fritzi Ritz, Abbie & Slats	2.85	8.50	20.00
10-26: 25-Peanuts app.	1.65	5.00	11.50

NOTE: *Abbie & Slats reprinted from Tip Top.*

UNITED NATIONS, THE (See Classics Illustrated Special Ed.)

UNITED STATES AIR FORCE PRESENTS: THE HIDDEN CREW
1964 (36 pages) (full color)
U.S. Air Force

	Good	Fine	Mint
Shaffenberger-a	.50	1.50	3.00

UNITED STATES FIGHTING AIR FORCE
Sept, 1952 - No. 29, Oct, 1956
Superior Comics Ltd.

	Good	Fine	Mint
1	3.50	10.50	24.00
2	1.70	5.00	12.00
3-10	1.00	3.00	7.00
11-29	.85	2.50	6.00
I.W. Reprint No. 1,9(nd)	.40	1.10	2.20

UNITED STATES MARINES
1943 - No. 4, 1944; No. 5, 1952 - 1953
William H. Wise/Life's Romances Publ. Co./Magazine Enterprises No. 5-8/Toby Press

	Good	Fine	Mint
nn-Mart Bailey-a	4.00	12.00	28.00
2-Bailey-a	3.00	9.00	21.00
3,4	2.65	8.00	18.00
5(A-1 55), 6(A-1 60), 7(A-1 68), 8(A-1 72)	2.35	7.00	16.00
7-11 (Toby)	1.00	3.00	7.00

NOTE: ***Powell** a-5-7.*

UNIVERSAL PRESENTS DRACULA (See Movie Classics)

UNKEPT PROMISE
1949 (24 pages)
Legion of Truth (Giveaway)

	Good	Fine	Mint
Anti-alcohol	5.35	16.00	32.00

UNKNOWN MAN, THE
1951 (Movie)
Avon Periodicals

	Good	Fine	Mint
nn-Kinstler-c	11.50	34.50	80.00

UNKNOWN SOLDIER (Formerly Star-Spangled War Stories) (See Brave & the Bold No. 146)
No. 205, Apr-May, 1977 - No. 268, Oct, 1982
National Periodical Publications/DC Comics

	Good	Fine	Mint
205-268: 251-Enemy Ace begins. 268-Death of Unknown Soldier. 248,249-Origin		.30	.60

NOTE: ***Evans** a-265-67; c-235. **Kubert** c-Most. **Miller** a-219p. **Severin** a-251-53, 260, 261, 265-67. **Simonson** a-254-256. **Spiegle** a-258, 259, 262-64.*

UNKNOWN WORLD (Strange Stories From Another World No. 2 on)
June, 1952
Fawcett Publications

	Good	Fine	Mint
1-Norman Saunders painted-c	8.50	25.50	60.00

UNKNOWN WORLDS (See Journey Into. . .)

UNKNOWN WORLDS
Aug, 1960 - No. 57, Aug, 1967
American Comics Group/Best Synd. Features

	Good	Fine	Mint
1	3.50	10.50	24.00
2-5	1.50	4.50	10.00
6-15: 15-Last 10¢ ish?	1.00	3.00	7.00
16-19	.85	2.50	6.00
20-Herbie cameo	1.00	3.00	7.00
21-35	.50	1.50	3.00
36-"The People vs. Hendricks" by Craig; most popular ACG story ever	.80	2.30	4.60
37-46	.30	.90	1.80
47-Williamson-a r-from Adventures Into the Unknown No. 96, 3 pgs.; Craig-a	.80	2.30	4.60
48-57		.60	1.20

NOTE: ***Ditko** a-49, 50p, 54. **Forte** a-3, 6, 11. **Landau** a-56(2). **Reinman** a-3, 9, 36. John Force, Magic Agent app.-No. 35, 36, 48, 50, 52, 54, 56.*

UNKNOWN WORLDS OF FRANK BRUNNER
Aug, 1985 - No. 2, Aug, 1985 ($1.75 cover)
Eclipse Comics

	Good	Fine	Mint
1,2-B&W-r in color	.30	.90	1.80

UNKNOWN WORLDS OF SCIENCE FICTION
12/74 - No. 6, 11/75; 12/76 (B&W Magazine) ($1.00)
Marvel Comics Group

	Good	Fine	Mint
1-Williamson/Wood/Torres/Frazetta r-/Witzend No. 1, Adams r-/Phase 1; Brunner & Kaluta-r	.50	1.50	3.00

Unearthly Spectaculars #2, © HARV

Unicorn Isle #1, © WaRP

Unknown Worlds #9, © ACG

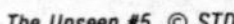
The Unseen #5, © STD

The Untouchables #01-879-207, © DELL

USA Comics #2, © MCG

UNKNOWN WORLDS OF S. F. (continued)

	Good	Fine	Mint
2	.40	1.20	2.40
3-6	.40	1.20	2.40
Special 1(12/76)-100 pgs.; Newton-c; Nino-a	.40	1.20	2.40

NOTE: ***Brunner*** *a-2; c-4, 6.* ***Chaykin*** *a-5.* ***Colan*** *a(p)-1, 3, 5.* ***Corben*** *a-4.* ***Kaluta*** *a-2; c-2.* ***Morrow*** *a-3, 5.* ***Nino*** *a-3, 6.* ***Perez*** *a-2, 3.*

UNSANE
June, 1954
Star Publications

	Good	Fine	Mint
15-Disbrow-a(2); L. B. Cole-c	8.50	25.50	60.00

UNSEEN, THE
1952 - No. 15, July, 1954
Visual Editions/Standard Comics

	Good	Fine	Mint
5-Toth-a	5.75	17.25	40.00
6,7,9,10-Jack Katz-a	4.00	12.00	28.00
8,11,13,14	3.15	9.50	22.00
12,15-Toth-a; Tuska-a, No. 12	5.00	15.00	35.00

NOTE: ***Fawcette*** *a-13, 14.* ***Sekowsky*** *a-7, 8(2), 10, 13.*

UNTAMED LOVE
Jan, 1950 - No. 5, Sept, 1950
Quality Comics Group (Comic Magazines)

	Good	Fine	Mint
1-Ward-c, Gustavson-a	10.00	30.00	70.00
2,4	6.00	18.00	42.00
3,5-Gustavson-a	6.50	19.50	45.00

UNTOLD LEGEND OF THE BATMAN, THE
7/80 - No. 3, 9/80 (mini-series)
DC Comics

	Good	Fine	Mint
1-Origin		.45	.90
2,3		.30	.60

NOTE: ***Aparo*** *a-1i, 2, 3.* ***Byrne*** *a-1p.*

UNTOUCHABLES, THE (TV)
No. 1237, 10-12/61 - No. 4, 8-10/62 (Robert Stack photo-c)
Dell Publishing Co.

	Good	Fine	Mint
4-Color 1237,1286	3.00	9.00	21.00
01879-207, 12-879-210(01879-210 on inside)	2.65	8.00	18.00
Topps Bubblegum premiums-2½x4½", 8 pgs. (3 different issues) "The Organization, Jamaica Ginger, The Otto Frick Story (drug), 3000 Suspects, The Antidote, Mexican Stakeout, Little Egypt, Purple Gang, Bugs Moran Story, & Lily Dallas Story"	1.35	4.00	9.00

UNUSUAL TALES (Blue Beetle & Shadow From Beyond No. 50 on)
Nov, 1955 - No. 49, Mar-Apr, 1965
Charlton Comics

	Good	Fine	Mint
1	4.65	14.00	32.00
2	2.15	6.50	15.00
3-5	1.65	5.00	11.50
6-8-Ditko c/a	5.00	15.00	35.00
9-Ditko c/a, 20 pgs.	5.75	17.25	40.00
10-Ditko c/a(4)	7.00	21.00	50.00
11-(68 pgs.); Ditko-a(4)	7.00	21.00	50.00
12,14-Ditko-a	3.75	11.25	26.00
13,16-20	1.00	3.00	7.00
15-Ditko c/a	4.00	12.00	28.00
21,24,28	.75	2.25	5.00
22,25-27,29-Ditko-a	2.00	6.00	14.00
23-Ditko-c	1.00	3.00	7.00
30-49	.50	1.50	3.00

NOTE: ***Colan*** *a-11.* ***Ditko*** *c-22,23,25-27, 31(part).*

UP FROM HARLEM (Tom Skinner. . .)
1973 (35-49 Cents)
Spire Christian Comics (Fleming H. Revell Co.)

	Good	Fine	Mint
		.50	1.00

UP-TO-DATE COMICS
No date (1938) (36 pgs.; B&W cover) (10 cents)
King Features Syndicate

	Good	Fine	Mint
nn-Popeye & Henry cover; The Phantom, Jungle Jim & Flash Gordon by Raymond, The Katzenjammer Kids, Curley Harper & others	15.00	45.00	90.00

(Variations to above contents exist.)

UP YOUR NOSE AND OUT YOUR EAR (Magazine)
April, 1972 - No. 2, June, 1972 (52 pgs.) (Satire)
Klevart Enterprises

	Good	Fine	Mint
V1No.1,2	.30	.90	1.80

USA COMICS (Gay Comics No. 18 on?)
Aug, 1941 - No. 17, Fall, 1945
Timely Comics (USA)

	Good	Fine	Mint
1-Origin Major Liberty (called Mr. Liberty No. 1), Rockman by Wolverton, & The Whizzer by Avison; The Defender with sidekick Rusty & Jack Frost begin; The Young Avenger only app.; S&K-c plus 1 pg.	265.00	795.00	1855.00
2-Origin Captain Terror & The Vagabond; last Wolverton Rockman	135.00	405.00	945.00
3-No Whizzer	105.00	315.00	735.00
4-Last Rockman, Major Liberty, Defender, Jack Frost, & Capt. Terror; Corporal Dix app.	87.00	260.00	610.00
5-Origin American Avenger & Roko the Amazing; The Black Widow, The Blue Blade & Victory Boys, Gypo the Gypsy Giant & Hills of Horror only app.; Sergeant Dix begins; no Whizzer	75.00	225.00	525.00
6-Captain America, The Destroyer, Jap Buster Johnson, Jeep Jones begin; Terror Squad only app.	80.00	240.00	560.00
7-Captain Daring, Disk-Eyes the Detective by Wolverton app.; origin & only app. Marvel Boy; Secret Stamp begins; no Whizzer, Sergeant Dix	68.00	205.00	475.00
8-10: 9-Last Secret Stamp. 10-The Thunderbird only app.	50.00	150.00	350.00
11,12: 11-No Jeep Jones	41.00	122.00	285.00
13-17: 13-No Whizzer; Jeep Jones ends. 15-No Destroyer; Jap Buster Johnson ends	30.00	90.00	210.00

U.S. AGENT (See Jeff Jordan. . .)

USAGI YOJIMBO SUMMER SPECIAL (See Critters 6&7)
1986 ($2.75, B&W)
Fantagraphics Books

	Good	Fine	Mint
1-r-/from Albedo	1.70	5.00	10.00

U.S. AIR FORCE COMICS (Army Attack No. 38 on)
Oct, 1958 - No. 37, Mar-Apr, 1965
Charlton Comics

	Good	Fine	Mint
1	1.00	3.00	7.00
2	.50	1.50	3.50
3-10	.35	1.00	2.00
11-20		.50	1.00
21-37		.30	.60

NOTE: ***Glanzman*** *c/a-9, 10, 12.* ***Montes/Bache*** *a-33.*

USA IS READY
1941 (68 pgs.) (One Shot)
Dell Publishing Co.

	Good	Fine	Mint
1-War propaganda	13.50	40.50	95.00

U.S. BORDER PATROL COMICS (Sgt. Dick Carter of the. . .) (See Holyoke One Shot)

U.S. FIGHTING MEN
1963 - 1964 (Reprints)
Super Comics

	Good	Fine	Mint
10-Avon's With the U.S. Paratroops	.50	1.50	3.00
11,12,15-18	.30	.80	1.60

U.S. JONES (Also see Wonderworld Comics)
Nov, 1941 - No. 2, Jan, 1942
Fox Features Syndicate

	Good	Fine	Mint
1-U.S. Jones & The Topper begin	40.00	120.00	280.00
2	26.00	78.00	180.00

U.S. MARINES
Fall, 1964 (One shot)
Charlton Comics

	Good	Fine	Mint
1	.30	.80	1.60

U.S. MARINES IN ACTION!
Aug, 1952 - No. 3, Dec?, 1952
Avon Periodicals

	Good	Fine	Mint
1-Louis Ravielli c/a	3.35	10.00	23.00
2,3: 3-Kinstler-c	1.65	5.00	11.50

U.S. 1
May, 1983 - No. 12, Oct, 1984
Marvel Comics Group

	Good	Fine	Mint
1		.30	.60
2-12		.25	.50

NOTE: ***Ditko*** *a-12p.* ***Golden*** *c-5-7,9,10,12.*

U.S. PARATROOPS (See With the . . .)

U.S. PARATROOPS
1964?
I. W. Enterprises

	Good	Fine	Mint
1-Wood-c r-/With the . . . No. 1	.50	1.50	3.00
8-Kinstler-c	.50	1.50	3.00

U.S. TANK COMMANDOS
June, 1952 - No. 4, March, 1953
Avon Periodicals

	Good	Fine	Mint
1-Kinstler-c	3.75	11.25	26.00
2-4: 2-Kinstler-c	2.15	6.50	15.00
I.W. Reprint No. 1,8	.40	1.10	2.20

NOTE: ***Kinstler*** *a-3, 4, I.W. No.1; c-1-4, I.W. No.1, 8.*

"V"
Feb, 1985 - No. 18, July, 1986
DC Comics

	Good	Fine	Mint
1-Based on TV movie & series	.25	.75	1.50
2-18		.45	.90

VACATION COMICS (See A-1 Comics No. 16)

VACATION IN DISNEYLAND (Also see Dell Giants)
Aug-Oct, 1959 - May, 1965 (Walt Disney)
Dell Publishing Co./Gold Key (1965)

	Good	Fine	Mint
4-Color 1025-Barks-a	5.35	16.00	37.00
1(30024-508)(G.K.)-Reprints Dell Giant No. 30 & cover to No. 1('58)	1.50	4.50	12.00

VACATION PARADE (See Dell Giants)

VALENTINO
Apr, 1985 ($1.70 cover; B&W)
Renegade Press

	Good	Fine	Mint
1	.30	.85	1.70

VALLEY OF THE DINOSAURS (TV) (Hanna-Barbera)
April, 1975 - No. 11, Dec, 1976
Charlton Comics

	Good	Fine	Mint
1-Howard inks		.40	.80
2-11: 2-Howard inks		.30	.60

VALLEY OF GWANGI (See Movie Classics)

VALOR
Mar-Apr, 1955 - No. 5, Nov-Dec, 1955
E. C. Comics

	Good	Fine	Mint
1-Williamson/Torres-a; Wood c/a	15.00	45.00	105.00
2-Williamson c/a; Wood-a	13.00	40.00	90.00
3-Williamson, Crandall-a	9.25	28.00	65.00
4-Wood-c	9.25	28.00	65.00
5-Wood c/a; Williamson/Evans-a	8.00	24.00	55.00

NOTE: ***Crandall*** *a-3, 4.* ***Ingels*** *a-1, 2, 4, 5.* ***Krigstein*** *a-1-5.* ***Orlando*** *a-3, 4; c-3.* ***Wood*** *a-1, 2, 5; c-1, 4, 5.*

VAMPIRELLA (Magazine)
Sept, 1969 - No. 112, Feb, 1983
Warren Publishing Co.

	Good	Fine	Mint
1-Intro. Vampirella	8.35	25.00	50.00
2-Amazonia series begins, ends No. 12	2.50	7.50	15.00
3 (Low distribution)	10.00	30.00	60.00
4-7	2.00	6.00	12.00
8-Vampi begins by Tom Sutton as serious strip (early issues-gag line)	1.35	4.00	8.00
9-Smith-a	2.00	6.00	12.00
10-No Vampi story	1.35	4.00	8.00
11-15: 11-Origin, 1st app. Pendragon. 12-Vampi by Gonzales begins	1.20	3.50	7.00
16-18,20-25: 17-Tomb of the Gods begins, ends No. 22	.85	2.50	5.00
19 (1973 Annual)	1.20	3.50	7.00
26,28-36,38-40: 30-Intro. Pantha. 31-Origin Luana, the Beast Girl. 33-Pantha ends	.70	2.00	4.00
27 (1974 Annual)	1.00	3.00	6.00
37 (1975 Annual)	.85	2.50	5.00
41-45	.35	1.00	2.00
46-Origin	.50	1.50	3.00
47-50: 50-Spirit cameo	.30	.90	1.80
51-99: 66,90-Pantha app. 93-Cassandra St. Knight begins, ends 103; new Pantha series begins, ends 108	.25	.75	1.50
100 (96pg. r-special)-Origin retold	.30	.90	1.80
101-112: 108-Torpedo series by Toth begins	.25	.75	1.50
Annual 1('72)-New origin Vampirella by Gonzales; reprints by Adams(No.1), Wood(No.9)	7.50	22.50	45.00
Special 1 ('77; large-square bound)	.85	2.50	5.00

NOTE: ***Adams*** *a-1, 10p, 19p.* ***Alcala*** *a-90, 93i.* ***Bode'/Todd*** *c-3.* ***Bode'/Jones*** *c-4.* ***Boris*** *c-9.* ***Brunner*** *a-10.* ***Corben*** *a-30, 31, 33, 54.* ***Crandall*** *a-1, 19.* ***Frazetta*** *c-1, 5, 7, 11, 31.* ***Jones*** *a-5, 9, 12, 27, 32, 33, 34, 50i.* ***Nino*** *a-59i, 61i, 67, 76, 85, 90.* ***Ploog*** *a-14.* ***Smith*** *a-9.* ***Sutton*** *a-11.* ***Toth*** *a-90i, 108, 110.* ***Wood*** *a-9, 10, 12, 19, 27; c-9.* ***Wrightson*** *a-33, 63. All reprint issues-37, 74, 83, 87, 91, 105, 107, 109, 111. Annuals from 1973 on are included in regular numbering. Later annuals are same format as regular issues.*

VAMPIRE TALES (Magazine)
Aug, 1973 - No. 11, June, 1975 (B&W) (75 cents)
Marvel Comics Group

	Good	Fine	Mint
1-Morbius, the Living Vampire begins by Pablo Marcos	.35	1.00	2.00
2-Intro. Satana; Steranko-r	.25	.75	1.50
3-11: 3-Satana app. 5-Origin Morbius. 6-1st Lilith app. 8-1st Blade app.		.60	1.20
Annual 1(10/75)	.25	.75	1.50

NOTE: ***Alcala*** *a-6, 8, 9i.* ***Boris*** *c-4, 6.* ***Chaykin*** *a-7.* ***Everett*** *a-1r.* ***Gulacy*** *a-7p.* ***Heath*** *a-9.* ***Infantino*** *a-3r.* ***Gil Kane*** *a-4, 5r.*

U.S. Paratroops #8, © I.W.

Valor #4, © WMG

Vampirella #30, © WP

Vault of Horror #13, © WMG

Venture #1, © AC Comics

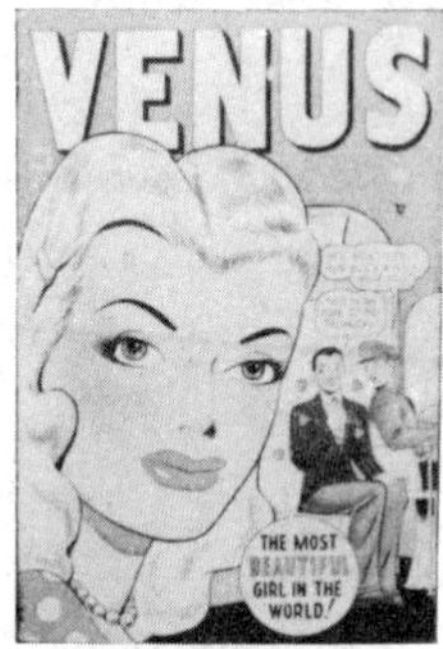

Venus #2, © MCG

VANGUARD ILLUSTRATED
Nov, 1983 - No. 7, July, 1984
Pacific Comics

	Good	Fine	Mint
1-Nudity scenes		.50	1.00
2-4 (Baxter paper)	.25	.75	1.50
5-7: 7-Mr. Monster app.	.25	.75	1.50

NOTE: ***Evans*** *a-7.* ***Kaluta*** *c-5, 7p.* ***Perez*** *a-6; c-6.* ***Rude*** *a-3-5; c-4.*

VANITY
Jun, 1984 - No. 2, Aug, 1984 ($1.50)
Pacific Comics

	Good	Fine	Mint
1,2-Origin	.25	.75	1.50

VARIETY COMICS
1944 - 1945; 1946
Rural Home Publications/Croyden Publ. Co.

	Good	Fine	Mint
1-Origin Captain Valiant	5.00	15.00	35.00
2-Captain Valiant	3.35	10.00	23.00
3(1946-Croyden)-Captain Valiant	2.50	7.50	17.50
4,5	2.15	6.50	15.00

VARIETY COMICS (See Fox Giants)

VARSITY
1945
Parents' Magazine Institute

	Good	Fine	Mint
1	1.75	5.25	12.00

VAUDEVILLE AND OTHER THINGS
1900 (10½x13") (in color) (18+ pgs.)
Isaac H. Blandiard Co.

	Good	Fine	Mint
By Bunny	16.00	48.00	110.00

VAULT OF DOOMNATION, THE
Oct, 1986 (One shot) ($1.70, B&W)
B-Movie Comics

	Good	Fine	Mint
1	.30	.90	1.70

VAULT OF EVIL
Feb, 1973 - No. 23, Nov, 1975
Marvel Comics Group

	Good	Fine	Mint
1 (Reprints begin)		.35	.70
2-23: 3,4-Brunner-c		.25	.50

NOTE: ***Ditko*** *a-14r, 15r, 20-22r.* ***Drucker*** *a-10r(Mystic No. 52), 13r(Uncanny Tales No.42).* ***Everett*** *a-11r(Menace No. 2), 13r(Menace No.4); c-10.* ***Krigstein*** *a-20r(Uncanny Tales No.54).*

VAULT OF HORROR (War Against Crime No. 1-11)
No. 12, Apr-May, 1950 - No. 40, Dec-Jan, 1954-55
E. C. Comics

	Good	Fine	Mint
12	105.00	315.00	735.00
13-Morphine story	48.00	145.00	335.00
14	42.00	125.00	290.00
15	35.00	105.00	245.00
16	27.00	80.00	190.00
17-19	20.00	60.00	140.00
20-22,24,25	15.00	45.00	105.00
23-Used in **POP**, pg. 84	16.00	48.00	110.00
26-B&W & color illos in **POP**	16.00	48.00	110.00
27-35	12.00	36.00	80.00
36-''Pipe Dream''-classic opium addict story by Krigstein; 'Twin Bill' cited in articles by T.E. Murphy & Wertham	12.00	36.00	80.00
37-Williamson-a	12.00	36.00	80.00
38-39: 39-Bondage-c	9.35	28.00	65.00
40-Low distribution	10.00	30.00	70.00

NOTE: ***Craig*** *art in all but No. 13 & 33; c-12-40.* ***Crandall*** *a-33, 34, 39.* ***Davis*** *a-17-38.* ***Evans*** *a-27, 28, 30, 32, 33.* ***Feldstein*** *a-12-16.* ***Ingels*** *a-13-20, 22-40.* ***Kamen*** *a-15-22, 25, 29, 35.* ***Krigstein*** *a-36, 38-40.* ***Kurtzman*** *a-12, 13.* ***Orlando*** *a-24, 31, 40.* ***Wood*** *a-12-14.*

V...-COMICS (Morse code for ''V'' - 3 dots, 1 dash)
Jan, 1942 - No. 2, Mar-Apr, 1942
Fox Features Syndicate

	Good	Fine	Mint
1-Origin V-Man & the Boys; The Banshee & The Black Fury, The Queen of Evil, & V-Agents begin	40.00	120.00	280.00
2-Bondage/torture-c	30.00	90.00	210.00

VECTOR
1986 - Present ($1.50, color)
Now Comics

	Good	Fine	Mint
1-3-Computer-generated-a	.30	.90	1.80

VENGEANCE SQUAD
July, 1975 - No. 6, May, 1976
Charlton Comics

	Good	Fine	Mint
1-Mike Mauser, Private eye begins by Staton		.40	.80
2-6: Morisi-a in all		.25	.50
5,6(Modern Comics-r, 1977)		.15	.30

VENTURE
Aug, 1986 - Present ($1.75, color)
AC Comics (Americomics)

	Good	Fine	Mint
1,2	.30	.90	1.80

VENUS
August, 1948 - No. 19, April, 1952
Marvel/Atlas Comics (CMC 1-9/LCC 10-19)

	Good	Fine	Mint
1-Venus & Hedy Devine begin; Kurtzman's ''Hey Look''	33.00	100.00	230.00
2	20.00	60.00	140.00
3,5	17.00	51.00	120.00
4-Kurtzman's ''Hey Look''	18.00	54.00	126.00
6-9: 6-Loki app.	16.00	48.00	110.00
10-S/F-horror ish. begin (7/50)	17.00	51.00	120.00
11-S/F end of the world(11/50)	21.00	62.00	146.00
12	15.00	45.00	105.00
13-19-Venus by Everett, 2-3 stories each; covers-No. 13,15-19	21.00	62.00	146.00

NOTE: *No. 3-5-content changes to teen-age. Bondage c-17.* ***Colan*** *a-12.*

VERI BEST SURE FIRE COMICS
No date (circa 1945) (Reprints Holyoke One-Shots)
Holyoke Publishing Co.

	Good	Fine	Mint
1-Captain Aero, Alias X, Miss Victory, Commandos of the Devil Dogs, Red Cross, Hammerhead Hawley, Capt. Aero's Sky Scouts, Flagman app.	10.00	30.00	70.00

VERI BEST SURE SHOT COMICS
No date (circa 1945) (Reprints Holyoke One-Shots)
Holyoke Publishing Co.

	Good	Fine	Mint
1-Capt. Aero, Miss Victory by Quinlan, Alias X, The Red Cross, Flagman, Commandos of the Devil Dogs, Hammerhead Hawley, Capt. Aero's Sky Scouts	10.00	30.00	70.00

VERY BEST OF DENNIS THE MENACE, THE
July, 1979 - No. 2, Apr, 1980 (132 pgs., Digest, 95 cents, $1.00)
Fawcett Publications

	Good	Fine	Mint
1,2-Reprints		.50	1.00

VERY BEST OF DENNIS THE MENACE, THE
April, 1982 - No. 3, Aug, 1982 (Digest Size) ($1.25)
Marvel Comics Group

	Good	Fine	Mint
1-3-Reprints		.65	1.25

NOTE: ***Hank Ketcham*** *c-all. A few thousand of No. 1 & 2 were printed with a DC emblem.*

VIC FLINT (Crime Buster...)
August, 1948 (Newspaper reprints; NEA Service)
St. John Publishing Co.

VIC FLINT (continued) — Good / Fine / Mint
1 — 4.00 12.00 28.00
2 — 2.35 7.00 16.00
3-5 — 2.00 6.00 14.00

VIC FLINT
Feb, 1956 - No. 2, May, 1956 (Newspaper reprints)
Argo Publ.
1,2 — 2.00 6.00 14.00

VIC JORDAN
April, 1945
Civil Service Publ.
1-1944 daily newspaper-r — 4.00 12.00 28.00

VICKI (Humor)
Feb, 1975 - No. 4, July, 1975 (No. 1,2: 68 pgs.)
Atlas/Seaboard Publ.
1-Reprints Tippy Teen — .50 1.50 3.00
2-4 — .30 .80 1.60

VICKI VALENTINE SUMMER SPECIAL
July, 1985 - Present ($1.70 cover; B&W)
Renegade Press
1-4: Woggon, Rausch-a; all have paper dolls. 2-Christmas ish. — .30 .85 1.70

VICKS COMICS (Also see Pure Oil Comics, Salerno Carnival of Comics, & 24 Pages of Comics)
nd (circa 1938) (68 pgs. in color) (Giveaway)
Eastern Color Printing Co. (Vicks Chemical Co.)
nn-Reprints from Famous Funnies (before No. 40). Contains 5 pgs. Buck Rogers (4 pgs. from F.F. No. 15, & 1 pg. from No. 16) Joe Palooka, Napoleon, etc. app. — 45.00 135.00 315.00
nn-16 loose, untrimmed page giveaway; paper-c; r-/Famous Funnies No. 14; Buck Rogers, Joe Palooka app. — 20.00 60.00 120.00

VICKY
Oct, 1948 - No. 5, June, 1949
Ace Magazine
nn(10/48) — 2.00 6.00 14.00
4(12/48), nn(2/49), 4(4/49), 5(6/49) — 1.65 5.00 11.50

VIC TORRY & HIS FLYING SAUCER
1950 (One Shot)
Fawcett Publications
Book-length saucer story by Powell; photo/painted-c — 20.00 60.00 140.00

VICTORY COMICS
Aug, 1941 - No. 4, Dec, 1941
Hillman Periodicals
1-The Conqueror by Bill Everett, The Crusader, & Bomber Burns begin; Conqueror's origin in text; Everett-c; No. 1 by Funnies, Inc. — 71.00 214.00 500.00
2-Everett-a — 40.00 120.00 280.00
3,4 — 28.00 84.00 195.00

VIC VERITY MAGAZINE
1945 - No. 7, Sept, 1946 (A comic book)
Vic Verity Publications
1-C. C. Beck-a — 4.65 14.00 32.00
2 — 3.35 10.00 23.00
3-7: 6-Beck-a. 7-Beck-c — 2.85 8.50 20.00

VIGILANTE, THE
Oct, 1983 - Present ($1.25; Baxter paper)
DC Comics — Good / Fine / Mint
1-Origin — .70 2.00 4.00
2 — .45 1.40 2.80
3-5: 3-Cyborg app. — .40 1.20 2.40
6-10: 6,7-Origin — .35 1.10 2.20
11-20: 20-Nightwing app. — .30 .85 1.70
21-30: 21-Nightwing app. — .25 .75 1.50
31-39: 35-Origin Mad Bomber — .65 1.30
40 — .25 .75 1.50
Annual 1 (10/85), 2(11/86) — .35 1.10 2.20
NOTE: *Newton a-4p.*

VIGILANTES, THE (See 4-Color No. 839)

VIKINGS, THE (See 4-Color No. 910)

VIRGINIAN, THE (TV)
June, 1963
Gold Key
1(10060-306)-Photo-c — 2.00 6.00 14.00

VISION AND THE SCARLET WITCH, THE
Nov, 1982 - No. 4, Feb, 1983 (mini-series)
Marvel Comics Group
1 — .25 .75 1.50
2-4: 2-Nuklo & Future Man app. — .50 1.00

VISION AND THE SCARLET WITCH, THE
Oct, 1985 - No. 12, Sept, 1986 (maxi-series)
Marvel Comics Group
1 (V2/1)-Origin — .25 .75 1.50
2-12: 2-West Coast Avengers x-over — .50 1.00

VISIONS ILLUSTRATED
1986 - Present
Fantasy General Comics
1 — .25 .75 1.50

VOID INDIGO
Nov, 1984 - No. 2, Mar, 1985 ($1.50, Baxter paper)
Epic Comics (Marvel)
1-Continues from Graphic Novel — .35 1.00 2.00
2-Sex, violence shown — .35 1.00 2.00

VOLTRON (TV)
1985 - No. 3, 1985
Modern Publishing
1-3: Ayers-a — .50 1.00

VOODA (Formerly Voodoo)
No. 20, April, 1955 - No. 22, Aug, 1955
Ajax-Farrell (Four Star Publications)
20-Baker c/a — 6.00 18.00 42.00
21,22-Baker-a plus Kamen/Baker story, Kimbo Boy of Jungle, & Baker-c (p) in all — 5.50 16.50 38.00
NOTE: *No. 20-Baker r-/Seven Seas No. 4.*

VOODOO (Vooda No. 20 on)
May, 1952 - No. 19, Jan-Feb, 1955
Ajax-Farrell (Four Star Publ.)
1-South Sea Girl-r by Baker — 11.50 34.50 80.00
2-Rulah story-r plus South Sea Girl from Seven Seas No. 2 by Baker (name changed from Alani to El'nee) — 9.50 28.50 65.00
3-Bakerish-a; man stabbed in face — 6.50 19.50 45.00
4,8-Baker-r — 6.50 19.50 45.00

Vicki Valentine Summer Special #2, © Renegade

The Virginian #1, © Revue Studios

Vooda #21, © AJAX

Voodoo #15, © AJAX

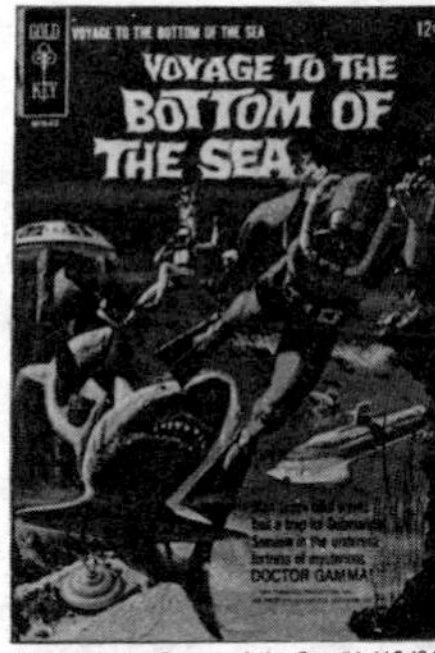

Voyage to the Bottom of the Sea #1 (12/64)
© Cambridge Prod. & 20th Century-Fox

Wagon Train #5, © Revue Prod.

VOODOO (continued)

	Good	Fine	Mint
5-7,9,10: 5-Nazi flaying alive. 6,8-Severed head panels	5.50	16.50	38.00
11-14,16-18: 14-Zombies take over America. 17-Electric chair panels	4.35	13.00	30.00
15-Opium drug story-r/Ellery Queen No. 3	4.65	14.00	32.00
19-Bondage-c; Baker-a(2)(r)	8.00	24.00	56.00
Annual 1(1952)(25 cents); Baker-a	26.00	78.00	180.00

VOODOO (See Tales of . . .)

VORTEX
1985 - Present
Vortex Publ.

	Good	Fine	Mint
1-12	.30	.90	1.80

VOYAGE TO THE BOTTOM OF THE SEA (TV)
No. 1230, 9-11/61 - No. 16, 4/70 (Painted covers)
Dell Publishing Co./Gold Key

	Good	Fine	Mint
4-Color 1230(Movie-1961)	2.65	8.00	18.00
10133-412(G.K.-12/64)	1.75	5.25	12.00
2(7/65) - 5: Photo back-c, 1-5	1.15	3.50	8.00
6-14	.75	2.25	5.00
15,16-Reprints	.45	1.35	3.00

VOYAGE TO THE DEEP
Sept-Nov, 1962 - No. 4, Nov-Jan, 1964
Dell Publishing Co.

	Good	Fine	Mint
1	1.50	4.50	10.00
2-4	1.00	3.00	7.00

WACKY ADVENTURES OF CRACKY (Also see Gold Key Spotlight)
Dec, 1972 - No. 12, Sept, 1975
Gold Key

	Good	Fine	Mint
1	.70	2.00	4.00
2	.35	1.00	2.00
3-12		.50	1.00

(See March of Comics No. 405,424,436,448)

WACKY DUCK (Formerly Dopey Duck?; Justice No. 7 on)
No. 3, Fall, 1946 - No. 6, Summer, 1947; 8/48 - No. 2, 10/48
Marvel Comics (NPP)

	Good	Fine	Mint
3	4.35	13.00	30.00
4-Infinity-c	5.75	17.25	40.00
5,6('46-47)	3.65	11.00	25.00
1,2(1948)	2.50	7.50	17.50
I.W. Reprint No. 1,2,7('58)	.30	.90	1.80
Super Reprint No. 10(I.W. on cover, Super on inside)	.30	.90	1.80

WACKY QUACKY (See Wisco)

WACKY RACES (TV)
Aug, 1969 - No. 7, Apr, 1972 (Hanna-Barbera)
Gold Key

	Good	Fine	Mint
1	.70	2.00	4.00
2-7	.45	1.25	2.50

WACKY WITCH
March, 1971 - No. 21, Dec, 1975
Gold Key

	Good	Fine	Mint
1	.85	2.50	5.00
2	.60	1.75	3.50
3-21	.35	1.00	2.00

(See March of Comics No. 374,398,410,422,434,446,458,470,482)

WACKY WOODPECKER (See Two Bit . . .)
1958; 1963
I. W. Enterprises/Super Comics

	Good	Fine	Mint
I.W. Reprint No. 1,2,7(no date-reprints Two Bit. . .)	.30	.90	1.80
Super Reprint No. 10('63)	.30	.90	1.80

WAGON TRAIN (1st Series) (TV) (See Western Roundup)
No. 895, Mar, 1958 - No. 13, Apr-June, 1962 (All photo-c)
Dell Publishing Co.

	Good	Fine	Mint
4-Color 895 (No.1)	3.50	10.50	24.00
4-Color 971,1019	2.65	8.00	18.00
4(1-3/60),6-13	2.35	7.00	16.00
5-Toth-a	2.85	8.50	20.00

WAGON TRAIN (2nd Series)(TV)
Jan, 1964 - No. 4, Oct, 1964 (All photo-c)
Gold Key

	Good	Fine	Mint
1	2.35	7.00	16.00
2-4: 3,4-Tufts-a	1.50	4.50	10.00

WAITING ROOM WILLIE (See Sad Case of . . .)

WALLY (Teen-age)
Dec, 1962 - No. 4, Sept, 1963
Gold Key

	Good	Fine	Mint
1	1.15	3.50	8.00
2-4	.75	2.25	5.00

WALLY THE WIZARD
Apr, 1985 - No. 12, Mar, 1986 (Children's comic)
Star Comics (Marvel)

	Good	Fine	Mint
1-12: Bob Bolling-c/a		.35	.70

WALLY WOOD'S T.H.U.N.D.E.R. AGENTS (See Thunder Agents)
Nov, 1984 - No. 2, Jan, 1985 (52 pgs.; $2.00)
Deluxe Comics

	Good	Fine	Mint
1,2	.35	1.00	2.00

NOTE: ***Giffen*** *a-1p, 2p.* ***Perez*** *a-1p, 2.*

WALT DISNEY CHRISTMAS PARADE (Also see Christmas Parade)
Winter, 1977 (224 pgs.) (cardboard covers, $1.95)
Whitman Publishing Co. (Golden Press)

	Good	Fine	Mint
11191-Barks-a r-/Christmas in Disneyland No. 1, Dell Christmas Parade No. 9, Dell Giant No. 53	.40	1.20	2.40

WALT DISNEY COMICS DIGEST
June, 1968 - No. 57, Feb, 1976 (50 cents) (Digest size)
Gold Key

	Good	Fine	Mint
1-Reprints Uncle Scrooge No. 5	3.00	9.00	18.00
2-4-Barks-r	1.70	5.00	10.00
5-Daisy Duck by Barks (8 pgs.); last published story by Barks (art only) plus 21 pg. Scrooge-r by Barks	2.00	6.00	12.00
6-13-All Barks-r	1.00	3.00	6.00
14,15	.70	2.00	4.00
16-Reprints Donald Duck No. 26 by Barks	1.35	4.00	8.00
17-20-Barks-r	.80	2.40	4.80
21-31,33,35-37-Barks-r; 24-Toth Zorro	.70	2.00	4.00
32	.50	1.50	3.00
34-Reprints 4-Color 318	1.35	4.00	8.00
38-Reprints Christmas in Disneyland No. 1	1.00	3.00	6.00
39-Two Barks-r/WDC&S No. 272, 4-Color 1073 plus Toth Zorro-r	.80	2.40	4.80
40-Mickey Mouse-r by Gottfredson	.50	1.50	3.00
41,45,47-49	.30	.90	1.80
42,43-Barks-r	.50	1.50	3.00
44-(Has Gold Key emblem, 50 cents)-Reprints 1st story of 4-Color 29, 256,275,282	2.00	6.00	12.00
44-Republished in 1976 by Whitman; not identical to original; slightly smaller, blank back cover, 69¢ cover price	.80	2.40	4.80
46,50-Barks-r	.50	1.50	3.00

WALT DISNEY COMICS DIGEST (continued) Good Fine Mint
51-Reprints 4-Color 71 .80 2.40 4.80
52-Barks-r/WDC&S No. 161,132 .50 1.50 3.00
53-Reprint/Dell Giant No. 30 .30 .80 1.60
54-Reprint/Donald Duck Beach Party No. 2 .30 .80 1.60
55-Reprint/Dell Giant No. 49 .30 .80 1.60
56-Reprint/Uncle Scrooge No. 32 (Barks) plus another Barks story .50 1.50 3.00
57-Reprint/Mickey Mouse Almanac('57) & two Barks stories .50 1.50 3.00

NOTE: *No. 1-10, 196 pgs.; No. 11-41, 164 pgs.; No. 42 on, 132 pgs. Old issues were being reprinted & distributed by Whitman in 1976.*

WALT DISNEY PRESENTS (TV)
No. 997, June-Aug, 1959 - No. 6, Dec-Feb, 1960-61 (All photo-c)
Dell Publishing Co.

4-Color 997 2.35 7.00 16.00
2(12-2/60)-The Swamp Fox(origin), Elfego Baca, Texas John Slaughter (Disney TV Show) 1.50 4.50 10.00
3-6 1.50 4.50 10.00

WALT DISNEY'S COMICS AND STORIES (Cont. of Mickey Mouse Magazine) (No. 1-30 contain Donald Duck newspaper reprints) (Titled 'Comics And Stories' No. 264 on)
10/40 - No. 263, 8/62; No. 264, 10/62 - No. 510, 1984; No. 511, 10/86 - Present
Dell Publishing Co./Gold Key No. 264-473/Whitman No. 474-510/ Gladstone No. 511 on

1(V1/1-c; V2/1-indicia)-Donald Duck strip-r by Al Taliaferro & Gottfredson's Mickey Mouse begin 300.00 1200.00 2900.00
(Prices vary widely on this book)
2 200.00 600.00 1400.00
3 82.00 246.00 575.00
4 64.00 192.00 450.00
4-Special promotional, complimentary issue; cover same except one corner was blanked out & boxed in to identify the giveaway (not a paste-over). This special pressing was probably sent out to former subscribers to Mickey Mouse Mag. whose subscriptions had expired. (Rare-five known copies) 115.00 345.00 800.00
5 50.00 150.00 350.00
6-10 40.00 120.00 280.00
11-14 36.00 108.00 250.00
15-17: 15-The 3 Little Kittens (17 pgs.). 16-The 3 Little Pigs (29 pgs.). 17-The Ugly Duckling (4 pgs.) 30.00 90.00 210.00
18-21 24.00 72.00 170.00
22-30: 22-Flag-c 21.00 62.00 150.00
31-Donald Duck by Carl Barks begins; see Four Color No. 9 for first Barks D.D. 121.00 362.00 850.00
32-Barks-a 86.00 258.00 600.00
33-Barks-a (infinity-c) 57.00 171.00 400.00
34-Gremlins by Walt Kelly begin, end No. 41; Barks-a 47.00 141.00 330.00
35,36-Barks-a 40.00 120.00 280.00
37-Donald Duck by Jack Hannah 18.00 54.00 125.00
38-40-Barks-a. 39-Christmas-c. 40-Gremlins by Kelly 27.00 81.00 190.00
41-50-Barks-a; 41-Gremlins by Kelly 21.00 62.00 150.00
51-60-Barks-a; 51-Christmas-c. 52-Li'l Bad Wolf begins, ends No. 203 (not in No. 55) 16.00 48.00 110.00
61-70: Barks-a. 61-Dumbo story. 63,64-Pinocchio stories. 63-c-swipe from New Funnies 94. 64-X-mas-c. 65-Pluto story. 66-Infinity -c. 67,68-M. Mouse Sunday-r by Bill Wright 13.00 40.00 90.00
71-80: Barks-a. 75-77-Brer Rabbit stories, no Mickey Mouse. 76-X-Mas-c 10.00 30.00 70.00
81-87,89,90: Barks-a. 82-84-Bongo stories. 86-90-Goofy & Agnes app. 89-Chip 'n' Dale story 8.50 25.50 60.00

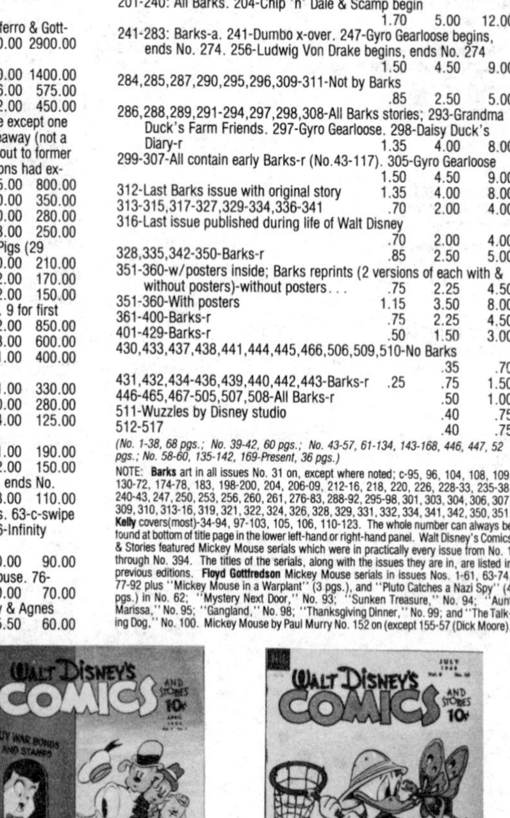

Good Fine Mint
88-1st app. Gladstone Gander by Barks 10.00 30.00 70.00
91-97,99: Barks-a. 95-1st WDC&S Barks-c. 96-No Mickey Mouse; Little Toot begins, ends No. 97. 99-X-Mas-c 7.00 21.00 48.00
98-1st Uncle Scrooge app. in WDC&S 11.50 34.50 80.00
100-Barks-a 7.35 22.00 50.00
101-106,108-110-Barks-a 5.75 17.25 40.00
107-Barks-a; Taliaferro-c. Donald acquires super powers 5.75 17.25 40.00
111,114,117-All Barks 4.35 13.00 30.00
112-Drug (ether) issue (Donald Duck) 5.15 15.50 36.00
113,115,116,118-123: Not by Barks. 116-Dumbo x-over. 121-Grandma Duck begins, ends No. 168; not in No. 135,142, 146,155 2.15 6.50 15.00
124,126-130-All Barks. 124-X-Mas-c 4.00 12.00 28.00
125-Intro. & 1st app. Junior Woodchucks; Barks-a 6.35 19.00 44.00
131,133,135-139-All Barks 4.00 12.00 28.00
132-Barks-a(2) (D. Duck & Grandma Duck) 5.15 15.50 36.00
134-Intro. & 1st app. The Beagle Boys 8.00 24.00 56.00
140-1st app. Gyro Gearloose by Barks 8.00 24.00 56.00
141-150-All Barks. 143-Little Hiawatha begins, ends No. 151,159 2.65 8.00 18.00
151-170-All Barks. 164-Has blank inside-c 2.35 7.00 16.00
171-200-All Barks 2.00 6.00 14.00
201-240: All Barks. 204-Chip 'n' Dale & Scamp begin 1.70 5.00 12.00
241-283: Barks-a. 241-Dumbo x-over. 247-Gyro Gearloose begins, ends No. 274. 256-Ludwig Von Drake begins, ends No. 274 1.50 4.50 9.00
284,285,287,290,295,296,309-311-Not by Barks .85 2.50 5.00
286,288,289,291-294,297,298,308-All Barks stories; 293-Grandma Duck's Farm Friends. 297-Gyro Gearloose. 298-Daisy Duck's Diary-r 1.35 4.00 8.00
299-307-All contain early Barks-r (No.43-117). 305-Gyro Gearloose 1.50 4.50 9.00
312-Last Barks issue with original story 1.35 4.00 8.00
313-315,317-327,329-334,336-341 .70 2.00 4.00
316-Last issue published during life of Walt Disney .70 2.00 4.00
328,335,342-350-Barks-r .85 2.50 5.00
351-360-w/posters inside; Barks reprints (2 versions of each with & without posters)-without posters. . . .75 2.25 4.50
351-360-With posters 1.15 3.50 8.00
361-400-Barks-r .75 2.25 4.50
401-429-Barks-r .50 1.50 3.00
430,433,437,438,441,444,445,466,506,509,510-No Barks .35 .70
431,432,434-436,439,440,442,443-Barks-r .25 .75 1.50
446-465,467-505,507,508-All Barks-r .50 1.00
511-Wuzzles by Disney studio .40 .75
512-517 .40 .75

(No. 1-38, 68 pgs.; No. 39-42, 60 pgs.; No. 43-57, 61-134, 143-168, 446, 447, 52 pgs.; No. 58-60, 135-142, 169-Present, 36 pgs.)

NOTE: **Barks** art in all issues No. 31 on, except where noted; c-95, 96, 104, 108, 109, 130-72, 174-78, 183, 198-200, 204, 206-09, 212-16, 218, 220, 226, 228-33, 235-38, 240-43, 247, 250, 253, 256, 260, 261, 276-83, 288-92, 295-98, 301, 303, 304, 306, 307, 309, 310, 313-16, 319, 321, 322, 324, 326, 328, 329, 331, 332, 334, 341, 342, 350, 351. **Kelly** covers(most)-34-94, 97-103, 105, 106, 110-123. The whole number can always be found at bottom of title page in the lower left-hand or right-hand panel. Walt Disney's Comics & Stories featured Mickey Mouse serials which were in practically every issue from No. 1 through No. 394. The titles of the serials, along with the issues they are in, are listed in previous editions. **Floyd Gottfredson** Mickey Mouse serials in issues Nos. 1-61, 63-74, 77-92 plus ''Mickey Mouse in a Warplant'' (3 pgs.), and ''Pluto Catches a Nazi Spy'' (4 pgs.) in No. 62; ''Mystery Next Door,'' No. 93; ''Sunken Treasure,'' No. 94; ''Aunt Marissa,'' No. 95; ''Gangland,'' No. 98; ''Thanksgiving Dinner,'' No. 99; and ''The Talking Dog,'' No. 100. Mickey Mouse by Paul Murry No. 152 on (except 155-57 (Dick Moore),

Walt Disney Presents #4, © WDC

Walt Disney's C & S #31, © WDC

Walt Disney's C & S #94, © WDC

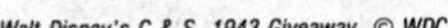
Walt Disney's C & S, 1943 Giveaway, © WDC

Walt Disney Showcase #30, © WDC

Walter Lantz Andy Panda #1, © Walter Lantz

WALT DISNEY'S C&S (continued)
327-29 (Tony Strobl), 348-50 (Jack Manning). **Al Taliaferro** Silly Symphonies in No. 5-''Three Little Pigs;'' No. 13-''Birds of a Feather;'' No. 14-''The Boarding School Mystery;'' No. 15-''Cookieland'' and ''Three Little Kittens;'' No. 16-''Three Little Pigs;'' No. 17-''The Ugly Duckling'' and ''The Robber Kitten;'' No. 19-''Penguin Isle;'' and ''Bucky Bug'' in Nos. 20-23, 25, 26, 28 (one continuous story from 1932-34; first 2 pgs. not Taliaferro).

WALT DISNEY'S COMICS & STORIES
1943 (36 pgs.) (Dept. store Xmas giveaway)
Walt Disney Productions

	Good	Fine	Mint
nn	45.00	135.00	300.00

WALT DISNEY'S COMICS & STORIES
Mid 1940's ('45-48), 1952 (4 pgs. in color) (slick paper)
Dell Publishing Co.(Special Xmas offer)

	Good	Fine	Mint
1940's version - subscription form for WDC&S - (Reprints two different WDC&S covers with subscription forms printed on inside covers)	8.35	25.00	50.00
1952 version	4.75	14.00	28.00

WALT DISNEY SHOWCASE
Oct, 1970 - No. 54, Jan, 1980 (No. 44-48, 68pp, 49-54, 52pp)
Gold Key

	Good	Fine	Mint
1-Boatniks (Movie)-Photo-c	1.00	3.00	6.00
2-Moby Duck	.50	1.50	3.00
3-Bongo & Lumpjaw-r	.35	1.00	2.00
4-Pluto-r	.35	1.00	2.00
5-$1,000,000 Duck (Movie)-Photo-c	.70	2.00	4.00
6-Bedknobs & Broomsticks (Movie)	.70	2.00	4.00
7-Pluto-r	,35	1.00	2.00
8-Daisy & Donald	.35	1.00	2.00
9-101 Dalmatians (cartoon feature); r-4-Color 1183	.50	1.50	3.00
10-Napoleon & Samantha (Movie)-Photo-c	.70	2.00	4.00
11-Moby Duck-r	.25	.75	1.50
12-Dumbo-r/4-Color 668	.35	1.00	2.00
13-Pluto-r	.30	.90	1.80
14-World's Greatest Athlete (Movie)-Photo-c	.70	2.00	4.00
15-3 Little Pigs-r	.25	.75	1.50
16-Aristocats (cartoon feature); r-Aristocats No. 1	.70	2.00	4.00
17-Mary Poppins; r-M.P. No. 10136-501-Photo-c	.70	2.00	4.00
18-Gyro Gearloose; Barks-r/4-Color No. 1047,1184	.70	2.00	4.00
19-That Darn Cat; r-T.D.C. No. 10171-602-Haley Mills photo-c	.50	1.50	3.00
20-Pluto-r	.25	.75	1.50
21-Li'l Bad Wolf & The Three Little Pigs	.30	.90	1.80
22-Unbirthday Party with Alice in Wonderland; r-4-Color No. 341	.50	1.50	3.00
23-Pluto-r	.25	.75	1.50
24-Herbie Rides Again (Movie); sequel to ''The Love Bug''-Photo-c	.35	1.00	2.00
25-Old Yeller (Movie); r-4-Color No. 869-Photo-c	.35	1.00	2.00
26-Lt. Robin Crusoe USN (Movie); r-Lt. Robin Crusoe USN No. 10191-601-Photo-c	.35	1.00	2.00
27-Island at the Top of the World (Movie)-Photo-c	.40	1.25	2.50
28-Brer Rabbit, Bucky Bug-r/WDC&S 58	.25	.75	1.50
29-Escape to Witch Mountain (Movie)-Photo-c	.35	1.00	2.00
30-Magica De Spell; Barks-r/Uncle Scrooge No. 36 & WDC&S No. 258	.85	2.50	5.00
31-Bambi (cartoon feature); r-4-Color No. 186	.50	1.50	3.00
32-Spin & Marty-r/F.C. 1026; Mickey Mouse Club (TV)-Photo-c	.50	1.50	3.00
33-Pluto-r/F.C. 1143	.25	.75	1.50
34-Paul Revere's Ride with Johnny Tremain (TV); 4-Color No. 822-r	.25	.75	1.50
35-Goofy-r/F.C. 952	.25	.75	1.50
36-Peter Pan-r/F.C. 442	.25	.75	1.50
37-Tinker Bell & Jiminy Crickett-r/F.C. 982,989	.25	.75	1.50
38-Mickey & the Sleuth, Part 1	.25	.75	1.50
39-Mickey & the Sleuth, Part 2	.25	.75	1.50
40-The Rescuers (cartoon feature)	.40	.90	1.80
41-Herbie Goes to Monte Carlo (Movie); sequel to ''Herbie Rides Again''-Photo-c	.25	.75	1.50
42-Mickey & the Sleuth	.25	.75	1.50
43-Pete's Dragon (Movie)-Photo-c	.35	1.00	2.00
44-Return From Witch Mountain (new) & In Search of the Castaways-r (Movies)-Photo-c; 68 pg. giants begin	.50	1.50	3.00
45-The Jungle Book (Movie); r-No. 30033-803	.50	1.50	3.00
46-The Cat From Outer Space (Movie)(new), & The Shaggy Dog (Movie)-r/F.C. 985-Photo-c	.50	1.50	3.00
47-Mickey Mouse Surprise Party-r	.50	1.50	3.00
48-The Wonderful Advs. of Pinocchio-r/F.C. 1203; last 68 pg. issue	.50	1.50	3.00
49-North Avenue Irregulars (Movie); Zorro-r/Zorro 11; 52 pgs. begin; photo-c	.25	.75	1.50
50-Bedknobs & Broomsticks-r/No. 6; Mooncussers-r/World of Adv. No. 1-Photo-c	.25	.75	1.50
51-101 Dalmatians-r	.25	.75	1.50
52-Unidentified Flying Oddball (Movie); r-/Picnic Party 8-Photo-c	.25	.75	1.50
53-The Scarecrow-r (TV)	.25	.75	1.50
54-The Black Hole (Movie)-Photo-c	.25	.75	1.50

WALT DISNEY'S MAGAZINE (Formerly Walt Disney's Mickey Mouse Club Magazine) (50 cents) (Bi-monthly)
V2No.4, June, 1957 - V4No.6, Oct, 1959
Western Publishing Co.

	Good	Fine	Mint
V2No.4-Stories & articles on the Mouseketeers, Zorro, & Goofy and other Disney characters & people	2.65	8.00	18.00
V2No.5, V2No.6(10/57)	2.65	8.00	18.00
V3No.1(12/57), V3No.3-6(10/58)	1.50	4.50	10.00
V3No.2-Annette photo-c	3.50	10.50	24.00
V4No.1(12/58) - V4No.2-4,6(10/59)	1.50	4.50	10.00
V4No.5-Annette photo-c	2.65	8.00	18.00

NOTE: *V2No.4-V3No.6 were 11½x8½'', 48 pgs.; V4No.1 on were 10x8'', 52 pgs. (Peak circulation of 400,000).*

WALT DISNEY'S MERRY CHRISTMAS (See Dell Giant No. 39)

WALT DISNEY'S MICKEY MOUSE CLUB MAGAZINE (Becomes Walt Disney's Magazine) (Quarterly)
Winter, 1956 - V2No.3, April, 1957 (11½x8½'') (48 pgs.)
Western Publishing Co.

	Good	Fine	Mint
V1No.1	7.00	21.00	50.00
2-4	3.65	11.00	25.00
V2No.1-3	2.85	8.50	20.00
Annual(1956)-Two different issues; ($1.50-Whitman); 120 pgs., cardboard covers, 11¾x8¾''; reprints	7.00	21.00	50.00
Annual(1957)-Same as above	5.00	15.00	35.00

WALT DISNEY'S WHEATIES PREMIUMS (See Wheaties)

WALTER LANTZ ANDY PANDA (Also see Andy Panda)
Aug, 1973 - No. 23, Jan, 1978 (Walter Lantz)
Gold Key

	Good	Fine	Mint
1-Reprints	.35	1.00	2.00
2-10-All reprints		.40	.80
11-23: 15,17-19,22-Reprints		.15	.30

WALT SCOTT'S CHRISTMAS STORIES (See 4-Color No. 959,1062)

WAMBI, JUNGLE BOY (See Jungle Comics)
Spring, 1942 - No. 3, Spring, 1943; No. 4, Fall, 1948 - No. 18, Winter, 1952-53
Fiction House Magazines

	Good	Fine	Mint
1-Wambi, the Jungle Boy begins	22.00	65.00	154.00
2 (1942)	11.00	33.00	76.00
3 (1943)	8.50	25.50	60.00
4(1948)-Origin in text	5.00	15.00	35.00
5-10	4.00	12.00	28.00
11-18	3.00	9.00	21.00
I.W. Reprint No. 8('64)-Reprints Fiction House No. 12 with new cover	1.00	3.00	6.00

WANTED COMICS
No. 9, Sept-Oct, 1947 - No. 53, April, 1953
Toytown Publications/Patches/Orbit Publ.

	Good	Fine	Mint
9	4.65	14.00	32.00
10,11: 10-Giunta-a; radio's Mr. D. A. app.	2.85	8.50	20.00
12-Used in **SOTI**, pg. 277	5.75	17.25	40.00
13-Heroin drug propaganda story	4.65	14.00	32.00
14-Marijuana drug mention story, 2 pgs.	2.65	8.00	18.00
15-17,19,20	2.00	6.00	14.00
18-Marijuana story, 'Satan's Cigarettes'; r-in No. 45 & retitled	9.00	27.00	62.00
21-Krigstein-a	2.65	8.00	18.00
22-Extreme violence	2.50	7.50	17.50
23,25-34,36-38,40-44,46-48,53	1.15	3.50	8.00
24-Krigstein-a; 'The Dope King,' marijuana mention story	4.65	14.00	32.00
35-Used in **SOTI**, pg. 160	4.65	14.00	32.00
39-Drug propaganda story ''The Horror Weed''	5.50	16.50	38.00
45-Marijuana story from No. 18	5.50	16.50	38.00
49-Has unstable pink-c that fades easily; rare in mint condition	1.85	5.00	11.50
50-surrealist-c; horror stys	4.65	14.00	32.00
51-''Holiday of Horror''-junkie story; drug-c	4.65	14.00	32.00
52-Classic ''Cult of Killers'' opium use story	4.65	14.00	32.00

NOTE: ***Lawrence** and **Leav** c/a most issues.*

WANTED: DEAD OR ALIVE (See 4-Color No. 1102,1164)

WANTED, THE WORLD'S MOST DANGEROUS VILLAINS
July-Aug, 1972 - No. 9, Aug-Sept, 1973 (All reprints)
National Periodical Publications (See DC Special)

	Good	Fine	Mint
1-Batman, Green Lantern, & Green Arrow		.60	1.20
2-Batman & The Flash		.40	.80
3-Dr. Fate, Hawkman, & Vigilante		.40	.80
4-Green Lantern & Kid Eternity		.40	.80
5-Dollman/Green Lantern		.30	.60
6-Starman/Wildcat/Sargon		.30	.60
7-Johnny Quick/Hawkman/Hourman		.30	.60
8-Dr. Fate/Flash		.30	.60
9-S&K Sandman/Superman		.30	.60

NOTE: ***Kubert** a-3i, 6, 7.*

WAR
7/75 - No. 9, 11/76; No. 10, 9/78 - No. 49?, 1984
Charlton Comics

	Good	Fine	Mint
1		.15	.30
2-49: 47-r		.15	.30
7,9(Modern Comics-r, 1977)		.15	.30

WAR ACTION
April, 1952 - No. 14, June, 1953
Atlas Comics (CPS)

	Good	Fine	Mint
1	2.85	8.50	20.00
2	1.50	4.50	10.00
3-6,8-10,14	1.35	4.00	9.00
7-Pakula-a	1.35	4.00	9.00
11-13-Krigstein-a	2.75	8.00	18.00

NOTE: ***Heath** a-1; c-7, 14. **Keller** a-6. **Maneely** a-1.*

WAR ADVENTURES
Jan, 1952 - No. 13, Feb, 1953
Atlas Comics (HPC)

	Good	Fine	Mint
1-Tuska-a	2.85	8.50	20.00
2	1.50	4.50	10.00
3-7,9-13	1.35	4.00	9.00
8-Krigstein-a	2.75	8.00	18.00

NOTE: ***Heath** c-4, 13. **Robinson** a-3; c-10.*

WAR ADVENTURES ON THE BATTLEFIELD (See Battlefield)

WAR AGAINST CRIME! (Vault of Horror No. 12 on)
Spring, 1948 - No. 11, Feb-Mar, 1950
E. C. Comics

	Good	Fine	Mint
1	35.00	105.00	245.00
2,3	20.00	60.00	140.00
4-9: 9-Morphine drug use story	19.00	57.00	132.00
10-1st Vault Keeper app.	52.00	155.00	365.00
11-2nd Vault Keeper app.	45.00	135.00	315.00

NOTE: *All have **Craig** covers. **Feldstein** a-4, 7-9. **Ingels** a-1, 2, 8.*

WAR AND ATTACK (Also see Special War Series No. 3)
Fall, 1964 - V2No.63, Dec, 1967
Charlton Comics

	Good	Fine	Mint
1-Wood-a	.85	2.50	5.00
V2No.54(6/66)-No. 63 (Formerly Fightin' Air Force)		.40	.80

NOTE: ***Montes/Bache** a-55, 56, 60, 63.*

WAR AT SEA (Formerly Space Adventures)
No. 22, Nov, 1957 - No. 42, June, 1961
Charlton Comics

	Good	Fine	Mint
22	1.00	3.00	7.00
23-30	.50	1.50	3.50
31-42	.35	1.00	2.00

WAR BATTLES
Feb, 1952 - No. 9, Dec, 1953
Harvey Publications

	Good	Fine	Mint
1	2.75	8.00	18.00
2	1.50	4.50	10.00
3-5,7-9	1.35	4.00	9.00
6-Nostrand-a	2.35	7.00	16.00

NOTE: ***Powell** a-1-3, 7.*

WAR BIRDS
1952
Fiction House Magazines

	Good	Fine	Mint
1	4.65	14.00	32.00
2	2.65	8.00	18.00
3-7	2.50	7.50	17.50

WAR COMBAT (Combat Casey No. 6 on)
March, 1952 - No. 5, Nov, 1952
Atlas Comics (LBI 1/SAI 2-5)

	Good	Fine	Mint
1	2.35	7.00	16.00
2	1.20	3.50	8.00
3-5	1.00	3.00	7.00

NOTE: ***Berg** a-2, 4, 5. **Henkel** a-5. **Maneely** a-1, 4.*

Wambi, Jungle Boy #8, © FH

War Against Crime #5, © WMG

War Birds #1, © FH

War Comics #26, © MCG

War Fury #4, © Comic Media

Warlock #12, © MCG

WAR COMICS (See Key Ring Comics)
May, 1940 (No mo. given) - No. 8, Feb-Apr, 1943
Dell Publishing Co.

	Good	Fine	Mint
1-Sikandur the Robot Master, Sky Hawk, Scoop Mason, War Correspondent begin	19.00	57.00	132.00
2-Origin Greg Gilday	9.50	28.50	65.00
3-Joan becomes Greg Gilday's aide	6.50	19.50	45.00
4-Origin Night Devils	8.50	25.50	60.00
5-8	5.00	15.00	35.00

WAR COMICS
Dec, 1950 - No. 49, Sept, 1957
Marvel/Atlas (USA No. 1-41/JPI No. 42-49)

	Good	Fine	Mint
1	4.00	12.00	28.00
2	2.00	6.00	14.00
3-10	1.70	5.00	12.00
11-20	1.00	3.00	7.00
21,23-32: Last precode (2/55). 26-Valley Forge story	.85	2.50	6.00
22-Krigstein-a	2.75	8.00	18.00
33-37,39-42,44,45,47,48	.70	2.00	5.00
38-Kubert/Moskowitz-a	2.00	6.00	14.00
43,49-Torres-a. 43-Davis E.C. swipe	2.00	6.00	14.00
46-Crandall-a	2.00	6.00	14.00

NOTE: ***Colan*** *a-4, 48, 49.* ***Drucker*** *a-37, 43, 48.* ***Everett*** *a-17.* ***Heath*** *a-7-9, 19.* ***G. Kane*** *a-19.* ***Orlando*** *a-42, 48.* ***Pakula*** *a-26.* ***Reinman*** *a-26.* ***Robinson*** *a-15.* ***Severin*** *a-26; c-48.*

WAR DOGS OF THE U.S. ARMY
1952
Avon Periodicals

	Good	Fine	Mint
1-Kinstler c/a	6.35	19.00	44.00

WARFRONT
9/51 - No. 35, 11/58; No. 36, 10/65; No. 37, 9/66 - No. 38, 12/66; No. 39, 2/67
Harvey Publications

	Good	Fine	Mint
1	3.00	9.00	21.00
2	1.50	4.50	10.00
3-10	1.35	4.00	9.00
11,12,14,16-20	.85	2.50	6.00
13,15,22-Nostrand-a	2.75	8.00	18.00
21,23-27,29,31-33,35	.70	2.00	5.00
28,30,34-Kirby-c	1.35	4.00	9.00
36-Dynamite Joe begins, ends No. 39; Williamson-a	1.35	4.00	9.00
37-Wood-a, 17pgs.	1.35	4.00	9.00
38,39-Wood-a, 2-3 pgs.; Lone Tiger app.	.85	2.50	6.00

NOTE: ***Powell*** *a-1-6, 9-11, 14, 17, 20, 23, 25-28, 30, 31, 34, 36.* ***Powell/Nostrand*** *a-12, 13, 15.* ***Simon*** *c-36?, 38.*

WAR FURY
Sept, 1952 - No. 4, March, 1953
Comic Media/Harwell (Allen Hardy Associates)

	Good	Fine	Mint
1-Heck c/a in all	2.65	8.00	18.00
2-4: 4-Morisi-a	1.35	4.00	9.00

WAR GODS OF THE DEEP (See Movie Classics)

WAR HEROES (See Marine War Heroes)

WAR HEROES
July-Sept, 1942 (no month); No. 2, Oct-Dec, 1942 - No. 10, Oct-Dec, 1944; No. 11, Mar, 1945
Dell Publishing Co.

	Good	Fine	Mint
1	7.00	21.00	50.00
2	3.50	10.50	24.00
3,5	3.00	9.00	21.00
4-Disney's Gremlins app.	7.00	21.00	50.00
6-11: 6-Tothish-a by Discount	2.65	8.00	18.00

NOTE: *No. 1 was to be released in July, but was delayed.* ***Cameron*** *a-6.*

WAR HEROES
May, 1952 - No. 8, April, 1953
Ace Magazines

	Good	Fine	Mint
1	2.65	8.00	18.00
2	1.35	4.00	9.00
3-8	1.20	3.50	8.00

WAR HEROES
Feb, 1963 - No. 27, Nov, 1967
Charlton Comics

	Good	Fine	Mint
1	.50	1.50	3.00
2-10	.30	.80	1.60
11-27: 27-1st Devils Brigade by Glanzman		.30	.60

NOTE: ***Montes/Bache*** *a-3-7, 21, 25, 27; c-3-7.*

WAR IS HELL
Jan, 1973 - No. 15, Oct, 1975
Marvel Comics Group

	Good	Fine	Mint
1-Williamson-a(r), 3pgs.		.40	.80
2-9-All reprints		.30	.60
10-15		.15	.30

NOTE: ***Bolle*** *a-3r.* ***Powell, Woodbridge*** *a-1. Sgt. Fury reprints-7, 8.*

WARLOCK (The Power of . . .) (See Strange Tales)
Aug, 1972 - No. 8, Oct, 1973; No. 9, Oct, 1975 - No. 15, Nov, 1976
Marvel Comics Group

	Good	Fine	Mint
1-Origin by Kane	.85	2.50	5.00
2,3	.40	1.20	2.40
4-8: 4-Death of Eddie Roberts	.35	1.00	2.00
9-15-Starlin-c/a in all. 10-Origin Thanos & Gamora. 14-Origin Star Thief	.35	1.00	2.00

NOTE: ***Buscema*** *a-2p; c-8p.* ***G. Kane*** *a-1p, 3-5p; c-1p, 2, 3, 4p, 5p, 7p.* ***Starlin*** *a-9-14p, 15; c-12p, 13-15.* ***Sutton*** *a-1-8i.*

WARLOCK
12/82 - No. 6, 5/83 ($2.00) (slick paper) (Direct Sales only)
Marvel Comics Group

	Good	Fine	Mint
1-Starlin Warlock r-/Str. Tales No. 178-180; Starlin-c	.35	1.00	2.00
2(1/83)-Starlin Warlock r-/Str. Tales No. 180,181 & Warlock No. 9; Starlin-c	.35	1.00	2.00
3-Starlin-a(r)/Warlock No. 10-12	.35	1.00	2.00
4-Starlin-a(r)/Warlock No. 12-15	.35	1.00	2.00
5-Starlin-a(r)/Warlock No. 15	.35	1.00	2.00
6	.35	1.00	2.00
Special Edition No. 1(12/83)	.35	1.00	2.00

NOTE: ***Byrne*** *a-5r.* ***Starlin*** *a-3-6r; c-1-4.*

WARLORD (See First Issue Special)
Jan-Feb, 1976; No.2, Mar-Apr, 1976; No.3, Oct-Nov, 1976 -Present
National Periodical Publications/DC Comics

	Good	Fine	Mint
1-Story cont'd. from 1st Issue Special No. 8	2.50	7.50	15.00
2-Intro. Machiste	1.25	3.75	7.50
3-5	.90	2.75	5.50
6-10: 6-Intro Mariah. 7-Origin Machiste. 9-Dons new costume	.85	2.50	5.00
11-20: 11-Origin-r. 12-Intro Aton. 15-Tara returns; Warlord has son	.60	1.80	3.60
21-30: 27-New facts about origin. 28-1st app. Wizard World	.45	1.25	2.50
31-36,39,40: 32-Intro Shakira. 39-Omac ends. 40-Warlord gets new costume	.35	1.00	2.00
37,38-Origin Omac by Starlin. 38-Intro Jennifer Morgan, Warlord's daughter	.35	1.00	2.00
41-47,49-52: 42-47-Omac back-up series. 49-Claw The Unconquered app. 50-Death of Aton. 51-r-/No.1.	.25	.75	1.50
48-(52pgs.)-1st app. Arak; contains free 16pg. Arak Son of Thunder; Claw The Unconquered app.	.35	1.00	2.00

53-80: 55-Arion Lord of Atlantis begins, ends No. 62. 63-The Barren

WARLORD (continued) — Good / Fine / Mint

Earth begins; contains free 16pg. Masters of the Universe .50 1.00
81-99,101-115: 91-Origin w/new facts .40 .80
100-Double size ($1.25) .65 1.30
Remco Toy Giveaway (2¾x4'') .50 1.00
Annual 1(11/82)-Grell c, a(p) .60 1.20
Annual 2(10/83) .50 1.00
Annual 3(9/84), 4(8/85), 5(9/86) .65 1.30

NOTE: ***Grell** a-1-15, 16-50p, 51r, 52p, 59p, Annual 1p; c-1-70, Annual 1. **Wayne Howard** a-64i. **Starlin** a-37-39p.*

WARLORDS (See DC Graphic Novel No. 2)

WARP
March, 1983 - No. 19, Feb, 1985 ($1.00-$1,25, Mando paper)
First Comics

1-Sargon-Mistress of War app. .30 .90 1.80
2-5: 2-Faceless Ones begins .65 1.30
6-10: 10-New Warp advs., & Outrider begin .50 1.00
11-19 .45 .90
Special 1(7/83, 36 pgs.)-Origin Chaos-Prince of Madness; origin of Warp Universe begins, ends No. 3 .50 1.00
Special 2(1/84)-Lord Cumulus vs. Sargon Mistress of War ($1.00) .50 1.00
Special 3(6/84)-Chaos-Prince of Madness .50 1.00

NOTE: ***Brunner** a-1-9p; c-1-9. **Chaykin** a(p)-Special 1; c-Special 1. **Ditko** a-2-4. **Staton** a-1i. No. 1-9 are adapted from the Warp plays.*

WARPATH
Nov, 1954 - No. 3, April, 1955
Key Publications/Stanmor

1 2.65 8.00 18.00
2,3 1.50 4.50 10.00

WARP GRAPHICS ANNUAL
Dec, 1985 ($2.50 cover)
WaRP Graphics

1-Elfquest, Blood of the Innocent, Thunderbunny & Myth-adventures app. .40 1.25 2.50

WARREN PRESENTS
Jan, 1979 - No. 14?, 1983?
Warren Publications

1-14-Eerie, Creepy, & Vampirella-r .50 1.00

WAR REPORT
Sept, 1952 - No. 5, May, 1953
Ajax/Farrell Publications (Excellent Publ.)

1 2.65 8.00 18.00
2 1.35 4.00 9.00
3,5 1.20 3.50 8.00
4-Used in **POP**, pg. 94 2.00 6.00 14.00

WARRIOR COMICS
1945 (1930's DC reprints)
H. C. Blackerby

1-Wing Brady, The Iron Man, Mark Markon 4.00 12.00 28.00

WAR ROMANCES (See True. . .)

WAR SHIPS
1942 (36 pgs.) (Similar to Large Feature Comics)
Dell Publishing Co.

Cover by McWilliams; contains photos & drawings of U.S. war ships 5.75 17.25 40.00

WAR STORIES
1942 - No. 8, Feb-Apr, 1943
Dell Publishing Co.

	Good	Fine	Mint
1	7.00	21.00	50.00
2	4.35	13.00	30.00
3,4,6-8: 6-8-Night Devils	4.00	12.00	28.00
5-Origin The Whistler	5.00	15.00	35.00

WAR STORIES (Korea)
Sept, 1952 - No. 5, May, 1953
Ajax/Farrell Publications (Excellent Publ.)

1 2.65 8.00 18.00
2 1.35 4.00 9.00
3-5 1.20 3.50 8.00

WAR STORIES (See Star Spangled. . .)

WART AND THE WIZARD
Feb, 1964 (Walt Disney)
Gold Key

1 (10102-402) 1.75 5.25 12.00

WARTIME ROMANCES
July, 1951 - No. 18, Nov, 1953
St. John Publishing Co.

1-All Baker-a 10.00 30.00 70.00
2-All Baker-a 6.00 18.00 42.00
3,4-All Baker-a 5.75 17.25 40.00
5-8-Baker c/a(2-3) each 5.15 15.50 36.00
9-12,16,18-Baker c/a each 3.75 11.25 26.00
13-15,17-Baker-c only 2.75 8.25 19.00

WAR VICTORY ADVENTURES (No. 1 titled War Victory Comics)
Summer, 1942 - No. 3, Winter, 1943-44 (5 cents)
U.S. Treasury Dept./War Victory/Harvey Publ.

1-(Promotion of Savings Bonds)-Featuring America's greatest comic art by top syndicated cartoonists; Blondie, Joe Palooka, Green Hornet, Dick Tracy, Superman, Gumps, etc.; (36 pgs.) 17.00 51.00 120.00
2-Powell-a 8.00 24.00 56.00
3-Capt. Red Cross (cover & text only); Powell-a 6.50 19.50 45.00

WAR WAGON, THE (See Movie Classics)

WAR WINGS
October, 1968
Charlton Comics

1 .50 1.00

WASHABLE JONES & SHMOO
June, 1953
Harvey Publications

1 8.00 24.00 56.00

WASH TUBBS (See 4-Color No. 11,28,53)

WATCHMEN
Sept, 1986 - No. 12, 1987 (12 issue mixi-series)
DC Comics

1-Alan Moore scripts in all .50 1.50 3.00
2,3 .35 1.00 2.00
4-8 .25 .75 1.50

WATCH OUT FOR BIG TALK
1950
Giveaway

Dan Barry-a (about crooked politicians) 2.35 7.00 14.00

WATER BIRDS AND THE OLYMPIC ELK (See 4-Color No. 700)

Warp #2, © First

Wartime Romances #6, © STJ

Watchmen #1, © DC

Web of Mystery #22, © ACE

Web of Spider-Man #1, © MCG

Weird Adventures #2, © P.L. Publ.

WAYFARERS, THE
Oct, 1986 - Present ($1.80, color)
Eternity Comics

	Good	Fine	Mint
1-Super-hero team	.30	.90	1.80

WEATHER-BIRD (See Comics From . . . & Free Comics to You . . .)
1958 - No. 16, July, 1962 (Giveaway)
International Shoe Co./Western Printing Co.

	Good	Fine	Mint
1	.50	1.50	3.00
2-16	.25	.75	1.50

NOTE: *The numbers are located in the lower bottom panel, pg. 1. All feature a character called Weather-Bird.*

WEATHER BIRD COMICS (See Comics From Weather Bird)
1957 (Giveaway)
Weather Bird Shoes

nn-Contains a comic bound with new cover. Several combinations possible; contents determines price (40 - 60 percent of contents).

WEB OF EVIL
Nov, 1952 - No. 21, Dec, 1954
Comic Magazines/Quality Comics Group

	Good	Fine	Mint
1-Used in **SOTI**, pg. 388. Jack Cole-a; morphine use story	12.00	36.00	84.00
2,3-Jack Cole-a. 2-Bra & slip panels	6.50	19.50	45.00
4,6,7-Jack Cole c/a	8.00	24.00	56.00
5-Electrocution-c; Jack Cole-c/a	9.50	28.50	65.00
8-11-Jack Cole-a	4.35	13.00	30.00
12,13,15,16,19-21	3.15	9.50	22.00
14-Part Crandall-c; Old Witch swipe	3.65	11.00	25.00
17-Opium drug propaganda story	3.85	11.50	27.00
18-Acid-in-face story	3.65	11.00	25.00

NOTE: ***Jack Cole** a(2 each)-2, 6, 8, 9. **Ravielli** a-13.*

WEB OF HORROR (Magazine)
Dec, 1969 - No. 3, Apr, 1970
Major Magazines

	Good	Fine	Mint
1-Jones-c; Wrightson-a	3.00	9.00	18.00
2-Jones-c; Wrightson-a(2), Kaluta-a	2.00	6.00	12.00
3-Wrightson-c; Brunner, Kaluta, Bruce Jones, Wrightson-a	2.00	6.00	12.00

WEB OF MYSTERY
Feb, 1951 - No. 29, Sept, 1955
Ace Magazines (A. A. Wyn)

	Good	Fine	Mint
1	7.00	21.00	50.00
2-Bakerish-a	4.35	13.00	30.00
3-10	3.50	10.50	24.00
11-18,20-26: 20-r/The Beyond No. 1	3.00	9.00	21.00
19-r-Chall. of Unknown No. 6 used in N.Y. Legislative Committee	3.50	10.50	24.00
27-Bakerish-a (r-/The Beyond No. 2); last pre-code issue	3.00	9.00	21.00
28,29: 28-All-r	2.35	7.00	16.00

NOTE: *This series was to appear as "Creepy Stories," but title was changed before publication. **Cameron** a-6, 8, 12, 13, 17, 18-20, 22, 24, 25, 27; c-8, 13, 17. **Colan** a-4. **Palais** a-28r. **Sekowsky** a-1-3, 7, 8, 11, 14, 21, 29. **Tothish** a-by Bill Discount No. 16. No. 29-all-r, 19-28-partial-r.*

WEB OF SPIDER-MAN, THE
Apr, 1985 - Present
Marvel Comics Group

	Good	Fine	Mint
1	.75	2.25	4.50
2,3	.45	1.40	2.80
4-8	.30	.90	1.80
9-13	.25	.70	1.40
14-20: 19-Intro Humbug & Solo		.50	1.00
21-25		.45	.90
Annual 1 (9/85)	.35	1.00	2.00
Annual 2 (9/86)-New Mutants app; Art Adams-a	.35	1.10	2.20

WEDDING BELLS
Feb, 1954 - No. 19, 1956
Quality Comics Group

	Good	Fine	Mint
1-Whitney-a	5.00	15.00	35.00
2	2.50	7.50	17.50
3-9	1.65	5.00	11.50
10-Ward-a, 9 pgs.	6.85	20.50	48.00
11-14,17	1.30	4.00	9.00
15-Baker-c	2.00	6.00	14.00
16-Baker-c/a	3.15	9.50	22.00
18,19-Baker-a each	2.65	8.00	18.00

WEEKENDER, THE
1945 - 1946 (52 pages)
Rucker Publ. Co.

	Good	Fine	Mint
V1No.4(1945)	7.00	21.00	50.00
V2No.1-36 pgs. comics, 16 in newspaper format with photos; partial Dynamic Comics reprints; 4 pgs. of cels from the Disney film Pinocchio; Little Nemo story by Winsor McCay, Jr.; Jack Cole-a	11.00	33.00	76.00

WEEKLY COMIC MAGAZINE
May 12, 1940 (16 pgs.) (Full Color)
Fox Publications

(1st Version)-8 pg. Blue Beetle story, 7 pg. Patty O'Day story; two copies known to exist. Estimated value. . . . $500.00
(2nd Version)-7 two-pg. adventures of Blue Beetle, Patty O'Day, Yarko, Dr. Fung, Green Mask, Spark Stevens, & Rex Dexter; one copy known to exist Estimated value. . . . $400.00

Discovered with business papers, letters and exploitation material promoting **Weekly Comic Magazine** for use by newspapers in the same manner of **The Spirit** weeklies. Interesting note: these are dated three weeks before the first **Spirit** comic. Letters indicate that samples may have been sent to a few newspapers. These sections were actually 15½x22" pages which will fold down to an approximate 8x10" comic booklet. Other various comic sections were found with the above, but were more like the Sunday comic sections in format.

WEIRD (Magazine)
1/66 - V8No.6, 12/74; V9No.1, 1/75 - V10No.3, 1977
(V1-V8, 52 pgs.; V9 on, 68 pgs.)
Eerie Publications

	Good	Fine	Mint
V1No.10(No.1)-Intro. Morris the Caretaker of Weird (ends V2No.10); Burgos-a	.70	2.00	4.00
11,12	.35	1.00	2.00
V2No.1-4(10/67), V3No.1(1/68), V2No.6(4/68)-V2No.7,9,10(12/68), V3No.1(2/69)-V3No.4	.35	1.00	2.00
V2No.8-Reprints Ditko's 1st story/Fantastic Fears No. 5	.50	1.50	3.00
5(12/69)-Rulah reprint; "Rulah" changed to "Pulah;" LSD story-reprinted in Horror Tales V4No.4, Tales From the Tomb V2No.4, & Terror Tales V7No.3	.35	1.00	2.00
V4No.1-6('70), V5No.1-6('71), V6No.1-7('72), V7No.1-6('73), V8No.1-6('74), V9No.1-4(1/75-'76)(no V9No.1), V10No.1-3('77)	.35	1.00	2.00

WEIRD ADVENTURES
May-June, 1951 - No. 3, Sept-Oct, 1951
P. L. Publishing Co. (Canada)

	Good	Fine	Mint
1-"The She-Wolf Killer" by Matt Baker, 6 pgs.	10.00	30.00	70.00
2-Bondage/hypodermic panel; opium den text story	6.50	19.50	45.00
3-Male bondage/torture-c; severed head story	5.75	17.25	40.00

WEIRD ADVENTURES
No. 10, July-Aug, 1951

WEIRD ADVENTURES (continued)
Ziff-Davis Publishing Co.

	Good	Fine	Mint
10-Painted-c	6.50	19.50	45.00

WEIRD CHILLS
July, 1954 - No. 3, Nov, 1954
Key Publications

	Good	Fine	Mint
1-Wolverton-a r-/Weird Mysteries No. 4; blood transfusion-c	15.00	45.00	105.00
2-Injury to eye-c	16.50	50.00	115.00
3-Bondage E.C. swipe-c	7.00	21.00	50.00

NOTE: *Baily c-1.*

WEIRD COMICS
April, 1940 - No. 20, Jan, 1942
Fox Features Syndicate

	Good	Fine	Mint
1-The Birdman, Thor, God of Thunder (ends No. 5), The Sorceress of Zoom, Blast Bennett, Typhon, Voodoo Man, & Dr. Mortal begin; Fine bondage-c	80.00	240.00	560.00
2-Lou Fine-c	40.00	120.00	280.00
3,4: 3-Simon-c. 4-Torture-c	28.00	84.00	195.00
5-Intro. Dart & sidekick Ace (ends No. 20); bondage/hypo-c	30.00	90.00	210.00
6,7-Dynamite Thor app. in each	28.00	84.00	195.00
8-Dynamo, the Eagle & sidekick Buddy & Marga, the Panther Woman begin	28.00	84.00	195.00
9	21.00	62.00	146.00
10-Navy Jones app.	21.00	62.00	146.00
11-16: 16-Flag-c	18.00	54.00	125.00
17-Origin The Black Rider	18.00	54.00	125.00
18-20: 20-Origin The Rapier; Swoop Curtis app; Churchill, Hitler-c	18.00	54.00	125.00

WEIRD FANTASY (Formerly A Moon, A Girl, Romance; becomes Weird Science-Fantasy No. 23 on)
No. 13, May-June, 1950 - No. 22, Nov-Dec, 1953
E. C. Comics

	Good	Fine	Mint
13(No.1) (1950)	80.00	240.00	560.00
14-Necronomicon story; atomic explosion-c	45.00	130.00	300.00
15,16: 16-Used in **SOTI**, pg. 144	35.00	105.00	245.00
17 (1951)	28.00	85.00	195.00
6-10	21.50	65.00	150.00
11-13 (1952)	16.00	48.00	110.00
14-Frazetta/Williamson(1st team-up at E.C.)/Krenkel-a, 7 pgs.; Orlando draws E.C. staff	30.00	90.00	210.00
15-Williamson/Evans-a(3), 4,3,&7 pgs.	18.00	54.00	125.00
16-19-Williamson/Krenkel-a in all. 18-Williamson/Feldstein-c	16.00	48.00	110.00
20-Frazetta/Williamson-a, 7 pgs.	18.00	54.00	125.00
21-Frazetta/Williamson-c & Williamson/Krenkel-a	30.00	90.00	210.00
22-Bradbury adaptation	12.50	37.50	85.00

NOTE: ***Crandall** a-22. **Elder** a-17. **Feldstein** a-13(No.1)-8; c-13(No.1)-18 (No.18 w/**Williamson**), 20. **Kamen** a-13(No.1)-16, 18-22. **Krigstein** a-22. **Kurtzman** a-13(No.1)-17(No.5), 6. **Orlando** a-9-22 (2 stories in No. 16); c-19, 22. **Severin/Elder** a-18-21. **Wood** a-13(No.1)-14, 17(2 stories ea. in No. 10-13). Canadian reprints exist; see Table of Contents.*

WEIRD HORRORS (Nightmare No. 10 on)
June, 1952 - No. 9, Oct, 1953
St. John Publishing Co.

	Good	Fine	Mint
1-Tuska-a	10.00	30.00	70.00
2	5.75	17.25	40.00
3-Finesque-a; hashish story	6.50	19.50	45.00
4,5-Finesque-a	5.50	16.50	38.00
6-Ekgren-c	11.50	34.50	80.00
7-Ekgren-c; Kubert, Cameron-a	12.00	36.00	84.00
8,9-Kubert c/a. 8-Bondage-c	8.50	25.50	60.00

NOTE: ***Cameron** a-7, 9. **Finesque** a-1, 2, 4. **Morisi** a-3.*

WEIRD MYSTERIES
Oct, 1952 - No. 14, Jan, 1955
Gillmore Publications

	Good	Fine	Mint
1-Partial Wolverton-c swiped from splash page ''Flight to the Future'' in Weird Tales of the Future No. 2; ''Eternity'' has an Ingels swipe	14.50	43.50	100.00
2-''Robot Woman'' by Wolverton; Bernard Baily-c-reprinted in Mister Mystery No. 18; acid in face panel	34.00	100.00	236.00
3,6: 3-Decapitation-c	8.00	24.00	56.00
4-''The Man Who Never Smiled'' (3 pgs.) by Wolverton; B. Baily skull-c	27.00	81.00	190.00
5-Wolverton story ''Swamp Monster,'' 6 pgs.; decapitation-c	27.00	81.00	190.00
7-Used in **SOTI**, illo-''Indeed'' & illo-''Sex and blood''	19.00	57.00	132.00
8-Wolverton-c panel reprint/No. 5; used in a 1954 Readers Digest anti-comics article by T. E. Murphy entitled ''For the Kiddies to Read''	8.00	24.00	56.00
9-Excessive violence, gore & torture	7.00	21.00	50.00
10-Silhouetted nudity panel	6.50	19.50	45.00
11-14 (No. 13,14-Exist?)	5.50	16.50	38.00

NOTE: ***Baily** c-2-8, 10-12.*

WEIRD MYSTERIES (Magazine)
Mar-Apr, 1959 (68 pages) (35 cents) (B&W)
Pastime Publications

	Good	Fine	Mint
1-Torres-a; E. C. swipe from TFTC No. 46 by Tuska-''The Ragman''	2.00	6.00	14.00

WEIRD MYSTERY TALES (See DC 100 Page Super Spectacular)

WEIRD MYSTERY TALES (See Cancelled Comic Cavalcade)
Jul-Aug, 1972 - No. 24, Nov, 1975
National Periodical Publications

	Good	Fine	Mint
1-Kirby-a		.50	1.00
2-24		.20	.40

NOTE: ***Alcala** a-5, 10, 13, 14. **Aparo** c-4. **Bolle** a-8. **Howard** a-4. **Kaluta** a-24; c-1. **G. Kane** a-10. **Kirby** a-1, 2p, 3p. **Nino** a-5, 6, 9, 13, 16, 21. **Redondo** a-9. **Starlin** a-2-4. **Wood** a-23. **Wrightson** c-21.*

WEIRD SCIENCE (Formerly Saddle Romances) (Becomes Weird Science-Fantasy No. 23 on)
No. 12, May-June, 1950 - No. 22, Nov-Dec, 1953
E. C. Comics

	Good	Fine	Mint
12(No.1) (1950)	82.00	245.00	575.00
13	45.00	135.00	315.00
14,15 (1950)	41.00	123.00	285.00
5-10	25.00	75.00	175.00
11-14 (1952)	16.00	48.00	110.00
15-18-Williamson/Krenkel-a in each; 15-Williamson-a. 17-Used in **POP**, pgs. 81,82	19.00	57.00	130.00
19,20-Williamson/Frazetta-a, 7 pgs each. 19-Used in **SOTI**, illo-''A young girl on her wedding night stabs her sleeping husband to death with a hatpin. . .''	25.00	75.00	175.00
21-Williamson/Frazetta-a, 6 pgs.; Wood draws E.C. staff; Gaines & Feldstein app. in story	25.00	75.00	175.00
22-Williamson/Frazetta/Krenkel-a, 8 pgs.; Wood draws himself in his story - last pg. & panel	25.00	75.00	175.00

NOTE: ***Elder** a-14, 19. **Evans** a-22. **Feldstein** a-12(No.1)-8; c-12(No.1)-8, 11. **Ingels** a-15. **Kamen** a-12(No.1)-13, 15-18, 20, 21. **Kurtzman** a-12(No.1)-7. **Orlando** a-10-22. **Wood** a-12(No.1), 13(No.2), 5-22 (No. 9, 10, 12, 13 all have 2 **Wood** stories); c-9, 10, 12-22. Canadian reprints exist; see Table of Contents.*

WEIRD SCIENCE-FANTASY (Formerly Weird Science & Weird Fantasy) (Becomes Incredible Science Fiction No. 30)

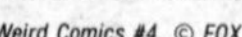
Weird Comics #4, © FOX

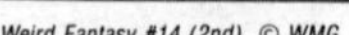
Weird Fantasy #14 (2nd), © WMG

Weird Horrors #1, © STJ

Weird Science-Fantasy Annual 1952, © WMG

Weird Tales of the Future #2, © S.P.M. Publ.

Weird Thrillers #2, © Z-D

WEIRD SCIENCE-FANTASY (continued)
No. 23 Mar, 1954 - No. 29, May-June, 1955
E. C. Comics

	Good	Fine	Mint
23-Williamson & Wood-a	18.00	55.00	125.00
24-Williamson & Wood-a; Harlan Ellison's 1st professional story, 'Upheaval!,' later adapted into a short story as 'Mealtime,' and then into a TV episode of *Voyage to the Bottom of the Sea* as 'The Price of Doom'	18.00	55.00	125.00
25-Williamson-c; Williamson/Torres/Krenkel-a plus Wood-a	22.00	65.00	154.00
26-Flying Saucer Report; Wood, Crandall, Orlando-a	17.00	51.00	120.00
27	18.00	55.00	125.00
28-Williamson/Krenkel/Torres-a; Wood-a	22.00	65.00	154.00
29-Frazetta-c; Williamson/Krenkel & Wood-a	42.00	125.00	295.00

NOTE: ***Crandall** a-26, 27, 29. **Evans** a-26. **Feldstein** c-24, 26, 28. **Kamen** a-27, 28. **Krigstein** a-23-25. **Orlando** a-in all. **Wood** a-in all; c-23, 27.*

WEIRD SCIENCE-FANTASY ANNUAL
1952, 1953 (Sold thru the E. C. office & on the stands in some major cities)
E. C. Comics

	Good	Fine	Mint
1952	104.00	312.00	725.00
1953	66.00	200.00	460.00

NOTE: *The 1952 annual contains books cover-dated in 1951 & 1952, and the 1953 annual from 1952 & 1953. Contents of each annual may vary in same year.*

WEIRD SUSPENSE
Feb, 1975 - No. 3, July, 1975
Atlas/Seaboard Publ.

	Good	Fine	Mint
1-Tarantula begins		.30	.60
2,3: 3-Buckler-c		.25	.50

WEIRD SUSPENSE STORIES (Canadian reprint of Crime SuspenStories No. 1-3; see Table of Contents

WEIRD TALES OF THE FUTURE
March, 1952 - No. 8, July, 1953
S.P.M. Publ. No. 1-4/Aragon Publ. No. 5-8

	Good	Fine	Mint
1-Andru-a(2)	23.00	70.00	160.00
2,3-Wolverton-a(3) each. 3 has LSD-like story	48.00	145.00	335.00
4-''Jumpin Jupiter'' satire by Wolverton; partial Wolverton-c	22.00	65.00	154.00
5-Wolverton-c/a(2)	48.00	145.00	335.00
6-Bernard Baily-c	10.00	30.00	70.00
7-''The Mind Movers'' from the art to Wolverton's ''Brain Bats of Venus'' from Mr. Mystery No. 7 which was cut apart, pasted up, partially redrawn, and rewritten by Harry Kantor, the editor; Bernard Baily-c	23.00	70.00	160.00
8-Reprints Weird Mysteries No. 1(10/52) minus cover; gory cover showing heart ripped out	8.50	25.50	60.00

WEIRD TALES OF THE MACABRE (Magazine)
Jan, 1975 - No. 2, Mar, 1975 (B&W) (75 cents)
Atlas/Seaboard Publ.

	Good	Fine	Mint
1-Jones-c	.35	1.00	2.00
2-Boris Vallejo-c, Severin-a	.30	.80	1.60

WEIRD TERROR (Also see Horrific)
Sept, 1952 - No. 13, Sept, 1954
Allen Hardy Associates (Comic Media)

	Good	Fine	Mint
1-''Portrait of Death,'' adapted from Lovecraft's ''Pickman's Model;'' lingerie panels, Hitler story	7.00	21.00	50.00
2	3.75	11.25	26.00
3,5,7,9,10	3.50	10.50	24.00
4,6-Dismemberment, decapitation	6.50	19.50	45.00
8-Decapitation story; Ambrose Bierce adapt.	5.50	16.50	38.00
11-End of the world story with atomic blast panels; Tothish-a by Bill Discount	5.50	16.50	38.00
12-Discount-a	3.35	10.00	23.00
13-Severed head panels	3.75	11.25	26.00

NOTE: ***Don Heck** a/c-most issues. **Landau** a-6. **Morisi** a-2-5, 7, 12. **Palais** a-1, 5, 8(2), 12. **Powell** a-10. **Ravielli** a-11, 20.*

WEIRD THRILLERS
Sept-Oct, 1951 - No. 5, Oct-Nov, 1952
Ziff-Davis Publ. Co. (Approved Comics)

	Good	Fine	Mint
1-Ron Hatton photo-c	12.00	36.00	84.00
2-Toth, Anderson, Colan-a	10.00	30.00	70.00
3-Two Powell, Tuska-a	7.00	21.00	50.00
4-Kubert, Tuska-a	9.50	28.50	65.00
5-Powell-a	7.00	21.00	50.00

NOTE: ***Anderson** a-2. **Roussos** a-4. No. 2, 3 reprinted in Nightmare No. 10 & 13; No. 4,5 r-/in Amazing Ghost Stories No. 16 & No. 15.*

WEIRD WAR TALES
Sept-Oct, 1971 - No. 124, June, 1983
National Periodical Publications/DC Comics

	Good	Fine	Mint
1	.25	.75	1.50
2-7,9,10: 5,6,10-Toth-a. 7-Krigstein-a		.30	.60
8-Adams c/a(i)	.30	.90	1.80
11-50: 36-Crandall, Kubert r-/No.2		.25	.50
51-63,65-67,69-124: 69-Sci-Fic ish. 93-Origin Creature Commandos. 101-Origin G.I. Robot		.20	.40
64,68-Miller-a		.40	.80

NOTE: ***Austin** a-51i, 52i. **Bailey** a-21, 33. **Crandall** a-2r, 36r. **Ditko** a-46p, 49p, 95, 99, 104-106. **Drucker** a-2, 3. **Evans** a-17, 22, 35, 46, 74, 82; c-73, 74, 82, 83, 85. **Giffen** a-124p. **Grell** a-67. **Heath** a-3, 59. **Howard** a-53i. **Kaluta** c-12. **Gil Kane** c-115, 116, 118. **Kubert** a-1-4, 7, 36, 68, 69; c-51, 60, 62-69, 72, 75-81, 84, 86-88, 90-96, 100, 103, 104, 106, 107, 123, 124. **Lopez** a-108. **Maurer** a-5. **Meskin** a-4r. **Morrow** c-54. **Newton** a-82p, 122p. **Nino** a-9. **Redondo** a-10, 13, 30, 38, 42, 52. **Rogers** a-51p, 52p. **Sekowsky** a-75p. **Simonson** a-10, 72. **Sparling** a-86p. **Spiegle** a-96, 97, 107, 109-112. **Starlin** c-89. **Staton** a-106p; c-108p. **Sutton** a-66, 87, 91, 92, 103. **Tuska** a-103p, 122p.*

WEIRD WESTERN TALES (Formerly All-Star Western)
No. 12, June-July, 1972 - No. 70, Aug, 1980 (No. 12: 52 pgs.)
National Periodical Publications/DC Comics

	Good	Fine	Mint
12-Bat Lash, Pow Wow Smith reprints; El Diablo by Adams/Wrightson	.25	.75	1.50
13,15-Adams-a; c-No. 15	.25	.75	1.50
14-Toth-a		.40	.80
16-28,30-70: 39-Origin/1st app. Scalphunter		.20	.40
29-Origin Jonah Hex		.40	.80

NOTE: ***Ditko** a-99. **Evans** inks-39-48; c-40. **G. Kane** a-15. **Kubert** c-12, 33. **Starlin** c-44, 45. **Wildey** a-26.*

WEIRD WONDER TALES
Dec, 1973 - No. 22, May, 1977
Marvel Comics Group

	Good	Fine	Mint
1-Wolverton-a r-from Mystic No. 6		.40	.80
2-22: 16-18-Venus r-by Everett/Venus No. 19,18 & 17. 19-22-Dr. Druid (Droom)-r		.25	.50

NOTE: *All Reprints: **Check** a-1. **Colan** a-17r. **Ditko** a-4, 5, 10-13, 19-21. **Drucker** a-12, 20. **Everett** a-3(Spellbound No.16), 6(Astonishing No.10), 9(Adv. Into Mystery No.5). **Kirby** a-6, 11, 13, 16-22; c-17, 19, 20. **Krigstein** a-19. **Kubert** a-22. **Maneely** a-8. **Mooney** a-7p. **Powell** a-7. **Torres** a-7. **Wildey** a-2.*

WEIRD WORLDS (See Adventures Into. . .)

WEIRD WORLDS (Magazine)
V1No.10(12/70), V2No.1(2/71) - No. 4, Aug, 1971 (52 pgs.)
Eerie Publications

	Good	Fine	Mint
V1No.10	.50	1.50	3.00
V2No.1-4	.35	1.00	2.00

WEIRD WORLDS
Aug-Sept, 1972 - No. 9, Jan-Feb, 1974; No. 10, Oct-Nov, 1974

WEIRD WORLDS (continued)
National Periodical Publications

	Good	Fine	Mint
1-Edgar Rice Burrough's John Carter of Mars & David Innes begin; Kubert-c		.50	1.00
2-7: 7-Last John Carter		.40	.80
8-10: 8-Iron Wolf begins by Chaykin		.30	.60

NOTE: ***Adams** a-2i, 3i. John Carter by **Anderson**-No. 1-3. **Chaykin** c-7, 8. **Kaluta** a-4; c-5, 6, 10. **Orlando** a-4i; c-2-4. **Wrightson** a-2i.*

WELCOME BACK, KOTTER (TV) (See Limited Collectors Ed. No. 57)
Nov, 1976 - No. 10, Mar-Apr, 1978
National Periodical Publications/DC Comics

	Good	Fine	Mint
1-Sparling a(p)		.40	.80
2-10: 3-Estrada-a		.30	.60

WELCOME SANTA (See March of Comics No. 63,183)

WELLS FARGO (See Tales of. . .)

WENDY PARKER COMICS
July, 1953 - No. 8, July, 1954
Atlas Comics (OMC)

	Good	Fine	Mint
1	2.50	7.50	17.50
2	1.30	4.00	9.00
3-8	1.15	3.50	8.00

WENDY, THE GOOD LITTLE WITCH
8/60 - No. 82, 11/73; No. 83, 8/74 - No. 93, 4/76
Harvey Publications

	Good	Fine	Mint
1	8.35	25.00	50.00
2	4.00	12.00	24.00
3-5	3.35	10.00	20.00
6-10	2.50	7.50	15.00
11-20	1.70	5.00	10.00
21-30	.85	2.50	5.00
31-50	.50	1.50	3.00
51-70	.40	1.20	2.40
71-93	.25	.75	1.50

(See Casper the Friendly Ghost & Harvey Hits No. 7,16,21,23,27,30,33)

WENDY WITCH WORLD
10/61; No. 2, 9/62 - No. 52, 12/73; No. 53, 9/74
Harvey Publications

	Good	Fine	Mint
1	5.35	16.00	32.00
2-5	2.75	8.00	16.00
6-10	1.70	5.00	10.00
11-20	1.00	3.00	6.00
21-30	.50	1.50	3.00
31-40	.35	1.00	2.00
41-53		.60	1.20

WEREWOLF (Super Hero)
Dec, 1966 - No. 3, April, 1967
Dell Publishing Co.

	Good	Fine	Mint
1	.35	1.00	2.00
2,3		.50	1.00

WEREWOLF BY NIGHT (See Marvel Spotlight)
Sept, 1972 - No. 43, Mar, 1977
Marvel Comics Group

	Good	Fine	Mint
1-Ploog-a-cont'd./Marvel Spotlight No. 4	.35	1.00	2.00
2-7-Ploog-a(p) in all		.40	.80
8-10		.30	.60
11-31: 15-New origin Werewolf		.25	.50
32-Origin & 1st app. Moon Knight	2.50	7.50	15.00
33-Moon Knight app.	1.70	5.00	10.00
34-36,38-43: 35-Starlin/Wrightson-c		.25	.50
37-Moon Knight app; part Wrightson-c	1.00	3.00	6.00
Giant Size 2(10/74, 68 pgs.)(Formerly G-S Creatures)-Frankenstein app; Ditko-a(r).		.30	.60
Giant Size 3-5(7/75, 68 pgs.); 4-Morbius the Living Vampire app.		.30	.60

NOTE: ***Bolle** a-6i. **Ditko** a-Gnt. Size 2r. **G. Kane** a-11p, 12p; c-21, 22, 24-30, 34p, Gnt. Size 3-5. **Mooney** a-7i. **Ploog** 1-4p, 5, 6p, 7p, 13-16p; c-5-8, 13-16. **Reinman** a-8i. **Sutton** a(i)-9, 11, 16, 35.*

WEREWOLVES & VAMPIRES (Magazine)
1962 (One Shot)
Charlton Comics

	Good	Fine	Mint
1	3.00	9.00	21.00

WEST COAST AVENGERS, THE
Sept, 1984 - No. 4, Dec, 1984 (mini-series; Mando paper)
Marvel Comics Group

	Good	Fine	Mint
1-Hawkeye, Iron Man, Mockingbird, Tigra	.75	2.20	4.40
2-4	.45	1.25	2.50

WEST COAST AVENGERS
Oct, 1985 - Present (regular series)
Marvel Comics Group

	Good	Fine	Mint
1 (V2/1)	.50	1.50	3.00
2,3	.35	1.00	2.00
4-6	.25	.75	1.50
7-10		.65	1.30
11-19		.50	1.00
Annual 1 (10/86)	.25	.75	1.50

WESTERN ACTION
1964
I. W. Enterprises

	Good	Fine	Mint
7-Reprint	.30	.90	1.80

WESTERN ACTION
February, 1975
Atlas/Seaboard Publ.

	Good	Fine	Mint
1-Kid Cody by Wildey & The Comanche Kid stories; intro. The Renegade		.30	.60

WESTERN ACTION THRILLERS
April, 1937 (100 pages)(Square binding)
Dell Publishers

	Good	Fine	Mint
1-Buffalo Bill, The Texas Kid, Laramie Joe, Two-Gun Thompson, & Wild West Bill app.	25.00	75.00	175.00

WESTERN ADVENTURES COMICS (Western Love Trails No. 7 on)
Oct, 1948 - No. 6, Aug, 1949
Ace Magazines

	Good	Fine	Mint
nn(No.1)-Sheriff Sal, The Cross-Draw Kid, Sam Bass begin	8.50	25.50	60.00
nn(No.2)(12/48)	4.65	14.00	32.00
nn(No.3)(2/49)-Used in **SOTI**, pgs. 30,31	5.50	16.50	38.00
4-6	3.85	11.50	27.00

WESTERN BANDITS
1952
Avon Periodicals

	Good	Fine	Mint
1-Butch Cassidy, The Daltons by Larsen; Kinstler-a; c-part r-/paperback Avon Western Novel 1	7.00	21.00	50.00

WESTERN BANDIT TRAILS (See Approved Comics)
Jan, 1949 - No. 3, July, 1949
St. John Publishing Co.

Weird Worlds #7, © DC

Wendy the Good Little Witch #3, © HARV

Western Action Thrillers #1, © DELL

Western Comics #5, © DC

Western Fighters, 3-D #1, © HILL

Western Hearts #2, © STD

WESTERN BANDIT TRAILS (continued)

	Good	Fine	Mint
1-Tuska-a; Baker-c; Blue Monk, Ventrilo app.	7.00	21.00	50.00
2-Baker-c	5.50	16.50	38.00
3-Baker c/a, Tuska-a	6.50	19.50	45.00

WESTERN COMICS (See Super DC Giant)
Jan-Feb, 1948 - No. 85, Jan-Feb, 1961 (52pgs., 1-18?)
National Periodical Publications

	Good	Fine	Mint
1-The Wyoming Kid & his horse Racer, The Vigilante (Meskin-a), The Cowboy Marshal, & Rodeo Rick begin	20.00	60.00	140.00
2	11.00	33.00	76.00
3,4-Last Vigilante	9.50	28.50	65.00
5-Nighthawk & his horse Nightwind begin (not in No. 6); Captain Tootsie by Beck	8.00	24.00	56.00
6,7,9,10	6.50	19.50	45.00
8-Origin Wyoming Kid; 2pg. pin-ups of rodeo queens	8.00	24.00	56.00
11-20	4.35	13.00	30.00
21-40: 27-Last 52 pgs.	3.35	10.00	23.00
41-60: 43-Pow Wow Smith begins, ends No. 85	2.65	8.00	18.00
61-85-Last Wyoming Kid. 77-Origin Matt Savage Trail Boss. 82-1st app. Fleetfoot, Pow Wow's girlfriend	1.30	4.00	9.00

NOTE: ***Gil Kane, Infantino*** *art in most.* ***Meskin*** *a-1-4.* ***Moreira*** *a-35, 37, 39.* ***Post*** *a-3-5.*

WESTERN CRIME BUSTERS
Sept, 1950 - No. 10, Mar-Apr, 1952
Trojan Magazines

	Good	Fine	Mint
1-Six-Gun Smith, Wilma West, K-Bar-Kate, & Fighting Bob Dale begin	9.50	28.50	65.00
2	5.75	17.25	40.00
3-5	5.35	16.00	37.00
6-Wood-a	14.50	43.50	100.00
7-Six-Gun Smith by Wood	14.50	43.50	100.00
8	4.65	14.00	32.00
9-Tex Gordon & Wilma West by Wood; Lariat Lucy app.	16.00	48.00	110.00
10-Wood-a	13.00	40.00	90.00

WESTERN CRIME CASES (The Outlaws No. 10 on?)
No. 9, Dec, 1951
Star Publications

	Good	Fine	Mint
9-White Rider & Super Horse; L. B. Cole-c	2.65	8.00	18.00

WESTERN DESPERADO COMICS (Formerly Slam Bang)
1940 (Oct.?)
Fawcett Publications

	Good	Fine	Mint
8-(Rare)	23.00	70.00	160.00

WESTERNER, THE (Wild Bill Pecos)
No. 14, June, 1948 - No. 41, Dec, 1951
"Wanted" Comic Group/Toytown/Patches

	Good	Fine	Mint
14	3.50	10.50	24.00
15-17,19-21: 19-Meskin-a	1.75	5.25	12.00
18,22-25-Krigstein-a	3.15	9.50	22.00
26(4/50)-Origin & 1st app. Calamity Kate, series ends No. 32; Krigstein-a	4.00	12.00	28.00
27-Krigstein-a(2)	4.65	14.00	32.00
28-41: 33-Quest app. 37-Lobo, the Wolf Boy begins	1.50	4.50	10.00

WESTERNER, THE
1964
Super Comics

	Good	Fine	Mint
Super Reprint No. 15,16(Crack West. No. 65), 17	.25	.75	1.50

WESTERN FIGHTERS
Apr-May, 1948 - V4No.7, Mar-Apr, 1953
Hillman Periodicals/Star Publ.

	Good	Fine	Mint
V1No.1-Simon & Kirby-c	8.50	25.50	60.00
2-Kirby-a(p)?	3.15	9.50	22.00
3-Fuje-c	2.85	8.50	20.00
4-Krigstein, Ingels-a	3.65	11.00	25.00
5,6,8,9,12	2.15	6.50	15.00
7,10-Krigstein-a	3.65	11.00	25.00
11-Williamson/Frazetta-a	13.50	40.50	95.00
V2No.1-Krigstein-a	3.65	11.00	25.00
2-12: 4-Berg-a	1.15	3.50	8.00
V3No.1-11	1.00	3.00	7.00
12-Krigstein-a	3.15	9.50	22.00
V4No.1,4-7	1.00	3.00	7.00
2,3-Krigstein-a	2.85	8.50	20.00
3-D 1(12/53, Star Publ.)-L. B. Cole-c	13.00	40.00	90.00

NOTE: ***Kinstlerish*** *a-V2/6, 8, 9, 12; V3/2, 5-7, 11, 12; V4/1(plus cover).* ***McWilliams*** *a-11.* ***Powell*** *a-V2/2.* ***Rowich*** *c-6.*

WESTERN FRONTIER
Apr-May, 1951 - No. 7, 1952
P. L. Publishers

	Good	Fine	Mint
1	3.00	9.00	21.00
2	1.65	5.00	11.50
3-7	1.30	4.00	9.00

WESTERN GUNFIGHTERS (1st Series) (Apache Kid No. 11-19)
No. 20, June, 1956 - No. 27, Aug, 1957
Atlas Comics (CPS)

	Good	Fine	Mint
20	2.65	8.00	18.00
21,25-27	1.50	4.50	10.00
22-Wood & Powell-a	6.75	20.25	47.00
23-Williamson-a	4.65	14.00	32.00
24-Toth-a	3.50	10.50	24.00

WESTERN GUNFIGHTERS (2nd Series)
Aug, 1970 - No. 33, Nov, 1975 (No. 1-6: 68 pgs.; No. 7: 52 pgs.)
Marvel Comics Group

	Good	Fine	Mint
1-Ghost Rider, Fort Rango, Renegades & Gunhawk app.		.40	.80
2-33: 2-Origin Nightwind (Apache Kid's horse). 7-Origin Ghost Rider retold. 10-Origin Black Rider. 12-Origin Matt Slade		.25	.50

NOTE: ***Baker*** *a-2r.* ***Everett*** *a-6i.* ***G. Kane*** *c-29, 31.* ***Kirby*** *a-1p(r), 10, 11.* ***Kubert*** *a-2r.* ***Maneely*** *a-2, 10r.* ***Morrow*** *a-29r.* ***Severin*** *c-10.* ***Smith*** *a-4.* ***Steranko*** *c-14.* ***Sutton*** *a-1, 2i, 3, 4.* ***Torres*** *a-26('57).* ***Wildey*** *a-8r, 9r.* ***Williamson*** *a-2r, 18r.* ***Woodbridge*** *a-27('57). Renegades in No. 4, 5; Ghost Rider-No. 1-7.*

WESTERN HEARTS
Dec, 1949 - No. 10, Mar, 1952
Standard Comics

	Good	Fine	Mint
1-Severin-a, Whip Wilson photo-c	5.00	15.00	35.00
2-Williamson/Frazetta-a, 2 pgs; photo-c	10.00	30.00	70.00
3	1.75	5.25	12.00
4-7,10-Severin & Elder, Al Carreno-a. 5,6-Photo-c	2.15	6.50	15.00
8-Randolph Scott/Janis Carter photo-c/'Santa Fe;' Severin & Elder-a	2.65	8.00	18.00
9-Whip Wilson photo-c; Severin & Elder-a	2.65	8.00	18.00

WESTERN HERO (Wow No. 1-69; Real Western Hero No. 70-75)
No. 76, Mar, 1949 - No. 112, Mar, 1952
Fawcett Publications

	Good	Fine	Mint
76(No.1, 52 pgs.)-Tom Mix, Hopalong Cassidy, Monte Hale, Gabby Hayes, Young Falcon (ends No. 78,80), & Big Bow and Little Arrow (ends No. 102,105) begin; painted-c begin	8.50	25.50	60.00

WESTERN HERO (continued)

	Good	Fine	Mint
77 (52 pgs.)	6.00	18.00	42.00
78,80-82 (52 pgs.): 81-Captain Tootsie by Beck	5.75	17.25	40.00
79,83 (36 pgs.): 83-Last painted-c	4.65	14.00	32.00
84-86,88-90 (52 pgs.): 84-Photo-c begin, end No. 112. 86-Last Hopalong Cassidy	5.00	15.00	35.00
87,91,95,99 (36 pgs.): 87-Bill Boyd begins, ends No. 95	4.00	12.00	28.00
92-94,96-98,101 (52 pgs.): 96-Tex Ritter begins. 101-Red Eagle app.	4.65	14.00	32.00
100 (52 pgs.)	5.00	15.00	35.00
102-111 (36pgs. begin)	4.00	12.00	28.00
112-Last issue	4.65	14.00	32.00

NOTE: *½-1 pg. Rocky Lane (Carnation) in 80-83,86,88,97.*

WESTERN KID (1st Series)
Dec, 1954 - No. 17, Aug, 1957
Atlas Comics (CPC)

	Good	Fine	Mint
1-Origin; The Western Kid, his horse Whirlwind & dog Lightning begin	4.35	13.00	30.00
2	2.15	6.50	15.00
3-8	1.65	5.00	11.50
9,10-Williamson-a in both, 4 pgs. each	3.85	11.50	27.00
11-17	1.30	4.00	9.00

NOTE: ***Maneely** c-2-7, 14. **Romita** a-1(2), 2(3)-7(3), 12, 14, 17; c-1, 12. **Severin** c-17.*

WESTERN KID, THE (2nd Series)
Dec, 1971 - No. 5, Aug, 1972
Marvel Comics Group

	Good	Fine	Mint
1-Reprints		.25	.50
2,4,5: 2-Severin-c. 4-Everett-r		.20	.40
3-Williamson-r		.25	.50

WESTERN KILLERS
1948 - No. 64, May, 1949; No. 6, July, 1949
Fox Features Syndicate

	Good	Fine	Mint
nn(nd, F&J Trading Co.)-Range Busters	4.35	13.00	30.00
60-Extreme violence; lingerie panel	6.00	18.00	42.00
61-64, 6: 61-J. Cole-a	3.50	10.50	24.00

WESTERN LIFE ROMANCES (My Friend Irma No. 3?)
Dec, 1949 - No. 2, Mar, 1950
Marvel Comics (IPP)

	Good	Fine	Mint
1-Photo-c	3.50	10.50	24.00
2-Spanking scene	5.00	15.00	35.00

WESTERN LOVE
July-Aug, 1949 - No. 5, Mar-Apr, 1950
Prize Publications

	Good	Fine	Mint
1-S&K-a; Randolph Scott "Canadian Pacific" photo-c (see Prize 76)	6.00	18.00	42.00
2,5-S&K-a	4.35	13.00	30.00
3,4-Photo-c	3.50	10.50	24.00

NOTE: ***Meskin** & **Severin/Elder** a-2-5.*

WESTERN LOVE TRAILS (Formerly Western Adventures)
No. 7, Nov, 1949 - No. 9, Mar, 1950
Ace Magazines (A. A. Wyn)

	Good	Fine	Mint
7	3.65	11.00	25.00
8,9	2.35	7.00	16.00

WESTERN MARSHAL (See Steve Donovan. . . & Ernest Haycox's 4-Color 534, 591, 613, 640 [based on Haycox's "Trailtown"])

WESTERN OUTLAWS (My Secret Life No. 22 on)
No. 17, Sept, 1948 - No. 21, May, 1949
Fox Features Syndicate

	Good	Fine	Mint
17-Kamen-a; Iger shop-a in all; 1 pg. 'Death and the Devil Pills' r-in Ghostly Weird 122	7.00	21.00	50.00
18-21	3.50	10.50	24.00

WESTERN OUTLAWS
Feb, 1954 - No. 21, Aug, 1957
Atlas Comics (ACI No. 1-14/WPI No. 15-21)

	Good	Fine	Mint
1-Heath, Powell-a	4.35	13.00	30.00
2	2.15	6.50	15.00
3-10: 9,10-Everett-a	1.75	5.25	12.00
11,14-Williamson-a in both, 6 pgs. each	3.85	11.50	27.00
12,18,20,21	1.30	4.00	9.00
13-Baker-a	2.15	6.50	15.00
15-Torres-a	2.35	7.00	16.00
16-Williamson text illo	1.65	5.00	11.50
17-Crandall-a, Williamson text illo	2.65	8.00	18.00
19-Crandall-a	2.00	6.00	14.00

NOTE: ***Bolle** a-21. **Colan** a-17. **Heath** c-4, 16. **Maneely** a-16, 17; c-9, 12. **Morisi** a-18. **Powell** a-3, 15, 16. **Romita** a-7. **Severin** a-16; c-17.*

WESTERN OUTLAWS & SHERIFFS (Formerly Best Western)
No. 60, Dec, 1949 - No. 73, June, 1952
Marvel/Atlas Comics (IPC)

	Good	Fine	Mint
60	4.00	12.00	28.00
61-65	2.75	8.25	19.00
66,68-73	2.15	6.50	15.00
67-Cannibalism story	2.75	8.25	19.00

NOTE: ***Maneely** c-69, 70, 73. **Robinson** a-68. **Tuska** a-69.*

WESTERN PICTURE STORIES (1st Western Comic)
Feb, 1937 - No. 4, June, 1937
Comics Magazine Company

	Good	Fine	Mint
1-Will Eisner-a	50.00	150.00	350.00
2-Will Eisner-a	30.00	90.00	210.00
3,4: 3-Eisner-c/a	25.00	75.00	175.00

WESTERN PICTURE STORIES (See Giant Comics Editions No. 6,11)

WESTERN ROMANCES (See Target. . .)

WESTERN ROUGH RIDERS
Nov, 1954 - No. 4, May, 1955
Gillmor Magazines No. 1,4 (Stanmor Publications)

	Good	Fine	Mint
1	2.35	7.00	16.00
2-4	1.15	3.50	8.00

WESTERN ROUNDUP (See Dell Giants)

WESTERN TALES (Formerly Witches. . .)
No. 31, Oct, 1955 - No. 33, July-Sept, 1956
Harvey Publications

	Good	Fine	Mint
31,32-All S&K-a; Davy Crockett app. in ea.	5.00	15.00	35.00
33-S&K-a; Jim Bowie app.	5.00	15.00	35.00

NOTE: *No. 32 & 33 Boy's Ranch-r.*

WESTERN TALES OF BLACK RIDER (Formerly Black Rider; Gunsmoke Western No. 32 on)
No. 28, May, 1955 - No. 31, Nov, 1955
Atlas Comics (CPS)

	Good	Fine	Mint
28 (No.1)	3.65	11.00	25.00
29-31	2.85	8.50	20.00

NOTE: ***Lawrence** a-30. **Maneely** c-29. **Severin** a-28. **Shores** c-31.*

WESTERN TEAM-UP
November, 1973
Marvel Comics Group

1-Origin & 1st app. The Dakota Kid; Rawhide Kid-r; Gunsmoke

Western Hero #78, © FAW

Western Kid #3 (1st Series), © MCG

Western Tales of Black Rider #29, © MCG

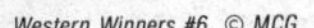
Western Winners #6, © MCG

Whack #1, © STJ

What If...? #2, © MCG

WESTERN TEAM-UP (continued)	Good	Fine	Mint
Kid-r by Jack Davis		.25	.50

WESTERN THRILLERS (My Past Confessions No. 7 on)
Aug, 1948 - No. 6, June, 1949
Fox Features Syndicate

1-"Velvet Rose"-Kamenish-a; "Two-Gun Sal," "Striker Sisters" (all women outlaws issue)	13.00	40.00	90.00
2	4.65	14.00	32.00
3,6: 3-Tuska-a, Heath-c	3.65	11.00	25.00
4,5-Bakerish-a; Butch Cassidy app. No. 5	5.50	16.50	38.00
52-(Reprint, M.S. Dist.)-1954? No date given (Becomes My Love Secret No. 53)	1.50	4.50	10.00

WESTERN THRILLERS (Cowboy Action No. 5 on)
Nov, 1954 - No. 4, Feb, 1955
Atlas Comics (ACI)

1-Severin-c	3.50	10.50	24.00
2-4	1.85	5.50	13.00

WESTERN TRAILS
May, 1957 - No. 2, July, 1957
Atlas Comics (SAI)

1	2.35	7.00	16.00
2-Severin-c	1.50	4.50	10.00

WESTERN TRUE CRIME (Becomes My Confessions)
No. 15, Aug, 1948 - No. 6, June, 1949
Fox Features Syndicate

15-Kamenish-a	7.00	21.00	50.00
16-Kamenish-a	3.75	11.25	26.00
3,5,6	2.35	7.00	16.00
4-Johnny Craig-a	6.00	18.00	42.00

WESTERN WINNERS (Formerly All-West. Winners; Black Rider No.8)
No. 5, June, 1949 - No. 7, Dec, 1949
Marvel Comics (CDS)

5-Two-Gun Kid, Kid Colt, Black Rider	6.50	19.50	45.00
6-Two-Gun Kid, Black Rider, Heath Kid Colt story; Captain Tootsie By Beck	5.00	15.00	35.00
7-Randolph Scott Photo-c w/true stories about the West	5.50	16.50	38.00

WEST OF THE PECOS (See 4-Color No. 222)

WESTWARD HO, THE WAGONS (See 4-Color No. 738)

WHACK (Satire)
Oct, 1953 - No. 3, May, 1954
St. John Publishing Co.

1-(3-D)-Kubert-a	13.00	40.00	90.00
2,3-Kubert-a in each	5.00	15.00	35.00

WHACKY (See Wacky)

WHAM COMICS (See Super Spy)
Nov, 1940 - No. 2, Dec, 1940
Centaur Publications

1-The Sparkler, The Phantom Rider, Craig Carter and the Magic Ring Detector, Copper Slug, Speed Silvers by Gustavson, Speed Centaur & Jon Linton (s/f) begin	48.00	145.00	335.00
2-Origin Blue Fire & Solarman; The Buzzard app.	34.00	100.00	236.00

WHAM-O GIANT COMICS (98 cents)
1967 (Newspaper size) (One Shot) (Full Color)
Wham-O Mfg. Co.

1-Radian & Goody Bumpkin by Wally Wood; 1 pg. Stanley-a; Lou Fine, Tufts-a; wraparound-c	1.50	4.50	10.00

WHAT DO YOU KNOW ABOUT THIS COMICS SEAL OF APPROVAL?
nd (1955) (4pgs.; color; slick paper-c)
No publisher listed (DC Comics Giveaway)

	Good	Fine	Mint
(Rare)	35.00	105.00	245.00

WHAT IF . . . ?
Feb, 1977 - No. 47, Oct, 1985 (All 52 pgs.)
Marvel Comics Group

1-Brief origin Spider-Man, Fantastic-4	1.00	3.00	6.00
2-Origin The Hulk retold	.70	2.00	4.00
3-5	.60	1.80	3.60
6-8,10	.45	1.25	2.50
9-Origins Venus, Marvel Boy, Human Robot, 3-D Man	.45	1.25	2.50
11,12	.35	1.10	2.20
13-Conan app.	.70	2.00	4.00
14-26: 22-Origin Dr. Doom retold	.30	.90	1.80
27-X-Men app.; Miller-c	.65	1.90	3.80
28-Daredevil by Miller	.85	2.50	5.00
29,30: 29-Golden-c	.25	.75	1.50
31-X-Men app.; death of Hulk, Wolverine & Magneto	.35	1.00	2.00
32,36-Byrne-a	.25	.75	1.50
33,34: 34-Marvel crew each draw themselves	.25	.75	1.50
35-What if Elektra had lived?; Miller/Austin-a	.25	.75	1.50
37-47: 37-Old X-Men app.	.25	.75	1.50

NOTE: ***Austin*** *a-27p, 32i, 34, 35i; c-35i, 36i.* ***J. Buscema*** *a-13p, 15p; c-10, 13p, 23p.* ***Byrne*** *a-32i, 36; c-36p.* ***Colan*** *a-21p; c-17p, 18p, 21p. .* ***Ditko*** *a-35.* ***Golden*** *c-40, 42.* ***Guice*** *a-40p.* ***Gil Kane*** *a-3p, 24p; c-2-4p, 7p, 8p.* ***Kirby*** *a-11p; c-9p, 11p.* ***Layton*** *a-32i, 33i; c-30, 32p, 33i, 34.* ***Miller*** *a-28p, 32i, 35p; c-27, 28p.* ***Mooney*** *a-8i, 30i.* ***Perez*** *a-15p.* ***Simonson*** *a-15p, 32i.* ***Starlin*** *a-32i.* ***Stevens*** *a-16i.* ***Sutton*** *a-2i, 18p, 28.* ***Tuska*** *a-5p.*

WHAT'S BEHIND THESE HEADLINES
1948 (16 pgs.)
William C. Popper Co.

Comic insert-''The Plot to Steal the World''	1.35	4.00	8.00

WHEATIES (Premiums) (32 titles)
1950 & 1951 (32 pages) (pocket size)
Walt Disney Productions

(Set A-1 to A-8, 1950)
A-1 Mickey Mouse & the Disappearing Island
A-2 Grandma Duck, Homespun Detective
A-3 Donald Duck & the Haunted Jewels
A-4 Donald Duck & the Giant Ape
A-5 Mickey Mouse, Roving Reporter
A-6 Li'l Bad Wolf, Forest Ranger
A-7 Goofy, Tightrope Acrobat
A-8 Pluto & the Bogus Money

each. . . .	2.00	6.00	12.00

(Set B-1 to B-8, 1950)
B-1 Mickey Mouse & the Pharoah's Curse
B-2 Pluto, Canine Cowpoke
B-3 Donald Duck & the Buccaneers
B-4 Mickey Mouse & the Mystery Sea Monster
B-5 Li'l Bad Wolf in the Hollow Tree Hideout
B-6 Donald Duck, Trail Blazer
B-7 Goofy & the Gangsters
B-8 Donald Duck, Klondike Kid

each. . . .	1.70	5.00	10.00

(Set C-1 to C-8, 1951)
C-1 Donald Duck & the Inca Idol
C-2 Mickey Mouse & the Magic Mountain
C-3 Li'l Bad Wolf, Fire Fighter
C-4 Gus & Jaq Save the Ship
C-5 Donald Duck in the Lost Lakes
C-6 Mickey Mouse & the Stagecoach Bandits

WHEATIES (continued)

	Good	Fine	Mint
C-7 Goofy, Big Game Hunter			
C-8 Donald Duck Deep-Sea Diver			
each....	1.70	5.00	10.00

(Set D-1 to D-8, 1951)

	Good	Fine	Mint
D-1 Donald Duck in Indian Country			
D-2 Mickey Mouse and the Abandoned Mine			
D-3 Pluto & the Mysterious Package			
D-4 Bre'r Rabbit's Sunken Treasure			
D-5 Donald Duck, Mighty Mystic			
D-6 Mickey Mouse & the Medicine Man			
D-7 Li'l Bad Wolf and the Secret of the Woods			
D-8 Minnie Mouse, Girl Explorer			
each....	1.70	5.00	10.00

NOTE: *Some copies lack the Wheaties ad.*

WHEE COMICS (Also see Tickle, Gay, & Smile Comics)
1955 (52 pgs.) (5x7¼'') (7 cents)
Modern Store Publications

	Good	Fine	Mint
1-Funny animal	.40	1.20	2.40

WHEELIE AND THE CHOPPER BUNCH (TV)
July, 1975 - No. 7, July, 1976 (Hanna-Barbera)
Charlton Comics

	Good	Fine	Mint
1,2-Bryne-a (1st work)	.70	2.00	4.00
3-7-Staton-a	.35	1.00	2.00

WHEN KNIGHTHOOD WAS IN FLOWER (See 4-Color No. 505, 682)

WHEN SCHOOL IS OUT (See Wisco)

WHERE CREATURES ROAM
July, 1970 - No. 8, Sept, 1971
Marvel Comics Group

	Good	Fine	Mint
1-Kirby/Ayers-r		.25	.50
2-8-Kirby-r		.20	.40

NOTE: ***Ditko** r-1, 2, 4, 7.*

WHERE MONSTERS DWELL
Jan, 1970 - No. 38, Oct, 1975
Marvel Comics Group

	Good	Fine	Mint
1-Kirby/Ditko-a(r)		.40	.80
2-10: 4-Crandall-a(r)		.30	.60
11,13-37		.20	.40
12-Giant issue		.30	.60
38-Williamson-r/World of Suspense No. 3		.30	.60

NOTE: ***Ditko** a(r)-4, 8, 10, 17, 19, 23, 24, 37. **Reinman** a-4r. **Severin** c-15.*

WHERE'S HUDDLES? (TV) (See Fun-In No. 9)
Jan, 1971 - No. 3, Dec, 1971 (Hanna-Barbera)
Gold Key

	Good	Fine	Mint
1	.85	2.50	5.00
2,3: 3 r-most No. 1	.50	1.50	3.00

WHIP WILSON (Movie star) (Formerly Rex Hart; Gunhawk No. 12 on)
No. 9, April, 1950 - No. 11, Sept, 1950 (52pgs., 9,10; 36pgs., 11)
Marvel Comics

	Good	Fine	Mint
9-Photo-c; Whip Wilson & his horse Bullet begin; origin Bullet; issue No. 23 listed on splash page; cover changed to No. 9	9.00	27.00	62.00
10,11-Photo-c	7.00	21.00	50.00
I.W. Reprint No. 1('64)-Kinstler-c; r-Marvel No. 11	.75	2.20	4.40

WHIRLWIND COMICS
June, 1940 - No. 3, Sept, 1940
Nita Publication

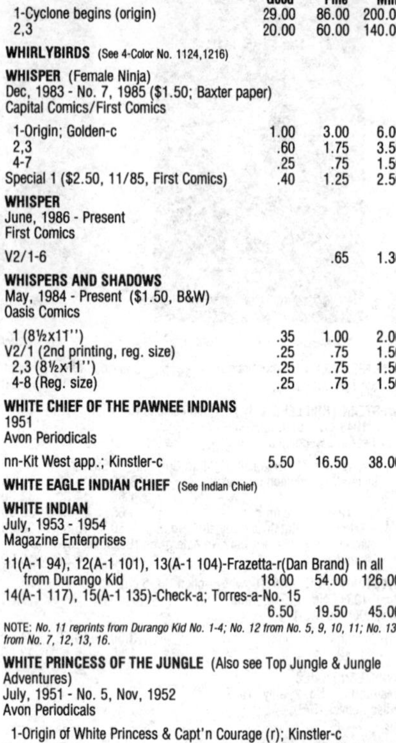

	Good	Fine	Mint
1-Cyclone begins (origin)	29.00	86.00	200.00
2,3	20.00	60.00	140.00

WHIRLYBIRDS (See 4-Color No. 1124,1216)

WHISPER (Female Ninja)
Dec, 1983 - No. 7, 1985 ($1.50; Baxter paper)
Capital Comics/First Comics

	Good	Fine	Mint
1-Origin; Golden-c	1.00	3.00	6.00
2,3	.60	1.75	3.50
4-7	.25	.75	1.50
Special 1 ($2.50, 11/85, First Comics)	.40	1.25	2.50

WHISPER
June, 1986 - Present
First Comics

	Good	Fine	Mint
V2/1-6		.65	1.30

WHISPERS AND SHADOWS
May, 1984 - Present ($1.50, B&W)
Oasis Comics

	Good	Fine	Mint
1 (8½x11'')	.35	1.00	2.00
V2/1 (2nd printing, reg. size)	.25	.75	1.50
2,3 (8½x11'')	.25	.75	1.50
4-8 (Reg. size)	.25	.75	1.50

WHITE CHIEF OF THE PAWNEE INDIANS
1951
Avon Periodicals

	Good	Fine	Mint
nn-Kit West app.; Kinstler-c	5.50	16.50	38.00

WHITE EAGLE INDIAN CHIEF (See Indian Chief)

WHITE INDIAN
July, 1953 - 1954
Magazine Enterprises

	Good	Fine	Mint
11(A-1 94), 12(A-1 101), 13(A-1 104)-Frazetta-r(Dan Brand) in all from Durango Kid	18.00	54.00	126.00
14(A-1 117), 15(A-1 135)-Check-a; Torres-a-No. 15	6.50	19.50	45.00

NOTE: *No. 11 reprints from Durango Kid No. 1-4; No. 12 from No. 5, 9, 10, 11; No. 13 from No. 7, 12, 13, 16.*

WHITE PRINCESS OF THE JUNGLE (Also see Top Jungle & Jungle Adventures)
July, 1951 - No. 5, Nov, 1952
Avon Periodicals

	Good	Fine	Mint
1-Origin of White Princess & Capt'n Courage (r); Kinstler-c	20.00	60.00	140.00
2-Reprints origin of Malu, Slave Girl Princess from Avon's Slave Girl Comics No. 1 w/Malu changed to Zora; Kinstler c/a(2)	14.50	43.50	100.00
3-Origin Blue Gorilla; Kinstler c/a	11.50	34.50	80.00
4-Jack Barnum, White Hunter app.; r-/Sheena No. 9	9.50	28.50	65.00
5-Blue Gorilla by Kinstler	9.50	28.50	65.00

WHITE RIDER AND SUPER HORSE (Indian Warriors No. 7 on)
Dec, 1950 - No. 6, Mar, 1951 (Also see Western Crime Cases)
Novelty-Star Publications/Accepted Publ.

	Good	Fine	Mint
1	4.00	12.00	28.00
2,3	2.75	8.00	18.00
4-6-Adapt. ''The Last of the Mohicans''	3.00	9.00	21.00
Accepted Reprint No. 5,6 (nd); L.B. Cole-c	1.70	5.00	12.00

NOTE: *All have **L. B. Cole** covers.*

WHITE WILDERNESS (See 4-Color No. 943)

Whisper #1, © Capital

Whispers & Shadows #1, © Oasis

White Rider & Super Horse #4, © STAR

Whiz Comics #1, © FAW

Who's Who: The Definitive . . . #1, © DC

Wilbur Comics #4, © AP

WHITMAN COMIC BOOKS
1962 (136 pgs.; 7¾x5¾''; hardcover) (B&W)
Whitman Publishing Co.

	Good	Fine	Mint
1-Yogi Bear, 2-Huckleberry Hound, 3-Mr. Jinks and Pixie & Dixie, 4-The Flintstones, 5-Augie Doggie & Loopy de Loop, 6-Snooper & Blabber Fearless Detectives/Quick Draw McGraw of the Wild West, 7-Bugs Bunny-reprints from No. 47,51,53,54 & 55 each. . . .	.50	1.50	3.00
8-Donald Duck-reprints most of WDC&S No. 209-213. Includes 5 Barks stories, 1 complete Mickey Mouse serial & 1 Mickey Mouse serial missing the 1st episode	7.75	22.00	44.00

NOTE: *Hanna-Barbera No. 1-6(TV), original stories. Dell reprints-No. 7, 8.*

WHIZ COMICS (Formerly Flash & Thrill Comics No. 1)
No. 2, Feb, 1940 - No. 155, June, 1953
Fawcett Publications

1-(nn on cover, No. 2 inside)-Origin & 1st newsstand app. Captain Marvel (formerly Captain Thunder) by C. C. Beck (created by Bill Parker), Spy Smasher, Golden Arrow, Ibis the Invincible, Dan Dare, Scoop Smith, Sivana, & Lance O'Casey begin

Good	Fine	VF-NM
2400.00	7200.00	15,000.00

(Only one known copy exists in Mint condition which has not sold)

1-Reprint, oversize 13½''x10''. **WARNING:** This comic is an exact duplicate reprint of the original except for its size. DC published it in 1974 with a second cover titling it as a Famous First Edition. There have been many reported cases of the outer cover being removed and the interior sold as the original edition. The reprint with the new outer cover removed is practically worthless.

	Good	Fine	Mint
2-(nn on cover, No. 3 inside); cover to Flash No. 1 redrawn, pg. 12 panel 4; Spy Smasher reveals I.D. to Eve	315.00	945.00	2200.00
3-(No. 3 on cover, No. 4 inside)-Spy Smasher reveals I.D. to Eve; 1st app. Beautia	190.00	570.00	1325.00
4-(No. 4 on cover, No. 5 inside)	161.00	483.00	1125.00
5-Captain Marvel wears button-down flap on splash page only	120.00	360.00	840.00
6-10: 7-Dr. Voodoo begins (by Raboy-No. 9-22)	86.00	258.00	600.00
11-14	55.00	165.00	385.00
15-Origin Sivana; Dr. Voodoo by Raboy	73.00	220.00	510.00
16-18-Spy Smasher battles Captain Marvel	73.00	220.00	510.00
19,20	35.00	105.00	245.00
21-Origin & 1st app. Lt. Marvels	40.00	120.00	280.00
22-24: 23-Only Dr. Voodoo by Tuska	31.00	92.00	215.00
25-Origin & 1st app. Captain Marvel Jr., x-over in Capt. Marvel; Capt. Nazi app; origin Old Shazam in text	90.00	270.00	630.00
26-30	23.00	70.00	160.00
31,32: 32-1st app. The Trolls	18.50	56.00	130.00
33-Spy Smasher, Captain Marvel x-over on cover and inside	23.00	70.00	160.00
34,36-40-The Trolls in No. 37	16.50	50.00	115.00
35-Captain Marvel & Spy Smasher-c	16.50	50.00	115.00
41-50: 43-Spy Smasher, Ibis, Golden Arrow x-over in Capt. Marvel. 44-Flag-c. 47-Origin recap (1pg.)	11.00	33.00	76.00
51-60: 52-Capt. Marvel x-over in Ibis. 57-Spy Smasher, Golden Arrow, Ibis cameo	8.00	24.00	56.00
61-70	6.50	19.50	45.00
71,77-80	5.00	15.00	35.00
72-76-Two Captain Marvel stories in each; 76-Spy Smasher becomes Crime Smasher	5.75	17.25	40.00
81-99: 86-Captain Marvel battles Sivana Family. 91-Infinity-c	5.00	15.00	35.00
100	6.50	19.50	45.00
101,103-105	4.00	12.00	28.00
102-Commando Yank app.	4.00	12.00	28.00
106-Bulletman app.	4.00	12.00	28.00
107-141,143-152: 112,139-Infinity-c	3.65	11.00	25.00
142-Used in **POP**, pg. 89	4.35	13.00	30.00
153-155-(Scarce)	8.50	25.50	60.00
Wheaties Giveaway(1946, Miniature)-6½x8¼'', 32 pgs.; all copies were taped at each corner to a box of Wheaties and are never found in fine or mint condition; ''Capt. Marvel & the Water Thieves,'' Golden Arrow, Ibis stories	13.00	40.00	80.00

NOTE: ***Krigstein*** *Golden Arrow-No. 75, 78, 91, 95, 96, 98-100.* ***Wolverton*** *½ pg. ''Culture Corner''-No. 65-68, 70-85, 87-96, 98-100, 102-109, 112-121, 123, 125, 126, 128-131, 133, 134, 136, 142, 143, 146.*

WHODUNIT
Aug-Sept, 1948 - No. 3, Dec-Jan, 1948-49
D. S. Publishing Co.

	Good	Fine	Mint
1-Seven pg. Baker-a	5.00	15.00	35.00
2-Old woman blackmails her doctor for morphine	3.00	9.00	21.00
3	2.65	8.00	18.00

WHODUNNIT?
June, 1986 - No. 2, 1986
Eclipse Comics

	Good	Fine	Mint
1,2	.35	1.00	2.00

WHO IS NEXT?
January, 1953
Standard Comics

	Good	Fine	Mint
5-Toth, Sekowsky, Andru-a	6.50	19.50	45.00

WHO'S MINDING THE MINT? (See Movie Classics)

WHO'S WHO IN STAR TREK
March, 1987 - No. 2, April, 1987
DC Comics

	Good	Fine	Mint
1,2-Chaykin-c	.25	.75	1.50

WHO'S WHO: THE DEFINITIVE DIRECTORY OF THE DC UNIVERSE
3/85 - No. 26, 4/87 (26 issue series) (no ads)
DC Comics

	Good	Fine	Mint
1-DC heroes from A-Z	.25	.75	1.50
2-5	.25	.70	1.40
6-10		.60	1.20
11-26		.50	1.00

NOTE: ***Kane*** *a-1,3.* ***Kirby*** *a-3.* ***Perez*** *c-1, 2, 3-5p, 13, 14p, 15, 16p, 17, 18p.*

WILBUR COMICS (Also see Zip Comics)
Sum', 1944 - No. 87, 11/59; No. 88, 9/63; No. 89, 10/64; No. 90, 10/65 (No. 1-46: 52 pgs.)
MLJ Magazines/Archie Publ. No. 8, Spr. '46 on

	Good	Fine	Mint
1	20.00	60.00	140.00
2 (Fall, '44)	10.00	30.00	70.00
3,4 (Wint, '44-'45; Spr, '45)	8.50	28.50	60.00
5-1st app. Katy Keene-begin series; Wilbur story same as Archie story in Archie No. 1 except that Wilbur replaces Archie	35.00	105.00	245.00
6-10 (Fall, '46): 7-Transvestite issue	8.50	25.50	60.00
11-20	5.00	15.00	35.00
21-30(1949)	4.00	12.00	28.00
31-50	2.00	6.00	14.00
51-69: 69-Last 10¢ ish?	1.15	3.50	8.00
70-90	.85	2.50	5.00

NOTE: *Katy Keene in No. 5-56, 58-69.*

WILD
Feb, 1954 - No. 5, Aug, 1954
Atlas Comics (IPC)

	Good	Fine	Mint
1	4.00	12.00	28.00
2	2.85	8.50	20.00
3-5	2.50	7.50	17.50

NOTE: ***Berg*** *a-5; c-4.* ***Colan*** *a-4.* ***Everett*** *a-1-3.* ***Heath*** *a-2, 3.* ***Maneely*** *a-1-3, 5; c-1, 5.* ***Post*** *a-2.*

WILD (This Magazine Is. . .) (Magazine)
Jan, 1968 - No. 3, 1968 (52 pgs.) (Satire)
Dell Publishing Co.

	Good	Fine	Mint
1-3	.85	2.50	5.00

WILD ANIMALS
Dec, 1982 (One-Shot)
Pacific Comics

1-Funny animal; Sergio Aragones-a		.50	1.00

WILD BILL ELLIOTT (Also see Western Roundup)
No. 278, 5/50 - No. 643, 7/55 (No No. 11,12) (All photo-c)
Dell Publishing Co.

4-Color 278(No.1, 52pgs.)-Titled "Bill Elliott;" Bill & his horse Stormy begin; photo front/back-c begin	5.75	17.25	40.00
2 (11/50), 3 (52 pgs.)	3.50	10.50	24.00
4-10(10-12/52)	2.85	8.50	20.00
4-Color 472(6/53),520(12/53)-Last photo back-c	2.85	8.50	20.00
13(4-6/54) - 17(4-6/55)	2.65	8.00	18.00
4-Color 643	2.65	8.00	18.00

WILD BILL HICKOK (Also see Blazing Sixguns)
Sept-Oct, 1949 - No. 28, May-June, 1956
Avon Periodicals

1-Ingels-c	11.00	33.00	76.00
2-Painted-c	5.50	16.50	38.00
3,5-Painted-c	3.00	9.00	21.00
4-Painted-c by Howard Winfield, not Frazetta	3.00	9.00	21.00
6-10,12: 8-10-Painted-c; 9-Ingels-a?	3.00	9.00	21.00
11,14-Kinstler c/a	3.65	11.00	25.00
13,15,17,18,20,23	2.15	6.50	15.00
16-Kamen-a; r-3 stories/King of the Badmen of Deadwood	3.00	9.00	21.00
19-Meskin-a	2.15	6.50	15.00
21-Reprints 2 stories/Chief Crazy Horse	2.15	6.50	15.00
22-Reprints/Sheriff Bob Dixon's. . ; Kinstler-a	2.15	6.50	15.00
24-27-Kinstler-c/a(r)	2.85	8.50	20.00
28-Kinstler-c/a (new); r-/Last of the Comanches	2.85	8.50	20.00
I.W. Reprint No. 1-Kinstler-c	.50	1.50	3.00
Super Reprint No. 10-12	.50	1.50	3.00

NOTE: *No. 23, 25 contain numerous editing deletions in both art and script due to code.* ***Kinstler*** *c-6, 7, 11-14, 17, 18, 20-22, 24-28.* ***Howard Larsen*** *a-1, 2(3), 4(4), 5(3), 7(3), 9(3), 11(4), 12(4), 17, 18, 21(2), 22, 24(3), 26.* ***Meskin*** *a-7.* ***Reinman*** *a-17.*

WILD BILL HICKOK & JINGLES (TV)(Formerly Cowboy Western)
March, 1958 - 1960 (Also see Blue Bird)
Charlton Comics

68,69-Williamson-a	3.15	9.50	22.00
70-Two pgs. Williamson-a	1.65	5.00	11.50
71-76 (No. 75,76, exist?)	.90	2.70	6.50

WILD BILL PECOS (See The Westerner)

WILD BOY OF THE CONGO (Also see Approved Comics)
No. 10, Feb-Mar, 1951 - No. 15, June, 1955
Ziff-Davis No. 10-12,4,5/St. John No. 6 on

10(2-3/51)-Origin; bondage-c by Saunders; used in **SOTI**, pg. 189	5.75	17.25	40.00
11(4-5/51),12(8-9/51)-Norman Saunders-c	3.50	10.50	24.00
4(10-11/51)-Saunders bondage-c	3.50	10.50	24.00
5(Winter,'51)-Saunders-c	2.65	8.00	18.00
6,8,9(10/53),10	2.35	7.00	16.00
7(8-9/52)-Baker-c; Kinstler-a	3.00	9.00	21.00
11-13-Baker-c(St. John)	3.00	9.00	21.00

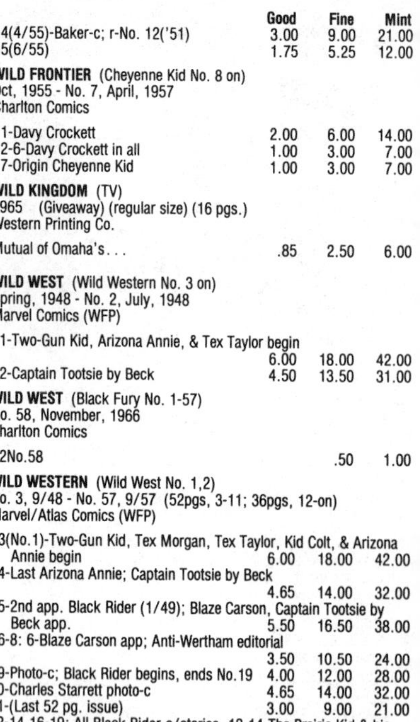

	Good	Fine	Mint
14(4/55)-Baker-c; r-No. 12('51)	3.00	9.00	21.00
15(6/55)	1.75	5.25	12.00

WILD FRONTIER (Cheyenne Kid No. 8 on)
Oct, 1955 - No. 7, April, 1957
Charlton Comics

1-Davy Crockett	2.00	6.00	14.00
2-6-Davy Crockett in all	1.00	3.00	7.00
7-Origin Cheyenne Kid	1.00	3.00	7.00

WILD KINGDOM (TV)
1965 (Giveaway) (regular size) (16 pgs.)
Western Printing Co.

Mutual of Omaha's. . .	.85	2.50	6.00

WILD WEST (Wild Western No. 3 on)
Spring, 1948 - No. 2, July, 1948
Marvel Comics (WFP)

1-Two-Gun Kid, Arizona Annie, & Tex Taylor begin	6.00	18.00	42.00
2-Captain Tootsie by Beck	4.50	13.50	31.00

WILD WEST (Black Fury No. 1-57)
No. 58, November, 1966
Charlton Comics

V2No.58		.50	1.00

WILD WESTERN (Wild West No. 1,2)
No. 3, 9/48 - No. 57, 9/57 (52pgs, 3-11; 36pgs, 12-on)
Marvel/Atlas Comics (WFP)

3(No.1)-Two-Gun Kid, Tex Morgan, Tex Taylor, Kid Colt, & Arizona Annie begin	6.00	18.00	42.00
4-Last Arizona Annie; Captain Tootsie by Beck	4.65	14.00	32.00
5-2nd app. Black Rider (1/49); Blaze Carson, Captain Tootsie by Beck app.	5.50	16.50	38.00
6-8: 6-Blaze Carson app; Anti-Wertham editorial	3.50	10.50	24.00
9-Photo-c; Black Rider begins, ends No.19	4.00	12.00	28.00
10-Charles Starrett photo-c	4.65	14.00	32.00
11-(Last 52 pg. issue)	3.00	9.00	21.00
12-14,16-19: All Black Rider-c/stories. 12-14-The Prairie Kid & his horse Fury app.	2.75	8.25	19.00
15-Red Larabee, Gunhawk (Origin), his horse Blaze, & Apache Kid begin, end No. 22; Black Rider c/story	3.50	10.50	24.00
20-29: 20-Kid Colt-c begin	2.15	6.50	15.00
30-Katz-a	2.50	7.50	17.50
31-37,39,40	1.50	4.50	10.00
38-War issue; Kubert-a	1.50	4.50	10.00
41-47,49-51,53,57	1.15	3.50	8.00
48-Williamson/Torres-a, 4 pgs; Drucker-a	3.85	11.50	27.00
52-Crandall-a	2.65	8.00	18.00
54,55-Williamson-a in both, 5 & 4 pgs., No. 54 with Mayo plus 2 text illos.	3.35	10.00	23.00
56-Baker-a?	2.00	6.00	14.00

NOTE: ***Annie Oakley*** *in No. 46, 47.* ***Arizona Kid*** *in No. 21, 23.* ***Arrowhead*** *in No. 34-39.* ***Black Rider*** *in No. 5, 9-19, 33-44.* ***Fighting Texan*** *in No. 17.* ***Kid Colt*** *in No. 4-6, 9-11, 20-47, 52, 54-56.* ***Outlaw Kid*** *in No. 43.* ***Red Hawkins*** *in No. 13, 14.* ***Ringo Kid*** *in No. 26, 41, 43, 44, 46, 47, 52-56.* ***Tex Morgan*** *in No. 3, 4, 6, 9, 11.* ***Tex Taylor*** *in No. 3-6, 9, 11.* ***Texas Kid*** *in No. 23-25.* ***Two-Gun Kid*** *in No. 3-6, 9, 11, 12, 33-39, 41.* ***Wyatt Earp*** *in No.47.* ***Ayers*** *a-41.* ***Berg*** *a-26; c-24.* ***Colan*** *a-49.* ***Forte*** *a-28, 30.* ***Heath*** *a-8; c-34, 44.* ***Keller*** *a-24, 26, 29-40, 44-46, 52.* ***Maneely*** *a-10, 15, 16, 28, 35, 40, 41, 43-45; c-18-22, 33, 35, 36, 39, 45.* ***Morisi*** *a-23, 52.* ***Pakula*** *a-52.* ***Powell*** *a-51.* ***Severin*** *a-46, 47.* ***Shores*** *a-30, 35, 36.* ***Sinnott*** *a-34-39.* ***Wildey*** *a-43. Bondage c-19.*

WILD WESTERN ACTION (Also see The Bravados)
March, 1971 - No. 3, June, 1971 (52 pgs.)

Wild Bill Hickok #2, © AVON

Wild Boy of the Congo #8, © Z-D

Wild Western #4, © MCG

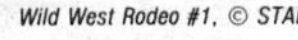
Wild West Rodeo #1, © STAR

Willie the Penguin #1, © STD

Wings Comics #5, © FH

WILD WESTERN ACTION (continued)
Skywald Publishing Corp. (Reprints)

	Good	Fine	Mint
1-Durango Kid, Straight Arrow; with all references to "Straight" in the story relettered to "Swift;" Bravados begin		.50	1.00
2-Billy Nevada, Durango Kid		.30	.60
3-Red Mask, Durango Kid		.30	.60

WILD WESTERN ROUNDUP
Oct, 1957; 1964
Red Top/Decker Publications/I. W. Enterprises

1(1957)-Kid Cowboy-r	.85	2.50	6.00
I.W. Reprint No. 1('60-61)	.25	.75	1.50

WILD WEST RODEO
1953 (15 cents)
Star Publications

1-A comic book coloring book with regular full color cover & B&W inside	2.15	6.50	15.00

WILD WILD WEST, THE (TV)
June, 1966 - No. 7, Oct, 1969
Gold Key

1,2-McWilliams-a	2.35	7.00	16.00
3-7	1.50	4.50	10.00

WILKIN BOY (See That . . .)

WILLIE COMICS (Formerly Ideal No. 1-4; Crime Cases No. 24 on; Li'l Willie No. 20 & 21) (See Wisco)
No. 5, Fall, 1946 - No. 19, 4/49; No. 22, 1/50 - No. 23, 5/50 (No No. 20 & 21)
Marvel Comics (MgPC)

5(No.1)-Nellie The Nurse, Margie begin	3.15	9.50	22.00
6,8,9	1.65	5.00	11.50
7(1),10,11-Kurtzman's "Hey Look"	2.65	8.00	18.00
12,14-18,22,23	1.30	4.00	9.00
13,19-Kurtzman's "Hey Look"	2.35	7.00	16.00

NOTE: *Cindy app.-17. Jeanie app.-17. Little Lizzie app.-22.*

WILLIE MAYS (See The Amazing . . .)

WILLIE THE PENGUIN
April, 1951 - No. 6, April, 1952
Standard Comics

1	1.15	3.50	8.00
2-6	.55	1.65	4.00

WILLIE THE WISE-GUY
Sept, 1957
Atlas Comics (NPP)

1: Kida, Maneely-a	.85	2.50	6.00

WILLIE WESTINGHOUSE EDISON SMITH THE BOY INVENTOR
1906 (36 pgs. in color) (10x16")
William A. Stokes Co.

By Frank Crane	13.00	40.00	90.00

WILL ROGERS WESTERN (Also see Blazing Comics)
No. 5, June, 1950 - No. 2, Aug, 1950
Fox Features Syndicate

5,2: Photo-c	6.00	18.00	42.00

WILL-YUM (See 4-Color No. 676,765,902)

WIN A PRIZE COMICS (Timmy The Timid Ghost No. 3 on?)
Feb, 1955 - No. 2, Apr, 1955
Charlton Comics

V1No.1-S&K-a; Poe adapt; E.C. War swipe	16.00	48.00	110.00
2-S&K-a	11.50	34.50	80.00

WINDY & WILLY
May-June, 1969 - No. 4, Nov-Dec, 1969
National Periodical Publications

	Good	Fine	Mint
1-4: r-/Dobie Gillis with some art changes		.50	1.00

WINGS COMICS
Sept, 1940 - No. 124, 1954
Fiction House Magazines

1-Skull Squad, Clipper Kirk, Suicide Smith, Jane Martin, War Nurse, Phantom Falcons, Greasemonkey Griffin, Parachute Patrol, & Powder Burns begin	50.00	150.00	350.00
2	25.00	75.00	175.00
3-5	20.00	60.00	140.00
6-10	16.00	48.00	110.00
11-15	13.00	40.00	90.00
16-Origin Captain Wings	14.50	43.50	100.00
17-20	11.00	33.00	76.00
21-30	10.00	30.00	70.00
31-40	8.50	25.50	60.00
41-50	7.00	21.00	50.00
51-60: 60-Last Skull Squad	6.00	18.00	42.00
61-67: 66-Ghost Patrol begins (becomes Ghost Squadron No. 71)	6.00	18.00	42.00
68,69: 68-Clipper Kirk becomes The Phantom Falcon-origin, Part 1; Part 2-No. 69	6.00	18.00	42.00
70-72: 70-1st app. The Phantom Falcon in costume, origin-Part 3; Capt. Wings battles Col. Kamikaze in all	5.00	15.00	35.00
73-80: 73-Bra & slip panels	5.00	15.00	35.00
81-99	5.00	15.00	35.00
100	6.00	18.00	42.00
101-114,116-124: 111-Last Jane Martin. 112-Flying Saucer c/story	3.75	11.25	26.00
115-Used in **POP**, pg. 89	4.35	13.00	30.00

NOTE: *Bondage covers are common. Captain Wings battles Sky Hag-No. 75, 76; . . . Mr. Atlantis-No. 85-92; . . . Mr. Pupin(Red Agent)-No. 98-103. Capt. Wings by* ***Elias****-No. 52-64; by* ***Lubbers****-No. 29-32,70-103; by* ***Renee****-No. 33-46.* ***Evans*** *a-85-103, 108(Jane Martin).* ***Larsen*** *a-52, 59, 64, 73-77. Jane Martin by* ***Fran Hopper****-No. 68-84; Suicide Smith by* ***John Celardo****-No. 76-103; by* ***Hollingsworth****-No. 105-109; Ghost Patrol by* ***Maurice Whitman****-No. 83-103; Skull Squad by* ***M. Baker****-No. 52-60; Clipper Kirk by* ***Baker****-No. 60, 61; Ghost Squadron by* ***Whitman****-No. 72-77, 104-110.* ***Tuska*** *a-5.*

WINGS OF THE EAGLES, THE (See 4-Color No. 790)

WINKY DINK (Adventures of . . .)
No. 75, March, 1957 (One Shot)
Pines Comics

75-Marv Levy c/a	1.30	4.00	9.00

WINKY DINK (See 4-Color No. 663)

WINNIE-THE-POOH
January, 1977 - No. 33, 1984 (Walt Disney)
(Winnie-The-Pooh began as Edward Bear in 1926 by Milne)
Gold Key No. 1-17/Whitman No. 18 on

1-New art	.25	.75	1.50
2-4,6-11		.40	.80
5,12-33-New material		.35	.70

WINNIE WINKLE
1930 - 1933 (52 pgs.) (B&W daily strip reprints)
Cupples & Leon Co.

1	6.00	18.00	42.00
2-4	4.35	13.00	30.00

WINNIE WINKLE
1941 - No. 7, Sept-Nov, 1949
Dell Publishing Co.

Large Feature Comic 2('41)	8.00	24.00	56.00
4-Color 94('45)	6.50	19.50	45.00
4-Color 174	3.50	10.50	24.00

WINNIE WINKLE (continued) **Good** **Fine** **Mint**

1(3-5/48)-Contains daily & Sunday newspaper-r from 1939-1941 3.00 9.00 21.00
2 (6-8/48) 1.75 5.25 12.00
3-7 1.50 4.50 10.00

WISCO/KLARER COMIC BOOK (Miniature)
1948 - 1964 (24 pgs.) (3½x6¾")
Given away by Wisco "99" Service Stations, Carnation Malted Milk, Klarer Health Wieners, Fleers Dubble Bubble Gum, Rodeo All-Meat Wieners, Perfect Potato Chips, & others; see ad in Tom Mix No.21
Vital Publications/Fawcett Publications

Blackstone & the Gold Medal Mystery(1948) 2.00 6.00 12.00
Blackstone "Solves the Sealed Vault Mystery"(1950) 2.00 6.00 12.00
Blaze Carson in "The Sheriff Shoots It Out"(1950) 2.00 6.00 12.00
Captain Marvel & Billy's Big Game (r-/Capt. Marvel Adv. No. 76) 24.00 70.00 145.00
(Prices vary widely on this book)
China Boy in "A Trip to the Zoo" No. 10 .85 2.50 5.00
Indoors-Outdoors Game Book .85 2.50 5.00
Jim Solar Space Sheriff in "Battle for Mars," "Between Two Worlds," "Conquers Outer Space," "The Creatures on the Comet," "Defeats the Moon Missile Men," "Encounter Creatures on Comet," "Meet the Jupiter Jumpers," "Meets the Man From Mars," "On Traffic Duty," "Outlaws of the Spaceways," "Pirates of the Planet X," "Protects Space Lanes," "Raiders From the Sun," "Ring Around Saturn," "Robots of Rhea," "The Sky Ruby," "Spacetts of the Sky," "Spidermen of Venus," "Trouble on Mercury" 2.00 6.00 12.00
Johnny Starboard & the Underseas Pirates('48) .70 2.00 4.00
Kid Colt in "He Lived by His Guns"('50) 2.35 7.00 14.00
Little Aspirin as "Crook Catcher" No. 2('50) .60 1.80 3.60
Little Aspirin in "Naughty But Nice" No. 6(1950) .60 1.80 3.60
Return of the Black Phantom 1.70 5.00 10.00
Secrets of Magic 1.00 3.00 6.00
Slim Morgan "Brings Justice to Mesa City" No. 3 1.00 3.00 6.00
Super Rabbit(1950)-Cuts Red Tape, Stops Crime Wave! 1.20 3.50 7.00
Tex Farnum, Frontiersman(1948) 1.30 4.00 8.00
Tex Taylor in "Draw or Die, Cowpoke!"('50) 2.00 6.00 12.00
Tex Taylor in "An Exciting Adventure at the Gold Mine"('50) 2.00 6.00 12.00
Wacky Quacky in "All-Aboard" .50 1.50 3.00
When School Is Out .50 1.50 3.00
Willie in a "Comic-Comic Book Fall" No. 1 .50 1.50 3.00
Wonder Duck "An Adventure at the Rodeo of the Fearless Quack-er!" (1950) .50 1.50 3.00
Rare uncut version of three; includes Capt. Marvel, Tex Farnum, Black Phantom Estimated value.... $250.00

WISE LITTLE HEN, THE
1934 (48 pgs.); 1935; 1937 (Story book)
David McKay Publ./Whitman

1st book app. Donald Duck; Donald app. on cover with Wise Little Hen & Practical Pig; painted cover; same artist as the B&W's from Silly Symphony Cartoon, The Wise Little Hen (1934)(McKay) 21.00 62.00 146.00
1935 Edition with dust jacket; 44 pgs. with color, 8¾x9¾" (Whitman) 18.00 54.00 126.00
888(1937)-9½x13", 12 pgs. (Whitman) Donald Duck app. 13.00 40.00 90.00

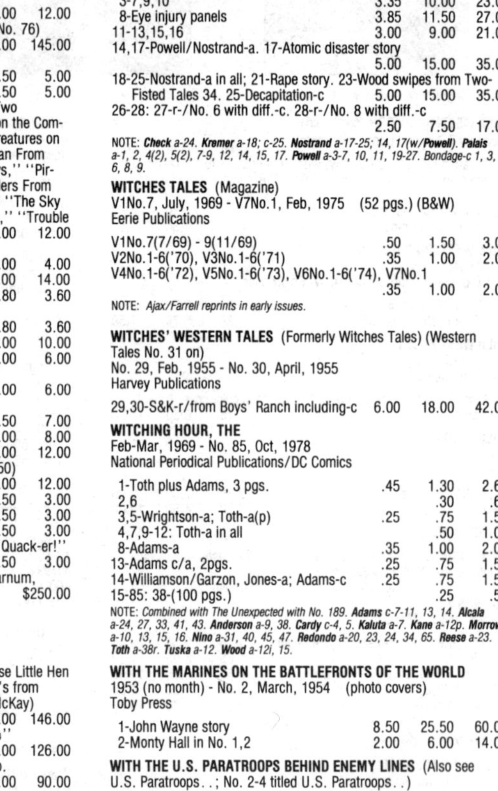

WITCHCRAFT
Mar-Apr, 1952 - No. 6, Mar, 1953
Avon Periodicals

	Good	Fine	Mint
1-Kubert-a; 1pg. check	20.00	60.00	140.00
2-Kubert & Check-a	11.50	34.50	80.00
3,6: 3-Kinstler, Lawrence-a	8.00	24.00	56.00
4-People cooked alive c/s	8.50	25.50	60.00
5-Kelly Freas-c	13.00	40.00	90.00

NOTE: ***Hollingsworth** a-4-6; c-4, 6.*

WITCHES TALES (Witches Western Tales No. 29,30)
Jan, 1951 - No. 28, Dec, 1954 (date misprinted as 4/55)
Witches Tales/Harvey Publications

1-1pg. Powell-a 11.50 34.50 80.00
2-Eye injury panel 4.00 12.00 28.00
3-7,9,10 3.35 10.00 23.00
8-Eye injury panels 3.85 11.50 27.00
11-13,15,16 3.00 9.00 21.00
14,17-Powell/Nostrand-a. 17-Atomic disaster story 5.00 15.00 35.00
18-25-Nostrand-a in all; 21-Rape story. 23-Wood swipes from Two-Fisted Tales 34. 25-Decapitation-c 5.00 15.00 35.00
26-28: 27-r-/No. 6 with diff.-c. 28-r-/No. 8 with diff.-c 2.50 7.50 17.00

NOTE: ***Check** a-24. **Kremer** a-18; c-25. **Nostrand** a-17-25; 14, 17(w/**Powell**). **Palais** a-1, 2, 4(2), 5(2), 7-9, 12, 14, 15, 17. **Powell** a-3-7, 10, 11, 19-27. Bondage-c 1, 3, 5, 6, 8, 9.*

WITCHES TALES (Magazine)
V1No.7, July, 1969 - V7No.1, Feb, 1975 (52 pgs.) (B&W)
Eerie Publications

V1No.7(7/69) - 9(11/69) .50 1.50 3.00
V2No.1-6('70), V3No.1-6('71) .35 1.00 2.00
V4No.1-6('72), V5No.1-6('73), V6No.1-6('74), V7No.1 .35 1.00 2.00

NOTE: *Ajax/Farrell reprints in early issues.*

WITCHES' WESTERN TALES (Formerly Witches Tales) (Western Tales No. 31 on)
No. 29, Feb, 1955 - No. 30, April, 1955
Harvey Publications

29,30-S&K-r/from Boys' Ranch including-c 6.00 18.00 42.00

WITCHING HOUR, THE
Feb-Mar, 1969 - No. 85, Oct, 1978
National Periodical Publications/DC Comics

1-Toth plus Adams, 3 pgs. .45 1.30 2.60
2,6 .30 .60
3,5-Wrightson-a; Toth-a(p) .25 .75 1.50
4,7,9-12: Toth-a in all .50 1.00
8-Adams-a .35 1.00 2.00
13-Adams c/a, 2pgs. .25 .75 1.50
14-Williamson/Garzon, Jones-a; Adams-c .25 .75 1.50
15-85: 38-(100 pgs.) .25 .50

NOTE: *Combined with The Unexpected with No. 189. **Adams** c-7-11, 13, 14. **Alcala** a-24, 27, 33, 41, 43. **Anderson** a-9, 38. **Cardy** c-4, 5. **Kaluta** a-7. **Kane** a-12p. **Morrow** a-10, 13, 15, 16. **Nino** a-31, 40, 45, 47. **Redondo** a-20, 23, 24, 34, 65. **Reese** a-23. **Toth** a-38r. **Tuska** a-12. **Wood** a-12i, 15.*

WITH THE MARINES ON THE BATTLEFRONTS OF THE WORLD
1953 (no month) - No. 2, March, 1954 (photo covers)
Toby Press

1-John Wayne story 8.50 25.50 60.00
2-Monty Hall in No. 1,2 2.00 6.00 14.00

WITH THE U.S. PARATROOPS BEHIND ENEMY LINES (Also see U.S. Paratroops..; No. 2-4 titled U.S. Paratroops..)

Witchcraft #2, © AVON

Witches Tales #1, © HARV

With the Marines... #1, © TOBY

Wolverine #4, © MCG

Wonder Comics #18, © BP

Wonder Duck #1, © MCG

WITH THE U.S. PARATROOPS... (cont'd.)
1951 - No. 6, Dec, 1952
Avon Periodicals

	Good	Fine	Mint
1-Wood-c & inside-c	7.00	21.00	50.00
2	4.35	13.00	30.00
3-6	3.65	11.00	25.00

NOTE: *Kinstler a-2, 5, 6; c-2, 4, 5.*

WITNESS, THE (Also see Amazing Mysteries, Captain America 71, Ideal 4, Marvel Mystery 92 & Mystic No. 7)
Sept, 1948
Marvel Comics (MjMe)

1(Scarce)-No Everett-c 33.00 100.00 230.00

WITTY COMICS
1945
Irwin H. Rubin Publ./Chicago Nite Life News No. 2

1-The Pioneer, Junior Patrol 3.65 11.00 25.00
2-The Pioneer, Junior Patrol 2.00 6.00 14.00
3-7-Skyhawk 1.65 5.00 11.50

WIZARD OF OZ (See Classics Ill. Jr. 535, Dell Jr. Treasury No. 5, 4-Color No. 1308, First Comics Graphic Novel, Marvelous..., & Marvel Treasury of Oz)

WIZARD OF TIME, THE
April, 1986 - Present ($1.50, B&W)
David House

1,2 .25 .70 1.40

WIZARD WORKS
1985 - No. 4 (4 issue mini-series)(B&W)
Fantasy General Comics

1-4 .30 .90 1.70

WOLF GAL (See Al Capp's...)

WOLFMAN, THE (See Book & Record Set & Movie Classics)

WOLVERINE (See Kitty Pryde &..., Incred. Hulk &... & Spider-Man vs...)
Sept, 1982 - No. 4, Dec, 1982 (mini-series)
Marvel Comics Group

1-Frank Miller-c/a(p) .65 1.90 3.80
2-4-Miller-c/a(p) .55 1.60 3.20

WOMAN OF THE PROMISE, THE
1950 (General Distr.) (32 pgs.) (paper cover)
Catechetical Guild

5.00 15.00 30.00

WOMEN IN LOVE (A Feature Presentation No. 5)
Aug, 1949 - No. 4, Feb, 1950
Fox Features Synd./Hero Books

1 10.00 30.00 70.00
2-Kamen/Feldstein-c 8.00 24.00 56.00
3 5.50 16.50 38.00
4-Wood-a 8.00 24.00 56.00

WOMEN IN LOVE
Winter, 1952 (100 pgs.)
Ziff-Davis Publishing Co.

nn-Kinstler-a (Scarce) 18.00 54.00 126.00

WOMEN OUTLAWS (My Love Memories No. 9 on)
July, 1948 - No. 8, Sept, 1949 (Also see Red Circle)
Fox Features Syndicate

1-Used in **SOTI**, illo-''Giving children an image of American womanhood''; negligee panels 21.00 62.00 145.00
2-Spanking panel 17.00 51.00 120.00
3-Kamen-a 13.00 40.00 90.00

	Good	Fine	Mint
4-8	10.00	30.00	70.00
nn(nd)-Contains Cody of the Pony Express	8.00	24.00	56.00

WOMEN TO LOVE
No date (1953)
Realistic

nn-(Scarce)-Reprint/Complete Romance No. 1; c-/Avon paperback 165 18.00 54.00 126.00

WONDER BOY (Formerly Terrific Comics) (See Bomber Comics)
No. 17, May, 1955 - No. 18, July, 1955
Ajax/Farrell Publ.

17-Phantom Lady app. Bakerish a/c 8.50 25.50 60.00
18-Phantom Lady app. 8.00 24.00 56.00

NOTE: *Phantom Lady not by Matt Baker.*

WONDER COMICS (Wonderworld No. 3 on)
May, 1939 - No. 2, June, 1939
Fox Features Syndicate

1-(Scarce)-Wonder Man only app. by Will Eisner; Dr. Fung (by Powell), K-51 begins; Bob Kane-a; Eisner-c 260.00 780.00 1820.00
2-(Scarce)-Yarko the Great, Master Magician by Eisner begins; 'Spark' Stevens by Bob Kane, Patty O'Day, Tex Mason app. Lou Fine's 1st-c; a(2pgs.) 140.00 420.00 980.00

WONDER COMICS
May, 1944 - No. 20, Oct, 1948
Great/Nedor/Better Publications

1-The Grim Reaper & Spectro, the Mind Reader begin; Hitler/Hirohito bondage-c 24.50 74.00 170.00
2-Origin The Grim Reaper; Super Sleuths begin, end No. 8,17 14.50 43.50 100.00
3-5 13.00 40.00 90.00
6-10: 6-Flag-c. 8-Last Spectro. 9-Wonderman begins 11.00 33.00 76.00
11-14-Dick Devens, King of Futuria begins No. 11, ends No. 14 13.00 40.00 90.00
15-Tara begins (origin), ends No. 20 13.50 40.50 95.00
16,18: 16-Spectro app.; last Grim Reaper. 18-The Silver Knight begins 12.00 36.00 84.00
17-Wonderman with Frazetta panels; Jill Trent with all Frazetta inks 15.00 45.00 105.00
19-Frazetta panels 13.50 40.50 95.00
20-Most of Silver Knight by Frazetta 16.50 50.00 115.00

NOTE: *Ingels c-11, 12. Schomburg (Xela) c-1-10; (airbrush)-13-20. Bondage-c 12, 13, 15.*

WONDER DUCK (See Wisco)
Sept, 1949 - No. 3, Mar, 1950
Marvel Comics (CDS)

1 3.00 9.00 21.00
2,3 2.00 6.00 14.00

WONDERFUL ADVENTURES OF PINOCCHIO, THE (See Movie Comics)
April, 1982 (Walt Disney)
Whitman Publishing Co.

3-(Continuation of Movie Comics?); r-/FC No. 92 .30 .60

WONDERFUL WORLD OF DUCKS (See Golden Picture Story Book)
1975
Colgate Palmolive Co.

1-Mostly-r .30 .60

WONDERFUL WORLD OF THE BROTHERS GRIMM (See Movie Comics)

WONDERLAND COMICS
Summer, 1945 - No. 9, Feb-Mar, 1947

WONDERLAND COMICS (continued)
Feature Publications/Prize

	Good	Fine	Mint
1	2.50	7.50	17.50
2	1.30	4.00	9.00
3-9	1.00	3.00	7.00

WONDER MAN
Mar, 1986 (One-Shot, 52 pgs.)
Marvel Comics Group

	Good	Fine	Mint
1	.25	.75	1.50

WONDERS OF ALADDIN, THE (See 4-Color No. 1255)

WONDER WOMAN (See Adventure, All-Star Comics, Brave & the Bold, DC Comics Presents, Legend of . . . , Sensation Comics, and World's Finest)

WONDER WOMAN
Summer, 1942 - No. 329, Feb, 1986
National Periodical Publications/All-American Publ.

	Good	Fine	Mint
1-Origin Wonder Woman retold (see All-Star No. 8); reprinted in Famous 1st Editions; H. G. Peter-a begins	250.00	750.00	1750.00
2-Origin & 1st app. Mars; Duke of Deception app.	85.00	255.00	595.00
3	62.00	185.00	435.00
4,5: 5-1st Dr. Psycho app.	45.00	135.00	315.00
6-10: 6-1st Cheetah app.	35.00	105.00	245.00
11-20	25.00	75.00	175.00
21-30	20.00	60.00	140.00
31-40	15.00	45.00	105.00
41-44,46-48	11.50	34.50	80.00
45-Origin retold	20.00	60.00	140.00
49-Used in **SOTI**, pgs. 234,236. Last 52 pg. ish	12.00	36.00	84.00
50-(44 pgs.)-Used in **POP**, pg. 97	9.50	28.50	65.00
51-60	8.50	25.50	60.00
61-72: 62-Origin of W.W. i.d. 64-Story about 3-D movies. 70-1st Angle Man app. 72-Last pre-code	7.00	21.00	50.00
73-90: 80-Origin The Invisible Plane	5.50	16.50	38.00
91-94,96-99: 97-Last H. G. Peter-a. 99-Origin W.W. i.d. with new facts	3.75	11.25	26.00
95-A-Bomb-c	4.35	13.00	30.00
100	4.65	14.00	32.00
101-104,106-110: 107-1st advs. of Wonder Girl; 1st Merboy; tells how W.W. won her costume	2.85	8.50	20.00
105-(Scarce)-Wonder Woman's secret origin; 1st app. Wonder Girl	5.75	17.25	40.00
111-120	1.85	5.50	13.00
121-126: 122-1st app. Wonder Tot. 124-1st app. Won. Wom. Family. 126-Last 10¢ ish.	1.20	3.50	8.00
127-130: 128-Origin The Invisible Plane retold	1.10	3.25	7.50
131-150	.85	2.50	5.00
151-158,160-170	.70	2.00	4.00
159-Origin retold	.85	2.50	5.00
171-178	.50	1.50	3.00
179-195: 179-No costume, plain clothes adventures to issue No. 203. 180-Death of Steve Trevor. 195-Wood inks?	.45	1.25	2.50
196 (52 pgs.)-Origin r-/All-Star 8	.50	1.50	3.00
197,198 (52 pgs.)-r	.50	1.50	3.00
199,200-Jones-c; 52 pgs.	.85	2.50	5.00
201-210: 204-Return to old costume; death of I Ching. 202-Fafhrd & The Grey Mouser debut		.40	.80
211-217: 211,214(100 pgs.), 217 (68 pgs.)		.35	.70
218-230: 220-Adams assist. 223-Steve Trevor revived as Steve Howard & learns W.W.'s I.D. 228-Both W. Women team up & New World War II stories begin, end No. 243		.35	.70
231-240: 237-Origin retold		.25	.50
241-260: 241-Intro Bouncer. 248-Steve Trevor Howard dies. 250-Intro/origin Orana, the new W. Woman. 251-Orana dies		.25	.50
261-286: 269-Last Wood a(i) for DC? (7/80). 271-Huntress & 3rd Life of Steve Trevor begin		.30	.60
287-New Teen Titans x-over	.25	.75	1.50
288-299: 288-New costume, logo. 291-93-Three part epic with Super-Heroines		.30	.60
300-Double-sized, 76 pg. anniversary issue; Giffen-a; New Teen Titans, JLA app.	.25	.75	1.50
301-309: 308-Huntress begins		.30	.60
310-328 (75¢ cover)		.40	.80
329-Double size		.65	1.30
Pizza Hut Giveaways (12/77)-Exact-r of No. 60,62		.40	.80

NOTE: ***Colan*** *a-288-305p; c-288-90p.* ***Giffen*** *a-300p.* ***Grell*** *c-217.* ***Kaluta*** *c-297.* ***Gil Kane*** *c-294p, 303-05, 307, 312, 314.* ***Miller*** *c-298p.* ***Morrow*** *c-233.* ***Nasser*** *a-232p; c-231p, 232p.* ***Perez*** *c-283p, 284p.* ***Spiegle*** *a-312.* ***Staton*** *a-241p, 271-287p, 289p, 290p, 294-99p; c-241p, 245p, 246p.*

WONDER WOMAN
Feb, 1987 - Present
DC Comics

	Good	Fine	Mint
1-New origin		.40	.80
2,3		.40	.75

WONDER WOMAN SPECTACULAR (See DC Special Series No. 9)

WONDER WORKER OF PERU
No date (16 pgs.) (B&W) (5x7")
Catechetical Guild (Giveaway)

	Good	Fine	Mint
	1.70	5.00	10.00

WONDERWORLD COMICS (Formerly Wonder Comics)
No. 3, July, 1939 - No. 33, Jan, 1942
Fox Features Syndicate

	Good	Fine	Mint
3-Intro The Flame by Fine; Dr. Fung (Powell-a), K-51 (Powell-a?), & Yarko the Great, Master Magician (Eisner-a) continues; Eisner/fine-c	57.00	171.00	400.00
4	43.00	130.00	300.00
5-10	40.00	120.00	280.00
11-Origin The Flame	45.00	135.00	315.00
12-20: 12-Dr. Fung ends	24.00	72.00	168.00
21-Origin The Black Lion & Cub	22.00	65.00	154.00
22-27	17.00	51.00	120.00
28-1st app/origin U.S. Jones; Lu-Nar, the Moon Man begins	20.00	60.00	140.00
29,31-33: 32-Hitler-c	12.00	36.00	84.00
30-Origin Flame Girl	23.00	70.00	160.00

NOTE: *Yarko by* ***Eisner****-No. 3-11.* ***Eisner*** *text illos-3.* ***Lou Fine*** *c/a-3-11; c-12, 13, 15; text illos-4.* ***Powell*** *a-3-12.* ***Tuska*** *a-5-9. Bondage-c 14, 15, 28, 31, 32.*

WONDERWORLD EXPRESS
1984
TrothDona Prod.

	Good	Fine	Mint
1	.35	1.15	2.30

WOODSY OWL (See March of Comics No. 395)
Nov, 1973 - No. 10, Feb, 1976
Gold Key

	Good	Fine	Mint
1	.25	.75	1.50
2-10		.50	1.00

Wonder Man #1, © MCG

Wonder Woman #14, © DC

Wonderworld Comics #20, © FOX

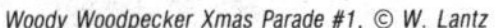
Woody Woodpecker Xmas Parade #1, © W. Lantz

Wordsmith #1, © Renegade

World Around Us #6, © GIL

WOODY WOODPECKER (Walter Lantz . . . No. 73 on?)
(See Dell Giants for annuals)
No. 169, 10/47 - No. 72, 5-7/62; No. 73, 10/62 - No. 201, 4/84 (nn 192)
Dell Publishing Co./Gold Key No. 73-187/Whitman No. 188 on

	Good	Fine	Mint
4-Color 169-Drug turns Woody into a Mr. Hyde	4.65	14.00	32.00
4-Color 188	3.65	11.00	25.00
4-Color 202,232,249,264,288	2.00	6.00	14.00
4-Color 305,336,350	1.50	4.50	10.00
4-Color 364,374,390,405,416,431('52)	1.30	4.00	9.00
16 (12-1/52-53) - 30('55)	1.00	3.00	7.00
31-50	.75	2.25	5.00
51-72	.55	1.65	4.00
73-75 (Giants, 84 pgs.)	1.50	4.50	12.00
76-80	.50	1.50	3.00
81-100	.35	1.00	2.00
101-120		.60	1.20
121-191,193-201		.40	.80
Christmas Parade 1(11/68-Giant)(G.K.)	1.50	4.50	10.00
Clover Stamp-Newspaper Boy Contest('56)-9 pg. story-(Giveaway)	.70	2.00	4.00
In Chevrolet Wonderland(1954-Giveaway)(Western Publ.)-20 pgs., full story line; Chilly Willy app.	2.00	6.00	14.00
Meets Scotty McTape(1953-Scotch Tape giveaway)-16 pgs., full size	1.75	5.25	12.00
Summer Fun 1(6/66-G.K.)(84 pgs.)	1.50	4.50	12.00

NOTE: *15 cents editions exist. Reprints-No. 92, 102, 103, 105, 106, 124, 125, 152, 153, 157, 162, 165, 194(⅓)-200(⅓).*

WOODY WOODPECKER (See Comic Album No. 5,9,13, Dell Giant No. 24, 40, 54, Dell Giants, The Funnies, Golden Comics Digest No. 1, 3, 5, 8, 15, 16, 20, 24, 32, 37, 44, March of Comics No. 16, 34, 85, 93, 109, 124, 139, 158, 177, 184, 203, 222, 239, 249, 261, 420, 454, 466, 478, New Funnies & Super Book No. 12, 24)

WOOLWORTH'S CHRISTMAS STORY BOOK
1952 - 1954 (16 pgs., paper-c) (See Jolly Christmas Book)
Promotional Publ. Co.(Western Printing Co.)

	Good	Fine	Mint
nn	2.00	6.00	14.00

NOTE: *1952 issue-**Marv Levy** c/a.*

WOOLWORTH'S HAPPY TIME CHRISTMAS BOOK
1952 (Christmas giveaway, 36 pgs.)
F. W. Woolworth Co.(Whitman Publ. Co.)

	Good	Fine	Mint
nn	2.00	6.00	14.00

WORDSMITH
Aug, 1985 - Present ($1.70, B&W)
Renegade Press

	Good	Fine	Mint
1-7	.30	.85	1.70

WORLD AROUND US, THE (Ill. Story of . . .)
Sept, 1958 - No. 36, Oct, 1961 (25 cents)
Gilberton Publishers (Classics Illustrated)

	Good	Fine	Mint
1-Dogs	1.50	4.50	10.00
2-Indians-Crandall-a	1.00	3.00	7.00
3-Horses; L. B. Cole-c	1.35	4.00	9.00
4-Railroads	.85	2.50	6.00
5-Space; Ingels-a	2.85	8.50	20.00
6-The F.B.I.; Disbrow, Evans, Ingels-a	2.00	6.00	14.00
7-Pirates; Disbrow, Ingels-a	2.35	7.00	16.00
8-Flight; Evans, Ingels, Crandall-a	2.00	6.00	14.00
9-Army; Disbrow, Ingels, Orlando-a	2.35	7.00	16.00
10-Navy; Disbrow, Kinstler-a	1.35	4.00	9.00
11-Marine Corps.	1.00	3.00	7.00
12-Coast Guard	1.00	3.00	7.00
13-Air Force; L.B. Cole-c	1.35	4.00	9.00
14-French Revolution; Crandall, Evans-a	2.65	8.00	18.00
15-Prehistoric Animals; Al Williamson-a, 6 & 10 pgs. plus Morrow-a	3.00	9.00	21.00
16-Crusades	1.75	5.25	12.00
17-Festivals-Evans, Crandall-a	2.00	6.00	14.00
18-Great Scientists; Crandall, Evans, Torres, Williamson, Morrow-a	2.35	7.00	16.00
19-Jungle; Crandall, Williamson, Morrow-a	3.50	10.50	24.00
20-Communications; Crandall, Evans-a	2.85	8.50	20.00
21-Presidents	1.75	5.25	12.00
22-Boating; Morrow-a	1.35	4.00	9.00
23-Great Explorers; Crandall, Evans-a	1.50	4.50	10.00
24-Ghosts; Morrow, Evans-a	1.50	4.50	10.00
25-Magic; Evans, Morrow-a	2.35	7.00	16.00
26-The Civil War	2.00	6.00	14.00
27-Mountains (High Advs.); Crandall/Evans, Morrow, Torres-a	1.75	5.25	12.00
28-Whaling; Crandall, Evans, Morrow-a; L.B. Cole-c	1.75	5.25	12.00
29-Vikings; Crandall, Evans, Torres, Morrow-a	2.00	6.00	14.00
30-Undersea Adventure; Crandall/Evans, Kirby-a	2.85	8.50	20.00
31-Hunting; Crandall/Evans, Ingels, Kinstler, Kirby-a	2.35	7.00	16.00
32-For Gold & Glory; Morrow, Kirby, Crandall, Evans-a	2.00	6.00	14.00
33-Famous Teens; Torres, Crandall, Evans-a	1.75	5.25	12.00
34-Fishing; Crandall/Evans, Ingels-a	1.50	4.50	10.00
35-Spies; Kirby, Evans, Morrow-a	1.75	5.25	12.00
36-Fight for Life (Medicine); Kirby-a	1.75	5.25	12.00

(See Classics Ill. Special Edition)

WORLD FAMOUS HEROES MAGAZINE
Oct, 1941 - No. 4, Apr, 1942 (a comic book)
Comic Corp. of America (Centaur)

	Good	Fine	Mint
1-Gustavson-c; Lubbers, Glanzman-a; Davy Crockett story; Flag-c	25.00	75.00	175.00
2-Lou Gehrig life story; Lubbers-a	14.50	43.50	100.00
3,4-Lubbers-a	13.50	40.50	95.00

WORLD FAMOUS STORIES
1945
Croyden Publishers

	Good	Fine	Mint
1-Ali Baba, Hansel & Gretel, Rip Van Winkle, Mid-Summer Night's Dream	4.00	12.00	28.00

WORLD IS HIS PARISH, THE
1953 (15 cents)
George A. Pflaum

	Good	Fine	Mint
The story of Pope Pius XII	3.50	10.50	22.00

WORLD OF ADVENTURE (Walt Disney's . . .)(TV)
April, 1963 - Oct, 1963
Gold Key

	Good	Fine	Mint
1-3-Disney TV characters; Savage Sam, Johnny Shiloh, Capt. Nemo, The Mooncussers	.75	2.25	5.00

WORLD OF ARCHIE, THE (See Archie Giant Series Mag. No. 148, 151, 156, 160, 165, 171, 177, 182, 188, 193, 200, 208, 213, 225, 232, 237, 244, 249, 456, 461, 468, 473, 480, 485, 492, 497, 504, 509, 516, 521, 532, 543, 554, 565)

WORLD OF FANTASY
May, 1956 - No. 19, Aug, 1959
Atlas Comics (CPC No. 1-15/ZPC No. 16-19)

	Good	Fine	Mint
1	6.00	18.00	42.00
2-Williamson-a, 4 pgs.	6.00	18.00	42.00
3-Sid Check, Roussos-a	2.65	8.00	18.00
4-7	2.35	7.00	16.00
8-Matt Fox, Orlando, Berg-a	3.00	9.00	21.00
9-Krigstein-a	3.00	9.00	21.00
10,13-15	1.65	5.00	11.50

WORLD OF FANTASY (continued) — Good / Fine / Mint

11-Torres-a 2.65 8.00 18.00
12-Everett-c 1.65 5.00 11.50
16-Williamson-a, 4 pgs.; Ditko, Kirby-a 4.75 14.25 33.00
17-19-Ditko, Kirby-a 3.50 10.50 24.00

NOTE: ***Berg*** *a-5, 6, 8.* ***Check*** *a-3.* ***Ditko*** *a-17, 19.* ***Everett*** *c-4, 5-7, 9, 13.* ***Kirby*** *c-15, 17-19.* ***Krigstein*** *a-9.* ***Maneely*** *c-14.* ***Morrow*** *a-7, 8, 14.* ***Orlando*** *a-8, 13, 14.* ***Powell*** *a-4, 6.*

WORLD OF GIANT COMICS, THE (See Archie All-Star Specials under Archie Comics)

WORLD OF JUGHEAD, THE (See Archie Giant Series Mag. No. 9, 14, 19, 24, 30, 136, 143, 149, 152, 157, 161, 166, 172, 178, 183, 189, 194, 202, 209, 215, 227, 233, 239, 245, 251, 457, 463, 469, 475, 481, 487, 493, 499, 505, 511, 517, 523, 531, 542, 553, 564)

WORLD OF KRYPTON, THE (World of . . . No. 3)
July, 1979 - No. 3, Sept, 1979 (mini-series)
DC Comics, Inc.

1-Jor-El marries Lara .40 .80
2,3: 3-Baby Superman sent to Earth; Krypton explodes; Mon-el app. .30 .60

WORLD OF MYSTERY
June, 1956 - No. 7, July, 1957
Atlas Comics (GPI)

1-Torres, Orlando-a 5.00 15.00 35.00
2-Woodish-a 1.75 5.25 12.00
3-Torres, Davis, Ditko-a 3.75 11.25 26.00
4-Davis, Pakula, Powell-a; Ditko-c 3.75 11.25 26.00
5,7: 5-Orlando-a 1.75 5.25 12.00
6-Williamson/Mayo-a, 4 pgs.; Ditko-a; Crandall text illo 4.00 12.00 28.00

NOTE: ***Colan*** *a-7.* ***Everett*** *c-3.* ***Romita*** *a-2.* ***Severin*** *c/a-7.*

WORLD OF SUSPENSE
April, 1956 - No. 8, July, 1957
Atlas News Co.

1-Orlando-a 5.00 15.00 35.00
2-Ditko-a 2.65 8.00 18.00
3,7-Williamson-a in both, 4 pgs. each; No. 7-with Mayo 3.85 11.50 27.00
4-6,8 1.75 5.25 12.00

NOTE: ***Berg*** *a-6.* ***Ditko*** *a-2.* ***Everett*** *a-1, 5; c-2, 6.* ***Heck*** *a-5.* ***Orlando*** *a-5.* ***Powell*** *a-6.* ***Roussos*** *a-6.*

WORLD OF WHEELS (Formerly Dragstrip Hotrodders)
Oct, 1967 - No. 32, June, 1970
Charlton Comics

17-32-Features Ken King .15 .30
Modern Comics Reprint 23('78) .15 .30

WORLD OF WOOD
1986 - No. 4 (mini-series)($1.75)
Eclipse Comics

1-4 .30 .90 1.80

WORLD'S BEST COMICS (. . . Finest No. 2 on)
Spring, 1941 (Cardboard-c)
National Periodical Publications

1-The Batman, Superman, Crimson Avenger, Johnny Thunder, The King, Young Dr. Davis, Zatara, Lando, Man of Magic, & Red, White & Blue begin (inside covers blank) 243.00 730.00 1700.00

WORLDS BEYOND (Worlds of Fear No. 2 on)
Nov, 1951
Fawcett Publications

Good / Fine / Mint

1-Powell, Bailey-a 7.00 21.00 50.00

WORLD'S FAIR COMICS (See N. Y. . . .)

WORLD'S FINEST COMICS (World's Best No. 1)
No. 2, Sum, 1941 - No. 323, Jan, 1986 (early issues-100 pgs.)
National Periodical Publ./DC Comics (No.1-17 cardboard covers)

2 114.00 342.00 800.00
3-The Sandman begins; last Johnny Thunder; origin & 1st app. The Scarecrow 100.00 300.00 700.00
4-Hop Harrigan app.; last Young Dr. Davis 70.00 210.00 490.00
5-Intro. & only app. TNT & Dan the Dyna-Mite; last King & Crimson Avenger 70.00 210.00 490.00
6-Star Spangled Kid begins; Aquaman app.; S&K Sandman with Sandy in new costume begins, ends No. 7 56.00 166.00 390.00
7-Green Arrow begins; last Lando, King, & Red, White & Blue; S&K art 56.00 166.00 390.00
8-Boy Commandos begin 50.00 150.00 350.00
9-Batman cameo in Star Spangled Kid; S&K-a; last 100pg. ish. 45.00 135.00 315.00
10-S&K-a 45.00 135.00 315.00
11-17-Last cardboard cover issue 38.00 115.00 265.00
18-20: 18-Paper covers begin; last Star Spangled Kid 36.00 107.00 250.00
21-30: 30-Johnny Peril app. 26.00 78.00 180.00
31-40: 33-35-Tomahawk app. 23.00 70.00 160.00
41-50: 41-Boy Commandos end. 42-Wyoming Kid begins, ends No. 63. 43-Full Steam Foley begins, ends No. 48. 48-Last square binding. 49-Tom Sparks, Boy Inventor begins 17.00 51.00 120.00
51-60: 51-Zatara ends. 59-Manhunters Around the World begins, ends No. 62 17.00 51.00 120.00
61-64: 63-Capt. Compass app. 15.00 45.00 105.00
65-Origin Superman; Tomahawk begins, ends No. 101 18.00 54.00 125.00
66-70-(15¢ issues)(Scarce)-Last 68pg. issue 19.00 57.00 132.00
71-(10¢ issue)(Scarce)-Superman & Batman begin as team 25.00 75.00 175.00
72,73-(10¢ issues)(Scarce) 19.00 57.00 132.00
74-80: 74-Last pre-code ish. 8.50 25.50 60.00
81-90: 88-1st Joker/Luthor team-up. 90-Batwoman's 1st app. in World's Finest 5.75 17.25 40.00
91-93,95-99: 96-99-Kirby Green Arrow 3.65 11.00 25.00
94-Origin Superman/Batman team retold 6.85 20.50 48.00
100 8.00 24.00 56.00
101-121: 102-Tommy Tomorrow begins, ends. No. 124. 113-Intro. Miss Arrowette in Green Arrow; 1st Batmite/ Mxyzptlk team-up. 121-Last 10¢ issue 2.65 8.00 18.00
122-141: 125-Aquaman begins, ends No. 139. 140-Last Green Arrow 1.50 4.50 9.00
142-Origin The Composite Superman(Villain); Legion app. 1.50 4.50 9.00
143-150: 143-1st Mailbag 1.00 3.00 6.00
151-160: 156-1st Bizarro Batman .70 2.00 4.00
161,170 (80-Pg. Giant G-28,G-40) .60 1.75 3.50
162-169,171-174: 168,172-Adult Legion app. .50 1.50 3.00
175,176-Adams-a; both r-Jonn' Jonzz' origin/Det. 225,226 .70 2.00 4.00
177,178,180-187,189-196,198-204: 182-Silent Knight-r/Brave & the Bold No. 6. 186-Johnny Quick-r. 187-Green Arrow origin-r/Adv. No. 256. 190-93-Robin-r. 198,199-3rd Superman/Flash race .25 .70 1.40
179,188,197 (80-Pg. Giant G-52,G-64,G-76) .30 .80 1.60

World of Mystery #6, © MCG

World's Best Comics #1, © DC

World's Finest Comics #44, © DC

World's Greatest Songs #1, © MCG

Worlds of Fear #7, © FAW

Wotalife Comics #1 (1959), © Norlen

WORLD'S FINEST COMICS (continued) — **Good** **Fine** **Mint**

205-6 pgs. Shining Knight by Frazetta/Adv. No. 153; 52 pgs.; Teen Titans x-over .35 1.10 2.20
206 (80-Pg. Giant G-88) .60 1.20
207-212 (52 pgs.) .40 .80
213-222: 215-Intro. Batman Jr. & Superman Jr. 217-Metamorpho begins, ends No. 220; Batman/Superman team-up begins .30 .60
223,226-Adams-a(r); 100 pgs.; Deadman origin in 223; 226-S&K, Toth-r; Manhunter part origin-r/Det. 225,226 .25 .75 1.50
224,225,227,228-(100 pgs.) .50 1.00
229-243: 229-r-/origin Superman-Batman team .25 .50
244-248: 244-Green Arrow, Black Canary, Wonder Woman, Vigilante begin; $1.00 size begins. 246-Death of Stuff in Vigilante; origin Vigilante retold. 248-Last Vigilante .40 .80
249-The Creeper begins by Ditko, ends No. 255 .50 1.00
250-The Creeper origin retold by Ditko .40 .80
251-262: 253-Captain Marvel begins. 255-Last Creeper. 256-Hawkman begins. 257-Black Lightning begins .40 .80
263-282 ($1.00): 268-Capt. Marvel Jr origin retold. 274-Zatanna begins. 279,280-Capt. Marvel Jr. & Kid Eternity learn they are brothers. 271-Origin Superman/Batman team retold .40 .80
283-297 (36 pgs.). 284-Legion app. .30 .60
298,299 (75¢ issues begin) .40 .80
300-(52pgs., $1.25)-New Teen Titans app. by Perez .60 1.20
301-323: 304-Origin Null and Void .40 .80
Giveaway (c. 1944-45, 8 pgs., in color, paper-c)-Johnny Everyman-r/W. Finest 10.00 30.00 60.00

NOTE: ***Adams*** *a-230r; c-174-176, 178-180, 182, 183, 185, 186, 199-205, 208-211, 244-246, 258.* ***Austin*** *a-244-246i.* ***Burnley*** *a-8, 10; c-7-9, 12.* ***Colan*** *a-274p.* ***Ditko*** *a-249-255.* ***Giffen*** *c-284p.* ***G. Kane*** *a-38, 174r, 282, 283; c-281, 282, 289.* ***Kirby*** *a-187.* ***Kubert*** *Zatara-40-44.* ***Miller*** *c-285p.* ***Morrow*** *a-245-248.* ***Nasser*** *a(p)-244-246, 259, 260.* ***Newton*** *a-253-281p.* ***Orlando*** *a-224r.* ***Perez*** *a-300i; c-271, 276, 277p, 278p.* ***Robinson*** *a-2, 9, 13-15; c-2-4, 6.* ***Rogers*** *a-259p.* ***Roussos*** *a-212r.* ***Simonson*** *c-291.* ***Spiegle*** *a-275-78, 284.* ***Staton*** *a-262p, 273p.* ***Toth*** *a-228r.* ***Tuska*** *a-230r, 250p, 252p, 254p, 257p, 283p, 284p, 308p.*

(Also see 80 Pg. Giant No. 15.)

WORLD'S FINEST COMICS DIGEST (See DC Special Series 23)

WORLD'S GREATEST ATHLETE (See Walt Disney Showcase No. 14)

WORLD'S GREATEST SONGS
Sept, 1954
Atlas Comics (Male)

1-(Scarce) Heath & Harry Anderson-a 9.50 28.50 65.00

WORLD'S GREATEST STORIES
Jan, 1949 - No. 2, May, 1949
Jubilee Publications

1-Alice in Wonderland 7.00 21.00 50.00
2-Pinocchio 6.00 18.00 42.00

WORLD'S GREATEST SUPER HEROES
1977 (3¾x3¾'') (24 pgs. in color) (Giveaway)
DC Comics (Nutra Comics) (Child Vitamins, Inc.)

Batman & Robin app.; health tips .25 .75 1.50

WORLDS OF FEAR (Worlds Beyond No. 1)
V1No.2, Jan, 1952 - V2No.10, June, 1953
Fawcett Publications

V1No.2-Classic Eyeball-c 7.00 21.00 50.00
3-Evans-a 5.50 16.50 38.00
4-6(9/52) 4.65 14.00 32.00
V2No.7-9 3.65 11.00 25.00
10-Saunders Painted-c; man with no eyes surrounded by eyeballs-c 9.50 28.50 65.00

NOTE: ***Powell*** *a-2, 4, 5.* ***Sekowsky*** *a-4, 5.*

WORLDS UNKNOWN
May, 1973 - No. 8, Aug, 1974
Marvel Comics Group — **Good** **Fine** **Mint**

1-Reprint from Astonishing No. 54; Torres, Reese-a .30 .60
2-8 .20 .40

NOTE: ***Adkins/Mooney*** *a-5.* ***Buscema*** *a/c-4p.* ***W. Howard*** *c/a-3i.* ***Kane*** *a(p)-1,2; c(p)-5, 6, 8.* ***Sutton*** *a-2.* ***Tuska*** *a(p)-7, 8; c-7p. No. 7, 8 has Golden Voyage of Sinbad movie adaptation.*

WORLD WAR STORIES
Apr-June, 1965 - No. 3, Dec, 1965
Dell Publishing Co.

1 1.00 3.00 6.00
2,3: 1-3-Glanzman-a .60 1.75 3.50

WORLD WAR II (See Classics Special Ed.)

WORLD WAR III
Mar, 1953 - No. 2, May, 1953
Ace Periodicals

1-(Scarce)-Atomic bomb-c 35.00 105.00 245.00
2-Used in **POP**, pg. 78 and B&W & color illos. 26.00 78.00 182.00

WORST FROM MAD, THE (Annual)
1958 - No. 12, 1969 (Each annual cover is reprinted from the cover of the Mad issues being reprinted)
E. C. Comics

nn(1958)-Bonus; record labels & travel stickers; 1st Mad annual; r-/Mad No. 29-34 8.50 25.50 60.00
2(1959)-Bonus is small 33⅓ rpm record entitled "Meet the Staff of Mad;" r-/Mad No. 35-40 13.00 40.00 90.00
3(1960)-20''x30''campaign poster "Alfred E. Neuman for President;" r-/Mad No. 41-46 5.75 17.25 40.00
4(1961)-Sunday comics section; r-/Mad No. 47-54 6.00 18.00 42.00
5(1962)-Small 33⅓ rpm record; r-/Mad No. 55-62 9.50 28.50 65.00
6(1963)-Small 33⅓ rpm record; r-/Mad No. 63-70 9.50 28.50 65.00
7(1964)-Mad protest signs; r-/Mad No. 71-76 3.65 11.00 25.00
8(1965)-Build a Mad Zeppelin 5.00 15.00 35.00
9(1966)-33⅓ rpm record 8.00 24.00 56.00
10(1967)-Mad bumper sticker 2.65 8.00 18.00
11(1968)-Mad cover window stickers 2.65 8.00 18.00
12(1969)-Mad picture postcards; Orlando-a 2.35 7.00 16.00

NOTE: *Covers:* ***Bob Clarke****-No. 8.* ***Mingo****-No. 7, 9-12.*

WOTALIFE COMICS
No. 3, Aug-Sept, 1946 - No. 12, July, 1947; 1959
Fox Features Syndicate/Norlen Mag.

3-Cosmo Cat 2.35 7.00 16.00
4-12-Cosmo Cat 1.30 4.00 9.00
1(1959-Norlen)-Atomic Rabbit, Atomic Mouse 1.00 3.00 7.00

WOTALIFE COMICS
1957 - No. 5, 1957
Green Publications

1 1.00 3.00 7.00
2-5 .55 1.65 4.00

WOW COMICS
May, 1936 - No. 4, Nov, 1936
David McKay Publications/Henle Publ.

1-Fu Manchu; Eisner-a 75.00 225.00 525.00
2-Ken Maynard, Fu Manchu, Popeye; Eisner-a 50.00 150.00 350.00

WOW COMICS (continued)

	Good	Fine	Mint
3-Eisner-c; Popeye, Fu Manchu	50.00	150.00	350.00
4-Flash Gordon by Raymond, Mandrake, Popeye; Eisner-a	75.00	225.00	525.00

WOW COMICS (Real Western Hero No. 70 on)
Wint, 1940-41; No. 2, Summer, 1941 - No. 69, Fall, 1948
Fawcett Publications

	Good	Fine	Mint
nn(No.1)-Origin Mr. Scarlet by S&K; Atom Blake, Boy Wizard, Jim Dolan, & Rick O'Shay begin; Diamond Jack, The White Rajah, & Shipwreck Roberts, only app.; the cover was printed on unstable paper stock and is rarely found in fine or mint condition; blank inside-c; bondage-c by Beck (Rare)	615.00	1850.00	4700.00
(Prices vary widely on this book)			
2-The Hunchback begins	53.00	160.00	370.00
3	32.00	95.00	225.00
4-Origin Pinky	39.00	117.00	272.00
5	26.50	80.00	185.00
6-Origin The Phantom Eagle; Commando Yank begins	21.50	64.50	150.00
7,8,10	21.50	64.50	150.00
9-Capt. Marvel, Capt. Marvel Jr., Shazam app.; Scarlet & Pinky x-over; Mary Marvel begins (cameo)	27.00	81.00	190.00
11-17,19,20: 15-Flag-c	12.00	36.00	84.00
18-1st app. Uncle Marvel (10/43); infinity-c	13.00	40.00	90.00
21-30: 28-Pinky x-over in Mary Marvel	8.00	24.00	56.00
31-40	5.50	16.50	38.00
41-50	4.35	13.00	30.00
51-58: Last Mary Marvel	3.65	11.00	25.00
59-69: 59-Ozzie begins. 65-69-Tom Mix app.	2.85	8.50	20.00

WRECK OF GROSVENOR (See Superior Stories No. 3)

WRINGLE WRANGLE (See 4-Color No. 821)

WULF THE BARBARIAN
Feb, 1975 - No. 4, Sept, 1975
Atlas/Seaboard Publ.

	Good	Fine	Mint
1-Origin		.40	.80
2-Intro. Berithe the Swordswoman; Adams, Wood, Reese-a		.30	.60
3,4		.25	.50

WYATT EARP (Hugh O'Brian Famous Marshal)
No. 860, 11/57 - No. 13, 12-2/1960-61 (Photo-c)
Dell Publishing Co.

	Good	Fine	Mint
4-Color 860 (No.1)-Manning-a	4.00	12.00	28.00
4-Color 890,921(6/58)-All Manning-a	3.00	9.00	21.00
4 (9-11/58) - 12-Manning-a	2.65	8.00	18.00
13-Toth-a	3.50	10.50	24.00

WYATT EARP
11/55 - No. 29, 6/60; No. 30, 10/72 - No. 34, 6/73
Atlas Comics/Marvel No. 23 on (IPC)

	Good	Fine	Mint
1	4.00	12.00	28.00
2-Williamson-a, 4 pgs.	3.85	11.50	27.00
3-6,8-11	1.50	4.50	10.00
7,12-Williamson-a, 4 pgs. each; No. 12 with Mayo	3.15	9.50	22.00
13-19	1.15	3.50	8.00
20-Torres-a	1.65	5.00	11.50
21-Davis-c	1.15	3.50	8.00
22-24,26-29: 22-Ringo Kid app. 23-Kid From Texas app. 29-Last 10¢ issue	.75	2.25	5.00
25-Davis-a	1.30	4.00	9.00
30-Williamson-r ('72)		.40	.80
31,33,34-Reprints		.25	.50
32-Torres-a(r)		.30	.60

NOTE: *Everett c-6. Kirby c-25, 29. Maneely c-12, 17, 20. Maurer a-4. Severin a-10; c-10, 14. Wildey a-5, 17, 24, 28.*

WYATT EARP FRONTIER MARSHAL (Formerly Range Busters; See Blue Bird)
No. 12, Jan, 1956 - No. 72, Dec, 1967
Charlton Comics

	Good	Fine	Mint
12	1.75	5.25	12.00
13-19	1.00	3.00	7.00
20-Williamson-a(4), 8,5,5, & 7 pgs.; 68 pg. issue	5.50	16.50	38.00
21-30	.55	1.65	4.00
31-72: 31-Crandall-r		.50	1.00

X-FACTOR
Feb, 1986 - Present
Marvel Comics Group

	Good	Fine	Mint
1-Double size; Layton/Guice-a	.40	1.25	2.50
2,3	.35	1.00	2.00
4,5	.25	.80	1.60
6-10		.60	1.20
11-15		.50	1.00
Annual 1 (10/86)	.25	.75	1.50

XMAS COMICS
12?/1941 - No. 2, 12?/1942 (324 pgs.) (50 cents)
No. 3, 12?/1943 - No. 7, 12?/1947 (132 pgs.)
Fawcett Publications

	Good	Fine	Mint
1-Contains Whiz No. 21, Capt. Marvel No. 3, Bulletman No. 2, Wow No. 3, & Master No. 18; Raboy back-c. Not rebound, remaindered comics—printed at same time as originals	120.00	360.00	840.00
2-Capt. Marvel, Bulletman, Spy Smasher	60.00	180.00	420.00
3-7-Funny animals	12.00	36.00	84.00

XMAS COMICS
Dec, 1949 - No. 7, Dec, 1952 (196 pgs.)
Fawcett Publications

	Good	Fine	Mint
4-Contains Whiz, Master, Tom Mix, Captain Marvel, Nyoka, Captain Video, Bob Colt, Monte Hale, Hot Rod Comics, & Battle Stories. Not rebound, remaindered comics—printed at the same time as originals	22.00	65.00	154.00
5-7-Same as above	19.00	57.00	132.00

XMAS FUNNIES
No date (paper cover) (36 pgs.?)
Kinney Shoes (Giveaway)

	Good	Fine	Mint
Contains 1933 color strip-r; Mutt & Jeff, etc.	10.00	30.00	50.00

X-MEN, THE (The Uncanny... No. 142 on; also see Classic X-Men, Heroes For Hope..., Marvel & DC Present, Marvel Team-up, Official Marvel Index To..., Special Edition... & The Uncanny...)
Sept, 1963 - Present
Marvel Comics Group

	Good	Fine	Mint
1-Origin X-Men; 1st app. Magneto	69.00	207.00	480.00
2-1st app. The Vanisher	31.00	92.00	215.00
3-1st app. The Blob	13.00	40.00	100.00
4-1st Quick Silver & Scarlet Witch & Brotherhood of the Evil Mutants	12.00	36.00	85.00
5	10.00	30.00	70.00
6-10: 8-1st Unus the Untouchable. 9-Avengers app. 10-1st Silver-Age app. Ka-Zar	6.50	20.00	46.00
11-15: 11-1st app. The Stranger. 12-Origin Prof. X. 14-1st app. Sentinels. 15-Origin Beast	3.50	10.50	24.00

Wow Comics #23, © FAW

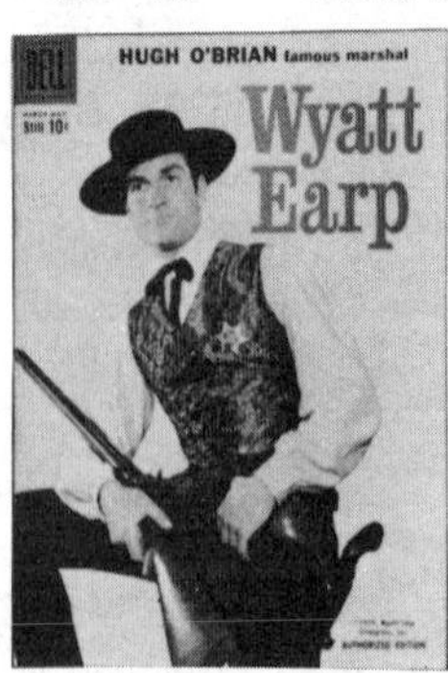

Wyatt Earp #6 (Dell), © Wyatt Earp Ent.

X-Factor #1, © MCG

X-Men #94, © MCG

X-Men #129, © MCG

Yakky Doodle & Chopper #1, © Hanna-Barbera

THE X-MEN (continued)

	Good	Fine	Mint
16-20: 19-1st app. The Mimic	2.65	8.00	18.00
21-27,29,30	2.00	6.00	14.00
28-1st app. The Banshee	2.65	8.00	16.00
31-37	1.50	4.50	9.00
38-Origin The X-Men feature begins, ends No. 57	1.85	5.50	11.00
39,40: 39-New costumes	1.35	4.00	8.00
41-48: 42-Death of Prof. X (Changeling disguised as). 44-Red Raven app. (G.A.)	1.15	3.50	7.00
49-Steranko-c; 1st app. Polaris	1.15	3.50	7.00
50,51-Steranko c/a	1.85	5.50	11.00
52	1.00	3.00	6.00
53-Smith c/a; 1st Smith comic book work	2.15	6.50	13.00
54,55-Smith-c	1.85	5.50	11.00
56-63,65-Adams-a. 56-Intro Havoc without costume. 65-Return of Prof. X. 58-1st app. Havoil	2.85	8.50	17.00
64-1st Sunfire app.	1.85	5.50	11.00
66	1.10	3.25	6.50
67-80: 67-All-r. 67-70,72-(52 pgs.)	.90	2.75	5.50
81-93-r-No. 39-45 with-c	.90	2.75	5.50
94(8/75)-New X-Men begin; Colossus, Nightcrawler, Thunderbird, Storm, Wolverine, & Banshee join; Angel, Marvel Girl, & Iceman resign	15.00	45.00	100.00
95-Death Thunderbird	7.35	22.00	44.00
96-99	5.00	15.00	30.00
100-Old vs. New X-Men; part origin Phoenix	5.85	17.50	35.00
101-Phoenix origin concludes	5.00	15.00	30.00
102-107: 102-Origin Storm. 104-Intro. Star Jammers. 106-Old vs. New X-Men	2.75	8.25	16.50
108-1st Byrne X-Men	5.00	15.00	30.00
109-1st Vindicator	4.60	13.75	27.50
110,111: 110-Phoenix joins	3.00	9.00	18.00
112-119: 117-Origin Prof. X	2.65	8.00	16.00
120-1st app. Alpha Flight (cameo), story line begins	4.50	13.50	27.00
121-1st Alpha Flight (full story)	4.85	14.50	29.00
122-128: 124-Colossus becomes Proletarian	1.70	5.00	10.00
129-Intro Kitty Pryde	1.70	5.00	10.00
130-1st app. The Dazzler by Byrne	2.15	6.50	13.00
131,138-Dazzler app. 138-Cyclops leaves; history of X-Men	1.30	4.00	8.00
132-136: 133-Wolverine goes solo. 134-Phoenix becomes Dark Phoenix	1.30	4.00	8.00
137-Giant; death of Phoenix	1.70	5.00	10.00
139-Alpha Flight app.; Kitty Pryde joins	1.85	5.50	11.00
140-Alpha Flight app.	1.85	5.50	11.00
141-Intro Future X-Men & The New Brotherhood of Evil Mutants; death of Frank Richards	.80	2.40	4.80
142,143: 142-Deaths of Wolverine, Storm & Colossus. 143-Last Byrne issue	.65	1.90	3.80
144-149: 145-Old X-Men app. 148-Spider-Woman, Dazzler app.	.55	1.60	3.20
150-Double size	.55	1.60	3.20
151-164: 161-Origin Magneto. 162-Wolverine app. 163-Origin Binary. 164-1st app. Binary as Carol Danvers	.40	1.20	2.40
165-Paul Smith-a begins	.60	1.75	3.50
166-Double size; Paul Smith-a	.45	1.40	2.80
167-174: 167-New Mutants x-over. 168-1st app. Madelyne Pryor. 171-Rogue joins. 174-Phoenix cameo	.35	1.00	2.00
175-Double size; anniversary issue; Phoenix returns? Paul Smith c/a	.40	1.20	2.40
176-185: 181-Sunfire app.	.30	.90	1.80
186-Double-size; Barry Smith/Austin-a	.35	1.10	2.20
187-192,194-199	.25	.70	1.40
193,200-Double size	.35	1.10	2.20
201-210		.60	1.20
211-220		.50	1.00
Annual 3(2/80)	.90	2.75	5.50
Annual 4(11/80)	.75	2.25	4.50
Annual 5(10/81)	.55	1.65	3.30
Annual 6(11/82)	.35	1.10	2.20
Annual 7(1/84)	.30	.85	1.70
Annual 8(12/84)		.60	1.20
Annual 9(1985)-New Mutants app.	.30	.85	1.70
Annual 10(1/87)	.25	.75	1.50
Giant-Size 1(Summer,'75, 50 cents)-1st app. new X-Men; Intro Nightcrawler, Storm, Colossus & Thunderbird; Wolverine app.	12.00	30.00	85.00
Giant-Size 2(11/75)-51 pgs. Adams-a(r)	2.65	8.00	16.00
Special 1(12/70)-Kirby-c/a; origin The Stranger	2.15	6.50	13.00
Special 2(11/71)	2.15	6.50	13.00

NOTE: ***Art Adams*** *a-Annual 9, 10p.* ***Adams*** *c-56-63.* ***Adkins*** *c-34.* ***Austin*** *a-108i, 109i, 111-17i, 119-43i, 196i, 204i, Annual 3i, 7i, 9i; c-109-111i, 114-22i, 123, 124-41i, 142, 143, Annual 3i.* ***Buscema*** *c-42, 43p, 45p.* ***Byrne*** *a-108p, 109p, 111-43p; c-113-16p, 127p, 129p, 131-41p.* ***Ditko*** *a-90r,* ***Everett*** *c-73.* ***Golden*** *a-Annual 7p.* ***G. Kane*** *c(p)-33, 74-76, 79, 80, 94, 95.* ***Kirby*** *a(p)-1-17 (No.12-17, 24, 27-29, 32, 67r-layouts); c(p)-1-22, 25, 26, 30, 31, 35.* ***Layton*** *a-105i; c-112i, 113i.* ***Miller*** *c-Annual 3.* ***Perez*** *c/a-Annual 3p; c-112p, 128p, Annual 3p.* ***Roussos*** *a-84i.* ***Simonson*** *a-171p; c-171.* ***B. Smith*** *a-198, 205, 214; c-186, 198.* ***Paul Smith*** *a-165-70p, 172-75p; c-165-70, 172-75.* ***Sparling*** *a-78p.* ***Steranko*** *a-50p, 51p; c-49-51.* ***Sutton*** *a-106i.* ***Toth*** *a-12p, 67p(r).* ***Tuska*** *a-40-42i, 44-46p, 88i(r); c-39-41, 77p, 78p.* ***Williamson*** *a-202i, 203i, 211i; c-202i, 203i, 206i.* ***Wood*** *c-14i. 25 cent & 30 cent issues of No. 98 & 99 exist.*

XMEN
Nov, 1986 (One-Shot)
Milky Way Graphics

	Good	Fine	Mint
1-X-Men parody	.25	.75	1.50

X-MEN AND ALPHA FLIGHT
Jan, 1986 - No. 2, Jan, 1986 ($1.50 cover; mini-series)
Marvel Comics Group

	Good	Fine	Mint
1,2: 1-Intro The Berserkers; Paul Smith-a	.40	1.25	2.50

X-MEN AND THE MICRONAUTS, THE
Jan, 1984 - No. 4, April, 1984 (mini-series)
Marvel Comics Group

	Good	Fine	Mint
1-Guice-c/a(p) in all	.30	.90	1.80
2-4		.60	1.20

X-MEN CLASSICS
Dec, 1983 - No. 3, Feb, 1984 ($2.00; Baxter paper)
Marvel Comics Group

	Good	Fine	Mint
1-3: Adams-r/X-Men	.40	1.25	2.50

X, THE MAN WITH THE X-RAY EYES (See Movie Comics)

X-VENTURE
July, 1947 - No. 2, Nov, 1947 (Super heroes)
Victory Magazines Corp.

	Good	Fine	Mint
1-Atom Wizard, Mystery Shadow, Lester Trumble	20.00	60.00	140.00
2	12.00	36.00	84.00

YAK YAK (See 4-Color No. 1186,1348)

YAKKY DOODLE & CHOPPER (TV)
Dec, 1962 (Hanna-Barbera)
Gold Key

	Good	Fine	Mint
1	1.75	5.25	12.00

YALTA TO KOREA
1952 (8 pgs.) (Giveaway) (paper cover)
M. Philip Corp. (Republican National Committee)

	Good	Fine	Mint
Anti-communist propaganda book	15.00	45.00	90.00

YANG (See House of Yang)
11/73 - No. 13, 5/76; V14/14, 9/85 - No. 17, 1/86

YANG (continued)
Charlton Comics

	Good	Fine	Mint
1-Origin		.50	1.00
2-5		.30	.60
6-13 (1976)		.20	.40
14-17 (1986)		.40	.80
3,10,11(Modern Comics-r, 1977)		.15	.30

YANKEE COMICS
Sept, 1941 - No. 4, Mar, 1942
Harry 'A' Chesler

	Good	Fine	Mint
1-Origin The Echo, The Enchanted Dagger, Yankee Doodle Jones, The Firebrand, & The Scarlet Sentry; Black Satan app.	30.00	90.00	210.00
2-Origin Johnny Rebel; Major Victory app.; Barry Kuda begins	19.00	57.00	132.00
3,4	15.00	45.00	105.00

YANKS IN BATTLE
Sept, 1956 - No. 4, Dec, 1956
Quality Comics Group

	Good	Fine	Mint
1	2.50	7.50	17.00
2-4	1.20	3.50	8.00

YANKS IN BATTLE
1963
I. W. Enterprises

	Good	Fine	Mint
Reprint No. 3	.25	.75	1.50

YARDBIRDS, THE (G. I. Joe's Sidekicks)
Summer, 1952
Ziff-Davis Publishing Co.

	Good	Fine	Mint
1-By Bob Oskner	3.00	9.00	21.00

YARNS OF YELLOWSTONE
1972 (36 pages) (50 cents)
World Color Press

	Good	Fine	Mint
Ill. by Bill Chapman	.50	1.50	3.00

YELLOW CLAW
Oct, 1956 - No. 4, April, 1957
Atlas Comics (MjMC)

	Good	Fine	Mint
1-Origin by Joe Maneely	17.00	51.00	120.00
2-Kirby-a	14.50	43.50	100.00
3,4-Kirby-a; 4-Kirby/Severin-a	13.00	40.00	90.00

NOTE: ***Everett*** *c-3.* ***Maneely*** *c-1.* ***Reinman*** *a-2i, 3.* ***Severin*** *c-2, 4.*

YELLOWJACKET COMICS (Jack in the Box No. 11 on)
Sept, 1944 - No. 10, June, 1946
E. Levy/Frank Comunale

	Good	Fine	Mint
1-Origin Yellowjacket; Diana, the Huntress begins	12.00	36.00	84.00
2	7.00	21.00	50.00
3,5	6.50	19.50	45.00
4-Poe's 'Fall Of The House Of Usher' adaptation	7.00	21.00	50.00
6-10: 7,8-Has stories narrated by old witch in 'Tales of Terror'	6.00	18.00	42.00

YELLOWSTONE KELLY (See 4-Color No. 1056)

YELLOW SUBMARINE (See Movie Comics)

YOGI BEAR (TV) (Hanna-Barbera)
No. 1067, 12-2/59-60 - No. 9, 7-9/62; No. 10, 10/62 - No. 42, 10/70
Dell Publishing Co./Gold Key No. 10 on

	Good	Fine	Mint
4-Color 1067	1.75	5.25	12.00
4-Color 1104,1162 (5-7/61)	1.30	4.00	9.00
4(8-9/61) - 6(12-1/61-62)	1.15	3.50	8.00
4-Color 1271(11/61), 1349(1/62)	1.00	3.00	7.00
7(2-3/62) - 9(7-9/62)-Last Dell	1.00	3.00	7.00
10(10/62-G.K.), 11(1/63)-titled "Y.B. Jellystone Jollies"-80 pgs.	1.50	4.50	12.00
12(4/63), 14-20	1.00	3.00	6.00
13(7/63)-Surprise Party, 68 pgs.	1.50	4.50	12.00
21-30	.55	1.65	4.00
31-42	.45	1.25	3.00
...Kite Fun Book('62, 8 pgs.)-paper cover; Pacific Gas & Electric giveaway; nn	1.00	3.00	6.00

YOGI BEAR (See Dell Giant No. 41, March of Comics No. 253, 265, 279, 291, 309, 319, 337, 344, Whitman Comic Books & Movie Comics under "Hey There It's...")

YOGI BEAR (TV)
Nov, 1970 - No. 35, Jan, 1976 (Hanna-Barbera)
Charlton Comics

	Good	Fine	Mint
1	.70	2.00	4.00
2-6,8-35: 28-31-partial-r	.35	1.00	2.00
7-Summer Fun (Giant); 52 pgs.	.35	1.00	2.00

YOGI BEAR (TV)
Nov, 1977 - No. 9, Mar, 1979
Marvel Comics Group

	Good	Fine	Mint
1-Flintstones begin		.40	.80
2-9		.20	.40

YOGI BEAR'S EASTER PARADE (See The Funtastic World of Hanna- Barbera No. 2)

YOGI BERRA (Baseball hero)
1951 (Yankee catcher)
Fawcett Publications

	Good	Fine	Mint
nn	17.00	51.00	120.00

YOSEMITE SAM (...& Bugs Bunny)
Dec, 1970 - No. 81, Feb, 1984
Gold Key/Whitman

	Good	Fine	Mint
1	.50	1.50	3.00
2-10	.35	1.00	2.00
11-30		.50	1.00
31-81: 81-r(⅓)		.30	.60

(See March of Comics No. 363,380,392)

YOUNG ALLIES COMICS (All-Winners No. 21)
Summer, 1941 - No. 20, Oct, 1946
Timely Comics (USA 1-7/NPI 8,9/YAI 10-20)

	Good	Fine	Mint
1-Origin The Young Allies; 1st meeting of Captain America & Human Torch; Red Skull app.; S&K-c/splash	195.00	585.00	1365.00
2-Captain America & Human Torch app.; Simon & Kirby-c	85.00	255.00	595.00
3-Fathertime, Captain America & Human Torch app.	70.00	210.00	480.00
4-The Vagabond & Red Skull, Capt. America, Human Torch app.	55.00	165.00	385.00
5-Captain America & Human Torch app.	40.00	120.00	280.00
6-10: 10-Origin Tommy Tyme & Clock of Ages; ends No. 19	30.00	90.00	210.00
11-20: 12-Classic decapitation story	24.00	72.00	166.00

YOUNG BRIDES
Sept-Oct, 1952 - No. 29, Jul-Aug, 1956 (Photo-c No. 1-13)
Feature/Prize Publications

	Good	Fine	Mint
V1/1-Simon & Kirby-a	5.00	15.00	35.00
2-S&K-a	2.65	8.00	18.00

Yellowjacket Comics #7, © E. Levy

Yogi Bear #10 (Dell), © Hanna-Barbera

Young Allies Comics #19, © MCG

Young Life #2, © QUA

Young Lover Romances #4, © TOBY

Young Men #27, © MCG

YOUNG BRIDES (continued)

	Good	Fine	Mint
3-6-S&K-a	2.35	7.00	16.00
V2/1,3-7,10-12 (No. 7-18)-S&K-a	2.00	6.00	14.00
2,8,9-No S&K	1.00	3.00	7.00
V3/1-3 (No. 19-21)-Last pre-code (3-4/55)	.85	2.50	6.00
4,6 (No. 22,24), V4/1,3 (No. 25,27)	.75	2.25	5.00
V3/5 (No. 23)-Meskin-c	1.15	3.50	8.00
V4/2 (No. 26)-All S&K ish	2.00	6.00	14.00
V4/4 (No. 28)-S&K-a, V4/5(No. 29)	1.15	3.50	8.00

YOUNG DR. MASTERS (See Advs. of Young Dr. Masters)

YOUNG DOCTORS, THE
January, 1963 - No. 6, Nov, 1963
Charlton Comics

	Good	Fine	Mint
V1No.1-6		.40	.80

YOUNG EAGLE
12/50 - No. 10, 6/52; No. 3, 7/56 - No. 5, 4/57 (Photo-c, 1-10)
Fawcett Publications/Charlton

	Good	Fine	Mint
1	4.65	14.00	32.00
2	3.15	9.50	22.00
3-9	2.65	8.00	18.00
10-Origin Thunder, Young Eagle's horse	2.35	7.00	16.00
3-5 (Charlton)-Formerly Sherlock Holmes?	1.00	3.00	7.00

YOUNG HEARTS
Nov, 1949 - No. 2, Feb, 1950
Marvel Comics (SPC)

	Good	Fine	Mint
1-Photo-c	2.85	8.50	20.00
2	1.50	4.50	10.00

YOUNG HEARTS IN LOVE
1964
Super Comics

	Good	Fine	Mint
17,18: 17-R/Young Love V5No.6, 4-5/62	.25	.75	1.50

YOUNG HEROES (Formerly Forbidden Worlds No. 34)
No. 35, Feb-Mar, 1955 - No. 37, June-July, 1955
American Comics Group (Titan)

	Good	Fine	Mint
35-37-Frontier Scout	1.15	3.50	8.00

YOUNG KING COLE (Becomes Criminals on the Run)
Fall, 1945 - V3/12, July, 1948
Premium Group/Novelty Press

	Good	Fine	Mint
V1/1-Toni Gayle begins	5.00	15.00	35.00
2	3.75	11.25	26.00
3-6	3.15	9.50	22.00
V2/1-7(7/47)	2.65	8.00	18.00
V3/1,3-6,12	2.00	6.00	14.00
2-L. B. Cole-a	2.65	8.00	18.00
7-L. B. Cole-c/a	4.00	12.00	28.00
8-11-L. B. Cole-c	3.35	10.00	23.00

YOUNG LAWYERS, THE (TV)
Jan, 1971 - No. 2, April, 1971
Dell Publishing Co.

	Good	Fine	Mint
1,2	1.15	3.50	8.00

YOUNG LIFE (Teen Life No. 3 on)
Spring, 1945 - No. 2, Summer, 1945
New Age Publ./Quality Comics Group

	Good	Fine	Mint
1-Skip Homeier, Louis Prima stories	3.00	9.00	21.00
2-Frank Sinatra c/story	2.00	6.00	14.00

YOUNG LOVE
2-3/49 - No. 73, 12-1/56-57; V3/5, 2-3/60 - V7/1, 6-7/63
Prize (Feature) Publ. (Crestwood)

	Good	Fine	Mint
V1/1-S&K c/a(2)	8.50	25.50	60.00
2-Photo-c begin; S&K-a; lingerie panel	3.85	11.50	27.00
3-S&K-a	2.85	8.50	20.00
4-6-Minor S&K-a	2.00	6.00	14.00
V2/1(No.7)-S&K-a(2)	2.85	8.50	20.00
2-5(No. 8-11)-Minor S&K-a	1.65	5.00	11.50
6,8(No. 12,14)-S&K-c only	2.00	6.00	14.00
7,9-12(No.13,15-18)-S&K c/a	2.85	8.50	20.00
V3/1-4(No. 19-22)-S&K c/a	2.00	6.00	14.00
5-7,9-12(No. 23-25,27-30)-Photo-c resume; S&K-a	1.65	5.00	11.50
8(No. 26)-No S&K	1.15	3.50	8.00
V4/1,6(No. 31,36)-S&K-a	1.65	5.00	11.50
2-5,7-12(No. 32-35,37-42)-Minor S&K-a	1.50	4.50	10.00
V5/1-12(No. 43-54), V6/1-9(No. 55-63)-Last pre-code; S&K-a-some	1.15	3.50	8.00
V6/10-12(No. 64-66)	1.00	3.00	7.00
V7/1-7(No. 67-73)	.55	1.65	4.00
V3/5(2-3/60), 6(4-5/60)(Formerly All For Love)	.45	1.35	3.00
V4/1(6-7/60)-6(4-5/61)	.45	1.35	3.00
V5/1(6-7/61)-6(4-5/62)	.45	1.35	3.00
V6/1(6-7/62)-6(4-5/63), V7/1	.35	1.00	2.00

NOTE: ***Severin/Elder*** *a-V2/3.* ***S&K*** *art not in No. 53, 57, 58, 61, 63-65.* ***Meskin*** *a-27. Photo c-V3/5-V5/11.*

YOUNG LOVE
No. 39, 9-10/63 - No. 120, Winter/75-76; No. 121, 10/76 - No. 126, 7/77
National Periodical Publ. (Arleigh Publ. Corp. No. 49-60)/DC Comics

	Good	Fine	Mint
39-50	.40	1.20	2.40
51-70: 64-Simon & Kirby-a		.50	1.00
71,72,74-77,80		.40	.80
73,78,79-Toth-a		.60	1.20
81-126: 107-114-(100 pgs.). 122-Toth-a		.30	.60

YOUNG LOVER ROMANCES (Formerly & becomes Great Lover. . . ?)
No. 4, June, 1952 - No. 5, Aug, 1952
Toby Press

	Good	Fine	Mint
4,5-Photo-c	1.15	3.50	8.00

YOUNG LOVERS (My Secret Life No. 19 on)
No. 16, 7/56 - No. 18, 5/57 (Formerly Brenda Starr?)
Charlton Comics

	Good	Fine	Mint
16,17('56)	1.15	3.50	8.00
18-Elvis Presley picture-c, text story (biography)	21.00	62.00	146.00

YOUNG MARRIAGE
June, 1950
Fawcett Publications

	Good	Fine	Mint
1-Powell-a; photo-c	3.85	11.50	27.00

YOUNG MEN (Formerly Cowboy Romances) (. . . on the Battlefield No. 12-20 (4/53); . . . In Action No. 21)
No. 4, 6/50 - No. 11, 10/51; No. 12, 12/51 - No. 28, 6/54
Marvel/Atlas Comics (IPC)

	Good	Fine	Mint
4	3.00	9.00	21.00
5-11	1.65	5.00	11.50
12-23	1.50	4.50	10.00
24-Origin Captain America, Human Torch, & Sub-Mariner which are revived thru No. 28. Red Skull app.	25.00	75.00	175.00
25-28	19.00	57.00	132.00

NOTE: ***Berg*** *a-7, 17, 20; c-17.* ***Colan*** *a-15. Sub-Mariner by* ***Everett****-No. 24-27.* ***Everett*** *a-18-20.* ***Heath*** *a-14.* ***Maneely*** *c-15.*

YOUNG REBELS, THE (TV)
January, 1971
Dell Publishing Co.

	Good	Fine	Mint
1	1.00	3.00	7.00

YOUNG ROMANCE COMICS (The 1st romance comic)
Sept-Oct, 1947 - V16/4, June-July, 1963
Prize/Headline (Feature Publ.)

	Good	Fine	Mint
V1/1-S&K c/a(2)	10.00	30.00	70.00
2-S&K c/a(2-3)	5.50	16.50	38.00
3-6-S&K c/a(2-3) each	4.75	14.25	33.00
V2/1-6(No.7-12)-S&K c/a(2-3) each	4.00	12.00	28.00
V3/1-3(No. 13-15)-Last line drawn-c; S&K c/a	2.00	6.00	14.00
4-12(No. 16-24)-Photo-c; S&K-a	2.00	6.00	14.00
V4/1-11(No. 25-35)-S&K-a	1.65	5.00	11.50
12(No. 36)-S&K, Toth-a; Ditko 1st published-a w/Bl. Magic 27	3.50	10.50	24.00
V5/1-12(No.37-48), V6/4-12(No.52-60)-S&K-a	1.50	4.50	10.00
V6/1-3(No. 49-51)-No S&K	1.30	4.00	9.00
V7/1-11(No. 61-71)-S&K-a in most	1.50	4.50	10.00
V7/12(No. 72), V8/1-3(No. 73-75)-Last pre-code (12-1/54-55)-No S&K-a	1.00	3.00	7.00
V8/4(No. 76, 4-5/55), 5(No. 77)-No S&K	.85	2.50	6.00
V8/6-8(No. 78-80, 12-1/55-56)-S&K-a	1.15	3.50	8.00
V9/3,5,6(No. 81, 2-3/56, 83,84)-S&K-a	1.00	3.00	7.00
4, V10/1(No. 82,85)-All S&K-a	1.30	4.00	9.00
V10/2-6(No. 86-90, 10-11/57)-S&K-a	1.00	3.00	7.00
V11/1,2,5,6(No. 91,92,95,96)-S&K-a	1.00	3.00	7.00
3,4(No. 93,94), V12/2,4,5(No. 98,100,101)-No S&K	.85	2.50	6.00
V12/1,3,6(No. 97,99,102)-S&K-a	1.00	3.00	7.00
V13/1(No. 103)-S&K, Powell-a	1.15	3.50	8.00
2-6(No. 104-108)	.45	1.35	3.00
V14/1-6, V15/1-6, V16/1-4(No. 109-124)	.35	1.00	2.00

NOTE: ***Meskin*** *a-16, 24(2), 47.* ***Robinson/Meskin*** *a-6.* ***Leonard Starr*** *a-11. Photo c-16-65.*

YOUNG ROMANCE COMICS
No. 125, Aug-Sept, 1963 - No. 208, Nov-Dec, 1975
National Periodical Publ. (Arleigh Publ. Corp. No. 127)

	Good	Fine	Mint
125-153,155-162	.40	1.20	2.40
154-Adams-c	.50	1.50	3.00
163,164-Toth-a		.50	1.00
165-196: 170-Michell from Young Love ends; Lily Martin, the Swinger begins		.40	.80
197(100 pgs.)-208		.25	.50

YOUR DREAMS (See Strange World of. . .)

YOUR TRIP TO NEWSPAPERLAND
June, 1955 (12 pgs.; 14x11½")
Philadelphia Evening Bulletin (Printed by Harvey Press)

	Good	Fine	Mint
Joe Palooka takes kids on tour through newspaper	2.35	7.00	14.00

YOUR UNITED STATES
1946
Lloyd Jacquet Studios

	Good	Fine	Mint
Used in **SOTI**, pg. 309,310; Sid Greene-a	9.00	27.00	62.00

YOUTHFUL HEARTS (Daring Confessions No. 4 on)
May, 1952 - No. 3, 1952
Youthful Magazines

	Good	Fine	Mint
1-"Monkey on Her Back" swipes E.C. drug story from Shock SuspenStories No. 12	8.50	25.50	60.00
2,3	4.35	13.00	30.00

NOTE: ***Doug Wildey*** *art in all.*

YOUTHFUL LOVE (Truthful Love No. 2)
May, 1950
Youthful Magazines

	Good	Fine	Mint
1	2.65	8.00	18.00

YOUTHFUL ROMANCES (Daring Love No. 15 & 17)
8-9/49 - No. 14, 10/52; No. 16, 3/53; No. 18, 7/53 - No. 8, 5/54
Pix-Parade No. 1-14/Ribage

	Good	Fine	Mint
1-(1st series)-Titled Youthful Love-Romances	6.00	18.00	42.00
2	3.65	11.00	25.00
3-5	3.15	9.50	22.00
6,7,9-14(10/52, Pix-Parade; becomes Daring Love No. 15)	2.15	6.50	15.00
8-Wood-c	8.00	24.00	56.00
16(3/53, Ribage; Formerly Daring Love No. 15; becomes Daring Love No. 17)	2.35	7.00	16.00
18 (7/53; Ribage; formerly Daring Love No. 17)	2.35	7.00	16.00
5 (9/53, Ribage)	1.85	5.50	13.00
6,7 (No. 7, 2/54)	1.50	4.50	10.00
8 (5/54)	1.50	4.50	10.00

ZAGO, JUNGLE PRINCE (My Story No. 5 on)
Sept, 1948 - No. 4, March, 1949
Fox Features Syndicate

	Good	Fine	Mint
1-Blue Beetle app.-partial r-/Atomic No. 4 (Toni Luck)	12.00	36.00	84.00
2,3-Kamen-a	10.00	30.00	70.00
4-Baker-c	9.50	28.50	65.00

ZANE GREY'S STORIES OF THE WEST
No. 197, 9/48 - 11/64 (All painted-c)
Dell Publishing Co./Gold Key 11/64

	Good	Fine	Mint
4-Color 197 (9/48)	4.00	12.00	28.00
4-Color 222,230,236('49)	3.50	10.50	24.00
4-Color 246,255,270,301,314,333,346	2.65	8.00	18.00
4-Color 357,372,395,412,433,449,467,484	2.00	6.00	14.00
4-Color 511-Kinstler-a	2.35	7.00	16.00
4-Color 532,555,583,604,616,632(5/55)	2.00	6.00	14.00
27(9-11/55) - 39(9-11/58)	1.75	5.25	12.00
4-Color 996 (5-7/59)	2.00	6.00	14.00
10131-411-(11/64-G.K.)-Nevada; r-4-Color No. 996	1.15	3.50	8.00

ZANY (Magazine) (Satire) (See Ratfink & Frantic)
Sept, 1958 - No. 4, May, 1959
Candor Publ. Co.

	Good	Fine	Mint
1-Bill Everett-c	2.00	6.00	14.00
2-4	1.35	4.00	9.00

ZAZA, THE MYSTIC (Formerly Charlie Chan; This Magazine Is Haunted V2No.12 on)
April, 1956 - No. 11, Sept, 1956
Charlton Comics

	Good	Fine	Mint
10,11	2.35	7.00	16.00

ZEGRA JUNGLE EMPRESS (Formerly Tegra) (My Love Life No. 6 on)
No. 2, Oct, 1948 - No. 5, April, 1949
Fox Features Syndicate

	Good	Fine	Mint
2	15.00	45.00	105.00
3-5	11.50	34.50	80.00

ZELL, SWORDANCER
1986 - Present?
Thoughts And Images

	Good	Fine	Mint
1	.40	1.25	2.50

ZERO PATROL, THE
Nov, 1984 - Present

Young Romance Comics #36, © PRIZE

Zago, Jungle Prince #2, © FOX

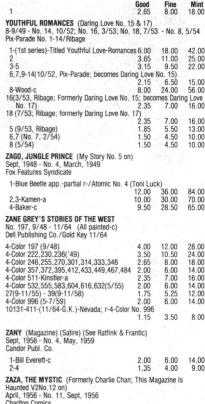

Zane Grey's Stories. . . #33, © DELL

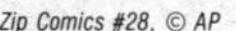
Zip Comics #28, © AP

Zoot #1, © FOX

Zorro #8 (Dell), © WDC

ZERO PATROL (continued)
Continuity Comics

	Good	Fine	Mint
1-5: Adams c/a	.35	1.00	2.00

ZIGGY PIG-SILLY SEAL COMICS (See Animated Movie-Tunes)
Fall, 1944 - No. 6, Fall, 1946 (See Krazy Komics)
Timely Comics (CmPL)

	Good	Fine	Mint
1-Vs. the Japs	5.75	17.25	40.00
2	2.85	8.50	20.00
3-5	2.65	8.00	18.00
6-Infinity-c	4.65	14.00	32.00
I.W. Reprint No. 1('58)-r/Krazy Komics	.50	1.50	3.00
I.W. Reprint No. 2,7,8	.25	.75	1.50

ZIP COMICS
Feb, 1940 - No. 47, Summer, 1944
MLJ Magazines

	Good	Fine	Mint
1-Origin Kalthar the Giant Man, The Scarlet Avenger, & Steel Sterling; Mr. Satan, Nevada Jones & Zambini, the Miracle Man, War Eagle, Captain Valor begins	77.00	231.00	540.00
2	38.00	115.00	265.00
3	30.00	90.00	210.00
4,5	25.00	75.00	175.00
6-9: 9-Last Kalthar & Mr. Satan	22.00	65.00	154.00
10-Inferno, the Flame Breather begins, ends No. 13	20.00	60.00	140.00
11,12: 11-Inferno without costume	17.00	51.00	120.00
13-17,19: 17-Last Scarlet Avenger	17.00	51.00	120.00
18-Wilbur begins (1st app.)	19.00	57.00	132.00
20-Origin Black Jack	27.00	81.00	190.00
21-26: 25-Last Nevada Jones. 26-Black Witch begins; last Captain Valor	17.00	51.00	120.00
27-Intro. Web	25.00	75.00	175.00
28-Origin Web	25.00	75.00	175.00
29,30	14.50	43.50	100.00
31-38: 33,34-Bondage-c. 34-1st Applejack app. 35-Last Zambini, Black Jack. 38-Last Web issue	11.00	33.00	75.00
39-Origin Red Rube (8/43)	11.00	33.00	75.00
40-47: 45-Wilbur ends	7.00	21.00	50.00

NOTE: ***Biro*** *a-5, 9, 17; c-5, 9.* ***Meskin*** *a-1-3, 5-7, 9, 10, 12, 13, 15, 16 at least. Bondage c-8, 9.*

ZIP-JET (Hero)
Feb, 1953 - No. 2, Apr-May, 1953
St. John Publishing Co.

	Good	Fine	Mint
1,2-Rocketman-r/Punch Comics; No. 1 cover from splash in Punch No. 10	12.00	36.00	84.00

ZIPPY THE CHIMP (CBS TV Presents. . .)
No. 50, March, 1957 - No. 51, Aug, 1957
Pines (Literary Ent.)

	Good	Fine	Mint
50,51	1.15	3.50	8.00

ZODY, THE MOD ROB
July, 1970
Gold Key

	Good	Fine	Mint
1	.55	1.65	4.00

ZOO ANIMALS
No. 8, 1954 (36 pages) (15 cents)
Star Publications

	Good	Fine	Mint
8-(B&W for coloring)	1.30	4.00	9.00

ZOO FUNNIES (Tim McCoy No. 16 on)
Nov, 1945 - No. 15, 1947
Charlton Comics/Children Comics Publ.

	Good	Fine	Mint
101(No.1) (1945)	3.50	10.50	24.00
2(9/45)	1.75	5.25	12.00
3-5	1.50	4.50	10.00
6-15: 8-Diana the Huntress app.	1.15	3.50	8.00

ZOO FUNNIES (Becomes Nyoka, The Jungle Girl No. 14 on?)
July, 1953 - No. 13, Sept, 1955; Dec, 1984
Capitol Stories/Charlton Comics

	Good	Fine	Mint
1-1st app.? Timothy The Timid Ghost; Fago-c/a	2.65	8.00	18.00
2	1.30	4.00	9.00
3-7	1.15	3.50	8.00
8-13-Nyoka app.	2.85	8.50	20.00
1 ('84)		.40	.80

ZOONIVERSE
Aug, 1986 - No. 6 ($1.25, color, mini-series)(Mando paper)
Eclipse Comics

	Good	Fine	Mint
1-6		.65	1.30

ZOO PARADE (See 4-Color No. 662)

ZOOM COMICS
December, 1945 (One Shot)
Carlton Publishing Co.

	Good	Fine	Mint
nn-Dr. Mercy, Satanas, from Red Band Comics; Capt. Milksop origin retold	12.00	36.00	84.00

ZOOT (Rulah No. 17 on)
nd (1946) - No. 16, July, 1948 (Two No. 13's & 14's)
Fox Features Syndicate

	Good	Fine	Mint
nn-Funny animal only	6.00	17.00	42.00
2-The Jaguar app.	5.75	17.25	40.00
3(Fall,'46)-6-Funny animals & teen-age	3.00	9.00	21.00
7-Rulah, Jungle Goddess begins(6/47); origin	24.50	72.50	170.00
8-10	18.00	54.00	125.00
11-Kamen bondage-c	20.00	60.00	140.00
12-Injury-to-eye panels	12.00	36.00	84.00
13(2/48), 14(3/48)	12.00	36.00	84.00
13(4/48), 14(5/48)	12.00	36.00	84.00
15,16	12.00	36.00	84.00

NOTE: ***Kamen*** *c-10-12; art-many issues.*

ZORRO (Walt Disney with No. 882)(TV)
May, 1949 - No. 15, Sept-Nov, 1961 (Photo-c 882-on)
Dell Publishing Co.

	Good	Fine	Mint
4-Color 228	12.00	36.00	84.00
4-Color 425,497	5.75	17.25	40.00
4-Color 538-Kinstler-a	6.50	19.50	45.00
4-Color 574,617,732	5.75	17.25	40.00
4-Color 882-Photo-c begin; Toth-a	4.35	13.00	30.00
4-Color 920,933,960,976-Toth-a in all	4.35	13.00	30.00
4-Color 1003('59)	3.50	10.50	24.00
4-Color 1037-Annette Funicello photo-c	6.00	18.00	42.00
8(12-2/59-60)	2.65	8.00	18.00
9,12-Toth-a	3.00	9.00	21.00
10,11,13-15-Last photo-c	2.00	6.00	14.00

NOTE: ***Warren Tufts*** *a-4-Color 1037, 8, 9, 13*

ZORRO (Walt Disney)(TV)
Jan, 1966 - No. 9, March, 1968 (All photo-c)
Gold Key

	Good	Fine	Mint
1-Toth-a	2.35	7.00	16.00
2,4,5,7-9-Toth-a	1.75	5.25	12.00
3,6-Tufts-a	1.50	4.50	10.00

NOTE: *No. 1-9 are reprinted from Dell issues.* ***Tufts*** *a-3,4. No. 3-r/No. 12-c & No. 8 inside; No. 4-r/No. 9-c & insides; No. 6-r/No. 11(all); No. 7-r/No. 14-c.*

ZOT!
April, 1984 - No. 10, July, 1985 ($1.50, Baxter paper)
Eclipse Comics

	Good	Fine	Mint
1-10: 4-Origin. 7-Spiegle-a	.25	.75	1.50

Z-2 COMICS (Secret Agent. . .) (See Holyoke One-Shot No. 7)

ZULU (See Movie Classics)

5 GOOD REASON
TO CHECK US OUT!

5 DIFFERENT COLLECTOR SERVICES

SATISFACTION GUARANTEED, OR YOUR MONEY REFUNDED!

WHAT TO SEND

13th YEAR SERVING FANDOM

1 COMIC BOOK INDEXING SYSTEM

COLLECTOR CARDS: The original & easiest way to keep track of comics and other serially numbered collectables.

- SEE WHAT YOU HAVE
- SEE WHAT YOU NEED
- 100 ISSUES PER CARD
- STANDARD GRADING
- HANDY POCKET-SIZE
- FITS 3"X 5" FILE BOX
- STURDY 110 lb STOCK
- INSTRUCTIONS

COLLECTORS: Spending $3-$5 to bag each 100 comics? Spend just pennies per 100 comics for an accurate & helpful record. Flexible system: new titles easily added.

POSTAGE & Handling: 1¢ per card, $4 maximum.

RETAILERS/DISTRIBUTORS/QUANTITY BUYERS: Proven staple seller in comics stores for over a decade. Discounts increase with quantity. Write or phone for details.

50/ $1.7
100/ $3.0
200/ $5.5
400/ $10.
600/ $14.
600/ $18.
+ P&H

SEND ORDER
SASE* SAMPL

2 ORDER COMICS FROM THE GUIDE

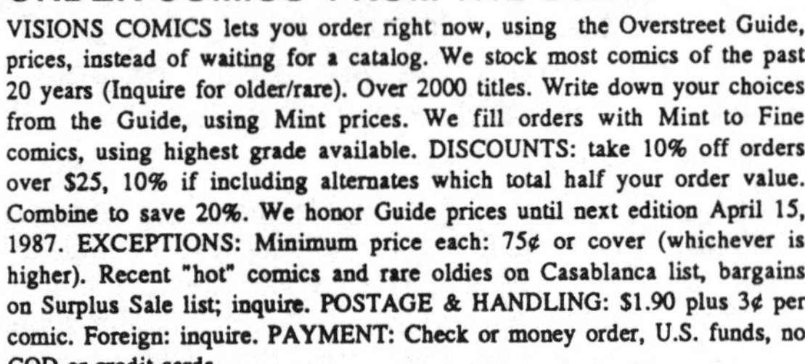
VISIONS COMICS lets you order right now, using the Overstreet Guide, prices, instead of waiting for a catalog. We stock most comics of the past 20 years (Inquire for older/rare). Over 2000 titles. Write down your choices from the Guide, using Mint prices. We fill orders with Mint to Fine comics, using highest grade available. DISCOUNTS: take 10% off orders over $25, 10% if including alternates which total half your order value. Combine to save 20%. We honor Guide prices until next edition April 15, 1987. EXCEPTIONS: Minimum price each: 75¢ or cover (whichever is higher). Recent "hot" comics and rare oldies on Casablanca list, bargains on Surplus Sale list; inquire. POSTAGE & HANDLING: $1.90 plus 3¢ per comic. Foreign: inquire. PAYMENT: Check or money order, U.S. funds, no COD or credit cards.

Visions Comics T.M.

- 100,000 COMICS
- GUIDE PRICES
- DISCOUNTS

SEND AN OR USING OVERS PRICE GUIDE

OR SA +25¢ F INFO & FLYER

3 ANOTHER EASY WAY TO ORDER COMICS

T.M. alternative comics

- POPULAR TITLES
- HUGE INVENTORY
- DISCOUNTS

ALTERNATIVE COMICS lets you order using current CBG Comics Price Guide. All terms, including discounts, are the same as with Visions Comics except you use CBG Guide prices (based on Near Mint), and we honor them until next edition 3 months later. Use our Phoenix address. CBG, fandom's weekly newspaper, includes new Guide every 3 months. Ask them for free sample CBG and mention us. Subscribe to receive next Guide.

The Comics Buyer's Guide
700 E. State St.
Iola, WI 54990

SEND AN OR USING CBG G

OR SA +25¢ F PRICE INFO

4 ROCKETS • SPACE • SF COLLECTABLES

"A grand old name in rocketry..."

ACME ROCKET COMPANY sells rocketry and spaceships, real and imaginary, for hobbyists & collectors. Catalog features plastic display model kits & Flying Model Rocket kits discontinued by manufacturers; memorabilia from space program, SF movies, TV; space-related SF comics, paperbacks, toys; space travel books.

SEND$ FOR B PICTU CATAL

5 UNIQUE COLLECTION LIQUIDATION

STAR WARS®

STAR WARS FOR SALE: Very large private collection selling by the piece. Collection started a year before first movie released; many quite rare.

SEND FOR B LISTIN

SEND TO
(Alternative Comics only): BOX 3556 - 087, PHOENIX, AZ
(All other services): BOX 28283 - 087, TEMPE, AZ 85282-0
Arizona residents: include 6% sales tax on merchandise.

*SASE means Self-Addressed Stamped Envelope (long).

PHONE (602) 838-3629 (not c

TROPIC
COMICS
"Special Advisor to the Overstreet Update."
South Florida's place for Golden Age,
Silver Age and recent comics...Over
250,000 comics in stock. We have
unlimited funds for quality collections.
New Comics 20% below cover. Now
with two locations to serve you...
313 S. STATE Rd. 7
Plantation Fl
33317
305 587-8878
742 NE 167 STREET
Miami Beach Fl
33162
305 940-8700
want lists
welcome

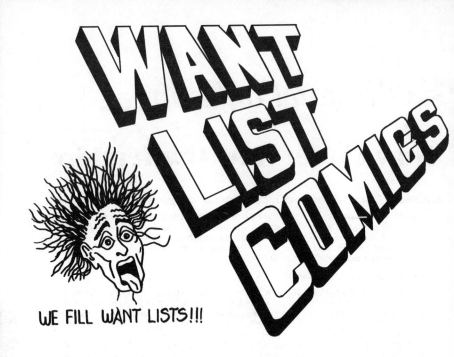

LOOK WHO'S NEW IN THE DC UNIVERSE!
DC BRINGS YOU THE RETURN OF THOSE CLASSIC CHARLTON HEROES...REVITALIZED FOR THE 80's
BLUE BEETLE • THE QUESTION • CAPTAIN ATOM • THE PEACEMAKER • SARGE STEEL
EACH IN THEIR OWN, HARD HITTING, ACTION PACKED SERIES!
ALL TITLES AND RELATED INDICIA AND THE DC BULLET ARE TRADEMARKS OF DC COMICS INC. © 1986 DC COMICS INC.

L.E.Cole
JOIN THE PARADE TO. . .

RARE and SCARCE COMICS
1938 — 1965
BOUGHT/SOLD/TRADED

"Undergrounds too"

O COLLECTION TOO LARGE OR SMALL! WE ARE .WAYS INTERESTED IN PURCHASING QUALITY BOOKS IN STRICT NE OR BETTER CONDITION.

REDBEARD'S BOOK DEN

1221 WEST COAST HWY., #409
NEWPORT BEACH, CALIFORNIA 92663
(714) 720-8757 (By Appointment only)

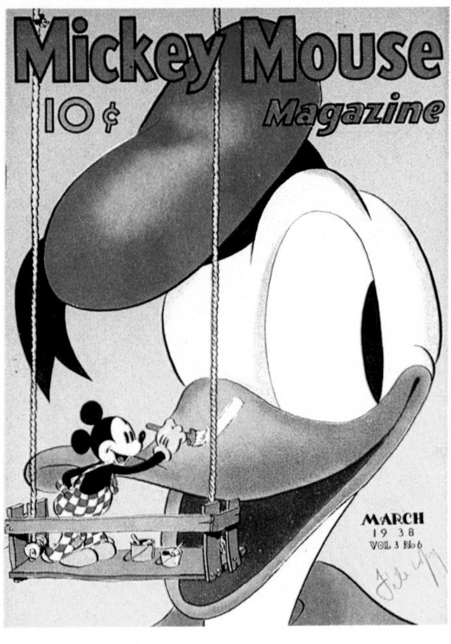

Mickey Mouse Magazine V3/6, 1938.
© WDC

Mickey Mouse Magazine V3/10, 1938.
© WDC

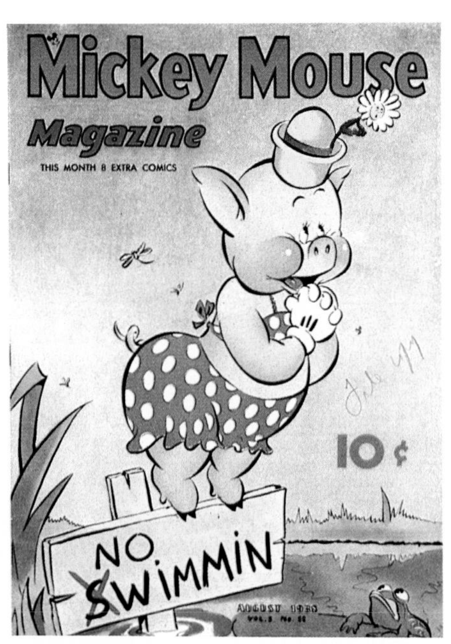

Mickey Mouse Magazine V3/11, 1938.
© WDC

Mickey Mouse Magazine V4/1, 1938.
© WDC

Mickey Mouse Magazine V4/2, 1938.
© *WDC*

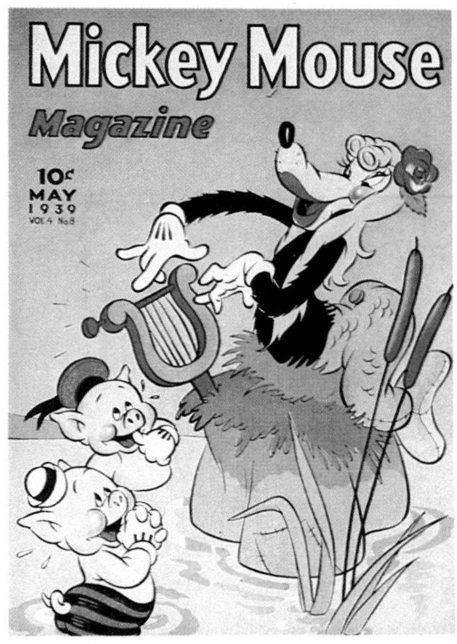

Mickey Mouse Magazine V4/8, 1939.
© *WDC*

Mickey Mouse Magazine V4/10, 1939.
© *WDC*

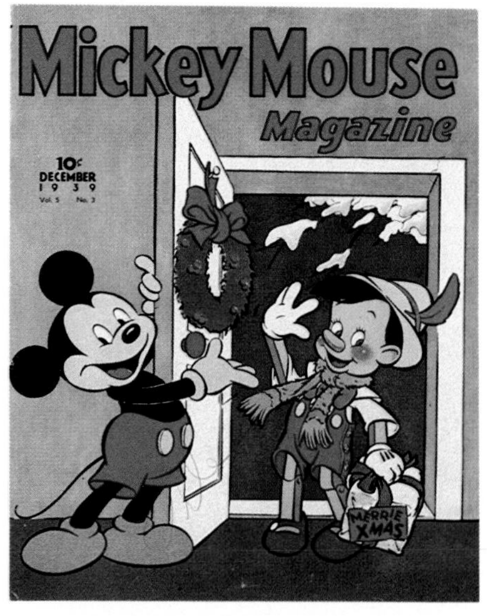

Mickey Mouse Magazine V5/3, 1939.
1st app. Pinocchio & only cover. © *WDC*

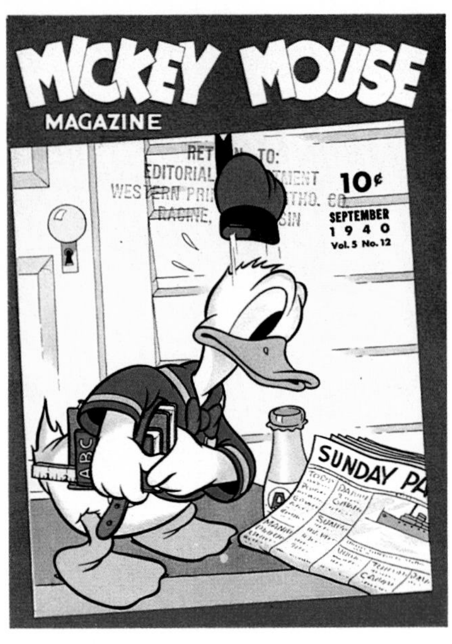

Mickey Mouse Magazine V5/12, 1940. The transition issue that changed the magazine into a comic book. © *WDC*

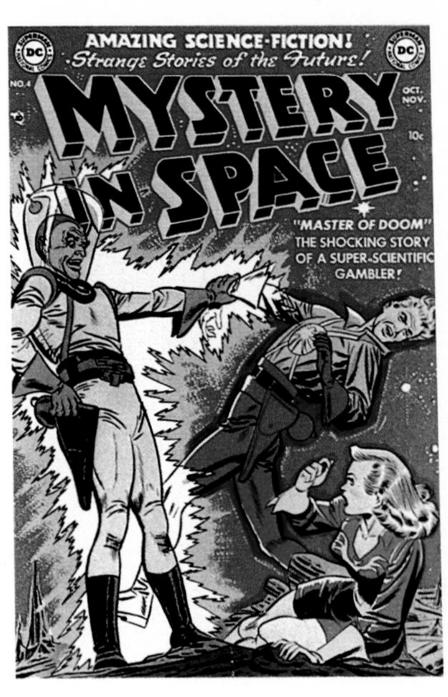

Mystery In Space No. 4, 1951. © *DC*

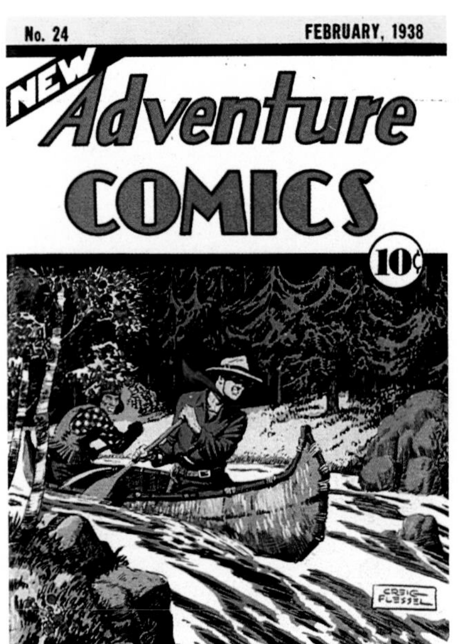

New Adventure Comics No. 24, 1938. © *DC*

100 Pages of Comics No. 101, 1937. © *Dell*

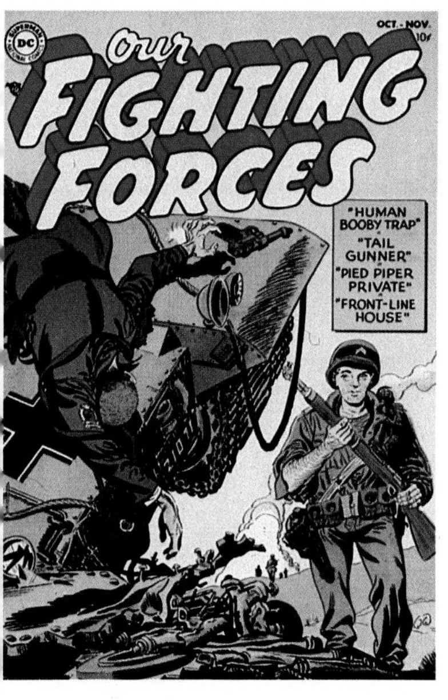

Our Fighting Forces No. 1, 1954. © *DC*

Peter Rabbit Comics No. 1, 1947. © *New York Herald Tribune*

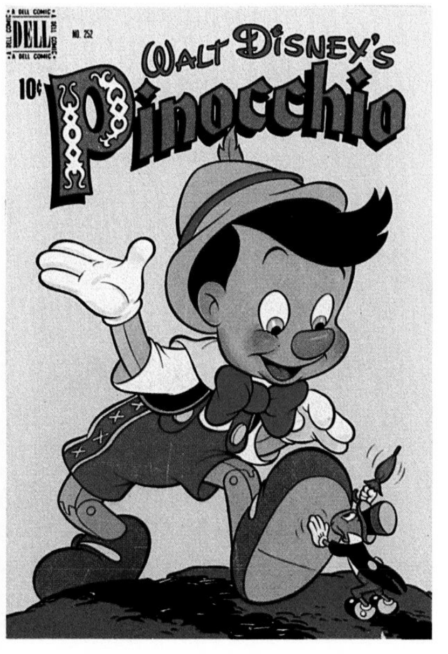

Four Color No. 252, 1949. © *WDC*

Police Comics No. 18, 1943. © *Qua*

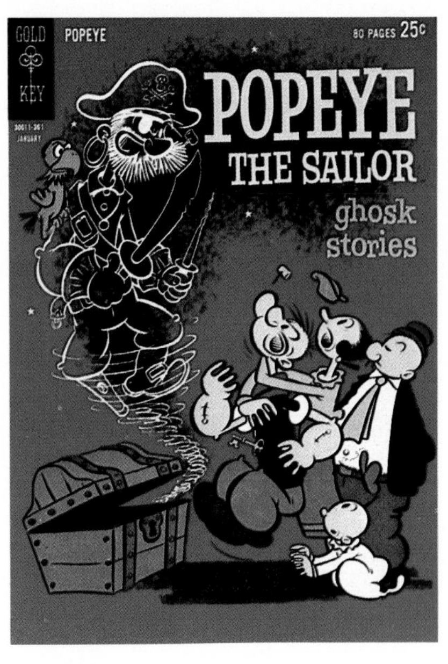

Popeye No. 67, 1963 (Giant). © *King Feat. Syndicate*

Four Color No. 1269, 1962. © *Columbia Broadcasting System*

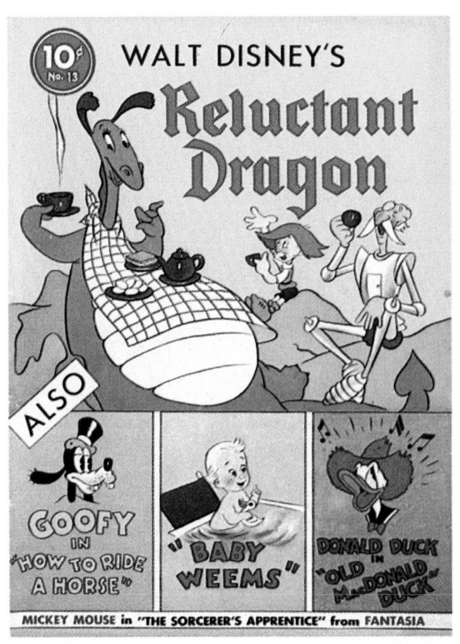

Four Color No. 13, 1941. © *WDC*

Four Color No. 434, 1952. © *Lee Duncan*

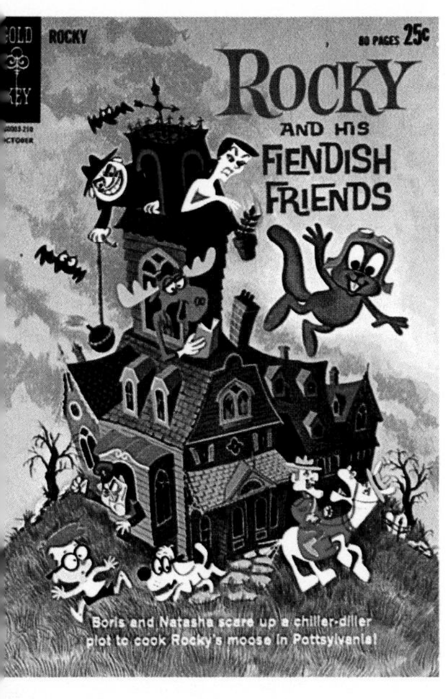

Rocky And His Fiendish Friends No. 1, 1962. (Giant). © *P.A.T—Ward Prods.*

Roy Rogers' Trigger No. 2, 1951. © *Roy Rogers Ent.*

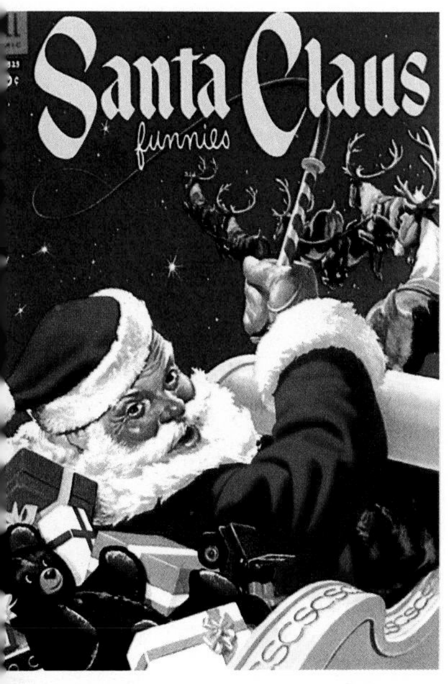

Four Color No. 525, 1953. © *West*

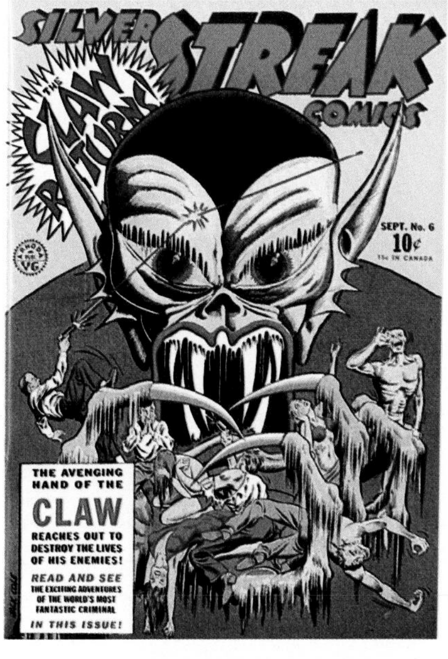

Silver Streak Comics No. 6, 1940. Classic Jack Cole-c; Origin & 1st app. Daredevil. © *Lev*

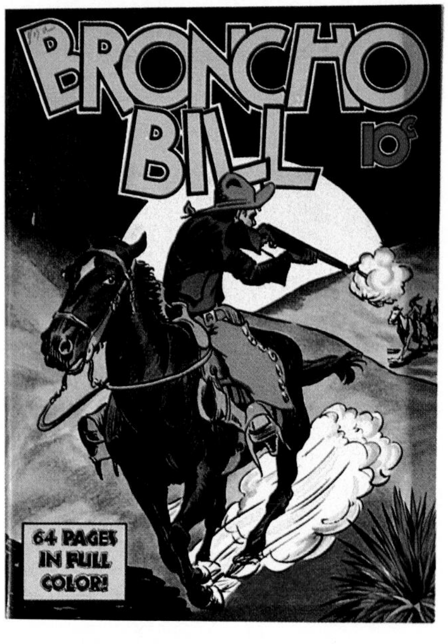

Single Series No. 2, 1939. © *UFS*

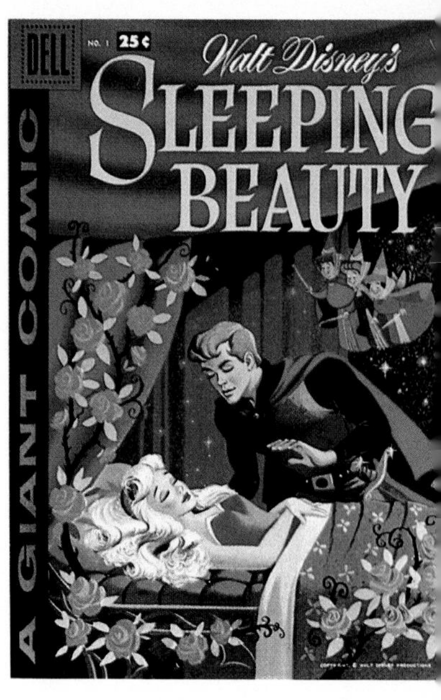

Sleeping Beauty No. 1, 1959 (Giant). © *WDC*

Four Color No. 49, 1944. © *WDC*

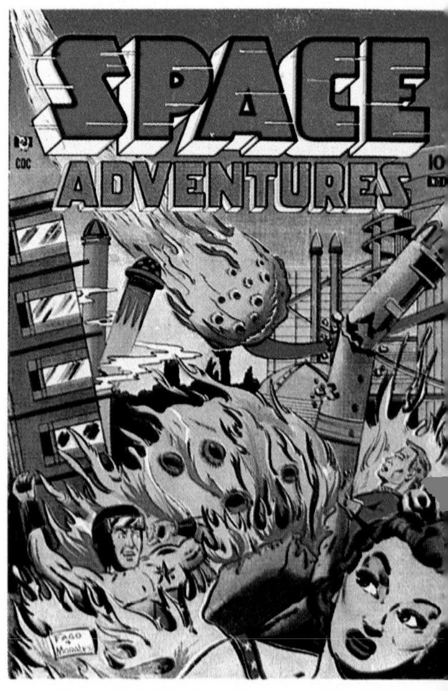

Space Adventures No. 1, 1952. © *CC*

Spy Smasher No. 2, 1941. © *Faw*

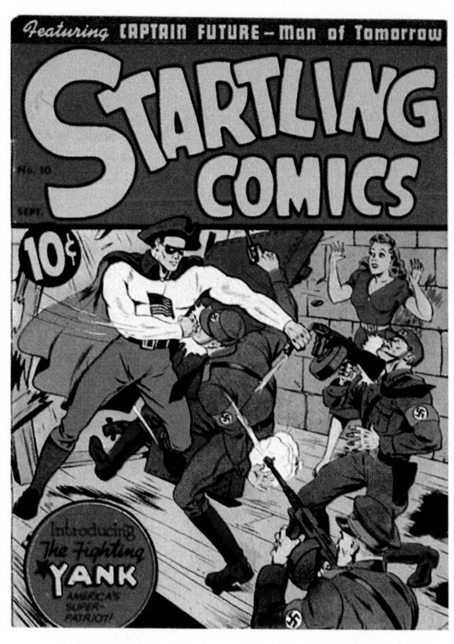

Startling Comics No. 10, 1941. Intro/origin The Fighting Yank. © *BP*

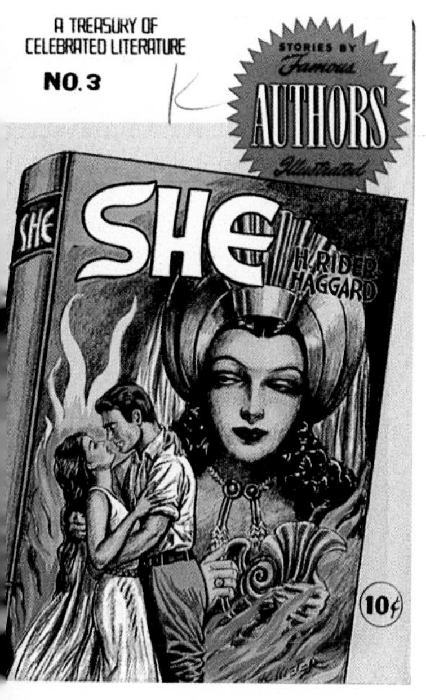

Stories by Famous Authors No. 3, 1950. © *Seaboard Publ.*

Straight Arrow No. 1, 1950. © *National Biscuit Co.*

Strange Terrors No. 7, 1953 (Giant). © *Stj*

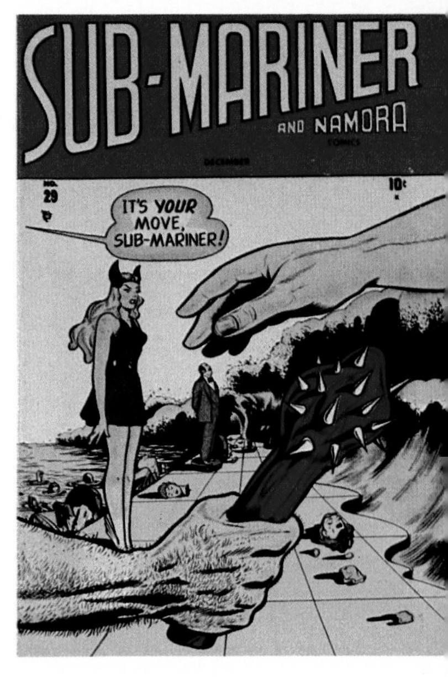

Sub-Mariner Comics No. 29, 1948. Note bizarre surrealistic-c. © *MCG*

Sunny No. 12, 1948. © *Fox*

Superman No. 2, 1939. © *DC*

Tex Ritter No. 1, 1950. © *Faw*

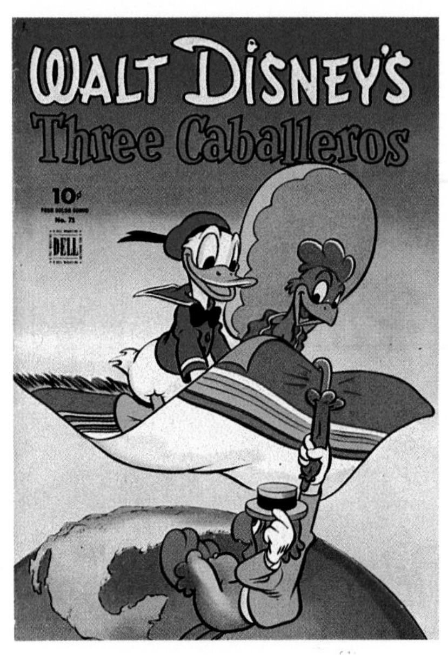

Four Color No. 71, 1945. © *WDC*

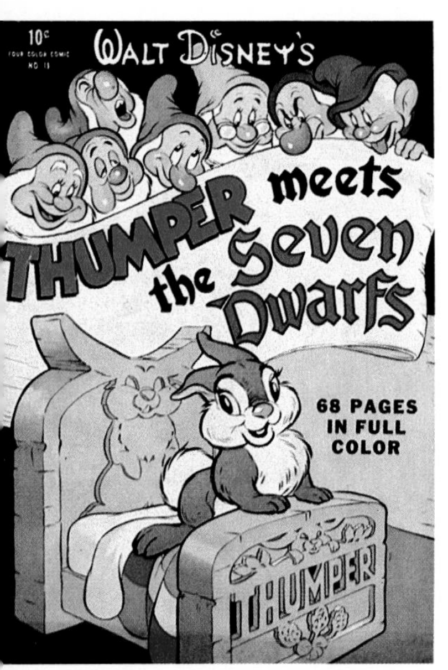

Four Color No. 19, 1943. © *WDC*

Tim Holt No. 25, 1951. 1st app. Black Phantom. © *ME*

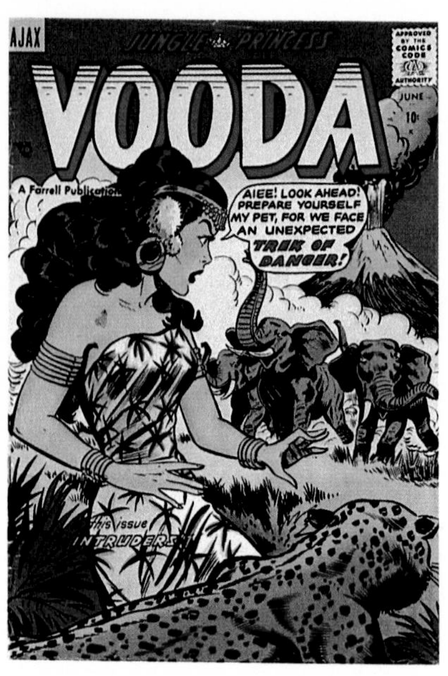

Vooda No. 21, 1955. © *Ajax*

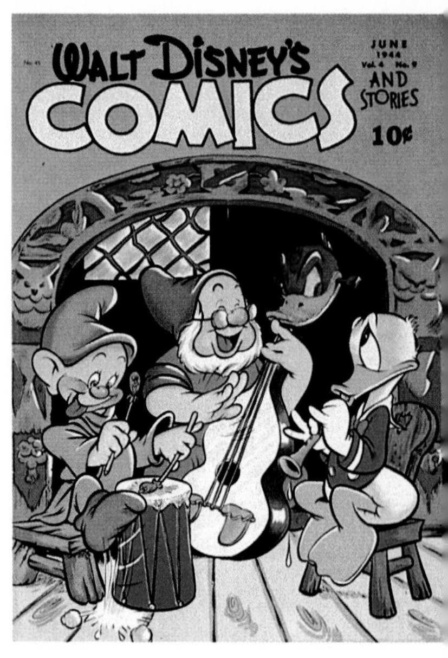

Walt Disney's Comics & Stories No. 45, 1944. © *WDC*

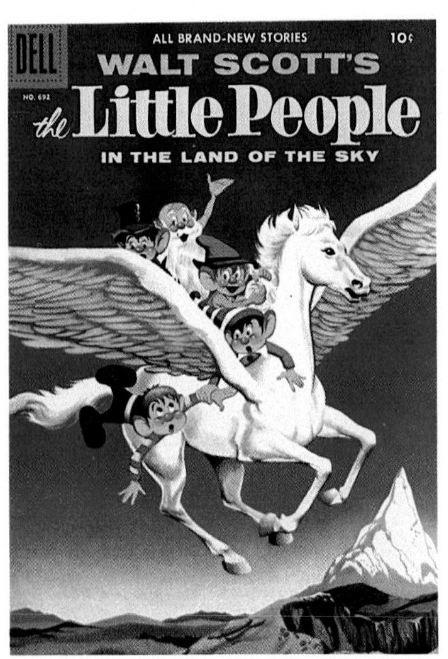

Four Color No. 692, 1956. © *NEA Service*

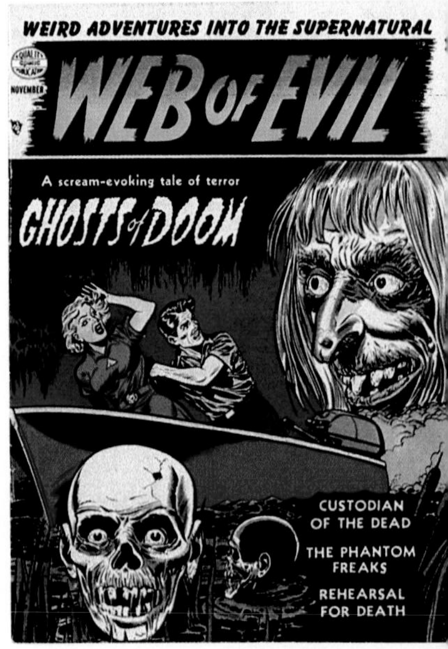

Web Of Evil No. 1, 1952. © *Qua*

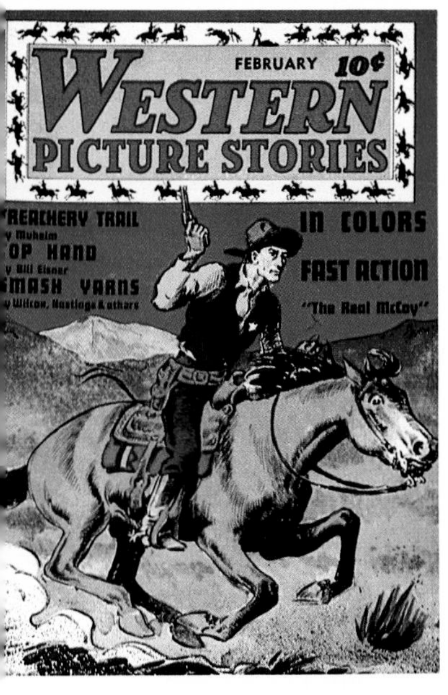

Western Picture Stories No. 1, 1937 (The first western comic book). © *CM*

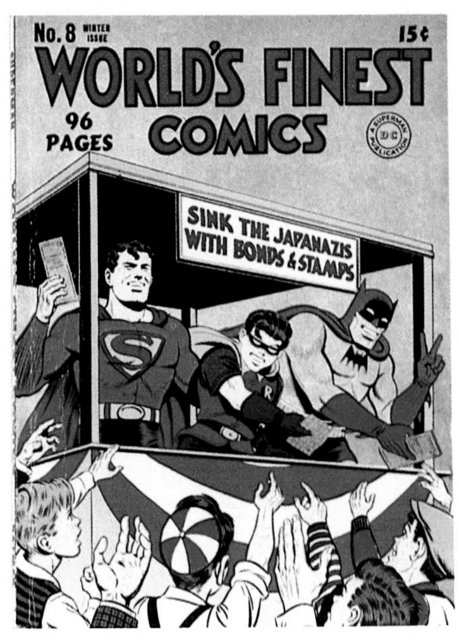

World's Finest Comics No. 8, 1942. © *DC*

Wow Comics No. 11, 1943. © *Faw*

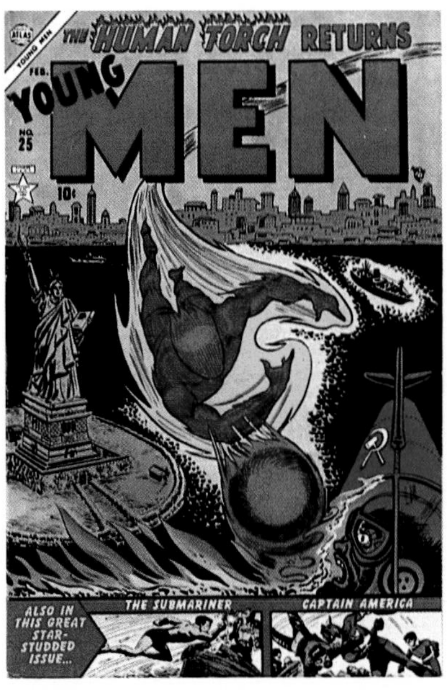

Young Men No. 25, 1954. © *MCG*

BUYING GOLDEN AGE AND SILVER AGE COMICS.

99 MT. AUBURN STREET CAMBRIDGE, MA 02138 617-492-6763

(Located in the heart of Harvard Square)

After twelve years we still have one of the best stocked and most interesting stores in America. Contact us if you have golden age or silver age comics for sale; we also buy original artwork, movie material, science fiction collections and other related material. Open Monday through Wednesday and Saturday, 10:00 to 6:00; Thursday & Friday, 10:00 to 8:00 and Sunday 12:00 to 6:00 and starting in January '87 we get our NEW COMICS on THURSDAY. New England customers come to us for great **discounts** on **subscriptions** and remarkable **discounts** on **back issue comics!** (We also do mail order.)

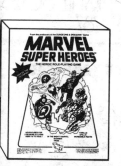

Classic
MOVIE
AND
COMIC
CENTER
19047 Middlebelt
Livonia, MI
Mid-7 Shopping Center
★ COMICS OLD AND NEW!
★ SCIENCE FICTION AND FANTASY BOOKS!
★ BUTTONS!
★ VIDEO CASSETTES!
★ T-SHIRTS!
★ MOVIE AND PERSONALITY POSTERS AND STILLS!
★ GUM CARDS!
★ OLD PLAYBOY MAGAZINES!
★ TONS OF NOSTALGIA ITEMS!
COMICSLINE
(313) 476-1255
SCIENCE FICTION
(313) 476-1256
MOVIES & RECORDS
(313) 476-1254
COMIX!
SPIDER-MAN AND THE THING © MARVEL COMICS GROUP
POPEYE © KING FEATURES SYNDICATE
BATMAN AND WONDER WOMAN ARE REGISTERED TRADEMARKS OF DC COMICS INC. © 1980
REALLY! HI, MOM!
austin
1980
© 1982

Ed Kalb, page 2

MAN FROM U.N.C.L.E.
2-22 .... 2.50
MARS PATROL (G.K.)
3-10 .... 2.50
MARVEL FANFARE
1,2 .... 8.00
3-5 .... 3.00
6-35, up 1.50
MARVEL TEAM UP
1 .... 15.00
2-4 .... 5.00
5-10 .... 3.50
11-20 .... 2.00
21-52,54-70,75,79,89 .... 1.50
53 .... 6.00
71-74,76-78,80-88,90-99 .... .75
100 .... 4.00
101-116,119-149 .... .75
117,118,150 .... 2.50
MARVEL TWO IN ONE
1 .... 8.50
2-10 .... 2.50
11-42,44-49 .... 1.00
43,50-55,83,84 .... 1.50
56-82,85-100 .... .75
MASTER OF KING FU
15 .... 4.00
16-50 .... 1.50
51-125 .... .75
METAL MEN
11-29 .... 2.50
30-44 .... 1.50
45-56 .... 1.00
MICRONAUTS
1 .... 4.00
2-12 .... 2.00
13-59 .... .75
MIGHTY COMICS PRESENTS
40-50 .... 2.50
MIGHTY CRUSADERS (1965)
1-7 .... 2.50
MIGHTY SAMSON
2-17 .... 2.50
MISTER MIRACLE
1 .... 4.50
2-25 .... 1.50
MOON KNIGHT
1 .... 3.00
2-15 .... 1.50
16-38 .... .75
MS. MARVEL
1 .... 3.00
2-23 .... 1.00
MY FAVORITE MARTIAN
1-7 .... 4.50
NEW MUTANTS
1 .... 3.00
2-19 .... 1.50
20-60, up .... .75
NEW TEEN TITANS (1980-87)
1 .... 17.50
2-4 .... 7.50
5-8 .... 4.50
9-19 .... 2.00
20-75, up 1.00
NEW TEEN TITANS (Baxter)
1 .... 4.00
2-35, up 1.50
NICK FURY (1968)
1 .... 7.50
2-7 .... 3.00
8-18 .... 2.00
NOT BRAND ECHH
1,9-13 .... 2.50
2-8 .... 2.00
NOVA
1 .... 3.00
2-25 .... 1.00
PETER PARKER THE SPEC. SPIDER-MAN
1 .... 4.00
2-26,29,30 .... 1.50
27,28 .... 6.50

31-63,65-68 .... 1.00
69,70 .... 4.00
71-130, up .... .75
PHANTOM (G.K./King)
5-28 .... 2.50
POWERMAN/IRON FIST (1972-87)
1 .... 5.00
2-19 .... 1.50
20-50 .... 1.00
51-56,58-125 .... .75
POWER PACK
1 .... 4.00
2-12 .... 1.50
13-35, up .... .75
PUNISHER
1 .... 6.00
2-5 .... 2.00
RAT PATROL (TV)
1-6 .... 4.00
RED RYDER
124-141 .... 5.00
ROM
1,17,18 .... 3.00
2-16 .... 1.50
19-75 .... .75
ROY ROGERS (Dell)
6-18 .... 15.00
SAGA OF THE SWAMP THING
1-19 .... 1.00
20,21 .... 15.00
22-29 .... 2.50
30-60, up .... .75
SAVAGE SWORD OF CONAN (Magazine)
1 .... 10.00
2-19 .... 4.00
20-125 .... 2.00
SEA DEVILS
12-35 .... 2.00
SECRET WARS I
1,2 .... 3.00
3-12 .... 1.50
SECRET WARS II
1-12 .... 1.50
SGT. FURY
10-13 .... 3.00
14-29 .... 2.00
30-69 .... 1.00
SHADOW (Archie)
1-8 .... 4.00
SILVER SURFER ('68)
1 .... 40.00
2,3,5-7 .... 12.00
8-18 .... 5.00
SPACE FAMILY ROBINSON
5-20 .... 2.50
21-36 .... 2.00
37-54 .... 1.50
SPECIAL MISSIONS (G.I. Joe)
1 .... 2.00
2-up 1.50
SPECTRE
1-10 .... 2.50
SPIDER-MAN (Amazing)
21-29 .... 10.00
30-40,50 .... 7.50
41-49 .... 4.00
51-95,99 .... 2.50
96-98,101,102 .... 6.00
100 .... 12.00
103-120,123-128 .... 2.00
121,122 .... 12.00
129 .... 6.00
130-150 .... 1.50
151-203 .... 1.25
204-237,240-248 .... 1.00
238,239,249-251 .... 2.00
252 .... 5.00
253-295, up .... .75
Annual 4-8 .... 3.00
9-19 .... 2.00
SPIDER-WOMAN
1,37,38 .... 2.50
2-36,39-50 .... .75

STARSLAYER
3-34 .... 2.00
STAR TREK (Gold Key)
1 .... 40.00
2-6 .... 15.00
31-60 .... 1.50
STAR WARS
1 .... 4.00
2-44 .... 1.50
45-115 .... .75
STRANGE ADVENTURES
205-216 .... 5.00
STRANGE TALES
116-130 .... 4.00
131-139 .... 3.00
140-168 .... 2.00
178-181 Warlock 2.00
SUB-MARINER
1 .... 10.00
2 .... 4.00
3-10 .... 2.00
11-39 .... 1.50
40-72 .... 1.00
SUPERBOY
102-120 .... 3.00
121-140 .... 2.00
141-210 .... 1.50
211-258 .... 1.00
SUPERMAN
216-254 .... 1.50
255-300 .... 1.00
301-430, up .... .75
SUPERMAN (New)
1-up 1.50
SUPERMAN FAMILY
164-222 .... 1.50
SWAMP THING ('72-76)
1 .... 7.50
2-10 .... 2.50
11-24 .... 1.50
TALES OF SUSPENSE
51-60 .... 5.00
61-69 .... 3.00
70-99 .... 2.00
TALES OF THE NEW TEEN TITANS (1982)
1-4 .... 1.50
TALES TO ASTONISH
37-42 .... 15.00
43-50 .... 7.50
51-62 .... 5.00
63-70 .... 3.00
71-101 .... 2.00
TARZAN (Dell)
58-119 .... 5.00
140-155 .... 3.00
156-206 .... 1.50
TARZAN (DC)
207-258 .... 1.00

TARZAN'S JUNGLE ANNUAL
2-7 .... 7.50
TEEN TITANS (Old)
24-53 .... 1.50
THING (Marvel)
1 .... 3.00
2-35 .... .75
THOR (Journey Into Mystery)
91-100 .... 10.00
101-111 .... 7.50
113-126 .... 4.00
127-139 .... 2.50
140-159 .... 2.00
160-179 .... 1.50
180,181 .... 2.50
182-200 .... 1.50
201-250 .... 1.00
251-336 .... .75
337 .... 3.50
338-350 .... 1.00
351-390, up .... .75
T.H.U.N.D.E.R. AGENTS (Tower)
1-20 .... 5.00
TOMB OF DRACULA
1 .... 7.50
2-10 .... 2.50
11-70 .... 1.00
TRANSFORMERS
1-3 .... 4.00
4-9 .... 1.50
10-30, up 1.00
TUROK
50-124 .... 1.00
TWISTED TALES
1-10 .... 2.00
TWO FISTED TALES (EC)
31-40 .... 30.00
UNCLE SCROOGE
111-157 .... 2.00
158-210 .... 1.50
VAMPIRELLA (Magazine)
16-39 .... 4.00
40-110 .... 2.00
VIGILANTE
1 .... 4.00
2-45, up 1.50
VOYAGE TO THE BOTTOM OF THE SEA (TV)
2-16 .... 2.50
WARLORD (DC)
1 .... 10.00
2 .... 6.00
3-10 .... 4.00
11-29 .... 2.00
30-50 .... 1.00
51-115, up .... .75

WATCHMEN
1 .... 2.50
2-12 .... 1.50
WEB OF SPIDER-MAN
1 .... 3.00
2-9 .... 1.50
10-35, up 1.00
WEIRD WESTERN TALES
19-70 .... .75
WEST COAST AVENGERS
1-4 (1984) 2.00
1 .... 2.00
2-9 .... 1.50
10-20, up 1.00
WHAT IF?
1 .... 5.00
2-13 .... 2.00
14-26,29,30,32-50 .... 1.50
27,28,31 .... 3.00
WHO'S WHO (DC Univ.)
1-24 .... 1.50
WOLVERINE
1-4 .... 3.00
WONDER WOMAN
140-159 .... 2.50
160-200 .... 1.50
201-220 .... 1.00
221-329 .... .75
WORLDS FINEST
151-179 .... 2.00
180-212 .... 1.50
213-282 .... 1.00
283-323 .... .75
X-FACTOR
1 .... 4.00
2-9 .... 1.50
10-25, up 1.00
X-MEN
21-29 .... 5.00
30-49, 52 .... 3.50
50,51,53-55,64 .... 5.00
56-63,65 .... 12.00
66-93 .... 2.50
94 .... 70.00
95 .... 35.00
96-101 .... 25.00
102-107 .... 12.00
108-111,120,121 .... 20.00
112-119,122 .... 10.00
123-130 .... 8.50
131-140 .... 7.50
141-143 .... 4.50
144-173 .... 2.50
174-186 .... 2.00
187-200 .... 1.25
201-230, up 1.00
Annual 5-10 .... 2.00
Giant Size 1 .... 45.00
2 .... 8.50

—WE ARE BUYING—

We are paying 80 to 100% of guide for many comics. Our new buying catalog consists of over 250 comic titles with prices we pay per issue. Publishers include (1935 - 1987): Marvel, DC, Timely, Atlas, EC, Fawcett, Fiction House, Standard, Dell, Gold Key and others.

We buy many ''off'' brand titles and can appreciate your lower grade material. If you're a dealer with overstock or a collector looking for cash -**write for our buying catalog No. 10.** Self addressed stamped envelope, please.

CBG
Customer Service Award — 1986

ED KALB
P.O. Box 4111, Mesa, Arizona 85201
1-602-832-5176

ANIMATION ARTWORK

VINTAGE ANIMATION is our specialty! Our collection includes beautiful painted cells from the earliest cartoon shorts to the classic **Disney** features such as **Pinocchio**, **Snow White** and **Fantasia**. We also have for sale original storyboard concept drawings and finished animation pencil drawings.

We have superb original daily strips and Sunday pages by many artists, including art from the **Disney** studio. We have Mickey Mouse, Donald Duck, Snow White, Pinocchio and Mickey's Christmas Carol.

SEND $2 FOR OUR ILLUSTRATED CATALOG LISTING 100s OF ART BUYS!

CARTOON CARNIVAL

408 BICKMORE DR. • WALLINGFORD PA 19086

FANTASY Illustrated
12531 HARBOR BLVD
GARDEN GROVE
CA. 92640
(714) 537-0087
1½ MI. SO. OF DISNEYLAN
AMAZING
X-MEN
2001
- SEND $1.00 FOR GIANT 1986 COMIC CATALOGUE. COVERS - MARVEL - D.C. - DELL
ARCHIE - HARVEY - DISNEY - GOLD and SILVER AGE PLUS ALL CONTEMPORARY PUBLISHERS
ALSO AVAILABLE: OUR 1987 PULP AND PAPERBACK CATALOGUES AT $1.00 EA.

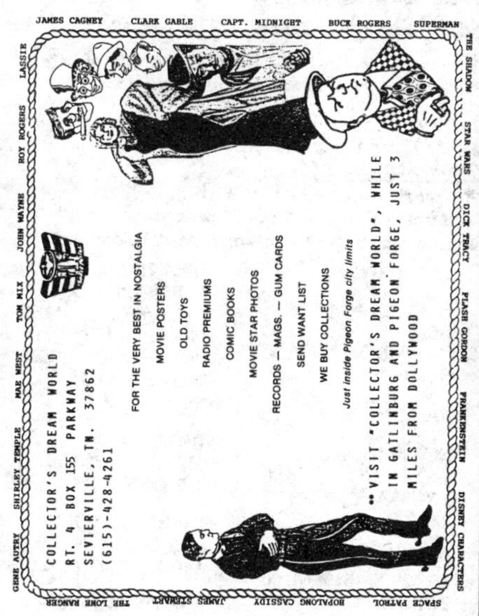

Curious

Book Shop

307 E. Grand River
East Lansing, MI 48823
(517) 332-0112

Mid-Michigan's Largest Selection of:
SCIENCE FICTION • PULPS • BOOKS
COMICS • B-L-B's • PAPERBACKS
MAGAZINES • ORIGINAL ART

ALWAYS BUYING QUALITY ITEMS!

VISIT OUR 2ND SHOP:
ARGOS BOOK SHOP
1405 Robinson Rd.
Grand Rapids, MI 49506
(616) 454-0111

THE COMPLEAT PAPERBACKER

15711 E. AMAR RD, LA PUENTE, CA 91744 phone (818)330-0400

• *WHEN IN SOUTHERN CALIF· VISIT THE* **NO.1** *STORE IN THE* **SAN GABRIEL VALLEY** *FOR A* **COMPLETE** *LINE OF* **COMICS, SCIENCE–FICTION** *AND* **OCCULT** *BOOKS.*

• *SITUATED AT* **15711 E. AMAR RD., LA PUENTE** *BETWEEN THE* **POMONA** *AND* **SAN BERNARDINO FREEWAYS**, *WE ARE ONE TRAFFIC LIGHT EAST OF* **HACIENDA**

OPEN 7 DAYS A WEEK, FROM 10:A.M. TO 8:P.M. WEEKDAYS, AND ON SAT. & SUN. FROM 10:A.M. TO 5:P.M. PHONE (818) 330-0400

WE ALSO HAVE THOUSANDS OF PAPERBACKS IN ALL CATEGORIES:-NOVELS, GOTHICS, MYSTERIES, WESTERNS, & LIGHT ROMANCES TOGETHER WITH NON-FICTION.

WHAT?

-STILL CAN'T SPELL "COMPLETE" EITHER!

REMEMBER- LOOK FOR THE STORE WITH THE MISSPELLED SIGN!

Help Me SPEND

$100,000.00 or MORE in '87

IN 1986 I FLEW **NORTH** TO BOSTON, **SOUTH** TO Ft. LAUDERDALE AND **WEST** TO DENVER.

TO BUY: • COMIC BOOKS • PULPS • BASEBALL CARDS • ORIGINAL ART • WAREHOUSE AND STORE STOCKS

Call Me Today — I'll Be There Tomorrow With **CASH**

FINDER'S FEE PAID **Up to $1,000 & More**

IF YOU KNOW OF SOMEONE WITH A NICE STOCK
I PAY 5 - 15% **CASH** AT TIME OF PURCHASE
CALL ME TODAY!! (NO COLLECT CALLS)

PETER KOCH • 176 Fort Lee Rd. • Leonia, NJ 07605

UNLIMITED CASH **201-585-2765** **UNLIMITED CASH**

25% DISCOUNT ON ALL NEW COMICS

Everything from Marvel and DC to all the independent companies–
Aircel, Blackthorne, Comico, Eclipse, First, Fantagraphics, Kitchen Sink, Mirage, Renegade, Sirius, Solson and more.

We also carry–

Fanzines
Posters
Role Playing Games
Comic Bags
A full line of back issues

EVERYTHING WE SELL IS DISCOUNTED FOR AT LEAST 25%

Minimum order is only $10 plus exact UPS shipping.
Orders are shipped weekly, bi-weekly or monthly.
Monthly order form filled with hundreds of items.
FREE Newsletter.
FREE Subscription to *Marvel Age* and *DC Releases*.
Comics are wrapped in plastic bags and shipped in specially constructed boxes.

Send for info and order form–

GEMINI COMICS
991 East 77th Street
Brooklyn, N. Y. 11236

STAR PHOTOS • MOVIE POSTERS • MAGAZINES

FREE CATALOG

JERRY OHLINGER'S®
MOVIE MATERIAL STORE, Inc.

242 W. 14th Street
New York, N.Y. 10011
(212) 989-0869

OPEN EVERY DAY 1:00-8:00pm
BETWEEN 8th AND 7th AVENUE
IND. SUBWAY W. 14th STREET STOP

HAVE YOU HEARD ABOUT IT?
THE JOE KUBERT SCHOOL OF CARTOON AND GRAPHIC ART, INC.
WHAT IS IT?
A THREE YEAR PROGRAM OFFERING A COMPLETE COURSE IN CINEMATIC ANIMATION AND CARTOON GRAPHICS!
SOME OF OUR GRADUATES INCLUDE:
STEVE BISSETTE—SWAMP THING FOR D.C.
RICK VEITCH—THE ONE FOR MARVEL
RON ZALME—FREELANCER FOR MARVEL
ANNA MARIE COLEMAN—HALLMARK
VINCENT ANDRIANI—HALLMARK
MARK PENNINGTON—HASBRO
JAN DURSEMA—CO-CREATOR OF ARION
ADAM KUBERT—HEAVY METAL
APPROVED BY: THE N.J. DEPT. OF EDUCATION
APPROVED FOR:
• VETERANS
• NON-RESIDENT ALIEN STUDENTS
ACCREDITED BY THE NATIONAL ASSOCIATION OF TRADE & TECHNICAL SCHOOLS
NATTS
Enrollments are limited—fill out this coupon and mail today.
Please send your free brochure, I am interested in:
☐ Cartoon Illustration · Graphic Arts
☐ Cinematic Animation
Please print clearly
Name ______ Age ______
Address ______
City ______ State ______ Zip ______
The Joe Kubert School of Cartoon and Graphic Art, Inc.
37 Myrtle Ave., Dover, NJ 07801 • 201-361-1327

Beginning our sixth fabulous year...
...FAT MOOSE COMICS !!
• We buy, sell and trade!
• Large selection of back issues!
• Comic bags, boxes, posters - supplies!
• Role playing and war game specialists!
- FAT MOOSE COMICS - GAMES -
235 RIDGEDALE AVE.
CEDAR KNOLLS, N.J. 07927
PH. (201)-898-4734

GEOFFREY'S

15530 CRENSHAW BLVD.

(213) 538-3198 **GARDENA, CA. 90249**

"Just a few miles from the LA airport"

GOLDEN AGE OUR SPECIALTY!!

TOP $$$ PAID FOR YOUR OLD COMICS!

Generous Finders fees paid

© WDC

We will pay a minimum of ⅓ Overstreet for **any** pre-1965 comics and we will pay a minimum of 50% for the more sought after early comics.

Send $1.00 for catalogue.

We purchased over $100,000 worth of Golden Age comics in the last year alone. We can get most comics for you!

© MCG

© BP

© DC

NEW COMICS AIRSHIPPED EVERY THURSDAY

Open Daily 11am—7pm. Late Thursdays

Posters, Cards, T-Shirts, Toys. Investment advice.

DARK
HORSE
COMICS
BRADRICK
STROMAN
SMITH
RON RANDALL
GULACY

MR. MONSTER'S
COMIC CRYPT
TM
347
FERRY
STREET
EASTON
PA, 18042
215-250-
0659
© 1987

Everything you need to collect

MARVEL

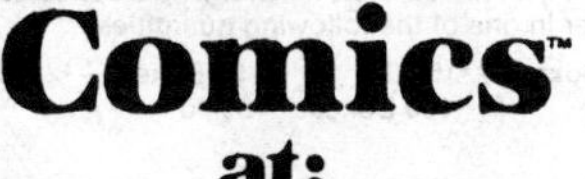

at:

COMIC BOOKS UNLIMITED

T.M.

21505 S. NORWALK BLVD.
HAWAIIAN GARDENS
(213) 865-4474

16344 BEACH BLVD.
WESTMINSTER
(714) 841-6646

the one-stop collectors' shop.

ROLE-PLAYING
GAMES

ROBOTECH
COMICS, MODELS, BOOKS & TOYS

BASEBALL CARDS
HAWAIIAN GARDENS STORE ONLY

WE BUY COMICS

NEW MARVEL COMICS EVERY FRIDAY

MARVEL
MYSTERY
COMICS

1289 PROSPECT AVENUE, BROOKLYN, N.Y. 11218
TELEPHONE: (212) 438-1335
BRAIN DAMAGE
COMICS

No. 14
SUPERMAN

ACTION
COMICS

BATMAN

Fantastic Four
THE AVENGERS
X-MEN
AMAZING FANTASY
THE INCREDIBLE HULK
THE AMAZING SPIDER-MAN

DARING
MYSTERY COMICS

The Best Work
By The Best Cartoonists In The World...

GILBERT HERNANDEZ

JAIME HERNANDEZ

RICK GEARY

FRIEDMAN BROTHERS

STAN SAKAI

E.C. SEGAR

PETER BAGGE

WM. MESSNER-LOEBS

STEVE DITKO

HAL FOSTER

MUNOZ & SAMPAYO

ROBERT CRUMB

From The Best Comics Publisher In The U.S.

At Fantagraphics Books, Comics Isn't A Commodity. It's An Art.

RETAILERS: Fantagraphics Books publications are the ideal way of cultivating a "cross-over" clientele among people who are not comics fans. Books like *The Complete Popeye, Any Similarity to Persons Living Or Dead*, and *Love and Rockets*, all of which have been reviewed in mainstream media, are perfect for attracting those hard-to-get "real-world" people with money to spend.

COLLECTORS: Because of their small print runs (compared to Marvels and DCs), Fantagraphics Books comics often shoot up in value soon after publication. Five-year-old copies of *Love and Rockets* #1 are now worth over $100, and one-year-old copies of *Critters* have increased by as much as 500%!

READERS: Fantagraphics Books offers the finest selection of comics in the U.S.: From Segar to Crumb, from Ditko to the Hernandez Bros., from Rick Geary to William Messner-Loebs. Send for our catalogue today—we *guarantee* you'll find something you'll like.

FOR A FREE CATALOGUE write to Fantagraphics Books, 4359 Cornell Road, Agoura CA 91301

© DC Comics Inc.

© Marvel Comics Inc.

© DC Comics Inc.

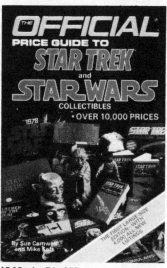

☐ *Please send me the following price guides –*
☐ *I would like the most current edition of the books listed below.*

THE OFFICIAL PRICE GUIDES TO:

☐ 199-3 **American Silver & Silver Plate** 5th Ed. 11.95
☐ 513-1 **Antique Clocks** 3rd Ed. 10.95
☐ 283-3 **Antique & Modern Dolls** 3rd Ed. 10.95
☐ 287-6 **Antique & Modern Firearms** 6th Ed. 11.95
☐ 738-X **Antiques & Collectibles** 8th Ed. 10.95
☐ 289-2 **Antique Jewelry** 5th Ed. 11.95
☐ 539-5 **Beer Cans & Collectibles** 4th Ed. 7.95
☐ 521-2 **Bottles Old & New** 10th Ed. 10.95
☐ 532-8 **Carnival Glass** 2nd Ed. 10.95
☐ 295-7 **Collectible Cameras** 2nd Ed. 10.95
☐ 277-9 **Collectibles of the Third Reich** 2nd Ed. 10.95
☐ 740-1 **Collectible Toys** 4th Ed. 10.95
☐ 531-X **Collector Cars** 7th Ed. 12.95
☐ 538-7 **Collector Handguns** 4th Ed. 14.95
☐ 290-6 **Collector Knives** 8th Ed. 11.95
☐ 518-2 **Collector Plates** 4th Ed. 11.95
☐ 296-5 **Collector Prints** 7th Ed. 12.95
☐ 001-6 **Depression Glass** 2nd Ed. 9.95
☐ 548-4 **'50s & '60s Collectibles** 1st Ed. 9.95
☐ 589-1 **Fine Art** 1st Ed. 19.95
☐ 311-2 **Glassware** 3rd Ed. 10.95
☐ 243-4 **Hummel Figurines & Plates** 6th Ed. 10.95
☐ 523-9 **Kitchen Collectibles** 2nd Ed. 10.95
☐ 291-4 **Military Collectibles** 5th Ed. 11.95
☐ 525-5 **Music Collectibles** 6th Ed. 11.95
☐ 313-9 **Old Books & Autographs** 7th Ed. 11.95
☐ 298-1 **Oriental Collectibles** 3rd Ed. 11.95
☐ 522-0 **Paperbacks & Magazines** 1st Ed. 10.95
☐ 297-3 **Paper Collectibles** 5th Ed. 10.95
☐ 529-8 **Pottery & Porcelain** 6th Ed. 11.95
☐ 524-7 **Radio, TV & Movie Memorabilia** 3rd Ed. 11.95
☐ 288-4 **Records** 7th Ed. 10.95
☐ 247-7 **Royal Doulton** 5th Ed. 11.95
☐ 280-9 **Science Fiction & Fantasy Collectibles** 2nd Ed. 10.95
☐ 299-X **Star Trek/Star Wars Collectibles** 1st Ed. 7.95
☐ 248-5 **Wicker** 3rd Ed. 10.95

THE OFFICIAL:

☐ 445-3 **Collector's Journal** 1st Ed. 4.95
☐ 549-2 **Directory to U.S. Flea Markets** 1st Ed. 3.95
☐ 365-1 **Encyclopedia of Antiques** 1st Ed. 9.95
☐ 369-4 **Guide to Buying & Selling Antiques** 1st Ed. 9.95
☐ 414-3 **Identification Guide to Early American Furniture** 1st Ed. 9.95
☐ 413-5 **Identification Guide to Glassware** 1st Ed. 9.95
☐ 448-8 **Identification Guide to Gunmarks** 2nd Ed. 9.95
☐ 412-7 **Identification Guide to Pottery & Porcelain** 1st Ed. 9.95
☐ 415-1 **Identification Guide to Victorian Furniture** 1st Ed. 9.95

THE OFFICIAL (SMALL SIZE) PRICE GUIDES TO:

☐ 309-0 **Antiques & Flea Markets** 4th Ed. 4.95
☐ 269-8 **Antique Jewelry** 3rd Ed. 4.95
☐ 737-1 **Baseball Cards** 7th Ed. 4.95
☐ 488-7 **Bottles** 2nd Ed. 4.95
☐ 544-1 **Cars & Trucks** 3rd Ed. 5.95
☐ 519-0 **Collectible Americana** 2nd Ed. 4.95
☐ 294-9 **Collectible Records** 3rd Ed. 4.95
☐ 545-X **Collector Guns** 3rd Ed. 5.95
☐ 306-6 **Dolls** 4th Ed. 4.95
☐ 520-4 **Football Cards** 6th Ed. 4.95
☐ 540-9 **Glassware** 3rd Ed. 4.95
☐ 526-3 **Hummels** 4th Ed. 4.95
☐ 279-5 **Military Collectibles** 3rd Ed. 4.95
☐ 278-7 **Pocket Knives** 3rd Ed. 4.95
☐ 527-1 **Scouting Collectibles** 4th Ed. 4.95
☐ 439-9 **Sports Collectibles** 2nd Ed. 3.95
☐ 494-1 **Star Trek/Star Wars Collectibles** 3rd Ed. 3.95
☐ 307-4 **Toys** 4th Ed. 4.95

THE OFFICIAL BLACKBOOK PRICE GUIDES OF:

☐ 743-6 **U.S. Coins** 26th Ed. 3.95
☐ 742-8 **U.S. Paper Money** 20th Ed. 3.95
☐ 741-X **U.S. Postage Stamps** 10th Ed. 3.95

THE OFFICIAL INVESTORS GUIDE TO BUYING & SELLING:

☐ 534-4 **Gold, Silver & Diamonds** 2nd Ed. 12.95
☐ 535-2 **Gold Coins** 2nd Ed. 12.95
☐ 536-0 **Silver Coins** 2nd Ed. 12.95
☐ 537-9 **Silver Dollars** 2nd Ed. 12.95

THE OFFICIAL NUMISMATIC GUIDE SERIES:

☐ 481-X **Coin Collecting** 3rd Ed. 9.95
☐ 254-X **The Official Guide to Detecting Counterfeit Money** 2nd Ed. 7.95
☐ 257-4 **The Official Guide to Mint Errors** 4th Ed. 7.95

SPECIAL INTEREST SERIES:

☐ 506-9 **From Hearth to Cookstove** 3rd Ed. 17.95
☐ 530-1 **Lucky Number Lottery Guide** 1st Ed. 4.95
☐ 504-2 **On Method Acting** 8th Printing 6.95

	TOTAL	

SEE REVERSE SIDE FOR ORDERING INSTRUCTIONS

© DC

© DC

© DC

© MCG

© Faw

© DC

CLASSIFIED ADVERTISING

TV GUIDES 1949-1987

Every issue available. Any article located. New 1987 Catalog (9th Edition, 52 pages) $3.00. (Includes a special section on KID'S SHOWS—the favorite shows you grew up with). TV GUIDE SPECIALISTS, Box 20-O, Macomb, IL 61455.

FREE Comic Catalogue. LOW PRICES. Golden-Silver Age, Marvels, DCs, Disneys, All Kinds. I like to TRADE, too. Money-Back Guarantee. SPECIAL BONUS WITH PURCHASE. Send an EXTRA 1st Class Stamp to: DAVE YARUSS, 7916 BLUE LAKE DR., SAN DIEGO, CALIF. 92119.

COMIC BOOKS FOR SALE

ONE OF THE WORLD'S LARGEST SELECTIONS OF GOLDEN AGE, DC, MARVEL, DELL AND CLASSICS ILLUSTRATED COMICS FOR SALE. I REGULARLY SEND OUT CATALOGUES OF COMICS AND SUNDAY PAGES I HAVE FOR SALE PLUS I HAVE A LARGE SUPPLY OF CONAN ORIGINAL ARTWORK FOR SALE. I AM THE ONLY CANADIAN DISTRIBUTOR OF MYLAR PLASTIC BAGS, CARTONS, CARDBOARD BACKING, ETC. ALL MANUFACTURED BY BILL COLE. ALL THESE ITEMS ARE LISTED FOR SALE IN MY CATALOGUES WHICH YOU CAN RECEIVE BY SENDING ME YOUR NAME AND ADDRESS. CALVIN SLOBODIAN, 859 - 4TH AVE., RIVERS, MANITOBA, CANADA R0K 1X0.

SUCCESSFUL COMIC DEALING—Ten page report with money making tips for dealers & collectors. Send $10.00 to: COLLECTIBLES, Box 481079, Niles, IL 60648.

Increase Sales! Black and White advertising photographs of your product. Fast service, reasonable prices. $3 for 'Quick-Print' sample photo and credit coupon. Free details. Jim Dapkus, Rt. 1, Box 247ea, Westfield, WI 53964.

$100,000.00 SEARCH!!

GOLDEN AGE COMICS WANTED! 1933-1955.

HIGHEST PRICES PAID!

Send lists or call. I am paying 40%-90% of guide. Phone 607-648-4025, Rick Semowich, RD8 Box 94, Binghamton, NY 13901.

BARGAIN BASEMENT'S BACK! MARVEL, DC, EC, DISNEY, ARCHIE, MORE! TOP ARTISTS, KEY ISSUES, LESSER GRADES, LOWEST PRICES! TRADING FOR COMICS, GAMES & GAMING MAGS TOO! SEND $1 (& SASE) FOR CATALOG #7! HM LEVY, BOX 197-S, EAST MEADOW, NY 11554.

SEND TO: E. K. WONG, 4282 10th Ave., Port Alberni, BC

• • • FREE NEWSLETTER!! • • •

Free copy of COMIX EMPORIUM NEWSLETTER. Monthly w/Marvel, DC & Independents news for the FAN. 4 iss/$1.25. Peter Drizhal, PO Box 663, Dept PG, Oxon Hill, MD 20745.

ORIGINAL ART WANTED!!!

GAHAN WILSON, ZIGGY, CREEPER, DOOM PATROL, METAL MEN, METAMORPHO, SPIDER-MAN BY DITKO, CHALLENGERS UNK., + OTHER 1960s MARVEL AND DC ART. RICK RANN, P.O. BOX 877, OAK PARK, IL 60303.

ORIGINAL ART WANTED!!!

BEATLES!!! BEATLES!!! BEATLES!!!

I want items on the Beatles like dolls, toys, records movie posters, promos, etc. Circus Boy, Monkees, & Rolling Stones items also wanted. RICK RANN, P.O BOX 877-PG, OAK PARK, IL 60303

WALT DISNEY ANIMATION ARTWORK WANTED!!

ALL OTHER STUDIO ARTWORK WANTED!!

Cels, backgrounds, drawings, etc., etc.

TOP PRICES PAID! Send listing with

prices or call: (818) 785-4080

COLLECTORS PARADISE GALLERY

P. O. BOX 1540

STUDIO CITY, CA 91604

★★ MULTINATIONAL COMIC DISTRIBUTION ★★

Send $1 (Refundable with 1st Purchase) for back issue catalog of Marvel, DC, Alternates, Golden-Age. 559 Place D'aiguillon, Montreal, Quebec, Canada H4J 1L8 (No cheques please).

COMIC BOOKS, MOVIE POSTERS, GUM CARDS, ROLE PLAYING GAMES, STAR TREK & STAR WARS ITEMS MAGAZINES AND GRAPHIC NOVELS AND MANY OTHER ITEMS. SEND 50¢ FOR CATALOG. BID TIME RETURN, 225 QUEENS AVE., LONDON, ONTARIO CANADA N6A 1J8.

COMIC CATALOG—Golden age, silver age and new comics. Send a 44¢ LSASE to: COLLECTIBLES, Box 481079, Niles, IL 60648

NEWER COMICS AT 50% O.P.G. (G.A. 75% & UP) SEND S.A.S.E. & 25¢ PER EACH LIST. ASK FOR THE LISTS YOU WANT. • COMIC BOOK LIST • BLB LIST N.P. COMIC STRIP LIST • PULP LIST • PAPERBACK LIST • MOVIE-TV ITEMS LIST • OLD LIFE -LOOK -POST - MISC. MAGAZINE LIST. I ALSO BUY THE ABOVE G. A. RAUCH, 3500 MANILA DR., WESTERVILLE, OHIO 43081

WORLDWIDE CLASSICS ILLUSTRATED NEWSLETTER Articles/Market Analysis—U.S. & Foreign Classics & Related Series. Free ads with Annual Subscription—$8.00 (6 issues) or send 39¢ stamp for sample copy. Dan Malan, 7519 Lindbergh Dr., St. Louis, MO 63117

COMIC BOOKS BOUGHT AND SOLD. 55,000 IN STOCK. MOST EVERYTHING PRICED 25% - 40% BELOW GUIDE! PHONE 607-648-4025. RICK SEMOWICH, RD8 BOX 94, BINGHAMTON, N.Y. 13901

SELLING Mattel Marvel SECRET WARS action figure mint in blister card: HOBGOBLIN & FALCON $9.9 each, includes postage & insurance. Need Iceman Electro, Constrictor for my own collection—will trade for those three too! Also SELLING talking LOST IN SPACE robots & Robby the Robots mint—send SASE Jim Carlo, 521 Ridge Rd. #10, Lyndhurst, NJ 07071.

VENTRILOQUISM ITEMS WANTED!!!

CHARLIE MCCARTHY, KNUCKLEHEAD SMIFF, DANNY O'DAY TEXACO KID, HUMPHREY HIGSBYE FARFEL DOG, JERRY MAHONEY, ETC... VENT DOLLS, DUMMIES, OR MEMORABILIA. RICK RANN PO BOX 877, OAK PARK, IL 60303

Full Color postcard, brochure, poster printing. Free samples. Jim Dapkus, Rt. 1, Box 247cs, Westfield, W 53964.

"THE MAD MAN" WISHES IT TO BE KNOWN THAT HE IS CELEBRATING HIS 11TH YEAR COLLECTING AND 6TH YEAR ADVERTISING IN OVERSTREET WITH THE MESSAGE HE IS STILL LOOKING FOR ITEMS RELATED TO MAD MAGAZINE AND ALFRED E. NEUMAN — LIKE T-SHIRTS, JEWELRY, RECORDS, ORIGINAL ART, ETC. PRICE & DESC. TO THE MAD MAN, 8422 - 149 STREET, EDMONTON, ALBERTA, CANADA T5R 1B4. TWO STAMPS FOR LIST OF DUPLICATES. HERE'S TO ANOTHER 11!

$•$•$• SUPERMAN COLLECTIBLES WANTED •$•$•$
I'LL BUY ANY SUPERMAN ITEM FROM 1938-1960: TOYS, GAMES, FIGURINES, PUZZLES, PREMIUMS, PINBACKS, WATCHES, NOVELTIES, ADV MATERIALS ... ANYTHING!! ALL LETTERS PROMPTLY ANSWERED. AND, I HAVE 1000'S OF ITEMS FOR TRADING!! DANNY FUCHS, 209-80p 18TH AVE., BAYSIDE, NY 11360. DEAL WITH CONFIDENCE WITH THE ORIGINAL "AMERICA'S FOREMOST SUPERMAN COLLECTOR" (D,M,J)

1987 IS OUR 11TH YEAR! Thousands of items. Comic books • Coins • Stamps • Trading Cards • Original Art. Phone (702) 359-7812. Visit or write soon. Stella Enterprises, 126 B St., P.O. Box 251, Sparks, NV 89432.

WANTED:
ORIGINAL COMIC BOOK AND NEWSPAPER STRIP ARTWORK. ESPECIALLY INTERESTED IN WORKS BY BARKS, CANIFF, FOSTER, HERRIMAN, RAYMOND AND SEGAR. I AM ALSO LOOKING FOR SUPERMAN COLLECTIBLES AND FIGURINES OF COMIC AND CARTOON CHARACTERS. TOM HORVITZ, 6511 MAR-OL ROAD #707, MAYFIELD HEIGHTS, OHIO 44124. 216-449-8965.

ATTENTION!

Mike & Pat's Exclusive Offerings

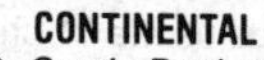

CONTINENTAL
Comic Books & Baseball Cards

True 3D 1952 #1 - N. Mint - $20.00
(A $40.00 Guide Value)

1964 Flintstones - New York World's Fair Comic. N. Mint $5.00
1965 Edition $10.00

Rare Find: **"The Amazing World of Superman"**
This is Issue #1 Metropolis Edition 1973 Preserved in Gem Mint Condition. Price Guide says $8.00 Our Price is $5.00!
(Includes giant Map of Krypton)

#1 Omega Men - Mint $1.00 per copy
Minimum order 5 copies - 200 copies $175.00

Baseball - N.Y. Mets Champions 8" X 10"'s
Ron Darling autographed photo $9.00

Complete Topps 1987 Baseball Set $32.00

For more information
see our full page ad in this issue.

Send for our Wholesale List
Postpaid Minimum Order $20.00

CONTINENTAL
Comic Books & Baseball Cards
71-05 Austin St., Forest Hills, N.Y. 11375
(718) 544-4487

PAPER AMERICANA FOR SALE
COMIC BOOKS—Marvels, Golden Age, EC's, DC's. Original comic art, SF items, Tarzan & Disney items, Pulps, Cartoon Books, Old Boys' Books, Old Magazines, Vintage Paperbacks, BLB's & MORE! I also BUY & TRADE. SSAE with your wants or what you have to sell or trade. As a collector, I pay more!
C. A. Hawk, 2622 Oregon St., Racine, WI 53405

WANTED
BY WORLD'S FOREMOST SUPERMAN COLLECTOR
Any and all SUPERMAN collectibles, art, and memorabilia: Toys, Games, Figurines, Jewelry, Puzzles, Paper Items, Gumcards, Ads, Promotional Material, Letters, Premiums, Etc. Anything from 1938 to 1987 pertaining to SUPERMAN. Gary Coddington, P.O. Box 5064, Pasadena, CA 91107. Overstreet Price Guide advisor. Superman Collector for 28 years. Memorabilia and art price advisor.

SELLING: INDEPENDENT COMICS, GOLDEN AGE, E.C.'S (SF), DISNEY, FANZINES, ORIG. ART, CELS, SPECIALIZE IN OLD MARVEL'S 1961-1963 BUY, SELL, TRADE. SEND YOUR WANT LIST AT ONCE TO: GUSTAVESON, 11684 VENTURA BL. #335, STUDIO CITY, CA 91604.

TV-MOVIE COMICS, OLD DELLS, GOLD KEY, MARVEL, DC, HARVEY, CLASSICS, DISNEY & ODDBALL COMICS FROM 1948-1986. SEND US YOUR WANTS (SASE). SAN FRANCISCO CARD EXCHANGE, 1316 - 18th AVE. SAN FRANCISCO, CA 94122. PH. 415-665-TEAM.

NON-SPORT & SPORT CARDS: OVER 1,000,000 CARDS IN OUR INVENTORY. YOUR WANTS—SASE. SAN FRANCISCO CARD EXCHANGE, 1316 - 18th AVE., SAN FRANCISCO, CA 94122. PH. 415-665-TEAM••••

WE'RE NO. 1 IN PHILADELPHIA

8110 BUSTLETON AVE., 19152
254 E. STREET RD., FEASTERVILLE

(215) 725—7705

BASEBALL CARDS
COMIC BOOKS
Bought - Sold - Traded

PAYING TOP DOLLAR FOR
LARGE COLLECTIONS

STORE HOURS:
DAILY 11-6, FRI. 11-9, SAT. 10-6, SUN 12-4